SIXTEENTH EDITION

SCHROEDER'S
ANTIQUES
PRICE GUIDE

Edited by Sharon & Bob Huxford

COLLECTOR BOOKS
A Division of Schroeder Publishing Co., Inc.

The current values in this book should be used only as a guide. They are not intended to set prices, which vary from one section of the country to another. Auction prices as well as dealer prices vary greatly and are affected by condition as well as demand. Neither the Editors nor the Publisher assumes responsibility for any losses that might be incurred as a result of consulting this guide.

Searching For A Publisher?

We are always looking for knowledgeable people considered experts within their fields. If you feel that there is a real need for a book on your collectible subject and have a large comprehensive collection, please contact Collector Books.

Additional copies of this book may be ordered from:

COLLECTOR BOOKS
P.O. Box 3009
Paducah, Kentucky 42002-3009

@$12.95. Add $2.00 for postage and handling.

Introduction

As the editors and staff of *Schroeder's*, our goal is to compile the most useful, comprehensive, and accurate background and pricing information possible. Our guide encompasses nearly five hundred categories, many of which you will not find in other price guides. Our sources are varied; we use auction results and dealer lists, and we consult with national collectors' clubs, recognized authorities, researchers, and appraisers. We have by far the largest Advisory Board of any similar publication on the market. Each year we add several new advisors and now have over 450 who cover almost all our categories. They go over our computer print-outs line by line, deleting listings that are misleading or too vague to be of merit; they often send background information and photos. We appreciate their assistance very much. Only through their expertise and experience in their special fields are we able to offer with confidence what we feel are useful, accurate evaluations that provide a sound understanding of the dealings in the market place today. Correspondence with so large an advisory panel adds months of extra work to an already monumental task, but we feel that to a very large extent this is the foundation that makes *Schroeder's* the success that it has become.

Our Directory, which you will find in the back of the book, lists each contributor by state. These are people who have allowed us to photograph various examples of merchandise from their show booths, sent us pricing information, or in any way have contributed to this year's book. If you happen to be traveling, consult the Directory for shops along your way. We also list clubs who have worked with us and auction houses who have permitted us to use photographs from their catalogs.

Our Advisory Board lists only names and home states, so check the Directory for addresses and telephone numbers should you want to correspond with one of our experts. Remember, when you do, **always** enclose a self-addressed, stamped envelope (SASE). Thousands of people buy our guide, and hundreds contact our advisors. The only agreement we have with our advisors is that they edit their categories. They are in no way obligated to answer mail. Some are dealers who do many shows a month. The time they spend at home may be very limited, and they may not be open to contacts. There's no doubt that the reason behind the success of our book is their assistance. We regret seeing them becoming more and more burdened by phone and mail inquiries. We have lost some of our good advisors for this reason, and when we do, the book suffers and consequently, so do our readers. Many of our listed reference sources report that they constantly receive long distance calls (at all hours) that are really valuation requests. If they are registered appraisers, they make their living at providing such information and expect a fee for their service and expertise.

If you find you need more information than *Schroeder's* provides, there are other sources available to you. Go to your local library; check their section on reference books. Museums are public facilities that are willing and able help you establish the origin and possibly even the value of your particular treasure. Check the yellow pages of your phone book. Other cities' phone books are available from either your library or from the telephone company office. Look under the heading *Antique Dealers*. Those who are qualified appraisers will mention this credit in their advertisement. But remember that if you sell to a dealer, he will expect to buy your merchandise at a price low enough that he will be able to make an appreciable profit when he sells it. Once you decide to contact one of these appraisers, unless you intend to see them directly, you'll need to take photographs. Don't send photos that are under or over exposed, out of focus, or shot against a background that detracts from important details you want to emphasize. It is almost impossible for them to give you a value judgement on items they've not seen when your photos are of poor quality. Shoot the front, top, and the bottom; describe any marks and numbers (or send a pencil rubbing), explain how and when you acquired the article, and give accurate measurements and any further background information that may be helpful.

The auction houses listed in the Directory nearly all have a staff of appraisal experts. If the item you're attempting to research is of the caliber of material they deal with, they can offer extremely accurate evaluations. Of course, most have a fee. Be sure to send them only professional-quality photographs. Tell them if you expect to consign your item to their auction. If you disagree with the value they suggest, you are under no obligation to do so.

Nearly 500 categories are included in our book. We have organized our topics alphabetically, following the most simple logic, usually either by manufacturer or by type of product. If you have difficulty in locating your subject, consult the index. Our guide is unique in that much more space has been allotted to background information than in any other publication of this type. Our readers tell us that these are features they enjoy. To be able to do this, we have adopted a format of one-line listings wherein we describe the items to the fullest extent possible by using several common-sense abbreviations; they will be easy to read and understand if you will first take the time to quickly scan through them.

The Editors

Editorial Staff

Editors
Sharon and Bob Huxford

Research and Editorial Assistants
Michael Drollinger, Nancy Drollinger, Linda Holycross, Donna Newnum, Loretta Woodrow

Layout
Beth Ray, Terri Stalions, Donna Ballard

Cover
Beth Summers

On the cover:

1937 Coca-Cola calendar, 12"x24", $525.00.

Mechanical Bank, Darktown Battery, $7,500.00.

Porcelain vase by Pickard with Cornflower Conventional pattern, 8¼" tall, $550.00.

Mickey Mouse bisque, 9½" tall, $4,500.00 – 5,000.00.

Jack-in-the-pulpit, Favrile Glass Vase, 20⅛" tall, $8,000.00 – 12.000.00.

Bisque socket head doll by Kammer & Reinhardt, 31" tall, $1,750.00.

Listing of Standard Abbreviations

The following is a list of abbreviations that have been used throughout this book in order to provide you with the most detailed descriptions possible in the limited space available. No periods are used after initials or abbreviations. When two dimensions are given, height is noted first. If only one dimension is listed, it will be height, except in the case of bowls, dishes, plates, or platters, when it will be diameter. The standard two-letter state abbreviations apply.

For glassware, if no color is noted, the glass is clear. Hyphenated colors, for example blue-green, olive-amber, etc., describe a single color tone; colors divided by a slash mark indicate two or more colors, i.e. blue/white. Teapots, sugar bowls, and butter dishes are assumed to be 'with cover.' Condition is extremely important in determining market value. Common sense suggests that art pottery, china, and glassware values would be given for examples in pristine, mint condition, while suggested prices for utility wares such as Redware, Mocha, and Blue and White Stoneware, for example, reflect the probability that since such items were subjected to everyday use in the home, they may show minor wear (which is acceptable) but no notable damage. Values for other categories reflect the best average condition in which the particular collectible is apt to be offered for sale without the dealer feeling it necessary to mention wear or damage. For instance, advertising items are assumed to be in excellent condition since mint items are scarce enough that when one is offered for sale the dealer will most likely make mention of that fact. The same holds true for Toys, Banks, Coin-Operated Machines, and the like. A basic rule of thumb is that an item listed as VG (very good) will bring 40% to 60% of its mint price — a first-hand, personal evaluation will enable you to make the final judgement; EX (excellent) is a condition midway between mint and very good, and values would correspond.

Am	American	dvtl	dovetail
appl	applied	emb	embossed, embossing
att	attributed to	embr	embroidered
bbl	barrel	eng	engraved, engraving
bk	back	EPNS	electroplated nickel silver
bl	bl	EX	excellent
blk	black	fr	frame, framed
brn	brown	Fr	French
bulb	bulbous	ft, ftd	foot, feet, footed
bsk	bisque	G	good
b3m	blown 3-mold	gr	green
C	century	grad	graduated
c	copyright	grpt	grain painted
ca	circa	H	high, height
cb	cardboard	hdl, hdld	handle, handled
CI	cast iron	HP	hand painted
compo	composition	illus	illustration, illustrated by
cr/sug	creamer and sugar	imp	impressed
c/s	cup and saucer	ind	individual
cvd	carved	int	interior
cvg	carving	Invt T'print	Inverted Thumbprint
dbl	double	irid	iridescent
decor	decoration	L	length, long
dk	dark	lav	lavender
Dmn Quilt	Diamond Quilted	ldgl	leaded glass
drw	drawer	litho	lithograph
dtd	dated	lt	light

M	mint	rpl	replaced
mahog	mahogany	rpr	repaired
mc	multicolor	rpt	repainted
MIB	mint in box	rstr	restored
MIG	Made in Germany	rtcl	reticulated
MIP	mint in package	rvpt	reverse painted
mk	mark	s&p	salt and pepper
MOP	mother-of-pearl	sgn	signed
mt, mtd	mount, mounted	SP	silverplated
NE	New England	sq	square
NM	near mint	std	standard
NP	nickel plated	str	straight
opal	opalescent	sz	size
orig	original	trn	turned, turning
o/l	overlay	turq	turquoise
o/w	otherwise	uphl	upholstered
Pat	patented	VG	very good
pc	piece	Vict	Victorian
ped	pedestal	W	width
pk	pink	wht	white
pkg	package	w/	with
pnt	paint	w/o	without
porc	porcelain	X, Xd	cross, crossed
prof	professional	yel	yellow
re	regarding	(+)	has been reproduced
rfn	refinished		
rnd	round		

A B C Plates

Children's plates featuring the alphabet as part of the design were popular from as early as 1820 until after the turn of the century. The earliest English creamware plates were decorated with embossed letters and prim moralistic verses, but the later Staffordshire products were conducive to a more relaxed mealtime atmosphere, often depicting playful animals and riddles or scenes of pleasant leisure-time activities. They were made around the turn of the century by American potters as well. All featured transfer prints, but color was sometimes brushed on by hand to add interest to the design.

Be sure to inspect these plates carefully for damage, since condition is a key price-assessing factor, and aside from obvious chips and hairlines, even wear can substantially reduce their values. Our advisor for this category is Dr. Joan George; she is listed in the Directory under New Jersey.

Ceramic

Aesop's Fables, Fox and Grapes, ABC rim, unmarked, 6¼", $225.00.

B for Bobby's Breakfast, blk transfer, Staffordshire 110.00
Blind Girl, blk transfer w/mc details, unmk, 6", EX 90.00
Bowl, boy, dog & toys, Pink Unity, Germany, 7½" 115.00
Canary, Bullfinch & Goldfinch, blk transfer w/mc, 7", EX 130.00
Cat & fan, flow bl, W Adams & Sons Tunstall England, 7" 165.00
Children's toys w/flowers, bl transfer, Germany 100.00
Children skating, emb letters, Staffordshire, hairline 50.00
Chinoga Watching Departure of Cavalcade, brn transfer, 7⅜" ..110.00
Couple on horses w/dogs, brn transfer w/mc, 7½" 90.00
Crusoe Finding the Footprints, 7¼" 130.00
End of the Chase, brn transfer w/mc details, unmk, 6⅝" 80.00
February, purple transfer w/mc, lt stain, 8" 120.00
Gathering Cotton, Blks in field, 6" 425.00
Hunters on elephants, bl transfer, Meakin, 5¼", NM 90.00
Iron Pier, Length 1000 Feet..., bl transfer, stain, 6⅞" 100.00
Iron Pier...West Brighton Beach, brn transfer w/mc, 7⅜" 80.00
L'Exercise (Drill), children play soldier, blk transfer, 6", EX 90.00
Lady & girl w/fruit basket, brn transfer w/mc, 6⅛" 70.00
Lady w/2 girls, blk transfer w/mc, 5¼" 70.00
Leaving Home, brn transfer, 6½" 110.00
Lincoln, 7¼" 500.00
Lone Fisherman, gr transfer, Staffordshire, 7" 110.00
Man & child on a donkey, gr transfer w/mc, unmk, 7" 70.00
Mug, A Is for Apple..., red transfer w/yel, 2¾" 100.00
Mug, ABCs along rim, mc rooster, gold trim, 2½" 100.00
Mug, cottage & milkmaid scene, gr transfer w/mc, 2⅞" 110.00
Mug, F Is for Fox, gr transfer, flake, 2¾" 90.00
Mug, hand signals for deaf, blk transfer, English, 2½" 475.00
Mug, K Is for Kitten..., blk transfer, Staffordshire, 2½" 150.00
Mug, V Is for Village Where..., 5 piggies, bl transfer, 3", NM 80.00
Peacock on a Banister, blk w/mc details, Elsmore, 7¼" 90.00

Public Buildings at Philadelphia, brn transfer w/mc, 7" 95.00
Punch & Judy, gr transfer, Allerton's, 7" 90.00
Riders jumping horses, bl transfer, Staffordshire 125.00
Slope Arms Our Defenders, lt bl transfer, 6½" 110.00
Stag & Hound, blk transfer w/mc details, 7½", EX 90.00
Steeple Chase, purple-gray transfer, England, 7¼" 95.00
Stilt Walking, blk transfer w/mc, Meakin, 5¼" 95.00
That Girl Wants the Pup Away..., blk transfer w/mc, 6", EX 100.00
Top-Whipping, blk transfer w/mc, Meakin, 6¼" 90.00
V & verse above 3 piggies, blk transfer, 3" 60.00
What Fruit Does Our Sketch Represent? answer on bk, 5⅛", VG ..150.00
2 scared children in wagon pulled by dog, bl transfer, 7", NM 90.00
3 Removes Are As Bad As a Fire..., blk transfer w/mc, 7¼" 90.00

Glass

Chicken emb in middle, 6" 65.00
Christmas Morn, frosted center 190.00
Clock, Thousand Eye, amber 90.00
Dog 85.00
Ducks, amber 65.00
Elephant w/howdah on bk, Ripley & Co, 6" 90.00
Garfield, ABC rim 100.00
Independence Hall, scalloped, 6¾" 110.00
Little Bo Peep, feeding dish 75.00
Mug, African Animals 68.00
Rabbit, frosted 45.00
Rooster, hen & chicks 65.00
Sancho Panza & Dapple 55.00

Tin

ABCs & Arabic numbers, scrolled foliage, 7⅝" 40.00
Brownies, ca 1893, 8⅞" 160.00
Bust of Washington, dents, 6⅛" 170.00
Eagle, 6¾" 270.00
Girl's portrait in oval medallion, Lava soap premium, 6¼" 85.00
Grinding Old Into Young, mini 165.00
Hi Diddle Diddle, 8¾" 85.00
Jumbo, elephant, dk gray, 6½" 125.00
Kittens 55.00
Lt Gen US Grant, 5½" 220.00
Mary Had a Little Lamb, 8" 135.00
Oscar & Josephine, 6½" 590.00
Victoria & Albert, 5⅞" 165.00
William Shakespeare, 6" 800.00

Abingdon

From 1934 until 1950, the Abingdon Pottery Co. of Abingdon, Ill., made a line of art pottery with a white vitrified body decorated with various types of glazes in many lovely colors. Novelties, cookie jars, utility ware, and lamps were made in addition to several lines of simple yet striking art ware. Fern Leaf, introduced in 1937, featured molded vertical feathering. La Fleur, in 1939, consisted of flowerpots and flower-arranger bowls with rows of vertical ribbing. Classic, 1939-40, was a line of vases, many with evidence of Chinese influence. Several marks were used, most of which employed the company name. In 1950 the company reverted to the manufacture of sanitary ware that had been their mainstay before the Art Ware Division was formed.

Highly decorated examples and those with black, bronze, or red glaze usually command at least 25% higher prices.

#116, vase, Classic, 10", from $18 to 22.50
#151, flowerpot, 5" 22.00
#305, bookends, sea gull, solid color, 6½" 70.00
#321, bookends, Cossack dancer, blk, pr 95.00
#363, bookends, colt, colors other than blk, 5¾" 85.00
#370, bookends, cactus, 6", pr 70.00
#388, pouter pigeon, 4½" 40.00
#3906, shepherdess & faun, blk, 11½" 220.00
#392, vase, morning glory, 5½" 25.00
#393, bowl, morning glory, 7" 35.00
#400, tea tile, geisha, sq, 5" 50.00
#408, bowl, leaf, beige, 1937, 6½" 40.00
#412, vase, Volute, wht, 1937-40, 15½" 125.00
#416, peacock, 7" 95.00
#422, vase, Fern Leaf, wht, 10" 30.00
#428, bookend, Fern Leaf, 5½" 45.00
#429, vase/candle holder, Fern Leaf, 8" 25.00
#435, wall pocket, Tri-Fern, 9", minimum value 135.00
#444, bookend/planter, dolphin, decor, 5¾", pr 50.00
#450, bowl, aster, oval, 11½" L 50.00
#452, bowl, aster, 9x14½" 45.00
#453, vase, aster, 8" 25.00
#460, bowl, Panel, 8" 25.00
#463, vase, star, 7" 18.00
#474, cornucopia, yel, 5½" 18.00
#497, Blackamoor, w/decor, 7½" 60.00
#501, bowl, shell, pk, sm 20.00
#505, candle holder, shell, dbl, 4" 20.00
#507, shell vase, oval, wht, 7½" 25.00
#509, ashtray, elephant, 5½" 50.00
#510, ashtray, donkey, 5½" 90.00
#512, vase, swirl, gr, 9" 20.00
#513, vase, swirl, 9", from $15 to 25.00
#522, vase, Barre 35.00
#532, bowl, console; gold trim 35.00
#532, bowl, console; lt bl 25.00
#533, bowl, shell, yel, med 22.00

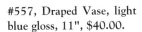
#557, Draped Vase, light blue gloss, 11", $40.00.

#564, bowl, scallop, pk, 11" 14.00
#568, mint compote, pk, ftd, 1942-47, 6" dia 28.00
#569D, cornucopia, bl w/decor 27.50
#571, goose, blk, 5" 35.00
#573, penguin, decor, 5½" 40.00
#593, vase, bow knot, bl, 9" 25.00
#610, bowl, shell, 9" 25.00
#616D, vase, cactus, w/sleeping Mexican man, 6½" 32.00
#629, vase, poppy, 6½" 30.00
#640, wall pocket, Triad, 5½" 30.00

#652, planter, puppy, decor, 6¾" 25.00
#654, vase, tulip, 6½" 20.00
#659, vase, Hackney, 8½" 30.00
#667, planter, gourd, 5½" 20.00
#669, planter, donkey, 7½" 25.00
#675D, wall pocket, match box form, 5½" 50.00
#676D, wall pocket, book form, 6½" 48.00
#681/#682, sugar bowl & creamer, daisy 27.50
#699, wall pocket, apron, 6" 50.00
#711, wall vase, carriage lamp, 10" 45.00
#714, candle holders, star, 4¼", pr 15.00
Cookie jar, #471, Old Lady, plain or decor, 1942 ....210.00
Cookie jar, #471, Old Lady, rare gr 195.00
Cookie jar, #549, Hippo, decor, 1942 ....225.00
Cookie jar, #561, Baby, Blk decor 300.00
Cookie jar, #588, Money Bag, 1947 ....70.00
Cookie jar, #602, Hobby Horse, from $185 to 225.00
Cookie jar, #611, Jack-in-Box 275.00
Cookie jar, #622, Miss Muffet 250.00
Cookie jar, #651, Choo Choo (Locomotive) 150.00
Cookie jar, #653, Clock, 1949, from $85 to 100.00
Cookie jar, #663, Humpty Dumpty, decor 250.00
Cookie jar, #674, Pumpkin, 1949 ....310.00
Cookie jar, #677, Daisy, 1949 ....45.00
Cookie jar, #678, Windmill 185.00
Cookie jar, #692, Witch, minimum value 350.00
Cookie jar, #693, Little Girl 60.00
Cookie jar, #694, Bo Peep 240.00
Cookie jar, #695, Mother Goose 295.00
Cookie jar, #696, Three Bears, from $90 to 120.00

Adams

Wm. Adams, whose potting skills were developed under the tutelage of Josiah Wedgwood, founded the Greengates Pottery at Tunstall, England, in 1769. Many types of wares including basalt, ironstone, parian, and jasper were produced; and various impressed or printed marks were employed. Until 1800 'Adams Co.' or 'Adams' impressed in block letters identified the company's earthenwares and a fine type of jasper similar in color and decoration to Wedgwood's. The latter mark was used again from 1845 to 1864 on parian figures. Most examples of their product found on today's market are transfer-printed dinnerwares with ornate backstamps which often include the pattern name and the initials 'W.A. & S.' This type of product was made from 1820 until about 1920. After 1890 the word 'England' was included in the mark; 'Tunstall' was added after 1896. From 1914 through 1940, a printed crown with 'Adams, Estbd 1657, England' identified their products. From 1900 to 1965, they produced souvenir plates with transfers of American scenes, many of which were marketed in this country by Roth Importers of Peoria, Illinois. In 1965 the company affiliated with Wedgwood. Although there were other Adams potteries in Staffordshire, their marks incorporate either the first name initial or a partner's name and so are easily distinguished from those of this company. See also Spatter; Staffordshire; Adams Rose.

Candlesticks, Cries of London, 3½", pr 80.00
Creamer, bl jasper, wht classical figures, 3¼" 50.00
Cup & saucer, Casino, lt bl transfer, mini 45.00
Plate, Monastery, red, att, 10½" 100.00
Plate, Seasons (Winter), pk transfer, 9½" 65.00
Plate, soup; Caledonia, red transfer, 11", EX 50.00
Plate, soup; The Sea, blk transfer, 10¾" 75.00
Plate, The Sea, red, hairline, 9½" 50.00

Relish, Woodland Lovers, dk bl, fruit hdls, unmk, rstr, 6⅝" **120.00**
Sugar shaker, bl jasper **200.00**

Adams, Matthew

In the 1950s a trading post located in Alaska contacted Sascha Brastoff to design a line of porcelain with scenes of Eskimos, Alaskan motifs, and animals indigenous to that country. These items were to be sold to the tourist trade.

Brastoff selected Matthew Adams to design the Alaska series. Pieces from the line he produced have the Sascha B mark on the front; some have a pattern number on the reverse. They did not have the rooster backstamp. (See the Sascha Brastoff category for information on this mark.)

After the Alaska series was introduced and proved to be successful, Matthew Adams left the employment of Sascha Brastoff and started his own business. Pieces made in his studio are signed Matthew Adams in script on the front. Some are stamped Alaska. The location of his studio or studios are unknown at the present time, but a 'Made in Alaska' paper label has been found. Our advisor for this category is Marty Webster; he is listed in the Directory under Michigan. Feel free to contact Mr. Webster if you have any further information.

Ashtray, hollow star shape, full Eskimo, 13" **75.00**
Ashtray, star shape, walrus, minor rstr, 10x12" **95.00**
Ashtray, walrus on gr, 6" dia **25.00**
Bowl, console; glacier, on blk, 12x21" **165.00**
Bowl, Eskimo on bl, 9" **25.00**
Bowl, seal, oval, 9" **60.00**
Bowl, walrus, yel, w/lid, 7" **75.00**
Box, glacier on blk, w/lid, 12" **95.00**
Charger, caribou on dk bl, 18" **150.00**
Charger, walrus, dk bl, 17" **150.00**

Covered dish, bear on yellow, $150.00; Vase, polar bear on blue, $75.00; Vase, polar bear on green, $75.00.

Cookie jar, mother & child on brn **75.00**
Cup & saucer, sled on bl **25.00**
Dish, Eskimo lady on gr, elbow shape, 12" **50.00**
Dish, igloo, unsgn, w/lid, 13" **60.00**
Jar, glacier on blk, w/lid **75.00**
Jar, polar bear, w/lid **98.00**
Lighter, glacier, 6" **50.00**
Pitcher, Eskimo, 13" **90.00**
Plate, Eskimo girl, #162, 7½" **30.00**
Platter, house, 12" **55.00**
Pot, walrus, w/lid, 8" **75.00**
Tankard, polar bear on blk, w/lid, 13" **235.00**
Tankard, ram on brn, 19", +6 lg mugs **250.00**
Tumbler, cabin **24.00**

Vase, mother & child on teal, cylindrical, 17" **185.00**
Vase, reindeer, 4½" **45.00**

Adams Rose, Early and Late

In the second quarter of the 19th century, the Adams and Son Pottery produced a line of hand-painted dinnerware decorated in large, red brush-stroke roses with green leaves on whiteware, which collectors call Adams Rose. Later, G. Jones and Son (and possibly others) made a similar ware with less brilliant colors on a gray-white surface.

Bowl, early, scalloped rim, 4¼x9½", NM **715.00**
Bowl, late, England, 5½" **70.00**
Bowl, soup; early, mk Adams, 10½", NM **145.00**
Bowl, vegetable; early, emb rim, w/lid, mk Adams, 12½" L, M ..**2,500.00**
Bowl, vegetable; late, 11", M **130.00**
Coffeepot, early, scroll hdl, dome lid, mk Adams, rpr, 12", EX ...**600.00**
Coffeepot, late, bulbous, rpr, 8¾" **260.00**
Creamer, early, 5¾", M **325.00**
Cup & saucer, handleless; early, scalloped rim, NM, 6 for **1,155.00**
Cup & saucer, handleless; late, M **125.00**
Plate, cup; early, scalloped, mk Adams, 4", EX **95.00**
Plate, early, 9", M **195.00**
Plate, toddy; early, plain rim, mk Adams, 5", EX **120.00**
Platter, late, 12", EX **135.00**
Sugar bowl, late, England, rpr, 6", EX **200.00**
Teapot, early, rnd body, 5", VG **300.00**
Teapot, late, M **325.00**

Advertising

The advertising world has always been a fiercely competitive field. In an effort to present their product to the customer, every imaginable gimmick was put into play. Colorful and artfully decorated signs and posters, thermometers, tape measures, fans, hand mirrors, and attractive tin containers (all with catchy slogans, familiar logos, and often-bogus claims) are only a few of the many examples of early advertising memorabilia that are of interest to today's collectors.

Porcelain signs were made as early as 1890 and are highly prized for their artistic portrayal of life as it was then . . . often allowing amusing insights into the tastes, humor, and way of life of a bygone era. As a general rule, older signs are made from a heavier gauge metal. Those with three or more fired-on colors are especially desirable.

Tin containers were used to package consumer goods ranging from crackers and coffee to tobacco and talcum. After 1880 can companies began to decorate their containers by the method of lithography. Though colors were still subdued, intricate designs were used to attract the eye of the consumer. False labeling and unfounded claims were curtailed by the Pure Food and Drug Administration in 1906, and the name of the manufacturer as well as the brand name of the product had to be printed on the label. By 1910 color was rampant with more than a dozen hues printed on the tin or on paper labels. The tins themselves were often designed with a second use in mind, such as canisters, lunch boxes, even toy trains. As a general rule, tobacco-related tins are the most desirable, though personal preference may direct the interest of the collector to peanut butter pails with illustrations of children, or talcum tins with irresistible babies or beautiful ladies. Coffee tins are popular, as are those made to contain a particularly successful or well-known product.

Perhaps the most visual of the early advertising gimmicks were the character logos, the Fairbank Company's Gold Dust Twins, the goose trademark of the Red Goose Shoe Company, Nabisco's ZuZu Clown and Uneeda Kid, the Campbell Kids, the RCA dog Nipper, and Mr.

Peanut, to name only a few. Many early examples of these bring high prices on the today's market.

Our listings are alphabetized by company name or, in lieu of that information, by word content or other pertinent description. When no condition is indicated, the items listed below are assumed to be in excellent condition, except glass and ceramic items, which are assumed mint. Remember that condition greatly affects value (especially true for tin items). For instance, a sign in excellent or mint condition may bring twice as much as the same one in only very good condition, sometimes even more. On today's market, items in good to very good condition are slow to sell, unless they are extremely rare. Mint (or near-mint) examples are high.

As a general rule, beer tip trays in near-mint condition are worth $150.00 to $250.00. Spool cabinets (depending on condition) may be evaluated at $100.00 to $150.00 per drawer.

We have several advertising advisors; see specific subheadings. For further information we recommend *Zany Characters of the Ad World* by Mary Jane Lamphier, *Advertising Character Collectibles* by Warren Dotz, *Value Guide to Advertising Memorabilia* by B.J. Summers, *The World of Beer Memorabilia* by Herb and Helen Haydock, and *Huxford's Collectible Advertising* by Sharon and Bob Huxford. All of these books are available at your local bookstore or from Collector Books. See also Advertising Dolls; Advertising Cards; Automobilia; Coca-Cola; Banks; Calendars; Cookbooks; Paperweights; Posters; Sewing Items.

Key:
cb — cardboard   ps — porcelain sign
cl — celluloid   sf — self-framed
lcs — litho on canvas sign   tc — tin container
pp — pre-prohibition   ts — tin sign

Ace High Cocoa, tc, sample, airplane, rectangular, EX 120.00
Action 5¢ Cigar, pocket mirror, tin w/paper insert, rnd, EX 35.00
Adam Scheidt Brewing Co, match safe, red/blk/gold on gr, EX ..110.00
Aero Eastern Motor Oil, can, Super Refined, plane, 2-gal, EX ...200.00
Aero Mayflower Transit Co, display, oak case, glass front, NM ..600.00
Aetna Life Ins Co, scorekeeper, Play Games & Enjoy Life, EX 30.00
Aetna Life Ins Co, stamp holder, bl & red, 2x1", EX 35.00
Air Float Talcum Powder, tc, gold shouldered top, EX 55.00
Alka-Seltzer, sign, sf cb, Listen to It Fizz, 29x30", EX 130.00
Allen's Coffee & Dainty Tea, toy plane, balsa, 1930s, NMIB 90.00
Allen's Ice Cream, tray, kids & dog, 13½" dia, G 130.00
Allstate Tire, menu board, Today's Special, 1930s, 35", VG 75.00
Amalie Motor Oil, clock, metal & glass, 15" dia, NM 275.00
American Crayon Co, Uncle Wiggly booklet, 1943, NM 10.00
American Eagle Tobacco, pocket tin, flat, sample, bl, EX 85.00
American-Maid Bread, fan, diecut cb, woman in hat, EX 30.00
Amherst Stoves & Furnaces, paperweight, glass, rectangular, M ..65.00
Amoco Anti-Freeze, thermometer, porc, oval, 11x15", EX+ 350.00
Anchor Brand Clothes Wringers, display rack, wood, 57x17", EX ...30.00
Anderson-Erickson Dairy Products, dbl-dome light-up clock, EX ..600.00
Angelus Marshmallows, mirror, winged angel, oval, ca 1900 ......145.00
Anheuser-Busch, bridge set, leather-type Amity case, 1973, EX ...50.00
Anheuser-Busch, charm bracelet, gold-plated A & eagle, EX 100.00
Anheuser-Busch, note holder, brass, emb A & eagle logo, EX 40.00
Anheuser-Busch, tray, couple & eagle tureen, 1900s, 18" 275.00
Arco Coffee, sign, 2-sided diecut cb keywind coffee tin, EX 55.00
Armour's Star Ham, ts on cb, The Ham What Am..., 13x19", NM ...550.00
Athletic Tea Co, sign, cb, 2-sided, boy & girl/text, 21", EX 80.00
Atlantic White Lead, string holder, boy in swing w/bucket, G- ...855.00
Bab-O Cleanser, can, cb & tin, sample, NM 30.00
Baby Ruth, beanbag, candy bar shape, Hasbro, 1971, VG 30.00
Baby Ruth, matchbook, Curtiss Candies...The Energy Sugar, NM ...3.00
Baby Ruth, ts, candy bar on yel, 1930s, rare, 16x35½", VG 250.00

Baby's Own Powder, canister, cb, full, 4", NM 60.00
Bambino Smoking Tobacco, pocket tin, vertical, red, EX+ 1,600.00
Barq's Root Beer, light-up clock, Pam, concave front, 1950s, 15" ..225.00
Beech-Nut Chewing Gum, alarm clock, girl's face, 1900, 6", EX ..525.00
Beech-Nut Chewing Tobacco, store bin, slant top, gr, EX+ 325.00
Beefeater Gin, bottle display, compo, English guard figure, VG ...25.00
Belding Bros & Co Spool Silk, cabinet, oak & glass, 7 drws, EX ...575.00
Bell Telephone, paperweight, NP silver, horseshoe form, M 50.00
Benson's Toffee, display, animated nodding man on base, EX ..2,310.00
Benson's Toffee, tc, red w/Toffee man, pry lid, 9x6", EX 155.00
Big Ben Chewing Tobacco, tc, red, litho graphics, keywind, EX+ ...30.00
Big Ben Pipe & Cigarette Tobacco, pocket tin, vertical, EX 950.00
Big Boy, Dolly, hands on hips, 1978, 14", M 30.00
Black Hawk Cigars, cigar box, ca 1894, EX+ 70.00
Blatz Beer, display, barrel banjo player on stage, EX 100.00
Blatz Beer, display, Bartender Joe, EX+ 90.00
Blatz Beer, display, running waiter, 19", EX 60.00
Blatz Old Heidleberg Beer, sign, plaster, girl on barrel, EX 120.00
Blue Bird Marshmallows, tc, triangular, 7", EX 115.00
Bond Bread, sign, paper, Easter Greetings, 1930s, 38x13", NM ..210.00
Boot Jack Plug Tobacco, box, wood, oval paper label, 4x13", EX ...35.00

Borden's Ice Cream, embossed tin sign, Elsie the Cow, 5-color, very minor rust and fading, 24x42", $160.00.

Borden's, creamer, ceramic, Elsie's head 75.00
Borden's, creamer, ceramic, Elsie standing 135.00
Borden's, creamer & sugar bowl, plastic, Elmer & Daisy, 3½", pr ..55.00
Borden's, pamphlet, The Story of Elsie, 1975, NM 5.00
Borden's, pin-bk button, Elsie's Bagel & Cream Cheese, NM 70.00
Borden's, sugar bowl, ceramic, Elmer's head, 2-pc 100.00
Briar Pipe Tobacco, sign, cb, Victorian lady, 10x8", NM+ 75.00
Bromo Seltzer, store dispenser, bl w/paper labels, EX 60.00
Brooks Soft Finish Machine Cotton, spool cabinet, 4-drw, EX ...775.00
BT Babbitt's Cleanser, can, sample, cb & tin, 3", NM 35.00
BT Babbitt's Cleanser, trolley sign, day/night image, 21", EX 275.00
Bubble Up, ts, Drink..., Kiss of Lemon/Kiss of Lime, 32", EX 85.00
Budweiser, charger, Say When, couple w/chafing dish, 16", EX .225.00
Budweiser, clock, mantel, 3-D Clydsdales & wagon, 16x17", EX ..85.00
Budweiser, display, 2 moving 6-packs & hand, 1950s, EX 100.00
Budweiser, sign, paper, Budweiser Girl, H King, 1913, EX 1,500.00
Budweiser, tray, docked R E Lee steamboat, 1930s, 13x18", VG+ ...140.00
Bull Dog Overalls, pocket mirror, bulldog, oval, EX 50.00
Bunnies Salted Peanuts, store tin, red, 10-lb, VG+ 245.00
Burgess Batteries, thermometer, tin, 13x5", EX 350.00

Buster Brown

Buster Brown was the creation of cartoonist Richard Felton; his comic strip first appeared in the *New York Herald* on May 4, 1902. Since then Buster and his dog Tige (short for Tiger) have adorned sundry commercial products but are probably best known as the trademark for the Brown Shoe Company established early in this century. Today hundreds of Buster Brown premiums, store articles, and advertising items bring substantial prices from many serious collectors.

Bank, BB & Tige atop red plastic ball shape, 1950s, 5", M 40.00
Birthday card, BB & Tige holding balloons, 1960s, EX 15.00

Book, BB Goes Fishing, muslin, Saalfield, EX 75.00
Book, BB Plays Cowboy, muslin, Saalfield, EX 75.00
Bowl, Stop Smiling...Come w/Me...Get Some Cake 535.00
Box, BB Stockings, 2 cartoon labels, 1910, NM 85.00
Box, Hosiery, BB & Tige, 1920s, 2½x12x7½", EX 45.00
Box, shoe; Daffyland graphics, suitcase design 35.00
Camera, box type, EX 100.00
Display, BB throwing bone to Tige, life sz, EX 325.00
Doll, BB, stuffed cloth, 1974, 14", NM 35.00
Fork, BB & Tige, SP, 1930s 45.00
Game, BB Shoe Game, ring toss, MIB 75.00
Match holder, Buster having party w/children, 7x2", EX 1,350.00
Pillow top, BB & Tige w/paint, c 1904, 23" sq, NM 185.00
Pin-bk button, BB Shoes, Brown Bilt Club, EX 10.00
Pin-bk button, Brown Bilt Club arched over BB & Tige, EX 10.00

Plate, Buster Brown and friend at tea, 7", with match-ing cup and saucer, ca 1910, 3-pc. set, NM, $175.00.

Pocket mirror, Vacation Days Carnival, w/bill hook 85.00
Postcard, early photo 30.00
Receipt book, Buster Brown & Tige, EX 135.00
Shaving mug 295.00
Shoe stretcher, figural BB & Tige, plastic, 1950s, 7½", NM 35.00
Sign, cb, diecut stand-up, BB Knitwear, tug of war, 12x18", EX ...65.00
Sign, dealer, hanging, 15x15", EX 115.00
Sign, particle brd, diecut, Quality Children's Shoes, 43", VG 120.00
Sign, tin, diecut, Tige pulls BB in shoe, 40", EX 12,100.00
Sign, tin, emb, BB Bread/Golden Sheaf Bakery, 1915, 20x28", G+ ..300.00
Tin, BB Cigar, sgn RP Outcult, slip lid, scarce, 5x5", EX 2,420.00
Tin, BB Mustard, paper label, sm pry lid, 2½", VG 90.00
Tote bag, BB & Tige, 1960s, NM 45.00
Whistle, BB & Tige, tin, rectangular, EX+ 32.00
Wrapping paper, BB Shoes, 30x19", EX 25.00

C.D. Kenny

C.D. Kenny was determined to be a successful man, and he was. Between 1890 and 1934, he owned seventy-five groceries in fifteen states. He realized his success in two ways: fair business dealings and premium giveaways. These ranged from trade cards and advertising mirrors to tin commemorative plates and kitchen items. There were banks and toys, clocks and tins. Today's collectors are finding scores of these items, all carrying Kenny's name.

Doll, pnt bsk, premium, printed mk, 4", NM 95.00
Figurine, Indian in canoe, EX 22.50
Pin-bk button, flags, Welcome United Singers, 1900s, 1½", EX ...15.00
Plate, tin, child in snow scene 90.00
Salt shaker, Geisha Girl 20.00
Stamp holder, cl, Dutch waitresses 16.50
Tape measure, retractable 48.00

Tin, Mammy's Favorite Brand Coffee, Mammy w/tray, 4-lb, NM ..500.00
Tin, Mammy's Favorite Brand Coffee, Mammy w/tray, 4-lb, VG ..295.00
Tin, red w/blk Victorian stenciling, 1880, EX 175.00
Tip tray, Thanksgiving Greetings, boy w/live turkey, 5", EX 240.00
Trivet 135.00

Calumet Baking Powder, tc, sample, 4-oz, NM 40.00
Calumet Baking Powder, thermometer, pnt wood, yel, 21", EX ..450.00
Campbell's Tomato Soup, thermometer, can, window dial, 12", NM .2,100.00
Campbell's Tomato Soup, trolley sign, Can't You Just..., EX 265.00
Campbell's Tomato Soup, trolley sign, Our Suggestion..., G 110.00

Campbell's Vegetable Soup, trolley sign, 22x21", NM, $265.00.

Canada Dry, clock, numbers & dots around crown, 15" sq, NM+ ..100.00
Canada Dry, pin-bk button, lg winking eye, NM 18.00
Canada Dry, push plate, emb tin, The Best of Them All, NM ...100.00
Canada Dry, ts, diecut, Canada Dry emb on crown, 15", EX 80.00
Capitol Fuel Co, paperweight, bronze, rnd, M 50.00
Capitol Milwaukee Beer, coaster, red/wht/bl, 4", EX 65.00
Carter's Knit Underwear, display, armless male figure, EX 725.00
Cascarets, pocket mirror, All Going Out..., rnd, VG 55.00
Cascarets, pocket mirror, Best for the Bowels..., rnd, EX 85.00
Caswell's Yellow & Blue Coffee, tc, slip lid, 1½-lb, NM 60.00
Chase & Sanborn's Teas, puzzle, Blk woman picking tea, 9x6", EX ..120.00
Chero-Cola, blotter, Drink...There's None So Good..., VG 12.00
Chero-Cola, tray, bottle on wood-grain, rectangular, EX+ 200.00
Cherry Smash, bottle topper, colonial gent, 1910-20s, NM+ 70.00
Cherry Smash Sundae, sign, cb hanger, circular, 12x13", EX+ ...110.00
Chicken Dinner Candy, sign, cb stand-up, rooster, 24", EX 220.00
CIL Ammunition, sign, cb stand-up, deer/snowy field, 27", NM ..95.00
Circus Club Marshmallows, tc, litho bulldog on cylinder, 7", EX ..210.00
Clark's Teaberry Gum, ts, Happy Thought!..., 1930s, 9x12", NM ..550.00
Climax Plug, tobacco pouch, leather, EX 18.00
Clover Brand Shoes, tip tray, Blk boy w/watermelon, oval, NM ...425.00
Clover Ice Cream, sign, neon, clover-shaped tubing, 20", NM ...210.00
Clover Ice Cream, sign, rvpt, chain hanger, 1930s, 5x9", EX+ ...550.00
Cooks Beer, ts, De Boss Sho Likes His Cook's..., sf, 21x13", VG ...140.00
Culture Crush Cut Smoking Tobacco, pocket tin, vertical, NM ...275.00
Cuticura Soap, sign, cb, Medicinal & Toilet Price 25¢, 16", EX ..60.00
Dad's Root Beer, crate, wood, EX 40.00
Dad's Root Beer, light-up clock, EX 75.00
Dairy Queen, paper cup, tall, 1956 ....20.00
Dan Patch Cut Plug, tc, yel, rnd corners, 4x6", VG+ 25.00
Derby Peter Pan Peanut Butter, tc, pry lid, 1-lb 12-oz, EX 30.00
Derby Peter Pan Peanut Butter, tc, sample, 2-oz, EX+ 100.00
Dial Smoking Tobacco, pocket tin, vertical, red & yel, NM 135.00
Diamond Dyes, cabinet, evolution of women, VG 450.00
Diamond Dyes, maypole w/lady & children dancing, EX 775.00
Diamond Dyes, ts, sf, A Busy Day in Dollyville, 1911, 11", G 850.00
Dick's Quincy Beer, tray, wht w/red rim, 11x15", VG+ 50.00
Diet-Rite Cola, ts, Sugar-Free.../bottle, bordered, 18x54", EX 65.00

Dilworth's Golden Urn Coffee, tc, sample, slip lid, 2½", VG 50.00
Dixie Cigarettes, tc, flat, gr, holds 100 cigarettes, EX 90.00
Dixie Queen Plug Cut Smoking Tobacco, lunch box, EX+ 400.00
Dixon's Stove Polish, sign, paper, girl/tree, 1890s, 16", EX 475.00
Donald Duck Bread, sign, tin, lg loaf on gr, 18x26", NM+ 410.00
Donald Duck Coffee, tc, sample, pry lid, yel, EX 400.00
Donald Duck Cola, sign, diecut cb, bottle cap & bottle, 26", NM ...180.00
Double Cola, clock, no lights, scarce, EX 285.00
Double Cola, menu board, tin, red & wht logo, 28x20", M 75.00
Douglas Aviation Tested Regular Gasoline, pump sign, 18", NM ..450.00
Dr AC Daniels' Horse Medicine, pocket mirror, 2" dia, VG 65.00
Dr Daniels' Remedies, display figure, papier-mache dog, VG+ ...750.00
Dr King's Liver Pills, store jar, rvpt label, 13x5x5", G 150.00
Dr Morse's Indian Root Pills, display, trifold, 27x40", EX 245.00
Dr Morse's Indian Root Pills, fan, cb w/wooden hdl, 8" dia, EX+ ...275.00

Dr. Pepper

A young pharmacist, Charles C. Alderton, was hired by W.B. Morrison, owner of Morrison's Old Corner Drug Store in Waco, Texas, around 1884. Alderton, an observant sort, noticed that the drugstore's patrons could never quite make up their minds as to which flavor of extract to order. He concocted a formula that combined many flavors, and Dr. Pepper was born. The name was chosen by Morrison in honor of a beautiful young girl with whom he had once been in love. The girl's father, a Virginia doctor by the name of Pepper, had discouraged the relationship due to their youth, but Morrison had never forgotten her. On December 1, 1885, a U.S. patent was issued to the creators of Dr. Pepper. Our advisors for Dr. Pepper listings are Craig and Donna Stifter; they are listed in the Directory under Illinois.

Apron, grocer's-type mfg's sample, logo on bib, NM 125.00
Belt buckle, chrome w/red/wht/blk enamel inlay, EX+ 160.00
Blotter, 1930s, EX to NM, from $40 to 60.00
Bottle, seltzer; 1930s 175.00
Bottle carrier, tin, 6-pack, 1930s, EX 65.00
Bottle opener, wall-mt, emb lettering, NM 25.00
Calendar, complete pad, 1937, EX 750.00
Calendar, complete pad, 1948, EX 200.00
Calendar, 1948, w/cover pg, 22x13½", NM 250.00
Calendar, 1951, NM 175.00
Clock, compo fr, glass front, 1930s, 15" dia, EX 225.00
Clock, lights up, Telechron, 1940s, 15" dia, NM 485.00
Clock, nonlighted, compo fr, 1930s, 15" dia, NM 300.00
Clock, oak, pendulum, 8-day store regulator, mirror, NM 500.00
Clock, 8-sided Deco design, red/blk/gold/wht, 1939, 18x18", EX ...950.00
Cookbook marker, celluloid 10.00
Drinking glass, Good for Life! appl label & 1-2-4 clock, M 220.00
Lapel pin, Route Salesman 50.00
Match holder, Keep DP in Your Home, 10-2-4 clock, NM+ 110.00
Match safe, wall hanging 175.00
Menu board, Baseball Tonight, pnt, 1930s, NM 295.00
Menu board, tin floor model, checked bkground, 34x21", NM+ ...155.00
Picnic cooler, 1940s, med sz 65.00
Radio, GE, wood cooler form, gr/yel/blk, 7½x12x7", VG 700.00
Sign, cb, A Lift for Life!, 1950s, 19x32", EX+ 400.00
Sign, cb, Energy Up!, Drink DP, w/clock, 1920s-30s, 13x13", EX ...2,750.00
Sign, cb, Madelon Mason, sign/bottle, sf, 1940s-50s, 15x25", NM 250.00
Sign, Glo Glass, Energy Up Drink DP Ice Cold, 1930s, 11x14", EX ...2,500.00
Sign, porc, brick look w/gr border, NM 550.00
Sign, porc, Good for Life!, wht/gr border, 1930s-40s, 11x27", NM ...225.00
Sign, tin, DP in slanted block lettering, EX 25.00
Sign, tin, 10-2-4 clock, bottle & logo, 1930s-40s, 54x18", EX 475.00
Thermometer, bottle cap, plastic, 1960s, NM 250.00

Thermometer, tin, Good for Life!, 1939, 17x5", EX+, $475.00.

Photo courtesy Gary Metz

Thermometer, 10-2-4 clock above bottle & logo, 1930s, EX 450.00
Tumbler, glass, name etched around flared top, 1910s 1,200.00

Dr Radway's R-R-R Remedies, sign, paper, Uncle Sam, 26", VG 1,100.00
Dr Swett's Root Beer, sign, cb stand-up, lady w/glass, 17", NM ..100.00
Dr Swett's Root Beer, sign, tin, boy w/glass & shadow, 9x24", EX ...425.00
Droste's Cocoa, tc, sample, couple on bench, 1⅞x1⅛", EX 75.00
Droste's Cocoa, tc, sample, dining car scene, 1⅞x1x1", EX 190.00
Drummond Tobacco Co, Christmas card, 7x5", VG 12.00
Dubble Ware Overalls..., tip tray/horse race game, 4" dia, EX 95.00
Dubuque Malting Co, coin purse, tooled leather/metal trim, VG ...140.00
Dubuque Malting Co, pin-bk button, name above logo, rnd, EX ..30.00
Duluth Imperial Flour, ts, Blk chef w/bread, 25x18", NM 2,600.00
Dunham's Concentrated Cocoanut, store bin, dome top, VG 350.00
Dunlap's Seeds, sign, paper, child w/oversized cabbage, EX 550.00
Dunnsboro Mild Pipe Tobacco, pocket tin, vertical, VG+ 1,000.00
DuPont Life Saving Service Powder, pocket mirror, rnd, EX 125.00
DuPont Smokeless Shotgun Powder, sign, paper, 1911, 27x18", NM ..650.00
Duquesne Pilsner, display, chalkware, uniformed figure, 11", EX ..125.00
Dutch Boy Paints, display, papier-mache figure, 15", VG 185.00
Dutch Boy Paints, match holder, diecut boy w/brush & pail, EX 475.00
Dutch Boy Products, display rack, Free Folders..., 22x15", EX 125.00
Dwinell-Wright Co Coffee, store bin, wood/paper label, 29", VG ...300.00
Dyer's Cough Drops, tc, Somers, EX 130.00
Dyer's Lime Juice Tablets, tc, gr, Somers, VG+ 85.00
E-Z Ball Gum, machine marque, cl over tin, 1920s, 7x10", EX ..425.00
Eagle Lye, pocket mirror, oval, EX+ 30.00
Early Times Whiskey, sign, 3-D altoplaster, 1920s, 28x23", NM ..500.00
Easthampton Spinning Co, paperweight, glass, rectangular, M 65.00
Eastside Bottled Beer, tray, eagle atop shield, 13" dia, G 75.00
Ebling's, foam scraper, gold on blk, VG+ 35.00
Eden Cube Cut, pocket tin, vertical, EX+ 275.00
Edgeworth Extra, pocket tin, sample, cut-down vertical, EX 70.00
Edison Mazda Lamps, tape measure, cl, mc M Parrish art, NM ...185.00
Egyptian Cigarettes, pocket tin, flat, rnd corners, EX+ 75.00
El Dallo Cigars, tip tray, dk bl, rectangular, EX 30.00
Elastilite Varnish, cabinet, can shape, bk opens, 34", EX 580.00
Elephant Salted Peanuts, jar, emb ball shape, 10" dia, EX 525.00
Elvo Pratt, rain gauge, tin litho, 6x6", EX+ 35.00
Empire Cream Separator, pocket mirror, oval, EX 100.00
Eskimo Pie, sign, porc, product name, 6x36", NM 140.00
Essex Mixture, pocket tin, vertical, poker hand, EX+ 6,050.00
Esso, bank, Esso Drop figure, plastic, 1960s, 7", EX 60.00
Esso, bank, Esso Tiger figure, vinyl, 1960s, G 15.00
Esso, bank, truck, plastic, red, 6¾", EX 35.00
Esso, drinking glasses, set of 6, 1955, EXIB 35.00
Esso, pocketknife, metal gas pump shape, 2½", EX 75.00

Esso, ps, 2-sided, Esso Credit Cards Honored, 14x18", NM 200.00
Esso Marine Gasoline, pump plate, porc, wht/red, 3" dia, EX+ 65.00
Essolube Motor Oil, puzzle, 1933, 12x17", EX 150.00
Eureka Centre Draft Mower, handbill, kids in field, 1880s, EX ..100.00
Eureka Harness Oil, tc, 1-gal, EX 45.00
Evans Reddy Waterless Cleanser, pail, press lid, bail hdl, VG 60.00
Ever-Ready Safety Razor, clock, metal, 18x12½", VG 850.00
Ever-Ready Safety Razor, clock, wood, w/pendulum, 22x18", EX ..2,200.00
Ever-Ready Safety Razor, display, tin/glass/wood, 12x10", VG ..1,100.00
Ever-Ready Safety Razor, sign, cb, DeLuxe Models, 11x27", EX ...400.00
Eveready Batteries, display case, metal/wood/plexiglass, EX 110.00
Everett Flour Mills, banner, wood staff, Miss Liberty, 45", EX .1,265.00
Eversweet Perspiration Deodorant, tip tray, 8x3", EX 65.00
Ex-Lax, push plate, rvpt plastic, bl, 8x4", EX+ 30.00
Fairbanks Dold Dust Washing Powder, sign, cb, 21x14", G+ 400.00
Fairy Soap, sign, cb, girl atop bar of soap, 1936, EX 275.00
Fairy Soap, tip tray, girl atop bar of soap, 4" dia, EX 65.00
Fan Tan Gum, tray, Oriental lady, 10½x13¼", G+ 250.00
Farmers Lager Beer, coaster, As Good as Ever, 4" dia, EX 40.00
Favorite Straight Cut Cigarettes, ts, dog on gr, 10x10", EX 1,500.00
Federal Fertilizers, ts, since 1884, 17x13", EX 45.00
Feen-a-mint Laxative, trifold, cb, man in chair, 5x30", VG 75.00
Fehr's Beer, ts, sf, nymph w/bottle & sleeping gent, 28x22", VG ..600.00
Fels-Naptha, trolley sign, Cleans & Cleans, 11x21", EX+ 50.00
Ferry's Seeds, sign, paper, A Word to the Wise/owl, 36x27", VG ..425.00
Fire Brigade Cigars, mirror, rvpt, ornate gold fr, 15x27", EX 360.00
Firestone Tires, sign, diecut porc, orange on bl, 31x36", EX 450.00
Firestone Tires, sign, rvpt glass, VG 275.00
Five Roses Flour, door push, porc, red & wht, 12x4", EX 260.00
Five Roses Flour, sign, diecut cb, girl chef, 20x18", NM 95.00
Five Roses Flour, sign, tin, ...All-Purpose Flour, 9x27", NM 25.00
Five Roses Flour, thermometer, porc, red on wht, 39", EX+ 180.00
Fleischmann's, sign, cb, boy/girl at fence, 1880s, 15x11", EX 450.00
Flit, display, 5-pc diecut cb stand-up, soldiers, 1928, VG 125.00
Florient Talcum Powder, tc, sample, gold shoulder top, 2", NM ...55.00
Flying A, pump sign, porc, winged A, red & wht, 8x15", M 200.00
Flying A Service, sign, diecut porc, winged A on rnd, 55", VG+ ..650.00
Folger's Coffee, jigsaw puzzle, orig tin container, NM 45.00
Folger's Coffee, sign, 2-sided diecut cb keywind tin, EX+ 50.00
Fontenac Brand Peanut Butter, tc, 12-oz, EX+ 65.00
Fort Garry Coffee, pail, Making Friends Everywhere, 5-lb, EX ...200.00
Fort Pitt Special Beer, sign, light-up, rvpt glass, 1940s, EX 175.00
Fort Pitt Special Beer, sign, tin, rnd w/name on shield, EX+ 65.00
Foster Hose Supporters, sign, cl, woman/corset, 17x9", EX 275.00
Fountain Fine Cut Tobacco, tc, gold on bl, 1-lb, EX+ 155.00
Four Roses Smoking Tobacco, pocket tin, vertical, EX+ 450.00
Four Roses Whiskey, ts, sf, 2 men at cockfight, 24x20", G 175.00
Frank E Davis Fish Co, pocket mirror, oval, EX+ 200.00
Frank's Quality Beverages, bottle topper, smiling girl, EX 8.00
Frank's Quality Beverages, sign, cb, flavor lift, 28x12", NM 75.00
Franklin Mills Wheatlet Cereal, thermometer/barometer, VG+ 50.00
Fred Krug Brewing Co, mug, ceramic, barrel shape, EX 155.00
Fred Krug Brewing Co, mug, clear glass, etched logo, 5", EX 100.00
Freedom Perfect Motor Oil, can, bulldog, 1-qt, NM 300.00
Freedom Perfect Motor Oil, sign, porc, 2-sided, 24" dia, VG 125.00
Friendship Cut Plug, alarm clock, man's face, ftd, 1885, EX 950.00
Frostie Root Beer, thermometer, tin, 30", EX 125.00
Full Dress, pocket tin, vertical, gold w/red oval, EX+ 360.00
Gail & Ax Tobacco, sign, paper, sailor, yel, 1915, 42x32", EX ...350.00
Garland Stoves & Ranges, broom holder, EX+ 150.00
Garland Stoves & Ranges, match holder, diecut tin, 7x4", EX+ ...225.00
Garland Stoves & Ranges, pocket mirror, oval, EX 20.00
Garrett's Snuff, tc, sample, w/contents, NM 15.00
Gayrock Clothing, ts, emb, dapper man, 40x28", VG 450.00

GE, clock, diecut porc, 2-sided, wht icebox w/bl trim, 36", VG+ .4,510.00
General Electric, display, wood drum major, M Parrish, 19", VG 400.00
General Motors, ts, emb, yel name vertical on bl, 29x3", EX 75.00
Genesee Beer, sign, cb, Enjoy the Holiday, Drive..., VG+ 15.00
Genessee Beer, sign, tin, couple bk to bk in cooler, 7x15", EX 50.00
George Washington Instant Coffee, tc, rectangular, 3-cup sz, NM ...25.00
Getup, ts, Drink Getup, It's King-Size, 14x24", NM 65.00
Ghirardelli Chocolate, clock, Baird, NM 3,500.00
Goebel Beer, display, plaster rooster on beveled base, 8", EX 100.00
Goebel Beer, tip tray, boy w/basket by boat, 4" dia, VG+ 65.00
Goebel Beer, tip tray, man at table, 4" dia, EX 100.00
Gold Dust Tobacco, pocket tin, vertical, VG+ 975.00
Golden Crown Table Syrup, tc, paper label, pry lid, 2", NM 25.00
Golden Eagle, pump sign, porc, name w/eagle, 13x13", NM 500.00
Golden Rod Coffee, tc, milk-can form, bail hdl, gr, 5-lb, NM 300.00
Golden Rule Blend Roasted Coffee, store bin, 16", EX 285.00
Golden Shell Motor Oil can, red/yel/wht, 1-qt, EX+ 65.00
Golden Voice Needles, tc, flat, Extra Loud, red/gold, EX 40.00
Golden Wedding Coffee, matchbox holder, 1½x2", EX+ 75.00
Golden Wedding Coffee, tc, sample, silhouette couple, EX 120.00
Golden Wedding Ginger, container, cb w/tin dial lid, red, EX 22.00
Golden West Coffee, tc, red, Regular, keywind, 1-lb, EX+ 135.00

Goodrich Sport Shoes, lithograph on cardboard, Indian studying footprints in the sand, damage and minor losses, 41x26", $260.00 at auction.

Grand Rapids Cabinet Co, pocket mirror, rnd, EX+ 80.00
Grandma's Cookies, bank, hard plastic, 1970s, M 35.00
Grapette, sign, cb, Enjoy..., tennis girl, 24x18", EX+ 125.00
Grapette, sign, cb, Thirsty or Not!, girl/flowers, 28x24", NM 140.00
Grapette, sign, neon counter-top, 1930s-40s, 13x22", VG 500.00
Grapette, sign, tin, Thirsty or Not, hand/bottle, 28x20", EX+ 280.00
Grapette, thermometer, tin, 15", EX 100.00
Great Atlantic & Pacific Tea Co, sign, cb, woman, 9x8", VG 75.00
Great Heart Coal, thermometer, porc, 1915, 39", NM 250.00
Great Hoods Co, puzzle, The Auto Race, 10x15", EX+ 70.00
Green River, sign, cb & tin, sunrise on red, 18x54", NM+ 300.00
Green River, sign, mirror, 1940s, EX+ 175.00
Green River, ts, In Bottles, emb silhouette river, 12x20", NM ...350.00
Green Spot, menu board, 35x22", NM 125.00
Green Spot, ts, name on circle above bottle, 42x12", M 135.00
Green Turtle Cigars, lunch box, wire hdl, EX+ 400.00
Greenback Tobacco, sign, paper, The Tug of War, 14x18", EX+ ..500.00
Greenback Tobacco, sign, paper, The Victory, 14x18", EX+ 500.00
Greyhound, sign, porc, 2-sided, dog/name, wht/bl, 24x40", EX ..375.00
Greyhound Lines, clock, dog & name on bl, 15" dia, EX 350.00
Griffith's Home Farm Butter, ts, Oh Boy It's Good, 11x35", EX .400.00
Gulf, sign, porc, Authorized Dealer, 1930s, 9x40", EX+ 130.00
Gulf, toy truck, friction tanker, Walt Reach, 2-pc, 13", EX+ 360.00
Half & Half, pocket tin, sample, cut-down vertical, EX 60.00
Hamm's Beer, bank, ceramic Hamm's bear holding sign, VG 355.00
Hamm's Beer, display, barrel w/scenes on flipping cards, EX 75.00

Hamm's Beer, sign, neon, bl lettering, 8x26", EX+ 90.00
Hamm's Beer, tap knob, chrome ball w/enamel insert, G+ 50.00
Happy Thought Tobacco, sign, paper roll-down, 29x12", EX ..1,100.00
Harley-Davidson, sign, neon, eagle atop emblem, 24x34", NM+ ..300.00
Hartford Fire Ins Co, ts, Live Stock Shipped..., 11x19", EX 55.00
Hartford Fire Ins Co, ts, Monarch of the Glen, sf oval, VG 140.00
Hartford Time Tested Insurance, clock, light-up, 15" dia, NM ..165.00
Harvard Pure Rye, ts, 2 couples partying, 22x30", G 385.00
Hawkeye Incubator Co, tray, woman by fireplace, rectangular, G 60.00
Hazle Club Cream Soda, sign, tin on cb, On tap/mug, 9" dia, NM .140.00
Hazle Club Sparkling Beverage, push plate, 1950s, NM+ 90.00
Hazle Club Sparkling Tru-Orange, sign, flange, 20x14", EX 130.00
Headlight Shrunk Overalls, sign, cb, train, 1930s, 10x21", EX ...150.00
Headlight Union Made Overalls, sign, neon, 1930s, 14x26", EX ..2,000.00
Headlight Union Made Overalls, sign, porc, 10x32", VG 450.00
Hecker's Cream Farina, sign, cb stand-up, 1920s, 28x19", EX 375.00
Heileman's Old Style Lager, coaster, I'm Asking For..., EX 30.00
Heileman's Old Style Lager, lcs, cavalier standing, 34x23", EX 60.00
Heileman's Old Style Lager, tap knob, ball/enamel insert, EX 55.00
Heinz Apple Butter, jar, pottery/paper label, lid/hdl, 8", VG 135.00
Heinz Cream Salad, display bottle, plastic, 19", G 55.00
Heinz Pure Foods/57 Varieties, string holder, 17x14", VG 3,400.00
Heinz's Tomato Preserves, crock, w/label, dtd 1883, NM 550.00
Heinz 57 Steak Sauce, display bottle, plastic, 20½", G 35.00
Heinz 57 Varieties, jigsaw puzzle, 1932, 12x10", EX 65.00
Henry George 5¢ Cigar, ts, emb, oval portrait, 20x14", EX+ ...1,750.00
Hercules Powder Co, sign, cb, Don't You Fool Me Dog, 1920, G .60.00
Hercules Powder Co, sign, cb, I'se Done Lost de Lunch, G+ 150.00
Hercules Powder Co, sign, cb stand-up, woman & dog, 1917, NM ..400.00
Hercules Powder Co, sign, cb, Sumpin's G'wine To Happen, VG ...200.00
Hercules Powder Co, sign, paper, Stowaways, 19x12", G+ 200.00
Hershey's Milk Chocolate, dispenser, 1¢, 19x9", VG 70.00
Hi-Plane Smooth Cut, pocket tin, vertical, red, 1-engine, VG+ ..65.00
Hi-Plane Smooth Cut, pocket tin, vertical, red, 2-engine, EX+ .150.00
Hi-Plane Smooth Cut, pocket tin, vertical, red, 4-engine, EX+ .720.00
High Grade Smoking Tobacco, pocket tin, vertical, gr, EX+ 625.00
High Grade Smoking Tobacco, pocket tin, vertical, silver, EX ..585.00
Hills Bros Coffee, thermometer, porc, 21", NM 450.00

Hires

Charles E. Hires, a drugstore owner in Philadelphia, became interested in natural teas. He began experimenting with roots and herbs and soon developed his own special formula. Hires introduced his product to his own patrons and began selling concentrated syrup to other soda fountains and grocery stores. Samples of his 'root beer' were offered for the public's approval at the 1876 Philadelphia Centennial. Today's collectors are often able to date their advertising items by observing the Hires boy on the logo. From 1891 to 1906, he wore a dress. From 1906 until 1914, he was shown in a bathrobe; and from 1915 until 1926, he was depicted in a dinner jacket. The apostrophe may or may not appear in the Hires name; this seems to have no bearing on dating an item. Our advisors for Hires are Craig and Donna Stifter; they are listed in the Directory under Illinois.

Ashtray, glass bottle form, EX+ 15.00
Ashtray holder (Hitchy Koo), cvd wood butler figure, 35", EX ..375.00
Banner, Mad About Moxie for Thanksgiving, NM 35.00
Book, puzzle; elephant on front, EX 35.00
Booklet, Hires Extracts, boy w/glass looking at sign, EX 15.00
Bookmark, pictures ducks, rare, EX 28.00
Bottle, Centennial, paper label, 1890s, NM 125.00
Bottle, concentrate; MIB 45.00
Bottle opener, slides in & out of hdl, Drink Moxie..., M 65.00

Bottle opener/ice pick, metal, the Best in the World, NM 35.00
Candy box, Moxie Candy Man on oval center, 4½-oz, EX+ 80.00
Checkerboard, Drank all the Year Round & Hires boy, 1892, VG ..185.00
Cigar box, wood w/paper labels, Food for the Brain, 8", G+ 415.00
Clock, Baird regulator, Compound for the Nervous System, VG ..7,000.00
Cooler, bottle form, Ice Cold Moxie, pre-1910s, 36x12", VG 550.00
Crate, wood 45.00
Dispenser, boy pointing, incomplete, 14x10½" dia, G 2,500.00
Dispenser, glass, Drink Moxie on red oval base, EX+ 350.00
Dispenser, hourglass shape, orig pump, 14x7" dia, EX 750.00
Dispenser, Muni Maker, marble base, SP fixtures, VG 2,750.00
Door push, Finer Flavor Because... & tilted bottle, 12x4", NM ..150.00
Drinking glass, str-sided, Drink Moxie Nerve Food, M 100.00
Ice-cream scoop, plastic, Only One Taste Says Hires to You, EX .10.00
Menu board, tin, Hires R-J Root Beer w/Real Root Juices..., EX+ ...200.00
Milk shake mixer, wht porc/iron, The Flavor For..., 1890s, EX ..1,050.00
Mug, ceramic, boy pointing, 4½", NM 375.00
Mug, ceramic, boy pointing, 5", NM 350.00
Mug, glass, Drink above Hires (on slanted band) Root Beer, M ...35.00
Notebook, salesman's, 1893 ....195.00
Pencil clip, cl, rnd head, gold/bl/blk, rare, EX 75.00
Pocket mirror, Put Roses in Your Cheeks, 1908, oval, rare, EX ..300.00
Punch bowl, boy in tuxedo, Villeroy & Boch, rpr, EX 35,500.00
Recipe booklet, Hires Food & Drink Recipes, EX 15.00
Sign, cb, Got a Minute?..., orig wood fr, 30x24", NM+ 375.00
Sign, cb, orig fr, 1940s, 20x36", EX 350.00
Sign, cb, Say Hires, Hires boy w/mug, 1880-90, oval, VG+ 1,000.00
Sign, cl, lady, Enjoy...Nature's..., 1920s, 8x11", EX 850.00
Sign, cl, 2 girls, Drink Hires, 10x6½", VG 1,200.00
Sign, paper, Say! Drink Hires 5¢, 1920s, 6x20½", EX 150.00
Sign, paper, trees form H, for extract, 1890s, 17x19", EX 425.00
Sign, rvpt glass, Drink..., Hires boy, chain fr, 8x7", NM 1,700.00
Sign, sf tin, boy w/mug pointing, 24x20", VG 4,500.00
Sign, sf tin, 2 girls w/glasses, ca 1915, 19½x23½", VG 6,500.00
Sign, tin, bottle diecut, wood bk, 48", EX 295.00
Sign, tin, bottle w/paper label, ...in Bottles, '20s, 10x28", EX 325.00
Sign, tin, diecut bottle, 1950s, 58x16", NM 425.00
Sign, tin, Drink Hires in Bottles, yel/bl/red, 1930s, 5x14", NM ..110.00
Sign, tin, emb bottle, Enjoy..., 1932, 11x28", EX 350.00
Sign, tin, Say Hires w/Hires boy, sf oval, 1907-08, 24x20", G+ ..600.00
Sign, trolley, Thirsts Gently Suffocated By..., 6x10", EX 275.00
Syrup bottle, For Malted Milk Flavored w/Hires, EX 660.00
Syrup dispenser, milk-glass globe on marble base, 1910, EX 7,500.00
Tip tray, girl w/glass, 6" dia, VG 200.00
Tip tray, I Just Love..., wood-grain rim, 6" dia, EX+ 275.00

Hires Root Beer, tray, lovely lady by Haskell Coffin, 13¼x10½", EX, $275.00.

Tray, Josh Slinger, ...Still a Nickel a Trickle, 1915, EX 650.00
Tray, soda jerk w/glass, 1914, 12" dia, VG 700.00

Holiday Pipe Mixture, pocket mirror, oval, NM 35.00
Hollywood Bread, sign, cb, Jan Sterling Says..., 31x22", EX 35.00
Home Brewing Co, mug, bl on tan, Compliments of..., VG+ 110.00

Homer's Ginger & Brandy, sign, rvpt glass, 6x10", EX 475.00
Homestead Brand Coffee, pail, plantation scene, 5-lb, VG+ 125.00
Honest Labor Cut Plug, pocket tin, flat, EX 45.00
Honest Scrap, store bin, tin, slant lid, EX+ 1,250.00
Honey-Fruit Gum, ts on cb, Nothing Like It..., 6x9", EX 1,300.00
Honey-Fruit Gum, whistle, paper, The Tastiest Chewing Gum, EX ...375.00
Hood Finest Linen Thread, tc, slip lid, 4x4" dia, NM 160.00
Hood's Sarsaparilla, jigsaw puzzle, 2-sided, 10x15", EX 145.00
Hood's Sarsaparilla, paper dolls, 2 dolls w/outfits, 1894, VG 80.00
Hood Tires, thermometer, wood, 15x4", G+ 215.00
Hoody's Peanut Butter, pail, bail hdl, VG+ 150.00
Hoosier Maid Cloves, tc, paper label, 2½", NM 22.00
Hoosier Poet Allspice, tc, paper label, 2¾", NM 45.00
Horlick's Malted Milk, jar, glass/blk lettering, lid, NM+ 35.00
Horlick's Malted Milk, pocket mirror, rnd, M 100.00
Horlick's Malted Milk, tc, sample, paper label, pry lid, NM 50.00
Hoster's, mug, ceramic, brn, script name, 5", EX+ 435.00
Howel's Orange Julep, sign, rvpt glass, 6x10", EX+ 755.00
Howel's Root Beer, ts, emb diecut bottle, VG 165.00
Howel's Root Beer, ts, red/blk/yel, 24" dia, NM+ 200.00
Hudepohl Brewing Co, paperweight, stein in clear Lucite, EX 20.00
Hull's, sign, molded compo, Hull's on Draught, 1950s, 13", NM ..55.00
Hulman's Quality Roasted Coffee, store bin, gold on bl, EX 125.00
Huntly & Palmers Biscuits, tin, sample, slip lid, EX 75.00
Imperial Cabinet Bourbon, ts, girl, octagon, 15x15", G+ 450.00
Imperial Ice Cream, tray, boy & girl, 13" dia, G 50.00
Ingersoll, display, space for 9 pocket watches, 16x10", G+ 120.00
Ingersoll, sign, porc, The Watch That Made..., 48x48", NM 475.00
International Fertilizers, sign, porc, product sack, 7x13", NM 200.00
International Louse Killer, sign, paper, can image, 28x21", EX ..175.00
International Tailoring Co, thermometer, wood, 23x7", G 135.00
Iodent Tooth Paste, clock, Correct Time To Buy..., 16x16", VG .75.00
Iodent Tooth Paste, trolley sign, Two Tubes For..., 13x23", EX ...85.00
Iroquois Beer, clock, dbl bubble, M 500.00
Iroquois Brewing Co, mug, salt-glazed stoneware, Indian, EX 165.00
Ithaca Guns, sign, paper, Nitro Powder, ca 1913, 27x16", G 600.00
Ivory Gloss Starch, tc, emb, gold on blk, 6-lb, EX+ 55.00
Ivory Soap, sign, cb, girl in bonnet, 33½x26", G 275.00
Jackie Coogan Salted Almonds, tc, blk on gr, 10-lb, VG+ 125.00
Jacob & Co's Biscuits, cabinet, oak/glass/marble, 38", VG+ 600.00
Jacob Schmidt Brewing Co, ts, aerial factory view, 28x40", G+ .1,250.00
Japp's Hair Rejuvenator, ts on cb, 7 hair samples, 13x10", NM ..135.00
Jas Hubbard & Son Oysters, sign, paper, Neptune, 24x15", EX ...1,750.00
Jenney Aero Solvenized, pump sign, porc, plane, 9" dia, NM .2,750.00
JI Case Threshing Machine Co, pocket mirror, oval, NM 110.00
John Finzer & Bros, clock, Baird, figure-8, VG 750.00
John Gilbert Jr Co, tip tray, store in wht ornate fr, 4x7", EX 25.00
John P Squire, puzzle, Squire's Pig Puzzle, 1899, 9x12", EX 100.00
Jolly Time Popcorn, box, EX graphics & color, 1930, EX 22.50
Juicy Fruit Gum, art plate, girl hugs dog & mule, 10" dia, EX .1,025.00
Juicy Fruit Gum, match holder, tin, 5x3¼", VG+ 250.00
Junges Bread, door push, yel w/pointed ends, 9x4", EX 55.00
Just Suits Cut Plug, lunch box, red, wire hdl, EX+ 75.00
Kellogg's Toasted Corn Flakes, sign, flange, baby in buggy, G 825.00
Kelly Tires, tire insert, diecut cb, lady motorist, 1915, NM 1,200.00
Kendall Motor Oil, clock, oil derrick face, lights up, 14", NM ...225.00
King Cole Tea & Coffee, door push, yel/wht on red/wht, 8x3", VG .300.00
King Cole Tea & Coffee, sign, porc, keyhole shape, 15x9", NM ...1,050.00
Kis-Me Gum, cutout, Blind Man's Bluff, 6x9", NM 10.00
Kis-Me Gum, cutout, In Fancy Dress, 6x9", NM 10.00
Kis-Me Gum, jar, emb glass w/paper label, glass stopper, EX 350.00
Kis-Me Gum, sign, cb, child's head pops up, 8½x6½", EX 700.00
Kis-Me Gum, sign, cb, lady w/hand on hip, 1896, 20x14", EX ..2,340.00
Kist Beverages, sign, cb stand-up, boy w/sack, 1940s, 50", NM ...460.00

Kist Beverages, sign, diecut tin bottle, 1950s, 55", NM+ 450.00
Kist Beverages, thermometer, Did You Get Kist Today?, EX 200.00
Kool Cigarettes, display carton, Mild Menthol/Cork Tipped, EX .45.00
Kool Cigarettes, display cigarette carton, w/Willy, EX 60.00
Kool Cigarettes, sign, paper, ...Derby Day..., 1934, 22", EX 225.00
La Belle Creole, pocket tin, flat, Ginna, pre-1901, EX+ 250.00
Lambertville Rubber Co, sign, paper roll-down, 22x15", VG+ ...900.00
Lawrence Barrett Cigar, sign, diecut porc, man's bust, 20", NM ...2,400.00
Leisy Brewing Premium Beer, sign, paper, girl, 1898, 18", EX .1,000.00
Lifesavers, display, tin box sectioned off by flavors, NM 2,530.00
Lifesavers, sign, tin, ...Always Good Taste, 1920s, 60", NM 1,900.00
Lily Beverage, tip tray, bottle & glass w/food, 5x7", NM 130.00
Lion Coffee, paper dolls, Little Boy Blue, 1900, 4-pc, NM 65.00

Log Cabin Syrup

Log Cabin Syrup tins have been made since the 1890s in variations of design that can be attributed to specific years of production. Until about 1914, they were made with paper labels. These are quite rare and highly prized by today's collectors. Tins with colored lithographed designs were made after 1914. When General Foods purchased the Towle Company in 1927, the letters 'GF' were added.

A Cartoon series, illustrated with a mother flipping pancakes in the cabin window and various children and animals declaring their appreciation of the syrup in voice balloons, was introduced in the 1930s. A Frontier Village series followed in the late 1940s. A schoolhouse, jail, trading post, doctor's office, blacksmith shop, inn, and private homes were also available. Examples of either series today often command prices of $75.00 to $200.00 and up.

Bank, glass, cabin figural, EX 35.00
Can opener, Towle's, metal 14.00
Container, plastic wigwam, yel letters, 1950s, 2x2" dia 7.50

Display, cardboard diecut, syrup camp scene, 28x22x7½", EX, $1,600.00.

Pin-bk button, log cabin & lettering, ca 1896-98, ⅞" dia, EX 20.00
Pull toy, Log Cabin Express, cabin form, tin, 5", VG 350.00
Spoon, silvered brass, 1908 in bowl, Golden Gate souvenir 35.00
Syrup bucket, tin, no lid or hdls 75.00
Syrup glass, dbl-spout, clear glass w/red panel, 2x1¾", EX 55.00
Syrup tin, bear in door, cartoon ends, Towle's, 5-lb 145.00
Syrup tin, blacksmith, 33-oz 140.00
Syrup tin, boy w/lasso, 1-lb 115.00
Syrup tin, cartoon all sides, sm 115.00
Syrup tin, child in doorway, 4¾x3¼x4¾" 115.00
Syrup tin, children, man by pump, Towle's, 33-oz 155.00
Syrup tin, dog at door, 12-oz 65.00
Syrup tin, Dr RU Well, cartoon style, rare 285.00
Syrup tin, Express Office, coach, Towle's, 33-oz 155.00
Syrup tin, Frontier Inn, cowboys & horse, 5-lb 225.00
Syrup tin, Frontier Jail, 12-oz 155.00
Syrup tin, hand w/finger pointing on top, Towle's, med 165.00
Syrup tin, Home Sweet Home, 12-oz 155.00

Syrup tin, pancakes, VG 15.00
Syrup tin, paper label, sample sz, rare, 2x1½" 375.00
Syrup tin, red, 5-lb 55.00
Syrup tin, red w/wht lettering, no lid, VG 35.00
Syrup tin, Stockade School, Towle's, 33-oz 155.00
Syrup tin, wigwam, 2-lb, very rare, 4x3¼x3½" 515.00

London Life Cigarettes, ts, sf, cricket players, 39x28", EX 550.00
Lucky Strike, fan, diecut cb, Sinatra on leaf shape, EX+ 250.00
Lucky Strike, pocket tin, green, It's Toasted, EX 100.00
Lucky Strike, pocket tin, vertical, sample, gr, VG 60.00
Lucky Strike, pocket tin, vertical, wht w/red logo, NM 645.00
Lucky Strike Roll Cut Tobacco, pocket tin, vertical, gr, VG+ 65.00
Luzianne Coffee & Chicory, tc, sample, wht/red/bl, 3", EX 150.00
Lyons All Purpose Grind Coffee, tc, aqua, keywind, ½-lb, EX ...100.00
Ma's Old Fashion Root Beer, thermometer, yel, 24x6", NM+ 130.00
Magnolene Penetrating Oil, tc, EX graphics, 1920s, 1-pt 75.00

Mail Pouch Tobacco, paper-board counter-top display, Panama Pacific Exposition, 3-D effect, Bloch Bros., 1915, 36x45", EX, $1,000.00.

Mail Pouch, porc thermometer, 1930s, 7", NM 600.00
Mail Pouch Tobacco, sign, cb, Seeing Through Stones, 21", EX ...100.00
Mail Pouch Tobacco, sign, cb, They Didn't Use Starch, 34", EX ..275.00
Mail Pouch Tobacco, store bin, tin, yel & wht on bl, VG+ 225.00
Mail Pouch Tobacco, string holder, 2-sided, 31", VG+ 7,700.00
Mail Pouch Tobacco, thermometer, tin, yel & wht on bl, 9", NM ..350.00
Mansfield's Choice Pepsin Gum, vendor, Automatic Clerk, EX ..1,000.00
Mansfield's Pepsin Gum, cabinet, counter-top, glass/oak, NM+ ...1,500.00
Master Padlocks, plaque, brass, emb lion head, 5½" dia, NM 65.00
McCormick LTD London & Canada, biscuit tin, golf bag, 11", EX .1,540.00
Mennen's Borated Talcum Powder, tc, sample, 1⅝", EX 150.00
Merrick's Spool Cotton, cabinet, oak/glass, 26x31x16", EX 1,450.00
Metropolitan Ins, ABC coloring book, 1930, NM 20.00
MGM Records, sign, rvpt glass, light-up, lion head, 6x24", EX ..575.00
Mobiloil, key holder, wood dmn shape, Pegasus logo, 7", EX 50.00
Mokaine Liqueur, tip tray, bar scene, 5x3½", EX 85.00
Mother Goose, Singing Action Circus, Kellogg's, complete, EX ..45.00
Mother's Oats, sign, paper, Mother's Boy, 1901, 23x16", EX 200.00
Mother's Oats, sign, paper, The Naughty Boy, 1903, 28x22", VG ...135.00
Motorola Radio, clock, neon, red/wht/bl, 21½" dia, EX 650.00

Moxie

The Moxie Company was organized in 1884 by George Archer of Boston, Massachusetts. It was at first touted as a 'nerve food' to improve the appetite, promote restful sleep, and in general to make one 'feel better!' Emphasis was soon shifted, however, to the good taste of the brew, and extensive advertising campaigns rivaling those of such giant competitors as Hires and Coca-Cola resulted in successful marketing through the 1930s. Today the term Moxie has become synonymous with courage and audacity, traits displayed by the company who dared compete with such well-established rivals. Our advisors for Moxie are Craig and Donna Stifter; they are listed in the Directory under Illinois.

Crate, wood 50.00
Fan, cb, diecut, Frances Pritchard/bottle at fair, 1916, VG 40.00
Fan, cb, diecut, Lillian MacKenzie/music graphics, 1918, EX 60.00
Fan, cb, diecut, Moxie girl/Moxie man, 1924, EX 35.00
Lamp shade, leaded glass Tiffany type, 1930s, NM+ 6,500.00
Match holder, diecut tin, str-sided bottle above crate, EX+ 300.00
Mobile toy, horse riding in car, tin diecut, 8" L, EX 1,400.00
Plate, china, logo & pointing man in center, gold rim, 6", M 45.00
Sign, cb, diecut, boy/dog w/3-pack Moxie Teers, 1928, 21", VG+ ..325.00
Sign, cb, diecut, girl peeking over top of carton, 24", VG 150.00
Sign, cb, diecut, He's Got Moxie 5¢, baseball boy, 18x8", NM ..250.00
Sign, cb, Learn To Drink Moxie..., girl in mirror, 1892, NM+ ...1,000.00
Sign, flange, Drink Moxie, red bkground, oval, 10x18", NM 275.00
Sign, tin, emb, Drink..., Braces First Chases Thirst, 7x20", VG 70.00
Sign, tin, Of Course You'll Have Some, woman pours, 20x28", EX ..4,000.00
Sign, tin, Old/New Moxie on bottle caps, red, 24x28", NM+ 200.00
Sign, tin, Yes! We Sell Moxie, Very Heathful..., oval, NM 1,200.00
Thermometer, tin, Drink Moxie It's Always a Pleasure..., NM ...485.00
Thermometer, tin, Old Fashion Moxie, Remember Those Days, EX 40.00
Tray, Drink Old Fashion Moxie on red, 12" dia, NM 65.00
Tray, glass & metal, I Like It, girl w/glass, hdld, 12" dia, EX 325.00

Munsing Union Suits, sign, cb stand-up, 6 kids in car, 11", NM 160.00
Munsingwear, sign, oil on canvas, twins & grandma, 22x30", G+ ...300.00
Munsingwear, sign, tin, sf, The Munsing Twins, 38x26", G 400.00
Murad Cigarettes, sign, Vanderbilt Cup Race, 1909, 11x14", EX ..550.00
Nabisco Log Cabin Brownies, box, cb cabin, PC Brownies, NM ...175.00
Nash Hardware Co, sign, brass, Est 1872, 12x18", EX 325.00
National Biscuit Co/Uneeda Bakers, jar, glass ball/tin lid, EX 145.00
Nehi, bottle topper, keyhole shape w/2 bathers, NM 115.00
Nehi, calendar, complete pad, Armstrong art, 1935, NM 275.00
Nehi, calendar, complete pad, 1936, EX 250.00
Nehi, menu board, 1930s-40s, 28x20", EX 100.00
Nehi, pocketknife, Remington, boot-shaped hdl, EX 110.00
Nehi, sign, cb stand-up, lady in gr w/bottle, 41", EX 1,000.00
Nehi, sign, flange, Drink Nehi Ice Cold/bottle, 1940s, 13", NM ...525.00
Nesbitt's, picnic cooler, aluminum, G 100.00
Nesbitt's, sign, cb, gloved lady w/bottle, 1950s, 23x21", VG 50.00
Nesbitt's, sign, tin, ...Real Oranges/bottle, 24x24", NM 200.00
Nesbitt's, sign, tin bottle shape, 84x24", NM+ 850.00
New Home Sewing Machine, sign, paper, boy/woman, 40x26", VG .1,200.00
New Home Sewing Machine, sign, paper, plantation, 22x16", VG 450.00
None Such Mince Meat, thermometer, pie-crust face, 9" dia, VG 145.00
None Such Mince Meat, ts, Indian chief, 28x20", EX+ 7,500.00
None Such Pumpkin..., lanterns, tin fr/glass inserts, 18", EX ..2,310.00
Nu-Grape, calendar, complete pad, 1925, NM 400.00
Nu-Grape, sign, cb diecut, girl & lg bottle, '20s, 14x24", NM 350.00
Occident Flour, thermometer, wood, 15", VG 160.00
Oceanic Cut Plug, cloth sack, wht w/graphics, NM 20.00
Ockwork Metal Polish/Texas Co, can, star logo, gr, 1-gal, EX .1,500.00
Oilzum Motor Oil, clock, Oilzum man's face, 14" dia, NM 650.00
Oilzum Motor Oil, thermometer, 15x7½", VG 375.00
Oilzum Motor Oil, ts, vertical Oilzum above Motor Oil, 61", EX ...775.00
Old Blue Ribbon, tray, bottle on woodgrain, 14x11", NM 75.00
Old Crow, cocktail glass, figural stem, 1970 ....15.00
Old Crow, decanter, Chessman, 1970s, EXIB 10.00
Old Crow, decanter, Royal Doulton, figural, EXIB 100.00
Old Crow, plate, ceramic, 3-Bird Toast, 10" 30.00
Old Crow, pourer, plastic, figural, EX 5.00
Old Crow, punch bowl w/10 cups & ladle, Hall, 1962 ....175.00
Old Crow, statue, plastic, blk-bordered wht base, 10", EX 35.00
Old Crow, swizzle stick, plastic, blk w/crow at end 1.00
Old Reading, sign, rvpt glass, light-up, arched panel, NM 1,900.00

Old Reading Beer, tray, deep-dish, dog begging, rnd, EX+ **80.00**
Old Schenley Whiskey, ts, I've Struck the Trail, 28x20", G **375.00**
Old Squire Pipe Tobacco, pocket tin, vertical, 10¢, EX **125.00**
Oliver Chilled Plows, ts, sf, storekeeper/horseman, 33x22", VG ...**880.00**
Orange Julep, window display, It's Julep Time, 1920s-30s, NM ..**750.00**
Orange-Crush, bottler opener/spoon, metal, EX **40.00**
Orange-Crush, display, cb stand-up bottle, glasses, 1930s, EX **350.00**
Orange-Crush, door push, tin, Come In!..., 1930s, EX **225.00**
Orange-Crush, sign, cl, Crushy singing, 9" dia, EX **500.00**
Orange-Crush, sign, diecut cb, bather/bottle, 1920s, 40", VG **500.00**
Orange-Crush, sign, flange, name/bottle in snow, 14x22", EX ...**250.00**
Orange-Crush, sign, neon, 1930s, 18" dia, NM **1,800.00**
Orange-Crush, sign, paper, ballerina, Otto, '36, 15x31", EX **425.00**
Orange-Crush, sign, tin bottle cap, Enjoy..., 36" dia, NM **525.00**
Orange-Crush, thermometer, dial type, 12" dia, NM+ **125.00**
Orange-Crush, thermometer, tin, 15", EX **275.00**
Orange-Crush, thermometer, wood, arched top, EX **415.00**
Orange-Crush, tray, Crushy squeezing oranges, 1930s, EX **275.00**
Orange-Crush, tray, Drink Orange-Crush..., raised rim, rnd, G **45.00**
Oscar Mayer, toy Wienermobile w/Little Oscar, 1950s, NM **75.00**
Osh Kosh B'gosh, ts, Union Made Work Clothes, red, 10x14", EX ..**115.00**
Owl Cigar Store, sign, rvpt glass, silver/blk/gold, 80x30", EX ..**2,000.00**
Pabst Blue Ribbon Beer, display, train engine/bottle, 1961, NM ...**200.00**
Pabst Blue Ribbon Beer, sign, cb, Blk waiter w/tray, 36", EX **650.00**
Pabst Blue Ribbon Beer, sign, diecut cb bottle, 34x10", VG+ **120.00**
Packard Brake Fluid, tc, unopened, M **35.00**
Pay Car Tobacco, sign, cb, 2 in boat, 1920-30s, 27x40", NM+ ...**700.00**
Payson's Indelible Ink, sign, paper, Blk boy w/pkg, 6x8", EX **275.00**
Pear's Soap, sign, paper, girl w/candle, 1905, 15x12", EX+ **600.00**

Pepsi-Cola

Pepsi-Cola was first served in the early 1890s to customers of Caleb D. Bradham, a young pharmacist who touted his concoction to be medicinal as well as delicious. It was first called 'Brad's Drink' but was renamed Pepsi-Cola in 1898. Various logos have been registered over the years. The familiar oval was first used in the early 1940s. At about the same time, the two 'dots' (indicated in our listings by '=') between the words Pepsi and Cola became one, though more recent items may carry the double-dot logo as well, especially when they're designed to be reminiscent of the old ones. The bottle cap logo came along in 1943 and with variations was used through the early '60s. Our advisors for Pepsi are Craig and Donna Stifter; they are listed in the Directory under Illinois.

Ashtray, ceramic, sq, bowed sides, bottle cap in rnd center, M **65.00**
Banner, canvas, Drink P=C Double Size 5¢, 1930s, 36x33", EX .**275.00**
Belt buckle, emb, P-C Hits the Spot, NM **15.00**
Blotter, Drink P-C Delicious Healthful, blk on brn, EX+ **120.00**
Bottle carrier, cb, striped bkground, 1951, VG **175.00**
Bottle carrier, tin, open bottom/sides, rnded hdl, VG+ **40.00**
Bottle carrier, wood, Buy P=C, cut-out hdl, 1940, EX **80.00**
Bottle opener, metal, flat bottle form, P=C 5¢, 1930s, VG **25.00**
Bottle opener, metal triangle, Drink Pepsi, 1950s, EX+ **20.00**
Calendar, Armstrong artwork, complete pad, 1921, 14x25" **2,300.00**
Calendar, lady w/glass by table, complete pad, 1909, 10x18" ..**3,250.00**
Calendar, support American Art series, 1944, 15x20", EX **65.00**
Calendar, 1920, sgn Rolf Armstrong, 7x5", EX **2,800.00**
Calendar, 1941, P-C Hits the Spot, girl w/bottle, 23x15", EX **275.00**
Calendar, 1947, Paintings of the Year, complete, EX+ **60.00**
Calendar, 1960, P-C Bottling Co, Lawson Wood art, EX+ **110.00**
Can, cone top, w/cap, 1940s-50s, 12-oz, EX **240.00**
Can, flat top, bottle cap on diagonal stripes, 1960s, VG+ **40.00**
Can, pull tab, stylized Pepsi logo on wht dmn, 1960s, VG+ **60.00**
Cash register topper, cb, Deco-style billboard, 1930s-40s, EX **550.00**

Clock, light-up, Drink P-C Ice Cold on cap, rnd, 1950s, NM **375.00**
Clock, light-up, Drink P-C Ice Cold on emb cap, 1945, sq, VG ..**180.00**
Clock, light-up, P=C on stylized cap w/lg #s, rnd, 1940s, EX+ ...**325.00**
Clock, light-up cash register, 1967, MIB **180.00**
Cooler, counter-top chest, P=C Ice Cold Sold Here, 1940s, EX+ ..**750.00**
Crate, wood, P=C logo **65.00**
Cuff links, sq w/P-C logo, M, pr **20.00**

Display, die-cut bottle, 16", EX+, $450.00.

Photo courtesy Gary Metz

Door handle, Enjoy P=C Bigger & Better, 1940s, 12x3", EX+ ...**210.00**
Door plate, tin, Pick a Pepsi, P=C bottle cap, yel, 14x4", EX **175.00**
Door push bar, porc, Have a Pepsi & logos, yel, 3x30", EX **115.00**
Fan, America Keeps Cool With.../Pepsi caps & bottle, 1930s, EX ...**100.00**
Menu board, tin, ...Bigger & Better, rope-like border, 1930s, G .**100.00**
Menu board, tin, Say Pepsi Please & bottle cap, 1950s, 30", G **60.00**
Paperweight, glass, rnd w/P-C in center, decorative rim, M **40.00**
Recipe booklet, Hospitality Recipes, 1940, NM **25.00**
Sign, cb, Be Sociable..., people & dalmatian, 1960s, 26x38", EX ..**145.00**
Sign, cb, diecut hanger, beach girl under umbrella, 1930s, NM .**1,100.00**
Sign, cb, Reputation Follows High Quality, 1930s, 16x8", NM ..**325.00**
Sign, cl, P=C bottle cap, 1945, 9" dia, EX **175.00**
Sign, porc, P=C on red on wht, blk border, 8x20", EX **365.00**
Sign, tin, paper label bottle at left, 1910, 14x38", EX **2,100.00**
Sign, tin, tapered-waist bottle, Here's Health, 1931, 13x39", EX ..**1,800.00**
Sign, trolley, Pepsi's Best..., glass & cap, 1940s, 11x21", G+ **550.00**
Thermometer, tin, Bigger & Better w/bottle, 1940s, 16x6", NM ...**525.00**
Thermometer, tin, P-C bottle cap, red, 1950s, 27", EX **110.00**
Tip tray, Compliments of P-C, banded rim, rectangular, NM **35.00**
Tip tray, roses in center, decorative rim, rectangular, NM **100.00**
Toy hot dog wagon, wooden cart w/tin umbrella, G **60.00**
Toy truck, Marx, plastic, dbl-decker, Drink P=C decals, EX+ **350.00**
Toy truck, Marx, plastic, flatbed, P=C decals, 7½", NM **250.00**
Toy truck, Nylint, snub-nose cab, open bays, 1950s, MIB **450.00**
Trash can, Pepsi can, early 1970s, 16", EX **20.00**
Tray, Enjoy P=C, Hits the Spot, music notes, 1940, 11x14", VG .**75.00**
Tray, lg bottle cap in center, 1945, 13¼" dia, EX+ **200.00**
Umbrella, red/wht, caps alternating w/Pepsi's Best, 1950s, EX ...**200.00**

Petoskey Chief 5¢ Cigar, sign, paper, Indian chief, 28", G+ **2,500.00**
Phillips 66, sign, diecut porc shield, orange/blk, 30x30", NM+ ..**250.00**
Pickwick Coffee, mask, diecut cb Mr Pickwick face, 1930s, NM ..**65.00**
Piedmont Cigarettes, folding chair, wood w/porc bk, '30s, rstr ...**225.00**
Pirate Cigarettes, alarm clock, swordsman/ship, ftd, 1890, EX **360.00**

Planters Peanuts

The Planters Peanut Co. was founded in 1906. Mr. Peanut, the dashing peanut man with top hat, spats, monocle, and cane, has represented Planters since 1916. He took on his modern-day appearance after the company was purchased by Standard Brands in 1961. He remains perhaps the most highly recognized logo of any company in the world. Mr. Peanut has promoted the company's products by appearing in ads; on product packaging; on or as store displays, novelties, and premiums; and even in character at promotional events (thanks to a special Mr. Peanut costume).

Among the favorite items of collectors today are the glass display jars which were sent to retailers nationwide to stimulate 'point-of-sale' trade. They come in a variety of shapes and styles. The first, distributed in the early 1920s, was a large universal candy jar (round covered bowl on a pedestal) with only a narrow paper label affixed at the neck to identify it as 'Planters.' In 1924 an octagonal jar was produced, all eight sides embossed, with Mr. Peanut on the narrow corner panels. On a second Octagon Jar, only seven sides were embossed, leaving one of the large panels blank to accomodate a paper label.

In late 1929 a Fishbowl Jar was introduced, and in 1932 a beautiful jar with a blown-out peanut on each of the four corners was issued. The Football shape was also made in the 1930s, as were the Square Jar, the large Barrel Jar, and the Hexagon Jar with yellow fired-on designs alternating on each of the six sides. All of these early jars had glass lids which after 1930 had peanut finials.

In 1937 jars with lithographed tin lids were introduced. The first of these was the slant-front Streamline Jar, which is also found with screened yellow lettering. Next was a squat version, the Clipper Jar, then the upright rectangular 1940 Leap Year Jar, and last, another upright rectangular jar with a screened, fired-on design similar to the red, white, and blue design on the cellophane 5¢ bags of peanuts of the period. This last jar was issued again after WWII with a plain red tin lid.

In 1959 Planters first used a stock Anchor Hocking one-gallon round jar with a 'customer-special' decoration in red. As the design was not plainly evident when the jar was full, the decoration was modified with a white under-panel. The two jars we've just described are perhaps the rarest of them all due to their limited production. After Standard Brands purchased Planters, they changed the red-on-white panel to show their more modern Mr. Peanut and in 1963 introduced this most plentiful, thus very common, Planters jar. In 1966 the last counter display was distributed: the Anchor Hocking jar with a fired-on large four-color design such as those that appeared on peanut bags of the period. Prior to this, a plain jar with a transfer decal in an almost identical but smaller design was used.

Some Planters jars have been reproduced: the Octagon Jar (with only six of the sides embossed), a small version of the Barrel Jar, and the Four Peanut Corner Jar. Some of the first were made in clear glass with 'Made in Italy' embossed on the bottom, but most have been made in Asia, many in various colors of glass (a dead giveaway) as well as clear, and carrying only small paper stickers, easily removed, identifying the country of origin. At least two reproductions of the Anchor Hocking jar with four-color designs have been made, one circa 1978, the other in 1989. Both, using the stock jar, are difficult to detect, but there are small differences between them and the original that will enable you to make an accurate identification. With the exception of several of the earliest and the Anchor Hocking, all authentic Planters jars have 'Made in USA' embossed on the bottom, and all, without exception, are clear glass. Unfortunately, several paper labels have also been reproduced, no doubt due to the fact that an original label or decal will greatly increase the value of an original jar.

In the late 1920s, the first premiums were introduced in the form of story and paint books. Late in the 1930s, the tin nut set (which was still available into the 1960s) was distributed. A wood jointed doll was available from Planters Peanuts Stores at that time. Many post-WWII items were made of plastic: banks, salt and pepper shakers, cups, cookie cutters, small cars and trucks, charms, whistles, various pens and

mechanical pencils, and almost any other item imaginable. In recent years the company, now a division of Nabisco, has continued to distribute a wide variety of novelties.

Note that there are many unauthorized Planters/Mr. Peanut items. Although several are reproductions or 'copycats,' most are fantasies and fakes. Our advisors for Planters Planters are Judith and Robert Walthall; they are in the Directory under Alabama.

Key:
cc — common colors	Mr P — Mr. Peanut
(green, blue, red, tan)	okl — octagon knob lid
(F) — fantasy	pfl — peanut finial lid
GW — gold wash	pl — plastic

Apron, Gold Measure, bl, 1991, M 6.00
Apron, Junior Chef w/hat, 1960, child's, MIP 100.00
Ashtray, chrome plated, Mr P in center, unauthorized, 1990s, M .12.50
Ashtray, GW metal, Mr P in center, '70s reissue (no date), MIB .20.00
Ashtray, GW metal, Mr P in center, 1906-56, w/booklet, MIB ..100.00
Bank, CI Mr P, blk/tan, 1987-90s, 5½"-11½", (F), from $6 to 20.00
Bank, pl Mr P, cc, 1950s-80, EX, from $10 to 25.00
Bank, pl Mr P, clear, 1950s-70s, EX 125.00
Bank, pl Mr P, orange, 1950s, EX 275.00
Bank, pl Mr P, yel/blk/wht, 1991, MIB, 19" 10.00

Barrel jar, embossed Mr. Peanut, original lid with peanut finial, original red and gold label, worn silver paint, with lid, 12¼", $250.00.

Cocktail glass, pl, Mr P stem, bl, gr, red, 1950s 25.00
Container, bl peanut, 1-lb, 11", M 15.00
Container, papier-mache peanut, 1940s, 1-lb, 12", NM 50.00
Containier, papier-mache Mr P, tan/blk/wht, 12½", NM 500.00
Display, pl Mr Peanut head, yel w/bl hat, 1979, 12" 15.00
Doll, jtd-wood Mr P, yel/blk/bl/wht, 1930s, 9", VG 150.00
Halloween mask, pl Mr P, 1950s, EX 100.00
Hand puppet, rubber Mr P, blk/tan, 1950s, EX 600.00
Jar, Barrel, pfl, paper label, 1935, 12¼", EX 250.00
Jar, Clipper, orig tin lid, 1938, EX 100.00
Jar, Fishbowl, okl, no label, 1929, 12½", EX 75.00
Jar, Football, pfl, 1931, 8½", EX 225.00
Jar, Four Peanut-Corner, pfl, 1932, 14" (+) 225.00
Jar, Octagon, 6 sides emb, pfl, clear & colors, repro 35.00
Jar, Octagon, 7 sides emb, okl, no label, 12", EX (+) 85.00
Jar, Octagon, 8 sides emb, okl, 1924, 12", EX (+) 250.00
Measuring scoop, tin litho w/Mr P, 1920s, 2¾", VG 75.00
Measuring spoon, pl, 4-in-1, Mr P hdl, 1950s, M 6.00
Night light, pl, dmn shape, Mr P on face, 1⅞", EX 25.00
Night light, pl, wht Mr P on aqua base, 1950s, 9½", NM+ 250.00
Nut dish set, tin litho, 1939 World's Fair, VG 25.00
Nut dish set, tin litho, 1940 World's Fair, VG 30.00
Peanut butter maker, pl, Broadway Toys, 1996, MIB 10.00
Peanut butter maker, pl, Emenee, 1967, MIB 65.00
Peanut butter maker, pl, Picam, 1970s, MIB 30.00
Pencil, mechanical, bl/yel, 1960s-91, M 10.00

Pencil, mechanical, blk/gold, 50th Anniversary, 1956, MIP 25.00
Pencil, mechanical, red/wht, Mr P in oil, 1949, EX 30.00
Santa mask, pl Mr P w/Santa cap, 1950s, EX 150.00
Shakers, kitchen; pl drinking cups w/snap-on lids, M, pr 45.00
Spoon, nut server; GW, Mr P on hdl, 1956-61, 5⅛", MIP 15.00
Spoon, nut server; SP, Mr P on hdl, 5⅛", 1941-61, MIP 15.00
Stick pin, pl Mr P, cc, aqua, yel, etc, 1950s, 1⅛" 3.00
Toy, walking Mr P, pl wind-up, blk/tan, 1984, 2¾", MIP 15.00
Toy, walking Mr P, pl wind-up, cc, blk/tan, 8½", 1950s, M 300.00
Victory pin, pl Mr P hangs on tin winged V, 1944, M 40.00
Whistle, pl Mr P, cc or yel, 1950s, 2½", M 4.00
Whistle, siren, pl Mr P, various colors, 1950s, 3⅜", M 30.00

Poll Parrot, neon and porcelain sign, multicolor paint, 41x21", EX, $950.00.

Poll Parrot Shoes, display, parrot flanked by shoes, 12", EX 285.00
Post Toasties, sign, cb, A Message for You!, 41", EX 800.00
Post Toasties, sign, cb, Sweet Memories, Bryson, 1909, 24", EX .535.00
Post Toasties, string holder, mechanical, ca 1916, 12" dia, VG ..625.00
Prexy Tobacco for Pipe & Cigarette, pocket tin, vertical, NM .1,700.00
Prince Albert Tobacco, ts, Chief Joseph, Nez Perce, 26x20", G .250.00
Quail Cigars, sign, paper, oval graphics, 1900, 10x13", EX 50.00
Quaker State Motor Oil, clock, It's a Lucky Day, 15" dia, VG ...175.00
Quandt Brewing Co, tray, cavalier w/frothy stein, 12" dia, VG ..110.00
Queen Quality Shoes, pocket mirror, oval, EX+ 150.00
Quick Meal Ranges, tip tray, 3½x4½", EX 45.00

RCA Victor

Nipper, the RCA Victor trademark, was the creation of Francis Barraud, an English artist. His pet's intent fascination with the music of the phonograph seemed to him a worthy subject for his canvas. Although he failed to find a publishing house who would buy his work, the Gramophone Co. in England saw its potential and adopted Nipper to advertise their product. The painting was later acquired and trademarked in the United States by the Victor Talking Machine Co., which was purchased by RCA in 1929. The trademark is owned today by EMI in England and by General Electric in the U.S. Nipper's image appeared on packages, accessories, ads, brochures, and in three-dimensional form. You may find a life-size statue of him; but all are not old. They have been manufactured for the owner throughout RCA history and are marketed currently by licensees, BMG Inc. and Thomson Consumer Electronics (dba RCA). Except for the years between 1968 and 1976, Nipper has seen active duty, and with his image spruced up only a bit for the present day, the ageless symbol for RCA still listens intently to 'His Master's Voice.' Our advisor for RCA Victor is Roger R. Scott; he is listed in the Directory under Oklahoma.

Bank, Nipper figural, flocked metal, 1940s 125.00
Buckle, His Master's Voice, brass, Nash Tiffany London 25.00
Chair, NP-pipe fr w/arm rest, plastic bk/seat, logo on bk, M 100.00

Curtains, RCA 40.00
Figure, Nipper, chalk, Victor, 4" 40.00
Figure, Nipper, crystal, Fenton, 4" 50.00
Figure, Nipper, molded plastic, 36", EX 235.00
Figure, Nipper, papier-mache, 14" 350.00
Figure, Nipper, papier-mache, 41" 1,000.00
Figure, Nipper, plaster, 12½x7½x5", VG 200.00
Magazine ad, 1903 Nat'l Geographic, trademk image, 13x15", NM ..90.00
Necktie, Nipper, M 35.00
Pin-bk button, I Support Nipper, 1930s, ½", EX 45.00
Plate, Nipper, collector's edition 50.00
Record brush, Nipper, 5½" L 25.00
Record display, dog & phonograph, chalk 150.00
Shakers, dog & RCA phonograph, plastic, pr 45.00
Shakers, Nipper, Lenox, 3", pr 55.00
Shakers, Radio Corp of Am, 1940s, pr 40.00
Sign, paper, His Master's Voice, texture, fr, 25x29", EX 675.00
Sign, plastic/metal, lights up, 1940s, 15x37", EX 200.00
Sign, tin, Nipper listening, fr, 13½x19", G 500.00
Watch fob, EX 30.00

Rainier Beer, tray, 1903, 12" dia, VG 325.00
Ralston Leather Wing Tip Shoes, display shoe, 25½", EX 660.00
Red Cross Stoves, Ranges & Furnaces, pocket mirror, rnd, EX 45.00
Red Crown Gasoline/Polarine, thermometer, porc, 73", EX+ 850.00

Red Goose Shoes

Realizing that his last name was difficult to pronounce, Herman Giesecke, a shoe company owner resolved to give the public a modified, shortened version that would be better suited to the business world. The results suggested the use of the goose trademark with the last two letters, 'ke,' represented by the key that this early goose held in his mouth. Upon observing an employee casually coloring in the goose trademark with a red pencil, Giesecke saw new advertising potential and renamed the company Red Goose Shoes. Although the company has changed hands down through the years, the Red Goose emblem has remained. Collectors of this desirable fowl increase in number yearly, as do prices. Beware of reproductions; new chalkware figures are prevalent.

Bank, CI goose form, 3¾", EX 85.00
Display, chalk, 12x9x5", EX 150.00
Display, diecut goose, boy & girl faces/box, M 325.00
Display, goose nodder, electric, 21", EX 450.00
Display rack, revolving, goose/monkey/organ grinder, 36", VG ..300.00
Note book, M 12.00
Pencil, mechanical; 5½", G 10.00
Pencil, w/pocket clip, NM 20.00
Pencil box, Half the Fun of Having Feet, 1½x8", VG 25.00
Pencil box, tin, cl top w/goose, 1920s, M 175.00
Sign, neon, 2-sided 3,750.00
Sign, neon, 24", M 2,800.00
String holder, diecut tin, name on goose form, 26x18", VG 1,500.00
Thermometer, pnt wood, It Takes Leather..., 22", VG 240.00
Top, tin, 1¼", NM 20.00
Whistle, tin, rnd, 1¼", NM 20.00
Whistle, wood w/paper label, cylindrical, 3½", EX 15.00

Red Hat Motor Oil, can, red/blk/wht, 1-qt, NM 750.00
Red Raven, tip tray, w/bottle & glass, gr & yel rim, 6x4", NM ...150.00
Red Raven Splits, sign, paper roll-down, nude child, 25", EX 450.00
Red Rooster Fruit & Produce, sign, porc, 20" dia, EX+ 1,600.00

Red Rose Tea, door plate, diecut porc, 9x3", NM 300.00
Red Rose Tea, ts, tea box on blk bkground, 19x29", NM 225.00
Red Seal Peanut Butter, pail, slip lid, 1-lb, EX 90.00
Reliance Coffee, tc, gr, keywind, 1-lb, EX+ 130.00
Remington Arms Co, sign, paper, Get Your Game..., 22x16", EX ..230.00
Remington Game Loads, display, trifold, 18x48", VG 230.00
Remington UMC, sign, cb, Let's Go, spaniel on box, 26x20", VG ..325.00
Richfield, weather vane, pnt metal, eagle on arrow, 43", EX+ ..1,000.00
Rinso Soap, trolley sign, Whiter Wash in Half the Time, G 80.00
Robert Burns 10¢ Cigar, sign, cb, oval portrait, 14x10", EX 60.00
Robin Hood Shoes, bank, tin & cb, 2¼x2", NM 30.00
Roelofs Hats, pocket mirror, oval, EX 110.00

Roly Poly

The Roly Poly tobacco tins were patented on November 5, 1912, by Washington Tuttle and produced by Tindeco of Baltimore, Maryland. There were six characters in all: Satisfied Customer, Storekeeper, Mammy, Dutchman, Singing Waiter, and Inspector. Four brands of tobacco were packaged in selected characters; some tins carry a printed tobacco box on the back to identify their contents. Mayo and Dixie Queen Tobacco were packed in all six; Red Indian and U.S. Marine Tobacco in only Mammy, Singing Waiter, and Storekeeper. Of the set, the Inspector is considered the rarest and in excellent condition may fetch more than $1,100.00 on today's market.

Dutchman, Dixie Queen, EX 400.00
Dutchman, Mayo, NM 675.00
Inspector, Dixie Queen, VG 500.00
Mammy, Mayo, NM+ 750.00
Mammy, Red Indian, EX+ 750.00
Satisfied Customer, VG+ 600.00
Singing Waiter, Mayo, VG+ 600.00
Storekeeper, Mayo, EX- 500.00

Round Oak Stoves, Ranges & Furnaces, ts, Doe-Wah-Jack, 10", EX ..200.00
Royal Crown Cola, Glo Glas, We Serve RC..., 10x12", EX+ ..1,100.00
Royal Crown Cola, sign, cb, Barbara Stanwyck, 11x28", VG 100.00
Royal Crown Cola, sign, cb, Bing Crosby, 26x32", NM 250.00
Royal Crown Cola, sign, tin, Take Home..., 1940, 16x24", EX+ ..600.00
Royal Crown Cola, thermometer, tin, bl, Drink..., EX 75.00
Royal Crown Cola, thermometer, tin, wht, 28", NM+ 100.00
Ruhstaller's, tip tray, girl w/city beyond, 4" dia, EX+ 225.00
Ruhstaller's, tip tray, lady w/dove on knee, 5" dia, VG+ 100.00
Runkels Pure Cocoa, tin, sample, 1½", EX 115.00
Samoset Chocolates, banner, 9x14", NM 150.00
Samoset Chocolates, display, plaster, Indian in canoe, 19", NM ..700.00
Sarony Cigarettes, roulette game, EX 30.00
Schrafft's Chocolates, trolley sign, scholar, 11x21", EX 200.00
Seal of North Carolina, sign, cb, My Old Man, 1910, 9x13", NM ...110.00
Sensible, lunch box, yel, slip lid, swing hdls, EX+ 45.00
Shamrock Cloud Master Premium, pump sign, porc, NM 85.00
Sharples Tubular Cream Separators, match safe, 7x2", NM 375.00
Sharples Tubular Cream Separators, pocket mirror, oval, EX 30.00
Shellzone Anti-Freeze, thermometer, tin litho, red, NM+ 250.00
Sign, tin, bottle at left on orange, 1920s, 9x19½", EX 475.00
Sign, tin, Drink & bottle on yel, 1930s, 12x4¾", EX 175.00
Sinclair HC Gasoline, clock, neon, metal fr, 20" dia, VG+ 1,300.00
Ski Club Beverage, ts, skiers, red/wht/bl, 1930s, 9x18", EX 35.00
Smoker's Dream, sign, cb, Granulated/Big John/Orphan Boy, NM ...165.00
Snider's Catsup, ts, 6-sided, bottle & tomatoes, 17x11", VG 300.00
Solarine Metal Polish, match holder, Wise Wives..., 5x4", VG ..125.00
Spalding Baseball Goods, sign, paper, 10x13", G 1,300.00

Spanish Blacking, clock, Baird regulator, figure-8, 27", G+ 850.00
Squeeze, fan pull, cb, ...The Snappy Drink, 1940s, 11", VG+ 175.00
Squeeze, sign, diecut cb, Will You Please Have..., 30x20", EX ...525.00
Squirrel Brand Peanut Taffy, display stand, 25", VG+ 685.00
Squirrel Peanut Butter, tc, orange, pry lid, 48-oz, EX 140.00
Standard Brewing Co, tray, execution of 38 Sioux, 12" dia, EX .465.00
Star's Linen Cabinet, sample box, Vel/Fab/Palmolive/etc, EX+ 65.00
Sterling Beer, ts, Know Your Army, 15x20", EX 95.00
Sun Crest, clock, lights up, NM 325.00
Sunbeam Bread, thermometer, dial type, 1950s, 13" dia, EX 225.00
Sweet-Orr Overalls, sign, curved porc, tug-of-war, 15x20", EX ..600.00
Sweethearts Talcum Powder, tc, gold shouldered top, VG+ 95.00
Swift's Premium Ham, sign, cb, chef frying, 1900, 18x10", NM .750.00
T Monegenon Pure Spices, store bin, tin, 21x24x14", G 775.00
Texaco Diesel Chief L, pump sign, porc, 18x12", scarce, NM 530.00
Texaco Fuel Chief 1 (Diesel Fuel), pump sign, rare yel, NM ...1,700.00
Texaco Motor Oil, blotter, Let Us Tell You What Brand..., M ..125.00
Texaco Products, tea towel, linen, 1940s, 28x16", NM 150.00
Traveler's Ins Co/Kellogg & Buckeley, letter folder, 13", G+ 225.00
Trolley Chewing Tobacco, store bin, gold on dk bl, rare, VG .1,150.00
Tuckett's Margurite Cigar, ts, sf, lady in gold, 28x22", EX 1,850.00
Tuxedo Tobacco, humidor, glass, 8-sided, paper label, NM 85.00
Uncle Sam Smoking Tobacco, pocket tin, vertical, EX 1,210.00
Uncle Sam Smoking Tobacco, pocket tin, vertical, NM 1,980.00
Uneeda Bakers, store bin, hinged glass front, 10x10", VG 65.00
Union Biscuit Co, bookmark, heart shape, 2¼x2", EX 30.00
Union Leader Smoking tobacco, ts, diecut pocket tin, 12", NM ...200.00
US Cartridge Co, sign, cb trifold, duck hunt, 34x48", EX 1,400.00
US Tires, clock, man's face w/goggles, 18" dia, EX 1,650.00
Van Camp's Concentrated Soups, ts, Dutch couple, 32x23", EX ...5,720.00
Van Dyke's Peanut Butter, pail, Mother Hubbard, rare, 4", EX 1,155.00
Vernor's Ginger Ale, display, automated Quaker man, rare, NM .4,500.00
Virgin Leaf Tobacco, alarm clock, man's face, ftd, 1885, EX ...1,760.00
Watkins Cocoa, tc, bl litho graphics, 1-lb, NM 70.00
Weatherbird Shoes, tin clicker, rooster weather vane, 1920s, M ..20.00

Wesson Oil, stoneware clock, blue and white, 5¼", $65.00 minimum value.

West Hair Nets, display, wood, lid opens w/3 drws in bk, VG+ 70.00
Whip Ready Rolled Tobacco, tc, 6-sided, slip lid, 5½", EX 350.00
Winchester, display, 2-sided 5-panel, hunting/kitchen, 39", EX ...1,000.00
Wood's Boston Coffees, store bin, tin, yel, dome top, VG 275.00
Wrigley's Gum, Mother Goose booklet w/Sprightly Spearmen, '15 ..35.00
Yankee Boy Plug Cut, pocket tin, vertical, red/wht, EX+ 880.00
Yellow Kid, cigar box, ad from Sunday NY Journal, EX 1,000.00
Yellow Kid, gum, 4 packs w/Pulver Co booklet, fr 1,200.00
Yellow Kid, plate, HP Yellow Kid w/parrot & cat, 1897 ....125.00
Yellow Kid, soap bar, NM w/partial box 185.00

7-Up

The Howdy Company of St. Louis, Missouri, was founded in 1920 by Charles L. Grigg. His first creation was an orange drink called Howdy. In the late 1920s Howdy's popularity began to wane so in 1929, Grigg invented a lemon-lime soda called Seven-Up as an alternative to colas. Grigg's Seven-Up became a widely accepted favorite. Our advisors on this category are Craig and Donna Stifter; they are listed in the Directory under Illinois.

Bottle, amber, appl color label, squat, 1930s 95.00
Display, cb bottle cutout w/peacock, 1930s, 7½x12¼", EX 75.00
Door push bar, Fresh Up Seven-Up, wht, 3x30", EX 65.00
Door push bar, porc, bilingual, 1950s, EX 50.00
Lighter, bottle on wht bkground, MIB 45.00
Menu board, tin, hand-held bottle & logo, 27x19", EX+ 85.00
Menu board, wood, First Against Thirst, EX+ 65.00
Patch, red sq cloth w/wht stitched logo, 5", EX+ 25.00
Picnic cooler, vinyl, wht w/gr straps, Fresh Up..., EX+ 15.00

7-Up, painted tin sign, orange, silver, and white, 40x30", EX, $295.00.

Sign, cb, ad w/liquor, easel bk, 1930s, 4x6", EX 35.00
Sign, cb, Enjoy a Seven-Up Float..., 1952, 16x12", EX 25.00
Sign, cb, We're a Fresh Up Family!, 1950s, vertical, EX 30.00
Sign, cb stand-up, Fresh Up w/the All Family Drink, EX+ 40.00
Sign, flange, Real 7-Up Sold Here & bubbles on disk, G 125.00
Sign, porc, Fresh Up With & bottle, 1951, EX, 16x40", EX 225.00
Sign, tin, First Against Thirst & logo, 10x28", NM 85.00
Sign, tin, Real 7-Up Sold Here, 1930s, 14" dia, EX 100.00
String holder sign, tin, 1930s, 13x15¾", EX 450.00
Thermometer, logo on gr dial, 12" dia, NM+ 125.00
Thermometer, porc, Fr, 1950s, 15x6", EX 60.00

Advertising Cards

Advertising trade cards enjoyed great popularity during the last quarter of the 19th century when the chromolithography printing process was refined and put into common use. The purpose of the trade card was to aquaint the public with a business, product, service, or event. Most trade cards range in size from 2" x 3" to 4" x 6"; however, many are found in both smaller and larger sizes.

There are two classifications of trade cards: 'private design' and 'stock.' Private design cards were used by a single company or individual; the images on the cards were designed for only that company. Stock cards were generics that any individual or company could purchase from a printer's inventory. These cards usually had a blank space on the front for the company to overprint their own name and product information. Values are given for cards in near-mint condition.

Four categories of particular interest to collectors are:

Mechanical — a card which achieves movement through the use of a pull tab, fold-out side, or movable part.

Hold-to-light — a card that reveals its design only when viewed before a strong light.

Diecut — a card in the form of something like a box, a piece of clothing, etc.

Metamorphic — a card that by folding down a flap shows a transformed image, such as a white beard turning black after use of a product.

For a more thorough study of the subject, we recommend *Reflections 1* and *Reflections 2* by Kit Barry; his address can be found in the Directory under Vermont.

Adams & Westlake Oil Stove, donkeys picnicking 15.00
Allan's Fly Brick, 1 boy showing 2 boys fly brick working 45.00
American Eagle Tobacco Co, National league, baseball pitcher ...300.00
Anti Tobacco, His Handicap, man carrying skeleton on bk 35.00
Arm & Hammer, insert, Bird — Wht-Winged Crossbill, 1896 ....3.00
Arm & Hammer, insert, Flower — Iris, 1895 ....3.00
Arrow Brand Oysters, diecut, elephants eating oysters 45.00
Austen's Forest Flower Cologne, girl in wht hat w/flowers 6.00
Baseball, A Brush w/the Ball, man running bases 23.00
Belding Thread, family saved from fire on spool of thread 35.00
Blasius Piano, Cleveland & Harrison endorsing piano 20.00
Bon Ami, 5 chicks in straw hat 8.00
Boss Pat Cases, scuba diver w/lg watch & shipwreck 10.00
Boston & Providence Clothing Co, mechanical, next president ..75.00
BT Babbit's Soap, boy & girl playing w/puppet 5.00
Buckeye Lawn Mower, foldover, boy & girl mowing 35.00
Carl Dunder Cigars, man reading to 4 children 20.00
Carters Little Liver Pills, 2 men looking at sign on tree 18.00
Chadwick's Spool Cotton, 2 girls pulling on apple tree 6.00
Cherokee Brewing, Indian w/bow & arrow ready to shoot 125.00
Clark's Root Cutter, humanized roots chopping roots 15.00
Clipper ship, Herald of the Morning 450.00
Clipper ship, Nor' Wester 175.00
Cottolene Shortening, wheel turns to show different products 40.00
Crawford Cooking Ranges, Maude Humphrey girl in bl 15.00
Currier & Ives, Fair Moon to Thee I Sing 75.00
Dr Hartshorn Cough Balsam, girl feeding ducklings w/dog 6.00
Dr Warner's Coralene Corset calendar, diecut, 1890 ....35.00
Drummond Tobacco Co, boy stepping through horseshoe 25.00
Eagle Brand Condensed Milk, 4 babies at table, 1 nurser 12.00
Edison Phonograph, baby from sad to happy because of music 35.00
Estey Organ Co, lady playing organ for guests 8.00
Fairbanks Soap, man getting a shave from barber 12.00
FE Meyers & Bro, Brownies w/pumps on the world 35.00
Fleischmann & Co, 5 kittens sitting on a bench 6.00
Flexible Flyers, sledders fly off cliff & turn into birds 35.00
Frank Miller's Crown Dressing, girl pushing doll in carriage 6.00
Goetting's Violets Perfumes, diecut, bouquet of violets 15.00
Gold Coin Stoves & Ranges, polar bear sleeping near stove 20.00
Gold Flake Tobacco, Gilbert & Sullivan's Dick Dead-Eye 35.00
Great Atlantic & Pacific Tea Co, 3 girls w/3 kittens 15.00
Hagan's Magnolia Balm, lady looking in mirror w/cherub 25.00
Herald Ranges, bust of girl in bl hooded jacket 8.00
Hires Root Beer, boy pointing, I Want Another Glass of... ....20.00
Hoods Pills, diecut, girl w/bonnet leaning on elbows 6.00
Hoyt's German Cologne, girl holding basket w/doves, 1894 ....12.00
Hoyt's German Cologne, girl in bonnet hugging sm dog 12.00
Hoyt's German Cologne, 5 children dancing around bottle 6.00
Ivers & Pond Piano Co, girl in hat & muff in snow storm 6.00
Ivory Soap, Maude Humphrey girl doing wash for her doll 25.00
J&P Coats Cord Thread, 2 girls w/a pony 5.00
Keystone Farm Machinery, Uncle Sam showing different machines .45.00
Keystone Watch Cases, diecut, monking hanging from clock 12.00
Lion Coffee, diecut doll, Sing a Song of Sixpence 10.00
Lion Coffee, diecut doll, the baker 10.00
Little Joker Tobacco, Munchausen & the Handsome Bear 35.00
Little Joker Tobacco, Munchausen's Astonishing Horse 35.00
Madame Alpanalb, gypsy palmist & fortune teller 20.00

Marshall Field & Co, linen department, handkerchiefs 20.00
Maurices Porceleine, diecut, paint can w/colors on bk 25.00
Merrick Thread Co, Liberty holding spool as the torch 8.00
Mirror Gloss Starch, girl looking at reflection in mirror 5.00
New Home Sewing Machine, house vignette w/pansies in front 5.00
New-Era Playing Cards, queen of dmns w/text 45.00

New Orleans Coffee Company, diecut of 3 children with product, $45.00.

Photo courtesy Kit Barry

Niagara Corn Starch, girl w/roses & dove on shoulder 5.00
One Hundred Years Hence, dispensing w/bridge & ferry 75.00
Paines Furniture, girl holding folding bed w/1 finger 20.00
Parker Gun, men shooting at targets, image of gun bbl 100.00
Perry Davis Pain Killer, angels carrying bottle around world 12.00
Perry Davis Pain Killer, boy caring for girl w/cut on finger 9.00
Planet Jr Seed Drill, drill standing alone 35.00
Plano Twine Binder, chickens pulling machine 35.00
Prof DM Bristol's, performing animals, Mattie catching balls 35.00
Quaker Oats, girl standing on rocks holding box of oats 25.00
Rough on Rats, Chinese man eating a rat, oversz card 350.00
RP Hall's Plasters, before & after using product w/verse 15.00
Runkel Brothers, girl in morning glory drinking cocoa 15.00
Santa Claus Soap, diecut, Santa holding tree & presents 35.00
Schenck's Pulmonic Syrup, girl & dog chasing butterfly 8.00
Schepp's Cocoanut, monkey pulling tail of other monkey on box ...45.00
Shaw Piano, diecut, dog begging w/ad in mouth 6.00
Spalding, diecut doll, bicycle rider 50.00
Spalding, diecut doll, golfer 75.00
Spalding, diecut doll, tennis player 75.00
Sterling Piano, girl looking at ad for organ mamma's buying 8.00
Sulphur Bitters, Mrs President Cleveland, photo 15.00
Syracuse Plows, man pushing child on ice using plow 20.00
Toy savings bank, Humpty Dumpty 600.00
Toy savings bank, Stump Speaker 500.00
Toy savings bank, Trick Pony 250.00
Tulip Soap, girl in snow w/bird on shoulder 8.00
Union Pacific Tea Co, well dressed lady on balcony 8.00
US Wind Engine & Pump Co, farmers & cow around windmill ...35.00
Van Houten's Cocoa, The Skylark 8.00
Van Houten's Cocoa, The Song Thrush 8.00
White Sewing Machines, 2 girls in tree looking at bird nest 6.00
Wise Furnaces, diecut, owl sitting on limb holding banner 25.00
Zeno Chewing Gum, diecut, vending machine for gum 35.00

Advertising Dolls and Figures

Whether your interest in ad dolls is fueled by nostalgia or strictly because of their amusing, often clever advertising impact, there are several points that should be considered before making your purchases. Condition is of utmost importance; never pay book price for dolls in poor condition, whether they are cloth or of another material. Restoring fabric dolls is usually unsatisfactory and involves a good deal of work. Seams must be opened, stuffing removed, the doll washed and dried, and then reassembled. Washing old fabrics may prove to be disastrous. Colors may fade or run, and most stains are totally resistant to washing. It's usually best to leave the fabric doll as it is.

Watch for new dolls as they become available. Save related advertising literature, extra coupons, etc., and keep these along with the doll to further enhance your collection. Old dolls with no marks are sometimes challenging to identify. While some products may use the same familiar trademark figures for a number of years (the Jolly Green Giant, Pillsbury's Poppin' Fresh, and the Keebler Elf, for example) others appear on the market for a short time only and may be difficult to trace. Most libraries have reference books with trademarks and logos that might provide a clue in tracking down your doll's identity. Children see advertising figures on Saturday morning cartoons that are often unfamiliar to adults, or other ad doll collectors may have the information you seek.

Some advertising dolls are still easy to find and relatively inexpensive, ranging in cost from $1.00 to $100.00. The hard plastic and early composition dolls are bringing the higher prices. Advertising dolls are popular with children as well as adults. For a more thorough study of the subject, we recommend *Advertising Dolls* by Joleen Robison and Kay Sellers. Our advisor for this category is Jim Rash; he is listed in the Directory under New Jersey.

Alka-Seltzer, Speedy, vinyl, 1960s, 8", M 500.00
Allied Van Lines, Buddy Lee, gr uniform & hat, EX 300.00
Atlas Van Line, Atlas Annie, print cloth, 1977, 15½", NM 10.00
Babbitt's Cleanser, Babbitt Boy, stuffed/compo, 15", EX 450.00
Baby Magic, Snuggly/Sammy/Suzie, uncut cloth, 1975, 24", M, ea .12.00
Baby Ruth, boy, stuffed print cloth, 1920s, 14½", EX 20.00
Baby Ruth, girl, bean-bag body, Hasbro, 1973, EX 35.00
Baby Ruth, girl, stuffed print cloth, 1920s, 16", EX 20.00
Baggies, alligator, inflatable, 1974-76, NM 5.00
Bazooka Bubble Gum, Bazooka Joe, print cloth, 1973, 18", NM 7.00
Big Boy, Nugget the Dog, stuffed cloth, 1978, MIP 35.00
Big Boy, stuffed cloth, 1978, 14", MIP 30.00
Bird's Eye, Merry, Minx or Mike, uncut cloth, 1953, NM, ea 15.00
Borden's, Elsie, stuffed brn body w/vinyl head & hooves, VG 70.00
Brach's Candy, Bracho Clown, stuffed print cloth, 17", NM 6.00
Brach's Candy, Scarecrow Sam, stuffed print cloth, 16", NM 5.00
Breck Hair Products, Bonnie Breck, vinyl, 1972, 9", NM 12.00
Brer Rabbit Molasses, Easter rabbit, plush, 1964, 27", NM 15.00
Bumble Bee Tuna, Yum Yum Bumble Bee, inflatable, 1974, M 6.00
Buster Brown, stuffed cloth, 1974, 14", NM 35.00
Campbell Soup Co, boy & girl, rag type, 1970s, MIB, pr 125.00
Campbell Soup Co, boy as chef, vinyl, 8", EX 50.00
Campbell Soup Co, boy or girl, Product People, 1974, 10", EX 30.00
Campbell Soup Co, girl cheerleader, vinyl, 1967, 8", EX 75.00
Caravelle Candy Bar, Caravelle Man, bendable, 1967, 10", EX .150.00
Carnation Milk, cow, plush, blk & wht w/red T-shirt, 7", NM 10.00
Ceresota Boy, print cloth, uncut 250.00
Chore Girl, stuffed print cloth, 1970s, 16", NM 100.00
Dolly Dear, print cloth, uncut 85.00
Dutch Boy, puppet, cloth/vinyl head, 1956, 12", NM 10.00
Dutch Boy, stuffed body/vinyl face/yarn hair, 1953, 15", NM 20.00
Esso, Attendant, bank, plastic, 1950s, 5", NM 12.00
Exxon/Humble Oil, tiger, stuffed plush, 1959, 16", NM 10.00
Exxon/Humble Oil, tiger, stuffed print cloth, 1960, 17", NM 12.00
Franklin Life Ins Co, Ben Franklin, print cloth, 12", NM 10.00
Fresca, dog, stuffed plush, brn & wht, 28", NM 15.00
Fresca, March Hare, stuffed plush, 28", NM 15.00
Gold Medal Flour, girl, stuffed print cloth, 1920s, 7½", NM 40.00

Gorton's, fisherman, jtd vinyl, slicker & hat, 7¼", NM **40.00**
Gulf, Buddy Lee, gray uniform, blk hat w/emblem, VG+ **350.00**
Henderson Glove Co, Indian, print cloth, 11", M **30.00**
Holland-American Lines, sailor, stuffed/compo head, 12½", NM ..**25.00**
Hood Dairy, Hood Dairyman, squeeze vinyl, 1981, M **65.00**
Istrouma Flour, Humpty Dumpty, lithoed on flour bags, 13", M ..**15.00**
Jolly Roger Restaurant, Jolly Roger, stuffed print cloth, M **9.00**
Keebler, Ernie the Keebler Elf, vinyl, 1974, 6½", EX **20.00**
Kellogg's, Dandy the Duck, doll kit, uncut cloth, 1935, NM+ **135.00**
Kellogg's, Dinky the Dog, doll kit, uncut cloth, 1935, VG+ **95.00**
Kellogg's, Goldilocks & Bears, uncut set **335.00**
Kellogg's, Little Bo Peep, doll kit, uncut cloth, 1928, EX+ **135.00**
Kellogg's, Snap!, Crackle! & Pop!, vinyl w/jtd arms, 1975, EX, set ...**105.00**
Kellogg's, Toucan Sam, stuffed print cloth, 1964, 9", M **25.00**
Kellogg's Papa Bear, uncut **120.00**
Levi's, boy or girl, cloth w/yarn hair, 1974, 10", ea **10.00**
Libby, cloth w/yarn hair, 1974, 14", M **15.00**
Lifesavers, figure, bendable, 1967, VG **150.00**
Mason Mints, Peppermint Patty, bean-bag doll, Hasbro, 1973, M ..**10.00**
Maxwell House Coffee, Papa Bear, plush, sleep shirt/hat, M **10.00**
Nestle, Little Hans, print cloth, 1970, M **20.00**
Nestle, Little Hans, vinyl, clothed, 1969, 12½", M **40.00**
Nestle, Quik Bunny, plush, 1976-77, 24", M **20.00**
Old Crow Whiskey, Old Crow, stuffed cloth, 1970, 28", M **25.00**
Peabody Guaranteed Overalls, man, print cloth, 17", M **65.00**
Pepperidge Farm, Gingerman, foam-filled pillow type, M **6.00**
Pepperidge Farm, goldfish, gold cloth pillow type, 16" L, M **6.00**
Peters Weatherbird Shoes, girl, cloth, compo head/arms, 22", M .**65.00**
Peters Weatherbird Shoes, girl, pnt bsk, 2½", M **40.00**
Philip Morris, Johnny the bellhop, cloth w/compo head, 15", M ..**125.00**
Phillips 66, Buddy Lee, tan shirt/brn pants, no hat, EX **275.00**
Pillsbury, Doughboy, stuffed cloth, 1972, 11", EX **15.00**
Pitti Sing, uncut **130.00**
Revlon, Little Miss Revlon, vinyl, clothed, 1950, 10½", M **25.00**
Revlon, Little Miss Revlon, vinyl, clothed, 1956, 18", M **50.00**
Seven-Up, Fresh Up Freddie, cloth w/rubber head, 1958, 24", M .**30.00**
Shakey's Pizza, Pizza Chef, vinyl, 9½", VG **75.00**
StarKist Tuna, Charlie Tuna, squeeze vinyl, 1974, EX **40.00**
Sunshine Animal Crackers, elephant, 3-D, print cloth, 7", M **55.00**
Toys R Us, Geoffrey the giraffe, plush, 1967, 25", M **15.00**
Trailways, bus hostess, stuffed nylon, clothed, 1970s, 12", M **5.00**
Welch's Grape Juice, Wally Welch, hand puppet, 9", EX **3.00**

African Art

African art does not consist of a single class of objects. Rather, these often-powerful sculptures are carved by many varying African tribes and groups across the central continent; each item represents specific cultural and spiritual functions and meanings. Many kinds of materials are used including wood, metal, fiber, ivory, and bone. Considerable numbers of these items are now being reproduced and sold to the tourist trade, but 'authentic' African art is generally considered to consist of objects which were used in cultural and religious activities. The items listed here are authentic, in good condition, and considered to be of average aesthetic quality. Scott Nelson, a collector of African art, is our advisor; his address is listed in the Directory under New Mexico.

Basket, Nigeria, open, fiber w/cowrie shells, 8x10" **125.00**
Beads, trade, ceramic, string of 20 ....**100.00**
Bracelet, Ashanti, bronze, knobs **30.00**
Cloth, Kuba, geometric design, 18" sq **175.00**
Comb, Ashanti, bird's head surmount, 4" **200.00**
Container, Luba, gourd, wooden figural stopper **60.00**

Container, Warega, ivory, 15" **200.00**
Divination board, Yoruba, animals, 20" dia **475.00**
Doll, Ewe, pnt figure, 5" **175.00**
Doll, Mossi, abstract human figure **275.00**
Door, Dogon, granary, human figures, 26" **1,500.00**
Drum, Hemba, geometric designs, 22" **275.00**
Earrings, Massai, beaded, 6" **275.00**
Figure, Baule, standing female, 14" **250.00**
Figure, Dogon, crouched male, 10" **650.00**
Figure, Yoruba, pnt Colonial, 12" **175.00**
Goldweight, Ashanti, bronze turtle **125.00**
Hat, Kuba, fiber, blk pnt **175.00**
Headdress, Bamana, Tchi-wara (antelope), horizontal **475.00**
Headrest, Luba, supporting human figure, 5" **375.00**
Heddle pulley, Semifo, bird surmount, 5" **375.00**
Ibejis, Yoruba, 9", pr **375.00**
Knife, Kuba, throwing, str blade, 14" **125.00**
Lock, Bamana, door, 2 figural surmounts, 14" **575.00**
Mask, Bamana, N'Tomo, 14" **275.00**
Mask, Dan, human face, 15" **375.00**
Mask, Dogon, Kamaga, 26" **800.00**
Mask, Karumba, polychrome, antelope, 21" **475.00**
Mask, Mende, helmet, female initiation, 12" **675.00**

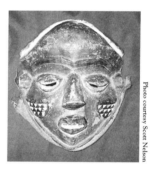

Mask, Pende, human face, 8", $275.00.

Pendant, Yoruba, ivory human figure, 4" **800.00**
Pipe, Cameroons, elephant, brass, 14" **275.00**
Ring, Dogon, bronze, horse & rider **275.00**
Slingshot, Baule, animal head, 5" **85.00**
Stool, Lega, human figural supports, 13" **475.00**
Whisk, Yoruba, human figure, wood & horsehair, 12" **275.00**

Agata

Agata is New England peachblow (the factory called it 'Wild Rose') with an applied metallic stain which produces gold tracery and dark blue mottling. The stain is subject to wear, and the amount of remaining stain greatly affects the value. It is especially valuable (and rare) when found on peachblow of intense color. Caution! Be sure to use only gentle cleaning methods.

Currently rare types of art glass have been realizing erratic prices at auction; until they stablize, we can only suggest an average range of values. In the listings that follow, examples are glossy unless noted otherwise. A condition rating of 'EX' indicates that the stain shows a slight amount of wear. Our advisors for this category are Betty and Clarence Maier; they are listed in the Directory under Pennsylvania. See also Green Opaque.

Bowl, finger; shiny, EX gold & mottling, 2½x5¼" **675.00**
Celery vase, scalloped, VG mottling, 6½" **975.00**

Celery vase, sqd/scalloped rim, M mottling, 6½" 1,950.00
Creamer, sq rim, mottled reed hdl, M mottling 1,800.00
Cruet, NM mottling 2,000.00
Pitcher, sq rim, sparce mottling, 6¼" 725.00
Pitcher, sq rim, tapered, M mottling, 6" 2,750.00
Punch cup, NM mottling, 12½" 350.00
Spooner, worn mottling, sq top, 4½" 350.00
Toothpick holder, sqd rim, EX color & mottling, 2¼" 1,000.00
Toothpick holder, tricorner, worn mottling, 2½" 525.00
Tumbler, EX color & mottling, 3¾" 1,000.00
Vase, lily; EX color & mottling 950.00
Vase, satin, M blk tracery, waisted, 10" 1,450.00
Vase, scalloped, M mottling, 6½" 1,200.00

Agate Ware

Clays of various natural or artifically dyed colors were combined to produce agate ware, a procedure similar to the methods used by Niloak in potting their Mission Ware. It was made by many Staffordshire potteries from about 1740 until about 1825.

Coffeepot, tankard form, strap hdl, rstr, 6½" 11,000.00
Creamer, mask & paw molded ft, rprs, 4⅝" 575.00
Mug, milk; fluted, cream w/brn marbleizing, 5¼" 1,000.00
Pitcher, brn/cream clays, ribbed strap hdl, 6½", NM 775.00
Tea caddy, sq w/canted corners, rpl lid, rim chips, 4" 2,600.00
Teapot, bl/brn/cream, Staffordshire, ca 1760, rstr, 3½" 500.00
Teapot, brn/red/cream/gr mottle, 1870s, 5⅝", +cr/sug/4 c/s 550.00

Akro Agate

The Akro Agate Co., founded in 1914 primarily as a marble maker, operated in Clarksburg, West Virginia, until 1951. Their popular wares included children's dishes, powder jars, flowerpots, and novelty items along with the famous 'Akro Aggies.' Much of their glass was produced in the distinctive marbleized colors they called Red Onyx, Blue Onyx, etc.; solid opaque and transparent colors were also produced. Most of the wares are marked with their trademark, a crow flying through the letter 'A' holding an Aggie in its beak and one in each claw. Other marks include 'J.P.' on children's pieces, 'J.V. Co., Inc.,' 'Braun & Corwin,' 'N.Y.C. Vogue Merc Co. U.S.A.,' 'Hamilton Match Co.,' and 'Mexicali Pickwick Cosmetic Corp.' on novelty items. In 1936 Akro obtained the molds from the Balmer-Westite Co. of Weston, West Virginia. Westite produced a similar line of products for several years. Their ware is drab in color when compared to Akro and is generally unmarked. The embossed Westite logo does appear occasionally on the bottoms of some pieces. Westite is commonly accepted as a companion collectible of Akro.

For more information we recommend *The Collector's Encyclopedia of Children's Dishes* by Margaret and Kenn Whitmyer, available at your local bookstore. Our advisor for miscellaneous Akro Agate is Albert Morin; he is listed in the Directory under Massachusetts.

Chiquita

Creamer, baked-on colors, 1½" 8.00
Creamer, crystal, 1½" 24.00
Creamer, transparent cobalt 16.00
Cup, transparent cobalt, 1½" 8.00
Saucer, baked-on colors, 3⅛" 2.00
Set, opaque colors other than gr, 12-pc, MIB 125.00
Set, transparent cobalt, 12-pc, MIB 130.00

Chiquita, 12-piece set (3 pieces shown), opaque colors other than green, $100.00 for set.

Sugar bowl (open), baked-on colors, 1½" 8.00
Sugar bowl (open), transparent cobalt, 1½" 16.00
Teapot, opaque gr, 3" 14.00

Concentric Rib

Creamer, sm, opaque colors other than gr or wht, 1¼" 16.00
Cup, sm, opaque colors other than gr or wht, 1¼" 8.00
Plate, sm, opaque colors other than gr or wht, 3¼" 7.00
Set, sm, opaque colors other than gr or wht, 8-pc 55.00
Set, sm, opaque gr or wht, 10-pc 53.00
Sugar bowl (open), sm, opaque colors other than gr or wht, 1¼" .16.00
Teapot, sm, opaque gr or wht, 3⅜" 12.00

Concentric Ring

Cereal bowl, lg, transparent cobalt, 3⅜" 40.00
Creamer, lg, opaque colors, 1⅜" 25.00
Creamer, sm, opaque colors, 1¼" 20.00
Cup, lg, yel, 1⅜" 50.00
Cup, sm, yel & lav, 1¼" 30.00
Plate, sm, transparent cobalt, 3¼" 20.00
Saucer, lg, marbleized bl, 3⅛" 15.00
Set, lg, transparent cobalt, 21-pc 560.00

Interior Panel, Stippled Interior Panel

Cereal bowl, lg, azure bl, 3⅜" 30.00
Cereal bowl, lg, marbleized gr & wht, 3⅜" 30.00
Creamer, lg, marbleized gr & wht, 1⅜" 25.00
Creamer, lg, opaque yel, 1⅜" 35.00
Creamer, sm, marbleized red & wht, 1¼" 35.00
Creamer, sm, opaque cobalt, wht lid, 1¼" 45.00
Creamer, sm, pk lustre, 1¼" 27.00
Cup, lg, marbleized bl & wht, 1⅜" 25.00
Cup, sm, azure bl, 1¼" 30.00
Cup, sm, pumpkin, 1¼" 20.00
Cup, sm, transparent gr or topaz, 1¼" 10.00
Plate, lg, lemonade & oxblood, 4¼" 15.00
Plate, lg, transparent gr, 4¼" 6.00
Plate, sm, marblcized bl & wht, 3¾" 16.00
Plate, sm, transparent gr 5.00
Saucer, lg, lemonade & oxblood, 3⅛" 10.00
Set, azure bl, 8-pc, MIB 135.00
Set, lg, azure bl, 21-pc, MIB 467.00
Set, lg, transparent topaz, 21-pc, MIB 200.00
Set, sm, marbleized red & wht, 16-pc 315.00
Sugar bowl, lg, gr lustre, w/lid, 1⅞" 35.00
Sugar bowl, lg, lemonade & oxblood, w/lid, 1⅞" 50.00
Sugar bowl, lg, transparent gr, w/lid, 1⅞" 32.00
Sugar bowl, sm, azure bl, 1¼" 35.00
Teapot, sm, marbleized gr & wht, 3⅜" 35.00
Teapot, sm, transparent gr, 3⅜" 30.00

Tumbler, sm, gr lustre, 2" 9.50

J.P. (Made for J. Pressman Company)

Cereal, lg, transparent red or brn, 3¾" 50.00
Creamer, lg, lt bl or crystal, 1½" 30.00
Cup, lg, transparent bl, ribbed, 1½" 25.00
Plate, lg, lt bl or crystal, 4¼" 10.00
Plate, lg, transparent, gr or brn, 4¼" 12.00
Set, lg, transparent gr or brn, 16-pc, MIB 300.00
Sugar bowl, lg, lt bl or crystal, 1½" 30.00

Miss America

Creamer, wht, 1¼" 50.00
Creamer, wht w/decal, 1¼" 65.00
Cup, wht, 1⅝" 40.00
Plate, forest gr, 4½" 45.00
Saucer, wht, 3⅝" 15.00
Set, wht, 17-pc, MIB 515.00
Sugar bowl, wht, w/lid, 2" 65.00
Sugar bowl, wht w/decal, w/lid, 2" 85.00
Teapot, orange & wht, 3¼" 140.00

Octagonal

Cereal bowl, lg, gr or wht, 3⅜" 10.00
Creamer, lg, lemonade & oxblood, closed hdl, 1½" 30.00
Creamer, lg, pumpkin, closed hdl, 1½" 30.00
Creamer, sm, dk gr, 1¼" 16.00
Cup, lg, lt bl, closed hdl, 1½" 15.00
Cup, sm, bl or wht, 1¼" 10.00
Pitcher, sm, lime gr, 2¾" 27.00
Plate, lg, opaque yel, 4¼" 6.50
Saucer, lg, dk bl, 4¼" 4.00
Set, lg, lemonade & oxblood, 17-pc, MIB 325.00
Set, lg, mixed colors (pk, yel, other opaques), 21-pc, MIB 185.00
Set, sm, gr & wht, 16-pc 140.00
Teapot, lg, pk, closed hdl, 3⅝" 25.00
Teapot, sm, dk gr, wht lid, 3⅜" 20.00
Tumbler, sm, bl or wht, 2" 14.00

Raised Daisy

Creamer, yel, 1¾" 50.00
Cup, bl, 1¾" 65.00
Plate, bl, 3" 14.00
Saucer, beige, 2½" 9.00
Sugar bowl, yel, 1¾" 50.00
Teapot, bl, w/lid, 2⅜" 85.00
Teapot, gr, 2⅜" 25.00
Tumbler, beige, 2" 30.00

Stacked Disc

Creamer, sm, opaque colors other than gr or wht, 1¼" 14.00
Cup, sm, opaque gr or wht, 1¼" 6.00
Pitcher, sm, opaque colors other than gr or wht, 2⅞" 16.00
Pitcher, sm, opaque gr or wht, 2⅞" 14.00
Plate, sm, opaque gr or wht, 3¼" 3.00
Set, sm, opaque colors other than gr or wht, 21-pc, MIB 195.00
Sugar bowl (open), sm, opaque colors other than gr or wht, 1¼" .14.00
Teapot, sm, opaque gr, w/wht lid, 3⅜" 15.00
Tumbler, opaque colors other than gr, 2" 14.00

Stacked Disc and Interior Panel

Cereal, lg, transparent gr, 3⅜" 22.00
Cereal, transparent cobalt, 3⅜" 30.00
Creamer, lg, opaque colors, 1⅜" 25.00
Creamer, sm, transparent amber, 1¼" 30.00
Cup, lg, transparent cobalt, 1⅜" 27.50
Cup, lg, transparent gr, 1⅜" 25.00
Cup, sm, opaque colors, 1¼" 12.00
Cup, sm, transparent gr, 1¼" 15.00
Pitcher, sm, transparent amber, 2⅞" 18.00
Pitcher, sm, transparent cobalt, 2⅞" 27.00
Plate, lg, marbleized bl, 4¾" 35.00
Plate, lg, transparent gr, 4¾" 12.00
Plate, sm, marbleized bl, 3¼" 35.00
Plate, sm, opaque colors, 3¼" 8.00
Saucer, lg, marbleized bl, 3¼" 15.00
Saucer, lg, opaque colors, 3¼" 6.00
Saucer, sm, transparent gr, 2¾" 8.00
Set, lg, transparent gr, 17-pc, MIB 160.00
Set, sm, transparent gr, 8-pc, MIB 100.00
Sugar bowl, lg, transparent gr, w/lid, 1⅞" 40.00
Sugar bowl, sm, marbleized bl, w/lid, 1¼" 65.00
Sugar bowl, sm, opaque colors, w/lid, 1¼" 18.00
Teapot, lg, opaque colors, 3¾" 50.00
Teapot, lg, opaque colors, 3¾" 45.00
Teapot, lg, transparent amber, 3¾" 40.00
Teapot, sm, marbleized bl, 3⅜" 125.00
Teapot, sm, transparent cobalt, 3⅜" 50.00
Tumbler, sm, opaque colors, 2" 50.00

Stippled Band

Creamer, lg, transparent amber, 1½" 22.00
Cup, lg, transparent amber, 1½" 15.00
Saucer, sm, transparent gr or amber, 2¾" 2.50
Set, lg, transparent gr, 21-pc, MIB 55.00
Set, sm, transparent gr, 8-pc, MIB 47.00
Sugar bowl, lg, transparent amber, w/lid, 1⅞" 30.00
Teapot, sm, transparent gr, 3⅜" 20.00
Tumbler, sm, transparent amber, 1¾" 11.00

Miscellaneous

Ashtray, Hamilton match holder, yel 135.00
Ashtray, heart card symbol, wht, 4" dia 195.00
Ashtray, heavy sq, bl/wht, lg 50.00
Ashtray, leaf, gr/wht 8.00
Ashtray, shell, orange/wht 8.00
Basket, bl/wht, 1-hdl 450.00
Basket, gr/wht, 2-hdl 45.00
Bell, bl 75.00
Bell, orange 275.00
Bowl, blk, Graduated Darts, #320 ....35.00
Bowl, cobalt, tab hdls, 7¼" 32.50
Bowl, finger; marbleized colors 10.00
Bowl, ivy design, bl, #323 ....28.00
Bowl, orange, tab hdl, #321 ....38.00
Bowl, oxblood/wht, #340 ....45.00
Candlesticks, gr/wht, 3¼", pr 395.00
Candlesticks, orange, 3¼", pr 275.00
Cornucopia, NYC Gogue Merc, bl/wht 16.00
Cornucopia, orange/wht, #765 ....15.00
Flowerpot, all colors, ribbed top, #291½, ea 8.00

Flowerpot, Banded Darts, orange/wht, #301 ....65.00
Flowerpot, blk, ribbed top, #300F 35.00
Flowerpot, combo, all colors, #295, ea 250.00
Flowerpot, factory decor, #1309 ....235.00
Flowerpot, Graduated Darts, orange, #307 ....45.00
Flowerpot, ivory, #1311 ....200.00
Flowerpot, Ribs & Flutes, orange, #296 ....24.00
J Vivaudou, mortar & pestle jar, blk, #331 ....24.00
J Vivaudou, puff box, bl, #334 ....195.00
J Vivaudou, shaving mug, blk 48.00
Knife, crystal, grid style, #739 ....45.00
Lamp, crystal, wall type, 3-pc 28.00
Lamp, ivory, 5-pc 65.00
Lamp, marbleized, 5-pc 95.00
Marble box, 100 #0 Akro Specials 400.00
Marble box, 100 #1 Moss Agates 350.00
Marble box, 25 #1 Akro Flinties 600.00
Planter, gr, rectangular w/rnd corners, #652 ....48.00
Planter, Japanese style, orange, #650 ....250.00
Planter, orange, oval, #654 ....18.00
Powder jar, apple form, orange 325.00
Powder jar, colonial lady, bl 75.00
Powder jar, Scottie dog figural, pk 75.00
Powder jar, treasure trunk form, orange/wht 125.00
Vase, Graduated Darts, royal bl, #312 ....125.00
Vase, orange, tab hdls, #317 ....95.00
Vase, Ribs & Flutes, yel, #311 ....135.00
Westite, bowl, fruit; marbleized, ftd 125.00
Westite, bud vase, brn/wht, #315 ....125.00
Westite, flowerpot, gr/wht, #305 ....20.00
Westite, vase, brn/wht, #312 ....65.00

Alamo Pottery

Operating for only a few years during the middle of the 20th century, Alamo Pottery Inc. was located in Texas where they produced dinnerware as well as some commercial art ware.

Flowerpot, gr 25.00
Planter, maroon, #829, 12" 100.00
Vase, sponged, 14" 50.00

Alexandrite

Alexandrite is a type of art glass introduced around the turn of the century by Thomas Webb and Sons of England. It is recognized by its characteristic shading, pale yellow to rose and blue at the edge of the item. Although other companies produced glass they called alexandrite, only examples made by Webb possess all the described characteristics and command premium prices. Amount and intensity of blue determines value. Our advisors for this category are Betty and Clarence Maier; they are listed in the Directory under Pennsylvania.

Compote, Optic Honeycomb, ftd, Webb, 1⅝x5" 975.00
Finger bowl, ribbed, reverse swirl ruffled rim, +6" plate 1,300.00
Punch cup, bbl shape, 2¾" 550.00
Toothpick holder, honeycomb pattern, 6-crimp rim, 2⅞" 1,100.00

Almanacs

The earliest evidence indicates that almanacs were used as long ago as Ancient Egypt. Throughout the Dark Ages they were circulated in great volume and were referred to by more people than any other book except the Bible. *The Old Farmer's Almanac* first appeared in 1793 and has been issued annually since that time. Usually more of a pamphlet than a book (only a few have hard covers), the almanac provided planting and harvesting information to farmers, weather forecasts for seamen, medical advice, household hints, mathematical tutoring, postal rates, railroad schedules, weights and measures, 'receipts,' and jokes. Before 1800 the information was unscientific and based entirely on astrology and folklore. The first almanac in America was printed in 1639 by William Pierce Mariner; it contained data of this nature. One of the best-known editions, Ben Franklin's *Poor Richard's Almanac*, was introduced in 1732 and continued to be printed for twenty-five years.

By the 19th century, merchants saw the advertising potential in a publication so widely distributed, and the advertising almanac evolved. These were distributed free of charge by drug stores and mercantiles and were usually somewhat lacking in information, containing simply a calendar, a few jokes, and a variety of ads for quick remedies and quack cures.

Today their concept and informative, often amusing, text make almanacs popular collectibles that may usually be had at reasonable prices. Because they were printed in such large numbers and often saved from year to year, their prices are still low. Most fall within a range of $4.00 to $15.00. Very common examples may be virtually worthless; those printed before 1860 are especially collectible. Quite rare and highly prized are the Kate Greenaway 'Almanacks,' printed in London from 1883 to 1897. These are illustrated with her drawings of children, one for each calendar month.

1898, Dr Harter's Almanac and Weather
Forecasts, Dayton O, color cover, EX, $12.00.

1833, Dr Miles, EX 8.00
1837, The Temperance, EX 20.00
1840, People's, EX 10.00
1856, Old Farmer's, EX 10.00
1862, Farmers & Planters, Croadsale, Campbell & Co, Phila, 18-pg .20.00
1865, Ayer's American, Lowell MA, 36-pg, 7¾x5", NM 20.00
1871, Farmers & Mechanics, AL Scovill & Co, EX 15.00
1873, Centaur, VG 8.00
1874, Hostetter's Illustrated US, Pittsburgh PA, 8x5¼", EX 16.00
1874, The Family, VG 8.00
1875, Jayne's Medical...& Guide to Health, 40-pg, 9x5¾", EX 12.50
1880, Rush's Almanac & Guide to Health, G 10.00
1881, Gargling Oil, EX 15.00
1882-83, Wakefield's Western Farmer's...& Account Book, 32-pg ...10.00
1889, Burdock Blood Bitters...& Key to Health, NY, 32-pg, EX 15.00
1889, Dr Harter's..., St Louis MO, 30-pg, 7½x5", VG 10.00
1890, Ayer's American, EX 10.00
1892, Ayer's American, VG 6.00
1893, Kickapoo Indian, NM 35.00

1894, Hostetter's Bitters	12.00
1894, Indianapolis News, EX	12.00
1895, Ayer's Sarsaparilla	7.00
1896, Dr King's Guide to Health & Household Instructor, 32-pg	16.00
1898, Old Farmer's, EX	6.00
1899, Peruna Drug Mfg, Columbus OH, EX	10.00
1902, Simmons Liver Regulator	10.00
1903, Ayer's American, lion & bottle litho on cover, 32-pg, NM	15.00
1903, Herrick's, NY, 32-pg, 8x5½", VG	10.00
1903, Peruna, Peruna Drug Co building on cover, 32-pg, EX	15.00
1905, Herrick's, G	6.00
1909, Ayer's American, lion on cover, 32-pg, NM	12.50
1916, Rev IR Hicks, many photos, Word & Works, 196-pg, 6x8½"	30.00
1925, NARD (National Association of Retail Druggists), EX	6.00
1927, Swamp Root, EX	15.00
1929, Dr Jayne's Medical...& Guide to Health, 32-pg, EX	10.00
1929, Dr Miles' New Weather...& Handbook, 32-pg, G	10.00
1931, Dr Pierce's Treasure Chest, NM	6.00
1933, The Herbalist/Indiana Botanic Gardens, VG+	12.00
1936, Dr Morse's...& Weather Forecaster, 32-pg, EX	12.00
1936, Herb Medicine Co, G	8.00
1938, Uncle Sam's, EX	10.00
1940, Swamp Root/Dr Kilmer & Co, VG	5.00
1941, De Laval Handy Reference Yearbook, 48-pg, VG	12.50
1941, Dr Miles, EX	5.00
1944, Flying Red Horse	6.00
1945, BF Goodrich Farmer's Handbook & Almanac, EX	12.00
1947, The Herbalist/Indiana Botanic Gardens, VG+	10.00

Aluminum

Aluminum, though being the most abundant metal in the earth's crust, always occurs in combination with other elements. Before a practical method for its refinement was developed in the late 19th century, articles made of aluminum were very expensive. After the process for commercial smelting was perfected in 1916, it became profitable to adapt the ductile, non-tarnishing material to many uses.

By the late thirties, novelties, trays, pitchers, and many other tableware items were being produced. They were often handcrafted with elaborate decoration. Russel Wright designed a line of lovely pieces such as lamps, vases, and desk accessories that are becoming very collectible. Many who crafted the ware marked it with their company logo, and these signed pieces are attracting the most interest. Wendell August Forge (Grove City, PA) is a mark to watch for; this firm produced some particularly nice examples and upwardly mobile market values reflect their popularity with today's collectors. In general, 'spun' aluminum is from the thirties or early forties, and 'hammered' aluminum is from the fifties.

For further information, refer to *Hammered Aluminum, Hand Wrought Collectibles*, by our advisor for this category, Dannie Woodard (listed in the Directory under Texas), and *Collectible Aluminum, An Identification and Value Guide*, by Everett Grist.

Water set: Pitcher, 7¼", 6 tumblers, each 5¼", $40.00 for the set.

Ashtray, bamboo, single rest, Everlast, 5" dia	30.00
Basket, flower/leaf band, fluted/serrated bowl, Everlast, 9"	15.00
Basket, mums, flared bowl, hdl w/twisted middle, Forman, 5"	20.00
Basket, poinsettia, fluted bowl, rnd hdl, Farber/Shelvin, 7"	10.00
Bowl, dogwood & butterflies, anodized gold, Armour, 8" sq	45.00
Bowl, tulip, hammmered ground, eared hdls, R Kent, 10" dia	30.00
Bowl, wheat, plain rim, Palmer/Smith, 14" dia	90.00
Buffet dish, polished, S-shaped tulip legs/finial, unmk, 9"	40.00
Candlesticks, S-shaped w/tulip, beaded edge, unmk, 8", pr	45.00
Casserole, floral band on lid, rolled hdls, Everlast, 9"	25.00
Casserole, hammered/beaded edges, loop finial, Buenilum, 8"	15.00
Cigarette box, dogwood, rectangular, W August, 5½"	75.00
Coasters, bamboo, Everlast, set of 8 w/ftd & hdld holder	30.00
Coasters, tulip-shaped, R Kent, set of 4 w/basket holder	35.00
Crumb brush & tray, tulip & ribbon, hammered ground, unmk	25.00
Dip server, bamboo structure w/3 hammered bowls, Everlast, 11"	60.00
Gravy boat w/plate, polished, beaded edges, Buenilum, 6"	20.00
Hurricane lamp, dbl, twisted/looped center hdl, Buenilum, 10"	30.00
Ice bucket, hammered beehive shape/sling hdl, unmk, 8"	15.00
Ice bucket, hammered rows, self-open lid, rnd hdl, unmk, 8"	10.00
Ice bucket (open), acorn/leaf, cane-shaped hdls, Continental	25.00
Lazy susan, acorn, flower & leaf hdls, unmk, 18" dia	25.00
Money clip, butterfly, DeMarsh	12.00
Pitcher, concentric bands, anodized copper, Color Craft, 8"	10.00
Pitcher, hammered, fluted flared rim, angled hdl, unmk, 6"	20.00
Pitcher, tulip, serrated edge, ice lip/ear hdl, R Kent, 9"	35.00
Plate, dogwood, plain edge, W August, 9"	30.00
Table, rnd tray top w/folding legs, W August	595.00
Teapot, hammered, NC Joseph, Stafford, England, 2-cup	20.00
Tray, bread; acorns & grapes, oval, W August, 7x11"	45.00
Tray, bread; floral spray, raised rim, unmk, 7x12"	20.00
Tray, sandwich; acorn, fluted edge, applied hdls, unmk, 11"	30.00
Tray, sandwich; berry & leaf, hammered ground, Farberware, 11"	10.00
Tray, sandwich; ivy ring, applied hdls, Everlast, 11" dia	15.00
Tray, sandwich; rose spray, crimped edge, Everlast, 12" sq	25.00
Tray, serving; mums, hammered, hdld, Continental, 8x11"	30.00
Tray, serving; thistle, fluted, loop hdls, Farber/Schlevin, 13"	10.00
Tray, serving; tulips, hammered, R Kent, 20x14"	40.00
Tray, 2-tier tidbit; roses, flared fluted edges, unmk, 11"	25.00
Tray, 2-tier tidbit; tulip spray/serrated edge, unmk, 10"	25.00
Trivet, acorn, fluted/serrated edge, Continental, 10" dia	30.00
Trivet, grapevine band, Everlast, 10" dia	15.00
Wastebasket, pine cone, fluted edge, W August, 11"	150.00

AMACO, American Art Clay Co.

AMACO is the logo of the American Art Clay Co. Inc., founded in Indianapolis, Indiana, in 1919, by Ted O. Philpot. They produced a line of art pottery from 1931 through 1938. The company is still in business but now produces only supplies, implements, and tools for the ceramic trade.

Values for AMACO have risen sharply, especially those for figurals, items with Art Deco styling, and pieces with uncommon shapes. Our advisor for this category is Virginia Heiss; she is listed in the Directory under Indiana.

Bowl, #58, Octagon, blk gloss, 4x9¾"	250.00
Deco head, #152, wht gloss, 6"	140.00
Vase, #S-3, bl/cream, 3"	45.00
Vase, #13, blood red, early mk, 8x7½"	145.00
Vase, #164, bl gloss, trumpet form, 12"	135.00
Vase, #22, gr matt, 2 sm hdls, 6"	45.00
Vase, #31, gray crystalline, 7½"	95.00

Vase, #39, bl matt, w/hdls, 6x4½" 85.00
Vase, #40, gr matt, w/hdls, 6x4" 45.00
Vase, #49, gr matt, w/hdls, 9" 125.00
Vase, #6, gr matt, 2 lg hdls, 9" 125.00
Vase, #75, yel matt, stick form, 5" 45.00
Vase, #95, blk gloss, 7" 120.00
Vase, #98, tan gloss, Deco globe shape, 6" 135.00

Amberina

Amberina, one of the earliest types of art glass, was developed in 1883 by Joseph Locke of the New England Glass Company. The trademark was registered by W.L. Libbey, who often signed his name in script within the pontil.

Amberina was made by adding gold powder to the batch, which produced glass in the basic amber hue. Part of the item, usually the top, was simply reheated to develop the characteristic deep red or fuchsia shading. Early amberina was mold-blown, but cut and pressed amberina was also produced. The rarest type is plated amberina, made by New England for a short time after 1886. It has been estimated that less than 2,000 pieces were ever produced. Other companies, among them Hobbs and Brockunier, Mt. Washington Glass Company, and Sowerby's Ellison Glassworks of England, made their own versions, being careful to change the name of their product to avoid infringing on Libbey's patent. Prices realized at auction seem to be erratic, to say the least, and dealers appear to be 'testing the waters' with prices that start out very high only to be reduced later if the item does not sell at the original asking price. Lots of amberina glassware is of a more recent vintage — look for evidence of an early production, since the later wares are worth much less than glassware that can be attributed to the older makers. Generic amberina with hand-painted flowers will bring lower prices as well. Our values are taken from auction results and dealer lists, omitting the extremely high and low ends of the range. See also Libbey.

Basket, swirled poke-bonnet shape w/amber hdl, 10¾x7" 395.00
Bowl, Daisy & Button, Hobbs, 2⅛x7⅛" sq 575.00
Bowl, Dmn Quilt, ruffled, 4x8¾" 465.00
Bowl, Dmn Quilt, 2x5" 195.00
Bowl, ruffled, 2½x5¼" 150.00
Bowl, sauce; Dmn Quilt, 1¼x4" 125.00
Bowl, swirled ribs, 4⅝" 125.00
Bowl, wavy rim, NE Glass, 2¾x5¼" 450.00
Celery vase, Dmn Quilt, sqd/scalloped rim, NE Glass, 6½" 400.00
Celery vase, Invt T'print, ribbed, 6¾" 200.00
Celery vase, sq, crimped rim, good color 275.00
Cruet, Invt T'print, amber faceted stopper, 6" 425.00
Cruet, Invt T'print, faceted stopper, NE Glass, 6¾" 850.00
Cruet, swirled w/tri-fold rim, amber faceted stopper, 6" 535.00
Custard cup, Dmn Quilt, amber reeded hdl, 2¾x2⅝" 175.00
Custard cup, paneled sides, reeded hdl, NE Glass, 2⅛x2½" 225.00
Finger bowl, Hobnail, 2⅞x4¼" sq 85.00
Goblet, water; internal ribs, 6⅛x3⅜" 300.00
Lamp, hall; Invt T'print, brass base & top, 12½" 350.00
Lamp globe, craquelle, 3" dia fitter, 6½x6½" 145.00
Mug, gold branches, swirled, amber rope hdl, 5½" 225.00
Nut dish, Daisy & Button, Gillinder, 1¾x6⅛x4¼" 375.00
Pitcher, Dmn Quilt, bulbous w/tricon rim, Midwestern, 4½" 350.00
Pitcher, Invt T'print, reeded hdl, NE Glass, 6" 450.00
Pitcher, Optic, cylindrical, 10x4¾", +8 5¼" tumblers 495.00
Pitcher, Swirl, amber hdl, 7½" 300.00
Pitcher, tankard; amber hdl, 4⅝x3" 400.00
Pitcher, tankard; Dmn Quilt, amberina hdl, 8½" 500.00
Pitcher, tankard; 10-panel, amber reeded hdl, 6¾" 645.00

Punch cup, 18 optic ribs, NE Glass, 2½" 185.00
Salt cellar, Daisy & Button yacht, Hobbs & Brockunier, 4½" 375.00
Spooner, Optic Dmn Quilt, NE Glass, 4½" 300.00
Toothpick holder, Daisy & Button, ftd, 3" 350.00
Toothpick holder, Dmn Quilt, sq top, NE Glass 475.00
Toothpick holder, Dmn Quilt, tricorner, 2⅜" 250.00
Toothpick holder, Venetian Dmn, tricorner, NE Glass, 2¼x3" 450.00
Trinket dish, Dmn Quilt w/flared rim, Mt WA, 4¾" dia 150.00
Tumbler, juice; amber loop reeded hdl, NE Glass, 3⅜x2½" 400.00
Tumbler, juice; Invt T'print, 3¾x2¾" 45.00
Tumbler, Swirl, 3⅞x2⅝" 150.00
Vase, Basketweave, amber ruffle, 9½x4¾" 195.00
Vase, calla-lily shape, ftd, appl spiral trim, 12¼x3¼" 175.00
Vase, elongated t'print, cylindrical, 7½" 175.00
Vase, HP florals, cylindrical, 6⅜x3⅞" 225.00
Vase, HP florals w/gold, ruffled, dimpled sides, 5¼x3⅝" 225.00
Vase, lily; faint ribs, NE Glass, 8" 650.00
Vase, lily; no ribbing, appl wafer base, 6¾" 700.00
Vase, lily; ribbed, 10" 275.00
Vase, optic dmns, roll-down rim, 6¾" 485.00
Vase, posy; Invt T'print, 3x2¼" 350.00
Vase, ribbed stem, flared pie-crust rim, rnd ft, 7" 250.00
Vase, ribbed trumpet on appl bulb stem, ped ft, 23¾" 700.00
Vase, trumpet; fold-over rim, 6" dia base, 20" 850.00

Plated Amberina

Cruet 8,500.00
Mug, amber hdl 2,300.00
Pitcher, bulbous w/tricorn rim, dk amber hdl, 6¼" 10,000.00
Pitcher, tankard, amber hdl, 7" 12,000.00
Plate, ruffled, 6⅜" 1,300.00
Tumbler, 4", M 2,450.00
Vase, lav to red to yel, NE Glass, 3½" 3,200.00
Vase, lily; slight swirl at 3-fold rim, 9½" 5,000.00

American Bisque

The American Bisque Pottery operated in Williamstown, West Virginia, from 1919 to 1982. The company was begun by Mr. B.E. Allen and remained an Allen-family business until its sale in 1982. Figural pottery was produced from approximately 1937 until about the time the pottery sold.

American Bisque pottery is often identified by the 'wedges' or dry-footed cleats on the bottom of the ware. Many cookie jar designs are unique to the American Bisque Company, such as cookie jars with blackboards and magnets, cookie jars with lids that doubled as serving trays, and cookie jars with 'action pieces' which show movement. American Bisque pieces are very collectible and are available in a broad variety of color schemes; some items are decorated with 22-24k gold. Many items are modeled after highly popular copyrighted characters.

For further information, we recommend American Bisque, Collector's Guide With Prices, by our advisor Mary Jane Giacomini; she is listed in the Directory under California.

Bank, Bedtime Pig, 6½" 40.00
Bank, Bow Pig, 5½" 30.00
Bank, chick w/neck bow, 6½" 40.00
Bank, Chicken Feed, 4½" 25.00
Bank, Circus Elephant, 6" 45.00
Bank, Humpty Dumpty, mk Alice in Philcoland, 6" 120.00
Bank, Mr Pig, 6" 30.00
Bank, polar bear, gold trim, 6" 38.00

Cookie jar, Bear & the Beehive (flasher), mk Corner Cookie Jar ...500.00
Cookie jar, Beehive, plain 50.00
Cookie jar, Butter Churn, w/flowering vine 30.00
Cookie jar, Castle, mk Cardinal 310 USA 175.00
Cookie jar, Cat, w/tail finial, (Ungemach) mk USA 145.00
Cookie jar, Collegiate Owl, mk Cookies, gold trim 150.00
Cookie jar, Cookieville Bus Co 350.00
Cookie jar, Cow & Moon (flasher) 995.00
Cookie jar, Cow/Lamb Turnabout 195.00
Cookie jar, Crank Telephone, mk Cardinal 311 USA 80.00
Cookie jar, Crowing Rooster, spaced tail 85.00
Cookie jar, Dancing Pig, mc dotted dress 195.00
Cookie jar, Farmer Pig 145.00
Cookie jar, French Chef 125.00
Cookie jar, Gift Box 150.00
Cookie jar, Jack-In-The-Box 150.00
Cookie jar, Kitten on Quilt Base, mk Cookies 175.00
Cookie jar, Moon Rocket, mk Cookies Out of This World 275.00
Cookie jar, Oaken Bucket, spoon finial, bail hdl 195.00
Cookie jar, Pennsylvania Dutch Boy, in straw hat 425.00
Cookie jar, Sad Clown, I Want Some Cookies, mk Cardinal USA ..125.00
Cookie jar, Seal on Igloo 350.00
Cookie jar, Sentry, in striped guard house 135.00
Cookie jar, Stern Wheeler, tugboat 250.00
Cookie jar, Sweethearts, 2 children under umbrella 350.00
Cookie jar, Yarn Doll, gold trim 250.00
Pitcher, apple, gold trim 75.00
Pitcher, pig, red bow & clover blooms 175.00

Photo courtesy Mary Jane Giacomini

Planter, Winter Couple, $30.00.

Planter, bear w/beehive, gold trim, 5¾" 35.00
Planter, bear w/beehive, 5¾" 25.00
Planter, circus horse, unmk, 7" 35.00
Planter, deer & stump, 5½" 14.00
Planter, deer reclining, 5¾" 14.00
Planter, Dutch girl w/wooden shoe, 6" 10.00
Planter, elephant head on basket, 3¾" 12.00
Planter, elephant seated by stump, 4" 12.00
Planter, fish, smiling, unmk, 4¾" 25.00
Planter, golf bag, 6" 14.00
Planter, kitten asleep w/slipper, 2¾" 8.00
Planter, kitten w/fishbowl, 6" 24.00
Planter, lamb sleeping, 3" 18.00
Planter, lamb w/watering can, 6½" 14.00
Planter, mare & foal, unmk, 5¾" 32.00
Planter, parakeet on bucket w/flowering vine, 6" 14.00
Planter, pig farmer w/lg ear of corn, 6½" 8.00
Planter, pig sleeping, 2½" 18.00
Planter, pig w/wooden basket, 4¾" 14.00
Planter, poodle, 7" 22.00
Planter, rabbit hugging head of cabbage, unmk, 5" 20.00

Planter, rabbit in log, unmk, 5¾" 24.00
Planter, sailfish, unmk, 8x10" 50.00
Planter, swan w/leaves, 7x9¾" 28.00
Refrigerator bottle, flower on wht swirl, w/stopper, 8¾" 150.00
Salt & pepper shakers, birds w/heads up, beaks open, 4½" 22.00
Salt & pepper shakers, chefs, 5" 30.00
Sprinkler bottle, elephant 85.00
Wall pocket, creamer & sugar bowl, 3" & 4", pr 28.00
Wall pocket, hurricane lamp, 6" 24.00

American Encaustic Tiling Co.

A.E. Tile was organized in 1879 in Zanesville, Ohio. Until closing in 1935, they produced beautiful ornamental and architectural tile equal to the best European imports. They also made vases, figurines, and novelty items with exceptionally fine modeling and glazes.

Desk pc, ram on stepped base w/pen troughs, 1922, 5½" L 200.00
Figurine, elephant, gunmetal on blk drip, 5½" 110.00
Figurine, elephant walking, gray/ivory matt, rpr, 6½x11" 70.00
Figurine, lady w/urn, ivory w/blk/gilt, 11¼x7½x6" 750.00
Figurine, panther, blk gunmetal matt, 7x14½" 150.00
Inkwell, bl/yel-mustard crystalline, 2 lids, 2x5¾" 225.00
Paperweight, ram w/lg horns, orange matt & gloss, 3½x5½" 125.00
Vase, bl metallic, ear hdls, incised 'bat' faces, 6x4" 400.00
Vase, gr & brn gloss, 7", NM 100.00
Vase, lime crystalline w/violet & bl irid, hdls, #734, 9" 150.00

American Indian Art

That time when the American Indian was free to practice the crafts and culture that was his heritage has always held a fascination for many. They were a people who appreciated beauty of design and colorful decoration in their furnishings and clothing; and because instruction in their crafts was a routine part of their rearing, they were well accomplished. Several tribes developed areas in which they excelled. The Navajo were weavers and silversmiths, the Zuni, lapidaries. Examples of their craftsmanship are very valuable. Today even the work of contemporary Indian artists — weavers, silversmiths, carvers, and others — is highly collectible. For a more thorough study we recommend *Arrowheads and Projectile Points*, *Indian Axes*, and *Indian Artifacts of the Midwest*. All three have been written by our advisor, Lar Hothem; you will find his address in the Directory under Ohio.

Key:
bw — beadwork   S — Southern
dmn — diamond   s-s — sinew sewn
E — Eastern   W — Western
NE — Northeastern   x — cross
p-h — prehistoric

Apparel and Accessories

Before the white traders brought the Indian women cloth from which to sew their garments and beads to use for decorating them, clothing was made from skins sewn together with sinew, usually made of animal tendon. Porcupine quills were dyed bright colors and woven into bags and armbands and used to decorate clothing and moccasins. Examples of early quillwork are scarce today and highly collectible.

Early in the 19th century, beads were being transported via pony pack trains. These 'pony' beads were irregular shapes of opaque glass imported from Venice. Nearly always blue or white, they were twice as large as the later 'seed' beads. By 1870 translucent beads in many sizes and colors had been made available, and Indian beadwork had become commercialized. Each tribe developed its own distinctive methods and preferred decorations, making it possible for collectors today to determine the origin of many items. Soon after the turn of the century, the craft of beadworking began to diminish.

Apron, Chippewa, blk velvet w/floral bw, wool fringe, 1890 ......**300.00**
Arm bands, Plains, blk/wht checked bw on red cloth, 1930, 3" W ..**50.00**
Belt, Nez Perce, super fine bw w/#16 cut beads, w/drop, 1890 ....**625.00**
Belt, Sioux, stair steps/circles, mc bw on bl, 1890, 3½x31" **125.00**
Breech cloth, Great Lakes, cloth w/bw & brass balls, 1890, 18" **525.00**
Coat, Pendleton, Western style, 5-color, 1930s **30.00**
Cuffs, Sioux, full bw on hide, trade cloth lined, 1930, 12" **425.00**
Dance kilt, Hopi, embr traditional motif ea side, 1940, 44x21" **75.00**
Dress, Blackfoot child's, red trade cloth w/bugle beads, 1900 ......**350.00**
Dress, Blackfoot lady's, cloth w/bugle beads & hawk bells, 1900 ...**475.00**

Dress, Cheyenne, hide with multicolor beadwork strips, overall fringe, red and black bead suspensions, replaced yoke, 18th century, 48" long, $2,300.00.

Dress, Cree, yel cloth w/rows of lg tin cones, 1940 ....**90.00**
Dress, Crow, red trade cloth w/cowrie shells & ribbon, 1930 ......**350.00**
Dress, Plains, velvet w/cowrie shell yoke, 1920 ....**500.00**
Dress, Plateau, gr trade cloth, cowrie shells/bugle beads 1940 .....**250.00**
Dress, Plateau, wht buckskin w/full bw yoke & fringe, 1920 ....**2,500.00**
Dress, Sioux, bl trade cloth w/dentellium shell yoke, 1900 ......**1,600.00**
Gloves, brain-tanned w/hourglass bw, 1930s, 9" **80.00**
Hat, Nez Perce, cornhusk, mc triangles in 2 bands, 1940, 8x7" ..**600.00**
Hat, Nez Perce lady's, fez w/brn stairsteps, 1935, 7x7" **180.00**
Leggings, Crow/Plateau, bw insert on 2 colors of cloth, 1900 .....**350.00**
Leggings, Nez Perce, geometric/floral bw, 1900, 16x8" **350.00**
Leggings, Nez Perce, trade cloth over buffalo, bw panels, 1890 ..**225.00**
Mittens, Huron, moose hide w/mc floral embr, 13½" L **325.00**
Moccasins, Arapaho, s-s buffalo w/full bw, 1900 ....**700.00**
Moccasins, Arapaho, s-s parfleche w/bw, 1870s **225.00**
Moccasins, Assiniboine, full bw, long fringe, 19th C, NM **2,400.00**
Moccasins, Blackfoot lady's, bw buckskin high-tops, sgn 1940 ..**250.00**
Moccasins, Cheyenne, full bw, bird on wht, 1900 ....**800.00**
Moccasins, Iroquois, floral bw, ankle flaps, 1880, 12" **145.00**
Moccasins, Oto, hide w/puckered toe, stylized floral bw, 1900 ...**175.00**
Moccasins, Plateau, floral bw/buckskin high-tops, 1900, 11" **700.00**
Moccasins, Pueblo, hard bent sole w/wht buckskin tops, 1935 ...**150.00**
Moccasins, Santee Sioux, mc floral bw front, 1920, 10" **175.00**
Moccasins, Shoshone, buckskin w/geometric bw toes, 1930, 10" ..**125.00**
Moccasins, Sioux, buffalo hide/full bw/pnt parfleche, 1910 ....**600.00**
Moccasins, Sioux, full bw geometrics, hard soles, 1940 ....**125.00**

Moccasins, Sioux child's, buffalo hide/full bw high-top, 1890 ....**500.00**
Vest, Blackfoot, full bw front on hide, partial bw bk, 1880 ......**2,200.00**
Vest, Chippewa, blk velvet w/floral bw front/bk, 1910 ....**350.00**
Vest, Navajo, woven w/centipede/dmns, 4-color, 1940, 21" **225.00**
War shirt, Crow boy's, ermines/horsehair/beads, made of Am flag ..**2,100.00**
War shirt, Plains, buffalo hide, full bw bands/human hair, 1900 ..**3,500.00**

Arts and Crafts

Ashtray, ingot silver, old pictorial stamps, 1940s, 5½" L **185.00**
Athabascan, box, bark w/floral bw, bw on lid, 1910, 5x5" dia **600.00**
Blanket strip, Nez Perce, 3 full bw discs/panels, 1890, 63x3" ...**3,700.00**
Bronze, long-horn steer, Tom Knapp, 1/40, Buckthorn, 10" L **125.00**
Canteen, Navajo, handwrought silver w/eng coyote & rabbit, 2" ..**125.00**
Canteen, tobacco; Navajo, heavy silver, 1900, 3" dia **260.00**
Cvg, NW Coast, wood, sitting bear w/masks on paws, 1900, 15" ..**450.00**
Ledger drawing, Kiowa, animals/man, 20th C, 10½x8½" **35.00**
Letter tray, Crow, parfleche w/pnt geometrics, 1950, 15x10" **120.00**
Oil painting, Mandan Buffalo Dancer, Tos-Que Wms, '64, 26x19" .**200.00**
Oil painting, 2 Kachinas/mule, sgn ND Shirley, 1978, 20x16" ...**165.00**
Painting, boy & colt, sgn Harrison Begay, 1965, 12x10" **275.00**
Painting, Hopi, Kachina dancer/Pueblo, Namoki, 1975, 19x15" ..**100.00**
Painting, Shields of Feathers, Dwatwa, 1978, 24x48" **200.00**
Whimsey, bw stars & From the Iroquois, 1920, 8x8" **200.00**
Whimsey, Iroquois, bw bird, 2 shades of bl, 1900 ....**80.00**

Bags and Cases

The Indians used bags for many purposes, and most display excellent form and workmanship. Of the types listed below, many collectors consider the pipe bag to be the most desirable form. Pipe bags were long, narrow, leather and bead or quillwork creations made to hold tobacco in a compartment at the bottom and the pipe, with the bowl removed from the stem, in the top. Long buckskin fringe was used as trim and complemented the quilled and beaded design to make the bag a masterpiece of Indian Art.

Apache, bw geometrics on hide, hide fringe, 1920, 9x5" **300.00**
Arapaho, strike-a-lite, s-s parfleche, beaded drops, 1880s, 3½x6" ..**450.00**
Cheyenne, knife case, s-s, tin cones, liner w/dk bl bw, 1880s **950.00**
Cheyenne, medicine case, pnt/twisted hide fringe, 1880, 15x7" .**550.00**
Cheyenne, pipe bag, bw hourglass, quilling/fringe, 1910, 26x6" ..**1,950.00**
Cheyenne, pipe bag, s-s/pnt antelope, bw bars, fringe, 20th C, 32" ...**1,100.00**
Cheyenne, strike-a-lite, hide w/bw & tin cone drops, 1890, 7x4" .**700.00**
Cree, gun case, moose hide/floral bw/wool suspensions, 1910 .....**375.00**
Cree, pipe bag, floral bw panel, fringe, 1920, 21x6" **250.00**
Crow, folded rawhide trunk w/pnt geometrics, 1900, 21x10" **325.00**
Crow, Indian in costume, full bw, contemporary, 14x6" **500.00**
Crow, medicine case, parfleche, trade cloth trim, 1900, 7x7" **300.00**
Crow, suitcase, pnt/folded parfleche, 1900, 27x14" **650.00**
Great Lakes, hand-woven wool w/geometrics, 1870, 18x17" ...**1,300.00**
Iroquois, pouch, floral bw on blk trade cloth, 1880s, 7x6" **90.00**
Iroquois, purse, floral bw on blk velvet, 1900, 7x8" **50.00**
Iroquois, purse, hide w/heavy bw floral, bw strap, 1900, 4x5" **220.00**
Micmac, document case, quilled floral on birchbark, 5", VG **60.00**
Nez Perce, belt pouch, contour bw w/society symbols, 1890, 8x7" ...**1,100.00**
Nez Perce, belt pouch w/flap, twined corn husk w/mc, 1940 ....**200.00**
Nez Perce, corn husk w/geometrics, rectangular, 1910, 11x9" **500.00**
Nez Perce, saddlebags, full bw, throw-over, 1930, 110x12" **650.00**
Nez Perce, twined corn husk w/trees & feathers, 1920, 14x11" ..**800.00**
Piegan, pipe, smoked moose hide/bw star/fringe, 1920, 24" **225.00**
Plains, knife case, full bw Am flag, fringe, 20th C, 16" **200.00**
Plains, medicine case, stitched leather w/cut-out hdls, 1890 ....**85.00**
Plateau, bw Indian lady in costume, 1930, 13" dia **165.00**

Plateau, End of Trail words/picture, 1940, 10x18" 125.00
Plateau, full bw flap w/fringe & tin cone drops, 1940, 21x6" 210.00
Plateau, full bw Indian/deer/plane/mtn, 1920, 24x16" 1,750.00
Plateau, full bw w/2 eagles & trees, 1930, 12x11" 175.00
Shoshone, bonnet case, pnt parfleche w/fringe, 1900, 16x4" 350.00
Sioux, awl case, allover bw/tin cones/horsehair, 1900, 15x¾" 300.00
Sioux, hide w/bw pinto horse, bw border, 1920, 7x4½" 125.00
Sioux, knife sheath, s-s w/allover bw, +knife, 1890, 9" 700.00
Sioux, medicine case, rawhide, blk-lined pnt motif, 1800s, 8x8" ...850.00
Sioux, medicine pouch, full bw keyhole on wht, bk: yel, 1890 ...225.00
Sioux, possible, bw on flaps, quilling on front, 1890, 20x14" ...2,400.00
Sioux, teepee, buffalo, quilled front/bw panels, 1870, 21x5" ...2,500.00
Sioux, teepee bag, bw/horsehair/tin cones, 1890, 23x16" 600.00
Sioux, woman's tobacco, both sides beaded, 1890, 6x3" 210.00
Tlingit, seal foot w/claws & floral bw at top, 1900, 10x6" 200.00
Yurok, purse, dentillum; made from antler, 1880, 4½x2" 250.00

Baskets

In the following listings, examples are basket form and coiled unless noted otherwise.

Apache, bowl, leaf/line motif, 1920, 2x12" 900.00
Apache, bowl, multiple stars, 1920, 3x11" 600.00
Apache, bowl, swirls/figures, oval, 1930, 3x14" 1,500.00
Apache, burden, twined, buckskin trim/fringe, 1900, 11x9" 200.00
Apache, burden, 3 bands, hide trim/drops/tin cones, 1989, 7x9" ..250.00

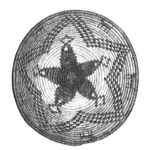

Apache, tray, radiating star elements with 5 stick-figure dogs, symmetrical designs, ca 1920, 2½x12½", $1,200.00.

Apache, tray, radiating snake motif, 1900, 18x3¼", NM 1,500.00
Apache, tray, 5-point star, ½-dmn rim motif, 1920, 12" 550.00
Apache, vertical bands w/floating coyote tracks, 1920, 3x9½" ...550.00
Apache, water basket, pitch covered, AZ, 1940, 18x10" 125.00
Apache, 5-point star w/in star, 1940, 11¼x7½" 250.00
Apache/Yavapai, tray, eagles at rim, blossom center, 1920, 12" .1,200.00
Cowlitz, embricated w/stair steps, EX quality, 1900, 13x14" 1,550.00
Haida, spruce root, twined/embricated geometrics, 1910, 8x5" 70.00
Hopi, Kachina face motif, 1910, 9x10", M 525.00
Hopi, 2nd Mesa, checkerbrd, w/swing hdl, 1940, 5x6" 140.00
Hopi, 2nd Mesa, connecting terraces, 1940, 6x9½" 150.00
Hopi, 2nd Mesa, plaque, 6 blk & red dogs, 1940, 10" 185.00
Hopi, 3rd Mesa, plaque, wicker w/eagle design, 1935, 12½" 275.00
Hupa, child's, ½-dmn spirals, 1920, 2x2" 150.00
Hupa, globular, twined conifer root w/false embr, 1910, 5x3" 350.00
Hupa, mush bowl, geometrics, half-twist, 1920, 3x6½" 90.00
Jacarilla Apache, mc geometric, woven carry holes, 1930, 6x9" .150.00
Klamath, bowl, twined, 1-band motif, 1920, 3x7" 85.00
Klickitat, berry basket, native rpr, 1890, 13x12" 75.00
Klickitat, mc embricated geometrics, 1930, 3x6" 275.00
Maidu, gambling basket, serrated/radiating motif, 1900, 16" 650.00
Makah, mc band, birds on lid, 1920, 3x6½" 125.00
Modoc, trinket basket, checkerbrd dbl lines/Xs, 1920s, 4x5" 400.00
Navajo, 18-point ceremonial wedding design, 1940, 2½x12" 125.00

Nootka, treasure, twined/geometrics, dome lid, 1920, 7x5" 125.00
Nootka, twined w/geometrics, dome lid, 1920, 7x5" 125.00
Oto, 3-band design, lg ring hdls, 1938, 10x9½" 100.00
Paiute, full bw w/geometrics on turq, 1950, 3½x2½" 350.00
Paiute, winnowing, 1900, 29x23" 200.00
Panamint, shoulder type, superfine, arrow/butterfly, 1900, 7x3" ...1,500.00
Papago, bowl, 4 human figures, 1925, 8x5" 100.00
Papago, horsehair, dogs frieze, fine wear, 1993, 2½" dia 135.00
Papago, mc cactus/birds/deer, 1960, 10x12" 175.00
Papago, storage, classic fret motif, w/lid, 1935, 11x9" 95.00
Papago, swirling stair steps, 1935, 4x9½" 60.00
Papago, tray, lg turtle in center, 1940, 12x10" 110.00
Papago, turtle motif, 1970, 7x5" 75.00
Pima, bowl, ladder design, flared sides, 1920s, 4x11" 400.00
Pima, olla, ladder motif, 1920, 10x12" 900.00
Pima, olla, spiraling checkerbrd, 1930, 6½x6" 325.00
Pima, plaque, 3-point star, fine stitch, 1930, 3" 325.00
Pima, stair step motif, fine weave, 1910, 2x5½" 450.00
Pima, stylized whirling logs, 1940, 3½x14", NM 900.00
Pima, tray, turtle bk/Xs motif, 1920, 18x5" 110.00
Pima, wine basket, fret motif, 1890, rare, 16x10" 375.00
Pima, 15 Xs on negative shapes, EX fine, 1930, mini, 3½x2" 550.00
Pit River, twined, bold geometrics, 1910, 6x6" 170.00
Pomo, bowl, blk triangles, 1900, 7x3" 1,000.00
Siletz, bowl, twined, 3 bands of line design, 1900, 5x9" 35.00
Tesque Pueblo, Kiva basket, red willow, 1930, 34" 225.00
Ute, tray, 3 rows of animals, 1990, 2x21" 300.00
Wasco, corn husk sally bag w/birds all around, 1935, 6x4" 55.00
Washo, burden, twined w/line design, 1920, mini, 8x7" 150.00
Washo, 4-dmn w/in dmn motif, mc tans, 1920s, 2½x6½" 175.00
Yavapai, birds/coyote tracks, star in bottom, 1930, 5x10" 400.00
Yokut, sifter, conical w/red designs, superfine, 1900, 6x7" 150.00
Yokut, stepped rectangles in lightning motif, 1900, 7x13" 1,000.00
Yokut, 2 bands of rattlesnake design, 1910, 13x20" 1,400.00

Blades and Points

Relics of this type usually display characteristics of a general area, time period, or a particular location. With study, those made by the Plains Indians are easily discerned from those of the West Coast. Because modern man has imitated the art of the Indian by reproducing these artifacts through modern means, use caution before investing your money in 'too good to be authentic' specimens.

Adena, Flint Ridge, Henry Co, OH, 4⅜" 495.00
Adena, Flint Ridge, MI, 5⅜" 385.00
Bi-pointed, hornstone, IN, 7" 265.00
Bi-pointed, mahog obsidian, N CA, 9½" 275.00
Candy Creek, dk pk, Yell Co, AR, 1⅞", EX 8.00
Clovis, lt tan, both sides fluted, IL, 3⅜" 165.00
Clovis spear, tan, good flutes, TX, 4" 245.00
Corner notch, Polk Co, MO, 4⅜" 50.00
Cumberland, midwest, 3" 50.00
Dalton type, colorful glossy flint, serrated, minor damage 15.00
Delhi, wht quartz, Stone Co, AR, 9" 20.00
Dovetail, OH, 4½" 135.00
Dovetail, Scioto Co, OH, 3¾" 200.00
Dovetail, Tazewell Co, IL, 3⅜" 135.00
Elora, tan & gray, Anderson Co, GA, 2⅞" 32.00
Karok, obsidian, 20th C, 10x1" 80.00
Klickitat, gemstone, from Klickitat River, p-h, 1x¾" 45.00
Osceola, midwest, 3½" 35.00
Paleo, brn, wide, 3" 75.00
Paleo, brn flint, 4" 150.00

Paleo, brn semitranslucent petrified wood, 4" **200.00**
Pedernales, Williamson Co, TX, 3⅜" **65.00**
Pickwick, red & tan, Shelby Co, TN, 2¼" **12.00**
Rheems Creek, wht quartz, NC, 1", EX **16.00**
Rose Springs, lt gray, Yell Co, AR, ¾", EX **18.00**
Sedelia, Cooper Co, MO, 7" **190.00**
Spear point, midwest, wht chert, p-h, 7x1" **40.00**
Thebes, William Co, TN, 4⅜" **120.00**
Triangular, gray stone, thin, TX, p-h, 2¾" **10.00**
Turkey tail, IN, 4¾" **1,000.00**

Blankets, Navajo

Pueblo Indians first made blankets centuries ago, but today most are made by Navajo Indians. Pendleton and Hudson's Bay blankets became widely available in the 1800s; around the turn of the century, rugs were developed because tourists were more likely to buy them as floor coverings and wall-hangings. Rugs or blankets are made in various regional styles; an expert can usually identify the area where it was made, sometimes even the individual who made it. The colors of wool are natural (gray-white, brown-black), vegetal (from plant dyes), or artificial (aniline, from synthetic chemicals). Value factors include size, tightness of weave, artistry of design, and condition. Examples by artists whose names are well known command the higher prices.

Child's wearing, stripes/serrated line design, 1880, 47x35" **100.00**
Hopi Pueblo, woven plaid/geometrics, 1930, 74x52" **250.00**
Saddle, dbl dmn motif, twill, 1900, 52x30" **300.00**
Saddle, dbl; Chief's, Chinle, 1920, 31x62" **150.00**
Sunday saddle, commercial yarn, 1940, 30x42" **100.00**
Trade/camp, geometric bands, w/fringe, 1920, 70x80" **150.00**
Transitional, butterfly design, soft weave, 1910, 97x57" **600.00**
Transitional, sawtooth design, soft weave, 1890, 44x72" **200.00**

Ceremonial Items

Club, Chippewa, cvd/pnt wood, 20th C, 22x9" **60.00**
Dance shield, Pueblo, thick hide w/pnt remnants, 1920, 20", pr ...**200.00**
Dance wand, Sioux, buffalo horn, hair-on-hide/bw trim, 1900 ...**135.00**
Dance wand, Zuni, pnt wood w/stars & moons, 1900, 15x3½", pr .**200.00**
Drum, Cochiti Pueblo, pnt hide, w/beater stick, 1940, 24" **300.00**
Drum, Crow (?), pnt decor, 19th C, 17" dia **1,600.00**
Drum, Plains, hide w/pnt Ghost Dance symbol, 1940, 25x19" ...**225.00**
Drum, Sioux, rawhide w/pnt designs, from Buffalo Bill show **425.00**
Drum, Tarahumara, hand-held w/pnt floral, 1960, 4x22" dia **60.00**
Fan, Peyote, mc feathers w/gourd, bw hdl/fringe, 1950, 14" **70.00**
Fetish, Sioux, turtle, full bw top, 1950 ....**100.00**
Fetish, Zuni, bear w/arrow-point prayer bundle, 20th C **425.00**
Fetish, Zuni, stone, bear w/prayer bundle on bk, 1960, 3x4½" ...**175.00**
Headdress, Blackfoot, wormy split horn/bw band/ermine, 1920 ..**1,450.00**
Headdress, Jemez Pueblo, antelope dance, pnt wood/horns, 1940 ..**150.00**
Mask, Iroquois, False Face Society, twined corn husk, 1920 ....**900.00**
Mask, Tlingit, cvd/pnt wood, 1900, w/provenance, 9x7" **600.00**
Medicine bundle, Blackfoot, w/several items included, 20th C ..**485.00**
Rain sash, Hopi, finger weave, wht, tassels/fringe, 1940, 46" **140.00**
Rattle, Hopi, gourd w/Kachina face ea side, 1940, 9x6" **100.00**
Shaman's charm, Mastodon ivory, eagle/wolf & baby, 1890, 4x2" ...**300.00**
Shaman's wand, Midiwin, bone, cvd skull/human hair, 1860, 8" ..**475.00**
Spoon, Sioux, horn w/crane effigy & s-s bw hdl & drop, 20th C ...**400.00**
Staff, Haida speaker's, cvd wood, totemic motif, 1900, 36" **450.00**
Staff, Plains, cvd wood w/horsehair on ends, 1960, 42" **70.00**
Tabletta, Hopi, lg butterflies etc, cottonwood, 17x20" **200.00**
War bonnet, Sioux, dyed turkey feather/bw/ermine, 1975, 16x22" ..**175.00**

Dolls

Kachinas, all Southwestern, polychrome on wood: Malo, 6¼", $1,000.00; Kweo Wolf, attributed to W. Tewaquaptewa (1870-1960), 8", $1,000.00; Heheya-aumutaqa, 6½", $425.00.

Kachina, Black Ogre, 1-pc, 1940, 10x4" **150.00**
Kachina, Crazy Rattle, cvd/pnt, sgn Broines, 1983, 22x13" **100.00**
Kachina, Deer, sgn A Sakiestewa, elaborate, 1986, 14x5" **200.00**
Kachina, Devil's Claw, cvd/pnt, sgn Rivera, 1983, 25x8" **100.00**
Kachina, Hopi, winged serpent in headdress, 1940, 12x14" **225.00**
Kachina, Koyemce (Mudhead w/child), sgn P Takala, 1980, 12x7" ...**150.00**
Kachina, Morning, cvd/pnt, sgn Hendricks, 1983, 23x10" **100.00**
Kachina, Munga, 1-pc, 1990, 12x4" **150.00**
Kachina, w/helmet, sgn N Talahongua, 1960, 12x5" **125.00**
Navajo, ea w/old jewelry, EX work, 1930, 13", EX, pr **500.00**
Nisqually, twined basketry w/facial features, 1900, 8x5" **250.00**
Sioux, bw on hide dress/leggings/mocs, buffalo hair, 1900, 8" **900.00**
Skookum, male/female, 1910, ea 11", +4" child **250.00**
Zuni, fully beaded, traditional attire/squash, 1970, 7" **95.00**

Domestics

Bowl, Zuni, wood w/HP water bird design, 20th C, 12x6½" **775.00**
Cradle, Apache, very basic work, w/old doll, 1920, 33x12" **500.00**
Cradle, Hupa, basketry, 1930, 11" **170.00**
Cradle, line bw, loom-bead strap, basketry visor, 1940, 33" **450.00**
Cradle, Mono, woven reed shaved bark w/hide, 1900, 13x6½" ..**225.00**
Cradle, toy, Nez Perce, floral bw on hide, 1900, 17x6" **400.00**
Scoop, Seneca or Iroquois, burl wood, eagle's beak form, 6" **725.00**
Spoon, Navajo, silver, o/l Kachina face & cornstalks, 1920 ....**325.00**
Spoon, Sioux, buffalo horn w/notches, rawhide thong, 1880, 8" ..**60.00**

Jewelry and Adornments

As early as 500 A.D., Indians in the Southwest drilled turquoise nuggets and strung them on cords made of sinew or braided hair. The Spanish introduced them to coral, and it became a popular item of jewelry; abalone and clam shells were favored by the Coastal Indians. Not until the last half of the 19th century did the Indians learn to work with silver. Each tribe developed its own distinctive style and preferred design, which until about 1920 made it possible to determine tribal origin with some degree of accuracy. Since that time, because of modern means of communication and travel, motifs have become less distinct.

Quality Indian silver jewelry may be antique or contemporary. Age, though certainly to be considered, is not as important a factor as fine workmanship and good stones. Pre-1910 silver will show evidence of hammer marks, and designs are usually simple. Beads have sometimes been shaped from coins. Stones tend to be small; when silver wire was used, it is usually square. To insure your investment, choose a reputable dealer.

Belt, Navajo, repousse, 6 3x2" conchos/7 spacers+buckle, 1950 .**225.00**
Belt, Navajo, stamped conchos/spacers/buckle, 1930s, 29" **100.00**
Belt, Navajo, 10 conchos w/heart-line bear & turq, 1985 ....**200.00**
Bolo, Zuni, Shalako Kachina, 4-color channel inlay, 1950, 3" .**135.00**
Bracelet, bangle; bone, full rnd, 1940, 12x1½" **45.00**

Bracelet, Haida, cvd silver w/wolf & salmon, 20th C, 1½" W 225.00
Bracelet, Navajo, appl dogs/stamped rattlesnake, gr turq 175.00
Bracelet, Navajo, hand-stamped links, 1940, 7x1" 80.00
Bracelet, Navajo, sand cast w/Blue Gem turq, 6x2" 220.00
Bracelet, Navajo, sq turq, shank w/stamping/wire twists, 1940 ...120.00
Bracelet, Navajo, turq/silver cluster, sgn Begay, 1975, 7x3" 110.00
Bracelet, Navajo, 13 silver/turq charms, 1940 ....110.00
Bracelet, watch; Navajo, 2 lg turq, 1980, 7x3" 150.00
Bracelet, Zuni, sunburst turq petit-point, 1950s 80.00
Bracelet, Zuni, 2-row turq petit-point, 26 stones, 1940 ....140.00
Buckle, Navajo, sand cast w/1 turq, 1940, 4x2½" 45.00
Buckle, Navajo, turq/much stamping, 1940, 4½x3" 200.00
Buckle set, Navajo, hand-stamped buckle/tip/holder, 1970 ....185.00
Choker, Sioux, bird-bone w/parfleche & bead separators, 1880 .100.00
Earrings, Navajo, drop style, ea w/31 coral cabs, 1940, 2½" 190.00
Earrings, Navajo, 13 rnd/triangle turq in ea, 1940, 3x1" 125.00
Earrings, Zuni, inlay dangles, EX work, 1940, 5x1" 130.00
Earrings, Zuni, 3 turq-inlaid horseshoe shapes in drop, 4" 85.00
Hair ornament, cvd rawhide wheel, bw drop/wht feather, 1920 ....80.00
Hair pipe breast plate, Piegan, rpl fringe, 1920, 17x8" 125.00
Hair pipe breast plate, Sioux, dbl row 4" bones, 20th C, 14x10" ..325.00
Hair pipe breast plate, Sioux lady's, w/trade beads, 1940, 34x7" ..350.00
Hair pipe necklace, Crow, mixed w/trade beads, 1900, 42" 100.00
Hair pipe necklace, Crow, 3-strand, brass/crow beads, 1900, 42" .175.00
Headband, Chippewa, crown style, porcupine quills, 1850 ....150.00
Heishi, Pueblo, rolled turq w/hanging jacklas, 1975, 32" 125.00
Heishi, Santo Domingo, turq, 2-strand w/shell pendant, 1975, 32" ..145.00
Jacklas, natural/grad turq w/shell 'corn,' 1940, 13", pr 50.00
Necklace, blk bear claws on buckskin, wht heart beads, 1930 ....800.00
Necklace, Buffalo Hunter, teeth & quill-wrapped hair, 1900 .....245.00
Necklace, coral bead choker, 25-strand w/silver cones, 18" 50.00
Necklace, Crow medicine man's, deer bones/hoofs, bear fur, 1900 ..245.00
Necklace, Hopi, pottery beads & spoons w/pnt bugs, 1940 ....85.00
Necklace, Navajo, bear paw pendant+3 sm, w/turq cabs, 1970 .....70.00
Necklace, Navajo, grad silver handmade beads, 1960 ....150.00
Necklace, Navajo, natural turq nuggets on turq heishi, 1940, 32" ..100.00
Necklace, Navajo, 37 natural turq/silver beads, 1950, 24" 200.00
Necklace, Pueblo, 2-strand, turq nuggets on heishi, 1940, 28" 35.00
Necklace, Pueblo, 3-strand, orange branch coral, 1960 ....90.00
Necklace, Santo Domingo, turq chunks w/pr of jacklas, 1950s ...110.00
Necklace, Toney Lualla (Zuni), 3-strand jet bears+fox spacers ..800.00
Necklace, Zuni, mixed turq fetish, ea w/arrowheads, 1875, 30" ..480.00
Necklace, Zuni, 3-strand, coral birds on wht heishi, 1964 ....140.00
Necklace, Zuni, 3-strand, mixed birds & bears, 1960, 24" 185.00
Pendant, Zuni, Kachina, shell/jet/coral/turq inlay, 1970, 3" 100.00
Pin, Navajo, serpent shape w/turq & coral, 1940 ....90.00
Pin, Zuni, Kachina Dancer, mc inlay, 1940, 5x3" 550.00
Pin, Zuni, thunderbird, 3-color channel inlay, 1950 ....50.00
Pin/pendant, Navajo, turq cluster, sgn LMB, 1980, 2" 45.00
Ring, Navajo, Bizbee stone & silver leaves, 1975 ....75.00
Ring, Navajo, lg Blue Gem oval turq, 1940 ....50.00
Ring, Navajo, lg Morenci rnd turq plaque, 1960 ....70.00
Ring, Navajo, lg turq, 1970 ....55.00
Ring, Navajo, turq/coral/MOP/jet stones, 1970 ....35.00
Ring, Navajo, ½-rnd gr turq, fancy bezel, 1930 ....65.00
Ring, Navajo, 4 leaves+3 Nevada gr turq cabs, 1975 ....95.00
Roach, dance; Nez Perce, mc deer/porcupine hair, 1920, 15x5" ..200.00
Roach, Plains, porcupine/deer hair, 1800s, 12" 325.00
Squash blossom, dime/quarter beads & drops, cast naja 225.00
Squash blossom, Navajo, Bizbee turq, 6 in naja, 1975, 32" 250.00
Squash blossom, Navajo, coral, 10 shadow-box blossoms, 1970 ..170.00
Squash blossom, Navajo, heavy, early style, 1930s, 19" 175.00
Squash blossom, Navajo, ornate naja, 1930, 26" 375.00
Trade beads, bl Venetians w/mc 'faces,' 1900, 27" 60.00

Trade beads, gr, rare color, museum quality, 1800, 24" 125.00
Trade beads, Lewis & Clark, blk/wht, 1800, 26" 85.00
Trade beads, matched Venetians w/mc dots, 1900, 29" 35.00
Trade beads, mixed cobalt, grad szs, 1880, 28" 45.00
Trade beads, Peking glass, red, 1880, 26" 65.00
Trade beads, red Venetians w/wht dots, 1840, 27" 125.00
Trade beads, very lg mixed-color chevrons, 1900, 36" 150.00

Pipes

Pipe bowls were usually carved from soft stone, such as catlinite or red pipestone, an argilaceous sedimentary rock composed mainly of clay. Steatite was also used. Some ceremonial pipes were simply styled, while others were intricately designed naturalistic figurals, sometimes in bird or frog forms called effigies. Their stems, made of wood and often covered with leather, were sometimes nearly a yard in length.

Apache, basalt bird effigy, gut-hide-wrap stem, 1880, 21" 250.00
Buffalo bone steme w/horse-head cvg, 16" 770.00
Cast w/chief & bear, eng, orig hdl, 1880s, 19" 495.00

Catlinite pipe with pewter inlays, outstanding condition, 5¼x12⅛", $1,100.00.

Catlinite, pewter inlay, historic, 6" 275.00
Chippewa lady's, pipestone elbow bowl, 1930, 1½x8½" 225.00
Human head form, red sandstone w/patina, Midwest, old, 6" 110.00
Mandan, catlinite, monster head form, 1860, 12x2" 300.00
Mimbres, brn stone, 2" 70.00
Pipe tomahawk, brass head, tacked wood stem, 20th C, 23x8" ...350.00
Pipe tomahawk, Plains, iron/wood shaft w/brass tacks, 13x4" 200.00
Plains, blk bowl, effigy stem w/fur & feathers, 20th C, 26x5" 100.00
Sioux, blk T-bowl (rpr), quill-wrap tacked stem, 1880, +tamp ...1,000.00
Sioux, catlinite, cvd/twisted mc stem, 1870, 37" 1,850.00
Sioux, inlaid blk T-bowl, quilled stem, 1880, 22x3½" 1,500.00
Sioux, pipestone elbow bowl, 1940s, 17x2" 60.00
Sioux, T-bowl w/pipestone stem, 2-part, 1900, 21x4" 300.00
Wood, cvd Indian head, w/stem, 1920s, 17½" 330.00

Pottery

Indian pottery is nearly always decorated in such a manner as to indicate the tribe that produced it or the pueblo in which it was made. For instance, the designs of Cochiti potters were usually scattered forms from nature or sacred symbols. The Zuni preferred an ornate repetitive decoration of a closer configuration. They often used stylized deer and bird forms, sometimes in dimensional applications.

Acoma, canteen, classic style, sgn Leno, 1950, 5x5" 35.00
Acoma, jar, thin walled, fine line deer, Rose Chino, 1970s, 8" ...250.00
Acoma, olla, fine lines/geometrics, 4-color, 1940, 6½x6" 120.00
Acoma, vase, fine line section/stars/geometrics, 1960, 6½x5" 50.00
Acoma, wedding vase, mc parrot/florals, 1950, 8x6" 115.00
Anasazi, bowl, snowflake, blk on wht, dmn motif, p-h, 7x4" 250.00
Anasazi, effigy, dog figure, pnt traces, 1100 AD, 5x5½" 165.00

Anasazi, jar, redware w/2 snake effigies, p-h, 6x6" **115.00**
Anasazi, mug, serrated bands/lines in blk/wht, 1200 AD, 4½" ...**225.00**
Anasazi, pitcher, blk on wht snowflake motif, p-h, 6x6" **550.00**
Anasazi, vessel, redware, shoe-shaped w/4 ft, p-h, 6x5" **115.00**
Catawba, jar, human face hdls, 1935, rare, 12x11" **70.00**
Cochiti, seed jar, stylized flowerheads, 1880, 11½", NM **450.00**
Cochiti, storyteller doll w/8 babies, sgn M Arquero, 7½x7" **175.00**
Cochiti, teapot, floral, w/spout & lugs, 1910, rare, 4x7" **275.00**
Gila, bowl, blk on red, geometrics w/in & w/out, p-h, 6x11" **185.00**
Hohokam, bowl, scrolls/lines, red on buff, sq form, 1200 AD, 4½" ..**200.00**
Hohokam, olla, buff spirals on red, provenance, p-h, 11x14" **725.00**
Hopi, bowl, Nampeyo designs, 1930, 3x9" **250.00**
Hopi, bowl, traditional rim design, sgn C Calayumptewa, 5x11" ...**125.00**
Hopi, jar, elaborate fine line motif, Adelle Nampeyo, 5x5" **270.00**
Hopi, plate, mc Kachina, sgn Marcella, 1980, 8½" **60.00**
Hopi, seed jar, cvd Kachina dancers, L Nampeyo, 1975, 5" **150.00**
Hopi, seed jar, elaborate mc decor, sgn Adelle Nampeyo, 3" **140.00**
Hopi, seed jar, stylized fine line bear paw, A Nampeyo, 4x5" **75.00**
Hopi, vase, lg stylized bird, swollen cylinder, 1920, 8x4" **275.00**
Maricopa, vase, ½-circle design, blk/red, fluted, 1940, 5" **80.00**
Mochica, effigy vessel, human head on hdl, grayware, 7½" **175.00**
Pinnewa, olla, blk on wht w/dmn motif, p-h, 5x6" **175.00**
Roosevelt, pitcher, blk on wht, p-h, 4x4", M **325.00**
Santa Clara, jar, blkware, sgn Petra, 1940, 6x5" **95.00**
Santa Clara, jar, cvd blkware w/avenu, Marcella, 1950, 5x4" **60.00**
Santa Clara, jar, cvd knife wing/etc, sgn Stella, 1960, 5" **220.00**
Santa Clara, vase, blkware, sgn Clara Suazo, 4½x5" **55.00**
Santa Clara, vase, blkware bear paws, Margaret & Luther, 3½" .**100.00**
Santo Domingo, wedding vase, geometrics, cream/red, 1940, 10" .**40.00**
Sikyatki, bowl, pnt int w/X, p-h, 9x4" **400.00**
St John, bowl, blk on red w/in, brn on buff w/out, p-h, 8x9" **125.00**
St John, bowl, blk on red w/wht outline, p-h, 4x9" **150.00**
Tanka Verde, mug, geometrics, brn/red, w/hdl, 1200 AD, 3" **170.00**
Tonto, olla, blk on gray w/geometrics & curvilinears, p-h, 12" ...**275.00**
Zia, jar, bird motif, H Gauchupin, 1960, 10x8" **145.00**
Zia, jar, birds all around, sgn Lois Medina, 1980, 7x7" **135.00**

Pottery, San Ildefonso

The pottery of the San Ildefonso pueblo is especially sought after by collectors today. Under the leadership of Maria Martinez and her husband Julian, experiments began about 1918 which led to the development of the 'black-on-black' design achieved through exacting methods of firing the ware. They discovered that by smothering the fire at a specified temperature, the carbon in the smoke that ensued caused the pottery to blacken. Maria signed her work (often 'Marie') from the late teens to the 1960s; she died in 1980. Today a piece with her signature may bring prices in the $500.00 to $4,500.00 range.

Jar, black-on-black stylized butterfly motif, signed Marie and Julian, 7x9", $2,200.00.

Bowl, blk on polished redware, tan bk, 1800s, 10½", EX **495.00**
Bowl, blkware, geometric, Juanita Vigil, 3½x5¼" **165.00**
Bowl, blkware, geometric band, Marie & Julian, 1935, 4", NM ..**550.00**

Bowl, blkware, polished, sgn Rose (Gonzales), 2x7" **175.00**
Corn meal container, blkware, simple design, Romona, 1930, 2½" ..**330.00**
Jar, blk on red, w/hdl, 1890s, 4x4" **165.00**
Jar, blkware, feathers, Carlos Dunlop (deceased), 1979, 12x10" ..**1,600.00**
Olla, mc stair-step panels, 1920, 10x10" **200.00**
Plate, blkware, feather motif, Marie Martinez/Santana, 6" **500.00**
Plate, blkware, polished, Marie & Julian, 11" **1,225.00**
Plate, blkware, polished, sgn Marie & Julian, 1940s, 7" **700.00**
Pot, blkware, water serpent, Marie, 4½x6" **650.00**

Rugs, Navajo

Chinle, dmns in 3 bands, vegetal, 1960, 50x37" **300.00**
Crystal, connecting dmns on wht, natural/vegetal, 1930, 105x57" ..**475.00**
Crystal, Storm pattern, natural/vegetal dyed, 1920, 66x49" **950.00**
Crystal, striking geometrics, natural wool, 1930, 102x68" **3,250.00**
Crystal Springs, dbl pattern, natural wool, 1940, 63x30" **150.00**
Dbl Maltese Xs, blk/red/wht on tan, 1930, 48x24" **135.00**
Eye Dazzler, Ganado, intricate 4-color motif, 1950, 60x32" **250.00**
Eye Dazzler, hand-combed, museum quality, 1920, 83x55", M ...**1,700.00**
Geometrics, brn/red on wht, 1920, 63x44" **250.00**
Geometrics, intricate/mc, fine weave, 1935, 73x43" **525.00**
Geometrics/lg optical illusion, 3-color on wht, 1960, 128x64" ..**1,250.00**
Regional, super fine, 1920, 56x34", M **500.00**
Serrated border/dmn motif, 4-color on wht, 62x38" **300.00**
Serrated dmns, banded ends, 4-color, 1930, 84x59" **900.00**
Serrated dmns, natural/vegetal dyed, 1940, 48x28" **200.00**
Storm, cornstalks/geometrics, 1935, 92x59" **900.00**
Storm pattern w/water bugs, 4-color on wht, 1970, 60x30" **225.00**
Stripes, gray/wht/blk/red, 1940, 46x38" **125.00**
Two Gray Hills, central lozenge, Xs/feathers, 1935, 76x44" **750.00**
Two Gray Hills, dbl central lozenge, 1970, 39x30" **500.00**
Two Gray Hills, natural wool, intricate design, 1970, 61x37" **800.00**
Two Gray Hills, natural/vegetal geometrics, 1950, 52x35" **175.00**
W Reservation, geometrics, 1935, 66x60" **600.00**
Wide Ruins, bands w/dmns, natural/vegetal, 1960, 48x31" **175.00**
Xed 'railroad track' design, 4-color on wht, 1930, 59x34" **175.00**
3 dmns w/chevron ends, red/brn/tan/wht, 1920, 60x34" **425.00**
5-part geometric, 3-color on wht, 1940, 51x33" **225.00**

Shaped Stone Artifacts

Bannerstone, Archaic, bow-tie, spotted stone, OH, 3x2" **225.00**
Bannerstone, Archaic, OH, hard stone, 2" **150.00**
Bannerstone, midwest, butterfly type, soft stone, 3x4" **100.00**
Bannerstone, saddle bk, porphyry, IL, 3¼" **1,300.00**
Bannerstone, tube type, slate, OH, 1½" **110.00**
Birdstone, midwest, elongated w/lg pop eyes, 1x3" **200.00**
Bowl, Diegueno, p-h, 2½x8" **65.00**
Bowl, Thimbres, pecked, w/knob hdl, oblong, 1200 AD, 9" L **150.00**
Discoidal, MO, 3" **275.00**
Discoidal, quartz, IL, 3¼" **185.00**
Figure, Hohokam-style animal, historic, 7x6" **55.00**
Gorget, midwest, gr slate w/2 drilled holes, p-h, 5½" **70.00**
Hammerstone, Hohokam, rnd/flat, 3" dia **10.00**
Metate, 3-walled, w/mano, p-h, 10x17x20" **200.00**
Mortar, Anasazi, p-h, 2x3" **80.00**
Mortar, Chumash, incised triangles at rim (chip), p-h, 3x4" **175.00**
Mortar, Chumash, spherical, w/rolling-pin pestle, p-h, 7x9" **200.00**
Mortar, Chumash, steatite, 19th C, 1½x2½" **130.00**
Mortar, N CA, flaring sides, w/pestle, p-h, 9x14" **160.00**
Pendant, anchor shape, Hardin Co, OH, 4" **550.00**
Pendant, pentagonal, Hardin Co, OH, 5" **700.00**
Pendant, pentagonal, OH, 4⅜" **220.00**

Plummet, CA, 4" 80.00

Tools

Adz, grooved, NY, 4¼" 80.00
Awl, gray flint, TX, 3" 7.50
Axe, full groove, brn garnet, polished bit, AZ, p-h, 7x4" 65.00
Axe, full groove, KY, 4½" 50.00
Axe, full groove, OH, 5½" 55.00
Axe, hematite, MO, 3½" 95.00
Axe, Hohokam, good polish, 9" 225.00
Axe, Hohokam, highly polished, 5½" 175.00
Axe, NW Coast, effigy head, very rare, 9½" 1,100.00
Axe, ¾-groove, gray stone, IA, p-h, 7" 125.00
Axe, ¾-groove, OH, 7" 300.00
Celt, Lenawee Co, MI, 5½" 35.00
Celt, OH, 8½" 330.00
Chisel, Delaware Co, OH, 3⅞" 35.00
Chisel, MI, 6" 135.00
Drill, 3" 25.00
Hoe, notched, IL, 5¾" 650.00
Maul, full-grooved human face effigy, OR, p-h, 6x4x4" 75.00
Maul, Hohokam, stone, 3" 35.00
Pick, slate, TN, 3½" 25.00
Pipe reamer, Dalton, MO, 3⅝" 60.00
Spade, flint, polished bit, IN, 11½" 220.00

Weapons

Bow, Plains, hand hewn w/pnt traces, 1890, 45" 200.00
Bow, Plains, single curve, horse-bk style, 1880s, 43" 150.00
Club, Plains, hide over stone, bw/fringe hdl, 20th C, 26x2" 150.00
Club, Plains, stone head, hide-wrap hdl/hair drop, 1890, 20" 190.00
Club, Sioux, brn egg shape w/bead trim, wood hdl, 1880, 22x7" ...300.00
Club, Sioux, rnd stone head, hide-covered/hair drop, 1900, 25" ...40.00
Dagger, hdl inlay, Mandan quilled/fringed case, 1870, 22x5" ..5,500.00
War club, Great Lakes, ball head, EX patina, 1870, 24x7" 1,600.00

Miscellaneous

Buffalo lap robe, cloth lined, hair on reverse, 1890, 69x78" 225.00
Gorget, trade silver, beaver motif, mk YA, 1800, 8x3" 575.00
Headstall, Seneca, bw stars, horse sz, 1900 ....125.00
Knife, skinning; Great Lakes, from file, effigy hdl, 1900, 8" 300.00
Martingale, Blackfoot, trade cloth/bw, bead/tin cone drops, 1890 ...350.00
Model canoe, Makah, cvd, w/seats & mast, pnt motif, 1940, 72" .1,500.00
Peace medal, Rutherford B Hayes, on beaded necklace, 3" 150.00
Photograph, ES Curtis, Oasis in Badlands, goldtone, fr, 8x10" ...3,500.00
Photogravure, ES Curtis, Jack Red Cloud, 1907, 15x12" 120.00
Photogravure, ES Curtis, Two Leggins - Absaroke, 15x12" 225.00
Photogravure, Kutenai Duck Hunter, ES Curtis, matted, 10x16" .70.00
Photogravure, Roland Reed, The Hunters - Ojibwa, 1910, 12x8" ..75.00
Photogravure, 3 Chiefs - Piegan, ES Curtis, matted, 12x16" 45.00
Quirt, Plains, leather w/brass-tacked hdl, leg shape, 20th C 175.00
Saddle throw, Nez Perce, buffalo hide w/bw & fringe, 1900, lg ...600.00
Snowshoes, Ojibway, rawhide/wood, 1930, 58x12" 290.00
Teepee, Nez Perce, canvas, 1920, rstr, lg 200.00
Teepee, Nez Perce, muslin w/pnt animals etc, 1900, lg 600.00
Totem, NW Coast, cvd, w/wings, mc, 1940, 19" 225.00
Totem, Tlingit, cvd, w/wings, pnt, sgn Gary Rice, 19" 550.00
Totem, Tlingit, 2-figure, 1890s, 15x2" 400.00
Trade axe, hand forged w/oval eye, 1860 ....45.00
Trade axe, hand-forged war style, wrap-around eye, 1800s, 6" 40.00
Trade axe, lady's, iron, orig hdl, 1800s, 19½" 110.00

Amethyst Glass

The term amethyst simply describes the rich color of this glassware, made by many companies both here and abroad since the 19th century.

Bottle, triangular, Deco decor w/gold, amethsyt stopper, 13" 225.00
Creamer, blown, appl hdl, folded lip, sm chip, 3¾" 285.00
Cuspidor, lady's 30.00
Honey dish, Arch, 4⅜" 25.00
Pitcher, free-blown, cut dmn bands, star-cut base, 6½" 500.00
Tumble-up, carafe & tumbler w/gold bands, 8½", on sm plate ...195.00
Vase, mc floral w/gold on blk, stick neck, 8¼" 385.00
Vase, yel & wht jonquils w/gold trim, 7⅞x3⅜" 175.00

Amphora

The Amphora Porcelain Works in the Teplitz-Turn area of Bohemia produced Art Nouveau-styled vases and figurines during the latter part of the 1800s through the first few decades of the 20th century. They marked their wares with various stamps, some incorporating the name and location of the pottery with a crown or a shield. Because Bohemia was part of the Austro-Hungarian empire prior to WWI, some examples are marked Austria; items marked with the Czechoslovakia designation were made after the war. Our advisor for this category is Jack Gunsaulus; he is listed in the Directory under Michigan.

Vase, Art Nouveau nymph with flowers in her hair, forest background, Reissner, Stellmacher & Kessel, marked Amphora, Turn, 13¼", $1,045.00.

Basket, flowers appl on woven look, rope hdl, porc, 7x9½" 495.00
Basket, rust, jewels, 12" 350.00
Bust, maiden, mc pnt w/gold trim, 14x15⅝x7⅛", NM 1,150.00
Candle holders, fish, brn, 3½", pr 400.00
Ewer, appl berries & foliage on mc irid, 11¼" 125.00
Ewer, appl grapes, gr & rose on ivory, rtcl hdl, #3583, 11½" 350.00
Figurine, lady w/water jug, long headdress/robe, 14½" 225.00
Jardiniere, jeweled cockerel w/cobalt trim, 6½" dia 195.00
Jug, lady medallion on brn, w/bl at rim/spout/hdl, #33148, 5" 60.00
Lamp base, leaf form, orange/gr/bl, mk, 24x5½" 175.00
Pitcher, grapes, gr irid on bl, waisted, earthenware, 11½" 315.00
Urn, appl cherries on cobalt, branch hdls, 14½" 300.00
Vase, appl grapes on dripping candle design, mk, 1887, 12½" ..3,800.00
Vase, appl stylized octopus on gr/brn w/blk, #4547, 8¾" 1,495.00
Vase, basketweave w/appl rose/child climbing up side, 11" 450.00
Vase, bats in relief, gold irid/dk red/dk lemon, #4660, 22" 5,000.00
Vase, berries & leaves, mc on earthenware, hdls, 6¾" 350.00
Vase, cherubs & flowers, pk/bl/gray, 20½" 1,400.00
Vase, children (2 heads above rim) appl/pnt on bulb top, 10" .1,500.00
Vase, floral, 5-color on bl sponged ground, 7⅞x5⅛" 140.00
Vase, floral & insects (stylized), mc w/gold, 8¼x5¼" 285.00

Vase, floral relief on bronze w/gold, hdls, ftd, 13½x7½" **635.00**
Vase, floral w/gold, earthenware, #3581/58 V, 8¾" **345.00**
Vase, floral w/jewels, rtcl top, 3 hdls, #8350/42, 7" **500.00**
Vase, gilt webs/butterflies/jewels, #8777/25, 7⅝" **865.00**
Vase, gold w/gr & violet irid & jewels, ovoid, 13½" **1,265.00**
Vase, Kingfisher, HP banded pk & bl geometrics, #15091, 10¼" ..**120.00**
Vase, lady's profile, flowers in hair, shaped top, 13½" **1,800.00**
Vase, lady's profile w/jewels on gr w/gold, mk, 6" **795.00**
Vase, lady w/flowers in hair, trees beyond, w/gold, HH, 6x6" **650.00**
Vase, leaves, mc enameling/gold, dimpled, #03023, 12⅜x5" **350.00**
Vase, lg peasant lady/sheep cvg, bk: landscape, 9x7" **150.00**
Vase, lg sqd hdls w/3 openings, rtcl rim, pearls, ftd, 15" **1,300.00**
Vase, peacock figural top on tall egg shape, 10" **650.00**
Vase, poppies, mc w/much gold on ivory, mk, #538/14, 13¼" **575.00**
Vase, Secessionist, pitted teal, rtcl mc dmn bands, 6¾" **475.00**
Vase, 4 matt colors, 4 skeletal buttresses, Edda, #3623, 7⅝" **375.00**

Animal Dishes with Covers

Covered animal dishes have been produced for nearly two centuries and are as varied as their manufacturers. They were made in many types of glass (slag, colored, clear, and milk glass) as well as china and pottery. On bases of nests and baskets, you will find animals and birds of every sort. The most common was the hen.

Some of the smaller versions made by McKee, Indiana Tumbler and Goblet Company, and Westmoreland Specialty Glass of Pittsburgh, Pennsylvania, were sold to food-processing companies who filled them with prepared mustard, baking powder, etc. Occasionally one will be found with the paper label identifying the product and processing company still intact.

Many of the glass versions produced during the latter part of the 19th century have been recently reproduced. As early as the 1960s, the Kemple Glass Company made the rooster, fox, lion, cat, lamb, hen, horse, turkey, duck, dove, and rabbit on split-ribbed or basketweave bases. They were made in amethyst, blue, amber, and milk glass, as well as a variegated slag. It is sometimes necessary to compare items in question to verified examples of older glass in order to recognize reproductions. Reproduction is continued today.

For more information, we recommend *Covered Animal Dishes* by our advisor, Everett Grist, whose address is in the Directory under Tennessee. In the listings below, when only one dimension is given, it is the greater one, usually length.

Atterbury Duck, milk glass, mk Patent Apld for, 11" **245.00**
Atterbury Duck repro, any color, Wright or Imperial, 11" **70.00**
Atterbury Hen on lacy base, milk glass w/amethyst head **295.00**
Atterbury Rabbit, milk glass, dtd Aug 6, 1889 on base, 9" **300.00**
Bull's head, wht opal, mustard jar, w/tongue ladle, Atterbury **250.00**
Cat on lacy base, milk glass, rectangular, WG on base **150.00**
Chicks on oblong basket, milk glass w/pnt details, 2¼x4¼" **325.00**
Dog (Chow), milk glass, condiment container, unmk McKee, 5½" ..**275.00**
Dolphin, Sawtooth; milk glass, repro by Kemple or St Clair **75.00**
Dolphin on sauce dish, milk glass, Westmoreland, 7¼" **100.00**
Donkey, pk, powder jar, att Jeannette **20.00**
Duck, Swimming; yel opaque, Vallerysthal, 5" or 5¾" **120.00**
Duck on cattail base, milk glass, unmk, 5½" **120.00**
Elephant w/rider, clear frosted, Vallerysthal, 7" **200.00**
Fish, Entwined; milk glass, Aug 6 1889 in lid, 6" dia **170.00**
Fish on collared base, clear frosted **150.00**
Fox (ribbed) on lacy base, milk glass, dtd Aug 6 1889 in lid **175.00**
Frog, milk glass, condiment container, unmk McKee, 5½" **550.00**
Hand & Dove, milk glass, rectangular, mk WG on base **110.00**
Hen, milk glass, mk Vallerysthal, 2" **20.00**
Hen, Str Head; clear w/HP details, unmk Imperial, sm **15.00**

Hen, Str Head; marigold carnival, Indiana Glass **25.00**
Hen w/chicks, milk glass, unmk McKee, 5½" **200.00**
Lamb on picket base, milk glass, Westmoreland Specialty **95.00**
Lion, British; milk glass, emb base, unmk, 6¼" **195.00**
Pekinese, milk glass, rectangular, att Sandwich, 4¾" **450.00**
Quail on scroll base, milk glass, unmk, 5½" **85.00**
Rabbit on basketweave base, milk glass, US Glass, 8" (+) **95.00**
Rabbit on wheat base, milk glass **350.00**
Rat on lg egg, milk glass, Vallerysthal **225.00**
Robin on ped base, any color, mk WG **60.00**
Rooster on Atterbury lacy base, milk glass, Westmoreland repro .**110.00**
Rooster on wide-rib base, bl opaque, Westmoreland, 5¼" **85.00**
Swan, bl to gr, powder jar, Jeannette, late 1960s **15.00**
Swan, Block; clear frosted, Challinor, Taylor & Co, 7" **145.00**
Swan, Closed-Neck; bl opaque, Westmoreland Specialty **110.00**
Swan, milk glass, condiment container, ea pc mk McKee, 5½" ..**250.00**
Swan, Raised Wing; molded eyes, milk glass, Westmoreland **85.00**
Turkey, Standing; milk glass, LE Smith **130.00**
Turtle, dk amber, knobby bk, LG Wright repro **45.00**

Appliances, Electric

Antique electric appliances represent a diverse field and are always being sought after by collectors. There were over one hundred different companies manufacturing electric appliances in the first half of the 20th century, some were making over ten different models under several different names at any given time in all fields: coffeepots, toasters, waffle irons, etc., while others were making only one or two models for extended periods of time. Today collectors and decorators alike are seeking those items to add to a collection or to use as accent pieces in a period kitchen.

Always check the cord before using and make sure the appliance is in good condition, free of rust and pitting. The prices below are for appliances in good to excellent condition. Prices may vary around the country.

If you have any questions regarding antique appliances, please contact our advisor, Jim Barker; he is listed in the Directory under Pennsylvania.

Blender, Knapp-Monarch Liquidizer, Deco style, 1940s, EX **55.00**
Blender, Waring, chrome base, heavy glass, EX **45.00**
Coffee set, Golden Pheasant #17050, EX **145.00**
Coffee set, Krome Kraft, gold Bakelite hdls **140.00**
Coffee set, Manning Bowman, EX **95.00**
Coffee set, Royal Rochester #17152, EX **75.00**
Coffee set, Royal Rochester #17161, EX **85.00**
Coffee set, Universal E817604, EX **95.00**
Coffee set, Universal E81804, EX **75.00**
Coffee set, Universal E915504, EX **95.00**
Fan, Emerson, brass cage, 6-blade, 1908 ....**150.00**

Photo courtesy Mary Frank Gaston

Fan, oscillating type with brass blades, marked Gilbert, 12" dia, EX, $135.00.

Fan, Emerson, oscillating, brass blade & cage, 8½" dia, EX 95.00
Fan, Emerson, 3-ftd, EX 275.00
Fan, Emerson #19645, EX 75.00
Fan, Emerson #5250 ....150.00
Fan, floor; Vornado, Deco, aluminum/steel, 24" dia, 72", VG 200.00
Fan, Fresh-N-Air, chrome w/black Bakelite blades, table model ...175.00
Fan, GE #78X593, EX 65.00
Fan, GE #78777 ....95.00
Fan, GE Whiz, EX 50.00
Fan, Gilbert, blk & brass blades, EX 55.00
Fan, Gilbert A-54, EX 95.00
Fan, Peerless, EX 125.00
Fan, R&M, EX 75.00
Fan, Robbing & Myers, brass blade, EX 125.00
Fan, Solar Cub, AC Gilbert, 6", EX orig 60.00
Fan, Westinghouse, 10" brass blade & cage 145.00
Fan, Westinghouse #165366, EX 100.00
Fan, Westinghouse #60673, EX 200.00
Foot massager, Dr Scholl's, enamel & metal, chrome base 40.00
Percolator, Hotpoint #114517 ....85.00
Percolator, Royal Rochester, creamic & metal, EX 150.00
Percolator, Universal, ftd, 12-cup 35.00
Refrigerator, General Electric, coil top 300.00
Toaster, Beardsly & Wolcott #T7090 ....45.00
Toaster, Bee Vac, T-14 ....55.00
Toaster, Bersted #73, EX 90.00
Toaster, Bersted #78 ....85.00
Toaster, Birtman Electric, single slice 85.00
Toaster, Coleman Electric #2, EX 125.00
Toaster, Dominion #1000, EX 45.00
Toaster, Edicraft Model H 75.00
Toaster, Fitzgerald Star Rite Auto Toaster #529 ....65.00
Toaster, Fitzgerald Star Rite Turn Around #75000, EX 85.00
Toaster, General Electric D-12, EX 375.00
Toaster, General Electric D-56, EX 85.00
Toaster, General Electric D-76, EX 95.00
Toaster, Gold Seal, all models, EX, ea 90.00
Toaster, Hot Point-GE #114T5, EX 65.00
Toaster, Hot Point-GE #115T17, EX 85.00
Toaster, L&H #205, EX 150.00
Toaster, Manning Bowman #K100 ....75.00
Toaster, Manning Bowman #K75 ....95.00
Toaster, National Stamping Works #227 ....55.00
Toaster, National Stamping works #230 ....45.00
Toaster, Red Top, electric 45.00
Toaster, Royal Rochester #E6412, EX 45.00
Toaster, Royal Rochester #13250, EX 50.00
Toaster, Royal Rochester #13406, EX 45.00
Toaster, Royal Rochester #13530, EX 55.00
Toaster, Samson Tri Matic 95.00
Toaster, Simples #215 ....95.00
Toaster, Toast O Matic #745, EX 150.00
Toaster, Trimble Auto Toaster 95.00
Toaster, Tscel Toastoy, child's, ca 1929, EX 95.00
Toaster, Universal #E9412, EX 55.00
Toaster, Universal #E942, EX 85.00
Toaster, Universal #E946, EX 45.00
Toaster, Universal #E947, EX 55.00
Toaster, Universal #7312, EX 45.00
Toaster, Universal #7822, EX 65.00
Toaster, Westinghouse, TTC-53 ....45.00
Toaster, Westinghouse TO-501 ....40.00
Toaster, Westinghouse TT-3, EX 55.00
Toaster, Westinghouse TTC-104 ....55.00

Toaster, Westinghouse TTC-43 ....45.00
Waffle iron, Lady Hibbard on ceramic insert, Bakelite hdls 135.00

Arc-En-Ciel

The Arc-En-Ciel Pottery Company operated in Zanesville, Ohio, from 1903 until 1907. Artware was produced only until 1905, typically finished in a high lustre gold glaze. Though not always marked, those pieces that are carry the half-circle rainbow logo containing the company name.

Vase, brn flecks in honey mustard gloss, long neck, #549, 6" 110.00
Vase, gold & yel gloss, twisted lobed form, mk, 7" 50.00
Vase, gold irid, purple & gr, mk, 12½", EX 60.00
Vase, striped rose, tan, yel & gray gloss, slim neck, 8½" 110.00

Arequipa

The Arequipa Pottery operated from 1911 until 1918 at a sanitorium near Fairfax, California. Its purpose was two-fold: therapy for the patients and financial support for the institution. Frederick H. Rhead was the originator and director. The ware, made from local clays, was often hand thrown, simply styled and decorated. Marks were varied but always incorporated the name of the pottery and the state. A circular arrangement encompassing the negative image of a vase beside a tree is most common.

Examples are evaluated according to quality of artwork; size and shape are less important. Those done by Rhead himself are most desirable.

Vase, incised leaves, 6", $750.00.

Bowl, gr gloss w/blk streak geometrics, #703/14, 2¼x7½" 200.00
Bowl vase, bl/gray streaked, 3550/9, 2¾x4¾" 200.00
Ewer, floral, mc on shaded gr, pinched spout, 10", EX 350.00
Vase, floral branch relief, terra cotta, long neck, 8x6" 975.00
Vase, leaves emb on lt to med brn mottle, #401, 10½x5½" 1,300.00
Vase, sculpted grapevines on shoulder, dk bl matt, 5x6", EX 300.00
Vase, stylized trees, brn/bl on wht, F Rhead, 3¾x3" 3,750.00

Argy-Rousseau, G.

Gabriel Argy-Rousseau produced both fine art glass and quality commercial ware in Paris, France, in 1918. He favored Art Nouveau as well as Art Deco and in the twenties produced a line of vases in the Egyptian manner, made popular by the discovery of King Tut's tomb. One of the most important types of glass he made was pate-de-verre. Most of his work is signed. Items listed below are pate-de-verre unless noted otherwise.

Bottle, scent; Fleurs et Feuilles band, gray/gr/amethyst, 5" 3,300.00

Lamp base, fern panels, red w/aubergine, 10" 2,000.00
Luminaire, tigers in grasses, blk/orange/raspberry/gray, 7⅞" 9,775.00
Night light, leaves/vines, cylindrical shade, iron base, 8" 4,800.00
Paperweight block, Joan d'Arc, Pate-de-Cristal, mk, 5½" 2,300.00
Pendant, Bouquet des Fleurs, purple/gr/red/brn, 2½" dia 1,265.00
Pendant, mc floral, GAR at disk edge, 2½" 1,380.00
Tray, sunflower to side, petal rim, 3½" dia 2,650.00

Vase, Le Jardin des Hesperides, pate-de-verre, classical maidens picking apples, Greek Key-relief base, 9½x5", $24,150.00 at auction.

Vase, apple blossom branches on wht, 5⅜" 4,025.00
Vase, red floral, gr & blk branches, 5⅜" 5,175.00
Vase, star flower panels w/raised cornflowers, 8½" 4,750.00

Art Deco

To the uninformed observer, 'Art Deco' evokes images of chrome and glass, streamlined curves and aerodynamic shapes, mirrored prints of pink flamingos, and statues of slender nudes and greyhound dogs. Though the Deco movement began in 1925 at the Paris International Exposition and lasted to some extent into the 1950s, within that period of time the evolution of fashion and taste continued as it always has, resulting in subtle variations.

The French Deco look was one of opulence — exotic inlaid woods, rich material, lush fur and leather. Lines tended toward symmetrical curves. American designers adapted the concept to cover every aspect of fashion and home furnishings from small inexpensive picture frames, cigarette lighters, and costume jewelry to high-fashion designer clothing and exquisite massive furniture with squared or circular lines. Vinyl was a popular covering, and chrome-plated brass was used for chairs, cocktail shakers, lamps, and tables. Dinnerware, glassware, theaters, and train stations were designed to reflect the new 'Modernism.'

The Deco movement made itself apparent into the fifties in wrought iron lamps with stepped pink plastic shades and Venetian blinds. The sheer volume of production during those twenty-five years provides collectors today with fine examples of the period that can be bought for as little as $10.00 or $20.00 up to the thousands. Chrome items signed 'Chase' are prized by collectors, and blue glass radios and tables with blue glass tops are high on the list of desirability in many areas.

Those interested in learning more about this subject will want to read *Collector's Guide to Art Deco* by our advisor, Mary Frank Gaston. She is listed in the Directory under Texas. See also Bronzes; Chase; Frankart; Furniture; Jewelry; Lalique; Radios; etc.

Armchair, blk lacquered cvd wood fr, uphl bk/seat, 37" 250.00
Ashtray, Howell, floor-standing, chrome, lift-out tray, 22½" 175.00
Bar, aluminum/formica/chrome, birch/lacquer int, 24" dia 2,100.00
Bar, walnut, sliding doors, 2 drws, mirrored int, 46x87" 1,495.00

Bust, lady w/birds, much detail, Werkstatte, 17¾x8" 2,530.00
Candle holders, chrome, stylized fish-form hdls, 4", pr 45.00
Carpet, Beauvais, geometric, 3-color wool, 62x36", VG 180.00
Carpet, flowering tree on tan w/pk border, 60x30" 220.00
Carpet, geometrics, brn tones on tan, 1930s, 128x144", EX 800.00
Carpet, machine-woven wool, mc sqs on brn, 126x105", VG 290.00
Chair, rnd bk cushion, octagonal arms/legs, 1920s, 33x23x20" ..140.00
Chest, Weber, 8-drw, burl w/blk pulls, glass/wood base, VG ...1,600.00
Cigar box, Aztec-style cloisonne decor, brass bands, 8⅞" L 1,035.00
Clock, Seth Thomas, stepped wood fr w/gold face, 8x9", EX 90.00
Clock, walnut, ceramic nudes, floral-emb pewter dial, 12" 500.00
Cornices, E Brandt, wrought-iron floral, 1925, 11½", 4 for 3,000.00
Desk, blk lacquer & mahog, 5 drws, ebonized plinths, 30x50" ...1,150.00
Figurine, aardvark, Primavera, mc on terra cotta, 6½x12⅜" ...1,100.00
Figurine, boy & dog, mc w/EX detail, WW mk, #311, 11½" ...1,000.00
Figurine, cat, Primavera, wht crackle on terra cotta, 12⅞" 1,100.00
Figurine, draped nude, ivory/orange/bl/gr, Werkstatte, 25⅜" ..3,000.00
Figurine, giraffe, Primavera, yel/mustard/brn glossy, 16" 1,050.00
Figurine, lady & child, modeled/sgraffito/mc, WW mk, 16⅛" .2,500.00
Figurine, mongoose, Primavera, #13866, 12⅝x6⅞" 1,100.00
Figurine, Pan, Lourioux, stoneware, 1925, 12½x9½x3½" 865.00
Figurine, stylized man, Gatelet/Primavera, 1930, 14⅝" 1,600.00
Frame, NP brass/burlwood w/2 glass panels, Paris, 14x14x5" 635.00
Hall tree, walnut & rosewood, central mirror, NP racks, 59" 920.00
Ice bucket, Hazel Atlas, chrome, cobalt glass insert, 11x8" 85.00
Jar, dresser; blk glass w/SP greyhound on lid 275.00
Lamp, desk; 2 patinated metal rams, blk marble base 200.00
Lamp, floor; 4-rod std converges on base, parchment shade, VG ..400.00
Lamp, nude in gray enamel, marble base, ball shade atop, 27" 600.00
Lamp, Salterini, std w/stylized bird, irreg-panel mica shade 1,300.00
Lamp, vanity; stylized nudes, wht metal w/bronze finish, pr 400.00
Lamp, 8-sided mica shade w/appl color, gilt post, CI base, 24" ...1,035.00
Luminaire, Becquerel, porc Chinese girl figural, 7⅝" 575.00
Pitcher, Peter Muller-Munk, Normandie by Revere, copper, 12" ...2,100.00
Rug, Whittall, Oriental, blk/gr/salmon, fringed, 144x105", VG .140.00
Sconce, 3-flare chome top, brass & frosted glass, 20x16", pr ...1,200.00
Shelf, Bakelite, on 3-tier step-down aluminum ½-rnd, 28" 700.00
Smoker's set, sterling box w/3 reed bars, +match box holder 200.00
Sofa, Fr, burl wood veneer w/velvet re-uphl, cubist, 72" 6,000.00
Table, blk lacquer 20" dia top, Xd chrome U-legs, 18", G 250.00
Tables, nesting; red/blk/silver leaf geometric tops, EX 950.00
Torchere, wrought iron w/hemispherical alabaster shade, 63" .1,840.00
Tumbler, Cartier, sterling, flared mouth, lg rnd base 125.00
Vase, C Faure Limoges, mc design on metal, 11⅞x8" 2,185.00
Vase, C Faure Limoges, mc scrolled tendrils on metal, 4⅜" 2,875.00
Vase, Jacques Douau, metal w/patinated deer, cone shape, 10" ..500.00
Vase, Sheherazade for Primavera, stylized mc scene, 13½" 920.00
Wall pocket, lady's head w/hat, pottery, wht glaze 70.00

Art Glass Baskets

A popular novelty and gift item during the Victorian era, these one-of-a-kind works of art were produced in just about any type of art glass in use at that time. They were never marked, since these were not true production pieces but 'whimsies' made by glassworkers to relieve the tedium of the long work day. Some were made as special gifts. The more decorative and imaginative the design, the more valuable the basket.

Amberina Swirl, amber ruffled rim, rosettes on hdl, 7x5" 400.00
Amethyst to clear, fine ribs, ornate rim, thorn hdl, 8" 195.00
Bl Basketweave w/emb florals, 5½x6½x4" 125.00
Bl o/l satin w/emb ribs, frosted spun rope hdl, 6½x6" 195.00
Bl swirl w/ruffled rim, clear hdl, 6x5¼" 145.00

Cranberry o/l, reverse swirl, crimped 4-lobe rim, 7½x6½" 225.00
Lime gr opal, ruffled, emb swirled ribs, clear hdl, 6½x6" 135.00
Mc spatter, ruffled rim, appl hdl, 6¾x5⅜" 175.00
Mc spatter, tricorner, clear thorn hdl, 8½x6" 175.00
Mc spatter cased, star-shaped top, clear twist hdl, 6¼x5⅜" 100.00
Mc spatter w/mica, ruffled rim, clear hdl, 6½x7⅝x6⅝" 195.00

Pink cased with crimped and scalloped rim, clear braid handle, 6½", $115.00.

Pk o/l w/mica, clear thorn hdl, 8-crimp, 7¼x4⅛" 185.00
Pk opal, Dmn Quilt, appl vaseline leaves & hdl, 6½x5" 160.00
Red Dmn Quilt, wht appl berries by clear hdl, 4 gr ft, 7" 425.00
Sapphire bl, swirled & ruffled, clear hdl, 6¼x5¼" 145.00
Sapphire bl swirl w/clear ruffle & thorn hdl, 7¼x5½" 175.00
Spangle, amber/wine swirl, 4-fold rim, Xd thorn hdl, 10x11" 400.00
Vaseline opal Dmn Quilt, appl spatter flowers, 7½" 225.00
Wht on pk, 4 gr/amber ferns form ft, amber X hdl, S&W, 13" ...500.00
Yel o/l satin, sq ruffled form, frosted braid hdl, 6" 155.00
Yel opaque, emb swirls & beads, clear thorn hdl, 6x4¾" 125.00

Art Nouveau

From the famous 'L'Art Nouveau' shop on the Rue de Provence in Paris, 'New Art' spread across the continent and belatedly arrived in America in time to add its curvilineal elements and asymmetrical ornamentations to the ostentatious remains of the Rococo revival of the 1800s. Nouveau manifested itself in every facet of decorative art. In glassware Tiffany turned the concept into a commercial success that lasted well into the second decade of this century and created a style that inspired other American glassmakers for decades. Furniture, lamps, bronzes, jewelry, and automobiles were designed within the realm of its dictates. Today's market abounds with lovely examples of Art Nouveau, allowing the collector to choose one or several areas that hold a special interest. Our advisor for this category is Steven Whysel; he is listed in the Directory under Arkansas. See also Bronzes; Galle; Jewelry; Loetz; Tiffany; Silver; specific manufacturers.

Bust, ceramic, maid weaves flowers into hair, 3388, 23" 1,400.00
Chandelier, wrought metal, bell harp w/leaves & 3-D monkey ..650.00
Clock, girl w/flowing hair, brass, Warner, 1898-04, 14" 300.00
Compote, ceramic, nude holds lily pad behind, Wahlis, 17" ...1,000.00
Crumb tray, copper, lady's head w/flowing hair, 5x6", EX 70.00
Curio cabinet, mahog w/floral inlay/stain glass, 2-door, VG 3,500.00
Dish, bronze, lady seated by lily blossom, sgn Cahuzac 300.00
Figurine, lady w/flowing hair/gown, SP, granite base, 7", EX 250.00
Fire screen, copper, iron fr/ceramic insert, English, 29x18" 330.00
Frame, brass stamped, lady's head at top, vines at side, 5x7" 100.00
Inkwell, SP over brass, stylized vines & leaves, 6" 175.00
Magnifying glass, lady w/flowing hair hdl, rpl glass 250.00
Paper embossing, lady's head, A Charpentier, fr, 5½x7½" 150.00
Pitcher, gr glass w/gold floral, concave style, +6 tumblers 420.00
Plaques, cvd oak relief: fisher woman & huntress, 13x23", pr 325.00

Sconce, bronze, 5 foliate arms w/crystal blossoms, 34x25" 800.00
Stand, ebonized wood w/whiplash legs, 3-shelf, cvd flowers 1,200.00
Tray, sterling, emb iris/naiad busts, Birmingham mks, 9x12" 625.00
Vase, ceramic, nude on melon figural, E Wahlis 1,350.00
Vase, pottery, winged lizard coils gr-blk bottle form, 12" 450.00

Arts and Crafts

The Arts and Crafts movement began in England during the last quarter of the 19th century, and its influence was soon felt in this country. Among its proponents in America were Elbert Hubbard (see Roycroft) and Gustav Stickley (see Stickley). They rebelled against the mechanized mass production of the Industrial Revolution and against the cumulative influence of hundreds of years of man's changing taste. They subscribed to a theory of purification of the styles: that designs be geared strictly to necessity. At the same time they sought to elevate these basic ideals to the level of accepted 'art.' Simplicity was their virtue; to their critics it was a fault.

The type of furniture they promoted was squarely built, usually of heavy oak, and so simple was its appearance that as a result many began to copy the style which became known as 'Mission.' Soon factories had geared production toward making cheap copies of their designs. In 1915 Stickley's own operation failed, a victim of changing styles and tastes. Hubbard lost his life that same year on the ill-fated *Lusitania*. By the end of the decade the style had lost its popularity.

Metalware was produced by numerous crafts people, from experts such as Dirk van Erp and Albert Berry to unknown novices. Prices for Arts and Crafts accessories rose dramatically in 1988, but by the beginning of 1991 leveled off and (in some cases) dropped. Metal items or hardware should not be scrubbed or scoured; to do so could remove or damage the rich, dark patina typical of this period. Our advisor for this category is Bruce Austin; he is listed in the Directory under New York. See also Furniture; Roycroft; Silver; Stickley; specific manufacturers.

Key: h/cp — hammered copper

Candelabrum, Jarvie, brass with original patina, #1 of only 4 made, 14", $9,000.00.

Armature, slag glass/wrought & cast fr, 4-light, 35" 2,185.00
Ashtray, Craftsman, h/cp, incised, no mk, 1x11" dia, VG 90.00
Ashtray, Heintz, silver on brass 50.00
Bookends, C Sorenson, h/cp, rnd tops, 5½" 150.00
Bookends, H Dixon, copper w/emb ship, mk, new patina, 6", VG ...210.00
Bookends, NEK, h/cp w/rtcl leafy tree, dk brn patina, 4½" 300.00
Bookends, Van Erp, h/cp sheet w/2-lobe 3-cutout top, 4½x6" 700.00
Bowl, Avon, h/cp, 6 lobes at rim, 1x10", VG 100.00
Bowl, Brossi, att; h/cp, incurvate, ftd, mk JB, 5½x7x9" 325.00
Bowl, Gebelein, h/cp, everted rim, ring ft, 2½x5", VG 170.00
Bowl, h/cp, rtcl flower/leaf on lid, 3½x9" dia, EX 180.00

Bowl, Handicraft Guild, stylized cut-out leaves, 1½x4", EX 375.00
Bowl, Liberty, h/pewter w/leaves, rtcl rim, #0546, 5" 100.00
Bowl, Tudric, pewter w/band motif, 3 pnt copper disks, 3x6" 230.00
Box, cigarette; oak, dvtl, orig finish, 3½x5x5½" 450.00
Box, cuff link; K Kipp, tooled flowers & W, semi-rnd, cleaned ..1,100.00
Box, h/cp, flared riveted legs, emb floral medallions, 10" L 900.00
Box, h/pewter w/tooled straps, 4 jewels, wood int, 9x6x3" 600.00
Box, Heintz, bronze w/geometric o/l, lt cleaning, 3x3½x9" 175.00
Box, Silver Crest, bronze w/A&C-motif lid, #B2271, 2x3½x6½" ..100.00
Candelabrum, Jarvie, 3 curved arms/conical holders, 10", VG ...2,600.00
Candlestick, Hurley, brass, 1 stem w/2 sea horse holders, 9" 500.00
Candlestick, Jarvie, Beta, mk, NM patina, 12" 1,200.00
Candlestick, Jarvie, tulip cup, tapered stem, rnd base, 6", VG 170.00
Candlesticks, bronze, mk, 14", VG, pr 1,000.00
Candlesticks, Hurley, bronze, sea horse/starfish base, 13", pr 650.00
Candlesticks, Jarvie, brass, w/bobeches, sgn, 11", pr 575.00
Candlesticks, Jarvie, bronze, ea w/bobeche, 14", pr 10,925.00
Candlesticks, Jarvie, bronze, sgn, 11", VG, pr 1,000.00
Centerpc, AE smith, tooled leather, chestnuts/leaves, 21" dia 275.00
Chafing dish, h/cp w/wood hdls, 3 extremely curled strap legs 800.00
Chamberstick, Craftsman, h/cp, hdl curved over oval base, 3x6" ..150.00
Chamberstick, Jarvie, brass, mk, cleaned, 6", VG 425.00
Clipboard, Shreve & Co, att; h/cp on to wood, arrowhead clip ..600.00
Clock, WMF, h/cp, dome top, incurvate strapped sides, 10½" ...1,600.00
Desk set, Heintz, silver floral on bronze, 5-pc, VG 200.00
Desk set, Van Erp, h/cp, 2 hinged boxes on pen tray, 12", VG ...400.00
Desk set, Van Erp, h/cp, 2 holders/blotter/letter opener 400.00
Frame, h/cp, arched top, oval window, 10½x6½", EX 140.00
Frame, h/cp, riveted picture slot & base, EX quality, 5x7" 650.00
Frame, h/cp w/tooled tree around window, EX work, 8x5½" 200.00
Frame, silver-tone metal w/etched pine cones, 3½x4½" 150.00
Gong, wood fr w/gr jewels & emb florals, 9x12x6" 1,200.00
Inkwell, Heinz, att; bronze w/silver o/l & stones, 3x7", VG 1,800.00
Inkwell, Hurley, bronze, w/lid, 1920, 3x5" dia 180.00
Jardiniere, D Van Erp, h/cp, incurvate, 10x14" 3,750.00
Lamp, Benedict, att; h/cp & mica, 19" cone shade, 24" 3,250.00
Lamp, D Van Erp, h/cp & mica 16" cone shade, flared base, 20" ...16,000.00
Lamp, Heintz, silver o/l, shade w/cut-out floral, rpl mica shade ..800.00
Lamp, Heintz, silver o/l bronze, cut-out cloth-bk 11" shade 700.00
Lamp, Heintz, silver o/l bronze, floral cut-out 9" shade 900.00
Lamp, Limbert, 2-post oak std, metal o/l mica shade, 24" W ..20,000.00
Lamp, Van Erp, h/cp & mica, orig font, rfn, 24x24" 11,000.00
Lamp, Van Erp, riveted h/c, 17" 4-panel mica shade, 18½", VG ..7,500.00
Letter opener, Hurley, bronze metal, sea horse/fish, 9" 150.00
Match holder, Van Erp, brass rectangle w/arched legs, 13x4", VG ..950.00
Plate, K Kipp, pewter, scalloped corners, 7½", set of 4 ....150.00
Rug, Celtic crosses in mc wool, tan border, 298x59" 900.00
Rug, Drugget, lt/dk gr diagonals on oatmeal, no mk, 9x12' 700.00
Rug, Drugget, orange/bl on oatmeal, fringe wear, 54x29", EX 160.00
Rug, Drugget, 4-color floral on oatmeal, no mk, EX, 6x4' 150.00
Salt dips, Kalo, h/cp, cleaned patina, 1½x3", set of 4, VG 130.00
Screen, 3-fold, brass-fr h/cp tree o/l on shell ground, 8x17" 1,400.00
Smoke stand, Van Erp, h/cp, dished top, str stem, 28x8" 1,900.00
Smoke stand, Van Erp, h/cp, 3-strap std, rfn, 31x8" 1,400.00
Smoking set, Heintz, silver geometrics on bronze, 3-pc, VG 300.00
Tray, Benedict Studios, h/cp, sides w/3 cutouts extend, 15" 110.00
Tray, Brosi, h/cp, stylized rectangle, EX work, 1x11x4" 190.00
Tray, Carence Crafters, leaf/berry motif on bronze, 5½" 130.00
Tray, h/cp, oval w/shaped well, 8½x16" 160.00
Tray, Liberty, Knox, pewter w/heart & trellis, #01259, 4½" 200.00
Tray, Van Erp, h/cp, EX rfn, 18" 800.00
Urn, Liberty, h/cp, leaf band w/turq jewels, trifoil ft, 6x12" 600.00
Vase, E Boston, h/cp, mk, bulbous, 7" 450.00
Vase, Heinrichs, h/cp, wide undulating rim, trumpet form, 16" ..200.00

Vase, Heintz, silver floral on bronze, slim/shouldred, 7½", VG ..260.00
Vase, Heintz, silver floral on gr-brn mottle, wide base, 12" 400.00
Vase, Heintz, silver leaf on bronze, mk, 4", EX 200.00
Vase, Heintz, silver tree on bronze, 1912, 8½" 275.00
Vase, made from artillery shell, emb poppies, dtd 1917, 13½" 260.00
Vase, Silver Crest, bronze w/gr patina, pine needle o/l, 5x5" 200.00
Vase, Strobl, gr textured matt, shouldered, 6" 290.00
Vase, Van Erp, h/cp, mk, 7x5", EX 850.00
Vase, Van Erp, h/cp, rolled rim, 8½x7", EX 1,600.00
Vase, Van Erp, h/cp 'warty' w/red & brn patina, 7x7" 8,500.00
Vase, Zark, trees, bl on bl to gr, drilled, 12½x8" 1,000.00
Vase, Zark, 4 cvd 'staves' extend above rim, bl-gr matt, 8" 850.00
Wall sconce, Jarvie, copper, shield w/2 candle cups, 14", VG 500.00
Wastebasket, Lakeside Craftshop, circle over linear cutouts 350.00
Wastebasket, Limbert, oak w/sq cutouts, brand, 18x11" sq 2,200.00
Wastebasket, oak, 5-sided w/cutouts at top, 14x7" 500.00
Wastebasket, oak w/leather connectors & copper tacks, VG 170.00

Austrian Glass

Many examples of fine art glass were produced in Austria during the time of Loetz and Moser that cannot be attributed to any glasshouse in particular, though much of it bears striking similarities to the products of both artists.

Centerpc, gr irid, HP florals, gilt/silvered metal fr, 15½" 460.00
Goblet, floral enamel, gr/pk w/gold outlines, 9" 250.00
Vase, amber w/purple feathering, pewter mt, 6¼", EX 325.00
Vase, amethyst w/mc irid wavy striations, globular, 9¾" 145.00
Vase, appl pk/wht tendrils on gr w/violet irid, 11" 200.00
Vase, chartreuse, ribbed/twisted, gooseneck, 15½" 345.00
Vase, fish form, amber irid & violet w/burgundy threads, 5⅜" ..1,035.00
Vase, free-blown, red w/gr splotches/dimples/gold lustre, 10½" ..400.00
Vase, yel w/pk streaks/splotches/irid, twisted, sq top, 13" 345.00

Austrian Ware

From the late 1800s until the beginning of WWI, several companies were located in the area known at the turn of the century as Bohemia. They produced hard-paste porcelain dinnerware and decorative items primarily for the American trade. Today examples bearing the marks of these firms are usually referred to by collectors as Austrian ware, indicating simply the country of their origin. Of those various companies, these marks are best known: M.Z. Austria; Victoria, Carlsbad, Austria (Schmidt and Company); and O. & E.G. (Royal) Austria.

Though most of the decorations were transfer designs which were sometimes signed by the original artist, pieces marked Royal Austria were often hand painted and so indicated alongside the backstamp.

Of these three companies, Victoria, Carlsbad, Austria, is the most highly valued. Collectors should note that in our listings transfer decorations showing 'signatures' (sgn), such as 'Wagner,' 'Kauffmann,' 'LeBrun,' etc., were not actually painted by those artists but were merely based on their original paintings.

Cake plate, roses 35.00
Chocolate set, roses on wht, pot+5 c/s 425.00
Ewer, calla lily, EX colors, turq int, mk, 15" 770.00
Figurine, dog, wht terrier w/mc mottle, 1930, 11⅛x9" 635.00
Figurine, horse, mc w/volcanic streaks, unmk/rstr, 20⅜" 1,500.00
Teapot, 18th-C couple w/gold/flowers, sgn Kauffmann, 7x7½" ..165.00
Vase, geometric mc deocr w/gold on tan, hdls, #1156, 12x5¼" ..345.00
Vase, HP florals w/gold, stick neck, crown/shield mk, 3¼" 40.00

Vase, Nouveau lady w/tambourine, gr/brn/cream, hdls, 11½" **300.00**
Vase, stylized holly/jeweled cartouches w/gold, 6¼x5¾" **375.00**

Autographs

Autograph collecting, also known as 'philography' or 'love of writing,' used to be a hobby shared by a few thousand dedicated collectors. But in recent years, autograph collecting has become a serious pursuit for more than 2,000,000 collectors worldwide. And in the past decade, more investors are adding rare and valuable autograph portfolios to their traditional investments. One reason for this sudden interest in autograph investing relates to the simple economic law of supply and demand. Rare autographs have a 'fixed' supply, meaning that unlike diamonds, gold, silver, stock certificates, etc., no more are being produced. There are only so many Abraham Lincoln, Marilyn Monroe, and Charles Lindbergh autographs available. In the meantime, it's estimated that more than 20,000 new collectors enter the market each year, thus creating an ever-increasing demand. Hence, the rare autographs generally rise steadily in value each year. Because of this scarcity, a serious collector will pay over $10,000 for a photograph signed by both Wilbur and Orville Wright, or as much as $25,000 for a handwritten letter of George Washington.

But by far, the majority of autograph collectors in the country do it for the love of the hobby. A polite letter and self-addressed, stamped envelope sent to a famous person will often bring the desired result. And occasionally one receives not only an autograph but a nice handwritten letter thanking the fan as well!

In terms of value, there are five general types of autographs: 1) mere signatures on an album page or card; 2) signed photographs; 3) signed documents; 4) typed letters signed; and 5) handwritten letters. The signatures are the least valuable, and handwritten letters the most valuable. The reasoning here is simple: with a handwritten letter, not only do you get an autograph but the handwritten message of the person as well. And this content can sometimes increase the value many times over. A handwritten letter of Babe Ruth thanking a fan for a gift might fetch a few thousand dollars. But if the letter were to mention Ruth's feelings on the day he retired, it could easily sell for $10,000 or more.

There are several major autograph collector organizations where members can exchange celebrity addresses or buy, sell, and trade their autographed wares. Philography can be a fun and rewarding hobby. And who knows! In ten or twenty years, those autographs you got for free could be worth a small fortune!

In the listings below, photos are assumed black and white unless noted color. Our advisor for autographs is Tim Anderson; he is listed in the Directory under Utah.

Key:
ADS — handwritten document signed	ins — inscription
	ISP — inscribed signed photo
ALS — handwritten letter signed	LH — letterhead
	LS — signed letter, typed or written by someone else
ANS — handwritten note signed	
AQS — autograph quotation signed	PLH — personal letterhead
	sig — signature
CS — counter signed	SP — signed photo
DS — document signed	

Alley, Kirsty; ISP, color, 8x10", EX **25.00**
Astaire, Fred; SP, bust portrait, matted/fr, 1935, 8x10", EX **300.00**
Autry, Gene; ISP, glossy, 1945, 5x7", EX **35.00**
Ball, Lucille; SP, Best & Cheers..., glossy, 1940, 8x6", EX **400.00**
Bara, Theda; SP, bust portrait, glossy, dtd 1918, 7x9", EX **400.00**
Barrymore, Ethel; SP, full-length, glossy, 1934, 7x9", EX **175.00**

Baxter, Warner; ISP, bust portrait, matt finish, 11x14", EX **145.00**
Bergman, Ingrid; SP, glamour portrait, 1956, 3x5", EX **150.00**
Bond, Lillian; SP, full-length, glossy, 1933, 8x10", EX **45.00**
Borden, Lizzie, sig on 7x4½" album leaf, EX **1,600.00**
Borgnine, Ernest; ISP, bust portrait, glossy, 8x10", EX **15.00**
Bowie, David; ISP, color, 8x10", EX **65.00**
Brook, Clive; SP, half-length, matt finish, 1930, 8x10", EX **75.00**
Brynner, Yul; SP, glossy, 8x10", EX **75.00**
Burke, Billie; ISP, half-length, glossy, 1932, 8x10", EX **150.00**
Burton, Harold H; LH, Jan 13, 1941, EX **135.00**
Burton, Richard; ISP, bust portrait, glossy, 8x10", EX **150.00**
Bush, George; sig on 1st day cover, EX **100.00**
Carillo, Leo; ISP, half-length, matt finish, 1937, 8x10", EX **75.00**
Carney, Art; sig on facial sketch, 3x5", EX **15.00**
Castle, Irene; ISP, seated, 1939, 11x14", EX **100.00**
Chaplin, Charlie; SP, sepia tone, 1917, 5x7", EX **750.00**
Cody, William F; ALS as Cousin Will, EX **600.00**
Coward, Noel; ISP, half-length, matt finish, 1930s, 7x9", EX **175.00**
Crosby, Bing; LS, 1-pg, Aug 31, 1946, EX **225.00**
Curtis, Jamie Lee; sgn check, 1980s, EX **35.00**
D'Angelo, Beverly; ISP, bust portrait, color, 8x10", EX **30.00**
Davis, Bette; ISP, bust portrait, 1940, 5x7", EX **80.00**
Davis, Tommy; SP, color, 8x10", EX **15.00**
Day, Doris; sgn check, 1947, EX **35.00**
Day, Leon; SP, 8x10", EX **30.00**
De Sade, Marquis; ADS, 5 lines, rare, 1812, 8x3", EX **2,000.00**
Depp, Johnny; sig on facial sketch, 8x10", EX **35.00**
Dickens, Charles; ALS, 1¼-pg, 1858, 5x7", EX **2,000.00**
Dietrich, Marlene; sig on 4x6" postcard, glossy, EX **45.00**
Donat, Robert; SP, bust portrait, 1936, 3x5", EX **50.00**
Douglas, Paul; SP, bust portrait, matt finish, 1931, EX **110.00**
Downing, Sir George; DS, manuscript, 1-pg, scarce, VG **800.00**
Dunaway, Faye; SP, shown w/cast, glossy, 8x10", EX **20.00**
Eastwood, Clint; SP, beside vehicle, glossy, 5x7", EX **15.00**
Edison, Thomas A; DS, sgn by 5 stockholders, Sept 26, 1917 ....**850.00**
Eisenhower, Dwight D; ISP, half-length, matt finish, 9x11" **500.00**
Fleming, Ian; SP, full-length in bedroom, scarce, 6x8", EX **1,800.00**
Ford, Gerald R; SP, color, 8x10", EX **85.00**
Fox, Nellie; sig on album pg, EX **75.00**
Gigli, Beniamino; SP, half-length, 1933, 3x5", EX **175.00**
Gosden, Freeman; ISP, glossy, 8x10", EX **30.00**
Griffith, Corinne; ISP, bust portrait, matt finish, 1927, EX **75.00**
Hackman, Gene; ISP, western portrait, color, EX **40.00**
Harrison, Rex; SP, scene from Anna Karenina, glossy, 8x10" **45.00**
Hayes, Helen; sgn check, 1960s, EX **35.00**
Hayward, Susan; ISP, To Pep..., 1942, 11x14", EX **400.00**
Hodges, Gil; sig on album pg, EX **95.00**
Holiday, Billie; ISP, bust portrait, matted/fr, 1945, EX **1,400.00**
Hoover, Herbert; ISP, bust portrait, 8x10", EX **300.00**
Irving, Washington; ALS, 1846, EX **450.00**
Jefferson, Thomas; DS, ship's passport, 1-pg, EX **1,600.00**
Jolson, Al; SP, bust portrait, matt finish, 1920, EX **300.00**
King, Stephen; ISP, portrait on movie set, color, 8x10", EX **50.00**
Lanza, Mario; ISP from That Midnight Kiss, rare, 1951, EX **500.00**
Marvin, Lee; SP, glossy, 8x10", EX **100.00**
Maxwell, Marilyn; ISP, glamour portrait, 1940s, EX **45.00**
Maynard, Ken; sig on album pg, lt toning **35.00**
McEnroe, John; SP, color, 8x10", EX **10.00**
McKinley, William; DS, military appointment, 1900, EX **500.00**
McNair, Ron; ISP, bust portrait, color, 8x10", EX **175.00**
Moody Blues, separate sigs on 3x5" cards, set of 4, EX **55.00**
Moore, Colleen; ISP, bust portrait, matt finish, 1928, EX **75.00**
Murray, Mae; inscr portrait by Hartsook, 1917, rare, 7x9", EX ...**100.00**
Peck, Gregory; ISP, glossy, 8x10", EX **20.00**

Phillips, Wendell; ALS, 2-pg, VG 75.00
Reagan, Ronald; SP as Governor of CA, glossy, 8x10", EX 200.00
Redford, Robert; SP, bust portrait, glossy, 8x10", EX 65.00
Robinson, Edward G; ISP, matt finish, 1935, EX 175.00
Rodgers, John; ALS, 1-pg, May 6, 1873, G 225.00
Roosevelt, Eleanor; ANS on 12mo sheet, VG 140.00
Roosevelt, Theodore; sig on postcard, 1908, EX 250.00
Russell, Rosalind; sgn check, 1940s, EX 40.00
Ryan, Nolan; SP, color, 8x10", EX 45.00
Scott, Winfield; ALS, 1-pg, Mar 2, 1853, VG 295.00
Seward, William H; ALS, 1-pg, Mar 9, 1849, VG 185.00
Seward, William H; DS, appointment, Mar 10, 1840, 15x10", VG ..140.00
Sheridan, Ann; ISP, matt finish, 1940s, 11x14", EX 250.00
Smith, Ozzie; SP, color, 8x10", EX 25.00
Steinbeck, John; SP, bust portrait, scarce, 7x8", EX 1,550.00
Storm, Gale; SP, bust portrait, glossy, 8x10", EX 15.00
Streep, Meryl; ISP, bust portrait, color, 8x10", EX 50.00
Swanson, Gloria; SP, 1920s, 3x5", M 45.00
Thomas, Danny; ISP, glossy, 8x10", EX 40.00

John Wayne, inscribed photo, black and white glossy, 9½x7", $350.00.

Verne, Jules; ins & sig on postcard, 1903, EX 1,000.00
Webber, Andrew Lloyd; ISP, bust portrait, scarce, 8x10", EX 250.00
Williams, Hank; sig on album pg, matted w/portrait, scarce 500.00
Young, Brigham; LS to Governor of NH, 1-pg, 1856, EX 1,300.00
Young, Gig; ISP, half-length, glossy, scarce, 8x10", EX 125.00

Automobilia

While some automobilia buffs are primarily concerned with restoring vintage cars, others concentrate on only one area of collecting. For instance, hood ornaments were often quite spectacular. Made of chrome or nickel plate on brass or bronze, they were designed to represent the 'winged maiden' Victory, flying bats, sleek greyhounds, soaring eagles, and a host of other creatures. Today they often bring prices in the $75.00 to $200.00 range. R. Lalique glass ornaments go much higher!

Horns, radios, clocks, gear shift knobs, and key chains with company emblems are other areas of interest. Generally, items pertaining to the classics of the thirties are most in demand. Paper advertising material, manuals, and catalogs in excellent condition are also collectible.

License plate collectors search for the early porcelain-on-cast-iron examples. First year plates (e.g., Massachusetts, 1903; Wisconsin, 1905; Indiana, 1913) are especially valuable. The last of the states to issue regulation plates were South Carolina and Texas in 1917, and Florida in 1918. While many northeastern states had registered hundreds of thousands of vehicles by the 1920s making these plates relatively common, those from the southern and western states of that period are considered rare. Naturally, condition is important. While a pair in mint condition might sell for as much as $100.00 to $125.00, a pair with

chipped or otherwise damaged porcelain may sometimes be had for as little as $25.00 to $30.00.

For more information we recommend *American Automobilia: An Illustrated History and Price Guide* by our advisors for this category, Jim and Nancy Schaut. They are listed in the Directory under Arizona. See also Gas Globes and Panels.

Ashtray, Champion, chrome plug in center, 1920s, 3x5", EX+ ..100.00
Ashtray, Champion, wht molded ceramic cupped hands w/logo, NM ..25.00
Ashtray, Fisk Tire, Fisk boy on rectangular marble base, EX 285.00
Ashtray, Ford V-8 hubcap base & camshaft pedestal, 26", EX 60.00
Ashtray, Sealed Power figure on rnd blk Bakelite dish, NM 110.00
Badge, chauffeur's, OH, 1949 ....28.50
Badge, office, Gulf Refining Co 45.00
Bank, Dodge Dart, cb/metal can, America's 1st Fine..., 4", EX 25.00
Banner, Chevrolet, First Showing...1935, bl/orange/tan, 36", EX ..150.00
Blotter, Gulf Gasoline, orange/bl/yel/brn, 3¾x6¼", EX 65.00
Blotter, Oilzum, yel/blk/wht, 1951, 6¼x3¼", EX 125.00
Book, Texaco, A Picture Story, hardcover, 1931, NM 350.00
Brochure, Chevrolet Trucks for 1941, EX 50.00
Brochure, Harley-Davidson, 4-pg color folder, 1975, 8½x11" 15.00
Brochure, Oldsmobile Six & Eight, full color, 10x7", VG+ 40.00
Brochure, 1922 Indian Scout, part color, 6x8½" 125.00
Calendar attachment, Chevrolet, metal base w/figural auto, EX ...275.00
Change purse, chauffer's hat w/emb car scene, 3", VG 120.00
Clock, Cadillac Service, neon, octagonal, 18", EX 950.00
Clock, dashboard, Elgin, 1920s, NM 80.00
Clock, Ford Sales & Service, Parts & Accessories, 18x18", VG+ ...750.00
Creeper, Pep Boys, oak board on swivel wheels, 36", EX 20.00
Door stop, Texaco, rnd CI sign on pedestal, 9½", VG 230.00
Drinking glasses, Mobil, red Pegasus logo, set of 6, NM 50.00
Emblem, Auburn Motor Car, blk/wht cloisonne chevron, 3", EX .75.00
Emblem, Crow Elk-Hart Motors, cloisonne heart, 2", NM+ 225.00
Emblem, Graham Paige, 3-color cloisonne oval, 2", NM+ 80.00
Emblem, Hudson Super Six, blk/wht cloisonne, 3", EX+ 75.00
Envelope, Indian Motorcycle logo in corner, 8x9", VG 15.00
Fan, Dodge-Plymouth, cb w/wicker hdl, 1936, 12x8" dia, EX 45.00
Fan, Ford, open car in mountain scene, 5 models on hdl, VG 85.00
First-aid kit, Mobil Flying Red Horse, complete 150.00
Flag, Gilmore Gasoline, cloth, lion on blk/wht check, 36", NM ...400.00
Hat, Yellow Cab, fabric/leatherette, 1930s, lg, EX+ 300.00
Hood ornament, Duesenberg, chrome-plated brass, 1931, EX 325.00
Hood ornament, Indian, Bakelite, lighted, 1950 ....150.00
Hood ornament, Lincoln, chrome-plated zinc dog, 1933, EX 275.00
Hood ornament, Mack bulldog 25.00
Hood ornament, Pontiac, chrome-plated Indian head, 2½", EX ..75.00
Horn, Sparton Chime Bugle air horn, 3 trumpets, 16", EX 75.00
Horn button, Custom Diamond T 45.00
Hubcaps, nude woman, 1950s, set of 4 ....250.00
Lamp, headlight, Model-T Ford, brass, 2 lenses, oil burner 85.00
Lamp shade, Chevrolet, plastic stained-glass look, 15", VG 250.00
Letter opener, Chevrolet, bronze, 1949 ....75.00
License plate, AZ, copper, 1934 ....75.00
License plate, CA, porc, 1914, M (unused), pr 325.00
License plate, steel, Sinners/dice/whiskey bottle, '50s 150.00
License plate attachment, Freedom Oil, red/cream, 5½", VG 75.00
License plate attachment, Goodrich Silvertown Safety League, EX ..15.00
License plate attachment, Harold's Club, EX+ 90.00
License plate attachment, Titusville PA, metal, 5x12", VG 110.00
License plate fr, AAA, metal, 1940s, 9¼x13¼", NM 135.00
Lighter, Dodge Trucks, barrel shape, Switch to..., 3", EX 60.00
Lighter, red metal pump w/rnd Gas globe & pump hdl, 4", EX ...175.00
Map holder, Esso Touring Service, metal, red/wht/bl, 24", VG 75.00
Notepad/calendar holder, Pontiac Motor Sales, metal, EX 145.00

Paperweight, Mack Truck, 50th Anniversary, bronze 75.00
Pin, AMA Gypsy Tour Participant, gold-tone, 1954 ....85.00
Pin, ARDC race car, diecut gold-tone metal, 1x1½", EX 25.00
Pin, Chevrolet Corvette Owner, metal, 1955-56, ½" dia, NM ...260.00
Pin, Chevrolet/50 Car Chapter 100 Car Club, 10k gold, NM 110.00
Pin, Packard Master Serviceman/Mechanic, metal, 2x1½", VG ...100.00
Pin-bk button, Chevrolet, I've Seen the 1953..., 1¾", NM 16.00
Pin-bk button, Chevrolet, Watch the Leader, ¾" dia, EX 10.00
Pin-bk button, 100% Ford, 1½" dia, VG 10.00
Plate, Ford, Shenango china, gr/wht, 6¼" dia, EX 45.00
Pocket mirror, Invincible Oil, celluloid, 1910s 75.00
Pocketknife, Chevrolet Parts & Accessories, metal & pearl, VG+ ..20.00
Pocketknife, Esso, metal gas pump shape, 2½", EX 100.00
Pocketknife, Goodyear Tires, tire shape, VG+ 115.00
Price sheet, Indian Motorcycles, 1922 models, 3½x8½" 25.00
Promotional car, 1954 Pontiac, plastic, blk, 2-door, 8", VG 90.00
Promotional car, 1955-56 T-Bird, AMT, plastic, red, 7¼", VG ...75.00
Promotional car, 1956 Chevrolet, plastic, 4-door, red/wht, VG .115.00
Promotional car, 1960 T-Bird, friction, yel/silver, 8", VG 75.00
Promotional car, 1964 Chevrolet Chevell Malibu, 2-door, M 150.00
Promotional car, 1966 Lincoln Continental, plastic, M 100.00
Promotional car, 1967 Cadillac El Dorado, plastic, M 75.00
Promotional car, 1970 Camaro Coupe, plastic, gr, 7", VG 75.00
Radiator cap, Chevrolet mascot, 4½", EX 90.00
Radiator cap, Model T, brass 35.00
Radio, Champion Spark Plugs, plastic plug on base, 14", VG+ 40.00
Sign, Chrysler, neon, encircled diagonal lettering, 25", EX 1,100.00
Sign, Ford Genuine Parts, porc, oval, 16x24", NM 675.00
Sign, Ford Parts Dept, porc, wht on bl, 18x24", EX 775.00
Sign, GMC Sales & Service, orange/bl, 42" dia, EX 950.00
Sign, Goodyear Balloon Tires, porc, tire/globe, 40x46", NM ..1,400.00
Sign, Guaranteed Cadillac Parts, tin on cb, 1910, sq, VG+ 2,000.00
Sign, Parts Dept, encased rvpt glass, light-up, 6x26", EX 300.00
Sign, Pontiac Sales & Service, porc, w/logo, 28x51", NM 1,225.00
Spark plug, Harley-Davidson, 1950s, unused, w/box 25.00
Thermometer, Buick Motor Cars, porc, wht on blk, 27", VG 200.00
Thermometer, Chevrolet, For Economical..., pnt wood, 10", EX ..250.00
Tire gauge, Buick, bl-gr, w/logo, 2x3", EX+ 75.00
Tire gauge, Dodge, yel w/orange & blk lettering, 2x3", EX+ 65.00
Tire gauge, Ford Model A, gr w/bl & red lettering, 2x3", NM 120.00
Weather vane, Pontiac, diecut metal, red/blk, 42", rstr, NM 250.00

Autumn Leaf

In 1933 the Hall China Company designed a line of dinnerware
for the Jewel Tea Company, who offered it to their customers as premiums. Although you may hear the ware referred to as 'Jewel Tea,' it was
officially named 'Autumn Leaf' in the 1940s. In addition to the dinnerware, frosted Libbey glass tumblers, stemware, and a melmac service
with the orange and gold bittersweet pod were available over the years,
as were tablecloths, plastic covers for bowls and mixers, and metal items
such as cake safes, hot pads, coasters, wastebaskets, and canisters. Even
shelf paper and playing cards were made to coordinate. In 1958 the
International Silver Company designed silverplated flatware in a pattern called 'Autumn' which was to be used with dishes in the Autumn
Leaf pattern. A year later, a line of stainless flatware was introduced.
These accessory lines are prized by collectors today.

One of the most fascinating aspects of collecting the Autumn Leaf
pattern has been the wonderful discoveries of previously unlisted pieces.
Among these items are two different bud-ray lid one-pound butter dishes; most recently a one-pound butter dish in the 'Zephyr' or 'Bingo'
style; a miniature set of the 'Casper' salt and pepper shakers; coffee, tea,
and sugar canisters; a pair of candlesticks; an experimental condiment

jar; and a covered candy dish. All of these china pieces are attributed to
the Hall China Company. Other unusual items have turned up in the
accessory lines as well and include a Libbey frosted tumbler in a pilsner
shape, a wooden serving bowl, and an apron made from the oilcloth
(plastic) material that was used in the 1950s tablecloth. These latter
items appear to be professionally done, and we can only speculate as to
their origin. Collectors believe that the Hall items were sample pieces
that were never meant to be distributed.

Hall discontinued the Autumn Leaf line in 1978. At that time the
date was added to the backstamp to mark ware still in stock in the Hall
warehouse. A special promotion by Jewel saw the reintroduction of
basic dinnerware and serving pieces with the 1978 backstamp. These
pieces have made their way into many collections. Additionally, in
1979 Jewel released a line of enamel-clad cookware and a Vellux blanket made by Martex which were decorated with the Autumn Leaf pattern. They continued to offer these items for a few years only, then all
distribution of Autumn Leaf items was discontinued.

It should be noted that the Hall China Company has produced
several limited edition items for the National Autumn Leaf Collectors
Club (NALCC): a New York-style teapot (1984); an Edgewater vase
(1987, different than the original shape); candlesticks (1988); a
Philadelphia-style teapot, creamer and sugar set (1990); a tea-for-two
set and a Solo tea set (1991), a donut jug, and a large oval casserole.
New items for the NALCC: small ball jug, 1-cup French teapot, and a
set of four chocolate mugs. The NALCC has also given their club members special items over the past few years made for them by Hall China:
a sugar packet holder, a chamberstick, and an oyster cocktail. Other
items are scheduled for production. All of these are plainly marked as
having been made for the NALCC and are appropriately dated. A few
other pieces have been made by Hall as limited editions for an Ohio
company, but these are easily identified: the Airflow teapot and the
Norris refrigerator pitcher (neither of which was previously decorated
with the Autumn Leaf decal), a square-handled beverage mug, and the
new-style Irish mug. A production problem with the square-handled
mugs halted their production. The company then issued a regular conic-
style mug with a round handle. Additional items available now are a
covered onion soup, tall bud vase, china kitchen memo board, and egg
drop-style salt and pepper shakers with a mustard pot. They have also
issued a deck of playing cards and Libbey tumblers.

Our advisor for this category is Gwynne Harrison; she is listed in
the Directory under California.

Bowl, covered vegetable; oval, 10", $75.00.

Baker, French; 2-pt 150.00
Baker, French; 3-pt 18.00
Baker, oval, Fort Pitt, 12-oz ind 200.00
Baker, souffle, 4⅛" 10.00
Baker/souffle, 4½" 50.00
Bean pot, 1-hdl 900.00
Bean pot, 2-hdl, 2¼-qt 250.00
Bowl, cereal; 6½" 12.00
Bowl, cream soup; 2-hdl 35.00
Bowl, flat soup; 8½" 20.00

Bowl, fruit; 5½" 6.00
Bowl, mixing; set of 3: 6¼", 7½", 9" 65.00
Bowl, refrigerator; plastic lids, 3 for 275.00
Bowl, Royal Glas-Bake, set of 4 ....145.00
Bowl, salad; 9" 20.00
Bowl, vegetable; divided, 10½" 120.00
Bowl, vegetable; oval, w/lid, 10" 65.00
Bowl, vegetable; oval, 10½" 25.00
Bowl, vegetable; rnd, 9" 125.00
Bowl cover set, plastic, 8-pc: 7 assorted covers in pouch 90.00
Bread box, metal 375.00
Butter dish, 1-lb, regular, ruffled top 300.00
Butter dish, ¼-lb, regular, ruffled top 200.00
Butter dish, ¼-lb, Square Top, rare 1,000.00
Butter dish, ¼-lb, Wings 1,400.00
Cake plate, 9½" 28.00
Cake safe, metal, motif on top & sides, 5" 50.00
Cake safe, metal, side decor only, 4½x10½" 45.00
Cake stand, metal base, orig box 175.00
Candy dish 400.00
Canister, metal, rnd, w/copper-tone lid, set of 4 ....200.00
Canister, metal, rnd, w/ivory plastic lid 10.00
Canister, metal, rnd, w/matching lids, set of 3 ....100.00
Canister, metal, sq, set of 4 ....225.00
Casserole, Royal Glas-Bake, rnd, w/clear glass lid 65.00
Casserole, Tootsie-hdl, w/lid 22.00
Cleanser can, metal, sq, 6", M 1,000.00
Clock, orig works 450.00
Coaster, metal, 3⅛" 7.50
Coffee dispenser/canister, metal, wall type, 10½x19" dia 300.00
Coffee maker, 9-cup, w/metal dripper, 8" 40.00
Coffee percolator, electric, all china, 4-pc 325.00
Coffee percolator/carafe, Douglas, w/warmer base, MIB 250.00
Cookie jar, Tootsie 250.00
Creamer, New Style 20.00
Creamer, Old Style, 4¼" 30.00
Cup & saucer, regular 12.50
Cup & saucer, St Denis 32.00
Custard cup 6.00
Flatware, silverplate, ea 32.00
Flatware, stainless, ea 28.00
Fruit cake tin, metal 10.00
Golden Ray base, to use w/candy dish or cake plate, pr 50.00
Gravy boat 25.00
Hot pad, metal, red or gr felt-like bking, rnd 18.00
Hot pad, oval 12.00
Hurricane lamp, Douglas, w/metal base, pr 400.00
Kitchen utility chair, metal, M 800.00
Marmalade jar, 3-pc 75.00
Mixer cover, Mary Dunbar, plastic 50.00
Mug, beverage 60.00
Mug, Irish coffee 125.00
Mustard jar, 3½", 3-pc 75.00
Napkin, ecru muslin, 6" sq 45.00
Pickle dish or gravy liner, oval, 9" 25.00
Picnic thermos, metal 350.00
Pie baker, 9½" 28.00
Pitcher, utility; 2½-pt, 6" 20.00
Place mat, paper, scalloped 35.00
Place mat, set of 8, MIP 325.00
Plate, 10" 15.00
Plate, 6" or 7", ea 6.00
Plate, 8" 15.00
Plate, 9" 10.00

Platter, 11½" 25.00
Platter, 13½" 28.00
Playing cards, regular or Pinochle, dbl deck, minimum value 160.00
Range set, shakers & covered drippings jar 65.00
Sauce dish, serving; Douglas, Bakelite hdl 350.00
Shakers, Casper, pr 25.00
Shakers, range, hdl, pr 25.00
Sugar bowl, New Style 25.00
Sugar bowl, Old Style, 3½" 40.00
Tablecloth, cotton sailcloth w/gold stripe, 54x54" 125.00
Tablecloth, cotton sailcloth w/gold stripe, 54x72" 135.00
Tablecloth, ecru muslin, 56x81" 300.00
Tablecloth, plastic 150.00
Teakettle, metal enamelware 225.00
Teapot, Aladdin 50.00
Teapot, long spout, 1935-42 ....50.00
Teapot, Newport 160.00
Teapot, Newport, dtd 1978, minimum value 160.00
Toaster cover, plastic, fits 2-slice toaster 40.00
Towel, dish; pattern & clock motif 50.00
Towel, tea; cotton, 16x33" 55.00
Trash can, metal, red 325.00
Tray, glass, wood hdl, 19½x11¼" 130.00
Tray, metal, oval 55.00
Tray, tidbit; 3-tier 100.00
Tumbler, Brockway, 13-oz 40.00
Tumbler, Brockway, 16-oz 40.00
Tumbler, Brockway, 9-oz 40.00
Tumbler, frosted, 9-oz, 3¾" 30.00
Tumbler, gold frost etched, flat, 10-oz 40.00
Tumbler, gold frost etched, flat, 15-oz 50.00
Tumbler, gold frost etched, ftd, 10-oz 60.00
Tumbler, gold frost etched, ftd, 6½-oz 60.00
Vase, bud; sm or regular decal, 6" 200.00
Warmer base, oval 185.00
Warmer base, rnd 175.00

Aviation

Aviation buffs are interested in any phase of flying, from early developments with gliders, balloons, airships, and flying machines to more modern innovations. Books, catalogs, photos, patents, lithographs, ad cards, and posters are among the paper ephemera they treasure alongside models of unlikely flying contraptions, propellers and rudders, insignia and equipment from WWI and WWII, and memorabilia from the flights of the Wright Brothers, Lindbergh, Earhart, and the Zeppelins. See also Militaria. Our advisor for this category is John R. Joiner; he is listed in the Directory under Georgia.

Airspeed indicator, Kollsman, 60 to 300 MPH, 1930-40s **95.00**

Creamer and sugar bowl, Graf Zeppelin, blue and gold on white, Heinrich & Co., 1928, $350.00.

Badge, hat; Delta, gold w/bl & wht enamel, 1929-53, EX 150.00
Badge, hat; Eastern, Ground Hostess, EX 25.00
Ballpoint pen, Western Airlines, New Non-Stop to San Diego, M ..10.00
Blanket, Air Canada, red, maple leaf logo, EX 20.00
Book, Curtiss Aviation, illus, 1912 ....40.00
Book, Flying Tiger Mechanic's Handbook, 1952, 300+ pgs, EX .125.00
Book, God Is My Co-Pilot, Robt L Scott (sgn), 1943, 277-pg 135.00
Book, Identification of Aircraft, civil defense, 1942, 145-pg 22.00
Book, Last Flight, Amelia Earhart, 1937, 226-pg, EX 45.00
Book, Zeppelin-Weltfahrten, 1933, folio sz, EX 100.00
Booklet, TWA, 1935, EX 15.00
Brochure, Pan Am System of the Flying Clippers..., 1948, EX 12.00
Brochure, Waco Aristocraft, 2-color, 4-fold, 1946, 16x11" 24.00
Certificate, Braniff Airlines, Equator Crossing, 1961, fr 40.00
Coasters, Continental Airlines, red plastic, set of 6 ....10.00
Coin, silver, Amelia Earhart emb portrait, 1928 ....45.00
Coin, silver, TWA Stratoliner Club, 1939-40, 1" dia 40.00
Cosmetic bag, Pan Am, bl w/emblem, zipper closure, NM 5.00
Cup, American, bl & wht, Syracuse China/Airlite, 1940s, EX 35.00
Decal, Nat'l Air Races, winged head logo, 1932, 2" dia 2.50
Emergency card, Eastern DC-9-31, Mar 1976, plastic, M 5.00
Flask, 1st Moon Landing, Neil Armstrong emb, Anchor Hocking ..175.00
Flatware, fork, Swissair 5.00
Flatware, fork/knife/spoon, Braniff International, set 15.00
Flatware, spoon, TWA 5.00
Flight computer, Am Airlines pilot's, P Dalton Mfg, 1933 ....135.00
Goggles, Luxor, mfg by EB Meyrowitz Co, 1918-20s, EX 295.00
Hatpin, Eastern, Flight Attendant 25.00
Key chain, Goodyear Airship, EX 10.00
Knife/corkscrew, Eastern 10.00
Lapel pin, Aircraft Industrial Service, brass propellers, 1918 ....65.00
Magazine, Aero Digest, Fairchild '45' photo cover, 1935, G 10.00
Magazine, Aero Digest, Howard DGA-9 on cover, May 1937, VG ...9.00
Magneto switch, F6F Grumman Hellcat, 2¼" magneto, 1940s 85.00
Map, Am Airlines, DC-6 on cover, 1953, opens to 22x32", EX 20.00
Mirror, emergency signalling, General Electric, 1940-50s, 3x6" ...30.00
Money clip, Capital Airlines, w/file & knife 65.00
Money clip, Goodyear Airship, EX 10.00
Pennant, World Fliers 1924 & biplane, gr felt, EX 20.00
Photo, DH-4 Barnstormer, sepia tone, 1920s, 3x4", EX 9.00
Pin, silver, Pan Am China clipper, pin-bk, '30s, 2" wingspan 40.00
Pin-bk, Apollo 11, US First to Moon, July 1969, 3½" 18.00
Pitcher, TWA, silver-tone, Oneida, 3" 20.00
Plate, American, bl & wht, Syracuse China/Airlite, 1940s, EX ..125.00
Plate, Apollo XIV commemorative, Wheaton glass, MIB 25.00
Postcard, American, DC-4, EX 10.00
Postcard, Hampden bomber, real photo, RAF markings, 1940, NM ..7.00
Poster, Douglas DC-3 'blueprint,' 1946, 24x36", EX 19.00
Propeller, laminated hardwood from biplane, 1930s, 84" 395.00
Report, pilot flight test, CAA form, Harrisburg, 1946 ....8.00
Ring, American, Junior Pilot, gold-tone, adjustable 15.00
Ring, pilot's, silver, eagle ea side, Air Corps emblem, 1930s 75.00
Ring, sterling, Air Corps Victory, V emblem, 1940s 65.00
Roly poly, United Air Lines, oval logo 5.00
Screwdriver, Swallow Aircraft Co, aluminum hdl, 1920s, 8" 145.00
Sheet music, Amelia Earhart's Last Flight, photo cover, 1939 ......40.00
Timetable, United, Hawaii Aug/Sept 1952, surfer on cover, EX ...15.00
Tray, American, w/coffee holder, silver, old logo, 6" dia, EX 35.00
Tumbler, highball; Continental, 3" 5.00
Tumbler, juice; Eastern, etched logo, early, EX 25.00
Wine, Braniff, stemmed, 5½" 5.00
Wine, Continental Air Lines, stemmed, 4½" 5.00
Wings, United, Jr Stewardess, metal, 2", MOC 12.00
Wings, United, Pilot, metal, upswept logo, 3" 40.00

Avon Works

In 1902 a firm based in Wheeling, West Virginia, absorbed several small local potteries; the Vance Avon Faience Co. of Tiltonville, Ohio, was one of them. They continued in operation at Tiltonville until 1905, when Avon moved to the Wheeling location. The production of art-ware was discontinued in an effort to produce a more commercially profitable semiporcelain ware; but by 1907 even that proved to be unsuccessful, and the Wheeling department closed in 1907. For more information on the earlier pottery, see Vance Avon.

Pitcher, squeezebag leaves on turq irid, dtd 1906, 6" 295.00
Tankard, decal portrait on brn, mk, +6 portrait mugs 600.00
Vase, grapevines, bl & brn on lime gr, 1902, 9" 850.00
Vase, incised stylized floral, bl/gr on dk bl gloss, mk, 5" 500.00
Vase, landscape, glossy, 6" 400.00
Vase, squeezebag 3-branch floral decor, Rhead, #126, 5x7" 1,200.00
Vessel, squeezebag crocus, red on bl to gr, hdls, 6" 400.00

Baccarat

The Baccarat Glass company was founded in 1765 near Luneville, France, and continues to this day to produce quality crystal tableware, vases, perfume bottles, and figurines. The firm became famous for the high-quality millefiori and caned paperweights produced there from 1845 until about 1860. Examples of these range from $300.00 to as much as several thousand. Since 1953 they have resumed the production of paperweights on a limited edition basis. Our advisors for this category are Randall Monsen and Rod Baer; their address is listed in the Directory under Virginia. See also Bottles, Commercial Perfume; Paperweights.

Tumbler, gilt and silver Legion d'honneur wreath suspended from a crown and ribbon, oval panels with cut laurel bands, ca 1835, 3½", $375.00.

Bottle, scent; Invitation, Jean Patou, sgn/labeled, 8" 795.00
Bottle, scent; Rose Tiente Sunburst, bulbous, w/stopper, 6¼" 110.00
Bottle, scent; Rose Tiente Sunburst, w/stopper, 5x2⅞" 95.00
Bottle, scent; Rose Tiente Swirl, cylindrical, 7¼x3⅛" 88.00
Bowl, centerpc; 8-pointed star w/prismatic properties, 15½" 200.00
Candlestick, Rose Tiente Swirl, sq, 8¼x3⅝" 195.00
Decanter, Remy, pinched shape w/spiked sides 140.00
Goblets, wheel-eng scrolls, 8 water, 4½"+4 wines, 4" 315.00
Ice bucket, Rose Tiente Swirl, 5⅜x5¼" 175.00
Lamp, fairy; Rose Tiente Sunburst, matching saucer base, 4⅛" ..245.00
Lamp, sapphire bl, emb ribs/scrolls, burner, w/shade, 10" 395.00
Lamp, spiral font & plinth on sq base, kerosene, 23", pr 4,400.00
Lamp base, Rose Tiente Sunburst, orig burner, 8x2⅞" 135.00
Lamp base, Rose Tiente Swirl, orig burner, 8½x3⅝" 145.00
Salt cellar, clear w/ornate gold band, gr scroll ft, 2" dia 75.00
Sculpture, Great Horned Owl, #767924, ca 1980 ....2,000.00

Tazza, Rose Tiente Swirl, ped ft, scalloped rim, 3¼x5" 110.00
Vase, eng Oriental foliage, on 4-leg ormolu base, 11" 800.00

Badges

The breast badge came into general usage in this country about 1840. Since most are not marked and styles have changed very little to the present day, they are often difficult to date. The most reliable clue is the pin and catch. One of the earliest types, used primarily before the turn of the century, involved a 't-pin' and a 'shell' catch. In a second style, the pin was hinged with a small square of sheet metal, and the clasp was cylindrical. From the late 1800s until about 1940, the pin and clasp were made from one continuous piece of thin metal wire. The same type, with the addition of a flat back plate, was used a little later. There are exceptions to these findings, and other types of clasps were also used. Hallmarks and inscriptions may also help pinpoint an approximate age.

Badges have been made from a variety of materials, usually brass or nickel silver; but even solid silver and gold were used for special orders. They are found in many basic shapes and variations — stars with five to seven points, shields, disks, ovals, and octagonals being most often encountered. Of prime importance to collectors, however, is that the title and/or location appear on the badge. Those with designations of positions no longer existing (City Constable, for example) and names of early western states and towns are most valuable.

Badges are among the most commonly reproduced (and faked) types of antiques on the market. At any flea market, ten fakes can be found for every authentic example. Genuine law badges start at $30.00 to $40.00 for recent examples (1950-1970); earlier pieces (1910-1930) usually bring $50.00 to $90.00. Pre-1900 badges often sell for more than $100.00. Authentic gold badges are usually priced at a minimum of scrap value (karat, weight, spot price for gold); fine gold badges from before 1900 can sell for $400.00 to $800.00, and a few will bring even more. A fire badge is usually valued at about half the price of a law badge from the same circa and material. Our advisor for this category is Gene Matzke; he is listed in the Directory under Wisconsin.

Fountain City F.D., silver metal, eagle on shield, $35.00.

Agricultural Volunteer, Conn, 1917 ....30.00
Board of Elections Inspector, silver-tone, pin-bk, early 65.00
Cincinnati OH Police, silver-tone shield w/state seal, 2¾" 65.00
Cleveland Police Sergeant, gold-tone metal shield, 3" 35.00
Jackson Co MO Deputy Constable, 6-point silver star, hallmk 70.00
Metropolitan Police Corporal, gold-tone shield w/blk letters 60.00
Milwaukee Police, SP shield w/blk lettering, EX 35.00
New Bedford Police, NP on brass, pin-bk, early, 2" dia 100.00
Pinkerton Special Services, shield w/eagle, hallmk 35.00
Reading PA Police, silver-tone w/state seal in center 30.00
Tamarac FL Police Officer, silver-tone w/enamel, 3" 40.00
US Capital Police 1993 Inauguration, gold-tone star 75.00

Banks

This year the continuing impact of auctions shows in the listings. Again, condition, condition, condition is what is driving the market. In addition, some banks with outstanding provenances were available, and they brought prices that reflect their individual value to a specific collector but distort the real market value of similar banks. The spread between a bank in good condition and an excellent or original condition example continues to widen. It is imperative that you realize the importance of paint and the completeness of a bank. Also some banks have a wide margin of value based on color variations. It becomes more and more important that you attend as many shows and auctions as possible. Direct contact with collectors and knowledgeable dealers is the only way you can get a feel for prices and the desirability of banks, both mechanical and still. Banks continue to hold their value. However, it is becoming extremely important for collectors to understand the market.

Let's take a look at the price variations possible on an Uncle Sam mechanical bank. If you find one with considerable paint missing but with some good color showing, the price would be around $1,000.00. If it has repairs or restoration, the value would drop to something like $800.00 or less. If you had another example, and it had two thirds of its original paint and no repairs, it would be priced around $1,800.00. One with minor nicks and 90% of the original paint could go as high as $3,500.00. Or if you find one that is in near-original paint and has no repairs, $5,000.00 would not be out of line. This should help you see what causes price variations. After considering all of these factors, remember the final price is always determined by what a willing buyer and seller agree on for a specific bank.

The category of mechanical banks is unique. Along with cast-iron toys, they are among the most outstanding products of the Industrial Revolution and are recognized as some of the most successful of the mass-produced products of the 19th century. The earliest mechanicals were made of wood or lead; but when John Hall introduced Hall's Excelsior, a cast-iron mechanical bank, it was an immediate success. J. & E. Stevens produced the bank for Hall and soon began to make their own designs. Several companies followed suit, most of which were already in the hardware business. They used newly developed iron-molding techniques to produce these novelty savings devices for the emerging toy market. Mechanical banks reflect the social and political attitudes of the times, racial prejudices, the excitement of the circus, and humorous everyday events. Their designers made the most of simple mechanics to produce banks with captivating actions that served not only to amuse but to promote the concept of thrift to the children. The quality of detail in the castings are truly remarkable. The most collectible examples were made during the period of 1870 to 1900; however, they continued to be made until the early days of World War II. J. & E. Stevens, Shepard Hardware, and Kyser and Rex are some of the more well-known manufacturers; most made still banks as well.

Still banks are widely collected, and you can literally choose from thousands of banks. No one knows exactly how many different banks were made, but at least three thousand have been identified in the various books published on the subject. Cast-iron examples still dominate the market, but the lead banks from Europe are growing in value. Tin and early pottery banks are drawing more interest as well. American pottery banks which were primarily collected by Americana collectors are becoming more important in the still bank field. This market has not been as volatile as the mechanical banks, but the number of collectors is growing. The auction market on still banks is not as extensive as with the mechanicals, but some nice examples do turn up. Collectors and dealers are still the best source.

Book of Knowledge Banks were produced by John Wright (Pennsylvania) from circa 1950 until 1975. Of the thirty models they made during those years, a few continued to be made in very limited numbers until the late 1980s; these they referred to as the 'Medallion' series. (Today the Medallion banks command the same prices as the earlier Book of Knowledge series.) Each bank was a handcrafted, hand-painted duplicate of an original as was found in the collection of The Book of Knowledge, the first children's encyclopedia in this country. Because the antique banks are often priced out of the range of many of today's collectors, these banks are being sought out as affordable substitutes for their very expensive counterparts.

As both value and interest continue on the increase, it becomes even more important to educate one's self to the fullest extent possible. We recommend these books for your library: *The Dictionary of Still Banks* by Long and Pitman, *The Penny Bank Book* by Moore, and *The Bank Book* by Norman. If you are primarily interested in mechanicals, *Penny Lane*, a book by Davidson, is considered the most complete reference available. It contains a cross-reference listing of numbers from all other publications on mechanical banks.

In the listings that follow, banks are identified by L for Long, G for Griffith, M for Moore, N for Norman, D for Davidson, and W for Whiting.

Our advisors for this category are Diane Patalano, listed in the Directory under New Jersey, and Dan Iannotti (for Book of Knowledge), listed under Michigan.

Key:
CI — cast iron   NPCI — nickel-plated cast iron
EPCI — electroplated cast iron

Advertising

Am Can Co, A Century of Progress, tin can 35.00
Amoco 586, can shape, 2¼" dia, NM 15.00
Big Boy, vinyl, slender, sm red & wht checks, 1970s, MIP 35.00
Borden's, Elsie's head, molded vinyl, 1970s, 9", EX 85.00

Calumet Baking Powder, cardboard cylinder with Kewpie-like child on a tin top, 4", EX, $145.00.

Calumet, N1650, pnt CI, 1924, M 385.00
Cap'n Crunch, vinyl Jean LaFoote figure, 1975, 7½", M 90.00
Cheesasarus Rex, mail-in premium, Kraft Macaroni & Cheese, M .35.00
Colonel Sanders, plastic figure, no base, 1970s, 8", EX 30.00
Decker's Iowana Pig, M603, CI, worn pnt, 2¾" 150.00
Eight O'Clock Coffee, red, NM 20.00
Ernie the Keebler elf, ceramic, recent 20.00
Florida Orange Bird, hard vinyl 35.00
Gerber's Orange Juice, tin can 28.00
Harley-Davidson Hog 80.00
Hush Puppies Hound, molded vinyl basset hound, '70s, 8", EX 30.00
Icee Polar Bear 35.00
Kellogg's Tony the Tiger, hard plastic figure, 1970s, 8½", NM 50.00
Ocean Spray Pure Cranberry Juice, tin can 55.00
Pillsbury Doughboy, cb tube w/repeated images, 1980s, 7", NM ...15.00

Red Goose Shoes, M610, pnt CI, 3¾", VG 75.00
Rival Dog Food, tin can 35.00
Sinclair Dinosaur, wht metal, 5½", EX 85.00
Smokey the bear, ceramic, seated figure w/pail, Japan, M 135.00
24-Hour Bug, gr vinyl bug w/pk eyes, Pepto Bismol, 1970s, 7", NM ..40.00

Book of Knowledge Banks

Artillery Bank, M 350.00
Boy on Trapeze, M 650.00
Bulldog, M 325.00
Butting Buffalo, M 350.00
Cabin Bank, M 315.00
Creedmoor Bank, M 395.00
Dentist, M 315.00
Eagle & Eaglets, M 450.00
Humpty Dumpty, M 335.00
Indian & Bear, M 425.00
Jonah & the Whale, M 325.00
Leap Frog, M 395.00
Magician Bank, NM 330.00
Milking Cow, M 345.00
Organ Bank, Boy & Girl, M 335.00
Owl Turns Head, M 275.00
Paddy & the Pig, M 385.00
Spise a Mule, Boy on Bench, M 395.00
Spise a Mule, Jockey Over, M 325.00
Tammany Bank, M 295.00
Teddy & the Bear, M 315.00
Trick Pony, w/orig box & documents, NM 345.00
Uncle Remus, M 395.00
Uncle Sam, M 375.00
US & Spain, M 325.00
William Tell, M 340.00

Mechanical

Always Did Spise a Mule, Bench; N-2940, pnt CI, EX 1,400.00
Artillery, N-1050, pnt CI, NM 4,400.00
Bad Accident, N-1150a, pnt CI, J&E Stevens, NM 3,750.00
Bear & Tree Stump, N-1210, CI, partial rpt, EX 415.00
Bill E Grin, N-1230, CI, rpt, VG 495.00
Boy on Trapeze, N-1350a, pnt CI w/some rpt, G 2,000.00
Boy Scout, N-1370, pnt CI, J&E Stevens, ca 1915, EX 6,000.00
Boy Scout, N-1370, pnt CI, J&E Stevens, ca 1915, M 11,550.00
Boy Stealing Watermelon, pnt CI, Kyser & Rex, 1894, EX 2,200.00
Boy Stealing Watermelon, pnt CI, Kyser & Rex, 1894, M 6,000.00
Butting Buffalo, pnt CI, Kyser & Rex, 1888, EX 9,900.00
Cabin, N-1610, pnt CI, J&E Stevens, 1885, EX 770.00
Chief Big Moon, seated Indian, pnt CI, NM- 3,700.00
Clown on Globe, N-1930, pnt CI, NM 5,000.00
Creedmoor, N-2000b, pnt CI, G- 275.00
Darktown Battery, M-2080, pnt CI, J&E Stevens, VG 2,800.00
Darktown Battery, N-2080, pnt CI, J&E Stevens, M 5,700.00
Dentist, D-152, pnt CI, J&E Stevens, 1880s-90s, VG 8,250.00
Dinah, N-2150b, pnt CI, short sleeves, 1891, EX 2,100.00
Dog on Turntable, N-2170a, pnt CI, Judd Mfg, EX 525.00
Elephant, N-2280, man pops out, pnt CI & wood, VG 230.00
Elephant, N-2280a, man pops out, pnt CI, Enterprise, 1884, EX ..625.00
Hall's Excelsior, N-2710, pnt CI, rpl monkey, 1869, VG 275.00
Hen & Chick, N-2790, pnt CI, NM 7,300.00
Hen & Chick, N-2790, pnt CI, G 450.00
Horse Race, N-2890, str base, pnt CI, 1870, M 24,200.00
Humpty Dumpty, N-2900, pnt CI, clown bust, 7½", EX 1,500.00

Indian Shooting Bear, N-2980, pnt CI, EX+ 2,900.00
Indian Shooting Bear, N-2980a, pnt CI, J&E Stevens, VG+ ..1,750.00
Jolly N, N-3110, pnt CI, English, VG 250.00
Jolly N, N-3330, Shepard, pnt CI, VG 275.00
Jonah & Whale, N-3490, pnt CI, Shepard Hardware, EX 4,000.00
Lion & 2 Monkeys, N-3650a, CI, worn pnt 775.00
Lion & 2 Monkeys (1 peanut), N-3650, pnt CI, EX 1,950.00
Magician, N-3760, pnt CI, EX 2,000.00
Mammy & Child, N-3790, CI, very worn pnt 2,400.00
Mason, N-3800, pnt CI, EX 2,300.00
Monkey (coin in stomach) pnt CI, VG 350.00
New Creedmoor, N-4220, pnt CI, EX 425.00
Organ Bank, N-4310, boy & girl, pnt CI, EX 975.00
Organ Grinder & Bear, N-4350, pnt CI, NM 7,200.00
Paddy & Pig, N-4400, pnt CI, VG 1,500.00
Paddy & Pig, N-4400, pnt CI, NM 5,100.00
Peg-Legged Begger, N-4480, pnt CI, VG 1,200.00
Santa Claus, N-5010, pnt CI, EX- 1,400.00
Toad on Stump, N-4470, pnt CI, EX 650.00
Tommy, N-5590, pnt CI, EX 4,700.00
Trick Buffalo, M-558, pnt CI, 5½", NM 1,150.00
Uncle Sam, N-5740, CI, worn pnt 1,050.00
Weeden's Plantation, N-5910, pnt tin, EX 1,000.00

Registering

Balfour Budget Bank, MC-249, tin, 3", VG 70.00
Battleship, tin litho, dime register, 2½" sq, G- 35.00
Captain Marvel, tin litho, dime register, Fawcett, '48, 2⅝", G 90.00
Daily Dime Cowboy, tin litho, Kalon Mfg, 2⅝", G 55.00
Davy Crockett, tin litho, dime register, 2⅝" sq, EX 300.00
Dime a Day, MC-229, tin litho, dime register, 3¾", EX 170.00
Jackie Robinson, MC-234, dime register, tin litho, 3", M 500.00
Keep 'Em Smiling, MC-219, dime register, tin litho, 3", EX 300.00
Little Orphan Annie, MC-215, tin litho, 3", EX 330.00
Mickey Mouse, tin litho, dime register, Disney, 1959, VG 415.00
Piggy Bank, tin litho, Kalon Mfg, dime register, 2⅝", NM 90.00
Prince Valiant, tin litho, King Features, 1954, 2⅝", G- 40.00
Sen Sen Gum, polished chrome, 1912, 2½x1¼", EX 135.00
Snow White, MC-215, tin litho, dime register, VG 85.00
Snow White, tin litho, dime register, Walt Disney, 2½" sq, M ..200.00
Superman, MC-216, dime register, tin litho, 3", EX 225.00
Vacation Daily Dime, tin litho, Kalon Mfg, 2⅝", NM 85.00
1964 World's Fair, tin litho, US Steel, 1961, MIP 70.00

Still

Baseball and Three Bats, M-1608, Hubley, 1914, VG+, $850.00; Camel, M-768, painted cast iron, Hubley, 1920s, EX, $325.00.

Alligator by Ball, M-728, pnt lead & tin, 2⅞", EX 435.00
Armoured Car, M-1424, pnt CI, 3¾", NM 2,200.00
Banque w/Rooster Finial, M-1152 (similar), brass, 6⅜", EX 450.00

Baseball & 3 Bats, M-1608, pnt CI, 5¼", NM 1,800.00
Baseball Player, M-18 variant, pnt CI, 5⅝", EX 275.00
Battleship Oregon, M-1439 variant, CI, worn pnt, 6" 200.00
Bear w/Staff on Base, M-712 (similar), brass, 6⅞", EX 135.00
Birth Bank, M1141 variant, brass, 7", EX 130.00
Blackpool Tower, M-984, pnt CI, 7⅜", EX 375.00
Boston Bull Terrior, M-421, pnt CI, 5¼", EX 300.00
Boston Statehouse, M-1209, pnt CI, 6¾", VG 1,250.00
Boxer Head, M-400, pnt lead, 2⅝", EX 250.00
Buffalo, M-560, pnt CI, 3⅛", VG 140.00
Building w/Gladiator, M-1154 (similar), pnt CI, 7½", NM 1,350.00
Bulldog w/Sailor's Cap, M-363, pnt lead, 4⅜", EX 875.00
Bungalo, M-999, pnt CI, 3¾", EX 325.00
Camel, M-768, pnt CI, 4¾", EX 325.00
Camel w/Bent Leg, M-757 (similar), pnt wht metal, 7⅛", EX ...260.00
Capitalist, M-5, pnt CI, 5", EX 2,200.00
Cat (Seated) w/Fine Lines, M-367, pnt CI, 4", NM 575.00
Cat w/Ball, M-352, pnt CI, 2½", EX+ 375.00
Cat w/Toothache, M-351, lead, worn pnt, 4" 175.00
City Bank, M-1111, CI, worn pnt, 4⅛" 230.00
Clown, M-211, pnt CI, 6¼", EX 85.00
Clown, N-1870, tin litho, Chein, EX 150.00
Clown w/Arched Top, N-1860, tin litho, NM 130.00
Clown w/Crooked Hat, M-210, pnt CI, 6¾", NM 3,700.00
Cologne Cathedral, M-980, lead, worn pnt, 4⅛" 450.00
Dina, N-2150a, pnt CI, short sleeves, VG 400.00
Dog w/Drum, pnt lead & tin, 1¾", NM 275.00
Dolphin, M-33, CI, worn pnt, 4½" 775.00
Domed Mosque, M-1177, pnt CI, 4¼", EX 340.00
Donkey w/Saddle, M-503, pnt lead, 5", EX 255.00
Dutch Boy on Barrel, M-180, pnt CI, 5⅝", EX 175.00
Dutch Girl (Standing), M-16, CI, worn pnt, 6½" 575.00
Eagle, M-1134, pnt CI, 9¾", EX+ 1,300.00
Elephant, 3 Stars; N-2340, pnt CI, NM 90.00
Elephant & 3 Clowns, N-2250, pnt CI, EX 1,100.00
Elephant on Tub, M-484, pnt CI, 5⅜", EX 215.00
Elephant w/Short Trunk, M-1630, pnt CI, 3¾", VG 105.00
Fez w/Tassle, M-1393 variant, pnt steel, 3⅛" 145.00
Finial Bank, M-1158, pnt CI, 5¾", EX 650.00
Football Player, M-11, pnt CI, 5⅞", EX 400.00
Frowning Face, M-12, pnt CI, 5⅝", EX 1,450.00
Globe Savings Fund, M-1199, pnt CI, 7⅛", EX 825.00
Goose, M-615, CI, gold pnt traces, 5" 150.00
Goose, M-615, pnt CI, 4⅞", EX 260.00
GOP Deco Elephant, M-450, pnt CI, 4⅜", EX 375.00
Graf Zeppelin, M-1428, CI, worn pnt, 1¾", VG 175.00
Hitler Pig, M-305, pnt compo, 4½", EX 125.00
Home Savings, M-1201, pnt CI, 10½", EX 1,100.00
Horse, Prancing; M-517, pnt CI, 4¼", VG 180.00
Horse, Rearing; M-521, bronze rpt, 6½", VG 55.00
Humpty Dumpty, M-338, tin litho, 5¼", NM 165.00
Independence Hall, M-1244, pnt CI, 8⅞", VG 550.00
Indiana Silo, M-1247, pnt CI, 3½", NM 725.00
Japanese Safe, M-883, pnt CI, 5⅜", EX 230.00
Jarmulowsky Building, M-1086, pnt CI, 7¾", EX 1,600.00
Junior Cash Register, M-930, pnt CI, 4¼", EX 250.00
King Midas, M-13, pnt CI, 4½", NM 3,500.00
Kitten w/Bow, M-349, pnt CI, 4¾", EX 125.00
Lichfield Cathedral, M-968, 6½", EX 425.00
Lincoln High Hat, M-1380, pnt CI, 2⅜", NM 170.00
Lion, M-742, pnt CI, 2½", EX+ 160.00
Lion (Quilted), M-758, pnt CI, 3¾", EX 370.00
Lion on Tub, M-746, CI, worn pnt, 5½" 130.00
Lion on Wheels, M760, pnt CI, 4½", EX 225.00

Lion w/Ears Up, M-757, pnt CI, 3⅝", EX 250.00
Little Joe, N-3690, pnt CI, VG 375.00
Made in Canada (Boy Scout), M-46, pnt CI, 5¾", EX 650.00
McKinley/Teddy Elephant, M-452, pnt CI, 2½", EX 1,450.00
New Deal Roosevelt, M-148, CI, worn pnt, 5" 200.00
New England Church, M-986, pnt CI, 7½", VG 350.00
New Heatrola, M-1354, CI & tin, worn pnt, 4½" 100.00
Old Doc Yak, M-30, pnt CI, 4½", VG 310.00
Organ Grinder, M-216, pnt CI, 6¼", EX 90.00
Pagoda, M-1153, pnt CI, 5", EX 390.00
Palace, M-1116, pnt CI, 7½", VG 850.00
People's Bank, M-1058, pnt CI & tin, 3⅝", EX 775.00
Pirate on Trunk, M-341, pnt wht metal, 6¼", EX 65.00
Possum, M-561, pnt CI, 2⅜", EX 675.00
Professor Pug Frog, M-311, pnt CI, 3¼", EX 450.00
Recording Bank, M-1062, pnt CI, 6⅝", VG 175.00
Rhino, M-721, pnt CI, 2⅝", NM 2,700.00
Roof Bank, M-1122, CI, NM, 5¼" 250.00
Rooster, M-547, pnt CI, 4⅝", NM 350.00
Rooster, N-4920, pnt CI, NM 560.00
Round Grenade, M-1429, CI, worn pnt, 2⅞" 160.00
Saddle Horse, M-523, pnt CI, 2¾", EX 290.00
Sailor, M-28, pnt CI, 5½", EX 400.00
Sailor, M-29, pnt CI, 5⅝", EX 550.00
Satchel, M-1268, pnt CI, 3⅜", NM 475.00
Save for a Rainy Day, M-616, pnt CI, 5⅜", EX 250.00
Scottie (Seated), M-419, CI, worn pnt, 4⅞" 100.00
Shell Out, M-1622, pnt CI, 2½", VG 360.00
Skyscraper, M-1241, CI, silver rpt, missing trap, 6⅝" 140.00
Songbird on Stump, M-664, pnt CI, 4¾", EX 450.00
Standing Indian, M-228, pnt CI, 5⅞", VG 150.00
State Bank, M-1080, CI, pnt traces, 5⅞" 200.00
State Bank, M-1633 (similar), pnt CI, 5½", EX 370.00
Steamboat, M-1459, pnt CI, 2½", EX+ 400.00
Stork Safe, M-651, pnt CI, 5½", NM 1,500.00
Swan, M-734, pnt lead, 4¼", EX 400.00
Tank, M-1419, pnt CI, 3⅝", EX 200.00
Thrifty Wise Pig, M-609, pnt CI, 6⅝", VG 120.00
Tower Bank, M-1198, pnt CI, 6⅞", EX 1,000.00
Tower Bank, M-1208 variant, pnt CI, 9¼", EX 325.00
Town Hall, M-998, pnt CI, 4⅝", NM 700.00
Uncle Sam Bust, N-5750, pnt CI, EX 1,450.00
Uncle Sam Hat, M-1382, pnt CI, 2", NM 140.00
US Tank Bank 1918, M-1437, pnt CI, 2⅜", EX 150.00
War Bonds Bullet, M-1403, pnt steel, 5¾", EX 200.00
Washington Monument, M-1049, pnt CI, 7½", EX 875.00
Westminster Abbey, M-973, CI, worn pnt, 6¼" 300.00
Westside Presbyterian Church, M-958, pnt CI, 3¾", EX 425.00
White City Safe #12, M-910, CI, worn pnt, 4⅞" 175.00
White City Safe #325, M-914, pnt CI, 4⅝", EX 300.00
Wisconsin Beggar Boy, M-307, pnt CI, 6⅞", EX 925.00
Wisconsin War Eagle, M-678, pnt CI, 2⅞", M 1,350.00
Young N, M-170, pnt CI, 4½", VG 225.00
1-Story House, M-1000, CI, worn pnt, 3" 125.00
100,000 Money Bag, M-1262, CI, worn pnt, 3⅝" 300.00
1890 Tower Bank, M-1198, pnt CI, 6⅞", EX 925.00
6-Sided Building, M-1007, pnt CI, 2⅜", EX 325.00

Barber Shop Collectibles

Even for the stranger in town, the local barber shop was easy to find, its location vividly marked with the traditional red and white striped barber pole that for centuries identified such establishments. As far back as the 12th century, the barber has had a place in recorded history. At one time he not only groomed the beards and cut the hair of his gentlemen clients but was known as the 'blood-letter' as well, hence the red stripe for blood and the white for the bandages. Many early barbers even pulled teeth! Later, laws were enacted that divided the practices of barbering and surgery.

The Victorian barber shop reflected the charm of that era with fancy barber chairs upholstered in rich wine-colored velvet; rows of bottles made from colored art glass held hair tonics and shaving lotion. Backbars of richly carved oak with beveled mirrors lined the wall behind the barber's station. During the late 19th century, the barber pole with a blue stripe added to the standard red and white as a patriotic gesture came into vogue.

Today the barber shop has all but disappeared from the American scene, replaced by modern unisex salons. Collectors search for the barber poles, the fancy chairs, and the tonic bottles of an era gone but not forgotten. See also Bottles; Razors; Shaving Mugs.

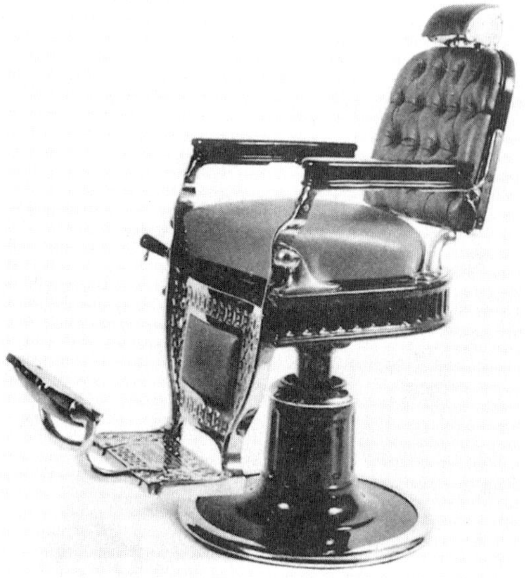

Chair, Koch, restored maroon porcelain and tan leather with renickeled parts, NM, $1,200.00.

Chair, gargoyle heads w/walnut panels, rstr, 1880s 1,500.00
Chair, Hercules, brass & oak, gr velour, swan supports, rstr 1,600.00
Chair, surgeon/barber; cvd oak, leather upholstery, G 1,250.00
Mug rack, dk wood, 24 holes, 46x22", EX 325.00
Mug rack, oak, 30 holes, 41x35", EX 575.00
Mug rack, oak w/raised acanthus leaves, 48 holes, 46x44" 625.00
Mug rack, wooden, 36 holes, scrolled crest, 45x32" 400.00
Mustache curler 27.50
Pole, cvd/trn wood w/ball finial, rpr, 80", VG 500.00
Pole, Koch, sidewalk type, model #909, 1921, NM 2,250.00
Pole, porc & glass, red & wht, 23½x5", EX 350.00
Pole, trn wood, old rpt w/gold, 19th C, 84", EX 865.00
Pole, wood w/old red/wht/bl pnt, mini, 10⅝" 375.00
Pole, wooden w/red/wht/bl/gold rpt, 24¼" 375.00
Sign, glass lens w/mc pnt in metal half-globe fr, 17" dia, EX 425.00
Sign, porc, Barber Shop, striped border, 12x24", VG+ 200.00
Sign, porc flange, red/wht/bl, 12x24", VG 150.00
Soap pot, wht ceramic w/gold name, w/lid, 2x3¾" dia 200.00
Stand, NP chrome, lights up, w/strap/brush/razor/cup/mirror, 62" 350.00
Token dispenser, Koken Barber Supply, NPCI, VG 75.00
Tube, Barbasol, w/box 27.50

Tube, Burma Shave, w/box **25.00**

Barometers

Barometers are instruments designed to measure the weight or pressure of the atmosphere in order to anticipate approaching weather changes. They have a glorious history. Some of the foremost thinkers of the 17th century developed the mercury barometer, as the discovery of the natural laws of the universe progressed. Working in 1644 from experiments by Galileo, Evangelista Torrecelli used a glass tube and a jar of mercury to create a vacuum and therefore prove that air has weight. Four years later, Rene Descartes added a paper scale to the top of Torrecelli's mercury tube and created the basic barometer. Blaise Pascal, working with Descartes, used it to determine the heights of mountains; indeed, only later was the correlation between changes in air pressure and changes in the weather observed and the term 'weatherglass' applied. Robert Boyle introduced it to England; and Robert Hook modified the form and designed the wheel barometer.

The most common type of barometer is the wheel or banjo type. Second is the stick type. Modifications of the plain stick would be the marine gimballed type, followed by the laboratory or kew or Fortin type. Others are the Admiral Fitzroys of which there are twelve or more types. The above types all have mercury contained in either glass tubing or wood-box cisterns.

Another type of barometer is the aneroid, working on atmospheric pressure changes. They come in all sizes ranging from 1" in diameter to 12" or larger. They may be in metal or wood cases. There is a Barograph which records on a graph that rotates around a drum powered by a 7-day clock mechanism. Pocket barometers (altimeters) vary in sizes from 1" diameter up to 6" diameter. One final type of barometer is the symphisometer, a modification of the stick barometer used for a limited time and not as accurate as a conventional marine barometer.

Our advisor for this category is Bob Elsner; he is listed in the Directory under Florida.

Gimbal stick, B Wood Liverpool, mahog/ebony, eng dial, 36" ...**2,100.00**
Stick type, DE Lent Rochester NY, allover cvd case, 36" **300.00**
Wheel or banjo, Atchison London, cvd/stained oak, 1880s, 29" ...**100.00**
Wheel or banjo, Carns...Liverpool, rosewood veneer & MOP, 38" ...**450.00**
Wheel or banjo, English mahog w/inlay, w/thermometer, 19th C **825.00**
Wheel or banjo, English rosewood, cvd bonnet/ivory finial, 39" ...**465.00**
Wheel or banjo, Leoni, NY, mahog w/eng eagle, ca 1840 ....**1,840.00**
Wheel or banjo, T Palmer & Gr, rosewood, 1870s, 41½" **300.00**

Barware

Back in the thirties when social soirees were very elegant affairs thanks to the influence of Hollywood in all its glamour and mistique, cocktails were often served up in shakers styled as miniature airplanes, zeppelins, skyscrapers, lady's legs, penguins, roosters, bowling pins, etc. Some were by top designers such as Norman Bel Geddes and Russel Wright. They were made of silverplate, glass, and chrome, often trimmed with colorful Bakelite handles. Today these are hot collectibles, and even the more common Deco-styled chrome cylinders are often priced at $25.00 and up. Ice buckets, trays, and other bar accessories are also included in this area of collecting. Our advisor for this category is Stephen Visakay, who is listed in the Directory under New Jersey.

Bottle opener, Cartier, Art Moderne, stainless steel/14k gold **100.00**
Set: shaker, chrome, Zeppelin, Henckes, 12", complete, EX ...**1,400.00**
Shaker, chrome, Bakelite cap w/scowling face relief, 11" **220.00**
Shaker, chrome, fire extinguisher w/emb recipes, 11", VG **90.00**

Photo courtesy Stephen Visakay

Golf-bag cocktail shaker, silverplate, International Silver Co., simulated cow-hide grain with leather straps and ball bag, Pat Sept. 7, 1926, 12½x3" dia, $1,200.00.

Shaker, chrome, penguin shape, twist-off cap/beak, 11", VG **250.00**
Shaker, chrome, upright dumbbell, disk base, blk cap, 13", VG .**250.00**
Shaker, chrome w/incised bands, Manning-Bowman, 8" **50.00**
Shaker, chrome w/incised verticals, yel Bakelite top, 12" **300.00**
Shaker, cobalt glass, dumbell shape, chrome cap, 13" **160.00**
Shaker, cobalt glass w/horizontal silver bands, 11", +2 glasses **325.00**
Shaker, cobalt glass w/silver bands, chrome cap, 16" **210.00**
Shaker, cranberry glass w/silver bands, 10", +6 3" glasses **150.00**
Shaker, glass, blk enamel penguins, shouldered/ftd, 14", VG **250.00**
Shaker, glass, blk/wht/silver geometrics, 11", VG **30.00**
Shaker, glass, dumbbell, chrome cap, 13", VG **190.00**
Shaker, glass, dumbbell w/ribbing, 12", VG **160.00**
Shaker, glass, hourglass shape in chrome housing, 9", EX **190.00**
Shaker, glass, World's Fair, bl letters etc on opaque, 5" **325.00**
Shaker, hammered sterling, Shreve & Co, early 20th C, 10½" ..**440.00**
Shaker, polished aluminum cylinder, 2 wheel hdls, 11", VG **100.00**
Shaker, silver/copper, Horn of Plenty, England, 1959, 15" **110.00**
Shaker, SP, bell shape, Asprey & Co, 1937, 10¾x6" **315.00**
Shaker, SP, bell shape, Dunhill, 11", EX **90.00**
Shaker, SP, bullet-nose cylinder, cup-dispenser base, 16" **950.00**
Shaker, SP, cylindrical, int rotates, drink recipes, 9", VG **200.00**
Shaker, SP, hammered barrel shape, Grogan, 7", VG **130.00**
Shaker, SP, lighthouse form w/flag, Meriden, 13", VG **950.00**
Shaker, SP, milk pail form, Reed & Barton, 1957, 10", VG **100.00**
Shaker, SP, stepped bell form w/wood hdl, England, 11" **230.00**
Shaker, SP, Thirst Extinguisher, England, 15", EX **325.00**
Shaker, SP, 2-hdl trophy shape, strainer bottom, 10", EX **160.00**

Basalt

Basalt is a type of unglazed black pottery developed by Josiah Wedgwood and copied by many other companies during the late 18th and early 19th centuries. It is also called 'Egyptian Black.' See also Wedgwood.

Coffeepot, classical scenes relief, flutes & scrolls, 8", EX **60.00**
Coffeepot, simple geometrics, unmk, 9⅝x12½", EX **50.00**
Creamer, emb floral, ornate hdl w/perched eagle, 4" **275.00**
Creamer, Wellington memorial relief, lion's head spout, 4x7" ...**225.00**
Pitcher, ewer w/band of vertical panels, Shorthose & Co, 6" **185.00**

Baskets

Basket weaving is a craft as old as ancient history. Baskets have been used to harvest crops, for domestic chores, and to contain the catch of fishermen. Materials at hand were utilized, and baskets from a specific region are often distinguishable simply by analyzing the natural fibers used in their construction. Early Indian baskets were made of corn husks or woven grasses. Willow splint, straw, rope, and paper were also used. Until the invention of the veneering machine in the late 1800s, splint was made by water-soaking a split log until the fibers were softened and flexible. Long strips were pulled out by hand and, while still wet and pliable, woven into baskets in either a cross-hatch or hexagonal weave.

Most handcrafted baskets on the market today were made between 1860 and the early 1900s. Factory baskets with a thick, wide splint cut by machine are of little interest to collectors. The more popular baskets are those designed for a specific purpose, rather than the more commonly found utility baskets that had multiple uses. Among the most costly forms are the Nantucket Lighthouse baskets, which were basically copied from those made there for centuries by aboriginal Indians. They were designed in the style of whale-oil barrels and named for the South Shoal Nantucket Lightship where many were made during the last half of the 19th century. Cheese baskets (used to separate curds from whey), herb-gathering baskets, and finely woven Shaker miniatures are other highly-prized examples of the basket-weaver's art.

In the listings that follow, assume that each has a center bentwood handle (unless handles of another type are noted) that is not included in the height. Unless another type of material is indicated, assume that each is made of splint.

For further information we recommend *Collector's Guide to Country Baskets* by Don and Carol Raycraft, available from Collector Books. See also American Indian; Eskimo; Sewing; Shaker.

Apple, wht oak splint, old dk gr pnt, VA, 1860s, 9x13½" 110.00
Buttocks, finely woven, minor damage, 2½x3¾x3½" 50.00
Buttocks, finely woven, some age, 3¼x4¾x6" 180.00
Buttocks, lt natural patina, some age, 9x16x13" 130.00
Buttocks, old patina, 8x11x9½" 165.00
Buttocks, old worn red pnt, 7x12x11" 575.00
Buttocks, 14 ribs, EX brn patina, 3x5x5½", rare sz 300.00
Buttocks, 14 ribs, wooden hdl, 3⅝x6x5¼" 195.00
Buttocks, 16 ribs, minor damage, 5½x12x12" 130.00
Buttocks, 28 ribs, 2-tone w/dk varnish, 4½x8½x7" 195.00
Buttocks, 30 ribs, EX patina, 4¾x9" 145.00
Buttocks, 32 ribs, dk red pnt, 4¾x9½x8½" 415.00
Buttocks, 32 ribs, minor damage, 9½x12" 100.00
Buttocks, 32 ribs, tightly woven, well shaped, 2x4½x4" 635.00
Cheese, mini, 3x7½" 250.00
Divided, 18th C, 31" L 275.00

Eye-of-God handle, 11½x12", $200.00.

Eye-of-God hdl, 1⅛x2¼x2⅛" 115.00
Goose feather, tightly woven swing, hdls & lid, 24" H 360.00
Gr-dyed splint on sides at rim & bottom, 3⅛x8" dia 160.00
Half buttocks, 11 ribs, old dk patina, 7" W 250.00
Nantucket, hinged bail hdl, oval, late 1800s, 11½", EX 575.00

Nantucket, solid wood bottom, hinged hdl, 4⅜x6" dia, EX 650.00
Nantucket, SP Boyer stamp on base, 5¼x7½" 1,350.00
Nantucket, swing hdl, Fred Chadwick, 9x12" 990.00
Nantucket, swing hdl, Mitchell Ray, 4¾x10" dia 770.00
Nantucket, swing hdl, MJ Hall...Penn, 7½x11¼" 1,100.00
Nantucket, swing hdl, oval, Fred Chadwick, 4¾x12x10" 1,100.00
Nantucket, swing hdl, 3x5" 400.00
Nantucket, swing hdl, 4x6"dia 385.00
Nantucket, swing hdl, 4x8¾" dia 440.00
Nantucket, swing hdl, 5¼x11¾" dia 440.00
Nantucket, swing hdl, 5x6¾" dia 440.00
Nantucket, swing hdl, 6¼x9" dia 500.00
Nantucket, swing hdl, 6x8½" dia 495.00
Nantucket purse, cvd ivory sea horse on lid, 7x11" 250.00
Oriental Export, rice straw, old varnish, woven hdl, 8x13x8" 85.00
Painted curliques w/faded bl, finely woven, 4½x8¾x7½" 25.00
Rectangular, dk worn finish, 4½x8¾x4½", EX 105.00
Rye straw bound w/wooden splint, coiled, early, 9½x19", VG ...110.00
Swing hdl, mini, 2¾x4" 500.00
Swing hdl, mini, 2¾x4", VG 225.00

Batchelder

Ernest A. Batchelder was a leading exponent of the Arts and Crafts movement in the United States. His influential book, *Design in Theory and Practice,* was originally published in 1910. He is best known, however, for his artistic tiles which he first produced in Pasadena, California, from 1909 to 1916. In 1916 the business was relocated to Los Angeles where it continued until 1932, closing because of the Depression.

In 1938 Batchelder resumed production in Pasedena under the name of 'Kinneola Kiln.' Output of the new pottery consisted of delicately cast bowls and vases in an Oriental style. This business closed in 1951. Tiles carry a die-stamped mark; vases and bowls are hand incised. Our advisor for this category is Jack Chipman, author of *Collector's Encyclopedia of California Pottery;* he is listed in the Directory under California.

Ashtray, lt bl matt, hexagonal w/emb advertising, 4½" 200.00
Bookends, 2¾" tiles set on Potter Studio brass mts, pr 350.00
Bowl, cobalt gloss, 1½x8" 95.00
Bowl, rose, oval, Kineloa Kiln mk, 4x12x7" 145.00
Tile, cherub in tree, bl semi-matt, 5¾x2½" 175.00
Tile, geometric design, blk & orange, 4" 65.00
Tile, La Mayan, terra cotta, 3½" 95.00
Tile, man w/horn emb on red/brn w/bl-wash ground, 5½", +fr ...210.00
Tile, stylized thistle, lt tan/bl bsk, 2¾" 70.00
Vase, caramel/brn gloss w/bl & gray highlights, 4" 260.00
Vase, teal over brn gloss, 5" 325.00

Battersea

Battersea is a term that refers to enameling on copper or other metal. Though originally produced at Battersea, England, in the mid-18th century, the craft was later practiced throughout the Staffordshire district. Boxes are the most common examples. Some are figurals, and many bear an inscription. Values are given for examples with only minimal damage, which is normal. Our advisor for this category is John Harrigan; he is listed in the Directory under Minnesota.

Bonbonniere, European scene on underside, 1½x2¾", EX 625.00
Box, Esteem the Giver, scenic lid w/mirror, ¾x1½x1" 275.00
Box, florals on bl, wht lid w/couple in landscape, oval, 2⅝" 195.00
Box, grisaille classical scene w/gold, 3½" dia 500.00

Box, lady's torso form, head forms lid, 3" **1,600.00**
Box, lt bl, wht lid w/Lafayette portrait, oval, 2⅜" **660.00**
Box, 2 boxers/10 spectators on lid, cobalt base, ¾x2x1½" **375.00**
Mirror holders, Gen Washington, pk w/pk banner, 2", pr **1,225.00**
Mirror knob, castle landscape, brass mt, late 1700s, 1½x2", pr ...**325.00**
Mirror knob, lady & dog, late 1700s, 1⅞", pr, VG **300.00**
Mirror knob, lady's portrait, late 1700s, 1⅜", pr, EX **350.00**
Mirror knob, man (lady) portrait, brass mts, 1780s, 1⅝", pr **525.00**
Mirror knob, putti artists, late 1700s, 1⅞" dia, pr, G **375.00**
Mirror knob, Sacred to Friendship monument, 2", EX, pr **675.00**
Needle case, floral & insects on yel, rstr, 4¾" L **550.00**

Bauer

Originally founded in Paducah, Kentucky, in 1885, the J.A. Bauer Company moved to Los Angeles where it was re-established in 1910. Until the 1920s, their major products were terra cotta gardenware, flowerpots, and stoneware and yellow ware bowls. During prohibition they produced crocks for home use. A more artful form of product began to develop with the addition of designer Louis Ipsen to the staff circa 1915. Some of his work, a line of molded vases, flowerpots, bowls, etc., was awarded a bronze medal at the Pacific International Exposition in 1916.

In 1930 the first of many dinnerware lines was tested on the market. Their initial pattern, Plain Ware, was well accepted and led the way to the introduction of the most popular dinnerware in their history and with today's collectors, Ring Ware. It was produced from 1932 into the early 1960s in solid colors of jade green, royal blue, dusty burgundy, ivory, Chinese yellow, Delph blue, orange-red, and (in very limited quantities) black or white. Its simple pattern was a design of closely-spaced concentric ribs, either convex or concave. Over the years, more than one hundred shapes were available. Some were made in limited quantities, resulting in rare items to whet the appetites of Bauer buffs today. Other patterns were La Linda, produced during the 1940s and 1950s, and Monterey Moderne, introduced in 1948 and remaining popular into the 1950s (made in pink, black, gray, brown, and green).

After WWII a flood of foreign imports and loss of key employees drastically curtailed their sales, and the pottery began a steady decline that ended in failure in 1962. Prices listed below reflect the California market. For more information we recommend *Collector's Guide to Bauer Pottery: Identification & Values* (Collector Books) and *The Collector's Encyclopedia of California Pottery* both by Jack Chipman, our advisor for this category. Mr. Chipman's address may be found in the Directory under California.

Ashtray, Monterey, wht, rare **175.00**
Bean pot, plain, all colors but blk, no hdl, 1-qt **60.00**
Bean pot, plain, blk, 2-hdl, 1-qt **125.00**
Beverage server, ice water; Monterey, w/lid **325.00**
Bird bath, jade gr or yel, 2-pc, rare, 22" **1,500.00**
Bowl, batter; Ring, blk, 1-qt **175.00**
Bowl, dessert; Monterey Moderne, blk, 5" **35.00**
Bowl, fruit; Monterey, wht, 6" **18.00**
Bowl, fruit; Monterey Moderne, all colors but blk, 4¼" **12.50**
Bowl, fruit/dessert; Al Fresco, speckled gr or gray, 5" **12.00**
Bowl, mixing; Atlanta, cobalt, #24 ....**150.00**
Bowl, mixing; Ring, lt bl, chartreuse or red-brn, #24, 1-qt **35.00**
Bowl, ramekin; Gloss Pastel Kitchenware, all colors **10.00**
Bowl, salad; Ring, blk, 9" **120.00**
Bowl, serving; Monterey, all colors, 9" **45.00**
Bowl, vegetable; Al Fresco, coffee brn or Dubonnet, 9¼" **20.00**
Bowl, vegetable; Contempo, all colors, 9½" **18.00**
Bowl, vegetable; Monterey Moderne, blk, oval, 9" **50.00**
Butter dish, Ring, dk bl, burgundy or ivory, oblong **250.00**
Butter dish, Ring, lt bl, rnd **225.00**

Candlestick, Ring, orange-red, dk bl or burgundy, 2½" **65.00**
Casserole, Gloss Pastel Kitchenware, all colors **45.00**
Casserole, Ring, blk, 8½" **180.00**
Casserole, Ring, dk bl, ivory or burgundy, 6½" **90.00**
Chop plate, Ringware, burgundy, 12" **75.00**
Chop plate, Ringware, orange, 12" **50.00**
Coffee server, Brusche Contempo, all colors, 8-cup **25.00**
Coffee server, plain, all colors but blk, open **65.00**
Coffee server, Ring, Delphinium w/copper hdl **95.00**
Coffeepot, Ring, orange-red, jade gr or yel (no later colors) **300.00**
Cookie jar, Brusche Al Fresco, all colors, rare **200.00**
Cookie jar, Ring, Delph bl, ivory or burgundy **500.00**
Creamer, Brusche Al Fresco, coffee brn or Dubonnet **10.00**
Creamer, La Linda, all matt colors, old shape **15.00**
Creamer & sugar bowl, Ring, ivory **95.00**
Cup, jumbo coffee; La Linda, all gloss colors (not made in matt) ...**50.00**
Cup & saucer, Brusche Contempo, all colors **10.00**
Cup & saucer, demitasse; Ring, yel **225.00**
Cup & saucer, El Chico, all colors **55.00**
Cup & saucer, Monterey, all colors but wht **33.00**
Custard cup, Gloss Pastel Kitchenware, all colors **8.00**
Flower bowl, Hi-Fire line, yel, fluted, deep, 10" **85.00**
Flowerpot, Ring Art & Gardenware, yel or orange-red, ruffled, 2" ..**20.00**
Gravy boat, Monterey, all colors but blk **40.00**
Gravy bowl, Ring, burgundy **125.00**
Honey jar, Ring, yel or bl, very rare **2,000.00**
Hostess tray & mug, Brusche Al Fresco, speckled gr or gray **35.00**
Jar, cigarette/cigar; Ring, blk, rare, 4" **500.00**
Jardiniere, Ring Art & Gardenware, dk bl or wht, 8" **85.00**
Marmalade, plain, blk **200.00**
Mug, Ring, blk, bbl shape, 12-oz **200.00**
Oil jar, all colors but blk, #129, 20" **900.00**
Pitcher, beer; Ring, blk, cylindrical, rare **800.00**
Pitcher, Gloss Pastel Kitchenware, gr, yel or turq, ice lip, 2-qt **50.00**
Plate, Al Fresco, speckled gr or gray, 8" **8.00**
Plate, Contempo, all colors, 10" **10.00**
Plate, grill; Monterey Moderne, all colors but blk, rnd **20.00**
Plate, grill; Monterey Moderne, blk, sq, rare **50.00**
Plate, Monterey Moderne, all colors but blk, 10½" **25.00**
Plate, salad; Ring, blk, 7½" **65.00**
Platter, La Linda, lt brn, pk or gray, oval, 12" **22.00**
Platter, Monterey Moderne, blk, oval, 12" **50.00**
Punch bowl, Ring, cobalt, 3-ftd, 14" **600.00**
Rack, holds Ring coffee server & 6 6-oz tumblers **65.00**
Relish plate, Monterey, all colors but wht, oval, 10½" **65.00**
Sherbet, Ring, dk bl, burgundy or ivory **95.00**
Souffle dish, Ring, jade gr or yel **200.00**
Stein, Ring, blk, cylindrical, 5" **250.00**
Sugar bowl, plain, blk, w/lid **100.00**
Swan, med turq **95.00**

Teapot, Gloss Pastel Kitchenware line, Aladdin design by Ray Murray, yellow, marked Bauer Los Angeles, 1940s, 8-cup, $200.00.

Teapot, Aladdin, yel, sm (6-cup) 125.00
Teapot, Contempo, all colors, 6-cup 45.00
Teapot, Monterey Moderne, all colors but blk, 6-cup 65.00
Teapot, plain, all colors but blk, 6-cup 150.00
Teapot, Ring, burgundy, 2-cup 100.00
Tumbler, La Linda, gr, yel or turq, 8-oz 22.00
Vase, jade, bulbous, Fred Johnson, 4¼" 40.00
Vase, jade, ruffled, Matt Carlton, 3½" 75.00
Vase, Rebekah, jade, Matt Carlton, 18" 1,650.00
Vase, Ring, blk, cylinder, 10" 200.00
Vase, Ring Gardenware, yel, jade or lt bl, cylinder, 8" 100.00

Bavaria

Bavaria, Germany, was long the center of that country's pottery industry; in the 1800s, many firms operated in and around the area. Chinaware vases, novelties, and table accessories were decorated with transfer prints as well as by hand by artists who sometimes signed their work. The examples here are marked with 'Bavaria' and the logos of some of the various companies which were located there.

Bonbon, floral transfer w/gold scrolls, 2-pc, 4x8¼" 40.00
Box, lady w/rose bouquet figural, 9" 135.00

Cake plate, multicolor roses in yellow center of wide rose-colored rim, crown and RC mark, $65.00.

Chocolate pot, wht w/gold band, +6 c/s 450.00
Creamer & sugar bowl, roses, lustre trim 40.00
Mug, bl flowers w/gold 35.00
Plate, lady's portrait, lacy gold rim, 6½" 35.00
Plate, swans & lily pads, scalloped cobalt border, 12½" 95.00
Punch bowl, floral w/in & w/o, mk, 8½x14", +porc stand 600.00
Teapot, alternating panels w/gold, +6 c/s 200.00
Tray, flower transfers, open lattice work, Schumann 100.00
Urn, floral spray w/gold, dome lid, Waldershof, 12x7" 55.00

Beer Cans

When the flat-top can was first introduced in 1934, it came with printed instructions on how to use the triangular punch opener. Cone-top cans, which are rare today, were patented in 1935 by the Continental Can Company. By the 1960s, aluminum cans with pull tabs had made both types obsolete.

The hobby of collecting beer cans has been rapidly gaining momentum over the past ten years. Series types, such as South African Brewery, Lion, and the Cities Series by Schmit and Tucker, are especially popular.

Condition is an important consideration when evaluating market price. Grade 1 must be in like-new condition with no rust. However, the triangular punch hole is acceptable. Grade 2 cans may have slight scratches or dimples but must be free of rust. For Grade 3, light rust, minor scratching, and some fading may be acceptable. When these

defects are more pronounced, a can is defaulted to Grade 4. Those in less-than-excellent condition devaluate sharply. In the listings that follow, cans are arranged alphabetically by brand name, not by brewery. Unless noted otherwise, values are for 11- to 12-oz. cans in Grade 1 condition.

Key: IRTP — Internal Revenue Tax Paid

ABC Extra Pale Dry Beer, flat top, red, wht & bl 30.00
Arrow Bock Beer, flat top, blk w/red label 500.00
Atlas Prager Bock Beer, flat top, gold & red, goat's head 60.00
Black Dallas Beer, flat top, red & wht, IRTP 400.00
Brew 66 Lighter, flat top, red w/yel labels & stripes 75.00
Brown Derby Pilsner, flat top, silver w/gr & brn stripes 75.00
Budweiser Bock Beer, flat top, red & wht, goat on B 600.00
Bull Dog Malt Liquor, flat top, metallic gold 25.00
Carling's Red Cap Ale, pull tab, gr w/yel oval label 15.00
Coors, flat top, yel, gold & red 40.00
Coors Golden Beer, flat top, gold w/blk band, IRTP 95.00
Croft All Malt Cream Ale, cone top, 3 heads 450.00
Croft Cream Ale, flat top, gr w/yel lettering 65.00
Dixie, flat top, gold w/wht label 350.00
Drewery's Lager, flat top, silver w/blk, instructional, IRTP 60.00
E&B Special Beer, cone top, NM 40.00
Edelweiss Bock Beer, flat top, brn w/wht label & bands 85.00
Edelweiss Light Beer, cone top, 1-qt, full, NM 85.00
Falstaff Draft Beer, pull tab, wht w/gold & maroon shield 10.00
Fisher Light Beer, pull tab, wht w/red label, gold trim 5.00
Gold Seal, low cone top, silver w/bl bottom band, IRTP 400.00
Great Falls Select Fine Beer, flat top, wht w/red 6, IRTP 25.00
Gretz, crowntainer, silver w/yel label, bl stripes, IRTP 150.00
Gunther's Premium Dry Lager, flat top, yel/brn stripes, IRTP 55.00
Hals Premium Beer, flat top, metallic bl, laughing man 150.00
Hamm's, flat top, gold w/bl band 10.00
Harvard Ale, flat top, silver w/red ball & trim, IRTP 125.00
Heidelberg Light Pilsner, pull tab, gold & wht w/blk 10.00
Holihan's Light Ale, flat top, gr w/wht label 30.00
Home Brew Lager Beer, flat top, gold w/red oval label 40.00
Home Olde Style Ale, flat top, wht w/gr label w/gold outline 30.00
Iron City Beer, 1975 Super Bowl Champs, pt 5.00
Kol Premium Quality, flat top, wht w/bl stripes & label 15.00
Lucky Lager, flat top, Aged For Flavor, yel w/gold label 10.00
Miller Ale, gr w/red, pt 4.00
National Bohemian Bock Beer, flat top, blk w/red label 95.00
Old Crown Ale, flat top, gold/yel label, instructional, IRTP 75.00
Old Milwaukee, flat top, bl, red/yel waiter label, IRTP 200.00
Old Mission Beer, flat top, orange 150.00
Old St Louis Ale, flat top, silver & red, IRTP 800.00
Olde Virginia, high cone top, bl w/wht label 150.00
Pabst Lodi, pull tab, wht w/bl label, gold-outlined Lodi 25.00
Padre Pale Lager, pull tab, yel & maroon 12.00
Pilgrim Ale, flat top, silver & red, instructional, IRTP 1,000.00
Primo Hawiian Beer, pull tab, gold & wht, map of islands 10.00
Rainier Famous Old Stock Ale, flat top, gr, maroon & wht 65.00
Reading Beer, Bicentennial, pt 3.00
Red Cap Ale, flat top, gr w/yel label, red cap 15.00
Regal Extra Special Ale, flat top, gr w/wht label, 3 steins 75.00
Regal Extra Special Ale, soft top, gr w/wht label, 3 steins 20.00
Schlitz Lager, low cone top, brn w/yel bands, IRTP 110.00
Schmidt City Club, high cone top, gold w/red label 65.00
Silver Bar Premium Beer, flat top, blk w/yel Silver Bar 150.00
Spearman Premium Quality, flat top, wht w/gold label 150.00
Sterling Pilsner, flat top, wht w/red oval, IRTP 50.00
Sterling Pilsner, flat top, wht w/red oval, non-IRTP 30.00
Tropical Golden All Grain, flat top, wht & red, gold bands 60.00

Valley Brew Pale Premium Beer, cone top, gray w/wht stripes **100.00**
Van Merritt Beer, windmill, pt **3.00**

Bellaire, Marc

Marc Bellaire, originally Donald Edmund Fleischman, was born in Toledo, Ohio, in 1925. He studied at the Toledo Museum of Art, under Ernest Spring, while employed as a designer for the Libbey Glass Company. During World War II, while serving in the Navy, he traveled extensively throughout the Pacific resulting in his enriched sense of design and color.

Marc settled in California in the 1950s where his work attracted the attention of national buyers and agencies who persuaded him to create ceramic lines of his own, employing hand-decorated techniques throughout. This resulted in the building of a studio in Culver City. He produced high-quality ceramics, often decorated with ultramodern figures or geometric patterns. His work was executed with a distinctive flair. His most famous line was Mardi Gras, decorated with slim dancers in spattered and striped colors of black, blue, pink, and white. Other major patterns were Jamaica, Balinese, Beachcomber, Friendly Island, Cave Painting, Hawaiian, Bird Isle, Oriental, Jungle Dancer, and Kashmir. Kashmir usually has the name Ingle on the front and Bellaire on the reverse.

It is to be noted that Marc was employed by Sascha Brastoff during the 1950s. Many believe that he was hired for his creative imagination and style.

During the period of 1951-1956, Marc was named one of the top ten artware designers by *Giftwares Magazine*. After 1956 he taught and lectured on art, design, and ceramic decorating techniques from coast to coast. Many pieces were one of a kind, commissioned throughout the United States.

During the 1970s he set up a studio in Marin County, California, and eventually moved to Palm Springs where he opened his final studio/gallery. There he produced large pieces with a Southwest style. Mr. Bellaire died in 1994. Our advisor for this category is Marty Webster; he is listed in the Directory under Michigan.

Ashtray, Bird Isle, blk birds on cream, 8" **85.00**
Ashtray, Clown, mc on cream, 7" **65.00**
Ashtray, Jamaica, musicians on brn, 10x14" **85.00**
Ashtray, Mardi Gras, figures on blk, 14x14" **225.00**
Ashtray, Still Life, matt fruits & leaves, 10x15" **100.00**
Compote, Cave Painting, 4-ftd, 6x12" **125.00**
Compote, Woman w/Bl Bird, 4-ftd, 8x17" **225.00**
Covered box, Mardi Gras, 10" dia **200.00**
Ewer, Mardi Gras, figures on blk, hdl, 18" **400.00**
Figurine, Mardi Gras, man reclining, very slim, 18" **1,000.00**
Figurine, Mardi Gras, man standing, very slim, 24" **1,000.00**
Figurine, Polynesian man standing, 12" **500.00**
Lamp, Mardi Gras, long-neck vase on wood base, 28" **350.00**
Platter, Hawaiian, 3 figures on orange, 7x13" **125.00**
Platter, Mardi Gras, figures on blk, 12x18" **250.00**
Platter, Polynesian Dancer, egg shaped, 11x15" **150.00**
Tray, Jungle Dancer, figure on blk/gr, 12" dia **200.00**
Vase, Balinese Women, hour-glass shape, 8" **125.00**
Vase, Black Cats, hourglass shape, 8" **125.00**
Vase, Mardi Gras, hourglass shape on 3 ft, 11" **125.00**

Belleek, American

From 1883 until 1930, several American potteries located in New Jersey and Ohio manufactured a type of china similar to the famous Irish Belleek soft-paste porcelain. The American manufacturers identified their porcelain by using 'Belleek' or 'Beleek' in their marks. American Belleek is considered the highest achievement of the American porcelain industry. Production centered around artistic cabinet pieces and luxury tablewares. Many examples emulated Irish shapes and decor with marine themes and other naturalistic styles. While all are highly collectible, some companies' products are rarer than others. The best-known manufacturers are Ott and Brewer, Willets, The Ceramic Art Company (CAC), and Lenox. You will find more detailed information in those specific categories. Our advisor for this category is Mary Frank Gaston; you will find her address in the Directory under Texas.

Key:
AAC — American Art China   CAP — Columbian Art Pottery
  Company   Works
ABC — American Beleek Works

Bowl, tiny flowers w/in & w/o, gold trim, AAC, 2½x5" **350.00**

Photo courtesy Mary Frank Gaston

Demitasse cup, nonfactory gold decoration on white porcelain, green 'Beleek' mark, 2¼" high, $110.00.

Creamer & sugar bowl, HP flowers, pk int, gold trim, AAC **650.00**
Cup & saucer, morning glories, Morgan **150.00**
Salt cellar, sponged gold on scalloped rim & base, AAC, 2½" ...**125.00**
Teapot, gold-paste decor on dragon shape, red CAP mk, 9" W ...**1,500.00**
Tumbler, Souvenir David's Society...1899, CAP, 4¼" **300.00**

Belleek, Irish

Belleek is a very thin translucent porcelain that takes its name from the village in Ireland where it originated in 1859. The glaze is a creamy ivory color with a pearl-like lustre. The tablewares, baskets, figurines, and vases that have always been made there are being crafted yet today. Shamrock, Tridacna, Echinus, and Thorn are but a few of the many patterns of tableware which have been made during some periods(s) of the pottery's history. Throughout the years, their most popular pattern has been Shamrock.

It is possible to date an example to within twenty to thirty years of crafting by the mark. Pieces with an early stamp often bring prices nearly triple that of a similar but current item. With some variation, the marks have always incorporated the Irish wolfhound, Celtic round tower, harp, and shamrocks. The first three marks (usually in black) were used from 1863 to 1946. A series of green marks identified the pottery's offerings from 1946 until the seventh mark (in gold/brown) was introduced in 1980 (it was discontinued in 1992). The most current mark, the eighth, is blue. Belleek Collector's International Society limited edition pieces are designated with a special mark in red. In the listings below, numbers designated with the prefix 'D' relate to the book *Belleek, The Complete Collector's Guide and Illustrated Reference, Second*

Edition, published by Wallace-Homestead Book Company, One Chilton Way, Radnor, PA 19098-0230. The author, Richard K. Degenhardt, is our advisor for Belleek; he is listed in the Directory under North Carolina.

Key:
A — plain (glazed only)
B — cob lustre
C — hand tinted
D — hand painted
E — hand-painted shamrocks
F — hand gilted
G — hand tinted and gilted
H — hand-painted shamrocks and gilted
J — mother-of-pearl
K — hand painted and gilted
L — bisque and plain
M — decalcomania
N — special hand-painted decoration
T — transfer design

I — 1863-1890
II — 1891-1926
III — 1926-1946
IV — 1946-1955
V — 1955-1965
VI — 1965-3/31/1980
VII — 4/1/1980-12/22/1992
VIII — 1/4/1993-current

Further information concerning Periods of Crafting (Baskets):
1 — 1865-1890, BELLEEK (three strand)
2 — 1865-1890, BELLEEK CO. FERMANAGH (three strand)
3 — 1891-1920, BELLEEK CO. FERMANAGH IRELAND (three strand)
4 — 1921-1954, BELLEEK CO. FERMANAGH IRELAND (four strand)
5 — 1955-1979, BELLEEK® CO. FERMANAGH IRELAND (four strand)
6 — 1980-1985, BELLEEK® IRELAND (four strand)
7 — 1985-1989, BELLEEK® IRELAND 'ID NUMBER' (four strand)
8-12 — 1990 to present (Refer to *Belleek, The Complete Collector's Guide and Illustrated Reference, 2nd Edition,* Chapter 5)

Acorn Covered Jam Pot, D1501-I, D, 4" 1,300.00
Amphora Lamp, D1502-I, K, 26¾" 1,950.00
Artichoke Tea Ware Covered Muffin Dish, D720-I, F, 9¼" dia .750.00
Artichoke Tea Ware Sugar Box, D711-I, F, 2¾" 450.00
Bird Vase, Flowered, D54-I, G, 10" 1,600.00
Blarney Tea Ware Bread Plate, D574-II, G, 10" dia 400.00
Blarney Tea Ware Tray, D571-II, K, 15x14¼" 1,400.00
Bust of Clytie, D14-II, L, 11" 3,200.00
Bust of Lord James Butler, D1128-I, L, 11½" 2,800.00
Cherub Candelabra, D341-VII, L, 3 removable holders, 15" ...4,800.00
Chinese Tea Ware Tea Saucer, D483(S)-I, K, 5" 200.00
Dolphin Candlestick, D343-I, K, 7½" 1,800.00
Dolphin Candlesticks, D343-VII, K, 8", pr 800.00
Dolphin Spill, D189-III, J, 6½" 240.00
Double Fish Vase, D1204-I, K, 12" 2,800.00
Double Photo Frame, D66-I, J, 12x11½" 5,800.00
Earthenware Foot Bath, D1021-I, F, 17x13¼" 375.00
Echinus Tea Ware Cream, D648-I, C, 3" 325.00
Echinus Tea Ware Egg Cup, D666-VI, B, 2½" 35.00
Erne Basket, D1688-5, J, 4-strand, 6" dia 500.00
Fern Flowerpot, D101-I, B, 8" dia 1,500.00
Figure of a Pig, D231-VI, B, 3" 75.00
Figure of Affection, D1134-II, L, 15" 2,350.00
Flowered Boston Basket, D1249-5, 4-strand, D, 12" 2,400.00
Gaelic Coffee Cup, D2007-VII, E, 4" 65.00
Grass Tea Ware Cream, D735-I, D, 2¼" 325.00
Harp Shamrock Butter Plate, D253-VI, B&E, 6¾" 60.00
Harp Vase, D1213-II, E, 6½" 250.00

Hexagon Tea Ware Floral Decorated Tray, D626-I, K, 16¼" ..2,200.00
Hexagon Tea Ware Teapot, D392-II, C, 5" 550.00
Imperial Centre, D96-II, G, 10¼" 4,800.00
Imperial Shell, D138 VI, B, 7½" 550.00
Irish Independent Tray, D2090-II, earthenware, 7½" 275.00
Lace Tea Ware Cream, D810-II, K, lg sz, 3¾" 775.00
Lace Tea Ware Sugar, D809-II, K, lg sz, 4" 725.00

Photo courtesy Richard Degenhardt

Lace Tea Ware Teapot, D2055-II, K, large size, 5¼", $1,400.00.

Lifford Cream, D301-VI, B, 3¼" 45.00
Lily of the Valley Frame, D135-I, A, lg sz, 16" L 3,700.00
Limpet Tea Ware Plate, D1372-III, B, 8" 75.00
Limpet Tea Ware Tea Cup, D549(C)-II, B 75.00
Lithophane, Child Looking in Mirror, D1539, 5½x5½" 600.00
Lithophane, Madonna, Child & Angel, D1544-unmk, 8⅞" 600.00
Lotus Sugar & Cream, D244-III/D245-III, B, 3¼" 125.00
Man w/Cat & Puppies, D1143-II, A, 7¾" 2,600.00
Mask Powder Bowl, D1547-V, B, ltd edition, lg sz, 5¼x4" 275.00
Nautilus on Coral, D131-I, C, 9" 1,000.00
Neptune Tea Ware Bread Plate, D425-VI, B, 10½" dia 75.00
Owl Spill, D1238-VI, B, 8¼" 70.00
Pierced Spill, Flowered, D49-VI, D, lg sz, 3½" 125.00
Quiver Vase, D151-I, K, 8" 2,400.00
Rathmore Oval Basket, D117-5, Belleek...Ireland, D, 12" dia .7,500.00
Ribbon Sugar & Cream, D243-III, B, 3½" 120.00
Richard K Degenhardt Basket, D1696-14, D, (1995), 8" 400.00
Rock Spill, D162-III, B, middle sz, 5½" 185.00
Saint Spill, D1223-III, A, 4½" 400.00
Seahorse & Shell, D129-I, K, 4" 1,200.00
Seahorse Flower Holder, D130-VI, B, 3" 125.00
Shamrock Milk Jug, D390-II, E, 6" 275.00
Shamrock Napkin Holder, D2021-VI, E 30.00
Shamrock Spill, D191-II, E, 5½" 165.00
Shamrock Tea Ware Coffeepot, D1319-III, E, 6¾" 375.00
Shamrock Tea Ware Covered Muffin Dish, D388-III, E, 4½x9" ...400.00
Shamrock Tea Ware Dejeuner Set, D371-II, E, 8-pc 2,650.00
Straw Basket, D79-II, B, 4¼" 500.00
Sunflower Vase, D188-II, J, 7½" 300.00
Swan, D254-VI, B, lg sz, 4½" 65.00
Sydenham Basket, D108-5, J, lg sz, 10¼" 1,400.00
Tridacna Tea Ware Teapot, D455-I, D, middle sz, 3¾" 500.00
Triple Fish Vase, D1231-VI, D, 15¾" 2,500.00
Triple Tulip Vase, D92-II, D, 9" 1,000.00
Victoria Shell, D128-III, B, 8" 500.00
Vine Tankard Jug, D1314-VI, D, 5½" 140.00
Violet Holder, D1185-I, C, 4¾" 850.00
Water Lily Vase on Rocks, D1235-I, D, 10" dia 3,500.00

Bells

Some areas of interest represented in the study of bells are history, religion, and geography. Since Biblical times, bells have announced morning church services, vespers, deaths, christenings, school hours, fires, and community events. Countries have used them en masse to peal out the good news of Christmas, New Year's, and the endings of World Wars I and II. They've been rung in times of great sorrow, such as the death of Abraham Lincoln.

Dorothy Malone Anthony is the author of a series of ten books entitled *World of Bells*. Her address is in the Directory under Kansas. All have over two hundred colored pictures covering many bell categories. See also Nodders; Schoolhouse Collectibles.

Blown, wht opaque w/red loopings, red rim, mercury hdl, 10" **275.00**
Brass, Dutch boy w/parasol figural, 4x2" **50.00**
Brass, emb angry god face ea side, fist finial, 3½x2¼" **65.00**
Brass, girl in hat w/arms outstretched figural, 3¾x1½" **65.00**
Brass, Jacobean head finial, emb figures around sides, 4x3¼" **100.00**
Brass, knight figural hdl, Hemony, 6¾x3⅜" **120.00**
Brass, lady w/fan figural, 5⅝x2¾" **75.00**
Brass, mushroom form w/2 pixies sitting on it, 3x3" **40.00**

Photo courtesy Dorothy Malone Anthony

**Brass, Old Mother Hubbard
figural, English, 4½", $85.00.**

Brass, warrior figural, Hemony, 6¾x3¼" **125.00**
School/town crier's, brass, trn apple wood hdl, 11" **100.00**
Sleigh, brass, 19 orig on leather strap, 1840s **350.00**
Sleigh, brass, 19 w/geometric decor on leather strap **350.00**
Sleigh, brass, 9 graduated on 83" leather strap **335.00**
Sleigh, metal, 25 graduated on 88" leather strap **250.00**
Table, sterling silver, mk RC for Crichton & hallmk, 4" **150.00**
Tea, hammered sterling, R Sunyer, 2 troy ozs, 3⅜" **175.00**
Watchman's, hand-held brass w/trn wood hdl, 9½x4¾" **140.00**

Bennett, John

Bringing with him the knowledge and experience he had gained at the Doulton (Lambeth) Pottery in England, John Bennett opened a studio in New York City around 1877, where he continued his methods of decorating faience under the glaze. Early wares utilized imported English biscuit, though subsequently local clays (both white and cream-colored) were also used. His first kiln was on Lexington Avenue; he built another on East Twenty-Fourth Street. Pieces are usually signed 'J. Bennett, N.Y.,' often with the street address and date. Later examples may be marked 'West Orange, N.J.,' where he retired. The pottery was in operation approximately six years in New York. Pieces signed with other initials are usually worth less. Please note: this John Bennett **did not** make patented syrup jugs! Our advisor for this category is Robert Tuggle; he is listed in the Directory under New York.

Charger, insects & flowers on honeycomb, sgn/1878, 14½" **4,625.00**

Jardiniere, apple blossoms on blk mottle, sgn, 6½x8" **2,090.00**
Jardiniere, magnolias, red & cream on blk, sgn, 7" **2,100.00**
Lamp, nasturtiums on turq mottle, brass base/font/burner, 15" ...**1,200.00**
Vase, cattleya orchids on gr mottle, sgn, 9½" **2,250.00**
Vase, crab apple blossoms on cobalt mottle, sgn/1880s, 20" **5,300.00**
Vase, floral, 4-color on mc, sgn Guild, rpr drilling, 8½x7" **500.00**
Vase, peonies on cobalt mottle, sgn/1882, 26" **22,000.00**
Vase, wht & rose blossoms on yel, sgn/1883, 9" **2,420.00**

Bennington

Although the term has become a generic one for the mottled brown ware produced there, Bennington is not a type of pottery, but rather a town in Vermont where two important potteries were located. The Norton Company, founded in 1793, produced mainly redware and salt-glazed stoneware; only during a brief partnership with Fenton (1845-47) was any Rockingham attempted. The Norton Company endured until 1894, operated by succeeding generations of the Norton family. Fenton organized his own pottery in 1847. There he manufactured not only redware and stoneware, but more artistic types as well — graniteware, scroddled ware, flint enamel, a fine parian, and vast amounts of their famous Rockingham. Though from an esthetic standpoint his work rated highly among the country's finest ceramic achievements, he was economically unsuccessful. His pottery closed in 1858.

It is estimated that only one in five Fenton pieces were marked; and although it has become a common practice to link any fine piece of Rockingham to this area, careful study is vital in order to be able to distinguish Bennington's from the similar wares of many other American and Staffordshire potteries. Although the practice was without the permission of the proprietor, it was nevertheless a common occurrence for a potter to take his molds with him when moving from one pottery to the next, so particularly well-received designs were often reproduced at several locations. Of eight known Fenton marks, four are variations of the '1849' impressed stamp: 'Lyman Fenton Co., Fenton's Enamel Patented 1849, Bennington, Vermont.' These are generally found on examples of Rockingham and flint enamel. A raised, rectangular scroll with 'Fenton's Works, Bennington, Vermont,' was used on early examples of porcelain. From 1852 to 1858, the company operated under the title of the United States Pottery Company. Three marks — the ribbon mark with the initials USP, the oval with a scrollwork border and the name in full, and the plain oval with the name in full — were used during that period.

Among the more sought-after examples are the bird and animal figurines, novelty pitchers, figural bottles, and all of the more finely-modeled items. Recumbent deer, cows, standing lions with one forepaw on a ball, and opposing pairs of poodles with baskets in their mouths and 'coleslaw' fur were made in Rockingham, flint enamel, and occasionally in parian. Numbers in the listings below refer to the book *Bennington Pottery and Porcelain* by Barret. Our advisors for Bennington (except for parian and stoneware) are Barbara and Charles Adams; they are listed in the Directory under Massachusetts.

Key: c/s — cobalt on salt glaze

Book flask, Bennington Battle, flint enamel, EX rstr, 11" **4,500.00**
Book flask, Ladies' Companion, flint enamel, 4-qt, 11x8¼" **2,800.00**
Bottle, Coachman, Rockingham, 1849 mk, 10⅜", EX **900.00**
Bottle, Toby, Rockingham, no tassels/ft showing, rstr, 10½" **475.00**
Bottle, Toby, Rockingham, w/mustache & tassels, mk, 11", VG ...**375.00**
Box, flint enamel, Alternate Rib, M w/VG lid, 3x8" L **450.00**
Candle holder, flint enamel, saucer base, scroll hdl, 4x6", EX **700.00**
Candlestick, flint enamel, 6⅝" **800.00**
Candlestick, olive mottle, prof rpr to lip, 8⅜" **360.00**

Candlestick, Rockingham, 7¾" 495.00
Candlestick, Rockingham w/blk flecks, 8" 495.00
Coffeepot, flint enamel, helmet shape, rstr, 12¾" 1,800.00
Cuspidor, scroddleware, 10" dia 1,100.00
Dish, flint enamel, 8-sided, hairlines, 8¾" L 500.00
Humidor, Rockingham, EX color, Alternate Rib, 1849 mk, 7", EX ...350.00
Lamp, flint enamel, 8-side step-ftd baluster std, prisms, 26" 8,000.00
Lion, flint enamel/coleslaw, paw on ball, tongue up, 11" L, EX ...3,500.00
Name plate, Rockingham w/1 wht letter, 7⅜" L 250.00
Paperweight, dog on pillow, Rockingham, 1849 mk, 4¼", VG ...500.00
Pie plate, flint enamel, EX color, 1849 mk, 10" 750.00
Pie plate, Rockingham w/yel highlights, 1849 mk, 11", EX+ 500.00
Pitcher, flint enamel, scalloped ribs, 12½" 770.00
Pitcher, flint enamel, yel/blk/brn w/ribs, 1849 mk, 8" 990.00
Pitcher, flint enamel w/cream, Alternate Rib, 1849 mk, 7" ...1,200.00
Pitcher, flint enamel w/EX color, Alternate Rib, 11", EX 1,200.00
Pitcher, flint enamel w/stripes, Tulip/Heart, mk, 10", VG 140.00
Pitcher, Rockingham, bust of Gen Stark form, EX rstr, 6" 1,850.00
Pitcher, Rockingham, emb hounds & stag, 9½" 600.00
Pitcher, Rockingham, Franklin's bust form, boot hdl, mk, 6, EX ...600.00
Pitcher, Rockingham, hound hdl, emb dogs/deer, 9", EX 850.00
Pitcher, Rockingham, Paneled Grapevine, limb hdl, 8¾", VG ..300.00
Pitcher & bowl, flint enamel, Alternate Rib, 12½", 13½" 3,900.00
Poodle, flint enamel, coleslaw, mc fruit/wht basket, 8x9", VG ...3,250.00
Snuff jar, Toby, flint enamel, mk, rstr, 4¼" 675.00
Soap dish, flint enamel, Alternate Rib, w/lid, 1849 mk, 5⅝", EX 800.00
Tiebacks, flint enamel, brns w/gr sprinkles, unmk, 4½", pr 400.00
Tile, flint enamel, emb intersections, mk, 7" 600.00
Toby jug, Rockingham, impressed mk, crack in hdl, 6¼" 325.00
Vase, eagle & stump figural w/turq/pk/gold enamels, 7¼" 200.00
Vase, flint enamel, tulip form, 10", NM 900.00

Stoneware

Cake crock, #1½/leaf, c/s, E&LP Norton, chips, 1870s, 7" 200.00
Churn, #2/leaf (dotted), c/s, E&LP Norton, rpr, 13½" 550.00
Churn, #5/peacock & tree, c/s, J Norton, rstr, 18" 2,200.00
Crock, #1½/leaf, c/s, J&E Norton, 10" 470.00
Crock, #1/leaf/dots, c/s, J Norton, prof rstr, 7" 175.00
Crock, #2/bird on plume, c/s, E&LP Norton, 1870s, 9", EX 500.00
Crock, #3/bird on plume, c/s, E&LP Norton, rstr, 12" 385.00
Crock, #3/deer/house/fence/tree, c/s, J&E Norton, rare, 12½" ...5,500.00
Crock, #3/deer/tree/fence, c/s, J&E Norton, rpr, 10½" 4,400.00
Crock, #3/parrot/plume, FB Norton..., flake/line, 1870s, 9½" 465.00
Crock, #4/chicken pecks corn, c/s, J Norton, sm chips, 11" 2,600.00
Crock, #4/flower vase, c/s, J&E Norton, flakes/line, 11" 715.00
Crock, #4/running rabbit, c/s, Norton & Fenton, rstr, 14½" 660.00
Jar, #3/floral, c/s, E&LP Norton, 14½", EX 575.00
Jar, #3/leaf (stylized/dotted), E&LP Norton, rstr, 13" 175.00
Jug, #1½/leafy floral, c/s, J&E Norton, 12½", EX 550.00
Jug, #1/bird, c/s, J Norton, drilled hole, 1860s, 11" 330.00
Jug, #1/bird on branch, c/s, J&E Norton, rstr hdl, 12" 220.00
Jug, #1/bird on twig, c/s, J&E Norton, 11½", NM 670.00
Jug, #1/floral (lg), c/s, J&E Norton, chip/mks, 11" 550.00
Jug, #1/leaf, c/s, E&LP Norton, 11½" 165.00
Jug, #2/bird on branch w/worm, c/s, J&E Norton, rstr, 13½" ...1,980.00
Jug, #2/bird on plume, c/s, E&LP Norton, line, 13½" 360.00
Jug, #2/floral, c/s, J&E Norton, stain/chip, 13½" 385.00
Jug, #2/floral (stylized), c/s, J Norton & Co, 13½", EX 300.00
Jug, #2/LWC in script, c/s, Norton & Co, chip, 13½" 175.00
Jug, #2/SWG in script/flower, J&E Norton, 13½", EX 220.00
Jug, #2/triple flower, c/s, Julius Norton, pings, 1850s, 14" 165.00
Jug, #3/dbl floral, c/s, J&E Norton, ca 1859, 15½" 745.00
Jug, #3/deer among pines, c/s, J&E Norton, rstr, 15½" 6,875.00

Jug, #3/floral (lg), c/s, J Norton & Co, ping/line, 16" 600.00
Jug, #3/geometrics, c/s, J&E Norton, line, 15" 190.00
Jug, #3/peacock on stump, c/s, J&E Norton, rstr, 15" 2,035.00
Pitcher, #2/flower basket, c/s, J&E Norton, chip, 12" 2,035.00
Pitcher, #2/plume, FB Norton..., chip/line, 1870s, 13½" 550.00

Beswick

In the early 1890s, James Wright Beswick operated a pottery in Longston, England, where he produced fine dinnerware as well as ornamental ceramics. Today's collectors are most interested in the figurines made since 1936 by a later generation Beswick firm, John Beswick, Ltd. They specialize in reproducing accurately detailed bone-china models of authentic breeds of animals. Their Fireside Series includes dogs, cats, elephants, horses, the Huntsman, and an Indian figure, which measure up to 14" in height. The Connoisseur line is modeled after the likenesses of famous racing horses. Beatrix Potter's characters and some of Walt Disney's are charmingly re-created and appeal to children and adults alike. Other items, such as character Tobys, have also been produced. The Beswick name is stamped on each piece. The firm was absorbed by the Doulton group in 1973. Our advisor for this category is Nicki Budin; she is listed in the Directory under New York.

Figurine, Amiable Guinea Pig, BP-3B mk 375.00
Figurine, Appley Dappley, 1st gold mk, discontinued 275.00
Figurine, Beaver on Log, #2194 ....195.00

Figurine, cat, sitting, brown striped tabby, bone china, 1950s, 6½", $75.00.

Figurine, Cheshire Cat, BP-3 mk 700.00
Figurine, Diggory, brn mk 50.00
Figurine, Duchess (pie), BP-3 mk 225.00
Figurine, Fierce Bad Rabbit, 1st gold mk, discontinued 150.00
Figurine, Flopsy, Mopsy & Cottontail, gold mk 225.00
Figurine, Foxy Whiskered Gentleman 75.00
Figurine, Ginger, BP-3 mk 650.00
Figurine, Hunca Munca, brn mk 65.00
Figurine, Hunca Munca, gold mk 200.00
Figurine, Little Pig Robinson, 1st gold mk 275.00
Figurine, Mallard Duck, #750 ....95.00
Figurine, Miss Moppet, gold mk 150.00
Figurine, Mr Jackson, 1st brn mk 225.00
Figurine, Mrs Rabbit, BP-2 mk 245.00
Figurine, Mrs Rabbit, gold mk 295.00
Figurine, Pheasant, #1226 ....125.00
Figurine, Pickles, BP-3B mk 350.00
Figurine, Pickles, gold mk 395.00
Figurine, Pig-Wig, brn mk 450.00
Figurine, Pigling Bland, 1st brn mk 200.00
Figurine, Pigling Bland, 1st paper label, gold mk 300.00
Figurine, Samuel Whiskers, discontinued 45.00

Figurine, Simkin, BP-3B mk **675.00**
Figurine, Squirrel Nutkin, BP-2 mk **45.00**
Figurine, Tiggy Winkle, gold mk **225.00**
Figurine, Timmy Tiptoes, gold mk **175.00**

Big Little Books

The first Big Little Book was copyrighted in 1932 and published in 1933 by the Whitman Publishing Company of Racine, Wisconsin. Its hero was Dick Tracy. The concept was so well accepted that others soon followed Whitman's example; and though the 'Big Little Book' phrase became a trademark of the Whitman Company, the formats of his competitors (Saalfield, Goldsmith, Van Wiseman, Lynn, and World Syndicate) were exact copies. Today's Big Little Book buffs collect them all.

These hand-sized sagas of adventure were illustrated with full-page cartoons on the right-hand page and the story narration on the left. Colorful cardboard covers contained hundreds of pages, usually totaling over an inch in thickness. Big Little Books originally sold for 10¢ at the dime store; as late as the mid-1950s when the popularity of comic books caused sales to decline signaling an end to production, their price had risen to a mere 20¢. Their appeal was directed toward the pre-teens who bought, traded, and hoarded Big Little Books. Because so many were stored in attics and closets, many have survived. Among the super heroes are G-Men, Flash Gordon, Tarzan, the Lone Ranger, and Red Ryder; in a lighter vein, you'll find such lovable characters as Blondie and Dagwood, Mickey Mouse, Little Orphan Annie, and Felix the Cat.

In the early to mid-'30s, Whitman published several Big Little Books as advertising premiums for the Coco Malt Company, who packed them in boxes of their cereal. These are highly prized by today's collectors, as are Disney stories and super-hero adventures. Our advisor for this category is Ron Donnelly; he is listed in the Directory under Alabama.

Note: At the present time, the market for these books is fairly stable — values for common examples are actually dropping. Only the rare, character-related titles are increasing.

Green Hornet Strikes!,
Whitman Better Little Book,
#1453, 1940, EX, $145.00.

Adventures of Pete the Tramp, Saalfield #1082, 1935, VG **32.00**
Adventures of Tim Tyler, #1053, EX **50.00**
Allen Pike of the Parachute Squad, #1481, 1941, VG **15.00**
Andy Panda & the Mad Dog Mystery, Walter Lantz, 1947, G **10.00**
Arizona Kid on the Bandit Tail, Whitman, #1192, 1936, NM **36.00**
Billy the Kid, Whitman, #773, 1935, NM **45.00**
Boss of the Chisholm Trail, #1153, NM+ **35.00**
Brad Turner in the Trans-Atlantic Flight, #1425, 1939, EX+ **25.00**
Bringing Up Father, #1133, EX **40.00**
Buck Rogers in the War w/Planet Venus, Whitman, 1938, VG ...**65.00**
Buck Rogers in the 25th Century AD, 1933, premium, EX **90.00**
Bullet Benton, Sapphire, 1939, NM **30.00**

Captain Easy Soldier of Fortune, #1128, EX **30.00**
Dan Dunn & the Border Smugglers, #1481, NM **45.00**
Dan Dunn & the Crime Master, #1171, EX **30.00**
Dick Tracy & the Boris Arson Gang, #1163, EX+ **45.00**
Donald Duck & the Mystery of the Double X, 1949, EX+ **45.00**
Donald Duck Headed for Trouble, #1430, G+ **20.00**
Down Cartridge Creek, Pinto Shane, #1140, 1938, VG **18.00**
Flash Gordon & the Monsters of Mongo, #1166, G+ **35.00**
G-Men on the Job, #1168, EX+ **25.00**
Gene Autry & the Riders of the Range, 1946, EX **25.00**
Gene Autry in the Law of the Range, #1353, VG+ **25.00**
Hairbrush Harry in Dept QT, #1101, EX **25.00**
Hall of Fame of the Air, #1159, EX **20.00**
Jane Withers in Keep Smiling, #1463, VG+ **25.00**
Jim Starr Border Patrol, Whitman, #1428, EX **28.00**
Jr G-Men, #1442, EX **25.00**
Just Kids, #1401, EX **35.00**
Kay Darcy & the Mystery Hideout, #1411, EX **20.00**
Kayo in the Land of Sunshine, #1180, EX **25.00**
Ken Maynard in Western Justice, #1430, M **45.00**
Li'l Abner in New York, Whitman, #1198, 1936, EX+ **50.00**
Little Orphan Annie & Punjab the Wizard, 1935, G **15.00**
Little Orphan Annie & the Ghost Gang, #1154, 1935, EX+ **32.00**
Lone Ranger & His Horse Silver, #1181, VG **20.00**
Lone Ranger & the Black Shirt Highway Man, 1939, VG **30.00**
Lost Patrol, Whitman, #753, EX **30.00**
Mickey Mouse & the Bat Bandit, #1153, 1935, VG **25.00**
Mickey Mouse in the Blaggard Castle, #762, 1934, VG **65.00**
Mickey Mouse in the Race for Riches, 1938, NM **75.00**
Mickey Mouse in the World of Tomorrow, 1948, EX+ **50.00**
Mickey Mouse on Sky Island, 1941, EX+ **55.00**
Mickey Rooney & Judy Garland, #1493, EX **35.00**
Moon Mullins & the Plushbottom Twins, #1134, EX **35.00**
Mutt & Jeff, #1167, VG **35.00**
Nancy & Sluggo, #1400, EX **30.00**
Oswald the Lucky Rabbit, 1934, VG **20.00**
Phantom & the Sky Pirates, #1468, 1948, VG+ **20.00**
Popeye in Puddleburg, 1934, G **20.00**
Popeye Sees the Sea, 1936, VG **20.00**
Powder Smoke Range, 1937, G- **15.00**
Practical Pig, Walt Disney, Whitman, #1058, EX **30.00**
Prairie Bill & the Covered Wagon, #758, NM **75.00**
Radio Patrol Trailing the Safeblowers, Whitman, #1173, VG **25.00**
Red Ryder & the Code of the West, #1427, EX **30.00**
Red Ryder & the Fighting Westerner, #1440, EX **25.00**
Roy Rogers at Crossed Feathers Ranch, 1945, VG **18.00**
Scrappy, Whitman, #1122, 1934, EX **40.00**
Secret Agent X-9, Whitman, #1144, 1936, EX **30.00**
Silver Streak, Whitman, #1155, NM **40.00**
Skippy, #761, VG+ **20.00**
Sombrero Pete, #1136, EX **15.00**
SOS Coast Guard, #1191, VG **22.00**
Story of Walt Disney's Snow White & 7 Dwarfs, #1460, 1938, VG ...**20.00**
Tailspin Tommy Great American Mystery, #1184, VG **45.00**
Tarzan Escapes, Whitman, #1182, NM **90.00**
Timid Elmer, Walt Disney, 1938, EX **35.00**
Tiny Tim of the Mechanical Men, 1937, EX **35.00**
Tom Mix & the Scourge of Paradise Valley, #4068, EX **80.00**
Tom Mix in the Range War, #1166, 1937, VG **20.00**
Walt Disney's Story of Minnie Mouse, Whitman, #1066, 1939, EX ..**30.00**
Wells Fargo, 1938, G- **37.50**
Will Rogers, #1096, 1935, VG **25.00**
Winning the Old Northwest, 1934, NM **30.00**
Woody Woodpecker & the Meteor Menace, 1967, NM **15.00**

Bing and Grondahl

In 1853 brothers M.H. and J.H. Bing formed a partnership with Frederick Vilhelm Grondahl in Copenhagen, Denmark. Their early wares were porcelain plaques and figurines designed by the noted sculptor Thorvaldsen of Denmark. Dinnerware production began in 1863, and by 1889 their underglaze color 'Copenhagen Blue' had earned them worldwide acclaim. They are perhaps most famous today for their Christmas plates, the first of which was made in 1895. See also Limited Edition Plates.

Nude seated at pool tray, #1532, 4½x8½", $225.00.

Bowl, Snow Flower	30.00
Dealer sign	40.00
Figurine, Alsatian pup, 3½"	75.00
Figurine, baby chick, #2914	35.00
Figurine, Bearded Titmouse birds, 31633 & #1634, ea	50.00
Figurine, boy playing flute, 11½"	295.00
Figurine, boy seated on book, #1742E	144.00
Figurine, boy w/flowerpot, 6"	90.00
Figurine, bulldog w/1 ear down, #1676, 4¼x3¼"	75.00
Figurine, cat, licking, standing, #2251, 7½"	110.00
Figurine, Fox Terrier, #1998	100.00
Figurine, girl w/arm raised, #2273	135.00
Figurine, girl w/tulips, #2298	160.00
Figurine, girl writes letter, 5"	110.00
Figurine, Hans C Anderson seated by standing girl, #2037	325.00
Figurine, lamb, #2171	50.00
Figurine, Lapwing bird, #2556	55.00
Figurine, Love Refused, #1614	155.00
Figurine, lovebird, #2341	55.00
Figurine, mouse, gray, #1801	55.00
Figurine, parrot on limb, bl & mauve, #2019, 5½"	140.00
Figurine, sea gull eats fish, 5½" L	75.00
Figurine, seal pup, #2472	50.00
Leaf dish, #356, pr	78.00
Planter, Snow Flower	40.00
Plate, Children's Day, 1995, w/box	35.00
Vase, magnolia spray, spherical, 7"	125.00

Binoculars

There are several types of binoculars, and the terminology used to refer to them is not consistent or precise. Generally, 'field glasses' refer to simple Galilean optics, where the lens next to the eye (the ocular) is concave and dished away from the eye. By looking through the large lens (the objective), it is easy to see that the light goes straight through the two lenses. These are lower power, have a very small field of view, and do not work nearly as well as prism binoculars. In a smaller size, they are opera glasses, and their price increases if they are covered with mother-of-pearl (fairly common but very attractive), abalone shell (more color-

ful), ivory (quite scarce), or other exotic materials. Field glasses are not valuable unless very unusual or by the best makers, such as Zeiss or Leitz. Prism binoculars have the objective lens offset from the eyepiece and give a much better view. This is the standard binocular form, called Porro prisms, and dates from around 1900. Another type of prism binocular is the roof prism, which at first resembles the straight-through field glasses, with two simple cylinders or cones, here containing very small prisms. These can be distinguished by the high quality views they give and by a thin diagonal line that can be seen when looking backwards through the objective. In general, German binoculars are the most desirable, followed by American, English, and finally French, which can be of good quality but are very common unless of unusual configuration. Japanese optics of WWII or before are often of very high quality. 'Made in Occupied Japan' binoculars are very common, but collectors prize those by Nippon Kogaku (Nikon). Some binoculars are center focus (CF), with one central wheel that focuses both sides at once. These are much easier to use but more difficult to seal against dirt and moisture. Individual focus (IF) binoculars are adjusted by rotating each eyepiece and tend to be cleaner inside in older optics. Each type is preferred by different collectors. Very large binoculars are always of great interest. All binoculars are numbered according to their magnifying power and the diameter of the objective in millimeters. 6 x 30 optics magnify six times and have 30 millimeter objectives.

Prisms are easily knocked out of alignment, requiring an expensive and difficult repair. If severe, this misalignment is immediately noticeable on use by the double-image scene. Minor damage can be seen by focusing on a small object and slowly moving the binoculars away from the eye, which will cause the images to appear to separate. Overall cleanliness should be checked by looking backwards (through the objective) at a light or the sky, when any film or dirt on the lenses or prisms can easily be seen. Pristine binoculars are worth far more than when dirty or misaligned, and broken or cracked optics lower the value far more. Cases help keep binoculars clean but do not add materially to the value. The following listings assume a very good overall condition, with generally clean and alligned optics.

Our advisor for this category is Peter Abrahams, who studies and collects binoculars and other optics. Please contact, especially to exchange reference material. Mr. Abrahams is listed in the Directory under Oregon.

Field Glasses

Folding, modern, hinged flat case, oculars outside	10.00
Folding or telescoping, no bbls, old	125.00
Goerz 5x40, military drab gr, WWI, IF, many other makers	40.00
Ivory covered, various sm szs & makers	180.00
LeMaire, bl leather/brass, various szs & makers	25.00
Metal, emb hunting scene, various sm szs & makers	35.00
Pearl covered, various sm szs & makers	90.00
Porc covered, delicate painting, various szs & makers	175.00
US Naval Gun Factory Optical Shop 6x30	75.00
Zeiss 'Galan' 2.5x34, modern design look, early 1920s	80.00

Prism Binoculars (Porro)

Barr & Stroud, 7x50, Porro II prisims, IF, WWII	110.00
Bausch & Lomb, 6x30, IF, WWI, Signal Corps	50.00
Bausch & Lomb, 7x50, IF, WWII, other makers same	80.00
Bausch & Lomb Zephyr, 7x35 & other, CF	150.00
Bausch & Lomb/Zeiss, Pat 1897, 8x17, CF	140.00
Crown Optical, 6x30, IF, WWI, filters	45.00
France, various makers & szs, if not unusual	30.00
Goertz Trieder Binocle, various szs, unusual adjustment	90.00
Leitz 6x30 Dienstglas, IF, good optics	65.00

Leitz 8x30 Binuxit, CF, 1950s 150.00
Nikon 9x35, 7x35, CF, 1950s 95.00
Nippon Kogaku, 7x50, IF, Made in Occupied Japan 150.00
Ross Stepnada, 7x30, CF, wide angle, 1930s 200.00
Sard, 6x42, IF, very wide angle, WWII 750.00
Toko (Tokyo Opt Co) 7x50, IF, Made in Occupied Japan 45.00
Universal Camera 6x30, IF, WWII, other makers same 50.00
US Naval Gun Factory Optical Shop 6x30, IF, filters, WWI 70.00
US Naval Gun Factory Optical 10x45, IF, WWI 140.00
US Navy, 20x120, various makers, WWII & later 3,000.00
Warner & Swasey (important maker) 8x20, CF, 1902 ....250.00
Zeiss, Starmobi 12/23/42x60, turret eyepcs, 1920s 2,000.00
Zeiss Deltrintem 8x30, CF, 1930s 95.00
Zeiss Teleater 3x13, CF, bl, leather 100.00
Zeiss 15x60, CF or IF, various models 600.00
Zeiss 8x40 Delactis, CF or IF, 1930s 200.00

Roof Prism Binoculars

Hensoldt, Dialyt, various szs, long tapered bbl, 1930s-80s 110.00
Hensoldt Universal Dialyt, 6x26, 3.5x26, cylindrical, 1920s 80.00
Leitz Trinovid, 7x42 & other, CF, 1960s-80s, EX 375.00
Zeiss Dialyt, 8x30, CF, 1960s 400.00

Birdcages

Birdcages can be found in various architectural styles and in a range of materials such as wood, wicker, brass, and gilt metal with ormolu mounts. Those that once belonged to the wealthy are sometimes inlaid with silver or jewels. In the 1800s, it became fashionable to keep birds, and some of the most beautiful examples found today date back to that era. Musical cages that contained automated bird figures became popular; today these command prices of several thousand dollars. In the latter 1800s, wicker styles came into vogue. Collectors still appreciate their graceful lines and find they adapt easily to modern homes.

Brass, arched top, openwork base, Fr, 1900s, 70x32x24" **1,650.00**
Chinese trade, porc/ivory/boxwood/jade/cloisonne mts, 1900s, 27" ..**400.00**
Dreamhouse, blk wire cage, table/umbrella/etc, 1950s, 35x24" **50.00**
Ebonized wood w/wire fork, Nouveau style, 1900s, 36x23½" **315.00**
Wood, plywood & wire, orange pnt over yel, duplex, 30" **80.00**
Wood w/wire bars, trn ft/posts, detailed cornice, pnt, 18" **325.00**

Bisque

Bisque is a term referring to unglazed earthenware or porcelain that has been fired only once. During the Victorian era, bisque figurines became very popular. Most were highly decorated in pastels and gilt and demonstrated a fine degree of workmanship in the quality of their modeling. Few were marked. See also Heubach; Nodders; Dolls; Piano Babies.

Boy & girl, ea w/dog, peach w/gold, 10½", EX, pr **65.00**
Boy & girl w/baskets, floral attire, Germany, 15", pr **450.00**
Boy w/flower basket by fence, pastels, Fr, 7¼" **125.00**
Bust of boy & girl, Fr, 10¾", pr **350.00**
Bust of young woman w/2 braids, shades of bl, 13½" **180.00**
Cherubs support rtcl vase, gold trim, 9" **195.00**
Classical couple holding hands, Germany, #21389, 10½" **135.00**
Girl in nightie w/kittens, dog & cat, Germany, 8½" **165.00**
Lady dancing, man w/mandolin, mc, ca 1880s, 16", pr **350.00**
Match striker, head of an old soldier, 3x1¾" **88.00**
Pastille burner, dog wearing hat w/feather, mc, 5" **225.00**

Youth in bl hat, holding purse, 16" 600.00

Black Americana

Black memorabilia is without a doubt a field that encompasses the most widely exploited ethnic group in our history. But within this field there are many levels of interest: arts and achievements such as folk music and literature, caricatures in advertising, souvenirs, toys, fine art, and legitimate research into the days of their enslavement and enduring struggle for equality. The list is endless.

In the listings below are some with a derogatory connotation. Thankfully, these are from a bygone era and represent the mores of a culture that existed nearly a century ago. They are included only to convey the fact that they are a part of this growing area of collecting interest. Black Americana catalogs featuring a wide variety of items for sale are available; see the Directory under Clubs, Newsletters, and Catalogs for more information. We also recommend *Black Collectibles* by P.J. Gibbs; and *Black Dolls, Books I and II*, by Myla Perkins, all published by Collector Books. See also Cookie Jars; Postcards; Posters; Sheet Music.

Humidor, man on stump, chalkware, 12", $650.00.

Ashtray, Coon Chicken Inn, smiling face on glass, 3½" 30.00
Bag, hickory chip; Ole Virginia, Mammy by grill 25.00
Biscuit jar, butler figural, basket hdl, ceramic, 7" 800.00
Book, A Day w/Noddy, Enid Blyton, EX 48.00
Book, Little Black Sambo, Platt & Munk, 1935, EX 50.00
Book, Little Black Sambo, pop-up, McLoughlin, 1942, EX 75.00
Book, Naughty Amelia Jane, Enid Blyton, EX 40.00
Book, Sambo & the Twins, H Bannerman, 1930s, EX 75.00
Book, Uncle Tom's Cabin, H Beecher Stowe, 1950s, EX 35.00
Book, Up From Slavery, Booker T Washington, 1907, EX 20.00
Bookends, Sambo & the tiger, wooden, pr 50.00
Booklet, Topsy, full-color, diecut, McLoughlin, 1897, EX 195.00
Bracelet, heavy sterling cuff type w/Blk head 1 end 285.00
Clothespin bag doll, golliwogg 60.00
Clothespin holder, Mammy, ceramic 495.00
Cookbook, Aunt Jemima Magical Recipes 35.00
Cookie jar, Aunt Jemima, plastic, F&F, NM 400.00
Cookie jar, Mammy, Pearl China, minimum 750.00
Cookie jar, Mammy, yel, Mosaic Tile 550.00
Creamer & sugar bowl, Aunt Jemima & Uncle Mose, F&F, w/lid ...150.00
Dexterity game, man w/cigar, 3 wht mini balls, 1900s 125.00
Dish, boy w/watermelon, chalkware, mc pnt, NM 75.00
Doll, golliwogg, Chad Valley, 12", EX 75.00
Doll, golliwogg, Dapper Dan style w/vest, etc, 21" 70.00
Doll, golliwogg, Robertson's Jam, English, 19" 68.00
Dolls, Wade & Diana, printed cloth, stuffed, 1950 premiums, pr ..140.00
Drinking straw, Coon Chicken Inn 25.00
Fan, paper on stick, man in top hat, Use Darky Toothpaste, EX ..55.00
Figurine, Billiken, compo, seated, 3¾" 130.00

Figurine, boy lying in alligator's mouth, ceramic, sm 115.00
Figurines, Rachel & Mushmouth, porc, Germany, pr 100.00
Film, Little Black Sambo, Castle, 8mm, EX 150.00
Film, Little Black Sambo, 35mm 200.00
Firecracker holder, Smoking Sambo, boy figural diecut 75.00
Game, Coontown Shooting Gallery, 4 target heads, ca 1920, NM ..285.00
Hitching post, boy w/bale of cotton, CI, mc pnt, 1850s, 44½" ...990.00
Hitching post, jockey, CI, mc pnt, 19th C, 37½", EX 775.00
Humidor, man w/straw hat, ceramic, M 450.00
Incense burner, boy screaming on potty, CI, 2-pc 135.00
Jar, dresser; Butler, heart shaped 350.00
Laundry bag, Mammy, w/sock & hankie holder pockets 60.00
Letter opener, celluloid alligator w/Blk-head pencil in mouth 55.00
Lingerie bag, Mammy face, oilcloth 50.00
Match book, Coon Chicken Inn, figural matches, M 35.00
Meat pick, Coon Chicken Inn 25.00
Memo board, Mammy, I'se Gots To Get, wooden 58.00
Napkin, Aunt Jemima Pancake Jamboree 10.00
Pail, Aunt Dina Molasses, Mammy, earliest version, 1908, EX ...125.00
Paint, Minstrel Black Face Paint, EX graphics 20.00
Pancake shaker, Aunt Jemima, yel plastic, F&F, NM 100.00
Pencil sharpener, boy's head, exaggerated features, early 60.00
Pin, Porter, Bakelite, burgundy 165.00
Place mat, Aunt Jemima Pancake Jamboree, EX 18.50
Place mat/map, Coon Chicken Inn 45.00
Plate, bread; Coon Chicken Inn 150.00
Plate, I'll Be Down To Get You in a Taxi Honey, 6½" 50.00
Plate, Mammy, Rockingham, wall hanging 155.00
Postcard, Pickaninny puzzle, M 65.00
Puzzle, Little Pickaninnies, wooden, Chubb, 9½x7" 295.00
Receipt, Armour Ham What Am, chef w/ham, 1938 ....18.00
Scouring pad holder, Chef, ceramic 200.00
Shakers, Aunt Jemima, F&F, 3½", pr 65.00
Shakers, Aunt Jemima & Uncle Mose, plastic, F&F, 5", pr 75.00
Shakers, Butler & Plaid Mammy, ceramic, 4¾", pr 125.00
Shakers, kids eating watermelon, bsk, pr 135.00
Shakers, Mammy, gr, Luzianne, old, pr 150.00
Shakers, Mammy & Chef, ceramic, Japan, pr 28.00
Sheet music, Ma Curly-Headed Baby, 1897, oversz, EX 25.00
Sheet music, Picaninny Picnic, banjo player cover, 1936, EX 25.00
Sheet music, Shortnin' Bread, Mammy cover, 1934, EX 22.50
Sheet music, That's My Mammy, Mammy cover, 1928, EX 17.50
Sheet music, Tuck Me To Sleep in My Old KY Home, 1921, G ..10.00
Sign, Table Reserved, Coon Chicken Inn 35.00
Skillet, CI, Mammy in relief, Dixie Land, mini 85.00
Spice shaker, Aunt Jemima, plastic, F&F, from set of 6, ea 50.00
String holder, big-face Mammy, ceramic 450.00
Syrup, Aunt Jemima, plastic, F&F, 5½" 70.00
Tin, Pender's Old VA Fruitcake, Mammy serving family, EX 45.00
Toaster cover, cloth Mammy doll, bright colors, 1950s 25.00
Toothpick holder, Coon Chicken Inn, pot-metal Porter's head .275.00
Tumbler, water; Coon Chicken Inn, smiling face on glass 65.00
Wall plaque, Mammy face, chalkware, NM 45.00

Black Cats

Made in Japan during the fifties, these novelty cats may be found bearing the labels of several different importers, all with their own particular characteristics. The best known and most collectible of these cats are from the Shafford line. Even when unmarked, they are easily identified by their red bows, green eyes, and white whiskers, eyeliners, and eyebrows. Relco/Royal Sealy cats are tall and slender, and their bow ties are gold with red dots. Wales is a wonderful line with yellow eyes

and gold detailing; Enesco cats have blue eyes, and there are other lines as well. When evaluating your black cats, be sure to inspect their paint and judge them accordingly. 50% paint should relate to 50% of our suggested values, which are given for cats in mint (or nearly mint) paint.

Ashtray, flat face shape, Shafford, 4½" 18.00
Ashtray, full figure, flat, 'Ashes' in body, 2½x3¾" 7.50

Cigarette lighter, Lucky Black Cat, green eyes, Shafford, 5½", $175.00.

Condiment set, 2 heads, J&M bows w/spoons, Shafford, 4" 75.00
Cookie jar, lg cat head, Shafford 85.00
Creamer & sugar bowl, cat-head lids are shakers, 5⅜" 50.00
Cruet, oil & vinegar, co-joined cats, 1-pc, Royal Sealy 40.00
Cruet, slender form, gold collar & tie, tail hdl 12.00
Cruets, he w/O eyes, she w/V eyes & hair bow, Shafford, pr 60.00
Decanter, upright, holds bottle w/cork stopper, Shafford 50.00
Demitasse pot, tail hdl, bow finial, Shafford, 7½" 95.00
Desk caddy, pen forms tail, spring body holds letters, 6½" 8.00
Egg cup, cat face on bowl, ped ft, Shafford 30.00
Grease jar, sm cat head, Shafford 75.00
Measuring cup, 4 cups on wood rack w/cat's face, Shafford 300.00
Mug, Shafford, rare lg sz 65.00
Mug, Shafford, 3½" 50.00
Pincushion, cushion on bk, tongue measure 25.00
Pitcher, milk; upright, Shafford 100.00
Pitcher, Shafford, scarce, mid-sz (1 of 3 szs), 5" 65.00
Pot holder caddy, 'teapot' cat, 3-hook, Shafford 125.00
Shaker, long cat, salt in 1 end, pepper in other end, Shafford 85.00
Shakers, seated, bl eyes, Enesco label, 5¾", pr 15.00
Spice rack, wireware face w/marble eyes, 4 shakers, Shafford 350.00
Spice set, gr eyes, 6 sq shakers w/appl red bows, wood rack 145.00
Spice set, yel eyes, 9 sq shakers w/appl red bows, wood rack 125.00
Stacking tea set, mamma pot, kitty creamer & sugar bowl, yel eyes ..65.00
Strainer, w/cat face, long wood hdl, Shafford 90.00
Teapot, bulbous body, head lid, gr eyes, Shafford, 6½" 45.00
Teapot, dbl-chamber, Shafford 125.00
Teapot, panther-like, gold eyes, sm 20.00
Teapot, upright, ovoid body (not ball-shaped), Shafford, 7" 175.00
Teapot, upright, paw spout, yel eyes, red bow, Wales, 8¼" 60.00
Toothpick holder, cat by vase atop book, Occupied Japan 12.00
Wall pocket, flattened 'teapot' cat, Shafford, scarce 95.00
Wall rack, long flat cat w/hooks for utensils, Shafford 90.00
Wine, emb cat's face, gr eyes, Shafford, sm 20.00

Black Glass

Black glass is a type of colored glass that when held to strong light usually appears deep purple, though since each glasshouse had its own formula, tones may vary. It was sometimes etched or given a satin finish;

and occasionally it was decorated with silver, gold, enamel, coralene, or any of these in combination. The decoration was done either by the glasshouse or by firms that specialized in decorating glassware. Crystal, jade, colored glass, or milk glass was sometimes used with the black as an accent. Black glass has been made by many companies since the 17th century. Contemporary glasshouses produced black glass during the Depression, seldom signing their product. It is still being made today.

To learn more about the subject, we recommend *A Collector's Guide to Black Glass,* written by our advisor, Marlena Toohey; she is listed in the Directory under Colorado. Look for her newly updated value guide. See also Tiffin, L.E. Smith, and other specific manufacturers.

Bowl, mixing; Hazel-Atlas, 5" 20.00
Bowl, oval, 1930s, 4¾x8" 48.00
Box, dresser; ormolu, 4 lion-paw ft, 7½" L 425.00
Candle holders, Basketweave base, 5" dia, pr 42.50
Candlestick, molded to resemble crackle, ca 1830, 7" 45.00
Candlesticks, Ellen, wide ft, pr 40.00
Celery dish, Greensburg's #681, ca 1930 ....32.50
Comport, Chatham (Bowman), openwork, 8½" 88.00
Comport, satin w/red & gold decor, 5½x5¾" 88.00
Creamer, Clover Leaf, Hazel-Atlas, ca 1930s 15.00
Creamer & sugar bowl, silver deposit decor, 1920s 40.00
Dresser tray, Dmn Optic, ca 1927, 8" 30.00
Flowerpot, molded band along rim, LE Smith, 1930s, 3" 15.00
Plate, Deco gazelle medallions & foliage w/silver o/l, 10¾" 320.00
Sauce boat, wide panels, 5¾" L 48.00
Saucer, Octagon, ca 1930s 7.50
Shakers, Snake Dance, LE Smith, 3½", pr 35.00
Sugar server, att Duncan & Miller, red plastic lid, 1930s, 6" 35.00
Toothpick holder, Guernsey Glass, 1980s, 2½" 12.00
Tumbler, clear bowl on blk ft, domed center, 1929-35, 12-oz 12.00
Tumbler, gold decor, 10-oz 20.00
Vase, baluster w/scalloped rim, Greensburg, 1925-35, 6" 15.00
Vase, bud; pnt floral decor, HC Fry, ca 1930 ....22.50
Vase, crimped top, ftd, LE Smith, 8" 35.00
Vase, flared top, hdls, ftd, LE Smith, #1900, 1930s, 7¼" 30.00
Vase, ftd, crimped top, LE Smith, 7" 30.00

Blown Glass

Blown glass is rather difficult to date; 18th and 19th century examples vary little as to technique or style. It ranges from the primitive to the sophisticated, but the metallic content of very early glass caused tiny imperfections that are obvious upon examination, and these are often indicative of age.

In America, Stiegel introduced the English technique of using a patterned, part-size mold, a practice which was generally followed by many glasshouses after the Revolution. From 1820 to about 1850, glass was blown into full-size three-part molds. In the listings below, glass is assumed clear unless color is mentioned. Numbers refer to a standard reference book, *American Glass* by Helen McKearin. See also Bottles and specific manufacturers. Our advisor for this category is Mark Vuono; he is listed in the Directory under Connecticut.

Basket, pierced sides, solid base, pontil, dbl hdls, 5x9½" 130.00
Blown, amber w/ornate pewter o/l, pewter stopper, 12" 300.00
Bottle, scent; Pillar mold, canary yel, pontiled, 5⅝" 375.00
Bottle, scent; sea-horse shape w/wht threading, 2¾" 110.00
Bottle, snuff; olive-amber, 8-sided, expanded mouth, 1800s, 4" ..125.00
Bowl, amethyst, floral eng body, pontil, 3½x4½" 40.00
Bowl, cobalt, appl ft/wafer stem, flared w/wht rim, 4⅝x5⅛" 154.00
Bowl, cobalt, 15-dmn pattern, appl ft, pontil scar, 2½x3½" 525.00

Bowl, cobalt, 19 ribs, folded rim, ftd, 3⅞" 115.00
Bowl, Expanded Dmn, cobalt, appl ft, 2¾x4½" 220.00
Bowl, golden amber, slant sides, folded rim, pontil, 3x7⅝" 550.00
Bowl, sapphire bl, swirled ribs, ftd, folded rim, 2¾x4¾" 220.00
Bowl & pan, aqua, pontil scars, folded rims, 5½", 6¼" 250.00
Candlesticks, Loop & Petal, canary, 7", pr, EX 360.00
Chalice, floral eng, Tempora Madantur..., ball knop, 10⅜" 500.00
Compote, folded rim, bladed knop stem, pontil, 4½x7" 145.00
Compote, ribbed ft & folded rim, hollow stem w/wafers, 10x9" ..550.00
Creamer, amethyst, bulbous w/cylindrical neck, solid hdl, 4" 110.00
Creamer, cobalt, appl ft & hdl, 3½" 220.00
Creamer, cobalt, lemon shape, hdl w/curl, solid base, pontil, 4" .300.00
Creamer, cobalt, 20-dmn, pontil scar, tooled rim/spout, 4" 525.00
Creamer, emerald gr, cylindrical neck, ftd, 4" 850.00
Creamer, med cobalt, pontil scar, appl base/hdl, 4¾" 1,000.00
Creamer, purple-amethyst, bulbous, ftd, 4⅛", NM 550.00
Cuspidor, starch bl, flared mouth, polished pontil, 3¾x9" 120.00
Decanter, appl threading at neck, pressed stopper, 11½" 70.00
Decanter, bl, pewter o/l w/serpents/faces, pewter stopper, 12" ...300.00
Decanter, cobalt, horizontal ribbed bbl form, ftd, 4⅝" 550.00
Decanter, cobalt, Pillar mold, seed bubbles, 10⅜" 1,000.00
Decanter, cobalt clambroth, Pillar mold, ped ft, 8¾" 950.00
Decanter, fiery wht opal cased, pontiled, 4 neck rings, 8½" 300.00
Decanter, Pillar mold, 8-rib, slender, pontiled, 12½" 50.00
Decanter, puce cased, Pillar mold, polished pontil, 9⅝" 3,300.00
Flip, eng scrolls/florals/birds, polished pontil, 8x6½" 225.00
Funnel, plain rim, sheared stem, 10½x7½", NM 30.00
Goblet, cobalt, invt-bell bowl, solid stem, pontil, 5¾" 225.00
Hat, golden amber, rnd crown, turned-up brim, 1½x2¾" 275.00
Hat, med red-amber, rolled rim, faint pontil, 4x8⅛" 65.00
Jar, apothecary, cobalt, appl ft, urn-shaped bowl, w/lid, 16" 1,155.00
Mug, tooled rim, flat hdl, pontil, 3½" 70.00
Mug, wht opal loopings, clear hdl, 6¼" 275.00
Pitcher, amber, bulbous, flared tooled rim, strap hdl, 6⅞" 575.00
Pitcher, aqua, flared mouth, solid hdl w/curl, pontil, 4⅝" 750.00
Pitcher, canary yel, Pillar mold, appl hdl, sm crack, 7¾" 300.00
Pitcher, clear w/gray-wht loopings, bulbous, appl hdl, 6¾" 800.00
Pitcher, clear w/wht loops, appl reverse hdl, ca 1905, 9⅝" 500.00
Pitcher, eng florals, appl ribs & hdl, pontil, 6½" 35.00

Pitcher, etched foliage, trefoil lip, striated neck, ribbon detail on handle, American, 19th century, 7¼", $600.00.

Pitcher, ewer form w/heavy rings, appl hdl w/curl, 10½", NM 275.00
Pitcher, flared tooled mouth, appl hdl w/curl, 2¼" 150.00
Pitcher, frosted opal milk glass, Pillar mold, crack, 9" 210.00
Pitcher, milk glass, red/bl vertical ribs, Pillar mold, 4⅝" 1,050.00
Pitcher, Pillar mold, 8-rib cylinder, wide mouth, 9½" 300.00
Rolling pin, cobalt w/red & blk florals, sheared end, 15¼" 170.00
Salt cellar, cobalt, pontil scarred ftd base, flared rim, 2" 180.00
Salt cellar, lt sapphire bl, bulbous w/flared rim, 2¾" 1,000.00
Salt cellar/egg cup, cobalt, folded rim, appl rnd base, 2⅞" 60.00
Sugar bowl, galleried & folded rim, tam finial, 7x4½" 1,700.00
Sugar bowl, Pillar mold, tooled/folded rim, ftd, w/lid, 7¼" 1,450.00
Sweetmeat, cut panels, cut scalloped rim, pontil, 11¼" 190.00

Syrup, milk glass cased, Pillar mold, pewter lid, 7½" 300.00
Tumbler, cobalt, Pillar mold, pontil scar, smooth rim, 4⅛" 800.00
Vase, canary, hexagonal Bigler variant bowl, sq ft, 12¼" 1,265.00
Vase, cobalt, 11-panel, rolled rim/rnd base, pontiled, 2½" 300.00
Vase, dk grass gr, appl ft & stem, ground pontil, 8¾" 150.00
Vase, fiery opal milk glass, Pillar mold, fluted rim, 10⅛" 7,700.00
Whimsey baton, clear 2/4-color alternating swirls, 58" 135.00
Whimsey horn, emb ribs, Am, 19th C, stain, 15½" 100.00
Whimsey pipe, red & wht drag loopings, infolded rim, 1860s 375.00
Wine, bell-shaped w/wht spiral ribbon/threads, 7⅝" 165.00

Blown Three-Mold Glass

A popular collectible in the 1920s, '30s, and '40s, blown three-mold glass has again gained the attention of many. Produced from approximately 1815 to 1840 in various New York, New England, and Midwestern glasshouses, it was a cheaper alternative to the expensive imported Irish cut glass.

Distinguishing features of blown three-mold glass are the three distinct mold marks and the concave-convex appearance of the glass. For every indentation on the inner surface of the ware, there will be a corresponding protuberance on the outside. Blown three-mold glass is most often clear with the exception of inkwells and a few known decanters. Any colored three-mold glass commands a premium price.

The numbers in the listings that follow refer to the book *American Glass* by George and Helen McKearin. Our advisor for this category is Mark Vuono; he is listed in the Directory under Connecticut.

Bird cage fountain, GI-12, bird finial, pontiled, 5¾" 250.00
Bottle, scent; GI-7, purple amethyst, vertical ribs, 6" 325.00
Bottle, toilet water; GI-7 type 4, cobalt, flared lip, 6¾" 280.00
Bottle, toilet; GI-3 type 1, sapphire bl, pontiled, 6", NM 100.00
Bottle, toilet; GI-3 type 2, cobalt, orig tam stopper, 6¼" 190.00
Bowl, GII-18, folded rim, 15-dmn base w/pontil, 1⅝x4¼" 120.00
Bowl, GIII-20, folded rim, rayed base w/pontil, 2x6⅝" 80.00
Bowl, GIII-6, slant sides, folded rim, rayed base, 1⅜x6" 130.00
Carafe/bottle, GI-29, aqua, rayed base, pontiled, 1-qt+ 1,300.00
Castor set, GI-10, 6-bottle, pewter fr mk Trask 115.00
Decanter, GI-27, orig b3m hollow stopper, 1-qt 150.00
Decanter, GI-8, emb Brandy, hollow stopper, pontil, 1-qt 400.00
Decanter, GII-16, 3 appl rigaree rings, w/wheel stopper, 7" 145.00
Decanter, GII-18, 18 dmn base w/pontil, hollow stopper, 1-pt ...150.00
Decanter, GII-24, rayed base w/pontil, hollow stopper, 1-qt 275.00
Decanter, GII-27, emb Brandy, 16-petal base, w/stopper 500.00
Decanter, GII-30, bright yel-olive w/chocolate splashes, 6½" .3,000.00
Decanter, GII-43, med yel-gr pineapple bbl, dbl lip, 8½" 3,000.00
Decanter, GII-7, bbl form w/shaped spout, wheel stopper, 7" 120.00
Decanter, GII-7, dk olive gr, dbl collar lip, 8¼" 2,300.00
Decanter, GIII-16, olive gr, funnel mouth, 7⅜", 1-pt 350.00
Decanter, GIII-2, dk olive gr, flared lip, pontiled, 1-qt 1,350.00
Decanter, GIII-2, med olive gr, flared lip, pontiled, 1-pt 1,600.00
Decanter, GIII-2, wine, flint, pontiled, 11" 525.00
Decanter, GIII-2 type 1, olive gr, flared rim, pontiled, 7" 2,400.00
Decanter, GIV-6, Baroque pattern, bulbous stopper, 9" 215.00
Flip, GII-18, tooled rim, 15-dmn base w/pontil, 6x4½" 180.00
Flip, GIII-22, tooled rim, smooth rim w/pontil, 6x4¼" 250.00
Hat, GII-18, folded rim, 15-dmn base w/pontil, 2x3⅛" 140.00
Hat, GIII-25, cobalt, flint, pontil scar 250.00
Hat, GIII-4, folded brim, rayed base, 2¼x2⅜" 100.00
Hat, GIII-7, rolled brim, rayed base w/pontil, 2¼x2½" 80.00
Pan, GI-30, aquamarine, flared sides, outfolded rim, ftd 1,500.00
Pan, GII-18, 12-dmn base, pontil, folded rim, 1¾x5¾" 85.00
Pitcher, GII-18, tooled rim, 16-dmn base w/pontil, 4⅝" 325.00

Pitcher, GII-25, bbl w/cylindrical neck, strap hdl, 5½" 1,600.00
Pocket flask, GII-18, clear, flattened chestnut, ribs & dmns ...1,300.00
Shot glass, clear, pontil scar, tooled rim, flake, 1⅝" 40.00
Sugar bowl, GII-22, gallcricd rim, rayed base, w/lid, 5¾"   4,500.00
Syrup, GV-II, star base, appl hdl w/curl, tin lid, 7⅞" 400.00
Tumbler, GI-24, sheared rim, smooth base w/pontil, 2⅞" 110.00
Tumbler, GII-33, plain rim & pontiled base, 3¾" 100.00
Tumbler, GIII-13, tooled rim, rayed base w/pontil, 2¾" 140.00
Tumbler, GIII-8, tooled rim, rayed base, 2⅞x2⅜" 120.00

Blue and White Stoneware

Salt glaze or molded stoneware was most commonly produced in a blue and white coloration, much of which was also decorated with numererous 'in-mold' designs (some 150 plus patterns). It was made by practically every American pottery from the turn of the century until the mid-1930s. Crocks, pitchers, wash sets, rolling pins, and other household wares are only a few of the items that may be found in this type of 'country' pottery, now one of today's popular collectibles.

Logan, Brush-McCoy, Uhl Co., and Burley Winter were among those who produced it; but very few pieces were ever signed. Naturally, condition must be a prime consideration, especially if one is buying for resale; pieces with good, strong color and fully molded patterns bring premium prices. Normal wear and signs of age are to be expected, since this was utility ware and received heavy use in busy households. In the listings that follow, crocks, salts, and butter holders are assumed to be without lids unless noted otherwise. For further information we recommend *Blue and White Stoneware* (1981) by Kathryn McNerny and *Collector's Encyclopedia of Salt Glaze Stoneware* (1997) by Terry Taylor and Terry and Kay Lowrance. See also specific manufacturers.

Photo courtesy Terry Taylor

Salt crock, Peacock, dark blue, with lid, 6x6", $500.00.

Batter jar, Wildflower, appl wood & wire hdl, 5x7" 275.00
Bean pot, Boston Baked Beans, Swirl, heavy diffused pattern 450.00
Bowl, Apricot, 9½" 95.00
Bowl, Daisy on Waffle, 10¾" 95.00
Bowl, mixing; Flying Bird, 4x7½" 300.00
Bowl, Reverse Pyramids w/Reverse Picket Fence, 2½x4½" 95.00
Bowl, Wedding Ring, 6 szs, $150 ea, or set of 6 for 800.00
Bowl, Wildflower, 4½x7" 100.00
Bowl (milk crock), Apricot, w/hdl 175.00
Butter crock, Apricot, appl wood & wire hdl, w/lid, 4x7" 250.00
Butter crock, Basketweave & Morning Glory, 4x7½" 400.00
Butter crock, Butterfly, orig lid & bail, 6½" 225.00
Butter crock, Cows, appl wood & wire hdl, w/lid, 4½x7¼" 500.00
Butter crock, Daisy & Lattice, 4x8", NM 175.00
Butter crock, Daisy & Trellis, orig lid & bail, 4½" 200.00
Butter crock, Dropped Windows, 4½x8" 225.00
Butter crock, Eagle, orig lid & bail, M 750.00

Butter crock, Grapes & Leaves, dbl ring around rim, 3x6½" **175.00**
Canister, Basketweave, Cereal, orig lid, 7½" **350.00**
Canister, Basketweave, Cloves, orig lid, 5" **200.00**
Canister, Basketweave, Coffee, orig lid, 7½" **350.00**
Canister, Basketweave, Pepper, orig lid, 5" **200.00**
Canister, Basketweave, Put Your Fist In, orig lid, 7½" **750.00**
Canister, Basketweave, Sugar, orig lid, 7½" **350.00**
Canister, Basketweave, Tobacco, orig lid, 7½" **750.00**
Canister, Snowflake, rpl lid, 6½x5¾" **150.00**
Chamberpot, Wildflower, stenciled pattern, 6x11" **135.00**
Coffeepot, Oval, Diffused Bl, bl-tipped knob, str sides, 11x4" .**1,500.00**
Coffeepot, Peacock, patterned sloped sides, 7x10" **2,500.00**
Coffeepot, Swirl, 'spurs' on hdl, acorn finial, 11½x6" **1,000.00**
Cookie jar, Brickers, flat button finial, 8x8" **500.00**
Cookie/biscuit jar, Flying Bird, orig lid, 9x6¾" **1,200.00**
Cooler, iced tea; Bl Band, flat lid, complete, 13x11" **295.00**
Cooler, water; Apple Blossom, brass spigot, 17x15" **2,000.00**
Cooler, water; Bl Band, orig lid **250.00**
Cooler, water; Cupid, brass spigot, patterned lid, 15x12" **700.00**
Cooler, water; Polar Bear, brass NP spigot, rare, 2-gal, 17x15" .**4,000.00**
Cooler, water; Polar Bear, Ice Water, no lid, 15¼" **385.00**
Crock, Lovebird, rstr bail & handgrip, 5½x9" **600.00**
Cup, measuring; Spearpoint & Flower Panels, 6x6¾" **400.00**
Cup, Wildflower w/emb Ribbon & Bow, 4½x2½" **85.00**
Cuspidor, Basketweave & Morning Glory, 5x7½" **125.00**
Cuspidor, Butterfly & Shield, 6x7½" **175.00**
Cuspidor, Flower Panels & Arches, 7x7½" **250.00**
Custard cup, Fishscale, 5x2½" **125.00**
Egg storage crock, Barrel Staves, bail hdl, 5½x6" **235.00**
Foot warmer, Diffused Bl, A Warm Friend, 12½x6½" **275.00**
Grease jar, Flying Bird, orig lid **650.00**
Ice crock, Barrel Staves, rope/tongs/ice block emb, 4½x6" **225.00**
Jardiniere, Flowers, hairline, 7⅞" **800.00**
Mug, Basketweave & Flower, 5x3" **150.00**
Mug, beer; advertising, Diffused Bl, sqd hdl **150.00**
Mug, Cattails **150.00**
Mug, Flying Bird, 5x3" **200.00**
Mug, plain **65.00**
Mug, Windy City (Fannie Flagg), Robinson Clay Products **200.00**
Pie plate, Bl Walled Brick-Edge star emb base, 10½" **150.00**
Pitcher, Acorns, stenciled, 8x6½" **150.00**
Pitcher, American Beauty Rose, 10" **500.00**
Pitcher, Apricot, 8" **250.00**
Pitcher, Avenue of Trees, allover bl, 9x7" **200.00**
Pitcher, Barrel, +6 mugs **395.00**
Pitcher, Basketweave & Morning Glory, 9" **250.00**
Pitcher, Bl Band, plain **200.00**
Pitcher, Bl Band Scroll **250.00**
Pitcher, Bluebird, 9x7" **450.00**
Pitcher, Butterfly, 9x7" **350.00**
Pitcher, Castle & Fishscale, 8" **195.00**
Pitcher, Cattails, 10" **300.00**
Pitcher, Cattails, 7" **250.00**
Pitcher, Cattails, 9½" **275.00**
Pitcher, Cherries & Leaves, w/printing, 9½" **375.00**
Pitcher, Cherry Cluster, 7½" **650.00**
Pitcher, Cherry Cluster & Basketweave, 10" **350.00**
Pitcher, Daisy Cluster, 7x7" **700.00**
Pitcher, Doe & Fawn, EX color **250.00**
Pitcher, Doe & Fawn, sparce bl, 8½" **185.00**
Pitcher, Dutch Boy & Girl by Windmill, 9" **175.00**
Pitcher, Dutch Landscape, stenciled, tall **150.00**
Pitcher, Eagle w/Shield & Arrows, rare, 8" **600.00**
Pitcher, Eagles & Shields in Ovals, 7" (rare sz) **1,200.00**

Pitcher, Fishscale & Wild Rose, 10" **160.00**
Pitcher, Flying Bird, 9" **500.00**
Pitcher, Garden Rose, 9", NM **500.00**
Pitcher, Girl & Dog, regular bl, 9" **675.00**
Pitcher, Girl & Dog, sponge, 9" **800.00**
Pitcher, Grape & Shield, 8½x5" **150.00**
Pitcher, Grape Cluster on Trellis, allover bl, 7x7" **225.00**
Pitcher, Grape w/Rickrack, any sz **250.00**
Pitcher, Grazing Cows, 6½" **500.00**
Pitcher, Grazing Cows, 7½" **400.00**
Pitcher, Grazing Cows, 8" **250.00**
Pitcher, Indian Boy & Girl, 6" **300.00**
Pitcher, Indian Good Luck (Swastika), 8½" **200.00**
Pitcher, Indian Head in War Bonnet, dl bl, waffled body, 9" **350.00**
Pitcher, Iris, 9" **225.00**
Pitcher, Leaping Deer, sponge, 8" **1,200.00**
Pitcher, Leaping Deer, 8½" **350.00**
Pitcher, Leeping Deer in 1 oval, Swan in other, 8" **1,200.00**
Pitcher, Lincoln, allover deep bl, 10x7" **600.00**
Pitcher, Lincoln, allover deep bl, 4¾x4¾" **175.00**
Pitcher, Lincoln, allover deep bl, 6x4" **250.00**
Pitcher, Lincoln, allover deep bl, 7x5" **300.00**
Pitcher, Lincoln, allover deep bl, 8x6" **350.00**
Pitcher, Lincoln w/Log Cabin **525.00**
Pitcher, Lovebird, arc bands, deep color, 8½" **450.00**
Pitcher, Lovebird, pale color, 8½", EX **300.00**
Pitcher, Monk, dk cobalt **350.00**
Pitcher, Peacock, 7¾x6½" **800.00**
Pitcher, Pine Cone, 9½" **500.00**
Pitcher, Poinsettia, 6½" **275.00**
Pitcher, Rose on Trellis **225.00**
Pitcher, Scroll & Leaf, advertising, 8" **450.00**
Pitcher, Shield, prof rpr, 8" **250.00**
Pitcher, Stag & Pine Trees, 9" **295.00**
Pitcher, Swan, in oval, deep color, 8½" **400.00**
Pitcher, Swan, lt bl, 8½" **350.00**
Pitcher, Tulip, 8x4" **350.00**
Pitcher, Wild Rose, solid bl, 9x6" **450.00**
Pitcher, Wild Rose, sponged bands, 9" **450.00**
Pitcher, Wildflower, stenciled **200.00**
Pitcher, Windmill & Bush, 9" **225.00**
Pitcher, Windmills, 7¼", EX **195.00**
Pitcher, Windy City (Fannie Flagg), Robinson Clay, 8½" **450.00**
Roaster, Diffused Bl, appl hdls, flat finial, 9x19" **225.00**
Roaster, Wildflower, domed lid, 8½x12" **195.00**
Rolling pin, Bl Band, advertising, 14x4" **550.00**
Rolling pin, Swirl, baker's sz, 16" **1,200.00**
Rolling pin, Swirl, orig wooden hdls, 13" **1,200.00**
Rolling pin, Wildflower, plain **350.00**
Rolling pin, Wildflower, w/advertising, 15x4½" **450.00**
Salt crock, Apricot, orig lid **225.00**
Salt crock, Butterfly, orig lid **250.00**
Salt crock, Daisy on Snowflakes, orig lid, 6½x6" **250.00**
Salt crock, Eagle, w/lid **575.00**
Salt crock, Grapevine on Fence, pale bl, orig lid, 6½x6¾" **300.00**
Salt crock, Lovebirds, orig lid, 9" **450.00**
Salt crock, Peacock, w/lid **550.00**
Soap dish, Beaded Rose **150.00**
Soap dish, cat's head **200.00**
Soap dish, Indian in War Bonnet **250.00**
Teapot, Swirl, dbl wire bail hdl, ball shape, 9x6½" **1,200.00**
Toothbrush holder, Bow Tie, stenciled flower **50.00**
Vase, Swirl, cone shape **250.00**
Wash set, Rose on Trellis, 2-pc **300.00**

Water bottle, Diffused Bl Swirl, stopper w/cork, 10x5½" **500.00**

Blue Ridge

Blue Ridge dinnerware was produced by Southern Potteries of Erwin, Tennessee, from the late 1930s until 1956 in twelve basic styles and two thousand different patterns, all of which were hand decorated under the glaze. Vivid colors lit up floral arrangements of seemingly endless variation, fruit of every sort from simple clusters to lush assortments, barnyard fowl, peasant figures, and unpretentious textured patterns. Although it is these dinnerware lines for which they are best known, collectors prize the artist-signed plates from the forties and the limited line of character jugs made during the fifties most highly. Examples of the French Peasant pattern are valued at double the prices listed below; very simple patterns will bring 25% to 50% less.

Our advisors, Betty and Bill Newbound, have compiled two lovely books, *Blue Ridge Dinnerware, Revised Third Edition*, and *The Collector's Encyclopedia of Blue Ridge*, both with beautiful color illustrations and current market values. They are listed in the Directory under Michigan. For information concerning the National Blue Ridge Newsletter, see the Clubs, Newsletters, and Catalogs section of the Directory.

Ashtray, advertising, w/rest **65.00**
Ashtray, ind, from $15 to **20.00**
Basket, aluminum edge, 10" **20.00**
Bonbon, divided, center hdl, from $90 to **100.00**
Bowl, divided, 8" **30.00**
Bowl, fruit; 5" **6.00**
Bowl, mixing; lg **35.00**
Bowl, mixing; sm **15.00**
Bowl, salad; 10½" **50.00**
Bowl, soup; flat **18.00**
Bowl, vegetable; divided, oval, 9" **25.00**
Bowl, vegetable; Premium, w/lid **80.00**
Box, candy; rnd w/lid, rare **125.00**
Box, Dancing Nudes, rare **450.00**
Box, Mallard, rare **550.00**
Box, powder; rnd **130.00**
Butter dish, Woodcrest **60.00**
Cake tray, Maple Leaf **60.00**
Carafe, w/lid **60.00**
Casserole, w/lid **40.00**
Celery, leaf chape, china **40.00**
Child's cereal bowl **45.00**
Child's feeding dish **40.00**
Child's mug **35.00**
Child's plate **40.00**
Coffeepot **150.00**
Counter sign **225.00**
Creamer, Colonial shape, no hdls **20.00**
Creamer, Fifties shape **18.00**
Creamer, Pedestal **55.00**
Creamer, regular **8.00**
Cup, dessert; glass **12.00**
Cup & saucer, Holiday **50.00**
Cup & saucer, Premium **45.00**
Cup & saucer, regular **12.00**
Custard cup **12.00**
Deviled egg dish **40.00**
Dish, baking; 13x8", w/metal stand **35.00**
Egg cup, Premium **30.00**
Gravy boat **28.00**
Jug, character; china, rare **600.00**

Jug, syrup; w/lid **90.00**
Lamp, china **135.00**
Lazy susan, complete **650.00**
Leftover, w/lid, lg **30.00**
Pitcher, Milady, china **125.00**
Pitcher, Sculptured Fruit, china **85.00**
Pitcher, Spiral shape, 7" **70.00**
Plate, aluminum edge, 12" **25.00**
Plate, Christmas Tree **70.00**
Plate, dinner; 9½" **18.00**
Plate, divided **25.00**
Plate, party; w/cup well & cup **30.00**
Plate, rnd, 6" **5.00**
Plate, sq, novelty pattern, 6" **50.00**
Plate, 11½" **60.00**
Platter, Thanksgiving Turkey **225.00**
Platter, Turkey w/Acorns **225.00**
Platter, 11" **18.00**
Ramekin, w/lid, 7½" **32.00**
Relish, Charm House **125.00**
Relish, crescent shape, ind **18.00**

Deep shell relish, Verna, from $70.00 to $80.00.

Relish, heart shape, sm **45.00**
Relish, loop handle, china **80.00**
Relish, Maple Leaf, china **65.00**
Salad spoon **40.00**
Server, center hdl **30.00**
Shakers, Apple, pr **18.00**
Shakers, Blossom Top, pr **35.00**
Shakers, Charm House, pr **95.00**
Shakers, chickens, pr **95.00**
Shakers, ftd, china, tall, pr **50.00**
Shakers, Palisades, pr **30.00**
Shakers, regular. short, pr **15.00**
Sherbet **22.00**
Sugar bowl, Charm House, china **75.00**
Sugar bowl, demitasse; china **40.00**
Sugar bowl, Rope hdl, w/lid **22.00**
Sugar bowl, Waffle, w/lid **20.00**
Sugar bowl, Woodcrest, w/lid **25.00**
Teapot, Chevron hdl **100.00**
Teapot, Colonial **100.00**
Teapot, demitasse; china **150.00**
Teapot, demitasse; earthenware **95.00**
Teapot, Fine Panel, china **125.00**
Teapot, Mini Ball, china **95.00**
Teapot, Piecrust **95.00**
Tidbit, 2-tier **30.00**
Tidbit, 3-tier **40.00**
Tile, rnd or sq, 6" **35.00**
Tray, chocolate pot; china **425.00**

Tray, demitasse; Skyline shape, 9½x7⅝" 90.00
Tray, flat shell, china 85.00
Tray, snack; Martha 95.00
Vase, boot, 8" 90.00
Vase, rnd, china, 5½" 80.00
Vase, tapered, china 95.00

Bluebird China

Made from 1910 to 1934, Bluebird china is lovely ware decorated with bluebirds flying among pink flowering branches. It was inexpensive dinnerware and reached the height of its popularity in the second decade of this century. Several potteries produced it; shapes differ from one manufacturer to another, but the decal remains basically the same. Among the backstamps you'll find W.S. George, Cleveland, Carrolton, Homer Laughlin, Limoges China of Sebring, Ohio; and there are others.

Because examples of this line are relatively scarce, we seldom find new listings. If you have some to add, let us hear from you.

Bowl, berry; Cleveland, ind 12.50
Bowl, deep, Deerwood, WS George, 4¾" 25.00
Bowl, deep, Homer Laughlin, 5½" 35.00
Bowl, ftd, 5" sq ribbed base w/canted corners, BSM, 3½x9x9" 80.00
Bowl, vegetable; Cleveland, 9¾" 45.00
Butter pat, no mk 15.00
Creamer, Deerwood, WS George 15.00
Creamer & sugar bowl, Knowles Taylor Knowles 45.00
Dish, oval, mk Hudson, Homer Laughlin, 5¼x4x1" 20.00
Plate, Cleveland, 6" 8.00
Plate, dinner; Knowles Taylor Knowles, 9¾" 22.50
Plate, Homer Laughlin, 9" 15.00
Plate, scalloped, Homer Laughlin, 7¼" 15.00
Platter, sqd oval, Carrollton, 17¾x12¾" 95.00
Teapot, Carrollton 125.00

Boch Freres

Founded in the early 1840s in La Louviere, Boch Freres Keramis became the foremost producer of art pottery in Belgium. Though primarily they served a localized market, in 1844 they earned worldwide recognition for some of their sculptural works on display at the International Exposition in Paris.

In 1907 Charles Catteau of France was appointed head of the art department. Before that time, the firm had concentrated on developing glazes and perfecting elegant forms. The style they pursued was traditional, favoring the re-creation of established 18th-century ceramics. Catteau brought with him to Boch Freres the New Wave (or Art Nouveau) influence in form and decoration. His designs won him international acclaim at the Exhibition d'Art Decoratif in Paris in 1925, and it is for his work that Boch Freres is so highly regarded today. He occasionally signed his work as well as that of others who under his direct supervision carried out his preconceived designs. He was associated with the company until 1950 and lived the remainder of his life in Nice, France, where he died in 1966. The Boch Freres Keramis factory continues to operate today, producing bathroom fixtures and other utilitarian wares. A variety of marks have been used, most incorporating some combination of 'Boch Freres,' 'Keramis,' 'BFK,' or 'Ch Catteau.' A shield topped by a crown and flanked by a 'B' and an 'F' was used as well.

Box, solid/floral rays, blk/gr/mc, 3x5" dia 300.00
Vase, abstract mc crackle decor on blk, #1833, 1930, 10⅛" 750.00

Vase, cvd geometrics, bl/blk/wht/yel crackle, Catteau, 12" 650.00
Vase, floral, mc on cream gloss, D1755, 13½", EX 375.00
Vase, lg exotic birds/florals, aqua/bl on wht, D1508, 10½" 1,100.00
Vase, lg floral/leaves, yel/wht orange on blk, D2072, 12" 375.00
Vase, lg penguins all around, mc on ivory crackle, 10x7" 1,900.00
Vase, mc drips & crystalline streaks on gr matt, 10⅞" 460.00
Vase, mc florals w/gr leaves on blk glossy, 5" 210.00
Vase, stylized bird/geometric bands, vivid colors, 8x8" 900.00
Vase, veined leaves, gr/tan matt, spherical, #906, 5½" 100.00

Boehm

Boehm sculptures were the creation of Edward Marshall Boehm, a ceramic artist who coupled his love of the art with his love of nature to produce figurines of birds, animals, and flowers in lovely background settings accurate to the smallest detail. Sculptures of historical figures and those representing the fine arts were also made and along with many of the bird figurines, have established secondary-market values many times their original prices. His first pieces were made in the very early 1950s in Trenton, New Jersey, under the name of Osso Ceramics. Mr. Boehm died in 1969, and the firm has since been managed by his wife. Today known as Edward Marshall Boehm, Inc., the private family-held corporation produces not only porcelain sculptures but collector plates as well. Both limited and non-limited editions of their works have been issued. Examples are marked with various backstamps, all of which have incorporated the Boehm name since 1951. 'Osso Ceramics' in upper case lettering was used in 1950 and 1951.

Owl, bone porcelain, ca 1980, limited edition, 18⅜", $865.00.

#100-11, Long Tail Tits, England 2,000.00
#100-19, Swallows w/Marsh Marigolds, England 2,000.00
#400-02, Verdins 1,000.00
#400-03, Black-Headed Grosbeak 1,000.00
#400-11, Orchard Orioles 1,450.00
#400-16, Yellow-Shafted Flicker w/chipmunk 950.00
#400-21, Snow Buntings 1,500.00
#400-35, Koala Baby 650.00
#40117, Cedar Waxwing & Cherries 350.00
#406, Mallards, pr 1,200.00
#429, Kestrels, pr 2,300.00
#438, Black-Capped Chickadee, Edward Marshall Boehm, 8½" ..250.00
#449, Fledgling Kingfisher, 6½" 200.00
#457, Goldfinches 1,200.00
#463, Ptarmigans, pr 1,850.00
#482, Tufted Titmice 1,100.00
#484, Parula Warblers 2,000.00
#486, Green Jays, pr 2,200.00

#487, Rufous Hummingbird w/Icelandic Poppy 1,450.00
#493, Roadrunner, pursuing a horned toad, 14x16" 900.00
#496, Hooded Merganser Ducks, male & female 850.00

Bohemian Glass

The term 'Bohemian glass' has come to refer to a type of glass developed in Bohemia in the late 16th century at the Imperial Court of Rudolf II, the Hapsburg Emperor. The popular artistic pursuit of the day was stone carving, and it naturally followed to transfer familiar procedures to the glassmaking industry. During the next century, a formula was discovered that produced a glass with a fine crystal appearance which lent itself well to deep, intricate engraving, and the art was further advanced.

Although many other kinds of art glass were made there, collectors today use the term 'Bohemian glass' to most often indicate clear glass overlaid or stained with color through which a design is cut or etched. (Unless otherwise described, the items in the listing that follows are of this type.) Red or yellow on clear glass is common, but other colors may also be found. Another type of Bohemian glass involves cutting through and exposing two layers of color in patterns that are often very intricate. Items such as these are sometimes further decorated with enamel and/or gilt work.

Goblet, red, engraved view of Patent Office, Washington, D.C., petal foot, 6½", $850.00.

Beaker, amethyst, facet-cut body, 1890s, 4" 170.00
Beaker, bl, cameo-cut fawn scene, 1850s, 4½" 1,450.00
Beaker, gr panels w/gold on facet-cut body, 1930s, 5¼" 115.00
Beaker, red, facet cut, 1930s, 5¼" 115.00
Beaker, red, facet-cut, ca 1860, flakes, 4½" 145.00
Beaker, red, facet-cut, ca 1875, 5" 135.00
Beaker, red, wheel-cut hunting dog, 1890s, 4" 150.00
Beaker, red, wheel-cut spa scene, ca 1875, 4¾", NM 150.00
Beaker, red & amber, wheel-cut florals, 1930s, 5½" 100.00
Beaker, red & amber panels, 1930s, 5¾" 150.00
Beaker, red circles, 1870s, 5½" 150.00
Bottle, scent; amethyst, cut florals/facets, 1860s, 4", NM 175.00
Bottle, scent; cobalt, facet-cut body/stopper, 1850s, 5" 300.00
Decanter, red, florals/scrolls, 1930s, 12½", +6 cordials 175.00
Mug, red, wheel-cut lamb, ca 1890, 4½", NM 125.00
Mug, wht, facet-cut design, 1860s, 4½" 150.00
Pokal, amber, heavily cut & faceted, 1850s, 7", NM 200.00
Server, clear w/ruby threaded stem, appl shell cups, 1750, 8⅜" ..400.00
Stein, bl opaline, HP florals w/gold, inlaid lid, 1840s, 6" 2,500.00
Vase, red, wht o/l panel w/bird scene, 1890s, 7½" 200.00

Bookends

Though a few were produced before 1880, bookends became a necessary library accessory and a popular commodity after the printing industry was revolutionized by Mergenthaler's invention, the linotype. Books became abundantly available at such affordable prices that almost every home suddenly had need for bookends. They were carved from wood, cast in iron, bronze, or brass, or cut from stone. Today's collectors may find such designs as ships, animals, flowers, and children. Patriotic themes, art reproductions, and those with Art Nouveau and Art Deco styling provide a basis for a diverse and interesting collection.

Recently, figural cast-iron pieces are in demand, especially examples with good original polychrome paint. This has driven the value of painted cast-iron bookends up considerably. See also Arts and Crafts; Bradley and Hubbard.

Abraham Lincoln, bronze, dtd 1925 ....95.00
Antique cars, redware, Japan, 1960s 18.00
Arabs praying & playing flute, bronze, Austrian 200.00
Bird (stylized), hand-hammered copper, pr 65.00
Bird in bas relief on rnd shape, pnt CI, #8-12 VM 200.00
Boy (girl) w/cat, CI, EX old pnt, Hubley #498 ....135.00
Bronco Rider, copper plated, NM 65.00
Camel, cast metal, mk 1928 ....95.00
Cardinal, pnt CI, NM 375.00
Colonial lady, pnt CI, blk & wht, EX 150.00
Dancing lady, bronze, Kindt, pr 195.00
Floral relief on crescent shape, #54 C Albany Fdy Co 60.00
Flower basket, CI, mc flowers in pk basket 125.00
Flowers in relief on crescent shape, pnt CI, unmk, EX 55.00
Fox terrier, sitting, pnt CI, Hubley, NM 400.00
Galleon ships, lead, pr 45.00
Gazelle, wht metal, gr pnt w/sparkles 45.00
Geese in flight, metal, EX pnt 45.00
George Washington, brass, dtd 1932, 7¾" 75.00
Ghoulish hooded face, pnt CI, EX 230.00
Horse head, wht onyx, lg 95.00
House, CI, all orig pnt 125.00
Ivy basket, pnt CI, NM 300.00
John F Kennedy, pewter look, mk FMC, 6" 30.00
Kittens in basket, CI, mc pnt, NM 325.00
Lady's head, futuristic, Frankart 175.00
Leaves, Deco style, copper, Vermont Copper Co 190.00
Leda & the Swan, Deco style, CI, orig gold pnt, 7½" 75.00
Leopard, copper plated, sgn Hentzel, dtd 1922 ....250.00
Liberty Bell, CI 12.50
Nouveau lady, cast bronze 100.00
Nude dancers, bronze, Kindt 375.00
Onyx, Deco-style dbl circles 145.00
Owl, Deco style, bronze, antique gr, sgn M Carr, pr 550.00
Owl on book, CI, NM orig brn pnt 200.00
Owl on book, CI, worn pnt, #587 ....35.00
Owl on stump, pnt CI, NM 225.00
Parrot on ring, pnt CI, NM 185.00
Robert E Lee in camp, CI, historical data on bk, VG 50.00
Roman soldier, cast metal 165.00
Sailboat, pnt CI, M 250.00
Ship, CI, fraternity letters, dtd 1927, VG 22.00
Spaniard w/guitar, Senorita w/fan, CI, orig pnt, 1930s, 5½" 55.00
Thinker, pnt metal, NM 35.00

Bootjacks and Bootscrapers

Bootjacks were made from metal or wood. Some were fancy figural shapes, others strictly business! Their purpose was to facilitate the otherwise awkward process of removing one's boots. Bootscrapers were handy gadgets that provided an effective way to clean the soles of mud and such. Our advisor for this category is Louis Picek; he is listed in the Directory under Iowa.

Bootjacks

Am Bull Dog, pistol shape, CI, blk pnt	75.00
Beetle, CI, orig worn pnt, Reading PA, 4x11x3", EX	120.00
Boss emb on shaft, lacy CI, 15" L	135.00
Cat silhouette, blk-pnt CI, 10½x10"	295.00
Cricket, CI, no pnt, Webster, Bros, Reading PA, 11"	55.00
Cricket, lacy CI, dtd 1878, 1½x4¾"	175.00
Heart figural, CI, scalloped sides, 13" L	135.00
Lee Riders advertising, wood w/leather trim, EX	75.00
Naughty Nellie, CI, VG orig pnt, 9½x5x2½"	165.00
Stylized fish, cvd wood, worn finish, 22" L	115.00
V-shape, ornate CI, VG	48.00

Bootscrapers

Beetle form, cast iron with original paint, 10½", $85.00.

Dachshund, CI, no pnt, tail forms ring, 20½x7½x7"	185.00
Duck, full bodied, scraper on bk, CI, 14½" L	350.00
Griffins jtd at wings & tails, CI, marble base, 18"	880.00
Pig silhouette, cut-out eye, CI, 8½x12"	200.00
Scottie, CI, orig pnt, EX	65.00
Scrolled harp shape, CI, 7⅞x7¼"	40.00
Wrought iron w/detailed scroll finial, 21x24"	500.00
Wrought iron w/scrolled finials, 11½"	75.00

Boru, Sorcha

Sorcha Boru was the professional name used by California ceramist Claire Stewart. She was a founding member of the Allied Arts Guild of Menlo Park (California) where she maintained a studio from 1932 to 1938. From 1938 until 1955, she operated Sorcha Boru Ceramics, a production studio in San Carlos. Her highly acclaimed output consisted of colorful, slip-decorated figurines, salt and pepper shakers, vases, wall pockets, and flower bowls. Most production work was incised 'S.B.C.' by hand.

Bowl, appl lilies at ruffled rim, 6½"	85.00
Bowl, maroon, appl peony on lid, 6"	85.00
Cup, 3 dinosaur hdls	55.00
Figurine, fawn, Penelope, 6"	85.00
Figurine, shepherdess	155.00
Pitcher, pk lustre florals w/gold centers, beading, 6½"	65.00
Shakers, bride & groom, pr	175.00
Shakers, elephants, pr	85.00
Shakers, sailor boy & girl, pr	150.00
Sugar shaker, lady figural, 6"	85.00

Bossons Artware

Bossons were originated in Congleton, Cheshire, England, in 1944 by the senior Mr. W.H. Bossons, an accredited potter. In 1946 he was joined in the business by his son Ray. Their first high-relief wall plaques depicting English scenes and floral subjects were released in 1948. Though they continued to make the floral plaques until 1994, it is Bossons's character wall masks (life-like sculptures) and figurines, conceived and developed in 1948 by Mr. W. Ray Bossons, that have become these unique gift-store collectibles. Ray Bossons is held in high regard as an acomplished artist and has sculpted several extremely popular Bossons including Don Quixote and Sancho Panza, Rolf, Sir Lancelot, Blackbeard, Pierre le Grand, the Parson, The Bossons Santa Claus, Shakespearean Collection, and the 'Briar Rose Collection' of comical animal studies.

Most often the Bossons's 'wall masks' (called 'heads') are subjects of men from all nations and walks of life. Female masks are rare. Two of the three 'Children Studies,' 1968, pictured in this article are the very rare 'Mimi and Rosa.' Some of the larger wall figurines include an animal (Desert Hawks, Desert Hunters, and Deccan Hunters). The most popular Bossons are made of a special gypsum (plaster) medium that is easily chipped or scuffed. Therefore mint or mint-in-box discontinued Bossons are few.

Since the mid-1960s, in nearly every case Bossons have the mask name incised under the collar (Smuggler, Tibetan, and Tyrolean are three recent exceptions, and Snake Charmer, Bengali, and Nigerian Women are three early exceptions) or at the base of the figurine with a date indicating when the mold was created. Also, on the reverse side of most Bossons sculptures will appear the following incision: 'Bossons Copyright Reserved,' and usually 'Congleton, England,' with date. **Those dates will not change though that model may be issued for years,** but collectors seek out the variations in color and sculptural changes that occur during the mask's span of production. Bossons released 'Shelf Ornaments' (1959); two extremely rare 12" pieces ('Afghan' and 'Berber'), and in 1963 four models ('Sikh,' Himalayan,' 'Moroccan,' and 'Serbian'), with no copyright markings or Bossons incisions. Collectors and dealers must be aware of many illegal directly molded copies. These can include 'Pancho,' 'Punjabi,' 'Syrian,' 'Rawhide,' 'Chef,' six original 'Military Masks,' and numerous fakes or look-alikes cast in everything from plaster, and rubber to even metal.

There are other English character masks and hand-painted gypsum artware products of fine quality produced by Naturecraft and the Legend Company. These products have a striking resemblance to Bossons in that Fred Wright, principal sculptor from 1957 to 1972, also did free-lance work for Legend (1950-1980). Much of his most prestigious pieces sculpted while at Bossons are inscribed with his initials. His Legend masks are often incised simply 'Made in England,' however some carry his initals as well.

As early as 1952, Mrs. Alice Brindley (or Miss Wilde as she was then known), sculpted some of the most outstanding Bossons ever created, including the three much loved 'Aboriginal Plaques.' She pursued her career as a free-lance artist until 1971 when she became an exclusive employee of the Bossons company, remaining there until 1995. Mrs. Brindley modeled nearly one hundred Bossons, including many wildlife masks, Scrooge, The Victorians, King Henry VIII, Catherine of Aragon and Anne Boleyn, Country-side Collection, The Americans, Seafarers, many of the Europeans, Tulip Time, Zapata, and Mozart. She now has her own 'AB Sculpture Studio' and recently completed a model of 'Cleopatra' for the Legend Company.

Molded in plaster, Bossons are frequently found in deplorable condition, and **avid collectors only pay the premium prices here for the most perfect examples,** either in factory 'mint' condition or perfectly returned to their original structural and coloring beauty by a recognized restoration artist recommended by Bossons.

In addition to a series of both domestic animals and wildlife in plaster, some Bossons were made of a hard plastic called 'Stonite.' This Fraser-Art Division of Bossons produced the unique and beautiful wildlife series of nine limited editions known as the 'Crown Collection,' including 'Bears and Bees' all modeled by Alice Brindley. Nearly indestructible, Fraser-Art works are also hand painted and therefore, in most cases, they are preserved in excellent condition. Produced from 1966 to 1995, they include 'Pony and Horse Heads,' many bird and fish studies, and the 'Copper Collection.' A limited number of Bossons collectors seek the clocks, mirrors, and other decorative items released during the late 1950s and early 1960s. Bossons also produced their 'Ivorex' plaques, formerly Osborne Editions.

Today many discontinued editions bring prices of several hundred dollars, a few (in perfect condition) go for several thousand. In 1966 the company announced what they termed a temporary closing for the purpose of restructuring. Though correspondence received by this author (Don Hardisty) stated they would resume operations in 1997, should this not come about, look for **all** Bossons to appreciate in value.

Our advisor for this category is Dr. Don Hardisty; since 1984 he has been recommended by Bossons to restore their products. He is listed in the Directory under New Mexico. The items below are all plaster products unless noted otherwise.

Key:

AC — American Collection
BR — Briar Rose Collection
CB — commonly found Bossons
CE — Collectors' Edition
CS — Country-side Collection
DC — Dickensian Collection
DCS — Dogs and Cats
DS — Dogs of Distinction
EC — European Collection
ER — extremely rare
FA — Fraser-Art (Stonite Products)
FAC — Fraser-Art Crown Collection
FP — floral plaques
FP14 — floral plaques, 14" dia
LRE — less recent edition
LWF — larger wall figure
MMD — Men of Mountains and Desert
NNUC — no name under the collar
OE — original edition
OEBR — older edition, becoming rare
OEC — older edition, common
PP — pottery products
RB — rare Bosson
RE — recent editions
Sa — Series A
Sb — Series B
SE — Second Edition
SF — Seafarers Collection
VC — Victorian Collection
VLWF — very large wall figures
VRB — very rare Bossons
WL — Wild Life

Mimi and Rose, no established value.

Aboriginal plaques, PP, ER, ea, from $175 to 350.00
Anemones, FP, OE & RE, 12" dia, ea 75.00
Anemones & Daffodils, rococo style, OE, ER, from $100 to 150.00
Anemones & Daffodils, rococo style, RE, from $45 to 60.00
Anne Hathaway's Cottage, 14" plaque, RB, from $40 to 75.00

Aruj Barbarossa, SF, Sb, RE, from $50 to 65.00
Autumn Gold, FP, OE & RE, 14" dia 100.00
Bargee, SF, Sb, LRE, from $65 to 85.00
Bears & Bees, FAC, LRE, from $350 to 500.00
Beefeater, EC, OEC, from $80 to 90.00
Bengali, 3 or 5 strips on hat, NNUC, LWF, MMD, VRB, $2,500 to .3,500.00
Betsey Trotwood, bl collar, DC, RB, from $200 to 300.00
Betsey Trotwood, pk collar, DC, OEBR, from $30 to 85.00
Bill Sikes, DC, OEBR, from $30 to 85.00
Blackbeard, SF, Sb, RE, from $30 to 40.00
Blk Panther (same mold as Golden Puma), SE, VLWF, RB, $275 to ..375.00
Boatman, SF, Sb, OEC, from $40 to 60.00
Boatman, SF, Sb, RE, CE (1994), from $150 to 200.00
Boxer, DCS, OEC, from $65 to 75.00
Boxer, DS, OEC, from $15 to 30.00
British Military Masks, OE (e w/eyes), EC, ER, from $600 to 700.00
British Military Masks, SE (3 w/o eyes), EC, RB, from $475 to ..500.00
Bruin, BR, OEC, unmk, from $75 to 125.00
Buccaneer, SF, LWF, OEC, from $65 to 85.00
Carnation (1 of 6), FP, OE, RE, 6" dia 35.00
Caspian Man, thick or thin sideburn, Sb, EC, RB, from $150 to ...175.00
Caspian Woman, w/o veil, NNUC, Sb, EC, VRB, from $1,000 to .1,800.00
Caspian Woman, w/veil, NNUC, Sb, EC, ER, from $1,500 to ..2,500.00
Cheyenne Indian, red-fringed jacket, SE, VLWF, OEC, $85 to ...125.00
Coolie, Sa, CB, LWF, from $100 to 150.00
Corsican (early examples have NNUC), Sb, CB, from $85 to 125.00
Coxswain, SF, LRE, from $65 to 90.00
Deccan Hunters, brn or gr-eyed cat, LWF, RB, from $175 to 225.00
Desert Hunters, dog's mouth closed, OE, MMD, RB, from $225 to ..265.00
Desert Hunters, dogs mouth open, SE, MMD, OEBR, from $175 to .185.00
Dogs (Mac, Pooch, Patch), PP, unmk, VRB, ea, from $350 to ...500.00
Don Quixote & Sancho Panza (composite), LWF, RE (ltd), $110 to ...125.00
Double Terriers, DCS, Series II, OEBR, from $75 to 125.00
Eskimo, Sa, AC, OEBR, from $75 to 125.00
Floral Spray, FP, RE, 10" dia 69.00
French Military Masks, LRE (3 w/eyes), EC, from $100 to 150.00
French Military Masks, OE (3 w/eyes), EC, ER, from $600 to 700.00
French Military Masks, SE (3 w/o eyes), EC, RB, from $500 to ..600.00
Golden Puma, OE, VLWF, RB, from $250 to 350.00
Highwayman, LWF, RB, from $185 to 245.00
Horatius Cocles, FA Copper Collection, LWF, RB, from $150 to ..175.00
Horse Heads, FA, OEBR, from $100 to 150.00
King Olaf, LRE, from $75 to 100.00
Kurd, Sb, OEC, from $40 to 60.00
Nigerian Man, Sb, RB, from $165 to 185.00
Nigerian Woman, NNUC, Sb, ER, from $1,400 to 1,800.00
Nuvolari, RE, from $45 to 65.00
Owl, WL, VRB, from $200 to 350.00
Owlet, WL, OEC 60.00
Owlets & Squirrel, WL, RE, from $85 to 100.00
Pancho, Sa, AC, OEBR, from $75 to 85.00
Pony Girl, part of 3 Children Studies, LWF, RB, from $450 to ..600.00
Pony Heads, FA, OEC, from $75 to 100.00
Rawhide, Sa, AC, OEC 65.00
Robin Hood, EC, Sb, CB 75.00
Romany, VLWF, SE, CB 100.00
Romany (Scandali w/gr or yel collar), LWF, OEBR, $175 to 225.00
Shelf Ornaments, unmk, RB, all 6", ea, from $150 to 300.00
Shepherd, CS, RE, from $65 to 75.00
Sherlock Holmes, VC, CB, from $65 to 75.00
Smuggler, NNUC, Sb, CB, from $40 to 60.00
Snake Charmer (thick or thin sideburns), NNUC, LWF, RB, $150 to ..300.00
Squirrel, BR, ER, from $200 to 400.00
Squirrel, Wl, OEC, LWF, from $65 to 75.00

Stag's Head, FA, WL, ER, unmk, from $350 to 475.00
Teals, RB, 14" plaque, from $75 to 125.00
The Bossons Santa Claus, RE, from $40 to 65.00
Tibetan, NNUC, EC, Sb, OEBR, NNUC, from $65 to 75.00
USAF Fighter Pilot, AC, LWF, RE, from $100 to 125.00
Warrior Panels, RB, 17x11" plaques, ea, from $300 to 475.00
Wood Anemones, 1 of 4, FP, RE, 4" dia 20.00
York, coonskin hat, yel shirt, AC, SE, from $75 to 85.00
York, hat w/brim, bl shirt, AC, OEBR, from $175 to 250.00
Zapata, AC, LWF, RE, from $65 to 75.00

Bottle Openers

Around the turn of the century, manufacturers began to seal bottles with a metal cap that required a new type of bottle opener. Now the screw cap and the flip top have made bottle openers nearly obsolete. There are many variations, some in combination with other tools. Many openers were used as means of advertising a product. Various materials were used including silver and brass.

A figural bottle opener is defined as a figure designed for the sole purpose of lifting a bottle cap. The actual opener must be an integral part of the figure itself. A base-plate opener is one where the lifter is a separate metal piece attached to the underside of the figure. The major producers of iron figurals were Wilton Products, John Wright Inc., Gadzik Sales, and L & L Favors. Openers may be free standing and three dimensional, wall hung or flat. They can be made of cast iron (often painted), brass, bronze, or aluminum.

Numbers within the listings refer to a reference book printed by the FBOC (Figural Bottle Opener Collectors) organization. Those seeking additional information are encouraged to contact FBOC, whose address can be found in the Directory under Clubs, Newsletters, and Catalogs.

Alligator & boy, CI, Wilton, F-134, EX 160.00
Auto jack, chrome, mk Duff Norton, F-211 ....32.00
Bulldog's head, CI, Wilton, wall mt, F-425, NM 110.00
Canada goose, CI, Wilton Pdts, F-105 ....68.00
Cockatoo, CI, J Wright, F-121, 1947, VG 190.00
Cowboy & signpost, CI, J Wright, F-14, EX 125.00
Cowboy w/guitar & cactus, hollow pot metal, F-28, 4⅞" 425.00
Dachshund, brass, F-83 ....32.00
Elephant, plated aluminum, F-49 ....28.00
Fish, pnt pot metal, hollow, Wright, F-158, 2¾" 110.00
Flamingo, hollow blown mold, Wilton Pdts, F-120 ....120.00
Foundryman, aluminum, F-29 ....18.00
Hanging drunk, Wilton Pdts, F-415 ....80.00
Hockey skate, pot metal 50.00
Horse's rear end, pot metal, base plate opener 45.00

Indian figural, brass, Iroquois Indian head Beer and Ale, Buffalo NY, 3½", $45.00.

Indian boy, Iroquois Beverages, pnt aluminum, F-197 ....35.00
Monkey, CI, Wright, F-89, EX 135.00
Palm tree drunk, CI, Wilton, F-20 ....45.00

Parrot, long bl tail, J Wright, F-108, 5¼" 35.00
Pretzel, aluminum, F-230, EX pnt 42.50
Quail, full figure, pot metal, on base 65.00
Rooster, pot metal, wht, hollow, F-98, VG 68.00
Sea gull, CI, EX pnt, Wright, F-123 ....60.00
Squirrel, J Wright, F-91 ....65.00
Squirrel, nickeled CI, Norlin Enterprises, F-91d, 1¾x3" 50.00
4-eyed man, CI, J Wright, F-413, EX 60.00

Bottles and Flasks

As far back as the 1st century B.C., the Romans preferred blown glass containers for their pills and potions. Though you're not apt to find many of those, you will find bottles of every size, shape, and color made to hold perfume, ink, medicine, soda, spirits, vinegar, and many other liquids. American business firms preferred glass bottles in which to package their commercial products and used them extensively from the late 18th century on. Bitters bottles contained 'medicine' (actually herb-flavored alcohol), and judging from the number of these found today, their contents found favor with many! Because of a heavy tax imposed on the sale of liquor in 17th-century England by King George, who hoped to curtail alcohol abuse among his subjects, bottlers simply added 'curative' herbs to their brew and thus avoided taxation. Since gin was taxed in America as well, the practice continued in this country. Scores of brands were sold; among the most popular were Dr. H.S. Flint & Co. Quaker Bitters, Dr. Kaufman's Anti-Cholera Bitters, and Dr. J. Hostetter's Stomach Bitters. Most bitters bottles were made in shades of amber, brown, and aquamarine. Clear glass was used to a lesser extent, as were green tones. Blue, amethyst, red-brown, and milk glass examples are rare. (Please note that color is a strong factor when pricing bottles. For example, an amber Hostetter's bitters sells for $25.00 or less, but a green variant can bring hundreds of dollars. An aqua scroll flask may bring $50.00, but a cobalt blue variation will command over $1,000.00.)

Perfume or scent bottles were produced abroad by companies all over Europe from the late 16th century on. Perfume making became such a prolific trade that as a result beautifully decorated bottles were fashionable. In America they were produced in great quantities by Stiegel in 1770 and by Boston and Sandwich in the early 19th century. Cologne bottles were first made in about 1830 and toilet-water bottles in the 1880s. Rene Lalique produced fine scent bottles from as early as the turn of the century. The first were one-of-a-kind creations done in the cire perdue method. He later designed bottles for the Coty Perfume Company with a different style for each Coty fragrance. Prices for commercial perfumes hinge on condition. Their values appreciate according to these factors: are they still sealed or full; do they retain all factory labels; is the original box or packing included? Deluxe versions bring premium prices. Example: blue flat Dans La Nuit cologne by Rene Lalique, value for 6" size, $250.00. Dans La Nuit, enameled with stars by Rene Lalique, 3" round ball, $900.00.

Spirit flasks from the 19th century were blown in specially designed molds with varied motifs including political subjects, railroad trains, and symbolic devices. The most commonly used colors were amber, dark brown, and green.

From the 20th century, early pop and beer bottles are very collectible as is nearly every extinct commercial container. Dairy bottles are a relatively new area of interest; look for round bottles in good condition with both city and state as well as a nice graphic relating to the farm or the dairy.

Bottles may be dated by the methods used in their production. For instance, a rough pontil indicates a date before 1845. After the bottle was blown, a pontil rod was attached to the bottom, a glob of molten glass acting as the 'glue.' This allowed the glassblower to continue to manipulate the extremely hot bottle until it was finished. From about 1845 until approximately 1860, the molten glass 'glue' was omitted. The rod was simply heated to a temperature high enough to cause it to afix itself to the bottle. When the rod was snapped off, a metallic residue was left on the base of the bottle; this is called an 'iron pontil.' A seam that reaches from base to lip marks a machine-made bottle from after 1903, while an applied or hand-finished lip points to an early mold-blown bottle. The Industrial Revolution saw keen competition between manufacturers, and as a result, scores of patents were issued. Many concentrated on various types of closures; the crown bottle cap, for instance, was patented in 1892. If a manufacturer's name is present, consulting a book on marks may help you date your bottle.

Among our advisors for this category are Madeleine France (see the Directory under Florida), Mark Vuono (Connecticut), Steve Ketcham (Minnesota), Monsen and Baer (Virginia), and John Tutton (Virginia). In the listings that follow (most of which have been taken from auction catalogs), glass is assumed to be clear unless color is indicated. Numbers refer to a standard reference book, *American Glass*, by George and Helen McKearin. See also Advertising, various companies; Avon; Barber Shop Collectibles; Blown Glass; Blown Three-Mold Glass; California Perfume Company; Czechoslovakia; De Vilbiss; Fire Fighting; Lalique; Medical Collectibles; Steuben.

Key:
am — applied mouth	grd — ground pontil
bbl — barrel	GW — Glass Works
bt — blob top	ip — iron pontil
b3m — blown 3-mold	ps — pontil scar
cm — collared mouth	rm — rolled mouth
fl — filigree	sb — smooth base
fm — flared mouth	sl — sloping
gm — ground mouth	sm — sheared mouth
gp — graphite pontil	tm — tooled mouth

Barber Bottles

Bay Rum pnt on milk glass, mc florals, ps, rm, 8⅞" 275.00
Bay Rum pnt on milk glass, mc florals, ps, 9⅛" 125.00
Bohemian-style decor, ruby to clear, sb, gm, 8½" 300.00
Cobalt bell form w/wht & gold decor, ps, rm, 8¾" 250.00
Cobalt w/gold bird on branch, sb, gm, pewter top, 8" 140.00
Cobalt w/mc florals, vertical ribs, ps, tm, 6¾" 140.00
Cobalt w/mc thistles, vertical ribs, ps, sm, 7¾" 350.00
Coin Spot, turq opal, sb, rm, 6⅞" 150.00
Cranberry opal w/vertical stripes, sb, rm, 7⅛" 190.00
Dk amethyst w/mc florals, ps, rm, 8" 150.00
Frank Bell Bay Rum, milk glass, mc florals, sb, gm, 9½" 125.00
Hobnail, cranberry opal, polished pontil, rm, 6⅝" 125.00
J Young Jr, Tonic, milk glass/florals, WT&C on sb, 9½" 400.00

Label under glass: Bay Rum and lady wearing hat, amber, smooth base, rolled mouth, 10½", $375.00.

Label under glass, JV Rice Tonic & lady, mc on clear, 7⅝" 375.00
Label under glass, LeVarn's...Tonic, wht/blk/gold on clear, 7½" ..70.00
Mary Gregory figure on gr-yel, vertical ribs, ps, rm, 7⅞" 240.00
Mary Gregory lady on cobalt, vertical ribs, ps, rm, 8¼" 500.00
Mary Gregory lady on gr bell form, vertical ribs, ps, 8" 210.00
Mary Gregory tennis player on cobalt, ps, rm, 8⅛" 230.00
Milk glass w/mc cherub, ps, sm, 7¾" 110.00
Milk glass w/mc dog & deer in brush, sb, rm, porc top, 11" 300.00
Milk glass w/opalescence, mc fox & hound scene, ps, 7½" 80.00
Sea Foam, milk glass w/mc florals, ps, rm, 9" 250.00
Silver o/l on emerald gr frost, ps, rm, chrome top, 7¾" 650.00
Spanish Lace, cranberry opal, rm, 8¼" 325.00
Spanish Lace, turq opal, rm, 8⅜" 325.00
Tiffany-style purple & bl art glass, sb, gm, 8" 650.00
Turq frost w/Nouveau floral & gold, ps, rm, 7¾" 425.00
Witch Hazel, milk glass w/mc florals, sb, rm, 9" 80.00
Witch Hazel, milk glass w/opalescence, deer scene, ps, 9⅛" 275.00

Bitters Bottles

Atwood's Vegetable Dyspeptic, aqua, sl cm, 1840s, 6½" 175.00
Bourbon Whiskey..., dk strawberry puce, bbl, 9¼", EX 375.00
Brown's Celebrated Indian...1868, med amber, Indian Queen, 12" ..475.00
C&C...PR Delany & Co, aqua, cm, sb, semicabin, 10⅛" 275.00
Clarke's Vegetable Sherry Wine...Mass, aqua, cm, 1840s, 14" 400.00
David Andrews Vegetable Jaundice..., aqua, tombstone, 8" 650.00
Doctor Fisch's Bitters...1866, golden yel-amber, fish, 11⅝" 200.00
Dr Bell's Golden Tonic, med amber, sb, sl cm, 9" 100.00
Dr Dimock's Tally-Ho..., golden yel-amber, sb, 8½" 325.00
Dr FA Mitchell's San Gento..., yel-amber, sb, am, 8⅜", EX 200.00
Dr Harter's Wild Cherry..., amber, sb, tm, 1890s, 7¼" 75.00
Dr Herbert John's Indian...Discoveries, amber, sb, am, 8½" 275.00
Dr John Bull's Compound Cedron..., amber, sb, sl cm, 9½" 275.00
Dr Lawrence's Wild Cherry Family..., amber, sb, tm, 8⅞" 100.00
Dr Marcus Universal, bl-aqua, ps, sl cm, 1840-55, 7⅞" 575.00
Dr Maton's Celebrated Stomach...PA, med amber, sb, cm, 9½" ...200.00
Dr Owen's European Life..., bl-aqua, ps, am, 7", NM 250.00
Dr Wheeler's Tonic Sherry..., dk aqua, roped corners, 9⅝" 925.00
ER Clarke's Sarsaparilla...Mass, dk bl-aqua, cm, 7¼", NM 240.00
FR Fleschhut's Celebrated...PA, dk bl-aqua, sb, cm, 8¾" 400.00
Germania...Wm C Oesting, yel-amber, sb, 8⅞" 125.00
Griffith's Opera...AR Griffith, golden yel-amber, sb, 8⅞" 120.00
Hertrich's, bright yel-gr, sb, tm, sample sz, 5¼" 170.00
Hygeia...Fox & Co, golden amber, sl cm, lt haze, 9¼" 110.00
Ishams Stomach..., med yel-amber, sb, cm, 9⅜" 140.00
Kaufmann's World Premium..., amber, sb, cm, 9⅝" 210.00
Keystone, amber, sb, cm, bbl, ca 1865-75, 9¾" 800.00
Loftus Peach..., dk olive-amber, sb, dbl cm, 11½" 95.00
National...Patent 1867, amber, sb, am, ear of corn, 12⅝" 350.00
Old Continental..., med amber, sb, am, semicabin, 10", NM 250.00
Old Homestead Wild Cherry..., med amber, am, log cabin, 9¾" ...325.00
Patented 1867 Old Cabin..., amber, sl cm, log cabin, 9¼", NM ..1,300.00
Royal Italian...Genova, med pk-amethyst, sb, am, 13½" 475.00
Rush's...AH Flanders, MD, NY, bl-aqua, sb, tm, 8¾" 175.00
Schroeder's...Louisville KY, med amber, lady's leg, 9" 375.00
Schroeder's...Louisville KY, orange-amber, lady's leg, 11¾" 350.00
Seaworth...Cape May NJ USA, med-amber, lighthouse, 6⅜" 3,000.00
Shedd's Spring..., med amber, sb, tm, labels, 9¾", NM 525.00
St Drake's 1860 Plant'n...1862, amber, 6-log cabin, 10" 125.00
St Drake's 1860 Plant'n...1862, dk cherry-puce, cabin, 10" 250.00
Suffolk...Philbrook & Tucker..., golden yel-amber, pig, 10" 775.00
W&Co NY, golden amber, ps, dbl cm, pineapple, 8⅝" 425.00
Wahoo & Calisaya...Pinkerton..., golden amber, semicabin, 10" ..750.00
WC Bitters Brobst & Rentschler..., amber, sb, tm, bbl, 10⅝" 275.00

Wm Allen's Congress..., deep bl-aqua, semicabin, 10¼" 300.00

Black Glass Bottles

Many early European and American bottles are deep, dark green or amber in color. Collectors refer to such coloring as black glass. Before held to light, the glass is so dark it appears to be black.

Mallet, olive gr, ps, deep kick-up, sm w/appl lip, 10" 130.00
Onion, olive gr, am, dug/even color, ca 1700, 6" 230.00
Seal: BB Co, olive gr, Patent on shoulder, b3m, 1830s, 9¼" 450.00
Seal: I Watson Esq Bilton, olive gr, cylindrical wine, 9" 400.00
Seal: JS 1798, dk olive gr, ps, am, chip, scarce ½-sz 450.00
Seal: MT&Co, deep olive-amber, ps, am, 9⅛" 200.00
Seal: RT 1789, dk olive gr, appl string rim, ps, 1770-90, 9" 1,000.00
Seal: S Philpol, dk olive-amber, ps, am, stain, 11⅜" 350.00
Utility, olive-amber, rectangle w/corner panels, ps, am, 8½" 165.00

Blown Glass Bottles and Flasks

Nurser, bl Oriental decor on wht, 1800s, 7" 325.00
Nurser, lt gr, chestnut shape, conical top, ps, 8¼" 100.00
Pitkin flask, lt gr, 32 broken swirl ribs, 6⅝" 285.00
Pitkin flask, yel w/olive tone, 36 broken swirl ribs, 6¾" 390.00

Cologne, Perfume, and Toilet Water Bottles

Bl opaque, slim form, ps, rm, 10⅞" 55.00
Cobalt, GI-7, type 4, b3m, ps, fm, 5¾" 170.00
Cobalt, 6-sided petal-form base, ps, 3⅞" 110.00
Column, dk gray-bl opal, ps, fm, shouldered, 2⅜" 230.00
Cranberry, star-cut base, gold stars, bubble stopper, 6" 175.00
Med lav-bl, GI-7, type 4, b3m, ps, fm, 5⅞" 200.00
Milk glass w/emb rose sprigs, roped corners, sb, 8¾" 120.00
Monument, emerald gr, tm, sb, Am, 1870s, 11⅞" 525.00
Peacock Eye, MOP, SP lid w/monogram, 3¾" 485.00
Scroll & Fern, flanged lip, ps, 4⅝" 35.00

Commercial Perfume Bottles

Fleurs de Rocaille (Rock Garden), Caron, flat urn shape, 2¼", sealed, with original paper wrapper, MIB, $77.00.

Added Attraction, Matchabelli, gold/red crown, 1⅝", +box 255.00
Attente, Verlayne, fan shape, Baccarat emblem, 3¼" 90.00
Carnegie Pink, Hattie Carnegie, Deco lady, empty, 3⅜" 230.00
Celui, Jeab Desses, gold-enamel ribbed shape, 2", +box 165.00
Chevalier de la Nuit, Ciro, blk frosted knight, 4⅝", +box 330.00
Deviltry, De Raymond, pk sphere w/red figural top, 5" 990.00
Fleur de France, D'Orsay, gold beads, R Lalique, 3¼", +box ...1,045.00
Jasmine, Lander, amber frosted lady in full gown, 4⅛" 385.00
L'Interdit, Givenchy, clear w/blk cap, held by compo bear, 3⅜" ..55.00
Miss Dior, Christian Dior, clear urn w/emb rings, 4½", +box 175.00

My Love, Elizabeth Arden, clear heart/brass cap, 2¾"+box 135.00
Note, Houbigant, clear flask, button stopper, 3¼", MIB 155.00
Ode, Guerlain, clear/frosted, rose-bud stopper, Baccarat, 7¼" 275.00
On Dit, Elizabeth Arden, frosted lady, worn label, 2⅞" 360.00
Orchidee, Renaud, violet opaque w/blk top, gold label, 2" 245.00
Royal Cyclamen, Houbigant, clear decanter, 4", +pk box 110.00
Sans Adieu, Worth, gr columnar shape, ring top, 2½" 310.00
Savoir Faire, Dorothy Gray, blk & gold masks on clear, 4" 420.00
Subtilite, Houbigant, clear Buddha, gold label, 3¼" 190.00
Vers le Jour, Worth, Worth emb on amber, frosted top, 2" 155.00
Zigane, Corday, clear violin w/gold, 3", +box 220.00
Zut, Schiaparelli, lady's lower torso w/gold, 5", +gr box 825.00

Dairy Bottles

Baker & Son, Atlanta MI, standing cow, yel-orange pyro, qt 15.00
Beltz Dairy, Palmerton PA, red pyro, rnd, qt 15.00
Boyles Dairy, Topeka KS, amber w/wht pyro, sq, qt 15.00
Cloverleaf, Stockton CA, Drive Safely, orange pyro, cream top, qt ..25.00
Dairydale Farms, Goshen NY & scene, orange pyro, sq, qt 7.50
Dashiell Dairy, Midland MD, red/gr/blk pyro, sq, qt 10.00
Ellerman Dairy, Athens WI, red pyro, rnd, qt 15.00
Greenacre Farms, gr pyro, rnd, ½-pt 7.50
Hilton Dairy, Madison ME, red pyro, rnd qt 18.00
Indian Hill Farm Dairy, Greenville ME & chief, orange pyro, qt ..27.00
Martin Farms, Rochester VT, cow's head, orange pyro, sq, qt 7.50
St Mary's...PA & barn scene, brn pyro, rnd, qt 15.00
Vermont Country, Shelburne VT, gr pyro w/cow's head, qt 7.00

Figural Bottles

Atterbury Duck, milk glass, Patd April 11th 1871, 11½" 275.00
Baby in egg, milk glass w/Blk pnt baby, sb, 2½" 250.00
Baby's face, milk glass, sb, gm, 2⅝" 375.00
Dice, 3 stacked, milk glass w/mc card transfers, 8⅞" 85.00
Ear of corn, golden amber, sb, am, 9⅝" 230.00
Eye, milk glass w/bl/blk/cream pnt, sb, gm, metal cap, 5⅛" 170.00
French woman, dk sapphire, tm, ps, 13½" 1,000.00
Hand, milk glass, sb, gm, roughness, 5⅜" L 160.00
Joan of Arc, milk glass, Jeanne D'Arc at base, sb, 16½" 250.00
Kummel bear, blk amethyst, sb, tm, silver o/l at base, 11⅛" 95.00
Kummel bear, milk glass, sb, am, 11⅛", NM 75.00
Lady holding water pitcher, milk glass, sb, gm, 11⅛" 190.00
Life preserver, milk glass, sb, tm, shallow chip, 5½" 230.00
Man's shoe, blk glass, Pat Appd For on sb, metal cap, 3½" 65.00
Man seated on bbl, golden yel, gm, sb, 11⅜" 70.00
Mermaid, brn & tan Rockingham type, 7¼", EX 110.00
Negro gentleman, formal attire, clear frosted w/mc pnt, 13" 600.00
Oriental man, milk glass, orig metal atomizer, 5½" 150.00
Pig, Good Old Bourbon, amber, tm, sb, 6¾" 160.00
Victorian lady, Coming Through the Rye, clear, pnt head, 13½" ..1,000.00

Flasks

Byron/Scott, GI-114, yel olive-amber, sm, ½-pt 190.00
Clasped Hands/Cannon, GXII-39, golden amber, sb, sm, 1-pt ...325.00
Columbus/Columbus, GI-127, clear, sm, grd, metal cap, ½-pt 230.00
Corn for World/Ear of Corn, GVI-4, golden to yel amber, 1-qt ..425.00
Cornucopia/Urn, GII-14, bl-emerald gr, open pontil, ½-pt 350.00
Cornucopia/Urn, GII-4, yel w/olive tone, ps, sm, 1-pt 300.00
Cornucopia/Urn, GII-7, olive gr, crude open pontil, ½-pt 120.00
Eagle w/Banner, GII-143, yel-gr, ip, sl cm, calabash 200.00
Eagle w/Shield/plain, GII-39, bright yel-gr, am, 1-pt 1,850.00
Eagle/Cluster of Grapes, GII-55, med root beer-amber, 1-qt ...1,550.00

Eagle/Eagle, GII-24, aqua, ps, sm, lt haze, 1-pt **95.00**
Eagle/Eagle, GII-24, dk bl-aqua, ps, sm, 1-pt 120.00
Eagle/Eagle, GII-30, aqua, ps, sm, ½-pt 210.00
Eagle/Eagle, GIII-1, bl-aqua, ps, sm, 1-pt 200.00
Eagle/Flag, GII-48, bl-gr, ps, sm, 1-qt 1,750.00
Eagle/Lafayette, GI-90, aqua, open pontil, sm, 1-pt 250.00
Eagle/Liberty, GII-64, med olive gr, sb, sm, ½-pt 230.00
Eagle/Louisville KY GW, GII-36, dk aqua, am, sb, 1-pt 170.00
Eagle/Masonic Arch, GIV-17, olive gr, ps, sm, 1-pt 325.00
Eagle/Masonic Arch, GIV-18, golden yel-amber, ps, sm, 1-pt 145.00
Eagle/Masonic Arch, GIV-32, aqua, ps, sm, 1-pt 160.00
Eagle/Masonic Arch, GIV-37, aqua, ps, sm, 1-pt 180.00
Eagle/New London GW, GII-67, golden honey-amber, ½-pt ..1,050.00
Eagle/Prospector, GXI-44, dk bl-aqua, sb, am, 1-pt 875.00
Flora Temple/Horse, GXIII-20, copper puce, no-hdl variant, 1-pt ...350.00
Flora Temple/Horse, GXIII-24, cherry puce, sb, am, hdl, 1-pt 450.00
Franklin/Masonic Arch, GIV-43, aqua, ps, sm, 1-pt 375.00
Hunter/Fisherman, GXIII-4, golden amber, ip, cm, calabash 240.00
Jenny Lind/Glass House, GI-99, yel-olive, ps, calabash 2,900.00
Jenny Lind/Lyre, GI-109, dk aqua, ps, sm, 1-qt 1,350.00
Kossuth/Tree, GI-113, lt to med apple gr, ip, cm, calabash 325.00
Prospector/Hunter, GXI-51, olive gr, sb, am, 1-pt 1,000.00
Prospector/Hunter, GXI-52, bl-aqua, sb, am, ½-pt 130.00
Scroll, GIX-10, med amber, ps, sm, 1-pt 400.00
Scroll, GIX-10b, dk olive amber, ps, sm, crude, 1-pt 400.00
Scroll, GIX-20, dk bl-aqua, ps, sm, open bubble, 1-pt 120.00
Scroll, GIX-34, cornflower bl, open pontil, sm, ½-pt 200.00
Scroll, GIX-34, yel-amber, ps, sm, ½-pt 550.00
Scroll, GIX-44, aqua, ps, sm, corset waist, 1-pt 425.00
Scroll, GIX-46, dk bl-aqua, ps, sm, dullness, 1-qt 650.00
Sheaf of Wheat/Traveler's Companion, GXV-1, dk olive-amber, 1-qt .135.00
Sheaf of Wheat/Westford, GXIII-37, med yel-amber, ½-pt 140.00
Sheaf of Wheat/5-pointed star, GXIII-39, bright yel-gr, 1-pt 850.00
Success to RR/Horse Pulling Cart, GV-3, yel-olive gr, 1-pt 350.00
Success to RR/Locomotive, GV-1, dk aqua, sm, 1-pt 240.00
Sunburst, GVIII-9, med yel w/amber tone, ½-pt 575.00
Washington, GI-41, med teal bl, ps, sm, 1-pt 200.00
Washington/Eagle, GI-11, dk bl-aqua, ps, sm, 1-pt, NM 575.00
Washington/Monument, GI-21, smoky clear, ps, sm, 1-qt 185.00
Washington/Taylor, GI-41, olive gr, ps, sm, ½-pt, NM 1,700.00
Washington/Taylor, GI-50, smoky clear, pontiled, sm, 1-pt 300.00
Washington/Tree, GI-35, aqua, ps, am, calabash 190.00

Food Bottles and Jars

Pickle jar, NM label reads New England Pickles Manufactured by Skilton...Mass., pictures 2 standing pilgrims, aqua with vertical ribs at shoulder, 1880-90, 11½", $160.00.

Cloverleaf, Stoddard, red-amber, rm, sb, 1870s, 8½", NM 400.00
Cloverleaf form, med bl-gr, rm, ip, 1860s, 7⅝" 150.00
Peppersauce, aqua, cathedral, 6-sided, ps, am, 8½" 90.00

Pickle, Landsdale & Bro, aqua, cathedral, ps, 8⅞" 625.00
Pickle, lt apple gr, cathedral, sb, am, 9⅛" 150.00
Pickle, lt gr, cathedral, beveled corners, ip, cm, 9¼" 250.00
Pickle, med emerald gr, sb, rm, potstone, 11" 475.00
Pickle, pale smoky olive, ip, am, hairline, 8¼" 400.00
Pickle, Skilton Foote...Bunker Hill, aqua, lighthouse, 8" 170.00
Pickle, Skilton Foote...Bunker Hill, clear, lighthouse, 11½" 170.00
Pickle, Skilton Foote...Bunker Hill, lt yel-gr, lighthouse, 11" 350.00

Ink Bottles

Bertinguiot, yel olive-amber, ps, sm, New England, 2⅛" 220.00
Cabin, aqua, tm, sb, 2⅜" 225.00
Carter's, cobalt, sb, am, master, 6¼" 220.00
Carter's, med cobalt, am, 2¾" 95.00
Cone, amber, rm, shouldered form, open pontil, 1850s, 2¼" 325.00
Conical, med yel-olive, lg X on ps base, sm, 2⅜" 240.00
E Waters Troy NY, aqua, am, master, 5⅛" 650.00
Estes NY Ink, dk aqua w/hint of gr, 8-sided, rm, 4" 1,100.00
Harrison's Columbian, aqua, 8-sided, open pontil, rm, 1⅝" 80.00
Harrison's Columbian, cobalt, ps, rm, 2" 600.00
Harrison's Columbian, lt to med sapphire bl, open pontil, 4¾" ..800.00
J&IEM, turtle, amber, sb, gm, 1⅝" 130.00
J&IEM, turtle, dk golden-amber, sb, 1870s, 1¾" 195.00
J&IEM, turtle, yel-olive, sb, gm, stress crack, 1⅝" 160.00
JS Dunham & Co, 12-sided umbrella, aqua, open pontil, 2⅜" ...260.00
S Fine Blk Ink, med olive gr, open pontil, rm, 3" 325.00
Teakettle, Ben Franklin bust, lt aqua, sb, sm, 2½" 350.00
Teakettle, blk amethyst w/silver o/l on lip, sb, 2" 300.00
Teakettle, bright yel-gr, sb, gm, 2", NM 425.00
Teakettle, clear, 8-sided, sb, gm, 2" 125.00
Teakettle, cobalt bbl, sb, gm, 2⅛", NM 800.00
Teakettle, lt to med yel-lime gr, appl finial, 1850s, 2¼" 375.00
Teakettle, milk glass, sb, gm, brass ring/lid, 2⅝" 375.00
Teakettle, milk glass w/mc florals, sb, gm, 2⅛", NM 325.00
Teakettle, smoky lav, sb, metal neck band, 2" 450.00
Umbrella, cobalt, 8-sided, rm, sb, 1870s, 2½", NM 425.00
Umbrella, dk yel-olive gr, open pontil, rm, 2½" 220.00
Umbrella, med bl-gr, 8-sided, open pontil, rm, 2⅛" 95.00
Umbrella, med emerald gr, 12-sided, rm, 2⅛" 230.00
Umbrella, rich purple amethyst, 8-sided, sb, tm, 2½" 800.00

Medicine Bottles

Allen's Lung Balsam, aqua, sb, 8" 10.00
Apothecary, dk cobalt w/pnt SYR: Scillae label, 6⅞" 90.00
Apothecary, pk-amethyst w/mc label under glass, 11⅝" 700.00
Cameron's Kephalia for the Hair, aqua, ps, am, 7⅜" 180.00
Chamberlain's Immediate Relief..., bl-aqua, ps, rm, 4¾" 80.00
Davis Vegetable Pain Killer, aqua, ps, 5" 25.00
Davis Vegetable Pain Killer, aqua, sb, 5" 5.00
Davis 3 Cornered Bottle Pile Remedy..., amber, triangular, 3½" ...100.00
Dodge Brothers Melanine Hair Tonic, dk purple-amethyst, 7¼" ..425.00
Dr D Jayne's Tonic Vermifuge, aqua, sb, 5¾" 5.00
Dr Kilmer's Swamp Root, aqua, sb, 8" 10.00
Dr King's New Discovery, aqua, sb, 6½" 7.00
Dr Shoop's Family Medicine, Racine Wis, aqua, SB, 7" 10.00
Dr Tebbetts'...Hair Regenerator, dk purple-amethyst, 7½" 150.00
Dr Townsend's Aromatic Hollands Tonic, golden amber, sb, 9" ..90.00
Dr WG Little's Ring Worm..., lt aqua, ps, rm, 3" 400.00
Genuine Swaim's Panacea..., aqua, ps, am, 7⅝" 725.00
Geo E Fairbanks No 10..., orange-amber, cylinder, 12⅛" 130.00
GW Merchant Lockport NY, dk emerald gr, sl cm, flake, 5" 120.00
HH Warner & Co Tippecanoe, root beer-amber, sb, am, 9" 80.00

J&C Maguire Chemist & Druggists, med cobalt, sb, 9⅜" **90.00**
James' Anodyne Expectorant..., dk bl-aqua, ps, rm, 2⅜" **275.00**
JL Giofray & Co Hair Renovator..., red-amber, sb, am, 8⅛" ...**1,800.00**
LQC Wishart's Pine Tree Tar Cordial..., med to dk bl-gr, 7¾" ..**250.00**
Lydia Pinkham's Vegetable Compound, aqua, sb, 8½" **5.00**
Marine Hospital Service 1798 USA 1871, amber, sb, 6", NM **160.00**
Mrs Winslow's Soothing Syrup, aqua, sb, 5" **8.00**
One Minute Cough Cure, aqua, sb, 5¾" **5.00**
Preston's Veg Purifying Catholicon..., aqua, pontiled, 9½" **200.00**
Psychine, aqua, sb, 5½" **10.00**
Sozodont for the Teeth, clear, sb, 2½" **3.00**
St Catherine's Chloride Calcium..., aqua, ps, am, 6" **100.00**
USA Hosp Dept, golden yel-amber, SOS on sb, dbl cm, 9¼" **325.00**
Vaseline, clear, sb, 3" **3.00**
Watkins Liniment, aqua, sb, 6½" **5.00**
Wayne's Diuretic Elixer..., med cobalt, sb, am, chip, 7½" **230.00**
WE Hagan & Co Troy NY, med cobalt, 8-sided, sb, 6¾" **70.00**

Mineral Water and Soda Bottles

CA Cole...North Howard, med cobalt, 10-pin, sb, cm, 8½" **425.00**
Caladonia Spring Wheelock VT, yel-amber, sb, dbl cm, 1-qt **500.00**
DG Hall, teal bl-gr, ip, am, 7¼" **130.00**
G Norris & Co City Bottling..., med cobalt, Hutchinson, 7" **160.00**
John Gardner & Son...Sharon Sulpher Water, teal bl, sb, 7½" ..**255.00**
JR Donaldson Newark NJ...Union GW, cobalt, mug base, 7¾" .**475.00**
Lynch & Clarke New York, med olive-amber, ps, sl cm, 1-pt **250.00**
McManus & Meade Bottlers..., aqua, sb, tm, Hutchinson, 6⅝" ..**1,050.00**
Middleton Mineral Spring..., emerald gr, sb, sl cm, 1-qt **500.00**

Poland Mineral Spring Water, H. Ricker & Sons Proprietors, aqua, figural man, smooth base, ca 1880-90, 11⅛", $195.00. (Many later variations of this bottle are available for under $50.00.)

Seymour & Co Buffalo NY, cobalt, ip, am, 7⅛" **425.00**
W Eagle's Superior..., med emerald gr, ip, am, 6¾" **80.00**
WP Knickerbocker Soda...NY 1848, sapphire bl, 8-sided, 7¾" ...**190.00**

Poison Bottles

Insecticide Vicat Brevete..., aqua, emb bug, sb, 4¼" **120.00**
Jacobs' Bed Bug Killer, skull & Xbones, golden-amber, 5½" ...**1,350.00**
Lattice & Dmns, cobalt, tm, cylindrical, sb, 11½" **600.00**
Poison, yel w/amber tone, sb, tm, 4¾" **250.00**
Poison/Poison, med amber, sb, tm, orig label, 5½", NM **50.00**
Skull figural, cobalt, tm, sb, 1870s, 4¼" **650.00**

Spirits Bottles

Adams Booth Co Sacramento Cal, clear, sb, tm, 12", EX **140.00**

AM Bininger...New York, med amber hdld urn, sb, sm, 8⅞" ...**2,000.00**
AM Bininger...New York, med amber jug, sb, am/hdl, 8⅞" **350.00**
AM Bininger...New York, med amber jug, sb, 7¾" **275.00**
Ambrosial BM&E AW & Co, yel-amber, ps, am, hdl, 9" **180.00**
Bininger's Night Cap...NY, amber, sb, am, 8" **340.00**
Bininger's Old Dominion Wheat Tonic..., dk olive gr, sb, 10" ...**200.00**
Bininger's Old KY Bourbon...NY, orange-amber, sb, 9¾" **80.00**
Bininger's Old Times Family Rye...NY, sb, am, 9¾" **230.00**
Bininger's Regulator...New York, aqua, rare, clock, 5¾" **900.00**
Bininger's Regulator...New York, yel-amber, clock, 6" **350.00**
Chesley's Jocket Club Whiskey, clear, sb, tm, crude, 12" **210.00**
Club (inside dmn), teal bl, ip, dbl cm, whittled, 9" **300.00**
Cutter OK Whiskey...Louisville KY..., yel-amber, sb, 11⅞" **75.00**
Distilled in 1848...AM Bininger...NY, amber, bbl, 8" **170.00**
Distilled in 1848...AM Bininger...NY, amber, bbl, 9½" **300.00**
Eagle Glenn Whiskey/eagle, lt amethyst, sb, tm, 11½", EX **70.00**
Geo Stinson Straight Rye..., yel-amber, strap-side flask, 8" **130.00**
Hall, Luhrs & Co Sacramento, sb, am, 12" **80.00**
HF&B NY (in shield), dk cherry puce w/melon ribs, sb, 9⅛" **475.00**
JN Kline & Co Aromatic...Cordial, med cobalt, teardrop, 5⅜" ..**275.00**
John B Drake Tremont House..., golden yel-amber, dug, ½-pt ...**180.00**
Kolbert & Cavagnaro...Stockton Cal, smoky clear, sb, am, 11½" ..**250.00**
Label under glass: Wm Foust Distiller..., clear/mc, 10" **775.00**
Palmer House Chicago, amber, Pat Aug 6th 1872 on sb, 7¼" **650.00**
Pepper Distillery Hand Made Sour Mash..., yel-amber, sb, 12" ...**180.00**
Pinch, cobalt w/Rye silver o/l, sb, tm w/o/l, haze **75.00**
Schlesinger & Bender...Cal, yel-amber, sb, tm, 11¾" **210.00**
Trade Mark GH Moore Old Bourbon Rye..., amber, sb, 12⅛" **85.00**
Wm H Spears...Pioneer Whiskey...SF, pale straw tint, sb, 12" **625.00**

Miscellaneous

Dresser, milk glass, emb grapes, long neck, sb, 9", pr **40.00**
Lavender Salts, Goetting & Co, See California Perfume Co
Sarsaparilla, Dr Guysott's Yel..., aquamarine, sl cm, ip, 10" **65.00**
Sarsaparilla, Old Dr J Townsend's, lt bl-gr, sl cm, ip, 9½" **125.00**
Snuff, olive-amber, ps, sm w/flared lip, whittled, 4" **85.00**
Utility, med yel-gr, ps, rm, 8" **300.00**
Utility, yel olive-amber, sb, folded rim, trn molded, 16" **330.00**

Boxes

Boxes have been used by civilized man since ancient Egypt and Rome. Down through the centuries, specifically designed containers have been made from every conceivable material. Precious metals, papier-mache, Battersea, Oriental lacquer, and wood have held riches from the treasuries of kings, snuff for the fashionable set of the last century, China tea, and countless other commodities. See also Toleware; specific manufacturers.

Bentwood, hardwood/pine w/pnt florals, dtd 1808, oval, 22½" ..**4,500.00**
Bentwood, worn gr pnt, lid branded w/initials, 10½" dia **270.00**
Bible, chestnut w/some curl, punched decor, wrought lock, 27" .**600.00**
Bible, tiger maple, book form, hinged lid, 19th C, 11¼" **385.00**
Bible, walnut Chpndl, dvtl, bracket ft, PA, 8½x14x24" **900.00**
Blk lacquer w/gilt decor, paw ft, brass hdls, 14" L **495.00**
Bride's, bentwood pine w/floral decor, laced seams, 15" L **660.00**
Candle, dvtl cherry w/walnut burl veneer, hangs, 12" **550.00**
Cash, brass & iron, 3-compartment, 1670s, 4x6" **625.00**
Document, Hepplwht figured mahog veneer w/inlay, 10½" **1,300.00**
Dome top, mahog w/marquetry geometric inlay, rfn, 9x20x12" ..**770.00**
Dome top, pin w/ink decor on dk varnish, staple hinges, 12" **495.00**
Dome top, pine w/pnt landscape, wire hinges, 15¾" **1,000.00**

Glass, cobalt w/HP birds & flowers, hinged lid, 3¾x4⅜" 265.00
Glove, mahog w/ivory inlay, ball ft, 1800s, 2x11x6" 275.00
Hanging, maple/pine w/chip-cvd & pierced front, 15x9x5" 2,000.00
Hide covered, leather trim & brass studs, 7½x10½" 330.00
Jewel, mc parrot & flowers w/gold on lacquer, 3½x9x6" 154.00
Jewel, Tunbridge, rosewood w/inlay, fading, 5x11x8" 275.00
Knife, dvtl mahog w/chestnut bottom, center divide, 14" 415.00
Knife, inlaid mahog Hepplewhite, 15x9" 650.00
Knife, tiger maple, trn hdl, early 1800s, 5½x14x10" 865.00
Mahog w/maple house & stars inlay, ftd, 12x8x5" 440.00
Pine, grpt, dome top, New England, early 1800s, 12x24x13" 430.00
Poplar w/brn vinegar grpt over mc ground, dvtl, 9x18x10" 2,000.00
Sea captain's, rosewood w/bone/ivory/wood inlays, tray, 14" L ...1,750.00
Shaving, mahog w/geometric inlay, fitted int, 10x6x3" 275.00
Spice, orig yel grpt w/gr, 5 dvtl drws, wire nails, 12x11x5" 1,700.00
Tea, Georgian banded mahog, domical lid, 5½x8x5½" 275.00
Tortoise shell, gilt brass mts & hdl, rpr, 5½" L 360.00
Walnut w/lt wood inlay, dvtl, heart escutcheon, 12" L 115.00
Writing, mahog w/brass mts, English handmade repro, 34x20x10" ..495.00
Writing, rosewood w/much brass banding, tooled leather top 400.00

Boyd Crystal Art Glass

Boyd Crystal Art Glass is a small but productive glass factory located in Cambridge, Ohio. It was established in 1978 when the Boyd family bought out the Degenhart factory. Over the years Boyd has produced more than two hundred molds; while many were their own design, they acquired others from glasshouses no longer in business. All the Boyd pieces are marked with a distinct logo of a 'B' in diamond. Further dating is possible because a line was added under the diamond in 1983, and an additional line was added above the diamond in 1988. In September 1993 another line was added, this one on the right of the diamond. Boyd's glass is prized because of the colors they formulated and the fact that once a piece is produced in a particular color it will not be produced in that color again, even if that color is brought back years later. All pieces are hand pressed from glass that is from a single-day tank. Colors are made for about ten weeks or less, thus limiting the number of pieces that can be produced in that color. More than three hundred different colors have been used and developed by the Boyds. Much like Degenhart glass, the colors can be confusing and difficult to identify. Exceptional slags and hand-painted pieces can command up to 50% higher prices. Satin glass variations are priced 10% to 30% higher when they can be found.

In the following listings, (N) indicates a mold that was new in 1996-97. (R) indicates the piece is retired. Our advisor for this category is Joyce Pringle; she is listed in the Directory under Texas.

Photo courtesy Joyce Pringle

Airplane, Cobalt, 3½x4", $21.00.

Airplane, Heather Gray 15.00
Airplane, Vanilla Coral 18.00
Airplane, Vaseline Carnival 25.00
Angel, Purple Frost (N) 18.00
Artie Penguin, Classic Black 8.25
Artie Penguin, Vaseline 15.00
Basket, Milk White, w/hdl, 4½" 15.00
Bernie the Eagle, Cardinal Red Carnival 10.00
Bird Salt, Cardinal Red 7.00
Bunny Salt, Golden Delight 20.00
Bunny Salt, Mirage 6.75
Cat Slipper, Classic Black Slag 10.00
Chick Salt, Nile Green 6.75
Chick Salt, Oxford Gray 22.00
Children's Lamb set, Classic Black 20.00
Chuckles the Clown, Baby Blue, (R) 9.00
Colonial Man Fredrick, Cobalt (R) 15.00
Debbie the Duck, Furr Green 6.00
Duck Salt, Cobalt 8.50
Duckling, Mardi Gras 3.00
Elizabeth Doll, Sunglow, miniature (R) 8.25
Freddie the Hobo Clown, Country Red (R) 8.00
Fuzzy the Teddy Bear, Oxford Gray (R) 10.00
Fuzzy the Teddy Bear, Plum 15.00
Hand Dish, Chocolate Carnival 5.00
Hen Dish, Champagne, 6" 35.00
JB Scotty, Cobalt (R) 52.50
JB Scotty, Daffodil (R) 20.00
JB Scotty, Mint Green (R) 21.50
JB Scotty, Mirage (R) 9.50
Joey the Horse, Bermuda (R) 32.50
Joey the Horse, Cashmire Pink (R) 22.00
Joey the Horse, Cobalt Carnival (R) 55.00
Joey the Horse, Pocono (R) 17.50
Joey the Horse, Vaseline Carnival (R) 16.00
Lamb Salt, Windsor Blue 8.50
Louise Doll, Ice Blue (R) 60.00
Louise Doll, Mother's Day 1996, HP 25.00
Louise Doll, Snow (R) 12.00
Lucky Unicorn, Lemonade 16.50
Marguerite Doll, Barely Pink (R) 20.00
Miss Cotton the Kitten, Mulberry Carnival 8.00
Miss Cotton the Kitten, Shasta White 8.00
Owl, Lime 12.00
Owl, Plumberry 13.50
Owl Bell, Lavender 10.00
Owl Bell, Spinnaker Blue 10.00
Parlour Pup, Bermuda 10.00
Patrick the Balloon Bear, Caramel (R) 8.00
Pooche, Buckeye 7.00
Pooche, Patriot White 8.00
Puff Box, Crown Tuscan 12.50
Rex the Dinasaur, Aqua Diamond 6.00
Rooster Holder, Heather Gray 10.00
Rose Puff Box, Kumquat 12.50
Sammy the Squirrel, Alexandrite (R) 8.50
Santa Bell, Cobalt 20.00
Scottie, Cornsilk (R) 30.00
Skippy, Golden Delight (R) 5.00
Taffy Carousel Horse, Purple Frost (N) 16.00
Teddy the Tugboat, Mint Green 12.50
Train, Cardinal Red Carnival, complete 110.00
Train Boxcar, Bamboo 7.00
Train Coal Tender, Seafoam 7.00

Train Set, Capri Blue, 6-pc **60.00**
Train Set, Easter 1996, 6-pc **110.00**
Tucker Car, Lime **10.00**
Willie the Mouse, Lime Carnival **9.00**
Woodchuck, Classic Black **12.00**
Zak the Elephant, Snow (R) **20.00**

Bradley and Hubbard

The Bradley and Hubbard Mfg. Company was a firm which produced metal accessories for the home. They operated from about 1860 until the early part of this century, and their products reflected both the Arts and Crafts and Art Nouveau influence. Their logo was a device with a triangular arrangement of the company name containing a smaller triangle and an Aladdin lamp. Our advisor for this category is Daniel Batchelor; he is listed in the Directory under New York.

Lamps

Floor, 8½" amber slag panel shade; cast metal std, 44", VG **650.00**
Hanging oil, crystal prisms, HP shade/font, ornate fr, mk **825.00**
Student, dbl; brass, rope-twist detail, electrified, 21" **1,155.00**

Table lamp, columnar base with patinated florals and palm leaves, 3-color slag glass panels, 4 bulbs, 11x21" diameter shade, 27" base, $1,870.00.

Table, bats in relief on metal dome shade w/jewels, #4328, 19" ..**1,265.00**
Table, 11" rvpt exotic fish shade; faux marble std, 14" **2,875.00**
Table, 17" fine-ribbed bent glass panel shade; metal std, 21" **625.00**
Table, 24" 8-sided tiered-panel glass shade; acanthus std, 30" .**1,725.00**

Miscellaneous

Andirons, brass/CI, sunburst finials, Pat 1886, 16½", pr **1,095.00**
Andirons, iron, stylized fighting bird forms, 20" **750.00**
Andirons, wrought iron, twisted/curled motif, mk, 29x16" **395.00**
Bookends, Boston Terriers, pnt CI, NM, pr **400.00**
Bookends, bust of Shakespeare, CI, orig label, EX **115.00**
Bookends, ship, CI, pr **100.00**
Desk set, brass, 4-pc **175.00**
Flue cover, lady w/gray hair holds red scarf **150.00**
Inkwell, cast metal deer & fence w/2 hobnail inserts, brass lids ..**275.00**
Mirror, cattails & roses, brass-finished CI, for table, 12x20" **375.00**
Plant stand, CI, 2-tier, late 1800s, 2 stamped mks, 31x12x16" ...**385.00**

Brass

Brass is an alloy consisting essentially of copper and zinc in vari-

able proportions. It is a medium that has been used for both utilitarian items and objects of artistic merit. Today, with the inflated price of copper and the popular use of plastics, almost anything made of brass is collectible. Our advisor, Mary Frank Gaston, has compiled a lovely book, *Antique Brass and Copper*, with full-color photos; you will find her address in the Directory under Texas. See also Candlesticks.

Basin, flat rim w/raised edge, early, rprs, 4x17" **30.00**
Bottle, scent; crest top w/dauber, unmk, 3½" **50.00**
Buckle, steel prongs, ornate stampings, Pat 1855, 1½" W **5.00**
Cauldron, wrought iron rim band, shaped hdl, 19th C, 14x21" ..**140.00**
Chamberstick, heart shape, England, 7¼" L **225.00**
Coach lantern, handmade, mid-to-late 1800s, 15½" **135.00**
Dipper, 4½" bowl, 13" L **80.00**
Dust pan, emb florals & wreaths, England, 8½x8" **60.00**
Fork, toasting; cast, British **18.00**
Kettle, gooseneck copper spout, English, 10x12" **285.00**
Lamp, student's, blk metal shade, Am, 1920s, 17½" **285.00**
Mold, for pewter spoons, 17" wrought-iron hinged hdl **425.00**
Pail, spun, iron bail hdl, Hayden's Pat, 11x17" **165.00**
Pie crimper, shaped wood hdl w/knob, 7" **45.00**
Skimmer, ornate wrought-iron hdl w/ram's horn finial, 21" **260.00**
Spittoon, graniteware pan fits beneath, all orig **60.00**
Taster, 3" bowl, hanger (bent), w/22" wrought-iron hdl **180.00**
Teapot, cvd wooden hdl, 4-ftd, 1800s, EX **275.00**
Tongs, simple style, 10½" L **55.00**
Watering can, hinged lid, European, 8x11", EX **75.00**

Brastoff, Sascha

The son of immigrant parents, Sascha Brastoff was encouraged to develop his artistic talents to the fullest, encouragement that was well taken, as his achievements aptly attest. Though at various times he was a dancer, sculptor, Hollywood costume designer, jeweler, and painter, it is his ceramics that are today becoming highly regarded collectibles.

Sascha began his career in the United States in the late 1940s. In a beautiful studio built for him by his friend and mentor, Winthrop Rockefeller, he designed innovative wares that even then were among the most expensive on the market. All designing was done personally by Brastoff; he also supervised the staff which at the height of production numbered approximately 150. Wares signed with his full signature (not merely backstamped 'Sascha Brastoff') were personally crafted by him and are valued much more highly than those signed 'Sascha B.,' indicating work done under his supervision. Until his death in 1993, he continued his work in Los Angeles, in his latter years producing 'Sascha Holograms,' which were distributed by the Hummelwerk Company.

Though the resin animals signed 'Sascha B.' were neither made nor designed by Brastoff, collectors of these pieces value them highly. According to the book cited in the last paragraph, after he left the factory in the 1960s, the company retained the use of the name to be used on reissues of earlier pieces or merchandise purchased at trade shows.

In the listings that follow, items are ceramic and signed 'Sascha B.' unless 'full signature' is indicated.

For further information we recommend *The Collector's Encyclopedia of Sascha Brastoff* by Steve Conti, A. DeWayne Bethany, and Bill Seay; available from Collector Books or your local book store. Our advisor for this category is Jack Chipman, author of *Collector's Encyclopedia of California Pottery*, another source of valuable information for Brastoff collectors. Mr. Chipman is listed in the Directory under California.

Ashtray, abstract, free-form, unmk, 10" **75.00**
Ashtray, abstract orange & brns, gloss, hooded, 4½" H **40.00**
Ashtray, amoebic design, chartreuse w/bl & yel, rnd **60.00**

Ashtray, Houses, gold stamp signature, 7¼" 45.00
Ashtray, leaf decor, full signature, rnd, lg 350.00
Ashtray, Rooftops, free-form, Sascha B, 7" 50.00
Ashtray, Star Steed, 5x13" 65.00
Ashtray, tulips, lg, 17" 150.00
Ashtray, Vanity Fair, #05, 5x9" 55.00
Ashtray/incense burner, fireplace w/chimney, bronze/gold, 7" 75.00
Bowl, abstract gr design, ftd, 8" 40.00
Bowl, Chi Chi Bird, #C3, 7" dia 65.00
Bowl, resin 50.00
Bowl, Rooftops, #F45, 6x11" 65.00
Bowl, Star Steed, 3-ftd, 10" 150.00
Box, cigarette; Star Steed 100.00
Box, Jewel Bird, #020 ....75.00
Box, Rooftops, pk on blk, rnd 65.00
Candle holders, bl & gr resin, 6", pr 100.00
Charger, Houses, enamel on copper, hangs, 15" 95.00
Dish, fish shape, House, 8½x8¼" 95.00
Dish, horse on gr, 6½" sq 55.00
Dish, Jewel Bird, #F40, 10" 65.00
Dish, 73rd Annual Convention of Master Brewers, #F42 ....65.00
Ewer, Star Steed, metallic 95.00
Fabric, 10 yards, rare 1,500.00
Figurine, bear, trn head, marigold resin, 7" L 350.00
Figurine, hippo, resin 400.00
Figurine, owl, gr resin, 14" 350.00
Figurine, polar bear, bl resin, 10" 300.00
Figurine, prancing horse, blk & gold, ceramic, 10½" 450.00
Figurine, rooster, gold, 22" 595.00
Figurine, seal, marigold resin, 9" L 300.00
Figurine, whale, bl resin, 12" 400.00
Flowerpot, Jewel Bird, #046B, 6" 65.00
Nut dish, bull's eye abstract 40.00
Planter, blk & gold pipe, lg 40.00
Plate, African Dancer, teal & green, full signature 595.00
Plate, fruit, 11" dia 65.00
Plate, vegetables, sq, full signature 375.00
Platter, Jewel Bird, gold on yel & gr, 17" dia 200.00
Shell, gold, 12" 100.00
Smoking set, gr floral, enameled on copper, 5-pc 200.00
Tray, florals, mk Sample under glaze, 7" sq 75.00
Vase, fruit on brn, rectangular, 9⅜" 100.00
Vase, Jewel Bird, #F20, 6" 85.00
Vase, Log Cabin, ovoid, 12" 195.00
Vase, Rooftops, w/gold, boat shape, 7x4" 175.00

Brayton Laguna

Durlin E. Brayton made handcrafted vases, lamps, and dinnerware in a small kiln at his Laguna Beach, California, home in 1927. He soon married, and with his wife, Ellen Webster Grieve, as his partner, the small business became a successful commercial venture. They are most famous for their amusing, well-detailed figurines, some of which were commissioned by Walt Disney Studios. Though very successful even through the Depression years, with the influx of imported novelties that deluged the country after WWII, business began to decline. By 1968 the pottery was closed. For more information on this as well as many other potteries in the state, we recommend *The Collectors Encyclopedia of California Pottery* by Jack Chipman; he is listed in the Directory under California.

Candlesticks, purple, hdld, early, pr 180.00
Chess piece, King & Queen, 12", pr 300.00
Cookie jar, Mammy, burgundy base, turq bandana (+) 1,300.00

Cookie jar, Matilda 475.00
Cookie jar, Wedding Ring Granny (+) 500.00
Creamer, Calico Cat 65.00
Creamer & sugar bowl, early Laguna colors 100.00
Figurine, abstract cat, blk, seated 145.00
Figurine, abstract cat, reclining, blk, 18" L 145.00
Figurine, Becky (Children series) 85.00
Figurine, bird, orange matt, 7½" 45.00
Figurine, Blackamoor kneels & holds cornucopia, 10" 175.00
Figurine, circus horse & ringmaster, pr 155.00
Figurine, cow family, purple, 3-pc set, from $350 to 450.00
Figurine, Dopey, Disney, rare 325.00
Figurine, duck, brn bsk/wht crackle 55.00
Figurine, Fifi & Zizi (cats), pr, 9" 200.00
Figurine, Figaro cat, Walt Disney 125.00
Figurine, fox, red, #H-57 ....75.00
Figurine, Gay Nineties Bedtime Couple 126.00
Figurine, gazelle, gold trim on woodtone 115.00
Figurine, grouse, red 75.00
Figurine, high-button shoe, brn & wht 25.00
Figurine, Hillbilly Wedding group, 6-pc set 2,000.00
Figurine, man w/pushcart 65.00

Figurines, opera singer, pianist and piano, stamped Copyright 1945 by Brayton Laguna Pottery, chanteuse: 7½", rare, $750.00.

Figurine, owl, woodtone & crackle, 6" 45.00
Figurine, Patti, Children series 95.00
Figurine, peasant lady, K-29B 70.00
Figurine, pelican, woodtone & crackle 45.00
Figurine, penguin, aqua, 7" 75.00
Figurine, Pluto, howling, Disney 175.00
Figurine, quail, turq, #B40 & #B41, pr 225.00
Figurine, shorebird, woodtone & crackle 50.00
Flower holder, Blackamoor figural, gold & blk, 8" 75.00
Flower holder, Frances 60.00
Flower holder, Sally, blond, bl flowered dress 50.00
Jelly jar, Mammy, red, rare 600.00
Pitcher, owl form, mk, dtd 1941 ....65.00
Planter, baby w/pillow 75.00
Plate, eggplant, hand fluted 75.00
Shakers, circus clown & dog, pr 250.00
Shakers, circus tent & animal, pr 375.00
Shakers, Gingham Dog & Calico Cat, pr 75.00
Shakers, Provincial peasant couple, pr 65.00
Shakers, rooster & hen, prof rstr, pr 100.00
Teapot, Provincial, brn, w/Tulip stand 125.00
Teapot, woman, teal & rose, early, rare 600.00
Toothbrush holder, dog 125.00
Vase, lady's head, 9x11" 450.00
Vase, Victorian boot, 4" 15.00
Wall hanger w/flowerpot, caballero, maroon & wht 95.00
Wall pocket, Blackamoor holds planter over his head, 2-pc, NM ...250.00

Bread Plates and Trays

Bread plates and trays have been produced not only in many types of glass but in metal and pottery as well. Those considered most collectible were made during the last quarter of the 19th century from pressed glass with well-detailed embossed designs, many of them portraying a particularly significant historical event. A great number of these plates were sold at the 1876 Philadelphia Centennial Exposition by various glass manufacturers who exhibited their wares on the grounds. Among the themes depicted are the Declaration of Independence, the Constitution, McKinley's memorial 'It Is God's Way,' Rememberance of Three Presidents, the Purchase of Alaska, and various presidential campaigns, to mention only a few.

'L' numbers correspond with a reference book by Lindsey; 'S' refers to a book by Stuart. Our advisor for this category is Darlene Yohe; she is listed in the Directory under Arkansas.

Angel Head, milk glass, B-7f 30.00
Banner Baking Powder 85.00
Be Industrious, beehive center, ornate border, 11½x8" 125.00
Bible 50.00
BPOE, elk center, flower border 85.00
Bunker Hill, Prescott/1775/Stark, L-44, 13¼x9" 120.00
Cleveland/Truman busts, clear/frosted, L-325, 9½x8½" 215.00
Columbus, milk glass, B-5A, 9½" 45.00
Continental Hall, hand hdls, 12¾" L 85.00
Cupid & Venus, 10½" dia 40.00
Egyptian, Cleopatra center, 13" L 50.00
Frosted Lion, Give Us This Day, 12½x9" 175.00
Garfield Drape, We Mourn, L-303, 11½" 75.00
Garfield Memorial, L-302, 10" L 40.00
George Washington, 1876 Centennial 140.00
Grand Army of the Republic, L-505, 11" 90.00
Grant, Let Us Have Peace 65.00
Horseshoe, single horseshoe hdls, 13" L 60.00
In Remembrance, 3 Presidents 75.00
Independence Hall 125.00
It Is Pleasant To Labor, grape & leaf center, 12¾" dia 55.00
Jewel Band, Bread Is Staff of Life 45.00
Knights of Labor, amber, oval, L-512, 12" 145.00
Liberty Bell, Signers 95.00
Lotus & Serpent 55.00
Memorial Hall 65.00
Merry Christmas, bells in center, shallow bowl shape 75.00
Minerva, w/motto & portrait 70.00
Nelly Bly, L-136, 12" 200.00
Railroad Train, L-134, 12x9" 85.00
Rock of Ages, clear w/opal center, Atterbury, 8¾" dia 180.00
Roosevelt, Teddy Bear Campaign, frosted center 225.00
Ruth the Gleaner, Gillinder 145.00
Sheridan Memorial 40.00
Washington & 13 stars, milk glass, B-1 ....50.00

Bretby

The Bretby Art Pottery was an English firm whose roots can be traced to the 1880s, an offspring of the earlier Tooth & Company Ltd. The Bretby mark was first used circa 1885. 'England' was added in later years of the 19th century, and by the 1920s, 'Made in England, Bretby,' was the standard mark.

Vase, ships scene w/jewels, 10" 475.00

Vase, 3-color, 3-hdl, 11" 110.00

Bride's Baskets and Bowls

Victorian brides were showered with gifts, as brides have always been; one of the most popular gift items was the bride's basket. Art glass inserts from both European and American glasshouses, some in lovely transparent hues with dainty enameled florals, others of Peachblow, Vasa Murrhina, satin, or cased glass, were cradled in complementary silverplated holders. While many of these holders were simply engraved or delicately embossed, others such as those from Pairpoint and Wilcox were wonderfully ornate, often with figurals of cherubs or animals. The bride's basket was no longer in fashion after the turn of the century.

Watch for 'marriages' of bowls and frames. To warrant the best price, the two pieces should be the original pairing. If you can't be certain of this, at least check to see that the bowl fits snuggly into the frame. Beware of later-made bowls (such as Fenton's) in Victorian holders.

In the listings that follow, if no frame is described, the price is for a bowl only.

Apricot satin, HP decor int; Meriden SP fr, 15" 795.00
Bl Herringbone MOP, pk int, mini, 4¼" 125.00
Bl o/l w/dainty florals & gold, ruffled rim, 3x10¾" 295.00
Butterscotch MOP w/pk int, aqua ruffle; Tufts fr, 13x10x4½" 600.00
Coralene, coral on wht to bl shaded; ftd Meriden fr 550.00
Cranberry to pk cased in wht; ornate Pairpoint acorn/leaf fr 465.00
Fuchsia/ruby swirl, crimped/ruffled; SP scrolled fr, 3½x10" 190.00

Gold coralene on bright blue ruffled basket, Wilcox silverplated frame, #5599, 12", M, $1,400.00.

Gold satin w/birds & floral, clear ruffle, 13"; mk fr 495.00
Gr o/l satin, heavily emb lattice at ruffled rim, 3¾x11½" 250.00
Hobnail, cranberry opal, ruffled rim; ornate SP fr, 7x14" 350.00
Lemon w/HP florals & dots, Mt WA; rstr SP fr, 12x10½" 425.00
Peachblow, glossy, ribbed body, ruffled rim, 4¼x10½" 225.00
Pk o/l w/dimples & hobnails, clear rim; floral SP fr, 14x10" 295.00
Pk satin w/HP decor, ruffled, NE Glass, 10½" 200.00
Pk w/mica flakes, ruffled, ornate Tufts fr w/figural fruit 650.00
Rose to pk o/l, ruffled, Mt WA; orig SP fr, 12¼x12" 400.00
Rose to wht, wht int, clear ruffle; SP Meriden fr, 4½x10" 345.00
Turq on wht w/griffin & urn cameo, Mt WA; SP Pairpoint fr, 9" ..1,000.00
Wht w/pk floral, bl ribbed int w/gold; Meriden fr w/bird, 15" 750.00
Yel satin w/decor, pk int, 12"; 3 cherubs hold Wilcox fr 2,500.00

Bristol Glass

Bristol is a type of semi-opaque opaline glass whose name was derived from the area in England where it was first produced. Similar glass was made in France, Germany, and Italy. In this country, it was made by the New England Glass Company and to a lesser extent by its contemporaries. During the 18th and 19th centuries, Bristol glass was imported in large amounts and sold cheaply, thereby contributing to the demise of the earlier glasshouses here in America. It is very difficult to distinguish the English Bristol from other opaline types. Style, design, and decoration serve as clues to its origin; but often only those well versed in the field can spot these subtle variations.

Box, lt bl w/mc hearts & flowers, 3½" 175.00
Box, patch; bl w/gold flowers & trim, 1½x2" dia 165.00
Dresser set, olive-gray w/enameled herons, 2 colognes+jar 85.00
Lustre, apple gr satin w/gold decor, 7 cut prisms, 9⅝", pr 395.00
Pitcher, turq bl opaque w/gold florals, 5¼x2⅝" 70.00
Salt cellar, gray opaque bucket w/SP rim & hdl, HP birds 60.00
Sweetmeat jar, gr opaque w/birds, SP trim & hdl, 4⅜" 135.00
Vase, aqua w/mc flowers, 9¼", pr 195.00
Vase, turq bl opaque, gold florals, ped ft, 3⅝x1⅜" 50.00

British Royalty Commemoratives

Royalty commemoratives have been issued for royal events since Edward VI's 1547 coronation through modern-day events, so it's possible to start collecting at any period of history. Many collectors begin with Queen Victoria's reign, collecting examples for each succeeding monarch and continuing through modern events.

Some collectors identify with a particular royal personage and limit their collecting to that era, ie., Queen Elizabeth's life and reign. Other collectors look to the future, expanding their collection to include the heir apparents Prince Charles and his first-born son, Prince William.

Royalty commemorative collecting is often further refined around a particular type of collectible. Nearly any item with room for a portrait and a description has been manufactured as a souvenir. Thus royalty commemoratives are available in glass, ceramic, metal, fabric, plastic, and paper. This wide variety of material lends itself to any pocketbook. The range covers expensive limited edition ceramics to inexpensive souvenir key chains, puzzles, matchbooks, etc.

Many recent royalty headline events have been commemorated in a variety of souvenirs. Buying some of these modern commemoratives at the moderate issue prices could be a good investment. After all, today's events are tomorrow's history.

For further study we recommend *British Royal Commemoratives* by our advisor for this category, Audrey Zeder; she is listed in the Directory under California.

Key:
anniv — anniversary	ILN — Illustrated London News
chr — christening	inscr — inscribed
com — commemorative	jub — jubilee
cor — coronation	LE — limited edition
EPNS — electro-plated nickel	mem — memorial
silver	wed — wedding

Album, George VI 1939 Canada Visit w/newspaper clippings 60.00
Book, Elizabeth II cor, prayer book, 3¼x4¾" 55.00
Book, Princess Elizabeth, text, pictures, hardbk, 1947 ....20.00
Booklet, Edward VIII, pictorial, w/abdication message 25.00
Booklet, Princess Margaret 19th birthday, Pitkins, 1949 ....15.00
Bookmark, Victoria jub, woven w/portrait, mc design 95.00
Bottle, Queen Alexandra 1901 baby feeder, gr glass 65.00
Bowl, Edward VIII 1937, mc portrait in cor clothing, 1x5" 55.00
Bowl, Elizabeth II cor, pressed glass crown shape, 4½x8" 110.00
Bust, Edward VII/Alexandra cor, bronze, weighted, 2¾", pr 175.00
Bust, Elizabeth II cor, lt bl parianware, 6¾" 95.00
Bust, Victoria 1897 jub, amber glass, 4x3⅝" 150.00

Charger, King George V portrait, floral border, Bavaria, 12½", $75.00.

Coin, George III 1818 sterling half crown 50.00
Compact, Elizabeth II cor, emb pearlized profile, gold-tone 65.00
Covered dish, George VI cor, mc transfer, Rington tea jar 195.00
Cup & saucer, Edward VII cor, mc, in cor robes, Grindley 60.00
Cup & saucer, George V jub, mc portrait, Deco style, Sutherland ...125.00
Doll head, Queen Elizabeth cor, bsk w/molded crown, HP 165.00
Egg cup, George V 1911 cor, mc king/queen, ftd, pr 135.00
Egg cup, George VI 1937 cor, mc portrait, ftd 50.00
Ephemera, Edward VII cor card, gold/mc party souvenir 20.00
Ephemera, Elizabeth II cor, unused scrapbook 25.00
Ephemera, Victoria 1901 mem, 5½x3½" 30.00
Figure, Elizabeth II cor, HP metal, 3¼" 45.00
First Day Cover, Duke of Windsor 1937 marriage 55.00
First Day Cover, Princess Elizabeth 1947 wed, Canadian issue 20.00
Framed picture, Elizabeth II silhouette, Enid Elliott, 5x6" 50.00
Glass, Victoria 1887 pitcher, pressed design, 4½" 150.00
Glass, Victoria 1897 dish, emb portrait, stippled, 10" 135.00
Horse brass, Queen Mary, relief portrait, cutouts, 3" dia 60.00
Jewelry, Edward VII cor pendant, silver w/red enamel, ¾" 60.00
Jewelry, George V cor shirt studs, brass w/photo, pr 75.00
Magazine, Elizabeth II cor, w/com souvenir article, Field 25.00
Magazine, George VI cor, Sphere record number 40.00
Matchbook, Elizabeth II, proof for palace use, wht w/red 25.00
Medal, Duke of Clarence 1892 death, ⅞" 45.00
Medal, Duke/Duchess York 1901 Canada Visit, pot metal, 1¾" ...25.00
Medal, George V cor, emb profile/design, silver, 1¼" 75.00
Medal, George V jug, emb profile/design, brass, 8-sided, 1½" 50.00
Medal, Victoria 1887 Royal Exhibit Manchester, bronze, 1¾" ...125.00
Medal, Victoria 1901 mem, Made for AA, silver, 1¼" 90.00
Miniature, Queen Mary cor jug, mc portrait, 2" 60.00
Mug, Charles 1953, sepia portrait by Marcus Adams, Paragon ...125.00
Mug, Edward VII 1902 cor, brn design, Royal Doulton, 4" 195.00
Mug, Edward VIII, sepia military portrait w/mc, 2⅝" 45.00
Mug, George V cor, mc portrait in uniform w/mc, 2¾" 65.00
Mug, George VI cor, porfile portrait w/mc, Royal Doulton, 3¼" ..95.00
Newspaper, Royal wedding luncheon 1871, Graphic 25.00
Novelty, Edward VII 1902 clay pipe, emb wht portrait 75.00
Novelty, Victoria 1897 jub, hinged napkin clip, brass 80.00
Photograph, Elizabeth II w/Winston Churchill, blk/wht, 6x8" 35.00
Photograph, George VI 1939 Canada Visit, w/queen in car, 4x3" 15.00
Pin-bk, Edward VII cor, mc portrait & King Flour ad, ¾" 45.00
Pin-bk, Elizabeth II 1959 Canada Visit, blk/wht portrait, 1¾" 20.00
Pitcher, Elizabeth II cor, mc emb ceremony, Burleigh, 8½" 225.00
Pitcher, Victoria 1897, emb bl decor on stoneware, Doulton, 9" ...875.00
Plate, Edward VII cor, mc portrait, Royal Doulton, 3½" 95.00
Plate, Edward VII cor, mc portrait, wide cobalt rim, 6" 150.00
Plate, Edward VIII cor, mc cor portrait, Grindley, 8" 60.00
Plate, Edward VIII 1937 accession, mc portrait, Belgium, 10" 225.00
Plate, Elizabeth II cor, sepia portrait, scalloped, Tuscan, 4" 25.00
Plate, Geo VI 1939 Canada Visit, w/family, Meakin 35.00
Plate, George VI cor, profile portrait w/mc, Royal Doulton, 6" ..125.00

Plate, Princesses Elizabeth/Margaret, from '37 toy set, 4½" 50.00
Plate, Victoria 1890s, HP portrait, 4¼" 125.00
Plate, Victoria 1897 jub, sepia portrait, Wagstaff, 9½" 250.00
Pocketknife, Elizabeth II cor, mc full figure, 2-blade 45.00
Postcard, Edward VII accession, blk/wht portrait, inscr 15.00
Postcard, Edward VIII 1937, military uniform, EX 12.00
Postcard, George V 1911 cor, Rotary, set of 6 ....30.00
Postcard, George VI 1939 Canada Visit 10.00
Postcard, Princess Elizabeth sitting /wCorgi dog, 1940 ....15.00
Postcard, Queen Mary 1911, embr dress, Beagles 10.00
Program, Elizabeth II cor, approved souvenir issue 25.00
Program, George VI 1939 Calgary, Canada Visit 25.00
Spoon, Edward VII/French President, gilt over sterling 80.00
Stamps, Edward VIII, stamp sheet overprinted Morocco Agencies .50.00
Stamps, Elizabeth II jub, stamp block Togolaise, silver/mc 15.00
Stickers, George VI cor, 60-pc, unused 35.00
Teapot, George V jub, mc portrait, Deco style, 3-cup 155.00
Teapot stand, Edward VII cor, gr glaze, Minton, 6" dia 200.00
Textile, Elizabeth II cor, hand-embr panel, 22x12" 45.00
Textile, Elizabeth II cor flag on stick, 16x12" 25.00
Textile, Elizabeth II jub full apron, brn decor, Irish linen 30.00
Textile, Elizabeth II jub towel, mc crowns/palace/etc 25.00
Tin, Elizabeth II cor, mc formal portrait, Hartley, 5x4x1" 40.00
Tin, George VI cor, sepia king & family, 2x7" dia 60.00
Tin, Prince Albert 1860, brass, Cachou Aromatise, 1½x¼" 80.00
Tin, Victoria 1897, mc transfer of queen/battleships, 6x3x4" 185.00
Trade card, George VI cor, Ceremonial Dress, Player, 50 for 35.00
Trade card, George VI cor, Our King & Queen, Wills, 50 for 40.00
Tray, George V jub, emb portrait, brass, 10½" 65.00
Urn, Princesses Elizabeth/Margaret, from toy set, 1937, 4½" 100.00

Broadmoor

In the October of 1933, the Broadmoor Art Pottery was formed and space rented at 217 East Pikes Peak Avenue, Colorado Springs, Colorado. Most of the pottery produced would not be considered elaborate and only a handful was decorated. Many pieces were signed by P.H. Genter, J.B. Hunt, Eric Hellman, and Cecil Jones. It is reported that this plant closed in 1936, and Genter moved his operations to Denver.

Broadmoor pottery is marked in several ways: a Greek or Egyptian-type label depicting two potters (one at the wheel and one at a tile-pressing machine) and the word Broadmoor; an ink-stamped 'Broadmoor Pottery, Colorado Springs (or Denver), Colorado'; and an incised version of the latter.

The bottoms of all pieces are always white and can be either glazed or unglazed. Glaze colors are turquoise, green, yellow, cobalt blue, light blue, white, pink, pink with blue, maroon red, black, and a copper lustre. Both matt and high gloss finishes were used.

The company produced many advertising tiles, novelty items, coasters, ashtrays, and vases for local establishments around Denver and as far away as Wyoming. An Indian head was incised into many of the advertising items, which also often bear a company or a product name. A series of small animals (horses, dogs, elephants, lamb, squirrels, a toucan bird, and a hippo), each about 2" high, are easily recognized by the style of their modeling and glaze treatments, though all are unmarked. Our advisors for this category are Carol and Jim Carlton, authors of *Collector's Encyclopedia of Colorado Pottery*; they are listed in the Directory under Colorado.

Ashtray, bl matt w/wht dog figure in center, 4 rests 45.00
Ashtray, pk w/wht ballerina figure in center, 4 rests 35.00
Bookends, Indian sits wrapped in blanket, 7", pr 200.00
Bowl, red, incurvate rim, 15" 55.00

Cornucopia, bl to mauve, 6" 45.00
Figurine, squirrel, brn, stamped mk, 2" 45.00
Mug, cylindrical, paper label, 5½" 50.00
Paperweight, scarab form, 3" to 4", ea, from $75 to 85.00
Relish tray, wht 3-petal flower form, center hdl, 10" 45.00
Vase, bl matt, pillow form, 6" 55.00
Vase, blk glossy, hdls, bulbous, w/label, 5" 65.00
Vase, bright yel, pillow form, 6x9" 55.00
Vase, dk gr, urn form, 8" 65.00
Vase, honeycomb glaze, slightly flared cylinder, ftd, 12" 140.00

Broadsides

Webster defines a broadside as simply a large sheet of paper printed on one side. During the 1880s, they were the most practical means of mass communication. By the middle of the century, they had become elaborate and lengthy with information, illustrations, portraits, and fancy border designs. Those printed on coated stock are usually worth more.

Grand Race for Benefit of Benevolent Associations, New Orleans, 1868, 14½x5", $350.00.

Am Cow Milker...Cure for Aching Hands..., 1865, 8x10" 60.00
Dr Ward's Vegetable Asthmatic Pills, MA, 1840s, 9x13", EX 50.00
Emancipation Proclamation, vignettes, Dimmick, 1864, fr, EX ..825.00
Go to Polls, Vote for (prohibition) Repeal, CT, 1933, 7x10" 28.00
Grand Excursion of Steamer Rockland, mid-1850s, 13x10+fr 650.00
McKinley assassination news, dtd, 1-pg, sm 435.00
Mr Villiers' Night, Boston theatrical, Apr 17, 1797, 19x12" 900.00
Oxygenated Bitters, blk on wht, early, 23x17½", VG 110.00
Sheriff's sale of PA property, Sept 1797, 8½x10½" 400.00
Thanksgiving proclamation, sgn Wm McKinney, 1897, 8x13" 20.00
White's Golden Tonic, illustrated, 1880s, 24x18", EX 20.00

Bronzes

Thomas Ball, George Bessell, and Leonard Volk were some of the earliest American sculptors who produced figures in bronze for home decor during the 1840s. Pieces of historical significance were the most popular, but by the 1880s a more fanciful type of artwork took hold. Some of the fine sculptors of the day were Daniel Chester French, Augustus St. Gaudens, and John Quincy Adams Ward. Bronzes reached the height of their popularity at the turn of the century. The American West was portrayed to its fullest by Remington, Russell, James Frazier, Hermon MacNeil, and Solon Borglum. Animals of every species were modeled by A.P. Proctor, Paul Bartlett, and Albert Laellele, to name but a few.

Art Nouveau and Art Deco influenced the medium during the '20s, evidenced by the works of Allen Clark, Harriet Frismuth, E.F. Sanford, and Bessie P. Vonnoh.

Be aware that recasts abound. While often esthetically satisfactory, they are not original and should be priced accordingly. In much the same manner as prints are evaluated, the original castings made under the direction of the artist are the most valuable. Later castings from the original mold are worth less. A recast is not made from the original mold. Instead, a rubber-like substance is applied to the bronze, peeled away, and filled with wax. Then, using the same 'lost wax' procedure as the artist uses on completion of his original wax model, a clay-like substance is formed around the wax figure and the whole fired to vitrify the clay. The wax, of course, melts away, hence the term 'lost wax.' Recast bronzes lose detail and are somewhat smaller than the original due to the shrinkage of the clay mold.

After Villanis, Sapho: Figure of a Maiden, brown patina, 28¼", $3,200.00.

Aizelin, Eugene Antoine; Pandora, Barbedienne mk, 12½" 660.00
Austrian, harlequin-style lady dancer, ivory inlay, 9¾" 980.00
Austrian, lamp, cast as market stall, cold pnt, 11" 1,849.00
Austrian, Richard Wagner on rouge marble socle base, 12" 195.00
Barbedienne, classical youth w/animal skin on shoulder, 25" ..1,600.00
Barbedienne, Venus, after the Classical, early 20th C, 26" 1,300.00
Bergmann, Arab couple by well, cold pnt, 11½" 1,100.00
Bitter, Pan w/flute/reclining nymphs, 13½x42" 3,450.00
Brutt, nude sword dancer, marble plinth, 1900s, 22¾" 1,365.00
Cavacos, dancing nude, lt brn patina, on base, 19½" 2,300.00
Chiparus, Les Amis de Toujours, gilt/ivory, 25" 13,800.00
Chiparus, Scarf Dancer, mc details, ca 1925, 26" 7,475.00
Chiparus, Thais, dancer, pnt/gilt/ivory, 1920s, 22" 38,750.00
Chiparus, Yambo, gilt & ivory, marble inlay base, 24" 18,400.00
Clara, Juan; girl pulls cat's tail, gr-brn patina, 10½x10" 1,600.00
Colinet, Danseuse D'Ankara, gilt/ivory, 25" 20,700.00
Continental, Angel w/Adam & Eve, plaque, late 1800s, 11" dia 200.00
Continental, eagle on marble plinth, late 1800s, 13x5¼" 140.00
Continental school, 2 nude male wrestlers, 15½x19" 2,400.00
Desca, matador, ca 1886 (on base), 25½" 2,500.00
Dumaige, classical maiden, 1872, 20" 1,980.00
French, Bust of Aristotle, gray marble base, 19th C, 7½" 385.00
French School, Joan of Arc in armor, early 1900s, 7¼" 220.00
French?, Geo Washington, standing, gilded, CI case, 1800, 17" ...2,500.00
Godet, ferocious bulldog tied to post, 32½x27x16" 1,650.00
Granger, nude dancing w/grapes, gr patina, 1930s, 19" 1,265.00
Guerbe, nude scarf dancer, gr patina/marble base, 23" 3,165.00
Guirande, draped nude dancer, marble base, 1920s, 18" 920.00
Habert, girl embracing boy, 1900s, 6½" 415.00
Houdon, bust of Geo Washington, Fr, 1820s, 8" 750.00

Kossowski the Younger, winged maiden, 38½" 27,000.00
Longman, Victory in form of classical athlete, marble base 3,750.00
Luducg, gull in flight on wave crest, 12½" 500.00
Masson, lion, patinated, ca 1900, 13x17" 2,200.00
McCarton, nude w/rose in hair, gr patina, 28" 3,165.00
Moreau, maiden carrying grape harvest, ca 1900, 25" 1,980.00
Rowan, kneeling nude w/child on shoulder, gr patina, 15x11" ...900.00
Russian, Troika group: peasants w/horse & cart, 30x38x15" ...1,300.00
Silvestre, woman & leaping lamb, early 20th C, 11½x32⅜" ...1,380.00
Somme, maiden in long gown w/sword, ivory mts, 9" 1,000.00
Szukalski, group of cobras & sm male figure, 27½x25" 2,875.00
Tereszcuk, boy & girl in boat, inkwell, 1925, 5½x15" 300.00
Unsgn, Nouveau recumbent nude on ped, 7¾x14½x8" 1,000.00
Unsgn, Venus de Milo, Musee de Louvre, 1890s, 12½" 250.00
Vannetti, tiger roaring w/2 cubs, lt brn patina, 10½x25" 1,600.00

Brouwer

Theophilis A. Brouwer, an accomplished artist even before his interests turned to the medium of pottery, started a small one-man operation in 1894 in East Hampton, New York. Two years later he relocated in Westhampton, where he perfected the technique of fire-painting, learning to control the effects of the kiln to produce the best possible results. In 1925 he founded the Ceramic Flame Company in New York, but it is for his earlier work that he is best known. Brouwer died in 1932.

Vase, dk brn metallic w/some copper, gr & purple irid, 5x6" 825.00
Vase, flame-pnt gr/orange/yel/brn mottle, can neck, hdls, 7" ..1,250.00
Vase, flame-pnt yel/orange/brn organic lustre, 7½x4", EX 650.00
Vase, gunmetal/grn/yel metallic, 3½x4" 450.00
Vase, streaky mc irid, bulbous w/long flaring neck, 7½" 1,500.00
Vase, yel/br/orange metallic w/mc irid, 5½x4" 950.00

Brownies by Palmer Cox

Created by Palmer Cox in 1883, the Brownies charmed children through the pages of books and magazines, as dolls, on their dinnerware, in advertising material, and on souvenirs. Each had his own personality, among them The Bellhop, The London Bobby, The Chairman, and Uncle Sam. But the oversized, triangular face with the startled expression, the protruding tummy, and the spindlelegs were characteristics of them all. They were inspired by the Scottish legends related to Cox as a child by his parents, who were of English descent. His introduction of the Brownies to the world was accomplished by a poem called The Brownies Ride. Books followed in rapid succession, thirteen in the series, all written as well as illustrated by Palmer Cox.

By the late 1890s, the Brownies were active in advertising. They promoted such products as games, coffee, toys, patent medicines, and rubber boots. 'Greenies' were the Brownies' first cousins, created by Cox to charm and to woo through the pages of the advertising almanacs of the G.G. Green Company of New Jersey. Perhaps the best-known endorsement in the Brownies' career was for the Kodak Brownie, which became so popular and sold in such volume that their name became synonymous with this type of camera. Our advisor for this category is Anne Kier; she is listed in the Directory under Ohio.

Almanac, G Green Woodbury, Palmer Cox illus, 1890 ....25.00
Basket, SP, Brownies w/chocolate advertising, Tufts 140.00
Book, Brownies & Other Stories, ca 1900, VG 55.00
Book, Brownies in Fairyland, Century Co 35.00
Book, Funny Stories About Funny People, 1905, EX 35.00

Book, The Brownies, Their Book, 1897, EX 175.00
Bottle, soda; emb Brownies, M 30.00
Brownie Portrait Cubes, McLoughlin Bros, c Cox 1892, VG 300.00
Cigar holder/ashtray, full-figure Brownie, Pairpoint SP 335.00
Comic sheet, 1907, lg, EX 25.00
Creamer, Little Boy Blue verse & 4 Brownies, gold trim, china 75.00
Cup & saucer, china 115.00
Dish, 2 Brownies w/golf clubs, 4" 95.00
Game, Ten Pins, 10 figures, c 1892, 12⅜" H, EX 1,150.00
Humidor, Bobby head figural, majolica, 6" 165.00
Magazine page, Ladies' Home Journal, Cox illus, ca 1890 ....18.00
Match holder, Brownie on striker, majolica 165.00
Mug, Policeman & Watchman w/lantern, SP 110.00
Package of needles, Policeman, 1893 Columbian Expo 50.00
Paper dolls, from 1895 paper supplement, 1-sheet 30.00
Paperweight, Brownie figural, SP 110.00
Pitcher, Brownies playing golf on tan, china, 6" 140.00
Pitcher, 2 Brownies on front, 3 on bk, china, 4½" 65.00
Plate, lobster chasing Brownies, china 95.00
Plate, 5 Brownies wrapped in tattered Am flag, china, 7½" 80.00
Rubber stamp, set of 12 ....100.00
Sheet music, Dance of the Brownies 25.00
Sign, emb Brownies on tin, Howell's Root Beer, EX 185.00
Table set, emb Brownies, SP, 3-pc (knife/fork/spoon), EXIB 70.00
Tray, 2 fencing Brownies, self hdls, china, 6¼x4½" 85.00

Brush

    George Brush began his career in the pottery industry in 1901 working for the J.B. Owens Pottery Co. in Zanesville, Ohio. He left the company in 1907 to go into business for himself, only to have fire completely destroy his pottery less than one year after it was founded. Brush became associated with J.W. McCoy in 1909 and for many years served in capacities ranging from general manager to president. (From 1911 until 1925, the firm was known as The Brush-McCoy Pottery Co.; see that section for information.) After McCoy died, the family withdrew their interests, and in 1925 the name of the firm was changed to The Brush Pottery. The era of hand-decorated art pottery had passed for the most part and would soon be completely replaced by the production of commercial lines. Of all the wares bearing the later Brush script mark, their figural cookie jars are the most collectible, and several have been reproduced.

    For additional information we recommend *The Collector's Encyclopedia of Brush-McCoy Pottery* (recently revised) by Sharon and Bob Huxford. Information on Brush cookie jars (as well as confusing reproductions) can be found in *The Collector's Encyclopedia of Cookie Jars* by Joyce and Fred Roerig; they are listed in the Directory under South Carolina. See also Brush-McCoy for information on a second reference book.

Cookie Jars

Cow, cat on her back, brown, #W10, $125.00.

Antique Touring Car, minimum value 700.00
Boy w/Balloons, minimum value 850.00
Chick in Nest 400.00
Cinderella Pumpkin, #W32 ....250.00
Circus Horse, gr 950.00
Clown, yel pants 250.00
Clown Bust, #W49, minimum value 325.00
Cookie House, #W31 ....125.00
Covered Wagon, dog finial, #W30, minimum value 550.00
Cow w/Cat on Bk, purple, minimum value 1,000.00
Davy Crockett, gold trim, minimum value 800.00
Davy Crockett, no gold, mk USA 300.00
Dog & Basket 300.00
Donkey w/Cart, ears down, #W33, gray 400.00
Donkey w/Cart, ears up, #W33, minimum value 800.00
Elephant w/Baby Bonnet & Ice Cream Cone, wht 500.00
Elephant w/Monkey on Bk, minimum value 5,000.00
Fish, #W52 ....500.00
Formal Pig, gr hat & coat (+) 300.00
Gas Lamp, K1 ....75.00
Granny, pk apron, bl dots on skirt 325.00
Granny, plain skirt, minimum value 400.00
Happy Bunny, wht, #W25 ....225.00
Hen on Basket, unmk 125.00
Hillbilly Frog, minimum value (+) 4,500.00
Humpty Dumpty, w/beany bow tie 275.00
Humpty Dumpty, w/peaked brn hat & shoes 250.00
Laughing Hippo, #W27 ....750.00
Little Angel 800.00
Little Boy Blue, gold trim, K25, sm 700.00
Little Boy Blue, K24 Brush USA, lg 800.00
Little Girl, #017 ....550.00
Little Red Riding Hood, gold trim, mk, lg, minimum value 850.00
Little Red Riding Hood, no gold, K24 USA, sm 550.00
Night Owl, from $115 to 125.00
Old Clock, #W10 ....165.00
Old Shoe, #W23 ....125.00
Panda, #W21 ....250.00
Peter, Peter Pumpkin Eater, #W24 ....300.00
Peter Pan, gold trim, lg 800.00
Peter Pan, sm 550.00
Puppy Police 585.00
Raggedy Ann, #W16 ....350.00
Sitting Pig 400.00
Smiling Bear, #W46 ....350.00
Squirrel on Log, #W26 ....100.00
Squirrel w/Top Hat, blk coat & hat 275.00
Squirrel w/Top Hat, gr coat 250.00
Stylized Owl 350.00
Stylized Siamese, #W41 ....400.00
Teddy Bear, ft apart 250.00
Teddy Bear, ft together 200.00
Treasure Chest, #W28 ....150.00
3 Bears 100.00

Miscellaneous

Bowl, emb mc flowers, #353, 1950s 20.00
Ewer, pk, slim neck, emb rings on body, 1950s, 7" 20.00
Flowerpot, Bittersweet, 1945, 6½" 25.00
Flowerpot, Rockcraft, emb pebble-look, 1933, 5½" 40.00
Mug, Santa's face, red hat 18.00
Pitcher, emb florals on tan, 1940s, 5½" 40.00
Planter, cat figural, yel w/pnt face details, 1952 ....55.00

Planter, lamb at corner of corral, 1950s **15.00**
Sugar bowl, Cloverleaf, mc on tan, w/lid, #K4 ....**40.00**
Vase, Bronze line, brn w/'seafoam' at rim, 1956, 10" **40.00**
Vase, Princess, scrolling gr leaves on cream, hdls, 1960s, 7" **30.00**
Vase, yel pitcher form, blk & gold paper label, 8" **30.00**
Window box, Stardust, wht streaky decor, 1957, 12" L **90.00**

Brush-McCoy

The Brush-McCoy Pottery was formed in 1911 in Zanesville, Ohio, an alliance between George Brush and J.W. McCoy. Brush's original pottery had been destroyed by fire in 1907; McCoy had operated his own business in Roseville, Ohio, since 1899. After the merger, the company expanded and produced not only their staple commercial wares but also fine artware. Lines such as Navarre, Venetian, Oriental, and Sylvan were of fine quality equal to that of their larger competitors. Because very little of the ware was marked, it is often mistaken for Weller, Roseville, or Peters and Reed.

In 1918 after a fire in Zanesville had destroyed the manufacturing portion of that plant, all production was contained in their Roseville (Ohio) plant #2. A stoneware type of clay was used there; and as a result, the artware lines of Jewel, Zuniart, King Tut, Florastone, Jetwood, Krakle-Kraft, and Panelart are so distinctive that they are more easily recognizable. Examples of these lines are unique and very beautiful, also quite rare and highly prized!

The Brush-McCoy Pottery operated under that name until after 1925 when it became the Brush Pottery. The Brush-Barnett family retained their interest in the pottery until 1981 when it was purchased by the Dearborn Company. For more information we recommend *The Collector's Encyclopedia of Brush-McCoy Pottery* by Sharon and Bob Huxford and *The Guide to Brush-McCoy Pottery*, written by Martha and Steve Sanford and edited by David P. Sanford, our advisors for this category. They are listed in the Directory under California. See also Brush.

Bank, frog figural, gr, #068, 1916, 3½" **85.00**
Bowl, Dandyline, gold, 1916, 3½x7½" **45.00**
Candlestick, King Tut, #032, 10½", ea **1,800.00**
Candlesticks, Onyx, 10½", pr **200.00**
Fern dish, Onyx, w/liner, #055, 2½x5" **65.00**
Jardiniere, bl birds on wht, #228, 1915, 7½" **450.00**
Jardiniere, floral swags on ivory, 1915, 9" **475.00**
Jardiniere, Pastel Ware, #248, 10" **275.00**
Pitcher, Colonial Jug, bl tinted, #27, 1911, rare, 4-pt **450.00**
Pitcher, Corn, #44, 1910, 6" **225.00**
Umbrella stand, Onyx (bl) , 1920s, 20½" **650.00**
Umbrella stand, Liberty Bell, #73, 22½" **700.00**
Vase, Colonial, matt, #080, 1924, 4" **200.00**
Vase, Navarre, wht decor on blk, integral hdls, 9" **600.00**
Vase, Onyx (gr), w/hdls, #063, 1920s, 12½" **225.00**
Vase, Vogue, blk geometrics on wht, cylindrical, 10" **225.00**

Buffalo Pottery

The founding of the Buffalo Pottery in Buffalo, New York, in 1901, was a direct result of the success achieved by John Larkin through his innovative methods of marketing 'Sweet Home Soap.' Choosing to omit 'middle-man' profits, Larkin preferred to deal directly with the consumer and offered premiums as an enticement for sales. The pottery soon proved a success in its own right and began producing advertising and commemorative items for other companies, as well as commercial tableware. In 1905 they introduced their Blue Willow line after extensive experimentation resulted in the development of the first successful underglaze

cobalt achieved by an American company. Between 1905 and 1909, a line of pitchers and jugs were hand decorated in historical, literary, floral, and outdoor themes. Twenty-nine styles are known to have been made. These have been found in a wide array of color variations.

Their most famous line was Deldare Ware, the bulk of which was made from 1908 to 1909. It was hand decorated after illustrations by Cecil Aldin. Views of English life were portrayed in detail through unusual use of color against the natural olive green cast of the body. Today the 'Fallowfield Hunt' scenes are more difficult to locate than 'Scenes of Village Life in Ye Olden Days.' A Deldare calendar plate was made in 1910. These are very rare and are highly valued by collectors. The line was revived in 1923 and dropped again in 1925. Every piece was marked 'Made at Ye Buffalo Pottery, Deldare Ware Underglaze.' Most are dated, though date has no bearing on the value. Emerald Deldare, made with the same olive body and on standard Deldare Ware shapes, featured historical scenes and Art Nouveau decorations. Most pieces are found with a 1911 date stamp. Production was very limited due to the intricate, time-consuming detail. Needless to say, it is very rare and extremely desirable.

Abino Ware, most of which was made in 1912, also used standard Deldare shapes, but its colors were earthy and the decorations more delicately applied. Sailboats, windmills, and country scenes were favored motifs. These designs were achieved by overpainting transfer prints and were often signed by the artist. The ware is marked 'Abino' in hand-printed block letters. Production was limited; and as a result, examples of this line are scarce today. Prices only slightly trail those of Emerald Deldare Ware.

The many uncataloged items that have been found over the years indicate that Buffalo Pottery decorators were free to use their own ideas and talents to create many beautiful one-of-a-kind pieces.

Our advisors for this category are Fred and Lila Shrader; they are listed in the Directory under California.

Key: C — commercial ware

Abino

Ashtray/match box, Windmills **895.00**
Candlestick, sailing scene, 9½" **685.00**
Cup & saucer, windmills & canal scene **390.00**
Mug, seascape w/sailing ship, 7" **550.00**
Pitcher, lighthouse scene, 8-sided, 8½" **1,160.00**
Plate, seascape & boats, 7¼" **450.00**
Plate, windmill & boat scene, 9¼" **500.00**
Sugar bowl, seascape, w/lid, 4¾" **525.00**
Tankard, lighthouse, wht int, 7½" **800.00**
Toothpick holder, seascape, 2½" **410.00**
Vase, scenic, basket style w/hdl, 12½" **2,650.00**

Deldare

Ashtray/matchbox holder, Fallowfield Hunt, 3¼x6" **1,600.00**
Bowl, cereal; Fallowfield Hunt, The Start, 6¼" **325.00**
Bowl, cereal; Ye Olden Days, 6½" **225.00**
Bowl, Emerald Ware, Dr Syntax Reading His Tour, 9" **1,400.00**
Bowl, Fallowfield Hunt, The Death, 9" **650.00**
Bowl, fruit; Emerald Ware, 8-sided, 10", w/14" tab-hdld tray ..**3,500.00**
Bowl, nut; Ye Lion Inn, 8⅛" **950.00**
Candle holder, Emerald Ware, butterfly decor, shield-bk, 6¾" ..**1,100.00**
Candle holder, untitled Village Scenes, shield-bk, 6¾" **1,400.00**
Candlesticks, untitled Village Scenes, 9½", pr **835.00**
Chamberstick/match holder, untitled Village Scenes, w/finger ring ..**575.00**
Chocolate pot, untitled Fallowfield Hunt scene, 6-sided, 8" ...**2,000.00**
Creamer, Fallowfield Hunt, Breaking Cover, 2½" **300.00**

Creamer & sugar bowl, Scenes of Village Life...Olden Days, w/lid ..425.00
Cup, punch; untitled Fallowfield Hunt scene 285.00
Cup & saucer, chocolate; untitled Fallowfield Hunt scene 575.00
Cup & saucer, chocolate; Ye Village Street 600.00
Cup & saucer, Emerald Ware, Art Nouveau decor 495.00
Hair receiver, Ye Village Street, w/lid, 5" 700.00
Humidor, Ye Lion Inn, 8-sided, 7" 1,100.00
Mug, Emerald Ware, allover geometrics/florals, wht int, 4½" 525.00
Mug, Fallowfield Hunt, Breaking Cover, 4½" 500.00
Mug, Fallowfield Hunt, untitled, 2½" 900.00
Mug, Scenes of Village Life in Ye Olden Days, 2½" 335.00
Mug, Ye Lion Inn, 4½" 250.00
Pitcher, Art Nouveau/arrowhead decor, 8-sided, 8" 1,250.00
Pitcher, Emerald Ware, Dr Syntax Setting Out to the Lake, 9" ..1,200.00
Pitcher, Fallowfield Hunt, The Return, 8" 695.00
Pitcher, Their Manner of Telling Stories..., 6" 375.00
Pitcher, To Spare an Old Broken Soldier, 7¾" 425.00
Pitcher, Ye Old English Village/Ye Lion Inn, 10" 685.00
Plaque, Fallowfield Hunt, Breakfast at Three Pigeons, 12" 650.00
Plate, At Ye Lion Inn, 6¼" 125.00
Plate, chop; Emerald Ware, Dr Syntax Sell's (sic) Grizzle, 13¾" ..1,800.00
Plate, chop; Fallowfield Hunt, The Start, 14" 700.00
Plate, Emerald Ware, Garden Trio, 9¼" 1,500.00
Plate, Emerald Ware, Misfortune at Tulip Hall (Dr Syntax), 8" .560.00
Plate, Fallowfield Hunt, Breaking Cover, 10" 295.00
Plate, Fallowfield Hunt, Death, 8½" 150.00
Plate, Fallowfield Hunt, Start, 8¼" 200.00
Plate, Hand Painted Deldare Ware Underglaze, 6½" 1,200.00
Plate, Ye Olden Times, 9½" 195.00
Plate, Ye Village Street, 7⅛" 125.00
Shaker, Emerald Ware, Art Nouveau decor 485.00
Sugar bowl, Fallowfield, 6-sided, 3½" 325.00
Tankard, Fallowfield Hunt, Hunt Supper, 12" 1,500.00
Tankard, Great Controversy, 10¼" 1,200.00
Tea tile, Traveling in Ye Olden Days, 6" 345.00
Teapot, Fallowfield Hunt, Breaking Cover, 6-sided, 3¾" 595.00
Teapot, Village Scenes, 6-sided, 4½" 500.00
Tray, calling card; Emerald Ware, Dr Syntax Robbed..., 7¾" 800.00
Tray, dresser; Emerald Ware, Dr Syntax Rural Sports..., 9x12" .1,900.00
Tray, pin; Ye Olden Days, 6¼x3½" 225.00
Vase, Great Controversy, cylindrical, 13¾" 2,000.00
Vase, untitled Village Scenes w/3 fashionable ladies, 8½" 975.00
Vase, untitled Village Scenes, 7" 550.00
Vase, Ye Village Parson/Ye Village Schoolmaster, 8½" 800.00

Miscellaneous

Ashtray/matchbox holder, Hotel Leighton, C 55.00
Bowl, berry; Blue Willow, ind, 5½" 35.00
Bowl, berry; Forget-Me-Not, ind, 5½" 18.00
Bowl, berry; Forget-Me-Not, 10½" 75.00
Bowl, rimmed soup; Blue Willow, 9" 77.00
Bowl, salad; Blue Willow, sq, 9" 135.00
Bowl, vegetable; Blue Willow, oval, 9x8" 135.00
Bowl, vegetable; Bonrea, teal gr w/gold, oval, 9x8" 55.00
Butter pat, bl floral border, mk Park Lane Hotel NY on bk, C 20.00
Butter pat, Blue Willow 35.00
Butter pat, Blue Willow, C 20.00
Butter pat, Bluebird 35.00
Butter pat, Empress, teal gr floral border w/gold 25.00
Butter pat, geraniums, mc, reverse: 1907 ....45.00
Butter pat, GP (over) O, teal gr & blk, C 25.00
Butter pat, Multifleure Lamelle, Sea Cave, C 50.00
Butter pat, West Point, C 35.00

Canister, wht w/gold, Pepper in blk, w/lid, 3" 45.00
Canister, wht w/gold, Tea in blk, w/lid, 7½" 75.00
Child's feeding dish, Campbell Kids w/o ABCs at rim, 7¾" 75.00
Cowboy hat, Blue Lune, C, 4½x2¾" 35.00
Creamer, Blue Willow, C, ind, 2½" 35.00
Creamer, Blue Willow, 5½" 65.00
Creamer, Gold Line, plain wht w/2 fine gold lines 15.00
Creamer, Vienna, rich bl & gold, 5½" 45.00
Cup & saucer, Blue Willow, C 45.00
Cup & saucer, Gaudy Willow 145.00
Egg cup, Blue Willow, C, 2¾" 35.00
Egg cup, Bluebird, dbl, 3½" 55.00
Mug, Celebration, Vacation, Meditation, etc, 4½", ea 65.00
Pitcher, Blue Willow, bulbous, 7" 200.00
Pitcher, Blue Willow, Chicago-style, cobalt & gold decor, 8" 255.00
Pitcher, Buffalo Hunt scene, teal gr & gold, 6½" 475.00
Pitcher, Cinderella, 6⅛" 550.00
Pitcher, George Washington, bl & wht w/gold, 7¾" 650.00
Pitcher, Geranium, bl & wht, 6½" 275.00
Pitcher, Geranium, teal gr, 4" 145.00
Pitcher, Hounds & Stag, mc, 6½" 625.00
Pitcher, Pilgrim, Miles Standish & John Alden, mc, 9" 800.00
Pitcher, Rip Van Winkle, mc, 6" 775.00
Pitcher, Robin Hood, mc, 8¾" 650.00
Pitcher, Roosevelt Bears, 8" 3,000.00
Plate, Bangor, brn tones w/cobalt & gold, 10" 55.00
Plate, Blue Willow, 10½" 55.00
Plate, cake; rose decor & gold, open hdls, 12" 65.00
Plate, chop; Blue Willow, 13" 235.00
Plate, chop; Rouge Ware, Morgan's Red Coach Tavern, C, 11½" ..300.00
Plate, Christmas, 1950-60, ea 50.00
Plate, Commemorative, New Bedford 50 Years Ago, bl/wht, 10" ..100.00
Plate, Commemorative; Washington's...Mt Vernon, bl/wht, 10" ...75.00
Plate, Dr Syntax Disputing His Bill..., bl/wht, 9¼" 325.00
Plate, fish set, 9", ea 65.00
Plate, Gaudy Willow, 10½" 165.00
Plate, historical scenes w/flower border, teal or bl, 10", ea 75.00
Plate, USFS, C, 8" 45.00
Platter, Blue Willow, 16x13" 225.00
Platter, Bonrea, 14x11" 145.00
Platter, Buffalo Hunt, teal border, 15x11" 300.00
Platter, fish set, 14x11" 175.00
Teapot, Blue Willow, sq, 5½" 185.00
Teapot, ivory w/platinum decor, w/orig metal tea ball 195.00
Teapot, roses & rosebud border, ornate hdl, 5½" 175.00
Teapot stand, Blue Willow, rnd, 6½" 225.00
Vase, Chrysanthemum, teal & wht, 5½" 45.00
Vase, Geranium, cobalt & wht, bulbous, 3¾" 290.00
Vase, Multifleure, pear shape, C, 8" 375.00

Buggy Steps

New and younger buggy step collectors have created a demand for original cast-iron buggy steps. They seek steps with design and pattern. Name steps still command good prices. The buggy era (1865-1910) produced vehicles from over forty-six different manufactures. What remains are treasured reminders of a past era. Prices shown are for original steps, mint to good. Rusty, broken, and pitted condition reduces the value. Many of the following listings are for name steps, however, there are numerous unmarked steps that are very desirable. Our advisor for this category is John Waddell; he is listed in the Directory under Texas.

Beebe Cart, sq, bolt-on, 3x3" 38.00

Cole, eared, oval, slot mt, 3½x2¼" 45.00
CW Co, sq shield, bolt-on, 3½x3½" 38.00
Dean & Co, oval, tee mt, 3½x2¼" 65.00
Deere, brass insert, rectangular, trifork mt, 4½x3" 70.00
Emerson, oval, tee mt, 5x3½" 65.00
Folding step, spring offset, open mt 36.00
Henney Buggy Co, oval, trifork mt, 5x3½" 60.00
Moon Bros, oval, 4½x3½" 60.00
NWS Co, open pad, bolt-on, 5x2½" 40.00
Open grate step, trifork mt, 4½x4" 60.00
Ornamental step, w/scraper & scroll, trifork mt 75.00
Peru, rnd, tee mt, 4½" dia 65.00
Staver, oval, trifork mt, 4½x3½" 60.00
Studebaker, rectangular, trifork mt, 5x3¼" 60.00
Surry step, oval, branch arm mt, 8½x6½" 135.00
Thompson Wagon Co, rectangular, w/shield & arm 65.00

Burmese

Burmese glass was patented in 1885 by the Mount Washington Glass Co. It is typically shaded from canary yellow to a rosy salmon color. The yellow is produced by the addition of uranium oxide to the mix. The salmon color comes from the addition of gold salts and is achieved by reheating the object (partially) in the furnace. It is thus called 'heat sensitive' glass. Thomas Webb of England was licensed to produce Burmese and often added more gold, giving an almost fuchsia tinge to the salmon in some cases. They called their glass 'Queen's Burmese,' and this is sometimes etched on the base of the object. This is not to be confused with Mount Washington's 'Queen's Design,' which refers to the design painted on the object. Both companies added decoration to many pieces. Mount Washington-Pairpoint produced some Burmese in the late 1920s and Gunderson and Bryden in the '50s and '70s, but the color and shapes are different. Our advisors for this category are Dolli and Wilfred Cohen; they are listed in the Directory under California. In the listings that follow, examples are assumed to have the satin finish unless noted 'shiny.' See also Lamps, Fairy.

Bonbon, smooth satin, rectangular, Mt WA, 2x5¼x4½" 385.00
Bonbon, 3 appl prunts, Mt WA, 2⅜x6½x4¾" 750.00
Bowl, console; Mt WA, 3½x11½" 1,500.00
Bowl, ruffled top, Mt WA, 2½x6" 225.00
Bride's basket, w/floral; emb Pairpoint fr w/3-D berries, 9½" ...1,400.00
Chimney, pk top/yel body, Mt WA, 9x4" 3,250.00
Compote, wavy shallow bowl on wafer base, Pairpoint, 4½x7" ..550.00
Creamer, appl Burmese hdl, Mt WA, 2½x1⅜" 550.00
Creamer, HP vintage, ruffled rim, 2⅝" 275.00
Creamer, tankard; crimped rim, 5½" 450.00
Cruet, shiny, melon ribs, mushroom stopper, Mt WA, 6½" 1,085.00
Epergne, Queen's, 7 ruffled bowls, clear frog, 14" 3,500.00
Epergne/fairy light, 2 lamps/2 bud vases, 10½x10½" 1,375.00
Finger bowl, shiny, ribbed, irregular scallops, Mt WA, +plate 595.00
Goblet, yel stem & wafer base, Mt WA, 6½x3½", pr 2,500.00
Match holder, mc florals, bulbous w/sq top, Webb, 2⅞x2½" 325.00
Mustard, ribbed bbl form, metal hinged lid, 4½" 375.00
Pickle jar, HP florals, melon ribs, Barbour Bros SP fr, +tongs 700.00
Pitcher, appl yel hdl, Mt WA, 2-qt, 7x6½" 1,100.00
Pitcher, HP poem by Thomas Hood/tea roses, Mt WA, 3½" ...1,650.00
Rose bowl, floral vine, Webb, 2¼" 300.00
Rose bowl, hexagonal, mc flowers, 3" 385.00
Rose bowl, prunus on yel, no blush, sq rim, Webb, 3¼" 345.00
Rose bowl, Queen's, shiny, berries, folded rim, Webb, 2" 375.00
Rose bowl, 8-crimp, Mt WA, 2½x2½" 335.00
Shakers, Mt WA, in SP holder, 2", pr 425.00

Shakers, ribbed cylinder, Mt WA, 4¼", pr 400.00
Spooner, Dmn Quilt, Mt WA, 4½x3½" 495.00
Sugar shaker, holly leaf & berries, Mt WA, 4⅝x3⅞" 995.00
Tazza, wafer base, Pairpoint, 1920s, 7" dia 550.00
Toothpick holder, Dmn Quilt, tricorner top, Mt WA, 2⅛" 585.00
Toothpick holder, HP chrysanthemums, tricorner top, Mt WA, 2½" ..585.00
Toothpick holder, HP florals, melon ribs, ruffled, 1¾" 650.00
Toothpick holder, pine cone, Webb, 2¾" 550.00
Toothpick holder, tricorner, Mt WA, 2" 395.00
Tumbler, juice; Mt WA, 3¾x2⅛" 285.00
Tumbler, juice; yel roses, Mt WA, 3¾" 465.00
Tumbler & saucer, whiskey; 2⅞", 4" 450.00
Vase, barn swallows, wht beaded top, ovoid, Mt WA, 9¾" 4,000.00
Vase, bl flowers/fall leaves, stick neck, 8" 975.00
Vase, bulbed rim, slim neck, ribbed body, Mt WA, 4¾", pr 700.00
Vase, bulbous, ruffled, unsgn Webb, 3½x2¾" 200.00
Vase, corseted, tightly crimped rim, 3" 325.00
Vase, Egyptian style, hdls, Mt WA, 10¼x3¾", pr 2,000.00

Vase, floral decoration, Webb, 9", $1,250.00.

Vase, gourd shape, Mt WA, 12x6½" 825.00
Vase, gourd shape, Mt WA, 8x4" 650.00
Vase, HP foliage & berries, flower-form top, 2¾x3½" 550.00
Vase, ivy decor, 8 ribs, flared rim, Webb, 3¾x4¼" 480.00
Vase, lg appl floral, icicles at sqd rim, ftd, glossy, 8x8" 4,600.00
Vase, lily; Mt WA, ca 1890, 23½" 1,250.00
Vase, lily; refired yel rim, Mt WA, 7" 335.00
Vase, lily; shiny, 12" 695.00
Vase, pentagonal mouth w/folded lip, Webb, 3½" 275.00
Vase, Queen's, HP ivy & tendrils, Webb, 8⅛" 700.00
Vase, Queen's, w/gold, bulbous, Mt WA, 12x6½" 2,950.00
Vase, shiny, mc leaves, 6-sided, bulbous, 3¾x3¼" 395.00
Vase, shiny, optic ribs, flower form, Webb, 7" 585.00
Vase, shiny, red florals, Webb, 8¼x4" 650.00
Vase, shiny, stemmed-flower form, Webb, 5" 750.00
Vase, 2 ibis in flight/pyramids/dunes/oasis, Mt WA, 12" 2,750.00

Butter Molds and Stamps

The art of decorating butter began in Europe during the reign of Charles II. This practice was continued in America by the farmer's wife who sold her homemade butter at the weekly market to earn extra money during hard times. A mold or stamp with a special design, hand carved either by her husband or a local craftsman, not only made her product more attractive but also helped identify it as hers. The pattern became the trademark of Mrs. Smith, and all who saw it knew that this was her butter. It was usually the rule that no two farms used the same mold within a certain area, thus the many variations and patterns available to the collector today. The most valuable are those which have animals, birds, or odd shapes. The most sought-after motifs are the eagle, cow, fish, and rooster. These works of early folk art are quickly disappearing from the market.

Molds

Acorn & fern, 4¾"	120.00
Cornflower, EX cvg, rnd case w/plunger, 4¾" dia	100.00
Cow, old scrubbed finish, 4¼" dia	145.00
Flower design in ea of 2 sqs, brass side hooks, ½-lb	85.00
Geometric decor, deep cvg, cherry wood, 4½x7", EX	115.00
Leaves in 2 sqs, dvtl hinges w/brass pins, ½-lb, 6x3½"	60.00
Pineapple, deeply cvd, stamped: Pat April 17, 1866, 3¾" dia	150.00
Rose & bud, 2-pc, rfn, 3½" dia	95.00
Roses & cherries, age cracks, rectangular, 2-part, 4x7"	110.00
Strawberry, staved hexagonal case w/pewter bands, 3-pc, 4¼", VG	225.00
Swan, old finish, 5" dia	125.00
Tulip & leaf, dbl, EX detailed cvg, 1¼x3¾x3⅜"	125.00

Stamps

Cow, trn inserted hdl, scrubbed patina, 4" dia	140.00
Cow (primitive), lollipop style, old worn patina, 9¼" L	245.00
Cow & tree, knotched band, 1-pc w/hdl, 4½" dia	300.00
Cow & tree, notched rim, 1-pc w/hdl, 3¾"	270.00
Cow & tree, poplar, EX patina, 1-pc trn hdl, 4⅜" dia	360.00
Dbl-tulip floral w/sawtooth edge, 1-pc w/hdl, 3x4⅝"	275.00
Eagle, poplar, old patina, semicircle, 7" L	660.00
Eagle, scrubbed poplar, 2-pc trn hdl, 4¼" dia	385.00
Eagle among leaves, deeply cvd, EX patina, 3⅜" dia	250.00
Fish, hardwood, scrubbed, lollipop hdl, 8"	190.00
Floral (stylized), worn patina, lollipop style, 7¾" L	250.00
Flower (5-petal) w/line decor, lollipop style, trn hdl, 4"	300.00
Foliage (stylized), scrubbed, 1-pc trn hdl, 4¼" dia	150.00

Heart design with leaves, notch-carved border, applied handle, 4½" dia, $325.00.

Heart & foliage, poplar w/chestnut hdl, age crack, 4⅜" dia	275.00
Heart & sunburst, lollipop style, worn patina, 6¾" L	215.00
Hearts & geometrics on almond shape, dk patina, curved hdl	350.00
Pineapple, poplar w/worn surface, semicircular, 7"	200.00
Pineapple, semicircular w/rpl trn hdl, 3⅜" dia	185.00
Pineapple (stylized), 1-pc w/trn hdl, worn patina, 4½x4¾"	165.00
Pinwheel w/in 2 circles, EX cvg, 4½"	145.00
Star (10-pointed), 1-pc hdl, 3⅝" dia	200.00
Star flower, deep cased sides, 1-pc w/trn hdl, scrubbed, 5"	415.00
Star flower, inserted hdl, EX patina, 4½"	300.00
Star w/6 points, lollipop style, 4⅞"+2" hdl	400.00
Swan, deeply cvd, old varnish, 5½" dia	150.00
Thistle w/dbl leaves, cvd ribbed border, stick hdl, 4" dia	110.00
Tulip, deeply cut, scrubbed poplar, 1-pc trn hdl, 4¼" dia	275.00
Tulip, stylized, 1-pc trn hdl, 3¾"	200.00
Tulip, walnut w/old patina, lollipop-like hdl, 7"	350.00
Tulip (primitive), 1-pc, trn hdl, scrubbed/age cracks, 5" dia	110.00
Tulip & star (stylized), notched band, 1-pc w/hdl, 4⅜" dia	250.00

Tulip-like flower w/lovebirds & rosettes, Peter Derr, 3⅞"	850.00
Tulips (3) w/vines, rectangular, 4½x3⅛"	270.00

Buttonhooks

The earliest known written reference to buttonhooks (shoe hooks, glove hooks, or collar buttoners) is dated 1611. They became a necessary implement in the 1850s when tight-fitting high-button shoes became fashionable. Later in the 19th century, ladies' button gloves and men's button-on collars and cuffs dictated specific types of buttoners, some with a closed wire loop instead of a hook end. Both shoes and gloves used as many as twenty-four buttons each. Usage began to wane in the late 1920s following a fashion change to low-cut laced shoes and the invention of the zipper. There was a brief resurgence of use following the 1948 movie 'High Button Shoes.' For a simple, needed utilitarian device, buttonhook handles were made from a surprising variety of materials: natural wood, bone, ivory, agate, and mother-of-pearl to plain steel, celluloid, aluminum, iron, lead and pewter, artistic copper, brass, silver, gold, and many other materials, in lengths that varied from under 2" to over 20". Many designs folded or retracted, and buttonhooks were often combined with shoehorns and other useful implements. Stamped steel buttonhooks often came free with the purchase of shoes, gloves, or collars. Material, design, workmanship, condition, and relative scarcity are the primary market value factors. Prices range from $1.00 to over $100.00. Buttonhooks are fairly easy to find, and they are interesting to display. Our advisor for this category is Richard Mathes; he is listed in the Directory under Ohio.

Buttonhook/penknife, ivory side plates, man's	40.00
Glove hook, gold plated, retractable, 3"	75.00
Glove hook, loop end, agate hdl, 2½"	45.00
Shoe hook, colored celluloid hdl, 8"	12.00
Shoe hook, faux ivory celluloid hdl, 8"	8.00
Shoe hook, lathe-trn hardwood hdl, dk finish, 8"	12.00
Shoe hook, stamped steel, advertising, 5"	8.00
Shoe hook, sterling, floral & geometrics	45.00
Shoe hook, sterling, Nouveau lady's face, 6½"	75.00
Shoe hook, sterling, W w/arrow, hammered Florentine decor, mk	45.00
Shoe hook/shoehorn combination, steel & celluloid, 9"	25.00

Bybee

The Bybee Pottery was founded in 1809 in the small town of Bybee, Kentucky. Their earliest wares were primarily stoneware churns and jars. Today the work is carried on by sixth-generation Cornelison potters who still use the same facilities and production methods to make a more diversified line of pottery. From a fine white clay mined only a few miles from the potting shed itself, the shop produces vases, jugs, dinnerware, and banks in a variety of colors, some of which are shipped to the larger cities to be sold in department stores and specialty shops. The bulk of their wares, however, is sold to the thousands of tourists who are attracted to the pottery each year.

Bowl, batter; brn-gr glossy, mk Bybee KY, 3¾x10x12"	25.00
Bowl, batter; wht glossy, tapered hdl, 1960s, 2¾x7¼x9¼"	25.00
Bowl, wht glossy, unsgn, mid-1960s, 3⅝x7¼"	20.00
Creamer, wht glossy, tapered hdl, w/lid, 4", NM	25.00
Flower frog vase, lav, 4¼x5¼"	25.00
Mug, bl, 16-oz	8.00
Pitcher, red-brn, 2 labels, w/lid, ca 1981, 11", NM	75.00
Plate, luncheon; wht, unmk, 1960s, ⅞x8", 4 for	25.00
Vase, orange-peel glaze, broad/waisted w/akimbo hdls, 8"	120.00
Vase, pk-red & dusty wht, 3-hdld, prof rstr, 7"	125.00

Calendar Plates

Calendar plates were advertising giveaways most popular from about 1906 until the late 1920s. They were decorated with colorful underglaze decals of lovely ladies, flowers, animals, birds and, of course, the twelve months of the year of their issue. During the 1950s they came into vogue again but never to the extent they were originally. Those with exceptional detailing or those with scenes of a particular activity are most desirable, so are any from before 1906 or after 1930.

1910, Compliments of Yosemite, lady within horse-shoe, very rare, $150.00.

1904, Happy New Year, Cupid & bell, 8" 50.00
1907, Santa & sleigh, 9" 55.00
1907, 4 ladies dressed as the 4 seasons, 10" 60.00
1908, lady, Detroit MI 38.00
1909, cherries, Merry Christmas to All, 9½" 35.00
1909, dog's head, Compliments of John S Stewart..., 9" 40.00
1909, Gibson Girl, 8½" 40.00
1909, 2 roses, Compliments of..., 8" 35.00
1910, angels 65.00
1910, Betsy Ross, Jersey City 38.00
1910, holly, Hitchcock Hardware, Woodbury CT 38.00
1910, horseshoe encircles hunter w/gun 40.00
1910, Niagara Falls, NY City 30.00
1910, Washington's Old Home at Mt Vernon, roses & ribbons 35.00
1910, water lilies on pond, 9" 35.00
1910, 2 cherubs, lg bell & hourglass, 8½", M 45.00
1911, cherub lighting candle, 8½" 40.00
1911, lg rose, calendar on horseshoe w/ribbons, 8½" 30.00
1911, Old Acquaintance 30.00
1911, turkey center, flower border 35.00
1912, cottage in meadow, 8", NM 25.00
1912, El Capitan Yosemite Valley CA, 8½" 25.00
1912, Indian maiden sits by fire & husks corn 40.00
1912, owl, JR Hess, Leesburg VA 35.00
1913, boy in rags under arch, 8" 35.00
1914, hunting scene, 8" 30.00
1914, 3 plums & 1 pear, 7¼" 25.00
1915, Panama Canal 35.00
1919, flag center, Lubbers Co...MI 35.00
1921, dove surrounded by 5 Allied flags, 7¼" 40.00
1924, flowers, holly berries & leaves around calendar, 9" 45.00
1930, Dutch boy & dog, 9" 70.00

Calendars

Calendars are collected for their colorful prints, often attributed to a well-recognized artist of the period. Advertising calendars from the turn of the century often have a double appeal when representing a company whose tins, signs, store displays, etc., are also collectible. See also Parrish, Maxfield.

1886, Grit, boy w/paper & 12 months, 11x8", EX 125.00
1886, Hood's Sarsaparilla, children sewing, rnd, NM 80.00
1890, Buckey Mowers, factory scene, 8-sheet, 6½x7" 245.00
1893, Hires, 2 girls w/kitten, complete, rare, NM 450.00
1894, Buckeye/Aultman-Miller, girls at stone wall, EX 140.00
1894, Hood's Sarsaparilla, Sweet Sixteen, complete, NM+ 85.00
1896, Grit (Pennsylvania), girl w/red fan & months, EX+ 150.00
1896, Honest Long Cut Tobacco, Papa Bear, complete, EX 75.00
1897, Hood's Sarsaparilla, sm girl in purple hat, complete, NM ...95.00
1899, American Seal Paint, Uncle Sam, etc, 1-sheet, 22x14", EX ..225.00
1899, Hood's Sarsaparilla, The American Girl, complete, NM+ .100.00
1899, P Kloppenburg, woman & kids at seashore, Nov, EX 50.00
1900, CB Youth's Companion, girls/months w/girl in circle, NM .75.00
1900, Kingsley Harness Co, diecut girl in gr, complete, NM+ 215.00
1901, Chas Ahlswede Clothier..., boy & girl, complete, VG+ 75.00
1903, Metropolitan Life Ins Co, children on trunk, 15x11", EX .235.00
1905, Atlantic & Pacific Tea Co, cb, girl & months, NM 160.00
1906, Harrington & Richardson Arms Co, complete, NM 400.00
1906, National Stoves & Ranges, girl w/puppy, 13x9¾", EX 200.00
1907, Necco Sweets, lady embroidering Necco logo, 12x8", EX+ .50.00
1907, Pickett Hardware Co, hanging fowl, complete, 16x10", EX ...75.00
1907, Village Scene, heart-shaped floral border, Feb, 14x11", EX ...130.00
1908, Union Ice & Coal Co, girl on phone, complete, 10x8", EX ..85.00
1909, Herman Giegling Meat Market, ship/roses, complete, 12", NM ...50.00
1909, Pompeian FG Co, Pompeian Beauty, 38x11", EX 375.00
1909, TF Maguire Groceries..., boy & girl behind bench, EX 55.00
1910, Champion Harvesting Machines, prairie, top only, VG+ ...65.00
1910, Hanson & Gilbertson, girl on red stool, Feb, EX 80.00
1910, Harrington & Richardson Arms Co, GM Arnold, 27x14", NM ...990.00
1911, HC Sattler..., boy & girl w/dog in garden, complete, EX ..275.00
1911, Kis-Me Gum, rowboat scene, complete, NM 1,075.00
1912, Chas H Dorsey, girl w/lamb, complete, 17x10", EX+ 310.00
1913, Hood's Sarsaparilla, The Dinner Bell, complete, EX+ 80.00
1914, GF Carls, cherubs/village/bird nest, complete, 15x11", EX .65.00
1914, Lady in Red Hooded Cape, diecut cb, complete, 11x8", M ..275.00
1914, Pabst Extract, American Girl, 41x11", VG+ 275.00
1915, H Favart Boots..., girl w/dog, complete, 7x4", EX 30.00
1916, Mrs LA Wellman, Cornell Il, diecut image, complete, EX ..80.00
1916, Pabst Extract, American Girl, 41x11", EX 325.00
1918, Bair Motor Co, romantic couple in car, complete, VG+ 75.00
1919, Dower Lumber Co, The Call, Indian in canoe, VG 40.00
1919, EJ Petru Java Coffee Mills, windmill on bark, EX+ 40.00
1922, Johnson Bros General Merchandise, Sunshine Girl, EX+ ...55.00
1924, Morrison Hotel & Terrace Garden, complete, 6x4", EX+ ...25.00
1927, Fisk Tires, Time-To-Re-Tire, emb wht on bl, complete, VG ...60.00
1928, Calendar of Champions Horse Review, 21x14", VG+ 15.00
1928, This Trip We All Go, Hercules Powder, complete, NM ...425.00
1930, We're Going Home, by Phillip Goodwin, 42x28", NM ...250.00
1931, Pontiac, logo & various symbols, incomplete, G 200.00
1934, Girl Scout, Hintermeister, 32x11", M 225.00
1935, Nehi, girl in yel w/fur cape, Rolf Armstrong art, EX 150.00
1936, Duplex Bread, Day After Day, shows baby, 9x17", EX 32.00
1937, M&W Mor, Toledo OH, grocery scene, complete, 23x15", EX ...75.00
1938, Nehi, sailor girl at helm, Rolf Armstrong art, EX+ 190.00
1939, Sailor w/Boyish Bob, Christy, 33x16", NM 150.00
1939, Trommer's Malt & Genuine Ale, elves, complete, EX 45.00
1940, Fox's Bread, boy/girl at stone wall, complete, 20x15", EX .170.00
1941, Budweiser, St Louis plant/Chicago, complete, EX 130.00
1944, Acme Beer, cb stand-up, lady w/glass, complete, EX 35.00
1944, John Deere, boy & girl at store window, complete, NM 90.00
1944, Triangle Filling Station, emb hunt scene, complete, VG 40.00

1946, Am Oil Co/Daley's Service Station, complete, 34x16", NM ...**100.00**
1949, Grapette, blond w/bottle, P Frush art, complete, NM+ **325.00**

Caliente

Caliente was a line of colored dinnerware made by the Paden City Pottery Company in Paden City, West Virginia. It was produced during the 1930s and 1940s in tangerine, yellow, blue, green, and cobalt blue.

Bowl, salad; 10" **25.00**
Bowl, 5¼" **10.00**
Bowl, 9" **20.00**
Candle holder **15.00**
Creamer **14.00**
Cup & saucer **15.00**
Plate, dinner; 10" **17.50**
Plate, 6" **5.00**
Plate, 9½" **10.00**
Platter, 12" **20.00**
Platter, 14" **25.00**
Shakers, pr **25.00**
Sugar bowl, w/lid **18.00**
Teapot **45.00**

California Faience

California Faience was the trade name used by William V. Bragdon and Chauncy R. Thomas on vases, bowls, and other artware produced at their pottery known as 'The Tile Shop' in Berkeley, California, from 1920 to 1930. Faience tile was the principal product of the business during these years and is the favorite with today's collectors. Items in a glossy glaze are rare and therefore more valuable. Tiles were marked 'California Faience' with a die stamp.

Book block, bear, plum-brn matt, 4x4½x6" **350.00**
Bowl, bl matt, str rim, 3x5½" **200.00**
Bowl, bl on turq, turq int, fluted, 2½x6" **150.00**
Bowl, Persian bl gloss, squat, 4½x6" **150.00**
Bowl, purple matt, shouldered, 1¾x5¼" **300.00**
Charger, golf scene, brn emb on celadon, VS on front, 11" **500.00**
Flower frog, 2 ducks, aqua glossy, mk, 5½" **100.00**

Tile, multicolor underglaze basket, in Dirk Van Erp hammered copper trivet frame, 5½", $1,500.00.

Tile, abstract pine tree, bl/yel gloss, 5¼" dia **250.00**
Tile, desert scene, mc, 5½" dia **450.00**
Tile, galleon, wine/dk bl/ochre on turq gloss, 5½" **150.00**
Tile, trees/road/bldgs/mtns, thin gr over brn, 5½", +fr **375.00**
Vase, bl matt, shouldered, 5x5½" **350.00**
Vase, gr-turq matt, squat, incurvate rim, 2¾x4" **275.00**
Vase, lovebirds & trees frieze on red, 6¼" **300.00**
Vase, stylized floral, wht slip trail on turq gloss, sgn, 4x4" **900.00**

California Perfume Company

D.H. McConnell, Sr., founded the California Perfume Company (C.P. Company; C.P.C.) in 1886 in New York City. He had previously been a salesman for a book company, which he later purchased. His door-to-door sales usually involved the lady of the house, to whom he presented a complimentary bottle of inexpensive perfume. Upon determining his perfume to be more popular than his books, he decided that the manufacture of perfume might be more lucrative. He bottled toiletries under the name 'California Perfume Company' and a line of household products called 'Perfection.' In 1928 the name 'Avon' appeared on the label, and in 1939 the C.P.C. name was entirely removed from the product. The success of the company is attributed to the door-to-door sales approach and 'money back' guarantee offered by his first 'Depot Agent,' Mrs. P.F.E. Albee, known today as the 'Avon Lady.'

The company's containers are quite collectible today, especially the older, hard-to-find items. Advanced collectors seek bottles and other items labeled Goetting & Co., New York; Goetting's; or Savoi Et Cie, Paris. Such examples date from 1871 to 1896. The Goetting Company was purchased by D.H. McConnell; Savoi Et Cie was a line which they imported to sell through department stores. Also of special interest are packaging and advertising with the Ambrosia or Hinze Ambrosia Company label. This was a subsidiary company whose objective seems to have been to produce a line of face creams, etc., for sale through drugstores and other such commercial outlets. They operated in New York from about 1875 until 1954. Because very little is known about these companies and since only a few examples of their product containers and advertising material have been found, market values for such items have not yet been established. Other items sought by the collector include products marked Gertrude Recordon, Marvel Electric Silver Cleaner, Easy Day Automatic Clothes Washer, pre-1915 catalogs, and California Perfume Company 1909 and 1910 calendars.

There are hundreds of local Avon Collector Clubs throughout the world that also have C.P.C. collectors in their membership. If you are interested in joining, locating, or starting a new club, contact the National Association of Avon Collectors, Inc., listed in the Directory under Clubs, Newsletters, and Catalogs. Those wanting a National Newsletter Club or price guides may contact Avon Times, listed in the same section. See also Avon. Inquiries concerning California Perfume Company items and the companies or items mentioned in the previous paragraphs should be directed toward our advisor, Dick Pardini, whose address is given under California. (Please send a large SASE; not interested in Avons, 'Perfection' marked C.P.C.'s, or Anniversary Keepsakes.)

Narcissus Perfume, 1925, 1-oz, M **120.00**
Narcissus Perfume, 1929-30, mc box, 1-oz, MIB **160.00**
Natoma Rose Perfume, 1914-15, glass bottle/stopper, ½-oz, M ..**160.00**
Natoma Rose Perfume, 1916, ½-oz, M **150.00**
Natoma Rose Talcum Powder, tin container, 1911, 3½-oz, MIB ..**160.00**
Olive Oil, glass bottle, 1895, 8-oz, M **75.00**
Perfection Coloring Set, 5 bottles in wood box, 1920, MIB **200.00**
Perfection Furniture Polish, can, 1916, 12-oz, M **70.00**
Perfection Kwick Cleaning Polish, can, 1922, 8-oz, M **50.00**
Perfection Liquid Spots Out, 1925, 4-oz, M **45.00**
Perfection Mothicide, can, 1925, ½-lb, M **40.00**
Perfume Sample Set, 1923, MIB **150.00**
Powder Sachet, bottle, ca 1915, M **45.00**
Powder Sachets, 1890s, M **90.00**
Powder tin, 2 nude babies play w/giant rose ea side, 1912, M **100.00**
Radiant Nail Powder, tin container, 1923, M **25.00**
Rose Pomade, jar, milk glass, 1914, M **65.00**
Shampoo Cream, milk glass, 1908, 4-oz, M **75.00**
Sweet Sixteen Face Powder, paper container, 1918, M **50.00**

Tooth Tablet, aluminum lid, clear or milk wht bottom, '20s, M ...50.00
Tooth Wash, emb bottle w/label, 1915, M 105.00
Trailing Arbutus Face Powder, paper container, 1925, MIB 40.00
Trailing Arbutus Talcum, tin container, 1914, sample sz, M 70.00
Trailing Arbutus Talcum, tin container, 1920, 1-lb, M 70.00
Verna Talc, mc container, 1928, 4-oz, MIB 95.00
Vernafleur Face Powder, tin container, 1925, M 20.00
Vernafleur Perfume, 1923, 1-oz, MIB 140.00
Violet Almond Meal, tin container, 1923, 4-oz, M 45.00
Witch Hazel Cream, 1904, 2-oz tube, MIB 50.00

Calling Cards, Cases, and Receivers

The practice of announcing one's arrival with a calling card borne by the maid to the mistress of the house was a social grace of the Victorian era. Different messages (condolences, a personal visit, or a good-by) were related by turning down one corner or another. The custom was forgotten by WWI. Fashionable ladies and gents carried their personally engraved cards in elaborate cases made of such materials as embossed silver, mother-of-pearl with intricate inlay, tortoise shell, and ivory. Card receivers held cards left by visitors who called while the mistress was out or 'not receiving.' Calling cards with fringe, die-cut flaps that cover the name, or an unusual decoration are worth about $3.00 to $4.00, while plain cards usually sell for around $1.00.

Cases

Abalone shell inlay, cvd wht floral medallion, 3⅝" 85.00
Ivory, China trade, ca 1860, 4x2⅜", in orig glass/paper box 75.00
Ivory, cvd figures in garden, 1800s, 3¾x2¾" 195.00
MOP, Dmn Quilt pattern, blk silk int, 3¾" L 85.00
Silver w/eng birds & flowers, 2½x4" 100.00
Sterling, chinoisere relief, grapevines, 3¾" 215.00
Sterling, Deco design & initial, w/link chain 75.00
Tortoise shell, fishing scene, canted corners, 4" L 82.50
Tortoise shell, ivory mts, English, 1800s 85.00
Tortoise shell, openwork cvgs, 2½x4" 90.00
Tortoise shell w/ivory & MOP inlays, 3⅝" 125.00
Tunbridge, mosaic florals, mid-1800s, EX 85.00

Receivers

Brass, girl's face w/bonnet, 4½x4½" 85.00
Brass, Nouveau lady across front, 3½x7" 125.00
Gilded silver, George V, mk London, 1913, 5" dia 100.00
Pewter, lady w/harp beside tray, Archibald Knox, EX 315.00
Pewter-like metal, lady w/flowing hair, 4½x7" 90.00
Porcelain, bust of armored knight, Derby, 3¾x5" 90.00
Pottery, Nouveau style, Hotel Astor/carriage scene, 6" L 75.00
Silverplate, dragon figure as ft, ca 1890 ....150.00
Silverplate, flower form w/stem & leaf base, ca 1880, 7" H 120.00
Silverplate, stag's head hdl, Middleton 195.00
Sterling, allover diapering w/monogram, ftd, Schultz, 6" 125.00
Sterling, repousse floral border, claw ft, Dominick & Haff 340.00
White metal, Art Nouveau lady emb on fan shape, 5x6" 85.00

Camark

The Camden Art and Tile Company (commonly known as Camark) of Camden, Arkansas, was organized in the fall of 1926 by Samuel J. 'Jack' Carnes. Using clays from Arkansas, John Lessell, who had been hired as art director by Carnes, produced the initial lustre and

iridescent Lessell wares for Camark ('CAM'den, 'ARK'ansas) before his death in December 1926. Before the plant opened in the spring of 1927, Carnes brought John's wife, Jeanne, and stepdaughter Billie to oversee the art department's manufacture of Le-Camark. Production by the Lessell family included variations of J.B. Owens' Soudanese and Opalesce and Weller's Marengo and Lamar. Camark's version of Marengo was called Old English. They also made wares identical to Weller's LaSa. Pieces made by John Lessell back in Ohio were signed 'Lessell,' while those made by Jeanne and Billie in Arkansas during 1927 were signed 'Le-Camark.' By 1928 Camark's production centered on traditional glazes. Drip glazes similar to Muncie Pottery were produced, in particular the green drip over pink. In the 1930s commercial castware with simple glossy and matt finishes became the primary focus and would continue so until Camark closed in the early 1960s. Between the 1960s and 1980s the company operated mainly as a retail store selling existing inventory, but some limited production occurred. In 1986 the company was purchased by the Ashcraft family of Camden, but no pottery has yet been made at the factory.

Our advisor for this category is David Edwin Gifford. He is listed in the Directory under Arkansas. Mr. Gifford is the author of *Collector's Encyclopedia of Camark Pottery*, and the editor of the *National Society of Arkansas Pottery Collectors Newsletter*.

Centerpiece bowl with bird frog, $50.00.

Basket, rope trim on edges, USA N49, 11" 40.00
Bowl, Iris, pk, #804R 110.00
Bowl, lt gr drip on butterscotch, 3½x9" 125.00
Candle holder, Iris, pk, pr 65.00
Candle holder/planter, dbl-fish, USA 014, 12" 75.00
Candy dish, 8-sided, w/lid, Camark die stamp, 5½" 55.00
Cookie jar, pumpkin shape, USA R58, 8" 45.00
Cookie jar, Ring, blk, rare 75.00
Figurine, cat climbing, w/sticker, 15" 100.00
Figurine, squirrel, standing/eating nut, USA N128, 8" 125.00
Planter, baby bassinet shape, 5½x4½" 30.00
Planter, deer, brn 45.00
Planter, elephant shape, Art Deluxe sticker, 11x8" 75.00
Planter, rolling pin shape, USA N1, 15x3½" 35.00
Planter/TV lamp, covered wagon shape, USA D23, 4x5" 30.00
Plate, chip & dip; petal design, USA R60, 12" dia 35.00
Plate, deviled egg, USA 015, 10½" dia 30.00
Scrub pad holder, Humpty Dumpty on window sill, HP, USA R33, 6" ..100.00
Soap dish, bathtub shape, USA 232, 4x2" 22.00
Soap dish, shell shape, unmk, 5½" 20.00
Teapot, Ring, cobalt, 6-cup 75.00
Vase, dbl water can, w/hdls, USA N-72, 8x6" 35.00
Vase, gladiola; pumpkin matt, #403, 8" 50.00
Vase, Iris, 11" 110.00
Vase, modeled rust matt, Deco styling, hdl on side, 6" 100.00
Vase, Morning Glory, yel & purple, 8" 95.00
Vase, pk & gr drip, 5" 75.00

Vase, water sprinkler bottle shape, USA 229, 13x8½" **45.00**
Vase, wht matt, high loop hdl, 8" **35.00**
Wall pocket, cup & saucer shape, HP flowers, unmk, 7½" **30.00**
Wall pocket, diaper shape, USA 837, 7x8" **30.00**

Cambridge Glass

The Cambridge Glass Company began operations in 1901 in Cambridge, Ohio. Primarily they made crystal dinnerware and well-designed accessory pieces until the 1920s when they introduced the concept of color that was to become so popular on the American dinnerware market. Always maintaining high standards of quality and elegance, they produced many lines that became best-sellers; through the '20s and '30s they were recognized as the largest manufacturer of this type of glassware in the world.

Of the various marks the company used, the 'C in triangle' is the most familiar. Production stopped in 1958. For a more thorough study of the subject, we recommend *Colors in Cambridge Glass* by the National Cambridge Collectors, Inc.; their address may be found in the Directory under Clubs. *Glass Animals and Figural Flower Frogs of the Depression Era* by Lee Garmon and Dick Spencer is a wonderful source for an in-depth view of their particular aspect of glass collecting. They are both listed in the Directory under Illinois. See also Carnival Glass; Glass Animals. In the listings below items are crystal unless noted otherwise.

Apple Blossom, crystal, bowl, fruit; tab hdld, 11" **35.00**
Apple Blossom, crystal, pitcher, #3130, 64-oz **135.00**
Apple Blossom, crystal, stem, water; #3135, 8-oz **14.00**
Apple Blossom, crystal, tumbler, ftd, #3135, 12-oz **17.50**
Apple Blossom, pk or gr, bowl, pickle; 9" **40.00**
Apple Blossom, pk or gr, pitcher, ball shape, 80-oz **275.00**
Apple Blossom, pk or gr, stem, cordial; #3130, 1-oz **125.00**
Apple Blossom, pk or gr, tumbler, #3025, 12-oz **40.00**
Apple Blossom, yel or amber, bowl, 4-ftd, 12" **70.00**
Apple Blossom, yel or amber, butter dish, w/lid, 5½" **225.00**
Apple Blossom, yel or amber, plate, dinner; 9½" **65.00**
Apple Blossom, yel or amber, vase, 2 styles, 8" **75.00**
Candlelight, bowl, #3900/34, 2-hdld, 11" **60.00**
Candlelight, candy dish, #3900/165, w/lid, rnd **95.00**
Candlelight, lamp, hurricane; #1617 ....**125.00**
Candlelight, pitcher, Doulton; #3400/141 ....**300.00**
Candlelight, plate, cake; #3900/35, 2-hdld, 13½" **60.00**
Candlelight, stem, cocktail; #3776, 3-oz **25.00**
Candlelight, stem, sherbet; #3776, low, 7-oz **16.50**
Candlelight, tumbler, juice; #3776, 5-oz **18.00**
Caprice, bl or pk, ashtray, #214, 3" **12.00**
Caprice, bl or pk, bowl, #81, shallow, 4-ftd, 11½" **100.00**
Caprice, bl or pk, bowl, salad; #57, 4-ftd, 10" **125.00**
Caprice, bl or pk, candlestick, #1338, 3-light, ea **75.00**
Caprice, bl or pk, cigarette box, #207, w/lid, 3½x2¼" **45.00**
Caprice, bl or pk, comport, #130, low ftd, 7" **50.00**
Caprice, bl or pk, mayonnaise, #129, 3-pc set, 6½" **115.00**
Caprice, bl or pk, nut dish, #93, 2½" **35.00**
Caprice, bl or pk, plate, #28, 4-ftd, 14" **100.00**
Caprice, bl or pk, stem, cordial; #300, blown, 1-oz **130.00**
Caprice, bl or pk, sugar bowl, #40, ind **25.00**
Caprice, bl or pk, tumbler, #14, str sides, 9-oz **87.50**
Caprice, bl or pk, tumbler, #310, flat, tall, 11-oz, 4¾" **80.00**
Caprice, bl or pk, vase, #246, 7½" **175.00**
Caprice, bl or pk, vase, #254, blown, 6" **350.00**
Caprice, crystal, ashtray, #213, shell form, 3-ftd, 2¾" **7.00**
Caprice, crystal, bowl, #50, 4-ftd, sq, 8" **40.00**
Caprice, crystal, bowl, #60, crimped, 4-ftd, 11" **35.00**

Caprice, crystal, bowl, jelly; #151, 2-hdld, 5" **15.00**
Caprice, crystal, candle reflector, #73 ....**250.00**
Caprice, crystal, candlestick, #74, 3-light, ea **35.00**
Caprice, crystal, candlestick, dbl; #69, 7½", ea **150.00**
Caprice, crystal, cracker jar, #202, w/lid **250.00**
Caprice, crystal, oil cruet, #101, w/stopper, 3-oz **30.00**
Caprice, crystal, plate, lemon; #152, hdld, 6½" **11.00**
Caprice, crystal, shakers, #92, flat, ind, pr **40.00**
Caprice, crystal, stem, parfait; #300, blown, 5-oz **80.00**
Caprice, crystal, tumbler, #15, str sides, 12-oz **37.50**
Caprice, crystal, tumbler, tea; #301, blown, 12-oz **17.00**
Caprice, crystal, vase, #338, crimped top, 6½" **100.00**
Chantilly, bowl, celery/relish; 3-part, 12" **35.00**
Chantilly, bowl, tab hdld, 11" **35.00**
Chantilly, butter bowl, ¼-lb **210.00**
Chantilly, creamer **14.50**
Chantilly, hat, sm **150.00**
Chantilly, mustard jar, w/lid **50.00**
Chantilly, pitcher, ball shape **120.00**
Chantilly, plate, bread & butter; 6½" **6.50**
Chantilly, stem, claret; #3625, 4½-oz **40.00**
Chantilly, stem, cocktail; #3600, 2½-oz **24.00**
Chantilly, stem, cordial; #3625, 1-oz **50.00**
Chantilly, stem, sherbet; #3600, tall, 7-oz **17.50**
Chantilly, stem, water; #3779, 9-oz **20.00**
Chantilly, stem, wine; #3775, 2½-oz **30.00**
Chantilly, tumbler, juice; #3775, ftd, 5-oz **14.00**
Chantilly, tumbler, water; #3625, ftd, 10-oz **17.50**
Chantilly, tumbler, 13-oz **22.00**
Cleo, bl, bowl, comport; 4-ftd, 6" **50.00**
Cleo, bl, bowl, console; 12" **75.00**
Cleo, bl, bowl, relish; 2-part **40.00**
Cleo, bl, planter, 12" **150.00**
Cleo, bl, salt cellar, 1½" **100.00**
Cleo, bl, stem, cordial; #3077, 1-oz **165.00**
Cleo, bl, tumbler, #3077, ftd, 8-oz **50.00**
Cleo, colors other than bl, candlestick, 1-light, 2 styles, ea **22.00**
Cleo, colors other than bl, decanter, w/stopper **225.00**
Cleo, colors other than bl, ice pail **60.00**
Cleo, colors other than bl, pitcher, w/lid, 22-oz **175.00**
Cleo, colors other than bl, sugar sifter, ftd, 6¾" **275.00**
Cleo, colors other than bl, syrup pitcher, w/glass lid **165.00**
Cleo, colors other than bl, tray, serving; hdld, 12" **150.00**
Cleo, colors other than bl, tumbler, #3115, ftd, 10-oz **37.50**
Cleo, colors other than bl, tumbler, #3115, ftd, 2½-oz **50.00**
Cleo, colors other than bl, vase, 9½" **110.00**
Crown Tuscan, bowl, shell; 3-ftd, 10" **95.00**
Crown Tuscan, candy dish, ftd, #6, w/lid **65.00**
Crown Tuscan, dolphin candlesticks, #67, 5", pr **275.00**
Crown Tuscan, urn, #3500/41, 10" **145.00**
Decagon, pastel colors, bowl, almond shape, ftd, 6" **22.00**
Decagon, pastel colors, bowl, berry; 10" **12.00**
Decagon, pastel colors, bowl, cream soup; w/liner **10.00**
Decagon, pastel colors, comport, tall, 7" **20.00**
Decagon, pastel colors, gravy boat, w/2-hdld liner **70.00**
Decagon, pastel colors, stem, cordial; 1-oz **40.00**
Decagon, pastel colors, stem, water; 9-oz **15.00**
Decagon, pastel colors, tray, service; oval, 12" **10.00**
Decagon, pastel colors, tumbler, ftd, 12-oz **20.00**
Decagon, red or bl, basket, upturned sides, 2-hdld, 7" **22.50**
Decagon, red or bl, bowl, cranberry; flat rim, 3¾" **20.00**
Decagon, red or bl, bowl, relish; 2-part, 11" **17.50**
Decagon, red or bl, bowl, relish; 2-part, 9" **15.00**
Decagon, red or bl, creamer, scalloped edge **18.00**

Decagon, red or bl, plate, salad; 8½" 10.00
Decagon, red or bl, salt cellar, ftd, 1½" 22.50
Decagon, red or bl, stem, sherbet; low, 6-oz 15.00
Decagon, red or bl, sugar bowl, ftd 20.00
Decagon, red or bl, tray, service; oval, 15" 40.00
Decagon, red or bl, tumbler, ftd, 8-oz 22.00

Diane, bowl, foot-
ed, 12", $50.00.

Diane, bowl, berry; 5" 20.00
Diane, bowl, celery/relish; 5-part, 12" 32.50
Diane, bowl, cereal; 6" 18.00
Diane, bowl, flared, 4-ftd, 12" 40.00
Diane, bowl, relish; 2-part, 7" 20.00
Diane, candlestick, keyhole shape, 1-light 17.50
Diane, creamer, #3400, scroll hdl 15.00
Diane, lamp, hurricane; keyhole base w/prisms 195.00
Diane, plate, bread & butter; sq, 6" 5.00
Diane, plate, dinner; 10½" 65.00
Diane, plate, torte; 14" 40.00
Diane, stem, cocktail; #3122, 3-oz 14.00
Diane, stem, sherbet; #1066, low, 7-oz 11.50
Diane, stem, water goblet; #3122, 9-oz 20.00
Diane, tumbler, juice; #3106, ftd, 5-oz 13.00
Diane, tumbler, sham bottom, 5-oz 30.00
Diane, tumbler, water; #1066, 9-oz 12.00
Diane, tumbler, 13-oz 30.00
Diane, vase, flower; ped ft, 11" 65.00
Elaine, bowl, pickle/relish; 5-part, 12" 37.50
Elaine, bowl, pickle/relish; 7" 20.00
Elaine, bowl, 3-ftd, 10" 30.00
Elaine, oil cruet, w/stopper, hdld, 6-oz 65.00
Elaine, plate, 2-hdld, ftd, 8" 15.00
Elaine, stem, claret; #3104, 4½-oz 75.00
Elaine, stem, cordial; #1402, 1-oz 57.50
Elaine, stem, cordial; #3500, 1-oz 57.50
Elaine, stem, sherbet; #1402, low 14.00
Elaine, stem, water, #3500, 10-oz 20.00
Flower frog, see Glass Animals and Figurines
Gloria, crystal, bowl, nut; ind, 4-ftd, 3" 45.00
Gloria, crystal, bowl, relish; 3-hdld, 3-part, 8" 22.50
Gloria, crystal, comport, low, 7" 30.00
Gloria, crystal, plate, cake; ftd, sq, 11" 60.00
Gloria, crystal, plate, 2-hdld, 6" 8.00
Gloria, crystal, saucer, sq 2.00
Gloria, crystal, sugar shaker, w/glass top 150.00
Gloria, crystal, tumbler, #3120, ftd, 10-oz 12.00
Gloria, crystal, tumbler, juice; #3115, ftd, 5-oz 12.00
Gloria, gr, pk or yel, bowl, cranberry; 4-ftd, 3½" 50.00
Gloria, gr, pk or yel, bowl, finger; flared rim, w/rnd plate 26.00
Gloria, gr, pk or yel, bowl, vegetable; 2-hdld, 9½" 90.00
Gloria, gr, pk or yel, creamer, ftd 17.50
Gloria, gr, pk or yel, cup, AD; rnd or sq 100.00
Gloria, gr, pk or yel, oil cruet, w/stopper, tall, ftd, hdld 175.00
Gloria, gr, pk or yel, stem, claret; #3035, 4½-oz 50.00
Gloria, gr, pk or yel, stem, cordial; #3120, 1-oz 125.00

Gloria, gr, pk or yel, tray, sandwich; center hdl, 11" 37.50
Gloria, gr, pk or yel, tumbler, juice; #3135, 5-oz 20.00
Gloria, gr, pk or yel, vase, keyhole base, 10" 120.00
Imperial Hunt Scene, colors, bowl, finger; #3085, w/plate 35.00
Imperial Hunt Scene, colors, pitcher, #711, w/lid, 76-oz 250.00
Imperial Hunt Scene, colors, stem, water; #3085, 9-oz 45.00
Imperial Hunt Scene, colors, stem, wine; #3085, 2½-oz 55.00
Imperial Hunt Scene, crystal, bowl, 3-part, 8½" 25.00
Imperial Hunt Scene, crystal, stem, #1402, 18-oz 60.00
Imperial Hunt Scene, crystal, stem, cordial; #1402, 1-oz 55.00
Imperial Hunt Scene, crystal, tumbler, #1402, flat, 15-oz 35.00
Imperial Hunt Scene, crystal, tumbler, #1402, flat, 7-oz 20.00
Mt Vernon, amber or crystal, ashtray, #68, 4" 12.00
Mt Vernon, amber or crystal, bowl, #118, crimped, oblong, 12" ...32.50
Mt Vernon, amber or crystal, bowl, #126, shallow, 11½" 30.00
Mt Vernon, amber or crystal, bowl, pickle; #65, 8" 17.50
Mt Vernon, amber or crystal, butter tub, #73, w/lid 65.00
Mt Vernon, amber or crystal, comport, #11, 7½" 25.00
Mt Vernon, amber or crystal, comport, #34, 6" 15.00
Mt Vernon, amber or crystal, comport, #99, 9½" 27.50
Mt Vernon, amber or crystal, decanter, #52, w/stopper, 40-oz 70.00
Mt Vernon, amber or crystal, ice bucket, #92, w/tongs 35.00
Mt Vernon, amber or crystal, pitcher, #91, 86-oz 115.00
Mt Vernon, amber or crystal, plate, bread & butter; #4, 6" 3.00
Mt Vernon, amber or crystal, plate, dinner; #40, 10½" 30.00
Mt Vernon, amber or crystal, saucer, #7 ....7.50
Mt Vernon, amber or crystal, sugar bowl, #4, ind 12.00
Mt Vernon, amber or crystal, tumbler, #13, bbl shape, 12-oz 15.00
Mt Vernon, amber or crystal, vase, #42, 5" 15.00
Mt Vernon, amber or crystal, vase, #46, ftd, 10" 50.00
Nude stem, amber, cigarette box 650.00
Nude stem, amber, cocktail 100.00
Nude stem, amber, wine 325.00
Nude stem, amethyst, banquet 300.00
Nude stem, amethyst, brandy 100.00
Nude stem, amethyst, claret 135.00
Nude stem, amethyst, cocktail 100.00
Nude stem, amethyst, cordial 450.00
Nude stem, carmen, claret 175.00
Nude stem, carmen, compote, cupped 160.00
Nude stem, carmen, cordial 650.00
Nude stem, carmen, goblet, water 135.00
Nude stem, Crown Tuscan, candlesticks, 9", pr 425.00
Nude stem, Crown Tuscan, shell compote, gold floral decor 175.00
Nude stem, Crown Tuscan/topaz, bowl 225.00
Nude stem, crystal, bowl, flying nude, 10" 450.00
Nude stem, crystal, claret, ribbed 110.00
Nude stem, crystal, compote, flared 120.00
Nude stem, crystal, shell mint 350.00
Nude stem, emerald, banquet 300.00
Nude stem, emerald, brandy 95.00
Nude stem, emerald, cigarette box, sm 450.00
Nude stem, emerald, cigarette box, tall 495.00
Nude stem, emerald, claret 120.00
Nude stem, emerald, cocktail 100.00
Nude stem, emerald, cordial 450.00
Nude stem, emerald, shell compote 250.00
Nude stem, forest gr, claret 150.00
Nude stem, forest gr, cocktail 95.00
Nude stem, Gold Krystol, brandy 110.00
Nude stem, Gold Krystol, cigarette box, tall 450.00
Nude stem, Gold Krystol, claret, ribbed 200.00
Nude stem, Gold Krystol, cocktail 145.00
Nude stem, pistachio, cocktail 145.00

Nude stem, royal bl, banquet 650.00
Nude stem, royal bl, claret 175.00
Nude stem, royal bl, cocktail 135.00
Nude stem, royal bl, compote, flared 185.00
Nude stem, royal bl, goblet, water 155.00
Nude stem, royal bl, hoch bowl on 6" stem 695.00
Nude stem, royal bl, wine 395.00
Portia, basket, upturned sides, 2-hdld 16.00
Portia, bowl, bonbon; 2-hdld, 5¼" 15.00
Portia, bowl, celery/relish; tab hdld, 3-part, 9" 30.00
Portia, bowl, finger; #3124, w/liner 32.00
Portia, bowl, flared, 4-ftd, 12" 45.00
Portia, bowl, sq, 8½" 15.00

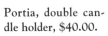

Portia, double candle holder, $40.00.

Portia, cocktail icer, 2-part 65.00
Portia, comport, 5½" 27.50
Portia, ice bucket, w/chrome hdl 65.00
Portia, puff box, ball shape, w/lid, 3½" 125.00
Portia, stem, claret; #3126, 4½-oz 37.50
Portia, stem, cordial; #3126, 1-oz 55.00
Portia, stem, cordial; #3130, 1-oz 55.00
Portia, stem, goblet; #3121, 10-oz 22.50
Portia, stem, parfait; #3121, 5-oz 35.00
Portia, stem, wine; #3121, 2½-oz 30.00
Portia, tray, celery; 11" 27.50
Portia, tumbler, tea; #3121, ftd, 12-oz 25.00
Portia, vase, ftd, 6" 45.00
Rosalie, amber, bowl, bonbon; 2-hdld, 5½" 12.00
Rosalie, amber, bowl, cream soup 20.00
Rosalie, amber, bowl, decagon; 12" 75.00
Rosalie, amber, candlestick, 2 styles, 4" 20.00
Rosalie, amber, comport, high ftd, 6½" 25.00
Rosalie, amber, comport, 2-hdld, 5½" 15.00
Rosalie, amber, mayonnaise, ftd, w/liner 25.00
Rosalie, amber, plate, dinner; 9½" 35.00
Rosalie, amber, stem, cordial; #3077, 1-oz 60.00
Rosalie, amber, sugar shaker 195.00
Rosalie, bl, pk or gr, bowl, basket; 2-hdld, 11" 45.00
Rosalie, bl, pk or gr, bowl, bouillon; 2-hdld 25.00
Rosalie, bl, pk or gr, bowl, w/lid, 3-part, 3⅝" 47.50
Rosalie, bl, pk or gr, bowl, 2-hdld, 8½" 25.00
Rosalie, bl, pk or gr, candy dish, w/lid, 6" 100.00
Rosalie, bl, pk or gr, creamer, ftd 17.00
Rosalie, bl, pk or gr, ice bucket 65.00
Rosalie, bl, pk or gr, plate, bread & butter; 6¾" 7.00
Rosalie, bl, pk or gr, platter, 15" 95.00
Rosalie, bl, pk or gr, tumbler, #3077, ftd, 2½-oz 35.00
Rosalie, bl, pk or gr, wafer tray 100.00
Rose Point, ashtray, #3500/129, sq, 3¼" 55.00
Rose Point, bell, dinner; #3121 ....145.00
Rose Point, bowl, #1401/122, 3-part, 10½" 245.00

Rose Point, bowl, #3400/1240, 4-ftd, oval, 12" 110.00
Rose Point, bowl, #3400/3, low ftd, 11" 145.00
Rose Point, bowl, #3500/115, ftd, w/hdl, 9½" 125.00
Rose Point, bowl, #3500/50, hdld, 6" 42.50
Rose Point, bowl, #993, 4-ftd, 12½" 85.00
Rose Point, bowl, cereal; #3400/53, 6" 77.50
Rose Point, bowl, nappy; #3400/56, 5½" 42.50
Rose Point, bowl, rimmed soup; #361, 8½" 250.00
Rose Point, butter dish, #506, w/lid, rnd 177.50
Rose Point, candlestick, #3900/72, 2-light, 6" 42.50
Rose Point, candlestick, #628, 3½" 35.00
Rose Point, candy box, #300, w/rose finial, 3-ftd, 6" ...265.00
Rose Point, cocktail shaker, #98, w/metal top, 46-oz ...150.00
Rose Point, comport, #3400/74, 4-ftd, 5" 67.50
Rose Point, comport, #3500/36, 6" 120.00
Rose Point, cup, punch; #488, 5-oz 37.50
Rose Point, decanter, #1380, sq, 26-oz 415.00
Rose Point, hat, #1702, 8" 475.00
Rose Point, marmalade jar, #147, 8-oz 135.00
Rose Point, pitcher, #3400/38, ball shape, 80-oz 195.00
Rose Point, pitcher, #3900/118, 32-oz 295.00
Rose Point, plate, bread & butter; #3400/1181, 2-hdld, 6" ...15.00
Rose Point, plate, dinner; #3900/24, 10½" 125.00
Rose Point, plate, torte; #3400/65, 14" 125.00
Rose Point, shakers, #3400/37, w/chrome tops, pr ...165.00
Rose Point, stem, cocktail; #3104, 3½-oz 275.00
Rose Point, stem, cocktail; #3106, 3-oz 35.00
Rose Point, stem, water; #3500, 10-oz 30.00
Rose Point, sugar bowl, #3400/16, ftd 85.00
Rose Point, tray, #3500/67, rnd, 12" 150.00
Rose Point, tray, celery; #3500/652, 12" 47.50
Rose Point, tray, celery/relish; #3900/126, 3-part, 12" ...60.00
Rose Point, tray, relish; #3400/67, 5-part, 12" 75.00
Rose Point, tray, relish; #3500/62, 4-part, 2-hdld, 7½" ...55.00
Rose Point, tray, relish; #3500/69, 3-part, 6½" 32.50
Rose Point, tumbler, #3106, 12-oz 32.00
Rose Point, tumbler, #3400/92, 2½-oz 100.00
Rose Point, tumbler, #7801, ftd, 5-oz 35.00
Rose Point, tumbler, juice; #3500, low ftd, 5-oz 35.00
Rose Point, vase, #1301, ftd, 10" 75.00
Rose Point, vase, #1620, ftd, 9" 115.00
Rose Point, vase, flower; #279, ftd, 13" 200.00
Valencia, basket, #3500/55, 2-hdld, ftd, 6" 22.00
Valencia, bottle, perfume; #3400/97, 2-oz 95.00
Valencia, bowl, finger; #1402/100, w/liner 30.00
Valencia, comport, #3500/36, 6" 27.50
Valencia, decanter, #3400/92, ball shape, 32-oz 125.00
Valencia, plate, #3500/39, ftd, 12" 27.50
Valencia, saucer, #3500/1 ....3.00
Valencia, shakers, #3400/18, pr 50.00
Valencia, stem, sherbet; #1402, low 12.50
Valencia, stem, wine; #3500, 2½-oz 27.50
Valencia, tumbler, #3400/100, 13-oz 20.00
Valencia, tumbler, #3500, ftd, 16-oz 20.00
Wildflower, candlestick, #3400/638, 3-light, ea 35.00
Wildflower, cocktail shaker, #3400/175 ....85.00
Wildflower, hat, #1704, 5" 165.00
Wildflower, lamp, hurricane; #1617, candlestick base ...150.00
Wildflower, pitcher, #3400/38, ball shape, 80-oz 135.00
Wildflower, plate, bread & butter; #3900/20, 6½" 7.50
Wildflower, plate, cake; #3900/35, 2-hdld, 13½" 37.50
Wildflower, stem, cordial; #3121, 1-oz 55.00
Wildflower, stem, parfait; #3121, low, 5-oz 32.50
Wildflower, vase, #1237, keyhole ftd, 9" 60.00

Wildflower, vase, flower; #279, ftd, 13" 110.00

Cameo

The technique of glass carving was perfected 2,000 years ago in ancient Rome and Greece. The most famous ancient example of cameo glass is the Portland Vase, made in Rome around 100 A.D. After glass blowing was developed, glassmakers devised a method of casing several layers of colored glass together, often with a light color over a darker base, to enhance the design. Skilled carvers meticulously worked the fragile glass to produce incredibly detailed classic scenes. In the 18th and 19th centuries Oriental and Near-Eastern artisans used the technique more extensively. European glassmakers revived the art during the last quarter of the 19th century. In France, Galle and Daum produced some of the finest examples of modern times, using as many as five layers of glass to develop their designs, usually scenics or subjects from nature. Hand carving was supplemented by the use of a copper engraving wheel, and acid was used to cut away the layers more quickly.

In England, Thomas Webb and Sons used modern machinery and technology to eliminate many of the problems that plagued early glass carvers. One of Webb's best-known carvers, George Woodall, is credited with producing over four hundred pieces. Woodall was trained in the art by John Northwood, famous for reproducing the Portland Vase in 1876. Cameo glass became very popular during the late 1800s, resulting in a market that demanded more than could be produced, due to the tedious procedures involved. In an effort to produce greater volume, less elaborate pieces with simple floral or geometric designs were made, often entirely acid etched with little or no hand carving. While very little cameo glass was made in this country, a few pieces were produced by James Gillinder, Tiffany, and the Libbey Glass Company. Though some continued to be made on a limited scale into the 1900s (and until about 1920 in France), for the most part, inferior products caused a marked reduction in its manufacture by the turn of the century. Beware of new 'French' cameo glass from Romania and Taiwan. Some of it is very good and may be signed with 'old' signatures. Watch for stencil-cut designs that are 'disconnected' and segmented. Know your dealer! Our advisor for this category is Don Williams; he is listed in the Directory under Missouri. See also specific manufactures.

Key: fp — fire polished

English

Basket, leaves, rainbow on wht, camphor ft, silver hdl, 5" 850.00
Vase, anemones, wht to cranberry frost, globular, 5" 630.00
Vase, apple blossoms, wht on red, 7¼" 1,000.00
Vase, clematis/butterfly, wht on pk & clear martele, 8¾" 3,000.00
Vase, florals & geometric bands, wht on bl, 10½" 2,450.00
Vase, florals/butterfly, orange & wht on lemon yel, 5½" 1,900.00
Vase, flower/foliage/butterfly, red/wht/yel, SP ft, 5¾" 220.00
Vase, honeysuckle vine, wht on yel to pk, stick neck, 6¾" 850.00
Vase, morning glories, leaf band, wht on red, bulbous, 5x3¼" ...1,220.00

French

Bottle, floral, gr on frosted/leafy ground, St Louis, 7½" 200.00
Bottle, floral/berries, ruby on gr, St Louis, 6x2" 325.00
Bottle, pine branches, eng/gold pnt on topaz, Rousseau, 8" 1,250.00
Bowl, daffodils, rust/dk bl on pk, acorn form, Degue, 8x11" 950.00
Vase, bellflowers, orange/burgundy on yel frost, Degue, 12" 700.00
Vase, blossoms/vines, brn on wht frost, Arsall, 12" 850.00
Vase, floral, purple/brn on cobalt/pk/frost, Degue, 20" 2,600.00
Vase, flowers/pods/leaves, purple/wht/pk on purple-pk, 3¾" 675.00

Vase, landscape cut/pnt on pk/gr/wht mottle, LeMartime, 3¾" ..550.00
Vase, morning glories, purple on chartreuse frost, Arsall, 13" 800.00
Vase, oasis/men by pool/pyramid, gr on peach, Arsall, 8x7" 1,095.00
Vase, raspberries, rose/gr/yel/wht, ovoid, Arsall, 16⅝" 1,725.00
Vase, sunflowers, orange/gr on wht mottle, ftd, Degue, 11x9" 750.00

Canary Ware

Canary ware was produced from the late 1700s until about the mid-19th century in the Staffordshire district of England. It was potted of yellow clay and the overglaze was yellow as well. More often than not, copper or silver lustre trim was added. Decorations were usually black-printed transfers, though occasionally hand-painted polychrome designs were also used.

Bowl, mc florals w/blk stripe, 2⅞x6¼", EX 75.00
Creamer, mc florals, silver striping, rpr, 4⅜" 55.00
Cup & saucer, Adam Buck transfer of lady & child, mini 450.00
Mug, boy asleep w/drum, dog beside, red transfer, 2¼", EX 160.00
Mug, child's, Lafayette/WA, blk transfer, Wood, EX color, 2½" ...1,600.00
Mug, Farmers Arms, blk transfer w/mc florals, rpt, 4⅝" 260.00
Mug, For My Dear Boy, lustre rim, wear, 1¾" 290.00
Mug, mc floral w/brn stripe on rim, rpr, 3½" 130.00

Pitcher, iron red cabbage roses with green and brown leaves, 7", $800.00.

Pitcher, 5-color floral, sm chip, 3¾" 275.00
Plate, blk spatter, 8-sided, English, 1800-40, 8" 325.00
Plate, Le Chat Botte (cat in boot), blk transfer, 8⅝", NM 110.00
Saucer, lady at pianoforte sepia transfer, rpr, 4" 160.00

Candle Holders

The earliest type of candlestick, called a pricket, was constructed with a sharp point on which the candle was impaled. The socket type, first used in the 16th century, consisted of the socket and a short stem with a wide drip pan and base. These were made from sheets of silver or other metal; not until late in the 17th century were candlesticks made by casting. By the 1700s, styles began to vary from the traditional fluted column or baluster form and became more elaborate. A Rococo style with scrolls, shellwork, and naturalistic leaves and flowers came into vogue that afforded the individual silversmith the opportunity to exhibit his skill and artistry. The last half of the 18th century brought a return to fluted columns with neoclassic motifs. Because they were made of thin sheet silver, weighted bases were used to add stability. The Rococo styles of the Regency period were heavily encrusted with applied figures and flowers. Candelabra with six to nine branches became popular. By the Victorian era when lamps came into general use, there was less innovation and more adaptation of the earlier styles. See also Silver; Tinware; specific manufacturers.

Key: QA — Queen Anne

Altar, Continental cvd rococo, trn column, trifid base, 35" **600.00**
Bell metal, paneled & waisted std, rnd base, 1700s, 10", pr **660.00**
Brass, bobeche above deep cup, trn std, sq base, 19th C, 12" **75.00**
Brass, cast baluster w/rnd base, w/ejector, 8x3¾", pr **95.00**
Brass, dbl baluster, domed ft, wax catcher, 1650s, 7½" **600.00**
Brass, Dmn Princess, w/push-up, Victorian, 10¾", pr **165.00**
Brass, Empire style, columnar std, urn-form support, 11", pr **360.00**
Brass, Fr, ca 1720-40, 9", pr **700.00**
Brass, Georgian, concave cup, hex base, 1710s, 6½", pr **440.00**
Brass, Good Luck pattern, 19th C, 12½", pr **300.00**
Brass, hex base w/cast cherubs, 11¼", pr **330.00**
Brass, Louis XV style, scroll decor, 12", pr **600.00**
Brass, QA, ca 1720, 6¾" **250.00**
Brass, QA, early, 7¼", pr **550.00**
Brass, QA, scalloped base, 8", pr **800.00**
Brass, QA style, old but not period, 8", pr **225.00**
Brass, Queen of Dmns, w/push-up, 11⅜", pr **275.00**
Brass, sq base, early, 6⅝" **140.00**
Brass, sq base w/paw ft, 8" **300.00**
Brass, tripod base w/paw ft, baluster stem, drip pan, 11½" **330.00**
Brass, w/side push-up, skillful rpr, early, 7⅜" **220.00**
Bronze, Neoclassical, sq base & stem, w/push-ups, 10¾", pr **375.00**
Bronze, Regency, silvered dolphin form, prisms, 1815, 9½" **250.00**
Bronze, scalloped base, early, 5¾" **220.00**
Bronze classical maiden figural w/scrolled arbor, 25", pr **440.00**
Bronze Deco-style nude w/amphora on her shoulder, 16", pr **500.00**
Candelabra, bronze, Charles X, 3-arm, paw ft, 19th C, 24", pr ...**1,700.00**
Candelabra, Louis XVI-style, bronze/marble, 6-light, 25", pr **500.00**
Candelabrum, Neoclassical-style gilt bronze, marble base, 30" ...**260.00**
Glass, amethyst, optic-ribbed shaft, cupped ped, 12", pr **230.00**
Glass, clambroth/alabaster, pressed crucifix form, 9⅛", EX **140.00**
Glass, pressed base, free-blown deep socket & extension, 9" **140.00**
Hogscraper, brass wedding band, w/push-up, lip hanger, 9", pr ...**900.00**
Hogscraper, sheet iron w/brass band, fan-shape ejector, 7½" **290.00**
Hogscraper, steel, w/push-up mk Shaw's, blk pnt, 7⅛" **145.00**
Hogscraper, steel w/worn tin wash, w/push-up & hanger, 6¼" ...**120.00**
Pricket, Continental Baroque-style cvd giltwood, 19th C, 29" ...**660.00**
Sconce, oak, cvd eagle bkplate, floral scrolling arms, 27", pr **250.00**
Sconce, sheet iron, heavy primitive, 10½" **140.00**
Silverplate, classic details, weighted base, bobeches, 9½" **150.00**
Sterling, Georgian, oval serpentine std/base, 9", pr **350.00**
Wrought iron, spiral adjusts, trn wooden base, 7", EX **190.00**

Candlewick

Candlewick crystal was made by the Imperial Glass Corporation, a division of Lenox Inc., Bellaire, Ohio. It was introduced in 1936, and though never marked except for paper labels, it is easily recognized by the beaded crystal rims, stems, and handles inspired by the tufted needlework called candlewicking, practiced by our pioneer women. During its production, more than 741 items were designed and produced. In September 1982 when Imperial closed its doors, thirty-four pieces were still being made.

Identification numbers and mold numbers used by the company help collectors recognize the various styles and shapes. Most of the pieces are from the #400 series, though other series numbers were also used. Stemware was made in eight styles — five from the #400 series made from 1941 to 1962, one from #3400 series made in 1937, another from #3800 series made in 1941, and the eighth style from the #4000 series made in 1947. In the listings that follow, some #400 items lack the mold number because that information was not found in the company files.

A few pieces have been made in color or with a gold wash. At least

two lines, Valley Lily and Floral, utilized Candlewick with floral patterns cut into the crystal. These are scarce today. Other rare items include gifts such as the desk calendar made by the company for its employees and customers; the dresser set comprised of a mirror, clock, puff jar, and cologne; and the chip and dip set.

Ashtray, #400/173, heart shape, 5½" **12.00**
Ashtray, #400/19, rnd, 2¾" **10.00**
Ashtray, #400/651, sq, 3¼" **32.00**
Ashtray set, #400/650, 3-pc nesting set, sq **102.00**
Basket, #400/73/0, hdld, 11" **225.00**
Bell, #400/108, 5" **85.00**

Birthday cake plate, 13", $395.00.

Bowl, #400/181, 2 hdls, 6½" **30.00**
Bowl, #400/182, 3-ftd, 8½" **110.00**
Bowl, #400/183, 3-ftd, 6" **60.00**
Bowl, #400/231, sq, 5" **85.00**
Bowl, #400/42B, rnd, 2 hdls, 4¾" **10.00**
Bowl, #400/75F, cupped edge, 10" **45.00**
Bowl, bouillon; #400/126, 2 hdls **40.00**
Bowl, butter/jam; #400/262, 3-part, 10½" **75.00**
Bowl, celery boat; #400/46, oval, 11" **55.00**
Bowl, cream soup; #400/50, 5" **40.00**
Bowl, fruit; #400/103F, beaded stem, 10" **140.00**
Bowl, lily; #400/74J, 4-ftd, 7" **65.00**
Bowl, relish; #400/215, 4 sections, oblong, 12" **115.00**
Bowl, relish; #400/60, 7" **25.00**
Bowl, sauce; #400/243, deep, 5½" **35.00**
Bowl, vegetable; #400/65/1, w/lid, 8" **265.00**
Butter dish, #400/161, beaded top, ¼-lb **30.00**
Cake stand, #400/67D, low ft, 10" **52.00**
Candle holder, #400/147, 3-light **25.00**
Candle holder, #400/280, flat, 3½" **20.00**
Candle holder, #400/40HC, heart shape, 5" **45.00**
Candle holder, #400/79R, rolled edge, 3½" **10.00**
Candle holder, #400/86, mushroom shape **22.00**
Candy box, #400/140, beaded ft, w/lid **225.00**
Candy box, #400/158, 3 sections, rnd, w/lid, 7" **165.00**
Candy box, #400/259, w/lid, 7" **135.00**
Cigarette box, #400/134, w/lid **30.00**
Coaster, #400/226, w/spoon rest **13.00**
Compote, #400/63B, 4½" **25.00**
Compote, #400/66B, plain stem, 5½" **18.00**
Compote, fruit; #400/103C, crimped, ftd, 10" **120.00**
Creamer, #400/126, beaded hdl, flat **32.00**
Creamer, #400/30, beaded hdl, 6-oz **8.00**
Cup, after dinner; #400/77 ....**18.00**
Decanter, #400/18, w/stopper, 18-oz **365.00**
Egg cup, #400/19, beaded ft **48.00**
Hurricane lamp, #400/76, candle base, hdld, 2-pc **150.00**
Icer, seafood/fruit cocktail; #3800, 1-bead stem, 2-pc **65.00**
Ladle, marmalade; #400/130, 3-bead stem **10.00**

Ladle, mayonnaise; #400/135, 6¼" 10.00
Marmalade set, #400/89, 4-pc 42.00
Mayonnaise set, #400/496, 3-pc 40.00
Oil, #400/164, beaded base, 4-oz 55.00
Oil, #400/278, bulbous bottom, hdld, 4-oz 65.00
Pitcher, #400/19, low ft, 16-oz 210.00
Pitcher, #400/419, plain, 40-oz 40.00
Plate, #400/124, oval, 12½" 75.00
Plate, #400/20V, cupped edge, 17" 42.00
Plate, #400/266, triangular, 7½" 85.00
Plate, #400/52C, crimped, 2 hdls, 6¾" 25.00
Plate, dinner; #400/10D, 10½" 35.00
Plate, luncheon; #400/7D, 9" 14.00
Plate, salad; #400/3D, 7" 8.00
Plate, torte; #400/17D, 14" 42.00
Plate, torte; #400/75D, cupped edge, 12½" 28.00
Platter, #400/131D, 16" 175.00
Punch set, #400/139/77, 10-pc 425.00
Salad set, #400/75B, 4-pc 85.00
Salt cellar, #400/19, 2¼" 9.00
Sauce boat, #400/169 ....100.00
Sauce boat liner, #400/169 ....35.00
Shakers, #400/116, bulbous w/beaded stems, plastic tops, pr 42.00
Shakers, #400/247, beaded ft, str sides, chrome tops, pr 16.00
Stem, cocktail; #3800, 4-oz 25.00
Stem, cocktail; #400/190, 4-oz 18.00
Stem, cordial; #400/190, 1-oz 70.00
Stem, parfait; #3400, 6-oz 50.00
Stem, wine; #3400, 4-oz 24.00
Stem, wine; #400/190, 5-oz 22.00
Stem, wine; #4000, 5-oz 25.00
Sugar bowl, #400/126, flat, beaded hdl 40.00
Sugar bowl, #400/31, plain ft 6.50
Tidbit set, #400/18TB, 3-pc 165.00
Tray, condiment; #400/148, 5¼x9¼" 42.00
Tray, fruit; #400/68F, center hdl, 10½" 55.00
Tray, relish; #400/102, 5 sections, 13" 65.00
Tumbler, #3400, ftd, 10-oz 14.00
Tumbler, #3800, 12-oz 25.00
Tumbler, juice; #400/18, 5-oz 38.00
Tumbler, parfait; #400/18, 7-oz 45.00
Tumbler, wine; #400/19, ftd, 3-oz 16.00
Vase, #400/138B, flared rim, ftd, 6" 80.00
Vase, #400/87C, fluted rim, beaded hdls, 8" 28.00
Vase, #400/87F, fan form w/beaded hdl, 8" 35.00
Vase, bud; #400/107, beaded ft, 5¾" 45.00
Vase, bud; #400/186, ftd, 7" 225.00
Vase, ivy bowl; #400/74J, 7" 50.00
Vase, rose bowl; #400/132, ftd, 7½" 165.00

Candy Containers

Figural glass candy containers were first created in 1876 when ingenious candy manufacturers began to use them to package their products. Two of the first containers, the Liberty Bell and Independence Hall, were distributed for our country's centennial celebration. Children found these toys appealing, and an industry was launched that lasted into the mid-1960s.

Figural candy containers include animals, comic characters, guns, telephones, transportation vehicles, household appliances, and many other intriguing designs. The oldest (those made prior to 1920) were usually hand painted and often contained extra metal parts in addition to the metal strip or screw closures. During the 1950s these metal parts

were replaced with plastic, a practice that continued until candy containers met their demise in the 1960s. While predominately clear, they are found in nearly all colors of glass including milk glass, green, amber, pink, emerald, cobalt, ruby flashed, and light blue. Usually the color was intentional, but leftover glass was used as well and resulted in unplanned colors. Various examples are found in light or ice blue, and new finds are always being discovered. Production of the glass portion of candy containers was centered around the western Pennsylvania city of Jeannette. Major producers include Westmoreland Glass, West Bros., Victory Glass, J.H. Millstein, J.C. Crosetti, L.E. Smith, Jack Stough, and T.H. Stough. While 90% of all glass candies were made in the Jeannette area, other companies such as Eagle Glass, Play Toy, and Geo. Borgfeldt Co. have a few to their credit as well.

Buyer beware! Many candy containers have been reproduced. Some, including the Camera and the Rabbit Pushing Wheelbarrow, come already painted from distributors. Others may have a slick or oily feel to the touch. The following list may also alert you to possible reproductions:

E&A #149/L #12 Chicken on Nest
E&A #184/L #17 Scottie Dog (Repro has a ice-like color and is often slick and oily)
E&A #180/L #24 Dog (clear and cobalt)
E&A #566/L #37, Owl (original in clear only, often painted. Repro found in clear, blue, green, and pink with a higher threaded base and less detail)
E&A #539/L #38 Mule and Waterwagon (original marked Jeannette, PA)
E&A #601/L #47 Rabbit Pushing Wheelbarrow (eggs are speckled on the repro; solid on the original)
E&A #618/L #55 Peter Rabbit
E&A #651/L #58 Rocking Horse (original in clear only)
E&A #342/L #76 Independence Hall (original is rectangular; repro has offset base with red felt-lined closure)
E&A #137/L #83 Charlie Chaplin (original has 'Geo. Borgfeldt' on base; reproduction comes in pink and blue)
E&A #208/L #89 Happifats on Drum (no notches on repro for closure to hook into)
E&A #345/L #90 Jackie Coogan (marked inside 'B')
E&A #349/L #91 Kewpie (must have Geo. Borgfeldt on base to be original)
E&A #546/L #94 Naked Child
E&A #674/L #103 Santa (original has plastic head; repro is all glass and opens at bottom)
E&A #162/L #114 Mantel Clock (originally in ruby flashed, milk glass, clear and frosted only)
#144 Amber Pistol (first sold full in the 1970s, not listed in E&A)
E&A #303/L #168 Uncle Sam's Hat
E&A #111/L #233 Santa's Boot
E&A #121/L #238 Camera (original says 'Pat Apld For' on bottom, (reproduction says 'B. Shakman' or is ground off)
E&A #132/L #242 Carpet Sweeper (currently being sold with no metal parts)
E&A #133/L #243 Carpet Sweeper (currently being sold with no metal parts)
E&A #177/L #246 Display Case (original should be painted silver and brown)
E&A #521/L #254 Mailbox
E&A #543/L #255 Drum Mug
E&A #661/L #268 Safe (original in clear, ruby flashed, and milk glass only)
E&A #577/L #289 Piano (original in only clear and milk glass, both painted)
E&A #60/L #356 Auto
E&A #33/L #377 Auto
E&A #56/L #378 Station Wagon

E&A #213/L #386 Fire Engine (repros in green and blue glass)

Others are possible. If in doubt, *do not buy* without a guarantee from the dealer and a return privilege in writing.

Our advisor for glass containers is Jeff Bradfield; he is listed in the Directory under Virginia. You may contact him with questions, if you will include an SASE. For more information we recommend *The Collector's Guide to Candy Containers* by Doug Dezso and Leon and Rose Poirier (Collector Books). See Clubs, Newsletters, and Catalogs for the address of the Candy Container Collectors of America. A bimonthly newsletter offers insight into new finds, reproductions, updates, and articles from over four hundred collectors and members, including all authors of books on candy containers. Dues is $18.00 yearly. The club holds an annual convention in June in Reading, Pennsylvania, for collectors of candy containers.

'L' numbers used in this guide refer to a standard reference series, *An Album of Candy Containers*, Vols 1 and 2, by Jennie Long. 'E&A' numbers correlate with *The Compleat American Glass Candy Containers Handbook* by Eikelberner and Agadjanian, revised by Adele Bowden. Values are given for undamaged examples with original paint and metal parts when applicable or unless noted otherwise. Repaired pieces (often repainted) are worth only a small fraction of one that is perfect. The symbol (+) at the end of some of the following lines was used to indicate items that have been reproduced.

Advice on papier-mache and composition candy containers comes from Jenny Tarrant; she is listed in the Directory under Maryland. See also Christmas; Halloween.

Alarm Clock, L #118 (E&A #161) 270.00
Apothecary Bottle #1, L #62 ....24.00
Apothecary Jar, L #450 ....75.00
Apothecary Lamp Base, L #558 (E&A #369) 40.00
Baby Chick, standing, G pnt, L #6 (E&A #145) 110.00
Barney Google on Pedestal, L #78 (E&A #72) 240.00
Baseball, frosted glass, w/o decals, L#222 (E&A #76b) 30.00
Baseball Player w/Bat, pnt traces, L #80 (E&A #77) 600.00
Bear, sitting, L #454 ....125.00
Bear in Auto, L #2 (E&A #84) 200.00
Big Shoe Circus Boxes, Elephant, Pat July 4, 1911, L #660 ....75.00
Boy Wearing Cap (Kayo), L #522 ....24.00
Cannon, all glass, L #538 ....360.00
Cannon, cobalt bbl, L #534 (E&A #122) 550.00
Cannon #2, 2 wheels, 6-spoke, L #138 (E&A #124) 500.00
Cash Register, fancy scroll design, L #614, rare 540.00
Cat, glass head, L #470 ....20.00
Chicken, rnd base, sm, L #474 (similar to E&A #146) 375.00
Chicken on Oblong Basket, L #10 (E&A #147) 60.00
Christmas Lamp, L #206 (E&A #368) 900.00
Circus Dog, w/hat, L #478 ....30.00
Circus Wagon, L #664 ....125.00
Clock, oval, clear glass, L #114 (E&A #62) (+) 120.00
Clock, oval, pnt milk glass, L #114 (E&A #62) (+) 210.00
Comic Characters, 3-pc set, L #530 ....300.00
Crystal Palace, L #517 (E&A #175) 200.00
Decorations, L #652 ....75.00
Defense Field Gun, L #142 (E&A #128) 360.00
Dog w/Glass Hat, lg, L #22 (E&A #182) 24.00
Dolly's Milk Bottle, L #66 (E&A #527) 48.00
Don't Park Here #2, L #589 (E&A #196-1) 270.00
Duck, blown, L #490 ....120.00
Duck on Rnd base, L #26 (E&A #200) 300.00
Duckling, G pnt, L #30 (E&A #197) 120.00
Felix by Barrel, EX pnt, L #86 (E&A #211) 720.00
Fish, L #34 ....400.00
Flossie Fisher Side Board, L #130 (E&A #237) 700.00

Goblin Head, EX pnt, L #162 (E&A #242) 480.00
Grocery Truck, L #458 (E&A #783) 700.00
Gun, Cambridge Automatic; L #542 (E&A #260) 175.00
Gun, Large; L #146 (E&A #269-B 24.00
Gun, Millstein's Plastic; L #154 (E&A #261) 35.00
Hand Bell, wooden hdl, L #494 ....250.00
Hat, w/tin brim, w/closure, L #166 (E&A #301) 100.00
Hat, w/tin brim, w/o closure, L #166 (E&A #301) 75.00
Horn, red tubes, L #620 ....24.00
Horn, striped tubes, L #618 (E&A #309) 24.00
Hot Doggie, L #14 (E&A #320) 600.00
Independence Hall, L #74 (E&A #342) (+) 360.00
Jack-O-Lantern Black Cat, L #158 (E&A #349-1) 540.00
Jackie Coogan #1, G pnt, L #90 (E&A #345) (+) 1,200.00
Kiddie's Breakfast Bell, L #18 (E&A #192) 30.00
Lamp, Mini Kerosene; Eagle Trademark, tall base, recent, L #566 ...10.00
Lamp, Mini Kerosene; Mail Box w/box, recent, L #562 ....10.00
Lamp, monkey, L #214 (E&A #533) 225.00
Lamp, ringed base, L #210 (E&A #374) 250.00
Lamp, tin top, L #462 ....40.00
Lantern, barn type #2, L #178 (E&A #427-B) 75.00
Lantern, Crossette-Ribbed base, L #198 (E&A #394-G) 18.00
Lantern, Dec 20, '04, L #174 (E&A #399) 30.00
Lantern, fancy trim, L #190 ....30.00
Lantern, Little Ball-Signal; clear globe, L #182 (E&A #439) 30.00
Lantern, oval panels, L #570 ....25.00
Lantern, Stough's #1, L #194 (E&A #447), lg 18.00
Lantern, twins on anchor, L #186 (E&A #385) 25.00
Lantern, w/tassels, L #574 ....36.00
Liberty Bell, pewter top, L #499 (E&A #86) 90.00
Locmotive, Stough's #3, L #426 (E&A #488) 24.00
Locomotive, dbl windows, L #414 (E&A #497) 90.00
Locomotive 888, Jeannette Glass, orig wheels, L #418 (E&A #483) (+) ..150.00
Locomotive 888, Victory Glass Co #3, L #422 (E&A #482) (+) ..20.00
Military Hat, w/closure, L #170 (E&A #131) 30.00

Miniature Battleship, E&A #97, L #338, 5½" long, $25.00.

Mounted Policeman, 90% pnt, L #551, very rare 3,000.00
Mule Pulling Barrel, L #38 (E&A #539) (+) 85.00
Naked Child, Victory Glass, L #94 (E&A #546) 40.00
Nurser Bottle, rnd, L #70 (E&A #549) 24.00
Planetorium, L #518 ....360.00
Rabbit, begging, pnt on head, L #50 (E&A #611) 90.00
Rabbit, extended hooked paws, L #486 (E&A #619) 240.00
Rabbit, Stough's, L #54 (E&A #617) (+) 42.00
Rabbit in Eggshell, orig pnt & lid, L #48 (E&A #608) 90.00
Rabbit on Dome, pnt on rabbit, L #46 (E&A #607) 360.00
Race Car w/driver, w/closure, L #430 (E&A #641b) 125.00
Rocking Horse #1, orig in clear only, L #58 (E&A 651) (+) 360.00
Rocking Settee, L #134 (E&A #653) 400.00
Santa Claus, leaving chimney, L #102 (E&A #673) 90.00
Santa Claus, panelled coat, L #98 (E&A #670) 150.00
Skookum, L #106 (E&A #681) 250.00
Squirrel on Tree Trunk, L #466 (E&A #699-1) 3,000.00
Statue of Liberty, bank slotted closure, L #526 ....3,000.00
Statue of Liberty, L #110 (E&A #700) 1,750.00

Suitcase, milk glass, bear decals, L #636 (E&A #707a) 175.00
Tank, WWI, L #434 (E&A #721) 120.00
Tank, 2-gun, L #438 (E&A #723) 24.00
Telephone, Bell & Crank #2, L #578 ....250.00
Telephone, desk type, tin, L #582 ....75.00
Telephone, flat-top hinge, wood receiver, L-301 (E&A #737c) ...50.00
Telephone, Kiddies Phone, L #586 ....24.00
Telescope, magnifying lens, L #632 (E&A #438) 180.00
Toy Town Dairy, L #656 (E&A #529) 90.00
Trunk, clear glass, L #219 (E&A #789) 110.00
Trunk, Laundry; L #606 (E&A #785) 700.00
Victor Opera Glasses, w/o box, L #624 (E&A #560) 360.00
Victor Opera Glasses, w/orig box, L #624 (E&A #560) 500.00
Wagon, tin, L #442 (E&A #820) 150.00
Watch, w/fob, L #122 (E&A #823) 420.00
Watch, w/o fob, L #122 (E&A #923) 275.00
Well-Oaken Bucket, amethystine, metal closure, L #237 (E&A #331) ..80.00
Wheelbarrow, lg wheel, L #610 (E&A #832) 140.00
Windmill, screw-on closure, L #446 (E&A #844) 275.00

Papier-Mache, Composition

Chick baby roly poly on wheels, 5", EX 215.00
Chicken & basket, EX pnt, Germany, sm 65.00
Clown rabbit, opens at neck, 6", EX 435.00
Duck emerging from egg, glass eyes, 4", EX 435.00
Football, Germany, ca 1910, 2½x3½", EX 85.00

Goose, wings lift, cotton batting over cardboard, 5¼", EX, $75.00 to $100.00.

Humpty Dumpty, mc, 5" 275.00
Rabbit, felt-covered, glass eyes, Germany, 10½", EX 200.00
Rabbit, felt-covered, glass eyes, 10¾", VG 145.00
Rabbit, full-bodied, glass eyes, flocked coat, 10", VG 200.00
Rabbit lady, glass eyes, 8", EX 345.00
Rabbit on carrot zeppelin, Japan, 5" 175.00
Rabbit on cb candy box, holds paper accordion, Germany, 9", EX ..330.00
Rabbit pulling wagon, glass eyes, Germany, rpr, 11", VG 100.00
Rabbit seated, Reutter label, 14", EX 325.00
Rooster, pewter ft, orig mc pnt, Germany, rprs, 6½" 195.00
Turkey, HP, wht metal ft, glass eyes, rpr, 15" 550.00
2 chickens, wood/papier-mache/cb, orig pnt, Germany, 3½" 145.00

Canes

Fancy canes and walking sticks were once the mark of a gentleman. Hand-carved examples are collected and admired as folk art from the past. The glass canes that never could have been practical are unique whimseys of the glass-blower's profession. Gadget and container sticks, which were produced in a wide variety, are highly desirable. Character, political, and novelty types are also sought after as are those with handles made of precious metals.

For more information we recommend *American Folk Art Canes, Personal Sculpture,* by George H. Meyer, Sandringham Press, 100 West Long Lake Rd., Suite 100, Bloomfield Hills, MI 48304. Other possible references are *Canes in the United States* by Catherine Dike and *Canes From the 17th – 20th Century* by Jeffrey Snyder. Our advisor for this category is Bruce Thalberg.

Bamboo root hdl opens to cigarette tube, Pat...1887 ....400.00
Boar's tooth hdl, rosewood shaft w/ivory dmn inlay, 1890s 300.00
Bone, hand w/rod, str wood shaft, brass collar, VG 480.00
Bone segmets cvd as bamboo, 12" wood as shaft base, 1890s 225.00
Gold filled, sm shepherd's crook, rosewood shaft, lady's 400.00
Hardwood, 1-pc, cvd snake/Verdon/1914-19, pistol grip hdl 120.00
Harmonica below rnd knob hdl, brass ferrule, 1900s, 36" 900.00
Horn, leaping frog T-style hdl, bamboo shaft w/brass collar 270.00
Horn, whistle in hoof hdl; trn cane shaft, pnt ferrule, VG 300.00
Ivory, brass & rosewood spy glass hdl, ebony shaft, 1890s 750.00
Ivory, horse head hdl, sterling collar, wood shaft 900.00
Ivory, Indian face hdl, wooden shaft w/cvd faces & bark 195.00
Ivory, lady's leg hdl, horn ferrule, malacca shaft 725.00
Malacca shaft opens/holds Toledo sword, horn ferrule, 1840s 500.00
Mechanical, hardwood shaft pcs: pen/pencil/ink pot, 1900s 325.00
Mechanical, 4-part: 2 dip pens/pencil/cap w/1904 Stanhope 850.00
Parade, brass finial opens/removes flag, hollow wood shaft 725.00
Pewter Anheuser-Busch eagle-head hdl, hardwood shaft, 1900s ..425.00
Porc hdl w/HP scenes, zebra wood shaft, Fr, 1880s 800.00
Rhino horn, dog w/glass eyes hdl, silver collor, wood shaft 400.00
Russian silver w/HP floral 1¼" dia hdl, ebony shaft 725.00
Staghorn, alligator bites Blk boy L-hdl, bark-on-wood shaft 1,550.00
Staghorn, grotesque comic face, metal collar, str wood shaft 210.00
Staghorn, skull-in-hand hdl, brass collar, hardwood shaft 1,500.00
Sterling, whippet head hdl w/glass eyes, brass ferrule, 1900s 600.00
Sterling knob w/hammered decor, metal ferrule, maple shaft 275.00
Sterling top screws open, hollow shaft w/14" glass flask 225.00
Walrus ivory, lady w/flowing hair, silver collar, wood shaft 375.00
Whale ivory crook, oak shaft w/brass ferrule, 1870s 275.00
Whale ivory w/baleen inlay/spacers, slim wood shaft, 1840s 880.00
Wood, bearded man's face hdl, silver collar, 1-pc, ca 1850 ....120.00
Wood, bearded man w/long hair, heavy shaft, 1-pc, G 90.00
Wood, Blk man's face w/ivory teeth hdl, natural wood, 1-pc 775.00
Wood, cvd hand holds baton hdl, 1-pc, spike ferrule, G 400.00
Wood, cvd hand w/metal fingernails, OH, 35" 195.00
Wood, cvd railroad theme allover, bone ferrule, 19th C 550.00
Wood, cvd wood snake, ball knob, brass ferrule, 1870s 150.00
Wood, cvd 2-tone animals/snakes/horseshoe/7 faces, 34" 385.00
Wood, dog's head hdl, crooked pnt shaft, G 100.00
Wood, knob hdl, 2 entwined snakes form shaft, scuffs, G 130.00
Wood, man's face w/skull cap hdl, natural, 1-pc, VG 95.00
Wood, plain hdl, cvd centipede on shaft, bark chipped, G 65.00
Wood, pnt cow's head w/inlay eyes/horns, natural shaft 625.00
Wood, reclining nude 5-style hdl, natural shaft, 1-pc, Am, VG ...1,450.00
Wood, vine & leaf cvg, brass ferrule, knot hdl, VG 55.00
Wood, well-dressed lady hdl, snake & frog on shaft, Am 575.00
Wood, 1-pc w/compass below gold-plated hinged lid, 1860s 350.00

Canton

Canton is a blue and white porcelain that was first exported in the 1790s by clipper ships from China to the United States, a practice that continued into the 1920s. Canton became very popular along the East Coast where the major ports were located. Its popularity was due to several factors: it was readily available, inexpensive, and (due to the fact that it came in many different forms) appealing to the housewife.

The porcelain's blue and white color and simple motif (teahouse, trees, bridge, and a rain-cloud border) have made it a favorite of people who collect early American furniture and accessories. Buyers of Canton should shop at large outdoor shows and up-scale antique shows. Collections are regularly sold at auction. Collectors usually prefer a rich, deep tone rather than a lighter blue. Cracks, large chips, and major repairs will substantially affect values. Prices of Canton have escalated sharply over the last twenty years, and rare forms are highly sought after by advanced collectors. Our advisor for this category is Hobart D. Van Deusen; he is listed in the Directory under Connecticut.

Basket, fruit; rtcl, w/mismatched undertray, 4½x11x9¾" **635.00**
Basket, fruit; rtcl, w/undertray, 4¾x11" **950.00**
Bidet, 19th C, 24" **800.00**
Bowl, fruit; ftd, cut corners, 9½" sq, EX **850.00**
Bowl, oyster; river scenic, berry finial, twisted hdls, 6¼" **200.00**
Bowl, river landscape, multi-borders, molded oval, 11x8½" **440.00**
Bowl, rtcl, w/8¾" undertray, 19th C **500.00**
Bowl, scalloped rim, 3x11", EX **425.00**
Bowl, vegetable; river landscape lid/berry finial, 8¼x7¼" **440.00**

Platter, 18" long, EX, $460.00.

Platter, canted corners, early 1800s, 20", NM **1,000.00**
Platter, well & tree, ft rpr, 17¼" **520.00**
Platter, well & tree, rain & cloud border, ftd, 14½x11" **770.00**
Platter, 19th C, 17⅜x14⅛" **880.00**
Punch bowl, river scene, rain & cloud border, 4x11½" **1,300.00**
Sugar bowl, berry finial, dbl twisted hdls, 19th C, 5" **225.00**
Teapot, rain cloud border **450.00**
Tile, river scene, octagonal, 1800s, 6⅛x6⅛" **425.00**
Tile, 6x6" sq **400.00**
Tureen, w/lid, 10¾" **900.00**

CapoDiMonte

In 1738 King Charles of Naples and the two Sicilies married the Princess Maria Amelia Christina of Saxony, the thirteen-year-old granddaughter of Agustus the Strong of Saxony, who was the founder of Meissen, the first porcelain factory in Europe. King Charles was so impressed by the beauty of the fine porcelain in her dowry, that he started a factory in 1743 on the grounds of the Royal Palace which stood on a hill overlooking Naples, Italy. He named his porcelain 'Capodimonte' which means 'top of the mountain.' The style was copied by Meissen, Dresden, Samson, and many others. The pieces available in today's marketplace are generally marked by a blue crown N (BCN). Twenty-two factories to this date in Italy alone still manufacture Capodimonte, the better known Porcellane Principe of Vicenza and Richord Ginori of Florence, the latter marked with crest and wreaths under a blue crown with R. Capodimonte. The style has also been called Doccia, Ginori, and Royal Naples.

As more collectors recognize and appreciate the quality of the older ware, buyer demand drives prices higher. Our advisor for this category is James Highfield; he is listed in the Directory under Indiana.

Ashtray, playful putti, R Capodimonte, 6" dia **35.00**
Bell, cherubs working in field, brn Crown C mk, 6" **45.00**
Box, Bacchic banqueting scene, BCN, 8¾x6¾" **1,725.00**
Box, cherubs/grape harvesting, BCN France, 3x3½" sq **140.00**
Box, couple reclining in landscape, BCN, 2x3½x2¾" **300.00**
Figurine, Harlequin, blk mask on base, BCN, recent, 5" **50.00**
Figurine, peasant man & lady, BCN, post WWII, 6½", pr **250.00**
Figurine group, Royal Carriage, 2 horses, BCN, 4x12" **250.00**
Plate, bathing river scene, cherub border, BCN, 9¼" dia **190.00**
Shield, ornate battle scene, figural & armor border, 23x17" **1,000.00**
Shoe, high-heeled pump w/cherub relief, blk Crown N mk, 5x6" ..**60.00**
Stein, battle scene, hinged helmet lid, BCN mk, 10½x5" dia **900.00**
Stein, drunken Bacchus carried by Pan, cherub finial, BCN mk ..**1,050.00**
Stein, religious figures scene, cherub lid, 1-liter, 11½" **1,039.00**
Tureen, figural ped, winged female hdls, BCN mk **900.00**
Urn, cherubs, ram-face hdls, w/lid, BCN Saxony, 10½" **300.00**
Urn, gods & goddesses in procession, baluster, BCN mk, 36" ..**3,500.00**
Vase, palace scenes, bl Crown C mk, 14", pr **1,250.00**

Carlton Ware

Carlton Ware was the product of Wiltshaw and Robinson, who operated in the Staffordshire district of England from about 1890. During the 1920s, they produced ornamental ware with enameled and gilded decorations such as flowers and birds, often on a black background. In 1958 the firm was renamed Carlton Ware Ltd. Their trademark was a crown over a circular stamp with 'W & R, Stoke on Trent' surrounding a swallow. 'Carlton Ware' was sometimes added by hand.

Biscuit barrel, Blush Ware, floral, SP lid & bail, 6¼" **225.00**
Bowl, coralbells on shell form w/cobalt/gold, pre-1921, 3x9¾" ..**270.00**
Bowl, Rouge Royale lustre, exotic birds & trees, 1¾x7½" **145.00**
Cheese dish, heather **325.00**
Cup & saucer, demi; wading birds, burgundy lustre w/gold **85.00**
Ginger jar, mc Oriental scenes on bl, mk, 10⅜x7¾" **695.00**
Jar, bl satin w/mc leafy branches & flowers, w/lid, 8¼x3¼" **395.00**
Mug, pilgrim hanging from gallows/poem about drinking **55.00**
Vase, blk w/boat scene on orange band w/gold, 6x3½" **165.00**
Vase, flowers on paneled fan w/gold on red ground, 7½" **925.00**
Vase, landscape on bl lustre w/gold, MOP int, mk, 6x3½" **450.00**
Vase, Persian ruler & servant scenes on bl, mk, 10½", pr **895.00**

Carnival Collectibles

Carnival items from the early part of this century represent the lighter side of an America that was alternately prospering and sophisticated or devastated by war and domestic conflict. But whatever the country's condition, the carnival's thrilling rides and shooting galleries were a sure way of letting it all go by — at least for an evening.

For further information on chalkware figures, we recommend *The Carnival Chalk Prize* by Thomas G. Morris, who is listed in the Directory under Oregon. Our advisors for shooting gallery targets are Richard and Valerie Tucker; their address is listed in the Directory under Texas.

Chalkware figure, Bell Hop, HP, mk 1934, 11½" **45.00**
Chalkware figure, Buddy Lee, pk chalk, unmk, 1920s, 13½" **90.00**
Chalkware figure, Captain Marvel, unmk, 1940-50, 14½" **95.00**
Chalkware figure, clown bank, ca 1940-50, 12" **50.00**

Chalkware figure, Donald Duck, 1934-50, 14" 85.00
Chalkware figure, Felix the Cat, ca 1922, rare, 12½" 230.00
Chalkware figure, Ferdinand the Bull, mk Liza, 1940s, 8½" 45.00
Chalkware figure, Hula Hula Girl, unmk, ca 1940-50, 16" 65.00
Chalkware figure, I Love Me Girl, HP, mohair wig, 11¼" 95.00
Chalkware figure, Kewpie-type Devil, unmk, 6½" 55.00
Chalkware figure, Lone Ranger & Silver, mk LR, 13¼" 80.00
Chalkware figure, Mae West, c Rainwater, 10½" 75.00
Chalkware figure, Majorette, JT Gittins, 1941, 10½" 40.00
Chalkware figure, Miss America, mk on base, 15¾" 65.00
Chalkware figure, Oriental lady bust, unmk, 5½" 40.00
Chalkware figure, Paul Revere, unmk, ca 1935-45, 14½" 40.00
Chalkware figure, sailor girl, unmk, 1930-40, 12¾" 45.00

Chalkware figure, Snow White, blue dress with gold glitter trim, 1940-50, 14½", M, $85.00.

Photo courtesy Tom Morris

Chalkware figure, Snow White, unmk, ca 1937-50, 15" 85.00
Chalkware figure, Tomboy, girl in pants, 1940, #1571, 14½" 45.00
Chalkware figure, Uncle Sam, unmk, 1935-45, 15" 85.00

Shooting Gallery Targets

Battleship, CI/worn wht pnt, Mangels, 6¼x11⅜", $200 to 300.00
Birds (8) on bar, CI/worn pnt, Mangels, 1½x41½", $700 to 800.00
Bull's-eye/pop-up duck, pnt CI, Quackenbush, 2¼x4", $300 to ..400.00
Cat w/bull's-eye, CI/worn pnt, Wurfflein, 14¼x19", minimum ..1000.00
Clown (Harlequin), CI/worn mc pnt, Hoffman, 20½", minimum ...1000.00
Dog, running, CI/worn pnt, AJ Smith, 6x11x⅜", $100 to 200.00
Duck, feather details, CI/red pnt, Parker, 3¾x5½", $100 to 200.00
Duck, feather details, CI/worn pnt, Evans, 5½x8½"', 100 to 200.00
Eagle, wings wide, CI/worn pnt, AJ Smith, 14¾x11x6", $500 to..600.00
Greyhound, running, CI/old patina, Parker, 12¾x26", minimum..1000.00
Monkey, standing, CI/old worn pant, 9¾x8½"x4¾", $300 to 400.00
Owl w/bull's-eye, CI/pnt traces, Evans, 10¾", $500 to................600.00
Pipe, CI/old patina, AJ Smith, 5⅜x1¾x⅜", under 50.00
Rabbit, running, CI/old patina, Parker, 12x25¼", minimum.....1000.00
Rabbit, standing, CI/worn pnt, AJ Smith, 18x10x8½", $900 to ..1000.00
Reindeer (elk), CI/worn pnt over wht, 10x9x6½", $300 to 400.00
Sabre-tooth tiger, CI/old patina, Mangels, 7¾x13", $500 to 600.00
Soldier, Hessian w/rifle, CI/pnt traces, Mueller, 9x5", $100 to 200.00
Squirrel, running, CI/old patina, Smith, 5⅛x9¼", $100 to 200.00
Star spinner, dbl; CI/worn pnt, Magnels, 8x2¾", $100 to...........200.00
Swan, CI/worn wht pnt, Mueller, 5¾x5⅜", $200 to....................300.00

Carnival Glass

Carnival glass is pressed glass that has been coated with a sodium solution and fired to give it an exterior lustre. First made in America in 1905, it was produced until the late 1920s and had great popularity in the average American household; for unlike the costly art glass produced by Tiffany, carnival glass could be mass produced at a small cost. Colors most often found are marigold, green, blue, and purple; but others exist in lesser quantities and include white, clear, red, aqua opalescent, peach opalescent, ice blue, ice green, amber, lavender, and smoke.

Companies mainly responsible for its production in America include the Fenton Art Glass Company, Williamstown, West Virginia; the Northwood Glass Company, Wheeling, West Virginia; the Imperial Glass Company, Bellaire, Ohio; the Millersburg Glass Company, Millersburg, Ohio; and the Dugan Glass Company (Diamond Glass), Indiana, Pennsylvania. In addition to these major manufacturers, lesser producers included the U.S. Glass Company, the Cambridge Glass Company, the Westmoreland Glass Company, and the McKee Glass Company.

Carnival glass has been highly collectible since the 1950s and has been reproduced for the last twenty-five years. Several national and state collectors' organizations exist, and many fine books are available on old carnival glass, including *The Standard Encyclopedia of Carnival Glass* by Bill Edwards.

Acorn (Fenton), plate, amethyst, scarce, 9" 600.00
Acorn Burrs (Northwood), punch cup, bl 75.00
Acorn Burrs (Northwood), tumbler, gr 100.00
Amaryllis (Northwood), compote, bl, sm 275.00
Apple & Pear Intaglio (Northwood), bowl, marigold, 10" 115.00
Apple Blossoms (Dugan), plate, amethyst, 8¼" 275.00
Apple Tree (Fenton), pitcher, water; bl 500.00
April Showers (Fenton), vase, pastel colors 200.00
Art Deco (English), bowl, marigold, 4" 38.00
Asters, bowl, marigold 60.00
Aurora Pearls, bowl, amethyst, w/decor, 2 szs, ea 700.00
Australian Panels (Crystal), creamer, amethyst 70.00
Australian Swan (Crystal), bowl, marigold, 5" 170.00
Baker's Rosette, ornament, amethyst 90.00
Ballard-Merced CA (Northwood), bowl, amethyst 950.00
Balloons (Imperial), vase, marigold, 3 szs, ea 75.00
Band of Roses, tumbler, marigold 150.00
Banded Drape (Fenton), tumbler, wht 95.00
Banded Portland (US Glass), puff jar, marigold 80.00
Beaded, hatpin, amethyst 45.00
Beaded Band & Octagon, lamp, kerosene; marigold 250.00
Beaded Cable (Northwood), candy dish, gr 80.00
Beaded Shell (Dugan), mug whimsey, amethyst 450.00
Beaded Stars (Fenton), bowl, marigold 40.00
Beaded Swirl (English), pitcher, milk; bl 90.00
Beads (Northwood), bowl, gr, 8½" 70.00
Bells & Beads (Dugan), bowl, gr, 7½" 115.00
Big Basketweave (Dugan), vase, peach opal, 6" 140.00
Bird w/Grapes, vase, wall; marigold 75.00
Birds & Cherries (Fenton), bonbon, gr 65.00
Blackberry Bramble (Fenton), bowl, bl 60.00
Blackberry Miniature (Fenton), compote, gr, sm 200.00
Blackberry Rays, compote, amethyst 350.00
Blackberry Wreath (Millersburg), plate, marigold, rare, 6" 2,250.00
Blossom & Palm (Northwood), bowl, amethyst, 9" 65.00
Boggy Bayou (Fenton), vase, bl, 15" 160.00
Border Plants (Dugan), bowl, peach opal, flat, 8½" 180.00
Bouquet (Fenton), pitcher, bl 550.00
Briar Patch, hat, amethyst 50.00
Brocker's (Northwood), plate, advertising; amethyst 1,700.00
Broken Arches (Imperial), punch bowl, marigold, w/base 365.00
Bull's Eye & Leaves (Northwood), bowl, gr, 8½" 50.00
Butterflies (Fenton), bonbon, bl 65.00
Butterflies & Waratah (Crystal), compote, amethyst, lg 300.00
Butterfly (Fenton), ornament, gr, rare 225.00

Butterfly (Northwood), bonbon, amethyst, ribbed exterior 250.00
Butterfly & Berry (Fenton), sugar bowl, amethyst, w/lid 160.00
Butterfly & Fern (Fenton), pitcher, marigold 395.00
Butterfly & Tulip (Dugan), bowl, amethyst, whimsey shape, rare ..1,500.00
Buttermilk, Plain (Fenton), goblet, gr 80.00
Buzz Saw (Cambridge), cruet, marigold, lg, rare, 6" 550.00
Captive Rose (Fenton), bonbon, bl 85.00
Captive Rose (Fenton), plate, amethyst, 9" 410.00
Captive Rose (Fenton), plate, marigold, 7" 140.00
Carolina Dogwood (Westmoreland), bowl, amethyst, 8½" 110.00
Cartwheel #411 (Heisey), compote, marigold 50.00
Cathedral (Sweden), compote, bl, 2 szs, ea 80.00
Chain & Star (Fostoria), tumbler, marigold, rare 900.00
Checkerboard (Westmoreland), tumbler, amethyst, rare 550.00
Cherry (Dugan), bowl, peach opal, ftd, 8½" 400.00
Cherry (Millersburg), bowl, marigold, 4" 60.00
Cherry (Millersburg), butter dish, amethyst, w/lid 375.00
Cherry & Cable (Northwood), spooner, bl, rare 500.00
Cherry & Daisies (Fenton), banana boat, marigold 950.00
Cherry Blossoms, tumbler, bl 40.00
Cherry Chain (Fenton), bowl, gr, 10" 90.00
Chrysanthemum (Fenton), bowl, bl, ftd, 10" 220.00
Circle Scroll (Dugan), tumbler, marigold, rare 400.00
Cluster of Grapes, hatpin, amethyst 250.00
Cobblestones (Imperial), bonbon, gr 70.00
Coin Dot (Fenton), basket whimsey, marigold, rare 75.00
Coin Dot (Fenton), plate, amethyst, rare, 9" 250.00
Coin Dot Vt (Westmoreland), bowl, rose; gr 60.00
Colonial (Imperial), toothpick holder, amethyst 110.00
Coral (Fenton), bowl, marigold, 9" 200.00
Corinth (Westmoreland), vase, peach opal 150.00
Corona, hatpin, amethyst 175.00
Cosmos (Millersburg), bowl, gr, 5" 70.00
Country Kitchen (Millersburg), creamer, gr 800.00
CR (Argentina), ashtray, marigold 90.00
Crab Claw (Imperial), bowl, amethyst, 10" 65.00
Crackle (Imperial), candy jar, marigold, w/lid 30.00
Crackle (Imperial), plate, amethyst 55.00
Crystal Cut (Crystal), compote, marigold 75.00
Cut Arcs (Fenton), compote, amethyst 60.00
Cut Sprays, vase, peach opal, 9" 75.00
Dahlia (Dugan), butter dish, marigold 120.00
Dahlia (Dugan), pitcher, amethyst, rare 950.00
Daisy (Fenton), bonbon, bl, scarce 300.00
Daisy Block (English), rowboat, marigold, scarce 250.00
Daisy Squares, rose bowl, gr 675.00
Dandelion (Northwood), mug, marigold 500.00
Deep Grape (Millersburg), compote, bl, rare 3,000.00
Diamond & Daisy Cut (US Glass), compote, bl 75.00

Diamond Band (Crystal), float set, amethyst 550.00
Diamond Checkerboard, butter dish, marigold 90.00
Diamond Flutes (US Glass), creamer, marigold 45.00
Diamond Point, basket, bl, rare 2,300.00
Diamonds (Millersburg), tumbler, gr 85.00
Dogwood Sprays (Dugan), bowl, peach opal, 9" 370.00
Dotted Daisies, plate, marigold, 8" 90.00
Double Diamonds, puff box, marigold 50.00
Double Dutch (Imperial), bowl, marigold, ftd, 9" 50.00
Double Scroll (Imperial), candlesticks, gr, pr 80.00
Double Star (Cambridge), pitcher, amethyst, scarce 650.00
Double Stem Rose (Dugan), bowl, gr, dome base, 8½" 115.00
Dragon's Tongue (Fenton), shade, peach opal 115.00
Dreibus Parfait Sweets (Northwood), plate, amethyst, hand-grip hdl, 6" ..550.00
Dugan Fan (Dugan), gravy boat, marigold, ftd 65.00
Dutch Mill, ashtray, marigold 65.00
Elephant, paperweight, marigold 1,250.00
Elks (Fenton), bowl, Detroit; amethyst, scarce 1,000.00
Elks (Fenton), plate, Atlantic City, gr, rare 1,800.00
Elks (Millersburg), paperweight, gr, rare 1,700.00
Enameled Panel, goblet, marigold 190.00
Engraved Floral (Fenton), tumbler, gr 95.00
Estate (Westmoreland), creamer, peach opal 90.00
Exchange Bank (Northwood), plate, amethyst, 6" 500.00
Fanciful (Dugan), plate, amethyst, 9" 550.00
Fancy Flowers (Imperial), compote, gr 175.00
Fashion (Imperial), bowl, gr, 9" 90.00
Fashion (Imperial), pitcher, marigold 250.00
Feather Stitch (Fenton), bowl, bl, 10" 80.00
Feathers (Northwood), vase, gr, 12" 95.00
Fentonia, bowl, bl, ftd, 9½" 70.00
Fentonia, tumbler, bl 75.00
Fern Panels (Fenton), hat, gr 60.00
Field Flower (Imperial), pitcher, milk; marigold, rare 180.00
File (Imperial & English), pitcher, amethyst, rare 445.00
Fine Cut & Roses (Northwood), rose bowl, bl, ftd 220.00
Fine Cut Rings (English), sugar bowl, marigold, stemmed 145.00
Fine Cut Rings Vt (English), cake stand, marigold, ftd 195.00
Fine Rib (Northwood, Fenton & Dugan), bowl, amethyst, 10" 60.00
Fine Rib (Northwood, Fenton & Dugan), vase, bl, 15" 80.00
Flannel Flower (Crystal), compote, amethyst, lg 155.00
Fleur-de-Lis (Millersburg), bowl, marigold, flat, 8½" 240.00
Flora (English), float bowl, bl 175.00
Floral & Grape (Dugan), pitcher, bl 270.00
Floral & Optic (Fenton), bowl, marigold, ftd, 10" 35.00
Floral & Wheat (Dugan), compote, amethyst 45.00
Flower & Beads, plate, amethyst, 6-sided, 7½" 115.00
Flowering Dill (Fenton), hat, marigold 40.00
Flute (Millersburg), bowl, marigold, 10" 65.00
Flute (Millersburg), vase, amethyst, rare 400.00
Flute (Northwood), sherbet, amethyst 50.00
Flute & Honeycomb (Millersburg), bowl, amethyst, rare, 5" 75.00
Flying Bat, hatpin, pastel colors, scarce 350.00
Footed Prism Panels (English), vase, bl 100.00
Forget-Me-Not (Fenton), pitcher, gr 300.00
Forget-Me-Not (Fenton), tumbler, amethyst 40.00
Four Flowers, plate, amethyst, 6½" 210.00
Four Flowers Vt, bowl, peach opal, on metal base, rare 300.00
Four Pillars (Northwood & Dugan), vase, bl 60.00
French Knots (Fenton), hat, bl 45.00
Frosted Block (Imperial), bowl, marigold, 9" 35.00
Frosted Block (Imperial), vase, smoke, 6" 100.00
Fruit & Flowers (Northwood), banana plate, amethyst, rare, 7" 350.00
Fruit & Flowers (Northwood), bowl, marigold, 9" 100.00

Photo courtesy Bill Edwards

**Diamond and Daisy Cut (U.S. Glass),
pitcher, amethyst, rare, $400.00.**

Fruit Basket (Millersburg), compote, amethyst, hdld, rare 1,950.00
Fruit Lustre, tumbler, marigold 40.00
Garden Mums (Northwood), bowl, bl, 10" 85.00
Garden Path Vt (Dugan), plate, peach opal, rare, 11" 3,300.00
God & Home (Dugan), tumbler, bl, rare 275.00
Goddess Athena, epergne, gr, rare 2,000.00
Golden Flowers, vase, marigold, 7½" 95.00
Golden Honeycomb (Imperial), plate, marigold, 7" 55.00
Graceful (Northwood), vase, gr 120.00
Grape, Heavy (Imperial), bowl, amethyst, 9" 265.00
Grape (Fenton's Grape & Cable), bowl, amethyst, ftd, 7¼" 115.00
Grape (Fenton's Grape & Cable), bowl, marigold, flat, 8" 50.00
Grape (Imperial), plate, bl, ruffled, 8½" 55.00
Grape (Northwood's Grape & Cable), candlesticks, gr, ea 210.00
Grape (Northwood's Grape & Cable), compote, amethyst, open ...375.00
Grape (Northwood's Grape & Cable), cup & saucer, marigold, rare ...400.00
Grape (Northwood's Grape & Cable), pin tray, gr 250.00
Grape (Northwood's Grape & Cable), plate, gr, ftd 110.00
Grape & Gothic Arches (Northwood), bowl, bl, 10" 80.00
Grape & Gothic Arches (Northwood), tumbler, pearl opal 170.00
Grape Wreath Multi-Star Vt, bowl, amethyst, 9" 90.00
Grape Wreath Multi-Star Vt, bowl, marigold, 5" 50.00
Grape Wreath Vt (Millersburg), bowl, gr, 7½" 80.00
Grapevine Lattice (Fenton), tumbler, bl, rare 95.00
Greek Key (Northwood), tumbler, amethyst, rare 295.00
Harvest Flower (Dugan), pitcher, marigold, rare 1,250.00
Harvest Poppy, compote, gr 400.00
Headdress, compote, gr 75.00
Hearts & Flowers (Northwood), bowl, gr, 8½" 750.00
Heavy Banded Diamonds (Crystal), bowl, amethyst, 9" 135.00
Heavy Hobnail (Fenton), vase, amethyst, rare 550.00
Heavy Prisms (English), celery vase, bl, 6" 95.00
Heisey Flute, punch cup, marigold 35.00
Heron (Dugan), mug, amethyst, rare 375.00
Hex Base, candlesticks, gr, pr 110.00
Hobnail (Millersburg), spooner, marigold, rare 275.00
Hobnail Soda Gold (Imperial), spittoon, gr, lg 75.00
Hobstar (Imperial), bowl, fruit; gr, w/base 75.00
Hobstar (Imperial), creamer, amethyst 85.00
Hobstar & Arches (Imperial), bowl, marigold, 9" 50.00
Hobstar & Feather (Millersburg), punch cup, bl, scarce 275.00
Hobstar & Fruit (Westmoreland), bowl, aqua opal, rare, 6" 300.00
Hobstar Flower (Northwood), compote, gr, scarce 270.00
Hobstar Reversed (English), butter dish, bl 70.00
Holly (Fenton), hat, amethyst 40.00
Holly & Berry (Dugan), nappy, bl 55.00
Holly Sprig or Whirl (Millersburg), bonbon, amethyst, plain 160.00
Holly Wreath Multi-Star Vt (Millersburg), bowl, gr, 7" 130.00
Honeycomb (Dugan), rose bowl, peach opal 250.00
Honeycomb Ornament, hatpin, amethyst 80.00
Horses' Heads (Fenton), rose bowl, bl, ftd 400.00
Humpty-Dumpty, mustard jar, marigold 75.00
Imperial #5 (Imperial), bowl, marigold, 8" 40.00
Imperial #9 (Imperial), compote, marigold 40.00
Intaglio Ovals (US Glass), bowl, aqua opal, 7" 70.00
Interior Flute, creamer, marigold 50.00
Interior Swirl, spittoon, peach opal 95.00
Inverted Coin Dot (Northwood-Fenton), pitcher, marigold 325.00
Inverted Feather (Cambridge), wine, marigold, rare 200.00
Inverted Strawberry, bowl, amethyst, 9" 300.00
Inverted Strawberry, celery dish, gr, rare 1,300.00
Inverted Thistle (Cambridge), tumbler, marigold, rare 425.00
Iris (Fenton), goblet, buttermilk; bl, scarce 160.00
Isaac Benesch, bowl, advertising; amethyst, 6½" 350.00

Jack-In-The-Pulpit (Dugan), vase, bl 80.00
Jacobean Ranger (Czech & English), wine, marigold 50.00
Jester's Cap (Westmoreland), vase, amethyst 275.00
Jeweled Heart (Dugan), bowl, peach opal, 10" 135.00
Jockey Club (Northwood), bowl, amethyst, 7" 600.00
Kangaroo (Australian), bowl, marigold, 5" 75.00
Keystone Colonial (Westmoreland), compote, amethyst, 6¼" ...295.00
Kittens (Fenton), bowl, bl, scarce, 4" 775.00
Kokomo (English), rose bowl, gr, ftd 60.00
Lacy Dewdrop (Westmoreland), banana boat, pastel colors 375.00
Late Enameled Strawberry, tumbler, marigold, tall 175.00

Lattice and Grape (Fenton), pitcher, marigold, $260.00; Tumbler, $38.00.

Photo courtesy Bill Edwards

Lattice (Dugan), bowl, amethyst, various szs, ea 70.00
Lattice & Leaves, vase, bl, 9½" 295.00
Lattice Heart (English), bowl, bl, 10" 70.00
Lattice Heart (English), compote, amethyst 90.00
Laurel Leaves (Imperial), plate, amethyst 55.00
Leaf & Beads (Northwood-Dugan), candy dish, amethyst, ftd 110.00
Leaf & Little Flowers (Millersburg), compote, gr, mini, rare 475.00
Leaf Swirl (Westmoreland), compote, amethyst 75.00
Lined Lattice (Dugan), vase, marigold, 5" 140.00
Little Flowers (Fenton), bowl, amethyst, rare, 5½" 80.00
Little Stars (Millersburg), bowl, bl, scarce, 7" 1,400.00
Loganberry (Imperial), vase, gr, scarce 395.00
Long Thumbprint (Dugan), vase, gr, 11" 40.00
Lotus & Grape (Fenton), bowl, gr, flat, 7" 55.00
Lovebirds, bottle, marigold, w/stopper 575.00
Lucille, tumbler, marigold, rare 750.00
Lustre & Clear (Fenton), vase, gr, fan shape 60.00
Lustre & Flute (Northwood), punch bowl, gr, w/base 150.00
Lustre Rose (Imperial), butter dish, marigold 60.00
Magpie (Australian), bowl, amethyst, 10" 560.00
Malaga (Dugan), bowl, marigold, scarce, 9" 160.00
Maple Leaf (Dugan), bowl, bl, stemmed, 4½" 30.00
Maple Leaf (Dugan), tumbler, amethyst 50.00
Marilyn (Millersburg), pitcher, marigold, rare 750.00
Mayan (Millersburg), bowl, gr, 10" 125.00
Maypole, vase, gr, 6¼" 60.00
Memphis (Northwood), bowl, amethyst, 10" 400.00
Mikado (Fenton), compote, bl, lg 400.00
Miniature Shell, candle holder, clear, ea 75.00
Mitered Diamond & Pleats (English), bowl, bl, 4½" 30.00
Mitered Ovals (Millersburg), vase, gr, rare 6,700.00
Moonprint (English), bowl, marigold, 8¼" 45.00
Morning Glory (Imperial), vase, funeral; gr 350.00
My Lady, powder jar, marigold, w/lid 150.00
Napoleon, bottle, pastel colors 85.00
Near Cut (Cambridge), decanter, gr, w/stopper, rare 3,500.00
Nesting Swan (Millersburg), rose bowl, marigold, rare 3,000.00
Nippon (Northwood), plate, bl, 9" 700.00
Northwood Jack-in-the-Pulpit, vase, bl, various szs, ea 50.00
Northwood's Poppy, bowl, peach opal, 7" 350.00

Nu-Art (Homestead) (Imperial), plate, bl, scarce 5,500.00
O'Hara (Loop), goblet, marigold 25.00
Octagon (Imperial), bowl, amethyst, 4½" 35.00
Octagon (Imperial), pitcher, milk; amethyst, scarce 200.00
Oklahoma (Mexican), tumbler, marigold, rare 500.00
Open Rose (Imperial), rose bowl, amethyst 60.00
Optic & Buttons (Imperial), bowl, marigold, 8" 30.00
Optic Flute (Imperial), bowl, amethyst, 10" 80.00
Orange Tree (Fenton), bowl, bl, ftd, 11" 130.00
Orange Tree (Fenton), powder jar, gr, w/lid 500.00
Orange Tree & Scroll (Fenton), pitcher, bl 900.00
Orange Tree Orchard (Fenton), tumbler, marigold 40.00
Oriental Poppy (Northwood), pitcher, marigold 500.00
Oval & Round (Imperial), bowl, gr, 4" 30.00
Oxford, mustard pot, marigold, w/lid 70.00
Palm Beach (US Glass), banana boat, marigold 100.00
Panelled Dandelion (Fenton), pitcher, gr 800.00
Panels & Ball (Fenton), bowl, wht, 11" 175.00
Pansy (Imperial), dresser tray, gr 80.00
Pansy (Imperial), plate, marigold, ruffled, rare 80.00
Panther (Fenton), bowl, marigold, ftd, 10" 135.00
Pastel Panels (Imperial), tumbler, pastel colors 75.00
Peach (Northwood), spooner, marigold 275.00
Peach Blossom, bowl, amethyst, 7½" 75.00
Peacock (Millersburg), bowl, gr, 5" 240.00
Peacock & Urn (Fenton), bowl, amethyst, 8½" 325.00
Peacock & Urn (Northwood), bowl, marigold, 5" 75.00
Peacock & Urn & Vts (Millersburg), bowl, amethyst, 9½" 400.00
Peacock at the Fountain (Northwood), punch bowl, marigold, w/base ..450.00
Peacock at the Fountain (Northwood), tumbler, gr 500.00
Peacock Tail (Fenton), plate, amethyst, 9" 225.00
Peacock Tail Vt (Millersburg), compote, marigold, scarce 90.00
Pebbles (Dugan), bowl, gr, 8" 55.00
Perfection (Millersburg), tumbler, gr, rare 650.00
Persian Garden (Dugan), plate, amethyst, rare, 6" 450.00
Petal Band, vase, compote; marigold, 6" 85.00
Petals (Dugan), banana bowl, amethyst 90.00
Pillar & Flute (Imperial), celery vase, amethyst 90.00
Pin-Ups (Australian), bowl, amethyst, rare, 8¾" 140.00
Pinched Swirl (Dugan), vase, marigold 90.00
Pineapple (English), bowl, bl, 7" 67.00
Plaid (Fenton), bowl, gr, 8¾" 350.00
Plain Petals (Northwood), nappy, gr, scarce 90.00
Plain Rays, bowl, amethyst, 9" 45.00
Poinsettia (Imperial), pitcher, milk; marigold 170.00
Poppy (Millersburg), compote, marigold, scarce 650.00
Poppy Show (Imperial), vase, amethyst, old only, 12" 3,500.00
Poppy Show (Northwood), plate, bl, rare, 9" 3,200.00
Premium (Imperial), candlesticks, red, pr 150.00
Primrose (Millersburg), bowl, ice cream; gr, scarce, 9" 190.00
Prism & Cane (English), bowl, amethyst, rare, 5" 65.00
Prism & Daisy Band (Imperial), bowl, marigold, 5" 18.00
Prism & Daisy Band (Imperial), sugar bowl, marigold 35.00
Prisms (Westmoreland), nappy, gr, hdld, rare 375.00
Pulled Loop (Dugan), vase, bl 110.00
Puzzle (Dugan), bonbon, peach opal, stemmed 100.00
Question Marks (Dugan), bonbon, amethyst 55.00
Radiance, tumbler, marigold 90.00
Rambler Rose (Dugan), tumbler, bl 45.00
Raspberry (Northwood), bowl, gr, 9" 75.00
Raspberry (Northwood), sauce boat, marigold, ftd 90.00
Rays & Ribbons (Millersburg), plate, marigold, rare 1,100.00
Regal Swirl, candlestick, marigold, ea 75.00
Rib & Panel, vase, peach opal 135.00

Ribbed Holly (Fenton), compote, amethyst 70.00
Ribbon Tie (Fenton), plate, bl, flat, 9½" 360.00
Rising Sun (US Glass), tumbler, marigold, rare 200.00
Robin (Imperial), tumbler, marigold, old only, scarce 60.00
Rococo (Imperial), vase, gr, 5½" 175.00
Rosalind (Millersburg), compote, jelly; gr, rare, 9" 2,000.00
Rose Bouquet, creamer, marigold 60.00
Rose Garden (Sweden), pitcher, communion; marigold, rare 600.00
Rose Garden (Sweden), rose bowl, bl, rare, lg 700.00
Rose Show Variant (Northwood), bowl, amethyst, 8¾" 750.00
Rose Tree (Fenton), bowl, bl, rare, 10" 1,200.00
Roses & Fruit (Millersburg), bonbon, gr, ftd, rare 1,100.00
Round-Up (Dugan), plate, amethyst, rare, 9" 225.00
Rustic (Fenton), vase, gr, various szs, ea 70.00
S-Repeat (Dugan), tumbler, marigold 300.00
Scale Band (Fenton), bowl, marigold, 6" 35.00
Scales (Westmoreland), bonbon, amethyst 48.00
Scroll & Flower Panels (Imperial), vase, bl, old only, 10" 150.00
Scroll Embossed (Imperial), compote, gr, sm 60.00
Scroll Embossed (Imperial), compote, marigold, lg 50.00
Seacoast (Millersburg), pin tray, clambroth, rare 900.00
Seaweed (Millersburg), bowl, marigold, rare, 5" 400.00
Shasta Daisy, pitcher, bl 495.00
Shell & Jewel (Westmoreland), creamer, amethyst, w/lid 65.00
Sheraton (US Glass), butter dish, pastel colors 130.00
Singing Birds (Northwood), mug, aqua opal 1,200.00
Singing Birds (Northwood), spooner, marigold 80.00
Single Flower (Dugan), bowl, pastel opal, 8" 80.00
Six Petals (Dugan), plate, marigold, rare 90.00
Ski-Star (Dugan), banana bowl, amethyst 125.00
Small Blackberry (Northwood), compote, marigold 50.00
Small Rib (Dugan), rose bowl, gr, stemmed 50.00
Smooth Panels (Imperial), pitcher, gr 175.00
Smooth Rays (Westmoreland), compote, gr 75.00
Soda Gold (Imperial), pitcher, marigold 240.00
Sowerby Flower Block (English), flower frog, marigold 60.00
Spearhead & Rib (Fenton's #916), vase, amethyst, 14" 250.00

Photo courtesy Bill Edwards

Split Diamond, butter dish, marigold, $65.00.

Springtime (Northwood), bowl, gr, 9" 250.00
Springtime (Northwood), tumbler, amethyst, rare 120.00
Square Diamond, vase, bl, rare 750.00
Stag & Holly (Fenton), plate, bl, ftd, 9" 1,800.00
Star & Fan (English), cordial set, marigold, 6-pc 1,500.00
Star & File (Imperial), vase, marigold, hdld 50.00
Star & Hobs (Northern Star), rose bowl, marigold, rare, 9" 250.00
Star Medallion (Imperial), celery tray, marigold 60.00
Star of David & Bows (Northwood), bowl, amethyst, 8½" 110.00
Star Spray (Imperial), bride's basket, smoke, complete, rare 125.00
Starburst, perfume, marigold, w/stopper 65.00
Starburst Lustre (Northwood), compote, gr 75.00
Stippled Mum (Northwood), bowl, amethyst, 9" 85.00

Stippled Rambler Rose (Dugan), bowl, nut; marigold, ftd **75.00**
Stippled Rays (Fenton), plate, amethyst, 7" **50.00**
Stippled Strawberry (Jenkins), bowl, amethyst, rare, 9" **200.00**
Stork & Rushes (Dugan), butter dish, marigold, rare **145.00**
Stork & Rushes (Dugan), cup, bl **35.00**
Strawberry, hatpin, gr **1,500.00**
Strawberry (Fenton), bonbon, amethyst **50.00**
Strawberry (Northwood), plate, bl, handgrip hdld, 7" **230.00**
Stream of Hearts (Fenton), bowl, marigold, ftd, 10" **80.00**
Style, bowl, amethyst, 8" **95.00**
Stylized Flower Center (Fenton), plate, gr **3,100.00**
Sunray, compote, amethyst **40.00**
Sweetheart (Cambridge), cookie jar, marigold, w/lid, rare **1,550.00**
Swirl (Imperial), mug, marigold, rare **90.00**
Swirl Hobnail (Millersburg), spittoon, amethyst, rare **750.00**
Sword & Circle, tumbler, marigold, rare **150.00**
Target (Fenton), vase, marigold, 11" **45.00**
Texas, tumbler, bl, giant sz **260.00**
Thin & Wide Rim (Northwood), vase, gr, ruffled **150.00**
Thistle (Fenton), compote, marigold **60.00**
Three Diamonds (Dugan), vase, bl, 10" **60.00**
Three Fruits (Northwood), plate, gr, rnd, 9" **475.00**
Three Row (Imperial), vase, amethyst, rare **1,200.00**
Thunderbird (Australian), bowl, marigold, 5" **60.00**
Tiger Lily (Imperial), tumbler, amethyst **60.00**
Top Hat, vase, pastel colors **50.00**
Top o' the Walk, hatpin, amethyst **200.00**
Tree Bark (Imperial), bowl, marigold, 7½" **20.00**
Tree Bark (Imperial), candy jar, marigold, w/lid **35.00**
Tree Bark Vt, planter, marigold **60.00**
Tree Trunk (Northwood), vase, bl, 12" **300.00**
Tufted Pillow, hatpin, amethyst **95.00**
Tulip Scroll (Millersburg), vase, amethyst, rare, 12" **400.00**
Twins (Imperial), bowl, gr, 9" **50.00**
Two Flowers (Fenton), bowl, amethyst, ftd, 8" **70.00**
Umbrella Prisms, hatpin, amethyst, sm **45.00**
Unshod, pitcher, marigold **85.00**
US Diamond Block (US Glass), compote, peach opal, rare **90.00**
Victorian, bowl, amethyst, rare, 12" **500.00**
Vineyard Harvest (Australian), tumbler, marigold, rare **250.00**
Vining Leaf & Vt (English), vase, gr, rare **350.00**
Vintage (Dugan), powder jar, bl, w/lid **150.00**
Vintage (Fenton), bowl, amethyst, 8" **45.00**
Vintage (Fenton), rose bowl, bl **60.00**
Vintage (Millersburg), bowl, amethyst, rare, 9" **900.00**
Vintage Banded (Dugan), mug, marigold **35.00**
Vintage Leaf (Fenton), bowl, amethyst, 7" **45.00**
Violet, basket, bl, either type **75.00**
Waffle Block (Imperial), basket, marigold, hdld, 10" **50.00**
Waffle Block & Hobstar (Imperial), basket, marigold **250.00**
War Dance (English), compote, marigold, 5" **120.00**
Water Lily & Cattails (Northwood), tumbler, amethyst **200.00**
Weeping Cherry (Dugan), bowl, peach opal, ftd **220.00**
Western Thistle, pitcher, cider; bl **350.00**
Wheels (Imperial), bowl, marigold, 9" **50.00**
Wide Panel Bouquet, basket, marigold, 3½" **75.00**
Wide Panel Shade, light shade, gr **175.00**
Wild Berry, jar, marigold, w/lid **250.00**
Wild Fern (Australian), compote, amethyst **240.00**
Wild Rose (Millersburg), lamp, gr, med sz **1,200.00**
Wild Strawberry (Northwood), plate, amethyst, rare, 9" **375.00**
Wildflower (Northwood), compote, gr, plain interior **350.00**
Windmill (Imperial), bowl, amethyst, 5" **25.00**
Wine & Roses (Fenton), wine, bl **95.00**

Wishbone (Northwood), epergne, wht, rare **1,700.00**
Wishbone & Spades (Dugan), plate, peach opal, rare, 10½" ...**1,350.00**
Woodlands, vase, marigold, rare, 5" **200.00**
Wreath of Roses (Fenton), punch bowl, gr, w/base **375.00**
Wreath of Roses Vt (Dugan), compote, marigold **55.00**
Wreathed Bleeding Hearts (Dugan), vase, marigold, 5¼" **110.00**
Wreathed Cherry (Dugan), bowl, amethyst, oval, 10½" **140.00**
Wreathed Cherry (Dugan), tumbler, wht **170.00**
Zig Zag (Fenton), pitcher, bl, w/decor, rare **450.00**
Zig Zag (Millersburg), card tray, gr, rare **900.00**
Zip Zip (English), flower frog holder, marigold **60.00**
474 (Imperial), bowl, gr, 9" **85.00**
474 (Imperial), pitcher, milk; marigold, scarce **225.00**
474 (Imperial), vase, gr, rare, 14" **1,100.00**

Carousel Figures

For generations of Americans, visions of carousel horses revolving majestically around lively band organs rekindle wonderful childhood experiences. These nostalgic memories are the legacy of the creative talent from a dozen carving shops that created America's carousel art. Skilled craftsmen brought their trade from Europe where American carvers took the carousel animal from a folk art creation to a true art form. The 'Golden Age of Carousel Art' lasted from 1880 to 1929.

There are two basic types of American carousels. The largest and most impressive is the 'park style' carousel built for permanent installation in major amusement centers. These were created in Philadelphia by Gustav and William Dentzel, Muller Brothers, and E. Joy Morris who became the Philadelphia Toboggan Company in 1902. A more flamboyant group of carousel animals was carved in Coney Island, New York, by Charles Looff, Marcus Illions, Charles Carmel, and Stein & Goldstein's Artistic Carousel Company. These park-style carousels were typically three, four, and even five rows with forty-five to sixty-eight animals on a platform. Collectors often pay a premium for the carvings by these men. The outside row animals are larger and more ornate and command higher prices. The horses on the inside rows are smaller, less decorated and of lesser value.

The most popular style of carousel art is the 'country fair style.' These carousels were portable affairs created for mobility. The horses are smaller and less ornate with leg and head positions that allow for stacking and easy loading. These were built primarily for North Tonawanda, New York, near Niagara Falls, by Armitage Herschell Company, Herschell Spillman Company, Spillman Engineering Company, and Allen Herschell. Charles W. Parker was also well known for his portable merry-go-rounds. He was based in Leavenworth, Kansas. Parker and Herschell Spillman both created a few large park-style carousels as well, but they are better known for their portable models.

Horses are by far the most common figure found, but there are two dozen other animals that were created for the carousel platform. Carousel animals, unlike most other antiques, are oftentimes worth more in a restored condition. Figures found with original factory paint are extraordinarily rare and bring premium amounts. Typically, carousel horses are found in garish, poorly applied 'park paint' and oftentimes are missing legs or ears. Carousel horses are hollow. They were glued up from several blocks for greater strength and lighter weight. Bass and poplar woods were used extensively.

If you have an antique carousel animal you would like to have identified, send a clear photograph and description along with a LSASE to our advisor, William Manns, who is listed in the Directory under New Mexico. Mr. Manns is the author of *Painted Ponies*, containing many full-color photographs, guides, charts, and directories for the collector.

Key:
IR — inside row   OR — outside row
MR — middle row   PTC — Philadelphia Toboggan
                             Company

Coney Island-Style Horses

Carmel, IR jumper, unrstr	6,000.00
Carmel, MR jumper, unrstr	8,900.00
Carmel, OR jumper w/cherub, rstr	40,000.00
Illions, IR jumper, rstr, from $5,000 to	6,500.00
Illions, MR stander, rstr	12,000.00
Illions, OR stander, eagle saddle, rstr	38,000.00
Looff, IR jumper, unrstr	6,000.00
Looff, OR jumper, unrstr	21,500.00
Stein & Goldstein, IR jumper, unrstr	5,000.00
Stein & Goldstein, MR jumper, rstr	13,000.00
Stein & Goldstein, OR stander w/bells, unrstr	42,000.00

European Horses

Anderson, English, unrstr	4,200.00
Bayol, French, unrstr	3,000.00
Heyn, German, unrstr	3,500.00
Hubner, Belgian, unrstr	3,000.00
Savage, English, unrstr	3,500.00

Menagerie Animals (Non-Horses)

Dentzel, bear, unrstr	28,000.00
Dentzel, cat, unrstr	42,000.00
Dentzel, lion, unrstr	52,000.00
Dentzel, pig, unrstr	9,000.00
Dentzel, rabbit, unrstr	40,000.00
E Joy Morris, deer, unrstr	13,500.00
Herschell Spillman, cat, unrstr	15,000.00
Herschell Spillman, chicken, portable, unrstr	9,500.00
Herschell Spillman, dog, portable, unrstr	10,000.00
Herschell Spillman, frog, unrstr	29,000.00
Looff, camel, unrstr	9,000.00
Looff, goat, rstr	17,000.00
Muller, tiger, rstr	37,000.00

Philadelphia-Style Horses

Philadelphia Toboggan Company, outside row stander, ca 1916, unrestored, $29,500.00.

Dentzel, IR 'topknot' jumper, unrstr	5,500.00
Dentzel, MR jumper, unrstr	14,000.00

Dentzel, OR stander, rstr	35,000.00
Dentzel, prancer, rstr	9,500.00
Morris, IR prancer, rstr	7,000.00
Morris, MR stander, unrstr	9,500.00
Morris, OR stander, rstr	18,000.00
Muller, IR jumper, rstr	8,900.00
Muller, MR jumper, rstr	16,000.00
Muller, OR stander, rstr	48,000.00
Muller, OR stander w/military trappings	75,000.00
PTC, chariot (bench-like seat), rstr	8,900.00
PTC, IR jumper, rstr	6,000.00
PTC, MR jumper, rstr	15,500.00
PTC, OR stander, armored, rstr	58,000.00
PTC, OR stander, unrstr	29,500.00

Portable Carousel Horses

Allan Herschell, all aluminum, ca 1950	550.00
Allan Herschell, half & half, wood & aluminum head	1,500.00
Allan Herschell, IR Indian pony, unrstr	2,500.00
Allan Herschell, OR, rstr	3,200.00
Allan Herschell, OR Trojan-style jumper	4,000.00
Armitage Herschell, track-machine jumper	2,600.00
Dare, jumper, unrstr	3,000.00
Herschell Spillman, chariot (bench-like seat)	3,500.00
Herschell Spillman, IR jumper, unrstr	3,000.00
Herschell Spillman, MR jumper, unrstr	3,200.00
Herschell Spillman, OR, eagle decor	5,500.00
Herschell Spillman, OR, park machine	14,000.00
Parker, MR jumper, unrstr	4,500.00
Parker, OR jumper, park machine, unrstr	10,000.00
Parker, OR jumper, rstr	6,800.00

Carpet Balls

Carpet balls are glazed china spheres decorated with intersecting lines or other simple designs that were used for indoor games in the British Isles during the early 1800s. Mint condition examples are rare. Our examples are for those in excellent to near-mint condition.

Blk intersecting lines on wht, ironstone, 3½"	110.00
Brn & wht plaid, 3⅜"	85.00
Brn stick spatter, 3¼"	55.00
Red intersecting lines on wht, 3½", EX	105.00
Yel stick spatter, 3¼"	55.00

Cartoon Art

Collectors of cartoon art are interested in many forms of original art — animation cels, sports, political or editorial cartoons, syndicated comic strip panels, and caricature. To produce even a short animated cartoon strip, hundreds of original drawings are required, each showing the characters in slightly advancing positions. Called 'cels' because those made prior to the 1950s were made from a celluloid material, collectors often pay hundreds of dollars for a frame from a favorite movie. Prices of Disney cels with backgrounds vary widely. Background paintings, model sheets, storyboards, and preliminary sketches are also collectible — so are comic book drawings executed in India ink and signed by the artist. Daily 'funnies' originals, especially the earlier ones portraying super heroes, and Sunday comic strips, the early as well as the later ones, are collected. Cartoon art has become recognized and valued as a novel yet valid form of contemporary art.

Key:
ab — airbrushed   WB — Warner Brothers
HB — Hanna-Barbera   WD — Walt Disney
KFS — King Features Syndicate

Animation Cel, Full Color

Aristocats, O'Malley, Disney seal, 1970 ....**475.00**
Baby Boop & Pudgy, King Features, ltd ed, Fleischer, 1991, fr **475.00**

Batman and Robin, cel from the TV series, gouache on celluloid, watercolor production ground, matted, 8½x12", $400.00.

Beauty & the Beast, WD, scene on stairway, 1992, fr, 17x20" **500.00**
Bugs Bunny, WB, baseball scene, ltd ed, Friz Freleng, fr **1,600.00**
Bugs Bunny's 1001 Rabbit Tales, WB, Friz Freleng, fr, 9x8" **975.00**
Casper the Ghost, ltd ed, Shamus Culhane, 1992, fr, 18x21" **475.00**
Charlie Brown Christmas, HP, sgn Bill Melendez, 1965 ....**795.00**
Dangerous Discovery, ltd ed, Carl Barks, fr, 17½x20" **800.00**
Dennis the Menace, ltd ed, Hank Ketchum, 1989, fr, 15x18" **300.00**
Donald Duck as Donald Applecore, gouache, '52, matted, 4½x3" **345.00**
Flintstones, HB, Barney holding Pebbles, print bkground, '70s ..**175.00**
Jetsons: The Movie, HB, all characters, 1989, fr, 17x19" **800.00**
Jonny's Golden Quest, HB, Jonny & Bandit, 1993, fr, 16x18" ...**475.00**
Jungle Book, WD, Vulture, color print bkground, 1967, 19x22" ...**375.00**
Party for Pebbles, HB, ltd ed, sgn, 1992, fr, 19x17" **725.00**
Peter Pan, WD, side-view of Wendy, gouache, fr, 6½x4" **1,380.00**
Scrappy Flips For Scooby, HB, ltd ed, sgn, 1989, fr, 17x19" **475.00**
Sleeping Beauty, WD, Briar Rose dancing, gouache, '59, fr, 6x4" ...**800.00**
Sleeping Beauty, WD, King Stefan, gouache, '59, matted, 6x6½" ..**430.00**
Snoopy Come Home, w/Woodstock on doghouse, 1969, 17x19" ..**825.00**
Snow White & Prince, WD, wishing well scene, ltd ed, fr, 13x16" **995.00**
Sword in the Stone, WD, Mime & Wizard dueling, 1963, fr, 14x17" ..**995.00**
Tom & Jerry in Two Little Indians, MGM, gouache, 1953, 9x12" ...**1,600.00**
Tweety's Great Escape, WB, HP, sgn Virgil Ross, 1993, fr **750.00**
Winnie the Pooh, WD, Owl, print bkground, 1960s, matted **475.00**
Winnie the Pooh, WD, w/Piglet/Christopher, ltd ed, 10½x14" .**1,495.00**
Yakky Doodle in All's Well..., gouache, ab bkground, 1961, fr ...**920.00**
Yogi Bear for Ranger, HB, ltd ed, sgn, 1992, fr, 19x24" **650.00**
Yosemite Pirate, WB, HP, ltd ed, sgn Friz, 1984, fr **975.00**
101 Dalmatians, WD, Pongo, gouache, 1961, fr, 7x5" **1,500.00**
101 Dalmatians, WD, watching TV, w/master bkground, 1991, fr ..**1,150.00**

Animation Drawing

Bugs Bunny in Rapid Transit, WB, gr/blk pencil, 1947, matted ...**2,300.00**
Garfield, pencil, 1980s, matted **200.00**
Goofy in Polar Trappers, WD, red/blk pencil, matted, 8x6" **1,265.00**
Gulliver's Travels, Max Fleischer, color shading **695.00**
Jetsons, HB, Dr Scarem, pencil, 1980s, matted, 11x14" **75.00**
Mickey as Captain, WD, red/gr/blk pencil, '40, matted, 4½x4" ..**865.00**
Mickey's Trailer, WD, red/orange/blk pencil, matted, 6½x7" .**1,600.00**
Minnie Mouse in Barn Dance, WD, pencil, 1928, rare, 5x7½" ..**1,095.00**
Peter Pan, WD, Capt Hook leaning on sword, pencils, 1953 ......**895.00**
Pinocchio, WD, Stromboli w/Pinocchio, pencil, 1940, 7½x9" ...**450.00**
Yogi & Boo Boo, HB, graphite, 1970s, matted **175.00**

Daily Newspaper Comic Strip

Bugs Bunny & Elmer Fudd, Armstrong, 1979 ....**235.00**
Dick Tracy, Chester Gould, w/villain, 1953 ....**485.00**
Flash Gordon, Barry, India ink on paper, 1962 ....**200.00**
Little Lulu, Armstrong, India ink on brd, 1964 ....**100.00**
Mutt & Jeff, Fischer, baseball theme, 1922 ....**600.00**
Pogo, Kelly, pencil/ink on paper, 1963 ....**475.00**
Popeye, Sagendorf, India ink on brd, 1976 ....**95.00**
Terry & the Pirates, Wunder, India ink on brd, 1951 ....**60.00**

Miscellaneous

Model sheet, Alice in Wonderland, carpenter, pencil, '51, 8x11" ..**725.00**
Model sheet, Double Dribble, Disney seal/sgn OK Jack Hannah ...**650.00**
Model sheet, George Jetson, pencil, 1980s, matted, 11x14" **75.00**
Model sheet, Mickey in Gulliver's Travels, Disney seal, 1934 ....**550.00**
Model sheet, Oopie, Columbia, gr/blk pencil, 1930s, fr, 9x10" **550.00**
Model sheet, Reluctant Dragon, Disney seal, 1940 ....**550.00**
Model sheet, Uncle Scrooge, Disney seal, 1930s **650.00**
Poster, Jerry & the Goldfish, MGM, 1-sheet, 1950, 41x27" **635.00**
Poster, Tomorrowland Submarine Voyage, silkscreen, 54x36" ..**975.00**
Story sheet, J Thaddeus, WD, conte crayon, 1949, matted, 5x5" ..**430.00**
Story sheets, Augie Doggie, red/blk pencil, 1960, set of 17 ....**865.00**
Story sheets, Quick-Draw McGraw, HB, pencil, 1960, 15 pgs .**1,035.00**
Storyboard, Bambi, WD, 2 mice in shelter, pastels, 1942, 15x17" **650.00**
Storyboard, Bambi, WD, 3 images by Garbutt, orange pencil, 7x7" ..**375.00**
Storyboard, Dumbo, 2 dancing crows, pastels, 1941, 5½x7" **225.00**

Cartoon Books

'Books of cartoons' were printed during the first decade of the 20th century and remained popular until the advent of the modern comic book in the late '30s. Cartoon books, printed in both color and black and white, were merely reprints of current newspaper comic strips. The books, ranging from thirty to seventy pages and in sizes from 3½" x 8" up to 11" x 17", were usually bound with cardboard covers and were often distributed as premiums in exchange for coupons saved from the daily paper. One of the largest of the companies who printed these books was Cupples and Leon, producer of nearly half of the two hundred titles on record. Among the most popular sellers were *Mutt and Jeff, Bringing Up Father,* and *Little Orphan Annie.*

Bringing Up Father, #2, Cupples & Leon, EX **80.00**
Bringing Up Father, #8, Cupples & Leon, VG **45.00**
Bringing Up Father, #18, Cupples & Leon, scarce, EX **75.00**
Charlie Chaplin Funny Stunts, color, Donohue, NM **110.00**
Charlie Chaplin in the Army, Donohue, EX **100.00**
Curly Tops on Star Island, Cupples & Leon, 1918, G **60.00**
Famous Comics, Captain & Kids, Whitman, 1934, EX **50.00**
Famous Comics, Captain Easy & Wash Tubbs, Whitman, EX **50.00**
Felix the Cat, McLoughlin, 1931, EX **200.00**
How Dick Tracy...Caught Rocketeers, Cupples & Leon, '33, EX ..**150.00**
Little Annie Rooney, McKay, 1943, 48-pg, NM **60.00**
Little Orphan Annie in Cosmic City, Cupples & Leon, VG **40.00**
Little Orphan Annie Never Say Die, Cupples & Leon, VG **45.00**
Little Orphan Annie Willing Helper, Cupples & Leon, 1932, VG ..**35.00**
Mutt & Jeff, #5, Ball, 1916, VG **80.00**
Mutt & Jeff Big Book, Cupples & Leon, hardcover, 1929, NM ..**165.00**
Popeye, Saalfield, 1934, 40-pg, EX+ **400.00**
Skeezix Out West, Reilly & Lee, hardcover, 1928, NM **75.00**
Smitty, Cupples & Leon, 1928, VG **35.00**
Tillie the Toiler, #2, Cupples & Leon, 52-pg, NM **40.00**

Tillie the Toiler, #4, Cupples & Leon, EX 30.00
Tricks of Katzenjammer Kids, 1905, NM 150.00
Winnie Winkle, #4, Cupples & Leon, EX 25.00

Cash Registers

By 1970 antique cash registers had risen to become blue chip collectibles, joining the ranks of fine paintings, bronzes, firearms, clocks, and other categories having permanent, established worth. Some extremely scarce and elegant cash registers will command up to $25,000.00 on today's market.

Register prices are determined by make, model, size, desirability of pattern, and accessories such as add-on clocks, topsigns, and personalized nameplates (which may be cast as topsigns or 'lid ovals' and on occassion cast into the register's front or back plates). Of immense consideration is the register's condition.

This column uses 'mint' condition (M) to indicate registers which have been cleaned, oiled, polished, and lacquered by a professional and have perfect glass, keytops, and indicators. Some restorers will replace the velvet underneath the lid (where applicable), which is an added touch of elegance. 'Very good' condition (VG) describes unrestored, unpolished registers which are complete and operating. Their values are usually about half of the restored model's value. All prices may vary as much as 20%, depending on geography and demand.

For further information we recommend the highly informative books *Antique Cash Registers, 1880-1920*, by Bartsch and Sanchez (Mr. Bartsch's address may be found in our Directory under Oregon); and *The Incorruptible Cashier*, Vols. I & II, currently available from our other advisor, John Apple, listed in our Directory under Wisconsin.

Dial, emb brass, emb pattern on drw, 25", EX 6,500.00
NCR #1, American detail adder, VG 2,650.00
NCR #1, w/rare topsign 2,800.00
NCR #1000, glass autographic box attachment, 1910-16, M ..1,200.00
NCR #1000, glass autographic box attachment, 1910-16, VG ...650.00
NCR #125 or #216, bronze fleur-de-lis, VG 950.00
NCR #129-130, bronze, VG 850.00
NCR #13 or #14, Ionic CI, 1899, G 750.00
NCR #130, Art Nouveau cabinet, M 1,600.00
NCR #135, Art Nouveau pattern, CI, 31-key, 1905, VG 600.00
NCR #2 or #3, detail adder, scroll pattern, VG 900.00
NCR #2 or #3, inlaid oak or mahog, scarce 2,250.00
NCR #226, rare bilingual topsign, EX orig 900.00
NCR #250 or #251, bronze, VG 900.00
NCR #3, mahog inlay, deep wood drw, ca 1886 .... 4,500.00
NCR #30, bronze, total adder, VG 1,400.00
NCR #312, #313, or #317, dolphin pattern, M 1,500.00
NCR #312, #313 or #317, dolphin pattern, VG 800.00
NCR #317 .... 450.00
NCR #322, #323, or #327, marble 3 sides, extended base, M ..1,800.00
NCR #322, #323, or #327, marble 3 sides, extended base, VG ..1,050.00
NCR #324 or #325 Woolworth sz, M 1,050.00
NCR #33, $5 maximum, CA, 1903, VG 900.00
NCR #332, #333, #349, or #356, orig topsign, VG 550.00
NCR #332, #333, #349 or #356, orig topsign, M 1,150.00
NCR #337, dolphin design, M 1,150.00
NCR #338, dogwood pattern, English numerals, CA, 1910-16, VG 475.00
NCR #356, 33 keys, rings to $20, 1908-16, M 1,300.00
NCR #360, 37 keys, rings to $60, 1908-09, M 1,500.00
NCR #441, #442, Empire design w/quartered-oak base, M 1,750.00
NCR #441-#452, Empire pattern, M 1,750.00
NCR #441-#452, Empire pattern, VG 800.00
NCR #441E-#452E, electric, M 2,250.00

NCR #441E-#452E, electric, VG 950.00
NCR #442E-L, EX orig 950.00
NCR #47, oak or mahog inlay, up to $6, VG 2,250.00
NCR #5, narrow scroll, glass topsign, EX orig 2,750.00
NCR #50, Renaissance design, orig clock, EX orig 2,500.00
NCR #52, Renaissance design, orig clock, extended base, M ..3,800.00
NCR #52 or #52¼, Renaissance design, extended base, VG ...2,900.00
NCR #52¼, dolphin design, extended base, M 2,200.00
NCR #522, 2-drw, electric bar model, 1910-16, M 2,500.00
NCR #522, 2-drw, electric bar model, 1910-16, VG 1,800.00
NCR #64, Bohemian pattern, iron, 25-key, 1901, VG 600.00
NCR #7 or #8, detail adder, fleur-de-lis, VG 850.00
NCR #711-#717, mahog-grain finish on steel, M 275.00
NCR #78, custom built to eliminate bk window, NP, 1902, VG ...950.00

Cast Iron

In the mid-1800s, the cast-iron industry was raging in the United States. It was recognized as a medium extremely adaptable for uses ranging from ornamental architectural filigree to actual building construction. It could be cast from a mold into any conceivable design that could be reproduced over and over at a relatively small cost. It could be painted to give an entirely versatile appearance. Furniture with openwork designs of grapevines and leaves and intricate lacy scrollwork was cast for gardens as well as inside use. Figural doorstops of every sort, bootjacks, trivets, and a host of other useful and decorative items were made before the 'ferromania' had run its course. Our advisor for this category is J.M. Ellwood; he is listed in the Directory under Arizona. See also Kitchen, Cast-Iron Bakers and Kettles; and other specific categories.

Armchairs, vintage detail, wht pnt, 20th C, 26½", pr 275.00
Armchairs, winged ornament, molded arms, hoofed ft, 32", pr ..1,980.00
Bench, curved foliage bk, griffin arms, rpt, 44" 500.00
Bench, EX fern detail, rprs, wht rpt, 58½" 770.00
Bench, fern design, Kramer Bros...Dayton O, wht rpt, 58" 900.00
Bench, semicircular, foliage/scrolls/berries, wht pnt, 43" 150.00
Bench, strapwork w/S-scrolled arms, late 1800s, 67½" L 275.00
Bench, vintage w/geometric grill seat, old wht rpt, 41", G 110.00
Cork press, figural dog hdl, 19th C, VG 125.00
Eagle, 3-part casting, old mc pnt, 16½" wingspan 385.00
Fountain, 4 birds among foliage at base, att Fiske, 40", VG 1,095.00

Garden chair, American Victorian Rococo, florals and scrolls, revolving seat with gadrooned skirt, mid-1800s, 32", $950.00.

High-top shoes, red & gold pnt, 6¾", facing pr 195.00
Lavabo, shell shape w/verdigris, 20x15", on oak 67" plaque 660.00
Lavabo stand, HP ceramic tiles, openwork base, 42x30x20" 500.00
Match striker, fly, wings lift to hold discarded matches 32.00
Mirror, scalloped fr w/old bl pnt traces, Victorian, 36x26x7" 650.00
Paperweight, salamander, worn gr pnt, Sherwin Williams..., 10" ..335.00
Pencil sharpener, automatic, table mounted, old, VG 150.00

Plaque, eagle in relief, old gold rpt, 12½x13" 300.00
Plaque, eagle/shield/arrows/etc in relief, inlaid fr, 7x10" 250.00
Shoe shine footrest, camel figure w/rest on bk, 7¼" 150.00
Spoon rest, pig w/curly tail, old gold pnt, 3x6" 85.00
Sprinkler, frog figural, orig pnt, 1900s, 4½x4½" 595.00
Tie rod element, S-curve, red pnt, 22" down to 18½", 3 for 40.00
Umbrella stand, pears/fruit on basketweave, Am, 1860s, 38½" ..700.00
Urn, Masonic emblems on base, wht rpt, Kramer Bros, 32" 140.00
Urn, old gr rpt, Stewart Iron Works, Cinci OH, 27x27" dia 375.00
Urn, ribbed reservoir, wht rpt, 21x15" dia, EX 250.00
Urn, w/ears, dk bl rpt, Kramer Bros, 31", pr 660.00
Wafer iron, J Savery's Sons NY 150.00
Wig curler, ball-shaped ends, scissors shape, 1700s, 10" 65.00

Castor Sets

Castor sets became popular during the early years of the 18th century and continued to be used through the late Victorian era. Their purpose was to hold various condiments for table use. The most common type was a circular arrangement with a center handle on a revolving pedestal base that held three, four, five, or six bottles. Some had extras; a few were equipped with a bell for calling the servant. Frames were made of silverplate, glass, or pewter. Though most bottles were of pressed glass, some of the designs were cut, and on rare occasion, colored glass with enameled decorations was used as well. To maintain authenticity and value, castor sets should have matching bottles. Prices listed below are for those with matching bottles and in frames with plating that is in excellent condition (unless noted otherwise).

Watch for new frames and bottles in both clear and colored glass; these have recently been appearing on the market.

Key: D&B — Daisy and Button

Seven-bottle, cast female ornament in center of silverplated Redfield and Rice frame, ca 1865-72, 21", $550.00.

3-bottle, cranberry, cut, SP tops; ornate SP fr, 5½x3¾" 200.00
3-bottle, D&B; SP fr w/toothpick holder finial 250.00
3-bottle, Gothic Arch, blown, orig stoppers; pewter fr 110.00
4-bottle, amberina w/eng decor; orig SP fr 985.00
4-bottle, Banded Ring; orig pewter fr, child sz 150.00
4-bottle, D&B (colors), orig stoppers; pressed glass fr 225.00
4-bottle, etched decor; SP fr mk Meriden, 14½" 150.00
4-bottle, King's Crown, ruby stained; orig glass stand 335.00
5-bottle, cut, Honeycomb, amberina; Meriden SP fr, 14" 900.00
5-bottle, etched amberina, cut amberina stoppers; gilt fr, EX ..2,000.00
5-bottle, etched floral w/cutting, much decor; Meriden fr 250.00
5-bottle, etched; Japanese-motif SP fr, bird at top 245.00
5-bottle, etched/cut; rotating Meriden fr, 14½x6¼" 150.00
5-bottle, wreath design w/cut dots; decor fr w/call bell 350.00
6-bottle, cut vintage; SP Rogers Smith & Co fr 235.00
6-bottle, cut; SP mechanical-door housing, Gleason 1,500.00

6-bottle, etched wreath; lg Reed & Barton fr w/cupid 350.00
6-bottle, Honeycomb; ornate Tufts fr, 18", EX 350.00
6-bottle, pressed, D&B; oversz 18" Meriden fr 375.00
6-bottle, Sawtooth; ornate Meriden fr, call bell, dtd 1888, EX ...450.00
7-bottle, cut crystal; gadrooned/shell-border Geo III fr 495.00

Catalina Island

Catalina Island pottery was made on the island of the same name, which is about twenty-six miles off the coast of Los Angeles. The pottery was started in 1927 at Pebble Beach, by Wm. Wrigley, Jr., who was instrumental in developing and using the native clays. Its principal products were brick and tile to be used for construction on the island. Garden pieces were first produced, then vases, bookends, lamps, ashtrays, novelty items, and finally dinnerware. The ware became very popular and was soon being shipped to the mainland as well.

Some of the pottery was hand thrown; some was made in molds. Most pieces are marked Catalina Island or Catalina with a printed incised stamp or handwritten with a pointed tool. Cast items were sometimes marked in the mold, a few have an ink stamp, and a paper label was also used.

The color of the clay can help to identify approximately when a piece was made: 1927 to 1932, brown to red clay; 1931 to 1932, an experimental period with various colors; 1932 to 1937, mainly white clay, but tan to brown were also used on occasion.

Items marked Catalina Pottery are listed in Gladding McBean. For further information we recommend *The Collector's Encyclopedia of California Pottery* by our advisor, Jack Chipman; he is listed in the Directory under California.

Dinnerware

Carafe, red, early red clay 125.00
Carafe, turq 135.00
Catalina Island, bowl, berry 30.00
Catalina Island, bowl, cereal 45.00
Catalina Island, bowl, fruit; ftd, sq, 13" 150.00
Catalina Island, bowl, vegetable; rnd, 8½" 75.00
Catalina Island, candle holder, low 80.00
Catalina Island, compote, ftd, lg 200.00
Catalina Island, cup, coffee/tea 45.00
Catalina Island, custard cup 25.00
Catalina Island, mug, 6" 45.00
Catalina Island, pitcher, squat base, 9" 125.00
Catalina Island, plate, bread & butter; coupe design, 6" 15.00
Catalina Island, plate, dinner; wide rim, 10½" 30.00
Catalina Island, plate, rolled rim, 12½" 75.00
Catalina Island, sugar bowl, w/lid 50.00
Catalina Island, teapot, traditional English style 250.00
Catalina Island, tumbler, 4" 22.50
Catalina Island, wine cup, hdld 25.00
Charger, red, #622, 17½" 175.00
Charger, 2 swans on water, mc matt, #907-65-B, 12½", NM 145.00
Coaster, bl, red clay 35.00
Rope Edge, casserole, w/lid 80.00
Rope Edge, chop plate, 13½" 70.00
Rope Edge, creamer 25.00
Rope Edge, cup & saucer 40.00
Rope Edge, plate, dinner; 10½" 25.00
Rope Edge, plate, salad; 8½" 20.00
Rope Edge, sugar bowl 35.00
Rope Edge, teapot 180.00
Shakers, Senorita & Peon, red & yel, pr 125.00

Miscellaneous

Ashtray, bear figural, souvenir: Catalina Island, gr, red clay 200.00
Bookends, frog, Monterey brn, prof rstr, rare 600.00
Bowl, Starlight, #709 ....160.00
Clamshell, pearly wht 100.00
Cowboy hat, Descanso gr 150.00
Flower vase, ivory, fluted, 10" 195.00
Step vase, Toyon red, red clay 350.00
Vase, lav w/flared rim, 5" 95.00
Vase, lt bl, sawtooth, 7¼" 165.00
Vase, trophy; red, hdls, 7½" 350.00

Catalogs

Catalogs are not only intriguing to collect on their own merit, but for the collector with a specific interest, they are often the only remaining source of background information available, and as such they offer a wealth of otherwise unrecorded data. The mail-order industry can be traced as far back as the mid-1800s. Even before Aaron Montgomery Ward began his career in 1872, Laacke and Joys of Wisconsin and the Orvis Company of Vermont, both dealers in sporting goods, had been well established for many years. The E.C. Allen Company sold household necessities and novelties by mail on a broad scale in the 1870s. By the end of the Civil War, sewing machines, garden seed, musical instruments, even medicine, were available from catalogs. In the 1880s Macy's of New York issued a 127-page catalog; Sears and Spiegel followed suit in about 1890. Craft and art supply catalogs were first available about 1880 and covered such varied fields as china painting, stenciling, wood burning, brass embossing, hair weaving, and shellcraft. Today some collectors confine their interests not only to craft catalogs in general but often to just one subject. There are several factors besides rarity which make a catalog valuable: age, condition, profuse illustrations, how collectible the field is that it deals with, the amount of color used in its printing, its size (format and number of pages), and whether it is a manufacturer's catalog verses a jobber's catalog (the former being the most desirable). Our advisor for this category is Richard M. Bueschel; he is listed in the Directory under Illinois.

AC Gilbert Co, toys, 1953, 52-pg, G 30.00
Aldens, Spring & Summer, 1966, VG 35.00
Allied Radio, 1938, 160-pg, VG 35.00
Avon Gifts, Christmas, 1956, 46-pg, VG 75.00
Babson Brothers, harnesses, 1923, 28-pg, G 20.00
Bailey's Beautician Supplies, 1969, 126-pg, VG 30.00
Beatrice Creamery Co, premiums, 1929, 26-pg, VG 8.00
Block Shop, toys, 1967, 38-pg, VG 25.00
Bobbink & Atkins Hardy Herbaceous Plants, 1932, 84-pg, VG ...30.00
Brazel Novelty Co, 1920s (?), 64-pg, VG 95.00
Brown & Sharpe Small Tools, 1941, 512-pg, VG 40.00
Brown & Williamson, premiums/general, 1974, 84-pg, VG 20.00
Buckeye Aluminum Co, aluminum ware, 1927, 32-pg, G 35.00
Butterwick Home Catalog Pattern Book, Spring, 1963, 64-pg, VG ...15.00
Carson Pirie Scott, 1924, 344-pg, EX 125.00
Cincinnati Iron Fence Co, 1921, 144-pg, VG+ 55.00
Colt Firearms & Pistols, 1977, 22-pg, VG 15.00
EE Southern Iron Co, housing materials, 1900, 20-pg, G 82.00
Electric Wheel Co, electric wheels & wagons, 1903, 48-pg, VG ..52.00
Enterprise Rubber Co, auto accessories, 1915, 44-pg, G 25.00
Florida Ladies' Holiday Fashions, 1960, 72-pg, VG 15.00
Gambles, Spring & Summer, general, 1955, 128-pg, VG 25.00
Gifford Wood Co, ice tools, 1896, 264-pg, G 165.00
Gimble Bros, women's & children's clothing, 1920, 280-pg, VG .30.00

Gold Metal Folding Furniture, 1929, 28-pg, VG 25.00
Gun Digest, 1964, 384-pg, VG 35.00
GW Flavell & Bro Inc, medical, 1915, 24-pg, G 30.00
Harrison Wholesale Christmas Gifts & Toys, 1929, 96-pg, VG 40.00
Henderson Desk Co, 1909, 32-pg, VG+ 48.00
Herbrand Quality Tools, 1939, 160-pg, VG 35.00
Herschell-Spillman Co, merry-go-rounds, 1907, 33-pg, G 190.00
Hoosier Stove Co, 1908, 64-pg, EX 90.00
International Stock Food, 1940s, 160-pg, VG 40.00
JC Penney, Spring & Summer, 1976, VG 25.00
John Plain, fashions/general/toys, 1970, 644-pg, VG 45.00
John Wanamaker, World's Greatest Organ, 1917, 24-pg, VG 38.00
King Sewing Machine Co, 1909, 56-pg, G 25.00
Lana Labell Holiday Fashions for JR/Misses, 1959, 48-pg, VG 15.00
Lane Bryant Baby Fashions, Spring & Summer, 1925, 38-pg, VG ...40.00
Larkin Co, NY & Paris fashions, 1910, 32-pg, G+ 32.00
Lee Wards Crafts & Supplies, Spring & Summer, 1964, 64-pg, VG ..15.00
Library Bureau, 1924, 40-pg, VG 35.00

McCall Book of Fashions, Spring of 1920, 13½x9½", EX, $40.00.

Mead Cycle Co, 'Ranger' bicycles & supplies, 1918, 64-pg, VG .100.00
Metal Arts Co, emblems & jewelry, 1922, 56-pg, G 15.00
Metropolitan Sewing Machine, 1910, 100-pg, VG 35.00
Monarch Machinery Co, 1903, 72-pg, VG 50.00
Montgomery Ward, cameras, 1849, VG 20.00
Montgomery Ward, Christmas, 1945, lg toy section, EX 55.00
Montgomery Ward, groceries, Sept/Oct, 1918, 96-pg, VG 40.00
Montgomery Ward, Summer Sale, 1965, VG 20.00
Montgomery Ward, wallpaper samples, 1926, 124-pg, VG 50.00
National Bella Hess, Fall & Winter, 1934, 154-pg, VG 50.00
National Bella Hess, Spring & Summer, 1941, VG 30.00
National Cloak & Suit, Fall & Winter, 1924, 430-pg, VG 100.00
Neiman Marcus, Christmas, 1965, VG 30.00
Nelson Doubleday Inc, book & magazine offers, 1927, 44-pg, VG ..10.00
Nelson Enterprises Magic Tricks & Supplies, 1950, 142-pg, VG ..40.00
Olson Rug Co, 1949, 40-pg, VG 25.00
Perfection Mfg Co, baby items, 1923, 32-pg, VG 35.00
Remington Firearms & Ammunition, Fall, 1958, 28-pg, VG 20.00
Robert Stoll, emblems & jewelry, 1921, 20-pg, VG 15.00
S&H Green Stamps, 1967, 186-pg, VG 20.00
Sears Roebuck Cameras & Supplies, 1940, 40-pg, VG 25.00
Sears Roebuck Electrical Power Tools, 1932, 32-pg, VG 30.00
Smith & Sons Harness Co, 1915, 95-pg, VG 55.00
South Bend Lathe Works, 1919, 64-pg, VG+ 15.00
Spiegel's Furniture Home Goods, 1929, 130-pg, VG 50.00
Strombecker, toy models, 1959, 8-pg, VG 50.00
Thornber Label Works, 1910, 32-pg, G+ 35.00
Underwood Typewriter Co, 1912, 24-pg, G 8.00
W Stokes Kirk, government surplus, 1919, 48-pg, G+ 28.00
Western Auto, Christmas, 1968, VG 30.00
Wm Corris & Co, price list of carriage parts, 1880, 14-pg, G 58.00

Caughley Ware

The Caughley Coalport Porcelain Manufactory operated from about 1775 until 1799 in Caughley, near Salop, Shropshire, in England. The owner was Thomas Turner, who gained his potting experience from his association with the Worcester Pottery Company. The wares he manufactured in Caughley are referred to as 'Salopian.' He is most famous for his blue-printed earthenwares, particularly the Blue Willow pattern, designed for him by Thomas Minton. For a more detailed history, see Coalport.

Cup & saucer, birds on floral branches, blk transfer w/mc, NM ..185.00
Cup & saucer, blk deer transfer w/mc, pearlware, EX 100.00
Cup & saucer, shepherd scene, gray transfer, EX 70.00
Mug, Liberty Cap & Pole/Lyre & Caduceus, blk w/mc, 3¾" 160.00
Pitcher, red to bl glossy, sq spout, broad base, 8", NM 100.00
Teapot, floral, bl w/gold, ca 1790, S mk, 5" 460.00
Teapot, pagoda, bl w/gold, porc, S mk, ca 1785, 5½", NM 460.00
Waste bowl, bl & wht Oriental decor, pearlware, C mk, 3x6¼" .195.00

Ceramic Art Company

Jonathan Coxon, Sr., and Walter Scott Lenox established the Ceramic Art Company in 1889 in Trenton, New Jersey, where they produced fine belleek porcelain. Both were experienced in its production, having previously worked for Ott and Brewer. They hired artists to hand paint their wares with portraits, scenes, and lovely florals. Today artist-signed examples bring the highest prices. Several marks were used, three of which contain the 'CAC' monogram. A green wreath surrounding the company name in full was used on special-order wares, but these are not often encountered. Coxon eventually left the company, and it was later reorganized under the Lenox name. See also Lenox. Our advisor for this category is Mary Frank Gaston; she is listed in the Directory under Texas.

Photo courtesy Mary Frank Gaston

Individual salt cellar and pepper shaker, mixed floral decoration with gold trim on white, pepper unmarked because of cork in base, $125.00 for the pair.

Bell, tulip shape, wht w/silver decor, unmk 165.00
Bowl, gold florals, pastel sponging, ruffled, 2x4½" 135.00
Creamer & sugar bowl, nautilus, gold-paste floral, w/lid 275.00
Cup, chocolate; bl beading & gold on ivory, ped ft 65.00
Cup, gold paste, ruffled rim, branch hdl, ped ft 95.00
Ewer, gold-paste florals on wht, ring hdl, mk, 7½" 485.00
Mug, holly leaves & berries w/gold, 1894 mk, 5¾", NM 120.00
Mug, monk on brn tones, sgn, ca 1894-96 ....125.00
Pitcher, lemonade; roses, red on gr, sgn Durr, 5½" 175.00
Pitcher, strawberries & leaves w/gold, sgn Leroy, 6" 340.00

Vase, violets & gold scrolls on cream, classic form, mk, 22½" 800.00
Vase, 3 heron reserves, iris on blk at neck, mk, 22" 550.00

Ceramic Arts Studio, Madison

The Ceramic Arts Studio Company began operations sometime prior to the 1940s, but it was about then that Betty Harrington started marketing her goods through this company. Betty Harrington was the designer primarily responsible for creating the line of figurines and knick-knacks that has become so popular with collectors. There were two others — Ulli Rebus, who not only designed several of the animals and various other pieces but taught Betty the art of mold-making as well; and Ruth Planter, who's work may have been very limited. About 65% of these items are marked, but even unmarked items become easily recognizable after only a brief study of their distinctive styling and glaze colors. At least eight different marks were used, among them the black ink stamp and the incised mark: 'Ceramic Arts Studio, Madison, Wisc.' A paper sticker was used in the early years.

After the 1955 demise of the company in Madison, the owner (Ruben Sand) went to Japan where he continued production under the same name using many of the same molds. After a short time, the old molds were retired, and new and quite different items were produced. Most of the Japan pieces can be found with a Ceramic Arts Studio backstamp. The Japan identification was often on a paper label and can be missing. Japan pieces are never marked Madison, Wisc., but not all Madison pieces are either. Red or blue backstamps are exclusively Japanese.

Another company that also produced figurines operated at about the same time as the Madison studio. It was called Ceramic Art (no 's') Studio; do not confuse the two.

A second and larger building in the C.A.S. complex in Madison was for the exclusive production of metal accessories. The creator and designer of this related line was Zona Liberace, Liberace's stepmother, who was art director for the line of figurines as well. These pieces are rising fast in value and because they weren't marked can sometimes be found at bargain prices. They were so popular that other ceramic companies bought them to complement their own lines, so they may also be found with ceramic figures other than C.A.S.'s.

Our advisor for this category is BA Wellman; his address can be found under Massachusetts. Mr. Wellman encourages collectors to write him with any new information concerning company history and/or production. He sends Jeff and Rosie a 'thank you' for helping us with this year's updates. See also Clubs, Newsletters, and Catalogs.

Note: We must regretfully inform you that Betty Harrington passed away on March 28, 1997.

Bank, Mr Blankety Blank, 4½" 75.00
Bell, Lillibelle, 6½" 75.00
Figurine, Autumn Andy, 5" 75.00
Figurine, bass viol boy, 4¾" 60.00
Figurine, birch bark canoe, 8" 125.00
Figurine, Bird of Paradise, male & female, pr 195.00
Figurine, bunny, 1¾" 24.00
Figurine, Burmese man, 5" 100.00
Figurine, Carmelita, 4¼" 40.00
Figurine, child w/towel, 5" 150.00
Figurine, chipmunk, brn, 2" 25.00
Figurine, Colonial man & woman, 6¾", 6½", pr 100.00
Figurine, Comedy & Tragedy, chartreuse, pr 180.00
Figurine, Cupid, 5" 150.00
Figurine, Dinky, girl skunk 25.00
Figurine, Dutch Love girl & boy, 5", pr 65.00
Figurine, Egyptian man & woman, rare, 9½", pr 500.00
Figurine, fawn, 4¼" 50.00

Figurine, flute lady, standing, rare, 8½" 195.00
Figurine, frog, 2" 25.00
Figurine, guitar man, sitting, 6½" 195.00
Figurine, Hans & Katrinka, chubby, 6½", 6¼", pr 110.00
Figurine, Harry & Lillibeth, pr 100.00
Figurine, Indian girl, 3¼" 30.00
Figurine, Lucindy & Col Jackson, pr 100.00
Figurine, Macabre dancers, 7¾", 9", pr 325.00
Figurine, Manchu lantern man, wht w/gold 65.00
Figurine, Modern Dance man, chartreuse 95.00
Figurine, Mr Monk, 4" 45.00
Figurine, Palomino colt, 5¾" 125.00
Figurine, Pansy (ballerina), standing, 5¾" 95.00
Figurine, Peter Rabbit, 3¾" 40.00
Figurine, pillow for sultan, 4½" 45.00
Figurine, Spanish rhumba couple, 7", 7½", pr 125.00
Figurine, Violet, ballerina, sitting, 3" 95.00
Head vase, Barbie, 7" 200.00
Head vase, Bonnie, 7" 200.00
Head vase, Manchu, beige w/blk 125.00
Jug, Aladdin, 2" 32.00
Jug, Diana the Huntress, 3" 40.00
Planter, flowerpot, rnd, 1" 20.00
Planter, sea shell only, 3" 48.00
Plaque, Chinese lantern man & woman, 8", pr 125.00
Plaque, Goosey Gander & Mary Contrary, 4½", 5", pr 165.00
Plaque, Harlequin & Columbine, blk & wht w/gr, pr 135.00
Plaque, Ophelia & Hamlet, holding lg masks, pr 200.00
Plaque, Zor, chartreuse 40.00
Razor bank, Tony the Barber 125.00
Shakers, bears, mom & baby, realistic, 3⅛", 2⅛", pr 250.00
Shakers, Blackamoor, 4¾", pr 95.00
Shakers, bunnies, running, 4½", 3½", pr 225.00
Shakers, Butch & Billy (pups), 3", 2", pr 125.00
Shakers, Calico Cat & Gingham Dog, pr 125.00
Shakers, cats, mom & baby, stylized, 4¼", 2⅝", pr 200.00
Shakers, Chinese boy & girl, 4¼", 4", pr 35.00
Shakers, Dem & Rep, 4½", pr 200.00
Shakers, Dutch boy & girl, 4", pr 35.00
Shakers, elephants, wee boy & girl, 3½", 3¼", pr 80.00
Shakers, Eskimos, wee boy & girl, 3¼", 3", pr 80.00
Shakers, Fifi & Fufu, 3", 2½", pr 225.00
Shakers, fighting cocks, pr 60.00
Shakers, fish on tails, 4" 75.00
Shakers, frog & toadstool, 2", 3", pr 75.00
Shakers, giraffe, mother & baby, 6½", 5½", pr 225.00
Shakers, leopards, fighting, 3½", 6¼", pr 225.00
Shakers, Minnehaha & Hiawatha, 6½", 3½", pr 300.00
Shakers, Mr & Mrs Penguin, 3¾", pr 75.00
Shakers, Native boy on alligator, pr 225.00
Shakers, ox & covered wagon, 3", pr 125.00
Shakers, pixie boy & toadstool, 2½", 3", pr 65.00
Shakers, Santa & evergreen, 2¼", 2½", pr 250.00
Shakers, snuggle bear & cub, blk, 4¼" overall, pr 225.00
Shakers, snuggle bear & cub, brn, pr 65.00
Shakers, snuggle boy in chair, 2¼" overall, pr 62.00
Shakers, snuggle chick in nest, 2¾" overall, pr 250.00
Shakers, snuggle cow & calf, 5¼" overall, pr 125.00
Shakers, snuggle doe & fawn, stylized, 3¾", 2", pr 125.00
Shakers, snuggle girl in chair, 2¼" overall, pr 62.00
Shakers, snuggle kitten & cream pitcher, 2½" overall, pr 195.00
Shakers, snuggle Oakie on spring leaf, 3" overall, pr 175.00
Shakers, snuggle sea horse in coral, 3½", 3", pr 95.00
Shakers, Spanish rhumba couple, 7", 7½", pr 295.00

Shelf sitter, boy w/dog, gr & grn 50.00
Shelf sitter, farm girl 45.00
Shelf sitter, harmonica boy, 4" 60.00
Shelf sitter, Jack & Jill, 4¾", 5", pr 70.00
Shelf sitter, Little Jack Horner, 4½" 75.00
Shelf sitter, Nip & Tuck, 4¼", 4", pr 45.00
Shelf sitter, Persian cats, pr 165.00
Shelf sitter, Pete parrot, maroon 65.00
Shelf sitter, setter, prone, paws hang over, 5" L 125.00
Shelf sitter, Tuffy cat, blk, 5¼" 100.00
Vase, Chinese, sq, 2" 20.00
Vase, Lu Tang on bamboo bud, 7" 45.00
Vase, rose motif, rnd, 2¼" 20.00

Metal Accessories

Arched window for Madonna & Child, 14" 75.00
Artist palette w/shelves, left & right, 13" across 95.00
Bean stalk for Jack, rare 95.00
Birdcage w/perch for birds, 14" 65.00
Diamond shadow box, for Attitude & Arabesque, 15½x13¾" 55.00
Frame w/shelf, 22" sq 55.00
Holder for planter 45.00
Pocket step shelf, w/planter, rnd, 8" 75.00
Pyramid shelf 75.00
Sofa, for Maurice & Michele, 10x3¾" 65.00
Triple ring shelves 125.00

Chalkware

Chalkware figures were a popular commodity from approximately 1860 until 1890. They were made from gypsum or plaster of Paris formed in a mold and then hand painted in oils or watercolors. Items such as animals and birds, figures, banks, toys, and religious ornaments modeled after more expensive Staffordshire wares were often sold door to door. Their origin is attributed to Italian immigrants. Today regarded as a form of folk art, 19th century American pieces bring prices in the hundreds of dollars. Carnival chalkware from this century is also collectible, especially figures that are personality related. For those, see Carnival Collectibles.

Cat, paint wear, 19th century, 7¼", $900.00; Stag, reclining, repairs, 16x15", $250.00.

Bank, seated dog, yel w/blk details, 7", NM 260.00
Bird, dk yel w/red & blk, on spherical plinth, 8" 165.00
Cat, red/yel/plk pnt, wear, 9½" 715.00
Cat, VG pnt, 19th C, 5½" 345.00
Dog on oval base, blk & wht w/red & yel, wear/damage, 5", pr ..220.00
Ewe & lamb, orig mc pnt, rpr cracks, 8¾" 525.00
Garniture, fruit & foliage, orig mc pnt, 14" 1,750.00
Rooster, orig red/yel/blk pnt, lt wear, 5¼" 485.00

Spaniel, wht w/red trim, hollow, late 19th C, 8½", M **165.00**
Squirrels, 4-color, on rnd base, nut to mouth, wear, 7", pr **330.00**

Champleve

Champleve, enameling on brass, differs from cloisonne in that the design is depressed or incised into the metal, rather than being built in with wire dividers as in the cloisonne procedure. The cells, or depressions, are filled in with color, and the piece is then fired.

Candlestick, onyx body & base w/metal neck/tripod ft, 8", pr **245.00**
Clock, mantel; gilt bronze w/enameling, urn surmount, 14½" ...**1,400.00**
Floor lamp, Chinese, no fixture, 61" **650.00**
Inkwell, onyx pots/hexagonal base, metal lids/base border **1,800.00**
Inkwell, urn form w/sea horse hdls, on ftd/shaped tray **345.00**

Urn, onyx and gilt bronze with champleve enamel, 10", $275.00.

Stand, gr onyx top w/champleve border, onyx ped, 30x18x18" ..**2,650.00**
Vase, figures in landscape, shouldered, 20th C, 16½" **290.00**
Vase, maidens & cherubs, crystal inserts, hdls, 1800s, 19", pr .**3,200.00**

Chase Brass & Copper Company

Americans were shocked in 1923 when an invitation to stage an exhibit at the first major postwar fair, The 1925 Exposition des Arts Deco-ratifs et Industriels, was declined by the American government because the U.S. could not comply with the exposition's requirement that only original work would be exhibited. Even though American industry produced a vast quantity of varied goods, there was very little 'original American' to show, since most design ideas were being brought in from Europe.

This blow to American prestige and the uproar that resulted prompted a dispatch of designers (among them Donald Deskey, Walter Dorwin Teague, and Russel Wright) to the Paris exhibition. They were to determine what steps would be necessary in order for U.S. designs to compete with European standards. They returned championing the new modernist style. By the mid-1930s, products were being designed and marketed that were attractive to the reluctant consumer insistent upon buying a streamline style that was uniquely American. During the decade of the '30s, the Chase Brass & Copper Company offered lamps, smoking accessories, and housewares similar to those Americans were seeing on the Hollywood screen at prices the average buyer could afford. These products are highly valued today not only because of their superior quality but also because of those who created them. Walter von Nessen, Gerth & Gerth, Rockwell Kent, Russel Wright, Laurelle Guild, and Dr. A. Reimann were some of Chases' well-known designers. Emily Post, who served as spokesperson for Chase, promoted a trend away from expensive silver and toward chromium serving pieces.

Besides chromium, Chase manufactured many products in brass, copper, nickel plate, or a combination of these metals; all are equally collectible. Some items had glass inserts which collectors also seek.

Nearly all Chase products were marked, either on the item itself or on a screw or rivet. On sets containing several pieces, the trademark may appear on only one. Be cautious. Check unmarked items to make sure they measure up to Chase's standard of quality, and lighting fixtures that are unmarked may be compared with pictures of verified examples. For safety's sake, replace both cords and internal wiring before attempting to use any electrical product. Not only will you be protected against possible loss from fire, but you will enhance the value of your collectible as well.

For more thorough study we recommend *Art Deco Chrome, The Chase Era,* and *Art Deco Chrome, Book 2, A Collector's Guide, Industrial Design in the Chase Era.* Both are authored by Richard J. Kilbride; Mr. Kilbride is listed in the Directory under Connecticut. In the listings that follow, examples are polished unless noted satin. For further information contact the Chase Collector's Society, listed in the Directory under Clubs, Newsletters, and Catalogs.

Bar caddy, chromium, jigger/opener/corkscrew/ice breaker **30.00**
Bell, Manchu, chrome, #13006 ....**80.00**
Bookends, brass/copper w/rivets & panels, 6½", G **350.00**
Bookends, figural soldiers, brass/blk plastic, von Nessen **325.00**
Bookends, ship's wheel, brass/walnut/Bakelite, pr **75.00**
Box, copper, imp Bacchus on lid, hinged, 1½x6x5", VG **550.00**
Box, Two-Tray, polished chromium or copper, #17106, 5" **45.00**
Butter dish, polished chromium w/wht knob, #17067, 2½x6" **65.00**
Cake & sandwich trowel, polished chromium w/wht knob, 8" **45.00**
Candlesticks, Taurex, copper, ca 1930, 9¾", pr **175.00**
Coffee service, 7¾" spherical percolator/cr/sug/15" tray **250.00**
Coffee service, Continental, #17054, 3-pc **225.00**
Coffee service, electric 8" pot/cr/sug/5 tumblers/rnd 12" tray **250.00**
Creamer & sugar bowl, Kent, chromium, wht hdl/knob, #17089 ..**75.00**
Dish, Tulip, polished chromium, ribbed scroll hdl, #90095 ....**50.00**
Duplex Jelly Dish, chrome basket w/glass insert, #90062, 5½" **30.00**
Flower bowl, Diana, chromium on fluted wht base, 10" **55.00**
Flower holder, Bubble, chromium w/glass liner, sq base, 3x3" **45.00**
Ice crusher, polished chromium, 6" **30.00**
Napkin holder, chromium or copper, wht plastic hdl, #90148 ......**50.00**
Percolator, Comet, chrome w/plastic hdls, #90120, 12" **145.00**
Pitcher, Sparta Water, chrome, wht plastic hdl, #90055, 8" **75.00**
Pitcher, Stir-It, polished chromium w/wht hdl, #17091, 8½" **65.00**
Relish dish, Fairfax, chromium w/wht hdls, glass liner, 8½" **60.00**
Sauce bowl, Lotus, chromium, blk hdl, +tray/ladle, #17045 ....**50.00**
Syrup jug, Jubilee, glass jug, chrome lid/tray, #26004 ....**35.00**
Tea ball, chromium w/wht hdl, #90118, 5" **50.00**
Tray, cracker & cheese; chromium w/walnut slicing board, #09016 ..**50.00**
Watering can, Niagara, brass/copper, Gerth, #05004, 8½" **175.00**

Chelsea

The Chelsea Porcelain Works operated in London from the middle of the 18th century, making porcelain of the finest quality. In 1770 it was purchased by the owner of the Derby Pottery and for about twenty years operated as a decorating shop. Production periods are indicated by trademarks: 1745-1750 — incised triangle, sometimes with 'Chelsea' and the year added; early 1750s — raised anchor mark on oval pad; 1752-1756 — small painted red anchor, only rarely found in blue underglaze; 1756-1769 — gold anchor; 1769-84 — Chelsea Derby mark with the script 'D' containing a horizontal anchor. Many reproductions have been made; be suspicious of any anchor mark larger than ¼".

Dish, floral w/insect, brn-trimmed wavy rim, 7", EX **600.00**
Figurine, boy w/flute & dog on plinth, gold anchor mk, 3¼" **225.00**
Figurine, gentleman (& lady), red anchor mk, 4¼", pr **325.00**
Figurine, lady w/lamb (male musician), boscage, 11", VG, pr **385.00**
Figurine, peacock, appl flowers & gold, anchor mk, 8", pr **435.00**

Figurine, seated gent (& lady), gold anchor mk, 7", pr **435.00**
Figurine, spotted dog & pup, gold anchor mk, 1700s, 3" **285.00**
Plate, fruit & nuts, wavy brn-trimmed rim, mk, 8" **500.00**
Tray, butterflies & insects, mc on wht, leaf shape, 10" **650.00**

Chelsea Dinnerware

Made from about 1830 to 1880 in the Staffordshire district of England, this white dinnerware is decorated with lustre embossings in the grape, thistle, sprig, or fruit and cornucopia patterns. The relief designs vary from lavender to blue, and the body of the ware may be porcelain, ironstone, or earthenware. Because it was not produced in Chelsea as the name would suggest, dealers often prefer to call it 'Grandmother's Ware.'

Grape, bowl, 8" **30.00**
Grape, coffeepot, stick hdl, 2-cup, 7" **65.00**
Grape, creamer **35.00**
Grape, cup & saucer **25.00**
Grape, egg cup **25.00**
Grape, pitcher, milk; 40-oz **50.00**
Grape, plate, 6" **12.00**
Grape, plate, 7" **18.00**
Grape, plate, 8" **20.00**
Grape, sauce boat **30.00**
Grape, sugar bowl, w/lid **50.00**
Grape, teacup **25.00**
Grape, teapot, octagonal, 10" **30.00**
Grape, teapot, 2-cup **65.00**
Grape, waste bowl **40.00**
Sprig, cake plate, 9" **40.00**
Sprig, cup & saucer **40.00**
Sprig, pitcher, milk **45.00**
Sprig, plate, dinner **25.00**
Sprig, plate, 7" **18.00**
Thistle, butter pat **15.00**
Thistle, cup & saucer **35.00**
Thistle, plate, 7" **15.00**

Chelsea Keramic Art Works

The Chelsea Keramic Art Works Robertson and Sons Pottery was established in 1872 in Chelsea, MA, by several members of the Robertson family, including Hugh C. Robertson who later formed the Dedham Pottery. Though their very early artware utilized a redware body, by the late 1870s it was replaced with yellow or buff burning clay. A line called Bourg-la-Reine (underglazed slip-decorated ware with primarily blue and green backgrounds) was produced, though not to any great extent. Other pieces were designed in imitation of Asian metalware, even to the extent that surfaces were 'hammered' to further enhance the effect. Occasionally live flora was pressed into the damp vessel walls to leave a decorative impression. They also made glazed plaques and tiles. Hugh C. Robertson ran the pottery alone after 1884 and labored to re-create the ancient Ming-era blood-red glaze. Although world acclaim greeted his rediscovery of what he then called 'Robertson's Blood,' his red-glazed vases cost too much to produce and bankruptcy followed in 1889. Supported by wealthy Boston art patrons, Hugh's pottery reopened in 1891 as the Chelsea Pottery U.S., and began using his other 1880s rediscovery, the crackle glaze, producing cobalt blue-decorated dinnerware. When this firm moved to Dedham in 1895 the ware became known as Dedham Pottery. From 1875 to 1880 the pottery was marked Chelsea Keramic Art Works Robertson and Sons in either two or three impressed lines. Earlier pieces were not marked. The impressed mark

CKAW, in a diamond formation, was also used between 1875 and 1889. From 1891 through 1895 the impressed letters CPUS in a clover leaf was utilized for the new firm. After the move to Dedham, only new Dedham Pottery marks were used. See also Dedham Pottery.

Ewer, gr & bl mottled gloss, mk on hdl, 14" **170.00**
Lamp base, emb floral branch on bl/gr glossy, 1880, 7¼x4¾" **175.00**
Plate, Clover, w/central medallion, imp CPUS clover mk, 8¼" ..**1,300.00**
Plate, pineapple, imp CPUS clover mk, 8½" **600.00**
Plate, pineapple band, bl on crackle gloss, sgn HCR, 10" **675.00**
Plate, Rabbit, imp clover mk, 10" **350.00**
Tile, emb floral on bl, 3-line mk, 12x6", pr **1,035.00**

Vase, fans and flowers in relief on blue gloss, signed GWF, marked CKAW, 7¾", $1,250.00; Pilgrim flask, floral relief on redware, signed with Robertson's early cojoined monogram, marked, 9½", $2,600.00.

Vase, appl wht flowers on butterscotch, squatty, 3½x5" **525.00**
Vase, bl & brn, flat ovoid w/hdls, chip, 13x8¾" **300.00**
Vase, brn/olive mottle, 4 shaped sides, elephant hdls, 7x3" **475.00**
Vase, cream crackle w/red flashing, hdld flask form, rpr, 10" **230.00**
Vase, floral relief on yel, Josephine Day, 1880, 4¾", EX **450.00**
Vase, sang-de-beouf, orange-peel texture w/gold lustre, 7½" ...**1,200.00**

Chicago Crucible

For only a few years during the 1920s, the Chicago (IL) Crucible Company made a limited amount of decorative pottery in addition to their regular line of architectural wares. Examples are very scarce today; they carry a variety of marks, all with the company name and location.

Vase, dk gr matt, twisted acorn shape, 9", EX **800.00**
Vase, gr matt, leaf-scalloped rim/low width, long hdls, 11" **600.00**
Vase, med bl, vertical leaves, high-fired/textured, 6½" **450.00**
Vase, med gr & brn matt, 4 lg leaves, bulbous, 5x3½" **475.00**
Vase, mint gr/olive matt mottle, twisted bottle form, 8", NM **350.00**
Vase, tobacco brn matt, vertical leaves, shouldered, 6½" **450.00**

Children's Books

Children's books, especially those from the Victorian era, are charming collectibles. Colorful lithographic illustrations that once delighted little boys in long curls and tiny girls in long stockings and lots of ribbons and lace have lost none of their appeal. Some collectors limit themselves to a specific subject, while others may be far more interested in the illustrations. First editions are more valuable than later issues, and condition and rarity are very important factors to consider before making your purchase. For further information we recommend *Collector's Guide to Children's Books, 1850-1950*, by Diane McClure Jones and Rosemary Jones; and *Whitman Juvenile Books Reference & Value Guide*, by David and Virginia Brown. Both are available from Collector Books or your local bookstore.

Adventures of Mr Toad, Big Golden Books, 1949, VG 20.00
Adventures of Poor Mrs Quack, TW Burgess, 1st ed, 1917 ....50.00
Adventures of Reddy Fox, Thornton W Burgess, 1917, EX 40.00
Alice's Further Adventures in Wonderland, linen cover, EX 38.50
Amazing Spider-Man, Lancer Books, 1966, paperbk, EX+ 15.00
Ancient Rhymes, McLoughlin, 1880s, EX 65.00
Arabian Nights, World, 1924, F Brundage illus, gilt cloth, VG 25.00
Aristocats, Little Golden Books, #D122, 1st ed, VG+ 12.00
Bedtime Stories, Little Golden Books, #2, 7th ed, VG+ 16.00
Big Book of Animal Stories, Kenosha, 1946 ....25.00
Billy Whiskers in the South, F Montgomery, Saalfield, 1917, G ..55.00
Black Arrow, NC Wyeth illus, EX 75.00

The Bobbsey Twins at the Seashore, Laura Lee Hope, Whitman, 1954, EX, $10.00.

Boys' Book of Sports & Outdoor Life, Century, 1st ed, 1886, VG 150.00
Bozo Helps Dinky Toot the Horn, McGraw-Hill, 1964, cb pgs, EX+ ..16.00
Buffalo Bill, D'Aulaire & Parin, Doubleday, 1st ed, 1952, VG ...125.00
Bugs Bunny Gets a Job, Little Golden Books, #136, 1st ed, VG+ .15.00
Candy Land, McLoughlin Little Color Classics, 1928, G+ 25.00
Charlotte's Web, EB White, Harper Bros, 1952, M 150.00
Cheery Scarecrow, Johnny Gruelle, Donohue, 1929, VG 65.00
Child's Geography of the World, Appleton, revised ed, 1951, VG ...20.00
Children's Stories in Am History, London, 1st ed, 1886, EX 35.00
Cinderella, Little Golden Books, #13, Disney, 1950, NM 12.00
Cinderella, McLoughlin Bros, 1896, linen, EX 38.50
Cotton in My Sack, Lippencott, 1st ed, 1949, VG 50.00
Dale Evans & the Lost Gold Mine, Little Golden Books, #213, VG+ ...18.00
Dick Tracy, Chester Gould, Whitman, 1943, EX+ 25.00
Donald Duck & the Wishing Star Story Book, Whitman, 1952, EX+ ...18.00
Dr Dolittle's Garden, Hugh Lofting, Stokes, 1st ed, 1927, VG+ ...75.00
Dr Seuss' Sleep Book, 1962 ....35.00
Fairy Stories, Merrill, 1953, EX+ 20.00
Felix the Cat, Wonder Books, #665, 1953, EX 10.00
Fighting Men of Mars, Edgar Rice Burroughs, VG 50.00
Gingerbread Man, Fuzzy Wuzzy series, Whitman, 1944, M 75.00
Goldilocks & the Three Bears, Blue Ribbon, 1934, pop-up, VG 200.00
Heidi, Johanna Spyri, Lippincott, 1919, VG 65.00
Howdy Doody Circus, Little Golden Books, #99, B ed, VG+ 16.00
J Fred Muggs, Little Golden Books, #234, A ed, EX 20.00
Jack & the Beanstalk, Duenewald Printing, 1944, pull-tab, NM ..60.00
Lassie & the Kittens, Tell-a-Tale, 1956, NM 10.00
Last of the Mohicans, NC Wyeth illus, EX 75.00
Little Mermaid, Disney, 1st ed, pop-up, M 15.00
Little Red Engine Gets a Name, Faber & Faber, ca 1940, VG 15.00
Little Red Hen, Macmillan, 1928, VG+ 30.00
Little Tom Tucker, McLoughlin Bros, 1923, linen, EX 35.00
Littlest Rebel, Shirley Temple ed, Random House, 1939, VG 25.00
Lone Ranger & War Horse, Cozy-Corner series, Whitman, 1951, NM ..30.00
Lost Princess of Oz, L Rank Baum, JR Neill illus 95.00
Mickey Mouse, Blue Ribbon, 1933, pop-up, EX+ 265.00
Mickey Mouse Stories, Walt Disney Studios, 1937, blk & wht, EX ...75.00
Miss Sniff the Fuzzy Car, Fuzzy Wuzzy series, Whitman, 1945, EX..75.00

Mister Ed, Little Golden Books, #483, A ed, EX 18.00
Mother Goose, Bowers Movie Flip Book #1, 1923, scarce, EX 85.00
Mother Goose, Franklin Watts, 1st Am ed, 1965, VG 30.00
Mother Goose, Her Best-Known Rhymes, Saalfield, 1st ed, VG ...55.00
Mother Goose, Tell-a-Tale, 1958, EX 8.00
Mother Goose, Vernon Grant illus, Kellogg's premium, 1934, EX ..60.00
My Pets, World, 1929, Mammoth series, EX 25.00
Night Before Christmas, C Moore, Lippincott, 1st Am ed, NM .185.00
Nursery Tales, Little Golden Books, #14, 3rd ed, EX 18.00
Old Granny Fox, Gr Meadow series, TW Burgess, 1st ed, 1920 ....60.00
Peter the Goat, David McKay, 1940, VG 25.00
Pets, McClure Phillips, 1st ed, 1906, VG 35.00
Puss-In-Boots, Blue Ribbon, 1934, pop-up, blk & wht illus, EX .200.00
Raggedy Ann in Cookie Land, J Gruelle, Voland, 1st ed, 1931, VG ..85.00
Roy Rogers Adventures No 3, Dean, VG 30.00
Runaway Robot Book, Scholastic Book Services, 1965, paperbk, EX ..15.00
Snuggy Bedtime Stories, Stokes, 1st ed, 1906, G 45.00
Stuart Little, Harper & Bros, 1st ed, 1945, VG 75.00
Surprise Package, Big Golden Books, Disney, 1948, VG 12.00
Teddy Bear & Other Songs, AA Milne, Dutton, 1st Am ed, 1926, G+ ..75.00
Tin Soldier, McLoughlin Bros, 1945, EX 10.00
Tom Corbett Trip to the Moon, Wonder Books, #713, 1953 ....10.00
Treasure Book of Best Stories, Saalfield, 1939, EX+ 25.00
Uncle Scrooge Rainbow Runaway, Whitman, 1965, EX+ 18.00
Walt Disney's Living Desert, Simon & Schuster, 1954, VG 10.00
Yearling, NC Wyeth illus, EX 95.00
Zorro, Little Golden Books, #D68, B ed, VG+ 14.00

Children's Things

Nearly every item devised for adult furnishings has been reduced to child size — furniture, dishes, sporting goods, even some tools. All are very collectible. During the late 17th and early 18th centuries, miniature china dinnerware sets were made both in China and in England. They were not intended primarily as children's playthings, however, but instead were made to furnish miniature rooms and cabinets that provided a popular diversion for the adults of that period. By the 19th century, the emphasis had shifted, and most of the small-scaled dinnerware and tea sets were made for children's play.

Late in the 19th century and well into the 20th, toy pressed glass dishes were made, many in the same pattern as full-scale glassware. Today these toy dishes often fetch prices in the same range as those for the 'grown-ups'!

Authorities Margaret and Kenn Whitmyer have compiled a lovely book, *The Collector's Encyclopedia of Children's Dishes,* with full-color photos and current market values; you will find their address in the Directory under Ohio. We also recommend *Children's Glass Dishes, China, and Furniture,* by Doris Anderson Lechler, available at your local bookstore or public library. See also A B C Plates; Canary Lustre; Clothing; Stickley; Willow Ware; etc.

Key:
ds — doll size   Fr — French
Emp — Empire

China

Bowl, Jumbo Elephant, Germany, 1910 ....65.00
Bowl, porridge; girls swinging, bl transfer, emb rim, 7⅛" 60.00
Creamer & sugar bowl, Blue Willow, w/lid, 2", 2¾" 40.00
Feeding dish, Baby Bunting, w/rhyme, gold trim, ca 1908, 8¾" 32.00
Feeding dish, Baby's Plate, girl in bl w/lg dog at table, 7¾" 28.00
Feeding dish, girls hang wash, Germany, 6" 75.00

Feeding dish, House That Jack Built, Germany, 7¼" 68.00
Feeding dish, 3 girls ice skating, unmk, 7" 65.00
Feeding set, Peter Rabbit, mug/dish/plate, Wedgwood 45.00
Feeding set, Raggedy Ann & Andy, Crooksville, 1941, 3-pc 60.00
Mug, Am Eagles on Shell/Prosper Freedom, brn transfer, 2½" ...325.00
Mug, begger & dog, brn transfer, 2¾" 60.00
Mug, Bible transfer, Path of Truth..., mc, 2½" 110.00
Mug, Bible transfer, Search the Scriptures, mc enamel, 2½" 90.00
Mug, Bow & Arrow/Playing at Horses, brn transfers, 2¾", NM 90.00
Mug, Carpenters & Iron Mongers, purple transfer, 2⅝" 90.00
Mug, children & man in boat, blk transfers w/mc, 2¾" 60.00
Mug, children at fence/others w/toy boats, brn transfer, 2½", EX .80.00
Mug, children playing games, brn transfer w/mc, 2½" 70.00
Mug, Christianity poem, blk transfer, pk lustre rim, 2½" 110.00
Mug, drum, marbles & badminton set, mc on porc, 20th C, 2⅝" .35.00
Mug, Dutch children, windmills & geese w/gold, Limoges 60.00
Mug, family scene, 1 of Temperance series, red transfer, 2¾" 90.00
Mug, florals/flags/leaves in pk lustre w/mc enamel, 2½" 90.00
Mug, Flowers That Never Fade..., blk transfer, 2⅞", EX 75.00
Mug, HMS Pinafore, blk transfer w/mc & gold, 3¼" 60.00
Mug, House in Which.../Church, 2 blk transfers, 2½" 70.00
Mug, Industry Is Fortune's Handmaid, blk transfer, 2⅜" 90.00
Mug, Juggle, brn transfer w/mc details, 2¾" 90.00
Mug, lady/child/old man/dog, brn transfer, 2⅞", NM 70.00
Mug, milking scene, blk transfer w/mc, 3", EX 90.00
Mug, Mr Pickwick & Mrs Bard, blk transfer, 3" 90.00
Mug, Northern Spell, blk transfer w/mc details, 2¾", EX 60.00
Mug, Partridge Shooting, brn transfer w/mc, 2½", EX 50.00
Mug, prayer transfer, mc w/pk lustre, 2½", EX 65.00
Mug, Seal of US over motto, red transfer on creamware, 2" 475.00
Mug, Under a 1st Rate Physician, blk transfer w/mc, 2¾" 90.00
Mug, Whip Top, children, blk transfer w/mc, 2¾" 90.00
Mug, 2 men in beached boat, dk bl transfer, 2½" 40.00
Plate, Against Lying, blk transfer w/mc, emb florals, 5¾" 60.00
Plate, Fishers, brn transfer, Edge Malkin & Co, 3⅞" 25.00
Plate, Franklin Maxims transfer, emb floral rim w/mc, 6½", NM .50.00
Plate, girl w/sheep, bl transfer, floral border, 7¼" 65.00
Plate, grill; children playing on cream, ca 1930, 7¼" 12.00
Plate, horseman slashing foot soldier, brn transfer, 7⅞" 60.00
Plate, Mr Caterwal Teaching His Children, blk transfer, 8", G 30.00
Plate, Robinson Crusoe, blk transfer w/mc, unmk, 6½" 70.00
Plate, Robinson Crusoe's Raft, blk transfer w/mc, 8-sided, 7", EX ...80.00
Plate, There Are No Gains w/o Pains, brn transfer w/mc, 5⅜" 70.00
Plate, They Took It Away..., blk transfer w/mc, 7½" 80.00
Plate, 2 boys w/dog, blk transfer, 8-sided, 7", NM 80.00
Plate, 2 girls playing game, blk transfer, Dawson, 6½", EX 70.00
Platter, emb/mc plum & leaves, Staffordshire, 4", NM 135.00
Soup, Franklin Flying a Kite, bl transfer, 3½" 45.00
Tea cup, Alice, Hammersley, 1920s 25.00
Tea set, Alice Tea Time, 1949, extra lg, MIB 55.00
Tea set, gr floral w/mc, C Meigh, ca 1840, 4½" pot+9 pcs 275.00
Tea set, May w/Apron, brn transfer, 5½" pot, 20 pcs, EX 180.00
Tea set, mc floral on pearlware, 4" pot+6 pcs, EX 350.00
Tea set, Merry Christmas, pk lustre & gold, 12-pc 395.00
Tea set, mixed fruit, beaded lustre, Germany, 1900s, 18-pc 245.00
Teapot, bl & red spatter, 8-sided, Staffordshire, rpr, 3¾" 60.00
Teapot, bl floral transfer, Staffordshire, 4½", EX 75.00
Teapot, dk bl & ochre floral, Staffordshire, rstr, 4¾" 150.00
Teapot, mc floral medallion, Staffordshire, 4⅜", EX 180.00
Warming dish, Hansel & Gretal, Holland, 1930s 65.00

Furniture

Examples with no dimensions given are child size unless noted doll size.

Armchair, Euro-style cvgs, cane seat, 20th C, 18" +settee 140.00
Armchair, ladderbk, woven splint seat, rfn, 25" 115.00
Armchair, wingbk, mauve uphl, modern, 21" 110.00
Armchair, 3-slat bk, red rpt, rpl splint seat, 21", EX 85.00
Armchair rocker, Adirondack style, bentwood w/old rpt, 25" 115.00
Bed, low post, rosewood grained, ME, 1830s, 41x72x32" 635.00
Bed, mahog Sheraton canopy, trn posts/spindles, 72x60x33" 770.00
Bed, painted Federal, 4-post tester, ca 1800, 14x15x11" 650.00
Bed, spindle type, folds, w/mattress & pillow, 25" 110.00
Blanket chest, pine, red pnt, bracket base, 19th C, 12½x20" ..1,250.00
Chair, side; country ladderbk; rpl rush seat, 22½" 85.00
Chair, side; grpt, 3 vignettes on bk slats, 19th C, 27" 140.00
Chest, tiger maple/ebonized, 2-drw, glass pulls, 1830s, 9x12" ..1,725.00
Chest of drws, pine, grpt, Isaac E Barnard, VT, 1800s, 8⅜x7" 500.00
Chest over drw, smoke grained, wood pulls, 1830s, 24x31x17" ..1,380.00

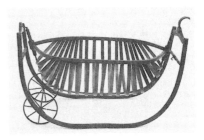

Cradle (sometimes referred to as a field cradle), slatted basket on bowed frame with two wheels opposing a bentwood handle, 19th century, EX original condition, $1,300.00.

Cradle, bl pnt w/red stripes/gilt stencil, ca 1875, 29x50x24" 635.00
Cradle, cherry, old worn red pnt, dvtl, 42" 300.00
Cradle, cherry, sq corner posts, trn finials, rfn/rstr, 43" 180.00
Cradle, grpt, 19th C, 7¾x17½", EX 230.00
Cradle, pine, hooded style, orig bl pnt, 18th C, 28½" 430.00
Cradle, pine w/old blk rpt, curved hood, 36" L 275.00
Cradle, pine w/old dk red, scalloped ends & sides, 9½x19" 105.00
Cradle, pine w/old red, renailed hood, 23" L 95.00
Cradle, pine w/old red pnt, wht flowers, landscape, 27" 165.00
Cradle, poplar, old grained rpt, dvtl, heart cutouts, 41" 150.00
Cradle, poplar w/gr int pnt, rnded hood, rfn, rprs, 43" 165.00
Cradle, walnut, trn finials, heart cutouts, gr rpt, 39" 200.00
Cupboard, dbl doors over bin & 4 drws, rfn/rprs, 43x33x14" 250.00
Cupboard, gr pnt, wire nails, primitive, 20" 75.00
Cupboard, pine w/wht rpt, dbl glass doors, sq nails, 27" 350.00
Cupboard, poplar w/red combed grpt, 1-brd door w/pane, 15x10" ..495.00
Desk, Country, rfn cherry & walnut, door & drw, 38x35x20" 385.00
Desk, poplar w/old red, 1-brd ends, nailed drw, OH, 31x23x16" ..550.00
Divan, walnut, trn/cvd details/reuphl, Victorian, 40" 195.00
Dresser, Eastlake Victorian, rfn walnut, marble top, 53" 550.00
Dresser, oak, 3-drw, wooden pulls, curved apron, 17", EX 150.00
Dresser, walnut w/dk finish, 3 drws & mirror, 9¼" 300.00
Highchair, Nantucket Chpndl, uphl seat, floral decor, EX 5,000.00
Highchair, red & blk grpt w/gold, rpt, 1900s, 29" 150.00
Highchair, Windsor, red pnt, A Folsom & Co, NH, 1830, 35" ..1,100.00
Rocker, Limbert #872, 2 curved bk slats, new seat/rfn, 23" 280.00
Rocker, w/arms, oak, Arts & Crafts, V slat+1 in bk, rfn, VG 400.00
Rocker, walnut w/cane seat & bk, Victorian, 26" 170.00
Rocker, Windsor w/mc pnt decor, bamboo trnings, 29" 330.00
Rocker, worn alligatored pnt, Peek-a-Boo decal on crest, 28" 195.00
Sofa, Am Rococo cvd rosewood, 1850, 47x33" 1,200.00
Table, drop leaf; oak/pine/poplar, rfn, 19x25x12" +leaves 85.00

Table, drop leaf; pine Co Hplwht, sq legs, 18x24x12"+leaves 200.00
Table, ice cream; wht rpt, 10x15" dia, +4 16" chairs 140.00
Table, walnut w/walnut burl 8-sided top, 4½x5x5" 380.00
Wash stand, wicker, old wht rpt, +4 porc enamel accessories 220.00

Glass

Panelled Cane, mug, cobalt, 2¾", $45.00.

Amazon (Mitered Sawtooth), creamer 50.00
American Beauty Rose, cake stand, 6⅝" 60.00
Arrowhead-In-Ovals, sugar bowl 35.00
Austrian No 200, butter dish 250.00
Baby Thumbprint, cake stand 125.00
Baby Thumbprint, compote, w/lid 200.00
Bead & Scroll, butter dish, w/flashing or clear 200.00
Bead & Scroll, spooner 70.00
Beaded Swirl Variant, sugar bowl 40.00
Braided Belt, sugar bowl, wht decor, w/lid 250.00
Bucket (Wooden Pail), butter dish 300.00
Bucket (Wooden Pail), creamer 75.00
Button Arches, creamer 70.00
Button Panel, butter dish, clear or w/o gold trim 125.00
Buzz Star (Whirligig), butter dish 35.00
Buzz Star (Whirligig), punch cup, 1¼x1⅜" 8.00
Colonial, butter dish, Cambridge 27.00
Daisy Band, cup & saucer 45.00
Diamond, cup & saucer, bl opaque 135.00
Diamond Ridge, sugar bowl, w/lid 150.00
Eastlake, mug, amber 22.00
Elephant, plate 200.00
Feeding Deer, mug, amber 45.00
Fine Cut Star & Fan, sugar bowl, w/lid 35.00
Grapevine w/Ovals, creamer 65.00
Hobnail, mug 50.00
Horizontal Threads, spooner 42.00
Inverted Strawberry, bowl, master berry 60.00
Kittens, bowl, marigold carnival 250.00
Lamb, butter dish 195.00
Lamb, creamer 80.00
Lion, cup & saucer 75.00
Loops & Ropes, cup & saucer 30.00
Martyrs, mug 75.00
Michigan, butter dish, gold trim 130.00
Michigan, sugar bowl, w/lid 60.00
Monkeys & Vines, mug 58.00
Nursery Rhyme, punch bowl, bl opaque, w/6 cups 800.00
Nursery Rhyme, punch cup, milk glass 25.00
Old Independence Hall, plate 75.00
Oval Star, bowl, berry; sm 10.00
Oval Star, butter dish 20.00
Oval Star, pitcher, w/4 tumblers 125.00
Oval Star, punch bowl 55.00
Oval Star, punch cup 9.00
Oval Star, tumbler 10.00
Pattee Cross, bowl, sauce 10.00
Pattee Cross, pitcher 90.00

Pattee Cross, punch bowl 100.00
Pattee Cross, tumbler 15.00
Pennsylvania, butter dish, gold trim 110.00
Pennsylvania, creamer, gold trim 40.00
Pennsylvania, spooner, gold trim 40.00
Quilted Center, plate 38.00
Rex (Fancy Cut), pitcher 75.00
Rex (Fancy Cut), spooner 35.00
Rex (Fancy Cut), tumbler 18.00
Rooster, creamer 140.00
Seated Dog, plate 95.00
Stippled Raindrop & Dewdrop, spooner 80.00
Stippled Vine & Beads, creamer 60.00
Stippled Vine & Beads, sugar bowl, w/lid 110.00
Style, creamer 18.00
Tulip & Honeycomb, punch bowl 25.00
Wheat Sheaf, punch bowl 35.00
Whirligig, butter dish 32.00
Wild Rose, butter dish, milk glass 85.00
Wild Rose, candlestick 150.00
Wild Rose, punch bowl, milk glass, w/6 cups 250.00
Wild Rose, spooner, milk glass 60.00
Wild Rose, sugar bowl, milk glass 100.00

Miscellaneous

Bicycle siren, Fire Chief, tin litho, push plunger, 1940s, MIB 100.00
Blocks, chromolitho paper on wood, 19 in orig 13x10½" box 165.00
Buckboard wagon, wood w/old rpt, spoke wheels w/rubber, 42" L ...300.00
Carriage, Haywood-Wakefield, wood & pnt enamel, bent chrome .500.00
Carriage, wood/bamboo, wire-spoke wheels, rpt, Gendron, 53" ..230.00
Crayons, Ding Dong School, NMIB 6.00
Doll stroller, iron w/fabric covering, wood hdl, 1890s, 27" 225.00
Kaleidoscope, brass cylinder, ped wood base, 19th C, G 395.00
Mantel lustre, clambroth w/gold florals/bands, prisms, 7" 225.00
Noah's Ark, wood w/orig mc pnt, 22", +94 figures, VG 825.00
Noah's Ark, wood/straw inlay, cvd wood/pnt, 37 animals/2 women ...330.00
Rattle/whistle, silver & coral, mk Birmingham, 1887, 3½" 300.00
Rocking horse, wood w/old mc pnt, saddle w/stirrups, 42", EX ...440.00
Slate, dbl, orig laces, opens like a book, sm 50.00
Sled, mc pnt decor on wood fr w/wrought fittings, 34" L 2,000.00
Sled, orig mc pnt on wood, steel-tipped runners, 32" 220.00
Sled, wood w/pnt rose, orig varnish, steel-tipped runners, 36" 225.00

Chintz

'Chintz' is the generic name for English china with an allover floral transfer design. This eye-catching china is reminiscent of chintz dress fabric. It is colorful, bright, and cheery with its many floral designs and reminds one of an English garden in full bloom. It was produced in England during the first half of this century and stands among other styles of china. Pattern names often found with the manufacturer's name on the bottom of pieces include Anemone, Chelsea, Chintz, Delphinium Chintz, June Roses, Mayfair, Hazel, Eversham, Royalty, Sweet Pea, Summertime, Springtime, and Welbeck, among others.

The older patterns tend to be composed of larger flowers, while the later, more popular lines can be quite intricate in design. And while the first collectors preferred the earthenware lines, many are now searching for the bone china dinnerware made by such firms as Shelley. Prices are already formidable and rising. You can concentrate on reassembling a favorite pattern, or you can mix two or more designs together for a charming, eclectic look. Another choice may be to limit your collection to teapots (the stacking ones are especially nice), breakfast sets, or cups and saucers. Our advisor for this category is Mary Jane Hastings; see the directory under Illinois. See also Egg Cups.

Anemone, biscuit barrel, Royal Winton 495.00
Anemone, cheese keeper, Lord Nelson 225.00
Apple Blossom, teapot, James Kent, 4-cup 595.00
Ascot, condiment set, Crown Ducal 165.00
Ascot, plate, 8-sided, Crown Ducal, 9" 90.00
Balmoral, creamer & sugar bowl, Royal Winton 145.00
Balmoral, cup & saucer, Royal Winton 95.00
Bedale, shakers, Royal Winton, pr 110.00
Bedale, trivet, Royal Winton 110.00
Beeston, jug, Royal Winton, 4" 295.00
Beeston, plate, dinner; Royal Winton, 10" 165.00
Black Beauty, butter dish, Lord Nelson 225.00
Black Beauty, cake plate, tab hdls, Lord Nelson 175.00
Blue Chintz, cup & saucer, Crown Ducal 95.00
Blue Chintz, jam pot & undertray, Crown Ducal 185.00
Brama/Spring Time, cake server, metal hdl, Midwinter 195.00
Briar Rose, plate, Lord Nelson, 4" sq 55.00
Butterfly Chintz, plate, Wade, 6" 65.00
Canton, vase, Crown Ducal, 9" 195.00
Cheadle, bonbon, Royal Winton 65.00
Cheadle, compote, ftd, Royal Winton 150.00
Chelsea, bowl, salad; chrome lid, Royal Winton 195.00
Chelsea, tennis set, Royal Winton 125.00
Chintz, bowl, Royal Winton, 5" 35.00
Clevedon, breakfast set 950.00
Clevedon, teapot, Royal Winton, 2-cup 450.00
Clyde, nut dish, Royal Winto 35.00
Clyde, relish, Royal Winton, sm 45.00
Coral, plate, Midwinter, 9" 115.00
Cotswold, cake stand, ped ft, Royal Winton, 8" sq 290.00
Cotswold, toast rack, 4-slice, Royal Winton 265.00
Cranstone, jug, Royal Winton, 5" 400.00
Cranstone, tray, Royal Winton, 7x12" 295.00
Crazy Paving, cup & saucer, demitasse; James Kent 50.00
Crocus, bowl, coupe; Royal Winton, 8" 95.00
Crocus, jug, hot water; Royal Winton 350.00
Cromer, creamer & sugar bowl w/tray, Royal Winton 135.00
Cromer, shakers, pr, w/tray, Royal Winton 145.00
Delphinium Chintz, egg cup, Royal Winton 140.00
Delphinium Chintz, plate, Royal Winton, 7" 75.00
Dorset, butter pat, Royal Winton 45.00
Dorset, plate, Royal Winton, 9" 100.00
DuBarry, butter dish, James Kent 165.00
DuBarry, creamer & sugar bowl, James Kent 145.00
Eleanor, teapot, Royal Winton, 6-cup 495.00
Eleanor, trivet, Royal Winton 110.00
English Rose, canoe, Royal Winton 350.00
English Rose, cup & saucer, Royal Winton 110.00
Estelle, egg cup, Royal Winton 140.00
Estelle, plate, Royal Winton, 6" 75.00
Esther, bud vase, Royal Winton 155.00
Esther, tennis set, Royal Winton 145.00
Evesham, teapot, Royal Winton, 6-cup 850.00
Evesham, teapot, stacking, Royal Winton 950.00
Fireglow Black, cup & saucer, Royal Winton 75.00
Fireglow White, cup & saucer, Royal Winton 85.00
Floral Feast, canoe, Royal Winton 225.00
Floral Feast, cheese keeper, Royal Winton, lg 225.00
Floral Garden (Jacobean), mug, Royal Winton, 4½" 175.00
Florence, plate, Royal Winton, 10" 200.00
Florence, plate, Royal Winton, 9" 175.00

Florida, jam pot & tray, James Kent 185.00
Florida, teapot, James Kent, 4-cup 600.00
Green Tulip, cake plate, Lord Nelson 200.00
Green Tulip, cake server, 3-tier, Lord Nelson 225.00
Grey Fruit, bowl, Crown Ducal 175.00
Harmony, bonbon, James Kent 55.00
Hazel, coffeepot, Royal Winton 950.00
Hazel, condiment set, Royal Winton 295.00
Heather, plate, Lord Nelson, 4" 45.00
Heather, teapot, stacking, Lord Nelson 550.00
Hydrangea Black, compote, James Kent 85.00
Hydrangea White, compote, James Kent 135.00
Ivory Chintz, candlestick, Crown Ducal 195.00
Ivory Chintz, vase, trumpet form, Crown Ducal, 6" 165.00
Ivory Fruit, vase, trumpet form, Crown Ducal, 6" 125.00
Joyce-Lynn, bowl, salad; chrome lid, Royal Winton 175.00
Joyce-Lynn, mint sauce & liner, Royal Winton 135.00
Julia, breakfast set, Royal Winton 1,200.00
Julia, teapot, stacking; Royal Winton 1,000.00
June Festival, bowl, soup; Royal Winton, 8" 70.00
June Festival, tray, Royal Winton, 7x12" 110.00
June Roses, butter dish, Royal Winton 225.00
June Roses, canoe, Royal Winton 325.00
Kew, cup & saucer, Royal Winton 95.00
Kew, salt & pepper shakers w/tray, Royal Winton 175.00
Kinver, toast rack, 2-slice, Royal Winton 225.00
Kinver, toast rack, 4-slice, Royal Winton 275.00
Lilac Time, plate, Empire, 7" 45.00
Lorna Doone, cake plate & server, Midwinter 195.00
Lorna Doone, sugar shaker, Midwinter 200.00
Majestic, hot-water jug, Royal Winton 450.00
Majestic, teapot, Royal Winton, 4-cup 700.00
Marguerite, creamer & sugar bowl, Royal Winton 145.00
Marguerite, relish, Royal Winton 75.00
Marigold, plate, Crown Ducal, 9" 100.00
Marigold, plate, James Kent, 9" 65.00
Marina, bud vase, Lord Nelson 85.00
Marina, nut dish, Lord Nelson 85.00
Marion, candy box, Royal Winton 350.00
Marion, tray, Royal Winton, 7x12" 250.00
Mauve Chintz, jug, Crown Ducal, 7" 175.00
May Festival, coaster, Royal Winton 35.00
May Festival, nut dish, Royal Winton 65.00
Mayfair, bonbon compote, Royal Winton 95.00
Mayfair, butter pat, Royal Winton 45.00
Mille Fleurs, bowl, James Kent, 6" 50.00
Mille Fleurs, creamer & sugar bowl, James Kent 125.00
Morning Glory, butter dish, Royal Winton 165.00
Morning Glory, teapot, Royal Winton, 4-cup 395.00
Nantwich, shakers, w/tray, Royal Winton 175.00
Nantwich, tray, Royal Winton, 6x10" 125.00
Old Cottage, breakfast set, Royal Winton 700.00
Old Cottage, tennis set, Royal Winton 90.00
Orient, condiment set, Royal Winton 195.00
Orient, shakers, Royal Winton, pr 75.00
Pansy, cheese keeper, Lord Nelson 225.00
Pansy, plate, Lord Nelson, 4" 35.00
Pekin, shakers, Royal Winton, pr 50.00
Pekin, trivet, Royal Winton 75.00
Pelham, breakfast set, Royal Winton 550.00
Pelham, compote, Royal Winton 100.00
Peony, cake plate, pierced hdls, Royal Winton 150.00
Pink Chintz, coffeepot, Crown Ducal, 3-cup 575.00
Pink Chintz, plate, Crown Ducal, 9" 115.00

Primula, bowl, James Kent, 9" 135.00
Primula, cup & saucer, demitasse; James Kent 85.00
Purple Chintz, bowl, Crown Ducal, 12" 150.00
Purple Chintz, vase, Crown Ducal, 9" 350.00
Queen Anne, coaster, Royal Winton 30.00
Queen Anne, creamer & sugar bowl, Royal Winton 75.00
Quilt, plate, Royal Winton, 10" 125.00
Quilt, plate, Royal Winton, 9" 95.00
Rapture, bowl, James Kent, 9" 100.00
Rapture, butter dish, James Kent 145.00
Richmond, egg cup, Royal Winton 85.00
Richmond, toast rack, 2-slice, Royal Winton 175.00
Rosalynde, coffeepot, James Kent 750.00
Rosalynde, jam pot, w/tray, James Kent 195.00
Rose & Motifs, jug, Crown Ducal, 5" 275.00
Rose & Motifs, spill vase, Crown Ducal, 8" 155.00
Rose DuBarry, cake plate, tab hdls, Royal Winton 145.00
Rose DuBarry, relish, Royal Winton 125.00
Rosetime, cheese keeper, Lord Nelson 250.00
Rosetime, teapot, stacking, Lord Nelson 650.00
Royal Brocade, bud vase, Lord Nelson 65.00
Royal Brocade, teapot, stacking, Lord Nelson 495.00
Royalty, jug, Royal Winton, 5" 425.00
Royalty, teapot, Royal Winton, 6-cup 800.00
Rutland, cup & saucer, Royal Winton 65.00
Rutland, jug, Royal Winton, 5" 250.00
Shrewsbury, cake plate, ped ft, Royal Winton, 8" 175.00
Shrewsbury, mint sauce boat w/tray, Royal Winton 175.00
Silverdale, nut dish, James Kent 35.00
Silverdale, tray, sandwich; James Kent 85.00
Skylark, jug, Lord Nelson, 7" 165.00
Skylark, shakers, Lord Nelson, pr, w/tray 135.00
Somerset, creamer & sugar bowl, w/tray, Royal Winton 175.00
Somerset, jug, Royal Winton, 4½" 350.00
Somerset, teapot, Royal Winton, 2-cup 425.00
Spring, biscuit barrel, Royal Winton 695.00
Spring, hot-water jug, Royal Winton 375.00
Spring Glory, butter dish, Royal Winton 155.00
Spring Glory, teapot, stacking, Royal Winton 650.00
Springtime, bowl, soup; Royal Winton, 8" 65.00
Springtime, creamer & sugar bowl, Royal Winton 110.00
Stratford, cup & saucer, demitasse; Royal Winton 125.00
Stratford, teapot, Royal Winton, 6-cup 900.00
Summertime, bowl, cream soup; w/tray, Royal Winton 140.00
Summertime, egg cup, Royal Winton, lg 95.00
Sunshine, canoe, Royal Winton 265.00
Sunshine, tray, Royal Winton, 7x12" 195.00
Sweet Nancy, plate, Royal Winton, 5" 55.00
Sweet Nancy, plate, Royal Winton, 7" 70.00
Sweet Pea, breakfast set, Royal Winton 950.00
Sweet Pea, plate, Royal Winton, 7" 100.00
Tapestry, plate, James Kent, 9" 85.00
Tapestry, tray, sandwich; James Kent 95.00
Tartan, plate, Royal Winton, 4" 35.00
Tartan, toast rack, 2-slice, Royal Winton 155.00
Victorian, compote, Royal Winton 100.00
Victorian, condiment set, Royal Winton 150.00
Victorian Rose, butter dish, Royal Winton 195.00
Victorian Rose, cake stand, 2-tier, Royal Winton 210.00
Welbeck, coffeepot, Royal Winton 1,100.00
Welbeck, tennis set, Royal Winton 195.00
Wild Flowers, compote, Royal Winton 135.00
Wild Flowers, cup & saucer, Royal Winton 85.00
Winifred, compote, Royal Winton 75.00

Winifred, jug, Royal Winton, 4" 135.00

Chocolate Glass

Jacob Rosenthal developed chocolate glass, a rich shaded opaque brown sometimes referred to as caramel slag, in 1900 at the Indiana Tumbler and Goblet Company of Greentown, Indiana. Later, other companies produced similar ware. Only the latter is listed here. See also Greentown. Our advisors for this category are Jerry and Sandi Garrett; they are listed in the Directory under Indiana.

Phenix-5 punch bowl, Property of Patent Applied Phenix Nerve Beverage Co inside, 6½x10½", $4,000.00.

Barber bottle (cologne), Venetian, w/stopper 650.00
Bonbon, Venetian, w/lid, rnd 400.00
Bowl, Aldine, w/lid, oval 1,650.00
Bowl, Chrysanthemum Leaf, 7" dia 575.00
Bowl, orange; Grape & Cable 3,500.00
Bowl, sauce; Cattail & Water Lily, Fenton 165.00
Bowl, 5-fluted 350.00
Box, Aurora, rectangular, 9x5½" 1,500.00
Butter dish, Cattail & Water Lily, Fenton 950.00
Butter dish, File 2,500.00
Candle holder, Griffin 2,000.00
Compote, Melrose, 7¾" 300.00
Cracker jar, Chrysanthemum Leaf, w/lid 2,500.00
Creamer, Rose Garland 1,350.00
Creamer, Touching Squares 1,250.00
Creamer, Wild Rose w/Scrolling, child sz 300.00
Mug, serenade; 5" 225.00
Pitcher, Geneva 1,000.00
Salt cellar, Honeycomb, master, rnd, 3½" 650.00
Sauce bowl, Melrose, smooth rim, 4¼" dia 250.00
Shaker, Wild Rose w/Bowknot 250.00
Sugar bowl, Rose Garland, w/lid 1,800.00
Toothpick holder, Geneva 650.00
Toothpick holder, Kingfisher 1,000.00
Tumbler, File 650.00
Tumbler, Wild Rose w/Bowknot 165.00
Vase, Beaded Triangle, tall, 6¼" 225.00
Vase, Masonic, tall, 6" 475.00

Christmas Collectibles

Christmas past... lovely mementos from long ago attest to the ostentatious Victorian celebrations of the season.

St. Nicholas, better known as Santa, has changed much since 300 A.D. when the good Bishop Nicholas showered needy children with gifts and kindnesses. During the early 18th century, Santa was portrayed as the kind gift-giver to well-behaved children and the stern switch-bearing disciplinarian to those who were bad. In 1822 Clement Clark Moore, a New York poet, wrote his famous *Night Before Christmas*, and the Santa he described was jolly and jovial — a lovable old elf who was stern with no one. Early Santas wore robes of yellow, brown, blue, green, red, white, or even purple. But Thomas Nast, who worked as an illustrator for *Harper's Weekly*, was the first to depict Santa in a red suit instead of the traditional robe and to locate him the entire year at the North Pole headquarters.

Today's collectors prize early Santa figures, especially those in robes of fur or mohair or those dressed in an unusual color. Some early examples of Christmas memorabilia are the pre-1870 ornaments from Dresden, Germany. These cardboard figures — angels, gondolas, umbrellas, dirigibles, and countless others — sparkled with gold and silver trim. Late in the 1870s, blown glass ornaments were imported from Germany. There were over 6,000 recorded designs, all painted inside with silvery colors. From 1890 through 1910, blown glass spheres were often decorated with beads, tassels, and tinsel rope.

Christmas lights, made by Sandwich and some of their contemporaries, were either pressed or mold-blown glass shaped into a form similar to a water tumbler. They were filled with water and then hung from the tree by a wire handle; oil floating on the surface of the water served as fuel for the lighted wick.

Kugels are glass ornaments that were made as early as 1820 and as late as 1890. Ball-shaped examples are more common than the fruit and vegetable forms and have been found in sizes ranging from 1" to 14" in diameter. They were made of thick glass with heavy brass caps, in cobalt, green, gold, silver, red, and occasionally in amethyst.

Although experiments involving the use of electric light bulbs for the Christmas tree occured before 1900, it was 1903 before the first manufactured socket set was marketed. These were very expensive and often proved a safety hazard. In 1921 safety regulations were established, and products were guaranteed safety approved. The early bulbs were smaller replicas of Edison's household bulb. By 1910 G.E. bulbs were rounded with a pointed end, and until 1919 all bulbs were hand blown. The first figural bulbs were made around 1910 in Austria. Japan soon followed, but their product was never of the high quality of the Austrian wares. American manufacturers produced their first machine-made figurals after 1919. Today figural bulbs (especially character-related examples) are very popular collectibles. Bubble lights were popular from about 1945 to 1960 when miniature lights were introduced. These tiny lamps dampened the public's enthusiasm for the bubblers, and manufacturers stopped providing replacement bulbs.

Feather trees were made from 1850 to 1950. All are collectible. Watch for newly manufactured feather trees that have been reintroduced.

For further information concerning Christmas collectibles, we recommend these highly informative books: *Christmas Collectibles* by Margaret and Kenn Whitmyer, and *Christmas Ornaments, Lights, and Decorations, A Collector's Identification and Value Guide, Volumes I through III*, by George Johnson. All books are available from Collector Books or your local bookstore.

Note: bulbs termed 'mini' measure no larger than 1½".

Bulbs

Banana w/face, yel w/red details on milk glass, from $20 to 30.00
Beach ball, mc pnt, 1930s-50s, Japan, mini 30.00
Bear, sitting w/paws up, mc on milk glass, 2¼" 45.00
Bell w/Santa face on ea side, mc on milk glass 12.00
Black boy squatting, mc on milk glass, Japan, from $45 to 55.00
Bubble light, various styles, Paramount Oil, ea, from $40 to 50.00
Candy cane, red & wht, 3", EX 32.00
Car, mc on milk glass, mini, from $30 to 40.00
Carriage lantern, mc on clear, w/exhaust tip, from $15 to 25.00
Cat, sitting, mc on clear, European, from $70 to 80.00
Cat in evening gown, mc on milk glass, Japan, from $70 to 80.00
Cat in suit w/glasses, mc on clear, from $70 to 80.00
Cat w/ball, mc on milk glass, Japan, from $70 to 80.00
Cat w/bowl, mc on clear, Japan, from $10 to 15.00

Choir girl, mc on milk glass, EX 45.00
Clown w/concertina, mc on milk glass, Japan, from $30 to 40.00
Cross, pk on milk glass, 3" 35.00
Dismal Desmond dog head, mc on milk glass, mini, from $30 to ..40.00
Dog in a polo outfit, mc on milk glass, from $25 to 35.00
Dog in basket, mc on milk glass, EX 50.00
Dwarf w/shovel, mc on clear, European, from $100 to 125.00
Ear of corn, yel to gr on clear, sm, from $125 to 150.00
Elephant on ball, mc on milk glass, Japan, from $30 to 40.00
Elephant w/trunk up, pnt details on milk glass, from $20 to 30.00
Flower, pnt on clear, common, from $8 to 10.00
Frog, gr on milk glass, from $22 to 27.00
Grapes, mc w/gr on milk glass, 3¼" 15.00
Hayseed farmer, mc on milk glass 95.00
Hippo girl, mc on clear, from $115 to 130.00
Horse head in horseshoe, mc on milk glass, Japan, from $30 to 40.00
Humpty Dumpty (bust), mc on milk glass 45.00
Indian Chief, EX HP details on clear, from $240 to 275.00
Indian chief, mc on clear, mini, from $70 to 80.00
Indian on a sq, mc on milk glass, Japan, from $20 to 25.00
Jack-o'-lantern, mc on clear, early, from $15 to 20.00
Jackie Coogan, mc on milk glass, Japan 75.00
Judy clown head or drama face, dbl-sided, mc, from $120 to 140.00
Kewpie w/flapper hat, mc on milk glass, Japan, from $20 to 25.00
Lantern, mc on milk glass, Japan, sm 12.00
Lion in suit w/pipe, mc on milk glass, Japan, lg, from $25 to 35.00
Little Orphan Annie, mc on milk glass, c 1935, 3⅛" 125.00
Log cabin, mc on milk glass, Japan, from $10 to 15.00
Monkey holding a vine, mc on clear, early, from $20 to 30.00
Mother Goose on goose, mc on milk glass, Japan, from $80 to 95.00
Mushroom, brn on wht on clear, from $20 to 25.00
Oceanliner, mc on milk glass, from $70 to 80.00
Olympic torch, mc on milk glass, from $15 to 25.00
Pear, yel shaded to red on clear, lg, from $15 to 25.00
Pig playing a drum, mc on milk glass, Japan, from $125 to 150.00
Puffed-Up Cat, mc on milk glass, Japan, from $60 to 70.00
Rabbit in a suit, mc on clear, mini, from $40 to 50.00
Raspberry, purple & gr on clear, exhaust tip, from $20 to 30.00
Rooster in a tub, mc on milk glass, from $30 to 50.00
Rose, open, red on milk glass, lg 40.00
Santa atop chimney, mc on milk glass, EX 50.00
Santa face in bell, mc on milk glass, type 1, from $10 to 15.00
Santa head, pnt details on milk glass, mini, from $15 to 20.00
Santa w/bag, mc on milk glass, lg, from $10 to 15.00
Santa w/hands in his sleeves, mc, exhaust tip, from $115 to 130.00
Seashell, mc on milk glass, from $40 to 50.00
Snow-covered cottage, mc on milk glass, sm, from $6 to 8.00
Songbird, bl on milk glass, common, from $8 to 12.00
Spaniel dog head, mc on celluloid, from $60 to 70.00
St Nicholas, type 1, slender, exhaust tip, from $100 to 125.00
Tom the Piper's Son, mc on milk glass, EX 125.00
Walnut, brn on clear, exhaust tip, from $20 to 30.00
Woman in shoe, mc on milk glass, NM 125.00

Candy Containers

Dwarf, cb, glitter, pnt face, 5" 45.00
Jockey cap, Dresden, blk brim, mk MIG, 1¾x4x2⅜" 150.00
Santa, Bakelite head, molded glass body, 1940s, 6½", EX 55.00
Santa, compo, cotton beard, red felt robe, twig tree, 7½", VG 130.00
Santa, compo/papier-mache, red cloth robe, twig tree, 32", EX ...2,750.00
Santa, papier-mache, flannel suit/fur beard, '20s, Germany, 8" ...300.00
Santa, papier-mache, fur beard, red cloth coat, Germany, 7" 55.00
Santa, papier-mache, red coat, bl pants, 4" 130.00

Santa, papier-mache, red hooded robe, rope belt, w/tree, 18", VG ..**1,760.00**
Santa, papier-mache & cb, bl & red clothes, 10", VG **285.00**
Santa, papier-mache & cb, cotton clothes, 14", EX **300.00**
Santa, papier-mache & cb, wire arms, bl pants, 17", EX **635.00**
Santa in boot, plaster face, cotton beard, Japan, 7" **100.00**
Santa on deer, compo, metal horns, Dresden trim, Germany, 10" ..**625.00**
Santa w/tree, compo, fur beard, Germany, 7" **22.00**
Snowball, celluloid, 2" **65.00**
Snowman w/cap, papier-mache, glass eyes, Germany, 5½" **20.00**
Snowman w/stick & bells, papier-mache, Germany, 4½" **40.00**
Star medallion, Dresden, cb w/glitter, 3" **120.00**
Turtle, Dresden, mc pnt, EX **425.00**
Wreath, Dresden, 4½", EX **200.00**

Ornaments

Blown glass ornaments: Patriotic lady, white and red with gold hair, EX paint, 3", $150.00; Owl, cream to pink, 1930s, EX paint, 3½", $95.00; Santa holding tree, pink and white with gold tree, ca 1930s, EX paint, $45.00.

Airplane, free-blown & wire-wrapped, 3½x6½" **95.00**
Aladdin, blown, turban & billowing pants, bronze colored, 3½" ...**150.00**
Angel, blown, emb on harp strings, Germany, 3½" **40.00**
Baby girl, blown, w/rattle in buggy w/folded hood, 3" **125.00**
Barney Google head, blown, sm hat, mustache & eyebrows, 2¼" **275.00**
Baseball, blown, w/stitching, emb anchor on top, 3" **200.00**
Basket of grapes, blown, oval woven basket, leaves show, 3½" **40.00**
Bear in clown suit, blown, ruffled collar, hat, 2½" **75.00**
Bear on motorcycle, blown, postwar, Germany **40.00**
Beetle, blown, pk or gr wings, 3" **165.00**
Bicycle, 3-D, beads & tubes, Czech, 3½" **35.00**
Boy's head, blown, in nightcap w/tassel, Czech, 3" **80.00**
Bulldog's head, blown, heavy facial features, 2½" **125.00**
Butterfly, Dresden, gold or silver, 3-D w/filigree wings, 2" **200.00**
Canary, blown, bright yel, spun glass tail, clip-on, 3½" **30.00**
Candle, blown, w/flame & wax dripping, clip-on, Germany, 4" ...**100.00**
Carousel, blown, 2 horses, 2 lions, w/riders, 2½" **25.00**
Carrot, free-blown, 3½" **35.00**
Castle tower, blown, rnd w/funnel-shaped roof, windows, 4" **90.00**
Cat in shoe, blown, Germany, 3½" **140.00**
Chain of acorns, blown, acorns 1¼", total length 18" **90.00**
Chain of crowns, blown, strung together, Germany, 1-1½ ft **100.00**
Chick on an egg, blown, cracked w/baby emerging, Germany, 3½" ...**150.00**
Cinderella shoe, blown, high-heeled slipper in colored glass **100.00**
Clown, blown, fat, mc, silvered, 3¼" **50.00**
Conestoga wagon, blown, Germany, 2" **35.00**
Corn cob, blown, sm ind kernels, no emb leaves, 4" **50.00**
Crane, free-blown, annealed bl wings/ft/beak, 1920s, 3" **30.00**
Daisy basket, blown, 6 woven panels & daisies, Germany, 2" **30.00**
Deep sea diver, blown, rnd helmet, sq weight on chest, 4½" **225.00**
Deer, free-blown, annealed legs/ears/antlers, 1920s, 3½" **35.00**
Dice, blown, emb circles & dots, hanger in corner, Germany, 2"..**35.00**

Dog, blown, sits blowing horn, molded fur, Germany, 3½" **175.00**
Dog, blown, w/basket of wine & fruit around neck, 5" **100.00**
Dragonfly, free-blown, pnt spun glass wings & tail, 6½" **150.00**
Duck, blown, annealed wings/top hat/tails, 1920s, 5" **40.00**
Eagle, blown, emb Liberty shield on chest, 3½" **150.00**
Elephant on ball, blown, trappings on head & bk, 2¾" **80.00**
Flower bowl, Sebnitz, scalloped edges, 2½" **55.00**
Football, blown, emb seams & stitching, 3¼" **90.00**
Frog, blown, sits playing banjo, Austrian, 3" **75.00**
Fruit basket, blown, mc fruit, 3" **35.00**
Giraffe, free-blown, annealed legs/ears/tail, 1920s, 2½" **30.00**
Giraffe, tin, eating out of tall tree, Germany, 2" **65.00**
Greyhound, Dresden, natural, 3-D, appl tail & ears, 3¼" **350.00**
Hansel, blown, cap, pants w/suspenders, holds cookie or book, 3" ...**80.00**
Heart, Dresden, gold or silver, emb flowers in center, 2" **110.00**
Hummingbird, blown, sides indented, spun-glass wings, 3½" **40.00**
Ice cream cone, free-blown, 1904 St Louis World's Fair, 4" **25.00**
Ice cream cone, spun cotton, 2½" **25.00**
Jack-O'-Lantern, blown, emb ribs/rnd eyes/nose/mouth, 2" **175.00**
Jesus on the Cross, blown, emb on sm disc, 1½" **55.00**
Lamb, blown, pk or gr, 4½" **95.00**
Lighthouse, blown, 6-sided, windows & walkway, 3" **45.00**
Lion head, blown, well detailed, mane around face & bk, 2¾" ...**300.00**
Locomotive, blown, engine, cab & coal car, Germany, 3" **100.00**
Ostrich, molded & free-blown, spun-glass tail, clip-on, 3¼" **125.00**
Owl head, blown, milk glass, lg beak, 3" **150.00**
Parrot head, blown, defined feathers, beak tucked in neck, 3" **250.00**
Pear, blown, split branch w/2 emb leaves, silvered, 3" **45.00**
Pear, free-blown, gold or amber glass, annealed leaves, 4" **35.00**
Peas in a pod, blown, split to show inner peas, Germany, 3" **425.00**
Penguin, free-blown, annealed flippers/beak/hook, mc, 4½" **40.00**
Pig in tuxedo, blown, w/vest/cummerbund/tie, no arms/legs, 2¾" ...**90.00**
Pocket watch, blown, emb w/Roman numerals, shows 10:00, 1¾" ..**45.00**
Polar bear, Dresden, naturalistic, 3-D, pnt wht, walking, 3½" **375.00**
Ringmaster, blown, silver w/red overcoat, 3¾" **150.00**
Sailboat, Dresden, gold or silver, paper sails & flag, 3" **125.00**
Santa, scrap, red robe, in oval, 5" **22.50**
Shark, blown, annealed hanger, spun glass tail, Japan, 4½" **125.00**
Snowman, blown, w/broom & top hat, 3¼" **75.00**
Snowman clown, blown, elbows bent, cone-shaped hat, 4¼" **25.00**
Songbird, Dresden, naturalistic, 3-D, 2¾" **200.00**
Spider in web, beaded, joined w/milk glass tubes, Czech, 3½" **40.00**
Squirrel, blown, sits w/nut in paw, Austrian, 3" **50.00**
Star, blown, 6-pointed star w/same emb in center, 2½" **15.00**
Strawberry, blown, gold **12.50**
Swan, molded & free-blown, milk glass, flat base, 1920s, 2¾" **35.00**
Swan, molded & free-blown, spun-glass tail & wings, 3½" **50.00**
Tree, beads & tubes, flat, Japan or Czech **8.00**
Turkey, blown, spread tail feathers, tucked beak, 2" **100.00**
Turtle, Dresden, gray, 3½" **250.00**
Wall clock, Sebnitz, weights & pendulum are glass tubes, 4½" ..**100.00**
Walnut, blown, emb w/flower or geometric designs, 1½" **5.00**
Windmill, blown, emb on disc, bumpy pattern under seams, 2¼" ..**40.00**
Witch, blown, in shawl, broom in hand, cat at ft, 3½" **400.00**
Zebra, free-blown, colored glass w/elongated stripes, 3" **40.00**

Miscellaneous

Bulb cover, Santa, early plastic, 3¼" **25.00**
Fence, pnt tin wire, 20" sq w/2-part 6" gate **110.00**
Fence, pnt wicker w/12 wooden posts, AW Drake...PA, 38" sq ..**265.00**
Fence, red wooden fr w/gr 4" pickets, w/gate, 18" sq **115.00**
Figure, angel, wax w/blond hair, spun glass wings, 4", pr **100.00**
Figure, reindeer, celluloid, hollow, w/glitter, 5" **25.00**

Figure, sheep, wooly w/wooden legs, 3¼" H 75.00
Kugel, ball, deep red, orig metal cap, 4" 200.00
Kugel, ball, med red, brass hanger, 3⅞" 200.00
Kugel, ball, pk-red, orig metal cap, 4¾" 200.00
Kugel, ball w/ribs, silver, orig metal cap, 2" 150.00
Kugel, grapes, amber, orig metal cap, 5½" 225.00
Kugel, grapes, cobalt, orig metal cap, 2¾" 250.00
Kugel, grapes, cobalt, orig metal cap, 6½" 400.00
Kugel, grapes, yel-gr, orig metal cap, 2¾" 225.00
Kugel, raspberry, cobalt, orig metal cap, 5" 1,000.00
Light, Bead & Rib, yel-orange, smooth base, 4" 450.00
Light, Expanded Dmn, cobalt, pontil scar, folded rim, 3¼" 140.00
Light, Expanded Dmn, cranberry, pontil scar, folded rim, 3½" ...130.00
Light, Expanded Dmn, cranberry flashed, smooth base, 3⅝" 120.00
Light, Expanded Dmn, dk ruby, smooth base, ground rim, 3½" ...50.00
Light, Expanded Dmn, emerald gr, pontil scar/folded rim, 3⅝" 95.00
Light, Expanded Dmn, med amethyst, pontil scar, 3" 45.00
Light, Expanded Dmn, pk amethyst, pontil scar, 3½" 75.00
Light, Expanded Dmn, teal bl-gr, pontil scar/folded rim, 3⅜" 45.00
Light, Expanded Dmn, yel-olive, pontil scar, crude, 3⅜" 65.00
Light, Expanded Dmn, yel-topaz, smooth base, ground lip, 3⅝" ...65.00
Light, Fern, cobalt, Hearn, Wright & Co, 3¾" 400.00
Light, Harlequin pattern, copper color, smooth base, 3⅜" 110.00
Light, Harlequin pattern, cranberry, smooth base, 3⅜" 150.00
Light, Harlequin pattern, dk amethyst, smooth base, 3⅜" 100.00
Light, Harlequin pattern, med cobalt, smooth base, 3⅜" 140.00
Light, Horizontal Rib, clear, England, 4½" 120.00
Light, Horizontal Rib, emerald gr, England, 4½" 425.00
Light, no pattern, ruby flashed, smooth base, 3⅝" 75.00
Light, Starburst, med pk amethyst, smooth base, 3⅞" 275.00
Santa, bsk, in mica sleigh, 1930s, 3½", EX 65.00
Santa, cloth face/satin suit/shredded beard, Am, '40s, 20", EX ...125.00
Santa, nodder, papier-mache, wool hair, rpl clothes, '30s, 26" ...1,265.00
Santa, papier-mache, Belsnickle, cloth trim, 11", G 300.00
Santa, papier-mache, Belsnickle, dk yel, w/tree, Japan, 11" 255.00
Santa, papier-mache, Belsnickle, gr robe, Germany, 9½" 825.00
Santa, papier-mache, Belsnickle, mica on coat, 6½", EX 450.00
Santa, papier-mache, Belsnickle, red w/gold, 9½", EX 1,200.00
Santa, papier-mache, red felt suit w/wht, 1920s, 6" 65.00
Santa, papier-mache & cb, paper belt, Japan, 13", EX 85.00
Santa, papier-mache/compo, w/lantern, red cloth robe, 14½", VG ..1,265.00
Santa, plastic, red & wht w/gr, lights up, lg, EX 75.00
Santa in sleigh, tin & plastic, battery-op, Japan, 17", EX 200.00
Santa nodder, compo/papier-mache, w/toy basket, w/up, 26", VG ..550.00
Sheep, wood & compo, orig pnt, wooly coat, Germany, 5" 40.00
Sheep, wood/papier-mache, wooly coat, ribbon/bell, Germany, 5"..135.00
Tree, feather; dk gr w/red berries, 1900s, 22", EX 225.00
Tree, feather; gr w/red berries & poinsettias, 1900s, 36" 285.00
Tree, feather; wht w/red berries, well made, 1930s, 32" 250.00
Tree stand, CI, gr pnt, gold star on ea leg (4), 3" opening 55.00
Tree stand, pnt tin, Santa scenes, VG 75.00

Chrysanthemum Sprig, Blue

This is the blue opaque version of Northwood's popular pattern, Chrysanthemum Sprig. It was made at the turn of the century and is today very rare, as its values indicate. Prices are influenced by the amount of gold remaining on the raised designs. Our advisors for this category are Betty and Clarence Maier; they're listed in the Directory under Pennsylvania.

Bowl, berry; sm 325.00
Bowl, master fruit; 10½" W 600.00

Butter dish 950.00
Compote, jelly 600.00
Condiment tray, rare, VG gold 750.00
Creamer 385.00
Cruet, EX gold, from $975 to 1,200.00

Pitcher, water size, $1,100.00.

Shakers, pr 450.00
Spooner, from $300 to 350.00
Sugar bowl, w/lid 600.00
Toothpick holder 450.00
Tumbler 350.00

Cincinnati Art Pottery

Established circa 1880, this pottery initially experimented in the newly developed underglaze Cincinnati faience, but soon abandoned these efforts and instead began producing a different kind of ware. Among its products were Hungarian Faience (embossed designs painted in various colors on light-toned grounds), Portland Blue Faience (named for the rich blue glaze used in its production), and the pottery's most famous line, Kenzota (an ivory faience primarily decorated with flowers). The company remained in business in Cincinnati, Ohio, until shortly after 1890.

Ewer, emb leaves, bl/wht/gold metallic, branch hdl, 9½", EX 100.00
Ewer, mc florals on cream w/gold, 11½" 210.00
Vase, floral, gold on aqua matt, mk, lt wear, 12" 200.00
Vase, floral, mc on wht to lt bl, sgn LR, 10½", NM 150.00

Circus Collectibles

The 1890s were the Golden Age of the circus. Barnum and Bailey's parades transformed mundane city streets into an exotic never-never land inhabited by trumpeting elephants with jeweled gold headgear strutting by to the strains of the calliope that issued from a fine red- and gilt-painted wagon extravagantly decorated with carved wooden animals of every description. It was an exciting experience. Is it any wonder that collectors today treasure the mementos of that golden era? See also Posters.

Key:
B&B — Barnum & Bailey   RB — Ringling Bros.

Book, B&B Circus, 100-pg, 1907 ....150.00
Book, RB B&B program, 80+ unnumbered pages, 1977, VG 10.00
Booklet, RB B&B, 1962, 50-pg 15.00
Calendar, B&B, circus scenes, 1973, 24x16", NM 25.00
Flashlight, RB, tiger figural, EX 20.00
Globe, RB B&B, paper, used for animals to jump through 30.00

Magazine, B&B Magazine of Wonders, mc cover, 1907, EX **150.00**
Photo, RB B&B, winter quarters, 1950s, 3¼x3¼", 50 for **30.00**
Photocard, Lorette Tattooed Lady **10.00**
Pitch card, Big Brute, fat man **5.00**
Program, Kelly Miller, sgn Zippo the Clown **15.00**
Program/magazine, RB B&B, 1951 edition, 76-pg, 11x8", NM **20.00**
Punch-out premium, RB B&B, 35-pc, Lever Brothers, M in mailer ...**135.00**
Season pass, Cole, 1964 ....**7.00**
Souvenir program, RB B&B, 1958 ....**25.00**
Ticket, Christian, Wallace Bros, 1966 ....**6.00**
Window card, 3 clowns **10.00**

Clarice Cliff

Between 1928 and 1935 in Burslem, England, as the director and part owner of Wilkinson and Newport Pottery Companies, Clarice Cliff and her 'paintresses' created a body of hand-painted pottery whose influence is felt to the present time.

The name for the oevre was Bizarre Ware, and the predominant sensibility, style, and appearance was Deco. Almost all pieces are signed and include the pattern names. There were over 160 patterns and more than 400 shapes, all of which are illustrated in *A Bizarre Affair — the Life and Work of Clarice Cliff*, published by Harry N. Abrams, Inc., written by Len Griffen and Susan and Louis Meisel.

Note: Non-hand-painted work (transfer printed) was produced after World War II and into the 1950s. Some of the most common names are 'Tonquin' and 'Charlotte.' These items, while attractive and enjoyable to own, have little value in the collector market.

Bowl, Rhodanthe, stylized plants, mc on cream, 2⅞x7⅝" **375.00**
Honey jar, Crocus, yel & orange flowers on gr, bee finial, 3" **345.00**
Jam jar, Crocus, mc w/gr stems on brn, B Rigers, 3½x3¼" **400.00**
Jug, Fantasque, orange & blk floral, 7¾x7" **750.00**
Jug, lotus; Anemone, floral, mc on cream, 11⅝x7¼" **350.00**
Jug, lotus; Autumn, houses & grees, ribbed, 11¾x8" **800.00**
Jug, lotus; Coral Firs, mc bands, 11⅝x7¼" **800.00**
Jug, lotus; Crocus, stylized florals w/bands, 11⅜x7⅛" **700.00**
Jug, lotus; Gardenia, mc floral bands, 11⅜x7⅛" **1,265.00**
Jug, My Garden, yel-brn w/red/wht/orange floral hdl, 9" **260.00**
Jug, Rhodanthe, stylized plants, mc on cream, 6⅝x3⅝" **430.00**
Jug, Secrets, stylized landscape, mc on cream, 7x4" **515.00**
Jug, Viscaria, mc flowers w/brn stems on cream, mk, 7½x6" **800.00**
Plate, Bizarre, magenta w/mc & gilt HP, L Knight, 1934, 10" **350.00**
Plate, Inspiration Lily, wht flowers w/bl stems on gr, 9" **700.00**
Teapot, Greetings From Canada, caribou/Indians/etc, 6½" **700.00**
Teapot, Harvest, fruit & floral, orange/yel/gr, 6½x9" **325.00**
Toast rack, Cabbage Flower, gr/brn/dk orange, 3x5" **350.00**
Vase, Blue Chintz, mc flowers, bl & gr bands, 7¾x6" **980.00**
Vase, Coral Firs, trees & landscape, 8¼x6" **700.00**
Vase, Delicia Citrus, oranges & lemons, blk & gr drips, 7¾x4" ..**575.00**
Vase, Inspiration, bl & wht flowers on bl to gr, mk, 7¼x8" **800.00**
Vase, Inspiration Lily, purple on bl-gr, 7x3" **375.00**
Vase, mc pansies on yel w/mc drips, 10½x4½" **575.00**
Wall pocket, dbl; Rhodanthe, yel/brn/orange flowers, 6½" dia ...**460.00**

Cleminson

A hobby turned to enterprise, Cleminson is one of several California potteries whose clever hand-decorated wares are attracting the attention of today's collectors. The Cleminsons started their business at their El Monte home in 1941 and were so successful that eventually they expanded to a modern plant that employed more than 150 work-ers. They produced not only dinnerware and kitchen items such as cookie jars, canisters, and accessories, but novelty wall vases, small trays, plaques, etc., as well. Though nearly always marked, Cleminson wares are easy to spot as you become familiar with their distinctive glaze colors. Their grayed-down blue and green, berry red, and dusty pink say 'Cleminson' as clearly as their trademark. Unable to compete with foreign imports, the pottery closed in 1963. Our advisor for this category is Jack Chipman, author of the *Collector's Encyclopedia of California Pottery*; he is listed in the Directory under California.

Ashtray, stylized fruit, 10" **36.00**
Ashtray, You're the Big Wheel **38.00**
Bell, French maid **65.00**
Butter dish, lady figure **65.00**
Canister, Cherry, tea sz **35.00**
Cleanser shaker, lady figure, 5 holes, 6½" **30.00**
Cookie jar, Carrot Head **165.00**
Cookie jar, Gingerbread House **200.00**
Cookie jar, heart shape, The Way to a Man's Heart **175.00**
Creamer & sugar bowl, Distlefink **30.00**
Cup & saucer, Gramma's **25.00**
Cup & saucer, My Old Man, lg **35.00**
Dish, clown w/pointed hat lid **45.00**
Egg cup, lady in apron, early **25.00**
Egg cup, man w/blk coat & striped pants **35.00**
Gravy boat, Distlefink, wht **35.00**
Hair receiver, girl w/folded hands, 2-pc **40.00**
Match holder, Cherry, wall mt **40.00**
Mug, Morning After, w/lid **35.00**
Pancake server, Big Top Circus, juvenile **75.00**
Pitcher, Cherry, oil-can shape, 9" **55.00**
Pitcher, Gala Gray, 7" **30.00**
Plaque, teapot, A Kitchen Bright... ....**35.00**
Plaque, Tom Sawyer **45.00**
Plate, Deco fruit, red on ivory **22.00**
Plate, rooster crowing, yel decor on rim, 9½" **30.00**

Razor blade bank, embossed man's face, brown on tan, 3¾", $25.00.

Ring holder, Chef **35.00**
Salt cellar, Cherry **40.00**
Shakers, Distlefink, lg, pr **25.00**
Shakers, kangaroo & baby, pr **45.00**
Shakers, Katrinka, pr **40.00**
Spoon rest, floral decor, 3-lobed **15.00**
Sprinkler, Chinese boy **35.00**
String holder, heart shape, You'll Always Have a Pull... ....**35.00**
Tray, Distlefink, leaf shape, 3-compartment **35.00**
Wall pocket, coffee grinder **30.00**
Wall pocket, frying pan **25.00**
Wall pocket, long johns, red/blk, 8" **30.00**
Wall pocket, Tea Time **40.00**

Clewell

Charles Walter Clewell was a metal worker who perfected the technique of plating an entire ceramic vessel with a thin layer of copper or bronze treated with an oxidizing agent to produce a natural deterioration of the surface. Through trial and error, he was able to control the degree of patina achieved. In the early stages, the metal darkened and, if allowed to develop further, formed a natural turquoise-blue or green corrosion. He worked alone in his small Akron, Ohio, studio from about 1906, buying undecorated pottery from several Ohio firms, among them Weller, Owens, and Cambridge. His work is usually marked. Clewell died in 1965, having never revealed his secret process to others.

Prices for Clewell have advanced rapidly during the past few years along with the Arts and Crafts market in general. Right now, good examples are bringing whatever the traffic will bear.

Bowl, brn patina, rivets/panels, 3x9" 260.00
Bowl, gr/brn, incurvate, #384-25, stress line to metal, 3x9" 200.00
Bud vase, gr/brn patina, #354, trumpet form, 6½" 260.00
Candlesticks, gr/brn, trumpet base, #414-2-6, 9½", pr 950.00
Candlesticks, orange/gr patina (exceptional), #415-3-6, 10", pr ...1,600.00
Cider set: pitcher, 6 mugs, 20" tray, riveted panels, EX 1,200.00
Lamp, gr/brn patina, cvd wood base, 23" overall 1,000.00
Mug, copper clad, rivet & panel decor, emb mark, 4½" 100.00
Mug, Utopian, gr/gold bronze patina, emb vines, #1035 ....210.00
Tankard, riveted, inscribed/1908, minor separation, 10" 350.00
Vase, bl/gr over orange patina, elongated gourd form, 14½" ...1,400.00
Vase, bl/gr patina, ftd cone form, #412-6, 9" 375.00
Vase, bl/gr striations on bronze, sgn/#d, 6½" 895.00
Vase, blk/dk gr/rust patina, #309, 5¼x4" 375.00
Vase, brn patina, lg fish/seaweed relief, no mk, 8x7" 1,200.00
Vase, brn/lt & dk gr patina, #466-147, shouldered, 5" 350.00
Vase, dk brn w/stylized floral, no mk, 5½" 400.00
Vase, dk gr patina, slim tapered cylinder, #349, 6½" 700.00
Vase, gr/brn patina, #277-26, shouldered, 16" 2,400.00
Vase, gr/brn patina, #305-2-6, 7¼x4" 650.00
Vase, gr/brn patina, bulbous w/flared collar neck, #471, 8½" ..1,900.00
Vase, gr/brn patina, chalice form, #412-2-6, 6½" 550.00
Vase, gr/brn patina, long neck, squat/angle base, #361-25, 10" ...850.00
Vase, gr/brn patina, ovoid w/collar neck, #272-6, 11x9" 1,200.00
Vase, gr/brn patina, swollen form, #256, lt wear, 13", EX 550.00
Vase, gr/brn patina, trumpet form on ped ft, #426-218, 9" 750.00
Vase, gr/brn patina (flaking), swollen cylinder, #60-2-6, 8" 325.00
Vase, gr/brn/blk patina, shouldered/incurvate, 3½x6" 400.00
Vase, gr/brn/orange patina, #442, 9½x8½" 3,500.00
Vase, gr/copper patina, spherical, #343, 3½x4" 450.00
Vase, gr/orange patina, #366-215, 15" 1,000.00
Vase, gr/orange patina, squat w/wide can neck, #167-215, 11" ...2,700.00
Vase, lt gr/bl/brn patina, trumpet neck, #364-6, 7" 800.00

Clews

Brothers Ralph and James Clews were potters who operated in Cobridge in the Staffordshire district from 1817 to 1835. They are best known for their blue and white transfer-printed earthenwares, which included American Views, Moral Maxims, Picturesque Views, and English Views. A series called *Three Tours of Dr. Syntax* contained thirty-one different scenes with each piece bearing a descriptive title. Another popular series was *Pictures of Sir David Wilkie* with seven prints. (Though we once thought that the Don Quixote series was made by Clews, new information seems to indicate that it was made instead by Davenport.)

Both printed and impressed marks were used, often incorporating the pattern name as well as the pottery. See also Staffordshire, Historical.

Creamer, Christmas, Wilkie's Designs, dk bl transfer, 5½" 250.00
Cup & saucer, Christmas Eve, Wilkie, dk bl transfer 225.00
Cup plate, Dr Syntax Bound to a Tree by Highwayman 325.00
Cup plate, Dr Syntax Drawing After Nature, dk bl transfer, 3½" ...340.00
Pitcher, Water Girl, dk bl transfer, rstr, 7⅜" 350.00
Plate, bl feather edge, emb rim, mk, 5¾" 70.00
Plate, bl floral transfer w/mc, 6", NM 40.00
Plate, Chinese Temple, dk bl transfer, mk, 8¾" 80.00
Plate, Coronation, floral, dk bl transfer, 10⅛", NM 170.00
Plate, Dr Syntax Mistakes Gentleman's Home..., 1830s, 10¼" ..185.00
Plate, Dr Syntax Reading His Tour, dk bl, emb rim, 8⅝", EX 100.00
Plate, Sancho Panza's Debate w/Teresa, dk bl transfer, 9½" 195.00
Platter, Advertisement for a Wife, dk bl transfer, 15¼" 1,500.00
Platter, Chinese landscape, cobalt transfer, 1830s, 14⅝" 220.00
Platter, gr feather edge, impressed mk, 6½" 170.00
Vase, Chameleon Ware, bl corset form, 5" 90.00
Vase, Chameleon Ware, HP geometrics, conical, 5⅜" 135.00

Clifton

Clifton Art Pottery of Clifton, New Jersey, was organized ca 1903. Until 1911 when they turned to the production of wall and floor tile, they made artware of several varieties. The founders were Fred Tschirner and William A. Long. Long had developed the method for underglaze slip painting that had been used at the Lonhuda Pottery in Steubenville, Ohio, in the 1890s. Crystal Patina, the first artware made by the small company, utilized a fine white body and flowing, blended colors, the earliest a green crystalline. Indian Ware, copied from the pottery of the American Indians, was usually decorated in black geometric designs on red clay. (On the occasions when white was used in addition to the black, the ware was often not as well executed; so even though two-color decoration is very rare, it is normally not as desirable to the collector.) Robin's Egg Blue, pale blue on the white body, and Tirrube, a slip-decorated matt ware, were also produced.

Bowl, stylized emb swirls on gr matt, sgn/mk, incurvate, 4½" 350.00
Humidor, Indian Ware, red w/blk & tan design, 7x5" 250.00
Jar, Indian Ware, geometric-emb rim/lid, 2-color band, 4", EX ..120.00
Pitcher, Indian Ware, geometrics, brn & brick red, #274, 4½" ...150.00
Teapot, Crystal Patina, yel to golden brn, 3¼x9½" 150.00
Teapot, Indian Ware, geometrics, brn & brick red, 4x8½" 175.00

Vase, thin green matt with raised stylized swirls on squat form, 1½x4½", $350.00.

Vase, Crystal Patina, yel/buff mottle, 4-side flared neck, 7" 275.00
Vase, gr matt, 2 integral akimbo hdls, 4½" 210.00
Vase, Indian Ware, interlocking waves, 2-color w/gold, 6x6" 150.00
Vase, Indian Ware, simple shoulder band, brn on red, 2½x4" 120.00
Vase, Indian Ware, swirls/geometrics, 3-color, #160, 4½x9" 450.00
Vase, Indian Ware, tan-outlined blk swirls on red, 6½x9" 475.00
Vase, streaky lime gr/buff matt, shouldered, #156, 10" 290.00
Vase, Tirrube, jonquils, yel/wht/gr on brick red, 8x4" 325.00

Clocks

In the early days of our country's history, clock makers were influenced by styles imported from Europe. They copied the European's cabinets and reconstructed their movements — needed materials were in short supply; modifications had to be made. Of necessity was born mainspring motive power and spring clocks. Wooden movements were made on a mass-production basis as early as 1808. Before the middle of the century, metal movements had been developed.

Today's collectors prefer clocks from the 18th and 19th centuries with pendulum-regulated movements. Bracket clocks made during this period utilized the shorter pendulum improvised in 1658 by Fromentiel, a prominent English clock maker. These smaller square-face clocks usually were made with a dome top fitted with a handle or a decorative finial. The case was usually walnut or ebony and was sometimes decorated with pierced brass mountings. Brackets were often mounted on the wall to accommodate the clock, hence the name. The banjo clock was patented in 1802 by Simon Willard. It derived its descriptive name from its banjo-like shape. A similar but more elaborate style was called the lyre clock.

The first electric novelty clocks were developed in the 1940s. Lux, who was the major producer, had been in business since 1912, making wind-up novelties during the '20s and '30s. Another company, Mastercrafter Novelty Clocks, first obtained a patent to produce these clocks in the late 1940s. Other manufacturers were Keebler, Westclox, and Columbia Time. The cases were made of china, Syroco, wood and plastic; most were animated and some had pendulettes. Prices vary according to condition and rarity.

Except for the novelty clocks whose values are on the increase, clock prices have been stable for several years. Unless noted otherwise, values are given for clocks in excellent condition. Clocks that have been altered, damaged, or have had parts replaced are worth considerably less.

Our advisor is Bruce A. Austin; he is listed in the Directory under New York. Our novelty clock advisors are Allegheny Mountain Antiques Gallery; their address is given under Pennsylvania.

Key:
br — brass	reg — regulator
dl — dial	rswd — rosewood
esc — escapement	T — time only
mcr — mercury	wt — weight
mvt — movement	vnr — veneer
og — ogee	2nds — seconds
pnd — pendulum	

Novelty Clocks

Photo courtesy Carole Kaifer

Pickanniny Pendulette #304 (aka Black Sambo, Dixie Boy and Colored Boy), eyes and tie move, painted carved/pressed wood, metal tie, Lux, 8¾x4½", M, $1,000.00; Clown with Tie, circus character Happy, eyes and tie move, painted carved/pressed wood, metal tie, Lux, 9¼x4", M, $800.00.

Ballerina dancing, w/music, United 125.00
Bird w/cage, Mastercrafters 150.00
Boy fishing, gold, United, 1950s 130.00
Carousel, Mastercrafters, electric 165.00
Children on a seesaw, Haddon 125.00
Church, gold, Mastercrafters 115.00
Couple swinging, ivory, United, 1950s 200.00
Cuckoo clock, grape & eagle, new bellows, German, 1900, 24" ...90.00
Enchanted Cottage, bird bobs/clock ticks, Lux, '05, 10" 100.00
Fireplace, gold cast metal, United 75.00
Fireplace, plastic, Mastercrafters, 1950s 65.00
Fireplace, w/figures, United Hearth, 1950s, NM 200.00
Frog band, 4 CI frogs around dial, Am, Pat date 1883, 11" 360.00
Girl, swinging, Mastercrafters, 1950s 125.00
Lighthouse w/sailboat scene, United, 1950s, NM 250.00
Majorette twirling baton, United, 1950s 100.00
Niagara Falls, plastic, Mastercrafters, 1950s, rare 115.00
Playmates, swinging, Mastercrafters, 1950s 125.00
Potbelly stove, white & gold (rare), NM 185.00
Rocking grandmother, Haddon 100.00
Ship's wheel & fish, United, 1950s 100.00
Starlight, glass, Deco face glows, Mastercrafters 75.00
Waterfall, old style, Mastercrafters 115.00

Shelf Clocks

Ansonia, steeple style, 30-hr/T/alarm, orig, 1860, 15" 125.00
Ansonia, walnut gingerbread, Berkeley model, 8-day, 1890s 150.00
Atkins, chain fusee w/center 2nds, orig finish & dl, 1860, 17" 2,400.00
Black, Star & Frost NY, bronze mtd, glass paneled, 1900, 13x8" 600.00
C&LC Ives...Conn, mahog Empire triple decker, rvpt/8-day, 37" ..500.00
Chauncey Jerome, mahog w/rswd finish, br trim, 16" 150.00
Chauncey Jerome, ogee w/mahog vnr, rvpt, 25¾" 150.00
Classical Revival, marble & basalt, incised decor, 1880s 300.00
Deemer, alarm, ornate ftd CI case, rnd dl, 30-hr, 1910, 10" 65.00
Eardley Norton, dbl fusee mahog bracket, 1780, 18", G 3,500.00
Eli Terry, pillar & scroll, mahog/mahog vnr, 31x17x5" 2,100.00
Eli Terry, pillar & scroll w/orig rvpt, pnd, 1832, 31" 1,800.00
Fr, blk marble/incised pattern, 8-day, chipped dl, 1890, 9" 95.00
Fr, brass bow-shaped front w/floral garland, pnd, 10¼" 325.00
Fr, gilded spelter figure on marble base, 1890, 11", G 190.00
Fr, gr onyx dome top, br finial, 8-day T&S, 1850s, EX 250.00
Fr, metal/glass/porc dl, top hdl, T/strike/repeat, 1910, 6" 425.00
Fr, reg, metal/glass panels/porc dl, mcr pnd, 1900, 11", G 450.00
Fr, rococo, br/MOP/ivory inlay, porc dl, 1890, 19½", G 450.00
Fr, rococo, br, porc dial, 8-day, 1880s 200.00
Fr, 4-column Empire, alabaster, orig mvt & pnd, 1870, G 235.00
Fr Classical Revival, blk marble/bronze, breakfront case 300.00
Fr Empire bronze/ormolu mtd, Czar Alexander/Victory, 1813, 19" ...2,700.00
Fr Neoclassical-style, bronze & wht marble, 1880s, 15x22" 350.00
German, blk marble w/columns, 30-hr, 1910, mini, 6", G 50.00
German, bracket, walnut, 8-day, T/strike, 1925, VG, 18" 145.00
Gilbert, cottage, rswd vnr, 30-hr, rstr dl/chips, 1880, 13½" 40.00
Gilbert, Pandia, walnut, 8-day/T/strike, rfn, 1890, 21½" 280.00
Gilbert, walnut gingerbread, T/strike/alarm, 1900, 20" 155.00
Ingraham, calendar, orig finish, 2 dls, 1869 Lewis Pat, 22" 1,175.00
Ingraham, golden oak/blk poplar finials, paper dl, 8-day, 17" 95.00
Ingraham, walnut gingerbread, T/strike/alarm, 20" 125.00
Japy Freres, Louis XVI-style, metal, Marly Horse group, 15x14" .650.00
John Smith & Sons, skeleton, York Minster fr, 2 fusee, 1865, 21" ...2,600.00
Munger & Benedict...NY, mahog vnr Empire, rvpt, pnd, 40" ..2,600.00
New Haven, birch, rnd enamel face, 1850s, 9½x16½x6" 450.00
New Haven, Electra, mahog w/tablet border, orig finish, pnd, 19" 100.00
New Haven, gilded bronze w/cherub, 9", VG 100.00

New Haven, La Lanza, oak, repapered dl, rpl hands, 1920, 22" **75.00**
New Haven, Shelf Referee reg, mk Standard Time, 1910, 35" **500.00**
New Haven, steeple, rswd vnr w/br works, pnd, 20" **200.00**
Sessions, mahog tambour w/burl inlay, porc dl, 1920, 10", VG **75.00**
Sessions, oak, 8-day, T/strike, rstr/rfn, 1920, 12" **65.00**
Seth Thos, Adamantine, gr & blk, ftd base, 1905, 11", G **80.00**
Seth Thos, Adamantine, 4-bell Sonora, minor wear, 1915, 13½" ...**275.00**
Seth Thos, Empire #303, wood/beveled glass, 1900, VG **375.00**
Seth Thos, Empire #40, crystal reg, 15-day, 1910, 8¾", G **280.00**
Seth Thos, inlaid mahog w/arched top, porc dl, 1920, 10", VG ..**170.00**
Seth Thos, mahog tambour, 8-day, Westminster chimes, 1930, 10", VG ...**125.00**
Seth Thos, Plymouth Hollow, 2-wt column, 30-hr, orig, 1850, 25" ..**225.00**
Seth Thos, student carriage alarm, NP, like-new dl, 1890, G **100.00**
Terhune & Edwards, CI, 8-day, repapered dl, no pnd, 1850, 15" **140.00**
Waterbury, mahog, dome top, 8-day T&S, Pat 1898 .....**250.00**
Welch, CI w/br trim & pnd, Patti-style mvt, 1890, 11½", VG ...**175.00**
Welch, mahog over pine, new dl/incorrect pnd, 1870, G, 12" **75.00**
Wm F Evans, skeleton, dbl-pillar design, 2 fusee, 1870, 19" **2,600.00**

Tall Case Clocks

Samuel Mulliken, Chippendale, mahogany, silvered engraved dial, refinished dial and case, ca 1780, 85", $9,000.00.

A Edwards Ashby, pine, arched doors & bonnet, pnd, rprs, 88" ..**1,700.00**
C French & Co...OH, cherry, broken arch pediment, 94" **7,500.00**
Charles P Herold, cherry Federal, motorized, 90x21x11" **1,800.00**
Cherry Country Sheraton, dvtl bonnet, pnd, rfn, 88" **1,700.00**
Cherry Country Sheraton w/curly walnut, rstr, 93½" **2,500.00**
Cherry Hplwht, Fr ft, waist door, dvtl bonnet, OH, 91" **1,400.00**
Curly maple Country w/walnut trim, wag-on-wall works, 89" .**2,100.00**
Federal cherry inlay, 8-day, floral iron dl, MA, 1810, 85" **4,300.00**
Federal mahog w/inlay, br wt 8-day mvt, 1790s, 95¼" **9,200.00**
Federal mahog w/inlay, rfn, 1790s, 104½" **9,200.00**
Fr boule, engr br/tortoise shell/ebony fr, 89", VG **1,600.00**
Frederick Wingate Augusta, mahog w/bird's-eye maple, 94" ...**2,500.00**
Herschede, #214, 3-wt/5-tube, dl w/rolling moon, 1935, 78", VG **1,250.00**
Herschede, #217, 3-wt/5 tube, mahog, dl w/rolling moon, '35, 80" ...**1,400.00**
Herschede, #276, 3-wt/5-tube chime, 1925, 78" **2,300.00**
Hplwht style, cherry w/inlay, wag-on-wall works, repro, 102" .**1,400.00**
James C Cole, 8-day, top fret w/3 finials, rfn, 1820, 89" **4,000.00**

L Watson Cincinnati, cherry Hplwht, broken-arch cornice, 92" ..**3,000.00**
Poplar w/old red pnt, wag-on-wall works, att Shakers, 78" **5,000.00**
Riley Whiting, CT, floral mc/gilt dl, 30-hr mvt, 1830s, 85" **1,900.00**
Wm Crane, Federal mahog, cornice, 3 br finials, 1780s, 93" ...**9,000.00**

Wall Clocks

Atkins, octagonal, rswd w/gilt trim, 30-day, rpt dl, 1857, 27" ..**1,500.00**
Chauncey Jerome, wood keyhole shape, rpt dl & tablet, 1850, 18" ...**900.00**
Differential, mahog vnr/glass insert, 1-yr, orig, 1920, 41", G ..**1,250.00**
Dutch, hood w/3 br figures, 30-hr, dl w/br 4 seasons, 1780, 43" ...**1,100.00**
German, free swinger, wood, Art Nouveau, rfn, 1910, 29" **150.00**
German, open-well Berliner, walnut, arched br dl, 1890, 48" ..**2,600.00**
Gilbert, Hollywood, ebony/nickel/beveled glass, 1920, 24", VG ...**300.00**
Gilbert, office calendar, decorative rnd top, 1885, 33½", G **700.00**
Gustav Becker, Berliner, wood, worm damage/warped, 1890, 35" ...**200.00**
Ingraham, gallery, old powdered gilding on rnd case, 1860, 26" .**750.00**
Ingraham, reg, Western Union w/calendar, cvd wood, 1910, 36" **350.00**
Junghans, reg, walnut w/ivorene dl, 8-day, 1919, 29", VG **150.00**
New Haven, banjo, eagle atop, minor wear, 1925, 24" **125.00**
New Haven, short drop calendar, octagonal top, EX vnr, 1890, 24" ..**350.00**
Phipps, Federal banjo, rvpt glass throat, 32", VG+ **900.00**
R Schneckenburger, 1-yr, ball torsion pnd, duplex esc, 1900, 34" ...**3,600.00**
Regulator, walnut w/compo Minerva crest, pnd, 42", VG **150.00**
Sessions, reg #2, oak w/rpl etched glass, T, 1910, 38", VG **250.00**
Seth Thos, banjo, maple w/bird's-eye vnrs, 1955, 19" **100.00**
Seth Thos, Brookfield banjo, wood, 8-day, minor wear, 1970, 28" ..**100.00**
Seth Thos, Cartel, rnd dl in ornate plaster fr, 1880, 42" **175.00**
Seth Thos, No 1 E Chevron, mahog, electric, 1950s **75.00**
Seth Thos, Queen Anne, oak, 8-day, 1880, 36", G **375.00**
Seth Thos, reg, rfn mahog case, br works, pnd, 36" **800.00**
Seth Thos, school, oak, sq dial w/pnd, orig finish, 1953, 26" **100.00**
Seth Thos, 12" drop, mahog, octagonal top, rfn/rstr, 1900, 23½" ...**200.00**
Vienna, reg, dbl-door, trn/cvd columns, 2-wt, 1885, 52" **1,850.00**
W Kolhner, reg, 1-weight (no springs) grand sonnerie, 1855, 53" ...**2,600.00**
Waltham, banjo, wood, Geo WA/Mt Vernon, 8-day, 1920, 19", VG ...**170.00**

Cloisonne

Cloisonne is a method of decorating metal with enameling. Fine metal wires are soldered onto the metal body following the lines of a predetermined design. The resulting channels are filled in with enamels of various colors, and the item is fired. The final step is a smoothing process that assures even exposure of the wire pattern. The art is predominately Oriental and has been practiced continuously, except during war years, since the 16th century. The most excellent examples date from 1865 until the turn of the century. The early 20th century export variety is usually lightweight and the workmanship inferior. Modern wares are of good quality and are produced in Taiwan as well as China.

Several variations of the basic art include plique-a-jour, achieved by removing the metal body after firing, leaving only the transparent enamel work; foil cloisonne, using transparent or semitranslucent enameling over a layer of embossed silver covering the metal body of the vessel; wireless cloisonne, made by removing the wire dividers prior to firing; and cloisonne executed on ceramic, wood, or lacquer rather than metal.

Box, wisteria/pines/exotic birds, Japan, 6" L **325.00**
Cigarette case, dragons, mc on gr, China **155.00**
Compote, floral, mc on bl, ped ft, scalloped, 5½x9½" **195.00**
Cup, butterflies & flowers, lappet borders, China, 19th C, 4" **100.00**
Ginger jar, wht florals repeat on cobalt, teakwood base, 8½" **125.00**
Jar, florals, mc on translucent red, Japan, 12" **395.00**

Jar, potpourri; birds/flowers/etc in panels, Japan, 4¼" 275.00
Plate, cranes & flowers in landscape on bl, Japan, 9¾" 300.00
Teapot, mc floral on turq, globular, China, 6" 145.00
Vase, bird & floral on turq, 8⅓" 80.00
Vase, irises, slender neck, 1860s, 7½" 700.00
Vase, peonies/mums/irises/birds/butterflies on bl, late, 13" 200.00
Vase, prunus tree on royal bl, 10x6" 235.00

Clothing and Accessories

'Second-hand' or 'vintage?' It's all a matter of opinion. But these days it's considered good taste (downright fashionable) to wear clothing from Victorian to styles from the sixties. Jackets with padded shoulders from the thirties are 'trendy.' Jewelry from the Art Deco era is just as beautiful and often less expensive than current copies. But why settle for new when the genuine article can be bought for the same price with exquisite lace that no reproduction can rival! When once the 'style' of the day was so strictly obeyed, today, in New York and the larger cities of California and Texas, in particular, nothing well-designed and constructed is 'out of style.' And though costumes by such designers as Chanel, Fortuny, and Lanvin may bring four-figure prices at fine auction houses, as a general rule, prices are very modest considering the wonderful fabrics one may find in vintage clothing, many of which are no longer available. Cashmere coats, elegant furs, and sequined or beaded gowns can be bought for only a small fraction of today's retail. Though some are strictly collectors, many do buy their clothes to wear. Care must be given to alterations, and gentle cleaning methods employed to avoid damage that would detract from their value. For any valuable garment requiring more than minimal repair, consult a professional restorer.

Prices in vintage clothing depend on condition, basic materials, trims, label (if available), construction, where found, scarcity of type, and desirability as a collectible item or a wearable historic artifact. For further information we recommend *Antique & Vintage Clothing* by Diane Snyder-Haug, available from Collector Books or your local bookstore. Our advisor for this category is Maryanne Dolan; she is listed in the Directory under California.

Key:
cap/s — cap sleeves
embr — embroidery
hs — hand sewn
l/s — long sleeves
ms — machine sewn
n/s — no sleeves
plt — pleated
s/s — short sleeves

Apron, bl & wht checks, ms, 33½" 70.00
Bathing trunks, men's, 1930s, unused 22.00
Bloomers, dk navy linen, tennis style, 1910s 85.00
Bloomers, girl's gym, 1900s, EX 40.00
Blouse, blk sateen w/net overall, mid-length/s, 1910s, EX 75.00
Blouse, pk silk, lace insets on shoulders, s/s, 1920s 32.00
Bonnet, Amish; ecru w/ribbon ties 35.00
Bonnet, blk velvet w/silk gathers & rosettes, 1910s, VG 75.00
Bonnet, interior style, purple ribbon trim, ca 1860s, EX 65.00
Bonnet, pioneer; patterned calico 15.00
Bonnet, pioneer; bl stripe, EX 35.00
Bonnet, quilted silk, 1850s 45.00
Camisole, pk silk & linen crochet 27.50
Camping outfit, lady's, khaki, 1920s 50.00
Cape, blk silk w/fringe, silk ties, 1910s, NM 125.00
Coat, blk velvet w/wht rabbit hood, full length, EX 115.00
Coat, dk cotton w/velvet trim, 1910s, EX 70.00
Coat, mohair, fur cuffs & collar, long, 1950s, NM 250.00
Coat, toddler's, Edwardian lace, EX 60.00

Collar, shirt; man's, Van Heusen, NY, M in wrapper 18.00
Corset, pk lace-up, 1930s, EX 25.00
Corset, Victorian era 55.00
Drawers, split style w/tucks & eyelet lace, button waist 30.00
Dress, bl moire faille w/satin tie, s/s w/cuffs, A-line, 1950s 30.00
Dress, blk chiffon, n/s, ostrich feathers on skirt, 1920s 175.00
Dress, blk silk undersheath w/chiffon, l/s, 1910s 135.00
Dress, blk w/net sleeves, beaded cuffs, full length, 1930s 100.00
Dress, brn patterned wool, high neck, button/s, 1915 ....145.00
Dress, child's, bl calico, l/s 75.00
Dress, child's, wht cotton w/lace trim, full skirt, l/s 55.00
Dress, child's, wool w/blk velvet trim, l/s, 1890s, EX 50.00
Dress, christening; pin-tucked lace, 1890s 65.00
Dress, Empire waist, 3-layer lace skirt, s/s, 1910s 100.00
Dress, flapper type, blk beads allover, 1920s, EX 175.00
Dress, navy, n/s, drop waist, plts & velvet flower, 1920s 75.00
Dress, rayon & velvet, n/s, A-line, short, 1940s 30.00
Dress, red chiffon, gathered bodice, long A-line skirt, 1960s 40.00
Dress, red w/glitter, Mandarin neck, s/s, 1950s 20.00
Dress, satin w/velvet cording, strapless, tea length, 1950s 38.00
Dress, silk, scoop neck, n/s, lace inserts in skirt, 1920s 100.00
Dress, silk chiffon, V neck, n/s, lace collar, 1920s, EX 90.00
Dress, silk chiffon w/net underskirt, scoop neck, n/s, 1920s 110.00
Dress, sm girl's, red calico w/growth plt, 1860s 55.00
Dress, striped voile, l/s, ca 1910, EX 95.00
Dress, velvet, dropped waist, lace collar, l/s, 1920s, EX 150.00
Dress, wedding; gauzey linen w/embr & lace, l/s, hs, 1890s, NM ...375.00
Dress, wht cotton, buttons to waist, l/s, cuffs, 1910s, VG 45.00
Dress, wht eyelet w/much embr, Edwardian 195.00
Dressing gown, Victorian wht w/lace/pintucks etc, EX 195.00
Driving duster, linen, EX 145.00
Dust cap, patterned silk w/crochet, EX 25.00
Gloves, ivory kid leather, elbow length, Schiaparelli, pr 40.00
Gloves, mc beads on wht, wrist length, 1950s, pr 25.00
Gloves, wht leather w/brn buttons, elbow length, pr, NM 50.00
Hat, beret, dk wool, 1910s 25.00
Hat, blk straw w/ostrich feather, Schiaparelli, 1920s 350.00
Hat, blk velvet w/coral beads at brim, Victorian 150.00
Hat, cloche w/felt flowers, 1920s 55.00
Hat, Edwardian plush w/plumes & coral flowers 250.00
Hat, golfer's, wool w/fur lining, EX 50.00
Hat, lady's, straw boater, 1900s 75.00
Hat, teen style, velvet w/gold lame & circular feathers 95.00
Hat, wht straw w/lg bouquet of forget-me-nots, ca 1900 ....110.00
Jabot, net w/wire stays, Victorian 17.50

Jacket, Levi blue denim, Big E red cloth label, metal buttons, 1960s, EX+, $175.00.

Jacket, Battenberg lace, EX lining 215.00
Jacket, blk silk, l/s, hip length, lapels, Victorian, EX 65.00
Jacket, blk velvet, glass buttons, l/s, collar, 1900s, EX 145.00

Jacket, cream wool w/much lace, fitted waist, stays, 1910s **45.00**
Jacket, dk wool, glass buttons, fur & ribbon trim, Victorian **165.00**
Jacket, gold brocade, stand-up collar, l/s, 1930s **30.00**
Jacket, letterman's; red & wht w/patches, leather sleeves, M **50.00**
Jacket, Levi Big E, dk bl denim, EX **135.00**
Jacket, motorcycle; blk leather, Harley-Davidson, w/belt, VG ...**135.00**
Jacket, 1st Edition Levi, silver buckle in bk, M **600.00**
Jacket, 2-tone brn, tailored, shoulder pads, l/s, 1940s **30.00**
Jeans, JC Penney, buckle-bk, crotch rivet, donut-hole buttons ..**250.00**
Jeans, Levi, single-stitch denim, EX **175.00**
Jeans, Levi Redline, dk denim, dbl-stitch, M **200.00**
Jeans, Levi XX 501, dk bl denim, M **300.00**
Jeans, Levi 501 XX War, donut-hole buttons, EX **185.00**
Nightgown, cotton, lace on puffed/s & neck, silk ribbon, EX **38.00**
Nightgown, crochet bodice w/cotton skirt, 1910s, 44" **25.00**
Nightgown, Edwardian, lacy **45.00**
Overalls, Lee, heavy tan canvas, union made, NM **25.00**
Pantaloons, cotton w/much wide lace **75.00**
Parasol, blk lace over wht silk, ivory hdl, 1860s **300.00**
Parasol, embr on wht linen, burl hdl, ca 1900 ....**150.00**
Parasol, gr brocade, folding, ca 1830, missing finial **55.00**
Petticoat, wht linen w/fancy handwork inserts, EX **40.00**
Robe, pk silk w/ostrich s/s, velvet tie, 1930s **110.00**
Scarf, silk w/beadwork & embr, center seam **30.00**
Shawl, cashmere, blk w/silver paisley, 70" sq **195.00**
Shawl, pk netting w/runching, blk bugle beads, 1920s, 120" **115.00**
Shawl, woven silk, ornate florals in golds & brns, 70x51" **165.00**
Shirt, Western style w/much embr, l/s, 1950s **24.00**
Shoes, high-top, brn lace-up, pr **85.00**
Shoes, lady's beach, red cotton w/wht laces, ca 1900, EX **85.00**
Skirt, bl velvet circle type, padded, 1950s **40.00**
Skirt, blk felt w/pnt flower, circle style, 1950s **40.00**
Skirt, cotton A-line, floor length, ca 1910s, EX **45.00**
Skirt, heavy cotton, blk buttons, pockets, floor length, 1910s **45.00**
Skirt, mc beads on flannel, Mexican style **40.00**
Slip, blk taffeta, 4 layers, zipper, 1950s **30.00**
Slip, peach silk, short style, 1920s, EX **25.00**
Top, sequins on wool, Valentina **50.00**
Trousers, child's, wht flannel, bib top, Victorian **95.00**
Uniform, chauffeur's, gr wool, jacket/pants/vest, 1920s, EX **250.00**
Veil, mourning; blk silk net, 1844 ....**55.00**

Cluthra

The name Cluthra is derived from the Scottish word 'clutha,' meaning cloudy. Glassware by this name was first produced by J. Couper and Sons, England. Frederick Carder developed Cluthra while at the Steuben Glass Works, and similar types of glassware were also made by Durand and Kimball. It is found in both solid and shaded colors and is characterized by a spotty appearance resulting from small air pockets trapped between its two layers. See also Steuben.

Vase, variegated orange and white with bubbles, charcoal handles, Kimball, #20144-12, 11", $425.00.

Vase, bl w/clear ft, tapered, Kimball, #2011, 8½" **300.00**
Vase, pk w/opal M hdls, classic form, #2939, 10" **2,700.00**
Vase, wht, Kimball, 6" **225.00**
Vase, wht/gr/red-brn in clear, beehive form, Kimball, 6¼" **260.00**
Vase, yel/wht in clear, long neck, Kimball, 1949, 16" **350.00**
Vase, yel/opal mottle, ftd cylinder, Kimball, 12½" **250.00**

Coca-Cola

J.S. Pemberton, creator of Coca-Cola, originated his world-famous drink in 1886. From its inception the Coca-Cola Company began an incredible advertising campaign which has proven to be one of the most successful promotions in history. The quantity and diversity of advertising material put out by Coca-Cola in the last one hundred years is literally mind-boggling. From the beginning, the company has projected an image of wholesomeness and Americana. Beautiful women in Victorian costumes, teenagers and schoolchildren, blue- and white-collar workers, the men and women of the Armed Forces, even Santa Claus have appeared in advertisements with a Coke in their hands. Some of the earliest collectibles include trays, syrup dispensers, gum jars, pocket mirrors, and calendars. Many of these items fetch prices in the thousands of dollars. Later examples include radios, signs, lighters, thermometers, playing cards, clocks, and toys — particularly toy trucks.

In 1970 the Coca-Cola Company initialed a multimillion-dollar 'image-refurbishing campaign' which introduced the new 'Dynamic Contour' logo, a twisting white ribbon under the Coca-Cola and Coke trademarks. The new logo often serves as a cut-off point to the purist collector. Newer and very ardent collectors, however, relish the myriad of items marketed since that date, as they often cannot afford the high prices that the vintage pieces command. For more information we recommend *Petretti's Coca-Cola Collectibles Price Guide*, 1994 edition (available from Nostalgia Publications whose address you will find under Auctions in the Directory); *Huxford's Collectible Advertising, Third Edition, BJ Summers' Guide to Coca-Cola;* and *Collectible Coca-Cola Toy Trucks* by our advisor Gael deCourtivron, who is listed in the Directory under Florida. For further information call the Cocaholics Hotline: 941-355-COLA or 941-359-COLA.

Key:
CC — Coca-Cola   tm — trademark
b/o — battery operated

Reproductions and Fantasies

Beware of reproductions! Prices are given for the genuine original articles, but the symbol (+) at the end of some of the following lines indicate items that have been reproduced. Warning! The 1924, 1925, and 1935 calendars have been reproduced. They are identical in almost every way; only a professional can tell them apart. These are *very* deceiving! Watch for frauds: genuinely old celluloid items ranging from combs, mirrors, knives, and forks to doorknobs that have been recently etched with a new double-lined trademark. Still another area of concern deals with reproduction and fantasy items. A fantasy item is a novelty made to appear authentic with inscriptions such as 'Tiffany Studios,' 'Trans Pan Expo,' 'World's Fair,' etc. In reality, these items never existed as originals. For instance, don't be fooled by a Coca-Cola cash register; no originals are known to exist! Large mirrors for bars are being reproduced and are often selling for $10.00 to $50.00.

Of the hundreds of reproductions (designated 'R' in the following examples) and fantasies (designated 'F') on the market today, these are the most deceiving.

Belt Buckle, no originals thought to exist (F), up to **10.00**

Bottle carrier, wood, yel w/red logo, holds 6 bottles (R) 10.00
Bottle dk amber, w/arrows, heavy, narrow spout (R) 10.00
Clock, Gilbert regulator, battery op, ¾-sz, NM+ (R) 175.00
Cooler, Glascock Jr, made by Coca-Cola USA (R) 350.00
Doorknob, glass etched w/tm (F) 3.00
Knife, bottle shape, 1970s, many variations (F), ea 5.00
Knife, fork or spoon w/celluloid hdl, newly etched tm (F) 5.00
Letter opener, stamped metal, Coca-Cola for 5¢ (F) 3.00
Pocket watch, often old watch w/new face (R) 10.00
Pocketknife, yel & red, 1933 World's Fair (F) 2.00
Sign, cb, lady w/fur, dtd 1911, 9x11" (F) 3.00
Soda fountain glass holder, word 'Drink' not orig (R) 5.00
Thermometer, bottle form, DONASCO, 17" (R) 10.00
Trade card, copy of 1905 'Bathtub' foldout, emb 1978 (R) 25.00

The following items have been reproduced and are among the most deceptive of all:

Pocket mirrors from 1905, 1906, 1908, 1909, 1910, 1911, 1916, and 1920.

Trays from 1899, 1910, 1913, 1914, 1917, 1920, 1923, 1925, 1926, 1934, and 1937.

Tip trays from 1907, 1909, 1910, 1913, 1914, 1917, and 1920.

Knives: many versions of the German brass model.

Cartons: wood versions, yellow with logo.

Calendars: 1924, 1925, and 1935.

These items have been marketed:

Brass thermometer, bottle shape, Taiwan, 24"

Cast-iron toys (none ever made)

Cast-iron door pull, bottle shape, made to look old

Poster, Yes Girl (R)

Button sign, has 1 round hole while original has four slots, most have bottle logo, 12", 16", 20" (R)

Bullet trash receptacles (old cans with decals)

Paperweight, rectangular, with Pepsin Gum insert

1949 cooler radio (reproduced with tape deck)

Tin bottle sign, 40"

Fishtail die-cut tin sign, 20" long

Straw holders (no originals exist)

Countless trays — most unauthorized (must read 'American Artworks; Coshocton, OH.')

Centennial Items

The Coca-Cola Company celebrated its 100th birthday in 1986, and amidst all the fanfare came many new collectible items, all sporting the 100th-anniversary logo. These items are destined to become an important part of the total Coca-Cola collectible spectrum. The following pieces are among the most popular centennial items.

Bottle, gold-dipped, in velvet sleeve, 6½-oz 60.00
Bottle, Hutchinson, amber, Root Co, ½-oz, 3 in case 375.00
Bottle, International, set of 9 in plexiglas case 450.00
Bottle, leaded crystal, 100th logo, 6½-oz, MIB 150.00
Medallion, bronze, 3" dia, w/box 100.00
Pin set, wood fr, 101 pins 450.00
Scarf, silk, 30x30" 40.00
Thermometer, glass cover, 14" dia, M 35.00

Coca-Cola Originals

Ashtray, 1940s, glass, Drink CC in Bottles on red dmn, NM 60.00
Bank, 1960, red can w/CC on wht dmn, VG 20.00
Banner, 1950s, Be Really Refreshed ...Around the Clock!, M 85.00
Baseball counter, 1907, keeps runs, hits & errors, EX+ 120.00

Blotter, undated, Carry a Smile Bk...Feeling Fit, NM 50.00
Blotter, 1913, Pure & Healthful Drink CC, 5¢, w/bottles, EX 35.00
Blotter, 1929, The Pause That Refreshes, couple toasting, EX 85.00
Blotter, 1930, The Pause That Refreshes, man in jacket, EX+ 50.00
Blotter, 1940, The Greatest Pause on Earth, clown, NM 60.00
Blotter, 1942, Wholesome Refreshment, 2 Scouts by cooler, EX ..10.00
Blotter, 1944, How About a Coke, 3 girls w/bottles, NM 10.00
Blotter, 1951, Drink CC, Sprite boy behind bottle, NM 10.00
Book, 1954, Bottle Manufacturer, 39 pgs, M 95.00
Bottle, Canadian, no city, aqua, str-sided, EX 25.00
Bottle, Nashville, amber, str-sided, logo on bottom, EX+ 60.00
Bottle, syrup; 1920s, foiled label, jigger cap, EX+ 665.00
Bottle, Woonsockett RI, lt gr, str-sided, block logo, VG 35.00
Bottle carrier, 1920s, cb, Six Bottles CC, NM 85.00
Bottle carrier, 1940s, wood, yel, wing logo, EX+ 200.00
Bottle carrier, 1950s, aluminum, lift hdl, 12-bottle, NM 125.00
Bottle carrier, 1950s, cb, Family Size, EX 10.00
Bottle case, 1950s, waxed cb, CC in 6-Bottle Cartons, M 60.00
Bottle opener, 1910-30, lion head, Drink CC, plain bk, NM+ ...125.00
Bottle topper, 1929, cb, Bathing Girl, 7x9¼", EX 1,000.00
Calendar, 1911, CC Girl, H King illus, full pad, 10½x17¾", NM ...3,500.00
Calendar, 1912, girl's profile, H King, full pad, 9¾x19¾", EX+ 3,500.00
Calendar, 1915, Elaine w/glass & folded parasol, 13x32", EX ..1,300.00
Calendar, 1918, June Caprice holding glass, full pad, NM 300.00
Calendar, 1925, girl w/wht stole, full pad, 12x24", EX (+) 800.00
Calendar, 1928, girl in gold dress, 12x24", EX 650.00
Calendar, 1931, fishing boy & dog under tree, Rockwell, EX 750.00
Calendar, 1935, Out Fishin', w/cover sheet, 10½x18⅝", EX (+) ..650.00
Calendar, 1942, Thirst Knows No Season, 6-pg, EX+ 250.00

Calendar, 1953, Santa with bottle on December 1952 page, 22x13", NM, $275.00.

Calendar, 1953, Work Better Refreshed, NM 150.00
Calendar, 1959, The Pause That Refreshes, basketball, NM 80.00
Calendar, 1967, For the Taste That You Never Get Tired Of, NM ..50.00
Calendar top, 1919, Elaine looking over shoulder, w/glass, G 450.00
Calendar top, 1936, old clam digger w/girl, G+ 150.00
Can, syrup; 1930s, gr w/rnd paper label, 1-gal, EX 275.00
Card set, 1923, Flowers of America, 20 w/envelope, EX 40.00
Change purse, 1919, gold-stamped Drink CC in Bottles..., VG 65.00
Clock, 1910, Gilbert regulator, Gibson girl decal, EX+ 4,000.00
Clock, 1910, leather bottle shape, 8x3", EX+ 800.00
Clock, 1942, neon, octagon, Drink.../bottle, 18", EX+ working ...1,500.00
Clock, 1950s, counter-top light-up, Please Pay..., sq or rnd, NM ..450.00
Clock, 1950s, light-up, rnd, Drink CC, bottle on yel dot, EX+ ..500.00
Clock, 1960s, light-up, sq, Drink CC on red fishtail, NMIB 200.00
Clock, 1960s, plastic/metal, Things Go Better..., 16x16", VG 80.00
Coin changer, 1950s, Vendo, ...Get Your Nickels Here, 15", NM ..650.00
Cooler, picnic; red vinyl box-type w/fishtail logo, NM 50.00

Cooler, 1929, Glascock Junior (single case), oval logos, EX **1,100.00**
Coupon, 1930s, Drink CC in Bottles, 6-pack on reverse, M **20.00**
Doll, 1950s, Buddy Lee, plastic, in uniform w/hat, w/tag, EX+ ...**500.00**
Door palm press, 1930s, porc, Have a CC, yel & wht on red, NM ..**250.00**
Door plate, 1930s, Thanks Call Again..., yel/wht on red, NM **225.00**
Door plate, 1940s-50s, Pull/Push, Refresh Yourself, NM+ **250.00**
Door push bar, 1930s, Come In! Have a CC, yel/wht on red, EX ...**200.00**
Door push bar, 1950s, Iced CC Here, yel/wht on red, EX **150.00**
Drinking glass, flared top, syrup line, NM **325.00**
Drinking glass, 1923-27, modified flared top, NM+ **140.00**
Fan, 1911, geisha girl in garden, Drink CC, 14", EX **150.00**
Fan, 1930s, Sprite Boy/bottle on yel dot, EX+ **65.00**
Festoon, 1930s, Icicles, The Pause..., 5-pc w/envelope, EX+ **650.00**
Festoon, 1939, Petunia, Thirst Stops Here, 5-pc, EX+ **800.00**
Game, Bingo set, orig box, VG+ **45.00**
Game, Streamlined Darts, EXIB **35.00**
Game, Table Tennis, complete, EXIB **60.00**
Game set, 1943, cards, cribbage, dominos & checkers, NMIB **500.00**
Ice pick, 1960s, Drink CC on wood hdl, NMIB **10.00**
Knife, 1960s-70s, 3 blades & opener, Krusius/Germany, NM+ **35.00**
Light fixture, 1930s, milk glass w/repeated Drink CC, NM+ (+) ..**1,500.00**
Light fixture, 1960s, 4 ad panels, roof-like top, 18x18", NM **325.00**
Lighter, flip-top, Enjoy CC, red/wht enamel, contour logo, M **45.00**
Lighter, 1963, musical, red, EX+ **125.00**
Lighter, 1984, silver/red logo, executive award, NM **30.00**
Magazine ad, 1923, flowers above Winter Girl, Drink CC, NM ...**20.00**
Match striker, 1939, porc, Drink CC, 4" sq, NM **500.00**
Matchbook cover, 1922, A Distinctive Drink..., EX **125.00**
Menu board, 1934, tin, Specials To Day, mc lines, 28x20", EX .**350.00**
Menu board, 1940, tin, Silhouette Girl, EX+ **300.00**
Menu board, 1950s, cb stand-up, Refreshing You Best..., EX **100.00**
Mirror, 1936, CC Memos/50th Anniversary, fr, vertical, EX **80.00**
Napkin holder, chrome, Sprite Boy & 5¢ glass/straw box, EX **500.00**
No-Drip Protector, 1938, A Great Drink..., NM **5.00**
No-Drip Protector, 1946, The Taste That Always Charms, NM **3.00**
Paper cup, 1960s, Things Go Better w/Coke, red & wht, NM+ **3.00**
Pitcher, glass w/red CC, pnt rim & 4 bottom rings, M **30.00**
Playing cards, 1943, Autumn Girl, 54 cards, complete, EXIB **75.00**
Playing cards, 1943, Silhouette Girl/Service Girl, NMIB **100.00**
Playing cards, 1951, Party Girl w/bottle, NMIB **80.00**
Playing cards, 1959, Sign of Good Taste, 1 deck, NMIB **75.00**
Playing cards, 1961, Coke Refreshes You Best!, NMIB **60.00**
Playing cards, 1971, It's the Real Thing, MIB (sealed) **20.00**
Pocket mirror, 1909, St Louis Fair, JB Caroll Chicago, EX- **400.00**
Pocket mirror, 1910, CC Girl, JB Caroll Chicago, EX+ **225.00**
Pocket mirror, 1920s, cat's head, diecut cb, 2½x2½", NM+ **425.00**
Postcard, 1911, Motor Girl w/bottle, unused, NM+ **1,200.00**
Pretzel dish, 1930s, aluminum, NM **180.00**
Puzzle, jigsaw; Crossing the Equator, EXIB **100.00**
Puzzle, jigsaw; Teen Age Party, Bill Gregg art, 11x18", NMIB ...**375.00**
Radio, 1960s, vending machine, wht/red, Drink CC, EX **100.00**
Record, 1970s, 45 rpm, Buy the World a Coke, New Seekers, M .**10.00**
Record carrying case, 1960s, Hi-Fi Club, vinyl, NM+ **85.00**
Sheet music, 1927, The CC Girl, EX **200.00**
Sign, arrow, 1920s, tin, 2-sided, Ice Cold CC Sold Here, EX (+) **350.00**
Sign, arrow, 1940s, masonite, red disk w/gold arrow, 17", EX+ ...**600.00**
Sign, button, 1950s, porc, red, CC over bottle, 36", NM **500.00**
Sign, button, 1950s, red, Drink CC Sign of Good Taste, 16", EX ..**225.00**
Sign, button, 1950s, wht, bottle, 24", EX **275.00**
Sign, button w/arrow, 1950s, red/silver, Drink CC, 12", M **475.00**
Sign, cb, 1931, It's a Family Affair, 20x36", NM **675.00**
Sign, cb, 1937, Face the Sun Refreshed, 50x29", EX **500.00**
Sign, cb, 1941, They All Want CC, waitress & food, 20x36", EX .**325.00**
Sign, cb, 1944, Coke Belongs, teen couple, 20x36", EX **325.00**

Sign, cb, 1944, Have a Coke, bottle on iceberg, 20x36", EX **150.00**
Sign, cb, 1945, For the Party, couple on bike, 27x16", EX **375.00**
Sign, cb, 1947, Party Pause, girl in clown suit, 20x36", VG+ **165.00**
Sign, cb, 1951, Pause!, clown & skater, gold fr, 27x16", NM **750.00**
Sign, cb, 1960, A Merry Christmas Calls for Coke, 27x16", VG ..**60.00**
Sign, cb, 1960s, Big Refreshment, Bowling Girl, 32x66", NM **350.00**
Sign, cb diecut, 1938, girl drinking from bottle, 22x15", EX **600.00**
Sign, cb diecut, 1946, Greetings..., Santa w/bottle, 12", EX **225.00**
Sign, cb diecut stand-up, 1954, Eddie Fisher, 19", EX **450.00**
Sign, cb hanger, 1940, bathing beauty on dmn, EX+ **1,000.00**
Sign, flange, 1952, Iced CC Here, yel/wht on red, vertical, NM ..**500.00**
Sign, flange, 1960s, Sign of... under CC fishtail, NM **225.00**
Sign, light-up, 1950s, ads on 2-sided globe, 21", EX **525.00**
Sign, neon, 1980s, Coke w/Ice, soda-glass shape, NM **350.00**
Sign, paper, 1920s, That Taste-Good Feeling, 20x12", VG **325.00**
Sign, paper, 1940s, We have CC 5¢, Sprite Boy, fr, 10x25", NM+ ..**200.00**
Sign, paper, 1950s, Now! Family Size Too!, Sprite Boy, 27", EX ...**115.00**
Sign, porc, 1940s, CC Sold Here Ice Cold, red, 12x29", EX+ **200.00**
Sign, porc, 1940s, Come In! Have a CC, yel/wht/red, 54", NM .**650.00**
Sign, tin, 1920s, Drink CC, Trade Mark under tail, 12x36", NM ..**725.00**
Sign, tin, 1940s, Drink CC, bottle on yel dot, 20x28", EX+ **325.00**
Sign, tin, 1940s, Take Home a Carton, yel on gr, 28x20", NM+ ...**475.00**
Sign, tin, 1950s, Serve CC at Home, 6-pack, 54x18", NM **300.00**
Sign, tin, 1954, diecut bottle, wet-look, 72", NM **575.00**

**Sign, 1960s, tin, Sign of Good Taste,
20x28", NM, $325.00.**

Sign, tin, 1960s, diecut CC fishtail, 12x26", G+ **100.00**
Sign, tin, 1982, Enjoy CC All Year Round, 33x24", NM+ **80.00**
Sign, trolley, 1912, girl in hammock, rstr, EX **2,600.00**
Standee, 1956, diecut cb, lady w/cart, 60", EX+ **600.00**
Thermometer, 1915, wood, Drink CC Delicious..., 21", VG+ **400.00**
Thermometer, 1944, masonite, Thirst Knows No Season, EX+ ..**300.00**
Thermometer, 1960s, dial, Things Go Better..., 12" dia, EX **150.00**
Tip tray, 1906, Juanita w/glass to mouth, 4" dia, EX (+) **650.00**
Tip tray, 1910, girl in wide-brimmed hat, EX (+) **300.00**
Tip tray, 1914, Betty, gr bkground, gold trim, EX+ (+) **200.00**
Tip tray, 1916, Elaine looking over shoulder, EX+ (+) **100.00**
Tip tray, 1920, Garden Girl in yel dress, EX (+) **300.00**
Toy car, Taiyo 1960s, Ford Sedan, friction, 9", EX+ **200.00**
Toy food stand, 1950s, Playtown Hot Dogs Hamburgers, NMIB ...**425.00**
Toy train set, Lionel, 1970s-80s, 027 guage, NMIB **350.00**
Toy truck, Buddy L #420C, 1978, EX **15.00**
Toy truck, Buddy L #4969, '70s, tractor-trailer, closed sides, NM .**65.00**
Toy truck, Buddy L #4973, 1970s, 7-pc set, NMIB **60.00**
Toy truck, Buddy L #5215, 1979s, Ford, 7½", NM **35.00**
Toy truck, Buddy L #5426, '60, Ford, yel steel/bumper, 15", NMIB ...**450.00**
Toy truck, Buddy L #5426, 1965-69, Ford, chrome bumper, EX .**125.00**
Toy truck, Buddy L #5546, 1956, Internat'l, orange steel, NMIB ..**825.00**
Toy truck, Buddy L #5646, 1957, GMC, yel steel, 14", NMIB ...**650.00**
Toy truck, Buddy L #666, 1980s, 15-pc set, MIB **45.00**
Toy truck, Goso #426-20, 1949, w/up, open bed, yel/red, 7½", NM ..**2,500.00**

Toy truck, Marx #1090, 1956-57, yel tin, w/cases, 17", M 850.00
Toy truck, Marx #21, 1954-56, yel tin, 12½", EX+ 250.00
Toy truck, Marx #991, 1950s, gray pressed steel, NMIB 1,000.00
Toy truck, Marx #991, 1950s, red pressed steel, EX+ 375.00
Toy truck, Marx #991, 1950s, yel steel, w/rear decal, NMIB 825.00
Toy truck, Metalcraft #171, 1932, A-fr, 10 glass bottles, 11", VG+ .575.00
Toy truck, Sanyo/A Haddock Co, 1960s, Route Truck, EX 375.00
Toy truck, Smith-Miller, 1944, A-fr, wood & aluminum, 14", EX .1,875.00
Toy van, Durham Industries (Hong Kong), 1970s-80s, NMIP 30.00
Toy van, Lemezarugyar, VW, 1970s, red plastic, friction, 7", MIB ...150.00
Toy van, Van Goodies (Canada), 1970s, Denimachine, 12", M .100.00
TV tray, 1956, party food w/fondue & Coke bottles, NM 10.00
TV tray, 1961, harvest table, scalloped rim, NM 15.00
Wallet, Whenever You See an Arrow..., snap closure, rare, NM ...175.00
Watch fob, 1907, Relieves Fatigue/Drink...Bottles 5¢, EX 120.00
Whistle, 1930s, wood, cylindrical, Pure as Sunlight, M 150.00
Window display, 1932, cb, lg clown & 3-D circus, complete, NM ..7,000.00

Trays

Values are given for trays in excellent plus condition (C8+). Those that have been reproduced are marked with a (+). The 1934 Weismuller and O'Sullivan tray has been reproduced at least three times. To be original, it must have a black back and must say 'American Artworks, Coshocton, Ohio.' It was not reproduced by Coca-Cola in the 1950s.

All 10½x13½" original serving trays produced from 1910-42 are marked with a date, Made in USA and the American Artworks Inc., Coshocton Ohio. All original trays of this format (1910-40) had REG TM in the tail of the C.

1897, Victorian lady, 9¼" dia 12,500.00
1901, Hilda Clark, 9¾" dia 4,000.00
1903, Hilda Clark, oval, 18½x15" 6,000.00
1905, Lillian Russell, glass or bottle, 10½x13¼" 3,500.00
1906, Juanita, glass or bottle version, oval, 13¼x10½" 2,200.00
1907, Relieves Fatigue, 10½x13¼", EX+ 3,000.00
1907, Relieves Fatigue, 13½x16½" 3,600.00
1908, Topless, Ginger Ale, 12¼" dia 6,500.00
1909, St Louis Fair, 10½x13¼" 1,800.00
1909, St Louis Fair, 13½x16½" 3,000.00
1910, Coca-Cola Girl, Hamilton King, 10½x13¼" (+) 850.00
1913, Girl in Lg Hat, Hamilton King, oval, 12¼x15¼" (+) 650.00
1914, Betty, oval, 12¼x15¼" (+) 575.00
1914, Betty, 10½x13¼" (+) 600.00
1916, Elaine, 8½x19" (+) 300.00
1920, Garden Girl, oval, 12¼x15¼" 800.00
1921, Autumn Girl, oval, 12¼x15¼" 800.00
1922, Summer Girl, 10½x15¼" 850.00
1923, Flapper Girl, 10½x13¼" 400.00
1924, Smiling Girl, brn rim, 10½x13¼" 650.00
1924, Smiling Girl, maroon rim, 10¼x13¼" 850.00

1926, Golfers, 10½x13¼" (+) 700.00
1927, Curbside Service, 10½x13¼" 750.00
1928, Bobbed Hair, 10½x13¼" 650.00
1929, Girl in Swimsuit w/Glass, 10½x13¼" 450.00
1930, Swimmer, 10½x13¼" 425.00
1930, Telephone, 10½x13¼" 400.00
1931, Boy w/Sandwich & Dog, 10½x13¼" 750.00
1932, Girl in Swimsuit on Beach, Hayden, 10½x13¼" 625.00
1933, Francis Dee, 10½x13¼" 500.00
1934, Weismuller & O'Sullivan, 10½x13¼" (+), from $650 to .900.00
1935, Madge Evans, 10½x13¼" 375.00
1936, Hostess, 10½x13¼" 350.00
1937, Running Girl, 10½x13¼" (+) 300.00
1938, Girl in the Afternoon, 10½x13¼" 275.00
1939, Springboard Girl, 10½x13¼" 285.00
1940, Sailor Girl, 10½x13¼" 350.00
1941, Ice Skater, 10½x13¼" 300.00
1942, Roadster, 10½x13¼" 350.00
1950, Girl w/Wind in Hair, screened bkground, 10½x13¼" (+) ..85.00
1950, Girl w/Wind in Hair, solid bkground, 10½x13¼" (+) 150.00
1955, Menu, 10½x13¼" 65.00
1957, Birdhouse, 10½x13¼" 100.00
1957, Rooster, 10½x13¼" 175.00
1957, Umbrella Girl, 10½x13¼" 325.00
1961, Pansy Garden, 10½x13¼" 20.00

Vendors

Though interest in Coca-Cola machines of the 1949-1959 era rose dramatically over the last few years, values currently seem to have leveled off and actually dropped 15% to 20%. The major manufacturers of these curved-top, 5¢ and 10¢ machines were Vendo (V), Vendorlator (VMC), Cavalier (C or CS), and Jacobs. Prices are for machines in excellent or better condition, complete and working. They vary greatly according to geographical location.

Cavalier, model #CS72, EX orig 1,200.00
Cavalier, model #CS72, M rstr 2,800.00
Cavalier, model #C27, EX orig 1,500.00
Cavalier, model #C27, M rstr 3,200.00
Cavalier, model #C51, EX orig 850.00
Cavalier, model #C51, M rstr 2,000.00
Jacobs, model #26, EX orig 1,800.00
Jacobs, model #26, M rstr 3,200.00
Vendo, model #23, EX orig 750.00
Vendo, model #23, M rstr 1,800.00
Vendo, model #39, EX orig 1,000.00
Vendo, model #39, M rstr 2,250.00
Vendo, model #44, EX orig 2,200.00
Vendo, model #44, M rstr 3,750.00
Vendo, model #56, EX orig 1,500.00
Vendo, model #56, M rst 3,500.00
Vendo, model #80, EX orig 650.00
Vendo, model #80, M rstr 1,600.00
Vendo, model #81, EX orig 1,500.00
Vendo, model #81, M rstr 3,500.00
Vendorlator, model #27, EX orig 1,800.00
Vendorlator, model #27, rstr (w/stand) 2,750.00
Vendorlator, model #27A, EX orig 800.00
Vendorlator, model #27A, M rstr 2,000.00
Vendorlator, model #33, EX orig 800.00
Vendorlator, model #33, M rstr 2,250.00
Vendorlator, model #44, Ex orig 1,800.00

Tray, 1925, Party, 10½x13¼", EX, $400.00. Beware of reproductions.

Vendorlator, model #44, M rstr 3,200.00
Vendorlator, model #72, EX orig 1,500.00
Vendorlator, model #72, M rstr 2,800.00

Coffee Grinders

The serious collector of kitchenwares and country store items rank coffee mills high on the list of desirable examples. A trend is developing toward preferring items whose manufacturers are easily identifiable. Names to look for include Adams, Arcade, Baldwin Bros., Daisy, Elgin National, Elma, Enterprise, Lane Bros., Parker, Regal, and Sun Mfg. Co.; there are many others. Any of these marks found on coffee mills represent companies who were in business at or before the turn of the century.

Side mills usually have a brass tag located on the tin hopper. If the hopper was made of cast iron, the name was usually cast into the metal. Some of the less expensive versions had no identification. Decals were often used on the front of lap mills and table styles, though sometimes you will find these decals on the inside of the drawer. Because decals are prone to flake off and fade, and since they are often destroyed when the mill is being refinished, lap and table mills are the most difficult types to attribute to a specific manufacturer. Canister mills had names and patent dates molded into the cast-iron housing or on the canister itself. Commercial mills used in country and general stores were made of cast iron. Important information such as manufacture and patent dates was usually cast into the wheels, housing, or base of the mill. Such identification contributes considerably toward value.

Good examples of early coffee mills are rapidly becoming difficult to find. Beware of the many imported imposters that are on the market today.

Key: adj — adjustment

A Kendrick & Sons No 1, lap, CI w/brass hopper, CI drw 155.00
Adams Pat, lap, pewter hopper, wood box, porc knob 145.00
AK & Sons #237707, CI, octagon base, rnd hopper, heavy 275.00
American Beauty, canister, CI & tin, orig cup & papers 85.00
American Duplex Model No 50, electric 45.00
American Duplex No 47, electric 45.00
Arcade, Crystal No 44, CI w/glass hopper, Arcade lid & cup 110.00
Arcade, Favorite No 30 ....180.00
Arcade, Favorite No 47, wood box, CI hopper 160.00
Arcade, Favorite No 74, CI hopper, wood box 155.00
Arcade, Imperial, table, closed CI hopper, wood box 95.00
Arcade, IXL, table, ornate CI hopper, hdl on side, 1-lb, EX 225.00
Arcade, lap, fancy CI top & hopper, wood box, EX 110.00
Arcade, Queen, glass canister & receiver, CI works 225.00
Arcade, Sunbeam, CI w/glass hopper, orig lid & cup, EX 95.00
Arcade, table, w/decal, Pat 6-5-1884, 1-lb 110.00
Arcade, Telephone, canister, CI front, Pat Sept 25 '88 ....525.00
Arcade, Telephone, Hoffman's advertising 925.00
Arcade, Telephone, no Pat dates, early 525.00
Arcade, Xray, canister, CI works, tin hopper w/glass, EX 165.00
Arcade No 147, lap, fancy CI closed hopper, wood box, EX 110.00
Arcade No 3, canister, CI w/glass hopper, orig lid 110.00
Arcade No 4, canister, CI, glass hopper, orig lid, wall mt 225.00
Arcade No 40, canister, CI/glass 110.00
Arcade No 5, side, CI, Pat June '94 ....85.00
Arcade No 700, lap, w/dust cover, Sears 1908 catalog, EX 125.00
Belmont, Lightning No 23, canister, tin & CI 155.00
Bronson-Walton Ever Ready No 2, canister, Pat 1905 ....115.00
Bronson-Walton Monitor, table, tin, ca 1909 ....75.00
Bronson-Walton, Silver Lake, canister, glass hopper 160.00
Caravan, canister, CI works, tin hopper, ca 1910, VG 95.00
Cavanaugh Bros, table, front fill, 1-lb 225.00

Chase & Sanborn, coffee bin 175.00
Coles Mfg No 7, counter, CI, Pat 1887, 16" wheels, 27", EX 750.00
Crescent, Rutland VT, CI, 15" wheels 225.00
Daisy No 667, miniature, CI top, wood box & drw, orig decal 85.00
DeVe, Holland made, lap, copper-plated hopper, decals 75.00
Elgin Nat'l, floor, silver hopper, 24" wheels 1,200.00
Elgin Nat'l No 44, CI/red pnt, w/eagle & pan, 5" wheels, 24" 575.00
Elgin Nat'l No 48, CI w/eagle, orig lily decal, 2 wheels 625.00
Elma, counter, CI, closed hopper, 10" single wheel, 17" 175.00
Elma No 0, CI, single wheel, 9¼" 125.00
Elma No 2, CI, single wheel, 12½" 145.00

Enterprise No. 5, cast iron with wood base and drawer, Pat. 1898, 29-lbs., 12" wheels, 18x13", VG, $525.00.

Enterprise, Baby No 2, orig pnt & decals, 2 wheels, 7½" 795.00
Enterprise, Champion No 1, single wheel, 19½" 825.00
Enterprise, floor, CI, CI hopper, Pat 1898, 39" wheels, VG 2,500.00
Enterprise No 00, CI 295.00
Enterprise No 100, wall mt 250.00
Enterprise No 116½, floor, Pat 1873, 39" wheels, 72", EX 3,675.00
Enterprise No 12, counter, w/eagle/decals, 2 wheels, Pat 1898 ...895.00
Enterprise No 12½, orig pnt & decals, 24¾" wheels 975.00
Enterprise No 212, floor, CI, 2 wheels, 30½" 2,900.00
Enterprise No 7, counter, CI, w/eagle, orig pnt, 17" wheels 825.00
Enterprise No 9, CI, brass eagle, Pat 1898, 19" wheels, 28", VG ...895.00
Golden Rule Blend Coffee, tin, gr & gold pnt, 10-lb, EX 125.00
Grand Union Tea, canister, red pnt, orig writing, Pat 1910 ....110.00
Griswold, coffee bean roaster, rnd, CI, wood hdl, 3-pc 595.00
Griswold, counter, CI, 2 wheels, Pat 1897 ....795.00
Hobart, gr w/hopper & catcher, electric 55.00
J Fisher, dvtl mahog, pewter hopper, handmade 225.00
J Fisher Warranted, lap, dvtl walnut, pewter hopper, unique 225.00
Japy Freres, ornate woodwork, brass hopper, ftd 145.00
L'il Tot, miniature, CI hopper & drw front, wood box 80.00
L&S, side, CI, on orig brd 80.00
Landers, Frary & Clark, CI, rnd, sq base, ornate, Pat 1875 ....475.00
Landers, Frary & Clark, Crown No 01, table, CI 85.00
Landers, Frary & Clark, Crown No 11, CI, decals, side crank 250.00
Landers, Frary & Clark, Regal, canister, wall mt 150.00
Landers, Frary & Clark, Standard, lap, 1878 ....145.00
Landers, Frary & Clark No 50, counter, CI, 12" wheels, EX+ 675.00
Lees, canister, CI works, rnd glass hopper, EX 85.00
Leslir & Krater, table, wood, Pat Oct 5, 1886, rare 550.00
Lightning, canister, CI works, tin hopper, 1-lb, EX 125.00
Mimosa, table mt, CI, open hopper, heavy 85.00
Miniature, canister, boy & girl, 5½x1½" 85.00
Nat'l, coffee & spice counter, CI, 17" wheels, 28", VG 625.00
Nat'l Specialty, CI, brass hopper, 2 12½" wheels 1,100.00
Nat'l Specialty No 0, table clamp-on, CI, covered hopper 125.00
Nat'l Specialty...Philadelphia, CI, 25" wheels, VG 625.00
None Such, Bronson Co Cleveland OH, table, tin, pnt 75.00
Parker, Charles; table, tall/thin, CI & tin top, hdl on top 125.00
Parker No 2, counter, CI w/orig decals, 9" wheels, EX 795.00
Parker No 350, side, CI, orig lid, Pat 4/1876 ....85.00

Parker No 449, canister, CI works, rnd glass hopper, VG 85.00
Parker No 49, side, tin hopper w/brass eagle, tin lid 110.00
Parker No 5005, counter, CI, 12½" wheels, 17", EX 695.00
Parker No 555, Challenge Fast Grind, table, 1-lb, orig, EX 95.00
Parker No 560, table, side crank, wood drw 375.00
Parker No 700, counter, CI, wood drw, 17" wheels 695.00
Parker Victor No 535, table, wood/tin hopper, hdl 135.00
Peck, Stow & Wilcox International #360, lap, unusual 155.00
Primitive, lap, dvtl, red buttermilk pnt, orig drw, pewter 175.00
Primitive, lap, dvtl walnut, wrought iron, brass hopper 175.00
PS&W No 3500, side, CI, orig lid, Britannia hopper 95.00
PS&W Vortex No 40, lap, CI hopper, wood box 145.00
PSW&Co No 6, side, orig CI lid, EX 75.00
Rock Hard, Garant-Sewaarborge, lap, imported 55.00
RR Kreiterr, Lewisberry, York Co PA, dvtl, pewter hopper 165.00
Russell & Erwin Mfg Co, lap, top adj, CI hopper, wood box 95.00
Russell & Erwin Mfg Co No 1008, CI hopper, wood box 90.00
S&H, counter, CI, w/drw, 19" wheels, 21", VG 525.00
Silvers No 1, CI, dbl-grind, w/cup 475.00
Simmons Hardware Co, Delmar Coffee, table, CI cover 295.00
Spong & Co No 1, table, CI w/tin cup, clamp mt 75.00
Star, canister, tin w/CI works, Pat 1910, VG 75.00
Star Model A, floor, 34½" wheels, G- 700.00
Steinfield, canister, CI works, glass jar 100.00
Strobridge, Brighton No 5, lap, open hopper, ca 1877 ....135.00
Sun, No 94, side, CI, Greenfield OH 75.00
Sun, Success No 25, cylinder, 2 different szs, ea 155.00
Sun Mfg No 1080, Challenge Fast Grind, Columbus OH, table ...80.00
Swift, drug mill, CI, open hopper, Pat June 30, 1874 ....525.00
Swift, side, CI, Pat 1845, Pat Aug 16, 1859, top missing 95.00
Swift No 13, counter, orig tin drw, red pnt, 12" wheels, 19" 475.00
Swift No 16, red w/lg decal, 2-wheel 795.00
Thomas Robert & Co, coffee bin 300.00
Turkish, brass cylinder, seal of sultan, folding hdl, old 75.00
Universal No 109, blk tin w/gr decal, Pat 1905, EX 95.00
W Cross & Sons, lap, CI w/orig CI drw, brass hopper & pull 85.00
Waddel Improved No 40, lap, CI hopper 115.00
Wilson, Increase, side, CI & tin 60.00
Wright, John; CI, red or gr pnt, 2-wheel, ca 1968, 6¾" 175.00
Wright's Hdwe Co, Brighton, table, 1-lb, 8" 85.00
WW Weaver Warranted, dvtl walnut, pewter hopper, ca 1830 ..225.00

Coin-Operated Machines

Coin-operated machines may be the fastest-growing area of collector interest in today's market. Many machines are bought, restored, and
used for home entertainment. Older examples from the turn of the century and those with especially elaborate decoration and innovative
accessories are most desirable.

Vending machines sold a product or a service. They were already
in common usage by 1900 selling gum, cigars, matches, and a host of
other commodities. Peanut and gumball machines are especially popular
today. The most valuable are those with their original finish and decals.
Older machines made of cast iron are especially desirable, while those
with plastic globes have little or no collector value. When buying unrestored peanut machines, beware of salt damage.

The coin-operated phonograph of the early 1900s paved the way
for the jukeboxes of the twenties. Seeburg was first on the market with
an automatic 8-tune phonograph. By the 1930s Wurlitzer was the top
name in the industry with dealerships all over the country. As a result
of the growing ranks of competitors, the '40s produced the most beautiful machines made. Wurlitzers from this era are probably the most popularly sought-after models on the market today. The model #1015 of

1946 is considered the all-time classic and often brings prices in excess
of $7,000.00.

Coin-Op Newsletter, Jukebox Collectors' Newsletter, and *Antique
Amusements, Slot Machine, and Jukebox Gazette* are excellent publications
for those interested in coin-operated machines; see the Clubs, Newsletters, and Catalogs section of the Directory for publishing information.

Jackie and Ken Durham are our advisors (for all but jukeboxes);
they are listed in the Directory under the District of Columbia. Our
advisor for jukeboxes is Norman Nelson; he is listed in the Directory
under Ohio.

Arcade Machines

Wizard Fortune Telling Machine,
aluminum and wood, colorful,
19x14x6", EX, $1,595.00.

Atlas 5¢ Tilt Test, formica case, flat-top game, EX 425.00
Cail-o-scope Peep Show, oak & CI floor model, EX orig 1,950.00
ESCo Rotary Merchandiser, EX orig 2,200.00
Exhibit Cupid's Post Office, ca 1920, EX orig 3,000.00
Exhibit Iron Claw Digger, oak case, 40", EX 3,500.00
Exhibit Kiss-O-Meter, EX orig 715.00
Exhibit Supply Crystal Palace Digger, EX orig 3,000.00
Exhibit Supply 1¢ Five Ball Shooter, rstr 1,800.00
Globe Amusement...Raise the Devil, strength tester, EX 4,350.00
Gottlieb Strength Test, hold grip to test, 15x8¼", EX 350.00
Hi Fly Coin Toss, baseball coin toss, 21", EX 600.00
Little Whirl Wind 1¢, flip ball game, counter-top, sm, VG 450.00
Mercury Strength Tester, rstr 600.00
Mills Punching Bag, ca 1900, EX orig 2,500.00
Mills 1¢ Grip Test, strength tester, 1920s, 52", rstr 2,000.00
Mutoscope, tin, 1940s style, EX orig 1,500.00
Mutoscope Love Analyst, fancy cabinet, EX orig 775.00
What Kind of Person Are You?, counter-top, 11x9x18", EX 550.00
Whiting Sculptoscope, EX orig 700.00

Jukeboxes

AMI A, EX orig 3,100.00
AMI Continental II, 1961, EX rstr 3,900.00
AMI D-80, 1951, EX rstr 1,200.00
Mills Throne of Music, ca 1939, EX orig 1,575.00
Rockola, #1448, 1954, EX rstr 3,000.00
Rockola, #1484, wall mt, EX orig 900.00
Rockola, #39, counter-top, EX orig 2,500.00
Rockola #1493, 1962, VG 900.00
Rockola #1495, 1961, EX rstr 2,500.00
Rockola #433, 1965, EX rstr 1,500.00
Seeburg #100R, 1954, EX rstr 3,500.00
Seeburg #147 Trash Can, 1947, EX rstr 3,500.00
Seeburg AY-100, 1961, EX rstr 1,600.00
Seeburg E, oak, w/xylophone, rstr 8,650.00
Seeburg G, 1953, EX rstr 2,750.00
Seeburg V, ca 1955, EX orig 3,000.00

Wurlitzer #1100, 24-selection, 1947, rstr **6,500.00**
Wurlitzer #1250, 1950, EX rstr **3,200.00**
Wurlitzer #1700, 1954, EX rstr **3,500.00**
Wurlitzer #1800, ca 1955, EX orig **2,000.00**
Wurlitzer #41, EX orig **5,750.00**
Wurlitzer #700, orig plastics, EX **3,500.00**
Wurlitzer #71, counter-top on #710 stand, 1941, rstr **8,000.00**
Wurlitzer #71, VG orig **5,750.00**
Wurlitzer #750, 24-selection, ca 1941, old rstr **6,500.00**
Wurlitzer #780, 1940, EX orig **3,500.00**
Wurlitzer #950, EX orig **20,000.00**
Wurlitzer P-12, 12-selection, 1937, EX orig **1,000.00**

Pinball Machines

All Am Football, 1 player, no flippers, 10 balls/1¢, 1935, VG ..**1,100.00**
Baker Target Skill, 1-player, no flippers, 5 balls/5¢, '41, VG **200.00**
Bally Blue Bird, 1 player, no flippers, cash drw, 1936, VG **700.00**
Bally Bull's Eye, 1 player, no flippers, 5 balls/5¢, VG **250.00**
Bally Cross Line, 1 player, no flippers, 1937, VG **450.00**
Bally Fleet Senior, 1 player, no flippers, 1934, VG **350.00**
Bally Rocket, 1 player, no flippers, 5 balls/5¢, 1933, G **350.00**
Bally Skipper, 1 player, counter-top, 3 balls/5¢, 23", VG **450.00**
Bingo Novelty, counter-top, 10 shots/1¢, 1931, VG **300.00**
Buckley Favorite, 1 player, counter-top, no flippers, 1932, VG ..**275.00**
Dudley-Clark Live Power, 1 player, no flippers, 1934, VG **300.00**
Genco Roly Poly, 1 player, no flippers, 10 balls/5¢, 1936, VG **225.00**
Gottlieb Baffle Ball, 1 player, counter-top, 1931, VG **550.00**
Gottlieb Big Broadcase, counter-top, 10 shots/1¢, 1933, VG **375.00**
Gottlieb Challenger, 2 players, flippers, 3 balls/25¢, VG **700.00**
Gottlieb Eye of Tiger, 2-player, 3 balls for 25¢, 69x52x22", VG .**200.00**
Gottlieb Jacks Open, 3 balls for 25¢, 1977, 69x52x22", VG **250.00**
Gottlieb Play Boy, 1 player, counter-top, 1932, G **400.00**
Hercules Roll-A-Ball, counter-top, 10 balls/1¢, 1931, G **200.00**
Keeny Big 6, 1 player, no flippers, 5 balls/5¢, VG **250.00**
Mills One-Two-Three, 1 ball for 5¢, 1938, 76x45x25", VG **500.00**
Mills Post Time, 1 player, battery-op, 1937, G- **600.00**
Mills Railroad, 1 player, no flippers, cash drw, 1936, VG **700.00**
Pierce Tool Hoop-Er-Doo, counter-top, 7 balls/1¢, 1932, G- **275.00**
Rock-Ola World's Fair Jigsaw, 1 player, no flippers, 1933, G ..**1,800.00**
Rock-Ola World's Series, 1-player, no flippers, 1934, VG **1,250.00**
Stoner Hold-Over, 1 player, no flippers, 5¢ play, 1940, VG **75.00**
Stoner Madcap, 1 player, no flippers, 6 balls/5¢, 1936, VG **200.00**
Stoner Ritz, 1 player, console, no flippers, 1938, G **200.00**
Stoner Super 8, 1 player, no flippers, 10 balls/5¢, 1934, VG **275.00**
Stoner 5&10, 1 player, no flippers, 10 balls/5¢, 1935, VG **250.00**
Western Shuffle Ball, 1 player, counter-top, 10 balls/1¢, VG **500.00**
Williams Peter Pan, 1 player, 5 shots/5¢, 1955, G **400.00**

Slot Machines

Bakers 5¢ Races, horserace, multiple slots, 1937, rstr **8,000.00**
Bally Reliance Dice, gold award payout, 1935, 17", rstr **4,000.00**
Bally 5¢ Royal Flush, 5-reel poker, ca 1935-38, 40", rstr **1,500.00**
Caille Peerless Roulette, floor model, all orig, NM **15,000.00**
Caille Puritan, 3-reel, coin entry at top, 1910, 12", G **550.00**
Caille 1¢ Superior, scrolled front, 1928, 22", VG **1,800.00**
Caille 25¢ Aristocrat Roulette, NM **9,200.00**
Caille 5¢ Superior, ornate CI front, ca 1928, 24", rstr **2,500.00**
Gabel's Leader, ca 1905, 65", rstr **8,000.00**
Gabels 25¢ Dewey, oak & ornate CI, ca 1805, 65", EX **9,000.00**
Groechen 5¢ Columbia, dbl jackpot, 18", VG **800.00**
Jenning 10¢ Standard Chief, EX orig **1,950.00**
Jennings Dutch Boy, ca 1929, 25", VG **1,850.00**

Jennings 1¢ Club Chief (Sun Chief), 1949, 27", VG **2,300.00**
Jennings 1¢ Little Duke Triplex, 1933, 24½", EX orig **2,000.00**
Jennings 1¢ Operator Bell, Rockola jackpot front, 1922, 25", VG ...**1,950.00**
Jennings 1¢ Silver Chief, chrome plated, rpt, 27", VG **2,200.00**
Jennings 1¢ Standard Chief, bronze head, 1946, 27", VG **2,400.00**
Jennings 25¢ Victoria, w/golf ball vendor, 24", rstr **5,500.00**
Jennings 5¢ Operator Bell, Roberts jackpot front, 1922, 24", G ..**1,900.00**
Mills Liberty Bell, CI, w/marque, ca 1909, 23", rstr **6,250.00**
Mills 1¢ Cherry Bell (Bursting Cherry), 1937, 26", G **1,850.00**
Mills 1¢ Mystery Golden 'Blue Front,' tokens, 1933, 25", G ...**1,850.00**
Mills 1¢ OK, w/gum vendor, 1930, 25", VG **1,850.00**
Mills 1¢ QT, ca 1935, 19", VG **1,850.00**
Mills 1¢ Silent War Eagle, dbl jackpot, 1932, 26", G **2,500.00**

Mills 10¢ Bursting Cherry, wood base, ca 1938-44, 25", EX original, $2,500.00.

Mills 10¢ Bluebell, EX orig **1,800.00**
Mills 25¢ Castle Front, EX orig **2,500.00**
Mills 25¢ Golden Nugget, 3-reel, 26", rstr **1,900.00**
Mills 25¢ Special Award 777, CI, 26x17", VG **1,800.00**
Mills 5¢ Chicago, oak/ornate CI, ca 1900, 66", VG **6,500.00**
Mills 5¢ Chicago, oak/ornate CI, 1903-10, 66", rstr **8,500.00**
Mills 5¢ Dewey, musical cabinet, ornate CI, rstr **12,000.00**
Mills 5¢ Silent Gooseneck (Lion Front), 1931, 25", G- **1,900.00**
Mills 5¢/25¢ Dewey Twins, floor model, rstr, 66" **22,500.00**
Pace 1¢ All Star Comet, ca 1936, 25", VG **1,850.00**
Watling 1¢ Baby, dbl jackpot, w/gum vendor, 1932, 25", VG .**1,800.00**
Watling 1¢ Treasury, EX orig **3,800.00**
Watling 1¢ Twin Jackpot (Blue Seal), 24½", G **1,800.00**
Watling 3¢ Roll-A-Top Coin Front, EX orig **2,800.00**
Watling 5¢ Cupid, oak & copper plate, ca 1910, 65", rstr **11,000.00**
Watling 5¢ Fox, color wheel, oak & NP, 1905-15, 65", rstr **8,000.00**

Trade Stimulators

Caille Log Cabin, ornate CI front, 1902, 10x14½x22", VG **2,700.00**
Caille 5¢ Winner Dice, CI dice popper, 11½", rstr **900.00**
Canda Jumbo, EX orig **4,200.00**
Cardinal 1¢, orig award card, rstr **600.00**
Daval 1¢ Penny Pack, w/gum vendor, ca 1940, 14", G- **500.00**
Decatur 5¢ Fairest Wheel, cigar vending, 1895, 22", VG **1,200.00**
Lion 1¢ Puritan Baby, w/gum vendor, EX orig **500.00**
Mills Commercial, 5-card type, 1904, 24" w/marque, rstr **6,000.00**
Mills Jockey, 5-reel poker game, ca 1900, 21", rstr **2,900.00**
Mills Upright Perfection, VG orig **1,500.00**
Puritan 1¢ Confection, w/mint vendor, 1933, EX orig **700.00**
Schall Star, horseshoe game, color wheel, oak case, EX **2,000.00**
Steeple Chase, all orig **1,200.00**
Wrigley 5¢ Daisy, coin drop, ca 1910, 9", VG **600.00**

Vendors

Ad-Lee Model D, gumball, globe machine, 1920s, 16", EX **450.00**

Adams' Pepsin Tutti-Fruiti Gum, side vendor, 1898, 18¼", VG ...**400.00**

Adams' Tutti-Fruiti Gum, wooden 4-column L shape, 1890s, 32", G- ...**600.00**

Advance, peanuts & gum, 1932 ....**350.00**

Advance HiLo Climax, slug rejector, 1905, 21", rstr **1,600.00**

Advance 1¢, gumball, CI w/metal lid, ca 1915, 17½", G **275.00**

Alexander Safety 1¢, matches, 5-column, ca 1910, 15", EX **450.00**

American 1¢, toilet paper, Pat Nov 27, 1903, 21", VG **1,200.00**

Atlas Van-Lite Lighter Fluid, side hdl, ca 1951, 19", VG **400.00**

Automatic Games Scoop 1¢, works like Old Mill, 1931, 22½", G **1,200.00**

Automatic Pepsin Gum, wooden pagoda-like top, 1903, 10", VG **4,000.00**

Betham's Pepsin Celery Gum, cobalt glass & wood, 1910, 14", VG .**1,650.00**

Black Diamond 1¢, Pepsin gum, orig decals, 1905, VG **700.00**

Breath Perfume, globe on 8-sided NP body, 1900s, 10½", EX ..**3,500.00**

Buffalo Pepsin Gum, 4-column, clockwork, 1907, 16", VG **6,000.00**

Bull's Head Perfume, spray from bull's mouth, 1908, 14", EX ..**3,350.00**

Butter-Kist 1¢, peanuts, Pat Dec 25, 1923, 22", rstr **750.00**

Caille Sunburst, gum, CI, Sunburst on globe, rpt, 1909, 20" ...**7,000.00**

Clovena Breath Pellets, rpl marque, 1908, 15½", EX **1,350.00**

Columbus #34, gumball, porc on CI, #4 globe, 1936, 14", VG ...**300.00**

Columbus Model A, gumball, w/stand, 1910, all orig **350.00**

Columbus Model D, gumball, Pat Sept 15, 1908, 14½", VG **500.00**

Columbus Model K 1¢, gumball, CI, prof rstr, 15" **350.00**

Columbus Model 2, packaged gum, 2-column, CI, 1920, 16", G .**500.00**

Crystal Breath Pellet, 2 sm globes on CI base, 1908, 10", EX **3,250.00**

Dentyne/Chiclets 1¢, gum, gr porc, ca 1900, 30½", G **950.00**

Detroit Free Press 1¢, matches, 2 wood columns, 1915, 15" **500.00**

Fleer's 1¢, Pepsin gum, ca 1898, rpt/rstr, 15" **1,300.00**

Freeport Goo Goo Gum, stick gum, CI, ca 1899, 16½", VG ...**5,500.00**

Freeport Twins, candy/peanuts, CI/wood, ca 1905, 18", EX ..**30,000.00**

Gabel Merchant, gumball, ornate CI, decals, 1901, 23", EX .**95,000.00**

Gravity Honey Breath Balls, orig decal, 1903, 13½", EX **3,750.00**

Great States Berkshire, emb panels, wht porc, 1938, 16", VG **250.00**

Hance Peerless 1¢, CI w/aluminum coin entry, ca 1915, 15", VG ..**4,500.00**

Hance Rex, peanuts, orig pnt, rare, EX orig **2,100.00**

Harry Woollen Wrigley's Gum, 5-column, 1920s, rstr, 17½" **750.00**

Hilo 1¢, Pepsin Rolls, rpl bk door/rstr, ca 1905, 18½" **500.00**

Honey Dew Bowling Alley, gumball, 1926, 23½", G **750.00**

Improved Hilo 1¢, peanuts, CI, metal lid, w/tray, 1908, 16", EX **950.00**

Ja Birsfield Capsule, stamps, 1915, 16", replated **4,000.00**

Kone Klutch 5¢, stamps, NP, 1911, 14", G **450.00**

Langley's Chiclemint Chewing Gum, pot metal, ca 1915, 14", G ..**400.00**

Lincoln Hot Nut, NP CI, stained-glass marque, 1915, 20½", G **900.00**

Mansfield Automatic Clerk 5¢, gumball, 2-column, 1902, 12", EX .**1,350.00**

Master No 2, gumball, wht porc, ca 1925, 16", VG **350.00**

Master Penny Drop, gumball, 1930, 24" **1,100.00**

Master's 1¢/5¢ Gooseneck, gum dispenser **450.00**

Midland Duplex 5¢, stamps, wood case, decals, 1912, 12", VG ..**950.00**

Miles Wrigley's, packaged gum, wall mt, 1920s, 21", VG **350.00**

Miles-Hi 1¢, packaged gum, ca 1927, 18½", EX **3,000.00**

Millard Breath Pellet, promotional machine, 1916, 8½", VG **850.00**

Millard Breath Pellet, rare CI version, 1916, 9", VG **1,250.00**

Mills American, stamps, patriotic decor, 1915, 22", EX **2,000.00**

National Colgan's Taffy Tolu, gum, Pat 1904, 14¼", VG **3,000.00**

National Peanut, wood w/metal container, 1910, 24", G **250.00**

National 5¢, Elgin pencils, ornate CI, marque, 1911, 17", EX+ .**1,900.00**

Northestern 33 Penny Drop, peanuts, CI, ca 1933, 23½", VG ...**600.00**

Northwestern, porc, gumballs, 1931, all orig **450.00**

Northwestern Sellem Matches, Nouveau-style CI, 1912, 14", VG ..**500.00**

Northwestern Try Some 1¢, gumballs, 1950s **85.00**

Northwestern 1¢, matches, rpt, 13", G **100.00**

Northwestern 1¢ Sq, gumball, CI, wht-duco lacquer, 1919, 15", EX ...**800.00**

Northwestern 3¢, matches, CI, rpt, 6x13x7", EX **250.00**

Northwestern 31 Merchandiser, gum, penny drop, '32, 24", VG ...**900.00**

Operators' Ace, Deco-style, aluminum, 1930s, 16½", VG **650.00**

Oriental Perfume Cabinet 10¢, wood, 3-column, 1920, 19½", G ...**200.00**

Pansy 1¢, gum/fortune card, aluminum, 1905, 11", VG **5,750.00**

Perfecto 1¢, gumball, wood, ca 1910, 19½", EX **750.00**

Pulver Chocolate Cocoa & Gum 1¢, gum, Buster Brown, rstr, 24" ..**1,850.00**

Pulver's Kola-Pepsin Gum, Foxy Grandpa, 1899, 24", rstr ...**1,700.00**

Pulver Too-Choos, gum, Foxy Grandpa, ca 1915, 24", VG **1,350.00**

Pulver 1¢ Clown, gum, short case, bl porc, 21", rstr **700.00**

Pulver 1¢ Clown, gum, short case, rpt brn & wht, 21", VG **700.00**

Pulver 1¢ Cop directing traffic, rpt, 21", VG **900.00**

Pulver 1¢ Yel Kid, gum, orange porc, 21", G **700.00**

Regina 17A, stick gum, oak cabinet, dbl comb, 1902, 21", VG ..**9,500.00**

Richardson's Liberty Drinks, emb grapes on globe, EX **500.00**

Santley Hot Nut, NP CI, stained glass marque, 1920, 19½", VG ..**700.00**

Scoopy Gum, baker w/scoop, ca 1950, 18½", EX **1,150.00**

Sentyu Wallflower Perfume, mahog/beveled mirror, '20, 19½", EX ...**150.00**

Shermack Sanitary 1¢/5¢/10¢ Postage, pnt CI, ca 1930, 8", VG ...**400.00**

Simpson Leebold 1¢, gumball, 10-sided, chromium, '23, 14", G ..**250.00**

Specialty Ideal Cold 1¢, peanuts, aluminum, 1930s, 16", VG **800.00**

Standard 1¢, Pepsin gum & fortune, floral decals, 21½", EX **400.00**

Stanley Hot Nuts, NP CI, ca 1920, 19", VG **1,150.00**

Stoner Twin Merchandiser, CI, 2 globes, ca 1941, 13", VG **300.00**

Towel & Soap 5¢, porc, bl & wht, ca 1904, 12x6", EX **325.00**

US Model D, stamps, CI/beveled glass, 1919, 10½", VG **700.00**

Velvet 1¢, mints, brass body & lid, ca 1912, 15", VG **950.00**

Vendex Chlorophyll 1¢, gumball, 1930s, rpt, 12", VG **150.00**

Vending Machine Co of Am, breath pellets, ca 1910, 12", VG ..**7,500.00**

White Happy Jap, gum, man's head form, Pat 1902, rpt, 14", EX .**950.00**

Wrigley's Gum, tab vendor, aluminum, 1927, rpt, 14½", G **325.00**

Yu-Chu Sweet Breath's, orig decal, Pat June 2, 1925, 10", VG ..**350.00**

Zeno 1¢, stick gum, clockwork, Pat May 5, 1908, 17", EX orig ...**200.00**

Miscellaneous

Duo Scope 1¢, oak case, cb insert, 19", EX **700.00**

Mills Electric Shock machine, 1930s, EX **850.00**

Mills Revelation See Yourself in Future, oak case, 61", VG **2,000.00**

Cole, A. R.

A second generation North Carolina potter, Arthur Ray Cole opened his own shop in 1926, operating under the name Rainbow Pottery until 1941 when he adopted his own name for the title of his business. He remained active until he died in 1974. He was skilled in modeling the pottery and highly recognized for his fine glazes.

Apothecary jar, Chrome-Red with split handles and incised decor, circular ink stamp, 5½", $250.00.

Vase, blk w/yel runs, incised lines, ftd cone, 1930s, 9½" **225.00**

Vase, lt bl w/mc at shoulder, pear shape, pre-1941, 5½", NM **85.00**

Vase, mc splotches, cylindrical, pre-1962, 9⅛" **200.00**

Vase, speckled turq, 3-hdld, 1930s, sgn/Rainbow Pottery, 5⅛" ...**105.00**

Wash pot, streaked matt/shiny gr, 3-leg, att, '50s, mini, 4⅛" **30.00**

Comic Books

For almost sixty years, the American public has been thrilled by the monthly adventures of everyone's favorite comic book heroes such as Superman, Captain Marvel, and Spiderman. Each 10¢ comic book issue, featuring a new saga of adventure and mystery, were usually met with excitement and anticipation by the youngsters who eagerly purchased them from their neighborhood candy store or newsstand. Unfortunately, the vast majority of these comic books were eventually discarded in favor of other worldly pursuits. Due to this fact, most comic books from the '30s and '40s did not survive, making them a very scarce and desirable collectible in today's world. Many comic books are worth very little, a few of the better examples are listed here.

Action Comics, #200, DC Comics, VG 95.00
Action Comics, #227, DC Comics, VG 50.00
Adventure Comics, #127, DC Comics, VG+ 135.00
Adventure Comics, #205, DC Comics, VG+ 75.00
Adventure Comics, #290, DC Comics, VG 32.00
Adventure Into Mystery, #2, Atlas, 1956, G 12.00
Adventures Into Weird Worlds, #4, Marvel Comics, G 18.00
Adventures of Rex the Wonder Dog, #14, DC Comics, VG+ 32.00
All-American Comics, #25, DC Comics, G+ 1,350.00
All-American Men of War, #15, DC Comics, VG 45.00
All-American Men of War, #51, DC Comics, VG+ 20.00
All-Flash, #17, DC Comics, G+ 100.00
All-Funny Comics, #8, DC Comics, G 10.00
All-Star Comics, #14, DC Comics, EX 675.00
All-Star Comics, #49, DC Comics, VG 210.00
All-Star Western, #59, DC Comics, NM 125.00
Amazing Spider-Man, #5, Marvel Comics, G 120.00
Animal Man, #1, DC Comics, NM 10.00
Anthro, #1, DC Comics, EX 18.00
Aquaman, #11, DC Comics, G+ 14.00
Archie & Me, #1, Archie, NM 125.00
Aristokittens, #8, Gold Key, NM 12.00
Astonishing, #4, Marvel Comics, VG 95.00
Astonishing Tales, #25, Marvel Comics, VG+ 30.00

Atom, #1, DC Comics,
EX, $300.00

Atom, #1, DC Comics, VG 165.00
Atom, #7, DC Comics, G+ 50.00
Atom & Hawkman, #42, DC Comics, EX 20.00
Avengers, #1, Marvel Comics, VG+ 400.00
Baby Huey the Baby Giant, #6, Harvey, NM 30.00
Barbie & Ken, #1, Dell, NM 145.00
Batman, #2, DC Comics, G+ 1,200.00
Batman, #6, DC Comics, EX 900.00
Batman, Annual, #1, DC Comics, VG 100.00
Blackhawk, #16, DC Comics, VG+ 125.00

Boy Commandos, #1, DC Comics, 1942 series, G 325.00
Brave & the Bold, #30, DC Comics, G 160.00
Brother Power the Greek, #1, DC Comics, VG+ 10.00
Bullwinkle, #2, Gold Key, NM 90.00
Captain America, #10, Timely/Atlas, 1941 series, EX+ 2,250.00
Captain America, #100, Marvel Comics, 1968 series, G+ 60.00
Captain Marvel, #26, Marvel Comics, VG+ 20.00
Captain Storm, #9, DC Comics, VG+ 3.50
Casper's Ghostland, #22, Harvey, NM 10.00
Challengers of the Unknown, #5, DC Comics, G+ 65.00
Comic Album/Donald Duck, #3, Dell, NM 50.00
Comic Cavalcade, #6, DC Comics, G+ 125.00
Congo Bill, #3, DC Comics, VG+ 120.00
Crackajack Funnies, #15, Dell, NM 230.00
Danger Trail, #2, DC Comics, G+ 175.00
Daredevil, #2, Marvel Comics, G 45.00
Date w/Millie, #4, Altas, EX 15.00
DC Special, #8, DC Comics, EX+ 12.00
Demon, #1, DC Comics, EX+ 21.00
Destroyer Duck, #1, Eclipse, NM 15.00
Detective, #100, DC Comics, VG+ 300.00
Detective, #298, DC Comics, G 25.00
Detective, #40, DC Comics, G- 450.00
Doctor Solar Man of the Atom, #3, Gold Key, NM 65.00
Doctor Strange, #170, Marvel Comics, EX 14.00
Doom Patrol, #19, DC Comics, NM+ 12.00
Eighty Page Giant, #1, DC Comics, G+ 35.00
Famous First Editions, #C-61, DC Comics, NM 10.00
Fantastic Four, #11, Marvel Comics, G+ 100.00
Fist Issue Special, #8, DC Comics, EX 12.00
Flaming Carrot, #18a, B&W/Dark Horse, NM 12.00
Flash Comics, #14, DC Comics, EX 250.00
Flash Comics, #169, DC Comics, EX 20.00
Frankenstein, Marvel Comics, #8, Marvel Comics, NM 10.00
Gabby Hayes Western, #2, Fawcett/Charlton Comics, NM 140.00
GI Combat, #17, DC Comics, VG 20.00
GI Combat, #68, DC Comics, G- 12.00
Green Lantern, #18, DC Comics, 1941, EX 300.00
Green Lantern, #23, DC Comics, 1960, VG+ 28.00
Groo, #2, Pacific, NM 12.00
Harvey Hits/Wendy the Witch, #7, Harvey, NM 80.00
Hawk & Dove, #4, DC Comics, G+ 6.00
Hawkman, #10, DC Comics, VG 16.00
Henry Aldrich Comics, #3, Dell, NM 28.00
Here's Howie, #18, DC Comics, VG 10.00
Hopalong Cassidy, #10, Fawcett, NM 155.00
House of Mystery, #22, DC Comics, VG+ 45.00
House of Secrets, #2, DC Comics, G 40.00
Incredible Hulk, #105, Marvel Comics, VG+ 25.00
Jimmy Olson, #8, DC Comics, G+ 50.00
Journey Into Mystery, #3, Marvel Comics, 1952 series, G 80.00
Justice Comics, #4, Atlas, VG+ 26.00
Justice League, #2, DC Comics, G+ 95.00
Kamandi, #1, DC Comics, EX+ 25.00
Leave It to Binky, #15, DC Comics, G+ 18.00
Lois Lane, #4, DC Comics, G+ 50.00
Marvel Mystery, #9, Marvel Comics, VG+ 4,500.00
Marvel Super-Heroes, #12, Marvel Comics, VG+ 32.00
Marvel Team-Up, #1, Marvel Comics, EX 25.00
Monster of Frankenstein, #1, Marvel Comics, NM 18.00
Mutt & Jeff, #24, DC Comics, VG+ 25.00
My Greatest Adventure, #14, DC Comics, EX+ 60.00
Mystery in Space, #53, DC Comics, VG 200.00
New Adventures of Charlie Chan, #4, DC Comics, VG 50.00

New Teen Titans, #1, DC Comics, 1980, NM+ 10.00
Our Army at War, #18, DC Comics, VG 55.00
Pat Boone, #3, DC Comics, VG+ 55.00
Sensation, #3, DC Comics, VG 240.00
Shadow, #1, DC Comics, EX+ 22.00
Showcase, #8, DC Comics, VG+ 1,450.00
Solar: Man of the Atom, #10, Valiant, NM 30.00
Star Spangled Comics, #74, DC Comics, VG 115.00
Star Spangled War Stories, #6, DC Comics, VG+ 85.00
Strange Adventures, #2, DC Comics, VG+ 280.00
Superboy, #9, DC Comics, G+ 85.00
Superman, #148, DC Comics, VG+ 20.00
Superman, #26, DC Comics, VG+ 215.00
Swamp Thing, #8, DC Comics, 1972 series, NM 12.00
Tales From the Crypt, #22, Golden Age, NM 725.00
Tales of Suspense, #8, Marvel Comics, G+ 55.00
Tales of the Unexpected, #3, DC Comics, VG 65.00
Tales To Astonish, #18, Marvel Comics, VG 50.00
Teen Titans, #1, DC Comics, EX+ 135.00
Terrifying Tales, #14, Star, NM 180.00
Thor, #165, Marvel Comics, EX 15.00
THUNDER Agents, #3, Archie, NM 25.00
Tom Terrific!, #1, Pines Comics, NM 130.00
Top Cat, #5, Charlton, NM 22.00
TV Casper & Co, #5, Harvey, NM 32.00
Tweety & Sylvester, #1, Gold Key, NM 20.00
Underdog, #2, Gold Key, NM 12.00
Warlord, #1, DC Comics, EX+ 10.00
Wonder Woman, #18, DC Comics, G+ 110.00
World's Finest, #6, DC Comics, VG+ 350.00
Wyatt Earp, #2, Dell, NM 25.00
X-Men, #2, Marvel Comics, G+ 210.00
Yogi Bear, #15, Charlton, NM 12.00

Compacts

The use of cosmetics before WWI was looked upon with disdain. After the war women became liberated, entered the work force, and started to use makeup. The compact, a portable container for cosmetics, became a necessity. The basic compact contains a mirror and a powder puff.

The vintage compacts were fashioned in a myriad of shapes, styles, materials, and motifs. They were made of precious metals, fabrics, plastics, and in almost any other conceivable medium imaginable. Commemorative, premium, patriotic, figural, Art Deco, plastic, and gadgetry compacts are just a few of the most sought-after types available today. Those that are combined with other accessories (music/compact, watch/compact, cane/compact) are also very much in demand. Vintage compacts are an especially desirable collectible since the workmanship, design, techniques, and materials used in their execution would be very expensive and virtually impossible to duplicate today.

Our advisor, Roselyn Gerson, has written four highly informative books, *Ladies' Compacts of the 19th and 20th Centuries*, *Vintage Vanity Bags and Purses*, *Vintage and Contemporary Purse Accessories*, and *Vintage Ladies' Compacts*. She is listed in the Directory under the state of New York. See Clubs and Newsletters for information concerning the compact collectors' club and their periodical publication, *The Powder Puff*.

Cara Norma, flower basket in spider web on gold-tone, 2x3" 85.00
Coro, half-moon shape, gold-tone w/enameled Persian design 60.00
Coty, gold-tone w/stylized wht puffs on orange, rnd 80.00
Czech, emb gold-tone decor w/mc stones, late 1800s, sq 200.00
De Corday, Silver Queen, resembles wht golf ball, 2" dia 50.00
Elgin, Am Beauty, gold-tone w/scalloped edge, 1930s, MIB 25.00

Elgin, gilt w/engr continents & compass, rnd, 1950s 175.00
Elgin, gold-tone w/allover harlequin masks, 2⅔" sq 60.00
Evans, compact/watch combo, silver-tone, oblong, 1950s 150.00
Evans, sterling gold wash w/pk, yel & wht basketweave, 5" dia ..250.00
Fan shape, gold-tone w/floral decor, pearl twist lock, 2x3" 60.00
Fan shape, MOP w/rhinestone floral decor, Japan 60.00
Girey, Kamra Pak, sparkling confetti plastic, 1930s-40s 80.00
Girl Scouts, satin gold-tone w/polished insignia, sq 80.00
Heart shape, gold-tone w/purple orchid on blk plastic lid 90.00
Heart shape, gold-tone w/rnd brocade lid, 1930s 60.00
Henriette, brass ball, 1930s 80.00
Horseshoe shape, gilt metal w/tooled leather inserts 125.00
Illinois Watch Case Co, gold-tone w/watch face, sq, 1930s 150.00
India, silver w/zigzags around cut-out map, octagonal 200.00
Ireland, gr enamel w/4 gold-tone scenes around emblem, rnd 50.00
K&K, dmn shape, satin & polished gold-tone dmn design 60.00
K&K, gray MOP w/rhinestones, oval, 1930s-40s 75.00
Kigu, Cherie, gold-tone heart w/jeweled crown, 1940s-50s 80.00
Kigu, heart-shaped flower on wht-dotted bl enamel, rnd 75.00
Lady Vanity, bl leather w/snap closure, oval 60.00
Lin-Bin, gr leather w/envelope-type coin holder on lid, 1940s ...100.00
Lucite, rnd beveled design w/inner & outer mirror, 1940s 100.00
Melba, gold-tone w/enameled tree scene, oblong, mini 60.00
Mondaine, maroon gold-tooled leather, 1930s 80.00
Nan Co-ed, leather horseshoe w/tooled cowboy motif, zippered .125.00
Officer's cap, bronzed, jeweled Air Force insignia, 1940s 100.00
Officer's cap, plastic, Army khaki, 1940s 80.00
Plastic, mc glitter stripes, rnd, 1920s 75.00
Plastic, red ladybug 125.00
Plastic, rhinestones on blk, rnd w/screw top, 1920s 80.00
Rex Fifth Aveneue, red, wht & bl w/military emblem, oval 75.00
Ronson, Art Deco enamel compact/lighter/cigarette case 150.00
Rowenta, petit-point floral decor on blk enamel, oval 50.00
Sabor, gilt & plastic w/kissing poodles in Lucite dome 80.00
Souvenir, California, oblong, wood w/cvd map & scenes 100.00
Souvenir, Pennsylvania Turnpike, sq w/view of tunnel & name ...60.00
Souvenir, Summit Pikes Peak, rnd, gold-tone w/wht plastic 80.00
Stratton, gold-tone & wht w/bl windmill, 2¾" dia 50.00
Stratton, gold-tone w/color images of beverages, 3" dia 60.00
Stratton, gold-tone w/leaf band around birds on branch, rnd 60.00
Stratton, Wedgewood, gold-tone w/3 Graces cameo, 3¼" dia 75.00
Until We Meet Again, sq, wood w/pnt GI & girl, 1940s 100.00
Vermeil, sterling silver w/bl cloisonne decor, rnd, w/chain 150.00

Photo courtesy Roselyn Gerson

Volupte, designed to resemble vanity table, collapsible cabriole legs (silvered metal opened, gold-tone closed), 3x2¼", MIB, $225.00.

Volupte, gold-tone w/raised spider-web design, sq, 3" 75.00
Volupte, hand shape, plain gold-tone, 1940s 125.00
Volupte, stippled gold-tone w/jeweled swing lock, 1940s, sq 100.00
Wadsworth, conductor's pocketwatch style, gold-tone, 2½" 60.00
Wadsworth, fan shape w/bird & flowers on yel enamel, 1940s 100.00
Yardley, gold-tone w/red, wht & bl commas, oval, 1940s 75.00

Computing Devices

Computing, calculating, and adding devices come in many shapes, sizes, and weights. Some are complex machines with many moving parts while others, such as slide rules, are quite simple in construction. These devices were used by scientists, accountants, engineers, and many other professionals when mathematical computations and exactness were required. Examples of devices and machines with early patent dates are usually of greatest interest to collectors. Our advisor for this category is Dale Beeks; he is listed in the Directory under Iowa.

Adder, Addometer, 7 numbered wheels, EX in case **35.00**
Adder, Gem, chain drive, pocket sz **45.00**
Adder, Webb, Pat 1867, wooden base, EX **400.00**
Adder, Webb, Pat 1889, all metal, EX **165.00**
Adder, Webb type, unsgn, all metal, EX **110.00**
Curta, pepper-grinder type, EX in case **250.00**
Machine, Brunsviga midget, wooden cover, EX **200.00**
Machine, Burroughs, push button, glass sides, lg **125.00**
Machine, Comptometer, copper case, push buttons **45.00**
Machine, Comptometer, wooden case, G **900.00**
Machine, Millionaire, metal case, heavy, lg, VG **750.00**
Slide rule, beginner's, EX in case **12.00**
Slide rule, circular, Gilson, EX in case **35.00**
Slide rule, demonstration, Pickett, 84" L, EX **120.00**
Slide rule, Keuffel & Esser NY, typical, EX **22.00**
Slide rule, Thachers, cylindrical, Pat 1882, EX in case **1,200.00**

Consolidated Lamp and Glass

The Consolidated Lamp and Glass Company of Coraopolis, Pennsylvania, was incorporated in 1894. For many years their primary business was the manufacture of lighting glass such as oil lamps and shades for both gas and electric lighting. The popular 'Cosmos' line of lamps and tableware was produced from 1894 to 1915. (See also Cosmos.) In 1926 Consolidated introduced their Martele line, a type of 'sculptured' ware closely resembling Lalique glassware of France. (Compare Consolidated's 'Lovebirds' vase with the Lalique 'Perruches' vase.) It is this line of vases, lamps, and tableware which is often mistaken for a very similar type of glassware produced by the Phoenix Glass Company, located nearby in Monaca, Pennsylvania. For example, the so-called Phoenix 'Grasshopper' vases are actually Consolidated's 'Katydid' vases.

Items in the Martele line were produced in blue, pink, green, crystal, white, or custard glass decorated with various fired-on color treatments or a satin finish. For the most part, their colors were distinctively different from those used by Phoenix. Although not foolproof, one of the ways of distinguishing Consolidated's wares from those of Phoenix is that most of the time Consolidated applied color to the raised portion of the design, leaving the background plain, while Phoenix usually applied color to the background, leaving the raised surfaces undecorated. This is particularly true of those pieces in white or custard glass.

In 1928 Consolidated introduced their Ruba Rombic line, which was their Art Deco or Art Moderne line of glassware. It was only produced from 1928-1932 and is quite scarce. Today it is highly sought after by both Consolidated and Art Deco collectors.

Consolidated closed its doors for good in 1964. Subsequently a few of the molds passed into the hands of other glass companies that later reproduced certain patterns; one such reissue is the 'Chickadee' vase, found in avocado green, satin-finish custard, or milk glass. Our advisor for this category is Jack D. Wilson, author of *Phoenix and Consolidated Art Glass, 1926 - 1980*; he is listed in the Directory under Illinois.

Key: mg — milk glass

Bird of Paradise, fan vase, yel wash, 10" **275.00**
Bird of Paradise, plate, gr wash, 12" **95.00**
Bittersweet, vase, amber irid over mg, rare, 9½" **475.00**
Bittersweet, vase, sepia cased, 9½" **350.00**
Blackberry, umbrella vase, wht wash, 18" **500.00**
Catalonian, vase, Reuben bl (rare color), #1100, 8" **300.00**

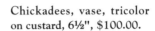
Chickadees, vase, tricolor on custard, 6½", $100.00.

Chickadee, vase, sepia wash on crystal, 6½" **135.00**
Chrysanthemum, vase, 3-color highlights on satin mg, 12" **175.00**
Cockatoo, console bowl, purple wash, 13" **225.00**
Con-Cora, cookie jar, violets on mg, orig label, 9" **145.00**
Dancing Girls, vase, straw opal, 12" **550.00**
Dancing Nymph, plate, pk frost, 10" **175.00**
Dancing Nymph, platter, gr wash, bowl shape, 16" **525.00**
Dogwood, vase, bl transparent over wht, 11" **400.00**
Dragon-Fly, vase, gold on glossy custard, 7" **175.00**
Dragon-Fly, vase, gr cased, orig Martele label, 7" **225.00**
Five Fruits, jug, yel wash, ½-gal **285.00**
Five Fruits, plate, purple wash, 14" **150.00**
Florentine, vase, gr, urn shape, 7" **250.00**
Foxglove, vase, 2-color highlighting on satin custard, 7" **145.00**
Hummingbird, puff box, bl wash on crystal, 5" **110.00**
Iris, jug, sepia wash **325.00**
Iris, mayonnaise bowl, purple wash **40.00**
Jonquil, vase, yel & gr highlights on satin custard, 6¼" **145.00**
Katydid, ashtray, gr **435.00**
Katydid, vase, purple wash, tumbler shape **170.00**
Line 700, lamp (7" vase), red slag **525.00**
Line 700, plate, service; bl frost, 10" **145.00**
Line 700, vase, bl w/ormolu mts, 6½" **375.00**
Line 700, vase, red w/satin bkground, 7" **500.00**
Lovebirds, banana boat, 3-color on custard, ormolu mts **625.00**
Lovebirds, powder jar, yel wash **80.00**
Lovebirds, vase, ruby stain on crystal, 11" **275.00**
Nuthatch, planter vase, 3-color highlights on mg, 10x5" **225.00**
Olive, bowl, reverse bl highlights, 8" **125.00**
Olive, vase, gold highlights on glossy mg, 4" **125.00**
Orchids, console bowl, gray wash, rare **275.00**
Pine Cone, vase, gr cased, 6½" **285.00**
Poppy, vase, bl wash, 10½" **275.00**
Regent Line, vase, ash-rose pk over wht opal, #1174-B, 4½" **125.00**
Ruba Rombic, bowl, topaz, cupped, 8" **800.00**
Ruba Rombic, candle holder, topaz **250.00**
Ruba Rombic, jug, wht opal, rare **2,500.00**
Ruba Rombic, nut dish, jungle gr, rare **225.00**
Ruba Rombic, plate, jade, 8" **145.00**
Ruba Rombic, plate, jungle gr, 15" **1,200.00**
Ruba Rombic, shot glass, gr, 2-oz **150.00**
Santa Maria, cigarette box, gr wash **235.00**

Screech Owls, vase, brn on satin mg, 5¾" 175.00
Screech Owls, vase, reverse ruby stain on crystal, 5¾" 175.00
Sea Gulls, orange highlighting on custard satin, 11" 475.00
Sea Gulls, vase, gr cased, 11" 750.00
Spanish Knobs, pinch vase, red, 6½" 210.00
Tropical Fish, vase, gr cased, 9" 375.00
Tropical Fish, vase, purple cased, 9" 375.00

Cookbooks

Cookbooks from the 19th century, though often hard to find, are a delight to today's collectors both for their quaint formats and printing methods as well as for their outmoded, often humorous views on nutrition. Recipes required a 'pinch' of salt, butter 'the size of an egg' or a 'walnut,' or a 'handful' of flour. Collectors sometimes specialize in cookbooks issued as advertising premiums. Especially desirable are the figurals that were shaped like a jar, a slice of bread, or some other form relative to the product. Others with unique features such as illustrations by well-known artists or references to famous people or places are priced in accordance. Cookbooks written earlier than 1874 are the most valuable and when found command prices as high as $200.00; figurals usually sell in the $10.00 to $15.00 range.

As is true with all other books, if the original dust jacket is present and in nice condition, a cookbook's value goes up by at least $5.00. Right now, books on Italian cooking from before circa 1940 are in demand, and bread-baking is important this year. For further information we recommend *A Guide to Collecting Cookbooks* by Col. Bob Allen and *Price Guide to Cookbooks and Recipe Leaflets* by Linda Dickinson. Our advisor for this category is Charlotte Safir; she is listed in the Directory under New York.

Key:
CB — cookbook   dj — dust jacket

A&P CB, 1975, 288-pg, EX 8.00
All About Baking, 1937, hardbk, 144-pg, EX 12.50
American Family CB, J Carson, 1898, VG 45.00
Baker's Best Chocolate Recipes, 1932, leaflet, EX 8.00
Best of Cooking, A Kruger, 1977, hardbk, 336-pg, VG 16.50
Better Cooking Library Cookie CB, 1964, hardbk, 126-pg, EX 8.00
Better Homes & Gardens Cookies & Candies, 1966, 126-pg, EX ..8.00
Better Homes & Gardens Cooking for Two, 1968, hardbk, VG 6.00
Better Homes & Gardens Heritage CB, 1975, hardbk, 400-pg 16.50
Betty Crocker CB, 1959, hardbk, EX 25.00
Betty Crocker Dinner for Two, 1964, hardbk, 156-pg, VG 10.00
Betty Crocker Good & Easy, 1954, 1st edition, sm, EX 10.00
Betty Crocker International CB, 1980, hardbk, 372-pg, VG 12.50
Betty Crocker New Outdoor CB, 1967, spiral, 160-pg, VG 10.00
Birds-Eye CB, 1941, paperbk, 63-pg, G 2.00
Bread Baking, L Pappas, 1975, paperbk, 183-pg, VG 6.00
Carnation CB, M Blake, 1941, 96-pg, G 8.00
Christmas Cookie CB, V Pasley, 1951, hardbk, 146-pg, EX 8.00
Cookie CB, D Clem, 1966, hardbk, 402-pg, EX 8.00
Cottolene Shortening, 52 Sunday Dinners; 1915, 192-pg, VG 4.00
Crown Cork & Seal Canning Book, 1936, paperbk, EX 5.00
Culinary Arts, Am Family CB; 1st edition, EX 25.00
Culinary Arts, Creole CB; 1956, paperbk, 68-pg, EX 3.00
Culinary Arts, Low Calorie Recipes; 1955, paperbk, 68-pg, EX 3.00
Culinary Arts, Scandinavian CB; 1956, paperbk, 68-pg, EX 3.00
Culinary Arts, 500 Delicious Salad Recipes; 1954, 48-pg, EX 5.00
D-Zerta, 1930, 32-pg, EX 10.00
Dole, Drink Dole's Pineapple; 1906, leaflet, G 3.00

Enterprising Housekeeper Recipe Book, 1902, 90-pg, EX 15.00
Entertaining w/Elegance, G Darioux, 1965, 404-pg, EX 8.00
Family Circle CB, 1974, hardbk, 189-pg, VG 15.00
Fannie Farmer, Food & Cookery of the Sick; 1906, 300-pg, EX ...28.00
Fannie Farmer CB, 1968, hardbk, 648-pg, EX 6.00
Fanny Farmer CB, 1906, EX 18.00
Flavor of France, Hasting, 1964, 232-pg, EX 20.00
Fleishmann, 65 Delicious Dishes Made From Bread; 1919, EX 10.00
For Men Only CB, Abdullah, 1937, hardbk, 205-pg, EX 10.00
From Garden to Kitchen, Middleton, 1937, 1st edition, EX 15.00
Graham Kerr CB, Doubleday, 1969, hardbk, 284-pg, EX 10.00
Great Sandwich Book, A Borghese, 1978, hardbk, 270-pg, VG 7.50
Helen Corbitt's CB, Houghton Mifflin, 1957, hardbk, 388-pg, VG ..7.50
Jell-O, What You Can Do w/Jell-O; 1933, 26-pg, G 12.00
Jell-O Ice Cream Powder, 1925, 4-pg, G 12.00
Julia Child's Kitchen, Knoph, 1977, hardbk, 687-pg, EX 18.00
Junket, Delicious Quick Desserts; 1929, leaflet, 24-pg, VG 3.00
Kraft, Food Favorites; 1951, paperbk, 32-pg, VG 2.00
Mary Jane's CB, 1916, hardbk, 307-pg, EX 100.00
Mary Meade's Country CK, RE Church, 1964, hardbk, 376-pg, EX ...12.00
Mayflower Recipes, 1932, 23-pg, VG 8.00
Maytag Dutch Oven CB, leaflet, 49-pg, EX 8.00
McNess CB, ca 1935, lady in gr, 79-pg, EX 6.00
Minute Tapioca, A Cook's Tour...; 1929, 40-pg, G 10.00
Mystery Chef, Be an Artist at the Gas Range; 1935, EX 10.00
National Biscuit, Biscuits for Salads; 1926, leaflet, 8-pg, G 2.00
Never Say Leftovers, M Loo, 1982, spiral, 106-pg, VG 5.00
New James Beard, Knopf, 1981, hardbk, 625-pg, VG 15.00
One Potato Two Potato, C Bollen, 1983, paperbk, 167-pg, VG 6.00
Pepsin Syrup, Dr Caldwell Home CB; ca 1910, 32-pg, G 3.00
Pillsbury, Best Cakes; ca 1960, paperbk, 48-pg, EX 4.00
Pillsbury, Best of Bake-off Collection; 1959, EX 35.00
Pillsbury's Diamond Anniversary Recipes, 1944, paperbk, EX 8.00
Pillsbury's 3rd Grand National 100...Recipes, 1952, 96-pg, VG 10.00
Royal Baking Powder, Best Wartime Recipes; 1917, leaflet, VG 2.00
Rumford CB, 1909, leaflet, w/wheat girl, EX 8.00
Science of Food & Cookery, H Anderson, 1926, hardbk, EX 18.00
Secrets of Good Cooking, Sister St Mary, 1928, 309-pg, EX 8.00
Sleepy Eye Mills CB, image in center, EX 300.00
Slumps Grunts & Snickerdoodles, L Perl, 1975, 125-pg, EX 6.50
Southern Cooking, Grosset, 1941, EX 20.00
Swans Down, Bake Like a Champion; 1936, 23-pg, VG 10.00
Trader Vic's Kitchen Kibitzer, Doubleday, 1956, 223-pg, VG 7.50
Watergate CB, Emporium, 1973, satirical, 96-pg, VG 7.00
Wesson Oil, Let's Enjoy Eating; 1932, 48-pg, EX 10.00
Woman's World Magazine, Salads & Sandwiches; 1924, 48-pg, EX 6.00

Cookie Cutters

Early hand-fashioned cookie cutters have recently been commanding stiff prices at country auctions, and the ranks of interested collectors are growing steadily. Especially valuable are the figural cutters; and the more complicated the design, the higher the price. A follow-up of the carved wooden cookie boards, the first cutters were probably made by itinerant tinkers from leftover or recycled pieces of tin. Though most of the 18th-century examples are now in museums or collections, it is still possible to find some good cutters from the late 1800s when changes in the manufacture of tin resulted in a thinner, less expensive material. The width of the cutting strip is often a good indicator of age; the wider the strip, the older the cutter. While the very early cutters were 1" to 1½" deep, by the '20s and '30s, many were less than ½" deep. Crude, spotty soldering indicates an older cutter, while a thin line of solder usually tends to suggest a much later manufacture. The shape of the backplate is another clue. Later cutters will have oval, round, or rectangular backs, while on the earlier type the back was cut to follow the lines of the design. Cookie cutters usually vary from 2" to 4" in size, but gingerbread men were often made as tall as 12". Birds, fish, hearts, and tulips are common; simple versions can be purchased for as little as $12.00 to $15.00. The larger figurals, especially those with more imaginative details, often bring $75.00 and up. The cookie cutters listed here are tin and handmade unless noted otherwise.

Bird, flying, strap hdl, 4x3" 22.00
Bird, standing, strap hdl, 3½x2½" 22.00
Cat, seated, w/hdl, 4x3" 30.00
Chicken, simple shape, flat bk, 5½" 55.00
Chicken w/fan-like tail, no hdl, 3⅝x3⅜" 50.00
Christmas tree, rectangular bk, strap hdl, 5½x4x1" 38.00
Deer, leaping, 8" 195.00
Deer, stylized antlers, flat bk finger holes, 6½" 160.00
Duck, arched ribbon hdl, 4⅛x3" 15.00
Duck, hdl missing, 3⅝x2⅜" 25.00
Eagle, flat bk, 4" 60.00
Elephant, good detail, strap hdl, 4¾" 70.00
Fish, strap hdl, 4" 20.00
Hatchet, strap hdl, 7" 55.00
Heart, strap hdl, 6½" 50.00
Hen, strap hdl, 3⅝x3⅞" 28.00
Horse, stylized, flat bk, loose seam, 4¾" 55.00
Horse, stylized, no hdl, 6½x6¼" 65.00
Horse, w/hdl, 2¾x3⅛" 50.00
Lady in long skirt, strap hdl, 4½" 58.00
Lady w/sawtooth edge on skirt, no hdl, lt rust, 4¼" 40.00
Leaf, feathery look w/curling edges, flat bk, 9½" 200.00
Lovebirds at heart, 7" 300.00
Man in the moon, flat bk, 4" 65.00
Man w/coat tails, strap hdl, 6¼" 70.00
Man w/hat, simple design, no hdl, 4⅞x2½" 60.00
Man w/hat, simple design, 6⅝" 100.00
Rabbit, flat bk w/2 finger holes, well made, 6" 100.00
Rabbit, running, strap hdl, 7¾" 42.00
Raggedy Ann & Andy, Hallmark, 1970s, MIP 27.50
Rocking horse, strap hdl, 4¼x4¾" 50.00
Rooster, flat bk, 7" 80.00
Rooster, ornate crimped details, flat bk, 6¼" 100.00
Rooster, sq hdl, 3⅝x3⅛" 35.00
Santa w/tree, strap hdl, 5" 38.00
Stag, flat bk, 5½" 65.00
Tulip & leaf (dbl) in crimped oval, strap hdl, 3¾x2¾" 25.00
Turkey, galvanized, flat bk, 4½" 65.00

Cookie Jars

The appeal of the cookie jar is universal; folks of all ages, both male and female, love to collect 'em! The early '30s heavy stoneware jars of a rather nondescript nature quickly gave way to figurals of every type imaginable. Those from the mid to late '30s were often decorated over the glaze with 'cold paint,' but by the early '40s underglaze decorating resulted in cheerful, bright, permanent colors and cookie jars that still have a new look fifty years later.

Stimulated by the high prices commanded by desirable cookie jars, a broad spectrum of 'new' cookie jars are flooding the marketplace in three categories: 1) Manufactures have expanded their lines with exciting new designs specifically geared toward attracting the collector market. 2) Limited editions and artist-designed jars have proliferated. 3) Reproductions, signed and unsigned, have pervaded the market, creat-

ing uncertainty among new collectors and inexperienced dealers. One of the most troublesome reproductions is the Little Red Riding Hood jar marked McCoy. Several Brush jars are being reproduced, and because the old molds are being used, these are especially deceptive. In addition to these reproductions, we've also been alerted to watch for cookie jars marked Brush-McCoy made from molds that Brush never used. Remember that none of Brush's cookie jars were marked Brush-McCoy, so any bearing the compound name is fraudulent. For more information on cookie jars and reproductions, we recommend *The Collector's Encyclopedia of Cookie Jars* by Fred and Joyce Roerig; they are listed in the Directory under South Carolina. Another good source is *An Illustrated Guide to Cookie Jars* by Ermagene Westfall. Our advisors for this category are Charlie and Rose Snyder; they are listed in the Directory under Kansas.

The examples listed below were made by companies other than those found elsewhere in this book; see also specific manufacturers.

Bambi, Twin Winton, squirrel finial, from $150 to 175.00
Barney Rubble, Certified International 45.00
Bartender, Pan Am Art, from $250 to 300.00

Basset Hound, Doranne of California, marked J1 USA, $50.00.

Photo courtesy Ermagene Westfall

Bear, California Originals, #2648 ....75.00
Beaver Fireman, Sigma, from $250 to 300.00
Benjamin Franklin for Strawbridge & Cothier/Treasure Craft ...160.00
Big Al, Treasure Craft, Disney, from $125 to 165.00
Bulldog Cafe, Treasure Craft, Disney, from $150 to 165.00
Bulldog on Safe, California Originals, from $35 to 50.00
C-3PO, Roman Ceramics 450.00
Candy Shack, Twin Winton, from $55 to 75.00
Carousel Horse, Hearth & Home, from $50 to 70.00
Case Steam Engine, 1993 for 150th Anniversary 125.00
Cathy, McMe 150.00
Cathy (Guisewite) Bust, Papel, very short run 95.00
Chicken Racer, Clay Art, from $50 to 65.00
Chipmunk, Norcrest 65.00
Circus Wagon, w/head, Sierra Vista 200.00
Circus Wagon, w/o head, Sierra Vista 135.00
Clown, wood grain, Deforest 90.00
Coffee Grinder, House of Webster 25.00
Cookie Chef, Treasure Craft, from $55 to 85.00
Cookie Monster, Newcor 45.00
Cow Jumped Over Moon, Robinson Ransbottom 275.00
Cowboy, Vandor 60.00
Cruisin' Dog, Treasure Craft, discontinued 95.00
Daffy Duck, Certified International, from $40 to 50.00
Daffy Duck Head, Warner Bros 85.00
Dalmatian, Schmid, musical 90.00
Disneyland's 40th Ann Sleeping Beauty Castle, Nestles' 75.00

Donkey, straw hat, Twin Winton 175.00
Dorothy & Toto (2-lidded) Star Jars 300.00
Dutch Girl, Delft, from $45 to 55.00
Dutch Girl, Pottery Guild, from $65 to 85.00
Elephant, Sierra Vista, from $95 to 110.00
Emmett Kelly Jr, Flambro 750.00
Ernie, w/blk or blond hair, Newcor 75.00
Fats, A Little Co, from $200 to 250.00
Garfield on Stack of Cookies, Enesco, from $285 to 310.00
Genie, full-bodied/sitting, Mexico/Disney theme park exclusive 150.00
Genie Bust, Thailand, Disney store exclusive 110.00
German Gentleman, W Germany, from $200 to 250.00
Girl Holding Chest, Pottery Guild, from $125 to 145.00
Goldilocks & the Three Bears, Home Collection, from $40 to 55.00
Grand Marshall, Treasure Craft for Mardi Gras Records 150.00
Grandfather Washington, JC Miller, from $100 to 135.00
Granny, Takahashi, from $45 to 60.00
Hen w/Chick, FAPCO, from $45 to 55.00
Hippo, Taiwan, from $40 to 50.00
Holiday Pooh Treehouse, 1994 exclusive to Disney stores 190.00
Hopalong Cassidy w/Topper (Happy Memories) 450.00
Human Bean, Enesco, from $140 to 150.00
Ice-Cream Cone, Treasure Craft, from $45 to 65.00
James Dean, Happy Memories 300.00
Kangaroo 'Champ,' Twin Winton 450.00
Katrina, Treasure Craft, from $450 to 475.00
King Kong 225.00
Kliban Cat in Long Pants, Sigma 175.00
Little Bo Peep, NAPCO, from $225 to 250.00
Little Green Sprout, Benjamin & Medwin 90.00
Little Red Riding Hood, Zimpleman, 1994, ltd edition 350.00
Mansion, bl roof, lady at door, from $85 to 115.00
Marilyn Monroe, Happy Memories 300.00
Mary & Her Lamb, Zimpleman, 1994 ltd edition 350.00
Maxine, Hallmark 125.00
Michael Jordan/Bugs Bunny, Warner Bros/Space Jam 150.00
Monkey w/Bananas, California Originals 160.00
Monkey w/Lollipop, Japan 30.00
Mother in Kitchen, wht & bl trim, Enesco 495.00
Mrs Owl, Treasure Craft, from $40 to 50.00
Mushroom House, Heritage Mint (recent grocery store premium) ..30.00
Mustang Car, Expressive Designs, from $85 to 115.00
Neiman-Marcus '93 Panda Bear Cowboy, Cert Int'l 125.00
Olympic Torch, Warner Bros 135.00
Owl, Am Pottery/Celadon, from $20 to 30.00
Pink Panther, w/certificate of authenticity, Treasure Craft 250.00
Pinocchio, Dayton Hudson 60.00
Pirate, Omnibus, from $50 to 75.00
Pluto (in doghouse), Disney, Treasure Craft Ltd Ed Gallery 250.00
Pumbaa, Schmid, musical 150.00
Quaker Grain Drops, Weiss 250.00
Rag Doll, Starnes, from $195 to 235.00
Raggedy Andy Bust, Japan 450.00
Rooster, Gilner, from $60 to 70.00
Roy Rogers or Dale Evans, McMe, ea 200.00
Sack 'O Cookies, Cardinal, from $45 to 60.00
Saks Fifth Ave Santa Calls, Treasure Craft, '94 or '95, ea 150.00
Santa's Cookie House, Otagiri, from $40 to 55.00
Santa w/Toy Sack, Sigma, from $60 to 75.00
Scarlett O'Hare, Fitz & Floyd, from $100 to 125.00
School Bus, Doranne 200.00
School Bus, Grant Howard, from $50 to 75.00
Sea Captain, head, Kreiss, from $125 to 175.00
Sheriff, Lane, from $650 to 700.00

Sister Chubby Cheeks, A Company of Two, from $135 to 170.00
Sister Ruth, JC Miller, from $115 to 140.00
Snoopy, brn, Holiday Designs (Not Schultz) 90.00
Snoopy on Doghouse, Benjamin & Medwin, from $45 to 60.00
Snowman, gold trim, NS Gustin 45.00
Stagecoach, Hearth & Home, from $60 to 75.00
Strawberry Jar, Californial Originals 25.00
Studebaker, Omnibus, from $80 to 110.00
Sylvester Head w/Tweety, Applause, from $75 to 90.00
Teddy Bear, wood tone, Twin Winton 85.00
Telephone, Cardinal, from $65 to 75.00
Tetley Tea, cylinder w/head, Wade China 180.00
Tin Man, Star Jars, from $175 to 200.00
Tin Soldier, Marsh, from $95 to 110.00
Train, Maurice of California, from $60 to 65.00
Transformer, Great Am Housewares, from $160 to 190.00
Trolley, Otagiri, from $65 to 80.00
Turtle, sitting, underglaze decor, Twin Winton 225.00
Wild 'Bull' Hickok, Hearth & Home, from $45 to 60.00
Wise Owl (Hootie), gold trim, Robinson Ransbottom, from $150 to ..175.00
Witch, Lotus 50.00
Wizard of Oz, Clay Art, from $75 to 110.00
Wyle E Coyote, Certified International, from $40 to 50.00

Cooper, Susie

A 20th-century ceramic designer whose works are now attracting the attention of collectors, Susie Cooper was first affiliated with the A.E. Gray Pottery in Henley, England, in 1922 where she designed in lustres and painted items with her own ideas as well. (Examples of Gray's lustreware is rare and costly.) By 1930 she and her brother-in-law, Jack Beeson, had established a family business. Her pottery soon became a success, and she was subsequently offered space at Crown Works, Burslem. In 1940 she received the honorary title of Royal Designer for Industry, the only such distinction ever awarded by the Royal Society of Arts solely for pottery design. Miss Cooper received the Order of the British Empire in the New Year's Honors List of 1979. She was the chief designer for the Wedgwood group from 1966 until she resigned in 1972. After 1980 she worked on a free-lance basis until her death in July 1995.

Pitcher, incised teasel design on light green, #149 on bottom, 6¼", $200.00.

Bowl, cream soup; Gardenias, 1960s 20.00
Bowl, fruit; Gardenias, 1960s, 5" 18.00
Bowl, fruit; washed red bands, earthenware, 1930s, 6" 18.00
Bowl, mc bands, Gray's period, 9" 125.00
Bowl, Peacock Feather, gr & bl, oval, 8½" 75.00
Bowl, wht band, 10" 225.00
Charger, HP leaves, 14" 280.00
Chocolate pot, Patricia Rose, pk wash, 7½" 100.00
Coffeepot, Nosegay, bl wash, 7¼" 120.00

Coffeepot, orange w/blk lines, Kestrel shape, 7¾" 160.00
Creamer & sugar bowl, Gardenias, 1960s, w/lid 45.00
Cup, silver lustre, Gray's period, 2¼" 40.00
Cup & saucer, Black Fruit (for Wedgwood), 6 for 225.00
Cup & saucer, demi; washed red bands, earthenware, 1930s 25.00
Cup & saucer, Gardenias, 1960s 20.00
Cup & saucer, washed red bands, earthenware, 1930s 20.00
Gravy boat, Gardenias, 1960s 45.00
Jam pot, Crayon Line, red & brn lines, w/lid, 4" 60.00
Jug, Cubist, Paris shape, Gray's Period, 4¼" 300.00
Jug, emb tulips on olive gr, 6½" 200.00
Jug, Paris, Tiger Lily 85.00
Plate, Corn Poppy, red/blk/brn, 10½" 30.00
Plate, Gardenias, 1960s, 8" 18.00
Plate, Swansea Spray, gr wash band, 7" 20.00
Plate, washed red bands, earthenware, 1930s, 10" 20.00
Platter, Gray's Pottery, Sunbuff Corona, oxblood bands, oval 225.00
Platter, Tiger Lily, 14" 75.00
Punch bowl, Wedding Ring, gray/brn/turq bands, 12½" dia 300.00
Vase, pk, appl buttons, 7½" 400.00

Coors

The firm that became known as Coors Porcelain Company in 1920 was founded in 1908 by John J. Herold, originally of the Roseville Pottery in Zanesville, Ohio. Though still in business today, they are best known for their artware vases and Rosebud dinnerware produced before 1939.

Coors vases produced before the late '30s were made in a matt finish; by the latter years of the decade, high-gloss glazes were also being used. Nearly fifty shapes were in production, and some of the more common forms were made in three sizes. Typical colors in matt are white, orange, blue, green, yellow, and tan. Yellow, blue, maroon, pink, and green are found in high gloss. All vases are marked with a triangular arrangement of the words 'Coors Colorado Pottery' enclosing the word 'Golden.' You may find vases (usually 6" to 6½") marked with the Colorado State Fair stamp and dated 1939. For such a vase, add $10.00 to the suggested values given below.

For further information we recommend *Collector's Encyclopedia of Colorado Pottery, Identification and Values*, by Carol and Jim Carlton, who provide miscellaneous listings. Our Rosebud advisor is Jo Ellen Winther. All are listed in the Directory under Colorado.

Rosebud

Baker, 9¼" 45.00
Bean pot, lg 65.00
Bowl, cream soup 30.00
Bowl, mixing; hdld, 3½ pt 80.00
Bowl, mixing; 1-pt 20.00
Bowl, mixing; 3-pt 45.00
Bowl, mixing; 6-pt 65.00
Bowl, pudding; 2-pt, sm 35.00
Bowl, sauce 15.00
Bowl, soup 40.00
Cake knife 75.00
Casserole, Dutch; w/lid, sm 65.00
Casserole, str-sided, 8" 65.00
Creamer, from $30 to 35.00
Custard 15.00
Egg cup, from $50 to 55.00
Muffin set 150.00
Plate, 4" 6.00
Plate, 7", from $12 to 18.00

Platter, from $35 to 40.00
Ramekin, hdld 35.00
Refrigerator set 110.00
Shakers, kitchen; pr 45.00
Teapot, sm 125.00
Tumbler, ftd, from $95 to 115.00

Miscellaneous

Bowl, pudding; Tulip, sm 50.00
Cake plate, Floree 55.00
Casserole, Fr; Open Window 95.00
Casserole, ind; Coorado, w/lid 45.00
Cup & saucer, Mello-Tone or Rockmont 15.00
Figurine, Laughing or Crying Monk, 6", ea 250.00
Gravy boat, Coorado, 1-pc 110.00
Lamp base, bl 150.00
Reamer, built-in strainer, 1920s 150.00
Shakers, Coorado, pr 65.00
Teapot, Tulip 150.00
Tumbler, Mello-Tone or Rockmont 35.00
Vase, Denver, matt bl, 10" 100.00
Vase, Florence, matt tan, 12" 125.00
Vase, Windsor, matt gr, 8" 70.00
Water server, Mello-Tone or Rockmont 40.00

Copper

Handcrafted copper was made in America from early in the 18th century until about 1850, with the center of its production in Pennsylvania. Examples have been found signed by such notable coppersmiths as Kidd, Buchanan, Babb, Bently, and Harbeson. Of the many utilitarian items made, teakettles are the most desirable. Early examples from the 18th century were made with a dovetailed joint which was hammered and smoothed to a uniform thickness. Pots from the 19th century were seamed. Coffeepots were made in many shapes and sizes and along with mugs, kettles, warming pans, and measures are easiest to find. Stills ranging in sizes of up to fifty-gallon are popular with collectors today. Our advisor, Mary Frank Gaston, has compiled a lovely book, *Antique Brass and Copper*, with many full-color photos and current market values; you will find her address in the Directory under Texas.

Architectural finial, spherical top, 6-sided base, 1800s, 90" 3,450.00
Architectural finial, verdigris surface, late 1800s, 33" 1,380.00
Box, painted & emb florals, 2" dia 60.00
Bucket, hearth; wrought iron arched hdl, 17½x15" 150.00
Bucket, rolled rim, dvtl/seamed, bell-metal cast hdls, 17" dia 325.00
Coal scuttle, helmet form, dvtl, battered, 10½" 70.00
Coal scuttle, helmet form, swing hdl, 16" W 300.00
Coffeepot, dvtl, hinged lid, old rpr, 10¾" 75.00
Coffeepot, oval canister w/gooseneck, English, 1800s, 9" 200.00
Jar, bl & gold jewel-like enamel, gilt-metal int & finial 85.00
Kettle, dvtl, iron bale hdl, minor splits at rim, 25" dia 275.00
Kettle, dvtl, wrought-iron bail, 20x30½" 350.00
Kettle, dvtl/hammered, iron bale hdl, 15" dia, w/tripod, 28" H ..225.00
Measure, tankard pitcher form w/hdl, ca 1860, 5" 55.00
Pitcher, dvtl, classic design, well made, 12" 160.00
Roaster, chestnut; wriggle-work decor, Am, 23x11½" dia 225.00
Sauce pan, dvtl w/CI hdl & label: Wrought Iron Range Co, 7" ..140.00
Skimmer, hammered, oval pierced spoon-shaped bowl, 17" L 145.00
Teakettle, dvtl, acorn finial, 11¼" 275.00
Teakettle, dvtl, gooseneck spout w/flap, swivel hdl, 7¾" 200.00
Teakettle, dvtl, oval, brass trim, milk glass hdl, 8" 250.00

Copper Lustre

Copper lustre is a term referring to a type of pottery made in Staffordshire after the turn of the 19th century. It is finished in a metallic rusty-brown glaze resembling true copper. Pitchers are found in abundance, ranging from simple styles with dull bands of color to those with fancy handles and bands of embossed, polychromed flowers. Bowls are common; goblets, mugs, teapots, and sugar bowls much less so. It's easy to find, but not in good condition. Pieces with hand-painted decoration and those with historical transfers are the most valuable.

Bowl, fruit; cobalt mid-band w/emb figures, ftd, 8¼" 200.00
Creamer, floral band, scrolled hdl, 4⅜" 70.00
Cup & saucer, House pattern, mini, 1¼" 25.00
Pitcher, clock & tea party transfers, hairlines, 7" 75.00
Pitcher, emb florals w/mc highlights, 7½" 65.00
Pitcher, General Jackson—Hero of Am, fishing scene, 5" 2,000.00
Pitcher, pastoral scenes on 2" band, lustre flower, 1810s, 8" 200.00
Pitcher, random dots, wide pk lustre band, 5½" 60.00
Pitcher, stylized florals, wide bl band, 6" 65.00
Plaque, Thou God Seest Me, blk transfer, 7" dia 255.00
Plate, mc florals on bl stripe, 6½" 45.00

Coralene Glass

Coralene is a unique type of art glass easily recognized by the tiny grains of glass that form its decoration. Lacy allover patterns of seaweed, geometrics, and florals were used, as well as solid forms such as fish, plants, and single blossoms. (Seaweed is most commonly found and not as valuable as the other types of decoration.) It was made by several glasshouses both here and abroad. Values are based to a considerable extent on the amount of beading that remains. Our advisors for this category are Betty and Clarence Maier; they are listed in the Directory under Pennsylvania.

Box, powder; allover gr beading w/gold & wht water lilies 165.00
Pitcher, acid peachblow w/seaweed motif, sqd rim, 8" 350.00
Vase, apricot Dmn Quilt MOP w/yel snowflakes & fleur-de-lis, 5" ...450.00
Vase, bl Dmn Quilt w/seaweed motif, 6½x7½" 395.00
Vase, bl Raindrop MOP w/pk seaweed & jeweled daisies, 7" 225.00
Vase, florals, mc beading, gold hdls, Pat mk on base, 9" 500.00
Vase, geometrics, yel on pk/wht/yellow, 7" 675.00
Vase, mums, purple & gr on purple & yel w/gold, 5x6" 350.00
Vase, pk Snowflake MOP w/yel star motif, shouldered, 4" 225.00
Vase, seaweed, mc on orange, 5" 475.00
Vase, seaweed on bl satin, cut rim, amber ft, 6½" 375.00
Vase, seaweed on bl satin, stick neck, 6" 150.00

Cordey

The Cordey China Company was founded in 1942 in Trenton, New Jersey, by Boleslaw Cybis. The operation was small with less than a dozen workers. They produced figurines, vases, lamps, and similar wares, much of which was marketed through gift shops both nationwide and abroad. Though the earlier wares were made of plaster, Cybis soon developed his own formula for a porcelain composition which he called 'Papka.' Cordey figurines and busts were characterized by old-world charm, Rococo scrolls, delicate floral appliques, ruffles, and real lace which was dipped in liquified clay to add dimension to the work.

Although on rare occasions some items were not numbered or signed, the 'basic' figure was cast both with numbers and the Cordey sig-

nature. The molded pieces were then individually decorated and each marked with its own impressed identification number as well as a mark to indicate the artist-decorator. Their numbering system began with 200 and in later years progressed into the 8000s. As can best be established, Cordey continued production until sometime in the mid-1950s. Boleslaw Cybis died in 1957, his wife in 1958. Our advisor for this category is Sharon A. Payne; she is listed in the Directory under Washington.

Key: ff — full figure

#1023, bowl, console; lg roses w/gold, oblong, 6x15x8" 185.00
#1028, box, pk & gr flower shape 65.00
#2307, robin on rose branch, 9" 150.00
#3008, man, Renaissance, dk gr, 7" 75.00
#302, lady, ff, flowing dress, 16" 195.00
#303, man, 14" 145.00
#325, Chinese wood duck, ornate base, EX colors, rare 400.00
#4001, lady, ruffled cap, 7" 85.00
#4002, man, ruffles at neck, bow at nape, 7" 85.00
#4049, child, Victorian, ff, much lace, 11" 150.00
#4050-A, man, blk top hat, cape & scarf, 7" 90.00
#4067, Oriental emperor & empress, ff, 8" 175.00
#4077, Oriental emperor & empress, ff, 15" 275.00
#4088, ballerina man & lady, 10", pr 205.00
#4101, ballerina, dancing, ff, 11" 250.00
#4153, man, ff, much lace, 14" 185.00

#5004, lady in green hat, shawl collar, 6½", $70.00.

#5026, bust of lady w/mantilla, Jr Miss Group 65.00
#5029, Elizabeth, high collar, Raleigh Group, 7½" 85.00
#5039, lady, Josephine, Raleigh Group 85.00
#5040, British guard, 8½" 100.00
#5054, lady w/roses, 9" 120.00
#5064, Caroline, 14" 245.00
#5066, Carmen, Spanish dress & mantilla, ff, 14" 150.00
#5069, lady, pearls at neck, gloves, many roses, 9" 135.00
#5085, Winter girl, lg hat, muff, ff, 11" 120.00
#5086, Summer girl, bonnet, shawl, ff, 11" 120.00
#5088, lady, ff, HP roses on dress, 11" 175.00
#5097, Oriental emperor, ff, 27¼" 225.00
#5099, Oriental empress, ff, 27¼" 225.00
#5360, poodle, pk, ribbon & rose collar, recumbent 100.00
#6004, bluebird on stump, lg 150.00
#6019, jar, buffalo design, bl, w/lid 95.00
#6037, box, appl cherubs/roses, cherub finial, ftd, 8x9", rare 300.00
#6046, ashtray 18.00
#627, ginger jar, w/lid, 7½x6" dia 150.00
#7000, plaque, primrose, Colonial lady, ff 100.00
#7060, box, pk b/bluebird finial, 7" dia 125.00
#7094, vase, Oriental figures & florals, gourd form, 9x8" 165.00
#8002, pin/ashtray, 4" sq 30.00

#8020, Oriental baby, no hat, ff, 15" 200.00
#902, wall pocket, lady's face, ringlets, 10¼" 200.00
#909, clock, bird & roses, rococo, wall hanging, 14½" 150.00
#926, picture frame w/cherubs, 15x10" 90.00
Cordey plaque 85.00
Dresser tray & 2 perfumes w/hdls, appl roses/morning glories 285.00
Lamp, lady in dk bl w/much lace, 12" figure, 17" overall 150.00
Lamp, pk roses w/gold on wht 85.00

Corkscrews

The history of the corkscrew dates back to the mid-1600s, when wine makers concluded that the best-aged wine was that stored in smaller containers, either stoneware or glass. Since plugs left unsealed were often damaged by rodents, corks were cut off flush with the bottle top and sealed with wax or a metal cover. Removing the cork cleanly with none left to grasp became a problem. The task was found to be relatively simple using the worm on the end of a flintlock gun rod. So the corkscrew evolved. Endless patents have been issued for mechanized models. Handles range from carved wood, ivory, and bone to porcelain and repousse silver. Exotic materials such as agate, mother-of-pearl, and gold plate were also used on occasion. Celluloid lady's legs are popular.

In the following descriptions, values are for examples in excellent condition, unless noted otherwise. Our advisor for this category is Roger Baker; he is listed in the Directory under California.

Brubaker, T-shaped, twisted wire shaft, wood hdl, 4¼" 15.00
England, 4-finger pull, w/button, ca 1895 ....23.00
Germany, Hercules, wood hdl 40.00
Lady's leg, tooled brass w/striped celluloid inlay, 2⅝" 150.00
Monkey (or dog), gold w/jewels, corkscrew tail 20.00
NP, Take a Peg of John Begg on sheath, pocket sz 18.00
Parrot, chrome plated, Negbaur USA Pat'd on ft, 5" 150.00
Plastic duplex (dbl worm), picnic type, modern 5.00
Twisted wire, helical worm, Henshall button, Clough, 4½" 12.50
Twisted wire, machine made, Pat WR Clough, ca 1875-76, 3" 12.00
US, Alaskan ivory tusk 30.00
US, brass band on boar's tooth hdl, 6", EX 85.00
US, Haff Mfg Co, NY, wooden hdl, mk Pat 4/14/86 ....135.00
US, James E Wolcott & Co, Cornhill Rye, bottle type, 1821 ....40.00
US, NP steel worm, cap lifter & wire breaker, EX 150.00
US, rnd steel shaft w/2" worm, wooden hdl 135.00
US, roundlet style, bullet shape, EX 50.00
US, walrus tusk w/sterling end, SP worm cap, mk Pat 1906 ....150.00
US, Williamson...Pat Sep 4 1900, brass pocket roundlet, 2¾" ...125.00
US, Woodward Tool Pat Aug 24, 1875, 10 tools in 1, EX 60.00
Weir's Pat 12804 25, Sept 1884, VG bronze finish 125.00

Cosmos

Cosmos, sometimes called Stemless Daisy, is a patterned glass tableware produced from 1894 through 1915 by Consolidated Lamp and Glass Company. Relief-molded flowers on a finely crosscut background were painted in soft colors of pink, blue, and yellow. Though nearly all were made of milk glass, a few items may be found in clear glass with the designs painted on. In addition to the tableware, lamps were also made.

Bottle, cologne; orig stopper, rare 300.00
Butter dish, 5x8" 275.00
Creamer 150.00
Lamp, banquet; kerosene, 24" 575.00
Lamp, banquet; slender base, rnd globe, all orig, 16" 525.00

Lamp, parlor; half-shade on matching base, 8" 375.00
Lamp, 10" 400.00
Pickle castor, mk SP fr 500.00
Pitcher, milk; 5" 250.00
Pitcher, syrup; 6" 300.00
Pitcher, water 350.00
Shakers, tall, orig lids, pr 175.00
Spooner 125.00
Sugar bowl, open 150.00
Sugar bowl, w/lid 185.00
Sugar shaker 400.00
Tumbler, 3¾" 75.00

Cottageware

You'll find a varied assortment of novelty dinnerware items, all styled as cozy little English cottages or huts with cone-shaped roofs; some may have a waterwheel or a windmill. Marks will vary. English-made Price Brothers or Beswick pieces are valued in the same range as those marked Occupied Japan, while items marked simply Japan are considered slightly less pricey. Our advisor for this category is Grace Klender; she is listed in the Directory under Ohio.

Bank, dbl slot, Price Bros, 4½x3½x5" 65.00
Bowl, salad; English 65.00
Butter dish, English 45.00
Butter pat, emb cottage, rectangular, Occupied Japan 18.00
Chocolate pot, English 135.00
Condiment set, mustard, 2½" s&p, on 5" hdld leaf tray 57.00
Condiment set, mustard pot, s&p, tray, row arrangement, 6" 45.00
Condiment set, mustard pot, s&p, tray, row arrangement, 7¾" 45.00
Condiment set, 2 shakers & mustard on tray, Occupied Japan 45.00
Condiment set, 3-part cottage on shaped tray w/appl bush, 4½" ..75.00
Cookie jar, pk/brn/gr, sq, Japan, 8½x5½" 65.00
Cookie jar/canister, cylindrical, English 85.00
Cookie or biscuit jar, Occupied Japan 85.00
Creamer & sugar bowl, English, 2½", 4½" 45.00
Cup & saucer, English, 2½", 4½" 45.00
Demitasse pot, English 100.00
Dish w/cover, Occupied Japan, sm 35.00
Egg cup set, 4 on 6" sq tray, English 60.00
Grease jar, Occupied Japan, from $25 to 35.00
Marmalade, English 40.00
Marmalade & jelly, 2-houses cojoined, Price Brothers 85.00
Mug, Price Brothers 50.00
Pin tray, English, 4" dia 20.00
Pitcher, water; English 150.00
Platter, oval, 11¾x 7½" 45.00
Sugar box, for cubes, English, 5¾" L 45.00

Teapot, English, unusual style, 4¾", $65.00.

Tea set, Japan, child's, serves 4 ....150.00
Teapot, English or Occupied Japan, 6½" 50.00
Toast rack, English 70.00
Tumbler, Occupied Japan, 3½", set of 6 ....60.00

Coverlets

The Jacquard attachment for hand looms represented a culmination of weaving developments made in France. Introduced to America by the early 1820s, it gave professional weavers the ability to easily create complex patterns with curved lines. Those who could afford the new loom adaptation could now use hole-punched pasteboard cards to weave floral patterns that before could only be achieved with intense labor on a draw-loom.

Before the Jacquard mechanism, most weavers made their coverlets in geometric patterns. Use of indigo-blue and brightly colored wools often livened the twills and overshot patterns available to the small-loom home weaver. Those who had larger multiple-harness looms could produce warm double-woven, twill-block, or summer-and-winter designs.

While the new floral and pictorial patterns' popularity had displaced the geometrics in urban areas, the mid-Atlantic and the Midwest by the 1840s, even factory production of the Jacquard coverlets was disrupted by cotton and wool shortages during the Civil War. A revived production in the 1870s saw a style change to a center-medallion motif, but a new fad for white 'Marseilles' spreads soon halted sales of Jacquard-woven coverlets. Production of Jacquard carpets continued to the turn of the century.

Rural and frontier weavers continued to make geometric-design coverlets through the 19th century, and local craft revivals have continued the tradition through this century. All-cotton overshots were factory produced in Kentucky from the 1940s, and factories and professional weavers made cotton-and-wool overshots during the past decade. Many Jacquard-woven coverlets have dates and names of places and people (often the intended owner — not the weaver) woven into corners or borders. In the listings that follow, examples are blue and white unless noted otherwise. When dates are included, they appear on the coverlet itself as part of the woven design.

Jacquard

Floral, 1-pc, single weave, red/wht, 1843, 68x79" 330.00
Floral & eagle, mulberry/wht, 1850s, 81x73" 260.00
Floral medallion w/eagles, rose border, 1-pc, red/wht, 79x72" 330.00
Floral medallions, eagle borders, 5-color, 2-pc, 78x88", EX 1,000.00
Floral medallions, gr/wht, dbl weave, 2-pc, 76x87", EX 220.00
Floral medallions, vintage border, 2-pc, OH/1852, 79x70" 580.00
Floral medallions, 2-pc, dbl weave, 1853, 85x76" 275.00
Floral medallions, 2-pc, single weave, 4-color, 1850, 85x71" 550.00
Floral medallions & stars, 2-pc, OH/1846, 88x66", EX 660.00
Floral medallions/bird corners, 3-color, 1854, 2-pc, 69x82", VG ...415.00
Floral medallions/dmns, 3-color, dbl weave, 2-pc, 82x90" 300.00
Floral medallions/eagle/trees, fringe, rpr, 80x72" 330.00
Floral medallions/rose border, 4-color, 2-pc, PA, 76x94" 1,100.00
Foliage medallions, president's border, 3-color, 1-pc, 82x86", G ..165.00
Rose medallions/snowflakes, 4-color, sgn/1841, 2-pc, 81x106" ...550.00
Star medallions/chanticleer borders, 2-pc, OH, 64x90" 495.00
4 rose medallions/bird/flowers, 3-color, 2-pc, 1843, 90x76" 385.00
4 rose medallions/bird/flowers, 5-color, 2-pc, 96x76" 385.00
4 rose medallions/foliage/vines, 4-color, 2-pc, 92x76" 525.00
4 rose medallions/vintage border, 1-pc, 1858, 90x70" 495.00

Overshot

Optical pattern, 2-color, 2-pc, 94x76" 225.00

Optical pattern, 3-color, fringe 1 end, 92x68", EX 180.00
Optical pattern, 3-color, 2-pc, 96x74", EX 115.00
Optical pattern, 5-color, appl fringe 3 sides, 2-pc, 92x78" 275.00

Cowan

Guy Cowan opened a small pottery near Cleveland, Ohio, ca 1909, where he made tile and artware on a small scale from the natural red clay available there. He developed distinctive glazes — necessary, he felt, to cover the dark red body. After the war and a temporary halt in production, Cowan moved his pottery to Rocky River, where he made a commercial line of artware utilizing a highly-fired white porcelain. Although he acquiesced to the necessity of mass production, every effort was made to insure a product of highest quality. Fine artists, among them Waylande Gregory, Thelma Frazier, and Viktor Schreckengost, designed pieces which were often produced in limited editions, some of which sell today for prices in the thousands. Most of the ware was marked 'Cowan' or 'Lakewood Ware,' not to be confused with the name of the 1930 mass-produced line called 'Lakeware.' Falling under the crunch of the Great Depression, the pottery closed in 1931.

The use of an asterisk (*) in the listing below indicates a nonfactory name that is being provided as a suggested name for the convenience of present-day collectors. One example is the glaze *Original Ivory, which is a high-gloss white that resembles undecorated porcelain. It was used on many of Cowan's lady 'flower figures' (Cowan's more graceful term for what some collectors call frogs).

Our advisor for this category is Mark Bassett; he is listed in the Directory under Ohio. With Victoria Naumann, Mark is the author of *Cowan Pottery and the Cleveland School*, a detailed history of Cowan Pottery and of Guy Cowan's students, colleagues, and designers. Prices quoted are for examples in mint condition, unless noted otherwise.

Key: Sp/I — Special Ivory

Vase, Larkspur (light blue lustre) with rainbow (or oilspot) effects, fluted, 11½", $200.00.

Ashtray, #T-2, gazelle on flat base, dk bl gloss, Eckardt, 5¼" 350.00
Ashtray, #77 , duck, April Gr, glossy, RG Cowan, 2¾" 95.00
Bookends, #E-864, pelicans, blk/bronze/silver, Jacobson, 4¾" .2,000.00
Bookends, #840-842, push-pull elephants, bronze, Postgate, 4½" ..1,250.00
Bowl, #X-43, Egyptian Bl/blk, Jazz designs, Schreckengost, 14" ...17,500.00
Bowl, #713-B, Columbine (April Gr w/Lapis int), 13" 175.00
Bowl, #733-B, April Gr w/Sp/I int, scalloped, 9¼" 75.00
Candlesticks, #??, Parchment Gr, grape hdls, Gregory, 7½", pr ..300.00
Candlesticks, #628, Sp/I, urn-shaped stem, 4¾", pr 75.00
Candlesticks, #744-L/#744-R, SP/I, nude by vine, RG Cowan, 12", pr ..1,750.00
Candlesticks, #777, April Gr, asymmetrical leafy base, 5½", pr ..125.00
Charger, #773, Russet Brn, racing nudes, floral center, 13" 1,250.00
Figure, #D-3, elephant paperweight, Blk, Postgate, 4½" 500.00

Figure, #793, Spanish Dancer (lady), Primrose, Anderson, 8½" .600.00
Figure, #869, Elephant, Oriental Red, rnd, Postgate, ltd ed, 10¾" 3,000.00
Flower frog, #680, (lady looking) Heavenward, *Orig Ivory, RGC, 8" ..300.00
Flower frog, #685, Duet, 2 ladies dancing, Sp/I, RG Cowan, 7½" 500.00
Flower frog, #686, Scarf Dancer, lady w/U-shape scarf, Sp/I, 6" ..350.00
Flower frog, #698, Pavlova, lady on 1 leg, *Orig Ivory, 6" 225.00
Flower frog, #709, Grace (bent left), Sp/I, RG Cowan, 6" 275.00
Lamp, #??, Chinese shape, Oriental Red (orange), no hardware, 8" ...150.00
Lamp, #??, curved Deco panels, Blk & Silver, 8¼" 750.00
Lamp, #??, squirrel/heron/flamingo, Peach, Gregory, 10" 500.00
Lamp, #594-B, twist-stem candlestick form, Marigold, 12½", pr 200.00
Pitcher, #X-11, Foliage (rust/yel mottle), lg hdl, 9" 300.00
Strawberry jar, #SJ-2, Azure (bl-gr mottle), sq, +tray, 1-pc 650.00
Strawberry jar, #SJ-6, Plum (purple/gr mottle), w/saucer, 7½" ...400.00
Vase, #V-39, Oriental Red (mc mottling/veins), ribbed, 6x8" 750.00
Vase, #V-48, Plum, bulbous shoulder, ftd, rope/twist ribs, 12" 750.00
Vase, #V-81, Pistachio (gr lining blend of rose & pk), 9" 350.00
Vase, #585, *Gunmetal drip on Marigold, Chinese shape, 9½" .650.00
Vase, Larkspur w/rainbow effects, emb flower, hdls, w/lid, 9", pr ..1,000.00
Wall pocket, #694, Delphinium, fluted w/lion head, RGC, 10" .400.00

Cracker Jack

Kids have been buying Cracker Jack since it was first introduced in the 1890s. By 1912 it was packaged with a free toy inside. Before the first kernel was crunched, eager fingers had retrieved the surprise from the depth of the box — actually no easy task, considering the care required to keep the contents so swiftly displaced from spilling over the side! Though a little older, perhaps, many of those same kids still are looking — just as eagerly — for the Cracker Jack prizes. Point of sale, company collectibles, and the prizes as well have over the years reflected America's changing culture. Grocery sales and incentives from around the turn of the century — paper dolls, postcards, and song books — were often marked Rueckheim Brothers (the inventors of Cracker Jack) or Reliable Confections. Over the years the company made some changes, leaving a trail of clues that often help collectors date their items. The company's name changed in 1922 from Rueckheim Brothers & Eckstein to The Cracker Jack Company. Their Brooklyn office was open from 1914 until it closed in 1923, and the first time the sailor Jack logo was used on their packaging was 1919. For packages and 'point of sale' dating, note that the word 'prize' was used from 1912 to 1925, 'novelty' from 1925 to 1932, and 'toy' from 1933 on.

The first loose-packed prizes were toys made of wood, clay, tin, metal, and lithographed paper. Plastic toys were introduced in 1946. Paper wrapped for safety purposes in 1948, subjects echo the 'hype' of the day — yo-yos, tops, whistles, and sports cards in the simple, peaceful days of our country, propaganda and war toys in the forties, games in the fifties, and space toys in the sixties. Few of the estimated 15 billion prizes were marked. Advertising items from Angelus Marshmallow and Checkers Confections (cousins of the Cracker Jack family) are also collectible. When no condition is indicated, the items listed below are assumed to be in excellent condition. 'CJ' indicates that the item is marked. Note: An often-asked question concerns the tin Toonerville Trolley called 'CJ.' No data has been found in the factory archives to authenticate this item; it is assumed that the 'CJ' merely refers to its small size. For further information see *Cracker Jack Toys, The Complete, Unofficial Guide for Collectors*, by Larry White. Our advisor for this category is Wes Johnson; he is listed in the Directory under Kentucky. Also look for *The Prize Insider* newsletter listed in the Directory under Clubs, Newsletters, and Catalogs.

Cast Metal Prizes

Badge, shield, CJ Jr Detective, silver, 1931, 1¼" 40.00

Badge, 6-point star, mk CJ Police, silver, 1931, 1¼" 44.00
Button, stud bk, Xd bats & ball, CJ pitcher/etc series, 1928 ....120.00
Chair, T (Tootsie), 3 different sectional pcs, pnt, mini, ea 12.00
Dollhouse items: lantern, mug, candlestick, etc; no mk, ea 6.50
Horse & wagon, CJ, 3-D, silver or gold, early, 2½", ea 250.00
Pistol, soft lead, inked, CJ on barrel, early, rare, 2⅛" 180.00
Ring, alphabet letter setting (series), unmk, ea 4.00
Rocking horse, no rider, 3-D, inked, early, 1⅛" 15.00
Rocking horse w/boy, 3-D, inked, early, 1½" 29.00
Spinner, early pkg in center, 'More You Eat...,' CJ, rare 295.00
Tootsietoy series: boats, cars, animals; 1931, ¾"-1½", ea 7.00

Dealer Incentives and Premiums

Badge, pin-bk, celluloid, lady w/CJ label reverse, 1905, 1¼" 65.00
Bat, baseball; wood, Hillerich & Bradsby, CJ, full sz 125.00
Book, pocket; jester on cover, CJ Riddles 73.00
Book, pocket; riddle/sailor boy/dog on cover, RWB, CJ, 1919 ......60.00
Book, Uncle Sam Song Book, CJ, 1911, ea 60.00
Cart w/2 movable wheels, wood dowel tongue, CJ 75.00
Corkscrew/opener, metal plated, CJ/Angelus, 3" 79.00
Golf tee set, wood tees in paper 'matchbook' folder, CJ, 1920s ...725.00
Harmonica, full scale, emb CJ, early, 5⅛" 385.00
Jigsaw puzzle, CJ or Checkers, 1 of 4, 7x10", in envelope 35.00
Marbles, Akro set of 12 in box w/instructions, CJ, 1929 ....950.00
Mask, Halloween; paper, CJ, series, 10" or 12", ea 22.00
Match holder, hinged, eng gold-tone case, CJ, 2½x1⅞" 650.00
Palm puzzle, mirror bk, CJ, mk Germany/RWB, 1910-14, 1½" ..110.00
Pen, ink; w/nib, tin litho bbl, CJ 550.00
Pencil top clip, metal/celluloid, oval boy & dog logo 220.00
Pencil top clip, metal/celluloid, tube shape w/package 220.00
Puzzle, metal, CJ/Angelus, 1 of 15, 1934, in envelope, ea 14.00
Riddle card, 2 series of 20, w/package/from factory, CJ, 1907, ea 7.00
Tablet, school; CJ, 1929, 8x10" 195.00
Thimble, aluminum, CJ Co/Angelus, red pnt, rare, ea 165.00
Wings, air corps type, silver or blk, stud-bk, CJ, 1930s, 3", ea 80.00

Packaging

Box, popcorn; Question Mark box end for CJ 'Toy,' 1923-27 ....85.00
Box, popcorn; red scroll border, CJ 'Prize,' 1912-25, ea 95.00
Box, popcorn; store display, CJ 'Novelty,' 1925-32, ea 90.00
Canister, tin, CJ Candy Corn Crisp, 10-oz 75.00
Canister, tin, CJ Coconut Corn Crisp, 1-lb 55.00
Canister, tin, CJ Coconut Corn Crisp, 10-oz 65.00
CJ Commemorative canister, mc scene, 1990s, ea 9.00
CJ Commemorative canister, wht w/red scroll, 1980s, ea 6.50
Crate, shipping; wood, CJ, Rueckheim Bros Eck, 1902-22, lg 150.00

Paper Prizes

Fortune-Telling wheel, 2-piece paper litho, turn for fortune, marked Cracker Jack, 1¾", $70.00 (same made of tin, $55.00).

Baseball CJ score counter, 3⅜" L 130.00
Book, Bess & Bill on CJ Hill, series of 12, 1937, mini 100.00

Book, Birds We Know, CJ, 1928, mini 85.00
Book, Chaplin flip book, CJ, 1920s, ea 115.00
Book, Twigg & Sprigg, CJ, 1930, mini 100.00
Booklet, stickers/wise cracks/riddles, Borden, CJ, 1965 on 2.50
Decal, cartoon or nursery rhyme figure, 1947-49, CJ 12.00
Disguise, ears, red (out of carrier), 1950, pr 30.00
Disguise, ears, red (still in carrier), CJ, 1950, pr 110.00
Disguise, glasses, hinged, cello lenses, CJ Where Ever..., '33 ....145.00
Disguise, glasses, hinged, w/eyeballs, unmk, 1933 ....6.00
Disguise, mustache, blk/brn, in carrier, CJ, 1949 ....60.00
Fortune Teller, boy/dog on film in envelope, CJ, '20s, 1¾x2½" ...75.00
Game, Midget Auto Race, wheel spins, CJ, 1949, 3⅜" H 45.00
Game spinner, ...baseball at home, unmk, 1946, 1½" dia 40.00
Hat, fold out, More You Eat/More You Want, CJ, early 75.00
Hat, Indian headdress, CJ, 1931, 2½" H 110.00
Hat, Indian headdress, CJ, 1950s, 5⅜" H 275.00
Hat, Me for CJ, early, ea 105.00
Hat visor, baseball, tie-on string, red or gr, CJ, 1931 ....120.00
Magic game book, erasable slate, CJ, series of 13, 1946, ea 35.00
Movie, Goofy Zoo, turn wheel(s): change animals, 1939 ....17.00
Movie, pull tab for 2nd picture, series, CJ, 1943, 1¼", ea 82.00
Movie, pull tab for 2nd picture, yel, early, 3", in envelope 125.00
Sand toy pictures, pours for action, series of 14, 1967, ea 9.00
Transfer, iron-on, sport figure or patriotic, CJ, 1939, ea 18.00
Transfer, iron-on, sport figure or patriotic, unmk, 1939, ea 6.00
Whistle, Blow for More, CJ box/boy/dog, yel, 1931, ea 55.00
Whistle, Blow for More, CJ/Angelus packages, 1928, '31 or '33, ea ..45.00
Whistle, pressed paper, series of 10, 1948-49, CJ, 1¼x2", ea 34.00
Whistle, Razz Zooka, C Carey Cloud design, CJ, 1949 ....32.00

Plastic Prizes

Animals, standup, letter on bk, series of 26, Nosco, 1953, ea 3.50
Animals, standup on base, assorted, Nosco or CJ, 1947 on, ea 1.50
Disc, emb comic character, series of 12, 1954, 1½" dia 16.00
Disc, emb fish plaque, oval, series of 10, 1956, ea 14.00
Dog, 3-D, hollow base, series of 10, CJCO, 1954, ea 6.00
Figure on rocking base, semi-flat, 1 of 9, Cloud design, 1956 ....3.00
Fob, alphabet letter w/loop on top, 1 of 26, 1954, 1½" 2.25
Magnifying glass, many designs/shapes, from 1961, ea 1.00
Palm puzzle, ball(s) roll into holes, dome or rnd, from 1966 ....2.50
Palm puzzle, ball(s) roll into holes, rectangle, CJ, 1920s, ea 37.00
Palm puzzle, ball(s) roll into holes, sq, CJ, 1920s, ea 22.00
Pinball game, lever shoots ball/score in holes, 1964 to recent 5.00
Signs, road; Stop, Caution, etc, yel, series of 10, 1954-60, ea 3.00
Spinner, tops varied colors, 10 designs, from 1948, ea 1.50
Toys, take apart/assemble, variety, from 1962, assembled, ea 1.00
Toys, take apart/assemble, variety, from 1962, unassembled, ea 3.00
Whistle, tube w/animals on top, CJ, series, 1950-53, 1⅜" 6.50

Tin Prizes

Badge, boy & dog diecut, complete w/bend-over tab, CJ 150.00
Badge, emb/plated CJ officer, 2⅜" or 1⅝", early, ea 110.00
Badge, litho, red/wht/bl, boy/dog, CJ, 1920s, 1¼" dia 150.00
Bank, 3-D book form, red/gr/or blk, CJ Bank, early, 2" 105.00
Bookmark, dogs, 4 different, 1941, 3", ea 22.00
Cash register, litho, More You Eat, CJ, early, 1⅞" 275.00
Clicker, 'Noisy CJ Snapper,' pear shape, aluminum, 1949 ....32.00
Clicker, CJ Telegraph, Pat 1897, inked, 1¾" dia, ea 145.00
Doll dishes, tin plated, CJ, 1931, 1¾", 1⅞", & 2⅛" dia, ea 35.00
Fortune Wheel, 2-pc litho, CJ, 1939-41, 1¾" 55.00
Helicopter, yel propeller, wood stick, unmk, 1937, 2⅝" 27.00
Horse & wagon, litho diecut, CJ & Angelus, 2⅛" 65.00

Horse & wagon, litho diecut, gray/red mks, CJ, 1914-23, 3⅛" ...395.00
Model T Ford, License: NY 1915 #999, blk/wht, CJ, rare, 2" 410.00
Pocket watch, silver of gold, CJ as numerals, 1931, 1½" 55.00
Sled, tin plated, CJ, 1931, 2" L 35.00
Small box shape: electric alarm clock litho, unmk, 1⅛" 85.00
Small box shape: electric stove litho, unmk, 1⅛" 90.00
Small box shape: radio litho, bl, unmk, 1⅛" 80.00
Soldier, litho, die-cut standup, officer/private/etc, unmk, ea 17.00
Spinner, wood stick, Always on Top, red/wht/bl, CJ, 1½" dia 25.00
Spinner, wood stick, Fortune-Teller Game, red/wht/bl, CJ, 1½" ...105.00
Spinner, wood stick, Question Mark Box at center, CJ 50.00
Spinner, wood stick, 2 Toppers, red/wht/bl, Angelus/Jack, 1½" ...70.00
Stand up, rectangle litho, boy & dog, ca 1916, lg or sm, ea 145.00
Tall box shape: Frozen Foods locker freezer, 1947, unmk, 1¾" 65.00
Tall box shape: grandfather clock, unmk, 1947, 1¾" 55.00
Tall box shape: radio, Tune in w/CJ, brn/yel, 1939, 1¾" 120.00
Train, engine & tender, litho, CJ Line/512 ....125.00
Train, litho coach only, red, unmk, 1941 ....24.00
Train, litho engine only, red, unmk, 1941 ....20.00
Tray, emb, litho w/early pkg, smaller version 115.00
Truck, litho, RWB, CJ/Angelus, 1931, ea 65.00
Wagon shape: Caterpillar tractor, unmk, 1931, 1¾" L 29.00
Wagon shape: Playtime Trailer (auto trailer), unmk, 1947 ....40.00
Wagon shape: tank, orange/red/gr camouflage, unmk 65.00
Wagon shape: Tank Corps No 57, gr & blk, 1941 ....30.00
Wheelbarrow, tin plated, bk leg in place, CJ, 1931, 2½" L 33.00

Miscellaneous

Ad, comic book, CJ, ea 9.00
Hat, ball park vendor cap, CJ, 1930s 30.00
Lunch box, tin, 2 hdls, CJ, 1980s, 4½x5x6" 25.00
Lunch box, tin emb, CJ, 1970s, 4x7x9" 30.00
Medal, CJ salesman award, brass, 1939, scarce 125.00
Sign, boy or girl w/box of CJ, 5-color cb, early, 17x22", ea 350.00
Sign, Jack & Bingo, die-cut litho, easel standup, CJ, early 310.00
Sign, Jack & Bingo, standing on early CJ pkg, mc cb, rare 385.00
Sign, Santa & prizes, mc cb, Angelus, early, lg 200.00
Sign, Santa & prizes, mc cb, Checkers, early, lg 1,000.00
Sign, Santa & prizes, mc cb, CJ, early, lg 250.00

Cranberry

Cranberry glass is named for its resemblance to the color of cranberry juice. It was made by many companies both here and abroad, becoming popular in America soon after the Civil War. It was made in free-blown ware as well as mold-blown. Today cranberry glass is being reproduced, and it is sometimes difficult to distinguish the old from the new. Ask a reputable dealer if you are unsure.

For further information we recommend *American Art Glass* by John A. Shuman III, available from Collector Books or your local bookstore. See also Cruets; Salts; Sugar Shakers; Syrups.

Bowl, Hobnail, white opalescent ribbon edge, flint, 3½x8¾", $175.00.

Bottle, gold stars, star cut in base, w/stopper, 6x3" 165.00
Bottle, gold vintage, orig cut faceted stopper, 7¾x2⅞" 165.00
Bottle, HP florals around middle, clear faceted top, 7½" 165.00
Bottle, wine; fancy gold scrolls/florals, cut stopper, 12" 195.00
Bowl, appl crystal ft & rim, 4-crimp, 5¼x5¼" 165.00
Bowl, clear scallops, mc florals w/gold, brass ft, 5x6⅜" 195.00
Bowl, coin in center, bl ruffled rim, 2⅜x8" 195.00
Bowl, SP shell fr w/hanging spoon, 10x6½" 145.00
Box, heavy mc enameling & gilt, 3⅝" dia 255.00
Box, HP lilies of valley/etc w/gold, 3x4" dia 145.00
Claret jug, emb Fr pewter lid & hdl, 11"+4 clarets/tray 395.00
Compote, mc florals & gold berries, clear ped, 4x6⅛" 135.00
Cup & saucer, gold florals & scallops, 2¼", 5½" 235.00
Decanter, clear wafer ft, eng decor, 10¼x3⅞" 165.00
Decanter, clear wafer ft, rope hdl, clear finial, 10¾" 195.00
Decanter, mc florals/gold, clear faceted stopper, 11½" 225.00
Mug, Baby Invt T'print, clear hdl, ped ft, 4x2¼" 60.00
Night light, HP vintage, gold-washed ormolu fr at ft, 6¼" 265.00
Pitcher, bl & lav pnt decor w/gold, clear hdl, 1⅞x1⅜" 125.00
Pitcher, clear glass ice bladder, 10x5" 210.00
Pitcher, Invt T'print, flowers & bee, 8¾x7" 585.00
Pitcher, Invt T'print, pnt bird on branch, wht hdl, 8x6" 585.00
Rose bowl, Optic, 5⅛x5¼" 100.00
Rose bowl, Ribbed Optic, 6-crimp, 4⅜x4¼" 95.00
Sugar bowl, clear ft, clear bubble finial, 6x4" 110.00
Sweetmeat jar, HP decor, rstr SP lid/hdl, 4½" dia 250.00
Vase, wht enamel decor w/gold, ormolu ft, 5⅞x3", pr 245.00

Creamware

Creamware was a type of earthenware developed by Wedgwood in the 1760s and produced by many other Staffordshire potteries, including Leeds. Since it could be potted cheaply and was light in weight, it became popular abroad as well as in England, due to the lower freight charges involved in its export. It was revived at Leeds in the late 19th century, and the type most often reproduced was heavily reticulated or molded in high relief. These later wares are easily distinguished from the originals since they are thicker and tend to craze heavily. See also Leeds; Wedgwood.

Candlestick, parrot on perch form, hex base, mc, English, 7" 500.00
Charger, magenta emb feather edge & scalloped rim, rstr, 16" ...325.00
Creamer, dolphin on satyr's head, gr/tan/manganese, rstr, 5¼" ..450.00
Cup plate, America, red transfer, bl feather edge, 4⅛" 325.00
Cup plate, stylized mc flowers, bl feather edge, 4¼", pr 130.00
Figurine, Elijah & the Raven, mc details, rstr wing, 10¼" 475.00
Jug, Death of the Bear..., blk transfer, 7¾" 100.00
Pitcher, mc landscapes, mini, 2⅜" 40.00
Pitcher, Oriental w/parasol, mc, English, 1770s, rstr, 6" 160.00
Plate, Our Lady of Kevelare, mc, ca 1780, 8½", NM 275.00
Plate, toddy; Hope, brn transfer, bl feather edge, unmk, 5¼" 110.00
Sauce boat, dolphin form w/emb scales, gr trim, 18th C, 4¼" 325.00
Soup, brn stylized leaf border, Wedgwood, 1780s, 9⅜" 60.00
Teapot, Chinaman in garden decor, rstr/rpl lid, 1785, 5¾" 300.00
Teapot, Dream Not of Joys..., 19th C, 6¼", EX 975.00
Teapot, Whieldon-type tortoise shell w/mc spots, 1780s, 5½" ...275.00
Toby jug, brn/yel/gr underglaze, 1770-1880, 7⅛", NM 550.00
Vase, ram's head hdls, slip fluting, Turner, 1790s, 8½" 575.00
Vase, 3 cornucopias & 2 dolphins, mc, 7½x6½", EX 375.00

Crown Ducal

The Crown Ducal mark was first used by the A.G. Richardson &

Co. pottery of Tunstall, England, in 1925. The items collectors are taking a particular interest in were decorated by Charlotte Rhead, a contemporary of Suzie Cooper and Clarice Cliff, and a member of the esteemed family of English pottery designers and artists.

Bowl, squeezebag floral on beige, C Rhead, 3⅜x10" 225.00
Jug, mc leaves on gray w/gr trim, C Rhead, 5¾" 345.00
Vase, floral, bl slip, mushroom shape, C Rhead, 6" 225.00
Vase, Indian Tree design on gold satin, C Rhead, 5x5" 175.00
Vase, leaf band on mushroom form, mc glossy, 6½x2" 125.00
Vase, poppies on blk, orange lustre int, mk, 7¾" 195.00

Crown Milano

Crown Milano was introduced in 1894 by the Mt. Washington Glass Company of New Bedford, Massachusetts. Along with Burmese, it was their bestselling line. The glass is very pale, almost ivory. It was blown, free-form or in molds, highly decorated with flowers and colored enamels, and fired. Made to compete with the English Porcelain Companies, Crown Milano required only about half as many steps to produce as the porcelain (for which it is often mistaken, especially when viewed from a distance). This enabled Mt. Washington to make very attractive pieces at competitive prices. Some of the very early pieces are referred to as 'Albertine'; these had a glossy finish. Satin pieces were marked 'CM,' and some were shipped with paper labels. One of the most outstanding Crown Milano decorators was Frank Guba, who preferred subjects such as flying ducks or other birds. Pieces decorated by him command very high prices.

In the descriptions that follow, the glassware is assumed to be satin unless noted glossy.

Atomizer, apple blossoms w/gold, gold cap, 5" 800.00
Atomizer, fall foliage & flora w/gold, 4x3½" 650.00
Atomizer, trumpet vines on swirled body, 6½" 595.00
Biscuit jar, ferns on shaded tan, blk/maroon fronds, #4413, 8" ...850.00
Bowl, Dmn Quilt w/HP raspberries/leaves, sq rim, 4½" 450.00
Box, gold lilies on beige, SP mts w/gold wash, PMC, 3x5x6" 900.00
Box, mc floral w/gold on cream, brass ring/latch, 3¼x4½" 280.00
Creamer, violets w/gold, 4x3¼" 475.00

Photo courtesy Henry and Geneva Tyler

Ewer, gold floral decor, rope handle, 1880-95, 10x8", $3,900.00.

Ewer, chrysanthemums w/gold scrolls, rope hdl, 10½x5" 1,950.00
Ewer, 18th-C couple/gold scrolls/rope hdl, Pairpoint trim, 12" ..2,600.00
Glue pot, flat metal hdl w/brush hdl, 2⅜" 285.00
Jar, temple; mixed floral sprays w/gold, orig stopper, 15½" 3,250.00
Jardiniere, chrysanthemums & gold scrolls on pk, #596, 6x8" 700.00

Mustard jar, pk apple blossoms, hinged lid 225.00
Pickle castor, Dmn Quilt, HP floral, Pairpoint fr, mk lid 1,495.00
Pitcher, gold & silver azaleas, pk & gold scrolls, 8½x6½" 2,000.00
Pitcher, gold pond lilies & buds, serpent hdl, #567, 9x7" 2,500.00
Pitcher, Grecian lady & sheep/birds, gold trim, 10½" 3,000.00
Pitcher, lilacs w/gold leaves on yel to wht w/gold, 12½" 1,600.00
Pitcher, mc tapestry florals w/gold swirls & hdl, 12" 950.00
Pitcher, wild roses w/gold, duckbill spout, rope hdl, 13x9" 2,000.00
Shaker, bl & wht daisies, ribbed cylinder, 4" 185.00
Shaker, HP hen (no decal), full shape w/orig top, 2½" 350.00
Shaker, ivy on bl egg form, orig lid, 2½" 60.00
Shakers, shiny, Lobe 4, mc floral, metal lid, 3", pr 225.00
Sugar shaker, fall leaves/bl berries, floral-emb lid, 3x4" 400.00
Sweetmeat jar, floral, SP lid & hdl, 5" 550.00
Sweetmeat jar, gold/jeweled sea urchins, pk sea flowers, 3" 900.00
Tray, mc irises, red/gold scrolled edge, 4 sides rolled, 10" 650.00
Tumbler, brn leaves w/yel coraline, pk shadow leaves, 3½" 525.00
Vase, apple blossoms on cream to gold, bulbous, 13¾x6½" 1,550.00
Vase, apple blossoms on shadowed brn w/gold, bulbous, 6¾" 600.00
Vase, daisies w/gold & jewels, melon ribs, bulbous, 12¾" 1,200.00
Vase, dancing couple medallion, gold scrolls, thorn hdls, 18" .2,050.00
Vase, floral, mc on swirled yel to wht, crimped rim, 6" 550.00
Vase, floral, red on wht w/yel trim, lily form, 17" 650.00
Vase, floral/scrolls, pk/amber on wht w/gold, hdls, 9" 925.00
Vase, florals w/gold on cream to turq, 13¼" 1,500.00
Vase, gold roses & buds trail around stick neck & body, 15" 900.00
Vase, jack-in-pulpit; children/landscape w/gold, 7¼" 1,500.00
Vase, leaves/acorns, mc/gold on pnt Burmese, ribbed, 9x7" 1,000.00
Vase, leaves/acorns, mc/gold on shadows, shell hdls, 8x7" 1,100.00
Vase, orchids (detailed) on pnt Burmese w/gold, 14½x6" 1,650.00
Vase, pansies, mc w/gold on shiny opal, #1037, 9" 1,150.00
Vase, peonies & bl scrolls w/gold, swirled form, 7½x3½" 800.00
Vase, thistles, cut/pulled rim, thorn hdls, #609, 7½x7", NM ..1,700.00
Vase, Venetian scene, gold scrolls/florals, bulbous, 10" 5,500.00
Vase, violets, opal sphere w/gold collar, 3 ball ft, #588, 6" 700.00
Vase, wild roses, pillow form, crown stopper, #580, 7½" 4,000.00
Vase, wild roses w/jewels, bulbous, 8¾" 1,200.00
Vase, wild roses w/jewels & gold, stick form, #565, 12¾" 1,200.00
Vase, 2 gold Cupid cartouches w/roses & scrolls, #593, 9x6¾" ..1,750.00

Cruets

Cruets, containers made to hold oil or vinegar, are usually bulbous with tall, narrow throats and a stopper. During the 19th century and for several years after, they were produced in abundance in virtually every type of glassware available. Those listed below are assumed to be with stopper and mint unless noted otherwise. Our advisor for this category is Elaine Ezell; she is listed in the Directory under Maryland.

Yellow satin glass, 6½", $225.00.

Alaska, vaseline opal w/decor 295.00
Argonaut Shell, custard w/EX gold, 6½" 850.00

Avocado gr w/dk Prussian bl hdl, sqd/dimpled, 7" 125.00
Bead Swag, milk glass w/gold beading 250.00
Beaded Swirl, gr w/EX gold 400.00
Beaumont's Columbia, vaseline 195.00
Bubble Lattice, bl opal 500.00
Bubble Lattice Paneled Sprig, wht opal 325.00
Caprice, bl 95.00
Cathedral, amber 95.00
Champion, ruby stain 250.00
Chrysanthemum Base Swirl, bl opal 350.00
Chrysanthemum Base Swirl, custard w/decor, 6¾" 365.00
Chrysanthemum Base Swirl, wht opal 225.00
Coinspot, bl opal, ringed neck 250.00
Cone, yel satin 275.00
Cornucopia, pk stain 95.00
Cranberry, clear ft & finial, flower prunt, 6¼x2¾" 230.00
Cranberry, HP florals, 3-way top, clear teardrop stopper, 8¼" ..295.00
Cranberry, spun-rope clear hdl, clear bubble stopper, 8¼" 195.00
Croesus, emerald gr, gr fan stopper, 6½" 350.00
Daisy & Fern, wht opal, Northwood 225.00
Duchess, maiden's blush 450.00
Empress, gr w/gold 350.00
Esther, gr w/EX gold, lg 350.00
Esther, gr w/gold, sm 175.00
Everglades, bl opal 500.00
Everglades, custard, EX gold 1,250.00
Fine Cut, vaseline 195.00
Flora, bl opal 650.00
Florette, pk satin 395.00
Georgia Gem, gr w/gold decor 275.00
Gonterman Hobnail, amber opal 750.00
Heart & T'print 110.00
Hobnail, cranberry opal, Hobbs 375.00
Hobnail, sapphire-bl opal, Hobbs, 7¾" 350.00
Intaglio, bl 165.00
Intaglio, custard w/decor 475.00
Intaglio, gr w/gold 350.00
Intaglio, vaseline opal 300.00
Intaglio, wht opal 175.00
Invt T'print, amberina, amber hdl, 6" 425.00
Jackson, vaseline opal 225.00
Jewel & Flower, vaseline opal 795.00
King's 500, cobalt w/EX gold 650.00
Louis XV, custard, good gold 365.00
Medallion Sprig, bl 450.00
Medallion Sprig, rubena 450.00
Nestor, bl w/EX decor 195.00
Panelled Sprig, wht opal 175.00
Prize, gr 225.00
Reverse Swirl, vaseline opal 450.00
Ribbed Drape, custard, no decor 565.00
Ribbed Herringbone, wht opal 300.00
Ribbed Opal Lattice, cranberry opal 525.00
S-Repeat, bl 165.00
S-Repeat, gr, w/shakers & tray 275.00
Seaweed, bl opal satin 475.00
Shoshone, gr 125.00
Stripe, bl opal, bl stopper & hdl, 6½" 285.00
Stripe, wht opal 175.00
Swag w/Brackets, bl opal 675.00
Thousand Eye, vaseline, acorn stopper 150.00
Tiny Optic, amethyst w/decor 125.00
Tokyo, bl opal 225.00
Tokyo, wht opal 120.00

Tortoise shell, melon ribbed, clear hdl, faceted stopper, 7" **195.00**

Wimpole, maiden's blush **125.00**

Windows (Swirled), cranberry opal **650.00**

Cup Plates, Glass

Before the middle 1850s, it was socially acceptable to pour hot tea into a deep saucer to cool. The tea was sipped from the saucer rather than the cup, which frequently was handleless and too hot to hold. The cup plate served as a coaster for the cup. It is generally agreed that the first examples of pressed glass cup plates were made about 1826 at the Boston and Sandwich Glass Co. in Sandwich, Cape Cod, Massachusetts. Other glassworks in three major areas (New England, Philadelphia, and the Midwest, especially Pittsburgh) quickly followed suit.

Antique glass cup plates range in size from 2⅝" up to 4¼" in diameter. The earliest plates had simple designs inspired by cut glass patterns, but by 1829 they had become more complex. The span from then until about 1845 is known as the 'Lacy Period,' when cup plate designs and pressing techniques were at their peak. To cover pressing imperfections, the backgrounds of the plates were often covered with fine stippling which endowed them with a glittering brilliance called 'laciness.' They were made in a multitude of designs — some purely decorative, others commemorative. Subjects include the American eagle, hearts, sunbursts, log cabins, ships, George Washington, the political candidates Clay and Harrison, plows, beehives, etc. Of all the patterns, the round George Washington plate is the rarest and most valuable — only four are known to exist today.

Authenticity is most important. Collectors must be aware that contemporary plates which have no antique counterparts and fakes modeled after antique patterns have had wide distribution. Condition is also important, though it is the exceptional plate that does not have some rim roughness. More important considerations are scarcity of design and color.

Our advisor for this category is John Bilane; he is listed in the Directory under New Jersey. The book *American Glass* by George and Helen McKearin has a section on glass cup plates. The definitive book is *American Glass Cup Plates* by Ruth Webb Lee and James H. Rose. Numbers in the listings that follow (computer sorted) refer to the latter. When no condition is indicated, the examples listed below are assumed to have only minor rim roughness as is normal. See also Staffordshire; Pairpoint.

R-101, scarce, G **42.00**

R-102, scarce, VG **50.00**

R-124A, VG **40.00**

R-151A, G- **28.00**

R-159A, scarce, VG **48.00**

R-169B, VG+ **35.00**

R-171, VG **34.00**

R-172A, EX **40.00**

R-174, EX **45.00**

R-177, VG+ **44.00**

R-199, G **28.00**

R-20, G **25.00**

R-216, G **52.00**

R-216B, VG **64.00**

R-236, G **28.00**

R-245, G- **24.00**

R-246, VG **38.00**

R-255, VG **20.00**

R-257, VG **30.00**

R-258, VG **30.00**

R-260, scarce, VG **75.00**

R-263, yel-gr (rare color), EX+ **425.00**

R-269, VG **30.00**

R-271A, VG **30.00**

R-272A, very rare, VG **75.00**

R-285, VG **34.00**

R-291, VG- **26.00**

R-311, VG- **20.00**

R-313, VG **20.00**

R-323, VG- **18.00**

R-324, purple amethyst, sunburst, 3¼", EX **300.00**

R-326, G+ **18.00**

R-327, G- **12.00**

R-332B, G- **12.00**

R-334, G+ **18.00**

R-334A, G **15.00**

R-339, VG **19.00**

R-340, G **15.00**

R-343B, scarce, VG+ **35.00**

R-367, G- **10.00**

R-379, VG- **12.00**

R-388, G+ **11.00**

R-390A, VG **13.00**

R-393, G **10.00**

R-396, VG **13.00**

R-402, VG **14.00**

R-41, scarce, EX **50.00**

R-425, G+ **23.00**

R-447, G **22.00**

R-447A, G **21.00**

R-456X1, G- **19.00**

R-465H, VG **23.00**

R-465HX1, G **19.00**

R-465N, G **16.00**

R-465X1, VG **26.00**

R-467A, G **15.00**

R-47, G **25.00**

R-476, G- **13.00**

R-50, rare, VG **125.00**

R-501, G **11.00**

R-508, G+ **15.00**

R-522, red-amber (rare color) **275.00**

R-546, G+ **15.00**

R-561A, clear w/gray striations, rare, NM **4,000.00**

R-565, G **25.00**

R-565A, G+ **26.00**

R-566A, scarce, G- **33.00**

R-570, rare, G+ **86.00**

R-590, G **28.00**

R-593, scarce, G- **48.00**

R-594, VG- **32.00**

R-605A, scarce, G **105.00**

R-610, VG **42.00**

R-610A, VG **34.00**

R-610C, G **35.00**

R-615, EX+ **1,600.00**

R-619, G **35.00**

R-619A, G **39.00**

R-62A, scarce, G **42.00**

R-624, scarce, G **48.00**

R-628, scarce, G **53.00**

R-636, VG- **42.00**

R-637, very rare, VG **275.00**

R-642, G+ **18.00**

R-654A, very rare, EX- **315.00**

R-655, rare, VG **260.00**

R-658, emerald gr, att Sandwich, EX+ 4,250.00
R-661, G- 15.00
R-665A, G 35.00
R-666, VG 35.00
R-670C, rare, G- 55.00
R-677, eagle, NM 70.00
R-677A, G- 25.00
R-679, G+ 26.00

R-689, plow (with crossbar), very rare, EX+, $325.00 at auction.

R-693, scarce, G+ 75.00
R-695, G- 40.00
R-79, G 32.00
R-800A, G- 33.00
R-812, G 14.00
R-97, scarce, VG- 48.00

Currier & Ives by Royal

During the 1950s dinnerware decorated with transfer-printed scenes taken from prints by Currier and Ives was manufactured by Royal China and given as premiums through A&P stores. Though it was also made in pink and green, the blue is by far the most popular. Pie plates in black and brown can be found, but no china sets in these colors have been reported. Today it is readily available at reasonable prices, and it has become a very popular collectible at malls and flea markets around the country. Included this year in our listings are pieces from hostess sets, which should be of great interest to collectors. New pieces which have been added to the price list include the clock, coffee mug with round handle, tall cup, snack plate, spoon rest/wall plaque, second-type gravy and underplate, and second-type sugar bowl with no handles. Our advisors for this category are Treva and Jack Hamlin; they are listed in the Directory under Ohio.

Ashtray, 5½" 15.00
Bowl, cereal; 6¼" 12.00
Bowl, cereal; 6⅝" 12.00
Bowl, cream soup; tab hdls, 6¼" 30.00
Bowl, dessert; 5½" 4.00
Bowl, soup; 8" 12.00
Bowl, vegetable; deep, 10" 28.00
Bowl, vegetable; 9" 24.00
Butter dish, Fashionable 38.00
Butter dish, Road Winter 30.00
Casserole, angle hdls 95.00
Casserole, tab hdls 150.00
Clock, 10" plate 75.00
Creamer, angle hdls 6.00
Creamer, rnd hdls, tall 20.00
Cup, angle hdl 3.50
Gravy boat, pour spout 16.00

Gravy boat, tab hdl 30.00
Gravy ladle 35.00
Lamp, candle; w/globe 125.00
Mug, coffee 27.00
Pie baker, 9 decals, 10" 28.00
Plate, bread & butter; 6½" 4.00
Plate, calendar; 10" 15.00
Plate, chop; 11½" 35.00
Plate, chop; 12¼" 28.00
Plate, dinner; 10" 6.00
Plate, luncheon; 9" 15.00
Plate, salad; 7¼" 12.00
Plate, snack; w/cup & well, 9" 25.00
Platter, meat; 13" dia 50.00
Platter, oval, 13" 30.00
Platter, tab hdls, 10½" 28.00
Saucer, 6⅛" 1.50
Shakers, pr 30.00
Spoon rest, wall hanging 30.00
Sugar bowl, hdld, w/lid 16.00
Sugar bowl, no hdl, str sides 35.00
Sugar bowl, no hdl, w/lid 25.00
Teapot 125.00
Tidbit tray, 3-tier 75.00
Tray, for gravy boat, 7¼" 18.00
Tray, gravy-like 7" plate 35.00
Tumbler, iced tea; 12-oz, 5½" 16.50
Tumbler, juice; 5-oz, 3½" 16.50
Tumbler, old fashioned; 7-oz, 3¼" 16.50
Tumbler, water; 8½-oz, 4¾" 16.50

Hostess Set Pieces

Bowl, dip; 4⅜" 18.00
Cake plate, flat, 10" 30.00
Cake plate, ftd, 10" 75.00
Candy bowl, 7¾" 25.00
Pie baker, 11" 35.00
Plate, serving; 7" 15.00
Tray, deviled egg 75.00

Custard

As early as the 1880s, custard glass was produced in England. Migrating glassmakers brought the formula for the creamy ivory ware to America. One of them was Harry Northwood, who in 1898 founded his company in Indiana, Pennsylvania, and introduced the glassware to the American market. Soon other companies were producing custard, among them Heisey, Tarentum, Fenton, and McKee. Not only dinnerware patterns but souvenir items were made. Today custard is the most expensive of the colored pressed glassware patterns. The formula for producing the luminous glass contains uranium salts which imparts the cream color to the batch and causes it to glow when it is examined under a black light.

Argonaut Shell, bowl, master berry; gold & decor, 10½" L 265.00
Argonaut Shell, bowl, sauce; ftd, gold & decor 65.00
Argonaut Shell, butter dish, gold & decor 350.00
Argonaut Shell, butter dish, no gold 275.00
Argonaut Shell, compote, jelly; gold & decor, scarce 145.00
Argonaut Shell, creamer, gold & decor 140.00
Argonaut Shell, creamer, no gold 110.00
Argonaut Shell, cruet, gold & decor 775.00

Argonaut Shell, pitcher, water; gold & decor 435.00
Argonaut Shell, shakers, gold & decor, pr 345.00
Argonaut Shell, spooner, gold & decor 140.00
Argonaut Shell, sugar bowl, w/lid, gold & decor 200.00
Argonaut Shell, tumbler, gold & decor 110.00
Bead Swag, bowl, sauce; floral & gold 50.00
Bead Swag, goblet, floral & gold 65.00
Bead Swag, tray, pickle; floral & gold, rare 260.00
Bead Swag, wine, floral & gold 60.00
Beaded Circle, bowl, master berry; floral & gold 245.00
Beaded Circle, butter dish, floral & gold 450.00
Beaded Circle, creamer, floral & gold 180.00
Beaded Circle, pitcher, water; floral & gold 675.00
Beaded Circle, shakers, floral & gold, pr 800.00
Beaded Circle, spooner, floral & gold 175.00
Beaded Circle, sugar bowl, w/lid, floral & gold 275.00
Beaded Circle, tumbler, floral & gold, very rare 125.00
Cane Insert, berry set, 7-pc 450.00
Cane Insert, table set, 4-pc 450.00
Cherry & Scales, bowl, master berry; nutmeg stain 130.00
Cherry & Scales, butter dish, nutmeg stain 230.00
Cherry & Scales, creamer, nutmeg stain 115.00
Cherry & Scales, pitcher, water; nutmeg stain, scarce 325.00
Cherry & Scales, spooner, nutmeg stain, scarce 110.00
Cherry & Scales, sugar bowl, w/lid, nutmeg stain, scarce 125.00
Cherry & Scales, tumbler, nutmeg stain, scarce 65.00
Chrysanthemum Sprig, bowl, master berry; gold & decor 275.00
Chrysanthemum Sprig, bowl, master berry; no gold 175.00
Chrysanthemum Sprig, bowl, sauce; ftd, gold & decor 50.00
Chrysanthemum Sprig, butter dish, gold & decor 300.00
Chrysanthemum Sprig, celery vase, gold & decor, rare 600.00
Chrysanthemum Sprig, compote, jelly; gold & decor 135.00
Chrysanthemum Sprig, compote, jelly; no decor 95.00
Chrysanthemum Sprig, creamer, gold & decor 125.00
Chrysanthemum Sprig, cruet, gold & decor, 6¾" 380.00
Chrysanthemum Sprig, pitcher, water; gold & decor 470.00
Chrysanthemum Sprig, pitcher, water; no decor 350.00
Chrysanthemum Sprig, shakers, gold & decor, pr 300.00
Chrysanthemum Sprig, spooner, gold & decor 130.00
Chrysanthemum Sprig, spooner, no gold 75.00
Chrysanthemum Sprig, sugar bowl, gold & decor 225.00
Chrysanthemum Sprig, toothpick holder, gold & decor 325.00
Chrysanthemum Sprig, toothpick holder, no decor 175.00
Chrysanthemum Sprig, tray, condiment; gold & decor, rare ..595.00
Chrysanthemum Sprig, tumbler, gold & decor 80.00
Dandelion, mug, nutmeg stain 165.00
Delaware, bowl, sauce; pk stain 65.00
Delaware, creamer, breakfast; pk stain 70.00
Delaware, tray, pin; gr stain 75.00
Delaware, tumbler, pk stain 55.00
Diamond w/Peg, bowl, master berry; roses & gold 215.00
Diamond w/Peg, bowl, sauce; roses & gold 40.00
Diamond w/Peg, butter dish, roses & gold 250.00
Diamond w/Peg, creamer, ind; no decor 30.00
Diamond w/Peg, creamer, ind; souvenir 45.00
Diamond w/Peg, creamer, roses & gold 75.00
Diamond w/Peg, mug, souvenir 50.00
Diamond w/Peg, napkin ring, roses & gold, rare 150.00
Diamond w/Peg, pitcher, roses & gold, 5½" 260.00
Diamond w/Peg, sugar bowl, w/lid, roses & gold 160.00
Diamond w/Peg, toothpick holder, roses & gold 150.00
Diamond w/Peg, tumbler, roses & gold 70.00
Diamond w/Peg, water set, souvenir, 7-pc 650.00
Diamond w/Peg, wine, roses & gold 55.00

Diamond w/Peg, wine, souvenir 50.00
Everglades, bowl, master berry; gold & decor 215.00
Everglades, bowl, sauce; gold & decor 60.00
Everglades, butter dish, gold & decor 395.00
Everglades, creamer, gold & decor 155.00
Everglades, shakers, gold & decor, pr 375.00
Everglades, spooner, gold & decor 160.00
Everglades, sugar bowl, w/lid, gold & decor 235.00
Everglades, tumbler, gold & decor 100.00
Fan, bowl, master berry; good gold 160.00
Fan, bowl, sauce; good gold 55.00
Fan, butter dish, good gold 235.00
Fan, creamer, good gold 110.00
Fan, ice cream set, good gold, 7-pc 500.00
Fan, pitcher, water; good gold 285.00
Fan, spooner, good gold 100.00
Fan, sugar bowl, w/lid, good gold 150.00
Fan, tumbler, good gold 75.00
Fan, water set, good gold, 7-pc 725.00
Fine Cut & Roses, rose bowl, fancy int, nutmeg stain 100.00
Fine Cut & Roses, rose bowl, plain int 85.00
Geneva, bowl, master berry; floral decor, ftd, oval, 9" L 110.00
Geneva, bowl, master berry; floral decor, rnd, 9" 130.00
Geneva, bowl, sauce; floral decor, oval 45.00
Geneva, bowl, sauce; floral decor, rnd 45.00
Geneva, butter dish, floral decor 225.00
Geneva, butter dish, no decor 135.00
Geneva, compote, jelly; floral decor 95.00
Geneva, creamer, floral decor 100.00
Geneva, cruet, floral decor 465.00
Geneva, pitcher, water; floral decor 250.00
Geneva, shakers, floral decor, pr 280.00
Geneva, spooner, floral decor 100.00
Geneva, sugar bowl, open, floral decor 85.00
Geneva, sugar bowl, w/lid, floral decor 150.00
Geneva, syrup, floral decor 475.00
Geneva, toothpick holder, floral w/M gold 375.00
Geneva, tumbler, floral decor 50.00
Georgia Gem, bowl, master berry; good gold 135.00
Georgia Gem, bowl, master berry; gr opaque 115.00
Georgia Gem, butter dish, good gold 190.00
Georgia Gem, celery vase, good gold 145.00
Georgia Gem, creamer, good gold 100.00
Georgia Gem, creamer, no gold 60.00
Georgia Gem, mug, good gold 45.00
Georgia Gem, powder jar, w/lid, good gold 80.00
Georgia Gem, shakers, good gold, pr 160.00
Georgia Gem, spooner, souvenir 55.00
Georgia Gem, sugar bowl, w/lid, no gold 95.00
Grape (& Cable), bottle, scent; orig stopper, nutmeg stain ..600.00
Grape (& Cable), bowl, master berry; nutmeg stain, ftd, 11" ..420.00
Grape (& Cable), bowl, nutmeg stain, 7½" 60.00
Grape (& Cable), bowl, sauce; nutmeg stain, ftd 50.00
Grape (& Cable), butter dish, nutmeg stain 275.00
Grape (& Cable), compote, jelly; open, nutmeg stain 145.00
Grape (& Cable), compote, nutmeg stain, 4½x8" 300.00
Grape (& Cable), cracker jar, nutmeg stain 800.00
Grape (& Cable), creamer, breakfast; nutmeg stain 80.00
Grape (& Cable), humidor, bl stain, rare 950.00
Grape (& Cable), humidor, nutmeg stain, rare 900.00
Grape (& Cable), nappy, nutmeg stain, rare 60.00
Grape (& Cable), pitcher, water; nutmeg stain 500.00
Grape (& Cable), plate, nutmeg stain, 7" 50.00
Grape (& Cable), plate, nutmeg stain, 8" 65.00

Grape (& Cable), powder jar, nutmeg stain 350.00
Grape (& Cable), punch bowl, w/base, nutmeg stain 1,750.00
Grape (& Cable), spooner, nutmeg stain 145.00
Grape (& Cable), sugar bowl, breakfast; open, nutmeg stain 75.00
Grape (& Cable), sugar bowl, w/lid, nutmeg stain 195.00
Grape (& Cable), tray, dresser; nutmeg stain, scarce, lg 350.00
Grape (& Cable), tray, pin; nutmeg stain 135.00
Grape (& Cable), tumbler, nutmeg stain 75.00
Grape & Gothic Arches, bowl, master berry; pearl w/gold 200.00
Grape & Gothic Arches, bowl, sauce; pearl w/gold, rare 80.00
Grape & Gothic Arches, butter dish, pearl w/gold 235.00
Grape & Gothic Arches, creamer, pearl w/gold, rare 100.00
Grape & Gothic Arches, favor vase, nutmeg stain 80.00
Grape & Gothic Arches, goblet, pearl w/gold 75.00
Grape & Gothic Arches, pitcher, water; pearl w/gold 300.00
Grape & Gothic Arches, spooner, pearl w/gold 85.00
Grape & Gothic Arches, sugar bowl, w/lid, pearl w/gold 135.00
Grape & Gothic Arches, tumbler, pearl w/gold 65.00
Grape Arbor, vase, hat form 90.00
Heart w/T'print, creamer 85.00
Heart w/T'print, lamp, good pnt, scarce, 8" 435.00
Heart w/T'print, sugar bowl, ind 80.00
Honeycomb, wine 65.00
Horse Medallion, bowl, gr stain, 7" 80.00
Intaglio, bowl, master berry; gold & decor, ftd, 9" 250.00
Intaglio, bowl, sauce; gold & decor 50.00
Intaglio, butter dish, gold & decor, scarce 300.00
Intaglio, compote, jelly; gold & decor 125.00
Intaglio, creamer, gold & decor 125.00
Intaglio, cruet, gold & decor 475.00
Intaglio, pitcher, water; gold & decor 395.00
Intaglio, shakers, gold & decor, pr 235.00
Intaglio, spooner, gold & decor 125.00
Intaglio, sugar bowl, w/lid, gold & decor 165.00
Intaglio, tumbler, gold & decor 85.00

Inverted Fan and Feather, fruit bowl, gold and decoration, $250.00.

Inverted Fan & Feather, bowl, master berry; gold & decor 250.00
Inverted Fan & Feather, bowl, sauce; gold & decor 65.00
Inverted Fan & Feather, butter dish, gold & decor 350.00
Inverted Fan & Feather, compote, jelly; gold & decor, rare 500.00
Inverted Fan & Feather, creamer, gold & decor 150.00
Inverted Fan & Feather, cruet, gold & decor, scarce, 6½" 1,100.00
Inverted Fan & Feather, pitcher, water; gold & decor 650.00
Inverted Fan & Feather, punch cup, gold & decor 250.00
Inverted Fan & Feather, shakers, gold & decor, pr 600.00
Inverted Fan & Feather, spooner, gold & decor 145.00
Inverted Fan & Feather, sugar bowl, w/lid, gold & decor 250.00
Inverted Fan & Feather, tumbler, gold & decor 100.00
Jackson, bowl, master berry; good gold, ftd 135.00
Jackson, bowl, sauce; good gold 45.00
Jackson, creamer, good gold 85.00
Jackson, pitcher, water; good gold 250.00

Jackson, pitcher, water; no decor 175.00
Jackson, shakers, good gold, pr 195.00
Jackson, tumbler, good gold 50.00
Louis XV, berry set, w/nutmeg, 7-pc 375.00
Louis XV, bowl, master berry; good gold 200.00
Louis XV, bowl, sauce; good gold, ftd 47.00
Louis XV, butter dish, good gold 200.00
Louis XV, creamer, good gold 80.00
Louis XV, pitcher, water; good gold 245.00
Louis XV, spooner, good gold 80.00
Louis XV, sugar bowl, w/lid, good gold 165.00
Louis XV, tumbler, good gold 65.00
Maple Leaf, bowl, master berry; gold & decor, scarce 335.00
Maple Leaf, bowl, sauce; gold & decor, scarce 95.00
Maple Leaf, butter dish, gold & decor 350.00
Maple Leaf, compote, jelly; gold & decor, rare 455.00
Maple Leaf, creamer, gold & decor 150.00
Maple Leaf, cruet, gold & decor, rare 3,000.00
Maple Leaf, pitcher, water; gold & decor 400.00
Maple Leaf, shakers, gold & decor, very rare, pr 800.00
Maple Leaf, spooner, gold & decor 155.00
Maple Leaf, sugar bowl, w/lid, gold & decor 230.00
Maple Leaf, tumbler, gold & decor 95.00
Panelled Poppy, lamp shade, nutmeg stain, scarce 800.00
Peacock & Urn, bowl, ice cream; nutmeg stain, sm 80.00
Peacock & Urn, bowl, ice cream; nutmeg stain, 10" 350.00
Punty Band, shakers, pr 175.00
Punty Band, spooner, floral decor 100.00
Punty Band, tumbler, floral decor, souvenir 65.00
Ribbed Drape, bowl, sauce; roses & gold 40.00
Ribbed Drape, butter dish, scalloped, roses & gold 375.00
Ribbed Drape, compote, jelly; roses & gold, rare 200.00
Ribbed Drape, creamer, roses & gold, scarce 180.00
Ribbed Drape, cruet, roses & gold, rare 650.00
Ribbed Drape, pitcher, water; roses & gold, rare 365.00
Ribbed Drape, shakers, roses & gold, rare, pr 360.00
Ribbed Drape, spooner, roses & gold 180.00
Ribbed Drape, sugar bowl, w/lid 235.00
Ribbed Drape, toothpick holder, roses & gold 475.00
Ribbed Drape, tumbler, roses & gold 65.00
Ribbed Thumbprint, wine, floral decor 80.00
Ring Band, bowl, master berry; roses & gold 150.00
Ring Band, bowl, sauce; roses & gold 45.00
Ring Band, butter dish, roses & gold 250.00
Ring Band, compote, jelly; roses & gold, scarce 195.00
Ring Band, creamer, roses & gold 115.00
Ring Band, cruet, roses & gold 450.00
Ring Band, pitcher, roses & gold, 7½" 350.00
Ring Band, shakers, roses & gold, pr 155.00
Ring Band, spooner, roses & gold 115.00
Ring Band, syrup, roses & gold 465.00
Ring Band, toothpick holder, roses & gold 135.00
Ring Band, tray, condiment; roses & gold 200.00
Singing Birds, mug, nutmeg stain 75.00
Tarentum's Victoria, bowl, master berry; gold & decor 200.00
Tarentum's Victoria, butter dish, gold & decor, rare 300.00
Tarentum's Victoria, celery vase, gold & decor, rare 275.00
Tarentum's Victoria, creamer, gold & decor, scarce 135.00
Tarentum's Victoria, pitcher, water; gold & decor, rare 375.00
Tarentum's Victoria, spooner, gold & decor 135.00
Tarentum's Victoria, sugar bowl, w/lid, gold & decor 160.00
Tarentum's Victoria, tumbler, gold & decor 75.00
Vermont, butter dish, bl decor 195.00
Vermont, toothpick holder, bl decor 155.00

Vermont, vase, floral decor, jeweled 110.00
Wide Band, bell, roses 195.00
Wild Bouquet, butter dish, gold & decor, rare 700.00
Wild Bouquet, creamer, no gold 145.00
Wild Bouquet, cruet, no decor, w/clear stopper 995.00
Wild Bouquet, sauce, gold & decor 60.00
Wild Bouquet, spooner, gold & decor 160.00
Wild Bouquet, tumbler, no decor 95.00
Winged Scroll, bowl, master berry; gold & decor, 11" L 200.00
Winged Scroll, bowl, sauce; good gold 45.00
Winged Scroll, butter dish, good gold 215.00
Winged Scroll, butter dish, no decor 160.00
Winged Scroll, celery vase, good gold, rare 400.00
Winged Scroll, cigarette jar, scarce 195.00
Winged Scroll, compote, ruffled, rare, 6¾x10¾" 495.00
Winged Scroll, cruet, good gold, clear stopper 375.00
Winged Scroll, hair receiver, good gold 135.00
Winged Scroll, pitcher, water; bulbous, good gold 350.00
Winged Scroll, shakers, bulbous, good gold, rare, pr ...400.00
Winged Scroll, shakers, str sides, good gold, pr 195.00
Winged Scroll, sugar bowl, w/lid, good gold 185.00
Winged Scroll, syrup, good gold 395.00
Winged Scroll, tumbler, good gold 75.00

Cut Glass

The earliest documented evidence of commercial glass cutting in the United States was in 1810; the producers were Bakewell and Page of Pittsburgh. These first efforts resulted in simple patterns with only a moderate amount of cutting. By the middle of the century, glass cutters began experimenting with a thicker glass which enabled them to use deeper cuttings, though patterns remained much the same. This period is usually referred to as Rich Cut. Using three types of wheels — a flat edge, a mitered edge, and a convex edge — facets, miters, and depressions were combined to produce various designs. In the late 1870s, a curved miter was developed which greatly expanded design potential. Patterns became more elaborate, often covering the entire surface. The Brilliant Period of cut glass covered a span from about 1880 until 1915. Because of the pressure necessary to achieve the deeply cut patterns, only glass containing a high grade of metal could withstand the process. For this reason and the amount of handwork involved, cut glass has always been expensive. Bowls cut with pinwheels may be either foreign or of a newer vintage, beware! Identifiable patterns and signed pieces that are well cut and in excellent condition bring the higher prices on today's market. See also Dorflinger; Hawkes; Libbey; Tuthill; Val St. Lambert; other specific manufacturers.

Key:
dmn — diamond   X-cut — crosscut
strw — strawberry   X-hatch — crosshatch

Basket, etched/cut florals, notched appl hdl, rayed base, 17" ...1,100.00
Basket, satin roses/deeply cut leaves, notched rim, 12x8x4" 250.00
Bowl, cane lappets above vesicas w/dmns, silver mtd, 7½" dia ...550.00
Bowl, flashed hobstars, shallow, 8" 50.00
Bowl, Harvard variant border, 4 floral-cut panels, 11¾" L 200.00
Bowl, Harvard-like cutting, 3-ftd, EX quality/work, 8½x6" 300.00
Bowl, hobstars/starred hobs/X-hatches/fans, 8" 115.00
Bowl, Jubilee, clear vesicas & hobstars, 9" 375.00
Bowl, lilies of the valley panels/florals/hobstars, hdls, 8" 250.00
Bowl, Murillo, leaves/butterfly/tulip/crocus, ca 1910, 8¾" 150.00
Bowl, notched rays/sunbust w/4 hobstars, 10x4½", NM 275.00
Bowl, pineapple/fan border, 26-point hobstar center, 1½x8" 170.00

Bowl, Pluto, Hoare, 2x9" 225.00
Bowl, triangular button fields/bars/prisms/fans, Taylor, 8" 170.00
Bowl, vesicas of flashed hobstars alternate w/hobstars, 9" 150.00
Cake plate, Nassua, 3 peg ft, J Hoare, 10" 375.00
Candlesticks, fluted panels & notches, rayed base, 7", pr 300.00
Candlesticks, rock crystal cutting, wafer connector, 7½", pr 95.00
Carafe, hobstars, 8" 130.00
Card receiver, lg hobstar fr w/fans, shell w/1 side folded 125.00
Celery vase, hobstars, incurvate rim, 12x4¾" 125.00
Celery vase, Russian, sawtooth rim, 6½" 245.00
Celery vase, strw dmns/fans/rayed roundels, star-cut base, 8¼" ..200.00
Champagne, hobnail, faceted knob w/teardrop in stem, 5", 4 for ..200.00
Champagne flute, strw dmns/fans, button stem, 7⅛", 6 for 550.00
Clock, boudoir; Harvard-type cuttings w/intaglio tulip ...145.00
Clock, boudoir; lg tulip, geometrics & leaves, working, 6¼" 225.00
Compote, band of 6 cut hobstars w/6 expanding stars, 8x6", pr ..200.00
Compote, Caroline, ruffled, petticoat base, Hoare, 5¼x6½" 145.00
Compote, hobstars/X-hatch lozenges/spirals, 5¾x5" 250.00
Compote, strw dmns & fans, ftd, 7½x9¼" 350.00
Compote, strw dmns & fans, ftd, 7¼x10½" 425.00
Creamer & sugar bowl, Acme, ped ft, Hoare 425.00
Creamer & sugar bowl, Pinwheel 95.00
Decanter, hobstars & fans, faceted stopper, 10½" 160.00
Decanter, strw dmn/fan, ped ft, cut stopper, 16x6" 375.00
Flower center, Harvard, 24-point base star, stepped neck, 8x9" ..700.00
Flower center, 3 lg hobstars, heavy/brilliant blank, 7x8" 450.00

Tazza, allover hobstars, notched and fluted stem, 24-point hobstar base, 9½x10", $285.00; Compote, Fan and Nailhead, notched and prism stem, 24-point hobstar base, 11x7", $450.00.

Ice pail, fans & hobstars, ca 1900, 7" 200.00
Jar, dmns w/in scallops, fct knop, star-cut base, w/lid, 8" 150.00
Lamp, honeycomb shaft, hobstar & fans base, cut cap shade, 21" ...1,800.00
Lamp, pinwheels/dmns/X-hatching/prisms, electrified, 22" 1,400.00
Loving cup, Am Brilliant period, 3-hdl, silver rim, 9½" 1,500.00
Loving cup, prism-cut, 3 triple-notched hdls, 6½" 575.00
Nappy, Expanding Star 135.00
Nappy, pinwheels/hobstars, prism center, dbl-notch hdls, 7" 125.00
Paperweight, bars of stars/X-hatch sqs, book form, 2¼x2¾" 300.00
Pitcher, champagne; Harvard variation, hobstar/step panel, 11" ..400.00
Pitcher, hobstars, squatty/bulbous w/flared base, 8" 400.00
Pitcher, tankard; hobstars w/canes & dmns, 11½" 525.00
Pitcher, thistle-like flowers, t'print hdl, 11½" 225.00
Plate, Bergen's White Rose, ca 1894, 7" 150.00
Plate, Pineapple/hobstars, sawtooth rim, center hdl, 4½x5" 225.00
Platter, ice cream; hobstars/fans/etc, sawtooth rim, 14x7" 245.00
Punch bowl, Am brilliant cuttings, 7x14", Gorham 1592 ladle ...1,600.00
Punch bowl, hobstars/lg bars of buttons, cut rim, 7x14" 600.00
Punch bowl, Poinsettia & Harvard, 3-part, 16x14" dia 4,600.00
Punch cup, hobstars/fans/etc, pr 60.00
Relish, pinwheels/fans/buttons, hobstar/cane center, 12x6½" 125.00

Rose bowl, band of 4 lg hobstars, EX quality/work, 8x8" 390.00
Rose bowl, Henry VIII, Clarke, 5x6" 225.00
Rose bowl, hobstars in dmn fields, fan/X-hatch vesicas, 6x7" 200.00
Sherry, strw dmn, 6 for 175.00
Spooner, hobstars/fans/cane banners, 16-point hobstar base, 5" .160.00
Tazza, floral/Harvard band, allover Harvard base, 11x10" 700.00
Tray, chrysanthemum variant, 7¾x11¾" 275.00
Tray, hobstar edge, central hobstar, fan tassels, 9" dia 140.00
Tray, ice cream; finely cut, Am Brilliant period, 16½x9½" 980.00
Tray, ice cream; hobstars/stars/dmns, 1890s, 3½x18x11" 360.00
Tray, ice cream; Russian cuttings, 17¾x10¼" 700.00
Tray, perfume; Chrysanthemum Variant, oval, 10x7" 225.00
Tray, pineapple & fan, 5¾" dia 60.00
Tray, pinwheels encircle hobstar, heart shape, 5½" 70.00
Tray, Russian border, cane/X-hatch center, serrated, 13x8" 450.00
Tray, sandwich, hobstars allover, 12" dia 625.00
Vase, allover cuttings/corset shape/sawtooth rim, Clarke, 11" 275.00
Vase, allover hobstars & fans, petticoat ft, 17" 2,200.00
Vase, Brunswick, corset shape, Hawkes, 14" 950.00
Vase, flower center, hobstars/honeycomb, conical, 5½x7¾" 195.00
Vase, flowers alternate w/button vesicas, bands, slim, 16½" 375.00
Vase, Harvard, flared top, 16x7" 950.00
Vase, hobstar dmns & feathers, dbl bulbous form, 18" 1,500.00
Vase, hobstars & dmns on star-cut ped ft, 12" 330.00
Vase, horizontal stepped neck, scalloped rim, Hoare, 10" 700.00
Vase, Irving Rose, bowling-pin shape, 12" 550.00
Vase, strw dmns, fluted ft, pontil scar, 8" 250.00

Cut Overlay Glass

Glassware with one or more overlying colors through which a design has been cut is called 'Cut Overlay.' It was made both here and abroad.

Bottle, scent; amethyst to wht opaque, brass holder, 12" 160.00
Bottle, scent; turq/wht/clear, teardrop stopper, 7¾" 375.00
Bowl, centerpc; gr/clear, oval canoe w/eng fruit/branches, 10" ...300.00
Bowl, red/clear, Russian variant, rayed base, 5x9½" 1,550.00

Compote, white cut to green with gold, 6x7" dia, $475.00.

Compote, wht to cranberry w/gold, goblet shape, 8⅞" 170.00
Decanter, red to clear, fans/dmns, bulbous, 8" 170.00
Tazza, gr to clear, dmn-cut bowl, star-cut base, 8¼" 635.00
Vase, amethyst to clear, facet-cut panels, heavy, 8½x6½" 350.00
Vase, bl to vaseline, fruit reserves, ornate borders, 15" 440.00
Vase, cranberry to clear, geometric canes/fans, scalloped, 12" 457.00

Cut Velvet

Cut Velvet glassware was made during the late 1800s. It is characterized by the effect achieved through the execution of relief-molded patterns, often ribbing or diamond quilting, which allows its white inner casing to show through the outer layer.

Bowl, Dmn Quilt, bl, 3-crimp, 4½x4⅛" 145.00
Cruet, Dmn Quilt, pk, clear hdl, tricorner spout, 6" 425.00
Ewer, Dmn Quilt, gr, knob neck, opal hdl, 10½" 200.00
Ewer, Dmn Quilt, pk, appl hdl, 8" 150.00
Pitcher, Dmn Quilt, pk, sq rim, bulbous, camphor hdl, 7x7" 525.00
Rose bowl, Dmn Quilt, bl, 6-crimp top, 3½x3½" 135.00
Rose bowl, Dmn Quilt, red, 6-crimp top, 3½x3½" 225.00
Vase, Dmn Quilt, bl, trumpet neck, 6½x3¾" 145.00
Vase, Dmn Quilt, chartreuse w/HP flowers & butterfly, 7½" 200.00
Vase, Dmn Quilt, gr, bulbous, 9" 295.00
Vase, Dmn Quilt, tan, bulbous, 5x5⅝" 175.00
Vase, Dmn Quilt, yel, crimped rim, Mt WA, 9½x6" 375.00
Vase, Rib, pk, 9⅜x4½" 125.00

Cybis

Boleslaw Cybis was a graduate of the Academy of Fine Arts in Warsaw, Poland, and was well recognized as a fine artist by the time he was commissioned by his government to paint murals in the Polish Pavillion's Hall of Honor at the 1939 World's Fair. Finding themselves stranded in America at the outbreak of WWII, the Cybises founded an artists' studio, first in Astoria, New York, and later in Trenton, New Jersey, where they made fine figurines and plaques with exacting artistry and craftsmanship entailing extensive handwork. The studio still operates today producing exquisite porcelains on a limited edition basis.

Apache 1,500.00
Appaloosa Colt 225.00
Cinderella at the Ball, 8" 450.00
Council Fire 4,000.00
First Flight 90.00
Funny Face, Carousel-Circus series, 1976, 10½" 295.00
Goldilocks & the 3 Bears (pandas), 6¼" 500.00
Great White Heron, #425 ....1,200.00
Little Bo Peep, 10½" 450.00
Madonna w/Bird 250.00
Peter Pan 628.00
Sandpiper, #40 ....425.00
Thumbelina 295.00
Wendy w/Doll, Children to Cherish series, 6¾" 550.00

Czechoslovakian Collectibles

Czechoslovakia came into being as a country in 1918. Located in the heart of Europe, it was a land with the natural resources necessary to support a glass industry that dated back to the mid-14th century. The glass that was produced there has recently captured the attention of today's collectors, and for good reason. There are beautiful vases — cased, ruffled, applied with rigaree or silver overlay — fine enough to rival those of the best glasshouses. Czechoslovakian art glass baskets are quite as attractive as Victorian America's, and the elegant cut glass perfumes made in colors as well as crystal are unrivaled. There are also pressed glass perfumes, molded in lovely Deco shapes, of various types of art glass. Some are overlaid with gold filigree set with 'jewels.' Jewelry, lamps, porcelains, and fine art pottery are also included in the field.

More than seventy marks have been recorded, including those in the mold, ink stamped, acid etched, or on a small metal nameplate. The newer marks are incised, stamped 'Royal Dux Made in Czechoslovakia' (see Royal Dux), or printed on a paper label which reads 'Bohemian Glass Made in Czechoslovakia.' (Communist controlled from 1948, Czechoslovakia once again was made a free country in December 1989. Today it no longer exists; since 1993 it has been divided to form the world's two newest countries, the Czech Republic and the Slovak Republic.) For a more thorough study of the subject, we recommend you refer to the books *Made in Czechoslovakia*, and *Made in Czechoslovakia, Book 2*, by Ruth A. Forsythe; she is listed in the Directory under Ohio. Another fine book is *Czechoslovakian Glass & Collectibles*, Volumes I and II, by Dale and Diane Barta and Helen M. Rose. In the listings that follow, when one dimension is given, it refers to height; decoration is enamel unless noted otherwise. See also Amphora; Erphila.

Candy Baskets

Bl mottled w/yel ruffled rim, blk rope hdl, 8"	250.00
Gr varicolored w/red opaque o/l, gr hdl, 8½"	250.00
Pk w/dk stripes, pk hdl, 8"	190.00
Red & gr mottle, crystal twisted thorn hdl, 6½"	240.00
Red varicolored w/red int, crystal twisted thorn hdl, 5½"	250.00
Yel w/blk rim, crystal hdl, 6½"	200.00

Cased Art Glass

Candlestick, blk w/red ring, slim w/flared ft, 8¼"	75.00
Egg, mc mottle, 3"	95.00
Pitcher, red & cobalt mottle, cobalt hdl, 9"	125.00
Pitcher, red w/blk hdl, flared cylinder, 10⅛"	175.00
Vase, mc canes on blk, red int, bulbous, ftd, 6"	185.00
Vase, mc mottle, slim form, 10½"	70.00
Vase, mc mottle, wht cased, bulbous, flared ft, 7¾"	75.00
Vase, orange w/mc stripes, 4-sided, 9½"	90.00
Vase, pk w/wht o/l spirals, ruffled rim, ftd, 8½"	125.00
Vase, red & wht mottle, red cased, blk serpentine decor, 8½"	200.00
Vase, red cylinder w/cobalt hdls, flared rim, 6"	95.00
Vase, red w/wht mottling, red int, blk trim, flared rim, 7"	95.00
Vase, varicolored w/gr aventurine, blk trim, wht int, 7"	150.00
Vase, varicolored w/ornate bl hdls, 8⅜"	145.00
Vase, wht w/pk int, bulbous, ruffled rim, 5½"	100.00
Vase, yel & brn variegated, 3 blk buttressed ft, 8⅜"	80.00
Vase, yel & wht mottle w/blk rim, trumpet form, 6¾"	130.00

Cut Glass Perfume Bottles

Amber shouldered base w/amber faceted teardrop stopper, 6⅛"	145.00
Amber w/gold cupid decor, amber stopper, 6½"	375.00
Amethyst flared base, frosted nude stopper, 6⅝"	800.00
Amethyst pyramid shape w/frosted stopper, 3⅜"	75.00
Bl shouldered base, rectangular floral intaglio stopper, 6¼"	145.00
Bl shouldered form w/matching tall slim stopper, 5½"	150.00
Blk opaque w/gold & jewels on shoulders, crystal stopper, 4⅛"	250.00
Crystal ball shape, rnd floral intaglio stopper, 5¼"	110.00
Crystal rnd base w/yel frost floral intaglio stopper, 5½"	80.00
Crystal sq form w/red Triomphe stopper, 3¾"	145.00
Crystal stepped base w/bl spear-shaped stopper, 6½"	110.00
Crystal w/fine cuttings, gr lovebirds intaglio stopper, 5"	225.00
Crystal w/frosted figure in base, crystal stopper, 5⅞"	225.00
Gr octagon w/jewels, gr frosted stopper, 4¾"	225.00
Gr sq shape w/tall slim stopper, 6¼"	125.00
Pk shouldered form w/lg pk flower-shaped stopper, 5½"	175.00
Pk stepped base, crystal spear-shaped stopper, 5⅝"	150.00
Pk stepped base, pk dmn-shaped stopper, 4¼"	120.00

Lamps

Basket, bl beaded, fruit, 8"	650.00
Basket, crystal beads, bl flowers, 8½"	675.00
Boudoir, lady figural, flower skirt, 10¼"	950.00

Desk, Deco figure stands by crystal bubbly paperweight, 9"	900.00
Perfume, cut bl shade, 4"	150.00
Sconce, clear w/prisms, 2-light, 14½"	250.00
Student, acid-cut shade w/floral decor, 21"	900.00
Table, Deco-style geometric decor on wht, 9"	900.00
Table, mottled satin base & shade, 12½"	450.00

Mold-Blown and Pressed Bottles

Cranberry opal hobnail, bulbous, wht opal stopper, 5½"	85.00
Crystal sq w/jeweled sq stopper, 4"	85.00
Crystal w/gold & red jewels, jeweled stopper, 4¾"	250.00
Crystal w/overall jewel decor, 2"	95.00
Crystal w/pnt decor, slim form, atomizer, 7¾"	75.00
Crystal/frosted cylinder w/pnt decor, faceted stopper, 5¼"	45.00
Frosted crystal w/enameled daisies, atomizer, 6½"	95.00
Gr, low shoulder, red sphere-shaped stopper, 7⅛"	40.00
Pk cased, slim form, atomizer, 5⅞"	75.00
Purple lustre, bulbous, flower stopper, 4½"	140.00

Opaque, Crystal, Colored Transparent Glass

Decanter, gr w/blk-pnt ring decor, 7⅝"	50.00
Pitcher, amber w/emb dmns & yel o/l, yel finial, 11½"	450.00
Pitcher, bl w/mc exotic bird on branch, 11¼"	350.00
Shakers, pk, cut decor, glass top, 4¾", pr	165.00
Tumbler, gr bubbly glass w/HP scene, 3⅜"	55.00
Vase, crystal w/canes & yel stripe decor, bulbous, 5¾"	275.00
Vase, crystal w/red spiral threads, cylindrical, 8¼"	150.00
Vase, dk bl cut to clear, floral eng in clear, 10¼"	350.00
Vase, mauve, acid etched, blk trim at ruffled rim, 5⅝"	200.00
Vase, orange w/yel o/l, fan form, 8"	185.00
Vase, varicolored mottle, stick neck, 8⅛"	85.00
Vase, wht frost, emb wild horses on ball form, 7"	75.00

Pottery, Porcelain, Semiporcelain

Basket, floral w/gr vines on wht, blk hdl & base, 5"	50.00
Basket, red w/blk & wht band around center, 4¼"	55.00
Bell, smiling face figural, hair forms hdl, 5¼"	40.00
Candlestick, wht lustre w/dk bl stripes, sq base, 4"	35.00
Creamer, moose figural, 4⅞"	45.00
Creamer, parrot figural, mc wings, 4½"	50.00
Figurine, elephant, blk w/pnt howdah & tusks, 4½"	50.00
Flower holder, bird on stump form w/multiple openings, 5½"	45.00

Photo courtesy Barta and Rose

Flower-sprinkling can, multicolor floral on glossy green, 6¼", $45.00.

Pitcher, Peasant Art, Fruit & Flower, red, w/lid, 7"	250.00
Pitcher, ram figural, Deco style, yel & red, 8½"	500.00
Sauce dish, lobster figural, w/lid, 3½"	35.00
Sugar bowl, orange to tan, petal style w/gr rim, 2½"	35.00
Teapot, pk lustre, ball form, 6⅛"	45.00

Vase, Egyptian figures in band, bulbous, 9⅛" 300.00
Vase, glossy red, 6-sided, slim, 4⅞" 25.00
Vase, lav irises w/cream, ring hdls, lustre, 6½" 55.00
Vase, lt gray pearl lustre, blk rim & angle hdls, 5½" 20.00
Vase, mc sawtooth pattern, blk rim, ftd, flared rim, 7¼" 125.00
Vase, mc 5-petal flowers on wht, blk rim, 6⅛" 30.00
Wall pocket, bird on bird-house perch, 5½" 45.00

D'Argental

D'Argental cameo glass was produced in France from the 1870s until about 1920 in the Art Nouveau style. Browns and tans were favored colors used to complement florals and scenic designs developed through acid cuttings. Our advisor for this category is Don Williams; he is listed in the Directory under Missouri.

Cameo

Dish, leaves/flowers, wine/caramel on tan frost, w/lid, 7" 750.00

Vase, exotic flowers, orange-amber double overlaid in brown tones, signed, 13½", $975.00.

Vase, floral, purple to lav frost, 6x8½" 975.00
Vase, rose bushes, red/maroon/amber opal, baluster, 10¾" 980.00
Vase, trees/river, fortress beyond, rose on yel, ftd, 14" 1,250.00
Vase, trumpet flowers/vines, dk red on dk yel, 13½x4½" 1,000.00
Vase, vineyard, orange-amber/brns, classic form, 13½" 1,035.00

Daum Nancy

Daum was an important producer of French cameo glass, operating from the late 1800s until after the turn of the century. They used various techniques — acid cutting, wheel engraving, and handwork — to create beautiful scenic designs and nature subjects in the Art Nouveau manner. Virtually all examples are signed. Our advisor for this category is Don Williams; he is listed in the Directory under Missouri.

Cameo

Bottle, scent; berry branches w/gold, silver mts, 6¼", pr 3,450.00
Bowl, floral/grass, purple on lt bl/yel, sqd form, 4½x6" 1,600.00
Bowl, fruit branches, gray-gr/apricot/frost, 5½x8" 1,500.00
Bowl, landscape, raspberry/peach/yel-gray, 5¼" H 2,300.00
Bowl, leaves/pods, cut/gold pnt on textured opal, 3⅝" 1,380.00
Bowl, leaves/vines, int w/grapes, mc on yel/amethyst, 5½" 1,000.00
Bowl, mistletoe, cut/HP on clear to gr, 5¾" 1,380.00
Bowl, swans in marsh, gr/wht/bl mottle w/HP details, 8⅜" 8,050.00
Bowl, trees/water/grasses, gr on gray, 3½x4" 1,200.00
Creamer, rain woodland on pk/gr, metal bark rim, twig hdl 3,000.00
Inkwell, vintage/pods, blk on gr/orange, dome lid, 4½x4" 2,300.00

Lamp, vintage 12" shade/base, blk on gr/orange mottle, 26" .11,000.00
Lamp, winter scene shade/vase, cut/pnt, sgn AR/DN, X mk, 15½" ...15,000.00
Pitcher, floral bands w/silver wire o/l on gr, 10" 2,200.00
Vase, berries/leaves, mc HP details on yel/purple, bulbous, 5" 900.00
Vase, berries/leaves on marmalade to purple, stick neck, 9¼" .1,900.00
Vase, birch trees, cut/pnt, fields/trees beyond, 3½x5" 2,000.00
Vase, bud; floral twigs, cut/pnt on lime mottle, bun ft, 7½" 1,400.00
Vase, catkins/leaves, brn/gold on bl/burgundy, 18" 2,750.00
Vase, clematis/butterfly, garnet red/frosted, 11⅜" 2,200.00
Vase, columbines, cut/pnt, rust red/gr/yel-gray/brn, 2" 865.00
Vase, columbines, cut/pnt on yel/lav mottle, 5" 1,300.00
Vase, currant berries/leaves, cut/pnt on 4-color mottle, 3½" 900.00
Vase, floral, cut/pnt, purple/bl-gray frost/orange/gr, 14½" 2,500.00
Vase, floral, wht/gr irid on emerald/purple, 3-sided, 8" 2,000.00
Vase, floral/pods, peach/brn on peach frost, 4-sided, 20x7" 3,750.00
Vase, Lady Slippers & webs, cut/pnt on yel/amethyst, 7x3½" 3,600.00
Vase, landscape, gr/yel/brn, trumpet form, 15¼" 3,000.00
Vase, leaves/berries, cut/pnt, dk red/yel mottle, slim, 8½" 1,650.00
Vase, leaves/berries, cut/pnt on yel/purple, bulbous, 5" 900.00
Vase, leaves/pods, yel/rust on ivory frost, bulb bottom, 17" 1,900.00
Vase, lg mums, amber on yel/orange frost, EX work, 21" 4,000.00
Vase, lilies/water, cut/pnt, yel/butterscotch/gray, 13⅝" 3,165.00
Vase, nuts/branch, gr/gilt on frost, bulbous shoulder, 7" 1,500.00
Vase, poppies/butterfly, cut/gold pnt on amethyst, 13¾" 2,700.00
Vase, rose branch, orange/gr on yel mottle, tapered, 6" 1,200.00
Vase, rose hips, rust-red/citron on yel/maroon mottle, 4¾" 750.00
Vase, roses/butterfly, pk/gr/yel/purple on gr mottle, 4" 950.00
Vase, stylized grapes/lg leaves, violet on orange, 5x10" 2,100.00
Vase, thistles, cut/gold pnt on lt bl, long neck, 19" 3,000.00
Vase, thorny vines/berries, gr/yel/red/orange, cylindrical, 5" 750.00
Vase, tobacco flowers/spear leaves, wine/orange, ftd, 18" 3,000.00
Vase, trees, cut/pnt on wht to lt gr frost, shouldered, 8" 3,500.00
Vase, trees/bushes, gr/brn/yel on bl/red/yel, X mk, 25" 3,250.00
Vase, trees/sailboats beyond, brn on orange/yel, slim, 20" 3,500.00
Vase, trees/water on pink/purple, 5x2¾" 1,500.00
Vase, vines, cut/pnt on peach mottle w/gr/purple splashes, 3¾" ..900.00
Vase, violets/inscription, cut/gilt on frost, 3¼" 1,500.00
Vase, winter trees allover, mini, 1¾" 800.00
Vase, winter trees on yel/wht, 2½" 1,800.00
Vase, 4 18th-C peasants/X of Lorraine insignias, sqd, 9" 4,500.00

Miscellaneous

Bowl, amber/rust mottle, 8" L, NM 325.00
Bowl, gr w/textured leaves, 7½" 225.00
Bowl, village/windmill, pnt blk on opal, 4-lobed rim, 3x6" 1,600.00
Bowl, violet/caramel mottle w/foil, crimped, 3½x7½" 750.00
Box, pate-de-verre, grasshopper sits on raspberries, rpr, 5" 1,900.00
Chandelier, red/yel/opal mottle, domical, 15" 175.00
Compote, chartreuse/royal bl mottle, 11" 825.00
Cordial, gold thistles on blk stems, ribbed, 5¼", pr 1,100.00
Figurine, frog, gr pate-de-verre, on crystal lily pad, 3x4" 1,600.00
Flask, strawberries, cut/gilt, silver ft/rim/lid, 5⅞" 1,500.00
Lamp, bl glass mushroom style w/chrome-trimmed base, 12" ..2,000.00
Lamp, orange mottled 20½" shade; wrought Brandt std, 68" ...4,500.00
Paperweight, tiny teal/brn frog on crystal lily pad, 4" 350.00
Salt cellar, lake w/boats pnt on opal, 1¼x2" 800.00
Sculpture, sparrow, crystal, eng mk, 2¾" 35.00
Tray, pate-de-verre, leaf w/snail, amber/gr/aubergine, 7" 260.00
Tumbler, windmill, blk on opal, bbl form, 3½" 1,050.00
Vase, florals/stems, gilt on textured opal, dmn form, 7" 350.00
Vase, gr overshot w/emb lozenges below, flared top, 11" 600.00
Vase, gr/cobalt mottle, oval w/flat sides, sqd collar, 4½x7" 325.00
Vase, royal bl stick neck shades to lt bl bulbous body, 6" 300.00

Vase, tangerine stick neck, mottled cobalt body, 24" 400.00
Vase, wavy scroll band etched on clear, globular, 6" 485.00

De Vez

De Vez was a type of acid-cut French cameo glass produced by Cristallerie de Pantin in Paris around the turn of the century. Our advisor for this category is Don Williams; he is listed in the Directory under Missouri.

Cameo

Lamp, fiddle-bk fern 11½" dome shade; matching base, 22" ...2,760.00
Vase, floral trees/water/sea gulls, tan on yel/rust, 6" 800.00
Vase, landscape scenic, red on yel opal, 5¼x3¾" 600.00
Vase, leaves/lake/trees/mtns, bl/yel/wht, prof rpr, 8" 850.00
Vase, mtn/water scene w/vines, dk & lt bl/yel on frost, 8" 950.00
Vase, palm trees & city by the sea, bl/red on cream, 4¾" 600.00
Vase, sailboats/river/trees/mtns, 3 cuttings, sgn, 6" 900.00
Vase, thistles, ships/mtns beyond, invt trumpet form, 6" 550.00

De Vilbiss

Perfume bottles, atomizers, and dresser accessories marketed by the De Vilbiss Company are appreciated by collectors today for the various types of lovely glassware used in their manufacture as well as for their pleasing shapes. Various companies provided the glass, while De Vilbiss made only the metal tops. They marketed their merchandise not only here but in Paris, England, Canada, and Havana as well. Their marks were acid stamped, ink stamped, in gold script, molded in, or on paper labels. One is no more significant than another. For more information we recommend *Bedroom and Bathroom Glassware of the Depression Years* by Margaret and Kenn Whitmyer; their address is listed in the Directory under Ohio. Our advisor for this category is Randy Monsen; he is listed in the Directory under Virginia.

Atomizer, alexandrite, Tiffin, mesh cord & bulb, 6" 250.00
Atomizer, bl, Deco-style brass base, 5⅞" 350.00
Atomizer, bl opal, Coin Spot, bulbous 65.00
Atomizer, blk cased w/gold stripes, all orig, 7" 145.00
Atomizer, blk w/gold Deco design, Bakelite crown top, 6½" 550.00
Atomizer, blk w/gold enamel flowers & base, all orig, 10¾" 600.00
Atomizer, clear & satinized w/coral & gold enamel, 9½" 600.00
Atomizer, clear w/rvpt blk, silver trim, all orig, 6½" +box 200.00
Atomizer, cranberry stain w/gold decor & ft, 7" 125.00
Atomizer, dk gr enamel w/blk flowers, octagonal, 5½" 65.00
Atomizer, gold crackle, beaded flower on top, 4¾" 85.00
Atomizer, gold irid opal, mk, 6½" 125.00
Atomizer, Kelly gr w/gold, 8" 350.00
Atomizer, King Tut, bl-gr irid on gr opaque, Durand, 7½" 770.00
Atomizer, lilac w/gold trim, mk, 6½" 320.00
Atomizer, lt gr oval windows, much gold enamel, all orig, 8" 300.00
Atomizer, lt pk in Deco holder w/curving brass hex base, 6" 440.00
Atomizer, orange satin enamel w/blk decor, frosted crystal stem, 7" ...145.00
Atomizer, orange stain over crystal, tall stem, 6" 165.00
Atomizer, ruby stain w/gold lustre, 8" 325.00
Atomizer, turq w/gold, Deco style, 7" 115.00
Bottle, scent; amber irid, ftd, 6½", MIB 175.00
Bottle, scent; amethyst, mk, 6" 325.00
Bottle, scent; caramel irid teardrop, long dauber, 6¼", +box 385.00
Bottle, scent; clear w/etched leaves, bl medallion dropper, 6½" .440.00
Bottle, scent; orange o/l w/Deco decor, 6¾", +7" atomizer 525.00

Bottle, scent; smoke gray, hand blown, sm 300.00
Dresser set, orange enamel w/blk & gold decor, 3-pc 195.00
Ginger jar, Chinese red w/gold flowers 250.00
Perfume dropper, crystal w/bl flowers 25.00
Perfume lamp, azurite bl w/blk-banded silver-tone base 250.00
Perfume lamp, Deco nude trio, blk on wht w/brass trim, 10¾" ...715.00
Perfume lamp, moonlit scene, blk & orange on opal, slim, 8" 275.00
Perfume lamp, nude figure on glass insert, 7" 250.00
Pin tray, blk matt w/gold trim 35.00

Decanters

Ceramic whiskey decanters were brought into prominence in 1955 by the James Beam Distilling Company. Few other companies besides Beam produced these decanters during the next ten years or so; however, other companies did eventually follow suit. At its peak in 1975, at least twenty prominent companies and several on a lesser scale made these decanters. Beam stopped making decanters in mid-1992. Now only a couple of companies are still producing these collectibles.

Liquor dealers have told collectors for years that ceramic decanters are not as valuable, and in some cases worthless, if emptied or if the federal tax stamp has been broken. Nothing is further from the truth. Following are but a few of many reasons you should consider emptying ceramic decanters:

1) If the thin glaze on the inside ever cracks (and it does in a small percentage of decanters), the contents will push through to the outside. It is then referred to as a 'leaker' and worth a fraction of its original value.

2) A large number of decanters left full in one area of your house poses a fire hazard.

3) A burglar, after stealing jewelry and electronics, may make off with some of your decanters just to enjoy the contents. If they are empty, chances are they will not be bothered.

4) It is illegal in most states for collectors to sell a full decanter without a liquor license.

Unlike years ago, few collectors now collect all types of decanters. Most now specialize. For example, they may collect trains, cars, owls, Indians, clowns, or any number of different things that have been depicted on or as a decanter. They are finding exceptional quality available at reasonable prices, especially when compared with many other types of collectibles.

We have tried to list those brands that are the most popular with collectors. Likewise, individual decanters listed are the ones (or representative of the ones) most commonly found. The following listing is but a small fraction of the thousands of decanters that have been produced.

These decanters come from all over the world. While Jim Beam owned its own china factory in the U.S., some of the others have been imported from Mexico, Taiwan, Japan, and elsewhere. They vary in size from miniatures (approximately 2-oz.) to gallons. Values range from a few dollars to more than $3,000.00 per decanter.

Most collectors and dealers define a 'mint' decanter as one with no chips, no cracks, and label intact. A missing federal tax stamp or lack of contents have no bearing on value. All values are given for 'mint' decanters. A 'mini' behind a listing indicates a miniature. All others are fifth or 750 ml unless noted otherwise. Our advisor for this category is Roy Willis; he is listed in the Directory under Kentucky.

Aesthetic Specialties (ASI)

Golf, Bing Crosby 38th 18.00
Truck, Cadillac, 1903, bl or wht 50.00
Truck, Chevrolet, 1914 ....85.00

Beam

Bobby Unser Gurney Eagle Racing Car, white with multicolor decals, ca 1975, MIB, $75.00.

Casino Series, Golden Gate, 1970 ....14.00
Casino Series, Harold's Club, Pinwheel 40.00
Casino Series, Reno; Horseshoe, Primadonna, or Cal-Neva 10.00
Centennial Series, Alaska Purchase 10.00
Centennial Series, Cheyenne 10.00
Centennial Series, Key West 8.00
Centennial Series, Lombard 8.00
Centennial Series, Statue of Liberty, 1975 ....20.00
Executive Series, 1979 Mother of Pearl 15.00
Executive Series, 1980 Titan 15.00
Executive Series, 1982 American Pitcher 24.00
Executive Series, 1983 Partridge Bell 35.00
Executive Series, 1984 Carolers Bell 28.00
Executive Series, 1991 Royal Filigree 18.00
Foreign Series, Australia, Galah Bird 25.00
Foreign Series, Australia, Kangaroo 18.00
Foreign Series, Australia, Koala 18.00
Foreign Series, Fiji Islands 10.00
Foreign Series, Kiwi Bird 8.00
Foreign Series, Samoa 10.00
Organization Series, Ducks Unlimited #10, 1984 ....95.00
Organization Series, Ducks Unlimited #6, 1980 ....45.00
Organization Series, Ducks Unlimited #7, 1981 ....35.00
Organization Series, Ducks Unlimited #8, 1982 ....60.00
Organization Series, Ducks Unlimited #9, 1983 ....60.00
Organization Series, Elks, 1968 ....6.00
Organization Series, Legion Music 8.00
Organization Series, Phi Sigma Kappa 15.00
Organization Series, Shriner, Raja Temple 25.00
Organization Series, VFW 10.00
Organization Series, 101st Airborne 12.00
People Series, Cowboy 20.00
People Series, Emmet Kelly 35.00
People Series, George Washington 20.00
People Series, Hank Williams, Jr 38.00
People Series, Martha Washington 14.00
People Series, Mr Goodwrench 40.00
State Series, Delaware 9.00
State Series, Kentucky, blk stopper 18.00
State Series, Maine 8.00
State Series, New Hampshire 7.00
State Series, Ohio 12.00
Wheel Series, Cable Car, 1968 ....7.00
Wheel Series, Cable Car, 1983 ....60.00
Wheel Series, Corvette, 1954, bl 110.00
Wheel Series, Corvette, 1955, bronze 100.00
Wheel Series, Corvette, 1963, red or silver 85.00
Wheel Series, Corvette, 1978, yel, red, or wht 75.00
Wheel Series, Ford, 1964 Mustang, blk 135.00

Wheel Series, Ford, 1964 Mustang, red 90.00
Wheel Series, Ford, 1964 Mustang, wht 80.00
Wheel Series, Golf Car 45.00
Wheel Series, Harold's Club Covered Wagon (1974) 45.00
Wheel Series, Locomotive, Grant 100.00
Wheel Series, Locomotive, JB Turner 150.00
Wheel Series, Mack Fire Engine 140.00
Wheel Series, Train, Caboose, gray 70.00
Wheel Series, Train, Caboose, red 65.00
Wheel Series, Train, Locomotive, General 125.00
Wheel Series, Train, Passenger Car 60.00
Wheel Series, Train, Tender, Coal for Grant 70.00
Wheel Series, Train, Tender, Wood (for General) 140.00
Wheel Series, Train, Tender, Wood for Turner 75.00
Wheel Series, 1913 Model T, blk or gr 65.00

Brooks

American Legion, Denver, 1972 ....15.00
Amvets 10.00
Car, '62 Mako Shark 35.00
Car, Auburn 25.00
Car, Duesenberg 35.00
Dog, w/bird, 1970 ....15.00
Elk 25.00
Fire Engine 25.00
Hambletonian 18.00
Indy Racer, #21 (1970) 55.00
Indy Racer, #21 (1971) 80.00
Keystone Cops 55.00
Man 'O War 25.00
Panda 18.00
Phonograph 25.00
Pistol, Dueling 12.00
Shrine, Fez 10.00
Shrine, King Tut Guard 22.00
Tennis Player 12.00
Ticker Tape 10.00
Trail Bike 15.00
Train, Iron Horse 10.00
Vermont Skier 12.00
Whale, Killer 22.00
Wichita Centennial 8.00

Dant, J.W.

American Legion 12.00
Field Birds, 8 different, ea 12.00
Indy 500 ....10.00

Dickel

Golf Club (glass) 12.00
Powder Horn, amber, qt 15.00
Powder Horn, dk, 4/5-qt 12.00

Famous Firsts

Coffee Mill 38.00
Roulette Wheel 35.00
Scale, Lombardy 30.00
Spirit of St Louis 125.00
Spirit of St Louis, midi 70.00
Spirit of St Louis, mini 48.00

Hoffman

Big Red Machine	50.00
Cats, 6 different, mini, ea	15.00
Children of the World, 6 different, ea	28.00
College Series, Helmet, Auburn	28.00
College Series, Helmet, Missouri	28.00
College Series, Mascot, 'Ol Miss Rebel	50.00
College Series, Mascot, Nevada Wolfpack	50.00
Mr Lucky Series, Mr Blacksmith	28.00
Mr Lucky Series, Mr Blacksmith, mini	15.00
Mr Lucky Series, Mr Fireman	75.00
Mr Lucky Series, Mr Fireman, mini	25.00
Mr Lucky Series, Mr Policeman	45.00
Mr Lucky Series, Mr Policeman, mini	20.00
Racecar, Foyt #2	120.00
Racecar, Johncock #20	70.00
Wildlife Series, Doe & Fawn	50.00
Wildlife Series, Fox & Rabbit	50.00

Kontinental

Dentist	35.00
Dockworker	30.00
Innkeeper	30.00
Statue of Liberty	25.00
Stephen Foster	28.00
Surveyor	35.00

Lionstone

Backpacker	28.00
Barber	45.00
Barber, mini	20.00
Buffalo Hunter	30.00
Camp Cook	20.00
Camp Follower	22.00
Canada Goose	55.00
Clown, 6 different, ea	40.00
Dancehall Girl, mini	15.00
Doctor, Country	18.00
Fisherman	40.00
Football Players	60.00
Goldpanner, mini	20.00
Johnny Lightning #1	100.00
Johnny Lightning #2	90.00
Laundryman, Chinese	22.00
Meadowlark	28.00
Photographer	60.00
Photographer, mini	22.00
Rainmaker	32.00
Rainmaker, mini	20.00
Revere, Paul	25.00
Riverboat Captain	22.00
Sheepherder	42.00
Sheepherder, mini	20.00
Telegrapher	26.00
Turbo Car STP, red	70.00

McCormick

Austin, Stephen	20.00
Bell, Alexander	25.00
Durante, Jimmy	55.00

Elvis, #1, 1977, wht	90.00
Elvis, #1, 1977, wht, mini	55.00
Elvis, #2, 1955, pk	80.00
Elvis, #2, 1955, pk, mini	50.00
Elvis, #3, 1968, blk	85.00
Elvis, #3, 1968, blk, mini	50.00
Elvis, Karate	350.00
Elvis, Karate, mini	100.00
Frontiersman, 4 different, ea	25.00
Iwo Jima	135.00
Iwo Jima, mini	75.00
King Arthur's Court, King Arthur	45.00
Lincoln, Abe	35.00
Monroe, Marilyn	475.00
Monroe, Marilyn; mini	160.00
Paul Bunyan	35.00
Peary, Robert	28.00
Pony Express	70.00
Rogers, Will	30.00
Shrine Dune Buggy	45.00
Telephone Operator	65.00
Williams, Hank Sr	140.00

O.B.R.

Engine, General	20.00
Guitar, Music City	18.00
Hockey Players	30.00
WC Fields, Bank Dick	45.00
WC Fields, Top Hat	40.00

Old Commonwealth

Coal Miner #1, w/Shovel	75.00
Coal Miner #1, w/Shovel, mini	25.00
Coal Miner #2, w/Pick	45.00
Coal Miner #2, w/Pick, mini	20.00
Firefighter, Fallen Comrade	70.00
Firefighter, Fallen Comrade, mini	25.00
Firefighter, Modern Hero #1	75.00
Firefighter, Modern Hero #1, mini	25.00
Firefighter, Nozzleman #2	70.00
Firefighter, Nozzleman 32, mini	24.00

Old Crow

Crow, red vest	25.00
Crow, Royal Doulton	95.00

Old Fitzgerald

Irish, Blarney	12.00
Irish, Leprechaun, 'Plase God'	30.00
Irish, Leprechaun, 'Prase Be'	23.00
Irish, Luck 1972	28.00
Irish, Wish 1975	22.00
Rip Van Winkle	30.00

Ski Country

Barrel Racer	75.00
Barrel Racer, mini	35.00
Bear, Brown	35.00
Birth of Freedom	95.00

Birth of Freedom, gallon 2,000.00
Birth of Freedom, mini 80.00
Bob Cratchit 60.00
Bob Cratchit, mini 34.00
Cardinals, Holiday 1991 ....70.00
Cardinals, Holiday 1991, mini 35.00
Deer, Whitetail 150.00
Deer, Whitetail, mini 50.00
Ducks Unlimited, Pintail, 1978 ....85.00
Ducks Unlimited, Pintail, 1978, mini 30.00
Ducks Unlimited, Pintail, 1978, ½-gallon 175.00
Ducks Unlimited, Widgeon, 1979 ....50.00
Ducks Unlimited, Widgeon, 1979, mini 30.00
Ducks Unlimited, Widgeon, 1979, ½-gallon 160.00
Eagle, Majestic 350.00
Eagle, Majestic, gallon 2,000.00
Eagle, Majestic, mini 140.00
Elk 195.00
Elk, mini 65.00
Indian, Cigar Store 50.00
Indian, Cigar Store, mini 32.00
Indian, North American, mini, set of 6 ....140.00
Indian, North American, set of 6 ....210.00
Indian, Southwest Dancers, set of 6 ....350.00
Indian, Southwest Dancers, set of 6, mini 200.00
Jaguar 160.00
Jaguar, mini 45.00
Koala 50.00
Owl, Barred; wall plaque 130.00
Owl, Barred; wall plaque, mini 40.00
Owl, Great Gray 80.00
Owl, Great Gray, mini 35.00
Pelican 50.00
Pelican, mini 35.00
Pheasant, Standing; mini 50.00
Phoenix Bird 60.00
Phoenix Bird, mini 30.00
Ram, Bighorn 60.00
Ram, Bighorn, mini 30.00
Ruffed Grouse 60.00
Ruffed Grouse, mini 25.00
Skunk Family 50.00
Skunk Family, mini 30.00
Wild Turkey 100.00
Wild Turkey, mini 110.00

Wild Turkey

Series I, #6, striding, $25.00.

Series I, #1, #2, #3, or #4, mini, ea 18.00
Series I, #1, 1971 ....260.00
Series I, #2 ....160.00
Series I, #3 ....70.00
Series I, #4 ....70.00

Series I, #5 ....30.00
Series I, #7 ....25.00
Series I, #8 ....45.00
Series I, set of #5, #6, #7 & #8, mini 150.00
Series II, Lore #1 ....25.00
Series II, Lore #2 ....35.00
Series II, Lore #3 ....45.00
Series II, Lore #4 ....50.00
Series III, #1, In Flight 120.00
Series III, #1, In Flight, mini 45.00
Series III, #10, Turkey & Coyote 95.00
Series III, #10, Turkey & Coyote, mini 45.00
Series III, #11, Turkey & Falcon 95.00
Series III, #11, Turkey & Falcon, mini 45.00
Series III, #12, Turkey & Skunks 95.00
Series III, #12, Turkey & Skunks, mini 45.00
Series III, #2, Turkey & Bobcat 140.00
Series III, #2, Turkey & Bobcat, mini 45.00
Series III, #3, Fighting Turkeys 150.00
Series III, #3, Fighting Turkeys, mini 50.00
Series III, #4, Turkey & Eagle 95.00
Series III, #4, Turkey & Eagle, mini 80.00
Series III, #5, Turkey & Raccoon 95.00
Series III, #5, Turkey & Raccoon, mini 45.00
Series III, #6, Turkey & Poults 95.00
Series III, #6, Turkey & Poults, mini 45.00
Series III, #7, Turkey & Red Fox 95.00
Series III, #7, Turkey & Red Fox, mini 50.00
Series III, #8, Turkey & Owl 100.00
Series III, #8, Turkey & Owl, mini 50.00
Series III, #9, Turkey & Bear Cubs 100.00
Series III, #9, Turkey & Bear Cubs, mini 50.00

Decoys

American colonists learned the craft of decoy making from the Indians who used them to lure birds out of the sky as an important food source. Early models were carved from wood such as pine, cedar, balsa, etc., and a few were made of canvas or papier-mache. There are two basic types of decoys: water floaters and shorebirds (also called 'stick-ups'). Within each type are many different species, ducks being the most plentiful since they migrated along all four of America's great waterways. Market hunting became big business around 1880, resulting in large-scale commercial production of decoys which continued until about 1910 when such hunting was outlawed by the Migratory Bird Treaty.

Today decoys are one of the most collectible types of American folk art. The most valuable are those carved by such artists as Laing, Crowell, Ward, and Wheeler, to name only a few. Each area, such as Massachusetts, Connecticut, Maine, the Illinois River, and the Delaware River, produces decoys with distinctive regional characteristics. Examples of commercial decoys produced by well-known factories — among them Mason, Stevens, and Dodge — are also prized by collectors. Though mass produced, these nevertheless required a certain amount of hand carving and decorating. Well-carved examples, especially those of rare species, are appreciating rapidly, and those with original paint are more desirable. Writer Carl F. Luckey has compiled a fully illustrated identification and value guide, *Collecting Antique Bird Decoys*; you will find his address in the Directory under Alabama. In the listings that follow, all decoys are solid-bodied unless noted hollow.

Key:
CG — Challenge Grade   RP — repaint
MDF — Mason's Decoy Factory   SG — Standard Grade

OP — original paint   WDF — Wildfowler Decoy Factory
ORP — old repaint   WOP — worn original paint
OWP — original working paint   WRP — working repaint
PG — Premier Grade

Blk Duck, Elmer Crowell, fluted tail, NM OP, artist brand 2,750.00
Blk Duck, Harry Shourds, swimming, old in-use RP 300.00
Blk Duck, Ken Gleason, hollow, NM OP, 1950 ....325.00
Blk Duck, Madison Mitchell, trn head, NM OP, sgn/dtd 1974 ...475.00
Blk Duck, WDF, hollow, 1 glass eye, WOP, Old Saybrook brand ..150.00
Blk-Bellied Plover, Elijah Burr, running, NM OP/VG patina .2,750.00
Blk-Bellied Plover, Mark McNair, raised wing tips, NM OP 600.00
Bluebill drake, Ira Hudson, rnd body, rpt in 1940 by Lem Ward ..500.00
Bluebill drake, MDF, CG, snakey head, NM OP/G patina 1,400.00
Bluebill drake, Reggie Marter, hollow, low head, WRP, ca 1930 ....450.00
Bluebill drake, Shang Wheeler, sleeping, NM OP/varnish 950.00
Bluebill hen, Stevens Factory, humpbk style, old in-use RP 225.00
Bluewing Teals, MDF, SG, glass eyes, EX OP, pr 1,550.00
Brant, Bill Bowman, hollow, EX OP, branded Edgar 1,150.00
Brant, Harry Shourds, hollow, EX OP w/tiger stripes, 1890-1900 ...5,000.00
Brant, Joseph Lincoln, old in-use RP, rpl bill, rare 350.00
Brant, WDF, NM OP, Point Pleasant brand 200.00
Canada Goose, Clarence Miller, fluted tail, NM OP, ca 1960 ...2,200.00
Canada Goose, Madison Mitchell, M OP, etched sgn, 1970 ....550.00
Canada Goose, Steve Ward, hollow, tack eyes, NM OP, 1964 ..1,800.00
Canvasback drake, Samuel Barnes, Upper Bay style, old WRP ..110.00
Canvasback hen, Norris Pratt, hollow, cvd wing tips, NM OP ...250.00
Curlew, Capt Jonas Sprague, OP, rpl bill, rare 500.00
Eider hen, Gus Wilson, inlet head, cvd eyes/bill, NM OP, rare ..500.00
Goldeneye drake, Willard Baldwin, hollow, in-use RP, 1923 .....300.00
Goldeneye hen, Bill Hammel, hollow & pegged, cvd eyes, WRP ...675.00
Greenwing Teal drake, MDF, NM OP, rare 850.00
Hooded Merganser drake, Miles Hancock, OP w/minor wear 825.00
Hooded Merganser hen, Doug Jester, EX OP, Mackey stamp ..1,600.00
Mallard drake, Charles Allen, hollow, artist brand, 1920s 800.00
Mallard drake, MDF, SG, tack eyes, NM OP, rare 500.00
Mallard drake, Robert Elliston, rnd body, OP, early 3,750.00
Mallard drake, Roswell Bliss, sleeping, NM OP, branded, rare ...450.00
Mallard drake, Ward Bros, balsa, cedar head/tail, NM OP, 1948 ....2,250.00
Mallard hen, MDF, PG, early style, EX OP, branded WHW 325.00
Mallard hen, MDF, PG, NM OP, never rigged 2,400.00
Mallards, WDF, hollow, inlet heads, Old Saybrook mk, NM OP, pr ..400.00
Pintail drake, Claude Trader, low head, old WRP, early 375.00
Pintail drake, Dodge Factory, EX OP, rare, ca 1880 ....675.00
Pintail drake, MDF, PG, early style, VG OP, rare 1,050.00
Pintail drake, Ridgeway Marter, hollow, EX OP/patina, 1920s ..2,250.00
Pintail hen, MDF, SG, rstr pnt w/traces of orig 150.00
Redhead drake, MDF, PG, slightly trn head, RP, branded WAS ..225.00
Robin Snipe, Crisfield, MD, running, Fall plumage, OP, rare 650.00
Robin Snipe, MDF, tack eyes, Spring plumage, EX OP, rare 500.00
Scaup drake, Henry Grant, hollow, glass eyes, NM OP, ca 1890 ...325.00
Sea gull, Ken Harris, full body, EX feather detail, NM OP, rare .600.00
Snow Plover, A Elmer Crowell, pnt loss, mini, 1¾" 260.00
Spotted Sandpiper, A Elmer Crowell, mini, 2⅛" 460.00
Widgeon drake, MDF, CG, G OP 700.00
Widgeons, WDF, OP/EX patina, Old Saybrook brand, 1939, pr .500.00
Willet, John Dilley, strong OP, G patina, rare 9,500.00

Dedham Pottery

Originally founded in Chelsea, Massachusetts, as the Chelsea
Keramic Works, the name was changed to Dedham Pottery in 1895
after the firm relocated in Dedham, near Boston, Massachusetts. The
ware utilized a gray stoneware body with a crackle glaze and simple
cobalt border designs of flowers, birds, and animals. Decorations were
brushed on by hand using an ancient Chinese method which suspended
the cobalt within the overall glaze. There were thirteen standard patterns, among them Magnolia, Iris, Butterfly, Duck, Polar Bear, and Rabbit, the latter of which was chosen to represent the company on their
logo. On the very early pieces, the rabbits face left; decorators soon
found the reverse position easier to paint, and the rabbits were turned
to the right. (Earlier examples are worth from 10% to 20% more than
identical pieces manufactured in later years.) In addition to the standard patterns, other designs were produced for special orders. These and
artist-signed pieces are highly valued by collectors today.

Though their primary product was the blue-printed, crackle-glazed
dinnerware, two types of artware were also produced: crackle glaze and
flambe. Their notable volcanic ware was a type of the latter. The mark
is incised and often accompanies the cipher of Hugh Robertson. The
firm was operated by succeeding generations of the Robertson family
until it closed in 1943. Our advisor for this category is Dale MacLean;
he is listed in the Directory under Massachusetts. See also Chelsea
Keramic Art Works.

Dinnerware

Ashtray, Rabbit, stamped, 1x6¼" 400.00
Ashtray, Rabbit, stamped registered, ¾x3¾" 250.00
Bacon rasher, Dolphin, Davenport rebus, stamped registered, 10" ...1,250.00

**Bacon rasher, Elephant, stamped/registered,
9¾x6", $1,100.00.**

Bacon rasher, Rabbit, stamped, 1⅛x9¾" dia 375.00
Boot, Bow & Band, unmk, 2⅛" 450.00
Bowl, nappy, Rabbit, flat rim, domed lid, stamped, 2¼x6" 325.00
Bowl, nappy, Rabbit, partial ink mk, 5¾" 225.00
Bowl, Rabbit, deep, stamped, rstr, 3⅜x8" 400.00
Bowl, Rabbit, stamped, 2⅜x9½" 375.00
Bowl, Rabbit, stamped, 2x4½" 200.00
Bowl, Rabbit, stamped, 3" 275.00
Bowl, Rabbit, stamped registered, 2¾x6" 325.00
Bowl, soup; Elephant & Baby (Rabbit), stamped registered/imp .600.00
Bowl, soup; Rabbit, flared rim, stamped/imp, 1½x9¼" 275.00
Bowl, Swan, stamped, 2¾x6⅛" 475.00
Bowl, whipped cream; Rabbit, stamped, 2½x7½" 325.00
Butter pat, petal design w/floral decor, stamped, 3¼" 400.00
Charger, Rabbit, stamped registered/imp, 12" 600.00
Chocolate pot, Rabbit, stamped/incised, 8¾x6" 1,200.00
Coaster, Polar Bear, stamped registered, 4" 600.00
Creamer, Rabbit, Davenport rebus, inscr, 3¼x5½" 600.00
Creamer, Rabbit, stamped, 3⅜" 350.00
Cup & saucer, demi; Rabbit, Davenport rebus, stamped 400.00
Cup & saucer, demi; Rabbit, stamped registered/imp 300.00
Cup & saucer, Iris, stamped registered, 2¼", 6", NM 350.00
Cup & saucer, Rabbit, stamped, 2", 6" dia 225.00

Cup plate, Rabbit, stamped registered, 4¼" 300.00
Egg cup, dbl; Butterfly & Flower, stamped, 3x3" 500.00
Egg cup, dbl; Rabbit, partial stamp, 3x3¼" 300.00
Egg cup, Rabbit, unmk, 2½" 200.00
Egg cup, Rabbit, w/lid, stamped, 4¼x4½" 600.00
Flower frog, rabbit figural, stamped registered, 1931 ....1,000.00
Mug, Chick, stamped, child sz, 3x4½" 2,500.00
Olive dish, Rabbit, stamped, 1½x8" 650.00
Pitcher, Mushroom, stamped/imp, 4¾x6" 1,150.00
Pitcher, Oak Block, unmk, 6x6" 700.00
Pitcher, Rabbit, stamped registered, 4½x5" 500.00
Plate, Azalea, stamped registered/imp, 10" 400.00
Plate, Azalea, stamped/imp, 8½" 325.00
Plate, Butterfly & Flower, stamped/imp, rstr, 10" 700.00
Plate, Butterfly & Flower, stamped/imp, 6" 475.00
Plate, Clover, stamped registered/imp, 8¼" 1,000.00
Plate, Crab & Seaweed, Davenport rebus, stamped/imp, 8½" 800.00
Plate, Day Lily, Davenport rebus, stamped/imp, 6⅛" 750.00
Plate, Double Turtle, stamped, 8½" 1,000.00
Plate, Duck, Davenport rebus, stamped/imp, 10" 450.00
Plate, Duck, stamped/imp, 6" 350.00
Plate, Elephant, stamped registered/imp, 7½" 600.00
Plate, Elephant & Baby, stamped registered/imp, 8¼" 750.00
Plate, emb cherubs/goats under gr (w/skips), stamped, 9" 575.00
Plate, Grape, att Davenport, stamped/imp, 6" 200.00
Plate, Grape, stamped/imp, 10" 375.00
Plate, Horse Chestnut, Davenport rebus, stamped, 8½" 325.00
Plate, Horse Chestnut, stamped registered/imp, 9¾" 300.00
Plate, Horse Chestnut, stamped/imp, 8½" 250.00
Plate, Iris, Davenport rebus, imp, 6" 225.00
Plate, Lobster, prof rstr, stamped/imp, 8¼" 400.00
Plate, Lobster, stamped, 6" 600.00
Plate, Luna Moth, stamped/imp, 8½" 700.00
Plate, Magnolia, stamped, 6" 200.00
Plate, Magnolia, stamped registered, 6¼" 200.00
Plate, Magnolia, stamped/imp, 8½" 275.00
Plate, Mushroom, Davenport rebus, stamped/imp, 9¾" 1,100.00
Plate, Mushroom, stamped/imp, 8½" 800.00
Plate, Polar Bear, stamped registered/imp, 7½" 600.00
Plate, Polar Bear, stamped/imp, 1931, 8⅛" 750.00
Plate, Pond Lily, Davenport rebus, stamped/imp, 9¾" 375.00
Plate, Pond Lily, stamped registered/imp, sgn HR, 6" 575.00
Plate, Pond Lily, stamped/imp, 6" 250.00
Plate, Poppy, stamped/imp, 8½" 325.00
Plate, Rabbit, att Davenport, imp, 6⅛" 250.00
Plate, Rabbit, stamped, 10" 275.00
Plate, Rabbit, stamped, 6¼" 200.00
Plate, Rabbit, stamped registered/imp, 7½" 225.00
Plate, Rabbit, stamped registered/imp, 8½" 250.00
Plate, Rabbit, stamped/imp, 8½" 250.00
Plate, Raised Pond Lily, imp, flake on ft, 8½" 130.00
Plate, Snowtree, Davenport rebus, stamped/imp, 8½" 425.00
Plate, Snowtree, stamped registered/imp, chip on ft, 7½" 150.00
Plate, Swan, stamped registered/imp, 8½" 500.00
Plate, Tufted Duck, imp, 8½" 500.00
Plate, Turkey, Davenport rebus, stamped, 8½" 450.00
Platter, Rabbit, stamped registered/imp, 14x8½" 1,200.00
Salt cellar, Rabbit, walnut on leaf form, mk DP, 3¼" dia 900.00
Shaker, pepper; Elephant & Baby, ink stamp, 2¾" 500.00
Shaker, Rabbit, unmk, open base w/cork, 2¾" 225.00
Shaker, Rabbit, unmk, 3½" 250.00
Spoon, Rabbit, hand thrown, ladle shape, stamped, 4½" L 750.00
Star dish, Elephant, 5-pointed, stamped, 1932, 1½x7½" 950.00
Stein, Rabbit, Davenport rebus, stamped, 4½x5¼" 500.00

Sugar bowl, Rabbit, stamped, w/lid, 4½" 350.00
Teapot, Rabbit, semibulbous, stamped registered, 1931, 6⅛" ..1,000.00
Teapot, Swan, bulging lid, stamped registered, 5¾x7" 1,300.00
Tile, Rabbit, stamped, 6" dia 400.00
Tile, Swan, stamped registered, 4¾" dia, NM 550.00

Miscellaneous

Candle holders, elephant decor, bl & wht, 1½", pr 950.00
Vase, brn/tan/dk bl/blk cratered drip glaze, shouldered, 8x6" ..1,000.00
Vase, buff-colored gloss, bulbous w/can neck, HCR, 3½x3¾" 700.00
Vase, sang-de-boeuf w/thick red mottle, 4½" 650.00
Vase, thick sang-de-boeuf metallic irid, can neck, mk, 5", NM ..550.00
Vase, thin gr/gray/yel, bulbous shoulder, incised mk, 6¾x5" 650.00

Degenhart

　　　The Crystal Art Glass factory in Cambridge, Ohio, opened in 1947 under the private ownership of John and Elizabeth Degenhart. John had previously worked for the Cambridge Glass Company and was well known for his superior paperweights. After his death in 1964, Elizabeth took over management of the factory, hiring several workers from the defunct Cambridge Company, including Zack Boyd. Boyd was responsible for many unique colors, some of which were named for him. From 1964 to 1974, more than twenty-seven different moulds were created, most of them resulting from Elizabeth Degenhart's work and creativity, and over 145 official colors were developed. Elizabeth died in 1978, requesting that the ten moulds she had built while operating the factory were to be turned over to the Degenhart Museum. The remaining moulds were to be held by the Island Mould and Machine Company, who (complying with her request) removed the familiar 'D in heart' trademark. The factory was eventually bought by Zack's son, Bernard Boyd. He also acquired the remaining Degenhart moulds, to which he added his own logo.

　　　In general, slags and opaques should be valued 15% to 20% higher than crystals in color.

Heart Toothpick, White Opalescent, $22.00.

Baby Shoe (Hobo Boot) Toothpick Holder, Caramel 15.00
Baby Shoe (Hobo Boot) Toothpick Holder, Custard Slag 40.00
Baby Shoe (Hobo Boot) Toothpick Holder, Nile Green 15.00
Baby Shoe (Hobo Boot) Toothpick Holder, Pearl Gray 20.00
Basket Toothpick Holder, Cobalt 15.00
Basket Toothpick Holder, Mint Green 20.00
Basket Toothpick Holder, Ruby 25.00
Beaded Oval Toothpick Holder, Amethyst 15.00
Beaded Oval Toothpick Holder, Bittersweet Slag 45.00
Beaded Oval Toothpick Holder, Concord Grape 25.00
Beaded Oval Toothpick Holder, Rubina 60.00
Beaded Oval Toothpick Holder, Tomato 45.00
Bell, Amber 12.00

Bell, Pink Lady	20.00
Bird Salt & Pepper, Antique Blue, pr	35.00
Bird Salt & Pepper, Canary, pr	20.00
Bird Salt & Pepper, Forest Green, pr	30.00
Bird Salt & Pepper, Peach Blo, pr	25.00
Bird Salt & Pepper, Persimmon, pr	25.00
Bird Toothpick Holder, Antique Blue	25.00
Bird Toothpick Holder, Bernard Boyd's Ebony	35.00
Bird Toothpick Holder, Gun Metal	20.00
Bird Toothpick Holder, Teal	15.00
Bow Slipper, Blue Jay Slag	27.50
Bow Slipper, Dark Amber	15.00
Bow Slipper, Heliotrope	45.00
Bow Slipper, Old Lavender	15.00
Bow Slipper, Peach (clear)	15.00
Bow Slipper, Smoky Heather	20.00
Bow Slipper, Willow Green	25.00
Buzz Saw Wine, Bloody Mary	65.00
Buzz Saw Wine, Pistachio	25.00
Chick Salt (Covered Dish), Apple Green, 2"	25.00
Chick Salt (Covered Dish), Concord Grape, 2"	35.00
Chick Salt (Covered Dish), Persimmon, 2"	20.00
Coaster, Amethyst	8.00
Coaster, Pearl Gray	15.00
Coaster, Sapphire	8.00
Colonial Drape Toothpick Holder, Forest Green	15.00
Colonial Drape Toothpick Holder, Sunset	20.00
Daisy & Button Creamer & Sugar, Amber	75.00
Daisy & Button Creamer & Sugar, Opal White	90.00
Daisy & Button Creamer & Sugar, Sapphire	75.00
Daisy & Button Hat, Aqua	20.00
Daisy & Button Hat, Nile Green	20.00
Daisy & Button Hat, Rose Marie	15.00
Daisy & Button Salt, Cambridge Pink	15.00
Daisy & Button Salt, Tomato	30.00
Daisy & Button Toothpick Holder, Bluebell	25.00
Daisy & Button Toothpick Holder, Elizabeth's Lime Ice	20.00
Daisy & Button Wine, Amber	20.00
Daisy & Button Wine, Milk Blue	40.00
Daisy & Button Wine, Sapphire Carnival	35.00
Elephant Head Toothpick Holder, Honey Amber	27.00
Elephant Head Toothpick Holder, Pink	25.00
Forget-Me-Not Toothpick Holder, Baby Pink Slag	25.00
Forget-Me-Not Toothpick Holder, Blue Fire Opal	25.00
Forget-Me-Not Toothpick Holder, Bluina	40.00
Forget-Me-Not Toothpick Holder, Chad's Blue	20.00
Forget-Me-Not Toothpick Holder, Gray Green Slag	20.00
Forget-Me-Not Toothpick Holder, Henry's Blue	15.00
Forget-Me-Not Toothpick Holder, Misty Green	22.50
Gypsy Pot Toothpick Holder, Bloody Mary	50.00
Gypsy Pot Toothpick Holder, Golden Glo	15.00
Gypsy Pot Toothpick Holder, Vaseline	20.00
Hand, Blue Fire	15.00
Hand, Caramel	25.00
Hand, Fog	20.00
Hand, Opalescent	7.00
Hand, Red	12.00
Hand, Willow Blue	10.00
Heart & Lyre Cup Plate, Custard Slag	25.00
Heart & Lyre Cup Plate, Forest Green	8.00
Heart & Lyre Cup Plate, Sunset	10.00
Heart Jewel Box, Amberina	25.00
Heart Jewel Box, Baby Green	25.00
Heart Jewel Box, Blue Marble Slag	45.00
Heart Jewel Box, Delft Blue	25.00
Heart Jewel Box, Heatherbloom	40.00
Heart Jewel Box, Nile Green	25.00
Heart Toothpick Holder, Blue & White Slag	25.00
Heart Toothpick Holder, Blue Slag	30.00
Heart Toothpick Holder, Elizabeth's Blue	45.00
Heart Toothpick Holder, Maverick	35.00
Heart Toothpick Holder, Pink Lady	20.00
Hen Covered Dish, 3", Amethyst & Cobalt	35.00
Hen Covered Dish, 3", Tiger	30.00
Hen Covered Dish, 5", Apple Green	65.00
Hen Covered Dish, 5", Cambridge Pink	50.00
Hen Covered Dish, 5", Rubina	225.00
High Boot, Crown Tuscan	45.00
High Boot, Emerald Green	25.00
Kat Slipper, Amberina	35.00
Kat Slipper, Dark Slag	30.00
Kat Slipper, Holly Green	20.00
Kat Slipper, Pigeon Blood	35.00
Kat Slipper, Tiger	40.00
Lamb Covered Dish, Amberina	75.00
Lamb Covered Dish, Custard	60.00
Lamb Covered Dish, Lavender	75.00
Lamb Covered Dish, Lemon Custard	70.00
Mini Pitcher, Amberina	20.00
Mini Pitcher, Frosted Crystal	9.00
Mini Pitcher, Jade	25.00
Mini Pitcher, Vaseline	15.00
Mini Slipper w/o Sole, Amberina	25.00
Mini Slipper w/o Sole, Custard	35.00
Mini Slipper w/Sole, Persimmon	35.00
Owl, Antique Blue	40.00
Owl, Baby Green Slag	75.00
Owl, Bloody Mary	150.00
Owl, Blue Jay	50.00
Owl, Daffodil	40.00
Owl, Dichromatic Blue Green	100.00
Owl, Dirty Sally	60.00
Owl, Green Maverick	75.00
Owl, Indigo Variant	100.00
Owl, January Blizzard w/Blue Slag	200.00
Owl, Light Amethyst	30.00
Owl, Midnight Sun	50.00
Owl, Mystery Suprise	300.00
Owl, Shamrock, Frosted	35.00
Owl, Tangerine	175.00
Owl, Toffee	40.00
Owl, Wonder Blue	45.00
Pooch, Blue & White Slag	35.00
Pooch, Crystal	15.00
Pooch, End of Blizzard	35.00
Pooch, Lavender Gray	25.00
Pooch, Opal Green Slag	30.00
Pooch, Powder Blue Slag	45.00
Portrait Plate, Cobalt	45.00
Portrait Plate, Frosted Green	36.00
Portrait Plate, Red	60.00
Priscilla, Baby Green	150.00
Priscilla, Blue Lady Variant	125.00
Priscilla, Fawn	95.00
Priscilla, Orchid	125.00
Robin Covered Dish, Aqua	65.00
Robin Covered Dish, Crystal	35.00
Robin Covered Dish, Fawn	65.00

Robin Covered Dish, Mint Green **60.00**
Robin Covered Dish, Rose Marie, dark **50.00**
Robin Covered Dish, Tomato **125.00**
Roller Skate (Skate Shoe), Custard Slag **75.00**
Roller Skate (Skate Shoe), Vaseline **35.00**
Seal of Ohio Cup Plate, Amberina **15.00**
Seal of Ohio Cup Plate, Brown **10.00**
Seal of Ohio Cup Plate, Honey Amber **10.00**
Seal of Ohio Cup Plate, Pine Green **15.00**
Seal of Ohio Cup Plate, Teal **10.00**
Star & Dew Drop Salt, Ivory **25.00**
Star & Dew Drop Salt, Lemon Opal **25.00**
Star & Dew Drop Salt, Tomato **50.00**
Stork & Peacock Child's Mug, Milk Blue **25.00**
Texas Boot, Baby Green **22.00**
Texas Boot, Chocolate Slag **25.00**
Texas Creamer & Sugar, Amethyst **50.00**
Texas Creamer & Sugar, Amethyst Carnival, hand stamped **100.00**
Texas Creamer & Sugar, Custard **100.00**
Tomahawk, Apple Green **30.00**
Tomahawk, Blue & White Slag **75.00**
Tomahawk, Dichromatic **45.00**
Turkey Covered Dish, Emerald Green **50.00**
Turkey Covered Dish, Ruby **90.00**
Wildflower Candle Holder, Bluebell, ea **25.00**
Wildflower Candy Dish, Amberina **40.00**
Wildflower Candy Dish, Green **20.00**
Wildflower Candy Dish, Rose Marie **20.00**

Delatte

Delatte was a manufacturer of French cameo glass. Founded in 1921, their style reflected the influence of the Art Deco era with strong color contrasts and bold design. Our advisor for this category is Don Williams; he is listed in the Directory under Missouri.

Cameo

Lamp, floral, red on butterscotch, bullet form, 15" **2,785.00**
Lamp, sea gulls on shade, ships on std, seaweed base, 18" **3,450.00**
Vase, fruit/vines, brn-lav mottle, tapered, 6" **500.00**
Vase, fuchsia vines, rose on wht/raspberry mottle, 11" **1,000.00**
Vase, rhododendron, wine on mc mottle, metal base, 16" **1,800.00**
Vase, Venetian cityscape, rose on pk/wht, frost hdls, 6x7" **1,250.00**

Miscellaneous

Vase, abstract Deco motif, mc on cased red, bottle form, 11" **475.00**
Vase, lt gr/dk bl mottle, flat-sided bulb, 15" **225.00**

Delft

Old Delftware, made as early as the 16th century, was originally a low-fired earthenware coated in a thin opaque tin glaze with painted-on blue or polychrome designs. It was not until the last half of the 19th century, however, that the ware became commonly referred to as Delft, acquiring the name from the Dutch village that had become the major center of its production. English, German, and French potters also produced Delft, though with noticeable differences both in shape and decorative theme.

In the early part of the 18th century, the German potter, Bottger, developed a formula for porcelain; in England, Wedgwood began pro-

ducing creamware — both of which were much more durable. Unable to compete, one by one the Delft potteries failed. Soon only one remained. In 1876 De Porcelyne Fles reintroduced Delftware on a hard white body with blue and white decorative themes reflecting the Dutch countryside, windmills by the sea, and Dutch children. This manufacturer is the most well known of several operating today. Their products are now produced under the Royal Delft label. Examples listed here are blue on white unless noted otherwise. See also specific manufacturers.

Bottle, English, Oriental coast, crimped rim, 1760, 9" **985.00**
Bowl, English, floral, mc, 1765, 9", EX **300.00**
Charger, Bristol, floral panels, ca 1740, 13¾" **360.00**
Charger, Dutch, floral landscape, medallions form border, 12" ...**330.00**
Charger, Dutch, landscape w/floral border, orange rim, 13¾" **330.00**
Charger, Dutch, mc floral, drilled for hanging, 16⅝" **770.00**
Charger, Dutch, mc floral w/birds in tree, 16½", EX **715.00**
Charger, English, lady w/cornucopia/mtns/trees, 1750s, 14", VG ..**600.00**
Charger, Fazakerly, floral, mc, ca 1760, 13" **900.00**
Charger, William & Mary, titled portraits, 1690, 13½" **990.00**
Dish, Dutch, Chinese style, early 1700s, 10⅛", EX **250.00**
Dish, Dutch, Oriental landscape, lobed, 18th C, 14", NM **900.00**
Figurine, Dutch, cow w/milkmaid, wht/mc, 1780s, 8", EX, pr **985.00**
Flower brick, English, Oriental landscape, 4½" L, pr **550.00**
Humidor, Dutch, floral cartouch titled St Vincent, 9", VG **220.00**
Jar, drug; Neopolitan, classical figures, mc, 1750s, 6⅝" **600.00**
Jar, Dutch, Chinese figures/landscape, late 1600s, 8½", G **650.00**
Jar, Dutch, Oriental scenes, brass lid, 11½" **625.00**
Plate, Bristol, Oriental figural scene, mc, 1760, 9", VG **300.00**
Plate, Bristol (att), Oriental landscape, 8⅞" **440.00**
Plate, Dutch, Oriental florals, octagonal, 9⅜" **225.00**
Plate, English, floral wheel, sm sqs in border, rstr, 14" **245.00**
Plate, Lambeth, house in landscape, bl & purple, 8½" **275.00**
Plate, Liverpool, Oriental coast, 1750, 8¾", EX **220.00**

Posset pot, Dutch, multicolor floral design, with lid, ca 1770, minor restorations, 10", $1,495.00.

Sculpture, bust of Napolean, sgn SB, dtd 1809, 11¾" **500.00**
Tile, Viking ship, deeply cvd, 5-color, 5x9" **350.00**
Tray, Oriental design, 4⅞x7¼" **195.00**
Vase, Dutch, floral panels/scroll, dome lid, 1780s, 16", EX **1,000.00**
Vase, Dutch, floral vases in panels, dog finial, 1800s, 25" **1,150.00**
Vase, Dutch, William of Orange, cut corners, 9", EX **435.00**
Wall pocket, Lambeth, cornucopia w/mask head, wht, 8", VG ..**465.00**

Denver

The Denver China and Pottery Company began production in 1901 in Denver, Colorado. The founder, William A. Long, used materials native to Colorado to produce underglaze-decorated brownware as well as other artware lines. Several marks were used: an impressed 'Denver' (often with the Lonhuda Faience cipher inside a shield), an imprinted 'Denaura,' and an arrow mark.

Bowl vase, gr, ftd form w/inverted rim, Denaura, 6x7" 250.00
Napkin ring, floral on brn, 2x2" 95.00
Vase, burro on brn, 9½x5½" 275.00
Vase, floral on brn, integral hdls, 6x9" 500.00
Vase, floral on shaded bl bsk, initialed by Long, 9½x5½" 1,000.00
Vase, long-stem poppies on gr matt, mushroom shape, 6x5" ...1,400.00

Denver Terra Cotta Pottery

While on his honeymoon in Colorado, a young chemist by the name of George Frackt became aware of the natural clay deposits there. As an employe of the St. Louis Terra Cotta Company in Missouri, he was impressed with the samples he had analyzed and decided to establish his own terra cotta plant in Denver.

Within a short time, he opened a two-story plant with twelve employes, where he made finished products in high-gloss colors. The company consolidated with Northwestern Terra Cotta Company in 1924. Artificial stone or concrete came into production in 1925 and continued into the late 1920s. The exact date of closing is unknown. Look for pieces of great weight with high-gloss colors and stamped marks.

Ashtray, gargoyle figural, gr glossy, minimum value 95.00
Bookends, elephant figural, 7x8", pr 500.00
Bookends, owl figual, gray, 7x5", pr 225.00
Planter, frog figural, blk, minimum value 125.00
Vase, 4 buttresses on slim form, clear over yel clay, 7x6" 125.00

Denver White

In 1894 Frederick and Frank White settled in Denver, Colorado, and formed the F.J. White & Son Pottery Company. They located at 1434 Logan Street. After the death of Frederick in 1919, Frank moved the pottery to 1560 South Logan, where he remained until the company closed. He had a kiln set up at home and worked each day on the pottery, often selling his products in his front yard. On many occasions he was commissioned to produce specialty items for customers.

Each piece is hand thrown and many are dated. They are usually incised with the name Denver and the letter 'W' inside the capital 'D.' Many items are decorated with Colorado scenery. Though most pieces are matt glazed with a glossy interior, some later examples were completely glossy. The Whites would also add a small band to some of the ware, similar to what you see on Wedgwood pottery today. They created a line with swirled colors as well. On March 6, 1960, Frank White died at the age of 91.

Our advisors for this category are Jim and Carol Carlton, authors of Collector's Encyclopedia of Colorado Pottery; they are listed in the Directory under Colorado.

Vase, pine cones on white, signed Stabler, brown hi-gloss interior, 6", $125.00 minimum value.

Jar, bl bsk w/wht geometric band, mk Denver, w/lid, 5½" 225.00
Jar, geometric shoulder band, wht on med bl, w/lid, 5" 80.00
Pitcher, dk gr, cylindrical, 7" 95.00
Teapot, turq gloss, minimum value 200.00
Vase, brn & bl swirl, bulbous, flared rim, 6" 125.00
Vase, brn & bl swirl, classic form, 6" 150.00
Vase, deer & trees among mtns, sgn Skiff, 10" 500.00
Vase, dk gr matt, 3-hdld, dtd 1917, 5½" 350.00
Vase, drip effect (unusual), cylindrical, 8" 100.00
Vase, linear band imp at shoulder, bl w/lav int, 5" 140.00
Vase, tan/brn swirls under opaque wht, 4½" 90.00
Vase, turq gloss, scalloped rim, flared cylinder, 10" 750.00

Depression Glass

Depression glass is defined by Gene Florence, author of several bestselling books on the subject, as 'the inexpensive glassware made primarily during the Depression era in the colors of amber, green, pink, blue, red, yellow, white, and crystal.' This glass was mass produced, sold through five-and-dime stores and mail-order catalogs, and given away as premiums with gas and food products.

The listings in this book are far from being complete. If you want a more thorough presentation of this fascinating glassware, we recommend The Collector's Encyclopedia of Depression Glass, The Pocket Guide to Depression Glass, Elegant Glassware of the Depression Era, and Very Rare Glassware of the Depression Years by Gene Florence, whose address is listed in the Directory under Kentucky.

Key:
AOP — allover pattern   PAT — pattern at top

Adam, ashtray, gr, 4½" 25.00
Adam, bowl, cereal; pk or gr, 5¾", ea 40.00
Adam, bowl, pk, no lid, 9" 30.00
Adam, bowl, pk or gr, oval, 10", ea 30.00
Adam, butter dish, gr, w/lid 325.00
Adam, candlesticks, Delphite, 4", pr 225.00
Adam, candlesticks, pk, 4", pr 85.00
Adam, coaster, gr, 3¼" 20.00
Adam, cup, yel 100.00
Adam, lamp, gr 300.00
Adam, plate, dinner; gr, sq, 9" 28.00
Adam, plate, salad; pk, rnd, 7¾" 60.00
Adam, plate, sherbet; pk, 6" 9.00
Adam, platter, pk, 11¾" 28.00
Adam, saucer, yel, 6" 85.00
Adam, shakers, gr, ftd, 4", pr 100.00
Adam, sugar bowl, pk 17.50
Adam, sugar bowl/candy dish lid, gr 40.00
Adam, vase, pk, 7½" 265.00
American Pioneer, bowl, crystal, pk or gr, hdld, 5", ea 20.00
American Pioneer, candlesticks, gr, 6½", pr 90.00
American Pioneer, lamp, gr, tall, 8½" 110.00
American Pioneer, lamp, gr, w/metal pole, 9½" 60.00
American Pioneer, pilsner, crystal, pk or gr, 11-oz, 5¾", ea 100.00
American Pioneer, pitcher, urn; gr, w/lid, 7" 225.00
American Pioneer, tumbler, juice; crystal or pk, 5-oz, ea 25.00
American Sweetheart, bowl, berry; cremax, rnd, 9" 35.00
American Sweetheart, bowl, berry; pk, rnd, 9" 50.00
American Sweetheart, bowl, cereal; monax, 6" 13.50
American Sweetheart, bowl, console; monax, 18" 425.00
American Sweetheart, bowl, soup; smoke & other trims, 9½", ea ..100.00
American Sweetheart, creamer, bl, ftd 115.00

American Sweetheart, creamer, pk, ftd 13.00
American Sweetheart, cup, red 75.00
American Sweetheart, lamp shade, cremax 450.00
American Sweetheart, pitcher, pk, 80-oz, 8" 695.00
American Sweetheart, plate, dinner; pk, 9¾" 37.50
American Sweetheart, plate, salver; monax, 12" 17.50
American Sweetheart, plate, salver; red, 12" 130.00
American Sweetheart, plate, server; bl, 15½" 375.00
American Sweetheart, saucer, smoke & other trims, ea 15.00
American Sweetheart, tidbit, red, 3 tiers: 8", 12" & 15½" 575.00
American Sweetheart, tumbler, pk, 5-oz, 3½" 75.00
Aunt Polly, bowl, berry; bl, lg, 7⅞" 45.00
Aunt Polly, bowl, berry; gr, 4¾" 8.00
Aunt Polly, bowl, pickle; gr, hdld, oval, 7¼" 15.00
Aunt Polly, butter dish, bl, w/lid 210.00
Aunt Polly, candy dish, bl, ftd, 2-hdld 30.00
Aunt Polly, creamer, bl 45.00
Aunt Polly, plate, sherbet; gr, 6" 6.00
Aunt Polly, shakers, bl 210.00
Aunt Polly, tumbler, bl, 8-oz, 3⅝" 28.00
Aunt Polly, vase, bl, ftd, 6½" 55.00
Aurora, bowl, cereal; cobalt or pk, 5⅜", ea 15.00
Aurora, bowl, cobalt or pk, deep, 4½", ea 50.00
Aurora, cup, gr 7.50
Aurora, plate, cobalt or pk, 6½", ea 12.00
Aurora, saucer, gr 2.50
Aurora, saucer, pk 6.00
Avocado, bowl, gr, deep, 3¼x9½" 135.00
Avocado, bowl, relish; crystal, ftd, 6" 9.00
Avocado, bowl, salad; pk, 7½" 35.00
Avocado, cup, pk, ftd, 2 styles, ea 30.00
Avocado, pitcher, pk, 64-oz 750.00
Avocado, plate, cake; crystal, 2-hdld, 10¼" 14.00
Avocado, saucer, pk, 8" 22.00
Avocado, tumbler, gr 265.00
Beaded Block, bowl, crystal, 1-hdl, 5½" 7.50
Beaded Block, bowl, jelly; ice bl, 2-hdld, 4⅞"-5" 16.00
Beaded Block, bowl, pickle; gr, 2-hdld, 6½" 13.00
Beaded Block, bowl, pk, rnd, deep, 6" 11.00
Beaded Block, bowl, vaseline, rnd, flared, 7¼" 18.00
Beaded Block, creamer, amber 16.00
Beaded Block, pitcher, crystal, jug style, 1-pt, 5¼" 80.00
Beaded Block, sugar bowl, red 25.00
Block Optic, bowl, berry; pk, lg, 8½" 30.00
Block Optic, bowl, cereal; gr, 5¼" 14.00
Block Optic, butter dish, gr, w/lid, 3x5" 45.00
Block Optic, candy jar, pk or gr, w/lid, tall, 2¼", ea 50.00
Block Optic, comport, mayonnaise; gr, 4" wide 30.00
Block Optic, creamer, any style, any color 13.00
Block Optic, goblet, wine; gr or pk, 4½", ea 35.00
Block Optic, ice/butter tub, pk, open 90.00
Block Optic, pitcher, gr or pk, 54-oz, 8½", ea 40.00
Block Optic, plate, grill; yel, 9" 40.00
Block Optic, plate, luncheon; gr, yel or pk, 8", ea 5.00
Block Optic, sherbet, yel, 5½-oz, 3¼" 9.00
Block Optic, tumble-up night set, gr 62.50
Block Optic, tumbler, gr or pk, 12-oz, 4⅞", ea 25.00
Block Optic, tumbler, gr or pk, 9½-oz, flat, 3⅞", ea 15.00
Block Optic, tumbler, pk, 3-oz, 2⅝" 22.50
Block Optic, tumbler, yel, ftd, 9-oz 22.00
Block Optic, whiskey, pk, 1-oz, 1⅝" 40.00
Bowknot, bowl, cereal; gr, 5½" 20.00
Bowknot, cup, gr 8.00
Bowknot, plate, salad; gr, 7" 12.00

Bowknot, sherbet, gr, low ftd 16.00
Bowknot, tumbler, gr, ftd, 10-oz, 5" 20.00
Cameo, bowl, berry; pk, lg, 8¼" 150.00
Cameo, bowl, cereal; gr or yel, 5½", ea 30.00
Cameo, bowl, console; yel, 3-legged, 11" 95.00
Cameo, bowl, soup; gr, rimmed, 9" 55.00
Cameo, butter dish, gr 210.00
Cameo, candy jar, pk, w/lid, low, 4" 475.00
Cameo, comport, mayonnaise; gr, 5" dia 30.00
Cameo, creamer, pk, 4¼" 110.00
Cameo, decanter, gr, frosted, w/stopper, 10" 32.00
Cameo, plate, grill; gr, closed hdls, 10½" 65.00
Cameo, plate, sherbet; yel, 6" 3.00
Cameo, platter, yel, closed hdls, 12" 40.00

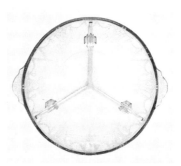

Cameo, green: 2-part relish tray, 7½" diameter, $30.00.

Cameo, sherbet, gr, molded, 3⅛" 13.00
Cameo, sugar bowl, yel, 3¼" 18.00
Cameo, tumbler, gr, 15-oz, 5¼" 70.00
Cameo, tumbler, pk, ftd, 11-oz, 5¾" 125.00
Cameo, tumbler, yel, ftd, 9-oz, 5" 16.00
Cherry Blossom, bowl, berry; pk or gr, rnd, 8½", ea 45.00
Cherry Blossom, bowl, fruit; pk or gr, 3-legged, 10½", ea 90.00
Cherry Blossom, butter dish, pk, w/lid 72.50
Cherry Blossom, cup, pk or Delphite, ea 18.00
Cherry Blossom, pitcher, pk or gr, PAT, flat, 42-oz, 8", ea 52.50
Cherry Blossom, plate, cake; pk or gr, 3-legged, 10¼", ea 30.00
Cherry Blossom, plate, dinner; gr, 9" 22.00
Cherry Blossom, plate, grill; gr, 9" 25.00
Cherry Blossom, plate, sherbet; pk or gr, 6", ea 8.00
Cherry Blossom, platter, pk, oval, 11" 37.50
Cherry Blossom, shakers, gr, scalloped bottom, pr 995.00
Cherry Blossom, sugar bowl, Delphite 18.00
Cherry Blossom, tumbler, pk, AOP, ftd, 4-oz, 3¾", ea ...18.00
Cherryberry, bowl, berry; pk or gr, deep, 7½", ea 20.00
Cherryberry, bowl, crystal, 2" deep, 6¼" 37.50
Cherryberry, butter dish, pk or gr, ea 165.00
Cherryberry, comport, pk or gr, 5¾", ea 24.00
Cherryberry, olive dish, crystal, 1-hdld, 5" 9.00
Cherryberry, pitcher, pk or gr, 7¾", ea 165.00
Cherryberry, plate, salad; crystal, 7½" 8.00
Cherryberry, sugar bowl, pk or gr, open, sm, ea 17.00
Chinex Classic, bowl, decal decor, 11" 35.00
Chinex Classic, bowl, vegetable; plain ivory, 7" 14.00
Chinex Classic, butter dish, castle decal, w/lid 125.00
Chinex Classic, cup, brnstone or plain ivory, ea 4.50
Chinex Classic, plate, sandwich/cake; castle decal, 11½" 25.00
Chinex Classic, plate, sherbet; decal decor, 6¼" 3.50
Circle, bowl, gr or pk, 4½", ea 8.00
Circle, bowl, gr or pk, 8", ea 16.00
Circle, goblet, wine; gr or pk, 4½", ea 12.50
Circle, pitcher, gr or pk, 80-oz, ea 27.50

Circle, plate, gr or pk, 9½", ea 12.00
Circle, plate, luncheon; gr or pk, 8¼", ea 4.00
Circle, sherbet, gr or pk, 3⅛", ea 6.00
Circle, tumbler, tea; gr or pk, 10-oz, 5", ea 16.00
Cloverleaf, ashtray, blk, match holder in center, 5¾" ...77.50
Cloverleaf, bowl, cereal; yel, 5" 35.00
Cloverleaf, bowl, dessert; pk, 4" 14.00
Cloverleaf, bowl, salad; gr, deep, 7" 40.00
Cloverleaf, bowl, salad; yel, deep, 7" 50.00
Cloverleaf, candy dish, yel, w/lid 100.00
Cloverleaf, plate, sherbet; blk, 6" 37.50
Cloverleaf, shakers, yel, pr 110.00
Cloverleaf, tumbler, gr, flat, 9-oz, 4" 52.50
Cloverleaf, tumbler, pk, flat, flared, 10-oz, 5¾" 22.00

Colonial, pink: Pitcher, 8", $65.00.

Colonial, bowl, berry; crystal, lg, 9" 22.00
Colonial, bowl, cream soup; pk, gr or crystal, 4½", ea 65.00
Colonial, butter dish, pk, w/lid 650.00
Colonial, cheese dish, gr 225.00
Colonial, goblet, wine; crystal, 2½-oz, 4½" 16.00
Colonial, plate, dinner; crystal, 10" 30.00
Colonial, plate, luncheon; pk or gr, 8½", ea 9.00
Colonial, spoon holder, pk 130.00
Colonial, tumbler, lemonade; gr, 15-oz 75.00
Colonial Block, bowl, pk or gr, 7", ea 17.00
Colonial Block, butter dish, pk or gr, ea 45.00
Colonial Block, butter tub, pk or gr, ea 40.00
Colonial Block, creamer, pk or gr, ea 12.00
Colonial Block, powder jar, pk or gr, w/lid, ea 17.50
Colonial Block, sugar bowl lid only, wht 4.50
Colonial Fluted, bowl, cereal; gr, 4" 9.00
Colonial Fluted, bowl, salad; gr, 2½x6½" 25.00
Colonial Fluted, creamer, gr 6.50
Colonial Fluted, plate, luncheon; gr, 8" 5.00
Colonial Fluted, sugar bowl, gr, w/lid 21.00
Columbia, bowl, soup; crystal, low, 8" 20.00
Columbia, butter dish, crystal, w/lid 20.00
Columbia, butter-dish bottom, crystal 12.50
Columbia, cup, pk 22.50
Columbia, plate, snack; crystal 35.00
Columbia, tumbler, water; crystal, 9-oz 27.50
Coronation, bowl, berry; Royal Ruby, hdld, lg, 8" 15.00
Coronation, bowl, berry; Royal Ruby, 4¼" 6.50
Coronation, bowl, gr, no hdls, 4¼" 30.00
Coronation, plate, luncheon; gr, 8½" 40.00
Coronation, plate, sherbet; pk, 6" 2.00
Coronation, sherbet, pk 4.50
Coronation, tumbler, pk, ftd, 10-oz, 5" 22.00
Cremax, bowl, vegetable; 9" 8.00
Cremax, cup, demitasse; bl 22.00
Cremax, plate, sandwich; ivory, 11½" 5.50

Cremax, saucer, demitasse; decor 9.00
Cube, butter dish, pk or gr, w/lid, ea 60.00
Cube, coaster, pk, 3¼" 7.00
Cube, cup, pk 7.50
Cube, powder jar, pk or gr, w/lid, 3-legged, ea 25.00
Cube, saucer, pk or gr, ea 3.00
Cube, tumbler, gr, 9-oz, 4" 70.00
Diamond Quilted, bowl, console; bl, rolled rim, 10½" 60.00
Diamond Quilted, cake salver, pk or gr, tall, 10" dia, ea .55.00
Diamond Quilted, compote, pk or gr, w/lid, 11½", ea 75.00
Diamond Quilted, ice bucket, bl or blk, ea 85.00
Diamond Quilted, pitcher, pk or gr, 64-oz, ea 50.00
Diamond Quilted, punch bowl & stand, pk or gr, ea 450.00
Diamond Quilted, sandwich server, bl or blk, center hdl, ea ...50.00
Diamond Quilted, vase, bl or blk, fan shape, dolphin hdls, ea ...75.00
Diana, bowl, console fruit; pk, 11" 40.00
Diana, bowl, salad; crystal, 9" 6.00
Diana, candy jar, amber, w/lid, rnd 35.00
Diana, plate, bread & butter; pk, 6" 4.00
Diana, saucer, amber 2.00
Diana, shakers, amber, pr 100.00
Dogwood, bowl, fruit; pk, 10¼" 495.00
Dogwood, cup, monax or cremax, thick, ea 40.00
Dogwood, pitcher, pk, American Sweetheart style, 80-oz, 8" ...575.00
Dogwood, saucer, monax or cremax, ea 20.00
Dogwood, tumbler, gr w/decor, 12-oz, 5" 110.00
Dogwood, tumbler, pk w/decor, 5-oz, 3½" 265.00
Doric, bowl, berry; Delphite, lg, 8¼" 125.00
Doric, bowl, cereal; pk, 5½" 50.00
Doric, bowl, cream soup; gr, 5" 395.00
Doric, pitcher, gr, flat, 32-oz, 5½" 40.00
Doric, pitcher, pk, ftd, 48-oz, 7½" 550.00
Doric, shakers, gr, pr 35.00
Doric, sherbet, Delphite, ftd 6.00
Doric, tumbler, pk, ftd, 12-oz, 5" 75.00
Doric, tumbler, pk, 9-oz, 4½" 65.00
Doric & Pansy, bowl, berry; gr or teal, lg, 8", ea 77.50
Doric & Pansy, bowl, pk or crystal, hdld, 9", ea 17.50
Doric & Pansy, butter dish, teal 450.00
Doric & Pansy, creamer, pk or crystal, ea 70.00
Doric & Pansy, plate, dinner; gr or teal, 9", ea 30.00
Doric & Pansy, saucer, pk or crystal, ea 4.00
Doric & Pansy, shakers, teal, pr 400.00
Doric & Pansy, sugar bowl, gr or teal, open, ea 110.00
English Hobnail, ashtray, pk or gr, sq, 4½", ea 20.00
English Hobnail, bonbon, ice bl, hdld, 6½" 37.50
English Hobnail, bowl, console; pk or gr, flanged, 12", ea ...40.00
English Hobnail, bowl, finger; ice bl, sq, ftd, 4½" 35.00
English Hobnail, bowl, nappy; pk or gr, cupped, 8", ea 30.00
English Hobnail, bowl, nappy; pk or gr, rnd, 6", ea 16.00
English Hobnail, bowl, pickle; pk or gr, 8", ea 27.50
English Hobnail, bowl, rose; pk or gr, 4", ea 45.00
English Hobnail, candlestick, pk or gr, rnd base, 3½", ea ...30.00
English Hobnail, candy dish, pk or gr, 3-ftd, ea 50.00
English Hobnail, cigarette box, ice bl, w/lid, 4½x2½" 50.00
English Hobnail, lamp, electric; pk or gr, 9¼", ea 110.00
English Hobnail, marmalade, ice bl, w/lid 65.00
English Hobnail, pitcher, pk or gr, rnd, 60-oz, ea 285.00
English Hobnail, pitcher, pk or gr, str sides, 32-oz, ea .165.00
English Hobnail, plate, torte; pk or gr, rnd, 14", ea 45.00
English Hobnail, saucer, pk or gr, rnd, ea 4.00
English Hobnail, stem, water goblet; ice bl, ftd, sq, 5-oz ...50.00
English Hobnail, tidbit, pk or gr, 2-tier, ea 42.50
English Hobnail, tumbler, iced tea; pk or gr, 12-oz, ea ...27.50

English Hobnail, vase, ice bl, flared top, 8½" 225.00
Fire-King Philbe, bowl, pk or gr, oval, 10", ea 50.00
Fire-King Philbe, bowl, vegetable; bl, oval, 10" 150.00
Fire-King Philbe, candy jar, crystal, w/lid, low, 4" 215.00
Fire-King Philbe, pitcher, bl, 56-oz, 8½" 1,175.00
Fire-King Philbe, pitcher, juice; crystal, 36-oz, 6" 295.00
Fire-King Philbe, plate, salver; pk or gr, 10½", ea 55.00
Fire-King Philbe, plate, sandwich; pk or gr, heavy, 10", ea 65.00
Fire-King Philbe, platter, pk or gr, closed hdls, 12", ea 125.00
Fire-King Philbe, sugar bowl, crystal, ftd, 3¼" 40.00
Fire-King Philbe, tumbler, crystal, ftd, 10-oz, 5¼" 30.00
Fire-King Philbe, tumbler, water; bl, flat, 9-oz, 4" 130.00
Floral, bowl, berry; Delphite, 4" 35.00
Floral, bowl, cream soup; pk or gr, 5½", ea 725.00
Floral, canister, jade-ite, 5¼" 50.00
Floral, comport, pk, 9" 800.00
Floral, lamp, gr 265.00
Floral, pitcher, lemonade; gr, 48-oz, 10¼" 250.00
Floral, plate, dinner; Delphite, 9" 135.00
Floral, tray, dresser set; gr, oval, 9¼" 185.00
Floral, tumbler, lemonade; pk, ftd, 9-oz, 5¼" 45.00
Floral, tumbler, water; Delphite, ftd, 7-oz, 4¾" 185.00
Floral, vase, gr, flared, 3-legged 475.00
Floral & Diamond Band, butter dish, pk, w/lid 130.00
Floral & Diamond Band, compote, pk, 5½" 15.00
Floral & Diamond Band, pitcher, gr, 42-oz, 8" 95.00
Floral & Diamond Band, sugar bowl, gr, w/lid, 5¼" 75.00
Floral & Diamond Band, tumbler, iced tea; gr, 5" 38.00
Floral & Diamond Band, tumbler, water; pk, 4" 20.00
Florentine No 1, ashtray, pk or yel, 5½", ea 28.00
Florentine No 1, bowl, berry; pk or yel, lg, 8½", ea 28.00
Florentine No 1, butter dish, crystal or gr, ea 125.00
Florentine No 1, creamer, yel 18.00
Florentine No 1, pitcher, crystal or gr, ftd, 36-oz, 6½", ea 40.00
Florentine No 1, plate, dinner; crystal or gr, 10", ea 16.00
Florentine No 1, platter, pk or yel, oval, 11½", ea 22.00
Florentine No 1, shakers, pk or yel, ftd, ea 55.00
Florentine No 1, sugar bowl, cobalt, ruffled 55.00
Florentine No 2, bowl, berry; pk, lg, 8" 30.00
Florentine No 2, bowl, crystal or gr, 5½", ea 32.00
Florentine No 2, bowl, vegetable; yel, w/lid, oval, 9" 65.00
Florentine No 2, butter dish, crystal or gr, ea 100.00
Florentine No 2, coaster, pk, 3¼" 16.00
Florentine No 2, cup, custard/jelly; crystal or gr, ea 60.00
Florentine No 2, pitcher, yel, ftd, 28-oz, 7½" 30.00
Florentine No 2, plate, crystal or gr, w/indent, 6¼", ea 17.50
Florentine No 2, plate, dinner; yel, 10" 14.00
Florentine No 2, platter, crystal or gr, oval, 11" ea 16.00
Florentine No 2, relish dish, pk, 3-part or plain, 10" 24.00
Florentine No 2, tumbler, crystal or gr, ftd, 5-oz, 3¼", ea 15.00
Flower Garden w/Butterflies, ashtray, amber, match pack holder ..165.00
Flower Garden w/Butterflies, bowl, blk, w/base, rolled edge, 9" ..200.00
Flower Garden w/Butterflies, candy dish, pk, w/lid, flat, 6" 155.00
Flower Garden w/Butterflies, cologne bottle, bl, w/stopper, 7½" ..275.00
Flower Garden w/Butterflies, compote, amber, fits 10" plate, 3" ...20.00
Flower Garden w/Butterflies, creamer, pk, gr or bl-gr, ea 70.00
Flower Garden w/Butterflies, plate, amber or crystal, 7", ea 16.00
Flower Garden w/Butterflies, powder jar, bl, ftd, 7½" 185.00
Flower Garden w/Butterflies, powder jar, pk or gr, flat, 3½", ea 75.00
Flower Garden w/Butterflies, tray, pk or gr, oval, 5½x10", ea 55.00
Flower Garden w/Butterflies, vase, pk or gr, 6¼", ea 125.00
Fortune, bowl, dessert; pk or crystal, 4½", ea 4.50
Fortune, candy dish, pk or crystal, w/lid, flat, ea 22.50
Fortune, plate, luncheon; pk or crystal, 8", ea 16.00

Fortune, tumbler, juice; pk or crystal, 5-oz, 3½", ea 8.00
Fruits, bowl, berry; gr, 8" 60.00
Fruits, bowl, berry; pk, 5" 20.00
Fruits, tumbler, gr, 12-oz, 5" 135.00
Fruits, tumbler, juice; gr, 3½" 30.00
Fruits, tumbler, pk, 1 fruit decor, 4" 15.00
Georgian, bowl, cereal; gr, 5¾" 22.50
Georgian, bowl, vegetable; gr, oval, 9" 60.00
Georgian, creamer, gr, ftd, 3" 11.00
Georgian, plate, luncheon; gr, 8" 9.00
Georgian, sugar bowl lid, gr, for 4" bowl 150.00
Georgian, tumbler, gr, flat, 12-oz, 5¼" 115.00
Hex Optic, bowl, berry; pk or gr, lg, 7½", ea 7.50
Hex Optic, bowl, mixing; pk or gr, 9", ea 22.00
Hex Optic, butter dish, pk or gr, w/lid, 1-lb size, ea 80.00
Hex Optic, pitcher, pk or gr, ftd, 48-oz, 9", ea 45.00
Hex Optic, plate, sherbet; pk or gr, 6", ea 2.50
Hex Optic, platter, pk or gr, 11", ea 12.50
Hex Optic, shakers, pk or gr, pr 27.50
Hex Optic, sugar shaker, pk or gr, ea 165.00
Hex Optic, tumbler, pk or gr, ftd, 7-oz, 4¾", ea 7.50
Hobnail, cup, pk 4.50
Hobnail, pitcher, crystal, 67-oz 25.00
Hobnail, tumbler, juice; crystal, 5-oz 4.00
Homespun, ashtray/coaster, pk or crystal, ea 6.50
Homespun, bowl, cereal; pk or crystal, closed hdls, 5", ea 25.00
Homespun, plate, dinner; pk or crystal, 9¼", ea 15.00
Homespun, sherbet, pk or crystal, low, flat, ea 16.00
Homespun, tumbler, pk or crystal, ftd, 15-oz, 6¼", ea 27.50
Homespun, tumbler, water; pk or crystal, flared top, 9-oz, 4", ea ...16.00
Indiana Custard, bowl, cereal; French Ivory, 6½" 20.00
Indiana Custard, bowl, vegetable; French Ivory, oval, 9½" 27.50
Indiana Custard, cup, French Ivory 37.50
Indiana Custard, plate, luncheon; French Ivory, 8⅞" 15.00
Indiana Custard, sherbet, French Ivory 90.00
Indiana Custard, sugar bowl, French Ivory, w/lid 30.00
Iris, bowl, berry; irid, beaded edge, 8" 20.00
Iris, bowl, fruit; crystal, straight edge, 11" 55.00
Iris, bowl, sauce; crystal, ruffled, 5" 9.00
Iris, candlestick, irid, pr 42.50
Iris, coaster, crystal 95.00
Iris, creamer, gr or pk, ftd, ea 110.00
Iris, goblet, irid, 8-oz, 5½" 195.00
Iris, goblet, wine; crystal, 3-oz, 4½" 16.00
Iris, irid, sugar bowl, crystal or irid, w/lid, ea 23.00
Iris, pitcher, crystal, ftd, 9½" 37.50
Iris, plate, dinner; irid, 9" 40.00
Iris, saucer, crystal 12.00
Iris, sherbet, irid, ftd, 4" 195.00
Iris, vase, gr or pk, 9", ea 130.00
Jubilee, bowl, fruit; yel, hdld, 9" 125.00
Jubilee, bowl, yel, 3-ftd, curved-in, 11½" 225.00
Jubilee, candy jar, pk or yel, w/lid, 3-ftd, ea 325.00
Jubilee, cup, pk, 2 styles 12.00
Jubilee, mayonnaise & plate, w/orig ladle, pk 310.00
Jubilee, plate, luncheon; yel, 8¾" 15.00
Jubilee, stem, sherbet/champagne; yel, 7-oz, 5½" 85.00
Jubilee, tray, sandwich; yel, center-hdld, 11" 200.00
Jubilee, tumbler, water; pk, 10-oz, 6" 75.00
Lace Edge, bowl, pk, ribbed, 9½" 30.00
Lace Edge, bowl, salad; pk, ribbed, 7¾" 45.00
Lace Edge, butter dish, pk, w/lid 65.00
Lace Edge, comport, pk, ftd, w/lid, 7" 47.50
Lace Edge, cup, pk 24.00

Lace Edge, plate, luncheon; pk, 8¼" 20.00
Lace Edge, relish dish, pk, deep, 3-part, 7½" 65.00
Lace Edge, relish plate, pk, 3-part, 10½" 25.00
Lace Edge, tumbler, pk, flat, 5-oz, 3½" 90.00
Laced Edge, bowl, opal, divided, oval, 11" 115.00
Laced Edge, bowl, opal, 5" 37.50
Laced Edge, bowl, soup; opal, 7" 80.00
Laced Edge, creamer, opal 40.00
Laced Edge, cup, opal 35.00
Laced Edge, mayonnaise, opal, 3-pc 135.00
Laced Edge, plate, salad; opal, 8" 32.00
Laced Edge, platter, opal, 13" 155.00
Laced Edge, tidbit, opal, 2-tiered, 8" & 10" plates 100.00
Lake Como, bowl, vegetable; wht, 9¾" 65.00
Lake Como, cup, St Denis, wht 27.50
Lake Como, plate, dinner; wht, 9¼" 30.00
Lake Como, saucer, St Denis, wht 12.00
Lake Como, shakers, wht, pr 42.50
Laurel, bowl, soup; wht opal or Jade Gr, 7⅞", ea 32.00
Laurel, bowl, vegetable; Poudre Bl, oval, 9¾" 45.00
Laurel, cheese dish, wht opal or Jade Gr, w/lid 52.50
Laurel, cup, French Ivory 7.00
Laurel, plate, dinner; wht opal or Jade Gr, 9⅛", ea 14.00
Laurel, plate, salad; French Ivory, 7½" 9.00
Laurel, shakers, French Ivory, pr 50.00
Laurel, sugar bowl, Poudre Bl, tall 30.00
Lincoln Inn, ashtray, cobalt or red, ea 17.50
Lincoln Inn, creamer, cobalt or red, ea 22.50
Lincoln Inn finger bowl; blk 12.50
Lincoln Inn, saucer, pk 3.50
Lorain, bowl, cereal; yel, 6" 60.00
Lorain, bowl, salad; crystal or gr, 7¼", ea 40.00
Lorain, bowl, vegetable; yel, oval, 9¾", ea 50.00
Lorain, cup, crystal or gr, ea 11.00
Lorain, plate, luncheon; yel, 8⅜" 26.00
Lorain, platter, crystal or gr, 11½", ea 25.00
Lorain, relish dish, yel, 4-part, 8" 35.00
Lorain, sherbet, crystal or gr, ftd, ea 20.00
Lorain, tumbler, yel, ftd, 9-oz, 4¾" 30.00
Madrid, bowl, berry; pk, lg, 9⅜" 19.00
Madrid, bowl, soup; gr, 7" 16.00
Madrid, butter dish, gr, w/lid 80.00
Madrid, candlestick, pk, 2¼", pr 20.00
Madrid, creamer, bl, ftd 20.00
Madrid, gravy boat & platter, amber 1,100.00
Madrid, jam dish, bl, 7" 35.00
Madrid, lazy susan, amber, wooden, w/cold-cut coasters 775.00
Madrid, pitcher, amber, ice lip, 80-oz, 8½" 60.00
Madrid, pitcher, amber, sq, 60-oz, 8" 45.00
Madrid, plate, dinner; gr, 10½" 35.00
Madrid, plate, luncheon; pk, 8⅞" 7.00
Madrid, plate, salad; bl, 7½" 20.00
Madrid, platter, pk, oval, 11½" 14.00
Madrid, shakers, gr, ftd, 3½", pr 90.00
Madrid, sugar bowl lid, gr 45.00
Madrid, tumbler, bl, 2 styles, 12-oz, 5½", ea 38.00
Manhattan, ashtray, crystal, sq, 4½" 18.00
Manhattan, bowl, crystal, closed hdls, 8" 20.00
Manhattan, candy dish, pk, 3-legged 12.00
Manhattan, comport, crystal or pk, 5¾", ea 32.00
Manhattan, creamer, pk, oval 11.00
Manhattan, pitcher, crystal, tilted, 80-oz 42.00
Manhattan, plate, dinner; pk, 10¼" 125.00
Manhattan, relish tray, crystal, 4-part, 14" 18.00

Manhattan, shakers, crystal, sq, 2", pr 27.50
Manhattan, sherbet, pk 15.00

Mayfair Federal, amber: Dinner plate, 9½", $14.00.

Mayfair Federal, bowl, cereal; gr, 6" 20.00
Mayfair Federal, bowl, cream soup; amber, 5" 18.00
Mayfair Federal, bowl, vegetable; crystal, oval, 10" 18.00
Mayfair Federal, cup, gr 8.50
Mayfair Federal, plate, grill; amber, 9½" 13.50
Mayfair Federal, plate, salad; amber, 6¾" 7.00
Mayfair Federal, platter, crystal, oval, 12" 20.00
Mayfair Federal, saucer, gr 4.50
Mayfair Federal, sugar bowl, crystal, ftd 11.00
Mayfair/Open Rose, bowl, gr, low, flat, 11¾" 40.00
Mayfair/Open Rose, bowl, vegetable; bl, oval, 9½" 67.50
Mayfair/Open Rose, bowl, vegetable; gr, 7" 125.00
Mayfair/Open Rose, butter dish, bl, w/lid, 7" 295.00
Mayfair/Open Rose, celery dish, gr or yel, divided, 9", ea 150.00
Mayfair/Open Rose, cookie jar, pk, w/lid 50.00
Mayfair/Open Rose, creamer, pk, ftd 27.50
Mayfair/Open Rose, goblet, bl, thin, 9-oz, 7¼" 180.00
Mayfair/Open Rose, goblet, cocktail; pk, 3-oz, 4" 85.00
Mayfair/Open Rose, pitcher, pk, 60-oz, 8" 55.00
Mayfair/Open Rose, plate, cake; gr, ftd, 10" 100.00
Mayfair/Open Rose, plate, cake; pk, w/hdls, 12" 40.00
Mayfair/Open Rose, plate, grill; bl, 9½" 52.50
Mayfair/Open Rose, shakers, pk, flat, pr 60.00
Mayfair/Open Rose, sherbet, gr or yel, ftd, 4¾", ea 150.00
Mayfair/Open Rose, tumbler, iced tea; pk, 13½-oz, 5¼" 57.50
Mayfair/Open Rose, tumbler, yel, ftd, 10-oz, 5¼" 180.00
Mayfair/Open Rose, whiskey, pk, 1½-oz, 2¼" 65.00
Miss America, bowl, cereal; crystal, 6¼" 10.00
Miss America, bowl, pk, curved in at top, 8" 72.50
Miss America, bowl, vegetable; pk, oval, 10" 28.00
Miss America, coaster, crystal, 5¾" 15.00
Miss America, cup, gr 12.00
Miss America, goblet, water; crystal, 10-oz, 5½" 21.00
Miss America, goblet, wine; Royal Ruby, 3-oz, 3¾" 250.00
Miss America, plate, salad; pk, 8½" 22.00
Miss America, plate, sherbet; gr, 5¾" 7.00
Miss America, platter, crystal, oval, 12¼" 14.00
Miss America, shakers, pk, pr 58.00
Miss America, sherbet, Royal Ruby 125.00
Moderntone, bowl, berry; cobalt, 5" 25.00
Moderntone, bowl, cereal; cobalt or amethyst, 6½", ea 75.00
Moderntone, butter dish, cobalt, w/metal lid 98.00
Moderntone, cup, cobalt or amethyst, ea 11.00
Moderntone, plate, dinner; cobalt, 8⅞" 17.50
Moderntone, plate, salad; cobalt, 6¾" 11.00
Moderntone, platter, amethyst, oval, 11" 37.50
Moderntone, saucer, cobalt 5.00
Moderntone, tumbler, amethyst, 9-oz 25.00
Moondrops, bowl, colors other than bl or red, hdld, oval, 9¾", ea 36.00

Moondrops, bowl, pickle; colors other than red or bl, 7½", ea 14.00
Moondrops, bowl, vegetable; bl or red, oval, 9¾", ea 45.00
Moondrops, butter dish, bl or red, w/lid, ea 450.00
Moondrops, candles, colors other than bl or red, ruffled, 2", pr 24.00
Moondrops, candlesticks, bl or red, metal stem, 8½", pr 40.00
Moondrops, comport, bl or red, 4", ea 27.50
Moondrops, cup, bl or red, ea 16.00
Moondrops, decanter, bl or red, rocket shape, 10¼", ea 450.00
Moondrops, goblet, water; bl or red, metal stem, 9-oz, 6¼", ea 23.00
Moondrops, mayonnaise, colors other than bl or red, 5¼", ea 32.00
Moondrops, pitcher, bl or red, 22-oz, 6⅞", ea 165.00
Moondrops, plate, salad; bl or red, 7⅛", ea 14.00
Moondrops, saucer, bl or red, ea 6.00
Moondrops, tumbler, bl or red, 7-oz, 4⅜", ea 16.00
Mt Pleasant, bonbon, pk or gr, rolled-up, hdld, 7", ea 16.00
Mt Pleasant, creamer, amethyst 19.00
Mt Pleasant, plate, grill; cobalt, 9" 12.00
New Century, bowl, berry; gr or crystal, 4½", ea 18.00
New Century, bowl, casserole; gr or crystal, w/lid, 9", ea 60.00
New Century, cup, pk 19.00
New Century, plate, breakfast; gr or crystal, 7⅛", ea 9.00
New Century, plate, dinner; gr or crystal, 10", ea 18.00
New Century, saucer, pk, cobalt or amethyst, ea 7.50
New Century, shakers, gr or crystal, pr 35.00
New Century, tumbler, gr or crystal, 5-oz, 3½", ea 12.00
New Century, tumbler, pink, cobalt or amethyst, 12-oz, 5¼", ea ..25.00
Newport, bowl, berry; amethyst, 4¾" 14.00
Newport, bowl, cereal; cobalt, 5¼" 35.00
Newport, cup, amethyst 10.00
Newport, plate, sandwich; cobalt, 11¾" 40.00
Newport, plate, sherbet; cobalt, 5⅞" 7.00
Newport, platter, amethyst, oval, 11¾" 35.00
Newport, shakers, cobalt, pr 47.50
Newport, sherbet, amethyst 13.00
Newport, tumbler, cobalt, 9-oz, 4½" 37.50
No 610 Pyramid, bowl, master berry; crystal, 8½" 16.00
No 610 Pyramid, bowl, pickle; pk or gr, 5¾x9½", ea 30.00
No 610 Pyramid, ice tub, gr 90.00
No 610 Pyramid, relish tray, crystal, hdld, 4-part 23.00
No 610 Pyramid, tray, pk, for creamer & sugar bowl 22.00
No 610 Pyramid, tumbler, yel, ftd, 2 styles, 8-oz 65.00
No 612 Horseshoe, bowl, cereal; gr or yel, 6½", ea 25.00
No 612 Horseshoe, bowl, salad; gr or yel, 7½", ea 23.00
No 612 Horseshoe, bowl, vegetable; yel, oval, 10½" 27.50
No 612 Horseshoe, butter dish, gr, w/lid 750.00
No 612 Horseshoe, creamer, gr, ftd 17.00
No 612 Horseshoe, plate, luncheon; yel, 9⅜" 13.50
No 612 Horseshoe, plate, salad; gr or yel, 8⅜", ea 10.00
No 612 Horseshoe, relish tray, gr, ftd, 3-part 20.00
No 612 Horseshoe, sherbet, yel 15.00
No 612 Horseshoe, tumbler, gr, 12-oz, 4¾" 160.00
No 612 Horseshoe, tumbler, gr or yel, ftd, 9-oz, ea 22.00
No 616 Vernon, creamer, gr or yel, ftd, ea 25.00
No 616 Vernon, cup, gr or yel, ea 15.00
No 616 Vernon, plate, luncheon; crystal, 8" 6.00
No 616 Vernon, sugar bowl, gr or yel, ftd, ea 25.00
No 616 Vernon, tumbler, gr or yel, ftd, 5", ea 35.00
No 618 Pineapple & Floral, bowl, berry; crystal, 4¾" 25.00
No 618 Pineapple & Floral, bowl, salad; amber or red, 7", ea 10.00
No 618 Pineapple & Floral, plate, sandwich; crystal, 11½" 17.50
No 618 Pineapple & Floral, plate, sherbet; amber or red, 8⅜", ea ..8.50
No 618 Pineapple & Floral, sherbet, amber or red, ftd, ea 18.00
No 618 Pineapple & Floral, tumbler, crystal, 12-oz, 5" 45.00
Normandie, bowl, cereal; amber, 6½" 25.00

Normandie, creamer, pk, ftd 11.00
Normandie, plate, grill; pk, 11" 17.00
Normandie, plate, salad; irid, 7¾" 52.50
Normandie, saucer, amber 4.00
Normandie, sugar bowl, irid 6.00
Old Cafe, bowl, crystal or pk, 5", ea 5.00
Old Cafe, candy dish, Royal Ruby, crystal or pk, low, 8", ea 11.00
Old Cafe, olive dish, crystal or pk, oblong, 6", ea 5.00
Old Cafe, pitcher, crystal or pk, 80-oz, ea 90.00
Old Cafe, tumbler, juice; Royal Ruby, 3" 10.00
Old English, bowl, fruit; pk, gr or amber, ftd, 9", ea 28.00
Old English, candy dish, pk, gr or amber, flat, w/lid, ea 50.00
Old English, compote, pk, gr or amber, 3½x7", ea 22.00
Old English, fruit stand, pk, gr or amber, ftd, 11", ea 40.00
Old English, pitcher, pk, gr or amber, w/lid, ea 120.00
Old English, sherbet, pk, gr or amber, 2 styles, ea 20.00
Old English, tumbler, pk, gr or amber, ftd, 4½", ea 22.50
Old English, vase, pk, gr or amber, 4½x8", ea 45.00
Ovide, bowl, cereal; wht w/decor, 5½" 13.00
Ovide, candy dish, blk, w/lid 40.00
Ovide, creamer, Art Deco 80.00
Ovide, fruit cocktail, gr, ftd 4.00
Ovide, plate, luncheon; Art Deco, 8" 45.00
Ovide, platter, wht w/decor, 11" 22.50
Ovide, sugar bowl, blk, open 6.50
Oyster & Pearl, bowl, crystal, 1-hdld, 5½" 8.00
Oyster & Pearl, bowl, fruit; Royal Ruby, deep, 10½" 50.00
Oyster & Pearl, plate, sandwich; crystal or pk, 13½", ea 18.00
Parrot, bowl, soup; gr, 7" 42.00
Parrot, bowl, vegetable; amber, oval, 10" 65.00
Parrot, butter dish, gr 350.00
Parrot, creamer, amber, ftd 60.00
Parrot, hot plate, gr, 5" 825.00
Parrot, plate, crystal, sq, 10¼" 26.00
Parrot, saucer, gr or amber, ea 15.00
Parrot, sugar bowl, gr 35.00
Parrot, tumbler, amber, 10-oz, 4¼" 100.00
Parrot, tumbler, gr, heavy, ftd, 5¾" 125.00
Patrician, bowl, berry; amber, crystal, pk or gr, 5", ea 12.00
Patrician, butter dish, gr, w/lid 110.00
Patrician, cookie jar, amber, w/lid 85.00
Patrician, cup, pk or gr, ea 11.00
Patrician, plate, grill; pk or gr, 10½", ea 15.00
Patrician, plate, salad; amber, crystal or pk, 7½", ea 15.00
Patrician, shakers, amber or crystal, pr 55.00
Patrician, sugar bowl lid, pk 60.00
Patrician, tumbler, gr, 9-oz, 4¼" 25.00
Patrick, bowl, console; pk, 11" 140.00
Patrick, candy dish, pk or yel, 3-ftd, ea 150.00
Patrick, creamer, pk 75.00
Patrick, goblet, cocktail; yel, 4" 80.00
Patrick, plate, luncheon; yel, 8" 27.50
Patrick, plate, sherbet; pk, 7" 20.00
Patrick, sherbet, pk, 4¾" 75.00
Patrick, tray, yel, 2-hdld, 11" 60.00
Petalware, bowl, berry; pk, lg, 9" 18.00
Petalware, bowl, cereal; crystal, 5¾" 4.00
Petalware, creamer, monax plain, ftd 6.00
Petalware, plate, salad; crystal, 8" 2.00
Petalware, plate, salver; pk, 11" 14.00
Petalware, plate, sherbet; cremax, 6" 6.00
Petalware, sugar bowl, cremax, ftd 10.00
Primo, bowl, yel or gr, 4½", ea 15.00
Primo, bowl, yel or gr, 7¾", ea 25.00

Primo, coaster/ashtray, yel or gr, ea 8.00
Primo, plate, grill; yel or gr, 10", ea 12.50
Primo, plate, yel or gr, 7½", ea 10.00
Primo, sherbet, yel or gr, ea 12.00
Primo, tumbler, yel or gr, 9-oz, 5¾", ea 20.00
Princess, bowl, berry; gr or pk, 4½", ea 25.00
Princess, bowl, salad; pk, octagonal, 9" 35.00
Princess, bowl, vegetable; topaz or apricot, oval, 10", ea 60.00
Princess, butter dish, gr or pk, ea 90.00
Princess, coaster, pk 65.00
Princess, cup, gr or pk, ea 12.00
Princess, plate, sandwich; gr, hdld, 10¼" 14.00
Princess, platter, gr or pk, closed hdls, 12", ea 24.00
Princess, shakers, topaz or apricot, 4½", pr 55.00
Princess, sugar bowl, gr 10.00
Princess, tumbler, topaz or apricot, ftd, 12½-oz, 6½", ea 150.00
Princess, tumbler, water; pk, 9-oz, 4" 25.00

Pyramid, green: Pickle dish, $30.00.

Queen Mary, ashtray, pk, oval, 2x3¾" 5.00
Queen Mary, bowl, berry; crystal, lg 8¾" 10.00
Queen Mary, bowl, berry; crystal, 5" 6.00
Queen Mary, bowl, cereal; pk, 6" 23.00
Queen Mary, bowl, pk, 1-hdl or none, 4" 5.00
Queen Mary, butter dish, pk 125.00
Queen Mary, candlesticks, crystal, dbl branch, 4½", ea 14.50
Queen Mary, cup, pk, lg 7.00
Queen Mary, relish tray, pk, 3-part, 12" 14.00
Queen Mary, tumbler, juice; pk, 5-oz, 3½" 9.00
Raindrops, bowl, cereal; gr, 6" 8.00
Raindrops, creamer, gr 7.50
Raindrops, shakers, gr, pr 295.00
Raindrops, sherbet, gr 6.50
Raindrops, sugar bowl lid, gr 40.00
Raindrops, tumbler, gr, 9½-oz, 4⅛" 9.00
Raindrops, whiskey, gr, 1-oz, 1⅞" 7.00
Ribbon, bowl, berry; blk, lg, 8" 35.00
Ribbon, bowl, cereal; gr, 5" 25.00
Ribbon, candy dish, gr, w/lid 35.00
Ribbon, cup, gr 5.00
Ribbon, plate, luncheon; blk, 8" 14.00
Ribbon, shakers, gr, pr 30.00
Ribbon, sugar bowl, gr, ftd 14.00
Ring, bowl, soup; crystal, 7" 10.00
Ring, butter/ice tub, w/decor or gr, ea 35.00
Ring, creamer, crystal, ftd 4.50
Ring, goblet, w/decor or gr, 9-oz, 7¼", ea 15.00
Ring, ice bucket, crystal 20.00
Ring, plate, sherbet; w/decor or gr, 6¼" 2.50
Ring, shakers, crystal, pr 20.00
Ring, sherbet, w/decor or gr, low, for 6½" plate, ea 15.00
Ring, tumbler, crystal, 10-oz, 4¾" 7.50
Ring, tumbler, crystal, 4-oz, 3" 4.00

Ring, tumbler, old fashioned; w/decor or gr, 8-oz, 4", ea 17.50
Ring, tumbler, water; w/decor or gr, ftd, 5½", ea 10.00
Rock Crystal, bowl, crystal, scalloped edge, 4½" 14.00
Rock Crystal, bowl, relish; crystal, 5-part, 12½" 45.00
Rock Crystal, bowl, salad; red, scalloped edge, 9" 110.00
Rock Crystal, candelabra, red, 3-light, pr 325.00
Rock Crystal, creamer, crystal, ftd, 9-oz 20.00
Rock Crystal, parfait, red, low ftd, 3½-oz 75.00
Rock Crystal, plate, red, scalloped edge, 9" 55.00
Rock Crystal, sandwich server, red, center hdl 145.00
Rock Crystal, spoon tray, crystal, 7" 20.00
Rock Crystal, spooner, crystal, ...40.00
Rock Crystal, stemware, goblet; red, ftd, lg, 8-oz 57.50
Rock Crystal, tumbler, red, concave or str sides, 9-oz, ea 52.50
Rock Crystal, vase, crystal, ftd 60.00

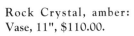

Rock Crystal, amber:
Vase, 11", $110.00.

Rose Cameo, bowl, berry; gr, 4½" 10.00
Rose Cameo, bowl, gr, str sides, 6" 20.00
Rose Cameo, sherbet, gr 12.00
Rose Cameo, tumbler, gr, 2 styles, ftd, 5", ea 20.00
Rosemary, bowl, berry; amber, 5" 6.00
Rosemary, bowl, cereal; pk, 6" 35.00
Rosemary, bowl, cream soup; gr, 5" 20.00
Rosemary, bowl, vegetable; amber, oval, 10" 14.00
Rosemary, cup, gr 9.50
Rosemary, plate, dinner; amber 9.00
Rosemary, platter, pk, oval, 12" 30.00
Rosemary, sugar bowl, pk, ftd 17.00
Rosemary, tumbler, amber or gr, 9-oz, 4¼", ea 30.00
Roulette, cup, crystal 36.00
Roulette, plate, sandwich; crystal, 12" 11.00
Roulette, plate, sherbet; pk or gr, 6", ea 4.50
Roulette, tumbler, iced tea; crystal, 12-oz, 5⅛" 16.00
Roulette, tumbler, juice; pk or gr, 5-oz, 3¼", ea 22.00
Roulette, tumbler, pk or gr, ftd, 10-oz, 5½", ea 27.50
Roulette, whiskey, crystal, 1½-oz, 2½" 8.00
Round Robin, bowl, berry; gr or irid, 4", ea 5.00
Round Robin, creamer, irid, ftd 6.50
Round Robin, plate, luncheon; gr or irid, 8", ea 4.00
Round Robin, plate, sandwich; irid, 12" 7.00
Round Robin, sugar bowl, gr 6.50
Roxana, bowl, berry; yel, 5" 10.00
Roxana, bowl, cereal; yel, 6" 15.00
Roxana, bowl, wht, 4½x2⅜" 14.00
Roxana, plate, sherbet; yel, 6" 7.50
Roxana, tumbler, yel, 9-oz, 4¼" 18.00
Royal Lace, bowl, berry; crystal, 5" 15.00
Royal Lace, bowl, gr, 3-legged, rolled edge, 10" 75.00
Royal Lace, bowl, pk, 3-legged, str edge, 10" 35.00
Royal Lace, butter dish, pk, w/lid 150.00
Royal Lace, candlestick, crystal, rolled edge, pr 45.00

Royal Lace, cookie jar, pk, w/lid 55.00
Royal Lace, pitcher, bl, str sides, 48-oz 155.00
Royal Lace, pitcher, crystal, w/lip, 68-oz, 8" 50.00
Royal Lace, pitcher, pk, w/lip, 96-oz, 8½" 95.00
Royal Lace, plate, luncheon; gr, 8½" 16.00
Royal Lace, platter, bl, oval, 13" 55.00
Royal Lace, sherbet, crystal, ftd 16.00
Royal Lace, tumbler, bl, 10-oz, 4⅞" 110.00
Royal Lace, tumbler, gr, 5-oz, 3½" 30.00
Royal Ruby, bowl, berry; 3¾" 5.50
Royal Ruby, bowl, heart shaped, 1-hdl, 5¼" 13.00
Royal Ruby, bowl, scalloped, 8" 37.50
Royal Ruby, bowl, 1-hdl, 5½" 13.00
Royal Ruby, candle holders, 4½", pr 65.00
Royal Ruby, cup 6.50
Royal Ruby, lamp 25.00
Royal Ruby, plate, sandwich; 13½" 45.00
Royal Ruby, tray, 6x4½" 12.50
S Pattern, bowl, berry; crystal, lg, 8½" 11.00
S Pattern, creamer, yel, amber or crystal w/trim, ea 7.00
S Pattern, pitcher, crystal, 80-oz, ea 52.50
S Pattern, plate, cake; crystal, heavy, 11¾" 40.00
S Pattern, plate, sherbet; monax, 6" 8.00
S Pattern, saucer, yel, amber or crystal w/trim, ea 2.50
S Pattern, sugar bowl, crystal, thick or thin, ea 5.50
S Pattern, tumbler, yel, amber or crystal w/trim, 12-oz, 5" 14.00
Sandwich, basket, amber or crystal, 10" tall, ea 35.00
Sandwich, bowl, console; amber or crystal, 9", ea 16.00
Sandwich, bowl, teal bl, hexagonal, 6" 14.00
Sandwich, creamer, red 45.00
Sandwich, cruet, pk or gr, w/stopper, 6½", ea 160.00
Sandwich, goblet, amber or crystal, 9-oz, ea 13.00
Sandwich, pitcher, red, 68-oz 130.00
Sandwich, plate, dinner; pk or gr, 10½", ea 20.00
Sandwich, plate, teal bl, indent for cup, oval, 8" 12.00
Sandwich, puff box, amber or crystal, ea 16.00
Sandwich, saucer, teal bl 4.50
Sandwich, sugar bowl, red, lg 45.00
Sandwich, wine, pk or gr, 4-oz, 3", ea 25.00
Sharon, bowl, cream soup; amber, 5" 27.50
Sharon, bowl, soup; amber or pk, flat, 1⅞x7¾", ea 50.00
Sharon, bowl, vegetable; gr, oval, 9½" 32.00
Sharon, butter dish, amber 46.00
Sharon, candy jar, gr, w/lid 160.00
Sharon, cup, amber 9.00
Sharon, pitcher, pk, w/o ice lip, 80-oz 145.00
Sharon, plate, salad; gr, 7½" 22.50
Sharon, shakers, amber, pr 40.00
Sharon, sugar bowl, pk 14.00
Sharon, tumbler, gr, thin, 9-oz, 4⅛" 70.00
Ships, cup, bl & wht, plain 11.00
Ships, ice bowl, bl & wht 35.00
Ships, plate, bread & butter; bl & wht, 5⅞" 22.00
Ships, plate, dinner; bl & wht, 9" 30.00
Ships, shot glass, bl & wht, 2-oz, 2¼" 155.00
Ships, tumbler, bl & wht, heavy bottom, 4-oz, 3¼" 27.50
Ships, tumbler, iced tea; bl & wht, 12-oz 22.00
Ships, tumbler, juice; bl & wht, 5-oz, 3¾" 12.00
Ships, tumbler, water; bl & wht, str sides, 9-oz, 3¾" 14.00
Sierra, bowl, berry; pk or gr, lg, 8½", ea 28.00
Sierra, butter dish, gr 65.00
Sierra, cup, pk 11.00
Sierra, plate, dinner; gr, 9" 22.00
Sierra, shakers, pk or gr, pr 37.50

Sierra, tumbler, pk, ftd, 9-oz, 4½" 55.00

Spiral, green: Pitcher, 7⅜", $30.00.

Spiral, bowl, mixing; gr, 7" 8.50
Spiral, creamer, gr, flat or ftd 7.50
Spiral, ice/butter tub, gr 26.00
Spiral, plate, sherbet; gr, 6" 2.00
Spiral, saucer, gr 2.00
Spiral, shakers, gr, pr 35.00
Spiral, sugar bowl, gr, flat or ftd, ea 7.50
Spiral, tumbler, water; gr, 9-oz, 5" 7.50
Starlight, bowl, cereal; pk, closed hdlds, 5½" 9.00
Starlight, bowl, crystal or wht, closed hdls, 8½", ea 10.00
Starlight, bowl, 2¾" deep, 12" wide 25.00
Starlight, plate, bread & butter; crystal or wht, 6", ea 3.00
Starlight, plate, sandwich; pk, 13" 15.00
Starlight, relish dish, crystal or wht, ea 14.00
Starlight, sherbet, crystal 13.00
Strawberry, bowl, crystal or irid, 2" deep, 6¼", ea 42.50
Strawberry, bowl, salad; pk or gr, deep, 6½", ea 18.00
Strawberry, butter dish, crystal or irid, ea 135.00
Strawberry, comport, pk or gr, 5¾", ea 19.00
Strawberry, pickle dish, oval, 8¼", ea 8.50
Strawberry, pitcher, pk or gr, 7¾", ea 150.00
Strawberry, plate, salad; crystal or irid, 7½", ea 10.00
Strawberry, tumbler, pk or gr, 8-oz, 3⅝", ea 30.00
Sunburst, bowl, berry; crystal, 4¾" 6.00
Sunburst, cup, crystal 6.00
Sunburst, relish dish, crystal, 2-part 12.00
Sunburst, tumbler, crystal, flat, 9-oz, 4" 17.50
Sunflower, ashtray, pk, center design only, 5" 9.00
Sunflower, cup, pk 12.00
Sunflower, saucer, gr 10.00
Sunflower, sugar bowl, pk 18.00
Sunflower, trivet, gr, 3-legged, turned-up edge, 7" 300.00
Swirl, bowl, cereal; pk, 5¼" 10.00
Swirl, bowl, lug soup; pk, tab hdls 24.00
Swirl, bowl, salad; ultramarine, rimmed, 9" 27.50
Swirl, butter dish, pk 190.00
Swirl, candle holders, Delphite, 1-branch, pr 115.00
Swirl, coaster, ultramarine, 1x3¼" 13.00
Swirl, plate, Delphite, 10½" 18.00
Swirl, plate, dinner; ultramarine, 9¼" 18.00
Swirl, plate, pk, 7¼" 6.50
Swirl, shakers, ultramarine, pr 42.00
Tea Room, bowl, banana split; gr, flat, 7½" 85.00
Tea Room, bowl, salad; pk, deep, 8¾" 67.50
Tea Room, candlesticks, gr, low, pr 48.00
Tea Room, cup, gr or pk, ea 50.00
Tea Room, marmalade, pk, notched lid 160.00
Tea Room, plate, sherbet; gr, 6½" 32.00
Tea Room, saucer, gr or pk, ea 28.00

Tea Room, sherbet, gr or pk, ftd, tall, ea 45.00
Tea Room, sugar bowl, gr, rectangular 20.00
Tea Room, tray, gr, center hdl 95.00
Tea Room, tumbler, gr, flat, 8-oz, 4⅛" 95.00
Tea Room, vase, gr, ruffled edge, 9½" 100.00
Thistle, bowl, berry; pk, lg, 10¼" 295.00
Thistle, bowl, cereal; gr, 5½" 22.00
Thistle, plate, grill; pk, 10¼" 17.50
Thistle, plate, luncheon; gr, 8" 18.00
Thistle, saucer, gr 9.50
Tulip, bowl, amethyst or bl, oblong, 13¼", ea 75.00
Tulip, creamer, amber, crystal or gr, ea 20.00
Tulip, ice tub, amethyst or bl, 3x4⅞", ea 60.00
Tulip, plate, amethyst or bl, 9", ea 14.00
Tulip, sherbet, amethyst or bl, flat, 3¾", ea 20.00
Tulip, tumbler, whiskey; amber, crystal or gr, ea 24.00
Twisted Optic, bowl, cereal; pk, 5" 5.50
Twisted Optic, bowl, console; canary yel, 10½" 35.00
Twisted Optic, bowl, cream soup; bl, 4¾" 16.00
Twisted Optic, candlesticks, gr, 2 styles, 3", pr 20.00
Twisted Optic, candy jar, amber, w/lid, ftd, flanged edge 30.00
Twisted Optic, candy jar, bl, w/lid, flat 50.00
Twisted Optic, creamer, bl 12.50
Twisted Optic, plate, pk, oval, w/indent, 7½x9" 5.00
Twisted Optic, plate, sandwich; bl, 10" 15.00
Twisted Optic, plate, sherbet; canary yel, 6" 4.00
Twisted Optic, sandwich server, gr, open center hdl 20.00
Twisted Optic, sherbet, canary yel 10.00
Twisted Optic, vase, amber, fan shape, 2-hdld, 7¼" 30.00
US Swirl, bowl, gr, 1-hdl, 5½" 9.50
US Swirl, bowl, gr or pk, oval, 2¾x8¼", ea 40.00
US Swirl, butter dish, gr or pk, ea 110.00
US Swirl, candy dish, pk, w/lid, 2-hdld 32.00
US Swirl, pitcher, gr or pk, 48-oz, 8", ea 50.00
US Swirl, shakers, gr or pk, pr 45.00
US Swirl, tumbler, gr, 12-oz, 4¾" 14.00
Victory, bowl, console; blk, 12" 65.00
Victory, bowl, soup; amber, flat, 8½" 20.00
Victory, comport, pk, 6" tall, 6¾" dia 15.00
Victory, gravy boat & platter, bl, set 325.00
Victory, plate, salad; gr, 7" 7.00
Victory, sandwich server, blk, center hdl 70.00
Victory, sugar bowl, amber 15.00
Vitrock, bowl, cereal; wht, 7½" 6.00
Vitrock, bowl, cream soup; wht, 5½" 15.00
Vitrock, bowl, soup; wht, flat 50.00
Vitrock, cup, wht 3.50
Vitrock, plate, luncheon; wht, 8¾" 4.50
Vitrock, platter, wht, 11½" 27.50
Waterford, bowl, cereal; crystal, 5½" 17.00
Waterford, butter dish, pk 220.00
Waterford, creamer, crystal, oval 5.00
Waterford, goblet, pk, Miss America style, 5½" 90.00
Waterford, plate, cake; pk, hdld, 10¼" 16.00
Waterford, plate, dinner; crystal, 9⅝" 11.00
Waterford, shakers, crystal, 2 types 8.50
Waterford, sugar bowl, crystal, Miss America style 35.00
Windsor, bowl, berry; pk, lg, 8½" 17.00
Windsor, bowl, crystal, pointed edge, 5" 5.00
Windsor, butter dish, gr, 2 styles, ea 85.00
Windsor, crystal, cup 3.50
Windsor, plate, dinner; gr, 9" 23.00
Windsor, plate, sherbet; pk, 6" 5.00
Windsor, powder jar, pk 55.00

Windsor, sugar bowl, crystal, like Holiday, w/lid 12.00
Windsor, tray, pk, w/o hdls, 8½x9¾" 85.00
Windsor, tumbler, gr, 12-oz, 5" 50.00

Derby

William Duesbury operated in Derby, England, from about 1755, purchasing a second establishment, The Chelsea Works, in 1769. During this period fine porcelains were produced which so impressed the King that in 1773 he issued the company the Crown Derby patent. In 1810, several years after Duesbury's death, the factory was bought by Robert Bloor. The quality of the ware suffered under the new management, and the main Derby pottery closed in 1848. Within a short time, the work was revived by a dedicated number of former employees who established their own works on King Street in Derby.

The earliest known Derby mark was the crown over a script 'D'; however this mark is rarely found today. Soon after 1782, that mark was augmented with a device of crossed batons and six dots, usually applied in underglaze blue. During the Bloor period, the crown was centered within a ring containing the words 'Bloor' above and 'Derby' below the crown, or with a red printed stamp — the crowned Gothic 'D.' The King Street plant produced figurines that may be distinguished from their earlier counterparts by the presence of an 'S' and 'H' on either side of the crown and crossed batons.

In 1876 a new pottery was constructed in Derby, and the owners revived the earlier company's former standard of excellence. The Queen bestowed the firm the title Royal Crown Derby in 1890; it still operates under that name today. See also Royal Crown Derby.

Figurine, Dr Syntax Departing in Calais, mc w/gold, 4½" 430.00
Figurine, Dr Syntax Reading, mc w/gold, 1820s, 3⅞" 260.00
Figurine, Dr Syntax Stretching, mc w/gold, ca 1865, 5", EX 700.00
Figurine, Dr Syntax Tied to a Tree, mc w/gold, ca 1820, 4" 520.00
Figurine, Dr Syntax Walking, mc w/gold, 5¼" 700.00
Figurine, Shepherdess, early 19th C, 9" 220.00
Potpourri, 3 goat-mask columns, hoof ft, baton mk, rprs, 9" 635.00
Stand, Imari pattern, factory mk, 1800-25, 14½" 550.00
Teapot, vines & bl band w/gold, #59, late 1700s, 7¼" 485.00
Vase, birds/foliage on bl, masks on loop hdls, 1870s, 6", pr 660.00
Vase, emb/HP/gilt floral, slim neck, scalloped, 1885, 5¼" 700.00

Desert Sands

As early as the 1850s, the Evans family living in the Ozark Mountains of Missouri produced domestic clay products. Their small pot shop was passed on from one generation to the next. In the 1920s it was moved to North Las Vegas, Nevada, where the name Desert Sands was adopted. Succeeding generations of the family continued to relocate, taking the business with them. From 1937 to 1962 it operated in Boulder City, Nevada; then it was moved to Barstow where it remained until it closed in the late 1970s.

Desert Sands pottery is similar to Mission Ware by Niloak. Various mineral oxides were blended to mimic the naturally occuring sand formations of the American West. A high-gloss glaze was applied to add intensity to the colorful striations that characterize the ware. Not all examples are marked, making it sometimes difficult to attribute. Marked items carry an ink stamp with the Desert Sands designation. Paper labels were also used.

Ashtray, 6½" 22.00
Bowl, console; hand thrown, 9½" 45.00
Bowl, incurvate rim, 3" 18.00

Bowl, 3", $15.00; Vase, inverted cylinder, 5", $25.00; Vase, flared rim, 3½", $25.00.

Butter dish 50.00
Shakers, pr 30.00
Tumbler 22.00
Vase, bulbous, flared rim, 3½" 35.00
Vase, inverted cylinder, slim, 5" 25.00

Devon, Crown Devon

Devon and Crown Devon were trade names of S. Fielding and Company, Ltd., an English firm founded after 1879. They produced majolica, earthenware mugs, vases, and kitchenware. In the 1930s they manufactured an exceptional line of Art Deco vases that have recently been much in demand.

Vase, goldfish on yel gloss, ink mk, 9" 260.00
Vase, mc geometric circles & lines, swollen form, Cooke, 9", NM ..130.00
Vase, petals w/in lg Vs, 5 stong colors, Hylan Cooke, 9x7" 550.00

Documents

Although the word 'document' is defined in the general sense as 'anything printed or written, etc., relied upon to record or prove something. . .,' in the collectibles market, the term is more diversified with broadsides, billheads, checks, invoices, letters and letterheads, land grants, receipts, and waybills some of the most sought after. Some documents in demand are those related to a specific subject such as advertising, mining, railroads, military, politics, banking, slavery, nautical, or legal (deeds, mortgages, etc.). Other collectors look for examples representing a specific period of time such as colonial documents, Revolutionary or Civil War documents, early western documents, or those from a specific region, state, or city.

Aside from supply and demand, there are five major factors which determine the collector-value of a document. These are:

1) Age — Documents from the eastern half of the country can be found that date back to the 1700s or earlier. Most documents sought by collectors usually date from 1700 to 1900. Those with 20th-century dates are still abundant and not in demand unless of special significance or beauty.

2) Region of origin — Depending on age, documents from rural and less-populated areas are harder to find than those from major cities and heavily populated states. The colonization of the West and Midwest did not begin until after 1850, so while an 1870s billhead from New York or Chicago is common, one from Albuquerque or Phoenix is not, since most of the Southwest was still unsettled.

3) Attractiveness — Some documents are plain and unadorned, but collectors prefer colorful, profusely illustrated pieces. Additional artwork and engravings add to the value.

4) Historical content — Unusual or interesting content, such as a letter written by a Civil War soldier giving an eyewitness account of the Battle of Gettysburg or a western territorial billhead listing numerous animal hides purchased from a trapper, will sell for more than one with mundane information.

5) Condition — Through neglect or environmental conditions, over many decades paper articles can become stained, torn, or deteriorated. Heavily damaged or stained documents are generally avoided altogether. Those with minor problems are more acceptable, although their value will decrease anywhere from 20% to 50%, depending upon the extent of damage. Avoid attempting to repair tears with scotch tape — sell 'as is' so that the collector can take proper steps toward restoration.

Foreign documents are plentiful; and though some are very attractive, resale may be difficult. The listings that follow are generalized; prices are variable depending entirely upon the five points noted above. Values here are based upon examples with no major damage. Common grade documents without significant content are found in abundance and generally have little collector value. These usually date from the late 1800s and early 1900s. It should be noted that the items listed below are examples of those that meet the criteria for having collector value. There is little demand for documents worth less than $5.00. For more information we recommend *Owning Western History* by our advisor Warren Anderson. His address and ordering information may be found in the Directory under Utah.

Key:
illus — illustrated   vgn — vignette

Assay certificate, Silverton CO, preprinted, 1896, 5x8" 28.00
Bank note, Canal Bank, New Orleans, $20, 1859, M 18.00
Bill of sale, 2 Negro boys & values, 1836, 6x9½" 175.00
Certificate, exchange; preprinted/filled in, 1864, EX 22.50
Check, depository; US Depository, Phila, fancy eng, 1865 ....8.00
Commission, MA, as sergeant, 1864, w/1869 Lieutenant discharge 200.00
Currency, Confederate, 1864, $20 bill 25.00
Currency, 25¢ note, Washington portrait, gr overprint, 1863 ....12.00
Discharge, Continental Army, sgn Brig Gen Enoch Poor, 1780 .225.00
Discharge, Revolutionary War, sgn twice, 1780 ....110.00
Estate appraisal, 1848, lists assets & slaves, 8x12", VG 100.00
Fractional note, 50¢, Edwin Stanton's portrait, 1866 ....12.00
Indenture, Bucks County, family & land, vellum, 1780 ....27.50
Indenture, NJ, preprinted, fancy printed title, 1908 ....15.00
Invoice, Boston, ships vgn, printed by Loring, 1849 ....12.00
Invoice, flour shipped on Britannia, NJ, 1772, EX 22.00
Invoice, Lone Star Gas Co, billed to Jack Ruby, 1956 ....20.00
Last will & testament, GA, bequests to slaves, 3-pg, 1861 ....75.00
Letter, Dept of War, re: money to widows, 1816 ....20.00
Letter, re: payment of inspector watching NY elections, 1845 ....6.50
Letter, VA, war news/talks of Gen Jackson/etc, 4-pg, EX 80.00
Letterhead, Major Gen GB McClellan, 5x8" sheet, EX 40.00
List, goods shipped to New Orleans, steamer vgn, 1861 ....4.00
Military Free Frank, Admiral JL Holloway Jr, 1945 ....20.00
Muster roll, preprinted, lists 38 soldiers/duties/etc, 1863 ....30.00
Oath, GA, promise not to sell liquor to Negroes, no date, 8x6" ...80.00
Oath of citizenship, Oct 1884, w/seal, EX 20.00
Orders, NH, Cavalry to report for duty, 1838 ....10.00
Patent papers, Spring Cat bank, CA Bailey, 2-pg, EX 95.00
Pension request, Confederate widow, details of service, 1900 ....5.00
Proclamation, death of B Harrison, blk border, 1901, 5x7" 10.00
Program, Official 1957 Miss America Pageant, 48-pg, NM 15.00
Receipt, arms/equipment w/costs, handwritten, dtd 1776, lg 75.00
Receipt, Gen Johnson's brigade receives cattle, 1864 ....15.00
Receipt, regimental needs, printed/filled in, 1776, G 65.00
Receipt, sale of animal skins, 1780s, 6x6" 45.00
Receipt, soldier's rations, 1829, 7½x2½", VG 10.00
Receipt, supplies to soldier's family, 1778, 6½x8½", G 35.00

Receipt, VA, food supplies, sgn Capt HL McKee, 1863, 3x5½" ...**15.00**
Report, tavern inspections in PA, 1887, 8½x12" **14.00**
Request, NH, listing for ammunition, 1864, 8x11" **12.00**
Subscription, New Orleans newspaper, 1865, 2½x9", G **15.00**
Tax receipt, VA, printed, section for slave tax, 1860s **15.00**
Warrant, MT, overprinted in red, Liberty vgn, 1893 ....**12.00**
Warrant, SD seal on left, vgn, 1905, check sz **6.50**
Writ, NH, summons for man, handwritten/printed, 1815 ....**22.50**

Dollhouses and Furnishings

Dollhouses were introduced commercially in this country late in the 1700s by Dutch craftsmen who settled in the East. By the mid-1800s, they had become meticulously detailed, divided into separate rooms, and lavishly furnished to reflect the opulence of the day. Originally intended for the amusement of adults of the household, by the latter 1800s their status had changed to that of a child's toy. Though many early dollhouses were lovingly hand fashioned for a special little girl, those made commercially by such companies as Bliss and Schoenhut are highly valued.

Furniture and furnishings in the Biedermeier style featuring stenciled Victorian decorations often sell for several hundred dollars each. Other early pieces made of pewter, porcelain, or papier-mache are also quite valuable. Certainly less expensive but very collectible, nonetheless, is the quality, hallmarked plastic furniture produced during the forties by Renwal and Acme, and the 1960s Petite Princess line produced by Ideal. In the listings that follow, dollhouses are litho paper on wood, unless otherwise noted. For more information, see *Schroeder's Collectible Toys, Antique to Modern.* Our advisor for this category is Barbara Rosen; she is listed in the Directory under New Jersey. See also Miniatures.

Furniture

Armoire, reddish-brn swirl, Ideal Young Decorator **25.00**
Bathinette, Renwal **15.00**
Bed, bright yel, hard plastic, Marx, ¾" scale **5.00**
Bed, turq spread, Ideal, 1969 ....**6.00**
Boudoir chaise lounge, bl, Ideal Petite Princess #4408-1 ....**18.50**
Chair, captain's; red, soft plastic, Marx, ½" scale **3.00**
Clock, mantel; red or ivory, Renwal #14 ....**10.00**
Cradle, pk, Best **6.00**
Crib, pk, soft plastic, Marx, ¾" scale **3.00**
Cupboard, ivory, Tootsietoy **20.00**
Fireplace w/andirons, brn & ivory, Plasco **12.00**

Grandfather clock, Ideal Petite Princess Fantasy Furniture, no folding screen (came without one), MIB, $36.00.

Grandfather clock, Ideal Petite Princess #4423-0 ....**18.00**
Hammock, Acme **20.00**
Highboy, yel, hard plastic, Marx, ½" scale **2.00**
Highchair, Ideal **22.00**

Hobby horse, metal, wht & gr, Durham Industries, ½" scale **8.00**
Hutch, pk, Superior, ¾" scale **5.00**
Ironing board, w/iron, Renwal **40.00**
Lamp, table; yel or brn w/ivory shade, Renwal #71 ....**8.00**
Laundry cart, Ideal **24.00**
Night stand, brn, Ideal **6.00**
Night stand, Strombecker, ¾" scale **5.00**
Potty chair, Renwal **10.00**
Refrigerator, yel, Imagination **2.00**
Rocker, Ideal **5.00**
Rocker, yel w/red trim, Acme **4.00**
Rocking horse, Acme **12.00**
Sewing machine, Renwal **35.00**
Sink, yel & bl, Ideal **35.00**
Sliding board, Acme **16.00**
Sofa, red, soft plastic, Marx, ¾" scale **3.00**
Stove, ivory w/blk door, Renwal #K69 ....**8.00**
Stroller, pk, Jeryco, MIB **8.00**
Sweeper, Ideal **22.00**
Table, dining; dk maroon swirl, Ideal **15.00**
Table, kitchen; lt bl, Plasco **5.00**
Table, wht, Allied **3.00**
Vanity, reddish-brn swirl, Ideal Young Decorator **20.00**
Vanity, yel, hard plastic, Marx, ¾" scale **5.00**
Victrola, gold, Tootsietoy **35.00**

Houses

Bliss, 2½ story/3 dormers/2 chimneys/balcony/porch, 1905, VG ..**3,100.00**
Bliss, 2-story/4-room, yel clapboard, porch & blacony, 23x20" ...**990.00**
Colonial style, wood/fiberboard, 4-room/attic, 1920s, 20x24x15" **350.00**
German, Butcher Shop, litho wood, complete w/figure/etc, 10x15" ..**3,500.00**
German, 2-story city building w/tower entrance, 17", EX **3,000.00**
German, 2-story/4-room/half-porch/balconies, 1890, 23x23", EX ..**990.00**
Marx, Colonial Doll House w/Disney characters, battery lights **70.00**
Marx, 2-story, red roof, patio above garage, ½" scale, EX **50.00**
McLoughlin, 2-story, Dolly's Playhouse, 1900, 18x12", EXIB **440.00**
Schoenhut, 2 columns, red tile roof, hinged side, 14x17x13", EX ...**900.00**
Schoenhut, 2-story/2-room, brick, red roof, columned porch, G ...**660.00**
Unknown, 3-story, wht slat-brd, gabled roof/balcony/porches, 34" ...**330.00**
Wolverine, Colonial Mansion, no garage, ½" scale, EX **45.00**

Dolls

Collecting dolls of any sort is one of the most rewarding hobbies in the United States. The rewards are in the fun, the search, and the finds — plus there is a built-in factor of investment. No hobby, be it dolls, glass, or anything else, should be based completely on investment; but any collector should ask: 'Can I get my money back out of this item if I should ever have to sell it?' Many times we buy on impulse rather than with logic, which is understandable; but by asking this question we can save ourselves a lot of 'buyer's remorse' which we have all experienced at one time or another.

Since we want to learn to invest our money wisely while we are having fun, we must become aware of defects which may devaluate a doll. In bisque, watch for eye chips, hairline cracks and chips, or breaks on any part of the head. Composition should be clean, not crazed or cracked. Vinyl and plastic should be clean with no pen or crayon marks. Though a quality replacement wig is acceptable for bisque dolls, composition and hard plastics should have their originals in uncut condition. Original clothing is a must except in bisque dolls, since it is unusual to find one in its original costume.

A price guide is only that — a guide. It suggests the average price for each doll. Bargains can be found for less-than-suggested values, and 'unplayed-with' dolls in their original boxes may cost more. Dealers must become aware of condition so that they do not overpay and therefore overprice their dolls — a common occurrence across the country. Quantity does not replace quality, as most find out in time. A faster turnover of sales with a smaller margin of profit is far better than being stuck with an item that does not sell because it is overpriced. It is important to remember that prices are based on condition and rarity. When no condition is noted, dolls are assumed to be in excellent condition with the exceptions of Armand Marseille, Cabbage Patch, Madame Alexander, Terri Lee, and Uneeda, which are priced in mint condition. In relation to bisque dolls, excellent means having no cracks, chips, or hairlines, being nicely dressed, shoed, wigged, and ready to to be placed into a collection. For a more thorough study of the subject, we recommend you refer to the many lovely doll books written by authority Pat Smith, available at your favorite bookstore or public library. If you're interested in Liddle Kiddles we recommend *Liddle Kiddles* (Collector Books) by Paris Langford.

Key:
bjtd — ball-jointed	OC — original clothes
blb — bent limb body	o/m — open mouth
bsk — bisque	p/e — pierced ears
c/m — closed mouth	pnt — painted
hh — human hair	pwt — paperweight eyes
hp — hard plastic	RpC — replaced clothes
jtd — jointed	ShHd — shoulder head
MIG — Made In Germany	ShPl — shoulder plate
NC — no clothes	SkHd — socket head
o/c/e — open closed eyes	str — straight
o/c/m — open closed mouth	trn — turned

American Character

Groom, hp, OC, 20"	500.00
Sweet Sue, hp, orig ballgown, 1958, 10½"	200.00
Sweet Sue, hp walker w/flat ft, saran wig, OC, 18", minimum	250.00
Sweet Sue, vinyl, curly brn hair, 1955, OC, 17"	300.00
Sweet Sue Bride, hp/vinyl, jtd knees/elbows, OC, 18", minimum	325.00
Sweet Sue Bridesmaid, hp/vinyl, pk gown, OC, 30", minimum	500.00
Tiny Tears, vinyl, RpC, 12"	55.00

Annalee

Barbara Annalee Davis has been making her dolls since 1950, originally as a hobby, but very soon on a commercial basis. Her creations range from tiny angels atop powder puff clouds to funky giant frogs. In between there are dolls for every occasion, with Christmas characters being her specialty. They're all characterized by their construction methods (felt over flexible wire framework) and their hand-painted faces with wonderful expressions. Naturally some of the older dolls are the most valuable (though more recent examples are desirable as well, depending on scarcity and demand), and condition, as usual, is very important. To date your doll, look at the tag. If made before 1986, that date is only the copyright date. (Dolls made after 1986 do carry the manufacturing date.) Dolls from the '50s have a long white red-embroidered tag with no date. From 1959 to '64, that same tag had a date in the upper right-hand corner. From 1965 until '70, it was folded in half and sewn into the seam. In 1970, a satiny white tag with a date preceded by a copyright symbol in the upper right-hand corner was used. In '75, the tag was a long white cotton strip with a copyright date. This tag was folded over in 1982, making it shorter. Our advisor for Annalees is Jane Holt; she is listed in the Directory under New Hampshire.

Windsurfer Mouse, Annalee birthdate on sail, 1982, 7", $150.00.

Photo courtesy Jane Holt

Angel w/star, 1988, 12"	50.00
Artist bunny, 1988, 18"	50.00
Ballerina bunny, 1981, 7"	65.00
Basketball player, 1993, 10"	50.00
Caroller girl, 1974, 10"	65.00
Caroller girl, 1974, 18"	100.00
Christmas Panda w/bag, 1985, 18"	100.00
Christopher Columbus in dome, 1991, 10"	225.00
Cowboy mouse, 1982, 7"	60.00
Cupid in hot-air balloon, 1987, 3"	60.00
Gnome w/mushroom, 1992, 7"	30.00
Hunter mouse w/rifle, 1974, 7"	140.00
Leprechaun, 1979, 10"	50.00
Logo Kid w/pin, 1989, 7"	80.00
Mark Twain in dome, 1986, 10"	225.00
Mrs Claus w/cape, 1971, 7"	30.00
Mrs Santa w/tray, 1979, 10"	50.00
Owl w/earmuffs, 1990, 5"	30.00
Reindeer, 1978, 36"	225.00
Reindeer w/Santa hat, 1985, 10"	20.00
Santa feeding reindeer, 1991, 10"	85.00
Santa frog w/bag, 1987, 10"	55.00
Santa on moon, 1983, 7"	50.00
Santa w/potbelly stove, 1984, 5"	50.00
Scrooge, 1988, 10"	75.00
Shepherd boy w/lamb, 1988, 7"	75.00
Slingshot angel, 1984, 12"	60.00
Stork w/baby in basket, 1987, 10"	95.00

Armand Marseille

Alma, ShHd, 12"	135.00
Alma, ShHd, 26"	485.00
AM, Darling Baby, 1906, 12"	350.00
AM, Floradora, ShHd, 23"	425.00
AM, Floradora, SkHd, 15"	250.00
AM, Floradora, SkHd, 17"	325.00
AM, Floradora 1374, ShHd, fur eyebrows, 21"	425.00
AM, Kiddiejoy, ShHd, 9"	225.00
AM, My Playmate (body), closed dome & c/m, 18"	1,800.00
AM, Roseland, 1910, 18"	485.00
AM, SkHd, c/m, 14"	950.00
AM, SkHd, o/m, blk, 12"	475.00
AM, SkHd, 17"	250.00
AM, SkHd, 8"	165.00
AM, trn ShHd, talks, 16"	500.00
AM 1894, SkHd, blk, 12"	375.00
AM 1894, SkHd, wht, 12"	200.00

AM 1894, SkHd, wht, 16½" 325.00
AM 1894, SkHd, 14" 250.00
AM 200, SkHd, googly eyes, 11½" 2,500.00
AM 231, Fany, baby, c/m, 1913, 25" 8,500.00
AM 250, mk GB (Geo Borgfeldt), SkHd, c/m, molded hair, 10½" ..500.00
AM 252, SkHd, googly eyes, 1915, 9½" 1,100.00
AM 253, SkHd, googly eyes, 6½" 750.00
AM 254, SkHd, googly eyes, molded hair, 8" 750.00
AM 257, baby, SkHd, 1914, 22" 550.00
AM 315, Queen Louise, SkHd, 27" 700.00
AM 3200, ShHd, some trn, 15" 275.00
AM 3200, ShHd, some trn, 1898, 16" 265.00
AM 3200, ShHd, some trn, 26" 600.00
AM 323, SkHd, googly eyes, 7½" 900.00
AM 327, SkHd, baby, fur hair, 1914, 12" 350.00
AM 327, SkHd, 1914, 20" 450.00
AM 329, girl, SkHd, 9" 275.00

AM 34¼ K Dream Baby, bisque socket head, blue sleep eyes, closed mouth, molded and painted hair, 5-piece bent limb body, in period clothing, 16", $500.00.

AM 341, My Dream Baby, flange, c/m, 15" 450.00
AM 341, My Dream Baby, flange, c/m, 1924, 7' 245.00
AM 341, My Dream Baby, SkHd, c/m, 16" 650.00
AM 3500, ShHd, 17" 400.00
AM 351, My Dream Baby, flange, o/m, 26" 900.00
AM 351, Wee One, rubber body, 1922, 7" 165.00
AM 3524, Baby Gloria, flange neck, 18" 1,200.00
AM 370, fur eyebrows (rare), 22½" 350.00
AM 370, 15" 225.00
AM 370, 19½" 350.00
AM 372, Kiddiejoy, ShHd, molded hair, 1926, 9" 350.00
AM 390, My Dearie, SkHd, 1908-22, 18" 400.00
AM 390, o/m, 7½" 175.00
AM 390, SkHd, 22" 385.00
AM 390, SkHd, 9½" 225.00
AM 390n, Patrice, 18" 500.00
AM 450, SkHd, c/m, provincial attire, 19" 1,650.00
AM 500, Infant Berry, molded hair, 1908, 5" 185.00
AM 500, Infant Berry, molded hair, 1908, 8" 265.00
AM 550, SkHd, c/m, 16" 1,700.00
AM 590, Hoopla Girl, o/c/e, o/c/m, 16" 1,800.00
AM 800, Baby Sunshine, 'Mama' talker in head, 1925, 16" 2,200.00
AM 95, trn ShHd, 20" 325.00
AM 970, Lady Marie, Otto Gans, 1916, 20" 700.00
AM 975, Sadie, baby, SkHd, 1914, 24" 800.00
AM 980, baby, SkHd, 14" 325.00
AM 990, Happy Tot, baby, SkHd, 13" 400.00
AM 990, Happy Tot, baby, SkHd, 1910, 21" 625.00
AM 991, Kiddiejoy, baby, SkHd, 14" 425.00
AM 995, baby, SkHd, 12" 300.00

AM 997, Kiddiejoy, baby, SkHd, 14" 425.00
Lily, ShHd, 1913, 17" 350.00
Mabel, ShHd, 1898, 17" 375.00
Queen Louise, 100, Germany, SkHd, 1910, 12" 25.00
Wonderful Alice, SkHd, fur eyebrows, 26" 650.00

Arranbee

Cloth w/compo head, arms & legs, bl sleep eyes, all orig, MIB ...145.00
Littlest Angel, hp, walker, jtd knees, o/c/e, OC, 10" 95.00
Miss Coty, rigid vinyl, rooted hair, o/c/e, 1957, OC, 10" 100.00
Nanette, hp, gold gown w/fur trim, 20", minimum 375.00
Nanette, hp, walker, head turns, OC, 21" 175.00
Nanette Bride, hp, 1950, OC, 21", minimum 375.00
Swiss Girl, compo, bl o/c/e, OC, 1946, 18" 250.00

Barbie Dolls and Related Dolls

Though the face has changed three times since 1959, Barbie is still as popular today as she was when she was first introduced. Named after the young daughter of the first owner of the Mattel Company, the original Barbie had a white iris but no eye color. These dolls are nearly impossible to find, but there is a myriad of her successors and related collectibles just waiting to be found. When no condition is indicated, the dolls listed below are assumed to be complete and mint in box unless otherwise specified. For further information we recommend *The World of Barbie Dolls* and *The Wonder of Barbie, 1976 — 1986*, by Paris, Susan, and Carol Manos; *The Collector's Encyclopedia of Barbie Dolls and Collectibles* by Sibyl DeWein and Joan Ashabraner, *Collector's Encyclopedia of Barbie Doll Exclusives and More* by Michael Augustyniak, *A Decade of Barbie Dolls and Collectibles, 1981-1991*, by Beth Summers, and *Barbie, The First Thirty Years*, by Stefanie Deutsch. *Barbie Fashion, Vol I, 1959 — 1967*, by Sarah Sink Eames, gives a complete history of the wardrobes of Barbie, her friends, and her family. Many of Patricia Smith's books contain chapters on Barbies as well as other dolls by Mattel.

Allan, 1964, pnt red hair, str legs, OC, M 70.00
Allan, 1965, bendable legs, bl trunks/red jacket 350.00
Barbie, 1958-59, #1, holes in ft, metal cylinders, 11½", MIB ..9,000.00
Barbie, 1959, #2, brunette hair, MIB 8,000.00
Barbie, 1960, #3, blond hair, orig swimsuit, NM+ 950.00
Barbie, 1960, #4, blond hair, replica swimsuit, NM 275.00
Barbie, 1960, #4, brunette hair, orig swimsuit, NM 425.00

Barbie, 1961, Ponytail, brunette, MIB, $475.00.

Barbie, 1961, Bubble-Cut, blond hair, orig swimsuit, EX 175.00
Barbie, 1961, Bubble-Cut, blond hair, orig swimsuit, MIB 450.00
Barbie, 1963, Fashion Queen, molded dk hair, 3 wigs/stand, MIB ..500.00
Barbie, 1964, Am Girl, blond hair w/side part, MIB 3,900.00

Barbie, 1971, Walk Lively, department-store special, MIB 200.00
Barbie, 1975, Deluxe Quick Curl, department-store special, MIB ...50.00
Barbie, 1979, Italian, MIB 200.00
Barbie, 1980, Parisienne, 1st in International series, MIB 200.00
Barbie, 1981, Magic Curl, department-store special, MIB 40.00
Barbie, 1983, Angel Face, M in worn box 35.00
Barbie, 1984, Irish, Dolls of the World series, MIB 135.00
Barbie, 1986, Dreamglo, orig outfit, VG 15.00
Barbie, 1987, California Dream, department-store special, MIB ...45.00
Barbie, 1988, Holiday, MIB 750.00
Barbie, 1989, Flight Time, MIB 25.00
Barbie, 1989, Ice Capades, MIB 30.00
Barbie, 1989, Mexican, Dolls of the World series, MIB 75.00
Barbie, 1990, Holiday, MIB 150.00
Barbie, 1991, Night Sensation, FAO Schwarz, MIB 225.00
Barbie, 1991, Platinum, Bob Mackie, MIB, from $600 to 700.00
Barbie, 1992, Benefit Ball, MIB 150.00
Barbie, 1992, Neptune Fantasy, Bob Mackie, MIB 1,000.00
Barbie, 1992, Pretty in Purple, K-Mart special, MIB 50.00
Barbie, 1993, Silver Screen, FAO Schwarz, MIB 200.00
Barbie, 1994, Holiday (Black), MIB 125.00
Christie, 1970, Twist 'N Turn, MIB 250.00
Christie, 1980, Golden Dream, department-store special, MIB 40.00
Courtney, 1990, Cool Tops, department-store special, MIB 30.00
Courtney, 1991, Pet Pals, department-store special, MIB 35.00
Francie, 1966, blond hair, bendable legs, orig swimsuit, NM 90.00
Francie, 1966, brunette hair, str legs, MIB 450.00
Francie, 1970, Malibu, orig outfit, VG 45.00
Ken, 1961, flocked blond hair, str legs, MIB 350.00
Ken, 1972, Busy, department-store special, MIB 35.00
Ken, 1975, Free Moving, pnt hair, OC, EX+ 35.00
Ken, 1979, Sport 'N Shave, MIB 35.00
Ken, 1980, Western, department-store special, MIB 35.00
Ken, 1991, Totally Hair, department-store special, MIB 55.00
Ken, 1994, Rhett Butler, Hollywood Legend series, MIB 65.00
Midge, 1963, blond hair, nude, NM 85.00
Midge, 1963, blond hair, str legs, freckles, MIB 200.00
Midge, 1963, blond hair, str legs, no freckles, MIB 500.00
Midge, 1965, titian hair, orig swimsuit, bendable legs, NM 250.00
Ricky, 1965, MIB 125.00
Skipper, 1965, blond hair, bendable legs, MIB 400.00
Skipper, 1970, titian hair, str legs, EX+ 60.00
Skipper, 1982, Horse Lovin', MIB 50.00
Skipper, 1986, Jewel Secrets, MIB 30.00
Skooter, 1965, brunette hair, str legs, orig swimsuit, NM 65.00
Skooter, 1976, Funtime, MIB 50.00
Stacey, 1967, Talking, titian hair, MIB 450.00
Stacey, 1967, Talking, titian hair, orig swimsuit, NM 165.00
Steffie, 1972, Walk Lively, brunette, bendable legs, OC, NM 125.00
Tuttie, 1966, blond or brunette hair, MIB 150.00

Barbie Gift Sets and Related Accessories

When no condition is indicated, the items listed below are assumed
to be mint and in the original box or package (if one was issued). Items
in only excellent condition may be worth 40% to 60% less.

Airplane, minimum value 1,000.00
Autograph book, 1962 ....30.00
Book, Barbie Color by Number, 1962, EX 25.00
Case, Barbie & Francie, bl, rnd, 1965, rare, EX 40.00
Clothes, Barbie Color Coordinates, #1832 ....750.00
Clothes, Campus Corduroys (Ken), #1410 ....75.00
Clothes, Country Clubbin' (Ken), #1400 ....135.00

Clothes, Drum Majorette, 1963 ....150.00
Clothes, Easter Parade, #900 series, 1958 ....900.00
Clothes, Enhanted Evening, pk gown, 1958 ....250.00
Clothes, Golden Glory, 1965 ....70.00
Clothes, Hollywood Premier, 1992 ....30.00
Clothes, Long 'N Short of It (Skipper), 1970 ....55.00
Clothes, Patio Party, 1966 ....100.00
Clothes, Pretty As a Picture, #1652 ....225.00
Clothes, Snow 'N Ride, 1988 ....55.00
Clothes, Sophisticated Lady, pk gown, red cape, 1963 ....300.00
Clothes, Travel Togethers, #1688 ....275.00

Barbie Color 'N Curl Set (Coiffure), European box marked 1966, MIB, $350.00.

Country Camper, 1970, #4994, NMIB 35.00
Dune buggy, 1970 ....300.00
Family House, minimum value 75.00
Game, Barbie Miss Lively Livin', Mattel, 1971, EXIB 25.00
Gift set, Barbie Foaming Beauty Bath, 1960s 110.00
Gift set, Barbie Perfectly Plaid, Sears, MIB (sealed) 350.00
Gift set, Ice Breaker, MIB, minimum value 600.00
Gift set, Olympic Gymnast, minimum value 85.00
Gift set, Round the Clock Wedding Party, 1965, minimum value ...850.00
Gift set, Tutti Nighty Night Sleep Tight, 1965 ....175.00
Horse, Dallas, palomino, M 60.00
Mercedes, gr, 1963, NMIB 150.00
Photo album 40.00
Record tote 25.00
Starcycle, #2149, 1978 ....12.00
Wristwatch, from $20 to 45.00

Belton

Concave head, 2 or 3 hole, EX bsk, o/c/m or c/m w/wig, 10" ...1,200.00
Concave head, 2 or 3 hole, EX bsk, o/c/m or c/m w/wig, 13" ...1,600.00
Concave head, 2 or 3 hole, EX bsk, o/c/m or c/m w/wig, 15" ...1,900.00
Concave head, 2 or 3 hole, EX bsk, o/c/m or c/m w/wig, 16" ...2,000.00
Concave head, 2 or 3 hole, EX bsk, o/c/m or c/m w/wig, 17" ...2,000.00
Concave head, 2 or 3 hole, EX bsk, o/c/m or c/m w/wig, 20" ...2,800.00
Concave head, 2 or 3 hole, EX bsk, o/c/m or c/m w/wig, 22" ...3,000.00
Concave head, 2 or 3 hole, EX bsk, o/c/m or c/m w/wig, 23" ...3,200.00
Concave head, 2 or 3 hole, EX bsk, o/c/m or c/m w/wig, 26" ...3,800.00
Concave head, 2 or 3 hole, EX bsk, o/c/m or c/m w/wig, 8" 800.00

Boudoir Dolls

Boudoir dolls, often called flapper dolls, were popular during the
1920s and 1930s, but they continued to be made up into the '40s as
well. These dolls are rarely marked, but most were made in the United
States, France, Italy, and Germany. Dolls of this type have silk or felt

painted face masks, elaborate cosumes, and are of excellent quality. The less expensive ones have composition heads and clothes that are stapled or nailed onto the body. Our advisor for this category is Bonnie Groves; she is listed in the Directory under Texas.

Anita, compo face/hands, inset lashes, silk OC, '20, 28", EX 135.00
Anita, nude & bald, 1920s, G 45.00
Cloth, pnt mask face, taffeta/lace dress, mohair wig, Fr, '20, 26" ...200.00
Compo, stapled clothes/hat, mohair wig, inset lashes, 1940s, VG ...50.00
Compo & cloth, mohair wig, inset lashes, mk Sterling, '30, EX 50.00
Finely pnt features, average clothes & quality, 16" 125.00
Finely pnt features, average clothes & quality, 28" 165.00
Finely pnt features, average clothes & quality, 32" 225.00
Finely pnt features, EX clothes & quality, 15", minimum 300.00
Finely pnt features, EX clothes & quality, 28", minimum 475.00
Finely pnt features, glass eyes, 28"-32", minimum 585.00
Finely pnt features, mini, 15", minimum 300.00
Finely pnt features, nude, 28"-32", ea, minimum 65.00
Harem girl, turban w/spit curls, harem pants, 27", minimum 600.00
Printed-on clothes, 27" 350.00
Silk face/floss hair, bsk limbs, lashes, silk OC, '20, Fr, 17", VG ..150.00
Smoking doll, cloth, 16"-17", minimum 285.00
Smoking doll, cloth, 25", minimum 465.00
Smoking doll, compo, 25", minimum 245.00
Smoking doll, compo, 28", minimum 375.00

Bru

Closed mouth, bisque socket head, blue paperweight eyes, pierced ears, composition body with straight wrists, 14", $12,000.00.

Closed mouth, all kid body, bsk lower arms; Bru, 13" 8,200.00
Closed mouth, all kid body, bsk lower arms; Bru, 18" 13,000.00
Closed mouth, all kid body, bsk lower arms; Bru 26" 26,000.00
Closed mouth, kid/wood body, bsk lower arms; Bru Jne, 14" .14,000.00
Closed mouth, kid/wood body, bsk lower arms; Bru Jne, 20" .21,000.00
Closed mouth, kid/wood body, bsk lower arms; Bru Jne, 28" .31,000.00
Closed mouth, mk Bru, circle dot, 16" 17,000.00
Closed mouth, mk Bru, circle dot, 19" 20,000.00
Closed mouth, mk Bru, circle dot, 26" 28,000.00
Open mouth, compo walker's body, throws kisses, 22" 9,600.00
Open mouth, nursing (Bebe), high color, late SFBJ, 12" 2,600.00
Open mouth, nursing (Bebe), high color, late SFBJ, 18" 4,500.00
Open mouth, nursing Bru (Bebe), early, EX bsk, 15" 7,000.00
Open mouth, SkHd, compo body; Bru, R, EX bsk, 14" 6,800.00
Open mouth, SkHd, compo body; Bru, R, EX bsk, 22" 8,800.00
Open mouth, SkHd, compo body; Bru, R, EX bsk, 28" 10,000.00

Cabbage Patch

Black boy or girl w/pacifier, 1984, MIB, minimum value 165.00

Black boy w/shaggy hair, freckles, 1983, MIB, minimum value ...400.00
Boy or girl w/no dimples, 1983, MIB, ea from $50 to 50.00
Boy w/tan shaggy hair & freckles, 1983, MIB 75.00
Coleco, astronaut, red signature, 1986, from $50 to 175.00
Coleco, Black freckled kid, 1983, from $225 to 175.00
Coleco, freckled girl or boy, 1983, minimum value 35.00
Coleco, popcorn hair, 1986, from $30 to 80.00
Coleco, red fuzzy-haired boys, 1983, from $175 to 300.00
Coleco, World Traveler, bl signature, 1985, from $40 to 45.00
Coleco, 1984-89, minimum value 35.00
Girl w/brunette ponytail, 1 tooth, 1985, MIB, minimum value ..150.00
Girl w/gray eyes, 1985, MIB, from $50 to 80.00
Girl w/2 blond ponytails, freckles, 1983, MIB, from $175 to 145.00
Hasbro, Teeny Tiny Preemie Twins (Oriental or Hispanic) 65.00
Hasbro, 16", from $25 to 50.00
Hasbro, 1989-94, minimum value 40.00
Lili Ledy, Mexico, from $75 to 175.00

Celebrity

Andy Gibb, Ideal, 1979, NMIB 35.00
Annie, porc, Applause, 1982, MIB 25.00
Barry Goldwater, Remco, 1964, NM 45.00
Betty Grable, compo, 1940s, OC, 21", NM 450.00
Boy George, vinyl, 1980s, 11½", MIB 50.00
Cheryl Tiegs, Matchbox, 1989, MIB 25.00
Deanna Durbin, compo, Ideal, 1939, OC, 14" 475.00
Diahann Carol (Julia), Mattel, as nurse, 11½", MIB 150.00
Dolly Parton, hp/vinyl, Eegee, 1987, 18", MIB 80.00
Dolly Parton, plastic/vinyl, red dress, Goldberger, '87, 17" 85.00
Elizabeth Taylor, World Dolls, 1988, 11½", M 50.00
Elvis Presley, Graceland, plastic/vinyl, 1984, MIB 75.00
Farrah Fawcett, jtd vinyl, Mego, 1977, 12¼", NM 25.00
Flying Nun, Hasbro, 12", MIB 95.00
General MacArthur, compo, all orig, 1930, 19", w/pin 285.00
Jackie Kennedy, plastic/vinyl, Horsman, 1961, OC, 25" 185.00
John Wayne, Effanbee Legend series, cowboy outfit, MIB 150.00
Judy Garland, compo, Ideal, 1939, OC, 14", minimum value ..1,000.00
Laurel & Hardy, Goldberger, 1986, 12", MIB, ea 45.00
Linda Evans (Crystal), jtd vinyl, World Doll, 1988, MIB 165.00
Mae West, Effanbee, Great Legends series, MIB 80.00
Marilyn Monroe, Tri-Str, 1982, 12", MIB, ea from $50 to 50.00
Mary Poppins, Horsman, Disney, 12", EXIB 75.00
Michael Jackson, LJN, Thriller outfit, 1984, 11½", MIP 30.00
Mr T, plastic/vinyl, Galoob, 1983, OC, 12" 25.00
Richard Chamberlain (Dr Kildare), rare, 11½", MIB 100.00
Sonja Henie, Madame Alexander, all orig, 18", M 450.00
Susan Dey (Laurie Partridge), Remco, 1973, OC, 19", MIB 150.00
Tiny Tim, felt features, wires in limbs for posing, 18" 50.00
Twiggy, Mattel, 1967, rare, 11½", MIB 250.00
Vanna White, World Dolls, w/accessories, 12" 45.00
Wayne Gretzky, Mattel, MIB 70.00

China, Unmarked

Adelina Patti, center part, curls at temples, 1860s, 14" 275.00
Adelina Patti, center part, curls at temples, 1860s, 18" 450.00
Adelina Patti, center part, curls at temples, 1860s, 22" 525.00
Biedermeier or Bald Head, takes wig, RpC, 14" 575.00
Biedermeier or Bald Head, takes wig, RpC, 20" 700.00
Brown Eyes (pnt), any hairstyle or date, 16" 575.00
Brown Eyes (pnt), any hairstyle or date, 20" 950.00
Common Hairdo, blond or blk hair, RpC, after 1905, 12" 145.00
Common Hairdo, blond or blk hair, RpC, after 1905, 23" 285.00

Common Hairdo, blond or blk hair, RpC, after 1905, 8" 80.00
Covered Wagon Style, sausage curls, RpC, 1840s-70s, 12" 285.00
Covered Wagon Style, sausage curls, RpC, 1840s-70s, 24" 900.00
Curly Top, loose ringlet curls, RpC, 1845-60s, 16" 500.00
Curly Top, loose ringlet curls, RpC, 1845-60s, 20" 700.00
Dolly Madison, modeled ribbon & bow, RpC, 1870-80s, 14" 275.00
Dolly Madison, modeled ribbon & bow, RpC, 1870-80s, 18" 500.00
Dolly Madison, modeled ribbon & bow, RpC, 1870-80s, 21" 600.00
Flat Top, blk hair, mid-part/short curls, RpC, ca 1860, 17" 300.00
Flat Top, blk hair, mid-part/short curls, RpC, ca 1860, 20" 350.00
Glass Eyes, various hairstyles, RpC, 1840s-70s, 14" 1,600.00
Japanese, blk or blond hair, mk or unmk, RpC, 1910-20s, 14" 185.00
Japanese, blk or blond hair, mk or unmk, RpC, 1910-20s, 17" 250.00
Man or Boy, glass eyes, side part, RpC, 14" 2,200.00
Man or Boy, pnt eyes, side part, RpC, 14", EX 1,200.00
Man or Boy, pnt eyes, side part, RpC, 16" 1,400.00
Man or Boy, pnt eyes, side part, RpC, 21½" 2,400.00
Peg Wood Body, early hairdo, 1840s, 16", EX 2,800.00
Pet Name, molded shirtwaist w/name on front, RpC, 1905, 19" .265.00
Pet Name, molded shirtwaist w/name on front, RpC, 1905, 8" ...125.00
Pierced Ears, various hairstyles, RpC, 14" 475.00
Pierced Ears, various hairstyles, RpC, 18" 675.00
Snood/Combs, any appl hair decor, RpC, 14" 650.00
Snood/Combs, any appl hair decor, RpC, 17" 800.00
Spill Curls, w/or w/out head band, RpC, 14" 400.00
Spill Curls, w/or w/out head band, RpC, 22" 850.00
Wood Body, articulated/slim hips, RpC, 1840s-50s, 12" 1,600.00
Wood Body, articulated/slim hips, RpC, 1840s-50s, 17" 3,500.00
Wood Body, jtd hips, covered-wagon hairdo, 1840s-50s, 12" ..1,000.00
Wood Body, jtd hips, covered-wagon hairdo, 1840s-50s, 15" ..1,900.00

Cloth

Chase, Black lady, pnt arms & legs, OC, 25" 7,200.00
Cotton cloth stuffed w/cotton, pencil face, 1880s, OC, 18" 225.00
Honey Lou, vinyl face mask, Gund, 1951, OC minus bonnet, 18" ..45.00
Litho on muslin girl, cotton stuffed, EX color, OC, 26" 285.00
Little Bo Peep, 1920s, EX 150.00
Little Lulu, pressed face, felt OC, Georgene Novelties, 15½" 300.00
Mary Had a Little Lamb, 1920s 200.00
Mask face, swivel head, yarn hair, 1940s, RpC, 24" 400.00
Merrie Marie, litho on cotton, jtd knees, 30", EX 125.00
Pitti Sing, 4 on uncut litho cloth sheet 300.00
Raggedy Ann & Andy, Mollye Goldman, 1920s, OC, 18", pr .1,200.00

Eegee

Baby Bunting, vinyl with molded hair,
sleep eyes, 2 upper teeth, clothes by
Mollye Goldman, 1956, 25½", $40.00.

Photo courtesy Pat Smith

Andy, hp/vinyl, pnt eyes to side, 1961, OC, 12" 35.00
Ballerina, plastic/vinyl, 1958, RpC, 20" 45.00
Bonnie Ballerina, plastic/vinyl, jtd, o/c/e, OC, 31" 185.00
Chubby Schoolgirl, hp/vinyl, bl o/c/e, walker, RpC, 10½" 15.00
Georgette, vinyl/cloth, gr o/c/e, orange hair, 1971, OC, 22" 45.00
Janie, vinyl, bl o/c/e, rooted hair, 1956, OC, 8½" 20.00
Kid Sister, plastic/vinyl, pnt features, blond hair, OC, 9¼" 15.00
Kiss Me, plastic/vinyl, raise arm for kiss, OC, 17" 25.00
Miss Debby, vinyl, bl o/c/e, 1948, OC (bride), 14" 30.00
Robert, latex/vinyl, bl o/c/e, molded/pnt hair, 1956, OC, 21" 60.00

Effanbee

Bernard Fleischaker and Hugo Baum became business partners in
1910, and after two difficult years of finding toys to buy, they decided to
manufacture dolls and toys of their own. The Effanbee trademark is a
blending of their names, Eff for Fleischaker and bee for Baum. The
company still exists today.

Alyssia, hp walker, vinyl head, 1958, OC, 20" 250.00
Ann Shirley, compo, 1936-40, OC, 17" 350.00
Baby Cup Cake, plastic/vinyl, o/c/e, dimples, RpC, 12" 20.00
Babyette, compo & cloth, sleeping, OC, 16" 350.00
Compo head & limbs, cloth body, o/c/m, 1920s, OC, 18" 165.00
Currier & Ives, plastic/vinyl, OC, 12" 40.00
Fluffy, vinyl, 1954, OC, 10" 45.00
Honey, compo, flirty eyes, 1947-48, 21" 450.00
Howdy Doody, compo/cloth, string-op mouth, 1947, OC, 17" ...185.00
Laurel (girl) by Jan Hagara, 1984, OC, 15" 50.00
Little Lady, compo, 1939-47, OC, 15" 350.00
Mae Starr, compo/cloth, record player inside, OC, 30" 465.00
Mary Jane, plastic/vinyl, walker, 1960, OC, 31" 265.00
Patsy, compo, 1927-30s, OC, 14" 365.00
Patsy Ann, vinyl, 1959, OC, 15" 200.00
Patsy Mae, 1932, OC, 20", minimum value 785.00
Patsy Ruth, compo/cloth, brn o/c/e, hh wig, OC, 27" 850.00
Santa Claus, compo, molded beard & hat, OC, 19", minimum ...1,200.00
WC Fields, compo/cloth, 1938, OC, 22" 500.00

Half Dolls

Half dolls were never meant to be objects of play. Most were modeled after the likenesses of lovely ladies, though children and animals
were represented as well. Most of the ladies were firmly sewn into pincushion bases that were beautifully decorated and served as the skirts of
their gowns. Other skirts were actually covers for items on milady's
dressing table. Some were used for parasol or brush handles or for tops
to candy containers or perfume bottles. Most popular from 1900 to
about 1930, they will most often be found marked with the country of
their origin, especially Bavaria, Germany, France, and Japan. You may
also find some fine quality pieces marked Goebel, Dressel and Kester,
KPM, and Heubach.

Germany, arms & hands attached, common type, 3" 25.00
Germany, arms & hands attached, common type, 5" 35.00
Germany, arms & hands attached, common type, 8" 55.00
Germany, arms & hands completely away, 12", $200 to 950.00
Germany, arms & hands completely away, 3", $85 to 145.00
Germany, arms & hands completely away, 5", $100 to 285.00
Germany, arms & hands completely away, 8", $165 to 650.00
Germany, arms extended, hands attached, 3" 50.00
Germany, arms extended, hands attached, 5" 85.00
Germany, arms extended, hands attached, 8" 125.00
Japan mk, 3" 20.00

Japan mk, 5" 30.00
Japan mk, 8" 50.00

Handwerck

#189, o/m, RpC, 14" 325.00
#421 21 Handwerk Germany, bsk head, o/m, jtd, RpC, 42" 3,200.00
#79 or #89, c/m, RpC, 21", minimum value 2,300.00
Bsk ShHd, o/m, kid body, RpC, 16" 350.00
Bsk SkHd, bjtd, brn o/c/e, o/m, p/e, hh wig, 28" 950.00
Child, bsk head, bjtd, set or o/c/e, after 1885, RpC, 25" 750.00
Child, bsk head, bjtd, set or o/c/e, after 1885, RpC, 36" 1,450.00
Child, bsk head, bjtd, set or o/c/e, mold mks, RpC, 12" 450.00

Hertel, Schwab and Company

#119, bsk head, pnt eyes, c/m, jtd compo, RpC, 16" 4,900.00
#126, Skippy, bsk head, molded hair, sleep eyes, o/c/m, 12" 1,000.00
#154, bsk head, c/m, RpC, 16" 2,400.00
#163, googly eyes, c/m, RpC, 12" 3,000.00
#217, googly eyes, c/m, wig, RpC, 7½" 875.00
#222, Our Fairy, molded hair, pnt eyes, RpC, 9" 1,500.00
#254, Patsy, bsk head, o/c/e, bent limbs, RpC, 14" 1,000.00
Prize Baby, bsk 1-pc body & head, glass eyes, 6" 300.00

Heubach

#1017, baby-faced toddler, bsk head, o/m, RpC, 18" 1,600.00

#5689, character doll, open mouth, set glass eyes, fully jointed, 26", $4,800.00.

Photo courtesy Pat Smith

#6692, ShHd, smiling, intaglio eyes, RpC, 15", minimum value 900.00
#7129, laughing character, ShHd, cloth body, RpC, 11" 675.00
#7602, long face pouty, pnt eyes & hair, c/m, RpC, 16" 2,200.00
#7781, baby, squinted eyes, yawning, RpC, 15" 1,800.00
#8197, ShHd, c/m, molded curls, kid body, RpC, 17", minimum ...8,700.00

Heubach-Koppelsdorf

#250-12/0 Germany, compo, o/c/e, o/m/teeth, RpC, 11", EX 125.00
#267, baby, o/m, flirty eyes, metal eyelids, Rpc, 17" 600.00
#300, baby, 5-pc bent-limb body, o/m, o/c eyes, 1910s, 10" 285.00
#300 3/0, SkHd, bl o/c eyes, 2 teeth, saran wig, RpC, 14" 250.00
#338, c/m, o/c eyes, pnt hair, cloth body, 1925, RpC, 13" 675.00
#339, o/c eyes, pnt hair, celluloid hands, cloth body, 9½" 425.00
Child, bsk ShHd w/bsk arms, kid body, o/m, Rpc, 14" 225.00

Horsman

Ballerina, vinyl, 1-pc body & legs, jtd elbows, 1957, OC, 18" 75.00
Betty Jane, compo, OC, 25" 450.00
Brother, compo/cloth, OC, 22", G, minimum value 300.00

Child, compo, 1930-40s, OC, 14" 145.00
Compo, mk EIH, 1910s-20s, RpC, 12" 185.00
Dimples, compo/cloth, 1928-33, RpC, 16" 225.00
Ella Cinders, compo/cloth, 1925, RpC, 14" 500.00
Linda, vinyl/plastic, rooted hair, o/c/e, 1959, OC, 36" 200.00
Mary Poppins, plastic/vinyl walker, o/c/e, 1966, OC, 26" 245.00
Mimi Thristy Baby, jtd, glassine eyes, OC, 6" 25.00
Peek-a-Boo, compo/cloth, G Drayton, OC, 7½", minimum 145.00
Pippi Longstocking, vinyl/cloth, 1972, OC, 18" 35.00
Pudgie Baby, plastic/vinyl, 1979, 12" 40.00
Renee Ballerina, stuffed vinyl, bl o/c/e, rooted hair, OC, 18" 45.00
Sleepy Baby, vinyl/cloth, molded closed eyes, 1965, 24" 50.00

Snow White, Disney, 1981, 8", M, $85.00.

Photo courtesy Pat Smith

Tuffie, vinyl, molded upper lip over lower, 1966, OC, 16" 50.00
Vinyl w/1-pc vinyl stuffed body, brn o/c/e, 1955, OC, 22" 30.00

Ideal

Baby Coos, cloth/plastic/vinyl, o/c/e, molded hair, 1948, 20" 85.00
Baby Giggles, vinyl, eyes to side, mechanical giggler, 28" 120.00
Baby Snooks Flexie, wire & compo, OC, 12", minimum value ...285.00
Betty Big Girl, plastic & vinyl, 1968, OC, 30" 245.00
Brother/Baby Coos, compo/hp/cloth, 1951, OC, 25" 100.00
Compo baby, cloth body, c/m, o/c/e, 1930s-40s, OC, 16" 200.00
Compo child, o/c/e, o/m, OC, 14" 165.00
Cousin Sue, vinyl/cloth, o/c/e, o/c/m w/teeth, RpC, 18" 85.00
Dina, hp/vinyl, pnt eyes, hair 'grows,' 1971, OC, 15" 90.00
Flossie Flirt, compo & cloth, flirty eyes, 1938-45, OC, 20" 265.00
Little Miss Revlon, hp/vinyl, bl o/c/e, jtd waist, OC, 10½" 125.00
Magic Lips, vinyl-coated cloth & vinyl, teeth, 1955, OC, 24" 95.00
Peter Playpal, 1961, OC, 36" 800.00
Pinocchio, compo & wood, 1938-41, OC, 10" 400.00
Sara Ann, hp, saran wig, 1952 on, OC, 14", minimum value 250.00
Tippy Tumbles, hp/plastic, does flips, battery-op, OC, 16½" 40.00
Uneeda Kid, compo & cloth, pnt eyes & hair, OC, 1914-19, 16" ..600.00

Jumeau

The Jumeau factory became the best known name for dolls during the 1880s and 1890s. Early dolls were works of art with closed mouths and paperweight eyes. When son Emile Jumeau took over, he patented sleep eyes with eyelids that drop down over the eyes. This model also had flirty (eyes that move from side to side) eyes and is extremely rare. Over 98% of Jumeau dolls have paperweight eyes. French doll industry from German competition.

Closed mouth, mk EJ (incised) Jumeau, rpr ft, 24" 8,700.00
Closed mouth, mk EJ (incised) Jumeau, 14" 5,800.00

Closed mouth, mk EJ (incised) Jumeau, 19" 6,800.00
Closed mouth, mk Tete Jumeau, 10" 3,000.00
Closed mouth, mk Tete Jumeau, 16" 4,100.00
Closed mouth, mk Tete Jumeau, 21" 4,800.00
Closed mouth, mk Tete Jumeau, 25" 5,600.00
Closed mouth, mk Tete Jumeau, 30" 6,800.00
Depose/Tete Jumeau, swivel head, p/e, long curls, adult, 22" ..7,400.00
Jumeau 1907, SkHd, appl ears, o/m, 18" 2,400.00
Jumeau 1907, swivel head, o/m, o/c/e, p/e, 23" 2,800.00
Long face, c/m, 21" 23,000.00
Long face, c/m, 30" 30,000.00
Open mouth, mk Tete Jumeau, 10" 2,300.00
Open mouth, mk Tete Jumeau, 16" 3,100.00
Open mouth, mk Tete Jumeau, 21" 3,100.00
Open mouth, mk Tete Jumeau, 25" 3,500.00
Open mouth, mk Tete Jumeau, 30" 4,600.00
Open mouth, mk Tete Jumeau, 30" 4,600.00
Open mouth, mk 1907 Jumeau, 17" 2,500.00
Open mouth, mk 1907 Jumeau, 25" 3,300.00
Open mouth, mk 1907 Jumeau, 32" 4,000.00
Phonograph in body, o/m, 25" 12,000.00
Portrait Jumeau, c/m, 20" 7,800.00

Kammer and Reinhardt

#100, baby, pnt hair & eyes, o/c/m, 15" 650.00
#101, boy or girl w/glass eyes, 12" 4,100.00
#101, boy or girl w/glass eyes, 20" 8,000.00
#101, boy or girl w/pnt eyes, 12" 2,000.00
#101, boy or girl w/pnt eyes, 20" 5,000.00
#107, Carl, pnt eyes, pouty mouth, orig mohair wig, 12½" ...13,000.00
#109, rare, w/glass eyes, 18" 26,000.00
#109, rare, w/pnt eyes, 18" 22,000.00
#112, rare, w/glass eyes, 18" 19,000.00
#112, rare, w/pnt eyes, 18" 17,000.00
#114, rare, w/glass eyes, 15" 5,900.00
#114, rare, w/pnt eyes, 11" 2,950.00
#114, rare, w/pnt eyes, 18" 5,500.00
#115 or #115a, c/m, 18" 4,900.00
#115 or #115a, o/m, 15" 1,400.00
#115 or #115a, o/m, 22" 2,600.00
#116 or #116a, c/m, 18" 3,500.00
#116 or #116a, o/m, 15" 1,400.00
#116 or #116a, o/m, 22" 2,600.00
#117, c/m, 24" 6,900.00
#117a, c/m, 18" 5,400.00
#117a, c/m, 30" 8,200.00
#126, sleeping/flirty glass eyes, o/m, silent, 28" 1,550.00
Dolly face, o/m, mold #400-403-102, etc, 24" 850.00
Dolly face, o/m, mold #400-403-109, etc, 16" 600.00
Dolly face, o/m, mold #400-403-109, etc, 38" 2,800.00

Kestner

Johannes D. Kestner made buttons at a lathe in a Waltershausen factory in the early 1800s. When this line of work failed, he used the same lathe to turn doll bodies. Thus the Kestner company began. It was one of the few German manufacturers to make the complete doll. By 1860, with the purchase of a porcelain factory, Kestner made doll heads of china and bisque as well as wax, worked-in-leather, celluloid, and cardboard. In 1895 the Kestner trademark of a crown with streamers was registered in the U.S. and a year later in Germany. Kestner felt the mark was appropriate since he referred to himself as the 'king of German dollmakers.'

A, ShHd, o/m, MIG/Kestner, 19" 685.00
B/6, ShHd, kid w/bsk ½-arms, o/m/teeth, o/c/e, 19" 685.00
Century Doll Co, flanged closed dome, c/m, 15" 685.00
D/8, SkHd & ShI Id, kid w/bsk ½-arms, c/m, 15" 800.00
E/9, SkHd, o/m, 1892, 26" 1,200.00
G/10, SkHd, c/m, JDK, 1912, 12" 600.00
G/11, Hilda, SkHd, o/c/e, o/m/teeth, 1920s, 15" 3,600.00
G/8, trn ShHd, o/m, MI/JDK, 19" 800.00
G11, SkHd, jtd, bl eyes, o/m, mohair wig, 19" 800.00
H/12, SkHd, o/c/m, JDK, 1892, 23" 3,000.00
Hilda, toddler, jtd body, o/m, o/c/e, 1914, rstr, 15" 4,800.00
I/13, SkHd, o/m, JDK, 1892, 26" 985.00
JDK, bsk head, glass eyes, c/m, appl ears, OC, 20", EX 4,800.00
JDK, bsk head on celluloid, R Gummi Co, turtle mk, 18" 500.00
JDK 12, SkHd, pwt, o/m, bent limbs, RpC, 15", VG 475.00
JDK/Kestner, Oriental, SkHd, o/m, 14" 4,800.00
K/12, ShHd, made for Century, o/c/m, molded hair, 21" 3,600.00
L/15, SkHd, bsk ShPl, c/m, 21" 3,000.00
N/17, SkHd, o/m, 1892, 17" 725.00
Trn ShHd, o/m, kid body, brn eyes, orig wig, 22", EX 750.00
10, SkHd, bsk ShPl, c/m, 21" 2,900.00
11, SkHd, pnt eyes to side, o/c/m, JDK/MIG, 11" 550.00
13, SkHd, o/m, JDK/MIG, 18" 700.00
143, ShHd, jtd compo, o/c/e, o/m, mohair wig, 14", EX 850.00
145, ShHd, kid w/bsk ½-arms, o/m, 17" 1,100.00
145 SkHd, c/m, 143/4/0/JDK, 11" 325.00
147, trn ShHd, o/m, JDK, 25" 900.00
148, ShHd, kid w/bsk ½-arms, o/m, 7½", 21" 700.00
150.1, bsk, Kestner seal on body, 8" 500.00
154, SkHd/ShHd, kid w/bsk ½-arms, o/m/teeth, DEP, 17" 725.00
154, SkHd/ShHd, kid w/bsk ½-arms, o/m/teeth, DEP, 21½" 750.00
167, SkHd, jtd compo, o/m, p/e, F 1/2,MI61/2,G, 16" 675.00
168, SkHd, o/m, MID/G7, 26" 1,000.00
169, SkHd, jtd compo, o/c/e, c/m, B1/2,BI61/2G, 18" 2,700.00
171, SkHd, jtd compo, o/c/e, o/m, 'Daisy,' F/M110, 18" 700.00
171, SkHd, jtd compo, o/c/e, o/m, 'Daisy,' F/M110, 32" 1,300.00
201, ShHd, celluloid on kid, o/m, set eyes/lashes, JDK, 19" 685.00
215, SkHd, jtd compo, fur eyebrows, o/m, MI9/GJDK, 21" 850.00
221, jtd compo, googly eyes, c/m smile, wig, JDK, 15" 5,200.00
235, toddler, kid body, 16" 750.00
245, SkHd, 5-pc baby, G/MIG/11/JDK Jr/1914 Hilda, 14" 3,300.00
257, SkHd, 5-pc baby, o/m, G/JDK, 10" 425.00
257, SkHd, 5-pc baby, o/m, G/JDK, 20" 850.00
260, flirty-eyed toddler, OC, 16" 1,900.00

Lenci

Characteristics of Lenci dolls include seamless, steam-molded felt heads, quality clothing, childishly plump bodies, and painted eyes that glance to the side. Fine mohair wigs were used, and the middle and fourth fingers were sewn together. Look for the factory stamp on the foot, though paper labels were also used. Dolls under 10" are known as mascots and usually sell for $150.00 to $200.00. The Lenci factory continues today, producing dolls of the same high quality.

African man w/sword & shield, 17", minimum value 2,000.00
Baby, 16", minimum value 1,800.00
Bali Dancer, 18" 1,800.00
Boy, side part, 18", minimum value 2,200.00
Boy, winking, o/c/m, pnt teeth, 1920s, 11" 2,800.00
Child, 14", minimum value 800.00
Child, 18", minimum value 1,200.00
Clown, 18" 1,600.00
Golfer, 16" 2,400.00

Lady w/adult face, flapper style, 14" **1,200.00**
Mascotte, 5", minimum value **250.00**
Pan, hooved ft, 9½" **2,100.00**
Surprise eyes, rnd pnt eyes, O-shaped mouth, 15" **1,900.00**

Liddle Kiddles

From 1966 to 1971, Mattel produced Liddle Kiddle dolls ranging in size from ¾" to 4". They were all poseable and had rooted hair that could be restyled. There were various series of the dolls, among them Animiddles, Zoolery Jewelry Kiddles, extraterrestrials, and Sweet Treets, as well as many accessories. To learn more about these dolls, we recommend *Liddle Kiddles, Identification and Value Guide*, by our advisor for this category, Paris Langford, who is listed in the Directory under Louisianna.

Alice in Wonderliddle, 1969, 3½", NM complete **100.00**
Beach Buggy, pk plastic & vinyl, 1967, 5½x5x6", NM complete .**25.00**
Beddy-Bye Biddle, no robe, 1968, 3", NM complete **65.00**

Cinderiddle, Storybook Kiddle, 3½", complete with 24-page book, M (never removed from box), $200.00.

Clothes, Orange Meringue, lace-trimmed outfit w/shoes, MIP **25.00**
Florence Niddle, nurse, 1966-67, 3", NM complete **50.00**
Heart Pin, 1½" doll w/crown in pin, 1968-70, NM **25.00**
Howard Biff Boodle, 1966, 3½", NM complete **60.00**
Kiddles Collectors Case, vinyl, 1968, 14½x10", M w/insert **25.00**
Lady Lavender, w/cup & saucer, 1970-71, M w/tag **100.00**
Laffy Lemon Kola, yel outfit, w/bottle, 1968-69, NM complete **35.00**
Liddle Kiddles Paper Dolls, Whitman, 1967, uncut, M **30.00**
Lilac Locket, lilac dress, gold frame w/chain, 1967, NM **25.00**
Lola Locket, platinum hair, in gold fr w/chain, 1967, NM **25.00**
Lucky Lion, 2-pc lion suit, felt ears/yarn bangs, 1969-70, NM **25.00**
Nappytime Baby, yarn hair, bunny cradle, 1970, NM **45.00**
Purple Gurple, Kozmic Kiddle, in spaceship, w/tag, 1969-70, NM ...**150.00**
Shirley Skediddle, blonde, 1968-70, 4", NM complete **25.00**
Sleeping Biddle Castle Playset, Sears, 1967, NM complete **150.00**
Teresa Touring Car, auburn hair, 1969-70, NM complete **55.00**
Tracy Trikediddle, orange pigtails, 1968-70, 4", NM complete **45.00**
Trikey Triddle, red hair, 1967, 2⅞", NM complete **55.00**
Zoolery Kiddles Frame-Tray Puzzle, Whitman, 1969, 14½x11½", M ...**100.00**

Madame Alexander

Beatrice Alexander founded the Alexander Doll Company in 1923 by making an all-cloth, oil-painted face, Alice in Wonderland doll. With the help of her three sisters, the company prospered; and by the late 1950s there were over six hundred employees making Madame Alexander dolls. The company still produces these lovely dolls today.

Agatha, hp, Jacqueline, bl dress, #2230, 1981 ....**250.00**
Alexander-Kins, hp, bend-knee walker, car coat, 1956-64, 8" **425.00**
Alexander-Kins, hp, nonwalker, party dress, 1965-66, 8", minimum .**1,000.00**
Alexander-Kins, hp, str-leg nonwalker, 1953 ....**475.00**
Alexander-Kins, hp, str-leg walker, Wendy Ann, nightie, 1955, 8" ...**150.00**
Alice in Wonderland, hp, Wendy Ann, 1955-36, 8", minimum ..**575.00**
Amish Boy, hp, Wendy Ann, bend-knee, 1966-69, 8" **265.00**
Ana McGuffey, compo, Tiny Betty, 1935-39, 7" **325.00**
Annabelle, hp, Barbara Jane, 1952, 29" **750.00**
Annette (Funicello), porc portrait by R Tonner, 1993, 14" **425.00**
Armenia, Wendy Ann, #507, 1989-90, 8" **52.00**
Astor, vinyl toddler, gold organdy, 1953 only, 9" **100.00**
Babs, hp, Maggie, 1949, 20" **750.00**
Baby Jane, compo, 1935, 16", minimum **850.00**
Ballerina, compo, Little Betty, 1935-41, 9" **300.00**
Belle of the Ball, Cissette, dk rose gown, #1120, 1989, 10" **68.00**
Betty, compo, 1936-37 only, 12" **425.00**
Binnie Walker, hp skater, 1955 only, 15" **550.00**
Bonnie Toddler, cloth/hp/vinyl, 1950-51, 18" **110.00**
Bride, Margaret, pk gown, 1953, 18"-21", minimum **800.00**
Bride, plastic/vinyl, Elise, 1966-88, 17" **125.00**
Butch, compo/cloth, 1949-51, 14"-16" **150.00**
Caroline, vinyl, 1961-62 only, 15" **285.00**
Christening Baby, cloth/vinyl, 1951-54, 11"-13" **75.00**
Claudette, Cissette, #1123, 1988-89, 10" **90.00**
Cuddly, cloth, 1943-44, 10½" **325.00**
December, Mary Ann, #1528, 1989 only, 14" **95.00**
Degas, compo, Wendy Ann, 1945-46, 21", minimum **1,900.00**
Dilly Dally Sally, compo, Tiny Betty, 1937-42, 7" **325.00**
Dottie Dumbunnie, cloth/felt, 1930s, minimum **800.00**
Dutch, hp, str leg, mk Alex, #777, 1972-73, 8" **45.00**
Estonia, str leg, Wendy Ann, #545, 1986-87 only, 8" **75.00**
Flowergirl, compo, Princess Elizabeth, 1939, 1944-47, 16"-18" ...**550.00**
Funny Maggie, yarn hair, Maggie, #140506, 1994, 8" **55.00**
Gibson Girl, hp, Cissette, eyeshadow, 1962, 10" **600.00**
Glenda the Good Witch, Wendy Ann, #473, 1992-93, 8" **60.00**
Godey Bride, hp, Margaret, 1950, 14", minimum **900.00**
Gretel, compo, Tiny Betty, 1935-42, 7" **275.00**
Guenivere, Portrette, forest gr/gold, #1146, 1992 only, 10" **95.00**
Heidi, hp, Maggie, #460, 1991-91, 8" **55.00**
Highland Fling, hp, Wendy Ann, #484, 1955 only, 8" **650.00**
Huckleberry Finn, hp, Wendy Ann, #490, 1989-91, 8" **60.00**
Hyacinth, vinyl toddler, bl clothes, 1953 only, 9" **100.00**
Isolde, Mary Ann, #1413, 1985-86, 14" **90.00**
Janie, toddler, #1156, 1964-66 only, 12" **285.00**
June Bride, compo, 1939, 1946-47, 21", minimum **1,800.00**
Kathy, compo, Wendy Ann, 1939, 1946, 17"-21", $750 to **900.00**
Kelly, hp, Lissy, 1959 only, 12" **425.00**
Letty Bridesmaid, compo, Tiny Betty, 1938-40, 7"-8" **275.00**
Little Cherub, compo, 1945-46, 11" **300.00**
Little Granny, plastic/vinyl, Mary Ann, floral gown, 1966, 14" ..**225.00**
Little Shaver, cloth, 1940-44, 10", minimum **475.00**
Little Victoria, Wendy Ann, #376, 1953-54, 7½"-8", minimum .**1,300.00**
Lively Huggums, knob makes limbs & head move, 1963, 25" **125.00**
Lord Nelson, vinyl, Nancy Drew, 1984-86, 12" **75.00**
Lucinda, plastic/vinyl, Janie, 1969-70, 12", minimum **345.00**
Lucy Bride, compo, Wendy Ann, 1937-40, 17" **475.00**
Madeline, hp/jtd elbows & knees, 1950-53, 17"-18", minimum .**950.00**
Mamie Eisenhower, Mary Ann, 1980-1990, 14" **100.00**
Mary Louise, compo, Wendy Ann, 1938, 1946-47, 21" **2,200.00**
Marybel, rigid vinyl, 1959-65, 16", doll only, minimum **165.00**
Melanie, compo, Wendy Ann, 1945-47, 21", minimum **675.00**
Mimi, hp, multi-jtd, formal clothes, 1961 only, 30" **800.00**
Mistress Mary, compo, Tiny Betty, 1937-41, 7" **285.00**

Mother Goose, str legs, 1986-92, 8" **55.00**
Muffin, cloth, 1966 only, 19" **100.00**
Nurse, hp, Wendy, all wht, 1956 only, 8", minimum **425.00**
Ophelia, Lissy, 1993 only, 12" **115.00**
Persia, compo, Tiny Betty, 1936-38, 7" **300.00**
Polly, plastic/vinyl, in ball gown, 1965 only, 17" **325.00**
Princess Elizabeth, compo, Tiny Betty, 1937-39, 7" **300.00**
Pussy Cat, cloth/vinyl, wht, 1965-85, 14" **95.00**
Queen, hp/vinyl, Jacqueline, gold dress, 1968, 21" **950.00**
Queen Elizabeth II, 40th anniversary of coronation, 1992, 8" **130.00**
Quizkin, hp, Wendy Ann, bald head, romper, 1953, 8", minimum ...**457.00**
Red Riding Hood, compo, Tiny Betty, 1935-42, 7" **285.00**
Romeo, compo, Wendy Ann, 1949, 18", minimum **1,200.00**
Rusty, cloth/vinyl, 1967-68 only, 20" **350.00**
Sally Bride, compo, Wendy Ann, 1938-39, 14", minimum **425.00**
Scarlett O'Hara, compo, Wendy Ann, 1941-43, 14"-15" **750.00**
Scarlett O'Hara, hp/vinyl, Jacqueline, gr gown, 1965, 21" **1,200.00**
Sleeping Beauty, compo, Tiny Betty/Little Betty, 1941-44, 7"-9" **650.00**
Sound of Music's Brigitta, Cissette, 1971-73, 10" **200.00**
Spanish Girl, hp, red polka-dot gown, #110545, 8" **65.00**
Sunbonnet Sue, compo, Little Betty, 1937-40, 9" **300.00**
Treena Ballerina, hp, Margaret, 1952 only, 15" **80.00**
Victoria, compo, Wendy Ann, 1939, 1941, 21", minimum **1,800.00**
Welcome Home Desert Storm, blk or wht, 1991 only, 8" **55.00**
Yolanda, Brenda Starr, 1965 only, 12" **325.00**

Mattel

Baby Beans, vinyl w/beanbag body, pnt eyes, 1971, OC, 11" **18.00**
Baby First Step, hp/vinyl, o/c, battery-op, 1968, RpC, 10" **35.00**
Baby Fun, vinyl, pnt eyes, rooted hair, 1968, OC, 8" **20.00**
Big Jack, hp/vinyl, pnt eyes & hair, fully jtd, OC, 9½" **75.00**
Bucky Love Notes, press for tunes, 1974, OC, 12" **30.00**
Casper the Talking Ghost, 1961, EXIB **100.00**

Chatty Cathy, pull-string talker, blond with blue eyes, 20", MIB, $185.00 minimum value. (Played with condition, $85.00.)

Photo courtesy Kathy Lewis

Chatty Cathy, bl eyes, blond curls, reissue **55.00**
Clown, o/c/m, molded hair or wig, 5-pc body, RpC, 10" **265.00**
Dr Doolittle, vinyl, molded & pnt features, OC, 6" **25.00**
Randy Reader, hp/vinyl, bl eyes, wht hair, battery-op, RpC, 19" ..**40.00**
Sister Belle, plastic/cloth, yarn hair, talker, OC, 17" **25.00**
Sweet 16, hp/vinyl, pnt eyes, blond hair, 1975, OC, 11½" **85.00**
Talking Baby Tenderlove, working, OC **20.00**
Wet Noodles, vinyl, pnt eyes, orange hair, 1969, OC, 3½" **15.00**

Mollye

Betty Elizabeth, hp, o/c, 1954, OC, 18" **445.00**
Chris Am Airlines Stewardess, hp, 1950s, OC, 14" **500.00**

International Doll, mask face, yarn hair, OC, 16" **125.00**
Lone Ranger, hp & latex, OC, 22" **350.00**
Mollye, cloth, OC w/wide-brimmed bonnet, 1920s, 12" **85.00**

Papier-Mache

Clown, o/c/m, molded hair or wig, 5-pc body, RpC, 10" **265.00**
Coiled braids over ears, RpC, 20", minimum **2,200.00**
Early type w/cloth body, wooden limbs, braids, RpC, 12" **135.00**
French/French type, o/m w/bamboo teeth, glass eyes, RpC, 15" ...**1,400.00**
German, molded hair, glass eyes, c/m, RpC, 14" **525.00**
German, molded hair, pnt eyes, c/m, RpC, 1870-1900, 23" **475.00**
German character head, glass eyes, c/m, fully jtd, RpC, 15" **1,100.00**
Greiner, molded hair, pnt eyes, cloth body, 19" **1,400.00**
M&S Superior, ShHd, molded hair, pnt eyes, RpC, 16" **400.00**
Milliner's model, braided bun, side curls, 1820-60, RpC, 10" **785.00**
Molded bonnet, kid body, wooden limbs, RpC, 15", minimum **2,000.00**
Motschmann type, glass eyes, c/m, solid dome, RpC, 15" **725.00**
ShHd, cloth body, blond wig, OC, 14" **250.00**
Trn ShHd, solid dome, glass eyes, c/m, compo arms, RpC, 17" ...**750.00**
1920s & later, cloth body, bright coloring, wig, RpC, 8" **80.00**

Parian

Bald solid-dome head, ear details, takes wigs, 1850s, RpC, 14" ...**775.00**
Man or boy, parted hair, cloth body, shirt & tie, 16" **900.00**
Molded comb, glass eyes, cloth body, RpC, 16" **1,700.00**
Molded hat, blond or blk hair, pnt eyes, 15" **2,200.00**
Molded hat, glass eyes, RpC, 16" **3,100.00**
Molded head band, Alice, RpC, 14" **400.00**
Molded head band, pnt eyes, unpierced ears, RpC, 18" **1,200.00**
Molded necklace, glass eyes, p/e, RpC, 21", minimum **2,500.00**
Molded scarf, pnt features, cloth body, RpC, 14", minimum ...**1,000.00**
Plain, no decor in hair or on shoulders, RpC, 10" **175.00**
Swivel neck, glass eyes, RpC, 21" **3,700.00**

Remco

Baby Grow-a-Tooth, 1969, OC, 14" **30.00**
Gingersnap, brn hp/vinyl, brn pnt eyes, curly hair, OC, 18" **50.00**
Hug-a-Bug, gr vinyl, pnt clothes/features, clip on bk, 3½" **6.00**
Jan, fully jtd, blk rooted hair, 1965, OC, 5½" **12.50**
Mimi, hp/vinyl, pnt eyes, blond hair, OC, 19" **65.00**
Sweet April, vinyl, stationary eyes, arms move, RpC, 5½" **6.00**
Tumbling Tomboy, hp/vinyl, 1969, OC, 16" **25.00**

Schoenhut

   Albert Schoenhut left Germany in 1866 to go to Pennsylvania to work as a repairman for toy pianos. He eventually applied his skills to wooden toys and later designed an all-wood doll which he patented on January 17, 1911. These uniquely jointed dolls were painted with enamels and came with a metal stand. Some of the later dolls had stuffed bodies, voice boxes, and hollow heads. Due to the changing economy and fierce competition, the company closed in the mid-1930s.

Baby, bent-limb body, pnt hair, decal eyes, OC, 12" **525.00**
Boy, cvd & pnt hair, bl pnt eyes, c/m, scuffed, RpC, 17" **2,600.00**
Boy, cvd hair, pnt bl intaglio eyes, c/m, RpC, 15", EX **2,000.00**
Boy, cvd hair, pnt eyes, walker, nude, 16½", VG **2,800.00**
Character child, intaglio eyes, o/c/m w/teeth, OC, 14" **1,600.00**
Child, cvd hair, molded ribbon, c/m, OC, 14" **2,500.00**
Child w/cvd hair, c/m, 14", EX **2,500.00**
Compo, molded curls, Patsy-style body, label, OC, 13" **1,600.00**

Dolly face, decal eyes, o/c/m w/teeth, OC, 14"	625.00
Dolly face, pnt eyes, o/c/m w/teeth, OC, 14"	675.00
Girl, bl pnt eyes, c/m, brn hh wig, RpC, 11"	250.00
Girl, brn decal eyes, o/c/m w/4 teeth, RpC, 17", EX	625.00
Girl, brn decal eyes, 4 pnt teeth, orig wig, 1911, RpC, 21½"	785.00
Girl, brn pnt eyes, brn hh wig, orig dress, 15", EX	500.00
Girl, intaglio eyes, cvd hair w/braids, c/m, RpC, 16"	600.00
Girl, intaglio eyes, pouty mouth, rpl wig, rpt, RpC, 21½"	785.00
Girl, pnt eyes, c/m, rpl wig, rpt, RpC, 15"	675.00
Girl, pnt eyes, 4 pnt teeth, cvd hair, rpt, RpC, 16"	700.00
Man, cvd hair, OC, 19", minimum	3,000.00
O/c/e, o/m w/cvd teeth, OC, 17"	1,350.00
Toddler, 12", EX	900.00
Tootsie Wootsie, pnt hair, o/c/m w/tongue/teeth, OC, 14"	2,100.00
Walker, pnt eyes, o/c or c/m, OC, 18"	1,100.00
Wood & compo, intaglio eyes, fully jtd, OC, 19", EX	1,400.00

SFBJ

By 1895 Germany was producing dolls at much lower prices than the French dollmakers could, so to save the doll industry, several leading French manufacturers united to form one large company. Bru, Raberry and Delphieu, Pintel and Godshaux, Fleischman and Bodel, Jumeau, and many others united to form the company Society Francaise de Fabrication de Bebes et Jouets (SFBJ).

Celestine, bsk SkHd on papier-mache, o/m, inset eyes, 18"	900.00
Tete Jumeau, p/e, o/m, o/c/e, lashes, 18"	1,600.00
15, o/c/e, o/m w/teeth, wood/compo body, RpC, 15", EX	1,500.00
203, 1900 bsk head on compo, o/m, inset eyes, 20"	3,000.00
223, bsk, closed dome, o/m w/8 teeth, molded hair, 17"	2,000.00
227, brn swivel closed-dome head, animal skin wig, 18"	2,500.00
228, toddler, papier-mache body, c/m, inset eyes, 16"	2,200.00
229, wood walker, o/c/m, inset eyes, 18"	4,000.00
230, SkHd, p/e, o/m, o/c/e, 23"	2,400.00
235, closed dome, molded hair, o/c/m, o/c eyes, 8"	500.00
236, laughing Jumeau, o/m, o/c/e, dbl chin, 17"	1,800.00
236, laughing Jumeau, o/m, o/c/e, dbl chin, 22"	2,300.00
239, Poulbot, street urchin, c/m, red wig, 14"	8,500.00
245, boy, o/c/m, lg googly glass eyes, pnt shoes, 12"	2,600.00
247, toddler, o/c/m w/2 inset teeth, 16"	2,400.00
247, toddler, o/c/m w/2 inset teeth, 24"	3,200.00
251, toddler, 25"	2,600.00
252, pouty, c/m, inset eyes, papier-mache body, 18"	6,200.00
257, 1900 toddler, o/c/m, inset eyes, 16"	2,500.00
301, bsk SkHd on compo, o/m, inset eyes, 16"	725.00
301, bsk SkHd on compo, o/m, inset eyes, 24"	1,400.00
301, bsk SkHd on compo, o/m, inset eyes, 30"	1,900.00
60, kiss-blower, cryer/walker, 22"	2,300.00
60, o/m w/teeth, o/c/e, jtd body & wrists, 25½"	950.00
60, SkHd, papier-mache/compo, plunger cryer, o/m, 1-pc, 11"	575.00

Shirley Temple

Prices are suggested for dolls complete and in mint condition. Add up to 25% (depending on her outfit) if mint with box.

Bsk, 6", pnt, molded hair, Japan	250.00
Celluloid, 5", Japan	185.00
Celluloid, 8", Japan	245.00
Compo, 11", 1934 to late '30s	900.00
Compo, 13"	700.00
Compo, 15-16"	800.00
Compo, 17-18"	950.00

Compo, 20"	1,100.00
Compo, 25", cowgirl	1,500.00
Compo, 7-8", Japan	300.00
Plastic/vinyl, 12", 1982-83	40.00
Plastic/vinyl, 8", 1982-83	30.00

Vinyl, 12", Ideal, hazel sleep eyes, 5-piece child body, original clothes, 1957, MIB, $250.00.

Vinyl, 12", 1950s	225.00
Vinyl, 15", 1950s	265.00
Vinyl, 16", 1973	125.00
Vinyl, 17", Montgomery Ward, 1972	165.00
Vinyl, 17", 1950s	325.00
Vinyl, 19", 1950s	400.00
Vinyl, 36", 1950s	1,600.00

Simon and Halbig

Simon and Halbig was one of the finest German makers to operate during the 1870s into the 1930s. Due to the high quality of the makers, their dolls still command large prices today. During the 1890s a few Simon & Halbig heads were used by a French maker, but these are extremely rare and well marked S&H.

AW, SkHd, o/m, SH/13, 21"	850.00
Baby Blanche, SkHd, o/m baby, S&H, 21"	950.00
CM Bergmann, SkHd, o/m, 1895, Halbig/S&H5, 30"	1,300.00
Elenore, SkHd, o/m, CMB/Simon & Halbig, 18"	650.00
Handwerck, SkHd, o/m, G/Halbig, 4, 26"	850.00
Handwerck, SkHd, o/m, S&H, 30"	1,100.00
Handwerck, SkHd, o/m, 1895, G/S&H/1, 16"	450.00
Handwerck, SkHd, o/m w/teeth, Simon & Halbig, rpl wig, 32"	1,300.00
10, SkHd, o/m, G/Halbig/S&H, 16"	600.00
10, SkHd, o/m, G/Halbig/S&H, 22"	900.00
100, SkHd, o/m, Simon & Halbig/S&C/G, 15"	500.00
1039, SkHd, flirty bl eyes, jtd walking body, p/e, wig, 22"	995.00
1078, SkHd, o/m, pwt, p/e, S&H, RpC, 18½"	725.00
1159, SkHd, adult, 1905, G/Simon & Halbig/S&H7, 18"	1,900.00
1159, SkHd, swivel on ShPl, wood w/kid fashion, o/m, 19"	2,000.00
1160, Louisa May Alcott, bsk head, cloth body, 7", EX	400.00
1296, SkHd, 1911, FS&Co/Simon & Halbig, 14"	525.00
156, SkHd, 1925, S&H, 18"	625.00
156, SkHd, 1925, S&H, 22"	725.00
179, SkHd, o/m, Simon & Halbig S11H DEP, 20"	700.00
282, SkHd, o/m, S&H, 18"	650.00
383, SkHd, flapper body, SH, 14"	1,200.00
409, SkHd, o/m, S&H, 26"	850.00
50, SkHd, c/m, Simon & Halbig, 16"	1,800.00
540, SkHd, o/m, G/Halbig/S&H, 16"	600.00
550, SkHd, o/m, Simon & Halbig/S&H, 16"	600.00
670, SkHd, o/m, Simon & Halbig, 16"	600.00

719, SkHd, c/m, S&H DEP, 16" 2,300.00
739, SkHd, c/m, brn, S 5 H DEP, 14" 1,600.00
739, SkHd, o/m/4 teeth, brn stationary eyes, p/e, DEP, OC, 17" ..1,300.00
769, SkHd, c/m, S&H DEP, 17" 2,600.00
908, SkHd, swivel on ShPl, c/m, SH, 16" 2,700.00
929, SkHd, c/m, S&H, DEP, 25" 4,900.00
939, SkHd, c/m, S 11H DEP, 23" 3,500.00
940, SkHd, closed dome, o/c/m, S 2 H, 26" 3,600.00
945, SkHd, c/m, S 2 H DEP, 16" 2,200.00
949, ShHd, o/m, o/c/e, S 10 H, bride clothes, 19½" 2,600.00

Steiner

Jules Nicholas Steiner established one of the earliest French manu-factoring companies (they made dishes and clocks) in 1855. He began with mechanical dolls with bisque heads, open mouths with two rows of bamboo teeth, and his patents grew to include walking and talking dolls. In 1880 he registered a patent for a doll with sleep eyes. This doll could be put to sleep by turning a rod that operated a wire attached to its eyes.

A Series, c/m, wire eyes, jtd, RpC, 21" 6,500.00
A Series Child, cb pate, c/m, pwt, jtd, RpC, 15" 4,400.00
A Series Child, cb pate, c/m, pwt, jtd, RpC, 25" 7,500.00
A Series Child, cb pate, o/m, pwt, jtd, RpC, 22" 6,500.00
A Series Le Parisien, c/m, RpC, 21" 6,400.00
A Series Le Parisien, c/m, RpC, 9" 2,800.00
A Series Le Parisien, o/m, RpC, 16" 2,400.00
B Series, c/m, pwt, jtd, RpC, 24" 5,400.00
Bourgoin, c/m, pwt, jtd, RpC, 20" 6,700.00
Bsk head & hip, Motschmann-style body, RpC, 18", minimum ..7,000.00
C Series, c/m, wire eyes, jtd, RpC, 17" 5,200.00
C Series Child, c/m, rnd face, pwt, ca 1880, RpC, 18" 5,400.00
Wht bsk, rnd face, o/m w/teeth, unmk, early, RpC, 16" 4,200.00

Terri Lee

Jerri Lee, in Spring Coat outfit 300.00
Jerri Lee, w/chaps & gun belt, all orig 375.00
Terri Lee, Brownie uniform, incomplete accessories 385.00
Terri Lee, early pk coat w/lt bl piping 325.00
Terri Lee, lt rose formal w/pk net skirt 450.00
Terri Lee, pedal-pusher outfit 250.00
Terri Lee, pk terry cloth bathrobe 250.00
Terri Lee, red school dress w/wht collar 300.00
Terri Lee, wht lace blouse & navy pleated skirt 300.00
Tiny Terri Lee, OC, 10", M in red/wht cb case 185.00

Uneeda

Baby Dana, plastic/vinyl, o/c/e, nurser, grows hair, OC, 20" 25.00
Chubby Toddler, plastic/vinyl, o/c/e, c/m, OC, 16½" 20.00
Coquette Bride, plastic/vinyl, o/c/e, 1961-67, OC, 16" 32.00
Grannykins, plastic/vinyl, gray hair, pnt eyes, OC, 6" 15.00
Tiny Penelope, vinyl, orange rooted hair, Hong Kong, OC, 6" 3.00
Twin, plastic/vinyl, molded hair, o/c/e, nurser, OC, 11" 10.00

Vogue

Angela, Debutant series, hp, 1953, OC, 8" 450.00
Boy & Girl Toodles, compo, complete & all orig in trunk 450.00
Ginny, hp, brn eyes, bent legs, wool wig, orig bunny suit, rare 1,400.00
Ginny, hp, molded lashes, walker, 1954-57, OC, minimum value ...300.00
Ginny, hp, pnt lashes, strung, OC, 8", minimum value 450.00

Ginny as Davy Crockett, 1953, 8" 400.00
Ginny Hawaiian, brn/blk, OC, 8", minimum value 725.00
Jeff, plastic/vinyl, OC (Phantom Skater), minimum value 200.00
Toodles, compo, dressed as Hansel, 1940s, 8" 300.00
Toodles, compo, pnt bl eyes, in Mexican dress, 1940s, 8" 300.00
Toodles Baby, compo, pnt eyes, orig dress/coat/bonnet, 7" 265.00
Toodles Boy, compo, orig striped outfit, 8" 365.00
Wee Imp, hp, red wig, OC, 8" 360.00

Wax, Poured Wax

Alice headband hairdo, RpC, 14" 475.00
Common type, worn wax, RpC, 12" 150.00
Lady, poured head & limbs, glass eyes, cloth body, RpC, 24" ..3,600.00
Lever-operated eyes, 1850s, RpC, 17" 950.00
Molded hat, RpC, 16" 3,200.00
Over compo, sleep eyes, cloth body, wood limbs, 1860s, RpC, 16" ..850.00
Poured head & limbs, glass eyes, cloth body, RpC, 16" 1,400.00
Poured head & limbs, glass eyes, cloth body, RpC, 22" 1,900.00
2-faced, laughing & crying, Bartenstein, 1890s, RpC, 16" 950.00

Door Knockers

Door knockers, those charming precursors of the doorbell, come in an intriguing array of shapes and styles. The very rare ones come from England. Cast-iron examples made in this country were often produced in forms similar to the more familiar doorstop figures.

Butterfly, mc w/pk rose, cream & purple bkplate, 3½" 115.00
Cardinal w/berries on branch, red w/blk, oval bkplate, 5" 200.00
Colonial woman, Waverly Studio, Wilmette IL, 4¾x2½" 150.00

Cupid, blond hair, flesh body, purple scarf and pink roses on blue background, #618 and #622, 4x3", EX/NM, $500.00.

Hand, old pnt, 9" 105.00
Ivy in basket, gr & yel, wht bkplate, 4¼x2½" 125.00
Lion head, ring in mouth, ca 1800, 7" 260.00
Morning Glory, purple on leaf bkground 225.00
Parrot, mc pnt 135.00
Peacock, blk w/mc feathers, wht bkplate, 3x3" 400.00
Snow owl, wht w/blk details, cream & gr bkplate, 4¾x3" 225.00

Doorstops

Although introduced in England in the mid-1800s, cast-iron doorstops were not made to any great extent in this country until after the Civil War. Once called 'door porters,' their function was to keep doors open to provide better ventilation. They have been produced in many shapes and sizes, both dimensional and flat-backed, and in the past few years have become a popular, yet affordable collectible. While cast-iron examples are the most common, brass, wood, and chalk were also used. An average price is in the $100.00 to $200.00 range, though some are valued at more than $400.00. Doorstops retained their usefulness and appeal well into the '30s.

The prices below reflect market values in the East where doorstops are at a premium. For other areas of the country, it may be necessary to adjust prices down about 25%. In the listings below, when no condition code is present, items are assumed to be in excellent original condition, flat-backed unless noted full-figured, and cast iron unless another material is mentioned. For further information we recommend *Doorstops, Identification and Values*, by Jeanne Bertoia.

Key:
B&H — Bradley & Hubbard ff — full-figured

Amish Man, standing w/right hand in pocket, ff, 8½x3¾" 225.00
Basset Hound, sitting, ff, Hubley, 7x6½" 325.00
Beagle, sitting, 8x6½" 200.00
Bear w/Honey, standing, 15x6½" 500.00
Boston Bulldog, glass eyes, Greenblatt Studios, 13x5½" 225.00
Boston Terrier, porcelainized, ff, 8¾x8" 125.00
Boston Terrier w/Paw Up, ff, 9½x7" 300.00
Camel, ff, 7x9" 300.00
Cape Cod Cottage, Hubley #444, 5½x7¾" 175.00
Charleston Dancers, Hubley, #270 FISH, 9x5", minimum value 500.00
Cocker Spaniel, ff, Hubley, 6¾x11" 225.00
Colonial Pilgrim, standing w/right arm extended, 8¾x5⅜" 375.00
Conestoga Wagon, mk No 100, 8x11" 150.00
Cosmos Vase, Hubley #455, 17¾x10¼" 350.00
Cottage in Woods, 8¼x7¼" 275.00
Cottage w/Fence, National Foundry #32, 5¾x8" 150.00
Covered Wagon, Hubley #375, 9½x5⅛" 175.00
Crocodile, wedge, 5¾x11½" 125.00
Dachshund, Taylor #8, 1930, 5½x7¼" 375.00
Doll on Base, pk dress & bonnet, ff 125.00
Dolly Dimple, yel dress, bl hat, ff, Hubley, 7¾x3¾" 300.00
Donald Duck, holding Stop sign, 8⅜x5¼" 200.00
Drum Major, red & wht outfit, ff, 13½x6½" 400.00
Elephant, Hubley, trunk over head, 8¼x10" 125.00
Frog on Mushroom, ff, 4½x3⅝" 175.00
Geisha, playing lute, ff, Hubley, 7x6" 250.00
German Shepherd, ff, Hubley, 9¾x13" 150.00
Giraffe, Hubley, 12½x9", minimum value 500.00
Giraffe, mk S-110, wedge, 13½x5¼" 275.00
Gnome Smoking Pipe, ff, 6½x10" 365.00
Heron, Albany Foundry #83, 7½x5⅛" 150.00
Huckleberry Finn, bl overalls, yel hat, Littco, 12½x9½" 500.00
Kitten, Hubley #38/National, 8x6" 150.00
Knight in Armor, 13¼x6" 225.00
Lamb, standing, ff, 6¾x9¼" 275.00
Lighthouse, National Foundry #95, 6¼x8" 250.00
Lil Red Riding Hood, Hubley #95, 9½x5" 450.00
Lil Red Riding Hood & Wolf, National Foundry #94, 7¼x5⅜" 375.00
Little Girl by Wall, ff, Albany, 5¼x3¼" 175.00
Lobster, 12½x6½" 425.00
Monkey, sitting, ff, 7x5" 225.00
Monkey on Barrel, Taylor #3, 1930, 8⅜x4⅞" 350.00
Nasturtiums, Hubley #221, 7¼x6½" 125.00
Olive Picker & Mule on Base, 7¾x8¾", minimum value 500.00
Owl, glass eyes, B&H #7797, 15½x5", minimum value 500.00
Owl on Books, Eastern, 9¼x6½" 475.00
Owl on Stump, facing left, 10x6" 225.00
Parrot, Blodgett Studios #1010, 12½x6½" 250.00
Peacock by Urn, Hubley #208, 7½x4¼" 225.00
Peacock on Fence, National Foundry #56, 13x7⅜" 250.00
Persian Cat, ff, Hubley, 8½x6½" 175.00
Peter Rabbit, Hubley #96, 9½x4¾" 400.00
Petunias & Asters, Hubley #470, 9½x6½" 150.00
Pied Piper, playing flute on mushroom, 7¼x5" 300.00
Pirate Girl, 13⅞x7¼" 275.00
Popeye, ff, Hubley, 9x4½", minimum value 500.00
Poppies & Cornflowers, Hubley #265, 7¼x6½" 125.00
Poppies & Snapdragons, Hubley #484, 7½x7¼" 125.00
Primrose, Hubley #488, 7⅜x6¼" 175.00
Putting Golfer, Hubley #34, 8⅜x7" 300.00
Rabbit w/Top Hat, red tux, Albany #94, 9⅞x4¾" 400.00
Reclining Kitten, ff, National Foundry, 8⅛x4" 225.00
Ship, mc, National Foundry, 10x12" 175.00
Show Horse, ff, Hubley, 8½x8" 175.00
Squirrel on Stump, 9x6⅜" 175.00
St Bernard, sm barrel around neck, 8x10½" 175.00
Swan, ff, National Foundry, 5¾x4½" 200.00
Tiger Lilies, Hubley #472, 10½x6" 200.00
Tulip Vase, Hubley #443, 10x8" 150.00
Twin Cats, Hubley #73, 7x5¼" 325.00
Uncle Sam, 12x5½" 500.00
Woman Holding Flowers, red dress, 8½x4¾" 125.00
Woman w/Hatbox, pk & gray dress, 6¾x5¼" 175.00

Dorchester Pottery

Taking its name from the town in Massachusetts where it was organized in 1895, the Dorchester Pottery Company made primarily utilitarian wares, though other types of items were made as well. By 1940 a line of decorative pottery was introduced, some of which was painted by hand with scrollwork or themes from nature. The buildings were destroyed by fire in the late 1970s, and the pottery was never rebuilt. In the listings that follow, the decorations described are all in cobalt unless otherwise noted. Our advisor for this category is Dale MacLean; he is listed in the Directory under Massachusetts.

Plate, farm mill and landscape, Knesseth Denisons, 7½", $200.00; Mug, clown and stripe motif, Dorchester/Cah/Ehh, 4½", $175.00.

Bowl, Apple, sgn CAH, stamped, 1776-1976, 2x5¾" 100.00
Bowl, Blueberry, sgn CAH, stamped, 2⅛x5¾", NM 75.00
Bowl, Blueberry, sgn CAH/N Ricci, stamped, 2x6½" 75.00
Bowl, Colonial Lace, sgn CAH, stamped, 2x5¾" 100.00
Bowl, Dragon-Bumblebee-Butterfly, sgn CAH, stamped, 2¼x9" ..275.00
Bowl, Grape, sgn CAH, stamped, 3⅛x7" 150.00
Bowl, Pinion, sgn CAH, 2x5¾", pr 125.00
Bowl, Ship & Seascape, sgn K Denisons, stamped, 2x5½" 150.00
Bowl, Teardrop, sgn CAH, stamped, 2¼x5¾" 150.00
Bowl & underplate, Whale, sgn CAH, 2¼x5½", 7½" 125.00
Candle holder, Pine Cone, sgn CAH, stamped, 2¼x5½", NM ..150.00
Candy dish, Whale, sgn CAH, ¾x5½" 150.00
Casserole, Geometric, sgn RT, stamped, 2½x7⅛" 300.00
Casserole, Half Scroll, sgn CAH/N Ricci, stamped, 4¾x7¼" 225.00

Casserole, Pine Cone, sgn CAH, stamped, 2¾x5½" 200.00
Casserole, Whale, sgn CAH/N Ricci, stamped, 4¾x8" 300.00
Charger, Blueberry, sgn CAH/N Ricci, stamped, 12⅛" 300.00
Charger, Ship, sgn JM/N Ricci, stamped, 12¼" 425.00
Charger, Whale, sgn CAH/N Ricci, stamped, 10½" 300.00
Cheese server, Half Scroll, sgn CAH, stamped, 2½x6" 275.00
Coffee set, Blueberry, sgn CAH, pot+mug+sugar bowl 150.00
Cup, Apple, sgn, CAH, 2¾x4¾", 2 for 100.00
Cup, Blueberry, sgn CAH, 2¾", 3 for 125.00
Dish, Grape, sgn CAH/N Ricci, stamped, 1½x8½" 100.00
Jar, Sacred Cod, w/lid, sgn CAH, stamped, 3¾x3¾" 125.00
Mug, Clown, All Gone inside, sgn CAH, stamped, 2¾" 175.00
Mug, Clown & Stripe, sgn CAH, stamped, 4½" 175.00
Mug, Grape, sgn CAH, stamped, 3x5¼" 75.00
Mug, Leprechaun, sgn CAH, stamped, 2¾x4½" 150.00
Mug, Pussy Willow, sgn CAH, stamped, 2¾x4¾" 100.00
Mug & saucer, Pine Cone, sgn CAH, stamped, 3", 6¼" 75.00
Pitcher, Full Scroll, w/lid, sgn CAH, 4½" 200.00
Pitcher, Grape, sgn CAH, stamped, 5½x7½" 225.00
Pitcher, Half Scroll, w/lid, sgn CAH, stamped, 5½" 200.00
Pitcher, Pine Cone, sgn CAH/N Ricci, 5½x5¼" 225.00
Pitcher, Pussy Willow, sgn CAH/N Ricci, stamped, 5½x4¼" 225.00
Pitcher, Whale, sgn CAH/N Ricci, stamped, 5½x7" 250.00
Plate, Acorn, sgn R Trotter, stamped, 7½" 225.00
Plate, Colonial Lace, sgn CAH/N Ricci, 10½" 275.00
Plate, Farm Mill & Landscape, sgn K Denisons, stamped, 7½" ...200.00
Plate, Pussy Willow, sgn CAH, stamped, 1776-1976, 7¼" 200.00
Toby jug, Quaker Oats replica, early orig label, 8x7½" 250.00

Dorflinger

C. Dorflinger was born in Alsace, France, and came to this country when he was ten years old. When still very young, he obtained a job in a glass factory in New Jersey. As a young man, he started his own glass-works in Brooklyn, New York, opening new factories as profits permitted. During that time he made cut glass articles for many famous people including President and Mrs. Lincoln, for whom he produced a complete service of tableware with the United States Coat of Arms. In 1863 he sold the New York factories because of ill health and moved to his farm near White Mills, Pennsylvania. His health returned, and he started a plant near his home. It was there that he did much of his best work, making use of only the very finest materials. Christian died in 1915, and the plant was closed in 1921 by consent of the family.

Dorflinger glass is rare and often hard to identify. Very few pieces were marked — many only carried a small paper label which was quickly discarded.

Carafe, Hobstars & Dmns 120.00
Decanter, flutes & bull's eyes, honeycomb at neck, 12" 295.00
Decanter, gr o/l, flute/ring cuttings, 9½"+4 2¼" wines 395.00
Decanter, sherry; cut decor, faceted stopper, 9" 125.00
Pitcher, tankard juice; hobstars, arches w/cane etc, 5" 325.00
Plate, cranberry to clear, Vintage, 8" 495.00
Relish, Dmn & Fan cutting w/stars, triple-cut hdl, 2-part 500.00
Wine, cranberry to clear, Renaissance 185.00

Dragon Ware

Dragon ware is fairly accessible and is still being made today. The new Dragon ware is distinguishible by the lack of detail in the dragon. In the older pieces, much care is given to the slipwork dragon's eyes, scales, and wings. In the new ware, the dragon is flat and lacks detail.

Colors are primary, referring to background color, not the color of the dragon. The primary color of a new piece has more shine than the older ware. Old colors are vibrant but for the most part not shiny (except for the lustre colors). New colors include green, lavender, yellow, pink, blue, pearlized, and orange as well as the classic blue/black. Old colors include orange, green, yellow, blue, pearlized, and blue/black. In addition to lustre finishes, you will find some background colors that are applied unevenly (and without shine), producing a cloud effect behind the dragon.

Many Dragon ware cups have lithophanes in the bottoms, often the face of a geisha girl. Nude lithophanes are more scarce but can sometimes be found in cups and saki cups. New pieces may also have lithophanes, but they are lacking in detail and tend to be flat.

Items listed below are unmarked unless noted otherwise. Ranges are given for pieces that are currently being produced. (Be sure to examine unmarked items well, in particular, looking for good detailing in the dragon. Remember, new pieces lack the quality of workmanship evident in items made earlier in the century and should not command the prices of the older ware.) Our advisor for this category is Suzi Hibbard; she is listed in the Directory under California.

Ashtray, gray, from $5 to 10.00
Ashtray, rectangular, gold trim, 4x3" 6.00
Bowl, dessert; gray, mk Kutani 25.00
Bowl, vegetable; gray, oblong, mk Kutani 35.00
Bowl w/frog, orange, mk MIJ, 9" 45.00
Box, cigarette; mk MIJ 25.00
Box, egg form, ftd, mk Saji, 3" 30.00
Castor set, 6-pc, on 10" tray 125.00
Chocolate set, bl lustre, 3-pc 55.00
Cracker jar, gray, mk Nippon, 7½" 425.00
Cup, coffee; bl cloud, mk Funatsuki 20.00
Cup & saucer, child sz, from $5 to 25.00
Cup & saucer, demitasse; from $5 to 20.00
Cup & saucer, demitasse; orange/peach, mk MIOJ 15.00
Cup & saucer, geisha lithophane 25.00
Cup & saucer, gold 15.00
Cup & saucer, lav, litho 15.00
Cup & saucer, no mk, from $7.50 to 30.00
Cup & saucer, whistling; orange, mk MIJ 25.00
Cup & saucer, 6-sided, child sz 15.00
Humidor, gray, mk Nippon, 7" 525.00
Incense burner, 3" 15.00
Incense jar, bl, mk MIJ, 5" 35.00
Incense jar, no mk, from $5 to 40.00

Mug, Nippon mark,
5½", $195.00.

Nappy, bl cloud 20.00
Oil lamp, bl, souvenir Crater Lake 15.00
Oil lamp, bl lustre, souvenir Oregon 15.00
Pitcher, mini; 1¾" 10.00
Planter, gray, hanging, mk MIJ 45.00
Plate, gold rim, M in wreath mk, 7½" 10.00
Plate, gray, mk Kutani, 10½" 40.00

Plate, gray, mk Kutani, 8" **25.00**
Plate, wht beading, brn flames, Japan, 7½" **10.00**
Plate, wht beads & lav rim, 6" **20.00**
Saki set, blk, litho, mk MIJ **60.00**
Saki set, 6 cups w/lithophanes **65.00**
Shakers, coffeepot/teapot, blk, pr **15.00**
Shakers, pr, from $5 to **20.00**
Snack set, gray, teapot+cr/sug+4 cups+4 plates **175.00**
Tankard set, gray, mk Nippon **1,500.00**
Tea set, demitasse; red cloud, 15-pc **125.00**
Tea set, gold dragons on cobalt, sgn Shofar on pot, 15-pc **425.00**
Tea set, gr cloud, dragon spout, litho, mk MIJ, 15-pc **200.00**
Tea set, no mk, 15-pc, $25 to **125.00**
Teapot, gold, mk Japan, child sz **20.00**
Teapot, gold hdl, 7" **45.00**
Teapot, gray w/dragon spout, mk MIJ **45.00**
Teapot w/stand, gray, dragon spout, MIJ **45.00**
Vase, amethyst glass, 6½" **15.00**
Vase, bl cloud, mk Nagoya China, 6½", pr **90.00**
Vase, gray, jeweled eyes, Nippon, 6" **175.00**
Vase, no mk, from $5 to **30.00**
Vase, orange, mk MIJ, 3" **10.00**
Vase, pearlized, 6" **45.00**
Vase, slender form, 6" **50.00**
Vase, wht, 8" **25.00**
Wall hanging, gray, mk MIJ **30.00**
Wall pocket, red, mk MIJ, 5½" **25.00**
Watering can, orange, 3" **10.00**

Dresden

The term Dresden is used today to indicate the porcelains that were produced in Meissen and Dresden, Germany, from the very early 18th century well into the next. John Bottger, a young alchemist, discovered the formula for the first true porcelain in 1708 while being held a virtual prisoner at the palace in Dresden because of the King's determination to produce a superior ware. Two years later a factory was erected in nearby Meissen with Bottger as director. There fine tableware, elaborate centerpieces, and exquisite figurines with applied details were produced. In 1731, to distinguish their product from the wares of such potters as Sevres, Worcester, Chelsea, and Derby, the Meissen company adopted their famous crossed-swords trademark. During the next century, several potteries were producing porcelain in the 'Meissen style' in Dresden itself. Their wares were often marked with imitations of Meissen's crossed swords.

The Carl Theime factory produced dinnerware as well as decorative pieces in the Meissen style from 1872 until 1972. Openwork pieces were their specialty. Their mark was an intertwined 'SP' with the word Dresden below. Other companies followed suit, and in 1883 began using the crown mark along with the Dresden indication. There were several variations of this mark employed over the years. Many of these companies produced Meissen-type wares well into the 20th century. See also Meissen.

Figurine, Beethoven at piano, surrounded by 5 listeners on oval base, 8½x22x11", $935.00.

Candelabra, pk & yel appl roses on wht, 10", pr **425.00**
Egg dish, mc floral w/gold, 8¾" **65.00**
Figurine, ballerina, in pk/wht dress w/appl flowers, 7" **225.00**
Figurine, boy feeding geese, mc w/gold, late, 5⅛" **145.00**
Figurine, dancer holds ruffled skirt wide, 10x10" **457.00**
Figurine, peasant & sleeping lover, lamb/kid/children/bee, 10" ..**675.00**
Figurine, pug dog, wht w/blk & pk, gold collar w/balls, 7x9" **550.00**
Plate, courting scene, rtcl border w/gold, 9", pr **355.00**
Urn, maidens in landscape/gold florals on red, w/lid, 19½" **1,300.00**
Vase, HP scenes, rtcl neck, ftd, 6½", pr **375.00**

Dresser Accessories

Dresser sets, ring trees, figural or satin pincushions, manicure sets — all those lovely items that graced milady's dressing table — were at the same time decorative as well as functional. Today they appeal to collectors for many reasons. The Victorian era is well represented by repousse silver-backed mirrors and brushes and pincushions that were used to display ornamental pins for the hair, hats, and scarves. The hair receiver — similar to a powder jar but with an opening in the lid — was used to hold long strands of hair retrieved from the comb or brush. These were wound around the finger and tucked in the opening to be used later for hair jewelry and pictures, many of which survive to the present day. (See Hair Weaving.)

Celluloid dresser sets were popular during the late 1800s and early 1900s. Some included manicure tools, pill boxes, and buttonhooks, as well as the basic items. Because celluloid tends to break rather easily, a whole set may be hard to find today. (See also Plastics.) With the current interest in anything Art Deco, sets from the '30s and '40s are especially collectible. These may be made of crystal, Bakelite, or silver, and the original boxes just as lavishly appointed as their contents.

Box, collar, celluloid, Pony Express rider scene on lid **160.00**
Curling iron, ornate sterling hdl **38.00**
Mirror, hand; SP, cupid figural hdl **175.00**
Set, faceted glass, cobalt & chrome tops, ca 1936, 6-pc **50.00**
Set, Fr ivory, 10-pc, M in faux reptile leather box **110.00**
Set, gr celluloid w/bl & topaz faux stones, 20-pc **400.00**
Set, ivory, clock/fr/vase/box, Dubarry, ca 1910 ....**135.00**
Set, silver, Baltimore Rose, Steiff, mirror/2 brushes/comb **200.00**
Set, sterling silver w/ornate emb, brush/comb/mirror **160.00**
Set, tortoise pyralin, 6-pc **50.00**
Tray, Fr bronze & champleve w/scrolling border, hdls, 14" **500.00**

Dryden

Dryden Pottery was founded fifty years ago in Ellsworth, Kansas, by Jim Dryden, WWII veteran with financing from a G.I. loan. A mention on the front page of the Wall Street Journal resulted in substantial orders from Macy's of New York and Fred Harvey Restaurants and gift shops in all the stations of the Santa Fe Railroad.

In the late 1940s and early 1950s, some six hundred stores stocked Dryden pottery. Stiff competition from occupied Japan and Europe forced wholesale prices so low that the only profit from the pottery was from direct sales to the traveling public. Tourists watched potters at work. These sales were profitable, but in 1955, the new transcontinental highway 70 through Kansas missed Ellsworth. The pottery had to move. Hot Springs, Arkansas, with its hundreds of thousands of tourists was chosen as the new location.

Since 1970 more and more of the production is wheel thrown and hand sculpted in an all-out attempt to follow the example of the world-famous Rookwood Pottery (1880-1967). Beautiful matt and gloss glazes plus one-of-a-kind originals make Dryden Pottery highly collectible.

Ashtray, #17A, blk 24.00
Berry set, C2, mustard 75.00
Bookends, #80, Scotty dogs 45.00
Boot, #90, souvenir 25.00
Boot, bl, 8" 35.00
Bowl, #40, brn, souvenir 35.00
Buffalo, souvenir 85.00
Elephant, #10 ....75.00
Flowerpot, #86, pr 25.00
Jug, H1, maroon 30.00
Lion, mustard 35.00

Mug, face relief, $30.00.

Panther, blk 85.00
Pitcher, #101, bl 37.00
Pitcher, #62, fish 50.00
Pitcher, #94, Messiah Chorus 25.00
Pitcher, #99, Brookville Hotel 30.00
Pitcher, H5, Lindsborg KS 20.00
Planter, #X, mustard, 10" 25.00
Planter, #5, pony 45.00
Planter, cow 35.00
Shakers, #70, blk, souvenir, pr 30.00
Spoon holder, yel, souvenir 30.00
Vase, #17, gr 16.00
Vase, #18, sq, souvenir 35.00
Vase, #50, souvenir 45.00
Vase, #95, navy 25.00
Vase, Ark, pk, 6" 50.00
Vase, Ark, 15" 85.00
Vase, leaf, bl 36.00

Duncan and Miller

The firm that became known as the Duncan and Miller Glass Company in 1900 was organized in 1874 in Pittsburgh, Pennsylvania, a partnership between George Duncan, his sons Harry and James, and his son-in-law Augustus Heisey. John Ernest Miller was hired as their designer. He is credited with creating the most famous of all Duncan's glassware lines, Three Face. (See Pattern Glass.) The George Duncan and Sons Glass Company, as it was titled, was only one of eighteen companies that merged in 1891 with U.S. Glass. Soon after the Pittsburgh factory burned in 1892, the association was dissolved, and Heisey left the firm to set up his own factory in Newark, Ohio. Duncan built his new plant in Washington, Pennsylvania, where he continued to make pressed glassware in such notable patterns as Bagware, Amberette, Duncan Flute, Button Arches, and Zippered Slash. The firm was eventually sold to U.S. Glass in Tiffin, Ohio, and unofficially closed in August 1955.

In addition to the early pressed dinnerware patterns, today's Duncan and Miller collectors enjoy searching for opalescent vases in many patterns and colors, frosted 'Satin Tone' glassware, acid-etched designs,

and lovely stemware such as the Rock Crystal cuttings. Milk glass was made in limited quantity and is considered a good investment. Ruby glass, Ebony (a lovely opaque black glass popular during the '20s and '30s), and, of course, the glass animal and bird figurines are all highly valued examples of the art of Duncan and Miller.

Expect to pay at least 25% more than values listed for other colors, for ruby and cobalt, as much as 50% more in the Georgian, Pall Mall, and Sandwich lines. Pink, green, and amber Sandwich is worth approximately 30% more than the same items in crystal. Milk glass examples of American Way are valued up to 30% higher than color, 50% higher in Pall Mall. Add approximately 40% to listed prices for opalescent items. Etchings, cuttings, and other decorations will increase values by about 50%. For further study we recommend *The Encyclopedia of Duncan Glass* by Gail Krause; she is listed in the Directory under Pennsylvania. Several Duncan and Miller lines are shown in *Elegant Glassware of the Depression Era* by Gene Florence. Also refer to *Glass Animals and Figural Flower Frogs of the Depression Era* by Lee Garmon and Dick Spencer; they are both listed under Illinois. See also Glass Animals.

Canterbury, crystal, ashtray, 5" 12.00
Canterbury, crystal, basket, crimped, 3x4" 27.50
Canterbury, crystal, basket, oval, 10x4½x8" 70.00
Canterbury, crystal, bowl, flared, 3½x12" 30.00
Canterbury, crystal, bowl, gardenia; 2x9" 25.00
Canterbury, crystal, bowl, star form, 1-hdl, 1¾x5½" 10.00
Canterbury, crystal, candle holder, low, 3" 12.50
Canterbury, crystal, candlestick, 3-light, 6" 25.00
Canterbury, crystal, cheese stand, 3½x5½" 10.00
Canterbury, crystal, comport, high std, 5½x6" 20.00
Canterbury, crystal, decanter, w/stopper, 32-oz, 12" 45.00
Canterbury, crystal, ice bucket/vase, 7" 37.50
Canterbury, crystal, pitcher, martini; no hdl, 32-oz, 9¼" 60.00
Canterbury, crystal, shakers, pr 22.50
Canterbury, crystal, tray, pickle & olive; 2-part, 9" L 17.50
Canterbury, crystal, tumbler, juice; ftd, #5115, 5-oz, 4¼" 12.00
Canterbury, crystal, vase, cloverleaf, 4½" 17.50
Canterbury, crystal, vase, flower arranger; 7" 35.00
Caribbean, bl, bowl, grapefruit; hdld, ftd, 7¼" 45.00
Caribbean, bl, creamer 25.00
Caribbean, bl, mustard, w/slotted lid, 4" 65.00
Caribbean, bl, relish, 5-part, 12¾" dia 90.00
Caribbean, bl, server, center hdl, 6½" 50.00
Caribbean, bl, stem, sherbet; ftd, 4¼" 17.50
Caribbean, bl, teacup 50.00
Caribbean, bl, vase, str sides, ftd, 8" 85.00
Caribbean, crystal, bowl, folded side, hdld, 3¾x5" 16.00
Caribbean, crystal, cocktail shaker, 33-oz, 9" 95.00
Caribbean, crystal, ice bucket, 6½" 75.00
Caribbean, crystal, plate, soup liner; rolled rim, 7¼" 5.00
Caribbean, crystal, shakers, metal lids, 3", pr 32.00
Caribbean, crystal, tray, 12¾" dia 25.00
Caribbean, crystal, tumbler, flat, 5-oz, 3½" 20.00
First Love, crystal, ashtray, #30, 3½x2½" 16.50
First Love, crystal, bowl, #117, 7x13" 62.50
First Love, crystal, bowl, #30, 1¾x11" 55.00
First Love, crystal, butter/cheese dish, #111, 7" sq 115.00
First Love, crystal, candle holder, 1-light, #111, 3" 25.00
First Love, crystal, candy jar, ftd, w/lid, #25, 7¼x5" 75.00
First Love, crystal, cocktail shaker, #5200, 32-oz 150.00
First Love, crystal, cup, #115 ....20.00
First Love, crystal, mayonnaise, ftd, hdls, #111, 2½x5½" 35.00
First Love, crystal, plate, #115, 14" 50.00
First Love, crystal, plate, #115, 8½" 20.00
First Love, crystal, relish, 5-part, #111, 12" 60.00

First Love, crystal, stem, ice cream; #5111½, 5-oz, 4" 14.00
First Love, crystal, tumbler, whiskey; #5200, 2" 55.00
First Love, crystal, vase, ftd, #506, 12" 145.00
Sandwich, crystal, bonbon, heart shape, hdls, 5½" 15.00
Sandwich, crystal, bowl, fruit; 3-part, 10" 80.00
Sandwich, crystal, bowl, nappy, ring hdl, 5" 12.00
Sandwich, crystal, bowl, salad; shallow, 12" 40.00
Sandwich, crystal, cake stand, plain ped ft, 13" 85.00
Sandwich, crystal, candlestick, 1-light, 4" 14.00
Sandwich, crystal, candlestick, 2-light, 5" 30.00
Sandwich, crystal, candy jar, ftd, w/lid, 8½" 55.00
Sandwich, crystal, epergne, threaded base, 7½" 70.00
Sandwich, crystal, pitcher, metal lid, 13-oz 60.00
Sandwich, crystal, relish, 2-part, oval, 7" 20.00
Sandwich, crystal, relish, 3-part, oblong, 10" 27.50
Sandwich, crystal, shakers, metal lids, 2½", pr 18.00
Sandwich, crystal, stem, parfait; ftd, 4-oz, 5¼" 30.00
Sandwich, crystal, tumbler, water; ftd, 9-oz, 4¾" 14.00
Sandwich, crystal, vase, fan form, ftd, 5" 25.00
Sandwich, crystal, vase, hat form, 4" 20.00
Spiral Flutes, amber, gr or pk, bowl, bouillon; 3¾", ea 15.00
Spiral Flutes, amber, gr or pk, bowl, nappy, 7", ea 15.00
Spiral Flutes, amber, gr or pk, cup, ea 9.00
Spiral Flutes, amber, gr or pk, ice tub, hdls, ea 50.00
Spiral Flutes, amber, gr or pk, plate, dinner; 10⅜", ea 22.50
Spiral Flutes, amber, gr or pk, platter, 13", ea 45.00
Spiral Flutes, amber, gr or pk, tumbler, ginger ale; 5½", ea 65.00
Spiral Flutes, amber, gr or pk, tumbler, water; ftd, 5⅛", ea 20.00
Tear Drop, crystal, ashtray, ind, 3" 6.00
Tear Drop, crystal, bowl, console; crimped, hdls, 10" 27.50
Tear Drop, crystal, bowl, fruit; 5" 6.00
Tear Drop, crystal, bowl, gardenia; 13" 35.00
Tear Drop, crystal, bowl, salad; 9" 25.00
Tear Drop, crystal, cake salver, ftd, 13" 55.00
Tear Drop, crystal, candlestick, 4" 9.00
Tear Drop, crystal, candy box, 3-part, 3-hdld, w/lid, 8" 60.00
Tear Drop, crystal, celery dish, 2-part, 2-hdls, 11" 18.00
Tear Drop, crystal, coaster/ashtray, rolled rim, 3" 7.00
Tear Drop, crystal, creamer, 6-oz 11.00
Tear Drop, crystal, lazy susan, 18" 90.00
Tear Drop, crystal, mustard jar, w/lid, 4¼" 35.00
Tear Drop, crystal, nut dish, 2-part, 6" 10.00
Tear Drop, crystal, pickle dish, 6" 15.00
Tear Drop, crystal, plate, torte; rolled rim, 14" 35.00
Tear Drop, crystal, relish, 5-part, 12" dia 27.50
Tear Drop, crystal, shakers, 5", pr 25.00
Tear Drop, crystal, stem, claret, 4-oz 17.50
Tear Drop, crystal, stem, sherbet, ftd, 5-oz 5.00
Tear Drop, crystal, sugar bowl, 3-oz 5.00
Tear Drop, crystal, teacup, 6-oz 8.00
Tear Drop, crystal, tray, hdls, 8" 12.50
Tear Drop, crystal, tumbler, flat, 9-oz, 4¼" 8.00
Tear Drop, crystal, tumbler, high-ball; flat, 14-oz, 5¾" 17.50
Tear Drop, crystal, tumbler, whiskey; flat, 2-oz 17.00
Tear Drop, crystal, vase, fan form, ftd, 9" 25.00
Terrace, amber or crystal, creamer, 3", ea 18.00
Terrace, crystal or amber, bowl, ftd, flared rim, 10", ea 55.00
Terrace, crystal or amber, celery tray, hdld, 2x8", ea 17.50
Terrace, crystal or amber, pitcher, ea 275.00
Terrace, crystal or amber, plate, torte; flat rim, 13", ea 50.00
Terrace, crystal or amber, plate, 11", ea 47.50
Terrace, crystal or amber, plate, 9" sq, ea 35.00
Terrace, crystal or amber, relish, 2-part, 6", ea 20.00
Terrace, crystal or amber, stem, cordial, #5111½, 3¾", ea 40.00

Terrace, crystal or amber, stem, wine, #5111½, 5¼", ea 32.50
Terrace, red or cobalt, cheese stand, 5¼x3", ea 40.00
Terrace, red or cobalt, plate, 11", ea 90.00
Terrace, red or cobalt, plate, 6" sq, ea 40.00
Terrace, red or cobalt, saucer, sq, ea 16.00
Terrace, red or cobalt, sugar bowl, 10-oz, 3", ea 35.00

Durand

Durand Art Glass was a division of Vineland Flint Glass Works in Vineland, New Jersey. This division was geared toward the manufacture of fine hand-blown art glass in the style of Tiffany and Steuben. Lustered glass and opal glass were used as a basis to create such patterns as King Tut, Heart and Vine, Peacock Feather, and Egyptian Crackle. Crystal, cased, and overlay glass were used to produce cut designs. Production began in 1924 and continued until 1931. Early art glass was unmarked. Later pieces were generally signed Durand, often written across a large 'V,' all in script. The numbers that sometimes appear along with the signature indicate shape and height of the object. Owner Victor Durand employed several employees as well as the owner of the failed Quezal Art Glass and Decorating Company, which explains why early Durand is often mistaken for Quezal. Note: Examples listed below are all signed unless noted otherwise. Our advisor for this category is Edward J. Meschi; he is listed in the Directory under New Jersey.

Bonbon, King Tut, bl irid w/swirled wht, amber finial/ft, 4¾" 700.00
Bowl, centerpiece; cobalt irid, folded rim, #2605, 2¼x14" 750.00
Bowl, coil, opal on bl irid, 3½x10½" 1,050.00
Bowl, peacock feathers, wht w/bl border on Spanish Yel, 15" 900.00
Bowl, red craquelle, 4x9", w/14" undertray 650.00
Candle lamp, feathers, gr & wht on gold irid bell form, 11x9" ...320.00
Candlesticks, feathers, wht on bl, flanged rim, 3x5", pr 650.00
Candlesticks, King Tut, bl irid w/opal, baluster stems, 10", pr .1,600.00
Compote, King Tut, bl irid w/amber ft & finial, 6¼" 700.00
Compote, King Tut, cobalt w/clear stem, att, 3½x6¾" 475.00
Console set, feathers, opal on cobalt, yel bases, 3-pc 1,700.00
Cup & saucer, feathers, opal on emerald gr 175.00
Ginger jar, marigold w/overall threading, 6" 950.00
Goblet, bl cup w/ambergris stem & ft 175.00
Goblet, feathers, opal on red cup, ambergris stem/ft 250.00
Goblet, ruby w/yel stem, ruby ft, scalloped, 8½" 550.00
Lamp, Egyptian craquelle, gr & wht, ginger jar, metal base 1,100.00
Lamp, feathers, gold w/gold threads on gold base, 10" 600.00
Lamp, King Tut, opal on bl irid, brass base, 15" 500.00
Lamp, red cut to clear, 14" 450.00
Plate, ambergris w/gr trim, 8" 100.00
Plate, feathers, opal on cobalt, 8" 225.00
Plate, ruby w/wht trim, 8" 125.00
Rose bowl, gold irid on bl-gold irid base, 5¼" 700.00
Rose bowl, hearts & vines, dk bl irid w/silver bl, irid ft, 5" 1,650.00
Tumbler, cobalt cut to clear 175.00
Tumbler, ruby cut to clear, 5" 175.00

Vase, deep gold iridescent with blue coils, 10⅝", $900.00.

Vase, ambergris (oil glass) w/3 wht opaque arches, 6¾" **460.00**
Vase, bl irid, appl gold irid ft, #20120, 12", pr **1,800.00**
Vase, bl irid, beehive form, #20177, 6½", pr **2,800.00**
Vase, bl irid, shouldered, 12" **900.00**
Vase, bl irid w/irregular mc lustre, oval sphere, #1995, 3¾" **435.00**
Vase, bl irid w/threaded body, gold irid ft, #2028½, 8¼" **1,250.00**
Vase, Coil, bl & marigold on opal, cylindrical, 9" **1,100.00**
Vase, Coil, gr/bl on gold, wide cylinder, no mk, 8" **850.00**
Vase, Coil, opal on gold irid, cylindrical, 10" **550.00**
Vase, dk bl irid w/allover threading, #1710, 8" **850.00**
Vase, Egyptian craquelle, red/wht on gold irid, 6¾" **1,000.00**
Vase, feathers, gold w/gold threading, #1812, 7" **450.00**
Vase, feathers, gr & gold on gold irid w/threading, 9½" **975.00**
Vase, feathers, opal on gold irid w/gold threads, #1710, 10" **1,600.00**
Vase, feathers, opal on marigold, allover threads, #20102, 14" ...**900.00**
Vase, feathers, wht on red, opal trim, hdls, 9" **850.00**
Vase, floral frieze/geometrics, red/wht opal, 10" **2,500.00**
Vase, gold, classic form, 9¾" **950.00**
Vase, gold irid, tapered w/beehive shoulder, sgn/#1978, 9" **900.00**
Vase, gold irid cased vasiform w/appl threading, 6¼" **460.00**
Vase, gold irid w/flared rim, #1770, 8" **700.00**
Vase, hearts & vines, bl on marigold irid, #1710, 6" **750.00**
Vase, hearts & vines, bl/gold on opal, gold threads, ftd, 9" **2,100.00**
Vase, hearts & vines, gr & bl on orange-gold, #1812, 7¾" **1,095.00**
Vase, hearts & vines, wht on bl irid, 6½" **865.00**
Vase, King Tut, opal on bl irid w/caramel inclusions, 7" **1,000.00**
Vase, lt/dk gr melon-stripe, hard ribbed, cup neck, 8x11" **1,500.00**
Vase, marigold w/allover threading, #1710, 8" **850.00**
Vase, opal cased to deep Lady Gay Rose, #1730, 6¾" **1,150.00**
Vase, Starburst, emerald cut to clear, #1710, 7" **950.00**

Durant Kilns

The Durant Pottery Company operated in Bedford Village, New York, in the early 1900s. Its founder was Mrs. Clarence Rice; she was aided by L. Volkmar to whom she assigned the task of technical direction. (See also Volkmar.) The artware and tableware they produced was simple in form and decoration. The creative aspects of the were carried on almost entirely by Volkmar himself, with only a minimal crew to help with production. After Mrs. Rice's death in 1919, the property was purchased by Volkmar, who chose to drop the Durant name by 1930. Prior to 1919 the ware was marked simply 'Durant' and dated. After that time a stylized 'V' was added.

Bowl, blk drip, bl int, flared, dtd 1914, 6x4" **400.00**
Bowl, Chinese plum, bl crackle int, oval, dtd 1917, 4x8x7" **315.00**
Vase, cobalt, exposed ft, flanged U-form, 1917, 6x7½" **185.00**
Vase, Persian bl matt, base/neck tapers, Volkmar/1927, 11x7" .**1,100.00**
Vase, purple/taupe/red, mottled/blistered, 1939, 7½x5½" **1,100.00**

Egg Cups

Egg cups, one of the fastest growing collectibles of the '90s, have been traced back to the ruins of Pompeii. Since then, they have been made in almost every country and in almost every conceivable material (ceramics, glass, metal, papier-mache, plastic, wood, ivory, even rubber and straw). Popular categories include Art Deco, Black Memorabilia, Chintz, Characters/Personalities, Golliwoggs, Railroadiana, Steamship, Souvenir Ware, etc.

Still being produced today in most countries, egg cups appeal to collectors on many levels. Prices can range from quite inexpen-

sive to many thousands of dollars. Those made prior to 1840 are scarce and sought after, as are the character/personality egg cups of the 1930s.

For a more thorough study of egg cups we recommend that you refer to *Egg Cups: An Illustrated History and Price Guide* (Antique Publications) by Brenda Blake, our advisor for this category. You will find her address listed in the Directory under Maine.

Key:
bkt — bucket, a single cup without a foot
dbl — 2-sided with small end for eating egg in shell, large end for mixing egg with toast and butter
fig — figural, an egg cup actually molded into the shape of an animal, bird, car, person, etc.
hoop — hoop, a single open cup with waistline
set — tray or cruet (stand, frame or basket) with 2 to 8 cups
sgl — single, with a foot; goblet shaped

Advertising/Souvenir

Bkt, Fanny Farmer, 2 facing yel chicks, scalloped rim **20.00**
Dbl, BPOE No 30, gr emblem **30.00**
Dbl, Caesar's palace, brn logo, recent **12.00**
Dbl, West Point, insignia **22.00**
Fig, Fanny Farmer, yel rooster, red trim worn away **14.00**
Fig, Fanny Farmer, yel rooster w/red trim **26.00**
Sgl, Crystal Palace London, pk lustreware, Germany, ca 1900 ......**35.00**
Sgl, Graceland, Japan **15.00**
Sgl, Moxie **125.00**
Sgl, Royal York Hotel, gold/blk border, porc, Royal Doulton **25.00**
Sgl, St Agnes Church...Mass, mc transfer, Germany, ca 1900 ......**32.00**
Sgl, Stanhope, vegetable ivory, Exhibition...Boston, 1883 ....**150.00**
Sgl, White House, WA, Mauchline **55.00**
Sgl, World's Fair, St Louis, transfer, 1904 ....**120.00**

American Dinnerware

Dbl, Autumn, bl/orange floral & fruit rim, Lenox, 1930s **45.00**
Dbl, Barkwood, brn bark-like design, Vernon Kilns, 1950s **15.00**
Dbl, Country Garden, emb pk flower w/gr, Stangl, 1950s-60s **12.00**
Dbl, Country Life, newly hatched yel chick, Stangl, late 1950s **65.00**
Dbl, Lu-Ray, Windsor Bl, Taylor, Smith & Taylor **14.00**
Dbl, Pk Lily, Stangl, 1950s **12.00**
Dbl, Rooster, Folk Art, caramel ground, Pennsbury, 1950s **20.00**
Dbl, Virginia Rose, Cable shape, Homer Laughlin, 1935-50s **28.00**
Sgl, Colonial Violet, integral saucer, Homer Laughlin, ca 1901 ...**22.00**
Sgl, Fiesta, red, 1936 ....**55.00**
Sgl, Tiffany, gold rim, Lenox **35.00**

Art Pottery

Bkt, trees & bl sky, SEG **300.00**
Dbl, Elephant, ftd, Dedham **550.00**
Dbl, Standing Rabbit, Juvenile series, Roseville, ca 1917 ....**165.00**
Dbl, tall ship, bl, MA Hadley **15.00**
Sgl, powder bl, Moorcroft, 1920s **40.00**

Black Memorabilia

Fig, child on potty attached to orange lustre cup, Japan, '30s **145.00**
Fig, female face, red lips, earrings, Goebel, 1968 ....**75.00**
Fig, male face, red lips, Germany, ca 1900 ....**130.00**

Characters/Personalities

Bkt, Katzenjammer Kids, early-looking Hans & Fritz, porc 95.00
Bkt, Lone Ranger, C Moore's emb face on stump, Keele..., 1961 .125.00
Bkt, Robert Burns, blk/wht transfer, porc w/gilt, Royal Stafford ...22.00
Bkt, Tonto, Silverheel's emb face on stump, Keele..., 1961 ....100.00
Fig, Betty Boop, lustreware face w/earrings, Japan, 1930s 400.00
Fig, Doc, standing by his signed egg cup, WD Ent, 1937 ....125.00
Fig, Hardy, face in relief, blond hair, brn Foreign mk, 1930s 150.00
Fig, Popeye standing, wht w/blk trim, Japan, 1930s 225.00
Fig, Snow White, standing by signed cup, WD Ent, 1937 ....275.00
Fig, Winston Churchill, toby face w/hdl & cigar, 1940s 200.00
Set, Muppets, figs: Statler/Waldorf/Zoot/Sam, Sigma..., '84, 4 for .160.00
Sgl, Edward VIII, Coronation, 1937 ....65.00

Chintz

Bkt, Rosalynde, James Kent 45.00
Dbl, Cheery Chintz, Warwick 70.00
Dbl, Fireglow, Royal Winton 110.00
Dbl, Hazel, Royal Winton 220.00
Dbl, Summertime, Royal Winton 110.00
Set, Nantwich, 4 buckets w/matching tray, Royal Winton 425.00
Sgl, Cheadle, Royal Winton 75.00
Sgl, Evesham, Royal Winton 120.00
Sgl, Royalty, Royal Winton 425.00

Glass

Dbl, Cape Cod, crystal, Imperial Glass Co, ca 1932 ....38.00
Fig, chicken, milk glass, John E Kemple 10.00
Fig, face, pk, Boyd 15.00

Figural, milk glass with painted details, 3½", $20.00.

Sgl, blown, cobalt w/flared rim, ca 1865 ....150.00
Sgl, Bohemian, o/l, wht to orange, ca 1890-1920 ....95.00
Sgl, Invt T'print, amberina 350.00
Sgl, mercury glass, etched w/gold-wash lining, ca 1900 ....70.00
Sgl, Yeoman, marigold, Bavarian shape, Heisey 55.00

Golliwoggs

Bkt, emb figure playing cricket, yel, Keele St Pott, ca 1960 ....38.00
Bkt, figure at doorway points to display window, English, 1960s ...55.00
Fig, Robertson's Golden Shred, plastic, ca 1959 ....65.00

Metal

Hoop, graniteware, wht w/blk rim trim, 1930s 80.00
Set, oak & SP, hdld stand w/6 bkt egg cups 325.00
Set, sterling, cruet w/8 cups, Geo Sharp, ca 1850 ....3,800.00
Sgl, brass, cherub ped supports cup 30.00
Sgl, brass, pierced, w/slot in base for spoon 25.00

Sgl, egg cutter, sterling, English, 1910, w/lid 175.00
Sgl, sterling, John Chandler Moore, 1850s 225.00
Sgl, sterling, Tiffany, 1930s 85.00

Staffordshire

Dbl, Bermuda, brn/gr floral, Myott, 1940s 25.00
Dbl, Cornish Kitchen Ware, bl molded bands, TC Green, 1930s .15.00
Dbl, Ferrare, boats, red transfer, Wedgwood 28.00
Dbl, Jenny Lind, red transfer, Royal Staffordshire 30.00
Dbl, Lily of the Valley, Shelley 80.00
Set, Geometric, duck egg stand, tray w/4 cups, Clarice Cliff 750.00
Sgl, bl/wht, landscape, flared rim, ca 1850 ....120.00
Sgl, Chelsea Ivory, floral, Grindley, goose-egg sz 15.00
Sgl, Drabware, olive-gray stoneware, Wedgwood mk, ca 1820 ....160.00
Sgl, Japan, Masons, ca 1820 ....200.00
Sgl, Mansfield, pierced, bl/wht, Worchester, ca 1760-65 ....1,300.00
Sgl, Mulberry, fluted, ca 1850 ....200.00
Sgl, Parian, emb design, Minton, ca 1850 ....275.00
Sgl, Regency, Shelley 45.00

Steamship/Cruiseship

Dbl, French Line, logo 135.00
Hoop, Cunard, blk border decor, Booths & Colcloughs..., 1950s ..45.00
Hoop, Dominion Line, bl transfer, ca 1890 ....100.00
Sgl, American Line, blk circular logo 50.00

Miscellaneous

Dbl, Doll Face, Nippon rising sun mk 135.00
Dbl, floral, HP, mc, sgn Russell, Hutschenreuther 65.00
Dbl, rooster, Holt Howard, Japan, 1961 ....15.00
Dbl, Tea Leaf, 3 copper-lustre leaves, late 19th C 350.00
Fig, boat, yel, Honiton 22.00
Fig, Cardinal Tuck, red robe, Goebel, stylized bee mk 150.00
Fig, duck, gr w/blk top hat, Occupied Japan, 1940s 20.00
Fig, rabbit pushing cup, plastic 20.00
Sgl, fruit, HP, mc, wet-look w/bl, Mennecy, DV mk, ca 1785 ....300.00
Sgl, Geisha Girl, red-orange border, Japan 14.00
Sgl, Lehn, salmon, floral & leaf decor 750.00
Sgl, Shamrock, Belleek, 2nd bl mk 100.00
Sgl, Shamrock, Belleek, 3rd gr mk 40.00
Sgl, spongeware, cut sponge, bl/wht, flared rim, ca 1870 ....200.00
Sgl, Wild Rose, Villeroy & Boch 14.00
Sgl, yellowware, ca 1880 ....300.00

Elfinware

Made in Germany from about 1920 until the 1940s, these miniature vases, boxes, salt cellars, and miscellaneous novelty items are characterized by the tiny applied flowers that often cover their entire surface. Pieces with animals and birds are the most valuable, followed by the more interesting examples such as diminutive grand pianos, candle holders, etc. Items covered in 'spinach' (applied green moss) can be valued at 75% to 100% higher than pieces that are not decorated in this manner. See also Salts, Open.

Basket, overall gr spinach w/appl red rose, 3½x5" 110.00
Box, cologne; appl roses, gr lustre, 8½" 60.00
Box, jewel; piano form 395.00
Candlestick, sm ring hdl, 2½" 55.00
Inkwell, 3x3¾" 60.00

Place card holder, appl roses on fan shape, Germany 30.00
Salt cellar, bl floral on basketweave, 2-hdld 35.00
Salt cellar, swan figural, Germany, 2¾x3" 100.00
Shoe, moss, etc, 4½" L 110.00
Vase, 3" 45.00
Watering can, 6" 60.00

Epergnes

Popular during the Victorian era, epergnes were fancy centerpieces often consisting of several tiers of vases (called lilies), candle holders, or dishes, or a combination of components. They were made in all types of art glass, and some were set in ornate plated frames.

Cased teal w/rigaree, 2 9" lilies, canes & baskets, 21x15" 1,250.00

Chartreuse opalescent with ruffle-edge bowl, 5 floral-form vases with applied rigaree, 20", $500.00.

Cranberry, 11" ruffled bowl, tall lily amid 3 sm, 3 canes, 21" 950.00
Cranberry, 2 sm trumpets+lg bowl, ruffled, rigaree 385.00
Crystal lily w/etched florals, Meriden SP mts, 17¾" 330.00
SP, English Egyptian Revival, frosted/cut tray & vase, 21" 1,600.00
Wht & bl opaline, center trumpet w/appl serpent, Fr, 19½" 330.00
Wht frosted w/pk scalloped rim, 2-lily, SP ped/ft, 21" 210.00
Wht opal, 4-lily, SP arms, shell trays on base, 16½" 500.00

Erickson

Carl Erickson of Bremen, Ohio, produced hand-formed glassware from 1943 until 1960 in artistic shapes, no two of which were identical. One of the characteristics of his work was the air bubbles that were captured within the glass. Though most examples are clear, colored items were also made. Rather than to risk compromising his high standards by selling the factory, when Erickson retired, the plant was dismantled and sold.

Ashtray, turq, controlled bubbles, pipe form 60.00
Bookend/vases, dk gr, controlled bubbles, 5", pr 295.00
Bottle, scent; gray w/crystal stopper, 9" 125.00
Compote, electric bl bowl, clear spherical ft, 5¾x8⅝" 105.00
Cruet, crystal, ground stopper, 9½" 60.00
Decanter, smoke, 6⅝", +clear bubble stopper 95.00
Paperweight vase, gr smear w/mica, controlled bubbles, 7" 125.00
Pitcher, Flame, dk gr, w/stirrer 185.00
Vase, cranberry, controlled bubbles, 7¼", NM 75.00
Vase, dk gr, hourglass shape, controlled bubbles, 10" 125.00
Vase, dk gr/crystal, controlled bubbles, 7¼" 125.00

Vase, smoke, ribbed, clear ped ft, controlled bubbles, 12" 120.00

Erphila

Ebeling and Ruess, an importing company in Philadelphia, began operations in 1886. The acronym 'Erphila' was frequently substituted for the manufacturer's mark on the imported items. It appears that the Erphila mark was used through the late 1930s and then again after WW II on products from U.S. Zone Germany as well as from other areas. The company imported from factories such as Fustenberg, W. Goebel, Villeroy and Boch, Heinrich, Keramos, and Schumann, to name a few. Figurines, art pottery, and some utilitarian items can be found bearing the Erphila mark. Examples are hard to find. Early German marks (those prior to 1900) often contain the word 'Fayence.' After the turn of the century, a rectangular mark in green ink was used. Following WW I, porcelain items were imported from Czechoslovakia. These sometimes carried gold and silver labels. A small variety of marks were used in the 1920s and '30s, but they all contained the name Erphila. Sticker labels were also used. 'Bavaria,' 'Black Forest,' and 'Italy' are sometimes found in combination with 'Erphila.'

Ebeling and Reuss continue the importing business, but it appears that since the 1940s they are also using an 'E' and 'R' on a bell-shaped mark. Because this mark does not contain the name 'Erphila,' we do not consider it to be such. We assume that they stopped using this name sometime in the 1950s.

Ashtray, bird & 2 chicks on rim, oval 20.00
Basket, rust, sm, MIG, 4½" 32.00
Bookends, Dutch couple, pr 60.00
Bookends, man & woman, mc, MIG, pr 75.00
Celery dish, leaf shape, wht, MIG 27.00
Charger, majolica, gr grapes in center, bl forest mk 120.00
Cracker jar, orange poppy 65.00
Dish, hen on nest, mc, Czech, 4x7" 85.00
Dish, triangular, gray & gr, w/dog, MIG, 2" 22.00
Dish, wheelbarrow shape w/child pushing, mc, MIG, 3x4" 50.00
Dresser doll, Nancy Pert, yel, MIG 145.00
Figurine, bear, gray, MIG, 1x3" 20.00
Figurine, bear standing on drum, MIG, 2½x3" 29.00
Figurine, bird on stump, yel & gray, MIG, 4¾" 35.00
Figurine, cat, sitting, blk & wht, MIG, 4½" 35.00
Figurine, dog, Chow, 4" 35.00
Figurine, dog, Scottie, gray & wht, MIG, 3" 35.00
Figurine, elephant, gray, 5" L 45.00
Figurine, elephant, red, MIG, orig sticker, 3⅛" 53.00
Figurine, elephant, red, MIG, 4¼" H 23.00
Figurine, elephant standing on drum, MIG, 2½x3" 29.00
Figurine, horse rearing, bl, Czech, 7" 30.00
Figurine, leopard, natural colors, MIG, 1¼x5" 85.00
Figurine, lion on stool, MIG, 2½x3" 29.00
Figurine, Madonna statue, wht & bl, 8½" 200.00
Figurine, Mrs Gamp, wht & orange, MIG, 3" 35.00
Figurine, pheasant, mc, MIG, 8x10" 72.50
Figurine, tiger, natural colors, MIG, 1x3" 20.00
Napkin holder, girl in orange hat figural, MIG, 3¾" 24.00
Planter, lady in pleated dress, Czech, 8" 45.00
Planter, ring hdls, wht & orange, Czech, 4x3½" dia 40.00
Plate, cake; carnations, MIG, 11" 30.00
Plate, cake; cherry chintz, MIG, 12" 52.00
Plate, emb fruit, mc, 8" 25.00
Teapot, cat figural, gray & blk, MIG, 8" 120.00
Teapot, dog figural, gray & blk, MIG, 8" 120.00
Teapot, pig figural, pk & blk, MIG, 8" 110.00

Teapot, rabbit figural, gray & blk, MIG, 8½" 120.00
Vase, bl iris, narrow neck, Czech, 6" 68.00

Eskimo Artifacts

While ivory carvings made from walrus tusks or whale teeth have been the most emphasized articles of Eskimo art, basketry and wood-working are other areas in which these Alaskan Indians excell. Their designs are effected through the application of simple yet dramatic lines and almost stark decorative devices. Though not pursued to the extent of American Indian art, the unique work of these northern tribes is beginning to attract the serious attention of today's collectors.

Snow goggles, wooden with visor-like rim above pierced viewing field, paint traces, EX patina, 5¼", $550.00.

Basket, alternating band motif, dome shape w/lid, 1930, 6x8" 125.00
Basket, checkerbrd motif, w/lid, 1920, 9x8" 80.00
Basket, geometrics, w/lid, 1920, 13x13", VG 100.00
Basket, Hooper Bay, fine quality, 1900, 7x12" 275.00
Basket, Hooper Bay, mc motif, museum quality, 1900, 13x16" ...850.00
Cribbage brd, eng ivory polar bear form w/seal ft, 1900, 10" 250.00
Cribbage brd, walrus tusk, hunting scenes/animals, 1900, 20" 400.00
Cvg, bear, EX detail, bone w/pnt features, 1940, 2x4" 60.00
Cvg, male figure in hooded parka, bone, 1930s, 13" 325.00
Cvg, walrus on rock, ivory, 1950, 2x2½" 185.00
Easel, 2 walrus tucks, 3-D walrus heads ea side, 1920, 16x11" 300.00
Kayak model, w/cvd paddle & bone-tipped accessories, 29" L 375.00
Mask, cvd, w/feather quill ray-like extensions, 1800s, 7x17" 300.00
Mask, finger puppet; thin wood w/2 finger openings, 1890, 10" ..1,000.00
Mask, Musk Ox ceremony, wood, fish protrusions 1920, 21" 700.00
Maul, stone head w/antler hdl, 1890, 7½" 30.00
Moccasins, child's, puckered hide soles, Alaska in beads, 1920 .....35.00
Mukluks, Historic design, pleated soles, rprs, 16", pr 65.00
Pouch, sealskin, highly decorated, w/flap, 1880, 7x8" 300.00
Shoes, hide soles, fur tops/trim, beadwork motif, 1930 ....45.00
Spindle-whirl weights, whalebone, excavated from tundra, 7", pr ..300.00
Spoon, horn w/bone & horn hdl, trade bead drop, 1920, 8" 35.00

Face Jugs, Contemporary

The most recognizable form of Southern folk pottery is the face jug. Rich alkaline glazes (lustrous greens and browns) are typical, and occasionally shards of glass are applied to the surface of the ware which during firing melts to produce opalescent 'glass runs' over the alkaline. In some locations clay deposits contain elements that result in areas of fluorescent blue or rutile; another variation is swirled or striped ware, reminiscent of 18th-century agateware from Staffordshire. Collector demand for these unique one-of-a-kind jugs is at an all-time high and is still escalating. Choice examples made by Burlon B. Craig and Lanier Meaders often bring over $1,000.00 on the secondary market. If you're interested in learning more about this type of folk pottery, contact the Southern Folk Pottery Collectors Society; their address is in the Directory under Clubs, Newsletters, and Catalogs. Our advisor for this category is Billy Ray Hussey; he is listed in the Directory under North Carolina.

China teeth, Albany slip, appl lashes/lids, '80s, M Rogers, 9" 325.00
China teeth, coleslaw details, gr-brn, Seagrove, 1960s, 7⅛" 450.00
China teeth, incised brows, dk gr alkaline, early 1900s, 5½" 350.00
China teeth/eyes, brn alkaline, att Brn Pottery, 1930s, 6", VG ..450.00
China teeth/pop-eyes, alkaline crushed glass glaze, Craig, 7⅜" ..500.00

Clay teeth, purple pupils, alkaline drip glaze, signed Lanier Meaders in script, mid-1980s, 9⅞", $1,000.00.

Clay teeth, cobalt pupils, alkaline, Lanier Meaders, 1980s, 10" ..1,000.00
Devil, red-brn glossy, tongue out, Brown Pottery, 1992, 15½" ...450.00
Double-faced, china teeth, alkaline, BB Craig, 1970s, 10⅛" ...1,200.00
Grotesque, glazed eyes, gr matt alkaline, Meaders, '70s, 9", EX ..1,900.00
Grotesque w/teeth, brns, Lanier Meaders, 1980s, 8¼" 675.00
Pottery teeth/eyes, incised beard, brn, Rogers Milansville, 9" 110.00
Rock teeth, 2-hdld, gr/brn alkaline, L Meaders, 1970s, 9" 2,400.00

Fairings

Fairings are small, brightly colored 19th-century hard-paste porcelain objects, largely figural groups and boxes. Most figural fairings portray amusing (if not risque) scenes of courting couples, marital woes, and political satire complete with appropriate base captions.

Fairing boxes, also referred to as trinket boxes, sometimes had captions similar to the figural fairings, and often there were similar figures on top. It was originally assumed that fairings were made in the Staffordshire area, and for many years, they were referred to as Staffordshire fairings. But soon there were many European makers producing them as well, especially the boxes, since the Europeans could make them more cheaply. England encouraged these makers by not charging import duties. Both the figural fairings and the box fairings were made with the same consumers in mind.

Many early fairings were not marked; those that were had only a small incised or painted mark. Before 1850 the makers, especially Conte and Boehme of Possneck, Germany (who became the major maker of the boxes), used hand-incised numbers (for one article) and Roman numerals (for the size number). The painter often added his painted-on mark or number. After the 1850s both the article number and the maker's mark were impressed. The Conte and Boehme mark is the most familiar — a bent elbow (arm) holding a sword, laying on a shield.

After 1891 all wares shipped to the U.S. had to be clearly marked by the name of the country. Our advisor for this category is Nancee Neely; she is listed in the Directory under Nebraska.

Bank, pk cottage w/Present From Scarborough in gold, 4" W 150.00
Before Marriage, couple on sofa 245.00
Box, baby asleep on pillow, ruffled edge, 2½" 150.00
Box, boy w/chicken on fireplace mantel w/mirror, 4¾" 165.00
Box, cat w/frog, English, 3" 90.00
Box, child in bed w/kitten, 4¼" 120.00
Box, child on bed pulls on pajamas, Conte & Boehme mk, 4" ...120.00
Box, child w/trumpet, doll in basket, 3¾" 175.00
Box, monkey playing instrument 200.00
Box, pigeon w/letter on lid, 2½x2½" 95.00
Girl peeking through bushes at rabbit 80.00

Happy Father, What 2?..., couple & twins, 1880s, 3½" **110.00**
I Am Starting for a Long Journey, man w/satchel & book **175.00**
Looking Down Upon His Luck, couple w/twins, Germany, 3½" ...**100.00**
Merry Widow, lady cat w/roses at ft **250.00**
O Do Leave Me a Drop, 2 cats at box **175.00**
Returning at One O'clock in the Morning, rare **150.00**
Tug of War, girl & dog by fence tugging at doll, 2¾x5¼" **185.00**
Wedding Night, man on knee to lady, gold trim, Germany **180.00**
Who Said Rats?, cat in draped bed, mice on table **165.00**
Will We Sleep First or How?, 5¼x4" **195.00**

Fans

The Japanese are said to have invented the fan. From there it went to China, and Portuguese traders took the idea to Europe. Though usually considered milady's accessory, even the gentlemen in 17th-century England carried fans! More fashionable than practical, some were of feathers and lovely hand-painted silks with carved ivory or tortoise sticks. Some French fans had peepholes. There are mourning fans, calendar fans, and those with advertising.

Fine antique fans (pre-1900) of ivory or mother-of-pearl have recently escalated in value. Those from before 1800 often sell for upwards of $1,000.00. Examples with mother-of-pearl sticks are most desirable; least desirable are those with sticks of celluloid. Our advisor for this category is Vicki Flanigan; she is listed in the Directory under Virginia.

Allegorical of marriage HP on silk, MOP sticks, 1870s, 11" **700.00**
Birds HP on silk, cvd/pierced ivory sticks, Burma, 1880s, 12" **300.00**
Brussels lace on cream silk, MOP sticks, 1870s, 10" **300.00**
Brussels lace w/appl decor on satin, MOP sticks, 1865, 10" **300.00**
Chick HP on silk, sequins, MOP sticks, ca 1905, 9", EX **450.00**
Dutch scenes HP on silk, ornate ivory sticks, 1750s, 10½" **1,200.00**
Gold & silver birds/flowers HP on blk gauze, wood sticks, 14" ...**150.00**
HP reserves on linen, pnt MOP sticks, 19th C, 15x26" **660.00**

International Exhibition of 1876, paper on wooden reeds, double sided, Japanese figures and main fair building, light wear, 11x22", $130.00.

Lady w/wand HP on bl gauze, MOP sticks, 1890s, 13" **225.00**
Leaf painted w/travelers, sgn Lasellaz, MOP sticks, 1885, 11" **995.00**
Lovers HP on silk, sgn Roland, tortoise-shell sticks, 1890s, 9" **200.00**
Marriage, 2 sm portraits HP on silk, ivory sticks, 1770s, 11" **900.00**
Mauve ostrich-feather waterfall, MOP sticks, 26" **300.00**
Oriental figures HP on silk, cvd/pierced ivory sticks, 1760s, 11" ...**500.00**
Palace scene & flowers HP on silk, ivory sticks, 1700s, 11½" ..**1,500.00**
Peacock HP & embr on bl gauze w/sequins, wooden sticks, 1900s ..**250.00**
Pierced ivory brise w/muses vignettes, ca 1790, old rprs, 11" ...**1,500.00**
Silk, HP lady w/dove, pnt wood sticks, Continental, 14x23" **160.00**
Tortoise-shell brise w/3 HP scenes & gold lacquer, 1860s, 12" ...**450.00**

Farm Collectibles

Country living in the 19th century entailed plowing, planting, and harvesting; gathering eggs and milking; making soap from lard rendered on butchering day; and numerous other tasks performed with primitive tools of which we in the 20th century have had little first-hand knowledge. Our

advisor for this category is Lar Hothem; his address is listed in the Directory under Ohio. See also Cast Iron; Woodenware; Wrought Iron.

Blueberry picker, tin/sheet iron, slide lid, Pat 1914 ....**50.00**
Book, Accounting...for Farmers, Chief Two-Moon on cover, 1923 ..**18.00**
Booklet, Massey Harris Buyers' Guide, 1955 ....**22.00**
Buckboard, dbl-horse, Shankford vertical supports, 19th C, EX ..**900.00**
Calf weaner, CI, mk Daisy, dtd **32.00**
Comb, horse's mane & tail, 1-pc all wood, ca 1840, 4x4" **75.00**
Corn sheller, CI, Gray Bros, Pat 1871, hand held **175.00**
Crackling squeezer, wood w/leather hinge, 21½" L **32.00**
Egg box, wide slats, wire hdl, sm, 2½-oz sz **40.00**
Hay rake, all wood, 62" **225.00**
Hinge, barn-door strap; wrought iron, 1700s, 24x33", pr **55.00**
Hobble, wrought iron, coiled spring type, 7" dia at center **30.00**
Implement seat, Bonanza, EX **125.00**
Implement seat, Empire, CI **50.00**
Implement seat, Jones Rake, CI **130.00**
Implement seat, Parlin & Orendorff, CI **125.00**
Implement seat, Peerless, CI **165.00**
Implement seat, Rock Island Plow Co, CI **140.00**
Lantern, barn; ash/hardwoods, pinned, glass 3 sides, 11" **480.00**
Lantern, barn; cherry, dk patina, pinned, glass 3 sides, 12", G **350.00**
Lantern, barn; pine & beech w/wrought-iron fittings, 7½" **440.00**
Meal grinder, Model No 1K...CB Bell...USA, CI, crank hdl, 14" ...**100.00**
Oxen yoke, tiger maple w/red wash, full sz, EX **250.00**
Pulley, well; iron, ornate wheel, iron hook, lg **22.50**
Rake, dump; horse-drawn, wooden tines, early, EX **150.00**
Rope maker, New Era, Patd 1911 ....**225.00**
Shovel, grain; maple, made from 1 pc, 1800s, 36" **325.00**
Sieve, bean sorting; wood w/brass, S Clouth...NH...1868, EX **195.00**
Sieve, winnowing; splint w/bentwood band, 15" dia, EX **250.00**
Wagon jack, wood & wrought iron, 1800s, 30" **45.00**
Wagon seat, arrow bk, wooden spring base, early 1800s, EX **700.00**
Wagon seat, splint, refinished, 29x33", EX **440.00**
Wrench, CI, 6-jaw form, mk Internat'l Harvester **7.00**

Fenton

Frank and John Fenton were brothers who founded the Fenton Art Glass Company in 1906 in Martin's Ferry, Ohio. The venture, at first only a decorating shop, began operations in July of 1905 using blanks purchased from other companies. This operation soon proved unsatisfactory, and by 1907 they had constructed their own glass factory in Williamstown, West Virginia. John left the company in 1909 and organized his own firm in Millersburg, Ohio.

The Fenton Company produced over 130 patterns of carnival glass. They also made custard, chocolate, opalescent, and stretch glass. This company has always been noted for its various colors of glass and has continually changed its production to stay attune with current tastes in decorating. In 1925 they produced a line of 'handmade' items that incorporated the techniques of threading and mosaic work. Because the process proved to be unprofitable, the line was discontinued by 1927. Even their glassware made in the past twenty-five years is already regarded as collectible. Various paper labels have been used since the 1920s; only since 1970 has the logo been stamped into the glass. For information concerning Fenton Art Glass Collectors of America, Inc., see the Clubs, Newsletters, and Catalogs section of the Directory. See also Carnival Glass; Custard Glass; Stretch Glass.

Apple Tree, vase, milk glass, #1561 ....**90.00**
Aqua Crest, bowl, 10" **45.00**
Aqua Crest, bowl, 7½" sq **38.00**

Aqua Crest, mayonnaise, 3-pc 45.00
Beaded Melon, rose bowl, Goldenrod, 3½" 50.00
Beaded Melon, vase, dk gr, #711, 8" 38.50
Beaded Melon, vase, gr o/l, 4½" 30.00
Big Cookies, basket, red, reeded hdl 75.00
Big Cookies, macaroon jar, blk, reeded hdl, #1681 .....90.00
Black Rose, vase, MOP, 10¾" 150.00
Blue Overlay, basket, 7½" 75.00
Blue Overlay, candy dish, crystal lid 72.50
Blue Overlay, cologne, w/stopper 45.00

Burmese, jack-in-the-pulpit vase, Louise Piper decoration, 10", $200.00.

Cactus, creamer, amber, #3408 ....25.00
Coin Dot, pitcher, cranberry opal, water sz 275.00
Daisy & Button, bowl, bl, oval, 4-leg, 5½x4" 25.00
Daisy & Button, cruet, bl, w/stopper 130.00
Daisy & Button, shakers, bl, pr 95.00
Daisy & Button, top hat, amber, 2½" 28.00
Daisy & Button, top hat, clear, 4½" 20.00
Daisy & Button, tray, amber, fan form, #957 ....29.00
Daisy & Button, vase, bl, crimped rim, 3⅛" 68.00
Daisy & Fern, tumbler, cranberry opal, flat, 4" 50.00
Diamond Optic, basket, ruby o/l, 7" 65.00
Diamond Optic, basket/top hat, mulberry, rare, 5" 145.00
Diamond Optic, bowl, ruby o/l, 7" 20.00
Diamond Optic, creamer, ruby o/l 20.00
Diamond Optic, jug, mulberry, hdld, 8" 200.00
Diamond Optic, plate, pk, octagonal, 7¾" 9.00
Diamond Optic, vase, cranberry o/l, 8" 65.00
Dot Optic, pitcher, cranberry opal, water sz 275.00
Dot Optic, pitcher, cranberry opal, 4" 60.00
Emerald Crest, cake stand, #7213 ....85.00
Emerald Crest, vase, 3½x4½" 17.50
Gold Crest, bowl, crimped, 7½" 30.00
Gold Crest, bowl, dbl-crimped, 6¾" 14.00
Gold Crest, bowl, dbl-crimped, 8" 20.00
Gold Crest, compote, ftd, 6½x8" 30.00
Gold Crest, jug, hdld, 9" 35.00
Hobnail, banana stand, milk glass, low ft 35.00
Hobnail, basket, Fr opal, 3¾x5" 42.00
Hobnail, bonbon, bl opal, ftd, hdls, 5" 18.00
Hobnail, bonbon, gr opal, 3-lobed, 5" 22.00
Hobnail, bottle, cologne; Fr opal, w/stopper 30.00
Hobnail, bowl, bl opal, dbl-crimped, 10" 65.00
Hobnail, bowl, cranberry opal, dbl-crimped, 10" 70.00
Hobnail, bowl, topaz opal, dbl-crimped, 9½" 72.50
Hobnail, cake plate, Fr opal, ftd 40.00
Hobnail, candlesticks, milk glass, 3", pr 28.00
Hobnail, candy dish, bl opal, ftd, w/lid 55.00

Hobnail, creamer & sugar bowl, bl opal, ind, 3½" 28.00
Hobnail, creamer & sugar bowl, Fr opal, ftd 28.00
Hobnail, creamer & sugar bowl, milk glass, #3906, w/tray ...25.00
Hobnail, creamer & sugar bowl, milk glass, ind 15.00
Hobnail, cruet, cranberry opal, w/stopper, 4⅞" 60.00
Hobnail, dresser set, bl opal, 3-pc 135.00
Hobnail, epergne, milk glass, 4-pc, mini 55.00
Hobnail, goblet, water; bl opal 24.50
Hobnail, goblet, water; Fr opal 38.00
Hobnail, hat vase, bl opal, 2½" 17.50
Hobnail, jug, bl opal, squat, uncrimped, 5½" 30.00
Hobnail, mustard, bl opal, w/lid 30.00
Hobnail, pitcher, milk; bl opal, 4⅝" 55.00
Hobnail, puff box, Fr opal, w/lid 35.00
Hobnail, shakers, bl opal, pr 28.00
Hobnail, shoe w/kitten, bl opal 14.00
Hobnail, tumbler, Fr opal, 9-oz 20.00
Hobnail, tumbler, juice; Fr opal 14.00
Hobnail, tumbler, water; bl opal, 11-oz 35.00
Hobnail, vase, bl opal, crimped, mini, 4" 25.00
Hobnail, vase, bl opal, crimped, 5¾" 38.00
Hobnail, vase, bl opal, fan form, 6¼" 42.00
Hobnail, vase, cornucopia; bl opal, 6" 30.00
Hobnail, vase, cranberry opal, dbl-crimped, 5" 65.00
Hobnail, vase, Fr opal, crimped, 3¼" 20.00
Ivory Crest, cornucopia candlesticks, 6", pr 70.00
Ivory Crest, plate, 8½" 30.00
Jacqueline, shakers, gr, pr 27.50
Jacqueline, sugar bowl, bl 24.50
Jacqueline, vase, yel, 6" 35.00
Lamp, G70, blk satin & crystal 175.00
Lamp, G70, gr opaque 175.00
Lamp, G70, pk, floral etch 175.00
Ming Green, bowl, octagonal, 8", w/14" underplate 325.00
Mosaic, vase, mandarin red/caramel on bl-blk w/dk threads, 8" ..1,200.00
Peach Crest, basket, crystal hdl, 7" 80.00
Peach Crest, basket, milk glass hdl, 7" 65.00
Plymouth, plate, luncheon; red, 8" 25.00
Plymouth, sherbet, red 25.00
Plymouth, tumbler, juice; red 25.00
Plymouth, tumbler, water; red 28.00
Rib Optic, top hat, Fr opal, 6¼x10½" 250.00
Rib Optic, wine bottle, cranberry opal, #1667, 14" 200.00
Rose Crest, vase, #186, 8" 50.00
Silver Crest, banana boat, low ft 50.00
Silver Crest, banana bowl, high std 65.00
Silver Crest, basket, 6" 28.00
Silver Crest, bowl, #7338, 8½" 50.00
Silver Crest, bowl, ftd, #7330, 9" sq 70.00
Silver Crest, cake salver, 12" 40.00
Silver Crest, candy box, ftd, tall 145.00
Silver Crest, chip & dip set, #7303 ....75.00
Silver Crest, mayonnaise, 3-pc 48.00
Silver Crest, plate, HP flowers, #7212, 12" 55.00
Silver Crest, plate, 8½" 20.00
Silver Crest, tidbit tray, 2-tier 55.00
Silver Crest, tidbit tray, 3-tier 50.00
Snow Crest, vase, aqua, #3153, 7½" 60.00
Stars & Stripes, tumbler, cranberry opal 50.00
Stretch, lemon tray, yel w/decor 35.00
Stretch, vase, bud; Florentine gr, #251, 12" 30.00
Vasa Murrhina, vase, Rose Mist, fan form, #6457, 7" ...60.00
Velva Rose stretch, candlestick, #316 ....22.00
Velva Rose stretch, sherbet, 75th anniversary 18.00

Fiesta

Fiesta is a line of dinnerware produced by the Homer Laughlin China Company of Newell, West Virginia, from 1936 until 1973. It was made in eleven different solid colors with over fifty pieces in the assortment. The pattern was developed by Frederick Rhead, an English Stoke-on-Trent potter who was an important contributor to the art-pottery movement in this country during the early part of the century. The design was carried out through the use of a simple band-of-rings device near the rim. Fiesta Red, a strong red-orange glaze color, was made with depleted uranium oxide. It was more expensive to produce than the other colors and sold at higher prices. Today's collectors still pay premium prices for Fiesta Red pieces. During the '50s the color assortment was gray, rose, chartreuse, and dark green. These colors are relatively harder to find and along with Fiesta Red and medium green (new in 1959) command the higher prices.

Fiesta Kitchen Kraft was introduced in 1939; it consisted of seventeen pieces of kitchenware such as pie plates, refrigerator sets, mixing bowls, and covered jars in four popular Fiesta colors.

As a final attempt to adapt production to modern-day techniques and methods, Fiesta was restyled in 1969. Of the original colors, only Fiesta Red remained. This line, called Fiesta Ironstone, was discontinued in 1973.

Two types of marks were used: an ink stamp on machine-jiggered pieces and an indented mark molded into the hollowware pieces.

In 1986 HLC reintroduced a line of Fiesta dinnerware in five colors: black, white, pink, apricot, and cobalt (darker and denser than the original shade). Since then yellow, turquoise, seafoam green, 'country' blue, lilac, persimmon, and sapphire blue have been added. Collectors have found that the new line poses no threat to their investments.

In the listings below, 'original colors' indicates only three of the original six — light green, turquoise, and yellow (or those remaining after specific original colors have been priced). Red, ivory, and cobalt values are listed separately. Turquoise was the last original color to be introduced, so the items that were discontinued in 1946 are harder to find in that color (since it had a shorter production run), and values fall into the upper price range along with red, cobalt, and ivory. For more information we recommend *The Collector's Encyclopedia of Fiesta, Harlequin, and Riviera* by Sharon and Bob Huxford, available at your local bookstore or from Collector Books.

Dinnerware

Creamer, red, individual, $240.00; Sugar bowl, yellow, individual, with lid, $120.00; Figure-8 tray, turquoise, $275.00.

Ashtray, '50s colors	88.00
Ashtray, orig colors	47.00
Ashtray, red, cobalt or ivory	60.00
Bowl, covered onion soup; cobalt or ivory	675.00
Bowl, covered onion soup; red	700.00
Bowl, covered onion soup; turq, minimum value	2,900.00
Bowl, covered onion soup; yel or lt gr	575.00
Bowl, cream soup; '50s colors	72.00
Bowl, cream soup; med gr, minimum value	4,000.00
Bowl, cream soup; orig colors	42.00
Bowl, cream soup; red, cobalt or ivory	60.00
Bowl, dessert; '50s colors, 6"	52.00
Bowl, dessert; med gr, 6"	475.00
Bowl, dessert; orig colors, 6"	38.00
Bowl, dessert; red, cobalt or ivory, 6"	52.00
Bowl, fruit; '50s colors, 4¾"	35.00
Bowl, fruit; '50s colors, 5½"	36.00
Bowl, fruit; med gr, 4¾"	450.00
Bowl, fruit; med gr, 5½"	68.00
Bowl, fruit; orig colors, 11¾"	250.00
Bowl, fruit; orig colors, 4¾"	25.00
Bowl, fruit; orig colors, 5½"	25.00
Bowl, fruit; red, cobalt, ivory or turq, 11¾"	285.00
Bowl, fruit; red, cobalt or ivory, 4¾"	32.00
Bowl, fruit; red, cobalt or ivory, 5½"	32.00
Bowl, ftd salad; orig colors	270.00
Bowl, ftd salad; red, cobalt, ivory or turq	330.00
Bowl, ind salad; med gr, 7½"	105.00
Bowl, ind salad; red, turq or yel, 7½"	85.00
Bowl, nappy; '50s colors, 8½"	62.00
Bowl, nappy; med gr, 8½"	140.00
Bowl, nappy; orig colors, 8½"	40.00
Bowl, nappy; orig colors, 9½"	52.00
Bowl, nappy; red, cobalt, ivory or turq, 8½"	52.00
Bowl, nappy; red, cobalt, ivory or turq, 9½"	65.00
Bowl, Tom & Jerry; ivory w/gold letters	260.00
Bowl, unlisted salad; red, cobalt or ivory	500.00
Bowl, unlisted salad; yel	105.00
Candle holders, bulb; orig colors, pr	95.00
Candle holders, bulb; red, cobalt, ivory or turq pr	130.00
Candle holders, tripod; orig colors, pr	465.00
Candle holders, tripod; red, cobalt, ivory or turq, pr	585.00
Carafe, orig colors	220.00
Carafe, red, cobalt, ivory or turq	280.00
Casserole, '50s colors	300.00
Casserole, French; standard colors other than yel	650.00
Casserole, French; yel	275.00
Casserole, med gr	725.00
Casserole, orig colors	140.00
Casserole, red, cobalt or ivory	195.00
Coffeepot, '50s colors	350.00
Coffeepot, demi; orig colors	340.00
Coffeepot, demi; red, cobalt, ivory or turq	435.00
Coffeepot, orig colors	195.00
Coffeepot, red, cobalt or ivory	245.00
Compote, orig colors, 12"	148.00
Compote, red, cobalt, ivory or turq, 12"	185.00
Compote, sweets; red, cobalt, ivory or turq	90.00
Creamer, '50s colors	40.00
Creamer, ind; turq or cobalt	345.00
Creamer, ind; yel	70.00
Creamer, med gr	80.00
Creamer, orig colors	22.00
Creamer, red, cobalt or ivory	35.00
Creamer, stick hdld, orig colors	45.00
Creamer, stick hdld, red, cobalt, ivory or turquoise	62.00
Cup, demi; '50s colors	350.00
Cup, demi; orig colors	60.00
Cup, demi; red, cobalt or ivory	75.00

Egg cup, '50s colors 160.00
Egg cup, orig colors 58.00
Egg cup, red, cobalt, or ivory 70.00
Lid, for mixing bowl #1-#3, any color, minimum value 785.00
Lid, for mixing bowl #4, any color, minimum value 900.00
Marmalade, orig colors 230.00
Marmalade, red, cobalt, ivory or turq 285.00
Mixing bowl, #1, orig colors 170.00
Mixing bowl, #1, red, cobalt, ivory or turq 205.00
Mixing bowl, #2, orig colors 110.00
Mixing bowl, #2, red, cobalt, ivory or turq 125.00
Mixing bowl, #3, orig colors 120.00
Mixing bowl, #3, red, cobalt, ivory or turq 130.00
Mixing bowl, #4, orig colors 130.00
Mixing bowl, #4, red, cobalt, ivory or turq 155.00
Mixing bowl, #5, orig colors 155.00
Mixing bowl, #5, red, cobalt, ivory or turq 175.00
Mixing bowl, #6, orig colors 200.00
Mixing bowl, #6, red, cobalt, ivory or turq 240.00
Mixing bowl, #7, orig colors 280.00
Mixing bowl, #7, red, cobalt, ivory or turq 325.00
Mug, Tom & Jerry; '50s colors 90.00
Mug, Tom & Jerry; ivory w/gold letters 65.00
Mug, Tom & Jerry; orig colors 58.00
Mug, Tom & Jerry; red, cobalt or ivory 78.00
Mustard, orig colors 95.00
Mustard, red, cobalt, ivory or turquoise 250.00
Pitcher, disk juice; gray, minimum value 2,500.00
Pitcher, disk juice; Harlequin yel 62.00
Pitcher, disk juice; red 450.00
Pitcher, disk juice; yel 45.00
Pitcher, disk water; '50s colors 275.00
Pitcher, disk water; med gr, minimum value 1,150.00
Pitcher, disk water; orig colors 115.00
Pitcher, disk water; red, cobalt or ivory 165.00
Pitcher, ice; orig colors 125.00
Pitcher, ice; red, cobalt, ivory or turq 150.00
Pitcher, jug, 2-pt; '50s colors 145.00
Pitcher, jug, 2-pt; orig colors 80.00
Pitcher, jug, 2-pt; red, cobalt or ivory 115.00
Plate, '50s colors, 10" 52.00
Plate, '50s colors, 6" 9.00
Plate, '50s colors, 7" 13.00
Plate, '50s colors, 9" 22.00
Plate, cake; orig colors 755.00
Plate, cake; red, cobalt or ivory 885.00
Plate, calendar; 1954 or 1955, 10" 45.00
Plate, calendar; 1955, 9" 50.00
Plate, chop; '50s colors, 13" 90.00
Plate, chop; '50s colors, 15" 115.00
Plate, chop; med gr, 13" 275.00
Plate, chop; orig colors, 13" 35.00
Plate, chop; orig colors, 15" 48.00
Plate, chop; red, cobalt or ivory, 13" 50.00
Plate, chop; red, cobalt or ivory, 15" 70.00
Plate, compartment; '50s colors, 10½" 75.00
Plate, compartment; orig colors, 10½" 40.00
Plate, compartment; orig colors, 12" 50.00
Plate, compartment; red, cobalt or ivory, 10½" 40.00
Plate, compartment; red, cobalt, ivory or turq, 12" ...60.00
Plate, deep; '50s colors 55.00
Plate, deep; med gr 120.00
Plate, deep; orig colors 40.00
Plate, deep; red, cobalt or ivory 52.00

Plate, med gr, 10" 110.00
Plate, med gr, 6" 20.00
Plate, med gr, 7" 32.00
Plate, med gr, 9" 45.00
Plate, orig colors, 10" 32.00
Plate, orig colors, 6" 5.00
Plate, orig colors, 7" 9.00
Plate, orig colors, 9" 12.00
Plate, red, cobalt or ivory, 10" 40.00
Plate, red, cobalt or ivory, 6" 7.00
Plate, red, cobalt or ivory, 7" 10.00
Plate, red, cobalt or ivory, 9" 18.00
Platter, '50s colors 58.00
Platter, med gr 140.00
Platter, orig colors 35.00
Platter, red, cobalt or ivory 45.00
Relish tray, gold decor, complete 250.00
Relish tray base, orig colors 65.00
Relish tray base, red, cobalt, ivory or turq 85.00
Relish tray center insert, orig colors 42.00
Relish tray center insert, red, cobalt, ivory or turq ...55.00
Relish tray side insert, orig colors 40.00
Relish tray side insert, red, cobalt, ivory or turq 48.00
Sauce boat, '50s colors 78.00
Sauce boat, med gr 155.00
Sauce boat, orig colors 45.00
Sauce boat, red, cobalt or ivory 68.00
Saucer, '50s colors 6.00
Saucer, demi; '50s colors 95.00
Saucer, demi; orig colors 18.00
Saucer, demi; red, cobalt or ivory 22.00
Saucer, med gr 12.00
Saucer, orig colors 4.00
Saucer, red, cobalt or ivory 5.00
Shakers, '50s colors, pr 45.00
Shakers, med gr, pr 140.00
Shakers, orig colors, pr 22.00
Shakers, red, cobalt or ivory, pr 30.00
Sugar bowl, ind; turq 350.00
Sugar bowl, ind; yel 120.00
Sugar bowl, w/lid, '50s colors, 3¼x3½" 72.00
Sugar bowl, w/lid, med gr, 3¼x3½" 160.00
Sugar bowl, w/lid, orig colors, 3¼x3½" 45.00
Sugar bowl, w/lid, red, cobalt or ivory, 3¼x3½" 55.00
Syrup, orig colors 320.00
Syrup, red, cobalt, ivory or turq 385.00

Syrup, yellow, $320.00.

Teacup, '50s colors 38.00
Teacup, med gr 58.00
Teacup, orig colors 25.00
Teacup, red, cobalt or ivory 35.00

Teapot, lg; orig colors 180.00
Teapot, lg; red, cobalt, ivory or turq 220.00
Teapot, med; '50s colors 310.00
Teapot, med; med gr, minimum value 1,000.00
Teapot, med; orig colors 155.00
Teapot, med; red, cobalt or ivory 195.00
Tray, figure-8; cobalt 82.00
Tray, utility; orig colors 38.00
Tray, utility; red, cobalt, ivory or turq 42.00
Tumbler, juice; chartreuse, Harlequin yel or dk gr 460.00
Tumbler, juice; orig colors 40.00
Tumbler, juice; red, cobalt or ivory 45.00
Tumbler, juice; rose 65.00
Tumbler, water; orig colors 60.00
Tumbler, water; red, cobalt, ivory or turq 75.00
Vase, bud; orig colors 80.00
Vase, bud; red, cobalt, ivory or turq 100.00
Vase, orig colors, 10" 720.00
Vase, orig colors, 12" 950.00
Vase, orig colors, 8" 560.00
Vase, red, cobalt, ivory or turq, 10" 800.00
Vase, red, cobalt, ivory or turq, 12", minimum value 1,100.00
Vase, red, cobalt, ivory or turq, 8" 640.00

Kitchen Kraft

Bowl, mixing; lt gr or yel, 10" 100.00
Bowl, mixing; lt gr or yel, 6" 65.00
Bowl, mixing; lt gr or yel, 8" 82.00
Bowl, mixing; red or cobalt, 10" 120.00
Bowl, mixing; red or cobalt, 6" 75.00
Bowl, mixing; red or cobalt, 8" 92.00
Cake plate, lt gr or yel 55.00
Cake plate, red or cobalt 65.00
Cake server, lt gr or yel 130.00
Cake server, red or cobalt 140.00
Casserole, ind; lt gr or yel 140.00
Casserole, ind; red or cobalt 155.00
Casserole, lt gr or yel, 7½" 85.00
Casserole, lt gr or yel, 8½" 100.00
Casserole, red or cobalt, 7½" 90.00
Casserole, red or cobalt, 8½" 110.00
Covered jar, lg; lt gr or yel 300.00
Covered jar, lg; red or cobalt 320.00
Covered jar, med; lt gr or yel 260.00
Covered jar, med; red or cobalt 280.00
Covered jar, sm; lt gr or yel 270.00
Covered jar, sm; red or cobalt 290.00
Covered jug, lt gr or yel 250.00
Covered jug, red or cobalt 275.00
Fork, lt gr or yel 100.00
Fork, red or cobalt 125.00
Metal frame for platter 26.00
Pie plate, lt gr or yel, 10" 40.00
Pie plate, lt gr or yel, 9" 40.00
Pie plate, red or cobalt, 10" 45.00
Pie plate, red or cobalt, 9" 45.00
Pie plate, spruce gr 290.00
Platter, lt gr or yel 68.00
Platter, red or cobalt 78.00
Platter, spruce gr 350.00
Shakers, lt gr or yel, pr 95.00
Shakers, red or cobalt, pr 105.00
Spoon, lt gr or yel 100.00

Spoon, red or cobalt 125.00
Stacking refrigerator lid, ivory 205.00
Stacking refrigerator lid, lt gr or yel 70.00
Stacking refrigerator lid, red or cobalt 80.00
Stacking refrigerator unit, ivory 195.00
Stacking refrigerator unit, lt gr or yel 45.00
Stacking refrigerator unit, red or cobalt 55.00

Fifties Modern

Postwar furniture design is marked by organic shapes and lighter woods and forms. New materials from war research such as molded plywood and fiberglass were used extensively. For the first time, design was extended to the masses and the baby-boomer generation grew up surrounded by modern shape and color, the perfect expression of postwar optimism. The top designers in America worked for Herman Miller and Knoll Furniture Company. These include Charles Eames, George Nelson, and Eero Saarinen.

Italian glass from the '50s represents some of the most beautiful designs of the period. The color and expressive forms that came from the island of Murano during this time were the perfect expression of Italian style and flair.

This information was provided to us by Richard Wright. See also Italian Glass.

Key:
uphl — upholstered   vnr — veneer

Stool, Sori Yanagi, rosewood veneer plywood with brass stretcher, elegant butterfly design, 1956, 16x16", $1,600.00.

Armchair, Cherner/Plycraft, laminated walnut, bikini bk, pr ..1,100.00
Armchair, Eames, chrome swivel base, leather chanel uphl 1,000.00
Armchair, Kagan, blk leather bbl on rnd chrome base, '70s 300.00
Armchair, Nelson/Miller, Kangaroo, re-uphl fiberglass, VG 1,700.00
Armchair, Nelson/Miller, Pretzel, birch/walnut bentwood 1,700.00
Armchair, Nelson/Miller, 2-part fiberglass w/wire base, VG 600.00
Armchair rocker, Eames/Miller, molded fiberglass & blk wire 700.00
Bench, Nelson/Miller, blk wood slatted top, 72" 700.00
Bookends, Von Nessen, stylized horse, brass tubing, 6x4" 425.00
Bottle, Fantoni, lady, mc on faux cane, part leather o/l, 15" 425.00
Bowl, Raymor, geometrics, mc matt/gloss, 2½x11" 270.00
Box, Gambone, geometrics, mc on plum, 3½x6x4" 300.00
Box, in/out; Nelson/Miller, walnut, 3-compartment, 32" L 250.00
Box, Waylande Gregory, wht w/red lid, 2x5x4" 200.00
Cabinet, Nelson, Thin Edge, well-grained rosewood vnr, 56" .3,500.00
Cabinet, Nelson/Miller, Basic Series, brn walnut, 2-door 250.00
Cabinet, Sarrinen/Johnson, birch 4-drw, birch/aluminum pulls .500.00
Catalog, Herman Miller, hardbound, 1952, 116-pg, EX 100.00
Centerpc, Andre Fau, rectangle base w/5 stacked bowls, 22" L ...300.00
Chair, child's; Bertoia/Knoll, 1-pc wht wire grid, blk base 225.00
Chair, Eames/Miller, uphl shaped seat/bk, bentwood legs 450.00

Chair, Gehry/Easy Edges, sculptural corrugated foam, 33x20" .2,300.00
Chair, Hovelskov, Harp, blk fr w/strung rope seat/bk, 53" 2,500.00
Chair, lounge; Morque, human body shape, red wool, 45x61x25" ...1,100.00
Chair, lounge; Wegner, tube chrome arm/bk fr w/rope bk/seat ..1,300.00
Chair, Panton, cone style, chrome X base, red uphl, 33" 900.00
Chair, Sarrinen/Knoll, Grasshopper, birch laminate, re-uphl ..1,600.00
Chair, side; Eames/Miller, blond bentwood, shaped seat/bk 550.00
Chair, side; Eames/Miller, red-stained bentwood, 27", EX 750.00
Chair, side; Spratling, leather sling in cvd wood fr w/cutout 500.00
Chairs, Panton/Miller, molded plastic, stacking, set of 6 ....950.00
Chaise lounge, Eames/Miller, leather pillows, pnt blk legs 1,900.00
Chest, Heywood-Wakefield, Sculptura birch, 4-drw, 40x38" 750.00
Chest, Nelson/Miller, Steel Frame, walnut fronts, 3-drw, pr 850.00
Chest of drw, Nelson/Miller, Thin Edge, rosewood, 34x67x18" ..3,600.00
Clock, Miller, blond wood balls on ea wire spoke, 13½" 425.00
Clock, Miller, kite w/center line, wht hands on gray/blk 850.00
Clock, Miller, thin chrome slats, blk dial, 24" dia 600.00
Clock, Miller, wood, orange blocks circle yel center, 11" 750.00
Clock, Miller, wood, 12 spokes, ea w/dmn-shape ends, 18" 1,200.00
Clock, Nelson/Miller, brn/wht checkerbrd, bl/wht dial, 20x9" ...125.00
Clock, Nelson/Miller, steering wheel, 12", EX 350.00
Clock, Rhode/Miller, chrome fr/base, blk #s on wht face, 6x8" ..325.00
Clock, table; Nelson/Miller, rosewood cube w/chrome X base 100.00
Desk, roll-top; Nelson, Action, 2-drw, 54" W, VG 350.00
Dresser, Heywood-Wakefield, Kohinoor, 6-drw, wheat, rfn, 56" ..425.00
Ewer, Fantoni, cvd cubist figure, mc on cratered blk, 25x4" 1,400.00
Figures, Fantoni, seated pr, mc on wht crackle, 15", pr 2,500.00
Figurine, WPA, woman in robe w/heavy boots walks dog, 9" 240.00
Lamp, Archille & Castiglioni/Flos, Toio, headlight atop, 62" 550.00
Lamp, cast ceramic C-shape, bl glaze, 19x16", VG 220.00
Lamp, floor; Aulenti/Artemide, wht plastic cylinder w/hood 260.00
Lamp, floor; Italian, 3 upright tubes vary in sz/height, 48" 400.00
Lamp, floor; Mouille, elliptical blk shade on pencil std, VG ...2,100.00
Lamp, floor; perforated adjustable metal shade, iron base, VG ...260.00
Lamp, pole; Italian (att), 3 arms w/adjustable shades, '50 ....800.00
Lamp, table; spun aluminum shade, cylinder base, 29x15" 150.00
Nightstand, Nelson/Miller, Thin Edge, rosewood, 1-drw, 23x19" .450.00
Ottoman, Girard/Miller, tufted/uphl, aluminum legs, 36" dia .3,000.00
Rocker, Eames/Miller, fiberglass shell, wire base, 28x25" 1,200.00
Rug, Miro, 2 human figures, primary colors on natural, 53x35" ..650.00
Rug, Pelletier, geometrics/circles, ivory/blk, 89x53" 275.00
Sculpture, Weinberg, minotaur w/bow, brass-plated, 17x7x4" 200.00
Settee, Jacobsen, Swan style, shaped fiberglass w/uphl, 57" 3,750.00
Sofa, Archizoom, Super Rhonda, sculptural foam, stacking, 88" ..1,100.00
Sofa, Heywood-Wakefield, 2-pc sectional, ea pc 53", EX 700.00
Sofa, Le Corbusier/Cassina, leather w/tube chrome base, 99" ..4,250.00
Sofa, Rohde/Troy-Sunshade, wraparound chanel uphl, 70", VG ..1,100.00
Stack hutch, Rhode/Heywood-Wakefield, bleached, 2-pc, 49x31" ..500.00
Stool, Chas Eames, walnut, trn spool form, no mk, 15x13" 800.00
Stool, vanity; Nelson/Miller, uphl seat, blk wood legs, VG 70.00
Table, card; Eames/Miller, folding, wht top, chrome leg, VG 250.00
Table, coffee; B Matthson/K Matthson, 37" dia teak top, VG 375.00
Table, coffee; Eames/Miller, blk plywood dished-out 34" top 375.00
Table, coffee; Lloyd, blk/yel laminate w/chrome tube U-base 400.00
Table, coffee; Nelson/Miller, rnd laminate top w/planter insert .600.00
Table, coffee; Robesjohn-Gibbings/Widdicomb, free-form wood, 72" ...950.00
Table, coffee; Wilkes/Miller, walnut, folding chrome legs, 59" 500.00
Table, dining; Ponti/Singer, walnut, brass-tip legs, 39" dia 425.00
Table, dining; Wormley, walnut vnr, dbl 3-leg ped, 98" 2,400.00
Table, Eames/Hiller, La Fonda, chrome open ped base w/4 legs .170.00
Table, end; Grossman, blk lacquer quadrangle top/sq shelf, VG .450.00
Table, Heywood-Wakefield, #M938G, wheat finish, 2-tier 175.00
Table, Heywood-Wakefield, pivot-top console, #M313G, VG ...325.00
Table, Nelson/Miller, 4-leg chrome ped base, 29" laminate top .400.00

Table, Noguchi, Xing wires support, wood base, 24" dia 950.00
Table, Platner/Knoll, base: thin steel rods, 24" walnut top 375.00
Table, Schultz/Knoll, floriform redwood 16" dia top 425.00
Table, Wendel Castle, walnut amoeba 22x14" top, cvd V base ..425.00
Table, 2½-rnd tiers, bent chrome strap supports, 22x24x12" 110.00
Tables, nesting; Heywood-Wakefield, rfn, set of 3, VG 375.00
Vanity system, Nelson, Thin Edge, 4-drw chest ea side, 88" 800.00
Vase, Cabat, aqua/blk drip over dk brn matt, 4½" 210.00
Vase, Cabat, caramel & brn drip over dk brn matt, 2½" 140.00
Vase, Cabat, dk bl drip w/gr highlights over dk brn, 3" 150.00
Vase, Fantoni, nude pr in panel, 4 dimpled sides, 15" 800.00
Vase, Fantoni, women, yel/wht/blk on mottle, bottle shape, 10" ..200.00
Vase, Gambone, geometric band, red on wht crackle, ftd, 16" 450.00
Vase, Memphis/Thun, wht, cone on ½-rnd w/3 gray/wht fins, 11" ..250.00
Vase, Raymor, dk mc bands, bulbous w/short neck, hdl, 12" 120.00

Finch, Kay

Kay Finch and her husband, Braden, operated a small pottery in Corona Del Mar, California, from 1939 to 1963. The company remained small, employing from twenty to sixty local residents who Kay trained in all but the most requiring tasks, which she herself performed. The company produced animal and bird figurines, most notably dogs, Kay's favorites. Figures of 'Godey' type couples were also made, as were tableware (consisting of breakfast sets) and other artware. Most pieces were marked.

After Kay's husband, Brandon, died in 1962, she closed the business. Some of her molds were sold to Freeman-McFarlin of El Monte, California, who soon contracted with Kay for new designs. Though the realism that is so evident in her original works is still strikingly apparent in these later pieces, none of the vibrant pastels or signature curliques are there.

Kay Finch died on June 21, 1993. Prices for her work have been climbing. Our advisor for this category is Jack Chipman, author of *The Collector's Encyclopedia of California Pottery*; he is listed in the Directory under California. Other sources of information include *Collectible Kay Finch* by Richard Martinez and Jean and Devin Frick (Collector Books) and *Kay Finch Ceramics, Her Enchanted World*, by Mike Nickel and Cynthia Horvath (Schiffer). Original model numbers are included in the following descriptions — three-digit numbers indicate pre-1946 models. After 1946 they were assigned four-digit numbers, the first two digits representing the year of initial production. *Kay Finch Ceramics Identification Guide* (published in 1992), containing many reprints of original catalog pages, is available from Frances Finch Webb; she is also listed in the Directory under California. See also Clubs and Newsletters.

Figurines: Mehitabel, #181, 8½",
$400.00; Hannibal (angry), #180,
10¼", $500.00; Jezebel, 6", $300.00.

Ashtray, swan, #4958, 3½" 75.00
Ashtray, teakwood matt, #115, oval, Talisman, 9" L 45.00
Box, cherry blossom relief, #4632, w/lid, 3½" dia 175.00
Cookie jar, Cookie Puss, ruffled collar, #4614, 12", minimum value ..2,000.00
Dog, Yorkie, #832, silver leaf, Freeman-McFarlin, 10½" 1,000.00
Figurine, Afghan angel, wht w/bl wings, #4911, sm 350.00
Figurine, angels, #114a, b, c; pastels, 4", ea 75.00
Figurine, bird, #846, gold leaf, Freeman-McFarlin, 7x7" 135.00
Figurine, bird, Dicky, #4905, 4" 150.00
Figurine, birds, Mr & Mrs, ##453 & #454, 4½" & 3", pr 175.00
Figurine, boxer dog, Dog Show, #5025 ....300.00
Figurine, bunny, Cottontail, #152, 2½" 150.00
Figurine, burro w/baskets, #4769, sm 100.00
Figurine, camel, #464, 5" 350.00
Figurine, cat, Baby Ambrosia, #5164, sm 200.00
Figurine, Chanticleer, #129, 10¾" 400.00
Figurine, cherub head, #212, 2¾" 75.00
Figurine, choir boy, kneeling, #211, 5½" 100.00
Figurine, cocker spaniel, Vicki, #455, 11¾" 700.00
Figurine, Court Lord, #451, & ladies, #400 & #401, 11", 3-pc ...650.00
Figurine, duck, Wacky, #472, 4½" 200.00
Figurine, ducks, Peep & Jeep, #178a & #178b, 3", pr 125.00
Figurine, elephant, seated or standing, no trappings, 4½", ea 175.00
Figurine, elephant, Violet, circus trappings, #190, 17", minimum ...2,500.00
Figurine, Godey couple, #122, 9½", pr 300.00
Figurine, guppy fish, #173, 2" 75.00
Figurine, horse, Free Spirit, #8, wood-tone, Freeman-McFarlin, 14" ..900.00
Figurine, kittens, Do no evil, See..., Hear..., #4834-35-36, 3", set 375.00
Figurine, lamb, kneeling, #136, sm 65.00
Figurine, monkey, Socko, #4841, 4½" 200.00
Figurine, monkey, standing/waving, #4962, 10" 600.00
Figurine, owl, #816, wood-tone, Freeman-McFarlin, 6" 125.00
Figurine, owl, Hoot, #187, 8¾" 200.00
Figurine, owl, Toot, #188, 6¾" 100.00
Figurine, Pekingese, lying down, #154, 14" L 550.00
Figurine, Percheron, #130, 3 styles, 4" to 6", ea, from $100 to 150.00
Figurine, pigs, Smiley or Grumpy, #164 & #165, 6¾" H, ea 300.00
Figurine, pigs, Winkie & Sassy, #166 & 185, 3¾", ea 115.00
Figurine, poodles, playful pr, #5203 & #5204, 10" 800.00
Figurine, rabbit, Cuddles, begging, #4623, 11" 450.00
Figurine, rooster & hen, Butch & Biddy, #177 & #176, he: 8½", pr ...250.00
Figurine, rooster & hen, Mr & Mrs Banty, #4844 & #4843, sm, pr ...175.00
Figurine, skunks, #4774 & #3775, playful pr, sm 450.00
Figurine, squirrels, #108a & #108B, 3" & 4", pr 175.00
Figurine, Yorky pups, #170 & #171, playful pr, 5½" & 6" 550.00
Garden seat, glossy purple, #5730, 15x17" 200.00
Mug, Missouri Mule, yel semimatt, 5" 75.00
Mug, Santa's face on side 100.00
Plaque, eagle, #5902, wht matt, 25x10" 300.00
Plaque, Virgo, silver & copper decor, 1960, 3¼" 85.00
Plate, rooster & hen decor, #4750, 9½" 95.00
Punch bowl, turq, 12" 295.00
Vase, tan semimatt, sqd form w/4 legs, 7" 50.00
Wall pocket, Ancestor Man, #5775, turq, 26" 275.00
Wall pocket, Santa face, #5373 ....325.00

Findlay Onyx and Floradine

Findlay, Ohio, was the location of the Dalzell, Gilmore, and Leighton Glass Company, one of at least sixteen companies that flourished there between 1886 and 1901. Their most famous ware, Onyx, is very rare. It was produced for only a short time beginning in 1889 due to the heavy losses incurred in the manufacturing process.

Onyx is layered glass, usually found in creamy white with a dainty floral pattern accented with metallic lustre that has been trapped between the two layers. Other colors found on rare occasions include a light amber (with either no lustre or with gilt flowers), light amethyst (or lavender), and rose. Although old tradepaper articles indicate the company originally intended to produce the line in three distinct colors, long-time Onyx collectors report that aside from the white, production was very limited. Other colors of Onyx are very rare, and the few examples that are found tend to support the theory that production of colored Onyx ware remained for the most part in the experimental stage. Even three-layered items have been found (they are extremely rare) decorated with three-color flowers. As a rule of thumb, using white Onyx prices as a basis for evaluation, expect to pay two to five times more for colored examples.

Floradine is a separate line that was made with the Onyx molds. A single-layer rose satin glassware with white opal flowers, it is usually priced in the general range of colored Onyx.

Chipping around the rims is very common, and price is determined to a great extent by condition. Our advisors for this category are Betty and Clarence Maier; they are listed in the Directory under Pennsylvania.

Floradine

Bowl, fluted, squat bulbous base, 4" 950.00
Celery vase, fluted cylinder neck, bulbous body, 6½", EX 1,000.00
Celery vase, NM 1,800.00
Creamer, bulbous, 4⅝" 950.00
Mustard pot, NM 1,550.00
Mustard pot, 3¾", EX 600.00
Spooner, 3¾" 1,000.00
Sugar bowl, bulbous, w/lid, 5½" 1,200.00
Sugar shaker 900.00
Syrup pitcher 1,750.00
Toothpick holder, 2½" 1,500.00
Tumbler, slightly bulbous, 3⅝" 1,000.00

Onyx

Bowl, wht w/raspberry decor, fluted top, 2½x4½" 1,300.00
Bowl, wht w/silver decor, 2½x5" 525.00
Butter dish, wht w/silver decor, 3x6" 1,150.00

Pitcher, white with silver decoration, 8", $1,200.00.

Creamer, wht w/silver decor, opal hdl, 4¾" 400.00
Salt shaker, wht w/silver decor, Pat 3/23/1889, 2⅝" 800.00
Spooner, wht w/silver decor, 4½x4" 525.00
Sugar bowl, wht w/silver decor, 5½", EX 475.00
Sugar shaker, wht w/silver decor, 5½" 545.00
Syrup pitcher, wht w/silver decor, pale opal hdl, 7¾" 985.00
Toothpick holder, wht w/silver decor, 2½" 500.00
Tumbler, bbl shape, 3½" 450.00

Fire Marks

The earliest American fire marks date back to 1752 when 'The Philadelphia Contributionship For the Insurance of Houses From Loss By Fire' (the official name of this company, still in business!) used a plaque to identify property they insured. The first fire marks were made of cast iron; later, sheet brass, lead, copper, tin, and zinc were also used. The insignia of the insurance company appeared on each mark, and they would normally reward the volunteer fire department who managed to be the first on the scene to battle the fire. (Altercations occasionally broke out between firefighting companies vying for the chance to earn the reward!)

Fire marks were first used in Great Britain about 1780 and were more elaborate than U.S. marks. The first English examples were made of lead and carried a policy number. They were used to identify insured property to the fire brigades maintained by the insurance companies.

During the latter half of the 19th century, municipalities replaced the volunteer fire companies and fire brigades with paid fire departments. No longer was there a need for fire marks, so the companies discontinued their use. Some companies still use fire marks for advertising purposes. Reproductions may be purchased for decorative purposes. Our advisor for fire marks is Glenn Hartley, Sr.; he is listed in the Directory under Georgia. See also *The Fire Mark Circle of America*, listed under Clubs, Catalogs, and Newsletters in the Directory.

Two cast-iron fire marks with polychrome paint: Fire Department Insurance, 11½" long, $375.00; City Insurance Co., Cin., 12½" long, $650.00.

Assoc Firemen's...Baltimore, pnt CI oval w/running man, 12", EX .320.00
FA, hydrant w/hose, CI, dk gr pnt, 10¾x7½" 85.00
German Freeport Ill, tin, lt pnt wear, 2½x7", EX 150.00
Green Tree Mutual Assurance, CI, NM orig pnt, 3¼" 125.00
Invicta & famous wht horse of Kent, lead, 8¾x6½" 350.00
Mutual Insurance, angel flying over Charleston, 9½x7½" 65.00
Northwestern National Service Strength Safety, tin, 3" 55.00
Phoenix Hartford, tin, lt pnt loss/rust, 8⅜x4¼" 250.00
UF, letter ea side eagle, pnt CI oval w/hobnail edge, 11" L 290.00
United Firemen's Ins Co of Phila PA, CI, 11¾x8¾", EX 150.00
Valiant Hose No 2, pnt CI, 1800s, minor pnt loss, rust, 10½" 400.00
4 clasped hands & #906, 7x10½" 365.00

Firefighting Collectibles

Firefighting collectibles have always been a good investment in terms of value appreciation. Many times the market will be temporarily affected by wild price swings caused by the 'supply and demand principle' as related to a small group of aggressive collectors. These collectors will occasionally pay well over market value for a particular item they need or want. Once their desires are satisfied, prices seem to return to their normal range. It has been noticed that during these periods of high prices, many items enter the marketplace that otherwise would

remain in collections. This may (it has in the past) cause a price depression (due again to the 'supply and demand principle' of market behavior). But when all is said and done, the careful purchase of quality, well-documented firefighting items has been an enjoyable hobby and an excellent investment opportunity.

Today there is a large, active group of collectors for fire department antiques (items over 100 years old) and an even larger group seeking related collectibles (those less than 100 years old). Our advisors for this category (except grenades) are H. Thomas and Patricia Laun; they are listed in the directory under New York.

Fire grenades preceded the pressurized metal fire extinguishers used today. They were filled with a mixture of chemicals and water and made of glass thin enough to shatter easily when thrown into the flames. Many varieties of colors and shapes were used. Not all the grenades listed contain salt-brine solution, some, such as the Red Comet, contain carbon tetrachloride, a powerful solvent that is also a health hazard and an environmental threat. (It attacks the ozone layer.) It is best to leave any contents inside the glass balls. The source of grenade prices are mainly auction results; current retail values will fluctuate. Our fire grenades advisor is Larry Meyer; he is listed in the Directory under Illinois.

Key:
ALF — American LaFrance   S&A — soda & acid
CCL4 — carbon tetrachloride

Alarm box, aluminum, style 51, quick-acting door, complete 135.00
Alarm box, CI, Gamewell, telegraph door, slant fist, complete ..245.00
Alarm box, CI, Utica...Alarm..., Excelsior sz/style, complete 750.00
Alarm box, CI & brass, Holtzer Cabot, 9½" dia 85.00
Alarm box, wooden, Std Electric Time, Springfield MA, early ..200.00
Alarm indicator, Gamewell, vibrating bell on top, complete ..2,850.00
Axe, early Viking style, orig 31" hdl, VG 225.00
Axe, fireman's, 8-lb flat pick head, early 65.00
Badge, ALFCo 577 Elmira, NP, scarce 65.00
Badge, Altona, 5 firemen in center, gold-tone metal 75.00
Badge, Brooklyn Fire Dept 1922, rnd, VG 150.00
Badge, Exempter Volunteer Firemen's Assoc, gold-tone shield 50.00
Badge, Fairmont Fire Assoc, coin-silver shield 150.00
Badge, Fire Line 91 Patterson NJ, NP alarm-box shape 175.00
Badge, Goodwill Steamer, NP, VG 60.00
Badge, Hoboken FD, NP, fire panoply center, VG 50.00
Badge, Hope Fire Co...PA on NP shield 100.00
Badge, MB Sherman Hose w/monogram on NP shield 80.00
Badge, Newark Fire Dept 909, NP, VG 120.00
Badge, Rockville Center FD, NP, VG 55.00
Badge, Southwark Hose 9 GWD, gold-tone coin-silver shield 160.00
Badge, Wm Penn H&L-1-&SFE Co, NP, VG 110.00
Bed key, hammered steel, EX 135.00
Bell, apparatus; brass, swinging cradle type, 10" 650.00
Bell, muffin; brass w/trn wooden hdl, Pat 1868, 3½" dia 375.00
Bell, muffin; solid brass, rpl hdl, 5½" dia 200.00
Bell, tapper, brass, acorn finial, 5" dia, on 9x5" slate base 295.00
Belt, wht leather w/red Cairns & Bros NY, EX 65.00
Book, Ahrens Fox, Rolls Royce..., Hass, hard cover, 1982 .....190.00
Book, Ahrens Fox Album, Sutsma, 1973 .....225.00
Book, ALF Operator's Manual, c 1921, 198-pg, EX 110.00
Book, American Fire House, Zorler, 1982, w/dust jacket 50.00
Book, History of New Bedford Fire Dept, VG 65.00
Book, Mack Fire Apparatus a Pictorial History, Eckart, 1991 .....50.00
Book, My 100 Favorite Fire Rigs, Sutsma, soft cover, 1977 .....225.00
Book, Seagrave - Pictorial History...Fire Apparatus, Lee, 1991 .....60.00
Book, Where's the Fire?, W Fochs, 1984 .....45.00
Book, Young Firemen of Lakeville, Webster, 1909 .....28.00
Books, As You Pass By, Dunshee, 1952, EX 35.00

Books, Firehouse, Dennis Smith, w/dust jacket, EX 35.00
Books, Foot Prints of Assurance, fire mark guide 50.00
Books, History of the Am Water Tower, Hass, 1988 ....110.00
Box, terminal; Gamewell, CI 70.00
Bracket, lantern; CI, bicycle clip, gooseneck, early 85.00
Bucket, leather, No 2 Trinity Church, 1831, VG 300.00
Bucket, leather, Protection Franklin Fire...1821, EX 850.00
Bucket, leather, red pnt, NM 100.00
Bucket, leather w/wrought-iron rim, old red rpt w/gold, 12" 220.00
Bucket, rubber, gr w/red maker's name & anchor, 12½"+hdl 80.00
Cane, firemantic/presentation, eng/emb, sterling top 800.00
Clamp, hose; steel, mk ALF 95.00
Container, battery acid; Gamewell, clear glass w/milk glass lid 80.00
Extinguisher, apparatus; Pirsch Std, w/hose, 2½-gal 200.00
Extinguisher, Badgers, S&A, pony sz, 1½-gal, EX 85.00
Extinguisher, Eclipse, tin, EX 85.00
Extinguisher, Junior Buffalo, S&A, pony sz, 1½-gal 100.00
Extinguisher, light-bulb shape, CCL4 ....20.00
Extinguisher, Pyrene, for home or auto, EX 40.00
Extinguisher, Rameses, tin tube, 22", VG 35.00
Extinguisher, Shur Stop, wall mt, bracket w/blank cartridge, EX ..50.00
Extinguisher, Ugasi, cb tube, 12", VG 15.00
Extinguisher, Underwriters Fire..., copper, S&A, 2½-gal 15.00
Frontispc, leather, Captain 1 AFD, 8" 80.00
Frontispc, leather, Foreman 5 SFD, fancy stitches, 8" 110.00
Frontispc, leather, Hook & Ladder...MA, 1870, 8", VG 65.00
Frontispc, leather, We Will Try 2 NSFE Co, 8" 140.00
Gauge, steam; Amoskeag Man Co, eng steam engine, 6½" dia, EX ...500.00
Gong, center-wind, Gamewell, brass, 6", EX 135.00
Gong, center-wind, Gamwell, brass, 10", w/key 235.00
Gong, chain-wind, Gamewell, brass plated, 10" 185.00
Gong, dbl-hammer alarm; 16" brass bell, 34x28", VG 450.00
Gong, Gamewell, Excelsior, oak case, 6" 975.00
Gong, Gamewell, Moses Crane oak case, patrol gong, 8½" 1,750.00
Gong, Gamewell, Moses Crane walnut case, complete/orig, 18" .4,500.00
Gong, Gamewell, Moses Crane walnut case, patrol gong, 8½" ..1,750.00
Gong, Gamewell, oak case, ball top, rfn, 18" 4,250.00
Gong, rotary, New Departure, brass, pull-chain type, 10" 325.00
Gong, single-stroke, Holtzer Cabot, heavy brass, 10", w/key 175.00
Gong, Star Electric, plain oak case, Binghamton NY, 8¾" 850.00
Gong, Star Gong, Boston, plain case, 14" 700.00
Grenade, American, clear, magenta contents 500.00
Grenade, Babcock, cobalt, Chicago 1,250.00
Grenade, Barnum's, aqua 550.00
Grenade, Carbona, amber, EX labels 65.00
Grenade, Diamond, amber 1,200.00
Grenade, Firex, cobalt, unemb, orig metal hanger, 4", M 65.00
Grenade, Hand...Extinguisher, clear, quilted, ftd, screw-top 500.00
Grenade, Harden's, cobalt, 3-pc 2,000.00
Grenade, Harden's Improved, clear, petal design 700.00
Grenade, Harden's Star, bl, complete w/contents 60.00
Grenade, Harden's Star, med cobalt, smooth base, full, 8" 625.00
Grenade, Harden's Star, yel-gr, potstone, 7⅞" 250.00
Grenade, Harkness Fire Destroyer, dk bl, ribbed, 6½" 200.00
Grenade, Hayward, 4-dmn panel, turq 450.00
Grenade, Hayward's, aqua, pleated, mid-sz 400.00
Grenade, Hayward's...Pat Aug 8 1871, amber, 6⅛" 120.00
Grenade, Heathman's Swift, amber 1,200.00
Grenade, HSN, clear 475.00
Grenade, Imperial, gr, garter, lg 575.00
Grenade, Prevoyante, amber 500.00
Grenade, PRR, aqua 800.00
Grenade, Pyrofite, aqua, EX label 65.00
Grenade, Santa Fe Route, clear 1,700.00

Grenade, Universal, bl 1,250.00
Grenade, WD Allen, gr 1,200.00
Hat, uniform; bl wool, bell top, no badge 10.00
Hat, uniform; bl wool, bell top, Syracuse NY badge 75.00
Helmet, aluminum, high eagle, CF Co 1 Carlisle PA, early, VG ...425.00
Helmet, aluminum, high eagle, metal frontpc 245.00
Helmet, aluminum, high front, Cairns Senator, red frontpc, VG ..220.00
Helmet, leather, high eagle, Bell & Siren Club, VG 400.00
Helmet, leather, high eagle, Cairns, Washington Foreman, EX .375.00
Helmet, leather, high eagle, Cairns, Washington 3 JPS, EX 375.00
Helmet, leather, high eagle, Engineer Natick FD, rpt, VG 275.00
Helmet, leather, high eagle, jockey style, Engineer MCVFD, VG ..400.00
Helmet, leather, high eagle, John Olson, VG 275.00
Helmet, leather, high eagle, Protection River, VG 375.00
Helmet, leather, high eagle, Roulstone, Boston, VG 375.00
Helmet, leather, high front w/fox, Cairns, EX 600.00
Helmet, leather, high front w/greyhound, Cairns, 1866 ....1,350.00
Helmet, leather, low front, Cairns, BFD in wht, G 75.00
Helmet, leather, low front, Cairns, Ladder 1 SFD, G 110.00
Inkwell, Fire Assoc of Phila, pewter, hinged hydrant w/hose, EX ..350.00
Lamp, engine; 2 red/2 bl/2 clear glass panels, eagle finial 1,500.00

Lantern, brass Dietz King, red paint, clear globe, EX, $175.00; Extinguisher, Shur Spray, ceiling mount, glass automatic type, 1-gallon, VG, $125.00.

Lantern, Dietz King, ALF, brass, NM 275.00
Lantern, Dietz King, brass, mk Seagrave, EX 375.00
Lantern, wrist; brass, DD Miller NY, Mohawk Chief, EX 600.00
Letter opener, brass, Gamewell Alarm Co, alarm box on hdl 325.00
Mask, breathing; leather w/mica eye shield, Pat Sept 1-86, VG .170.00
Nozzle, Akron, brass, 2-man, shut off, Pat 1930, 21" 125.00
Nozzle, Akron, rubber hdls, 2½" 95.00
Nozzle, brass, w/shut off, 8" 30.00
Nozzle, Bresnan, brass, cellar distributor 230.00
Nozzle, combination; Fog Nozzle Co, brass, 1½" 35.00
Nozzle, early shut-off type, brass w/leather hdls, 38" 200.00
Nozzle, Eureka Fire Hose, early hand type w/leather hdl, 36" 60.00
Nozzle, Hunneman & Co, brass, mk Protector on tip, 48" 550.00
Nozzle, Santa Rosa, aluminum, 2½" 125.00
Paperweight, Fireman's Ins Co, Newark NJ, brass, ca 1955 ....50.00
Paperweight, hydrant shape, VBM Co, Lou KY, 4" 85.00
Playing cards, Firefighter Equipment Co, Schenectady NY, MIB .18.00
Playing cards, Gamewell, Police/Fire Box on bks, 1910s, EXIB ..495.00
Rack, fire grenade; metal wire, holds 3 pt-sz grenades 75.00
Rattle, brass weight on end, EX 180.00
Rattle, dbl reed w/weighted end, EX 75.00
Stamp, time & date; Gamewell, Chelsea clock, EX working 600.00
Station, Gamewell, pull box w/orig instructions, on oak panel ...225.00
Telephone, Utica Fire Alarm Tel Co, oak wall type, VG 300.00
Torch, parade; brass on trn pole, 30" 100.00
Toy, Texaco helmet, plastic, w/amplifier, EX 65.00
Trumpet, nickel, octagonal, Cairns, Pat 1877, VG 800.00

Trumpet, presentation; brass, sm crack in bell, dtd 1846, 17" **650.00**
Trumpet, presentation; SP, JO Mead & Sons, dtd 1859, 24", EX ..**650.00**
Trumpet, speaking; toleware, AST Foreman Central Falls, 17", VG ..**400.00**
Tumbler, hi-ball, Seagrave w/picture of engine & truck **3.00**

Fireglow

Fireglow is a type of art glass that first appears to be an opaque cafe au lait, but glows with rich red 'fire' when held to a strong source of light.

Ewer, tan w/mc flowers, 10½" **150.00**
Vase, bud; florals/berries/firefly, ftd, Mt WA, 5¾" **110.00**
Vase, portrait, 10" **185.00**

Fireplace Implements

In the colonial days of our country, fireplaces provided heat in the winter and were used year round to cook food in the kitchen. The implements that were a necessary part of these functions were varied and have become treasured collectibles, many put to new use in modern homes as decorative accessories. Gypsy pots may hold magazines; copper and brass kettles, newly polished and gleaming, contain dried flowers or green plants. Firebacks, highly ornamental iron panels that once reflected heat and protected masonry walls, are now sometimes used as wall decorations. By Victorian times the cookstove had replaced the kitchen fireplace, and many of these early utensils were already obsolete; but as a source of heat and comfort, the fireplace continued to be used for several more decades. See also Wrought Iron.

Andirons, brass, baluster shafts, scroll legs, ball ft, 12" **225.00**
Andirons, brass, dbl rings, ball finial, 1800s, 20" **300.00**
Andirons, brass, Regency, pointed finials, 19th C, 27" **1,155.00**
Andirons, brass, steeple tops, sgn J Davis Boston, 19" **1,600.00**
Andirons, brass, trn shafts/spurred legs/ball tops, 1800s, 17" **330.00**
Andirons, brass, trn tops/stds, scrolled legs, PA, 1800s, 18" **660.00**
Andirons, brass, trn/faceted shafts, scrolled legs, Phila, 19" **825.00**
Andirons, brass, urn top, sgn Morgan's 5, 20" **850.00**
Andirons, brass, urn top, spurred legs, ball ft, 18½" **350.00**
Andirons, brass, 1st Empire Classical, ball tops, 16" **1,200.00**
Andirons, brass w/multi-trn shafts, scroll ft, acorn finials **500.00**
Andirons, bronze, ornate Renaissance style, 19th C, 36" **2,300.00**
Andirons, CI, Spanish Baronial, spiral supports, 33" **500.00**
Andirons, copper, owl w/glass light-up eyes on branch, 21" **650.00**
Andirons, wrought iron, EX detail, ea w/crane, 1890s, 32½" **165.00**
Andirons, wrought-iron Gothic style, flat disk top, 36" **150.00**

Bellows, carved walnut panels with remnants of red Moroccan leather, brass nozzle, early 1800s, 20", $450.00.

Broiler, wrought iron, penny ft, adjusts, 12x18" **250.00**
Bucket, hearth; wrought copper, rolled rim, dvtl, 17" dia, EX **325.00**
Coal scuttle, japanned metal, wire bail, 1880s, 11x16", VG **35.00**
Dutch oven, tin w/iron spit, 19" L **330.00**
Fender, brass, bow front, rtcl mid section, 1830s, EX **500.00**
Fender, brass, early 19th C, 10x38", EX **400.00**
Fender, brass, English, 8x50", +3 brass tools w/ebony hdls **1,750.00**
Fender, brass, rtcl Greek key & fluted decor, 9x47x14" **440.00**
Fender, brass w/curved grill, 48" **220.00**
Fender, iron & brass w/spiral wire decor, 1810s, 15¼x40¾" **500.00**
Fender, ribbed & molded brass, late Georgian, 7x43x11" **220.00**
Fender, steel, eng serpentine shape, English, 1790s, 52" **400.00**
Flue rake, sheet iron & wire, hook finial, 1870s **7.00**
Kettle shelf, wrought iron, 10½x14" **35.00**
Logs fork, wrought & CI, twisted hdl, 1800s, 42" **45.00**
Pipe tongs, brass scissors type, 1800s, 8¼" **65.00**
Screen, brass, Louis XV Revival style, scroll legs, 38x38" **500.00**
Screen, Louis XV style, 3-panel, pnt leather, 36x47" **600.00**
Shovel & tongs, bell metal, lemon-top brass & iron, 33", 32" **700.00**
Spit, CI w/wrought-iron spikes, 31" L **165.00**
Spit, wrought iron, geared lever action, 8" L **300.00**
Toaster, wrought hoop w/stand, 18th C, EX **525.00**
Toaster, wrought iron loop w/stand, 1700s, 21½" **525.00**
Toaster, wrought iron w/scroll work, 17" **275.00**
Trammel, wrought iron, sawtoothed, adjusts from 36" **165.00**
Trivet, wrought iron, rnd w/3 ft, 7⅝" dia, 23" hdl **70.00**

Fishing Collectibles

Collecting old fishing tackle is becoming more popular every year. Though at first most interest was geared toward old lures and some reels, rods, advertising, and miscellaneous items are quickly gaining ground. Values are given for examples in excellent or better condition and should be used only as a guide. For more information contact our advisor Randy Hilst, an appraiser and collector whose address and phone number are listed in the Directory under Illinois.

Key:
BE — bead eyes   PE — painted eyes
GE — glass eyes   TE — tack eyes

Bucket, minnow; Falls City Angler's Choice, 1862, 8", EX **15.00**
Canoe paddles, minor end cracks, 1945, VG **65.00**
Catalog, Abercrombie & Finch, 293-pgs, 1911, G cover, EX inside ...**100.00**
Creel, trout; split willow, leather bound, strap, med sz, EX **100.00**
Decoy, Yel Perch, Oscar Peterson, 2 weights, 7" L, EX **375.00**
Float, pike; wooden, HP, early design, 12½", VG **75.00**
Fly, dry; Mallard Quill, by Edward Hewitt, mtd in glass dome **200.00**
Hook, Stanley's Prefection Weedless, M on card **25.00**
Line dryer, by Hardy, aluminum, hand-held, folding, EX **115.00**
Lure, Bass Hog, TJ Boulton, yel/orange body, red head, C1911, 4" ..**120.00**
Lure, Bate's Pat Spinner, copper & SP, EX **400.00**
Lure, Bottlenose Tad Polly, Heddon, yel w/red & brn spots, 4" **70.00**
Lure, Bucktail Surface Minnow, Heddon #400, rainbow finish, 2⅝" ...**325.00**
Lure, cork frog, Pflueger, HP, C1900, 3" **120.00**
Lure, Creek Chub Bait, Husky Pikie minnow, #2300, 1920s **15.00**
Lure, James Heddon SOS wounded minnow #140, ca 1928 ....**35.00**
Lure, Kusky Darter, Creek Chub, frog finish, 5⅛", NM **1,500.00**
Lure, Little Egypt Pork Rind, Al Foss (1st lure), VG **35.00**
Lure, Mud Puppy, Roberts, gray, 6¼", VG (blk & wht box) **45.00**
Lure, Musky Injured Minnow, Creek Chub, in silver flash, 5", NM ...**1,500.00**
Lure, Musky Jitterbug, Gr Perch scale, Arbogast Co, 4½" **25.00**
Lure, Musky Pikie, Creek Chub, golden shiner finish, 6", NM ...**1,000.00**

Lure, Pflueger, tandem spinner, 1897 ....**30.00**
Lure, Submerged Minnow, early Shakespeare #33, mc, 3", EX- ..**250.00**
Lure, Trout Caster Plug, Paw Paw, M **50.00**
Lure, Vamp, Heddon, rare Goldfish finish, orange, mk, NM **600.00**
Net, landing; Abercrombie & Fitch Troutster, maple hdl, 20" ...**250.00**

Reel, 12/0 Big Game, Arthur Kovalovsky & Sons, plated stainless or brass hardware, unused, in leather case, $2,200.00.

Reel, bait casting; Pflueger #1895, free spool, MIB **60.00**
Reel, bait; Winchester #2142, raised pillar, 1¾" dia **125.00**
Reel, fly; Hardy Uniqua, brass ft, 2⅝" **130.00**
Reel, Heddon Automatic, free-stripping, #87, MIB **30.00**
Reel, Horton #33 Bluegrass **185.00**
Reel, interocean; Pflueger 1885, leather thumb brake, MIB **110.00**
Reel, Pennell Supra, brass, 1890s, EX **30.00**
Reel, Shakespeare Hoosier, 1922 ....**90.00**
Reel, surf; Policansky's Monitor, 2¾" dia, VG **110.00**
Rod, bait casting; Heddon's #103, 2-pc, 5½', VG **75.00**
Rod, bass; FE Thomas, Dirigo, 3-pc, 9½', VG in bag/tube **145.00**
Rod, fly; Heddon #10 Blue Waters, 3-pc, 9', M in bag/tube **150.00**
Rod, fly; Orvis Battenkill, 2-pc, 8', EX in bag/labeled tube **275.00**
Rod, salmon; Classic Payne, 3-pc, 12', EX in rpl canvas case **500.00**
Rod, spinning; Orvis Special, 1950s, 2-pc, 7', EX in bag/tube **200.00**
Rod, trout; Leonard, 2-pc, Catskill 38H, 7', M in bag/tube **1,700.00**
Rod, trout; Leonard Model 700-2 Duracane, M in bag & tube ...**750.00**
Rod, trout; Paul H Young, Ace, 2-pc, 7½', EX in bag & tube **400.00**
Rod, trout; Rueben Barkly; 2-pc, 2-tip, 7½', M in bag/tube **425.00**
Rod, trout; Winchester, 3-pc, 9', ferrule rpl, VG in bag/tube **100.00**
Rod/reel, salt water; wood, 7', Shakespeare Juniper reel, VG **50.00**

Flags of the United States

The brevity and imprecise language of the first Flag Act of 1777 allowed great artistic license for America's early flag makers. This resulted in a rich variety of imaginative star formations which coexisted with more conventional union patterns. In 1912 inviolate design standards were established for the new 48-star flag, but the banners of our past history continue to survive:

The 'Great Star' pattern — configured from the combined stars of the union, appeared in various star denominations for about 50 years, then gradually disappeared in the post-Civil War years.

The utilitarian 'scatter' pattern — created through the random placement of stars, is traceable to the formative years of our nation and remained a design influence through most of the 19th century.

The 'wreath' pattern — first appearing in the form of simple single-wreath formations, eventually evolved into the elegant double- and triple-wreath medallion patterns of the Centennial period.

Acquisition of specific star denominations is also a primary consideration in the collecting process. Pre-Civil War flags of 33 stars or less are very scarce and are typically treated as 'blue chip' items. Civil War-era flags of

34 and 35 stars also stand among the most sought-after denominations. Market demand for 36-, 37-, and 38-star flags is strong but less broad-based, while interest in the unofficial 39-, 40-, 41-, and 42-star examples is largely confined to flag aficionados. The very rare 43 remains in a class by itself and is guaranteed to attract the attention of the serious collector.

Row-patterned flags of 44, 45, and 46 stars still turn up with some frequency and serve as a source of more modestly priced vintage flags. Ordinary 48-star flags flood the flea markets and are priced accordingly, while the short-lived 49 is regarded as a legitimate collectible. 13-star flags, produced over a period of more than 200 years, surface in many forms and must be assessed on a case-by-case basis.

Many flag buffs favor sizes that are manageable for wall display while others are attracted to the more monumental proportions. Allowances are typically made for the normal wear and tear — it goes with the territory. But sever fabric deterioration and other forms of excessive physical damage are legitimate points of negotiation.

The dollar value of a flag is by no means based upon age alone. The wide price swings in the listing below have been influenced by a variety of determining factors related to age, scarcity, and aesthetic merit. In fact, almost any special feature that stands out as unusual or distinctive is a potential asset. Imprinted flags and inscribed flags; 8-point stars, gold stars, and added stars; extra stripes, missing stripes, tri-color stripes, and war stripes are all part of the pricing equation. And while political and military flags may rank above all others in terms of prestige and price, any flag with a significant and well-documented historical connection has 'star' potential (pardon the pun). Our advisor for this category is Robert Banks; he is listed in the Directory under Maryland.

11 stars, wreath pattern, hand-sewn flannel, 1840s, 31x40" **650.00**
13 stars, (4-5-4), sea captain's, ca 1860s, 74x140" **500.00**
13 stars, hand/machine sewn, Centennial, 60x86" **250.00**
13 stars, in semi-wreath, hand sewn, 1870s, 54x102" **325.00**
13 stars, printed glazed muslin, 1880s, 7x11" **20.00**
13 stars, 9 stripes, hand sewn, 1860s, 27x50" **700.00**
19 stars, 16 orig+3, sewn scrap fabric, 39x66" **1,500.00**
20 stars, hand-embr into Great Star, rare, 24x32" **1,800.00**
26 stars, Great Star, embr on sewn silk, 30x43" **1,100.00**
29 stars, entirely hand sewn, poor condition, 43x68" **575.00**
30 stars, gold stars/fringe, silk, delicate, 52x68" **550.00**
31 stars, Great Star, Lincoln related, printed, 11x14" **285.00**
31 stars, row pattern, hand-stitched bunting, 104x247" **850.00**

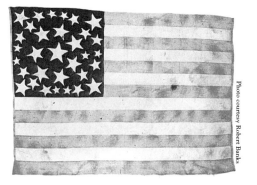

32-Star, hand-stitched cotton in variant wreath pattern, 42x60", $700.00.

32 stars, dbl wreath of inset stars, hand sewn, 36x48" **700.00**
33 stars, Great Star, hand-sewn muslin, 60x96" **825.00**
33 stars, hand-/machine-sewn wool bunting, 66x92" **600.00**
33 stars, in rows, printed bunting, 28x44", G- **325.00**
34 stars, dbl-wreath pattern, printed silk, 18x28" **300.00**
34 stars, Great Star, mixed fabrics, sewn, 91x154" **1,100.00**

34 stars, printed linen, 3 sewn sections, 22x48" 250.00
34 stars, random pattern, hand sewn, 66x140" 710.00
35 stars, dbl-wreath pattern, printed, sized muslin, 19x28" 190.00
35 stars, recruiting flag, sewn bunting, 50x116" 750.00
35 stars, row pattern, hand/machine sewn, 96x180" 625.00
36 stars, cut-in, in rows, machined stripes, 25x50" 300.00
36 stars, inscr parade flag, muslin print, 6x9" 90.00
36 stars, sailing ship's, inscr & dtd, 75x142" 375.00
37 stars, medallion pattern, printed/sewn muslin, 48x87" 280.00
37 stars, printed silk, 32x40" 85.00
37 stars, row pattern, hand-sewn silk, poor condition, 60x80" 230.00
37 stars, row pattern, stitched bunting, 30x48" 325.00
38 stars, medallion-wreath pattern, printed cotton, 12x17" 120.00
38 stars, printed silk w/ribbon ties, 30x47" 100.00
38 stars, row pattern, clamp dyed in 3 sections, 60x120" 220.00
38 stars, row pattern, hand/machine-stitched bunting, 71x116" .250.00
38 stars, unique wreath pattern, sewn, 89x134" 375.00
38 stars, 1776-1876 pattern, printed linen, 27½x46" 625.00
39 stars, Centennial 'International Flag,' 16x24" 90.00
39 stars, row pattern, all machine-stitched bunting, 40x84" 350.00
39 stars, row pattern variation, printed silk, 12x24" 85.00
39 stars (6-5 pattern), printed gauze bunting, 19x34" 70.00
40 stars, row pattern, hand-sewn bunting, lg, 98x204" 270.00
40 stars, row pattern, printed/sewn British import, 55x106" 185.00
41 stars (rare), printed cotton sheeting, 15x24" 140.00
42 stars, row pattern, printed silk/fringe, poor, 24x36" 70.00
42 stars, sewn cotton, from Ft Hamilton NY, 120x177" 275.00
42 stars, 7-row pattern, printed cotton, 27x47" 80.00
43 stars, machine-sewn bunting, extremely rare, 29x70" 675.00
44 stars, machine-sewn cotton bunting, 53x82" 90.00
44 stars, triple-wreath pattern, printed cotton, 23x26" 100.00
45 stars, HP w/sewn stripes, 38x70" 120.00
45 stars, machine-sewn cotton bunting, 80x108" 55.00
45 stars, printed silk w/red ribbon ties, 32x46" 45.00
45 stars, row pattern variant, printed muslin, 9x13" 25.00
46 stars, machine-sewn wool bunting, 72x138" 60.00
46 stars, printed silk, GAR Post in gold, 32x45" 350.00
47 stars, unofficial, sewn bunting, 108x137" 200.00
48 stars, all crocheted, dtd 1941, 20x38" 85.00
48 stars, machine-sewn cotton bunting, 60x96" 30.00
48 stars, printed cotton w/GAR surprint, 11x16" 25.00
48 stars, sewn to form 'USA,' unauthorized WWI, 45x69" 300.00
48 stars, USN Union Jack, machine-sewn wool, 23x33" 35.00
48 stars in gold, sewn WWII casket flag, 58x118" 150.00
49 stars, embr, sewn stripes, 36x60" 45.00
49 stars, 3 uncut flags, printed cottonsheet, 37x36" 25.00
50 stars, early prototype 'June 1959,' 52x66" 220.00
50 stars, hand-knitted coverlet w/fringe, 30x51" 30.00
51 stars, printed flaglette for DC statehood, 4x6" 15.00

Florence Ceramics

Figurines marked 'Florence Ceramics' were produced in the '40s and '50s in Pasadena, California. The quality of the ware and the attention given to detail are prompting a growing interest among today's collectors. The names of these lovely ladies, gents, and figural groups are nearly always incised into their bases. The company name is ink stamped. Examples are evaluated by size, rarity, and intricacy of design. For more information we recommend *The Florence Collectibles* by Doug Foland, our advisor for this category. You will find him listed in the Directory under Oregon. Another source is *The Collector's Encyclopedia of California Pottery* by Jack Chipman; he is listed in the Directory under California.

Abigail, bl, 8½" 195.00
Adeline, bl & pk 295.00
Amber, pk gown, w/parasol, 9¼", from $250 to 425.00
Amelia, rust & tan 250.00
Ann, wht fancy basket 150.00
Ava, gr & gray 225.00
Barbara, 8½", from $200 to 325.00
Belle, flower holder, gray 125.00
Beth, flower holder, tan 135.00
Blondie & Sandy, beach boy & girl, 7½", pr 500.00
Blossom Girl & Lantern Boy, 8¼", pr, from $150 to 200.00
Camille, dk red gown, 9", from $130 to 300.00
Carmen, Spanish dancer, 12½", from $700 to 850.00
Catherine, purple, on couch, 6¾x7¾" 595.00
Cindy, purple, 8" 435.00
Colleen, moss gr, w/fingers, 8" 265.00
Cynthia, 9¼", from $275 to 300.00
David, bust 250.00
Don & Judy, 7¼", 7", pr, from $300 to 350.00
Douglas, tan & gr, 8" 195.00
Edward, gray w/gr chair, 7" 430.00
Ethel, 7¼", from $95 to 150.00
Eugenia, 9", from $250 to 350.00
Fair Lady, rose 1,200.00
Fall Reverie & Companion, yel & gr, ea w/basket of fruit, pr ..1,800.00
Gibson Girl w/Gold Muff, early, 9½", from $95 to 125.00
Jim, gray, 6¼" 90.00
Joy & Jerry, flower holders, wht & bl, pr 295.00
Karen, rose & wht 500.00
Kiu & She-Ti, 11", pr, from $$400 to 500.00
Lady Diana, sea foam 650.00
Lantern Boy & Blossom, flower holders, gr & blk, pr 250.00

Photo courtesy Doug Foland

Lillian Russell, minimum value, $1,200.00.

Linda Lou, child, 7¾", from $160 to 180.00
Madame Pompadour & Louis XV, gold/wht, 12¼", pr 850.00
Marianne, hat in hand, 8¾", from $275 to 300.00
Martin, long red coat & hat, 10½", from $175 to 250.00
Mimi, flower holder, bl & wht 50.00
Musette, burgundy, 9½", from $200 to 250.00
Nita, 8", from $100 to 150.00
Pamela, bust 250.00
Pat & Mike, bl/gr & burgundy, pr 595.00
Patrice, holding fan, 7¼", from $100 to 250.00
Patsy, flower holder, 6" 50.00
Peg, tying hat, 7", from $50 to 75.00

Peter, bl coat, hat in hand, 9¼", from $175 to 250.00
Pheasant, wht, tail down 225.00
Pouter pigeon, wht matt 325.00
Pouter pigeon, wht w/gray base 450.00
Princess, wht & gold 800.00
Reggie & Carol, 7¼", pr, from $500 to 550.00
Rita, flower holder 225.00
Roberta, 8½", from $200 to 275.00
Rosalie, 9½", from $200 to 300.00
Rosemarie, 8¼", from $250 to 300.00
Sherri, pk gown, hands away, 8", from $175 to 200.00
Sherri, sea foam 450.00
Shirley, 8", from $135 to 195.00
Spring Reverie & Companion, pr 1,800.00
Story Hour, w/boy 1,100.00
Story Hour, w/o boy 950.00
Suzette, flower holder 65.00
Swan, planter 450.00
Taka, w/parasol, 11", from $150 to 185.00
Wynken & Blynken, bedtime boy & girl, 5½", pr 600.00
Yvonne, gr dress, 8¾" 300.00

Florentine Cameo

Although the appearance may look much like English cameo, the decoration on this type of glass is not wheel cut or acid etched. Instead a type of heavy paste — usually a frosty white — is applied to the face to create a look very similar to true cameo. It was produced in France as well as England; it is sometimes marked 'Florentine.'

Pitcher, bird/grasses on med bl, w/camphor hdl, 7" 225.00
Vase, berry vines on apricot satin, stick neck, 7¾" 200.00
Vase, berry vines on bl satin, knob neck, 9" 225.00
Vase, birds/grasses/flowers/seedlings on yel satin, 3½" 75.00
Vase, flowers & leaves on bl, ruffled, bulbous, 8" 265.00
Vase, trumpet flowers on red, 6" 175.00

Flow Blue

Flow Blue ware was produced by many Staffordshire potters; among the most familiar were Meigh, Podmore and Walker, Samuel Alcock, Ridgway, John Wedge Wood (who often signed his work Wedgewood), and Davenport. It was popular from about 1825 through 1860 and again from 1880 until the turn of the century. The name describes the blurred or flowing effect of the cobalt decoration, achieved through the introduction of a chemical vapor into the kiln. The body of the ware is ironstone, and Oriental motifs were favored. Later issues were on a lighter body and often decorated with gilt.

Our advisor, Mary Frank Gaston, has compiled a lovely book, *The Collector's Encyclopedia of Flow Blue China,* with full-color illustrations and current market values; you will find her address in the Directory under Texas.

Albany, platter, Johnson Bros, 16" 285.00
Amoy, creamer, Davenport 525.00
Amoy, flanged soup, Davenport 200.00
Amoy, pitcher & bowl, Davenport 3,195.00
Amoy, plate, Davenport, 9½" 150.00
Amoy, sauce bowl, Davenport 65.00
Amoy, sugar bowl, Davenport, w/lid 700.00
Arabesque, plate, 11" 165.00
Argyle, bowl, fruit; Grindley, 5" 40.00

Argyle, bowl, vegetable; oval, Grindley, 10" 100.00
Argyle, plate, Grindley, 10½" 130.00
Argyle, plate, Grindley, 9" 95.00
Argyle, platter, Grindley, 15" 325.00
Ashburton, pitcher, Grindley, 2-qt 495.00
Astoria, bowl, New Wharf Pottery, 9¼" 150.00
Beaufort, platter, Grindley, 12" 95.00
Belport, platter, 17" 195.00
Brush Stroke, wash pitcher & bowl, 10", 13½" 850.00

Candia, plate, Cauldon, 10", $95.00.

Carlton, teapot, Alcock 1,095.00
Cavendish, platter, 18" 625.00
Cecil, butter pat 55.00
Chapoo, sugar bowl, Wedge Wood 495.00
Chapoo, teapot, Wedge Wood 895.00
Chusan, cup & saucer 110.00
Chusan, wash pitcher 475.00
Colonial, cup & saucer 65.00
Conway, bowl, soup; New Wharf Pottery 65.00
Conway, plate, New Wharf Pottery, 10" 90.00
Conway, plate, New Wharf Pottery, 8" 70.00
Crumlin, cup & saucer, Myott 75.00
Crumlin, gravy boat & underplate, Myott 210.00
Dainty, bowl, vegetable; Maddock, w/lid 295.00
Daisy, pitcher, Maastrich, 8" 210.00
Dorothy, bone dish 65.00
Duchess, cup & saucer, demitasse; Grindley 28.00
Dundee, bowl, cereal; Ridgway, 6¼" 45.00
Early, gravy boat, floral, prof rpr 325.00
Fairy Villas, bowl, Adams, 10" 200.00
Fairy Villas, plate, Adams, 8¾" 75.00
Festoon, wash pitcher, bowl & slop jar, Grindley 2,500.00
Florence, butter pat, Wood & Son 45.00
Geisha, cake plate, 10¼", +4 6¾" plates 285.00
Gironde, soap dish, Grindley 110.00
Gothic, platter, 18x14" 895.00
Granada, gravy boat w/underplate, Alcock 175.00
Hamilton, butter pat 45.00
Hamilton, cup & saucer, Meakin 45.00
Hamilton, platter, Burgess & Leigh, 15½x12" 135.00
Harvest, bowl, Hancock, 5x15¼" 285.00
Hawthorne, plate, Mercer, 7" 35.00
Hindustan, cup & saucer, Maddock 225.00
Holfburg, platter, 14" 100.00
Hong Kong, platter, Meigh, 16x12", EX 525.00
Hong Kong, sugar bowl, Meigh, w/lid 750.00
Indian, teapot, lg 1,095.00
Indian Jar, creamer, Furnival, 5½" 750.00
Iris, creamer & sugar bowl 225.00
Ivanhoe, plate, Ivanhoe & Rowena 175.00
Japanese, potty, w/lid 695.00
Jeddo, wash pitcher & bowl 2,500.00

Kelvin, platter, 18" 325.00
Kinworth, bowl, Johnson, 5½" 19.00
La Belle, bowl, loop hdls, Wheeling 395.00
La Belle, celery, Wheeling 295.00
La Belle, creamer, Wheeling 215.00
La Belle, plate, Wheeling, 9½" 85.00
La Belle, syrup, hinged silver lid, Wheeling, 4½" 395.00
La Francaise, gravy boat, w/undertray, French China ... 95.00
La Francaise, plate, French China, 9" 35.00
Lahore, plate, Phillips, 9¾" 110.00
Lancaster, teacup & saucer, New Wharf Pottery 65.00
Linda, butter pat 55.00
Linda, egg cup 125.00
Lonsdale, plate, Ridgway, 8" 65.00
Lonsdale, plate, Ridgway, 9" 70.00
Lonsdale, platter, Ridgway, sm 87.50
Lorne, bowl, vegetable; Grindley 90.00
Lorne, bowl, vegetable; oval, w/lid, Grindley 295.00
Lorne, creamer, Grindley 210.00
Lorne, plate, Grindley, 10" 100.00
Lorne, platter, Grindley, 14" 275.00
Marechal Niel, bowl, vegetable; w/lid 375.00
Marechal Niel, butter pat 55.00
Marechal Niel, platter, 16" 215.00
Margot, chamber pot, w/lid, Grindley 300.00
Margot, spooner, Grindley 225.00
Marguerite, bone dish, Grindley 40.00
Marie, platter, Grindley, 14" 145.00
Marie, platter, Grindley, 15¾" 175.00
Melbourne, gravy boat, w/underplate, Grindley 175.00
Melbourne, platter, 17" 240.00
Non Pareil, bowl, Burgess & Leigh, 8¾" 85.00
Non Pareil, cup & saucer, Burgess & Leigh 85.00
Non Pareil, plate, Burgess & Leigh, 6" 75.00
Non Pareil, plate, Burgess & Leigh, 9⅞" 100.00
Non Pareil, platter, Burgess & Leigh, 16x13" 650.00
Normandy, bowl, flanged rim, Johnson Bros, 9½" 90.00
Normandy, bowl, Johnson Bros, 7⅝" 60.00
Normandy, bowl, soup; flanged rim, Johnson Bros, 10" ... 100.00
Normandy, plate, dessert; Johnson Bros, 7" 50.00
Normandy, plate, luncheon; Johnson Bros, 9" 70.00
Normandy, plate, salad; Johnson Bros, 8" 60.00
Oregon, plate, Mayer, 8½" 125.00
Oregon, plate, Mayer, 9½" 150.00

Oriental, plates, New Wharf Pottery, 8⅞", 8 for $800.00 (minimum value).

Paisley, bowl, soup; flat, Mercer, 7¼" 40.00
Paisley, plate, Mercer, 7" 35.00
Paisley, platter, Mercer, 14" 275.00
Paisley, soup tureen, Mercer 575.00
Pelew, teapot, Challinor 775.00
Prussia, bowl, vegetable; Libertas, 10" 95.00

Rose, bone dish, Grindley 65.00
Rose, plate, Grindley, 10" 40.00
Royal Blue, bone dish, Burgess Campbell 95.00
Sabraon, bowl, vegetable; w/lid 385.00
Sabraon, pitcher, milk sz 795.00
Sabraon, platter, 13x10" 575.00
Scinde, bowl, vegetable; Alcock 450.00
Scinde, bowl, vegetable; Alcock, w/lid 750.00
Scinde, cup & saucer, Alcock 175.00
Scinde, cup plate 185.00
Scinde, gravy boat 395.00
Scinde, plate, 10½" 170.00
Scinde, platter, mc, Ridgway, 1838, 19¼x16" 875.00
Scinde, platter, 14x10¼" 675.00
Scinde, platter, 16" 700.00
Scinde, platter, 20¼" 1,150.00
Scinde, sauce dish, rimmed, 5" 55.00
Scinde, sauce tureen & undertray, pagoda finial 750.00
Scinde, sugar bowl, w/lid 750.00
Scinde, tea set, 3-pc 2,000.00
Scinde, teapot 1,095.00
Scinde, waste bowl, lg 750.00
Shanghai, platter, Grindley, 16x12" 225.00
Syrian, toothbrush holder 220.00
Temple, cup & saucer, Podmore Walker 225.00
Tivoli, soup tureen, RH&S, 8½x13½" 225.00
Togo, butter pat, Colonial Pottery 55.00
Tonquin, plate, Adams, 10½" 185.00
Tonquin, platter, Adams, 13" 550.00
Tonquin, soup, Adams 125.00
Touraine, bowl, vegetable; oval, Stanley, 9¾" 125.00
Touraine, creamer, lg 475.00
Touraine, cup & saucer, Stanley 95.00
Touraine, pitcher, Stanley, milk sz 1,095.00
Touraine, plate, Alcock, 8" 65.00
Touraine, plate, 10" 125.00
Touraine, platter, Stanley, 12½" 200.00
Touraine, platter, 15" 300.00
Touraine, platter, 16" 375.00
Touraine, waste bowl 225.00
Trilby, pitcher, hot water; Wood & Son 175.00
Trilby, toothbrush holder, Wood & Son 165.00
Trilby, wash pitcher & bowl, Wood & Son, NM 895.00
Turin, casserole, Johnson Bros, w/lid 200.00
Vermont, bone dish, Burgess & Leigh 38.00
Vermont, butter pat, Burgess & Leigh 55.00
Virginia, butter pat 45.00
Waldorf, cup & saucer, New Wharf Pottery 125.00
Warwick, dresser tray, Podmore Walker 225.00
Warwick, punch cup, Podmore Walker 175.00
Warwick, wash bowl, Podmore Walker 325.00
Watteau, bowl, New Wharf Pottery 125.00
Watteau, cup & saucer, New Wharf Pottery 65.00
Watteau, plate, New Wharf Pottery, 10½" 75.00
Waverly, soup tureen, Maddock 575.00

Flue Covers

When spring housecleaning started and the heating stove was taken down for the warm weather season, the unsightly hole where the stovepipe joined the chimney was hidden with an attractive flue cover. They were made with a colorful litho print behind glass with a chain for hanging. In a 1929 catalog, they were advertised at 16¢ each or six for

80¢. Although scarce today, some scenes were actually reverse painted on the glass itself. The most popular motifs were florals, children, animals, and lovely ladies. Occasionally flue covers were made in sets of three — one served a functional purpose, while the others were added to provide a more attractive wall arrangement. They range in size from 7" to 14", but 9" is the average. Our advisor for this category is Cara J. Washburn; her address is in the Directory under Wisconsin.

Blond lady in bl dress, shoulder up, bl-gr bkground, 4" dia, EX ...125.00
Blue jay on branch, HP on brass, 10" dia 36.00
Brunette in jeweled dress & helmet, 8½", EX 85.00
Brunette in red dress, wht wicker fr, 14" 75.00
Cherries in basket, chain, 8" dia fr, G 45.00
Father Christmas w/doll & child litho, 7" dia 70.00
Girl in pk dress w/brn hair, chain, 8"dia, G 75.00
Giving Thanks, crimped pewter edge, orig chain, 12", EX 35.00
Greek scenic w/couple in foreground, 8½" 25.00
Ladies (2) in bl & gr on gray in gold-tone fr, 9", G 22.50
Mother peeling apples w/daughter in kitchen, 8" dia, G 50.00
Oriental boy w/bouquet, tin border, orig chain, 8½x7½", EX 125.00
Remember the Maine, Spanish Am War, chain border, 8" sq, EX ...100.00
Steamship, rvpt, brn & gold border, G 30.00
Strawberries, grapes, roses, 8" dia fr, EX 75.00
Victorian girl in wht dress w/gold, 8" dia, EX 100.00
2 dogs & horse, artist sgn, chain, 8" dia, G 50.00

Folk Art

That the creative energies of the mind ever spark innovations in functional utilitarian channels as well as toward playful frivolity is well documented in the study of American folk art. While the average early settler rarely had free time to pursue art for its own sake, his creative energy exemplified itself in fashioning useful objects carved or otherwise ornamented beyond the scope of pure practicality. After the advent of the Industrial Revolution, the pace of everyday living became more leisurely, and country folk found they had extra time. Not accustomed to sitting idle, many turned to carving, painting, or weaving. Whirligigs, imaginative toys for the children, and whimsies of all types resulted. Though often rather crude, this type of early art represents a segment of our heritage and as such has become valued by collectors.

Values given for drawings, paintings, and theorems are 'in frame' unless noted otherwise. See also Baskets; Decoys; Frakturs; Samplers; Trade Signs; Weathervanes; Wood Carvings.

Smoker's stand, bent hickory twig furniture, 31", $125.00.

Birdhouse, Deco style w/porch, pnt wood, 1930s, 12x16", EX 85.00
Birdhouse, ship form, wood/sheet metal, weathered, 58" L 990.00
Birdhouse, wooden 2-unit motel w/TV antennas etc, 1950s, 22" ..130.00
Bust, long-haired lady, cvd sandstone, early 1900s, 18x11x9" 650.00

Figure, Blk preacher, cvd wood, paper/fabric/cloth, 9¼" 160.00
Frame, made from natural growth of burl, 23x14" 30.00
Log cabin model, bark-covered branches, 1940s, 24x15x14" 165.00
Oil on academy board, rural scene, cleaned, fr, 15x27" 110.00
Oil on board, lady in wht by horse & dog, late 1800s, 25x19" ...165.00
Painting, pastel of fruit, in oak Arts & Crafts fr, 26x21" 225.00
Pen/ink drawing on wove paper, flowers/birds, sgn, fr, 14x12" 120.00
Picture, burned maple, cabin, girl & dog, 1900s, 15x10" 60.00
Plaque, cvd flapper-style lady w/parrot on arm, 1930s, 18x14" ...225.00
Spencerian drawing, birds/nest/scroll, OH, 1903, 20x25" 495.00
Theorem on paper, flowers in vase, creases/stains, fr, 18x14" 360.00
Theorem on paper, fruit in basket, 8x10" 110.00
Theorem on paper, stone bridge/castle/etc, 1850s, 12x10" 185.00
Theorem on paper, 2 blk chickens, primitive, fr, 11½x8" 470.00
Theorem on velvet, flower basket, sgn, matted & fr, 19x22" 495.00
Theorem on velvet, fruit & exotic birds, sgn, 16x18" 165.00
Theorem on velvet, fruit on a Canton plate, sgn, 19x22" 275.00
Theorem on velvet, lady in landscape, 19th C, 10x11¼" 775.00
Theorem on velvet, mc roses, old gilt fr, 8¼x11½" 470.00
Toy, fire truck, open cab, 2-part ladder, red pnt, 1880s, 27" 185.00
Whirligig, ancient Roman warrior, cvd/pnt wood, 1890s, 16½" .700.00
Whirligig, Mammy washer woman, pnt wood, 1930s, 14x18", EX ...150.00
Whirligig, 4 rowers in 2 boats, Harvard/Yale, mc pnt, 43" 220.00

Fostoria

The Fostoria Glass Company was built in 1887 at Fostoria, Ohio, but by 1891 it had moved to Moundsville, West Virginia. During the next two decades, they produced many lines of pressed patterned tableware and lamps. Their most famous pattern, American, was introduced in 1915 and was produced continuously until 1986 in well over two hundred different pieces. From 1920 to 1925, top artists designed tablewares in colored glass — canary (vaseline), amber, blue, orchid, green, and ebony — in pressed patterns as well as etched designs. By the late thirties, Fostoria was recognized as the largest producer of handmade glassware in the world. The company ceased operations in Moundsville in 1986.

Many items from both the American and Coin Glass lines are currently being reproduced by Lancaster Colony. In some cases the new glass is superior in quality to the old. Since the 1950s, Indiana Glass has produced a pattern called 'Whitehall' that looks very much like Fostoria's American, though with slight variations. Because Indiana's is not handmade glass, the lines of the 'cube' pattern and the edges of the items are sharp and untapered in comparison to the fire-polished originals. Three-footed pieces lack the 'toe' and instead have a peg-like foot, and the rays on the bottoms of the American examples are narrower than on the Whitehall counterparts. The Home Interiors Company offers several pieces of American look-alikes which were not even produced in the United States. Be sure of your dealer and study the books suggested below to become more familiar with the original line.

Coin Glass reproductions are flooding the market. Among items you may encounter are an 8" round bowl, 9" oval bowl, 8¼" wedding bowl, 4½" candlesticks, urn with lid, 6¼" candy jar with lid, footed comport, sugar, and creamer; there could possibly be others. Colors in production are crystal, green, blue, and red. The red color is very good, but the blue is not the original color, nor is the emerald green. Buyer beware!

For further information see *Elegant Glassware of the Depression Era* by Gene Florence; *Fostoria, the Popular Years, Third Edition Price Guide*, by Jo Ann Schliesman; and *Fostoria, An Identification and Value Guide of Pressed, Blown & Hand Molded Shapes*, by Ann Kerr. *Glass Animals and Figural Flower Frogs of the Depression Era* by Lee Garmon and Dick Spencer offers an in-depth look at that particular aspect of Fostoria's production. (See also Glass Animals.) Their addresses are listed in the Directory under Illinois. Items with (+) at the end of the lines are currently being reproduced; prices are for original issues. Our advisor is Debbie Maggard; she is listed in the Directory under Ohio.

American, ashtray, oval, 3⅞" 12.50

American, crystal, basket, reeded handle, 9", $110.00.

American, bowl, banana split; 9x3½" 350.00
American, bowl, centerpc; 9½" 42.50
American, bowl, deep, 8" 55.00
American, bowl, float; 11½" 75.00
American, bowl, nappy; 4½" 12.00
American, bowl, rose; 5" 25.00
American, box, w/lid, 4½x4½" 200.00
American, candlestick, 2-light, bell base, 6½" 90.00
American, comport, jelly; 4½" 15.00
American, creamer, tea; #2056½, 3-oz, 2⅜" 12.00
American, goblet, tea; #2056, low ftd, 12-oz, 5¾" 15.00
American, hat, tall, 4" 45.00
American, ice bucket, w/tongs 60.00
American, oil cruet, 5-oz 35.00
American, pitcher, flat, 1-qt 40.00
American, plate, dinner; 9½" 40.00
American, shaker, 3", ea 10.00
American, spooner, 3¾" 35.00
American, syrup, w/drip-proof top 50.00
American, tray, oval, hdld, 6" 35.00
American, tumbler, water; #2056, ftd, 9-oz, 4⅞" 18.00
American, urn, ped ftd, sq, 6" 30.00
American, vase, swung; 10" 165.00
American, wash bowl & pitcher, hotel sz 2,500.00
Baroque, bl, bowl, cereal; 6" 35.00
Baroque, bl, cup 30.00
Baroque, bl, platter, oval, 12" 60.00
Baroque, bl, tumbler, juice; 5-oz, 3¾" 37.50
Baroque, crystal, bowl, cream soup 35.00
Baroque, crystal, bowl, 10x7½" 25.00
Baroque, crystal, candy dish, w/lid, 3-part 15.00
Baroque, crystal, plate, 8½" 6.00
Baroque, yel, bowl, jelly; w/lid, 7½" 50.00
Baroque, yel, candlestick, 4" 30.00
Baroque, yel, pitcher, 6½" 450.00
Baroque, yel, tumbler, tea; 14-oz, 5¾" 100.00
Buttercup, bowl, lily pond; #2364, 12" 55.00
Buttercup, bowl, salad; #2364, 9" 50.00
Buttercup, cigarette holder, #2364, 2" 35.00
Buttercup, plate, crescent salad; #2364, 7¼x4½" 35.00
Buttercup, stem, cocktail; #6030, 3½-oz, 5¼" 22.50
Buttercup, tray, pickle; #2350, 8" 25.00
Buttercup, tray, relish; #2364, 2-part, 6½x5" 22.50
Buttercup, vase, #2614, 10" 120.00
Century, ashtray, 2¾" 10.00
Century, bowl, flared, 12" 35.00
Century, bowl, flared, 8" 25.00

Century, bowl, salad; 10½" 35.00
Century, candlestick, dbl; 7" 30.00
Century, oil cruet, w/stopper, 5-oz 45.00
Century, pitcher, 48-oz, 7⅛" 95.00
Century, plate, luncheon; 8½" 12.50
Century, stem, cocktail; 3½-oz, 4⅛" 20.00
Century, sugar bowl, ind 9.00
Century, tray, relish; 2-part, 7⅛" 15.00
Century, tray, utility; hdld, 9⅛" 25.00
Century, vase, oval, 8½" 65.00
Chintz, bowl, #2496, hdld, 5" 25.00
Chintz, bowl, ftd, #6023 ....37.50
Chintz, bowl, vegetable; #2496, oval, 9½" 185.00
Chintz, comport, cheese; #2496, 3¼" 25.00
Chintz, creamer, #2496, ftd, 3¾" 17.50
Chintz, ice bucket, #2496 ....130.00
Chintz, plate, dinner; #2496, 9½" 50.00
Chintz, saucer, #2496 ....5.00
Chintz, stem, claret/wine; #6026, 4½-oz, 5⅜" 40.00
Chintz, sugar bowl, ftd, #2496, 3½" 16.00
Chintz, tray, #2375, center hdl, 11" 40.00
Chintz, tray, pickle; #2496, 8" 32.50
Chintz, tray, relish; #2419, 5-part 40.00
Chintz, vase, #4108, 5" 85.00
Coin, amber or olive gr, ashtray, #115, oblong, 3x4" 15.00
Coin, amber or olive gr, ashtray, #124, 10" 31.00
Coin, amber or olive gr, bowl, nappy; #495, 4½" 38.00
Coin, amber or olive gr, candlestick, #326, 8" 31.00
Coin, amber or olive gr, cigarette urn, #381, ftd, 3⅜" 20.00
Coin, amber or olive gr, compote, #199, ftd, 8½" 54.00
Coin, amber or olive gr, goblet, #2, 10½-oz 34.00
Coin, amber or olive gr, pitcher, #453, 1-qt, 6½" 81.00
Coin, amber or olive gr, punch bowl, #602, ftd, 14" 94.00
Coin, amber or olive gr, shaker, #652, chrome lid, 3¼", pr ...31.00
Coin, amber or olive gr, tumbler, iced tea; #64, 12-oz, 5⅛" ...46.00
Coin, amber or olive gr, urn, #829, w/lid, ftd, 12¾" 85.00
Coin, amber or olive gr, wine, #26, 5-oz, 5⅛" 44.00
Coin, crystal, bowl, #189, oval, 9" 36.00
Coin, crystal, bowl, wedding; #162, w/lid, 8¼" 50.00
Coin, crystal, candlestick, #316, 4½", pr 42.00
Coin, crystal, candy box, #354, w/lid, 6⅜" 35.00
Coin, crystal, cigarette holder & ashtray, w/lid 25.00
Coin, crystal, creamer, #680, 3½" 16.00
Coin, crystal, dbl old fashion, #23 ....20.00
Coin, crystal, jelly, #448, ftd, 3¾" 16.00
Coin, crystal, punch bowl, #600, 1½-gal, 14" 250.00
Coin, crystal, salver, cake; #630, 10" 80.00
Coin, crystal, sugar bowl, #673, w/lid, 5⅜" 25.00
Coin, crystal, tumbler, juice; #81, 9-oz, 3⅝" 27.00
Coin, empire gr, red or bl, ashtray, #123, 1-coin, 5" 36.00
Coin, empire gr, red or bl, bowl, #189, oval, 9" 108.00
Coin, empire gr, red or bl, candlesticks, #326, 8", pr 75.00
Coin, empire gr, red or bl, decanter, #400, w/stopper 270.00
Coin, empire gr, red or bl, iced tea, #58, 14-oz 84.00
Coin, empire gr, red or bl, plate, #550, 8" 54.00
Coin, empire gr, red or bl, punch cup, #615, 3½" 40.00
Coin, empire gr, red or bl, sherbet, #7, 9-oz, 5⅝" 52.00
Coin, empire gr, red or bl, tray, condiment; #738, 9⅝" 105.00
Coin, empire gr, red or bl, tumbler, water; #73, 9-oz, 4¼" ...90.00
Coin, empire gr, red or bl, vase, bud; #799, 8" 45.00
Colony, ashtray, rnd, 4½" 12.50
Colony, bowl, bonbon; 3-ftd, 7" 12.00
Colony, bowl, ftd, oval, 11" 37.50
Colony, bowl, salad; 9¾" 35.00

Colony, butter dish, ¼-lb 32.50
Colony, creamer, ind, 3¼" 6.50
Colony, pitcher, milk; 16-oz 85.00
Colony, plate, luncheon; 8" 10.00
Colony, stem, oyster cocktail; 4-oz, 3⅜" 12.00
Colony, tray, for ind creamer/sugar bowl 10.00
Colony, vase, cupped, 7" 35.00
Fairfax, amber, candlestick, flattened top 10.00
Fairfax, amber, cup, ftd 6.00
Fairfax, amber, plate, salad; 7½" 3.00
Fairfax, amber, sauce boat liner 15.00
Fairfax, amber, sugar bowl, tea 6.00
Fairfax, gr or yel, cheese & cracker set, 2 styles, ea 35.00
Fairfax, gr or yel, ice bucket 35.00
Fairfax, gr or yel, plate, grill; 10¼" 22.00
Fairfax, gr or yel, tumbler, ftd, 9-oz, 5¼" 13.00
Fairfax, rose, bl or orchid, baker, oval, 9" 25.00
Fairfax, rose, bl or orchid, creamer, ftd 11.00
Fairfax, rose, bl or orchid, plate, whipped cream 11.00
Fairfax, rose, bl or orchid, stem, water; 10-oz, 8¼" 30.00
Heather, bowl, flared, 8" 22.50
Heather, bowl, fruit; 5" 14.00
Heather, bowl, lily pond; 11¼" 50.00
Heather, candlestick, 4½" 15.00
Heather, creamer, 4¼" 8.00
Heather, mayonnaise, 4-pc, divided, w/2 ladles 35.00
Heather, plate, crescent; 7½" 32.50
Heather, shakers, 3⅛", pr 17.50
Heather, stem, goblet; #6037, low, 9-oz, 6⅜" 22.00
Heather, tray, muffin; hdld, 9½" 35.00
Heather, tumbler, #6037, ftd, 12-oz, 6⅛" 25.00
Hermitage, amber, gr or yel, bowl, cereal; #2449½, 6" 9.00
Hermitage, amber, gr or yel, decanter, #2449, w/stopper, 28-oz 50.00
Hermitage, amber, gr or yel, plate, #2449½, 7⅜" 6.00
Hermitage, amber, gr or yel, stem, claret; #2449, 4-z, 4⅝" 15.00
Hermitage, amber, gr or yel, tumbler, #2449, ftd, 9-oz, 4⅛" 10.00
Hermitage, bl or wisteria, bowl, salad; #2449½, 7½" 20.00
Hermitage, bl or wisteria, tray, relish; #2449, 3-part, 7¼" 25.00
Hermitage, bl or wisteria, tumbler, #2449½, 2-oz, 2½" 15.00
Hermitage, bl or wisteria, tumbler, iced tea; #2449, 5¼" 25.00
Hermitage, crystal, bottle, oil; #2449, 3-oz 17.50
Hermitage, crystal, coaster, #2449, 5⅝" 5.00
Hermitage, crystal, plate, #2449½, 6" 3.00
Hermitage, crystal, salt shaker, individual, #2449 ......4.00
June, crystal, bowl, baker; oval, 9" 35.00
June, crystal, bowl, soup; 7" 40.00
June, crystal, candlestick, 2" 10.00
June, crystal, goblet, cocktail; 3-oz, 5¼" 20.00
June, crystal, oil cruet, ftd 200.00
June, crystal, plate, cheese; hdld, w/indent, 10" 20.00
June, crystal, sauce boat liner 15.00
June, crystal, sugar bowl, tea 20.00
June, pk or bl, bowl, bouillon; ftd 35.00
June, pk or bl, bowl, 10" 100.00
June, pk or bl, candlestick, Grecian; 3" 85.00
June, pk or bl, comport, #2375, 7" 90.00
June, pk or bl, goblet, wine; 3-oz, 5½" 95.00
June, pk or bl, plate, chop; 13" 95.00
June, pk or bl, plate, luncheon; 8¾" 15.00
June, pk or bl, shakers, ftd, pr 165.00
June, pk or bl, tumbler, ftd, 2½-oz 85.00
June, yel, bowl, cream soup; ftd 32.50
June, yel, bowl, mint; 3-ftd, 4½" 20.00
June, yel, ice bucket 75.00

June, yel, plate, bread & butter; 6" 6.00
June, yel, plate, grill; 10" 65.00
June, yel, platter, 15" 105.00
June, yel, tumbler, ftd, 12-oz, 6" 30.00
Kashmir, bl, bowl, baker; 9" 45.00
Kashmir, bl, cup 20.00
Kashmir, bl, plate, bread & butter; 6" 6.00
Kashmir, bl, plate, grill; 10" 50.00

Kashmir, blue, sand-wich server, center handle, $55.00.

Kashmir, bl, stem, cocktail; 3-oz 25.00
Kashmir, bl, stem, sherbet; low, 5-oz 20.00
Kashmir, yel or gr, bowl, fruit; 5" 13.00
Kashmir, yel or gr, comport, 6" 35.00
Kashmir, yel or gr, ice bucket 65.00
Kashmir, yel or gr, plate, sandwich; center hdl 35.00
Kashmir, yel or gr, stem, cordial; ¾-oz 85.00
Kashmir, yel or gr, stem, 11-oz 22.50
Navarre, bowl, #2496, flared, 12" 62.50
Navarre, bowl, #2496, tricornered, 4⅝" 15.00
Navarre, bowl, bonbon; #2496, ftd, 7⅜" 27.50
Navarre, candlestick, dbl; #2496, 4½" 35.00
Navarre, comport, cheese; #2496, 3¼" 27.50
Navarre, creamer, #2440, ftd, 4¼" 20.00
Navarre, dinner bell 45.00
Navarre, pitcher, #5000, ftd, 48-oz 325.00
Navarre, plate, cake; #2440, oval, 10½" 47.50
Navarre, sauce dish, mayonnaise; #2496, divided, 6½" 37.50
Navarre, shakers, #2364, flat, 3¼", pr 57.50
Navarre, stem, claret; #6106, 4½-oz, 6½" 40.00
Navarre, sugar bowl, #2440, ftd, 3⅝" 18.00
Navarre, tray, #2496½, for ind creamer & sugar bowl 22.00
Navarre, tray, relish; #2496, 2-part, sq, 6" 32.50
Romance, ashtray, #2364, ind, 2⅝" 12.50
Romance, bowl, #2594, hdld, oval, 13½" 55.00
Romance, bowl, #2596, shallow, oblong, 11" 47.50
Romance, bowl, #6023, ftd, blown, 9¼" 75.00
Romance, candlestick, #2594, 5½" 25.00
Romance, comport, #2364, 8" 40.00
Romance, ladle, mayonnaise; #2364 ....5.00
Romance, plate, #2337, 7" 10.00
Romance, plate, torte; #2364, 14" 42.50
Romance, shakers, #2364, 2⅝" 50.00
Romance, stem, sherbet; #6017, low, 6-oz, 4½" 14.00
Romance, tray, relish; #2364, 8" 22.50
Romance, tumbler, #6017, ftd, 12-oz, 6" 25.00
Romance, vase, #2614, 10" 75.00
Romance, vase, #2619½, ground bottom, 6" 50.00
Royal, amber or gr, bowl, #2315, ftd, 10½" 45.00
Royal, amber or gr, bowl, #2324, ftd, 10" 40.00
Royal, amber or gr, bowl, bouillon; #2350½, ftd 12.50
Royal, amber or gr, bowl, fruit; #2350, 5½" 12.00
Royal, amber or gr, bowl, nappy; #2350, 8" 30.00
Royal, amber or gr, candlestick, #2324, 9" 45.00
Royal, amber or gr, creamer, ftd 14.00

Royal, amber or gr, cup, #2350½, ftd 13.00
Royal, amber or gr, ice bucket, #2378 ....45.00
Royal, amber or gr, plate, dinner; #2350, 10½" 30.00
Royal, amber or gr, plate, soup (underplate); deep, 8½" 35.00
Royal, amber or gr, platter, #2350, 10½" 30.00
Royal, amber or gr, saucer, #2350/#2350½ 3.00
Royal, amber or gr, stem, cocktail; #869, 3-oz 22.50
Royal, amber or gr, stem, sherbet; #869, high, 6-oz 16.00
Royal, amber or gr, tray, celery; #2350, 11" 25.00
Seville, amber, bowl, bouillon; #2350, flat 15.00
Seville, amber, bowl, ftd, 10" 35.00
Seville, amber, bowl, grapefruit; #945½, blown 40.00
Seville, amber, bowl, soup; #2350, 7¾" 17.50
Seville, amber, comport, #2337, twisted stem, 7½" 20.00
Seville, amber, plate (cream soup liner), #2350 ....5.00
Seville, amber, sauce boat, #2350 ....55.00
Seville, amber, stem, sherbet; #870, low 12.50
Seville, amber, sugar bowl, #2350½, ftd 12.50
Seville, gr, bowl, baker; #2350, oval, 9" 30.00
Seville, gr, bowl, console; #2329, rolled edge, 11" 32.50
Seville, gr, candy jar, #2331, w/lid, 3-part, flat 80.00
Seville, gr, cup, #2350, flat 12.50
Seville, gr, plate, dinner; #2350, 10½" 40.00
Seville, gr, platter, #2350, 15" 80.00
Seville, gr, stem, water; #870 ....22.50
Seville, gr, tray, pickle; #2350, 8" 15.00
Seville, gr, tumbler, #5084, ftd, 9-oz 16.50
Trojan, pk, ashtray, #2350, sm 30.00
Trojan, pk, bowl, #2395, 10" 90.00
Trojan, pk, candlestick, #2375, flared, 3" 20.00
Trojan, pk, creamer, #2375, ftd 22.50
Trojan, pk, goblet, water; #5299, 10-oz, 8¼" 37.50
Trojan, pk, plate, chop; #2375, 13" 65.00
Trojan, pk, plate, salad; #2375, 7½" 12.00
Trojan, pk, sugar bowl, tea; #2375½ 55.00
Trojan, pk or yel, saucer, AD; #2375 ....10.00
Trojan, yel, bowl, bouillon; #2375, ftd 18.00
Trojan, yel, bowl, centerpc; #2394, ftd, 12" 40.00
Trojan, yel, bowl, cereal; #2375, 6½" 27.50
Trojan, yel, candy jar, #2394, w/lid, ½-lb 135.00
Trojan, yel, decanter, #2439, 9" 750.00
Trojan, yel, parfait, #5099 ....65.00
Trojan, yel, plate, dinner; #2375, sm, 9½" 25.00
Trojan, yel, sherbet, #5099, low, 4¼" 16.00
Trojan, yel, tray, relish; #2375, 8½" 20.00
Trojan, yel, tumbler, #5099, ftd, 2½-oz 40.00
Versailles, bl, ashtray, #2350 ....30.00
Versailles, bl, bowl, cereal; #2375, 6½" 45.00
Versailles, bl, candlestick, #2395½, scroll decor, 5" 40.00
Versailles, bl, comport, #2375, 7" 55.00
Versailles, bl, mayonnaise, #2375, w/liner 50.00
Versailles, bl, plate, luncheon; #2375, 8¾" 12.50
Versailles, bl, plate, sauce boat; #2375 ....35.00
Versailles, bl, sugar pail, #2378 ....225.00
Versailles, pk or gr, bowl, #2394, ftd, 12" 35.00
Versailles, pk or gr, bowl, baker; #2375, 10" 55.00
Versailles, pk or gr, bowl, lemon 15.00
Versailles, pk or gr, cheese & cracker set, #2375 or #2368, ea 75.00
Versailles, pk or gr, decanter, #2439, 9" 900.00
Versailles, pk or gr, ice bucket, #2375 ....62.50
Versailles, pk or gr, plate, canape; #2375, 6" 20.00
Versailles, pk or gr, tumbler, #5098 or #5099, ftd, 2½-oz 45.00
Versailles, yel, bowl, baker; #2375, 10" 40.00
Versailles, yel, bowl, bouillon; #2375, ftd 20.00

Versailles, yel, bowl, grapefruit; #5082½ 40.00
Versailles, yel, candlestick, #2394, 2" 17.50
Versailles, yel, creamer, tea; #2375½ 42.50
Versailles, yel, tray, #2375, center hdl, 11" 35.00
Versailles, yel, whipped cream pail, #2378 ....110.00
Vesper, amber, bowl, cereal; #2350, sq or rnd, 6½" 30.00
Vesper, amber, bowl, console; #2329, rolled edge, 11" 45.00
Vesper, amber, bowl, soup; deep, 8¼" 35.00
Vesper, amber, creamer, #2350½, flat 22.00
Vesper, amber, platter, #2350, 12" 60.00
Vesper, amber, stem, sherbet; #5093, low 17.00
Vesper, amber, urn, lg 90.00

Vesper, blue, candy jar, #2331, with lid, $200.00.

Vesper, bl, cup, AD; #2350 ....70.00
Vesper, bl, plate, #2287, center hdl, 11" 50.00
Vesper, bl, saucer, AD; #2350 ....20.00
Vesper, bl, stem, cordial; #5098, ¾-oz 110.00
Vesper, bl, tumbler, #5100, ftd, 9-oz 40.00
Vesper, gr, bowl, baker; #2350, oval, 9" 60.00
Vesper, gr, bowl, bouillon; #2350, ftd 12.00
Vesper, gr, candlestick, #2324, 2" 17.50
Vesper, gr, comport, 8" 40.00
Vesper, gr, plate, salad; #2350, 7½" 6.00
Vesper, gr, plate, w/indent for cheese, 11" 18.00
Vesper, gr, sugar bowl, #2350½, ftd 18.00

Frakturs

Fraktur is a German style of black letter text type. To collectors the fraktur is a type of hand-lettered document used by the people of German descent who settled in the areas of Pennsylvania, New Jersey, Maryland, Virginia, North and South Carolina, Ohio, Kentucky, and Ontario. These documents recorded births and baptisms and were used as bookplates and as certificates of honor. They were elaborately decorated with colorful folk-art borders of hearts, birds, angels, and flowers. Examples by recognized artists and those with an unusual decorative motif bring prices well into the thousands of dollars, in fact, some have sold at major auction houses in excess of $5,000.00. Frakturs made in the late 1700s after the invention of the printing press provided the writer with a prepared text that he needed only to fill in at his own discretion. The next step in the evolution of machine-printed frakturs combined woodblock-printed decorations along with the text which the 'artist' sometimes enhanced with color. By the mid-1800s, even the coloring was done by machine. The vorschrift was a handwritten example prepared by a fraktur teacher to demonstrate his skill in lettering and decorating. These are often considered to be the finest of frakturs. Those dated before 1820 are most valuable.

The practice of fraktur art began to diminish after 1830 but hung on even to the early years of this century among the Pennsylvania Germans ingrained with such customs. Our advisor for this category is Frederick S. Weiser; he is listed in the Directory under Pennsylvania. (Mr. Weiser has provided our text, but being unable to physically examine the frakturs listed below cannot vouch for their authenticity, age, or condition.) These prices were realized at a very reputable Midwest auction house but are low average compared to the East where prices are noticeable higher. Note: Be careful not to confuse fracturs with prints, calligraphy, English-language marriage certificates, Lord's Prayers, etc.

Key:
lp — laid paper
pr — printed
p/i — pen and ink
wc — watercolored
wp — wove paper

P/i/wc, flowers/heart, S Baumann (Ephrata), 1799, 14½x16½" ..330.00
P/i/wc/lp, floral wreath/birds, 4-color, OH, 1781, 8x12" 770.00
P/i/wc/lp, flowers/trees/etc, PA, 1798, 8½x13⅛" 2,475.00
P/i/wc/lp, flowers/tulips/birds/eagle, PA, 12x11" 550.00
P/i/wc/lp, mc florals/English text, OH, 1929, 7¾x12¾" 4,730.00
P/i/wc/lp, PA, 1825, fr, 8½x9½" 440.00
P/i/wc/lp, stylized floral, att M Brechal, in fr 770.00
P/i/wc/lp, tulip/compass designs/etc, 9¾x7¾" 660.00
P/i/wc/lp, tulips/flowers/birds, PA, 1810, rpr, fr, 15x18" 440.00
P/i/wc/wp, Adam & Eve in Paradise, mc scenes, PA, 20x16", G ...330.00
P/i/wc/wp, stylized mc tulips, 1848, 10¾x9¾", VG 500.00
P/i/wc/wp, vining tulips, PA, 1834, 13x11" 385.00
P/i/wp, geometric border, OH, 1829, fr, 9½x11½" 990.00
Pr, Geburts..., 3-color, Peters, 1828, fr, 19x15" 140.00
Pr/p/i/wc/lp, hearts/etc, Frederick Krebs, 1788, rpr, 14x17" 335.00
Pr/wc, hearts/flowers/etc, G Miller, PA, 1806, 18x16", G 120.00
Pr/wc, hearts/vines/etc, Frederick Krebs, 1787, 17x19" 550.00
Wc/pr, birth in PA, Kaufmann/OH, 1866, modern fr, 18x16" 440.00
Wc/pr, Geburts und Taufschein, PA, Ritter, 1843, 19x16" 110.00

Miscellaneous

Bookplate, p/i/wc/wp, tulips, 4-color, PA, 1827, 10x12" 330.00
Bookplate, p/i/wc/wp, 3-color, PA, 1859, 9⅝x6¾" 110.00
Bookplate, p/i/wp, name/1813, stains, 11¼x9" 330.00
Valentine, pencil/crayon/p/i/ledge paper, verses, 12x12" 1,750.00
Vorschrift, p/i/lp, 2-color, 9x13", G 75.00
Vorschrift, p/i/wc/lp, PA, 1790, fr, 12x17" 495.00

Frames

Styles in picture frames have changed with the fashion of the day, but those that especially interest today's collectors are the deep shadow boxes made of fine woods such as walnut or cherry, those with Art Nouveau influence, and the oak frames decorated with molded gesso and gilt from the Victorian era. Our advisor for this category is Michael Hinton; he is listed in the Directory under Pennsylvania.

Photo courtesy Michael Hinton

Black walnut and gold leaf, back stamped with 1871 patent date, 24x20" oval, 34½x30½" overall, EX, $1,150.00.

Anglo-Indian sterling silver, cast piercework, 16x13", 25 oz ...2,500.00
Architectural, wood, Florentine Gothic w/angel Gabriel, 29" 500.00
Beveled pine w/pnt blk/brn/yel on red ground, 17x12½" 220.00
Beveled pine w/red rosewood grpt, 12x16" 150.00
Brass filigree, gilt, 5" dia, pr 300.00
Brass filigree w/mc faceted glass jewels, 1900s, 9x7" 195.00
Cherry w/pearl heart at ea cross corner, folky style, 15x11" 100.00
Chip cvd, old red pnt & natural, easel bk, 7x6" 250.00
Chip cvd, worn red pnt w/blk strip, 4" molding, 18x21" 125.00
Giltwood & gesso, fluted rim, cast berry edge, 53x65" 550.00
Leather, tooled vines, irregular curved outline, 15x12" 90.00
Oak, gesso, emb florals, 18x24" 150.00
Pine w/orig blk pnt & gold stenciling, 14x18" 165.00
Poplar, blk pnt, 1⅝" molding, 18x14" 75.00
Silverplate, crown/Cupid crest, scroll ft, easel bk, 8½" 275.00
Sterling, etched flowers in ea corner, standing, 2x3" 75.00
Sterling w/chased foliate border, 8x6" 150.00
Walnut, oval liner, incised decor, dtd 1871, 20x30" 950.00
Walnut shadow box, deep oval, late 1800s, 21x17", pr 500.00
Walnut w/gilt & marbleized inner borders, 15x17" 150.00

Frances Ware

Frances Ware, produced in the 1880s by Hobbs, Brockunier and Company of Wheeling, West Virginia, is either clear or frosted with amber-stained rim bands. The most often found pattern is Hobnail, but Swirl was also made. Our advisors for this category are Betty and Clarence Maier; they are listed in the Directory under Pennsylvania.

Hobnail, clear; bowl, 7½" 65.00
Hobnail, clear; butter dish 95.00
Hobnail, clear; creamer 60.00
Hobnail, clear; finger bowl, 4" 35.00
Hobnail, clear; pitcher, 8½" 125.00
Hobnail, clear; spooner 40.00
Hobnail, frosted; bowl, ftd, berry pontil, 6x10" 150.00
Hobnail, frosted; bowl, oblong, 8" 75.00
Hobnail, frosted; bowl, sq, 7½" 70.00
Hobnail, frosted; bowl, 2½x5½" 40.00
Hobnail, frosted; bowl, 4½" 30.00
Hobnail, frosted; bowl, 8" dia 75.00
Hobnail, frosted; bowl, 9" 85.00
Hobnail, frosted; butter dish 120.00
Hobnail, frosted; celery vase 75.00
Hobnail, frosted; chandelier, amber font, brass fr, 14" dia 950.00
Hobnail, frosted; creamer & sugar bowl, amber rims, lg 250.00
Hobnail, frosted; cruet 550.00
Hobnail, frosted; marmalade 125.00
Hobnail, frosted; pitcher, milk 150.00
Hobnail, frosted; pitcher, water; sq top, 8½" 175.00
Hobnail, frosted; plate, sq, 5¾" 25.00
Hobnail, frosted; sauce dish, sq, 4" 28.00
Hobnail, frosted; shakers, very rare, pr 180.00
Hobnail, frosted; spooner 70.00
Hobnail, frosted; sugar bowl, w/lid 80.00
Hobnail, frosted; syrup, pewter lid 165.00
Hobnail, frosted; toothpick holder 60.00
Hobnail, frosted; tray, cloverleaf, 12" 125.00
Hobnail, frosted; tray, oblong, 14" 150.00
Hobnail, frosted; tumbler, water 45.00
Swirl, clear; shakers, pr 55.00
Swirl, clear; syrup 90.00
Swirl, frosted; bowl, 3¾" H 40.00

Swirl, frosted; cruet 175.00
Swirl, frosted; cruet, orig stopper, mini 295.00
Swirl, frosted; mustard jar 140.00
Swirl, frosted; pitcher, water 120.00
Swirl, frosted; shakers, pr 105.00
Swirl, frosted; sugar bowl, w/lid 80.00
Swirl, frosted; sugar shaker, orig lid 125.00
Swirl, frosted; syrup, Pat dtd 145.00
Swirl, frosted; tumbler 35.00

Franciscan

Franciscan is a trade name used by Gladding McBean and Co., founded in northern California in 1875. In 1923 they purchased the Tropico plant in Glendale where they produced sewer pipe, gardenware, and tile. By 1934 the first of their dinnerware lines, El Patio, was produced. It was a plain design made in bright, attractive colors. El Patio Nouveau followed in 1935, glazed in two colors — one tone on the inside, a contrasting hue on the outside. Coronado, a favorite of today's collectors, was introduced in 1936. It was styled with a wide, swirled border and was made in pastels, both satin and glossy. Before 1940 fifteen patterns had been produced. The first hand-decorated lines were introduced in 1937, the ever-popular Apple pattern in 1940, Desert Rose in 1941, and Ivy in 1948. Many other hand-decorated and decaled patterns were produced there from 1934 to 1984.

Dinnerware marks before 1940 include 'GMcB' in an oval, 'F' within a square, or 'Franciscan' with 'Pottery' underneath (which was later changed to 'Ware'). A circular arrangement of 'Franciscan' with 'Made in California USA' in the center was used from 1940 until 1949. At least forty marks were used before 1975; several more were introduced after that. At one time, paper labels were used.

The company merged with Lock Joint Pipe Company in 1963, becoming part of the Interpace Corporation. In July of 1979 Franciscan was purchased by Wedgwood Limited of England, and the Glendale plant closed in October 1984.

Our advisors for this category are Mick and Lorna Chase (Fiesta Plus); they are listed in the Directory under Tennessee. Authority Delleen Enge has compiled an informative book, *Franciscan Ware* (self-published, available from the author). See also Gladding McBean.

Coronado

Bowl, cereal 12.00
Bowl, cream soup 23.00
Bowl, vegetable; serving, oval 20.00
Bowl, vegetable; serving, rnd 15.00
Butter dish 45.00
Candlesticks, pr 28.00
Casserole, w/lid 35.00
Cigarette box 40.00
Coffeepot, demitasse 95.00
Creamer & sugar bowl, w/lid 30.00
Cup & saucer 12.00
Cup & saucer, demitasse 22.00
Gravy boat, w/attached plate 28.00
Nut cup, ftd 16.00
Plate, chop; 12" 25.00
Plate, chop; 14" 35.00
Plate, 6½" 8.00
Plate, 7½" 10.00
Plate, 8½" 12.00
Platter, 11½" 25.00
Platter, 15½" 35.00

Saucer, cream soup 35.00
Shakers, pr 15.00
Sherbet 10.00
Teapot 65.00

Desert Rose

Photo courtesy Mick and Lorna Chase

Desert Rose, Long 'n Narrow, 15½x7¾", $495.00.

Ashtray, ind 20.00
Ashtray, oval 125.00
Ashtray, sq, no established value
Bell, Danbury Mint 125.00
Bell, dinner 125.00
Bowl, bouillon; w/lid 325.00
Bowl, cereal; 6" 15.00
Bowl, divided vegetable 45.00
Bowl, fruit 12.00
Bowl, mixing; lg 195.00
Bowl, mixing; med 175.00
Bowl, mixing; sm 125.00
Bowl, porringer 295.00
Bowl, rimmed soup 28.00
Bowl, salad; 10" 115.00
Bowl, soup; ftd 32.00
Bowl, vegetable; 8" 32.00
Bowl, vegetable; 9" 40.00
Box, cigarette 125.00
Box, egg 195.00
Box, heart shape 165.00
Box, rnd 165.00
Butter dish 45.00
Candle holders, pr 75.00
Candy dish, oval, no established value
Casserole, 1½-qt 85.00
Casserole, 2½-qt 195.00
Coffeepot 95.00
Coffeepot, ind 395.00
Compote, lg 75.00
Compote, low, no established value
Cookie jar 295.00
Creamer, ind 40.00
Creamer, regular 22.00
Cup & saucer, coffee; no established value
Cup & saucer, demitasse 55.00
Cup & saucer, jumbo 65.00
Cup & saucer, tall 45.00
Cup & saucer, tea 18.00
Egg cup 35.00
Ginger jar 225.00
Goblet, ftd 165.00
Gravy boat 32.00

Heart	145.00
Hurricane lamp, no established value	
Jam jar	75.00
Microwave dish, oblong, 1½-qt	275.00
Microwave dish, sq, 1-qt	215.00
Microwave dish, sq, 8"	245.00
Mug, bbl, 12-oz	50.00
Mug, cocoa; 10-oz	135.00
Mug, 7-oz	25.00
Napkin ring	35.00
Piggy bank	250.00
Pitcher, jug; no established value	
Pitcher, milk	95.00
Pitcher, syrup	75.00
Pitcher, water; 2½-qt	125.00
Plate, chop; 12"	75.00
Plate, chop; 14"	175.00
Plate, coupe dessert	75.00
Plate, coupe party	295.00
Plate, coupe steak	195.00
Plate, divided; child's	195.00
Plate, grill	125.00
Plate, side salad	40.00
Plate, TV	175.00
Plate, 10½"	25.00
Plate, 6½"	6.00
Plate, 8½" or 9½", ea	18.00
Platter, turkey; 19"	295.00
Platter, 12¾"	45.00
Platter, 14"	65.00
Porringer, no established value	
Shaker & pepper mill, pr	295.00
Shakers, rose bud, pr	24.00
Shakers, tall, pr	65.00
Sherbet	25.00
Soup ladle, no established value	
Sugar bowl, open, ind	125.00
Tea canister	225.00
Teapot	85.00
Thimble	45.00
Tidbit tray, 2-tier	195.00
Tile, in fr	75.00
Tile, rnd, fluted	195.00
Tile, sq	65.00
Toast cover	195.00
Trivet, fluted, rnd	125.00
Tumbler, juice; 6-oz	35.00
Tumbler, 10-oz	32.00
Tureen, soup; flat bottom	495.00
Tureen, soup; ftd, either style	695.00
Vase, bud	75.00

Apple Pieces Not Available in Desert Rose

Bowl, batter	395.00
Bowl, str sides, lg	55.00
Bowl, str sides, med	45.00
Casserole, stick hdl & lid, ind	65.00
Jam jar, redesigned	125.00
Shaker & pepper mill, wooden top, pr, no established value	
½-apple baker, from $195 to	225.00

For other hand-painted patterns, we recommend the following general guide for comparable pieces (based on current values):

Cafe Royal	-30%
Daisy	-20%
October	-20%
Forget-Me-Not	-10%
Meadow Rose	-10%
Desert Rose	Base Line Values
Apple	+10%
Ivy	+30%
Strawberry Fair	+20%
Strawberry Time	+20%
Fresh Fruit	+20%
Bountiful	+20%
Poppy	+35%
Original (small) Fruit	+50%
Wild Flower	+100% to 200%

There is not an active market in Bouquet, Rosette, or Twilight Rose, as these are scarce, having been produced only a short time. Our estimate would place Bouquet and Rosette in the October range (-20%) and Twilight Rose in the Ivy range (+30%).

Photo courtesy Mick and Lorna Chase

Ivy, teapot, $295.00.

El Patio

Bowl, cereal	12.00
Bowl, fruit	12.00
Bowl, salad; 3-qt	25.00
Bowl, vegetable; oval	30.00
Butter dish	40.00
Creamer	10.00
Cup	10.00
Cup, jumbo	18.00
Cup & saucer, demitasse	40.00
Gravy boat, w/attached underplate	35.00
Plate, bread & butter	7.00
Plate, 10½"	15.00
Plate, 8½"	12.00
Platter, 13"	45.00
Saucer	4.00
Saucer, jumbo	8.00
Sherbet	10.00
Sugar bowl, w/lid	18.00
Teapot, w/lid, 6-cup	65.00

Franciscan Fine China

The main line of fine china was called Masterpiece. There were at least four marks used during its production from 1941 to 1977. Almost every piece is clearly marked. This china is true porcelain, the body having been fired at a very high temperature. Many years of research and experimentation went into this china before it was marketed. Production was temporarily suspended during the war years. More than 170 patterns and many varying shapes were produced. All are valued about the same with the exception of the Renaissance group, which is 25% higher.

Bowl, vegetable; serving, oval	50.00
Cup	20.00
Plate, bread & butter	18.00
Plate, dinner	30.00
Plate, salad	25.00
Saucer	12.00

Starburst

Ashtray, ind	20.00
Bonbon/jelly dish	22.00
Bowl, crescent salad	40.00
Bowl, divided, 8"	25.00
Bowl, salad; ind	25.00
Butter dish	45.00
Candlesticks, pr, from $175 to	200.00
Chop plate, from $55 to	65.00
Coffeepot	135.00
Creamer & sugar bowl	25.00
Gravy boat, from $20 to	25.00
Jug, water; 10"	90.00
Mug	60.00
Oil cruet	65.00
Pepper mill	150.00
Pitcher, 7½", from $50 to	65.00
Plate, dinner	12.00
Shakers, sm, pr	20.00
Tumbler, 6-oz, from $40 to	50.00
TV tray	75.00
Vinegar cruet	65.00

Frankart

During the 1920s Frankart, Inc., of New York City, produced a line of accessories that included figural nude lamps, bookends, ashtrays, etc. These white metal composition items were offered in several finishes including verde green, jap black, and gunmetal gray. The company also produced a line of caricatured animals, but the stylized nude figurals have proven to be the most collectible today. With few exceptions, all pieces were marked 'Frankart, Inc.' with a patent number or 'pat. appl. for.' All pieces listed are in very good original condition unless otherwise indicated. Our advisor for this category is Walter Glenn; he is listed in the Directory under Georgia.

Lamp, kneeling nude gazes into 5" diameter amber globe, 7", $650.00.

Photo courtesy Walter Glenn

Ashtray, monkey w/curled tail, 6" ceramic insert, 8½"	275.00
Ashtray, nude on tiptoe, arched bk, holds 4" tray	450.00
Ashtray, nude sits atop column/leg extends over sq tray, 9½"	450.00
Ashtray, nude stands, 3" ashball on geometric base, 10"	425.00
Ashtray, nude stands on copper ball, holds 6" tray, 24"	650.00

Ashtray, striding satyr holds 3" ceramic tray, 8"	350.00
Bookends, nude sits atop metal book, 10", pr	350.00
Bookends, nude sits atop mushrooms, 8", pr	325.00
Bookends, nudes dancing, frog on base, 10", pr	450.00
Bookends, nudes in headstand support books, 10", pr	350.00
Bookends, stylized parrot on arched perch, 7", pr	250.00
Clock, 2 nudes kneel & hold 10" rnd glass clock, 12½"	1,800.00
Lamp, nude seated, leg extended, 3" globes on sides, 7½"	750.00
Lamp, seated nude holds 3" crackle globe in lap, 9"	585.00
Lamp, seated nude silhouettes against 3" sq glass cylinder, 12"	1,150.00
Lamp, 2 nudes kneel bk to bk, 8" crackle globe between, 9"	750.00
Lamp, 2 nudes sit either side of glass skyscraper, 13"	900.00
Lamp, 2 nudes stand either side rectangular glass panel, 10½"	1,050.00
Lamp, 2 nudes stand either side 8" crackle globe, 9"	750.00
Vase, dancing nude beside amber trumpet form, #77197, 9¾"	1,600.00

Frankoma

The Frank Pottery, founded in Oklahoma in 1933 by John Frank, became known as Frankoma in 1934. The company produced decorative figurals, vases, and such, marking their ware from 1936-38 with a pacing leopard 'Frankoma' mark. These pieces are highly sought. The entire operation was destroyed by fire in 1938, and new molds were cast — some from surviving pieces — and a similar line of production was pursued. The body of the ware was changed in 1955 from a honey tan (called 'Ada clay,' referring to the name of the town near the area where it was dug) to a red brick clay (known as Sapulpa), and this, along with the color of the glazes (over fifty have been used), helps determine the period of production. A Southwestern theme has always been favored in design as well as in color selection.

In 1965 they began to produce a limited-edition series of Christmas plates, followed by a bottle vase series in 1969. Considered very collectible are their political mugs, bicentennial plates, Teenagers of the Bible plates, and the Wildlife series. Their ceramic Christmas cards are also very popular items with today's collectors.

Frankoma celebrated their 50th anniversary in 1983. On September 26 of that same year, Frankoma was again destroyed by fire. Because of a fire-proof wall, master molds of all 1983 production items were saved, allowing plans for rebuilding to begin immediately.

Frankoma filed for Chapter 11 in April 1990, and eventually sold to a Maryland investor in February of 1991, thereby ending the family-ownership era. For a more thorough study of the subject, we recommend that you refer to *Frankoma Treasures* and *Frankoma and Other Oklahoma Potteries* by Phyllis and Tom Bess, our advisors; you will find their address in the Directory under Oklahoma.

Bookend, sea horse, leopard mk	400.00
Bookends, Bucking Bronco, Prairie Gr, 6", pr	300.00
Bookends, Setters, Osage Brn, pr	150.00
Bottle vase, Chinese Red, gray & Terra Cotta, #14	250.00
Bowl, Dogwood, brn & Flame, oval, 13½"	45.00
Carafe, w/lid, any color	22.50
Casserole, gray & Terra Cotta, hdls, w/lid, 4x11½"	35.00
Catalog, 1950	30.00
Christmas card, Donna Frank, 1952	100.00
Christmas card, 1944	110.00
Christmas card, 1947-48	85.00
Christmas card, 1949	65.00
Christmas card, 1950-51	75.00

Christmas card, 1952 ....85.00
Christmas card, 1953-56 ....75.00
Christmas card, 1957 ....70.00
Christmas card, 1958-60 ....65.00
Christmas card, 1961-66 ....60.00
Christmas card, 1967-68 ....50.00
Christmas card, 1969-71 ....40.00
Christmas card, 1972 ....35.00
Christmas card, 1973-75 ....30.00
Christmas card, 1976-77 ....85.00
Christmas card, 1980-82 ....25.00
Christmas plate, 1965 ....310.00
Christmas plate, 1967 ....70.00
Christmas plate, 1977-82 ....35.00
Creamer, Wagon Wheel 8.00
Flower holder, boot, star on sides, Ada clay, #507, 3½" 20.00
Honey jar, Beehive, Wisteria (lav), #803, 1983 ....40.00
Jar, cvd, Prairie Gr, #70 ....70.00
Jar, Indian, gr matt, rare, lg 225.00
Jug, Prairie Gr, w/stopper, 3-cup 75.00
Lazy susan, Wagon Wheel, Prairie Gr, #94FC 85.00
Mug, Donkey, Carter/Mondale, 1977 ....45.00
Mug, Donkey, 1975, Autumn Yel 45.00
Mug, Donkey, 1980, Terra Cotta 40.00
Mug, Elephant, Nixon-Agnew, Flame, 1969 ....75.00
Mug, Elephant, 1968 ....95.00
Mug, Elephant, 1970, bl 65.00
Mug, Elephant, 1973 ....50.00
Mug, Wagon Wheel 5.00
Planter, Madonna of Grace, Gracetone, #231-B, 6" 75.00
Plate, Bob White Quail, 1972 ....100.00
Plate, David, Teenager of the Bible, 1974 ....40.00
Plate, Jesus the Carpenter, Teenager of the Bible 40.00
Plate, Symbols of Freedom 25.00
Plate, White-Tail Deer, 1973 ....90.00
Plate, Wild Turkey, 1978 ....85.00
Sculpture, Bear Family, ltd edition by Joniece Frank, 8" 50.00
Sculpture, Bucking Bronco, no stepped base, #121, 5" ...300.00
Sculpture, cat reclining, blk gloss, 4½x9" 25.00
Sculpture, Circus Horse, blk 165.00
Sculpture, Gardener Boy, Prairie Gr 125.00
Sculpture, Gardener Girl, bl, Ada clay, 1942-52 ....95.00
Sculpture, Indian chief, Ada clay, #142, 7½" 100.00
Sculpture, puma, sitting, blk, Ada clay, #114 ....95.00
Sculpture, swan, Peacock Bl, mini 50.00
Sculpture, White Buffalo, ltd edition by Joniece Frank, 5½" 50.00
Sculpture, Wolf Family, ltd edition by Joniece Frank, 4" 50.00
Sugar bowl, Wagon Wheel, w/lid 18.00
Trivet, Spanish Iron, 6" sq 20.00
Vase, collector; V-1, 1969, 15" 105.00
Vase, collector; V-12, 13" 65.00
Vase, collector; V-13, blk & Terra Cotta, 1981, 13" 65.00
Vase, collector; V-15, 2-pc, last of series 70.00
Vase, collector; V-2, turq, 1970, 12" 70.00
Vase, collector; V-4, blk & Terra Cotta, 1972 ....85.00
Vase, collector; V-5, Flame Red, 1973, 13" 85.00
Vase, collector; V-6, Celadon & blk, 13" 85.00
Vase, collector; V-7, 13" 80.00
Vase, collector; V-8, red & wht, red stopper, 13" 75.00
Vase, collector; V-9, blk & wht, w/stopper, 13" 75.00
Vase, Cowboy Boot, Ada clay, #133, mk Frankoma Pottery 20.00
Vase, goose, Ada clay, #60-B 30.00
Wall masks, Tragedy & Comedy, wht, #118T&C, pr 65.00
Wall pocket, Phoebe, Prairie Gr, Ada clay, #730, 7½" 125.00

Fraternal Organizations

Fraternal memorabilia is a vast and varied field. Emblems representing the various organizations have been used to decorate cups, shaving mugs, plates, and glassware. Medals, swords, documents, and other ceremonial paraphernalia from the 1800s and early 1900s are especially prized. Our advisor for Odd Fellows is Greg Spiess; he is listed in the Directory under Illinois. Information on Masonic and Shrine memorabilia has been provided by David Smies, who is listed under Kansas.

Masons

Ashtray, brass, sq & compass, 1934 ....20.00
Ballot box, walnut, w/marbles, ca 1900 ....85.00
Bible, gold trim, ca 1950, 12x9x3" 25.00
Bookends, sq & compass, bronze finish 25.00
Chalice, cranberry glass w/silver sword hdls, 1908 ....125.00
Cuff links, sq & compass, 14k w/ruby 100.00
Cup, Indian head in relief, mc pnt on glass, 1903 ....60.00
Lapel pin, dmn, 14k, 32nd degree 25.00
Magazine, Life cover, October 1956 ....10.00
Plate, Los Angeles, gold & pnt on clear glass, May 1906 ....48.00
Print block, lead, sq & compass, ca 1930s 18.00
Ring, 14k, dmn, 32nd degree, 1948 ....125.00
Sword, Knights Templar, celluloid hilt, named 125.00

Odd Fellows

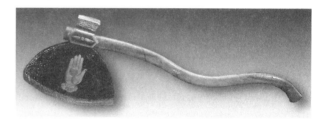

Parade axe, paint-decorated wood, 19th century, 10¼x33", EX, $865.00.

Mask, ceremonial; molded mesh wire, man's face, 1900s, 8" 65.00
Match safe, brass, symbols & emb ribbon, late 1800s, 2¼" 95.00
Miniature, wooden ax, orig blk/wht/silver pnt, 11¼" 38.00
Needlework panel, heart in hand w/seeing eye, 21x20" 155.00
Ring, eng symbols on 10k, w/color highlights, man's 250.00
Tankard, Justice/allegorical gray transfer w/mc, 4" 50.00
Trivet, heart in hands & ivy, 3-ring hdl, 1800s, 5" dia+3" hdl ...130.00

Shrine

Book, Shrine History, Prince Hall, 1993 ....20.00
Bowl, soup; Kosair Temple, ca 1920s 8.00
Cane, wood, Nile Temple, Seattle, 1936 ....40.00
Figure, in tux & fez, McCormick decanter 20.00
Pin, sword w/set-in rhinestones, sterling 4.00

Miscellaneous

Eastern Star, plate, cr/sug, c/s, matching set 17.00
Eastern Star, spoon, sterling, ca 1950s 35.00
Elks, medal, 1901 convention, 2x4" 18.00
Knights of Columbus, sword, w/canvas case 95.00

Moose, fob, 14k w/tooth 45.00

Fruit Jars

As early as 1829, canning jars were being manufactured for use in the home preservation of foodstuffs. For the past twenty-five years, they have been sought as popular collectibles. At the last estimate, over four thousand fruit jars and variations were known to exist. Some are very rare, perhaps one-of-a-kind examples known to have survived to the present day. Among the most valuable are the black glass jars, the amber Van Vliet, and the cobalt Millville. These often bring prices in excess of $3,000.00 when they can be found. Aside from condition, values are based on age, rarity, color, and special features. Our advisor for this category is John Hathaway; he is listed in the Directory under Maine.

Mason's Patent Nov 30th 1858, medium yellow with olive tone, smooth base, correct zinc screw lid, 1-quart, $275.00.

Acme Seal (script), regular mouth, clear, qt 50.00
Air Tight (arched), clear, pt 100.00
Am (eagle & flag) Fruit Jar, lt gr, lip chip, ½-gal 75.00
Am (NAGCo), aqua, porc lined, sm lip crack, midget 120.00
Amazon Swift Seal (in circle), bl, pt 22.00
Anchor (block letters) below slanting anchor, clear, qt 48.00
ARS (fancy script), aqua, lip chip, qt 58.00
Atlas E-Z Seal, amber, qt 50.00
Atlas E-Z Seal, aqua, 48-oz 15.00
Atlas E-Z Seal, aqua, 58-oz 43.00
Atlas E-Z Seal (in circle), lt bl, qt 32.00
Atlas-Mason Improved Pat'd, gr, qt 25.00
Atlas-Mason's Pat, gr, qt 20.00
Atlas-Mason's Pat Nov 30th 1858, aqua, ½-gal 10.00
Automatic Sealer, aqua, ½-gal 185.00
Ball Eclipse, clear, wide mouth, ½-gal 10.00
Ball Improved (dropped A), aqua, pt 10.00
Ball Improved Ghost Mason, aqua, pt 20.00
Ball Mason, lt olive gr, pt 30.00
Ball Pat Apl'd For, aqua, qt 198.00
Ball Perfect Mason, amber, ribbed, ½-gal 45.00
Ball Perfect Mason, dk aquamarine, qt 35.00
Ball Perfect Mason, emerald gr, qt 75.00
Ball Perfect Mason, lt aqua, qt 12.00
Bambergers 'The Always Busy Store' Newark, aqua, qt 100.00
Banner (circled by Pat dates), aqua, ½-gal 175.00
Calcutt's Pat Apr 11 Nov 7th 1893 (on lid), clear, qt 35.00
Canton Fruit Jar, clear, chip on lid ear, ½-gal 125.00
CF Spencer's Pat'd Rochester NY, aqua, qt 78.00
Clarke Fruit Jar Co Cleveland O, aqua, qt 80.00
Cohansey (arched), aqua, pt 65.00
Cohansey Mfg Co Pat Mch 20 77 (base), aqua, barrel shape, qt .128.00
Cross Gem, aqua, midget 40.00

Crown (no dot), aqua, qt 15.00
Crystal Jar CG, clear, glass screw-on lid, qt 35.00
Decker's Iowana Mason City, Iowa, Pat'd July 14 1908, qt 25.00
Dexter (circled by fruit & vegetables), aqua, lid chips, qt 88.00
Drey Pat'd 1920 Improved Everseal, clear, ½-gal 18.00
Eagle, aqua, repro cast brass, qt 175.00
Eclipse Jar, aqua, early zinc lid, qt 268.00
Empire, aqua, repro clamps, qt 88.00
Eureka Pat'd Dec 27th 1864, aqua, qt 73.00
Excelsior Improved, aqua, no closure, qt 40.00
Federal (drape flag) Fruit Jar, aqua, qt 98.00
Franklin Dexter Fruit Jar, aqua, qt 32.00
Gem CFJ (fancy mono), aqua, midget 150.00
Genuine Boyds Mason, lt gr, ½-gal 20.00
Gimbel Brothers Pure Food Store Phil, clear, pt 50.00
Glassboro Trade Mark Improved, aqua, pt 22.00
Globe, amber, pt 100.00
Griffen's Patent Oct 7 1862, aqua, orig clamp, qt 175.00
H&C (in circle), aqua, pt 18.00
Haines Combination, aqua, no lid/sm inner lip chip, qt 138.00
Haines Improved Mar 1st 1870, aqua, qt 90.00
Hansee's Palace Home Jar, clear, qt 88.00
Hero (over cross), clear, qt 48.00
Heroine, aqua, 2-pc zinc lid, pt 120.00
Howe Jar Scranton, PA, clear, qt 75.00
Improved Crown (script), lt gr, ½-gal 18.00
Improved Jewel Made in Canada, clear, qt 8.00
J&B Fruit Jar Pat'd July 14th 1898, aqua, pt 135.00
Jewel Jar (block letters in fr), clear, pt 15.00
Kerr Self Sealing Mason, amber, qt 20.00
King Pat Nov 2, 1869, aqua, sm lid chip, qt 275.00
Lafayette (script), aqua, qt 150.00
Marion Jar (fancy) Mason's Pat Nov 30th 1858, gr, qt 25.00
Mason, aqua, porc lined, ½-gal 150.00
Mason (arched), dk aquamarine, qt 50.00
Mason (block letters), amber, pt 75.00
Mason (lg letters on slant), bl, qt 60.00
Mason CFJ Improved, aqua, midget 20.00
Mason Fruit Jar (2 lines), amber, pt 150.00
Mason's (cross) Improved, aqua, midget 50.00
Mason's (cross) Patent Nov 30th 1858, amber, ½-gal 150.00
Mason's (cross) Patent Nov 30th 1858, lt apple gr, qt 70.00
Mason's (keystone in circle), Pat Nov 30th 1858, aqua, midget ...40.00
Mason's (keystone) Improved, aqua, pt 35.00
Mason's CFJ Pat Nov 30th 1858, rev: Clyde NY, midget 150.00
Mason's III Pat Nov 30th 1858, aqua, midget 150.00
Mason's III Pat Nov 30th 1858, aqua, qt 125.00
Mason's Improved, aqua, midget 25.00
Mason's Pat Nov 30th 1858, yel-gr, qt 40.00
Mason's Pat Nov 30th 58, aqua, midget 58.00
Mason's 2 Patent Nov 30th 1858, aqua, midget 45.00
Millville Atmosphere Fruit Jar, aqua, qt 45.00
Mission (bell) Mason Made in California, aqua, ½-pt 95.00
My Choice, aqua, repro clamp, ½-gal 200.00
Ostite (in dmn), clear, rare, no clamp, qt 135.00
Peerless, aqua, qt 150.00
Potter & Bodine Philadelphia (script), aqua, qt 123.00
Queen (circled by Pat dates), aqua, rough lip, qt 33.00
Safety, aqua, repro wire, qt 118.00
Smalley Nu-Seal Trade Mark (in dmns), clear, ½-pt 50.00
Solidex (in oval), deep gr, ½-gal 40.00
Swasey Double Safety (in fr), clear, ½-gal 25.00
Thompson, aqua, incorrect lid, qt 300.00
Trade Mark Advance, aqua, orig wire, qt 375.00

Trade Mark Mason's CFJ Improved, aqua, midget 25.00
Vacuum Seal Pat'd Nov 1st 1904 Detroit, clear, no lid, qt 98.00
Victor Pat 1899 (around M in dmn), aqua, qt 48.00
Victory (in shield on lid), clear, twin side clamps, ½-pt 20.00
Victory the Victory Jar (on lid), clear, ½-pt 15.00
Wears Jar (in stippled oval), clear, twin wire clamps, ½-pt 58.00
Woodbury, aqua, qt 33.00
Woodbury, aqua, ½-gal 45.00

Fry

Henry Fry established his glassworks in 1901 in Rochester, Pennsylvania. There, until 1933 when it was sold to the Libbey Company, he produced glassware of the finest quality. In the early years they produced beautiful cut glass; and when it began to wane in popularity, Fry turned to the manufacture of occasional pieces and oven glassware. He is perhaps most famous for the opalescent pearl glass called 'Foval.' It was sometimes made with blue or jade green trim in combination. Because it was in production for only a short time in 1926 and 1927, it is hard to find. Our advisor for this category is Ron Damaska; he is listed in the Directory under Pennsylvania. See also Kitchen Collectibles, Glassware.

Baker, clear opal, oval, #1917, 6" 15.00
Bowl, Basket of Flowers cutting, str sides, heavy, 4x10" 265.00
Bowl, Foval, opal w/bl festooning, bl ft, 4½" H 365.00
Candle holder, Royal Bl 18.00
Candlesticks, Foval, bl trim, 10½", pr 275.00
Candy dish, Foval, bl ft & stem, 4¾" 165.00
Casserole, crystal lime glass, oval, #1932-8 ....50.00
Casserole, gr, w/lid, #1938, 7" 78.00
Champagne, Rose etching, hollow stem 45.00
Compote, Foval, rolled rim, bl stem, 5¾x10¾" 250.00
Creamer & sugar bowl, Monaca cutting, pr 185.00
Cup & saucer, Azure Bl 22.00
Cup & saucer, Foval, bl hdl 60.00
Cup & saucer, Foval, gold o/l 50.00
Goblet, Vienna cutting, stemmed 95.00
Loaf pan, Pearl Ovenware, rectangular, 10½" 45.00
Nappy, Wilhelm cutting, hdls 145.00
Plate, canape; emerald gr 20.00
Plate, Dmn Quilt, emerald gr, 7½" 15.00
Plate, Foval, jade gr rim, 8½" 38.00
Roaster, Pearlware, w/lid, #1946, 14" L 78.00

Tea set, Foval, applied green handles, service for 6, $450.00.

Teapot, Foval, gr spout & hdl, w/6 matching c/s 450.00
Tumbler, conical w/silver o/l, 10-oz 110.00
Tumbler, floral cutting 58.00
Vase, Azure Bl reeding on crystal, #2565 ....155.00
Vase, Foval, silver o/l on body & rim, jade base, 4½" 195.00
Vase, Golden Glow, str sides, 12" 195.00
Vase, Ivy cutting, slim form, 14" 275.00

Vase, Poppy lower half, 4" 78.00

Fulper

The Fulper Pottery was founded in 1899, after nearly a century of producing utilitarian stoneware under various titles and managements. Not until 1909 did Fulper venture into the art pottery field. Vasekraft, their first art line, utilized the same heavy clay body used for their utility ware. Although shapes were unadorned and simple, the glazes they developed were used with such flair and imagination (alone and in unexpected combined harmony) that each piece was truly a work of art. Graceful Oriental shapes were produced to complement the important 'famille rose' glaze developed by W.H. Fulper, Jr. Other shapes and glazes were developed in line with the Arts and Crafts movement of the same period.

During WWI, doll's heads and Kewpies were made to meet the demand for hard-to-find imports. Figural perfume lamps and powder boxes were made both in bisque and glazed ware. Examples prized most highly by collectors today are those made before a devastating fire destroyed the plant in 1929, resulting in an operations takeover by Martin Stangl later that same year.

Several marks were used: a vertical 'Fulper' in a line reserve, a horizontal mark, a Vasekraft paper label, 'Rafco,' 'Prang,' and 'Flemington.' Fulper values are to a major degree determined by the desirability of the glazes and forms. And, of course, larger examples command higher prices. Lamps with colored glass inserts are rare and highly prized. Our advisor for this category is Douglass White; he is listed in the Directory under Florida.

Bookends, ladies in full skirts, mc glossy, 7", pr, NM 210.00
Bookends, open book resting on another, 4¾", EX 200.00
Bowl, bl/lav crystalline w/olive, ribbed, #4012, 3x12" 190.00
Bowl, bl/violet/gr on rose drip, inverted, 4½x12", NM 280.00
Bowl, effigy; amber flambe over mustard w/brn matt base, 8" 475.00
Bowl, effigy; bl flambe on bl matt, 3-figure base, 8x11" 600.00
Bowl, mc crystalline gloss, 2½x8", +lily pad frog, NM 200.00
Bowl, mc flambe, early mk, #408 ....150.00
Bowl, olive/bl gloss, 2x9" 110.00
Candle shield, gr crystalline, hdl, 7½x5" 175.00
Candlestick, bl/tan/cream flambe, wide rim, fluted form, 11" 260.00
Candlesticks, mint gr crystalline on olive, twist stem, 8", pr 200.00
Candlesticks, yel matt w/gr, ink mk, 10½", pr 350.00
Flower frog (cherub)+ 9" bowl, cream/mint gloss over oatmeal ..170.00
Lamp, ldgl 16½" shade w/foliate insets; 2-socket base, 17" 26,450.00
Lamp, mushroom; Chinese bl flambe w/inlaid glass, EX 6,500.00
Lamp, shade w/ldgl geometric apron (EX), crystalline, 23" 6,000.00
Pilgrim flask, gunmetal w/flowing silver stars, 10x7½" 425.00
Vase, appl rose & leaves, lav & bl gloss, 3½x8" 110.00
Vase, bl & olive crystalline, unmk, 7" 275.00
Vase, bl flambe, concave sides w/geometric mid-band, 14" 550.00
Vase, bl flambe on blk w/cream patches, 12" 865.00
Vase, bl/gr matt above bl gloss, ftd sphere w/2 sm hdls, 7½" 325.00
Vase, brn/tan flambe, 4 buttresses, 8¾x6" 260.00
Vase, butterscotch flambe, flaring sides, 7½" 400.00
Vase, caramel on bl gloss, asymmetrical hdls/design, ftd, 9½" 400.00
Vase, caramel/bl/brn crystalline, rnd w/3 loop rim hdls, 7" 270.00
Vase, Chinese metallic flambe over mahog/ivory, 7-sided, 10" ...550.00
Vase, cobalt/gr/ivory flambe, ovoid w/can neck, 9x5" 350.00
Vase, cream on gray w/bl highlights, ogee sides, 13½" 425.00
Vase, famille rose matt, hdls, 4½x5½" 190.00
Vase, Flemington gr w/silver threading, incurvate, 8½x6" 200.00
Vase, gr crystalline gloss, 3 hdls at incurvate neck, 7" 210.00
Vase, gr/gunmetal lustre, teardrop shape, 13x7" 1,600.00

Vase, gray-gr/tan crystalline gloss, squat, sq hdls, 3x6½" **225.00**
Vase, gray/gr/bl/olive matt, broad base, ink mk, 3x4½" **100.00**
Vase, gunmetal flambe over frothy ivory & brn, classic, 12" **325.00**
Vase, gunmetal to caramel Cat's Eye, mk, 8" **175.00**
Vase, ivory/mahog/purple/bl-gr flambe, 7-sided, tapering, 9½" ...**425.00**
Vase, lav crystalline on cream gloss, shouldered, 6½" **150.00**
Vase, lav/bl crystalline w/olive angle rim hdls, 6x7½" **270.00**
Vase, lt gr crystalline, 4 buttresses above wide base, 9" **290.00**
Vase, mint gr crystalline on olive & caramel, 3-hdl, 6½" **240.00**
Vase, olive/bl on rose drip, tapered w/2 ring hdls, 12½" **900.00**
Vase, olive/rose flambe w/aqua highlights, 4½" **80.00**
Vase, pk matt, bulbous, 5x6" **150.00**
Vase, rose matt, buttressed, 8½" **325.00**
Vase, rose matt, classic form, 10½" **225.00**
Vase, rose matt, curving rim-to-width hdls, short neck, 7½" **300.00**
Vase, rose/gr flambe w/aqua, rnd w/3 sm upright hdls, 6x7½" **350.00**
Vase, tan/gr/caramel flambe, appl 4-ftd platform, rpr, 16" **1,400.00**

Furniture

American 17th- and 18th-century furniture played an important role in its environment. Aside from the utility, furniture was a symbol indicating wealth, taste, and station in life of the owner. Each period brought about distinct design changes that created a recognizable form for that particular time frame. Our earliest furniture was handmade by the cabinetmaker with apprentices and journeymen who learned every phase of the craft of the master cabinetmaker. The end of the Civil War brought the Industrial Revolution and mechanization of furniture manufacturing. With it came the ornate Victorian period and the many revival styles. These were followed in the 20th century by Art Deco and Art Nouveau and more revival of our earliest periods.

It is important for the buyer of antique and collectible furniture to approach each piece from the point of view of the prevailing taste of that particular time frame. Pieces from lesser cabinetmakers should be recognized simply as makers of old furniture, as age alone does not equal value.

The marketplace is showing a definite recovery from the recession, however some categories are still selling below their market value. Because of this, items that have sold at auction for at least 25% lower than their normal market values will be designated with (*). Items listed in the lines that are designated with (**) are pieces in the best of form and of museum quality. Traditional mahogany furniture from the 20th century and machine made in the style of Hepplewhite, Sheraton, and Duncan Phyfe is still enjoying great popularity as are their English counterparts. Turn-of-the-century European inlaid and carved furniture is also rising in value. Commonplace oak furniture is still selling well below its highs of a few years ago.

Condition is the most important factor to consider in determining value. It is also important to remember that *where* a piece sells has a definite bearing on the price it will realize, due simply to regional preference. Our advisor for this category is Suzy McLennan Anderson, ISA, of Heritage Antiques, whose address is listed in the Directory under New Jersey. To learn more about furniture, we recommend *The Collector's Encyclopedia of American Furniture* by Robert and Harriet Swedberg. See also Fifties Modern; Nutting, Wallace; Shaker; Stickley.

Note: When only one dimension is given for blanket chests, dry sinks, tables, settees, and sofas, it is length.

Key:
Am — American	Geo — Georgian
bj — bootjack	grpt — grainpainted
brd — board	hdbd — headboard
Chpndl — Chippendale	hdw — hardware
Co — Country	Hplwht — Hepplewhite

cvd — carved	mar — marriage
cvg — carving	NE — New England
c&b — claw and ball	QA — Queen Anne
do — door	trn — turning
drw — drawer	uphl — upholstered/upholstery
Emp — Empire	vnr — veneer
Fed — Federal	Vict — Victorian
Fr — French	W/M — William and Mary
ftbd — footboard	: — over (example: 1 do: 2 drw
G — good	— 1 door over 2 drawers)

Armoires

Fruitwood Euro, 2 panel do, 2 dvtl drw, 77x44" **600.00**
Fruitwood Fr Provincial, cvd rosette:dbl do:scroll ft, 68x48" ...**2,000.00**
Fruitwood Louis XV, shell-cvd cornice, 1852, 77" **4,950.00**
Oak Vict, cornice w/appl decor:2 panel do:2 drw, 97x40x16" **900.00**
Oak Vict, ornate cornice:2 figured paneled do:2 drws, 84x51" .**1,295.00**
Walnut Am, panel do, stepped/molded cornice, 1840s, 85" **1,045.00**

Beds

Colonial Revival, low post, hdbd w/cvd crest, cvd finials **800.00**
Day, Biedermeier fruitwood, scrolled crest rails, 35x84x41" **990.00**
Day, cvd hardwood Anglo-Indian w/floral arabesques, 72" **1,045.00**
Day, Federal bird's-eye maple, trn ends/legs, Am, 1800s **300.00**
Field, threaded wooden pins, rope rails, trn posts, 54x82x58" **465.00**
Hired man's, pine w/dk over red, peaked crest, 29x73x26" **110.00**
Jenny Lind, cherry/poplar, orig rails, 39x72x34", VG **65.00**
Mahog Fr Emp, dore bronze mts/paneled sides, 1810s, 58x47x72" ..**5,250.00**
Maple gr-pnt Classical trn post, NE, 1830, 48x72x40" **1,600.00**
Maple 4-post, trn posts w/bar & paneled hdbd, 1830s **500.00**

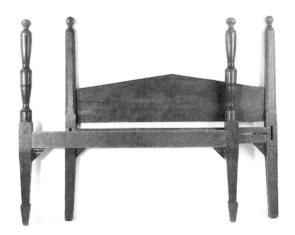

Painted and turned low-post bed with original red stain, New England, early 1800s, 48½x52¼x79½", $500.00.

Recamier, mahog Am Classical, well cvd ft, uphl, 1820s **715.00**
Rope, cherry & maple w/curly maple, trn posts, 48x75x51" **330.00**
Rope, curly maple, trn posts, rfn/rpl rails, 76x58" **1,100.00**
Rope, curly maple/poplar, trn posts/trumpet finials, 52x69x52" ..**500.00**
Rope, poplar, trn posts, acorn finials, rfn/rpl, 63x75x54" **165.00**
Rope, poplar w/orig grpt on wht, goblet finials, PA, 63x70x50" .**770.00**
Rope, poplar w/red traces, trumpet finials, 48x75x50" **250.00**
Tall post, cvd mahog, pineapple finials, 1900s **750.00**
Tall post, tiger maple, New England, 1800s, 82x80x48½" **2,400.00**
Tester, Scandinavian, pnt decor, 19th C **1,375.00**
Tester, 4-post/arched, figured maple Fed, ME, 1830, 86x80x55" ...**3,000.00**

Trundle, 1700s, 18x54x42", EX **200.00**

Benches

Bucket bench w/drw, grpt over early gr, 1800s, 39x26x14" **1,600.00**
Church pew, pine w/walnut scroll arms & bk, rfn, 52" **165.00**
Fruitwood Louis XV-style, cvd apron, floral uphl, 18x61x19" **660.00**
Limbert, drop-arm, 5-slat sides/12 in bk, rfn, no mk, 70" **2,100.00**
Mammy's, arrowbk, scrolled arms, alligatored pnt, OH, 47" **900.00**
Michigan Chair Co, oak, 3 cutouts ea side, 40", VG **2,500.00**
Oak Gothic style, EX cvg, lion arms/etc, Belgium, 54" **1,375.00**
Pine, primitive w/old gray pnt, bj ends, 68" L **140.00**
Pine Co, 1-brd ends w/cut-out ft & arms, lift-top seat, 72" **550.00**
Pine Co, 1-brd top, old tan pnt, 20x68x14" **260.00**
Poplar/Co w/old rpt, mortised legs, 77x12" **300.00**
Settle, Lifetime, 2-slat sides/7 in bk, label, 75", VG **1,900.00**
Settle, PA stenciled/freehand flowers/wings on yel, 78" **9,400.00**
Settle, Sheraton bamboo Windsor, old dk brn, 1-brd seat, 73" ..**4,600.00**
Settle, spindle bk/rolled crest, rpt grpt w/decor, 75" **165.00**
Water, pine Co, 1-brd ends, 2 panel do, open shelf, 51x42" **1,875.00**
Water, poplar Co, red traces, 30x38x16" **715.00**
Water, softwood Co, old pnt, beaded-edge bk brds, rpr, 45x36" .**440.00**
Window seat, mahog Am Classical, trapezoidal, uphl, 1825 ....**1,375.00**

Blanket Chests, Coffers, Trunks, and Mule Chests

Cherry Co Sheraton, paneled case, w/till, rstr, 27x42x20" **385.00**
Cherry/poplar, paneled, trn ft, rprs, 30x56x24" **330.00**
Curly maple Co, 6-brd, wrought strap hinges, 25x48x18", EX **550.00**
Curly maple w/red traces, 6-brd w/cut-out ft, drw, 31x42x17" **500.00**
Mule, rfn pine, 6-brd type, trn ft, 2 dvtl drw, 37x40x19" **550.00**
Pine/poplar w/brn sponging, tulips/hex signs, PA/1806, 52" ** ..**19,250.00**
Pine/poplar w/old gr rpt, dvtl, strap hinges, till, 24x41x20" **715.00**
Poplar, orig brn vinegar grpt on yel w/blk trim, 24x38x19" **385.00**
Poplar w/orig grpt & tulips in wht reserves, PA, 22x44x19" **1,400.00**
Poplar w/orig red stripe grpt on yel, dvtl, 25x44x19" **165.00**
Scandinavian pine, pnt decor, iron hdls, 1860s, 21x50x24" **470.00**
Walnut Chpndl, dvtl case, ogee ft, w/till, rfn, 22x41x18" **440.00**
Walnut PA Chpndl, 2 dvtl drw, ogee ft, rpl/rstr, 28x53" **1,650.00**

Bookcases

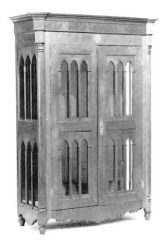

Cherry wood bookcase with chevron string inlay, Gothic arched panels, scalloped skirt, American, early 1800s, 73x54", $2,400.00.

Golden oak era, 2 leaded glass do, 54x60x12½", EX **500.00**
Limbert #347, 3 shelves:glass do, shaped sides, 47x17" **2,400.00**
Limbert #358, 2 do, ea w/2 vertical panes, corbels, VG **2,600.00**
Mahog Am Classical, dbl glazed do:3 sm drw, 92x54½" **6,600.00**

Quarter-sawn oak, stacked, drw in base, cornice, 6-shelf, 81" **775.00**
Revolving, mahog, orig finish, Trade Mark Danner label, 43x21" .**495.00**
Stack, poplar/birch w/stain, 3-part, Globe Wernicke, 47x34" **550.00**
Walnut Vict, dbl 1-pane do:low base w/2 drw, 72x39" **495.00**
Walnut/burl vnr Vict breakfront, shelves:4 drw:2 do, 90" **3,000.00**

Cabinets

China, Fed style w/inlay, 2 do:2 drw:2 do, 1880s, 97" **1,400.00**
China, Lifetime #6435, 2-do, ea w/6 panes of glass at top, VG ..**1,600.00**
China, Limbert, 1-do w/3 panes atop, side shelves, rpl bk **6,000.00**
China, Limbert #448, 2-do, ea w/2 sm panes:1, 63x46", VG ...**2,400.00**
China, oak bow front w/lion's head cvgs, 58x44x16" **2,100.00**
China, Shop of the Crafters, 1 do w/sqs made w/mullions, 64" ..**4,750.00**
Magazine, inlay: birds/leaves, Arts & Crafts, 3 open shelves ...**1,300.00**
Vernis Martin, glass sides/do, pnt gardens etc, 56" **2,100.00**
Vitrine, giltwood Louis XVI style, 2 glass do, Fr, 69x52" **2,850.00**

Candlestands

Birch Co Chpndl, tripod base, rpl top, rfn, 25x14x14½" **440.00**
Birch Co Chpndl, tripod base w/snake ft, NH, 28x17x16" **990.00**
Bird's-eye maple Emp, 8-sided top, trn std, 4 legs, 1850s **300.00**
Cherry Co Chpndl, trn column, tripod base, 3-brd top, 17" dia .**330.00**
Hardwood Chpndl, tilt top, old rpt, rprs, 27x19" dia **150.00**
Hardwood/pine/poplar Co Chpndl, tripod base, 28x19" dia **385.00**
Mahog Fed, 8-sided top:ring, vase & trn std, 1800s, 28" **330.00**
Mahog Hplwht, oval tilt top, tripod base, 30x21x14" **1,045.00**
Mahog w/gallery top, twisted vase/ring std, 3-leg, 1700s, 36" **550.00**
Mahog/birch Am Fed, spiral-trn support, tripod base, 28" **385.00**
Walnut Chpndl, trn column, tripod base, 1-brd top, 27" **1,550.00**

Chairs

Arm, Chpndl-style wing-bk, worn uphl, 20th C, 43" **320.00**
Arm, Fed wing-bk, reeded mahog fr, reuphl, castors, 42" **7,150.00**
Arm, Jacobean style, cvd fr, velvet reuphl, 1900s, 50" **770.00**
Arm, mahog fr, cabriole legs/open arms, reuphl, 20th C, 48" **715.00**
Arm, mahog George III, pierced ribbon bk, uphl seat, 1780s **500.00**
Arm, mahog Louis XV style w/uphl seat, open arms, much cvg ...**1,800.00**
Arm, maple, 4 grad arched slats, rush seat, rfn, 45" **525.00**
Arm, walnut Co, canted bk w/vase splat, slip seat, 48" **550.00**
Arm, walnut QA style, velvet uphl, rprs, 20th C, 36" **165.00**
Arm, Windsor, brace-bk, continuous arm, repro, rprs, 38x17" **165.00**
Arm, Windsor, 11-spindle low-bk, shaped seat, old rpt, 29" **990.00**
Arm, Windsor, 5-spindle bow-bk, splayed base, oval seat, 34" **360.00**
Arm, Windsor, 7-spindle comb-bk, w/cvd ears, rstr seat, 47" ..**2,500.00**
Arm, Windsor sack-bk w/knuckle arms, pnt, MA, 1780s, 38x17" ..**5,175.00**
Arm, yew English, 5-slat ladder-bk, shaped arms, 43" **300.00**
Armchair, Old Hickory, 7-twig spindle-bk, splint seat, sgn **350.00**
Chaise lounge, Louis XVI style, cvd/pnt, uphl, 59" L **1,300.00**
Chpndl-style mahog, wing-bk, cabriole legs, c&b ft, 20th C **315.00**
Club, Deco style, bird's-eye maple arms, orig uphl, EX **1,150.00**
Corner, Chpndl maple, pierced slats, rush seat, trn legs **350.00**
Desk, Limbert, #85, 3-slat bk, arched rungs, recovered, 42" **800.00**
Edwardian-style marquetry w/MOP, bbl bk, 20th C **230.00**
Highchair, mc PA florals on salmon pnt, spindle bk, 36" **715.00**
Highchair, 2-slat ladder-bk, splint seat, blk pnt, 32" **465.00**
Lolling, mahog Hplwht style, uphl, 46½" **200.00**
Lolling, mahog Sheraton style w/inlay, brocade uphl, repro **330.00**
Mahog English Chpndl w/figured vnr, b&c ft, rprs, 38½" **1,200.00**
Mahog W&M style, much cvg, wing-bk, Albano Co, ca 1950 ...**520.00**
Potty, walnut QA, scrolled apron, trn legs, 1-brd lid, 18x18" ..**1,400.00**
QA style, shell-cvd apron, cabriole legs, c&b ft, 20th C **260.00**

Rocker, Adirondack, roots & twigs w/hewn slat seat, 40" **650.00**
Rocker, hardwood w/5 arched maple slats, rpr, 37" **65.00**
Rocker, Limbert #842, 5-slat sides, rpl pads, brand, VG **3,000.00**
Rocker, sewing; gr pnt w/mc flowers/stripes, 31" **90.00**
Rocker, 4-slat ladder-bk, trn posts, rush seat, 43" **250.00**
Rocker arm, JM Young, vertical bk slats, new leather, no mk **750.00**
Rocker arm, maple Co, 4-slat bk, rpl splint seat, 43" **300.00**
Rocker arm, walnut Emp w/scrolled arms, reuphl, 40" **50.00**
Rocker arm, walnut fr w/gooseneck arms, worn uphl, rprs, 40" ...**150.00**
Side, bamboo Windsor, 9-spindle bow-bk, blk rpt, 38¾" **360.00**
Side, Co QA, mixed woods w/red traces, rush seat, 41" **745.00**
Side, Co QA, vase splat/shaped crest, rush seat, rpt, 40" **635.00**
Side, hardwood, 5 grad arched slats, rush seat, 42" **275.00**
Side, mahog Vict w/cvd floral crest, worn uphl seat, 34" **85.00**
Side, maple Co Chpndl, sq legs, arched crest, rpl seat, 37" **195.00**
Side, Michigan Chair Co, att; wide+narrow horizontal bk slat ...**425.00**
Side, Sheraton w/pnt decor, balloon rush seat, 33½" **440.00**
Side, walnut E PA QA, cabriole legs/vase splat/slip seat, 41" ..**2,970.00**
Side, walnut Phila QA, cabriole legs, vase splat, uphl, 39" **3,500.00**
Side, walnut QA, cabriole legs, vase splat, slip seat, 39" **1,100.00**
Side, Windsor, bamboo trn-spindle hoop-bk, gr pnt, 1800s **675.00**
Side, Windsor, bamboo 7-spindle bow-bk, shaped seat, rprs, 36" ..**195.00**

Chair Sets

Arm, elm English Regency, open arms, uphl seat, 33", pr **1,650.00**
Arm, Windsor, bamboo, branded IB Ackley, old blk rpt, 37", pr **3,000.00**
Arm, Windsor, Phila bow-bk w/branded G&R Gaw label, gr rpt, pr ...**2,400.00**
Dining, mahog Fed style, cvd fan/scroll bk, uphl seat, 4 for **660.00**
Dining, mahog Regency style, bowed crest, uphl seat, 6 for **650.00**
Euro Renaissance Revival, rfn/reuphl, 37", 2 arm+6 sides * **300.00**
Mahog Chpndl style w/cvg, reuphl, early 20th C, 39½", pr **2,200.00**
Side, Baroque Revival, cvd/trn, mahog stain, reuphl, 37", pr **200.00**
Side, Co 3-slat ladder-bk, trn finials, tape seat, rfn, 34", pr **110.00**
Side, gr pnt w/yel stripes/gold floral stencil, PA, 34", 6 for **3,600.00**
Side, mahog Chpndl, beaded edge outlines crest/stiles, 6 for ...**4,000.00**
Side, mahog vnr Classical, 1840s, 31¼", 8 for **1,955.00**
Side, maple QA style, shape crest, vase splat, rush seat, 31", pr ..**550.00**
Side, oak baroque style, cvd spiral-twist columns/uphl, 42", pr ...**385.00**
Side, rod-bk Windsor, old rfn, early 19th C, 34", 6 for **3,450.00**
Side, tiger maple, 2-slat bk, rstr cane seat, 5 for **880.00**
Tiger maple QA, orig blk pnt, rpl seats, 1790s, 40", 4 for **6,325.00**
Walnut George II style, shaped crests, slip seat, 10 for **7,500.00**

Chests

Classical carved mahogany and veneer chest, replaced brasses, old finish, ca 1825, 52x40x20", $1,495.00.

Am pine & cherry, bonnet drw:3 full drw, bracket base, 1850s ..**230.00**
Birch Chpndl, 6 dvtl overlapping grad drw, sm rprs, 53x39" ...**3,400.00**

Birch Fed, 4-drw, rope-trn columns, ball ft, 1830s, 43x42" **990.00**
Bird's-eye maple Co, 4-drw, ½-trn columns, ca 1825, 42" **2,500.00**
Campaign, mahog vnr w/brass corners/flush hdw, 3-drw, VG * ..**220.00**
Cherry Chpndl, 7 dvtl overlapping drw, rfn/rpl, 39x36x18" **1,400.00**
Cherry Co, 4 dvtl drw, paneled ends, rfn, 47x43x21" **850.00**
Cherry Co, 4 dvtl drw, 1-brd ends, rprs/rpl, 38x42" **880.00**
Cherry Fed w/inlay, 4 grad drw, New England, 1790s, 38x42" **4,400.00**
Cherry Sheraton, old blk combed grpt, 4-drw, rpl pulls, 44x40" .**1,800.00**
Cherry Sheraton, 2 drw:3, rpl oval brasses, 45x41" **1,595.00**
Cherry Sheraton, 5 dvtl drw w/cockbeading, trn ft, 48x42" **965.00**
Cherry Sheraton, 9 dvtl drw w/beading, cornice, PA, 67x43" .**6,600.00**
Cherry w/curly maple facade Emp, 4 dvtl drw, 50x43" **1,540.00**
Cherry/mahog Sheraton, 4 dvtl drw, rpl pulls/rfn, 42x45" **990.00**
Continental red lacquer w/gilt, 2-drw/cabriole legs, 1700s, 35x40" .**1,200.00**
Curly maple Emp w/walnut pilasters, 4 dvtl drw, 48x44" **440.00**
Curly maple/mahog Sheraton, 4 bow-front drw, rprs, 40x40" **660.00**
Curly maple/poplar Emp, 7 dvtl drw, trn ft, rfn, 47x42" **990.00**
Mahog Chpndl style bow-front, 4-drw, modern repro, 32x38" ...**330.00**
Mahog Emp w/flame vnr, 5 dvtl drw, cvd columns, 42x45" **300.00**
Mahog vnr Emp, 2 step-bk:3 dvtl drw, ring pulls, rprs, 44" **550.00**
Maple/Chpndl, 5 overlapping dvtl drw, rfn/rpl, 54x36" **4,180.00**
On chest, cherry Chpndl, early stain, orig brasses, 68x39" **4,600.00**
On chest, mahog English Chpndl, bail brasses, 18th C, 78" **6,000.00**
On chest, tiger maple QA, 10-drw, cabriole legs, 1780s, 83" .**15,000.00**
Pine w/folky pnt decor, 5-drw, modern repro, 36x26x15" **275.00**
Walnut Chpndl, 3 sm drw:2:4 grad drw, PA, rprs, 72x37" **6,325.00**
Walnut Hplwht w/inlay, 4 grad dvtl drw, Fr ft, 39x40", EX **880.00**
Walnut PA, 3 sm:5 grad drw, bracket ft, ca 1765, 61x39" **2,800.00**
Walnut QA on fr, 3 sm:5 grad drw, ca 1760, 70x43x22" **8,500.00**
Walnut Vict w/Eastlake detail, do/3-drw, marble top, 38x30" **330.00**

Cupboards (See also Pie Safes)

Butternut/poplar Co 1-pc step-bk, 4 shelves:2 drw:2 do, 78" **250.00**
Cherry/flame mahog vnr Emp Gothic Revival, 2-pc step-bk, 80" **880.00**
Cherry/poplar Co, 2 6-pane do:2 drw:2 panel do, OH, 84x45" ..**1,950.00**
Continental, crown molding: cvd do w/rosettes, 1800s, 64x33" **550.00**
Corner, burled yew English, raised panels, ca 1800, 83x38" **3,200.00**
Corner, butternut Co w/inlay, 4-do, 2-pc, rpl/rprs, 91" **1,650.00**
Corner, cherry Co, dbl arched do:2 drw:2 do, 2-pc, 85" **1,870.00**
Corner, cherry Co, 2 6-pane do:2 drw:2 do, 1-pc, 79x51" **1,595.00**
Corner, cherry Co, 2 8-pane do:2 panel do, apron, 80x48" **485.00**
Corner, cherry Emp w/pnt striping, rstr, 2-pc, 87x61" **4,180.00**
Corner, cherry Fed, 2 do:3 drw:2 drw, 2-pc, 1800s, 94x52" **3,800.00**
Corner, chery Co, 8-pane dbl do:2 panel do, rpr, 84x45" **3,400.00**
Corner, pine, 2 6-pane do:2 panel do, 1-pc, 74x49" **1,400.00**
Corner, pine architectural, arched dbl do, 1-pc, 102x52" **3,300.00**
Corner, pine w/gr stain, 2 panel do:2, apron, 1-pc, 80x46" **4,125.00**
Corner, pine w/red grpt rpt, 12-pane do:2 shelves:do, 89x43" .**2,575.00**
Corner, poplar Co, 6-pane do:panel do, 1-pc, 85x38" **1,750.00**
Corner, rfn cherry, 2 12-pane do:2 drw:2 panel do, OH, 88x45" ..**4,300.00**
Corner, walnut Chpndl architectural, 2 arch do, 2-pc, 99" **1,600.00**
Corner, walnut Co, 4 panel do, 2 dvtl drw, 1-pc, 92x46" **990.00**
Court, Euro w/decor, pine w/olive & mc rpt, 1-pc, 80x52" **1,265.00**
Hanging, pine Euro, rpt grpt, 1-drw, raised-panel do, 27x22" **250.00**
Hanging corner, Euro bow-front, pine, old wht rpt, 44x31" **770.00**
Hanging corner, pine down to old red, 1 do:3 drw, 24x13" **465.00**
Hardwood/pine Continental, 2 drw:1 do, damage, 38x26" **1,200.00**
Jelly, cherry/poplar w/old red, dbl do/nailed drws, 61x39" **825.00**
Jelly, pine Fed, splashbrd, 2 drw:2 panel do, 42x41x18" **375.00**
Jelly, primitive, pine, old pnt, step-bk shelves, 45x42" **385.00**
Jelly, walnut Co, dbl 1-brd do, dvtl drw, rpl ft, 61x44x19" **1,100.00**
Jelly, walnut Co, 2-brd ends, 2 panel do, dvtl drw, 56x41" **990.00**
Oak Jacobean w/vine cvgs, ring-trn columns, 17th C, 54x48" ...**2,000.00**

Pewter, pine Co, open top w/2 shelves, bl/red rpt, 71x51" **2,200.00**
Pewter, pine w/architectural details, 1-pc, rfn/rstr, 84x42" **1,985.00**
Pewter, pine w/old rpt, open top, 1-brd ends, 75x48x16" **2,000.00**
Pine Co, old red pnt, pr 1-brd do w/pilasters, 37x30x9" **935.00**
Pine Co Emp w/old grpt, 2 do:2 drw:3 drw:4 do, 2-pc, 86" **2,200.00**
Pine Co 2-pc step-bk w/old red, raised panels, 85x46" **2,200.00**
Pine/poplar Co 1-pc step-bk, dbl do/2 nailed drw, 77x39x17" **230.00**
Poplar Co, old red rpt w/yel drws & do panels, 2-pc, 81x43" **850.00**
Spice, walnut/poplar, 48-drw, sq nails, rpl knobs, 15x24" **1,128.00**
Walnut Co, 2 panel do, pie shelf, cornice, 2-pc, 75x46" **2,300.00**
Walnut Co, 2 panel do:shelf:2 drw:2 do, 2-pc, 84x47x18" **1,650.00**
Walnut Co, 4 panel do, cornice, 1-pc step-bk, 78x43" **1,300.00**

Desks

Burl walnut vnr Georgian, 4 grad drw, bracket base, 42x33" ...**2,750.00**
Butler's, curly maple/poplar Co Hplwht, rfn/rpl, 47x41" **3,200.00**
Butler's, mahog flame-grain vnr Emp, 4-drw/fitted int, 48" **413.00**
Cherry Chpndl, slant front, 4 dvtl drw, fitted int, 41x38" **2,600.00**
Cherry Co, slant front, fitted int, 5 dvtl drw, rfn, 38x37" **1,550.00**
Clerk's, pine w/grpt, 2 dvtl drw, damage/rprs, 44x40x21" **600.00**
Invalid's, pine w/brn/cream grpt, metal escutcheons, 31" L **385.00**
Lady's, cherry/maple Sheraton, fitted top, 3-drw, 2-pc, 60" **1,550.00**
Lady's, cherry/walnut/curly maple Co Emp, fitted top, 55x39" ...**1,300.00**
Lap, burlwood ebony & brass w/MOP inlay, 1870s **200.00**
Limbert #719, kneehole, fitted gallery, rfn, 42" **1,600.00**
Limbert #735, 2 3-drw banks, 2 drw:kneehole, gallery, mk **2,000.00**
Mahog Boston Chpndl w/serpentine front, slant lid, 45x42" ..**5,000.00**
Mahog Chpndl style, slant lid, 4 grad serpentine drw, c&b ft **450.00**
Mahog Chpndl style, slant lid, 4-drw, c&b ft, 20th C **400.00**
Mahog English Hplwht w/inlay, slant front, fitted int, 48" **2,200.00**
Oak, c&b ft, flat top, 2 banks of 2 drw, 1 drw on end, 48" **600.00**
Pine Co on fr, lift lid/pigeon holes, gallery top, 42"+crest **465.00**
Plantation, cherry Co, rpl bookcase top, dvtl drw, 72x36" **550.00**
Plantation, cherry/ash/poplar, fitted int/drw, 2-pc, 58x36" **550.00**
Plantation, walnut Co, bookcase top, fitted int, 1-drw, 78" **1,045.00**
Plantation, walnut Co, slant lid, fitted int, rfn, 64x36" **1,000.00**
Roll top, quarter-sawn oak, 5-drw, cvd pulls, 50x42x32" **1,650.00**
Roll top, quarter-sawn oak, 5-drw base, fitted int, 60" **2,400.00**
Tiger maple Chpndl style, slant lid, 4 grad drw, bracket ft **1,955.00**
Walnut Co Emp, lift lid, fitted int, dvtl gallery, 39x34x23" **250.00**
Walnut Phila Chpndl, slant front, 4 dvtl drw, 44x40" **4,290.00**
Walnut vnr English QA w/inlay, slant lid, 4-drw, 40x36" **2,900.00**
Writing, English Sheraton w/satinwood inlay, 30x52x23" **990.00**
Writing, walnut Chpndl, fitted int, 4-drw, PA ca 1780 ....**4,300.00**

Dressers

Cherry Fed w/inlay, 4 grad drw, fan decor, 1790s, 38x42x21" .**4,400.00**
Henderon, mahog Vict style, serpentine, mirror, cvgs, 27" **850.00**
Heywood-Wakefield, 2 banks of 4 drw, long wood pulls, 54" W .**325.00**
Mahog Am Emp, 4-drw, flame grpt, ogee mirror, 75" **850.00**
Mahog w/cvg, shaped marble top, urn finials, candle shelves ..**1,800.00**
Oak, curved facade, swivel mirror, press/cvd decor **595.00**
Vict Eastlake walnut/walnut burl, 3-drw, marble top, 48x43" **300.00**

Dry Sinks

Ash/poplar, 2 cvd panel do, drw/shelf top, rfn, 1900, 43x47" **600.00**
Butternut Co, 2 panel do, nailed drw, bksplash, rfn, 43" **715.00**
Cherry/poplar Amish Co, old gray patina, hutch top, IN, 44" **880.00**
Cut-out ft, 2 panel do, nailed well/old mellow finish, 33x46" **825.00**
Mustard grpt softwood, 2-shelf bk, 2 nailed drw, 52x62" **1,150.00**
Oak Co hutch top, porc knobs, rstr, 49x44x18" **275.00**

Pine Co, 2 panel do, CI latch, rfn, 34x36" **385.00**
Pine/poplar, w/crest, worn bl-gray rpt, OH, 36x36x14½" **635.00**

Hall Pieces

Bench, pine, pedimented crest rail, 3-plank seat, 43x71x27" **880.00**
Bench, quarter-sawn golden oak, mirror & hooks, 75x36x19" **990.00**
Chair, walnut Renaissance Revival, uphl seat, 1850s **250.00**
Tree, quarter-sawn oak, lift-lid seat, mirror/hooks, 83" **880.00**

Highboys

Cherry bonnet-top highboy, short drawers flank fan-carved drawer over 4 graduated drawers, lower section with 1 long drawer over 3 short drawers, scalloped apron, old varnish, Connecticut, 81x40x22", $8,500.00.

Curly maple QA, 6 drw:4, cabriole legs, 71x36x19" ** **13,750.00**
Mahog Chpndl style, arch crest, drw:4:base drw, c&b ft **980.00**
Maple QA, cvd scroll top, orig brasses, rfn, 1770s, 89x40x19" ...**9,200.00**
QA maple, 5 grad drw:drw:3 short drw, cabriole legs, 1790s* ..**2,750.00**
Walnut Chpndl, open bonnet, 3 short drw:3 long, 1770s, EX * ..**7,500.00**
Walnut Chpndl, 3 grad drws:2 short:3 long, PA, 1850s, rstr * .**7,500.00**
Walnut QA, 5 drw (vnr fronts):3, rstr/rfn, 67x37" **1,550.00**
Walnut QA, 5 grad drw:3, rstr, New England, 68x39x20" **5,750.00**

Lowboys

Cherry QA, 3 dvtl drw overlap, 2-brd top, rpl/rfn, 34" L **2,200.00**
Mahog Chpndl style, 20th C handmade repro, 32x34" **550.00**
Mahog QA, 5 dvtl drw, rpl brasses/top, rprs, 30x34x21" **990.00**
Oak Jacobean style, Canfield top, molded drw front, 1940s **200.00**
Red walnut George II, frieze drw, cvd apron, cabriole legs **4,800.00**
Walnut English QA, old bleached finish, old rprs, 27x27x19" **1,200.00**

Pie Safes

Cherry Co, dbl do w/12 tin panels: drw, rfn, 53x40x16" **1,550.00**
Pine Co, worn bl pnt:gr, 12 punched tin panels, 55x39" **660.00**
Poplar, 12 punched panels, mortised, red stain, OH, 47x39" ...**1,980.00**
Poplar Co, dbl do w/punched tin:dvtl drw, rfn, 57x38" **575.00**
Poplar Co, sq corner posts, 16 tin panels, bl rpt, 64x40" **1,870.00**
Poplar Co, 14 punched tin panels, mortised/pinned, 52x50" ...**2,500.00**
Poplar Co, 2 drw:dbl do w/punched panels, old red, 48x53" **1,650.00**
Poplar w/red rpt, sq posts, dvtl drw, 12 tin panels, 53x37" **715.00**
Poplar/cherry Co, dbl do w/punched tin:2 drw, 1-pc, 78" **695.00**
Redwood/pine, 8 punched tin panels, sq corner posts, 49x37" ...**2,860.00**
Walnut, 2 dvtl drw: dbl do, 6 punched tin panels, 75x53x17" .**3,300.00**

Walnut, 4 tin panels, sq posts, Shenandoah Valley, 53x50x23" ..**2,500.00**

Secretaries

Cherry Chpndl, 2 do:slant lid:4 drw, 2-pc, rfn, 80x40" **3,575.00**
Cherry Co w/bird's-eye vnr drw fr, 3-pc, rstr, 83x48" **600.00**
Curly walnut Emp, 2 dvtl drw in base, 2-pc, rprs, 81x44" **700.00**
Mahog Emp, 3 open shelves, 2 lattice do, ball ft, 1830s, 76" ...**2,100.00**
Mahog English Hplwht w/inlay, old finish, 2-pc, 87x45" **4,180.00**
Mahog vnr Emp w/figure, 3 dvtl drw, bookcase top, 2-pc, 86" **600.00**
Pine Emp, 2 do:split drw/writing space:3 drw, 1850s **635.00**
Poplar Co w/red pnt, bookcase w/2 do:slant lid:2 drw, 81" **3,500.00**
Walnut Vict, paneled, appl cvgs, slant lid, fitted int, 96" **1,650.00**

Settees

Am pnt/stenciled ½-spindle bk w/trn legs, ca 1825, 72" **1,000.00**
Austrian cvd & gilded, velvet uphl, 19th C, 39x77x20" **3,600.00**
Chpndl, uphl triple chair cvd-ribbon bk, serpentine seat rail .**3,250.00**
Emp-style mahog, arched bk, scrolled arms, EX uphl, 1890s **750.00**
Fed-style mahog w/inlay, str crest rail, 20th C, EX **435.00**
Louis XV style, camel bk, damask uphl, 40x70x28" **1,100.00**
Old Hickory style, twig built, woven splint bk, 52" **800.00**
PA German pnt decor, ½-spindle bk, scalloped crest, 72" **950.00**
Pine Sheraton ½-spindle bk, ca 1835, 72" **175.00**
Rococo Revival walnut, floral cvd crest, molded skirt, 1850s **350.00**
Rosewood (laminated) Am Rococo, scrolled arms, uphl, 41x62" ..**5,500.00**
Walnut Italian Neoclassical, overall cvg, uphl, 82½" **3,000.00**
Walnut Renaissance Revival, appl crest decor, Am, 1850s **150.00**
Walnut Vict w/cvd detail, reuphl/rprs/rfn, 58" **330.00**
Windsor, arrow bk,open arms, plank seat, 1820s, 72" **2,100.00**
Windsor, open arms, bamboo-trn spindles, 19th C, 74" **1,800.00**

Shelves

Bracket, giltwood, cvd flowers, Phila, 1830s, 11x20", pr **4,400.00**
Butternut, wall mt, 1850s, 44x30x9" **500.00**
Etagere, birch Classical, red stain, 5-shelf, 1800s, 60x18x13" ..**2,300.00**
Etagere, ebonized cherry, wall mt, NY, 1880s, 34x23" **440.00**
Etagere, mahog Regency style, 4-shelf/2-drw, 46x17x15" **525.00**
Etagere, rosewood Am Rococo, ornate cvg, 1850s, 118x54x15" ..**10,450.00**
Etagere, rosewood grained Rococo, marble top, NY, 1850s, 90x37" .**3,575.00**
Mahog, block & trn posts ea w/3 shelves, wall mt, 1800s, pr **150.00**
Pine, grad/step-bk type, 7-shelf, New England/1840s, 93x37" **700.00**
Pine w/old red-brn rpt, 4-shelf, wall mt, 48x41" **660.00**

Sideboards

Am oak, cvd bksplash, split drw:drw:2 do, paw ft **400.00**
Cherry Sheraton w/vnr, 2 flat/2 curved do, 3-drw, 72" L **3,500.00**
Huntbrd, cherry Sheraton, 4 dvtl drw/reeded top, rpl, 41" **2,750.00**
Huntbrd, mahog English Chinese Chpndl style, rprs, 30x51x24" **715.00**
Limbert, #2420, Ebon-Oak, 3 cabinets:long drw, 43", EX **2,500.00**
Limbert, orig gr finish, long corbels support mirror bk, 59" **5,000.00**
Limbert #459¾, mirror, 3 drw:3 drw w/do ea side:long drw **2,300.00**
Mahog Emp w/flame vnr, paw ft, trn columns, 3-part, 58x74x27" ...**900.00**
Mahog Emp w/some figure, paw ft, 3 drw:4 panel do, 56x75", VG ..**440.00**
Mahog Euro, blk rpt w/gold florals, marble top, 38x74", VG **880.00**
Mahog Fed style w/inlay, bow-front w/concave sides, 1900s **1,265.00**
Mahog Hplwht, serpentine front, string inlay, 39x66x24" **2,600.00**
Mahog Hplwht style w/fan & flower inlay, demilune, 34x60x25" ..**2,700.00**
Mahog Hplwht w/inlay, serpentine w/5 dvtl drw/dbl do, 67" L ..**3,850.00**
Mahog vnr Hplwht style, modern repro, 68" **850.00**
Shop of the Crafters #323, geometric floral inlay, 54", VG **2,100.00**

Sofas

Empire w/lyre fr w/cvd shell crest/flower/foliage, rstr, 92" **200.00**
Flame mahog vnr Emp, brocade reuphl, 85" **220.00**
Mahog, Classical cvd shells on columnar arms, satin uphl, 69" ..**1,980.00**
Mahog & mahog vnr Emp, lyre arms, paw ft, leather uphl, 86" ..**385.00**
Mahog Am Classical, much cvg, cornucopia legs, Morristown, 91" ...**2,860.00**
Mahog Chpndl style, camel-bk, cvd sq legs, 20th C, EX **600.00**
Mahog Chpndl style camel-bk w/salmon brocade uphl, repro, 76" ..**330.00**
Mahog Chpndl style w/flame stitch uphl, modern repro, 66" **250.00**
Mahog Classical Revival, rolled crest w/cvg, paw ft, 1860s **1,100.00**
Mahog Emp bench shape, sabre legs/appl medallions, reuphl, 72" ...**990.00**
Mahog Emp style, cvd arm supports, Am, 20th C **200.00**
Mahog Emp style, silk uphl, rolled arms, paw ft, 89" **1,500.00**
Mahog Fed, flat crest rail, curved arms w/cvgs, 1790s, 75" **2,100.00**
Mahog Philadelphia Chpndl, true centennial camel-bk, EX ...**2,000.00**
Mahog Sheraton, brocade reuphl, trn/reeded legs, 75½" **1,300.00**
Mahog Sheraton w/cvd details, reuphl, PA, 34¾x76x26" **4,400.00**
Walnut Renaissance Revival, w/red plush, trn ft, Am, 1850s **200.00**
Walnut Vict, medallion bk w/burl vnr trim, reuphl, 29x29x16" .**500.00**
Walnut Vict Louis XV, serpentine bk, reuphl, 84", EX **400.00**

Stands

Sheraton stand, maple and poplar nightstand, pegged construction, stripped and waxed, circa 1850, 29x22x21", $750.00.

Book, mahog, vertical box w/crest over 2 shelves, 1800s, 39" **385.00**
Cherry Co, dvtl drw, rpl 2-brd top, rfn, 28x20x20" **220.00**
Cherry Co Emp w/mahog vnr, dvtl drw, rpl top, 29x22x18" **165.00**
Cherry Co Hplwht, dvtl drw, 2-brd top, rpl pulls, 33x19" **550.00**
Cherry Co Sheraton, 2 dvtl drw, 2-brd top, rfn, 29x21" **465.00**
Cherry Co Sheraton, 3 dvtl drw, 2-brd top, 30x22x18" **450.00**
Cherry Hplwht w/bird's-eye vnr drw, 2-brd top, 29x18x19" ** ..**3,900.00**
Cherry/birch Hplwht, trn column/tripod legs/1-brd top, 15x20" ...**660.00**
Curly maple Co, dvtl drw, 2-brd top, rfn, 29x19x20" **385.00**
Curly maple Sheraton, 2 dvtl drw, 2-brd top, 28x31x18" **2,035.00**
Magazine, Limbert #300, shaped slab cut-out sides, 45x26" **1,600.00**
Magazine, Michigan Chair Co, 4-slat sides, 33x16" sq, VG **850.00**
Mahog Sheraton, shaped top, 2-drw, 29½" **600.00**
Mahog Sheraton, 2 drw w/rnded fronts, 1-brd top, 28x20x17" ...**220.00**
Mahog vnr Emp, dvtl drw, tripod base, trn column, 30x20x16" .**300.00**
Mahog/mahog vnr Sheraton, 3 dvtl drw, rfn/rpl, 29x19x18" **360.00**
Night, cherry Co, dvtl drw, 2-brd top, trn legs, 29x18" sq **250.00**
Plant, Arts & Crafts, rnd w/slatted top bin, MacMurdo ft **425.00**
Plant, ebonized softwood w/floral cvgs, 6-leg, 30x12" dia **85.00**
Plant, oak, Arts & Crafts, sq box top of curved slats, 35" **650.00**
Plant, onyx & gilt brass, Fr Vic+, 34" **715.00**
Poplar Co Sheraton, orig red grpt, dvtl drw, 1-brd, 39x19x18" ...**300.00**
Sewing, burl walnut Vict, mirrored top, 1870s, 30x22x16" **400.00**
Sewing, mahog Fed style w/inlay, demilune lift lid, 19th C **200.00**

Shaving, Am inlaid mahog, swell-front base w/2 drws, 19" **100.00**
Walnut Co, 2 dvtl drws, 1-brd top, trn legs, rfn, 29x19x20" **385.00**
Walnut Co Hplwht, mortised/pinned apron, 3-brd top, 20" sq ...**250.00**
Work, mahog Sheraton, 2-drw, brass paw ft, 1850s, 33x22x18" .**550.00**

Stools

Footstool, Hubbard & Eldridge, Mission oak, cushion top, 20" ..**475.00**
Footstool, Limbert #225, tacked leather, 1 drw, 18" L **1,100.00**
Footstool, poplar, orig blk pnt w/dots & dogs, 13" hexagon **150.00**
Footstool, Windsor, splayed & bamboo trn legs, uphl, 13" L **75.00**
Gout, mahog Regency, adjustable, brass castors, uphl **330.00**
Old Hickory, att; twig built, woven top, no mk, 18" **250.00**
Piano, mahog, shaped crest, cvd/pierced, uphl, 1840s **600.00**
Piano, Vict, needlepoint seat, cabriole legs, 1870s, EX **385.00**
QA style, velvet uphl seat, cvd legs, late 1800s **350.00**
W&M style, uphl seat, 4 red/gilt legs, decor on stretcher **385.00**

Tables

Ash Co Hplwht w/red, 1-drw/breadbrd top/stores leaves, 48" **935.00**
Banquet, cherry Hplwyt style w/inlay, 2-section, open: 104" ...**1,425.00**
Banquet, cherry/walnut Sheraton style w/figured vnr, open: 145" ..**990.00**
Breakfast, Am mahog, reeded hinged top, ped base/4 brass ft **935.00**
Card, cherry Emp w/mahog flame vnr, lyre ped, open: 35x36" ...**300.00**
Card, Euro style w/figured vnr & ebonized trim, folding, repro ...**275.00**
Card, mahog Hplwht style w/inlay, modern repro, 30x36x18" ..**415.00**
Card, mahog Hplwht w/inlay, ovolo decor apron, swing leg **1,980.00**
Card, Old Hickory, grooved oak top, 4 twig legs, mk, EX **450.00**
Corner drop leaf, mahog English QA, triangular apron, 35" sq ...**770.00**
Dining, curly maple Co Sheraton, dvtl drw, 2-brd, 29x24x33" ..**2,500.00**
Dining, mahog Chpndl-Hplwht transitional Pembroke, 35"+leaves **650.00**
Dining, mahog Hplwht w/inlay, serpentine apron (VG), 31x42x20" ..**1,500.00**
Dressing, Biedermeier Hplwht-style curly/burl maple, 2-drw **300.00**
Dressing, butternut/poplar Sheraton, pnt decor, mirror, 58x38" ...**4,800.00**
Dressing, cherry Sheraton w/vnr, much cvg, 3-drw, 43" **2,300.00**
Drop leaf, birch Co Chpndl butterfly gate-leg, 42"+leaves **770.00**
Drop leaf, birch Sheraton, orig red varnish, 36"+leaves **550.00**
Drop leaf, birch/curly birch Co Sheraton, 42"+leaves **440.00**
Drop leaf, cherry Co, swing legs, rpl drw/top, 38"+2 leaves **165.00**
Drop leaf, cherry Co Sheraton, 6-leg, rfn/rpl, 44"+leaves **330.00**
Drop leaf, cherry w/old rfn, 6 trn legs, 46"+2 leaves **330.00**
Drop leaf, cherry/birch Co QA, swing legs, rfn, 37"+leaves **1,485.00**
Drop leaf, mahog Emp, ped w/acanthus knees/paw ft, 39"+leaves **770.00**
Drop leaf, mahog Hplwht Pembroke w/inlay, 1-drw, 32"+leaves ...**635.00**
Drop leaf, mahog Hplwht style w/inlay, repro, 25"+leaves **300.00**
Drop leaf, maple Co Chpndl, worn red, swing leg, 45"+leaves ...**990.00**
Drop leaf, walnut Chpndl swing leg, rpr, 47+17" leaves **1,650.00**
Drop leaf, walnut QA swing, cabriole legs, rstr, 42"+2 leaves ..**3,400.00**
Golden Oak era, trn/reeded legs, oversz c&b ft, 28" sq **465.00**
Hutch, pine Co, hinged lid in base, 3-brd top, 45" **1,320.00**
Library, Limbert, #1141, corbels on legs, 2-drw, V apron, mk .**2,600.00**
Library, Limbert, #120, 4 slat legs w/spade cutouts, 45" dia **4,750.00**
Library, Limbert, 1-drw over kneehole, shelves to side, rfn **1,000.00**
Library, mahog Emp style, hairy paw ft, rfn/rstr, 48" **535.00**
Library, walnut, 2-drw, vinyl insert in top, rfn/rstr, 48" **250.00**
Library table/desk, cherry, 3-drw, apron, 1900s, 39x42x28" **220.00**
Limbert, shelf:base w/2 cutouts ea side, V aprons, 34x30" sq ..**15,000.00**
Mahog Regency style, ped w/4 splayed legs, Baker, 29x96x46" ...**475.00**
Refectory, oak, 6-leg, cvd apron, 3-brd, scrubbed, 123" **2,200.00**
Sawbuck, pine Co, old gr rpt over red, 2-brd top, 37x27" **1,100.00**
Sawbuck, pine Co, weathered gray, sq nails, 2-brd top, 66" **600.00**
Server, Limbert #445, 1-drw, bk splash, curved apron, 33" **900.00**
Shop of the Crafters, floral inlay in slab legs, 36" dia, G **1,600.00**

Side, Limbert #101, octagonal 20" top, wide cut-out legs **800.00**
Tall ped, mahog w/line inlay on column, 1900s, 59x11½" dia ...**385.00**
Tap, grpt pine, rectangular, sq legs, molded edge, 1820s **920.00**
Tavern, maple Co QA, dk red stain, oval top, rprs, 27x30x22" **2,300.00**
Tavern, maple/ash Co QA w/pine top, trn legs, mortised/pinned ..**1,100.00**
Tavern, QA, mixed hard & soft woods, damage/rprs, 44" **1,950.00**
Tavern, walnut, plank top w/drw, rnd legs, ball ft **5,500.00**
Tea, Lifetime, 18" rnd top, sm rnd shelf, 24", VG **850.00**
Tea, mahog Emp influence, birdcage, 1-brd tilt-top, 36" dia **450.00**
Tea, New England QA, cherry tilt-top, tripod base, 34" dia **4,400.00**
Tea, pine QA w/dk stain w/red grpt, 1-brd top, RI, 26x33x22" ..**4,125.00**
Tea, walnut Chpndl, cvd fr/trn column/2-brd tilt-top, 38" **5,600.00**
Tea cart, mahog, drop leaf, 1 drw, 1900s, 30x35x17"+leaves **110.00**
Tilt top, birch Co Hplwht, 2-brd top, tripod base, 39x31x23" **95.00**
Tilt top, papier-mache w/nacre inlay, trn ped, 27x28x23" **220.00**
Trestle, oak, plank top, pierced terminal supports, 78" **2,100.00**
Work, poplar Co Hplwht, sq legs, 2-brd top, 29x29x39" **500.00**
Work, poplar/hardwood Co Hplwht, dvtl drw, 2-brd top, 39" **525.00**
Work, rfn walnut w/inlay on drws, apron, 3-brd top, PA, 53" **2,500.00**

Wardrobes

Cherry Co, break-down case, 2 panel do, 2-section int, 78" **990.00**
Cherry/curly cherry, panel do:2 dvtl drw, OH, 80x47x25" **4,290.00**
Fruitwood Louis XV Provincial, 2-do, 1890s, 89x56" **2,750.00**
Kas, pine, orig rose-mulled decor & brn grpt, 1806, 62x44" **1,100.00**
Kas, pine w/mc sponging on bl, red moldings, 72x50" **990.00**
Kas, poplar w/orig brn grpt & blk trim, OH, 72x48" **4,950.00**
Mahog English campaign, flush brass hdw, breaks down, 75x58" ..**1,700.00**
Walnut Co, 1-brd ends/base/moldings, raised panels, 73x48" ..**1,100.00**
Walnut w/cvd pine capitals, panel do, rfn, 63x33" **1,155.00**

Washstands

Sheraton galleried pine, scalloped back splash and eared arms, single drawer, lower shelf, American, ca 1820, 37x25x17", $500.00.

Bird's-eye maple/pine Co Sheraton, 1-drw, 1-brd top, rfn, 30" ...**220.00**
Corner, Co, medial shelf w/drw, gallery top, sq legs **300.00**
Corner, mahog English Hplwht, dvtl drw, shelf, 34x24" **935.00**
Corner, mahog Fed style, medial shelf w/drw, curved legs **200.00**
Maple/cherry Fed academy work pnt (scenes), ca 1800, 36x17x16" ..**1,250.00**
Walnut Vict w/panel do, 1-drw, shelf on bk splash, 31"+crest **385.00**

Miscellaneous

Cellaret, Fed mahog w/inlay, false drw, 1800s, 31x32x18" **3,300.00**
Chiffonier, bird's-eye maple w/serpentine front, 6-drw, mirror ...**350.00**
Coat rack, oak, quarter-sewn figure w/cvd crest, mirror, 25x25" .**220.00**
Costumer, oak, dbl-pole w/iron hooks, Arts & Crafts, 72x24" **700.00**
Library steps, mahog Regency-style, English, 22x15x19" **700.00**
Linen press, Hplwht mahog, 3-part w/fitted int, bracket ft **2,750.00**

Linen press, mahog Geo III w/inlay, 2-pc, 18th C, 74x48" **3,300.00**
Linen press, mahog Georgian style, 2 panel do, 83x49x26" **3,300.00**
Linen press, oak English QA, pegged, 2-pc, 1750s, 72x44", VG .**750.00**
Linen press, pine Co Chpndl, dbl do:5 drw, 2-pc, 75x50" **2,750.00**
Pedestal, Limbert, Ebon-Oak, X-base w/heavy corbels & inlay ..**2,300.00**
Screen, hardwood Co pole type, tripod base, snake ft, 54" **660.00**
Screen, Regency rosewood & brass pole, needlework screen **770.00**
Spice rack, hardwood, drw labels/porc pulls/wire nails, 35x10" ...**275.00**
Tea cart, mahog, folding, Am, 20th C **90.00**

Galle

Emile Galle was one of the most important producers of cameo glass in France. His firm, founded in Nancy in 1874, produced beautiful cameo in the Art Nouveau style during the 1890s, using a variety of techniques. He also produced glassware with enameled decoration, as well as some fine pottery — animal figurines, table services, vases, and other objets d' art. In the mid-1880s he became interested in the various colors and textures of natural woods and as a result began to create furniture which he used as yet another medium for expression of his artistic talent. Marquetry was the primary method Galle used in decorating his furniture, preferring landscapes, Nouveau floral and fruit arrangements, butterflies, squirrels, and other forms from nature. It is for his furniture and his cameo glass that he is best known today. All Galle is signed.

In the listings below, 'fp' indicates items that have been fire polished. Our advisor for this category is Don Williams; he is listed in the Directory under Missouri.

Cameo

Atomizer, floral/lg leaves, caramel/coral on ivory, 10" **600.00**
Bottle, floral vines, caramel/coral on yel, w/stopper, 6" **750.00**
Bottle, lay-down; daisies w/gold stems pnt on citron, 5½" **1,400.00**
Bowl, maple leaves/pods, med/lt gr on peach, 4 rim points, 7½" .**1,100.00**
Box, berries/butterfly on yel frost, 4-panel peaked lid, 8" L **5,000.00**
Jar, floral, caramel/coral on yel, w/lid, 3½x3½" **650.00**
Lamp, boudoir; floral, red on yel w/bl & gr streaks, 10" **6,000.00**
Lamp, hibiscus on pk/magenta shade & base, brass arms, 12" ..**6,800.00**
Lamp, hydrangeas, conical 11" shade/tapered ftd base, 23" ...**10,000.00**
Lamp base, berry pods/vines, orange on yel frost, 8½" **600.00**
Lamp base, irises/foliage, amethyst on wht frost, 17½" **1,500.00**
Shade, ceiling; pine needles, brn on pastel frost, 20" dia **5,000.00**
Shot glass, seed pods/leaves, 2-tone gr on apricot, 2½" **550.00**
Vase, apple blossoms, red/citron, slim ovoid w/wide rim, 8" **1,025.00**
Vase, azaleas, wine on citron, tapered/ftd, 8" **1,400.00**
Vase, berry clusters, orange on citron, fp, banjo form, 7" **900.00**
Vase, clematis, lilac on gold-gray, banjo form, 5½" **575.00**
Vase, clematis, purple on butterscotch, everted rim, 10⅞" **6,900.00**
Vase, clematis vines, lav-bl on frost, bottle shape, 7¾" **1,250.00**
Vase, daffodils, distant trees, fp, ftd/tapered, 10½" **1,200.00**
Vase, fern fronds, med/lt gr on yel/frost, ftd/slim, 27½" **3,750.00**
Vase, floral, amber on pk/citron, stick neck, 4½" **525.00**
Vase, floral, lav on pk/violet, wht hdls, 5½x5" **1,100.00**
Vase, floral, lav/gr on pk/wht, cylinder w/wide base, 10" **700.00**
Vase, floral, lime gr on frost w/pk splashes, long neck, 12" **2,500.00**
Vase, floral, olive gr-beige to yel-orange, 16" **2,100.00**
Vase, floral, orange on frost, long cylindrical neck, 24" **3,750.00**
Vase, floral, purple on peach/purple, rnd w/long neck, 12" **2,500.00**
Vase, floral, red on frost, cylindrical neck w/hdls, 8" **3,450.00**
Vase, grapes, red-amber on opal/amber, fp, stick neck, 8½" **900.00**
Vase, grapes/vines, tan/dk brn on rose/gray, 12" **1,100.00**
Vase, leaves, brn on yel, slim ovoid, 4" **600.00**

Vase, lilies/pads, salmon on lt gr, fp, incurvate/slim, 22" **4,600.00**
Vase, lily plant, med/dk purple on lt purple mottle, 9" **2,000.00**
Vase, lotus, orange on almond/orange, fp, egg form, lid, 6" **1,500.00**
Vase, nasturtiums/pods, orange on frost, ribbed, 3¾" **350.00**
Vase, pine cones, brn on frost, long cylinder neck, 23¼" **2,875.00**
Vase, poppies, orange on wht frost, cylindrical, 17⅜" **2,300.00**
Vase, roses, amber/brn on yel, slim/ftd, 13" **3,000.00**
Vase, thistles, gr on peach frost, star mk, 5x5" **600.00**
Vase, trees, tan on peach/frost, 7" **1,000.00**
Vase, trees/man on bridge, brn on ivory to cream, slim, 19" **4,000.00**
Vase, trees/man on bridge, violet/brn on yel/gr, 10½" **1,800.00**
Vase, trees/river bank, violet/brn/gr/tan on wht frost, 8" **1,600.00**
Vase, trees/shrubs/lake, dk brn/tan/lt gr/gray, slim, 7" **2,200.00**
Vase, trumpet flowers, bl/lav on citron frost, sqd, 11½" **6,600.00**

Vase, wind-blown tulips and leaves, purple to lavender on amber to orange with internal multicolor decoration, 3-petal flower-form top, signed, 12", $13,000.00.

Vase, warrior/horse reserve on leaf-cvd ground, 5x5" **500.00**
Vase, water lilies, amber in bl water on ivory/bl, 11x3" **1,800.00**
Vase, water lilies/etc, butterscotch on wht, stick neck, 6⅝" **1,500.00**
Vase, wisteria, lav/gr on pk frost, rnd/flat sided, 3" **600.00**
Vase, wisteria, purple on wht to yel, cylindrical, 17½" **2,875.00**

Enameled Glass

Bowl, floral, mc/gold on gray, irregular rim, 4¾x8" **690.00**
Carafe, spade devices, blk on topaz, twist hdl, 6¼" **865.00**
Cordial, thistles on amber cup & stem, 3½" **425.00**
Decanter, lg floral spray, mc/gilt on ribbed amber, 7" **2,300.00**
Ewer, poppy pods/ferns/dragonfly on lt amber, gilt, 7", EX ...**1,150.00**
Flask, winged griffin/crown on ribbed bl, 6x4" **2,185.00**
Tray, fleur-de-lis plumes, red/blk/wht on topaz, 5¾" **635.00**
Tumbler, fleur-de-lis, wht on amber, ribbed, 5" **350.00**
Tumbler, vignette, mc on clear ribbed body, 4½" **300.00**
Vase, field flowers on topaz, ruffled U-form, 5" **1,200.00**
Vase, nasturtiums, mc on amber frost, hexagonal, 10" **1,950.00**
Vase, tiger lilies, mc w/gold, lobed cylinder, 12¾" **1,600.00**

Marquetry, Wood

Music stand, gladiolas, scalloped top+2 tiers, rtcl notes, 34" ...**2,000.00**
Stand, shaped 16x16" top/2nd tier w/inlay, thin arched legs ...**2,400.00**
Table, daffodils, 14" sq top on 2 curved 3-part legs **2,400.00**
Table, 2-tier, daffodils/grasses, scrolling legs, 32x36" **4,600.00**
Table a ecriere, foliage in inlaid int, inlaid drw, 31x21" **5,000.00**
Vitrine, flowers: top/side/front panel, glass door, 53x24" **9,000.00**
Waste basket, flowerheads/foliage, early 1900s, 51x35" **2,530.00**

Pottery

Centerpiece, dbl swan form, bl-gray w/red, mk, 14½" L **925.00**

Centerpiece bowl, 3 geese with intertwined necks, multicolor with butterflies, grasses, and flowers, G Depose, 15x6½", $2,000.00.

Flagon, man's portrait, lid w/3-D cherries, rope hdl, 13" 1,200.00
Jar, molded as bag tied w/2 pk bows, birds atop, #113, 11x7" ..1,100.00
Pitcher, 2 men on bench, 3rd w/bagpipes on bronze C-shape, 8" .1,500.00
Plate, floral/insects/inscription on wht, laced rim, 9", pr 935.00
Tray, bachelor buttons emb/pnt on wht, 3x6" 200.00
Vase, lighthouse scene, bl/wht, faience, teardrop, 16" 1,100.00
Vase, man's portrait, pillow form w/dbl ring hdls, sgn, 12" 1,600.00
Wall pocket, ribbons/pine cones/bows/grasshoppers/etc, mk, 10" ..900.00

Gambling Memorabilia

Gambling memorabilia from the infamous casinos of the West and items that were once used on the 'Floating Palace' riverboats are especially sought after by today's collectors.

Book, Handbook for Bicycle...Cards, Robinson, 1955, 48-pg, EX .80.00
Card shuffler/dealer, automatic, common, 1940s, 5x5x5" 20.00
Casino in Box, roulette, dice, blackjack, gun hideaway 2,500.00
Chip, Bakelite, US Anchor, 1½" dia, 100 in orig box 65.00
Chip, bone, plain, solid color, set of 100 ....35.00
Chip, bone, w/design or color border, 1mm thick, set of 100 ....75.00
Chip, clay, emb, inlaid, or eng, ea, from $1 to 7.00
Chip, clay or metal, w/casino name, minimum value 3.00
Chip, cvd ivory, initialed, EX 55.00
Chip, dealer; clay w/goat head in relief, ea 50.00
Chip, MOP, eng, oval 20.00
Chip, plastic, wood or rubber, no design, set of 100 ....5.00
Chip rack, wood chest w/lid & pull-out rack, no chips, minimum ...70.00
Chip rack, wood lazy susan (carousel) type, w/lid, no chips 10.00
Dice, ivory, ⅝", pr 80.00
Dice, red Lucite, 2", pr, EXIB 125.00
Dice cage, chuck-a-luck, 10", w/dice & rack, VG 80.00
Dice cage, hide drums, heavy chrome, 9x14" 300.00
Dice cup, ivory 100.00
Dice cup, leather, w/5 celluloid die 55.00
Gambling marker, eng MOP 10.00
Keno goose, polished walnut bowl between posts, 13x24" 750.00
Playing cards, faro; poker sq w/sq edges, set of 52, minimum 60.00
Punch board, Best Hand, 240 punches, 7½x10½", M 35.00
Table, black jack; casino style, felt top, 1930s, rstr 2,000.00
Table, crap; casino style, felt layout, ca 1930, VG rstr 3,500.00
Wheel, roulette; w/felt-top table w/brass banding, VG 600.00
Wheel, roulette; wood, table-top type, 21" dia, EX 900.00

Game Calls

Those interested in hunting and fishing collectibles are beginning to take notice of the finer specimens of game calls available on today's market. Our advisor for this category is Randy Hilst; he is listed in the Directory under Illinois.

Faulks WA-33A, duck call 20.00
Herter's Predator 20.00
Lindsey Pied Piper Predator 25.00
Oliveros Duc-Em 75.00
Pull-Em, crow 50.00
Weems Wild Call 20.00

Gameboards

Gameboards, the handmade ones from the 18th and 19th century, are collected more for their folk art quality than their relation to games. Excellent examples of these handcrafted 'playthings' sell well into the thousands of dollars; even the simple designs are often expensive. If you are interested in this field, you must study it carefully. The market is always full of 'new' examples. Well-established dealers are often your best sources; they are essential if you do not have the expertise to judge the age of the boards yourself. Our advisor for this category is Louis Picek; he is listed in the Directory under Iowa.

Checkers, cherry & walnut w/inlay, compartments, 13" sq 275.00
Checkers, pine w/cream/tan pnt, 3-brd, 19½x25¾" 250.00
Checkers, pine w/old mustard & blk pnt, 15x20" 400.00
Checkers, pine w/olive-gold & blk pnt, 18½x30¾" 275.00
Checkers, pine w/red & blk pnt, appl gallery, 13x16" 330.00
Checkers, plywood w/appl gallery, blk pnt/varnish, 19x30" 100.00
Checkers, rvpt w/oak fr border, 20" sq 225.00
Checkers, softwood w/orig blk & wht pnt, 12" sq 230.00
Checkers, walnut w/dk gr & blk pnt sqs, ca 1900, 32" L 185.00
Checkers, walnut w/ebony/maple inlay, 8¼" sq, +sm chess pcs 35.00
Fox & Geese, maple, 33 holes w/clay marbles, 7¾" dia, EX 110.00
Italian specimen marble, circular, 1830s, 27" 2,200.00

Games

Collectors of antique games are finding it more difficult to find their treasures at shows and flea markets. Most of the action these days seems to be through specialty dealers and auctions. The appreciation of the art on the boards and boxes continues to grow. You see many of the early games proudly displayed as art, and they should be. The period from the 1850s to 1910 continues to draw the most interest. Many of the games of that period were executed by well-known artists and illustrators. The quality of their lithography cannot be matched today. The historical value of games made before 1850 has caused interest in this period to increase. While they may not have the graphic quality of the later period, their insights into the social and moral character of the early 19th century are interesting.

20th-century games invoke a nostalgic feeling among collectors who recall looking forward to a game under the Christmas tree each year. They search for examples that bring back those Christmas-morning memories. While the quality of their lithography is certainly less than the early games, the introduction of personalities from the comic strips, radio, and later TV created new interest. Every child wanted a game that featured their favorite character. Monopoly, probably the most famous game ever produced, was introduced during the Great Depression.

For further information, we recommend *Schroeder's Collectible Toys, Antique to Modern*, available from Collector Books. Our advisor for personality-related games in Norm Vigue; he is listed in the Directory under Massachusetts.

Aerial Contest, JW Spear & Sons, early 1900s, EX in G cb box ...**145.00**
Aerial Contest Up-to-Date Game, 3-fold board, Spear, EX in box ..**2,860.00**
Aggravation Deluxe, Lakeside, 1982, EX in box **22.00**
Air Race Around the World, Lido, 1950s, EX in box **22.50**
All Star Baseball, Cadaco, #183, 1962, MIB **75.00**
All the King's Men, Parker Bros, 1979, EX in box **30.00**
Amazing Dunninger Mind Reading, Hasbro, 1967, NMIB **25.00**
Assembly Line, Selchow, MIB **45.00**
Automobile Race, wood pcs, LH Mace, ca 1905, EX in VG box ...**635.00**
Baseball, McLoughlin Bros, board game, 1886, litho box, EX .**1,600.00**
Baseball & Checkers, Milton Bradley, 1900, EX in cb litho box ..**230.00**
Bermuda Triangle, Milton Bradley, 1976, EX in box **37.50**
Black Cat Fortune Telling, Parker Bros, 1930s, NMIB **22.50**
Bowl & Score, ES Lowe, 1974, VG in box **22.50**
Boy Scouts Progress, Parker Bros, 1924, EX in box **220.00**
Canoga, casino type, 1972, M **25.00**
Checkered Game of Life, Bradley, ca 1911, EX in box **220.00**
Chopper Strike, Milton Bradley, 1976, EX in box **37.50**
Clue, Parker Bros, 1972, EX **12.00**
Clue the Great Detective Game, Parker Bros, 1949, EX in box **30.00**
Commercial Crazies, Mattel, 1986, EX in box **35.00**
Cowboy Round Up, Parker Bros, 1953, M **33.00**
Cross Country Race by Land..., Chicago, 1911, EX in box **575.00**
Dollars & Sense, Better Games, 1980, EX in box **25.00**
Eastern Front Solitaire, Omega Games, 1986, EX in box **25.00**
Errand Boy-An Amusing Game, McLoughlin, 1891, NMIB **300.00**
Finance, Parker Bros, 1962, EX **30.00**
Flinch, Parker Bros, 1934, M **25.00**
Funny Bones, Parker Bros, 1968, EX in box **30.00**
Gambler, Parker Bros, 1977, EX **25.00**
Game of Bagatelle, McLoughlin, 1890, NMIB **580.00**
Game of Bicycle Race, McLoughlin, EX in box **495.00**
Game of Christmas Jewel, McLoughlin, 1899, EX in box **660.00**
Game of District Messenger Boy, McLoughlin, 1886, VG in box .**250.00**
Game of Fish Pond (boat), McLoughlin, 1890, EX in boat **200.00**
Game of Hare & Hounds, McLoughlin, 1891, EX in box **550.00**
Game of Magnetic Fish Pond, McLoughlin, 1891, EX in box **385.00**
Game of Mother Goose's Xmas Party, McLoughlin, 1898, VG in box ..**470.00**
Game of Red Riding Hood Adventure..., Parker Bros, EX in box .**470.00**
Game of Stubborn Pig, Bradley, EX w/partial box **210.00**
Game of Tobogganing at Christmas, McLoughlin, 1899, G in box ...**1,650.00**
Game of Uncle Sam's Mail, McLoughlin, NMIB **580.00**
Gingerbread Man, Selchow & Righter, 1964, EX in box **30.00**
Gladiator, Avalon Hill, 1981, M **27.00**
Go to the Head of the Class, Milton Bradley, 1986, EX **22.00**
Grand Bicycle Race Game, 4-fold board, EX in box **415.00**
Hangman, Milton Bradley, 1976, EX **25.00**
Hold the Fort, Parker Bros, 1895, G in box **200.00**
How To Succeed in Business..., M Bradley, 1967, MIB **25.00**
India-An Oriental Game, McLoughlin, 1895, EX in box **75.00**
Junior Bicycle Game, Parker Bros, 1897, EX in box **185.00**
Junior Executive, Whitman, 1955, EX in box **30.00**
Junk Yard Game, Ideal, 1975, EX in box **35.00**
Li'l Stinker, cards, Schaper, 1946, NMIB **18.00**
Life, Milton Bradley, 1985, EX **25.00**
Little Am-Admiral Byrd's S Pole Game, Parker Bros, EX in box ..**580.00**
Little Cowboy Game, Parker Bros, VG in box **440.00**
Little Red Riding Hood, McLoughlin, 1900, EX in box **550.00**
Luftwaffe, Avalon Hill, 1971, M in VG box **23.00**
Mail Express & Accomodation, McLoughlin, 1895, EX in box ..**525.00**
Mansion of Happiness, McLoughlin, 1895, VG in box **415.00**
Masterpiece, Parker Bros, 1970, EX **45.00**
Merry Hunt, Singer, EX in box **415.00**
Merry-Go-Round Game, Whitman, 1965, EX in box **25.00**

Mid-Life Crisis, Game Works, 1982, EX in box **25.00**
New Pilgrim's Progress, McLoughlin, 1893, VG in box **245.00**
Office Boy Good Old Game, Parker Bros, 1889, VG in box **230.00**
Option, Parker Bros, 1983, EX in box **30.00**
Owl & Pussy Cat Game, Edgar Clark Tokalon Series, VG in box ...**400.00**
Payday, Parker Bros, 1976, VG in box **27.50**

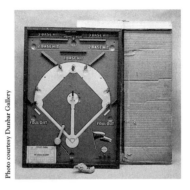

Pennant Winner, Wolverine, 25x18", NM $665.00.

Phalanx Game of Strategy, war game, Whitman, 1964, NMIB **25.00**
Pin Tail on Donkey, Milton Bradley, folder dtd 1932 ....**30.00**
Pit, Parker Bros, 1904, M in long box **18.00**
Playing Department Store, Bradley, McLoughlin image on cover, VG .**330.00**
Race for Presidency, cards & board, WS Reed, 1889, EX **260.00**
Rack-O, Milton Bradley, 1961, VG **15.00**
Rich Uncle, Parker Bros, 1962, VG in box **35.00**
Ripley's Believe It or Not, Whitman, 1979, M **35.00**
Risk, Parker Bros, 1965, EX **25.00**
Rook, Parker Bros, 1934, EX **15.00**
Rook, Parker Bros, 1957, EX in VG box **24.00**
Scan, Parker Bros, 1970, EX in box **27.50**
Scotland Yard, Milton Bradley, 1985, M **35.00**
Scrabble, Selchow & Righter, 1976, NM **25.00**
Seige, hand puppet knights & plastic castle board, 1966, NM **30.00**
Sorry!, Parker Bros, 1964, VG in box **30.00**
Spill & Spell, Parker Bros, 1971, EX **22.00**
Star Reporter, board game, Parker Bros, 1954, EX in box **50.00**
Sting, Ideal, 1976, EX **40.00**
Susceptibles-Parlor Amusement, McLoughlin, 1891, VG in box ..**360.00**
Thinking Man's Football, 3M, 1973, EX **35.00**
Tiddley Winks, Transogram, 1939, EX in VG box **24.00**
Video Village, Milton Bradley, 1960, EX **25.00**
Wonderful Game of Oz, Parker Bros, 1922, VG **210.00**
Yacht Race, cb sailboats/etc, McLoughlin, 1887, VG in box **470.00**
Yankee Doodle Game of Am History, Parker Bros, 1895, VG in box ...**220.00**

Personalities, Movies, and TV Shows

All in the Family, cards, Milton Bradley, 1972, VG in EX box **12.00**
Annie, Parker Bros, 1981, EX **15.00**
Annie Oakley, board game, Milton Bradley, 1955, NMIB **45.00**
Barbie Queen of the Prom, 1960, EX **45.00**
Batman, board game, Hasbro, 1973, NMIB, scarce **65.00**
Batman, board game, Milton Bradley, 1966, NMIB **75.00**
Battlestar Galactica, board game, Parker Bros, 1978, EX **15.00**
Black Beauty, Transogram, 1958, NM in G box **25.00**
Blondie, board game, Parker Bros, 1969, EX in box **25.00**
Close Encounters, Parker Bros, 1978, EX **15.00**
Columbo Detective, Milton Bradley, 1973, EX in box **15.00**
Dark Shadows Mysterious Maze, 1968, NMIB **65.00**

Dear Abby, Ideal, 1972, nearly complete, EX in box 22.00
Dick Tracy, Mystery Card Game, Whitman, 1941, NM 45.00
Dick Tracy Detective, Whitman, 1937, NMIB 95.00
Donald Duck's Party Game for Young Folks, Parker Bros, 1938, EX .150.00
Dragnet Badge 714 Puzzle Game, Transogram, 1955, NMIB 28.00
Drew Pearson's Predict-A-Word, 1949, EX in 6x8" box 17.50
Eddie Cantor's Tell It to the Judge, Parker Bros, 1930s, NMIB 45.00
Electronic Batman, Lisbeth-Whiting, 1966, EX 70.00
Elsie the Cow, Selchow & Righter, 1941, NMIB 145.00
Family Feud, Milton Bradley, 1985, M 10.00
Felix the Cat, board game, Milton Bradley, 2nd ed, 1968, NMIB .45.00
Felix the Cat's Dandy Candy, Built-Rite, 1947, NMIB 65.00

Flintstones Stone Age Game, board game, Transogram, color litho box, 17½" long, EX, $60.00.

Flintstones' Big Game Hunt, Whitman, 1962, NMIB 90.00
Flintstones Break Ball Game of Skill, Whitman, 1962, MIB 90.00
Flying Nun, board game, Milton Bradley, 1968, NMIB 35.00
Garfield, Parker Bros, 1981, M in EX box 12.00
GI Joe Adventure Board, Hasbro, 1982, NM in torn box 10.00
Gomer Pyle, board game, Transogram, 1966, NMIB 48.00
Hardy Boys Mystery, Parker Bros, 1978, EX 25.00
Huckleberry Hound Bumps, Transogram, 1961, NMIB 45.00
Jetson's, Milton Bradley, 1985, EX 10.00
Jonny Quest, cards, Milton Bradley, 1964, NMIB 70.00
Laurel & Hardy...Monkey Business, Transogram, 1962, VG in box ...35.00
Laverne & Shirley, Making Your Dreams Come True, 1977, M ...15.00
Legend of the Lone Ranger, Milton Bradley, 1980, EX 15.00
Linus the Lionheart Critter card game, EX in box 22.50
Lippy the Lion Flips Game, Transogram, 1962, NMIB 75.00
MAD's Spy Vs Spy, board game, Milton Bradley, 1986, NMIB 12.00
Man From UNCLE, board game, Ideal, 1965, NMIB 50.00
Man From UNCLE, playing cards, 1965, M on card (sealed) 40.00
Mandrake the Magician, board game, Transogram, 1966, NMIB .45.00
Mr T, card game, Milton Bradley, 1983, M 10.00
Peter Rabbit's Race Game, tin litho, F Warne & Co, EX in box ...245.00
Quick Draw McGraw, card game, Ed-U, 1961, NMIB 12.00
Quick Draw McGraw Private Eye, Milton Bradley, 1960, NMIB 55.00
Rifleman, board game, Milton Bradley, 1955, NMIB 45.00
Six Million Dollar Man, Parker, 1975, NM 25.00
Snow White & the Seven Dwarfs, Cadaco, 1977, MIB (sealed) ...20.00
Starsky & Hutch Detective, board game, M Bradley, 1977, MIB (sealed) ...25.00
Steve Canyon Air Force, Lowell, 1950s, NMIB 65.00
Superboy, board game, Hasbro, 1965, NMIB 115.00
That Girl, board game, Remco, 1968, NMIB 170.00
Tom & Jerry Game, Milton Bradley, 1977, EX in box 12.00
Walton's, board game, Milton Bradley, 1974, MIB (sealed) 28.00
Wild Bill Hickok Cavalry & Indians, Built-Rite, 1956, NMIB 42.00

G. A. R. Memorabilia

The 'The Grand Army of the Republic' was first conceived by Chaplain W.J. Rutledge and Major B.J. Stephenson early in 1864 when they were tent-mates during our own Civil War. These men vowed to each other that if they were spared they would establish an organization that would preserve friendships and memories formed during this time. Shortly after the war ended, Rutledge and Stephenson made their desires a reality. The first National Convention of the Grand Army of the Republic was held in Indianapolis, Indiana, on November 20, 1866. The purpose of the organization was to provide aid and assistance to the widows and orphans of the fallen Union dead and to care for the hospitalized veterans as needed. The last comrade of the G.A.R. died in 1949.

Many items are surfacing from the early encampments which were held on both state and national levels, which resulted in a wide variety of souvenir items having been made.

Badge, hat; gold-tone on brass wreath w/silver GAR, 2½" 65.00
Booklet, Women's Relief Corp rules, 1889 ....15.00
Canteen, ceramic, Stanton on obverse, 1891 ....110.00
Canteen, molded stoneware, 26th Annual...IA, 1900, 3¾" 245.00
Cup, tin, red, wht & bl enameling, 1908 ....95.00
Hat badge, gold-tone shell wreath silver-tone initials, 2¼" 55.00
Sword, model 1860, GAR eng 195.00
Watch fob, SP canteen form w/symbols, dtd 1861-65 ....110.00

Gas Globes and Panels

Gas globes and panels, once a common sight, have vanished from the countryside but are being sought by collectors as a unique form of advertising memorabilia. Early globes from the 1920s (some date back to as early as 1912), now referred to as 'one-piece globes,' were made of molded milk glass and were globular in shape. The gas company name was etched or painted on the glass. Few of these were ever produced, and this type is valued very highly by collectors today.

A new type of pump was introduced in the early 1930s; the old 'visible' pumps were replaced by 'electric' models. Globes were changing at the same time. By the mid-teens a three-piece globe consisting of a pair of inserts and a metal body was being produced in both 15" and 16½" sizes. Collectors prefer to call globes that are not one-piece or plastic 'three-piece glass' (Type 2) or 'metal body, glass inserts' (Type 3). Though metal-body globes (Type 3) were popular in the 1930s, they were common in the 1920s, and some were actually made as early as 1915. Though rare in numbers, their use spans many years. In the 1930s Type 2 and Type 3 globes became the replacements of the one-piece globe. The most recently manufactured gas globes are made with a plastic body that contains two 13½" glass lenses. These were common in the fifties but were actually used as early as 1932.

Note: Standard Crowns with raised letters are one-piece globes that were made in the 1920s; those made in the 1950s (no raised letters), though one-piece, are not regarded as such by today's collectors. Both variations are listed below. Our advisor for this category is Scott Benjamin; he is listed in the Directory under Ohio.

Type 1, Plastic Body, Glass Inserts (Inserts 13½") — 1931-1950s

Ashland Diesel 200.00
Dixie, plastic band 200.00
DX Ethyl 250.00
Falcon 850.00
Frontier Gas, Rarin' To Go, w/horse 450.00
Hornet, Capcolite body, 13½", NM 225.00
Kendall Polly Power, Capcolite body, 13½" dia, NM 225.00
Marathon, no runner 150.00
Marine, sea horse, EX color 550.00
Shamrock, oval body 250.00
Texaco Diesel Chief, Capcolite body, 13½", NM 650.00

Texaco Sky Chief 275.00
Viking, pictures Viking ship 650.00
66 Flite Fuel, Phillips, shield shape, all plastic 450.00

Type 2, Glass Frame, Glass Inserts (Inserts 13½") — 1926-1940s

Aerio, gr gill ripple body, 13½", NM 5,000.00
American, gill body, 12½", NM 375.00
Amoco, gill body, 13½", NM 375.00
Atlantic, glass body, 13½" dia, NM 325.00
Champlin Preston, 3-pc glass 400.00
Derby 375.00
Esso 325.00
Frontier Gas, Double Refined 325.00
Golden 97 Ethyl, hull glass body, 12½", NM 375.00
Guyler Brand, milk glass, EX 700.00
Indian Gas, Red Dot 600.00
Kanotex, w/sunflower, gill body 450.00
Koolmotor, clover shape 1,350.00
Mobil Gas 425.00
Pitman Streamlined, bl gill rippled body, 13½", NM 5,000.00
Red Crown, milk glass 350.00
Sinclair Dino, milk glass, EX 250.00
Skelly Anomarx w/Ethyl 450.00
Sky Chief, gill body, 13½", NM 400.00
Standard Crown, bl 650.00
Standard Crown, gr or orange, ea 900.00
Standard Flame 400.00
Texaco Diesel Chief 850.00
Texaco Star, blk outline on 'T' 400.00
White Flash, gill body 375.00

Type 3, Metal Frame, Glass Inserts (Inserts 15" or 16½") — 1915-1930s

Lubrite Sky-Hy, 15", $750.00.

Atlantic Ethyl, 16½" 600.00
Atlantic White Flash, 16½" 500.00
Cities Services Oils, 1929, 15" fr 500.00
Esso Extra, 15" 425.00
General Ethyl, 15" fr, complete 700.00
Kendal Gasoline, airplane, metal body, rare, 15", NM 5,000.00
Mobil Gas, winged horse, 15" or 16½" metal fr, NM 600.00
Mobilfuel Diesel, lg horse, high profile 800.00
Phillips Benzo, low profile metal body, 15", NM 3,500.00
Purol Gasoline, w/arrow, porc body 850.00
Purol Pep, porc body 750.00
Red Crown Ethyl 950.00
Rocor, w/eagle 650.00
Signal, old stoplight, 15", VG 3,800.00
Socony, milk glass inserts on metal 1,200.00
Sunland Ethyl, 15" 550.00
Tidex, 16½" 475.00

Tydol, 16½" 500.00
White Star, 15" fr, complete 850.00

Type 4, One-Piece Glass Globes, No Inserts, Co. Name Etched, Raised, or Enameled — 1912-1931

Atlantic, chimney cap 2,800.00
Diamond 850.00
Dixie, etched 1,600.00
Musgo 4,800.00
Pierce Pennant, etched 2,800.00
Republic, 3-sided 2,200.00
Shell, rnd, etched 750.00
Sinclair, etched, milk glass 1,100.00
Skelly 750.00
Super Shell, rnd, etched 3,500.00
Texaco, milk glass, emb letters, brass collar 1,200.00
That Good Gulf..., emb, orange & blk letters, EX 900.00
White Eagle, some feather detail, 20¾", EX 1,500.00
White Rose, boy pictured, pnt 2,800.00

Gaudy Dutch

Inspired by Oriental Imari wares, Gaudy Dutch was made in England from 1800 to 1820. It was hand decorated on a soft-paste body with rich underglaze blues accented in orange, red, pink, green, and yellow. It differs from Gaudy Welsh in that there is no lustre (except on Water Lily). There are seventeen patterns, some of which are: War Bonnet, Grape, Dahlia, Oyster, Urn, Butterfly, Carnation, Single Rose, Double Rose, and Water Lily. For further information we recommend *The Collector's Encyclopedia of Gaudy Dutch & Welsh* by John Shuman, available from Collector Books. Unless otherwise noted, values are given for items with minimal wear and no obvious damage.

Butterfly, coffeepot, 11" 4,000.00
Butterfly, cream pitcher 1,500.00
Butterfly, creamer 900.00
Butterfly, cup & saucer, butterfly on side 750.00
Butterfly, plate, 6⅜" 625.00
Butterfly variant, cup & saucer, NM 525.00
Carnation, cream pitcher, 4⅛" 800.00
Carnation, plate, deep, sm feather border, 10" 775.00
Carnation, plate, 7¼" 550.00
Carnation, sugar bowl 800.00
Dahlia, creamer 900.00
Dahlia, plate, 8" 800.00
Dahlia, sugar bowl 900.00
Double Rose, creamer 600.00
Double Rose, cup & saucer 525.00
Double Rose, cup plate 700.00
Double Rose, toddy plate, 4½" 750.00
Double Rose, waste bowl, 6" 625.00
Dove, plate, 6⅜" 500.00
Dove, sugar bowl, w/lid 500.00
Dove, teapot 850.00
Dove, toddy plate 700.00
Grape, cup & saucer, 4-color, 1830s, 2½", 5¾" 525.00
Grape, cup plate 600.00
Grape, plate, 6" 300.00
Grape, platter, 15" 900.00
Grape, soup plate, 8¾" 550.00
Grape, waste bowl 465.00
Leaf, tea bowl & saucer 800.00

Oyster, creamer 400.00
Oyster, cup & saucer 375.00
Oyster, plate, 5⅝" 385.00
Oyster, teapot 500.00
Primrose, plate, mk Riley, 8¾" 550.00
Primrose, tea bowl & saucer 700.00
Single Rose, coffeepot 725.00
Single Rose, cup plate 400.00
Single Rose, plate, 6¼" 425.00
Single Rose, plate, 7¼" 500.00
Single Rose, soup plate 375.00
Single Rose, waste bowl, 6⅛" 550.00
Strawflower, plate, mk Riley, 10" 1,900.00
Strawflower, plate, 9" 700.00
Strawflower, soup plate 800.00
Sunflower, plate, 7½" 675.00
Sunflower, sugar bowl, w/lid 600.00
Sunflower, tea bowl & saucer 800.00
Urn, cup & saucer, waisted cup, rpt/rpr 180.00
Urn, cup plate 425.00
Urn, plate, 4-color, 1820s, 7½", VG 750.00
Urn, soup plate, 8⅞" 500.00
Urn, waste bowl, 5½" 825.00
War Bonnet, cup & saucer, 1830s, 2½", 5½", EX 750.00
War Bonnet, plate, shallow, 8⅛" 875.00
War Bonnet, plate, 8¼", NM 825.00
War Bonnet, sugar bowl, w/lid 850.00
War Bonnet, teapot, oval w/arched hdl, scroll finial, EX 525.00
War Bonnet, toddy plate, 8" 800.00
Zinnia, plate, deep, 9¾" 1,125.00

Gaudy Ironstone

Gaudy Ironstone was produced in the mid-1800s in Staffordshire, England. Some of the ware was decorated in much the same colors and designs as Gaudy Welsh, while other pieces were painted in pink, orange, and red with black and light blue accents. Lustre was used on some designs, omitted on others. The heavy ironstone body is its most distinguishing feature.

Key: pc — polychrome

Platter, orange blossoms, Imari border, 17", $600.00.

Coffeepot, Seeing Eye, Walley, Niagara shape, 11", EX 650.00
Cup & saucer, bl band/gr stripes/red & gr balls, mini, pr 55.00
Cup & saucer, floral, mc/gold/yel accents, paneled, mk, EX+ 200.00
Cup & saucer, Seeing Eye, registry mk, NM 130.00
Pitcher, molded design, bl highlights & lustre, 8" 200.00
Pitcher & bowl, floral, mc enamel, mk, 10½", 14" 575.00
Plate, floral, pc w/lustre, Ironstone, 8⅜" 115.00
Plate, mc florals w/cobalt & gold, 9¼" 95.00
Plate, Morning Glory, red & gr, 8⅝", EX 125.00

Plate, Pinwheel, mk Ironstone, EX 50.00
Plate, Rose, red/gr/blk, 7⅜" 85.00
Plate, Strawberry, gold lustre, flower border, 12-sided, 8" 225.00
Plate, Strawberry, gold lustre, mk, 10", NM 325.00
Plate, Strawberry, scalloped, 8½" 95.00
Plate, tulips & berries, pc, 8¾" 150.00
Plate, Urn of Flowers, 9⅜" 250.00
Platter, Imari floral, red & gold, 20¾", EX 225.00
Platter, Rose, 4-color, mk England, 13" 200.00
Platter, Strawberry & Rose, 3-color, wear/stains, 14¾" 325.00
Sugar bowl, Urn of Flowers, stain/rprs, 7⅜" 225.00
Teapot, Morning Glory, gr, 8-sided, mk D, 9" 875.00
Waste bowl, Seeing Eye, emb foliage at rim, 5¼", EX 230.00

Gaudy Welsh

Gaudy Welsh was an inexpensive hand-decorated ware made in both England and Wales from 1820 until 1860. It is characterized by its colors — principally blue, orange-rust, and copper lustre — and by its uninhibited patterns. Accent colors may be yellow and green. (Pink lustre may be present, since lustre applied to the white areas appears pink. A copper tone develops from painting lustre onto the dark colors.) The body of the ware may be heavy ironstone, creamware, earthenware, or porcelain; even style and shapes vary considerably. Patterns, while usually floral, are also sometimes geometric and may have trees and birds. Beware! The Wagon Wheel pattern has been reproduced.

Our advisor for this category is Cheryl Nelson; she is listed in the Directory under Minnesota. For further information we recommend *The Collector's Encyclopedia of Gaudy Dutch & Welsh* by John Shuman, available from Collector Books.

Note: The Bethedsa pattern is very similar to a Davenport jug pattern. No porcelain Gaudy Welsh was made in Wales.

Bryn Pistyll, jug, 5" 175.00
Buckle, plate, 10" 135.00
Cambrian Rose, jug, 8" 425.00
Chain, jug, flow bl, 7¼" 385.00
Chinoiserie, mug, 2" 180.00
Columbine, cup & saucer 85.00
Columbine, teapot 275.00
Feather, cup & saucer 95.00
Flower Basket, plate, 8" 225.00
Forget-Me-Not, jug, 6" 220.00
Glamorgan, jug, 7" 375.00
Grape, jug, 7" 150.00
Grape, plate, 10" 110.00
Grape & Lily, cup & saucer 145.00
Grape & Lily, plate, 10" 175.00
Grape & Lily, sugar bowl 185.00
Gwent, jug, 5" 295.00
Herald, cup & saucer 175.00
Herald, plate, 10" 215.00
Hexagon, plate, 10" 135.00
Japan, jug 475.00
Japan, teapot 425.00
Morning Glory, creamer, 5" 165.00
Oyster, cup & saucer 85.00
Oyster, jug, 7" 100.00
Oyster, teapot 295.00
Pagoda, bowl, 10" 785.00
Pot de Fleurs, vase, 7" 575.00
Rainbow, plate, 10" 275.00
Rhondda, jug, 5" 395.00

Rhondda, jug, 7¼" 475.00
Strawberry, teapot 495.00
Tulip, creamer, 5" 150.00
Tulip, mug, 2½" 125.00
Tulip, plate, 10" 95.00
Tulip, waste bowl 90.00
Village, cup & saucer 185.00
Village, plate, 7½" 215.00
Welsh War Bonnet, cup & saucer 235.00

Geisha Girl

Geisha Girl Porcelain was one of several key Japanese china production efforts aimed at the booming export markets of the U.S., Canada, England, and other parts of Europe. The wares feature colorful, kimono-clad Japanese ladies in scenes of everyday Japanese life, surrounded by exquisite flora, fauna, and mountain ranges. Nonetheless, the forms in which the wares were produced reflected the late 19th- and early 20th-century Western dining and decorating preferences: tea and coffee services, vases, dresser sets, children's items, planters, etc.

Over one hundred manufacturers were involved in Geisha Girl production. This accounts for the several hundred different patterns, well over a dozen border colors and styles, and several methods of design execution. Geisha Girl Porcelain was produced in wholly hand-painted versions, but most were hand painted over stenciled outlines. Be wary of Geisha ware executed with decals. Very few decalled examples came out of Japan. Rather, most were Czechoslovakian attempts to hone in on the market. Czech pieces have stamped marks in broad, pseudo-Oriental characters. Items with portraits of Oriental ladies in the bottom of tea or sake cups are *not* Geisha Girl Porcelain, unless the outside surface of the wares are decorated as described above. These lovely faces are formed by varying the thickness of the porcelain body and are called lithophanes.

The height of Geisha Girl production was between 1910 and the mid-1930s. Some post-World War II production has been found marked Occupied Japan.

The ware continued in minimal production through the 1980s, but point of origin was Hong Kong. These productions are discerned by the pure whiteness of the porcelain; even, unemotional borders; lack of background washes and gold enameling; and overall sparseness of detail. A new wave of Nippon-marked reproduction Geisha emerged in 1996. If the Geisha Girl productions of the 1860s-80s were overly plain, the mid-1990s repros are overly ornate. Original Geisha Girl porcelain was enhanced by brush strokes of color over a stenciled design; it was never the 'color within the lines perfectly' type of decoration found on current reproductions. Original Geisha Girl porcelain was decorated with color washes; the reproductions are in heavy enamels. The backdrop decoration of the current reproductions feature solid, thick colors, and the patterns feature too much color; peroid Geisha ware had a high ratio of white space to color. The new pieces also have bright shiny gold in proportions greater than most period Geisha ware. The Nippon marks on the reproductions are wrong. Some of the Geisha ware created during the Nippon era bore the small precise decaled green M-in-Wreath mark, a Noritake registered trademark. The reproduction items feature an irregular facsimile of this mark. Stamped onto the reproductions is an unrealistically large M-in-Wreath mark in shades of green ranging from an almost neon to pine green with a wreath that looks like it has seen better days, as it does not have the perfect roundness of the original mark. Reproductions of mid-sized trays, chunky hatpin holders, an ornate vase, a covered bottle, and a powder jar are among the current reproductions popping up at flea and antique markets.

Many of our descriptions contain references to border colors and treatments. This information is given immediately preceding the mark and/or size. Our advisor for this category is Elyce Litts; she is listed in the Directory under New Jersey.

Key:
#2 — Torii
#4 — T in Cherry Blossom
#11 — diaper mk
#12 — Royal Kaga
#16 — SNB
#19 — Japan
#20 — Made in Japan
#35 — Plum Blossom
#42 — Vantine

#68 — SGK China, Occupied Japan
J #1 — Yachi
J #6 — Tashiro
J #16 — Kutani
J #19 — Ozan
J #36 — Made by Kato
J #46 — Yasutera

Biscuit jar, Basket of Mums B, melon ribs, red w/gold 65.00
Biscuit jar, Oni Dance B, red-orange w/gold chrysanthemums, ftd ..85.00
Bonbon, Bamboo Trellis, red w/gold 45.00
Bowl, berry; Boat Festival, cobalt, ind, #35 ....12.00
Bowl, Footbridge B, red w/yel, 8" 35.00
Bowl, Mother & Son C, red-orange w/gold, J#44 ....30.00
Bowl, nut; Feather Fan, ftd, mc border 48.00
Bowl, Pointing D, red-orange w/gold buds, 5¼" 12.00
Bowl, soup; Geisha in Sampan A, brn w/gold, #21 ....28.00
Butter pat, Flower Gathering B, red-orange, 3¼" 12.00
Cocoa pot, Garden Bench C, cobalt w/gold, 6½" 55.00
Cocoa pot, Lesson, cobalt w/gold, conical, #19, 8" 35.00

Cocoa pot, Parasol variant in reserve, pink and blue flowers, dark red-orange trim, 9½", $45.00.

Cocoa pot, Parasol B: Torii & Parasol, cobalt w/gold, #16 ....55.00
Cocoa pot, To the Teahouse, gold rim, #2 ....65.00
Creamer, Boy w/Scythe, cobalt w/gold, #20 ....15.00
Creamer, Kite B, red w/gold lacing, J#16 ....16.00
Creamer, Paper Carp, red-orange w/gold, J#16 ....20.00
Creamer & sugar bowl, Ribbon Parasol, red-orange w/gold 30.00
Cup & saucer, demi; Basket A, curved sides, allover pattern 20.00
Cup & saucer, demi; Paper Carp, red-orange, #15 ....15.00
Cup & saucer, tea; Peacock on Flowered Stone Roof, cobalt/gold ...25.00
Egg cup, Cherry Blossom Ikebana, flowers in pot, cobalt 18.00
Egg cup, Duck Watching, gold border, mk 22.00
Egg cup, Parasol Modern: Processional Parasol, pale cobalt 7.00
Hatpin holder, Rendezvous, vine & leaves, J#16 ....100.00
Humidor, Battledore, scalloped bl w/gold line 85.00
Jug, Battledore, fluted edge & base, ribbed, 5" 35.00
Manicure jar, Parasol C: Parasol, red, #19, 2¼" 20.00
Mint dish, Bamboo Trellis, red-orange w/gold buds 12.00
Mug, Gardening, red w/gold line, 3" 45.00
Nappy, Leaving the Teahouse, mc border, J #16a 22.00
Nappy, Mother & Daughter, dk turq w/gold, lobed 35.00
Pin tray, Duck Watching B, pine gr w/wht, uneven edge, #34 ......10.00
Plate, Bamboo Tree, chrysanthemum shape, 7" 15.00
Plate, Battledore, red-orange, scalloped swirl, 6¼" 15.00
Plate, Duck Watching, gold, #62, 7" 18.00
Plate, Fan A, red-orange w/gold, 7" 15.00

Plate, Flute & Koto, bl-gr w/gold buds, #19, 7" 24.00
Plate, Inside the Treehouse, apple gr, fluted swirl, 8½" 35.00
Plate, Kite B, red w/gold lacing, scalloped edge, J #16 ....28.00
Plate, Visitor to the Court, bl w/gold, scalloped, #19, 7¼" 22.00
Powder jar, Processional, mc border, J316 ....38.00
Powder jar, Pug, brick red, 4¼" 35.00
Shakers, Blind Man's Bluff, lt apple gr, fluted, pr 25.00
Shakers, Bouncing Ball, bl-gr, pr 22.00
Sugar bowl, Garden Bench G, cobalt w/gold, J #16 ....30.00
Sugar bowl, Mother & Daughter, 2 reserves, red w/gold 15.00
Tea set, Visitor to the Court, cobalt w/gold trim, #19, 3-pc 65.00
Teacup & saucer, Bicycle Race, red-orange w/gold 30.00
Teacup & saucer, Bouncing Ball, bl-gr w/gold buds 25.00
Teacup & saucer, Child Reaching for Butterfly, red-orange, #20 ....8.00
Teacup & saucer, Circle Dance, scalloped cobalt w/gold 12.00
Teacup & saucer, Cloud B, red-orange w/yel 12.00
Teacup & saucer, Geisha in Sampan A, gold 15.00
Teapot, Bamboo Trellis, red-orange w/gold buds, ftd 35.00
Teapot, Bouncing Ball, bl-gr w/gold buds 55.00
Teapot, Flute & Koto, red 30.00
Teapot, Garden Bench C, cobalt w/gold, melon ribbed, 4¾" 30.00
Teapot, Grape Arbor, red w/gold 26.00
Toothpick holder, Circle Dance, red, cylindrical 15.00
Tray, dresser; Bird Cage, red-orange w/gold, J#28 ....35.00
Vase, Bamboo Trellis, red-orange, #14, 4½", pr 25.00

German Porcelain

Unless otherwise noted, the porcelain listed in this section is marked simply 'Germany.' Products of other German manufactures are listed in specific categories. See also Bisque; Pink Paw Bears; Pink Pigs; Elfinware.

Vase, large roses on shaded green with gold trim at rim and handles, marked P.T. Germany, 9½", $325.00.

Bowl, mc fruit w/gold, rtcl, 4-lobed, crown mk, 2x8½" sq 38.00
Candelabrum, 3-arm, appl foral, mother/child std, 20" 135.00
Candle holder, blk cat figural, tail hdl, 5x4" 125.00
Figurine, boy & girl dancing, older mk, 7" 95.00
Figurine, boy in knee pants/girl in bonnet, mc, unmk, 14⅝", pr .110.00
Figurine, nude lying on clam shell, mc irid, unmk 100.00
Plaque, Girl at Fountain, HP, fr, 9½x5⅞" 1,150.00
Plate, floral transfer w/gold, emb scroll & poppy rim, 12¼" 35.00
Slipper, emb flowers, wht w/gold trim, 2½x4x1¼" 20.00
Tile, pk & wht water lilies w/orange & gr lustre rim, 6" dia 28.00

Gladding McBean and Company

This company was established in 1875 in Lincoln, California. They first produced only clay drainage pipes, but in 1883 architectural terra cotta was introduced, which has been used extensively in the United States as well as abroad. Sometime later a line of garden pottery was added. They soon became the leading producers of tile in the country. In 1923 they purchased the Tropico Pottery in Glendale, California, where in addition to tile they also produced huge garden vases. Their line was expanded in 1934 to included artware and dinnerware.

At least fifteen lines of art pottery were developed between 1934 and 1942. For a short time they stamped their wares with the Tropico Pottery mark; but the majority was signed 'GMcB' in an oval. Later the mark was changed to 'Franciscan' with several variations. After 1937 'Catalina Pottery' was used on some lines. (All items marked 'Catalina Pottery' were made in Glendale.) For further information we recommend *The Collector's Encyclopedia of California Pottery*, by our advisor for this category, Jack Chipman. He is listed in the Directory under California.

Bowl, lt yel, molded ribs, mk Sunkist, 4x10" 40.00
Clam shell, ivory w/peach int, 7x4" 45.00
Cup & saucer, demi; salmon pk w/turq inside 25.00
Pitcher, orange, str sides, flared rim, mk, 9x9", NM 80.00
Vase, assorted shells on turq, 12" 195.00
Vase, head form, terra cotta, glazed decor, #C801 ....165.00
Vase, head form, turq satin matt, #C801 ....135.00
Vase, ivory w/peach int, satin matt, #C338, 12" 125.00
Vase, ivory w/turq int, satin matt, #C312, 8" 75.00
Vase, ivory/bl, ribbed Deco style, 8x8" 65.00
Vase, lt brn w/lt bl int, melon ribs, slim, 6x3" 40.00
Vase, oxblood, #105, 6", pr 450.00
Water set, red-orange, carafe+2 tumblers on tray 65.00

Glass Animals and Figurines

These beautiful glass sculptures have been produced by many major companies in America, in fact, some are still being made today. Heisey, Fostoria, Duncan and Miller, Imperial, Paden City, Tiffin, and Cambridge made the vast majority, but there were many others involved on a lesser scale. Some, but not all, marked their animals.

As many of the glass companies went out of business, molds were often sold to others still active who used them to reproduce their own line of animals. While some are easy to recognize, others can be very confusing. For example, Summit Art Glass now owns Cambridge's 6½", 8½", and 10" swan molds. We recommend *Glass Animals of the Depression Era* by Lee Garmon and Dick Spencer, if you're thinking of starting a collection or wanting to identify and evaluate the glass animals you already have. Both are our advisors for this category and are listed in the Directory under Illinois.

Note: Heisey Collectors of America stopped using the plug horse as a mascot and have adoped the rabbit paperweight as the new yearly mascot. In our descriptions, unless a color is mentioned, values are for clear examples.

Cambridge

Bashful Charlotte, flower frog, lt emerald, 11½" 350.00
Bashful Charlotte, flower frog, peachblo, 6½" 150.00
Bashful Charlotte, flower frog, 6½" 100.00
Bird on stump, flower frog, gr, 5¼" 275.00
Blue Jay, flower block 135.00
Bridge hound, ebony, 1¼" 35.00
Draped Lady, flower frog, amber, 8½" 195.00
Draped Lady, flower frog, Dianthus, 8½" 175.00
Draped Lady, flower frog, lt emerald, 8½" 225.00
Draped Lady, flower frog, lt pk frost, 13¼" 300.00
Draped Lady, flower frog, pk frost, 8½" 150.00
Eagle, bookend, 5½x4x4" 80.00

Heron, lg, 12" 135.00
Lion, bookend, ea 135.00
Mandolin Lady, flower frog, dk amber 450.00
Melon Boy, flower frog, pk 400.00
Pouter Pigeon, bookend, milk glass, 5½" 95.00
Rose Lady, flower frog, dk amber, tall base, 9¾" ...275.00
Rose Lady, flower frog, gr satin, 8½" 200.00
Rose Lady, flower frog, lt pk, 8½" 175.00
Scottie, bookends, hollow, pr 175.00
Sea gull, flower block 60.00
Swan, carmen, 6½" 225.00
Swan, Crown Tuscan, 3" 50.00
Swan, ebony, 10½" 250.00
Swan, ebony, 3" 65.00
Swan, emerald, 3" 40.00
Swan, milk glass, 3" 60.00
Swan, milk glass, 8½" 275.00
Turkey, gr, w/lid 475.00
Turtle, flower holder, ebony 225.00
Two Kids, flower frog, amber satin, 9¼" 400.00

Duncan and Miller

Donkey, cart & peon, 3-pc set 475.00
Duck, ashtray, red, 7" 90.00
Goose, fat, 6x6" 325.00
Mallard duck, cigarette box, #30, w/lid, 3½x4½" ...45.00
Silvan swan, 12" 85.00
Swan, ashtray, crystal w/bl neck, 4" 35.00
Swan, candle holder, red w/crystal neck, 7" 80.00
Swan, crystal bowl, 10½" 24.00
Swan, dk gr bowl, 10½" 65.00
Swan, red bowl, 7½" 60.00
Swan, solid, 3" 25.00
Swan, solid, 7" 75.00
Swan, wht milk glass w/red neck, 10½" 450.00
Swordfish, bl opal, rare 500.00
Sylvan swan, yel opal, 5½" 120.00
Tropical fish, candle holder, 5½" 500.00

Fenton

Airedale, rosalene 110.00
Bear, blk, sitting on font 38.00
Bear, wht irid, sitting 15.00
Bunny, lt bl 16.00
Bunny, pale yel 20.00

Butterfly, blue, round base, 4¾", $30.00.

Butterfly, candle holder, ruby carnival, 1989 souvenir, 7½" 85.00
Elephant, whiskey bottle, periwinkle, 8" 450.00

Filly, rosalene, head front 115.00
Fish, red w/amberina tail & fins, 2½" 55.00
Fish, rosalene, bookend 95.00
Gazelle, rosalene 115.00
Happiness Bird, red, 6½" 28.00
Hen, rosalene 85.00
Rabbit, rosalene, paperweight 65.00
Turtle, flower block, amethyst, 4" L 85.00

Fostoria

Bird, candle holder, 1½" 20.00
Buddha, bookends, blk, pr 525.00
Cat, lt bl, 3¾" 35.00
Chinese Lute, ebony w/gold, 12½" 300.00
Deer, sitting or standing, bl 55.00
Deer, sitting or standing, Silver Mist 40.00
Duck, mama 30.00
Duckling, head bk (+) 20.00
Duckling, walking (+) 15.00
Eagle, bookend, 7½", ea 150.00
Goldfish, horizontal, rare 125.00
Horse, bookend, 7¾", ea 45.00
Madonna, Silver Mist, w/base, orig issue, 11¾" (+) ...80.00
Polar bear, 4⅝" 65.00
Seal, topaz, 3⅞" 125.00
Squirrel, amber, sitting 35.00
Whale 25.00

Heisey

Angelfish 140.00
Bull, sgn, 4x7½" 1,600.00
Chick, head down or up, ea 95.00
Colt, kicking 185.00
Colt, kicking, cobalt 1,200.00
Colt, rearing, amber 650.00
Colt, standing 90.00
Colt, standing, cobalt 1,000.00
Cygnet, baby swan, 2½" 200.00
Doe head, bookend, 6¼" 800.00
Dolphin, candlesticks, Moongleam, #110, pr ...700.00
Donkey 295.00
Duck, ashtray 90.00
Duck, ashtray, Marigold 195.00
Duck, flower block, Flamingo 200.00
Elephant, amber, lg or med 1,850.00
Elephant, lg or med 425.00
Filly, H head bkwards 1,800.00
Filly, head forward 1,000.00
Fish, bowl, 9½" 500.00
Fish, match holder, 3x2¾" 175.00
Flying mare 3,000.00
Frog, cheese plate, Marigold 285.00
Giraffe, head bk 225.00
Giraffe, head to side 225.00
Goose, wings half 95.00
Hen, 4½" 400.00
Horse head, bookend, frosted, ea 130.00
Horse head, cigarette box, #1489, 4½x4" 55.00
Irish setter, ashtray 30.00
Irish setter, ashtray, Moongleam 55.00
Kingfisher, flower block, Moongleam 200.00
Mallard, wings half 185.00

Piglet, sitting	100.00
Plug horse	145.00
Plug horse, cobalt	1,200.00
Rabbit, paperweight, 2¾x3¾"	180.00
Ram head, stopper, 3½"	150.00
Ringneck pheasant	160.00
Rooster, amber, 5⅜"	2,500.00
Rooster, vase, 6½"	90.00
Rooster head, cocktail	50.00
Rooster head, stopper, 4½"	45.00
Sea horse, cocktail	140.00
Sow, 3x4½"	600.00
Swan	1,450.00
Swan, ind nut, #1503	25.00
Swan, pitcher	700.00
Tiger, paperweight, 2¾x8"	1,100.00
Tropical fish, 12"	1,800.00
Wood duck	750.00

Imperial

Asiatic pheasant, amber	425.00
Bulldog-type pup, milk glass, 3½"	65.00
Chick, head down, milk glass	10.00
Clydesdale, amber	400.00
Clydesdale, Verde Gr	150.00
Colt, balking, caramel slag	125.00
Colt, standing, amber	125.00
Cygnet, blk, 2½"	55.00
Cygnet, Horizon Bl	25.00
Dog, Airedale, Ultra Bl	65.00
Donkey, Meadow Gr Carnival	65.00
Elephant, caramel slag, med	65.00
Elephant, caramel slag, sm	85.00
Elephant, Nut Brn, sm	120.00
Fish, bookend, ruby, ea	340.00
Fish, match holder, Sunshine Yel satin, 3"	20.00
Gazelle, blk, 11"	400.00
Horse head, bookend, pk, rare, ea	300.00
Mallard, wings down, Horizon Bl, HCA, 4½"	35.00
Mallard, wings half, caramel slag	35.00
Marmote Sentinel (woodchuck), caramel slag, 4½"	60.00
Owl, jar, caramel slag, 16½"	65.00
Piglet, sitting, amber	40.00
Piglet, standing, ruby	35.00
Rabbit, paperweight, Horizon Bl, 2¾"	110.00
Rooster, amber	475.00
Scottie, milk glass, 3½"	55.00
Terrier, Parlour Pup, Sunshine Yel carnival	45.00
Tiger, paperweight, caramel slag	150.00
Wood duck, Ultra Bl satin	45.00
Wood duckling, sitting, caramel slag, 4½"	75.00
Wood duckling, standing, Sunshine Yel satin	15.00

L.E. Smith

Cock, Fighting; bl, 9"	45.00
Goose, 2½"	25.00
Goose Girl, orig, 6"	25.00
Horse, bookend, rearing, amber	30.00
Horse, bookend, rearing, blk, ea	65.00
Horse, recumbent, amberina, 9" L	125.00
Queen fish, aquarium, gr, 7x15"	225.00
Scottie, pipe rest, fired-on blk, 5½" L	10.00

Swan, milk glass, w/decor, 8½"	45.00
Thrush, bl frost	20.00

New Martinsville

Russian wolfhound, 7¼", $95.00.

Bear, baby	55.00
Bear, mama, 4x6"	225.00
Bear, papa	250.00
Chick, frosted, 1"	25.00
Eagle, 8"	85.00
Gazelle, leaping, frosted base, 8¼"	65.00
Hen, 5"	75.00
Porpoise on wave, orig	600.00
Rooster w/crooked tail, 7½"	85.00
Seal, baby w/ball	60.00
Seal, candle holders, pr	125.00
Seal w/ball, bookends, 7", pr	140.00
Swan, ruby, candle holders, pr	70.00
Tiger, head up, 6½"	225.00
Wolfhound	125.00
Woodsman, sq base, 7⅜"	135.00

Paden City

Bunny, cotton-ball dispenser, ears bk, bl frosted	90.00
Bunny, cotton-ball dispenser, ears bk, milk glass	95.00
Dragon swan, 9¾" L	215.00
Pheasant, Chinese; crystal, 13¾"	85.00
Pheasant, head turned, lt bl, 12" L	175.00
Pony, blk, 12"	350.00
Pouter pigeon, bookend, 6¼"	85.00
Rooster, Chanticleer; lt bl, 9¼"	200.00
Rooster, head down, 8¾"	80.00

Tiffin

Cat, Sassy Susie, blk satin w/pnt decor, #9448, 11"	175.00
Fish, solid, crystal, 8¾x9"	350.00
Owl, lamp, cobalt, 1934-29	1,250.00

Viking

Angelfish, amber, 7x7"	125.00
Angelfish, milk glass, pr	150.00
Bird, moss gr, tail up, 12"	25.00
Bird, orange, long tail, 9½"	25.00
Cat, gr, sitting, 8"	55.00
Dolphin, candle holders, pink, hexagonal ft, 9½", pr	150.00
Duck, ashtray, dk bl, 9"	45.00
Duck, dk teal, Viking's Epic Line, 9"	35.00
Duck, fighting, head up or down, Viking's Epic Line	45.00

Duck, orange, rnd, ftd, 5" 25.00
Duck, ruby, rnd, ftd, 5" 35.00
Egret, orange, 12" 45.00
Hound dog, crystal, 8" 50.00
Jesus, crystal w/crystal mist, flat bk, 6x5" 65.00
Mouse, crystal mist, 4" 35.00
Owl, amber, Epic series 45.00
Penguin, 7" 25.00
Pony, aqua bl, tall 95.00
Rabbit (Thumper), 6½" 35.00
Seal, persimmon, 9¾" L 15.00
Swan, bowl, amber, 6" 45.00
Swan, orange, fluted, 6½x4" 45.00
Swan, yel mist, paper label, 6" 50.00

Westmoreland

Bulldog, Crystal Mist, pnt collar, rhinestone eyes, 2½" 35.00
Butterfly, 4½" 27.00
Owl, Crystal Mist, 5½" 30.00
Porky Pig, milk glass, hollow, 3" L 15.00
Robin, pk, 5⅛" 25.00
Robin, 3¼" L 20.00
Starfish, candle holders, milk glass, 5", pr 45.00
Turtle, flower block, gr, 7 holes, 4" L 55.00
Wren, Crystal Mist, 2½" 17.50
Wren, pk, 2½" 20.00
Wren, red, 2½" 22.50

Miscellaneous

Haley, horse, jumping 45.00
Haley, horse, jumping, milk glass 50.00
Haley, Lady Godiva, bookend, 1940s 40.00
Haley, pheasant, 1940s, 12" 30.00
Indiana, panther, walking, amber 225.00
Indiana, panther, walking, bl 250.00
Mosser, lady's leg, bookend, custard, pr 175.00
New Martinsville by Mirror Images, mama bear, ruby 85.00
New Martinsville by Mirror Images, police dog, ruby 75.00
New Martinsville by Mirror Images, wolfhound, ruby carnival 125.00

Glass Knives

Glass knives were manufactured from about 1920 to 1950, with distribution at its greatest in the late thirties and early forties. Colors generally followed Depression glass dinnerware: crystal, light blue, light green, pink (originally called rose), and more rarely amber, forest green, and white (opal). Many glass knives were hand painted in fruit or flower designs. Knife blades were ground to a sharp edge. Today knives are usually found with blades nicked through years of use or bumping in silverware drawers or reground, which is acceptable to collectors as long as the original knife shape is maintained.

Many glass knives were engraved for gift-giving, personalized with the recipient's name and on occasion, with a greeting. Originally presented in boxes, most glass knives were accompanied by a paper insert extolling the virtues of the knife and describing its care.

Boxes printed with World's Fair logos are fun to find, though not rare. Butter knives, which are smaller than other glass knives, typically were made in Czechoslovakia and sometimes match the handle patterns of glass salad sets. Knife lengths often vary slightly because the knives were snapped off the molded glass during manufacture.

Our advisor for this category is Adrienne Escoe; she is listed in the Directory under California. For information concerning the Glass Knife Collectors Club, see the Clubs, Newsletters, and Catalogs section of the Directory.

Values reflect knives with minor blade roughness or resharpening.

Aer-Flo, pink, NMIB, $55.00.

BK, gr 50.00
Block, gr 35.00
Butter knife, bl & crystal, 5¾" 30.00
Butter knife, gr & crystal, 6¼" 25.00
Dagger, crystal, HP, 9¼", MIB 155.00
JCW, crystal, 9" 30.00
Plain hdl, crystal 100.00
Rose Spray, crystal 25.00
Rose Spray, gr 80.00
Rose Spray, pk, MIB 85.00
Star, bl, 9" 35.00
Steel-ite, crystal, 8½" 25.00
Stonex, amber, 8⅜" 140.00
Stonex, gr, MIB 90.00
Vitex (3-Star), bl, 9¼", MIB 32.00
3-Leaf, gr, 9" 35.00
3-Leaf, pk, 8½", MIB 35.00
5-Leaf, bl, 9" 35.00

Glass Shoes

Little shoes made of glass can be found in hundreds of styles, shapes, and colors. They've been made since the early 1800s by nearly every glasshouse, large and small, in America. To learn more about them, we recommend *Shoes of Glass* by our advisor Libby Yalom, who is listed in the Directory under Maryland. Numbers in the listings refer to her book.

#111, Daisy & Square, boot, bl, buttons on left, 3⅛x3" 45.00
#116, milk glass, bow on front, slightly concave sole, 2⅜x4¾" 45.00
#12, Daisy & Button, amber, Patd Oct 19/86, med 40.00
#128, crystal w/scalloped edge, tassel, 4⅜x4¼" 70.00
#136, blk w/cuff, t'print in sole, shield outline on vamp, 4" 55.00
#17, Daisy & Button, bl, no lace holes, mesh sole, 3x5⅞" 50.00
#20, Daisy & Button, milk glass, ribbed band, 2⅜x4⅞" 40.00
#203, baby's, crystal w/gold pnt laces, bow & flowers, 3⅞" 30.00
#274, crystal, plain w/hollow sole, solid heel, 2⅝x4¾" 30.00
#3, Daisy & Button, bl, mesh sole, Duncan, lg 45.00
#322, mc spangle w/wht int, crystal rigaree, 3¾x5" 120.00
#359, frosted Burmese color w/ruffled edge, 2½x6⅜" 98.00
#371, pk & wht latticino, crystal ruffle/heel, wht sole, 6⅜" 100.00
#385, Dutch style, crystal w/3 ridges on vamp, 3 buttons, 7" 60.00
#408, Daisy & Button, apple gr, 2½x11¾" 150.00
#489, boot w/strap & spur, crystal, R on side, 2½x2¼" 20.00
#50, Finecut, crystal, dmn mesh sole mk HT, 2¾x5⅛" 42.00
#566, boot, ruby cut to crystal, ca 1980, 7¾x5½" 130.00

#65, Cane, pointed-toe slipper, crystal, 1¾x4¾" **40.00**
#77, bottle, crystal w/metal top, lg toe showing, 4¾x5¾" **100.00**
#94, frosted crystal w/pk & wht pnt flowers on vamp w/gold **75.00**

Glidden

Genius designer Glidden Parker established Glidden Pottery in 1940 in Alfred, New York, having been schooled at the unrivaled New York State College of Ceramics at Alfred University. Glidden pottery is characterized by a fine stoneware body, innovative forms, outstanding hand-milled glazes, and hand decoration which make the pieces individual works of art. Production consisted of casual dinnerware, artware, and accessories that were distributed internationally.

In 1949 Glidden Pottery became the second ceramic plant in the country to utilize the revolutionary Ram pressing machine. This allowed for increased production and for the most part eliminated the previously used slip-casting method. However, Glidden stoneware continued to reflect the same superb quality of craftsmanship until the factory closed in 1957. Although the majority of form and decorative patterns were Mr. Parker's personal designs, Fong Chow and Sergio Dello Strologo also designed award-winning lines.

Glidden will be found marked on the unglazed underside with a signature that is hand incised, mold impressed, or ink stamped. Interest in this unique stoneware is growing as collectors discover that it embodies the very finest of Mid-Century High Style. Our advisor is David Pierce; he is listed in the Directory under Ohio.

Ashtray, Loop Artware, #904-U **65.00**
Ashtray, SafeX, dbl, rectangular, 12½x6½" **30.00**
Ashtray, Teardrop, Garden, #184 ....**30.00**
Ashtray, Teardrop, Zig-Zag, #183 ....**30.00**
Bottle, dressing; Alfred Stoneware, #812 ....**45.00**
Bowl, cobalt, #17 ....**25.00**
Bowl, Early Pink, #15 ....**30.00**
Bowl, Leaf, engobe #27 ....**17.00**
Bowl, Turquoise Matrix, #38 ....**20.00**
Bowl, Yellowstone, #17 ....**15.00**
Candle bench, Chi Chi Poodle, 8¾x3¾x2" **30.00**
Candle bench, Mexican Cock, 8¾x3¾x2" **35.00**
Casserole, Menagerie, Hippo, #163 ....**45.00**
Casserole, Ric-Rac, bl-gray, #165 ....**35.00**
Casserole, Sage & Sand, #167 ....**10.00**
Casserole, Will O' the Wisp, #165 ....**30.00**
Charger, Leaf, dk cobalt, #68 ....**140.00**
Coaster, Flourish, #19 ....**10.00**
Coaster, Turquoise Matrix, #19 ....**5.00**
Creamer & sugar bowl, Boston Spice, #1430/#1440 ......**40.00**
Creamer & sugar bowl, Flourish, #144/#143 ....**55.00**
Creamer & sugar bowl, High Tide, #1430/#1440 ....**40.00**
Creamer & sugar bowl, Sage & Sand, #144/#143 ....**20.00**
Creamer & sugar bowl, Turquoise Matrix, #144/#143 ....**25.00**
Cup & saucer, 'W,' #141/#142 ....**17.00**
Cup & saucer, Flourish, #141/#142 ....**20.00**
Cup & saucer, High Tide, #441/#442 ....**17.00**
Cup & saucer, Pear, #141/#142 ....**15.00**
Cup & saucer, Yellowstone, #141/#142 ....**10.00**
Pitcher, Boston Spice, #617 ....**65.00**
Pitcher, Feather, #617 ....**50.00**
Pitcher, Glidden Blue, #615 ....**85.00**
Pitcher, High Tide, #615 ....**65.00**
Pitcher, Yellowstone, #615 ....**45.00**
Planter, cobalt, #89 ....**30.00**
Planter, Yellowstone, #122 ....**12.00**

Photo courtesy David Pierce

Plate, Mexican Cock, 5½", $15.00.

Plate, Canape Capers Canines, #35 ....**25.00**
Plate, Snowdrop, #33 ....**55.00**
Teapot, Turquois Matrix, #619 ....**50.00**
Vase, cobalt, #128 ....**30.00**
Vase, Flourish, #5 ....**40.00**
Vase, Gulfstream Blue, #4020 ....**175.00**
Vase, Loop Artware, #935 ....**150.00**
Vase, Turquoise Matrix, #49 ....**35.00**
Vase, Yellowstone, #86 ....**30.00**

Goebel

F.W. Goebel founded the F&W Goebel Company in 1871, located in Rodental, West Germany. They produced thousands of different decorative and useful items over the years, the most famous of which are the Hummel figurines first produced in 1935 based on the artwork of a Franciscan nun, Sister Maria Innocentia Hummel.

The Goebel trademarks have long been a source of confusion because **all** Goebel products, including Hummels, of any particular time period bear the same trademark, thus leading many to believe all Goebels are Hummels. Always look for the Hummel signature on actual Hummel figurines (these are listed in a separate section).

There are many, many other series — some of which are based on artwork of particular artists such as Disney, Charlot Byj, Janet Robson, Harry Holt, Norman Rockwell, M. Spotl, Lore, Huldah, and Schaubach. Miscellaneous useful items include ashtrays, bookends, salt and pepper shakers, banks, pitchers, inkwells, perfume bottles, etc. Figurines include birds, animals, Art Deco pieces, etc. The Friar Tuck monks and the Co-Boy elves are especially popular.

The date of manufacture of a particular piece is determined by the trademark. The incised date found underneath the base on many items is the **mold copyright** date. Actual date of manufacture may vary as much as twenty years or more from the copyright date.

Most Common Goebel Trademarks and Approximate Date Used:
Crown mark (may be incised or stamped, or both) 1923 — 1950
Full bee (complete bumble bee inside the letter 'V') 1950 — 1957
Stylized bee (dot with wings inside letter 'V') 1957 — 1964
3-Line (stylized bee with 3 lines of copyright info to the right of the trademark) 1964 — 1972
Goebel bee (word Goebel with stylized bee mark over the last letter 'e') 1972 — 1979
Goebel (word Goebel only) 1979 — Present

Our advisors for this category are Gale and Wayne Bailey; they are listed in the Directory under Georgia.

Photo courtesy Gale and Wayne Bailey

Golfer salt and pepper shakers on a tray, M28 A-C, full bee trademark, $95.00.

Artist Signed

Dis 150, Bambi perfume spender, full bee 150.00
Dis 8, Thumper ashtray, full bee 185.00
Hul 702, lady in yel dress, stylized bee 125.00
Hul 709, lady dresser box, stylized bee 185.00
Lore 250, boy w/wheelbarrow, 3-line mk 135.00
Rob 405/A, Flight Into Egypt, Goebel bee 125.00
Rob 434, Janet Robson plaque, 3-line mk 95.00
Rock 202, boy w/dog, 3-line mk 250.00
Rock 205, First Love, 3-line mk 275.00
Schau 12, lady w/lg dog, full bee 250.00
Schau 19, lady dancing, full bee 150.00
Schau 6, boy w/lamb, full bee 95.00
Spo 37, Madonna w/Child, full bee 85.00
Spo 48, angel ringing bell, stylized bee 45.00

Cardinal Tuck (Red Monk)

Ashtray, ZF43/0, stylized bee 175.00
Condiment set & tray, stylized bee 300.00
Mustard jar, S183, stylized bee 125.00
Sugar bowl, Z37, stylized bee 125.00

Charlot BYJ Redheads and Blonds

Byj 1, Strike, Goebel 65.00
Byj 16, Bless Us All, stylized bee 50.00
Byj 17, A Child's Prayer, 3-line mk 50.00
Byj 19, Spellbound, Goebel bee 110.00
Byj 24, Daisies Won't Tell, Goebel 75.00
Byj 3, Oops, Goebel 110.00
Byj 38, Evening Prayer, Goebel bee 75.00
Byj 4, Little Miss Coy, Goebel bee 60.00
Byj 40, Guess Who, Goebel bee 110.00
Byj 51, Let It Rain, Goebel bee 150.00
Byj 67, Trouble Shooter, Goebel 75.00
Byj 68, Say A-a-aah, Goebel 125.00
Byj 79, Camera Shy, Goebel 135.00
Byj 86, Once Upon a Time, Goebel 125.00
Byj 9, E-e-eek, Goebel 85.00
10 088 13, Something Tells Me, Goebel 100.00
10 092 11, Dear Sirs, Goebel 120.00
10 093 10, Yeah Team, Goebel 150.00
10 101 13, Come Along, Goebel 60.00

Co-Boy Figurines

Al the Trumpet Player, Goebel 70.00
Co-Boy dealer plaque, Goebel bee 85.00

Dod the Doctor, Goebel 80.00
Ted the Tennis Player, Goebel 70.00
Tommy Touchdown, Goebel 70.00
Toni the Skier, Goebel 70.00
Utz the Banker, Goebel bee 80.00

Fashion Ladies

13 018 21, Southern Belle 1860, Goebel 75.00
16 280 21, The Cosmopolitan, Goebel 75.00
16 327 21, Katharina, Goebel 125.00

Friar Tuck (Brown Monk)

Bank, SD29, full bee 75.00
Condiment set & tray, stylized bee 85.00
Cookie jar, full bee 350.00
Mug, T74/0, full bee 35.00
Mug, T74/1, full bee 45.00
Pitcher, S141/0, full bee 45.00
Sugar bowl, Z37, full bee 45.00

Miscellaneous

Ashtray, w/bird, RT174, stylized bee 40.00
Ashtray, w/cat, RT182, full bee 45.00
Ashtray, w/duck, RT894, crown mk 65.00
Bank, chimney sweep, Goebel bee 45.00
Candle holder, blk dog, L53, crown mk 65.00
Decanter, Afghan hound dog, KL861, crown mk 85.00
Honey pot, beehive, Goebel 45.00
Match holder/striker, blk bird, S49, stylized mk 35.00
Perfume spender, owl, ET4, Goebel bee 150.00
Pitcher, Colonial man w/book, S129 ....50.00
Pitcher, Dutch girl, S484, crown mk 55.00
Pitcher, elephant, S487, 6" 75.00
Pitcher, parrot, S485, crown mk 65.00

Goldscheider

The Goldscheider family operated a pottery in Vienna for many generations before seeking refuge in the United States following Hitler's invasion of their country. They settled in Trenton, New Jersey, in the early 1940s where they established a new corporation and began producing objects of art and tableware items. (No mention was made of the company in the Trenton City Directory after 1950, and it is assumed that by this time the influx of foreign imports had taken its toll.) In 1946 Marcel Goldscheider established a pottery in Staffordshire where he manufactured bone china figures, earthenware, etc., marked with a stamp of his signature. Larger artist-signed examples are the most valuable with the Austrian pieces bringing the higher prices. Our advisors are Randy and Debbie Coe; they are listed in the Directory under Oregon.

A wide variety of marks has been found. Listed here are several of that correspond with numbers in the listings that follow.

Key:
1 — Goldscheider USA Fine China
2 — Original Goldscheider Fine China
3 — Goldscheider USA
4 — Goldscheider-Everlast Corp.
5 — Goldscheider Everlast Corp. in circle
6 — Goldscheider Inc. in circle
7 — Goldcrest Ceramics Corp. in circle
8 — Goldcrest Fine China

9 — Goldcrest Fine China USA
10 — A Goldcrest Creation
11 — Created by Goldscheider USA

Bust, lady in ruffled bonnet, hands to face, 1930, 15¼" 1,380.00
Bust, lady in winter outfit, hand on hat, #824, mk #3, 6¼" 95.00
Bust, lady's head/hands, Austria/#33/092, 12" 550.00
Bust, lady w/brick red face, mc details, wood base, 12½" 800.00
Figurine, Balinese Dancer, 16" 275.00
Figurine, boy angel, bl & gray, #322, mks #6 & #8, 4" 75.00
Figurine, boy seated w/pot on shoulder, mc, #d, 6⅞" 230.00
Figurine, Chinese boy w/fan, wht & pk, #1255, mk #10, 12" 145.00
Figurine, Chinese boy w/lute, wht & pk, #1254, mk #10, 8" 145.00
Figurine, cockatoo, gr & bl, #860, mk #5, 14" 295.00
Figurine, draped nude, 5-color, sgn/#d, rstr, 19" 1,450.00
Figurine, foal, grazing 95.00
Figurine, German shepherd, lg 185.00
Figurine, lady in winter outfit w/umbrella, #508, mk #11, 11½" .160.00
Figurine, Madonna, pk & gray, #225, mks #6 & #8, 5" 85.00
Figurine, rooster, wht, #880, mk #9, 10½" 145.00
Figurine, Royal Blackamoors (couple), Barbara Loveday, 15", pr 650.00
Figurine, Southern Bell, #800-438, Everlast mk, 8" 95.00
Mask, lady, orange/cream on terra cotta, #6427, 12½" 575.00

Gonder

Lawton Gonder grew up with clay in his hands and fire in his eyes. Gonder's interest in ceramics was greatly influenced by his parents who worked for Weller and a close family friend and noted ceramic authority, John Herold. In his early teens Gonder launched his ceramic career at the Ohio Pottery Company while working for Herold. He later gained valuable experience at American Encaustic Tile Company, Cherry Art Tile, and the Florence Pottery. Gonder was plant manager at the Florence Pottery until fire destroyed the facility in late 1941.

After years of solid production and management experience, Lawton Gonder established the Gonder Ceramic Art Company, formerly the Peters and Reed plant, in South Zanesville, Ohio. Gonder Ceramic Arts produced quality art pottery with beautiful contemporary designs which included human and animal figures and a complete line of Oriental pottery. Accentuating the beautiful shapes were unique and innovative glazes developed by Gonder such as flambe (flame red with streakes of yellow), 24k gold crackle, antique gold, and Chinese crackle.

All Gonder is marked with the company name and mold number. They include 'Gonder U.S.A' in block letters, 'Gonder' in script, 'Gonder Original' in script, and 'Gonder Ceramic Art' in block letters. Paper labels were also used. Some of the early Gonder molds closely resemble RumRill designs that had been manufactured at the Florence Pottery; and because some RumRill pieces are found with similar (if not identical) shapes, matching mold numbers, and Gonder glazes, it is speculated that some RumRill was produced at the Gonder plant. In 1946 Gonder started another company which he named Elgee (chosen for his initials LG) where he manufactured lamp bases until a fire in 1954 resulted in his shifting lamp production to the main plant. Operations ceased in 1957.

Basket, L-19 ....95.00
Bowl, console; bl, J-55 ....55.00
Bowl, dolphin, #556 ....75.00
Candle holders, F-14, pr 25.00
Cookie jar, yel, P-24, no lid 50.00
Cornucopia, gr, #521 ....85.00
Creamer, beige, P-33 ....30.00
Creamer & sugar bowl, gr or purple, P-33 ....65.00

Ewer, gr shell, #508 ....175.00
Figurine, Chinese woman, purple 125.00
Figurine, panther, gr/yel blended, 19" 175.00
Figurine, sea horse, bl crackle, lg 150.00
Figurine, swan, gr, #511, lg 85.00
Lamp, horse head 50.00
Pitcher, #917 ....60.00
Pitcher, gr/wht, #365 ....85.00
Pitcher, wht, E-60 ....45.00
Planter, #738 ....25.00
Planter, red flambe, E-5 ....75.00
Teapot, purple, P-31 ....85.00
Teapot, yel, P-31 ....85.00
TV lamp, ship, gr 85.00
Vase, gold crackle, E-4 ....95.00
Vase, gr, E-82 ....45.00
Vase, H-56 ....25.00
Vase, H-69 ....50.00
Vase, leaf, E-67 ....60.00
Vase, pk, J-61 ....85.00
Vase, swan form, #511 ....75.00
Vase, yel, dbl hdl, J-69, 9½" 42.00
Vase, yel, H-84 ....45.00

Goofus Glass

Goofus glass is American-made pressed glass with designs that are either embossed (blown out) or intaglio (cut in). The decorated colors were aerographed or hand applied and not fired on the pieces. The various patterns exemplify the artistry of the turn-of-the-century glass crafters. The primary production dates were ca 1908 to 1918. Goofus was produced by many well-known manufacturers such as Northwood, Indiana, and Dugan. Our advisor for this categor is Leon Travis of the *Goofus Glass Gazette*; he is listed in the Directory under Virginia. See also Clubs and Newsletters.

Bowl, Butterfly, pattern decor, Dugan, 9", M 65.00
Bowl, Carnation, 9", M 25.00
Bowl, Daisy & Web, opal, M 65.00
Bowl, Deer & Carnation, Northwood, 9", M 65.00
Bowl, Greek Key & Sunflower, gr, Northwood, 9", M 65.00
Bowl, Jeweled Heart, Dugan, 9", M 55.00
Bowl, Monk Drinking From Tankard, 7", M 65.00
Bowl, Moth, pattern decor, rare, M 65.00
Bowl, Nasturtium, Indiana, 9", M 30.00
Bowl, Pears, brn on gold, allover decor, M 75.00
Bowl, Rose on Crackle, ftd, M 45.00
Bowl, Two Fruits & Olympic Torch, pattern decor, rare, 9", M 95.00
Bowl, Wheel & Block, opal, M 45.00

Bread tray, scene from Last Supper, 7x11", EX, $90.00.

Decanter, Cabbage Rose, M 65.00
Dish, Sunflower, gr, Northwood, 7", M 65.00
Hair receiver, Rose on Basketweave, rare, M 125.00
Hatpin holder, Rose on Basketweave, rare, M 65.00
Lamp, Cabbage Rose, matching chimney, 12", M 150.00
Lamp, Cabbage Rose, umbrella shade, 18", M 400.00
Lamp, Daisy, matching chimney, 18", M 300.00
Lamp, Poppy, ball shade, 18", M 275.00
Nappy, Poppy, pattern decor, Northwood, M 35.00
Plate, Butterfly, Dugan, rare, 11", M 125.00
Plate, Carnation, 11", M 25.00
Plate, chop; Bird & Strawberry, 12", M 125.00
Plate, Chrysanthemum, 3-color, 11", M 65.00
Plate, Monk Drinking From Tankard, 7", M 125.00
Plate, Rose-in-Snow, Goofus version, 11", M 35.00
Plate, Thistle, rare, 5", M 65.00
Powder jar, Cabbage Rose, M 30.00
Powder jar, Gibson Girl, M 50.00
Shakers, Cabbage Rose, orig lids, M, pr 75.00
Syrup, Cabbage Rose, M 150.00
Vase, Asters in Basket, 12½", M 95.00
Vase, Bird in Berry Patch, 12", M 95.00
Vase, Cabbage Rose, milk glass, 7", M 25.00
Vase, Cabbage Rose, 15", M 95.00
Vase, Lady w/Veil, rare, 12", M 125.00
Vase, Lovebirds in Hollyhock, 12", M 85.00
Vase, Peacock in Tree, 15", M 150.00
Vase, Poppy, 5", M 15.00
Vase, Statue of Liberty, rare, 12", M 150.00

Goss and Crested China

William Henry Goss received his early education at the Government School of Design at Somerset House, London, and as a result of his merit was introduced to Alderman William Copeland, who owned the Copeland Spode Pottery. Under the influence of Copeland from 1852-1858, Goss quickly learned the trade and soon became their chief designer. Little is known about this brief association, and in 1858 Goss left to begin his own business. After a short-lived partnership with a Mr. Peake, Goss opened a pottery on John Street, Stoke-on-Trent, but by 1870 he had moved his business to a location near London Road. This pottery became the famous Falcon Works. Their mark was a spread-wing falcon (goss-hawk) centering a narrow, horizontal bar with 'W.H. Goss' printed below.

Many of the early pieces made by Goss were left unmarked and are difficult to discern from products made by the Copeland factory, but after he had been in business for about fifteen years, all of his wares were marked. Today unmarked items do not command the prices of the later marked wares.

Adolphus William Henry Goss (Goss's eldest son) joined his father's firm in the 1880s. He introduced cheaper lines, though the more expensive lines continued in production. Shortly after his father's death in 1906, Adolphus retired and left the business to his two younger brothers. The business suffered from problems created by a war economy, and in 1936 Goss assets were held by Cauldon Potteries Ltd. These were eventually taken over by the Coalport Group, who retained the right to use the Goss trademark. Messrs. Ridgeway Potteries bought all the assets in 1954 as well as the right to use the Goss trademark and name. In 1964 the group was known as Allied English Potteries Ltd. (A.E.P.), and in 1971 A.E.P. merged with the Doulton Group. Now it remains to be seen if Goss ware will ever be produced again. Our advisor for this category is Patrick Herley; he is listed in the Directory under New York.

Ann Hathaway's Cottage, sm 45.00
Beaconsfield Bust, parian, on sq base 90.00
Blackpool Tower, Blackpool 55.00
Bottle, leather, Canterbury 6.50
Flask, conical, Conway 4.50
Jack, Lincoln, Margate 12.50
Jug, Reading, State of NY 9.50
Jug, Roman, Newcastle 8.50
Jug, Scarborough, Margate 6.00
Lamp, Caerleon, Glasgow 9.00
Lloyd George's Early Home (no annex) 128.00
Loving cup, 3-hdls, Devon, Lydford, Wm the Conqueror, sm, 2" .15.00
Market Cross, Richmond 50.00
Mather, Irish, Bognor, sm 7.00
Pope's Pipe, Twickenham 30.00
Pot, Guys Porridge, Hurstmonceux 15.00
Queen Elizabeth's Riding Shoe, South Sea 32.50
Queen Victoria's First Shoe, Wembley 25.00
Reculver's Towers, Kent/Herne Bay 120.00
Salt pot, Stockton, Maidenhead 7.00
Shakespeare's House, separate base 95.00
Tank, Eastbourne 45.00
Teapot stand, circular, Eastbourne 11.50
Tyg, Leeds 6.50
Urn, Nottingham, Chichester 6.50
Vase, Cirencester, Battle Abbey 7.50
Wall pocket, Blackpool, sm 10.00

Crested China

Arcadian model figures: Aristocrat, taking pinch of snuff, 80.00; Cavalier, Van Dyke-style beard, $65.00; Tulip boy in Dutch costume, $75.00.

Arcadian, elephant, standing, Matlock, Bath 18.50
Arcadian, Old Curiosity Shop 25.00
Arcadian, terrier, Buxton 15.00
Arcadian, The Globe, Swanage 25.00
Arcadian, vase, Ashover, 2" 8.50
Carlton, ewer, Wembley, 2" 7.50
Carlton, HMS Lion (battleship), Burntisland 45.00
Carlton, vase, 2-hdl, Cornwall 6.00
Carlton, Winchester Bushel, Winchester 17.00
Grafton, Fireman's Helmet 15.00
Grafton, HMS Landship (tank), Newcastle-on-Tyne ...25.00
Grafton, vase, Banbury, 2" 5.50
Victoria, Parakeet, Matlock Bath 14.00
Victoria, pig, Matlock Bath 12.50
Willow Art, Bakewell Cross, Bakewell, 4½" 45.00
Willow Art, elephant, trumpeting, Long Eaton 21.00
Willow Art, man in the moon, pearl lustre, Cardinal Wolsey 21.50
Willow Art, Match striker, Great Yarmouth 9.50
Willow Art, Windsor Castle, Windsor, 6" L 35.00

Gouda

Since the 18th century the main center of the pottery industry in Holland was in Gouda. One of its earliest industries, the manufacture of clay pipes, continues to the present day. The artware so easily recognized by collectors today was first produced about 1885. It was decorated in the Art Nouveau manner. Stylized florals, birds, and geometrics were favored motifs; only rarely are they naturalistic. The Nouveau influence was strong until about 1915. Art Deco was attempted but with less success. Though most of the ware is finished in a matt glaze, glossy pieces in both pastels and dark colors are found on occasion and command higher prices. Decoration on the glossy ware is usually very well executed. Most of the workshops failed during the Depression, though earthenware is still being made in Gouda and carries the Gouda mark. Until very recently Regina was still making a limited amount of the old Gouda-style pottery in a matt finish. Watch for the Gouda name, which is usually a part of the backstamp of the various manufacturers.

Candle holder, bl flowers w/gold & rust, House mk, 2¼x6½" 110.00
Ewer, Nouveau portrait, high glazed, 9½" 190.00
Jar, ginger; Nouveau mc design on blk matt, House mk, 10" 300.00
Jar, Persian floral, cloisonne style, dome lid, #1054, 20" 800.00
Jardiniere vase, Deco designs, 4-hdl, mk Schoonhoven, 8" 250.00

Lamp base, Nouveau multicolor tulips on high gloss, handles, 36", EX, $500.00.

Vase, blk w/mc floral & border, bl mk, 6¼" 125.00
Vase, floral on gr matt w/heavy silver o/l, 7" 350.00
Vase, lions & vines, 12" 350.00
Vase, mc florals, turq int, tan rim, mk, 2¾x2¾" 30.00

Graniteware

Graniteware, made of a variety of metals with enamel coatings, derives its name from its appearance. The speckled, swirled, or mottled effect of the vari-colored enamels may look like granite — but there the resemblance stops. It wasn't especially durable! Expect at least minor chipping if you plan to collect.

Graniteware was featured in 1876 at Phily's Expo. It was mass produced in quantity, and enough of it has survived to make at least the common items easily affordable. Condition, color, shape, and size are important considerations in evaluating an item; cobalt blue and white, green and white, brown and white, and old red and white swirled items are unusual, thus more expensive. Pieces of heavier weight, seam constructed, riveted, and those with wooden handles and tin or matching graniteware lids are usually older.

For further study we recommend *The Collector's Encyclopedia of Graniteware, Colors, Shapes, and Values*, Books I and II, by our advisor, Helen Greguire. Both are available from the author. For information on how to order, see her listing in the Directory under New York. For the address of the National Graniteware Society, see the section on Clubs, Newsletters, and Catalogs.

Baking pan, bl & wht lg mottle, wht int, molded hdls, oblong, M .140.00
Baking pan, bl & wht lg swirl, wht int, molded hdls, oblong, EX ..85.00
Baking pan, brn & wht lg swirl, wht int, molded hdls, oblong, NM .285.00
Baking pan, cobalt & wht lg mottle, molded hdls, oblong, NM 250.00
Baking pan, gray lg mottle, appl wire hdl, oblong, M 55.00
Batter jug, bl & wht relish pattern, wht int, wire bail, NM 550.00
Bowl, cereal; bl & wht relish pattern w/pewter trim, M 185.00
Bowl, fruit; bl w/fancy cutouts, 9" dia, G+ 110.00
Bowl, mixing; gray med mottle, side hdl, G+ 65.00
Bowl, mixing; yel & wht lg mottle w/blk trim, wht int, '60s, NM .30.00
Bowl, serving; bl & wht med swirl w/blk trim, wht int, NM 65.00
Bowl, soup; bl & wht lg swirl w/blk trim, wht int, M 75.00
Bread pan, bl & wht lg mottle w/blk trim, seamed ends, G+ 225.00
Bread pan, cobalt & wht med swirl, wht int, oblong, G+ 245.00
Bread pan, gray lg mottle, seamed ends, NM 45.00
Bucket, bl & wht lg swirl w/touch of gray, tin lid, NM 185.00
Bucket, bl & wht med mottle, tin lid, EX 135.00
Bucket, bl shading, matching lid, M 195.00
Bucket, blk & wht lg mottle, tin lid, M 455.00
Bucket, gr & wht lg swirl, Emerald Ware, matching lid, NM 350.00
Bucket, lt bl & wht wavy mottle w/blk trim, tin lid, NM 285.00
Butter dish, bl & wht lg mottle, spun knob, G+ 750.00
Butter dish, wht w/cobalt trim, M 165.00
Cake turner, wht w/blk hdl, perforated, NM 110.00
Churn, bl & wht swirl, blk hdls, wood dasher & cover, 18", EX .1,995.00
Coaster, bl & wht lg swirl w/blk trim, Bl Diamond Ware, NM ...225.00
Coaster, red insert, mk Towle Sterling 101, M 85.00
Coffee biggin, daisies & leaves on lt gr, pewter trim, 5-pc, M 595.00
Coffee biggin, lt bl shading to wht, tall, 4-pc, NM 295.00
Coffee biggin, lt bl w/gold bands, glass cover, 3-pc, NM 210.00
Coffee biggin, red & wht checked pattern w/red trim, 4-pc, G+ ..595.00
Coffee biggin, red & wht lg mottle w/red trim, 4-pc, G+ 565.00
Coffee biggin, yel w/blk trim, Bakelite knob, 5-pc, M 195.00
Coffee boiler, bl shading to wht, Bluebelle Ware, M 265.00
Coffee boiler, brn & wht lg swirl, NM 525.00
Coffee boiler, brn & wht relish pattern, NM 225.00
Coffee boiler, dk bl & wht relish pattern, NM 325.00
Coffee boiler, wht w/blk trim, Belmont label, M 165.00
Coffee flask, bl relish pattern, metal top, 6¾", NM 310.00
Coffee roaster, blk & wht mottle, screen-style drum, lg, M 425.00
Coffeepot, aqua & wht lg swirl w/blk trim, NM 265.00
Coffeepot, bl & wht lg swirl, NM 295.00
Coffeepot, bl & wht lg swirl w/blk trim & hdl, rare, NM 395.00
Coffeepot, brn & wht mottle, brass-plated lid, wood hdl, M 395.00
Coffeepot, brn shading to gold, Enamel Art Ware label, NM 325.00
Coffeepot, cobalt & wht mottle, wood hdl & knob, NM 225.00
Coffeepot, gr & wht lg swirl, Emerald Ware, NM 595.00
Coffeepot, gray lg mottle w/pewter trim, copper bottom, M 325.00
Coffeepot, pk & wht relish pattern, NM 295.00
Coffeepot, pk & yel flowers on bl to wht, Stewart Ware, M 225.00
Coffeepot, yel & wht lg swirl w/blk trim, glass knob, M 195.00
Colander, gr & wht lg mottle w/dk bl trim & hdls, ftd, NM 395.00
Colander, gray mottle, strap hdls, 3 appl ft, M 75.00
Colander, wht w/cobalt trim & hdls, fancy perforations, ftd, M 45.00
Cream can, bl & wht lg swirl w/blk trim, wire bail, NM 395.00
Cream can, brn shading, wire bail/wood hdl, M 195.00
Cream can, gray lg mottle, Boston style, mk Granite Iron Ware, M .195.00
Creamer, aqua shading to wht, squatty, G+ 110.00
Creamer, gray lg mottle w/pewter trim, M 625.00
Creamer, mc lg swirl w/blk trim & hdl, squatty, G+ 325.00
Creamer, morning glories on wht, pewter trim, M 395.00
Cup, brn & wht lg swirl w/blk trim, NM 100.00
Cup & saucer, bl & wht lg swirl w/blk trim, NM 145.00
Cup & saucer, bl & wht sm mottle w/blk trim, NM 100.00

Cup & saucer, gr & wht lg swirl w/blk trim, Chrysolite, G+ 235.00
Cup & saucer, yel & wht lg swirl w/blk trim, 1960s, M 75.00
Cuspidor, bl & wht sm mottle, wht int, 2-pc, NM 265.00
Dbl boiler, aqua & wht lg swirl w/cobalt trim, flared, NM 300.00
Dbl boiler, bl & wht mottle w/blk trim, Snow on the Mtn, M 275.00
Dbl boiler, gr & wht lg mottle w/gr trim, Elite Austria, EX 245.00
Dipper, bl & wht swirl w/blk trim & hdl, w/eyelet, EX 95.00
Dishpan, bl & wht lg mottle, wht int, oval, NM 295.00
Egg cup, wht w/blk trim, Polar Ware Co, M 110.00
Fish kettle/poacher, gray lg mottle, w/insert, NM 235.00
Fry pan, cobalt & wht lg swirl, wht int, M 295.00
Funnel, bl & wht mottle, wht int, mk Elite Austria, G+ 65.00
Funnel, cobalt & wht swirl w/blk trim, wht int, lg squatty, NM .295.00
Gravy boat, bl & wht swirl w/blk trim & hdl, Bl Diamond Ware, NM .255.00
Kettle, bl & wht lg swirl w/blk trim & hdls, convex, M 295.00
Kettle, brn & wht lg swirl, wht int, Berlin style, NM 300.00
Kettle, cobalt & wht lg swirl w/blk trim, convex, NM 325.00
Ladle, bl & wht lg swirl w/blk hdl, G+ 75.00
Ladle, red & wht lg swirl w/bl trim & hdl, foreign, old, NM 495.00
Measure, aqua & wht lg mottle w/cobalt trim, EX 295.00
Measure, bl & wht lg mottle w/lt bl trim, EX 235.00
Measure, gray mottle, riveted spout/hdl, NM 225.00
Measure, red, wht & bl lg swirl w/dk bl trim, EX 595.00

Melon mold, mottled gray, marked Extra Agate, L&G
Mfg. Co., 4x7¾", M, $125.00 (unmarked, M, $100.00).

Milk can, cobalt & wht lg swirl, wht int, wire bail/wood hdl, NM .995.00
Mold, flower imprint w/scalloped edges, lt bl w/wht int, M 135.00
Mold, ring shape w/tubular center, bl & wht mottle w/cobalt, M .295.00
Mold, shell form, wht, oblong, G+ 85.00
Mold, strawberry imprint w/fluted edges, bl & wht mottle, G+ ..250.00
Muffin pan, cobalt & wht lg swirl, blk trim/wht int, 8-cup, NM ..525.00
Muffin pan, cobalt & wht lg swirl w/in & w/o, 8-cup, M 595.00
Muffin pan, gray lg mottle, 6-cup, M 65.00
Muffin pan, wht w/cobalt trim, mk L&G Mfg Co, 9-cup, NM ...275.00
Mug, bl & wht lg mottle w/blk trim, barrel shape, NM 185.00
Mug, cobalt & wht lg swirl, wht int, NM 110.00
Mug, gr & wht lg swirl w/blk trim, Emerald Ware, EX 145.00
Mug, mc flowers on dk bl, wht int, G+ 65.00
Mug, red & wht lg swirl w/blk trim, 1960s, NM 30.00
Mug, turq swirl, wide strap hdl, EX 55.00
Mug, yel & wht lg swirl w/dk bl trim, 1960s, M 30.00
Pail, bl & wht lg swirl w/blk trim, wire bail/wood hdl, sm, M 235.00
Pail, brn shading w/blk trim, wire bail/wood hdl, M 135.00
Pie plate, gr & wht lg swirl w/blk trim, Chrysolite, NM 135.00
Pie plate, wht w/gr trim, Savory Ware, M 35.00
Pitcher, milk; bl & wht mottle w/blk trim & hdl, M 195.00
Pitcher, milk; bl shading w/bl trim & hdl, Bluebelle Ware, M 180.00
Pitcher, molasses; brn shading, wht int, NM 295.00
Pitcher, water; bl & wht wavy mottle w/blk trim & hdl, M 650.00
Pitcher, water; brn & wht swirl w/blk trim & hdl, EX 550.00
Pitcher, water; dk gr & wht swirl w/blk trim, EX 395.00
Pitcher, water; wht, mk L&G Mfg Co, NM 75.00

Pitcher & bowl, wht w/cobalt trim, M 110.00
Plate, bl & wht med mottle w/bl trim, 9" dia, NM 65.00
Plate, brn & wht lg swirl w/blk trim, 9" dia, M 145.00
Plate, cobalt & wht lg swirl w/blk trim, M 145.00
Platter, blk swan on wht, blk trim, octagon, M 155.00
Platter, cobalt & wht lg swirl, oval, NM 395.00
Platter, mc lg swirl on both sides, oval, G+ 1,195.00
Pudding pan, brn & wht lg swirl w/blk trim, wht int, M 225.00
Roaster, bl & wht lg swirl w/blk trim & hdls, oval, 2-pc, M 395.00
Roaster, bl & wht lg swirl w/blk trim & hdls, rnd, 2-pc, M 195.00
Roaster, gray mottle, oval, 2-pc, M 195.00
Salt box, gray lg mottle, G+ 575.00
Saucepan, bl & wht lg swirl w/blk trim & hdl, Berlin style, EX ..165.00
Saucepan, brn & wht lg swirl w/blk trim & hdl, wht int, EX 145.00
Saucer, gray lg mottle, 6⅞" dia, M 75.00
Scoop, thumb; wht w/cobalt hdl, NM 115.00
Skimmer, bl, perforated, hdld, NM 140.00
Skimmer, wht w/fancy perforation, tubular hdl, G+ 125.00
Soap dish, shell form, gray lg mottle, holes for hanging, EX 185.00
Spatula, bl & wht sm mottle w/blk hdl, G+ 185.00
Spatula, gray med mottle, NM 85.00
Spoon, cream w/gr hdl, NM 35.00
Spoon, gr & wht swirl, Chrysolite, G+ 195.00
Spooner, brn & wht lg swirl w/blk trim, NM 2,000.00
Strainer, gray & dk bl sm mottle, wire ft, w/cover, EX 135.00
Strainer, gray med mottle w/fancy perforations, hdld, ftd, M 165.00
Sugar bowl, apple blossoms on bl, pewter trim, M 425.00
Sugar bowl, red & wht lg mottle, mk Japan, 1960s, M 60.00
Syrup, gray med mottle, NP copper top, G+ 495.00
Syrup, wht w/NP lid & thumb rest, VG 195.00
Tart pan, gray mottle, M 45.00
Tea strainer, bl & wht lg swirl, screen bottom, NM 255.00
Tea strainer, gray, perforated, NM 75.00
Teakettle, bl w/blk Art Deco pattern, gold trim, Alaska hdl, M .120.00
Teakettle, cobalt & wht lg swirl w/blk trim, EX 495.00
Teakettle, gr & wht lg swirl, Alaska hdl, Chrysolite, EX 750.00
Teakettle, gr & wht lg swirl w/blk trim, wht int, squatty, M 525.00
Teakettle, gr & wht sm mottle w/gr trim, EX 165.00
Teakettle, red & wht lg mottle w/blk trim & hdl, 1960s, M 145.00
Teakettle, wht w/bl veining, Snow on the Mountain, EX 180.00
Teakettle, yel w/blk trim & hdl, EX 75.00
Teapot, bl, gr & orange sponge design, mk Elite, 6-sided, NM ...175.00
Teapot, bl & wht sm mottle, NM 225.00
Teapot, bl & wht sm mottle, tall squatty, mk Elite, M 395.00
Teapot, bl lg swirl w/blk trim, Columbian Ware, NM 525.00
Teapot, brn & wht lg swirl, NM 675.00
Teapot, brn shading, riveted hdl, rare, NM 275.00
Teapot, calla lilies on wht, pewter trim, M 295.00
Teapot, castle scene on wht, pewter trim, M 325.00
Teapot, cobalt & wht lg swirl, wood hdl, ribbed cover, M 525.00
Teapot, daisies & leaves on lt gr, pewter trim, M 395.00
Teapot, gr & wht lg mottle, Chrysolite, NM 525.00
Teapot, gr ribbed body w/glass cover, lg & squatty on ped, NM .165.00
Teapot, gray med mottle, dmn cutouts on tubular hdl, M 185.00
Teapot, gray mottle, pewter trim, scalloped top edge, M 295.00
Teapot, mc fruit on yel & wht shading, blk trim, 1970s, M 60.00
Teapot, mc lg swirl w/blk hdl & spout, squatty, G+ 495.00
Teapot, red w/blk & wht dots, squatty, mk Czechoslovakia, sm, M ..195.00
Teapot, violet shading, squatty, Thistle Ware, G+ 225.00
Tray, aqua & wht lg mottle, w/brass eyelet, oblong, NM 375.00
Tray, gray med mottle, oval, NM 145.00
Tray, red & wht lg mottle w/bl trim, 1960s, rnd, NM 55.00
Tumbler, bl & wht lg mottle w/blk trim, M 85.00
Tumbler, bl shading to gray w/blk trim, wht int, G+ 75.00

Tumbler, brn & wht lg swirl w/blk trim, NM 550.00
Tumbler, gray med mottle, M 200.00
Tureen, soup; gray med mottle, blk wooden hdls, ftd, oval, G+ ..595.00
Tureen, soup; lt bl & wht mottle, rnd, ftd, NM 595.00
Vegetable dish, cobalt w/wht interior, oval, M 85.00
Vegetable dish, yel & wht lg swirl w/blk trim, oblong, M 165.00
Wash basin, gr & wht swirl w/blk trim, w/eyelet, Emerald Ware, EX .195.00
Waste bowl, brn & wht relish pattern w/pewter trim, ring hdls, M .395.00

Green Opaque

Introduced in 1887 by the New England Glass Company, this ware is very scarce due to the fact that it was produced for less than one year. It is characterized by its soft green color and a wavy band of gold reserving a mottled blue metallic stain. It is usually found in satin; examples with a shiny finish are extremely rare.

Bowl, 4x8", M 1,150.00
Box, powder; NM gold mottling on bowl & lid, 4x6¼" 1,150.00
Cruet, orig stopper 1,150.00
Mug, 2¼" 500.00
Punch cup 550.00
Punch cup, worn decor, 2½" 225.00
Shaker, 2½" 400.00
Toothpick holder, gold trim 1,150.00
Tumbler, EX gold & mottling 665.00
Tumbler, lemonade; w/hdl, 5" 950.00
Tumbler, M mottling, 3½" 800.00
Vase, flared, M gold & mottling, 6" 900.00
Vase, 14-rib ovoid w/flaring rim, VG gold & mottling, 6" 500.00

Greenaway, Kate

Kate Greenaway was an English artist who lived from 1846 to 1901. She gained worldwide fame as an illustrator of children's books, drawing children clothed in the styles worn by proper English and American boys and girls of the very early 1800s. Her book, *Under the Willow Tree*, published in 1878, was the first of many. Her sketches appeared in leading magazines, and her greeting cards were in great demand. Manufacturers of china, pottery, and metal products copied her characters to decorate children's dishes, tiles, and salt and pepper shakers as well as many other items. Our advisor is James Lewis Lowe, Director of the Kate Greenaway Society; he is listed in the Directory under Pennsylvania. See also Napkin Rings.

Almanac, 1886, wht leather, Sangorski/Sutcliffe 475.00
Almanac, 1892, London, 1st edition, VG 135.00
Book, A Apple Pie, Warne, 1940, w/dust jacket, VG 28.00
Book, Kate Greenaway's Birthday Book, 1970, w/jacket, NM 12.00
Book, Mother Goose, London, later print of 1st edition, VG 150.00
Bowl, Daisy & Button, amber; R&B SP holder w/girl & dog 525.00
Butter pat, children playing transfer, pre-1910 ....40.00
Cup & saucer, pk lustre trim, pre-1910 ....125.00
Engraving, Harper's Bazaar, Jan 1879, full-pg 25.00
Figurine, seated girl tugs on lg hat, bsk, pre-1910, sm 75.00
Paperweight, CI, Victorian girl in lg bonnet, pre-1910, 3x2¾" ..110.00
Pencil holder, pnt porc, pre-1910 ....100.00
Plate, ABC, girl in lg hat, Staffordshire, 7" 95.00
Plate, children at play, fruits, birds & flowers, 9" 100.00
Scarf, Greenway illus on silk, early, EX 65.00
Tea set, semiporc, floral motif, pre-1910, 3-pc 70.00
Toothpick holder, bsk, girl sits on stump, basket on bk 40.00

Toothpick holder, clear glass, 2 girls by basket 100.00
Wall pocket, ceramic, 6 girls on open book form, 6x9x3" 125.00

Greentown Glass

Greentown glass is a term referring to the product of the Indiana Tumbler and Goblet Company of Greentown, Indiana, ca 1894 to 1903. Their earlier pressed glass patterns were #11, a pseudo-cut glass design; #137, Pleat Band; and #200, Austrian. Another line, Dewey, was designed in 1898. Many lovely colors were produced in addition to crystal. Jacob Rosenthal, who was later affiliated with Fenton, developed his famous chocolate glass in 1900. The rich, shaded opaque brown glass was an overnight success. Two new patterns, Leaf Bracket and Cactus, were designed to display the glass to its best advantage, but previously existing molds were also used. In only three years Rosenthal developed yet another important color formula, Golden Agate. The Holly Amber pattern was designed especially for its production. The dolphin covered dish with a fish finial is perhaps the most common and easily recognized piece ever produced. Other animal dishes were also made; all are highly collectible. There have been many repros — not all are marked! The symbol (+) at the end of some of the following lines was used to indicate items that have been reproduced.

Our advisors for this category are Jerry and Sandi Garrett; they are listed in the Directory under Indiana. See the Pattern Glass section for clear pressed glass; only colored items are listed here.

Animal dish, bird w/berry, cobalt 650.00
Animal dish, bird w/berry, Nile gr 1,950.00
Animal dish, cat on a hamper, canary, tall (+) 650.00
Animal dish, cat on hamper, chocolate, low 700.00

Animal dish, cat on hamper, cobalt, tall, $750.00.

Animal dish, cat on hamper, Nile gr, tall (+) 1,500.00
Animal dish, dolphin, amber, sawtooth edge (+) 750.00
Animal dish, dolphin, chocolate, smooth edge 450.00
Animal dish, dolphin, cobalt, beaded edge 850.00
Animal dish, dolphin, Golden Agate, beaded edge 950.00
Animal dish, fighting cocks, amber 1,400.00
Animal dish, fighting cocks, chocolate 2,000.00
Animal dish, fighting cocks, wht opaque 1,750.00
Animal dish, hen on nest, canary 450.00
Animal dish, hen on nest, Golden Agate 1,500.00
Animal dish, rabbit, amber (+) 200.00
Animal dish, rabbit, wht opaque (+) 200.00
Austrian, bowl, canary, rectangular, 8¼x5¼" 225.00
Austrian, butter dish, canary, child's 525.00
Austrian, compote, canary, 4½" dia 225.00
Austrian, creamer, canary, ped base, sm 190.00
Austrian, creamer, cobalt, child's 300.00
Austrian, punch cup, amber 225.00

Austrian, tumbler, amber 300.00
Beehive, vase, bud; amber 300.00
Brazen Shield, cake stand, bl, 9⅜" or 10⅜", ea 300.00
Brazen Shield, relish tray, bl 150.00
Brazen Shield, sugar bowl, bl, w/lid 225.00
Cactus, bowl, chocolate, 5¼" 135.00
Cactus, butter/cheese dish, chocolate, ped ft 800.00
Cactus, compote, chocolate, 8¼" 225.00
Cactus, mug, chocolate, hdld 75.00
Cactus, syrup, chocolate, metal lid 200.00
Cactus, tumbler, bl-wht opal rim 350.00
Cord Drapery, bowl, cobalt, hand-fluted, 8¼" 250.00
Cord Drapery, cake plate, amber, ftd 180.00
Cord Drapery, goblet, emerald gr 280.00
Cord Drapery, spooner, amber 150.00
Cord Drapery, toothpick holder, cobalt 400.00
Cord Drapery, water tray, emerald gr 275.00
Cupid, butter dish, Nile gr 500.00
Cupid, creamer, chocolate 375.00
Cupid, spooner, wht opaque 125.00
Cupid, sugar bowl, wht opaque, w/lid 150.00
Cut glass, bowl, unknown pattern, chocolate, 6" 475.00
Cut glass, plate, Dmn & Bow, chocolate, 6" sq 750.00
Dewey, bowl, chocolate, 8" 285.00
Dewey, bowl, emerald gr, 8" 90.00
Dewey, butter dish, cobalt, 4" 275.00
Dewey, butter dish, Nile gr, 4" dia 250.00
Dewey, creamer, canary, 5" 100.00
Dewey, creamer, wht opaque, 4" tall 100.00
Dewey, cruet, chocolate, w/stopper 2,000.00
Dewey, mug, teal bl 200.00
Dewey, plate, amber 90.00
Dewey, serpentine tray, Golden Agate 1,650.00
Dewey, sugar bowl, emerald gr, w/lid, 2½" dia 85.00
Early Diamond, dish, cobalt, rectangular, 8x5" 200.00
Early Diamond, tumbler, emerald green 150.00
Greentown Daisy, butter dish, frosted clear 65.00
Greentown Daisy, creamer, frosted emerald gr, w/lid ...115.00
Greentown Daisy, mustard pot, chocolate, w/lid 225.00
Greentown Daisy, sugar bowl, wht opaque, w/lid 90.00
Herringbone Buttress, bowl, clear w/bl opal edge, 5¼" ...775.00
Herringbone Buttress, bowl, emerald gr, 7¼" 250.00
Herringbone Buttress, butter dish, emerald gr, ped ft ...600.00
Herringbone Buttress, cordial, olive gr, 3⅜" 200.00
Herringbone Buttress, mug, chocolate 85.00
Herringbone Buttress, punch cup, emerald gr 165.00
Herringbone Buttress, shaker, emerald gr 325.00
Herringbone Buttress, sugar bowl, emerald gr 325.00
Herringbone Buttress, vase, emerald gr, 8" 275.00
Holly, toothpick holder, Wht Agate 3,650.00
Holly Amber, bowl, oval 475.00
Holly Amber, bowl, rectangular, 10x4" 1,500.00
Holly Amber, compote, made from 4½" & 6½" lids ...1,500.00
Holly Amber, cruet 2,250.00
Holly Amber, mustard pot, open, 3¼" 850.00
Holly Amber, plate, sq, 7½" 950.00
Holly Amber, tray, 9¼" 1,500.00
Holly Amber, vase, ped ft, 8" 2,200.00
Leaf Bracket, butter dish, chocolate 175.00
Leaf Bracket, celery tray, chocolate, 11" 135.00
Leaf Bracket, nappy, wht opaque 190.00
Leaf Bracket, shaker, chocolate 165.00
Leaf Bracket, toothpick holder, chocolate 350.00
Mug, dog & child, chocolate 750.00

Mug, indoor drinking scene, Nile gr, 5¾" 165.00
Mug, Serenade, emerald gr 135.00
Novelty, buffalo, Nile gr, no date (+) 750.00
Novelty, Connecticut skillet, Nile gr 600.00
Novelty, Dewey bust, wht opaque, w/base 215.00
Novelty, ribbed covered dish (Dewey base w/lid), teal bl ...200.00
Pattern #75 (formerly #11), bowl, bl, 6¼" dia 190.00
Pattern #75 (formerly #11), bowl, emerald gr, rectangular, 8x6½" .90.00
Pattern #75 (formerly #11), toothpick holder, emerald gr 90.00
Pattern #75 (formerly #11), tumbler, iced tea; clear 15.00
Pitcher, Paneled, chocolate 600.00
Pitcher, Ruffled Eye, emerald gr 200.00
Pleat Band, cordial, canary 250.00
Scalloped Flange, vase, chocolate 95.00
Shuttle, butter dish, chocolate 1,250.00
Shuttle, creamer, chocolate 650.00
Shuttle, mug, amber 375.00
Shuttle, tumbler, canary 400.00
Teardrop & Tassel, bowl, sauce; chocolate, 4" 235.00
Teardrop & Tassel, compote, Nile gr, w/lid, 4⅝" 475.00
Teardrop & Tassel, pitcher, amber 325.00
Teardrop & Tassel, sugar bowl, wht opaque, w/lid 150.00
Toothpick holder, dog's head, frosted amber 325.00
Toothpick holder, picture fr, amber 275.00
Toothpick holder, sheaf of wheat, chocolate (+) 900.00
Toothpick holder, witch head, Nile gr (+) 190.00
Tumbler, Paneled, chocolate 500.00
Tumbler, Sawtooth, chocolate 125.00
Tumbler, Uneeda Biscuit, chocolate, tall 145.00

Grueby

William Henry Grueby joined the firm of the Low Art Tile Works at the age of fifteen and in 1894, after several years of experience in the production of architectural tiles, founded his own plant, the Grueby Faience Company, in Boston, Massachusetts. Grueby began experimenting with the idea of producing art pottery and had soon perfected a fine glaze (soft and without gloss) in shades of blue, gray, yellow, brown, and his most successful, cucumber green. In 1900 his exhibit at the Paris Exposition Universelle won three gold medals.

Grueby pottery was hand thrown and hand decorated in the Arts and Crafts style. Vertically thrust stylized leaves and flowers in relief were the most common decorative devices. Tiles continued to be an important product, unique (due to the matt glaze decoration) as well as durable. Grueby tiles were often a full inch thick. Obviously incompatible with the Art Nouveau style, the artware was discontinued soon after 1910. The ware is marked in one of several ways: 'Grueby Pottery, Boston, USA'; 'Grueby, Boston, Mass.'; or 'Grueby Faience.' The artware is often artist signed. Our advisor for this category is David Rago; he is listed in the Directory under New Jersey.

Bowl, bl, upright leaves, 3½x7" 700.00
Bowl, gr, appl leaves, 2x5½" 650.00
Jar, bl w/yel & cream leaf neck band, w/lid, sgn/1-4-07, 8" 2,700.00
Jar, curdled bl matt w/dk bl speckling, w/ lid, 6¾x5¾" 2,530.00
Tile, candlestick, 3-color, 6" 2,200.00
Tile, chicken in red clay, 4" sq in wide oak fr 100.00
Tile, elephant, red clay, in oak fr, 4" 240.00
Tile, goose, cream/yel on bl to gr, 4", +fr 500.00
Tile, Grueby Tile & chamberstick, 3-color, Seaman, rstr, 6x4½" .1,300.00
Tile, lg rabbit/grasses, 3-color, 6", +fr 1,100.00
Tile, mermaid relief, brn on bl, 6", +fr, EX 350.00
Tile, pelican, red clay, in oak fr, 4" 140.00

Tile, pine trees/mtns, 5-color, 6", +fr 1,800.00
Tile, reindeer in red clay, 4" sq in wide oak fr 120.00
Tile, row of 4 penguins on ice in water, mc, 4", +fr 1,800.00
Tile, ship w/full sails, 4-color, 4", in oak fr 450.00
Tile, stylized bud/leaf, 4-color, 6", +fr 500.00
Tile, trees arch above swans, 4-color/squeezebag, 4", +fr 650.00
Tile, trees/bldg, 6-color, 4", in oak fr 650.00
Tile, trees/mtns beyond, 6-color, sgn MCM, 6" 2,200.00

Vase, yellow iris on green, 13", $22,000.00.

Vase, bl, repeating-leaf band, bulbous, inverted rim, 7", NM ..1,380.00
Vase, bl-gr mottle, 3¼x2½" 200.00
Vase, curdled gr, wide ribs, bulbous/sq, #155, 5½x7" 2,900.00
Vase, curdled med gr, long neck, low angle shoulder, 8" 950.00
Vase, dk gr, emb wide leaves, WP/#155, 5¾x6½" 3,600.00
Vase, dk gr, leaves w/curled tips, gourd form, 8" 4,000.00
Vase, dk gr, 4 cvd/appl leaves, tips/buds form rim, 8" 2,800.00
Vase, gr, cvd panels, artist sgn, bulbous base, 7", EX 600.00
Vase, gr, leaves w/narrow spines, shouldered, sm prof rstr, 5" ..1,300.00
Vase, gr, long neck, shouldered body, 6" 800.00
Vase, gr, long/short leaves alternate, bbl shape, rpr, 9x7" 3,400.00
Vase, gr, sculpted/appl leaves at bulb bottom, long neck, 8" ...1,800.00
Vase, gr, tips of 2 appl leaves curl out at rim, 8½", NM 1,100.00
Vase, gr, tooled/appl leaves on body & neck, 12½x9" 19,000.00
Vase, gr, trumpet neck, 3¾x3" 500.00
Vase, gr, upright leaves, 5½x9" 1,800.00
Vase, gr, wide leaves w/curled tops, rstr, 3x5¼" 1,100.00
Vase, gr, 2 rings at shoulder, 3x5½" 400.00
Vase, gr, 3-sided: leaf panels, 3-lobe rim, WP, 8¼x4½" 3,000.00
Vase, gr (EX glaze), long neck, squat body w/leaves, JE, 8½" ..3,000.00
Vase, gr (EX glaze), wide leaves, 23x9" 8,000.00
Vase, gr mottle, hdls from rim to angle shoulder, 9½x5" 1,100.00
Vase, gr mottle, tall broad leaves, ovoid, ERF, 9¾x6½" 6,000.00
Vase, gr mottle, 2 rows tooled/appl leaves, SW/#158, 5x7" 1,800.00
Vase, gr w/wht buds between wide leaves, cylinder, 5½", EX ..1,000.00
Vase, gr w/yel buds, wide leaves w/top curl, shouldered, 12½" 9,000.00
Vase, gr w/yel buds between wide leaves, 4x4" 3,300.00
Vase, gr w/yel clover above row of leaves, EX work, WP, 5x5" 3,900.00
Vase, gr w/yel trefoils, rows of leaves, MS, 12x9", EX 12,000.00
Vase, mustard, angle shoulder, 10x8", NM 1,900.00
Vase, ochre, overlapping upright leaves, rpr, 11x8" 2,800.00
Vase, ochre-brn, bulbous w/long wide cylinder neck, 13x8" 1,900.00
Vase, olive gr, 5 wide cvd leaves, MS, rstr rim, 7½x5" 1,800.00
Vase, organic gr, 3 rows of leaves/flowers/buds, WP, 13x9" 7,750.00

Gustavsberg

Gustavsberg Pottery, founded near Stockholm, Sweden, in the late

1700s, manufactured faience, creamware, and porcelain in the English taste until the end of the 19th century. During the 20th century, the factory has produced some inventive modernistic designs, often signed by their artists. Wilhelm Kage (1889-1960) is best remembered for Argenta, a stoneware body decorated in silver overlay, introduced in the 1930s. Usually a mottled green, Argenta can also be found in cobalt blue and white. Other lines included Cintra (an exceptionally translucent porcelain), Farsta (copper-glazed ware), and Farstarust (iron oxide geometric overlay). Designer Stig Lindberg's work, which dates from the 1940s through the early 1970s, includes slab-built figures and a full range of tableware. Some pieces of Gustavsberg are dated.

Bowl, Argenta, fish & trailing bubbles, silver rim, 2x7" 365.00
Box, Argenta, silver o/l, nude smoking mk, 1930, 6x4½" 550.00
Covered dish, gold w/red & bl irid, 1928, 3¾x4" 110.00
Sculpture, blond boy in bl pants holds teddy/sucks thumb, 7" 210.00
Sculpture, smiling tiger, Lisa L, 10" L 90.00
Tip tray & match holder, Swedish Am Lines, silver o/l, pr 95.00
Vase, Argenta, detailed fish w/bubbles in sterling, 4¾" 195.00
Vase, Argenta, silver o/l floral on gr mottle, #1076, 7⅝" 490.00
Vase, Argenta, silver o/l floral on sea gr, 8¼x7" 350.00
Vase, Argenta, silver o/l linear design w/foliage on gr, 9¼" 460.00
Vase, brn crystalline, squat bottle form, Friberg, 5½" 375.00
Vase, cameo cut, bl floral o/l on bl mottle, 1913, 4½x6¼" 450.00
Vase, cityscape, mc on gray, Stig Lindberg, cylinder, 16" 275.00

Hagen-Renaker

Best known for their line of miniature animal figures, Hagen-Renaker was founded in Monrovia, California, in 1946. It is estimated that perhaps as many as eighty different dogs were produced. In addition to the animals, they made replicas of characters from several popular Disney films under license from the Disney Studio. The firm relocated in San Dimas in 1966, where they remain active to the present time. Their wares are sometimes marked with an incised 'HR,' a stamped 'Hagen-Renaker' or part of the name, or paper labels. For more information, we recommend *The Collector's Encyclopedia of California Pottery* by Jack Chipman. Another source of information is Hagen-Renaker Collectors Club (HRCC), listed in the Directory under Clubs, Newsletters, and Catalogs.

Figurine, Ranger, brown and white spotted dog, gold and black sticker on back, 1953, 5" long, $65.00.

Figurine, Adelaide donkey, glossy, hat removes, San Marcos, 5½x6" ...80.00
Figurine, Baron, German Shepherd dog, Monrovia 60.00
Figurine, Black Bisque, bull 90.00
Figurine, Bobby, bulldog pup, glossy, Monrovia 30.00
Figurine, Butch, Mustang foal, bay, Monrovia 250.00
Figurine, Fez, recumbent Arabian foal, wht, Monrovia 225.00
Figurine, Friar, St Bernard 85.00

Figurine, His Nibs, Cocker Spaniel, Monrovia 50.00
Figurine, Lady & Tramp's Pedro 95.00
Figurine, Lippit, Morgan stallion, chestnut, Dan Dimas 90.00
Figurine, Moonbeam, playing Persian kitten, Monrovia 40.00
Figurine, Nobby, bulldog pup, glossy, Monrovia 60.00
Figurine, Patsy, standing Cocker Spaniel puppy, Monrovia 40.00
Figurine, Peggy, squirrel 40.00
Figurine, Siamese cat, glossy, sitting, 8" 70.00
Figurine, Son John, matt lamb, San Marcos 15.00
Figurine, Sparky, Dalmatian, San Marcos 75.00
Figurine, Starlight 45.00
Figurine, stylized cat 65.00
Plaque, Hippon River, 3 mini hippos at river 35.00

Hagenauer

Carl Hagenauer founded his metal workshops in Vienna in 1898. He was joined by his son Karl in 1919. They produced a wide range of stylized sculptural designs in both metal and wood.

Bookends, leaping gazelles, brass, 3-scallop bk, 5", VG 200.00
Bookends, native w/spear & shield, blk/red, wood mts, 5x8" 290.00
Bookends, seated dogs, chrome, scalloped side, 5", EX 650.00
Bookends, stylized pelicans, brass, mks, 5¼x5" 460.00
Candlesticks, brass, long beaded stems, 1930, 11⅝", pr 700.00
Figure, buffalo, mahog w/brass horns, ft rpr, 12" 450.00
Figure, bunnies w/long ears, bronzed patina, 1½", set of 4 ....280.00
Figure, giraffe, bronze finish w/gold highlights, 7½" 110.00
Figure, golfer, blk w/gold highlights, Austria, 3½", pr 400.00
Figure, hunter on horse w/dog, bronze/wood, '30, 8½x13⅜" 700.00
Figure, Madonna, cvd teak, silver face/hands, sgn Vienna, 6" 400.00
Figure, native boy sits, blk w/gold spear & shield, 3½" 180.00
Figure, native dancing w/spear & shield, blk, grass skirt, 7" 200.00
Figure, native girl strikes pose, hair in knot, blk, 9½" 270.00
Figure, native head, wood w/brass earring & oval base, 6" 325.00
Figure, native rowers, brass/wood, mk, ca 1925, 4⅝x19⅞" 800.00
Figure, native striding, blk w/gold spear & shield, 5½" 160.00
Mask, lady, hammered metal w/silver finish, #1045, 20x14¼" 4,485.00
Mask, native lady w/scarf, bronze w/blk finish, 10x6¾" 865.00
Mirror, brass, stylized fish, openwork hdl, mk, 10¼x6" dia 435.00
Sculpture, stylized buffalo, mahog w/brass horns, 6½x12" 575.00

Hair Weaving

A rather unusual craft became popular during the mid-1800s. Human hair was used to make jewelry (rings, bracelets, lockets, etc.) by braiding and interlacing fine strands of hair into hollow forms with pearls and beads added for effect. Hair wreaths were also made, often using hair from deceased family members as well as the living. They were displayed in deep satin-lined frames along with mementoes of the weaver or her departed kin. The fad was abandoned before the turn of the century. The values suggested below are for mint condition examples. Any fraying of the hair greatly lowers value.

Bracelet, dk hair in dbl fancy braid, 15k gold mts, 6½x½" 280.00
Bracelet, finely woven hair w/gold fittings, locket end 125.00
Earrings, ¼" brunette tube in love knot, 14k gold mts 250.00
Necklace, box-link chain w/15k gold mts/clasp, 46" 145.00
Necklace, brass slide & clip for locket, 1880s, 44" 225.00
Necklace, long & thin woven hair, gold mts & sliding heart 100.00
Ring, belt & buckle motif w/gold band, covered w/hair 190.00
Watch fob, lg gold fittings, ornate, Victorian 195.00

Watch fob, 10k yel gold mts, plain 50.00
Wreath, Victorian, orig shadow-box fr, 24x24" 325.00

Hall

The Hall China Company of East Liverpool, Ohio, was established in 1903. Their earliest product was whiteware toilet seats, mugs, jugs, etc. By 1920 their restaurant-type dinnerware and cookware had become so successful that Hall was assured of a solid future. They continue today to be one of the country's largest manufacturers of this type of product.

Hall introduced the first of their famous teapots in 1920; new shapes and colors were added each year until about 1948, making them the largest teapot manufacturer in the world. These and the dinnerware lines of the '30s through the '50s have become popular collectibles. For more thorough study of the subject, we recommend *The Collector's Encyclopedia of Hall China* by Margaret and Kenn Whitmyer; their address may be found in the Directory under Ohio.

Blue Bouquet, bowl, flat soup; 8½" 18.00
Blue Bouquet, bowl, Radiance, 9" 25.00
Blue Bouquet, casserole, Thick Rim 45.00
Blue Bouquet, gravy boat 30.00
Blue Bouquet, leftover, rectangular 75.00
Blue Bouquet, platter, oval, 11¼" 24.00
Blue Bouquet, saucer 2.50
Cameo Rose, bowl, cereal; 6¼" 9.50
Cameo Rose, bowl, oval, 10½" 22.00
Cameo Rose, cup 9.00
Cameo Rose, plate, 7¼" 6.50
Cameo Rose, platter, oval, 15½" 25.00
Cameo Rose, tidbit tray, 3-tier 42.00
Christmas Tree & Holly, bowl, oval 30.00
Christmas Tree & Holly, coffeepot 145.00
Christmas Tree & Holly, plate, 10" 25.00
Christmas Tree & Holly, tidbit, 2-tier 55.00
Crocus, baker, French, fluted 30.00
Crocus, bread box, metal 40.00
Crocus, creamer, Meltdown 40.00
Crocus, gravy boat 30.00
Crocus, plate, 10" 45.00
Crocus, sugar bowl, Art Deco, w/lid 30.00
Crocus, tray, metal, rnd 22.00
Eggshell, host jug, Red Dot 50.00
Eggshell, mug, Tom & Jerry, Red Dot 10.00
Game Bird, bowl, fruit; 5½" 8.00
Game Bird, casserole 30.00
Game Bird, cup 14.00
Heather Rose, bowl, oval, 9¼" 16.00
Heather Rose, bowl, vegetable; w/lid 30.00
Heather Rose, plate, 6½" 3.50
Heather Rose, platter, oval, 11¼" 12.00
Homewood, drip jar, Radiance 20.00
Homewood, plate, 9" 8.00
Mums, bowl, cereal; 6" 12.00
Mums, bowl, oval, 10¼" 27.00
Mums, casserole, Medallion 40.00
Mums, jug, Simplicity 125.00
Mums, platter, oval, 13¼" 25.00
Mums, sugar bowl, Medallion, w/lid 22.00
No 488, baker, French 25.00
No 488, bowl, fruit; 5½" 8.00
No 488, jug, Simplicity 150.00

No 488, plate, 8¼" 10.00
No 488, platter, oval, 13¼" 25.00
No 488, pretzel jar 150.00
No 488, shakers, Medallion, ea 50.00
No 488, stack set, Radiance 100.00
Orange Poppy, ball jug, #3 ....70.00
Orange Poppy, bowl, fruit; 5½" 8.00
Orange Poppy, bowl, vegetable; rnd, 9¼" 32.00
Orange Poppy, casserole, oval, 13" 90.00
Orange Poppy, coffeepot, S-lid 60.00
Orange Poppy, pie baker 32.00
Orange Poppy, plate, 9" 14.00
Orange Poppy, shakers, Novelty Radiance, rare, ea 100.00
Orange Poppy, soap dispenser, metal 45.00
Pastel Morning Glory, bean pot, New England, #4 ....110.00
Pastel Morning Glory, cake plate 22.00
Pastel Morning Glory, creamer, New York 14.00
Pastel Morning Glory, leftover, sq 65.00
Pastel Morning Glory, saucer, St Denis 7.50
Pert, jug, Chinese Red 12.00
Pert, sugar bowl, Chinese Red 8.00
Piggly Wiggly, baker, French, fluted 25.00
Piggly Wiggly, marmite, petite 35.00
Primrose, bowl, flat soup; 8" 10.00
Primrose, cup 6.00
Primrose, plate, 7¼" 5.00
Primrose, sugar bowl, w/lid 14.00
Red Poppy, baker, French, fluted 15.00
Red Poppy, bowl, Radiance, 9" 18.00
Red Poppy, bread box, metal, 3 styles 40.00
Red Poppy, cup 10.00
Red Poppy, drip jar, #1188, open 25.00
Red Poppy, plate, 10" 35.00
Red Poppy, saucer 3.00
Red Poppy, sifter, metal 35.00
Red Poppy, sugar bowl, Daniel, w/lid 22.00
Red Poppy, toaster cover, plastic 24.00
Sears' Arlington, bowl, cereal; 6¼" 5.50
Sears' Arlington, bowl, vegetable; w/lid 28.00
Sears' Arlington, pickle dish, 9" 5.00
Sears' Fairfax, bowl, oval, 9¼" 15.00
Sears' Fairfax, plate, 8" 4.50
Sears' Fairfax, saucer 2.00
Sears' Monticello, bowl, fruit; 5¼" 5.00
Sears' Monticello, cup 6.00
Sears' Monticello, plate, 10" 7.00
Sears' Monticello, platter, oval, 13¼" 16.00
Sears' Mount Vernon, bowl, cereal; 6¼" 7.00
Sears' Mount Vernon, gravy boat, w/underplate 20.00
Sears' Mount Vernon, plate, 8" 4.00
Sears' Mount Vernon, sugar bowl, w/lid 15.00
Sears' Richmond/Brown-Eyed Susan, bowl, cereal; 6¼" 7.00
Sears' Richmond/Brown-Eyed Susan, bowl, oval, 9¼" 15.00
Sears' Richmond/Brown-Eyed Susan, plate, 6½" 3.00
Serenade, bowl, cereal; 6" 7.00
Serenade, bowl, fruit; 5½" 5.00
Serenade, coffeepot, Terrace 45.00
Serenade, creamer, Art Deco 14.00
Serenade, plate, 8" 4.00
Serenade, platter, 11¼" 18.00
Serenade, sugar bowl, Art Deco, w/lid 22.00
Silhouette, ball jug, #3 ....95.00
Silhouette, bowl, Radiance, 9" 22.00
Silhouette, bowl, salad; 9" 18.00

Silhouette, bowl, vegetable; rnd, 9¼" 30.00
Silhouette, clock, electric 75.00
Silhouette, gravy boat 25.00
Silhouette, pie baker 30.00
Silhouette, plate, 9" 18.00
Silhouette, shakers, Medallion, ea 25.00
Silhouette, tea tile, 6" 95.00

Photo courtesy Margaret and Kenn Whitmyer

Silhouette, teapot, Medallion, $65.00.

Silhouette, wax paper dispenser 45.00
Springtime, bowl, fruit; 5½" 6.00
Springtime, cup 7.00
Springtime, plate, 6" 4.00
Springtime, platter, oval, 15" 25.00
Teapot, Airflow, cobalt w/gold trim, 6-cup 65.00
Teapot, Aladdin, Morning Glory bl, infuser, 6-cup 135.00
Teapot, Aladdin, red, oval, 6-cup 145.00
Teapot, Albany, mahog w/gold trim, 6-cup 65.00
Teapot, Apple, blk w/gold trim 200.00
Teapot, Baltimore, red, 6-cup 200.00
Teapot, Birdcage, maroon w/gold trim 275.00
Teapot, Boston, red, 2-cup 125.00
Teapot, Carraway, bl, gold label, 6-cup 65.00
Teapot, Damascus, turq, 6-cup 150.00
Teapot, Donut, red, 6-cup 300.00
Teapot, Football, maroon, 6-cup 600.00
Teapot, French, cadet bl w/gold fowers 55.00
Teapot, Hollywood, red, 8-cup 225.00
Teapot, Los Angeles, red, 4-cup 150.00
Teapot, Manhattan, warm yel, 6-cup 85.00
Teapot, McCormick, brn w/gold, 6-cup 50.00
Teapot, Melody, red & Hi-White, 6-cup 250.00
Teapot, Moderne, turq w/gold trim, 6-cup 50.00
Teapot, Musical, bl, 6-cup 175.00
Teapot, New York, cobalt bl w/gold trim, 6-cup 50.00
Teapot, New York, red, 6-cup 125.00
Teapot, Pert, maroon w/gold trim, 6-cup 65.00
Teapot, Star, Chinese red 175.00
Teapot, Streamline, bl w/gold, 6-cup 75.00
Teapot, Surfside, emerald gr w/gold, 6-cup 125.00
Teapot, Thorley Grape, wht w/gold jewels, 6-cup 100.00
Teapot, Windshield, cobalt, 6-cup 125.00
Teapot, Windshield, Game Bird, 6-cup 175.00
Teapot, Windshield, red, 6-cup 200.00
Teapot, Windshield, warm yel, 6-cup 75.00
Tulip, bowl, Radiance, 7½" 14.00
Tulip, bowl, rnd, 9¼" 30.00
Tulip, creamer, Modern 12.00
Tulip, plate, 10" 25.00
Tulip, sugar bowl, Modern, w/lid 20.00
Wild Poppy, ball jug, #3 ....125.00

Wild Poppy, coffeepot, Washington, 6-cup 175.00
Wild Poppy, tea tile 75.00
Wildfire, bowl, cereal; 6" 10.00
Wildfire, bowl, str-sided, 6" 12.00
Wildfire, bowl, Thick Rim, 8½" 25.00
Wildfire, gravy boat 25.00
Wildfire, jug, Pert, 5" 70.00
Wildfire, saucer 2.50
Wildfire, shakers, Pert, ea 30.00
Yellow Rose, baker, French, fluted 15.00
Yellow Rose, bowl, cereal; 6" 6.00
Yellow Rose, coffeepot, Norse 50.00
Yellow Rose, onion soup 32.00
Yellow Rose, plate, 6" 3.00
Yellow Rose, plate, 9" 7.00

Zeisel Designs, Hallcraft

Arizona, butter dish 55.00
Arizona, cup 6.00
Arizona, egg cup 25.00
Arizona, vase 35.00
Bouquet, ashtray 10.00
Bouquet, casserole, 2-qt 27.50
Bouquet, cup, AD 10.00
Bouquet, percolator, electric 115.00
Bouquet, shakers, pr 20.00
Buckingham, bowl, celery; oval 16.00
Buckingham, cereal; 6" 7.50
Caprice, ashtray 5.00
Caprice, butter dish 37.50
Caprice, coffeepot, 6-cup 42.50
Caprice, onion soup, w/lid 17.50
Caprice, plate, 11" 12.00
Fantasy, ashtray 10.00
Fantasy, basket 55.00
Fantasy, bowl, celery; oval 18.00
Fantasy, cup & saucer 10.00
Fantasy, ladle 10.00
Fantasy, platter, 15" 18.00
Fern, ashtray 10.00
Fern, bowl, vegetable; divided 18.00
Fern, casserole 25.00
Fern, gravy boat 15.00
Fern, plate, 6" 4.00
Fern, relish, 4-part 20.00
Fern, shakers, ea 10.00
Fern, sugar bowl, w/lid 12.00
Frost Flowers, creamer & sugar bowl, w/lid 22.50
Frost Flowers, plate, 8" 6.00
Harlequin, butter dish 60.00
Harlequin, vinegar bottle 25.00
Holiday, bowl, vegetable; open, sq, 8¾" 15.00
Holiday, creamer 10.00
Lyric, coffeepot, 6-cup 50.00
Lyric, egg cup 20.00
Mulberry, bowl, vegetable; 8¾" sq 18.00
Mulberry, creamer 10.00
Mulberry, marmite, w/lid 22.00
Peach Blossom, bowl, salad; 14½" 27.50
Peach Blossom, vinegar bottle 30.00
Pinecone, plate, E-style, 9¼" 7.50
Pinecone, tidbit tray, 3-tier, E-style 40.00
Spring, gravy boat 18.00

Sunglow, ashtray 10.00
Sunglow, butter dish 35.00
Sunglow, casserole 20.00
Sunglow, cup 5.00
Sunglow, ladle 10.00
Sunglow, plate, 6" 3.00

Hallmark

Hallmark introduced a line of artplas (molded plastic) ornaments in 1973 that have quickly become popular with collectors. They also have produced miniature ornaments since 1988, which are very collectible, as well as limited edition ornaments produced for members of the Hallmark Keepsake Ornament Collectors' Club.

The magazine, *The Ornament Collector*, edited by Rosie Wells, our advisor for this category, is available if you want more information on ornament collecting. Rosie also publishes a yearly official Secondary Market Price Guide on Hallmark Ornaments. Her address is listed in the Directory under Clubs, Newsletters, and Catalogs and again under Illinois. Values are for ornaments in mint condition and with their original boxes.

1973, Manger Scene, XHD 102-2, 3¼" 90.00
1974, Angel, QX 110-1, 3¼" 78.00
1975, Adorable Ornaments: Betsy Clark, QX 157-1, 3½" 235.00
1976, Chickadees, QX 204-1, 2⅝" 60.00
1976, Yesteryears: Train, QX 181-1, 4" 120.00
1977, Beauty of America: Seashore, QX 160-2, 2⅝" 55.00
1977, Grandma Moses, QX 150-2, 3¼" 55.00
1978, Colors of Christmas: Merry Christmas, QX 207-6, 4⅛" 80.00
1978, Tree Trimmers: Santa, QX 135-6, 2¼" 55.00
1979, Behold the Star, QX 255-9, 3¼" 35.00
1979, Christmas Heart, QX 140-7, 3½" 95.00
1980, A Spot of Christmas Cheer, QX 153-4, 2½" 145.00
1981, Candyville Express, QX 418-2, 3" 110.00
1981, Frosted Images: Angel, QX 509-5, 1½" 55.00
1982, Little Trimmers: Christmas Owl, QX 131-4, 2" ...45.00
1983, Angel Messenger, QX 408-7, 2" 95.00
1983, Kermit the Frog, QX 495-6, 3½" 95.00
1984, White Christmas, QX 905-1, 4½" 90.00
1985, Candy Apple Mouse, QX 470-5, 3¾" 60.00
1985, Heavenly Trumpeter, QX 405-2, 5" 95.00
1986, Christmas Sleigh Ride, QLX 701-2, 3¾" 125.00
1987, Goldfinch, QX 464-9, 2½" 65.00
1988, Rocking Horse, QX 402-4, 8th in series, 3¼" 45.00
1989, Backstage Bear, QLX 721-5, 3½" 35.00

1990, QX 473-6, Merry Olde Santa, 1st in series, MIB, $65.00.

1989, Cool Swing, QX 487-5, 3½" 30.00
1990, Keepsake Club: Armful of Joy, QXC 445-3, 2¾" ...40.00
1991, Baby's First Christmas, QLX 724-7, 4½" 80.00

1992, Angel of Light, QLX 723-9, 10¼" **34.00**
1993, Dollhouse Dreams, QLX 737-2, 3¼" **48.00**
1994, Gingerbread Fantasy, QLX 738-2, 4¼" **80.00**
1995, Jumping for Joy, QLX 734-7 ....**50.00**

Halloween

The origin of Halloween can be traced back to the ancient practices of the Druids of Great Britain who began their New Year on the 1st
of November. The Druids were pagans, and their New Year's celebrations involved pagan rites and superstitions. They believed that as the
old year came to an end the devil would gather up all the demons and
evil in the world and take them back to Hell with him. Witches were
women who had sold their souls to the devil and, with their black cat in
attendance, flew up through their chimneys on brooms. When the
Roman Catholic Church came into power in 700 A.D., they changed
the holiday into a religious event called 'All Saints Day,' or 'Allhallows.'
The evening before, October 31, became 'Allhallows Eve' or 'Halloween.' Today Halloween is strictly a fun time, and Halloween items
are fun to collect. Pumpkin-head candy containers of papier-mache or
pressed cardboard, noisemakers, postcards with black cats and witches,
costumes, and decorations are only a sampling of the variety available.

Our advisor for this category is Jenny Tarrant; she is listed in the
Directory under Missouri. See also Candy Containers.

Candy box, Pug's Halloween Candies, wood w/paper label, EX ..**800.00**
Cheroot holder w/case, witch on broom, NM **300.00**
Costume, hanging witch, Ben Cooper, 1960s, EX **30.00**
Costume, Wolfman, Groovy Ghoolies, M **20.00**
Crank toy, jack-o'-lantern drummer, cloth outfit, Germany, EX **1,800.00**

Photo courtesy Dunbar Gallery

**Decorations, embossed die-cut jack-o'-lanterns,
Germany, 1920s, $85.00 each.**

Decoration, cat, heavy emb paperboard, Germany, early, 12" **95.00**
Decoration, witch, paper, 4", EX **40.00**
Diecut, cat, blk, pressed cb, Germany, 1920s, 10x11" **75.00**
Diecut, cat on moon, cb, HE Lehrs, 14" **75.00**
Diecut, cat w/saxaphone, emb, Germany, 12", NM **100.00**
Diecut, devil, emb, Germany, 15", EX **125.00**
Diecut, jack-o'-lantern goblin face, Germany, 1920s, 11", EX **160.00**
Diecut, pumpkin lady, emb cb, Germany, 7½", EX **125.00**
Diecut, witch, stock paper, orange, 5", VG **45.00**
Figure, owl, pulp, orange/gr, Am, 4", EX **75.00**
Figure, witch, plaster, 3½", EX **55.00**
Hat, blk/orange paper w/witch/cat/moon/etc, Germany, 1930s, NM **20.00**
Hat, orange & blk felt w/appliqued cat, pointed style, 15" **65.00**
Horn, carrot face, Germany, 1920s, 6½", EX **200.00**
Horn, jack-o'-lantern face, Germany, 7½", NM **375.00**
Horn, jack-o'-lantern w/hat, Germany, 1920s, 8", NM **425.00**

Incense burner, skull figural, nodder jaw **48.00**
Jack-o'-lantern, cb, Germany, 1920s, 5", EX **200.00**
Jack-o'-lantern, cb, w/face insert, Germany, 3" **125.00**
Jack-o'-lantern, cb, w/face insert, Germany, 4" **175.00**
Jack-o'-lantern, cb, w/face insert, Germany, 5" **225.00**
Jack-o'-lantern, cb, w/face insert, Germany, 6" **255.00**
Jack-o'-lantern, cb, w/face insert, Germany, 7" **300.00**
Jack-o'-lantern, compo, Germany, rpl teeth, 3", EX **315.00**
Jack-o'-lantern, egg carton, growling face insert, Am, 6" **155.00**
Jack-o'-lantern, egg carton, smiling face insert, Am, 4½" **110.00**
Jack-o'-lantern, egg carton, smiling face insert, Am, 5" **125.00**
Jack-o'-lantern, egg carton, smiling face/cut-out nose, Am, 7½" .**165.00**
Jack-o'-lantern, for parade, tin w/paper face, Am, 1900s, 7", EX **1,000.00**
Jack-o'-lantern, pulp, growling face, Am, 6", NM **135.00**
Lantern, blk cat, cb, Germany, 1930s, 4", M **350.00**
Lantern, blk cat face on fence, papier-mache, Am, 1940s-50s **225.00**
Lantern, blk cat head, egg carton w/face insert, Am **225.00**
Lantern, cat arching on base, ceramic, Germany, 1930s, 8", M ..**265.00**
Lantern, cat head, cb or compo, face insert, Germany, 5-7" **365.00**
Lantern, cat head, cb or compo, w/face, rnd, Germany, 3-4" **295.00**
Lantern, cat head, molded nose, cb or compo, Germany, 3-4" **325.00**
Lantern, cat head, molded nose, cb or compo, Germany, 5-7" **450.00**
Lantern, cat w/full body, egg carton, w/face insert, Am **475.00**
Lantern, devil head, pulp, Am, 8", EX **450.00**
Lantern, orange cat head, egg carton, w/face insert, Am **225.00**
Lantern, orange cat on fence, egg carton, w/face insert, Am **195.00**
Lantern, red devil, egg carton, w/face insert, Am **395.00**
Lantern, skull, cb, face insert, Am, 1950s-60s, EX **95.00**
Lantern, skull, cb or compo, w/insert, Germany, minimum value **450.00**
Lantern, skull on pole, plastic, plug-in base, 12", EX **55.00**
Lantern, vegetable person, cb, Germany, 1920s, 6½", EX **395.00**
Lantern, watermelon, cb or compo, w/face, Germany, 5-8", minimum value .**650.00**
Lantern, watermelon jack-o'-lantern, cb, Germany, 3", EX **550.00**
Lantern, witch, papier-mache, Germany, 1920s, 4½", EX **375.00**
Lantern, witch head, cb or compo, Germany, minimum value ...**650.00**
Light bulb, skull & cross bones, milk glass, EX **35.00**
Mask, devil, papier-mache over head mold, EX **265.00**
Mask, man's head w/lg wound, papier-mache, 9½" **85.00**
Match box, blk cat, pnt wood, 1920s, 13x5x4", NM **85.00**
Match/cigarette holder, cat on box, ceramic, Germany, 4", NM **180.00**
Noisemaker, pumpkin face w/fringe hair, cb w/wood ratchet, EX .**95.00**
Noisemaker, witch face on metal frying pan shape **35.00**
Noisemaker, witches/bats/cats, tin, oval, 1940s, 4", EX **150.00**
Noisemaker, wooden ratchet style, orange/blk, Japan, 7x7x2" **55.00**
Panel, crepe paper, brownies/jack-o'-lanterns, 1920s, 32", EX **95.00**
Rattle, tin litho w/wood hdl, Kirchof, 1950s, 4½" L, NM **35.00**
Rattle/Whistle, jack-o'-lantern face, Germany, 1920s, 11", EX ..**275.00**
Scissors toy, vegetable man, compo, wood base, 1920s, 12", NM **700.00**
Scrap picture, cat, emb cb w/gr eyes, Germany, 6x9" **35.00**
Shakers, jack-o'-lantern & witch, ceramic, EX, pr **20.00**
Tambourine, blk cat face, tin, EX **50.00**
Tiara, cat w/bats on side, emb, Germany, 4½x10", EX **155.00**
Tiara, pumpkin man w/cats, emb, Germany, 4½x10", EX **165.00**
Treat bucket, cat, hard plastic, orange, 3½", EX **45.00**
Treat bucket, witch, hard plastic, orange/blk, 5", EX **100.00**

Candy Containers

Black cat w/pumpkin on bk, hard plastic, 1950s, 3" **35.00**
Boot w/jack-o'-lantern, face on front, Germany, 1920s, 5" **225.00**
Cat, papier-mache, blk & yel, West Germany, 1950s, 7½" **45.00**
Cat in sweater holding jack-o'-lantern, hard plastic, 1950s, 5" **65.00**
Cat pushing pumpkin on wheels, hard plastic, 1950s, 6" **120.00**
Clown w/hat, hard plastic, 1950s, 5" **65.00**

Devil, papier-mache, red/blk/yel, West Germany, 1950s, 7" **45.00**
Horse, orange hard plastic, 1950s, 5" **65.00**
Jack-o'-lantern w/hat, Germany, 5", M **175.00**
Lemon-head man, compo, Germany, 7" **725.00**
Owl, pulp, glass eyes, blk base, Am, 11", EX **235.00**
Pear, compo, yel w/mc details, Germany, 3" **425.00**
Pumpkin, lights up, hard plastic, 1950s, 4" **45.00**
Pumpkin, lights up, hard plastic, 1950s, 5" **55.00**
Pumpkin, papier-mache, orange & gr, West Germany, 1950s, 6" .**45.00**
Pumpkin man, bsk, jtd, orange & gr, 7" **825.00**
Pumpkin man, papier-mache, orange & gr, West Germany, 5½" .**22.50**
Pumpkin queen w/crown/ears, hard plastic, 1950s, 4" **65.00**
Pumpkin w/witch's head & cat's head on sides, hard plastic, 3" **35.00**
Scarecrow, hard plastic, 1950s, 5" **55.00**
Snowman, orange hard plastic, w/hat & pipe, 1950s, 5" **65.00**
Tambourine, orange & blk hard plastic, 1950s, 5" **85.00**
Veggie man, compo, Germany, 5" **675.00**
Witch, cb, Germany, 1940s, 8½", NM **350.00**
Witch, papier-mache, West Germany, 1950s, 7½", EX **65.00**
Witch on motorcycle, hard plastic, 1950s **265.00**
Witch on pumpkin, pulp, Am, 1940s-50s, 5", EX **125.00**
Witch on rocket, hard plastic, 1950s, 3" **75.00**

Hampshire

The Hampshire Pottery Company was established in 1871 in Keene, New Hampshire, by James Scollay Taft. Their earliest products were redware and stoneware utility items such as jugs, churns, crocks, and flowerpots. In 1878 they produced majolica ware which met with such success that they began to experiment with the idea of manufacturing art pottery. By 1883 they had developed a Royal Worcester type of finish which they applied to vases, tea sets, powder boxes, and cookie jars. It was also utilized for souvenir items that were decorated with transfer designs prepared from photographic plates.

Cadmon Robertson, brother-in-law of Taft, joined the company in 1904 and was responsible for developing their famous matt glazes. Colors included shades of green, brown, red, and blue. Early examples were of earthenware, but eventually the body was changed to semiporcelain. Some of his designs were marked with an M in a circle as a tribute to his wife, Emoretta. Robertson died in 1914, leaving a void impossible to fill. Taft sold the business in 1916 to George Morton, who continued to use the matt glazes that Robertson had developed. After a temporary halt in production during WWI, Morton returned to Keene and re-equipped the factory with the machinery needed to manufacture hotel china and floor tile. Because of the expense involved in transporting coal to fire the kilns, Morton found he could not compete with potteries of Ohio and New Jersey who were able to utilize locally available natural gas. He was forced to close the plant in 1923.

Interest is highest on examples in the monochrome glazes, and it is the glaze, not the size or form, that dictates value. The souvenir pieces are not particularly of high quality and tend to be passed over by today's collectors.

Bowl, ivory & aqua mottle, artichoke form, mk, 2¾x4¼" **200.00**
Bowl, ivory mottle w/brn at neck w/lt brn at base, mk, 3x5" **175.00**
Bowl, lt gr-gray w/lav mottle, hemispherical, #151, 3x4¼" **175.00**
Chamberstick, gr matt, hooded bk w/hdl, 7" **270.00**
Fairy lamp, gr matt, ped form, dtd 1911, 3½x6½" **600.00**
Jar, dk gr gloss, flared neck, mk, 8½x2¾" **225.00**
Jug, peanut; gr matt w/dk lav-gray mottle, #43, 4½x6" **250.00**
Pitcher, dk gray w/aqua mottle, emb floral, gr hdl, #81, 9¾" **225.00**
Pitcher, gr matt w/gray flecks, scroll hdl, #3, 11" **350.00**
Pitcher, tankard, stylized band decor on gr matt, mk, 7" **100.00**
Vase, aqua mottle on steel gray, tapered base, #66, 6¾" **600.00**
Vase, bl/gray mottle, shouldered, #90, 8½" **200.00**

Vase, bud; dk aqua w/mauve mottle, serpent head on hdl, 6¼" ..**175.00**
Vase, cocoa-brn mottle, flower form, M in O mk, 3x1¾" **150.00**
Vase, collie on grass, EX art, sgn ADF, rpr, 7½x8" **1,500.00**
Vase, dk cocoa-brn matt, bulbous, #165, M in O mk, 4¾" **200.00**

Vase, green matt with embossed leaves and vine handles, 8¼x6", $575.00.

Vase, gr matt, Arts & Crafts form, M in O mk, 7x5¾" **650.00**
Vase, gr matt, cylinder neck, bulbous bottom, #107, 7" **350.00**
Vase, gr matt, cylindrical, emb swirls, incised mk, 7½x4" **400.00**
Vase, gr matt, hand-thrown ovoid, unmk, 6x3½" **150.00**
Vase, gr matt, upright tulips/leaves, 8½x7" **750.00**
Vase, gr matt urn form, hdls, 4" **220.00**
Vase, gr matt w/feathered gray drip, hdls, #35, 5¾x7½" **400.00**
Vase, gr matt w/gray drip, long neck, hand thrown, unmk, 4½" ..**225.00**
Vase, gr matt w/gray flecks, trumpet form, mk, 4½x3¼" **250.00**
Vase, gray mottle w/cobalt flecks on cobalt to aqua, 7¼x3½" **350.00**
Vase, ivory mottle on aqua, squat, #133, M in O mk, 3x5¼" **400.00**
Vase, lt aqua drip on dk aqua, emb floral, #78, mk, 4¼x5" **475.00**
Vase, med bl matt, emb cattails/leaves, 7x4" **350.00**
Vase, mint gr mottle w/feathered gray & matt gr, #110, 4¼x3" ..**375.00**
Vase, sage gr mottle w/gr & brn specks, trumpet neck, #92, 9" ...**750.00**
Vase, sage gr/mint gr/multi-brn matt, ovoid, 4¼x3" **300.00**
Vase, sea gr & aqua on steel bl matt, blk int, mk, 5½x7" **450.00**
Vase, steel bl to cobalt semilustre, bulbous, 3¼x5" **150.00**
Vase, 2-tone gr matt w/gray veins, trumpet neck, 6¼x4¼" **275.00**

Handel

Philip Handel was best known for the art glass lamps he produced at the turn of the century. His work is similar to the Tiffany lamps of the same era. Handel made gas and electric lamps with both leaded glass and reverse-painted shades. Chipped ice shades with a texture similar to overshot glass were also produced. Shades signed by artists such as Bailey, Palme, and Parlow are highly valued.

Teroma lamp shades were created from clear blown glass blanks that were painted on the interior (reverse painted), while Teroma art glass (the decorative vases, humidors, etc. in the Handel Ware line) is painted on the exterior. This type of glassware has a 'chipped ice effect' achieved by sand blasting and coating the surface with fish glue. The piece is kiln fired at 800 degrees F. The contraction of the glue during the cooling process gives the glass a frosted, textured effect. Some shades are sand-finished, adding texture and depth.

Both the glassware and chinaware decorated by Handel are rare and command high prices on today's market. Many of Handel's chinaware blanks were supplied by Limoges. Our advisor for this category is Daniel Batchelor; he is listed in the Directory under New York.

Key: chp — chipped/lightly sanded

Handel Ware

Compote, dragonflies, base: lotus, yel stem w/plants, 7½" 325.00
Humidor, apple blossom branch on lid, pk on earthtones, 4" 800.00
Humidor, Cigars/monk on lid, monks/steins on dk ground, 6" 800.00
Humidor, gr enamel on opalware, bulbed cover, #4050, 7½" 450.00
Humidor, gr w/wht lining, lg knob on lid, mk, 7½" 450.00
Humidor, monk portrait on gr & brn opalware, #104/279, 6x3" .900.00
Jar, HP duck/dragonfly/lilies on clear, #H091, 7½" 700.00
Jar, hunting dog w/bird on brn & gr opalware, brass rim, 3½" 400.00
Mug, monk w/stein transfer on brn opalware, 2¼" 125.00
Vase, Teroma, autumn landscape, 11¾" 1,380.00
Vase, Teroma, birds/trees, amber-gold on clear, #4256, 9x4" ..1,750.00
Vase, Teroma, dog on gr & brn opalware, metal rim/hdls, 4x4" .325.00

Lamps

Boudoir, rvpt 7" bamboo/foliage shade; bronze woodland std, 14" ...2,500.00
Boudoir, rvpt 7" Teroma wisteria #6709 shade; bronze std, 13" 3,000.00
Boudoir, rvpt Teroma windmill #5882 shade; mk std, 14" 1,500.00
Boudoir, rvpt 8" mixed floral on red hex shade; bronze std, 14" 3,500.00
Boudoir, rvpt/chp 7" floral shade, candlestick std, 14" 2,500.00
Boudoir, rvpt/chp 7" sailing scene #6450 shade; hex std, 14" ..2,300.00
Boudoir, rvpt/chp 8" scenic shade; branch-cast #6457 std, 14" 2,000.00
Chandelier, metal geometric o/l 8-sided 22" shade, VG 2,800.00
Desk, caramel 10" cylinder shade on arched stem, #678.5 ....900.00
Desk, rvpt 10" Teroma gr-cased-to-wht shade; rnd std, 16" 1,200.00
Floor, chp 10" dk gr dome shade; bronzed harp base, 57" 1,700.00
Floor, overlaid slag shade, curved-neck/arch-ftd std, 44" 2,700.00
Floor, slag 24" tropical sunset shade; mk dome std, 24" 15,000.00
Hanging, craquelle 10" amber opal globe w/HP parrot, all mts 1,100.00
Lantern, iron, conical shade; bracket w/ship silhouette, 15" 850.00
Mini, rvpt 6" conical frosted shade, 3-arm mk base, 9¾" 475.00
Piano, chp cylinder #6786 ½-shade (EX); bronzed base 750.00
Shade, marbleized Arts & Crafts design, mushroom form, 12" ...550.00
Shade, pnt 6" globe shape w/parrot on branch; bronzed mts, 12" .1,800.00
Shade, rvpt chrysanthemums, tam-o'-shanter form, #2558, 12" .750.00
Table, amber 17" paneled shade; bronze water-lily std, 20¾" ..2,200.00
Table, chp 14" dome shade #5384; fluted bronze base, 21" 1,800.00
Table, ldgl 16" apple blossom dome shade; #1856 I std, 22" 1,950.00
Table, ldgl 16" floral band/brickwork shade; slim std 1,100.00
Table, ldgl 18" floral drop-apron shade; foliate std, 22" 4,025.00
Table, ldgl 18" floral shade; bronze ribbed std, 23" 2,200.00
Table, o/l floral on 7-panel 16" shade; 3-socket std, 22" 2,415.00
Table, o/l metal band 4-panel slag-glass 11" shade; 20" 900.00
Table, pnt 15" windmill scenic shade; bean-pot form std, 20" .2,000.00
Table, rvpt 12" floral tam-o'-shanter shade; mk std, 19" 700.00
Table, rvpt 16" Teroma poppy shade; 3-socket std, 22½" 4,600.00
Table, rvpt 16" Teroma tropical island shade; rpt std, 20½" 3,900.00
Table, rvpt 16" woodland #6519 shade; slender std, 23" 3,000.00
Table, rvpt 18" Arts & Crafts 5-color shade; bronzed std, 24" .7,500.00
Table, rvpt 18" landscape shade; vase std w/emb leaves 6,000.00
Table, rvpt 18" roses/butterflies shade; std w/leaf braces 12,500.00
Table, rvpt 18" scenic #7111 shade, EX; baluster std, 22½" 4,370.00
Table, rvpt 18" Teroma #6750 shade w/foliage; cast std, 24" ...3,335.00
Table, rvpt 18" trees #7118 sgn Bedigie shade; brn-pnt std 6,500.00
Table, rvpt 18" trees 8-sided shade; floral & bird emb std 5,000.00
Table, rvpt/chp Roman ruins #6825 shade sgn HB; tagged std .9,000.00
Table, rvpt/chp 16" floral shade; bean-pot form std, 20" 7,000.00
Table, rvpt/chp 16" scenic shade; #6282 std, 21½" 4,000.00
Table, rvpt/chp 18" birch trees shade; bronze urn-form std, 24" ...7,000.00
Table, rvpt/chp 18" birds in flight shade; vase std, 22" 5,500.00
Table, rvpt/chp 18" jungle bird shade; dk foliate std, 24" 8,500.00
Table, rvpt/chp 18" scenic #6534 shade; baluster std, 26" 8,200.00

Table, rvpt/chp 18" trees sgn/#d shade; swirled bronzed std 8,000.00
Table, 3 ldgl lily shades; flower-form mk bronze base, 21" 4,600.00
Torchere, rvpt 4" floral shade; bronze stick std, 59", pr 4,500.00

Harker

The Harker Pottery was established in East Liverpool, Ohio, in 1840. Their earliest products were yellowware and Rockingham produced from local clay. After 1900 whiteware was made from imported materials. The plant eventually grew to be a large manufacturer of dinnerware and kitchenware, employing as many as three hundred people. It closed in 1972 after it was purchased by the Jeannette Glass Company. Perhaps their best-known lines were their Cameo wares, decorated with white silhouettes in a cameo effect on contrasting solid colors. Floral silhouettes are standard, but other designs were also used. Blue and pink are the most often found background hues; a few pieces are found in yellow. For further information we recommend *The Collector's Guide to Harker Pottery* by Neva Colbert.

Amy, casserole, w/lid 40.00
Amy, lifter 22.00
Amy, pepper shaker 12.00
Amy, pie plate 26.00
Amy, platter, 12" 20.00
Amy, range shakers, pr 45.00
Antique Auto, ashtray 20.00
Cactus, cake plate 24.00

Calico Tulip, Condiment jars, metal lids, $9.00 each; Utility plate on Virginia shape, 12", $28.00.

Calico Tulip, pie plate 20.00
Calico Tulip, pitcher, batter 32.00
Calico Tulip, spooner 28.00
Calico Tulip, syrup 29.00
Carnival, cake plate 20.00
Coronet, platter 20.00
Deco Dahlia, cake plate 22.00
Deco Dahlia, condiment set, complete in rack 60.00
Deco Dahlia, custard cup 15.00
Deco Dahlia, range shakers, pr 45.00
Duchess, condiment set, in rack 28.00
Duchess, creamer 8.00
Godey Print, bowl, flat soup 8.00
Godey Print, bowl, fruit 3.00
Godey Print, bowl, vegetable 12.00
Godey Print, creamer 8.00
Godey Print, cup & saucer 4.00

Godey Print, plate, 10"	8.00
Godey Print, plate, 8¼"	4.00
Godey Print, platter, 11¾"	15.00
Godey Print, sugar bowl, w/lid	12.00
Ivy Vine, bowl, mixing	24.00
Ivy Vine, plate, 10"	15.00
Ivy Vine, spoon	28.00
Mallow, custard cup	15.00
Mallow, lifter	22.00
Mallow, spoon	28.00
Modern Tulip, bowl, mixing	15.00
Modern Tulip, cookie jar	48.00
Modern Tulip, fork	36.00
Modern Tulip, lifter	24.00
Modern Tulip, pie plate	24.00
Modern Tulip, platter	24.00
Modern Tulip, syrup	24.00
Petit Point I, casserole, stacking; w/lid	44.00
Petit Point II, casserole, stacking; w/lid	44.00
Petit Point II, pie plate	28.00
Provincial Tulip, plate, 10"	10.00
Red Apple, casserole, w/lid, 9"	40.00
Red Apple, fork	36.00
Red Apple, pie plate	28.00
Red Apple, plate, 10"	15.00
Red Apple, spoon	32.00
Red Apple, swirl bowl	23.00
Springtime, platter	20.00

Harlequin

Harlequin dinnerware, produced by the Homer Laughlin China Company of Newell, West Virginia, was introduced in 1938. It was a lightweight ware made in maroon, mauve blue, and spruce green, as well as all the Fiesta colors except ivory (see Fiesta). It was marketed exclusively by the Woolworth stores, who considered it to be their all-time bestseller. For this reason they contracted with Homer Laughlin to reissue Harlequin to commemorate their 100th anniversary in 1979. Although three of the original glazes were used in the reissue, the few serving pieces that were made were restyled, and collectors found the new line to be no threat to their investments.

The Harlequin animals, including a fish, lamb, cat, penguin, duck, and donkey, were made during the early 1940s, also for the dime-store trade. Today these are very desirable to collectors of Homer Laughlin china.

In the listings that follow, use the values designated 'high' for all colors other than turquoise and yellow. *The Collector's Encyclopedia of Fiesta* by Sharon and Bob Huxford contains a more thorough study of this subject. It is available from Collector Books or your local library.

Animals, maverick, gold trim	55.00

Animals: Standard colors, $175.00 each; Non-standard Fiesta red penguin, $275.00.

Ashtray, basketweave, high	58.00
Ashtray, basketweave, low	35.00
Ashtray, regular, high	53.00
Ashtray, regular, low	38.00
Bowl, '36s oatmeal; high	26.00
Bowl, '36s oatmeal; low	16.00
Bowl, '36s; high	40.00
Bowl, '36s; low	26.00
Bowl, cream soup; high	30.00
Bowl, cream soup; low	20.00
Bowl, cream soup; med gr, minimum	600.00
Bowl, fruit; high, 5½"	11.00
Bowl, fruit; low, 5½"	8.00
Bowl, ind salad; high	35.00
Bowl, ind salad; low	20.00
Bowl, mixing; Kitchen Kraft, mauve bl, 8"	125.00
Bowl, mixing; Kitchen Kraft, red or lt gr, 6", ea	90.00
Bowl, mixing; Kitchen Kraft, yel, 10"	125.00
Bowl, nappy; high, 9"	40.00
Bowl, nappy; low, 9"	26.00
Bowl, oval baker, high	40.00
Bowl, oval baker, low	27.00
Butter dish, cobalt, ½-lb	300.00
Butter dish, high, ½-lb	135.00
Butter dish, low, ½-lb	115.00
Candle holders, high, pr	250.00
Candle holders, low, pr	210.00
Casserole, w/lid, high	160.00
Casserole, w/lid, low	95.00
Creamer, high lip, any color, ea	130.00
Creamer, ind; high	35.00
Creamer, ind; low	20.00
Creamer, novelty, high	40.00
Creamer, novelty, low	28.00
Creamer, regular, high	20.00
Creamer, regular, low	14.00
Cup, demitasse; high	110.00
Cup, demitasse; low	42.00
Cup, lg, any color, ea	180.00
Cup, tea; high	11.00
Cup, tea; low	9.00
Egg cup, dbl, high	28.00
Egg cup, dbl, low	20.00
Egg cup, single, high	35.00
Egg cup, single, low	25.00
Marmalade, high	240.00
Marmalade, low	200.00
Nut dish, basketweave, high	18.00
Nut dish, basketweave, low	13.00
Perfume bottle, any color, ea	120.00
Pitcher, service water; high	105.00
Pitcher, service water; low	70.00
Pitcher, 22-oz jug, high	68.00
Pitcher, 22-oz jug, low	40.00
Pitcher, 22-oz jug, med gr	250.00
Plate, deep; high	30.00
Plate, deep; low	20.00
Plate, deep; med gr	75.00
Plate, high, 10"	36.00
Plate, high, 6"	5.50
Plate, high, 7"	8.00
Plate, high, 9"	14.00
Plate, low, 10"	24.00
Plate, low, 6"	4.00

Plate, low, 7"	6.00
Plate, low, 9"	10.00
Platter, high, 11"	25.00
Platter, high, 13"	32.00
Platter, low, 11"	18.00
Platter, low, 13"	22.00
Platter, med gr, 11"	200.00
Platter, med gr, 13"	250.00
Sauce boat, high	35.00
Sauce boat, low	22.00
Saucer, demitasse; high	28.00
Saucer, demitasse; low	15.00
Saucer, demitasse; med gr	125.00
Saucer, high	4.00
Saucer, low	2.00
Saucer/ashtray, high	63.00
Saucer/ashtray, low	50.00
Shakers, high, pr	26.00
Shakers, low, pr	18.00
Sugar bowl, w/lid, high	32.00
Sugar bowl, w/lid, low	20.00
Sugar bowl, w/lid, med gr	100.00
Syrup, red or yel	175.00
Syrup, spruce gr or mauve	300.00
Teapot, high	145.00
Teapot, low	85.00
Tray, relish; mixed colors	300.00
Tumbler, car decal	65.00
Tumbler, high	58.00
Tumbler, low	45.00

Hatpin Holders

Most hatpin holders were made from 1860 to 1920 to coincide with the period during which hatpins were popularly in vogue. The taller types were required to house the long hatpins necessary to secure the large hats that were in style from 1890 to 1914. They were usually porcelain, either decorated by hand or by transfer with florals or scenics, although some were clever figurals. Glass examples are rare, and those of slag or carnival glass are especially valuable.

If you are interested in collecting or dealing in hatpins or hatpin holders, you will find that authority Lillian Baker has several fine books available on the subject, including her most recent publication, *Hatpins and Hatpin Holders,* complete with beautiful color illustrations and current market values. Our advisor for this category is Robert Larsen; he is listed in the Directory under Nebraska.

Photo courtesy Robert Larsen

Schafer & Vater, applied poppies, rare, $575.00 to $650.00.

Bisque, bell form w/cameo motif, 12-hole, 2¼"	225.00
Bisque, cone-shaped wall mt, cameo, rtcl top, 6-hole, 6¾"	250.00
Bisque, wall-mt, conical basket w/emb roses, 11-hole, 6½"	275.00
Carnival glass, Grape & Cable, purple, 7x2½"	355.00
Daisy & Button, clear, silver top, rare, 8"	450.00
Jasperware, Strawberries on Brick Tower, mk S&V, 12-hole, 5"	325.00
Jasperware, wht relief ancient figures on gr, 5¼"	300.00
Limoges, floral, attached trinket box, w/lid, 4½"	325.00
Limoges, roses on wht w/gold, sq top, 5¼"	100.00
Nippon, berries, purple & bl w/gold	180.00
Pickard, HP Nouveau motif w/gold top, 4¾"	225.00
Porc, cylindrical, wht w/classical figure & peacock, 3⅝"	350.00
Royal Bayreuth, Goose Girl	375.00
Royal Bayreuth, lt brn dachshund figural	1,050.00
Royal Bayreuth, man w/turkey, bl mk	375.00
Royal Bayreuth, wht poppy figural	850.00
Royal Doulton, hunt scene, 4¾"	185.00
Royal Doulton, Ophelia in lav/pk on cream, 7-hole, 5"	350.00
RS Germany, orange poppy, gr mk	125.00
RS Prussia, calla lilies, gr	200.00
RS Prussia, pk carnation, bulbous, red mk	250.00
Ruby glass, HP daisies & gold sprays	150.00
Silver, plush velvet cushion, Art Nouveau, 6½x1¾"	165.00
Willow Art China, Jewish symbol transfer, Jerusalem, 5½"	125.00

Hatpins

A hatpin was used to securely fasten a hat to the hair and head of the wearer. Hatpins, measuring from 4" to 12" in length, were worn from approximately 1850 to 1920. During the Art Deco period, hatpins became ornaments rather than the decorative functional jewels that they had been. The hatpin period reached its zenith in 1913 just prior to World War I, which brought about a radical change in women's headdress and fashion. About that time, women began to scorn the bonnet and adopt 'the hat' as a symbol of their equality. The hatpin was made of every natural and manufactured element in a myriad of designs that challenge the imagination. They were contrived to serve every fashion need and complement the milliner's art. Collectors often concentrate on a specific type: hand-painted porcelains, sterling silver, commemoratives, sporting activities, carnival glass, Art Nouveau and/or Art Deco designs, Victorian Gothics with mounted stones, exquisite rhinestones, engraved and brass-mounted escutcheon heads, gold and gems, or simply primitive types made in the Victorian parlor. Some collectors prefer the long pin-shanks while others select only those on tremblants or nodder-type pin-shanks.

If you are interested in collecting or dealing in hatpins, see the information in the Hatpin Holders introduction concerning reference books. For further study we recommend *The Collector's Encyclopedia of Hatpins and Hatpin Holders* by Lillian Baker, available at your local bookstore or from Collector Books. Our advisor for this category is Robert Larsen; he is listed in the Directory under Nebraska.

Key: cab — cabochon

Brass, bust of Victorian lady	75.00
Brass, cat's head w/red stone eyes	90.00
Brass Nouveau fr w/faceted amethysts, 1½x2¾"	125.00
Brass sphere w/4 coral stones	95.00
Brass w/conical topaz stone in center	85.00
Carnival glass, butterfly, gr irid	175.00
Enamel, Nouveau flower & leaves on sterling mt, ca 1900, 1⅛"	75.00
Garnet, cab-cut, 1" overall head on 5½" gilt pin	150.00
Ivory, cvd elephant standing atop ball, 1⅛" on 7⅜" pin	175.00

Photo courtesy Robert Larsen

Left to right: Amethyst stone surrounded by rhinestones, from $275.00 to $325.00; Amethyst with filigree and ring of rhinestones, from $250.00 to $300.00; Heart-shaped with rhinestones, $175.00 to $225.00.

Ivory, hollow-cvd chrysanthemum, 1" on 7⅜" steel pin 150.00
Mercury glass, cased, Bohemia, ca 1905, 2¼" 125.00
Mosaic, heart shape, 8" 225.00
Plastic, flame form w/tiny pnt plastic bugle beads, 3¼" 45.00
Plique-a-jour, gr, flattened-dome shape 725.00
Porc, irid, ceramic transfer w/HP accents & gold overlay, 1¼" ...150.00
Porc, rnd molded & pnt Eye-of-Horis motif, ca 1925, 1¼" 100.00
Porc, teardrop w/HP Victorian couple, gold o/l, 1¾" 190.00
Rhinestone, faceted gr stone circled w/15 brilliants, 1" 125.00
Rhinestone, 4 dmn shapes of mc brilliants form star, 1¾" 150.00
Satsuma, HP bl & gold floral design, 1¾" on 10" pin 225.00
Satsuma, 2 HP kimono-clad women, heavy gold beading, 1¾" ..250.00
Silver, eagle head w/red stone eye & rhinestones, 1¾" 175.00
Sterling, Charles Horner 175.00
Sterling, cherub, ⅜" 125.00
Sterling, faceted amethyst atop baroque design, dtd '66, 2⅞" 175.00
Sterling, hand-wrought Dutch shoe, Netherlands hallmk, ¾" 75.00
Sterling, Nouveau head w/hair forming heart shape, ca 1905, 1" 150.00
Sterling, Nouveau lady w/repousse work, 1" on 9" pin 125.00
Sterling apple blossom 58.00
Sterling w/oval amethyst, braced bk 80.00
Tortoise shell teardrop w/fancy pique work, 1½" on 7¼" pin 135.00
Turquoise stone (triangular) on brass & wire filigree mt, 1¾" 150.00
Vanity, red stone on brass mt, ornate filigree, w/puff/mirror 1,200.00

Haviland

The Haviland China Company was organized in 1840 by David Haviland, a New York china importer. His search for a pure white, nonporous porcelain led him to Limoges, France, where natural deposits of suitable clay had already attracted numerous china manufacturers. The fine china he produced there was translucent and meticulously decorated, with each piece fired in an individual sagger.

It has been estimated that as many as 60,000 chinaware patterns were designed, each piece marked with one of several company backstamps. 'H. & Co.' was used until 1890 when a law was enacted making it necessary to include the country of origin. Various marks have been used since that time including 'Haviland, France'; 'Haviland & Co. Limoges'; and 'Decorated by Haviland & Co.' Various associations with family members over the years have resulted in changes in management as well as company name. In 1892 Theodore Haviland left the firm to start his own business. Some of his ware was marked 'Mont Mery.' Later logos included a horseshoe, a shield, and various uses of his initials and name. In 1941 this branch moved to the United States. Wares produced here are marked 'Theodore Haviland, N.Y.' or 'Made In America.'

Though it is their dinnerware lines for which they are most famous, during the 1880s and 1890s they also made exquisite art pottery using a technique of underglaze slip decoration called Barbotine, which had been invented by Ernest Chaplet. In 1885 Haviland bought the for-

mula and hired Chaplet to oversee its production. The technique involved mixing heavy white clay slip with pigments to produce a compound of the same consistency as oil paints. The finished product actually resembled oil paintings of the period, the texture achieved through the application of the heavy medium to the clay body in much the same manner as an artist would apply paint to his canvas. Primarily the body used with this method was a low-fired faience, though they also produced stoneware.

Drop Rose: Ramekin and underplate, 3¼", 5¼", $128.00; Sherbet, $195.00.

Ashtray, man in tux & advertising, 1920-36, 4½" 62.50
Bonbon basket, Fantaisie Romeo form, floral w/gold, 1920s mk .185.00
Cake plate, narrow tan rim, pierced hdls, 1865-76 mk, 10" 90.00
Cake stand, floral on wht, Marseille form, 1888-96 mk, 9" 120.00
Chamberstick, rosebuds & gold on Marseille form, 1888-96, 3" .185.00
Chocolate pot, floral on shaded gr w/gold, 1893-1930 mk, 5¼" .100.00
Chocolate pot, floral on wht, St Germaine form, 1903-25 mk, 11" .215.00
Coffeepot, floral on wht, sq Pompadour form, 1888-96 mk, 8½" ..220.00
Compote, wht rtcl lace form on ped ft, 1876-89 mk, 7½x9" 300.00
Creamer, bird figural, bl/wht/yel, Sandoz, 4½" 500.00
Cup & saucer, demi; floral w/gold, Silver form, 1893-1930 ....68.00
Cup & saucer, pk floral w/gold, Ranson form, 1893-1930 ....105.00
Egg cup, floral on wht w/gold, 1904-1920s mk, 3" 65.00
Ferner, HP floral, sgn Henri, 6-sided, 1893-1930 mk, 7½" 350.00
Foot bath, ornate handles w/gold, gold band decor, 1850-65 mk 800.00
Jug vase, appl floral on terra cotta, E Lindeneher, 14" 2,200.00
Knife rest, 2 fish joined at mouth, Sandoz, 5" 400.00
Mayonnaise, leaf shape w/gold, 1804-1920s mk, w/underplate ...110.00
Pitcher, HP/emb floral decor w/gold, imp mk, 1850s-60s, 10" 175.00
Plate, Josephine portrait, gold decor/emb rim, 9" 225.00
Teapot, simple gold band decor on wht, appl mk, 7½" 90.00
Vase, floral on brn sgn R, terra cotta, ftd, 1873-82 mk, 5" 625.00
Vase, non-factory floral w/3 gold hdls, 1893-1930 mk, 12" 300.00
Wash pitcher & bowl, red band w/gold on wht, 1870s mks 1,000.00

Hawkes

Thomas Hawkes established his factory in Corning, New York, in 1880. He developed many beautiful patterns of cut glass, two of which were awarded the Grand Prize at the Paris Exposition in 1889. By the end of the century, his company was renowned for the finest in cut glass production. The company logo was a trefoil form enclosing a hawk in each of the two bottom lobes with a fleur-de-lis in the center. With the exception of some of the very early designs, all Hawkes was signed. (Our values are for signed pieces.)

Bottle, scent; Venetian, faceted stopper, 8x4½" 495.00
Bowl, berry; cut, hobstars & fans, 9", NM 225.00

Candlesticks, heavy fluting, rayed star bases, 9", pr **475.00**
Creamer & sugar bowl, eng satin bands, sterling ped bases **125.00**
Inkstand, Gravic, central well w/hinged metal lid, 4¼x5" **1,725.00**
Tray, overall hobnails, hdls, 14¾x7¾" **425.00**
Tumbler, Gravic, polished chrysanthemum decor, sgn **75.00**
Vase, Brunswick Variant, hobstar ft, trumpet form, 8" **295.00**
Vase, chain of hobstars, bull's-eyes, 10" **200.00**
Vase, florals eng on slim form, trefoil mk, 12" **155.00**

Head Vases

Vases modeled as heads of lovely ladies, delightful children, clowns, Madonnas — even some animals — were once popular as flower containers. Today they represent a growing area of collector interest. Most of them were imported from Japan, although some American potteries produced a few as well.

For more information, we recommend *Head Vases, Identification and Values,* by Kathleen Cole and *The World of Head Vase Planters* by Mike Posgay and Ian Warner. Our advisors for this category are Phil and Nila Thurston; they are listed in the Directory under New York.

Baby boy hugging bottle, Sampson #313A, 5½" **48.00**
Baby girl holding phone, pk & bl bonnet, Enesco #2185, 5" **48.00**
Baby girl w/pk bow in hair, ruffled collar, Inarco #E3156, 5½" **55.00**
Boy in bl beret, blond hair, Relpo #2010, 7" **80.00**
Boy in fireman's hat, Inarco paper label, 5" **40.00**
Boy praying, red hair, Inarco #E978, 5" **35.00**

Christmas girl with present, Napco, 1947, 4", $75.00.

Clown in crumpled blk hat, polka-dot tie, unmk, 5¼" **40.00**
Clown in tiny blk hat, Inarco #E-5071, 4½" **27.50**
Florabelle, Betty Lou Nichols, 11" **900.00**
Girl in bl bonnet w/gold trim & bow, unmk, 5" **40.00**
Girl in Christmas outfit, blond hair, Napco #CS2348B, 5½" **60.00**
Girl in orange turtleneck, blond hair, Inarco #E6211, 5" **48.00**
Girl in pk beret, matching blouse, hand up, Relpo #1694-L, 7½" .**80.00**
Girl in pk bonnet w/flowers, hand to cheek, Royal Crown #3411, 7" ...**75.00**
Girl in tam, hand to face, Relpo #K1694/S, 5½" **48.00**
Girl praying, blond hair, Inarco #E1579, 5" **40.00**
Girl w/blk headband, long blond hair, Relpo #K1931, 8½" **120.00**
Girl w/blond side ponytail, gr bodice, pearl earrings, Japan, 7" **60.00**
Girl w/bows in wraparound braid, pearl necklace, Rubens #4121, 6" **40.00**
Girl w/braids in yel scarf, Inarco #E2965, 7" **55.00**
Girl w/phone to ear, yel headband, Inarco #E3548, 5½" **40.00**
Girl w/pigtails & yel scarf, Inarco #E2965, 7" **55.00**
Girl w/umbrella, flowers in hair, unmk, 4½" **65.00**
Lady in bl hat w/side bow, gold jewelry, unmk, 4" **40.00**
Lady in bright yel hat w/wht bow, gr blouse, Japan, 5½" **35.00**
Lady in gr scarf, matching blouse, blond hair, unmk, 3" **27.50**
Lady in lg yel beret, matching blouse, blk hair, unmk, 7½" **40.00**
Lady in pale bl scarf, blond hair, Lefton paper label, 6" **48.00**

Lady in pk bonnet w/yel rose, Napco #S126B, paper label, 5½" ...**55.00**
Lady in pk scarf, blk blouse, Relpo #K1615, 5½" **40.00**
Lady in plumed hat, pearl jewelry, Inarco #E-191, 5½" **55.00**
Lady in top hat, hand up, pearl jewelry, unmk, 6½" **48.00**
Lady in wht flat-rimmed hat, blk blouse, blond hair, Thames, 6" .**55.00**
Lady in yel hat, hand to ear, red necklace, Lefton #1736, 5½" **48.00**
Lady w/blk bow in hair, pearl jewelry, Enesco paper label, 6½" **75.00**
Lady w/flower in hair, hand to chin, bl glove, Inarco #E2104, 7" .**55.00**
Lady w/upswept hair, ruffled collar, pearl jewelry, #3854, 6½" **60.00**
Teenage girl, sunglasses on top of head, 7" **400.00**

Heisey

A.H. Heisey began his long career at the King Glass Company of Pittsburgh. He later joined the Ripley Glass Company which soon became Geo. Duncan and Sons. After Duncan's death Heisey became half-owner in partnership with his brother-in-law, James Duncan. In 1895 he built his own factory in Newark, Ohio, initiating production in 1896 and continuing until Christmas of 1957. At that time Imperial Glass Corporation bought some of the molds. After 1968 they removed the old 'Diamond H' from any they put into use. In 1985 HCA purchased all of Imperial's Heisey molds with the exception of the Old Williamsburg line.

During their highly successful period of production, Heisey made fine handcrafted tableware with simple, yet graceful designs. Early pieces were not marked. After November 1901 the glassware was marked either with the 'Diamond H' or a paper label. Blown ware is often marked on the stem, never on the bowl or foot.

Our advisor for this category is Debbie Maggard; she is listed in the Directory under Ohio. For information concerning Heisey Collectors of America, see the Clubs, Newsletters, and Catalogs section of the Directory. See also Glass Animals.

Charter Oak, comport, #3362, low ft, 6" **45.00**
Charter Oak, gr, finger bowl, #3362 ....**20.00**
Charter Oak, marigold, stem, sherbet; #3362, low ft, 6-oz **40.00**
Charter Oak, orchid, stem, parfait; #3362, 4½-oz **65.00**
Charter Oak, pk, tumbler, #3362, flat, 12-oz **17.50**
Chintz, bowl, pickle/olive; 2-part, 13" **25.00**
Chintz, celery tray, 10" **25.00**
Chintz, grapefruit, Duquesne, #3389, ftd **40.00**
Chintz, plate, luncheon; sq, 8" **15.00**
Chintz, stem, cocktail; #3389, 3-oz **20.00**
Chintz, stem, sherbet; #3389, 5-oz **15.00**
Chintz, tumbler, iced tea; #3389, 12-oz **22.50**
Chintz, yel, creamer, 3-dolphin ftd **45.00**
Chintz, yel, finger bowl, #4107 ....**25.00**
Chintz, yel, pitcher, dolphin ft, 3-pt **275.00**
Chintz, yel, plate, hors d' oeuvre, 2-hdld, 13" **45.00**
Chintz, yel, stem, parfait; #3389, 5-oz **45.00**
Chintz, yel, sugar bowl, 3 dolphin ft **42.50**
Chintz, yel, tray, celery; 13" **35.00**
Crystolite, bottle, bitters; w/short tube, 4-oz **175.00**
Crystolite, bowl, conserve; hdld, 2-part, 8" **16.00**
Crystolite, bowl, jelly; oval, 4-ftd, 6" **16.00**
Crystolite, candlestick, 2-light **25.00**
Crystolite, candy dish, swan form, 6½" **35.00**
Crystolite, creamer, ind **17.00**
Crystolite, hurricane block, sq, 1-light **25.00**
Crystolite, mayonnaise, shell form, 3-ftd, 5½" **32.00**
Crystolite, oil bottle, 3-oz **50.00**
Crystolite, plate, dinner; 10½" **80.00**
Crystolite, plate, shell form, 7" **24.00**

Crystolite, 3-part relish tray, 12", $35.00.

Crystolite, puff box, w/lid, 4¾" 60.00
Crystolite, tray, relish; leaf form, 4-part, 9" 25.00
Crystolite, urn, flower; 7" 75.00
Empress, alexandrite, saucer 25.00
Empress, cobalt, bowl, floral; dolphin ftd, 11" 400.00
Empress, cobalt, bowl, nasturtium; dolphin ftd, 7½" 325.00
Empress, gr, bowl, relish; triplex, 7" 45.00
Empress, gr, comport, oval, 7" 75.00
Empress, gr, jug, flat 165.00
Empress, gr, jug, ftd, 3-pt 225.00
Empress, gr, plate, 10½" 125.00
Empress, gr, saucer, AD 10.00
Empress, gr, stem, sherbet; 4-oz 35.00
Empress, gr, tumbler, dolphin ftd, 8-oz 195.00
Empress, pk, bowl, floral; ftd, 2-hdld, 8½" 40.00
Empress, pk, bowl, jelly; ftd, 2-hdld, 6" 17.00
Empress, pk, comport, ftd, 6" 50.00
Empress, pk, plate, hors d'oeuvre; 2-hdld, 13" 40.00
Empress, pk, tray, relish; 3-part, 10" 35.00
Empress, yel, bowl, frappe; w/center 60.00
Empress, yel, bowl, vegetable; oval, 10" 45.00
Empress, yel, cup 31.00
Empress, yel, plate, bouillon liner 13.00
Empress, yel, plate, 12" 55.00
Empress, yel, sugar bowl, ind 35.00
Empress, yel, tray, sandwich; center hdl, 12" 57.00
Greek Key, bowl, banana split; ftd, 9" 27.50
Greek Key, bowl, jelly; hdld, 5" 75.00
Greek Key, bowl, nappy; 4" 20.00
Greek Key, bowl, nappy; 6" 25.00
Greek Key, bowl, punch; ftd, 12" 300.00
Greek Key, coaster 15.00
Greek Key, creamer & sugar bowl, oval, ind 75.00
Greek Key, jar, crushed fruit; w/lid, 1-qt 300.00
Greek Key, oil bottle, w/#6 stopper, 6-oz 125.00
Greek Key, pitcher, 3-pt 165.00
Greek Key, plate, 7" 35.00
Greek Key, puff box, #3, w/lid 100.00
Greek Key, stem, sherry; 2-oz 200.00
Greek Key, tumbler, flared rim, 7-oz 22.00
Ipswich, candy jar, w/lid, ¼-lb 150.00
Ipswich, cobalt, bowl, floral; ftd, 11" 250.00
Ipswich, gr, plate, sq, 7" 40.00
Ipswich, pk, stem, oyster cocktail; ftd, 4-oz 37.50
Ipswich, pk, tumbler, soda; ftd, 8-oz 40.00
Ipswich, yel, stem, goblet; knob in stem, 10-oz 45.00
Ipswich, yel, sugar bowl 40.00
Lariat, basket, ftd, 10" 195.00
Lariat, bowl, gardenia; 13" 39.00
Lariat, bowl, nappy; 7" 15.00
Lariat, candlestick, 3-light 35.00

Lariat, cigarette box 45.00
Lariat, platter, oval, 15" 50.00
Lariat, stem, oyster cocktail/fruit; 4½-oz 15.00
Lariat, stem, pressed, 9-oz 20.00
Lariat, stem, wine; blown, 2½-oz 25.00
Lariat, swing vase 125.00
Lodestar, dawn, ashtray 80.00
Lodestar, dawn, bowl, crimped, 11" 95.00
Lodestar, dawn, pitcher, #16126, 1-qt 150.00
Lodestar, dawn, sugar bowl 50.00
Lodestar, dawn, vase, crimped, #1626, 8" 175.00
Minuet, bell, dinner; #3408 ....75.00
Minuet, bowl, #1514, oval, 12" 60.00
Minuet, bowl, sauce; ftd, 7½" 30.00
Minuet, candlestick, #112, 1-light 30.00
Minuet, cup 37.50
Minuet, plate, luncheon; 8" 15.00
Minuet, shakers, #10, pr 65.00
Minuet, stem, oyster cocktail; #5010, 4½-oz 20.00
Minuet, tumbler, fruit juice; #5010, 5-oz 32.50
Minuet, vase, urn; #5012, 6" 70.00
New Era, creamer 35.00
New Era, saucer, AD 10.00
New Era, stem, cocktail; high, 3½-oz 10.00
New Era, sugar bowl 35.00
New Era, tumbler, soda; ftd, 14-oz 15.00
Octagon, cheese dish, #1229, 2-hdld, 6" 7.00
Octagon, gr, basket, #500, 5" 300.00
Octagon, gr, plate, sandwich; #1229, 10" 30.00
Octagon, marigold, bowl, nut; ind, 2-hdld 65.00
Octagon, orchid, bowl, mint; #1229, 6" 25.00
Octagon, orchid, plate, cream-soup liner 12.00
Octagon, orchid, sugar bowl, hotel sz 30.00
Octagon, pk, bowl, flat soup; 9" 15.00
Octagon, pk, creamer, hotel sz 15.00
Octagon, pk, plate, muffin; #1229, sides up, 12" 27.00
Octagon, yel, cup, #1231 ....20.00
Octagon, yel, plate, 10½" 30.00
Old Colony, bowl, mint; dolphin ftd, 6" 16.00
Old Colony, bowl, salad; 2-hdld, sq, 10" 30.00
Old Colony, comport, oval, ftd, 7" 40.00
Old Colony, gr, bowl, nappy; dolphin ftd, 7½" 75.00
Old Colony, gr, plate, bouillon 15.00
Old Colony, gr, stem, cordial; #3380, 1-oz 155.00
Old Colony, gr, stem, wine; #3390, 2½-oz 35.00
Old Colony, gr, tray, center hdl, sq, 12" 85.00
Old Colony, marigold, grapefruit; #3380, ftd 30.00
Old Colony, marigold, stem, parfait; #3380, 5-oz 40.00
Old Colony, marigold, tumbler, soda; #3380, ftd, 8-oz ...32.50
Old Colony, pk, bowl, nappy; 4½" 10.00
Old Colony, pk, comport, #3368, ftd, 7" 57.50
Old Colony, pk, cruet, oil; ftd, 4-oz 70.00
Old Colony, pk, plate, sandwich; 2-hdld, sq, 13" 40.00
Old Colony, pk, stem, oyster cocktail; #3390, 3-oz 15.00
Old Colony, pk, tumbler, juice; #3390, 5-oz 15.00
Old Colony, plate, sq, 9" 15.00
Old Colony, yel, bowl, salad; 2-hdld, rnd, 10" 57.50
Old Colony, yel, creamer, ind 40.00
Old Colony, yel, finger bowl, #4075 ....11.00
Old Colony, yel, plate, muffin; 2-hdld, rnd, 12" 70.00
Old Colony, yel, plate, rnd, 4½" 7.00
Old Colony, yel, stem, oyster cocktail; #3380, 4-oz 15.00
Old Colony, yel, stem, water; #3390, 11-oz 25.00
Old Sandwich, beer mug, 18-oz 50.00

Old Sandwich, cobalt, stem, claret; 4-oz 150.00
Old Sandwich, cobalt, tumbler, bar; ground bottom, 1½-oz 100.00
Old Sandwich, decanter, w/#98 stopper, 1-pt 75.00
Old Sandwich, gr, parfait, 4½-oz 60.00
Old Sandwich, gr, sundae, 6-oz 35.00
Old Sandwich, pk, candlestick, 6" 100.00
Old Sandwich, yel, ashtray, ind 35.00
Old Sandwich, yel, pilsner, 10-oz 37.00
Orchid, bottle, French dressing; 8-oz 250.00
Orchid, bowl, gardenia; 13" 70.00
Orchid, bowl, jelly; ftd, 7" 40.00
Orchid, bowl, jelly; Queen Ann, 2-hdld, 6" 30.00
Orchid, cocktail shaker, #4225, 1-pt 275.00
Orchid, mayonnaise, 1-hdl, 6½" 50.00
Orchid, pitcher, ice tankard; 64-oz 525.00
Orchid, plate, cheese & cracker; 14" 100.00
Orchid, plate, dinner; 10½" 135.00
Orchid, plate, torte; rolled edge, 14" 75.00
Orchid, shakers, pr 60.00
Orchid, sugar bowl, ind 25.00
Orchid, tray, celery; 13" 50.00
Orchid, vase, fan form, ftd, 7" 85.00
Orchid, vase, 14" 650.00
Plantation, bowl, gardenia; 9½" 85.00
Plantation, bowl, jelly; flared, 6½" 45.00
Plantation, bowl, relish; oval, 5-part, 13" 65.00
Plantation, comport, w/lid, deep, 5" 100.00
Plantation, mayonnaise, rolled ft, 4½" 55.00
Plantation, plate, cake salver; ftd, 13" 135.00
Plantation, stem, claret; pressed, 4½-oz 65.00
Plantation, stem, cordial; 1-oz 125.00
Plantation, sugar bowl, ftd 30.00
Pleat & Panel, crystal, bowl, jelly; 2-hdld, 5" 9.00
Pleat & Panel, crystal, bowl, vegetable; oval, 9" 12.50
Pleat & Panel, crystal, marmalade, 4¾" 12.50
Pleat & Panel, gr, bowl, nappy; 4½" 12.00
Pleat & Panel, gr, bowl, nappy; 8" 35.00
Pleat & Panel, pk, pitcher, w/ or w/o ice lip, 3-pt 130.00
Pleat & Panel, pk, platter, oval, 12" 35.00
Pleat & Panel, pk, sugar bowl, w/lid, hotel sz 25.00
Pleat & Panel, pk, tumbler, tea; ground bottom, 12-oz 17.50
Pleat & Panel, plate, bouillon liner, 6¾" 4.00
Provincial, cigarette box, w/lid 50.00
Provincial, crystal, ashtray, sq, 3" 12.50
Provincial, crystal, bowl, floral; 12" 30.00
Provincial, crystal, plate, cheese; ftd, 5" 10.00
Provincial, crystal, stem, wine; 3½-oz 15.00
Provincial, crystal, vase, pansy; 6" 35.00
Provincial, limelight, bowl, nut/jelly; ind 35.00
Provincial, limelight, bowl, relish; 4-part, 10" 195.00
Provincial, limelight, creamer, ftd 95.00
Provincial, limelight, sugar bowl, ftd 95.00
Queen Ann, bowl, floral; rolled edge, 9" 22.00
Queen Ann, bowl, salad; 2-hdld, sq, 10" 30.00
Queen Ann, creamer, ind 15.00
Queen Ann, jug, ftd, 3-pt 70.00
Queen Ann, mayonnaise, w/ladle, ftd, 5½" 20.00
Queen Ann, plate, sq, 10½" 40.00
Queen Ann, plate, 7" 8.00
Queen Ann, platter, 14" 25.00
Queen Ann, stem, sherbet; 4-oz 15.00
Queen Ann, tumbler, ground bottom, 8-oz 15.00
Ridgeleigh, ashtray, sq, 6" 20.00
Ridgeleigh, bowl, floral; oblong, 14" 50.00

Ridgeleigh, bowl, floral; 10" 35.00
Ridgeleigh, bowl, jelly; 2-hdld, 6" 14.00
Ridgeleigh, bowl, nut; ind, 2-part 10.50
Ridgeleigh, cigarette box, w/lid, 6" 30.00
Ridgeleigh, plate, ice-tub liner, 2-hdld 30.00
Ridgeleigh, plate, torte; ftd, 13½" 45.00
Ridgeleigh, stem, saucer champagne; blown, 5-oz 20.00
Ridgeleigh, stem, sherbet; pressed 12.00
Ridgeleigh, tray, celery; 12" 35.00
Rose, bell, dinner; #5072 ....150.00
Rose, bowl, honey; Waverly, ftd, 7" 60.00
Rose, bowl, honey/cheese; Waverly, ftd, 6½" 75.00
Rose, bowl, mint; Cabochon, ftd, 5¾" 75.00
Rose, bowl, salad; Waverly, 9" 95.00
Rose, candlestick, Cascade, #142, 3-light 80.00
Rose, chocolate dish, Waverly, w/lid, 5" 150.00
Rose, comport, Waverly, oval, ftd, 7" 130.00
Rose, ice tub, Waverly, 2-hdld 295.00
Rose, pitcher, #4164, 73-oz 575.00
Rose, stem, cocktail; #5072, 4-oz 45.00
Rose, vase, #4198, 8" 120.00
Saturn, crystal, bowl, floral; rolled edge, 13" 45.00
Saturn, crystal, marmalade, w/lid 45.00
Saturn, crystal, pitcher, w/ice lip, blown, 70-oz 75.00
Saturn, crystal, rose bowl, lg 40.00
Saturn, crystal, stem, parfait; 5-oz 15.00
Saturn, zircon/limelight, ashtray 150.00
Saturn, zircon/limelight, bowl, salad; 11" 140.00
Saturn, zircon/limelight, oil bottle, w/#1 stopper, 2-oz 350.00
Saturn, zircon/limelight, stem, cocktail; 3-oz 60.00
Saturn, zircon/limelight, vase, flared, 8½" 175.00
Stanhope, creamer, w/ or w/o rnd knobs, 2-hdld 35.00
Stanhope, finger bowl, #4080, blown or plain 10.00
Stanhope, oil bottle, w/ or w/o rnd knob, 3-oz 275.00
Stanhope, stem, goblet; #4083, 10-oz 22.50
Stanhope, tumbler, soda; #4083, 12-oz 25.00
Stanhope, vase, w/ or w/o rnd knob, 2-hdld, 9" 65.00
Twist, crystal, bowl, nut; ind 5.00
Twist, crystal, comport, tall, 7" 25.00
Twist, crystal, saucer 3.00
Twist, gr, bowl, floral; 9" 40.00
Twist, gr, plate, Kraft cheese, 8" 40.00
Twist, marigold or alexandrite, ice bucket 300.00
Twist, pk, bowl, mint; 2-hdld, 6" 20.00
Twist, pk, cup, zigzag hdls 25.00
Twist, pk, tray, celery; 13" 30.00
Twist, yel, bowl, 2-hdld, 6" 20.00
Twist, yel, stem, saucer champagne; 2-block stem, 5-oz 25.00
Victorian, bottle, rye; 27-oz 150.00
Victorian, candlestick, 2-light 110.00
Victorian, decanter, w/stopper, 32-oz 50.00
Victorian, plate, sandwich; 13" 80.00
Victorian, stem, oyster cocktail; 5-oz 15.00
Victorian, tumbler, bar; 2-oz 35.00
Waverly, bowl, gardenia; 10" 20.00
Waverly, bowl, relish; rnd, 4-part, 9" 25.00
Waverly, box, sea-horse hdl, w/lid, ftd, tall, 5" 85.00
Waverly, candle holder, block form, 1-light, rare 100.00
Waverly, comport, low ft, 6" 12.00
Waverly, plate, cake salver; ftd, 13½" 65.00
Waverly, plate, luncheon; 8" 8.00
Waverly, stem, cordial; #5019, 1-oz 50.00
Waverly, sugar bowl, ftd 20.00
Waverly, vase, violet; 3½" 45.00

Yeoman, green, cup and saucer, $40.00.

Yeoman, clear, bottle, cologne; w/stopper 55.00
Yeoman, clear, bowl, lemon; rnd, 5" 6.00
Yeoman, clear, plate, oyster cocktail; 9" 10.00
Yeoman, cobalt, salt tub, ind 35.00
Yeoman, crystal, bowl, fruit; oval, 9" 20.00
Yeoman, crystal, tray, hors d'oeuvre; w/covered center, 13" 32.00
Yeoman, crystal, tumbler, whiskey; 2½-oz 5.00
Yeoman, crystal; bowl, banana split; ftd 10.00
Yeoman, gr, bowl, cream soup; 2-hdld 30.00
Yeoman, gr, bowl, lemon; w/lid, rnd, 5" 45.00
Yeoman, gr, creamer 22.00
Yeoman, gr, pitcher, 1-qt 75.00
Yeoman, gr, stem, champagne; 6-oz 22.00
Yeoman, marigold, bowl, pickle/olive; rectangular, 8" 35.00
Yeoman, marigold, saucer 10.00
Yeoman, orchid, bowl, berry; 2-hdld, 8½" 55.00
Yeoman, orchid, egg cup 52.00
Yeoman, orchid, plate, cream soup liner 14.00
Yeoman, orchid, sugar bowl, w/lid 40.00
Yeoman, pk, bowl, jelly; low ftd, 5" 20.00
Yeoman, pk, bowl, vegetable; 6" 10.00
Yeoman, pk, marmalade jar, w/lid 35.00
Yeoman, pk, plate, 7" 8.00
Yeoman, pk, salver, low ftd, 10" 30.00
Yeoman, pk, tray, oblong, 12" 19.00
Yeoman, yel, ashtray, bow-tie form, hdld, 4" 22.00
Yeoman, yel, bowl, floral; low, 12" 35.00
Yeoman, yel, plate, 6" 8.00
Yeoman, yel, stem, oyster cocktail; ftd, 2¾-oz 10.00

Heubach

Gebruder Heubach is a German porcelain company that has been in operation since the 1800s, producing quality figurines and novelty items. They are perhaps most famous for their doll heads and piano babies, most of which are marked with the circular rising sun device containing an 'H' superimposed over a 'C.' Our advisor for this category is Grace Ochsner; she is listed in the Directory under Illinois. See also Dolls, Heubach.

Baby crawling on tummy, wht gown, 8" 450.00
Baby seated in pk dress, 5", ea 250.00
Baby sits w/ice skates, night light, 3½" 425.00
Bicyclist, 11½" 450.00
Blond boy straddling bench blowing bubbles, 9" 500.00
Blond girl in pk pleated skirt w/gr sash, mk, ¾" 375.00
Boy (nude) w/hand over eye, brn shoes, vase at bk, 4" 300.00
Boy in dk bl sweater, tan pants, on tummy, holds ball, 5" L ...375.00
Boy in gr knicker suit w/pocket linings trn out, 9" 425.00
Boy in tattered suit, broom resting between ft, 8" 375.00
Boy w/monkey on arm, lav suit, 13" 450.00
Boy w/parasol, 5" 235.00

Dutch boy & girl stand bk to bk, unmk, 5¼x3" 150.00
Dutch boy in wht suit pulling cap down w/both hands, 8" 500.00
Dutch boy sitting w/basket behind, mk, 5x4¾" 425.00
Dutch children sitting, mk, 7¼", pr 425.00
Dutch girl w/attached basket, flirty pose, mk, 7½" 375.00
Girl in bunny costume before lg pk egg, eyes to side, 7½" 525.00
Girl stands beside vase, mk, 6½" 225.00
Humidor, Jasper, gr, Indian chief on lid, 5" 150.00
Lady in lt gr dress w/floral design, lacy eyes, mk, 12" 400.00
Planter, figural shepherdess w/flock, mk, 4x10¾x2¾" 195.00
Plaque, Jasper, Indian on horse attacks bear, wht/lav, 9" L ...215.00
Pup w/muzzle, impressed mk, 5" 225.00
Snow baby dressed as bear, seated, 3" 225.00
Vase, anemones, pk on gray, gr mk, 8⅝x3" 125.00
Vase, roses, pk on gr w/gold, mk, 4x1½" 125.00

Hickman, Royal Arden

Born in Willamette, Oregon, Royal A. Hickman was a genius in all aspects of design interpretation. Mr. Hickman's expertise can be seen in the designs of the lovely Heisey figurines, Kosta crystal, Bruce Fox aluminum, Three Crowns aluminum, Vernon Kilns, and Royal Haeger Pottery (as well as handcrafted silver, furniture, and paintings).

Because Mr. Hickman moved around during much of his lifetime, his influence has been felt in all forms of the media. Designs from his independent companies include 'Royal Hickman Pottery and Lamps' (sold through Ceramic Arts Inc., of Chattanooga, Tennessee), 'Royal Hickman's Paris Ware,' 'Royal Hickman — Florida,' and 'California Designed by Royal Hickman.' The following listings will give examples of pieces bearing the various trademarks. Our advisors for this category are Lee Garmon and Doris Frizzell; both are listed in the Directory under Illinois (only S.A.S.E. inquiries answered). See also Royal Haegar; Vernon Kilns, Melinda pattern.

Bruce Fox Aluminum

Banana leaf, sgn Royal Hickman-RH 6, 22½" L 25.00
Dish, lobster, lg 65.00
Dish, 3-point leaf, sgn Royal Hickman, 15½" L 25.00
Ivy tray, #362, 13" 20.00
Platter, fish, EX detail, sgn Royal Hickman-RH3, 13x9" 65.00
Silent butler, dog's head, sgn, 8x5½" 65.00
2-acorn oak tray, 14½" 25.00
5-point leaf tray, 14" 25.00
7-point leaf tray, sgn Royal Hickman, 14" 25.00

California, Designed by Royal Hickman

Bowl, red w/blk highlights, #607, 9½" 40.00
Figurine, deer, apple gr w/wht spots, appl eyes, 15" 45.00
Figurine, giraffe & young, pk w/blk spots 65.00

Gravy boat and leaf tray, $75.00.

Lamp base, flying geese, 17" 250.00
Punch bowl, Tom & Jerry, w/8 mugs 350.00
Swan, red w/blk highlights, #643, 17" 95.00

Miscellaneous Signatures

Sea horse vase, sgn Royal Hickman USA, #468, 8" 35.00
Vase, fish figurine, Petty Crystal Glaze, #467 ....35.00
Vase, lg heart, sgn Royal Hickman, Italy, #3774 ....95.00
Vase, rooster figurine, Petty Crystal Glaze, #565 ....95.00

Royal Hickman — Florida

Vase, free-form, #578, 14" 40.00
Vase, horse's head, gray w/wht mane, 13¾" 125.00
Vase, pouter pigeon, blk cascade, #599, 8½" 45.00
Vase, swan, head down, blk cascade, #3624-R, 14" 75.00

Royal Hickman — Guadalajara, Mexico

Vase, 3 dolphin figures, 13" 125.00

Higgins

Contemporary glass artists Frances and Michael Higgins have been designing high-quality glassware since the late 1940s. Their designs are often created by fusing layers of glass together, though sometimes colored ground glass is used to 'paint' the decoration onto the surface. Molds are used, and through a process called 'slumping,' the glass is fired to a very high temperature, causing it to soften and take on the predetermined shape. Their work is ultramodern and is more readily found in metropolitan areas.

The earliest mark was an engraved signature on the bottom of the glass — either 'Frances Stewart Higgins' or 'Michael Higgins' or both, which was dropped in favor of just 'Higgins' with a raised 'Higgins Man.' From approximately 1957 to 1964, the Higgins signature was embossed in gold on top. After 1964 up to the present the signature again appears on the bottom and is engraved in the glass. Our advisor is Dennis Hopp; he is listed in the Directory under Illinois.

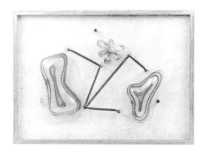

Sculpture, 3 geometric pieces of glass mounted on canvas in wooden frame, 22x29", $1,200.00.

Ashtray, fish, orange, yellow & gold, 14x10" 165.00
Ashtray, flowers, gold signature, sq 40.00
Ashtrays, gray & gold triangles on orange, 10x14", 10x7", 7x5" .250.00
Bowl, fruit decor, 6" 65.00
Centerpc/ashtray, orange & red w/lt bl rays, 10x14" 95.00
Clock, blk/wht/gold w/red/gold hands, rnd, for GE, 1954 ....550.00
Posy pocket, orange stripes, metal chain hanger 195.00

Tray, red & orange w/lt bl rays fron center, 10x14" 95.00

Historical Glass

Glassware commemorating particularly significant historical events became popular in the late 1800s. Bread trays were the most common form, but plates, mugs, pitchers, and other items were also pressed in clear as well as colored glass. It was sold in vast amounts at the 1876 Philadelphia Centennial Exposition by various manufacturers who exhibited their wares on the grounds. It remained popular well into the 20th century.

In the listings that follow, L numbers refer to a book by Lindsey, a standard guide used by many collectors. Our advisor for this category is Darlene Yohe; she is listed in the Directory under Arkansas. See also Bread Plates; Pattern Glass.

Bottle, Columbus, milk glass, w/stopper 600.00
Bottle, Granger, L-266 ....110.00
Bottle, Statue of Liberty, milk glass, rpr stopper 500.00
Bowl, Frosted Eagle (Old Abe), braid trim, w/lid, 8" 395.00
Covered dish, Battleship Oregon, milk glass, L-469, 6½" L, EX ...75.00
Covered dish, Covered Wagon, frosted, L-128 ....150.00
Cup, Harrison & Morton, bl 235.00
Cup, McKinley, w/lid, L-355 ....60.00
Flask, Grover Cleveland, etched, flat-side rectangle, 7" 475.00
Flask, Washington & Jackson, dk amber 495.00
Goblet, Emblem Centennial, L-61 ....45.00
Goblet, Liberty Bell, Bicentennial, 5" 9.00
Goblet, Pittsburgh Centennial 95.00
Goblet, Shield, 1876 Centennial 50.00
Hat, Uncle Sam, no pnt, L-110 ....35.00
Hat, 1908 Presidential Campaign, milk glass w/red pnt 125.00
Jar, Statue of Liberty, L-530 ....70.00
Jefferson Davis, milk glass 68.00
Lamp, oil; Goddess of Liberty, 1987 Centennial 125.00
Match holder, T Roosevelt, etched, top hat form 90.00
Mug, Assassination 60.00
Mug, Centennial, waisted 90.00
Mug, Garfield Born...Assassinated...., clear, mini, 2¼" 80.00
Mug, Knights of Labor, knight & worker, L-513 ....55.00
Mug, Lincoln & Garfield, Our Country's Martyrs, L-272 ....95.00
Mug, Tennessee, L-102 ....55.00
Paperweight, Director Goshorn, 1876, Gillinder, L-449 ....155.00
Paperweight, Lincoln, L-275 ....175.00
Paperweight, Plymouth Rock, L-18 ....90.00
Paperweight, Washington Monument, milk glass 175.00
Pitcher, Dewey, L-400 ....65.00
Plate, Bust of McKinley, Protection & Plenty, clear, 7¼" 50.00
Plate, CA Gold Rush, Eureka 50.00
Plate, Columbia Shield, sapphire bl 225.00
Plate, Columbus, milk glass, 9½" 65.00
Plate, emb cannon balls, bicentennial dates, 8" 9.00
Plate, For President Winfield S Hancock, 8" 110.00
Plate, Garfield, frosted head, star border, 6" 35.00
Plate, George Washington, milk glass 45.00
Plate, Grant, Patriot & Soldier, amber, sq, 9½" 50.00
Plate, Grant Peace, maple leaf 45.00
Plate, Niagara Falls, milk glass 35.00
Plate, Old State House, L-32 ....50.00
Plate, Pope Leo, milk glass, L-240 ....40.00
Plate, President Taft, flags & eagles, milk glass, 7" 85.00
Plate, Texian Campaign, lt bl, 9½" 195.00
Platter, Carpenter's Hall 65.00

Shaker, Centennial, boot 27.00
Spooner, Log Cabin, L-184 ....115.00
Statue, Ruth the Gleaner, frosted, 1876 Phila Expo, Gillinder ...175.00
Statuette, Lincoln, Gillinder & Sons, L-277 ....385.00
Stein, Centennial 65.00
Sugar shaker, Proclaim Liberty Throughout the Land 195.00
Tumbler, Admiral Dewey, Battle of Manila Bay, 1898 ....30.00
Tumbler, bar; Bumper to the Flag, Civil War, L-480 ....150.00
Tumbler, eagle, flags, cannon, L-148, 4¾" 125.00
Tumbler, Eagle & dates enameled on yel, short 4.00
Tumbler, Lincoln Tribute, L-282 ....25.00
Tumbler, Louisiana Purchase, L-107 ....35.00
Tumbler, St Louis Expo, milk glass, L-379 ....15.00
Tumbler, Union Forever, Bumper to the Flag, 3⅛" 80.00
Tumbler, whiskey; flag w/13 stars, eagle on shield, 3¼" 135.00

Hobbs, Brockunier & Co.

Hobbs and Brockunier's South Wheeling Glass Works was in operation during the last quarter of the 19th century. They are most famous for their peachblow, amberina, Daisy and Button, and Hobnail pattern glass. The mainstay of the operation, however, was druggist items and plain glassware — bowls, mugs, and simple footed pitchers with shell handles. See also Frances Ware.

Bowl, Hobnail, peachblow color, crimped, SP base, 6x11x6" 350.00
Celery, Gonterman Swirl, bl crimped rim, wht opal base, 5⅝" ...235.00
Pitcher, Hobnail, wht opal, sq top, 5¾x5" 225.00
Pitcher & tumbler, bl w/silver mica, dimpled mold 165.00

Holt Howard

Novelty ceramics marked Holt Howard represent one of the newest areas of collectibles on today's market, and dealers report a good amount of market activity. Made from the '50s into the '70s, they're not only marked, but most are dated as well. There are several lines to reassemble — the rooster, the white cat, figural banks, Christmas angels and Santas, to name only a few — but the one that most Holt Howard collectors seem to gravitate toward is the Pixie line.

Rooster egg cup, $18.00; Salt and pepper shakers, large, $30.00 for the pair.

Airwick, holly girl figural 38.00
Bank, Coin Clown, bobbing head 185.00
Bell, holly decor 15.00
Candle holder, chick 25.00
Candle holders, angel figures, pr 35.00
Candle holders, rooster figural, pr 25.00
Candlesticks, Santa hdl 22.00
Cherry jar, Cherries If You Please on sign held by butler 260.00
Coffeepot, emb rooster 85.00

Cookie jar, wht cat-head form 50.00
Creamer & sugar bowl, emb rooster 45.00
Honey jar, Pixie Ware, rare 190.00
Instant coffee jar, Pixie Ware, brn-skinned/blond-head finial 190.00
Jam & jelly jar, Pixie Ware, flat-head finial 60.00
Letter holder, wht cat w/coiled-wire bk 25.00
Lipstick holder, ponytail girl 75.00
Mug, Santa 12.00
Mustard jar, Pixie Ware, yel-head finial 60.00
Note pad holder, 3-D lady's hand 45.00
Pitcher, emb rooster 50.00
Pitcher, Santa winking, fan-like beard, +6 sm mugs 85.00
Planter, camel 15.00
Plate, Rake 'N Spade, MIB 20.00
Platter, emb rooster, oval 25.00
Razor bank, barber figure 30.00
Scouring powder shaker, wht lady cat figural w/apron & broom ...95.00
Shakers, mice in wicker baskets, pr 35.00
Shakers, Pixie Ware, pr 65.00
Shakers, ponytail girl, pr 45.00
Shakers, rooster figural, tall, pr 30.00
Shakers, tomatoes, pr 15.00
Shakers, wht cat's head, pr 20.00
Shakers, wht cats, tall, pr 20.00
Snack set, tomato, 1 cup & 1 plate, 1962 ....14.00
Spoon rest, rooster figural 35.00
String holder, wht cat's head only 45.00
Vase, bud; rooster 22.00
Vase, bud; wht cat in plaid cap & neckerchief 75.00
Wall pocket, wht cat's head 45.00

Homer Laughlin

The Homer Laughlin China Company of Newell, West Virginia, was founded in 1871. The superior dinnerware they displayed at the Centennial Exposition in Philadelphia in 1876 won the highest award of excellence. From that time to the present, they have continued to produce quality dinnerware and kitchenware, many lines of which are becoming very popular collectibles. Most of the dinnerware is marked with the name of the pattern and occasionally with the shape name as well. The 'HLC' trademark is usually followed by a number series, the first two digits of which indicate the year of its manufacture. For further information we recommend *The Collector's Encyclopedia of Fiesta, Revised Seventh Edition,* by Sharon and Bob Huxford; *The Collector's Encyclopedia of Homer Laughlin China* by Joanne Jasper; and *Collector's Guide to Homer Laughlin's Virginia Rose* by Richard G. Racheter (all available from Collector Books).

Our values are base prices. Very desirable patterns on the shapes named in our listings may increase values by as much as 70%. See also Fiesta; Harlequin; Riviera.

Cavalier, casserole, w/lid 40.00
Cavalier, creamer 12.00
Cavalier, plate, 10" 10.00
Cavalier, sauce boat 16.00
Debutante, dish, 15" 20.00
Debutante, nappy, 8" 12.00
Debutante, pie server 25.00
Debutante, plate, 7" 6.00
Debutante, shakers, pr 12.00
Debutante, sugar bowl, w/lid 15.00
Debutante, teapot 40.00
Eggshell Georgian, bowl, 5" 10.00

Eggshell Georgian, casserole, w/lid **40.00**
Eggshell Georgian, plate, 8" sq **8.00**
Eggshell Georgian, sauce boat **15.00**
Eggshell Georgian, shakers, pr **14.00**
Eggshell Georgian, teacup & saucer **8.00**
Eggshell Nautilus, baker, 10" **16.00**
Eggshell Nautilus, bowl, deep, 5" **8.00**
Eggshell Nautilus, creamer **12.00**
Eggshell Nautilus, nappy, 10" **16.00**
Eggshell Nautilus, plate, chop; 14" **20.00**
Eggshell Nautilus, plate, 10" **10.00**
Eggshell Nautilus, teapot **60.00**
Empress, baker, 10" **15.00**
Empress, butter dish **50.00**
Empress, nappy, 10" **15.00**
Empress, plate, 8" **6.00**

Photo courtesy Joanne Jasper

Jade: Plate, 9", $12.00; Fruit bowl, $6.00; Teacup and saucer, $10.00. These are base prices for this shape, see narrative.

Jade, baker, 10" **20.00**
Jade, jug, w/lid, sm **50.00**
Jade, plate, 8" **8.00**
Jade, sauce boat **18.00**
Jade, sugar bowl, w/lid **18.00**
Jade, teapot **70.00**
Liberty, plate, 10" **12.00**
Liberty, plate, 6" **5.00**
Liberty, sugar bowl, w/lid **15.00**
Liberty, teacup & saucer **10.00**
Liberty (Historical America), casserole, w/lid **55.00**
Liberty (Historical America), creamer **16.00**
Liberty (Historical America), plate, 7" **8.00**
Liberty (Historical America), sauce boat **24.00**

Hull

The A.E. Hull Pottery was formed in 1905 in Zanesville, Ohio, and in the early years produced stoneware specialities. They expanded in 1907, adding a second plant and employing over two hundred workers. By 1920 they were manufacturing a full line of stoneware, art pottery with both airbrushed and blended glazes, florist pots, and gardenware. They also produced toilet ware and kitchen items with a white semiporcelain body. Although these continued to be staple products, after the stock market crash of 1929, emphasis was shifted to tile production. By the mid-'30s interest in art pottery production was growing, and over the next fifteen years, several lines of matt pastel floral-decorated patterns were designed, consisting of vases, planters, baskets, ewers, and bowls in various sizes.

The Red Riding Hood cookie jar, patented in 1943, proved so successful that a whole line of figural kitchenware and novelty items was added. They continued to be produced well into the '50s. (See also Little Red Riding Hood.) Through the '40s their floral artware lines flooded the market, due to the restriction of foreign imports. Although best known for their pastel matt-glazed ware, some of the lines were high gloss. Rosella, glossy coral on a pink clay body, was produced for a short time only; and Magnolia, although offered in a matt glaze, was produced in gloss as well.

The plant was destroyed in 1950 by a flood which resulted in a devastating fire when the floodwater caused the kilns to explode. The company rebuilt and equipped their new factory with the most modern machinery. It was soon apparent that the matt glaze could not be duplicated through the more modern processes, however, and soon attention was concentrated on high-gloss artware lines such as Parchment and Pine and Ebb Tide. Figural planters and novelties, piggy banks, and dinnerware were produced in abundance in the late '50s and '60s. By the mid-'70s dinnerware and florist ware were the mainstay of their business. The firm discontinued operations in 1985.

Our advisor, Brenda Roberts, has compiled a lovely book, *The Collector's Encyclopedia of Hull Pottery*, with full-color photos and current values. You will find her address in the Directory under Missouri. Another informative book is *Collector's Guide to Hull Pottery, The Dinnerware Lines*, by Barbara Loveless Gick-Burke, available from Collector Books or your bookstore.

Blossom Flite, basket, #T-2, 6" **80.00**
Blossom Flite, candle holder, #T-11, 3" **60.00**
Blossom Flite, teapot, #T-14, 8¼" **145.00**
Bow-Knot, basket, #B-12, 10½" **800.00**
Bow-Knot, bell, loop hdl, unmk, 6" **325.00**
Bow-Knot, console bowl, #B-16, 13½" **395.00**
Bow-Knot, jardiniere, #B-18, 5¾" **225.00**
Bow-Knot, vase, #B-10, 10½" **500.00**
Bow-Knot, wall plaque, cup & saucer, #B-24, 6" **260.00**
Bow-Knot, wall pocket, iron, unmk, 6¼" **280.00**
Butterfly, ashtray, matt, #B-3, 7" **45.00**
Butterfly, ewer, glossy, #B-15, 13½" **235.00**
Butterfly, lavabo, matt, w/orig hanger, #B-25/#B-24, 2-pc, 16" ..**245.00**
Butterfly, teapot, glossy, B-18, 8½" **145.00**
Calla Lily, cornucopia, bl, #570/33, 8" **145.00**
Calla Lily, ewer, bl/pk, #506, 10" **425.00**
Calla Lily, vase, #520/33, 8" **170.00**
Calla Lily, vase, #530-33, 7" **145.00**
Calla Lily, vase, #540/33, 6" **140.00**
Camellia, cornucopia, #101, 8½" **175.00**
Camellia, creamer, #111, 5" **125.00**
Camellia, hanging basket, #132, 7" **315.00**
Camellia, sugar bowl (open), #112, 5" **125.00**
Camellia, vase, #131, 4¾" **90.00**
Capri, basket, sea gr, matt, #48, 12¼" **75.00**
Capri, ewer, pine cone in relief, coral, matt, #87, 12" **110.00**
Capri, swan, coral, matt, #23, 8½" **65.00**
Capri, urn, lion's head in relief, #50, 9" **60.00**
Cinderella Kitchenware (Blossom), casserole, #21, 7½" **45.00**
Cinderella Kitchenware (Blossom), teapot, #26, 42-oz **170.00**
Cinderella Kitchenware (Bouquet), grease jar, #24, 32-oz **55.00**
Cinderella Kitchenware (Bouquet), pitcher, #29, 32-oz **65.00**
Classic, vase, floral, bl on pk, #5, 6" **35.00**
Classic, vase, floral, pk on pk, #4, 6" **35.00**
Continental, basket, persimmon w/yel stripes, #55, 12¾" **210.00**
Continental, bud vase, bl, #66, 9½" **40.00**
Continental, candle holder/planter, gr, unmk, 4" **30.00**
Continental, ewer, gr, #56, 12½" **225.00**

Crescent Kitchenware, bowl, #B-1, 9½" 35.00
Crescent Kitchenware, mug, dk gr, #B-16, 4¼" 20.00
Crescent Kitchenware, teapot, burgundy, #B-13, 7½" 85.00
Debonair, cookie jar, chartreuse, #0-8, 8¾" 95.00
Dogwood, basket, #501, 7½" 375.00
Dogwood, cornucopia, #522, 3¾" 100.00
Dogwood, ewer, #519, 13½" 700.00
Dogwood, vase, #516, 4¾" 200.00
Dogwood, window box, #508, 10½" 225.00
Early Art, candle holder, lav, lustreware, unmk, 3" 75.00
Early Art, vase, ribbed body, #39, 8" 100.00
Early Art, vase, vertical stripes, #32, 8" 85.00
Early Art, wall pocket, lustreware, unmk, 8½" 100.00
Early Utility, bowl, gr, #421, 7" 40.00
Early Utility, flowerpot w/saucer, #538, 4" 36.00
Early Utility, mug, brn, Happy Days Are Here Again, #265, 4½" .30.00
Early Utility, salt box, bl bands, porc, #111, 6" 150.00
Ebb Tide, basket, #E-5, 6¼" 140.00
Ebb Tide, candle holders, gold trim, #E-13, ¾", pr 32.00
Ebb Tide, console bowl, sea shell form, #E-12, 15¾" 175.00
Ebb Tide, ewer, #E-10, 14" 260.00
Fiesta, basket, leaf & berry design, #51, 12½" 70.00
Fiesta, cornucopia, fancy scalloped top, #49, 8½" 80.00
Fiesta, flowerpot, rose in relief, ped ft, #43, 6" 60.00
Floral, cookie jar, #48, 8¾" 145.00
Floral, salad bowl, #49, 10" 75.00
Floral, shaker, #44, 3½" 20.00
Imperial, basket, #F-38, 6¾" 35.00
Imperial, ewer, #F-480, 10½" 55.00
Imperial, planter, praying hands, #F-475, 6" 30.00
Imperial, urn, gold lustre trim, #F-88, 5¾" 40.00
Iris, basket, #408, 7" 365.00
Iris, candle holder, #411, 5" 110.00
Iris, ewer, #401, 13½" 525.00
Iris, planter, #412, 7" 225.00
Iris, vase, #402, 7" 195.00
Iris, vase, bud; #410, 7½" 195.00

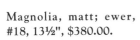
Magnolia, matt; ewer,
#18, 13½", $380.00.

Magnolia, glossy; basket, #H-14, 10½" 425.00
Magnolia, glossy; candle holder, #H-24, 4" 45.00
Magnolia, glossy; ewer, #H-3, 5½" 60.00
Magnolia, glossy; sugar bowl, w/lid, #H-22, 3¾" 40.00
Magnolia, glossy; vase, #H-13, 10½" 170.00
Magnolia, glossy; vase, #H-16, 12½" 250.00
Magnolia, matt; basket, #10, 10½" 450.00
Magnolia, matt; candle holder, #27, 4" 50.00
Magnolia, matt; console bowl, #26, 12" 210.00
Magnolia, matt; cornucopia, #19, 8½" 145.00
Magnolia, matt; teapot, #23, 6½" 210.00

Magnolia, matt; vase, #20, 15" 500.00
Mardi Gras, mixing bowl, pk, unmk, 10¼" 45.00
Mardi Gras, vase, yel, unmk, 6" 25.00
Mirror Almond, bowl, vegetable; 11" L 20.00
Mirror Almond, French casserole, w/lid, sm 15.00
Mirror Almond, mug, 3¼" 4.00
Mirror Almond, plate, dinner; 10" 8.00
Mirror Almond, plate, salad; 6½" 5.00
Mirror Brown, bank, pig, Jumbo, #197 ....130.00
Mirror Brown, bowl, salad; #569, 6½" 5.00
Mirror Brown, butter dish, ¼-lb, 7" L 25.00
Mirror Brown, canister set, rnd, 4-pc 375.00
Mirror Brown, carafe, #502, 2-cup 65.00
Mirror Brown, casserole, w/chicken lid, 8" 55.00
Mirror Brown, cookie jar, cylinder, 8" 40.00
Mirror Brown, cookie jar, gingerbread man, 12" 300.00
Mirror Brown, pitcher, w/ice lip, #514, 2-qt 25.00
Mirror Brown, shakers, mushroom form, 4", pr 25.00
Mirror Brown, spoon rest, oval, 6½" 30.00
Mirror Brown, teapot, 6" 40.00
Novelty, bank, figural pig w/cork nose, pk & bl, 5" 105.00
Novelty, bank, turnabout stylized male/female cat, gr, #198, 11" 270.00
Novelty, figurine, basket girl, glossy, #954, 8" 45.00
Novelty, figurine, dachshund, glossy blk, 6x14" 225.00
Novelty, figurine, swing band accordionist, unmk, 6" 135.00
Novelty, kitten w/spool, #89, 6" 25.00
Novelty, planter, knight, #55, 8" 75.00
Novelty, planter, lovebirds, #93, 6" 45.00
Novelty, planter, pig, #60, 5" 45.00
Novelty, planter, poodle, #114, 8" 55.00
Novelty, planter, telephone, #50, 9" 65.00
Novelty, vase, twin deer, 362, 11½" 75.00
Novelty, vase, unicorn, #98, 9½" 65.00
Novelty, wall pocket, goose, #67, 6½" 65.00
Novelty, wall pocket, ribbon, #71, 6" 40.00
Nuline Bak-Serv, casserole, w/lid, #D-13, 7½" 60.00
Nuline Bak-Serv, cookie jar, peach, #D-20, 2-qt, 8" 115.00
Nuline Bak-Serv, pitcher, bl, #C-29, 7" 80.00
Orchid, basket, #305, 7" 800.00
Orchid, candle holder, #315, 4" 115.00
Orchid, ewer, #311, 13" 725.00
Orchid, vase, #307, 4¾" 155.00
Orchid, vase, #308, 4½" 100.00
Parchment & Pine, ashtray, #S14, 14" 165.00
Parchment & Pine, candle holders, unmk, 5" L, pr 35.00
Parchment & Pine, console bowl, unmk, 16" L 135.00
Parchment & Pine, teapot, #S-15, 8" 125.00
Pine Cone, vase, pk, #55, 6½" 185.00
Poppy, ewer, #610, 4¾" 160.00
Poppy, planter, #602, 6½" 255.00
Poppy, vase, #607, 6½" 150.00
Poppy, wall pocket, #609, 9" 400.00
Rosella, basket, #R-12, 7" 280.00
Rosella, cornucopia, #R-13, 8½" L 140.00
Rosella, ewer, #R-7, 9½", rare 1,200.00
Rosella, lamp base, #L-3, 11" 425.00
Rosella, vase, #R-15, 8½" 135.00
Rosella, vase, #R-2, 5" 40.00
Rosella, wall pocket, heart shape, #R-9, 6½" 175.00
Royal Ebb Tide, vase, pk, unmk, 10¾" 95.00
Royal Imperial, window box, pk, #82, 12½" 35.00
Royal Woodland, wall pocket, shell form, aqua, #W-13, 7½" ...105.00
Serenade, ashtray, #S-23, 13x10½" 130.00
Serenade, basket, #S-14, 12" 450.00

Serenade, candy dish, #S-3, 8¼" 165.00
Serenade, vase, #S-1, 6½" 65.00
Sun-Glow, casserole, w/lid, #51, 7½" 80.00
Sun-Glow, flowerpot, #97, 5½" 40.00
Sun-Glow, grease jar, #53, 5¼" 55.00
Sun-Glow, pitcher, #55, 7½" 145.00
Sun-Glow, wall plaque, whisk broom, #82, 8¼" 100.00
Thistle, vase, #52, 6½" 125.00
Tokay, candy dish, #9, 8½" 145.00
Tokay, cornucopia, #10, 11" 75.00
Tokay, ewer, #13, 12" 290.00
Tokay, leaf dish, #19, 13" 50.00
Tropicana, basket, #55, 12¾" 850.00
Tropicana, vase, #54, 12½" 495.00
Tulip, basket, #102-33, 6" 345.00
Tulip, ewer, #109, 8" 295.00
Tulip, jardiniere, #115-33, 7" 310.00
Tulip, vase, #107-33, 8" 175.00
Tulip, vase, #111-33, 6" 145.00
Water Lily, basket, #L-14, 10½" 400.00
Water Lily, console bowl, #L-21, 13½" 220.00
Water Lily, cornucopia, #L-7, 6½" 100.00
Water Lily, ewer, # L-3, 5½" 80.00
Water Lily, jardiniere, #L-24, 8½" 340.00
Wildflower, basket, #W-16, 10½" 360.00
Wildflower, candle holder, unmk 45.00
Wildflower, cornucopia, #W-10, 8½" 135.00
Wildflower, lamp base, #W-17, 12½" 400.00
Wildflower (# series), teapot, #72, 8" 1,000.00
Wildflower (# series), vase, #51, 9½" 260.00
Wildflower (# series), vase, #52, 5¼" 165.00
Woodland, glossy; basket, #W-22, 10½" 265.00
Woodland, glossy; cornucopia, #W-10, 11" 95.00
Woodland, glossy; dbl bud vase, #W-15, 8½" 120.00
Woodland, glossy; flowerpot, w/attached saucer, #W-11, 5¾" 125.00
Woodland, matt; candle holder, #W-30, 3½" 120.00
Woodland, matt; cornucopia, #W-2, 5½" 75.00
Woodland, matt; ewer, #W-6, 6½" 155.00
Woodland, matt; hanging basket, #W-31, 5½" 235.00
Woodland, matt; vase, #W-17, 7½" 365.00
Woodland, matt; wall pocket, #W-13, 7½" 250.00
Woodland, matt; window box, #W-14, 10" 170.00
Yellowware, baker, bl banded, w/lid, #455, 9" 155.00
Yellowware, batter bowl, #25-3, 9" 140.00
Yellowware, bowl, bl banded, #421, 12" 100.00
Yellowware, cup, custard, brn banded, #114, 3" 18.00
Yellowware, pitcher, brn banded, #107, 5" 80.00

Hummel

Hummel figurines were created through the artistry of Berta Hummel, a Franciscan nun called Sister M. Innocentia. The first figures were made about 1935 by Franz Goebel of Goebel Art Inc., Rodental, West Germany. Plates, plaques, and candy dishes are also produced, and the older, discontinued editions are highly sought collectibles. Generally speaking, an issue can be dated by the trademark. The first Hummels, from 1934-1949, were either incised or stamped with the 'Crown WG' mark. The 'full bee in V' mark was employed with minor variations until 1959. At that time the bee was stylized and represented by a solid disk with angled symmetrical wings completely contained within the confines of the 'V.' The three-line mark, 1964-1972, utilized the stylized bee and included a three-line arrangement, 'c by W. Goebel, W. Germany.' Another change in 1970 saw the 'stylized bee in V' suspended between

the vertical bars of the 'b' and 'l' of a printed 'Goebel, West Germany.' Collectors refer to this mark as the 'last bee' or 'Goebel bee.' The mark in use from 1979 to 1990 omits the 'bee in V.' The current mark in use since 1991 is a crown with 'WG' initials with a large 'Goebel' and a small 'Germany' signifying a united Germany. For further study we recommend *Hummel, An Illustrated Handbook and Price Guide* by Ken Armke, *Hummel Figurines and Plates, A Collector's Identification and Value Guide,* by Carl Luckey, and *The No. 1 Price Guide to M.I. Hummel* by Robert L. Miller. These books are available through your local book dealer. Idiosyncrasies in the numerical order of the following listings are due to computer sorting. See also Limited Edition Plates.

Key:
ce — closed edition   SB — stylized bee
CM — crown mark   LB — last bee
FB — full bee   MB — missing bee

#105, Adoration With Bird, closed edition, limited production, 4¾", $6,000.00.

#II/112, Just Resting, table lamp, SB, ce, 7½" 255.00
#III/110, Let's Sing, candy box, 3-line mk, ce, 5¼" 125.00
#III/38/0, Angel, Joyous News w/Lute, candle holder, CM, ce, 2" 90.00
#III/53, Joyful, candy box, FB, ce, 6½" 380.00
#III/63, Singing Lesson, candy box, CM, ce, 5¾" 470.00
#1, Puppy Love, SB, ce, 5" 310.00
#109/II, Happy Traveler, FB, ce, 7½" 540.00
#11/2/0, Merry Wanderer, CM, ce, 4½" 290.00
#110, Let's Sing, FB, ce, 4" 220.00
#111/I, Wayside Harmony, CM, ce, 5¼" 435.00
#112 3/0, Just Resting, FB, ce, 4" 180.00
#113, Heavenly Song, candle holder, LB, ce, 3½x4¾" 2,160.00
#114, Let's Sing, ashtray, SB, ce, 3½x6¼" 145.00
#118, Little Thrifty, bank, SB, ce, 5¼" 145.00
#119 2/0, Postman, MB, ce, 4½" 100.00
#12/I, Chimney Sweep, SB, ce, 6" 220.00
#123, Max & Moritz, CM, ce, 5¼" 435.00
#124, Hello, FB, ce, 6½" 290.00
#125, Vacation Time, plaque, SB, ce, 4x4¾" 180.00
#126, Retreat to Saftey, plaque, CM, ce, 5x5" 360.00
#127, Doctor, FB, ce, 5" 200.00
#128, Baker, 3-line mk, ce, 5" 165.00
#13/0, Meditation, LB, ce, 5½" 160.00
#130, Duet, CM, ce, 5" 540.00
#131, Street Singer, FB, ce, 5" 235.00
#132, Star Gazer, FB, ce, 4¾" 270.00
#135, Soloist, FB, ce, 5" 175.00
#136, Friends, FB, ce, 10½" 1,450.00
#137B, Child in Bed (child looking right), CM, ce, 3x3" 215.00
#139, Flitting Butterfly, wall plaque, FB, ce, 2½" sq 145.00
#14 A&B, Book Worm, boy & girl bookends, ce, 5½" 360.00
#140, The Mail Is Here, plaque, FB, ce, 4¼x6¾" 290.00
#141, Apple Tree Girl, CM, ce, 6½" 540.00
#142, Apple Tree Boy, FB, ce, 6½" 400.00
#143/0, Boots, SB, ce, 5¼" 200.00

#144, Angelic Song, CM, ce, 4" 270.00
#145, Little Guardian, FB, ce, 4" 180.00
#146, Angel Duet, font, FB, ce, 3½x4¾" 110.00
#147, Angel Shrine, font, SB, ce, 3x5" 60.00
#150, Happy Days, CM, ce, 6¼" 940.00
#151, Madonna Holding Child, brn, CM, ce, 12½" 6,500.00
#152A, Umbrella Boy, FB, ce, 8" 1,585.00
#152B, Umbrella Girl, CM, ce, 8" 2,550.00
#154, Waiter, CM, ce, 6½" 580.00
#16/I, Little Hiker, FB, ce, 5¾" 255.00
#163, Whitsuntide, CM, ce, 7" 720.00
#165, Swaying Lullaby, wall plaque, CM, ce, 4½x5¼" 540.00
#166, Boy w/Bird, ashtray, CM, ce, 3¼x6" 290.00
#167, Angel Sitting, font, CM, ce, 3¼x4⅛" 180.00
#168, Standing Boy, plaque, CM, ce, 4⅛x5½" 540.00
#17/0, Congratulations, FB, ce, 5¾" 220.00
#170, School Boys, CM, ce, 10" 1,900.00
#171, Little Sweeper, SB, ce, 4¼" 130.00
#173/0, Festival Harmony (w/flute), 3-line mk, ce, 8" 255.00
#174, She Loves Me, She Loves Me Not, SB, ce, 4¼" 180.00
#177, School Girls, FB, ce, 9½" 2,200.00
#179, Coquettes, SB, ce, 5" 290.00
#182, Good Friends, SB, ce, 4" 200.00
#183, Forest Shrine, FB, ce, 9" 650.00
#184, Latest News, FB, ce, 5¼" 360.00
#186, Sweet Music, FB, ce, 5½" 255.00
#192, Candlelight, candle holder, FB, ce, 7" 505.00
#193, Angel Duet, candle holder, 3-line mk, ce, 5" 180.00
#195, Barnyard Hero, CM, ce, 6" 650.00
#196, Telling Her Secret, CM, ce, 6¾" 795.00
#197, Be Patient, FB, ce, 6¼" 360.00
#198, Home From Market, CM, ce, 6" 435.00
#199, Feeding Time, FB, ce, 5¾" 360.00
#2/0, Little Fiddler, CM, 6" 435.00
#201, Retreat to Saftey, CM, ce, 6" 650.00
#203, Signs of Spring, FB, ce, 5¼" 400.00
#205, MI Hummel Dealer's Plaque (in German), FB, ce, 5½x4¼" 720.00
#206, Angel Cloud, CM, ce, 3¼x4¾" 255.00
#21/I, Heavenly Angel, FB, ce, 7" 290.00
#218, Birthday Serenade, FB, ce, 5¼" 615.00
#22/0, Angel w/Bird, font, ce, 3x4" 145.00
#223, To Market, table lamp, SB, ce, 9½" 325.00
#224, Wayside Harmony, table lamp, SB, ce, 9½" 345.00
#226, The Mail Is Here, FB, ce, 4½x6¼" 760.00
#228, Good Friends, table lamp, 3-line mk, ce, 7½" 235.00
#23/III, Adoration, CM, ce, 9" 1,080.00
#230, Apple Tree Boy, table lamp, FB, ce, 7½" 575.00
#234, Birthday Serenade, table lamp, SB, ce, 7¾" 720.00
#235, Happy Days, table lamp, FB, ce, 7¾" 575.00
#24/I, Lullaby, candle holder, SB, ce, 3½x5¼" 180.00
#240, Little Drummer, FB, ce, 4¼" 200.00
#241, Angel Lights, candle holder, LB, ce, 10¼x8¼" 215.00
#243, Madonna & Child, font, SB, ce, 3⅛x4" 65.00
#25, Angelic Sleep, candle holder, FB, ce, 3½x5¼" 235.00
#252 A&B, Apple Tree Girl (A) & Boy (B), SB, ce, 5", pr 255.00
#255, Stitch in Time, 3-line mk, ce, 6¾" 255.00
#26/0, Child Jesus, font, 3-line mk, ce, 2¾x5¼" 35.00
#28/II, Wayside Devotion, FB, ce, 7¼" 470.00
#29, Guardian Angel, font, CM, ce, 2⅞x6" 935.00
#3/I, Book Worm, LB, ce, 5½" 215.00
#32/I, Little Gabriel, CM, ce, 6" 1,440.00
#33, Joyful, ashtray, FB, ce, 3½x6" 180.00
#34, Singing Lesson, ashtray, LB, ce, 6¼" 110.00
#36/0, Child w/Flowers, font, CM, ce, 3¼x4¼" 145.00

#42/0, Good Shepherd, FB, ce, 6½" 270.00
#44A, Culprits, table lamp, CM, ce, 9" 435.00
#47/0, Goose Girl, CM, ce, 5" 435.00
#48/V, Madonna, plaque, FB, ce, 8¾x10¾" 900.00
#49/0, To Market, SB, ce, 5¼" 270.00
#5, Strolling Along, FB, ce, 5¼" 310.00
#50, Volunteers, CM, ce, 7" 865.00
#51/0, Village Boy, SB, ce, 6½" 135.00
#52/I, Going to Grandma's, FB, ce, 6" 540.00
#53, Joyful, 3-line mk, ce, 4" 100.00
#54, Silent Night, candle holder, FB, ce, 3½x4¾" 360.00
#55, Saint George, SB, ce, 6¾" 310.00
#56/A, Culprits, 3-line mk, ce, 6½" 240.00
#56/B, Out of Danger, CM, ce, 6½" 325.00
#58/I, Playmates, CM, ce, 4¼" 505.00
#59, Skier, SB, ce, 5½" 215.00
#6/II, Sensitive Hunter, FB, 7¼" 685.00
#60 A&B, Farm Boy & Goose Girl, bookends, FB, ce, 4¾", pr ..435.00
#62, Happy Pastime, ashtray, FB, ce, 3½x6¼" 180.00
#63, Singing Lesson, 3-line mk, ce, 3" 100.00
#65, Farewell, CM, ce, 5" 505.00
#67, Doll Mother, FB, ce, 4½" 255.00
#68, Lost Sheep, CM, ce, 6" 400.00
#69, Happy Pastime, FB, ce, 3½" 200.00
#7/II, Merry Wanderer, SB, ce, 10" 1,225.00
#70, Holy Child, FB, ce, 7¼" 200.00
#71, Stormy Weather, CM, ce, 6½" 720.00
#72, Spring Cheer, FB, ce, 5¼" 215.00
#73, Little Helper, SB, ce, 4½" 120.00
#74, Little Gardener, FB, ce, 4¼" 145.00
#79, Globe Trotter, 3-line mk, ce, 5" 180.00
#80, Little Scholar, FB, ce, 5½" 255.00
#81 2/0, School Girl, SB, ce, 4½" 140.00
#82, School Boy, CM, ce, 5" 400.00
#83, Angel Serenade (w/lamb), FB, ce, 5½" 325.00
#84, Worship, wht, CM, ce, 5¼" 325.00
#86, Happiness, SB, ce, 4¾" 130.00
#87, For Father, CM, ce, 5½" 435.00
#88, Heavenly Protection, FB, ce, 9¼" 865.00
#89, Little Cellist, CM, ce, 7½" 830.00
#91 A&B, Angels at Prayer, font, FB, ce, 3⅜x5", pr 145.00
#92, Merry Wanderer, plaque, SB, ce, 4½x5" 150.00
#93, Little Fiddler, plaque, CM, ce, 5x5½" 290.00
#94, Surprise, CM, ce, 5¾" 540.00
#95, Brother, SB, ce, 5½" 195.00
#96, Little Shopper, FB, ce, 4¾" 180.00
#97, Trumpet Boy, FB, ce, 5" 155.00
#98, Sister, FB, ce, 5¾" 225.00
#99, Eventide, CM, ce, 4¼x5" 650.00

Imari

Imari is a generic term which covers a broad family of wares. It was made in more than a dozen Japanese villages, but the name is that of the port from whence it was shipped to Europe. There are several types of Imari. The most common features a design with panels of birds, florals, or people surrounding a central basket of flowers. The colors used in this type are underglaze blue with overglaze red, gold, and green enamels. The Chinese also made Imari wares which differ from the Japanese type in several ways — the absence of spur marks, a thinner-type body, and a more consistent control of the blue. Imari-type wares were copied on the continent by Meissen and by English potters, among them Worcester, Derby, and Bow. Unless noted otherwise, our values are for Japanese ware. Our advisor is Norma Angelo; she is listed in the Directory under New York.

Bowl, apple blossoms/foliage, mc, scalloped, 19th C, 11" L **195.00**
Bowl, bamboo/clouds/apple blossom, 19th C, 6½", 8 for **850.00**
Bowl, birds & foliage, flower petal border, 19th C, 9¼" **385.00**

Bowl, carp on blue with gold, with lid, late 19th century, 12x11", $850.00.

Bowl, dragon central reserve on chrysanthemum form, 9" **275.00**
Bowl, floral central reserve/garden reserves, 18th C, 11½" **625.00**
Bowl, flowers & vase w/in gold floral panels w/cobalt, 10¼" **275.00**
Charger, central floral reserve/6 border reserves, 12" **190.00**
Charger, floral & bird reserves, 11¾" **140.00**
Charger, floral reserves, shallow, 19th C, 24" dia, VG **1,750.00**
Charger, flower urn & prunus sprays, 18th C, 15½" dia, EX ...**1,750.00**
Charger, foo lion among peonies/blossoms, 19th C, 17¾" **385.00**
Charger, phoenix, dragon & foo dog reserves, 18½" **750.00**
Charger, pine & flower reserve, sm rim reserves, ca 1900, 16" ..**1,150.00**
Charger, wisteria/florals/fruit, late 17th C, 12½", EX **1,500.00**
Charger, 3 lady-in-garden reserves on porc, 12½" **120.00**
Plate, Chrysanthemum, bl/red/gr w/gold, mk, 6", 8 for **70.00**
Plate, Chrysanthemum, bl/red/gr w/gold, mk, 9½", 6 for **400.00**
Plate, floral reserves, ribbed, scalloped, early 19th C, 7½" **165.00**
Plate, floral vase & sprigs, 2 borders, gilt, 18th C, 9" **140.00**
Umbrella stand, birds & florals, cylindrical w/cobalt, 24" **1,100.00**

Imperial Glass Company

The Imperial Glass Company was organized in 1901 in Bellaire, Ohio, and started manufacturing glassware in 1904. Their early products were jelly glasses, hotel tumblers, etc., but by 1910 they were making a name for themselves by pressing quantities of carnival glass, the iridescent glassware that was popular during that time. In 1914 NuCut was introduced to imitate cut glass. The line was so popular that it was made in crystal and colors and was reintroduced as Collector's Crystal in the 1950s. From 1916 to 1920 they used the lustre process to make a line called Imperial Jewels. Free-Hand ware, art glass made entirely by hand using no molds, was made from 1922 to 1928.

The company entered bankruptcy in 1931 but was able to continue operations and reorganize as the Imperial Glass Corporation. In 1936 Imperial introduced the Candlewick line, for which it is best known. In the late thirties the Vintage Grape Milk Glass line was added, and in 1951 a major ad campaign was launched, making Imperial one of the leading milk glass manufacturers.

In 1940 Imperial bought the molds and assets of the Central Glass Works of Wheeling, West Virginia; in 1958 they acquired the molds of the Heisey Company and in 1960 the molds of the Cambridge Glass Company of Cambridge, Ohio. Imperial used these molds, and after 1951 they marked their glassware with an 'I' superimposed over the 'G' trademark. The company became a subsidiary of Lenox in 1973; subsequently an 'L' was added to the 'IG' mark. In 1981 Lenox sold Imperial

to Arthur Lorch, a private investor (who modified the L by adding a line at the top angled to the left, giving rise to the 'ALIG' mark). He in turn sold the company to Robert F. Stahl, Jr., in 1982. Mr. Stahl filed for Chapter 11 to reorganize, but in mid-1984 liquidation was ordered, and all assets were sold. A few items that had been made in '84 were marked with an 'N' superimposed over the 'I' for 'New Imperial.'

For more information, we recommend *Imperial Glass Encyclopedia, Vol I and II*, edited by James Measell. Our advisor is Joan Cimini; she is listed in the Directory under Ohio. See also Candlewick; Carnival Glass; Glass Animals and Figurines; Stretch Glass.

Baked apple, Tradition, crystal **8.00**
Bonbon, Pillar Flutes, bl, crimped, 7" **22.50**
Bottle, cologne; Early American Hobnail, pk **45.00**
Bowl, berry; Katy, bl opal, flat rim **30.00**
Bowl, cereal; Katy, bl opal, deep **65.00**
Bowl, cereal; Katy, bl opal, flared rim **60.00**
Bowl, Katy, bl opal, #749B, 9¼" **125.00**
Bowl, Katy, bl opal, low, 8" **65.00**
Bowl, Pillar Flutes, lt bl, 10" **35.00**
Bowl, Rose, caramel slag, 8" **34.00**
Bowl, Rose, red slag, #62C, 9" **54.00**
Bowl, soup; Katy, bl opal **85.00**
Cake server, Cape Cod, #160/220, 10" sq **95.00**
Cake stand, Cape Cod, crystal, ftd, #160/167D **55.00**
Cake stand, Cape Cod, crystal, multi-server top, #160/93, 12" ...**110.00**
Candle cake plate, Cape Cod, crystal, 72-candle, #160/72 ....**350.00**
Candlesticks, duo; Katy, bl opal, pr **250.00**
Candlesticks, duo; Katy, gr opal, pr **195.00**
Candlesticks, Tradition, crystal, sq base, 3¼", pr **28.00**
Candy jar, Cape Cod, crystal, ftd, w/lid, #160/110, 10" **75.00**
Celery tray, Cape Cod, crystal, #160/189, 10½" **65.00**
Celery tray, Huckabee, pk, oval, 8¼" **32.50**
Champagne, Cape Cod, Verde, #1602, 6-oz **16.50**
Cigarette lighter, Cape Cod, milk glass, #1602 ....**30.00**
Claret, Cape Cod, Azalea, #1602 ....**20.00**
Claret, Cape Cod, crystal, #1602, 5-oz **10.00**
Claret, Cape Cod, Verde, #1602 ....**16.00**
Cocktail, Reeded (Spun), teal, ftd **17.50**
Comport, Katy, milk glass, 4¾" **45.00**
Compote, Cape Cod, crystal, ftd, #160/48B, 7" **45.00**
Creamer & sugar bowl, Cape Cod, crystal, flat, #160/30 ....**20.00**
Creamer & sugar bowl, Cape Cod, crystal, ftd, #160/31 ....**30.00**
Cruet, Cape Cod, crystal, #160/119, 4-oz **30.00**
Cruet, Octagon, jade, w/stopper **90.00**
Cup & saucer, Katy, crystal **15.00**
Cup & saucer, Pillar Flutes, lt bl **25.00**
Decanter, Big Shots (Shot Gun Shells), red w/EX gold, #711, 40-oz ..**210.00**
Decanter, Cape Cod, crystal, #160/163, 30-oz **65.00**
Decanter, Cape Cod, crystal, sq, #160/212, 24-oz **70.00**
Finger bowl, Cape Cod, crystal, #1602 ....**12.00**
Goblet, water; Cape Cod, crystal, #1602, 11-oz **10.00**
Goblet, water; Dew Drop, opal, #1886 ....**25.00**
Goblet, water; Hoffman House, bl, #46 ....**16.00**
Goblet, water; Turn O' the Century, Azalea, #612 ....**22.00**
Ivy ball, Early American Hobnail, amber, ftd, #742 ....**24.00**
Ivy ball, Reeded (Spun), red, crystal ft, 4" **65.00**
Jar, Ipswich, Heather, #1405, 2-pc **55.00**
Jar, mustard; Cape Cod, crystal, #160/156 ....**30.00**
Jar, owl form, gr slag **90.00**
Jar, pokal, caramel slag, #464, 2-pc **85.00**
Jar, 3-in-1 Diamond, ruby, #1, lg **65.00**
Lamp, Dew Drop, wht opal, #1886/350 ....**175.00**
Mayonnaise, Katy, bl opal, w/underplate **120.00**

Mayonnaise, Laurel, cut, Rose Pk, #256, w/ladle 30.00
Mayonnaise ladle, Katy, lt bl opal 45.00
Mint dish, Cape Cod, crystal, heart shape 20.00
Mug, Dumbo, gr, 1974 ....75.00
Nappy, Early American Hobnail, Ritz Bl, #7145B, 7" sq 26.00
Nappy, Pansy, caramel slag, hdl, 5" 30.00
Pickle dish, Pillar Flutes, bl, hdl, #682 ....25.00
Pitcher, Early American Hobnail, crystal, #742, 55-oz 30.00
Pitcher, Reeded (Spun), teal, ice lip, 80-oz 95.00
Pitcher, Tradition, crystal, ice lip, #165, 54-oz 60.00
Pitcher, Windmill, purple slag, glossy 45.00
Pitcher, Windmill, red slag, glossy 55.00
Plate, Collector's Crystal, #5059D, 13" 30.00
Plate, Katy, bl opal, 6" 20.00
Plate, Mum, Peacock carnival, #524, 10½" 55.00
Plate, Niagara, crystal, 9½" 10.00
Plate, Old English, crystal, 7" 16.00
Plate, torte; Provincial, gr, #1506, 13" 35.00
Plate, Tradition, crystal, 6¾" 6.00
Plate, Tradition, crystal, 8" 10.00
Punch set, Cape Cod, crystal, #160/20, 12" bowl+14 pcs 225.00
Punch set, Crocheted Crystal, bowl, +12 cups & ladle 130.00
Punch set, Mt Vernon, crystal, complete 150.00
Relish, Cape Cod, crystal, oval, 3-part, #160/55, 9½" 35.00
Rose bowl, Reeded (Spun), cobalt, metal fr 35.00
Rose bowl, Reeded (Spun), red 45.00
Saucer, Tradition, crystal, 5½" 6.00
Shakers, Cape Cod, crystal, #160/213, 3-pc set 55.00
Shakers, Cape Cod, crystal, ftd, #160/116, pr 22.50
Sherbet, Cape Cod, amber, #1602 ....12.00
Sherbet, Huckabee, pk, ftd 15.00
Sherbet, Mt Vernon, crystal, low 7.00
Toothpick holder, Octagon, caramel slag 12.00
Trivet, milk glass, #1950/450, 4-pc set 35.00
Tumbler, Big Shot, gr w/EX gold, #711, 11-oz 25.00
Tumbler, Crown Concord decor, Grape, #995, 10-oz 18.00
Tumbler, Gypsy Rings, Antique Bl, #116, 16-oz 14.00
Tumbler, iced tea; Reeded (Spun), teal, 14-oz 22.00
Tumbler, juice; Cape Cod, amber, ftd, #1602, 6-oz 16.00
Tumbler, juice; Cape Cod, Azalea, ftd, #1602, 6-oz 18.00
Tumbler, Shaeffer, cobalt, #4511, 9½-oz 12.50
Tumbler, Voo Doo, bl/gold, #760, 16-oz 18.00
Tumbler, whiskey; Cape Cod, crystal, flat, 2½" 15.00
Vase, bud; Free-Hand, hearts/vines, lt gr on opal, 8½" 350.00
Vase, bud; peach & butterscotch w/mirror finish, 10" 225.00
Vase, Cathay Crystal, Ku ribbon, #5012 ....800.00
Vase, drape design, brn irid on orange, baluster, label, 8" 450.00
Vase, drape design, red on amber irid, ped ft, 7x8½" 450.00
Vase, Egyptian form, mirror bl irid, orig label, 8¼" 450.00
Vase, Free-Hand, drape design, wht on mustard, orange int, 8½" 170.00
Vase, Free-Hand, gold w/pk & orange irid, ovoid, 10" 350.00
Vase, Free-Hand, hearts/vines, bl on orange irid, 9" 350.00
Vase, Free-Hand, hearts/vines, cobalt on opal, 6½" 375.00
Vase, Free-Hand, hearts/vines, gr/gray on opal, bulbous, 6" 600.00
Vase, Free-Hand, hearts/vines, orange on cobalt, bulbus, 6" 600.00
Vase, Free-Hand, hearts/vines, purple on gr-tint opal, 4" 175.00
Vase, Free-Hand, hearts/vines, violet on gr, no mk, 9" 650.00
Vase, Free-Hand, hearts/vines, white on cobalt, label, 45⁄8x6" 650.00
Vase, Free-Hand, hearts/vines, wht on bl, 5¾" 400.00
Vase, Free-Hand, hearts/vines, wht on cobalt, 10" 650.00
Vase, gold irid w/opal swags, ruffled, 10½" 375.00
Vase, Katy, cobalt, #743B 65.00
Vase, Katy, gr opal, #743N, 5½" 65.00
Vase, Katy, red, #743B 65.00

Vase, marigold irid, flared, 8" 125.00
Vase, Reeded (Spun), red, 9" 65.00

Imperial Porcelain

The Blue Ridge Mountain Boys were created by cartoonist Paul Webb and translated into three-dimension by the Imperial Porcelain Corporation of Zanesville, Ohio, in 1947. These figurines decorated ashtrays, vases, mugs, bowls, pitchers, planters, and other items. The Mountain Boys series was numbered 92 through 108, each with a different and amusing portrayal of mountain life. Imperial also produced American Folklore miniatures, twenty-three tiny animals one inch or less in size, and the Al Capp Dogpatch series. Because of financial difficulties, the company closed in 1960.

American Folklore Miniatures

Cat, 1½" 40.00
Cow, 1¾" 35.00
Hound dogs 50.00
Plaque, store ad, Am Folklore Porcelain Miniatures, 4½" 450.00
Sow 35.00

Blue Ridge Mountain Boys by Paul Webb

Ashtray, #101, man w/jug & snake 95.00
Ashtray, #103, hillbilly & skunk 95.00
Ashtray, #105, baby, hound dog, & frog 125.00
Ashtray, #106, Barrel of Wishes, w/hound 75.00
Ashtray, #92, 2 men by tree stump, for pipes 125.00
Box, cigarette; #98, dog atop, baby at door, sq 115.00
Dealer's sign, Handcrafted Paul Webb Mtn Boys, rare, 9" 650.00
Decanter, #100, outhouse, man, & bird 95.00

Decanter, Ma leaning over stump with baby and skunk, #104, $95.00.

Decanter, man, jug, snake, & tree stump, Hispch Inc, 1946 ....75.00
Figurine, #101, man leans against tree trunk, 5" 90.00
Figurine, man on hands & knees, 3" 95.00
Figurine, man sitting, 3½" 95.00
Figurine, man sitting w/chicken on knee, 3" 95.00
Jug, #101, Willie & snake 75.00
Mug, #94, Bearing Down, 6" 95.00
Mug, #94, dbl baby hdl, 4¼" 95.00
Mug, #94, ma hdl, 4¼" 95.00
Mug, #94, man w/bl pants hdl, 4¼" 95.00
Mug, #94, man w/yel beard & red pants hdl, 4¼" 95.00
Mug, #99, Target Practice, boy on goat, farmer, 5¾" 95.00
Pitcher, lemonade 200.00
Planter, #100, outhouse, man, & bird 75.00
Planter, #105, man w/chicken on knee, washtub 125.00

Planter, #110, man, w/jug & snake, 4½" 65.00
Planter, #81, man drinking from jug, sitting by washtub 75.00
Shakers, Ma & Old Doc, pr 95.00

Miscellaneous

Items in this section that are designated 'IP' are miscellaneous novelties made by Imperial Porcelain; the remainder are of interest to Paul Webb collectors, though made by an unknown manufacturer. Prints on calendars and playing cards are signed 'Paul Webb.'

Artist board, babies or mtn women, sgn Paul Webb, 30x30" 275.00
Artist board, mtn boys only, sgn Paul Webb, 30x30" 225.00
Calendar, 1954, 12 sgn scenes, Brown & Bigelow, complete 48.00
Figurine, cat in high-heeled shoe, 5½" L 40.00
Hot pad, Dutch boy w/tulips, rnd, IP 30.00
Ink blotters, sgn scenes, ea 12.00
Mug, #29, man hdl, sgn Paul Webb, 4¾" 45.00
Planter, #106, dog sitting by tub, IP 75.00
Playing cards, ad: Rafe Oiling Gun, Brown & Bigelow, MIB 75.00
Shakers, pigs, 5", pr 95.00
Shakers, standing pigs, IP, 8", pr 95.00

Indian Tree

Indian Tree is a popular dinnerware pattern produced by various potteries since the early 1800s to recent times. Although backgrounds and borders vary, the Oriental theme is carried out with the gnarled, brown branch of a pink-blossomed tree. Among the manufacturers' marks, you may find represented such notable firms as Coalport, S. Hancock and Sons, Soho Pottery, and John Maddock and Sons.

Bowl, rimmed soup; Maddock, 9" 20.00
Bowl, soup; Johnson Bros, 7¼" 13.00
Bowl, vegetable; Johnson Bros, 8½" 25.00
Bowl, vegetable; rnd, Morley 22.00
Creamer, Johnson Bros 17.00
Cup & saucer, AD; Minton 25.00
Cup & saucer, Maddock 12.50
Gravy boat, Maddock 32.00
Gravy tureen, English, w/lid & ladle 85.00
Pitcher, Coalport, milk sz 75.00

Plate, Staffordshire, 9", $12.00.

Plate, dinner; Woods, set of 6, +6 c/s 180.00
Plate, Maddock, 7¾" 8.00
Platter, Johnson Bros, 12½" 26.00
Platter, Spode, 15" 165.00
Sugar bowl, Johnson Bros, w/lid 22.00
Teapot, Burgess & Lee 60.00
Tureen, gravy; w/lid 145.00

Inkwells and Inkstands

Receptacles for various writing fluids have been used since ancient times. Through the years they have been made from countless materials — glass, metal, porcelain, pottery, wood, and even papier-mache. During the 18th century, gold or silver inkstands were presented to royalty; the well-known silver inkstand by Philip Syng, Jr., was used for the signing of the Declaration of Independence, and impressive brass inkstands with wells and pounce pots (sanders) were proud possessions of men of letters. When literacy vastly increased in the 19th century, the dip pen replaced the quill pen; and inkwells and inkstands were widely used and produced in a broad range of sizes in functional and decorative forms from ornate Victorian to flowing Art Nouveau and stylized Art Deco designs. However, the acceptance of the ballpoint pen literally put inkstands and inkwells 'out of business.' But their historical significance and intriguing diversity of form and styling fascinate today's collectors. See also Bottles, Ink.

Brass, seated elephant between pineapple wells, w/tray 385.00
Brass, 2 wells w/cut glass lids, pen holder, w/dip pen 135.00
Brass w/goat horns, cut glass well, pen/opener shelves, 9" L 160.00
Bronze, gold dore, crown lid, emb florals, arms for pen, 6" 85.00
CI, leaping stag w/dogs in pursuit, glass wells, 5x9x5" 350.00
CI, man eating turkey, mc pnt, late 1800s, 5", EX 330.00
CI stag's head w/antler pen holders, glass well, 5⅛", EX 75.00
MOP & tortoise shell, 2 wells 400.00
Pottery, head of a screaming lady, dk brn, 3" 50.00
Pottery, poodle dog, mc on wht, Staffordshire, 5¼x5" 150.00
Pottery, shoe form, brn Rockingham, 3x5½", EX 50.00
Pottery, whippet figural, mc w/gold, Staffordshire, 5x8" 120.00
Sheffield plate, beaded edges, 2 lift panels, claw ft 300.00

Ship captain's, brass with hand-blown ink bottle insert, marked Geselzlich GF Schutzt on base, ca 1890, 2", NM, $170.00.

Silver w/hinged lid, ftd, clear insert, Walker & Hall, 3½x6" 165.00
Sterling, 8-sided bombe shape on conforming tray, 39-oz 600.00
Wht metal & brass, Queen Victoria bust, 1897 Jubilee, 7¼" 350.00

Insulators

The telegraph was invented in 1844. The devices developed to hold the electrical transmission wires to the poles were called insulators. The telephone, invented in 1876, intensified their usefulness; and by the turn of the century, thousands of varieties were being produced in pottery, wood, and glass of various colors. Even though it has been rumored that red glass insulators exist, none have ever been authenticated. Many insulators are embossed with patent dates.

Of the more than 3,000 types known to exist, today's collectors evaluate their worth by age and rarity of color. Aqua and green are the most common colors in glass, dark brown the most common in ceramic. Threadless insulators (for example, CD #701.1), made between 1850 and 1865, bring prices well into the hundreds, if in mint condition.

In the listings that follow, the CD numbers are from an identification system developed in the late 1960s by N.R. Woodward.

Those seeking additional information about insulators are encouraged to contact Line Jewels NIA #255 (whose address may be found in the Directory under Clubs, Newsletters, and Catalogs) or attend a club-endorsed show. For information, contact Len Linscott, listed in the Directory under Florida. In the listings that follow those stating 'no name' have no company identification, but have embossed numbers, dots, etc. Those stating 'no embossing' are without raised letters, dots, or any other markings.

Key:
* (asterisk) — Canadian   SDP — sharp drip points
CB — corrugated base   RB — rough base
CD — Consolidated Design   RDP — round drip points
SB — smooth base

Threaded Pin-type Glass Insulators

CD 102, Westinghouse No 3, SB, lt gr 250.00
CD 103, Brookfield, SB, aqua 5.00
CD 106, Maydwell-9, SB, lt pk 5.00
CD 107, Armstrong No 9, SB, clear 1.00
CD 108, Whitall Tatum Co No 9, SB, lt straw 2.00
CD 110, Brookfield, SB, aqua 100.00
CD 112, Lynchburg 31, RDP, gr 5.00
CD 114, Hemingray, SDP, gr-aqua 3.00
CD 114, Hemingray No 11, SDP, lt bl 6.00
CD 115, Armstrong No 3, SB, clear 3.00
CD 117, no name, SB, dk aqua 15.00
CD 118, no name, SB, Carnival 200.00
CD 120, CEW, SB, bl 125.00
CD 120, Patent/Dec 19, 1871, SB, ice bl 10.00
CD 121, C&P Tel Co, SB, gr 20.00
CD 123, EC&M Co, SB, gr-aqua 75.00
CD 127, WU, SB, bl-aqua 150.00
CD 128, Hemingray, SB, off-clear 2.00
CD 133, BGMCo, SB, lt purple 40.00
CD 135, Chicago Insulator Co, SB, bl 50.00
CD 137, Hemingray, SB, clear 1.00
CD 138, Brookfield Postal Tel Co, SB, lt aqua 12.00
CD 139, McLaughlin USLD, SB, aqua 125.00
CD 142, Hemingray, RDP, Carnival 15.00
CD 143.5, THE Co, SB, lt gr 60.00
CD 144*, no name, horizontal ridges, SB, gr 75.00
CD 147, Hemingray Pat Oct 8, 1907, SB, aqua 1.00
CD 154, Gayner No 44, SB, bl-aqua 2.00
CD 155, Kerr Dp 1, SB, off clear 3.00
CD 158.1, Chester, (inner skirt emb), SB, aqua 1,250.00
CD 160, Armstrong's No 14, SB, clear 20.00
CD 162, Hamilton Glass Co, RDP, lt gr 40.00
CD 163, Armstrong, SB, clear 1.00
CD 166, California, SB, sage-gr 5.00
CD 168, Hemingray No 510, CB, Carnival 30.00
CD 169, Whitall Tatum No 4, SB, ice-bl 3.00
CD 170, no name, SB, gr-aqua 10.00
CD 175, Hemingray-25, SB, clear 10.00
CD 180, Liquid Insulator, SB, lt aqua 1,000.00
CD 182, Dry Spot No 10, SB, straw 750.00
CD 188, B, SB, gr 25.00
CD 188, Brookfield, SB, emerald gr 30.00
CD 196, HGCo, Pat May 2, 1893, SDP, ice aqua 75.00
CD 197, Whitall Tatum No 15, SB, clear 3.00
CD 202, Hemingray 53, SDP, aqua 20.00

CD 206, no name, SDP, straw 250.00
CD 210, Postal, SB, emerald gr 10.00
CD 213, Hemingray 43, RDP, bl 15.00
CD 230, Hemingray 512, SB, lt citrine 25.00
CD 235, Pyrex 662, SB, Carnival 30.00
CD 240, Pyrex 131, SB, clear 15.00
CD 245, 9200 (no name), SB, gr 300.00
CD 251, NEGM Co, SB, ice bl 20.00
CD 254, No 3 Cable, SB, lt bl 50.00
CD 257, Hemingray No 60, RDP, clear 15.00

Photo courtesy Len Linscott

CD 263, Columbia, smooth base, aqua, $60.00.

CD 269, Jumbo, SB, dk aqua 300.00
CD 282, Knowles Boston, SB, aqua 200.00
CD 286, Locke, SB, lt bl 50.00
CD 294, NEGMCo, SB, aqua 40.00
CD 299.1, prism, SB, lt aqua 250.00
CD 306, Lynchburg, SDP, aqua 200.00
CD 317, Chambers, SB, gr 300.00
CD 325, Pyrex 401, SB, clear 15.00

Threadless Pin-type Glass Insulators

CD 1038, Cutter, SB, aqua 200.00
CD 728, no emb, SB, lt bl 125.00
CD 734, McMicking, SB, lt aqua 60.00
CD 742, no emb, SB, lt gr 100.00

Irons

History, geography, art, and cultural diversity are all represented in the collecting of antique pressing irons. The progress of fashion and invention can be traced through the evolution of the pressing iron.

Over seven hundred years ago, implements constructed of stone, bone, wood, glass, and wrought iron were used for pressing fabrics. Early ironing devices were quite primitive in form, and heating techniques relied on inserting a hot metal slug into a cavity of the iron, adding hot burning coals into a chamber or pan, and by placing the iron directly on hot coals or a hot surface.

To the pleasure of today's collectors, some of these early irons, mainly from the period of 1700 to 1850, were decorated by artisans who carved and painted them with regional motifs typical of their natural surroundings and spiritual cultures.

Beginning in the mid-1800s, new cultural demands for fancy wearing apparel initiated a revolution in technology for types of irons and methods to heat them. Typical of this period is the fluter which was essential for producing the ruffles demanded by the 19th-century ladies. Hat irons, polishers, and numerous unusual iron forms were also used during this time, and provided a means to produce crimps, curves, curls, and special fabric textures. Irons from this era are characterized by their unique shapes, odd handles, latches, decorations, and even revolving mechanisms.

Also during this time, irons began to be heated by burning liquid and gaseous fuels. Gradually the new technology of the electrically heated iron replaced all other heating methods, except in the more rural areas and undeveloped countries. Even today the Amish communities utilize gasoline fuel irons.

In the listings that follow, prices are given for examples in very good to excellent condition. Damage, repairs, plating, excessive wear, rust, and missing parts can dramatically reduce value. For further information we recommend *Irons By Irons* and *More Irons By Irons* by our advisor Dave Irons; his address and information for ordering these books are given in the Directory under Pennsylvania.

Billiard table, G Wright, English, 10", VG 125.00
Charcoal, all brass, cutwork vents, Indian, 10", VG 125.00

Photo courtesy Dave Irons

Charcoal, European box irons: Helmeted soldier head as front latch, hinged at back, late 1800s, 8¼", $100.00 to $150.00; L. Lawton (name punched), all-brass body with rivets, 1700s, 9", $500.00 to $700.00.

Charcoal, box, head latch, rainbow hdl, European, VG 150.00
Charcoal, dbl chimney, NE Plus Ultra, Pat 1902, VG 225.00
Charcoal, Jr Carbon Iron, 1911, 6", EX 250.00
Charcoal, trn chimney, brass heat shield, European 150.00
Cold hdl, Enterprise #55, Phila, 2-pc, EX 35.00
Cold hdl, slant hdl, 2-pc, 7⅜", EX 160.00
Cold hdl, Universal Thermo Cell Sad Iron, 2-pc 145.00
Egg, all CI, standing, English, 2-pc, VG 180.00
Fluter, clamp-on, Companion, orig blk pnt, EX 350.00
Fluter, combination, charcoal, Eclipse, side plate, VG 160.00
Fluter, combination, Hewitt, revolving, clamp-on plate 400.00
Fluter, fine fluting, brass rolls, box body, English, EX 250.00
Fluter, machine, American, Phila PA, orig pnt, EX 130.00
Fluter, rocker, The Star, all cast, 2-pc, VG 120.00
Fluter, roller, Clark's, blk pnt, 2-pc, EX 175.00
Goffering, English, Queen Anne style w/tripod ft, EX 325.00
Goffering, wrought, penny ft, 18th C, 4" bbl, VG 350.00
Hat, shackle, movable brim clamp, EX 150.00
Hat, tolliker, wood, brim form, 4½", EX 150.00
Iron heater, pyramid, all cast, holds 3 irons, VG 150.00
Liquid fuel, Diamond Iron Akron Lamp Co, EX 65.00
Liquid fuel, Imperial Self heating Flat Iron, w/pump 85.00
Little, charcoal, front latch, European, 4⅝", VG 225.00
Little, cold hdl, Ober, dbl pointed, 4", EX 150.00
Little, cold hdl, Sensible No 0, 4", VG 95.00
Little, cross rib, all CI, 2¾", EX 40.00
Little, ox tongue, all brass, L hdl, European, 4½" 250.00
Little, rope hdl, dbl-pointed, NP, 3⅜", EX 45.00
Little, swan, orig pnt, 2⅛", w/trivet, EX 200.00

Little, wire grip, star symbol, 3⅜", VG 80.00
Little, WP mk, thin base, all CI, Fr, 3" 60.00
Natural gas, The Fletcher Laurel, gray agate, English 225.00
Natural gas, The Swing, many vent slots, Pat 1904, VG 125.00
Polisher, Carron, rnd bottom, English, 5", VG 90.00
Polisher, Sweeney 1896, Biard Co, 7", VG 160.00
Sad iron, Keystone, dbl-pointed, 8½", EX 160.00
Sad iron, Le Gaulois No 5, thin base, Fr, VG 80.00
Sad iron, Ober #6, Pat Mar 19 '12, VG 65.00
Sleeve, long hdl, flower decor, oval, Fr, VG 160.00
Sleeve, Sherman's Improved, all CI, EX 140.00
Slug, box, all brass, cut-work hdl, Danish, 5" 225.00
Slug, box, all brass, leather-wrapped hdl, European, VG 200.00
Slug, box, Kenrick, w/slug, English, EX 125.00
Slug, drop-in-the-bk, rnd bk, European, w/trivet 350.00

Ironstone

During the last quarter of the 18th century, English potters began experimenting with a new type of body that contained calcinated flint and a higher china clay content, intent on producing a fine durable whiteware — heavy, yet with a texture that would resemble porcelain. To remove the last trace of yellow, a minute amount of cobalt was added, often resulting in a bluish-white tone. Wm and John Turner of Caughley and Josiah Spode II were the first to manufacture the ware successfully. Others, such as Davenport, Hicks and Meigh, and Ralph and Josiah Wedgwood, followed with their own versions. The latter coined the name 'Pearl' to refer to his product and incorporated the term into his trademark. In 1813 a 14-year patent was issued to Charles James Mason, who called his ware Patented Ironstone. Francis Morley, G.L. Asworth, T.J. Mayer, and other Staffordshire potters continued to produce ironstone until the end of the century. While some of these patterns are simple to the extreme, many are decorated with in-mold designs of fruit, grain, and foliage on ribbed or scalloped shapes. In the 1830s transfer-printed designs in blue, mulberry, pink, green, and black became popular; and polychrome versions of Oriental wares were manufactured to compete with the Chinese trade. See also Mason's Ironstone. Our advice for this category comes from Home Place Antiques, whose address is listed in the Directory under Illinois.

Bowl, berry/sauce; Rolling Star, Edwards 30.00
Bowl, Full Ribbed, Pankhurst, 9½" 36.00
Bowl, soup; Prairie Flowers, Livesley Powell & Co, 10" 30.00
Bowl, vegetable; Boote's 1851, T&R Boote, 8⅞" 145.00
Bowl, vegetable; President, oval, w/lid 145.00
Bowl, vegetable; Prize Bloom, w/lid, TJ&J Mayer 225.00
Bowl, vegetable; Wheat & Blackberry, Taylor, w/lid, 10¼" L 145.00
Butter dish, Panelled Grape, w/lid and drain 235.00
Chamberpot, President, J Edwards, w/lid 125.00
Coffeepot, Lily, H Burgess 175.00
Compote, New York, unmk, 5½x9½" 165.00
Creamer, Wheat & Clover, Turner & Tompkinson, 7⅜" 125.00
Creamer & sugar bowl, Victor, Jones 265.00
Cup & saucer, handleless; Niagara, Paris 45.00
Cup & saucer, Western, Hope & Carter, mini 55.00
Cup plate, Niagara Fan, Shaw, 3⅞", EX 70.00
Ladle, sauce tureen; Boote's 1851, unmk, 7¼" 60.00
Pitcher, milk; Olympic, Elsmore & Forster, 9⅜" 145.00
Pitcher, Panelled Leaves, Meakin, 8¾" 165.00
Pitcher, President, J Edwards, 8⅝" 155.00
Plate, Ceres, Turner & Goddard, 10" 35.00
Plate, Cherry Scroll, J&G Meakin 50.00
Plate, Ivy Wreath, Meir & Son, 8¾" 30.00
Plate, Rolling Star, Edwards, 9½" 25.00

Plate, Sharon Arch, Wedgwood, 10⅝" 38.00
Plate, Sydenham, T&R Boote, 10¼" 42.50
Plate, Virginia, Bougham & Mayer, 9½" 22.50
Platter, Nosegay, Baker & Co, 13½" 50.00
Platter, Ribbed Raspberry, w/bloom, J&G Meakin, 12x9⅛" 65.00
Platter, well & tree; J&G Meakin, 16⅜" 85.00
Relish, Laurel Wreath, unmk 45.00
Relish, Wheat, Meakin 30.00
Sugar bowl, Niagara, Walley, 6¾" 185.00
Syrup, plain, pewter lid, unmk, 5⅜" 95.00
Tea saucer, Full Ribbed, Pankhurst, 6" 12.00
Tea set, Square Ridged, Johnson Bros, 3-pc 275.00
Teapot, Ceres, Elsmore & Forster 245.00
Teapot, Corn & Oats 275.00
Teapot, Wheat & Hops, sm 245.00
Toothbrush holder, Columbia, vertical, unmk, 5" 125.00
Tureen, sauce; Lily of the Valley, w/lid & underplate 165.00
Tureen, sauce; President, oval, J Edwards, 3-pc 245.00
Tureen, sauce; Sevres, Edwards, +underplate & lid 175.00
Tureen, soup; Lafayette, w/lid, Clementson, 10x14x8" 325.00
Wash bowl, Scalloped Decagon, Davenport, 13¼" 95.00
Wash bowl, Victory, John Edwards 115.00
Wash bowl & pitcher, Ceres, Elsmore & Forster, 14", 14" 345.00
Wash bowl & pitcher, Fig, Wedgwood 395.00
Wash bowl & pitcher, Wheat & Hops, Meakin 300.00
Wash pitcher, Corn & Oats 175.00
Wash pitcher, Vintage, Challinor 150.00
Wash pitcher, Wheat & Hops 125.00
Waste bowl, Tuscan, unmk, 3⅛x5¼" 80.00

Patterned Ironstone

Bowl, vegetable; No 21, purple transfer, 2x9⅜x6⅝" 45.00
Coffeepot, Challinor Ardennes, hexagonal, ftd, 10", EX 190.00
Coffeepot, Tyrol, purple transfer, Wedgewood, rpr, 10" 75.00
Creamer, Rose, purple transfer, 5⅞" 70.00
Cup & saucer, Lucerne, bl transfer, Pankhurst 35.00
Cup & saucer, mc floral w/gold lustre & yel accents, 5⅞", NM ..200.00
Cup & saucer, Roselle, pk transfer, Meir 50.00
Cup plate, Gipsy, bl transfer, 4" 35.00
Cup plate, Versailles, bl transfer, unmk, 4⅛" 40.00
Cup plate, Zamara, purple transfer, yel/gr accents, 4" 50.00
Plate, Ailanthus, purple transfer, C&WHK, 6¼", pr 40.00
Plate, Corinthia, pk transfer, Challinor, 10" 30.00
Plate, Paradise, gr transfer, LP&Co, 8½" 25.00
Plate, pastoral scene, floral border, dk bl transfer, 9½" 95.00
Plate, Strawberry, red & gr w/gold lustre, 12-sided, unmk, 7¾" ..175.00
Plate, Venus, purple transfer, Podmore Walker, 8⅝" 25.00
Plate, Yale College, lt bl transfer, England, 19th C, 9⅜" 45.00
Platter, Gipsy, bl transfer, 15x11¾" 80.00
Punch bowl, mc flower basket transfer w/gold, 1850s, 14¼" 250.00
Sugar bowl, Tyrol, purple transfer, w/lid, rpr, 8½" 85.00
Waste bowl, Roselle, pk transfer, Meir, 3¾x5½" 40.00

Italian Glass

Throughout the 20th century, one of the major glassmaking centers of the world was the island of Murano. From the Stile Liberte work of Artisi Barovier (1890-1920s) to the early work of Ettore Sottsass in the 1970s, they excelled in creativity and craftsmanship. The 1920s to '40s featured the work of glass designers like Ercole Barovier for Barovier and Toso and Vittorio Zecchin, Napoleone Martinuzzi, and Carlo Scarpa for Venini. Many of these pieces are highly prized by collectors.

The 1950s saw a revival of Italy as a world-reknown design center for all of the arts. Glass led the charge with the brightly colored work of Fulvio Bianconi for Venini, Dino Martens for Aureliano Toso, and Ercole Barovier for Barovier and Toso. The best of these pieces are extremely desirable. The '60s and '70s have also seen many innovative designs with work by the Finnish Tapio Wirkkala, the American Thomas Stearns, and many other designers.

Unfortunately, amongst the great glass, there was a plethora of commercial ashtrays, vases, and figurines produced that, though have some value, do not compare in quality and design to the great glass of Murano. These pieces are listed as 'Murano' glass rather than by maker.

Venini: The Venini company was founded in 1921 by Paolo Venini, and he led the company until his death in 1959. Major Italian designers worked for the firm, including Vittorio Zecchin, Napoleone Martinuzzi, Carlo Scarpa, and Fulvio Bianconi. After his death, his son-in-law, Ludovico de Santillana, ran the factory and employed designers like Toni Zucchieri, Tapio Wirkkala, and Thomas Stearns. The company is known for creative designs and techniques including Inciso (finely etched lines), Battuto (carved facets), Sommerso (controlled bubbles), Pezzato (patches of fused glass), and Fascie (horizontal colored lines in clear glass). Until the mid-'60s, most pieces were signed with acid-etched 'Venini Murano ITALIA.' In the '60s they started engraving the signatures. The factory still exists.

Barovier: In the late 1920s, Ercole Barovier took over the Artisti Barovier and started designing many different vases. In the 1930s he merged with Ferro Toso and became Barovier and Toso. He designed many different series of glass including the Barbarico (rough, acid-treated brown or deep blue glass), Eugenio (free-blown vases), Efeso, Rotallato, Dorico, Egeo (vases incorporating murrine designs), and Primavera (white etched glass with black bands). He designed until 1974. The company is still in existence. Most pieces were unsigned.

Aureliano Toso: The great glass designer Dino Martens was involved with the company from about 1938 to 1965. It was his work that produced the very desirable Oriente vases. This technique consisted of free-formed patches of green, yellow, blue, purple, black and white stars, and pieces of zanfirico canes fused into brilliantly colored vases and bowls. His El Dorado series was based on the same technique but was not opaque. He also designed pieces with alternating groups of black and white filigrana lines. Pieces are unsigned.

Seguso: Flavio Poli became the artistic director of Seguso in the late 1930s and remained until 1963. He is known for his Corroso (acid-etched glass) and his Valve series (elegant forms of two to three layers of colored glass with a clear glass casing).

Archimede Seguso: In 1946 Archimede Seguso left the Seguso Vetri D'Arte to open a new company and designed many innovative pieces. His Merlatto (thin white filigrana suspended three dimensionally) series is his most famous. The epitome of his work is where a colored glass (yellow or purple) is windowed in the merlotti. His Macchia Ambra Verde is yellow and spots on a gold base encased in clear glass. The A Piume series contained feathers and leaves suspended in glass. Pieces are unsigned.

Alfredo Barbini: Barbini was a designer known for his sculptures of sea subjects and his amorphic-shaped vases with an inner core of red or blue glass with a heavy layer of finely incised outer glass. He worked in the 1950s to 1960s, and some pieces are signed.

Vistosi: Although this glassworks was started in the 1940s, fame came in the 1960s and '70s with the birds designed by Allesandro Pianon and the early work of the Memphis school designer, Ettorre Sottsass. Pieces may be signed.

AVEM: This company is known for its work in the 1950s and '60s. The designer, Ansolo Fuga, did work using a solid white glass with inclusions of multicolored murrines.

Cenedese: This is a postwar company led by Gino Cenedese with Alfredo Barbini as designer. When Barbini left, Cenedese took over the design work and also used the free-lanced designs of Fulvio Bianconi. They are known for their figurines and vases with suspended murrines.

Cappellin: Venini's original partner (1921-25), Giacomo Cappellin, opened a short-lived company (1925-32) that was to become extremely important. His chief designer was the young Carlo Scarpa who was to create many masterpieces in glass both for Cappellin and then Venini.

Ettore Sottsass: Sottsass is a modern designer who founded the Memphis School of Design in the 1970s. He is an extremely famous designer who designed several series of glass for the Vistosi Glass Company. The pieces were created in limited editions, signed and numbered, and each piece was given a name.

Our advisor for this category is Howard Lockwood, publisher of *Vetri: Italian Glass News.* For further information concerning Mr. Lockwood or this publication, see the Directory under New Jersey.

Seguso Vetri d'Arte, sommerso vase, Flavio Poli, clear cased over red and purple, ca 1950, 5½x7", $1,000.00; Venini, clessidre, Paolo Venini, light plum and ocean blue vessels joined incalmo, ca 1950s, 6", $1,100.00; Barovier & Toso, Eugeneo series vase, clear with gold leaf, pulled and pierced handles, amethyst foot, rim and handles, ca 1951, 5½", $800.00.

Venini Glass

Bottle, A Canne, bl vertical canes, red stopper 1,320.00
Bottle, bl & blk vertical canes, stopper, 13" 1,650.00
Bottle, bl & gr, ribbed, pointed stopper, 18¼" 715.00
Bottle, blk, wht mezza-filigrana band, 13½" 550.00
Bottle, gr w/2 appl red bands, 14" 2,750.00
Bottle, gray & wht vertical canes, ball stopper, 20" 770.00
Bottle, gray w/yel & blk bands, yel stopper, 16½" 1,430.00
Bottle, Inciso, orange stopper, 10½" 715.00
Bowl, Fasce Orrizontali, yel & red bands, 6" dia 209.00
Bowl, Pezzato, Paris colors, 5¾" H 2,990.00
Bowl, sqd corroso in clear, 2¼x4" 319.00
Carafe, red & pk opaque stripes, 12½" 740.00
Figurine, Blackamoor holding flower, 7½" 207.00
Figurine, Commedia Dell Arte, Arlechinno/bk stand 2,185.00
Figurine, Commedia Dell Arte, Meneghino, 15½" 1,430.00
Figurine, Costume, woman, yel & bl zanfirico skirt, 13" 2,530.00
Figurine, Pantalone, 13½" 1,610.00
Figurine, Sirene, gr irid, arms thrown bk, 6¾" 3,240.00
Goblet, A Canne, red/bl/yel/purple/amber/gr canes 440.00
Handkerchief, clear w/red & blk vertical stripes 830.00
Handkerchief, deep red w/wht int, 3½" 143.00
Handkerchief, red w/wht int, 7½" 478.00
Hourglass, bl & avocado, 10" 1,210.00
Obelisk, clear, bl core, wht ribbon spiral, 7¼" 121.00
Paperweight, clear w/turq band, sq, 5" 460.00
Pigeon, gr corroso, 7" 1,900.00
Pigeon, red body, appl irid wings, 8" L 1,160.00
Tumbler, A Canne, red/bl/yel/amethyst stripes, 6" 253.00

Vase, amber sommerso w/gold inclusions, 8¾" 3,150.00
Vase, amethyst-colored battuto, 9½" 1,942.00
Vase, Cinesi, bl irid 3,900.00
Vase, Cinesi, yel w/wht opaque ft, 14" 640.00
Vase, Fan, clear base, wht/amethyst/yel fan, 8x12" 2,420.00
Vase, Filigrana clear/yel spiral threads, 14" 690.00
Vase, Forati, brn & bl, pierced center, 12" 696.00
Vase, Forati, clear bl & gr, 2 asymetrical holes, 11¾" 1,300.00
Vase, Inciso, teardropped, amber & bl layers, 14" 880.00
Vase, occhi cylinder, blk & clear murrines, 5¼" 2,300.00
Vase, Pennallate, pale bl & sky bl stripes, 9¾" 14,950.00
Vase, Pezzato, gr/eggplant/yel/clear, flared, 7½" 4,025.00
Vase, Pulegoso, dk gr, ribbed hdls/ft/neck, 6" 880.00
Vase, red & blk tessuto sqd form, 8" 2,530.00
Vase, Spicchi, bl/red/yel triangles, circular, 7½" 12,150.00
Vase, Stearns cylinder, gunmetal/clear top, bl stripes, 9½" ...4,075.00
Vase, Stearns Doges Hat, 6½" 6,900.00
Vase, Veronese, topaz, 13" 388.00

Non-Venini Glass

A Seguso, A Piumme vase, amber w/gr/yel/wht feathers, 16" ..2,260.00
A Seguso, A Piumme vase, yel, 5 suspended feathers, 9¾" 2,530.00
A Seguso, bowl, shadow ribbed, pk & bl bubbles, 12" dia 385.00
A Seguso, bowl, tan murrines, wht center/aubergine outline, 7" ..1,380.00
A Seguso, Bullicante bowl, cranberry, gold inclusions, 10½" L ..209.00
A Seguso, Fantasia Bianca Nera bowl, 4½" H 1,210.00
A Seguso, Merletto Incalmo, gr & amber, 2 merletto, 7½" 6,600.00
A Seguso, sculpture, owl head, amber, 10" 230.00
A Toso, Bianca Nera vase, colorless disk base, 9¾" 696.00
A Toso, bowls, blk & wht striped, pr 192.00
A Toso, Mezza filigrana bowl, 6" dia 151.00
A Toso, Mezza filigrana vase, 24½" 825.00
A Toso, Oriente bowl, 2" H 238.00
A Toso, Oriente jug-shaped pitcher, 12¼" 6,075.00
A Toso, Oriente vase, pinwheel design, 8½" 5,200.00
A Toso, vase, translucent amethyst, 2 hdls, 13" 935.00
A Toso, vase, wht cased, mustard & red spiral band, 8¾" 195.00
A Toso, vase, wht opaque, yel & pk stripes, 12½" 440.00
A Toso, Zanfirico vase, 19½" 715.00
AVEM, Anse Volante vase, red irid, 4 hdls, 7¼" 1,059.00
AVEM, Con Effetti vase, red, burst silver & gold, 8½" 9,260.00
AVEM, patchwork vase, wht flower form w/gr dots, 15½" 3,450.00
AVEM, vase, bl hourglass, band of mc canes, 13½" 4,160.00
AVEM, vase, gr w/lg appl rings, 11" 935.00
AVEM, vase, red & bl, lozenge filigrana/murrines, 13½" 4,160.00
AVEM, vase, triple-necked, 2 bands of red & gr, 11" 3,800.00
Barbini, Aquarium block, 2 whimsical fish, 7½" 1,265.00
Barbini, Aquarium bookends, single fish, 6½" 660.00
Barbini, Bull, transparent corroso, 12½" L 2,600.00
Barbini, figurines, male & female, trays of fruit, 7", pr 330.00
Barbini, Scavo Bear, 5¾" 825.00
Barovier, A Canne vase, bl/gr/aubergine stripes, 15¼" 2,300.00
Barovier, Ambrati vase, amber marbleized, 8" 1,320.00
Barovier, Barbarico bowl, 3¼" 920.00
Barovier, Clam Shell, irid candle holder, 6½" 412.00
Barovier, Cordonato D'Oro lamp base, 30" 110.00
Barovier, Cordonato D'Oro vase, gr, ribbed, 13" 165.00
Barovier, Cordonato D'Oro vase, pulled hdls, 13" 565.00
Barovier, Corinto bowl 19,600.00
Barovier, Crepuscolo bowl, 9" 1,550.00
Barovier, Dorico bowl, wht & bl murrines, 5½" 3,190.00
Barovier, Eugeneo pitcher, bl, 7½" 1,955.00
Barovier, garniture, pr red vases & bowl, gold grape hdls 575.00

Barovier, Graffito vase, 11½" 1,265.00
Barovier, Intarsia bowl, red & gray, 10" W 1,480.00
Barovier, Intarsia vase, aqua w/pumpkin-colored stripes 2,990.00
Barovier, Intarsia vase, orange & clear, 11½" 2,600.00
Barovier, Intarsia vase, red & bl sqs, drilled, 14" 1,430.00
Barovier, Lenti lamp base, pk, 11¾" 1,760.00
Barovier, Lenti vase w/gold inclusions, 11½" 4,600.00
Barovier, Murrino vase, purple/wht/clear, sq, 6½" 4,770.00
Barovier, Oriente vase, 12" 2,760.00
Barovier, Rostrato vase, 9½" 1,420.00
Barovier, Rugiada bowl, open hdls, 4¼" H 920.00
Barovier, Saturneo vase, bl & wht, 11" 2,587.00
Barovier, Sidero vase, clear w/wht & bl outlined circles, 8" 1,610.00
Barovier, Tessere vase, wht & red pattern, 11¾" 2,430.00
Cappellin, Soffiati, yel vase, appl red chain, 7" 660.00
Cenedese, Aquarium block, 4 fish, 9" 2,110.00
Cenedese, Aquarium bookends, 6" 345.00
Cenedese, Aquarium luminaire, 2 fish, jellyfish, 7" W 1,760.00
Cenedese, Bird, clear, red & yel murrines, 7½" 825.00
Cenedese, leaf bowl, bl int, aqua ext, 5¾" 435.00
Cenedese, Momento vase, blk & yel w/bl stripe, 11½" 1,210.00
Cenedese, Scavo Corroso, sqd bottle, bl, 13" 230.00
F Toso, bottle, bl & clear, ball stopper, 13" 715.00
F Toso, lamp base, fused gr & bl murrines, 24" 495.00
F Toso, Murrine vase, flower blossoms, 2 hdls, 12¼" 483.00
F Toso, Nero Rosso vase, 4" 1,100.00
F Toso, vase, gr, cracked ext, appl blk decor, 9" 440.00
F Toso, vase, gr w/gold inclusions, appl teardrops, 11" 1,045.00
F Toso, vase, orange & wht latticino, ruffled, 13" 192.00
F Toso, vase, polychromed canes, 8" 440.00
F Toso, vase, red, wht casing, appl bl hdls, 11½" 550.00
F Toso, vase, red canes, cylindrical, 8½" 1,300.00
Seguso Vetri, candlesticks, clear, palm-tree shape, 11½", pr ...1,050.00
Seguso Vetri, corroso fish, red w/blk eyes & ft, 16½" L 238.00
Seguso Vetri, corroso mirror, clear w/gold inclusions, 15¼" 1,390.00
Seguso Vetri, figurine, woman, clear irid w/bl base, 9" 990.00
Seguso Vetri, picture fr, pk tinted, 12½" 1,020.00
Seguso Vetri, sommerso basket vase, gr w/yel int, 11½" 66.00
Seguso Vetri, sommerso jar, red & bl layers, w/lid, 5" 405.00
Seguso Vetri, sommerso vase, amethyst & red layers, 9½" 780.00
Seguso Vetri, sommerso vase, bl & alexandrite layers, 10½" ...1,980.00
Seguso Vetri, sommerso vase, bl & aquamarine layers, 6¾" 870.00
Seguso Vetri, sommerso vase, clear w/gr core, 9" 286.00
Sottsass, Amitie, wht/gr/red/blk/clear cylinder, 15" 2,200.00
Sottsass, Dench vase, bl w/purple base, 3 loop hdls, 8" 8,700.00
Sottsass, Diodata vase, bl & gr w/blk disk foot, 11" 2,420.00
Sottsass, Fililla compote, bl, 6 hanging pendants, 13½" 2,300.00
Sottsass, Mizar vase, bl w/mc hdls, 12" 2,750.00
Sottsass, Moceniga vase, yel 1,100.00
Sottsass, Morosina, 4-tiered wht cylinder w/bl decor, 15" 2,310.00
Tagliapietra, handkerchief vase, gr & red threaded, 11" 510.00
Tagliapietra, Tessuto vase, red & bl caning, 8½" 550.00
Vistosi, bird, bl cube, 10½" 1,650.00
Vistosi, bird, bl flat triangle, red stripes, 6¾" 2,295.00
Vistosi, bird, J shaped, bl 1,100.00
Vistosi, bird, J shaped, gr, 12" 2,030.00
Vistosi, bird, orange, appl spots, 8" 1,045.00
Vistosi, vase, amber w/3 red murrine bands, 13½" 880.00

Ivory

Technically, true ivory is the substance composing the tusk of the elephant; the finest type comes from Africa. However, tusks and teeth of other animals — the walrus, the hippopotamus, and the sperm whale, for instance — are similar in composition and appearance and have also been used for carving. The Chinese have used this substance for centuries, preferring it over bone because of the natural oil contained in its pores, which not only renders it easier to carve but also imparts a soft sheen to the finished product. Aged ivory usually takes on a soft caramel patina, but unscrupulous dealers sometimes treat new ivory to a tea bath to 'antique' it! A bill passed in 1978 reinforced a ban on the importation of whale and walrus ivory. All examples listed here are Oriental in origin unless noted otherwise.

Boat w/rooster head & 2 passengers, 5¼" 415.00
Brush pot, cvd bamboo branches, China, 5½" 190.00
Brush pot, cvd Chinese landscape & text, 5¾" 325.00
Chop block, cvd elephant & attendant, China, 18th C, 2½" 120.00
Cribbage board, Chinese Export, late 19th C, 10x3" 175.00
Cribbage board, Chinese Export, lion paw ft, 19th C, 9¾" 375.00
Death's head w/serpent/frog/etc, age crack, 3¼" 85.00
Fisherman & child, 6¾"+base 150.00
Goddess reclines on cvd wood couch, China, 13½" 900.00
Man w/2 devils, age crack, 3¼" 330.00
Needle case, umbrella shape, screw-off hdl & lid, 4" 135.00
Recline nude w/bound feet, flower between breasts, China, 9" L ..225.00

Study of armored samurai on knoll, sepia wash, signed Koshun, Meiji Period, small repairs, 18⅝", $3,700.00.

Table screen panel, cvd landscape, teapot/peaches on bk, 8" 110.00
Tusk, family scenes in relief, old rpr, 7" 220.00
Vase, boar hunt scene, Japan, 5" 425.00
Vase, lotus blossom & branch lid w/cranes, w/lid, Japan, 7½" 400.00

Jack-in-the-Pulpit Vases

Popular novelties at the turn of the century, jack-in-the-pulpit vases were made in every type of art glass produced. Some were simple, others elaborately appliqued and enameled. They were shaped to resemble the lily for which they were named.

Bl & wht stripes, frosted ft, 12¼x5⅛" 195.00
Bl Hobnail w/wine ruffled rim, 7x6½" 110.00
Chartreuse gr opal, ruffled edge, 7¼x4½" 75.00
Maroon & wht spatter, vaseline opal appl top, 11x6" 110.00
Pk opal to vaseline, 11¼x4⅞" 135.00
Red to opal, appl yel flowers & leaves, appl ft, 8" 135.00
Rubena verde opal, crimped rim, 12" 225.00
Sapphire bl, Dmn Quilt w/HP florals & gold, 9¾x4⅝" 250.00

Wht opaque w/rose int, wishbone ft, 5x3¼" 85.00

Jalan

During the second quarter of the century, both hand-thrown and molded pottery were produced by Manuele Jalanivich and Olsen Ingvardt, most of which were marked 'Jalan.' Their studio was located in San Francisco until the late '30s and after that in Belmont. Their wares were low-fired earthenware, and crackle glazes were favored.

Bowl, bl gloss, ped ft, mk/dtd 1928, 2x11" 165.00
Bowl, chevron panels cut-bk on lime crackle, conical, 5x9" 325.00
Bowl, purple, Chinese bl crackle int, mk, 2x8" 210.00
Vase, plum purple w/turq lip, pillow form, 8" 350.00

Japanese Lustreware

Imported from Japan during the 1920s, novelty tableware items, vases ashtrays, etc. — often in blue, tan, and mother-of-pearl lustre glazes — were sold through five-and-dime stores or given as premiums for selling magazine subscriptions. The Occupied Japan Club is listed in the Directory under Clubs, Newletters, and Catalogs.

Ashtray, clown figural, card-suit buttons on tan lustre, 3" 20.00
Ashtray, wht lustre Deco rabbit beside red & bl tray, 2¾" 35.00
Creamer & sugar bowl, exotic bird w/tan & bl lustre, on tray 50.00
Creamer & sugar bowl, mc Deco decor w/tan lustre ft & int, 3½" ..45.00
Flask, A Little Scotch, man figural, tan lustre, blk mk, 4" 40.00
Flask, cat figural, yel, red mk, 6½" 12.00
Flower bowl, circle of swans along rim, tan & bl, 8" 75.00
Pincushion, calico dog w/tan lustre top hat, blk mk, 3¾" 35.00
Pincushion, penguin figural, bl & wht, blk mk, 3" 18.00
Snack set (plate & cup) 25.00
Tea set, tan & bl, teapot+cr/sug+6 c/s 100.00
Toothbrush holder, bull figural, bl & tan lustre w/blk, 4¼" 60.00
Toothbrush holder, cat figural, tan & wht, red mk, 4¼" 55.00

Jervis

W.P. Jervis began his career as a potter in 1898. By 1908 he had his own pottery in Oyster Bay, New York. His shapes were graceful; often he decorated his wares with sgraffito designs over which he applied a matt glaze. Many pieces were incised 'Jervis' in a vertical arrangement. The pottery closed around 1912.

Vase, mint gr & brn gloss, 3½" 140.00
Vase, squeeze-bag flower, corseted, mk, 10" 400.00

Jewelry

Jewelry as objects of adornment has always been regarded with special affection. Whether it be a trinket or a costly ornament of gold, silver, or enameled work, jewelry has personal significance to the wearer. The art of the jeweler is valued as is any art object, and the names of Lalique or Faberge on collectible pieces bring prices demanded by the signed works of Picasso. Once the province of kings and noblemen, jewelry now is a legacy of all strata of society. The creativity reflected in the jeweler's art has resulted in a myriad of decorative adornments for men and women, and the modern usage of 'lesser' gems and base metals has elevated the value and increased the demand for artistic merit, so

that now it is considered by collectors to be on a par with intrinsic value. Luxuriously appointed pieces of Victorian splendor and Edwardian grandeur now compete with the unique, imaginative renditions of jewelry produced in the exciting Art Nouveau period as well as the adventurous translation of jewelry executed in man-made materials versus natural elements. Today prices for gems and gemstones crafted into antique and collectible jewelry are based on artistic merit, personal appeal, pure sentimentality, and intrinsic value. Note: Diamond prices vary greatly depending on cut, color, clarity, etc., and to assess the value of any diamond of more than a carat in weight, you will need to have information about all of these factors. Values given here are for diamond jewelry with a standard commercial grade of diamonds that are most likely to be encountered.

Our advisor for fine jewelry in this category is Rebecca Dodds; her address may be found in the Directory under Florida. If you are interested in collecting or dealing in jewelry, you will find that authority Lillian Baker has several fine books available on the subject — *100 Years of Collectible Jewelry: 1850-1950; Art Nouveau and Art Deco Jewelry;* and *Fifty Years of Collectible Fashion Jewelry: 1925-1975.* These books are complete with beautiful full-color illustrations and current market values. Another fine source of information is *Christmas Pins, Past and Present* (Collector Books) by Jill Gallina. See also Plastics.

Key:
cab — cabochon	gw — gold washed
ct — carat	k — karat
dmn — diamond	plat — platinum
dwt — penny weight	r/stn — rhinestone
Euro — European cut	stn — stone
fl — filigree	wg — white gold
gf — gold filled	yg — yellow gold
grad — graduated	ygf — yellow gold filled

Brooch, Georgian facet-cut aquamarine surrounded by eight oval aquamarines with gold 14k beadwork; Earrings, four oval aquamarines suspending a cluster of nine with gold 14k beadwork, very large, $2,500.00 for the set.

Bar pin, 14k yg w/sm pearl 30.00
Bracelet, bangle, 14k gold w/eng 275.00
Bracelet, bangle, 14k openwork buckle type, sm dmns/enamel .1,250.00
Bracelet, bangle, 14k yg, hinged 175.00
Bracelet, bangle, 14k yg w/dbl heart ends & 30 sm dmns 250.00
Bracelet, bangle, 14k yg w/7 cut sapphires & 8 .8ct dmns 625.00
Bracelet, bangle, 14k yg w/9 sm dmns, 1960s 200.00
Bracelet, charm; 14k yg w/2 oval Victorian lockets/4 charms 625.00
Bracelet, gutta percha links w/gold studs, 1870s 285.00
Bracelet, Kalo, silver, leaf/berry rtcl rnd links 700.00
Bracelet, seed pearls, flexible, 6 rose dmns in clasp 425.00
Bracelet, 14k yg, dbl links, flexible, 23dwt 450.00
Bracelet, 14k yg, dbl links, gold coin charm, 17dwt 340.00
Bracelet, 14k yg, flexible, 49 dmns 1ct tw 500.00
Bracelet, 14k yg, flexible mesh, 14k charm w/pearl, 38.5dwt 500.00
Bracelet, 14k yg links, 39dwt, 7½" 600.00
Bracelet, 14k yg w/floral eng, ½" W, hinged, 20 grams 195.00
Bracelet, 14k yg w/2ct tw dmns, 1.75ct tw emeralds 2,200.00

Bracelet, 14k yg w/30 dmns 1ct tw 525.00
Bracelet, 14k yg w/38 dmns 2ct tw 1,000.00
Bracelet, 9k yg, flexible w/'padlock' clasp 200.00
Brooch, plat, flower sprays w/dmns 11.75ct tw 7,200.00
Brooch, rose & yg scrolls w/8 aquamarines/25 rubies, 35dwt tw ..800.00
Brooch, Taxco/Wm Spratling, silver clown w/gw, 4½" 1,200.00
Brooch, yg/wg w/ruby/sapphire/16 emeralds/124 dmns, 6ct tw ...4,250.00
Brooch, 14k textured yg w/3 5-petal coral flowers 125.00
Brooch, 14k wg w/lg pearl & 6 sm dmns 150.00
Cross, 14k yg 'nugget' style, 7 grams 85.00
Cross, 14k yg, 3 grams 55.00
Earrings, Geo Jensen, sterling doves, pr 130.00
Earrings, obsidian cvd frog dangles, ear wires, pr 125.00
Earrings, plat, .70ct dmn at post w/.60ct dmn drop, pr 3,300.00
Earrings, plat w/rnd .65ct tw dmn, pr 1,500.00
Earrings, wg w/.25ct tw dmn, pr 575.00
Earrings, 14k yg, ea w/1.50ct oval amethyst, posts, pr 90.00
Earrings, 14k yg, Star Ruby sapphire over 1ct ea, drops, pr 285.00
Earrings, 14k yg, wheel w/3 sm rubies in center, clip, pr 375.00
Earrings, 14k yg dangle, shield motif, granulation, pr 285.00
Earrings, 14k yg oval fct amethyst w/6 sm dmns, pr 350.00
Earrings, 14k yg w/mabe pear center, pr 210.00
Earrings, 14k yg w/1.5ct citrine, pierced, pr 75.00
Locket, 14k yg heart w/.35ct dmn, 13dwt tw 500.00
Necklace, amethyst, 3-strand grad beads, gold/amethyst clasp 495.00
Necklace, crystal grad beads & carnelians, opera length 50.00
Necklace, cultured pearls, 1-strand, 6mm, 14k clasp, 25" 900.00
Necklace, cultured pearls, 1-strand, 7mm, 14k yg clasp, 20" 1,100.00
Necklace, cultured pearls 1-strand, 3.15-8mm, gold clasp, 15" ...175.00
Necklace, cultured pearls 69 in 1-strand, 5.5 to 5mm, yg clasp ...165.00
Necklace, cultured pearls 1-strand, 54 7mm, clasp w/dmns, 16" .200.00
Necklace, jet, 51 6mm Whitby fct beads w/50 spacers, 24" 135.00
Necklace, lapis lazuli, 61 grad rnd beads 250.00
Necklace, Liberty, 5 gold 'spades' w/opals, gr stn spacers 1,300.00
Necklace, 14k yg, mesh w/buckle & tassel center, 36.5dwt 800.00
Necklace, 14k yg, oval & dbl U links, 15", 22dwt 450.00
Necklace, 14k yg, styled as snake, 14", 23dwt 400.00
Necklace, 14k yg, 3 rope strands, oval clasp, 55dwt 1,100.00
Necklace, 14k yg choker styled as snake, 41.5dwt 850.00
Pendant, 14k yg w/seed pearls in center 200.00
Pendant, 14k yg w/2ct fct amethyst 50.00
Pin, Art Silver Shop, floral-rtcl bar w/blister pearl, 2" 260.00
Pin, Georg Jensen, 14k yg circle, circle mk, 1½" dia 460.00
Pin, Kalo, sterling acorn & leaf, 2" 200.00
Pin, plat w/dmns of 1.90ct tw 1,500.00
Pin, wg w/6 7mm pearls & 30 seed pearls in circle 120.00
Pin, 14 yg scroll w/9 sm grad dmns 200.00
Pin, 14k rose & yg bow knot w/2 sm sq rubies & 2 sm dmns 325.00
Pin, 14k yg bow w/2.40ct aquamarine 325.00
Pin, 14k yg leaf w/52 grad dmns 1.75ct tw, Van Cleef & Arpels ..3,250.00
Pin, 14k yg w/garnet & semiprecious stones, 7.5dwt tw 100.00
Pin, 14k yg w/jet & seed pearls 180.00
Pin, 14k yg w/10ct oval citrine 150.00
Pin, 14k yg w/5 sm dmns in circle 140.00
Ring, man's, 14k yg, 2 rectangular citrines tw 10.75dwt 150.00
Ring, man's, 14k yg w/emerald-cut 10.50dwt smoky topaz 150.00
Ring, man's, 14k yg w/onyx bust of Mercury, 10.50dwt 150.00
Ring, man's, 14k yg w/oval cab blk star 13dwt sapphire 170.00
Ring, man's, 14k yg w/10dwt cab garnet 90.00
Ring, man's, 14k yg w/26dwt lapis lazuli 225.00
Ring, man's, 14k yg w/3 turq stones 26dwt tw 200.00
Ring, plat, .70ct dmn w/4 sm side dmns 750.00
Ring, yg w/2 oval dmns .25ct ea 450.00
Ring, yg w/28 grad rnd dmns 2.85ct tw in cluster 1,500.00

Ring, yg/wg, 1ct emerald/12 sm rose dmns 950.00
Ring, 12k yg w/7.75dwt jade stone 150.00
Ring, 14k wg w/13ct oval fct amethyst & 14 dmns 1.40ct tw ..1,000.00
Ring, 14k yg w/1ct rectangular cut tourmaline 75.00
Ring, 14k yg w/.60ct rnd solitaire dmn 330.00
Ring, 14k yg w/center .70ct dmn w/9 sm, 1ct tw 750.00
Ring, 14k yg w/emerald-cut .50ct emerald 150.00
Ring, 14k yg w/emerald-cut faux ruby, modern style 70.00
Ring, 14k yg w/oval fct amethysts tw 3.50cts 90.00
Ring, 14k yg w/oval fct citrine in claw setting 80.00
Ring, 14k yg w/oval sapphire, 20 sm sapphires/20 sm dmns 260.00
Ring, 14k yg w/pear-shape 10ct aquamarine 300.00
Ring, 14k yg w/10ct tourmaline & 2 tiers of sm dmns 825.00
Ring, 14k yg w/2.25ct emerald-cut emerald w/4 sm dmns 500.00
Ring, 14k yg w/5x8mm dk gr emerald 245.00
Ring, 14k yg w/7.5mm cultured pearl 60.00
Ring, 14k yg wedding band, 9.5dwt 100.00
Ring, 18k yg fl w/7 dmns tw .50ct 330.00
Ring, 18k yg w/emerald-cut 2.50ct dmn & 2 baguettes 5,250.00
Ring, 18k yg w/3 calibre-cut & 4 cab sapphires & 6 sm dmns 300.00

Costume Jewelry

Rhinestone jewelry has become a very popular field of collecting. Copyrighting jewelry came into effect in 1955. Pieces bearing a copyright mark (post-1955) are considered 'collectibles,' while pieces (with no copyright) made before then are regarded as 'antiques.' Rhinestones are foil-backed leaded crystal stones with a sparkle outshining diamonds. Look for signed and well made, unmarked pieces for your collections and preserve this American art form. Our advisor for costume jewelry is Marcia Brown; she is listed in the Directory under Oregon.

Bracelet, HAR, hinged style with purple brilliants and rhinestones, $195.00.

Bracelet, Eisenberg, rhodium r/stns, wide, 1950 ....145.00
Bracelet, Eisenberg Ice, ⅞" W 140.00
Bracelet, Nettie Rosenstein, sterling, infinity motif, 2" W 400.00
Brooch, Cini, star w/moonstone center 60.00
Brooch, Cini, sterling Libra 45.00
Brooch, Coro, enameled iris, lg 125.00
Brooch, Corocraft Sterling, leaf w/red & bl stns 95.00
Brooch, Eisenberg Ice, 2½", w/matching earrings 110.00
Chain, Sarah Coventry, rhodium, ca 1960 ....10.00
Cross, Emmons, Regency, antiqued rhodium fl w/beading 45.00
Dress clip, Eisenberg, lg fct/cut r/stns on gold vermeil, '30s 155.00
Earrings, Chr Dior/Germany, faux jade & sapphires on gold-tone 85.00
Earrings, Emmons, faux pearls set in rhodium, 1960, clip-on 35.00
Earrings, Hobe, gemstones on gold-tone leaf form, 1¾x1" 95.00
Earrings, Robert, pearl & crystals in ornate button style 40.00
Fur clip, De Rosa, sterling winged feather, w/earrings 115.00
Pendant, Kramer, bl & wht pronged rhinestones 40.00
Pin, Boucher, fish form w/enamel stripes on gold-tone, 1955 ....75.00
Pin, Cini, dogwood, sterling, lg 180.00
Pin, Coro, peacock form, enamel on gold plate, 1950 ....75.00
Pin, Coro Craft, spray of faux sapphires/dmns, 4½" 165.00
Pin, Corocraft Sterling, bird in flight, pnt details 195.00
Pin, Emmons, bobcat's gold-tone face w/gr eyes, 1954 ....75.00

Pin, Emmons, Lambkin, oxidized brass & pnt enamel lamb, 1960 .....**35.00**
Pin, Hobe, tricolored gemstones, in gold-tone fl, 2¾x1½" **250.00**
Pin, Ledo, pear shape/baguette-cut faux gemstones on gold-tone .**55.00**
Pin, scarf; Boucher, gold-tone & wht enamel bamboo design **55.00**
Pin, scarf; Trifari, gold-tone feather design, 1960 ....**25.00**
Pin, Schreiner NY, poodle, jet blk stones **125.00**
Pin, sweater guard; horses, brass **28.00**
Pin, Trifari, molded mc glass flowers on rnd shape, rhodium **30.00**
Pin, Trifari, poodle w/MOP body **25.00**
Pin, Trifari, sterling feather, pave **45.00**
Pins, swag; Corocraft Sterling, sword & sheath, HP & jewels **145.00**
Ring, Emmons, aurora borealis r/stns set in gold-tone, 1970 ....**30.00**

Josef Originals

Figurines of lovely ladies, charming girls, and whimsical animals marked Josef Originals were designed by Muriel Joseph George of Arcadia, California, from 1945 to 1985. Until 1960 they were produced in California, but costs were high and copies of her work were being made in Japan. To remain competitive, she and her partner, George Good, contracted with the Katayama Company in Japan to build a factory and produce her designs to her approval. Muriel retired in 1982; however, George Good continued production of her work as well as new ones of his staff's creation. The company was sold in late 1985, and the name is currently owned by Applause. A limited amount of figurines bear the name. Those made during the ownership of Muriel George are the most collectible. They can be recognized by these characteristics: The girls have a high-gloss finish, black eyes, and most are signed. Brown eyes date from 1982-85. Applause uses a red-brown eye. The animals were mainly done in a matt finish and have labels. Later animals have a flocked coat. Prices are given for figurines in perfect condition only. Our advisors, Jim and Kaye Whitaker, are the authors of two books, *Josef Originals, Charming Figurines* and *Josef Originals, A Second Look.* They are listed in the Directory under Washington.

Happiness Is Series: Happiness Is Rain, Japan, 4¾" $27.00; and Happiness Is Mud Puddles, Japan, 5¼", $28.00.

Angel, character cat, wht w/nylon whiskers, Japan, 3¼" **22.00**
Birthday girls, #1-#16, Japan, 2" through 6", ea **20.00**
Birthstone doll music box, 12 in series, plays tune, Japan, 5¼" **45.00**
Bridal group figure, Bride, Japan, 4½" **30.00**
Bridal group figure, Flower Girl, Japan, 4" **30.00**
Bridal group figure, Groom, Japan, 4½" **30.00**
Bridal group figure, Ring Bearer, Japan, 3½" **30.00**
Buggy Bugs series, various bugs w/wire antenna, Japan, 3¼", ea ...**20.00**
Candle holders, Christmas mice, pr **55.00**
Dalmatian, Kennel Club, Japan, 3½" **22.00**
First Date, gr gown, w/fan, Japan, 9" **110.00**

Flower Sprites, varied poses, Japan, 3¾", ea **32.00**
Frogs, varied poses, Japan, 3-4", ea **15.00**
Joseph II, California, 5½" **40.00**
Little Tutu, various colors, California, 4" **30.00**
Marie Antoinette, California, 5½" **40.00**
Musicale series, Robin at harp, Japan, 6" **65.00**
Raindrops Keep Falling music box, children/umbrella, Japan, 6¾" **75.00**
Rose Garden series, 6 poses, Japan, 5", ea **60.00**
Rosemary, pk, w/parasol, Japan, 7¼" **95.00**
Santa w/toy bag & martini, Japan, 6" **55.00**

Judaica

The items listed below are representative of objects used in both the secular and religious life of the Jewish people. They are evident of a culture where silversmiths, painters, engravers, writers, and metal workers were highly gifted and skilled in their art. Most of the treasures shown in recently displayed exhibits of Judaica were confiscated by the Germans during the late 1930s up to 1945; by then eight Jewish synagogues and fifty warehouses had been filled with Hitler's plunder. Judaica is currently available through dealers, from private collections, and the annual auction held in Israel.

Breastplate, E European parcel-gilt silver, 1866, 12" **3,000.00**
Breastplate, Polish parcel-gilt silver, late 1700s, 11" **5,000.00**
Bridal mirror, N Africa silver over brass, 1890s, 18⅛" L **900.00**
Candelabra, Polish brass, 3-candle, early 1800s, 17", pr **800.00**
Carpet, Rachel's Tomb, Bezalel, early 1900s, 23x44½", EX **650.00**
Charity container, Lithuanian silver, mug form, 1800s, 8½" ...**1,000.00**
Collection box, cast bronze, Seccessionist style, 1930s, 8" **2,600.00**
Etrog basket, silver filigree, Zhitomir, 1856-57, 7" L **650.00**
Etrog container, Austrian silver, hinged lid, 1844, 5½x5½" **600.00**
Etrog container, Continental parcel gilt silver, 1900s, 3" **300.00**
Etrog container, Continental silver, eng oval, 1900s, 5¼" **500.00**
Etrog container, Palestinian wood, cvd scenes, 1900, 3½x7" **700.00**

Hannukah lamp, Bezalel silver, lions flanking a lit Menora, eight candle sockets, ca late 1930s, 9¾", $1,200.00.

Hannukah lamp, Bezalel silver, Biblical design, 1930s, 18" **2,600.00**
Hannukah lamp, Bezalel silver, medieval style, 1930s, 8¼" **4,000.00**
Hannukah lamp, brass, sgn B Griedst, 8-socket, 1900s, 12½" .**3,250.00**
Hannukah lamp, bronze, anthropomorphic, Italy/17th C, 10¼" ..**4,250.00**
Hannukah lamp, Damascene silver/brass, lions, 1900s, 14" ...**1,600.00**
Hannukah lamp, German silver, Nouveau style, 1900s, 12¼" ..**2,600.00**
Hannukah lamp, Italian bronze, ornate scrolls, 17th C, 7" **1,100.00**
Hannukah lamp, N Africa brass, 8 oil pans, 1900, 10½" **300.00**
Hannukah lamp, N Eastern brass, bird surmounts, 18th C, 10" ..**300.00**
Hannukah lamp, Polish brass, palms/lions/crown, 19th C, 11" ...**550.00**
Hannukah lamp, Polish silver, foliage/lions, 1920s, 11" **1,100.00**
Hannukah lamp, Russian-Polish silver, 8-socket, 1890s, 11" ...**1,800.00**
Hannukah lamp, Ukranian silver & filigree, dtd 1895, 10½" .**4,750.00**
Havdallah compendium, Austro-Hungarian silver, 19th C, 6" .**1,300.00**

Havdallah cup, Bohemian glass, yel w/HP symbols, 1890s, 3¼" .650.00
Hevrah Kadishah comb, Russian silver, 1860, ¼" L 1,200.00
Kiddush cup, Bezalel silver, vintage/filigree, 1920, 6½" 650.00
Kiddush cup, Bohemian glass, etched tulip form, 1800s, 11" ...1,300.00
Kiddush cup, festival; German parcel gilt, 1730s, 5*1/8*" 8,500.00
Kiddush cup, German silver, 8-sided, rnd base, 18th C, 4⅞" ...4,000.00
Kiddush cup, Polish silver, much eng, gilt int, 1863, 2⅝" 700.00
Kiddush goblet, Bezalel silver, emb Moses scene, 1940s, 6" 1,300.00
Kiddush goblet, German silver, chased fruit, ca 1900, 4⅞" 1,100.00
Kiddush goblet, Polish silver, chased foliage, 19th C, 5¼" 550.00
Laver set, Hungarian SP, inscr, 1862, 15" basin/9" laver 2,500.00
Marriage belt, German silver-gilt, 2-strand, 1600s, 38" 8,000.00
Marriage cup, German silver, emb/etched foliage, 1880s, 3½" 2,500.00
Miniature, Torah crown, Continental silver, 19th C, 9½" 2,900.00
Miniature, Torah finials, gold, Dutch form, 20th C, ¾", pr ...3,250.00
Passover condiment dish, Bohemian glass & brass, 1900s, 9½" 4,000.00
Passover seder plate, Palestinian brass/copper, 1930s, 13" 750.00
Sabbath candelabra, Ukranian brass, 5-candle, 1850s, 19", pr 425.00
Sabbath candelabrum, E European brass, 5-candle, 19th C, 20" .375.00
Sabbath candlesticks, Polish silver, roses/etc, 1868, 10", pr 1,000.00
Sabbath candlesticks, Polish silver, vintage, 1881, 12", pr 600.00
Sabbath candlesticks, Polish silver, vintage, 1885, 13", pr 700.00
Sabbath candlesticks, Russian silver, emb decor, 1863, 13", pr .1,100.00
Sabbath lamp, French brass, 6-part star, 19th C, 31" 1,200.00
Sabbath lamp, German brass, tulip form, ca 1790, 34½" 1,000.00
Sabbath lamp, German brass, 8-part star form, 1800s, 16½" 450.00
Sabbath lamp, Polish brass, 6-arm, star shape, 18th C, 21" 800.00
Sabbath lamp, Polish brass, 8 detachable arms, 1800s, 36½" ...4,500.00
Sabbath lamp, Russian-Polish silver, 5-point star, 1879, 24" .10,000.00
Seder plate, Russian silver, openwork rim, 1900s, 12½" 2,500.00
Spice tower, Austro-Hungarian silver, 2-tier, 1890s, 8¼" 350.00
Spice tower, German silver, clock tower form, 19th C, 9" 1,600.00
Spice tower, German silver, 1 lg/4 sm towers, 1900s, 7" 1,200.00
Spice tower, Polish silver, eng panels, bells, 19th C, 8¾" 1,200.00
Spice tower, Polish silver, sq filigree section, 1850s, 6½" 400.00
Spice tower, Polish silver filigree, late 19th C, 10¾" 450.00
Spice tower, Polish silver filigree, pennant, 1880s, 9" 500.00
Spice tower, Polish-Ukranian silver, 6 pennants, 1850s, 9½" 900.00
Tefillin cases, Continental silver, 19th C, 3½x2¼", pr 425.00
Tora binder, France, pnt scenes on linen, 1879, 124" 400.00
Tora case, Egyptian, velvet covered, silver mtd, 1925, EX 500.00
Torah finials, Moroccan silver/hammered gold, 18th C, 15", pr ...7,000.00
Torah finials, N African silver, early 1900s, 10¼", pr 800.00
Torah finials, Russian silver, 3-tier w/bells, 1881, 16", pr 1,500.00
Torah pointer, E European silver, late 19th C, 10¾" 200.00
Torah pointer, German silver, twisted wire stem, 19th C, 11" 200.00
Torah pointer, W Europe, cvd ivory, porc finial, 1850s, 14" ...2,200.00
Vase, Bezalel brass, 3 classic scenes, 1916, 7½" 500.00
Wall laver, Bezalel copper, convex emb basin, 1900s, 27" 30,000.00
Yom Kippur belt buckle & belt, Polish-Russian silver, 1894 ....600.00

Jugtown

The Jugtown Pottery was started about 1920 by Juliana and Jacques Busbee, in Moore County, North Carolina. Ben Owen, a young descendant of a Staffordshire potter, was hired in 1923. He was the master potter, while the Busbees experimented with perfecting glazes and supervising design and modeling. Preferred shapes were those reminiscent of traditional country wares and classic Oriental forms. Glazes were various: natural-clay oranges, buffs, 'tobacco-spit' brown, mirror black, white, 'frog-skin' green, a lovely turquoise called Chinese blue, and the traditional cobalt-decorated salt glaze. The pottery gained national recognition, and as a result of their success, several other local potteries were established. Jugtown is still in operation; however, they no longer use their original glaze colors which are now so collectible.

Bowl, blue and red Chinese translation glaze, circular stamp, 6½x13" (rare large size), $2,500.00.

Bowl, cobalt stars & stripes on salt glaze, 2⅝x4¼", NM 95.00
Candlesticks, bl mottle & blk gloss, tapered stems, 4½", pr 110.00
Cup & saucer, cobalt on salt glaze, glossy, 2⅜", 5¾", NM 65.00
Inkwell, Chinese bl, Albany slip int, 3" 375.00
Pitcher, gr (rare), scroll around collar, 1920s-30s, 5½" 550.00
Pitcher, tobacco spit brn, 8" 125.00
Teapot, cobalt brushwork on salt glaze, glossy, 6½x10", EX 750.00
Vase, blk gloss, flaring wide rim, narrow platform ft, 6½" 220.00
Vase, Chinese bl, bulbous, hdls, 10" 1,200.00
Vase, Chinese bl, ovoid, 4" 300.00
Vase, Chinese bl, teardrop form, 5½" 400.00
Vase, gray & wht gloss, 5½" 190.00
Vase, thick wht, 4-hdld, 7" 325.00

K. P. M. Porcelain

The original KPM wares were produced from 1823 until 1847 by the Konigliche Porzellan Manfaktur, located in Berlin, Germany. Meissen used the same letters on some of their porcelains, as did several others in the area. In addition to the initials, the mark sometimes contains a crowned eagle with a scepter. Watch for items currently being imported from China; they are marked KPM with the eagle, but the scepter is not present. Our advisor for this category is Don Williams; he is listed in the Directory under Missouri.

Basket, floral sprays w/much gold, 2-part, 4x12½x8½" 130.00
Bowl, centerpc; HP florals w/gold, 6½x14x11" 350.00
Group, sm girl w/bouquet being crowned by another, 1925, 8" ...700.00
Panel, lady w/locket, sgn, gilt fr, 10¼x8" 4,000.00

Plaque, girl with basket of books and folio, scepter mark, late 19th century, 9¼x6½" plus gilt frame, $4,000.00.

Plaque, bl bird pr on nest w/3 eggs, 14" dia 2,500.00
Plaque, draped nude & horse, Walther, gold fr, 9¼x6¼" 3,500.00
Plaque, Jesus at the Age of 12, 1860-80, 3¼x2½"+fr 495.00
Plaque, Louis Le Brun Selbstbildnis, Dittrich, 10½x8½" 4,000.00

Plaque, man in doorway holds baby, girl/rabbits aside, 9x11" ..6,500.00
Plate, floral HP on wht, ca 1840, 10" 35.00

Kayserzinn Pewter

J.P. Kayser Sohn produced pewter decorated with relief-molded Art Nouveau motifs in Germany during the late 1800s and into the 20th century. Examples are marked with 'Kayserzinn' and the mold number within an elongated oval reserve. Items with three-dimensional animals, insects, birds, etc., are valued much higher than bowls, plates, and trays with simple embossed florals, which are usually priced at $100.00 to about $200.00, depending on size.

Beaker, poppies, #436, 4½" 155.00
Bonbon, shell form w/Art Nouveau nude, sgn/#4136, 8x6¾" 200.00
Bowl, appl floral, hdls, 34227, 13½" 110.00
Candelabrum, 2-arm, T-form std, #4531, 10½" 1,225.00
Covered dish, Art Nouveau decor, sm 95.00
Flagon, flowers & vines, dog & horse head, 12" 375.00
Ice bucket, emb foliage, cylindrical, #4860, 8" 250.00
Mug, trophy; 1902 Women's Tournament, Nouveau decor 55.00
Pitcher, floral, 9" 235.00
Stein, poppies, #436, 4½" 125.00
Tray, lily-of-valley on spade shape, #4294, 9⅜" 70.00
Vase, antelope skulls w/horns on chalice form, 14¼" 475.00
Vase, rabbits holding fruit, ftd, oval, #4490, sm 240.00

Keeler, Brad

Keeler studied art for a time in the 1930s; later he became a modeler for a Los Angeles firm. By 1939 he was working in his own studio where he created naturalistic studies of birds and animals which were marketed through giftware stores. They were decorated by means of an airbrush and enhanced with hand-painted details. His flamingo figures were particularly popular. In the mid-'40s, he developed a successful line of Chinese Modern housewares glazed in Ming Dragon Blood, a red color he personally developed. Keeler died of a heart attack in 1952, and the pottery closed soon thereafter. For more information, we recommend *The Collector's Encyclopedia of California Pottery* by Jack Chipman.

Figurine, bird on branch, #720, 5½" 45.00

Blue Jay, #735, 9", $65.00.

Photo courtesy Jack Chipman

Figurine, bluebird, #18 ....40.00
Figurine, canary, tail up or tail down, 8¼" or 6", ea 40.00
Figurine, cocker spaniel pup, #735 ....40.00
Figurine, cowboy, hat in left hand, Pride & Joy line, 7" 60.00
Figurine, peacock, Fantasy line, #747, 11" 165.00

Figurine, sea gull, wings up, wave as base, #29, 10½" 90.00
Figurine, Siamese cat, #798 ....50.00
Figurine, tropical bird (like flamingo), Fantasy line #702, 15" 195.00
Lobster dish, 18" 85.00
Planter, baby booties, Pride & Joy line 25.00
Planter, baby carriage, Pride & Joy line 25.00
Planter, hobby horse, Pride & Joy line 25.00
Relish, lobster, divided, 12x10" 65.00

Keen Kutter

Keen Kutter was the brand name chosen in 1870 by the Simmons Firm for a line of high-grade tools and cutlery. The trademark was first applied to high-grade axes. A corporation was formed in 1874 called Simmons Hardware Company. In 1923 Winchester merged with Simmons and continued to carry a full line of hardware plus the Winchester brand. The merger dissolved. On July 1, 1940, the Simmons Company was purchased by Shapleigh Hardware Company. All Simmons Hardware Co. trademark lines were continued, and the business operated successfully until closing in 1962. Today the Keen Kutter logo is owned by the Val-Test Company of Chicago, Illinois. For further study we recommend *Keen Kutter Collectibles*, an illustrated price guide by our advisors for this category, Jerry and Elaine Heuring, available at your favorite bookstore or public library. The Heurings are listed in the Directory under Missouri. See also Knives.

Auger bits, KS9, w/wooden box & paper label 120.00
Awl, scratch; stamped logo on wood hdl 75.00
Axe, #5 plain pattern 30.00
Axe, fireman's 350.00
Axe, hunter's 30.00
Axe box, wooden, dovetailed corners 35.00
Bit, screwdriver; for a brace, set of 3 ....30.00
Bit, twist drill, 13/32 ....10.00
Bottle, oil; clear or bl 60.00
Bottle, oil; orig paper label, w/orig box 250.00
Brace, KA6, 6" sweep 55.00
Brace, KB, 12" 25.00
Carpenter pinchers 18.00
Carving set, stag hdls, 2-pc 35.00
Chisel, socket corner, ¾" 40.00
Chisel, 1½" 25.00
Clock, logo in center, glass w/metal fr, electric, 15" sq, EX 875.00
Concrete tool, groover, solid brass w/wood hdl, K01 ....110.00
Concrete tool, radius, solid brass w/wood hdl 125.00
Corkscrew 30.00
Draw knife, blade w/offset hdls, KLP, 8" 90.00
File box 15.00
Fork, bailing; KHB44½, 8-tine 35.00
Fork, spading; long bent hdl, 4-tine 35.00
Gauge, screw pitch 225.00
Gouge, 1½" 35.00
Grinder, corn mill; CI 120.00
Grinder, hand; logo on stone & CI holder, 7" wheel 200.00
Grinder, tool; hand crank 75.00
Hammer, ball pein; 16-oz 40.00
Hammer, saw setting; orig sticker on hdl, 7-oz 150.00
Hammer, tinner's 30.00
Hammer, upholstery 30.00
Hatchet, broad or bench, 5" to 6", ea 55.00
Hatchet, lathing 30.00
Hatchet sheath 75.00
Hoe, grub 30.00

Hoe, weeding; K3C4½ 40.00
Knife, key-chain 100.00
Knife, linoleum; K64, 3½" blade 18.00
Knife, rechargable electric, cordless, Val-Test, w/box 65.00
Knife, switchblade; Pat 1909-1910 ....400.00
Knife steel, K540, 8" 20.00
Level, wooden, KK104, 12" 45.00
Level, wooden, KK2, 28" 30.00
Mallot, wooden 65.00
Nail apron 90.00
Picnic jug, insulated w/cup on lid, bail hdl, spigot 150.00
Plane, bull-nose rabbet; K75, nonadjustable, 4" 175.00
Plane, cabinet scraper; KK79 ....50.00
Plane, corrugated bottom, K2 ....1,000.00
Plane, iron, K6 ....70.00
Plane, scrub; K240, 9½" 100.00
Plane, smooth bottom, K5½" 75.00
Plane, wooden, sawtoothed half-moon logo, 15" 55.00
Pliers, channel lock; K57 ....85.00
Pliers, combination; K160 ....25.00
Pocketknife, 2-blade, K02235N 80.00
Rake, dandelion; KLDR 30.00
Rake, garden; 12 teeth 30.00
Router, K171 ....150.00
Ruler, 8-fold zigzag, yel, K504, 48" 225.00
Saw, buck 100.00
Saw, compass; 14" 25.00
Saw, dehorning; CI w/wooden hdl 65.00
Saw, hack; K188 ....45.00
Saw, hand; K88 ....45.00
Saw set, K10 ....12.00
Screwdriver, machinist's 25.00
Screwdriver, ratchet 75.00
Screwdriver, wooden hdl, brass ferrules, 8" 30.00
Shears, pruning 25.00
Shovel, KRD2B 30.00
Shovel, scoop; all wood hdl 45.00
Speed indicator for revolving axes or spindles, K40 ....100.00
Square, K3 Blue Brand 30.00
Square, long tongue, K10, 8" 45.00
Square, sliding T-bevel; CI hdls, 10" 45.00
Tack claw, K5 ....20.00
Tape measure, Jr Steel Tape, K82 ....100.00
Weed cutter, KWCS-K 40.00
Wrench, adjustable crescent; K8 ....25.00
Wrench, adjustable S 175.00
Wrench, cape-screw; K727, ⅜ & 7/16 ....25.00
Wrench, combination alligator & screwdriver wrench, K15 ....75.00
Wrench, pipe; 18" 20.00

Kellogg Studio

Stanley Kellogg (1908-1972) opened the Kellogg Studio in Petoskey, Michigan, in 1948. It remained in operation until 1976, producing a wide range of both decorative and functional ceramics including dinnerware, vases, and figurines. Most pieces are glazed in rich, solid colors and are marked 'Petoskey' as well as 'S. Kellogg Studio' or 'Kellogg's.' Stanley Kellogg began as a sculptor, and it was while working with the great Swedish-American sculptor, Carl Milles, on an outdoor monument that Stanley suffered the back injury which forced him to turn to studio work. In addition to naturalistic treatments of Michigan wildlife, Kellogg developed some angular, architectural forms in his molded art pottery. Our coadvisors for this category are Walter P. Hogan and Wendy L. Woodworth; they are listed in the Directory under Michigan.

Bowl, burgundy gloss, 3¼", w/separate flower frog lid, 4" 25.00
Bowl, pear tree theme, 10" 20.00
Figure, Great-Horned owl on branch, brn & ivory, 7¼" 50.00
Flower frog vase, matt wht, spherical w/pentagonal rim, 3¼" 25.00
Mug, matt gr mottle, pr lake trout in relief, sq hdl, 5" 55.00
Pitcher, blk gunmetal irid, 8" 65.00
Plate, grapevine theme, 10" 8.00
Vase, lav gloss, bulbous w/tall cylinder neck, 7" 25.00
Wall plaques, 4 bluegill, plaster, 6½" & 3¼" 30.00

Kelva

Kelva was a trademark of the C.F. Monroe Company of Meriden, Connecticut; it was produced for only a few years after the turn of the century. It is distinguished from the Wave Crest and Nakara lines by its unique Batik-like background, probably achieved through the use of a cloth or sponge to apply the color. Large florals are hand painted on the opaque milk glass; and ormolu and brass mounts were used for the boxes, vases, and trays. Most pieces are signed. Our advisors for this category are Dolli and Wilfred Cohen; they are listed in the Directory under California.

Whisk broom holder, floral on red, $1,150.00.

Box, Crown mold, floral w/beadwork, ftd, 6½" dia 995.00
Box, floral, mc on autumn gr, oval, hinged, 3x5¼" 550.00
Box, floral on bl reserves w/ivory & gold, 8" sq 1,450.00
Box, floral w/beading & pastels, hexagonal, 3x3¼" 475.00
Box, lily sprays, wht on brick red, 4" dia 500.00
Box, roses on gr, rococo border, 2¾x4½" 400.00
Box, wild roses on bl w/Cigars in gold, 5" H 500.00
Box, wild roses on gray-bl mottle, 2¼x4½" dia 375.00
Ferner, floral on fuchsia, 4½x7½" 650.00
Ferner, pk flowers & emb borders, w/liner, 8½" 875.00
Ferner, wild roses on gr, 8" dia 595.00
Match holder, floral on wht, ornate hdls, 1½x2½" 500.00
Vase, floral, pk & wht on gr w/beading, ftd, 13½" 1,150.00
Vase, floral on gr, ornate SP hdls & ft, 18½" 1,595.00
Vase, tulips, purple on bl, ormolu mts, 11" 850.00

Kentucky Derby Glasses

Kentucky Derby glasses are the official souvenir glasses sold at Churchill Downs filled with mint juleps on Derby Day. Many folks who attend the Derby from all over the country take home the souvenir glass, and thus the collecting begins. The first glass (1938) is said to have either been given away as a souvenir or used for drinks among the elite at the Downs. This glass, the 1939 glass, two glasses from 1940, the 1940-41 aluminum tumbler, the 'Beetleware' tumblers from 1941-44, and the 1945 short, tall, and jigger glasses are the rarest, most sought after glasses, and they command the highest prices. In order to identify the year of a pre-1969 glass, as the year was not on the front of the glass prior to that year, simply add one year to the last date listed on the back of the glass. This is somewhat confusing, however the current year's glass is produced long before the Derby winner is determined. Our advisor for this category is Betty Hornback; she is listed in the Directory under Kentucky.

1941, aluminum 800.00
1941, French Lick 800.00
1941-44, Beetleware, from $2,500 to 4,000.00
1945, jigger 1,000.00
1945, regular 1,200.00
1945, tall 425.00
1946-47, ea 100.00
1948 ....180.00
1948, frosted bottom 200.00
1948, Iron Leige 185.00
1949 ....180.00
1950 ....425.00
1951 ....550.00
1952, Gold Cup 190.00
1953 ....135.00
1954 ....175.00
1955 ....135.00
1956, 4 variations, ea, from $150 to 250.00

1957, gold and black on frosted glass, $110.00

1958, Gold Bar 175.00
1959-60, ea 80.00
1961 ....100.00
1962 ....65.00
1963 ....50.00
1964 ....50.00
1965, from $55 to 60.00
1966, from $50 to 60.00
1967-68, ea 50.00
1969 ....47.00
1970 ....55.00
1971 ....45.00
1972-73, ea 40.00
1974, Federal (both), from $125 to 150.00
1974, mistake 18.00
1974, regular 16.00
1975, from $10 to 12.00
1976 ....14.00
1976, plastic 12.00
1977 ....10.00

1978-79, ea 12.00
1980 ....18.00
1981-82, ea 12.00
1983 ....9.00
1984 ....7.00
1985 ....9.00
1986 ....10.00
1986 (1985 copy) 18.00
1987-89, ea 9.00
1990-92, ea 7.00
1993-95, ea 5.00
1996-97, ea 3.00

Kew Blas

Kew Blas was a trade name used by the Union Glass Company of Summerville, Massachusetts, for their iridescent, lustered art glass produced from 1893 until about 1920. The glass was made in imitation of Tiffany and achieved notable success. Some items were decorated with pulled leaf and feather designs, while others had a monochrome lustre surface. The mark was an engraved 'Kew Blas' in an arching arrangement.

Bottle vase, leaves, gold irid on golden opal, 4" 675.00
Candlestick, gold irid, swirled baluster stem, wide base, 8" 250.00
Compote, gold irid, 3½x6" 300.00
Goblet, amber irid, raised rim, 5" 115.00
Goblet, golden-orange irid, baluster stem, disk ft, 7⅝" 200.00
Salt cellar, gold irid 175.00
Vase, draped loops, gold on yel, 5¼" 700.00
Vase, feathers, gr & gold irid on oyster wht, gold int, 4½" 700.00
Vase, feathers, gr & gold on dk orange irid, hdls, 5¼" 750.00
Vase, feathers, gr & gold on gold irid, ovoid, hdls, 5¾" 1,265.00
Vase, feathers, gr on gold irid cased opal, 6¾" 925.00
Vase, feathers, opal on gold, shouldered, 6" 650.00
Vase, feathers on opal/yel/gold cased, baluster, ruffled, 6" 700.00
Vase, gold irid w/pk int & swirl on base, floriform, 12⅝" 500.00
Vase, jack-in-pulpit; amber w/stretched gold irid, 12¼x8" 1,495.00
Vase, jack-in-pulpit; irid opal/pulled threads on opal, att, 9" 550.00
Vase, leaves, gold on golden opal, bottle neck, 4" 800.00
Vase, leaves, gr on gold irid, 10" 750.00
Vase, leaves, gr on wht, gold int, scalloped/incurvate, 11½" ...1,000.00
Vase, snakeskin, gr on gold irid, scalloped, 4½" 650.00

King's Rose

King's Rose was made in Staffordshire, England, from about 1820 to 1830. It is closely related to Gaudy Dutch in body type as well as the colors used in its decoration. The pattern consists of a full-blown, orange-red rose with green, pink, and yellow leaves and accents. When the rose is in pink, the ware is often referred to as Queen's Rose.

Various designs and borders, descriptions and values follow.

Coffeepot, dome lid, minor wear, 11¾" 950.00
Creamer, Queen's, geometric band at ewer-type spout, 4", EX 70.00
Creamer, Queen's, red stripe at rim & arched hdl, unmk, 4⅜" ...200.00
Creamer, 3-color, red & gr vine border, 4¼x6", EX+ 275.00
Cup & saucer, handleless; Queen's, 4-color, vine/rose rim, EX ...150.00
Cup & saucer, Queen's, swirl mold, saucer w/bl dot border 225.00
Cup & saucer, solid border, M 250.00
Cup & saucer, 3 floral reserves in rim band, NM 180.00
Cup plate, lustre-decor rim, 4½" 165.00
Plate, basketweave border, 6½" 85.00
Plate, orange rose, pk lustre X-hatched rim, 5¾", pr 120.00
Plate, pk rose, vine border, 8", NM 170.00
Plate, Queen's, 3-color, red/gr vine border, unmk, 5¼", NM 200.00
Plate, sectional border, lt wear, 9¾" 165.00
Plate, soup; 3-color, pk band w/dmn decor, unmk, 9⅞" 400.00
Plate, vine border, 9¾", EX 180.00
Plate, 3-color, pk band w/dmn decor, imp mk, 7¼", NM 125.00
Plate, 3-color, pk border w/dmn decor, imp mk, 5⅝", M 120.00
Sugar bowl, Queen's, vine border, scalloped, 5½" 185.00
Teapot, prof rpr, 6" 325.00
Teapot, Queen's, geometric border, Staffordshire, 6¼", EX 210.00
Waste bowl, solid border, minor wear, 2¾x5⅝" 200.00

Kitchen Collectibles

During the last half of the 1850s, mass-produced kitchen gadgets were patented at an astonishing rate. Most were ingeniously efficient. Apple peelers, egg beaters, cherry pitters, food choppers, and such were only the most common of hundreds of kitchen tools well designed to perform only specific tasks. Today all are very collectible. For further information we recommend *Kitchen Glassware of the Depression Years* by Gene Florence and *Kitchen Antiques, 1790-1940*, by Kathryn McNerney. See also Appliances; Glass Knives; Molds; Primitives; Reamers; Tinware; Wooden Ware.

Cast Kitchen Ware

Be aware that cast-iron counterfeit production is on the increase. Items with phony production numbers, finishes, etc., are being made at this time. Many of these new pieces are the popular cornstick pans. To command the values given below, examples must be free from damage of any kind or excessive wear and tear. Waffle irons must be complete with all three pieces and the handle. The term 'EPU' in the description lines refers to the Erie PA, USA mark. The term 'block mark' refers to the lettering in the large logo that was used ca 1920 until 1940; 'slant logo' refers to the lettering in the large logo ca 1900 to 1920. Our advisor is Grant S. Windsor; he is listed in the Directory under Virginia. See also Clubs, Newsletters, and Catalogs.

Aebleskiver pan, Griswold #32 ....35.00
Bread stick pan, Wagner #1326 ....35.00
Cake mold, lamb, Griswold #866 ....125.00
Cake mold, rabbit, Griswold 295.00
Cake mold, Santa, Griswold 600.00
Cornstick pan, Griswold #273 ....35.00
Cornstick pan, Wagner, Krusty Korn Kob, July 6, 1920 ....35.00
Dutch oven, Griswold #8 Tite Top, w/lid 50.00
Dutch oven, Griswold #9, Erie, 4¼x9¾" 60.00
Dutch oven, Wagner #6 ....100.00
Gem pan, Griswold #6, full writing 300.00
Gem pan, Griswold #8, Erie USA 250.00
Gem pan, Wagner D, solid broad center bar 45.00
Golf ball pan, Griswold #9, full writing 150.00

Griddle, Griswold #10, slant logo 50.00
Griddle, Griswold #12, lg logo, rnd 85.00
Griddle, Griswold #9, block logo 35.00
Griddle, Griswold #9, oval, slant logo 175.00
Kettle, Griswold, Erie #812X 75.00
Meatloaf pan, Griswold #977, 2¾x10⅛x5½" 450.00
Muffin pan, GF Filley #5, 8-cup 100.00
Muffin pan, Griswold #3, slant logo 500.00
Muffin pan, Griswold #9, golf ball (947 on 1 cup only) 100.00

Muffin pan, Harvest, ca 1890, 1¾x16¼x8", $200.00.

Muffin pan, R&E Pat 1856, 11-cup 50.00
Muffin pan, Wagner, cups in heart/club/dmn/spade (3 ea) 200.00
Muffin pan, Wagner, model B 35.00
Plett pan, Griswold #34 ....35.00
Popover gem pan, Wagner #2 ....350.00
Popover pan, Griswold #10, USN 125.00
Popover pan, Griswold #18 ....85.00
Roaster, Griswold #5, oval 500.00
Roaster, Wagner #7, raised letters, oval 275.00
Saucepan, Griswold, lg emblem, 2-qt 45.00
Skillet, breakfast; Griswold 5 in 1 ....200.00
Skillet, egg; Griswold #53, sq 45.00
Skillet, Griswold #14, block logo 200.00
Skillet, Griswold #15, oval 375.00
Skillet, Griswold #3, sq, rare 200.00
Skillet, Griswold #4, block logo, no smoke ring 50.00
Skillet, Griswold #4, lg logo, no smoke ring 40.00
Skillet, Griswold #5, slant logo/EPU 45.00
Skillet, Griswold #6, block logo, smoke ring 100.00
Skillet, Griswold #6, slant logo 40.00
Skillet, Griswold #8, slant logo/EPU, no smoke ring 45.00
Skillet, Griswold #8, sq, pattern #2108 ....50.00
Skillet, Griswold #9, slant logo/Erie 45.00
Skillet, Griswold #9, Victor 45.00
Skillet, Victor #7 ....50.00
Skillet, Wapak #3, Indian head medallion 125.00
Skillet lid, Griswold #11, raised letters 550.00
Skillet lid, Griswold #8, high-dome, top writing 50.00
Teakettle, Wagner #0, child's 200.00
Teakettle, Wagner #8 ....50.00
Vienna roll pan, Griswold #6 ....200.00
Waffle iron, Andersen, heart shape 125.00
Waffle iron, Griswold #11, sq 150.00
Waffle iron, Griswold #13, hotel type 1,000.00
Waffle iron, Griswold #18, Heart & Star 175.00
Waffle iron, Griswold #8, Pat 1901 ....50.00
Waffle iron, Griswold #8, Pat 1908 ....45.00
Waffle iron, Stover #7 ....85.00
Waffle iron, unmk, Am eagle design, 5½"+31" hdl 150.00
Waffle iron, Wagner, mini 225.00

Waffle iron, Wagner #8, tall stand, wood hdls, Pat 1910 ....**45.00**

Egg Beaters

Egg beaters are an unbeatable collectible. Ranging from hand helds to rotary cranks, to squeeze power, to Archimedes up-and-down models, egg beaters are America's favorite kitchen gadget. A mainstay of any kitchenware collection, egg beaters in recent years have come into their own — nutmeg graters, spatulas, and can openers will have to scramble to catch up. At the turn of the century, everyone in America owned an egg beater. Every household did its own mixing and baking — there were no processed foods. And every inventor thought he/she could make a better beater. Thus American ingenuity produced more than one thousand egg beater patents, dating back to 1856, with several hundred different models being manufactured over the years. As a true piece of Americana, egg beaters have risen in value over the past couple of years, with a half dozen mixers valued at $2,000.00 and more. But the vast majority are under $40.00, while the values of the super rare beaters continue upward. And just when you think you've seen them all, new ones always — always — turn up, usually at flea markets or garage sales. For further information, we recommend our advisor (author of the definitive book on egg beaters) Don Thornton, who is listed in the Directory under California. See also Clubs, Newsletters, and Catalogs for Kollectors of Old Kitchen Stuff (KOOKS).

A&J, tin w/wood hdl, Pat 1923, w/bowl, EX **30.00**
Art-Beck, rachet type, NMIB **40.00**
Cyclone **80.00**
Dover, hotel, 1915, 12½", EX **40.00**
Dover #11, tiny beaters **65.00**
Holts, Pat Aug 22, 1899-Ap 3, 1900, CI, 12" **40.00**
Improved Keystone, EX **175.00**
KC USA, dbl circle **75.00**
Keystone, wall mt **425.00**
Ladd Beater #0, oval metal hdl, dtd Oct 10, 1921 ......**15.00**
Silver, CI, glass bottom **250.00**
Taplin's Dover Pattern-Improved, Pat 1903 ....**45.00**
Taplin Tumbler **75.00**
Wasburn Co, turbine type **25.00**
1898 Perfection, 2 propeller blades, NM **300.00**

Glassware

Batter bowl, gr, vertical ribs, Anchor Hocking **25.00**
Batter bowl, jadite, Anchor Hocking **18.00**
Batter jug, amber, sq sides & lid, Paden City **50.00**
Batter jug, cobalt, Paden City **70.00**
Batter jug, Liberty Am Pioneer, pk **165.00**
Bottle, water; gr, flask form w/emb panels, Hocking, 32-oz **25.00**
Bottle, water; gr, flattened moon shape, Hocking **35.00**
Bottle, water; red, emb horizontal ribs below shoulder **85.00**
Bowl, cobalt, Hazel Atlas, 8½", w/metal holder **35.00**
Bowl, custard, McKee, 8" **18.00**
Bowl, Delphite, horizontal ribs, Jeannette, 5½" **60.00**
Bowl, Delphite, Jeannette, 9" **75.00**
Bowl, gr, Tufglas, 4" **10.00**
Bowl, gr, 7¾" **12.50**
Bowl, Hex Optic, pk, flat rim, 9" **25.00**
Bowl, jadite, w/decor, Hocking, 7½" **15.00**
Bowl, mixing; blk, emb rings, 9⅜" **45.00**
Bowl, mixing; gr, paneled sides, plain rim, Hocking, 11½" **25.00**
Bowl, mixing; gr, 9" **20.00**
Bowl, mixing; gr clambroth, 8¾" **25.00**
Bowl, mixing; pk, Federal Glass, 9½" **18.00**

Bowl, mixing; yel, Rest-Well, Hazel Atlas, 8¾" **40.00**
Butter dish, amber, rectangular, Federal Glass, 1-lb **35.00**
Butter dish, blk base w/crystal lid, rectangular **75.00**
Butter dish, custard, emb vertical ribs, rectangular, McKee **40.00**
Butter dish, dk amber, emb fine ribs, rectangular **60.00**
Butter dish, gr, emb Butter Cover on lid, Hazel Atlas **40.00**
Butter dish, gr, rectangular, Hocking **30.00**
Butter dish, gr, 2-lb box form **150.00**
Butter dish, pk, rectangular, bow finial on lid **60.00**
Butter dish, Red Ships on wht, rectangular, McKee **25.00**
Butter tub, amber, emb ribs, Federal **30.00**
Cake plate, pk, Snowflake pattern **22.00**
Canister, blk fired-on w/emb ribs & paper label, glass lid **25.00**
Canister, caramel, matching lid, 40-oz **75.00**
Canister, caramel w/blk letters, blk metal lid, 48-oz **100.00**
Canister, clear waffled w/blk letters & fleur-de-lis, tin lid **22.50**
Canister, cobalt w/NM wht letters, w/lid, Hazel Atlas **400.00**
Canister, cobalt w/worn wht letters, w/lid, Hazel Atlas **300.00**
Canister, custard w/blk letters, sq w/metal lid **40.00**
Canister, Delphite w/blk letters, Jeannette, 40-oz **350.00**
Canister, Delphite w/blk letters, metal lid, 48-oz **200.00**
Canister, dk amber, emb Coffee, tin lid **95.00**
Canister, Dutch boy on clear, red tin lid **20.00**
Canister, gr, emb vertical ribs, blk/wht paper label, 47-oz **45.00**
Canister, gr, sq w/rnd metal top, McKee, rare **65.00**
Canister, gr 'Taverne' scene on clear, metal lid, lg **30.00**
Canister, gr clambroth, matching lid, Hocking, 47-oz **50.00**
Canister, jade-ite w/blk letters, sq w/matching lid, 48-oz **45.00**
Canister, milk glass w/blk letters, metal lid, 48-oz **50.00**
Canister, Skokie Gr, screw-on lid, McKee, 48-oz **55.00**
Canister, wht clambroth, sq w/rnded corners, blk tin lid **35.00**
Canister, yel opaque w/blk letters, metal lid, 40-oz **75.00**
Casserole, clear w/gr finial, Pyrex, sm **14.00**
Cheese dish, clear, Sanitary Preserver **40.00**
Coaster, cobalt, Hazel Atlas **7.00**
Cocktail shaker, cobalt, barbell form, Hazel Atlas **85.00**
Cocktail shaker, dk amber, pitcher form w/emb rnd top **95.00**
Cocktail shaker, gr, chrome lid **20.00**
Coffeepot, red, Silex, metal stand, lid & hdl **200.00**
Cookie jar, blk, LE Smith **85.00**
Cookie jar, gr, bbl form **60.00**
Cup, gr, slick hdl **10.00**
Cup, soup; fired-on color, sq **4.00**
Custard cup, Skokie Gr, McKee **6.00**
Decanter, yel opaque, pinched-in sides (3), glass stopper **110.00**
Egg cup, Chalaine Bl **15.00**
Fork & spoon set, red **200.00**
Funnel, gr, Tufglas **95.00**
Gravy boat, amber, 2-spout, Cambridge **25.00**
Gravy boat & undertray, gr, Cambridge **75.00**
Grease jar, yel opaque w/blk stripe, Hocking, w/lid **45.00**
Ice bucket, blk amethyst **50.00**
Ice bucket, gr, w/metal drainer **35.00**
Ice bucket, mc rings on clear, Hocking **15.00**
Ice bucket, pk elephants on clear **25.00**
Ladle, Chalaine Bl, screw-on hdl **200.00**
Measuring cup, amber, no hdl **37.50**
Measuring cup, clear, McKee Glasbake Scientific **20.00**
Measuring cup, dk amber, 2-cup **275.00**
Measuring cup, gr fired-on, 2-cup **12.00**
Measuring cup, milk glass, Glasbake **50.00**
Measuring pitcher, Chalaine Bl, no hdl, 4-cup **1,300.00**
Measuring pitcher, pk, emb ribs, Hocking, 2-cup **40.00**
Measuring pitcher, Skokie Gr, no hdl, McKee, 4-cup **350.00**

Measuring pitcher, yel opaque, ftd, w/hdl, 4-cup 130.00
Mug, Chalaine Bl 30.00
Mug, gr clambroth 35.00
Mustard jar, Twist, pk, Heisey, w/spoon 80.00
Parfait glass, gr, emb rings, ftd, Paden City 12.00
Pickle jar, gr 100.00
Pitcher, amber, Chesterfield, paneled cylinder 90.00
Pitcher, gr, emb dmn band & vertical ribs, loop hdl 45.00
Pitcher, jade-ite, Hocking, 16-oz 20.00
Pitcher, milk; cobalt, Hazel Atlas 100.00
Pitcher, utility; pk 60.00
Pretzel jar, pk, emb ribs, matching pk lid, Hocking 75.00
Refrigerator dish, Chalaine Bl, 4x5" 50.00
Refrigerator dish, jade-ite w/matching lid, triangular 10.00
Rolling pin, clear w/cobalt hdls 250.00
Rolling pin, custard, McKee 345.00
Rolling pin, forest gr 150.00
Rolling pin, Peacock Bl 275.00
Rolling pin, Seville Yel, McKee 345.00
Rolling pin, Silvers, glass, doweled middle, wood hdls, lg 60.00
Rolling pin, wht clambroth w/wooden hdls 125.00
Scoop, gr, sm 35.00
Shaker, blk, hobnails, metal top, Fenton 30.00
Shaker, blk fired-on, sq w/rnd metal screw-on lid 10.00
Shaker, blk fired-on w/vertical ribs & paper label, metal lid 7.00
Shaker, dk gr, metal top, Owens-Illinois, sm 8.00
Shaker, fired-on color w/screw-on lid 6.00
Shaker, Skokie Gr, Roman Arch side panel, McKee 25.00

Shakers, Delfite blue, square, Jeannette, $150.00 for the pair.

Shakers, lady w/apron on custard, McKee, red metal lid 20.00
Shakers, pk, Jennyware, flat, pr 50.00
Skillet, clear, McKee Range Tec 10.00
Skillet, jadite, Fire-King, mini 40.00
Soap dish, gr clambroth 17.50
Straw holder, Peacock Bl, 1950s 250.00
Sugar bowl, Emerald-Glo, w/lid & liner 20.00
Sugar shaker, amber, metal lid, Paden City 175.00
Sundae, gr, fluted 18.00
Syrup, gr, angular hdl, metal top, Paden City 35.00
Toast holder, clear 65.00
Tray, wht clambroth, 10⅝" sq 15.00
Tumble-up set, red, pitcher+tumbler 175.00
Tumbler, gr clambroth, emb horizontal ribs, sm ft 10.00
Tumbler, Mission Juice emb on pk 25.00
Tumbler, Skokie Gr, McKee 12.00
Vase, Chalaine Bl, ruffled rim, 12" 125.00
Water dispenser, custard, McKee 140.00

Miscellaneous

Apple corer, Atceco-Std, tin, tube type, 6¾" 20.00

Apple corer, tin, rnd wood knob hdl, ca 1877 ....25.00
Apple peeler, Geo R Thompson, CI, lever action 165.00
Apple peeler, Goodell, ca 1880 ....70.00
Apple peeler, Goodell...Pat 1898, CI, turntable, EX 110.00
Apple peeler, Lockey Howland, CI, 1856, EX 110.00
Apple peeler, Reading Hdw, CI, last Pat May 22, 1877 ....95.00
Apple peeler, Reading PA 1878, CI, turntable, EX 120.00
Apple peeler, Thompson, New England Butt Co, CI, Pat 1877 ..175.00
Apple peeler, White Mountain #3, Goodell, ca 1898 ....70.00
Apple peeler, wood & iron, 1860s, 4½x3¾" on brd 195.00
Apple peeler, wrought w/wood hdl, straddle seat, 1790s, 25" L ..200.00
Apple peeler, 7" maple wheel, leather belts, on brd, 1800s 175.00
Apple peeler, 7" walnut wheel w/string pulleys on brd, 1700s 400.00
Apple peeler/corer/slicer, Tippecanoe, CI, 3-prong fork 95.00
Bean sieve, wood w/slats, moves from sq to dmn shape 195.00
Bowl scraper, plastic, Am Beauty Cake Flour, 6x6" 25.00
Box, knife scouring; wood w/sq nails, 1840s, 14½" H 110.00
Bread maker, Universal #4, Landers Frary & Clark, 1904, EX 65.00
Bread maker, Universal #8, metal, Pat Dec 25, 1906 ....65.00
Bread slicer, wood & iron, Pat Dec 20, 1867, 9x10" base 185.00
Caker turner/spatula, metal w/trn wood hdl, ca 1890, 14" 22.50
Can opener, Dazey, electric 28.00
Can opener, Never-Slip, CI w/loop hdl, Pat Nov 12, '02 ....20.00
Can opener, Vaughan's Easy Cutter, steel w/wood hdl, 1900s 7.00
Can/cap bottle opener, A&J, cast steel/wood/brass, 1920, 6" 15.00
Candy hatchet, CI, ca 1900, 8¾" 25.00
Cheese scoop/tester, narrow tin blade, maple hdl, 10¾" 70.00
Cheese slicer, iron w/fine wire blade, 1920s, 6⅞" 18.00
Cherry seeder, Champion, chrome, multiple action 45.00
Cherry seeder, Duke, Reading Hdw, Pat Pend, ca 1890, 11" 95.00
Cherry seeder, Enterprise, CI, clamp type, 1883 ....65.00
Cherry seeder, New Standard Wobbly Wheel 110.00
Cherry seeder, Rollman #8, CI/wood, clamps on, 12" 65.00
Chopper, iron, kidney-shaped 8½" blade, 22" 85.00
Chopper, sheet-iron blade, forged nails, oak hdl, 1870s, 6½" 60.00
Chopper, Starrett, Pat 5/23/1865, iron/tin on wood base 350.00
Chopper, wide crescent blade, wood hdl, 8¾", EX 140.00
Chopper, wrought blade, cast tube iron hdl, Pat Feb 1887 ....55.00
Chopper, wrought iron blade w/wood hdl, 1800s 55.00
Chopper, wrought steel, dbl blade, wood hdls, 12¼" 110.00
Churn, Dazey, 8-qt 210.00
Churn, Dazey #10, 1-qt 1,350.00
Churn, Dazey #20, words in circle, VG 300.00
Churn, Dazey #40, w/Pat date, 4-qt 140.00
Churn, Dazey #60, w/Pat date, 6-qt 140.00
Churn, Lightning, 1-qt 295.00
Churn, Lightning Butter Machine, Pat Feb 6, 1917, 2-qt 120.00
Churn, staved drum shape w/dk tin bands, crank hdl, 15x13" 135.00
Cleanser dispenser, Kleanser Kate, lady figural, ceramic 30.00
Clothes sprinkler bottle, clothespin, HP, ceramic, from $50 to 60.00
Clothes sprinkler bottle, Dutch boy, gr & wht, ceramic 135.00
Clothes sprinkler bottle, elephant w/clover, ceramic 75.00
Clothes sprinkler bottle, iron shape w/lady ironing, ceramic 70.00
Clothes sprinkler bottle, iron w/ivy, ceramic 40.00
Clothes sprinkler bottle, Mammy, ceramic, possibly Pfaltzgraff ..250.00
Clothes sprinkler bottle, Mary Maid, any color, plastic, from $15 to 35.00
Clothes sprinkler bottle, rooster, red & gr, ceramic 125.00
Cream stirrer, Bennett...Co, tin/iron, 4¾" dia, 22" L 18.00
Cutter, biscuit; Kreamer, strap hdl 10.00
Egg whisk/whip, tinned wire, paddle fr, 1930s, 10½" 10.00
Fork, cooking; Rumford, lg loop hdl 20.00
Grater, All in One Pat Pend, tin, ca 1940, 10⅝x4¼" 25.00
Grater, brass, hand-fashioned, half-rnd, 1-pc fr, 1800s, 13" 225.00
Grater, cheese; pine fr w/punched tin front, 12x8x4"+hdl 175.00

Grater, cornmeal; punched tin on pine brd, 1700s, 30x8½" **45.00**
Grater, Gilmore Pat, japanned tin, half-rnd, 1800s, 9" **15.00**
Grater, ironstone, lt gray, curved top, 5½" **55.00**
Grater, nutmeg; Edgar, bar-closed hdls **100.00**
Grater, nutmeg; Edgar, mechanical, 1896 ....**75.00**
Grater, nutmeg; Gem, Caldwell, CI/tin/wood, 1890s **125.00**
Grater, nutmeg; Rapid **395.00**
Grater, nutmeg; Snyder, 1904 ....**475.00**
Grater, nutmeg; tin & wood, mechanical, w/crank, 6" **275.00**
Grater, nutmeg; wood/CI/tin, hand-held, 7" **185.00**
Grater, tin w/heavy wire fr, 3 surfaces, hinged door, 1910 ....**32.00**
Grater, tin/nickel/wood, revolving drum type, 1930s, 8⅞" **25.00**
Grinder, meat; Regal, CI, clamps on, 1900s, 8⅞"x2½" **35.00**
Grinder, Pomeroy's #10, CI, table-top type, EX **15.00**
Grinder/grater, CI/aluminum, Germany, clamps on, NM **28.00**
Grinder/spice mill, blk CI, crank hdl, 1890s **45.00**
Ice crusher, Dazey, chrome & blk, standing style **22.00**
Juicer, Dazey Churn Co, aluminum, wall mt **17.00**
Juicer, Wearever, aluminum, counter-top, EX, EX **7.00**

**Knife holder, Nuway, red and white,
box dated 1939, M, $15.00.**

Photo courtesy Fran Carter

Knife sharpener, CI & wood, hdl trns gears, 1900s **22.00**
Kraut cutter, pine, cut-out crest w/heart, EX patina, 22" L **120.00**
Lemon squeezer, King's, CI w/glass insert, 1882 ....**95.00**
Lemon squeezer, Newman's Drum..., CI/wood, Pat...1883, 9" **95.00**
Masher, heavy wire w/wood hdl, brass collar, 9¼" **25.00**
Masher, iron bottom w/holes, wood hdl, 16" **20.00**
Masher, trn tiger-striped maple hdl, 1850s, 12½" **90.00**
Masher, trn wood w/mushroom finial, 1800s, 10¾" **25.00**
Masher, zigzag mashers work w/fulcrum action, 11½" **85.00**
Mixer, Robert's Lightning, glass bottom, w/dasher, Pat 1913 ....**45.00**
Pan, angelfood cake; Swans Down Cake Flour, tin **30.00**
Pan, chicken; Griswold #8, chrome, self-basting lid **95.00**
Pan scraper, Am-Maid Bread **75.00**
Pastry blender, NP iron, gr pnt wood hdl, 1900s, 9½" **32.00**
Pea sheller, Vaughan, hand-crank table model, EX **55.00**
Pie crimper, bone wheel, wood hdl, 5¼" **30.00**
Pie crimper, maple, 6" **30.00**
Pineapple corer, scissors type, 5½" **20.00**
Potato baker, Rumford **85.00**
Potato peeler, Hamlinite, 1920 ....**55.00**
Raisin seeder, Blk Lightning, CI, clamps on **95.00**
Raisin seeder, Enterprise #36, clamps on, Pat '05, EX **70.00**
Raisin seeder, Everett, wood w/7 curved wires, 1889-93 ....**75.00**
Raisin seeder, Gem, dtd Dec 24, 1895 ....**95.00**
Rolling pin, wht stoneware, maple hdls, 19x3" dia **200.00**
Sausage stuffer, tin, wood plunger, hand-held, ca 1860 ....**110.00**
Seive, tin, Foley Food Mill, wood hdls **12.00**
Sifter, Blood's, wooden, Pat Sept 17, 1861 ....**350.00**

Sifter, Bromwell's Measuring Sifter, tin, gr hdl, 1930s **18.00**
Sifter, Ernshaw, tin, scoop shape w/crank hdl **120.00**
Sifter, Lee's Favorite Flour, tin, crank hdl, 6x5", EX **28.00**
Sifter, Made in USA, tin & wire, gr wood knob, 1900s, 3" **15.00**
Skillet, Wearever #2510, aluminum, gr wood hdl, EX **12.50**
Slicer, vegetable; bird's-eye maple w/iron blade, 14x7" **90.00**
Slicer, vegetable; tin, str cutter w/wire fr, 1900s, 12x4" **3.00**
Slicer, vegetable; wood, 6 blades, wire pusher, 1898, 18" **95.00**
Spatula, griddle; Swans Down Cake Flour, knife style, 12½" **35.00**
Spatula, Wholesome Baking Powder, open hdl, 11½" **12.00**
Spoon, steel, pierced hole in hdl, 15½" **5.00**
Strawberry huller, Boston Huller 1894, NP brass **18.00**
Sugar nippers, wrought iron, pliers type, lines/rings, 10" **200.00**
Thermometer, candy or maple syrup; copper **60.00**
Tool, Woodward Tool Kitchen Gadget, CI, 1874, 5 uses, 5¾" L .**65.00**
Whip, cream; Fries **100.00**
Whip, cream; Horlick Cream Whipper, blk wire, 1920s, 9½" **32.00**
Whip, mayonnaise; Universal, rare **400.00**
Whisk, blk tin & wire, coiled & str, 1880s, 7½" **10.00**
Whisk, Rex Past Flour, heavy wire w/iron hdl **18.00**

Knives

Knife collecting as a hobby began in earnest during the 1960s when government regulations required for the first time that knife companies mark their product with the country of origin. The few collectors and dealers cognizant of this change at once began stockpiling the older knives made before this law was enacted. Another impetus to the growing interest in this area came with the Gun Control Act of 1968, which severely restricted gun trading. Frustrated gun dealers transferred their attention to knives. Today there are collectors clubs in many of the states.

The most sought-after pocketknives are those made before WWII. However, Case, Schrade, and Primble knives of a more recent manufacture are also collected. Most collectors prefer knives 'as found.' Do not attempt to clean, sharpen, or in any way 'improve' on an old knife.

The prices quoted here are for knives in mint condition. If a knife has been used, sharpened, or blemished in any way, its value decreases. Knives in excellent condition generally are valued at half the prices listed below. The newer the knife, the greater the reduction in value. For further information refer to *The Standard Knife Collector's Guide, 2nd Edition*, by Ron Stewart and Roy Ritchie, and *Sargent's American Premium Guide to Knives and Razors, Identification and Values, 3rd Edition*, by Jim Sargent. Our advisor for this category is Bill Wright; he is listed in the Directory under Indiana.

Key:
a/s — acorn shield	lp — long pull
bd — blade	jack — jackknife
b/s — bullet shield	LVNY — Little Valley New York
g/b — grooved bolster	s/b — slant button
imi — imitation	wb — winterbottom

Case, BM2086, pyralin hdl, 2-bd, WR Case & Sons, 3¼" **400.00**
Case, C61050, gr bone hdl, 1-bd, Tested XX, 5⅜" **450.00**
Case, G1095, gr swirl hdl, 2-bd, WR Case & Sons, Bradford PA, 5" ..**350.00**
Case, S2, sterling silver hdl, 2-bd, Tested XX, 2¼" **175.00**
Case, W1216, wire hdl, 1-bd, Case Tested, Pat 9-21-26, 3¼" **150.00**
Case, 1103ISH, walnut hdl, 1-bd, Tested XX, 1920-40, 3⅛" **110.00**
Case, 3252, hobo, yel compo hdl, 1-bd, 1 fork, Tested XX, 3¾" .**450.00**
Case, 4100SS, citrus, wht compo hdl, 1-bd, USA, 5½" **75.00**
Case, 4200SS, citrus, wht compo hdl, 2-bd, USA, 5½" **85.00**
Case, 5205½, stag hdl, 2-bd, Tested XX, 1920-40, 3¾" **400.00**
Case, 5224½, stag hdl, 2-bd, Tested XX, 3" **175.00**

Case, 53131, canoe, stag hdl, 3-bd, Tested XX, 1920-40, 3⅝" ..**1,000.00**
Case, 53131PU, stag hdl, 3-bd, lp, WR Case & Sons, 3⅝" **1,400.00**
Case, 5364TF, stag hdl, 3-bd, Tested XX, 1920-40, 3⅛" **250.00**
Case, 5391, stag hdl, 3-bd, XX, 1940-42, 4½" **1,500.00**
Case, 61048SP, Rogers bone hdl, 1-bd, XX, 1940-64, 4⅛" **100.00**
Case, 6111½, gr bone hdl, 1-bd, Case (rare), 1920-40, 4⅜" **500.00**
Case, 61213, gr bone hdl, 1-bd, Tested XX, 1920-40, 5⅜" **550.00**
Case, 6185, bone hdl, 1-bd, 10 Dot, 1970, 3⅝" **70.00**
Case, 62009RAZ, bone hdl, 2-bd, lp, XX, 3⅜" **55.00**
Case, 62042, gr bone hdl, 2-bd, XX, 1940-55, 3" **100.00**
Case, 62087, red bone hdl, 2-bd, XX, 1940-64, 3¼" **55.00**
Case, 6217R, gr bone hdl, 2-bd, Tested XX, 4" **250.00**
Case, 6227, bone hdl, 2-bd, XX, 2¾" **35.00**
Case, 6250, Rogers bone hdl, 2-bd, Case Bradford PA, 4⅜" **650.00**
Case, 6258, bone hdl, 2-bd, WR Case & Sons LVNY, 2⅞" **300.00**
Case, 6268, gr bone hdl, 2-bd, bomb shield, Tested XX, 3¼" **400.00**

Case, #6285, doctor's knife, 2-blade, Tested XX, 3⅝", $275.00.

Case, 63045, gr bone hdl, 3-bd, Tested XX, 1920-40, 3⅝" **225.00**
Case, 63092, gr bone hdl, 3-bd, Tested XX, 1920-40, 4" **325.00**
Case, 64052, bone hdl, 4-bd, XX, 1940-64, 3½" **90.00**
Case, 6445R, rough blk hdl, 4-bd, Tested XX, 1920-40, 3¾" **200.00**
Case, 6488, red bone hdl, 4-bd, XX, 4⅛" **150.00**
Case, 8151LSAB, pearl hdl, 1-bd, Tested XX, 5¼" **1,200.00**
Case, 82058, pearl hdl, 2-bd, Case Bros Cutlery Co, 2⅞" **250.00**
Case, 82063½, pearl hdl, 2-bd, Tested XX, 1920-40, 3⅛" **135.00**
Case, 8225LP, pearl hdl, 2-bd, WR Case & Sons, Bradford PA, 3" ..**350.00**
Case, 8233, letter opener, pearl hdl, 2-bd, 6¾" **225.00**
Case, 8268, pearl hdl, 2-bd, lp, Case Bros LVNY, 3¼" **250.00**
Case, 8271, pearl hdl, 2-bd, lp, XX, 3¼" **225.00**
Case, 83102SS, pearl hdl, 3-bd, XX, 1940-64, 2¾" **150.00**
Case, 8347LP, pearl hdl, 3-bd, Case & Sons Bradford PA, 4" **500.00**
Case, 84052, pearl hdl, 4-bd, Case Bros LVNY, 3¾" **900.00**
Case, 92058, bird's eyes, Fr pearl hdl, 2-bd, Tested XX, 3¼" **125.00**
Queen, 11, wb bone hdl, 1-bd, Queen Steel, 4⅛" **25.00**
Queen, 1450, blk Delrin hdl, 1-bd, Bicentennial ed w/flag, 5" **30.00**
Queen, 15, Rogers bone hdl, 2-bd, Queen Stainless, 3½" **40.00**
Queen, 19, fisherman, Rogers bone hdl, 2-bd, Big Q, 5" **80.00**
Queen, 26, serpentine, burnt orange imi bone hdl, 3-bd, 3¼" **35.00**
Queen, 48, whittler, wb bone hdl, 3-bd, Queen Steel, 3½" **45.00**
Queen, 56, smoked pearl hdl, 3-bd, Queen, 3⅜" **125.00**
Queen, 60, Barlow, wb bone hdl, 1-bd, Queen, 3½" **35.00**
Queen, 62, wb bone hdl, 1-bd, easy open, Queen Steel, 5⅜" **50.00**
Queen, 63, wb bone hdl, 2-bd, Queen Steel, 4" **30.00**
Queen, 7, Senator, wb bone hdl, 2-bd, Big Q, 2½" **35.00**
Remington, R102, blk compo hdl, 3-bd, w/chain, 3½" **140.00**
Remington, R105A, onyx hdl, 3-bd, 3⅜" **150.00**
Remington, R1073, bone hdl, 2-bd, 3⅜" **150.00**
Remington, R1233, jack, bone hdl, 2-bd, 4½" **285.00**
Remington, R1243, Barlow, blk compo hdl, 1-bd, 5" **300.00**
Remington, R1437, ivory hdl, 1-bd, 3½" **140.00**
Remington, R1630, bone hdl, 1-bd, lock-back, rare **600.00**
Remington, R165, jack, yel scale hdl, 2-bd, 3½" **125.00**
Remington, R1751, redwood hdl, 2-bd, 3½" **80.00**

Remington, R2203, bone hdl, 2-bd, 3⅜" **100.00**
Remington, R3050, jack, buffalo horn hdl, 2-bd, 4" **300.00**
Remington, R325, pyremite hdl, 2-bd, lp, b/s, 3⅞" **170.00**
Remington, R3274, cattle, pearl hdl, 3-bd, lp, g/b, 3¾" **400.00**
Remington, R3333, scout, brn bone hdl, 3-bd, a/s, bail, 3¾" **300.00**
Remington, R3443, brn bone hdl, 2-bd, 3¼" **175.00**
Remington, R3485, equal end, gold swirl hdl, 3-bd, 3⅜" **200.00**
Remington, R3555G, stockman, pyremite hdl, 3-bd, 3⅞" **250.00**
Remington, R3565, stockman, brn swirl pyremite hdl, 3-bd, a/s, 4" ...**300.00**
Remington, R3573, bone hdl, 3-bd, a/s, 3⅞" **240.00**
Remington, R3620BU, buffalo hdl, 3-bd, 4" **140.00**
Remington, R3644, pearl scale hdl, 3-bd, s/b, 4" **450.00**
Remington, R3693, whittler, brn bone hdl, 3-bd, a/s, s/b, 3½" ...**550.00**
Remington, R3843, utility, brn bone, multi-bd, bail, 4" **350.00**
Remington, R3855, pruner, imi ivory hdl, 2-bd, 4" **250.00**
Remington, R3926, stag hdl, 4-bd, a/s, 3⅞" **400.00**
Remington, R563, brn bone hdl, 2-bd, a/s, 3¼" **150.00**
Remington, R682, gunstock, blk compo hdl, 2-bd, 3" **450.00**
Remington, R706, Hawkbill, stag hdl, 1-bd, 4" **150.00**
Remington, R71, redwood hdl, 3-bd, 3⅛" **100.00**
Remington, R738, Hawkbill, cocobolo hdl, 1-bd, 4½" **120.00**
Remington, R963, Scout, imi bone hdl, 2-bd, easy open, 4¼" **350.00**
Remington, R993, blk compo hdl, 2-bd, 3¼" **115.00**
Western States, C208, jack, candy stripe hdl, 2-bd, 3⅝" **75.00**
Western States, dog-leg jack, Christmas tree hdl, 2-bd, 3" **75.00**
Western States, P319, pearl compo hdl, 2-bd w/gaff, 5" **60.00**
Western States, whittler, pearl compo hdl, 3-bd, 3⅞" **75.00**
Western States, 13208, brn & blk swirl compo hdl, 2-bd, 3⅜" **25.00**
Western States, 2106BH, pearl o/l hdl, 1-bd, 5¼" **150.00**
Western States, 2206, imi pearl hdl, 2-bd, drilled bolster, 5⅛" **65.00**
Western States, 2230, pearl o/l compo hdl, 2-bd, 4½" **125.00**
Western States, 241, pen knife, imi pearl hdl, 2-bd, 2⅝" **25.00**
Western States, 3100, pearl o/l compo hdl, 1-bd, 5¼" **125.00**
Western States, 342, red sparkle hdl, 3-bd, 3⅝" **45.00**
Western States, 4149F, florist, imi ivory hdl, 1-bd, w/bail, 3⅞" **40.00**
Western States, 6100, bone hdl, 1-bd, etched buffalo skull, 5⅜" ...**300.00**
Western States, 6206, bone hdl, 2-bd, blk iron bd/cap pins, 5⅛" **65.00**
Western States, 643, whittler, pearl comp hdl, 3-bd, 3¼" **35.00**
Western States, 7256F, agate compo hdl, 3-bd, 2⅞" **45.00**
Western States, 8244, pearl hdl, 2-bd, etched 2nd bd, 3" **40.00**

Kosta

Kosta glassware has been made in Sweden since 1742. Today they are one of that country's leading producers of quality art glass. Two of their most important designers were Elis Bergh (1929-1950) and Vicke Lindstrand, artistic director from 1950 to 1973. Lindstrand brought to the company knowledge of important techniques such as Graal, fine figural engraving, Ariel, etc. He influenced new artists to experiment with these techniques and inspired them to create new and innovative designs. Today's collectors are most interested in pieces made during the 1950s and '60s. Our advisor for this category is Abby Malowanczyk; she is listed in the Directory under Texas.

Bowl, Colora, int amethyst/gr lines, gr ft, Lindstrand, 3x6" **950.00**
Bowl, Kraka fishnet, bl/amber/dk bl, Palmquist, #495, 3½x7½" .**750.00**
Plate, 1972 Christmas, cobalt, Sgn V Lindstrand **65.00**
Vase, compressed circular form w/mc appl ribbon, Valien, 12" ...**125.00**
Vase, encased algae/eng fish, Lindstrand/#42348, rstr rim, 6¾" ..**175.00**
Vase, eng feathers, oval rim & ft, Lindstrand #52451, 8½" **400.00**
Vase, frosted w/scenic enameling, slim, 12" **125.00**
Vase, gr-cased bl & clear, int trails, Lindstrand, #1590, 8 ....**700.00**
Vase, int wht trails, Lindstrand/LH1153, 1955, 12" **400.00**

Vase, thick gr layer in clear w/cut window, #55171, 6½"	600.00
Vase, thick gr-bl w/clear layers/diagonals, Lindstrand, 6"	450.00
Vase, Trad I Dimma, trees in fog, Lindstrand, LU2005, 13"	2,990.00
Vase, Unikate, blk trails at bottom, Lindstrand, #2004, 14"	300.00
Vase, yel w/bl rim, clear thick ft w/1 bubble, #01845, 5x5"	300.00

Kutani

Kutani, named for the Japanese village where it originated, was first produced in the seventeenth century. The early ware, Ko Kutani, was made for only about thirty years. Several types were produced before 1800, but these are rarely encountered. In the 19th century, kilns located in several different villages began to copy the old Kutani wares. This later, more familiar type has large areas of red with gold designs on a white ground decorated with warriors, birds, and flowers in controlled colors of red, gold, and black.

Bowl, fish among waves int/ext, 19th C, 3⅛x5¼", EX	250.00
Cup, gods of good fortune, calligraphy inscription, 2", pr	135.00
Plate, karako/birds/flowers in rust red, 1880s, 8½"	90.00
Vase, 2 ladies in outdoor scene in oval panel, flask form, 5"	150.00
Vase, 2 reserves on brocade ground, foliage hdls, rpr, 20"	325.00

Labels

Before the advent of the cardboard box, wooden crates were used for transporting products. Paper labels were attached to the crates to identify the contents and the packer. These labels often had colorful lithographed illustrations covering a broad range of subjects. Eventually the cardboard box replaced the crate, and the artwork was imprinted directly onto the carton. Today these paper labels are becoming collectible — primarily for the art, but also for their advertising appeal. Our advisor for this category is Cerebro; their address is listed in the Directory under Pennsylvania.

Unless otherwise noted, values are given for examples in excellent to near-mint condition.

Apple, Chief Josef, Indian portrait, 1940, M	7.50
Apple, L-Z, boy taking bite of apple, M	15.00
Apple, Oregon Apples, bl/red/yel	5.00
Apple, Page, bellboy holding plate of apples, M	8.00
Apple, Tennis, lg tennis racket, 1930, M	30.00
Blackberries, Menlo, tropical road & berries, M	10.00
Cigar box, Adam & Eve, couple running through garden, 6x9", M	4.00
Cigar box, Belle Ami, buxom woman, 4½" sq, M	14.00
Cigar box, Ben Tracy, male portrait & naval ships, 6x9", M	17.00
Cigar box, Checkers, men playing checkers, 6x9", M	35.00
Cigar box, Clitus, 3 Greek runners, 4½" sq, M	15.00
Cigar box, Darby, ram & gold coins, 6x9", M	15.00
Cigar box, Eureka, woman & flowers, 6x9"	20.00
Cigar box, First National, bank, cars & trolley, 6x9", M	18.00
Cigar box, Florine, pretty girl, 4½" sq, M	10.00
Cigar box, Golden Grit, bundle of tobacco leaves, 6x9", M	3.00
Cigar box, Grey Horse, man on horse, 4½" sq, M	6.00
Cigar box, Herco, Arab desert scene w/camel & pyramids, 6x9"	12.00
Cigar box, Indio, Art Deco image of Indian head, 6x9", M	10.00
Cigar box, Javotte, 1930 image of pretty woman, 6x9", M	15.00
Cigar box, Lilia, woman holding box of cigars, 4½" sq, M	15.00
Cigar box, Little African, stone litho, 4x4"	140.00
Cigar box, Meisterschaft, rower, 4½" sq, M	40.00
Cigar box, Nabors, boys on fence, 4½" sq, M	50.00
Cigar box, Our Sport, hunter & 2 dogs, 4½" sq	50.00

Cigar box, Radio Queen, stone litho	100.00
Cigar box, Remus, bust of Roman w/condor on shoulder, 6x9", M	17.00
Cigar box, Ribble, yacht on open seas, 4½" sq, M	35.00
Cigar box, Sam Houston, bust portrait, 4½", M	7.00
Cigar box, Sheik, sphinx, pyramids & star, 6x9", M	5.00
Cigar box, Taft, presidential portrait, 4½" sq, M	35.00
Cigar box, William Penn, portrait w/signature, 4½" sq	12.00
Citrus, Boss, wht-bearded southerner, M	7.50
Citrus, Crescent Moon, orange grove at night, 1930	6.00
Citrus, Florida Cowboy, cowboy on bucking bronco, 1930, M	10.00

Citrus, Flyer, Cucamonga Citrus Fruit Growers Assn. Cucamonga, Cal., $600.00 minimum.

Citrus, Kiss-Me, 2 children, 1940, M	8.00
Corn, Just the Cob, lady cleaning ears of corn, M	12.00
Corn, Sailor Brand, sm mountainous creek, VG	15.00
Elderberries, Epicure, man holding can, fruit & berries, G	8.00
Honey, Lone Star, view of Alamo through star, M	5.00
Lemon, Basketball, women playing basketball, 1920	50.00
Lemon, Index, hand pointing at lemons, 1920, M	7.00
Lemon, Montecito Valley, orange grove, stone litho, 1920, M	24.00
Orange, Atlas, Atlas w/globe on bk, 1930, M	35.00
Orange, Double Brand, orange train, 1930, M	4.00
Orange, Home of Ramona, southwest hacienda, 1900, M	175.00
Peaches, Bonner Brand, packing house & peach	25.00
Peaches, Sun-Lite, jars, bottles & bowl of peaches	15.00
Pear, Big City, NYC skyline at night, 1930, M	3.00
Pear, Placer, view of gold mining camp, 1930, M	15.00
Pear, Westside, view of valley, M	4.00
Peas, West Shore, tropical village & bowl of peas	12.00
Pineapple, Golden Sheaf, pineapple plate & emb wheat, 1931, M	15.00
Pumpkin, Marshall, seal on pumpkin	3.00
Salmon, Yacht, sailboat & salmon, M	10.00
Tomatoes, Boris, lg tomato & crest of sm eagle, M	5.00
Tomatoes, OK Brand, lg tomato & country scene w/buck	18.00
Vegetable, Larsen's Veg-All, vegetables & bowls, 1929	5.00

Labino

Dominick Labino was a glass blower who until mid-1985 worked in his studio in Ohio, blowing and sculpting various items which he signed and dated. A ceramic engineer by trade, he was instrumental in developing the heat-resistant tiles used in space flights. His glassmaking shows his versatility in the art. While some of his designs are free-form and futuristic, others are reminiscent of the products of older glasshouses. Because of problems with his health, Mr. Labino became unable to blow glass himself; he died January, 10, 1987. Work coming from his studio since mid-1985 has been signed 'Labino Studios, Baker,' indicating ware made by his protegee, E. Baker O'Brien. In addition to her own compositions, she continues to use many of the colors developed by Labino.

Bowl, gr & opal free-form, 1981, 3½"	700.00

Bowl, opaque pulls in amber, 1977, 7" **800.00**
Bowl, silver schmeltz, 1982, 6½" **850.00**
Cordial, red to amber, twisted air-bubble stem, 1969, 6½" **1,000.00**
Cup, smoky w/red rim, 1967, 3½" **450.00**
Decanter, amber, 4 prunts ea on bottle & stopper, 1977, 11½" ..**1,400.00**
Emergence, cylinder w/2 pinched/pulled rings, 1983, 4½" **6,250.00**
Emergence, dbl veil & encased air, 1976, 6" **6,100.00**
Figurine, duck, bl, 1983, 4" **275.00**
Figurine, owl, apple gr irid, 1981, 4" **400.00**
Figurine, owl, swirled opal, 1973, 4½" **700.00**
Panel, clear, cast by Labino, from mold by Carder, 1983, 5x6½" ...**350.00**
Panel, gr w/brn, 18x18" **800.00**
Paperweight, clear gr w/tulips, 1968 ....**450.00**
Paperweight, floral, 1967, sm **425.00**
Pitcher, silver-red, 1984, 4½" **450.00**
Sculpture, gr w/brn ribbon, 1968, 5" **1,300.00**
Sculpture, pear form, pk veil, pencil-neck opening, '77, 5½" ..**1,000.00**
Vase, amber irid, spherical w/4 prunts, 1968, 4½" **600.00**
Vase, amber w/clear bubbles, spherical, 1983, 3" **550.00**
Vase, amber-gr w/red/yel/bl sprays, 1970, 9" **1,800.00**
Vase, amethyst, bulbous, 1969, 6½" **700.00**
Vase, amethyst w/encased air bubble, bulbous, 1967, 7½" **1,700.00**
Vase, bl w/air bubbles, 1983, 3½" **550.00**
Vase, bl w/brn design & bubbles, 1968, 5½" **750.00**
Vase, bl w/free-hand sculptured loops, bulbous, 1982, 6" **425.00**
Vase, brn-bl Copper Glass, sgn, 1967, 10" **425.00**
Vase, bud; copper-red, 1982, 6½" **450.00**
Vase, clear opal w/prunts, 1980, 8" **750.00**
Vase, clear w/mc motif & bl veil, sq, 1984, 5½" **800.00**
Vase, clear w/silver loopings, 1968, 10" **1,700.00**
Vase, clear w/yel & bl swirled festoons, 1972, 4½" **900.00**
Vase, copper-red, pear form, 1973, 3½" **300.00**
Vase, copper-red, 1985, 2¼x6" **350.00**
Vase, copper-red w/amber tones, wide rim, paneled sides, '67, 6" ..**850.00**
Vase, gr opal w/2 elongated prunts, 1965, 8" **950.00**
Vase, gr w/aventurine, 1970, 4¾" **2,800.00**
Vase, gr w/gr & bl festoons, ovoid, 1970, 5½" **1,000.00**
Vase, hobnails, amber w/red rim, 1963, 3½x5" **2,000.00**
Vase, lt bl w/wht dinosaur, 1979, 3¾" **1,100.00**
Vase, lt milky bl, narrow base, 1966, 6" **375.00**
Vase, mc cased in clear, sq, 1982, 4¾" **600.00**
Vase, mc design w/veil, sq, 1984, 4½" **650.00**
Vase, opaque to brn w/gr flecks, 1965, 4½" **550.00**
Vase, purple w/everted rim, 1966, 7½" **400.00**
Vase, red irid w/clear elongated paneled sides, 1983, 6¼" **650.00**
Vase, silver schmeltz, wide rim, 1968, 6" **1,500.00**
Vase, silver w/mottled surface, squat, 1970, 3¼" **950.00**
Vase, smoky bl, encased air, 1968, 8¼" **1,950.00**
Vase, smoky w/brn design, bulbous, 1968, 7¾" **700.00**
Vase, wht texture on amber w/4 gr prunts, 1968, 4½" **900.00**
Vase, yel encased in clear, bottle form, 1979, 5¾" **525.00**
Vase, yel festooning w/bl vertical stripe, ovoid, 1975, 4" **1,000.00**
Vase, yel opal, pinched, 1966, 5½" **1,000.00**

Lace, Linens, and Needlework

Two distinct audiences vie for old lace and linens. Collectors seek out exceptional stitchery like philatelists and numismatists seek stamps or coins — simply to marvel at its beauty, rarity, and ties to history. Collectors judge lace and linens like figure skaters and gymnasts are judged: artist impression is half the score, technical merit the other. How complex and difficult are the stitches and how well are they done? The 'users' see lace and linens as recyclables. They seek pretty wearables or decora-

tive materials. They want fashionable things in mint condition, and have little or no interest in technique. Both groups influence price.

Undiscovered and underpriced are the 18th-century masterpieces of lace and needle art in techniques which will never be duplicated. Their beauty is subtle. Amazing stitches often are invisible without magnification. To get the best value in any lace, linen, or textile item, learn to look closely at individual stitches and study the design and technique. The finest pieces of any lace, linen, or textile are wonderfully constructed. The stitches are beautiful to look at and do a good job of holding the thing together. Our advisor for this category is Elizabeth M. Kurella; she is listed in the Directory under Michigan.

Key:
embr — embroidered   ms — machine sewn
hs — hand sewn

Photo courtesy Lace Merchant

Detail of 19th-century needle lace and embroidery tablecloth, 66x123", with fifteen napkins, $925.00.

Bedspread, bl chintz w/mc birds & flowers, braid trim, 114x60" .**140.00**
Bedspread, linen & crochet panels, dbl sz, NM **175.00**
Bedspread, Marseilles lace, cutouts for bed posts, full sz **250.00**
Bedspread, silky damask, pnt cherubs/urns/etc, dbl sz **250.00**
Blanket, pk silk w/embr flowers, baby's **25.00**
Bonnet, baby; Ayrshire bk, needle lace & embr, ca 1830 ....**65.00**
Bridal veil, 8" long teardrop, 14" needle-lace border, rprs **1,100.00**
Collar, Battenberg, full circle, button circles, lg, EX **125.00**
Collar, crochet, tightly worked modern style, ivory **25.00**
Coverlet, lindsey woolsey, red/blk plaid w/red/bl edge, 2-pc **440.00**
Cuffs, Battenberg, graceful points in front, wht, pr **25.00**
Doily, Battenberg, grapes & leaves, 10" dia **75.00**
Doily, crochet, Cupid center, 11½" sq **45.00**
Doily, linen center w/2" lace border, 10" **25.00**
Doily, needle lace, solitary rose design, beige, 5½" dia **10.00**
Fichu (sm shawl), machine lace, wht, 19th C, 10½x36", VG **75.00**
Flounce, lace dbl-headed eagles/scrolls/etc, 18th C, 8½x36" **950.00**
Handkerchief, hairpin lace **45.00**
Handkerchief, 2" deep tatted edge, medallions w/picots, 20th C ..**25.00**
Handkerchief, 5" Point-de-Gaze needle lace, 1870s, 18" sq **350.00**
Lace fragment, English Honiton bobbin edging lace, 20" L **175.00**
Lace fragment, Mechlin bobbin lace, 18th C, 2½x8" **55.00**
Lace panel, filet, ecru, Grecian lady & cherubs, 10x23" **75.00**
Lappet, Argentan needle lace, joined, ca 1740, G **475.00**
Lappet, Brussels bobbin lace, ca 1740, 22" dia, damaged, pr **650.00**
Lappet, Point-de-Gaze needle lace, joined, ca 1870, 32" **150.00**
Mattress cover, bl/red/wht plaid homespun, wear, 56x60" **135.00**
Mattress cover, bl/wht gingham homespun, machine sewn, 72x60" ..**75.00**
Needle lace fragment, cherubs/bows/flowers/etc, 19th C, 11x14" .**75.00**
Needle lace initial, set in lacy oval, 2x1½" **10.00**

Needlework panel, bird on floral branch, petit point, 14½" fr **95.00**
Needlework panel, flowers/trees/etc, silk embr, 1811, 16x19" **495.00**
Needlework panel, lady & child, English, 1800s, 21x16" **275.00**
Needlework panel, man at door, lady at window, fr, 27x26" **275.00**
Parasol, cream silk w/embr mc flowers/gold accents, 18th C ...**2,500.00**
Pillowcase, crochet edge, pr **35.00**
Pillowcase, drawnwork florals, 15x13", pr **35.00**
Runner, Battenberg, 17x54" **135.00**
Runner, filet lace, cherubs in center, 18x42" **145.00**
Runner, filet lace, ladies w/flower baskets, 16x50" **135.00**
Runner, wht, 6" Hardanger border, 15½x40" **135.00**
Sham, bleached homespun w/embr flowers, knotted fringe, 1825 ..**110.00**
Shams, Battenberg, buttoned bk, lace edge, 16" sq, pr **165.00**
Shams, 16" Battenberg center, buttoned bk, 30x30"+ruffle, pr ..**155.00**
Shawl, machine-mace Chantilly lace, ca 1860s, from $45 to **75.00**
Sheet, bl & wht check homespun, rolled hem, 70x57", EX **370.00**
Sheet, wht homespun, folded top hem, rolled bottom, 89x76" ..**100.00**
Show towel, homespun, drawnwork flower panel, 59x14" **115.00**
Show towel, homespun w/cutwork stars/ladies & embr, 60x18" .**360.00**
Show towel, X-stitch embr of flowers/etc, sgn/1836, 51x20" **400.00**
Show towel, X-stitch flowers/animals/birds/name/1847, 8x18" ...**165.00**
Show towel, X-stitch flowers/hearts/etc, sgn/1849, 55x19" **140.00**
Tablecloth, Battenberg inserts, 110", +12 napkins **350.00**
Tablecloth, Battenberg trim, 40x40", EX **135.00**
Tablecloth, Battenberg vintage pattern, 49" dia **175.00**
Tablecloth, crochet, ecru floral, fringed border, 36" dia **60.00**
Tablecloth, homespun, brn/natural, machine hemmed, 74x58" .**135.00**
Tablecloth, homespun, gold & wht check, hand hemmed, 40x68" ..**220.00**
Tablecloth, homespun cotton w/stitched wool florals, 36x36" ...**115.00**
Tablecloth, homespun linen, wht-on-wht pattern, 38x71", EX **85.00**
Tablecloth, homespun w/woven bird's-eye dmns, 52x74" **55.00**
Tablecloth, homespun w/woven geometrics, fringed, 51x70" **75.00**
Tablecloth, Irish linen, 84x70", +10 napkins **70.00**
Tablecloth, linen, Cluny lace inserts & edge, 92" dia **325.00**
Tablecloth, linen, ecru, Cluny lace medallions, 136" L **225.00**
Tablecloth, linen w/wht & natural floral designs, 60x76", pr **100.00**
Tablecloth, Madeira lace, 72" dia **150.00**
Tablecloth, needle lace, beige, 19th C, 70x104", +10 napkins ...**725.00**
Tablecloth, wht lawn, 82x65", +6 napkins w/cutwork & embr ..**115.00**
Tablecloth, wht linen, woven floral, fringe, 1900s, 100x54" **100.00**
Tablecloth, wht w/floral needle lace openwork, banquet sz **450.00**
Tablecloth, 5" Cluny lace border, scalloped center, 22" dia **195.00**

Lacy Glassware

Lacy glass became popular in the late 1820s after the development of the pressing machine. It was decorated with allover patterns — hearts, lyres, sheaves of wheat, etc. — and backgrounds were completely stippled. The designs were intricate and delicate, hence the term 'lacy.' Although Sandwich produced this type of glassware in abundance, it was also made by other Eastern glassworks as well as in the Midwest. By 1840, its popularity on the wane and a depressed economy forcing manufacturers to seek less expensive modes of production, lacy glass began to be phased out in favor of pressed pattern glass.

Reference numbers correspond with *Sandwich Glass* by Ruth Webb Lee. When no condition is indicated, the items listed below are assumed to be without obvious damage; minor roughness is normal. See also Salts, Open.

Bowl, Beaded Scale, flake, 1¼x4½" **20.00**
Bowl, Crossed Swords, violet-bl, 4½", NM **120.00**
Bowl, flower baskets/Gothic arches/stars, scalloped, 2¼x10" ..**2,750.00**
Bowl, Gothic Arch, w/lid, 5½x7", NM **1,200.00**

Bowl, Industry, att NE Glass, 6⅜", EX **150.00**
Bowl, Oak Leaves, scalloped, 7¼", EX **50.00**
Bowl, Peacock Eye w/Rayed center, ftd, 6½", NM **375.00**
Bowl, Princess Feather Medallion, 7⅜", NM **80.00**

Bowl, Scotch Plaid, 7¾", $100.00.

Bowl, steamboat center, 8-sided, 6" dia, NM **775.00**
Casket, Gothic Arch, w/undertray, 5½x7" overall, EX+ **3,250.00**
Compote, paneled/scalloped wafer, lobed base, 4½x7" **50.00**
Compote, Petticoat Dolphin, fiery wht opal, tooled rim, 5⅝" **145.00**
Compote/sweetmeat, Oak Leaves/geometrics, 1830-40, 3¼x5¼" ...**200.00**
Creamer, Heart & Scale, att NE Glass, 4½", EX **60.00**
Dish, Roman Rosette, purple amethyst, 5½" **275.00**
Honey dish, Lee/Rose #301, lt sapphire bl, 3⅞" **70.00**
Mustard pot, Peacock Feather, 1830-45, 2½x2⅞", EX **350.00**
Nappy, Tulip & Acanthus Leaf, 7½" dia, EX **75.00**
Plate, Eagle, 8-sided, scalloped, 6", NM **80.00**
Plate, Hairpin, flake, 6¼" **60.00**
Plate, heart design, sapphire bl, 5⅞", EX **350.00**
Plate, Oak Leaves, canary, att NE Glass, 4¾" **500.00**
Plate, pine tree & shield motif at border, 6", NM **100.00**
Plate, Roman Rosette, dk amethyst, ca 1835-50, 5⅜" **200.00**
Plate, Roman Rosette center, fiery wht opal, chip, 6" **30.00**
Plate, scallops, points, dmns & fans, att NE Glass, 6¼" **300.00**
Platter, locomotive & 3 passenger cars, 9x12" **85.00**
Sand shaker, vertical beading, pierced pewter top, 2⅞" **900.00**
Sugar bowl, feather & dmn design, milk glass, w/lid, 6" dia **850.00**
Sugar bowl, Gothic Arch, canary, w/lid, 1840-60, 5¼" **750.00**
Sugar bowl, Gothic Arch, dk amethyst, 5½", EX **3,500.00**
Sugar bowl, Loop, wafered std, w/lid, 9¾" **350.00**
Sugar bowl, Providence, w/lid, 6", EX+ **1,500.00**
Tumbler, Gothic Arch, 2⅝" **950.00**

Lalique

Beginning his lengthy career as a designer and maker of fine jewelry, Rene Lalique at first only dabbled in glass, making small panels of cire perdue (wax casting) to use in his jewelry. He also made small flacons of gold and silver with his glass inlays, which attracted the attention of M.F. Coty, who commissioned Lalique to design bottles for his perfume company. The success of this venture resulted in the opening of his own glassworks at Combs-la-Ville in 1909. In 1921 a larger factory was established at Wingen-sur-Moder in Alsace-Lorraine. By the '30s Lalique was world renown as the most important designer of his time.

Lalique glass is lead based, either mold blown or pressed. Favored motifs during the Art Nouveau period were dancing nymphs, fish, dragonflies, and foliage. Characteristically the glass is crystal in combination with acid-etched relief. Later some items were made in as many as ten colors (red, amber, and green among them) and were occasionally accented with enameling. These colored pieces, especially those in black, are highly prized by advanced collectors.

During the '20s and '30s, Lalique designed several vases and bowls reminiscent of American Indian art. He also developed a line in the Art Deco style decorated with stylized birds, florals, and geometrics. In addition to vases, clocks, automobile mascots, stemware, and bottles, many other useful objects were produced. Most items made before his death in 1945 were marked 'R. Lalique'; later the 'R' was deleted even though some of the original molds were still used. Numbers found on the bases of some pieces are catalog numbers. Beware of fraudulent pieces that have begun to surface in increasing numbers. Our advisor for this category is John Danis; he is listed in the Directory under Illinois.

Key:
cl/fr — clear and frosted   RL — signed R. Lalique
L — signed Lalique   RLF — signed R. Lalique, France
LF — signed Lalique France

Ashtray, dog figure at center, smoked glass, RLF, #290, 3½" **325.00**
Ashtray, Vezelay, dmn w/leaves, amber fr, RL, 4½x4½" **275.00**
Blotter, Faun et Nymphe, fr w/silver metal, RL, 2x6½x3⅜" **850.00**
Bottle, Helene, scarf dancers/fr chanels, RLF, 9" **750.00**
Bottle, scent; Amphritite, nymph, bl, RL, 4" **2,100.00**
Bottle, scent; Camille, lappets, emerald gr, RLF, 2¼" **750.00**
Bottle, scent; Clairefontaine, cl/fr, flower stopper, LF, 4½" **100.00**
Bottle, scent; Duncan, dancing females, cl/fr, LF, 7½" **350.00**
Bottle, scent; Panier de Roses, clear w/gray enamel, RL, 4" **1,000.00**
Bottle, scent; tulips, cl/fr, RL, 6½" **200.00**
Bowl, coupe; Oeillets, carnations, cl/fr, LF, 2½x14" **350.00**
Bowl, Gui #1, berries/branches, gr, RL, 3⅜x8" **900.00**
Bowl, Lys, lilies, opal, 4-ftd, 4⅞x9⅜" **500.00**
Bowl, Ondines Ouverte, 6 nymphs, opal, RLF, #380, 8" **800.00**
Bowl, Pinsons, birds among grasses, cl/fr, LF, 3¾x9¼" **150.00**
Bowl, Poissons #1, fish & bubbles, opal, RL, 9½" **500.00**
Bowl, Raisins & Pans, paneled grapes, cl/fr, 2x5", 6 for **350.00**
Box, Fleurettes, brn enamel patina at edges, RLF, #580, 3¼" **375.00**
Box, powder; Fleurs d'Amour, metal, R Gallet, RLF **125.00**
Box, powder; Girland de Graines, seed border, fr, RL, 1⅞x4" **375.00**
Box, Quatre Papillons, fr/opal, Lalique, 1½x3⅛", NM **350.00**
Box, Roger, birds & circles, cl/fr, LF, 5¼" dia **140.00**
Box, Trois Figurines, fr, for D'Orsay, RL, 1½x3¾", EX **150.00**
Cordial, Pouilly, bl tint, RL, 3¼" **50.00**
Goblet, Le Souvenir de Reims, angel, cl/fr, LF, 8¼" **100.00**
Lamp base, Mesanges, wreath w/birds, cl/fr, LF, 6½" **125.00**

Luminaire, Gross Poisson Vagues, R. Lalique, France, without base, 12", $3,850.00.

Luminaire, Oiseau de Feu, bird-woman, cl/fr, RLF, 17" **10,000.00**
Mascot, Archer, cl, NP mt, RLF **1,000.00**
Mascot, Coq Nain, rooster, #1135 ....**395.00**
Mascot, Levrier, greyhounds, cl/fr, RLF, 2¾x7½" **2,200.00**
Mascot, Longchamps, horse head, cl w/blk base, RLF **1,500.00**
Plate, Asters, concentric beaded ovals, cl/fr, RLF, 10¾" **400.00**
Plate, Caravelle, nautical, cl/fr, LF, 8½" **125.00**
Sculpture, cat, seated, fr, LF, 8¼" **500.00**
Sculpture, Chouette, owl, RL, #1193 ....**325.00**
Sculpture, Crucifixion, on heavy pyramidal lighted stand, 20x11" ..**500.00**

Sculpture, Putto, fr, block Lalique mk, 3¾" **100.00**
Statuette, Source de Fontaine Calypso, fr, RLF, 27⅛" **4,000.00**
Statuette, Suzanne, outstretched arms w/drapery, RLF/#822, 9" ...**5,500.00**
Tumbler, Chinon, scrolls, cl/fr, RL, 4¾" **50.00**
Vase, Acanthus motif, red bulging sides, RLF, #929, 7" **6,000.00**
Vase, Avalon, bird & berry, fr on yel, RLF, 6x5½" **1,850.00**
Vase, Bacchantes, nudes, fr, RLF, 4¾" **550.00**
Vase, Bacchantes, nudes, opal, RLF, 9¾" **5,500.00**
Vase, Bandes de Roses, bl wash on cl, LF, 9¼" **575.00**
Vase, Borromee, peacock heads, bl, ovoid, RLF, 9" **1,950.00**
Vase, Chevals, stallions, fr, LF, 6x7¾" **300.00**
Vase, Coquille, scallop shells, fr, RLF, 7" **200.00**
Vase, Davos, sharkskin pattern, amber, RLF, 11½" **1,000.00**
Vase, Domremy, thistle pods, fr, RLF, 8¾" **600.00**
Vase, Domremy, thistle pods, gray fr, RLF, 8½" **1,500.00**
Vase, Espalion, fern fronds, opal, RLF, #996, 7" **600.00**
Vase, Ferrieres, cl/fr, RLF #848019, 7½x5" **900.00**
Vase, Formose, goldfish, red, spherical, RLF, #934, 6¾" **1,200.00**
Vase, Gui, berries/foliage, fr opal, RLF, H 9948, 6½" **600.00**
Vase, Laurier, laurel, fr/gr wash, RL, 7" **635.00**
Vase, Le Mans, rooster, gr w/fr, RLF, 4" **1,600.00**
Vase, Lizards et Bluets, blk, RL emb/F eng, 13x9" **3,100.00**
Vase, Malines, leaves, cl/fr, spherical, 11", EX **1,600.00**
Vase, Marisa, fish, fr/bl wash, globular, RLF/#1002, 9" **2,800.00**
Vase, Mimosa, leaves, brn stain, #953 ....**925.00**
Vase, Oleron, swirling fish, fr, spherical, RLF, #1008, 3½" **575.00**
Vase, Oursin, sea urchin, sepia wash on fr, RLF, 7⅛" **750.00**
Vase, Pallissy, mollusks, bl wash/fr, RLF, #980, 4½" **1,100.00**
Vase, Papillon, butterflies, cl/fr, LF, 3¾" **90.00**
Vase, Perruches, lovebirds on branches, bl, 10x9" **2,875.00**
Vase, Pinsons, birds/berries, wht opal/cl, RL, 7¼x9" **1,500.00**
Vase, Piriac, fish band, cl/fr, #1043, 6½" **550.00**
Vase, Poissons, fish, bright gr, spherical, RL, 9¼" **5,500.00**
Vase, St Cloud, leaves, cl/fr, urn form, Cristal LF, 4⅝" **150.00**
Vase, St Marc, cl/fr, ca 1950, 6½" **445.00**
Vase, Tournai, fr/opal, RLF, 5¾" **800.00**

Lamps

The earliest lamps were simple dish containers with a wick that hung over the edge or was supported by a channel or tube. Grease and oil from animal or vegetable sources were the first fuels used. Ancient pottery lamps, crusie, and Betty lamps are examples of these early types. In 1784 Swiss inventor Ami Argand introduced the first major improvement in lamps. His lamp featured a tubular wick and a glass chimney. During the first half of the 19th century, whale oil, burning fluid (a highly explosive mixture of turpentine and alcohol), and lard were the most common fuels used in North America. Many lamps were patented for specific use with these fuels.

Kerosene was the first major breakthrough in lighting fuels. It was demonstrated by Canadian geologist Dr. Abraham Gesner in 1846. The discovery and drilling of petroleum in the late 1850s provided an abundant and inexpensive supply of kerosene. It became the main source of light for homes during the balance of the 19th century and for remote locations until the 1950s.

Although Thomas A. Edison invented the electric lamp in 1879, it was not until two or three decades later that electric lamps replaced kerosene household lamps. Millions of kerosene lamps were made for every purpose and pocketbook. They ranged in size from tiny night or miniature lamps to tall stand or piano lamps. Hanging varieties for homes commonly had one or two fonts (oil containers), but chandeliers for churches and public buildings often had six or more. Wall or bracket lamps usually had silvered reflectors. Student lamps, parlor lamps (now called Gone-With-the-Wind lamps), and patterned glass lamps were designed to complement the popular furnishing trends of the day. Gaslight, introduced in the early 19th century, was used mainly in homes of the wealthy and public places until the early 20th century. Most fixtures were wall or ceiling mounted, although some table models were also used.

Few of the ordinary early electric lamps have survived. Many lamp manufacturers made the same or similar styles for either kerosene or electricity, sometimes for gas. Top-of-the-line lamps were made by Pairpoint, Phoenix, Tiffany, Bradley and Hubbard, and Handel. See also these specific sections.

When buying lamps that have been converted to electricity, inspect them very carefully for any damage that may have resulted from the alterations; such damage is very common, and when it does occur, the lamp's value may be lessened by as much as 50%. Lamps seem to bring much higher prices in some areas than others, especially the larger cities. Conversely, in rural areas they may bring only half as much as our listed values. One of our advisors for lamps is Carl Heck; he is listed in the Directory under Colorado. See also Stained Glass.

Key:
ab — acorn burner   Ob — O burner
hb — hornet burner   pb — pinafore burner
nb — nutmeg burner   Vb — P&A Victor burner

Aladdin Lamps, Electric

From 1908 Aladdin lamps with a mantle became the mainstay of rural America, providing light that compared favorably with the electric light bulb. They were produced by the Mantle Lamp Company of America in over eighteen models and more than one hundred styles. During the 1930s to the 1950s, this company was the leading manufacturer of electric lamps as well. Still in operation today, the company is now known as Aladdin Industries Inc., located in Nashville, Tennessee. For those seeking additional information on Aladdin Lamps, we recommend *Aladdin — The Magic Name in Lamps; Aladdin Electric Lamps;* and *A Collector's Manual and Price Guide,* all written by our advisor for Aladdins, J. W. Courter; he is listed in the Directory under Kentucky. Mr. Courter has also published a book called *Angle Lamps, Collector's Manual and Price Guide.*

Bed lamp, #909SS, Whip-o-lite fluted shade, EX 200.00
Bed lamp, B-45, Whip-o-lite shade, EX 85.00
Bedroom, P-52, ceramic, EX 30.00
Bedroom, P-68, ceramic, EX 35.00
Boudoir, E-410, glass, early, EX 60.00
Boudoir, G-203R, Alacite, EX 40.00
Boudoir, G-36, Alacite, floral base, 1946, EX 75.00
Boudoir, M-91, metal, 1937, EX 50.00
Bridge, #2062, EX 225.00
Bridge, #2079, walnut, EX 300.00
Bridge/table, #7091, EX 225.00
Figurine, G-16, lady, etched crystal, EX 600.00
Figurine, G-375, Dancing Ladies Urn, EX 950.00
Figurine, G-79, rooster, EX, minimum value 1,200.00
Floor, #1005, MOP glass bowl, w/night light, EX 375.00
Floor, #3348, Type A, EX 150.00
Floor, #3358, IES reflector, EX 225.00
Floor, #3460, reflector, EX 175.00
Floor, #3690, reflector, candle arms, EX 200.00
Floor, #3767, 2 15" florescent tubes, EX 175.00
Floor, #3994, Alacite ring, candle arms, w/night light, EX 300.00
Glass Urn, G-213A, Alacite, closed urn, EX 225.00

Glass Urn, G-379, Alacite, tall ribbed urn w/top, EX 150.00
Jr floor (lounge), #1060, candle arms, EX 175.00
Magic Touch, MT-507, ceramic base, EX 350.00
Magic Touch, MT-520, cherry & brass base, EX 500.00
Pin-Up, G-351, Alacite, wall medallion, EX 100.00
Pin-Up, P-57, Gun-'n-Holster, ceramic, EX 125.00
Ranch House, G-335C, Topper horse head w/shade, Alacite, EX .750.00
Table, #785, Lg Vase, tan, EX 225.00
Table, E-201, Vogue ped, gr, EX 450.00
Table, G-U, brass & marble, EX 100.00
Table, G-179, Opalique, EX 100.00
Table, G-197, illuminated base, EX 80.00
Table, G-2, marble-like glass, EX 325.00
Table, G-255, Alacite, illuminated base, EX 70.00
Table, G-308, Alacite, EX 60.00
Table, G-60, short harp, EX 100.00
Table, G-85, EX 150.00
Table, G-97, crystal, EX 125.00
Table, M-1, metal, bronze, EX 100.00
Table, M-448, metal, tripod base, EX 30.00
Table, M-495, brass metal, EX 25.00
Table, P-401, ceramic, EX 40.00
Table, P-430, ceramic, EX 40.00
Torchier floor, #3760, EX 300.00
Torchier floor, #4598, EX 250.00
TV lamp, M-367, blk iron base w/shade, EX 30.00
TV lamp, TV-384, shell, ceramic, EX 75.00

Aladdin Lamps, Kerosene

Aladdin Vase Model #12, ebony, 10¼", EX 500.00
Aladdin Vase Model #12, tan, 12", EX 200.00
Caboose Model B, B-400, brass font, EX 200.00
Floor Model B, #1257, ivory & gold, EX 175.00
Floor Model B, B-284, silver & gold, EX 200.00
Floor Model B, B-425, gold plated & ivory lacquer, EX 200.00
Florentine Vase Model #12, gr moonstone, 8½", EX 2,200.00
Hanging, Model #3, w/#203 shade, EX 700.00
Hanging, Model C, aluminum hanger & font, w/paper shade, EX ..100.00
Practicus, parlour lamp, polished brass or Old English, EX 600.00
Shelf, Model #23, Lincoln Drape, clear, EX 100.00
Table, Model #11, nickel, EX 120.00
Table Model #23, Short Lincoln Drape, amber, 1981, EX 100.00
Table Model A, Venetian, peach, EX 150.00

Photo courtesy J.W. Courter

Table Model B, Tall Lincoln Drape, with 14" Whip-o-lite shade, old, M, $275.00.

Table Model B, B-53, clear, EX **75.00**
Table Model B, Beehive, B-83, EX **550.00**
Table Model B, Corinthian, B-126, wht & rose moonstone, EX ...**250.00**
Table Model B, Orientale, B-131, gr, EX **175.00**
Table Model B, Quilt, B-91, wht & rose moonstone, EX **325.00**
Table Model B, Short Lincoln Drape, B-60, EX **500.00**
Table Model B, Simplicity, B-29, gr, EX **125.00**
Table Model B, Washington Drape, B-49, amber crystal, EX **375.00**
Wall Bracket Model #6, complete **200.00**

Angle Lamps

The Angle Lamp Company of New York City developed a unique type of kerosene lamp that was a vast improvement over those already on the market; they were sold from about 1896 until 1929 and were expensive for their time. Our Angle lamp advisor is J.W. Courter; he is listed in the Directory under Kentucky. See the narrative for Aladdin Lamps for information concerning popular books Mr. Courter has authored.

Hanging, #224, nickel, rose floral, no glass, EX **750.00**
Hanging, #263, polished brass, old glass, EX **475.00**
Hanging, #284, antique brass, no glass, EX **500.00**
Hanging, #352, polished brass, 3-burner, no glass, EX **600.00**
Hanging, Classic #2, antique gold, no glass, EX **1,400.00**
Hanging, EG-22, nickel, old glass, EX **550.00**
Wall, #102, nickel, old glass, EX **350.00**
Wall, #104, nickel, grape pattern, no glass, EX **275.00**
Wall, #163, polished brass, old glass, EX **275.00**
Wall, #285, antique brass, old glass, EX **1,000.00**
Wall, Classic #3, antique gold, no glass, EX **1,000.00**
Wall, EG-12, nickel, extended grape, no glass, EX **275.00**
Wall, Leaf & Vine, nickel, old glass, EX **400.00**
Wall, plain grape, nickel, old glass, EX **425.00**

Chandeliers

Baccarat-style cut glass, 6-light, electrified, Fr, 40x39" **1,980.00**
Blk metal, cut crystal, 10-light, lg prisms, Fr, 31x29" dia **450.00**
Colonial trn cherry & wrought iron, 5 lights for candles **350.00**
Continental Rococo style, 18-light, lg prisms/crystals, 26x24" ...**1,200.00**
Empire-style gilt/patinated bronze, 4-light, 21½x17½" **700.00**
Gilt bronze, 5-light, scrolled arms, electrified, 19th C, 26x21" ...**770.00**
Louis XV style, brass, 6-light, prisms, 28x28", pr **1,875.00**
Louis XVI style, gilt/pnt bronze, 20-light, cage form, 29x19" **880.00**
Neoclassical-style brass & crystal, 8-light, 5-tier, 36x34" **550.00**
QA, brass, 5 removable S-scroll arms, 21x27½" dia **3,080.00**
Venetian glass, 6-light, floral std & sphere pendant, 33" **1,900.00**
Victorian-style gilt ormolu mts/8-branch/putti supports, 48" ...**1,800.00**
Wrought iron, 8-sided, amber inserts, 4 sets of 3 arms, EX **300.00**

Decorated Kerosene Lamps

Amethyst to clear, brass shaft, marble/brass base, 1860s, 11" **650.00**
Amethyst to clear, wht opaque base, Sandwich, 1860s, 9½", G ...**350.00**
Bl cut to clear font, scalloped hex base, NE Glass, 11¼" **1,100.00**
Bl cut to wht to clear, 3-dolphin base, Sandwich, 12½", EX ...**2,000.00**
Blown bucket-like font on pressed flower base, Sandwich, 8½" .**125.00**
Blown/pressed, wht opaque shades, NE Glass, 1850s, 11½", pr ...**2,185.00**
Canary, loop font, sq monument base, 2-burner, Sandwich, 12½" ..**550.00**
Clear w/gray mahog base, Sandwich, 1875-78, 9x3½", EX **400.00**
Cobalt cut to clear/frosted flowers, brass ft, 7" shade **900.00**
Cranberry cut to clear, dbl-step marble ft, Sandwich, 21", EX ...**2,500.00**
Cranberry cut to clear, wht opaque base w/gilt, 12½" **385.00**
Fiery opal cut to clear, marble base, brass stem, 7¾" **300.00**

Milk glass cut to pk font w/pnt decor, wht marble base, 15" **330.00**
Onion, lav, orig brass collar/connector, 1865-80, Sandwich, 12" ..**5,000.00**
Pk cut to clear, milk glass stem/ft, Sandwich, 18½", EX **1,250.00**
Red cut to clear, wht sq base, Sandwich, 8½x3½", EX **500.00**
Sanded clambroth font w/acanthus decor, marble base, 11½" **100.00**
Tulip cuttings, clear/frosted, turned-over rim, Sandwich, 6½" ...**160.00**
Vaseline w/opal swirls, finger lamp **335.00**

Fairy Lamps

Baby's head, emerald gr frost, pyramid sz, 4½x2⅝" **175.00**
Bl frost w/cut flowers, clear ribbed Clarke base, 4¾x3⅝" **175.00**
Bl nailsea 8" dome shade, ruffled base, Clarke insert, 6½" **695.00**
Bl verre moire frost, mk Clarke insert, 5¼x6¼" **600.00**
Burmese, Clarke base, 4¾x3⅞" **295.00**
Burmese, clear base, Webb, pyramid sz, 3¾" **245.00**
Burmese, crimped skirt, mk Webb & Sons, #138 shape, 5½" **950.00**
Burmese, flat/crimped base, Webb, Cricklite insert, 3½" **750.00**
Canary yel to wht MOP, Herringbone, ball shade, 5¼" **1,250.00**
Coralene, yel wheat on turq to wht, Clarke insert, 5½" **375.00**
Cranberry Dmn Quilt, clear Clarke base, 4¾" **275.00**
Custard w/HP floral branch, cup-shaped base, 5" **385.00**
Owl figural, bsk w/brn & gold pnt, Noritake, 7", EX **350.00**
Red nailsea, domed shade on ribbed base, camphor ft, 6" **450.00**
Red nailsea w/clear Cricklite insert, 5½x6¾" **935.00**
Rubena, Dmn Quilt, ruffled, clear Clarke base, 6¼x3¾" **225.00**
Turq Dmn Quilt, clear Clarke base, 4¾" **195.00**
Yel Dmn Quilt, clear Clarke base, 4¾" **195.00**

Gone-With-the-Wind and Banquet Lamps

Victorian pattern in red satin, electrified, EX plating, 27", $500.00.

Floral on pk rpt ball shade, brass & onyx fr, 33", EX **250.00**
Floral rpt on yel, bl & pk, wht metal & onyx body, 32½", EX **200.00**
Indian w/dead goose on milk glass, 10" ball shade/std, 27", EX ...**800.00**
Pk cased font, emb cranberry to clear shade, 3-tier, 24½" **500.00**
Red satin w/emb dragon, 26", VG+ **350.00**
Victorian scene on wine & gold porc std; cranberry shade, 25" ..**600.00**

Hanging Lamps

Bl Dmn Quilt MOP w/butterfly & floral, brass mts, 18" **550.00**
Ceiling, Rayo, brass, kerosene, gilt metal fr, 38x14", pr **250.00**
Cranberry Invt T'print, complete, 9x6" **350.00**
Cranberry Optic Expanded Bull's Eye shade, red brass fr, 11½" ..**125.00**
Cranberry swirl shade in red brass fr, 12½", EX **150.00**
Peachblow melon-rib 14" shade/font, rtcl brass fr, Sandwich ..**2,000.00**
Pk opal bell-shape shade, clear orig font, brass fr, 14" **240.00**
Pk opal swirl shade in red brass fr, 11½", EX **150.00**

Red satin, Coin Spot, ball shade, brass fr, pressed font, 27" 250.00
Wht font/ball shade w/mc bird in rushes, CI fr mk Pat 1875 ......900.00

Lanterns

Brass bell shape w/blown/etched globe, 19th C, 18x9¾" 900.00
Pierced tin w/clear paneled globe, Am, late 1800s, 11", EX 175.00
Pierced tin w/cobalt blown globe, Am, 19th C, 10¾" 750.00
Pierced tin w/ruby NE Glass globe, 10¾"+hdl, EX 750.00
Skater's, tin w/gr glass globe, Am, late 1800s, 6½" 375.00
Street, copper, England, 19th C, electrified, 21x16", EX 275.00
Tavern, copper, 8-sided, glass panels, faceted top, 32x15" 330.00
Tin, beveled glass sides, brass kerosene burner, 8¾", VG 250.00
Tin w/pierced florets, clear insert mk NE Glass Co, 17¼" 250.00

Lard Oil/Grease Lamps

Betty, miner's, wrought w/heart finial, gold pnt, 4" w/hanger 200.00
Betty, wrought iron, bird finial on lid, 4", w/hanger 150.00
Betty, wrought iron, heart finial, swivel lid, 4½", EX 110.00
Crusie, dbl, iron w/lacy scrollwork, delicate hanger, 12½" 325.00
Crusie, dbl, wrought iron, twisted hanger, 6" 125.00
Kettle, brass, heavy iron gimbal hanger, 6½" 215.00
Kettle, iron/brass, pencil std, 3-ftd saucer base, 9" 300.00
Pottery, bright gr glaze, lg hdl, European, 9½" 125.00
Rush, iron, 3-leg, shoe ft, spring-operated, 9½" 465.00
Rush, wrought, w/counterbalance, rpl burl base, 12½" 165.00
Rush, wrought iron, blk pnt, ca 1900, 8¼x4x4" 230.00
Rush, wrought iron, w/candle socket counterweight, 9½" 385.00

Miniature Lamps, Kerosene

Amber Log Cabin, hb, 3⅝", EX 500.00
Amber shoe form, hb, 3" 900.00
Amberina ball shade/bell-shaped base, lt ribbing, nb, 9", EX 500.00
Amberina umbrella shade/ball base w/amber ft & 'leaves,' 8", EX ...1,050.00
Amberina w/amber ruffle, silver ribbed std mk EPBM/#d, 10" 800.00
Bl crackle o/l swirl ball shade/base w/clear shell ft, nb, 8" 700.00
Bl Dmn Quilt MOP, sq base, orig brass mts, 10⅛x4½" 1,250.00
Bl opaque swag/acanthus-emb umbrella shade/sqd base, nb, 8" ..550.00
Bl opaque w/emb swirl-rib onion shade/squat base, hb, 7¾" 225.00
Bl Raindrop MOP, cobalt chimney, ruffled bowl shade, ftd, nb, 8" ..550.00
Bl satin tulip-shaped shade/emb ogee base, 9", EX 800.00
Bl satin umbrella shade/shouldered base w/emb florals, nb, 8" 800.00
Canary satin Dmn Quilt, brass burner, 2¾" 165.00
Clear opal Snowflake, allover intricate silver filigree, 7" 1,050.00
Clear w/opal swirls in pyriform shade/base, 6¼" 350.00
Cobalt o/l w/Bohemian-cut vintage to chimney & hdld base, 9" 450.00
Cranberry opal Coin Spot ball shade/font, clear stem/ft, nb, 8" ..2,300.00
Cranberry swirl, rnd silver swirl base mk JB TD&S/EPBM #, 9" .450.00
Cranberry swirl ovoid shade w/flared rim, ball base, hb, 8", EX ..425.00
Dk amethyst Twinkle, collar ball shade/onion base, ac, 7" 225.00
Figural bsk base: girl w/cart, wicker shade, nb, 9" 250.00
Gr opaque ball shade/base w/emb floral & fishnet, nb, 7½" 350.00
Gr opaque ball shade/shouldered base w/emb scrolls & floral, 8" ..500.00
Gr satin Beaded Drape ball shade/shouldered base, nb, 9½" 250.00
Gr satin undulating/veined ball shade/sq base, nb, 8", EX 345.00
Log Cabin, Pat Sept 30 1868, rpl collar, 3⅜" 200.00
Milk glass, emb umbrella shade/ovoid base w/red & gr floral, 8" ..250.00
Milk glass, pk/bl pnt, emb eagle, ball shade/gourd base, nb, 8" ...300.00
Milk glass Artichoke, pk/gr pnt, ribbed/shouldered base, nb, 8" .100.00
Milk glass ball shade w/bl Delft pnt, sq porc base, 6", EX 350.00
Milk glass ball shade/base emb as owl body, nb, 8" 1,450.00
Milk glass Pan-Am Expo, bl-gr ball shade/base, nb, 9", EX 450.00

Milk glass w/bl & gray Delft, ball shade, ab, Pairpoint, 8" 600.00
Milk glass w/pnt owl face on ball shade, body on base, nb, 8" 800.00
Owl figural, bsk w/naturalistic pnt, Capo di Monte, 5¼" 4,000.00
Owl head-shape base, porc w/bl & tan, gilt, Dietz Doyle, 4" 400.00
Parrot, wht porc, amber eyes, tan beak, brn base, SP/L #d, 6½" .750.00
Pk Dmn Quilt MOP, sqd/ruffled/dimpled, camphor ft, 10" 950.00
Pk opal Rib, sqd base, brass burner, Monot & Stumpf, 9¾" 1,300.00
Pk opal shade w/ruffled crown, acorn base w/clear ft, 7½", EX ..1,300.00
Pk-cased ball shade/cylinder base emb w/ribs & sprigs, 8" 650.00
Pk-cased melon rib umbrella shade/shouldered base, nb, 7", NM ..250.00
Pk-cased satin ball shade w/emb pansy faces, ribbed base, 7" 300.00
Red satin, tulip-shape shade/emb shouldered base, nb, 9", EX 325.00
Santa Claus figural, red/bl pnt, ab, 9½", EX 2,300.00
Sapphire bl to clear ball shade, orig brass burner, 10x3½" 450.00
Sapphire bl w/floral, ribbed, ftd urn base w/crimp edge, 6½" 900.00
Skeleton bust, wht bsk w/pastel trim, glass eyes, 5½" 4,000.00
Spatter Beaded Swirl ovoid shade w/flared crown, squat base, 8" ..300.00
Spatter swirl-emb ovoid shade w/flared rim, petal ft, 9", EX 1,050.00
Wht opal Reverse Swirl rnd shade/font, brass saucer base, 7½" ..700.00
Yel-cased acorn shade/shouldered bombe-shaped base, nb, 7" 500.00
Yel-cased Cone-emb umbrella shade/ball base, nb, 8" 500.00
Yel-cased umbrella shade/cylinder base w/floral & gold, nb, 8" ..800.00

Motion Lamps

Animated motion lamps were made as early as 1920 and as late as 1980s. They reached their peak during the 1950s when plastic became widely used. They are characterized by action created by the heat of a light bulb which causes the cylinder to revolve and create the illusion of an animated scene. Some of the better-known manufacturers were Econolite Corp., Scene in Action Corp., and LA Goodman Mfg. Co. As with many collectible items, prices are guided by condition, availability, and collector demand. Values are given for lamps in mint condition. Any damage or flaws seriously reduce the price. Our advisors for motion lamps are Kaye and Jim Whitaker; they are listed in the Directory under Washington.

Bar Is Open, blk plastic, 1970, 13" 40.00
Budweiser, advertising, blk w/lights, 12" 35.00
Butterflies, Econolite, 1954, 11" 105.00
Carousel, plastic, 1960s, 5" 55.00
Christmas tree, plastic, LA Goodman, 1952, 17" 55.00
Colonial fountain, glass/metal, Scene in Action, 1931, 10" 150.00
Flames, metal/plastic, Scene in Action, 1931, 10" 135.00
Forest fire, LA Goodman, 1956, 11" 95.00
Fountain of Youth, Econolite (Roto-Vue Jr), 1950, 10" 125.00
Indian Chief, plaster/glass, Gritt Inc, 1920, 11" 95.00
Mateus Wine, blk w/lights, 1980s, 12" 50.00
Mill scene, Econolite, 1956, 11" 95.00
Niagara Falls, Econolite, 1955, 11" 85.00
Ships, bronze/plastic, Rev-O-Lite, 1930, 10" 110.00
Snow scene, Econolite, 1957, 11" 115.00
Spirit of '76, Creative Light Prod, 1973, 11" 35.00
Steam boats, Econolite, 1957, 11" 110.00
White Christmas, flat front, Econolite, 11" 95.00

Pattern Glass Lamps

Acanthus, bl opaque font on wht base, dbl burner, 1830s, 13" 1,600.00
Allover Bull's Eye, stand lamp 165.00
Apollo, amber, nb, 9" 95.00
Aquarius, amber, stem lamp, #2 burner, 10" 125.00
Arch font on hexagonal tiered base, reattached collar, 11¼" 75.00
Atterbury Head, emb faces, hb, finger lamp, flat, 4", EX 225.00
Berkshire, appl hdl, 2¾" 70.00

Bull's Eye, clear font on emerald gr stem/ft, 9¼" 250.00
Chapman, milk glass font, Atterbury base, dtd 1868, 10" 130.00
Checkered Star Band, stand lamp, 6½" 185.00
Dmn & Fan, amber, finger lamp, flat, 3¾", EX 55.00
Dmn Sawtooth & Sheath, w/hdl, 3⅜", EX 85.00
Heart, gr opaque, stem lamp, #2 burner, 9¾", EX 175.00
Heart, opaque custard, finger lamp, ftd 425.00
Leaf & Jewel, ftd, w/hdl, 5" 200.00
Peacock Feather, amber, #1 burner, stem lamp, 8" 190.00
Pompeian Swirl, verre-de-soie, Harrach, 1890s, 22x8½" 550.00
Prince Edward, pk cased, 4 medallions, all orig, 16½" 955.00
Princess Feather, brass collar & burner, w/chimney, 13" 125.00
Riverside Fern, gr font, clear beaded ft, stand lamp 200.00
Sheldon Swirl, vaseline, #1 burner, stem lamp, 8", EX 225.00
Shield & Star, finger lamp, flat 175.00
Star & Punty, bl opaque to sapphire bl, hex base, Sandwich, 8½" ...3,000.00
Star & Punty, orig brass collar, 9¾", EX 100.00
Sweetheart, brass columnar stem, sq marble base, 10¾" 75.00
Sweetheart front on hexagonal base, orig collar, 9½" 135.00
Triple Flute & Bar font, blk glass base, stem lamp, #1, 9¾" 150.00
Venetian, bl opal, #1 burner & chimney, finger lamp, 6", NM ...250.00

Peg Lamps

Cranberry glass w/HP florals, orig burner, 5⅝x3⅜" 125.00
Cranberry w/frosted rubena cut shade, orig burner, 13" 295.00
Cut glass font: frosted w/stars, Adelphi SP stick, 11", pr 775.00
Dmn Quilt, rubena, gilt wht metal figural candlestick, 17x5" 450.00
Gr w/HP floral & gilt, bronze Rococo std, Paris burner, 16" 295.00
Robin's egg bl shade & font w/emb decor, brass base, 15", pr ..1,500.00
Ruby font, brass std, 12" 160.00
Yel swirl MOP, orig burner, 6x3⅜" 165.00

Reverse-Painted Lamps

Phoenix Lamp Company
(attributed), 17" peacock
shade, gilt-metal 2-socket base,
22", $1,200.00.

Classic, 19" bell shade w/trees; bronze hex urn std, 23" 1,300.00
Jefferson, 22" landscape/ducks/moon shade; emb gilt std, 22" ..1,500.00
Moe Bridges, 15" trees/water blk-on-orange shade; blk std 1,800.00
Moe Bridges, 17" landscape pebbled shade; mk urn std, 24" 975.00
Pittsburgh, att; 18" Taj Mahal shade; 2-socket std, 22" 1,600.00
Pittsburgh, 14" palm scenic on chipped glass; bronze std, 22" 700.00
Pittsburgh, 16" water lily shade; urn-form metal base, 20½" 900.00
Pittsburgh, 16½" swan scenic shade; 2-socket bronze std, 22" .1,150.00
Unmk, 14" autumn sailing scene shade; Deco std, 21" 1,250.00
Unmk, 14" floral 4-panel shade; VG pnt-CI fluted std, 19" 230.00
Unmk, 16" Lakes of Killarney shade; leaf/swag-emb std, 23" 850.00
Unmk, 16" Phoenix-type windmill shade; on VG std, 23" 750.00
Unmk, 17" cottage scene shade; mc/gilt-metal std, 24" 1,150.00
Unmk, 17" peacock on wall shade; gilt-metal 2-socket std, 22" ..1,200.00
Unmk, 18" evening landscape; blk rose-emb stem std, 24" 1,500.00
Unmk, 18" fall scene on peachblow sky shade; urn std, 24" 2,040.00

Unmk, 18" man in coastal scene shade; gilt metal std, 26" 1,350.00
Unmk, 8" floral frosted #3114C shade; pnt opal std, 13" 500.00
Unmk, 8" rural scenic shade; pnt #148 std, 16½" 320.00

Student Lamps, Kerosene

Brass with old 6" milk glass
shade, 16", EX, $250.00;
Nickel-plated brass with old
10" milk glass shade, $550.00
minimum value.

Brass, gr ribbed 7" dia shade, Manhattan, electrified, 22" 450.00
Brass, Miller's Ideal No 0 burner, later milk glass shade 110.00
Double, GA Kleeman, NY, NP brass, 19½" 600.00
Double, Miller, 2-arm, verdigris on metal, 21½" 550.00
Double, yel brass w/cased shades, electrified, 27x23", EX 500.00

Whale Oil/Burning Fluid Lamps

Blown bell-shaped font, aqua, brass collar, 4⅝" 200.00
Blown conical font, lemon-squeezer stem, sq base, 10" 160.00
Blown conical font on lacy base, rpl brass collar, 9", EX 65.00
Blown font on ball stem, pressed stepped base, 6", EX 80.00
Blown font on knopped stem, rnd ft, pontil scar, 1830s, 6¼" 125.00
Blown rnd font, dbl-ball solid stem, dbl burner, 9" 650.00
Blown rnd font attached w/peg, hollow stem, rnd base, 7⅝" 160.00
Blown rnd font joined by wafers to pressed sq base, 5¾" 80.00
Blown rnd font w/appl lip, hollow stem, rnd base, 9⅛", EX 80.00
Blown urn shape w/wafers, lacy base, dbl burner, 9", EX 150.00
Blown wht opaque globe, wht opal lion-head base, Sandwich, 8½" 400.00
Pressed, acanthus, orig brass collar, 12¾", NM 170.00
Pressed, cobalt, sq base w/8-sided paneled font, 1850s, 9½" 920.00
Pressed, emerald gr, sq base, 8-sided paneled font, 1850s, 9½" ...1,840.00
Pressed, Waffle & T'print, hex star base, dbl burner, 9⅝" 300.00
Pressed canary yel font, acanthus leaf base, Sandwich, 13" 925.00
Pressed/blown, scroll std/paw-ft base, Sandwich, 10½", pr 635.00

Lang, Anton

Anton Lang was a German studio potter and an actor in the Ober-ammergau Passion Plays early in the 20th century. Because he played the role of Christ three times, tourists brought his pottery back to the U.S. in suitcases, which accounts for the prevalence of smaller examples today. During 1923-1924 Anton Lang and the other 'Passion Players' toured the U.S. selling their crafts. Lang would occasionally throw pot-tery when the cast passed through a pottery center such as Cincinnati, where Rookwood was located. His pottery, marked with his name in script, is fairly scarce and highly valued for its artistic quality. His son Karl designed most of the Art Deco shapes and conducted glaze experi-ments. Only pieces bearing a hand-written signature (not a facsimile) are certain to be Anton Lang originals instead of the work of Karl or the Langs' assistants. Postcards, programs, and photographs depicting Lang are also collectible. The pottery is now owned and operated by Karl's daughter, Barbara Lampe. Our advisor for this category is Clark Miller; he is listed in the Directory under Minnesota.

Bowl, decor, Germany, 4x5½" 160.00
Chamberstick, windmill, HP blk/gr on tan, hand sgn, 6x4½" 150.00
Leaf dish, w/hdl 45.00
Pitcher, feathered bl bands on beige, 4½" 75.00
Pitcher, floral, mc/HP on tan, hand sgn, 6¾x6" 150.00
Pitcher, flower emb on gunmetal, 4¾x4¾" 75.00
Pitcher, gr drip over oxblood, indents on body, 6½x6" 225.00
Vase, bulb, mustard w/brn int, hand sgn, 5x5" 75.00
Wall pocket, Art Deco, brn, 7½x3½" 175.00

Le Verre Francais

Le Verre Francais was produced during the 1920s by Schneider at Epinay-sur-Seine in France. It was a commercial art glass in the cameo style composed of layered glass with the designs engraved by acid. Favored motifs were stylized leaves and flowers or geometric patterns. It was marked with the name in script or with an inlaid filigrane. Our advisor for this category is Don Williams; he is listed in the Directory under Missouri.

Key: fp — fire polished

Cameo

Bowl, roses, red on ivory/bl, dk knobbed bun ft, 9x9" 850.00
Box, sunflowers/geometrics, gr/orange/amethyst, 2⅝" 900.00
Ewer, carnations, orange/brn on bl/yel mottle, angle hdl, 13" 950.00
Lamp, berries/leaves, red/bl/orange/frost, 10" shade, 17" 3,000.00
Lamp, floral 18" dome shade; matching base, 18½" 4,885.00
Lamp, fruit, red frost/maroon 9" shade, wrought fr, hanging 1,600.00
Lamp, perfume; Deco floral, pk/bl/rose/maroon, leaf base, 6" 920.00
Lamp, poppies, dk pk on lt pk/purple frost, hanging, 12" L 1,500.00
Pitcher, grapes/leaves, red/maroon on yel, trailing hdl, 12" 1,100.00
Vase, floral, golden orange/amber/yel/orange, oviform, 6½" 775.00
Vase, floral, orange/clear/variegated yel, 1920s, 8" 600.00
Vase, floral, orange/purple on ivory/purple, bun ft, 22x6" 1,100.00
Vase, floral, pk-lav/orchid/purple, heavy walls, 11¼" 1,950.00
Vase, floral, red on yel mottle, blk ft, 12" 850.00
Vase, free-forms, red/gr/mc mottle, bottle form, 14" 635.00
Vase, fruit repeats, red/maroon, tricorner rim, 7" 635.00
Vase, geometrics, lt bl/gr on amber, no mk, bottle form, 5½" 300.00
Vase, poppies, red on yel, 13½" 1,000.00
Vase, 3 fruit baskets, brn on yel/orange, tapering/ftd, 21" 1,800.00

Leeds, Leeds Type

The Leeds Pottery was established in 1758 in Yorkshire and under varied management produced fine creamware, often highly reticulated and transfer printed, shiny black-glazed Jackfield wares, polychromed pearlware, and figurines similar to those made in the Staffordshire area. Little of the early ware was marked; after 1775 the impressed 'Leeds Pottery' mark was used. From 1781 to 1820, the name 'Hartley Greens & Co.' was added. The pottery closed in 1898.

Today the term 'Leeds' has become generic and is used to encompass all polychromed pearlware and creamware, wherever its origin. Thus similar wares of other potters (Wood for instance) is often incorrectly called 'Leeds.' Unless a piece is marked or can be definitely attributed to Leeds by confirming the pattern to be authentic, 'Leeds-Type' would be a more accurate nomenclature.

Key:
cw — creamware   pw — pearlware

Bowl, allegorical & ships w/verse, blk transfer, 8¾" 250.00
Bowl, mc floral, hairline, 4¼x9¼" 140.00
Cup & saucer, handleless; mc foliage, flakes 180.00
Cup plate, mc floral, gr feather edge, 4½", NM 185.00
Jug, lion pattern, silver resist, ca 1810, 4½" 500.00
Pitcher, pw, bl & wht Leeds decor, 7½", EX 330.00
Plate, Am Eagle crest, molded gr shell rim, 8" 650.00
Sauce boat, flowers & berries, bl on wht, mk, 1800s, 4½" 180.00

Tea caddy, creamware, flower clusters and vines, face within flower on front and back, flowering tree on sides, late 18th century, 8½x5¼x4", $1,000.00.

Teapot, cw, floral, leaf spout, twined hdl, rpr, 4½" 375.00
Teapot, cw, floral swags, leaf spout, twined hdl, rstr, 3½" 345.00
Teapot, cw, gr/yel stripes, brn dots, leaf spout, 1780s, 5¾", EX ...2,645.00
Teapot, cw, magenta florals/beadwork, twined hdl, 1770, 4¾", EX 800.00
Teapot, cw, mc floral, scalloped/pierced gallery, 5¼", EX 750.00
Teapot, pw, bl & wht floral, 7½", EX 200.00
Tureen, cw, emb leaves, 1800s, rstr, 13½" hdl to hdl 500.00
Tureen, sauce; basketweave, floral finial, w/tray, 1800s 450.00
Urn, cw, rtcl body, angel caryatid hdls, 7¼", pr 300.00
Urn, silver lustre, rtcl, graduated rnd base, 1810s, 15", pr 740.00

Lefton China

Lefton China is one of the most desirable, most sought-after collectibles in the market place today. The company was founded in the early 1940s by Mr. Geo Zoltan Lefton who had migrated to the United States from Hungary. In the 1930s he was a designer and manufacturer of sportswear, and his hobby of collecting fine china and porcelain led him to the creation of his own ceramic business.

When Pearl Harbor was bombed in December of 1941, Mr. Lefton befriended a Japanese-American and helped him protect his property from being destroyed by groups of anti-Japanese. Soon after, Mr. Lefton became associated with a Japanese factory owned by Kowa Toki K.K. Until 1980 this factory produced thousands of items that were sold by the Lefton Company, all bearing the initials of KW before the item number. These and many of the whimsical pieces from lines such as as Bluebirds, Girl Face, Miss Priss, Cabbage Cutie, Mr. Toodles, and the Dutch Girl are eagerly sought by collectors today. As with any antique or collectible, prices vary depending on location, condition, and availability. For the history of Lefton China, information about Lefton factories, marks and other identification methods, we highly recommend the *Collector's Encyclopedia of Lefton China, Books I and II*, by our advisor, Loretta DeLozier, who is listed in the Directory under Iowa. You may also contact her regarding the National Society of Lefton Collectors.

Animal, bear, #131, 6½" 50.00
Animal, dog, setter breed, #80521 ....52.00
Animal, mice, #02477, 2½" 12.00

Animal, reindeer lying down, Green Holly, #5218 ....15.00
Ashtray, pk porc w/bird, oval, #262, 5" 30.00
Bird, duck in grass, #628 ....35.00
Bird, musical, #02143, 6" 45.00
Bird, owl, #7566, 12" 75.00
Bird, sea gull, #02715, 7" 60.00
Bone dish, Brown Heritage, Floral, #563, 8" 18.00
Bone dish, Poinsettia, #4398, 6" 18.00
Bowl, swan center, Only a Rose, #425, 7½" 85.00
Box, candy; Berry Harvest, #297, 5¼" 65.00
Box, candy; pk w/pk rose trim, china, #2151, 5½" 85.00
Box, candy; Santa on roof of house, #06533, 8½" 55.00
Box, music; canary, bsk, #2142, 6" 55.00
Box, pin; Flowers of the Month, #2260, 2¼" 7.00
Box, powder; hand w/sm flowers in pk, #964, 4¼" 50.00
Box, Rose Garden, #6581 ....55.00
Box, swan, Only a Rose, #428 ....75.00
Card holders, flower decor, Flower Garden, #3147 ....4.00
Coffeepot, Blue Paisley, #1972 ....135.00
Coffeepot, fleur-de-lis, #2910 ....65.00
Cookie jar, bluebirds, #289 ....275.00
Cookie jar, Mr Toddles, #3236 ....250.00
Cookie jar, mushroom w/caterpillar on lid, Made in Italy, #130 ...40.00
Cookie jar, Pink Daisy, #4856 ....45.00
Cup & saucer, gr & wht trimmed in gold, #546 ....35.00
Decanter set, dk gr w/gold, 8-pc set, #4107 ....85.00
Dish, Red Cardinal, leaf shape, #01239 ....18.00
Egg cup, Elegant Rose, #2048 ....35.00
Figurine, boy w/dog, #3503, 6" 30.00
Figurine, Colonial man & lady w/musical instruments, #3658, ea pr ..250.00
Figurine, Four Seasons, bsk, #3210, 5¾", ea 65.00
Figurine, modern, all wht, #1129, 5¼" 50.00
Jam jar, Mr Toodles, #3290, 4¼" 50.00
Pitcher set, Dutch Line, shelf w/4 cups, #3705 ....75.00
Planter, blk matt, gold design, blk velvet, #425, 6x4" 32.00

Planter, girl figural, white dress and hat with yellow trim, #3138, 7", $40.00.

Plate, Fruit Basket, w/plastic hdl, #1893, 9" 45.00
Plate, magnolia, #2522, 7½" 22.00
Plate, salad; Berry Harvest, #305, 8" 28.00
Plate, Sweet Violets, #2864, 10¼" 25.00
Shakers, Americana, #955, pr 28.00
Shakers, Daisytime, #3362, pr 18.00
Shakers, turkeys, #1991, pr 28.00
Snack set, Rose, #100, 8" 30.00
Switch plate, single; Flowers & Stones, pk, #077 ....25.00
Teapot, Honey Bee, #1278 ....125.00
Teapot, Rustic Daisy, #3855 ....85.00
Tray, Rose Garden, 2-tier, #6587 ....65.00

Wall plaque, Christy, #448 ....18.00
Wall plaque, sm girl praying, Lord's Prayer verse, #3215 ....15.00
Wall plaques, Mermaids in Shells, #4489, 7¼", pr 80.00

Legras

Legras and Cie was founded in St. Denis, France, in 1864. Production continued until the 1930s. In addition to their enameled wares, they made cameo art glass decorated with outdoor scenes and florals executed by acid cuttings through two to six layers of glass. Their work is signed 'Legras' in relief and in enamel. Our advisor for this category is Don Williams; he is listed in the Directory under Missouri.

Cameo

Vase, aquatic plants, brn/gr on tan/apricot, stick neck, 11" 350.00
Vase, aquatic plants, wine/gr on rust/tan, amber hdls, 10" 700.00
Vase, bud; foliage, fiery opal/dk & olive gr, 8¼" 635.00
Vase, Deco roses/ribbons, blk on red/blk mottle, 15x8" 750.00
Vase, floral, lt/dk maroon on lt maroon/opal mottle, 16" 850.00
Vase, floral branches, cut/pnt, maroon/frost, oviform, 7¾" 550.00
Vase, leaves on gr w/gold enamel, globular, 9½" 600.00
Vase, lg autumn leaves on burgundy mottle, ftd cylinder, 20" .1,100.00
Vase, shepherd/sheep landscape, orange/yel sky, cylinder, 9" 800.00

Enameled Glass

Rose bowl, floral, 3-color on pnt yel ground on clear, 3¾x4" 200.00
Rose bowl, trees on orange sky w/birds & snow, 4" H 400.00
Rose bowl vase, snow scene on orange/gold, 10x9" 1,250.00
Vase, floral, etched/pnt, red-orange/clear, w/blk enamel, 13" 925.00
Vase, landscape, naturalistic tones, cylindrical, 12" 700.00
Vase, Nouveau mc poppies on emerald gr, 12" 700.00
Vase, riverscape at sunset, etched trees, ovoid, 14" 1,200.00
Vase, sailing landscape, metal base mk Depose, 11¾", pr 1,200.00

Lenox

Walter Scott Lenox, former art director at Ott and Brewer, and Jonathan Coxon founded The Ceramic Art Company of Trenton, New Jersey, in 1889. By 1906 Cox had left the company and to reflect the change in ownership, the name was changed to Lenox Inc. Until 1930 when the production of American-made Belleek came to an end, they continued to produce the same type of high-quality ornamental wares that Lenox and Coxon had learned to master while in the employ of Ott and Brewer. Their superior dinnerware made the company famous, and since 1917 Lenox has been chosen the official White House China. Our advisor for this category is Mary Frank Gaston; she is listed in the Directory under Texas. See also Ceramic Art Company.

Bonbon, pk shell, gr mk, 4½" 25.00
Bowl, cereal; Maywood, 5¾" 23.00
Bowl, cream soup; Westfield 35.00
Bowl, fruit; Oakleaf 20.00
Bowl, soup; Poppies on Blue 9.00
Bowl, vegetable; Eternal, oval, lg 66.00
Bowl, vegetable; Hancock, w/lid 195.00
Bowl, vegetable; Holiday, oval, 9⅝" 50.00
Bowl, vegetable; Kelly, oval 90.00
Candy dish, Holiday, 9¾" 35.00
Cheese dish, Holiday, 7⅝" 30.00
Cigarette holder, cup shape, gr mk, 2¾x2⅝" 30.00

Cigarette lighter, pk w/gold, Ronson wick type, gold wreath mk ..75.00
Creamer, Autumn 50.00
Creamer, Eternal 45.00
Creamer, Kelly 60.00
Creamer, Noblesse 62.00
Creamer, Oakleaf 35.00
Cup, Westfield 34.00
Cup & saucer, Citation Gold 26.00
Cup & saucer, Citation Lace 27.00
Cup & saucer, Classic Edition 50.00
Cup & saucer, Eternal 24.00
Cup & saucer, Fruits of Life 35.00
Cup & saucer, Hannah 30.00
Cup & saucer, Harvest 30.00
Cup & saucer, Hayworth 22.00
Cup & saucer, Holiday 40.00
Cup & saucer, Kelly 35.00
Cup & saucer, Kingsley 33.00
Cup & saucer, Maywood 14.00
Cup & saucer, Noblesse 42.00
Cup & saucer, Oakleaf 38.00
Cup & saucer, Poppies on Blue 16.00
Cup & saucer, Wyndcrest 36.00

Dish, hand-painted purple clematis on
white Belleek, gold trim, 5", $65.00.

Figurine, swan, coral, 4½" 50.00
Flower holder, Celadon, #1781, 12" 95.00
Gravy boat, Belvidere 110.00
Gravy boat, Oakleaf 95.00
Leaf dish, heavy gold, #3005, 2x10½" 75.00
Nut dish, wht swan form, gr wreath mk, 5" L 50.00
Plate, bread & butter; Belvidere, 6⅛" 10.00
Plate, bread & butter; Citation Gold 9.00
Plate, bread & butter; Eternal 8.00
Plate, bread & butter; Fruits of Life 12.00
Plate, bread & butter; Hannah 10.00
Plate, bread & butter; Harvest, 6¼" 11.00
Plate, bread & butter; Holiday 14.00
Plate, bread & butter; Kelly 12.00
Plate, bread & butter; Kingsley, 6½" 15.00
Plate, bread & butter; Maywood, 6½" 5.00
Plate, bread & butter; Oakleaf 17.00
Plate, dinner; Belvidere, 10½" 24.00
Plate, dinner; Citation Gold 17.00
Plate, dinner; Citation Lace 33.00
Plate, dinner; Eternal 16.00
Plate, dinner; Fruits of Life 24.00
Plate, dinner; Hannah 18.00
Plate, dinner; Harvest, 10½" 26.00
Plate, dinner; Hayworth 16.00
Plate, dinner; Kelly 24.00

Plate, dinner; Kingsley, 10⅝" 30.00
Plate, dinner; Oakleaf 25.00
Plate, dinner; Olympia, 10" 26.00
Plate, dinner; Wyndcrest 30.00
Plate, salad; Belvidere, 8⅜" 14.00
Plate, salad; Citation Gold 12.00
Plate, salad; Citation Lace 12.50
Plate, salad; Eternal 12.00
Plate, salad; Fruits of Life 16.00
Plate, salad; Harvest, 8¼" 15.00
Plate, salad; Hayworth 10.00
Plate, salad; Holiday 19.00
Plate, salad; Kingsley, 8⅜" 18.00
Plate, salad; Lenox, 8¼" 15.00
Plate, salad; Maywood, 8¼" 7.00
Plate, salad; Oakleaf 22.00
Plate, salad; Wyndcrest 19.00
Platter, Belvidere, 13⅞" 80.00
Platter, Eternal, lg 100.00
Platter, Holiday, 16" 90.00
Platter, Kelly, lg 140.00
Platter, Oakleaf, 15½" 175.00
Relish, Holiday, 8" 21.00
Sugar bowl, Eternal 58.00
Sugar bowl, Kelly 75.00
Sugar bowl, Oakleaf, w/lid 58.00
Vase, band of lg birds/mtns, porc, gr ink mk, 10½" 260.00
Vase, emb lilies, gold trim, gold wreath mk, 4⅜x1⅝" 50.00
Vase, red rose w/gold leaves, long neck, #27, 8" 65.00
Vase, Romeo & Juliet, from Ispanky sculpture, ltd ed, 9½" ...195.00

Letter Openers

Made in a wide variety of materials and designs, letter openers make an interesting collection, easy to display and easy on the budget as well. Our advisor for this category is Ron Damaska; he is listed in the Directory under Pennsylvania.

Celluloid, Indianapolis Brush & Broom advertising 24.00
Celluloid, W Atlee Burpee & Co advertising 20.00
Ebony w/sterling cap, 14" 195.00
Eskimo ivory cvd umbrella hdl w/seals, silver ferrule, 1902 ....250.00
Ivory dagger shape w/cvd elephants & flowers 30.00
Metal, Burrough's Adding Machine Co advertising 10.00
Silver, hand hammered, marked Lebolt, 10" 325.00
Stainless steel, Miller's Forge Am Made Manicure Cutlery 45.00
Walnut w/cvd snake hdl, old soft patina, 8¾" 85.00
Walrus tooth, dagger shape, heavy 175.00

Libbey

The New England Glass Company was established in 1818 in Boston, Massachusetts. In 1892 it became known as the Libbey Glass Company. At Chicago's Columbian Expo in 1893, Libbey set up a ten-pot furnace and made glass souvenirs. The display brought them world-wide fame. Between 1878 and 1918 Libbey made exquisite cut and faceted glass, considered today to be the best from the brilliant period. The company is credited for several innovations — the Owens bottle machine that made mass production possible and the Westlake machine which turned out both electric light bulbs and tumblers automatically. They developed a machine to polish the rims of their tumblers in such a way that chipping was unlikely to occur. Their glassware carried the patented Safedge guarantee. Libbey also made glassware in numerous colors, among them cobalt, ruby, pink, green, and amber. Our advisor for this category is Mike Roscoe; he is listed in the Directory under Ohio.

Champagne, squirrel stem, wht opal, 6" 200.00
Claret, bear stem, blk, 5½" 155.00
Claret, bear stem, wht opal 165.00
Cocktail, kangaroo stem, ruby experimental, 6" 325.00
Cocktail, kangaroo stem, wht opal, 6" 165.00
Cocktail, Symphony, ruby connecting bubble, 4⅞", 8 for 800.00
Compote, amberina, scalloped, ped base, mk, 6x7" 1,375.00
Compote, clear optic ribs w/gr dots, twist stem, Nash, 6¾x7" 635.00
Compote, elephant stem, wht opal, 11" dia, from $850 to 950.00
Cordial, kangaroo stem, blk 110.00
Cordial, monkey stem, blk 150.00
Cordial, monkey stem, wht opal, 5" 130.00
Cordial, whippet stem, wht opal 175.00
Dinner bell, 1893...Xposition (sic), frosted hdl, 5¾" 285.00
Goblet, cat stem, wht opal 200.00
Maize, butter dish, bl husks on irid 650.00
Maize, butter dish lid, gr husks on custard 165.00
Maize, celery vase, clear w/amber staining & bl leaves, 6" 235.00
Maize, celery vase, gr husks on custard 200.00
Maize, condiment set, custard, 3 pcs on tray w/metal lid 600.00
Maize, pickle castor, amber stain 595.00
Maize, pickle castor, gr husks on custard, SP fr 550.00
Maize, pitcher, bl husks on clear w/amber irid, clear hdl, 9" 600.00
Maize, pitcher, clear irid w/amber stain, 8½" 550.00
Maize, shakers, gold-edged bl husks on custard, pr 250.00
Maize, sugar shaker, yel/gold leaves on custard, 5¾" 345.00
Maize, toothpick holder, gold-edged gr husks on custard 400.00
Maize, tumbler, bl husks on irid 235.00
Maize, vase, yel/gold leaves on custard, 6½" 250.00
Mayonnaise, allover hobstars, oval, 6", +undertray 425.00
Pitcher, cut flowering branches, etched mk, 1920s, 7x6½" 195.00
Pitcher, Kingston, lg hobstars/mitres/fans, 13" 550.00
Pitcher, opal w/pk stripes, cased pk-striped hdl, 5½" 345.00
Punch bowl, cut, hobstars/buttons/cane, 2-part, 11½x12" 650.00
Punch cup, inscr World's Fair 1893 in blk, gold trim 85.00
Sherbet, rabbit stem, wht opal, 2½" 160.00
Sherbet, squirrel stem, wht opal, 4" 125.00
Sherbet, Symphony, ruby connecting bubble, Nash, 5⅝", 8 for ...800.00
Tumbler, juice; fuchsia amberina, ribbed, 4¼" 215.00
Vase, amberina, flared 6" dia rim, #3102, 5" 950.00
Vase, amberina, ribbed, elongated/ftd, 11½" 1,200.00
Vase, amberina, ribbed bottle form, 9" 1,050.00
Vase, amberina, ruffled conical shape, 1917 stamp, 10¾" 575.00
Vase, clear w/gr zipper-pattern dots, Nash, K-542, 10" 375.00
Vase, gr, spiral, ftd, 13⅞" 165.00
Vase, jack-in-the-pulpit; amberina, #3014, 5x5¾" 1,200.00

Lightning Rod Balls

Used as ornaments on lightning rods, the vast majority of these balls were made of glass, but ceramic examples can be found as well. Their average diameter is 4½" but can vary from 3½" up to 5½". Only a few of the many available pattern-and-color combinations are listed here. The most common measure 4½" and are found in sun-colored amethyst and milk glass. Our advisor is Rod Krupka, author of a book on this subject. Anyone interested in receiving a hobby-related newsletter may write to him for more information; he is listed in the Directory under Michigan.

Amber, Swirl, 5½x5" 100.00
Amethyst (sun-colored), Mast, emb swirls, 5¾x4⅞" 150.00
Bl opaque, Electra, rnd, 5⅛x4½" 30.00
Bl opaque, Ribbed Grape, 5⅛x4⅜" 55.00
Bl opaque w/dk bl swirls, Diddie Blitzen 50.00
Cobalt, rnd, 4½" dia 50.00
Dk amber, WC Schinn Mfg Co, lt stain, 4¾x4¼" 100.00
Dk bl opaque, Onion, 4⅛x3⅜" 125.00

W.C. Shinn Mfg Co., gold, belted, sheared ends, original metal center shaft and ends, 5", M, $300.00.

Gr, rnd pleat, 5x4½" 175.00
Red, Electra, cone, 5⅜x4⅝" 300.00
Wht opaque, Moon & Star pattern 30.00

Limited Edition Plates

Currently values of some limited edition plates have risen dramatically while others have drastically fallen. Prices charged by plate dealers in the secondary market vary greatly; we have tried to suggest an average.

Bing and Grondahl

1895, Behind the Frozen Window 6,250.00
1896, New Moon 1,950.00
1897, Christmas Meal of Sparrows 1,100.00
1898, Roses & Star 685.00
1899, Crows Enjoying Christmas 1,500.00
1900, Church Bells Chiming 895.00
1901, 3 Wise Men 425.00
1902, Gothic Church Interior 395.00
1903, Expectant Children 425.00
1904, View of Copenhagen From Fredericksberg Hill 225.00
1905, Anxiety of the Coming Christmas Night 215.00
1906, Sleighing to Church 165.00
1907, Little Match Girl 225.00
1908, St Petri Church 110.00
1909, Yule Tree 110.00
1910, Old Organist 110.00
1911, Angels & Shepherds 110.00
1912, Going to Church 110.00
1913, Bringing Home the Tree 110.00
1914, Amalienborg Castle 105.00
1915, Dog on Chain Outside Window 175.00
1916, Prayer of the Sparrows 105.00
1917, Christmas Boat 105.00
1918, Fishing Boat 105.00
1919, Outside the Lighted Window 95.00
1920, Hare in the Snow 95.00
1921, Pigeons 95.00
1922, Star of Bethlehem 95.00
1923, Hermitage 95.00
1924, Lighthouse 105.00

1925, Child's Christmas 105.00
1926, Churchgoers 105.00
1927, Skating Couple 155.00
1928, Eskimos 95.00
1929, Fox Outside Farm 105.00
1930, Tree in Town Hall Square 115.00
1931, Christmas Train 115.00
1932, Lifeboat at Work 115.00
1933, Korsor-Nyborg Ferry 105.00
1934, Church Bell in Tower 105.00
1935, Lillebelt Bridge 105.00
1936, Royal Guard 110.00
1937, Arrival of Christmas Guests 135.00
1938, Lighting the Candles 175.00
1939, Old Lock-Eye, The Sandman 235.00
1940, Delivering Christmas Letters 285.00
1941, Horses Enjoying Meal 325.00
1942, Danish Farm on Christmas Night 275.00
1943, Ribe Cathedral 225.00
1944, Sorgenfri Castle 115.00
1945, Old Water Mill 185.00
1946, Commemoration Cross 115.00
1947, Dybbol Mill 165.00
1948, Watchman 115.00
1949, Landsoldaten 170.00
1950, Kronborg Castle at Elsinore 175.00
1951, Jens Bang 145.00
1952, Old Copenhagen Canals & Thorsvaldsen Museum 145.00
1953, Royal Boat 155.00
1954, Snowman 155.00
1955, Kaulundborg Church 155.00
1956, Christmas in Copenhagen 165.00
1957, Christmas Candles 175.00
1958, Santa Claus 140.00
1959, Christmas Eve 155.00
1960, Village Church 185.00
1961, Winter Harmony 115.00
1962, Winter Night 90.00
1963, Christmas Elf 115.00
1964, Fir Tree & Hare 75.00

1965, Bringing Home the Tree, $60.00.

1966, Home for Christmas 55.00
1967, Sharing the Joy 49.00
1968, Christmas in Church 35.00
1969, Arrival of Guests 35.00
1970, Pheasants in Snow 32.00
1971, Christmas at Home 30.00
1972, Christmas in Greenland 30.00
1973, Country Christmas 30.00
1974, Christmas in the Village 30.00
1975, The Old Water Mill 30.00

1976, Christmas Welcome 27.00
1977, Copenhagen Christmas 27.00
1978, A Christmas Tale 27.00
1979, White Christmas 27.00
1980, Christmas in the Woods 32.00
1981, Christmas Peace 32.00
1982, The Christmas Tree 42.00
1983, Christmas in Old Town 45.00
1984, Christmas Letter 50.00
1985, Christmas Eve, Farm 45.00
1986, Silent Night 47.00
1987, Snowman's Christmas 65.00
1988, In King's Garden 55.00
1989, Christmas Anchorage 55.00
1990, Changing Guards 65.00
1991, Copenhagen Stock Exchange 85.00
1992, Pastor's Christmas 85.00
1993, Father Christmas in Copenhagen 85.00

M. I. Hummel

The last issue for M.I. Hummel annual plates was made in 1995. Values listed here are for plates in mint condition with original boxes.

1971, Heavenly Angel 525.00
1972, Hear Ye, Hear Ye 55.00
1973, Glober Trotter 95.00
1975, Ride Into Christmas 60.00
1976, Apple Tree Girl 65.00
1977, Apple Tree Boy 70.00
1978, Happy Pastime 50.00
1979, Singing Lesson 40.00
1980, School Girl 49.00
1981, Umbrella Boy 49.00
1982, Umbrella Girl 80.00
1983, The Postman 165.00
1984, Little Helper 60.00
1985, Chick Girl 80.00
1986, Playmates 140.00
1987, Feeding Time 105.00
1988, Little Goat Herder 100.00
1989, Farm Boy 110.00
1990, Shepherd's Boy 185.00
1991, Just Resting 135.00
1992, Meditation 130.00
1993, Doll Bath 185.00
1994, Doctor 200.00
1995, Come Back Soon 225.00

Royal Copenhagen

1908, Madonna & Child 3,500.00
1909, Danish Landscape 225.00
1910, Magi 170.00
1911, Danish Landscape 170.00
1912, Christmas Tree 165.00
1913, Frederik Church Spire 165.00
1914, Holy Spirit Church 185.00
1915, Danish Landscape 205.00
1916, Shepherd at Christmas 145.00
1917, Our Savior Church 145.00
1918, Sheep & Shepherds 135.00
1919, In the Park 135.00

1920, Mary & Child Jesus 135.00
1921, Aabenraa Marketplace 115.00
1922, 3 Singing Angels 115.00
1923, Danish Landscape 115.00
1924, Sailing Ship 150.00
1925, Christianshavn Street Scene 110.00
1926, Christianshavn Canal 105.00
1927, Ship's Boy at Tiller 175.00
1928, Vicar's Family 115.00
1929, Grundtvig Church 115.00
1930, Fishing Boats 140.00
1931, Mother & Child 145.00
1932, Frederiksberg Gardens 150.00
1933, Ferry & Great Belt 160.00
1934, Hermitage Castle 165.00
1935, Kronborg Castle 215.00
1936, Roskilde Cathedral 195.00
1937, Main Street of Copenhagen 265.00
1938, Round Church of Osterlars 325.00
1939, Greenland Pack Ice 415.00
1940, Good Shepherd 450.00
1941, Danish Village Church 375.00
1942, Bell Tower 415.00
1943, Flight Into Egypt 575.00
1944, Danish Village Scene 305.00
1945, Peaceful Scene 450.00
1946, Zealand Village Church 200.00
1947, Good Shepherd 255.00
1948, Nodebo Church 225.00
1949, Our Lady's Cathedral 255.00
1950, Boeslunde Church 245.00
1951, Christmas Angel 395.00
1952, Christmas in Forest 165.00
1953, Frederiksberg Castle 165.00
1954, Amalienborg Palace 195.00
1955, Fano Girl 215.00
1956, Rosenborg Castle 195.00
1957, Good Shepherd 145.00
1958, Sunshine Over Greenland 145.00
1959, Christmas Night 155.00
1960, Stag 155.00
1961, Training Ship 165.00
1962, Little Mermaid 225.00
1963, Hojsager Mill 85.00
1964, Fetching the Tree 75.00
1965, Little Skaters 74.00
1966, Blackbird 55.00
1967, Royal Oak 52.00
1968, Last Umiak 42.00
1969, Old Farmyard 39.00
1970, Christmas Rose & Cat 52.00
1971, Hare in Winter 32.00
1972, In the Desert 26.00
1973, Train Home Bound 37.00
1974, Winter Twilight 32.00
1975, Queens Palace 26.00
1976, Danish Watermill 43.00
1977, Immervad Bridge 28.00
1978, Greenland Scenery 28.00
1979, Choosing Tree 60.00
1980, Bringing Home Tree 38.00
1981, Admiring Tree 40.00
1982, Waiting for Christmas 95.00
1983, Merry Christmas 57.00

1984, Jingle Bells 52.00
1985, Snowman 65.00
1986, Wait for Me 62.00
1987, Winter Birds 67.00
1988, Christmas Eve Copenhagen 75.00
1989, Old Skating Pond 85.00
1990, Christmas in Tivoli 120.00
1991, St Lucia Basilica 60.00
1992, Royal Coach 70.00
1993, Arrival Guests by Train 75.00

Limoges

From the mid-18th century, Limoges was the center of the porcelain industry of France, where at one time more than forty companies utilized the local kaolin to make a superior quality china, much of which was exported to the United States. Various marks were used; some included the name of the American export company (rather than the manufacturer) and 'Limoges.' After 1891 'France' was added. Pieces signed by factory artists are more valuable than those decorated outside the factory by amateurs. For a more thorough study of the subject, we recommend you refer to *The Collector's Encyclopedia of Limoges Porcelain, 2nd Edition,* by our advisor, Mary Frank Gaston, who is listed in the Directory under Texas. Her book has beautiful color illustrations and current market values.

Biscuit jar, bl & gold florals, relief scrolls, 7½x5½" 145.00
Bowl, centerpc; peaches w/in & w/o, 8-sided, on 4-leg base, 12" ...495.00
Box, floral medallions on bl, ormolu mts, 2¾" 100.00
Box, forget-me-nots & foliage on pk, T&V, 3¾x13x4¾" 395.00
Box, Nouveau free-form w/scrolls, violets & gold, 9x6½" 165.00
Charger, lady's portrait on gold w/poppies, T&V, 13" 295.00
Coffeepot, mc florals on fluted pear shape, C hdl, 10" 150.00
Dish, mc roses w/much gold, 3-compartment, unmk, 11¼" dia ..150.00
Figurine, nude lady on tree branch w/flowers & bird, sgn, 13" 900.00
Fish set, fish, mc w/gold, 12" platter+10 8½" plates 650.00
Plaque, Helios & horses, wht on gr pate-sur-pate, 6" dia 120.00

Plaque, lady's portrait, imperfections, 7½", $445.00.

Plaque, officer & lady, sgn Clair, 1880, 23½" 975.00
Plaque, Venus & Cupid by water, gilt scrolls, sgn, 13" 245.00
Plaque, 2 cows grazing w/mtns, T&V, 7x9½" 295.00
Plate, country church scene, gold rim, 12¼" 195.00
Plate, duck in flight, sgn Burg, gold rococo rim, 11¼" 225.00
Plate, game birds, gold rococo border, HP mk, 15⅝", pr 695.00
Plate, lady in mtn landscape, sgn Wantzel, gold border, 13" 110.00
Plate, luncheon; gold medallion/filigree/cobalt band, 9½" 30.00
Plate, oyster; dainty floral, 7½" 80.00
Plate, oyster; seaweed w/gold, 5-hole, T&V, 8¼" 90.00
Plate, oyster; violets on wht w/gold, ca 1900, 9", 6 for 715.00
Plate, pastoral scene, gold rococo border, 12½", pr 450.00

Plate, peaches on branches w/gold, gold rococo, mk, 12⅞" 265.00
Plate, shepherdess & nobleman, gold rococo border, 10⅜" 135.00
Punch bowl, purple berries, 6x13", +5 cups & tray 800.00
Punch bowl, vintage, sgn EDW, gold rim/ft, 14¼" 500.00
Toothpick holder, gold collar & hdl, floral top, blk below 35.00
Tray, dresser; Dutch shoreline scene w/windmill, 1870s 165.00
Tray, dresser; lady in field thick gold border, 11" 150.00
Vase, lakeside landscapes on yel, scroll hdls, 1890s, 14", pr 220.00
Vase, pk hibiscus w/trailing stems & gold, 12½x6¼" 350.00

Lithophanes

Lithophanes are porcelain panels with relief designs of varying degrees of thickness and density. Transmitted light brings out the pattern in graduated shading, lighter where the procelain is thin and darker in the heavy areas. They were cast from wax models prepared by artists and depict views of life from the 1800s, religious themes, or scenes of historical significance. First made in Berlin about 1803, they were used as lampshade panels, window plaques, or candle shields. Later steins, mugs, and cups were made with lithophanes in their bases. Japanese wares were sometimes made with dragons or geisha lithophanes. Our advisor for this category is Lucille Malitz; she is listed in the Directory under New York. See also Dragon Ware; Steins.

Candle lamp, volcano scenic, bronze, rare 195.00
Cup & saucer, lady's portrait, moriage dragons allover, unmk 28.00
Lamp, fairy; 3-panel, bamboo base/fr, mk Longwi, 8" 550.00
Panel, boy & girl pray before shrine, PPM #1179, 6¼x4½" 300.00
Panel, girl at trellis, bl & gr glass border, 10½x8¾" 450.00

Little Red Riding Hood

Though usually thought of as a product of the Hull Pottery Company, research has shown that a major part of this line was actually made by Regal China. The idea for this popular line of novelties and kitchenware items was developed and patented by Hull, but records show that to a large extent Hull sent their whiteware to Regal to be decorated. Little Red Riding Hood was produced from 1943 until 1957. Values have risen sharply over the past several months. For further information we recommend *Collecting Hull Pottery's Red Riding Hood* by Mark Supnick. Watch for the announcement of another book on this subject by Joyce and Fred Roerig, authors of *The Collector's Encyclopedia of Cookie Jars*. Our advisors for this category are Rose and Charlie Snyder; they are listed in the Directory under Kansas. Note: Beware of reproductions.

Cookie jar, open basket, red shoes, $850.00.

Bank, standing 600.00
Bank, wall hanging 1,900.00
Butter dish 425.00

Canister, cereal 900.00
Canister, salt 1,200.00
Canisters, coffee, sugar or flour; ea 800.00
Cookie jar, closed basket, minimum 360.00
Cookie jar, open basket, gold stars on apron, minimum 675.00
Cookie jar, poinsettia 1,050.00
Cookie jar, red spray w/gold bows, red shoes 850.00
Cookie jar, wht 200.00
Cracker jar, unmk 900.00
Creamer, top pour, no tab hdl 450.00
Creamer, top pour, tab hdl 500.00
Creamer & sugar bowl, side pour 500.00
Grease jar, flower basket, gold trim 1,200.00
Lamp 2,100.00
Match holder, wall hanging 800.00
Match holder, wall hanging, overglaze pnt gone, EX 450.00
Mug, emb figure, wht (no color), minimum value 450.00
Mustard jar, no spoon 300.00
Mustard jar, w/spoon 400.00
Pitcher, batter 575.00
Pitcher, milk; standing, 8" 375.00
Planter, hanging 475.00
Shakers, 3¼", pr 150.00
Shakers, lg, 5½", pr 200.00
Shakers, Pat Design 135889, med sz, pr 950.00
Spice jar, sq base 750.00
Sugar bowl, crawling 250.00
Sugar bowl, side pour 475.00
Sugar bowl, w/lid 675.00
Sugar bowl lid 225.00
Teapot 365.00
Wall pocket 550.00
Wolf jar, yel 900.00

Liverpool

In the late 1700s Liverpool potters produced a creamy ivory ware, sometimes called Queen's Ware, which they decorated by means of the newly perfected transfer print. Made specifically for the American market, patriotic inscriptions, political portraits, or other States themes were applied in black with colors sometimes added by hand. (Obviously their loyalty to the crown did not inhibit the progress of business!) Before it lost favor in about 1825, other English potters made a similar product. Today Liverpool is a generic term used to refer to all ware of this type. Our advisor for this category is William Kurau; he is listed in the Directory under Pennsylvania.

Jug, Britains Glory.../Fox Hunt, mc, rstr, 9½" 375.00
Jug, Commodore Preble's squadron at Tropoli/portrait, blk, 8" ..1,500.00
Jug, Emblem of Am/Coming Into Port..., blk, 9¾", NM 1,900.00
Jug, Jefferson Liberty/Farmers Arms, blk, rstr, 11¼" 8,500.00
Jug, Madison & 15 states' names/ship, blk, 6¾" 5,400.00
Jug, sailor/lady in tavern/legend, mc w/pk lustre, 6¼" 1,100.00
Jug, ship Caroline/coat of arms, mc w/copper lustre, 9¼" 1,600.00
Jug, Tom Bowling funeral scene w/verse/warship, blk, 7" 990.00
Jug, Tythe Pig/Emblem of Lamb..., blk w/mc, 10", EX 225.00
Jug, Washington w/Chain of States..., blk, Herculaneum, 8" 550.00
Jug, 2 Cupids Weep...Sally Currier...1802, blk, rpr, 8" 275.00
Jug, 3-masted ship/city of WA, blk w/mc, early 1800s, 10¼" ..1,600.00
Plaque, Duke of Wellington ship, mc w/pk lustre, 8x9" 440.00
Plate, Hope, blk transfer w/mc, ca 1800, rprs, 10" 175.00
Tankard, Tythe Pig/poem, blk w/mc, 6", VG 170.00
Teapot, British 3-masted vessel, blk w/mc, rstr, 5¼" 900.00

Lladro

Lladro porcelains are currently being produced in Labernes Blanques, Spain. Their retired and limited edition figurines are popular collectibles on the secondary market. Prices seem especially volatile; our values are gleaned from dealer inventories around the country.

Afghan Hound Bongo Player, #1156 ....400.00
Afternoon Prom 225.00
Bell, Christmas, 1988 ....25.00
Beth, #1358 ....175.00
Bouquets, club pc 600.00
Boy Meets Girl, #1188 ....250.00
Boy w/Smoking Jacket, #4900 ....175.00
Can I Play? 375.00
Chinese Noble Woman 1,750.00
Clean Up Time 35.00
Comforting Daughter 295.00
Dancing Partner, #5093 ....375.00
Daughters, 13" 545.00
Donkey in Love, #4524 ....325.00
Dress Maker, #4700, 14½" 375.00
Dress Rehearsal 365.00
Embroiderer 425.00
Exquisite Scent, girl w/hand to face leans forward, 11" 425.00
Garden Classic 395.00
Garden of Dreams 995.00
Garden Treasure 175.00
Gentleman Equestrian, #5329 ....320.00
Girl w/Dice, #1176 ....200.00
Girl w/Flowers, #1172 ....250.00
Grandma Talking to Child, 1985, 9" 495.00
Heather, #1359 ....175.00
Lady at Dressing Table, #1242 ....2,995.00
Lady w/Baby in Carriage, 12½x9½x3¾" 425.00
Land of Giants 225.00
Languid Clown, #4924, retired 800.00
Lhasa Apso, #4642 ....295.00
Lovers in the Park, couple on bench, 11" 725.00
Madonna, #4586 ....285.00
Mariko, #1429, retired, 16", w/base & box 1,290.00
Oriental Girl, matt, #4840 ....225.00
Oriental Spring, #4988, 11½" 225.00
Palls, club pc 2,200.00
Poodle, #1259 ....200.00
Practice Makes Perfect, Rockwell 600.00
Promenade 225.00
Ride in the Country, #5354 ....325.00
Rosalinda, matt, #4836 ....195.00
Sisters, #5031 ....775.00
Sleeping Beauty Dance, 37560 ....1,695.00
Soldier w/Gun, #1164 ....350.00
Spring Bouquets 600.00
Summer Stock, Rockwell 600.00
Summer Stroll 225.00
Ten & Growing 375.00
Traveler, club pc 1,250.00
Young Bach, #1801 ....675.00

Lobmeyer

J. and L. Lobmeyer, contemporaries of Moser, worked in Vienna, Austria, during the last quadrant of the 1800s. Much of the work attributed to them is decorated with distinctive enameling; favored motifs are people in 18th-century garb.

Tumbler, man in tricorner hat and greatcoat, 3", $400.00.

Goblet, man in greatcoat & tricorner hat, mk No VII, ftd 485.00
Goblet, wht opaline, cut florals w/gold, wht pnt dots, 5½" 385.00
Vase, gold scrolls, yel/orange pnt ruffles, mc vines, 18" 950.00
Wine, lady in mc floral fr, 5⅜" 750.00
Wine, mc florals w/gold, 12-panel, ftd, 5⅜" 750.00

Locke Art

Joseph Locke already had proven himself many times over as a master glassmaker, working in leading English glasshouses for more than seventeen years. He came to America where he joined the New England Glass Company. There he invented processes for the manufacture of several types of art glass — amberina, peachblow, pomona, and agata among them. In 1898 he established the Locke Art Glassware Co. in Mt. Oliver, Pittsburgh, Pennsylvania. Locke Art Glass was produced using an acid-etching process by which the most delicate designs were executed on crystal blanks. Most examples are signed simply 'Locke Art,' often placed unobtrusively near a leaf or a stem. Other items are signed 'Jo Locke,' some are dated, and some are unsigned. Most of the work was done by hand. The business continued into the 1920s. For further study we recommend *Locke Art Glass, Guide for Collectors*, by Joseph and Janet Locke, available at your local bookstore.

Bowl, dessert; Grape & Line, ftd 110.00
Goblet, Poppy, 8-oz, 6½", 5 for 600.00
Pitcher, Grape & Line, corset shape, 8¼x6" 670.00
Sherbet, Grape & Line, ftd, 3¼x3¾" dia 110.00
Vase, sailboat etch, sgn, 10" 3,500.00

Locks

The earliest type of lock in recorded history was the wooden cross bar used by ancient Egyptians and their contemporaries. The early Romans are credited with making the first key-operated mechanical lock. The ward lock was invented during the Middle Ages by the Etruscans of Northern Italy; the lever tumbler and combination locks followed at various stages of history with varying degrees of effectiveness. In the 18th century the first precision lock was constructed. It was a device that utilized a lever-tumbler mechanism. Two of the best-known of the early 19th-century American lock manufacturers are Yale and Sargent, and today's collectors value Winchester and Keen Kutter locks very highly. Factors to consider are rarity, condition, and construction. Brass and bronze locks are generally priced higher than those of steel or iron. Our advisor for this section is Joe Tanner; he is listed in the Directory under Washington.

Key:
bbl — barrel   st — stamped

Brass Lever Tumbler

Winchester incised (stamped) on front and back, 2" wide, $145.00.

Ames Sword Co, Perfection st on shackle, 2¾" 65.00
Anchor, 6-lever, emb, 3⅛" 38.00
Belknap, emb, 3⅛" 25.00
Blue Grass, emb, 3" 85.00
Chubbs Patent London, st, 6⅛" 350.00
Cotterill, st High Security key, 5⅛x3⅛" 290.00
Cotterill Birmingham Eng, st, 5⅛" 350.00
Duplex Yale & Towne Mfg Co, st, 2⅞" 125.00
Geo B Bahr & Co Lou KY, st, 3⅛" 45.00
Good Luck, emb, 2¾" 45.00
GW Co, 1929, emb, 3" 60.00
GW Nock, fancy etch, st, 2⅞" 160.00
JWM, emb, bbl key, 2⅝" 25.00
Mercury, Mercury emb on body, 2¾" 75.00
Motor, Motor emb on body, 3¼" 35.00
P Fister Cin O, st, 2½" 60.00
Roeyonoc, Roeyonoc st on body, 3¼" 30.00
Ruby, Ruby emb in scroll on front, 2¾" 20.00
Siberian, Siberian emb on shackle, 2½" 110.00
Simmons, emb, 2¼" 18.00
Tooker & Reeves (seal lock), st, 5¼" 400.00
Tower & Lyon NY, st, 3" 25.00
W Bohannan & Co, SW emb in scroll on front, 2⅜" ...30.00
Watch, emb, flat key, 3" 30.00
1898, emb, 2¾" 30.00

Combinations

Canton Lock Co, emb, iron, 3⅜" 425.00
Clark, st, brass, 2¼" 300.00
Edwards Mfg Co No-Key, st on lock, brass, 2¾" 60.00
Karco st on body, 2½" 50.00
Miller Keyless, st, iron, 3¼" 70.00
No Kee, st, brass, 2" 45.00
Number or letter disk, st, 3-disk, brass, 1½" 100.00
Number or letter disk, st, 3-disk, iron, 2" 20.00
Number or letter disk, st, 4-disk, brass, 3½" 170.00
Number or letter disk, st, 4-disk, brass, 4½" 250.00
Number or letter disk, st, 4-disk, iron, 4½" 275.00
Permutation Lock Den Co, emb, brass, 3⅝" 400.00
Quaint Mfg Co, st on lock case, 4¼" 200.00
Sorel Limited Canada, st, brass, 3¼" 200.00
Sutton Lock Co st on body, 3" 200.00
Turman's Keyless, st, brass, 2¼" 160.00
WA Harrison, Inc, st, brass, 2½" 60.00

Eight-Lever Type

Blue Chief, st, steel, 4½" 25.00
Excelsior, st, steel, 4¾" 30.00
Goliath, steel, Goliath 8-Lever st on front 25.00
Mastodon, st, brass, 4½" 30.00
Mastodon, st, steel, 4½" 15.00
Reese, st, steel, 4¾" 15.00
Samson, brass, 8-Lever st on front 18.00

Iron Lever Tumbler

Airplane, st, 2¾" 40.00
Automobile, st, 2⅞" 35.00
Bear, emb, 2⅝" 25.00
Bronco, emb, 3¼" 45.00
Caesar, emb, 2¾" 15.00
Eagle, 4 dice emb on front, 2¾" 40.00
G Merkel, st, 3" 30.00
HC Jones (trick lock), st, 4¼" 470.00
Jupiter, word Jupiter/star & moon emb on front, 3¼" ...18.00
King Korn, words King Korn emb on body, 2⅞" 40.00
Lever Buckle Co, emb, 4½" 45.00
Mars, emb, 2¼" 20.00
Moose head, emb, 2¾" 20.00
Owl, emb, 2¼" 30.00
Rough Rider (horse & rider), emb, 3" 50.00
S Andrews, st, 2⅝" 200.00
Star Lock Works, st, 3⅛" 50.00
Thoroughbred, emb, 2⅛" 12.00
Victory, emb, 3⅛" 45.00
W Bohannon, Brook NY WB, st, 3¼" 35.00
W Hall & Co, st, 4½" 300.00
Woodland, emb, 2⅜" 30.00

Lever Push Key

Achilles, emb, iron, 3⅝" 50.00
Aztec, emb, 6-lever, 2⅛" 50.00
Belknaps 6-Lever, emb, iron, 2¼" 40.00
California, emb, brass, 2½" 20.00
Cherokee, emb, 6-lever, iron, 2½" 170.00
Crank, emb, iron, 2⅞" 25.00
Crescent 4-Lever, emb, iron, 2" 40.00
Eagle 3-Lever, emb, brass, 2" 50.00
Eclipse, emb, 6-lever, brass, 2½" 20.00
Elm City 4-Lever, emb, brass, 2" 35.00
Empire, emb, 6-lever, brass, 2½" 20.00
Fordloc, emb, iron, 3¼" 40.00
HS&Co 6-Lever, emb, brass, 2¼" 70.00
Jewett Buffalo, emb, brass, 2¼" 150.00
McIntosh, emb, 6-lever, iron, 2½" 90.00
Morley, emb, iron, 2½" 30.00
National Lock Co, emb, brass, 2½" 120.00
Nugget 4-Lever, emb, brass, 2" 50.00
Supplee, emb, iron, 2½" 20.00
Vulcan, emb, iron, 2¾" 20.00

Logo — Special Made

Anaconda, st, brass, 2⅞" 60.00
Canada Custom, emb, iron, 2¾" 130.00
City of Boston Dept of Schools, st, brass, 2⅞" 40.00
Coca-Cola, st, brass, 2⅝" 40.00

Conoco, st, brass, 2⅝" 25.00
D&H, emb, brass, 2½" 170.00
Delco Products, st, brass 20.00
Georgia Power Co, st, brass, 3" 15.00
Hawaiian Elec, st, brass, 3" 30.00
International Harvester Co, emb, brass, 2½" ..100.00
John Deere, st, brass 50.00
Lilly, st, brass, 2½" 15.00
Okla State Pen, st, brass, 2⅝" 50.00
Oliver, emb, iron, 2½" 80.00
Ordnance Dept, st, brass, 2⅞" 20.00
Property of Syracuse Univ, st, brass, 2⅝" 40.00
Public Service Co, st, brass, 2⅞" 20.00
Standard Oil Co, st, brass, 2⅝" 25.00
Swift & Co, st, iron, 2¼" 20.00
Texaco, emb, brass, 2¾" 60.00
University of Notre Dame, emb, brass, 2½" ...160.00
University of Okla, st, brass, 2⅞" 40.00
USBIA, st, brass, 3¾" 80.00
USBIR, st, brass, 3¾" 80.00
USGS, emb, iron, 2½" 40.00
USMC, st, brass, 2½" 20.00
West Baking Co, emb, brass, 2½" 90.00
Winchester, emb, iron, 2⅞" 140.00
Zoo, st, iron, 2½" 25.00

Pin-Tumbler Type

Corbin, emb, iron, 2¾" 20.00
Eagle, emb, iron, 2¾" 20.00
Fulton, emb Fulton on body, 2⅝" 30.00
Hickory, emb, iron, 2¾" 60.00
Il-A-Noy, emb, iron, 2¾" 35.00
Il-A-Noy, emb Il-A-Noy on body, 2½" 40.00
Rich-Con, emb, iron, 2⅞" 50.00
Sargent, emb, iron, 2¾" 15.00
Shapleigh, emb Shapleigh on body, 2⅝" 30.00
Simmons, emb, iron, 2⅝" 30.00
Yale, brass, emb Yale on body, Yale & Towne on shackle, 2⅝" 25.00
Yale, emb, iron, 2½" 20.00

Scandinavian (Jail House) Type

Backalaphknck (Russian), st, iron, 5" 200.00
Bull Dog, emb, brass, 2½" 80.00
Corbin, st, brass, 2½" 50.00
Nrarvck (Russian), st, iron, 4" 160.00
Pear, emb, iron, 3½" 40.00
R&E Co, emb, iron, 3¼" 40.00
Romer, st, iron, 4" 70.00
Star, emb line on bottom, iron, 3¾" 100.00
Star, iron, 2½" 70.00
99 Miller, emb 99, brass, 1¾" 80.00

Six-Lever Type

Bon-Ton, st, iron, 3" 15.00
Edwards, iron, Edwards st on body 18.00
Miller Six Lever, st, brass, 3⅞" 20.00
Oak Leaf Six Lever, st, iron, 3¼" 15.00
Olympiad Six Lever, st, iron, 3¾" 25.00
Safe, brass, Safe st on body 18.00
SHCo Simmon Six Lever, emb, iron, 3⅞" 70.00

Story and Commemorative

AYPEX Seattle (Alaska Yukon Pacific Expo), emb tin/iron, 3" .235.00
Canteen, US emb on canteen-shape lock, 2" ...500.00
CI, emb ornate scroll motif throughout body of lock, 3½" 170.00
CI, emb skull/X-bones w/florals, NH Co on bk, 3¼" 200.00
Dan Patch, iron, 1⅞" 125.00
Eagle/stars/shield & stars, emb CI, Eagle Liberty, 2½" 300.00
Missouri Seal, brass, 2¼" 150.00
National Hardware Co (NHCo), emb, iron, 2½" 200.00
National Hardware Co (NHCo), emb Mercury figure, iron, 2" ..170.00
National Hardware Co (NHCo), emb SK, iron, 3½" 425.00
New York to Paris, brass, 2⅝" 200.00
North Pole, brass, 2⅞" 150.00
Russell & Erwin (R&E), emb Aztec figure, iron, 2¼" 200.00
Russell & Erwin (R&E), emb bird, iron, 2⅞" 400.00
Russell & Erwin (R&E), emb Ganesha form, iron, 3" 325.00
Russell & Erwin (R&E), emb mailbox, iron, 3⅛" 300.00
Russell & Erwin (R&E), emb vase, iron, 3¼" 600.00
1901 Pan Am Expo, brass, emb w/buffalo, 2⅝" ...175.00
1904 World's Fair, iron & brass, 3⅝" 300.00

Warded Type

Aetna, emb, brass, 2¼" 35.00
Army, iron pancake ward key, emb letters, 2½" ...40.00
Cruso Chicken, emb, brass, 2¾" 35.00
Enders, st, brass, 1½" 25.00
G&B, st, brass, 3" 15.00
Hex, iron, sq lock case, emb US on bk, 2⅛" 95.00
Jewel, emb, iron, 2½" 18.00
Kirby, emb, brass, 2¼" 20.00
Lucky, emb, brass, 2½" 45.00
Red Cross, brass sq case, emb letters, 2" 10.00
Red Seal, emb, brass, 2" 20.00
Ruby, emb, brass, 2⅛" 20.00
Safe, brass sq case, emb letters, 1⅞" 8.00
Safety First, brass pancake type, emb letters, 2¾" ...15.00
Sampson, emb, iron, 2½" 20.00
Shapleigh, st, brass, 2" 18.00
Sprocket, brass oval shape, emb letters, 2⅛" 50.00
Texas, emb, brass, 2½" 50.00
Twister, st, brass, 2⅞" 12.00
Van Guard, emb, iron, 2⅞" 18.00
Winchester, brass sq case, st letters, 2¾" 125.00

Wrought Iron Lever Type (Smokehouse Type)

Bramah's Patent VR, 5" 60.00
Improved Warranted, 3½" 35.00
MW&Co, flat key, 3½" 20.00
R&E, 4½" 40.00
VR, 3½" 30.00
Waines, 4⅜" 40.00
WT Patent, 3¼" 20.00

Loetz

The Loetz Glassworks was established in Klostermule, Austria, in 1840. After Loetz's death the firm was purchased by his grandson, Johann Loetz Witwe. Until WWII the operation continued to produce fine artware, some of which made in the early 1900s bears a striking resemblance to Tiffany's, with whom Loetz was associated at one time.

In addition to the iridescent Tiffany-style glass, he also produced threaded glass and some cameo. The majority of Loetz pieces will have a polished pontil. Our advisor for this category is Don Williams; he is listed in the Directory under Missouri.

Biscuit jar, gr irid w/maroon threads, basket hdl 350.00
Bowl, eng/gilt florals on irid w/mc swirls, 5x10½" 1,100.00
Bowl, gr w/draped amber threads, gold irid rim wrap, 3½x5½" ...635.00
Bowl, pk slag marbleized, HP bl leaves w/gold, 3¾x5" 300.00
Bowl, purple irid to gr w/random oil spots, hdls, gilt fr, 8" 575.00
Bowl, purple irid w/random oil spots & gr irid, 4½x11¾" 300.00
Bowl, ruby to gr irid, 3 metal studs, 4-ftd metal fr, 8x4" 495.00
Bowl, yel w/gold irid/gr combed streaks, scalloped, 2¾x6" 1,265.00
Bowl, yel w/violet irid, chanel-molded oval, 12" 525.00
Box, cobalt irid, appl gr vines, hinged lid, 3½x5½" 450.00
Bride's bowl, Hobnail, red irid, ruffled, brass fr, 10x13" 325.00
Cigarette lighter, gr irid w/dimples, metal top w/eagle, 10" 425.00
Compote, honey-amber to lav w/gold ruffled rim, dimpled, 9½" ...525.00
Cracker barrel, oil spots w/entwined vines, SP rim/lid, 5½" 350.00
Inkwell, brass lotus flowers/pods on gr irid, devil lid, 3" sq 550.00
Inkwell, peacock eyes on emerald gr, brass pod lid, 1½x5" 210.00
Jar, bl irid w/floral silver o/l, w/lid, 4¾" 2,000.00
Rose bowl, oil spots, cobalt w/gold irid, 5¼x7" 700.00
Shade, clear w/amber & gr lustre design, ca 1910, 5", EX 150.00
Sweetmeat, emerald w/purple threading, silver hdl/lid, 3" 200.00
Syrup, Prussian bl irid w/embedded threading, silver mts, 7½" ...150.00
Vase, bl irid, pitted, ruffled tricon rim, 5" 200.00
Vase, copper Secessionist-style o/l & jewels on amber, 9" 1,100.00
Vase, cranberry w/gold, pinched/ruffled, ca 1910, 4½" 675.00
Vase, gold irid oil spots on 3-knothole trunk form, 10¼" 800.00
Vase, gold w/rust-red oval random dots, 4" 625.00
Vase, gold w/snake winding 4 X about neck & shoulder, 6" 700.00
Vase, gr irid w/bl/silver spots & lines, bulbous/crimped, 5" 500.00
Vase, gr irid w/lg appl red tendrils & globs, 9½" 1,000.00
Vase, gr irid w/molded depressions w/bl-silver lustre, 9⅝" 750.00
Vase, gr irid w/textured int, waisted drum form, 4⅜" 300.00
Vase, gr irid w/thread wrap, squat w/cylinder neck, 14" 225.00
Vase, gr/bl/silver stretched canes, cloverleaf top, 7x5" 1,500.00
Vase, gray-gr w/pulled swirls w/rainbow irid, trefoil rim, 13" 300.00
Vase, hearts & arrows, gr/pk/purple irid, brass collar, 6" 260.00
Vase, honeycomb irid w/3 gr swirls, waisted, 6¾" 345.00
Vase, lt gr irid, long neck w/appl dk gr spiral & disks, 23" 2,100.00
Vase, Octopus, pk MOP w/gold, quatrefoil rim, 6x5" 2,875.00
Vase, oil spots, amethyst on peacock irid, flared rim, 8x4½" 220.00
Vase, oil spots, dk purple w/bl & gr irid, bottle form, 10" 1,100.00
Vase, oil spots, gold/purple irid on gold-oyster, 3-hdl, 5¾" 1,700.00
Vase, oil spots, lt amber on cobalt, dbl-gourd form, 9¾" 2,070.00
Vase, oil spots, red w/bl irid, Secessionist-type hdls, 7x11" 1,380.00
Vase, oil spots, silver on silvery-gr, corseted, 4¼" 1,000.00
Vase, oil spots on gr, 2 looping above-rim hdls, 7" 300.00
Vase, paperweight technique, dk purple/lav irid, 5x6" 1,500.00

Vase, pull-ups, bl on overall silver o/l, 5½" 2,500.00
Vase, pulled design, amber w/lav irid, 7½x5" 2,000.00
Vase, pulled design, bl/gold/gr on gr w/platinum spots, 8" 1,800.00
Vase, pulled design, silvery-gr w/amber irid on amber, 7¾" 1,150.00
Vase, pulled feathers, silvery-bl irid on red, Spaun, 10" 2,000.00
Vase, pulled waves, bl on red irid w/silver floral o/l, 4¾" 2,250.00
Vase, pulled waves, dk brn on gr w/gold irid, silver o/l, 9" 5,350.00
Vase, pulled waves, gr w/gold & purple irid, shouldered, 7½" 850.00
Vase, purple irid, cylindrical, flared lip, 11¼" 385.00
Vase, purple irid w/cobalt swirls, mtd in fr, 7½" 450.00
Vase, purple irid w/dimples & threading, scalloped, 5½" 650.00
Vase, red/wht/pk opal cased, aubergine-blk threads, 12" 400.00
Vase, silver o/l tulips, gr/bl/silver, paperweight base, 7½" 2,700.00
Vase, swirls, gold irid/tan on caramel, squatty/crimped, 13¼" 850.00
Vase, waves & zippers, gr/bl/purple on oyster wht, 5" 1,850.00
Vase, 10 cranberry spots, gold circles, pinched form, 5" 1,500.00

Lomonosov Porcelain

Founded in Leningrad in 1744, the Lomonosov porcelain factory produced exquisite porcelain miniatures for the Czar and other Russian nobility. One of the first factories of its kind, Lomonosov's products consisted largely of vases and delicate sculptures. In the 1800s Lomonosov became closely involved with the Russian Academy of Fine Arts, a connection which has continued to this day as the company continues to supply the world with these fine artistic treasures. In 1992 the backstamp was changed to read 'Made in Russia,' instead of 'Made in USSR.' Some dealers may be pricing items marked 'Made in USSR' at 75% to 100% above prices listed below.

Afghan hound, #3548 ....30.00
Buck, #6545 ....122.00
Camel, young offspring, #6576 ....25.00
Doe, #6546 ....102.00
Elephant, #6573 ....25.00
Ermine, standing, #6432 ....19.00
Ermine w/egg, #6562 ....28.00
Fawn, #6450 ....34.00
Foal, wht, #6512, lg 53.00
Gazelle 10.00
Giraffe, #6492, lg 92.00
Lion cub, recumbent, #6441 ....12.00
Panda, #6531, sm 14.00
Poodle, playing, #2746 ....15.50
Seal, #6481 ....16.00
Spaniel, #6500 ....25.00
Tiger cub, #6480 ....25.00
Yakut w/flower, #6194 ....75.50
Yakut woman w/fish, #6195 ....75.00

Longwy

The Longwy workshops were founded in 1798 and continue today to produce pottery in the north of France near the Luxembourg-Belgian border under the name 'Societe des Faienceries de Lonswy et Senelle.' The ware for which they are best known was produced during the Art Deco period, decorated in bold colors and designs. Earlier wares made during the first quarter of the 19th century reflected the popularity of Oriental art, cloisonne enamels in particular. The designs were executed by impressing the pattern into the moist clay and filling in the depressions with enamels. Examples are marked 'Longwy,' either impressed or painted under glaze.

Vase, Papillon, red with blue iridescent and spotted decor, in Secessionist-style pewter handled mount, 6¾x10½", $1,400.00.

Bowl, Rehausse-Decor a la Main, florals/birds, cobalt lid/hdls **140.00**
Box, mc parrot on lid, 7½" dia **225.00**
Charger, Arab musicians/foliage, D985, 17x17⅛" **490.00**
Charger, floral/insects, mc on lt bl, sgn/mk, 14½" **500.00**
Charger, stag in forest/circles, bl/blk matt, Primavera, 15" **400.00**
Plaque, cranes in marsh, cobalt field, 8x6½" **90.00**
Plate, bird on branch in wht panel among mc florals, 8" dia **200.00**

Vase, stylized tropical forest scene in multicolor enamels on spherical form, signed Emaux de Longwy, #5660, 14¼x13", $6,000.00.

Vase, floral, mc/brn-lined wht top & orange skirt, #5505, 9" **210.00**
Vase, floral, red-orange on red crackle, Primavera, 12x9½" **1,265.00**
Vase, floral, yel/tan/caramel on vivid bl, #1810, 8" **250.00**
Vase, Hispano-Moresque decor on crackle, #D570, 14⅝x9½" ...**345.00**
Vase, mc tropical design on blk, #3427/#F3487, 8¾x7" **460.00**

Lonhuda

William Long was a druggist by trade who combined his knowledge of chemistry with his artistic ability in an attempt to produce a type of brown-glazed slip-decorated artware similar to that made by the Rookwood Pottery. He achieved his goal in 1889 after years of long and dedicated study. Three years later he founded his firm, the Lonhuda Pottery Company. The name was coined from the first few letters of the last name of each of his partners, W.H. Hunter and Alfred Day. Laura Fry, formerly of the Rookwood company, joined the firm in 1892, bringing with her a license for Long to use her patented airbrush-blending process. Other artists of note, Sarah McLaughlin, Helen Harper, and Jessie Spaulding, joined the firm and decorated the ware with nature studies, animals, and portraits, often signing their work with their initials. Three types of marks were used on the Steubenville Lonhuda ware. The first was a linear composite of the letters 'LPCO' with the name 'Lonhuda' impressed above it. The second, adopted in 1893, was a die-stamp representing the solid profile of an Indian, used on ware patterned after pottery made by the American Indians. This mark was later replaced with an impressed outline of the Indian head with 'Lonhuda' arching above it. Although the ware was successful, the business floundered due to poor management. In 1895 Long became a partner of Sam Weller and moved to Zanesville where the manufacture of the Lonhuda line continued. Less than a year later, Long left the Weller company. He was associated with J.B. Owens until 1899, at which time he moved to Denver, Colorado, where he established the Denver China and Pottery Company in 1901. His efforts to produce Lonhuda utilizing local clay were highly successful. Examples of Denver Lonhuda are sometimes marked with the LF (Lonhuda Faience) cipher contained within a canted diamond form. For further information we recommend *Collector's Encyclopedia of Colorado Pottery* by Carol and Jim Carlton; they are listed in the Directory under Colorado.

Pitcher, floral, mc on caramel & dk brn, Upjohn, #208, 9½" **160.00**
Vase, broad leaves, caramel & brn on dk brn, 14" **180.00**
Vase, daisies, cream/tan/brn on dk brn to gray-gr, 6" **400.00**

Vase, floral, mc on purple to gray, mks, 8½" **190.00**

Losanti

Mary Louise McLaughlin, who had previously experimented in trying to reproduce Haviland faience in the 1870s and 'American faience' (a method of inlaying color by painting the inside of the mold before the vessel was cast) in the mid-1890s, developed a type of hard-paste porcelain in which the glaze and the body fused together in a single firing. Her efforts met with success in 1900, and she immediately concentrated on glazing and decorating techniques. The ware she prefected was called Lonsanti, most of which was decorated with Nouveau florals, either carved or modeled. By 1906 she had abandoned her efforts. Examples are marked with several ciphers, one resembling a butterfly, another with the letters MCL superimposed each upon the other, and L McL in a linear arrangement. Other items were marked Lonsanti, sometimes in the Oriental manner.

Vase, cobalt metallic, bulbous w/closed horizontal hdls, 4½" **550.00**
Vase, narcissus on thick bl/cream mottle, mfg flaw, 5x3½" **1,900.00**
Vase, Nouveau floral, bl on wht to lt bl, porc, 1889, 5" **11,250.00**

Lotus Ware

Isaac Knowles and Issac Harvey operated a pottery in East Liverpool, Ohio, in 1853 where they produced both yellowware and Rockingham. In 1870 Knowles brought Harvey's interests and took as partners John Taylor and Homer Knowles. Their principal product was ironstone china, but Knowles was confident that American potters could produce as fine a ware as the Europeans. To prove his point, he hired Joshua Poole, an artist from the Belleek Works in Ireland. Poole quickly perfected a Belleek-type china, but fire destroyed this portion of the company. Before it could function again, their hotel china business had grown to the point that it required their full attention in order to meet market demands. By 1891 they were able to try again. They developed a bone china, as fine and thin as before, which they called Lotus. Henry Schmidt from the Meissen factory in Germany decorated the ware, often with lacy filigree applications or hand-formed leaves and flowers to which he added further decoration with liquid slip applied by means of a squeeze bag. Due to high production costs resulting from so much of the fragile ware being damaged in firing and because of changes in tastes and styles of decoration, the Lotus Ware line was dropped in 1896. Some of the early ware was marked 'KT&K China'; later marks have a star and a crescent with 'Lotus Ware' added. For further information we recommend *Collector's Encyclopedia of Knowles, Taylor & Knowles China* by Mary Frank Gaston, our advisor for this category; she is listed in the Directory under Texas.

Bonbon/nappy, sm floral on wht w/gold, ftd, 8" L **325.00**
Bottle, scent; pierced/scrolled, twig hdls, folded rim, 3½" H **650.00**
Bowl, appl floral branches, netting, 3¾x4¾" **175.00**
Bowl, Columbia, appl bl florals w/gold, 4x5" **550.00**
Bowl, Columbia, appl lacy openwork w/gold, 4¾" H **900.00**
Bowl, floral, mc w/gold, rtcl ornaments, sgn, gr mk, 2½" H **800.00**
Bowl, floral branches w/gold, fishscale shoulder, mk, 4¾" H **400.00**
Bowl, gold appl florals on tan matt, beaded rim, pk int, 4½" **350.00**
Bowl, gold emb floral branches, beaded ruffled rim, 4x4¾" **175.00**
Bowl, gold emb floral panels on netting, 3¾" H **400.00**
Bowl, gold floral & rtcl ornaments on yel, gr mk, 4" H **500.00**
Bowl, gold florals on gr w/netting, beaded/ruffled rim, 5" **300.00**
Bowl, gold rtcl medallions, HP florals, gold netting, 6½" L **600.00**
Bowl, lady's portrait, swirled/scalloped rim w/gold, 3x10" **1,100.00**

Bowl, pastel cornflowers, sgn, gold ruffled rim, 4½" H 450.00
Chocolate jug, emb florals, no enameling or gold, 9" 550.00
Chocolate jug, gold-paste florals, 9" 750.00
Cracker jar, emb fishnet & beadwork panels, 7½" 550.00
Creamer & sugar bowl, Chestnut design, gold-paste florals 500.00
Cup & saucer, AD; Mecca, lt gr geometrics w/gold, 2½", 5" 135.00
Cup & saucer, tea; Sonoma, sculped leaf design, ftd cup 135.00
Finger bowl, gold sponging on ruffled rim, 2¾x5¼" 175.00
Flower bowl, gold leaves w/red & bl highlights, 4½" 650.00
Jug, emb leaves, no pnt or gold, 5x7" 650.00
Jug, Globe, roses w/much gold, 5x7" 750.00
Match holder, openwork body w/beadwork, gold at rim, 4" L 800.00
Pin tray, draped nude, fan behind her, HP, rare, 6" L 1,300.00
Pitcher, emb floral at neck, scalloped base, no decor, 7" 500.00
Pitcher, netting, 2¾" 100.00
Salt cellar, gold lustre int, ⅜x½" dia 80.00
Shell tray, roses & garland transfer, 5x5½" 350.00
Syrup, acanthus leaf shoulder, scroll hdl, floral rim, 4½" 225.00
Syrup, morning glories, pk/wht on pk, serpentine hdl, 3" 225.00
Tea set, pk/bl floral panels/bl panels, gold florals, 3-pc 650.00
Teapot, emb floral, gilt cut-out rim, 3¾", +cr/sug 525.00

Vase, white porcelain ewer form with raised jewels and applied handles, 15", $4,200.00; Vase, white porcelain with applied chains, bowl shape with ruffled mouth, 7½", $1,000.00.

Vase, lily form, bl/pk/ivory shaded w/gold trim, 8" 1,100.00
Vase, roses, red on red, gold hdls, stick neck, 7½" 400.00
Vase, roses in yel & pk, blk hdls w/emb masks below, 8" 425.00

Lu Ray Pastels

Lu Ray Pastels dinnerware was introduced in the early 1940s by Taylor, Smith, and Taylor of East Liverpool, Ohio. It was offered in assorted colors of Persian Cream, Sharon Pink, Surf Green, Windsor Blue, and Gray in complete place settings as well as many service pieces. It was a successful line in its day and is once again finding favor with collectors of American dinnerware. For further information we recommend *Collector's Guide to Lu Ray Pastels* by Bill and Kathy Meehan. Our advisor for this category is Shirley Moore; she is listed in the Directory under Oklahoma.

Bowl, '36s oatmeal 33.00
Bowl, coupe soup; flat 13.00
Bowl, cream soup 42.00
Bowl, fruit; Chatham Gray, 5" 12.50
Bowl, fruit; 5" 5.00
Bowl, lug soup; tab hdld 19.00
Bowl, mixing; 10" 75.00
Bowl, mixing; 7" 70.00
Bowl, salad 42.00
Bowl, vegetable; oval, 9½" 16.00
Bowl, 10¼" 85.00

Bowl, 8¾" 75.00
Butter dish, Chatham Gray, rare color, w/lid 90.00
Calendar plates, 8", 9" & 10", ea 40.00
Casserole 70.00
Chocolate cup, AD; str sides 60.00
Chocolate pot, AD; str sides 360.00
Coaster/nut dish 65.00
Coffee cup, AD 18.00
Coffeepot, AD 135.00
Creamer 8.00
Creamer, AD, ind 40.00
Creamer, AD, ind, from chocolate set 92.00
Egg cup, dbl 18.00
Epergne 110.00
Gravy boat 22.00
Jug, water; ftd 60.00
Muffin cover 90.00
Muffin cover, w/8" underplate 105.00
Nappy, vegetable; rnd, 8½" 15.00
Pitcher, bulbous w/flat bottom 55.00
Pitcher, juice 115.00
Plate, cake 63.00
Plate, Chatham Gray, rare color, 7" 16.00
Plate, chop; 15" 25.00
Plate, grill; compartment 22.00
Plate, 10" 16.00
Plate, 6" 3.00
Plate, 8" 15.00
Plate, 9" 10.00
Platter, oval, 11½" 13.50
Platter, oval, 13" 16.00
Relish dish, 4-part 75.00
Sauce boat, fixed stand 23.00
Saucer, coffee; AD 8.50
Saucer, coffee/chocolate 22.50
Saucer, cream soup 22.50
Saucer, tea 3.00
Shakers, pr 13.00
Sugar bowl, AD; w/lid, from chocolate set 92.00
Sugar bowl, AD; w/lid, ind 40.00
Sugar bowl, w/lid 11.00
Teacup 8.00
Teapot, curved spout, w/lid 55.00
Teapot, w/lid, flat spout 75.00
Tray, pickle 24.00
Tumbler, juice 35.00
Tumbler, water 50.00
Vase, bud 215.00

Lunch Boxes

Early 20th-century tobacco companies such as Union Leader, Tiger, and Dixie sold their products in square, steel containers with flat, metal carrying handles. These were specifically engineered to be used as lunch boxes when they became empty. (See Advertising, specific companies.) By 1930 oval lunch pails with colorful lithographed decorations on tin were being manufactured to appeal directly to children. These were made by Ohio Art, Decoware, and a few other companies. In 1950 Aladdin Industries produced the first 'real' character lunch box — a Hopalong Cassidy decal-decorated steel container now considered the beginning of the kids' lunch box industry. The other big lunch box manufacturer, American Thermos (later King Seely Thermos Company) brought out its 'blockbuster' Roy Rogers box in 1953, the first fully lithographed steel lunch box and matching bottle. Other companies (ADCO Liberty; Landers, Frary & Clark; Ardee Industries; Okay Industries; Universal; Tindco; Cheinco) also produced character pails. Today's collectors often tend to specialize in those boxes dealing with a particular subject. Western, space, TV series, Disney movies, and cartoon characters are the most popular. There are well over five hundred different lunch boxes available to the astute collector. For further information we recommend *The Illustrated Encyclopedia of Metal Lunch Boxes* by Allen Woodall and Sean Brickell. Our advisor for this category is Allan Smith; he is listed in the Directory under Texas. In the following listings, lunch boxes are metal unless noted vinyl or plastic, and values include thermoses only when they are mentioned within the descriptions.

Roy Rogers and Dale Evans, Double R Bar Ranch, American Thermos, 1953, EX with thermos, $175.00.

Adam-12, Aladdin, metal, 1972, EX 50.00
Alvin & the Chipmunks, vinyl, gr, 1963, EX 250.00
Annie, vinyl, w/thermos, 1981, NM 40.00
Astronaut, metal, dome top, 1960, NM 210.00
Battlestar Galactica, metal, w/thermos, 1978, EX 40.00
Black Hole, metal, w/plastic thermos, 1979, NM 55.00
Bonanza, metal, w/thermos, Aladdin, 1965, EX/NM 215.00
Boston Red Sox, vinyl, 1960, EX 60.00
Bozostuffs, plastic, red, w/thermos, 1988, M 30.00
Buccaneer, metal, dome top, 1957, VG 100.00
Captain Kangaroo, vinyl, 1964, EX 375.00
Chan Clan, metal, w/thermos, 1973, EX 130.00
Curiosity Shop, metal, 1972, VG 50.00
Daniel Boone, metal, red rim, w/thermos, 1955, EX 170.00
Davy Crockett, metal, gr rim, 1955, VG 50.00
Deputy Dog, Thermos, vinyl, 1962, EX 350.00
Dick Tracy, metal, 1967, EX 145.00
Disneyland Monorail, metal, 1960, VG 185.00
Donnie & Marie, vinyl, 1978, EX 75.00
Drag Strip, metal, w/plastic thermos, 1975, EX 55.00
Ecology, plastic, dome top, w/thermos, 1980, EX 35.00
ET, Aladdin, metal, w/thermos, 1982, M 30.00
Family Affair, metal, w/thermos, 1969, EX 90.00
Flintstones, Canadian, metal, yel rim, w/thermos, EX 125.00
GI Joe, metal, 1967, VG 75.00
Grizzly Adams, Aladdin, metal, dome top, w/thermos, 1977, EX ..100.00
Hair Bear Bunch, metal w/plastic thermos, 1971, EX 75.00
Hogan's Heroes, metal, dome top, 1966, EX 235.00
Hot Wheels, metal, 1969, EX 60.00
Howdy Doody, metal, 1954, EX 400.00
Jetsons: The Movie, plastic, w/thermos, 1990, M 25.00
Julia, Thermos, metal, 1969, EX 90.00
Krofft Supershow, Aladdin, metal, 1976, EX 60.00
Land of the Giants, Aladdin, metal, 1969, NM 155.00
Liddle Kiddles, vinyl, bl, w/metal thermos, 1968, EX 200.00
Lion in the Van, vinyl, 1978, M 170.00
Marvel Comics Super Heroes, metal, 1976, VG 15.00
Mod Tulips, metal, dome top, 1962, EX 275.00
Mr T, plastic, orange, w/thermos, 1984, EX 18.00

Muppets, plastic, dome lid, w/thermos, 1981, EX 18.00
Partridge Family, metal, 1971, VG 35.00
Peanuts, metal, tan rim, 1966, G+ 20.00
Peanuts, vinyl, red, 1969, NM 90.00
Popeye, Aladdin, metal, w/plastic thermos, 1980, NM 80.00
Punky Brewster, plastic, w/thermos, 1984, EX 15.00
Rat Patrol, Canadian, metal, yel rim, w/thermos, VG 75.00
Return of the Jedi, plastic, red, 1983, EX 30.00
Robin Hood, metal, 1956, VG 75.00
Roy Rogers Saddlebag, vinyl, brn, 1960, EX 200.00
Satellite, metal, 1958, VG+ 45.00
Scooby Doo, metal, 1973, EX 45.00
Strawberry Shortcake, metal, w/thermos, 1980, EX 15.00
Superman, metal, w/thermos, 1978, VG 30.00
Thundercats, metal, w/thermos, 1985, M 30.00
Tic Tac Toe, vinyl, red, 1970, VG 35.00
Tom Corbett Space Cadet, metal, bl, 1952, EX 125.00
Twiggy, vinyl, 1967, EX 200.00
Universal's Movie Monsters, Aladdin, metal, 1979, EX 70.00
Wagon Train, metal, 1964, VG 75.00
Welcome Back Kotter, 1976, VG+ 40.00
Wizard of Oz, plastic, w/thermos, 1989, VG 25.00
Woody Woodpecker, metal, 1972, EX 90.00
Yogi Bear, metal, purple rim, 1974, EX 75.00
Yogi's Treasure Hunt, plastic, w/thermos, 1987, NM 30.00

Lutz

From 1869 to 1888, Nicholas Lutz worked for the Boston and Sandwich Company where he produced the threaded and striped art glass that was so popular during that era. His works were not marked; and since many other glassmakers of the day made similar wares, the term Lutz has come to refer not only to his original works but to any of this type.

Basket, pk threading, appl pk & clear tooled hdl, 6" 235.00
Cup & saucer, yel/wht/gold striping, gold in hdl, 2½", 4½" 90.00
Finger bowl, threaded cranberry, +5" plate 200.00
Smoke bell, pk/wht/gold striping, ruffled, triangular, iron mt 100.00
Tumbler, lemonade; cranberry threads, 2 appl berries 150.00

Maddux of California

One of the California-made ceramics now so popular with collectors, Maddux was founded in the late 1930s and during the years that followed produced novelty items, TV lamps, figurines, planters, and tableware accessories. Our advisor for this category is Doris Frizzell; she is listed in the Directory under Illinois.

#1019, swan console bowl (set), porc wht, 11½" 20.00
#1047, Contempo bowl (set), wht satin, 16½" 15.00
#1051, candlestick, dbl, 11" 25.00
#1067, shell console bowl (set), pk, 16" 15.00
#2015, vase, Antique Gold, hdls, 12" 15.00
#206A, planter, Chinese Bell Tower, 8" 20.00
#2102, bowl, ftd 10.00
#221, vase, swan, wht, 12" 20.00
#225, vase, horse's head top, str-sided body, aqua, 12" 18.00
#3006, TV lamp/planter, half circle 25.00
#3009, serving tray/lazy suzan, pearlized, 2-tiered, 6-pc 25.00
#3017, seashell bowl, wht 15.00
#3095A, bowl, ped w/6 ind servers 25.00
#3251-L, tray, serving; 2-tier 20.00

#3275, gr pepper relish, w/lid & side bowls 12.00
#3304, planter, bird 20.00
#400/401, flamingo, pr 35.00
#510, planter, swan, blk, 11" 18.00
#515, planter, flamingo, pk, 10½" 45.00
#527, Chinese pheasant, 11½" 20.00
#528, planter, 2 birds in flight, pk & blk, 10" 20.00
#529, vase, 2 flamingos, 5" 40.00
#536, planter, bird in flight, 11½" H 20.00
#7001, ashtray, 12" dia 10.00
#7134, ashtray, fish, 6" L 20.00
#7204, ashtray, pig form, natural color, 7" L 12.00
#808, TV lamp, pearltone shell, 13" 40.00
#810, TV lamp, stallion, prancing, on base, 12" 20.00
#826, TV lamp, cockatoos 50.00
#828, TV lamp, swan planter, wht porc, 12½" 20.00
#829, TV lamp, deer (2), running, natural, 10½" 20.00
#839, TV lamp, mallard, flying, natural colors, 11½" 35.00
#841, TV lamp, head of Christ, 3-D planter 25.00
#844, TV lamp, prairie schooner (covered wagon), 11" 30.00
#846, TV lamp, nativity scene, 3-D planter, 12" 25.00
#859, TV lamp, Toro (bull), ft on mound, 11½" 20.00
#887, TV lamp, Persian Glory (horse head), 11½" 20.00
#889, TV lamp, Malibu shell, pearltone, 10¼" 20.00
#892, TV lamp, Colonial ship, 10½" 30.00
#894, TV lamp, Toro (bull), charging, walnut, 11½" 20.00
#895, TV lamp, dbl swan, 11½" 30.00
#896, TV lamp, bassett hound, 12½" 55.00
#897, TV lamp, mare & foal, wht porc 30.00
#907, doe, walnut, wht porc, tangerine, 12½" 15.00
#911/#913, Chinese pheasants, air-brushed colors, 11", pr 30.00
#914, stag, standing, natural colors, 12½" 15.00
#923, swans (2), blk matt, 10½" 25.00
#924, stag, standing, natural colors, 12½" 15.00
#925/#926, horses, rearing/charging, pr 20.00
#928/#929, mallards, male/female, natural colors, 9½", pr 40.00
#932, rooster, 10½" 30.00
#969, Early Birds, blk matt, tangerine, 14½", pr 25.00
#970, flamingo, flying, natural colors, 11" 45.00
#971, flamingo, winging, natural colors, 12" 45.00
#972/#973, bull, red, head up/head down, 11" L, pr 50.00
#982, horse, prancing 20.00
#984, elephant, sitting, 18" 25.00
Ashtray set, yel & red, metal caddy w/6 ind ashtrays 20.00
Bank, smiling piggy, red or gr, 12" L 25.00
Cats, Deco style, blk matt, 12½", facing pr 50.00
Cockatoo, on branch w/appl flower, 11" 35.00
Cookie jar, Bear, #2101 .... 75.00
Cookie jar, Beatrix Potter Rabbit, c Maddux of Calif 100.00
Cookie jar, Calory Hippy 300.00
Cookie jar, Clown, very lg, from $325 to 395.00
Cookie jar, Grape Cylinder 45.00
Cookie jar, Humpty Dumpty, #2113, from $250 to 300.00
Cookie jar, Koala 75.00
Cookie jar, Queen, #2104, from $125 to 140.00
Cookie jar, Raggedy Andy, #2108, Raggedy Andy, from $250 to .. 300.00
Cookie jar, Scottie 75.00
Cookie jar, Snowman 75.00
Cookie jar, Squirrel, Maddux of Calif, C Romanelli, #2110 .... 100.00
Cookie jar, Strawberry 35.00
Cookie jar, Walrus 65.00
Ducklings, 3 on grassy base 20.00
Flamingo Line, single flamingo planter, 6" 20.00
Planter, rearing horse, 10x7½" 22.00

Magazines

Magazines are collected for their cover prints and for the information pertaining to defunct companies and their products that can be gleaned from the old advertisements. In the listings that follow, items are assumed to be in very good condition unless noted otherwise. See also Movie Memorabilia; Parrish, Maxfield.

Key:
 M — mint condition, in original wrapper
 EX — excellent condition, spine intact, edges of pages clean and straight
 VG — very good condition, the average as-found condition

American Magazine, 1918, November, Rockwell art, EX 30.00
Collier's, 1956, March 2, Grace Kelly & Prince Rainier 15.00
Cosmopolitan, 1953, August, Janet Leigh cover, EX 7.50
Cosmopolitan, 1953, May, Marilyn Monroe/Oklahoma, EX 45.00
Country Gentleman, 1917, September 8, Rockwell art, EX 30.00
Esquire, 1941, November, Vargas & Petty art 20.00
Esquire, 1958, October, Silver Anniversary 25.00
Fortune, 1949, Ben Shahn, EX 30.00
Good Housekeeping, 1959, July, Ingrid Bergman, NM 10.00

Harper's Weekly, 1883, August 23, W.A. Rogers cover only, EX, $25.00.

Harper's Weekly, 1858, July 24, Hudson Bay Gold Fields, EX 35.00
Harper's Weekly, 1901, September, McKinley 20.00
Ladies Home Journal, 1912, December, Parrish art, EX 75.00
Ladies Home Journal, 1924, November, Wyeth art, EX 20.00
Ladies Home Journal, 1933, December, choir singers, NM 15.00
Ladies Home Journal, 1941, July 1941, Bette Davis 15.00
Life, 1938, July 2, Gary Cooper 20.00
Life, 1939, May 22, World's Fair Guide 20.00
Life, 1941, September 9, Ted Williams, EX 50.00
Life, 1943, July 12, Roy Rogers & Trigger 35.00
Life, 1954, September 13, Judy Garland 20.00
Life, 1958, April 21, Kennedy family 15.00
Life, 1962, September 28, Don Drysdale cover, VG 12.50
Life, 1966, April 15, Louis Armstrong, EX 35.00
Life, 1966, March 11, Batman 25.00
Life, 1968, April 12, Dr Martin Luther King shooting 15.00
Life, 1972, December 29, Year in Pictures, last weekly issue 32.00
Life, 1978, November, Mickey Mouse's 50th Birthday, EX 15.00
Look, 1927, December, Shirley Temple & Santa, EX 35.00
Look, 1950, August 29, Hopalong Cassidy, EX 30.00
Look, 1957, May 14, Frank Sinatra, His Life Story, EX 10.00
Look, 1963, December, Kennedy & family, Special Edition 15.00
Look, 1971, April 6, Walt Disney World Opening, EX 15.00
McCall's, 1921, April, paper dolls, EX 20.00
McCall's, 1932, August, Mickey Mouse's Father, EX 30.00

McCall's, 1949, July, Eleanor Roosevelt Tells Her Story, EX **6.00**
Newsweek, 1937, October 4, Hitler & Mussolini, EX **25.00**
Newsweek, 1944, May 29, Dionne Quintuplets, EX **15.00**
Newsweek, 1972, January 10, Who Can Beat Nixon? **12.00**
Playboy, 1955, February, Jayne Mansfield, EX **150.00**
Playboy, 1960, May, Ginger Young, EX **18.00**
Playboy, 1967, March, Fran Gerard/Sharon Tate, Vargas art, EX ..**20.00**
Redbook, 1956, September 9, Gina Lollobrigida, EX **15.00**
Rolling Stone, 1969, #36, Jim Morrison/Janice Joplin, EX **100.00**
Rolling Stone, 1971, #88, Morrison Memorial, EX **100.00**
Saturday Evening Post, 1916, May 20, Rockwell's 1st cover, EX ..**50.00**
Saturday Evening Post, 1930, May 24, Gary Cooper, EX **45.00**
Saturday Evening Post, 1947, March 2, Rockwell cover, VG **20.00**
Saturday Evening Post, 1956, May, 19, Eye Doctor, Rockwell, EX ...**20.00**
Saturday Evening Post, 1956, May 19, Rockwell cover, VG **15.00**
Saturday Evening Post, 1957, June 29, Rockwell cover, EX **18.00**
Saturday Evening Post, 1960, October 29, JFK, Rockwell, VG **15.00**
Saturday Evening Post, 1968, June 1, Bobby Kennedy, EX **35.00**
Sports Illustrated, 1955, February 14, Autopilot cover, VG **10.00**
Sports Illustrated, 1956, June 18, Mickey Mantle, EX **150.00**
Sports Illustrated, 1959, April 15, Willie Mays **45.00**
Sports Illustrated, 1963, June 10, Cassius Clay, EX **95.00**
Sports Illustrated, 1965, January 18, Swimsuit, EX **65.00**
Sports Illustrated, 1984, December 10, Michael Jordan, EX **40.00**
Sports Magazine, 1969, April, Mickey Mantle, EX **20.00**
Sports Magazine, 1978, January 16, Beauties of Brazil, EX **20.00**
Time, 1939, April 10, Ginger Rogers, NM **35.00**
Time, 1963, May 17, James Baldwin, NM **40.00**
Time, 1964, January 3, Martin Luther King, EX **30.00**
TV Guide, 1953, July 17, Lucy & Desi, EX+ **35.00**
TV Guide, 1955, October 3, Rock Hudson, EX+ **15.00**
TV Guide, 1961, March 25, Alfred Hitchcock, EX+ **10.00**
TV Guide, 1963, March 30, Cast of Bonanza, EX+ **45.00**
TV Guide, 1965, September 18, Adrianne, EX+ **22.00**
TV Guide, 1970, April 25, Raquel Welch & John Wayne, EX+ ..**20.00**
TV Guide, 1977, June 11, Grizzly Adams, EX+ **12.00**
TV Guide, 1982, January 9, Michael Landon, EX+ **14.00**
TV Guide, 1988, August 13, Alf, EX+ **10.00**
TV Guide, 1990, September 8, Women of Twin Peaks, EX+ **25.00**
Yank, 1944, December 22, Sad Sack & Santa **10.00**

Majolica

Majolica is a type of heavy earthenware, design-molded and decorated in vivid colors with either a lead or tin type of glaze. It reached its height of popularity in the Victorian era; examples from this period are found in only the lead glazes. Nearly every potter of note, both here and abroad, produced large majolica jardinieres, umbrella stands, pitchers with animal themes, leaf shapes, vegetable forms, and nearly any other design from nature that came to mind. Few, however, marked their ware. Among those who did were Minton, Wedgwood, Holdcroft, and George Jones in England; Griffin, Smith, and Hill (Etruscan) in Phoenixville, Pennsylvania; and Chesapeake Pottery (Avalon and Clifton) in Baltimore.

Color and condition are both very important worth-assessing factors. Pieces with cobalt, lavender, and turquoise glazes command the highest prices. For further information we recommend *The Collector's Encyclopedia of Majolica* by Mariann Katz-Marks (see Directory, Pennsylvania). Values below are for pieces in mint condition. Our advisor for this category is Hardy Hudson; he is listed in the Directory under Florida.

Bottle, monk w/jug & glass figural, 10½" **350.00**
Bowl, acanthus leaves on bl, Geo Jones, 1870s, 10" **500.00**
Bowl, centerpc; Della Robbia, putti support ea end, Holdcroft .**1,500.00**

Bowl, centerpc; 2 putti ea side, gr mottle, pk int, 15x20" **1,760.00**
Bowl, cobalt shell w/dolphin ft, Holdcroft, 14" H **1,200.00**
Bowl, fruit; Oak Leaf, Etruscan, 12¼" **600.00**
Bowl, fruit; Oak Leaf w/Acorn, Etruscan **300.00**
Bowl, leaf form, pk border, 10" **165.00**
Bowl, salad; Shell & Seaweed, ftd, Etruscan **600.00**
Bowl, sauce; Sunflower, Albino, Etruscan **110.00**
Bowl, sauce; Sunflower, pk, Etruscan **220.00**
Bowl, Shell & Seaweed, Etruscan, 8½" **475.00**
Butter dish, Shell & Waves **375.00**
Butter pat, Begonia, Etruscan **100.00**
Butter pat, Bird on Branch **150.00**
Butter pat, Blackberry on wht **110.00**
Butter pat, Pansy, mc, Etruscan **175.00**
Cake stand, Maple Leaf on lt pk, Etruscan **275.00**
Cake stand, Pond Lily, 3 storks on ft, 6x9¼" **450.00**
Candle holder, boy figural, Continental, 6½" **100.00**
Candle holder, Victorian lady w/flower basket, 8" **90.00**
Centerpc, Putto in lg shell holds up sm shell, Copeland, 12" **980.00**
Charger, Roman legions, grotesque border, mc, 16" dia **400.00**
Cheese bell & stand, florals & basketweave, G Jones, 10" H ...**2,300.00**
Cheese keeper, bird on branch on yel, flower finial, 7" **1,155.00**
Cheese keeper, floral on turq, wedge, Holdcroft, 9½" **900.00**
Cheese keeper, lovebirds/dragonfly/prunus on wht, G Jones ...**1,000.00**
Coffeepot, Shell & Seaweed, Etruscan, NM **800.00**
Compote, Classical, solid color, Etruscan, 9½" dia **125.00**
Compote, Daisy on cobalt, Etruscan **500.00**
Compote, Fern & Bow, Banks & Thorley **350.00**
Compote, Shell & Seaweed, ftd, Etruscan, 6½x9¼" **1,750.00**
Creamer, Corn, unmk, 4½" **125.00**
Creamer, Shell & Seaweed, Etruscan, 3¾" **275.00**
Cup & saucer, Basket & Fern **200.00**
Cup & saucer, Cauliflower, Etruscan **440.00**
Cup & saucer, Flying Crane & Water Lily on cobalt **300.00**
Cup & saucer, Holly & Basketweave, red & gr on yel **175.00**
Cup & saucer, pineapple form **250.00**
Dish, Begonia Leaf w/lizard, Palissy style, 6½" L **300.00**
Garden seat, elephant, mc on brn, rim chip, Chinese, 17", pr **440.00**
Garden seat, toadstool form, Continental, 19½" **1,250.00**
Humdior, frog in red jacket/bl hat plays mandolin, 7½" **500.00**
Humidor, alligator w/red cape, 5" **600.00**
Humidor, boy seated on rope, 7½" **220.00**
Humidor, cat w/bandage on head holds fish, 7½" **500.00**
Humidor, man w/clown hat & collar **175.00**
Humidor, man w/handlebar mustache & hat **175.00**
Humidor, monkey in pk jacket figural, 10" **600.00**
Lamp, dolphin figural, European, 22" **750.00**
Match holder, boot maker figural, w/striker, 8½" **220.00**
Match holder, man by tree stump, w/striker, 6½" **150.00**
Match holder, man sings/plays mandolin figural, w/striker **165.00**
Match holder, mountain lion figural **580.00**
Match holder, rabbit at tree stump figural **440.00**
Nut dish, squirrel on leaf form, G Jones, ca 1875, 10½" **750.00**
Pitcher, bear figural, red int, 8½" **450.00**
Pitcher, Begonia Leaf, pk int, 7¼" **225.00**
Pitcher, birds feeding young in nest on brn, 7¼" **250.00**
Pitcher, Calla Lily, gray, yel, wht & gr, 5" **150.00**
Pitcher, castle tower form w/medieval figures, Minton, 13" **800.00**
Pitcher, cat w/mandolin figural, red int, 9", NM **770.00**
Pitcher, Corn, metal lid, English Registry mk, 8½" **400.00**
Pitcher, dog figural, brn & wht w/lav int, 9½" **600.00**
Pitcher, Dogwood on mottled ground, 5½" **175.00**
Pitcher, duck figural, EX color/detail, St Clement, 17" **495.00**
Pitcher, English Rose on cobalt, 7½" **220.00**

Pitcher, fish figural, open mouth, tail hdl, Morley & Co, 8" 275.00
Pitcher, flowers, mc on cobalt, brn hdl, 5¾" 225.00
Pitcher, flowers & lily pads, mc on brn, Holdcroft, 5½" 175.00
Pitcher, Flying Crane, 8½" 350.00
Pitcher, game birds on lav, Holdcroft, 7" 450.00
Pitcher, Ivy on Tree Bark, mc, 6" 250.00
Pitcher, Lily of Valley on wht, Lear, 10¼" 250.00
Pitcher, lily on brn, unmk Holdcroft, 5" 220.00
Pitcher, lotus & lily plants, sq rim, Copeland, ca 1877, 7½" ...3,500.00
Pitcher, monkey figural, bamboo hdl, 8" 450.00
Pitcher, owl figural, 10" 400.00
Pitcher, Pineapple, pk int, 5½" 225.00
Pitcher, rooster figural, St Clement, 11¼" 415.00
Pitcher, roses on yel & brn, English, 6" 150.00
Pitcher, Sunflower & Urn on wht, Wedgwood, 6½" 450.00
Pitcher, wheat on cobalt, Copeland, 7½" 400.00
Planter, Bamboo, lav int, ftd, G Jones, 5¼x6½" sq 880.00
Plaque, dog & stag, WS&S, 10x8" 470.00
Plaque, 2 lizards & alligator, unsgn Palissy, 8½" 550.00
Plate, Asparagus, mc, Fr, 9½" 210.00
Plate, Bellflower on cobalt, 8" 250.00
Plate, Cauliflower, 9" 250.00
Plate, Dogwood on Basketweave, twig border, Holdcroft, 9" 300.00
Plate, leaves, brn & gr, Etruscan, GSH, 8" 225.00
Plate, Ocean, mc w/gray border, Wedgwood, 9" 325.00
Plate, Overlapping Begonia, Etruscan, 9" 200.00
Plate, Pond Lily, 9¼" 200.00
Plate, Shell & Fishnet on turq, Fielding, 8½" 300.00
Platter, Asparagus w/Basketweaver, 16½x10" 300.00
Platter, Begonia Leaf on cobalt w/pk rim, 12" 385.00
Platter, Bird & Fan, Eureka, 16½x11" 350.00
Platter, bread; Rose & Rope, cobalt center, 15½x10½" 400.00
Platter, Eat Thy Bread w/Thankfulness 350.00
Platter, Fan & Floral w/Bird & Butterfly, 13½" 275.00
Platter, Leaves & Fern on turq, 12" 300.00
Platter, Maple Leaf on brn, 11½" 200.00
Platter, Sunflower & Begonia, mc, hdls, 11x8" 330.00
Sardine boat, fish on lid, lav int, 12½" 1,300.00
Sardine box, pointed leaves on cobalt, G Jones 1,600.00
Spittoon, Begonia Leaf on yel basket, pk int, 5½" 250.00
Spittoon, Flower on Basket, mc on wht 225.00
Spittoon, Shell & Seaweed, Etruscan, 6½" 900.00
Strawberry server, berries & flowers, vine hdl, Minton 1,200.00
Strawberry server, birds on branches form hdl, G Jones, 8x15" ..1,750.00
Sugar bowl, Shell & Seaweed, Etruscan, 5¼" 440.00
Syrup, Sunflower on cobalt, Etruscan 550.00
Teapot, appl leaves & berries, frog finial, Palissy style, EX 770.00
Teapot, Bird & Fan, Wardle 350.00
Teapot, Fan & Scroll w/insect, EX color, 7½", NM 275.00
Teapot, Shell & Seaweed, Etruscan 800.00
Tobacco box, rectangular basket w/boy on lid, 7x6x4" 275.00
Tray, Corn, gr & yel, oval, 12¾" 350.00
Vase, bird on bulrush form, bug on base, G Jones, 9¼" 1,500.00
Vase, Blk lady w/basket figural, Continental, 11½" 500.00
Vase, bud; Maize, gr & cobalt on brn, Wedgwood, 5" 330.00
Vase, monkey plays beside bamboo stalk, Minton, 7¼" 2,100.00
Vase, Nouveau lady seated on rim, mc & cobalt, 15½" 880.00
Vase, 3 lions form ft, brns & cobalt, pk int, Etruscan 500.00
Waste bowl, Shell & Seaweed, Etruscan 770.00

Malachite Glass

Malachite is a type of art glass that exhibits strata-like layerings in

shades of green, similar to the mineral in its natural form. Some examples have an acid-etched mark of Moser/Carlsbad, usually on the base. However, it should be noted that in the past fifteen years there have been reproductions from Czechoslovakia with a paper label.

Basket, lady & cherubs, loop hdl, 6x6½" 165.00
Box, nudes on lid & base, 2x3½" dia 110.00
Egg, on sterling tripod stand, 8" H 160.00
Vase, Ingrid (draped women), Schlevogt, 9½" 300.00

Mantel Lustres

Mantel lustres are decorative vases or candle holders made from all types of glass, often highly decorated, and usually hung with one or more rows of prisms. In the listings that follow, values are given for a pair.

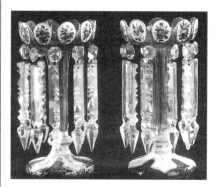

Ruby and white overlay with painted floral sprays within oval panels forming scalloped top, cut prisms, hollow circular feet with cut decoration, gold trim, late 1800s, 10", $400.00 for the pair.

Cranberry w/HP floral, scalloped, long prisms, 14" 600.00
Gr w/wht star flowers/beads/gold bars, prisms, 14½", pr 250.00
Pk & wht cased w/gilt & wht florals, prisms, 1890s, 12", pr ..165.00
Pk Bristol w/HP florals & gold, cased, prisms, 12" 375.00

Maps and Atlases

Maps are highly collectible, not only for historical value but also for their sometimes elaborate artwork, legendary information, or data that since they were printed has been proven erroneous. There are many types of maps including geographical, military, celestial, road, and railroad. Nineteenth-century maps, particularly of U.S. areas, are increasing in popularity and price. Rarity, area depicted (i.e. Texas is more sought after than North Dakota), and condition are major price factors. Our advisor for this category is Murray Hudson; he is listed in the Directory under Tennessee.

Key:
b/w — black/white   J&B — Johnson and Browning
hc — hand colored

Atlases

Appleton's Library...Modern Geography, 103 maps, 1892, EX ...500.00
Atlas of World & Gazetter, Funk & Wagnall, 1924, 191-pg, EX ..20.00
Century of Progress, 1933 World's Fair, 108-pg, VG 20.00
Cram's Universal, 159 countries/etc, 1888, EX 175.00
Rand McNally Std...of World, 138 maps+engravings, 1890, EX ...150.00

Maps

Africa, R de Vaugondy, hc, 1756, 19x25"+mat & fr 300.00
AK, Klondike Region, mc, 1900, 15x21", VG 40.00

AL & GA, hc, w/2 vignettes, J&B, 1862, 18x26", EX 95.00
Charlston & Savannah, hc, by street, Colton, 1855, 15x18", EX .75.00
Cuba, Official Map, color, 1900, 14x22", VG 40.00
Dallas, mc, 1900, 11x14", VG 50.00
France, Guillaume de L'Isle, Amsterdam, hc, early, 20x25"+fr ...300.00
Holy Land, Ortelius, hc, ca 1570, 14½x19¾"+margins 600.00
KS, dbl-pg, mc, 1883, 14x21", VG 35.00
KY & TN, hc, w/3 vignettes, J&B, 1862, EX 85.00
LA & New Orleans, hc, 3 segments, Gray, 1878, 16x26", EX 85.00
MI, GW&CB Colton, hc, Lake Superior on bk, single folio, 1855 ...75.00
Morian or Jerusalem & Adjacent Country, b/w, 1816, 8x11", G ..75.00
N America, Chapman & Hall, 1853, 12x16½" in fr, EX 85.00
NC & SC, AJ Johnson, dbl folio w/hc insets, 1865 .... 65.00
NC & SC, hc, 2 vignettes & Charlston, J&B, 1862, 18x26", VG ...75.00
New England (including NY/NJ), Homann, 1759, 19½x23¼" ..900.00
New Foundland, dbl-pg, mc, 1900, VG 40.00
North Am, dbl-pg, mc, 1900, 14x22", VG 35.00
NY, NJ, PA; mc, dbl-pg, Zell's Atlas, 1852, VG 30.00
Palestine, mc, dbl-pg, 1888, 14x21", EX 45.00
Philippine Islands, dbl-pg, color, 1900, 14x22", VG 30.00
Puerto Rico, mc, dbl-pg, 15x21", VG 25.00
Southern States, 1883, 12x17", VG 35.00
TX, hc, w/Galveston Bay & Sabine Lake, J&B, 1862, 18x26", EX ..175.00
US, Johnson, dbl folio w/hc, 1864, EX 90.00
USA, mc, dbl-pg, 1900, 14x22", VG 35.00
VA (Undivided), hc, 1852, 5x7", VG 40.00
VA & West VA, mc, dbl-pg, 1900, 14x22", VG 40.00
Western Hemisphere, Bertius, eng, 1624, 18x23", EX 1,550.00
WI, J&B, hc by counties, single folio w/border 50.00
WI & MI, AJ Johnson, dbl folio w/hc counties, 1864 .... 60.00
WY, mc, 1883, 11x14", VG 35.00

Marblehead

What began as therapy for patients in a sanitarium in Marble-head, Massachusetts, has become recognized as an important part of the Arts and Crafts movement in America. Results of the early experiments under the guidance of Arthur E. Baggs in 1904 met with such success that by 1908 the pottery had been converted to a solely commercial venture. Simple vase shapes were often incised with stylized animal and floral motifs or sailing ships. Some were decorated in low relief; many were plain. Simple matt glazes in soft yellow, gray, wisteria, rose, tobacco brown, and their most popular, Marblehead blue, were used alone or in combination. The Marblehead logo is distinctive — a ship with full sail and the letters 'M' and 'P.' The pottery closed in 1936.

Bookends, sailing ships, cvd/pnt, 6-color, rpr, 5½" 375.00
Bowl, dk bl, 2x6" dia 425.00
Bowl, gray, lt ribbing, incurvate w/collar neck, 3x6" 210.00
Bowl, gray, lt violet int, 4x9" 200.00
Bowl, gray w/brn int, 1½x7½" 160.00
Bowl, oak leaf/berry band, gr/red on dk bl, 2½x6" 1,000.00
Bowl, spades, blk on dk gr, AB, 1½x7" 700.00
Candlesticks, geometrics, gray on dk gr, HJH, 7½", pr 2,500.00
Chamberstick, bl, inverted cone w/hdl, 4" 260.00
Chamberstick, gr, #1917, 4" 250.00
Creamer, dk bl w/lt bl int, 3" 135.00
Cup, dk bl w/hdl & rim band in subtle gr, Baggs/Tutt, 3½" 200.00
Tile, galleon, 4-color, 4½" 275.00
Tile, peacock, dk bl/red/gr on lt bl, oak fr, 4¾" 850.00
Tile, ship at sea, 4-color, 6", +fr 500.00
Tile, steamship on sea, 3-color, 4½", +fr 375.00

Vase, allover stylized florals, pk & bl on gray & bl, rpr, 9" 1,900.00
Vase, bl, flaring sides, 6" 350.00
Vase, brn, 2½x2¼" 170.00
Vase, butterflies/flowers/berries cvg, 5-color, 4x4" 1,400.00
Vase, dk bl, baluster w/short neck, 5" 230.00
Vase, dk bl, teardrop, 6x6" 500.00
Vase, dk gr, rim-to-wide base, 2½x4½" 250.00
Vase, dk pebbly bl, tapering w/flared rim, 8x4½" 450.00
Vase, floral band cvg, 4-color, 6x5" 2,600.00
Vase, florals on upright stems (4 repeats), 3-color, HT, 5½" ...2,600.00
Vase, gr, cylindrical, 7½", NM 375.00
Vase, gr, squat, 3x4¼" 375.00
Vase, grapevines, 3-color on gray & bl, 5½" 1,700.00
Vase, grapevines, 4-color (EX art), HT, 3½" 1,500.00
Vase, gray, short neck, shouldered, 5" 150.00
Vase, lav, concave cylinder, 6½" 280.00
Vase, leaf panels, gray on dk gr, cylinder, 9½x4½", NM 4,750.00
Vase, lt bl gloss w/pk int, 3" 160.00
Vase, lt purple, flaring sides, 5" 170.00
Vase, lt purple, incurvate cylinder, 8" 400.00
Vase, mustard w/incised ribs & diagonals, 6" 270.00
Vase, olive gr, 3x6½" 250.00
Vase, pk, flared rim, narrow flat ft, 3" 100.00
Vase, purple, cylindrical w/inverted rim, 3½x2¼" 200.00
Vase, purple, tapered form, 7½" 350.00
Vase, purple matt, tapered form, mk, 4" 250.00
Vase, seaweed cvg, brn on periwinkle, AEG, 3x3½" 550.00

Vase, stylized squared leaves on swollen form, 5-color, EX artwork, 7", $5,000.00.

Vase, sqd leaves/berries/tendrils, 4-color, swollen form, 6" 3,500.00
Vase, swirl/dots rim band, blk/brn/tan on olive, HT, 7½x6" ...4,250.00
Vase, upright berried branches, 4-color (EX art), 4½" 2,000.00
Vase, yel/rust/tan speckle, heavy finger ridges, flared, 5" 375.00
Wall pocket, bl gloss, bulbous w/flared & crimped top, 5" 270.00
Wall pocket, med gr, bulbous, 5" 160.00

Marbles

Marbles have been popular with children since the mid-1800s. They've been made in many types from a variety of materials. Among some of the first glass items to be produced, the earliest marbles were made from a solid glass rod broken into sections of the proper length which were placed in a tray of sand and charcoal and returned to the fire. As they were reheated, the trays were constantly agitated until the marbles were completely round. Other marbles were made of china, pottery, steel, and natural stones.

Below is a listing of the various types, along with a brief description of each.

Agates: stone marbles of many different colors — bands of color alternating with white usually encircle the marble; most are translucent.

Ballot Box: handmade (with pontils), opaque white or black, used in lodge elections.

Bloodstone: green chalcedony with red spots, a type of quartz.

China: with or without glaze, in a variety of hand-painted designs — parallel bands or bull's-eye designs most common.

Clambroth: opaque glass with outer evenly spaced swirls of one or alternating colors.

Clay: one of the most common older types; some are painted while others are not.

Comic Strip: a series of twelve machine-made marbles with faces of comic strip characters, Peltier Glass Factory, Illinois.

Crockery: sometimes referred to as Benningtons; most are either blue or brown, although some are speckled. The clay is shaped into a sphere, then coated with glaze and fired.

End of the Day: single-pontil glass marbles — the colored part often appears as a multicolored blob or mushroom cloud.

Goldstone: clear glass completely filled with copper flakes that have turned gold-colored from the heat of the manufacturing process.

Indian Swirls: usually black glass with a colored swirl appearing on the outside next to the surface, often irregular.

Latticinio Core Swirls: double-pontil marble with an inner area with net-like effects of swirls coming up around the center.

Lutz Type: glass with colored or clear bands alternating with bands which contain copper flecks.

Micas: clear or colored glass with mica flecks which reflect as silver dots when marble is turned. Red is rare.

Onionskin: spiral type which are solidly colored instead of having individual ribbons or threads, multicolored.

Peppermint Swirls: made of white opaque glass with alternating blue and red outer swirls.

Ribbon Core Swirls: double-pontil marble — center shaped like a ribbon with swirls that come up around the middle.

Rose Quartz: stone marble, usually pink in color, often with fractures inside and on outer surface.

Solid Core Swirls: double-pontil marble — middle is solid with swirls coming up around the core.

Steelies: hollow steel spheres marked with a cross where the steel was bent together to form the ball.

Sulfides: generally made of clear glass with figures inside. Rarer types have colored figures or colored glass.

Tiger Eye: stone marble of golden quartz with inclusions of asbestos, dark brown with gold highlights.

Vaseline: machine-made of yellowish-green glass with small bubbles.

Prices listed below are for marbles in near-mint condition unless noted otherwise. When size is not indicated, assume them to be of average size, ½" to 1". Polished marbles have greatly reduced values. (We do not list tinted marbles because there is no way of knowing how much color the tinting has, and intensity of color is an important worth-assessing factor.

For a more thorough study of the subject, we recommend *Antique and Collectible Marbles, 3rd Edition; Machine-Made and Contemporary Marbles, 2nd Edition;* and *Big Book of Marbles,* all by our advisor, Everett Grist; you will find his address in the Directory under Tennessee.

Agate, contemporary, carnelian, 1¾"	160.00
Banded Opaque, gr & wht, 2"	1,200.00
Banded Opaque, red & wht, 1¾"	1,200.00
Banded Opaque, red & wht, ¾"	95.00
Banded Transparent Swirl, bl, ¾"	75.00
Banded Transparent Swirl, lt gr, 1¾"	750.00

Banded opaque, semi-opaque milky white with pink stripes, ¾" to ⅜", set of 3, $310.00; Indian Swirls, ¾" to ⅞", set of 3, $340.00.

Bennington, bl, 1¾"	40.00
Bennington, bl, ¾"	3.00
Bennington, brn, 1¾"	30.00
Bennington, fancy, 1¾"	80.00
Bennington, fancy, ¾"	5.00
China, decorated, glazed, apple, 1¾"	1,200.00
China, decorated, glazed, rose, 1¾"	2,000.00
China, decorated, glazed, wht w/geometrics, 1¾"	125.00
China, decorated, unglazed, geometrics & flowers, ¾"	200.00
Clambroth, opaque, bl & wht, 1¾"	2,600.00
Clambroth, opaque, bl & wht, ¾"	250.00
Clambroth Swirl, red/wht, Germany, 1900, ⅞"	475.00
Comic, Andy Gump	100.00
Comic, Betty Boop	200.00
Comic, Cotes Bakery, advertising	900.00
Comic, Kayo, rare	300.00
Comic, Little Orphan Annie	100.00
Comic, Moon Mullins	300.00
Comic, set of 12	1,500.00
Comic, Skeezix	150.00
Comic, Tom Mix	2,000.00
Cork Screw, machine-made, common, ⅝"	5.00
End of Day, bl & wht, 1¾"	1,200.00
Goldstone, ¾"	35.00
Indian Swirl, 1¾"	2,500.00
Indian Swirl Lutz-type, gold flakes, ¾"	600.00
Line Crockery, clay, 1¾"	75.00
Mica, bl, ¾"	35.00
Mica, gr, 1¾"	800.00
Onionskin, w/mica, 1¾"	1,500.00
Onionskin, w/mica, ¾"	110.00
Onionskin, 16-lobe, unusual, 1¾"	1,800.00
Onionskin, ¾"	90.00
Onionskin, 4-lobe, 1¼"	450.00
Opaque Swirl, gr, ¾"	75.00
Opaque Swirl Lutz-type, bl, yel, gr, ¾"	325.00
Peppermint Swirl, opaque, red, wht, & bl, 1¾"	2,000.00
Peppermint Swirl, opaque, red, wht, & bl, ¾"	125.00
Pottery, 1¾"	75.00
Ribbon Core Lutz-type, red, 1¾"	1,800.00
Slag, bl, machine-made, sm	3.00
Slag, bl, machine-made, 1½"	150.00
Solid Opaque, gr, 1¾"	800.00
Solid Opaque, ¾"	75.00
Sulfide, alligator, 1¾"	250.00
Sulfide, baboon playing bass fiddle, 2⅛"	1,200.00
Sulfide, bear cub on all 4s, detailed, 1¼", NM+	175.00
Sulfide, bird, 2", EX	150.00
Sulfide, cat, 1¼"	100.00
Sulfide, child sitting, 1¾"	600.00

Sulfide, child w/sailboat, 1¾" 800.00
Sulfide, cow, detailed, 1⅞", NM+ 210.00
Sulfide, crane w/fish, 1¾" 600.00
Sulfide, deer, 1¼" 175.00
Sulfide, dog howling, 1⅜", M 140.00
Sulfide, dog on grass mound, HP/3-color, pontil, 1¼", NM 3,500.00
Sulfide, eagle w/closed wings, 1⅞" 150.00
Sulfide, elephant, 1¾" 175.00
Sulfide, elephant w/long trunk, 1¼", NM 140.00
Sulfide, face of angel w/wings, 1¾" 1,000.00
Sulfide, figure-8, 1¾" 400.00
Sulfide, fish, 1¾" 175.00
Sulfide, fox, 1½", EX 130.00
Sulfide, frog, 1⅞", NM+ 150.00
Sulfide, goat, 1¾" 125.00
Sulfide, hen, 1⅛" 150.00
Sulfide, Jenny Lind bust, 1¾" 900.00
Sulfide, lamb, 1¾", NM 125.00
Sulfide, lion, standing male, 1½", NM 85.00
Sulfide, owl, w/closed wings, 1¾" 150.00
Sulfide, pig, 1¾" 150.00
Sulfide, pony, 1¾" 200.00
Sulfide, rabbit running, lg/offset/sm bubble, 1½", M- 110.00
Sulfide, razor-bk hog, 1½" 150.00
Sulfide, rooster, lg/detailed, polished (no pontil), 1¾" 110.00
Sulfide, rooster, 1¾" 150.00
Sulfide, Santa Claus, 1¾" 1,200.00
Sulfide, sheep grazing, 1¼", NM 85.00
Sulfide, sheep standing, detailed, 1½", M 130.00
Sulfide, squirrel, standing, 1¾", EX 170.00

Marine Collectibles

Vintage tools used on sea-going vessels, lanterns, clocks, and memorabilia of all types are sought out by those who are interested in preserving the romantic genre that revolves around the life of the sea captains, their boats, and their crews; ports of call; and the lure of far away islands. See also Steamship Collectibles; Telescopes; Scrimshaw; Tools.

Alarm gong, mk USN, polished brass, w/dbl striker, 18" dia 550.00
Anchor, CI fluke style, 12x9" 40.00
Auger, boatyard; 22" wood hdl w/2" bit, worn 20.00
Bell, tugboat; brass, w/striker, 8½x12" dia 525.00
Binnacle, J Morton Ltd, brass & wood, complete, 56", EX 1,800.00
Binnacle, Norwegian work boat, no hood, 27" 525.00
Box, folding, canvas w/wood bottom, fits in 16x36" bag, NM 575.00
Chair, captain's; military, vinyl w/aluminum fr, EX 300.00
Chest, captain's; wood w/iron bands, Oriental, 1850s, 30x34" ...1,900.00
Clock, WW II cargo, S Thomas, Bakelite body/brass rim, 10" 375.00
Compass, US Coast Guard, WM Welch Mfg, model #2, brass ...250.00
Gauge, pressure; Bakelite, 0-200 psi, 4½" face 15.00
Gauge, pressure; brass, mk 0-450 LB Per Sq In, 11½" face 200.00
Lantern, brass w/onion-shaped globe, British MM, 10x7" 150.00
Lantern, dbl-caged steamboat style, steel/clear globe, 11" 120.00
Lifeboat chart dividers, stainless steel, WWII era, 4" 18.00
Lifeboat parallel chart ruler, Livanos Shipping Co 25.00
Model, whaling ship, detailed, Bennet, 19th C, 23" L, +case ..3,200.00
Navigation light, pnt steel w/onion-shaped globe, 23x12" 200.00
Navigation light, port; galvanized steel w/brass top ring, 18" 175.00
Net float, Japanese, w/portions of orig net, 12" dia 140.00
Propeller, acorn-style lock nut mk STD 1, brass 110.00
Propeller, brass & copper, 3-blade, 12" dia 90.00
Sextant, FW Lincoln, Boston, 19th C, EX 460.00

Telephone, Hose-McCann Type A Model N, hand-crank 125.00
Wheel, iron & wood w/fold-out steering stick, 54" **3,500.00**
Whistle, steam; brass flat-top single-note, w/o valve, 20x4" **300.00**

Martin Bros.

The Martin brothers were studio potters who worked from 1873 until 1914, first at Fulham and later at London and Southall. There were four brothers, each of whom excelled in their particular area. Robert, known as Wallace, was an experienced stonecarver. He modeled a series of grotesque bird and animal figural caricatures. Walter was the potter, responsible for throwing the larger vases on the wheel, firing the kiln, and mixing the clay. Edwin, an artist of stature, preferred more naturalistic forms of decoration. His work was often incised or had relief designs of seaweed, florals, fish, and birds. The fourth brother, Charles, was their business manager. Their work was incised with their names, place of production, and letters and numbers indicating month and year.

Vessel, grotesque birds embracing, moss green, gray, and brown, mounted on wooden base, signed, dated 10.6.1908, 7½x6¾x3", $13,800.00.

Bird jar, head cocked, mustard/bl/gr/brn matt, 1898, 10½" ...**16,250.00**
Bird jar, open mouth, Xd-eyes, 1911, rstr, 11x6½" **16,250.00**
Bird jar, smiling, blk/bl/gray/brn, 1898, 14¼x5½" **22,750.00**
Bird jar, triangular brn beak, brn/gr/beige, 1895, 9½x6" **10,400.00**
Bird vessel, grotesque, brn/bl/gr/gray, wood base, 8x3½" **7,475.00**
Bowl, satyrs & grape leaves, bl/brn, touch-ups, 3½x10¼" **7,800.00**
Humidor, 2-faced, orange-brn tones, rstr lid, 1903, 7x6¼" **6,800.00**
Jug, dbl-face, gr/brn salt glaze, brn spout, RW Martin, 5x4" **2,900.00**
Jug, sea creatures/plants, grays/brns/bl, 4-sided, 1896, 9½" **3,250.00**
Jug, single leering face, brn mottle, RW Martin, 1909, 6½" **3,900.00**
Jug, toothy fish/creatures, brn on mottled gray, 1900, 12", EX **3,900.00**
Paperweight, dragon w/curled tail, brn/gr, 1882, 2½x4½" **2,600.00**
Pitcher, iguanas & lizards, 4-sided, 1875, rstr, 7½x6½" **2,300.00**
Pitcher, mischevious face ea side, brn/caramel flambe, 5½" **1,900.00**
Salt cellar, toothy fish & flowers, bl/brn/gr, sq, 3¼x5" **3,000.00**
Spoon warmer, gargoyle w/open mouth, RW Martin, 5¼x5" ..**6,500.00**
Toby jug, seated man, brn & caramel, RW Martin, 1903, 10x5½" .**4,900.00**
Vase, bud; 2 storks, brn & ivory, 4-sided, 1904, 5½x1¾" **1,300.00**
Vase, dragons, blk & gray on copperdust, slim, 1901, 11½" **2,900.00**
Vase, dragons & gargoyles, brn/wht/blk on dk brn, 1896, 8" ...**1,300.00**
Vase, flying dragons, gray on brn, classic form, 1896, 8¾" **2,300.00**
Vase, incised snails/jelly fish, mc on gray & brn, 1903, 9¼" **3,250.00**

Mary Gregory

Mary Gregory glass, for reasons that remain obscure, is the namesake of a Boston and Sandwich Glass Company employee who worked for the company for only two years in the mid-1800s. Although no evidence actually exists to indicate that glass of this type was even produced there, the fine colored or crystal ware decorated with figures of children in white enamel is commonly referred to as Mary Gregory. The glass, in fact, originated in Europe and was imported into this country where it was copied by several eastern glasshouses. It was popular from the mid-1800s until the turn of the century. It is generally accepted that examples with all-white figures were made in the U.S.A., while gold-trimmed items and those with children having tinted faces or a small amount of color on their clothing are European. Though amethyst is rare, examples in cranberry command the highest prices. Blue ranks next; and green, amber, and clear items are worth the least. Watch for new glass decorated with screen-printed children and a minimum of hand painting. The screen effect is easily detected with a magnifying glass.

Bottle, scent; cranberry, girl, rnd, rnd gold stopper, 3½" 300.00
Bottle, scent; emerald gr, boy, clear faceted stopper, 3½" 175.00
Bottle, scent; lt bl, lady & flowers, 3"+stopper 275.00
Box, cranberry, boy w/flowers, dome top, 5¾x6" dia 1,065.00
Box, gr, child on lid, 2½x3½" dia 125.00
Box, lime gr, boy w/flower, 4" H 255.00
Box, patch; bl, boy points at birds, 1½x3" dia 225.00
Box, powder; emerald gr, boy among flowers & gr leaves 255.00
Creamer, cranberry, boy w/butterfly net, 3½" 325.00
Decanter, gr, boy in pk suit, tooled hdl/acorn stopper, 11½" 295.00
Goblet, amber, girl w/flower spray, 5⅛x2⅜" 125.00
Jar, amethyst, girl blowing bubbles, tulip finial w/gold, 8" 150.00
Lamp, blk amethyst, boy by fence, complete/orig, 20½x6½" 895.00
Mug, amber, girl, Mother 1890, 3" 85.00
Pitcher, bl, girl w/flower & staff, gold rim, 9½" 325.00
Pitcher, blk amethyst, girl swinging, reeded hdl, 9" 530.00
Pitcher, cranberry, boy, trees & bird, 10" 325.00
Pitcher, olive, youth w/staff, ribbed tankard, 8½" 150.00
Pitcher, Prussian bl, lady in long gown, pnt features, 9½" 325.00
Tea warmer, lav, boy w/net & sailboats, metal fr, 4¼" 250.00
Urn, blk, girl & boy pick apples, ped base, 9¾" 350.00
Vase, blk amethyst, girl w/tray, 8¼" 175.00
Vase, bud; emerald gr; Cupid, 7" 150.00
Vase, cranberry, girl w/basket, ped ft, 5" 225.00
Vase, emerald gr, girl w/flower, gold trim, 8" 135.00
Vase, gr opaque bristol, boy w/flower tray, ruffled, 11x4¼" 225.00
Vase, honey-amber, girl w/rod & hoop, clear ped ft, 12" 235.00
Vase, lime gr, girl w/butterfly net, cylindrical, 10⅝x4" 195.00
Vase, lime gr satin, elegant lady, lipped, 7" 125.00

Mason's Ironstone

In 1813 Charles J. Mason was granted a patent for a process said to 'improve the quality of English porcelain.' The new type of ware was in fact ironstone which Mason decorated with colorful florals and scenics, some of which reflected the Oriental taste. Although his business failed for a short time in the late 1840s, Mason re-established himself and continued to produce dinnerware, tea services, and ornamental pieces until about 1852 at which time the pottery was sold to Francis Morley. Ten years later, Geo. L. and Taylor Ashworth became owners. Both Morley and the Ashworths not only used Mason's molds and patterns but often his mark as well. Because the quality and the workmanship of the later wares do not compare with Mason's earlier product, collectors should take care to distinguish one from the other. Consult a good book on marks to be sure. The Wedgwood Company now owns the rights to the Mason patterns and is reproducing the Vista pattern. Note: Blue Vista is generally valued at 15% to 20% above prices for pink/red. Our advisor for this category is Susan Hirshman; she is listed in the Directory under Oregon.

Ashtray, Vista, bl, mk, 3½x3½" 10.00

Bowl, Vista, brown with sea-serpent handles, 11", $275.00.

Bowl, dessert; Fruit Basket, mc on wht, mk, 5½" 40.00
Bowl, dessert; Regency, mc on cream, mk, 5½" 50.00
Bowl, Oriental scenes, mc on cream, 8-sided, mk, 3¾x6¾" 60.00
Bowl, soup; Regency, mc on cream, scalloped, mk, 9", 6 for 80.00
Bowl, soup; Willow, Oriental landscape, flow bl, mk, 9½" 90.00
Bowl, vegetable; Vista, red, sq, mk, 9x9" 175.00
Bowl, Vista, bl, mk, 5x11" 90.00
Bowls, Vista, red, 8-sided, mk, nesting set of 3 ....650.00
Casserole, Vista, red, w/lid, mk, 11x10" 275.00
Creamer, Cow Bells, brn, mk, 3x4¾", EX 30.00
Creamer, Oriental flowers, mc on wht, 4x3½" 350.00
Jug, Cow Bells, brn, 8-sided, mk, 5½x6¾", EX 50.00
Jug, floral, mc on wht w/gold, bl snake hdl, 8-sided, mk, 3½" 150.00
Jug, floral, mc on wht w/gold, bl snake hdl, 8-sided, mk, 7½" 225.00
Jug, floral & butterflies, gold on cobalt, 8-sided, mk, 8" 2,000.00
Jug, Fountain, mulberry & cream, w/mc HP details, mk, 6½" 200.00
Jug, Fruit Basket, mc on wht, serpent hdl, mk, 6x7" 150.00
Jug, Fruit Basket, mc on wht, 8-sided, mk, 5½x5" 175.00
Jug, milk; The Kill, wild boar/3 dogs, stag/3 dogs, mk, 7½" 400.00
Jug, Oriental scenes, mc on wht w/gold, mk, 11x10" 325.00
Jug, Oriental scenes w/cobalt & gold, 8-sided, mk, 6½" 325.00
Jug, Regency, mc on cream, scalloped rim, 8-sided, mk, 6¼" 225.00
Jug, Vista, bl, 8-sided, mk, 7x6½" 200.00
Jug, Vista, mc on cream, 8-sided, 6½" 225.00
Jug, 2 birds among flowers, mc on wht, 8-sided, mk, 4½" 175.00
Perfume holder, Oriental mc flowers on cobalt w/gold, mk, 7" ...250.00
Pitcher, Oriental couple & flowers on blk, mk, 4x5½" 500.00
Pitcher, Oriental scenes w/cobalt & gold, 6-sided, mk, 9" 1,700.00
Plate, Am Marine, red on cream, red mk, 9½" 100.00
Plate, courtyard scene, mulberry w/mc florals, mk, 8" 60.00
Plate, dinner; Regency, mc on cream, scalloped, 10½" 35.00
Plate, dinner; Vista, red, mk, 10½" 35.00
Plate, Oak, mc on cream, mk, 1910, 8½" 30.00
Plate, Strathmore, mc on cream w/HP details, mk, 9" 15.00
Plate, Willow, Chinese landscape, flow bl, mk, 10¼" 100.00
Platter, Chinoiserie, lt bl transfer, crown mk, 20" 200.00
Platter, Oriental design, orange/cobalt/gr 40.00
Platter, Regency, mc on cream, scalloped rim, mk, 16x13" 300.00
Platter, Vista, red, scalloped rim, mk, 17x14" 200.00
Vase, Chinese Dragon, flow bl, 8-sided, mk, 5½" 100.00
Vase, flowers & butterflies, mc on blk, 6-sided, mk, 9" 600.00
Vase, Oriental flowers, mc on wht, 8-sided, mk, 5½x2½" 200.00
Vase, Oriental scenes in panels on cobalt, 8-sided, mk, 6" 225.00
Vase, red pheasant & mc floral on wht, sq, mk, 8x3½" 375.00

Massier

Clement Massier was a French artist-potter who in 1881 established a workshop at Golfe Juan, France, where he experimented with metallic lustre glazes. (One of his pupils was Jacques Sicardo, who brought the knowledge he had gained through his association with

Massier to the Weller Pottery Company in Zanesville, Ohio.) The lustre lines developed by Massier incorporated nature themes with allover decorations of foliage or flowers on shapes modeled in the Art Nouveau style. The ware was usually incised with the Massier name, his initials, or the location of the pottery. Massier died in 1917.

Charger, pines by lake, burgundy irid ground, 12½" **1,400.00**
Vase, gr opaque gloss, lg bat's-wing hdls, 9x10½" **450.00**
Vase, sunflowers, flat/irid yel on irid violet/gr, hdls, 14" **980.00**
Vase, thistles, gold/blk on bl mottled w/gold, mk, 6½" **230.00**

Match Holders

Before the invention of the safety match in 1855, matches were kept in matchboxes and carried in pocket-size match safes because they ignited so easily. John Walker, an English chemist, invented the match more than one hundred years ago, quite by accident. Walker was working with a mixture of potash and antimony, hoping to make a combustible that could be used to fire guns. The mixture adhered to the end of the wooden stick he had used for stirring. As he tried to remove it by scraping the stick on the stone floor, it burst into flames. The invention of the match was only a step away! From that time to the present, match holders have been made in amusing figural forms as well as simple utilitarian styles and in a wide range of materials. Both table-top and wall-hanging models were made — all designed to keep matches conveniently at hand. Our advisor for this category is Ron Damaska; he is listed in the Directory under Pennsylvania. See also Advertising.

Brass, devil figure, scrolled wall mt, early **55.00**
Brass, dog at the window **65.00**
Brass, man swinging on fence, desk type, lg **250.00**
Bsk, boy w/butterfly net **50.00**
Bsk, monkey in bow tie, hat at ft, striker on head, Germany **150.00**
Bust of lady in plumed hat, pnt CI, LB17 Iron Art, EX **55.00**
China, chamberstick, w/matchbox holder, Dresden **110.00**
China, gaudy decor, wall mt, Japan **25.00**
China, saucer type, box holder, Mayer **25.00**
CI, C Parker, Pat Oct 1868, EX **215.00**
CI, dbl urn pockets, hangs, dtd 1867, w/striker, 5x7½" **70.00**
CI, fly figural, hinged body, old blk/gold pnt, 4½" **115.00**
CI, grapes/leaves, lacy openwork, old **55.00**
CI, hatchet, NP, wall hanging, 1908 ....**42.50**
CI, rtcl bkplate, 2-compartment, 7" **45.00**
CI, self-closing, Pat 12/20/1864, rare sm version **90.00**
CI, urn, dbl; mk Bradley & Hubbard, Pat 1/28/1868 ....**100.00**
CI, urn form w/hdls on sq base, 3" **65.00**
CI, 2 urns w/scrollwork **100.00**
Compo, Indian in full headdress, mc pnt, 7½x4⅞x3½" **50.00**
Farmer's head, Iron Art, wall mt, 6x4½" **75.00**
Glass, Miss Liberty's head, 4½", NM **100.00**
Milk glass, Indian **68.00**
Pottery, saucer base on low stem, unglazed sides, 3½" **25.00**
Redware, acorns/leaves around pocket in wht/gr, 7" dia **150.00**
Tin, crest w/crimped & cut-out decor, pnt traces, 4x7", EX **32.00**

Match Safes

Match safes, aptly named cases used to carry matches in the days before cigarette lighters, were used during the last half of the 19th century until about 1920. Some incorporated added features (hidden compartments, cigar cutters, etc.), some were figural, and others were used by retail companies as advertising giveaways. They were made from every type of material, but silverplated styles abound. Both the advertising and common silverplated cases generally fall in the $50.00 to $100.00 price range. Our advisor for this category is Ron Damaska; he is listed in the Directory under Pennsylvania. See also Advertising.

Advertising, Indian Motorcycle, embossed graphics on brass, minor tarnish, 2¼x2½", $300.00.

Brass w/emb horse head & horseshoe, 2⅝x1½x2½" **45.00**
Brass w/overall emb florals, interior tip cutter, 2¼" **35.00**
Celluloid, Neverslips Horseshoes **125.00**
German silver, Art Nouveau flowers, 1½x2¾x½" **50.00**
NP brass, bow-tie shaped button pushes to open flaps, 3¾" **70.00**
NP brass turtle form w/button latch, 2⅞x1⅝" **125.00**
NP brass w/MOP sides & HP florals, 1⅜x2⅝", EX **45.00**
Prohibition Brewer Workmen, celluloid **125.00**
Sterling, Art Nouveau Cupid kissing sleeping maiden, ca 1900 .**130.00**
Tin & NP brass, Nouveau reserves of deer & Gibson girl, 2¼" **40.00**

Mauchline Ware

Mauchline ware is the generic name for small, well-made, and useful wooden souvenirs and giftware from Mauchline, Scotland, and nearby locations. It was made from the early 19th century into the 1930s. Snuff boxes were among the earliest items, and tea caddies soon followed. From the 1830s on, needlework, stationery, domestic, and cosmetic items were made by the thousands. Today, needlework items are the most plentiful and range from boxes of all sizes made to hold supplies to tiny bodkins and buttons. Napkin rings, egg cups, vases, and bowls are just a few of the domestic items available.

The wood most commonly used in the production of Mauchline ware was sycamore. Finishes vary. Early items were hand-decorated with colored paints or pen and ink. By the 1850s, perhaps even earlier, transferware was produced, decorated with views associated with the place of purchase. These souvenir items were avidly bought by travelers for themselves as well as for gifts. Major exhibitions and royal occasions were also represented on transferware. An alternative decorating process was initiated during the mid-1860s whereby actual photos replaced the transfers. Because they were finished with multiple layers of varnish, many examples found today are still in excellent condition.

Tartan ware's distinctive decoration was originally hand painted directly on the wood with inks, but in the 1840s machine-made paper in authentic Tartan designs became available. Except for the smallest items, each piece was stamped with the Tartan name. The Tartan decoration was applied to virtually the entire range of Mauchline ware, and because it was favored by Queen Victoria, it became widely popular. Collectors still value Tartan ware above other types of decoration, with transferware being their second choice. Other types of Mauchline decorations include Fern ware and Black Lacquer with floral or transfer decoration.

When cleaning any Mauchline item, extreme care should be used to avoid damaging the finish! Mauchline ware has been reproduced for at least twenty-five years, especially some of the more popular pieces and finishes. Collectors should study the older items for comparison and to learn about the decorating and manufacturing processes.

Bookmark, Weymouth, 4½x¾" 45.00
Box, spool; Llangollen..., orig label, spool pegs, 9¼x5" 225.00

Box, Holyrood Palace, 2¼x2x3½", $60.00; Kaleido-scope, City Hall Hamilton, 2½x1¾" dia, $115.00.

Cotton holder, Clark & Co transferware 185.00
Flask holder, Present From Dunoon, Xmas scene, 3" 60.00
Lap desk, Balmoral Castle+2 scenes, opens, mini, 7x9" 195.00
Needle case, Loch Tay From Killin, cylindrical, 5½" L 67.00
Pin disk, Glascow 165.00
String holder, Burns Cottage Interior, 2" 125.00
Tatting shuttle, McLean Tartan 345.00
Watch stand, Glasgow Green & Suspension Bridge, 5½" 150.00

McCoy

The third generation McCoy potter in the Roseville, Ohio, area was Nelson, who with the aid of his father, J.W., established the Nelson McCoy Sanitary Stoneware Company in 1910. They manufactured churns, jars, jugs, poultry fountains, and foot warmers. By 1925 they had expanded their wares to include majolica jardinieres and pedestals, umbrella stands and cuspidors, and an embossed line of vases and small jardinieres in a blended brown and green matt glaze. From the late '20s through the mid-'40s, a utilitarian stoneware was produced, some of which was glazed in the soft blue and white so popular with collectors today. They also used a dark brown mahogany color and a medium to dark green, both in a high gloss. In 1933 the firm became known as the Nelson McCoy Pottery Company. They expanded their facilities in 1940 and began to make the novelty artware, cookie jars, and dinnerware that today are synonomous with 'McCoy.' More than two hundred cookie jars of every theme and description were produced.

More than a dozen different marks have been used by the company; nearly all incorporate the name 'McCoy,' although some of the older items were marked 'NM USA.' For further information consult *The Collector's Encyclopedia of McCoy Pottery* (with recently updated values) by Sharon and Bob Huxford or *McCoy Pottery Collector's Reference & Value Guide* by Margaret Hanson, Craig Nissen, and Bob Hanson (both published by Collector Books).

Stimulated by the high prices commanded by desirable cookie jars, a broad spectrum of 'new' cookie jars are flooding the market place in three categories: 1) Manufacturers have expanded their lines with exciting new designs to attract the collector market. 2) Limited editions and artist-designed jars have proliferated. 3) Reproductions, signed and unsigned, have pervaded the market, creating uncertainty among new collectors and inexperienced dealers.

Alert! It should be noted that the original Nelson McCoy Pottery has closed its doors. Now an entrepreneur has emerged and has adopted the McCoy Pottery name and mark. This company is reproducing old McCoy designs as well as some classic designs of other defunct American potteries. Their wares are signed 'McCoy' with a mark which very closely approximates the old McCoy mark.

Cookie Jars

Animal Crackers 120.00
Apollo Age, minimum value 1,400.00
Apple, 1950-64 ....65.00
Apple on Basketweave 70.00
Astronauts 650.00
Bananas 125.00
Barnum's Animals 400.00
Baseball Boy 225.00
Basket Eggs 60.00
Bear, cookie in vest, no 'Cookies' 95.00
Betsy Baker 275.00
Black Kettle, w/immovable bail, HP flowers 40.00
Black Vase, w/flowers on lid 220.00
Bobby Baker 100.00
Bugs Bunny, cylinder 225.00
Caboose 165.00
Cat on Coal Scuttle 200.00
Chairman of the Board, minimum value 400.00
Chef 140.00
Chilly Willy 85.00
Chinese Lantern 85.00
Chipmunk 150.00
Circus Horse 250.00
Clown Bust 85.00
Clown in Barrel 150.00
Clyde Dog 200.00
Coalby Cat 450.00
Coffee Grinder 45.00
Coffee Mug 45.00
Colonial Fireplace 95.00
Cookie Barrel 45.00
Cookie Boy 225.00
Cookie Cabin 125.00
Cookie Jug, dbl loop 30.00
Cookie Jug, single loop, 2-tone gr rope 25.00
Cookie Jug, w/cork stopper, brn & wht 30.00
Cookie Log 75.00
Cookie Safe 65.00
Cookstove 60.00
Corn 200.00
Covered Wagon 150.00
Cylinder, w/red flowers 45.00
Dalmatians in Rocking Chair 450.00
Dog on Basketweave 90.00
Drum 100.00
Duck on Basketweave 100.00
Dutch Boy 55.00
Dutch Girl, boy on reverse, rare 125.00
Dutch Treat Barn 75.00
Elephant w/Split Trunk, rare, minimum value 450.00
Engine, blk 175.00
Flowerpot, plastic flower on top 500.00
Football Boy 225.00
Forbidden Fruit 75.00
Freddy Gleep 500.00
Friendship 250.00
Frontier Family 60.00
Fruit in Bushel Basket 80.00
Gingerbread Boy 75.00
Globe 325.00
Grandfather Clock 80.00
Granny 85.00

Granny, gold trim	125.00
Hamm's Bear	225.00
Happy Face	100.00
Hen on Nest	95.00
Hillbilly Bear, rare, minimum value	900.00
Hobby Horse	175.00
Hocus Pocus, wht	60.00
Honey Bear	120.00
Hot Air Balloon	60.00
Indian	400.00
Jack-O'-Lantern	750.00
Kangaroo, bl	300.00
Keebler in tree	95.00
Kettle, jumbo sz	60.00
Kissing Penguins	110.00
Kitten on Basketweave	90.00
Kittens (2) on Low Basket, minimum value	800.00
Kittens on Ball of Yarn	150.00
Kookie Kettle, blk	45.00
Lamb on Basketweave	90.00
Leprechaun, minimum value	1,200.00
Liberty Bell	100.00
Little Clown	100.00
Lollipops	100.00
Mac Dog	95.00
Mammy, Cookies on base	300.00
Mammy w/Cauliflower, G pnt, minimum value	1,100.00
Modern	50.00
Monk	75.00
Mother Goose	175.00
Mr & Mrs Owl	110.00
Nursery, decal of Humpty Dumpty	100.00
Oaken Bucket	35.00
Old Churn	40.00
Pears on Basketweave	70.00
Pelican	195.00
Pepper, yel	40.00
Picnic Basket	85.00
Pineapple	100.00
Pineapple, Modern	100.00
Pirate's Chest	110.00
Popeye Cylinder	225.00
Potbelly Stove, blk	40.00
Puppy, w/sign	125.00
Quaker Oats, rare, minimum value	450.00
Red Barn, cow in door, rare, minimum value	350.00
Rooster, wht, 1970-1974	75.00
Rooster, 1955-1957	175.00
Round w/HP Leaves	65.00
Sad Clown	100.00
Smiley Face	50.00
Snoopy on Doghouse	300.00
Snow Bear	100.00
Spaniel in Doghouse, pup finial	295.00
Stagecoach, minimum value	1,000.00
Strawberry, 1955-57	65.00
Strawberry, 1971-75	60.00
Teapot, 1971	95.00
Tepee, str top	350.00
Tilt Pitcher, blk w/roses	40.00
Timmy Tortoise	35.00
Tomato	55.00
Touring Car	130.00
Traffic Light	65.00

Tudor Cookie House	125.00
Tulip on Flowerpot	225.00
Turkey, gr, rare color	300.00
Upside Down Bear, panda	75.00
WC Fields	250.00
Wedding Jar	125.00
Windmill	150.00
Wishing Well	65.00
Woodsy Owl	300.00
Wren House	175.00
Yosemite Sam, cylinder	250.00

Miscellaneous

Basket, leaves & berries form bowl, smooth branch hdl, 1948	65.00
Basket, metallic glaze, 1970 reissue	65.00
Bean pot, emb leaves on lt brn, hdl, 1943	50.00
Bean pot, Suburbia, emb horizontal bands on tan, mk, 1964, 2-qt	45.00
Birdbath, Greystone finish, unmk, 1930-40, 25"	400.00
Bookends, lilies on leafy base, mk, 1948, pr	125.00
Bowl, nested shoulder; shield w/in circle mk, 5½"	30.00
Cache pot, dbl; bird between 2 flower forms, mk, 1948	45.00
Figurine, panther, blk, no mk, 1950s	50.00
Figurine, rooster, brn w/red comb, USA, 1941	30.00
Flowerpot, emb leaves & berries on ivory, no mk, 1935	45.00
Flowerpot, Greek Key borders on gr, mk	20.00
Jardiniere, emb holly leaves & berries on gr, no mk, 1935, lg	80.00
Novelty, basketball, no mk	100.00
Novelty, cornucopia, Sunburst Gold, mk	50.00
Novelty, peacock, wht, no mk	60.00
Novelty, pigeon, pk, mk USA	40.00
Pitcher, donkey figural, tail hdl, mk, 1940s	250.00
Pitcher, emb cloverleaves on yel-tan, mk, 1948	45.00
Pitcher, floral on brn, tilt style, 1939	50.00
Pitcher, parrot figural, mc, mk, 1952	200.00
Pitcher, water; emb water lilies on gr, fish hdl, no mk, 1935	75.00

Planter, fish figural, pink and green, 1955, $500.00.

Planter, cradle, pk, no mk	30.00
Planter, dog w/cart, mk, 1952	35.00
Planter, 3-lily form, mk, 1950	60.00
Shakers, gr pr form head of cabbage, 1954	75.00
Sugar bowl, Sunburst Gold, w/lid, 1947	40.00
Tankard, brn staved-barrel form, shield mk, 1926	70.00
Tankard, Indian Peace Sign (swastika) on brn, 1926	125.00
Tea set, Pine Cone, emb pine cones on gr, 1946, 3-pc	100.00
Vase, cornucopia; gr, no mk, 1926, lg	50.00
Vase, emb leaves on lt gr, angle hdls, no mk, 1942, 12"	125.00
Vase, emb wheat on gr 6-sided form, hdls, 1953	35.00
Vase, wht waisted form w/rim-to-base hdls, mk, 1941, 9"	40.00

McCoy, J. W.

The J.W. McCoy Pottery Company was incorporated in 1899. It operated under that name in Roseville, Ohio, until 1911 when McCoy entered into a partnership with George Brush, forming the Brush-McCoy Company. During the early years, McCoy produced kitchenware, majolica jardinieres and pedestals, umbrella stands, and cuspidors. By 1903 they had begun to experiment in the field of art pottery and, though never involved to the extent of some of their contemporaries, nevertheless produced several art lines of merit. Their first line was Mt. Pelee, examples of which are very rare today. Two types of glazes were used, matt green and an iridescent charcoal gray. Though the line was primarily mold formed, some pieces evidence the fact that while the clay remained wet and pliable it was pulled and pinched with the fingers to form crests and peaks in a style not unlike George Ohr.

The company rebuilt in 1904 after being destroyed by fire, and other artware was designed. Loy-Nel Art and Renaissance were standard brown lines, hand decorated under the glaze with colored slip. Shapes and artwork were usually simple but effective. Olympia and Rosewood were relief-molded brown-glaze lines decorated in natural colors with wreaths of leaves and berries or simple floral sprays. Although much of this ware was not marked, you will find examples with the die-stamped 'Loy-Nel Art, McCoy' or an incised line identification.

Corn, tankard, unmk, 1910 ....**350.00**
Grape, canister, covered cereal; unmk, 1912 ....**250.00**
Loy-Nel-Art, bowl, floral on brn, hdls, 1905, 2" H **200.00**
Loy-Nel-Art, jardiniere, floral on brn, 4-ftd, 1905, 6" **300.00**
Loy-Nel-Art, vase, floral on brn, hdls, unmk, 1905, 8" **300.00**
Olympia, punch bowl, grapes on brn, 1905 ....**600.00**
Olympia, vase, corn on brn, initialed S, slim form, 1905, 11" **500.00**
Onyx, candlesticks, no mk, 6", pr **100.00**
Rosewood, ewer, grapes on brn, 1905, 10" **450.00**

Medical Collectibles

The field of medical-related items encompasses a wide area from the primitive bleeding bowl to the X-ray machines of the early 1900s. Other closely related collectibles include apothecary and dental items. Many tools that were originally intended for the pharmacist found their way to the doctor's office, and dentists often used surgical tools when no suitable dental instrument was available. A trend in the late 1700s toward self-medication brought a whole new wave of home-care manuals and 'patent' medical machines for home use. Commonly referred to as 'quack' medical gimmicks, these machines were usually ineffective and occasionally dangerous. Our advisor for this category is Jim Calison; he is listed in the Directory under New York.

Bleeder, trigger loaded, MIB **350.00**
Book, Abortion, Thomas, 1890, EX **45.00**
Book, Electricity & Roentgen Rays, Tousy, 1910, EX **55.00**
Book, Painless Childbirth for Healthy Mothers, Dye, 1896, EX ...**35.00**
Book, Treatise on Human Physiology, HC Chapman, 1887, leather .**48.00**
Book, Treatment & Prophylaxis of Syphillis, Fournier, 1907, EX .**35.00**
Book, Triumphs of Medicine, Hartzog, 1st ed, 1927, 317-pg **10.00**
Craniotomy set, 1909, complete in orig box **400.00**
Curette, bone; steel shaft, ivory hdl, Linden a Rotterdam **85.00**
Curetting instrument, steel w/ivory hdl, Linden, 8½" **70.00**
Dental elevator, steel shaft, ebony hdl, Galante, 1860s, 5½" **85.00**
Drill, bone; silver, hand-operated, Drapier France, 11½" **850.00**
Ear spoon, teaspoon w/half cover, AF Sherley, 5⅞" **48.00**
Ear trumpet, leather-covered brass w/curved end, 1800s, 8½" .**1,250.00**

Ear-viewing device, silver, Kellogg...CT, Pat 1852, 5" **650.00**
Ether mask, silver, foldable **135.00**
Forceps, embryotomy; steel, scissors like, Hausman, 1860s, 11" ..**135.00**
Forceps, unplated steel w/sharp ends, Jouet Fils, 1860s, 4⅝" **65.00**
Hammer, autopsy; steel, hooked hdl, Mathieu Paris, 7⅜" **125.00**
Knife, amputation; ebony hdl, Mathieu Paris, 1860s, 11¼" **98.00**
Lancet, ivory hdl, 1860s, 5" **45.00**
Leech carrier, blown glass, globular shape w/everted lip **60.00**
Mirror, dental; swiveling oval w/ebony hdl, 1860s, 4⅝" **225.00**
Needle, arterial; steel shaft, ebony hdl, Down London, 1860s **35.00**
Needle, peritoneal; steel ½-rnd needle, London, 1860s, 7" **35.00**

Pill cutter or separator, American, handled blade attached to wooden base by brass hinge, ca 1870, 12½" long, EX, $190.00.

Pill maker, brass & steel, SuperXpress No 2, 1900s, 12½" **325.00**
Pill press, brass, Whiteall Tatum Pill & Suppository #6 ....**575.00**
Press, iron & brass, late 1800s, 13" L **180.00**
Quack machine, Wms 20th Century Battery, wooden box, 7½" L ..**175.00**
Retractor, steel shaft/dbl claws, ebony hdl, 1850s, 6⅜" **35.00**
Saw, amputation; steel & ebony, Charrier a Paris, 1860s, 15" **250.00**
Saw, metacarpal; checkered ebony hdl, thin blade, 1860s, 7" **75.00**
Scalpel, ebony hdl, 1860s, 6" **25.00**
Scalpel, ivory hdl, mk Coxeter, 1860s, 5⅝" **60.00**
Scissors, surgical; unplated steel, Galante, 1860s, 6½" **75.00**
Scraper, dental; ivory hdl w/silver mt, steel shaft, 4⅝" **60.00**
Sponge holder, ebony hdl, forceps-shaped shaft, 1860s, 9" **60.00**
Sterilizer, copper & brass w/porc knobs, Paris, 1900s, 13½" **325.00**
Stethoscope, binaural, mk Dr Cammann's...Tiemann & Co, EX .**1,200.00**
Stethoscope, monoral, ebony shaft w/flaring chest pc, 5¼" **325.00**
Stethoscope, monoral, fruitwood, flat ear pc, 5" **200.00**
Syringe, ivory nozzle, for ear irrigation, 7½" **125.00**
Table, overbed; folds bk, raises/lowers, Victorian, 1880s **950.00**
Tongue depressor, wht metal w/emb decor, 5" **60.00**
Tooth key, ivory hdl, R&L, 1800s **395.00**
Tooth key, 8-sided ebony hdl, steel shaft, 1-claw, 1850s, 6" **235.00**
Tourniquet, brass, no strap, 1850s **225.00**
Tourniquet, brass w/central screw, 1860s, 3" H **170.00**
Tracheotomy perforator, sterling & agate, 1800s **395.00**

Meissen

The Royal Saxon Porcelain Works was established in 1710 in Meissen, Saxony. Under the direction of Johann Frederick Bottger, who in 1708 had developed the formula for the first true porcelain body, fine ceramic figurines with exquisite detail and tableware of the highest quality were produced. Although every effort was made to insure the secrecy of Bottger's discovery, others soon began to copy his ware; and in 1731 Meissen adopted the famous crossed swords trademark to identify their own work. The term 'Dresden ware' is often used to refer to Meissen porcelain, since Bottger's discovery and first potting efforts were in nearby Dresden. See also Onion Pattern.

Bowl, bl floral, rtcl, bl arrow mk, 11x8½" 125.00
Bowl, vegetable; Princess Feather, Xd swords, 2x11" 800.00
Box, powder; roses, pk on wht, Xd swords 190.00
Bust, child in bonnet, 9", NM 950.00
Candlestick, appl/HP flowers on rococo vase stem, 9½", pr 700.00
Chamberstick, red/pk flowers w/gilt, +cone-form snuffer 500.00
Cup & saucer, courting scenes on cobalt w/gilt, 3½" 345.00
Desk set, harbor view/gilt, 1880s, 7x11" tray, bell, +2 pcs 1,000.00
Figurine, cherub w/scythe & wheat, Xd swords, 5" 575.00
Figurine, Cupid by fluted column, Jes Les Unis, 5½", NM 450.00
Figurine, Cupid on skull, mk, 8" 1,100.00
Figurine, Happy Family, couple admiring baby, 8½" 1,850.00
Figurine, lady in apron, shell in hand/tray on head, mk, 6¼" 450.00
Figurine, man holding grapes, Xd swords mk, 4¾" 495.00
Figurine, 3 putti: 1 riding horse/2 lead w/gravevines, 5¾" 1,350.00
Inkwell, floral & insect reserves on cobalt, 1800s, 2½" dia 265.00
Plate, floral medallions on cobalt & wht, 11½" 575.00
Tray, bl waves w/mermaid at edge, 3½" 350.00
Vase, cobalt w/wht & gold, serpent hdls, 11" 250.00
Vase, florals on cobalt, swan-head hdls, urn form, 20" 1,350.00
Vase, lovers reserve on cobalt, snake hdls, rtcl lid, 12" 1,500.00

Mercury Glass

Mercury glass was made popular during the 1850s when the New England Glass Company displayed an assortment of items at the New York Crystal Palace Exhibition. It enjoyed a short revival at the turn of the century. Mercury glass was made with two thin layers, either blown with a double wall or joined in sections, with the space between the walls of the vessel filled with a mixture of tin, lead, bismuth, and perhaps some mercury, though some authorities say that because mercury was so costly, it was soon replaced with silver nitrate. The opening was sealed to prevent air from dulling the bright color. Though most examples are silver, red, blue, green, and gold can be found on occasion. Remember that the value of this type of glass hinges greatly on the condition of the mercury lining. In the listings that follow, all examples are silver unless noted another color.

Compote, gilt int, wht leaf decor, 6x6⅜" 95.00
Curtain pins, eng vintage, pewter collars, NE Glass, 3½", pr 300.00
Vase, tapered beaker form, 8¼x6¼" 60.00
Wig stand, 2-pc, 10¼" 330.00

Merrimac

Founded in 1897 in Newburyport, Massachusetts, the Merrimac Pottery Company primarily produced gardenware. In 1901, however, they introduced a line of artware that is now collectible. Marked examples carry an impressed die-stamp or a paper label, each with the firm name and the outline of a sturgeon, the Indian word for Merrimac.

Vase, dk gr mottle, 12¾x10½" 2,100.00
Vase, dk gr/gunmetal flambe, tapering, ring ft, 14x7" 500.00
Vase, dk gr/gunmetal satin, rim-to-width akimbo hdls, 6½" 450.00
Vase, lt gr matt, slim gourd form, no mk, base flakes, 6" 90.00
Vase, thick dk/med gr matt, shouldered, 5½" 375.00

Metlox

Metlox Potteries was founded in 1927 in Manhattan Beach, California. Before 1934 when they began producing the ceramic housewares for which they have become famous, they made ceramic and neon outdoor advertising signs. The company went out of business in 1989.

Well-known sculptor Carl Romanelli designed artware in the late 1930s and early 1940s (and again briefly in the 1950s). His work is especially sought after today.

Some Provincial dinnerware lines can be confusing. There are two 'rooster' lines, Red Rooster (red, orange, and brown) and California Provincial (dark green and burgundy), and there are two 'homestead' lines, Colonial Homestead (red, orange, and brown like the Red Rooster pieces) and Homestead Provincial (dark green and burgundy like California Provincial). For further information we recommend *Collector's Encyclopedia of Metlox Potteries* by our advisor Carl Gibbs, Jr.; he is listed in the Directory under Texas.

Cookie Jars

Photo courtesy Carl Gibbs

Lamb Head, says 'Baa,' $135.00.

Apple, Golden Delicious, 9½", from $125 to 150.00
Barn, Mac's, minimum value 400.00
Barrel, green apple lid, from $100 to 125.00
Barrel, squirrel & nuts lid, 11", from $125 to 150.00
Basket, natural, gr apple lid, from $40 to 50.00
Basket, natural, w/cookie lid, 10½", from $45 to 55.00
Basket, wht, w/basket lid, from $35 to 45.00
Bear, ballerina, from $125 to 150.00
Bear, Koala, from $150 to 175.00
Bear, Roller, from $150 to 175.00
Bear, Teddy, brn (color glazed), from $45 to 50.00
Beaver, Bucky, from $150 to 175.00
Bluebird on stump, glaze decor, from $150 to 175.00
Candy Girl, 9", from $325 to 350.00
Cat, Calico, gr w/pk ribbon, from $300 to 325.00
Clown, wht w/bl accents, 3-qt, from $225 to 250.00
Cookie Boy, 9", from $325 to 350.00
Cow, purple w/pk flowers & butterfly, yel bell, from $600 to 700.00
Cow, yel, no flowers, w/butterfly & bell, minimum value 500.00
Cub Scout, minimum value 750.00
Daisy Topiary, 2¾-qt, from $65 to 75.00
Dina-Stegasaurus, any color except lav, from $150 to 175.00
Dog, Bassett Hound, minimum value 650.00
Dog, Gingham, cream w/bl collar, from $140 to 150.00
Dog, Scottie, wht, from $175 to 200.00
Duck, Francine, from $175 to 200.00
Duck, Puddles, yel raincoat, from $50 to 60.00
Dutch Boy, from $300 to 325.00
Frog Prince, from $225 to 250.00
Gingerbread, color glazed, from $150 to 175.00
Granada Green, 3-qt, from $35 to 45.00
Grapefruit, 3-qt, from $175 to 200.00
Happy the Clown, 11", minimum value 350.00
Hippo, Bubbles, yel & gr, minimum value 450.00

Hippo, Dottie, wht w/yel dots, minimum value 500.00
Humpty Dumpty, seated w/ft, from $275 to 300.00
Kangaroo, 11¼", minimum value 1,000.00
Lamb, wht, from $275 to 300.00
Lion, yel, 2-qt, from $150 to 175.00
Loveland, from $65 to 75.00
Mammy, Cook, yel, from $450 to 500.00
Mammy, Scrub Woman, minimum value 2,000.00
Merry Go Round, bl, wht & gr, from $200 to 225.00
Mouse, Chef Pierre, from $100 to 125.00
Mouse Mobile, color glazed, from $175 to 200.00
Noah's Ark, bsk, 2½-qt, from $125 to 150.00
Orange, 3½-qt, from $60 to 70.00
Owls on stump, color glazed, from $85 to 95.00
Pear, yel, from $150 to 175.00
Penguin, Frosty, short or long coat, from $125 to 150.00
Piggy, Little; bsk, 2-qt, from $150 to 175.00
Pinocchio, 3-qt, 11", from $375 to 400.00
Pumpkin, boy on lid, minimum value 500.00
Pumpkin, stem on lid, from $150 to 175.00
Rabbit, Easter Bunny, color glazed, from $300 to 325.00
Rabbit, w/carrot, glaze decor, minimum value 450.00
Rabbit, w/carrot, stain finish, from $300 to 325.00
Rag Doll, boy, 1¾-qt, from $200 to 225.00
Rex-Tyrannosaurus Rex, rose, from $150 to 175.00
Rooster, bl, 2-qt, from $325 to 350.00
Santa, standing, solid chocolate, minimum value 900.00
Schoolhouse, 11", minimum value 475.00
Space Rocket, 12⅞", minimum value 1,000.00
Squirrel on Pine Cone, glaze decor, 3-qt, 11", from $80 to 90.00
Squirrel on stump, stain finish, from $65 to 75.00
Strawberry, 3½-qt, 9½", from $60 to 70.00
Sunflowers, Cookie Creations Series, 2-qt, from $65 to 85.00
Topsy, red polka dots, minimum value 800.00
Topsy, solid bl apron, from $500 to 550.00
Tulip, minimum value 500.00
Walrus, brn & wht, from $350 to 375.00
Wells Fargo, 11x9", from $675 to 700.00
Wheat Shock, 4-qt, from $100 to 125.00
Woodpecker on Acorn, 3-qt, from $375 to 400.00

Dinnerware

Photo courtesy Carl Gibbs

**California Provincial, 3-tier tray
with wooden stem, $125.00.**

California Aztec, butter dish 99.00
California Aztec, cofffepot 250.00
California Aztec, cup & saucer 20.00
California Aztec, jam & jelly 60.00
California Aztec, juice cup 45.00

California Aztec, platter, 13" 65.00
California Geranium, bowl, divided vegetable 40.00
California Geranium, bowl, salad 65.00
California Geranium, cup & saucer 13.00
California Geranium, gravy ladle 20.00
California Geranium, plate, dinner 12.00
California Geranium, platter, med 35.00
California Geranium, sauce boat 30.00
California Golden Blossom, bowl, soup 18.00
California Golden Blossom, bowl, vegetable 45.00
California Golden Blossom, celery dish 45.00
California Golden Blossom, platter, 13" 50.00
California Golden Blossom, shakers, pr 30.00
California Ivy, bowl, divided vegetable; oval, 11" 55.00
California Ivy, bowl, salad; 11¼" 90.00
California Ivy, coaster, 3¾" 20.00
California Ivy, pepper mill 48.00
California Ivy, plate, salad; 8" 12.00
California Ivy, platter, oval, 13" 55.00
California Ivy, salt shaker, barbeque; lg 32.00
California Ivy, shakers, sm, pr 28.00
California Ivy, teapot, 6-cup 110.00
California Ivy, tray, 1-tier 45.00
California Peach Blossom, creamer 28.00
California Peach Blossom, cup 12.00
California Peach Blossom, plate, dinner 15.00
California Peach Blossom, platter, sm 40.00
California Peach Blossom, shakers, pr 30.00
California Peach Blossom, sugar bowl, w/lid 30.00
California Peach Blossom, tumbler 28.00
California Provincial, bowl, lug soup; 5" 28.00
California Provincial, bowl, vegetable; 10" 55.00
California Provincial, butter dish 95.00
California Provincial, coffee carafe, 7-cup 145.00
California Provincial, creamer, 6-oz 30.00
California Provincial, cup & saucer 18.00
California Provincial, egg cup 35.00
California Provincial, kettle casserole, w/lid, 2-qt 12-oz 135.00
California Provincial, pitcher, milk; 1-qt 70.00
California Provincial, shakers, hdld, pr 30.00
California Provincial, spice-box planter 95.00
California Provincial, tumbler, 11-oz 40.00
California Provincial, turkey platter, 22½" 285.00
California Strawberry, coffeepot, 8-cup 90.00
California Strawberry, creamer, 10-oz 22.00
California Strawberry, plate, bread & butter; 6⅜" 8.00
California Strawberry, plate, dinner; 10¼" 13.00
California Strawberry, platter, oval, 9½" 30.00
California Strawberry, shakers, pr 24.00
Colonial Heritage, bread server 65.00
Colonial Heritage, casserole, w/chicken figural lid 140.00
Colonial Heritage, cup & saucer 15.00
Colonial Heritage, egg cup 28.00
Colonial Heritage, pitcher, lg 80.00
Colonial Heritage, sugar bowl, w/lid 30.00
Colonial Heritage, sugar canister, w/lid 70.00
Homestead Provincial, bowl, cereal; 7¼" 18.00
Homestead Provincial, bowl, soup; 8" 28.00
Homestead Provincial, bowl, vegetable; basket design, 8⅛" 59.00
Homestead Provincial, coffee carafe warmer, metal, sm 40.00
Homestead Provincial, gravy boat, 1-pt 49.00
Homestead Provincial, mug, lg, 1-pt 38.00
Homestead Provincial, pipkin set, minimum value 475.00
Homestead Provincial, plate, bread & butter; 6⅜" 10.00

Homestead Provincial, creamer and sugar bowl, $65.00.

Homestead Provincial, soup tureen, w/lid, minimum value 850.00
Homestead Provincial, sugar bowl, w/lid 35.00
Navajo, bowl, salad; 12" 90.00
Navajo, chop plate, 13" 65.00
Navajo, mug, cocoa; 8-oz 20.00
Navajo, pitcher, milk; 1-qt 55.00
Navajo, plate, dinner; 10½" 15.00
Navajo, shakers, pr 36.00
Provincial Fruit, bowl, salad; 11⅛" 70.00
Provincial Fruit, bowl, soup; 8½" 18.00
Provincial Fruit, coffeepot, 7-cup 100.00
Provincial Fruit, gravy boat, 1-pt 35.00
Provincial Fruit, shakers, pr 24.00
Provincial Fruit, sugar bowl 22.00
Provincial Fruit, teapot 100.00
Provincial Rose, bowl, cereal 14.00
Provincial Rose, butter dish 60.00
Provincial Rose, mug, 8-oz 20.00
Provincial Rose, plate, dinner 14.00
Provincial Rose, salad fork & spoon 55.00
Provincial Rose, teapot 120.00
Red Rooster Provincial, bowl, divided vegetable; 12" 65.00
Red Rooster Provincial, bowl, lug soup; 5" 25.00
Red Rooster Provincial, buffet server, 12¼" 75.00
Red Rooster Provincial, butter dish 75.00
Red Rooster Provincial, egg cup 32.00
Red Rooster Provincial, pepper shaker, rooster 32.00
Red Rooster Provincial, pitcher, 1-qt 70.00
Red Rooster Provincial, plate, bread & butter; 6⅜" 10.00
Red Rooster Provincial, plate, dinner; 10" 16.00
Red Rooster Provincial, tea canister, w/lid 55.00
Red Rooster Provincial, tumbler, 11-oz 34.00
Red Rooster Provincial, turkey platter, 22½" 275.00
Sculptured Daisy, bowl, cereal; 7¼" 14.00
Sculptured Daisy, bowl, vegetable; sm, 7" 35.00
Sculptured Daisy, casserole, w/lid, 1½-qt 90.00
Sculptured Daisy, mug, 8-oz 20.00
Sculptured Daisy, oval baker, 11" 50.00
Sculptured Daisy, plate, dinner; 10½" 13.00
Sculptured Daisy, platter, oval, 9½" 35.00
Sculptured Daisy, teapot, 7-cup 100.00
Sculptured Daisy, tumbler, 11-oz 30.00
Sculptured Grape, bowl, soup; 8⅛" 25.00
Sculptured Grape, compote, ftd, 8½" 80.00
Sculptured Grape, creamer, 10-oz 28.00
Sculptured Grape, pitcher, 1¼-qt 65.00
Sculptured Zinnia, butter dish 60.00
Sculptured Zinnia, cup & saucer 14.00
Sculptured Zinnia, mug, 8-oz 22.00
Sculptured Zinnia, platter, oval, 12½" 40.00
Sculptured Zinnia, salad fork & spoon 55.00

Sculptured Zinnia, sugar bowl, w/lid, 10-oz 28.00
Sculptured Zinnia, teapot, 6-cup 100.00

Miniatures

Bear, paw upraised, 5" 65.00
Bird, sitting w/tail up, 6¼" 35.00
Bird, wings outstretched, sm 30.00
Bird on branch, 4⅝" 70.00
Chimpanzee, on all fours, 4½" 95.00
Chinese Lady, various szs, ea, from $65 to 125.00
Crocodile, 9" 110.00
Dog, Abstract; running 55.00
Duck, head down, 3" 35.00
Fawn, 5½" 50.00
Flamingo, head upright, 6¼" 50.00
Frog, head up, 3" 35.00
Giant Anteater 125.00
Goose, head forward, 6½" 45.00
Horse, Circus; front legs raised, 6" 100.00
Indian Elephant, Baby, balancing on ball, 6½" 125.00
Indian Elephant, Baby, walking, 6½" 95.00
Otter 95.00
Sea Horse, 4½" 75.00
Swan, 3" 45.00
Terrier, 12½" 95.00

Nostalgia Line

Modeled after items reminiscent of the late 19th and early 20th centuries, the Nostalia line contained models of locomotives, gramaphones, early autos, stage coaches, and baby carriages. There were also wagons and carts pulled by horses or donkeys, sometimes with separate drivers and passengers. The line was produced from the late 1940s through the 1960s.

Blitzen 155.00
Cannon 55.00
Doctor's buggy, 9" 70.00
Horse, med gaited, 3x4" 95.00
Horse, Morgan, 8½x7¾" 130.00
Horse, Palomino, 6x6" 135.00
Horse, saddle bred, lg, 8x9" 145.00
Locomotive 65.00
Mail wagon 80.00
Mary Jane 55.00
Old Ford 85.00
Pony, 7½x6" 110.00
Powder horn w/strap 50.00
Train car 40.00
Trolley car 95.00
Victorian carriage, 11x5x5½" 100.00
Victrola 65.00

Poppets

From the mid-'60s through the mid-'70s, Metlox produced a line of 'Poppets,' eighty-six in all, representing characters ranging from royalty and professionals to a Salvation Army group. They came with a name tag; some had paper labels, others backstamps.

American boy, 5¾" 35.00
Charlie, seated man, 5⅞" 55.00
Donald & David, group 55.00

Herb planter w/seeds, 8⅝"	60.00
Jenny, seated, girl, 8¾"	45.00
Johnnie, seated sailor boy, 7⅛"	45.00
Kitty, sm girl, 6⅝"	35.00
Melinda, girl tennis player, 6¼"	45.00
Monica, nun, 8"	45.00
Mother Goose, w/4" bowl	65.00
Mother Nature, 6¾"	60.00
Pamela, girl in gown	45.00
Penelope, w/4" bowl	45.00
Zelda, choral lady #2, 7⅝"	45.00

Mettlach

In 1836 Nicholas Villeroy and Eugene Francis Boch, both of whom were already involved in the potting industry, formed a partnership and established a stoneware factory in an old restored abbey in Mettlach, Germany. Decorative stoneware with in-mold relief was their specialty, steins in particular. Through constant experimentation, they developed innovative methods of decoration. One process, called chromolith, involved inlaying colorful mosaic designs into the body of the ware. Later underglaze printing from copper plates was used. Their stoneware was of high quality, and their steins won many medals at the St. Louis Expo and early world's fairs. Most examples are marked with an incised castle and the name 'Mettlach.' The numbering system indicates size, date, stock number, and decorator. Production was halted by a fire in 1921; the factory was not rebuilt. Our advisor for this category is Ron Fox; he is listed in the Directory under New York.

Key:
L — liter   PUG — print under glaze
POG — print over glaze   tl — thumb lift

#1028, stein, relief: tan & brn, inlaid lid, .5L	145.00
#1044/127, plaque, PUG: hunting dog, worn gold, 17"	300.00
#1044/147, plaque, PUG: Lichtenstein, 14"	400.00
#1044/352, plaque, transfer/HP: Orientals, rpt gold, 17½"	300.00
#1044/81, plaque, PUG/HP: cavalier, rpt gold, 17"	350.00
#1266, stein, relief: 4 archway scenes, bl, inlaid lid, .5L	170.00
#1266, stein, relief: 4 archway scenes, terra cotta, .25L	120.00
#1370, stein, relief: cream & tan, pewter lid, .5L	110.00
#1394, stein, etched: German cards, SP lid, .5L, NM	300.00
#1396, stein, etched: cherub drinking, Warth, inlaid lid, .5L	715.00
#1411, plaque, etched: lady in lg hat, Warth, 16"	530.00
#1478, stein, etched: dwarfs build bbls, inlaid lid, .5L	665.00
#1526, stein, etched: Augustiner Brau, pewter lid, .3L	350.00
#1526/1098, stein, PUG/HP: Uncle Sam/leaders, pewter lid, .5L	400.00
#1526/1108, stein, PUG: Bock w/beaker, Schlitt, pewter lid, 1L	435.00
#1526/1145, stein, PUG: barmaid, Schlitt, pewter lid, .5L	245.00
#1526/1271, stein, PUG: man w/drunk, barmaid pewter lid, 1L	345.00
#1526/1281, stein, PUG: hunter drinking, pewter lid, .5L	340.00
#1526/599, stein, PUG/HP: trumpeter, pewter lid, 1L	300.00
#1539, stein, threading & glaze, inlaid lid, .25L	465.00
#1668, vase, etched & glazed: repeating design, 5", pr	435.00
#1737, stein, relief: hops/malt/wheat, inlaid lid, 2L	460.00
#1786, stein, etched: St Florian, dragon hdl/pewter lid, .5L	825.00
#1909-1008, stein, PUG: man at harp, Schlitt, pewter lid, .5L	315.00
#1909-1009, stein, PUG: dwarfs, Schlitt, pewter lid, .25L	230.00
#1909-1174, stein, PUG: man smokes, Schlitt, pewter lid, .5L	310.00
#1909-949, PUG: comic man smokes in heart, pewter lid, .5L	230.00
#1947, stein, etched: man in vines, inlaid lid, .5L, NM	335.00
#1968, stein, etched: lovers, inlaid lid, .25L	280.00
#1968, stein, etched: lovers, inlaid lid, .5L	415.00

#2001A, stein, etched/relief: lawyer, inlaid lid, .5L	600.00
#2002, stein, etched: Munchen & verse, inlaid lid, .5L	465.00
#2028, stein, etched: Gasthaus scene, inlaid lid, .5L	530.00
#2035, stein, etched; festive Greek scene, inlaid lid, .5L	465.00
#2035, stein, etched: festive Greek scene, inlaid lid, .3L	250.00
#2089, stein, etched: fairy tale scene, inlaid lid, .5L	800.00
#2093, stein, etched: cards, inlaid lid, .5L	700.00
#2100, stein, etched: Germans/Romans, inlaid lid, .3L, NM	450.00

#2134, stein, etched; dwarf in nest, inlaid lid, H. Schlitt, .5L, NM, $1,375.00; #2003, stein, etched; 3 scenes of men, inlaid lid, .5L, $580.00.

#2170, pass cup, etched: 3 scenes, 3-hdl, 6¼"	575.00
#2176/954, stein, PUG: party scene, pewter lid, 2.1L, NM	745.00
#2177-959, PUG: knight drinking, Schlitt, pewter lid, .25L	230.00
#2192, stein, etched: Etruscan scene, inlaid lid, .5L	870.00
#2204, stein, etched/relief: Prussian eagle, inlaid lid, 1L	1,200.00
#2231, stein, etched: Gasthaus scene, inlaid lid, .5L, NM	415.00
#2277, stein, etched: Nurnberg, inlaid lid, .25L	380.00
#228, stein, relief: 4 archway scenes, inlaid lid, rpr, .5L	165.00
#2327-1290C, beaker, PUG: Bavarian crest, .25L	130.00
#2382, stein, etched: Thirsty Rider, Schlitt, 1L	1,200.00
#2602, punch bowl, cameo: women & children, Stahl, 5.75L	255.00
#2626, plaque, etched: cavalier drinking, terra cotta, 7½"	175.00
#2714, stein, cameo/etched: 3 indoor scenes, inlaid lid, .3L	580.00
#2778, stein, etched: carnival scene, inlaid lid, .5L	1,275.00
#2936, stein, etched: elk/Art Nouveau, inlaid lid, .5L	400.00
#2959, stein, etched: bowling scene, inlaid lid, .5L	365.00
#2960II, tray, etched: Art Nouveau, gold/bl/wht, 12"	275.00
#2994, stein, etched: Art Nouveau design, inlaid lid, .25L	755.00
#3099, stein, etched: Diogenes in bbl, inlaid lid, 3L	2,500.00
#3135, stein, etched: Am eagle w/flags, inlaid lid, .5L	1,000.00
#3149, punch bowl, cameo: ladies/cherubs/etc, rpr, 5L	370.00
#3243, stein, etched: Art Deco design, inlaid lid, .5L	1,115.00
#3321, cup & saucer, Art Deco, red/gr/wht, 1½", 6¼"	290.00
#3321, trivet, etched: gr/yel/wht, 8", EX	125.00
#3321II, pitcher, etched: Art Deco, gr/yel/wht, 6½", NM	110.00
#3352, bowl, etched: Art Nouveau, 3-color, 4½x9", NM	200.00
#3437, candlestick, etched: Art Nouveau, mc, 6½"	275.00
#375, punch bowl, relief/figural: animals, cow finial, 10L	175.00
#485, stein, relief: musical scene, 3-color, pewter lid, 1L	200.00
#6, stein, relief: gray, earlier version, pewter lid, 2.5L	165.00
#7040, plaque, Phanolith: mythological figures, rpr, 21"	340.00
#876, stein, relief: bl salt glaze, Das Kellerfest, 1.5L	90.00

Microscopes

The microscope has taken on many forms during its 250-year evolutionary period. The current collectors' market primarily includes examples from England, those surplused from institutions, and continental beginner and intermediate forms which sold through Sears Roebuck & Company and other retailers of technical instruments. Earlier examples have brass maintubes which are unpainted. Later, more common examples are all black with brass or silver knobs and horseshoe-shaped bases. Early and more complex forms are the most valuable; these always had hardwood cases to house the delicate instruments and their accessories. Instruments were never polished during use, and those that have been polished to use as decorator pieces are of little interest to most avid collectors. Our advisor for this category is Dale Beeks; he is listed in the Directory under Iowa.

Bausch & Lomb, 1885, brass, tripod base, 15", EX in case 600.00
Bausch & Lomb, 1897, blk base, brass tube, 14", EX 200.00
Bausch & Lomb, 1915, blk, horseshoe base, EX 95.00
Drum or furnace form, Fr, 6", EX in case 55.00
Grunow, J&W NY student form, EX w/case & accessories 550.00
Gundlach, Y base, brass, 1879, 14", EX 325.00
Leitz, blk base, brass tube, EX in case 200.00
Queen, Y base, brass & iron, 14", G in case 325.00
Spencer Lens Co, brass, horseshoe base, 13", EX 95.00
Stamp magnifier, 3-leg, brass, 1½", G 40.00

Student microscope, Continental form, ca 1870, 11", w/case, $350.00.

Student form, Fr, ca 1910, 9", G in case 65.00
Swift, brass/steel, 19th C, EX, w/case & accessories 600.00
Zeiss IIa, EX, w/case & accessories 400.00
Zentmeyer, Columbian, student form, EX in case 375.00
Zentmeyer, professional form, 18", EX in case 1,650.00

Midwestern Glass

As early as 1814, blown glass was made in Ohio. By 1835 glasshouses in Michigan were producing similar pattern-molded types that have long been highly regarded by collectors. During the latter part of the 19th century, all six of the states of the Northwest Territory were mass producing the pressed-glass tableware patterns that were then in vogue. Various types of art glass were produced in the area until after the turn of the century. Items listed here are attributed to the Midwest by certain physical characteristics known to be indigenous to that part of the country. See also Findlay Onyx; Greentown Glass; Libbey; Zanesville Glass. Our advisor for this category is Mark Vuono; he is listed in the Directory under Connecticut.

Bottle, globular, amber, 24 vertical ribs (even in neck), 8" 3,700.00
Bottle, globular, aqua, 24 swirled ribs, 7⅞" 220.00
Bottle, globular, dk amber, 24 swirled ribs, 7⅞" 400.00
Bottle, globular, golden yel-amber, 24 swirled ribs, 7⅝" 700.00
Bottle, globular, golden yel-amber, 24 vertical ribs, 7½" 375.00
Bottle, globular, med amber, no pattern, 8⅛" 325.00
Bottle, globular, med amber, 14 swirled ribs, 8½" 400.00
Bottle, globular, med amber, 24 swirled ribs, 8½" 400.00

Bottle, globular, med amber, 24 swirled ribs, 9¼" 625.00
Bottle, globular, med yel-amber, 24 swirled ribs, 7" 525.00
Bottle, globular, med yel-gr, 14 swirled ribs, 7½" 275.00
Bottle, golden-amber, globe w/rolled rim, pontilled, 11" 450.00
Bowl, milk; med amethyst, slant sides, folded rim, 3x9" 225.00
Bowl, red-amber, free-blown, tubular pontil, 2¼x5¼" 70.00
Creamer, amethyst, horizontal rings, strap hdl, scalloped, 4" 270.00
Creamer, 16 swirled ribs, appl hdl, open pontil, 3½" 450.00
Cruet, med yel-gr, 18 swirled ribs, 7¼" 350.00
Flask, chestnut; aqua, 24 broken-swirl ribs, 4¾" 160.00
Flask, chestnut; gold-amber, bulbous, pontiled, 4¾" 325.00
Flask, chestnut; golden-amber, 24 swirled ribs, ¼-pt 225.00
Flask, chestnut; lt apple gr, 16 vertical ribs, sm chip, 5¾" 375.00
Flask, chestnut; med amber, 18 swirled ribs, 6½" 240.00
Flask, chestnut; yel w/hint of olive, 14 vertical ribs, 5¼" 375.00
Flask, chestnut; yel-olive, 20 vertical broken ribs, 6⅞" 300.00
Flask, chestnut; yel-olive, 24 vertical ribs, 4¾" 500.00
Flask, grandfather's; dk amber, 24 broken swirled ribs, 7¾" 850.00
Flask, grandfather's; med amber, 24 vertical ribs, 8" 700.00
Flask, pitkin; med gr, 32 broken swirled ribs, 6⅝" 475.00
Flask, pocket; chocolate-amber, 24 vertical ribs, pontiled, 5" 850.00
Flask, pocket; gold-amber, broken swirls, pontiled, 4¾" 725.00
Pan, gold-amber, folded lip, 6⅜" 300.00
Pan, lt gold-amber, folded lip, 2x5¾" 385.00
Pitcher, yel-topaz, 32 vertical ribs, crimped hdl, 5¾" 3,250.00
Salt cellar, amethyst, ogee w/24 vertical ribs, ftd, 2½" 1,350.00
Salt cellar, cobalt, 12-dmn, ogee w/rnd ft, pontiled, 3" 195.00
Tumbler, gold-amber, plain rim, smooth base w/pontil, 3⅞" 35.00

Militaria

Because of the wide and varied scope of items available to collectors of militaria, most tend to concentrate mainly on the area or areas that interest them most or that they can afford to buy. Some items represent a major investment and because of their value have been reproduced. Extreme caution should be used when purchasing Nazi items. Every badge, medal, cap, uniform, dagger, and sword that Nazi Germany issued is being reproduced today. Some repros are crude and easily identified as fakes, while others are very well done and difficult to recognize as reproductions. Purchases from WWII veterans are usually your safest buys. Reputable dealers or collectors will normally offer a money-back guarantee on Nazi items purchased from them. There are a number of excellent Third Reich reference books available in bookstores at very reasonable prices. Study them to avoid losing a much larger sum spent on a reproduction. Our advisor for this category is Ron Willis; he is listed in the Directory under Oklahoma.

Key: insg — insignia

Imperial German

Badge, wound; Navy, NM orig blk finish, EX+ 45.00
Badge, wound; silver pierced planchet, EX 35.00
Boots, Infantry enlisted, blk leather, EX, pr 200.00
Buckle, enlisted, gray metal, brn leather tab dtd 1916, EX 26.00
Buckle, troop enlisted, silvered crown on brass, EX 50.00
Helmet, Model 1918, field gray, 3-pad liner, Otto Koch Co, EX ...300.00
Helmet, spike; Baden Ersatz, gray felt & metal, EX 300.00
Helmet, spike; Baden Infantry, brass w/gilt, w/liner, NM 350.00
Helmet, spike; Pioneer Guard Battalion, eagle frontplate, EX 400.00
Helmet, trench; Model 1916, field gray, EX 125.00
Jacket, dress; Navy enlisted, dk bl wool, dbl breasted, EX 290.00
Medal, Bavarian...Military Merit, 4th class, silver/enamel 50.00

Medal, Iron Cross, 1st class, 1914, EX 75.00
Medal, Iron Cross, 2nd class, 1870, rpl ribbon, EX 180.00
Medal, Red Cross, gray metal planchet, EX 20.00
Medal, SW Africa Service, gilded brass planchet, ribbon, M 65.00
Shoulder board, Police, red-flecked silver braid on bl, EX 20.00

Third Reich

Armband, Werkluftschutz, wht embr on bl cotton, M 50.00
Badge, General Assault, gray metal, solid bk, JFS hallmk, EX 50.00
Badge, German Youth Proficiency, silver planchet, EX 45.00
Badge, Luftwaffe Flak Artillery, gray metal, solid bk, EX 125.00
Badge, Navy Destroy Combat, gilt wreath, solid bk, hallmk, EX ...150.00
Badge, Navy Submarine Combat, gray metal w/gold wash, G 150.00
Bar, Close Combat, 2nd class, silver, hallmk, EX 185.00
Belt, Army, blk leather, metal hook, EX 25.00
Brooch, Red Cross nurse, oval, mc enameling, EX 80.00
Canteen, Army, aluminum, blk lacquer, brn wool cover, NM 32.00
Cap, folding side; Army enlisted, gray wool, eagle insg, EX 90.00
Cap, visor; SA M43, brn wool w/silver piping, eagle insg, EX 225.00
Collar tabs, Army Sonderfuhrer, gray w/silver, EX, pr 25.00
Document, Navy Mine Sweeper Badge Award, eagle stamp, '44 ..80.00
Flag, Hitler Youth, dbl-sided, dmn swstika, 52x30", EX 125.00
Gas mask, Luftschutz Civilian, gr rubber w/filter/carton, M 25.00
Haversack, Hitler Youth, olive gray canvas, EX 38.00
Helmet, M35 style, desert camo, w/liner/strap, EX 230.00
Helmet, pith; Africa Corps, dk olive wool, eagle/insg, EX 175.00
Helmet, protective; Luftwaffe SSK 90 'Jet Pilot,' steel, M 1,000.00
Helmet, Waffen SS, M42 style, field gray, insg, EX+ 1,495.00
Insignia, cap; Army Mtn Edelweiss, yel/wht on gr, EX 20.00
Insignia, sleeve; Army Turkistan Volunteer, machine woven, EX ...30.00
Leggings, Army, field gray canvas w/blk leather, NM 25.00
Medal, Mother's Cross, gold, w/bowed ribbon, EX+ 60.00
Shirt, Hitler Youth, brn cotton twill, yel piping, EX 115.00
Tunic, Forestry Assoc, gr wool, 4-pocket, 1942, EX 130.00
Tunic, Waffen SS Artillery Kanonier, gray wool, insg, EX 1,200.00

Japanese

Badge, WWII, Military Veteran, silver w/gilt star insg, G 40.00
Badge, WWII, pilot's wings, embr silver bullion/yel on bl 60.00
Banner, wht & purple silk, war flags/cherry blossom, 9x30", EX ...35.00
Bayonet frog, WWII, brn leather, brass buckle, EX 40.00
Booklet, WWII identity, Japanese character inscription, EX 25.00
Bugle, WWII, Army, brass, w/brn lacquered mouthpc, EX 135.00
Coat, WWII, Army, khaki twill w/fur lining, G 85.00
Flag, red ball on wht silk, dtd 1946, 29x34", EX 40.00
Goggles, WWII pilot's, aluminum fr, velvet padding, G 200.00
Handcuffs, WWII Era, side locks, 3-link chain, EX 125.00
Medal, Order of Sacred Treasure, 6th class, silver/enamel, EX ...200.00
Medal, Order of Sacred Treasure, 8th class, silver, w/ribbon 545.00

Medal, China Incident Commemorative, ca 1942, NM, $50.00.

Medal, Red Cross Golden Order of Merit, silver cross/enamel ...120.00
Medal, WWII Era, Red Cross, silver planchet, w/ribbon, EX 25.00
Rifle grenade, WWII, hollow charge type w/stabilizer, inert 170.00

Russia

Badge, hat; eagle & St George slaying dragon, bronze, EX 20.00
Banner, Navy, red star & sickle on wht w/bl stripe, 53x102" 150.00
Belt, WWII, Army, dk brn leather, iron roller buckle, EX 40.00
Binoculars, brass w/worn blk lacquer, clear optics, 1915 ....95.00
Booklet, Identification, brn cloth cover, unissued, M 20.00
Buckle, brass, hammer, sickle & star designs, 1980s, EX 20.00
Buckle, Imperial Era, Artillery, brass, eagle, VG 60.00
Hat, Army officer Papakha, gray fur/star insg/red wool crown, NM ..55.00
Hat, Navy enlisted, blk wool, red star, ca 1980, EX 30.00
Helmet, Army, NM gr finish, compo fabric liner, 1960, EX 35.00
Helmet, Ballistic, titanium w/khaki cover, ca 1991, M 600.00
Helmet, Tank Crew, blk cotton w/padded lining, VG 42.00
Medal, Imperial Era, Bravery, 3rd class, silvered planchet 110.00
Medal, Naval Aviator, gilt wings w/red, ca 1980, EX+ 130.00
Medal, Order of Bogdan Khmelnitsky, breast star, silver, NM 300.00
Medal, Order of Lenin, gold/silver/platinum, #d bk, EX 1,000.00
Medal, Order of Red Banner of Labor, gilt/silver, w/ribbon 50.00
Medal, Red Star, #d on bk, silver/enamel 35.00
Medal, 200th Anniversary of St Petersburg, bronze, ca 1903 ....30.00
Medallion, Imperial Era, Czar Nicholas II Commemorative, bronze ..30.00
Medallion, Imperial Era, War of 1812 Commemorative, bronze .150.00
Shoulder boards, Naval Aviation Lieutenant, bl flecked, 1990, M ..20.00
Tunic, Navy enlisted, wht cotton pullover w/bl & wht trim, M ...30.00
Uniform, enlisted, khaki cotton tunic/trousers/hat, 1980s, NM 45.00

United States

Armband, WWI, Stretcher Bearer, red cross on wht, G 30.00
Badge, WWII, PT Boat, mk Sterling, tie clip bar on reverse 50.00
Bag, ammunition; WWII, Army, for M2A1, khaki canvas, EX 20.00
Blanket, WWI, Marine Corps, gr wool, rpr, G 55.00
Boots, field; WWI officer, knee-high brn leather, laces, EX 50.00
Boots, WWII, Paratrooper, brn leather, cloth laces, EX 150.00
Bullet mold, Civil War era, iron, 2-cavity, .30 caliber 40.00
Canteen, Spanish-Am War Era, pnt canvas, mc motifs, EX 300.00
Chevrons, Army Hospital Steward, gr wool, 1901-02, NM 25.00
Field glasses, Indian War Era, telescoping brass tubes, EX 80.00
Gas mask, WWI, rubberized face w/hose & filter, w/bag, G 25.00
Helmet, WWI, Army, worn khaki finish, w/liner, G 20.00
Insignia, collar; Medical Department, silver cross, M1902 ....20.00
Insignia, collar; WWII, General Staff officer, eagle/star, pr 100.00
Insignia, shoulder; Vietnam War Era 334 Armed Helicopter 50.00
Jacket, bomber; WWII Era, Air Force, fleece-lined leather, NM ...485.00
Jacket, flak; Vietnam War Era, Army, khaki nylon, EX 20.00
Jacket, flight; WWII, Airforce CBI A-2, brn leather, insg, EX ...975.00
Jacket, Vietnam War era, leather, G-1, EX 150.00
Map, survival; WWII, Air Force, printed silk, Japan, 1945, EX 27.00
Medal, Army of Occupation, bronze planchet, w/ribbon, EX 20.00
Medal, Vietnam Service, bronze planchet w/worn ribbon 20.00
Shako, Infantry enlisted, 1881, 3rd Regiment, EX 350.00
Shako, Span-Am War Era, MD Nat'l Guard, blk wool/pompon, VG+ ...500.00
Shirt, WWI, Army, khaki wool flannel, commercial pattern, EX ..30.00
Shoulder boards, WWII, Coast Guard Lieutenant, gray cloth, EX ..20.00
Trousers, female fatigue; WWII, Army, khaki cotton, NM 30.00
Trousers, WWII, Army officer, dk khaki wool, EX 25.00
Tunic, Spanish-Am War Era enlisted, khaki twill, 4-pocket, EX ..160.00
Tunic, WWI, Army Tank Corps enlisted, khaki wool, w/cap 300.00
Uniform, Gulf War, Army, desert camo, shirt/trousers, NM 25.00

Uniform, WWI, wool, shirt/pants/belt/overseas cap, VG **225.00**

Milk Glass

Milk glass is the current collector's name for milk-white opaque glass. The early glassmaker's term was Opal Ware. Originally attempted in England in the 18th century with the intention of imitating china, milk glass was not commercially successful until the mid-1800s. Pieces produced in the U.S.A., England, and France during the 1870-1900 period are highly prized for their intricate detail and fiery, opalescent edges.

For further information we recommend *Collector's Encyclopedia of Milk Glass, An Identification & Value Guide,* by Betty and Bill Newbound. Our advisor for this category is Rod Dockery; he is listed in the Directory under Texas. Several standard collectors' books have been referenced in our listings: Belknap (B), Collector's Encyclopedia by Newbound (CE), Ferson (F), Grist (G), Imperial's Vintage Milk Glass by Garrison (I), Lindsey (L), Millard (M), and Warman (W). See also Animal Dishes with Covers; Bread Plates; Historical Glass; Westmoreland.

Basket, scrolls, M-196B **50.00**
Bottle, gargoyle head w/stopper, W-62A **48.00**
Bowl, crinkled lacy edge, B-137, 8¾" **35.00**
Bowl, lacy edge, Atterbury, B-139A, 7" **40.00**
Bowl, lacy edge, B-136, 9½x8½" **45.00**
Bowl, Scroll & Eye, M-70A, 7½" **30.00**
Bowl, Wicket, 6½" **24.00**
Box, Rabbit, F-131, 3¾" H **110.00**
Butter dish, lacy edge, rnd, Atterbury, CE-296 ....**40.00**
Candle holders, Scroll & Lace, ftd, CE-63, 4½", pr **60.00**
Candlestick, Jesus on cross, Imperial, I-135, 9½" **85.00**
Compote, Blackberry, B-121, 8" **160.00**

Covered dish, Battleship Maine, CE-172, 8" long, $100.00.

Covered dish, cherry cluster, Vallerysthal, 4¼" sq **65.00**
Covered dish, dog on wide-rib base, B-174B **55.00**
Covered dish, Santa on sleigh, robed, F-456 ....**225.00**
Covered dish, Uncle Sam on battleship, F-552 ....**75.00**
Creamer, Ceres, F-309 ....**90.00**
Creamer, Owl, bl, eyes, F-6 ....**40.00**
Creamer, Paneled Wheat, F-255 ....**75.00**
Egg cup, Basketweave, dtd, F-347 ....**35.00**
Egg cup, Bird, F-130, 4½" **175.00**
Fruit jar, owl w/eagle top, F-510 ....**125.00**
Inkwell, Horseshoe, F-449 ....**75.00**
Jar, owl figural, F-513, tall **135.00**
Jar base, Tyrolean Bears, orig pnt, CE-190A **150.00**
Mustard tureen, w/lid, CE-177C **20.00**
Pitcher, Fish, F-328 ....**200.00**
Pitcher, Sheaf of Wheat, F-278 ....**180.00**
Plate, ABC, CE-274, 7" **50.00**
Plate, Abe Lincoln, CE-272, 9¼" **55.00**
Plate, Angel Head, much pnt & gilt, B-7F **30.00**
Plate, Bear, California, F-543 ....**125.00**
Plate, Cupid & Psyche, B-6B, 7½" **40.00**

Plate, Diamond & Shell, B-8D, 7" **20.00**
Plate, Eagles & Am Flag, gold & colors, B-6D **25.00**
Plate, Easter Greeting w/chick, F-492 ....**37.50**
Plate, Easter Greeting w/rabbit & egg, B-3C **70.00**
Plate, Easter Opening, B-7D, 7½" **75.00**
Plate, Fish, Atterbury, F-574B **500.00**
Plate, Forget-Me-Not, single roll, 7" **12.50**
Plate, Frank Brothers, F-460 ....**50.00**
Plate, He's All Right, cat & dog, rare, B-20D, 6" **115.00**
Plate, Indian Chief, lacy edge, B-4F **75.00**
Plate, No Easter Without Us, rooster, CE-268 ....**50.00**
Plate, Owl Lovers, CE-272, 7½" **45.00**
Plate, Ring & Dot **10.00**
Plate, Robin, closed lattice, F-156 ....**100.00**
Plate, Stamp w/Wicket border, F-469 ....**25.00**
Plate, Star, lacy edge **15.00**
Relish, Blackberry **40.00**
Salt cellar, goose, master, M-164D **20.00**
Spooner, Blackberry, F-253 ....**50.00**
Sugar bowl, Blooming Rose (Wild Rose), W-113A, mini **55.00**
Sugar shaker, Grape, w/lid, M-187C **40.00**
Syrup, Tree of Life, w/lid, F-145 ....**100.00**
Toothpick holder, monkey figural on stump, F-218 .....**35.00**
Tray, Question Mark, 8x4¾" **18.00**
Tray, ribbed edge, 3x5" **8.00**
Vase, Masque, Imperial, I-128, 8½" **45.00**
Vase, Mephistopheles, Vallerysthal, CE-368, 9½" **75.00**

Miniatures

There is some confusion as to what should be included in a listing of miniature collectibles. Some feel the only true miniature is the salesman's sample; other collectors consider certain small-scale children's toys to be appropriately referred to as miniatures, while yet others believe a miniature to be any small-scale item that gives evidence to the craftsmanship of its creator. For salesman's samples, see specific category; other types are listed below. See also Dollhouses and Furnishings; Children's Things.

Bench, mahog Classical, scrolled arms, silk uphl, 9x18" **935.00**
Blanket chest, butternut, dvtl, cut-out ornament, rprs, 9" **575.00**
Blanket chest, cherry w/ebonized trim, hinged lid, 12x15x8" ..**1,300.00**
Blanket chest, pine, bracket ft, 2 false drws, wood hinges, 12" **440.00**
Blanket chest, poplar w/grpt, dvtl, wear, 5½x10½x7" **495.00**
Blanket chest, 1-drw, ivory knobs, early 1800s, 14x14x8" **2,750.00**
Bucket, staved, bl over wht pnt, metal bands, wire bail, 4½" **750.00**
Butler's chest, Chpndl style, mahog veneer w/inlay, 30" **495.00**
Candlestand, English mahog, adjustable, 1790s **250.00**
Carriage clock, Waterbury, brass, porc/enamel face, 2¼" **220.00**
Chest, Federal, 2 short drws over 3 graduated drws, 1800s, 18" ..**300.00**
Chest, mahog/mahog vnr, 4-drw, wht opal glass pulls, 15x14x9" ..**800.00**
Chest, pine, 2-tone grpt, 5 dvtl drws, cornice, 19½" **880.00**
Chest, poplar/pine Sheraton, cvd legs, 5 dvtl drws, 18½" **600.00**
Chest of drws bank, glazed earthenware, J Jones, 1869, 6¼" **285.00**
Pitcher, chinoisere on pearlware, rstr, 2¾" **50.00**
Pitcher & bowl, paneled, att NE Glass, 1840s, 2½", 3⅛" **185.00**
Tea service, bl dmns/dots on pearlware, English, 1820s, 12-pc ..**475.00**
Teakettle, copper, 4" **60.00**

Minton

Thomas Minton established his firm in 1793 at Stoke on Trent and within a few years began producing earthenware with blue-printed patterns similar to the ware he had learned to decorate while employed by the Caughley Porcelain Factory. The Willow pattern was one of his most popular. Neither this nor the porcelain made from 1798 to 1805 was marked (except for an occasional number series), making identification often impossible.

After 1805 until about 1816, fine tea services, beehive-shaped honey pots, trays, etc., were hand decorated with florals, landscapes, Imari-type designs, and neoclassic devices. These were often marked with crossed 'L's. It was Minton that invented the acid gold process of decorating (1863), which is now used by a number of different companies. From 1816 until 1823, no porcelain was made. Through the '20s and '30s, the ornamental wares with colorful decoration of applied fruits and florals and figurines in both bisque and enamel were usually left unmarked. As a result, they have been erroneously attributed to other potters. Some of the ware that was marked bears a deliberate imitation of Meissen's crossed swords. From the late '20s through the '40s, Minton made a molded stoneware line (mugs, jugs, teapots, etc.) with florals or figures in high relief. These were marked with an embossed scroll with an 'M' in the bottom curve. Fine parian ware was made in the late 1840s, and in the '50s Minton experimented with and perfected a line of quality majolica which they produced from 1860 until it was discontinued in 1908. Their slogan was 'Majolica for the Millions,' and for it they gained widespread recognition. Leadership of the firm was assumed by Minton's son Herbert sometime around the middle of the 19th century. Working hand in hand with Leon Arnoux, who was both a chemist and an artist, he managed to secure the company's financial future through constant, successful experimentation with both materials and decorating methods. During the Victorian era, M.L. Solon decorated pieces in the pate-sur-pate style, often signing his work; these examples are considered to be the finest of their type. After 1862 all wares were marked 'Minton' or 'Mintons,' with an impressed year cipher.

Many collectors today reassemble the lovely dinnerware patterns that have been made by Minton. Perhaps one of their most popular lines was Minton Rose, introduced in 1854. The company itself once counted forty-seven versions of this pattern being made by other potteries around the world. In addition to less expensive copies, elaborate hand-enameled pieces were also made by Aynsley, Crown Staffordshire, and Paragon China. Solando Ware (1937) and Byzantine Range (1938) were designed by John Wadsworth. Minton ceased all earthenware production in 1939.

Dinnerware values given in the following listings are for items that were produced from 1870-1950. Current production pieces bring lower prices on the resale market. See also Majolica.

Tray, pate-sur-pate, female figures with Cupid behind curtain, Louis Solon Hildesheim, made for the Paris Exhibition of 1878, 13", $4,255.00.

Coffeepot, Ancestral 250.00
Creamer, Ancestral 45.00
Figurine, Miranda, parian, molded by John Bell, 15" 425.00
Figurine, Shakespeare w/scroll, parian, ca 1865, 17½" 880.00

Flask, moon; pate-sur-pate, child reserve w/gold, 10½", pr 7,200.00
Jardiniere, floral, yel/brn on gr, sgn C, #4, 8½x12", NM 900.00
Lamp base, pate-sur-pate, Ronde by Louis Solon, 1871, 21" 2,070.00
Plaque, pate-sur-pate, classical figures, L Solon, 8½x16" 6,900.00
Plate, Armorial, gilt laurel band, 10¼" 55.00
Platter, Ancestral, 12½" 100.00
Sugar bowl, Ancestral, w/lid 75.00
Teapot, Ancestral 225.00
Urn, exotic birds/grapes & fruit, rose/gilt decor, 10½" 575.00
Vase, incised flowers under dk bl on mottled gr, bulbous, 7½" ...345.00
Vase, pate-sur-pate, Cupid medallions w/gold, w/lid, 9¼" 2,750.00
Vase, pate-sur-pate, lady & Cupid/2 children, L Solon, 13" 3,100.00
Vase, pate-sur-pate, oval Cupid medallions, L Birks, 7¾" 2,500.00
Vase, Secessionist, 5" 200.00

Mirrors

The first mirrors were made in England in the 13th century of very thin glass backed with lead. Reverse-painted glass mirrors were made in this country as early as the late 1700s and remained popular throughout the next century. The simple hand-painted panel was separated from the mirrored section by a narrow slat, and the frame was either the dark-finished Federal style or the more elegant, often-gilded Sheraton.

Mirrors changed with the style of other furnishings; but whatever type you purchase, as long as the glass sections remain solid, even broken or flaking mirrors are more valued than replaced glass. Careful resilvering is acceptable if excessive deterioration has taken place. In the listings that follow, the term 'style' (example: Federal style) is used to indicate a mirror reminiscent of but made well after the period indicated. Obviously these repro styles will be valued much lower than their original counterparts. Our advisor for this category is Michael Hinton; he is listed in the Directory under Pennsylvania.

Key:
Chpndl — Chippendale	Fed — Federal
Emp — Empire	QA — Queen Anne

Architectural, Fed mahog, rope-cvd columns, rvpt, 38x18" 770.00
Architectural, gilt gesso on wood Emp w/acorn cornice, 46x25" ...415.00
Architectural, hardwood/mahog vnr Fed 2-part, rvpt house, 22" ..160.00
Architectural, mahog & curly maple Fed, rvpt, 2-part, 31x17" ...415.00
Architectural, mahog w/reeded pilasters, rvpt, 2-part, 27x14" 220.00
Biedermeier mahog, plain top w/crown molding & chip cvg, 39x24" ...990.00
Bull's-eye, cvd florals/scrolls, eagle finial, gilt, 50x26" 9,350.00
Bull's-eye girandole, cvd dragon/gilt, 2 candle sockets, 38" 3,300.00
Cheval, birch w/mahog finish, CI/glass ball & claw ft, 79" 525.00
Cheval, mahog Late Regency, rope-cvd, paw ft, 1830s, 70x29" .2,500.00
Cheval, mahog/hardwood Fr Emp style w/ormolu, 80x33" 1,265.00
Chpndl, cvd scrolls/rosettes, ball/leaf finial, gilt, 54x28" 3,000.00
Chpndl mahog vnr, gilt/gessoed phoenix, late 1700s, 37x21" .1,000.00
Chpndl scroll mahog, appl phoenix crest, regilded, 40x20" 495.00
Chpndl scroll mahog, cvd phoenix crest, rprs/rpl, 28x17" 440.00
Chpndl scroll mahog, old finish, gilt liner & eagle, 44x21" 2,400.00
Chpndl scroll walnut, worn silvering, old rpr, 22½" 415.00
Chpndl style giltwood, shell acanthus crest, floral fr, 54x30" 850.00
Chpndl style mahog & gilt gesso, phoenix cartouch, 61x31" ..1,050.00
Chpndl style mahog w/gilt/florals/scrolls, eagle finial, 42" 660.00
Convex, cvd wooden foliage/eagle crest, gold rpt, 1890s, 48" ..1,400.00
Convex oval fr w/much cvg, gilt eagle finial, 42x27" 770.00
Courting, cvd fr w/rvpt floral panels/8-sided scene, 17x13" 600.00
Courting, wood fr w/gessoed baroque scroll crest, rpt, 15x11" 220.00
Dressing table, mahog w/cvd dolphin stds, on sm chest, 27x24" .495.00
Emp, blk & gold rpt w/brass rosettes in corner blocks, 30x14" 440.00

Emp, trn pilasters/corner blocks, rpt w/gold, 2-part, 34x16" **275.00**
Fed mahog 2-part, rope-cvd pilasters, cornice, rvpt, 22x13" **220.00**
French, 3 cvd urn finials, fluted half-columns w/gilt, 44x20" **660.00**
French Emp style, ebonized & gilded, 20th C, 36x19" **495.00**
Giltwood Adams-style, urn finial on oval, swag pendant **260.00**
Giltwood Regency, eagle crest, ebonized rabbet, 45x29" **2,300.00**
Gothic style walnut, urn crest, foliate scrolls, 1860s, 62x70" ...**2,500.00**
Hplwht pine & gesso, worn gilt, urn finial, Phila, 50x26" **8,525.00**
Italian, rope trn fr w/appl birds/etc, gilt, 1700s, 42x37" **4,400.00**
Mahog fret scroll, rstr, 19th C, 48x25" **325.00**
Mahog vnr English style w/gilt, eagle finial, repro, 60x29" **935.00**
Maple faux bamboo, Am, 19th C, 23½x18½" **165.00**
Over-the-mantle, Emp style, corner blocks, gold rpt, 60x24" **165.00**
Pier, Vict Eastlake walnut w/burl vnr, marble shelf, 94x29x13" .**825.00**
Pier, Vict Eastlake walnut w/gilt, marble shelf, 94x32" **1,100.00**
Pier, Vict rococo, pierced scrolled crest, 1850s, 117x38" **1,300.00**
QA walnut, all orig, 20" L **400.00**
Rosewood vnr w/molded figure, beveled glass, 21x19" **440.00**
Shaving, mahog Emp, 2 dvtl drws, cvd brackets, 29x22" **300.00**
Trumeau, giltwood Louis XV style, shell crest, 61x15", pr **660.00**
William IV, cvd/gilded, etched glass, 1840s, 19½" dia **360.00**

Mocha

Mochaware is utilitarian pottery made principally in England (and to a lesser extent in France) between 1780 and 1840 on the then prevalent creamware and pearlware bodies. Initially, only those pieces decorated in the seaweed pattern were called 'Mocha,' while geometrically decorated pieces were referred to as 'Banded Creamware.' Other types of decorations were called 'Dipped Ware.' During the last thirty to forty years the term 'Mocha' has been applied to the entire realm of 'Industrialized Slipware' — pottery decorated by the turner on his lathe using coggle wheels and slip cups.

Mocha was made in numerous patterns — Tree, Seaweed or Dandelion, Rope (also called Worm or Loop), Cat's-eye, Tobacco Leaf, Lollypop or Balloon, Marbled, Marbled and Combed, Twig, Geometric or Checkered, Banded, and slip decorations of rings, dots, flags, tulips, wavy lines, etc. It came into its own as a collectible in the latter half of the 1940s and has become increasingly popular as more and more people are exposed to the rich colorings and artistic appeal of its varied forms of abstract decoration.

The collector should take care not to confuse the early pearlware and creamware Mocha with the later kitchen yellow ware, graniteware, and ironstone sporting mocha-type decoration that was produced in America by such potters as J. Vodrey, George S. Harker, Edwin Bennett, and John Bell. This type was also produced in Scotland and Wales and was marketed well into the 20th century.

Bowl, earthworm, bl/brn band above 4 thin brn lines, 3x6" **450.00**
Bowl, earthworm on wide bl band, 3¾x7¼", EX **325.00**
Bowl, gr ribbed w/marbleized 4-color band, 3½x7½" **550.00**
Castor, earthworm on bl, 4¾", EX **700.00**
Castor, earthworm on tan, 4½", EX **350.00**
Cup, spit; earthworm, gr ground w/yel glaze, 4⅝", VG **920.00**
Cup & saucer, handleless; seaweed, blk on orange, EX **550.00**
Mug, earthworm, 2 bands on gray, 5" **400.00**
Mug, earthworm, 3-color on gray band w/blk stripe, 3⅝" **250.00**
Mug, earthworm, 4-color stripes, leaf hdl, rpr, 4⅞" **215.00**
Mug, earthworm, 4-color w/brn band & bl stripes, 3½", EX **210.00**
Mug, marbleized, 3-color, 2½x5¼", NM **70.00**
Mug, seaweed, brn on pumpkin, 6", EX **635.00**
Mustard pot, cat's eye, brn & wht on bl, 3¾", NM **430.00**
Mustard pot, seaweed, brn on pumpkin, 4" **700.00**

Pitcher, bl/gr-gray/dk brn bands, emb spout, hairline, 7⅛" **190.00**
Pitcher, bl/wht/brn running dots, lt yel/bl/brn stripes, 7" **195.00**
Pitcher, earthworm, 3-color, bl bands & blk stripes, 7⅝" **360.00**
Pitcher, seaweed, brn w/alternating bands of 4 colors, 7⅛", VG ..**300.00**
Pitcher, vertical marbleized decor in blk w/bl & gr, 6¾" **75.00**
Tankard, wide gray band amid 2 bl/2 thin blk bands, 5⅝" **160.00**
Tumbler, allover marbleized decor, 7-color, 3¾", EX **170.00**
Tumbler, 2 narrow gr bands/wide brn marbled band, 3¼", EX ...**425.00**

Molds

Food molds have become popular as collectibles — not only for their value as antiques, but because they also revive childhood memories of elaborate ice cream Santas with candy trim or barley sugar figurals adorning a Christmas tree. Ice cream molds were made of pewter and came in a wide variety of shapes and styles. Chocolate molds were made in fewer shapes but were more detailed. They were usually made of tin, copper, and occasionally of pewter. Hard candy molds were usually metal, although primitive maple sugar molds (usually simple hearts, rabbits, and other animals) were carved from wood. (Unless otherwise indicated, those in our listings are cast aluminum or stainless steel.) Cake molds were made of cast iron or cast aluminum and were most common in the shape of a lamb, a rabbit, or Santa Claus. Our advisors for this category are Dale and Jean Van Kuren; they are listed in the Directory under New York.

Chocolate Molds

Astronaut **75.00**
Bear, standing, 5" **175.00**
Bear, 2-part, tin clips, 9" **220.00**
Boy on bicycle, 9" **295.00**
Bride or groom, 10", ea **140.00**

Car, ET Meiro Deurne-Anvers, no clip, 2¼x6½", $50.00.

Cat, cartoon style w/long neck **295.00**
Charlie Chaplin **255.00**
Chick w/hat, 5½" **45.00**
Duck swimming, 2-pc w/clamp, 4¼x3½" **80.00**
Easter bunny, late 1800s, 12" **375.00**
Easter egg, Randle & Smith, 6½" **70.00**
Egg w/emb stork & baby medallion, 3x2x2" **55.00**
Fish, mk GMT Co Germany, 10" **75.00**
Girls (3), folding, US Pat Pending, 9½" **75.00**
Hen, folding, 2½" **50.00**
Indian, 5¼" **85.00**
Jack-o'-lantern, mk USA, 3¼" **60.00**
Lions standing, 4 sections **135.00**
Little Red Riding Hood **175.00**
Mickey Mouse **65.00**
Owl **55.00**
Rabbit, 11¼" **175.00**
Rabbit in convertible **145.00**

Rabbit in suit, 6" 40.00
Rabbit on grassy mound, 10x7x2½" 110.00
Rabbit on lg egg, 8½" 75.00
Rabbit smoking pipe, 7" 65.00
Rabbits (3), German, 5x8" 95.00
Rooster, 3-part, USA, 5½x6½" 75.00
Santa, side hinge, 4½" 95.00
Santa, 4" 95.00
Scottish girl in kilt, 10" 140.00
Sheep, 4½" 68.00
Squirrel, tin, 9½" 100.00
Teddy bear, 11½" 395.00
Train 95.00

Hard Candy Molds

Soldier, tin, groove for stick,
1-piece, 5½", $30.00.

Battleship in waves, TM-256, groove for stick, 2½x1¼" 75.00
Castle w/flag, groove for stick, 1¾x1½" 80.00
Hand, TM-31, groove for stick, 1¾x1¼" 60.00
Lion, 3-part, TM-40, groove for stick, 4x5" 130.00
Locomotive, 3-part, TM-14, groove for stick, 3½x6" 145.00
Mouse, TM-37, groove for stick, 2¼x1¼" 100.00
Rabbits, baby in cart, TM-41, groove for stick, 4½x3½" 130.00
Rat, TM-238, groove for stick, 2½x1" 90.00
Teddy bear, walnut, rctl, 2-part, makes 6, 1½x12" 145.00

Ice Cream Molds

Apple, E-239 ....40.00
Bell, #605 ....35.00
Black boy killing turkey, L&Co, 4" 60.00
Bonnet w/face, E-968 ....125.00
Chick in egg, vertical, #600, 4" 35.00
Cow, #659 ....60.00
Cupid sits on rose, full figure, E-959 ....60.00
Drum, 2½" 30.00
Easter egg, E-906 ....30.00
Engagement ring, pewter 72.00
Football, E-1159 ....28.00
George & Martha Washington, 5½", pr 250.00
Gourd, 4" 25.00
Heart w/cupid, E&Co, 3¾" 45.00
Horse, 3" 30.00
Masonic emblem, Shrine, #1081 ....35.00
Mum, E-355 ....35.00
Peach half w/stone, #160 ....30.00
Potato, K-154 ....35.00
Pumpkin, E-309 ....30.00
Soldier, 5⅝" 50.00
Strawberry 30.00
3 pears, L&Co, 3⅝" 35.00

Maple Sugar Molds

Beaver, hand cvd, EX detail, 5x9" 90.00
Fruit & foliage, hardwood, 2-part, 5½x8" 40.00
Hearts (2), varnished, 3x18" 140.00
House w/cvd-in windows & doors, seperate sides & roof, 5½" 110.00
Openwork on rnd fluted cups, CI, 1840s, 12 in 11x16" fr 115.00
6 cutouts, birds/fish/etc, 1-pc, 16x3" 170.00

Miscellaneous

Aluminum, lamb, 12" 65.00
CI, bird on branch, oval, 5" 225.00
CI, cloverleaf, for doughnuts, Pat The Ace Co 115.00
Copper/tin, cabbage rose, 4¼x5½x3¼" 125.00
Copper/tin, ear of corn, worn, 6x4" 125.00
Copper/tin, fish, 8½x9" 120.00
Pewter, 4-parts: grapes/eagles & swags/rabbit/basket, 5x6" 250.00
Tin, cheese, heart shape, tubular fr, 2¾x5⅞x5¾" 170.00
Tin, fish shape, 2½x10½x7½", EX 135.00
Tin, flower w/fluted sides, wire hanging loop, sm 40.00
Tin, overlapping circles, fluted sides, 3¾x7x5" 45.00
Tin, pear, lt rust, 5¼x3½" 75.00
Wood, cvd floral, high tin sides, curved heart form, 7" 275.00
Wood, Scottish shortbread, cvd zigzag edge, 1¼x9½x7" 50.00

Monmouth

The Monmouth Pottery Company was established in 1892 in Monmouth, Illinois. Their primary products were salt-glazed stoneware crocks, churns, jugs, bristol, spongeware, and brown glaze. In 1906 they were absorbed by a conglomerate called the Western Stoneware Company. Monmouth became their #1 plant and until 1930 continued to produce stoneware marked with their maple leaf logo. Items marked 'Monmouth Pottery Co.' were made before 1906. Western Stoneware Co. introduced a line of artware in 1926. The name chosen was Monmouth Pottery. Some stamps and paper labels add ILL to the name.

Bowl, bread; Albany & salt glazes, 2-gal 150.00
Chicken waterer, Bristol glaze, Maple Leaf mk, 1-gal 150.00
Churn, Bristol glaze, 2-gal 250.00
Churn, Bristol glaze, 3-gal 250.00
Churn, Bristol glaze, 5-gal 250.00
Churn, salt glaze, early cobalt stencil, no maple leaf 300.00
Cooler, ice water; bl & wht sponge, w/lid & spigot, 8-gal 2,000.00
Crock, Albany slip, cobalt mk, 6-gal 400.00
Crock, Bristol glaze, 2 men in a crock stamp, 5-gal 600.00
Crock, Bristol glaze, 2 men in a crock stamp, 20-gal 500.00
Crock, cobalt on salt glaze, Albany slip int, 3-gal, from $200 to .250.00
Crock, early dull Bristol glaze, cobalt stencil 300.00
Crock, salt glaze, bottom mk, 2-gal 75.00
Jar, bl mottled, Newcomb look-alike trim, 16" 250.00
Jar, preserve; Bristol, maple leaf mk, 3-gal 150.00
Statue, cow & calf, Albany glaze, mk Monmouth Pottery Co .2,000.00

Monot and Stumpf

The firm of Monot and Stumpf was organized in 1868, the merger of the E.S. Monot and F. Stumpf glassworks. It was located in Pantin, France. They produced fine art glass of various types until ca 1892, when the company reorganized and became known as the Cristallerie de Pantin.

Bowl, pink opaline, in ormolu holder with claw feet, 6", $395.00.

Bride's bowl, pk opal w/gold lustre int, 3¾x7½" 195.00
Finger bowl, pk opal stripes, ribbed/ruffled, 2¼x5" 80.00
Salt cellar, chocolate opal, gold lustre int, petal top, 1⅜" 65.00
Salt cellar, pk opal, gold lustre int, ⅞x2" 65.00
Salt cellar, pk opal striped, gold lustre int, fluted, 1⅜" 65.00

Mont Joye

Mont Joye was a type of acid-cut French cameo glass produced by Cristallerie de Pantin in Paris around the turn of the century. It is accented by enamels. Our advisor for this category is Don Williams; he is listed in the Directory under Missouri.

Bowl, iris, lav & wht w/gold leaves on textured frost, 5¼" H 450.00
Jug, claret; floral, 4-color on frost, metal hdl/spout, 10" 650.00
Tray, iris, lav & wht w/gold leaves on frost, ftd, 3x11½" L 750.00
Vase, floral, amethyst stain, ca 1900, 10" 700.00
Vase, mistletoe, gold on gr metallic, wide mouth, 11" 1,150.00
Vase, mums & leaves on wht opal, cylindrical neck, mk, 15" ..1,200.00
Vase, spider mum, gold on textured gr, sq sides, 7" 750.00
Vase, violets, lav w/gilt on textured frost, waisted, 4¾" 325.00
Vase, violet bouquet & gold leaf on textured gr, 7½" 750.00

Moon and Star

Moon and Star was originally produced in the 1880s by John Adams & Company of Pittsburgh. In the 1960s, Joseph Weishar of Wheeling, West Virginia, owner of the Island Mould & Machine Company, reproduced some of the original molds and incorporated the pattern into approximately forty new and different items. Two of the largest distributors of this line were L.E. Smith of Mt. Pleasant, Pennsylvania, who pressed their own glass, and L.G. Wright of New Martinsville, West Virgina, who had theirs pressed by Fostoria, Fenton, and Westmoreland. Both companies carried a large and varied assortment of shapes and colors. Several other companies were involved in its manufacture as well, especially of the smaller items.

Over the years the glassware has been pressed in amberina (yellow shading to orange- or ruby-red), green, amber, crystal, light blue, and ruby. Pieces in ruby and light blue are most collectible and harder to find than the other colors, which seem to be abundant. Purple, pink, cobalt, amethyst, tan slag, and light green and blue opalescent were made, too, but on a lesser scale.

Current L.E. Smith catalogs contain a small assortment of pieces that are still available in crystal, pink, cobalt (lighter than the old shade), and these colors with an iridized finish. A new color, teal green, was introduced in 1992, a water set in sapphire blue opalescent was pressed in 1993, and the new color in 1994 was cranberry ice. Items are currently being pressed in various colors by the Weishar Company, who add their mark to the new glassware made primarily for collectors. Our

values are given for ruby and light blue. For amberina, green, and amber, deduct 20%.

Ashtray, moons at rim, star in base, 6-sided, 5½" 18.00
Butter dish, allover pattern, scalloped ft, 6x5½" dia 50.00
Candle holders, allover pattern, flared & scalloped ft, 6", pr 35.00
Compote, allover pattern, ftd, scalloped rim, 5½x8" 35.00
Compote, allover pattern, ftd, scalloped rim, 7x10" 45.00
Compote, allover pattern, w/lid, 10x8" 65.00
Creamer & sugar bowl, open, disk ft, sm 28.00
Creamer & sugar bowl, w/lid, 5¾", 6", pr 75.00
Decanter, bulbous w/allover pattern, plain neck, 32-oz, 12" 60.00
Goblet, water; plain rim & ft, 5¾" 15.00
Jelly dish, plain flat rim, disk ft, patterned lid, 6¾x3½" 35.00
Nappy, allover pattern, crimped rim, 2¾x6" 18.00
Relish bowl, 6 lg scallops form allover pattern, 1½x8" 25.00
Salt cellar, allover pattern, scalloped, sm flat ft 8.00
Shakers, allover pattern, metal lids, 4x2", pr 25.00
Sherbet, plain rim & stem, 4¼x3¾" 15.00
Soap dish, allover pattern, oval, 2x6" 12.00
Sugar shaker, allover pattern, metal lid, 4½x3½" 40.00
Syrup, allover pattern, metal lid, 4½x3½" 40.00
Toothpick holder, allover pattern, scalloped rim, ftd 10.00
Tumbler, iced tea; no pattern at rim or ft, 11-oz, 5½" 20.00
Tumbler, juice; no pattern at rim or on disk ft, 5-oz, 3½" 14.00
Tumbler, no pattern at rim or disk ft, 7-oz, 4½" 15.00

Moorcroft

William Moorcroft began to work for MacIntyre Potteries in 1897. At first he was the chief designer but very soon took over their newly created art pottery department. His first important design was the Aurelian Ware, part transfer and part hand painted. Very shortly thereafter, around the turn of the century, he developed his famous Florian Ware, with heavy slip, done in mostly blue and white. Since the early 1900s there has been a sucession of designs, most of them very characteristic of the company. Moorcroft left MacIntyre in 1913 and went out on his own. He had already well established his name, having won prizes and gold medals at the St. Louis World's Fair as well as in Paris. In 1929 Queen Mary, who had been collecting his pottery, made him 'Potter to the Queen,' and the pottery was so stamped up until 1949. William Moorcroft died in 1945, and his son Walter ran the company until recent years. The factory is still in existence. They now produce different designs but continue to use the characteristic slipwork. Moorcroft pottery was sold abroad in Canada, the United States, Australia, and Europe as well as in specialty areas such as the island of Bermuda.

Moorcroft went through a 'Japanese' stage in the early teens with his lovely lustre glazes, Oriental shapes, and decorations. During the mid-teens he began to produce his most popular Pomegranate Ware and Wisteria (often called 'Fruit'). Around that time he also designed the popular Pansy line as well as Leaves and Grapes. Soon he introduced a beautiful landscape series called variously Hazeldine, Moonlit Blue, Eventide, and Dawn. These wonderful designs along with Claremont (Mushrooms) seem to be the most sought after by collectors today. It would be possible to add many other designs to this list.

During the 1920s and '30s, Moorcroft became very interested in highly fired Flambe (red) glazes. These could only be achieved through a very difficult procedure which he himself perfected in secret. He later passed the knowledge on to his son.

Dating of this pottery is done by knowledge of the designs, shapes, signatures, and marks on the bottom of each piece; an experienced person can usually narrow it down to a short time frame. Prices escalated for this 'rediscovered' pottery in the late 1980s but has now leveled off. This is true mainly of the pre-1935 designs of William Moorcroft, as it is items from that era that attract the most collector interest. Prices in the listings below are for pieces in mint condition unless noted otherwise; no reproductions are listed here. Advisors for this category are Wilfred and Dolli Cohen; they are listed in the Directory under California.

Bottle, orchids, mc on ivory & bl, bulbous, 6" 375.00
Bowl, Eventide landscape, imp mk, ca 1925, 8¼" 775.00
Bowl, mtn landscape, bl/gr tones, cylindrical, #18, 12½" 1,600.00
Bowl, pansies on dk bl, shallow, mks, ca 1945, 4½" 150.00

Bowl, spring flowers on washed blue, signed and impressed marks, ca 1936, 12¾", $635.00.

Candlesticks, pomegranates, Tudric pewter mts, 7¾", pr 1,495.00
Candlesticks, wisteria on bl, pewter bobeches/ft, ca 1925, 6", pr 750.00
Compote, pomegranates on dk bl, 2 mks, ca 1925, 5½" 550.00
Egg cup, dk bl speckles in lt bl, 2¼" 50.00
Lamp, orchids, mc on bl, brass base/finial, 27½" 695.00
Match striker, forest scene, incised base rings, MacIntyre, 3" 500.00
Pitcher, Deco peacock feathers, flambe, 2 mks, 1940s, 9¼" 695.00
Plate, Eventide landscape, 2 mks, ca 1925, 8½" 850.00
Sweet dish, Moonlit Blue, Tudric, pewter mts, '25, 4½x2¾" 575.00
Tankard, Florian, stylized floral on khaki, angle hdl, 11" 1,000.00
Vase, anemones, bl/red on lt to dk gr, 5¼x4½" 175.00
Vase, anemones, bl/red/cream/brn on cobalt, ovoid, 5" 345.00
Vase, anemones on bl, mk/label, ca 1932, 4" 320.00
Vase, anemones on dk bl, classic form, mid-1900s, 12", pr 550.00
Vase, Aurelian, floral transfer, tapered w/hdls, 8", pr 1,100.00
Vase, Aurelian, MacIntyre, slim form, ca 1897, 9" 520.00
Vase, Claremont, hdls at bulbous shoulder, tapering body, 9" .1,900.00
Vase, Claremont, toadstools on ruby, mk, 1913, rstr, 10" 1,380.00
Vase, Flaminian, red flambe, shouldered, 6" 750.00
Vase, floral transfer, bl/gold/ivory, MacIntyre, 8" 400.00
Vase, Florian, flowers, mc on cream, MacIntyre, hdls, 10" 1,300.00
Vase, Florian, flowers, wht on bl, sm rpr, 8x7½" 900.00
Vase, Florian, poppies on bl, 2 mks, ca 1900, 5½" 750.00
Vase, grapes/leaves, purple/crimson on cobalt, 1930s, 7⅛" 575.00
Vase, hibiscus, mc on pea gr, 7" 150.00
Vase, leaves & berries on gr, 2 mks, ca 1945, 6¼" 290.00
Vase, Natural, celadon, finger rings, shoulder band, 9" 230.00
Vase, pansies on bl, classic shape, 2 mks, ca 1930, 7" 350.00
Vase, pansies on bl, hdls, ca 1930, 8" 550.00
Vase, pansies on bl, 2 mks, ca 1930, 6" 250.00
Vase, peacock feathers, 3-color squeeze-bag decor, 11x3½" 950.00
Vase, Persian, floral, red/bl/ivory/gr panels on gr, 9½" 2,100.00
Vase, pomegranates, mc on dk bl, MIE, 4" 150.00
Vase, pomegranates, mc on eggplant, shouldered ovoid, 10¼" 1,035.00
Vase, poppies, rose/caramel/tan/teal on dk bl, bulbous, 9½" 1,300.00
Vase, wisteria, mc on bl, W Moorcroft, MIE, 9" 550.00

Moravian Pottery and Tile Works

Dr. Henry Chapman Mercer was an author, anthropologist, historian, collector, and artist. One of his diversified interests was pottery. In 1898 he established the Moravian Pottery and Tile Works in Doylestown, Pennsylvania, the name inspired by his study and collection of decorative stove plates made by the early Moravians. Because the red clay he used there proved to be unfit for tableware, he turned to the production of handmade tile which he himself designed. Though he never allowed it to become more than a studio operation, the tile works was nevertheless responsible for some important commercial installations, one of which was in the capitol building at Harrisburg.

Mercer died in 1930. Business continued in the established vein under the supervision of Mercer's assistant, Frank Swain, until his death in 1954. Since 1968 the studio has been operated by The Bucks County Commission, and tiles are still fashioned in the handmade tradition. They are marked 'Mercer' and are dated.

Inkwell, cvd tree of life/inscriptions, gr, 4x4", NM 450.00
Tile, Centaur or Nuremberg, gr on ivory, no mk, 4½" 95.00
Tile, Doctor, from Canterbury Tales, bl & wht, 4" 90.00
Tile, Knight of Nuremburg, gr on ivory, 4½" 95.00
Tile, pomegranate brocade dk gr glass, unmk, 4x3¾" 95.00
Tile, Rain, Am Indian, rtcl, dk gr semimatte, 4"+fr, NM 180.00
Tile, Zodiac, glazed red clay, no mk, 4" 115.00

Morgantown Glass

Incorporated in 1899, the Morgantown Glass Works experienced many name changes over the years. Today 'Morgantown Glass' is a generic term used to identify all glass produced there. Purchased by Fostoria in 1965, the factory was permanently closed in 1971. Our advisor for this category is Jerry Gallagher, longtime researcher of the company and author of *A Handbook of Old Morgantown Glass, Volume I*. He is listed in the Directory under Minnesota. See Clubs, Newsletters, and Catalogs for information concerning Mr. Gallagher's book, The Morgantown Collectors of America (a research society founded by him), and *The Morgantown Newscaster,* a triannual M.C.A. journal with research updates and reports of current trends.

Adair etch, crystal/gold; stem, goblet; #7604½, 10-oz 125.00
Adam etch, crystal; stem, champagne; #7810 Monaco, 5-oz 38.00
Adonis etch, crystal; stem, goblet; #7604½ Heirloom, 9-oz 50.00
Adonis etch, crystal/gr; stem, goblet; #7606½ Athena, 9-oz 110.00
Adonis etch, rose; stem, goblet; 7604½ Heirloom, 9-oz 65.00
Adonis etch, topaz; stem, goblet; #7604½ Heirloom, 9-oz 65.00
Am Beauty etch, crystal; jug, no lid, #2 Arcadia, 54-oz 350.00
Am Beauty etch, crystal; stem, champagne; #7695 Trumpet, 6-oz 48.00
Am Beauty etch, crystal; stem, wine; #7668 Galaxy, 5-oz 48.00
Am Beauty etch, crystal; stem, wine; #7695 Trumpet, 2½-oz 65.00
Am Beauty etch, crystal; tumbler, iced tea; #8701 Garret, 14-oz ..45.00
Am Beauty etch, crystal; tumbler, juice; #7668 Galaxy, 6-oz 34.00
Am Beauty etch, crystal; tumbler, water; #9715 Calhoun, 10-oz ..42.00
Am Beauty etch, rose; finger bowl, #2927, 4¼" 65.00
Am Beauty etch, rose; stem, goblet; #7565 Astrid, 10-oz 55.00
Am Beauty etch, rose-amber; jug, w/lid, #39 Milton, 54-oz 425.00
Aquaria etch, crystal/gr; stem, goblet; #7643 Oceana, 9-oz 95.00
Arctic etch, crystal; stem, goblet; #7640 Art Moderne 135.00
Art Moderne, cobalt/crystal; stem, cordial, #7640, 1½-oz 145.00
Art Moderne, crystal/blk; stem, goblet; #7640, 9-oz 100.00
Art Moderne, crystal/frost; stem, icer; sgn DC Thorpe, 2-pc 245.00
Baden etch, blk filament; stem, goblet; #7606½ Athena, 9-oz 95.00

Baden etch, crystal/blk; jug, ftd; #49 Jubilee, 54-oz 385.00

Baden etch, crystal/blk; tumbler, ftd, #7661 Camilla, 6-oz 55.00

Barry #37, crystal/rose; jug, hdld/ftd, Palm Optic, 48-oz 335.00

Barry #37, Meadow Gr/Jade; jug, hdld/ftd, 84-oz 495.00

Bartley #7637, gr/cased Alabaster/gr; tumbler, ftd, 13-oz 95.00

Biscayne etch, crystal/gold; tumbler, bar; #9715, 2½-oz 68.00

Bramble Rose etch, crystal; stem, champagne; #7577 Venus, 5½-oz ...58.00

Bramble Rose etch, rose; plate, luncheon; #1500, 8½" 32.00

Candlespheres, Old Amethyst; #8 Mars, pr 225.00

Carlton, platinum Marco; bowl, flared, #4355 Janice, 13" 215.00

Carlton, platinum Marco; stem, goblet, #7653 Cantata, 9-oz 78.00

Carlton, etch, crystal/blk; stem, sherbet; #7606½, 5½-oz 65.00

Carlton Frostie etch, crystal; punch bowl, #21, 12" 465.00

Carlton Milan, crystal; stem, goblet; #7668 Galaxy, 10-oz 32.50

Cathay etch, crystal; stem, champagne; #7711, Callahan, 5½-oz .50.00

Cherry Blossom etch, topaz; stem, champagne; #7577, 5½-oz 45.00

Cherry Blossom etch, topaz; stem, goblet; #7577 Venus, 9-oz 60.00

Corinth etch, crystal/gold; stem, wine; #7654 Lorna, 3-oz 68.00

Courtney #7637, crystal/DC Thorpe decor; stem, claret; 4½-oz .255.00

Crinkle, amberina; tumbler, water; flat, #1962, 10-oz 68.00

Crinkle, amethyst; San Juan, tankard, #1962, 54-oz, 9" 75.00

Crinkle, crystal; Tia Juana, juice/martini; #1962, 34-oz, 6½" 50.00

Crinkle, gr; Ockner jug, #1962, 54-oz 72.00

Crinkle, lt bl frosted; tumbler, flat, #1962, 20-oz 38.00

Crinkle, peacock bl; Ockner jug, #1962, 54-oz 98.00

Crinkle, peacock bl; tumbler, juice; flat, #1962, 6-oz 22.00

Crinkle, peacock bl; tumbler, water; flat, #1962, 10-oz 22.00

Crinkle, ruby; Ockner jug, #1962, 54-oz 135.00

Crinkle, ruby; Owl tumbler, highball; flat, #1969, 16-oz 85.00

Eileen etch, crystal/gold #32 band; goblet, #7673 Lexington, 9-oz ...125.00

Elizabeth, azure; stem, goblet; #7630 Ballerina, 9-oz 100.00

Elizabeth, crystal; stem, wine; #7630 Ballerina, 2¾-oz 65.00

Fairwin, bl filament; stem, goblet; #7673 Lexington, 9-oz 110.00

Faun etch, crystal/blk; champagne, #7640 Art Moderne, 5½-oz .160.00

Faun etch, crystal/blk; stem, goblet; #7640 Art Moderne, 9-oz ...185.00

Fernlee, crystal/blk; stem, goblet; #7640 Art Moderne, 9-oz 135.00

Florence etch, crystal; stem, cocktail; #300 Touraine, 3-oz 45.00

Floret etch, crystal; stem, goblet; #7684 Yale, 9-oz 85.00

Floret etch, crystal; stemmed icer & insert, #7589 Laurette 65.00

Golf Ball, cobalt/crystal; candlestick, 2 styles, #7643, 4", pr 225.00

Golf Ball, cobalt/crystal; stem, champagne, #7643, 5½-oz 48.00

Golf Ball, cobalt/crystal; stem, goblet; #7643, 9-oz 55.00

Golf Ball, pastel/crystal; stem, goblet; from $48 to 60.00

Golf Ball, rose/gr finial; candy dish, flat, #2938 Helga, 5" 685.00

Golf Ball, ruby/crystal; candy dish, #9074 Maureen, 4½" 375.00

Golf Ball, ruby/crystal; candy dish, flat, #1212 Michael, 7" 315.00

Golf Ball, ruby/crystal; compote, low, w/lid, #7643 Celeste 375.00

Golf Ball, ruby/crystal; stem, goblet; #7643 Celeste, 9-oz 50.00

Guest set, Anna Rose; Palm optic, #25 Trudy, 2-pc 70.00

Guest set, Azure; Festoon optic, #25 Trudy, 2-pc 85.00

Guest set, Baby Bl opaque; Hollyhock decor, #23 Margaret 185.00

Guest set, Golden Iris; hdls, pulled spout, #23 Margaret 295.00

Guest set, yel opaque bottle/blk tumbler, #25 Trudy 235.00

Hollywood, blk band; tumbler, highball; flat, #8701, 12-oz 48.00

Kyoto etch, crystal/gr; stem, champagne; #7634 Tiburon, 6-oz ...120.00

Kyoto etch, crystal/gr; stem, goblet; #7634 Tiburon, 9-oz 145.00

Labelle etch, crystal/gold band; stem, goblet; #7640 Art Moderne ..95.00

Lace Bouquet etch, crystal; stem, goblet; #7668 Galaxy, 10-oz 47.50

LeMons, cobalt/gold; stem, goblet; #7640 Art Moderne, 9-oz 255.00

LeMons, cobalt/platinum; stem, goblet; #7640 Art Moderne, 9-oz ...185.00

LMX (El Mexicano), Hyacinth; Ockner jug, #1933, 54-oz 350.00

LMX (El Mexicano), Ice; candle holder, bulbous, #1933, 4", pr .280.00

LMX (El Mexicano), Rose Quartz; ice tub, #1933 ....295.00

LMX (El Mexicano), Rose Quartz; Ockner jug, #1933, 54-oz 340.00

LMX (El Mexicano), Rose Quartz; tumbler, ftd, #1933, 13-oz 68.00

LMX (El Mexicano), Seaweed; decanter, liquor; w/stopper, #1933 ..225.00

Marilyn etch, crystal/gr; stem, goblet; #7636 Square, 5½-oz 120.00

Marilyn etch, crystal/rose; stem, champagne; #7636 Square, 5½-oz 135.00

Mayfair etch, crystal; stem, goblet; #7668 Galaxy, 10-oz 38.00

Maytime etch, topaz; stem, champagne; #7664½ Vernon, 5½-oz .40.00

Melon, alabaster/cobalt hdl; beverage set, #20069, 7-pc 850.00

Melon, frosted/blk hdl, Aurora etch; jug, #20069 ....695.00

Mikado etch, crystal; stem, goblet; #7711 Callahan, 10-oz 48.50

Monroe #7690, cobalt or ruby/crystal; stem, champagne; 6-oz 75.00

Monroe #7690, Golden Iris/crystal; stem, cordial, 1½-oz 120.00

Monroe #7690, Old Amethyst/crystal; stem, cordial; 1½-oz 145.00

Nantucket etch, crystal; stem, goblet; Queen Anne, 10-oz 95.00

Nantucket etch, crystal/gr; stem, goblet; #7654 Lorna, 9-oz 85.00

Nasreen etch, crystal/blk; tumbler, #9074 Belton, 9-oz 58.00

Nasreen etch, topaz/crystal; stem, claret; #7665 Laura, 5-oz 95.00

Old Bristol, cobalt w/opal rim; plate, unknown #, 7½" 88.00

Old English #7678, cobalt/crystal; stem, champagne; 6½-oz 50.00

Old English #7678, Stiegel Gr/crystal; stem, goblet; 10-oz 58.00

Old English #7678, Stiegel Gr/crystal; stem, iced tea; 12-oz 58.00

Palm Optic, Alexandrite; stem, iced tea; #7667 Georgian, 12-oz ..195.00

Palm Optic, Anna Rose; stem, goblet; #7477 Venus, 9-oz 45.00

Palm Optic, Anna Rose/gr; stem, goblet; #7646 Sophisticate, 9-oz 90.00

Palm Optic, Anna Rose/gr; stem, wine; #7614 Hampton, 3-oz 95.00

Palm Optic, Azure; salver, ftd, unknown #, 7" 195.00

Palm Optic, Azure; stem, parfait; #7536 Alycia, 5½-oz 50.00

Palm Optic, crystal/Anna Rose; jug, #37 Barry, 48-oz 295.00

Palm Optic, Venetian Gr; stem, goblet; #7577 Venus, 9-oz 50.00

Paragon #7624, crystal/blk; stem, goblet; 9-oz 170.00

Paragon #7624, crystal/blk; stem, sherbet; 5½-oz 95.00

Paula #7675, Stiegel Gr/crystal; stem, goblet; 10-oz 125.00

Peacock Optic, gr or rose; stem, goblet; #7638 Avalon, 9-oz 45.00

Peacock Optic, gr; tumbler, bar; flat, #9051 Zenith, 1½-oz 85.00

Persian etch, crystal; marmalade jar, glass lid, #106 Willett 145.00

Picardy etch, crystal; champagne, #7646 Sophisticate, 5½-oz 38.00

Picardy etch, crystal; stem, goblet; #7646 Sophisticate, 9-oz 55.00

Pineapple Optic, gr; stem, goblet; #7644½ Vernon, 9-oz 52.00

Prairie Rose, crystal/gr; stem, goblet; #6046 Kirby 55.00

Priscilla, blk filament; stem, champagne; #7620 Fontanne, 6-oz ...95.00

Pygon #7623, crystal/blk; sherbet, 5-oz 85.00

Pygon #7623, crystal/frosted; champagne, sgn Thorpe, 5½-oz 155.00

Pygon #7623, frosted; wine, Thorpe HP bird decor, 3½-oz 235.00

Reyer Thistle, crystal; stem, goblet; #7713 Scotia, 9-oz 55.00

Reyer Thistle, crystal; stem, wine; #7668 Galaxy, 2½-oz 45.00

Richmond etch, crystal; stem, goblet; #7570 Horizon, 10-oz 30.00

Rosalie etch, crystal; bowl, console; #4355 Janice, 13" 225.00

Rosalie etch, topaz/crystal; stem, goblet; #7662 Majesty, 10-oz ...110.00

Rosamonde etch, pnt crystal/Golden Iris; tumbler, #9074, 10-oz ..145.00

Saranac etch, crystal; stem, champagne; #7690 Monroe, 5½-oz ...48.00

Sea Gulls enamel decor, jug, #545 Pickford, 60-oz 425.00

Sea Gulls enamel decor, tumbler, ftd, #9093, 120-oz 80.00

Sharon etch, crystal/platinum; candlespheres, #8 Mars, pr 265.00

Sharon etch, crystal/platinum; vase, ball shape, #8 Luna 185.00

Sonoma etch, crystal; stem, goblet; #7659 Cynthia, 10-oz 68.00

Sonoma etch, topaz; stem, goblet; #7659 Cynthia, 10-oz 85.00

Square #7636, claret, DC Thorpe decor, 4½-oz 235.00

Square #7636, crystal; champagne, 5½-oz 160.00

Superba, blk filament; champagne, #7664 Queen Anne, 6½-oz .145.00

Superba, blk filament; goblet, #7664 Queen Anne, 10-oz 215.00

Tinker Bell, crystal; guest set, #24 Maria, 4-pc, very rare 675.00

Tinker Bell, gr; vase, bud; ftd, #53 Serenade, 10" 345.00

Toulon gold stencil, rose; stem, goblet; #7604½, 10-oz 135.00

Toulon gold stencil, rose; stem, parfait; #7604½, 6-oz 150.00

Versailles, crystal; stem, goblet; #7711 Callahan, 10-oz 50.00

Victoria, crystal; goblet; #300 Touraine, 9-oz **55.00**
Virginia etch, amber; stem, goblet; #7614 Hampton, 9-oz **55.00**
Virginia etch, crystal; stem, goblet; #7587 Hampton, 9-oz **45.00**
Yale #7684, cobalt or ruby; stem, goblet; 9-oz **125.00**
Yale #7684, Stiegel Gr; stem, goblet; 9-oz **115.00**

Continental Line

Ashley #4354, Golden Iris/crystal rim; basket, ftd, 10" dia **365.00**
Clayton #4357½, Spanish Red; basket, 10" dia **375.00**
Electra #35½, Spanish Red; vase, flower; hdls, 10" **350.00**
Irene #4356, amber/crystal rim; basket, 8-crimp, 10½" dia **365.00**
Jennie #20, Aquamarine/crystal hdl; basket, bonbon; 4½" dia ...**485.00**
Jupiter #71, Ritz Bl/crystal; vase, flower; Italian base, 6" **345.00**
Lyndale #64, Confetti; kerosene lamp, Italian base, 6" **475.00**
Neapolitan #64, blk amethyst; ivy ball, Italian base, 6" **400.00**
Patrick #4358, all crystal; basket, flower; 8-crimp, 6" dia **285.00**
Roma #68, Indian Blk; vase, flower; Italian base, 10" dia **350.00**
Vienna #71, Stiegel Gr; bowl, console; Italian base, 12" **785.00**
Ziegfeld #61, Spanish Red; witch ball, Italian base, 8" **850.00**

Silk-Screen Color Printing on Crystal

Manchester Pheasant, cocktail, #7664 Queen Anne, 3½-oz **165.00**
Manchester Pheasant, goblet, #7664 Queen Anne, 10-oz **210.00**
Queen Louise, crystal/rose; stem, cocktail; #7614 Hampton, 6-oz **165.00**
Queen Louise, crystal/rose; stem, goblet; #7614 Hampton, 9-oz .**225.00**

Sunrise Medallion Etch

#37 Barry, Azure; jug, ftd, 84-oz **595.00**
#37 Barry, crystal; jug, ftd, 80-oz **500.00**
#45 Catherine, gr or rose; vase, bud; ftd, 10" **370.00**
#53 Serenade, Azure; vase, bud; bulbous, ftd, 10" **425.00**
#7630 Ballerina, Azure; stem, goblet; 9-oz **85.00**
#7630 Ballerina, rose; stem, goblet; 9-oz **75.00**
#7630 Ballerina, topaz; stem, goblet; 9-oz **70.00**
#7654½ Legacy, crystal/Moonstone; stem, cocktail; 3-oz **155.00**
#7654½ Legacy, crystal/Moonstone; stem, goblet; 9-oz **225.00**
#7664 Queen Anne, crystal; stem, goblet; 10-oz **90.00**

Moriage

The term 'moriage' refers to certain Japanese wares decorated with applied slipwork designs. There are several methods used to achieve the characteristic relief effect. The decorative devices may be designed separately and applied to the vessel, piped on in narrow ribbons of clay (slip-trailed), or built up by brushing on successive layers of liquified slip. See also Dragon Ware; Nippon.

Ewer, white stylized flowers on green, 7", $195.00.

Bowl, purple flowers w/much beading, 3-ftd, 2x6" **75.00**

Box, floral reserves, 2x4" dia **135.00**
Chocolate pot, floral reserves, lacy netting, 9" **325.00**
Ewer, floral medallions, mc slipwork, bulbous bottom, 12" **365.00**
Ginger jar, roses w/teal bottom, 4-sided, emb heart **150.00**
Hair receiver, bl flowers w/moriage trim at top & on lid **75.00**
Plaque, fronds & pods, ornate border, 8½" **210.00**
Sugar shaker, roses on gr, bbl form **110.00**
Vase, Nouveau iris & lilies, beading, 12" **285.00**
Vase, pastel florals over shadow flowers, flared rim, 4½" **235.00**
Vase, roses reserve, hdls, 9½" **195.00**

Mortars and Pestles

Mortars are bowl-shaped vessels used for centuries for the purpose of grinding drugs to a powder or grain into meal. The masher or grinding device is called a pestle.

Brass, side hdls, 3⅝", w/pestle **40.00**
Burl, EX figure, old soft patina, 7¾", w/pestle **275.00**
Burl, 7¾x6¾", rpl pestle **225.00**
CI, chalice shape, 14", w/pestle **125.00**
CI, flared ft, 6¾", w/pestle **55.00**
CI crescent shape in wooden fr, 19¼", disk-shaped pestle **1,485.00**
Hardwood w/old varnish, w/table clamp, 5¾" **300.00**
Tiger maple, 7x6", w/ball-finial pestle **250.00**
Trn wood, red stain, 7¾", w/pestle **215.00**
Wooden bowl shape, figured, dk finish, 3¾x7", w/pestle **165.00**

Mortens Studio

Oscar Mortens was already established as a fine sculptural artist when he left his native Sweden to take up residency in Arizona. During the 1940s he developed a line of detailed animal figures which were distributed through the Mortens Studios, a firm he co-founded with Gunnar Thelin. Thelin hired and trained artists to produce Mortens's line, which he called Royal Designs. More than two hundred dogs were modeled and over one hundred horses. Cats and wild animals such as elephants, panthers, deer, and elk were made, but on a much smaller scale. Bookends with sculptured dog heads were shown in their catalogs, and collectors report finding wall plaques on rare occasions. The material they used was a plaster-type composition with wires embedded to support the weight. Examples were marked 'Copyright by the Mortens Studio' either in ink or decal. Watch for flaking, cracks, and separations. Crazing seems to be present in some degree in many examples. When no condition is indicated, the items listed below are assumed to be in near-mint condition, allowing for minor crazing.

Bloodhound, #877 ....**150.00**
Borzoi, brn or blk, #749 ....**125.00**
Boxer, #556, mini **65.00**
Chihuahua, #865 ....**85.00**
Cocker Spaniel, blk, early, #786 ....**85.00**
Cocker Spaniel, brn, #786 ....**75.00**
Cocker Spaniel, brn & wht, early, #730A **65.00**
Collie pup, #818, mini **55.00**
Dalmatian, #854 ....**95.00**
Dalmatian, plaque, #636 ....**165.00**
Dalmatian pup, #812, mini **55.00**
Doberman, #783 ....**95.00**
Doberman, #785 ....**95.00**
Fox Terrier, blk, #766 ....**95.00**
German Shepherd, #556, mini **65.00**

German Shorthair Pointer, #849	175.00	Dinnerware, creamer, apple gr	20.00
Irish Setter, #856	95.00	Dinnerware, plate, apple gr, 10"	25.00
Palomino, rearing, 9"	110.00	Dinnerware, sugar bowl, apple gr, w/lid	25.00
Pekinese, #553, mini	65.00	Dinnerware, sweetmeat bowl, gr/yel drip, w/lid	50.00
Pekinese, #740, mini	85.00	Figurine, elephant, gray drip, rare, mini, 3¼x6"	75.00
Pointer, tail to leg, #851	95.00	Figurine, elephant, trumpeting/extended tusks, mulberry, 9½" L	55.00
Pointer pup, recumbent, #503	75.00	Flower frog, Lorelei figural, gr, 6½"	60.00
Pomeranian, #739	95.00	Radio speaker, 3 animal paw ft, brn drip, 16¾"	100.00
Pomeranian, mouth open, #739, mini	85.00	Vase, floral spray HP on cobalt, #116, 7"	22.00
Poodle, gray, 4"	70.00	Wine jug, musical, plays polka, brn drip, 9"	125.00
Pug, #738	125.00		
Samoyed, #744, mini	85.00		
Spaniel, blk & wht, #560, mini	65.00		
Springer Spaniel, #745	95.00		

Morton Pottery

Midwest Potteries, Inc. (1940-1944)

Figurine, canary pr on stump, yel/gold decor, 4½"	30.00
Figurine, cock, fighting, bl/brn, 6"	18.00
Figurine, deer, stylized, brn/gr, 12"	25.00
Figurine, heron, bl/wht w/gold decor, 11"	35.00
Figurine, horse, rearing, brn drip, 10¾"	35.00
Figurine, hunting dog w/pheasant, natural colors, 9x5"	35.00
Figurine, race horse, mahog, 5½x6½" on base, 7½x2"	100.00
Figurine, September Morn, nude female, 14k gold, 11½"	100.00
Figurine, stallion (wild horse), rearing, 14k gold, 10¾"	40.00
Figurine, swan, swimming position, brn/gold decor, 4½"	24.00
Shadow lamp base for lg figurals, yel/gr drip, 17½x7½x5½"	60.00

Six potteries operated in Morton, Illinois, at various times from 1877 to 1976. Each traced its origin to six brothers who immigrated to America to avoid military service in Germany. The Rapp brothers established their first pottery near clay deposits on the south side of town where they made field tile and bricks. Within a few years, they branched out to include utility wares such as jugs, bowls, jars, pitchers, etc. During the ninety-nine years of pottery operations in Morton, the original factory was expanded by some of the sons and nephews of the Rapps. Other family members started their own potteries where artware, gift-store items, and special-order goods were produced. The Cliftwood Art Pottery and the Morton Pottery Company had showrooms in Chicago and New York City during the 1930s. All of Morton's potteries were relatively short-lived operations with the Morton Pottery Company being the last to shut down on September 8, 1976. For a more thorough study of the subject, we recommend *Morton's Potteries: 99 Years, Vols. I and II*, by Doris and Burdell Hall; their address can be found in the Directory under Illinois.

Morton Pottery Company (1922-1976)

Christmas item, fawn, figurine, wht, #645	14.00
Christmas item, lollipop tree, holes for sticks, gr, 9¼"	30.00
Christmas item, Mrs Claus, planter/vase, 9½"	30.00
Christmas item, Santa Claus, cranberry/nut/ashtray	15.00

Morton Pottery Works — Morton Earthenware Co. (1877-1917)

Baker, deep, yellowware, 11" dia	65.00
Bowl, banded yellowware, 4½"	30.00
Churn, brn Rockingham, 4-gal	175.00
Milk boiler, yellowware, 3½-pt	55.00
Miniature, coffeepot, brn Rockingham, 3-pc, 3"	60.00
Miniature, jug, brn Rockingham, 1½"	50.00
Miniature, pitcher, gr, 1¾"	25.00
Teapot, acorn shape, brn Rockingham, 3¾-cup	80.00
Teapot, pear shape, brn Rockingham, ind, 1½-cup	35.00

Christmas items, all Santa: punch bowl,
16-cup, rare, $125.00; Mugs, $18.00 each.

Cliftwood Art Potteries, Inc. (1920-1940)

Figurine, tiger, solid cast, natural colors, 5x16", $125.00.

Christmas item, Santa Claus, nut cup	12.00
Christmas item, Santa Claus, planter/vase, 9½"	35.00
Christmas item, Santa Claus on chimney, planter, #870	25.00
Christmas item, sleigh, red, #772	30.00
Easter item, bunny, figural planter, brn/pk, #430, 5"	10.00
Easter item, bunny (boy) in top hat/vest, figurine, brn/bl, 9½"	18.00
Easter item, bunny (girl) w/umbrella, planter, pk/bl, 9½"	18.00
Easter item, bunny w/carrot, basket/planter, wht/pk, #435, 5¼"	20.00
Easter item, chick on decorated egg, planter, 4½x4"	12.00
Thanksgiving item, turkey, cookie jar, chick finial, yel/brn spatter	90.00
Thanksgiving item, turkey, figurine, wht, mini, rare, 2½"	12.00
Thanksgiving item, turkey, planter, natural colors, #3335, lg	35.00
Thanksgiving item, turkey, planter, natural colors, #619, sm	12.00
Valentine item, heart vase, red, #428, 5¾"	12.00
Valentine item, heart vase, red, #571, 5¾"	12.00
Valentine item, heart vase, red, #953, 3½"	8.00

Ashtray, w/cigarette & match holders, brn drip	35.00
Dinnerware, compote, mint matt ivory, 4x6½"	24.00

American Art Potteries (1947-1961)

Bowl, water lily blossom, bl/pk spray, 3¼x5" 15.00
Console set, petals, pk/gray spray, 10" bowl+2 candle holders 25.00
Creamer, bird figural, tail hdl, blk/gr spray 15.00
Doll parts, 1½" head & appendages, HP natural colors 70.00
Doll parts, 3" head & appendages, HP natural colors 60.00
Doll parts, 7¼" head & appendages, HP natural colors 90.00
Figurine, hog, Hampshire, natural colors, 5½" 35.00
Figurine, hog, Poland China, natural colors, 5½" 40.00
Mint dish, flat flower blossom, gr/brn/mauve spray, 5½" dia 7.00
Planter, bluebird on bent branch, bl/cobalt spray, 7¼" 18.00
Planter, hog, Hampshire, blk w/wht band, 5½" 20.00
Planter, parrot on tall stump, brn/gr spray, 8½" 18.00
Planter, rabbit beside stump, brn/wht/pk/gr spray, 4¾" 15.00
Planter, swan, gr/yel spray w/gold decor, 10½" 27.00
Vase/flower frog, invt mushroom form, gr/yel spray, 4¾" 15.00

Mosaic Tile Co.

The Mosaic Tile Company was organized in 1894, in Zanesville, Ohio, by Herman Mueller and Karl Langenbeck, both of whom had years of previous experience in the industry. They developed a faster, less-costly method of potting decorative tile, utilizing paper patterns rather than copper molds. By 1901 the company had grown and expanded with offices in many major cities. Faience tile was introduced in 1918, greatly increasing their volume of sales. They also made novelty ashtrays, figural boxes, bookends, etc., though not to any large extent. Until they closed during the 1960s, Mosaic used various marks that included the company name or their initials — 'MT' superimposed over 'Co.' in a circle. See also Tiles.

Tile, sailing ship in low relief, 4-color, impressed mark, ca 1910, 6x6", $375.00.

Box, dog figure reclines on lid, gr gloss/rust matt, 3½x8" 260.00
Figurine, bear, blk on dk gr matt, 5½x9½" 150.00
Figurine, buffalo, wht matt, rpr, 8x14", pr 175.00
Figurine, tray supports pointer dog, copper metallic, 5x8x6" 135.00

Moser

Ludwig Moser began his career as a struggling glass artist, catering to the rich who visited the famous Austrian health spas. His talent and popularity grew, and in 1857 the first of his three studios opened in Karlsbad, Czechoslovakia. The styles developed there were entirely his own; no copies of other artists have ever been found. Some of his original designs include grapes with trailing vines, acorns and oak leaves, and richly enameled, deeply cut or carved floral pieces. Sometimes jewels were applied to the glass as well. Moser's animal scenes reflect his careful attention to detail. Famed for his birds in flight, he also designed stalking tigers and elephants, all created in fine enameling.

Moser died in 1916, but the business was continued by his two

sons who had been personally and carefully trained by their father. The Moser company bought the Meyr's Neffe Glassworks in 1922 and continued to produce quality glassware.

When identifying Moser, look for great clarity in the glass; deeply carved, continuous engravings; perfect coloration; finely applied enameling (often covered with thin gold leaf); and well-polished pontils. Our advisor for this category is Don Williams; he is listed in the Directory under Missouri. Items described below are enameled unless noted otherwise.

Beaker, gr, florals, 4⅞" 115.00
Bottle, scent; cranberry, wht floral w/gold, acorn form, 5" 350.00
Bowl, amber, florals, appl bl rigaree & ft, 4", NM 300.00
Bowl, cranberry w/gold, 16-panel base, 8x9½" 485.00
Bowl, dk amber, cut geometric panels, gold panel, oval, 5x9" 350.00
Bowl, gr vaseline, cut geometric panels/gold cameo, low, 13" 495.00
Bowl, tangerine, gold oak leaves/appl acorns, 4 yel ft, 10" L 800.00
Bowl & saucer, amberina, florals/insects, w/lid, 7¾x7½" 1,565.00
Box, blk amethyst w/gold warriors/creatures, 3¼x5¾" 475.00
Box, clear w/cranberry stain, cut florals, 1930s, 3½x6" 815.00
Box, cranberry, florals w/gold & jewels, 3x3½x11½" 1,000.00
Cordial, cranberry, dogs & florals, ca 1900, 2½" 110.00
Cordial, cranberry stain, gold trim, ca 1900, lt wear, 3⅝" 120.00
Decanter, amethyst to clear w/gold, bubble stopper, 7½" 195.00
Decanter, clear w/gr stain, florals, 1890s, 7¾" 465.00
Finger bowl, clear w/mc roses & gold, +6" plate 200.00
Finger bowl, electric bl w/mc ferns & gold, unsgn, 4½" 100.00
Goblet, amethyst, cut floral & stem w/gold, 7" 520.00
Goblet, clear, 2-tone gold/silver floral on bowl, ca 1900, 6" 220.00
Goblet, cranberry, ferns/leaves w/gold, ca 1900, 4⅝" 170.00
Goblet, cranberry, gold florals, ca 1900, 5½" 325.00
Jar, dresser; Ciodi medallion, gr panels w/gold & florals 375.00
Mug, cranberry stain & HP w/gold, ca 1900, 5", NM 75.00
Pitcher, cranberry w/bugs, dragonfly & leaves, 4¼" 795.00
Pitcher, sapphire bl Dmn Quilt w/wht floral, reed hdl, 7" 250.00
Salt cellar, Prussian bl, mc leaves/appl acorn, 1¼x1½" 550.00
Sherbet, gr, gold floral/dots, scissored edges, +plate 400.00
Tumbler, clear, nude parents & 2 children w/gold, 4" 400.00
Tumbler, clear, nude w/flowing hair & gold trim, 4" 400.00
Vase, Alexandrite, ribbed floral form w/stem, 8½" 450.00
Vase, amber, florals, presentation inscription, 10½", NM 185.00
Vase, amber spangle w/bl rigaree, lizard & florals, 4½" 185.00
Vase, amberina, appl/pnt parrot w/acorns & gold, 14", NM 3,500.00
Vase, bl, florals & bugs, appl flower, gold trim, 7½", NM 775.00
Vase, bl w/mc florals, elephant-head hdls, 13¼", pr 3,165.00
Vase, bl w/mc florals, 2 appl alligators, 9¾", NM 700.00
Vase, cameo jungle scene, amber/red/gr, trumpet form, 14x8¼" ...2,070.00
Vase, clear w/2-toned gold floral, diagonal cuttings, 6" 200.00
Vase, clear/ribbed w/gold scrolls & wht storks, cylinder, 9" 220.00
Vase, dk amethyst w/cut panels, gold ACB band, sgn, 7¾" 275.00

Vase, emerald green with acid-cut stylized flowers and leaves, beaker form, 7¼", $450.00.

Vase, gr, mums, 10" 250.00
Vase, gr w/cut panels, gold cut band, cylindrical, sgn, 9¼" 300.00
Vase, purple w/mc Harlequin & gold traces, 6" 250.00
Vase, tangerine craquelle, mc meadow flowers, cylinder, 12" 195.00
Vase, teal, cut sea horses/aquatic plants, ftd, 10" 650.00
Vase, wht opaque to cranberry, florals, 8 cut-bk panels, 6½" 165.00
Vase, yel panels alternate w/clear, intaglio florals, 10½" 500.00

Moss Rose

Moss Rose was a favorite dinnerware pattern of many Staffordshire and American potters from the mid-1800s. In America the Wheeling Pottery of West Virginia produced the ware in large quantities, and it became one of their best sellers, remaining popular well into the nineties.

Bowl, HP, gold rim, ped ft, unmk, 5x9¾" 35.00
Butter pat, Meakin, EX 15.00
Coffeepot, child sz 45.00
Coffeepot, dolphin hdl, 7" 70.00
Creamer, child sz 25.00
Creamer, Meakin 38.00
Cup & saucer, child sz 20.00
Cup & saucer, demitasse; ornate hdl & ft 15.00
Cup & saucer, ped ft, scalloped saucer, gold trim 12.00

Gravy tureen with lid and undertray, Haviland, $125.00.

Plate, unmk, 7½" 10.00
Platter, rectangular, Meakin, 14x10" 38.00
Shaving mug, unmk 35.00
Tea set, 15-pc, child size 275.00
Tea set, Japan, 16-pc+lids 75.00
Tray, tiered, unmk 32.00
Wash set, unmk, 11" pitcher+13½" bowl 300.00

Mother-of-Pearl Glass

Mother-of-Pearl glass was a type of mold-blown satin art glass popular during the last half of the 19th century. A patent for its manufacture was issued in 1886 to Frederick S. Shirley, and one of the companies who produced it was the Mt. Washington Glass Company of New Bedford, Massachusetts. Another was the English firm of Stevens and Williams. Its delicate patterns were developed by blowing the gather into a mold with inside projections that left an intaglio design on the surface of the glass, then sealing the first layer with a second, trapping air in the recesses. Most common are the Diamond Quilted, Raindrop, and Herringbone patterns. It was made in several soft colors, the most rare and valuable is rainbow — a blend of rose, light blue, yellow, and white. Occasionally it may be decorated with coralene, enameling, or gilt. Watch for 20th-century reproductions, especially in the Diamond Quilted pattern. Our advisors for this category are Betty and Clarence Maier; they are listed in the Directory under Pennsylvania. See also Coralene.

Basket, Dmn Quilt, rainbow, ruffled, invt-V camphor hdl, 8" .1,050.00
Bonbon, Dmn Quilt, wht & clear, ruffled, Pat, 1¼x8½" 450.00
Bottle, scent; Dmn Quilt, bl, lay-down teardrop, 5½" 495.00
Bottle, scent; Peacock Eye, wht, orig glass stopper, 3¾" 485.00
Bowl, Dmn Quilt, bl, scalloped, 3 branch ft, pontil, 5x8" 200.00
Bowl, jack-in-pulpit; Dmn Quilt, rainbow, Pat, 3½" H 1,285.00
Bowl vase, Dmn Quilt, chartreuse, bl int, ruffled, 4¼" 395.00
Celery vase, Dmn Quilt, lt bl, crimped rim, 4¾x3½" 235.00
Creamer, Dmn Quilt, rainbow, sq top, frosted hdl, 2¾" 950.00
Creamer, Ribbon, bl, frosted hdl/ft, 2⅛x2¾" 245.00

Cruet, Diamond Quilt, rainbow, with stopper, 7¼", $750.00 (watch for reproductions).

Cruet, Herringbone, pk, camphor/frosted hdl, bulbous, 5½" 850.00
Ewer, Herringbone, pk, ruffled rim, thorn hdl, 8½" 385.00
Finger bowl, Dmn Quilt, apricot, crimped, +6½" plate 180.00
Finger bowl, Dmn Quilt, chartreuse, scalloped, mk Pat, +plate ..325.00
Jam dish, Ribbon, dk chartreuse, SP holder, 5x4¼" 265.00
Rose bowl, Dmn Quilt, bl, dimpled sides, 8-crimp, 3⅝x4⅛" ...185.00
Rose bowl, Dmn Quilt, bl, pleated, Stevens & Wms, 3¾x4" 225.00
Rose bowl, Ribbon, bl, 2½" +gr Ribbon lily pad underplate 400.00
Rose bowl, Ribbon, bl, 3-pinch top, 3⅛x2⅝" 165.00
Rose bowl, Ribbon, bl, 9-crimp, 2¾x3½" 245.00
Rose bowl, Ribbon, chartreuse, 8-crimp top, 2⅞x3¼" 195.00
Rose bowl, Ribbon, lt gr, 2¾x5", w/lily pad underplate 300.00
Shakers, Coin Spot, bl, 3½", pr 600.00
Spooner, Raindrop, apricot, 3-lobe top, Webb 195.00
Sugar shaker, Raindrop, bl, SP lid, 6¼" 325.00
Sweetmeat, Flower & Acorn, red w/gold flowers, SP trim, 5½" ..945.00
Tumbler, Dmn Quilt, rainbow, HP florals, 3½" 885.00
Tumbler, Herringbone, pk, 3¾x2⅝" 175.00
Vase, bud; Ribbon, bl shades w/ruffled rim, metal fr, 8¼" 125.00
Vase, Dmn Quilt, bl, wht int, bottle shape, 7½x3½" 125.00
Vase, Dmn Quilt, bl, wht int, 6¾x3⅝" 170.00
Vase, Dmn Quilt, bl, 4½x3¼", pr 235.00
Vase, Dmn Quilt, pk, bulbous, rnd mouth, 5⅛x4¾" 145.00
Vase, Dmn Quilt, pk, crimped/ruffled, camphor trim/hdls, 5" 210.00
Vase, Dmn Quilt, rainbow, knob neck, 3-petal ruffled rim, 6" 850.00
Vase, Dmn Quilt, yel, stick neck, 10" 200.00
Vase, Federzeichnung/Octopus, pearly scrolls w/brn & gold, 8½" 2,100.00
Vase, Flower & Acorn, bl, waisted, clear wafer ft, 7x6" 735.00
Vase, Herringbone, bl, melon ribs, 6½x3" 325.00
Vase, Herringbone, bl w/mc threads, gourd form, Northwood, 8" ..450.00
Vase, Herringbone, pk, bulbous melon w/fan-shaped top, 6½" ...175.00
Vase, Herringbone, pk, ruffled rim, 5½x3½" 175.00
Vase, Herringbone, red gloss, clear thread o/l, hdls, 11" 300.00
Vase, Pompeian Swirl, powder bl w/pk air traps, 7½", NM 545.00
Vase, Raindrop, apricot, melon ribs, ruffled rim, Mt WA, 5½" ..250.00
Vase, Raindrop, bl, fan-shaped ruffled top, 5½x2¾" 150.00
Vase, Ribbon, bl, wht int, 3-pearl top, dimpled, 4¾x5¾" 395.00
Vase, Ribbon, chartreuse, wafer ft, 2½x2¾" 195.00
Vase, Ribbon, chartreuse, w/gold prunus, 4⅛x3¼" 395.00
Vase, Verre Moire, pk, ruffled rim, wht int, 8¼x5" 450.00

Water set, Dmn Quilt, apricot, 7" pitcher+6 3⅝" tumblers **1,285.00**

Movie Memorabilia

Movie memorabilia covers a broad range of collectibles, from books and magazines dealing with the industry in general to the various promotional materials which were distributed to arouse interest in a particular film. Many collectors specialize in a specific area — posters, pressbooks, stills, lobby cards, or souvenir programs (also referred to as premiere booklets). In the listings below, a one-sheet poster measures approximately 27" x 41", three-sheet: 41" x 81", and six-sheet: 81" x 81". Window cards measure 14" x 22". See also Autographs; Cartoon Art; Paper Dolls; Personalities; Sheet Music.

Book, National Velvet, E Taylor, hardbk, 305-pg, 1945, EX **25.00**
Book, Seven Year Itch, M Monroe on cover, paperbk, 1955, EX ..**15.00**
Book, Story of How West Was Won, Random House/MGM, '63, EX ..**10.00**
Calendar, Marilyn Monroe, Golden Dreams, 1955, M **55.00**
Calendar, Marilyn Monroe, 1974, G **15.00**

Campaign book, Gone With the Wind, MGM, 1939, NM, $4,370.00 at auction.

Fan club kit, Three Stooges, 1959, EX **35.00**
Game, Godfather, Family Games Inc, 1971, VG+ **25.00**
Hand puppet, Dean Martin, cloth body/vinyl head, 1950s, EX **40.00**
Insert card, Born Yesterday, W Holden/J Holliday, 1951, EX **65.00**
Insert card, Cowboy & Lady, G Cooper/M Oberon, 1954, EX **35.00**
Insert card, Defiant Ones, T Curtis/S Portier, 1958, EX **20.00**
Insert card, Iron Petticoat, K Hepburn/B Hope, 1956, EX **36.00**
Insert card, Johnny Belinda, Jane Wyman, 1948, EX **45.00**
Insert card, Last Time I Saw Paris, E Taylor/V Johnson, '54, VG .**40.00**
Insert card, Machine Gun Kelly, Charles Bronson, 1958, EX **40.00**
Insert card, Saint's Girl Friday, L Hayward/D Dors, 1954, EX **50.00**
Insert card, VIPS, E Taylor/R Burton, 1963, EX **25.00**
Insert card, Voodoo Island, Boris Karloff, 1957, EX **65.00**
Lobby card, Gay Divorcee, Horton/E Lancaster, 1933, EX **25.00**
Lobby card, Go West Young Lady, Ford/Singleton/Miller, '41, EX ...**25.00**
Lobby card, Hell's Angels, Jean Harlow, '37 (reissue), rare, EX ..**175.00**
Lobby card, Love Story, R O'Neal/A McGraw, 1970, set of 4, EX ..**25.00**
Lobby card, Place in the Sun, M Clift/S Winters, 1951, EX **20.00**
Lobby card, Sun Also Rises, Errol Flynn, '57, set of 7, EX **50.00**
Lobby card, Two Lost Worlds, James Arness, 1950, set of 7, EX ..**50.00**
Magazine, Modern Screen, Elizabeth Taylor, June 1961, EX **12.00**
Magazine, Motion Picture, Clara Bow, April 1931, EX **55.00**
Magazine, Motion Picture, Hayworth & daughter, Jan '46, VG ...**35.00**
Magazine, Movie Life, Doris Day, July 1949, VG+ **18.00**
Magazine, Movie Story, B Davis/G Brent, May 1941, VG+ **25.00**
Magazine, Movie Story, Gregory Peck, Dec 1946, EX **30.00**
Magazine, Movie Story Yearbook, #7, Loretta Young, 1948, VG ..**20.00**
Magazine, Movieland, Marilyn Monroe, July 1952, NM **100.00**

Magazine, Movies, Joan Fontaine, May 1942, VG+ **20.00**
Magazine, Photoplay, Irene Dunn, June 1953, EX **30.00**
Magazine, Photoplay, Tuesday Weld, Aug 1961, VG **15.00**
Magazine, Picture Play, Myrna Loy, April 1937, EX **18.00**
Magazine, Screenland, Veronica Lake, Dec 1944, VG+ **20.00**
Magazine, Silver Screen, Sept 1944, VG+ **15.00**
Match book, Betty Grable, Down Argentine Way, 1940s, M **12.00**
Movie slide, Laurel & Hardy/Pack Up Your Troubles, cb mt, EX ..**110.00**
Movie slide, Marx Bros/The Cocoanuts, O Shaw/M Eaton, VG ...**65.00**
Pencil box, Charlie Chaplin, tin, 1930s, EX **60.00**
Plate, Marilyn Monroe, Royal Orleans, MIB **65.00**
Playbill, Raisin in the Sun, Sidney Portier cover, 1959, EX **22.00**
Pocket mirror, Marilyn Monroe in swimsuit, 2x3", M **5.00**
Poster, Barbarella, Jane Fonda, '66, 60x40", rare, VG **65.00**
Poster, Betrayal, silent, Jannings/G Cooper, '29, 1-sheet, EX **100.00**
Poster, Breakfast at Tiffany's, A Hepburn, '61, 3-sheet, EX **700.00**
Poster, Bridge on River Kwai, '58, style-B/1-sheet, rare, EX **200.00**
Poster, Enforcer, Clint Eastwood, 1977, 1-sheet, EX **50.00**
Poster, Family Plot, B Durn, Hitchcock film, '76, 1-sheet, EX **35.00**
Poster, Farmer's Daughter, L Young/J Cotton, '47, 1-sheet, EX **75.00**
Poster, Fat Spy, Jayne Mansfield, 1966, ½-sheet, EX **25.00**
Poster, Invasion USA, destruction of NY, 1952, 3-sheet, EX **150.00**
Poster, It's a Mad Mad Mad World, Jack Davis art, 6-sheet, VG ...**100.00**
Poster, Killer's Kiss, Kubrick film, 1955, ½-sheet, rare, EX **75.00**
Poster, Lion in Winter, P O'Toole/K Hepburn, '68, ½-sheet, VG **35.00**
Poster, Love on a Pillow, Bridget Bardot, 1964, 1-sheet, EX **40.00**
Poster, Manchurian Candidate, Sinatra/Harvey, '62, 1-sheet, EX ...**65.00**
Poster, Miracle Worker, P Duke/A Bancroft, 1962, ½ sheet, EX ..**50.00**
Poster, My Son John, H Hayes/R Walker, 1952, 1-sheet, EX **60.00**
Poster, One Flew Over Cuckoo's Nest, 1975, 1-sheet, EX **50.00**
Poster, Racket, Mitchum/L Scott/R Ryan, '51, 3-sheet, EX **100.00**
Poster, Raintree County, E Taylor/M Clift, '57, 1-sheet, EX **90.00**
Poster, Run Silent Run Deep, Gable/Lancaster, '58, 1-sheet, EX ..**50.00**
Poster, Speedway, Elvis/N Sinatra, 1968, 60x40", EX **85.00**
Poster, Untamed, T Power/S Hayward, 1955, ½-sheet, VG **50.00**
Poster, View To Kill, Roger Moore, 1985, 1-sheet, rare, EX **65.00**
Press book, Haunted Honeymoon, Robert Montgomery, 1940, EX ..**25.00**
Press book, Mogambo, C Gable/A Gardner, 1953, EX **45.00**
Press book, Separate Tables, B Lancaster/R Hayworth, EX **35.00**
Program, Cyrano de Bergerac, Jose Ferrer, 1947, VG+ **25.00**
Program, Diamond Lil, Mae West, 1956, EX **30.00**
Program, Some Like It Hot, Dutch, 1954 ....**50.00**
Program, 50th Annual Academy Awards, 1978, M **60.00**

Poster, Some Like It Hot, Marilyn Monroe, Tony Curtis, and Jack Lemmon, United Artists, 1959, 41x27", NM, $660.00.

Standee, Marilyn Monroe in windblown dress, diecut cb, EX **30.00**
Still, Lucille Ball, The Long Long Trailer, '63, 8x10", NM **12.00**
Token, James Dean, phrase & portrait on wood, 1½", EX **25.00**
Tray, Pinky Lee, Pinky doing splits, 1950, 10x14", EX **30.00**
Window card, An Affair To Remember, Grant/Kerr, 1957, EX **65.00**
Window card, China, A Ladd/L Young, 1943, EX **75.00**
Window card, Dangerous Blondes, E Keyes, 1943, EX **35.00**
Window card, Lady Refuses, Betty Compson, 1931, EX **75.00**

Window card, M*A*S*H, Donald Sutherland, 1970, M 25.00
Window card, Man of All Seasons, Paul Scofield, 1967, EX 25.00
Window card, Mr Roberts, H Fonda/J Cagney/J Lemmon, '55, EX 50.00
Window card, No Business Like Show Business, M Monroe, '54, VG ..50.00
Window card, Rear Window, J Stewart/G Kelly, 1954, EX 50.00
Window card, Spinout, Elvis/S Fabray, 1966, EX 35.00
Window card, Tom Thumb, R Tamblyn, 1958, EX 35.00
Window card, Voyage to the Bottom of the Sea, 1961, EX 40.00

Mt. Washington

The Mt. Washington Glass Works was founded in 1837 in South Boston, Massachusetts, but moved to New Bedford in 1869 after purchasing the facilities of the New Bedford Glass Company. Frederick S. Shirley became associated with the firm in 1874. Two years later the company reorganized and became known as the Mt. Washington Glass Company. In 1894 it merged with the Pairpoint Manufacturing Company, a small Brittania works nearby, but continued to conduct business under its own title until after the turn of the century. The combined plants were equipped with the most modern and varied machinery available and boasted a working force with experience and expertise rival to none in the art of blowing and cutting glass. In addition to their fine cut glass, they are recognized as the first American company to make cameo glass, an effect they achieved through acid-cutting methods. In 1885 Shirley was issued a patent to make Burmese, pale yellow glassware tinged with a delicate pink blush. Another patent issued in 1886 allowed them the rights to produce Rose Amber, or amberina, a transparent ware shading from ruby to amber. Pearl Satin Ware and Peachblow, so named for its resemblance to a rosy peach skin, were patented the same year. One of their most famous lines, Crown Milano, was introduced in 1893. It was an opal glass either free blown or pattern molded, tinted a delicate color, and decorated with enameling and gilt. Royal Flemish was patented in 1894 and is considered the rarest of the Mt. Washington art glass lines. It was decorated with raised, gold-enameled lines dividing the surface of the ware in much the same way as lead lines divide a stained glass window. The sections were filled in with one or several transparent colors and further decorated in gold enamel with florals, foliage, beading, and medallions.

Our advisors for this category are Betty and Clarence Maier; they are listed in the Directory under Pennsylvania. See also Amberina; Cranberry; Salt Shakers; Burmese; Crown Milano; Royal Flemish; etc.

Biscuit jar, gold/mc floral on wht/tan swirls, lid w/turtle 800.00
Biscuit jar, pulled-drape pk satin w/HP florals, SP trim, 8" 725.00
Biscuit jar, spider mums w/gold beads on opalware, 6½x7" 550.00
Candlesticks, canary, lotus socket, lobed stem, 7½", pr 325.00
Candlesticks, petal socket, dolphin std, sq base, 11", pr 375.00
Compote, Napoli, grapes w/gold, 3½x7⅜" 575.00
Cracker barrel, boy & girl blow bubbles, gold trim, 5" 1,000.00
Cracker barrel, cornstalks, pastel w/gold, puffy lid, 6½" 550.00
Cracker barrel, pansies, mc on biscuit ground, ornate lid, 5" 500.00
Cracker barrel, poppies, yel/red on tan & yel, emb leaves, 5" 450.00
Cruet, Rose Amber, trefoil spout, 5½" 450.00
Cup & saucer, demi; pansies w/gold on clear, 2¼", 4⅝" 750.00
Lamp, Dutch scene, mk Delft, Pairpoint burner, 8¾" 875.00
Peg lamp, violets/gold scrolls on shade & body, silver mt, 22" ...2,200.00
Pitcher, floral, mc w/gold on bl wash, sq mouth, 9x7½" 550.00
Pitcher, orchids, mc w/gold lines on clear, 7" 400.00
Punch cup, Napoli, Palmer Cox Brownies/cat, 2x2¾" 2,000.00
Rose bowl, daisies, mc w/gold on bl wash, #620, 2¾x3¼" 435.00
Rose bowl, floral, pk/mauve on apricot/cream, 4" 275.00
Rose bowl, floral, pk/yel w/ivy, folded rim w/gold, 4x4½" 485.00
Rose bowl, pansies w/gold on beige satin, crimped, 3½x4" 395.00

Shaker, floral clusters, mc on textured peach, fig style 200.00
Shaker, lay-down egg, Columbian 1893 Exhibition 185.00
Shaker, lay-down egg w/HP violets 185.00
Shaker, stand-up egg w/HP pecking hen, 2½" 350.00
Sugar shaker, ostrich egg form w/pastel nasturtiums, 4" 250.00
Sugar shaker, tomato form w/bl flowers on biscuit, 2½" 425.00
Sweetmeat jar, mc spangle w/gold mica, HP dogwoods, SP trim .285.00
Vase, floral w/gold, ribbed, waisted, 10½x5" 635.00
Vase, jack-in-pulpit; lustreless wht w/scattered floral, 9½" 385.00
Vase, Lava, global, reeded hdls, 4½" 2,900.00
Vase, Lava, mc inclusions in blk, flared rim, reed hdls, 3½" 2,250.00
Vase, Lava, mc inclusions in blk, spherical, 5" 2,400.00
Vase, mc florals & leafy scrolls, stick neck, 7¼" 650.00
Vase, mums, gold on emerald gr, sqd cylinder, 8", pr 500.00

Photo courtesy Clarence and Betty Maier

Vase, Verona, floral, clear with green wash, gold trim, 10", $1,570.00.

Vase, Verona, knight, gold & silver on clear w/pk wash, 14" ..1,950.00
Vase, yel-gr, trumpet form, polished pontil, ca 1880, 11¾" 300.00

Mulberry China

Mulberry china was made by many of the Staffordshire area potters from about 1830 until the 1850s. It is a transfer-printed earthenware or ironstone named for the color of its decorations, a purplish-brown resembling the juice of the mulberry. Some pieces may have faded out over the years and today look almost gray with only a hint of purple. (Transfer printing was done in many colors; technically only those in the mauve tones are 'mulberry'; color variations have little effect on value.) Some of the patterns (Corean, Jeddo, Pelew, and Formosa, for instance) were also produced in Flow Blue ware. Others seem to have been used exclusively with the mulberry color. Our advisor for this category is Mary Frank Gaston; she is listed in the Directory under Texas.

Abbey, creamer 195.00
Athens, cup & saucer, handleless 70.00
Athens, gravy boat, Meigh 85.00
Athens, plate, 10½" 55.00
Avon, teapot, lg 385.00
Bochara, bowl, vegetable; w/lid 375.00
Bochara, platter, 14" 110.00
Bochara, soup tureen & tray, EX 895.00
Brunswick, platter, w/polychrome, 17" 385.00
Bryonia, tureen, soup; rnd w/lid 110.00
Calcutta, cup & saucer, handleless 175.00
Calcutta, plate, 8½" 60.00
Calcutta, teapot 275.00

Castle Scenery, pitcher, 8" 395.00
Chusan, plate, Podmore Walker, 8¼" 30.00
Chusan, platter, 18" 220.00
Corean, bowl, vegetable; w/lid 435.00
Corean, creamer 195.00
Corean, pitcher, 10" 330.00
Corean, platter, 16x12" 260.00
Corean, platter, 18x14" 350.00
Cyprus, bowl, vegetable; w/lid 300.00
Cyprus, creamer 200.00
Cyprus, plate, 11" 55.00
Cyprus, platter, 15½" 215.00
Cyprus, teapot 275.00
Delhi, soap box, w/lid 140.00
Flora, creamer 170.00
Flora, soap dish, Walker, 3-pc 160.00
Foliage, plate, 9" 30.00
Heath's Flower, soup plate, 10½" 75.00
Hong, pitcher, 2-qt 335.00
Hong, plate, 5" 40.00
Hyson, sugar bowl 165.00
Jeddo, bowl, vegetable; Adams, w/lid 535.00
Jeddo, creamer 215.00
Jeddo, pitcher, Adams, 2-qt 435.00
Jeddo, platter, 15½" 245.00
Jeddo, sugar bowl 195.00
Jeddo, teapot 415.00

Longport, plate, T&J Mayer, 9½", $25.00.

Lozere, cup & saucer, handleless 55.00
Madras, plate, 10" 145.00
Marble, pitcher, 8" 325.00
Medina, cup & saucer 65.00
Medina, pitcher & bowl set, JP&Co, EX 295.00
Medina, sugar bowl, Furnival 195.00
Nankin, creamer 225.00
Neva, plate, 10⅞" 80.00
Ning-Po, creamer, Hall 375.00
Panama, creamer 245.00
Pelew, bowl, vegetable; w/lid 380.00
Pelew, teapot 350.00
Peruvian, cup & saucer, handleless 70.00
Peruvian, pitcher, 8½" 400.00
Peruvian, teapot, Wedge Wood 300.00
Rhone Scenery, coffeepot, Podmore Walker 400.00
Rhone Scenery, cup plate 50.00
Rhone Scenery, tureen, sauce; w/underplate 250.00
Rose, pitcher, 2-qt 375.00
Savoy, platter, Walker, 15½" 300.00
Scinde, platter, Podmore Walker, 15½" 200.00
Seaweed, potty 270.00
Shannon, plate, 8" 20.00

Shapoo, cup plate 65.00
Singanese, toddy plate, J Wedge Wood, 5" 30.00
Temple, pitcher 125.00
Temple, tea tile, Podmore Walker 95.00
Tonquin, cup & saucer 95.00
Tonquin, platter, 10¾" 120.00
Tonquin, sauce bowl 50.00
Udina, cup & saucer, Clementson 80.00
Udina, teapot, Clementson 440.00
Venture, creamer 95.00
Vincennes, bowl, vegetable; w/lid 380.00
Vincennes, creamer 225.00
Vincennes, platter, 15½" 200.00
Vincennes, relish 180.00
Washington Vase, bowl & pitcher 695.00
Washington Vase, creamer 225.00
Washington Vase, platter, 13½" 250.00
Washington Vase, teapot 525.00
Washington Vase, waste bowl 215.00
Wreath, cup & saucer, handleless 75.00

Muller Freres

Henri Muller established a factory in 1900 at Croismare, France. He produced fine cameo art glass decorated with florals, birds, and insects in the Art Nouveau style. The work was accomplished by acid engraving and hand finishing. Usual marks were 'Muller,' 'Muller Croismare,' or 'Croismare, Nancy.' In 1910 Henri and his brother Deseri formed a glassworks at Luneville. The cameo art glass made there was nearly all produced by acid cuttings of up to four layers with motifs similar to those favored at Croismare. A good range of colors was used, and some later pieces were gold flecked. Handles and decorative devices were sometimes applied by hand. In addition to the cameo glass, they also produced an acid-finished glass of bold mottled colors in the Deco style. Examples were signed 'Muller Freres' or 'Luneville.' Our advisor for this category is Don Williams; he is listed in the Directory under Missouri.

Cameo

Vase, large rose in orange, yellow, and dark red with brown leafy branch on frost, 6½", $2,200.00.

Bowl, trees/shrubs, blk/raspberry/gr, sgn, 3¾" 800.00
Vase, poppies, red/blk on yel/bl/frost, 5¼" 2,100.00
Vase, trees/river, blk ruby/red on pastel mottle, tapered, 5" 1,800.00
Vase, 3 ladies by seashore on purple, 4" 750.00

Miscellaneous

Chandelier, yel & purple mottle w/gilt-bronze fr, 3-arm, 24" ..1,800.00
Hanging fixture, 3 dbl wrought pendants, mc mottled shade, 45" ...1,200.00
Luminiere, mc mottle w/foil inclusions, wrought fr, 16½" 5,450.00
Vase, mc mottle/gold & silver inclusions, bl knop base, 19" 1,600.00

Vase, willows/fall grasses pnt on dk gr to yel, hdls, 5" 800.00

Muncie

Muncie Pottery, established in Muncie, Indiana, by Charles O. Grafton, was produced from 1922 until about 1935. It is made of a heavier clay than most of its contemporaries; the styles are sturdy and simple. Early glazes were bright and colorful. In fact, Muncie was advertised as the 'rainbow pottery.' Later most of the ware was finished in a matt glaze. The more collectible examples are those modeled after Consolidated Glass vases — sculptured with lovebirds, grasshoppers, and goldfish. Their line of Art Deco-style vases bear a remarkable resemblance to the Consolidated Glass company's Ruba Rombic line. Vases, candlesticks, bookends, ashtrays, bowls, lamp bases, and luncheon sets were made. A line of garden pottery was manufactured for a short time. Items were frequently impressed with MUNCIE in block letters. Letters such as A, K, E, or D and the numbers 1, 2, 3, 4, or 5 often found scratched into the base are finishers' marks.

Bookends, Leda & the Swan, 5x7", pr 195.00
Dutch shoe, bl gloss/peachskin, 6½" L 275.00
Jug, brn gloss, w/music box, hdld, 8½" 185.00
Lamp, nude panels, gr matt, orig finial 450.00
Vase, gr on rose, #143, 7" 75.00

Vase, goldfish, green and tan, 8½", $275.00.

Vase, hat w/folded brim, matt lt gr, 7" 185.00
Vase, pillow form, gloss yel, 6" 75.00
Vase, pillow form, matt bl/rose, 9" 110.00
Vase, Ruba Rombic fan shape, matt bl/rose, 8" 210.00
Vase, ruffled top, gr/lav, 7" 75.00
Vase, ruffled top, hdls, matt gr/rose, 6" 65.00
Vase, stick form, matt gr, 8" 65.00

Musical Instruments

The field of automatic musical instruments covers many different categories ranging from watches and tiny seals concealing fine early musical movements to huge organs and orchestrions which weigh many hundreds of pounds and are equivalent to small orchestras. Music boxes, first made in the early 19th century by Swiss watchmakers, were produced in both disk and cylinder models. The latter type employs a cylinder with tiny pins that lift the teeth in the comb of the music box (producing a sound much like many individual tuning forks), and music results. The value of a cylinder music box depends on the length and diameter of the cylinder, the date of its manufacture, the number of tunes it plays (four or six is usually better than ten or twelve), and its manufacturer. Nicole Freres, Henri Capt, LeCoultre, and Bremond are among the most highly regarded, and the larger boxes made by Mermod Freres are also popular. Examples with multiple cylinders,

extra instruments (such as bells or an organ section), and those in particularly ornate cabinets or with matching tables bring significantly higher prices. While smaller cylinder boxes are still being made, the larger ones (over 10" cylinders) typically date from before 1900. Disk music boxes were introduced about 1890 but were replaced by the phonograph only twenty-five years later. However, during that time hundreds of thousands were made. Their great advantage was in playing inexpensive interchangeable disks, a factor that remains an attraction for today's collector as well. Among the most popular disk boxes are those made by Regina (USA), Polyphon, Mira, Stella, and Symphonion. Relative values are determined by the size of the disks they play, whether they have single or double combs, if they are upright or table models, and how ornate their cases are. Especially valuable are those that play multiple disks at the same time or are incorporated into tall case clocks.

Player pianos were made in a wide variety of styles. Early varieties consisted of a mechanism which pushed up to a piano and played on the keyboard by means of felt-tipped fingers. These use sixty-five note rolls. Later models have the playing mechanism built in, and most use eighty-eight note rolls. Upright pump player pianos have little value in unrestored condition because the cost of restoration is so high. 'Reproducing' pianos, especially the 'grand' format, can be quite valuable, depending on the make, the size, the condition, and the ornateness of the case. 'Reproducing' pianos have very sophisticated mechanisms and are much more realistic in the reproduction of piano music. They were made in relatively limited quantities. Better manufacturers include Steinway and Mason & Hamlin. Popular roll mechanism makers include Ampico, Duo-Art, and Welte. The market for all types of player pianos has been weak for several years.

Coin-operated pianos (Orchestrions) were used commercially and typically incorporate extra instruments in addition to the piano action. These can be very large and complex, incorporating drums, cymbals, xylophones, bells, and hundreds of pipes. Both American and European coin pianos are very popular, especially the larger and more complex models made by Wurlitzer, Seeburg, Cremona, Weber, Welte, Hupfeld, and many others. These companies also made automatically playing violins (Mills Violin Virtuoso, Hupfeld), banjos (Encore), and harps (Whitlock); these are quite valuable.

Mechanical organs range all the way from parlor pump organs and roll-operated reed organs to band organs found on carousels and giant fairground and dance hall organs. Pump organs made by Estey, Wilcox, and others are often very ornate but also very common and bulky; as a result, the market is very limited. The more sophisticated roll-playing reed organs are collectible but still find a limited market due to the cost of restoration. They are very undervalued and have been for a long time. Carousel-type band organs, especially those made by well-known manufacturers such as Wurlitzer and Artizan, continue to sell well. The highest values are reserved for the larger Welte, Gavioli, Bruder, and other organs used in fairgrounds, dance halls, and private residences that incorporate hundreds of pipes. With a harder-to-find, larger instrument, a good supply of rolls contributes much to its value, since in many cases rolls cannot be found.

Unless noted, prices given are for instruments in fine condition, playing properly, with cabinets or cases in well-preserved or refinished condition. In all instances, unrestored instruments sell for much less, as do those with broken or missing parts, damaged cases, and the like. On the other hand, particularly superb examples in especially ornate case designs and those that have been particularly well kept will often command more. Our advisor for mechanical instruments is Martin Roenigk; he is listed in the Directory under Connecticut. Fred Oster advises us on non-mechanical instruments; he is listed under Pennsylvania.

Key:
c — cylinder   d — disk

Mechanical

Box, B&M Etouffoirs en Acier, 10¾" c, 6-tune 800.00
Box, Baker, Troll & Fils, 17¼" c, 12-tune, 31" case 2,400.00
Box, Criterion 15½", dbl combs, w/matching base, EX 5,500.00
Box, German Symphonion, 13¾" d, walnut veneer 22" case ..2,300.00
Box, Imperial Symphonion, 17⅝" upright, 2 c, EX 7,000.00
Box, interchangeable 11" c, w/writing table, EX 6,500.00
Box, Langdorf & Fils, 17¼" c, 6-tune, 29" case 3,500.00
Box, Langdorf Longue Marche, 7 12½" C, EX 12,000.00
Box, Lochmann Orig, 24½" c, tubular bells, upright, EX 18,000.00
Box, Mandoline Quatuor, 17¼" c, ornate 28" case 5,000.00
Box, Mermod Freres, 11¼" c, 2½" d, 10-tune 1,500.00
Box, Mermod Freres, 17½" c, 8-tune, 35" case 4,500.00
Box, Mermod Freres Ideal Soprano, 14¾" c, 6-tune 3,400.00
Box, Mermod Freres Interchangeable, 4 13" c, rprs/rstr 5,000.00
Box, Nicole Freres, 13¼" c, 8-tune, ebony wood case 1,700.00
Box, Nicole Freres (att), 10¾" c, 6-tune, VG 1,300.00
Box, Perfection, 14" single comb, 4 d, EX orig 1,800.00
Box, Regina, 11" d, oak case, VG, +16 d 1,100.00
Box, Regina, 12" d, mahog cabinet 1,600.00
Box, Regina, 15½" d, curved front, changer, oak case, EX 18,000.00
Box, Regina, 15½" d, cvd mahog case, 10½x21x19", +60 d 5,700.00
Box, Regina, 15½" d, single comb, pinstriped case, EX 2,400.00
Box, Regina, 20¾" d, dbl comb, oak desk style, ca 1910 ....12,000.00
Box, Regina, 20¾" d, walnut 29" case 4,500.00
Box, Regina, 27" d, 2 c, eng mahog case 9,000.00
Box, Regina Sublima Corona Style 31, 20¾" d, EX 16,000.00
Box, Regina 27 Dragon Front, 12-tune, ca 1899-1902, rstr ...22,500.00
Box, Stella, 17¼" d, dbl comb, mahog case, table model, EX ..5,000.00
Box, Stella Concert, 15½" d, w/table 4,000.00
Box, Swiss, sewing necessaire, 2½" c, single comb, 1830s 2,200.00
Box, Swiss, 11⅛" c, 3-tune, key wind, 1850s 1,700.00
Box, Swiss, 12⅞" c, 4-tune, ca 1850, 21" case 1,600.00
Box, Swiss, 13" c, 6-tune, Louis XV case, 43x29" 2,000.00
Box, Swiss, 6½" c, 3-tune, veneer 21" case 850.00
Box, Swiss Bells & Drum in Sight, 13" c, 8-tune, 24" 2,400.00
Box, Swiss Flutes Voix Celestes, 11" c, 6-tune, 20¾" 2,200.00
Box, Swiss Sublime Harmony, 8⅛" c, dbl comb, 17" case 1,100.00
Box, Swiss Sublime Harmony Piccolo Zither, 18½" c, 10-tune ...3,700.00
Box, Symphonian Musical Automaton, VG, w/28 d 3,500.00
Box, Symphonium, 17⅝" d, dbl comb, mahog table model 5,800.00
Box, Troll & Baker, 13" c, brass & silver inlay, 9 bells, EX 5,500.00
Calliope, Tangley, roll operated, EX 7,500.00
Nickelodeon, Capital, oak case w/violin pipes & rolls, EX 8,000.00
Nickelodeon, Coinola CX, walnut case, w/xylophone, EX orig ..7,000.00
Nickelodeon, Seeburg A, EX orig 3,500.00
Nickelodeon, Seeburg A, w/xylophone, NM 9,800.00
Nickelodeon, Seeburg C, oak w/beveled glass panels, EX orig 5,000.00
Nickelodeon, Seeburg E, w/xylophone, rstr 10,500.00
Nickelodeon, Seeburg K, w/flute pipes, EX orig 12,000.00
Nickelodeon, Seeburg K, w/xylophone, eagle front 12,000.00
Nickelodeon, Seeburg L, EX orig 6,500.00
Nickelodeon, Wurlitzer CX, Grecian style, rstr 23,500.00
Orchestrelle, Aeolian, heavily cvd mahog, EX orig 2,000.00
Orchestrelle, Aeolian V, oak, EX orig 3,500.00
Orchestrelle, Aeolian W, EX, +200 rolls 4,900.00
Orchestrion, Coinola C-2, EX 27,000.00
Orchestrion, Coinola CX, w/11 instruments 18,000.00
Orchestrion, Cremona, Marquette, 10-tune, A rolls, 64", EX ...3,750.00
Orchestrion, Cremona J, rstr 45,000.00
Orchestrion, Nelson Wiggins style 8, rstr 11,000.00
Orchestrion, Seeburg G, NM 45,000.00
Orchestrion, Western Electric, 10-tune G roll, 1920s, rstr 7,500.00

Band organ, Wurlitzer 150, 18 brass horns, drum, cymbal, snare drum, and many internal pipes, in red case with gold trim, two inlaid mirrors, missing original side wings, with 10 paper rolls, ca 1920, 79x89", NM, $30,000.00.

Organ, band; Artizan, 46-key, +15 rolls 16,000.00
Organ, band; Wellershaus, 56-key/191 pipes/2 drums, 1875 ..18,000.00
Organ, band; Wurlitzer #146, rstr 18,000.00
Organ, band; Wurlitzer #153, rstr 40,000.00
Organ, concert; Cabinetto, walnut case w/gilt, 17½" 550.00
Organ, dance; Arburo, rstr 15,000.00
Organ, dance; Bursen, rstr 17,500.00
Organ, Dutch street; Limonaire, 34-key, w/music book/1 figure ..22,000.00
Organ, fairground; Gasparini, 52-key, early 1900s, rstr 16,000.00
Organ, fairground; Gavioli, 65-key, 240 pipes, EX 42,000.00
Organ, fairground; Ruth-Voigt, 56 keyless, 5 figures, EX 55,000.00
Organ, monkey; Molinari, 26-key, EX 4,000.00
Organ, monkey; Molinari, 47-key, w/orig cart, EX 11,500.00
Organ, monkey; Molinari & Sons, 7-tune bbl, EX 4,500.00
Organ, Wilcox & Wht Symphony, oak, w/shutters, rstr 1,500.00
Organette, Organina, walnut case, paper rolls 375.00
Piano, grand; Ampico, art case, 74", EX orig 22,000.00
Piano, grand; Chickering Ampico #65, 77", EX orig 16,000.00
Piano, grand; Knabe Ampico, 62", EX orig 1,200.00
Piano, grand; Knabe Ampico, 64", EX orig 1,250.00
Piano, grand; Marshall & Wendall Ampico, 60", EX orig 1,200.00
Piano, grand; Steinway Louis XV Duo-Art XR, mahog, 73", rstr ..18,500.00
Piano, grand; Wurlitzer Recordo, retubed, rfn, 56" 1,500.00
Piano, push-up; Harrand Cecilian, EX 500.00
Piano, upright; Ampico, Marshall & Wendall, rstr 3,700.00
Piano, upright; Ampico B, Marshall & Wendall, EX 2,200.00
Piano, upright; Charles Steiff Welte, M orig 1,200.00
Piano, upright; Chickering Ampico, EX orig 1,500.00
Piano, upright; George Steck Duo-Art, EX 1,400.00
Piano, upright; Melville Clark Apollophone, scarce, EX 800.00
Piano, upright; Steinway Duo-Art, brn mahog, M rstr 9,800.00
Piano, upright; Symphony, oak w/art glass, 10-tune, 61", EX ..7,000.00
Piano/organ, Reproduco Duplex, rare 8,000.00
Piano/pipe organ, Reproduco, EX orig 6,500.00
Piano/pipe organ, Reproduco, orig Seeburg Swan Glass, rstr ...9,500.00
Pianocorder, Marantz, w/50 cassettes, EX 3,000.00
Violano, Mills Violano Virtuoso, single violin, rfn, EX 22,500.00
Violano-Virtuoso, Mills, oak case, ca 1920 ....24,000.00

Non-Mechanical

Accordion, Hohner, 3-row buttons, red, Corona #HA3522, MIB ...375.00

Accordion, Tanzbar, EX **1,800.00**
Banjo, Bacon Peerless Plectrum, 1920, rstr, M **1,500.00**
Banjo, GC Dobson, 5-string, maple, fretless, 11" rim **350.00**
Banjo, Gibson RB-175, long neck, 5-string, 1954, NM, +case ...**550.00**
Banjo, Lyons & Healy, 5-string, open bk, ca 1920, G **100.00**
Banjo/mandolin, Weymann #40, maple shell, dk-stained neck ..**125.00**
Bass saxhorn, German, upright, 3 Berliner valves, 1870s **350.00**
Fife, Am, B flat, German silver, ebonite band/inlays, 14" **45.00**
Fife, H Wrede London, boxwood, 1 sq brass key, 1830s **125.00**
Flugelhorn, CW Moritze, brass w/German-silver trim, 1880s **850.00**
Flute, E Baack, cocuswood, German silver mts, 1939-72, 21" **385.00**
Flute, Graves, fruitwood, ivory mts, 1 brass key, 1850s, 21" **1,200.00**
Flute, Rohe NY, boxwood, horn mts, brass key, 1840s, 21" **400.00**
Guitar, classical; Solar-Gonzalez, rosewood, 1965, +case **1,350.00**
Guitar, flamenco; M Ramirez, 3-pc cyprus bk, 1914, G, +case ...**8,500.00**
Guitar, Gibson L-12, sunburst, 1939, EX, w/hard case **1,650.00**
Guitar, Gibson SJ, natural finish, sm pick guard, 1955, VG **1,600.00**
Guitar, Guild F-47, 1972, VG, orig hard case **1,200.00**
Guitar, Martin D-28, 1952, EX, G- orig hard case **4,600.00**
Guitar, Martin 00-18G, classic w/X-brace, 1938, EX **950.00**
Guitar, steel lap; Harmony, gray pearloid, EX, orig case **140.00**

Harp, French, ca 1850, no strings, case marked: Pleyel, Wolff and Lion, $3,500.00.

Harpsichord, Am, rosewood, scroll & lyre rest, 1860s, 38x81" ...**2,500.00**
Mandolin, Bruno, inlaid, 1880s, w/case, EX **95.00**
Mandolin, Gibson Style A-Jr, snakehead, brn face, NM **675.00**
Piano, grand; WM Knabe, walnut, Renaissance Revival, 68", EX ...**3,850.00**
Piano, J Osborn, Boston, classical mahog/mahog vnr, 1820, 67" **1,850.00**
Piano, spinet; Queen Anne style, mahog, EX orig, w/bench **430.00**
Piccolo, unstamped German Grenadilla, ivory band, NP mts **50.00**
Tuba, Besson & Co, SP, 3 piston valves, G **100.00**
Ukelele, Wayman Soprano, mahog, EX **150.00**

Mustache Cups

Mustache cups were popular items during the late Victorian period, designed specifically for the man with the mustache! They were made in silverplate as well as china and ironstone. Decorations ranged from simple transfers to elaborately applied and gilded florals. To properly position the 'mustache bar,' special cups were designed for 'lefties.' These are the rare ones!

A Present written w/gold, gold bands & trim, Germany, w/saucer **40.00**
Emb florals w/gold trim, mc beadwork, lt wear **30.00**
Gr & gold paisley w/sm pk flowers, rpr, Germany, VG **35.00**
Mc florals w/emb decor, Germany, w/saucer **60.00**
Pk & wht flowers w/bright gr leaves, gold scrolls, w/saucer **40.00**

Pk flower garlands & gold lettering on porc, unmk, w/saucer **48.00**
Roses w/much gold on porc, scalloped, w/saucer **35.00**

Roses on white with gold, unmarked, $65.00.

Sheep & buildings landscape, EX gold trim, 4½" dia **35.00**
Violet bouquets on wht w/gold, left-handed, Germany, w/saucer .**70.00**
Violets on turq w/gold swirls, unmk, w/saucer **45.00**

Nailsea

Nailsea is a term referring to clear or colored glass decorated in contrasting spatters, swirls, or loops. These are usually white but may also be pink, red, or blue. It was first produced in Nailsea, England, during the late 1700s but was made in other parts of Britain and Scotland as well. During the mid-1800s a similar type of glass was produced in this country. Originally used for decorative novelties only, by that time tumblers and other practical items were being made from Nailsea-type glass. See also Lamps; Witch Balls.

Bottle, gemel, clear w/wht loopings, gr lip rings, 11¼" **100.00**
Bowl, olive gr w/wht flecks, folded-out rim, 3½x6½" **900.00**
Finger bowl, amber, pk threading, clear ft, berry pontil **250.00**
Flask, pocket; olive gr w/wht loopings, open pontil, 6¼" **155.00**
Flask, red & bl loopings on wht, pontiled, 1-pt **290.00**
Flask, red & wht loopings, 7" **100.00**
Pitcher, olive-gr w/wht flecks & appl threads, ca 1820, 7¾" ...**1,000.00**
Salt cellar, dk gr w/wht flakes, appl ft, master, 2¾" **400.00**
Vase, bud; clambroth w/bl loopings, pontil, 7¼" **400.00**
Vase, dk olive gr w/wht flecks & rim, bulbous, 6½" **600.00**
Vase, olive gr w/wht flecks, cylindrical, ftd, 6½" **575.00**

Nakara

Nakara was a line of decorated opaque milk glass produced by the C.F. Monroe Company of Meriden, Connecticut, for a few years after the turn of the century. It differs from their Wave Crest line in several ways. The shapes were simpler; pastel colors were deeper and covered more of the surface; more beading was present; flowers were larger; and large transfer prints of figures, Victorian ladies, cherubs, etc., were used. Ormolu and brass collars and mounts complemented these opulent pieces. Most items were signed; however, this is not important since the ware was never reproduced. Our advisors for this category are Dolli and Wilfred R. Cohen; their address is listed in the Directory under California.

Ashtray, flowers on gr hexagonal bowl, ormulu mts, sm **200.00**
Bonbon, daisies/beaded scrolls on pk to yel, wire hdl, 6" dia **350.00**
Bowl, trinket; flowers/beading on pk, ormulu hdls, 2x4" **175.00**
Box, Bishop's Hat, portrait transfer, 4½" **550.00**
Box, blown-out pansy on lid, 3¾" dia **695.00**
Box, cartouche of 2 ladies in garden on gr, 8½" **1,695.00**
Box, Collars & Cuffs, pansies/beaded scrolls on bl to ivory **1,850.00**
Box, Crown mold, peonies on moss gr, 8½" dia **1,595.00**

Box, Crown mold, sailing scene panels, ftd, 6½" dia 1,495.00
Box, Crown mold, 6 roses on top, mirror inside, 5½x6" 1,295.00
Box, floral/scrolls, wht/bl on Burmese color, 7½" 1,145.00
Box, flowers on gr shaded to pk, plain mold, 2¾x3½" dia 350.00
Box, Greenaway figures & beading, uncmb, 6" dia 900.00
Box, roses, pk/wht on gr to pk, fancy ft, oval, 3½x5½" 400.00
Box, 2 cherubs on lid, bl, 2x3¾" dia 350.00
Box, 2 cherubs on pnt Burmese, 3½x8½" 1,250.00
Box, 2 pk lilies/spiked leaves on turq, hinged, 4½" dia 475.00

Card holder, embossed scrolls and flowers on blue, $450.00;
Box, roses and beadwork on blue, 6" dia, $650.00; Tray, Egg
Crate (rare mold for Nakara), florals on blue, $450.00.

Hair receiver, children having tea, dmn shape 585.00
Humidor, floral & 'Tobacco' banner on dk rust, 6x6" 800.00
Humidor, Indian in headdress on red-brn, brass lid, 6x6" 1,275.00
Humidor, Old Sport, bulldog w/stein & pipe, 7¾x4½" 695.00
Humidor, owl on tree transfer, 5½x4" 1,200.00
Jar, lady's portrait/dotted enamel on caramel, 4½" dia 425.00
Match holder, tiny beaded flowers on gr, ormolu rim, 2" dia 275.00
Pin tray, scrolls/wht dots on pk, orig lining, 2¼x4¾" 175.00
Plaque, Queen Louise in wht reserve on bl, ormolu mt 2,500.00
Umbrella stand, emb scrolls/flowers, Indian portrait, 20½" 3,500.00
Vase, daisies in pk fr, lav/tan Nouveau design, cylindrical, 11" ..875.00
Vase, wild roses/scrolls on beige, 4-ftd ormolu base, 9" 795.00

Napkin Rings

Napkin rings became popular during the late 1800s. They were made from various materials. Among the most popular and collectible today are the large group of varied silverplated figurals made by American manufacturers. Recently the larger figurals in excellent condition have appreciated considerably. Only those with a blackened finish, corrosion, or broken and/or missing parts have maintained their earlier price levels. When no condition is indicated, the items listed below are assumed to be all original and in very good to excellent condition. Check very carefully for missing parts, solder repairs, or marriages.

A timely warning: inexperienced buyers should be aware of excellent reproductions on the market, especially the wheeled pieces. However, these do not have the fine detail and patina of the originals and tend to have a more consistent, soft pewter-like finish. These are appearing at the large, quality shows at top prices, being shown along with authentic antique merchandise. Beware! For further information we recommend *Figural Napkin Rings* (Collector Books) by Lillian Gottschalk and Sandra Whitson.

Key:
gw — gold washed　　　　　SH&M — Simpson, Hall, & Miller
R&B — Reed & Barton

Acorns at side of ring, rnd base, Meriden #163 ....65.00
Barrel ring held by Xd branches & leaf 65.00

Beaver sits on leaves & branches, Toronto #110 ....125.00
Bird w/long tail on leaf, ring attached to wings 95.00
Boy in harness pulls ring on wheels, Wilcox #01577 ....500.00
Boy plays w/dog atop ring, rectangular base, Rogers #19 ....250.00
Boy removing sock sits beside ring, Derby #341 ....275.00
Boy rolls ring, lady watches, oblong base, Tufts #1597 ....500.00
Boy w/ball & bat by ring, rectangular base, Babcock #202 ....250.00
Boy w/rope pulls 4-wheeled cart, Rogers #128 ....500.00
Bulldog sits chained to doghouse, sq base, SH&M #207 ....350.00
Cat atop ring arches bk at dog, rnd base, Rogers #296 ....295.00
Cherries & leaves on side of ring, leafy base, Standard #732 ......125.00
Cherub holds spear while riding on bk of fish, Meriden #157 .....395.00
Cherubs (2) w/ring on bks, rectangular base, JW Tufts #1544 ....500.00
Chick on wishbone, rococo base, elevated ring, NM 65.00
Chick pulls cart holding ring 245.00
Conquistador leans on rifle, rectangular base, Toronto #1337 ....350.00
Crocodile carries ring on bk, Meriden #0202 ....195.00
Dog chases bird up ring, oval base, R&B #1110 ....150.00
Dog on ea side of satchel-shaped ring, Van Bergh #97 ....265.00
Dog on haunches after bird atop ring, Aurora #27 ....225.00
Dog w/ring hdl in mouth, rnd base, SH&M #014 ....195.00
Fan forms base for 2 butterflies holding ring 95.00
Fans support ring, butterfly below, Meriden #208 ....200.00
Frog w/glass eyes on sm leaf, fly on hammered ring 350.00
Giraffe nibbles vine tied to ring, Manhattan #239 ....395.00
Girl teaches lg poodle ABCs, ball-ft base, JW Tufts 450.00
Girl w/pigtails holds ring, no base, Meriden Britania #280 ....315.00
Girl w/rifle on shoulders, sq-ft base, SH&M #205 ....450.00
Goat on rectangular base beside ring, Knickerbocker #181 ....165.00
Greenaway boy w/cookie, dog begs, rectangular base, Rogers 350.00
Greenaway girl w/muff on sled, bk to ring, Meriden-Britania 350.00
Horse stands by fence that juts out from ring, Meriden #0284 ....350.00
Horseshoe on ring, w/emb horse's head & Good Luck, SH&M 95.00
Jester before ring points & holds torch, Meriden #0258 ....250.00
Knight, raised arm w/torch, rnd base, Barbour #59 ....140.00
Lion rests paws on ring, rectangular base, Meriden #153 ....255.00
Monkey playing saxaphone attached to ring 205.00
Napoleon between ring, salt cellar & pepper shaker, Miller 385.00
Owl on sq base w/leaves, sm owls on ring, SH&M #204 ....395.00
Owl perched on wishbone attached to ring, Van Bergh #39 ....65.00
Parrot w/glass eyes on loop hdl by ring, #4338 ....195.00
Pheasant on nest by ring, rectangular base, Southington #209 ...135.00
Rabbit sitting under log tree, ring above, R&B #1520 ....210.00
Rifles crossed on ea side of ring, Meriden #355 ....200.00
Rip Van Winkle stands on rocky base, ring on shoulder, EX 700.00
Sailor w/anchor beside ring, R&B #1346 ....395.00
Sled w/ring atop, old-fashioned type, Wilcox #01532 ....65.00
Sphinx, lg ft, holds up ring w/bud vase atop, Aurora #45 ....140.00
Sqirrel climbs tree, ring atop, rnd base, R&B #1150 ....195.00
Sunflower base, octagonal, Meriden #37 ....75.00
Tennis racquet & ball support ring, EX 165.00

Wheelbarrow holds ring, Tufts #1537, 2⅞", $225.00.

Wolf baying at moon, fancy Barbour base w/ball ft 295.00

New England Glass Works

Founded in 1818 by Deming Jarves in Boston, Massachussetts, the New England Glass Company produced cut, blown three-mold, free-blown, and pressed glass of the highest quality. They were recognized for their fine decorative accomplishments, using etching, gilding, and engraving to emphasize their wares. For more than fifty years, they produced prize-winning pressed glass dinnerware sets. Because they refused to compromise the quality of their product by using the cheaper lime-based glass that flooded the market in the 1860s, the company fell into financial trouble and by 1877 was forced to close. However, William Libbey, who had been the sales manager there since 1870, leased the premises and resumed operations with his father, Edward Drummond Libbey, as full partner. In 1892 the firm became known as The Libbey Glass Company. See also Amberina; Libbey.

Flask, deep olive green, 20 vertical ribs, pontil scar, 7⅜", EX, $235.00.

Bottle, cologne; opaque opal, hexagonal, pontiled, 4¾", NM 100.00
Bottle, scent; bl to clear w/flower medallion, 6¾" 165.00
Celery dish, Dmn Quilt, amber, crimped top, 6" 325.00
Decanter, olive-amber, str sides, cylindrical, 7" 1,400.00
Vase, camphor w/stork, Locke design, 4½x2¼" sq 385.00
Vase, canary, Elongated Loop, gauffered rim/marble base, 12" ...400.00
Vase, canary, Elongated Loop, hexagonal base, 1-pc, 9⅝" 300.00
Vase, canary, 3-printie, hexagonal base, 9¼", NM, pr 250.00
Vase, wht fiery opal w/pk rim, flared rim, pontiled, 6¾" 625.00

New Martinsville

The New Martinsville Glass Company took its name from the town in West Virginia where it began operations in 1901. In the beginning years, pressed tablewares were made in crystal as well as colored and opalescent glass. Considered an innovator, the company was known for their imaginative applications of the medium in creating lamps made entirely of glass, vanity sets, figural decanters, and models of animals and birds. In 1944 the company was purchased by Viking Glass, who continued to use many of the old molds, the animals molds included. They marked their wares 'Viking' or 'Rainbow Art.' Viking recently ceased operations and has been purchased by Kenneth Dalzell, President of the Fostoria Company. They, too, are making the bird and animal models. Although at first they were not marked, future productions are to be marked with an acid stamp. Dalzell/Viking animals are in the $50.00 to $60.00 range. Values for cobalt and red items are two to three times higher than for the same item in clear. See also Depression Glass; Glass Animals and Figurines.

Basket, Janice, blk, #4552, 11" 195.00
Basket, Janice, crystal w/red hdl, 6½" 65.00
Bowl, Prelude, crystal, 12" 50.00
Bowl, Radiance, lt bl, 10" 145.00

Bowl, Radiance, red, 7", gold filigree metal basket 145.00
Bowl, swan; crystal w/red neck, 10" 125.00
Cake stand, Prelude, ped ft, 11" 85.00
Candlestick, Janice, lt bl, #4554, 5" 42.50
Champagne, Prelude 22.00
Cup, punch; Radiance, red 18.00
Cup & saucer, Mildred, Hostmaster, amber 22.50
Goblet, water; Prelude 25.00
Jug, ruby 90.00
Plate, Mildred, Hostmaster, amber, 8½" 450.00
Plate, torte; Prelude, 14" 30.00
Relish, Janice, lt bl, hdld, 6" 37.50
Relish, Prelude, 3-part, 10" 45.00
Relish, Radiance, lt bl, #4228, 8½" 65.00
Tumbler, Oscar, ruby, 4⅝", 6 for 135.00

Newcomb

The Newcomb College of New Orleans, Louisiana, established a pottery in 1895 to provide the students with first-hand experience in the fields of art and ceramics. Using locally dug clays — red and buff in the early years, white-burning by the turn of the century — potters were employed to throw the ware which the ladies of the college decorated. Until about 1910 a glossy glaze was used on ware decorated by slip painting or incising. After that a matt glaze was favored. Soft blues and greens were used almost exclusively, and decorative themes were chosen to reflect the beauty of the South. The year 1930 marked the end of the matt-glaze period and the art-pottery era.

Various marks used by the pottery include an 'N' within a 'C,' sometimes with 'HB' added to indicate a 'hand-built' piece. The potter often incised his initials into the ware, and the artists were encouraged to sign their work. Among the most well-known artists were Sadie Irvine, Henrietta Bailey, and Fannie Simpson.

Newcomb pottery is evaluated to a large extent by two factors: design and condition. In the following listings, items are assumed matt unless noted otherwise. Our advisor for this category is David Rago; he is listed in the Directory under New Jersey.

Vase, pine landscape, green and dark blue on shaded glossy ground, AF Simpson, 1908, 12½x5", $16,000.00; Vase, bulb flowers, cobalt on green and blue striated glossy ground, Harriet Joor, 1902, 9x5", $6,500.00.

Bowl, berries/leaves, att S Irvine, ca 1920, 3x5" 865.00
Bowl, daffodils, S Irvine, #259, 1910, 4½x8⅜" 1,100.00
Bowl, floral band on shoulder, purple body, Simpson, 8" 1,400.00
Bowl, floral on bl, Bailey, 2½x7" 850.00
Bowl, lg iris/vertical lines, mc gloss, McKee, 1890s, 6½", EX .3,500.00
Bowl, lizard band, gr on dk bl on lt bl, Ryan, 3x9", EX 4,750.00
Bowl, stylized irises, H Bailey, #LZ28, 1915, 2⅜x6¾" 500.00
Bowl vase, floral band at incurvate top half, Irvine, 3x5½" 750.00
Chocolate pot, floral on med bl, HB/FE76, w/lid, 10½" 4,000.00
Plaque, moon/moss/oak trees, Bailey, 5½" 2,100.00
Plaque, shrubs/oaks w/moss, bl & gr on pk, S Irvine, fr, 5" 4,000.00

Tankard, thistles/leaves on red, LeBlanc, 1903, 8x6", NM **1,500.00**
Trivet, floral, bl/yel on bl w/gr, Irvine, 5" dia **750.00**
Vase, bl mottled gloss, 2½x3" **300.00**
Vase, cypress trees on bl, AF Simpson, 1917, 9x7" **9,200.00**
Vase, cypress trees on bl, Irvine, 1916, 6x4" **1,400.00**
Vase, emb verticals, blk gloss, TR78, 5", NM **200.00**
Vase, floral, bl/yel/gr on med bl, bulb bottom, Irvine, 9x4½" ..**2,700.00**
Vase, floral at incurvate rim, glossy, S Irvine, #DL59, 12" **3,250.00**
Vase, floral on bl, gourd form, S Irvine, OR79, #214, 6" **1,100.00**
Vase, floral on bl, incurvate, AF Simpson, MH82, #71, 9" **2,500.00**
Vase, fruit, pk/gr on bl, S Irvine/NC PP50, incurvate, 9" **2,200.00**
Vase, jasmine border at neck on bl, AF Simpson, 1921, 8" **1,400.00**
Vase, jonquils on bl, Irvine, flaring cylinder, 4½" **1,600.00**
Vase, landscape/cloud band, bl on lt bl gloss, Scudder, 7x4" ..**2,600.00**
Vase, lg irises/combed leaves, glossy, LeBlanc, 7x4¼" **6,750.00**
Vase, lg wht flowers at shoulder on bl, Simpson/IH26, 6x5" ...**1,700.00**
Vase, long-stem blossoms form shoulder band, Bailey, 8" **2,300.00**
Vase, long-stem floral, glossy, incurvate, Irvine, 1908, 6" **2,000.00**
Vase, long-stem irises cvd on bl, AF Mason, 1914, 9x5" **3,500.00**
Vase, moon/lg oak trees, S Irvine, LD52, ovoid, 6" **2,100.00**
Vase, moon/moss/oak trees, AF Simpson, paper label, 1928, 8" ..**2,800.00**
Vase, moon/moss/oak trees, AF Simpson, 1925, 7x4" **2,600.00**
Vase, moon/moss/oak trees, Irvine/SF14, baluster, 5½" **1,900.00**
Vase, moon/moss/oak trees, S Irvine, NC RF81, 11" **5,500.00**
Vase, moon/moss/oak trees, sgn F, AA, 6" **1,800.00**
Vase, moon/moss/oak trees (EX art), AF Simpson, baluster, 6½" ..**6,600.00**
Vase, moon/moss/oak trees (EX color), Bailey, 1933, 4½x5" ..**2,200.00**
Vase, moon/moss/oak trees (EX color/art), Irvine/OV29, 11" ..**9,000.00**
Vase, moss/oak trees (EX art/detail), NC/JM/JA45/150, 11x7" ..**8,000.00**
Vase, overlapping leaves, S Irvine, 1915, 4⅝x2" **750.00**
Vase, pine cones, Bailey, cylinder, #320, 10" **2,800.00**
Vase, pine cones, Bailey, RZ38, #24, 5½" **1,200.00**
Vase, pine cones, unusually wide shoulder, Bailey, 7x7" **2,500.00**
Vase, pine trees, cvd/HP bl/gr on bl, Simpson, 1915, 11x5" **6,500.00**
Vase, sm flowers w/long stems, wht on dk bl/lt gr, Irvine, 4" **850.00**
Vase, stylized floral, wht/gr on bl gloss, Roman, w/lid, 3x4" **5,000.00**
Vase, stylized swamp lilies, glossy, A Urquart, 1902, 7x5" **7,500.00**
Vase, trees, bl/gr w/pk sky, Irvine, 1918, 4¼x2¾" **1,300.00**

Newspapers

People do not collect newspapers simply because they are old. Age has absolutely nothing to do with value — it does not hold true that the older the newspaper, the higher the value. Instead, most of the value is determined by the historic event content. In most cases, the more important to American history the event is, the higher the value. In over two hundred years of American history, perhaps as many as 98% of all papers *do not* contain news of a significant historic event. Newspapers not having news of major events in history are called 'atmosphere.' Atmosphere papers have little collector value. (See price guide below.)

To learn more about the hobby of collecting old and historic newspapers, be sure to visit the mega-Web sight on the Internet at: http://www.historybuff.com/. Within this sight you will find a more extensive price guide to old and historic newspapers; an extensive, searchable, 300,000-word reference library of American history with an emphasis on newspaper-publishing speeches; interactive crossword puzzles; regular auctions of ephemera, historic documents, and newspapers; a mall with over 100 different online catalogs of paper collectibles; and much, much more! The e-mail address for the NCSA is: rbrown@tir.com.

1800-1820, Atmosphere editions **7.00**
1821-1859, Atmosphere editions **5.00**

1836, Texas declares independence **60.00**
1845, Annexation of Texas **35.00**
1846, Start of Mexican War **30.00**
1846-1847, Major battles of Mexican War **20.00**
1847, End of Mexican War **30.00**
1848, Gold discovered in California **60.00**
1859, John Brown's raid on Harper's Ferry **45.00**
1860, Lincoln elected 1st term **150.00**
1861, Lincoln's inaugural address **175.00**
1861-1865, Atmosphere editions: Confederate titles **50.00**
1861-1865, Atmosphere editions: Union titles **7.00**
1861-1865, Major battles of Civil War **75.00**
1862, Emancipation Proclamation **135.00**
1863, Gettysburg Address **250.00**
1865, April 29 edition of Frank Leslie's **350.00**
1865, April 29 edition of Harper's Weekly **300.00**
1865, Capture & death of J Wilkes Booth **100.00**
1865, Fall of Richmond **100.00**
1865, NY Herald, Apr 15 (Beware: reprints abound) **900.00**
1865, Titles other than NY Herald, Apr 15 ....**400.00**
1866-1900, Atmosphere editions **4.00**
1876, Custer's Last Stand **150.00**
1881, Billy the Kid killed **200.00**
1881, Garfield assassinated **50.00**
1881, Gunfight at OK Corral **225.00**
1882, Jesse James killed **200.00**
1898, Sinking of Maine **40.00**
1901, McKinley assassinated **60.00**
1903, Wright Brother's flight **300.00**
1906, San Francisco earthquake, other titles **30.00**
1906, San Francisco earthquake, San Francisco title **500.00**

1912, April 16, first account of the sinking of the Titanic, New York Times, $250.00.

1915, Sinking of Lusitania **125.00**
1927, Babe Ruth hits 60th home run **70.00**
1927, Lindbergh arrives in Paris **75.00**
1929, St Valentine's Day Massacre **150.00**
1929, Stock market crash **90.00**
1931, Al Capone found guilty **35.00**
1931, Jack 'Legs' Diamond killed **35.00**
1933, Machine Gun Kelley captured **35.00**
1934, Baby Face Nelson killed **40.00**
1934, Bonnie & Clyde killed **125.00**
1934, Dillinger killed **150.00**
1934, Pretty Boy Floyd killed **35.00**
1937, Hindenbergh explodes **65.00**
1941, Honolulu Star-Bulletin, Dec 7, 1st extra (+) **600.00**
1941, Other titles, Dec 7, w/Pearl Harbor news **35.00**
1948, Chicago Daily Tribune, Nov 3, Dewey Defeats Truman ...**900.00**
1961, Alan Shephard 1st astronaut in space **20.00**

1961, Roger Maris hits 61st home run **25.00**
1962, Death of Marilyn Monroe **30.00**
1962, John Glenn orbits Earth **18.00**
1963, JFK assassination, Nov 22, Dallas title **60.00**
1963, JFK assassination, Nov 22, titles other than Dallas **8.00**
1968, Assassination of Martin Luther King **12.00**
1968, Assassination of Robert Kennedy **12.00**
1969, Moon landing **22.00**
1974, Nixon resigns **12.00**

Nicodemus

Chester Nicodemus moved from Dayton, Ohio, to Columbus in 1930 and started teaching at the Columbus Art School. During this time he made vases and commissioned sculptures, water fountains, and limestone and wood carvings. In 1941 Chester left the field of teaching to pursue pottery making full time, using local red clay containing a large amount of iron. Known for its durability, he called the ware Ferro-stone. He made teapots and other utility wares, but these goods lost favor, so he started producing animal and bird sculptures, nativity sets, and Christmas ornaments, some bearing Chester's and Florine's names as personalized cards for his customers and friends. Chester died in 1990.

His glaze colors were turquoise or aqua, ivory, green mottle, (pink) pussy willow, and golden yellow. The glaze was applied so that the color of the warm red clay would show through, adding an extra dimension to each piece. Examples are usually marked with his name incised in the clay, but paper labels were also used. Our advisor for this category is James Riebel; he is listed in the Directory under Ohio.

Ashtray, Indianapolis 500, race car, sgn **50.00**
Bottle, bright turq, ceramic stopper, 4½" **85.00**
Creamer, w/lid, 4" **50.00**
Creamer & sugar bowl, mustard, 2½" **95.00**
Figurine, Joseph **75.00**
Figurine, 3 Wise Men **125.00**
Jug, tan, 4" **80.00**
Pitcher, gr, 6" **185.00**
Pitcher, 4" **90.00**
Plate, 3" **15.00**
Teapot, sm **100.00**
Urn, mustard, 3-hdld, 6x6" **200.00**
Vase, bulbous, 4½" **100.00**
Vase, Ferro-stone, yel, 5¼" **125.00**
Vase, gr, twist hdls, 8" **175.00**
Vase, gr & brn, hdls, 8½" **200.00**
Vase, 3-hdld urn form, mustard, 6x6" **175.00**
Vase/cigarette holder, 3" **40.00**
Wall pocket, incised floral, golden yel, 9½" **350.00**

Niloak

During the latter part of the 1800s, there were many small utilitarian potteries in Benton, Arkansas. By 1900 only the Hyten Brothers Pottery remained. Charles Hyten, a second generation potter, took control of the family business around 1902. Shortly thereafter he renamed it the Eagle Pottery Company. In 1909 Hyten and former Rookwood potter Arthur Dovey began experimentation on a new swirl pottery. Dovey previously worked for the Ouachita Pottery Company of Hot Springs and produced a swirl pottery there as early as 1906. In March 1910 the Eagle Pottery Company introduced Niloak, kaolin spelled backwards. During 1911 Benton businessmen formed the Niloak Pottery corporation. Niloak, connected to the Arts and Crafts Movement

and known as 'mission' ware, had a national representative in New York by 1913. Niloak's production centered on art pottery characterized by accidental, swirling patterns of natural and artificially colored clays. Many companies through the years have produced swirl pottery, yet none achieved the technical and aesthetic qualities of Niloak. Hyten received a patent in 1928 for the swirl technique. Although most examples have an interior glaze, some early Mission Ware pieces have an exterior glaze as well; these are extremely rare. Swirl/Mission Ware production continued steadily until the Depression when hard times and sagging sales caused Hyten to produce more traditional wares. In 1931 Niloak introduced Hywood Art Pottery, a glazed ware (sometimes similar in shape to Weller's Nile) of mostly hand-thrown vases. Soon thereafter, Niloak introduced castware as its primary production and renamed the line Hywood by Niloak. Throughout its existence, the company produced utilitarian items as well as artware. In 1934 Hyten's company found itself facing bankruptcy. Hardy L. Winburn, Jr., along with other Little Rock businessmen, raised the necessary capital and were able to provide the kind of leadership needed to make the business profitable once again. Both lines (Eagle and Hywood) were renamed 'Niloak' in 1937 to capitalize on this well-known name. The pottery continued in production until 1947 when it was converted to the Winburn Tile Company, which exists to this day in Little Rock. Be careful not to confuse the swirl production of the Evans Pottery of Missouri with Niloak. The significant difference is the dark brown matt interior glaze of Evans pottery.

Our co-advisors for this category are Lila and Fred Shrader (see the Directory under California) and David Edwin Gifford (see Arkansas). Mr. Gifford is the author of *Collector's Encyclopedia of Niloak Pottery*, and the editor of the *National Society of Arkansas Pottery Collectors Newsletter*.

Mission Ware

Ashtray, rolled rim w/3 rests, 2nd art mk, 1½x5" dia **225.00**
Bookends, resembles stacked books, pr **425.00**
Bottle, water; 7½", +3½" tumbler **465.00**
Bowl, fruit; 4¼x11½" **300.00**
Bowl, lg art mk, 3" **80.00**
Bowl, Patent Pend'g, rolled rim, 3¼" **125.00**
Candlesticks, flared base, 1st art mk, 9", pr **450.00**
Candlesticks, invt trumpet form, 8", pr **400.00**
Chamberstick, hdl, 5½" **225.00**
Cigarette box, w/lid, 4½x3½" **255.00**
Cigarette jar, 2nd art mk, 4½x3¾" dia **250.00**
Compote, ped w/flared ft, 6½x8½" **325.00**
Cup, punch; 3¾" **80.00**
Fern dish, w/insert, 3x7½" **285.00**

Flower bowls, 3x5¾", $275.00; 2x4¾", $225.00.

Flower bowl, lg art mk, 4¾x4½" **300.00**
Flower frog, unmk, 3x1½" **80.00**
Humidor, predominantly red, 1st art mk, 6" **450.00**
Humidor, w/matchbox holder lid, 5x7" **395.00**

Inkwell, Patent Pend'g, 2½" 150.00
Jardiniere, rolled rim, 1st art mk, 7" 400.00
Jardiniere, w/bull's-eye, 8¼" 410.00
Jug, w/finger ring, no stopper, 6" 385.00
Lamp base, bull's-eye motif, unmk, 6½" 350.00
Lamp base, drilled, 12" 400.00
Mug, barrel shape, 1st art mk, 4½" 200.00
Mug, Patent Pend'g, 5½" 250.00
Paperweight, 2nd art mk, 1½x3" dia 175.00
Pin tray, 2nd art mk, 1¼x3¾" dia 80.00
Pitcher, ewer shape, 8½" 295.00
Planter, 1st art mk, ftd, 2½x7½" dia 225.00
Planter, 1st art mk, 4½" 250.00
Puff box, flared base, 1st art mk, 4½x3¼" dia 350.00
Thimble, ⅞" 195.00
Tile, unmk, 4¼x4¼" 400.00
Tray, rolled edge, cut-out hdls, 9x7" 400.00
Tumbler, Patent Pend'g, flared rim, 5" 150.00
Tumbler, shot sz, 2" 110.00
Tumbler, 5½" 65.00
Vase, bud; dbl-groove motif, flared base, 1st art mk, 8¾" 150.00
Vase, bulbous, early Niloak, 10¾" 280.00
Vase, bulbous, Patent Pend'g, 5¼" 120.00
Vase, bulbous w/flared rim, mini, 2½" 120.00
Vase, bulbous w/flared rim, 1st art mk, 5½" 90.00
Vase, bulbous w/rolled rim, 1st art mk, 10" 300.00
Vase, bulbous w/rolled rim, 2nd art mk, 10¼" 300.00
Vase, cabinet; 2nd art mk, 3" 80.00
Vase, conical, blk ink stamp, 8" 250.00
Vase, conical w/flared ft, predominantly red, 1st art mk, 9" 275.00
Vase, conical w/flared ft, 1st art mk, 9½" 275.00
Vase, cylindrical, Patent Pend'g, 7½" 210.00
Vase, cylindrical, 1st art mk, 4½" 70.00
Vase, cylindrical, 1st art mk, 9¾" 275.00
Vase, cylindrical w/slightly flared base, 1st art mk, 8¼" 250.00
Vase, cylindrical w/waisted neck, 8½" 250.00
Vase, elongated teardrop form, 6" 200.00
Vase, fan form, lg art mk, 7¼" 275.00
Vase, ogee shape, 13" 750.00
Vase, ogee sides, 6½" 160.00
Vase, pear shape, 1st art mk, 8" 250.00
Vase, waisted cylinder form, 1st art mk, 10¼" 300.00
Wall pocket, cone shape, unmk, 6" 350.00
Wall pocket, rolled collar, 6½" 275.00

Miscellaneous

Ashtray, duck, matt, 2¾" L 22.00
Basket, Dolly Varden shape w/basketweave, matt, 5½" 35.00
Basket, hanging, w/3 sm loops, 4½" dia 35.00
Bean pot, hi-gloss, w/lid, mini, 2¾" 35.00
Bowl, attached 7" Peter Pan figurine peers into bowl, matt 65.00
Candlestick, hand thrown, matt, paper label, 6¾" 85.00
Canoe, matt, w/flower frog, 3½x11" 95.00
Console set, matt, oval 3x12" bowl+pr 7" candlesticks 165.00
Cookie jar, tab hdls, matt, 10½" 100.00
Creamer, cow, hi-gloss, 5" 55.00
Figurine, bulldog, sleeping, matt, 2x6" 50.00
Figurine, donkey (stubborn), matt, 4" 45.00
Figurine, Fr poodle, matt, 3½" 45.00
Figurine, razorback hog w/or w/o U of A, matt 85.00
Figurine, Southern Belle, ruffled skirt/hands by side, matt, 11" ..110.00
Figurine, wishing well, matt, 8" 45.00
Figurine, wooden shoe, matt, 4½" 25.00

Jar, matt, pierced lid, 4¾" 55.00
Jug, hand thrown, hi-gloss, mini, 2½" 35.00
Juice set, pitcher, emb flowers on wht matt, +4¾" tumblers 55.00
Mug, cylindrical, matt, 4½" 35.00
Paperweight, brick shape, matt, top-mk Niloak, 3x6½x1¾" 125.00
Pitcher, ball shape, matt, w/stopper, 7½" 75.00
Pitcher, ewer shape, matt, 11" 55.00
Pitcher, simple design, hi-gloss, 2" to 3", from $10 to 20.00
Planter, attached saucer, att, 6" 35.00
Planter, camel in resting position, over-glaze decor, 4" 55.00
Planter, deer, free standing, matt, 10" 85.00
Planter, deer standing in tall grass, matt, 7" 35.00
Planter, doughnut shape, matt, 3" center hdl, 9½" dia 65.00
Planter, elephant standing on drum, trunk up, matt, 7½" 45.00
Planter, half-circle, matt, 3" center hole, 9½" dia 45.00
Planter, Southern Belle, matt, 7" 75.00
Planter, squirrel w/nuts, hi-gloss, 5" 32.00
Planter, Trojan Horse on base, gloss, 9" 45.00
Plate, salad/dessert; petal design, matt, 8" 45.00
Shakers, airplane, matt, 2", pr 75.00
Shakers, various animal shapes, matt, 2" to 2½", pr, from $25 to .35.00
Strawberry jar, w/4 bud-shaped openings, matt, 10½" 48.00
Teapot, ball shape, matt, 6½" 75.00
Teapot, Fr-style, slender w/S-curve spout, matt, 9" 90.00
Toothpick holder, elephant w/baskets, gloss, 3½" 45.00
Toothpick holder, frog w/open mouth, hi-gloss, 2½" 28.00
Tray, relish; 3-part, triangular, hi-gloss, 10x10x10" 55.00
Vase, braid-like hdls, matt, 9½" 45.00
Vase, bud; stacked ring-like design, hi-gloss, 8½" 22.00
Vase, fan shape w/flared ft, delicate hdls, 5" 35.00
Vase, fan shape w/flared ft, matt, 7" 45.00
Vase, hand-thrown, delicate S-shape snake-head hdls, matt, 8" ...85.00
Wall pocket, basket design w/hdl, hi-gloss, 8" 65.00

Nippon

Nippon generally refers to Japanese wares made during the period from 1891 to 1921, although the Nippon mark was also used to a limited extent on later wares (accompanied by 'Japan'). Nippon, meaning Japan, identified the country of origin to comply with American importation restrictions. After 1921 'Japan' was the acceptable alternative. The term does not imply a specific type of product and may be found on items other than porcelains. For further information we recommend *The Collector's Encyclopedias of Nippon Porcelain* (there are four in the series) by our advisor, Joan Van Patten; you will find her address in the Directory under New York. In the following listings, items are assumed hand painted unless noted otherwise. Numbers included in the descriptions refer to these specific marks:

Key:
#1 — China E-OH
#2 — M in Wreath
#3 — Cherry Blossom
#4 — Double T Diamond in Circle
#5 — Rising Sun
#6 — Royal Kinran
#7 — Maple Leaf
#8 — Royal Nippon, Nishiki
#9 — Royal Moriye Nippon

Ashtray, owl on branch, 3 rests, #2, 5½" 160.00
Ashtray, river scenic on rectangular form, 2 rests, #2, 4½" 85.00
Basket vase, yel floral, blk trim, #2, 6x7¼" 250.00
Bowl, fruit; fruit in relief, mc, hdls, #2, 7½" 200.00
Bowl, mc roses w/cobalt & gold, scalloped, #7, 7¾" 275.00
Box, trinket; mc butterflies on wht w/gold, #2, 3¼" dia 100.00
Box, trinket; piano form w/Deco-style decor, #2, 2½x5" 325.00

Candlestick, floral w/heavy gold beading, #7, 10¾" 280.00
Candy dish, hunt scene along rim, #7, 12" 250.00
Chocolate, roses band/reserves, much gold, angle hdl, #7, 14" ...300.00
Chocolate pot, floral reserve on gold, angle hdl, #7, 10½" 425.00
Chocolate set, floral w/gold, 5-sided, mk, 10¾" pot+6 c/s 500.00
Compote, scenic w/cobalt & gold rim, tub hdls, #7, 2¼x5" 225.00
Cookie/cracker jar, florals, gold trim, bulbous, ftd, #2, 7" 250.00
Cruet, sampan scenic, flat stopper, #2, 7¼" 325.00
Egg server, floral rim, 6 indents, center hdl, #5, 6¼" 155.00
Ewer, river scenic reserve w/cobalt & gold, conical, #7, 5¾" 275.00
Ferner, Egyptian decor, 6-sided, #2, 7" 375.00
Ferner, gold lion decor on wht, 4-ftd, #7, 5½" L 225.00
Ferner, Indian on running horse in relief, brn tones, #2, 6¾" 900.00
Ferner, river scenic, column ea corner, #2, 5" 300.00
Ferner, roses on wht w/gold, 4-ftd, scalloped, #2, 6½" 175.00
Game set, game birds, floral reserve rim, 16½" lg+6 sm 2,400.00
Hatpin holder, lg roses on flared cylinder, #2, 5" 125.00
Humidor, owl in relief, brn tones, #2, 7" 900.00
Humidor, playing cards, brn lid, #2, 4½" 450.00
Humidor, river & bridge, bl & brn tones, #2, 4" H 500.00
Humidor, scenic reserves/Deco florals, triangular, #2, 6½" 450.00
Humidor, tiger in relief, brn tones, #2, 7" 1,800.00
Humidor, 3 Indian chiefs in relief, #2, 7¼" 5,200.00
Jar, moriage trees in landscape, sq sides, #2, 6" 500.00
Lamp base, floral on gr, gold trim & ring hdls, #7, 14½" 300.00
Match holder & striker, floral, bell shape, #2, 3½" 175.00
Mug, man on camel scene, moriage trim, #2, 4¾" 300.00
Mug, river scenic, autumn colors, #2, 5" 250.00
Mug, roses on wht w/gold, w/lid, #7, 5¾" 185.00
Mug, windmill scenic, flared cylinder, #2, 5½" 250.00
Nut set, irises on wht, gold scallops, #5, lg+4 sm 150.00
Pitcher, Deco floral band on wht w/gold, w/lid, #2, 5½" 125.00
Pitcher, mc roses w/cobalt & gold, unmk, 7¾" 600.00
Plaque, bird on pine branch, #2, 7¾" 250.00
Plaque, eagle in relief, brn tones, #2, 10½" 2,200.00
Plaque, farmer sewing seeds in relief, #2, 12" 2,200.00
Plaque, fox-hunt scene, natural colors, #2, 9" 375.00
Plaque, lady's portrait & floral reserves w/gold, #7, 12½" 800.00
Plaque, sampan scenic, earth tones, mk, 10" 250.00
Plaque, watermelon slice & fruit, sgn, #2, 12" 375.00
Plaque, 3 horses in landscape relief, #2, 10" 1,100.00
Plate, windmill scene, smooth cobalt & gold rim, #2, 6½" 275.00
Relish, roses on wht, Wedgwood trim, boat shape, #2, 7½" 250.00
Serving tray, Wedgwood, cream on bl, 3-part, center hdl, #2 .....350.00
Stein, man w/pipe & glass, vintage border, #2, 7" 725.00
Sugar bowl, floral band on cream, angle hdls/finial, #2, 6½" 110.00
Sugar shaker, floral band on wht w/gold, arched hdl, #2, 5¼" 90.00
Tankard, lg florals on slim form, gold hdl, #7, 14½" 525.00
Tankard, lg roses on cobalt w/gold, slim, unmk, 18" 700.00
Tea set, tomato figural, #2, 4" pot/cr/sug/6 c/s 900.00
Teapot, Wedgwood, cream on bl, #2, 4¾", +cr/sug 700.00
Toast rack, florals on wht, #5, 8¼" L 140.00
Urn, florals w/moriage foliage, #9, 12" 600.00
Urn, landscape reserve w/gold on cobalt, bolted, #7, 19" 6,000.00

Vase, bird on moriage branch, urn form, #7, 9¼" 400.00
Vase, camel scenic w/cobalt & gold, hdls, #2, 8½" 450.00
Vase, castle tapestry w/gold, cylindrical, #7, 6¼" 700.00
Vase, chrysanthemums on bl, gold hdls, #2, 10½" 325.00
Vase, Classical maiden reserve w/gold, cylindrical, #7, 18¼" ..2,200.00
Vase, exotic mc birds & vines on wht w/gold, mk, 7" 135.00
Vase, figures walking dog, ftd ewer form, #2, 7½" 400.00
Vase, figures/seaside band, shouldered, angle hdls, #2, 8¼" 400.00
Vase, floral reserve & decor, Oriental style, sq sides, #2, 16" 850.00
Vase, floral reserve w/cobalt & gold, cylinder, unmk, 15" 1,800.00
Vase, floral reserve w/moriage trim, 3-hdl, unmk, 6" 300.00
Vase, florals, pastel, classic form, #2, 13" 250.00
Vase, florals, yel on lav, sm yel hdls, #2, 6½" 175.00
Vase, florals & gold beading, hdls, bottle neck, #7, 8½" 325.00
Vase, geisha panels, gold hdls, #8, 9½" 250.00
Vase, gold floral o/l, slim form w/flared base, #7, 10" 225.00
Vase, gold o/l reserve & band on cobalt, sm hdls, #7, 8½" 650.00
Vase, irises on pk w/much gold, hdls, #2, 14½" 425.00
Vase, lady's portrait, full length, gold hdls, #7, 12½" 1,000.00
Vase, lady's portrait reserve, gold uptrn hdls, #7, 7¼" 800.00
Vase, leafy swags on gourd shape, sea horse hdls, #7, 8½" 425.00
Vase, man & horse-drawn cart, gold hdls, #2, 13" 1,100.00
Vase, man on camel, brn tones, ftd, angle hdls, #2, 5½" 250.00
Vase, man on camel scene, gold angle hdls, #2, 18" 1,600.00
Vase, moose in relief, cylindrical, #2, 13½" 1,300.00
Vase, moriage butterflies w/jewels, sm hdls, #7, 9" 425.00
Vase, moriage dragon, ring hdls, ruffled rim, #7, 8½" 250.00
Vase, moriage dragon on brn, ring hdls, bottle neck, #2, 9½" 350.00
Vase, moriage gulls in landscape, cylindrical, #7, 11¾" 600.00
Vase, river reserve w/flowers & gold, angle hdls, #2, 6½" 175.00
Vase, river scenic, loving cup form, #2, 4¼" 125.00
Vase, river scenic, ornate uptrn hdls, #2, 8¼" 275.00
Vase, river scenic, ruffled rim, ring hdls, #2, 12" 600.00
Vase, river scenic reserve & band, 6-sided, sm hdls, #2, 9½" 300.00
Vase, roses, lg wht w/gold trim on cobalt, gold hdls, #7, 10½" ...275.00
Vase, roses, mc w/cobalt, gold hdls, bulbous, #7, 7¾" 450.00
Vase, roses on dk yel, gold angle hdls, #2, 12" 300.00
Vase, sampan scenic, earth tones, angle hdls, #2, 5" 125.00
Vase, scenic reserve w/cobalt & gold, integral hdls, #7, 9" 550.00
Vase, swan tapestry, gr hdls, #7, 6" 700.00
Vase, tapestry reserve, gold ring hdls, #3, 7" 650.00
Vase, Wedgwood, cream on bl, angle hdls, #2, 6¾" 500.00
Whiskey jug, grapes & vines, Noritake Nippon mk, 5¾" 550.00
Wine jug, Indian in canoe, gold hdl, #2, 8¾" 900.00
Wine jug, roses w/moriage trim, #7, 8" 900.00
Wine jug, sampan scenic reserve, Deco band, #2, 9½" 900.00

Nodders

So called because of the nodding action of their heads and hands, nodders originated in China where they were used in temple rituals to represent deity. At first they were made of brass and were actually a type of bell; when these bells were rung, the heads of the figures would nod. In the 18th century, the idea was adopted by Meissen and by French manufacturers who produced not only china nodders but bisque as well. Most nodders are individual; couples are unusual. The idea remained popular until the end of the 19th century and was used during the Victorian era by toy manufacturers. For further informations we recommend *Figural Nodders, Indentification & Value Guide*, by Hilma R. Irtz, available from Collector Books or your local bookstore.

Betty Boop, hula hip nodder, rare 175.00
Boy in clown suit w/cobalt trim, w/puppet doll, 7" 175.00

Vase, man holding bowls in landscape in relief, handles, green M mark, 10", $2,800.00; Vase, house by stream in landscape, large gold handles, green M mark, 10½", $350.00.

Canadian Mounty	80.00
Charlie Weaver	125.00
Cow, papier-mache w/hide covering, glass eyes, horn horns, 12"	325.00
Davy Crockett	300.00
Donald Duck	125.00
Dr Kildare	150.00
Elephant or donkey, celluloid political symbols, Japan, ea	35.00
Girl & kitten in chair, porc, Thuringia, 1870-1937, 6¾"	250.00
Girl in pk holding match-striker basket, porc, Heubach type, 4"	150.00
Japanese elder seated on mat, terra cotta body, oval mk, 7½"	450.00
Mammy Yokum	150.00
Mandarin, seated, pnt/fired bsk, unmk, 4½"	125.00
Maynard	275.00
Mickey Mouse	125.00
Pig, pk plastic, emb Germany, 2x4"	75.00
Victorian boy on nodding donkey, unmk Germany, 6½x7¾"	375.00
Winnie the Pooh	200.00
Yosemite Sam	250.00

German Comic Characters

During the early 1930s, Germany produced a collection of small figure dolls, approximately 2" to 4" high, representing the most popular comic strip and cartoon characters of that time. They were made of bisque with brightly painted details and clearly stamped with their appropriate names and 'Germany' on their backs. Generally, their movable heads were attached with an elastic string going through their bodies, hence the name 'nodders,' but there were some characters produced earlier that were frozen with no movable parts. The most popular ones came in boxed sets, but the lesser-known characters were sold separately, making them rarer and harder to find today. We have listed the most valuable characters from the series here; those not mentioned below are valued at $125.00 and under. Our advisor for German character nodders is Doug Dezso; he is listed in the Directory under New Jersey. He will answer questions (as long as an SASE is included) on German character nodders only.

Ambrose Potts	350.00
Aunt Mamie & Uncle Willie, ea	350.00
Auntie Blossom	150.00
Bill, Dock, Avery, Max or Pop Jenks, ea	200.00
Buttercup	250.00
Chubby Chaney	250.00
Corky	475.00
Ferina	350.00
Grandpa Teen	350.00
Happy Hooligan	600.00
Harold Teen	150.00

Photo courtesy Doug Dezso

Jeff Regus, small, $175.00, medium or large, $250.00 each.

Junior Nebbs	500.00

Lillums	150.00
Little Andy Rooney, arms move	250.00
Little Egypt	350.00
Lord Plushbottom	150.00
Ma & Pa Winkle, ea	350.00
Majory, Patsy, Lilacs or Josie, ea	400.00
Mary Ann Jackson	250.00
Min Gump	150.00
Mr Bailey	150.00
Mr Bibb	400.00
Mr Winker	250.00
Mushmouth	350.00
Mutt or Jeff, ea	250.00
Nicodemus	350.00
Pat Fannigan	400.00
Pete the Dog	250.00
Rudy or Fanny Nebbs, ea	250.00
Scraps	250.00
Widow Zander	400.00
Winnie Winkle	150.00

Noritake

The Noritake Company was first registered in 1904 as Nippon Gomei Kaisha. In 1917 the name became Nippon Toki Kabushiki Toki. The 'M' in wreath mark is that of the Morimura Brothers, distributors with offices in New York. It was used until 1941. The tree crest mark is the crest of the Morimura family.

The Noritake Company has produced fine porcelain dinnerware sets and occasional pieces decorated in the delicate manner for which the Japanese are noted. (Two dinnerware patterns are featured below, and a general range is suggested for others.)

Authority Joan Van Patten has compiled two lovely books, *The Collector's Encyclopedia of Noritake, Vols. I and II*, with many full-color photos and current prices; you will find her address in the Directory under New York. In the following listings, examples are hand painted unless noted otherwise. Numbers refer to these specific marks:

Key:
#1 — Komaru   #3 — M in Wreath
#2 — M in Wreath

Azalea

The Azalea pattern was produced exclusively for the Larkin Company, who gave the lovely ware away as premiums to club members and their home agents. From 1916 through the '30s, Larkin distributed fine china which was decorated in pink azaleas on white with gold tracing along edges and handles. Early in the '30s, six pieces of crystal hand painted with the same design were offered: candle holders, a compote, a tray with handles, a scalloped fruit bowl, a cheese and cracker set, and a cake plate. All in all, seventy different pieces of Azalea were produced. Some, such as the fifteen-piece child's set, bulbous vase, china ashtray, and the pancake jug, are quite rare. One of the earliest marks was the Noritake M in wreath with variations. Later the ware was marked 'Noritake, Azalea, Hand Painted, Japan.' Our advisor is Peggy Roush; she is listed in the Directory under Florida.

Basket, mint; Dolly Varden, #193	195.00
Bonbon, #184, 6¼"	50.00
Bowl, #12, 10"	42.50

Bowl, candy/grapefruit; #185 ....195.00
Bowl, deep, #310 ....68.00
Bowl, fruit; shell form, #188, 7¾" 385.00
Bowl, oatmeal; #55, 5½" 28.00
Bowl, vegetable; divided, #439, 9½" 295.00
Bowl, vegetable; oval, #101, 10½" 60.00
Bowl, vegetable; oval, #172, 9¼" 58.00
Butter chip, #312, 3¼" 145.00
Butter tub, w/insert, #54 ....48.00
Cake plate, #10, 9¾" 40.00
Candy jar, w/lid, #313 ....695.00
Casserole, gold finial, w/lid, #372 ....540.00
Casserole, w/lid, #16 ....115.00
Celery/roll tray, #99, 12" 55.00
Cheese/butter dish, #314 ....135.00
Child's set, #253, 15-pc 2,500.00
Coffeepot, AD; #182 ....595.00
Compote, #170 ....98.00
Condiment set, #14, 5-pc 65.00
Creamer & sugar bowl, #122 ....158.00
Creamer & sugar bowl, #7 ....45.00
Creamer & sugar bowl, AD; open, #123 ....140.00
Creamer & sugar bowl, gold finial, #401 ....155.00
Creamer & sugar bowl, ind, #449 ....395.00
Cruet, #190 ....195.00
Cup & saucer, #2 ....20.00
Cup & saucer, AD; #183 ....150.00
Cup & saucer, bullion; #124, 3½" 24.50
Gravy boat, #40 ....48.00
Jam jar set, #125, 4-pc 155.00
Match/toothpick holder, #192 ....130.00
Mayonnaise set, scalloped, #453, 3-pc 495.00
Mustard jar, #191, 3-pc 60.00
Pickle/lemon set, #121 ....24.50
Pitcher, milk jug; #100, 1-qt 195.00
Plate, #4, 7½" 10.00
Plate, bread & butter; #8, 6½" 10.00
Plate, cream soup; #363 ....175.00
Plate, dinner; #13, 9¾" 28.00
Plate, grill; 3-compartment, #38, 10¼" 165.00
Plate, scalloped sq, salesman's sample 950.00
Plate, soup; #19, 7⅛" 25.00
Platter, #17, 14" 60.00
Platter, #186, 16" 475.00
Platter, #56, 12" 58.00
Platter, cold meat/bacon; #311, 10¼" 215.00
Refreshment set, #39, 2-pc 48.00
Relish, #194, 7⅛" 85.00
Relish, loop hdl, 2-part, #450 ....425.00
Relish, oval, #18, 8½" 20.00
Relish, 2-part, #171 ....58.00
Relish, 4-part, #119, rare, 10" 150.00
Saucer, fruit; #9, 5¼" 10.00
Shakers, bell form, #11, pr 30.00
Shakers, bulbous, #89, pr 30.00
Shakers, ind, #126, pr 27.50
Spoon holder, #189, 8" 115.00
Spoon holder, #339, 2-pc 35.00
Syrup, #97, w/underplate & ladle 135.00
Teapot, #15 ....110.00
Teapot, gold finial, #400 ....495.00
Vase, bulbous, #452 ....1,150.00
Vase, fan form, ftd, #187 ....185.00
Whipped cream/mayonnaise set, #3, 3-pc 38.50

Tree in the Meadow

Another of their dinnerware lines has become a favorite of many collectors. Tree in the Meadow features a hand-painted scene with a large dark tree in the foreground, growing near a lake. There is usually a cottage in the distance. Sometimes referred to as Tree by the Lake, this line was made during the 1920s and '30s and seems today to be in good supply. Various interesting forms are seen, and reassembling a complete set should be an enjoyable undertaking. Our advisor is Peggy Roush; she is listed in the Directory under Florida.

Basket, Dolly Varden 125.00
Bowl, cream soup; 2-hdl 35.00
Bowl, fruit; shell form, #210 ....300.00
Bowl, oatmeal 15.00
Bowl, soup 20.00
Bowl, vegetable; 9" 35.00
Butter pat 15.00
Butter tub, open, w/drainer 35.00
Candy dish, 5½" 400.00
Celery dish 35.00
Cheese dish 45.00
Coffeepot 200.00
Compote 50.00
Condiment set, 5-pc 45.00
Creamer & sugar bowl, demitasse 40.00
Cruets, vinegar & oil; cojoined, #319 ....360.00
Cup & saucer, breakfast 25.00
Cup & saucer, demitasse 35.00
Egg cup 30.00
Gravy boat 50.00
Jam jar/dish, 4-pc 70.00
Lemon dish 15.00
Mayonnaise set, 3-pc 50.00

Miscellaneous

So many lines of dinnerware have been produced by the Noritake company that to list them all would require a volume in itself. In fact, just such a book is available — *The Collector's Encyclopedia of Early Noritake* by Aimee Neff Alden (Collector Books). And while many patterns had specific names, others did not, so you'll probably need the photographs the book contains to help you identify your pattern. Outlined below is a general guide for the more common pieces and patterns. The high side of the range will represent lines from about 1933 until the mid-'60s (including those marked 'Occupied Japan), while the higher side should be used to evaluate lines made after that period.

Photo courtesy Joan Van Patten

Match holder, Deco-style lady with dog, red #3 mark, $130.00.

Ashtray, Deco lady in red & blk, 4 rests, #3, 5" 210.00

Ashtray, Deco-style clown sits at side, lustre, #3, 5" **295.00**
Basket vase, Deco flowers on yel & blk, twig hdl, #3, 10" **230.00**
Bottle, scent; lady in gr w/dog, floral stopper, #3, 6¼" **250.00**
Bowl, Deco florals on wht to tan lustre, pierced hdls, #3, 9½" **90.00**
Bowl, lg wht flower on bl lustre, scalloped, #3, 5½" **90.00**
Bowl, red/wht/blk Oriental landscape on yel w/gold, #1, 5½" **90.00**
Bowl, sauce; swans on bl, wht band, w/tray, #3, 3½" H **60.00**
Bowl w/attached mermaid flower frog, gr #3, 5" **375.00**
Butter dish, Deco florals/birds on wht, bl band, #3, 6½" **85.00**
Butter tub, sm floral on wht, gold rim, tub hdls, #3, 5¼" **30.00**
Cake plate, floral center, turq rim w/hdls, #3, 9½" **55.00**
Cake plate, floral reserve on wht, ped ft, #3, 10½" **55.00**
Candlesticks, flowers/butterfly on flower form, #3, 5¼", pr **200.00**
Candy dish, butterfly on tan lustre, flowers 1 side, #3, 9¼" **60.00**
Candy dish, Deco florals on wht, blk hdl, #3, 3" H **65.00**
Candy dish, Deco-style geometrics on yel, w/lid, #3, 6¼" **150.00**
Candy dish, exotic birds, gold rim, 3 pierced hdls, #3, 9½" **60.00**
Candy dish, grapes on bl, lav int, boat shape, #3, 9" **75.00**
Candy dish, river scenic, center hdl, #3, 8½" L **95.00**
Chambersticks, floral on bl lustre, ring hdls, #3, 2", pr **80.00**
Cigarette/playing card holder, lady in flower, #3, 3¾" **185.00**
Compote, butterflies on wht lustre, scalloped, #3, 10½" **85.00**
Compote, Deco floral int, orange lustre, hdls, ftd, #3, 8¼" **75.00**
Compote, exotic bird/flowers on wht w/gold, hdls, #3, 9¾" **75.00**
Cookie/biscuit jar, Oriental landscape, pail form, #3, 8" **160.00**
Creamer, lady w/fan, orange/purple lustre, #3, 3½" **70.00**
Creamer & sugar bowl, butterfly/flowers on blk, lustre int, #3 ......**85.00**
Cruet set, river scenic, #3, pr on center-hdld 8" tray **125.00**
Inkwell, lady figural, lustre dress, red #3, 4¼" **350.00**
Lemon dish, fruit reserve, blk center hdl, #3, 5¼" **60.00**
Lemon dish, lemon & buds on red, flower form, #3, 6" **60.00**
Lemon dish, river scenic, sm hdl, #3, 5½" **60.00**
Pin dish, dog at side of tray, lustre, red #3, 2¾" **60.00**
Plaque, silhouette-style lady at dressing table, #3, 8½" **235.00**
Plate, lg butterfly center, bl rim, #3, 7¾" **35.00**
Plate, man in top hat & long cape, lustre rim, #3, 7¾" **235.00**
Plate, river & mtn scene, lustre rim, #3, 7¾" **40.00**
Plate, 2 ladies drinking tea, red rim, sq, #3, 9" **300.00**
Powder box, Deco-style lady figural, #3, 5" **325.00**
Powder puff box, bird on floral branch, 8-sided, #3, 4¾" **175.00**
Powder puff box, exotic bird on lid, red #3, 4" **195.00**
Relish, florals on wht, pk floral band, 2-part, #3, 8½" L **55.00**
Rouge, lady w/lg red fan on wht, #3, 2½" **215.00**
Sandwich plate, Deco florals, center hdl, #3, 7¾" **75.00**
Sugar shaker & creamer, Deco lady/orange lustre, red #3 ....**150.00**
Syrup, floral on wht w/gold trim, #3, 4½" **70.00**
Vase, dancing nude on pk, uptrn hdls, ftd, #3, 8½", pr **300.00**
Vase, fruit baskets on wht, lustre/gold trim, #3, 6" **80.00**
Vase, lg bl flowers on orange lustre, #3, 10" **110.00**
Vase, mc florals on lustre, gold hdls, #3, 6½" **80.00**
Vase, pastoral scenic, slim, ruffled rim, red #3, 8" **150.00**
Vase, peacock figural, mc lustre, red #3, 5¼" **150.00**
Vase, roses w/gold on wht, ornate gold hdls, #3, 6¼" **220.00**
Vase, 2 exotic birds on red, gold tub hdls, #3, 6" **95.00**
Wall pocket, exotic bird on red, gr #3, 8" **130.00**

Norse

The Norse Pottery was established in 1903 in Edgerton, Wisconsin, by Thorwald Sampson and Louis Ipson. A year later it was purchased by A.W. Wheelock and moved to Rockford, Illinois. The ware they produced was inspired by ancient bronze vessels of the Norsemen. Designs were often incised into the red clay body. Dragon handles and feet were favored decorative devices, and they achieved a semblance of patina through the application of metallic glazes. The ware was marked with model numbers and a stylized 'N' containing a vertical arrangement of the remaining letters of the name. Production ceased after 1913. Our advisor for this category is John Danis; he is listed in the Directory under Illinois.

Bowl, 2 serpents incised on side, gr on blk, 3-ftd, 4" **210.00**
Bowl/vase, geometrics, metallic copper, 5¼x7½" **455.00**
Chamberstick, cvd edges, high-bk cupped form w/hdl, #69, 6" ...**425.00**
Jug, cvd snake band at shoulder, curved hdls, w/gold, #47, 8" **550.00**
Jug, sea horses in verdigris on blk metallic, 1903-13, 7x5½" **400.00**
Vase, emb ferns, gr on blk, rolled-out rim, 9x9" **475.00**

Vase, grotesque lizard on shoulder, black matt with gold and green highlights, 12", $1,200.00.

Vase, stylized cvg, gr/blk/gold, ftd/hdld classic form, 14" **800.00**
Vase, 2 creatures w/long tails as hdls, 3 squat ft, 4x6" **325.00**

North Dakota School of Mines

The School of Mines of the University of North Dakota was established in 1890, but due to a lack of funding it was not until 1898 that Earle J. Babcock was appointed as director, and efforts were made to produce ware from the native clay he had discovered several years earlier. The first pieces were made by firms in the east from the clay Babcock sent them. Some of the ware was decorated by the manufacturer; some was shipped back to North Dakota to be decorated by native artists. By 1909 students at the University of North Dakota were producing utilitarian items such as tile, brick, shingles, etc., in conjunction with a ceramic course offered through the chemistry department. By 1910 a ceramic department had been established, supervised by Margaret Kelly Cable. Under her leadership, fine artware was produced. Native flowers, grains, buffalo, cowboys, and other subjects indigenous to the state were incorporated into the decorations. Some pieces have an Art Nouveau — Art Deco style easily attributed to her association with Frederick H. Rhead, with whom she studied in 1911. During the '20s the pottery was marketed on a limited scale through gift and jewelry stores in the state. From 1927 until 1949 when Miss Cable announced her retirement, a more widespread distribution was maintained with sales branching out into other states. The ware was marked in cobalt with the official seal — 'Made at School of Mines, N.D. Clay, University of North Dakota, Grand Forks, N.D.' in a circle. Very early ware was sometimes marked 'U.N.D.' in cobalt by hand.

Bookends, sheaf of wheat, #171, pr **550.00**
Bowl, bl matt w/brn highlights, J Wallace, incurvate, 4" **170.00**
Bowl, floral band cvd on lt gr, K Harris, 4x6" **400.00**
Figurine, girl w/basket, brn/bl/rust, E Shabert, 1942, 6½" **210.00**

Lamp, rose matt, sgn ALM, 1928, pottery: 9½" **280.00**
Plaque, bust of man, gray & bl, 1933, rpr, 5x3½" **60.00**
Plaque, Grand Council of Masters, 1933 ....**185.00**
Plate, morning glories cvd on bl, sgn M Jacobson, 8" **595.00**
Vase, artichoke leaves cvg, tobacco brn matt, 6x5" **650.00**
Vase, band of wolves, gray-bl on ivory, rpr, 3½x3¾" **500.00**
Vase, brn to gr gloss, sgn, bulbous w/dome lid, 7" **180.00**

Vase, carved and painted birds on cut-back ground banded with red and aqua berries, signed Mary E., blue mark, 8¼", $4,000.00.

Vase, cherry red gloss, hand-thrown, angle shoulder, 5" **130.00**
Vase, cowboy rider/mtns, bl/textured cream, Hattson, 5", EX **290.00**
Vase, deer/trees/Indian designs, brn on tan, Rudset, 7½" **1,300.00**
Vase, die-stamp designs/3-line bars, med bl, Summers, 4x6½" ...**260.00**
Vase, dk gr metallic, bulbous w/collar rim, JM/217, 8x6" **375.00**
Vase, floral, pk w/gr centers & leaves, cvd, Huck, 3x3" **550.00**
Vase, floral band cvd at shoulder, ivory matt, Cable, 8x6" **1,200.00**
Vase, floral on pk w/gr on tan, cvd, Huck, sgn/#1385, 2x4" **180.00**
Vase, geometrics cvd on lt gr semigloss, 4" **140.00**
Vase, groundhogs/wheat, brn/yel on gr to brn, Huck, 5x5" **1,600.00**
Vase, gunmetal matt, finger ridges, Seamen, 7½x5" **260.00**
Vase, Indians on horses/geometrics cvd on brn, Huck, 6¾x6" ...**1,300.00**
Vase, lt yel w/dk bl int, 3¾" **125.00**
Vase, oatmeal to yel semigloss, wide waisted, JM, 5" **375.00**
Vase, rose band, pk/gr on gray, rose ground, Huck, 4x5½" **250.00**
Vase, simple floral shoulder band, pk/gr/tan, Huck, 2½x5" **250.00**
Vase, standing Dutch women, 2-tone brn, Van Camp, 3½x4" ...**325.00**
Vase, tepees/mtns band cvd on caramel gloss, Cable, 7x4½" ..**2,000.00**
Vase, triangles in band, 4-color gloss, HO, BD 16, 8x5½" **550.00**
Vase, Viking ships/gulls, 3-color, Mattson '49A, 5x5" **1,200.00**
Vase, wheat, cream w/gr trim, Huckfield, 3x3" **175.00**

North State

In 1924 the North State Pottery of Sanford, North Carolina, began small-scale production, the result of the extreme fondness Mrs. Rebecca Copper had for potting. With the help of her husband and the abundance of suitable local clay, the pottery flourished and became well known for lovely shapes and beautiful glazes. The pottery was in business for thirty-five years; most of its ware was sold in gift and craft shops throughout North Carolina.

Ashtray, burnt orange/gr, imp mk, 1¾" H, NM **30.00**
Candle lantern, gr, 9½", NM **75.00**
Ewer, bl over red clay, 8½" **95.00**
Pitcher, copper lustre, slender form, 6½" **60.00**
Vase, oxblood w/gr patches, shouldered, early, 10½" **750.00**

Northwood

The Northwood Company was founded in 1896 in Indiana, Penn-

sylvania, by Harry Northwood, whose father, John, was the art director for Stevens and Williams, an English glassworks. Northwood joined the National Glass Company in 1899 but in 1901 again became an independent contractor and formed the Harry Northwood Glass Company of Wheeling, West Virginia. He marketed his first carnival glass in 1908, and it became his most popular product. His company was also famous for its custard, goofus, and pressed glass. Northwood died in 1923, and the company closed. See also Carnival; Custard; Goofus; Opalescent; Pattern Glass.

Bowl, berry; emerald gr intaglio w/gold ft, 7½" **60.00**
Bowl, berry; Leaf Medallion, purple w/EX gold, lg+4 sm **150.00**
Bowl, berry; Leaf Mold, canary spatter **150.00**
Bowl, berry; red berries on gold branches, lg+4 sm **150.00**
Bowl, Leaf Medallion, emerald, ftd, 9" **75.00**
Bowl, sauce; Alaska, emerald gr **40.00**
Bowl, sauce; Leaf Umbrella, Rose DuBarry **45.00**
Butter dish, Gold Rose **75.00**
Butter dish, Leaf Mold, lime gr satin **175.00**
Butter dish, Memphis, gr w/gold **175.00**
Butter dish, Royal Oak, rubena frost **300.00**
Butter dish, Teardrop Flower, gr w/gold **175.00**
Butter dish, Utopia Optic (Venetian), gr **200.00**
Celery tray, Alaska, emerald gr **125.00**
Celery vase, Leaf Umbrella, bl cased **325.00**
Compote, Intaglio, emerald gr w/EX gold, ftd, 8" dia **125.00**
Creamer, Alaska, emerald gr **75.00**
Creamer, Leaf Mold, spatter, shiny **185.00**
Creamer, Leaf Mold, vaseline frost **245.00**
Creamer, Memphis, gr w/gold **85.00**
Creamer, Peach, gr w/gold **85.00**
Creamer, Royal Ivy, rubena frost **300.00**
Cruet, Leaf Umbrella, cranberry **995.00**
Cruet, Royal Ivy, cased rainbow spatter, clear stopper, 6" **895.00**
Cruet, Royal Ivy, frosted rubena **375.00**
Cruet, Royal Ivy, rainbow craquelle **725.00**
Lamp base, Royal Ivy, frosted rubena **325.00**
Pickle castor, Royal Ivy, frosted & clear, EX SP fr & tongs **175.00**
Pitcher, Leaf Mold, canary rainbow spatter satin, w/4 tumblers ..**550.00**
Pitcher, Leaf Umbrella, mauve cased, water sz **425.00**
Pitcher, Leaf Umbrella, shiny bl cased, water sz **375.00**
Pitcher, Peach, clear w/ruby & gold, water sz **150.00**
Pitcher, Peach, gr w/gold, water sz, +6 tumblers **400.00**

Pitcher, Regent, cobalt with gold, with six tumblers (four shown), $800.00.

Pitcher, Rope & Cable, amethyst, lg **300.00**
Pitcher, Royal Ivy, clear frosted, no decor, water sz **90.00**
Pitcher, Royal Ivy, frosted rubena, water size, +6 tumblers **650.00**
Rose bowl, Leaf Mold, canary rainbow spatter, crimped rim, lg ..**110.00**

Rose bowl, Leaf Mold, vaseline frost 285.00
Rose bowl, Royal Ivy, rainbow craquelle cased 225.00
Rose bowl, Royal Ivy, rubena frost 140.00
Rose bowl, Threaded Swirl, rubena, lg 75.00
Rose bowl, wht w/3-color pull-ups, 8-crimp, 3⅛x2⅞" 295.00
Shaker, Cactus, cranberry, blown, ca 1895, 3⅜" 145.00
Shaker, Royal Oak, cranberry rubena, blown, ca 1888, 2½" 80.00
Shakers, Leaf Mold, vaseline, pr 150.00
Shakers, Leaf Umbrella, ruby w/wht spatter, pr 375.00
Shakers, Royal Oak, rubena frost, MOP lids, pr 250.00
Shot glass, Grape & Cable, crystal 25.00
Spooner, Alaska, emerald gr 70.00
Spooner, Cherry & Cable, clear w/gold & purple 45.00
Spooner, Leaf Mold, lime gr 150.00
Spooner, Memphis, gr w/gold 85.00
Spooner, Peach, gr w/gold 95.00
Spooner, Royal Ivy, rubena frost 100.00
Sugar bowl, Leaf Mold, lime gr 165.00
Sugar bowl, Memphis, gr w/gold 140.00
Sugar bowl, Peach, gr w/gold 125.00
Sugar bowl, Royal Ivy, rubena frost, w/lid 225.00
Sugar shaker, Leaf Mold, bl satin 350.00
Sugar shaker, Leaf Umbrella, bl cased 300.00
Sugar shaker, Leaf Umbrella, cranberry, orig lid 495.00
Sugar shaker, Netted Oak, EX decor 135.00
Sugar shaker, Royal Ivy, frosted rubena 250.00
Sugar shaker, Royal Oak, frosted rubena 295.00
Sweetmeat jar, wht satin w/pk & bl pull-ups, SP lid, 5¼" 450.00
Syrup, Leaf Mold, canary rainbow spatter 475.00
Syrup, Leaf Umbrella, cranberry, rare 650.00
Toothpick holder, Leaf Mold, canary rainbow spatter 125.00
Toothpick holder, Royal Ivy, rainbow cased 225.00
Toothpick holder, Royal Ivy, rubena frost 85.00
Tumbler, Leaf Mold, canary rainbow spatter 100.00
Tumbler, Leaf Umbrella, shiny bl cased 85.00
Vase, Grapevine Cluster, purple 75.00
Vase, pull-up dbl-gourd w/camphor leaf hdls, pk/yel/wht, 8½" ...325.00
Water set, Peach, gr & gold, 7-pc 385.00

Norweta

Norweta pottery was produced by the Northwestern Terra Cotta
Company of Chicago, Illinois. It was made for approximately ten
years, beginning sometime before 1907. Not all was marked. Both
matt and crystalline glazes were employed, and terra cotta vases were
also produced.

Bookends, seated elves, 1 reading book/1 w/mug, 8½", EX 325.00
Tile, cherub w/sign: Northwestern..., red clay, 5x4", EX 60.00

**Vase, blue crystalline on
ivory, 5¾", $475.00.**

Vase, cvd leaves/prominent veins, mint gr/dk brn matt, 4x6" 500.00
Vase, textured lav over cream matt, #10003, 5½" 140.00

Nutcrackers

The nutcracker, though a strictly functional tool, is a good example
of one to which man has applied ingenuity, imagination, and engineering skills. Though all were designed to accomplish the same end, hundreds of types exist in almost every material sturdy enough to withstand
sufficient pressure to crack the nut. Figurals are popular collectibles, as
are those with unusual design and construction. Patented examples are
also desirable. Our advisor for this category is Earl MacSorley; he is listed
in the Directory under Connecticut. For more information, we recommend *Ornamental and Figural Nutcrackers* by Judith A. Rittenhouse.

Alligator, CI, no pnt, 13½" 50.00
Alligator, heavy brass 100.00
Bearded elf, CI, 10" 400.00
Black pirate, cvd wood, mc pnt, glass eyes, Germany, EX 475.00
Cherub, brass, old, 6½", EX 100.00

**Dog, cast iron with
black paint, 5¼x9x4½",
EX, $75.00.**

Dog on ftd base, CI, brn & wht pnt, 5¾x11½" 75.00
Dome shape, CI, fits over knee, ca 1870 ....100.00
Elephant, CI, old red pnt, twine tail, 5x9¾" 175.00
Home, table clamp, dtd 1915, M 40.00
Parrot, brass 60.00
Perfection, NP CI, Pat 1914 ....40.00
Ram, cvd wood, glass eyes, 8½" 150.00
Squirrel, CI, Pat 1913 ....30.00
Squirrel on branch, bronze 40.00

Nutting, Wallace

Wallace Nutting (1861-1941) was America's most famous photographer of the early 20th century. A retired minister, Nutting took
more than 50,000 pictures, keeping 10,000 of his best and destroying
the rest. His popular and bestselling scenes included *Exterior Scenes*
(apple blossoms, country lanes, orchards, calm streams, and rural
American countrysides), *Interior Scenes* (usually featuring a colonial
woman working near a hearth), and *Foreign Scenes* (typically thatch-
roofed cottages). His poorest selling pictures, which have become
today's rarest and most highly collectible, are classified as *Miscellaneous
Unusual Scenes* and include categories not mentioned above: animals,
architecturals, children, florals, men, seascapes, and snow scenes. *Process Prints* are 1930s machine-produced reprints of twelve of Nutting's
most popular pictures. These have minimal value and can be detected
by using a magnifying glass.

Nutting sold literally millions of his hand-colored platinotype pictures between 1900 and his death in 1941. Starting first in Southbury,
Connecticut, and later moving his business to Framingham, Massachusetts, the peak of Wallace Nutting picture production was 1915-
25. During this period Nutting employed nearly two hundred people,
including colorists, darkroom staff, salesmen, and assorted office person-

nel. Wallace Nutting pictures proved to be a huge commercial success and hardly an American household was without one by 1925.

While attempting to seek out the finest and best early American furniture as props for his colonial interior scenes, Nutting became an expert in early American antiques. He published nearly twenty books in his lifetime, including his ten-volume *State Beautiful* series and various other books on furniture, photography, clocks, stools, chairs, settles, settees, tables, stands, desks, mirrors, beds, chests of drawers, cabinet pieces, and treenware. His furniture was clearly marked with a distinctive paper label (which was glued directly onto the piece) or a block or script signature brand, which was literally branded into the furniture.

The overall synergy of the Wallace Nutting, name — pictures, books, and furniture — has made anything 'Wallace Nutting' quite collectible.

Prices below are for pictures in good to excellent condition. Mat stains or blemishes, poor picture color or frame damage can decrease value significantly.

Our advisor for this category is Michael Ivankovich, author of many books concerning Nutting. Those currently available are *The Collector's Guide to Wallace Nutting Pictures; The Wallace Nutting Expansible Catalog; The Alphabetical and Numerical Index to Wallace Nutting Pictures; The Guide to Wallace Nutting Furniture, Wallace Nutting General Catalog, Supreme Edition; Wallace Nutting: A Great American Idea; Wallace Nutting's Windsors: Correct Windsor Furniture;* and *The Guide to Wallace Nutting-Like Photographers of the Early 20th Century.* Also available through Mr. Ivankovich is *The History of The Sawyer Pictures* by Carol Begley Gray. Mr. Ivankovich's address and ordering information are listed in the Directory under Pennsylvania.

Untitled path through the apple orchard, miniature, about 3x4" in large frame, $65.00.

Wallace Nutting Pictures

Afternoon Tea, 14x17"	175.00
Barre Brook, 13x16"	125.00
Bit of Sewing, 11x14"	95.00
Chair for John, 12x16"	195.00
Colonial Days, 14x17"	1,125.00
Comfort & a Cat, 14x17"	325.00
Coming Out of Rosa, 14x17"	195.00
Confidences, 13x16"	185.00
Decked as a Bride, 11x14"	75.00
Eventful Journey	650.00
Five O'Clock, 11x17"	175.00
Four O'Clock, 14x17"	1,275.00
Fruit Luncheon, 16x20"	295.00
Garden of Larkspur, 13x16"	85.00
Going for the Doctor, 13x16"	1,100.00
Greeting, 11x14"	165.00
Hollyhock Cottage, 13x16"	135.00
Hollyhocks (floral scene), 8x10"	525.00
LaJolla, 13x16"	275.00
Larkspur, 11x14"	75.00

Listless Day, 13x16"	325.00
Litchfield Minster, 11x14"	165.00
Maple Sugar Cupboard, 14x17"	150.00
Mary's Little Lamb, 13x16"	250.00
Meeting Place, 18x22"	2,420.00
Mission Corner, 10x12"	275.00
Nest, 12x15"	150.00
Old Drawing Room, 11x17"	185.00
Pergola Amalfi, 13x16"	160.00
Plymouth Curves, 11x17"	145.00
Process print, All Sunshine, 16x20"	25.00
Process print, Barre Brook, 12x15"	15.00
Process print, Decked As a Bride, 16x20"	20.00
Roses & Larkspur, 13x16"	1,200.00
Sea Ledges, 10x16"	265.00
Slack Water, 11x17"	150.00
Stitch in Time, 14x17"	220.00
Sunshine & Music, 13x16"	225.00
Swimming Pool, 11x17"	165.00
Tea for Two, 13x16"	225.00
Untitled blossoms (blossoms & stone wall), 7x9"	75.00
Untitled foreign (girl in garden), 7x9"	65.00
Untitled foreign (3-spired cathedral), 7x9"	85.00
Untitled interior (girl by fire), 8x12"	125.00
Untitled interior (girls having tea), 8x10"	110.00
Untitled stream (stream & birches), 7x9"	85.00
Warm Spring Day, 11x17"	275.00
Watersmeet, 13x16"	125.00
Way It Begins, 14x17"	625.00

Wallace Nutting Books

American Windsors, w/dust jacket	100.00
Clock Book, 2nd edition	40.00
Connecticut Beautiful, gr cover, 1st edition	45.00
England Beautiful, gr cover, 1st edition	55.00
Furniture of the Pilgrim Century	100.00
Furniture Treasury, bl cover, 1954 edition, Volumes I & II	35.00
Furniture Treasury, 1st edition, 3 volumes	300.00
Ireland Beautiful, gr cover, 1st edition	50.00
Maine Beautiful, tan cover, 2nd edition	35.00
Massachusetts Beautiful, gr cover, 1st edition	35.00
New Hampshire Beautiful, gr cover, 1st edition	40.00
New York Beautiful, tan cover, 2nd edition	45.00
Pennsylvania Beautiful, gr cover, 1st edition	40.00
Photographic Art Secrets	125.00
Vermont Beautiful, gr cover, 1st edition	45.00
Virginia Beautiful, tan cover, 2nd edition	40.00
Wallace Nutting Biography	85.00

Wallace Nutting Furniture

#101 Windsor rnd stool, block brand	300.00
#102, Windsor oval stool, paper label	250.00
#164 Brewster rushed 3-legged stool, script brand	385.00
#166 rushed maple stool, block brand, 15"	300.00
#168 rushed maple stool, block brand, 22"	425.00
#17 Windsor tripod candlestand, block brand	525.00
#21 maple screw (whirling) candlestand, block brand	990.00
#22, cross-based candlestand, block brand	575.00
#28 treenware open salt dish, impressed brand, 1½"	155.00
#301 Windsor side chair, block brand	525.00
#305 Windsor bent-rung bowbk side chair, bamboo trns, block brand	800.00
#31 curly maple candlestick (single), impressed brand	175.00

#31 curly maple candlestick (single), unmk **95.00**
#310 Windsor slipper side chair, paper label **550.00**
#326, Windsor fan-bk side chair, script brand/paper label **550.00**
#377 3-slat bk side chair, block brand **385.00**
#392 4-rung ladderbk side chair, block brand **475.00**
#393 Pilgrim side chair, block brand **360.00**
#401 Windsor continuous-arm chair, block brand, from $650 to ...**1,200.00**
#411 Brewster armchair, script brand **1,000.00**
#412 Pennsylvania Windsor comb-bk armchair, block brand ..**1,400.00**
#414 Windsor low-bk armchair, block brand/paper label **525.00**
#415 Windsor comb-bk armchair, block brand, from $750 to .**1,500.00**
#419 Windsor dbl comb-bk armchair, paper label, from $750 to ..**1,500.00**
#421 Windsor rocking armchair, script brand **1,100.00**
#440 Windsor writing armchair, PA trnings w/drw, block brand ...**2,800.00**
#601 oak refractory table, block brand **935.00**
#616 pine trestle bable, block brand **750.00**
#619 maple crane bracket table, script brand **685.00**
#761 gold 3-feather mirror, impressed brand **575.00**
Unnumbered treenware pen & pencil tray, impressed brand **250.00**

Major Wallace Nutting-Like Photographers

Although Wallace Nutting was widely recognized as the country's leading producer of hand-colored photographs during the early 20th century, he was by no means the only photographer selling this style of picture. Throughout the country literally hundreds of regional photographers were selling hand-colored photographs from their home regions or travels. The subject matters of these photographers was very comparable to Nutting's, including interior, exterior, foreign, and miscellaneous unusual scenes. The key determinants of value include the collectibility of the particular photographer, subject matter, condition, and size. Keep in mind that only the rarest pictures, in the best condition, will bring top prices. Discoloration and/or damage to the picture or matting can reduce value significantly.

Several photographers operated large businesses and, although not as large or well known as Wallace Nutting, they sold a substantial volume of pictures which can still be readily found today. The vast majority of their work was photographed in their home regions and sold primarily to local residents or visiting tourists. It should come as little surprise that three of the major Wallace Nutting-like photographers — David Davidson, Fred Thompson, and the Sawyer Art Co. — each had ties to Wallace Nutting.

David Davidson: Second to Nutting in overall production, Davidson worked primarily in the Rhode Island and Southern Massachusetts area. While a student at Brown University around 1900, Davidson learned the art of hand-colored photography from Wallace Nutting, who happened to be the minister at Davidson's church. After Nutting moved to Southbury in 1905, Davidson graduated from Brown and started a successful photography business in Providence, Rhode Island, which he operated until his death in 1967.

Barefoot Boy, 9x16" **195.00**
Daughter of Sheffield, 13x16" **275.00**
Diadem Aisle, 10x12" **50.00**
Dropt Stitch, 13x16" **185.00**
Echo Lake, 8x10" **65.00**
Her House in Order, 12x16" **45.00**
Prize Pewter, 12x16" **45.00**
Puritan Lady, 12x16" **75.00**
Rambler Rose, 12x16" **170.00**
Shattered Wave, 12x15" **85.00**
Sunset Point, 12x16" **45.00**
Village Maiden, 14x17" **180.00**

Welcome Guest, 9x15" **155.00**
Wisteria, 13x16" **95.00**
Ye Olden Tyme, 13x16" **300.00**

Sawyer: A father and son team, Charles H. Sawyer and Harold B. Sawyer, operated the very successful Sawyer Art Company from 1903 into the 1970s. Beginning in Maine, the Sawyer Art Company moved to Concord, New Hampshire, in 1920 to be nearer their primary market of New Hampshire's White Mountains. Charles H. Sawyer briefly worked for Nutting in 1902-03 while living in southern Maine. Sawyer's production volume ranks #3 behind Wallace Nutting and David Davidson.

Afterglow, 6x8" **25.00**
Autumn Glory, 9x12" **50.00**
Camel's Hump, 7x9" **50.00**
Chapel, San Juan Capsitrano, 13x16" **155.00**
Echo Lake, Franconia Notch, 13x16" **55.00**
Elephant's Head, 5x7" **35.00**
Gateway to the Adirondacks, 13x20" **155.00**
Joseph Lincoln's Garden, 16x20" **185.00**
Lafayette Slides, 13x15" **90.00**
Mt Lafayette, 7x9" **35.00**
Old Man of the Mountains, 11x14" **45.00**
Peaceful Sentinels, 11x14" **60.00**
Rock Garden, Cape Cod, 16x20" **165.00**
Sunset on the Kennebec, 12x20" **70.00**
Surf at Pinnacle Rock, 13x20" **90.00**

Fred Thompson: Frederick H. Thompson and Frederick M. Thompson were another father and son team that operated the Thompson Art Company (TACO) from 1908-1923, working primarily in the Portland, Maine, area. We know that Thompson and Nutting had collaborated because Thompson widely marketed an interior scene he had taken in Nutting's Southbury home. The production volume of the Thompson Art Company ranks #4 behind Nutting, Davidson, and Sawyer.

Bridal Blossoms, 8x15" **60.00**
Covered Bridge, 9x12" **75.00**
Dixie Apple Blossoms, 16x20" **65.00**
Fireside Fancies, 11x14" **85.00**
Neath the Blossoms, 7x9" **65.00**
New England Blossoms, 8x14" **65.00**
Old Mill Dam, 9x12" **25.00**
Pine Grove, 14x17" **40.00**
Roasting Apples, 10x12" **55.00**
Roller, 8x14" **85.00**
Sailing Ship, 8x10" **240.00**
Sea Foam, 7x11" **75.00**
Sentinels, 6x12" **25.00**
Spinning Days, 14x17" **95.10**
Tired of Spinning, 7x9" **55.00**

Charles Higgins: Working out of Bath, Maine, some of Higgins's finest pictures rivaled Nutting's best. No firm connection has been found between Higgins and Wallace Nutting.

Apple Blossom Lane, 8x12" **35.00**
By the Fireplace, 11x14" **125.00**
Fall Days, 8x14" **35.00**
Lane, 9x12" **95.00**
Near Sugar Hill, 8x12" **55.00**
Pine Road, 8x10" **30.00**
Rocky Shore, 8x14" **55.00**

Untitled exterior 20.00
Untitled interior, 7x9" 35.00
Untitled seascape, 7x11" 65.00

Minor Wallace Nutting-Like Photographers

Hundreds of other smaller local and regional photographers attempted to market hand-colored pictures comparable to Nutting's during the 1900-30s time period. Although quite attractive, most were not as appealing to the general public as Wallace Nutting pictures. However, as the price of Wallace Nutting pictures has escalated, the work of these lesser-known Wallace Nutting-like photographers have become increasingly collectible.

A partial listing of some of these minor Wallace Nutting-like photographers include Babcock; J.C. Bicknell; Blair; Ralph Blood (Portland, Maine); Bragg; Brehmer; Brooks; Burrowes; Busch; Carlock; Pedro Cacciola; Croft; Currier; Depue Bros; Derek; Dowly; Eddy; May Farini (hand-colored colonial lithographs); Geo. Forest; Gandara; Gardner (Nantucket, Bermuda, Florida); Gibson; Gideon; Gunn; Bessie Pease Gutmann (hand-colored colonial lithographs); Edward Guy; Harris; C Hazen; Knoffe; Haynes (Yellowstone Park); Margaret Hennesey; Hodges; Homer; Krabel; Kattleman; La Bushe; Lake; Lamson (Portland, Maine); M. Lightstrum; Machering; Rossiler Mackinae; Merrill; Meyers; William Moehring; Moran; Murrey; Lyman Nelson; J. Robinson Neville (New England); Patterson; Owen Perry; Phelps; Phinney; Reynolds; F. Robbins; Royce; Fred'k Scheetz (Phila...Pennsylvania); Shelton; Standley (Colorado); Stott; Summers; Esther Svenson; Florence Thompson; Thomas Thompson; M.A. Trott; Sanford Tull; Underhill; Villar; Ward; Wilmot; Edith Wilson; and Wright.

A very general breakdown of prices for works by these minor Wallace Nutting-like photographers would be as follows.

Larger pictures, greater than 14x17", from $75 to over 200.00
Medium pictures, from 11x14" to 14x17", from $50 to 200.00
Smaller pictures, 5x7" to 10x12", from $10 to 75.00

The same pricing guidelines that apply to Wallace Nutting pictures also typically apply to Wallace Nutting-like pictures
1.) Exterior scenes are the most common.
2.) Some photographers sold colonial interior scenes as well.
3.) Subject, matter, condition, and size are all important determinants of value.

Miscellaneous Nutting Memorabilia

Advertising sign, glass, 8x10" 550.00
Advertising sign, paper, 11x16" 125.00
Calendar, in thin metal fr 75.00
Colorist's photograph, 8x10" 110.00
Furniture catalog, final edition, 1937 ....125.00
Furniture catalog, supreme edition, 1930 ....110.00
Greeting card, w/exterior scene, 4x5" 75.00
Miniature exterior scene, 4x5" 65.00
Miniature floral scene, 4x5" 175.00
Miniature interior scene, 4x5" 110.00
Pirate print, Swimming Pool, unsgn 10.00
Silhouette, George & Martha Washington, pr 85.00
Silhouette, Girl by Garden Urn, 4x4" 40.00
Silhouette, Girl Sits at Vanity, 4x4" 35.00
Silhouette, Girl Stands by Cheval Mirror, 5x5" 45.00
Silhouette, Lamb Follows Girl to School, 7x8" 65.00
Silhouette, Mother's Day Card 45.00

Occupied Japan

Items marked 'Occupied Japan' have become popular collectibles in the last few years. They were produced during the period from the end of World War II until April 18, 1952, when the occupation ended. By no means was all of the ware exported during that time marked 'Occupied Japan'; some was marked 'Japan' or 'Made In Japan.' It is thought that because of the natural resentment felt by the Japanese toward the occupation, only a fraction of these wares carried the 'Occupied' mark. Even though you may find identical 'Japan'-marked items, because of its limited use, only those with the 'Occupied Japan' mark are being collected to any great extent. Values vary considerably, based on the quality of workmanship. Generally, bisque figures command much higher prices than porcelain, since on the whole they are of a finer quality.

For those wanting more information, we recommend *The Collector's Encyclopedia of Occupied Japan Collectibles* by Gene Florence; he is listed in the Directory under Kentucky. Our advisor for this category is Florence Archambault; she is listed in the Directory under Rhode Island. She represents the Occupied Japan Club, whose mailing address may be found in the Directory under Clubs, Newsletters, and Catalogs. All items described in the following listings are assumed ceramic unless noted otherwise.

Ashtray, frog w/open mouth 14.00
Ashtray, horse pulling wagon, red dmn on side, 3¼" 8.00
Ashtray, Statue of Liberty in center, metal 15.00
Ashtray, Wedgwood-type, Niagara Falls souvenir, 4½" dia 15.00
Bookends, penguins, 4", pr 35.00
Bowl, fruit decor on wht, cut-out design on rim, 7" 15.00
Bowl, pk flowers on wht, scalloped rim, tab hdls, Ucagco 10.00
Bowl, salad; wood, 10" 25.00
Child's set, cup & saucer/sugar bowl/creamer, elephant w/flag 32.00
Child's set, teapot/cup & saucer/sugar bowl, tomato form 42.00
Cigarette box, Colonial ladies on lid, wht w/gold, w/ashtray 25.00
Cigarette box, pk flowers on wht, w/4 ashtrays 22.50
Cigarette lighter, champagne bucket, metal 18.00
Cigarette lighter, gun form, metal, 2½" 15.00
Cigarette lighter, Indian in profile, metal 22.50
Cigarette lighter, urn type, metal, 2¾" 10.00

Cocktail shaker, lacquerware with morning-glory vine on front, metal base, 11¼", $60.00.

Cup & saucer, crab apples on wht, gold trim 12.50
Cup & saucer, dancing girls, gold trim 25.00
Cup & saucer, demitasse; floral medallion on rust, Kato 12.50
Cup & saucer, demitasse; flowers on wht, gold trim 12.50
Cup & saucer, demitasse; lacy flower on blk 14.00
Cup & saucer, demitasse; wht w/flowers & red panels 14.00
Cup & saucer, flower on wht shading to yel, gold trim 15.00

Cup & saucer, river scene w/gold trim, Aurger design 24.00
Cup & saucer, thatch house & river scene, gold trim 18.00
Cup & saucer, yel w/gold trim, floral int, Jyoto 12.50
Dinnerware set, dogwood on ivory w/gold trim, set for 8 ....300.00
Dinnerware set, Livonia (Dogwood), serves 12+casserole+platter ...450.00
Dinnerware set, Livonia (Dogwood), serves 6+gravy boat & platter ..250.00
Dinnerware set, Rochelle, Grace China, serves 4+serving pcs 200.00
Dinnerware set, simple pattern, serves 4 ....225.00
Dinnerware set, simple pattern, serves 8+platter+2 lg bowls 350.00
Dinnerware Set, Wild Rose, Fuji China, serves 8+serving pcs 300.00
Dinnwerware set, apples or crab apples, serves 6+gravy+platter .250.00
Doll, celluloid, baby in snowsuit 45.00
Doll, celluloid w/pk crocheted dress, 6" 45.00
Figurine, angel w/horn, bsk, 5" 25.00
Figurine, ballerina, gold net skirt, 4½" 30.00
Figurine, Colonial man w/violin, bsk, 9" 60.00
Figurine, Cupid on sled, bsk, 5" 35.00
Figurine, frog w/accordion, bsk, 4" 20.00

Figurine, girl with book, 6", $30.00.

Figurine, girl w/song book, Ucagco China, 5¾" 30.00
Figurine, Hummel-type, boy w/begging dog, 5" 40.00
Figurine, nude on sea horse, 3½" 20.00
Figurine, Oriental dancer, 7½" 30.00
Figurine, Oriental lady w/muff, 8" 32.00
Figurine, peacock, 3" 8.00
Figurine, puppies in basket, 2½" 15.00
Flower frog, mc polka dots on wht, ftd, 4½" dia 12.50
Lamp base, Colonial lady lifting skirt, porc, 10" 40.00
Lamp base, Mary & lamb, bsk 100.00
Lamp base, musician & singer, porc, 11½", pr 150.00
Lamp base, Wedgwood-type, bsk 50.00
Match safe, brn w/yel, wht & bl flower design, 6¼" 38.00
Pencil trimmer, elephant on world globe, metal 20.00
Planter, bird on tree branch, 3" 10.00
Planter, boot, 6½" 14.00

Planter, boy and bird beside basket, red mark, 6¼x4¼", $75.00.

Photo courtesy Leon Travis

Planter, boy beside cactus, 4" 8.00
Planter, elf w/cart, 7½" 20.00
Planter, lady & shell, bsk, 5½x6½" 75.00
Planter, rabbit w/cart, 2½x6" 15.00
Planter, rooster w/cart, 3x4½" 10.00
Planter, Santa figure, 6" 35.00
Planter, zebra, 5¼x6¼" 15.00
Plate, cabin scene w/chickens, gold trim 20.00
Plate, dinner; crab apples on wht, gold trim 20.00
Plate, snack; gr leaf form w/wht flowers & gold trim, 9" 10.00
Plate, yel flower on wht, gold trim, Ucagco China 15.00
Plate, yel hibiscus on wht, cut-out design on rim 22.50
Powder jar, bl w/rose finial, 3½" 15.00
Powder jar, heart shape w/windmill scene, 2¾" 12.50
Ring box, heart shape, orange trim 15.00
Shakers, bellhop w/suitcases, pr 22.50
Shakers, chicks in basket, pr 22.50
Shakers, corn cobs, pr 15.00
Shakers, Humpty Dumpty, mk Ardalt...No 6343, pr 55.00
Shakers, Indians in canoe, pr 25.00
Shakers, Scottish couple, pr 18.00
Shelf sitter, ballerina, net skirt, 5" 30.00
Shelf sitter, fishing couple, bsk, 2½" 20.00
Toby mug, winking man, 4" 25.00
Tray, divided; Statue of Liberty/Empire State Building, metal 15.00
Vase, amber glass, 2¾" 20.00
Vase, boy ready for picnic at base, 5" 15.00
Vase, emb flower, ruffled rim, wavy hdls, 5½" 8.00
Vase, pagoda in relief, ftd, sm hdls, 5¼" 25.00
Vase, Wedgwood-type, 6⅛" 30.00
Wall plaque, Colonial lady, bsk, oval, 7x4¾" 30.00
Wall plaque, cup & saucer, 3¼" 8.00
Wall plaque, duck in flight, 5" 25.00

Ohr, George

George Ohr established his pottery in the 1880s in Biloxi, Mississippi. The unusual style of the ware he produced and his flamboyant personality earned him the title of 'the mad potter of Biloxi.' Though acclaimed by some of the critics of his day to be perhaps the most accomplished thrower in the history of the industry, others overlooked the eggshell-thin walls of his vessels, each a different and often contorted shape, and saw only that the ware's 'tortured' appearance contradicted their own sedate tastes.

Ohr worked alone. His work was typically pinched and pulled, pleated, crumpled, dented, and folded. Lizards and worms were often applied to the ware, each with detailed, expressive features. He was well recognized, however, for his glazes, especially those with a metallic patina. The ware was marked with his name, alone or with 'Biloxi' added. Ohr died in 1918. Our advisor for this category is Fer-Duc, Inc.; whose address is listed in the Directory under New York.

Bowl, blk wash on brn, crimped/crumpled, 3½x8" 3,000.00
Chamber pot, speckled ochre, holds realistic contents, 2½" 600.00
Pitcher, bl wash, cut-out hdl, body seam forms spout, 4x5½" ..2,250.00
Pitcher, brn w/blk mottle, twist at neck/dimpled, rpr, 7" 2,200.00
Pitcher, emb nudes/florals in panels, brn mottled, 7¾" 1,155.00
Pitcher, gr mottled matt, ear hdl extends to neck band, 8x3" ..4,300.00
Pitcher, red matt w/gr drip, cut-out hdl, pinched body, 5" 4,750.00
Plaque, gr, figural crab on 6-sided base, 2½x9½" 2,750.00
Vase, blk gloss, waisted neck, 3¼x3¼" 550.00
Vase, blk speckled, ovoid w/crimped rim, 4½x4" 990.00
Vase, bsk, cylindrical w/twist at base & rim, 7½x4", EX 900.00

Vase, bsk, long/flat in-body folds, star-folded rim, 5x5" **1,000.00**
Vase, dk gr spotted, cone w/twisted neck, hdls, rstr, 9x4½" **3,750.00**
Vase, dk gunmetal, crimped rim, rprs/hairlines, 5½x4" **650.00**
Vase, dripped/mottled brn/gr on ochre, pinched/dimpled, 6x5" ..**1,840.00**
Vase, gunmetal spots on orange clay w/gloss glaze, 5x5" **1,600.00**
Vase, mc streaks on thin-walled form, crimped rim, 1901, 6" ..**1,495.00**
Vase, red & orange pinched form, verse on bottom, rpr, 6" **500.00**
Vase, rose neck w/twist on bl matt body, bottle form, 5x4" **2,500.00**
Vase, sponged ochre/blk on raspberry, 4-lobe rim, 4x5¼" **3,200.00**

Old Ivory

Old Ivory dinnerware was produced during the late 1800s by Herman Ohme, of Lower Salzbrunn in Silesia. The patterns are referred to by the numbers stamped on the bottom of many items. (Though not every piece is numbered, the vast majority bears the tiny blue fleur-de-lis/crown mark with Silesia or Germany beneath. Handwritten numbers signify something other than pattern.) Patterns #16 and #84 are the easiest to find and come in a wide variety of table items. Values are about the same for both patterns. Other floral designs include pink, yellow, and orange roses; holly; and lavender flowers — all on the same soft ivory background. The ware was not widely distributed; its two main distribution points were in Maine and, to a lesser extent, Chicago. Our prices are intended to represent a nationwide average, though you may have to pay a little more in some areas. Novice collectors should be aware of copy-cat versions from the turn of the century that are much heavier and of a coarser material. They are marked 'Old Ivory' without the blue trademark. They are not included in this listing. Our advisor for this category is Glen Horn; see the Directory under Texas.

Chocolate pot, colored roses on dark rusty red, 10", $150.00; Berry bowl, Holly pattern, light gold wear, 9" dia, $225.00; Chocolate pot, flower sprigs, no number, 10", $275.00.

Biscuit jar, #16 or #84, 8" **450.00**
Bonbon, #76, round, fancy hdl, 6½" **115.00**
Bowl, #16 or #84, 6½" **65.00**
Bowl, berry; #16 or #84, 5" **35.00**
Bowl, nappy, #15, 6½" **95.00**
Bowl, serving; #15, 9¼" **195.00**
Bowl, serving; #200, 9¼" **195.00**
Bowl, vegetable; #16 or #84, 9⅛", from $65 to **85.00**
Butter dish, #16 or #84, w/lid & liner **695.00**
Butter pat, #16 or #84 ....**90.00**
Cake plate, #15, open hdls, 10¾" **125.00**
Casserole, #16 or #84, w/lid **1,095.00**
Celery tray, #16 or #84, 11x5½" **150.00**
Chocolate set, #11, pot+6 c/s **495.00**
Chocolate set, #16 or #84, 10¼" pot+4 c/s, from $800 to **850.00**
Creamer & sugar bowl, #16 or #84, w/lid **195.00**
Cup & saucer, #75 ....**75.00**
Cup & saucer, #76 ....**75.00**

Demitasse pot, #16 or #84 ....**395.00**
Gravy bowl, #16 or #84, scalloped **695.00**
Hair receiver, 2½x4" dia **250.00**
Ladle holder, #16 or #84 ....**95.00**
Plate, #15, 7¾" **95.00**
Plate, #16 or #84, 6" **30.00**
Plate, bread & butter; #16 or #84 ....**75.00**
Plate, chop; #15, 13" **150.00**
Plate, dinner; #16 or #84, 10" **150.00**
Plate, dinner; Apple Blossoms, 8¼" **135.00**
Plate, luncheon; #76, 4 for **125.00**
Shakers, #16 or #84, 2½", pr **195.00**
Teapot, #15 ....**395.00**
Tile, #16 or #84, 6¼" dia **225.00**
Toothpick holder, #16 or #84 ....**250.00**
Waste bowl, #7, mk, 2½x9x7" **225.00**

Old Paris

Old Paris porcelains were made from the mid-18th century until about 1900. Seldom marked, the term refers to the area of manufacture rather than a specific company. In general, the ware was of high quality; characterized by classic shapes, colorful decoration, and gold application.

Bowl, bl cornflowers on wht, red mks, 5⅛x12⅛" **600.00**
Bulb pot, people/flowers w/gold, mask hdls, 1850s, 7¾" **1,400.00**
Compote, gilt & magenta gothicized decor, 1830s, 4¼x9", pr **250.00**
Corbielle, porc wickerwork, navette form, 10x14¼x7¾" **770.00**
Cup & saucer, mc florals w/lacy gold, generous sz **85.00**
Flasks, exotic Eastern man & woman figurals, 1850s, 11½", pr ..**470.00**

Garniture vases, large mixed flowers on cobalt with much gold, foliate handles, ca 1850, 24", each with losses, $1,500.00 for the pair.

Inkstand, mc floral w/gold, 2-covered pots/pen tray, 1860s **250.00**
Jar, apothecary; gilt decor, knopped lid, 1840, 10½" **325.00**
Shell dish, flowers on gr w/gold, early, 1⅝x9½x8¾", pr **440.00**
Vase, gardening trophies & flowers on red, 1860s, 19", pr **440.00**
Vase, nobleman portrait, gold hdls, 1840s, 11¼" **220.00**
Vielleuse, seascapes, gold anthemion borders, 1850s, 9" **660.00**

Old Sleepy Eye

Old Sleepy Eye was a Sioux Indian chief who was born in Minnesota in 1780. His name was used for the name of a town as well as a flour mill. In 1903 the Sleepy Eye Milling Company of Sleepy Eye, Minnesota, contracted the Weir Pottery Company of Monmouth, Illinois, to make steins, vases, salt crocks, and butter tubs which the company gave away to their customers. A bust profile of the old Indian and his name decorated each piece of the blue and gray stoneware. In addition to these four items, the Minnesota Stoneware Company of Red Wing made a mug with a verse which is very scarce today.

In 1906 Weir Pottery merged with six others to form the Western Stoneware Company in Monmouth. They produced a line of blue and white ware using a lighter body, but these pieces were never given as flour premiums. This line consisted of pitchers (five sizes), steins, mugs, sugar bowls, vases, trivets, and mustache cups. These pieces turn up only rarely in other colors and are highly prized by advanced collectors. Advertising items such as trade cards, pillow tops, thermometers, paperweights, letter openers, postcards, cookbooks, and thimbles are considered very valuable. The original ware was made sporadically until 1937. Brown steins and mugs were produced in 1952. Our advisor for this category is Jim Martin; he is listed in the Directory under Illinois.

Stein, brown, 1952, 7¾", $300.00.

Banner, center portrait & western scenes, 22" sq, EX 1,450.00
Barrel, flour; orig paper label, 1920s 1,800.00
Barrel, grapevine-effect banding 3,500.00
Barrel, oak w/brass bands 4,500.00
Butter crock, Flemish 625.00
Calendar, 1904, NM 375.00
Calendar, 1904, VG 150.00
Cookbook, EX 185.00
Cookbook, Indian on cover, Sleepy Eye Milling Co, 4¾x4" 300.00
Cookbook, loaf of bread shape, EX 115.00
Cookbook, loaf of bread shape, NM 210.00
Coupon, for ordering cookbook 250.00
Coupon, for ordering pillow top 200.00
Dough scraper, tin/wood, To Be Sure, EX 435.00
Fan, Indian chief, die-cut cb, 1900 ....1,200.00
Flour sack, cloth, mc Indian, red letters 345.00
Flour sack, paper, Indian in blk, blk lettering, NM 125.00
Ink blotter 125.00
Label, barrel end; mc Indian portrait, 16", NM 160.00
Label, barrel; Indian chief, Whilmann's Bros, 16" dia, EX 250.00
Letter opener, bronze 900.00
Match holder, pnt 1,875.00
Match holder, wht 1,050.00
Mug, bl & gray, 4¼" 360.00
Mug, bl & wht, 4¼" 220.00
Mug, verse, Red Wing, EX 1,625.00
Paperweight, bronzed company trademk 560.00
Pillow cover, Sleepy Eye & tribe meet President Monroe 750.00
Pillow cover, trademk center w/various scenes, 22", NM 1,600.00
Pin-bk button, Indian, rnd face 350.00
Pitcher, #1, 4" 300.00
Pitcher, #2 ....350.00
Pitcher, #3 ....315.00
Pitcher, #3, w/bl rim 1,375.00
Pitcher, #4 ....400.00
Pitcher, #5 ....435.00
Pitcher, bl & gray, 5" 325.00
Pitcher, bl on cream, 8", M 345.00
Pitcher, standing Indian, good color, #5 size 1,560.00

Postcard, colorful trademk, 1904 Expo Winner 185.00
Ruler, wooden, 15" 700.00
Salt crock, Flemish, 4x6½" 600.00
Sheet music, in fr 300.00
Sign, self-fr tin, Old Sleepy Eye Flour, 20x24" 2,500.00
Sign, tin litho die-cut Indian, ...Flour & Cereals, 13½" 1,650.00
Spoon, demitasse; emb roses in bowl, Unity SP 105.00
Spoon, Indian-head hdl 125.00
Stein, bl & wht, 7¾" 800.00
Stein, brn, 1952, 22-oz 300.00
Stein, brn & wht 1,500.00
Stein, brn & yel, Western Stoneware 1,500.00
Stein, cobalt 1,250.00
Stein, Flemish, bl on gray 700.00
Stein, ltd edition, 1979-84, ea 125.00
Sugar bowl, bl & wht, 3" 750.00
Thermometer, front rpl 800.00
Vase, cattails, all cobalt 1,450.00
Vase, cattails, bl & wht, good color, 9" 800.00
Vase, cattails, brn on yel, rare color 1,500.00
Vase, cattails, gr & wht 5,000.00
Vase, Indian & cattails, Flemish, 8½" 470.00

O'Neill, Rose

Rose O'Neill's Kewpies were introduced in 1909 when they were used to conclude a story in the December issue of *Ladies' Home Journal*. They were an immediate success, and soon Kewpie dolls were being produced worldwide. German manufacturers were among the earliest and also used the Kewpie motif to decorate chinaware as well as other items. The Kewpie is still popular today and can be found on products ranging from Christmas cards and cake ornaments to fabrics, wallpaper, and metal items.

Our advisor for this category is Kitty Watson; she is listed in the Directory under Oklahoma. In the following listings, 'sgn' indicates that the item is signed Rose O'Neill. © is also a good mark on items. Unsigned items are of little interest to collectors.

Ad, Jell-O, blk & wht, ca 1915 ....6.00
Bank, Kewpie, chalk w/metal glasses, 1966, 11¾" 75.00
Bell, Kewpie figural hdl, brass, 3" 95.00

Book, Kewpies Their Book, Crowell Publishing, 1913, VG, $325.00.

Book, Kewpie primer, Rose O'Neill, 1916 ....195.00
Book, Kewpies in Action, M Leuzzi, 1971 ....125.00
Book, The One Rose, Rowena Ruggles, 1st ed, 1964 ....150.00
Booklet, Jell-O, Jell-O Girl & Kewpie-like fairies, 1910s, NM 60.00
Bottle, scent; Kewpie figural, bent knees, Germany, 3½" 895.00
Bowl, cereal; 5 action Kewpies, Royal Rudolstadt, sgn, 6¼" 115.00

Cards, Kewpies & mtn scene, advertising, 1970s, complete, EX ...**20.00**
Clock, bl & wht jasper, Kewpie, sgn, Germany, 5½x5½" **600.00**
Clock, pk & gr jasper, sgn, 3½x4½", EX **485.00**
Cup, 5 action Kewpies, Royal Rudolstadt, sgn O'Neill Wilson, lg ..**100.00**

Dresser set, marked Royal Rudolstadt (Prussia), rare, EX, from $1,850.00 to $2,000.00.

Hatpin holder, bl/wht jasper, Kewpies, mk, 4½", NM, minimum **425.00**
Hood ornament, Kewpie, metal, mk, rare, 6½" **2,500.00**
Jewelry box, Kewpie Blunderboo, cast metal, mk, $1,200 to **1,400.00**
Kewpie, brass door knocker, mk Elpec England, 5" **150.00**
Kewpie, bsk, Buttonhole, arms up, sticker, 2", $225 to **250.00**
Kewpie, bsk, Confederate Soldier, w/rifle, sgn, 3" or 4½", ea **500.00**
Kewpie, bsk, Confederate Soldier, w/rifle, sgn, 5½" **600.00**
Kewpie, bsk, Farmer w/flowers, sgn, 4½" **500.00**
Kewpie, bsk, frozen arms, Japan mk, 3¼" **85.00**
Kewpie, bsk, Governor, in tan 'wicker' chair, sgn, 3½" **500.00**
Kewpie, bsk, Governor, Japan, lg **250.00**
Kewpie, bsk, Hottentot, jtd arms, sgn, 7¾", $875 to **925.00**
Kewpie, bsk, Huggers, sgn, 3½", $300 to **350.00**
Kewpie, bsk, jtd arms, sgn ft, 12", EX **1,300.00**
Kewpie, bsk, jtd hips & shoulders, sgn, 4" **525.00**
Kewpie, bsk, lady bug on toe, sgn, w/orig bug, 3½" **750.00**
Kewpie, bsk, lady bug on toe, sgn, w/orig bug, 4½" **900.00**
Kewpie, bsk, Lawyer, sgn, 3½" **800.00**
Kewpie, bsk, on inkwell, sgn, 3½" **625.00**
Kewpie, bsk, on tummy, heart sticker, sgn, 4" **550.00**
Kewpie, bsk, playing drum, sticker, mk, sgn, 3½" **1,800.00**
Kewpie, bsk, reading book, unmk (German quality), 2" **400.00**
Kewpie, bsk, reading book on lap, sgn, 3½" **825.00**
Kewpie, bsk, seated w/mandolin, sgn, 2" **300.00**
Kewpie, bsk, sgn on ft, 12", EX **1,300.00**
Kewpie, bsk, sitting, attached to basket, sgn, 3" **800.00**
Kewpie, bsk, sitting, heart label, sgn, 3½" **525.00**
Kewpie, bsk, sitting, holding rose, sgn, 1¾" **350.00**
Kewpie, bsk, sitting at tea table, mk Goebel, 4½", minimum ..**2,000.00**
Kewpie, bsk, Soldier, Kaiser helmet/rifle, sgn, 4½", minimum **850.00**
Kewpie, bsk, standing, heart sticker on chest, 5" **125.00**
Kewpie, bsk, standing, sgn, German, 4½", EX **115.00**
Kewpie, bsk, Sweeper, sgn, 3½", EX **400.00**
Kewpie, bsk, Thinker, sgn, 5" **425.00**
Kewpie, bsk, Thinker, sgn, 6" **500.00**
Kewpie, bsk, Traveler, sgn, 3½" **450.00**
Kewpie, bsk, w/baby chick, 1913 sticker on bk, 2" **350.00**
Kewpie, bsk, w/blk cat, Germany, sgn, 1920s, lg **525.00**
Kewpie, bsk, w/blk cat, Japan, 1920s, lg **375.00**
Kewpie, bsk, w/Doodle Dog, Japan, 2½" **400.00**
Kewpie, bsk, w/guitar beside tall vase, sgn, EX, $825 to **950.00**
Kewpie, bsk, w/rabbit, sgn, 2½" **400.00**

Kewpie, bsk, w/teddy bear, sgn, $525 to **700.00**
Kewpie, bsk, w/umbrella & Doodle Dog, sgn, 3½" **1,650.00**
Kewpie, bsk head, jtd, chubby toddler, JDK, 10" **4,200.00**
Kewpie, bsk head/glass eyes, cloth body, sgn, 12", minimum ...**3,000.00**
Kewpie, bsk head/glass eyes, compo body, mk Kestner, 10", NM ..**4,200.00**
Kewpie, bsk head/pnt eyes, cloth body, sgn, 12", $1,600 to **2,000.00**
Kewpie, bsk shoulder head, cloth body, sgn, 6-7", $600 to **700.00**
Kewpie, celluloid, Blk, German, sticker, 5", $140 to **200.00**
Kewpie, celluloid, Japan, 2" **45.00**
Kewpie, celluloid, Japan, 5" **90.00**
Kewpie, celluloid, Japan, 9" **175.00**
Kewpie, cloth, mask face, original clothes, Kreuger, 12" **250.00**
Kewpie, cloth, 1-pc body w/face mask, Kreuger, 16" **300.00**
Kewpie, compo, Hottentot, red wings, heart, 11", $450 to **500.00**
Kewpie, red plush, vinyl face, Knickerbocker, lg **80.00**
Kewpies, bsk, 2 give roses to girl (flocked dress), Goebel, minimum ..**4,500.00**
Magazine cover, Santa w/11 Kewpies, Ladies' Home Journal, '27 ....**55.00**
Napkin ring, SP Kewpie, mk, $250 to **275.00**
Paper dolls, Ragsy & Ritzy, c O'Neill, 1930s, EX+ **350.00**
Place-card holder, Kewpie, bsk, playing mandolin, mk, 3" **325.00**
Plate, child's tea; tumbling bare Kewpies, gold trim, 5¼" **68.00**
Plate, 6 Kewpies, Royal Rudolstadt, 7" **115.00**
Plate, 7 action Kewpies, Royal Rudolstadt, sgn **115.00**
Poster, Kewpie Baseball Team, O'Neill, 9x6"+½" border, M **55.00**
Puzzle, Hallmark Kewpie Puzzle, Springbok, 20¼" sq, M **30.00**
Shakers, Kewpie Thinker, porc, Japan, pr **50.00**
Shakers, Kewpies on tummies, pr **60.00**
Shakers, Thinkers, pr **75.00**
Spoon, SP, Kewpie **150.00**
Stickpin, sterling, Kewpie Thinker, mk, ⅝", $85 to **100.00**
Talcum container, china, Kewpie/wreath/roses, not O'Neill, old **90.00**
Talcum container, tin, 8", EX **195.00**
Tea cup & saucer w/plate, Army Kewpies, sgn, Germany **175.00**
Tea set, Action Kewpies, c O'Neill Wilson, Germany, 22-pc ...**1,300.00**
Tea set, Kewpies, Germany, service for 2, doll sz, MIB **975.00**
Tea set, Kewpies w/gold, O'Neill/Bavaria, child's, 15-pc **550.00**
Tea set, Royal Rudolstadt, sgn O'Neill Wilson, 12-pc, EX **900.00**
Tray, Kewpie makes lemonade, tin litho, 13x10½", VG, $500 to **575.00**
Tray, W/Kewpish Love From Rose O'Neill, Kewpie, 3½", $275 to .**750.00**

Onion Pattern

The familiar pattern known to collectors as Onion acquired its name through a case of mistaken identity. Designed in the early 1700s by Johann Haroldt of the Meissen factory in Germany, the pattern was a mixture of earlier Oriental designs. One of its components was a stylized peach, which was mistaken for an onion; as a result, the pattern became known by that name. Usually found in blue, an occasional piece may also be found in pink and red. The pattern is commonly associated with Meissen, but it has been reproduced by many others including Villeroy and Boch and Royal Copenhagen.

Blue Danube is a modern line of Onion-patterned dinnerware produced in Japan and distributed by Lipper International of Wallingford, Connecticut. One hundred twenty-five items are available in porcelain; it is sold in most large stores with china departments.

Basket, rtcl, shallow, Meissen, 1890s, 7" **165.00**
Bouillon cup & saucer, Meissen **45.00**
Bowl, divided; Meissen 'imperfect' mk, 13½" dia **225.00**
Bowl, Meissen, 8½" **295.00**
Bowl, notched corners, Meissen Xd swords, sq, 9" **220.00**
Bowl, serving; Meissen, 8x13" dia, NM, pr **250.00**
Butter pat, Germany **28.00**

Cake plate, 10" dia 155.00
Cake stand, Meissen, 4½x13" 300.00
Canister, Zucker, stenciled, ped base 70.00
Chamberstick, 6" 80.00
Charger, Meissen late Xd-swords mk, 16" dia, EX ..225.00
Compote, rnd openwork bowl w/5 floral medallions, Meissen, 9" ..375.00
Creamer, Meissen, 3½" 60.00
Cup & saucer, Germany 35.00
Funnel, loop hdl 125.00
Gravy boat, Meissen, 4½x12" 100.00
Jar, instant coffee; Japan 20.00
Letter opener, brass blade, Germany 40.00
Masher, lg 185.00
Plate, bread & butter; Hutschenreuther 15.00
Plate, bread & butter; Meissen, 6¼" 28.00
Plate, dessert; Meissen, 8¼", 10 for 250.00
Plate, dinner; Meissen, 1900s, 10½" 70.00
Plate, dinner; Meissen, 9½" 60.00

Platter, scalloped rim, Meissen, 17x11", $350.00.

Platter, fish; Meissen, 24¾" 500.00
Platter, Meissen, 13½x8¾" 85.00
Platter, Meissen crown mk, 18½x13", EX 150.00
Platter, rolled ends, Meissen, 16½x12" 250.00
Platter, scalloped, Meissen Xd swords, 21x15" 300.00
Platter, stamped Meissen w/a star, 20x10" 170.00
Rolling pin, heavy porc, unmk, Germany, 18" 300.00
Salt box, rnd, wood lid, wall mt, Made in Japan, 7" 100.00
Spoon, 10" 95.00
Tray, bread; 16x11" 175.00
Tureen, Meissen crown mk, 8½x13" 300.00
Tureen, Meissen Xd swords, 11x15" across hdls 400.00
Utensil holder, wall mt, 15-slot, 5½x12x10" 495.00
Vase, ftd, Meissen Xd swords, 5" 140.00

Opalescent Glass

First made in England in 1870, opalescent glass became popular in America around the turn of the century. Its name comes from the milky-white opalescent trim that defines the lines of the pattern. It was produced in table sets, novelties, toothpick holders, vases, and lamps. For further information we recommend *The Standard Encyclopedia of Opalescent Glass* by Bill Edwards (Collector Books).

Abalone, bowl, wht 26.00
Acorn Burrs (& Bark), bowl, sauce; wht 40.00
Alaska, bride's basket, bl 295.00
Alaska, creamer, bl 90.00
Alaska, tumbler, vaseline 75.00
Arabian Nights, tumbler, wht 50.00
Argonaut Shell (Nautilus), bowl, master; wht 120.00
Argonaut Shell (Nautilus), shakers, vaseline, rare, pr (+) 250.00

Argonaut Shell (Nautilus), sugar bowl, bl 250.00
Ascot, bowl, vaseline 45.00
Astro, bowl, gr 35.00
Autumn Leaves, banana bowl, wht 50.00

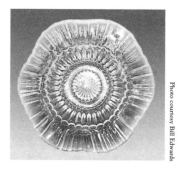

Barbells, bowl, white opalescent, $30.00.

Basketweave (Open Edge), bowl, vaseline 25.00
Basketweave (Open Edge), console set, wht, 3-pc 150.00
Beaded Cable, bowl, bl, ftd 50.00
Beaded Cable, rose bowl, wht, ftd 45.00
Beaded Drapes, bowl, gr, ftd 40.00
Beaded Drapes, rose bowl, wht, ftd 40.00
Beaded Fan, rose bowl, bl, ftd 50.00
Beaded Fleur-de-Lis, compote, bl 50.00
Beaded Moon & Stars, bowl, bl, recent 40.00
Beaded Ovals in Sand, creamer, gr 80.00
Beaded Ovals in Sand, sauce bowl, bl 35.00
Beaded Ovals in Sand, shakers, gr, pr 90.00
Beaded Ovals in Sand, tumbler, bl 95.00
Beaded Stars, advertising bowl, bl 240.00
Beaded Stars, bowl, gr 55.00
Beads & Bark, vase, wht, ftd 60.00
Beatty Honeycomb, bowl, master; wht 45.00
Beatty Honeycomb, butter dish, wht 135.00
Beatty Honeycomb, celery vase, wht 75.00
Beatty Honeycomb, sugar bowl, bl 120.00
Beatty Rib, celery vase, bl 80.00
Beatty Rib, creamer, wht 40.00
Beatty Rib, shakers, wht, pr 60.00
Beatty Swirl, butter dish, wht 150.00
Beatty Swirl, celery vase, wht 60.00
Beatty Swirl, pitcher, vaseline 190.00
Beatty Swirl, spooner, bl 75.00
Blocked Thumbprint & Beads (Fishscale & Beads), nappy, wht ...30.00
Blown Twist, pitcher, bl 550.00
Blown Twist, sugar shaker, wht 130.00
Blown Twist, tumbler, gr 175.00
Brideshead, creamer, bl 65.00
Brideshead, tumbler, bl 90.00
Bubble Lattice, finger bowl, bl 45.00
Bubble Lattice, sugar bowl, wht 70.00
Bubble Lattice, tumbler, gr 50.00
Bull's Eye, water bottle, wht 135.00
Buttons & Braids, pitcher, water; cranberry 495.00
Buttons & Braids, tumbler, gr 40.00
Carousel, bowl, wht 25.00
Cashews, bowl, bl 35.00
Chippendale, basket, bl 60.00
Christmas Pearls, shakers, wht, pr 175.00
Chrysanthemum Base Swirl, bowl, master; cranberry 160.00

Chrysanthemum Base Swirl, celery vase, bl 135.00
Chrysanthemum Base Swirl, mustard pot, cranberry 225.00
Chrysanthemum Base Swirl, sugar bowl, bl 200.00
Circled Scroll, jelly compote, bl 150.00
Circled Scroll, pitcher, gr 395.00
Circled Scroll, sugar bowl, wht 85.00
Coin Spot, bowl, master; gr 40.00
Coin Spot, tumble-up, cranberry 275.00
Consolidated Crisscross, butter dish, wht 425.00
Consolidated Crisscross, finger bowl, cranberry 120.00
Consolidated Crisscross, tumbler, wht 100.00
Cornucopia, vase, bl, hdls 75.00
Curtain Optic, pitcher, vaseline 140.00
Daffodils, tumbler, gr, rare 200.00
Dahlia Twist, epergne, wht 100.00
Daisy & Fern, creamer, wht 60.00
Daisy in Crisscross, pitcher, cranberry 850.00
Daisy in Crisscross, tumbler, bl 60.00
Diamond & Daisy, basket, bl, hdld 50.00
Diamond Spearhead, jelly compote, wht 75.00
Diamond Spearhead, sugar bowl, wht 95.00
Diamond Spearhead, tumbler, gr 70.00
Dolly Madison, pitcher, gr 400.00
Dolly Madison, sauce bowl, wht 25.00
Double Greek Key, bowl, master; wht 60.00
Double Greek Key, mustard pot, bl 300.00
Double Greek Key, sugar bowl, bl 175.00
Dragon Lady, rose bowl, bl 45.00
Duchess, butter dish, wht 150.00
Duchess, lamp shade, wht 75.00
Duchess, pitcher, canary 175.00
Everglades, butter dish, bl 360.00
Everglades, sauce bowl, bl, oval 40.00
Fan, bowl, master; bl 75.00
Fan, butter dish, gr 385.00
Fern, celery vase, cranberry 145.00
Fern, pitcher, wht 175.00
Fern, sugar bowl, bl 200.00
Flora, butter dish, bl 275.00
Flora, jelly compote, canary 140.00
Flora, spooner, wht 90.00
Fluted Scrolls (Klondyke), bowl, master; canary 70.00
Fluted Scrolls (Klondyke), epergne, wht, sm 55.00
Fluted Scrolls (Klondyke), pitcher, bl 240.00
Gonterman (Adonis) Swirl, creamer, amber 125.00
Gonterman (Adonis) Swirl, shade, bl 100.00
Gonterman (Adonis) Swirl, tumbler, bl 90.00
Greek Key & Ribs, bowl, bl 60.00
Hearts & Flowers, compote, wht 60.00
Hobnail, butter dish, cobalt, 4-ftd 100.00
Hobnail, finger bowl, bl 65.00
Hobnail, tumbler, bl 70.00
Hobnail, water tray, wht 110.00
Hobnail & Panelled Thumbprint, bowl, master; bl 75.00
Hobnail & Panelled Thumbprint, butter dish, vaseline 170.00
Hobnail in Square (Vesta), sugar bowl, wht 130.00
Honeycomb (Blown), cracker jar, cranberry 395.00
Honeycomb & Clover, spooner, bl 150.00
Honeycomb & Clover, sugar bowl, gr 175.00
Idyll, creamer, gr 130.00
Idyll, sauce bowl, bl 30.00
Idyll, tumbler, wht 50.00
Inside Ribbing, bowl, master; bl 65.00
Inside Ribbing, jelly compote, bl 65.00

Inside Ribbing, sugar bowl, wht 90.00
Intaglio, spooner, wht 40.00
Intaglio, tumbler, bl 110.00
Inverted Fan & Feather, pitcher, wht 300.00
Inverted Fan & Feather, rose bowl, vaseline 85.00
Inverted Fan & Feather, sugar bowl, bl 250.00
Iris with Meander, jelly compote, bl 55.00
Iris with Meander, pickle dish, canary 75.00
Jackson, epergne, bl, sm 145.00
Jackson, spooner, wht 60.00
Jackson, tumbler, canary 65.00
Jewel & Fan, bowl, gr 55.00
Jewel & Flower, creamer, vaseline 150.00
Jewel & Flower, novelty bowl, bl 50.00
Jewel & Flower, sugar bowl, wht 90.00
Jewel & Flower, tumbler, bl 90.00
Jewelled Heart, compote, wht 45.00
Jewelled Heart, creamer, bl 80.00
Jewelled Heart, novelty bowl, gr 40.00
Jolly Bear, bowl, bl, rare 250.00
Lady Chippendale, compote, cobalt, tall 90.00
Laura (Single Flower Framed), bowl, bl, scarce 55.00
Linking Rings, bowl, bl 60.00
Little Nell, vase, gr 35.00
Lords & Ladies, sugar bowl, bl 70.00
Lorna, vase, wht 30.00
Lustre Flute, butter dish, wht 200.00
Lustre Flute, custard cup, wht 40.00
Lustre Flute, pitcher, bl 375.00
Maple Leaf, jelly compote, canary 65.00
Mary Ann, vase, bl 95.00
Melon Optic Swirl, bowl, gr, rare 90.00
Melon Swirl, pitcher, bl 450.00
Netted Roses, bowl, bl 70.00
Northern Star, banana bowl, wht 50.00
Northern Star, bowl, wht 60.00
Old Man Winter, basket, gr, sm 100.00
Opal Spiral, sugar bowl, bl 195.00
Over-All Hob, butter dish, bl 240.00
Over-All Hob, finger bowl, vaseline 55.00
Over-All Hob, spooner, wht 50.00
Overlapping Leaves (Leaf Tiers), bowl, wht, ftd 40.00
Overlapping Leaves (Leaf Tiers), rose bowl, gr, ftd 75.00
Palisades, novelty vase, wht 35.00
Palm & Scroll, bowl, bl, ftd 45.00
Palm Beach, creamer, vaseline 135.00
Palm Beach, jelly compote, bl, rare 175.00
Palm Beach, pitcher, bl 450.00
Panelled Flowers, nut cup, wht, ftd 50.00
Panelled Holly, bowl, master; wht 135.00
Panelled Holly, sugar bowl, bl 350.00
Panelled Sprig, cruet, wht 135.00
Peacock Tail, tumbler, gr 90.00
Pearl Flowers, nut bowl, gr, ftd 45.00
Pearl Flowers, rose bowl, wht, ftd 45.00
Pearls & Scales, compote, gr 60.00
Pearls & Scales, rose bowl, canary, rare 55.00
Piasa Bird, bowl, bl 55.00
Piasa Bird, spittoon whimsey, wht 80.00
Pine Cones & Leaves, bowl, wht 70.00
Pineapple & Fan, vase, canary 400.00
Poinsettia, pitcher, bl, from $350 to 375.00
Poinsettia, tumbler, cranberry 125.00
Polka Dot, toothpick holder, wht 295.00

Polka Dot, tumbler, bl 70.00
Primrose (Daffodils Variant), pitcher, wht 300.00
Prince Albert & Victoria, creamer, bl, ftd 65.00
Prince William, creamer, canary 60.00
Prince William, tumbler, bl 40.00
Princess Diana, creamer, bl 55.00
Princess Diana, plate, vaseline, crimped edge 60.00
Princess Diana, salad bowl, bl 55.00
Queen's Petticoat, vase, bl 85.00
Quilted Pillow Sham, creamer, bl 70.00
Reflecting Diamonds, bowl, gr 60.00
Regal (Northwood's), butter dish, wht 125.00
Regal (Northwood's), celery vase, gr 175.00
Reverse Drapery, bowl, gr 45.00
Reverse Swirl, butter dish, wht 135.00
Reverse Swirl, cruet, canary 170.00
Reverse Swirl, custard cup, cranberry 150.00
Reverse Swirl, spooner, bl 120.00
Ribbed Coin Spot, pitcher, cranberry 1,050.00
Ribbed Coin Spot, sugar shaker, cranberry 550.00
Ribbed Lattice, butter dish, bl 215.00
Ribbed Lattice, creamer, cranberry 400.00
Ribbed Lattice, tumbler, wht 40.00
Ribbed Spiral, jelly compote, canary 65.00
Ribbed Spiral, sauce bowl, bl 30.00
Ribbed Spiral, sugar bowl, wht 150.00
Richelieu, jelly compote, bl 75.00
Richelieu, nappy, wht, hdld 70.00
Rose Spray, compote, amethyst 60.00
Scottish Moor, pitcher, rubena 400.00
Scottish Moor, vase, bl, fluted 140.00
Scroll w/Acanthus, sauce bowl, canary 25.00
Scroll w/Acanthus, sugar bowl, bl 145.00
Scroll w/Acanthus, tumbler, canary 75.00
Seaweed, celery vase, cranberry 175.00
Seaweed, creamer, wht 95.00
Seaweed, pitcher, bl 350.00
Shell, Beaded; bowl, master; bl 125.00
Shell, Beaded; sugar bowl, wht 150.00
Shell & Wild Rose, novelty bowl, gr, open edge 55.00
Sir Lancelot, bowl, bl, ftd 67.00
Somerset, tumbler, bl, 3" 30.00
Spanish Lace, butter dish, canary 395.00
Spanish Lace, cracker jar, bl 700.00
Spanish Lace, creamer, cranberry 175.00
Spanish Lace, water bottle, cranberry 425.00
Spokes & Wheels, bowl, wht 37.00
Squirrel & Acorn, vase, wht 75.00
Squirrel & Acorn, whimsey, bl 90.00
Star & Stripes, pitcher, wht 240.00
Stripe, vase, wht 60.00
Stripe, Wide; pitcher, bl 250.00
Sunburst on Shield (Diadem), bowl, master; bl 140.00
Sunburst on Shield (Diadem), pitcher, canary 475.00
Surf Spray, pickle dish, wht 40.00
Swag w/Brackets, bowl, wht 30.00
Swag w/Brackets, cruet, bl 500.00
Swag w/Brackets, spooner, wht 55.00
Swag w/Brackets, tumbler, gr 65.00
Swirl, cheese dish, wht 240.00
Swirl, sguar shaker, bl 135.00
Swirl, spooner, wht 40.00
Swirl, sugar bowl, gr 95.00
Swirling Maize, salad bowl, bl 95.00

Thousand Eye, celery vase, wht 90.00
Thousand Eye, tumbler, wht 25.00
Thread & Rib, epergne, bl 800.00
Three Fruits, bowl, bl, scarce 200.00
Tokyo, creamer, wht 40.00
Tokyo, jelly compote, bl 55.00
Tokyo, tumbler, gr 70.00
Tree Trunk, vase, wht 75.00
Twist, butter dish, wht, mini 170.00
Twist, spooner, canary, mini 80.00

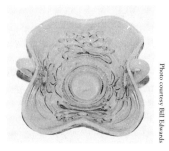

Photo courtesy Bill Edwards

Waterlily and Cattails, bonbon, blue opalescent, $35.00.

Water Lily & Cattails, pitcher, wht 200.00
Water Lily & Cattails, plate, bl 45.00
Water Lily & Cattails, sauce bowl, amethyst 35.00
Water Lily & Cattails, sugar bowl, bl 200.00
Wild Bouquet, bowl, master; bl 195.00
Wild Bouquet, jelly compote, gr 130.00
Wild Bouquet, tumbler, wht 40.00
William & Mary, compote, canary 90.00
Windows (Plain), finger bowl, bl 50.00
Windows (Plain), tumbler, cranberry 110.00
Windows (Swirled), mustard jar, bl 75.00
Windows (Swirled), plate, cranberry, 2 szs, ea 250.00
Windows (Swirled), spooner, wht 70.00
Wreath & Shell, novelty bowl, bl 70.00
Wreath & Shell, rose bowl, canary 80.00
Wreath & Shell, sauce bowl, bl 27.00
Wreath & Shell, sugar bowl, canary 150.00

Orientalia

The art of the Orient is an area of collecting currently enjoying strong collector interest, not only in those examples that are truly 'antique' but in the 20th-century items as well. Because of the many aspects involved in a study of Orientalia, we can only try through brief comments to acquaint the reader with some of the more readily available examples. We suggest you refer to specialized reference sources for more detailed information. See also specific categories.

Key:
Ch — Chinese	FV — Famille Verte
ctp — contemporary	gb — guard border
cvg — carving	hdwd — hardwood
drw — drawer	Jp — Japan
Dy — Dynasty	Ko — Korean
E — export	lcq — lacquer
FJ — Famille Juane	mdl — medallion
FN — Famille Noire	rswd — rosewood
FR — Famille Rose	tkwd — teakwood

Bronze

Candle holders, dragon & phoenix, lotus drip pan, Jp, 20", pr **160.00**
Crane pr, 2 w/head trn, 2nd w/neck out, detailed, 71", 64" **2,750.00**
Figure, Sumo wrestler w/hands up holding bowl, 20th C, 19½" .**290.00**
Koro, twin beast-head hdls, bird reserves, Jp, 16" **250.00**
Sculpture, Buddha on open throne, Ch, 19th C, 13¾" **200.00**
Vase, birds & foliage, baluster, Jp, 14½", pr **260.00**
Vase, spherical, bamboo branch hdl w/birds, drilled, Jp, 12" **220.00**

Furniture

Fire screen, cvd tkwd & lcq w/appl ivory/bone, Ch, 1900s, 42" ..**125.00**
Screen, 4 hinged blk lcq panels: pagoda scene, 19th C, 72x64" ..**550.00**
Stand, cvd wood, bamboo-like hexagonal, Jp, 13" H **110.00**
Table, tkwd cvd animal apron, cvd supports, Ch, 40x50x17" **625.00**

Lacquer

Lacquerware is found in several colors, but the one most likely to be encountered is cinnabar. It is often intricately carved, sometimes involving hundreds of layers built one at a time on a metal or wooden base. Later pieces remain red, while older examples tend to darken.

Figure, Buddha before ornate madorla, Jp, 17½" **225.00**
Figure, dignitary w/long mustache & beard, cvd wood/gilt, 15" ..**150.00**
Shrine, cvd exterior w/gilt, text on diaper ground, Ch, 17½" **325.00**
Shrine, int w/seated Bodhisattva on lotus, gilt, Jp, 14" **300.00**
Tea caddy, cut pewter inserts, Ch E, 19th C, 5¾x9¼x6½" **400.00**

Netsukes

A netsuke is a miniature Japanese carving made with two holes called the himitoshi, either channeled or within the carved design. As kimonos (the outer garment of the time) had no pockets, the Japanese man hung his pipe, tobacco pouch, or other daily necessities from his waist sash. The most highly valued accessory was a nest of little drawers called an inro, in which they carried snuff or sometimes opium. The netsuke was the toggle that secured them. Although most are of ivory, others were made of bone, wood, metal, porcelain, or semiprecious stones. Some were inlaid or lacquered. They are found in many forms — figurals the most common, mythological beasts the most desirable. They range in size from 1" up to 3", which was the maximum size allowed by law. Many netsukes represented the owner's profession, religion, or hobbies. Scenes from the daily life of Japan at that time were often depicted in the tiny carvings. The more detailed the carving, the greater the value.

Careful study is required to recognize the quality of the netsuke. Many have been made in Hong Kong in recent years; and even though some are very well carved, these are considered copies and avoided by the serious collector. There are many books that will help you learn to recognize quality netsukes, and most reputable dealers are glad to assist you. Use your magnifying glass to check for repairs. In the listings that follow, netsukes are ivory unless noted otherwise; 'stain' indicates a color wash.

Baby crawling, sepia washes, sgn Ryomin, late 1800s, 2" **635.00**
Boar on beafy bed, inlaid eyes/stain, Kaigyokusai, 1¾" **10,700.00**
Camellia cvd in manju form, dk stain, 19th C, 1½" dia **350.00**
Dbl masks w/blk pnt & red pigment, 19th C, 2¾", 1¾" **550.00**
Man milling grain, mouse at his ft, 19th C, 2" **315.00**
Monkey seated, sad face, inlay/pigment, 1800s, 1¼" **575.00**
Monkey w/fruit protects baby, EX stain/inlay, Kaigyoku, 1⅜" ..**5,175.00**
Oni striding, boxwood, EX details, sgn Masakazu, 1850s, 2" **1,840.00**

Professional sneezer w/feather in hand, wood, Maiji, 1⅜" **465.00**
Shoki subduing Oni, 19th C, minor damage, 2¼" **130.00**
Shoki w/lg pipe on lion, sgn Kazumasa, late 19th C, 1½" **700.00**
Skeleton holding skull, sepia/blk wash, 19th C, 1⅜" **550.00**
Tigress & cub at play, red/blk stain, 19th C, 1½" **460.00**
3 seated karako w/instruments, sgn Innan, 1¼", EX **435.00**

Porcelain

Chinese export ware was designed to appeal to Western tastes and was often made to order. During the 18th century, vast amounts were shipped to Europe and on westward. Much of this fine porcelain consisted of dinnerware lines that were given specific pattern names. Rose Mandarin, Fitzhugh, Armorial, Rose Medallion, and Canton are but a few of the more familiar.

Vase, Famille Noire, multicolor lotus decoration, China, late 1800s, restored, 46", $1,200.00.

Basket, seascape/floral, bl on wht, Jp, 4½x6⅝" **90.00**
Bowl, Ch, dragons, bl underglaze, Kangxi, 1700s, 3½x7", VG **850.00**
Bowl, court scenes, diapering, Mandarin palette, 1890s, 10⅜" ...**385.00**
Bowl, E, clouds, purple diapering, ca 1900, 9½" **220.00**
Bowl, E, court scenes, Mandarin palette, 18th C, rstr, 10" **110.00**
Bowl, E, figures in panels, diapering, Mandarin palette, 9" **300.00**
Bowl, E, flowers in basket & sprays, ca 1900, 7½" **170.00**
Bowl, E, FR, nobles in landscapes, ca 1900, 10¼" **385.00**
Bowl, E, FR, nobles/animals/birds, late 1700s, rstr, 5x10½" **220.00**
Bowl, figures/diapering/cracked ice, Kangxi, ca 1700, 3¾x7" ..**1,350.00**
Bowl, FV, 5-petal lotus form, center reserve, 15½" **1,100.00**
Bowl, punch; E, Bl Fitzhugh, scalloped, rstr, 11" **500.00**
Bowl, punch; E, landscape reserves/florals, rstr, 9" **650.00**
Bowl, salad; E, landscape, cut corners, mc festoons int, 9½" ...**1,800.00**
Brush pot, 2 ladies' portraits, early 1800s, 5⅛", G **150.00**
Charger, E, FR, turq reverse, Qianlong, 15½", EX **600.00**
Ewer, Arita, figures/landscapes, bl-gray, late 1600s, 7¼" **1,200.00**
Incense burner, robed man on rock base, seal mks, 1880s, 12" ...**150.00**
Jar, E, FR, nobles in procession, 8x9¼", pr **165.00**
Jar, wine; garden scenes, Ch, 19th C, 7½x7½" **165.00**
Jardiniere, landscape, bl on wht, Ch, 19th C, 8½x11" **700.00**
Jug, Arita, figures in landscape/flowers, 1600s, Jp, 8¼", EX **650.00**
Mug, E, floral, cylindrical, twisted hdl, 18th C, 6" **330.00**
Mug, E, floral sprays & swags, bbl form, rstr, 6¼" **450.00**
Mug, E, florals/swags, bbl form, Ch, 6½", EX **450.00**
Oil/vinegar pots, E, arms of De Wendt, Holland/1752, 5⅛", pr ..**920.00**
Planter, landscape reserves stenciled in cobalt, Jp, 16" **220.00**
Plate, E, armorial decor, pierced rim, 7½", pr **1,350.00**
Plate, E, figures in garden, 9" **130.00**
Plate, Rose Canton, Ch, 8¼", pr **175.00**
Platter, E, Arms of Grant, FR enamels w/court scene **3,300.00**
Platter, E, Bl Fitzhugh, late 1700s, 16¾" **950.00**
Platter, E, Bl Fitzhugh, late 1700s, 18½", NM **1,200.00**
Platter, E, garden pattern, crest & motto, w/drain, 18¾" **2,100.00**

Platter, E, lady on boat, Ch, 1770, 13⅛" **700.00**
Platter, E, Thousand Butterflies, 1850s, 15" **400.00**
Punch bowl, E, figure reserves, diapering, 1770, 10¼", VG **800.00**
Punch bowl, E, figures/birds in reserves, 9¼" **400.00**
Punch bowl, E, palace vignettes, bl quilted border, 10½" **500.00**
Shrimp dish, Bl Fitzhugh, 10½", EX **500.00**
Sugar bowl, E, Nanking w/gold, strawberry finial, 6½" **325.00**
Tea service, E, grisaille decor, 18th C, partial set, 17-pc **660.00**
Tea set, E, Mandarin palette, child's, ca 1780, 17-pc set **3,300.00**
Tea/coffee set, E, sepia decor, 1800s, 8½" pot+cr/sug+15 pcs **750.00**
Teapot, E, Armorial, De Wendt, w/gold, Holland/1752, 5½" .**1,725.00**
Teapot, E, drum form, braided hdl, berry lid, 1790s, 6" **400.00**
Teapot, E, figures in garden, braided hdl, 1840s, 6½" **270.00**
Teapot, E, floral, swan's neck spout, pagoda finial, 1700s **360.00**
Teapot, E, mc landscape reserves, bamboo spout/hdl, 7½" **1,100.00**
Teapot, E, reserves on blk diaper ground, rstr hdl, 6" **260.00**
Teapot, E, wood-like spout/hdl, peach finial, 18th C, 6" **600.00**
Tureen, E, Bl Fitzhugh, braided hdls, pineapple finial, 14" **1,400.00**
Undertray, Orange Fitzhugh, 8¼", EX **260.00**
Urn, E, FV, figures on baluster form, 14½" **275.00**
Vase, appl dragons w/pearl, florals, bulbous, Ch, 14½", EX **600.00**
Vase, E, figures in reserves, dragon hdls, ca 1900, 11¼" **550.00**
Vase, E, landscape/floral panels on cobalt, 16" **770.00**
Vase, E, landscape panels/red scrollwork, Jp, 19th C, rprs, 13" ...**140.00**
Vase, FR, mandarin scenes, gr/gold diapering, 1860s, 24" **3,000.00**
Vase, Ming-style flowers, mask/ring hdls, Ch, 18th C, 15" **600.00**
Vase, warriors on crackle, foo dog hdls, 19th C, 13", pr **500.00**
Warming dish, E, Nanking, 19th C, 11½" **180.00**

Rugs

The 'Oriental' or Eastern rug market has enjoyed a renewal of interest in recent years as collectors have become aware of the fact that some of the semiantique rugs (those sixty to one hundred years old) may be had at a price within the range of the average buyer.

Baluch, vining colums on camel, red border, late 1800s, 72x36" ...**460.00**
E Persian Meshad, ivory mdl on navy & red, 1930s, 110x129" ...**2,000.00**
Ersari, 3 columns of 8 Tauk Noska guls on red, 1890s, 116x42" **700.00**
Ersari, 3 rows of 6 8-sided guls on rust, 1890s, 114x90" **750.00**
Hamadan, Herati on navy, gold/rust borders, 1905, 40x104" ...**1,300.00**
Hamadan, lg hex mdl on Herati design on ivory, 1890s, 78x64" ...**865.00**
Heriz, sm star mdl/vines on red, bl border, 1940s, 69x56" **575.00**
Karabagh, flowering plants, mc on camel, 1899, 68x41" **1,600.00**
Karabagh, rows of boteh on navy, red dmn border, 108x48" **800.00**
Karadja, 3 mdls/sm motifs on red, bl border, 1900s, 54x44" **550.00**
Kazak, 3 columns of dmns on red, ivory border, 1880s, 64x44" ...**700.00**
Kazak, 3 gabled mdls/6 octagons on navy, 1899, 92x50" **1,380.00**
Kazak, 4 bl dmn mdls w/gold & bl-gr on red, 1890s, 116x70" ..**2,185.00**
Kazak, 4 dmn mdls on red, bl border, ca 1890, 84x40" **865.00**
Kirman, bl/rose mdl on ivory, bl borders, 1900s, 120x165" **1,500.00**
Kirman, mc mdl/border on ivory, 185x118" **2,200.00**
Kirman, mc overall design on bl, mc border, ca 1900, 115x170" ...**400.00**
Kurd, dmn flowerhead lattice on bl, red border, 1890s, 67x52" ..**700.00**
Kurd, overall Herati on dk bl, flowerhead border, 74x50" **460.00**
Kurd, stepped 6-sided mdls w/anchor pendants, 1900s, 76x44" ..**1,150.00**
NW Persia, rows of filigree-style boteh on red, 1900s, 140x36" ..**865.00**
NW Persia, 3 dmn mdls on camel, rust border, 1890s, 140x46" ..**635.00**
NW Persia, 3 indented mdls on bl, ivory border, 1890s, 69x42" .**700.00**
Oushak, sm mdl on gold, bl/gold borders, 1900, 104x139" **2,000.00**
Oushak, 2 mdls on salmon w/gr borders, wool on wool, 108x156" ...**5,000.00**
Persian, Mihrab design, late 1800s, 140x108" **3,250.00**
S Caucasian, 2 lg mc mdls on med bl, 2 borders, 1880s, 78x50" **500.00**
S Caucasian, 4 sq mdls on navy, ivory border, 1890s, 140x42" ..**1,100.00**

Shiraz, navy mdl on red, brn borders, 61x102" **650.00**
Shirvan, Afshan variant on bl, w/border, early 1900s, 122x67" ..**1,035.00**
Shirvan, palmets & shields on navy, tan border, 60x45" **500.00**
Shirvan, 3 8-sided mdls on dk bl, ivory border, 1890s, 74x45" ...**1,035.00**
Tekke, 4 columns of 8-sided guls on dk red, ca 1940, 120x76" ...**1,150.00**
Tekke Ensi, bl plants on rust, tree border, 1880s, 60x45" **460.00**

Snuff Bottles

The Chinese were introduced to snuff in the 17th century, and their carved and painted snuff bottles typify their exquisite taste and workmanship. These small bottles, seldom measuring over 2½", were made of amber, jade, ivory, and cinnabar; tiny spoons were often attached to their stoppers. By the 18th century, some were being made of porcelain, others were of glass with delicate interior designs tediously reverse painted with minuscule brushes sometimes containing a single hair. Copper and brass were used but to no great extent.

Bohemian glass, Snowflake pattern, blk to wht, ca 1900, 2½" **75.00**
Cloisonne, mc floral, seal on underside, 20th C, 2⅝" **300.00**
Glass, brn w/tiny gold specks to imitate goldstone, 19th C, 3" ...**650.00**
Glass, peacock bl, 19th C, 2¾" **100.00**
Ivory, flat flask w/cvd mtn scene, 2" **100.00**
Ivory, 2 figures/bird/pine tree, gr stopper, 2¼" **100.00**
Lacquer, cinnabar red, relief cvgs, 19th C, 3¼" **550.00**
Lapis lazuli, overall cvg, 19th C, 2⅝" **300.00**
Moss agate w/gr inclusions, 19th C, 2⅝" **125.00**

Peking glass, red overlay snuff bottles with green glass stoppers, ca 1800-1880: Carved sages crossing footbridges to rustic dwellings, $990.00; Carved carp, $1,100.00.

Quartz agate w/brn-blk inclusions, 19th C, 3⅛" **450.00**
Rock crystal, cvd dragon in clouds, 18th C, 3" **300.00**
Rvpt pandas & tigers, sgn, 2⅝" **175.00**

Woodblock Prints, Japanese

Framed prints are of less value because one can not inspect their condition or tell if they have borders or are trimmed.

Actor, Kunichika, 19th C, 13¼x9", VG **275.00**
Figure & bird/seated couple, Kuniyoshi, 1849, diptich, 20x14" ..**350.00**
Samurai & old man in landscape, Toyokuni, 1850s, 14x19¾" ...**350.00**
Samurai w/sword/2nd w/teapot, Toyokuni, 1850, diptich, 20x14", G ..**400.00**
2 Samurai in water w/fish, Kunisada, 1890s, 14½x19½" **475.00**

Miscellaneous

Badge of office, embr wood duck & symbols, 14" L **90.00**
Carving, man & fish, boxwood, Jp, 19th C, 5⅝" **150.00**
Carving, root figure of sage holding a peach, Ch, rprs, 9" **50.00**
Jewelry box, cvd wood w/bone inlay, Ch, 14x14½" **725.00**
Jewelry case, cvd ivory w/stone inlay & gilt, 8½" sq **775.00**
Pipe, silver w/gold diapers, Jp, 8¼" **270.00**
Plaque, Kwan Yin, CI, Ch, 13⅜" **350.00**

Stirrup, Ch, CI w/inlaid bats & shou symbols, 7" **110.00**
Teapot, CI, calligraphy, Jp Provincial, 19th C, +stand/vessel **150.00**
Teapot, silver, urn w/dragon/etc panels, Ch, +cr/sug, 42-oz **800.00**
Tsuba, iron w/inlay brass & silver, Jp, ca 1800, 3½x3¼" **350.00**
Tsuba, Myochin style, iron w/gilt copper inlay, 16th C, 3" **400.00**

Orrefors

Orrefors Glassworks was founded in 1898 in the Swedish province of Smaaland. Utilizing the expertise of designers such as Simon Gate, Edward Hald, Vicke Lindstrand, and Edwin Ohrstrom, it produced art glass of the highest quality. Various techniques were used in achieving the decoration. Some were wheel engraved; others were blown through a unique process that formed controlled bubbles or air pockets resulting in unusual patterns and shapes. Our advisor for this category is Abby Malowanczyk; she is listed in the Directory under Texas.

Bowl, Ariel, stripes & bubbles, Ohrstrom, #1711E, 8" dia **700.00**
Bowl, Graal, aubergine spiral stripes, S/268L E Hald, 9¼" **550.00**
Bowl, Graal, purple stripes on crystal, Hald/#841, 3¼x5½" **950.00**
Bowl, Kantara, lt bl to aubergine, Landberg/NU33001, 5" **200.00**
Bowl, Ravenna, int red geometrics, Palmquist/nr1182, 3½" **700.00**

Cup, Negerhyddan, clear with engraved jungle scene, lid with teardrop finial, designed by Edward Hald, signed Orrefors Hald 65. 25. H., ca 1918, 10½", $3,000.00.

Fish bowl, Graal, fish/plants, Hald/#158E, 5" H **490.00**
Paperweight, Ariel, bubble image of king, Ohrstrom, 4½x6" **600.00**
Vase, clear to gray, appl blk neck, Lundin/DU 9-59, 12x13" ...**1,100.00**
Vase, Diana w/deer & pheasant eng, Lindstrand/#2696, 9¾" **550.00**
Vase, eng, Edward Hald/#256-29R, 1929, 12¼" **400.00**
Vase, eng fish/bubbles, thick U-form, Lindstrand/#2644, 8" **350.00**
Vase, eng fish/bubbles, wavy beaker form, HE/#199, 10" **400.00**
Vase, eng girl w/basket & flowers, Palmquist/#2653, 8" **100.00**
Vase, gr/clear, 3-sided, NU3583/3, 8" **175.00**
Vase, Graal, int fish/plant life, thick walls, 4x4" **450.00**
Vase, Kraka, swags of fine bubbles in bl/clear, Palmquist, 13" **800.00**
Vase, Slip Graal, gray w/clear loops, blk ft, Landberg, 5½" **850.00**
Vase, Slip Graal, int swirls, rim folds, blk disk ft, Hald, 3" **220.00**
Vase, topless dancer in skirt eng, Lindstrand/1648 R-3 Hj, 9" **600.00**
Vase, Tulpenglaser, clear to aubergine, Landberg/NU311-57, 20" ...**1,600.00**

Ott and Brewer

The partnership of Ott and Brewer began in 1865 in Trenton, New Jersey. By 1876 they were making decorated graniteware, parian, and 'ivory porcelain' — similar to Irish belleek though not as fine and of different composition. In 1883, however, experiments toward that end had reached a successful conclusion, and a true belleek body was introduced. It came to be regarded as the finest china ever produced by an American firm. The ware was decorated by various means such as hand painting, transfer printing, gilding, and lustre glazing. The compa-

ny closed in 1893, one of many that failed during that depression. In the listings below, the ware is belleek unless noted otherwise. Our advisor for this category is Mary Frank Gaston; she is listed in the Directory under Texas.

Vase, gold-slip vine decor on cream, reticulated 4-footed base with gold leaves and seashells, gold handles, crown and sword mark, 19x10", $10,000.00.

Basket, crisscross indents, gold leaves, twig hdl, mk, 4" **550.00**
Bowl, Cactus, gold thistles inside & out, mk, 3¼x10½" **1,000.00**
Cup & saucer, Echinus, wht w/gold, mk **150.00**
Cup & saucer, pearl w/gold accents, shell shape, set of 10 ....**850.00**
Humidor, wht w/brn staves, gold hdl, Tiffany & Co/mk **415.00**
Pitcher, gold floral, bark base, horn shape, branch hdl **375.00**
Pitcher, Tridacna, wht w/gold, mauve lustre int, mk, 1¾" **85.00**
Plate, 2 game birds on shelf, ruffled rim w/gold, mk **725.00**
Teapot, Tridacna, yel w/gold, wht loop hdl, mk, 4" **400.00**
Vase, floral w/gold, ornate crimped & ruffled rim, 5" **525.00**

Overbeck

The Overbeck Studio was established in 1911 in Cambridge City, Indiana, by four Overbeck sisters. It survived until the last sister died in 1955. Early wares were often decorated with carved designs of stylized animals, birds, or florals with the designs colored to contrast with the background. Others had tooled designs filled in with various colors for a mosaic effect. After 1937, Mary Frances, the last remaining sister, favored handmade figurines with somewhat bizarre features in fanciful combinations of color. Overbeck ware is signed 'OBK,' frequently with the designer's and potter's initials under the stylized 'OBK.'

Bowl, pk/yel/aqua, 3½", +1½" blossom/seed flower frog **130.00**
Figurine, blue jay, bl & brn on wht, 3¼x5½" **145.00**
Figurine, girl, pk bonnet/shawl, 3-color plaid skirt, 3½" **200.00**
Figurines, musicians w/instruments, 1 rpr, 4½", set of 8 ....**2,100.00**
Vase, cvd bird medallions, gray glossy, 6½" **2,455.00**
Vase, pk mottle, shouldered, 7¾x2¾" **500.00**
Vase, stylized butterfiles cvd on cocoa matt, MO, 4x4½" **650.00**
Vase, 3 landscape panels, rose on gray, sgn EF, 5½x4" **4,500.00**

Overshot

Overshot glass is characterized by the beaded or craggy appearance of its surface. Earlier ware was irregularly textured, while 20th-century examples tend to be more uniform.

Bouquet holder, clear, 4 joined/lipped ball shapes, Sandwich, 4" ..**425.00**
Bowl, bl opaque w/amber scallops, appl floral branch, 6" **225.00**
Bowl, cased bl, scalloped rim, crystal ft, 5½" **70.00**
Pitcher, amber w/Prussian bl hdl, drip rim & spout, 8¾" **400.00**
Pitcher, lt bl w/amber hdl, bulbous, Sandwich, 6" **175.00**
Pitcher, tankard, clear, Sandwich, 9¾" **225.00**

Pitcher, tankard, clear, 8x5" 100.00
Pitcher, tankard, cranberry, clear reeded hdl, Sandwich, 6¾" 230.00
Pitcher, tankard, cranberry w/clear reeded hdl, 9⅛x4½" 165.00

Owen, Ben

Ben Owen worked at the Jugtown Pottery of North Carolina from 1923 until it closed in 1959. He continued in the business in his own Plank Road Pottery, stamping his ware 'Ben Owen, Master Potter.' His pottery closed in 1972. He died in 1983 at the age of 81.

Bean pot, red-brn variations, rolled hdls, D Garner, 1960s, 8½" ..85.00
Bowl, yel-buff, dbl-corded hdl, mk, '60s, 3¼x9x10½", NM 225.00
Candlestick, buff-yel gloss, mk, 1960s, 9¾", EX 45.00

Pitcher, glossy brown/orange, 1960s, 3½", $65.00.

Pitcher, brn-orange gloss, grooved hdl, mk, 1960s, 3½" 65.00
Pot, red-orange, 2-hdld, w/lid, mk, 1960s, 4", NM 75.00
Ring jug, glossy salt glaze, F Craven, 1960s, 10" W 350.00
Vase, wht gloss, mk, 8" 425.00

Owens Pottery

J.B. Owens founded his company in Zanesville, Ohio, in 1891, and until 1907, when the company decided to exert most of its energies in the area of tile production, made several quality lines of art pottery. His first line, Utopian, was a standard brown ware with underglaze slip decoration of nature studies, animals, and portraits. A similar line, Lotus, utilized lighter background colors. Henri Deux, introduced in 1900, featured incised Art Nouveau forms inlaid with color. (Be aware that the Brush McCoy Pottery acquired many of Owens' molds and reproduced a line similar to Henri Deux, which they called Navarre.) Other important lines were Opalesce, Rustic, Feroza, Cyrano, and Mission, examples of which are rare today. The factory burned in 1928, and the company closed shortly thereafter. Values vary according to the quality of the artwork and subject matter. Examples signed by the artist bring higher prices than those that are not signed. For further information we recommend *Owens Pottery Unearthed* by Kristy and Rick McKibben and Jeanette and Marvin Stofft. Mrs. Stofft is listed in the Directory under Indiana.

Aborigine, vase, jug form, 9½" 315.00
Feroza, vase, brn to gunmetal, 6" 175.00
Feroza, vase, emb floral on gunmetal, hdls, #1099 ....225.00
Lightweight, stein, grapes on brn, sgn Herold, #795, 8" 475.00
Lightweight, vase, floral on brn, sgn Cecil Excel, #870, 9" 525.00
Lotus, pitcher, stork in water, mc on gray to cream, 6", NM 275.00
Lotus, vase, poppies, purple/wht on bl-gr, Chilcote, #1248 ....950.00
Matt Green, pitcher, banded decor, bulbous, 3½" 150.00
Matt Green, vase, Arts & Crafts band, 6x5" 350.00
Matt Green, vase, cvd Greek Key at rim, #10, 11½x9" 650.00

Matt Green, vase, emb vertical leaves, 4½" 230.00
Tile, acorns/oak leaves, 6-color, 6", +fr 500.00
Tile, grapes/stylized foliage, purple/gr on lt rn, 6", +fr 500.00
Tile, 3 flying geese, wht/gray/yel on lt bl, 11½x17", +fr 1,700.00
Umbrella stand, lighthouse scene, shaded gr gloss, 23½" 1,500.00
Utopian, jug, corn, mc on dk brn, 8" 450.00
Utopian, jug, Indian portrait (EX art), 10¾x5" 2,800.00
Utopian, lamp base, floral, mc on brn, 10" 325.00
Utopian, mug, berries & stems, autumn tones on brn, sgn TS, 5" 150.00
Utopian, pitcher, tankard; dog portrait, Timberlake, #1015, 12" ..2,750.00
Utopian, vase, broad leaves, caramel & tan on brn, 3½" 100.00
Utopian, vase, daisies, yel & caramel on dk brn & caramel, 5" ...150.00
Utopian, vase, floral, yel & teal on brn & gr, 8" 200.00
Utopian, vase, pansies, mc on dk brn gloss, #947, 2½" 120.00

Pacific Clay Products

The Pacific Clay Products Company got its start in the 1920s as a consolidation of several smaller southern California potteries. The main Los Angeles plant had been founded in 1890 to make kitchen stoneware, ollas, and similar items. Terra cotta and brick were later produced.

In 1932 Hostess Ware, a vividly colored line of dinnerware, was introduced to compete with Bauer's Ring Ware. Coralitos, a lighter-weight, pastel-hued dinnerware line was first marketed in 1937, and a similar but less expensive line called Arcadia soon followed. Art ware including vases, figurines, candlesticks, etc., was produced from 1932 to 1942, at which time the company went into war-related work and pottery manufacture ceased. A limited amount of hand-decorated dinnerware was also made. For further information we recommend *The Collectors Encyclopedia of California Pottery* by our advisor, Jack Chipman; he is listed in the Directory under California.

Photo courtesy Jack Chipman

Pacific artware: Vase, white, 6¼", $50.00; Bust, white, by Bernita Lundy, 7¾", $60.00; Bud vase, yellow, 7", $45.00; Vase, blue, 7½", $65.00.

Bowl, orange, Ring-style, 5x11" 85.00
Carafe, red 65.00
Casserole, ind; orange, 3x7", w/lid & underplate 70.00
Casserole, Ring, orange, w/lid, in metal rack 68.00
Cheese server, orange, 15" dia 95.00
Creamer, demitasse; Ring, gr 35.00
Egg cup, early design, flat ft 50.00
Goblet, Hostessware, gr 100.00
Swan, rust, lg 75.00
Teapot, sapphire, flat base, 6x12" 125.00
Teapot, yel, 3-ftd, rare 175.00
Tray, Hostessware, Ring, 15" 95.00
Tumbler, Ring-style 24.00
Tumbler, tall, matching set of 5 ....145.00
Vase, olive gr & turq, stick neck, 8x4" 150.00

Vase, sapphire, 4 buttresses, domed ft, 7x4" **65.00**

Paden City

The Paden City Glass Company began operations in 1916 in Paden City, West Virginia. The company's early lines consisted largely of the usual pressed tablewares, but by the 1920s production had expanded to include colored wares in translucent as well as opaque glass in a variety of patterns and styles. The company maintained its high standards of handmade perfection until 1949, when under new management much of the work formerly done by hand was replaced by automation. The Paden City Glass Company closed in 1951; its earlier wares, the colored patterns in particular, are becoming very collectible.

Paden City Glass is not always easily recognized by collectors or dealers, as it was almost never marked. It is believed this was so the glass could be sold to decorating companies. The company assigned both line numbers and names to many of its blanks or sets of glassware. Colors were sometimes given more than one name, and etchings were named as well. All this makes identification of items offered for sale through mail order difficult, and labels prepared by dealers are often confusing.

A review of literature available on Paden City reveals the following names for the company's plate etchings: Ardith; California Poppy; Cupid; Delilah Bird (Peacock Reverse); Eden Rose; Frost; Gazebo; Gothic Garden; Lela Bird; Nora Bird; Orchid (three variations); Peacock and Rose (Peacock and Wild Rose); Samarkand; Trumpet Flower; Utopia. Names given to cuttings made on Paden City blanks are Yorktown and Lazy Daisy. It is not clear whether the names originated with Paden City or with secondary decorating companies.

Our advisors for this category are George and Mary Hurney; they are listed in the Directory under Illinois. (Note: their interest is only in Paden City glassware, not the pottery.) See also Glass Animals and Figurines; Kitchen Collectibles, Glass.

This list gives company line numbers with corresponding line names. This information was obtained from Hazel Marie Weatherman's *Price Trends 2* and Jerry Barnett's *Paden City: The Color Company*.

#69, #69½ — Georgian, Aristocrat
#90 — Breton, Chevalier
#154 — Rena
#191 — Party Line
#198 — Ross
#199 — Inna
#202 — Virginia
#203 — Webb
#204 — Etta
#205 — Estelle
#206 — Pineapple
#209 — Edna
#210 — Skidoo, Spire
#215 — Hotcha
#220 — Cantina, Largo
#221 — S.S. Dreamship, Maya
#300 — Archaic
#330 — Luli
#400 — City Lights
#411 — Vaara, Mrs B
#412 — Crow's Foot (Square)
#444 — Vale
#555 — Vermillion
#700 — Simplicity
#701 — Lazy Daisy
#777 — Secrets
#836 — Future
#881 — Wotta Line, Gadroon
#890 — Crow's Foot (Round)
#895 — Lucy
#900 — Nadja
#991 — Penny Line
#994 — Popeye and Olive
#1503 — Trance
#1504 — Chaucer
#2000 — Mystic

And, finally, a listing of colors with alternate names or descriptive phrases:

Amber — (dull)
Cheriglo — (delicate) pink
Cobalt Blue — Royal Blue
Crystal — (clear, no tint)
Dark Green — forest green
Dark Amber — (honey color)
Light Blue — Copen, Neptune
Mulberry — amethyst
Opal — opaque white
Primrose — (amber with reddish tint)
Red — ruby
Rose — (dark pink)
Yellow — (pale, soft)

Ardith, bowl, yel, ftd, #411, 9¼" **57.00**
Ardith, cake plate, gr, ftd, #300, 11¼" **72.00**
Ardith, tray, yel, center hdl, #411, 10" **50.00**
Black Forest, creamer, gr **60.00**
Black Forest, ice tub, pk **160.00**
Black Forest, pitcher & tumble night set, pk **625.00**
Black Forest, sandwich tray, pk, hdls **65.00**
Black Forest, vase, blk, 10" **295.00**
Crow's Foot, bowl, blk, ftd, 10½" **75.00**
Crow's Foot, bowl, red, 6" **30.00**
Crow's Foot, bowl, yel, sq, 11" **30.00**
Crow's Foot, candlestick, blk or bl, 5¾", ea **30.00**
Crow's Foot, cup & saucer, ruby **15.00**
Crow's Foot, plate, cracker; amber, 10⅜" **35.00**
Crow's Foot, plate, red, 5¾" **2.25**
Crow's Foot, plate, red, 6" sq **5.00**
Crow's Foot, platter, blk or bl, 12", ea **32.50**
Crow's Foot, vase, crystal, Erwin Etch, 10" **35.00**
Crow's Foot, vase, red, 11¾" **195.00**
Cupid, bowl, fruit; gr or pk, 10¼", ea **150.00**
Cupid, cake plate, gr or pk, ftd, ea **230.00**
Cupid, cake stand, gr **245.00**
Cupid, candy dish, gr or pk, w/lid, 3-part, ea **200.00**
Cupid, ice bucket, gr or pk, 6", ea **190.00**
Cupid, mayonnaise, gr, 3-pc set **275.00**
Cupid, vase, gr or pk, fan shaped, ea **225.00**
Della Robbia, basket, 9" **175.00**
Della Robbia, candle, 4" **32.00**
Della Robbia, plate, 18" **165.00**
Della Robbia, tumbler, ftd, 8-oz **30.00**
Gazebo, tray, lt bl, center hdl **75.00**
Georgian, old fashioned, ruby, 3¼" **15.00**
Georgian, sherbet, ruby **12.50**
Georgian, tumbler, ruby, ftd V shape, 3½" **10.00**
Largo, bowl, red, hdls, 9" **50.00**
Largo, plate, red, hdls, 11⅜" **50.00**
Lela Bird, candle holders, pk, pr **125.00**
Lela Bird, tray, pk, center hdl, 10½" **110.00**
Lela Bird, vase, blk, elliptical, 8½" **175.00**
Nora Bird, candy dish, gr, flat, w/lid **375.00**
Nora Bird, mayonnaise, gr, w/ladle **110.00**
Nora Bird, sugar bowl, pk, rnd hdl **60.00**
Nora Bird, vase, blk, elliptical **295.00**
Orchid, bowl, console; yel, Crow's Foot blank, 11" **185.00**
Orchid, bowl, pk, ped ft, 9¾" **165.00**

Orchid, comport, yel, Crow's Foot blank, 6⅝" 175.00
Party Line, compote, pk, ftd, 11" 35.00
Peacock & Wild Rose, bowl, all colors, flat, 8½", ea 75.00
Peacock & Wild Rose, bowl, gr, ftd, 10½" 160.00
Peacock & Wild Rose, bowl, pk, 11" 160.00
Peacock & Wild Rose, cake plate, pk 140.00
Peacock & Wild Rose, candlesticks, all colors, 5", ea pr 125.00
Peacock & Wild Rose, compote, pk, 6" 110.00
Peacock & Wild Rose, ice bucket, all colors, 6", ea 145.00
Peacock & Wild Rose, ice tub, gr 185.00
Peacock & Wild Rose, plate, gr, 10½" 75.00
Peacock & Wild Rose, plate, pk, center hdl, 10½" 110.00
Peacock & Wild Rose, plate, 10⅜" 110.00
Peacock & Wild Rose, vase, blk, 6½" 160.00
Peacock & Wild Rose, vase, gr, bulbous, 12" 250.00
Peacock & Wild Rose, vase, gr, 10" 140.00
Peacock & Wild Rose, vase, gr, 12" 190.00
Peacock & Wild Rose, vase, pk, 10" 170.00
Peacock Reverse, bowl, all colors, sq, 8¾", ea 85.00
Peacock Reverse, bowl, rolled rim, any color, #701 ....90.00
Peacock Reverse, creamer, all colors, flat, 2¾", ea 77.50
Peacock Reverse, saucer, all colors, ea 20.00
Penny Line, decanter, cobalt, w/stopper, +5 2½-oz tumblers 120.00
Penny Line, shot glass, ruby 30.00
Star Cut, condiment set, w/lids & spoons 45.00
Trance, server, crystal, center hdl 35.00

Paintings on Ivory

Miniature works of art executed on ivory from the 1800s are assessed by the finesse of the artist, as is any fine painting. Signed examples and portraits with an identifiable subject are usually preferred.

Portrait of a small girl with flowers, attributed to Mrs. Moses Russell (Clarissa Peters), ca 1830-40, in Union case, light wear to pigment, 2½x2", $8,625.00 at auction.

Duchess D'Orlians, floral-draped bodice, 3½" in 6" fr 125.00
Fr lady in plumed hat by Gothic column, sgn, 5¾x4¾" 135.00
Lady, in gold oval fr w/hair braid on bk, 2¾" 600.00
Lady, pastels, artist sgn, gilt brass fr, 4½" 165.00
Lady in red chair, in hinged case, 3¼" 385.00
Madonna & Child, sgn/dtd 1617, 3¼x2½", matted in fr 295.00
Man, identified, artist sgn, gilt on brass fr w/velvet, 7x6" 360.00
Man, unsgn, fr, 2¼x1¾" 260.00
Man, unsgn, 19th C, in pendant/brooch fr, 2½x2" 230.00
Man in bl tie, in oval gilded case w/lock of hair in bk, 2½" 275.00
Marie Antoinette, plumed hat, sgn, sectioned ivory fr, 5x4" 100.00

Military officer, blk lacquer fr w/brass trim, 5x4⅜" 140.00
2 brothers w/riding crop & apple, unsgn, 4½x3½" 1,500.00

Pairpoint

The Pairpoint Manufacturing Company was built in 1880 in New Bedford, Massachusetts. It was primarily a metalworks whose chief product was coffin fittings. Next door, the Mt. Washington Glassworks made quality glasswares of many varieties. (See Mt. Washington for more information concerning their artware lines.) By 1894 it became apparent to both companies that a merger would be to their best interest.

From the late 1890s until the 1930s, lamps and lamp accessories were an important part of Pairpoint's production. There were three main types of shades, all of which were blown: puffy — blown-out reverse-painted shades (usually floral designs); ribbed — also reverse painted; and scenic — reverse painted with scenes of land or seascapes (usually executed on smooth surfaces, although ribbed scenics may be found occasionally). Cut glass lamps and those with metal overlay panels were also made. Scenic shades were sometimes artist signed. Every shade was stamped on the lower inside or outside edge with 1) The Pairpoint Corp., 2) Patent Pending, 3) Patented July 9, 1907, or 4) Patent Applied For. Bases were made of bronze, copper, brass, silver, or wood, and are always signed.

Because they produced only fancy, handmade artware, the company's sales lagged seriously during the Depression; and, as time and tastes changed, their style of product was less in demand. As a result, they never fully recovered; consequently part of the buildings and equipment was sold in 1938. The company reorganized in 1939 under the direction of Robert Gundersen and again specialized in quality hand-blown glassware. Isaac Babbit regained possession of the silver departments, and together they established Gundersen Glassworks, Inc. After WWII, because of a sharp decline in sales, it again became necessary to reorganize. The Gundersen-Pairpoint Glassworks was formed, and the old line of cut, engraved artware was reintroduced. The company moved to East Wareham, Massachusetts, in 1957. But business continued to suffer, and the firm closed only one year later. In 1970, however, new facilities were constructed in Sagamore under the direction of Robert Bryden, sales manager for the company since the 1950s.

In 1974 the company began to produce lead glass cup plates which were made on commission as fund-raisers for various churches and organizations. These are signed with a 'P' in diamond and are becoming quite collectible. Our advisor for Pairpoint lamps is Daniel Batchelor; he is listed in the Directory under New York. See also Napkin Rings.

Glass

Bell, dk amethyst w/cotton candy stem hdl, HP decor, 12" 85.00
Bottle, scent; dk amethyst cut to clear, 8" 175.00
Cake plate, red w/blk stem, floral silver o/l, 5½x10" 1,095.00
Candlesticks, cobalt w/eng vintage, bubble knop, 10¾", pr 635.00
Candy jar, Aurora, silver base & finial, bubble-ball stem, 12" 650.00
Chalice, blown w/cut/eng florals, bubble-ball stem, Bryden, 12" ..85.00
Chalice, eng eagle, crystal, loop hdls, Bryden, 10¾" 85.00
Chalice, pulled loops, bl & wht, controlled bubble stem, 12" 295.00
Compote, blk w/clear bubble-ball connector, 6¼x6¼" 75.00
Compote, forest gr, clear bubble-ball stem, 7¾x8¼" 145.00
Vase, Adelaide, cobalt cut to clear, bubble-ball stem, 12" 1,100.00
Vase, Adelaide, Rosaria cut to clear, bubble-ball connector, 12" ...1,300.00
Vase, cornucopia; cut border, bubble-ball shaft/ped ft, 12½" 400.00
Vase, dk cranberry w/wht loops, clear ft, Bryden, 8" 95.00
Vase, gold ruby, clear bubble-ball connector, 12½" 150.00
Vase, gold ruby, crystal base, flared rim, 8x7" 95.00
Vase, gold ruby, trumpet form w/bubble-ball stem, 13" 145.00

Vase, jack-in-pulpit; mc floral on amethyst, Bryden, 9½" **185.00**
Vase, Rosaria w/eng grapes & Dmn Quilt, bubble-ball stem, 12" **550.00**
Vase, ruby, bubble-ball connector, Bryden, 12½" **75.00**
Vase, Tavern; sailing ship on wavy sea, many bubbles, 6" **385.00**

Lamps

Puffy 10" Papillon 4-lobe shade; #B3048 std, 13¾" **5,750.00**
Puffy 13½" red rose shade; blossoms arms, #3055 std, 21½" ..**11,500.00**
Puffy 14" florals & birds Stratford shade; Nouveau std, 22" **3,500.00**
Puffy 14" Papillon shade; 4-arm gilded #B3006 std, 21½" **8,000.00**
Puffy 14" peony domical shade; #3086 std w/sq base, 18½" **7,000.00**
Puffy 16" mixed floral sq Torino shade; sq base, 20" **7,475.00**
Puffy 18" pilgrims sq Tavenna shade; 4-arm B3056 std, 23½" .**9,200.00**
Puffy 8" rose tree shade w/mc roses border; brass std, 15¾" **3,000.00**
Puffy 9" butterfly & floral shade; #B3050 metal std, 16¾" **7,000.00**
Puffy 9" floral Papillon shade; #C3057 std, 16" **2,990.00**
Puffy 9" mixed floral Stratford shade; #B3080 std, 14" **3,000.00**
Rvpt, 6½" floral medallions sq Vassar shade; #E3018 std, 14" .**1,035.00**
Rvpt 10" abstract floral Vienna shade; 3-ftd std, 19½" **1,800.00**
Rvpt 10" autumn village landscape shade; mk urn std **1,600.00**
Rvpt 10" iris Vienna shade; floral std, 20" **1,850.00**
Rvpt 12" tulip Venice shade; metal std w/sq ft, 29" **3,000.00**
Rvpt 13" floral Florence shade; floral metal base, 23" **3,000.00**
Rvpt 14" nasturtiums Vienna shade; invt vasiform std, 22" **3,000.00**
Rvpt 15" floral shade w/spatterwork; #3099 candelabrum std, 26" ..**1,500.00**
Rvpt 15" Garden of Allah shade; dbl-hdld amphora-style std, 20" ..**2,750.00**
Rvpt 15" seascape Directorie shade sgn Guba; candelabrum st, 26" ...**6,000.00**

Reverse-painted 16" Lansdowne shade with Spanish galleon on heavy seas, signed Durand, D-3076½ gilt bronzed metal base with 3 dolphins, 22½", $4,800.00.

Rvpt 16" Genoa Rose shade; copper-finished std, 21" **8,500.00**
Rvpt 18" harbor scene Berkley shade; SP dolphin std, 22" **4,500.00**
Rvpt 18" harbor scene Carlisle shade; #D3034 std, 22½" **3,680.00**
Rvpt 8" daffodil Bryn Mawr hex shade; copper-bronze std, 15" ..**2,185.00**

Paper Dolls

No one knows quite how or when paper dolls originated. One belief is that they began in Europe as 'pantins' (jumping jacks) and were frequently worn as part of the costume. By the late 1790s, they were being mass produced. During the 19th century, most paper dolls portrayed famous dancers and opera stars such as Fanny Elssler and Jenny Lind. In the late 1800s, the Raphael Tuck Publishers of England produced many series of beautiful paper dolls; retail companies used them as advertisements to further the sale of their products. Around the turn of the century, many popular women's magazines began featuring a page of paper dolls.

Most familiar to today's collectors are the books with dolls on cardboard covers and clothes on the inside pages. These made their appearance in the late 1920s and early '30s. The most collectible (and the most valuable) are those representing celebrities, movie stars, and comic-strip characters of the '30s and '40s.

When no condition is indicated, the dolls listed below are assumed to be in mint, uncut, original condition. Cut sets will be worth about half price if all dolls and outfits are included and pieces are in very good condition. If dolls were produced in die-cut form, these prices reflect such a set in mint condition with all costumes and accessories.

For further information we recommend *A Collector's Guide to Magazine Paper Dolls* (Collector Books) and *Tomart's Price Guide to Lowe and Whitman Paper Dolls*, both by Mary Young, our advisor for this category; she is listed in the Directory under Ohio. We also recommend *Schroeder's Collectible Toys, Antique to Modern* (Collector Books).

Am Beauties (M Monroe), Saalfield Artcraft #1338, uncut, M ..**115.00**
Animated Alice in Wonderland, Milton Bradley #4109, 1950s, MIB ...**45.00**
Annette Funicello, Walt Disney, 1950s, uncut, M **55.00**
Baby Jane, jtd w/fasteners, 1927 design by G Breed, unused **95.00**
Baby Sparkle Plenty, Saalfield #2500, 1948, uncut, M **50.00**
Baby Tender Love, Whitman #1960, 1971, uncut **15.00**
Betty Grable, Whitman #989, 1941, cut **65.00**
Beverly Hillbillies, Whitman #1955, 1964, partially cut, EX+ **38.00**
Brother & Sister, Whitman #4105, NMIB **30.00**
Brother/Sister, Whitman #1182-15, 1950, unused, M **47.50**
Chuck & Di Have a Baby, Simon & Schuster, 1982, M **15.00**
Cradle Baby, Saalfield #5214, cut clothes, 1948, cradle book **32.00**
Dearie Dolls, 20" doll w/3 costumes/hats, MT Sheahan, 1915, NM ..**125.00**
Debbie Reynolds Cut-Outs, Whitman #1956, 1960, cut in folder, NM ..**35.00**
Dolly Darlings, 6 dolls+clothing, cut, Whitman #1963, G **20.00**
Dress Me Cut Out Dolls, Whitman #1177, 1943, uncut, M **60.00**
Flying Nun, Saalfield #5121, 1968, uncut, M **40.00**
Four Sleeping Dolls, eyes open/close, Whitman #2060, 1945, uncut, M ..**70.00**

Gale Storm, Whitman #2089, uncut, 1959, M, $110.00.

Happy Days, Fonzie, Toy Factory #105, 1976, MIP **25.00**
Judy & Jim Paper Doll Storybook, Simon & Schuster, 1948, M ...**58.00**
Judy Garland, Whitman #980, cut **65.00**
Julia, Saalfield #6055, 1968, MIB **50.00**
Let's Play w/the Baby, Merrill #1550, 1948, M **35.00**
Little LuLu, Whitman #1987, 1974, unused, M **30.00**
Mary Poppins, Whitman #1967, 1973, uncut, M **25.00**
My Fair Lady, Ottenheimer, #2060-5, 1965, uncut, lg book, M **50.00**
Outdoor Pals, 4 dolls, Whitman #5347, MIB **45.00**
Partridge Family, Artcraft #5137, 1971, uncut, M in NM folder ...**40.00**
Princess Di Paper Doll Book, #1985-50, 1985, M **15.00**
Queens (Rose, Ice, etc), Saalfield #295, 1944, uncut **30.00**
Raggedy Ann & Andy, w/color book, Saalfield #4409, Gruelle, '44, M ..**95.00**
Ricky Nelson, Whitman #2081, 1959, NM **75.00**
Rosemary Clooney, sm soft-cover book, #1806, 1959, uncut **35.00**
Shirley Temple, Saalfield #1715, uncut, NM **195.00**
Shirley Temple, Saalfield #290, 6 pgs of clothes, uncut **135.00**

Shirley Temple, Saalfield Artcraft #1789, 1960, M 75.00
Sisters, Gabriel #D135, NMIB 56.00
Sonny & Sue, Abbott #1387, 1950s, uncut 20.00
Trim Dotty's Dresses, Whitman #5336, unused, EXIB 30.00
Twiggy, Whitman #1999, 1967, uncut, NM 35.00
3 Little Girls Who Grew, 6 dolls, Whitman #990, 1945, uncut, M ..60.00
4 Playmates, Lowe #125, 1940, uncut 18.00

Paperweights

All paperweights listed here are made totally of glass (including the lampwork flowers, fish, birds, snakes, lizards, and millefiori rods). The only elements that are not glass are the clay sulfides encased within some of the Baccarat and St. Louis weights. Today, antique weights (1845 to ca 1870s) and those made by contemporary artists attract the most attention and are the most expensive. Lower-priced 'gift' weights come from American glasshouses and studios, China, Murano, Italy, and Scotland. But because of the expenses involved in their manufacture (fuel, material, and labor), even they are not cheap. There is an international association of paperweight collectors with many state and regional chapters. (For information see Clubs, Newsletters, and Catalogs in the Directory.) Many books are currently available on the subject of paperweights. For the beginner we recommend *All About Paperweights* by L.H. Selmen.

Probably inspired by the work of Pierre Bigaglia (Venice), the French factories of Baccarat, Clichy, and St. Louis turned their attention to paperweight making in the 1840s. They first made millefiori paperweights, the technique a revival of methods used in Alexandria, Damascus, Rome, and Byzantium before the time of Christ. (This art form had faded out but had been revived in 16th-century Venice.) The French Classic period was 1845 to 1860; English (Whitefriars and Bacchus) and American (Sandwich and New England) glasshouses followed their lead about ten years later. Gradually, as the paperweight's popularity declined, production began to wane; Clichy closed in the 1880s, as did a few American factories. Baccarat made weights as late as 1910; in the '20s and '30s, a worker by the name of Dupont revived the art. Then in the 1950s St. Louis and Baccarat sparked a renewal of interest in weight making that is still going strong today. Some of the most desirable weights from American artists were made by the Banfords, Randall Grubb, Rick Ayotte, Chris Buzzini, Ken Rosenfeld, Gordon Smith, Paul Stankard, Charles Kaziun (d), Del (d) and Debbie Tarsitano, and the Trabuccos. From Scotland, Paul Ysart (d), Perthshire and Caithness/Whitefriars are also well known.

Note: Prices reflect the usual buyer's fee charged by most auction houses. Furthermore, there are many factors which determine value, particularly of antique weights. Auction-realized prices of contemporary weights are usually different from issue price; 'list price' may be for weights issued earlier and reduced for clearance or influenced by market demand and other factors. The competition for antique weights has been increasing dramatically over this decade. New collectors entering the field have greatly influenced prices. As the numbers of collectors increase, available antique weights decrease per capita, forcing prices upwards. Since the 1930s antique paperweights have steadily increased in value, making them one of today's best investments. The dimension given at the end of the description is diameter.

Key:

con — concentric	mill — millefiori
fct — faceted	o/l — overlay
gar — garland	pm — pastry mold
grd — ground	pwt — paperweight
jsp — jasper	sil — silhouette
latt — latticinio	

Ayotte, Rick

Breath of Life, 3 yel roses (bud to open), leaves/wht flowers 950.00
Pk & brn butterfly w/3 lilac clematis flowers, ltd ed, 3⅝" 900.00
Springtime in Manoraga, European robin on floral branch, 3⅝" ...900.00
2 lg lampwork apples & blossoms, ltd ed, 3¾" 750.00

Baccarat, Antique

Antique Baccarat, blue, red, green and white millefiori garland with central medallion on claret ground, 2¾", $1,495.00.

Close pack mill canes w/arrows/stars/shamrocks/etc, 3" 1,250.00
Con mill mushroom, wht star rods/red whorl/complex canes, 3¼" ..2,000.00
Mushroom w/bl & wht torsade, star-cut base, 3⅛" 1,850.00

Baccarat, Modern

Lime gr canes w/alternate mc canes forming rings, 1977, 3⅜" 450.00
Pansy w/5 gr leaves on clear grd, star-cut base, 2⅜" 550.00
Spaced mill in muslin grd w/18 complex canes, 1973, 3" 400.00
Wht cog canes/12 Zodiac canes on carpet grd, 1972, 3⅛" 550.00
3 pears & 5 leaves on wht opaque grd, 1973 ltd ed, 3¼" 400.00

Banford, Bob

Bee over red flower & 2 buds on azure bl grd, fct, 3¼" 800.00
Palargonium blooms & buds w/leaves on cobalt, 3¼" 600.00
Triple pansies w/dmn-cut base, 3¼" 750.00
7 different flowers w/buds on dmn-cut base, 2 bees, 4" 2,000.00

Banford, Bobby

Orange flower on leafy bed on blk grd, 2¼" 250.00
Pk flower/6 mc buds, wht knotweeds & leaves, 3" 600.00
2 violets & bud on stems, star-cut base, 3" 400.00
3 red flowers w/blk centers, wht knotweed & leaves, 2¼" 250.00
4 mc flowers & buds w/knotweeds on honey grd, 2½" 300.00

Banford, Ray

Iris & 3 buds w/leaves on star-cut base, 3" 500.00
Pk rose w/trellis on bl grd, 1 top/7 oval fcts, '70s, 2" 95.00
Red rose amid 6 buds on azure bl grd, fct, 3⅛" 750.00

Buzzini, Chris

Acorn, Yosemite Series, ltd ed, 3⅜" 1,200.00
Complex pk-gray flower w/roots amid pebbles, ltd ed, 3½" 1,200.00
Mock orange blossoms on rocky slopes, 3¼" 900.00
Perennial among granite cliffs, ltd ed, 3⅜" 1,200.00
Wallflower, catchfly, sky pilot & lessingia blossoms, 3⅜" 1,500.00
5 bl blossoms on plant w/root system, ltd ed, 3⅜" 1,200.00

Caithness

Christmas candle & mistletoe on bl, fct, 3⅜" 325.00
Rapture, red rose, pineapple cutting, gr o/l on top, 4¾" 995.00
Water lily on gr grd, fct, mini, 2¼" 210.00
3 wise men & camels etched on surface, blk/wht core, 3¾" 225.00

Clichy, Antique

C scroll on turq w/con center & C gars, 3⅛" 2,850.00
Pansies w/bud & 6 leaves, 2½" 1,800.00
Spaced con w/stardust & pastry mold canes, moss grd, bubbles ..800.00
Star canes form whorl in center of mc canes, 2" 750.00

Deacons, John

Antique-style primrose in clear crystal, 2¼" 225.00
Butterfly, purple & wht dbl o/l w/fancy cutting, 3⅛" 395.00
Dahlia w/21 pk & wht petals, 3" 275.00
Pansy w/leaves & stem on wht latt grd, 2¾" 250.00
Pk & wht dbl o/l w/bl dbl clematis in latt crown, 3⅜" 395.00
Pk dahlia on wht strip & 5 gr leaves, 3" 275.00
Wht dbl clematis w/leaves on bl latt grd 225.00

Donofrio, Jim

Beaded breastplate, 2 pots & shards on natural grd, 3⅜" 1,000.00
Giraffe dines on leaves, 2 pears on branch, 3⅜" 1,000.00
Purple-spotted frog w/blk & yel striped frog, 3⅜" 1,000.00
Purple-spotted poisonous dart frog & flower, 2¾" 475.00
2 copper-brn frogs on bambo, 3⅜" 1,000.00
2 gr frogs, branch w/2 5-petal flowers on sand grd, 3⅜" 1,000.00
3 Indian pots & hatchet on natural grd, 3⅜" 1,000.00

Kaziun, Charles

Pansy w/bl & brn on wht petals, yel-gr grd, gold bee mk, 2¼" 750.00
Pk/wht center cane w/gr & yel canes set w/red heart, sgn, 2" 400.00
Red/wht center cane/6 assorted on bl opaque, sgn/early, 2⅛" 400.00
Tilted spider lily/leaves on aqua grd w/gold mica, ped, 1¼" 450.00
Yel spider lily on sparkled turq grd, sgn, ped, 1¾" 300.00

Lundberg Studios

Bl Nosegay, bl flower w/in 2 rows of flowers on wht muslin 400.00
Cupid's Messenger, pk/wht flowers on pk muslin w/mc canes 500.00
Independence (Summer of 4 Seasons), crown type, 3¼" 250.00
Spring (of 4 Seasons), yel & gr twists/yel latt twists, 3¼" 250.00
Wht crane w/bamboo on irid yel grd, 3¾" 400.00

New England Glass, Antique

Bl/wht/ruby canes in scramble, 2⅝" 200.00
Pear on clear rnd base, 2⅝" 1,200.00
Red poinsettia w/complex center cane on bl/wht jasper, 3" 750.00
Spaced con mc canes on latt, 2¾" 300.00

Parabelle

Con mill w/bl pansy & ring of pansies on latt, ltd ed, 3⅛" 850.00
Con mill w/central wht rose on X-hatched latt, ltd ed, 3⅛" 900.00
Dbl trefoil of gr/red loops on upset muslin grd, ltd ed 215.00
Pk & gr rose, complex arrow/cog canes on wht grd, 3" 625.00
Primrose center cane, complex arrow/primrose/pk & wht canes, 2½" ..250.00

Rose canes amid leaf canes, pansy cane gar, ltd ed 650.00
Wht mill canes on cobalt grd, 1996 ltd ed 225.00
6 cane loops resemble flower on violet-bl grd, ltd ed, 3" 185.00

Parsley, Johne

2 pk dogwood w/4 buds, variegated leaves on cobalt grd, 2⅞" 750.00
3 wht dogwoods w/red ties & gr leaves on gr grd, 2¾" 825.00
3 yel flowers w/red stamens & pk flower w/leaves, fct 850.00

Perthshire

Bl & wht mini swirl w/pk flower, 1989 ltd ed, 2¼" 300.00
Christmas bells & mistletoe w/in gar on gr grd, top fct, 2⅞" 350.00
Lampwork flower & daisy canes on lace grd, 6&1 fcts, 3" 285.00
Lampwork flowers on cushion grd, gr/wht dbl o/l, 1/12 fcts, 3" ...680.00
Pear/plums/lemon/orange in latt basket, 1980 ltd ed, 2½" 400.00
3 flowers w/gr leaves & lady bug, 1/12 fcts, ltd ed, 2¾" 465.00

Rosenfeld, Ken

Blk & dichroic gold disk w/Yin & Yang sign, flower gar, 3" 400.00
Fiesta, 4 ears of corn/12 red chili peppers, 1992, 3⅜" 450.00
Mc flowers among assorted rocks & wht moss grd, 3" 425.00
Pk camellia, yel flower & bl cluster of flowers, 2½" 250.00
Radishes, carrots, asparagus & turnips 300.00
2 lav flowers & bud w/2 bl & 1 yel flower sandy grd, 3¼" 300.00
6 Christmas ball, 4 w/bl aventurine, on bed of holly, 2½" 250.00

St. Louis, Antique

Antique St. Louis, colorful fruit bouquet on white latticinio ground, 2¾", $1,450.00.

Bl clematis w/bud, 3 cane flowers on leafy bead, fct, 3¼" 1,700.00
Mc scramble of rods/twists/tubes/lengths of complex canes, 2" ...375.00
Mc spaced mill canes w/alternating colors on outer rows 600.00

St. Louis, Modern

Fancy, pk dahlia w/center cane, 5 layers of petals, 3⅛" 570.00
Mc flowers in latt mushroom shape basket, fct, 1978, 3¼" 500.00
Memory, 18 mc flowers in yel latt basket, fct, l993 ltd ed 1,900.00
Oriental, 5-color canes on mc carpet grd, ltd ed, 3" 1,140.00
Red cherries on latt, fct, mini, 1985 ltd ed, 2¼" 400.00
Sarah, mill on red & wht carpet grd, ltd ed, 3⅛" 1,080.00
Wht clematis w/red-tipped petals & mill stamens on bl latt 500.00

Stankard, Paul

Buttercups & buds on bl cased to wht, sgn, 1974, 2½" 750.00
Wht flower w/leafy stem & roots, bl opaque grd, 1971, 2¼" 800.00
Wht stylized floral w/gr stem & roots, sgn cane, 1972, 1¼" 635.00
Yel flower w/leaves, emerald gr cased to wht, sgn, 1973, 2¾" ..1,035.00
Yel wild rose w/4 leaf clusters, sgn, 1974, 2¾" 865.00

Tarsitano, Debbie

Butterfly in blk & bl w/pk over 3 pk flowers, fct, 3¾" 1,450.00
Purple 17-petal flower & 3 knotweed sprays in crystal, 2⅜" 600.00
Red dahlia w/7 layers of petals, w/bud & leaves, 3½" 1,100.00
Speckled flower w/gr leaves & bud on star-cut grd, 6&1 fcts ...1,200.00
3 flowers on stems w/3 buds & leaves, star-cut base, 2¾" 600.00

Tarsitano, Delmo

Butterfly & 4 blossoms on sand, Earth Life, 3¼" 950.00
Dragonfly & plants, Earth Life, 3¼" 800.00
Mc rings of stars/flowers/turtle canes, 3¼" 1,265.00
Salamander on rocky sand w/plants, Earth Life, 3½" 1,500.00

Whitefriars

Bl & wht con mill, 5/1 fcts, 3" dia 110.00
Con mill w/bl/wht/red/gr complex canes, fct, 3" 200.00
Con mill w/circles of pk/wht, red/wht, bl/wht cog canes, 2⅞" 200.00
Con mill w/red/bl/wht/gr canes, fct, mini, 2⅜" 175.00
Multi-fct con mill on clear, ca 1960s, 3¼" 225.00

Ysart, Paul

Clematis w/mill center on turq sanded grd, sgn, ped, 3½" 375.00
Mill heart w/complex cane & gar on dk purple, early, 3⅛" 450.00
Pattern mill forms loose star design on bl/wht jsp grd, 3¼" 425.00
Robert Burns sulfide on bl jsp grd w/gar, spall, 3" 295.00

Miscellaneous

Gooderham, J; Victorian lady w/fan on cushion, fct o/l, 2⅛" 300.00
Lundberg, Steven; wht trillium/leaves/3 pk butterflies, 3⅜" 440.00
Lundberg, Steven; yel iris w/5 buds on bl grd, 3¾" 320.00
Orient & Flume, butterfly & 2 pk stemmed buds, ltd ed, 3¾" 700.00
Pairpoint, swirl, controlled bubbles/eng florals, ftd, 4x3⅛" 250.00
Whittemore, FD; yel rose on ped, early, 2¾x1⅞" 450.00

Parian Ware

Parian is hard-paste unglazed porcelain made to resemble marble. First made in the mid-1800s by Staffordshire potters, it was soon after produced in the United States by the U.S. Pottery at Bennington, Vermont. Busts and statuary were favored, but plaques, vases, mugs, and pitchers were also made.

Bust of Sir Walter Scott, Copeland, ca 1875, on base, 8¼", $230.00; Figure of Miranda, Minton, modeled by John Bell, ca 1866, 15", $430.00; Bust of Dickens, attributed to Robinson & Leadbeater, late 19th century, on base, 11¼", $260.00.

Bust, Bismark, sgn Warth, dtd 1879, 7¼" 125.00
Bust, maiden in bonnet, 1850s, on Neoclassical base, 18" 2,000.00
Bust, Shakespeare, sgn JT&B 45.00
Figurine, draped nude couple embrace on base, unmk, 17⅝" 160.00
Pitcher, Garibaldi relief, mc, 3⅜" 160.00
Pitcher, pk/wht w/appl vintage, ewer form, twist hdl, 14", NM ..130.00
Sculpture, Geo Washington, full standing figure, 13½" 2,250.00

Parrish, Maxfield

Maxfield Parrish (1870-1966), with his unique abilities in architecture, illustrations, and landscapes, was the most prolific artist during 'The Golden Years of Illustrators.' He produced art for more than one hundred magazines, painted girls on rocks for the Edison-Mazda division of General Electric, and landscapes for Brown & Bigelow. His most recognized work was 'Daybreak' that was published in 1923 by House of Art and sold nearly two million prints. Parrish began early training with his father who was a recognized teacher, was schooled in architecture at Dartmouth, and became an active participant in the Cornish artist colony in New Hampshire where he resided. Due to his increasing popularity, reproductions are now being marketed. Bobby Babcock, our advisor for this category, is listed in the Directory under Texas.

Ad, Jell-O, Polly Put the Kettle On, matted & fr, 10½x8", NM ...95.00
Book, Arabian Nights, 12 illus, 1909, NM 275.00
Book, Dream Days & Golden Age, 1902 ....195.00
Book, Golden Treasury of Songs & Lyrics, 1st ed, 1911 ....295.00
Book, Italian Villas & Their Gardens, 1st edition, 1904 ....395.00
Book, Knave of Hearts, hardbound, 1925 ....1,500.00
Book, Knickerbocker' History of NY, 1st edition, 1900 ....450.00
Book, Mother Goose in Prose, 1905 ....750.00
Book, Poems of Childhood, 9 illus, 1904, NM 295.00
Book plate, Fool in Green, Knave of Hearts, 1925, matted & fr, NM ..100.00
Book plate, Pompdebile..., Knave of Hearts, 1925, fr, NM 100.00
Calendar, Contentment, Edison/Mazda, trimmed to image, '27, sm ...300.00
Calendar, Dreamlight, Edison/Mazda, cropped to border, 1923, sm ..575.00
Calendar, Ecstasy, Edison/Mazda, 1930, no pad, lg, NM 1,200.00
Calendar, Enchantment, Edison/Mazda, 1926, no pad, sm 575.00
Calendar, Evening, 1947, 4x5¾", EX 155.00
Calendar, Golden Hours, Edison/Mazda, full pad 750.00
Calendar, Primitive Man, Edison/Mazda, 1921, full pad, sm ...2,200.00
Calendar, Reveries, Edison/Mazda, cropped, 1927, lg 1,200.00
Calendar, Venetian Lamplighter, Edison/Mazda, full pad, 8½x19" ..1,400.00
Calendar top, Early Autumn, 1939, orig fr, 13x17", EX 350.00
Calendar top, Thy Rocks & Hills, 1944, 17x21½", EX 495.00
Calendar top, Twilight, 1937, matted & fr, 11x15", EX 350.00
Check, to Lydia Parrish, March 28, 1916, NM 300.00
Cigar box lid, Old King Cole, 1910s, fr, 6x10", NM 650.00
Cookbook, Jell-O, 1924, 6⅛x4¼", NM 135.00
Frontispiece, Aladdin, Collier's, 1907, matted & fr 125.00
Frontispiece, Philosopher, Colliers, 1912, matted & fr 200.00
Magazine cover, Collier's, May 1909, Old King Cole, rare, NM .200.00
Magazine cover, Collier's, May 1913, man fishing, NM 195.00
Magazine cover, Ladies' Home Journal, June 1901, matted & fr .150.00
Magazine cover, Life, October 1921, Evening, 10½x8", NM 195.00
Magazine page, Botanist, Collier's, matted & fr 100.00
Magazine page, Grand Canyon, Century, matted & fr 75.00
Magazine page, Hiawatha, Collier's 75.00
Magazine page, Knickerbocker Days, Cosmopolitan, 1901, NM ...60.00
Pamphlet, You & Your Work, Parrish illus, 1944 ....125.00
Photo, Parrish in his studio, blk/wht, unfr, 5x3½", NM 175.00
Playing cards, Contentment, Edison/Mazda, 1928, unopened 325.00
Playing cards, New Moon, Edison/Mazda, 1958, unopened 175.00

Poster, The Christmas Scribner's, man in burgundy coat on green background, red and black lettering, 22x14", NM, $3,000.00.

Poster, National Authority on Amateur Sports, rare 3,900.00
Print, Aladdin, 1907, 9x11", new mat & fr 275.00
Print, Atlas, EX 300.00
Print, Autumn Afternoon, matted, no fr 200.00
Print, Brazen Boatmen, new mat & fr 225.00
Print, Cassim, rpl mat & fr 200.00
Print, Christmas, Harper's Monthly, 1896 ....195.00
Print, Daybreak, Brown & Bigelow, 1922, 18x13" 500.00
Print, Dreaming, 10x18", 1928 ....650.00
Print, Evening, 1922, 12x15" 325.00
Print, Evening Shadows, 1989, M 75.00
Print, Fisherman & Genia, 1906, new mat & fr 200.00
Print, Garden of Allah, sm 195.00
Print, Garden of Allah, 1918, 15x30" 550.00
Print, Idiot, Original Collier's, 1910, 11x13½" 325.00
Print, Peaceful Valley, Pomegranate, 1989, 19x25" 75.00
Print, Peaceful Valley, 1936, complete, new mat & fr, sm 250.00
Print, Perfect Day, Brown & Bigelow, new mat & fr, sm 75.00
Print, Perfect Day, Brown & Bigelow, 1943, lg, EX 385.00
Print, Prince Codadad, 1906, 9x11" 225.00
Print, Rocks & Rills, 1981, 12½x15½" 45.00
Print, Royal Gorge, rare, 1925, 16½x20" 750.00
Print, Rubaiyat, 1917, unfr, sm, NM 300.00
Print, Rybaiyat, rare R&N seal, verse on bk, ornate fr, 8x30" 775.00
Print, Sheltering Oaks, Brown & Bigelow, 1960, matted, lg 225.00
Print, Sheltering Oaks, Parrish signature, 16x12+", matted 995.00
Print, Sinbad Plots Against the Giant, matted, 1907 ....200.00
Print, Twilight, Brown & Bigelow, matted, 1937 ....325.00
Print, Twilight Hour, matted & fr, 1951, 11x8½", EX 395.00
Print, Villa Chigi, Century, matted, 1915, 10½x14" 175.00
Print, Villa Gori, Century, matted, 1915, 10½x14" 175.00
Print, Village Brook, Brown & Bigelow, matted & fr, 1941, med 295.00
Print, Village Church, Brown & Bigelow, newer fr, 1949, med, EX 295.00
Print, W/Trumpet & Drum, 1905, 11x16" 395.00
Print, When Day Is Dawning, Brown & Bigelow, matted, 1954 ......375.00
Print, Young King of Black Isle, 1907, 11x9" 225.00
Puzzle, Daybreak, 1970, NM 125.00
Puzzle, Jig of Jigs, The Prince; 1926, NMIB 295.00
Tin, Edison Mazda Lamps ad, very rare 200.00
Triptych, Daybreak, Wild Geese, Canyon, rare, 20x56" 2,500.00

Pattern Glass

Pattern Glass was the first mass produced fancy tableware in America and was much prized by our ancestors. From the 1840s to the Civil War, it contained a high lead content and is known as 'Flint Glass.' It is exceptionally clear and resonant. Later glass was made with soda lime and is known as non-flint. By the 1890s pattern glass was produced in great volume in thousands of patterns, and colored glass came into vogue. Today the highest prices are often paid for these later patterns flashed with rose, amber, canary, and vaseline; stained ruby; or made in colors of cobalt, green, yellow, amethyst, etc. Demand for pattern glass declined by 1915, and glass fanciers were collecting it by 1930. No other field of antiques offers more diversity in patterns, prices, or pieces than this unique and historical glass that represents the Victorian era in America.

Our advisor for this category is Darlene Yohe; she is listed in the Directory under Arkansas. For a more thorough study on the subject, we recommend *The Collector's Encyclopedia of Pattern Glass* by Mollie Helen McCain, available from Collector Books. See also Bread Plates; Cruets; Historical Glass; Salt and Pepper Shakers; Salts, Open; Sugar Shakers; Syrups; specific manufacturers such as Northwood.

Note: Values are given for open sugar bowls and compotes unless noted 'w/lid.'

Actress, butter dish 100.00
Actress, cake stand, frosted stem, 10" 135.00
Actress, creamer 85.00
Actress, tray, dresser 65.00
Admiral Dewey, See Dewey; See Also Greentown Dewey
Alabama, butter dish, ruby stained 145.00
Alabama, pitcher, water 145.00
Allover Diamond, egg cup 22.00
Allover Diamond, ice cream tray 32.00
Allover Diamond, ice tub 38.00

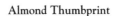

Almond Thumbprint

Almond Thumbprint, cordial 42.50
Almond Thumbprint, sugar bowl, w/lid, flint 65.00
Almond Thumbprint, tumbler, ftd 38.00
Amazon, butter dish, etched decor 75.00
Amazon, champagne 32.50
Amazon, creamer 38.00
Amberette, See Klondike
Apollo, pitcher, water 80.00
Apollo, salt cellar 20.00
Arched Ovals, cake stand 36.00
Arched Ovals, mug 20.00
Arched Ovals, punch cup 7.50
Arched Ovals, spooner, ruby stain 32.00
Arched Ovals, wine 15.00
Argus, ale glass, flint 80.00
Argus, champagne, flint 70.00
Argus, mug, flint 68.00
Art, celery vase, ruby stain 95.00
Art, goblet 65.00
Art, relish 22.50
Art, sugar bowl, w/lid, ruby stain 125.00
Art, tumbler 32.50
Ashburton, carafe 178.00
Ashburton, egg cup, dbl 100.00
Ashburton, goblet 45.00

Ashburton, honey dish 17.50
Atlas, butter dish 75.00
Atlas, marmalade 50.00
Atlas, tray, water 72.50
Atlas, tumbler 27.50
Aurora, pitcher, water; ruby stain 95.00
Aurora, waste bowl 30.00
Aurora, wine, ruby stain 48.00
Austrian, goblet 40.00
Austrian, tumbler 22.50
Balder, See Pennsylvania
Baltimore Pear, bowl, 8" 22.00
Baltimore Pear, creamer 30.00
Baltimore Pear, relish, 8¼" 24.00
Baltimore Pear, water tray 30.00

Bar and Diamond

Bar & Diamond, tumbler 22.50
Bar & Diamond, wine 18.00
Barberry, celery vase 38.00
Barberry, compote, high std, shell finial on lid, 6"....50.00
Barberry, sugar bowl, shell finial 42.50
Barley, celery vase 22.50
Barley, goblet 35.00
Barrel Huber, See Huber
Basket Weave, cup & saucer, amber 30.00
Basket Weave, goblet, amber 30.00
Basket Weave, mug, 3" 20.00
Basket Weave, water tray 35.00
Beaded Band, creamer 32.00
Beaded Band, pitcher, water 78.00
Beaded Band, relish, sm 15.00
Beaded Grape, bread plate 25.00
Beaded Grape, pickle dish 22.50
Beaded Grape, vase, gr, 6" 45.00
Beaded Grape, wine 32.00
Beaded Grape Medallion, egg cup 35.00
Beaded Grape Medallion, pitcher, water 150.00
Beaded Grape Medallion, plate, 6" 30.00
Beaded Grape Medallion, tumbler, ftd 48.00
Beaded Medallion, butter dish 45.00
Beaded Medallion, compote, low std 90.00
Beaded Mirror, See Beaded Medallion
Beaded Swirl, creamer, flat 25.00
Beaded Swirl, egg cup 15.00
Beaded Swirl, mug 12.00
Beaded Swirl, sugar bowl, flat, w/lid 38.00
Beaded Tulip, goblet 38.00
Beaded Tulip, pitcher, water 60.00
Beaded Tulip, plate, 6" 24.00
Beaded Tulip, wine 30.00
Bearded Head, See Viking
Bellflower, creamer 50.00

Bellflower, egg cup 40.00
Bellflower, goblet, water 70.00
Bigler, celery vase 90.00
Bigler, decanter, 1-qt 115.00
Bigler, wine 50.00
Bird & Strawberry, butter dish 85.00
Bird & Strawberry, punch cup 20.00
Bird & Strawberry, sugar bowl 55.00
Bleeding Heart, bowl, 8" 36.00
Bleeding Heart, pitcher, water 100.00
Bleeding Heart, sauce dish 12.50
Bleeding Heart, sugar bowl, w/lid 75.00
Block & Fan, butter dish, ruby stain 90.00
Block & Fan, cake stand, 10" 45.00
Blue Jay, See Cardinal Bird
Bohemian, mug, rose stained w/gold 80.00
Bohemian, tumbler, rose stain 48.00
Bow Tie, goblet 65.00
Bow Tie, pitcher, 5½" 50.00
Broken Column, carafe 80.00
Broken Column, cracker jar 95.00
Broken Column, pitcher, water 100.00
Broken Column, tumbler 50.00
Buckle, lamp, brass/iron base 185.00
Buckle, salt cellar, flat, flint 32.50
Buckle, wine, flint 125.00
Buckle w/Star, mustard jar 80.00
Buckle w/Star, relish 18.00
Buckle w/Star, tumbler 55.00
Bull's Eye, carafe 50.00
Bull's Eye, cordial 78.00
Bull's Eye, mug, appl hdl, 3½" 110.00
Bull's Eye, spooner 38.00
Bull's Eye, whiskey 78.00
Bull's Eye & Fan, relish 22.50
Bull's Eye Band, See Reverse Torpedo
Bull's Eye in Heart, See Heart w/Thumbprint
Bull's Eye w/Diamond Point, honey dish 35.00
Bull's Eye w/Diamond Point, wine 125.00
Button Arches, cake stand, ruby stain 175.00
Button Arches, pitcher, milk 38.00
Button Arches, plate, 7" 15.00
Button Arches, spooner, ruby stain 40.00
Button Band, bowl, 10" 32.00
Button Band, cordial 40.00
Button Band, goblet 42.50
Button Band, tumbler 28.00
Cabbage Rose, wine 40.00
Cable, cake stand, 9" 110.00
Cable, egg cup 65.00
Cable, plate, 6" 75.00
Cable, tumbler, ftd 215.00
California, See Beaded Grape
Cane, goblet, amber 35.00
Cane, relish, 8" 22.00
Cane, spooner, apple gr 38.00
Cape Cod, bowl, hdls, 6" 38.00
Cape Cod, decanter 175.00
Cape Cod, goblet 48.00
Cape Cod, platter, hdls 50.00
Cape Cod, wine 36.00
Cardinal Bird, butter dish, 3 birds in base 125.00
Cardinal Bird, pitcher, water 160.00
Cardinal Bird, spooner 40.00

Cathedral, creamer, amber, sq 50.00
Cathedral, tumbler 25.00
Centennial, See Liberty Bell
Chain, goblet 24.00
Chain, sugar bowl, w/lid 35.00
Chain & Shield, bread plate 18.00
Chain & Shield, platter, oval 27.50
Chain w/Diamonds, See Washington Centennial
Chain w/Star, cake stand, 8¾" 35.00
Chain w/Star, creamer 27.50
Chain w/Star, pickle dish, oval 12.50
Chain w/Star, sauce bowl, flat 12.50
Chain w/Star, spooner 26.00
Chandelier, celery vase 20.00
Chandelier, creamer 35.00
Chandelier, pitcher, water; etched 135.00
Chandelier, violet bowl 42.50
Classic, goblet 285.00
Classic, plate, 10" 195.00
Coin, See US Coin
Colorado, banana stand, gr 45.00
Colorado, butter dish, bl 195.00
Colorado, mug 25.00
Colorado, mug, gr 35.00
Colorado, plate, bl, 8" 72.50
Colorado, punch cup 20.00
Columbian Coin, mug, frosted coins 125.00
Columbian Coin, pitcher, milk; golden coins 200.00
Columbian Coin, relish, frosted coins, 8" 60.00
Columbian Coin, spooner, golden coins 80.00
Comet, compote, low std 180.00
Comet, goblet 88.00
Comet, tumbler, bar 90.00
Compact, See Snail
Connecticut, celery vase 28.00
Cord & Tassel, egg cup 40.00
Cord & Tassel, wine 45.00
Cord Drapery, mug 40.00
Cord Drapery, pickle dish, amber 80.00
Cord Drapery, sugar bowl, gr, w/lid 185.00
Cordova, bowl, berry; w/lid 32.00
Cordova, creamer 35.00
Cordova, finger bowl 20.00
Cordova, pitcher, milk 35.00
Cordova, tumbler 17.50
Cottage, cake stand, bl 90.00
Cottage, plate, 7" 22.50
Croesus, bowl, master berry; amethyst, +6 ind 795.00
Croesus, butter dish 90.00
Croesus, compote, amethyst, high std, 7" 175.00
Croesus, jelly compote 22.50
Croesus, pitcher, water; gr 200.00
Croesus, pitcher, water; gr, w/6 tumblers 850.00
Croesus, plate, gr, ftd, 8" 70.00
Croesus, spooner 60.00
Crow's Foot, See Yale
Crown Jewels, See Chandelier
Crystal Wedding, banana stand 95.00
Crystal Wedding, nappy 27.50
Crystal Wedding, relish, 7½" L 25.00
Cube w/Fan, See Pineapple & Fan
Cupid & Venus, cake stand 55.00
Cupid & Venus, creamer 38.00
Cupid & Venus, goblet 78.00

Cupid & Venus, wine, 3¾" 85.00
Currant, butter dish 70.00
Currant, celery vase 45.00
Currant, pitcher, water 95.00
Currant, relish 15.00
Currier & Ives, butter dish 60.00
Currier & Ives, creamer 35.00
Currier & Ives, lamp, 9½" 75.00
Currier & Ives, plate, 10" 20.00
Currier & Ives, tray, 9½" dia 50.00
Curtain, creamer 32.00
Cut Log, mug 22.50
Cut Log, tankard 75.00
Dahlia, bowl, bl 30.00
Dahlia, bread plate, amber 58.00
Dahlia, champagne 55.00
Dahlia, egg cup, bl 68.00
Dahlia, pickle dish 22.50
Dahlia, spooner, amber 55.00
Daisy & Button, ashtray, ftd 6.00
Daisy & Button, egg cup, bl 22.50
Daisy & Button, parfait, amber 28.00
Daisy & Button, plate, vaseline, 7" sq 38.00
Daisy & Button, sugar bowl, bl, w/lid 85.00
Daisy & Button, wine 28.00
Daisy & Button w/Crossbar, punch cup 15.00
Daisy & Button w/Crossbar, tray, amber 55.00
Daisy & Button w/Crossbar, wine 27.50
Daisy & Button w/Thumbprint Panels, goblet, amber stain 50.00

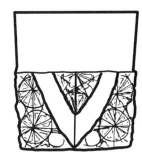

Daisy & Button w/V Ornament

Daisy & Button w/V Ornament, celery vase 32.00
Daisy & Button w/V Ornament, match holder 25.00
Daisy & Button w/V Ornament, mug 25.00
Daisy & Button w/V Ornament, tumbler 15.00
Dakota, celery tray, clear 48.00
Dakota, compote, high std, eng, w/lid, 8" 200.00
Dakota, pitcher, milk; jug type, 1-pt 200.00
Dakota, spooner, etched 35.00
Dakota, tumbler, ruby stain 45.00
Dakota, waste bowl 60.00
Deer & Dog, spooner, etched 100.00
Deer & Dog, wine 80.00
Deer & Pine Tree, goblet 60.00
Deer & Pine Tree, sugar bowl, w/lid 60.00
Delaware, creamer 50.00
Delaware, dresser tray 35.00
Delaware, spooner, gold trim 70.00
Dew & Raindrop, bud vase 28.00
Dew & Raindrop, punch cup 9.00
Dewey, butter dish, vaseline 78.00
Dewey, parfait 48.00
Dewey, See Also Greentown, Dewey

Dewey, tumbler 48.00
Diagonal Band, creamer 32.00
Diagonal Band, goblet 30.00
Diagonal Band, pitcher, water 45.00
Diamond Horseshoe, See Aurora
Diamond Medallion, See Grand
Diamond Point, champagne, flint 130.00
Diamond Point, cordial, vaseline 36.00
Diamond Point, spill holder, flint 50.00
Diamond Quilted, champagne, turq 40.00
Diamond Quilted, cordial, amber 35.00
Diamond Quilted, creamer, amber 40.00
Diamond Quilted, relish, vaseline, leaf shape 18.00
Diamond Thumbprint, bowl, 8" 88.00
Diamond Thumbprint, butter dish 215.00
Diamond Thumbprint, pitcher, milk 465.00
Dinner Bell, See Cottage
Doric, See Feather
Double Leaf & Dart, See Leaf & Dart
Drapery, butter dish 42.50
Drapery, creamer 24.00
Drapery, goblet 27.50
Egg in Sand, goblet 28.00
Egg in Sand, pitcher, water; bl 100.00
Egg in Sand, relish 12.50
Egg in Sand, water tray, flat 24.00
Egyptian, creamer 50.00
Egyptian, plate, 12" 88.00
Egyptian, spooner 18.00
Elephant, See Jumbo
Emerald Green Herringbone, See Florida
Empress, butter dish 65.00
Empress, spooner, gr 75.00
Empress, tumbler 35.00
Esther, butter dish 68.00
Esther, creamer, gr 120.00
Esther, goblet 55.00
Esther, goblet, ruby stain 80.00
Esther, plate, 10" 28.00
Esther, wine, gr 55.00
Etched Dakota, See Dakota
Eureka, bread plate, 11¾" 30.00
Eureka, cordial 45.00
Eureka, wine 32.00
Excelsior, cordial 45.00
Excelsior, creamer, molded hdl 88.00
Eyewinker, bowl, 6½" 28.00
Eyewinker, butter dish 65.00
Eyewinker, compote, high std, 9½" 145.00
Eyewinker, goblet 32.00
Eyewinker, tumbler 30.00
Fairfax Strawberry, See Strawberry
Feather, cake plate 60.00
Feather, cordial 120.00
Feather, tumbler, gr 88.00
Feather, wine 48.00
Festoon, bowl, berry, rectangular, 8" 25.00
Festoon, butter dish 45.00
Festoon, marmalade 35.00
Festoon, water tray, 10" 35.00
Fine Cut, cake stand 40.00
Fine Cut, pitcher, water; amber 80.00
Fine Cut & Block, champagne, amber 60.00
Fine Cut & Block, cordial 65.00

Fine Cut & Block, punch cup, yel blocks 45.00
Fine Cut & Block, wine 20.00
Fine Cut & Diamond, See Grand
Fine Cut & Feather, See Feather
Fine Cut & Panel, bowl, oval, 8" 20.00
Fine Cut & Panel, compote, high std, amber, w/lid ...125.00
Fine Cut & Panel, plate, amber, 6" 25.00
Fine Cut & Panel, platter, bl 55.00
Fine Cut & Panel, spooner 12.00
Fine Cut & Panel, waste bowl, vaseline 38.00
Fine Rib, goblet, flint 78.00
Fine Rib, wine 45.00
Fingerprint, See Almond Thumbprint
Fishscale, cake stand 38.00
Fishscale, creamer 25.00
Fishscale, pickle dish 30.00
Fishscale, water tray 40.00
Flamingo Habitat, creamer 45.00
Flamingo Habitat, goblet 35.00
Flamingo Habitat, wine 45.00
Florida, butter dish 55.00
Florida, mustard pot, w/lid 28.00
Florida, nappy 15.00
Florida, sauce bowl, gr 8.00
Florida, tumbler, gr 42.00

Flower Pot

Flower Pot, goblet 45.00
Flower Pot, sugar bowl 48.00
Flute, claret 25.00
Flute, goblet, flint 28.00
Frosted Circle, compote, 7x7½" 25.00
Frosted Circle, wine 42.50
Frosted Leaf, egg cup 90.00
Frosted Leaf, goblet 120.00
Frosted Leaf, tumbler 45.00
Frosted Lion, See Lion
Frosted Ribbon, See Ribbon
Frosted Roman Key, butter dish, flint 55.00
Frosted Roman Key, champagne, flint 80.00
Frosted Stork, sauce bowl 30.00
Frosted Stork, waste bowl 185.00
Galloway, finger bowl 25.00
Galloway, goblet 60.00
Galloway, punch cup 12.50
Garfield Drape, cake stand 80.00
Garfield Drape, goblet 40.00
Gem, See Nailhead
Georgia, bonbon, ftd 28.00
Georgia, cake stand, 10" 55.00
Georgia, creamer 35.00
Georgia, mug 30.00

Georgia, tumbler 32.50
Good Luck, See Horseshoe
Grand, goblet 32.00
Grand, pitcher, water 45.00
Grand, spooner 20.00
Grape & Festoon, w/Stippled Leaf, sugar bowl, w/lid 50.00
Grape & Festoon w/Shield, mug, sapphire, bl, 2½" 55.00
Grape & Festoon w/Shield, mug, 1⅞" 20.00
Grape & Festoon w/Stippled Leaf, goblet 38.00
Grape & Festoon w/Stippled Leaf, plate, 6" 20.00
Grape & Festoon w/Stippled Leaf, wine 45.00
Grasshopper, celery vase 65.00
Grasshopper, plate, ftd, 10½" 30.00
Grasshopper, salt cellar 50.00
Grasshopper, sugar bowl, w/insect, w/lid 75.00
Greek Key, celery tray, 9" 42.00
Greek Key, goblet 90.00
Greek Key, punch cup 18.00
Guardian Angel, See Cupid & Venus
Hairpin, celery vase 65.00
Hairpin, tumbler 55.00
Halley's Comet, creamer 42.00
Halley's Comet, marmalade 58.00
Halley's Comet, spooner 55.00
Hamilton, egg cup 45.00
Hamilton, tumbler, water 80.00
Hand, compote, high std, 7" 60.00
Hand, honey dish 15.00
Hand, mug 42.00
Hand, sugar bowl, w/lid 80.00
Hawaiian Lei, cake stand 40.00
Hawaiian Lei, cup & saucer 40.00
Heart w/Thumbprint, finger bowl 42.50
Herringbone Band, See Ripple
Herringbone Buttress, See Greentown, Herringbone Buttress
Hickman, butter dish 38.00
Hickman, goblet 42.00
Hickman, plate, 6" 12.50
Hickman, rose bowl 30.00
Hidalgo, celery vase 30.00
Hidalgo, pitcher, water 45.00
Hidalgo, tumbler 27.50
Hinoto, egg cup 40.00
Hinoto, whiskey, flint 140.00
Holly, butter dish 150.00
Holly, pitcher, water 235.00
Holly, wine 150.00
Holly Amber, See Greentown, Holly Amber
Honeycomb, champagne, flint 45.00
Honeycomb, goblet 22.50
Hops & Barley, See Wheat & Barley
Horn of Plenty, butter pat, flint 24.00
Horn of Plenty, cordial, flint 150.00
Horn of Plenty, pitcher, water; flint, minimum value 600.00
Horn of Plenty, wine, flint 125.00
Horseshoe, creamer 45.00
Horseshoe, plate, 10" 100.00
Huber, egg cup 30.00
Huber, goblet 42.00
Hummingbird, goblet, bl 68.00
Hummingbird, water tray 55.00
Hummingbird, wine 95.00
Idaho, See Snail
Illinois, olive dish 20.00

Illinois, pitcher, tankard, SP rim 90.00
Illinois, plate, sq, 7" 27.50
Illinois, sauce bowl 28.00
Iris w/Meander, See Opalescent Glass
Ivy in Snow, cake stand, 10" 45.00
Ivy in Snow, creamer 22.00
Ivy in Snow, tumbler, ruby stain 45.00
Jacob's Ladder, butter dish 70.00
Jacob's Ladder, creamer 38.00
Jacob's Ladder, marmalade 10.00
Jersey Swirl, salt cellar, canary 24.00
Jewel Band, pitcher, milk 48.00
Jewel w/Dewdrop, compote, 6" 38.00
Jewel w/Dewdrop, mug, 3½" 35.00
Jewel w/Festoon, creamer 27.50
Jewel w/Festoon, punch cup 24.00
Jewel w/Moondrop, mug 50.00
Jewel w/Moondrop, tumbler 42.50
Jewelled Moon & Star, butter dish 70.00
Jewelled Moon & Star, spooner, amber stain 65.00
Jewelled Moon & Star, wine 35.00
Job's Tears, See Art

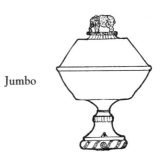

Jumbo

Jumbo, butter dish, Barnum, w/lid 550.00
Jumbo, butter dish, oblong 725.00
Jumbo, butter dish, sq 650.00
Jumbo, compote, Barnum, oval, 7" 1,800.00
Jumbo, compote, Barnum, oval, 8" 1,000.00
Jumbo, compote, w/lid, 5¾" 1,000.00
Jumbo, creamer 165.00
Jumbo, pitcher, amber 400.00
Jumbo, pitcher, bl, ribbed, water sz 425.00
Jumbo, pitcher, PT Barnum, water sz 850.00
Kentucky, cup, gr 22.50
Kentucky, olive dish, handles 28.00
Kentucky, punch cup 12.50
Kentucky, spooner 35.00
King's Crown, banana stand, ftd, ruby stain 150.00
King's Crown, cordial 30.00
King's Crown, goblet 32.50
King's Crown, preserve dish, 10" 38.00
King's Crown, sugar bowl, 2¾" 32.00
Klondike, bowl, amber stain, scalloped, 7" 200.00
Klondike, pitcher 250.00
Klondike, tumbler, amber stain 140.00
La Clede, See Hickman
Lace, See Drapery
Lawrence, See Bull's Eye
Leaf, See Maple Leaf
Leaf & Dart, egg cup 18.00
Leaf & Dart, salt cellar, master 25.00
Leaf & Dart, wine 28.00

Leaf Bracket, See Greentown, Leaf Bracket
Leaf Medallion, See Northwood, Leaf Medallion
Liberty Bell, bowl, ftd, 8" 100.00
Liberty Bell, creamer 95.00
Liberty Bell, mug, mini 120.00
Lily of the Valley, cake stand 68.00
Lily of the Valley, honey dish 12.50
Lily of the Valley, pitcher, water 140.00
Lily of the Valley, sugar bowl 38.00
Lincoln Drape, egg cup 70.00
Lincoln Drape, sugar bowl, w/lid, flint 125.00
Lion, champagne 195.00
Lion, cordial 195.00
Lion, pitcher, water 325.00
Lion, spooner 85.00
Log Cabin, bowl, 3⅝x8x5¼", w/lid 425.00
Log Cabin, creamer, 4½" 125.00
Log Cabin, sugar bowl, w/lid 295.00
Long Spear, See Grasshopper
Loop, compote, flint, 8½" L 35.00
Loop, cordial, nonflint 38.00
Loop, creamer, flint 38.00
Loop & Dart, goblet 35.00
Loop & Dart, sugar bowl, w/lid 50.00
Loop w/Stippled Panels, See Texas
Magnet & Grape, butter dish, frosted leaf, flint 195.00
Magnet & Grape, egg cup, clear leaf, nonflint 22.00
Magnet & Grape, pitcher, milk; clear leaf, nonflint 80.00

Maine

Maine, cake stand, emerald gr 60.00
Maine, mug 37.50
Maine, pitcher, milk 68.00
Maine, tumbler 32.00
Manhattan, basket, 11½x10x7" 150.00
Manhattan, celery tray 25.00
Manhattan, creamer, ind 25.00
Manhattan, goblet 30.00
Maple Leaf, pitcher 48.00
Maple Leaf, tumbler 37.50
Maryland, bowl, berry; gold trim 17.50
Maryland, celery vase 32.00
Maryland, compote, high std, ruby stain, w/lid 110.00
Maryland, creamer, gold trim 27.50
Maryland, relish, ruby stain, oval 60.00
Mascotte, butter pat 12.00
Mascotte, cheese dish 67.50
Mascotte, compote, w/lid, 5" 45.00
Mascotte, spooner, eng decor 40.00
Mascotte, tumbler 30.00
Massachusetts, goblet 45.00
Massachusetts, punch cup 17.50
Massachusetts, sugar bowl, w/lid 40.00

Medallion, sugar bowl, amber, w/lid 45.00
Melrose, compote, 5¾x7½" 27.50
Michigan, butter dish, bl stain 185.00
Minerva, honey dish 20.00
Minnesota, basket 68.00
Minnesota, bonbon, 5" 17.50
Minnesota, creamer, sm 22.00
Minnesota, nappy, 4½" 15.00
Minnesota, olive dish, ruby stain 28.00
Minnesota, spooner 25.00
Minor Block, See Mascotte
Mirror, See Galloway
Missouri, butter dish 48.00
Missouri, cordial, gr 60.00
Missouri, creamer 25.00
Missouri, goblet 55.00
Missouri, tumbler 32.00
Monkey, mug 115.00
Moon & Star, carafe, frosted, flint 55.00
Moon & Star, champagne 70.00
Moon & Star, claret, frosted, flint 60.00
Moon & Star, egg cup, flint 40.00
Morning Glory, salt cellar, flint, master 235.00
Morning Glory, wine, flint 95.00
Nail, cake stand 45.00
Nail, decanter 37.50
Nail, tumbler 18.00
Nail, tumbler, ruby stain 60.00
Nailhead, goblet 22.50
Nailhead, wine 38.00
Nestor, butter dish, clear w/gold 70.00
Nestor, tumbler, gr 32.00
New England Pineapple, champagne, flint 265.00
New England Pineapple, decanter, flint, qt 180.00
New England Pineapple, pitcher, water 325.00
New England Pineapple, wine, flint 200.00
New Hampshire, cake stand, gold trim, 8¼" 32.00
New Hampshire, mug, rose stain, lg 48.00
New Hampshire, tumbler, gold trim 27.00
New Jersey, goblet 42.50
New Jersey, jelly compote, high std 50.00
New Jersey, pitcher, water 100.00
O'Hara Diamond, bowl, berry; sm 12.00
O'Hara Diamond, compote, high std, w/lid 42.50
O'Hara Diamond, plate, 7" 22.50
O'Hara Diamond, tumbler 28.00
Oaken Bucket, See Wooden Pail
One Hundred & One, goblet 50.00
One Hundred & One, sauce dish 20.00
One Hundred & One, spooner 40.00
One-O-One, See One Hundred & One
Open Rose, salt cellar, master 25.00
Open Rose, spooner 32.50
Oregon, creamer, flat 32.00
Oregon, goblet 32.50
Oregon, relish 18.00
Palmette, celery vase 50.00
Palmette, cup plate 45.00
Palmette, goblet 38.00
Palmette, relish 18.00
Panelled Daisy, celery vase 36.00
Panelled Daisy, goblet 28.00
Panelled Forget-Me-Not, celery dish 48.00
Panelled Forget-Me-Not, mustard jar 42.50

Panelled Star & Button, mug, mini	18.00
Panelled Star & Button, salt cellar, master	15.00
Panelled Thistle, basket	75.00
Panelled Thistle, bread plate	48.00
Panelled Thistle, doughnut stand, 6"	32.00
Panelled Thistle, sugar bowl, w/lid	50.00
Pavonia, creamer, eng	40.00
Pavonia, pitcher, lemonade; plain	115.00
Pavonia, salt cellar, ind, plain	15.00
Pavonia, waste bowl, ruby stain	60.00
Pennsylvania, biscuit jar, gr	135.00
Pennsylvania, bowl, berry; 8"	28.00
Pennsylvania, decanter	110.00
Pennsylvania, relish	10.00
Pennsylvania, tumbler, gr	42.50
Pigmy, See Torpedo	
Pillow Encircled, sauce dish	12.50
Pillow Encircled, sugar bowl, w/lid	38.00
Pineapple & Fan, pitcher, water	80.00
Pioneer, See Westward Ho	
Pleat & Panel, bowl, rectangular, ftd, 8"	38.00
Pleat & Panel, goblet	35.00
Pleat & Panel, marmalade	98.00
Pleat & Panel, plate, sq, 7"	20.00
Plume, bowl, w/lid, 8"	45.00
Plume, sugar bowl	22.50
Polar Bear, bread tray	160.00
Polar Bear, goblet	100.00
Popcorn, butter dish, w/lid	55.00
Popcorn, wine	32.00
Portland, butter dish	55.00
Portland, celery tray	20.00
Portland, goblet	38.00
Portland, ring tree	88.00
Powder & Shot, creamer, bulbous, flint	98.00
Powder & Shot, egg cup, flint	60.00
Prayer Rug, See Horseshoe	
Pressed Leaf, spooner	22.50
Pressed Leaf, wine	42.00
Primrose, pitcher	45.00
Primrose, tray, wafer; 11" dia	32.00
Princess Feather, butter dish	45.00
Princess Feather, creamer	40.00
Princess Feather, egg cup	38.00
Princess Feather, goblet	48.00
Priscilla, creamer, ind	25.00
Priscilla, goblet	40.00
Priscilla, rose bowl, 3¾"	35.00
Psyche & Cupid, celery vase	30.00
Psyche & Cupid, pitcher, water	90.00
Question Mark, bowl, oblong, 7"	20.00
Question Mark, bread tray	32.00
Question Mark, cordial	22.50
Recessed Pillared Red Top, See Nail	
Red Block, cheese dish	135.00
Red Block, creamer, sm	48.00
Red Block, goblet	36.00
Red Block, rose bowl	75.00
Red Top, See Button Archres	
Reverse Torpedo, biscuit jar, w/lid	130.00
Reverse Torpedo, goblet	90.00
Reverse Torpedo, pitcher, tankard, 10¼"	165.00
Ribbed Ivy, egg cup	40.00
Ribbed Palm, egg cup	40.00

Ribbed Palm, tumbler	120.00
Ribbed Palm, wine, flint	75.00
Ribbon, butter dish	80.00
Ribbon, platter, 13"	55.00
Ribbon Candy, butter dish, ftd	60.00
Ribbon Candy, cake stand, 10½"	50.00
Ribbon Candy, cordial	58.00
Ribbon Candy, goblet	70.00
Ripple, ice tub	60.00
Ripple, wine	35.00
Ripple Band, See Ripple	
Rochelle, See Princess Feather	
Roman Rosette, butter dish	50.00
Roman Rosette, creamer	32.00
Rose in Snow, bottle, bitters; orig stopper	110.00
Rose in Snow, creamer, sq	40.00
Rose in Snow, goblet, amber	55.00
Rose in Snow, pitcher	130.00
Rose Sprig, cake stand, 10"	150.00
Rose Sprig, relish, sq, 6"	30.00
Rose Sprig, wine	32.00
Rosette, pitcher, water	55.00
Rosette, plate, 7"	17.50
Royal Ivy, See Northwood	
Royal Oak, See Northwood	
Ruby Thumbprint, See King's Crown	
S-Repeat, sauce bowl, apple gr w/gold	32.00
S-Repeat, wine, gr	45.00
Sandwich Star, compote, low std, 6½"	65.00
Sandwich Star, decanter, bar lip, 1-pt	75.00

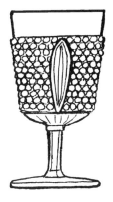

Sawtooth

Sawtooth, cordial, flint	55.00
Sawtooth, egg cup, nonflint	27.50
Sawtooth, goblet, flint	60.00
Sawtooth, goblet, nonflint	22.50
Sawtooth, sugar bowl, w/lid, flint	65.00
Sawtooth Band, See Amazon	
Scalloped Daisy Red Top, See Button Arches	
Scroll w/Flowers, compote, w/lid	75.00
Scroll w/Flowers, sugar bowl, w/lid	55.00
Sedan, See Panelled Star & Button	
Seneca Loop, See Loop	
Shell & Jewel, bowl, 8"	35.00
Shell & Jewel, tumbler, amber	36.00
Shell & Tassel, bowl, canary, w/lid, 8"	125.00
Shell & Tassel, compote, 7½" sq	98.00
Shell & Tassel, creamer, sq	60.00
Shell & Tassel, spooner, sq	55.00
Sheraton, wine	22.00

Shoshone, mug 25.00
Shuttle, tumbler 48.00
Skilton, goblet 35.00
Skilton, pitcher, tankard, ruby stain 125.00
Skilton, relish 18.00
Snail, banana stand 160.00
Snail, compote, ruby stain, high std, 7" 110.00
Snail, custard cup 30.00
Snail, plate, 5" 35.00
Snail, wine 68.00
Spades, See Medallion
Spirea Band, spooner, vaseline 32.50
Spirea Band, sugar bowl, w/lid 25.00
Sprig, pickle dish 18.00
Sprig, pickle jar 68.00
Sprig, relish 17.50
Sprig, tumbler 30.00
Star & Feather, creamer 35.00
Star & Stripes, creamer 22.50
Star Rosetted, plate, 7" 12.00
States, goblet, clear w/gold 40.00
States, nappy, hdls, clear w/gold 25.00
Stippled Chain, goblet 24.00
Stippled Chain, sugar bowl, w/lid 20.00
Stippled Forget-Me-Not, cup & saucer 40.00
Stippled Forget-Me-Not, plate, 7" 70.00
Stippled Grape & Festoon, goblet 35.00
Stippled Grape & Festoon, pitcher, water 110.00
Strawberry, spooner 35.00
Strigil, celery tray 20.00
Strigil, punch cup 15.00
Strigil, wine 30.00
Sunk Honeycomb, cup & saucer, ruby stain 40.00
Sunk Honeycomb, goblet, ruby stain 47.50
Sunken Primrose, See Florida
Swan, cake stand 110.00
Swan, mustard, amber 75.00
Tarentem's Thumbprint, pitcher, water; etched 45.00
Teardrop & Tassel, bowl, 8¼" 50.00
Teardrop & Tassel, creamer 42.50
Teardrop & Tassel, pitcher, water 65.00
Teardrop & Tassel, See Also Greentown, Teardrop & Tassel
Teardrop & Tassel, spooner 45.00
Tennessee, bread plate, colored jewels 80.00
Tennessee, butter dish 58.00
Tennessee, cake stand, 8" 40.00
Tennessee, mug 38.00
Texas, goblet 95.00
Texas, horseradish 45.00
Texas, vase, 6½" 27.50
Theatrical, See Actress
Thousand Eye, celery dish, hat shape, amber 55.00
Thousand Eye, compote, bl, 6" 42.50
Thousand Eye, cordial, gr 58.00
Thousand Eye, inkwell 35.00
Thousand Eye, plate, 10" 35.00
Thousand Eye, wine, vaseline 42.50
Three Face, celery vase 125.00
Three Face, champagne 175.00
Three Face, compote, high std, 7" 98.00
Three Face, cracker jar 1,350.00
Three Face, spooner 80.00
Three Face, sugar bowl, w/lid 150.00
Three Panel, compote, low std, 7" 30.00

Three Panel, goblet, bl 42.50
Three Panel, mug, vaseline 38.00
Three Panel, tumbler, bl 40.00
Thumbprint, See Argus
Thumbprint Band, See Dakota
Thunderbird, See Hummingbird
Torpedo, banana stand 60.00
Torpedo, compote, jelly; w/lid 40.00
Tree of Life, See Portland
Tree of Life w/Hand, butter dish 135.00
Tree of Life w/Hand, spooner 38.00

Triangular Prism

Triangular Prism, goblet 22.00
Triangular Prism, spooner, flint 55.00
Tulip w/Sawtooth, creamer, flint 88.00
Tulip w/Sawtooth, goblet, flint, 6⅝" 65.00
Two Panel, compote amber, w/lid 65.00
Two Panel, goblet, amber 30.00
Two Panel, wine 30.00
US Coin, cake stand, frosted 435.00
US Coin, creamer, clear 375.00
US Coin, epergne, clear 1,100.00
US Coin, pitcher, milk; clear 625.00
US Coin, tray, clear, 8" dia 295.00
US Coin, tumbler, ale; clear 265.00
US Coin, waste bowl, frosted 265.00
Utah, bowl, 6" 22.50
Utah, creamer 32.00
Utah, pickle dish 15.00
Valencia Waffle, bread plate 35.00
Valencia Waffle, compote, lt bl, 7" sq 55.00
Valencia Waffle, pitcher, water; amber, 7½" 70.00
Valencia Waffle, relish, amber, 9x5⅜" 22.50
Vermont, basket, clear w/gold 35.00
Vermont, pitcher, water; gr w/gold 130.00
Viking, bowl, sq, 8" 48.00
Viking, butter dish 80.00
Waffle, bar tumbler 100.00
Waffle, celery vase 85.00
Waffle, egg cup, flint 45.00
Waffle & Thumbprint, decanter, flint, 1-pt 350.00
Waffle & Thumbprint, tumbler, whiskey; flint 95.00
Waffle & Thumbprint, wine, flint 98.00
Washington, butter dish 165.00
Washington, creamer 195.00
Washington, tumbler, lemonade 80.00
Washington, wine 120.00
Washington Centennial, egg cup 42.50
Washington Centennial, sugar bowl 30.00

Wedding Ring, goblet, flint **90.00**
Wedding Ring, tumbler **82.50**
Westward Ho, creamer **98.00**
Westward Ho, goblet **115.00**
Westward Ho, marmalade, w/lid **188.00**
Westward Ho, pitcher, water **265.00**
Westward Ho, spooner **95.00**
Wheat & Barley, goblet, amber **25.00**
Wheat & Barley, pitcher, water; amber **80.00**
Wheat & Barley, tumbler **22.50**
Wildflower, butter dish, apple gr **50.00**
Wildflower, champagne **30.00**
Wildflower, creamer, bl **37.50**
Willow Oak, creamer **35.00**
Wisconsin, banana stand **72.50**
Wisconsin, cup & saucer **55.00**
Wisconsin, relish **28.00**
Wooden Pail, match holder, amber **30.00**
Wooden Pail, pitcher **100.00**
Wooden Pail, spooner, bl **50.00**
Wyoming, bowl, 4" **12.50**
Wyoming, cake stand, 11" **75.00**
Wyoming, mug **40.00**
X-Ray, carafe, gr w/gold **145.00**
X-Ray, marmalade, gr w/gold **75.00**
X-Ray, pitcher, clear w/gold trim, 9½" **55.00**
Yale, cake stand **55.00**
Yale, goblet **32.00**
Yale, spooner **22.50**
Yale, sugar bowl, w/lid **45.00**
Zipper, butter dish **42.50**
Zipper, goblet **25.00**
Zipper, wine, ruby stain **40.00**
3-Face, butter dish **175.00**
3-Face, goblet **140.00**
3-Face, pitcher, water; etched **550.00**
3-Face, sugar bowl **150.00**

Paul Revere Pottery

The Saturday Evening Girls were a social group of young Boston ladies who met to pursue various activities, among them pottery making. Their first kiln was bought in 1906, and within a few years it became necessary to move to a larger location. Because their new quarters were near the historical Old North Church, they chose the name Paul Revere Pottery. With very little training, the girls produced only simple ware. Until 1915 the pottery operated at a deficit; then a new building with four kilns was constructed on Nottingham Road. Vases, miniature jugs, children's tea sets, tiles, dinnerware, and lamps were produced, usually in soft matt glazes often decorated with incised, hand-painted designs from nature. Examples in a dark high gloss may also be found on occasion.

Several marks were used: 'P.R.P.'; 'S.E.G.'; or the circular device, 'Boston, Paul Revere Pottery' with the horse and rider.

The pottery continued to operate; and even though their product sold well, the high production costs of the handmade ware caused the pottery to fail in 1946.

Bowl, brn mocha, w/8-sided matching frog, SEG/4-4/17/TM, 8¼" ..**125.00**
Bowl, fish on chicory bl band on ivory, SEG/EG/RB, 1½x3½" ..**650.00**
Bowl, flower; steel bl, heavy, SEG/5-17/RB, 1½x8½" **125.00**
Bowl, lav-mauve satin, SEG/9-17/LS, 2¾x8¼" **125.00**
Bowl, lotus flowers, blk on jade gr, SEG/466-1-10/SMB, 6½" **900.00**

Bowl, porridge; Greek Key, hdls, EG/5-3-25, 6¼", +spoon **225.00**
Bowl, porridge; wht band on bl, SEG/9-20/AM, 2½", +plate, NM .**150.00**
Bowl, wht rosette band on chickory bl, SEG/9-2-11/TS..., 4¼" .**200.00**
Box, lotus flowers on steel bl, SEG/12-19/Lucy..., 3x4½" **650.00**
Box, trinket; tulip band on ivory, SEG/4-8-14/JG, 2¾" **200.00**
Child's set, trees, gr/bl/yel on lt & dk bl, c/s+6" bowl **750.00**
Creamer, Greek Key band on sage gr, SEG/1-19/IMA, 1¾" **125.00**
Creamer, lt sage & tan, wht speckled int, SEG, 1¾x3¾" **60.00**
Cup & saucer, coffee; bl band on wht, bl int, SEG/6-20/ELW/LS ...**75.00**
Cup & saucer, coffee; crouching rabbit on wht w/bl band, SEG .**450.00**
Cup & saucer, demi; lotus flowers on ivory, SEG/1-20/EG **200.00**
Egg cup, landscape band on ivory, sgn EG, SEG, 1½x1¾" **325.00**
Egg cup, lotus flower band, bl band at top, SEG/TM, 1½" **325.00**
Jar, ivory rabbits on turq grass, yel sky, SEG/12-15, 4¼" **600.00**
Jar, tulip on lid, wht/gr on yel, PRP, 3x5" dia **350.00**
Mug, chicory bl, PRP, 3¾", 4 for **100.00**
Mug, Stanley-His-Mug, bl rabbit on gr, yel sky, PRP/1-38/LS ..**450.00**
Nut dish, squirrel band on ivory, SEG/5-15/JG, ¾x3" **300.00**
Paperweight, mc tulips w/yel sky, 8-sided form, unmk, 1x2½" ...**325.00**
Paperweight, swan on mc waves, 8-sided, SEG/12-13/TB, 2½" ..**250.00**
Paperweight, tree, gr on bl, hexagonal, PRP, 3" **210.00**

Pitcher, multicolor band of Viking ships, signed IG (Ida Goldstein), SEG/138/11-10, ca 1910, 10x8", $2,000.00.

Pitcher, bl & gr mottle on tan gloss, 7", NM **130.00**
Pitcher, gray & lt bl gloss, paper label, 4½" **110.00**
Pitcher, owl & moon repeats on bl, wht band, SEG/1-11/EG, 4" ..**1,500.00**
Pitcher, wht duck, bl sky, yel mtns, PRP/7-?/EB/LS, 4", EX **275.00**
Pitcher, 2 wht rabbits, gr shrubs, bl sky, logo/11-24/#B, 3" **400.00**
Pitcher, 4 ivory swans & lotus flowers, SEG/10-3-12/FL, 2¾" **850.00**
Pitcher, 8 squirrels on narrow band, SEG, 2¾x4¾", EX **500.00**
Plate, broad wht mottled band on bl, SEG/10-20/ELW, 7¾", pr ..**90.00**
Plate, Greek Key, SEG/10-12/AM, 6½", pr **350.00**
Plate, house & landscape repeating, SEG/10-14/FL, 6¼" **800.00**
Plate, lotus flowers on ivory, yel band, SEG/11-10/RB, 6¼" **200.00**
Plate, lt bl wide band on chicory bl, SEG/3-24/H, 6½", 3 for **125.00**
Plate, rabbit, wht on turq w/yel sky, logo/10-25/Fl, 8½" **425.00**
Plate, rosettes, wht on speckled bl, SEG/348-9-10/FL, 10" **250.00**
Plate, steel bl speckles, SEG/5-20/11-17, 7½", 6½", pr **50.00**
Plate, tulip band on ivory, gr border, SEG/5-20/LG, 7½" **300.00**
Plate, water lily band on yel, PRP, 6" **450.00**
Salt cellar, narrow gr band on ivory, SEG/10-12/TB/IK, 2" **70.00**
Sponge pot, landscape on steel bl, SEG/5-17/EG, 1¾x3¾" **600.00**
Teapot, crouching rabbit, mc on wht w/bl band, PRP, 7x8" **650.00**
Teapot, jade gr to turq, spherical, logo/JW, 3¾x9¼" **175.00**
Teapot, pineapple-like design on ivory, SEG/5-16, 4¾x5½" **900.00**
Teapot, wht mottle band on chicory bl, SEG/11-23/M, 4¼x8¾" ..**275.00**
Tile, building & street scene, 5-color, SEG/51-5-11/RB, 3¾" **550.00**
Tile, gr mottled center, purple border, glossy, SEG, fr, 5" **350.00**
Tray, tulips on ivory, gr band, SEG/4-18-14/JG, 15" **500.00**
Trivet, Badger House-Corner..., mc scene, PRP, 3¾" dia **475.00**
Trivet, 3-masted ship, mustard/olive on bl, SEG, 5½" **600.00**

Vase, blk w/silver highlights, SEG, 4" 160.00
Vase, incised ship, speckled bl band, SEG/5-20/AM, 10" 1,500.00
Vase, teal matt, wide rim, SEG, 6½" 180.00
Vase, tulip band, mc & brn on yel & wht, 1926, 7½" 865.00
Wall pocket, lotus flowers, mc on royal bl, SEG/10-22/EB, 9" 500.00

Pauline Pottery

Pauline Pottery was made from 1883 to 1888 in Chicago, Illinois, from clay imported from the Ohio area. The company's founder was Mrs. Pauline Jacobus, who had learned the trade at the Rookwood Pottery. Mrs. Jacobus moved to Edgerton, Wisconsin, to be near a source of suitable clay, thus eliminating shipping expenses. Until 1905 she produced high-quality wares, able to imitate with ease designs and styles of such masters as Wedgwood and Meissen. Her products were sold through leading department stores, and the names of some of these firms may appear on the ware. Not all were marked; unless signed by a noted local artist, positive identification is often impossible. Marked examples carry a variety of stamps and signatures: 'Trade Mark' with a crown, 'Pauline Pottery,' and Edgerton Art Pottery' are but a few.

Charger, gold-traced flowers, excellent artwork, 10", M, $650.00.

Ginger jar, leaves cvg w/gold on tan & gr, rtcl lid, 9", EX 800.00
Jar, florals/stylized bands, ivory/brn/gr/gold, w/lid, 8" 260.00
Pitcher, lg jonquils on lt yel, grotesque hdl, rpr, 8" 800.00
Teapot, leaves, caramel/gr/yel/gold, 5x6½", EX 350.00
Vase, gr mottled gloss, wide angle width, 2½", EX 100.00

Peachblow

Peachblow, made to imitate the colors of the Chinese Peachbloom porcelain, was made by several glasshouses in the late 1800s. Among them were New England Glass; Mt. Washington; Webb; and Hobbs, Brockunier and Company (Wheeling). Its pink shading was achieved through action of the heat on the gold content of the glass. While New England's peachblow shades from deep crimson to white, Mt. Washington's tends to shade from pink to blue-gray. Many pieces were enameled and gilded. While by far the majority of the pieces made by New England had a satin (acid) finish, they made shiny peachblow as well. Wheeling glass, on the other hand, is rarely found in satin. In the 1950s Gundersen-Pairpoint Glassworks initiated the reproduction of Mt. Washington peachblow, using an exact duplication of the original formula. Though of recent manufacture, this glass is very collectible. Our advisors for this category are Betty and Clarence Maier; they are listed in the Directory under Pennsylvania.

Bottle, scent; Webb, HP florals, silver atomizer, 5½" 430.00
Bowl, Webb, heavy gold prunus, 2⅝x3⅞" 365.00
Celery vase, Webb, corset shape w/HP florals & gold, 5¼" 310.00

Creamer, NE Glass, ribbed, appl wht hdl, 2¾x3½" 600.00
Creamer & sugar bowl, Libbey, traces of 1893 Fair decor, 2½" ...525.00
Cruet, HP floral, pinched sides, amber hdl, shiny, 6½" 450.00
Cruet, Wheeling, tepee shape, 6½" 1,350.00
Cup, punch; Wheeling, amber loop hdl, 2½" 375.00
Finger bowl, Mt WA, ruffled, acid, 2½x5¾" 1,200.00
Finger bowl, NE Glass, ruffled, 2½x5½" 250.00
Pear w/long stem, NE Glass, 5½" 150.00
Pitcher, tankard, Wheeling, amber reeded hdl, 11" 2,400.00
Pitcher, Wheeling, fuchsia to amber & cased to wht, 3" 635.00
Pitcher, Wheeling, ovoid w/waisted neck, sqd mouth, water sz ..1,350.00
Punch cup, Wheeling, amber loop hdl, 3½" 400.00
Rose bowl, NE Glass, gilt World's Fair 1893, scalloped, 2½" H ..575.00
Rose bowl, NE Glass, 2¾x2⅞" 335.00
Salt cellar, NE Glass, ribbed, EX color, 1¼x2" 750.00
Shaker, NE Glass, Wild Rose, 2-part lid, 4" 950.00
Spittoon, lady's; NE Glass, bulbous, 2¾x5¼" 750.00
Toothpick holder, NE Glass, SP Greenaway fr, 5" 835.00
Tumbler, English, eng name, 3¾" 150.00
Tumbler, NE Glass, 3¾" 475.00
Tumbler, Wheeling, 3⅞x3" 450.00
Vase, English, mc hummingbird on gold branch, cylindrical, 9" ..260.00
Vase, lily; Gundersen, tricon rim, 9" 300.00
Vase, Morgan; Wheeling, no stand, 7½" 1,200.00
Vase, Morgan; Wheeling, on EX griffin stand, 10" overall 1,765.00
Vase, Mt WA, apple blossoms, gourd form, 8¼x4" 1,900.00
Vase, Mt WA, pk to powder bl, gourd form, 8x4" 2,750.00
Vase, NE Glass, waisted, 5½" 485.00
Vase, stick neck, Mt WA, 8" 2,100.00
Vase, Webb, bird among vines/pine branches, stick neck, 14" ...375.00
Vase, Webb, gold & silver florals, 5x3" 295.00
Vase, Webb, gold floral, 11" 600.00
Vase, Webb, gold flowers & butterfly, 3¼x2¾" 325.00
Vase, Webb, gold leaves/vines, 8" 375.00
Vase, Webb, owl on tree w/acorns, flying bat, 14¼" 2,500.00
Vase, Webb, stick neck, 8¼" 300.00
Vase, Wheeling, long neck, ca 1886, 10½" 1,250.00
Vase, Wheeling, stick neck, 9¼" 985.00
Vase, Wheeling, tapered, 3½" 450.00

Pearlware

Developed by Wedgwood in the late 1770s primarily for their dinnerware lines, pearlware was soon being made by many other Staffordshire potteries as well. Much of it made for export to America. It is characterized by its blue-white body, similar in appearance to true porcelain. During the first decade of the 1800s, pearlware with chinoiserie decorations and hand-painted flowers became popular. See also Leeds.

Coffeepot, blue transfer of garden/music party, applied ochre line at top, unmarked, 4", NM, $250.00.

Bowl, bl floral, 2¾", EX 80.00
Bowl, Oriental design in bl, England, late 1700s, 3x6⅜" 300.00
Bowl, Wared, bl feather edge, Wedgwood, 2x8¾" 155.00

Bust, Wm Pitt the Younger, mc details, 8⅞" 450.00
Chamber pot, emb eagle & florals, 1820-40, 5¼x9" 325.00
Coffeepot, bl chinoiserie, entwined hdl w/florals, 10" 450.00
Coffeepot, bl floral, scroll hdl, button finial, 11", EX 245.00
Coffeepot, Faith/Hope purple transfers, dome lid, 9½", EX 160.00
Coffeepot, mc rose decor, emb ribs, dome top, 10¾", NM 550.00
Creamer, emb strawberry band w/mc & brn striping, 4½", EX ...140.00
Creamer, mc floral, leaf hdl on cup shape, 3¼" 140.00
Cup & saucer, bl floral, EX 70.00
Cup & saucer, handleless; Oriental bl transfer w/gold 110.00
Dish, Wared, bl feather edge, Wedgwood, 1½x8" sq 155.00
Gravy tureen, bl feather edge, Wedgwood, 7½x9, +8¾" tray ..1,100.00
Pitcher, satyr's head form w/mc details, rstr, 5⅜" 140.00
Pitcher, T Denman & H Brougham emb portraits w/mc, 5", EX ..650.00
Plate, bl feather edge, unmk, 10" 160.00
Plate, bl pagoda scene, bl feather edge, unmk, 8½", NM 140.00
Plate, Chinese landscape, bl feather edge, 8", NM, pr 145.00
Plate, emb acanthus leaves along bl feather edge, 10¼", EX 45.00
Plate, emb drape w/bl pagoda scene, bl feather edge, 9¾" 150.00
Plate, emb rim w/bl feather edge, Rogers, 9½", NM 135.00
Plate, Seal of US, mc w/gr feather edge, unmk, 6½" 550.00
Plate, stylized plants, mc w/bl feather edge, rstr, 7" 125.00
Plate, Wared, bl feather edge, Wedgwood, 9½" 145.00
Plate, yel & blk tulip w/gr leaves, brn stripe, 7⅜" 370.00
Plate, yel & brn flower w/mc leaves, mc vine border, 7⅜" 375.00
Platter, emb basketweave, gr feather edge, oval, 10" 175.00
Punch bowl, Chinese landscape, rstr rim, 4½x10¾" 160.00
Shaker, coggled band at base, bl feather edge, 4⅝" 130.00
Soup, Cabbage Rose, scalloped, 8" dia, NM 50.00
Soup, Seal of US, mc w/gr feather edge, unmk, 7⅞" 475.00
Sugar bowl, bl chinoisere & geometrics, rstr, 4½" dia 100.00
Tankard, underglaze bl chinoisere, cylindrical, 5½", NM 160.00
Tankard/mug, emb bands & checks w/lt bl, hairline, 4¾" 80.00
Tea caddy, bl chinoiserie, chamfered corners, 5" 160.00
Tea caddy, blk transfer of flowers, fluted cylinder, 5", NM 225.00
Teapot, bl chinoiserie, globular, unmk, 4⅜", +cr/sug 900.00
Toby jug, detailed modelling, Pratt-style colors, 9⅞", NM 800.00
Vase, coggled band at shoulder, gr feather enamel, 10x7" 800.00
Wash bowl & pitcher, mc peafowl in tree, 9⅝", 12" dia, EX 350.00

Peking Cameo Glass

The first glasshouse was established in Peking in 1680. It produced glassware made in imitation of porcelain, a more desirable medium to the Chinese. By 1725 multilayered carving that resulted in a cameo effect lead to the manufacture of a wider range of shapes and colors. The factory was closed from 1736 to 1795, but glass made in Po-shan and shipped to Peking for finishing continued to be called Peking glass. See also Orientalia.

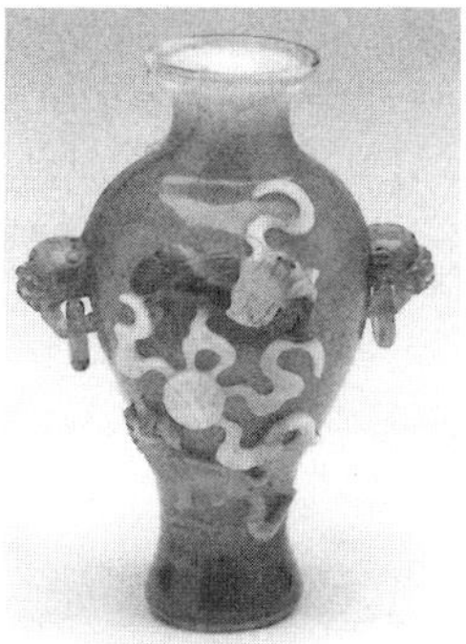

Vase, foo dogs at play, red and white on transparent green, loose ring handles, 1700s, 6", $6,600.00.

Bottle, scent; floral, turq on wht, disk stopper, 5¼" 150.00
Bowl, lotus form w/peony branch panels, bright yel, 6¼" 800.00
Jar, flowering vines, gr on wht opal, 5x5" 575.00
Vase, floral, bl on wht, bulbous, 5⅝" 280.00
Vase, floral, bl on wht, classic shape, 7¾", pr 350.00
Vase, lotus blossoms/butterflies, ruby on wht, 9½" 325.00
Vase, rams in landscape, lappet bands, cobalt/wht, 1800, 9" ...1,750.00

Peloton

Peloton glass was first made by Wilhelm Kralik in Bohemia in 1880. This unusual art glass was produced by rolling colored threads onto the transparent or opaque glass gather as it was removed from the furnace. Usually more than one color of threading was used, and some items were further decorated with enameling. It was made with both shiny and acid finishes.

Biscuit jar, clear w/mc strings, ribbed, SP lid/etc, 7x6½" 785.00
Celery vase, clear w/mc strings, flowers & bee 335.00
Rose bowl, pk w/mc stringing, clear ft, 6-crimp, 2⅝" dia 175.00
Sweetmeat, wht satin w/pastel strings, SP mts, 6½x5½" 600.00
Vase, clear w/mc strings, tricorner rim, 4x4¾" 295.00
Vase, pk w/mc strings, pinched middle, 3½x3⅞" 225.00
Vase, posy; mc florals, clear w/bl strings, 4¼x2½" 100.00
Vase, posy; mc florals, clear w/bl strings/gold, 4¼x2½" 175.00
Vase, yel w/wht strings, hdls, 5" 100.00

Pennsbury

Established in the 1950s in Morrisville, Pennsylvania, by Henry Below, the Pennsbury Pottery produced dinnerware and novelty items, much of which was sold in gift shops along the Pennsylvania Turnpike. Henry and his wife, Lee, worked for years at the Stangl Pottery before striking out on their own. Lee and her daughter were the artists responsible for many of the early pieces, the bird figures among them. Pennsbury pottery was hand painted, some in blue on white, some in multicolor on caramel. Pennsylvania Dutch motifs, Amish couples, and barbershop singers were among their most popular decorative themes. Sgraffito (hand incising), was used extensively. The company marked their wares 'Pennsbury Pottery' or 'Pennsbury Pottery, Morrisville, PA.'

In October of 1969 the company closed. Contents of the pottery were sold in December of the following year; and, in April of 1971, the buildings burned to the ground. Items marked Pennsbury Glenview or Stumar Pottery (or these marks in combination) were made by Glenview after 1969. Pieces manufactured after 1976 were made by the Pennington Pottery. Several of the old molds still exist, and the original Pennsbury Caramel process is still being used on novelty items, some of which are produced by Lewis Brothers, NJ. Production of Pennsbury dinnerware was not resumed after the closing. Our advisor for this category is Shirley Graff; she is listed in the Directory under Ohio. Note: prices may be higher in some areas of the country — particularly on the East Coast, the southern states, and Texas.

Candle holders, Rooster and Hen, 3½", $120.00 for the pair.

Ashtray, Outen the Light 30.00
Bowl, Dutch Talk, scarce, 9" 70.00
Bowl, Red Rooster, pie-crust edge, 6½" 50.00
Bowl, vegetable; Red Rooster, 2-part, 9½x6¼" 50.00
Candy dish, Hex, heart shape, 6x6" 35.00
Coffee mug, eagle 20.00
Coffeepot, Hex, 2-cup 50.00
Coffeepot, Hex, 6-cup 75.00
Cookie jar, Red Barn 200.00
Creamer, Amish man, 2½" 30.00
Creamer, Hex, 2½" 20.00
Creamer, Red Rooster, 2½" 30.00
Creamer, Red Rooster, 4" 30.00
Cup, Red Rooster 25.00
Figurine, chicadee, 3½" 150.00
Figurine, hen, any color, 10½" 250.00
Figurine, ring-neck pheasant, minimum value 600.00
Figurine, rooster, any color, 11½" 250.00
Mug, beer; Amish 45.00
Mug, beer; Barbershop Quartet 45.00
Mug, beer; eagle 35.00
Mug, beer; Gay Ninety 45.00
Mug, beer; Hex 35.00
Mug, coffee; Black Rooster 30.00
Mug, coffee; Red Barn 35.00
Pie plate, Amish couple by apple tree, 9" 65.00
Pitcher, eagle, 6" 45.00
Pitcher, Folk Art, bl on wht, rare, 5" 50.00
Pitcher, Hex, 6¼" 55.00
Plaque, Bucks Co Commemorative, map of county ..100.00
Plaque, fish, bl, gray & red w/gr fins, 17x10" ...95.00
Plaque, Pennsbury, church 150.00
Plate, dinner; Red Rooster, 10" 35.00
Plate, picking apples, fr 85.00
Plate, salad; Red Rooster, 8" 15.00
Saucer, Red Rooster 10.00
Shakers, Hex, 2½", pr 30.00
Sugar bowl, Red Rooster, 4" 30.00
Teapot, Red Rooster 95.00
Wall pocket, God Bless Our Mortgaged Home 90.00
Wall pocket, w/Tin Lizzie, 4-seater 125.00

Pens and Pencils

The first metallic writing pen was patented in 1809, and soon machine-produced pens with steel nibs gradually began replacing the quill. The first fountain pen was invented in 1830; but due to the fact that a suitable metal for the tips had not yet been developed, they were not manufactured commercially until the 1880s. The first successful commercial producers were Waterman in 1884 and Parker with the Lucky Curve in 1888.

The self-filling pen of 1890 featured the soft, interior sack which filled with ink as the metal bar on the outside of the pen was raised and lowered. Variations of the pumping mechanism were tried until 1932 when Parker introduced the Vacumatic, a sackless pen with an internal pump. Our advisors for this category are Judy and Cliff Lawrence; they are listed in the Directory under Florida. For those seeking additional information, a catalog is published monthly by the Pen Fancier's Club, whose address can be found in the Directory under Clubs, Newsletters, and Catalogs. In the listings that follow, all pens are lever-filled unless otherwise noted.

Key:
AF — aeromatic filler
BF — button filler
GPM — gold-plated metal
GPT — gold-plated trim
CF — cartridge filler
CPT — chrome-plated trim
ED — eyedropper filler
GFM — gold-filled metal
GFT — gold-filled trim
HR — hard rubber
NPT — nickel-plated trim
PF — plunger filler
TD — touchdown filler
VF — vacumatic filler

Ballpoint Pens

Cross, 1955, GFM, EX 60.00
Everhard Faber, 1945, brn/GF cap, EX 65.00
Eversharp, CA, 1945, bl/GF cap, M 75.00
Eversharp, CA, 1947, GFM, EX 115.00
Eversharp Skyline, CA, 1944, maroon w/striped cap, EX ..50.00
Eversharp Skyline, CA, 1948, brn/gold-striped cap, M ..50.00
Parker, Arrow, 1980, GFM, GFT, initials, EX 45.00
Parker, T-Ball Jotter, 1959, sterling filigree, initials, EX ..200.00
Reynold's, #400, 1946, aluminum, EX 200.00
Reynold's, Internat'l, 1945, aluminum, M 150.00
Reynold's, Rocket, 1946, bl w/GFT, dried up, otherwise EX ..80.00
Sheaffer, Lady Sheaffer Stratowriter, 1948, bl, GFT, NM ..75.00
Sheaffer, Stratowriter, 1946, GFM, M 85.00
Sheaffer, Wht Dot Tuckaway Stratowriter, 1948, maroon, GFT, M .60.00

Fountain Pens

Camel, 1938, gold-silver streaked marbleized, GFT, LF, EX ..200.00
Carter, INX 2117, 1928, blk, GFT, LF, NM 550.00
Conklin, #20 Crescent Filler, 1920, blk chased HR, GFT, EX ..150.00
Conklin, #30 Crescent Filler, 1924, blk chased HR, GFT, EX ..190.00
Conklin, Crescent Filler, 1920, GFM filigree, EX ...400.00
Conklin, Endura, 1931, blk, GFT, LF, NM 250.00
Conway, Stewart #1209, 1935, blk w/gold bands, AF, EX ..165.00
Conway, Stewart #286, 1938, blk, GFT, LF, EX 90.00
Edison, Universal #6, 1926, red mottled HR, GFT, LF, EX ..400.00
Eversharp, Gold Seal Doric, 1932, blk, GFT, LF, G ..250.00
Eversharp, Gold Seal Doric, 1936, blk, GFT, PF, EX ..500.00
Eversharp, Skyline, 1942, maroon, GFT, LF, EX 60.00
Gold Bond, Stoniet #8, 1928, blk w/yel, GFT, LF, NM ..400.00
Hick & Sons, 1935, blk, gold-over-sterling cap, GFT, AF, G ..300.00
Inkograph Stylographic, 1926, GFM, GFT, LF, NM 150.00
Parker, #41 Lucky Curve, 1906, gold filigree, ED, M ..7,500.00
Parker, #47, 1908, pearl bbl, GFM cap, GFT, ED, M ..7,500.00
Parker, Bl Dmn Vacumatic, 1936, gold pearl stripes, GFT, VF, EX ..65.00
Parker, Duofold Sr, 1925, blk, GFT, BF, EX 325.00
Parker, Jack Knife Safety #20, 1915, red mottled HR, ED, M ..550.00
Parker, Lady Duofold, 1924, red HR, GFT, BF, EX 125.00
Parker, Lucky Curve, 1915, GFM, ED, EX 420.00
Parker, Lucky Curve Baby, 1912, blk HR, ED, NM 350.00
Parker, Red Giant, 1904, red HR, ED, rare, M 7,800.00
Parker, Royal Challenger, 1939, Gold Herringbone, GFT, BF, EX .100.00
Parker, Super 21, 1959, pk w/wht gold-lined cap, GFT, AF, EX ..45.00
Parker, 17 Super, 1964, blk, GFT, AF, EX 95.00
Parker, 51 Demi-sz, 1948, bl w/Lustraloy cap, wht GFT, VF, NM ..60.00
Parker, 51 Flighter, 1949, stainless, GFT, AF, G ...190.00

Photo courtesy Judy and Cliff Lawrence

Sheaffer, Lifetime Autograph, 1929, black with solid 14k gold trim, lever filler, initial, EX, $215.00.

Sheaffer, Lifetime, 1925, jade gr marbleized, GFT, LF, EX ..100.00
Sheaffer, Lifetime, 1928, jade gr marbleized, GFT, LF, EX ..250.00

Sheaffer, Lifetime, 1939, blk, GFT, LF, EX 190.00
Sheaffer, Lifetime Autograph, 1939, blk w/14k gold, LF, EX 225.00
Sheaffer, No 2 Self-Filling, 1919, blk chased HR, NPT, LF, EX ...80.00
Sheaffer, No 22 Student Special, 1919, blk HR, NPT, LF, M 90.00
Sheaffer, Target, 1971, pk w/chrome cap, GFT, CF, M 22.00
Sheaffer, Triumph TM, 1949, maroon, GFT, TD, EX 50.00
Wahl Eversharp, Gold Seal, 1928, red woodgrain HR, GFT, LF, EX .250.00
Wahl Eversharp, Signature, 1928, jade gr marbleized, GFT, EX .115.00
Waterman, #0754, 1925, blk HR, GFT, EX 140.00
Waterman, Emblem, 1947, blk, GFT, LF, EX 180.00
Waterman, Ideal 'Tree Trunk,' 1910, sterling, ED, EX 4,900.00
Waterman, Ideal, 1939, blk-lined silver marbleized, GFT, EX 200.00
Waterman, Ideal #15 VS Safety, 1915, blk HR, ED, G 265.00
Waterman, Ideal #3, 1934, blk, NPT, LF, EX 50.00
Waterman, Ideal #42½ VS Baby Safety, 1909, sterling, ED, EX .250.00
Waterman, Ideal #452, 1928, sterling filigree, LF, G 395.00
Waterman, Ideal #46, 1915, red ripple HR, GFT, LF, EX 490.00
Waterman, Ideal #58, 1921, blk chased HR, NPT, LF, NM 1,200.00
Waterman, Ideal #58, 1925, red ripple HR, GFT, LF, M 2,500.00
Waterman, Ideal #7, 1936, Emerald Ray, GFT, LF, EX 450.00
Waterman, Ideal Patrician, '32, moss agate marbleized, GFT, M ..2,495.00
Waterman, 100 Yr, 1942, blk, GFT, LF, EX 200.00
Waterman, 100 Yr Supersz, 1941, maroon, GFT, LF, EX 400.00
Waterman, 100 Yr Supersz, 1944, blk, GFT, LF, EX 350.00

Mechanical

Carter, 1928, lapis bl marbleized, GFT, EX 70.00
Cross, Century, 1946, GFM, EX 80.00
Parker, Dufold Sr, 1929, Moderne pearl & blk, GFT, EX 230.00
Parker, Duofold, 1922, blk, GFT, BF, EX 130.00
Parker, Duofold, 1922, red-enameled metal, GFT, G 90.00
Parker, Duofold Big Bro, 1922, blk HR, GFT, G 110.00
Parker, Duofold Jr, 1929, gr jade marbleized, GFT, EX 120.00
Parker, Duofold Sr, 1923, red, GFT, EX 290.00
Parker, Duofold Sr, 1928, red, GFT, EX 250.00
Parker, Duofold Sr, 1931, jade gr marbleized, GFT, EX 240.00
Parker, Golf, 1933, sea gr pearl marbleized, GFT, EX 175.00
Parker, Vest Parker, 1933, jade gr marbleized, EX 150.00
Parker, 51, 1948, gray w/GFM top, GFT, EX 120.00
Parker, 51 Demi-sz, 1950, bl w/Lustraloy top, wht GFT, M 50.00
Sheaffer, Junior, 1939, brn & MOP, GFT, M 40.00
Sheaffer, Lifetime, 1920, GFM, EX 22.00
Sheaffer, Lifetime, 1949, bl, GFT, EX 15.00
Sheaffer, Target, 1959, bl, GFT, M 35.00
Sheaffer, 1934, emerald pearl stripes, GFT, EX 25.00
Sheaffer, 1934, gold pearl stripes, GFT, EX 22.00
Sheaffer, 1939, gold pearl stripes, GFT, EX 70.00
Sheaffer, 1940, red & MOP, GFT, M 40.00
Sheaffer, 1949, maroon w/14k gold band, GFT, M 42.00
Sheaffer, 1950, brn, GFT, EX 15.00
Sheaffer, 1959, blk, GFT, EX 15.00
Wahl Eversharp, Gold Seal, 1931, gr jade marbleized, EX 100.00
Wahl Eversharp, 1925, red HR, GFT, G 75.00
Wahl Eversharp, 1928, red woodgrain HR, NPT, EX 85.00
Wahl Eversharp, 1938, red HR, NPT, G 65.00
Waterman, Ideal, 1925, red HR, GFT, EX 32.00
Waterman, Ideal, 1932, scarlet-gold marbleized, GFT, EX 50.00

Sets

Eversharp, Command Performance, 1944, solid 14k gold, LF, EX .490.00
Eversharp, Gold Award, 1945, GF over sterling, GFT, LF, EX ...250.00
Eversharp, 64 Skyline, 1943, bl w/14k gold caps/trim, LF, EX 250.00

Parker, 51, 1948, blk w/GFM caps, GFT, VF, M 175.00
Parker, 51, 1950, gr w/GFM caps, GFT, AF, EX 135.00
Sheaffer, Admiral Snorkel, 1955, gr, GFT, TD 40.00
Sheaffer, Triumph Crest Lifetime, 1945, blk, GFT, LF, NM 175.00
Sheaffer, Triumph Lifetime 2000, 1946, blk w/14k trim, LF, EX ...235.00
Wahl-Eversharp, 1934, GFM, GFT, LF, NM 300.00

Personalities, Fact and Fiction

One of the largest and most popular areas of collecting today is character-related memorabilia. Everyone has favorites, whether they be comic-strip personalities or true-life heroes. The earliest comic strip dealt with the adventures of the Yellow Kid, the smiling, bald-headed Oriental boy always in a nightshirt. He was introduced in 1895, a product of the imagination of Richard Fenton Outcault. Today, though very hard to come by, items relating to the Yellow Kid bring premium prices.

In 1902 Buster Brown and Tige, his dog and constant companion (more of Outcault's progenies), made it big in the comics as well as in the world of advertising. Shoe stores appealed to the younger set through merchandising displays that featured them both. Today items from their earlier years are very collectible.

Though her 1923 introduction was unobtrusively made through only one newspaper, New York's *Daily News*, Little Orphan Annie, the vacant-eyed redhead in the inevitable red dress, was quickly adopted by hordes of readers nationwide, and before the demise of her creator, Harold Gray, in 1968, she had starred in her own radio show. She made two feature films, and in 1977 'Annie' was launched on Broadway.

Other early comic figures were Moon Mullins, created in 1923 by Frank Willard; Buck Rogers by Philip Nowlan in 1928; and Betty Boop, the round-faced, innocent-eyed, chubby-cheeked Boop-Boop-a-Doop girl of the early 1930s. Bimbo was her dog and KoKo her clown friend.

Popeye made his debut in 1929 as the spinach-eating sailor with the spindly-limbed girlfriend, Olive Oyl, in the comic strip *Thimble Theatre,* created by Elzie Segar. He became a film star in 1933 and had his own radio show that during 1936 played three times a week on CBS. He obligingly modeled for scores of toys, dolls, and figurines, and especially those from the '30s are very collectible.

Tarzan, created around 1930 by Edgar Rice Burroughs, and Captain Midnight, by Robert Burtt and Willfred G. Moore, are popular heroes with today's collectors. During the days of radio, Sky King of the Flying Crown Ranch (also created by Burtt and Moore) thrilled boys and girls of the mid-1940s. Hopalong Cassidy, Red Rider, Tom Mix, and the Lone Ranger were only a few of the other 'good guys' always on the side of law and order.

But of all the fictional heroes and comic characters collected today, probably the best loved and most well known is Mickey Mouse. Created in the late 1920s by Walt Disney, Micky (as his name was first spelled) became an instant success with his film debut, Steamboat Willie. His popularity was parlayed through wind-up toys, watches, figurines, cookie jars, puppets, clothing, and numerous other products. Items from the 1930s are usually copyrighted 'Walt Disney Enterprises'; thereafter, 'Walt Disney Productions' was used.

For more information we recommend *Schroeder's Collectible Toys, Antique to Modern,* by Sharon and Bob Huxford. For those interested in Disneyanna, we recommend *Stern's Guide to Disney Collectibles; Character Toys and Collectibles* (there are two volumes); and *The Collector's Encyclopedia of Disneyana.* All are available from Collector Books. Our advisor for this category is Norm Vigue; he are listed in the Directory under Massachusetts. See also Autographs; Banks; Big Little Books; Children's Books; Comic Books; Cookie Jars; Dolls; Games; Lunch Boxes; Movie Memorabilia; Paper Dolls; Pin-Back Buttons; Posters; Puzzles; Rock 'N Roll Memorabilia; Toys.

Al Jolson, hand puppet, molded rubber/cloth, 1950, NM **175.00**
Alice in Wonderland, book, Alice in Philcoland, 1948 ....**65.00**
Alice in Wonderland, Little Nipper...record album, 1951, EX **50.00**
Alice in Wonderland, marionette, 1950s, EX **85.00**
Alice in Wonderland, mug, milk glass, 1930s **60.00**
Alice in Wonderland, planter, Leeds, WDP, ceramic, 7", NM ...**135.00**
Aristocats, Colorforms, 1960s, NMIB **38.00**
Bambi, animated alarm clock, Bayard/France, WDP, 1964, VG .**225.00**
Bart Simpson, wristwatch, Nelsonics, LCD, 5-function, MOC **12.00**
Bat Masterson, cane, chromed plastic, 1958, EX **25.00**
Batman, air freshener, mc diecut, 1970s, MIP **6.00**
Batman, Batmobile 1966 license plate **20.00**
Batman, electric toothbrush, 1977, NM **35.00**
Batman, figure, bendable, 1973, NM **25.00**
Batman, magic slate, Golden, 1989, MIP **3.00**
Batman, pencil, w/Penguin topper, NM **2.00**
Batman, snow-cone cup, cb, 1950s, 5½", M **4.00**
Batman & Robin, alarm clock, wind-up, 1980s, 4½", M **15.00**
Batman & Robin, Teen Wonder Book, hardcover, BC Comics, 1982 ..**75.00**
Batman & Robin, trash can, 1966 ....**40.00**
Beany & Cecil, music box, Mattel, MIB **150.00**
Betty Boop, child's quilt, 1930s, 14x11" **95.00**
Big Bad Wolf, bsk figure, Disney, 1930s, 3½", EX **65.00**
Big Bad Wolf, planter, gold trim, Brechner, 1939 ....**145.00**
Bionic Woman, Paint-By-Number Set, MIB **35.00**
Bonzo, figure, chalkware w/mc details, 1930s, 7", EX **60.00**
Buck Jones, cb standup diecut, blk/wht, 7x7½" **85.00**
Buck Rogers, pencil box, 12 characters/etc, Dille, 1935, 10", EX ..**85.00**
Buck Rogers, Space Ranger Kit, Sylvania premium, '52, M **140.00**
Buck Rogers, Strato Kite, 1948, MIP **85.00**
Buck Rogers, Sunday comics, color pg, 1937 ....**25.00**
Buck Rogers, 25th Century pencil case, bl, EX+ **110.00**
Buffalo Bill Jr, premium ring, 1950 ....**45.00**
Buggs Bunny, cookie mold, 1978, EX **5.00**
Bugs Bunny, invitations, Warner Bros, 1981, MOC **6.00**
Bugs Bunny, planter, Shaw, 1940s, 5x4", EX **125.00**
Bugs Bunny, wristwatch, carrot hands, Timex/Warner Bros, 1955 ...**250.00**
Buzz Sawyer, Christmas card, 1950s, unused, NM+ **8.00**
Capt Marvel, wristwatch, orig band, unused, M **350.00**
Captain Kangaroo, color book, 1956, NM **15.00**
Captain Midnight, Code-O-Graph badge, 1946 radio premium, EX ..**95.00**
Captain Midnight, mug, Ovaltine, M **35.00**
Casper the Ghost, candy bucket, plastic, EX+ **30.00**
Casper the Ghost, figure, bendable, 1970s, EX **12.00**
Charlie Chaplin, pencil box, tin, 1930s, EX **60.00**
Charlie McCarthy, book, Speaking for Myself, 1939, EX **22.00**
Charlie Tuna, pencil sharpener, battery operated **30.00**
Chip 'N Dale, wristwatch, quartz, Disney, Lorus **21.00**
Cinderella, sheet music, A Dream Is a Wish..., 1950, M **20.00**
Clarabelle, inflatable figure, 1950, 26" **95.00**
Daffy Duck, place mat, Warner Bros, Pepsi, EX **7.00**
Dan Dare, pocketwatch, NM **350.00**
Dan Quayle, wristwatch, runs backwards, M in egg-carton box ..**150.00**
Davy Crockett, bank, bronze **68.00**
Davy Crockett, bedspread, poplin, many scenes, EX **225.00**
Davy Crockett, bowl, milk glass, Indians/whts in canoes, 5" **30.00**
Davy Crockett, neckerchief, yel, early, NM **25.00**
Davy Crockett, pin, long rifle form, EX+ **20.00**
Davy Crockett, shirt, cotton flannel, curled fringe, VG+ **75.00**
Dennis the Menace, helmet, Ideal, 1950s, MIB **75.00**
Dick Tracy, book, Exploits of DT, 1946, EX **40.00**
Dick Tracy, candy wrapper, Schutter Candy Co, early 1950s, NM ...**25.00**
Dick Tracy, decoder, red cb, Post premium, late 1940s, M **25.00**
Dick Tracy, flashlight, bl w/red top, 1950s, 3", EXIB **50.00**

Dick Tracy, Secret Service Patrol Flagship, balsa plane, MIB **250.00**
Dick Tracy, Sparkle Paints, Kenner, 1963, MIB (sealed) **55.00**
Dick Tracy, suspenders/hand cuffs/whistle, 1940s, EXIB **80.00**
Donald Duck, brush, metal on wood, Henry L Hughes, 1930s, EX+ ..**115.00**
Donald Duck, child's ring, sterling silver, NM **65.00**
Donald Duck, lamp, ceramic figural, Leeds, 1940s, EX+ **125.00**
Donald Duck, pocketwatch, Mickey decal on bk, 1934, EXIB ...**1,100.00**
Donald Duck, slippers, WD, 1930s-40s, child sz, EX **75.00**
Donald Duck, squeeze toy, DD as baby, Disney, 1986, 7", EX **8.00**
Donald Duck, sweeper, wood & tin, Disney, 1940, EX **65.00**
Dr Ben Casey, bobbin' head figure, Vince Edwards, 1950s, M **100.00**
Dr Dolittle, hat, beany type, Jacobson Hat Co, NMIP **20.00**
Dr Dolittle, periscope, Bar-Zim #609, NMIP **20.00**
Dr Kildare, color book, 1968, M **20.00**
Dracula, figure, bendable, Universal Studios, MOC **8.00**
Dudley Do-Right, Fan Club card, 1970 ....**8.00**
Elmer Fudd, wristwatch, Sheraton, 1972, M **85.00**
ET, key chain, figural, M **3.00**

Photo courtesy Dunbar Gallery

Felix the Cat, chocolate pot, Germany, 1920s, 5½", $650.00.

Felix the Cat, figure, jtd wood w/leather, 1920s-30s, VG+ **395.00**
Felix the Cat, pin, blk enamel on brass **75.00**
Felix the Cat, tin litho clicker, Germany, 1920s, EX **85.00**
Ferdinand the Bull, bsk figure, 1930s, 3" **35.00**
Flintstones, Fred bank, Homecraft, 1973, NM **25.00**
Flintstones, Fred bank, vinyl figural, BBI toys, 1986, 6", MIB **15.00**
Flintstones, Fred earring tree, EX+ **20.00**
Flintstones, tablecloth, 1974, MIB (sealed) **12.00**
Gabby Hayes, sheriff's set, 1950s, unused, NMOC **80.00**
Gene Autry, Cowboy Paint Book, 1940, NM **50.00**
Gene Autry, lariat flashlight, 1950, MIB **65.00**
Gene Autry, sheet music, Silver Haired Daddy, EX **15.00**
Gene Autry, song book, 1946, 46-pg, EX **20.00**
Ghost Busters, iron-on transfers, 1984, MOC **5.00**
Green Hornet, color book, Whitman, 1966, NM **45.00**
Green Hornet, rub-ons, Hasbro, M in NM box, rare **425.00**
Groucho Marx, goggles & cigar, 1955, MOC **65.00**
Harlem Globetrotters, wristwatch, c CBS, 1960s, NM **200.00**
Hector Heathcote, Colorforms, 1964, EXIB **28.00**
Hopalong Cassidy, Bar-20 director's chair, M **800.00**
Hopalong Cassidy, bedspread, gr chenille, NM **275.00**
Hopalong Cassidy, Canasta set, 2 decks & saddle tray, MIB **175.00**
Hopalong Cassidy, cowboy hat, blk felt, VG **85.00**
Hopalong Cassidy, cup, milk glass **20.00**
Hopalong Cassidy, hair trainer bottle, full, sm, EX **20.00**
Hopalong Cassidy, ice cream container, O'Fallon Dairy, 1-qt **30.00**
Hopalong Cassidy, ice-cream cup, Sealright, 1950, 3" dia, EX+ **100.00**
Hopalong Cassidy, mug, china **45.00**
Hopalong Cassidy, neckerchief slide, steer head w/red glass eyes ..**35.00**
Hopalong Cassidy, place mat, plastic, 1950, 12x18", EX **30.00**

Hopalong Cassidy, plate, WS George, 1950s, 9" **65.00**
Hopalong Cassidy, potato chip can, M **250.00**
Hopalong Cassidy, Ranch punch-out set, 1950, M **75.00**
Hopalong Cassidy, sweater, cardigan style, child sz **175.00**
Howdy Doody, alarm clock, It's HD Time, rnd dial, 2-bell, 6", EX **65.00**
Howdy Doody, Bandage Strips, 1950, MIB **60.00**
Howdy Doody, bank, ceramic, HD on TV, Vandor **145.00**
Howdy Doody, bank, HD on bbl, Lefton, 1950s, 6", NM **335.00**
Howdy Doody, Christmas stencil, uncut **50.00**
Howdy Doody, crayon set, 1950, lg sz, complete, NMIB **200.00**
Howdy Doody, handkerchief, 1950s, M **35.00**
Howdy Doody, ice cream spoon, long hdl **15.00**

Howdy Doody Marionette, Peter Puppet Playthings, 1950s, MIB, $250.00.

Howdy Doody, night light, plastic HD figural, M **95.00**
Howdy Doody, plate, Taylor, Smith & Taylor **65.00**
Howdy Doody, Puppet Show punchout book, 1952, NM **100.00**
Howdy Doody, puzzle/key chain, M **18.00**
Howdy Doody, shoe polish, Kunkle, NMIB **20.00**
Howdy Doody, sweatshirt, 1950s, MIB **125.00**
Howdy Doody, teaspoon, SP, EX **15.00**
Howdy Doody, wallpaper border, HD w/friends, 1950s, 9-ft, EX ...**270.00**
Huckleberry Hound, bubble bath, 1961, MIB (sealed) **40.00**
Huckleberry Hound, Wonder Slate, Hamlyn, 1973, MIP (sealed) **20.00**
Incredible Hulk, figure, rubber, 1979, 5", EX **8.00**
Incredible Hulk, Rub 'N Play Set, Colorforms, 1979, MIB **12.00**
Jack Armstrong, Magic Answer Box, EX **50.00**
Jack Armstrong, pedometer, cereal premium, NM **25.00**
Jack Armstrong, radio premium, Write a Fighter Corps, +mailer .**35.00**
Jack Armstrong, Torpedo flashlight, EX **50.00**
James Bond, beach towel, portrait w/facsimile autograph, 1964 ....**85.00**
James Bond, talcum powder, 1960s, NM **75.00**
Jiminy Cricket, figurine, pewter, 1970s, M **75.00**
Joe Palooka, bsk figure, Germany, 7" **30.00**
Keystone Cop, fan, cb diecut, dtd 1908, w/advertising **65.00**
Lady & the Tramp, napkin ring, emb sterling, Disney, NM **125.00**
Li'l Abner, slide puzzle/key chain, plastic, 1950, M **24.00**
Li'l Abner, tray, Dogpatch USA, 1968, EX **45.00**
Little House on the Prairie, Paint-By-Number Set, 1979, MIB **45.00**
Little Lulu, color book, Whitman #1663, 1974, M **20.00**
Little Lulu, Sticker Fun Book, Whitman #1695, 1974, oversz, NM ..**10.00**
Little Orphan Annie, decoder badge, 1938 ....**65.00**
Little Orphan Annie, ID bracelet, 1934 radio premium **80.00**
Little Rascals, wristwatch, LCD, MOC **30.00**
Lone Ranger, bolo tie, Half a Century, M **22.00**
Lone Ranger, boots, 1948, MIB w/papers **700.00**
Lone Ranger, chaps/pants/shirt, NM **375.00**
Lone Ranger, chuck wagon lantern, NMIB **175.00**
Lone Ranger, crayon tin, 1940s, EX **35.00**

Lone Ranger, Deputy badge, gray metal star, MOC **35.00**
Lone Ranger, figural pen, 1940s, EX **75.00**
Lone Ranger, Herald Examiner pin-bk, 1939, NM **35.00**
Lone Ranger, movie film ring **75.00**
Lone Ranger, pedometer, cereal premium, 1950s, w/strap, MIP **38.00**
Ludwig Von Drake, mug, ceramic, Disney, 1961, 4", NM **22.50**
Man From UNCLE, Secret Cap Shooting Lighter, EX **45.00**
Mickey Mouse, alarm clock, MM on rnd dial, 1940, 5", EXIB **300.00**
Mickey Mouse, bsk figure, as conductor, Germany, 3", M **185.00**
Mickey Mouse, color book, WD, 1948, NM **40.00**
Mickey Mouse, Joke Book, Wheatings, WDP **18.00**
Mickey Mouse, mechanical pencil, MM head, Bakelite, 1930s ..**135.00**
Mickey Mouse, Mickey Canasta Jr card game, MIB **38.00**
Mickey Mouse, Old Maid game, 1935, EXIB **65.00**
Mickey Mouse, pencil sharpener, Bakelite, WDE **125.00**
Mickey Mouse, pin, MM as drummer, Syrocco, 1930s, EX **65.00**
Mickey Mouse, rubber figure, Seiberling, 1930s, 3½", NM **100.00**
Mickey Mouse, Shooting Gallery, 1970s, MOC **12.00**
Mickey Mouse, Silly Symphonies Songbook, England, NM **35.00**

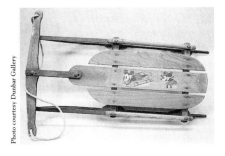

Mickey Mouse sled, American, 1930s, EX, $375.00.

Mickey Mouse, wristwatch, Bradley, Disney, 1960s, NM **35.00**
Mickey Mouse, wristwatch, metal band, Ingersoll, 1930s, EXIB ..**635.00**
Mickey Mouse & Donald Duck, fork & spoon set, stainless, MOC ...**8.00**
Mickey Mouse & Pluto, pin, mc enamel, 1930s, EX **125.00**
Minnie Mouse, wristwatch, MM on face, Timex, 1958, MIB **355.00**
Mork & Mindy, Magic Show, Colorforms, MIB **30.00**
Mork & Mindy, tote bag, 1979, NM **30.00**
Mr Magoo, alarm clock, Magoo w/fishing pole, China, 5", EX ...**30.00**
Mr Magoo, doll, rubber & cloth, 1962, 16" **65.00**
Mummy, head, glow-in-the dark, 2", M **15.00**
Muppets, Miss Piggy oven mitt, 1981, EX **8.00**
Nightmare Before Christmas, PVC figures, set of 5, M **18.00**
Olive Oyl, ponytail holder, King Features, 1958, MOC **30.00**
Pink Panther, jewelry set, 1989, MOC **12.00**
Pinocchio, bank, ceramic, on whale, Schmid Musical **60.00**
Pinocchio, bsk figure, Disney, 1940s, EX+ **50.00**
Pinocchio, night light, ceramic figural, 1980s, M **45.00**
Planet of the Apes, bank, plastic, M **25.00**
Pluto, jump rope, Disney, 1970s, MOC **12.00**
Popeye, belt, leather, 1930s, M on display card **175.00**
Popeye, bowl, cereal; plastic, 1979, EX **8.00**
Popeye, Colorforms, The Weatherman, 1959, NMIB **30.00**
Popeye, Dynamite Music Machine record player, EX **25.00**
Popeye, Eagle pencil, mechanical, 1929, NMIB **65.00**
Popeye, figural charm, hard celluloid, 1930s, EX **18.00**
Popeye, jtd/pnt wood figure, 1930s, 5", EX **65.00**
Popeye, lamp, cast lamppost, orig pipe & shade, 1935 ....**650.00**
Popeye, lamp, sitting, vinyl, 1959, M **95.00**
Popeye, note pad, graphic front & bk covers, 1929, EX **38.00**
Popeye, paint set, Am Crayon, 1933, MIB **130.00**

Popeye, tie bar, enameled, 1930s 150.00
Popeye, wallet, vinyl w/flasher sq, NM 55.00
Porky Pig, cookie mold, 1978, EX 5.00
Raggedy Ann, figure, bsk, 1988, 4", M 15.00
Raggedy Ann, footstool, Knickerbocker, all orig, EX 135.00
Rat Finks, ring, M, sm 10.00
Red Ryder, medallion, Lucky Coin, Penney's ad on bk, VG+ 7.00
Red Ryder, medallion, silver-tone metal, Daisy Mfg, '38, 2" 15.00
Rin-Tin-Tin & Rusty, belt buckle, EX 65.00
Rocketeer, Fan Club membership button 2.00
Rocketeer, wallet, Pyramid Handbag Co, Disney 18.00
Rockey Squirrel, figure, pnt ceramic, 2½", NM 45.00
Roy Rogers, bedspread, tan, NM 210.00
Roy Rogers, curtains, beige panels, 78x30", EX 250.00
Roy Rogers, Deputy Sheriff badge, whistle on bk, VG+ 40.00
Roy Rogers, Flash Camera, Herbert George, complete, EXIB 195.00
Roy Rogers, gloves, orig store tags, NM 125.00
Roy Rogers, harmonica, Reed, 1955, 4", NMOC 65.00
Roy Rogers, horseshoe set, rubber w/litho bases, VG+ 95.00
Roy Rogers, Microscope ring, 1949 radio premium 115.00
Roy Rogers, saddle ring, sterling silver, premium, M 225.00
Roy Rogers, Tru Vue magic eyes, 1956, NMOC 45.00
Roy Rogers & Trigger, alarm clock, Ingraham, 1950s, 5", EXIB .200.00
Schmoo, savings bond certificate, Al Capp, 1949, M 30.00
Scooby Doo, bank, vinyl w/felt vest, NM 25.00
Shirley Temple, carriage, gray, ST hubcaps, decals, EX 675.00
Shirley Temple, plate, Baby Take a Bow 65.00
Shirley Temple, Wheaties box, 1936, M 150.00
Shirley Temple, 78 rpm record, ST Reads Disney's Bambi, EX 45.00
Simpsons, Fun Dough Model Maker, Rose Art, MIB 10.00
Skippy, handkerchief, 1930, NM 58.00
Sleeping Beauty, musical figurine, Schmid, 7" 40.00
Sleeping Beauty, sewing set, Transogram, Disney, EX+IB 75.00
Smitty, wristwatch, red band, New Haven, 1935, EXIB 575.00
Smokey the Bear, ashtray, ceramic, Norcrest 125.00
Smokey the Bear, blotter, 1954, 6¼x2½" 13.00
Smokey the Bear, Dakin squeeze doll, 5½" 25.00
Smokey the Bear, mug, Prevent Forest Fires 22.00
Smokey the Bear, pin-bk, I'm Smokey's Helper 12.00
Smokey the Bear, shakers, w/bbl & w/shovel, pr 30.00
Smurfs, record player, 1982, EX 20.00
Snoopy, alarm clock, Blessing/Germany, 1972, 5", EX 55.00
Snoopy, bank, SP, Leonard #9669, MIB 30.00
Snoopy, bookends, red plastic hearts, Hong Kong, EX, pr 18.00
Snoopy, fishing rod, Zebco, VG 10.00
Snoopy, pajama bag, w/button, EX 28.00
Snoopy, wristwatch, tennis ball second hand, Timex #86211, M .65.00
Snoopy & Woodstock, doormat, wht & yel on gray, 14x26", M ...15.00
Snoopy bell, Snoopy atop doghouse, Schmid, Christmas 1973, EX ..60.00
Snow White, biscuit tin, Disney, Belgium, early, VG+ 185.00
Snow White, sewing cards, WDP, early, EXIB 65.00
Snow White, wooden pin, 1938, MOC 65.00
Snow White & 7 Dwarfs, bsk musical figures, Schmid, 1989, MIB ..425.00
Snow White & 7 Dwarfs, Dopey squeeze toy, Disney, 1960s, 4", EX ...45.00
Snow White & 7 Dwarfs, ironing board, Wolverine, 1940s, 24", EX ..35.00
Snow White & 7 Dwarfs, pocket dime-register bank 275.00
Snow White & 7 Dwarfs, soap, WDE, in storybook box 75.00
Speedy Gonzalez, bank, ceramic figural, on wedge of cheese, M ...35.00
Speedy Gonzalez, cloth doll, Mighty Star, 1971, NM 10.00
Spider-Man, book bag, canvas, EX 12.00
Spider-Man, wallet, 1978, MOC 18.00
Spiro Agnew, wristwatch, Dirty Time, M 75.00
Superman, bedspread, 1978, unused 50.00
Superman, belt buckle, heavy bronze, 1970s, 4", M 7.50

Superman, Crusader ring, 1940s, M 500.00
Superman, kite, 1971, MIP 22.00
Superman, Krypto ray gun, w/films/box/insert, M 1,250.00
Superman, Paint-By-Number Set, 1977, MIB 28.00

Superman record player with book and record, ca 1978, EX, $45.00.

Superman, wallet, brn leather, 1976, M 10.00
Superman, wristwatch, New Haven, lg, EX+ 475.00
Superman, wristwatch, Return of..., ltd ed, 1993, MIB 70.00
Tarzan, Viewmaster reel set, B-580, 1950, MIP 35.00
Thumper, bank, ceramic, pk, Schmid Musical 65.00
Tinkerbell, varivue button, I Tink It's Great 12.00
Tom Corbett Space Cadet, book bag, 1950s, EX 150.00
Tom Mix, cigar box labels, 1920s, 3 different, ea 20.00
Tom Mix, compass/magnifier, glow-in-the-dark arrowhead, 1947 ...65.00
Tom Mix, cowboy boots box, EX 60.00
Tom Mix, Magnet ring, 1946 radio premium 60.00
Tom Mix, Ralston dealer promo postcard, 1940s 60.00
Tom Mix, silver badge, premium, Tom on horse, 2", EX 50.00
Tom Mix, watch fob, gold ore, 1940 ....40.00
Tonto, figure w/horse, Gabriel, 1973, M 45.00
Uncle Scrooge, bank, Brechner, M pnt 125.00
Underdog, pillow, wht inflatable vinyl, EX 23.00
WC Fields, red-nose battery tester, 1974, MIP 5.00
Wild Bill Hickok, poster, 1950s premium, M in envelope 25.00
Wimpy, pressed wood figure, Syroco, 1944, 4", EX 95.00
Winnie the Pooh, bank, ceramic figural, Disney, Enesco, 5" 45.00
Winnie the Pooh, rug, mc cotton, Disney/Sears, 1964, 34x62", EX ..95.00
Winnie the Pooh, switch plate, WDP, EX+ 6.00
Wizard of Oz, foaming bath beads, Ansehi, 1975, complete, EX+ ...25.00
Wizard of Oz, wastebasket, Cheinco, 1975, 10x13", G 65.00
Woody Woodpecker, flannel board set, VG 45.00
Yogi Bear, camera, 1976, NMOC 20.00
Zorro, gloves, 1958, EX, pr 50.00
3 Stooges, flicker ring, any character, NM 20.00

Peters and Reed

John Peters and Adam Reed founded their pottery in Zanesville, Ohio, just before the turn of the century, using the local red clay to produce a variety of wares. Moss Aztec, introduced about 1912, has an unglazed exterior with designs molded in high relief and the recesses highlighted with a green wash. Only the interior is glazed to hold water. Pereco (named for Peters, Reed and Company) is glazed in semi-matt blue, maroon, cream, and other colors. Orange was also used very early, but such examples are rare. Shapes are simple with in-mold decoration sometimes borrowed from the Moss Aztec line. Wilse Blue is a line of high-gloss medium blue with dark specks on simple shapes. Landsun, characterized by its soft matt multicolor or blue and gray combinations, is decorated either by dripping or by hand brushing in an effect sometimes called Flame or Herringbone. Chromal, in much the same colors as Landsun, may be decorated with a realistic scenic, or the swirling application of colors may merely suggest one. Vivid, realistic Chromal scenics command much higher prices than weak, poorly drawn examples. (Brush-McCoy made a very similar line called Chromart. Neither will be marked; and due to the lack of documented background material available, it may be impossible make a positive identification. Collectors nearly always attribute this type of decoration to Peters and Reed.) Shadow Ware is usually a glossy, multicolor drip over a harmonious base color but is occasionally seen in overall matt glaze. When the base is black, the effect is often iridescent.

Perhaps the most familiar line is the brown high-glaze artware with the 'sprigged'-type designs. Although research has uncovered no positive proof, it is generally accepted as having been made by Peters and Reed. It is interesting to note that many of the artistic shapes in this line are recognizable as those made by Weller, Roseville, and other Zanesville area companies. Several other lines were produced including Mirror Black, Persian, Egyptian, Florentine, Marbleized, etc., and an unidentified line which collectors call Mottled-Marbleized Colors. In this high-gloss line, the red clay body often shows through the splashed-on multicolors.

In 1922 the company became known as the Zane Pottery. Peters and Reed retired, and Harry McClelland became president. Charles Chilcote designed new lines, and production of many of the old lines continued. The body of the ware after 1922 was light in color. Marks include the impressed logo or ink stamp 'Zaneware' in a rectangle.

Umbrella stand, blue, yellow and caramel marbleized on black ribbed form, 23", EX, $850.00.

Bowl, centerpc; Wilse Bl, w/candlesticks **125.00**
Ewer, grape clusters, Brn Ware, 6" **85.00**
Ewer, lion's head w/grapevine, Brn Ware, 11" **250.00**
Flower frog, lily pad, Landsun, 2x6½" **38.00**
Planter, Marbleized, lg **200.00**
Vase, brn w/bl & gr drip, Shadow Ware, Zane, 10½x8½" **275.00**
Vase, bud; Landsun, 9½" **125.00**
Vase, caramel/tan/dk bl drip over sponged ground, Zane, 9" **200.00**
Vase, Chromal scenic (impressionistic), 11" **400.00**
Vase, Chromal scenic (realistic), 11" **800.00**
Vase, Landsun, flame, 3¾x3½" **100.00**
Vase, Marbleized, bl, 9" **200.00**
Vase, monks portraits, Brn Ware, 3-hdld, 7" **150.00**
Vase, Moss Aztec, lg flowers, brn w/gr wash, Ferrell, 8" **180.00**
Vase, Wilse Bl, #612, 8½" **80.00**
Vase, wreath, Brn Ware, 10" **175.00**
Wall pocket, Marbleized, 8" **135.00**

Pewabic

The Pewabic Pottery was formally established in Detroit, Michigan, in 1907 by Mary Chase Perry Stratton and Horace James Caulkins. The two had worked together since 1903, firing their ware in a small kiln Caulkins had designed especially for use by the dental trade.

Always a small operation which relied upon basic equipment and the skill of the workers, they took pride in being commissioned for several important architectural tile installations.

Some of the early artware was glazed a simple matt green; occasionally other colors were added, sometimes in combination, one over the other in a drip effect. Later Stratton developed a lustrous crystalline glaze. (Today's values are determined to a great extent by the artistic merit of the glaze.) The body of the ware was highly fired and extremely hard. Shapes were basic, and decorative modeling, if used at all, was in low relief. Mary Stratton kept the pottery open until her death in 1961. In 1968 it was purchased and reopened by Michigan State University. Several marks were used over the years: a triangle with 'Revelation Pottery' (for a short time only); 'Pewabic' with five maple leaves; and the impressed circle mark.

Bowl, turq drip over irid gloss, incurvate, 2¼x4¾" **350.00**
Dish, bl/violet/gold, short narrow ft rim, w/sterling lid, 6½" ...**1,500.00**
Dish, gray/gr matt over metallic aqua, swirled shell form, 4½" ...**200.00**
Plate, rim w/5 repeats of castle & tree, mc metallics, 10" **700.00**
Tile, Detroit Business Women's Club 1912-62, MI outline, 4" dia ..**50.00**
Tile, turkey, orange on bl, 3¼" sq **125.00**
Vase, aqua/lt bl mottled gloss, 4x5½", NM **250.00**
Vase, bl metallic gloss, wide teardrop on ring ft, 9½" **1,200.00**
Vase, bl w/violet/gunmetal/gold irid, wide gourd form, 6½" **500.00**
Vase, bl/gr irid w/emb bands, short narrow ft rim, 4x6" **650.00**

Vase, bronze and red warty iridescent with cream interior, obscured mark, 15½x7", $4,000.00.

Vase, chocolate/brick brn over red clay, 5½x7" **500.00**
Vase, gold/pk to orange metallic, shouldered, mk, 7" **1,100.00**
Vase, gr metallic drip over silver/purple irid, 3½", NM **325.00**
Vase, gr metallic w/platinum & rose, shouldered, rpr, 10" **425.00**
Vase, irid purple/bl drip over blk matt, 10x8½" **2,800.00**
Vase, purple irid splotches on blk gunmetal, drilled, 13x6" **1,400.00**
Vase, purple/bl mottled irid, ovoid w/flared rim, 5¾x4" **650.00**
Vase, thick med bl crackle, shouldered ovoid, 3", NM **220.00**

Pewter

Pewter is a metal alloy of tin, copper, very small parts of bismuth and/or antimony, and sometimes lead. Very little American pewter contained lead, however, because much of the ware was designed to be used as tableware, and makers were aware that the use of lead could result in poisoning. (Pieces that do contain lead are usually darker in color and heavier than those that have no lead.) Most of the fine examples of American pewter date from 1700 to the 1840s. Many pieces were melted down and recast into bullets during the American Revolution in 1775; this accounts to some extent why examples from this period are quite difficult to find. The pieces that did survive may include buttons, buckles, and writing equipment as well as the tableware we generally think of.

After the Revolution makers began using antimony as the major alloy with the tin in an effort to regain the popularity of pewter, which glassware and china was beginning to replace in the home. The resulting product, known as britannia, had a lustrous silver-like appearance and was far more durable. While closely related, britannia is a collectible in its own right and should not be confused with pewter.

Key: tm — touch mark

Basin, eagle tm, 7¾" 300.00
Basin, eagle tm w/B Barns, 3x10⅜" 330.00
Basin, Humphrey Evans tm, ca 1730-80, 11", EX 230.00
Basin, unmk Am, 8" 215.00
Beaker, Boardman & Hart tm, ca 1830-50, 5¼", EX 375.00
Beaker, Oliver Trask tm, dents/nicks, 1832-47, 5¼", pr 1,150.00
Beaker, TD & Sherman Boardman tm, ca 1810-30, 5⅛" 700.00
Beaker, Timothy Boardman & Co tm, ca 1825, 5⅛" 635.00
Bowl, baptismal; Boardman BX tm, 4⅜" 400.00
Bowl, eagle tm of T Danforth, shallow, 11½", VG 110.00
Bowl, lion tm of T Danforth II, shallow, 13¼" 360.00
Bowl, TD Boardman tm (Laughlin), deep, 9⅜" 800.00
Bowl, vegetable; Continental angel tm, pear finial, 13½" 220.00

Candlestick, England (rubbed touchmark), with provenance (having belonged to Reverend Job Cushing of Massachusetts), ca 1675, 8½", $7,700.00.

Candlesticks, Roswell Gleason tm, 8¾", pr 980.00
Candlesticks, unmk (att Homan), 7⅜", pr 275.00
Chalice, unmk, 7½" 125.00
Charger, crowned rose & London tms, 12¼" dia 55.00
Charger, faint tm (English), 16½" 385.00
Charger, Yates & Made in London tms, 15" 275.00
Coffeepot, Ashbil Griswold tm, 10½", EX 500.00
Coffeepot, Boardman & Hart tm, 12", VG 350.00
Coffeepot, Boardman tm, triple-belly, ca 1830, 11½" 550.00
Creamer, unmk Am, ear hdl, 4⅝" 275.00

Flagon, Samuel Danforth touchmark, domed cylinder with C-shaped handle, ca 1800, old repairs, 12", $500.00.

Flagon, TD & Sherman Boardman tm, 14" 1,740.00
Ice bucket, Continental angel tm, 8"+hdl 440.00

Ladle, TD Boardman tm, curved hdl, 13" 250.00
Ladle, unmk, trn wood hdl, 15" 165.00
Lamp, Capen & Molineux NY tm, rpl collar, w/burner, 7⅞" 165.00
Lamp, hand; M Hyde tm, cast ear hdl, w/burner & snuffers, 3" ..195.00
Lamp, oil; dbl bull's eye, unmk, 19th C, 8¼" 750.00
Loving cup, James Dixon & Sons, Sheffield tm, 5¾" 115.00
Mug, Boardman & Hart tm (2), cast ear hdl, 3⅛" 275.00
Plate, B&C London tm, dents/wear, 7¾" 50.00
Plate, crowned rose & London tms, scratches, 7⅞" 125.00
Plate, eagle tm of Boardman Warranted, 8⅝" 95.00
Plate, eagle tm of Jacob Eggleston, rare, 7⅞", NM 515.00
Plate, eagle tm of S Kilbourn, 7¾" 415.00
Plate, eagle tm of T Danforth III, lt wear, 6⅛" 550.00
Plate, eagle tm of Thomas Boardman, wear, 7¾" 275.00
Plate, J Martine tm, 9" 965.00
Plate, London tm (indistinct), 7⅞" 95.00
Plate, Love tm, 7⅞" 195.00
Plate, Roswell Gleason tm, 9⅜" 165.00
Plate, TD (Thomas Danforth, Phila) tm, split, 7¾" 165.00
Plate, Townsend & Compton tm, 8⅜" 65.00
Platter, John Watts tm, 1850s, 9⅜", pr 230.00
Platter, Townsend & Compton tm, pierced insert, 28¾x22" ..2,415.00
Porringer, cast crown hdl, 4¾", EX 140.00
Porringer, G Jones tm, dent/spits, ca 1774-1809, 4⅜" 955.00
Porringer, SE Hamlin tm, dents/scratches, 1801-56, 5⅜" 750.00
Spoons, WT&Co tm, 19th C, 8", 6 for 230.00
Tall pot, HB Ward & Co tm, rpr to spout, 10⅜" 75.00
Tall pot, R Dunham tm, 11¾" 470.00
Tall pot, Roswell Gleason tm, split, 9⅜" 185.00
Tall pot, unmk Am, rprs, 10¼" 220.00
Teapot, Calder tm, sm split, 8½" 220.00
Teapot, crown tm w/5M, pear shape, soldered rpr, 6¾" 195.00
Teapot, E Brown & Co tm, machine tooled-band, rpr, 6½" 80.00
Teapot, eagle Calder tm, 7½" 385.00
Teapot, G Richardson Warranted tm, 8" 500.00
Teapot, I Vickers tm, vintage & rose tooled band, rpr, 5½" 150.00
Teapot, JW Cahill & Co tm, 7¾", EX 235.00
Teapot, R Gleason tm, 7" 275.00
Teapot, Smith & Co tm, soldered rpr, 7" 175.00
Teapot, unmk Am, 8" 110.00
Teapot, Willis Humiston NY tm, 6¾" 225.00

Pfaltzgraff

Pfaltzgraff has operated in Pennsylvania since the early 1800s making redware at first, then stoneware crocks and jugs, yellow ware, and spongeware in the '20s, artware and kitchenware in the '30s, and stoneware kitchen items through the '40s. To collectors, they're best known for their Gourmet Royal (circa 1950s), a high-gloss dinnerware line of solid brown with frothy white drip glaze around the rims, and their giftware line called Muggsy, comic-character mugs, ashtrays, bottle stoppers, children's dishes, a pretzel jar, a cookie jar, etc. It was designed in the late 1940s and continued in production until 1960. The older versions have protruding features, while the features of later examples were simply painted on.

For more information on Gourmet Royal dinnerware, we recommend *The Flea Market Trader* and *The Garage Sale and Flea Market Annual*, both by Collector Books.

Gourmet Royale, ashtray, #321, 7¾", from $10 to 12.00
Gourmet Royale, baker, #323, oval, 9½", from $20 to 22.00
Gourmet Royale, bean pot, #11-3, 3-qt, w/warmer, from $48 to ...50.00
Gourmet Royale, bowl, mixing; 10", from $15 to 17.00

Gourmet Royale, bowl, spaghetti; #391, 14", from $30 to **35.00**
Gourmet Royale, casserole, stick hdl, 1-pt, from $12 to **14.00**
Gourmet Royale, chip 'n dip, #211, 12", from $18 to **20.00**
Gourmet Royale, fondue pot, w/holder & wood trim, from $35 to ..**40.00**
Gourmet Royale, marmalade, from $18 to **20.00**
Gourmet Royale, plate, dinner; 10", from $6.50 to **8.00**
Gourmet Royale, shakers, owl shape, pr, from $25 to **35.00**
Gourmet Royale, soup tureen, #393, 5-qt, w/underplate **70.00**
Gourmet Royale, tray, snack; 8⅜x11⅝", from $17 to **20.00**

Mugs, character faces, $38.00 each.

Muggsy, ashtray **125.00**
Muggsy, cigarette server **125.00**
Muggsy, cookie jar, character face, minimum value **250.00**
Muggsy, mug, action figure (golfer, etc), any, from $65 to **85.00**
Muggsy, tumbler **60.00**

Phoenix Bird

Blue and white Phoenix Bird china has been produced by various Japanese potteries from the early 1900s. With slight variations the design features the Japanese bird of paradise and scroll-like vines of Kara-Kusa, or Chinese grass. Although some of their earlier ware is unmarked, the majority is marked in some fashion. More than one hundred different stamps have been reported, with 'Made in Japan' the one most often found. Coming in second is Morimura's wreath and/or crossed stems (both having the letter 'M' within). The cloverleaf with 'Japan' below very often indicates an item having a high-quality transfer-printed design. Among the many categories in the Phoenix Bird pattern are several shapes; therefore (for identification purposes), each has been given a number, i.e. #1, #2, etc. Newer items, if marked at all, carry a paper label. Compared to the older ware, the coloring of the new is whiter and the blue more harsh; the design is sparse with more ground area showing. Although collectors buy even 'new' pieces, the older is of course more highly prized and valued.

For further information we recommend *Phoenix Bird Chinaware, Books I — IV*, written and privately published by our advisor, Joan Oates; her address is in the Directory under Michigan. Join Phoenix Bird Collectors of America (PBCA) and receive the *Phoenix Bird Discoveries* newsletter, an informative publication that will further your appreciation of this chinaware. See Clubs, Newsletters, and Catalogs for ordering information.

Bowl, ice-cream; scalloped, 10" **110.00**
Bowl, nut; scalloped, ftd, #1 ....**45.00**
Butter chip/pat **15.00**
Castor set, 8-pc **250.00**
Chocolate pot, scalloped **135.00**
Coffee cann/mug, str sides, hdls, old **18.00**
Creamer & sugar bowl, #4, curled hdls **45.00**

Gravy tureen, #1, w/lid **95.00**

Photo courtesy Joan Oates

Grill plate with Phoenix Bird in center, Blue Willow border, $45.00.

Honey pot, rattan hdl **35.00**
Jar, marmalade; #1, w/lid **55.00**
Pitcher, buttermilk; oval **75.00**
Pitcher, iced tea; scalloped **80.00**
Plate, toast; w/lid **145.00**
Reamer, 2-pc **175.00**
Sauce boat, English, #3 ....**40.00**
Shakers, fat, squatty, #4, pr **28.00**
Soap dish, w/lid & drain **150.00**
Spoon stacker, oval **185.00**
Tea caddy, w/lid, 6½" **135.00**

Phoenix Glass

Founded in 1880 in Monaca, Pennsylvania, the Phoenix Glass Company became one of the country's foremost manufacturers of lighting glass by the early 1900s. They also produced a wide variety of utilitarian and decorative glassware, including art glass by Joseph Webb, colored cut glass, Gone-with-the-Wind style oil lamps, hotel and bar ware, and pharmaceutical glassware. Today, however, collectors are primarily interested in the 'Sculptured Artware' produced in the 1930s and 1940s. These beautiful pressed and mold-blown pieces are most often found in white milk glass or crystal with various color treatments or a satin finish.

Phoenix did not mark their 'Sculptured Artware' line on the glass; instead, a silver and black (earliest) or gold and black (later) foil label in the shape of the mythical phoenix bird was used.

Quite often glassware made by the Consolidated Lamp and Glass Company of nearby Coraopolis, Pennsylvania, is mistaken for Phoenix's 'Sculptured Artware.' Though the style of the glass is very similar, one distinguishing characteristic is that perhaps 80% of the time Phoenix applied color to the background leaving the raised design plain in contrast, while Consolidated generally applied color to the raised design and left the background plain. Also, for the most part, the patterns and colors used by Phoenix were distinctively different from those used by Consolidated.

In 1970 Phoenix Glass became a division of Anchor Hocking which in turn was acquired by the Newell Group in 1987. Phoenix has the distinction of being one of the oldest continuously operating glass factories in the United States. For more information refer to *Phoenix and Consolidated Art Glass, 1926-1980*, written by our advisor, Jack D. Wilson, who is listed in the Directory under Illinois. See also Consolidated Glass.

Key: mg — milk glass

Ashtray, Phlox, slate bl pearlized 225.00
Ashtray, 100th Anniversary Commemorative, amber 45.00
Banana boat, Diving Girl, aqua frost 350.00
Bowl, Tiger Lily, amethyst frost, 11½" 425.00
Candle holders, Strawberry, gr over mg, 4¼", pr 275.00
Candy dish, Phlox, bl frost 200.00
Cigarette box, Phlox, aqua wash 150.00
Console bowl, Lily, gr wash w/frosted design 475.00
Umbrella vase, Thistle, slate bl pearlized, 18" 575.00
Vase, Aster, lt tan w/pearlized design, 7" 85.00
Vase, Bluebell, florist gr, KR Haley, 7" 250.00
Vase, Cosmos, bl over mg, 7½" 175.00
Vase, Cosmos, brn shadow, 7½" 145.00
Vase, Dancing Girl, tan pearlized, 12" 550.00
Vase, Freesia, pk w/frosted design, 8" 150.00
Vase, Jewel, wht w/lt bl design, 4¾" 110.00
Vase, Lily, aqua wash, str sides, 8" 225.00
Vase, Madonna, brn shadow, 10½" 275.00
Vase, Madonna, med gr on mg, 10½" 225.00
Vase, Olive, lt bl wash, orig Rueben Line label (rare), 4" 275.00
Vase, Philodendron, slate bl over mg, 11½" 200.00
Vase, Primrose, brn shadow, 8¾" 325.00
Vase, Star Flower, bl & mg, 7" 145.00

Photo courtesy Jack D. Wilson

**Vase, Wild Geese, red pearlized,
9¼", $285.00.**

Vase, Wild Rose, aqua w/frosted design, 10½" 250.00
Vase, Wild Rose, wht frost, 10½" 150.00
Vase, Zodiac, med bl w/frosted design, 10" 750.00
Vase, Zodiac, tan over mg, 10" 800.00

Phonographs

The phonograph, invented by Thomas Edison in 1877, was the first practical instrument for recording and reproducing sound. Sound wave vibrations were recorded on a tinfoil-covered cylinder and played back with a needle that ran along the grooves made from the recording, thus reproducing the sound. Very little changed to this art of record making until 1885, when the first replayable and removable wax cylinders were developed by the American Graphaphone Company. These records were made from 1885 until 1894 and are rare today. Edison began to offer musically recorded wax cylinders in 1889. They continued to be made until 1902. Today they are known as brown wax records. The first disc records and disc machines were offered by the inventor Berliner in 1894. They were sold in America until 1900, when the Victor company took over. In the 1890s, all machines played 7" diameter disc records; the 10" size was developed in 1901. By the early 1900s there existed many disc and cylinder phonograph companies, all offering their improvements. Among them were Berliner, Columbia, Zonophone, United States Phono, Wizard, Vitaphone, Amet, and others.

All Victor I's through VI's originally came with a choice of either brass bell, morning-glory, or wooden horns. Wood horns are the most valuable, adding $1,000.00 (or more) value to the machine. Spring models were produced until 1929 (and even later). After 1929, most were electric (though some electric motor models were produced as early as 1910). Unless another condition is noted, prices are for complete, original phonographs in at least fine to excellent condition. Note: Edison coin-operated cylinder players start at $7,000.00 and may go up to $20,000.00 each. All outside-horn Victor phonographs are worth at **least** $1,000.00 or more, if in excellent original condition. Machines that are complete, still retaining all their original parts, and with the original finish still in good condition are the most sought after. Our advisor for this category is J.R. Wilkins; he is listed in the Directory under Texas. Unless noted, values are for examples in excellent condition, sold at popular, repeated buying prices.

Key:
cyl — cylinder   NP — nickel plated
mg — morning glory   rpd — reproducer

Berliner B Ideal, disc, Auto grand rpd, 16" brass bell, oak **1,200.00**
Berliner Trade Mark, disc, Johnson rpd, blk bell horn, M **3,750.00**
Bing Kiddyphone, disc, Bing rpd, cone horn, circular case **250.00**
Brunswick, cvd upright case w/moldings, lg **350.00**
Brunswick, plain upright case, sm **200.00**
Busy Bee Grand, disc, orig rpd, red mg horn, w/decal **700.00**
Cameraphone, disc, orig rpd, tortoise-shell resonator, oak **550.00**
Columbia A, cyl, eagle rpd, NP bell horn, oak case **500.00**
Columbia AA, cyl, eagle rpd, sm NP horn, sm oak cabinet **500.00**
Columbia AH, disc, Columbia rpd, brass bell horn, no decal ..**1,000.00**
Columbia AJ, disc, Columbia rpd, brass bell horn, rear crank **900.00**
Columbia AJ, disc, Columbia rpd, brass bell horn, top crank ..**2,000.00**
Columbia AK, disc, orig rpd, brass bell horn, 7¼" turntable **800.00**
Columbia AO, cyl, D rpd, brass bell horn **500.00**
Columbia AU, disc, rpd attached to horn, open works, turntable ..**600.00**
Columbia AZ, cyl, Lyric rpd, repro blk/brass horn **500.00**
Columbia BC 20th C, cyl, 4" Higham rpd, brass bell/5" mandrel ..**1,200.00**
Columbia BE Leader, cyl, Lyric rpd, mg, 6" mandrel, serpentine ...**650.00**
Columbia BF Peerless, cyl, Lyric rpd/brass horn/6" mandrel, oak ...**650.00**
Columbia BG Sovereign, cyl, orig rpd & horn/6" mandrel, mahog ..**900.00**
Columbia BI Sterling, disc, Columbia rpd, oak horn **2,250.00**
Columbia BK Jewel, cyl, Lyric rpd, copper horn, wicker basket ..**460.00**
Columbia BQ Rex, cyl, Lyric rpd, orig mg horn, oak case **600.00**
Columbia BS Coin-op, cyl, eagle rpd, rpl horn **3,000.00**
Columbia Grafonola, disc, orig rpd, inside horn, mahog, upright **200.00**
Columbia Q, cyl, Q rpd, blk cone horn, keywind **300.00**
Columbia Q Busy Bee, cyl, D rpd, 10" blk cone horn, key wind .**300.00**
Columbia Regent Desk, disc, Columbia rpd, inside horn, mahog ..**400.00**
Edison Amberola B-VI, cyl, Dmn B rpd, inside horn, mahog **350.00**
Edison Amberola VI, cyl, Dmn B rpd/inside horn, oak table top ...**350.00**
Edison Amberola X, cyl, Dmn B rpd, inside horn, NM **330.00**
Edison Amberola 30, cyl, Dmn C rpd, inside horn, oak, NM **375.00**
Edison Amberola 50, cyl, Dmn C rpd, inside horn, oak case **450.00**
Edison Concert, cyl, D rpd, brass horn/stand, 5" mandrel **2,500.00**
Edison Concert C, cyl, B rpd, 30" brass bell, floor stand, M ...**2,500.00**
Edison Dmn Disc A100, DD rpd, inside horn, Moderne golden oak ...**350.00**
Edison Dmn Disc B80, DD rpd, inside horn, table model **350.00**
Edison Dmn Disc C150, DD rpd, inside horn, Sheridan floor model ..**200.00**
Edison Fireside, cyl, H rpd, cygnet horn **1,150.00**
Edison Fireside, cyl, K rpd, blk metal cygnet horn, 2/4 min **850.00**
Edison Fireside A, cyl, Dmn B rpd, oak Music Master horn **2,250.00**
Edison Fireside A, cyl, K rpd, maroon horn/crane **1,000.00**
Edison Fireside B, cyl, Dmn B rpd, blk cygnet horn, 4 min **1,000.00**
Edison Gem A, cyl, B rpd, cone horn, label & decal **400.00**
Edison Gem D Maroon, cyl, K rpd, 20" maroon horn **1,800.00**
Edison Gem E Maroon, cyl, all orig **2,000.00**

Edison Home combination type, plays wax cylinders, oak horn and base, ca 1900, 39x20", EX restored, $1,650.00.

Victor V, oak case and horn, VG/EX, $3,500.00.

Edison Home, cyl, C rpd, 14" brass bell horn, ribbon decal 650.00
Edison Home, cyl, H rpd, metal cygnet horn, 2/4 min 675.00
Edison Home A, cyl, C rpd, 14" blk/brass horn, gr oak/banner ...500.00
Edison Home A Suitcase, cyl, C rpd, 14" repro horn, decal 550.00
Edison Home B, cyl, H rpd, lg brass bell, 2/4 min, rfn 550.00
Edison Home E, cyl, O rpd, oak cygnet horn, oak case 1,800.00
Edison Opera A, cyl, L rpd, mahog Music Master horn, mahog ..5,000.00
Edison Standard, cyl, C rpd, brass bell horn 475.00
Edison Standard A Suitcase, cyl, old-style rpd, 14" brass bell 550.00
Edison Standard B, cyl, C rpd, rpt mg horn, heavy crane 650.00
Edison Standard C, cyl, C rpd, mg horn, repeating attachment ..700.00
Edison Standard D, cyl, K rpd, blk cygnet horn 1,000.00
Edison Triumph, cyl, C rpd, 7" brass bell, 2-min 950.00
Edison Triumph, cyl, O rpd, oak cygnet horn, NM 2,500.00
Edison Triumph, cyl, O rpd, wood cygnet, 2/4 min repeater 2,800.00
Edison Triumph D, cyl, H rpd, 23" bell horn, 2/4-min 725.00
Edison Triumph G, cyl, opera case 4,000.00
Edison/Amet, spring motor, 1893-95, ea, from $2,500 to 8,000.00
Excelsior, cyl, aluminum rpd & horn, open works 500.00
Fern-O-Grand Baby Grand, disc, inside horn, piano shape 950.00
Kalamazoo Duplex, disc, Kalamazoo rpd, 2 lg horns 3,300.00
Mae Star Phonograph Doll, cyl, MS rpd, internal horn 500.00
Pathe Actuelle, disc, cone horn, oak console 750.00
Puck Lyre, cyl, floating rpd, red mg horn 400.00
Standard A, disc, Standard rpd, bl mg horn, decal 650.00
Standard X, disc, Standard rpd, blk mg horn, spindle model 650.00
Thorens Excelda, disc, Excelda rpd, internal horn, camera type .285.00
United Symphony, disc, United rpd, inside horn, table model ...250.00
Victor E Monarch Jr, disc, Concert rpd, brass horn, rear mt 1,200.00
Victor E Monarch Jr, disc, Exhibition rpd, brass bell horn 1,100.00
Victor I, disc, Exhibition rpd, repro brass bell, oak case 1,000.00
Victor II, disc, Exhibition rpd, metal horn 1,200.00
Victor II, disc, Exhibition rpd, oak horn & case 2,500.00
Victor II, dsic, Exhibition rpd, 18" brass bell horn, oak 1,000.00
Victor III, disc, Exhibition rpd, blk mg horn, oak case 1,200.00
Victor IV, disc, Exhibition rpd, mahog horn & case 2,200.00
Victor M Monarch, disc, Exhibition rpd, 11" horn, oak case ..1,500.00
Victor M Monarch, disc, lg brass bell, oak case 1,500.00
Victor MS Monarch Specialty, disc, Exhibition rpd, oak horn ..2,500.00
Victor P Premium, disc, Exhibition rpd, 18" brass bell horn 1,000.00
Victor R Royal, disc, Exhibition rpd, 9½" brass bell, oak 1,000.00
Victor Schoolhouse XXV, disc, oak horn, oak upright case 3,000.00
Victor VI, disc, Exhibition rpd, mahog horn & case 5,000.00
Victor VV-IV, disc, Exhibition rpd, inside horn, oak table top ..200.00
Victor VV-VI, disc, Exhibition rpd, inside horn, oak table top ..200.00
Victor VV-X, disc, Exhibition rpd, inside horn, table top 500.00
Victor VV-XII, disc, Exhibition rpd/inside horn/mahog table top ...550.00
Victor VV-50, disc, #2 prd, inside horn, oak portable 150.00
Victor VV-70, disc, #4 rpd, inside horn, table top 325.00

Victor VV-8-30, disc, Orthophonic rpd, inside horn, credenza ..1,000.00
Victor Z, disc, Exhibition rpd, brass bell horn, front mount ..12,000.00
Vitaphone, disc, w/horn, minimum value 1,000.00
Zonophone, disc, front mt w/horn, from $1,000 to 3,000.00
Zonophone, disc, rear mt, w/horn, from $800 to 1,500.00
Zonophone Champion, disc, Exhibition rpd, sm gr mg horn ...1,200.00
Zonophone Parlor, disc, brass bell horn, rear crank 1,100.00

Photographica

Photographic collectibles include not only the cameras and equipment used to 'freeze' special moments in time but also the photographic images produced by a great variety of processes that have evolved since the daguerrean era of the mid-1800s. For the most part, good quality images have either maintained or increased in value. Poor quality examples (regardless of rarity) are not selling well. Interest in cameras and stereo equipment is down, and dealers report that average-priced items that were moving well are often completely overlooked. Though rare items always have a market, collectors seem to be buying only if they are bargain priced.

Our advisor for this category is John Hess; he is listed in the Directory under Massachusetts.

Albumens

Abraham Lincoln portrait, J Gurney stamp, oval, 1860s, 8x6" ...460.00
African man w/scarred face & tasseled hat, 1869, EX 55.00
Blk soldier w/identified Southern officers, 6x8¼", EX 450.00
General Robert E Lee on horse Traveler, M Miley, 1868, EX 285.00
I'm Not Afraid, girl w/lg shovel & torn clothes, 15x20" 125.00
Little Bear, Cheyenne warrior, JK Hillers, 1875, 9¾x7¼" 490.00
Nude study of 2 women, 1850s, 3⅛x1⅛" 745.00
NY State Militia guard, stands in greatcoat, oval, 9x6" 175.00
Pike's Peak Hanging Rock, Manitou & Pike's Peak Ry, 5x8" 75.00
Thomas A Edison, V Daireaux Paris, 1880s, 5½x3¾" 375.00
Union general composite, prof rpr, 1862, 8½x10" 160.00
Union soldier, full-length, WL Germon, Phila, in 17x20" fr 145.00

Ambrotypes

An ambrotype is a type of photograph produced by an early wet-plate process whereby a faint negative image on glass is seen as positive when held against a dark background.

Half plate, farmhouse w/clothes on line, ME, MOP case 235.00
Whole plate, 8-member missionary family in Hawaii 350.00
6th plate, policeman, hand-tinted, 1850s, w/leather case 335.00

6th plate, postmortem, baby in wht, 1855, +case 45.00
6th plate, Union soldier w/beard seated by wife, EX, +case 95.00
9th plate, dk-skinned lady, tinted cheeks & lips, VG 22.50
9th plate, seated Confederate w/percussion pepperbox, EX 300.00
9th plate, sheriff w/5-pointed star badge in rnd disk, EX 30.00

Cabinet Photos

Actress Ullie Akerstrom seated in wht gown, Eisenmann, VG 14.50
Amy Arlington holding 2 python snakes, Eisenmann, VG 32.50
Chester A Arthur, bust portrait, EX 16.50
Edwin Thomas Booth, seated, J Notman, EX 32.50
Felix Wehrle, elastic skin man, Eisenmann, rare, EX 70.00
Fireman holding fire trumpet, Buckholz, EX 30.00
Indian Wars infantryman holding musician's sword, EX 25.50
John L Sullivan, boxing history to 1889 on bk, VG+ 40.00
Man playing fife w/US flag in 1 end, river bkdrop, EX 18.50
Officer wearing 1850s baldric device, EX 12.50
Oliver Wendell Holmes, bust portrait, Warren, EX 15.50
Outdoor scene of palomino trick horse, Eisenmann, G+ 25.50
Ralph Waldo Emerson, bust portrait, Chas Taber, 1882, VG 16.50
USMC soldier, bust portrait, 1880s, VG+ 20.00
2 coyotes seated, close-up view, WH Jackson, EX 30.00
4 giants in military uniform, full-length, Eisenmann, G+ 30.00

Cameras

Among the earliest daguerrean cameras was the sliding box-on-a-box camera. It was focused by sliding one box in and out of the other, thus adjusting the distance of the lens to the ground glass. This was replaced on later models with leather bellows. These were the forerunners of the multilens cameras developed in the late 1870s, which were capable of recording many small portraits on a single plate. Double-lens cameras produced stereo images which, when viewed through a device called a stereoscope, achieved a 3-dimensional effect. In 1888 George Eastmann introduced his box camera, the first to utilize roll film. This greatly simplified the process, making it possible for the amateur to enjoy photography as a hobby. Detective cameras, those disguised as books, handbags, etc., are among the most sought after by today's collectors.

Nikon F2S Photomic camera, with DS12 automatic aperture control, NM, $300.00.

Baby Hawk-Eye, box camera, 1896-98 ....165.00
Baldamatic I, 35mm rangefinder, ca 1959 ....55.00
Beirette, folding compact, 35mm, metal w/leather bellows, '30s .180.00
Boots Special, compact folding field type, 1911 ....80.00
Certo Champion II, 35mm, lever advance, West Germany 20.00
Contessa Piccolette, folding vest pocket, ca 1919-26 ....90.00
Eastman Kodak #4 Kodak Jr, Universal lens, 48 exposures, 1890s ..385.00
Eastman Kodak Bull's-Eye #4, side loading, 1896-04 ....50.00
Eastman Kodak Folding Brownie #2, maroon bellows, 1904-07 ....40.00
Ernemann Mignon-Kemera, folding type, cross-swing struts, 1910s ...120.00
Fuji Baby Balnet, early version w/folding viewfinder, 1940s 130.00
Goltz Mentor Dreivier, 127 film, eye-level style, 1930s 650.00
Graflex Anniversary Speed Graphic, drop bed, chrome trim 125.00
Houghton Ensigne Carbine, tropical model, 1937-36 ....150.00

Isoflex I, cast metal reflex box type, 1952 ....20.00
Kodak Petite, pk, w/mirrored compact case, EX 635.00
Kodak Vest Pocket, trellis struts, common lens, 1912-14 ....45.00
Leica IIf, no slow speeds, red dial, 1951-56 ....165.00
Merlin, cast-metal mini w/crackle finish, 1936 ....125.00
Olympus Flex BII, click stops on shutter, 1950s 120.00
Pocket Magda, metal folding type, ca 1920 ....185.00
Praktica Nova, 35mm, eye-level type, 1965 ....50.00
Rocamco, metal box type, special 35mm film, 1936 ....185.00
Semi Minolta II, folding type, 16 exposures, 1937 ....60.00
Standard Star-Lite, 35mm, 1960s 20.00
Super Kodak Six-20, coupled electric eye, 620 film, 1938-44 ..1,100.00
Uni-Fex, blk plastic box type, telescoping front, 1949 ....12.50
Utility Falcon Jr, folding vest pocket, Bakelite case 15.00
Voigtlander Bessamatic M, no meter, ca 1964 ....90.00

Carte De Visites

Among the many types of images collectible today are carte de visites, known as CDVs, which are 2¼" x 4" portraits printed on paper and produced in quantity. The CDV fad of the 1800s enticed the famous and the unknown alike to pose for these cards, which were circulated among the public to the extent that they became known as 'publics.' When the popularity of CDVs began to wane, a new fascination developed for the cabinet photo, a larger version measuring about 4½" x 6½". Note: A common portrait CDV is worth only about 50¢ unless it carries a revenue stamp on the back; those that do are valued at about $1.00 each.

Red Stocking Baseball Club, Cincinnati, NM, $700.00.

Albino woman, Eisenmann, VG 16.00
Benjamin F Kelly seated w/sword on his lap, Brady-Anthony, EX 40.00
Boy & greyhound dog on stuffed lounge, 1880s, EX 10.00
Boy in sailor suit seated on tree stump, EX 20.00
Boy riding lg tricycle, Stevens, EX 12.50
Capt O'Brian, Buford Staff, Moulthrop & Williams, EX 32.50
Cat seated on photographer's chair, close-up view, EX 20.00
Chinese girl seated in mandarin robe beside table, EX 12.50
Circus performer Zalumma Agra, full-length, E Anthony, VG 22.50
Civil War cavalry sgt leaning on sword, Claflin image, EX 95.00
Civil War soldier holding album on marble table, Hopkins, EX ...30.00
Civil War soldier holding rifled musket, seated, VG 45.00
Civil War soldier w/arm in sling, Steiger image, VG 85.00
Civil War soldiers, 1 standing/1 leaning on crutches, VG+ 85.00
Civil War soldiers & Irish friend playing cards, EX 75.00
Confederate officer, vignetted chest view, VG 40.00
Dolly Varden Carroll, midget portrait, full-length, rare, EX 22.00
Dudley Foster atop table, midget portrait, Eisenmann, G+ 26.00
Edwin M Stanton, vignetted view, scarce, EX 45.00
Gamblers playing cards, close-up of 2 men, Roberts, 1864, EX 24.50
General Charles Ferguson Smith, full-length, Brady, 1862, EX 30.00

General George G Meade, bust portrait, Gutenkunst, EX **40.00**
General Nathaniel Banks seated in frock, Case & Getchell, EX ..**40.00**
General Winfield S Hancock, chest pose, Gutenkunst, EX **40.00**
Giant Capt Bates & his manager w/epaulets, EX **25.00**
Girl w/china-head doll on her lap, Black & Chase, 1865, VG **12.00**
Henriette Moretz, age 16, midget portrait, Eisenmann, EX **25.00**
James Garfield, bust portrait, VG **12.50**
John Stratton seated w/sleeves folded up, EX **95.00**
John Wilkes Booth seated w/cane & arm on hip, VG **40.00**
Little girl w/blue jay in her lap, Currier, EX **16.00**
Lucretia Coffin Mott seated w/book in lap, rare, VG **30.00**
MA Militia soldier holding artillery sword, rare, 1850, EX **50.00**
Major B Kennicott, chest pose in frock coat, EX **40.00**
Man riding bicycle w/man running alongside, NM **55.00**
Mary Todd Lincoln in blk satin dress facing right, EX **55.00**
Miss Jennie Quigley, age 20, midget portrait, 1860s, VG **24.00**
Outdoor scene of Castle Thunder, Richmond VA, VG **25.50**
Outdoor scene of mansion w/gambrel roof, Loomis, EX **12.00**
Schuyler Coffax seated w/hands on his lap, VG **9.50**
Seth Kinman holding rifle on his lap, Brady, rare, VG **225.00**
Union musician in frock coat, full-length, VG **40.00**
William T Lander in frock coat, bust portrait, EX **25.50**
Winfield S Hancock, bust portrait, looking left, EX **22.00**
Woman holding gymnastic stick, full-length, EX **15.00**
Zouave cadets, standing, Miller, EX **95.00**

Daguerreotypes

Among the many processes used to produce photographic images are the daguerreotypes (made on a plate of chemically treated metal) — the most-valued examples being the 'whole' plate which measures 6½" x 8½". Other sizes include the 'half' plate, measuring 4½" x 5½", the 'quarter' plate at 3¼" x 4¼", the 'sixth' plate at 2¾" x 3¼", the 'ninth' at 2" x 2½", and the 'sixteenth' at 1⅜" x 1⅝". (Sizes may vary slightly, and some may have been altered by the photographer.)

4th plate, man w/long wht hair looking right, full case, EX **95.00**
4th plate, seated man holding wire-fr glasses, VG **22.50**
6th plate, girl in print dress w/book, 1840s, full case, VG **22.50**
6th plate, lady w/cross in hand, gold trim, VG **50.00**
6th plate, man & wife, horizontal image, full case, EX **22.50**
6th plate, man in cowboy-type hat, full case, VG+ **24.50**
6th plate, woman in plaid dress & lg scarf, encased, EX **22.50**
9th plate, seated young girl w/her elderly mother, full case **22.50**

Stereoscopic Views

Stereo cards are photos made to be viewed through a device called a stereoscope. The glass stereo plates of the mid-1800s and photo prints produced in the darkroom are among the most valuable. In evaluating stereo views, the subject, date, and condition are all-important. Some views were printed over a thirty- to forty-year period; 'first generation' prices are far higher than later copies, made on cheap card stock with reprints or lithographs, rather than actual original photographs.

It is relatively easy to date an American stereo view by the color of the mount that was used, the style of the corners, etc. From about 1854 until the early 1860s, cards were either white, cream-colored, or glossy gray; shades of yellow and a dull gray followed. While the dull gray was used for a very short time, the yellow tones continued in use until the late 1860s. Red, green, violet, or blue cards are from the period between 1865 until about 1870. Until the late 1870s, corners were square; after that they were rounded off to prevent damage. Right now, quality stereo views are at a premium.

Set of six Shaker views (one shown by Kimball), two interiors, one view of school, others buildings, EX, $200.00.

Adalaide Neilson in Romeo & Juliet costume, Gurney, 1872, EX **20.00**
Apache Canyon, close-up view of train, Henry Brown #189, EX ...**110.00**
Balloon w/crowd of people, E Pluribus emblem, Hacker, G+ **100.00**
Broadway, NY, Anthony New Gelatine-Bromide Process, set of 3 ..**60.00**
Broadway Near Wall St, J Gurney & Son, ca 1868, VG **25.00**
City of Worcester, F Jay Haynes #364, EX **150.00**
Floyd Gibbons, close-up in wht suit, Keys #32797, NMIB **45.00**
Graff Zeppelin, Keys #32277, VG **30.00**
Great Eastern in Southampton Water, GW Wilson #219, VG+ ..**40.00**
Hunter's Paradise, Kilburn #12820, EX **10.00**
Indian talking to cowboy in sign language, Keys #V23247, VG **15.00**
Interior St Francis Church, GW Pach #491, EX **20.00**
Looking Up 5th Ave From 23rd, Bierstadt #991, VG **20.00**
Main St, Wrangel, AK, boardwalk view, Keys #V21039, EX **35.00**
Prof Wise Inflating His Balloon Ganymede, Anthony #221, VG ..**165.00**
Refining Oil, refinery scene, Frank Robbins #53, VG+ **35.00**
San Francisco Earthquake, Kilburn #16881/#16882, VG+ **30.00**
Sitting Bull's Deserted Teepee, F Jay Haynes #844, VG **145.00**

Tintypes

Tintypes, contemporaries of ambrotypes, were produced on japanned iron and were not as easily damaged.

Indian war cavalry trooper w/carbine/sword/side arm, 3¾x2½" ..**300.00**
4th plate, soldier w/arm in sling in front of camp scene **130.00**
6th plate, Union soldier w/scarce E Whitney revolver, EX **300.00**
9th plate, seated soldier w/musket, M&P, encased, EX **200.00**

Union Cases

From the mid-1850s until about 1880, cases designed to house these early images were produced from a material known as thermoplastic, a man-made material with an appearance much like gutta percha. Its innovator was Samuel Peck, who used shellac and wood fibers to create a composition he called Union. Peck was part owner of the Scoville Company, makers of both papier-mache and molded leather cases, and he used the company's existing dies to create his new line. Other companies, among them A.P. Critchlow & Company, Littlefield, Parsons & Company, and Holmes, Booth & Hayden soon duplicated his material and produced their own designs. Today's collectors may refer to cases made of this material as 'thermoplastic,' 'composition,' or 'hard cases,' but the term most often used is 'Union.' It is incorrect to refer to them as gutta percha cases.

Sizes may vary somewhat, but generally a 'whole' plate case measures 7" x 9⅛" to the outside edges, a 'half plate 4⅞" x 6", a 'quarter' plate 3¾" x 4¾", a 'sixth' 3⅛" x 3⅝", a 'ninth' 2⅜" x 2⅞", and a 'sixteenth' 1¾" x 2". Clifford and Michele Krainik and Carl Walvoord have written a book, *Union Cases*, which we recommend for further study. Another source of information is *Nineteenth Century Photographic Cases and Wall Frames* by Paul Berg.

The Landing of Columbus, whole plate, ca 1858, VG, $2,000.00.

Half plate, geometrics, K-16, NM 400.00
16th plate (dbl), Children w/Toys, K-574, EX 150.00
4th plate, Capture of Major Andre, by S Peck & Co, ca 1856, EX ..150.00
4th plate, Geometric Scroll, K-66, EX+ 135.00
4th plate, Parting of Hafed & Hinda, K-35, VG 200.00
4th plate, Roger deCoverly & Gypsies Fortune, K-30, EX 125.00
4th plate, Sir Roger de Coverly & Gypsies, K-30, EX, $100 to ...125.00
6th plate, Calmady Children, K-129, EX 200.00
6th plate, Crossed Cannons & Liberty Cap, K-112, NM 200.00
6th plate, Eagle at Bay, K-111, EX 125.00
6th plate, Fireman Saving Child, K-118, EX 150.00
6th plate, Geometric, K-270, VG 75.00
6th plate, Geometric, w/glass window, K-355, EX 95.00
6th plate, Geometric, w/ruby ambro portrait 50.00
6th plate, Hidden Pearl, w/ambro portrait, VG 45.00
6th plate, Magnified Circle, R-233, EX, +dag 25.00
6th plate, Profile of Learned Man, K-146, EX 150.00
6th plate, Shield, Crossed Cannon & Flags w/Liberty Cap, EX ..175.00
6th plate, Union & Constitution, K-373, lt wear, EX 100.00
6th plate, 10-Pointed Star w/arabesque border, R-20 ....20.00
9th plate, American Gothic, K-374, EX 50.00
9th plate, Angel w/Trumpet, R-49, EX, w/image 65.00
9th plate, Blind Beggar, K-388, EX+ 75.00
9th plate, Chess Players, R-41 variant, NM...................90.00
9th plate, Geometric, VG 45.00
9th plate, Profile of Liberty, K-367, EX 125.00
9th plate, Scroll, Constitution & Laws, R-76, G 100.00
9th plate (dbl), Children w/Toys, R-29 ....135.00
9th plate (dbl), Family Party, K-560, EX 150.00
9th plate (dbl)/16th plate (triple), Lovers Going to the Well, K-35 ...575.00

Miscellaneous

Stereoscope, Mascher's Improved, folding type with daguerreotype portrait of young man, ¼-plate size, EX, $370.00.

Book, Principles of Stereography, McKay, 189-pg, VG 35.00
Magic lantern, metal w/pierced decor, Auguste Lapierre 125.00
Magic lantern, wood w/lacqured brass fittings, w/illuminant 250.00
Peep box, wood, single viewing lens, litho sheets, 1850s 900.00
Projection lamp, metal body, carbon arc, brass fittings 150.00
Projector, EP; blk-pnt tin, lit w/mini kero lamp, German, 10" ...140.00
Projector, postcard; USA Radio Jr, HC White, 11x9x10½"+case .100.00
Stereo viewer, burl walnut, binocular-style eyepc, 7" 225.00
Stereo viewer, ebonized/pale wood, folds, Paris, 2¾x11x6¾" 200.00
Stereo viewer, figured walnut, Alex Beckets NY, 1857/1859, 18½" ...400.00
Stereo viewer, Little Rocket, blk pnt, metal stand/wood base, 9" .75.00
Stereo viewer, walnut, folding stand, Pat 1866/1877/1878, 12½" ..125.00

Piano Babies

A familiar sight in Victorian parlors, piano babies languished atop shawl-covered pianos in a variety of poses: crawling, sitting, on their tummies or on their backs playing with their toes. Some babies were nude, and some wore gowns. Sizes ranged from about 3" up to 12". The most famous manufacturer of these bisque darlings was the Heubach Brothers of Germany, who nearly always marked their product; see Heubach for listings. Watch for reproductions. These guidelines are excerpted from one of a series of informative doll books by Pat Smith, published by Collector Books.

Baby on tummy with arms around puppy, EX painted details and touches of lustre, Germany, 4¾x11", $810.00.

Blk, bsk, 12", EX quality 995.00
Blk, bsk, 12", med quality 425.00
Blk, bsk, 16", EX quality, minimum value 1,085.00
Blk, bsk, 16", med quality 975.00
Blk, bsk, 4", EX quality 425.00
Blk, bsk, 4", med quality 325.00
Blk, bsk, 8", EX quality 525.00
Blk, bsk, 8", med quality 375.00
Bsk, molded hair, unjtd, molded-on clothes, 12", EX quality 975.00
Bsk, molded hair, unjtd, molded-on clothes, 15", med quality 495.00
Bsk, molded hair, unjtd, molded-on clothes, 4", EX quality 325.00
Bsk, molded hair, unjtd, molded-on clothes, 4", med quality 225.00
Bsk, molded hair, unjtd, molded-on clothes, 8", EX quality 895.00
Bsk, molded hair, unjtd, molded-on clothes, 8", med quality 435.00
Bsk, w/animal/pot/flowers/etc, 12", EX quality 995.00
Bsk, w/animal/pot/flowers/etc, 16", EX quality, minimum 1,100.00
Bsk, w/animal/pot/flowers/etc, 4", EX quality 395.00
Bsk, w/animal/pot/flowers/etc, 8", EX quality 615.00

Picasso Art Pottery

Pablo Picasso created some distinctive pottery during the 1940s, marking the ware with his signature.

Handled vessel, impressed Medur
Plein Feu and signed in black Edition
Picasso, Medura, 11½", $2,300.00;
Bowl, stamped Edition Picasso,
Medura, 2x6½", EX, $400.00.

Dish, bird in profile, blk/bl on wht, 6" dia 600.00
Pitcher, owl form, blk & wht w/bl & red, Madoura, 1955, 10¼" ...1,840.00
Plate, horse & rider, unglazed on wht crackle, 7½" 550.00
Tile, eye impression, unglazed, 6" 110.00

Pickard

Founded in 1895 in Chicago, Illinois, the Pickard China Company
was originally a decorating studio, importing china blanks from European manufacturers. Some of these early pieces bear the name of those
companies as well as Pickard's. Trained artists decorated the wares with
hand-painted studies of fruit, florals, birds, and scenics and often signed
their work. In 1915 Pickard introduced a line of 23k gold over a dainty
floral-etched ground design. In the 1930s they began to experiment with
the idea of making their own ware and by 1938 had succeeded in developing a formula for fine translucent china. Since 1976 they have issued
an annual limited edition Christmas plate. They are now located in
Antioch, Illinois.

The company has used various marks. The earliest (1893-1894)
was a double-circle mark, 'Edgerton Hand Painted' with 'Pickard' in the
center. Variations of the double-circle mark (with 'Hand Painted
China' replacing the Edgerton designation) were employed until 1915,
each differing enough that collectors can usually pinpoint the date of
manufacture within five years. Later marks included the crown mark,
'Pickard' on a gold maple leaf, and the current mark, the lion and
shield. Work signed by Challinor, Marker, and Yeschek is especially
valued by today's collectors. For further information we recommend
Collector's Encyclopedia of Pickard China by Alan B. Reed, available from
Collector Books.

Bonbon, Nouveau violets on airbrushed gr, 1903-05, 9" 185.00
Bowl, amaryllis & etched gold, Beutlich, ftd, 1905-10, 10" 425.00
Bowl, nasturtiums w/gold, EC Challinor, gold rim, mk, 10½" 325.00
Bowl, pastel grapes, gold rim, Beutlich, 1905-10, 9¼" 225.00
Box, trinket; gold scrolls, flower border, 1905 mk, 3" dia 145.00
Charger, red & yel tulips, sgn H Michel-Stouffer, 12½" 250.00
Coffee set, Aura Mosaic, much gold, sgn C Rosl, 1910-12, 3-pc ..500.00
Cup & saucer, Blackberry Conventional, sgn Fisch, 1903-05 .....125.00
Ferner, Pond Lily, sgn Leach, 1903-05, Limoges blank, 7" 425.00
Mug, cherries on bl w/gold, sgn LeRoy, ca 1898-1903, 5¼" 400.00
Mug, monk w/tankard & candle, Aldrich, 1898-1903, 6" 300.00
Mustard pot, pk & bl pnt flowers w/gold, 1912 mk 60.00
Pitcher, dahlias & raised gold w/lustre, Arno, 1910-12, 6¾" 425.00
Plate, poppies sprays on gr ring on wht, Luken, 1912-18, 6" 55.00
Plate, Tulip Moderne, sgn Chahn, ca 1898-1903, 8" 150.00

Plate, 3 pk daisy sprays w/gold border, Tolley, 1905-10, 8½" 125.00
Platter, poppy sprays on cream w/gold, hdls, 1905-10, 14¾" 180.00
Shaker, purple pansies w/gold, 1910 mk 85.00
Shakers, Lemon Tree, sgn E Tolpin, 1910-12 mk, pr 125.00
Tea set, Moorish design, sgn Hessler, 1905-10, 3-pc 500.00

Vases, all ca 1912-1918: Fall Birches,
signed Challinor, 12", $1,450.00; Red-
haired sylph, signed M, 11", $1,500.00;
Everglades, signed Challinor, 10", $900.00.

Vase, Cherokee Rose, sgn Walt, wishbone hdls, 1910-12, 8½" ..375.00
Vase, Evening Spreads Her Mantle, allegorical, Grane, 9½" ...2,500.00
Vase, lakeside forest, Challinor, gold hdls, 1912-18, 7¼" 500.00
Vase, violets on cream, sgn, gold neck, bulbous, 7" 145.00

Pickle Castors

Pickle castors, which were both functional and decorative,
became popular after the Civil War, reaching their peak about 1885.
By 1900 they had virtually disappeared from factory catalogs.
Numerous styles were available. They consisted of a decorated, silverplated frame that held either a fancy clear pressed-glass insert or
one of decorated colored art glass — the latter being popular in the
more affluent Victorian households and more desirable with collectors today.

In the listings below, the description prior to the semicolon
refers to the jar (insert), and the remainder of the line describes the
frame. When no condition is indicated, the silverplate is assumed
to be in very good to excellent condition; glass jars are assumed
near-mint.

Key:
rsl — resilvered   3-D — three-dimensional

Amberina, diagonal ribs; cherub-ftd SP fr 425.00
Amethyst craquelle w/HP gold orchids; SP fr w/bird finial 650.00
Barrel; ornate Reed & Barton SP fr, fancy fork 295.00
Bead & Drape, red satin; ftd SP fr, +tongs 395.00
Burmese; Rogers-Smith fr w/2 Greenaway boys, +fork 750.00
Clear, emb diagonal Xs/cone flowers; ornate fr,+tongs, 13" 175.00
Clear w/etched decor; Meriden #250 SP fr, +tongs 275.00
Cobalt w/gold scrolls & florals; orig SP fr, +tongs 500.00
Cone, pk satin cased; rstr Tufts SP fr 450.00
Coreopsis, mc florals on wht satin; SP fr, + tongs 400.00
Cranberry optic Invt T'print, bulbous; ornate Tufts SP fr 475.00
Cranberry w/HP floral & gold; ornate SP fr, 10x8" 950.00
Cranberry w/HP windmill & foliage; Pairpoint SP fr 450.00

Cranberry; emb Barbour SP fr, 6½", +fork 395.00
Cupid & Venus; orig SP fr, +tongs 250.00
Daisy & Button, amber; ornate SP fr w/scrolled ft, +tongs 350.00
Daisy & Button, canary; bird finial, scroll-top fr, +tongs 350.00
Daisy & Button, topaz; ornate SP fr w/side ornaments, +tongs ... 350.00
Daisy & Button w/V Bar ornament, amber; plain SP fr 375.00
Drape, pigeon blood; EX SP fr 595.00
Eng florals in 6 panels; rstr Rogers #345 fr, 9" 350.00
Fine Cut & Panel, sapphire bl; rsl SP fr, 11", +tongs 325.00
Florette, pk; rstr Tufts fr 400.00
Fostoria's Victoria; orig SP fr 175.00
Frosted, emb birds/insects; Reed & Barton dbl-hdl fr, +fork 350.00
Hobstar, vaseline, Imperial; mk Pairpoint fr, rare 750.00
Honeycomb, rubena w/coralene florals; SP fr w/flower finial 525.00
Invt T'print, amber w/bl HP berries; Meriden fr, 12" 625.00
Invt T'print, clear, HP flowers/birds; 12½" fr w/Cupid 495.00

Inverted Thumbprint, cranberry with multicolor florals, ornate silver-plated frame, with tongs, $595.00.

Invt T'print, cranberry, gold butterfly etc; Meriden fr 550.00
Invt T'print, cranberry w/floral; scroll fr/cutout ft, +tongs 300.00
Invt T'print, rubena w/pk & gr coralene; rstr fr 920.00
Invt T'print, sapphire bl, flowers/leaves; orig SP ftd fr 495.00
Jacob's Ladder; SP fr, +tongs, scarce 350.00
Open Heart Arches, pigeon blood satin; orig fr 450.00
Raindrop satin, wht to pk; Simpson Hall Miller fr, 12" 1,395.00
Red Dmn Quilt MOP; SP ftd Empire fr, 9¾", +fork 850.00
Royal Ivy, rubena frost; chased fr, +tongs 550.00
Rubena, HP florals; rstr SP fr 525.00
Shell & Seaweed, pk cased, HP florals; Aurora fr, 9½" 1,150.00
Spatter, (mc cased); ornate Wilcox ftd fr 495.00
Swirl; low ftd Meriden fr w/hdls 150.00
Torquay, pigeon blood; orig SP fr 350.00
Victoria, Fostoria; ornate SP fr, +tongs 275.00
Wht satin, HP rose apple blossoms; rstr fr 325.00
Zipper & Beads, emerald gr; SP fr w/birds 395.00

Pierce, Howard

Howard Pierce, a talented artist, began his studio work in 1941 in Claremont, California. His lifelong career would focus on creating porcelain wildlife pieces. Formal training for his chosen field was completed at the Chicago Art Institute, California's Pomona College, and the University of Illinois. While in National City, California, he met Ellen Van Voorhis whom he married a short time later.

William Manker, a talented, multifaceted craftsman in his own right, hired Mr. Pierce to help in his studio. When Pierce went out on his own, some of Manker's training was reflected in his early products. In particular, the two-color, high-gloss bowls and small vases can be attributed to this liaison. Their business relationship lasted about three years.

From the beginning, Howard concentrated on wildlife and animals. Initially he made some polyurethane pieces, mostly birds or roadrunners on bases, which caused him to have an allergic reaction and forced him to discontinue work in that medium. Those pieces are highly collectible on today's market.

Some items, mostly wall pockets, cups and saucers, sugar bowls and creamers, were produced in a Wedgwood-type Jasper ware in mint green or pink. Later Mr. Pierce would use the same Jasper ware in white to create porcelain bisque animals and plants (horses and trees in particular) that he inserted or placed close to open areas of some of his vases (which were predominately glazed in glossy light or dark green).

Pierce's abilities enabled him to work with widely diversified materials. When Mount St. Helens erupted, he was one of the first artists to include its ash in his formulas. The inclusion of this grain-like substance created a rough, sandy texture in the finished products. Lava was another appealing treatment used for some of his items and should not be confused with the Mount St. Helens textures. 'Lava,' Mr. Pierce explained, 'caused a bubbling up from the bottom.' Until you have seen a lava item it is difficult to understand the scope of his vision and talent.

Gold leaf was a beautiful addition to his line. In fact, Pierce created two 'gold' lines. The gold leaf was exquisite as well as elegant. But there was another gold treatment that Pierce was not proud of, and his name does not appear on many of those products. Sears, Roebuck and Company ordered (through Pierce's distributor) a large assortment of items, all of which were to be finished in an overall gold. Unfortunately much of the gold flaked off over time, exposing a red body underneath. Collectors who know the Pierce line will quickly recognize a 'Sears gold' piece.

In the late 1970s, Pierce introduced a system wherein a number was assigned to each piece he designed. This number was incised directly into the ware, then recorded in a ledger which gave the formula for the particular glaze treatment he had used. He considered these glazes 'experimental.' From the numbering system, Pierce was able to re-create glazes he liked and those that were good sellers. Generally these were in varying shades of blue, green, yellow, purple, and pink. Pierce felt the gray, white, and brown were more suitable for wildlife, and therefore he regarded the 'experimental' colors as 'seconds.' Collectors have taken a special interest in experimentals, making their values a little higher.

So talented was he that many companies and nonprofit organizations solicited his work to display outside their place of business or to beautify their city. These items were made from cement and would sometimes be from ten to fifteen feet high. Later, Howard might create the same item in a life-size form, again using cement. Today many collectors utilize these pieces to adorn their gardens and patios.

Mr. Pierce believed that everyone who wanted a product of his should have it, so he successfully managed throughout the years to keep his costs (and ultimately, the selling prices) low.

In November 1992, Howard and Ellen Pierce destroyed all the molds he had created over the years, citing Howard's health problem as the major reason for this move. Still, he wanted to work; so in 1993, he purchased a small kiln and on a limited basis created smaller versions of his past products. These pieces were simply stamped 'Pierce.' In February 1994, Howard Pierce passed away. Our advisor for this category is Susan Cox; she is listed in the Directory under California.

Bowl, Lava, brn & wht, 2½x9" 100.00
Bowl, lt gr & pk, flared, early mk, 1¾x5" 25.00
Figurine, big-horned sheep on base, wht, 7¼" 45.00
Figurine, chickadee, bl, 3¾", 2½", pr 38.00
Figurine, circus horse on base, wht & brn, 6½" 145.00
Figurine, dove, brn & tan, mk Pierce, 1993, 3½" 29.00
Figurine, duck, Sears gold, mk, 7¾" 48.00
Figurine, elephant seated w/trunk up, pk, 4¾" 50.00
Figurine, Eskimo, brn & wht, #206P, 7" 95.00

Figurines, fish, purple with black stripes, 4¾", 3¼", pair, $115.00.

Figurine, horse, brn w/tan, mottled tail, 9" 155.00
Figurine, Madonna & Child, modern, wht, 5" 65.00
Figurine, panther, dk brn, 11½" 100.00
Figurine, penguin, blk & wht, 3¾", 3¼", pr 75.00
Figurine, polar bear walking, wht, 7¼" 75.00
Figurine, porcupine, rough-textured blk w/wht, 4" 110.00
Figurine, raccoon, brn, tail w/4 stripes, 9" 80.00
Figurine, roadrunner on base, polyurethane, 8" 200.00
Magnet, owl, bl glaze, 2" 28.00
Sign, dealer; tree bark surface, brn, 2½" 130.00
Vase, bud; experimental bl, 3½" 65.00
Vase, deer & tree on base, wht w/blk base, 7½" 135.00
Wall plaque, 2 raccoons on branch, brn cement, 16" 410.00
Wall pocket, 5 wht deer, bsk lt & dk pk, 7¾" 170.00
Whistle, snake, brn & wht, 3½" 45.00

Pigeon Blood

Pigeon blood glass, produced in the late 1800s, may be distinguished from other dark red glass by its distinctive orange tint.

Biscuit jar, Florette, metal lid 310.00
Biscuit jar, Little Shrimp 325.00
Biscuit jar, Open Heart Arches 325.00
Bowl, berry; Open Heart Arches 225.00
Butter dish, Coreopsis 275.00
Carafe, Coreopsis, water sz 295.00
Creamer, Beaded Drape 150.00
Creamer, Coreopsis 125.00
Pitcher, water; Bulging Loop 400.00
Pitcher, water; Coreopsis, pnt flowers, metal lid 400.00
Sugar bowl, Torquay, glass top 165.00
Syrup, Beaded Drape 600.00

Pilkington

Founded in 1892 in Manchester, England, the Pilkington pottery

experimented in wonderful lustre glazes that were so successful that when they were diplayed at exhibition in 1904, they were met with critical acclaim. They soon attracted some of the best ceramic technicians and designers of the day who decorated the lustre ground with flowers, animals, and trees; some pieces were more elaborate with scenes of sailing ships and knights on horseback. Each artist signed his work with his personal monogram. Most pieces were dated and carried the company mark as well. After 1913 the company became known as Royal Lancastrian.

Their Lapis Ware line was introduced in the late 1920s, featuring intermingling tones of color under a matt glaze. Some pieces were very simply decorated while others were painted with designs of stylized leafage, scrolls, swirls, and stripes. The line continued into the '30s. Other pieces of this period were molded and carved with animals, leaves, etc., some of which were reminiscent of their earlier wares.

The company closed in 1938 but reopened in 1948. During this period their mark was a simple P within the outline of a petaled flower shape. Our advisor for this category is David Ehrhard; he is listed in the Directory under California.

Bowl, stylized mc shamrocks, 3 closed hdls, 2x4½" 325.00

Vase, fish and seaweed in lustre gold and blue, globular, Richard Joyce cipher, marked, #3184, 6½x5½", $1,700.00.

Vase, gr & bl mottled, matt, mks, 5" 80.00
Vase, gr under rose mottling, dimpled shoulder, 10¾x6¾" 200.00
Vase, lt gr/lt bl flambe froth, #2462, 8½x5½" 150.00
Vase, orange mottle, bulbous, finger rings, ETR/#3185, 6x5" 80.00
Vase, Sunstone, metallic gold/caramel-lined flambe, 4½", EX ...100.00
Vase, yel floral on bl irid, wht leaf band, 1920, 4¾x5¼" 435.00

Pillin

Polia Pillin was born in Poland in 1909. She came to the U.S. as a teenager and showed an interest and talent for art which she studied in Chicago. She married William Pillin, who was a poet and potter. They ultimately combined their talents and produced her very distinctive pottery from the 1950s to the mid-1980s. She died in 1993.

Polia Pillin won many prizes for her work, which is always signed Pillin with the loop of the 'P' over the full name. Some undecorated pieces are signed W&P, due to her husband's collaboration.

Her work is prized for its art, not for the shape of her pots, which for the most part are simple vases, dishes, bowls, and boxes. Wall plaques are rare. She pictured women with hair reminiscent of halos, girls, an occasional boy, horses, birds, and fish. After viewing a few of her pieces, her style is unmistakable. Some of her early work is very much like that of Picasso.

Her pieces are somewhat difficult to find, as all the work was done without outside help, and therefore limited in quantity. In the last few years, more and more people have become interested in her work, resulting in escalating prices. Our advisors for this category are Dolli and Wilfred Cohen; they are listed in the Directory under California.

Photo courtesy Dolli and Wilfred Cohen

Tray, Easter Island look, large, $775.00.

Bowl, lady/rooster/horse, mc on lt bl & wht, 3½x5" 475.00
Box, lady w/bird, mc on gr & brn, 2x4" dia 375.00
Covered dish, lady w/mandolin, mc on shaded bl, 2x4" dia 375.00
Jug, blistered yel/brn gloss, sgn, 7¾x5" 275.00
Plate, lady & bird, 7¾" 850.00
Vase, abstract figure on all 4 sides, 11½x3¾" 975.00
Vase, dancing women, mc on mottled pk & yel, 7½" 650.00
Vase, dbl portraits of girls & rooster on dk yel, pinched, 5" 450.00
Vase, dk gr/bl crystalline, 1950s, 9¾" 175.00
Vase, gr/olive matt texture, wide gourd w/tiny neck, 13" 375.00
Vase, horse & 2 ladies, wht on peacock & rust, 9x7" 850.00
Vase, horses, lady w/balloons, mc on bl, can form, 4½" 495.00
Vase, horses, mc on wht to brn, pear form, 6" 550.00
Vase, ladies, mc on bl, rectangular, 9", NM 850.00
Vase, lady & horse, 6" 625.00
Vase, lady w/bird, 2 ladies dance, mc on bl, 4½x5" 495.00
Vase, lady w/birds, ball form, 6" 550.00
Vase, lt to dk brn crystalline, bulbous w/can neck, 8½" 270.00
Vase, lt to dk gr gloss, bulbous w/sm opening, 6½" 200.00
Vase, nudes, 6" 750.00
Vase, scarlet flambe gloss, spherical w/short neck, 9½x7" 425.00
Vase, 2 full-length ladies, mc on yel/brn, slim form, 15" 1,500.00

Pin-Back Buttons

Buttons produced up to the early 1920s were made of a celluloid covering held in place by a ring (or collet) to the back of which a pin was secured. Manufacturers used these 'cellos' to advertise their products. Many were of exceptional quality in both color and design. Buttons were produced in sets featuring a variety of subjects. These were given away by tobacco, chewing gum, and candy manufacturers, who often packed them with their product as premiums. Usually the name of the button maker or the product manufacturer was printed on a paper placed in the back of the button. Often these 'back papers' are still in place today. Much of the time the button maker's name was printed on the button's perimeter, and sometimes the copyright was added. Beginning in the 1920s, a large number of buttons were lithographed on tin; these are referred to as tin 'lithos.'

Nearly all pin-back buttons are collected today for their advertising appeal or graphic design. There are countless categories to base a collection on.

The following listing contains non-political buttons representative of the many varieties you may find. All are celluloid unless described otherwise. Values reflect buttons in excellent, well-centered condition, with bright color and only the very slightest of wear, if any.

Adams Trucks, Deliver the Goods, truck, bl/blk/wht, 1¼" 100.00
Apollo XI, America Salutes First Men...Moon, mc, 1969, 1¾" 15.00
Baby Bear Bread, bear, eyeballs move, mc, 1920s, 1½" 110.00
Baer Family Reunion, 3 cartoon bears, 1908, 1½" 135.00
Ben-Hur Cigars, Get the Habit, Smoke..., man's face, 1¼" 35.00
Big Boy, National Club Member, mc, ca 1960, 1⅛" 40.00
Blue Bonnet, Vote for...Little Sister, yel, litho, 1" 12.00
Buster Brown Shoes, winking Buster & Tige, mc, 1900-10, 1⅜" ...150.00
Butter-Nut, I Say..., baker w/loaf, red/wht litho, 1930s, 1¼" 18.00
Chase & Sanborn's Seal Brand Coffee, red/wht, 1910s, 1⅜" 10.00
Colgate Sunny Smile Club, dog pictured 20.00
Columbia Graphophone, graphophone image, bl/wht, 1920s, 1⅜" ..60.00
Cracker Jack, Me for.../The Famous Confection, 1930s, 1¼" 100.00
Daisy Air Rifles, boy w/rifle, mc, 1910, ⅞" 125.00
Daisy Rubbers, Wear..., lg daisy image, mc, 1910-20, 1⅛" 20.00
Dead Shot Smokeless Powder, wounded duck, mc, 1900-1910, ⅞" .65.00
Detroit Electric, 1910 above early auto, blk/wht, 1¼" 100.00
Dixie Boy Shoes, Lynchburg VA, boy w/shoes, mc, 1" 45.00
Dominion Cleanser, cow's head, 1910s, 1¼" 15.00
Dubuque Malting Co, logo in center, mc, 1900-1910, 1¼" 35.00
Ducks Unlimited, duck in flight, 1938, 1" 80.00
Dupont Smokeless, mc, ⅞" 75.00
DuPont Smokeless Powder, grouse image, mc, 1900-1910, 1⅛" ...75.00
Edison Mazda Lamp, His Only Rival, globe/sun/bulb, mc, 1½" 55.00
Emmarts, 4 piglets riding on bk of mother, 1⅝" 50.00
Fleischmann's Yeast, rhyme/horse-drawn coach, mc, 1¾" 110.00
General Lee car, Iowa Jaycees 50.00
Happy Daisy Boy, w/rifle, mc, 1914, 1⅜" 250.00
Honey & Sonny Bread, boy & girl, mc, 1" 12.00
Howdy Doody, I'm For above cartoon head, mc, 1948, 1¼" 65.00
Huber Economy/Power/Durability, mc, 1½" 125.00
John Glenn, America's First Orbital Space Man, 1960s, 3⅜" 35.00
Kellogg's, child w/box of flakes, mc, 1920s, 1¼" 40.00
Li'l Abner, blk/wht on bl, ca 1950, 1¼" 45.00
Liberty Flour, mc, Statue of Liberty, 1900-10, 1⅛" 35.00
Lois Lane, bust portrait, red/wht/bl, 1960s, ⅜" 20.00
Marble Champion, wht lettering on dk bl, 1¼" 100.00
Miller High Life, girl/moon, mc, '30s, 1"+3" celluloid hanger 115.00
Miller High Life, girl/moon, mc, 1930s, 1" 50.00
Miller's Cocoa, mc, windmill, 1900, 1¼" 30.00
Mirro Aluminum, Jack Paar Advertises..., mc, 1950s, 2" 30.00
Model A Ford Club, oval, early 18.00

Morton's/Buster Brown Bread, from 1909 button series, each with different baseball player featured, multicolor with black and white photo, 1¼", $300.00.

Mutt & Jeff, images on gr, Tangle Comics, 1940s, 1¼" **50.00**
My Friend Shirley Temple, orig **50.00**
Ocean Wave Washer, lettering around image, mc, 1900-1910, 4" **150.00**
Pat Boone Fan, I Am A, blk/wht, 1⅜" **15.00**
Peter's Shells, celluloid, mc duck hunter, ⅞" **85.00**
Peters Shells/Cartridges, man aiming at lg P, mc, ⅞" **85.00**
Pingree Shoe, The Girl of the..., profile, mc, 1900, 1¼" **50.00**
Raymond's Pectoral Plaster for All Coughs, 2 boys, mc, 1¼" **85.00**
RCA Victor, Little Nipper/Club Member, bl/wht, 1940s, 1⅜" **45.00**
Region 4 BSA, 1956, 3½" **65.00**
Rin-Tin-Tin, King of the Canines, head, blk/wht, 1½" **35.00**
Roy Rogers, My Pal, blk /wht, red rim, 1950s, 1¾" **150.00**
Safety Captain, MO Pacific Lines **45.00**
Santa, in early auto, mc, w/store advertising, 1¼" **100.00**
Shapleigh Dmn Edge, dmn trademk **65.00**
Skippy, Detroit Times, 1930s **30.00**
Skippy Racer Club, bust image, 1930s, 1⅛" **50.00**
Sun-Times Comic Capers Club, 4 cartoon figures, '40s, 2⅜" ..**1,200.00**
Tarzan, Club Member, Vita Hearts, head image, gr, 1930s, 1¼" **200.00**
Veteran National Indian War **45.00**
Western Amesbury Line Pontiac Buggy Co, Indian, mc, 1⅛" **95.00**
Wonder-Cut Bread, Feel It.../It's Fresh, loaf, mc, 1930s, 2" **20.00**

World War II mechanical, Uncle Sam hangs Hitler, 1½" dia, $85.00.

Yale, The Everlasting Motorcycle, mc, 1900-1910, 1¼" **65.00**
Yellow Kid, standing, holding shirt out on sides, 1¼" **40.00**

Pink Lustre Ware

Pink lustre was produced by nearly every potter in the Staffordshire district in the late 18th and first half of the 19th centuries. The application of gold lustre on white or light-colored backgrounds produced pinks, while the same over dark colors developed copper. The wares ranged from hand-painted plaques to transfer-printed dinnerware. Design features in the phrase immediately following the item (i.e. cup, plate, etc.) are in pink lustre unless otherwise specifically described within the line.

Bough pot, House pattern, w/lid, ca 1815, rpr, 9¼" **1,265.00**
Bust, John Wesley, enamel decor, ca 1825, 10½" **1,035.00**
Compote, man gives children food/He That Refuseth..., 4x5", EX ..**65.00**
Cup & saucer, Durham cathedral/city, blk transfer, Davenport **95.00**
Cup & saucer, Moses in Bulrushes, magenta transfer w/mc **30.00**
Cup & saucer, 3-color swags at rim, allover lustre **60.00**
Desk set, Greek Key borders, tray & 3 covered pots, 1810s **635.00**
Figure, Charity, gr & yel details, ca 1820, 9" **1,035.00**
Furniture rests, lion heads w/front paws, 1820s, 3¾", pr **1,100.00**
Jug, bear figural holds man w/'Boney' on hat, 1810s, 10" **2,300.00**
Jug, commemorative; Princess Charlotte/Prince Leopold, 6" **375.00**
Loving cup, Nicholl Gascoine/iron monger's tools, 1815, 5¼" ...**700.00**
Mug, brn transfer of religious poem, lustre band, 3", EX **130.00**
Mug, House pattern, emb basketweave, fluted band, 3¾" **175.00**

Pitcher, Abbey w/tower/church/etc, unmk, 7⅜" **275.00**
Pitcher, dog w/bird ea side in pk/gr, emb neck vine, 5¾" **700.00**
Pitcher, HP florals, 1820s, 8¼" **520.00**
Pitcher, Memory of Princess Charlotte, blk transfer, 4¾", NM ...**1,200.00**
Pitcher, stag, doe/fawn, gr/brn trees, some red, 6", EX **600.00**
Pitcher, vintage w/overall lustre & band at mouth, 5", EX **30.00**
Pitcher, 4 portrait busts in relief, mc enameling, 6" **325.00**
Plaque, Queen Caroline, rectangle, 1820s, 4½x5¼" **375.00**
Plaque, theatrical scene, lustre scrolled border, rpr, 6", pr **700.00**
Punch bowl, HP floral int & ext, ca 1820, 6¾x10¼" **300.00**
Shaving mug, David Snowdon, hunt scene, w/insert & lid, 1820s ..**1,150.00**
Teapot, scenic landscape decor, 5½x10¼", NM **150.00**

Tray, English country church, unmarked, 7½", M, $135.00.

Tray, landscape by waterfall, lustre leaf-molded hdls, 15½" **460.00**
Vase, quintal; mottled enamel, leaf spout, 8¾" **700.00**
Vase, quintal; mottled enamel, 1820s, rprs, 7½" **250.00**

Pink Paw Bears

These charming figural pieces are very similar to the Pink Pigs described in the following category. They were made in Germany during the same time frame. The cabbage green is identical; the bears themselves are whitish-gray with pink foot pads. You'll find some that are unmarked while others are marked 'Germany' or 'Made in Germany.' In theory, the unmarked bears are the oldest, made prior to 1890 when the McKinley Tariff Act required imports to be marked with the country of origin. Those marked 'Made In' were probably produced after the revision of the Act in 1914.

1 by bean pot **135.00**
1 by graphaphone **135.00**
1 by honey pot **145.00**
1 by top hat **110.00**
1 in roadster (car identical to pk pig car) **165.00**
1 on binoculars **150.00**
1 peeking out of basket **135.00**
1 sitting in wicker chair **150.00**
2 in front of basket **135.00**
2 in hot-air balloon **150.00**
2 in purse **165.00**
2 in roadster **150.00**
2 on pin dish **120.00**
2 peering in floor mirror **150.00**
2 sitting by mushroom **125.00**
2 standing in wash tub **150.00**
3 in roadster **175.00**
3 on pin dish **145.00**

Pink Pigs

Pink Pigs on cabbage green were made in Germany around the

turn of the century. They were sold as souvenirs in train depots, amusement parks, and gift shops. 'Action pigs' (those involved in some amusing activity) are the most valuable, and prices increase with the number of pigs. Though a similar type of figurine was made in white bisque, most serious collectors prefer only the pink ones. They are marked in two ways: 'Germany' in incised letters, and a black ink stamp 'Made in Germany' in a circle.

2 on cotton bale, 1 inside, 1 peering over top, 2¾x2½", $135.00.

1 beside gr drum, wall-mt match holder	95.00
1 beside purse	75.00
1 beside shoe	75.00
1 beside stump, camera around neck, toothpick holder	145.00
1 beside waste basket	75.00
1 coming out of cup	95.00
1 coming out of suitcase	95.00
1 coming through gr fence, post at sides, open for flowers	95.00
1 driving touring car	165.00
1 going through purse	90.00
1 in case looking through binoculars	145.00
1 in gr Dutch shoe	75.00
1 in gr suitcase bank, head 1 side, bk other, gold trim	110.00
1 in Japanese submarine, Japan imp on both sides	125.00
1 in money sack bank	85.00
1 in roadster	145.00
1 lg pig sitting behind 3" trough	95.00
1 on binoculars	95.00
1 on binoculars, gold trim	125.00
1 on chair	110.00
1 on gr trinket dish, leg caught in lobster claw	110.00
1 on horseshoe-shaped dish w/raised 4-leaf clover	75.00
1 on keg playing piano	150.00
1 on shoulder of gr ink bottle	115.00
1 playing accordion on side of tray, wht bear ea side	150.00
1 pushing head through wooden gate	95.00
1 putting letter in mailbox	95.00
1 reclining on horseshoe ashtray	70.00
1 riding train, 4½"	150.00
1 sits, holds orange Boston Baked Beans pot match holder	125.00
1 sits by high-top boot	110.00
1 sitting in bathtub	135.00
1 sitting on log, mk Germany	110.00
1 standing in gr tub	95.00
1 w/attached toothpick holder	75.00
1 w/front ft in 3-part dish containing 3 dice, 1 ft on dice	125.00
1 w/tennis racket stands beside vase, Lawn Tennis, 3¾"	125.00
1 wearing chef's costume, holds frypan, w/basket	125.00
2, mother & baby in bl blanket in tub, rabbit on board atop	110.00
2, mother in tub gives baby a bottle, lamb looks on, 4x3½"	125.00
2, 1 at telephone booth, 1 inside, 4½"	125.00
2 at confession, 4½"	90.00
2 at wishing well	110.00

2 behind trough, unmk	75.00
2 by eggshell	95.00
2 dancing, in top hat, tux & cane	110.00
2 in basket, Merry Squeelers, 3½x3"	90.00
2 in bed, Good Night on footboard, 4x3x2½"	145.00
2 in carriage	95.00
2 in open car	145.00
2 in open trunk, 3¾"	95.00
2 in purse	95.00
2 on basket, head raising lid, plaque on front	110.00
2 on seesaw on top of pouch bank	90.00
2 on top hat	95.00
2 on tray hugging, 3x4½"	90.00
2 sitting at table playing card game 'Hearts'	170.00
2 under toadstool	125.00
3, 1 on lg slipper playing banjo, 2 dancing on side	145.00
3, 2 sit in front of coal bucket, 3rd inside	125.00
3 at trough, 4½" L	98.00
3 dressed up on edge of dish	80.00
3 sm pigs behind oval trough, mk, 2¾x2½x1¾"	95.00
3 w/baby carriage, father & 2 babies, Wheeling His Own	125.00
3 w/carriage, mother & 2 babies, Germany	95.00

Pisgah Forest

The Pisgah Forest Pottery was established in 1920 near Mount Pisgah in Arden, North Carolina, by Walter B. Stephen, who had worked in previous years at other locations in the state — Nonconnah and Skyland (the latter from 1913 until 1916). Stephen, who was born in the mountain region near Asheville, was known for his work in the Southern tradition. He produced skillfully-executed wares exhibiting an amazing variety of techniques. He operated his business with only two helpers. Recognized today as his most outstanding accomplishment, his Cameo line was decorated by hand in the pate-sur-pate style (similar to Wedgwood Jasper) in such designs as Fiddler and Dog, Spinning Wheel, Covered Wagon, Buffalo Hunt, Mountain Cabin, Square Dancers, Indian Campfire, and Plowman. Stephen is known for other types of wares as well. His crystalline glaze is highly regarded by today's collectors.

At least nine different stamps mark his wares, several of which contain the outline of the potter at the wheel and 'Pisgah Forest.' Cameo is sometimes marked with a circle containing the line name and 'Long Pine, Arden, NC.' Two other marks may be more difficult to recognize: 1) a circle containing the outline of a pine tree, 'N.C.' to the left of the trunk and 'Pine Tree' on the other side; and 2) the letter 'P' with short uprights in the middle of the top and lower curves. Stephen died in 1961, but the work was continued by his associates. Our advisor for this category is R.J. Sayers; he is listed in the Directory under North Carolina.

Vase, Cameo, light blue background over aqua gloss, signed Stephen in cameo, wafer mark, 1953, 10", NM, $1,100.00 at auction.

Bowl, Cameo, Christmas dinner, wht/bl, Stephen, 2⅜x6½" 500.00
Bowl, ivory/beige crystalline, 1951, 5x5½" 200.00
Ewer, crazed turq w/blk streaks, pk int, dtd 1936, 8⅜" 195.00
Jar, turq/gr mottle, D1936, w/lid, 3" 35.00
Mug, man w/violin, wht on gr matt, 3½" 140.00
Pitcher, maroon & bl w/crystals, 8x4" 145.00
Pitcher, turq w/rose int, mk, 1930-40s, 3" 45.00
Tea set, Cameo, carriage/horse, wht on olive, Stephen, 3-pc 700.00
Teapot, Cameo, pioneer/cabin/etc, wht on bl, Stephen, 4½" 210.00
Vase, bl, hdls, 6x6¼" 125.00
Vase, bl crystals on wht to caramel, 5½" 325.00
Vase, brn/ochre flambe w/bl crystalline, Stephen/1948, 6x6" 425.00
Vase, Cameo, bl matt w/wht wagon scene, Stephen/1940s, 7½" ...475.00
Vase, Cameo, scenic neck band on olive, aqua/gr mottle, 4½" ...375.00
Vase, caramel to wht w/bl & wht crystals, bulbous, 4½" 550.00
Vase, cream/lt bl crystalline over gr/dk bl matt mottle, 5½" 220.00
Vase, gray/ivory/lt gr w/wht & bl crystals, shouldered, 9" 450.00
Vase, turq crackle w/pk int, 5½" 125.00
Vase, wht w/random lg bl crystals, shouldered, 6½" 450.00
Vase, yel gloss, hand-thrown, trumpet form, 6" 60.00
Vase, yel w/bl & gr crystals, bulbous neck, hdls, 1937, 8½" 700.00

Pittsburgh Glass

As early as 1797, utility window glass and hollow ware were being produced in the Pittsburgh area. Coal had been found in abundance, and it was there that it was first used instead of wood to fuel the glass furnaces. Because of this, as many as one hundred fifty glass companies operated there at one time. However, most failed due to the economically disastrous effects of the War of 1812. By the mid-1850s those that remained were producing a wide range of flint glass items including pattern-molded and free-blown glass, cut and engraved wares, and pressed tableware patterns. Our advisor for this category is Mark Vuono; he is listed in the Directory under Connecticut.

Bottle, canary yel, 8-panel, appl bar lip, 1850s, 10¼" 1,000.00
Bottle, cobalt, 8 vertical ribs, appl bar lip, 10¾" 2,400.00
Bottle, puce-amethyst, tapered, 16 right-swirl ribs, 7⅜" 350.00
Bottle, sapphire, 8-panel blob-top, bl stopper w/cork, 12½" 1,000.00
Bowl, str sides, folded rim, 12-panel, funnel ft, 5½x8" 375.00
Candlesticks, clambroth/alabaster, emb thistles, 9⅝", pr 400.00
Candlesticks, fiery opal, pewter inserts, 1840s, 9⅜", pr 550.00
Candlesticks, free-blown, rnd base, long hollow stem, 12", pr .1,000.00
Canister, clear w/appl bl rings & finial, 12¼" 660.00
Compote, folded rim, 12-panel base, funnel ft, 5½x8" 375.00
Compote, Pillar mold, 8-rib, baluster stem, w/lid, 11x9" 825.00
Compote, Pillar mold, 8-rib, flared rim, ftd, 1830s, 9x10⅛" 650.00
Condiment set, 7 cut bottles, silver stand w/seal of US/etc 2,750.00

Creamer, sapphire blue, 12 vertical ribs, pattern molded, 5", $900.00.

Creamer, emerald gr, bulbous, rnd ft, pontiled, ca 1800, 4" 850.00
Creamer, purple-amethyst, bulbous, pontiled, 1820s, 4⅛" 550.00

Creamer, 14 vertical ribs, pear shape, 5", 4¾", pr 170.00
Cuspidor, pk/wht/bl loops encased in clear, pontiled, 6¾" 1,200.00
Decanter, cut, strawberry dmns & fans, hollow stopper, 9½" 170.00
Decanter, purple amethyst, appl rim, 8-sided mug base, 11" 550.00
Decanter, strawberry dmns & fan cuttings, 9½" 225.00
Goblet, 12-panel, thick rnd base, rough pontil, 5" 70.00
Jigger, sapphire bl, 6-panel, 2¼" 35.00
Pitcher, dk sapphire bl, much tooling at rim, appl hdl, 6" 1,900.00
Pitcher, strawberry dmns/ovals/starburst cuttings, 7¾" 450.00
Sugar bowl, emerald gr, appl ft & knob (on lid), 5½" 3,300.00
Sugar bowl, sapphire bl, 12 ribs, tam finial, 7½" 5,500.00
Sugar bowl, 12 vertical ribs, domed lid, pontiled, 7⅜" 600.00
Tumbler, amethyst, 8-panel, 3¼" 220.00
Tumbler, clambroth, 9-panel, 3⅛" 110.00
Tumbler, grass gr, 6 panels & arches, 3⅜" 300.00
Tumbler, lt violet-bl, 7-panel, 3⅝" 127.00
Tumbler, peacock bl w/amber streak, 9-panel, 3½" 230.00
Vase, baluster stem, thick base w/pontil, eng florals, 9½" 325.00
Vase, blown, flared rim, eng florals, knop stem, pontil, 8¾" 400.00
Vase, frosted opal clambroth w/sapphire bl rim & ft, 10", NM ...375.00
Whiskey taster, canary, pressed 9-panel, pontil, 1⅝" 40.00
Wine, blown, bell-shaped bowl w/wht twisted thread, 6⅜" 115.00

Plastics

The term 'collectible plastics' is defined as those types produced between 1868 (when synthetic plastics were invented) and the period immediately following WWII. There are several, and we shall mention each one and attempt briefly to acquaint you with their characteristics:

1) Pyroxylin (Celluloid, Loalin, French Ivory, Pyralin). Chemical name: cellulose nitrate. Earliest form, invented in 1868 by John Wesley Hyatt; highly flammable; yellows with age; much used in toiletry articles. Fairly lightweight, many articles of pyroxylin were made by heating and molding thin sheets.

2) Cellulose Acetate (Tenite, Similoid). Made in attempt to produce a product similar to cellulose nitrate but without the flammability. Had limited use in the costume jewelry trade; most often encountered as car knobs and handles of the '30s and '40s. Surfaces tend to crack with age and exposure to light. Always molded, never cast. Colors varied; imitation horn and marble were most popular; imitation coral is seen in molded 'floral' jewelry.

3) Casein Plastics (Ameroid, Galalith, Dorcasine, Casolith). Invented in 1904 using milk proteins. Use limited to buttons and buckles due to warping and lengthy curing time. Made in a wide range of colors; very easy to laminate or to carve from stock rods or sheets, but never molded.

4) Phenol Formaldehyde (Bakelite, Catalin, Marblette, Agatine, Gemstone, Durite, Durez, Prystal). Invented by L.H. Baekland in 1908; used extensively in the '30s. There are two major types: cast and molded. Molded types include Durez and Bakelite, dark-toned, wood flour-filled plastics that were used extensively for early telephones (still used when non-conductivity of heat and electricity is vital). The most popular name in cast phenolics was Catalin, trade name of the American Catalin Corporation of New York. Made in a wide range of colors; widely used for costume jewelry, cutlery handles, decorative boxes, lamps, desk sets, etc. Heavyweight material with a slightly 'greasy' feel; very hard but can be carved with files, grinding tools, and abrasive cutters. Buffs to high, durable polish. Cast phenolics were used primarily from 1930 to around 1950 when they proved too labor-intensive to be economical.

5) Urea Formaldehyde (Beetleware, Plaskon, Duroware, Hemocoware, Uralite). Invented around 1929, this was lighter in color than phenol formaldehyde, thus used for injection-molded products in pastel colors. Lightweight, not strong; shiny rather than glossy. It cannot be carved and was used mainly for cheap radio and clock cases, never for jewelry.

The period between the two World Wars produced acrylic resins such as Lucite and vinyl. Polystryene made its appearance then, and furfural-phenols were in use in industrial applications. Though a great future was predicted for ethyl cellulose, by the late '30s it was still in the experimental phase. For most purposes the field of decorative plastics from the first half of the century can be narrowed down to the five major types listed above. Of these, cellulose acetate is rarely encountered. Casein is limited to button and belt buckle manufacture; urea is easily identifiable as a cheap, brittle material. Pyroxylin is the celluloid of which so many vanity sets were made. Molded phenolics such as Bakelite were dark in color and used for utilitarian objects; cast phenolics such as Catalin were used most notably for jewelry (please don't call it Bakelite), cutlery handles, desk sets, and novelties.

Dealers and collectors should be aware of '70s reproduction Marblette animal napkin rings (they have no eye rods and no age patina) and molded acrylic bracelets in imitation of carved Catalin ones (look for a seam line or lack of definition in carved areas). As prices rise, copies become more common. 1986 saw the mass production of inlaid polka-dot bracelets using old-stock findings but without the precision fit (or patina) of the originals.

In 1988 and continuing to the present, a large number of 'collage' pieces appeared in vintage clothing and antique stores on the West and East Coasts. These are over-sized, glued-together assemblages of old Catalin stock parts including buttons with the shanks filed off, poker chips, etc., made into brooches or pendants, sometimes hung on necklaces of re-strung Catalin beads. They can be recognized by their aesthetically jumbled, 'put-together' look; and although some may claim they are old, they are not.

Our advisor for this category is Catherine Yronwode, who also publishes an informative newsletter, *The Collectible Plastics*; she is listed in the Directory under California. Our thanks to Benjamin Rose for help with radio prices.

Bakelite

Cigarette box, half-cylinder, rotates open, dk brn	45.00
Clock, electric, alarm, Deco design, blk or dk brn	65.00
Clock, mantel, wind-up alarm, Deco design, dk brn	60.00
Inkwell, streamlined, blk, w/lid	25.00
Penholder, streamlined, blk	22.50
Radio, Majestic #55, dk brn, 1939	250.00
Radio, Silvertone Compact, Sears, dk brn, 1936-1937	250.00
Radio, Stewart Warner Varsity College, dk brn, 1938-1939	250.00
Roulette wheel, dk brn, 1930s	80.00
Roulette wheel, mc Catalin chips, wood rack, w/box, 1930s	200.00
Watch, lady's handbag; Westclox, blk, 2¾" dia	100.00

Catalin

Ashtray, marbleized lt gr, sq, 4½"	30.00
Barometer, Taylor, amber & dk gr, rectangular, 4"	45.00
Blotter, Carvacraft, Great Britain, amber/blk	45.00
Bottle opener, chrome plate, red, gr, or amber hdl	10.00
Bracelet, bangle; apple-juice clear, figural bk-cvg	175.00
Bracelet, bangle; apple-juice clear, floral bk-cvg	150.00
Bracelet, bangle; apple-juice clear, geometric bk-cvg	130.00
Bracelet, bangle; deep cvg, w/rhinestones	90.00
Bracelet, bangle; elaborate floral cvg, narrow	60.00
Bracelet, bangle; elaborate floral cvg, wide	85.00
Bracelet, bangle; lt geometric cvg, narrow	30.00
Bracelet, bangle; lt geometric cvg, wide	45.00
Bracelet, bangle; novelty, mc, figural or animal cvg	250.00
Bracelet, bangle; scratch cvd, narrow	22.00
Bracelet, bangle; scratch cvd, w/rhinestones	35.00

Bracelet, bangle; scratch cvd, wide	27.00
Bracelet, bangle; stylized floral cvg, narrow	28.00
Bracelet, bangle; stylized floral cvg, wide	45.00
Bracelet, bangle; uncvd, narrow	8.00
Bracelet, bangle; uncvd, wide	11.00
Bracelet, bangle; 12 inlaid polka dots, wide	225.00
Bracelet, bangle; 2-color stripes	80.00
Bracelet, bangle; 3-color stripes	100.00
Bracelet, bangle; 4-color (or more) stripes	150.00
Bracelet, bangle; 6 inlaid polka dots, narrow	200.00
Bracelet, cellulose acetate chain, 7 cvd figural charms	250.00
Bracelet, clamper; figural, animal, or novelty applique	250.00
Bracelet, clamper; inlaid geometric designs	200.00
Bracelet, clamper; stylized floral cvg	95.00
Bracelet, clamper; w/inlaid rhinestones	50.00
Bracelet, curved/flat links, deeply cvd	65.00
Bracelet, curved/flat links, uncvd	45.00
Bracelet, stretch; orig elastic, Catalin & metal	50.00
Bracelet, stretch; orig elastic, deeply cvd	65.00
Bracelet, stretch; orig elastic, mc, uncvd	50.00

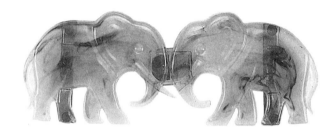

Buckle, marbleized amber elephants, ca 1935, 2-piece, $55.00.

Buckle, latch type, mc, novelty or figural applique	65.00
Buckle, latch type, mc, stylized floral or geometric, cvd	40.00
Buckle, latch type, mc, uncvd	25.00
Buckle, latch type, 1-color, novelty or figural	55.00
Buckle, latch type, 1-color, stylized floral or geometric	30.00
Buckle, latch type, 1-color, uncvd	8.00
Buckle, latch type, 1-color w/rhinestones, Deco	30.00
Buckle, slide type, mc, stylized floral or geometric, cvd	35.00
Buckle, slide type, mc, uncvd	20.00
Buckle, slide type, 1-color, stylized floral or geometric, cvd	9.00
Buckle, slide type, 1-color, uncvd	6.00
Butter mold, gr/amber/brn, floral cvg, 2½"	45.00
Buttons, card of 6, red or blk laminated, 1½" rod	18.00
Buttons, card of 6, scotty, fruit, or cvd floral figural	28.00
Buttons, card of 6, uncvd octagonal, amber, 1" dia	10.00
Cake breaker, CJ Schneider, red, gr, or amber hdl	4.00
Carving set, knife, fork, steel	30.00
Carving set, 3-pc w/wood wall rack	40.00
Checkers, red & blk, full set, in box	35.00
Cheese slicer, scotty hdl, wood & chrome base	20.00
Chess set, hand cvd, red & blk, leather box	300.00
Chopsticks, ivory, pr	5.00
Cigarette box, chrome inserts, cylindrical, 4½"	45.00
Cigarette box, lt gr, wood bottom, rectangular, 5½x3¾"	40.00
Cigarette holder, imitation amber, sterling tip, orig case	25.00
Cigarette holder, long, mc or w/rhinestones	25.00
Cigarette lighter, Arco-Lite devil's head, red or blk	175.00
Cigarette lighter, mc stripes or inlay	45.00
Clock, New Haven, wind-up alarm, amber, Deco, 3⅝"	60.00
Clock, Sessions, electric alarm, scalloped case, 4¼" dia	60.00

Clock, Seth Thomas, wind-up alarm, maroon case, 3½" 60.00
Clock, Westclox, Moonbeam, electric flashing light alarm 90.00
Clothesline, Jigger, red anchors, 10 pins, metal box 10.00
Cocktail recipes, Ben Hur, mtd on drunk, red w/blk base 50.00
Cocktail recipes, Ben Hur, mtd on fighting roosters 45.00
Cork, Ben Hur, w/red fighting roosters, blk base 25.00
Corkscrew, chrome, red, gr, or amber hdl 12.50
Corn holder, Kob Knobs, diamond shape or lathe trn, 8 +box 50.00
Crib toy, Tykie Toy, boy, girl, clown, kitten, etc, ea 195.00
Crib toy, Tykie Toy, clown, loalin head/Catalin body 195.00
Crib toy, Tykie Toy, elephant, laolin head/Catalin body 195.00
Crib toy, Tykie Toy, 11 mc spools on string, 1940s 100.00
Crib toy, Tykie Toy, 12-1½" rings on 2⅞" ring, 1940s 100.00
Crib toy, Tykie Toy catalogue, 1946 ....35.00
Crib toy, Tykie Toy Tales (book about these toys), 1946 ....45.00
Dice, ivory or red, 2½", pr 15.00
Dice, ivory or red, ¾", pr 2.00
Dice cage, metal/red Catalin, blk Lucite base, w/dice 100.00
Dice cup, leather or cork lined 40.00
Dominoes, ivory or blk, full set, w/wood box 40.00
Dominoes, red or gr, full set, w/wood box 50.00
Drawer pull, 1-color, w/pnt inlay stripe 2.00
Drawer pull, 2-color, octagon, w/inlaid dot 3.00
Dress clip, mc inlaid Deco design 30.00
Dress clip, novelty, figural, animal, or vegetable 50.00
Dress clip, scratch cvd 25.00
Dress clip, stylized floral cvg 30.00
Dress clip, 1-color, w/rhinestones, Deco design 30.00
Earrings, lg drop style, pr 10.00
Earrings, novelty, figural, animal, or vegetable, pr 35.00
Earrings, stylized floral cvg, pr 15.00
Earrings, uncvd disks, pr 8.00
Egg beater, red, gr, or amber hdl 16.00
Flatware, chrome plate, 1-color hdl 2.00
Flatware, chrome plate, 3-pc matched place setting 8.00
Flatware, stainless, 1-color hdl 3.00
Flatware, stainless, 1-color hdl, leatherette box, 36-pc 180.00
Flatware, stainless, 1-color hdl, 3-pc matched place setting 10.00
Flatware, stainless, 2-color hdl 4.00
Flatware, stainless, 2-color hdl, wood box, 36-pc 250.00
Flatware, stainless, 2-color hdl, 3-pc matched place setting 15.00
Gavel, lathe turned, ivory 25.00
Gavel, lathe turned, red, blk, & ivory 35.00
Gavel, lathe turned, red, w/presentation box, dtd 1946 ....40.00
Ice cream scoop, stainless, red hdl 20.00
Inkwell, Carvacraft Great Britain, amber, dbl well 115.00
Inkwell, Carvacraft Great Britain, amber, single well 90.00
Knife, cvd red, gr, or amber hdl 6.00
Lamp base, brass & amber, Deco design, 10" 30.00
Lamp base, red, amber, & blk, Deco design, 8" 44.00
Letter opener, blk & amber stripes, Deco design 20.00
Letter opener, chrome/Catalin, Deco design 20.00
Letter opener, marbleized gr, dagger shape 20.00
Mah-Jong set, tiles, rails, 6-color, complete, w/box 150.00
Memo pad, Carvacraft Great Britain, amber 55.00
Nail brush, Ducky, duck shape, translucent eye rod 50.00
Nail brush, marbleized lt gr, 2½x1½" 9.00
Nail brush, Masso, amber octagon, 2" dia 9.00
Nail brush, turtle shape, dark amber, 3½" 20.00
Napkin ring, amber, red, or gr, 2" dia band 8.00
Napkin ring, animal or bird, no inlaid eye or ball on head 30.00
Napkin ring, chicken w/inlaid beak 35.00
Napkin ring, elephant w/ball on head 35.00
Napkin ring, lathe turned, amber, red, or gr, 1¾" dia 10.00

Napkin ring, Mickey Mouse or Donald Duck shape w/decal 60.00
Napkin ring, rabbit w/inlaid eye rod 40.00
Napkin ring, rocking horse or camel w/inlaid eye rod 72.00
Napkin ring, scotty, w/inlaid eye rod 40.00
Napkin ring set, 6-colors, 2" band, orig box 40.00
Necklace, cellulose acetate chain, animal figurals 300.00
Necklace, cellulose acetate chain, Deco dangling pcs 200.00
Necklace, cvd red & amber beads, 18" 65.00
Necklace, uncvd gr beads, 20" 40.00
Ozone generator, Air-Clear, dk amber, streamlined case 75.00
Pencil sharpener, Disney character decal, silhouette shape 45.00
Pencil sharpener, gun, tank, or plane shape w/decal 40.00
Pencil sharpener, orange, no decal, ¾x1" 8.00
Pencil sharpener, red, Mickey Mouse decal, ¾x1" 30.00
Pencil sharpener, scotty, red, cvd details, blk base 30.00
Pencil sharpener, scotty, yel, silhouette shape 20.00
Pencil sharpener, Trylon & Perisphere, 1939 World's Fair 50.00
Penholder, amber & blk striped, Deco design 35.00
Penholder, marbleized amber, Deco design 25.00
Penholder, scotty, red w/blk base 45.00
Picture frame, amber & red Deco design, 6x7" 45.00
Picture frame, red, gr, or amber, sq, 6" 35.00
Pin, animal, resin wash w/glass eye, lg 150.00
Pin, animal, resin wash w/glass eye, sm 90.00
Pin, animal or vegetable, inlaid or appl in several colors, lg 210.00
Pin, animal or vegetable, inlaid or appl in several colors, sm 125.00
Pin, animal or vegetable, 1-color, lg 90.00
Pin, animal or vegetable, 1-color, sm 80.00
Pin, mc Deco design, lg 80.00
Pin, mc Deco design, sm 60.00
Pin, novelty or patriotic figural, resin wash/inlay/appl, lg 200.00
Pin, novelty or patriotic figural, resin wash/inlay/appl, sm 135.00
Pin, novelty or patriotic figural, 1-color, lg 95.00
Pin, novelty or patriotic figural, 1-color, sm 65.00
Pin, stylized floral cvg, lg 50.00
Pin, stylized floral cvg, sm 40.00
Pin, w/danglers, animal or vegetable, resin wash/inlay/appl 200.00
Pin, w/danglers, animal or vegetable, 1-color 135.00
Pin, w/danglers, geometric form, mc 60.00
Pin, w/danglers, geometric form, 1-color 50.00
Pin, w/danglers, novelty or patriotic, resin wash/inlay/appl 250.00
Pin, w/danglers, novelty or patriotic, 1-color 150.00
Pipe, amber & gr, bowl lined w/clay 30.00
Pitcher, syrup; glass, red, gr, or amber hdl, ...18.00
Pocket watch, Debonaire, yel Deco case, 1⅞" dia 60.00
Poker chip rack, cylindrical, w/50 chips, 2½" 85.00
Poker chip rack, rectangular, w/200 chips, 4" 120.00
Powder box, amber & blk fluted cylinder, 2½" 50.00
Powder box, amber & gr fluted cylinder, 4" 60.00
Radio, AMC 'Peaktop,' amber, maroon trim 2,500.00
Radio, Emerson Cathedral (AU190), amber 1,200.00
Radio, Emerson Cathedral (AU190), bright red, very rare 13,000.00
Radio, Emerson Cathedral (AU190), gr marbled 2,200.00
Radio, Emerson College model, amber or gr, 1938 ....1,000.00
Radio, Emerson College model, red, 1938 ....1,200.00
Radio, Fada Streamliner, amber, amber knobs/bezel, 1941 ......1,000.00
Radio, Fada Streamliner, amber, red knobs/bezel, 1941 ....1,100.00
Radio, Fada Streamliner, red, amber knobs/bezel, 1941, rare ...9,800.00
Radio, Kadette Klockette, amber, gr, or maroon, 1937 ....1,200.00
Radio, Kadette Klockette, red, 1937 ....1,500.00
Ring, inlaid Deco stripe design, 2-color 45.00
Ring, stylized floral cvg, 1-color 35.00
Ring, uncvd, 1-color 20.00
Ring, uncvd, 2-color 30.00

Ring case, hinged-lid style, amber or maroon 150.00
Ring case, open-top style, amber, red, or blk, Deco design 90.00
Safety razor, Schick Injector, amber hdl 18.00
Safety razor, Schick Injector, extra blades, orig box, 1939 ....45.00
Salad servers, Chase chrome, ivory, blk, or brn, pr 45.00
Salad servers, chrome, red, gr, or amber hdls, pr 12.00
Shakers, ball shape or half-cylinder shape, 1½", pr 30.00
Shakers, glass, in 3⅛" Catalin holder, pr 30.00
Shakers, mushroom shape, amber & ivory, 1⅞", pr 35.00
Shakers, stepped cylinder shape, 3½", pr 30.00
Shakers, Washington Monument, 3¼", pr 35.00
Shaving brush, red, gr, or amber 20.00
Shaving brush, red, gr, or amber, w/holder 40.00
Spatula, stainless, red, gr, or amber hdl 6.00
Spoon, iced tea, chrome, w/Catalin knob, 6-pc set 25.00
Spoon, slotted, stainless, red, gr, or amber hdl 5.00
Steering knob, chrome clamp 18.00
Stirrer, iced tea; Chase, chrome ball/mint leaf, 6-pc set 35.00
Stirrer, iced tea; shovel blade, Catalin hdl, 6-pc set 45.00
Strainer, red, gr, or amber hdl, 2¾" dia 5.00
Strainer, red, gr, or amber hdl, 5" dia 6.00
Swizzle stick, baseball-bat shape, amber or red 5.00
Swizzle stick holder, amber or red, Rheingold Lager decal 95.00
Thermometer, BT Co, amber & blk, 2¾" dia 45.00
Thermometer, Taylor, amber & dk gr, rectangular, 4" 45.00
Writing set, blk, amber, or gr marble, Deco, 5-pc, orig box 175.00

Celluloid

Photo courtesy Mike's General Store

Rattles, 10", $120.00 each.

Bracelet, imitation tortoise w/inlaid rhinestones 40.00
Bracelet, snake w/inlaid rhinestones 48.00
Bridge marker, pnt ivoroid animal or figure, France 25.00
Bridge pencil holder, animal, pearlescent ivory on blk 70.00
Buttons, ivoroid or pearlescent, ¾" dia, card of 6 ....8.00
Carving set, ivoroid, knife/fork/steel, eng blade 30.00
Clock, Greek temple facade, wind-up alarm, ivoroid 50.00
Crib toy, TykieToy or similar, man in the moon, laolin 250.00
Dresser set, amberoid & gr marbleized, 7-pc 80.00
Dresser set, ivoroid, 10-pc, w/9" bevel glass mirror 110.00
Dresser set, ivory pearlescent or amberoid, 5-pc 60.00
Flatware, gr pearl on blk hdl, 3-pc set 9.00
Flatware, ivoroid hdl, table knife, fork, or spoon, ea 2.00
Hair receiver, ivoroid, pearlescent or amberoid, w/2-part lid 12.00
Manicure set, ivoroid, pearlescent or amberoid, 10-pc, +case 30.00
Manicure set, ivoroid, 18-pc, roll-up leather case 25.00
Manicure set, 4 mini-tools in coral-color tube, Germany 22.00
Manicure set, 4 mini-tools in tube holder w/pnt florals 35.00
Mirror, dresser; ivoroid, cut-out hdl, bevel glass, 8" 25.00
Mirror, dresser; ivoroid, oval bevel glass, 13" 35.00
Mirror, dresser; pearlescent or amberoid, bevel glass, 12" 28.00

Picture frame, easel bk, ivoroid, 2" dia 15.00
Powder box, ivoroid, pearlescent or amberoid 15.00
Shaving stand, ivoroid, 5-pc, w/razor 75.00

Lucite

Bottle, perfume; w/atomizer, rose inclusion 20.00
Bracelet, stretch, orig elastic, clear, bk-cvd 27.00
Picture frame, Deco, clear, sq, 6" 18.00
Purse, box style, clear, pearl, ivory, or tortoise 45.00
Shakers, translucent red, 4", pr 12.00

Playing Cards

Playing cards can be an enjoyable way to trace the course of history. Knowledge of the art, literature, and politics of an era can be gleaned from a study of its playing cards. When royalty lost favor with the people, Kings and Queens were replaced by common people. During the periods of war, generals, officers, and soldiers were favored. In the United States, early examples had portraits of Washington and Adams as opposed to Kings, Indian chiefs instead of Jacks, and goddesses for Queens.

Tarot cards were used in Europe during the 1300s as a game of chance, but in the 18th century they were used to predict the future and were regarded with great reverence.

The backs of cards were of no particular consequence until the 1890s. The marble design used by the French during the late 1800s and the colored wood-cut patterns of the Italians in the 19th century are among the first attempts at decoration. Later the English used cards printed with portraits of royalty. Eventually cards were decorated with a broad range of subjects from reproductions of fine art to advertising.

Although playing cards are becoming popular collectibles, prices are still relatively low. Complete decks of cards printed earlier than the first postage stamp can still be purchased for less than $100.00. Our advisor for this category is Ray Hartz; he is listed in the Directory under Pennsylvania. Another fine source of information is the Antique Deck Collectors Club, 52 Plus Joker; see Directory under Clubs, Newsletters, and Catalogs.

Key:
AC — ad card
C — complete
cts — courts
hc — hand colored
J — joker

OB — original box
SC — score card
std — standard
XC — extra card
WF — World's Fair

James J. Jeffries on fronts, 52 famous fighters and fights of the early 1900s on backs, 54 cards (complete), NM in EX box, $500.00.

Advertising

Franklin Cigars, wide, ca 1908, 52+J+AC, EX-, VG box 55.00
Gold Medal Flour, wide, flour bag bks, 1912, 52+J, EXIB 45.00
Green River Whiskeys, wide, man & horse, 1927, G, G box 35.00
H Jackson Co, wide, 1905, 50 of 52, VG in aluminum case 50.00

Hamm's Beer, bear cards, wide, non-std, 1968, 52+J, MIB **88.00**

Harvard, wide, Ward's, 1900, 52+special J, VG- **55.00**

Ingalls, Christmas, blk/wht employee photos, 52+15J, NMIB **165.00**

Iron Fireman, dbl deck, orange/bl, NMIB **35.00**

Kelly Springfield Tires, wide gr bks, 1915, 52+J, VGIB **65.00**

Kissproof, Kissproof Girl, narrow, 52+AC, VG-, torn box **20.00**

Marlboro Texan #45, wide, dbl deck, ea: MIB, sealed **10.00**

Prince of Wales Relief Fund, wide, 1914, 52+J+AC+XC, MIB **65.00**

Spalding, Great Am Golf Holes, non-std, 52+2J, MIB, sealed **32.00**

United Carpenters & Joiners, wide, 1920s, 52+J, G, G- box **99.00**

Walk-Over Shoes, brn monotone, wide, 1912, 52+AC, VG, G box ...**22.00**

Fortune Telling, Games, and Magic

Deland's Automatic, Adams, 1920, 52+J, VG, G- box **25.00**

Deland's Nifty, wide, 51 of 52, 1920s, EX-, partial box **28.00**

Gavitt's Stock Exchange, RR theme, 1903, 48C+XC+rules, MIB **55.00**

Magic Circle, Zodiac, De La Rue, M in wrapper **5.00**

Mystic, Anna Riva, 1980, 50C+instructions, NM, G- box **12.00**

Modern Decks

Anma II, 4 branches of service, 2nd version, 1941, 52+2XC, NMIB ..**50.00**

Baraja Maya, Mexico, narrow non-std, 52+SC, EX **23.00**

Cards of War, Gulf War ltd ed, 1991, 52+2XC+booklet, MIB **35.00**

Citicards 90, EM Lewis, ltd ed, 52+mc J+plain J, MIB **88.00**

De La Rue, 150th Anniversary, narrow, non-std, 52+J+XC, MIB ...**35.00**

Death on Drugs, Weedon Enterprises, 1985, 52+2J, MIB **55.00**

Finger Alphabet, finger positions, 1987, whist, 52+2J+4XC, EX ..**22.00**

Goldwater, non-std cts, 1965, MIB, sealed **35.00**

Hermes, Cassandre, wide, 1950, 52+2J+XC, MIB **85.00**

Ripley's Believe It or Not, facts on faces, 1963, 54C, MIB **22.00**

Russia-Maya, non-std cts/aces, narrow, 1979, 52+2J+XC, MIB **37.00**

Unisex, Canadian, dbl-headed cts, 1980s, 52+2J+2XC, NMIB ..**165.00**

Victory, non-std, issued after VE day, 1945, 52+2J, VG, G box ...**85.00**

Western PC, Canteen Capers on J, WWII issue, 52+J+XC, M **22.00**

Older Decks, Bridge or Whist

Argentina-Fourvel #9, motorcycles, 48C+2 blanks, M in wrapper ..**45.00**

Belgium-Eagle Brand #2, gr bks, 52C, 1890, M in wrapper **35.00**

Dougherty-Rad Bridge, gr bks, narrow, 1920s, MIB **20.00**

England-Society, butterflies on bks, Goodall, 52+J, M, G box **17.00**

France-Jeu Moyen Age #555, Grimaud, 52C, 1915?, NM, G- box ..**450.00**

Germany-Swiss Landscapes & Costumes, 52C, EX, no box **500.00**

Iceland's 1000 Anniversary, Magnusen, 1930, 42+2J+booklet, MIB ..**35.00**

Italy-Vannini, girl & Hitler/Mussolini Js, 52+2J, EX, VG box ...**300.00**

National-Tennis #144, bl bks, narrow, 1885, 52, VG, G- box **25.00**

Spain-Naypes Refinos, wavy-line bks, 48C, 1850-80, NM **120.00**

USPC-Congress, Gorge, purple border, narrow, MIB, sealed **27.00**

Older Decks, Narrow, Odd Sizes or Shapes

Circular Coon, Blk racist type, 1900s, 52+J, NM, G tin **1,430.00**

Circular Waterprooff PCC, 5-way cts, 1890s, 52+globe J, NMIB **450.00**

Golden Dmn, Hanzel, 1925, 52+J+AC, MIB **85.00**

India-Erotic, circular, erotic couples, 52C, EX **40.00**

India-Erotic, HP couples on real ivory, ca 1880, 52+2J, NM ...**1,600.00**

Mlle From Armentiers, non-std cts, Butler, 1933, 52+XC, NM **500.00**

USPC-Skat, German suits/European cts, ca 1889, 32C, VG **55.00**

Older Decks, Wide

Bicycle USPC #808, League, red bks, 52+J, G, G box **33.00**

Bicycle USPC #808, Wheel #2, bl bks, 52+J+blank, 1917, MIB ..**97.00**

Cabinet USPC #707, 32C+4XC, VG in rpl box **50.00**

Congress USPB #606, Laughing Water, 1915, MIB, sealed **140.00**

Congress USPC #606, Liberty, gold edges, 52+J, 1918, NM, G box ...**20.00**

Cougherty-Climax #14, bl bks, 1920s, 52, EX-, NM box **25.00**

Freedom PC, patriotic cts, 1917, 52+J, NM, G- box **535.00**

Jumbo Bridge USPC #88, 52+special J+XC, VG+, G box **10.00**

National CC Steamboat #9, brn bks, 52+J, 1885, NM, no box ..**300.00**

NYCC-Bee #92, bl bks, 51 of 52, 1923, VG, G- box **20.00**

NYCC-Hart's Crown #444, bl bks, 52+J, NM, EX box **40.00**

Royal, NYCC, European ruler cts, 1895, 52+J, G, partial box **250.00**

Russell PCC Steamboat, pattern bks, 52+J, EX, 1918 case **200.00**

Std PCC Society #1001, It Listens Good, 52+J+AC, '15, NM, G box ..**70.00**

Steamboat USPC #999, 52+J, 1907, NM, VG box **75.00**

Pinups

Elvgren, Essex Shoe Supply, topless girl, dbl deck, EXIB **40.00**

Elvgren, lady in gr hat, red gloves, 1950, MIB, sealed **70.00**

Elvgren, 52 pinups on faces, special J, bio card, MIB, sealed **110.00**

MacTherson, Not According to Hoyle, brunette, 52+J, EXIB **25.00**

Miss Pondel Queen Rayon, '47 Textile Expo, dbl deck, EXIB **45.00**

Petty Pippins, lady in band uniform, USPCC, 52+J+XC, NMIB ..**12.00**

Petty Pippins, redhead w/tennis racket, 52+J, VG, G- box **17.00**

Piatnik, Austria, Vargas style, 52C, EX+, EX box **38.00**

Quick Draw, cowgirl, dbl deck, 52/52+J, VG, EXIB **38.00**

Rolf Armstrong, draped nude on bl, 1930s, 52+J+SC, VG, G box ...**40.00**

Vargas, Comme Ci, Comme Ca!, 1953, dbl deck ea 52, EXIB **165.00**

Vargas, Esquire, redhead on floor, rare Esquire J, 52C, EXIB **88.00**

Souvenir and Expositions

Bermuda, Light & Shadows, narrow, 51 of 52, EX- in case **20.00**

Black Hills SD, Fr Creek bks, narrow, 52+Chief J, VG, G- box ...**22.00**

Boston, Bunker Hill Monument, 1904, 52+J+2XC, EX+, G box ..**55.00**

Canada Ocean to Ocean, scenic, wide, 1910, 52+J+XC, VG+, G- box ...**55.00**

Columbian Expo, Hayner, bl bks, SX8 format, 1893, 52, EX- **250.00**

Columbian Expo, mc sketches, Clark, 1893, 52+J+XC, VG, G- box ..**100.00**

Cuba, 53 views, wide, 1930s, 52+J, VG, partial box **45.00**

Great Lakes-Western, St Issaac Jacques bk, 52+J+2XC, EX, EX box ...**110.00**

Intermountain, CO/UT, wagon train, 52+J, EX, EX box **160.00**

Jamestown Expo, wide, photo bks, 1906, 52+J, M, EX box **445.00**

NY City, Statue of Liberty, 1915, 52+special J, EX-, G box **35.00**

Pan-Am Expo, blk/wht photos, wide, 1904, 52+J, NMIB **42.00**

Sesquicentennial, narrow, Philadelphia, 1926, 52+J+XC, NM **55.00**

St Louis, Meyer Drugs, Louis XVI bks, 1905, 52+J, G, G- box **50.00**

Texas Sesquicentennial, narrow, W Cook, 52+2J+booklet, MIB ...**15.00**

Washington & Pacific NW, Mt Ranier, 1900, 52+J+XC, EX in box ...**125.00**

White Mountains, old man on bk, 1910, 52+J+2XC, M, EX box .**35.00**

Transportation: Airline, Steamship, Railroad

Air India, maharaja bks, non-std, 1974, 52+J+SC, M, no box **28.00**

Atlantic Coast, Engine 525, MIB, sealed **28.00**

Cunard Line, color steamer bks, 52+J, NMIB **12.50**

Delta, Bahamas, 2nd series, 52+2J, MIB **16.00**

Fred Harvey-Great SW, Apache chief ace, 52+J+XC, VG, G- box ...**80.00**

Great Northern, Crow Chief, W Reiss, 1939, 52+J+XC, M, G box ..**85.00**

Milwaukee Rd, scenic, wide, 1916, 52+scenic J, VG, G box **48.00**

Missouri Pacific, Scenic Limited, 1930, 52+J, MIB **138.00**

Pacific Mail, buck & logo on red, ca 1911, 52, VG-, G box **66.00**

Pan Am, Hawaii, 52+2J, MIB **15.00**

Penn, American on viaduct, 42+SC/52+J+SC, ea G in slipcase ..**60.00**

Rio Grande, scenic, narrow, 52 photos, 1952, 52+J, MIB **26.00**

S Pacific, yel engine/brn cottonfield, 1950, 52+J, NMIB **17.50**
Savannah Line, steamer photo, 1927, 52+J+SC, EX, EX box **78.00**
TWA, Douglas DC-9, MIB, sealed **12.00**
Wht Pass & Yukon, AK photos, 1905, 52+2XC+timetable, G+, G box ...**70.00**

Political

The most valuable political items are those from any period which relate to a political figure whose term was especially significant or marked by an important event or one whose personality was particularly colorful. Posters, ribbons, badges, photographs, and pin-back buttons are but a few examples of the items popular with collectors of political memorabilia.

Political campaign pin-back buttons were first mass produced and widely distributed in 1896 for the president-to-be William McKinley and for the first of three unsuccessful attempts by William Jennings Bryan. Pin-back buttons have been used during each presidential campaign ever since and are collected by many people. The most scarce are those used in the presidential campaigns of John W. Davis in 1924 and James Cox in 1920.

Contributions for this category were made by Michael J. McQuillen, monthly columnist of *Political Parade*, which appears in *AntiqueWeek* newspapers; he is listed in the Directory under Indiana. Our advisor for this category is Paul J. Longo; he is listed under Massachusetts. See also Autographs; Broadsides; Historical Glass; Watch Fobs.

Badge, Al Smith for Governor/Wagner for Senate, silk ribbon ..**150.00**
Badge, Cleveland/Hendricks, brass rooster/silk ribbon **80.00**
Badge, McKinley/Hobart on brass 6-point star w/gold wreath **95.00**
Badge, Our President Harry S Truman, celluloid w/silk ribbon **35.00**
Badge, Robert A Taft, celluloid, red/wht/bl silk ribbon, EX **35.00**
Bandana, Grover Cleveland, red/blk, incomplete print, VG **125.00**

Banner, celebrating George Washington 1889 centennial, 17x24", EX, **$250.00.**

Book, Harding Memorial Dedication Program, soft cover, 48-pg ..**20.00**
Book, Issues & National Leaders, Taft/Bryan cover, 480-pg, EX ...**20.00**
Book, Teddy Roosevelt Patriot & Statesman, Meyers, 1901, VG .**35.00**
Booklet, Fremont Songs for the People, w/photo, VG **95.00**
Booklet, Greatest Show on Earth...LBJ, 9-pg, EX **25.00**
Bookmark, Woodrow Wilson, aluminum heart shape, EX **65.00**
Brooch, JFK, red stones on gilt donkey, NM **12.00**
Button, Hancock/English, brass, EX **25.00**
Button, Harrison Reform, brass, 1840, EX **25.00**
Button, Willkie, red/wht/bl enamel on brass, 2x2", EX **10.00**
Button, Zachary Taylor image/Rough & Ready, brass/metal, EX ..**35.00**
Cartoon, Teddy & Civil Service Reform, Puck, 1890s, 19x13" **40.00**
Charm bracelet, JFK & family, NP, 7½", EX **25.00**
Charm bracelet, Nixon, letters/elephant/state of Ohio, NMIP **25.00**
Cloth, Washington Bicentennial 1732-1932, bust image, 17x22" **50.00**
Coin, McClellan campaign, 1864 ....**45.00**
Coin, Stephan Douglas campaign, 1860 ....**30.00**
Coin purse, President Harding, Compliments NY Bakery..., EX ...**45.00**
Doorstop, US Grant, mc enamel on iron, 8", EX **50.00**

Ferrotype, Grant/Colfax, image in brass fr, NM **250.00**
Ferrotype, Lincoln/Johnson, image in brass fr, silk ribbon, EX **300.00**
Figurine, John John, saluting, Inarço, F-1844, 6", M **50.00**
Handkerchief, McKinley/Hobart, Protection/Prosperity, silk, EX ..**90.00**
License plate, Al Smith for President, EX **45.00**
License plate, Herbert Hoover for President, 3x5", VG **35.00**
License plate, Hoover in lg letters, pnt tin, ca 1928, 5x14¾" **60.00**
License plate, LBJ for the USA, red/wht/bl, EX **30.00**
Medal, Daniel Webster/Liberty & Union..., orig case, EX **90.00**
Medal, For President Gen US Grant 1868, copper, ¾" dia **50.00**
Medal, Grant portrait, For President...1868, copper, ¾" dia **50.00**
Medal, McKinley/Roosevelt Second Inauguration, M **150.00**
Medal, Rutherford B Hayes for President..., NM **50.00**
Medal, T Roosevelt Awarded by the Philadelphia Press, brass **15.00**
Medallion, McKinley Memorial, silver, 1907 ....**35.00**
Money clip, Kennedy Dollar After Taxes, NP, 2", NM **12.00**
Needle case, Hoover/Curtis, heavy paper, red/wht/bl, 3x5", EX ...**30.00**
Padlock, Bryan 1908 Holds the Key, blk enamel on brass, EX **55.00**
Paperweight, Herbert Hoover, metal, 1928, EX **45.00**
Paperweight, McKinley/Hobart, glass, blk/wht faces, EX **65.00**
Pendant, mechanical; Harding, gilt, 1½", EX **65.00**
Pennant, Ike/elephant photo, cloth, red/wht/bl, 17", NM **25.00**
Pennant, Nixon's the One, photo, cloth, red/wht/bl, 29", NM **20.00**
Pin-bk, Barkley/Roosevelt/Truman (words), 1944, ⅞", EX **25.00**
Pin-bk, Dewey, Mothers, Sisters, Wives..., 1944, 1¼", EX **45.00**
Pin-bk, Dewey portrait, My Choice, 1920, 1¼", EX **10.00**
Pin-bk, Dewey portrait, We Want Dewey, 1948, 1¼", EX **15.00**
Pin-bk, Dewey/Bricker jugate, 1944, ⅞", EX **30.00**
Pin-bk, Dewey/Creighton/Warren (words), 1948, 1¼", EX **15.00**
Pin-bk, Dewey/Warren jugate, flag bkground, 1948, 1¼", EX **30.00**
Pin-bk, Edith Willkie portrait, For First Lady, 1940, 1¼", EX **37.00**
Pin-bk, Hoover, Speed Recovery, Re-elect..., ⅝", EX **10.00**
Pin-bk, Hoover portrait, gr/wht, 1932, ⅞", EX **40.00**
Pin-bk, Hoover/Curtis jugate, Hoover & Curtis, 1932, ⅞", EX ..**145.00**
Pin-bk, Ike, I Like..., 1952, ⅞", EX **3.00**
Pin-bk, Ike, I Still Like..., 1945, ⅞", EX **3.00**
Pin-bk, Ike portrait, For the Love of Ike..., 1956, 2¼", EX **25.00**
Pin-bk, Ike portrait, Man of the Hour, 1952, 1¾", EX **15.00**
Pin-bk, Ike/Nixon jugate, Don't Change the Team..., 1956, 3", EX ...**100.00**
Pin-bk, Ike/Nixon jugate, Ike & Dick Junior Club, 1952, 2¼", EX **35.00**
Pin-bk, Ike/Nixon jugate, They're for You..., 1952, 1¼", EX **15.00**
Pin-bk, Landon in plane, Land-on Washington, 1936, 1¼", EX .**2,500.00**
Pin-bk, Landon portrait, sunflower ground, 1936, 1¾", EX **25.00**
Pin-bk, Landon-Knox GOP, elephant, '36, ⅞", +felt sunflower, EX .**5.00**
Pin-bk, Landon/Knox jugate, sunflower & elephant, 1936, ⅞", EX ...**18.00**
Pin-bk, Roosevelt, America Calls..., shield ground, 1932, ⅞", EX **40.00**
Pin-bk, Roosevelt, Carry On, FDR, 1940, 1", EX **8.00**
Pin-bk, Roosevelt, I Want Roosevelt Again, 1936, 1¼" **20.00**
Pin-bk, Roosevelt portrait, For President, 1932, ⅞", EX **10.00**
Pin-bk, Roosevelt portrait, I Want...Again, 1944, 1¼", EX **12.00**
Pin-bk, Roosevelt portrait, Souvenir of Inauguration, '41, 1¼", EX ..**30.00**
Pin-bk, Roosevelt portrait, We Need You, 1936, 1¼", EX **40.00**
Pin-bk, Roosevelt/Garner jugate, For President..., 1932, ⅞", EX **125.00**
Pin-bk, Roosevelt/Garner jugate, red/wht/bl shield, 1936, ⅞", EX ..**30.00**
Pin-bk, Roosevelt/Truman jugate, brn/wht, 1944, 1", EX **85.00**
Pin-bk, Roosevelt/Wallace jugate, red/bl, 1940, 1¼", EX **20.00**
Pin-bk, Stevenson portrait, Adlai, Best in View, '52, 1½", EX **70.00**
Pin-bk, Stevenson portrait, All the Way w/Adlai, '56, 1", EX **15.00**
Pin-bk, Stevenson-Kefauver jugate, Dollars for..., '56, 1¼", EX **50.00**
Pin-bk, Stevenson/Sparkman jugate, Go Forward..., '52, 1¼", EX ...**35.00**
Pin-bk, Truman, Confidentially I'm for..., 1948, 1¼", EX **40.00**
Pin-bk, Truman portrait, Inauguration...1949, name, '48, 1¼", EX ...**25.00**
Pin-bk, Truman portrait, Truman for Me, 1948, ⅝", EX **50.00**
Pin-bk, Truman/Barkley jugate, flag bkground, 1948, 1¼", EX ..**200.00**

Pin-bk, Underwood/Stevenson/Sparkman (words), '52, ⅞", EX ...18.00
Pin-bk, Williams/Stevenson/Kefauver (words), 1956, 1", EX 10.00
Pin-bk, Willkie, I Want To Be a Captain Too, 1940, 1¼", EX 10.00
Pin-bk, Willkie portrait, red/wht/bl border, 1940, 1¼", EX 25.00
Pin-bk, Willkie/McNary jugate, Am Way of Life, 1", EX 150.00
Plate, FD Roosevelt image/Flags of Nations border, 11" dia 50.00
Plate, James A Garfield for President, 8" dia, EX 50.00
Plate, McKinley, mc image w/cobalt border, 9½" dia, EX 50.00
Plate, Taft/Sherman inauguration, tin 150.00
Pocket mirror, William McKinley Memorial, mc, EX 15.00
Pocketknife, W Wilson 1913, lists Presidents, NP grips, NM 150.00
Postcard, John & Jackie Kennedy, full-color photo, 9x6", M 5.00
Postcard, President Warren G Harding, mc, unused, NM 6.00
Postcard, T Roosevelt photo, The Need in Public & Private... ......22.00
Postcard booklet, Homage to the President-JFK, 1964, M 12.00
Poster, Al Smith campaign, photo, brn/tan, 1928, 22x14", NM ...45.00
Poster, Alf Landon campaign, photo, brn/wht, 13x10", M 30.00
Poster, Charles E Hughes, blk/wht, c 1908, 27x20½", EX 50.00
Poster, Lyndon Johnson campaign, photo, 1964, red/wht/bl, NM ...20.00
Print, FD Roosevelt, De Nevers, 1933, 16x20", EX 40.00
Print, McKinley family, Kurz Art, 1901, ornate fr, 21x18" 30.00
Print, US Grant, ornate blk/gilt frame, 24x20", EX 80.00
Program, Democratic Nat'l Convention, July 12, 1948, 80-pg 20.00
Program, Eisenhower Inauguration, 48-pg, NM 25.00
Program, Eisenhower/Nixon, Inaugural Festival 1957, blk/gold 20.00
Puzzle, FDR, 1933, complete w/orig box, EX 75.00
Ribbon, His Country's Friend...Henry Clay, silk, 8x2½", NM 350.00
Ribbon, Lincoln, silk, red/wht/bl, 1860, 8x2", EX 250.00
Ribbon, Our Choice...Harrison/Reed, silk, 6x2", EX 75.00
Ribbon, President Wilson, mc woven silk, 4½x3", NM 60.00
Ribbon, Teddy Roosevelt, portrait, blk on pk, 1904 ....65.00
Ribbon, Wm H Taft for President, mc litho on silk, 6x2", EX 40.00
Ribbon, Wm J Bryan for President, mc litho on silk, 6x2", EX 40.00
Sheet music, Eisenhower Inauguration, 1953 ....8.00
Sheet music, Go GOP, PA Governor John Fine, 1952 ....8.00
Steel engraving, Benjamin Harrison, blk/wht, fr, 8x11", NM 15.00
Stickpin, Harrison/Morton, United We Stand..., bl/wht, EX 90.00
Stickpin, Roosevelt/Fairbanks, photo in twisted brass fr, EX 40.00
Stickpin, Uncle Sam profile, brass, EX 10.00
Stud, Hoover 1928 Campaign, elephant figure, wht metal, NM ...12.00
Stud, McKinley/Protection 96, red/wht/bl, EX 30.00
Textile, Harrison/Morton 1888 Protect Home Industry, 22x25" ...165.00
Textile, McKinley/Hobart 1896 Protection, blk/wht, 22x22" 200.00
Ticket, Hayes/Wheeler, blk/wht, 8½x3", EX 50.00
Ticket, James G Blaine for President, 1884, EX 50.00
Tie clip, FD Roosevelt, red/wht/bl enamel on NP brass, EX 15.00
Tie tac, flasher; Vote Adlai, EX 15.00
Tobacco tab, Benjamin Harrison, red/wht/bl litho on tin, EX 15.00
Token, Hancock/English, rooster in center, brass, EX 25.00
Token, James Buchanan, No Sectionalism/USA, brass, 28mm, EX ..25.00
Token, Winfield Scott/First in War..., brass, EX 30.00
Tray, FD Roosevelt image/White House in center, 10x13", EX 50.00

Pomona

Pomona glass was patented in 1885 by the New England Glass Works. Its characteristics are an etched background of crystal lead glass often decorated with simple designs painted with metallic stains of amber or blue. The etching was first achieved by hand cutting through an acid resist. This method, called first ground, resulted in an uneven feather-like frost effect. Later, to cut production costs, the hand-cut process was discontinued in favor of an acid bath which effected an even frosting. This method is called second ground. Our advisors for

this category are Betty and Clarence Maier; they are listed in the Directory under Pennsylvania.

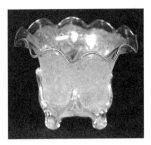

Vase, Expanded Diamonds, wishbone feet, 3¾", $350.00.

Bowl, berry; Cornflower, 1st ground, amber/bl stain, 3½x8⅝" ...650.00
Bowl, berry; Cornflower, 1st ground, amber/bl stain, 4¼x9¾" ...675.00
Bowl, 2nd ground, folded & crimped rim, 4" 50.00
Butter dish, Acanthus Leaf, 1st ground, gold stain, 4½x8" 1,265.00
Celery vase, Acanthus Leaf, 1st ground, gold stain, 6⅛x4½" 550.00
Champagne, 2nd ground, amber stain, 4¼x3⅝" 325.00
Creamer, 1st ground, amber stain, 3¼" 245.00
Creamer, 1st ground, sqd rim, 2¾" 175.00
Creamer & sugar bowl, Cornflower, 1st ground, amber stain 485.00
Finger bowl, Cornflower, 1st ground, gold stain, 2½" 175.00
Finger bowl, Cornflower, 2nd cround, ruffled, +6" crimped plate ...150.00
Finger bowl, Cornflower, 2nd ground, bl stain, 2½x5½" 155.00
Finger bowl, 1st ground, ruffled, 2¼" H, +5¼" plate 150.00
Rose bowl, 2nd ground, bl flowers, 5x5¼" 480.00
Sugar bowl, 2nd ground, ruffled, hdls 110.00
Toothpick holder, 1st ground, fan form, amber stain, 2¾" 475.00
Tumbler, Cornflower, 1st ground, amber/bl stain, 4 for 500.00
Tumbler, Cornflower, 2nd ground 90.00
Tumbler, Cornflower, 2nd ground, amber stain, 3¾x2⅝" 145.00
Tumbler, 2nd ground, butterfly/pansy, ribbed, 3¾" 75.00
Vase, Acanthus Leaf, 1st ground, ftd, amber/bl stain, 5¼" 625.00
Vase, Cornflower, 1st ground, bl stain w/gold, ftd, 5¼" 375.00

Porcelier

The Porcelier Company, originally from East Liverpool, Ohio, started business in the late 1920s and moved to Greensburg, Pennsylvania, in the early 1930s. The company flourished until the late 1940s and finally closed its doors due to labor disputes in 1954.

They produced an endless line of vitrified porcelain products including furniture coasters, electric appliances, dripolators, and light fixtures. These products were sold in many stores under a variety of names and carried over ten different types of marks and labels.

The prices below are for items in excellent condition. To learn more about this subject, we recommend *Collector's Guide to Porcelier China* by Susan F. Grindberg (Collector Books). If you have any questions or information regarding Porcelier, please contact our advisor, Jim Barker; he is listed in the Directory under Pennsylvania.

Daisy Chain pot, $38.00; Tankard, solid green, $48.00; Liquid dispenser, $65.00.

Ball jug, Mexican 80.00
Casserole, Basketweave Cameo, w/lid, 8½" 55.00
Ceiling fixture, floral, 3-socket 55.00
Coffee boiler, Rope Bow, 6-cup 45.00
Creamer, Dbl Floral 15.00
Creamer, Silhouette 25.00
Creamer & sugar bowl, Cottage 45.00
Decanter, Oriental Deco 60.00
Fireplace andirons, 23" 300.00
Percolator, Cattail, electric 80.00
Percolator, Scalloped Wild Flowers, electric 150.00
Perculator, electric; Golden Wheat 85.00
Pitcher, batter; Barock-Colonial, gold dots 75.00
Pitcher, disc; Flight 85.00
Pitcher, Floral Rope, 2-cup 35.00
Sugar bowl, American Beauty Rose 12.00
Sugar bowl, Orange Poppy 12.00
Sugar bowl, Rope Bow 12.00
Teapot, Barock-Colonial, ivory, red, or bl dots 65.00
Teapot, Beehive Crisscross, 8-cup 40.00
Teapot, Diamond Leaf, 2-cup 32.00
Teapot, Dutch boy & girl, 6-cup 30.00
Teapot, Hearth, 6-cup 30.00
Waffle iron, Scalloped Wild Flowers, from $225 to 300.00
Wall sconce, floral decal, single 35.00

Postcards

Postcards are distinguished from almost any other collectible due to the fact that nearly any topic can be found represented on cards! For this reason, postcard collecting is considered the 'all-encompassing hobby'! A German by the name of Emmanuel Herrman is credited for inventing the postcard, first printed in Austria in 1869. They were eagerly accepted by the Continentals and the English alike, who saw them as a more economical way to send written messages.

The first to be printed in the United States were on U.S. government postals. The Columbian Exposition of 1892-1893 served as the spark that ignited the postcard phenomenon. Souvenir cards by the thousands were sent to folks back home — expo scenes, transportation themes, animals, birds, and advertising messages became popular. There were patriotic themes, Black themes, and cards for every occasion and holiday. Scenics, cards with small-town railroad depots, and views of U.S. towns (especially photos) are very sought after.

Some of the earliest postcard publishers were Raphael Tuck, Nister, and Gabriel. Early 20th-century illustrators such as Frances Brundage and Ellen Clapsaddle designed cards that are especially collectible.

Although the postcard rage waned at the onset of WWI, they rank today among the most sought-after items of ephemera, second only to stamps. While postcards are abundant, they're one of the hardest collectible categories to evaluate and price. Literally millions are available worldwide, and values range from pennies on up. To evaluate your postcards, it is suggested that you contact the IFPD for a dealer in your area. This roster contains the names of hundreds of dealers who deal in postcards. You should expect the dealer to need to look at the cards to judge their condition, scarcity, etc. Some dealers offer evaluations by mail as well, but please make these arrangements before sending your cards. **Do not** expect a dealer to price cards from a list or written description, as this is not possible. For a dealer list, contact the International Federation of Postcards Dealers, P.O. Box 1765, Manassas, VA 20108, or contact our advisor Jeff Bradfield, 90 Main St., Dayton, VA 22821, (540)-879-9961.

A few examples are listed below. When no condition is indicated, these postcards are assumed to be in excellent condition whether used or unused.

Key:
p/ — publisher   s/ — signed

Advertising, Anheuser-Busch, The Relief Train, VG+ 45.00
Advertising, Best Bros Keene's Cement, bank image, 1910, VG ..45.00
Advertising, Cherry Smash, Mt Vernon lawn, VG 100.00
Advertising, Duryea's Maizena, girl behind boxes, EX+ 30.00
Advertising, Economy King Separators/Sears Roebuck & Co, NM ..65.00
Advertising, Elgin Watches, tattered boy, 1914, VG+ 40.00
Advertising, Emerson's Bromo Seltzer, Uncle Sam/bottle, NM+ ..115.00
Advertising, Falstaff Beer, Easter Greetings, scarce, VG 125.00
Advertising, Fry's Cocoa/Fry's Milk Chocolate, British, NM 125.00
Advertising, Golden Rod Coffee, Camping Out, EX 65.00
Advertising, Heinz, ext/int views of building, NM 40.00
Advertising, Heinz Baked Beans, people conversing, EX+ 35.00
Advertising, Keen Kutter Store, photo of 3 girls, M 115.00
Advertising, Kellogg's, Circumstances Alter Faces, NM 35.00
Advertising, Prudential Ins, milk bottle/meat/food, NM 40.00
Advertising, Shell Gasoline, Mutt & Jeff, 1934, VG 35.00
Advertising, Silvertone Phonograph, family music scene, NM 65.00
Artist, A Mucha, Languid Woman, Champenois/Paris, 1900, NM ..250.00
Artist, F Laskoff, Horseback Riding, 1903, NM 105.00
Artist, H Fisher, Cynthia, Cosmopolitan #971, EX+ 85.00
Artist, H Matisse, The Fish, 1913, NM 200.00
Artist, SL Schmucker, She Listened w/a Flitting Blush, NM 285.00
Black, By the Sand Road, sepia photo, EC Eddy, 1914 ....250.00
Black, cartoon of boy & girl kissing, Hungary, 1908, VG 40.00
Black, Golliwog's Auto-Co-Car, s/Florence Upton, Canada, VG+ ..35.00
Black, Josephine Baker w/dog, sepia photo, L Aubert, EX+ 175.00
Black, Not Bad! Eh?, dapper gent, Tuck, #6813, EX+ 400.00
Black, Song & Their Singers/After the Ball, VG+ 35.00
Christmas, A Joyful Christmas, hold-to-light, 1908, EX+ 150.00
Christmas, A Merry Christmas to You, hold-to-light, EX+ 220.00
Christmas, Kid's Kristmas Kontest, A Bushnell & Co, 1913, VG ..35.00
Christmas, Santa on sleigh, transparency, Schwerdtfeger, EX+ ..115.00
Christmas, snowy church/pond scene, hold-to-light, 1908, EX 35.00
Fantasy, Tie That Binds, Photocraft/Newark NJ, EX 125.00
Halloween, All Halloween Carnival, 1905, Ideal Adv Co, VG 50.00
Halloween, Happy Hallowe'en, Gibson Art Co, NM 30.00
Hold-to-Light, Gardens/Grand Basin, St Louis, 1904, 6x9", NM ..220.00
Hold-to-Light, Gruss aus Berlin, town hall, German, 1902, VG ...35.00
Hold-to-Light, The Promenade/Coney Island, Koehler, #1601, EX ...75.00

Leather, I'm Having Too Much Fun To Leave Salt Lake City, NM, $5.00.

Mechanical, B Gotthelf ad, mill wheel rotates, #308T, 1908, EX 125.00
Mechanical, Chas L Trout & Co ad, When You Go Fishing, VG .100.00
Mechanical, girl's arm w/bouquet raises & lowers, 1909, EX 65.00
Mechanical, mix & match yokels w/nude statues, German, EX 40.00
Mechanical, 2 boxers w/1 swinging arm, EX 85.00
Photo, A Passing Pastime Reno NV, casino scene, sepia, VG+ ..225.00
Photo, Dead Motor-Dixon's Dirigible at Latonia KY, 1919, NM ..150.00
Photo, Guarding Car Barns...OH, police guard street, EX 120.00
Photo, Indian Family at Home/Council-Bluffs IA, 1912, VG 40.00
Photo, men & children in early US Mail truck w/open sides, EX+ .140.00

Photo, Most Prominent Aviators of the Day, 1911, NM **125.00**
Photo, Sheldon Barn Raisers, JH Cave/Detroit, EX **105.00**
Photo, Stoney Indian Chief, Canadian Pacific RR, Harmon, NM ..**80.00**
Photo, street scene, Harvard NB, blk & wht, 1907 ....**12.00**
Photo, street scene, Harvard NB, color, 1910 ....**5.00**
Photo, Titanic, Tom Harvey, NM **600.00**
Photo, train wreck scene on the NY, New Haven & Hartford, EX+ ...**130.00**
Photo, woman dressed in Am flags, 1910, VG **350.00**
Political, Deserves a Second Term..., Taft, 1912, VG+ **200.00**
Political, Keep Cool-idge, blk & wht, 1924, EX **185.00**
Political, Marx/Lenin/Stalin in octagonal fr, blk & wht, NM **30.00**
Political, National Platform of the Prohibition Party, VG+ **45.00**
Political, Ohio's 7 Presidents, oval portraits & flags, NM **85.00**
Political, Salt River Ticket/Landon & Knox, anti-GOP, 1936, G ..**125.00**
Political, T Roosevelt arm-in-arm w/Blk dandy, EX+ **375.00**
Poster Art, Canadian Pacific Railway, promotional, NM **90.00**
Poster Art, Cunard Line to Canada, seashore scene, EX+ **75.00**
Poster Art, Mid-Pacific Carnival Honolulu, Star-Bulletin, VG+ ..**725.00**
Poster Art, Penna Dutch Folk Festival, Dorothy E Kalback, EX ...**45.00**
Poster Art, Siam National Exhibits..., Canada, 1933, VG **50.00**
Poster Art, St Paul Outdoor Sports Carnival, s/Moen, 1919, NM ...**105.00**
Poster Art, The Electric Circus, s/Jacqui Morgan, ca 1960, EX **75.00**
Silk, Cathedral of Coln, brn & wht, Germany, 1899, VG **85.00**
Silk, Ye Peeping Tom of Conventre, court gesture, British, EX+ ..**85.00**
Social, End of the World, anti-atomic war, Germany, 1959, NM .**65.00**
Social, Waiting, man strapped in electric chair, 1908, EX **40.00**
Sports, Columbia, America's Cup Defender 1899, #233, EX+ **35.00**
Sports, Olympic Village, photo, 1932, NM **40.00**
Transparency, Imperial Pavilion of Austria, Paris, 1900, VG **30.00**
Transparency, Paris — 18 Place Vendome, day-to-night, EX+ **30.00**
Transparency, Queen Wilhelmina/husband of Netherlands, NM .**45.00**
Valentine, To My Valentine, silk/emb, Schmucker/Winsch, NM **65.00**

Posters

Advertising posters by such French artists as Cheret and Toulouse-Lautrec were used as early as the mid-1800s. Color lithography spurred their popularity. Circus posters by the Strobridge Lithograph Co. are considered to be the finest in their field, though Gibson and Co. Litho, Erie Litho, and Enquirer Job Printing Co. printed fine examples as well. Posters by noted artists such as Mucha, Parrish, and Hohlwein bring high prices. Other considerations are good color, interesting subject matter and, of course, condition. The WWII posters listed below are among the more expensive examples; 80% of those on the market bring less than $50.00. See also Movie Memorabilia; Political.

Advertising

Standard Fireworks, man with body made up of fireworks, color litho, 60x40", EX, $285.00.

Beacon Shoes for Men, sailboat & lighthouse, 24x20", EX **300.00**

Columbia Bicycles, early cycling scene, 27x12", VG **350.00**
Crosman Bros Peerless Watermelon, 2 Blk boys, 24x17", VG .**1,800.00**
Deering Grass Cutting Machinery, boaters watch, 22x29", EX ..**3,000.00**
Ithaca Guns, pheasant on stump, 1913, 27x16", G **600.00**
Jacob Hoffman Brewing Co, bouquet/beer glass/cigar, 31x21", NM ..**75.00**
Lefevre-Utile Biscuits, girl & dogwood, 1907, 27x20", VG **300.00**
Peters Big Game Ammunition, moose by lake, 29x18", G **700.00**
Tipper's '3 Tips!,' snorting bull w/products, 45x34", G **200.00**

Circus

Beatty-Cole Bros, lion & trainer, 36x21", NM **200.00**
Beatty-Cole Bros, lions & tigers w/trainer, 29x28", VG- **20.00**
Beatty-Cole Bros, 2 rows of marching elephants, 29x28", VG- **20.00**
Christy Bros Big 5 Ring Wild Animal Circus, 79x80½", G- **800.00**
Clyde Beatty, Big Otto...Hippo..., 28x21", EX **85.00**
Miller Bros, clown & elephants, 41x13", EX **20.00**
RB B&B, Circus World Showcase, 1973, 28x22", EX **25.00**
RB B&B, close-up of clown tipping hat, 21x28", EX **200.00**
RB B&B, clown bust lower left, 28x41", EX **150.00**
RB B&B, Dorothy Herbert on horse, 40x28", EX **100.00**
RB B&B, Gunther Gebel-Williams Farewell Tour, 33x24", EX ...**15.00**
RB B&B, yel lettering on bl w/globe, 1945, 21x28", EX **140.00**
Vargas, tiger's head w/mouth open, 24x17", EX **20.00**
Wondercade Illusion Spectacular, Live on Stage, 28x23½", EX ...**35.00**

Travel

Air France, Afrique Du Nord, plane over city, 40x26", EX+ **345.00**
Air France, Amerique Du Nord, NY/Paris, 1950, 40x25", M **800.00**
Autriche, man in lederhosen standing rowing boat, 37x25", NM ..**200.00**
Bermuda, couple on bikes & sailboat at night, 40x24", EX+ **460.00**
Bremen-New York, 3 ships against NY skyline, 1930s, 34x24", NM ...**975.00**
Brissago, cactus flower against desert sky, 39x26½", EX+ **745.00**
Central Hudson Line, couple watch shoreline, 1925, 46x30", NM **690.00**
Cunard Line, blk Deco ocean liner w/4 red stacks, 37x26", M ...**1,955.00**
Deauville, male diver against bl sky, 60½x46½", NM **400.00**
Egypt, cat w/bl scarab around neck on magenta, 40x28", M **350.00**
Hungary, 2 angelic girls in wht against bl, 38x25", M **315.00**
Motor-Road to the Gaisberg, car & mountain town, 37x25", NM ..**375.00**
Norway The Home of Ski-ing, couple rest on snow, 39x24", EX+ ..**750.00**

Ocean liner Normandie on the high seas, color lithograph, A.M. Cassandre, 1935, 39¼x24¼", EX, $9,500.00.

St Moritz, lg wht rabbit against dk bl ground, 50x36", NM **575.00**
State Parks, stylized family over grill, 1935, 40x27", EX+ **460.00**

War

WWI, Help Them Keep Your Savings Pledge, 29x19", VG **100.00**

WWI, I Want Your...Army..., Uncle Sam, Flagg, 1917, 39x30", NM ..**1,800.00**
WWII, 'Till We Meet Again/Buy War Bonds, 14x10", M **65.00**
WWII, Bonds Build Ships/Buy More Bonds, 16x11", G **30.00**
WWII, Do With Less So They'll Have Enough!..., 40x28", M ...**125.00**
WWII, Doing All You Can Brother? Buy War Bonds, 40x28", NM ...**140.00**
WWII, Fire Away! Buy Extra Bonds, 28x20", EX **135.00**
WWII, Give It Your Best!, Am flag, horizontal, VG **180.00**
WWII, Guide the Fighter Planes, Join..., 28x20", EX **75.00**
WWII, Let's Hit Bull's Eye! Everybody At Least 10%, 20x15", M ..**50.00**
WWII, Men Working Together, GI/war worker/sailor, G **125.00**
WWII, Miles of Hell to Tokyo! Work..., 26x18", G **100.00**
WWII, The United Nations Fight for Freedom, 28x22", M **100.00**
WWII, They Did Their Part, 5 Sullivan brothers, 28x22", G **150.00**
WWII, You Buy 'Em We'll Fly 'Em!..., 60x40", EX **385.00**

Miscellaneous

Cannstatter Park, split image of park festival, 29x18", EX **300.00**
Helping Hoover in Our US School Garden, 1920s, 30x20", NM ...**275.00**
Minstrel, Geo Thatcher's, Darktown/Blackville..., 29x40", G+ ..**4,500.00**
Montana Frank Shows, cowboy on horse, 27½x20½", VG+ **200.00**
Pimlico Course, horse race in progress, 18x25", G **650.00**
Safety, 2 kids & dog at corner w/Play Zone sign, 41x31", EX ..**2,050.00**
Theatre, Human Hearts, group around slain man, 1901, 27x40", VG+ ..**400.00**

Pot Lids

Pot lids were pottery covers for containers that were used for hair dressing, potted meats, etc. The most desirable were decorated with colorful transfer prints under the glaze in a variety of themes, animal and scenic. The first and probably the largest company to manufacture these lids was F. & R. Pratt of Fenton, Staffordshire, established in the early 1800s. The name or initials of Jesse Austin, their designer, may sometimes be found on exceptional designs. Although few pot lids were made after the 1880s, the firm continued into the 20th century.

American pot lids are very rare. Most have been dug up by collectors searching through sites of early gold rush mining towns in California. Minor rim chips are expected and normally do not detract from listed values. When no condition is given, assume that the value reflects on examples in such condition.

American

Art Gallery exhibition building, multicolored, 1½x4¼", with matching base marked Philadelphia Exhibition 1876, very rare, exceptional condition, $800.00.

Bazin's Ambrosial Shaving Cream, purple, 3", EX, + base **375.00**
Bazin's Ambrosial Shaving Cream, purple, 3", VG, +base **160.00**
Bazin's Odontine...Xavier Bazin..., blk, 2¾", EX, +base **550.00**
Capitol at Washington Worsley..., lav, 3½", EX, +base **850.00**
Caswell Massey & Co Cold Cream..., gr, 2½x3¼" **160.00**
Cha's E Haley...Cherry Tooth Paste, blk, 2½", EX, +base **625.00**
Dr Allport's Dentifrice...Chicago, blk, 3¼" **770.00**

Dr Buchanan's Universal Vegetable..., blk, 1⅞", +base **85.00**
Dr EJ Coxe's Extract...Sarsaparilla..., blk, 3¼", EX, +base **450.00**
Dyer's Orange Flowers & Orris Toothpaste, bl-blk on wht, 2¾" ...**800.00**
Elixer Should Be Used At Night..., blk, 3½", EX **100.00**
Genuine Bears' Grease...Jules Hauel..., blk, 3¼", EX **800.00**
Genuine Beef Marrow...X Baxin..., blk, 3", EX **600.00**
Glenn's Aromatic Rose Tooth Paste, blk, 3", EX, +base **500.00**
Harrison's Columbian..., clambroth glass, 3¼", +base **300.00**
Highest Premiums Awarded...X Bazin Phila, purple, 3⅜", EX **550.00**
Highly Perfumed Bears' Grease...X Bazin..., blk, 2¾", EX **950.00**
Occidental Tooth Paste, Vennard...NY, blk, 3", +mismatched base ..**625.00**
Odonto or Oak Bark...Tooth Paste..., red, 3¼", +base **475.00**
Oriental Tooth Paste Bazin & Sargent..., blk, 3", EX, +base **700.00**
Otondo or Oak Bark & Orris Tooth Paste, red, 3¼" **475.00**
Premium Ambrosial Cream...Jules..., purple, 3½", EX, +base **500.00**
Purified Charcoal Tooth Paste...X Baxin..., blk, 3¾" **100.00**
Taylor's Saponoceous Compound..., purple, 3½", EX, +base **575.00**
Taylors' Saponaceous Compound..., bl, 3¼", EX **280.00**
Washington Crossing Delaware...Taylor..., lav, 3½", EX **425.00**
Wild Cherry Blossom Dentifrice..., blk, 2¾", EX, +base **500.00**

English

Am Indians Hunting Buffalo, mc, Pratt, 4½", EX **260.00**
Bear on throne, lion/crowing rooster, mc, 3", EX **110.00**
Bellevue, Pegwell Bay, lg estate, mc, 5", EX **140.00**
Cherry Toothpaste...F Newbury..., sailboat, blk/wht, 2¾", EX **75.00**
Dentifrice Velvetis E Rimmel Ltd..., mc, 4", EX, +base **1,100.00**
Dutch battle, windmill burning, Pratt, Wouvermann, 6" L **85.00**
Examining the Nets, mc, hairline, 4", EX **150.00**
Grand Internat'l Bldg 1851 Exhibition..., mc, rare, 5", EX **300.00**
Kettle of Fish, dogs spill kettle, Pratt, mc, 4", EX **130.00**
Landing the Catch, mc, 4", EX **70.00**
Lobster Saucer, lobster/cat/fish, mc, 4½", EX **135.00**
Messrs Read Dentists...Brighton, blk, 3¼", EX **1,000.00**
Queen's Own Cherry Tooth Paste, queen, red/wht, 3⅜", VG **350.00**
Shirtliff's...Tooth Paste..., blk/wht, rectangular, 3¾" **150.00**
Shrimpers, fisherman & children, mc, Pratt, 4⅛" **115.00**
Swinton's English Primrose, cobalt/wht, 2⅝", +base **185.00**
Uncle Toby, Pratt, 4" **105.00**
White Clover Tooth Paste..., floral, blk/wht, 2⅝", EX **150.00**

Powder Horns and Shot Flasks

Though powder horns had already been in use for hundreds of years, collectors usually focus on those made after the expansion of the United States westward in the very early 1800s. While some are basic and very simple, others were scrimshawed and highly polished. Especially nice carvings can quickly escalate the value of a horn that has survived intact to as high as $400.00. Those with detailed maps, historical scenes, etc. bring even higher prices.

Metal flasks were introduced in the 1830s; by the middle of the century they were produced in quantity and at prices low enough that they became a viable alternative to the powder horn. Today's collector regards the smaller flasks as the more desirable and valuable, and those made for specific companies bring premium prices.

Flask, brass, emb eagle, broken spring, varnish traces, 4¾" **100.00**
Flask, brass, emb percussion revolver, unmk, 4¾", VG **300.00**
Flask, brass, MA Arms Co emb in circle ea side, 4½", VG **275.00**
Flask, copper, emb circle & star, 2¾", NM **150.00**
Flask, copper, emb foliage/eagle/shield/etc, 4⅝", G **50.00**
Flask, copper/brass, Colt's Patent over stars/eagle/banner, EX **250.00**

Horn, cvd, Alaskan totem symbols allover, wood plug, 1900s, 14" ..**225.00**
Horn, cvd, Arms of MA & vines, wood plug, ca 1763, 10", VG ...**2,000.00**
Horn, cvd, bird/foliage/geometrics, name/1775, 9¾" **1,150.00**
Horn, cvd, birds in tree/sun/moon, dtd 1811, primitive, 15¾" ...**675.00**
Horn, cvd dbl-rib near spout, primitive figures, early, 17", G **175.00**
Horn, cvd, Dutch hex symbols, sgn, ca 1800, 5½" **375.00**
Horn, cvd, Ft Lauderdale FL, 1800s, 13½" **450.00**
Horn, cvd, owner's name, Philadelphia, 1836, 9½" **300.00**
Horn, cvd, Will You Take a Drink..., NY, ca 1870, 5½" **375.00**

Pratt

Prattware has become a generic reference for a type of relief-molded earthenware with polychrome decoration. Scenic motifs with figures were popular; sometimes captions were added. Jugs are most common; but teapots, tableware, even figurines were made. The term 'Pratt' refers to Wm. Pratt of Lane Delph, who is credited with making the first examples of this type, though similar wares were made later by other Staffordshire potters. Pot lids and other transfer wares marked Pratt were made in Fenton, Staffordshire, by F. & R. Pratt & Co. (See Pot Lids).

Figurines, Elijah and Widow of Zarephath, titled 'Eliga' and 'Wido' on bases, late 1700s, 9½", $660.00 for the pair; Watch stand, central clock flanked by draped classical figures, early 1800s, restored, 11⅛", $1,200.00.

Bottle, scent; bl arrows & yel panels, 1790-1820, 1¾" **300.00**
Figurine, baby in cradle, yel & bl, early 19th C, 4½", EX **350.00**
Figurine, Billy Waters, mc on pearl glaze, 7¼" **1,400.00**
Figurine, Winter, allegorical, mc enamels, rstr, 8½" **390.00**
Pipe, lady's face bowl, coiled w/decor, pearlware, 9½" **750.00**
Pipe, serpent form w/lady on neck, mc, rstr, 10¾" **5,000.00**
Pipe bowl, Turk's head shape, mc, 2½" **170.00**
Pitcher, emb hearts w/children ea side, early 1800s, 4¾", G **300.00**
Pitcher, Mischievous Sport/Sportive Innocence, pearlware, 7" ..**535.00**
Pitcher, Miser ea side, mc trim, att, rstr, 5¼" **350.00**
Pitcher, scenic, pearlware, mc, prof rstr, 7½" **425.00**
Plate, child & pet, emb floral rim, mc enamels, 2¾" **80.00**
Sauce boat, fox's head forms body & spout, swan hdl, 5x7" **850.00**
Toby jug, pearlware, underglaze enamels, w/lid, 1790s, 10" **750.00**
Wall pocket, cornucopia form w/Cupid in relief, 11½", EX **1,500.00**

Precious Moments

Known as 'America's Hummels,' Precious Moments™ are a line of well-known collectibles created by Samuel J. Butcher and produced by Enesco, Inc. These pieces have endeared themselves to many because of the inspirational messages they portray. Over 300,000 club members have joined the national club in thirteen years.

The collection was fifteen years old in 1993. Each piece is pro-

duced with a different mark each year. This mark, not the date, is usually the link to the values of the piece. Most mold changes result in increased values, and when a piece is retired or suspended, its price increases as well. As an example, 'God Loveth a Cheerful Giver' retailed for $9.50 in 1980; it was retired in 1981 and has a secondary market price now of $850.00 to $950.00. The majority of the collection has increased in value from its original retail.

Rosie Wells Enterprises, Inc., our advisor for this category, has published the Precious Moments™ collector magazine, *Precious Collectibles*®, as well as a secondary market price guide. She has hosted International Conventions for Precious Moments™ collectors since 1983. Her address is in the Directory under Clubs, Newsletters, and Catalogs. Items listed below are assumed to be in mint condition with the original box.

Baby's First Trip, #16012, Dove mk, suspended 1989 ....**300.00**
Bringing God's Blessing to You, E-0509, Fish mk, suspended 1987 .....**90.00**
But Loves Goes on Forever, E-0001, no mk, charter member club **175.00**
First Noel ornament, E-2368, Hourglass mark, retired 1984 ....**75.00**

God Loveth a Cheerful Giver, girl with puppies in cart, E-1378, no mark, retired in 1981, $850.00 to $950.00.

Join in on the Blessing, E-0404, Fish mk, new member club **55.00**
Let Us Call Club..., E-0103, Hourglass mk, charter member club .**65.00**
Make a Joyful Noise, E-1374G, unmk **130.00**
My Guardian Angel, musical, E-5205, no mk, suspended 1985 ..**120.00**
Nobody's Perfect, E-9268, Hourglass mk w/smile, retired 1990 ...**550.00**
Onward Christian Soldier, E-0523, decaled Fish mk **130.00**
Sharing Our Season Together, E-0501, Fish mk, suspended 1986 ..**175.00**
To a Special Dad ornament, E-0515, Fish mark, suspended 1988 .**60.00**
To Tell the Tooth..., #105813, Cedar Tree mk, suspended 1990 ..**185.00**
Unicorn ornament, E-2371, missing mk, retired 1988 ....**60.00**

Primitives

Like the mouse that ate the grindstone, so has collectible interest in primitives increased, a little bit at a time, until demand is taking bites instead of nibbles into their availability. Although the term 'primitives' once referred to those survival essentials contrived by our American settlers, it has recently been expanded to include objects needed or desired by succeeding generations — items representing the cabin-'n-cornpatch existence as well as examples of life on larger farms and in towns. Through popular usage, it also respectfully covers what are actually 'country collectibles.'

From the 1600s into the latter 1800s, factories employed carvers, blacksmiths, and other artisans whose handwork contributed to turning out quality items. When buying, 'touchmarks,' a company's name and/or location and maker's or owner's initials, are exciting discoveries.

Primitives are uniquely individual. Following identical forms, results more often than not show typically personal ideas. Using this as a guide (combined with circumstances of age, condition, desire to own, etc.) should lead to a reasonably accurate evaluation. For items not listed, consult comparable examples. Authority Kathryn McNerney has compiled several lovely books on primitives and related topics: *Primitives, Our American Heritage; Collectible Blue and White Stoneware;* and *Antique Tools, Our American Heritage.* You will find her address in the Directory under Florida. See also Butter Molds and Stamps; Boxes; Copper; Farm Collectibles; Fireplace Implements; Kitchen Collectibles; Molds; Tinware; Weaving; Woodenware; and Wrought Iron.

Bed warmer, brass, pierced & eng lid, trn walnut hdl, 49" 195.00
Bed warmer, brass w/copper nail heads, walnut hdl, 44" 160.00
Bed warmer, brass w/eng (simple) lid, trn wood hdl, 43", EX 185.00
Bed warmer, brass w/pnt-decor wooden hdl, Am, 19th C, 41" 490.00
Bed warmer, copper, hinged pierced lid, trn wood hdl, 7¼" dia .290.00
Bed warmer, copper w/brass ferrule, trn/pnt hdl, 41" 195.00
Bed warmer, simple punched deisgn on lid, chestnut hdl, 42" 275.00
Board, corn cutting; yel pnt, tin prongs & slicer, 27x6" 60.00
Candle box, pine/poplar, old grpt w/gilt starflowers, 7½" 290.00

Photo courtesy Aston Americana

Candle mold, 18 pewter tubes, wooden case with bootjack feet marked H. Tiebe, Nauvoo (a Mormon settlement in Illinois, ca 1838-1845), with wick spools and rods intact, 18x6x22", $1,650.00; Tallow candles, set of 6, wicks intact, 9", $290.00.

Candle mold, copper, 1-tube, arched ribbon hdl, 11x2x3" 195.00
Candle mold, pewter, 24-tube, in wooden fr, 18x6½x22½" 965.00
Candle mold, pewter, 30-tube, pine fr, crude, 16x21" 770.00
Candle mold, tin, 12-tube, ear hdls, 5¾" 285.00
Candle mold, tin, 12-tube, lg ear hdl, 10⅞" 100.00
Candle mold, tin, 24-tube, dbl hdls, ca 1830, 11" 350.00
Candle mold, tin, 24-tube, ear hdl, 20" 300.00
Candle mold, tin, 3-tube, appl ribbon hdl, 10x3⅝x2½" 110.00
Candle mold, tin, 36-tube, EX wooden fr/pnt, rprs, 17x29x8½" ..1,650.00
Candle mold, tin, 5-tube, arched base, scroll hdls, 9x9x3½" 270.00
Candle mold, tin, 8-tube, ear hdl, 10⅜" 120.00
Candle snuffer, scissors shape, w/tin tray, ca 1820 ....75.00
Churn, pine w/wrought crank hdl, sq nails, 16½x12x11" 165.00
Churn, wooden box shape w/sq nails, orig bl pnt, 16x16x12" 350.00
Clothes wringer, wooden, Wyeth, Pat June 10, 1898, rfn, VG 65.00
Cookie mold, basket of flowers, iron, oval, 4x6" 210.00
Cookie mold, bird on branch in oval w/fancy border, CI, 5" 165.00
Dough scraper, wrought iron, 1-pc 60.00
Foot warmer, hardwood w/holes forming hearts/etc, 9½" L 250.00
Foot warmer, hardwood w/punched tin, dtd 1800, 8x9" 225.00
Foot warmer, mortised wood fr w/punched tin panel, 9x10" 250.00
Foot warmer, stoneware pig, cork stopper, 1900s, 11", EX 90.00
Foot warmer, walnut w/sliding door, tin insert, 1820s, EX 350.00
Pie crimper, copper wheel w/wood hdl, 1810s, 1⅜" dia 110.00
Pie crimper, tin, 2⅛" wheel w/hollow tube hdl, 9" 110.00

Pie crimper, walnut w/ivory inlay, 1⅜" wheel, 8" 120.00
Quilting fr, mortised/pinned, old red/brn pnt, ca 1800, 47" 250.00
Rack, apple drying; dvtl corners, thin slats in center, 39x19" 85.00
Rack, drying; 4 wood slats fold out ea side, 1880s, 30x8" 220.00
Scoop, cranberry; FL Buckingham Mfg...Mass, 19¾x20½" 385.00
Scrub stick, hand-cvd wood w/hook end, 10¼" 75.00
Sock dryers, heavy wire, lg, pr 28.00
Sock stretchers, wooden, Fairway Store...Boston, pr 35.00
Sugar nippers, wrought iron, 8½" 70.00
Sugar nippers, wrought steel, cast rectangular base, wood hdl 275.00
Tinder lighter, tin, old gr pnt traces, w/flint, 4½" dia 240.00
Tongs, maple sugar; wrought iron, rivet hinge/loop hdls, 8½" 180.00
Tray, apple sorting; boat shape, shallow, 83x34½" 450.00
Washboard, hand cvd w/wide grooves, 1-pc, 11x4⅛"+hdl 90.00
Washboard, wood fr w/Rockingham insert, worn wht pnt, 23x12" ..450.00
Yoke, bucket-carrying; softwood w/old gr, pnt, 38", G 65.00

Prints

The term 'print' may be defined today as almost any image printed on paper by any available method. Examples of collectible old 'prints' are Norman Rockwell magazine covers and Maxfield Parrish posters and calendars. 'Original print' refers to one achieved through the efforts of the artist or under his direct supervision. A 'reproduction' is a print produced by an accomplished print maker who reproduces another artist's print or original work. Thorough study is required on the part of the collector to recognize and appreciate the many variable factors to be considered in evaluating a print. Prices vary from one area of the country to another and are dependent upon new findings regarding the scarcity or abundance of prints as such information may arise. Although each collector of old prints may have their own varying criteria by which to judge condition, for those who deal only rarely in this area or newer collectors, a few guidelines may prove helpful. Staining, though unquestionably detrimental, is nearly always present in some degree and should be weighed against the rarity of the print. Professional cleaning should improve its appearance and at the same time help preserve it. Avoid tears that affect the image; minor margin tears are another matter, especially if the print is a rare one. Moderate 'foxing' (brown spots caused by mold or the fermentation of the rag content of old paper) and light stains from the old frames are not serious unless present in excess. Margin trimming was a common practice; but look for at least ½" to 1½" margins, depending on print size.

When no condition is indicated, the items listed below are assumed to be in very good to excellent condition. See also Nutting, Wallace; Parrish, Maxfield.

Audubon, John J.

Audubon is the best known of American and European wildlife artists. His first series of prints, 'Birds of America,' was produced by Robert Havell of London. They were printed on Whitman watermarked paper bearing dates of 1826 to 1838. The Octavo Edition of the same series was printed in seven editions, the first by J.T. Bowen under Audubon's direction. There were seven volumes of text and prints, each 10" x 7", the first five bearing the J.J. Audubon and J.B. Chevalier mark, the last two, J.J. Audubon. They were produced from 1840 through 1844. The second and other editions were printed up to 1871. The Bien Edition prints were full size, made under the direction of Audubon's sons in the late 1850s. Due to the onset of the Civil War, only 105 plates were finished. These are considered to be the most valuable of the reprints of the 'Birds of America Series.'

In 1971 the complete set was reprinted by Johnson Reprint Corp. of New York and Theaturm Orbis Terrarum of Amsterdam. Examples of the latter bear the watermark G. Schut and Zonen. In 1985 a second reprint was done by Abbeville Press for the National Audubon Society.

Although Audubon is best known for his portrayal of birds, one of his less-familiar series, 'Vivaparous Quadrupeds of North America,' portrayed various species of animals. Assembled in corroboration with John Bachman from 1839 until 1851, these prints are 28" x 22" in size. Several octavo editions were published in the 1850s. In the following listing, all measurements are actual print size unless stated otherwise.

Bl-Winged Yel Swamp Warbler, #111, Bowen, 1st ed, 1841, 20x13" .135.00
Black Vulture, #106, Havell, 25½x37½" 5,500.00
Booby, #207, Amsterdam Edition, 39x26" 400.00
Cardinal, #203, Bowen, 1st ed, 6½x10" 700.00
Carolina Squirrel, #7, Bowen Octavo, 7x11" 250.00
Couger, Male; #96, Bowen, 1846, 21½x27⅛" 4,500.00
Florida Comorant, #252, Havell, 1835, 19½x26½" 2,500.00
Fork-Tail Flycatcher, #168, Amsterdam, 26x39" 750.00
Franblin's Marmot, #84, Bowen Folio, 22x27" 1,200.00
Gannet, #326, Havell, 26x39" 14,000.00
Glossy Ibis, #348, Bowen, 1st edition, 7x11" 600.00
Golden-Winged Woodpecker, #273, Bowen, 1850s, 6½x10" 125.00
Great Footed Hawk, #20, Bien, 27x39" 3,500.00
Grey Fox, #21, Bowen Folio, 22x27" 12,000.00
Iceland Falcon, #366, Amsterdam, 26x39" 3,000.00
Key-West Dove, #167, Havell, 25x38" 5,000.00
King Duck, #276, Havell, 1835, 26¼x38½" 4,500.00
Mallard Duck, #385, Bien, 26¾x37½" 8,000.00
Moose Deer, Bowen, lg folio 3,000.00
Oyster Catcher, #223, Havell, 26x38" 4,500.00
Prairie Wolf, Bowen Octavo, 7x11" 400.00
Raccoon, #61, Bowen Octavo, 7x11" 600.00
Red-Breasted Sandpiper, #315, Havell, 1836, 12¼x19½" 750.00
Red-Shouldered Hawk, #56, Amsterdam, 26x39" 900.00
Robin, #131, Amsterdam Edition, 39x26" 725.00
Swamp Hare, #37, Bowen, 1850s, 7x10" 250.00
Swamp Sparrow, #175, Bowen, 1st edition, 6½x11" 200.00
Turkey Cock, Plate 1 or #1, Havell, 27x38" 90,000.00
Velvet Duck, Male & Female; #247, Havell, 1835, 24x38⅛" ..4,500.00
White Wolf, #27, Bowen Folio, 22x27" 3,500.00
Wood Thrush, #144, Bowen, 1st edition, 6x11" 250.00

Currier and Ives

Nathaniel Currier was in business by himself until the late 1850s when he formed a partnership with James Merrit Ives. Currier is given credit for being the first to use the medium to portray newsworthy subjects, and the Currier and Ives views of 19th-century American culture are familiar to us all. In the following listings, 'C' numbers correspond with a standard reference book by Conningham. Values are given for prints in very good condition; all are colored unless indicated black and white. Unless noted 'NC' (Nathaniel Currier), all prints are published by Currier and Ives. Our advisors for this category are John and Barbara Rudisill (Rudisill's Alt Print Haus); they are listed in the Directory under Maryland.

A Crack Team at a Smashing Gait, 1869, C-1282, large folio, $1,500.00.

Abigail, NC, 1846, C-9, sm folio 85.00
Accommodation Train, 1876, C-32, sm folio 400.00
Alnwick Castle, Scotland; undtd, C-87, med folio 125.00
Am Country Life, Pleasures of Winter; NC, 1855, C-123, lg folio ..2,300.00
Am Farm Scenes/No 3, NC, 1853, C-133, lg folio 3,600.00
Am Game, 1866, C-163, lg folio 900.00
Am Prize Fruit, 1862, C-183, lg folio 1,800.00
Autumn in Adirondacks (Lake Harrison), undtd, C-323, sm folio ..350.00
Autumn on Lake George, undtd, C-324, sm folio 250.00
Battle of Gettysburg, undtd, C-407, sm folio 300.00
Bear Hunting, Close Quarters (summer); undtd, C-447, sm folio ..750.00
Beauty of New England, undtd, C-462, sm folio 65.00
Benjamin Franklin, Statesman...; NC, 1847, C-499, sm folio 500.00
Between Two Fires, 1879, C-511, sm folio 225.00
Black-Eyed Susan, NC, 1848, C-551, sm folio 300.00
Blue Fishing, undtd, C-578, sm folio 950.00
Brook Trout Fishing, 1872, C-704, sm folio 900.00
Burning of Clipper...Golden Light, NC, undtd, C-740, sm folio 455.00
Camping Out, Some of Right Sort; NC, 1856, C-777, lg folio 3,500.00
Cares of a Family, NC, 1856, C-814, lg folio 3,500.00
Central Park, NY, The Bridge; undtd, C-950, sm folio 300.00
Chicky's Diner, undtd, C-1029, sm folio 150.00
Children in the Woods, undtd, C-1033, sm folio 150.00
Christ Walking on the Sea, undtd, C-1071, sm folio 30.00
City of New York, NC, 1855, C-1102, lg folio 3,000.00
Clipper Ship in a Hurricane, 1855, C-1154, med folio 2,000.00
Clipper Ship in a Snow Squall, undtd, C-1157, sm folio 900.00
Cork Castle & Black Rock Castle, undtd, C-1253, sm folio 90.00
Cozzen's Dock, West Point, undtd, C-1277, med folio 800.00
Darktown Yacht Club, Hard...Breeze; 1885, C-1439, sm folio 250.00
Day Before Marriage, NC, 1847, C-1459, sm folio 100.00
Declaration Committee, 1876, C-1530, sm folio 300.00
Distanced, 1878, C-1589, sm folio 225.00
Drive Through the Highlands, undtd, C-1627, med folio 700.00
Dude Belle, 1883, C-1634, sm folio 230.00
Dude Swell, 1883, C-1635, sm folio 230.00
Dutchman & Hiram Woodruff, 1871, C-1640, sm folio 700.00
Easter Offering, 1871, C-1659, sm folio 30.00
Enchanted Isles, 1869, C-1740, sm folio 90.00
English Winter Scene, undtd, C-1745, sm folio 525.00
Express Train, 1870, C-1792, sm folio 2,000.00
Family Pets, NC, undtd, C-1840, sm folio 100.00
First Ride, NC, 1849, C-1987, sm folio 130.00
First Trot of the Season, 1870, C-1998, lg folio 2,000.00
Fording the River, NC, undtd, C-2081, med folio 550.00
Fr Revolution, Burning...Carriages...; NC, 1848, C-2139, sm folio .120.00
Fruits of Temperence, 1870, C-2195, sm folio 200.00
General Lewis Cass, NC, 1846, C-2288, sm folio 80.00
General Shields at the Battle..., 1862, C-2294, sm folio 195.00
Georgie, Quite Tired; undtd, C-2359, sm folio 90.00
Girl I Love, 1870, C-2376, sm folio 75.00
Good Times on the Old Plantation, undtd, C-2451, sm folio 700.00
Got the Drop on Him, 1881, C-2455, sm folio 250.00
Grand National Whig Banner, NC, 1844, C-2511, sm folio 200.00
Grand Pacer Richball, 1890, C-2519, sm folio 300.00
Great Salt Lake, Utah; undtd, C-2649, sm folio 400.00
Group of Lilies, undtd, C-2670, sm folio 130.00
Happy Little Pups, undtd, C-2717, sm folio 135.00
Harbor for the Night, undtd, C-2724, sm folio 300.00
Harvesting, The Last Load; undtd, C-2750, sm folio 325.00
Henry Clay of Kentucky, NC, undtd, C-2791, sm folio 120.00
Home of the Deer, undtd, C-2867, med folio 500.00
Homeward Bound, NC, C-2885, 1845, sm folio 750.00
Hooked, 1874, C-2928, sm folio 500.00

Hudson From West Point, 1862, C-2972, med folio 1,050.00

Hues of Autumn on Racquet River, undtd, C-2982, sm folio 300.00

Imported Messenger, 1880, C-3042, sm folio 300.00

Inviting Dish, 1870, C-3124, sm folio 150.00

Italian Landscape, undtd, C-3139, sm folio 75.00

Just Married, undtd, C-3321, sm folio 100.00

King of the Forest, undtd, C-3333, sm folio 200.00

Lakeside Home, 1869, C-3423, med folio 350.00

Leaders, 1888, C-3471, lg folio 1,000.00

Life in the Country, Evening; 1862, C-3508, med folio 850.00

Life in the Woods, Returning; 1860, C-3513, lg folio 3,500.00

Life of a Fireman, Ruins; NC, 1854, C-3520, lg folio 2,500.00

Lincoln Family, 1867, C-3546, sm folio 80.00

Little Ellen, undtd, C-3614, sm folio 95.00

Little Mary & Lamb, 1877, C-3670, sm folio 150.00

Little May Blossom, 1874, C-3671, sm folio 85.00

Little Students, undtd, C-3720, sm folio 150.00

Loss of Steamship Swallow, NC, 1845, C-3779, sm folio 425.00

Maggie, undtd, C-3864, sm folio 95.00

Marriage Certificate, NC, 1848, C-4000, sm folio 100.00

May Queen, NC, undtd, C-4089, sm folio 90.00

Mill-Cove Lake, undtd, C-4123, sm folio 350.00

Mink Trapping, Prime; 1862, C-4139, lg folio 10,000.00

Moose & Wolves, A Narrow Escape; undtd, C-4185, sm folio ...300.00

Mother's Pet, NC, undtd, C-4237, sm folio 100.00

Mother's Wing, 1866, C-4239, med folio 250.00

Mountain Rumble, undtd, C-4244, sm folio 175.00

My Highland Boy, NC, undtd, C-4305, sm folio 95.00

My Pet Bird, undtd, C-4348, med folio 175.00

My Pony & Dog, undtd, C-4350, sm folio 150.00

My Three White Kitties, ...Their ABCs; undtd, C-4357, sm folio ..150.00

New Fashioned Girl, undtd, C-4422, sm folio 225.00

New Suspension Bridge, Niagara Falls; undtd, C-4432, sm folio ..300.00

Niagara Falls, undtd, C-4457, med folio 350.00

Nosegay, 1870, C-4512, sm folio 125.00

Old Ford Bridge, undtd, C-4559, sm folio 225.00

Old Mill in Summer, undtd, C-4571, sm folio 300.00

On a Point, NC, 1855, C-4592, med folio 600.00

On the Coast of California, undtd, C-4598, sm folio 350.00

Outward Bound, Going Out Under...; undtd, C-4666, sm folio ..700.00

Parson's Colt, 1879, C-4706, sm folio 225.00

Patriot of 1776, 1876, C-4725, sm folio 200.00

Peaceful River, undtd, C-4736, sm folio 175.00

Perry's Victory on Lake Erie, NC, undtd, C-4754, sm folio 650.00

Pigeon Shooting, Playing the Decoy; 1862, C-4780, lg folio ...2,975.00

Pride of the Garden, 1873, C-4914, sm folio 175.00

Prince & Princess of Wales, C-4926, undtd, sm folio 90.00

Quail Shooting, NC, 1852, C-4989, lg folio 3,000.00

Quails, NC, C-4992, sm folio 350.00

Queen of Beauty, undtd, C-4997, sm folio 75.00

Rabbits in Woods, undtd, C-5036, sm folio 250.00

Raspberries, 1870, C-5065, sm folio 150.00

Roadside Mill, 1870, C-5175, sm folio 350.00

Robinson Crusoe..., 1874, C-5189, sm folio 175.00

Royal Mail Steamship Persia, NC, 1856, C-5240, lg folio 1,150.00

Scene on the Susquehanna, undtd, C-5415, sm folio 300.00

See-Saw, undtd, C-5457, med folio 350.00

Shall I?, undtd, C-5477, very sm folio 750.00

Silver Cascade, Wht Mountains; undtd, C-5521, sm folio 275.00

Soldier's Adieu, NC, 1847, C-5593, sm folio 125.00

Soldier's Home, 1862, C-5599, sm folio 125.00

Source of the Hudson..., undtd, C-5627, sm folio 325.00

Spring, NC, 1849, C-5671, sm folio 225.00

Stable Scene No 2, NC, undtd, C-5686, sm folio 500.00

Stella & Alice Grey, ...Whalebone; NC, 1855, C-5811, lg folio ..1,750.00

Summer Evening, undtd, C-5853, sm folio 175.00

Summer Ramble, undtd, C-5874, med folio 350.00

Sunrise on Lake Saranac, 1860, C-5895, lg folio 2,800.00

Surrender of General Lee..., 1865, C-5909, sm folio 250.00

Through to the Pacific, 1870, C-6051, sm folio 1,200.00

Trolling for Bluefish, 1866, C-6158, lg folio 10,000.00

Trotting Cracks at the Forge, 1869, C-6169, lg folio 8,000.00

US Frigate Independence, 64 Guns; NC, 1841, C-6307, sm folio ..465.00

Valley Forge VA, undtd, C-6355, sm folio 250.00

Velocipede, 1869, C-6365, sm folio 1,400.00

View on Rondout, undtd, C-6451, med folio 600.00

Village Blacksmith, 1864, C-6462, lg folio 3,000.00

Washington at Prayer, NC, undtd, C-6517, sm folio 125.00

Washington at Princeton, NC, 1846, C-6518, sm folio 400.00

Water Jump at Jerome Park, undtd, C-6564, sm folio 465.00

Water Rail Shooting, NC, 1855, C-6567, sm folio 800.00

Wedding Day, NC, undtd, C-6599, sm folio 125.00

Why Don't He Come?..., undtd, C-6653, sm folio 125.00

William Tell, Son's Head; undtd, C-6712, sm folio 95.00

Woodcock Shooting, 1870, C-6775, sm folio 550.00

Woodlands in Summer, undtd, C-6778, sm folio 250.00

Yacht Vesta..., undtd, C-6817, sm folio 400.00

Young Brood, 1870, C-6840, sm folio 250.00

Zachary Taylor, Nation's..., NC, 1847, C-6874, sm folio 150.00

Fox, R. Atkinson

A Canadian who worked as an artist in the 1880s, R. Atkinson Fox moved to New York about ten years later, where his original oils were widely sold at auction and through exhibitions. Today he is best known, however, for his prints, published by as many as twenty printmakers. More than thirty examples of his work appeared on Brown and Bigelow calendars, and it was used in many other forms of advertising as well. Though he was an accomplished artist able to interpret any subject well, he is today best known for his landscapes. Fox died in 1935. Our advisor for Fox prints is Pat Gibson whose address is listed in the Directory under California.

Aces All, 1929, 10x8" 245.00

Andrew Jackson, 1923 calendar, #742, 8x5" 80.00

At the Pool, cows, #579, 7½x10" 175.00

Benjamin Franklin, 1923 calendar, #744, 8x5" 80.00

Day Dreams, #410, 10x14" 250.00

Dreamy Paradise, 9x7" 95.00

English Garden, #57, fr, 14x20" 95.00

Faithful & True, old couple, #533, 7½x5½" 265.00

Flanders Field, #76, 6x12" 95.00

Girl of the Golden West, sgn Geo White (pseudonym), 6x8" 85.00

Grover Cleveland, 1923 calendar, #711, 5x3½" 80.00

Guardian of the Valley, mountain puzzle, #591 ....80.00

Heart's Desire, #55, fr, 12¼x22¼" 175.00

Love's Paradise, #13, 18x30" 275.00

Mirror Lake, #488, 5¼x3½" 95.00

Monarch of the North, polar bears, #613, 14½x10" 250.00

Mount Shasta, #486, 5¼x3½" 95.00

Music of the Waters, #218, 20x16" 150.00

October Days, birch trees & flowers, #44, 6x8" 65.00

Repairing of All Kinds, blksmith, #640, 13x10" 375.00

Seeking Protection, horses & fire, #363, 9½x8" 195.00

Spirit of Youth, #4, 18x10" 95.00

Tom & Jerry, horses, #583, 9x12" 165.00

When Evening Calls Them Home, cows by stream, #353, 9x7" .175.00

Gutmann, Bessie Pease

Delicately tinted prints of appealing children sometimes accompanied by their pets, sometimes asleep, often captured at some childhood activity are typical of the work of Gutmann; she painted lovely ladies as well and was a successful illustrator of children's books. Her career spanned the earlier decades of this century. Our advisor for this category is Earl MacSorley; he is listed in the Directory under Connecticut.

Afternoon Tea, Colonial	75.00
Awakening, #664	75.00
Baby's 1st Christmas, #158	150.00
Book, Through the Looking Glass	150.00
Butterfly, #632	150.00
Chuckles, #799	60.00
Contentment, #781, oval fr, 4½x8"	90.00
Daddy's Coming, #644	300.00
Double Blessing, #643	300.00
Dreamland's Border, #692	125.00
Feeling, #19	125.00
First Step, #815	150.00
Goldilocks, #771	450.00
Home Builders, #655	150.00
In Disgrace, orig oval fr	150.00
Kitty's Breakfast, #805	125.00
Little Bit of Heaven, #650	75.00
Little Bo Peep, blk & whte, #200	125.00
Message of the Roses, #641	250.00
Mighty Like a Rose, #642	150.00
Miss Flirt, #217	60.00
On the Up & Up, #796	125.00
Our Alarm Clock, #626	345.00
Priceless Necklace, #744	600.00
Reward, #794	150.00
Sonny Boy, #784	110.00
Sunbeam, #730, & Mischief, #729, matching frs, pr	400.00
Symphony, #702	395.00
Tasting, #21	125.00
Thank You God, #822	75.00
Tom Tom the Piper's Son, #219	200.00
Wedding Breakfast, Colonial	75.00
Winged Aureole, #700	350.00

Icart, Louis

Louis Icart (1888-1950) was a Parisian artist best known for his boudoir etchings in the '20s and '30s. In the '80s prices soared, primarily due to Japanese buying. The market began to readjust in 1990, and most etchings now sell at retail between $1,400.00 and $2,500.00. Value is determined by popularity and condition, more than by rarity. Original frames and matting are not important, as most collectors want the etchings restored to their original condition and protected with acid-free mats.

Beware of the following repro and knock-off items: 1. Pseudo engravings on white plastic with the Icart 'signature.' 2. Any bronzes with the Icart signature. 3. Most watercolors, especially if they look similar in subject matter to a popular etching. 4. Lithographs where the dot-matrix printing is visible under magnification. Some even have phony embossed seals or rubber stamp markings. Our advisor is William Holland, author of *Louis Icart: The Complete Etchings*; and *The Collectible Maxfield Parrish*; he is listed in the Directory under Pennsylvania.

Autumn Swirls, 1924, 17x12", orig fr	1,200.00
Basket of Apples, 1924, 17x12", orig fr	1,200.00
Bathers, 1926, 21x17", orig fr	1,400.00

Belle Rose, 1933, 16x21", M	2,200.00
Bluebirds, 1925, 19x15", orig fr	1,100.00
Casanova, 1928, 21x14"	1,265.00
Chronicles of Women: Strategist, 1917, 10x6⅞", EX	700.00
Cigarette Memories, 1931, 14½x17½", EX	4,000.00
Conchita, 1929, 20¼x13¼", EX	1,380.00
Coursing I, 1914, 12x16⅝", orig fr	5,465.00
Coursing II, 1929, 15¼x25¼", EX	3,575.00
Coursing III, 1930, 16x25¾"	4,300.00
Eve, 13x19", EX	1,850.00
Fair Dancer, HP touches, 1939, 19½x22⅞", EX	2,000.00
Faust, HP touches, 1928, 21x13", orig fr	800.00
French Doll, lady smoking & admiring doll, 14x18", EX	1,150.00
Gay Senorita, 1939, 17½x21½", orig fr	1,500.00
Guest, 1941, 17x11", EX	3,450.00
Hiding Place, 1927, 19x15", orig fr	1,150.00
Japanese Goldfish, 1924, 14x18", EX	1,500.00
Joan of Arc, 1929, 19x15", EX	1,500.00
Lady of the Camelias, prof fr & matted, 17x21", EX	1,500.00
Lady of the Camelias, 1927, 17x21", VG, orig fr	1,000.00
Laughing, 1930, 12x17", EX	1,650.00
Lilies, 1934, 28x19", EX	3,800.00
Look, 1928, 19x14", orig fr	1,000.00
Lou Lou, 1921, 17x12", EX	1,950.00
Love Letters, 1926, 14½x19", EX	1,500.00
Madame Butterfly, 1927, 20x13", EX	1,495.00
Masks, 1926, 18½x14½", M	1,400.00
Mealtime, 1927, 19x14", M, prof fr & matted	2,200.00
Miss California, 1927, rpr, 21x16¾"	1,725.00
Modern Eve, 1933, 21x16½", M	5,000.00
New Grapes, 1922, 20x13½", orig fr	1,100.00
Old Yarn, 1924, 17x21", orig fr	700.00
On the Champs Elysees, 1938, 15¾x22", orig fr	1,600.00
Orange Seller, 1929, 18½x14", orig fr	800.00
Perfect Harmony, 1932, 13x17", EX, orig fr	3,450.00
Pink Alcove, 1929, 10¼x12½", M	1,500.00
Pink Lady, HP touches, 1933, 8⅝x11", orig fr	800.00
Poem, 1928, 18¾x22¼", M	2,500.00
Salome, 19¾x13¾", EX, prof fr & matted	1,400.00
Sapho, 1929, 16¾x20⅝", EX	1,500.00
Seville, HP touches, 1928, 20x13¼", EX	1,150.00
Sleeping Beauty, 1927, 15x18½", orig fr	1,300.00
Smoke, 1926, 14x19", orig fr	1,200.00
Snow, 1922, 29½x14¼", orig fr	1,150.00
Spanish Dance, HP touches, 1929, 20⅞x14"	950.00
Speed, ca 1927, 15x25", EX, orig fr	3,000.00
Springtime, 1924, 18x14¼", orig fr	1,265.00
Springtime Promenade, 1948, 14½x19½", orig fr	2,000.00
Sweet Caress, 1924, 18x12", orig fr	1,400.00
Swimsuit, 14x10", orig fr	1,350.00
Symphony in Blue, lady by vase of flowers, 22x19", orig fr	1,650.00
Thieves, ca 1926, 16½x12", EX	2,000.00
Venus, 1928, 13¾x19", EX, orig fr	1,200.00
Victory, 1945, 10⅛x7⅞", M	700.00
Werther, lady by garden wall, 1928, 21x14"	2,000.00
Winter Bouquet, 1924, 16½x11¾"	1,900.00
Youth, 1930, 24½x16", EX, orig fr	4,000.00

Kurz and Allison

Louis Kurz founded the Chicago Lithograph Company in 1833. Among his most notable works were a series of thirty-six Civil War scenes and one hundred illustrations of Chicago architecture. His company was destroyed in the Great Fire of 1871, and in 1880 Kurz formed a partnership with Alexander Allison, an engraver. Until both retired in 1903, they produced hundreds of lithographs in color as well as black and white.

Assault on Fort Sanders, lg folio 275.00
Battle of Bull Run, Fought July 21, 1861, lg folio 190.00
Battle of Cedar Creek, Sheridan's Cavalry; lg folio 285.00
Battle of Champion Hills, lg folio 130.00
Battle of Five Forks, VA; lg folio 275.00
Battle of Fort Donnelson, lg folio, EX 185.00
Battle of Nashville, on brd, rstr tears, 17½x25" 275.00
Capture of Fort Fisher, lg folio 260.00
Fort Pillow Massacre, lg folio 315.00
Great Connemaugh...Disaster (Johnston flood), lg folio 335.00
Last Charge & Capture of Port Arthur, lg folio 200.00
Siege of Vicksburg, lg folio 275.00
Trial of Robert Emmett, His Closing Remarks; lg folio 200.00

McKenney and Hall

Ahyouwaighs Chief of 6 Nations, 1845, 8½x6½" 415.00
Anacamegisca/Foot Prints, Chippewa chief, Biddle, 1838, 18x13" .235.00
Ap-Pa-Noo-Se, Sauke chief, 1838, 18x13" 825.00
Chittee-Yoholo, Seminole chief, 1845, 9¼x6" 200.00
Chon-man-I-Case, Otto half chief, 1836, 16x10"+modern fr 600.00
Foke-Luste-Hajo, Seminole chief, 1845, 8x6½" 360.00
Jackepa or The Six, Chippewa chief, Rice/Clark, 1843, 18x13" .325.00
Katawabeda, Chippewa chief, Bowen, 1841, 18x13" 295.00

Keokuk, Chief of the Sacs and Foxes, 1836, 18½x12¾", matted in contemporary frame, $1,600.00.

Little Crow, Sioux chief, Greenough, 1838, lg folio 200.00
Micanopy, Seminole chief, Greenough, 1838, 18x13" 395.00
Mistippee, 1845, 9¼x6" 250.00
Mon-Ka-Ush-Ka, Sioux chief, 1845, 8½x6½" 330.00
Nah-Et-Iuc-Hopie, 1843, 16x10"+modern fr 350.00
Nea Mathla, Seminole chief, 1838, lg folio 380.00
Neomonie, Iowa chief, Greenough, 1838, 18x13" 195.00
No-Tin, Chippewa chief, 1845, 9¼x6" 150.00
On-Ge-Wae, Chippewa chief, 1843, 16x10"+modern fr 400.00
Peah-Mus-Ka, Musquakee chief, 1843, 9x6" 330.00
Pee-Che-Kir, Chippewa chief, 1843, 16x10"+modern fr 400.00
Petalesharro, Pawnee brave, 1845, 9x6" 330.00
Push-Ma-Ta-Ha, Choctaw warrior, 1838, 18x13" 935.00
Red Jacket, Seneca war chief, 1837, 18x13" 1,300.00
Se-Loc-Ta, Creek chief, 1845, 9¼x6" 200.00
Shau-Hau-Napo-Tinia, Iowa chief, 1845, 9x6" 200.00
Tishcohan, Delaware chief, Biddle, 1837, 18x13" 145.00
Waapashaw, Sioux chief, 1836, 18x13" 200.00
Watchemone, Iowa chief, Greenough, 1838, 18x13" 295.00
Wesh Cubb or The Sweet, Chippewa chief, Biddle, 1838, 18x13" ..215.00

Mucha, Alphonse

Mucha became famous for his beautiful Art Nouveau lithographs featuring Sarah Bernhardt and Job cigarette papers, which he issued in the 1890s. Born in Prague in 1860, he studied there as well as in Paris and for a time taught at the New York School of Applied Design for women before returning to Prague.

Automne, 1903, 27¾x12" 6,400.00
Biscuits Lefevre Utile-Flirt, young couple, 24½x10½" 3,500.00
Figures Decoratives, 1905, 14x10⅜" 300.00
Gismonda, Les Maitres de L'Affice, 14x5½" 865.00
Job, lady w/blk hair on mc ground, fr, 1898, 57x38", EX 7,300.00
Lorenzaccio, 1896, 12⅞x4½", EX 1,265.00
Monaco Monte-Carlo, 1897, 41¼x27¾", VG 9,200.00

Monaco-Monte-Carlo, lady within a halo of flowers and birds, 1897, 42¼x29¼", $9,000.00.

Monaco Monte-Carlo, 1897, 43¾x29¾", VG 6,900.00
Precious Stones: La Topaz, 1900, 23¾x9½", VG 5,175.00
Reverie, 1896, 25x18¾" 1,400.00
Russian Restituenda, 1922, 30x17" 1,200.00
Wiener Chic, lady in wht, 1900, 15x11", VG 1,200.00
Zodiac La Plume, maid in profile, 1896, 25¾x19" 10,350.00

Prang, Louis

Battle of Antietam, lg folio 140.00
Battle of Manila, colorful sea battle, 1896, 16x20" 125.00
Battle of Port Hudson, lg folio 170.00
Sheridan's Final Charge at Winchester, lg folio 170.00
Siege of Vicksburg, The Assault on Fort Hill; sgn, fr, 1880 ....395.00

Yard Longs

Values for yard-long prints are given for examples in **near mint** condition, full length, nicely framed, and with the original glass. To learn more about this popular area of collector interest, we recommend *Those Wonderful Yard-Long Prints and More, More Wonderful Yard-Long Prints,* Book 2, and *Yard-Long Prints,* Book 3, by our advisors Bill and June Keagy, and Charles and Joan Rhoden. They are listed in the Directory under Indiana and Illinois respectively. A word of caution: watch for reproductions; **know your dealer.**

American Farming Magazine, WH Lister, 1918, info on bk 350.00
Battle of the Chicks, sgn Ben Austrian, ca 1920 ....250.00
Beatrice, advertising Belle of Drexel cigar, c 1911 ....450.00
Carnation Symphony 200.00
Carrier's Greeting, 1907 Peoria Evening Journal 400.00
Cats & Kittens on a Seesaw, c 1893 by Art Interchange Co 275.00

Dogwood & Violets, Paul DeLongpre 250.00
Ducklings by WM Carey, baby ducks in & around pool water 250.00
Easter Greetings, Paul DeLongpre, c 1894 ....400.00
Girl w/the Laughing Eyes, F Carlyle, c 1910 ....250.00
Harvest Moon, sgn Frank H Desch, John Clay & Co, 1922 ....400.00
Hope, Union Pacific Tea Co, c 1898, 16x40" 350.00
Hula Girl on Surfboard, sgn Gene Pressler 350.00
In Sunny Africa, Jos Hoover, #1038, 4th in series, c 1904 ....350.00
Kittens w/Mother 250.00
Metropolitan Life Ins Co, 4 stages of life, 1907 ....400.00
Pabst Extract, different baby for ea month, 1904 ....350.00
Pabst Extract American Girl, sgn CW Hennnig, 1912 ....350.00
Priscilla, Schlitz Malt Extract, 1910 ....450.00
Selz Good Shoes, lady in wht gown & shoes, sgn Christy 350.00
Winter Solace, sgn Changler lower left corner 350.00
Yard of Cherries & Flowers, sgn Leroy 200.00
Yard of Dogs, c 1903 ....250.00

Purinton

Founded in 1936 in Wellsville, Ohio, Purinton Pottery relocated in 1941 in Shippenville, Pennsylvania, and began producing hand-painted wares that are today attracting the interest of collectors of 'country-type' dinnerware. Using bold brush strokes of vivid color, simple yet attractive patterns such as Apple, Fruits, Tea Rose, and Pennsylvania Dutch were manufactured in tableware sets and accessory pieces. For more information we recommend *Purinton Pottery* by Susan Morris; she is listed in the Directory under Oregon. Our advisor for this category is Pat Dole; she is listed in the Directory under Alabama.

Ashtray, Apple, wire in middle for cigarettes, 5½" 40.00
Ashtray, blindman's; Intaglio, 4½" 75.00
Baker, Petals, 7" 35.00
Baker, Turquoise, 7" 30.00
Bank, Uncle Sam, 4½" 50.00
Banks, piggy; mini, 4" 25.00
Bean pot, Intaglio, 3¾" 30.00
Bottle, vinegar; Fruit, cobalt trim, 1-pt, 9½" 35.00
Bottle, water; turq or yel, 9", ea 35.00
Bowl, fruit; Cactus Flower, 12" 85.00
Bowl, fruit; Normandy Plaid, 12" 35.00
Bowl, fruit; Petals, 12" 50.00
Bowl, range; Grapes, w/lid, 5½" 45.00
Bowl, spaghetti; Normandy Plaid, 14½" 55.00
Butter dish, Apple, 6½" 65.00
Candle holder, Intaglio, brn, aqua or coral, 6x2", ea 55.00
Candle holder, Saraband, 6x2" 50.00

Photo courtesy Pat Dole

Pennsylvania Dutch, 4-piece canister set, $450.00.

Canister, Fruit, rnd, wooden lids, 7½" 65.00
Coaster, Crescent Flower, 3½" 40.00
Cocktail dish, Fruit, 11¾" 55.00
Coffee server, Seaform, 9" 125.00

Coffeepot, Petals, 8-cup 75.00
Cookie jar, Fruit, red trim, oval, 9" 60.00
Cookie jar, Heather Plaid, oval, 9½" 60.00
Cookie jar, Pennsylvania Dutch, sq shape, w/pottery lid, 9½" 125.00
Creamer & sugar bowl, mini; Mountain Rose, 2" 50.00
Cup, Ming Tree, 2½" 15.00
Decanter, book; set of 3, metal rack, 7¾" 125.00
Decanter, mini; Intaglio, 5" 35.00
Decanter, Mountain Rose, 5" 45.00
Dish, Apple, w/lid, 9" 65.00
Dish, candy; Peasant House, 6" 60.00
Dish, jam & jelly; Apple, 5½" 45.00
Dish, jam & jelly; Pennsylvania Dutch, 5½" 65.00
Dish, pickle; Maywood, 6" 15.00
Dish, relish; 3-section, metal or pottery hdl, 10", ea 45.00
Dutch shoes, plain or decor, 4" to 5", ea 10.00
Ewer, souvenir; Cook Forest, 9" 150.00
Heather Plaid, salt & pepper shakers, pr 32.00
Jar, biscuit; Ivy-Blossom, 8" 55.00
Jar, grease; Apple, w/lid, 5½" 85.00
Jar, marmalade; Mountain Rose, 4½" 65.00
Jar, marmalade; Palm Tree, 4½" 125.00
Jardiniere, Ivy-Bl & Red Blossom, 5" 30.00
Jug, Dutch; Mountain Rose, 2-pt, 5¾" 85.00
Jug, honey; Apple, 6¼" 55.00
Jug, honey; Petals, 6¼" 45.00
Jug, Kent; Ivy-Red Blossom, 1-pt, 4½" 30.00
Jug, Kent; Turquoise, 1-pt, 4½" 40.00
Jug, oasis; Desert Scene, 9½x9½", minimum value 500.00
Jug, Rebecca; Mountain Rose, 7½" 45.00
Lamp, table; Leaves, 6¼" (pottery section) 65.00
Lamp, TV; Red Feather, 8½" 75.00
Mug, beer; Palm Tree, 16-oz, 4¾" 85.00
Mug, beer; Saraband, 16-oz, 4¾" 30.00
Mug, Heather Plaid, w/hdl, 8-oz, 4" 30.00
Mug, juice; Apple, 6-oz, 2½" 15.00
Mug, juice; Chartreuse, 6-oz, 2½" 15.00
Pitcher, beverage; Normandy Plaid, 2-pt, 6¼" 55.00
Planter, basket; Palm Tree, 6¼" 100.00
Planter, basket; Pennsylvania Dutch, 6¼" 85.00
Planter, rum jug; Heather Plaid, 6½" 40.00
Planter, sprinkler shape, Red Tulip, 5½" 65.00
Planter, Tea Rose, 5" 65.00
Plate, breakfast; Sunflower, 8½" 45.00
Plate, chop; Fruit; 12" 35.00
Plate, chop; Maywood, 12" 30.00
Plate, lap; Apple, 8½" 15.00
Plate, salad; Saraband, 6¾" 6.00
Plate, souvenir; Alpha Chalet, 9¾", minimum value 175.00
Platter, chop; Intaglio, 12" 25.00
Platter, grill; Apple, 12" 45.00
Platter, meat; Pennsylvania Dutch, 12" 50.00
Saucer, Chartreuse, 5½" 3.00
Saucer, Seaform, 5½" 8.00
Shakers, Crescent Flower, rnd, 2¾", pr 65.00
Shakers, range; Daisy, red trim, 4", pr 50.00
Shakers, stacking; Pennsylvania Dutch, 2¼", pr 60.00
Shakers, Tea Rose, mini jug style, 2½", pr 50.00
Soup & sandwich set, Intaglio, plate, 11", cup, 2¼x4" 50.00
Teapot, Ivy-Red Blossom, w/drip filter, 6-cup, 9" 75.00
Teapot, Normandy Plaid, 6-cup, 6" 50.00
Teapot, Three Pansies, triangular hdl, 6-cup, 5¾" 125.00
Toothpick holder, rolling pin shape, 5" 25.00
Tray, roll; Apple, 11" 35.00

Tray, tidbit; Seafoam, 9x10" dia **75.00**
Tumbler, Chartreuse, 12-oz, 5" **20.00**
Tumbler, Provincial Fruit, 12-oz, 5" **20.00**
Vase, cornucopia; Ivy-Red Blossom, 6" **20.00**
Vase, Crescent Flower, hdld, 7½" **125.00**
Vase, pillow; Maywood, 6¾" **25.00**
Vase, Shooting Star, 6" **25.00**
Wall pocket, Heather Plaid, 3½" **35.00**
Wall pocket, Mountain Rose, 3½" **65.00**
Wall pocket, Sunny, 3½" **40.00**

Purses

Beaded purses and bags represent an area of collecting interest that is very popular today. Purses from the early 1800s are often decorated with small, brightly colored glass beads. Cut steel beads were popular in the 1840s and remained stylish until about 1930. Mesh purses are also popular. In the 1820s mesh was woven. Chain-link mesh came into usage in the 1890s, followed by the enamel mesh bags carried by the flappers in the 1920s. Purses are divided into several categories by (a) construction techniques — whether beaded, embroidered, or a type of needlework; (b) material — fabric or metal; and (c) design and style. Condition is very important. Watch for dry, brittle leather or fragile material. For those interested in learning more, we recommend *Antique Purses, A History, Identification, and Value Guide, Second Edition*, by Richard Holiner; *More Beautiful Purses*, and *Combs and Purses*, both by Evelyn Haertigi of Carmel, California. Our advisor for this category is Veronica Trainer; she is listed in the Directory under Ohio.

Beaded, bl & red flowers on wht, silver filigree fr, fringe, 11x7" ...**300.00**
Beaded, blk geometric design on ivory, silver filigree fr, 7x6" **90.00**
Beaded, blk/gr/wht checked design, blk/wht fringe, gilt fr, 9x7" ...**90.00**
Beaded, castle scene w/jeweled fr, chain hdl, fringe, 11x7" **225.00**
Beaded, floral tapestry, daisies on gilt fr, chain hdl w/swans **225.00**
Beaded, floral tapestry w/jeweled fr, chain hdl, fringe, 13x9" **300.00**
Beaded, flowers/geometric design on gr, gilt fr, fringe, 15x8" **300.00**
Beaded, gold w/allover fringe, rope closure, 8½x6" **75.00**
Beaded, gold w/mc rhinestones on gilt fr, fancy closure, 8x7" **100.00**
Beaded, lav w/allover fringe, matching hdl, 6x5" **70.00**
Beaded, mc flowers on blk, clutch style, 5x8½" **75.00**
Beaded, mc w/basket bottom, drawstring closure, Japan, 7x8" **75.00**
Beaded, orange dmn-shape w/fringe, gilt fr, 12x7" **130.00**
Beaded, orange w/fringe, tassel at bottom, rope closure, 11x5" **75.00**
Beaded, pearlized w/ivory fringe, drawstring closure, 8½x5" **65.00**
Beaded, scenic tapestry w/jeweled fr, fringe, 11x7½" **240.00**
Beaded, scrolls on shades of bl, chain hdl, fringe, 13x9" **270.00**
Crocheted, ivory, elongated oval w/2 hdls, Japan, 5x8½" **75.00**

Lucite, tortoise shell with rhinestones and brass trim, 4x8" (excluding handle), $115.00.

Lucite, brn burl-like w/carryall, swing hdl, Wilardy, 7¾x8" **350.00**
Lucite, marbleized gray, w/carryall, swing hdls, Wilardy, 4x7" **225.00**

Lucite, wht sparkle confetti w/carryall, swing hdl, 3¼x10" **275.00**
Mesh, blk leaf design on orange, orange fr, Whiting & Davis, 7" ..**115.00**
Mesh, butterfly & flowers, silver filigree fr, Mandalian, 7x4" **150.00**
Mesh, Deco-style geometrics, fringe, Mandalian, 9x5" **175.00**
Mesh, floral abstract, gilt fr/ornate closure, Whiting & Davis **100.00**
Mesh, German .800 fine silver w/int change purse, 1900 ....**100.00**
Mesh, German silver w/floral-emb gilt fr, fringe, lg, EX **155.00**
Mesh, gold Beadlite, chain hdl, Whiting & Davis, 5x3½" **45.00**
Mesh, gold dmn design on bl, gilt fr, Mandalian, 7x4½" **90.00**
Mesh, gold-tone, bl cabochon thumb pc, Whiting & Davis, 8x3" ..**225.00**
Mesh, gold-tone, cloisonne lid w/HP roses on compact, Evans, 10x5" .**275.00**
Mesh, gr enameled costume bag w/compact, Whiting & Davis, 6x5" ..**600.00**
Mesh, peacocks/feather design, silver fr, fringe, Mandalian, 8" ...**115.00**
Mesh, SP w/emb fr, tassel & chain hdl, 1920s, 8x3½" **400.00**
Suede, brass fr decorated w/swirls & rhinestones, clutch, 4x9" ...**225.00**
Suede (antelope), brass fr w/transparent beads, Argentina, 6x4" ...**225.00**

Puzzles

'Jigsaw' puzzles have been around almost as long as games. The first examples were handcrafted from wood, and they are extremely difficult to find. Most of the early examples featured moral subjects just as the board games did. By the 1890s jigsaw puzzles had become a major form of home entertainment. During the Depression years jigsaw puzzles were set up on card tables in almost every home. The early wood examples are the most valuable.

Cube puzzles, or blocks, were often made by the same companies as the board games. Again, early examples display the finest quality lithography. While all subjects are collectible, some (such as Santa blocks) often command prices higher than games from the same period. Our advisor for this category is Norm Vigue; he is listed in the Directory under Massachusetts. In the listings all items are jigsaw puzzles unless noted otherwise.

After the Rain, 80 wooden pcs, Parker Bros, ca 1909, EX **15.00**
Blossom Time, plywood, HC MacDonald, 1930s, 556-pc, EXIB .**100.00**
Child's Companion ABC Picture Blocks, London, 11x7", EXIB ...**465.00**
Cowboys, cb, 50 interlocking pcs, Platt & Munk, '40s, 9x11", EXIB ...**15.00**
Ducks & Geese, Springbok, 500 pcs, 1966, 20x20", EXIB **5.00**
Fire Engine, jigsaw, McLoughlin, 1894, EXIB **200.00**
Home Memories, cb, Big Star, 250 pcs, 1930s, 13½x10", EXIB **4.00**
Leaving the Inn, J Straus, 300 pcs, 1940s, 16x12", EXIB **20.00**
Mediterranean Villa #120, Perfect, 1940s, EXIB **10.00**
Old Windmill at Sunset, Parker Bros, 302 pcs, 1939, EXIB **85.00**
Pirate's Sweetheart, Tuco/Art Picture Puzzle, 1933, EXIB **6.00**
Pulling the Splinter, Stoughton Stud/Tiz-A-Teeze, 1930s, EXIB ..**22.00**
Seaman's Joy & Sorrow, Weigel/GW Faber, 1850s, EXIB **1,350.00**
Three O'Clock in the Morning, Perfect, 1950, 16x120", EXIB **8.00**
Victorian block type, makes 6 scenes, late 1800s, EXIB **250.00**
Young Ship Builder's Picture Blocks, McLoughlin Bros, 1892, EXIB .**385.00**

Personalities, Movies, and TV Shows

Alice in Wonderland, fr tray, unmk (not Disney), 1950s, EX **25.00**
Bat Masterson, Giant Jigsaw, Colorforms, 1960, NMIB **35.00**
Batman, jigsaw, chasing Penguin, Whitman, 1966, EXIB **10.00**
Bozo, jigsaw, on high wire, 1969, NMIB **10.00**
Cisco Kid, fr tray, on horse, Saalfield, 1951, EX **25.00**
Deputy, Milton Bradley, 1950, set of 3, NMIB **50.00**
Disneyland Frontierland, cb litho, Jaymar, 1950s, EXIB **20.00**
Donald Duck, fr tray, Whitman, 1950, 15x11½", NM **20.00**
Donald Duck in Disneyland, jigsaw, Jaymar, 1960s, NMIB **12.50**
Family Affair, jigsaw, Whitman, 1970, 100-pc, 14x18", NMIB **12.00**

Flintstones, 4 7x10" jigsaws, Warren, 1976, NMIB **12.00**
Frankenstein Jr, jigsaw, Whitman, 1968, EXIB **20.00**
Gunsmoke, fr tray, 1959, NM **20.00**
Hobbit, jigsaw, Giant, 1971, 500+pcs, 25x21", EXIB **15.00**
Howdy Doody, fr tray, 1953, NM **35.00**
Huckleberry Hound, fr tray, 1961, EX **22.50**
Jemima Puddleduck, figural, Warne, 1930s, NMIB **130.00**
Katzenjammer Kids, jigsaw, Jaymar, 1950s, NMIB **22.00**
King Leonardo, fr tray, Jaymar, 1961, 11x13", EX **20.00**
Little LuLu, fr tray, Whitman #4428, 1959, EX/NM **35.00**
Little LuLu, jigsaw, Whitman #4404, late 1940s, NMIB **45.00**
Man From UNCLE, Micro-Film Affair, M Bradley, 600+ pcs, NMIB ..**35.00**
Mother Goose, wooden, Little Jack Horner, NMIB **125.00**
Raggedy Ann & Andy, fr, tray, Milton Bradley, 1955, EX **15.00**
Rootie Kazootie, fr tray, NM **20.00**
Ruff 'N Reddy, fr tray, early, NM **20.00**
Shotgun Slade, jigsaw, Milton Bradley, 1960, 100 pcs, NMIB **18.00**
Superman, jigsaw, Whitman, 1966, 150-pc, 14x18", NMIB **15.00**

Welcome Back Kotter, frame tray, Whitman, 1977, M in sealed package, $12.50.

Woody Woodpecker, fr tray, NM **12.00**
Yogi Bear, fr tray, 1961, NM **15.00**
20,000 Leagues Under the Sea, fr tray, Jaymar, 1954, NMIB **18.00**
6 Million Dollar Man Bionic Crisis, Parker Bros, MIB **10.00**

Pyrography

Pyrography, also known as wood burning, Flemish art, or poker work, is the art of burning designs into wood or leather and has been practiced over the centuries in many countries.

In the late 1800s pyrography became the hot new hobby for thousands of Americans who burned designs inspired by the popular artists of the day including Mucha, Gibson, Fisher, and Corbett. Thousands of wooden boxes, wall plaques, novelties, and pieces of furniture that they purchased from local general stores or from mail-order catalogs were burned and painted. These pieces were manufactured by companies such as The Flemish Art Company of New York and Thayer & Chandler of Chicago, who printed the designs on wood for the pyrographers to burn.

This Victorian fad developed into a new form of artistic expression as the individually burned and painted pieces reflected the personality of the pyrographers. The more adventurous started to burn between the lines and developed a style of 'all-over burning' that today is known as Pyromania. Others not only created their own designs but even made the pieces to be decorated. Both these developments are particularly valued today as true examples of American folk art.

By the 1930s its popularity had declined and, like Mission furniture, was neglected by generations of collectors and dealers. The recent appreciation of Victoriana, the Arts and Crafts Movement, the American West, and the popularity of turn-of-the-century graphic art has rekindled interest in pyrography which embraces all these styles.

A new book, *The Burning Passion — Antique and Collectible Pyrography,* by Carole and Richard Smyth, our advisors for this category, is currently available from the authors; they are listed in the Directory under New York.

Key: hb — hand burned

Photo courtesy Carole and Richard Smyth

Combination chair-table, allover hand-burned and painted poinsettia designs and Rest-Ye and Thankful-Be on chair back with velvet to center of table top, EX, $950.00.

Book rack, hb/pnt girl w/book, 5¾" W, extends to 15¾" L **150.00**
Box, floral decor, 14½" **40.00**
Chest, blanket; hb/pnt swans/lady's head/flowers/etc, ca 1890 ....**850.00**
Coat hanger, hb/pnt poppies & leaves, Mother Dearest **80.00**
Cue holder, hb pool-hall scene, folk art, unique **650.00**
Egg cups, hb/pnt, pr **60.00**
Flatware box, factory burned/pnt poinsettias, Rogers, 9x11x5" ...**195.00**
Footstool, hb/pnt allover w/owl/branches/leaves **250.00**
Frame, hb/pnt flower garland, Thayer-Chandler, 8" dia **85.00**
Frame, triple; hb fox/dogs/etc, +3 orig hunt prints, 16x33" **365.00**
Gameboard, hb/pnt ea side/edges, Flemish Art, 15" sq (open) **200.00**
Knife rack, hb Lizzie Borden w/axe, 5 hooks below, rare **550.00**
Magazine stand, 4-shelf, burned/pnt florals, Thayer-Chandler, 48" ..**800.00**
Medicine chest, hb/pnt Nouveau lady & vines, wall mt **450.00**
Mirror, hand; hb/pnt lady's head w/flowing hair, 13¼x6¾" **180.00**
Nut bowl, hb/pnt squirrel on branch, Flemish Art Co #816, 5" **65.00**
Panel, basswood, burned/pnt orange, Thayer-Chandler, 16x30" ...**465.00**
Panel, hp panel after pnting: To the Feast, minor gold, 9x34" **500.00**
Pedestal, hb/pnt Nouveau flowers & vines, 45" **400.00**
Plaque, cvd/burned/pnt strawberry basket, 3-ply, 12" dia **70.00**
Plaque, girl bathing puppies, #854, 14½" **125.00**
Plaque, hb orange cat w/bow, paper 1912 calendar, 5¾" dia **50.00**
Plaque, Nouveau lady w/cherries, 19½" **150.00**
Ribbon holder, hb/pnt Sunbonnet babies (3), 5x12" **160.00**
Spoon holder, geometric florals, wall hanging, 1915, 10x8" **45.00**
Tie rack, factory stamp, HP soldier/nurse/sailor, WWI motto **125.00**

Quezal

The Quezal Art Glass and Decorating Company of Brooklyn, New York, was founded in 1901 by Martin Bach. A former Tiffany employee, Bach's glass closely resembled that of his former employer. Most pieces were signed 'Quezal,' a name taken from a Central American bird. After

Bach's death in 1920, his son-in-law, Conrad Vohlsing, continued to produce a Quezal-type glass in Elmhurst, New York, which he marked 'Lustre Art Glass.' See also that particular category. Examples listed here are signed unless noted otherwise.

Bowl, centerpc; amber w/silver-bl stretch irid, 11¼" 460.00
Lamp, feathers on gold irid 10" shade; bronze std, 19" 1,725.00
Shade, feathers on gold, 6", pr 200.00
Shade, leaves, yel & gr on gold-threaded opal, 5½x5" 115.00
Shade, wht opal w/gold int bell form, 4⅝x4" dia, 6 for 635.00
Sherbet, feathers, gr w/gold on opal irid, gold int, 3¾" 1,300.00
Vase, amber, cylindrical w/disk ft, 9⅞" 350.00
Vase, amber w/bl irid, lt stain, 4¼" 400.00
Vase, amber w/gold irid, classic oval body, 7" 485.00
Vase, entwined swirls, gold on opal, 12½" 1,100.00

Vase, gold feathers pulled and hooked on pale yellow, violet, and blue highlights and wide green outlining, #A145, 9", $2,100.00.

Vase, feathers, gr & gold on golden-amber irid, #669, 6¾" 2,300.00
Vase, feathers, gr on gold irid, #P353, 7¾" 1,265.00
Vase, feathers, gr on ivory w/gold, ftd trumpet form, 8" 800.00
Vase, feathers, gr w/gold on opal, trumpet form, 14" 1,300.00
Vase, feathers, gr & gold, gold ft/int, petaled/ruffled, 10½" 2,000.00
Vase, floral, gr & gold w/gold vertical vines on opal irid, 8¾" .1,900.00
Vase, gold, ovoid, 5¾" 450.00
Vase, gold w/mc irid, flared/ruffled trumpet form, #358, 5" 650.00
Vase, hearts & vines, aubergine w/gold irid, teardrop, 5¼" 4,600.00
Vase, jack-in-pulpit; feathers, wht on gold irid, 11" 3,000.00
Vase, leaves, gold & bl on opal irid, gold threads, 6½" 850.00
Vase, leaves, gold irid on opal, gold top, flared neck, 9" 2,000.00
Vase, leaves, gr w/gold irid on opal irid, 5½" 850.00
Vase, leaves etc, silver o/l on rainbow irid, dbl gourd, 8½" 3,000.00
Vase, lily; gold w/allover rainbow irid, squatty base, 4" 600.00
Vase, swirls, bl & gold on wht, bullet-nose base w/3 ft, 8" 2,500.00

Quilts

Quilts, while made of necessity, nevertheless represent an art form which expresses the character and the personality of the designer. During the 17th and 18th centuries, quilts were considered a necessary part of a bride's hope chest; the traditional number required to be properly endowed for marriage was a 'baker's dozen'! American Colonial quilts reflect the English and French taste of our ancestors. They would include the classifications known as Lindsey-Woolsey and the central medallion applique quilts fashioned from imported copper-plate printed fabrics.

By 1829 spare time was slightly more available, so women gathered in quilting bees. This not only was a way of sharing the work but also gave them an opportunity to show off their best work. The hand-dyed and pieced quilts emerged, and they are now known as Sampler, Album, and Friendship quilts. By 1845 American printed fabric was available.

In 1793 Eli Whitney developed the cotton gin; as a result, textile production in America became industrialized. Soon inexpensive fabrics were readily available, and ladies were able to choose from colorful prints and solids to add contrast to their work. Both pieced and appliqued work became popular.

Pieced quilts were considered utilitarian, while appliqued quilts were shown with pride of accomplishment at the fair or used when itinerant preachers traveled through and stayed for a visit. Today many collectors prize pieced quilts and their intricate geometric patterns above all other types. Many of these designs were given names: Daisy and Oak Leaf, Grandmother's Flower Garden, Log Cabin, and Ocean Wave are only a few. Appliqued quilts involved stitching one piece — carefully cut into a specific form such as a leaf, a flower, or a stylized device — onto either a large one-piece ground fabric or an individual block. Often the background fabric was quilted in a decorative pattern such as a wreath or medallions.

Amish women scorned printed calicos as 'worldly' and instead used colorful blocks set with black fabrics to produce a stunning pieced effect. To show their reverence for God, the Amish would often include a 'superstition' block which represented the 'imperfection' of Man!

One of the most valuable quilts in existence is the Baltimore Album quilt. Made between 1840-1860 only three-hundred or so still exist today. They have been known to fetch over $100,000.00 at prominent auction houses in New York City. Usually each block features elaborate applique work such as a basket of flowers, patriotic flags and eagles, the Oddfellow's heart in hand, etc. The border can be sawtooth, meandering, or swags and tassels.

During the Victorian period the crazy quilt emerged. This style became the most popular quilt ever in terms of sheer numbers produced and popularity. The crazy quilt was formed by random pieces put together following no organized lines and was usually embellished by elaborate embroidery stitches. Fabrics of choice were brocades, silks, and velvets.

Another type of quilting, highly prized and rare today, is trapunto. These quilts were made by first stitching the outline of the design onto a solid sheet of fabric which was backed with a second having a much looser weave. White was often favored, but color was sometimes used for accent. The design (grapes, flowers, leaves, etc.) was padded through openings made by separating the loose weave of the underneath fabric; a backing was added and the three layers quilted as one.

Besides condition, value is judged on intricacy of pattern, color effect, and craftsmanship. Examine the stitching. Quality quilts have from ten to twelve stitches to the inch. A stitch is defined as any time a needle pierces through the fabric. So you may see five threads but ten (stitches) have been used. In the listings that follow, examples rated excellent have minor defects, otherwise assume them to be free of any damage, soil, or wear. Values given here are auction results; retail may be somewhat higher. Our advisor is Craig Ambrose; he is listed in the Directory under Iowa.

Key:
dmn — diamond	mp — machine pieced
embr — embroidered	ms — machine sewn
hs — hand sewn	Vt — variant
hq — hand quilted, quilting	X — cross

Amish

Blk rectangle in borders of purple & blk, purple binding, lg 750.00
Fence Row Vt, band border, sawtooth edge, 1910, 82x64", EX ..1,100.00
Flower Garden, 3-color, PA, 1910, 78x89" 375.00
Red & gr bars, late 1800s, 85x80", EX 850.00
Tumbling Block Vt, mc w/dk brn bking, crib sz, 34" sq 600.00
9-Patch, 24 blocks, vine/diagonal stitching, 1900, lg 765.00

Appliqued

Photo courtesy Marie Miller's American Quilts

Poinsettia Applique, small appliqued berries add fine detailing, ca 1860, 86x86", $1,295.00.

Animals/people/ladder/house/Baby/etc, mc wools, 1880s, 32x46" .1,750.00
Baltimore Album, Broderie perse style, fancy quilting, 1852, M ..18,500.00
Butterfly Charm, mc on wht, hs, 1920s, 75x61" 350.00
Eagle, yel on wht, hs, hq grid, 1930s, 94x78", EX 350.00
Floral designs (9/stylized), red/bl on wht, 1916, 84" sq, EX 375.00
Floral medallions, 4-color on wht, hs/embr, 1930s, 86x74" 750.00
Floral medallions (16), border swags, well quilted, 1930, 81" sq ...335.00
Floral medallions (9), red/gr on wht, worn, 87" sq 275.00
Floral medallions (9), red/gr on wht, 70x70", EX 330.00
Floral medallions (9), red/gr/yel/bl on wht w/gr, 86" sq 415.00
Floral medallions (9), vining border, solids on wht, 97" sq 660.00
Floral medallions (9), vining border, 4-color, 80x84", EX 575.00
Floral sprays & border on wht, EX quilting, 19th C, 67x80" 475.00
Floral wreaths (12), mc calicos on wht w/red binding, 96x72" ...575.00
Friendship, flowers/birds on wht, gr border, 1844-47, 104x106" ..2,300.00
Garden Bouquet, mc prints/wht, hs, ltweight, 1930s, 74x62" 350.00
Roses & vining border, gr calico/solid red, hs, 1880, 96" sq 750.00
Tulips, red/gr on yel calico w/gr piping, 1880, 98" sq, NM 995.00
Tulips, yel/goldenrod/gr on wht, 79x79", EX 935.00

Pieced

Adirondack Log Cabin, 6-color, ms/quilted, 1940, 78x90" 225.00
Around the World, silk bking, 86x86", EX 300.00
Bear Tracks in a Square, 30 blocks on cranberry, 1800s, 55x71" ...385.00
Bow Tie, navy/wht, ms binding, 88x70", NM 275.00
Bricks patchwork, bl border, hs, 1940s, lg, EX 275.00
Carpenter's Square, indigo (bl) dbl border, 1920s 875.00
Checkerboard, mc w/red & wht stripe border, 73x73", EX 330.00
Corduroy-Lone Star pastels on navy, starry border, ca 1940 ....450.00
Crazy, multiple fabrics w/much embr, ca 1885, lg, EX 625.00
Crazy, multiple fabrics w/much embr, 2-sided, ca 1880s, VG 450.00
Crazy, multiple fabrics w/red velvet border, dtd 1908, lg 675.00
Crazy, silks, velvets, cottons, sm pcs, Victorian, lg, EX 750.00
Crazy Fan, wool tied/floral embr, 1800s, 73x81", EX 1,045.00
Double Irish Chain, quilted scrolls & wreaths, 1940, 72x84", EX ..350.00
Double Irish Chain w/sawtooth edge, mc calicos, 92x80", EX 180.00
Drunkard's Path, bl/wht, lt wear, 76x76", EX 330.00
Feathered Star, Indigo Dbl Sawtooth border, 1930s, 82x86", M ..1,250.00
Flower Garden, wht border, old but newly quilted, 87x95" 350.00
Irish Chain, bl/wht, circle quilting, 76x79", EX 385.00

Log Cabin, mc wool/silk/cotton, 19th C, 60x70", EX 750.00
Medallions (25), mc calico on wht, wreath quilting, 106x107" ..800.00
Ocean Waves, bl/wht, appliqued border, hs, 70x80", NM 350.00
Sawtooth, mc prints/wht, fine quilting, ms binding, 80x86" 415.00
Sawtooth medallions (12), yel/gr calicos on wht, 88x66", EX 225.00
Stars, gr/red calico on wht, fading, 88x100" 150.00
Stars, 8-pointed, navy on wht, 70x76", EX 440.00
Tulips, mc calicos on pk ground, homespun bking, 82x81" 440.00
Tumbling Blocks, red/bl/pk calicos on wht, 74x86", EX 450.00
Tumbling Blocks, 3-D look, ¼" silk strips, 1930s, 68x74" 575.00
World's Fair, female medallion center, lav silks, 1933 kit 450.00
4 Stars in a Block, 20 cubes/turkey track intersections, lg 550.00
9-Patch Vt, mc/wht patches on red, 19th C, 76" sq, EX 330.00

Quimper

Quimper is a type of pottery produced in Quimper, France. A tin enamel-glazed earthenware pottery with hand-painted decoration, it was first produced in the 1600s by the Bousquet and Caussy Factories. Little of this early ware was marked. By the late 1700s, three factories were operating in the area, all manufacturing the same type of pottery. The Grande Maison de HB, a company formed as a result of a marriage joining the Hubaudiere and Bousquet families, was a major producer of Quimper pottery. They marked their wares with various forms of the 'HB' logo; but of the pottery they produced, collectors value examples marked with the 'HB' within a triangle most highly.

Francois Eloury established another pottery in Quimper in the late 1700s. Under the direction of Charles Porquier, the ware was marked simply 'P.' Adolph Porquier replaced Charles in the 1850s, marking the ware produced during that period with an 'AP' logo. 'PB' (for Porquier-Beau) was used ca 1875 until 1900.

Jule HenRiot began operations in 1886, using molds he had purchased from Porquier. His mark was 'HR,' and until the 20th century he was in competition with The Grande Maison de HB. In 1926 he began to mark his wares 'HenRiot Quimper.' In 1968 the two factories merged. They are still in operation under the name Les Faenceries de Quimper. The factory sold in the fall of 1983 to Sarah and Paul Janssens from the United States, making it the first time the owners were not French. For those interested in learning more about Quimper, we recommend *Quimper Pottery: A French Folk Art Faience* by Sandra V. Bondhus, our advisor for this category, whose address can be found in the Directory under Connecticut.

Fish platter, Naive couple with a-la-touche floral sprays, HR Quimper, 21x9¼", $550.00.

Bannette, piper, mc florals, HRQ, 8¼" 425.00
Basket, biniou player/lady spinning flax, HBQ, 6¼" 325.00
Bell, man w/cane figural, sgn AG, HQF, 4⅞x3⅛" 130.00
Bell, peasant man, bagpipe form, unglazed clapper, HQF, 3½" ...110.00
Bottle, snuff; crowing rooster, book form, late 1800s, 3" 200.00
Bowl, Breton lady, scalloped rim, hdl, HBQF, 5x13½x8½" 165.00
Bowl, Breton man, floral garland, HBQ, 2½x7¼" 85.00
Box, bonboniere; boys & toy boat, PB, 19th C, 2½x4½" sq 995.00

Butter dish, man w/bagpipes, Decor Riche, HBQ, 4x7" 300.00
Butter pat, Eskimos on gr ground, scalloped rim, HenRiot 17.50
Cake plate, man w/walking stick, flat, hdls, unmk, 12" 175.00
Candlesticks, figural man & lady, HQF, 8", pr 950.00
Coffeepot, man & lady, hexagonal, HQF, 8", EX 195.00
Cruet, lady & florals, peach-shaped finial, HBQ, 6½" 105.00
Cup & saucer, Breton lady/floral garland, trefoil shape, AP 145.00
Cup & saucer, demitasse; peasant man, HQF, 2", 4" 35.00
Font, holy water; ermine tail form, man by cross, HQF, 9¼" 275.00
Inkwell, star shape, complete w/inslet & lid, HQF 295.00
Jam pot, peasant man & fir tree, straw hdl, HB, rstr, 2½" 65.00
Jardiniere, swan form, lady seated on breast, HRQ, 6¾x8" 265.00
Pitcher, Breton lady, florals at sides, HQF, 6" 150.00
Pitcher, lady, geometric panels, HRQ, fading/wear, 6" 130.00
Pitcher, man w/cane, floral sprays, HRQ, 8½" 165.00
Plate, Breton fisherman & daughter, mc, PB, 19th C, 9¼" 835.00
Plate, exotic bird on branch, mc, HQ, rstr, 8" 35.00
Plate, lady, a-la-touche floral sprig, scalloped, HRQ, 6", NM 50.00
Plate, lady knits, girl holds yarn, mc, wire hanger, HR, 8" 565.00
Platter, Breton lady, oval, HBQF, recent, 23x11½" 175.00
Platter, Broderie Breton couple, HBQ, 14¾x11¼", NM 365.00
Porringer, lady knitting, Malicorne, pierced, PBX, 7½" 45.00
Salt cellar, dbl; swan form, man & lady, HQF, 3½" 105.00
Shakers, Breton couple, HBQF, ca 1930s, 3½", pr 95.00
Teacup & saucer, man w/walking stick & pipe, HBQ, 2½" 65.00
Teapot, man & lady, bl striped hdl, HQ, 8" 200.00
Teapot, Ordinaire, man on front, floral on bk, HQF, 7¾", NM .165.00
Tureen, peasant lady, Ordinaire, HQF, new, 9½x10¼" 100.00
Umbrella stand, peacocks/florals, HB Quimper, rstr, 10x9½" 225.00
Vase, Broderie Breton couple, 4 sunflower panels, HBQ, 10" 335.00
Vase, bud; lady, a-la-touche sprays, HBQ, 6x5" 55.00
Vase, quintal; man w/flute, HQ, 3½", EX 95.00
Wall pocket, Breton lady, cornucopia form, HQF, 10¾" 150.00
Wall pocket, Breton lady, slipper form, HB, 7¾x2¾" 355.00
Wall pocket, lady w/basket, cone form, HQF, #118, 10½" 200.00
Wall pocket, man & lady, dbl-cone form, Belle-Ile, HQF, 10" ...220.00

Radford

Pottery associated with Albert Radford (1882-1904) can be categorized by three periods of production. Pottery produced in Tiffin, Ohio, (1896-1899) consists of bone china (no marked examples known) and high-quality jasperware with applied Wedgwood-like cameos. Tiffin jasperware is often impressed 'Radford Jasper' in small block letters. At Zanesville, Ohio, Radford jasperware was marked only with an incised, two-digit shape number, and the cameos were not applied but rather formed within the mold and filled with a white slip. Zanesville Radford ware was produced for only a few months before the Radford pottery was acquired by the Arc-en-Ciel company in 1903. Production in Zanesville was handled by Radford's father, Edward (1840-1910), who remained in Zanesville after Albert moved to Clarksburg, West Virginia, where the Radford Pottery Co. was completed shortly before Albert's death in 1904. Jasperware was not produced in Clarksburg, and the molds appear to have been left in Zanesville, where some were subsequently used by the Arc-en-Ciel pottery. The Clarksburg, West Virginia, pottery produced a standard glaze, slip-decorated ware, Ruko; Thera and Velvety, matt glazed ware often signed by Albert Haubrich, Alice Bloomer, and other artists; and Radura, a semimatt green glaze developed by Albert Radford's son, Edward. The Clarksburg plant closed in 1912. Our advisor for this category is James L. Murphy; he is listed in the Directory under Ohio.

Vase, Thera, multicolor floral decoration on green matt, #1453, 12½", $700.00.

Jasper

Ewer, appl grapes & raspberries, Old Man Winter hdl, #17, 9" ...350.00
Mug, floral relief, 4½" 165.00
Pitcher, tankard, vintage, lt bl, #28, 12" 200.00
Vase, cherubs & lion, #15, 6½" 325.00
Vase, cherubs on flying eagles, #23, 9½" 475.00
Vase, lady beside fire, grapes reverse, #55, 3½" 100.00
Vase, lady kneels w/arms up, bird in hand, bark trim, #24, 9" 600.00
Vase, lady sits, trees & dog, bark trim, #14, 7" 310.00

Miscellaneous

Jardiniere, Ruko, tulips, 8½x9" 250.00
Pitcher, dog & goose scenic panels, pine tree hdl, 10½" 160.00
Vase, Radura, 4 hdls, scalloped rim, 10" 400.00
Vase, Thera, gr w/nasturtium decor, cylindrical, 12" 250.00

Radios

Vintage radios are very collectible. There were thousands of styles and types produced, the most popular of which today are the breadboard and the cathedral. Consoles are usually considered less marketable, since their size makes them hard to display and store. For those wishing to learn more about antique radios, we recommend *The Collector's Guide to Antique Radios, Volumes I through IV*, by Sue and Marty Bunis, available from your local bookstore or Collector Books. They are also the authors of *A Collector's Guide to Transistor Radios*. For information on novelty radios, refer to *Collector's Guide to Novelty Radios* by Marty Bunis and Robert Breed. Values are given for radios in near mint to mint condition.

Key:
pb — push button   SW — short wave
phono — phonograph   tbl/m — table model
s/r — slide rule

Adler #201-A, tbl/m, ftd rectangular wood case, 3-dial, 1925 .....125.00
Admiral #CL-684, console, wood, 1936 ....110.00
Admiral #113-5A, tbl/m, blk plastic, 1938 ....100.00
Admiral #5Z22, tbl/m, plastic, center trapezoid dial, 1952 ....30.00
Admiral #78-P6, portable, leatherette, AC/DC/battery, 1941 ......25.00
Air Castle #106B, tbl/m, streamline, cream plastic, 1947 ....100.00
Air Castle #9904, tombstone tbl/m, wood, 1934 ....140.00
Air-Way #41, tbl/m, wood, rectangular, lift top, battery, 24" 140.00
Airline #62-306, tbl/m, wood, rotary phone-type dial, 1938 ....75.00
Airline #84KR-1520A, red metal, AC/DC, 1949 ....60.00
Airline #93WG-604A, tbl/m, plastic, 1946 ....115.00
Am Bosch #16, Amborola tbl/m, wood, 1925, battery 250.00
Am Bosch #200-A, Treasure Chest tbl/m, cvd wood, 1932 ....250.00

Apex #8A, cathedral tbl/m, wood, 1931 ....200.00
Arvin #417, Rhythm Baby tombstone tbl/m, wood, 1936 ....175.00
Arvin #444AM, tbl/m, yel metal, AC/DC, 1947 ....80.00
Arvin #518DW Phantom Pal, tbl/m, wood, 1937 ....70.00
Atwater Kent, cathedral tbl/m, wood, 1932 ....350.00
Atwater Kent #40, console, wood, 4-legged, 1928 ....150.00
Automatic #F-790, console w/pull-out phono, wood, 1947 ....100.00
Bendix, #111W, tbl/m, ivory plastic, AC/DC, 1949 ....50.00
Bendix #646A, end tbl, wood drop leaf, AC/DC, 1946 ....125.00
Bremer-Tully #7-71, console, wood, highboy, 1928 ....135.00
Browning-Drake #5-R, tbl/m, wood, rectangular, battery, 1926 ..150.00
Case #1015, console, wood, 1935 ....150.00
Channel Master #6536, tbl/m, walnut, AM/FM, 1960 ....25.00
Clarion #90, tombstone, wood, 1931 ....160.00
Climax #35, Ruby tbl/m, ultra-streamlined walnut veneer, 37" ..300.00
Clinton, #1102, console, wood, 1937 ....135.00
Colonial #16, tbl/m, wood, low rectangle, battery, 1925 ....125.00
Coronado #05RA4-43-9876A, portable, leatherette, AC/DC, 1950 ..30.00
Coronado #43-7651, console w/pull-out phono, wood, 1946 ....85.00
Crosley #127, tombstone, wood, 1931 ....260.00
Crosley #46FA, tbl/m, plastic, 1947 ....45.00
Crosley #5-38, tbl/m, wood, slant front, battery, 1926 ....100.00
Crosley #899, console, wood, 1936 ....135.00
Delco #R-1230A, tbl/m, ivory plastic, AC/DC, 1947 ....75.00
Delco #R-1410, portable, AC/DC/battery, 1948 ....35.00
Detrola #302, cathedral-C, wood, triangular, 1938 ....325.00
Dewald #406, tbl/m, plastic, 1938 ....95.00
Emerson #DB-315, tbl/m, walnut, AC/DC, 1939 ....75.00
Emerson #25A, wood, curved top, 1933 ....100.00
Emerson #370, console w/inner phono, walnut, 1940 ....120.00
Emerson #400, Aristocrat tbl/m, Catalin, 1940, minimum value .400.00
Eveready #20, tbl/m, wood, high rectangle, battery, 1928 ....100.00

Photo courtesy Sue and Marty Bunis

Fada #366T, wood with right front dial, wraparound grill, six station-indicator lights, five knobs, AC, 1937, $100.00.

Fada #PL41, portable, leatherette, AC/DC/battery, 1941 ....30.00
Fada #53, tbl/m, Catalin, 1938, minimum value 750.00
Farnsworth #AC-55, console, wood, 1939 ....120.00
Farnsworth #BK-73, chairside w/inner phono, 1940 ....125.00
Firestone 4-A-42, Georgian console w/phono, wood, 1947 ......100.00
Freed-Eisemann #NR-12, tbl/m, wood, battery, 1924 ....200.00
Freshman #G-4, Equaphase console, wood, 1927 ....185.00
Freshman #21, Earl tbl/m, metal, 1929 ....85.00
Freshman #6-F-12, Masterpiece console, walnut, battery, 1926 ..200.00
Garod #6AU-1, Commander tbl/m, Catalin, 1946, minimum value ..650.00
GE #E-61, tombstone, wood, curved top, 1936 ....150.00
GE #K-63, cathedral, wood, ftd, 1933 ....250.00
GE #L-678, tbl/m, inner phono, wood, 1941 ....35.00
GE #45, Musaphonic console w/pull-out phono, wood, 1948 .....100.00
GE #636, portable, red plastic, battery, 1955 ....30.00
Gloritone #99, cathedral, wood, 1931 ....225.00
Gruno #450, tombstone, wood, 1934 ....185.00

Hallicrafters #TW-2000, portable, leatherette, 1955 ....125.00
Howard #60, console w/inner phono, wood, 1931 ....145.00
Jackson-Bell #25, Peter Pan tombstone, wood, 1932 ....300.00
Jewel #955, tbl/m, plastic, AC/DC, 1950 ....50.00
Kadette #S947, Jr tbl/m, plastic pocket-sz, AC/DC, 1933 ....300.00
Kennedy #164, console, wood, 6-legged lowboy, 1932 ....175.00
Knight #6D-360, console w/pull-out phono, wood, 1948 ....110.00
Lafayette #C-121, portable, leatherette, AC/DC/battery, 1940 ....25.00
Lafayette #D73, tbl/m, plastic, AC/DC, 1939 ....100.00
Lafayette #60, tombstone, wood, 1935 ....135.00
Magnavox #75, console, mahog, battery, 1925 ....275.00
Majestic #15A, tombstone, wood, 1932 ....120.00
Majestic #344, console, wood, 4-legged lowboy, 1932 ....125.00
Majestic #651, tbl/m, wht plastic, AC/DC, 1937 ....125.00
Majestic #7T11, tbl/m, plastic, AC/DC, 1942 ....125.00
Midland #M6A, tbl/m, wood, 1946 ....55.00
Mohawk #115, console, wood, highboy, battery, 1925 ....215.00
Motorola #45P1, Pixie portable, plastic, battery, 1956 ....250.00
Motorola #75F21, console, wood, 1947 ....100.00
Music Master #140, tbl/m, wood, rectangular, battery, 1925 ....400.00
Olympic #7-724, console w/inner phono, wood, 1947 ....75.00
Packard-Bell #100A, tbl/m, ivory plastic, AC/DC, 1949 ....45.00
Pfanstiehl #10-C, console, wood, highboy, battery, 1924 ....185.00
Philco #A-801, console, wood Deco style, 1941 ....120.00
Philco #16B, tombstone, 2-tone wood, 1933 ....200.00
Philco #37-60, cathedral, wood, 1937 ....175.00
Philco #41-231, tbl/m, wood Deco style, AC/DC, 1941 ....85.00
Philco #41-316, console, wood, 1941 ....215.00
Philco #48-200-I, Transitone tbl/m, plastic, AC/DC, 1948 ....40.00
Philco #70 grandfather clock, wood, colonial style, 1932 ....400.00
Pilot #53, tombstone, wood, 1934 ....150.00
RCA #1X, tbl/m, plastic, AC/DC 50.00
RCA #100, cathedral, wood, 1933 ....175.00
RCA #4T, cathedral, wood, 1935 ....125.00
RCA #6-T, tombstone, wood, 1936 ....125.00
RCA #6-XF-9, tbl/m, plastic, AM/FM, 1956 ....35.00
RCA #9K3, console, wood, 1936 ....130.00
RCA #9SX8, Little Nipper tbl/m, marbled plastic, AC/DC, 1939 ..400.00
RCA #96E2, chairside, 2-tone wood, 1939 ....175.00
Silvertone #16, tbl/m, plastic, AC/DC, 1951 ....30.00
Silvertone #1822, console, wood Deco style, 1935 ....185.00
Sonora #RBU-176, tbl/m, wht plastic, AC/DC, 1946 ....40.00
Sonora #WDU-249, portable, plastic, AC/DC/battery, 1948 ....40.00
Sparton #987, console, wood, 1936 ....200.00
Sterling #B-2-60, Imperial console, walnut, 1929 ....150.00
Stewart-Warner #1401, tombstone, 2-tone wood, 1935 ....140.00
Stromberg-Carlson, chairside, wood Deco style, 1937 ....350.00
Stromberg-Carlson #641-A, tbl/m, walnut finish, 1929 ....100.00
Sylvania #3303TA, portable, leather, AC/DC/battery, 1957 ....45.00
Truetone #D-2610, tbl/m, plastic, 1946 ....75.00
Westinghouse #H-210, portable, plastic, AC/DC, 1949 ....45.00
Westinghouse #WR-14, cathedral, 2-tone wood, 1931 ....200.00
Westinghouse #WR-368, console, wood, 1938 ....165.00
Woolaroc #3-1A, tbl/m, red & wht plastic, AC/DC, 1946 ....65.00
Wurlitzer Lyric #SA-99, console, wood, 6-legged lowboy, 1934 .145.00
Zenith #4-B-131, tombstone, walnut, battery, 1937 ....130.00
Zenith #5-G-003, portable, plastic, AC/DC/battery, 1947 ....30.00
Zenith #6-D-315, tbl/m, plastic Deco style, 1938 ....160.00
Zenith #6-S-546, chairside, wood, 1941 ....135.00
Zenith #8-S-563X, console, wood, 1942 ....200.00

Novelty

Adding machine, Commodore #202 ....65.00

Alka-Seltzer, screw-top can shape, 1971 ....75.00
Cabbage Patch, 1985 ....12.00
Cannon on carriage 40.00
Coors Beer can, EX 25.00
Double Cola, EX 25.00
Dr Pepper vending machine, open leather case w/strap, MIB 300.00
Evel Knievel Motorcycle Tire, blk w/decaled wheel, 6" dia 50.00
Good News/Bad News, Concept 2000 #80 ....50.00
King Kong, plush w/vinyl face, Amico Inc, 1986 ....35.00
Kool-Aid Bursts bottle 16.50
Lazy Susan, plastic tray w/6 mc dishes, Windsor/Hong Kong 80.00
Pepsi-Cola vending machine, M in G box 175.00
Rock-a-Walker binoculars, AM receiver 35.00
Rolls Royce, 1931 model, gold/silver/blk, EX 50.00
Smiley Face, rnd 3-D head w/hands & shoes, Sentinel Elect 75.00
Spider-Man, 2-D w/outlined decal front, Marvel Comics, 1979 ...50.00
Tony's Pizza Bag, AM/FM 40.00

Photo courtesy Bunis and Breed

Toy soldier, made in Hong Kong but distributed by General Electric, 7x2¾", M, $75.00.

Tropicana Orange, EX 20.00
Windsor Jukebox 25.00
10-4 Good Buddy Teddy Bear, Dakin, 1976 ....35.00

Transistor

Post-World War II baby boomers, now approaching their fiftieth year, are rediscovering prized possessions of youth, their pocket radios. The transistor wonders, born with rock 'n roll, were at the vanguard of miniaturization and futuristic design in the decade which followed their introduction to Christmas shoppers in 1954. The tiny receiving sets launched the growth of Texas Instruments and shortly to follow abroad, Sony and other Japanese giants.

The most desirable sets include the 1954 four-transistor Regency TR-1 and colorful early Sony and Toshiba models. Certain pre-1960 models by Hoffman and Admiral represented the earliest practical use of solar technology and are also highly valued. To avoid high tariffs, scores of two-transistor sets, boys' radios, were imported from Japan with names like Pet and Charmy. Many early inexpensive transistor sets could be heard only with an earphone. The smallest sets are known as shirt-pocket models while those slightly larger are called coat pockets. Early collectible transistor radios all have civil defense triangle markings at 640 and 1240 on the frequency dial and nine or fewer transistors. Very few desirable sets were made after 1963. Model numbers are most commonly found inside sets. Our advisor for this category is Mike Brooks; he is listed in the Directory under California and welcomes questions. Please include a SASE.

Admiral #4P21, horizontal, 4 transistors, AM, battery 35.00
Americana #FP80, vertical, 8 transistors, AM, battery 25.00

Angel, 2-transister 45.00
Automatic Tum Thumb 125.00
Barlow GT-180 ....100.00
Braun T3 ....60.00
Emerson #838 ....110.00
Emerson #888 Vanguard, vertical, 8 transistors, AM, battery 75.00
GE #677, horizontal, 5 transistors, AM, battery 125.00
Harpers #GK-900 ....100.00
Hoffman Solaradio 300.00
Jupiter, watch radio 90.00
Lafayette #FS-91 ....150.00
Lincoln #TR-970, vertical, 9 transistors, SW/LW/MW, battery ...45.00
Mantola #M4D 250.00
Matsushita #T-92 Portalarm, 6 transistors, AM, battery 100.00
Minute Man 60.00
Monarch #90 ....110.00
Motorola #56T1 ....150.00
Motorola #7X24W, horizontal, 7 transistors, AM, battery 150.00
NEC #NT-620, horizontal, 6 transistors, AM, battery 50.00
Olympic #666 ....45.00
Raytheon #T-100-3, horizontal, AM, battery 200.00
Realtone #TR-1088 ....120.00
Regency #TR-1, vertical, blk, AM, battery 250.00
Regency #TR-1, vertical, jade gr, AM, battery 600.00
Truetone #D3614A, horizontal, 4 transistors, AM, battery 150.00
Zenith Royal 200, vertical, 7 transistors, AM, battery 45.00

Railroadiana

Collecting railroad-related memorabilia has become one of America's most popular hobbies. The range of collectible items available is almost endless, considering the fact that more than 175 different railroad lines are represented. Some collectors prefer to specialize in only one, while others attempt to collect at least one item from every railway line known to have existed. For the advanced collector, there is the challenge of locating rarities from short-lived railroads; for the novice there are abundant keys, buttons, passes, and playing cards. Among the most popular specializations are dining-car collectibles — flatware, glassware, dinnerware, etc., in a wide variety of patterns and styles.

Good lanterns are appreciating on today's market. Lantern prices are based on the scarcity of the railroad, the color and shape of the globe, and whether the railroad name is embossed rather than being simply acid etched. Note: Two-color lantern globes are now being reproduced.

Fred Harvey items have really come in to their own. Anything Fred Harvey sells, from swizzle sticks to stationery and mint-in-wrapper pencils. Railroad matchbooks are also heavily in demand, most are bringing from $1.00 to $1.50 with some of the more scarce roads bringing from $3.00 to $5.00 each, including the California Zephyr at $5.00. Some railroads have become polarized. In Pennsylvania the PRR items are purchased in a frenzy while the Rio Grande is ignored. This is reversed in the western states. Also remember that the Rio Grand and Southern Pacific are no more, having been bought out by Union Pacific.

Since we've mentioned reproductions, collectors should be made aware that there is a brass spittoon currently coming out of Taiwan that is about 12" high, could be in two sections, and has a pinched waist. The wording 'Union Pacific Railroad' and a train are embossed on the front and the back. Unscrupulous dealers are passing these off as old and asking exorbitant prices. To continue this sad story, other reproductions abound in the many areas of railroadiana, from minimally priced paper items to dining car china and glassware. Some pieces are beautifully executed while others are quite crude. Additionally, lanterns, locks, and keys are being cleverly altered to affect a more desirable piece. Railroad police badges are also being reproduced. They're on the market with high asking prices, being presented as authentic badges by dishonest dealers. Buyer beware! Remember the eleventh commandment: Know Thy Dealer. (Prices stated below are for authentic pieces.)

For a more thorough study, we recommend *Railroad Collectibles, Third Revised Edition*, by Stanley L. Baker and *Dining on Rails* by Richard Luckin, available at your local library or bookstore. Because prices are so volatile, the best pricing sources are often monthly or quarterly 'For Sale' lists. Two you may find helpful may be ordered from Golden Spike, P.O. Box 422, Williamsville, NY 14221, and Grandpa's Depot, 1616 17 St., Suite 267, Denver, CO 80202. Our advice for the dinnerware section comes from Fred and Lila Shrader (Shrader's Antiques); they are listed in the Directory under California. John White (Grandpa's Depot, see Colorado) advises us for the remainder.

Key:
BL — bottom logo
BS — bottom stamped
FBS — full back stamp
NBS — no bottom stamp
NTL — no top logo
SL — side logo
SM — side mark
TL — top logo
TM — top mark

Dinnerware

Child's set, Great Northern, Rocky pattern, animal characters, 5" oatmeal bowl, side logo, $450.00; 8" plate, top logo, $450.00; 3" mug, side logo, $550.00.

Ashtray, GN, Glory of the West, BS, 4" 125.00
Ashtray/match holder, MP, Cobalt Blue, SL 89.00
Bowl, berry; CN, Bonaventure, TL, 5½" 25.00
Bowl, berry; Glacier, BS, 5¼" 65.00
Bowl, berry; NKP, Bellevue, TL, 5" 49.00
Bowl, berry; SP, Sunset, TL, NBS, 5¼" 95.00
Bowl, cereal; B&O, Centenary, BS, 6½" 65.00
Bowl, cereal; C&O, Staffordshire, BS, 6½" 135.00
Bowl, cereal; CB&Q, Violets & Daisies, NBS, 6½" 55.00
Bowl, cereal; GN, Mtns & Flowers, BS, 7¼" 60.00
Bowl, cereal; SP, Prairie Mtn Wildflowers, BS, 6¼" 80.00
Bowl, vegetable; UP, Harriman Blue, oval, BS, 6¼x5" 25.00
Butter pat, ATSF, Mimbreno, NBS 55.00
Butter pat, C&O, Silhouette, NBS 75.00
Butter pat, CB&Q, Violets & Daisies, NBS 22.00
Butter pat, CN, Continental, TL, BS 35.00
Butter pat, CP, Green Band, TL 67.00
Butter pat, EH&A, Hampton, TL 225.00
Butter pat, FEC, Mistic, NBS 18.00
Butter pat, N&W, Cavalier, TM 75.00
Butter pat, N&W, Dogwood, NBS 35.00
Butter pat, NYC, Commodore, TM, BS 55.00
Butter pat, NYC, Hudson, BS 135.00
Butter pat, PRR, Liberty, TL, NBS 110.00
Butter pat, PRR, Purple Laurel 25.00
Butter pat, Pullman, Indian Tree, TM 110.00
Butter pat, SP, Prairie Mtn Wildflower, NBS 98.00
Chocolate pot, ATSF, California Poppy, NBS, w/lid 125.00

Chocolate pot, ATSF, Mimbreno, NBS, w/lid 210.00
Compote, FEC, Carolina, BS, 6½" w/2¾" ped 85.00
Creamer, ATSF, Mimbreno, w/hdl, BS, ind 385.00
Creamer, B&O, Centenary, BS, 3¾" 225.00
Creamer, PRR, Keystone, SL, NBS, ind 85.00
Creamer, Pullman, Indian Tree, SM, NBS, ind 75.00
Creamer, SP, Montello, BS, 3½", ind 75.00
Cup & saucer, bouillon; CN, Quetico, SL 45.00
Cup & saucer, C&O, Train-Ferry, SL (cup) 110.00
Cup & saucer, CM&PS, Olympian (To Puget Sound Electrified), TM ...135.00
Cup & saucer, CMStP, Olympian, TM 110.00
Cup & saucer, CP, Dominion, SL, NBS 75.00
Cup & saucer, demitasse; B&O, Centenary, BL 110.00
Cup & saucer, demitasse; C&O, Silhouette, NBS (cup), BS (saucer) ...385.00
Cup & saucer, demitasse; CN, Queen Elizabeth, SL (cup) 75.00
Cup & saucer, Fred Harvey, Trend, NBS 25.00
Cup & saucer, L&N, Regent, NBS 175.00
Cup & saucer, Pullman, Indian Tree, both TM 125.00
Cup & saucer, SP, Prairie Mtn Wildflowers, both BS 95.00
Egg cup, dbl; C&NW, Flambeau, NBS 30.00
Egg cup, dbl; D&RGW, Blue Adam, NBS 28.00
Egg cup, dbl; GN, Oriental, BS 225.00
Egg cup, dbl; SP, Prairie Mtn Wildflowers, NBS 185.00
Egg cup, dbl; SP&S, American, NBS 21.00
Egg cup, GN, Mtns & Flowers, BS, sm 225.00
Egg cup, WP, Feather River, SL, NBS, sm 295.00
Gravy boat, Southern, Peach Blossom, SL 165.00
Gravy boat, StL&SF, Denmark, NBS 22.00
Gravy boat, WP, Feather River, SL, NBS 300.00
Hot food cover, CMStP&P, Peacock, NBS 150.00
Hot food cover, WP, Feather River, SL 250.00
Ice cream dish, ATSF, Mimbreno, w/tab hdl, FBS, 5" 135.00
Ice cream dish, CN, Bonaventure, w/tab hdl, TL, 5" 50.00
Plate, Alaska, McKinley, TL, 7¼" 175.00
Plate, ATSF, Bleeding Blue, TL, 9½" 145.00
Plate, ATSF, Mimbreno, FBS, 10" 197.00
Plate, ATSF, Mimbreno, FBS, 7½" 75.00
Plate, CMStP&P, Hiawatha, TM & BS, 7½" 235.00
Plate, CMStP&P, Traveler, NBS, 9½" 10.00
Plate, divided; Pullman, Indian Tree, TM, 12½" 135.00
Plate, Fred Harvey, Webster, NBS, 9" 95.00
Plate, NYC, Commodore, TL, BS, 9" 60.00
Plate, NYC, Country Gardens, NBS, 11¼" 75.00
Plate, Prairie Mtn Wildflowers, NBS, 9½" 58.00
Plate, PRR, Mtn Laurel, FBS, 9½" 55.00
Plate, SP, Imperial, TL, BS, 7¼" 85.00
Plate, SP, Prairie Mtn Wildflowers, BS, 5½" 50.00
Plate, SSW, Cotton Belt, TM, BS, 10" 270.00
Plate, UP, Circus (monkey smoking pipe), NBS, 9½" 255.00
Plate, UP, Desert Flower, BS, 10½" 78.00
Plate, UP, Historical, TL, BS, 7¼" 110.00
Plate, UP, Zion, BS, 10" 350.00
Plate, WAB, Banner, TL, 9½" 178.00
Plate, WP, Feather River, TL, NBS, 7¼" 59.00
Platter, ACL, Flora of the South, BS, 11x8" 145.00
Platter, CM&PS, Puget, TM, 13x9½" 165.00
Platter, CMStP&P, Peacock, NBS, 8x6½" 35.00
Platter, D&RG, Curecanti, TL, 10½x7" 395.00
Platter, D&RGW, Prospector, TL, 11½x9½" 45.00
Platter, GN, Mtns & Flowers, BS, 9x7" 67.00
Platter, KCS, Flying Crow, TL, 11¾x8" 655.00
Platter, NP, Yellowstone, TL, 7½x5" 75.00
Platter, UP, Harriman Blue, TL, 12½x9" 110.00
Platter, WAB, Lafayette, TL, 13½x9" 230.00

Relish dish, L&N, Green Leaf, NBS, 7½x4" 42.00
Relish dish, UP, Portland Rose, BS, 9½x4½" 295.00
Sauce boat, UP, Desert Flower, BS 85.00
Service plate, C&NW, Flambeau, 'The 400,' TM, 10½" 525.00
Service plate, IC, Panama Ltd, BS, 10¼" 550.00
Service plate, MKT, Alamo, BS, 10½" 395.00
Service plate, MP, State Capitols, BS, 10½" 395.00
Service plate, MP, State Flowers, BS, 10½" 225.00
Service plate, N&W, Dogwood (w/legend on reverse), BS, 10½" ...135.00
Soup plate, ACL, Flora of the South, flat w/rim, BS, 9" 210.00
Soup plate, CMStP&P, Peacock, flat w/rim, NBS, 8" 65.00
Soup plate, CN, Queen Elizabeth, TL, 9½" 38.00
Soup plate, MKT, Bluebonnet, BS, 9" 145.00
Sugar bowl, GN, Oriental, NBS, w/lid 175.00
Teapot, ATSF, California Poppy, NBS 110.00
Teapot, B&O, Centenary, BS 385.00
Teapot, NP, Verde Green, SL: Monad+YPL 250.00
Teapot, NYNH&H, Platinum Blue, BS 255.00

Glassware

Ashtray, B&O Railroad, 5", $17.00 to $25.00.

Ashtray, ATSF (Sante Fe frosted in cursive in bottom), 4½x3¼" ..35.00
Ashtray, Erie, winged logo/100th Anniversary, bl & gold, 3½" sq ..20.00
Ashtray, GN, entwined wht letters, BS, 4" dia 18.00
Ashtray, McCloud RR, red logo, 3½" dia 18.00
Ashtray, NP (Northern Pacific YPL, red & blk), 4½" sq 10.00
Ashtray, Rock Island, clear w/blk or red bearskin logo 10.00
Bottle, milk; MP buzz-saw logo, ½-pt 35.00
Bottle, whiskey, empty, w/label: for___ RR, from $9 to 15.00
Champagne, AT&SF, cut banner w/Santa Fe, 3½" 150.00
Champagne, Santa Fe, hock style, heavy base, 5" 60.00
Champagne, Southern Ry, gr logo, 4½" 25.00
Cordial, ATSF, etched Sante Fe in cursive, stem, 3¼" 45.00
Cordial, NP, etched YPL Monad logo, 3½" 65.00
Cordial, Santa Fe, 4" 60.00
Cruet, Santa Fe, Daylight w/ball & wing logo 180.00
Double shot, Pullman (in base), 8-sided base, 3¼" 45.00
Double shot, Santa Fe, str sides, weighted base, 2-oz 50.00
Goblet, UP, frosted shield, pinstripe, ped ft, 5½" 15.00
Goblet, UP, stemmed, tall 18.00
Pitcher, water; M&StL, SP fr, Albert Pick & Co, 1928 ....365.00
Platter, ATSF, Chico w/train & US map in silver & blk, 14" 67.00
Roly-poly, PRR, frosted train encircles glass, 3½" 10.00
Roly-poly, UP, frosted shield & pinstripe, 2¾" 11.00
Roly-poly, Wabash, flag & train, red & bl, 3¼" 12.00
Shot glass, D&H in shield, 2¾" 20.00
Shot glass, UP, frosted shield & pinstripe, 2¼" 11.00
Tumbler, ATSF, Santa Fe wht enamel in script, 5½" 15.00
Tumbler, B&O, etched dome logo below 4 etched lines, 4½" 42.00
Tumbler, Burlington Rte, 4½" 12.00
Tumbler, juice; WAB, frosted flag logo, 3¼" 55.00
Tumbler, LV, wht enamel flag logo w/wreath, 5¾" 45.00

Tumbler, MP, eagle logo, 4¼" 8.00
Tumbler, NYC, wht enamel, 5½" 15.00
Tumbler, NYC, wht logo, flanged base, 5" 10.00
Tumbler, NYC, 1964 World's Fair w/train in blk & gold, 6¾" 9.00
Tumbler, SF, SM, 5½x2½" 14.00
Tumbler, StL&SF, Frisco cutting, 3¾" 50.00
Wine, CN, Canadian National etched w/3 pinstripes, stem, 3½" .65.00
Wine, CN, etched logo, 4½" 38.00
Wine, IC, etched IC dmn logo, stem, 3¾" 65.00
Wine, IC, frosted dmn logo, stemmed 17.50
Wine, Santa Fe, tulip style, 6", 4 for 150.00

Keys

A companion to the switch locks would be the switch keys (that fit in the same lock) or similar keys that have straight bits and open box car locks (requiring 'car' keys). Switch keys and/or car keys are brass with hollow barrels and round heads with holes for attaching to a key ring. In order to be collectible, the head must be marked with a name, initials, or a railroad with 'switch' generally designated by 'S' and 'car' as 'C' markings. Railroad, patina 'not polished,' and a manufacturer other than Adlake all affect the price and collectibility.

A new precedent was set in 1995 when a Denver and South Park 'car' key went at a Missouri auction for $2,500.00. The key was marked DSP&P (an early Colorado road that quit in 1898), brass, and had a hollow barrel and straight bit. Switch keys that only recently brought $15.00 to $17.00 are now bringing $30.00.

Switch, AT&SF, Adlake 30.00
Switch, B&O, brass 30.00
Switch, Burlington Northern 24.00
Switch, Burlington Rte, Adlake 30.00
Switch, C&NW, Adlake, brass, NM 30.00
Switch, Clinchfield, brass 40.00
Switch, D&RGW, NM 35.00
Switch, Erie, brass 28.00
Switch, Grand Trunk, brass 35.00
Switch, MKT 30.00
Switch, MOPAC, brass 40.00
Switch, NY Central, Adlake, brass 42.50
Switch, Santa Fe, Adlake & Weston, brass 32.00
Switch, Soo Line 32.00
Switch, SP, Adlake & Weston, brass 35.00

Lamps

Caboose marker, Adlake, glass lenses, M 225.00
Switch, Adlake, electric, day targets, 4½" lenses 225.00
Switch, Adlake, no RR mks, glass lenses, shields, 16½" 225.00
Switch, Adlake, nonsweating, oil burning, 5" lens 225.00
Switch, Adlake, short rnd top w/day targets 225.00
Switch, CC&O, Adlake, oil burner, 5½" lenses, pr 500.00
Switch, Handlan #150, 5½" lenses, M 225.00
Switch marker, Adlake, diver's helmet style, late version 300.00
Switch target, Adlake, w/snow shields, M 225.00

Lanterns

Before 1920 kerosene brakemen's lanterns were made with tall globes, usually 5⅜" tall. These are the most desirable and are usually found at the top of the price scale. Short globes from 1921 through 1940 normally measure 3½" in height, except for those manufactured by Dietz, which are 4" tall. (Soon thereafter, battery brakemen's lanterns came into widespread usage; these are not popular with collectors and are generally not railroad marked.)

All should be marked with the name or initials of the railroad. Look on the top, the top apron, or the bell base (if it has one). Globes may be found in these colors (listed in order of popularity): clear, red, amber, aqua, cobalt, and two-color.

Adams Express, Star Headlight..., gr unmk globe, tall, 1870 ....475.00
Adlake, clear unmk globe, short, M 45.00
B&O, Keystone the Casey, red cast globe, tall 365.00
BR&P, Dietz No 39, clear cast globe, EX 400.00
CC&O, Adams & Westlake, clear mk globe, brass burner, tall ..450.00
Clinchfield, Adlake, clear etched globe, tall 350.00
Clinchfield, Adlake, red globe, short, G 125.00
Clinchfield, Adlake Kero, cobalt unmk globe, short 135.00
D&RG, Adlake, clear cast globe, tall, EX 1,200.00
D&RG, Dietz, bell bottom, etched melon globe, wood hdl 250.00
ET&WNC, Adams & Westlake Adlake #250, Adlake Kero, short 750.00
ME Central, Dietz Vesta, bl unmk globe 285.00
MOPAC, Handlan-Buck, bell bottom, cast globe, mk base 525.00
N&W, Armspear, clear unmk globe, short, 1926, EX 85.00
NY Central, Dietz Vesta, clear cast globe, EX 295.00
PA Lines, Adlake, cast globe, brass burner, tall, 1908 ....265.00
Penn Central, Adlake, red globe, short 115.00
Presentation, Adams & Westlake, NP, clear globe, Pat 1860s, EX .725.00
Presentation, Adams & Westlake Queen, NP, gr/clear globe 165.00
Presentation, CT Hamm, NP brass, etched name/etc, M 1,425.00
Presentation, ETV&GRR, brass top, etched globe, EX 1,400.00
PRR, Keystone Casey, clear cast globe, 1903, EX 275.00
SCL, Adlake, red unmk globe, short 115.00
SCL, brass plated, bl globe 390.00
SR, Adlake, clear cast globe, short, 1925, M 265.00
SR, Adlake, red unmk globe, short, NM 125.00
SR, Adlake, unmk globe, short 125.00
StL&SW, Handlan Buck, dome w/etched globe, Cotton Belt logo ...250.00
Unmk, Adams & Westlake, clear globe, short 50.00
UP, Adams & Westlake Adams, mk globe, brass burner, tall 575.00
Wabash Terminal, Adlake, clear etched globe, short 225.00

Linens

Apron, CA Zephyr imprinted over red Pullman label 15.00
Blanket, GN, goat logo 300.00
Blanket, GN, w/name 250.00
Blanket, Pullman, cinnamon (solid color) wool 150.00
Blanket, Pullman, dk bl wool, for Blk passengers, 1920s-30s 175.00
Blanket, Pullman, wool, cross-stitch pattern, 1920s-30s 175.00
Blanket, Soo Line, wool, lg logo 225.00
Blanket, UP in gray, lg blk Overland logo 275.00
Headrest, SCL, beach scene, yel & gr 17.00
Headrest, SR, khaki w/lg logo, button-down style 17.00
Napkin, Ft Worth & Denver City, red letters on wht 10.00
Napkin, Santa Fe, wht on wht, 19½" sq 10.00
Napkin, UP, yel, bl or pk 7.00
Pillowcase, CA Zephyr imprinted over Pullman logo 10.00
Pillowcase, Pullman, regular sz 7.00
Sheet, CA Zephyr imprinted over Pullman, berth sz 15.00
Sheet, Pulman, berth or twin sz 12.00
Tablecloth, Amtrak, wht, stamped NRPC, 32x45" 10.00
Tablecloth, FL East Coast, Car 90, wht, 65x67" 50.00
Tablecloth, NY Central, wht letters on rust, 40x43" 18.00
Tablecloth, Rio Grande, wht speed letters on plum, 40" sq 18.00
Tablecloth, SCL, lg logo, 48½"x52", G 25.00
Tablecloth, UP, pk, 31½x46" 12.00

Towel, CA Zephyr, red stripe, EX 20.00
Towel, dish; Burlington Rte, bl on wht 10.00
Towel, dish; Pullman logo (lg), wht on wht, ca 1900 ....10.00
Towel, GN, imprinted on red stripe 20.00
Towel, hand; Burlington Rte, EX 15.00
Towel, Pullman, bl stripe 12.00

Locks

Brass switch locks (pre-1920) were made in two styles: heart-shaped and Keen Kutter style. Values for the heart-shaped locks are determined to a great extent by the railroad represented and just how its name appears on the lock. Most in demand are those with large embossed letters; if the letters are small and incised, demand is minimal. For instance, one from the Union Pacific line (even with heavy embossed letters) may go for only $45.00, while the same from the D&RG railroad could go easily sell for $250.00. Old Keen Kutter styles (brass with a 'pointy' base) from Colorado & Southern and Denver & Rio Grande could range from $600.00 to $1,200.00.

Steel switch locks (circa 1920 on) with the initials of the railroad incised in small letters — for example BN, L&H, and PRR — are usually valued at $20.00 to $28.00.

Signal, Clinchfield, brass, w/steel key 30.00
Signal, Seaboard, brass, w/key 30.00
Switch, AT&SF, steel, shanty type, no key 35.00
Switch, CC&O, brass, w/mk brass key 250.00
Switch, Clinchfield, Slaymaker, steel, w/mk brass key 55.00
Switch, ETN&VA, brass, ca 1850s, rare 975.00
Switch, N&W, Slaymaker, brass, w/mk brass key 120.00
Switch, UP, Adlake Adams, brass, w/mk brass key 225.00

Silverplate

The value of a hollow ware item is affected by where the logo and/or railroad name was stamped; a side-marked piece is much preferred to one with the mark on the bottom. Note: Some railroad silver from early private cars has recently surfaced. Marks such as Denver & Salt Lake car 101 (called the 'Pheasant') and FECRy's 'Alicia' (Henry Flagler's car) are good examples and might today be considered 'museum quality' by railroadiana buffs.

Bowl, melon ice; SF, Harrison & Howland, 5½" dia 195.00
Bowl, melon; MOPAC, BS, 1946, 7¼" 75.00
Bowl, MOPAC, very plain, 12-oz, 7" dia 35.00
Butter pat, Pullman, bias corners, Internat'l, 3" sq 45.00
Change tray, Milwaukee, BS, R Wallace, 12-oz, 6¼" 65.00
Change tray, UP, BS, 1946, 6½" 95.00

Photo courtesy Stanley Baker

Coffeepot, Northern Pacific, side and bottom marks, ca 1888, 1-pint, 7", $250.00.

Coffeepot, Santa Fe, flip lid, SM, 11-oz, G	150.00
Coffeepot, UP, acorn finial, BS, Internat'l, 1954, 14-oz	55.00
Compote, T&P, BS, Reed & Barton, 1930, 4½x6½"	225.00
Creamer, MOPAC, flip lid, BS, 1927, 6-oz	75.00
Creamer, UP, pagoda finial, hinged lid, BS, Reed & Barton	55.00
Finger bowl, NC&StL, BS, Reed & Barton, 1¾x4⅞"	95.00
Fork, place; ACL, Zephyr	12.00
Fork, place; Burlington Rte, Modern	12.00
Gravy boat, UP, 4-oz, G	75.00
Hot food cover, UP, BS, Reed & Barton, 6"	55.00
Knife, place; Burlington Rte, Belmont	15.00
Knife, place; Burlington Rte, Modern	10.00
Knife, place; CA Zephyr	15.00
Menu holder, UP, half-moon shape, BS, 1954	125.00
Plate, NC&StL, logo on rim, BS, Reed & Barton, 6½"	75.00
Saucer, ice cream; CMStP&P, BS, Internat'l, 1936	65.00
Sherbet, New Haven, stemmed, BS, 4"	50.00
Spoon, iced tea; Burlington Rte, Modern	15.00
Spoon, iced tea; CA Zephyr, BM	18.00
Spoon, iced tea; D&SL, Century	12.00
Spoon, iced tea; SF, Albany, BS	15.00
Spoon, serving; SF, Albany, BS	15.00
Spoon, soup; CA Zephyr	15.00
Sugar bowl, Fred Harvey, w/lid, BS, Reed & Barton, 6-oz	75.00
Sugar bowl, MOPAC, compote style, Wallace, BS, w/lid, 9-oz	95.00
Sugar bowl, NC&StL, SM, Gorham	120.00
Sugar bowl, UP, pagoda finial, BS, Reed & Barton, 12-oz	55.00
Syrup, NC&StL, hinged lid, SL, BS, Reed & Barton, 10-oz	130.00
Teaspoon, ACL, Internat'l Silver, NM	20.00
Tray, bread; MOPAC, fancy edge, oval, BS, Reed & Barton, 13"	85.00
Tray, bread; NC&StL, TM, Gorham, 11⅛x6¾"	120.00
Tray, buzz saw logo, silver on copper, BS, 11"	55.00
Tray, CM&StP, 1927 BS, 5½" dia	65.00
Tray, CMStP&P, BS, sm	55.00
Tray, Pullman, fancy edge, Internat'l, 7x10"	75.00
Tray, T&P, eagle logo, BS, 7" dia	125.00
Tray (underliner), CMStP&P, BS, 1929, 5¼"	50.00
Turkey cover, Fred Harvey, top hdl, BS, 18"	125.00

Miscellaneous

Annual passes are skyrocketing in popularity (as opposed to trip or one-time passes, which are not very desirable in the field of pass collecting). Their values are contingent upon the specific railroad, its length of run (whether it was a short one or a major line), and their appearance. Many were tiny works of art lettered with fancy calligraphy and decorated with vignettes.

Timetables are climbing rapidly in popularity, and pins with the names of railroad companies are very good right now. On the other hand, 'Brotherhood' pins (or any item) hold little interest for collectors. Watch for reproduction signs; most are small in size, about 5" x 12", on aged cardboard under glass in black frames. These will read 'Public Telephone,' 'Waiting Room,' etc.

Badge, hat; Conductor (no RR name), blk letters on silver	35.00
Badge, hat; D&RGW Conductor, gold w/blk letters	65.00
Badge, hat; D&RGW Parlor Car Conductor, gold w/blk letters, M	125.00
Badge, hat; D&RGW Trainman, mc logo w/silver & blk, M	85.00
Badge, hat; Penn Central Asst Conductor, red on brass	65.00
Badge, ID; Ry Express Agency Employee, celluloid, 1930s, 1½"	10.00
Baggage tag, NY Central, speeding train, 2x4"	7.00
Baggage tag, Yellowstone, Over the Top..., bl	10.00
Blotter, Burlington Rte, combination tour, 4x9", M	100.00
Blotter, GN, goat logo, BS, 3x6", NM	15.00

Blotter, Milwaukee, 2 Hiawathas & schedule, 3x8½"	10.00
Blotter, MP, red buzz saw logo, 3x9", M	7.00
Blotter, Santa Fe, La Bosada, red letters, 3½x6¼", M	15.00
Blueprint, D&RG, narrow gauge engine type 2-8-0, 1882, 7x12"	10.00
Bond coupon, Rio Grande Southern, 1900, 1x2½"	5.00
Book, Cripple Creek Road, McFarland (sgn), w/jacket, 1944	75.00
Book, Over Range to Golden Gate, Wood, 1902, 283-pg, EX	75.00
Book, Trains in Transition, Beebe, 1941, w/jacket	25.00
Booklet, C&S, Picturesque CO, 1910, 7x10", M	60.00
Booklet, CO Midland, Through the Rockies, 27 photos, 7x10"	100.00
Booklet, Pullman Progress, mc, info from 1859 to 1942, 4x10"	25.00
Booklet, Rock Island, CO...Under Turq Sky, 1921, 32-pg, 6x9"	30.00
Booklet/almanac, Rock Island, multiscene cover, 1883, 6x9"	45.00
Brochure, Burlington Rte, w/NB map, 1900, opens to 17x32"	50.00
Brochure, C&A w/MOPAC & T&P, Rotary convention, 1929	10.00
Brochure, C&NW, summer fares to West, 1936, opens to 18"	7.00
Brochure, C&NW 400, color photo, 1945, opens to 16"	10.00
Brochure, D&RG, Expo & Summer Schedules, 1915, 5x10", EX	35.00
Brochure, D&RG, Klondike Gold Fields, w/maps, 1898, 4x8"	50.00
Brochure, Fred Harvey, Indian Detour, bl cover, w/maps, 1929	35.00
Brochure, Milwaukee, Liberty Guide, 3x7"	10.00
Brochure, Rio Grande, Engine 165 Presented to CO Springs, '38	10.00
Brochure, Twin Zephyrs, 8-car Zephyr, lt bl, 1940, 4x6"	10.00
Brochure, UP Forty Niner, mc, 1937, 3¼x5½"	10.00
Brochure, UP/C&NW, The Challenger, lime gr, 1937, 3x6"	10.00
Builders' card, Vandalia Line, locomotive #36, 6¼x9¼"	45.00
Caboose marker, Handlan, yel, 15"	225.00
Calendar, steam; SP, 12 blk/wht locomotive pictures, 1987, M	10.00
Calendar, UP, 1958, dbl-sided mc pictures, 12x22"	15.00
Can, B&O, Lamptender's Fuel Can, 1-gal, EX	50.00
Card, On Board, C&NW/UP/SP Overland Ltd, 4-pg, 3½x4½"	10.00
Clothes brush, Pullman, 6¾"	45.00
Coat, conductor's frock; brass Rio Grande buttons, 1800s	100.00
Coat hanger, Pullman, wood	12.50

Conductor's hat, Chesapeake & Ohio Railway, NM, $225.00.

Contract/lease, Co Midland, booklet form, 1899, 1-pg, 5x8"	25.00
Dater die, CO Orestod & D&RGW, brass, sq center, complete	250.00
Dater die, D&RGW Co Gypsum CO, brass, rnd center, complete	250.00
Dater die, D&RGW RR Moffatt CO, brass, rnd center, complete	300.00
File, employees'; SP, 1914, 4-pg, 9x12"	5.00
Flyer, BR/D&RG/WP, CA Via the Exposition Flyer, color, 1941	25.00
Flyer, SP, automated buffet car, yel sheet, 5x6"	10.00
Hammock, berth, gr cord & mesh, 61" L	65.00
Jacket, Amtrak agent's; royal bl w/gold buttons, M	35.00
Jacket, cook's; C&NW, M	25.00
Jacket, waiter's; NY Central, wht w/bl lapels	18.00
Light, caboose marker; Adlake, glass lenses, M	225.00
Light, switch target; Adlake, w/snow shields, lenses, M	230.00
Magazine, IL Central Gulf News, Dec, 1972, 33-pg	3.50
Magazine cover, IL Central, leather, 9x10", G	30.00
Menu, Fred Harvey, CA Ltd, dbl-fold, 1931, 5½x8"	15.00
Menu, Fred Harvey, Final Rail Fan Tour, 1938, 9x12"	10.00
Menu, MP, 20th Anniversary, Rotary convention, Dallas, '29, 5x7"	10.00

Menu, Union News Co, from Penn Station in NJ, 1945, 7x11" ...25.00
Newsletter, D&RG & Rio Grande Southern, 1911, 4-pg, 9x12" ..20.00
Pants, waiter's; Milwaukee, purple stripe, string ties 10.00
Pants, waiter's; Rio Grand, yel stripe down legs 25.00
Pass, AL Great Southern, 1927 ....10.00
Pass, annual; Rock Island Lines, 1909 ....25.00
Pass, Cincinnati Hamilton & Dayton, 1910 ....10.00
Pass, Fred Harvey, Eating House, employees' rates, 1921 ....22.00
Pencil, Rock Island, bearskin logo, wht on blk, M 1.00
Photo, CO Midland, 11-mile canyon, ca 1888, 9x12" 10.00
Pick head, Clinchfield, 22" 22.50
Playing cards, D&RGW, 53 in maroon box, NM 25.00

Postcard, Cross Crossings Cautiously, letter on back about joining club, ca 1923, 3½x5½", EX, $5.00.

Postcard, SP, rotary snow plow, mc, 1981, 5x7" 1.50
Poster, Atlantic Coast RR, 2 men w/Florida poster, 21x14", VG+ ..1,200.00
Poster, Prompt Movement of Armed Forces, WWII, 8x9" 20.00
Punch, pinhole (prestapler); blk CI, ca 1900 ....25.00
Receipt, Wells Fargo Express, filled in, 1890 ....10.00
Schedule, D&RG, Hotel Men's Special, Denver-Salt Lake, 1909 ...15.00
Schedule/brochure, C&NW MN 400, orange, 1937, 4x8" 10.00
Sign, Diner, stainless steel, blk letters, 2½x14" 45.00
Sign, Dining...Opposite Direction, brass grommet, 5x7" 18.00
Sign, Kindly Flush..., aluminum, wht letters, 3x11" 40.00
Sign, Meal Service Car Foward, steel grommet, blk/wht, 8x9" 10.00
Sign, Push, stainless steel, blk letters, 3½x7" 40.00
Sign, Quiet Is Requested/Have You..., brass grommet, 5x6" 15.00
Sign, Rock Island Freight Sales, enamel on steel, 11x27", EX 45.00
Sign, Telegraph Money Orders...Accepted Here, pnt tin, 8x12" ...125.00
Step box, UP, gr base, silver top, NM 250.00
Swizzle stick, GNRy, wht plastic w/bl letters 3.00
Swizzle stick, Grand Central Terminal, bl glass, gold letters 25.00

Tie tack, Pennsylvania Railroad, red and yellow enameling on metal, 2", $50.00.

Timetable, CA Zephyr, bright orange, 1949 ....20.00
Timetable, D&RGW w/WP, red cover, 1925, 54-pg 20.00
Timetable, Grand Trunk Ry, local, blk/wht, 1947 ....5.00
Timetable, Pere Marquette, gr, 1950, EX 4.00
Timetable, Santa Fe, Big System Map, 1888, EX 50.00
Timetable, Southwest Ltd, blk/wht, 1948 ....10.00
Timetable, Wabash, flag logo, 1941, G 10.00
Timetable/brochure, RGW, bl cover, 1899, 38-pg, EX+ 100.00
Toilet paper holder, UP, silvered metal & wood 65.00
Token, IL Central, bronze, For 100 years..., 1⅜" 35.00
Viewbook, D&SL, Over the Moffat Road, w/map, 1906, 10x15" .40.00
Voucher, Co Springs-Cripple Creek District, 1909, 7x8" 10.00

Voucher, treasurer's; UP Denver & Gulf, 1897, 7x9" 10.00
Waybill, baggage; Central Pacific, filled out, 1879, 7x8" 15.00
Wrench, Southern Ry, adjustable, early, lg 40.00

Razors

As straight razors gain in popularity, prices of those razors also increase. This carries with it a lure of investment possibilities which can encourage the novice or speculator to make purchases that may later prove to be unwise. We recommend that before investing serious money in razors, you become familiar with the elements which make a razor valuable. As with other collectibles, there are specific traits which are desirable and which have a major impact on the price of a piece.

The following information is based on the book *The Standard Guide to Razors* by Roy Ritchie and Ron Stewart (available from R&C Books, P.O. Box 151, Combs, KY 41729, @ $9.95 +$2.50 S&H, autographed). It describes the elements most likely to influence a razor's collector value and their system of calculating that value. (Their book is a valuable reference guide to both the casual and serious collector of razors.)

There are four major factors which determine a razor's collector value. These are the brand and country of origin, the handle material, the art work found on the handles or blades, and the condition of the razor. Ritchie and Stewart freely admit that there are other facters that may come into play with some collectors, but these are the major players in determining value. They have devised a system of evaluation which is based on these four factors.

The most important factor is the value placed on the brand and country of origin. This is the price of a common razor made by (or for) a particular company. It has plain handles, probably made of plastic, no art work except perhaps a simple blade etch and is in collectible condition. It is the beginning value. Hundreds (thousands?) of these values are provided in the 'Listings of Companies and Base Values' chapter in the book.

The second category is that of handle material. This covers a wide range of materials, from fiber on the low end to ivory on the high end. The collector needs to be able to identify the different handle materials when he sees them. This often takes some practice since there are some very good plastics that can mimic ivory quite successfully. Also, the difference between genuine celluloid and plastic can become significant when determining value. A detailed chart of these values is supplied in the book. The listing below can be used as a general guide.

The third category is the most subjective. Nevertheless, it is an extremely important factor in determining value. This category is artwork, which can include everything from logo art to carving and sculpture. It may range from highly ornate to tastefully correct. Blade etching as well as handle artistry are to be considered. Perhaps what some call the 'gotta have it' or the 'neatness' factors properly fall into this category. You must determine just where your razor falls in evaluating it in this category. Again, this book provides a more complete listing of considerations than is used here.

Finally, the condition is factored in. The book's scales run from 'parts' (10% +) to 'Good' (150% +/-). Average (100% +/-) is classified as 'Collectible.'

Samplings from charts:

Chart A: Companies and Base Value:

Abercrombie & Finch, NY 11.00
Aerial, USA 20.00
Boker, Henri & Co, Germany 12.00
Brick, F, England 10.00
Case Mfg Co, Spring Valley, NY 35.00
Chores, James 8.00
Dahlgren, CW; Sweden 12.00

Diane, Japan 10.00
Electric Co, NY 14.00
ERN, Germany 11.00
Faultless, Germany 10.00
Fox Cutlery, Germany 12.00
Golden Rule Cutlery, Chicago 11.00
Griffon XX, Germany 9.00
Henckels, Germany 15.00
Holley Mfg Co CT 27.00
International Cutlery Co NY/Germany 8.00
IXL, England 14.00
Jay, John; NY 12.00
KaBar, Union Cut Co, USA 28.00
Kanner, J; Germany 9.00
Kern, R&W; Canada/England 9.00
LeCocltre, Jacque; Switzerland 14.00
Levering Razor Co, NY/Germany 18.00
McIntosh & Heather, OH 12.00
Merit Import Co, Germany 9.00
National Cut Co, OH 12.00
Oxford Razor Co, Germany 10.00
Palmer Brothers, Savannah, GA 20.00
Primble, John; India Steel Works, Louisville, KY 22.00
Queen City, NY 30.00
Quigley, Germany 11.00
Rattler Razor Co, USA 25.00
Robeson Cut Co, USA 25.00
Salamander Works, Germany 11.00
Soderein, Ekilstuna, Sweden 11.00
Taylor, LM; Cincinnati, OH 14.00
Tower Brand, Germany 10.00
Ulmer, Germany 10.00
US Barber Supply, TX 14.00
Vinnegut Hdw Co, IN 11.00
Vogel, ED; PA 12.00
Wade & Butcher, England 24.00
Weis, JH; Supply House, Louisville, KY 15.00
Yankee Cutlery Co, Germany 11.00
Yazbek, Lahod, OH 12.00
Zacour Bros, Germany 10.00
Zepp, Germany 9.00

Chart B, as described below, is an abbreviated version of the handle materials list in *The Standard Guide to Razors*. It is an essential category in the use of the appraisal system developed by the authors.

Ivory	550%
Tortoise Shell	500%
Pearl	400%
Stag	400%
Bone	300%
Celluloid	250%
Compostion	150%
Plastic	100%

Chart C deals with the artistic value of the razor. As pointed out earlier, this is a very subjective area. It takes study to determine what is good and what is not. Taste can also play a significant role in determining the value placed on the artistic merit of a razor. The range is from superior to nonexistent. Categories generally are divided as follows:

Superior	550%
Good	400%
Average	300%

Minimal	200%
Plain	100%
Nonexistant	0%

Chart D is also very subjective. It determines the condition of the razor. You must judge accurately if the appraisal system is to work for you.

Good	150%

Does not have to be factory mint to fall within this cagegory. However, there can be no visible flaws if it is to be calculated at 150%.

Collectible	100%

May have some flaws that do not greatly detract from the artwork or finish.

Parts	10%

Unrepairable, valuable as salvageable parts.

Razors may fall within any of these categories, ie. collectible + 112%.

Now to determine the value of your razor, multiply A times B, then multiply A times C. Add your two answers and multiply this sum times D. The answer you get is your collector value. See the example below.

(a) Brand and Origin Base Value	(b) Handle Material % Value	(c) Artwork % Value	(d) Condition % Value	(e) Collector Value
Wade & Butcher England **$24.00**	Iridescent Pearl Handles 24 x400% **$96.00**	Carved handles 24 x 350% **$84.00**	Cracked handle at pin Collectible- 80%	$96+$84=$180 $180 x 80%= **$144.00**

Reamers

The reamer market is very active right now, and prices are escalating rapidly. Reamers have been made in hundreds of styles and colors and by as many manufacturers. Their purpose is to extract the juices from lemons, oranges, and grapefruits. The largest producer of glass reamers was McKee, who pressed their products from many types of glass — custard; delphite and Chalaine blue; opaque white; Skokie green; black; caramel and white opalescent; Seville yellow; and transparent pink, green, and clear. Among these, the black and the caramel opalescents are the most valuable.

The Fry Glass Company also made reamers that are today very collectible. The Hazel Atlas Crisscross orange reamer in pink often brings in excess of $275.00; the same in blue, $375.00. Hocking produced a light blue orange reamer and, in the same soft hue, a two-piece reamer and measuring cup combination. Both are considered rare and very valuable with currently quoted estimates at $400.00 and up for the former and $800.00 and up for the latter. In addition to the colors mentioned, red glass examples — transparent or slag — are rare and costly. Prices vary greatly according to color and rarity. The same reamer in crystal may be worth three times as much in a more desirable color.

Among the most valuable ceramic reamers are those made by American potteries. The Spongeband reamer by Red Wing is valued in excess of $500.00; Coorsite reamers with gold or silver trim are worth $300.00 and up. Figurals are popular — Mickey Mouse and John Bull may bring $600.00 to $1,000.00. Others range from $55.00 to $350.00. Fine china one- and two-piece reamers are also very desirable and command very respectable prices.

A word about reproductions: A series of limited edition reamers is being made by Edna Barnes of Uniontown, Ohio. These are all marked with a 'B' in a circle. Other repoductions have been made from old molds. The most important of these are Anchor Hocking two-piece two-cup measure and top, Gillespie one-cup measure with reamer top, Westmoreland with flattened handle, Westmoreland four-cup measure embossed with orange and lemons, Duboe (hand-held darning egg), and Easley's diamonds one-piece.

Our advisor for this category is Dee Long; she is listed in the Directory under Illinois. For more information concerning reamers and reproductions, contact our advisor or the National Reamer Collectors Association (see Clubs, Newsletters, and Catalogs). Be sure to include an SASE when requesting information.

Ceramic

Baby's, chicks jumping rope, pk 150.00
Clown Face 'Mug' 98.00
Clown figural, mc, Japan, 6½" 75.00

Clown, multicolor on white,
Japan, 5½", $80.00.

Clown figural, white w/blk/orange/red, Japan, 2-pc, 6½" 95.00
Dog figural, beige w/red & blk trim, 2-pc, 8" 225.00
Floral w/gold, Nippon, 2-pc 195.00
Floral w/gold, Royal Rudolstadt, 2-pc 250.00
House, beige w/tan & orange trim, 2-pc, Japan, 5½" 100.00
Lustre w/flowerpots, toy, 2½" 250.00
Mexican w/cactus figural, mc, Japan 200.00
Moss Rose 50.00
Paisley, wht on bl, England 70.00
Pitcher form, mc flowers on beige, tan trim at top 50.00
Puddinhead, 6" 175.00
Rosebuds on gr, Japan, 2-pc 60.00
Saucer form, cream w/yel bees, Japan, 3¾" 45.00
Teapot style, wht w/bl sailboat, Germany, 2-pc, 3¼" 65.00
Toby-style man figural, gray hair, gr coat, lav hat, 4¾" 175.00
Windmill form, Japan, 4½" 75.00

Glass

Anchor Hocking, gr panelled 20.00
Anchor Hocking, gr, pitcher form, ftd, 4-cup 40.00
Cambridge, gr, tab hdl, sm 200.00
Fleur-de-lis, mustard 600.00
Fleur-de-lis, red 600.00
Fry, Azure bl, str sides, open tab hdl 1,300.00
Hazel Atlas, Criss Cross, bl, orange reamer 375.00
Hazel Atlas, Criss Cross, gr, lg 32.00
Hazel Atlas, Criss Cross, pk, lemon reamer 325.00

Hazel Atlas, Criss Cross, pk, orange reamer 275.00
Hocking, Vitrock, loop hdl, orange reamer 30.00
Jeannette, delphite, sm 110.00
Jeannette, ultramarine, sm 115.00
LE Smith, pk, 2-pc, baby sz 150.00
Lindsay, pk 475.00
McKee, blk, grapefruit reamer 925.00
Orange Juice Extractor, pk, unemb 60.00
Sunkist, blk 600.00
Sunkist, caramel 400.00
Sunkist, Chalaine Bl 275.00
Sunkist, Crown Tuscan 400.00
Sunkist, jade-ite 65.00
Sunkist, milk glass, Westmoreland 25.00
Sunkist emb on milk glass 20.00
Tufglas, gr 150.00
Unmk, cobalt, tab hdl, sm 275.00
US Glass, pk, tub form w/reamer top, 4-pc 220.00
US Glass, yel, pitcher form 500.00
Westmoreland, amber, 2-pc, baby sz 195.00

Records

Records of interest to collectors are often not the million-selling hits by 'superstars.' Very few records by Bing Crosby, for example, are of any more than nominal value, and those that are valuable usually don't even have his name on the label! Collectors today are most interested in records that were made in limited quantities, early works of a performer who later became famous, and those issued in special series or aimed at a limited market. Vintage records are judged desirable by their recorded content as well; those that lack the quality of music that makes a record collectible will always be 'junk' records in spite of their age, scarcity, or the obsolescence of their technology.

Records are usually graded visually rather than by audio quality, since it is seldom if ever possible to first play the records you buy at shows, by mail, at flea markets, etc. Condition is one of the most important value-assessing factors. For example, a truly mint-condition Elvis Presley 45 of Milk Cow Blues (Sun 215) has a potential value of over $1,000.00. If that same 45 had a sticker on it that was one-eighth of an inch square, it could lose up to half of that value! To be judged mint, a record and sleeve must be in original, unsealed condition. It must show absolutely no evidence of use. Excellent condition is a rating applied to a record that may show slight signs of wear and use but will have almost no audible defect.

While the value of most 78s does not depend upon their being in appropriate sleeves or jackets (although a sleeveless existence certainly contributes to damage and deterioration!), this is not the case with many 45s, most EPs (extended play 45s) and LPs (long-playing 33⅓s). Often, common and otherwise minimally valued 45s might be collectible if they are in appropriate 'picture sleeves' (special sleeves that depict the artist/group or other fanciful or symbolic graphic and identify the song titles, record label, and number), e.g. many common records by Elvis Presley, The Beatles, and The Beach Boys. In order for most EPs and LPs to be saleable, they *must* be in their original jackets and in nice condition — indeed, excellent or better — unless they are very scarce and sought after. Sleeves may show marginal deterioration but no repairs, pen or pencil marks, stickers, or physical damage. A Good record has both visual and audible distractions but is still playable. Sleeves will show ring wear but will not be physically damaged, and Fair indicates a record that is both visually and audibly distracting, one that has obvious damage — no skips, but possible 'play through' scratches. It can still be usable. Sleeves will show heavy ring wear and some minor physical damage. A Poor record may or may not play. Sleeves are faded, torn, marked, or otherwise damaged beyond pleasurable viewing.

Many promo records being discarded by radio stations today are finding their way into collections. These may say 'Not for Sale,' 'Audition Copy,' 'D.J.,' etc. These radio station versions are sometimes different than commercial issues and sometimes more sought after than their commercial twins. Promos by certain 'hot' artists, such as Elvis Presley and The Beach Boys are usually premium disks.

Our advisor for this category is L.R. Docks, author of *American Premium Record Guide*, which lists 60,000 records by over 7,000 artists, now in its fourth edition. He is listed in the Directory under Texas. In the listings that follow, prices are suggested for records that are in excellent condition.

Key:
Bru — Brunswick
Ch — Champion
Col — Columbia
Edi — Edison

Para — Paramount
Orch — Orchestra
Vi — Victor
Vo — Vocalion

Blues, Rhythm and Blues, Rock 'N Roll, Rockabilly

Photo courtesy Les Docks

Reb's Legion Club 45s, Steppin' High, Hollywood, from $200.00 to $300.00.

Ace, Johnny; Midnight Hours Journey, Flair 1015, 45 rpm 20.00
Amos, Muddy Water Blues, Bluebird 5862, 78 rpm 20.00
Anderson, Elton; Roll on Train, Vi 1001, 45 rpm 8.00
Audrey, Dear Elvis, Plus 104, 45 rpm 15.00
Bartholomew, Dave; Another Mule, Imperial 5322, 45 rpm 10.00
Bee, Willie; Ramblin' Mind Blues, Vo 03907, 78 rpm 15.00
Big Four, Out of Tune, Moon 306, 45 rpm 15.00
Bluejacks, Late Hour Blues, Dot 1000, 78 rpm 10.00
Bowser, Donnie; Stone Heart, Era 3029, 45 rpm 10.00
Brown, Billy; Lost Weekend, Republic 2007, 45 rpm 10.00
Brown, Ora; Jinx Blues, Para 12481, 78 rpm 100.00
Bruce, Edwin; Rock Boppin' Baby, Sun 276, 45 rpm 10.00
Byrne, Jerry; Lights Out, Specialty 635, 45 rpm 10.00
Calicott, Joe; Fare Thee Well Blues, Bru 7166, 78 rpm 400.00
Campbell, Charlie; Pepper Sauce Mama, Vo 03571, 78 rpm 100.00
Carl, Steve; Curfew, Meteor 5046, 45 rpm 40.00
Cassell, Tommy; Go Ahead On, Cassell 58½, 45 rpm 20.00
Chatman, Christine; Wino's Lament, Million 2002, 45 rpm 10.00
Cobras, Sindy, Modern 964, 45 rpm 40.00
Cole, Lucy; Empty Bed Blues, Ch 15549, 78 rpm 100.00
Contours, Funny, Motown 1012, 45 rpm 15.00
Craig, Pee Wee; Ramblin' Man, Choice 1000, 45 rpm 15.00
Crawford, Fred; Rock Hard Candy, Starday 243, 45 rpm 30.00
Crow, Hank; Crazy 'Bout You, Southwest 204, 45 rpm 20.00
Curry, Earl; Try & Get Me, R&B 1313, 45 rpm 15.00
Curry, Elder; Memphis Blues, Okeh 8857, 78 rpm 80.00
Dallas, Chuck; Come On Let's Go, K-C 102, 45 rpm 10.00
Dean, Frank; Bubblin', Trend 30-008, 45 rpm 10.00

Delaney, Mattie; Tallahatchie River Blues, Vo 1480, 78 rpm 400.00
Dippers, Such a Fool Was I, Epic 9453, 45 rpm 12.00
Dixon, Webb; Rock Awhile, Astro 101, 45 rpm 20.00
Dreamlovers, Zoom, Zoom, Zoom, Heritage 107, 45 rpm 12.00
Drivers, My Lonely Prayer, De Luxe 6104, 45 rpm 15.00
Elmore, Johnny; War Chant Boogie, Jar 105, 45 rpm 15.00
Ervin, Leroy; Rock Island Blues, Swing 415, 78 rpm 20.00
Everett, Vince; I'm Snowed, Royalty 505, 45 rpm 12.00
Fabulous Four, Betty Ann, Chancellor 1085, 45 rpm 20.00
Fisher, Sonny; Pink & Black, Starday 244, 45 rpm 40.00
Five Chords, Red Wine, Cuca 1031, 45 rpm 20.00
Five Jets, Crazy Chicken, De Luxe 6064, 45 rpm 20.00
Flames, Together, GM 2107, 45 rpm 30.00
Flamingos, Golden Teardrops, Chance 1145, 45 rpm 150.00
Four Blazes, Night Train, United 125, 45 rpm 10.00
Four Gents, On Bended Knee, Park 133, 45 rpm 60.00
Four Seasons, Bermuda, Gone 5122, 45 rpm 20.00
Four Troys, In the Moonlight, Freedom 40013, 45 rpm 15.00
Framer, Eli; Framer's Blues, Vi 23409, 78 rpm 700.00
Franklin, Buck; Crooked World Blues, Vi 23310, 78 rpm 200.00
Frost, Frank; Hey Boss Man, Phillips Int, LP 120.00
Gilley, Mickey; Susie-Q, Astro 104, 45 rpm 20.00
Glad Rags, My China Doll, Excello 2121, 45 rpm 15.00
Gray, Geneva; Fortune Teller's Blues, Okeh 8449, 78 rpm 50.00
Guitar Frank, Wild Track, Bridges 2203/2204, 45 rpm 20.00
Hadley, Jim; Midnight Train, Buddy 117, 45 rpm 30.00
Hardy, Bill; Rockin' at the Zoo, Rita 1001, 45 rpm 20.00
Harmonica Slim, Drop Anchor, Vita 146, 45 rpm 10.00
Harris, Wm; Bull Frog Blues, Gennett 6661, 78 rpm 700.00
Hart, Hattie; You Wouldn't Would You Papa?, Vi 23273, 78 rpm ..500.00
Henry, Lena; Sinful Blues, Vo 14902, 78 rpm 30.00
Hightower, Willie; If I Had a Hammer, Fury 5002, 45 rpm 8.00
Hill, Charlie; Pappa Charlie Hill Blues, Gennett 6904, 78 rpm .850.00
Houston, David; Hackin' Around, RCA Vi 6917, 45 rpm 8.00
Howard, John Henry; Black Snake, Gennett 3124, 78 rpm 40.00
Ivy Three, Bagoo, Shell 306, 45 rpm 8.00
Jackson, Odis; Pretty Baby, Fechi 90, 78 rpm 10.00
Jackson, Wanda; Mean Mean Mean, Capitol 4026, 45 rpm 15.00
James, Skip; Cherry Ball Blues, Para 13065, 78 rpm 700.00
James, Skip; Hard Luck Child, Para 13106, 78 rpm 850.00
Johnson, Buddy; Rock 'N Roll, Mercury 20209, LP 30.00
Johnson, Kiki; Lone Grave, QRS 7001, 78 rpm 150.00
Jones, Sonny; Dough Roller, Vo 05056, 78 rpm 30.00
Killen, Billy J; Georgia Boy, Meridian 1510, 45 rpm 15.00
King, Ray; A Date At Night, Karl 222, 45 rpm 100.00
Lee, Harry; Rockin' on a Reindeer, Igloo 101, 45 rpm 60.00
Lewis, Kate; Mercy Blues, Broadway 5016, 78 rpm 75.00
Lillie, Lonnie; Truck Driver's Special, Marathon 5003, 45 rpm 75.00
Little Joe Blue, Dirty Work Going On, Movin' 132, 45 rpm 10.00
Lumpkin, Bobby; One Way Ticket, Felco 102, 45 rpm 50.00
Martin, Jimmy; Rock the Bop, Jaxon 501, 45 rpm 40.00
Martin, Sara; Alabamy Bound, Okeh 8262, 78 rpm 75.00
McDonald, Tee; Beef Man Blues, Decca 7018, 78 rpm 75.00
McVoy, Carl; Tootsie, Vi 2001, 45 rpm 12.00
Mellow Keys, I'm Not a Deceiver, Gee 1014, 45 RPM 20.00
Mint Juleps, Bells of Love, Herald 481, 45 rpm 25.00
Mississippi Mud Mashers, Tiger Rag, Bluebird 7316, 78 rpm 25.00
Moonlighters, Glow of Love, Tara 100, 45 rpm 30.00
Murphy, Jimmy; Baboon Boogie, Col 21569, 45 rpm 50.00
Newman, Jack; Blackberry Wine, Vo 04265, 78 rpm 15.00
Nichols, Nick; Frankie & Johnny, Col 2071-D, 78 rpm 50.00
Nite Riders, Doctor Velvet, Apollo 466, 45 rpm 20.00
Patton, Charley; Pea Vine Blues, Para 12877, 78 rpm 500.00
Patton, Charley; Some Summer Day, Para 13080, 78 rpm 800.00

Pickett, Dan; Lemon Man, Gotham 201, 78 rpm 25.00
Pierce, Webb; Teenage Boogie, Decca 30045, 45 rpm 10.00
Pine Top Smith, I'm Sober Now, Vo 1266, 78 rpm 150.00
Pratt, Lynn; Tom Cat Boogie, Hornet 1000, 45 rpm 30.00
Presley, Elvis; Milkcow Blues Boogie, RCA Vi 6382, 45 rpm 20.00
Pretty Boy, Rockin' the Mule, Big 617, 45 rpm 20.00
Prodigals, Marsha, Falcon 1011, 45 rpm 20.00
Quinteros, Eddie; Slow Down Sally, Brent 7014, 45 rpm 20.00
Renowns, Wild One, Everest 19369, 45 rpm 15.00
Roberts, Gip; Sandman, JVB 29, 78 rpm 15.00
Ross, Lee; Candy Lips, Liberty 55127, 45 rpm 8.00
Satellites, Linda Jean, Cupid 5004, 45 rpm 35.00
Shaul, Lawrence; Tutti Fruitti, Reed 1049, 45 rpm 30.00
Shaw, Allen; Moanin' the Blues, Vo 02844, 78 rpm 250.00
Short, Jaydee; Telephone Arguin' Blues, Para 13043, 78 rpm 500.00
Sims, Henry; Be True Be True Blues, Para 12940, 78 rpm 500.00
Singleton, Charlie; Alligator Meat, Decca 48193, 45 rpm 15.00
Smithson, Lonnie; Me & the Blues, Starday 330, 45 rpm 25.00
Son House, Dry Spell Blues, Para 12990, 78 rpm 700.00
Spencer, Mamie; Scrubbin' Blues, Oriole 795, 78 rpm 30.00
Stewart, Sandy; Playmates, Atco 6137, 45 rpm 8.00
Taskiana Four, Dixie Bo-Bo, Vi 20852, 78 rpm 30.00
Tate, Joe; Satellite Rock, Roulette 4059, 45 rpm 10.00
Thomas, Elvis; Motherless Child Blues, Para 12977, 78 rpm 500.00
Thompson, Hank; Rockin' in the Congo, Capitol 3623, 45 rpm 6.00
Tucker, Bessie; The Dummy, Vi 21708, 78 rpm 100.00
Washburn, Alberta; Pig Meat Mama, Superior 2739, 78 rpm 250.00
Wayne, Scott; Roobie Doobie, Talent 1011, 45 rpm 12.00
Western Kid, Western Blues, Gennett 7230, 78 rpm 250.00
Wilkins, Robert; Falling Down Blues, Bru 7125, 78 rpm 400.00
Wilkins, Tim; Black Rat Blues, Vo 03176, 78 rpm 185.00
Williams, Lee; Centipede, Imperial 5429, 45 rpm 20.00
Willis, Hal; Walkin' Dream, Athens 704, 45 rpm 20.00
Winston, Edna; Peepin' Jim, Vi 20407, 78 rpm 40.00
Wray, Lucky; Teenage Cutie, Starday 608, 45 rpm 30.00
Young, Man; Let Me Ride Your Mule, Old Swing Master 19l 78 rpm ..50.00
Young, Nelson; Rock Old Sputnick, Lucky 0002, 45 rpm 40.00
Zeppa, Ben Joe; Topsy Turvy, Era 1042, 45 rpm 12.00

Country and Western

Allen, Lee & Austin; Chattanooga Blues, Col 14266-D, 78 rpm ..100.00
Bailey, Green; Santa Barbara Earthquake, Gennett 6702, 78 rpm ..75.00
Baker, Charlie; Just Plain Folks, Ch 16614, 78 rpm 30.00
Burnett Brothers, Rockin' Chair, Vi 23745, 78 rpm 20.00
Carson, Rosa Lee; Drinker's Child, Okeh 45005, 78 rpm 12.00
Conlon, Peter J; Barn Dance, Okeh 45030, 78 rpm 8.00
Davenport, Emmett; Virginia Moonshiner, Supertone 9539, 78 rpm 12.00
Davis, Charlie; Down in Southern Town, Timely Tunes 1559, 78 rpm ..50.00
Earl & Bill, Oregon Trail, Vo 15014, 78 rpm 8.00
Fletcher & Foster, Working So Hard, Ch 16121, 78 rpm 75.00
Gaydon, Whit; Tennessee Coon Hunt, Vi V40315, 78 rpm 20.00
Harris, JD; Cackling Hen, Okeh 45024, 78 rpm 20.00
Hickory Nuts, Louisville Burglar, Okeh 45169, 78 rpm 15.00
Hopkins, Doc; Methodist Pie, Broadway 8337, 78 rpm 10.00
Johnson, Edward; Sand Cave, Ch 15048, 78 rpm 7.00
Kirby, Fred; In the Shade of the Pine, Bluebird 6325, 78 rpm 8.00
Locke, Rusty; Milk Cow Blues, TNT 1012, 78 rpm 8.00
MacBeth, WW; Red Wing, Bru 443, 78 rpm 8.00
Marlow & Young, My Carolina Home, Ch 15732, 78 rpm 30.00
Martin & Hobbs, Havana River Glide, Ch 16536, 78 rpm 150.00
McKinney Brothers, Old Uncle Joe, Ch 16830, 78 rpm 15.00
Moonshiners, Midnight Waltz, Vi V40284, 78 rpm 25.00
New Arkansas Travelers, Handy Man, Vi 21288, 78 rpm 12.00

Newman, Fred; San Antonio, Para 3177, 78 rpm 15.00
Oak Mountain Boys, Medley, Ch 15874, 78 rpm 10.00
Pine Ridge Boys, Railroad Boomer, Bluebird 8671, 78 rpm 8.00
Prairie Ramblers, Go Easy Blues, Bluebird 5320, 78 rpm 50.00
Quinn, Frank; Pop Goes the Weasel, Okeh 45030, 78 rpm 10.00
Red Mountain Trio, Carolina Sunshine, Col 15462-D, 78 rpm 20.00
Roanoke Jug Band, Home Brew Rag, Okeh 45393, 78 rpm 125.00
Rose, Jack; Jack & Babe Blues, Okeh 45370, 78 rpm 15.00
Scott, Jimmie; Rocky Road, Star Talent 781, 78 rpm 10.00
Skyland & Scotty, Great Grandad, Bluebird 5357, 78 rpm 35.00
Spooney Five, Chinese Rag, Col 15234-D, 78 rpm 20.00
Swamp Rooters, Swamp Cat Rag, Bru 556, 78 rpm 20.00
Turner, Cal; Only a Tramp, Ch 15587, 78 rpm 18.00
Wanner, Enos; Strawberry Roan, Superior 2722, 78 rpm 30.00
Weems String Band, Greenback Dollar, Col 15300-D, 78 rpm 30.00
White Mountain Orch, Leather Britches, Vi V40185, 78 rpm 30.00
Wilkins, Frank; The Last Mile, Broadway 8205, 78 rpm 12.00
Zack & Glen, Gambler's Lament, Okeh 45240, 78 rpm 8.00

Jazz, Dance Bands, Personalities

Alabama Serenaders, Alabama Stomp, Ch 15140, 78 rpm 30.00
Arkansas Trio, Boll Weevil Blues, Edi 51373, 78 rpm 10.00
Atlanta Merrymakers, Black Stomp, Madison 1935, 78 rpm 15.00
Barbecue Pete, Avenue Strut, Ch 15904, 78 rpm 50.00
Bernard, Mike; 1915 Rag, Col A1427, 78 rpm 20.00
Blues Chasers, Sweet Georgia Brown, Perfect 14428, 78 rpm 10.00
Broadway Pickers, Salty Dog, Broadway 5069, 78 rpm 300.00
Campus Boys, Rainbow Man, Banner 6425, 78 rpm 10.00
Candy & Coco, Kingfish Blues, Vo 2833, 78 rpm 20.00
Checker Box Boys, Outside, Broadway 1262, 78 rpm 8.00
Coleman, EL; Steel String Blues, Okeh 8216, 78 rpm 50.00
Cotton Club Orch, Riverboat Shuffle, Col 374-D, 78 rpm 50.00
Crosby, Bing; Cabin in the Cotton, Bru 6329, 78 rpm 12.00
Crosstown Ramblers, River Bottom Glide, Ch 15030, 78 rpm 60.00
Deppe, Louis; Southland, Gennett 20021, 78 rpm 30.00
Dixie Rhythm Kings, Easy Rider, Bru 7115, 78 rpm 120.00
Eaton, Charlie; Bucket of Blood, Herwin 93017, 78 rpm 150.00
English, Peggy; Sweet Man, Vo 15132, 78 rpm 10.00
Finnie, Ethel; Hula Blues, Ajax 17027, 78 rpm 50.00
Fuller, Bob; Alligator Crawl, Banner 7151, 78 rpm 15.00

Gene Autry, That's Why I Left the Mountains, Q.R.S., from $200.00 to $300.00.

Glascoe, Percy; Stomp 'em Down, Col 14088-D, 78 rpm 30.00
Golden Gate Serenaders, Oh! Baby, Gennett 6487, 78 rpm 12.00
Hamp, Charles W; I'm in Seventh Heaven, Okeh 41266, 78 rpm ..12.00
Harlem Footwarmers, Jungle Jamboree, Okeh 8720, 78 rpm 50.00
Harlem Stompers, Jammin' in Georgia, Decca 7616, 78 rpm 10.00
Henderson, Bertha; Jamboree Blues, Okeh 8265, 78 rpm 75.00

High Hatters, Wipin' the Pan, Vi 21835, 78 rpm 8.00
Hudson Trio, Twelfth Street Rag, Famous 3024, 78 rpm 10.00
Jamaica Jazzers, West Indies Blues, Okeh 40117, 78 rpm 75.00
Jolly Three, Ain't Got a Dime Blues, Vo 03955, 78 rpm 30.00
Karle, Art & His Boys; Moon Over Miami, Vo 3146, 78 rpm 20.00
Kay, Dolly; Hot Lips, Col A3758, 78 rpm 10.00
King, Frances; She's Got It, Okeh 40854, 78 rpm 15.00
Langford, Frances; Moon Song, Bluebird 5016, 78 rpm 12.00
Lee, Ruth; Maybe Someday, Sunshine 3002, 78 rpm......................300.00
Lill's Hot Shots, Drop That Sack, Vo 1037, 78 rpm 120.00
Lynch's Rhythm Aces, She's My Baby Now, Challenge 742, 78 rpm ..10.00
Marigold Entertainers, Jeoulos, Vo 15800, 78 rpm 10.00
Marvin, Johnny; My Pet, Vi 21435, 78 rpm 15.00
Melody Sheiks, Indian Nights, Okeh 40438, 78 rpm 8.00
Memphis Bell-hops, Animal Crackers, Challenge 135, 78 rpm 70.00
Midnight Ramblers, Too Busy, Broadway 1175, 78 rpm 8.00
Moonlight Revelers, Memphis Stomp, Grey Gull 1786, 78 rpm ...50.00
Moskowitz, Joseph; Operatic Rag, Vi 17978, 78 rpm 20.00
New Orleans Owls, Goose Pimples, Coo 1261-D, 78 rpm 30.00
New Yorkers, Under a Texas Moon, QRS 1003, 78 rpm 15.00
Original Jazz Hounds, Slow Down, Col 14094-D, 78 rpm 100.00
Palmer, Gladys; I'm Livin' in a Great Big Way, Decca 7106, 78 rpm ..10.00
Pinkie's Birmingham Five, Carolina Stomp, Gennett 3208, 78 rpm ...40.00
Rambler, Lonely Eyes, Romeo 315, 78 rpm 8.00
Rhythm Aces, Jazz Battle, Bru 4244, 78 rpm 100.00
Robinson, Elzadie; Houston Bound, Para 12420, 78 rpm 150.00
Rocky Mountain Trio, Blowin' Off Steam, Gennett 3288, 78 rpm ..15.00
Roye, Ruth; Hotsy Totsy Town, Col A3881, 78 rpm 12.00
Searcy Trio, Kansas Avenue Blues, Okeh 8360, 78 rpm 75.00
Sioux City Six, Flock O' Blues, Gennett 5569, 78 rpm 150.00
Snodgrass, Harry; Maple Leaf Rag, Bru 3239, 78 rpm 10.00
Spencer Trio, John Henry, Decca 1873, 78 rpm 10.00
Sullivan, Joe; Gin Mill Blues, Col 2876-D, 78 rpm 40.00
Texas Ten, Charleston, Regal 9835, 78 rpm 10.00
Thomas, Hersal; Suitcase Blues, Okeh 8227, 78 rpm 100.00
Triangle Harmony Boys, Sweet Patooties, Gennett 6275, 78 rpm .300.00
Vagabonds, Ukelele Lady, Gennett 3100, 78 rpm 12.00
Virginians, Low Down, Vi 21680, 78 rpm 10.00
Washington, Buck; Old Fashion Love, Col 2925-D, 78 rpm 40.00
West, Mae; Easy Rider, Bru 6495, 78 rpm 15.00
Wiley, Lee; Let's Do It, Liberty 297, 78 rpm 10.00
Williams, Mary Lou; Clean Pickin', Decca 1155, 78 rpm 12.00
Young, Margaret; High Brown Blues, Bru 2253, 78 rpm 8.00

Red Wing

The Red Wing Stoneware Company, founded in 1878, took its name from its location in Red Wing, Minnesota. In 1906 the name was changed to the Red Wing Union Stoneware Company after a merger with several of the other local potteries. For the most part they produced utilitarian wares such as flowerpots, crocks, and jugs. Their early 1930s catalogs offered a line of art pottery vases in colored glazes, some of which featured handles modeled after swan's necks, snakes, or female nudes. Other examples were quite simple, often with classic styling.

Dinnerware lines were added in 1935, and today collectors scramble to rebuild extensive table services. Many lines were decorated by hand. Among the most popular hand-painted lines are Bob White, Tropicana, and Round-up. Town and Country, designed by Eva Zeisel, was made for only one year late in the 1940s. Today many collectors regard Zeisel as one of the most gifted designers of that era and actively seek examples of her work. Town and Country was a versatile line, adaptable to both informal and semiformal use. Irregular, often eccentric shapes characterize the line, as handles of pitchers and serving

pieces are usually extensions of the rim. Bowls and platters are free-form comma shapes or appear tilted, with one side slightly higher than the other. Although the ware is unmarked, it is recognizable by its distinctive shapes and glazes. White is often used to complement interiors of bowls and cups, Bronze (metallic brown) enjoys favored status, and gray is unusual. Other colors include rust, dusk blue, sand, chartreuse, peach, and forest green.

After the addition of their dinnerware lines, 'Stoneware' was dropped from the name, and the company became known as Red Wing Potteries, Inc. They closed in 1967. For further study we recommend *Red Wing Stoneware, An Identification and Value Guide,* and *Red Wing Collectibles* by Dan and Gail DePasquale and Larry Peterson, available at your bookstore or from Collector Books. Our advisor for the general dinnerware lines is Doug Podpeskar; he is listed in the Directory under Minnesota. Our artware advisors are Wendy and Leo Frese (Three Rivers Collectibles); they are listed under Texas. Karen Silvermintz (see Texas) and Charles Alexander (see Indiana) advise on the Town and Country dinnerware.

Key:
c/s — cobalt on stoneware   RW — Red Wing
MN — Minnesota   RWUS — Red Wing Union
NS — North Star   Stoneware

Commercial Art Ware and Miscellaneous

Vase, orange with pelican handles, 1930s, 10", $95.00.

Ashtray, horse head, Fleck Zepher Pk (pk speckled), M-1472 ......75.00
Ashtray, Red Wing, maroon 40.00
Ashtray, wing shape, 75th Anniversary, maroon 50.00
Bowl, console; gray over burgundy, #2307, 1953 ....150.00
Bowl, console; Regular Line, #852, 7½x12" 35.00
Bowl, red w/wht, #6004, shallow, 11" 550.00
Bowl, wht, scalloped (referred to as daisy), #1620, 10" 14.00
Candle holders, Magnolia, 2-light, #1029, pr 55.00
Cigarette holder, horse head lid, M-1474 ....200.00
Compote, Cherub, lav, #761 ....55.00
Ewer, Magnolia, #1028, 1940s, 6" 25.00
Figurine, Cowboy & Cowgirl, HP, B-1414/B-1415, pr 400.00
Figurine, Oriental man, solid gr, B-1389 ....75.00
Flower frog, angelfish, #1045 ....200.00
Leaf vase, buff & gr, #1166 ....20.00
Pitcher, Dutch Bl, #768, 6½x7½" 90.00
Pitcher, Dutch Bl, dbl spout, #766 ....120.00
Pitcher, Magnolia, #1219, 11" 145.00
Planter, emb leaf, burgundy w/gray int, sq, B-1404 ....40.00
Planter, Nakomis, #198, 7½" 175.00
Planter/bookends, Belle 100 Line, dk brn mottling on brn, pr 85.00
Plate, African drummer on lt bl, 14" 360.00
Plate, African lady on lt bl, 14" 580.00
Vase, brushware acorn & oak veaves, #149, 7" 100.00
Vase, cherub appl to cylinder, wht, #821, ca 1963 ....330.00

Vase, cream lustre w/Rachel lustre int, #888, 7" 30.00
Vase, deer figural, tan w/no HP decor, #1120 ....40.00
Vase, floral, gr/mauve, minor flake, #1107, 8" 75.00
Vase, Gardenia, #1319, 12" 100.00
Vase, gr & wht, #145, 9" 66.00
Vase, gray on burgundy, 75th Anniversary sticker, B-2317, 10" .100.00
Vase, lady on a swing w/2 cherubs, #776, 12" 90.00
Vase, leaf & dot decor, mint gr w/brn int, #840, 1938, 11" 40.00
Vase, Lotus, HP decor, H-511, 10" 120.00
Vase, lt bl, #155, 9" 100.00
Vase, Magnolia, #1215, 10" 60.00
Vase, Magnolia, bulbous, #1222, 7" 65.00
Vase, Murphy bl crystalline, Decorator line, M-3014, 12¼" 175.00
Vase, Murphy, orange crystalline, Decorator Line, M-3007, 12" ..100.00
Vase, pk w/wht int, loop hdls w/balls below, #1207, 10" 30.00
Vase, Prismatique, #794, 11" 105.00
Vase, seashell form, #1066 ....190.00
Wall pocket, violin, #907 ....50.00

Cookie Jars

Queen of Tarts, marked
Red Wing USA, $550.00.

Bob White, unmk 125.00
Carousel, unmk 900.00
Crock, wht 60.00
Dutch Girl, yel w/brn trim 140.00
Friar Tuck, cream w/brn, mk 195.00
Friar Tuck, gr, mk 295.00
Friar Tuck, yel, unmk 175.00
Grapes 225.00
Grapes, cobalt or dk purple, ea 450.00
Jack Frost, unmk 750.00
King of Tarts, mc, mk 975.00
King of Tarts, pk w/bl & blk trim, mk 950.00
King of Tarts, wht, unmk 675.00
Peasant design, emb/pnt figures on brn 85.00
Pierre (chef), brn, unmk 195.00
Pierre (chef), gr, unmk 350.00
Pierre (chef), pk, mk 450.00
Pineapple, yel 200.00

Dinnerware

Bob White, bowl, cereal 22.00
Bob White, bowl, fruit 12.00
Bob White, butter dish, ¼-lb 75.00
Bob White, casserole, w/lid, 2-qt 45.00
Bob White, casserole, 4-qt 50.00
Bob White, cup & saucer 20.00
Bob White, hors d'oevres holder 50.00
Bob White, pitcher, water; sm 45.00

Bob White, pitcher, water; 60-oz 50.00
Bob White, plate, 10½" 12.50
Bob White, plate, 6½" 6.00
Bob White, plate, 8" 8.00
Bob White, platter, 13" 80.00
Bob White, shakers, quail form, pr 40.00
Bob White, teapot 100.00
Capistrano, bowl, berry; 5½" 8.00
Capistrano, bowl, divided vegetable 28.00
Capistrano, bowl, salad; 12" 45.00
Capistrano, plate, 10½" 10.00
Capistrano, plate, 6½" 5.00
Capistrano, platter, 13" 35.00
Crazy Rhythm, creamer & sugar bowl 45.00
Fondoso, cookie jar, yel, 8½" 100.00

Lotus, Beverage pot,
$32.50; Dinner plate,
$10.00; Cup and
saucer, $8.00.

Lotus, casserole, w/lid 30.00
Lotus, cup & saucer 10.00
Lotus, gravy boat 10.00
Lotus, platter 35.00
Lotus, spoon rest 20.00
Lotus, sugar bowl 15.00
Lute Song, butter dish 38.00
Lute Song, casserole 35.00
Magnolia, plate, dinner 12.00
Magnolia, platter, 13" 30.00
Midnight, bowl, divided vegetable 22.50
Midnight Rose, teapot 125.00
Midnight Rose, tidbit, 3-tier 26.00
Random Harvest, bowl, salad; lg 85.00
Random Harvest, tidbit tray, paper label 27.50
Round-Up, bowl, salad; 10" 95.00
Round-Up, bread tray, long 150.00
Round-Up, butter dish 200.00
Round-Up, carafe, w/stopper 295.00
Round-Up, cookie jar, off-color lid 400.00
Round-Up, creamer 50.00
Round-Up, cup & saucer 55.00
Round-Up, plate, 10½" 35.00
Round-Up, plate, 7½" 20.00
Round-Up, relish, 3-compartment 95.00
Smart Set, cup & saucer 38.00
Smart Set, plate, 10" 35.00
Smart Set, platter, 20" 120.00
Tampico, bowl, cereal 16.00
Tampico, bowl, divided vegetable 45.00
Tampico, bowl, salad; 12" 85.00
Tampico, cup & saucer 12.50
Tampico, gravy bowl w/stand 50.00
Tampico, mug, coffee 45.00
Tampico, pitcher, 13" 85.00
Tampico, plate, 10½" 14.00
Tampico, plate, 6½" 5.00

Tampico, plate, 8½"	9.50
Tampico, water cooler & stand	385.00
Tip-Toe, trivet	65.00
Town & Country, bean pot, rust, w/lid	400.00
Town & Country, bowl, mixing; dusk bl	100.00
Town & Country, bowl, vegetable; sand, 8"	35.00
Town & Country, bowl, 5"	15.00
Town & Country, casserole, marmite, chartreuse, ind	25.00
Town & Country, casserole, stick hdl, w/lid, lg	95.00
Town & Country, creamer & sugar bowl, w/lid, minimum value	50.00
Town & Country, cruets, mixed colors, orig stoppers, sm, pr	150.00
Town & Country, cup & saucer, forest gr w/wht int	27.50
Town & Country, mug, coffee	48.00
Town & Country, pitcher, peach, 3-pt	125.00
Town & Country, pitcher, sand, 2-pt	85.00
Town & Country, plate, bronze, 10½"	45.00
Town & Country, plate, gray, 8"	20.00
Town & Country, plate, rust, 6½"	7.50
Town & Country, plate, 10½"	25.00
Town & Country, platter, peach, comma shape, 9"	35.00
Town & Country, shakers, Shmoo shape, mixed colors, pr	75.00
Town & Country, sugar bowl, bronze, w/lid	65.00
Town & Country, syrup, chartreuse	95.00
Town & Country, teapot, sand	250.00
Village Green, casserole, lg	28.00
Village Green, shakers, pr	22.50

Stoneware

Photo courtesy DePasquale and Peterson

Beehive jug, Albany slip, hand-turned style with wall stamp, M, 2-gal, $700.00.

Bean pot, Albany slip, Boston style, RW, 1-gal	250.00
Bean pot, Albany slip, cup type, NS, ind	150.00
Bean pot, Albany slip, short neck, NS, 1-gal	140.00
Bean pot, Albany slip & wht, bail hdl, RW, 1-qt	95.00
Bowl, Greek Key, bl & wht, 12"	225.00
Bowl, shoulder; wht, RW, 1-pt	55.00
Casserole, Spongeband, RW, w/lid, sm	375.00
Chamber pot, bl spongeware, unmk	375.00
Churn, bird/#6, c/s, unmk, 6-gal	1,500.00
Churn, butterfly/#6, c/s, RW, 6-gal	1,500.00
Churn, molded seam, leaf/#3, c/s, MN, 3-gal	1,100.00
Churn, P/#4, c/s, RW, 4-gal	950.00
Churn, P/#4, c/s, unmk, 4-gal	450.00
Churn, red wing/#2/union oval, c/s, 2-gal	275.00
Churn, 2 birch leaves/#8, c/s, unmk, 8-gal	800.00
Churn, 2 birch leaves/#10, c/s, RW, 10-gal	1,000.00
Combinette, emb lily on wht w/bl bands, complete, unmk	275.00
Cooler, butterfly/#6, c/s, RW, 6-gal	2,400.00
Cooler, daisy/#6, c/s, RW, 6-gal	2,000.00

Cooler, Ice Water/#3/birch leaves, wht, old shape	800.00
Cooler, Ice Water/#6/flower, c/s, RW, 6-gal	8,000.00
Cooler, 2 birch leaves/#4, c/s, RW, 4-gal	2,400.00
Crock, birch leaves/#25, c/s, MN, 25-gal	1,200.00
Crock, birch leaves/#40, c/s, unmk, 40-gal	1,000.00
Crock, butter; Albany slip, high style, NS, 1-qt	150.00
Crock, butter; Albany slip, low style, MN, 2-lb	50.00
Crock, butter; Albany slip, low style, RW, 1-lb	80.00
Crock, butter; salt glaze, low style, RW, 10-lb	80.00
Crock, butter; wht, high style, MN, ½-gal	50.00
Crock, butter; wht, low style, MN, 10-lb	50.00
Crock, butterfly/#20, c/s, 20-gal	1,000.00
Crock, butterfly/#30/stencil, c/s, RW, 30-gal	2,200.00
Crock, drop-8/#3, c/s, RW, 3-gal	450.00
Crock, lily/#30/stencils, c/s, RW, 30-gal	2,400.00
Crock, red wing/#15, wht, RWUS, 15-gal	100.00
Crock, red wing/#40, wht, RWUS, 40-gal	350.00
Crock, target/#2, c/s, RW	200.00
Crock, 4 leaves/#10, c/s, stamped/handwritten, RW, 10-gal	700.00
Cuspidor, brn & wht, fancy style, MN, lg	450.00
Cuspidor, molded seam, Albany slip, unmk	125.00
Jar, fruit; Stone Mason, blk or bl label on wht, 1899, 1-gal	600.00
Jar, packing; wht, bail hdl, MN, 5-lb	75.00
Jar, preserve; Albany slip, RW, 1-gal	500.00
Jar, preserve/snuff; Albany slip, MN, ½-gal	60.00
Jar, preserve/snuff; Albany slip, RW, 4-gal	250.00
Jar, preserve/snuff; wht, RW, 1-qt	100.00
Jar, safety valve; wht, bail hdl, RW, 1-qt	200.00
Jar, wax sealer; Albany slip, MN, 1-qt	60.00
Jug, beehive threshing; red wing/#5/oval, c/s, RWUS, 5-gal	1,000.00
Jug, beehive; birch leaf/#5, c/s, RW, 5-gal	2,500.00
Jug, beehive; birch leaves/#3, c/s, RW oval, 3-gal	350.00
Jug, beehive; elephant-ear leaves/#5, wht, RW oval, 5-gal	1,500.00
Jug, beehive; red wing/#4, c/s, RW Union oval, 4-gal	700.00
Jug, bl banded; cone top, RW, 1-gal	450.00
Jug, common; Albany slip, bottom seam, MN, 1-gal	75.00
Jug, common; Albany slip, molded at bottom, 1895, NS, 1-gal	200.00
Jug, common; salt glaze, MN, 1-gal	325.00
Jug, common; wht, MN, 1-gal	70.00
Jug, fancy; red wings on wht, brn top, 2-gal	750.00
Jug, fancy; wht w/brn ball top, MN, ¼-pt	225.00
Jug, fancy; wht w/brn ball top, RW, 1-gal	200.00
Jug, fancy; wht w/brn ball top, RW, ½-pt	175.00
Jug, fancy; wht w/brn ball top, RW, 2-gal	275.00
Jug, fancy; wht w/brn ball top, unmk, 1-pt	50.00
Jug, molded seam, Albany slip, bail hdl, MN, ½-gal	250.00
Jug, molded seam, Albany slip, bail hdl, RW, 1-gal	400.00
Jug, molded seam, Albany slip, bird mk, RW, 2-gal	225.00
Jug, molded seam, bl mottle, bail hdl, MN, 1-gal	1,300.00
Jug, molded seam, wht, bail hdl, MN, 1-gal	100.00
Jug, molded seam, wht, bail hdl, RW, 1-gal	150.00
Jug, molded seam, wht, wide mouth, MN, ½-gal	70.00
Jug, shoulder; Albany slip, cone top, RW, 2-gal	650.00
Jug, shoulder; birch leaf/#3/Union oval, c/s, MN, 3-gal	175.00
Jug, shoulder; brn & salt glaze, ball top, RW, 1-gal	225.00
Jug, shoulder; brn & salt glaze, cone top, RW, 2-gal	350.00
Jug, shoulder; brn & salt glaze, dome top, MN, 2-gal	175.00
Jug, shoulder; brn & salt glaze, funnel top, MN, 1-gal	125.00
Jug, shoulder; brn & salt glaze, funnel top, MN, ½-gal	200.00
Jug, shoulder; brn & salt glaze, funnel top, MN, 2-gal	175.00
Jug, shoulder; brn & salt glaze, standard top, NS, ½-gal	375.00
Jug, shoulder; brn & salt glaze, wide mouth, NS, 1-gal	400.00
Jug, shoulder; red wing on wht, brn top, 1930s, 2-gal	500.00
Jug, shoulder; salt glaze w/brn drips, pear top, NS, 2-gal	900.00

Jug, shoulder; wht, cone top, RW, ½-gal **95.00**
Jug, shoulder; wht, funnel top, MN, 2-gal **75.00**
Jug, shoulder; wht, standard top, MN, 1-qt **90.00**
Jug, shoulder; wht, standard top, MN, 2-gal **75.00**
Jug, tomato or fruit; Albany slip, wide mouth, MN, ½-gal **75.00**
Pan, milk; wht, NS **100.00**
Pipkin, Albany slip & wht, MN, 4-pt **300.00**
Pipkin, Albany slip or wht, unmk, 4-pt **90.00**
Pitcher, mustard; wht, MN or RW **90.00**
Pitcher, Russian; Albany slip, unmk, 1-gal **100.00**
Spittoon, Albany slip, MN **650.00**
Spittoon, German style, bl bands on salt glaze, emb decor, RW ..**600.00**
Spittoon, German style, bl bands on salt glaze, MN **800.00**
Spittoon, salt glaze, RW **800.00**
Spittoon, salt glaze, unmk **275.00**
Syrup, wht, shouldered, pouring spout, MN, 1-gal **60.00**
Syrup, wht, shouldered cone top, MN, ½-gal **70.00**
Umbrella stand, bl spongeware, unsgn **1,400.00**
Wash bowl & pitcher, emb lily on wht w/wide lt bl bands, RW ..**850.00**

Redware

The term redware refers to a type of simple earthenware produced by the Colonists as early as the 1600s. The red clay used in its production was abundant throughout the country, and during the 18th and 19th centuries redware was made in great quantities. Intended for utilitarian purposes such as everyday tableware or use in the dairy, redware was simple in design and decoration. Glazes of various colors were used, and a liquid clay referred to as 'slip' was sometimes applied in patterns such as zigzag lines, daisies, or stars. Plates often have a 'coggled' edge, similar to the way a pie is crimped or jagged, which is done with a special tool. In the following listings, EX (excellent condition) indicates only minor damage. Our advisor for this category is Barbara Rosen; she is listed in the Directory under New Jersey.

Birdhouse, creamy opaque w/yel highlights, 7½" **50.00**
Bowl, orange int, str sides w/slight flare, 2¼x7½" **200.00**
Bowl, 3-line yel slip, coggled rim, 2⅝x13½" **825.00**
Creamer, yel slip design w/gr, ribbed strap hdl, 4⅜" **435.00**
Dish, dk glaze w/yel slip spots, rim flake, 7⅝" **275.00**

Flask, shades of orange, red, and olive, molded concentric rings each side, ca 1760-1800, 6¾", $180.00.

Jar, brn manganese, vertical hdl, Am, early 1800s, 8", EX **225.00**
Jar, brushed brn swirls on shiny clear, 1863 label, 5", EX **85.00**
Jar, dk tan, ovoid, w/lid, 11¼", EX **375.00**
Jar, gr w/orange spots, flakes, 8¼" **220.00**
Jar, gr w/orange spots, wooden lid, hdls, lg flake, 10⅝" **195.00**
Jar, mottled amber, tooled band, flared lip, 8⅜" **195.00**
Jar, orange/brn w/manganese decor, w/lid, 11", EX **250.00**
Jar, tooled lines, appl hdls, flared lip, ovoid, 8¾" **275.00**

Jar, yel-amber w/brn sponging & flecks, gr dots, rope hdls, 7" .**1,800.00**
Jug, brn w/amber spots, incised str & wavy lines, strap hdl, 5" **165.00**
Jug, dk amber w/brn, strap hdl, ovoid, 8½", EX **165.00**
Jug, dk brn, ovoid w/ribbed strap hdl, 10¾" **110.00**
Jug, gr-orange w/brn flecks, strap hdl, chips, 8¼" **165.00**
Jug, orange w/dk brn splotches, strap hdl, 5¾", EX **275.00**
Loaf pan, 3-line yel slip, coggled rim, 3x16x11" **1,425.00**
Mold, Turk's head, amber & gr w/dk brn sponging, 9" **165.00**
Mold, Turk's head, gr w/amber & orange spots, 5x10¾", EX **50.00**
Pie plate, brn mica int, unglazed exterior, 5⅛" **75.00**
Pie plate, orange int, unglazed exterior, 4¼" **100.00**
Pie plate, yel slip, coggled rim, 12¼", EX **300.00**
Pie plate, 3-line yel slip, coggled rim, chips/line, 10" **220.00**
Pie plate, 3-line yel slip, coggled rim, 8" dia **525.00**
Pie plate, 3-line yel slip, coggled rim, 9½", EX **330.00**
Pitcher, milk; orange/brn w/brn manganese & speckling, 6½" ...**225.00**
Pitcher, orange w/brn sponging, strap hdl, chips, 6½" **195.00**

Plate, yellow slip squiggle pattern on brick orange-red, ca 1800-30, 7½" dia, NM, $250.00.

Plate, Distlefink among floral branches, 10½", EX+ **2,200.00**
Plate, Lafayette & squiggles in yel slip, 11¼", NM **400.00**
Plate, Mince Pie in yel slip, 10", EX **250.00**
Plate, orange w/yel slip crow's foot decor, coggled rim, 4" ...**475.00**
Plate, toddy; dk orange w/brn spatter, 6¾", EX **70.00**
Plate, toddy; lt amber w/brn splotches, 4⅞" **165.00**
Plate, 3-line yel slip, coggled rim, 12", VG **330.00**
Teapot, clear orange w/dk brn splotches, molded ribs, rpr, 7" .**385.00**
Teapot, engine trn, glazed, 1750s, 5", EX **350.00**
Umbrella stand, ivy on tree bk, orig brn & wht, red int, 21" ..**110.00**

Regal China

Located in Antioch, Illinois, the Regal China Company began its business in 1938. Products of interest to collectors are James Beam decanters, cookie jars, salt and pepper shakers, and similar novelty items. The company closed its doors sometime in 1993. The Old Mac-Donald Farm series listed below is becoming especially collectible. Prices are based on excellent gold trim. (Gold trim must be 90% intact or deductions should be made for wear.) See also Decanters.

Alice in Wonderland

Cookie Jar **3,200.00**
Creamer, White Rabbit **600.00**
Pitcher, King of Hearts, milk sz **650.00**
Shakers, matching colors, rare, pr **675.00**
Shakers, Tweedledee & Tweedledum, pr **850.00**
Shakers, wht w/gold trim, pr **675.00**
Sugar bowl, White Rabbit, w/lid **600.00**

Teapot, Mad Hatter 2,500.00

Cookie Jars

Cat 425.00
Churn Boy 275.00
Clown, gr collar 675.00
Davy Crockett 550.00
Diaper Pin Pig 525.00
Dutch Girl, peach trim 800.00
Fifi Poodle 650.00
Fisherman 650.00
French Chef 375.00
Goldilocks 375.00
Hobby Horse 250.00
Hubert Lion 775.00
Humpty Dumpty, red wall 325.00
Little Miss Muffett 385.00
Oriental Lady w/Baskets 600.00

Photo courtesy Ermagene Westfall

Peek-a-boo, $1,500.00.

Quaker Oats 125.00
Three Bears 285.00
Toby Cookies 750.00
Tulip 300.00
Uncle Mistletoe 850.00

Old McDonald's Farm

Creamer and sugar bowl, $235.00 for the pair.

Butter dish, cow's head 220.00
Canister, flour, cereal, coffee; med, ea 220.00
Canister, pretzels, peanuts, popcorn, chips, tidbits; lg, ea ...300.00
Canister, salt, sugar or tea; med, ea 220.00
Cookie jar, barn 275.00
Creamer, rooster 110.00
Grease jar, pig 175.00
Pitcher, milk 400.00
Shakers, boy & girl, pr 75.00
Shakers, churn, gold trim, pr 90.00
Shakers, feed sacks w/sheep, pr 195.00

Spice jar, assorted lids, sm, ea 100.00
Sugar bowl, hen 125.00
Teapot, duck's head 250.00

Shakers

A Nod to Abe, 3-pc 250.00
Bendel, bears, wht w/pk & brn trim, pr 100.00
Bendel, bunnies, wht w/blk & pk trim, pr 135.00
Bendel, kissing pigs, gray w/pk trim, lg, pr 375.00
Bendel, love bugs, burgundy, lg, pr 165.00
Bendel, love bugs, gr, sm, pr 65.00
Cat, pr 225.00
Clown, pr 450.00
Dutch Girl, pr 275.00
FiFi, pr 450.00
Fish, C Miller, pr 60.00
French Chef, wht w/gold trim, pr 175.00
Humpty Dumpty, pr 140.00
Peek-a-Boo, peach trim, rare, lg, pr 575.00
Peek-a-Boo, red dots, lg, pr 500.00
Peek-a-Boo, red dots, sm, pr 220.00
Peek-a-Boo, w/burgundy trim, rare, sm, pr 350.00
Peek-a-Boo, wht solid, lg, pr 400.00
Peek-a-Boo, wht solid, sm, pr 200.00
Peek-a-Boo, wht w/gold trim, lg, pr 450.00
Pig, pk, mk C Miller, 1-pc 95.00
Tulip, pr 50.00
Van Telligen, bears, brn, pr 20.00
Van Telligen, boy & dog, blk, pr 120.00
Van Telligen, boy & dog, wht, pr 60.00
Van Telligen, bunnies, solid colors, pr 22.00
Van Telligen, ducks, pr 30.00
Van Telligen, Dutch boy & girl, pr 40.00
Van Telligen, Mary & lamb, pr 55.00
Van Telligen, sailor & mermaid, pr 195.00
Vermont Leaf People, 3-pc 150.00

Miscellaneous

Banks, kissing pigs, Bendel, lg, pr 425.00
Creamer & sugar bowl, cat form, ea 175.00
Creamer & sugar bowl, Tulip 100.00
Teapot, Tulip, tall 125.00

Relief-Molded Jugs

Early relief-molded pitchers (ca 1830s-40s) were made in two-piece molds into which sheets of clay were pressed. The relief decoration was deep and well defined, usually of animal or human subjects. Most of these pitchers were designed with a flaring lip and substantial footing. Gradually styles changed, and by the 1860s the rim had become flatter and the foot less pronounced. The relief decoration was not as deep, and foliage became a common design. By the turn of the century, many other types of pitchers had been introduced, and the market for these early styles began to wane.

Watch for recent reproductions; these have been made by the slip-casting method. Unlike relief-molded ware which is relatively smooth inside, slip-cast pitchers will have interior indentations that follow the irregularities of the relief decoration. Values below are for pieces in excellent condition. Our advisor for this category is Kathy Hughes; she is listed in the Directory under North Carolina.

Key: Reg — Registered

Argos, gr, Brownfield, Apr 29, 1864, 8" **175.00**
Bacchanalian Dance, wht, Meigh, 1844, 7⅝" **450.00**
Chrysanthemum, gr & wht, Ridgway, ca 1860, 9¼" **275.00**
Diana, Edward Walley, June 21, 1850, 10" **450.00**
Garibaldi, unknown, ca 1870, 13" **250.00**

Gipsey (sic), pictorial white body in raised relief, unglazed, Edward Walley, mid-1800s, 10", $350.00.

Gipsy (sic), lav on parian, Alcock, Reg July 1, 1842, 4¾" **250.00**
Good Samaritan, buff & tan, Jones & Walley, 1841, 8" **375.00**
Hunters & Hounds, gray-gr w/wht vintage, Wedgwood, 1810, 6⅞" ..**475.00**
Julius Caesar, gray, appl laurel wreath, Meigh, 1839, 8¼" **450.00**
Love & War, Samuel Alcock, ca 1845, 7¾" **400.00**
Mermaid & Cupid, Minton, parian, wht on gr, ca 1911, 6" **700.00**
Moses & the Rock, Ridgway & Abington, Jan 1, 1859, 5½" **250.00**
Now I'm Grandpapa, unknown, ca 1850, 8½" **400.00**
Prince Consort, Old Hall Earthenware Co, Apr 9, 1862, 8" **500.00**
Punch, Samuel Alcock & Co, ca 1845, 8¾" **450.00**
Rose, parian, unmk, ca 1850, 6½" **175.00**
Sir Walter Scott commemorative, gray-gr, Minton, 8" **350.00**
Sleeping Beauty, teal & wht, Dudson, ca 1860, 5¼" **185.00**
Tulip, bl & wht, Dudson, 1860, 7" **175.00**
Victoria Regina, Sanford Pottery, July 6, 1860, 9¾" **450.00**
Youth & Old Age, ca 1845, Copeland-Garret, gray-gr, 8¾" **250.00**

Restraints

Since the beginning of time, many things from animals to treasures have been held in bondage by hemp, bamboo, chests, chains, shackles, and other constructed devices. Many of these devices were used to hold captives who awaited further torture, as if the restraint wasn't torturous enough. The study and collecting of restraints enables one to learn much about the advancement of civilization in the country or region from which they originated. Such devices at various times in history were made of very heavy metals — so heavy that the wearer could scarcely move about. It has only been in the last sixty years that vast improvements have been made in design and construction that afford the captive some degree of comfort. Our advisor for this category is Joseph Tanner; he is listed in the Directory under Washington.

Key:
bbl — barrel
d-lb — double lock button
K — key
Kd — keyed

lc — lock case
NST — non-swing through
ST — swing through
stp — stamped

Foreign Handcuffs

Australian, Saf Lock, ST, takes pin-tumbler K in side, stp **145.00**
Czechalaviak, ST, Ralken flat key, modern ST **90.00**

Deutsche Polizei, ST, middle hinge, folds, takes bbl-bit K **80.00**
East German, aluminum, single lg hinge, ST, bbl K **60.00**
East German, heavy steel, NP single lg hinge, NST, bbl K **90.00**
English, Chubb, NST, hi-security 10-slider lock mechanism **275.00**
English, Chubb Arrest, steel, ST, multi-bit solid K **225.00**
English, Latrobe, aluminum alloy, center chain, ST, dbl-bit K ...**160.00**
French Lapegy, ST, aluminum alloys, takes flat bitted K **75.00**
French Revolved, oval, ST, takes 2 Ks: bbl & pin tumbler **150.00**
German, 3-lb steel set, 2⅝" thick, center chain, bbl K **175.00**
German Clejuso, oval design, ST, dbl-cuff weight, 22-oz **100.00**
German Clejuso, sq lc, adjusts/NST, d-lb on side, bbl K **100.00**
German Darby, adjusts, well finished, NST, sm **120.00**
German Hamburg 8, non-adjust NST, center bar/post w/K-way ..**250.00**
Hiatt, English Darby, like US CW Darby, stp Hiatt & #d **75.00**
Hiatt, solid state, 2 separate cuffs joined bk to bk, stp/#d **165.00**
Hiatt English non-adjust screw K Darby style, uses screw K **100.00**
Hiatt Figure 8, swings open to insert/withdraw wrists **125.00**
Italian, stp New Police, modern Peerless type, ST, sm bbl K **35.00**
Plug 8, remove plug before inserting external threaded K **200.00**
Russian modern ST, blued bbl key, unmk, crude **80.00**
Spanish, stp Alcyon/Star, modern Peerless type, flat K **65.00**
Spanish, stp Alcyon/Star, modern Peerless type, ST, sm bbl K **45.00**

Foreign Leg Shackles

East German, aluminum, lg hinge, cable amid 4 cuffs, bbl key **80.00**
German Clejuso, sq lc, adjusts/NST, d-bl on side, bbl K **125.00**
German Clejuso Darby type, adjusts/NST/plated, uses screw K ..**160.00**
Hiatt English combo manacles, handcuff/leg irons w/chain **275.00**
Hiatt English non-adjust screw K Darby style, uses screw K **100.00**
Hiatt Plug leg irons, same K-ing as Plug-8 cuffs, w/chain **225.00**

U.S. Handcuffs

Smith & Wesson model 100, hinged in middle, barrel key, double-lock slider, $50.00.

Adams, teardrop lc, bbl Kd, NST, usually not stp **170.00**
American Munitions, modern/rnd, sm bbl Kd, ST bow, stp **45.00**
Bean Giant, sideways figure 8, solid center lc, dbl-bit K **400.00**
Bean Patrolman, kidney-bean form, d-lb on lc, NST, stp T **100.00**
Bean-Cobb, sm rnd lc, removable cylinder, d-lb, NST, 1899 ....**80.00**
Cavenay, looks like Marlin Daley but w/screw K, NST **160.00**
Civil War padlocking type, various designs w/loop for lock **170.00**
Colt, modern ST bow, sm bbl Kd, stp w/Colt & Co name **160.00**
Flash Action Manacle, like Bean Giant w/ST, K-way center **225.00**
Flexibles, steel segmented bows, NST Darby type, screw K **150.00**
H&R Super, ST, shaft-hinge connector takes hollow titted K ...**100.00**
Harvard, takes sm bbl K, ST, stp Harvard Lock Co **65.00**
Judd, NST, used rnd/internally triangular K, stp Mattatuck **120.00**
Lilly Hand Iron, 2" strap iron (8" L), oval bands, NST, sq K **400.00**
Marlin Daley, NST, bottle-neck form, neck stp, dbl-titted K **200.00**
Mattatuck, NST, propeller-like K-way, stp Mattatuck/etc **90.00**
Palmer, 2" steel bands, 2 K-ways (top & center), NST stp **300.00**

Peerless, ST, takes sm bbl K, stp Mfg'ered by Peerless Co **40.00**
Peerless, ST, takes sm bbl K, stp Mfg'ered by S&W Co **75.00**
Peerless Big Guy, modern ST, bbl K **50.00**
Phelps, NST, twist chain between cuffs, Tower look-alike **225.00**
Pratt combo, 1 cuff connects w/nipper/claw, ST, mk Pratt   **250.00**
Providence Tool Co, stp, NST, Darby screw K style **120.00**
Rankin, steel NST, mk screw K **225.00**
Romer, NST, takes flat K, resembles padlock, stp Romer Co **250.00**
S&W 94 Maximum Security, ST, takes Ace-type K, stp S&W **90.00**
Strauss, ST, takes lg solid bitted K, stp Strauss Eng Co **85.00**
Tower, NST, bottom K, solid/flat-fitted K goes in cuff edge **100.00**
Tower bar cuffs, cuffs separate by 10-12" steel bar **120.00**
Tower Dbl Lock, NST, takes bbl-bitted K, usually stp Tower **60.00**
Tower Detective Pinkerton, NST, sq lc, bbl-bitted K, no stp **120.00**
Tower Single Lock, NST, bbl-bit K, K-way slanted on lc, sm **70.00**
Tower-Bean, NST, sm rnd lc, takes tiny bbl-bitted K, stp **75.00**
Tri-lock, heavy polymer & stainless steel, ST, triple lock **60.00**
Walden 'Lady Cuff,' NST, takes sm bbl K, lightweight, stp **250.00**

U.S. Leg Shackles

American Munitions, as handcuffs **55.00**
Civil War or prison ball & chain, padlocking or rivet type **250.00**
Cloc spike, 30" L opening for ankle w/padlock & 2 spikes **500.00**
H&R Supers, as handcuffs **400.00**
Harvard, as handcuffs **75.00**
Judd, as handcuffs **135.00**
Leg lock brace, metal brace, ankle to knee, lever locked **225.00**
Oregon boot, break-apart shackle on above ankle support **400.00**
Palmer, as handcuffs but w/detachable chain, NST **400.00**
Peerless Big Guy, modern ST, bbl K **60.00**
Providence Tool Co, stp, NST **150.00**
Strauss, as handcuffs **125.00**
Tower, bottom K, as handcuffs **100.00**
Tower ball & chain, leg iron w/chain & 6-lb to 50-lb ball **250.00**
Tower Dbl-Lock, as handcuffs **90.00**
Tower Detective, as handcuffs **150.00**

Various Other Restraining Devices

African slave Darby-style cuffs, heavy iron/chain, handmade **130.00**
African slave Darby-style leg shackles, heavy/hand forged **160.00**
African slave padlocking or riveted forged iron shackles **135.00**
Argus iron claw, twist T to open & close **40.00**
Darby neck collar, rnd steel loop opens w/screw K **150.00**
English figure-8 nipper, claws open by lifting top lock tab **80.00**
Gale finger cuff, knuckle duster, non-K, mk GFC **125.00**
German nipper, twist hdl opens/closes cuff, stp Germany/etc **75.00**
Jay Pee, thumb cuffs, mk solid body, bbl K **15.00**
Mighty-Mite, thumb cuffs, solid body, ST, mk, bbl K **75.00**
Phillips nipper, claw, flip lever on top to open **80.00**
Thomas Nipper, claw, push button top to open **80.00**
Tower Lyon, thumb cuffs, solid body, NST, dbl-bit center K **150.00**

Reverse Painting on Glass

Verre eglomise is the technique of painting on the underside of glass. Dating back to the early 1700s, this art became popular in the 19th century when German immigrants chose historical figures and beautiful women as subjects for their reverse glass paintings. Advertising mirrors of this type came into vogue at the turn of the century.

Chinese nobles w/servants in landscape, ca 1800, 15x12" **440.00**

Figures on beach, sailboat offshore, 18th C, 7x10" **165.00**
George Washington portrait, mahog veneer fr, 12x10" **220.00**
Lady in low-cut gown, German inscription, fr, 15x12" **300.00**
Lady playing harp, Chinese Export, 13½x19½" **125.00**

Lafayette silhouette (titled), black, red, and gold, black and gold painted matt, simple frame, ca 1825-45, 6½x4⅞", $475.00.

Lafayette silhouette portrait, blk/red/gold, 1830s, 6½x5" **475.00**
Man's portrait, bl coat w/ornate collar, flakes, 11½x9" **415.00**
Peacock & flowers, Averil, Chinese Export, ca 1885, 27x29" **750.00**
Village scene w/Mt Fuji beyond, Japan, 19th C, 12x16", pr **660.00**

Richard

Richard, who at one time worked for Galle, made cameo art glass in France during the 1920s. His work was often multilayered and acid cut with florals and scenics in lovely colors. The ware was marked with his name in relief. Our advisor for this category is Don Williams; he is listed in the Directory under Missouri.

Cameo

Atomizer, berries/leaves, brn/bl, trumpet form, gold mts, 12" **700.00**
Lamp, boudoir; navy on orange & yel mottle, domed shade, 9½" ..**2,600.00**
Vase, berries, blk on orange, elongated w/bun ft, 11½" **550.00**
Vase, branches/carnations, burgundy on pk, stick neck, 8½" **525.00**
Vase, landscape/water mill, amber on orange, 10½x4½" **800.00**
Vase, vines/berry pods, pk on yel, invt trumpet form, 6" **350.00**

Riviera

Riviera was a line of dinnerware introduced by the Homer Laughlin China Company in 1938. It was sold exclusively by the Murphy Company through their nationwide chain of dime stores. Riviera was unmarked, lightweight, and inexpensive. It was discontinued sometime prior to 1950. Colors are mauve blue, red, yellow, light green, and ivory. On rare occasions, dark blue pieces are found, but this was not a standard color. For further information we recommend *The Collector's Encyclopedia of Fiesta* by Sharon and Bob Huxford, available from Collector Books.

Baker, 9x7", $20.00.

Batter set, complete 285.00
Batter set, ivory, w/decals, complete 170.00
Bowl, baker; 9" 28.00
Bowl, cream soup; w/liner, ivory 95.00
Bowl, fruit; 5½" 12.00
Bowl, nappy; 7¼" 28.00
Bowl, oatmeal; 6" 40.00
Bowl, utility; ivory 50.00
Butter dish, cobalt, ¼-lb 250.00
Butter dish, colors other than cobalt or turq, ¼-lb 135.00
Butter dish, turq, ¼-lb 290.00
Butter dish, ½-lb 140.00
Casserole 110.00
Creamer 12.00
Cup & saucer, demitasse; ivory 80.00
Jug, open, ivory, 4½" 95.00
Jug, w/lid 130.00
Pitcher, juice; mauve bl 210.00
Pitcher, juice; yel 120.00
Plate, deep 24.00
Plate, 10" 55.00
Plate, 6" 8.00
Plate, 7" 12.00
Plate, 9" 18.00
Platter, closed hdls, 11¼" 28.00
Platter, cobalt, 12" 70.00
Platter, 11½" 25.00
Platter, 15" 60.00
Sauce boat 22.00
Saucer 4.00
Shakers, pr 20.00
Sugar bowl, w/lid 20.00
Teacup 11.00
Teapot 145.00
Tidbit, ivory, 2-tier 75.00
Tumbler, hdl 75.00
Tumbler, hdl, ivory 145.00
Tumbler, juice 52.00

Robertson

Fred H. Robertson, clay expert for the Los Angeles Brick Company and son of Alexander Robertson of the Roblin Pottery, experimented with crystalline glazes as early as 1906. In 1934 Fred and his son George established their own works in Los Angeles, but by 1943 they had moved operations to Hollywood. Though most of their early wares were turned by hand, some were also molded in low relief. Fine crackle glazes and crystallines were developed. Their ware was marked with 'Robertson,' 'F.H.R.,' or 'R.,' with the particular location of manufacture noted. The small pottery closed in 1952.

Chamberstick, rose matt, dish base, hdl, 2¼x5¾" 125.00
Lamp, HP floral on wht crackle, 1945, Hollywood, 11½" 235.00
Lamp, ldgl butterflies on 12" shade, crystalline mc drip, 16" ...2,800.00
Pitcher, emb flying geese, gr matt, angle hdl, mk FHR/LA, 6" 235.00
Vase, bl crackle, flattened ftd dish form, sgn, 4½" 110.00
Vase, crystalline, bl flakes on gold-yel, Los Angeles, mk, 5" 1,375.00

Robineau

After short-term training in ceramics in 1903, Adelaide Robineau (with the help of her husband Samuel) built a small pottery studio at

her home in Syracuse, New York. She was adept in mixing the clay and throwing the ware, which she often decorated by incising designs into the unfired clay. Samuel developed many of the glazes and took charge of the firing process. In 1910 she joined the staff of the American Women's League Pottery at St. Louis, where she designed the famous Scarab Vase. After this pottery failed, she served on the faculty of Syracuse University. Her work was and is today highly acclaimed for the standards of excellence to which she aspired.

Vases: Porcelain bottle shape, taupe and celadon flambe, AR medallion mark, #327, 6x2¾", $4,250.00; Bulbous, light brown crystalline, AR mark, broken and reglued, 2½x2¼", $450.00.

Vase, bl crystalline over gr on porc, sgn RP#153, 5", NM 3,000.00
Vase, celadon gloss to yel matt flambe over wht porc, 2" 1,300.00
Vase, celadon w/red wash, cvd ribs, bottle shape, 1916, 5½" ...2,700.00
Vase, pk/wht blotchy flambe gloss, bottle form, rpr, 8x2½" 2,700.00

Robj

Robj was the name of a retail store that operated in Paris for only a few years, from about 1925 to 1931. Robj solicited designs from the best French artisans of the period to produce decorative objects for the home. These objects were produced mostly in porcelain but also in glass and earthenware. The most well known are the figural bottles which were particularly popular in the United States. However, Robj also produced tea sets, perfume lamps, chess sets, ashtrays, bookends, humidors, powder jars, cigarette boxes, figurines, lamps, and milk pitchers. Robj objects tend to be whimsical, and all embody the Art Deco style. Items listed below are ceramic unless noted otherwise. Our advice for this category comes from Randall Monsen and Rod Baer, their address is listed in the Directory under Virginia.

Figurines, three musicians, white with gold, maroon and black details, tallest: 11⅜", $2,550.00 for the group.

Atomizer, 4 Seasons, glass, eng gilt top, ca 1925, 6" 600.00
Bottle, man in gray coat & blk hat figural, 10" 325.00
Box, dresser; Deco Maiden, 8½" 295.00
Cup & saucer, gold bands & int, mk/Limoges, 2½"/6", 4 for 175.00
Decanters, figures in cloaks, 1 blk/1 wht, 10½", pr 345.00
Figurine, Deco lady seated, 1 knee bent, gray, 11x10" 750.00
Figurine, jockey & leaping horse, wht crackle, 10x17x2½" 1,150.00

Jar, powder; lady in tiered gown, yel/blk, mk, 5½x5⅜" 375.00
Vase, enameled glass, medallion ea side, ovoid, 9" 800.00

Rock 'N Roll Memorabilia

Memorabilia from the early days of Rock 'n Roll recalls an era that many of us experienced firsthand; these listings are offered to demonstrate the many and various aspects of this area of collecting. Items indicated by this symbol (+) have been reproduced. Beware! Many are so well done even a knowledgeable collector will sometimes be fooled.

Our advisor for Elvis memorabilia is Rosalind Cranor, author of *Elvis Collectibles* and *Best of Elvis Collectibles* (Overmountain Press); she is listed in the Directory under Virginia. The remainder is under the advisement of Bob Gottuso, author of Beatles and KISS sections in *Garage Sale Gold* by Tomart; see Pennsylvania.

Aerosmith & Ted Nugent, poster, blk/wht, 17x11½" 30.00
Alice Cooper, cup, clear plastic w/Trash in red, 4", EX 10.00
Andy Gibb, flip book, Shadow Dancin', EX 25.00
Beatles, alarm clock, photo/Yel Submarine on face, Sheffield 720.00
Beatles, Beatlemaniac Fan Club Kit, EX in orig envelope 175.00
Beatles, bedspread, UK, wht chenille w/sewn image, 1964, EX ..250.00
Beatles, belt buckle, metal w/photo under plastic, EX 40.00
Beatles, book, Beatles Forever, 1978, NM 20.00
Beatles, book, Love Letters to the Beatles, 1964, EX 25.00
Beatles, book binder, UK, gray cloth over cb, blk faces, EX 250.00
Beatles, book covers, set of 7 w/insert card, VG+ 85.00
Beatles, booklet, concert; 1965, 12x12", EX 25.00
Beatles, bookmark, Sgt Pepper's Lonely..., 1968 ....5.00
Beatles, bookmarks, cb figures, Yel Submarine, 1968, 9", EX, ea 8.00
Beatles, bracelet, blk/wht photos on brass mt, EX 90.00
Beatles, brooch, blk/wht photo in gold metal, 2" dia, EX 70.00
Beatles, bulletin brd, Yel Submarine, group photo, NMIP 140.00
Beatles, cap, brn corduroy w/Ringo image, EX 100.00
Beatles, cigar labels, Holland, 1964, set of 4 ....55.00
Beatles, Collectors' stamps, 1964 Hallmark Edition, 5 for 10.00
Beatles, coloring book, Saalfield, unused, M 90.00
Beatles, commemorative coin, 1964 visit to US, brass 30.00

Beatles, Sgt Pepper costume figures (Ringo Starr and George Harrison), 22", with original tags & stands, EX, $65.00 each.

Beatles, greeting cards, Yel Submarine, MIB 190.00
Beatles, guitar string, Hofner, MIP 75.00
Beatles, handkerchief, UK, With Love From Me to You, VG 35.00

Beatles, headband, Love the Beatles, MIP (sealed), minimum value ..55.00
Beatles, hummer, cb w/faces & signature on tube, 11", EX 150.00
Beatles, Kaboodle Kit, yel vinyl, EX 700.00
Beatles, lapel tag, Hard Day's Night, giveaway 24.00
Beatles, magnet, From Me to You, 2x3", EX 5.00
Beatles, mobile, 4 punch-outs/stage on cb sheet, Whitman, EX .150.00
Beatles, mug, ceramic w/fired-on decal, hdld, UK, EX 120.00
Beatles, nodders, compo, Carmascots, 1964, VG/orig box, set of 4 ...550.00
Beatles, nodders, Hong Kong, 1960s, 3½", set of 4 (+) 35.00
Beatles, notebook, photo in Palladium doorway, spiral-bound, EX ...60.00
Beatles, panty hose, Holland, MIB 55.00
Beatles, paperweight, Official Beatles Fan, mc, 1970s, EX 95.00
Beatles, pencil case, SPP, tan vinyl, 8½x3½", VG+ 125.00
Beatles, pennant, blk cartoon drawings on gold felt, 27", VG 170.00
Beatles, pillow, full figures on red, House Pillows, rare, EX 350.00
Beatles, pins, Yel Submarine, cloisonne, set of 15 ....75.00
Beatles, pins, Yel Submarine, HP brass, 8 for 25.00
Beatles, plate, Washington Pottery, 1964, NM 90.00
Beatles, playing cards, orig single deck w/orange bkground 390.00
Beatles, pop-up book, Yel Submarine, NM 45.00
Beatles, postcards, 1 of ea member +Yel Sub/Sgt Pepper, EX 85.00
Beatles, press book, Let It Be, 6-pg, EX 75.00
Beatles, print, Live at the Cavern Club, sgn Pete Best, EX 100.00
Beatles, record box, gr w/wht top, blk hdl, Airflite, VG+ 315.00
Beatles, scarf, red w/blk photos, leatherette cord, EX 70.00
Beatles, scrapbook, color photos front/bk, Whitman, unused, EX .70.00
Beatles, stamp booklet, complete, M 45.00
Beatles, stationery, Sgt Pepper's..., 4 sheets/envelopes 20.00
Beatles, stick pin, Yel Submarine, diecut tin, 1968, EX 35.00
Beatles, talcum powder tin, UK/Margo of Mayfair, EX 490.00
Beatles, thimble, Fenton, baked-on image, EX 15.00
Beatles, wallet, vinyl w/photos, VG 65.00
Beatles, watercolor set, set of 6, lg, sealed 160.00
Beatles, Yel Submarine, diecast, Corgi, 5", EX 200.00
Bee Gees, jigsaw puzzle, 1979, 2 styles, sealed, ea 20.00
Bee Gees, pin-bk, 1979 tour 6.00
Bill Haley & the Comets, pin-bk button 20.00
Blondie, ashtray, Parallel Lines, acrylic w/color photo, EX 35.00
Canned Heat, concert poster, Dinosaurs, bl/red/wht, 23x18", M ..35.00
Cheap Trick, bow tie, wht print on blk, promo, EX 28.00
Crosby, Stills & Nash, matchbook, EX 15.00
Culture Club, cup, plastic w/blk image of Boy George, 5", EX 20.00
Dave Clark 5, jigsaw puzzle, Canadian, 1965, 180-pc, VG 120.00
David Cassidy, Colorforms, 1972, NM 35.00
Donny & Marie Osmond, Dress-Up Kit, Colorforms, 1977, NMIB 35.00
Donny & Marie Osmond, record player, mk Sing Along Radio..., MIB ...60.00
Elvis Presley, beach hat, w/orig photo hang tag, 1956, EX 125.00
Elvis Presley, button, flasher; Love Me Tender, blk/wht, EX 20.00
Elvis Presley, figure, Aloha jumpsuit, resin, Hamilton, 9", M 65.00
Elvis Presley, key chain, flasher; full figure on yel, EX 18.00
Elvis Presley, lipstick, Hound Dog Orange, 1956, M on card 340.00
Elvis Presley, menu, Las Vegas, 1972, 10¾" dia 65.00
Elvis Presley, music box, Love Me Tender, resin, Hamilton, 10", M .80.00
Elvis Presley, music box w/jewelry drw, Hound Dog, 8", NM 125.00
Elvis Presley, necklace, 1956, M on photo card 175.00
Elvis Presley, Paint By Number set, EP Enterprises, 1956 ....1,800.00
Elvis Presley, pencil sharpener, EP Enterprises, 1956 ....210.00
Elvis Presley, photo album, 1956, concert souvenir, EX 175.00
Elvis Presley, pin-bk button, I'm a Kissin' Cousin w/ribbons 100.00
Elvis Presley, poster, Easy Come, Easy Go, 1-sheet, EX 90.00
Elvis Presley, poster, Girl Happy, 1964, 27x41" 100.00
Elvis Presley, promo hat, GI Blues, bl/red on brn paper, EX 100.00
Elvis Presley, standee, Love Me Tender, 72", minimum value .1,000.00
Elvis Presley, toy guitar, Lapin, 1984, sealed on orig card 75.00

Elvis Presley, toy guitar, Selcol, 1959, rare, EX 1,000.00

Elvis Presley, wallet, vinyl (came in various colors), Elvis Presley Enterprises, All Rights Reserved, M, $485.00.

Elvis Presley, wristwatch, Elvis stamp face 17.00
Elvis Presley, 45 record, A Fool Such As I, w/picture sleeve, NM ...55.00
Elvis Presley, 45 record, Love Me Tender, blk/gr picture sleeve, NM 80.00
Elvis Presley, 45 record, Love Me Tender, blk/pk picture sleeve, NM 50.00
Elvis Presley, 45 record, Love Me Tender, blk/wht picture sleeve, NM ..150.00
Elvis Presley, 45 record, Teddy Bear, w/picture sleeve, NM 60.00
Elvis Presley, 78 rpm record, Sun label, VG 225.00
Everly Brothers, tin, Belgian 55.00
Grateful Dead, concert poster, skulls & bones, blk/wht, 23x15" ...65.00
Gregg Allman, slingshot, I'm No Angel, Epic promo, EX 35.00
Hollies, LP record, Greatest Hits, NM 15.00
Jefferson Airplane, poster, Other Half, blk/red/wht, 1967, M 50.00
KISS, bracelet, gold chain w/red inset, orig card 36.00
KISS, Colorforms, complete, orig box, VG+ 80.00
KISS, comb, Australia, several colors available, ea 10.00
KISS, letter from Gene Simmons on KISS stationery 100.00
KISS, make-up kit, Kiss Your Face, Remco, MIB 95.00
KISS, model kit, Custom Chevy Van, complete, w/decals, VG+ .90.00
KISS, necklace, Peter Criss, gold autograph style, orig pkg 32.00
KISS, necklace, 3-D logo in silver or gold finish, ea 10.00
KISS, pencils, set of 4, MIP 45.00
KISS, picture disk, solo LPs, 1 of ea member, ea 50.00
KISS, puffy stickers, Rockstics, set of 4, MOC 60.00
KISS, tour program, Lick It Up, World Tour '84, 24-pg, VG+ 45.00
Led Zeppelin, poster, blk on lt gray, 22½x17", M 40.00
Madonna, notebook, Desperately Seeking Susan, 1985, EX 20.00
Madonna, poster, Blond Ambition World Tour 90, 28x17", NM .30.00
Michael Jackson, Colorforms, 1984, MIB 25.00
Michael Jackson, microphone, LJN, 1984 ....25.00
Monkees, board game, Transogram, 1967, NMIB 100.00
Monkees, bracelet, group photo in brass-colored disk, EX 30.00
Monkees, flip books, ea 14.00
Monkees, gum card box, series 3, colorful cartoons, VG 60.00
Monkees, gum cards, Hit Songs, complete set of 30 ....60.00
Monkees, playing cards, complete w/full-color box, EX 35.00
Monkees, Private Picture Book, fan club offer, Laufer, NM 75.00
Monkees, ring, flasher; chrome, VG 20.00
Monkees, Show Biz Baby, complete, 4", ea member 78.00
Monkees, sunglasses, orig tag, EX 44.00
Monkees, tablet, photo cover, unused, 8½x11" 40.00
Monkees, tambourine, complete, hard to find, EX 85.00
Mother Earth, poster, Kaleidoscope, blk/wht, 22x15", NM 25.00
Paul McCartney & Wings, card set, Back to the Egg, set of 5 ....15.00
Pink Floyd, 16mm film, MGM 20.00
Poison, first aid kit, Unskinny Bop, promo, EX 25.00
Prince, tambourine, from Love God tour 125.00
Rolling Stones, flasher button display, 1960s-early '70s, EX 100.00
Rolling Stones, key ring, 1983, sealed on orig card 10.00

Rolling Stones, poster, Steelwheels Tour, mc, 15x19", NM 20.00
Rolling Stones, press kit & lobby card, 1970s, EX 50.00
Tom Petty, poster, blk/wht, artist sgn, 17x12" 50.00
Uriah Heep, matchbox, Warner Bros promo, 1975, VG 18.00
Van Halen, binoculars, w/logo, EX 15.00
Van Halen, program, 1980 concert tour, ticket on bk, EX 35.00

Rockingham

In the early part of the 19th century, American potters began to prefer brown- and buff-burning clays over red because of their durability. The glaze favored by many was Rockingham, which varied from a dark brown mottle to a sponged effect sometimes called tortoise shell. It consisted in part of manganese and various metallic salts and was used by many potters until well into the 20th century. Over the past two years, demand and prices have risen sharply, especially in the east. For further information we recommend *Collector's Guide to Rockingham, The Enduring Ware*, by Mary Brewer. See also Bennington.

Bottle, Coachman Toby, dk brn, 8⅞" 495.00
Bottle, Toby barrel, brn, 9¼" 95.00
Bottles, shoe form, pinpoint flakes, 6⅝", pr 220.00
Bowl, shallow, 2½x10½x8¾" 195.00
Bowl, vegetable; oblong, octagonal, 10⅜" 140.00
Bowl, vegetable; oblong, octagonal, 12½" 175.00
Foot warmer, shell & scroll emb on bk, 9" 400.00
Humidor, emb floral medallions, sm chip, 8" 80.00
Humidor, molded vintage, 7½" 225.00
Paperweight, brn dog on unglazed oval base, 3½x6½" 275.00
Pen holder, boy reclining figural, 19th C, 5¼" 295.00
Pie plate, 10" 135.00

Pitcher, tulips in relief, 9½", $200.00.

Pitcher, emb corn, mid-1800s, 11¼", NM 350.00
Pitcher, emb Geo Washington w/in wreath, ca 1876, 8" 150.00
Pitcher, emb panels w/lotus base, 8" 150.00
Pitcher, emb sheaf & grain, w/lid, 10", EX 220.00
Pitcher, gr & brn, paneled, mask spout, 9" 395.00
Plate, rayed center, scalloped rim, 8", pr 220.00
Salt crock, w/crest & emb peacocks, no lid, 6" dia 125.00
Teapot, emb Chinaman ea side, 9½", EX 165.00

Rogers, John

John Rogers (1829-1904) was a machinist from Manchester, New Hampshire, who turned his hobby of sculpting into a financially successful venture. From the originals he meticulously fashioned of red clay, he had bronze master molds made from which plaster copies were cast. He specialized in five different categories: theatrical, Shakespeare,

Civil War, everyday life, and horses. His large detailed groupings portrayed the life and times of the period between 1859 and 1892. When no condition is indicated, examples are assumed to be in very good to excellent condition. Our advisor for this category is George Humphrey; he is listed in the Directory under Maryland.

Bath 2,000.00
Bubbles 2,000.00
Bushwacker 2,000.00
Checkers Players, sm 1,500.00
Checkers Up at the Farm 450.00
Country Post Office 750.00
Courtship in Sleepy Hollow, Pat date 550.00
Fairy's Whisper, ca 1881 ....1,400.00
Faust & Marguerite, Leaving the Garden 1,200.00
Fetching the Doctor 750.00
Fighting Bob, ca 1889 ....1,100.00
First Ride 725.00
Frolic at the Old Homestead, 1887, 22½" 800.00
Going for the Cows 450.00
Madam Your Mother Craves a Word 700.00
Mail Day 2,000.00
Matter of Opinion 600.00
Neighboring Pews 475.00
One More Shot 550.00
Parting Promise 475.00
Playing Doctor 500.00
Rip Van Winkle at Home, 18½" 425.00
Shaughraun & Tatters 700.00
Speak for Yourself John 500.00
Taking the Oath & Drawing Rations, sgn, 23" 525.00
Tap on the Window 525.00
Traveling Magician, ca 1877 ....750.00
Village Schoolmaster 850.00
Watch on the Santa Maria 750.00
Wounded Scout, ca 1864 ....750.00

Rookwood

The Rookwood Pottery Company was established in 1879 in Cincinnati, Ohio. Its founder was Maria Longworth Nichols Storer, daughter of a wealthy family who provided the backing necessary to make such an enterprise possible. Mrs. Storer hired competent ceramic workers who through constant experimentation developed many lines of superior art pottery. While in her employ, Laura Fry invented the airbrush-blending process for which she was issued a patent in 1884. From this, several lines were designed that utilized blended backgrounds. One of their earlier lines, Standard, was a brown ware decorated with underglaze slip-painted nature studies, animals, portraits, etc. Iris and Sea Green were introduced in 1894 and Vellum, a transparent mat-glaze line, in 1904. Other lines followed: Ombroso in 1910 and Soft Porcelain in 1915. Many of the early artware lines were signed by the artist. Soon after the turn of the 20th century, Rookwood manufactured 'production' pieces that relied mainly on molded designs and forms rather than freehand decoration for their esthetic appeal. The Depression brought on financial difficulties from which the pottery never recovered. Though it continued to operate, the quality of the ware deteriorated, and the pottery was forced to close in 1967.

Unmarked Rookwood is only rarely encountered. Many marks may be found, but the most familiar is the reverse 'RP' monogram. First used in 1886, a flame point was added above it for each succeeding year until 1900. After that a Roman numeral added below indicated the year of manufacture. Impressed letters that related to the type of clay utilized

for the body were also used — G for ginger, O for olive, R for red, S for sage green, W for white, and Y for yellow. Artware must be judged on an individual basis. Quality of the artwork is a prime factor to consider. Portraits, animals, and birds are worth more than florals; and pieces signed by a particularly renowned artist are highly prized. Our advice for this category comes from Fer-Duc Inc., whose address is listed in the Directory under New York.

Iris

Vase, apple blossoms (detailed), S Coyne, 1905, #906E, 4½" .1,100.00
Vase, branches on blk to wht, CC Lindeman, 1906, #9355, 6" ..800.00
Vase, clovers, OG Reed, 1902, #919, 4" 475.00
Vase, crocus blooms & buds, F Rothenbusch, 1904, #935D, 7½" .2,000.00
Vase, crows (3) on gr, KV Horne, 1907, #900DW, 6½", NM 950.00
Vase, daisies w/stems, initialed, 1905, #951D, 8½" 1,200.00
Vase, dogwood blossoms, CA Baker, 1901, #30E, 8" 800.00
Vase, floral, Oriental-style, SE Coyne, 1908, #905D, 8" 2,500.00
Vase, floral (EX art), JE Zettel, 1902, #937, 9" 800.00
Vase, floral branches, CC Lindeman, 1908, #941, 8" 1,200.00
Vase, floral on blk to bl, Carl Schmidt, 1909, #1126C, 8½" .13,000.00
Vase, grapes, Sara Sax, ca 1900, #876C, 10x4½" 1,150.00
Vase, holly berries, pk on blk to ivory, Hurley, 1906, 6x3½" 700.00
Vase, iris on gray to pk, L Lindeman, 1903, #922D, 7" 900.00
Vase, jonquils, Irene Bishop, 1907, #952, 6" 950.00

Vase, mushrooms on dark brown to cream, Carl Schmidt, #917B, 1903, 9", $4,000.00.

Vase, orchid w/leaves, C Schmidt, 1903, #907D, 10½", NM ..1,700.00
Vase, orchids, C Schmidt, 1900, #892C, 5⅝x4¼" 1,150.00
Vase, orchids on pk to gr, AR Valentien, 1903, #940B, 12½" ...7,500.00
Vase, pine branches, Lenore Asbury, 1906, #935C W, 9" 800.00
Vase, rooks on bl to cream, SE Coyne, 1906, #951D, 8½" 2,600.00
Vase, rose on gr to pk, AR Valentien, 1902, #904B, 14", NM ...1,200.00
Vase, roses, J Jensen, 1946, #6359, 7½" 600.00
Vase, roses, pk on pastel, JE Zettel, 1925, 9x3¾" 900.00
Vase, roses & buds w/branches, I Bishop, 1904, #926, 7" 1,000.00
Vase, roses on yel to bl, Sara Sax, 1906, #913 C, rstr, 8" 800.00
Vase, sailboats, Lenore Asbury, 1911, #907E, 8½", NM 900.00
Vase, violets, mc on bl to cream, CA Baker, 1896, #792E, 6" 900.00
Vase, violets w/wide leaves, R Fechheimer, 1901, #614F, 6½" ...1,100.00

Limoges

Jar, soaring birds among rushes, AR Valentien, 1882, #97, 5" 850.00
Jug, birds in bamboo, AR Valentien, 1882, #61, 4⅝x2¾" 490.00
Pitcher, soaring birds, AR Valentien, 1886, #101 A, 11½", EX .700.00
Porringer, reeds against sky w/gold, M Rettig, 1882, 2x7" 250.00
Vase, bird on branch before moon, M Rettig, 1882, 4x4", NM ..250.00
Vase, birds on branches, AR Valentien, 1882, 14½" 4,750.00
Vase, emb/pnt fish w/gold, att ML Nichols, 1882, rpr, 13x13" ...2,000.00

Mat

Note: Both incised mat and painted mat are listed here. Incised mat descriptions are indicated by the term 'cvd' within the line; the others are for the hand-painted mat ware.

Bowl, red hibiscus flowers, Sallie Coyne, 1925, #1929, 6½" **550.00**
Dish, overlapping leaves & acorns, 1910, #1692, 1x6½x7½" **325.00**
Ewer, peach blossoms w/gold, Matt A Daly, 1887, #333S, 9½" ..**600.00**
Pin tray, fish swimming on shell form, 1906, #1207, 5½" **225.00**
Plaque, Arts & Crafts landscape, 1904, 12" sq **3,250.00**
Plaque, sailing ship in churning sea, 1904, 12x8" **3,500.00**

Vase, Arts & Crafts-style finely molded leaves, green mat, William P. McDonald, #2492, 1920, 12x7", $900.00.

Vase, berries & leaves on purple, CS Todd, 1920, #942C, 7½" ..**550.00**
Vase, butterflies (3), dk bl, 1921, #2325, 9½" **850.00**
Vase, cvd Arts & Crafts waves, OG Reed, 1903, #40DZ, 6½" ...**850.00**
Vase, cvd bellflowers, wine/gr/bl/brn, Hentshell, 1914, 15" **4,250.00**
Vase, cvd daffodils on long stems, yel on gr, Fechheimer, 6" ..**2,200.00**
Vase, cvd floral, purple on gr, CS Todd, hdls, 1915, 15x10" ...**1,200.00**
Vase, cvd floral, 5-color, hdls, Hentschel, 1915, #339B, 15" **950.00**
Vase, cvd floral band, mc on bl, CS Todd, 1919, 8x3" **700.00**
Vase, cvd grapes, bl/gr on yel, SC Todd, 1918, #339B, 14" **750.00**
Vase, cvd pinwheel band, med gr, W McDonald, 1900, 5½" **550.00**
Vase, cvd/pnt Arts & Crafts florals, A Pons, 1907, #906E, 4x5" ...**900.00**
Vase, cvd/pnt berries & leaves, CS Todd, 1914, #826D, 7" **475.00**
Vase, cvd/pnt daffodils, Fechheimer, 1905, #942, 6½", NM ...**1,000.00**
Vase, cvd/pnt nude, gr, AM Valentien, 1901, #160Z, 2½x3½" ..**1,800.00**
Vase, cvd/pnt pine cones, ET Hurley, 1905, #969C, 6" **900.00**
Vase, emb Arts & Crafts leaves, mottled brn, 1915, #984, 13" ..**1,200.00**
Vase, floral, C Covalenco, 1924, #2724, 6" **550.00**
Vase, floral, CS Todd, 1920, #654C, 5½" **475.00**
Vase, floral, Elizabeth Barrett, 1924, #2039C, 11½" **650.00**
Vase, floral, EN Lincoln, 1926, #2822, 7" **800.00**
Vase, floral, EN Lincoln, 1928, #6079, 18½" **2,100.00**
Vase, floral, MH McDonald, 1928, #2785, 12½" **1,500.00**
Vase, floral, red on bl, MH McDonald, 1926, #926C, 9" **600.00**
Vase, floral, SE Coyne, 1931, #914E, 5" **500.00**
Vase, floral branches, MH McDonald, 1928, #1357, 7½" **550.00**
Vase, floral branches on gr, W Hentschel, 1921, #2191, 5½" **900.00**
Vase, floral on bl to aqua, K Shirayamadani, 1933, S, 7½" **1,200.00**
Vase, floral on pk, K Shirayamadani, 1936, S, 6" **800.00**
Vase, floral w/twisted stems, C Covalenco, 1925, #1045, 5½" ...**600.00**
Vase, fruity branches, Olga G Reed, 1908, #1356 E, 7" **1,900.00**
Vase, horse, mc on dk bl, Jens Jensen, 1935, 5" **3,250.00**
Vase, irises (EX art), K Shirayamadani, 1938, S, 7" **2,200.00**
Vase, mushrooms/geometric panels, Hentschel, '11, #932, 6½" .**400.00**

Porcelain

Jar, tropical birds, bright mc, ET Hurley, 1934, #2301E, 9½" ..**1,900.00**

Jug, floral on cream, Lorinda Epply, 1926, #2974, 8½" **750.00**
Potpourri jar, floral w/gold, A Van Briggle, 1887/#326, 6" **700.00**
Vase, berries & leaves, K Shirayamadani, 1925, #2720, 6½" **2,600.00**
Vase, birch trees, ET Hurley, 1945, #6197C/#5053, 8½" **6,000.00**
Vase, Chinese plum blossoms, Harriet Wilcox, 1927, #2308, 7" ..**1,600.00**
Vase, fish & flowers, 2-hdld, Sara Sax, 1922, #2634, 10", EX ..**1,100.00**
Vase, fish on dk bl, J Jensen, 1934, S, 5" **1,900.00**
Vase, floral, tan/bl on wht, J Jensen, Jewel, 1946, 9x6" **500.00**
Vase, floral (EX art), WE Hentschel, 1931, #2032D, 9½" **1,100.00**
Vase, floral & fruit, K Shirayamadani, 1922, #295C, 11" **5,500.00**
Vase, floral & wide V, WE Hentschel, 1921, #214 C, 3x5½" **300.00**
Vase, floral branch, peach on celadon, Holtkamp, 1952, 8" **450.00**
Vase, floral on bl to yel, MH McDonald, 1940, #2918E, 6½" **600.00**
Vase, floral on brn & gray, J Jensen, 1945, #6640, 6½" **1,300.00**
Vase, floral on gray, CS Todd, 1920, #2368, rstr, 16½" **2,400.00**
Vase, floral on gray, Jens Jensen, 1948, #6920, rpr, 12" **800.00**
Vase, floral shoulder, Shirayamadani, 1928, #2381, 5½x5½" ..**1,600.00**
Vase, floral w/long stems, C Stegner, 1946, #775, 10" **850.00**
Vase, florals/plumes/swirls, L Epply, 1929, #914E, 5½" **750.00**
Vase, geometrics, mc on yel, Sara Sax, 1930, #6143, 4" **900.00**
Vase, gnarled trees, A Conant, 1919, #2040E, 7½" **2,500.00**
Vase, grapes, mc on wht, Lorinda Epply, 1931, #6184E, 7" **850.00**
Vase, irises, K Shirayamadani, 1946, #6314/#6586, 7½" **900.00**
Vase, landscape, hazy, MH McDonald, '40, #614D, drilled, 10½" ...**1,400.00**
Vase, lilies, wht/amber on bl, Shirayamadani, 1946, 7½x5" **700.00**
Vase, nude & snake amid florals, J Jenson, 1944, #6875, 6½" .**5,500.00**
Vase, roses, wht/gr on lt bl, Ed Diers, 1925, 5x4" **475.00**
Vase, swans & blossoms, J Jensen, 1934, #2783, 9½" **1,800.00**
Vase, trees on pk, J Jensen, 1931, #6199D, 5" **1,100.00**
Vase, tropical birds on bl, ET Hurley, 1924, #2785, 13" **2,200.00**
Vase, wheat & bowed leaves, MH McDonald, 1939, #9358, 11½" .**1,000.00**
Vase, 3 bands of flowers & leaves on yel, Jewel, Hentschel, 11" ..**1,000.00**

Sea Green

Mug, comic figure/rook on perch, HE Wilcox, 1898, #837 G, 5" ..**1,500.00**
Vase, carp (6), ET Hurley, 1898, #744C G, rstr, 7¼" **1,500.00**
Vase, cyclamens, Sallie Toohey, 1902, #932D, 8½" **1,600.00**
Vase, fish in swirling sea, ET Hurley, G#982F, 6" **2,500.00**
Vase, floral, bl on gr, M Mitchell, 1901, #921 G, rstr, 6" **400.00**
Vase, floral, EN Lincoln, 1905, #951E, 6½" **3,750.00**
Vase, floral on bl, LE Lindeman, 1901, #536E, 3" **950.00**
Vase, frog & plant, OG Reed, 1898, #816E, 6" **3,000.00**
Vase, sea gulls (5)in storm, ET Hurley, 1901, #922C G, 8" **4,750.00**

Standard

Ewer, daisies on brick shaded to green, K. Shirayamadani, #391, 1888, 13x6", $1,250.00.

Ewer, floral w/ornate silver o/l, M Nourse, 1893, #387C, 11" ..**9,000.00**
Jug, Chief White Man Kuawa, C Baker, 1899, #512B, 10" **4,500.00**

Mug, figure in overcoat & hat, S Toohey, 1892, #259C, 6" **850.00**
Pitcher, cavalier, silver o/l, 1894, #259B, +6 #259E mugs **29,000.00**
Pitcher, floral, 1886, #259, 8½" **350.00**
Plaque, children & animals, 2-tile, B Horsfall, 7½x20" **8,500.00**
Plaque, 2 jovial monks at table, MA Daly, rstr, 9½x12" **4,250.00**
Vase, acorns w/Gorham silver o/l, 1891, R1044/#589DW, 10½" ..**5,500.00**
Vase, autumn leaves, Irene Bishop, 1900, #568E, 4½" **450.00**
Vase, dogwood blossoms, Adeliza D Sehon, #S1442, 9½" **650.00**
Vase, Eagle Deer Sioux (chief), A Sehon, 1901, #604D, 7" **4,250.00**
Vase, floral, E Bertha/I Cranch, 1895, #741C, 5½" **450.00**
Vase, floral w/silver floral o/l, E Diers, 1901, #442, 7½" **3,750.00**
Vase, floral w/silver o/l, M Nourse, 1903, #926A, 13" **5,500.00**
Vase, floral w/silver o/l, McDonald, 1892, #524/#664C, 8½" ..**5,500.00**
Vase, fruit/flowers on sage gr, L Fry, 1885, #46, rstr, 9¼" **550.00**
Vase, leaves, initialed, 1899, #614F, 6" **425.00**
Vase, lily of the valley, Irene Bishop, 1905, #605E, 5" **750.00**
Vase, orange blossoms, Amelia Sprague, 1889, #395 S, 4" **375.00**
Vase, pine cones, Matt Daly, 1902, #907B, 17", NM **1,400.00**
Vase, pine cones & needles, Shirayamadani, 1898, #S1405C, 13" ..**9,000.00**

Tiger Eye

Vase, bird on brn metallic, S Toohey, 1899, #792C, 11½", EX ..**900.00**
Vase, floral/olive branches, AR Valentien, 1889, #216R, 13½" .**950.00**
Vase, leafy floral, Matt Daly, 1886, #39B, 13½", NM **950.00**
Vase, plums on branches, AR Valentien, 1891, #589C W, 12½" ...**750.00**

Vellum

Plaque, Dutch landscape, ET Hurley, 1914, 9x12"+orig fr **6,000.00**
Plaque, Early Dawn, hazy landscape, ET Hurley, label, 6x8" ...**2,100.00**
Plaque, Evening Glow, Ed Diers, 1915, 8x10½" **5,000.00**
Plaque, Evening Sunset, river scene, SE Coyne, 4½x8½" **3,000.00**
Plaque, landscape, Sara Sax, 1916, 7x9" **4,250.00**
Plaque, mtn landscape (EX art), ET Hurley, 1945, 12x10" ...**5,500.00**
Plaque, Sunset Through Birches, Hurley, '13/#5133, 10½x8⅜" ..**3,565.00**
Plaque, trees & mtns, ET Hurley, 1945, 12x10" **4,000.00**
Plaque, trees in landscape, EF McDermott, 1926, 8½x10½" ...**5,000.00**
Plaque, winding stream landscape, F Rothenbusch, 5½x7½" .**2,000.00**
Vase, abstract floral branches, Rothenbusch, 1923, 5¾x3" **850.00**
Vase, apple blossoms on bl & brn, C Steinle, 1917, 8x4" **650.00**
Vase, bamboo stems & leaves, L Epply, 1908, #1124E V, 7" ..**1,500.00**
Vase, bl jays & flowers, Lorinda Epply, 1917, #703, 5½" **850.00**
Vase, daisies, Kay Ley, 1955, #2724/#4013, 6" **1,200.00**
Vase, fish swimming, ET Hurley, 1904, partial label, 8", NM **800.00**
Vase, flamingos, K Shirayamadani, 1907, #1369D V, 9" **6,500.00**
Vase, floral, bl on lt gray, L Eppley, 1924, #900A, 13" **8,500.00**
Vase, floral, EN Lincoln, 1908, #1278 E, 7½" **700.00**
Vase, floral, Katherine Van Horne, 1914, #1663 V, 9" **650.00**
Vase, floral, pk/gr on shaded pk, M Nourse, 1905, 6¾x3" **400.00**
Vase, floral (delicate), Fred Rothenbusch, 1925, 31356F V, 6" ..**1,900.00**
Vase, floral (detailed), MH McDonald, 1921, #938D, 7" **700.00**
Vase, floral branches, E Diers, 1913, #950D V, 9½" **850.00**
Vase, floral branches, Lenore Asbury, 1930, #80C V, 7" **850.00**
Vase, floral branches (gnarled), ET Hurley, 1924, #2544 V, 8" ..**1,400.00**
Vase, floral branches & vines, Ed Diers, 1925, #1356F V, 6" ..**1,500.00**
Vase, floral on bl to tan, F Rothenbusch, 1929, #915E, 6" **1,200.00**
Vase, floral on bl to wht, ET Hurley, 1927, #494B, 5" **550.00**
Vase, floral on pk to cream, Sara Sax, 1905, 6", NM **250.00**
Vase, floral w/berries, ET Hurley, 1927, #491, 8½" **900.00**
Vase, floral w/stems & leaves, WH McDonald, 1920, #915E V, 6" ..**950.00**
Vase, floral w/vines, Ed Diers, 1912, #1843, 5" **450.00**
Vase, floral/band on shoulder, ET Hurley, 1942, 5x3½" **1,000.00**
Vase, florals atop branches, ET Hurley, 1918, #2305, 9½" **900.00**

Vase, grapes, purple/gr on gr to purple, C Todd, 1910, 6x4" **750.00**
Vase, harbor scene, Carl Schimdt, 1922, #1930, 7" **3,750.00**
Vase, irises, Arts & Crafts, AM Valentien, 1905, #906D, 5½" ..**1,600.00**
Vase, irises, yel on celadon, M Nourse, 1904, 8½x3¾" **1,500.00**
Vase, mistletoc on bl to cream, HM Lyons, 1913, #913 V E, 6" ...**475.00**
Vase, poppies (EX art), R Fechheimer, 1904, #707 V, 5½" **1,500.00**
Vase, Queen Anne's lace, Sara Sax, 1910, #1655E V, 8" **1,900.00**
Vase, roses, Edward Diers, 1914, #295D, 9" **800.00**
Vase, roses, pk/gr on pastels, EG Diers, 1918, 10½x5" **1,100.00**
Vase, sailboats on gr, Sallie E Coyne, 1909, #1369E GV, 7½" ...**2,000.00**

Vase, snow scene, Sallie Coyne, 1919, 10", $4,250.00.

Vase, snowscape, Lenore Asbury, 1914, 3925c V, 11" **3,000.00**
Vase, snowscape, Sara Sax, 1910, #952E V, 7½" **4,000.00**
Vase, stag & 2 does in snow, ET Hurley, 1947, #5419, 10½" ...**2,350.00**
Vase, trees & hills, Sallie Coyne, 1917, #892B V, 11" **2,300.00**
Vase, trees & lake landscape, Ed Diers, 1916, #1664D V, 11" .**2,900.00**
Vase, trees & lake landscape, ET Hurley, 1955, 8x5" **2,200.00**
Vase, trees & mtn landscape, Sara Sax, 1915, #988D, 7" **1,600.00**
Vase, trees in landscape, ET Hurley, 1920, #2033C, 12½" **2,400.00**
Vase, trees in landscape, Lorinda Epply, 1926, #1661 V, 8½" **900.00**
Vase, Venetian harbor scene, C Schmidt, 1921, #900A V, 13" ..**11,000.00**
Vase, violets w/overlapping stems, C Baker, '04, #33EZ, 5½" **850.00**

Wax Mat

Vase, apple blossoms, yel on orange, LN Lincoln, 1924, 6½" **450.00**
Vase, floral, purple/gr on feathered mauve, Crofton, 1925, 8" **800.00**
Vase, floral, red/gr on dk bl, C Crofton, 1923, #1920, 9½" **675.00**
Vase, geometric butterfat design, 3-color, J Jensen, 1930, 5½" ...**1,000.00**
Vase, hollyhock, pk/gr on feathered pk, K Jones, 1930, 8½x6" ...**600.00**
Vase, thistles, purple/gr on purple, LN Lincoln, 1922, 9½" **1,000.00**

Miscellaneous

Bookends, #2275, 1950, rook, gr opaque hi-glaze, 5½", pr **260.00**
Bookends, #2444D, 1921, elephant, standing, 5x5¾", pr **450.00**
Bookends, #2446, 1920, peacock against fence, 5", NM, pr **260.00**
Bookends, #2503, 1929, sphinx w/book, brn/tan drip, 7½", pr ...**650.00**
Bookends, #2564, 1940, panther on open book, brn hi-glaze, pr ..**270.00**
Bookends, #2629, 1935, bird on leaves, caramel drip, 5½", pr **300.00**
Bookends, #2998, 1945, hounds, gr hi-glaze, 5", pr **280.00**
Bookends, #3444D, 1921, elephant, avocado mat, 5", NM, pr ...**260.00**
Bowl, #1770, 1923, paneled, pk matt, 3x5½" **180.00**
Bowl, #2151, 1921, floral emb, gr & bl mat, 4x9" **110.00**
Bowl, #2153, 1919, emb holly band, bl mat, 3x7½" **120.00**
Bowl, #2157, 1920, stylized waves, dk bl mat, 3x7½" **140.00**
Bowl, #2256B, 1922, aqua & blk hi-glaze, 4½x9½", NM **90.00**
Bowl, #2923, 1927, ladies in flowing skirts at edge, 13" **700.00**
Candlesticks, #508, 1922, lt bl mat, 6", pr **150.00**
Candlesticks, #822D, 1920, lt bl mat, 6½", pr **160.00**

Covered dish, #2505, 1921, open design, lt bl matt, 3" 110.00
Figurine, #6080, 1928, rooster, bl mottled on cocoa mat, 5" 240.00
Figurine, #6241, 1936, young donkey, wht mat, Asbury, 6" 240.00
Figurine, #6972, 1952, tropical bird, gr hi-glaze, 9" 160.00
Figurine, donkey, 1939, brn w/lt brn details, E Abel, 4x5¾" 300.00
Flower frog, #2256B, 1924, bird on stump, blk hi-glaze, 6" 190.00
Flower frog, nude w/frog, blk hi-glaze, 5" 220.00
Jar, #2641B, 1923, bl mat, w/lid, 1½x5" 210.00
Paperweight, #2777, 1928, pup, wht mat, 5x3½" 220.00
Paperweight, #2777, 1934, pup, gunmetal, 5x3½" 240.00
Paperweight, #6160, 1935, long-eared rabbit, aqua mat, 3" 160.00
Paperweight, #6437, 1940, rose, pk mat, 5½" 130.00
Pin tray, #2595, 1947, sleeping nude, cocoa opaque, 2x4½" 140.00
Plate, #87, 1888, cameo mc daisies on pk & gray, Sprague, 6" 190.00
Plate, #87, 1888, cameo mc floral, S Toohey, 6" 660.00
Potpourri, #1321E, 1925, floral, E Barrett, 3-pc, 4" 700.00
Potpourri, #1321E, 1938, pierced floral, aqua hi-glaze, 4" 260.00
Sculpture, #972, 1953, egret, blk & wht hi-glaze, 9" 160.00
Tile, #1987, 1916, bird among plants, cream & bl mat, 5½" 300.00
Tile, #3210, 1925, ferns & geometrics, 3-color, mat, 5½" 190.00
Tile, gnarled tree in rnd reserve, 4-color, 6", +fr 950.00
Tile, lg tree, cream sketch on 6-color ground, 5½" 600.00
Tile, poppy cvd on bl-gr nottle, 7¾" 300.00
Tile, ship w/flags & full sail, 7-color (EX glaze), 12", +fr 1,600.00
Tile, trees/riverbank, 5-color, 12", +fr 2,400.00
Tile, 1920, 2 birds among vines, mc, 5½" sq 400.00
Trivet, #2350, 1919, sea gulls/waves, wht/bl on gr, 6" dia 125.00
Trivet, #3077, 1929, parrot & morning glories, 6-color, 6" sq 220.00
Vase, #1307, 1916, tulips buds, curdled bl on lt bl mat, 5" 350.00
Vase, #1343, 1922, stylized floral branches, CS Todd, 5" 750.00
Vase, #1370, 1911, dogwood on tall stems, gr/brn mat, 7x4" 450.00
Vase, #1674, 1921, buds/leaves, 4x1½" 140.00
Vase, #1681, 1914, vertical leaves & pods, gr on pk, 4½" 140.00
Vase, #1681, 1921, vertical floral, yel mat, 4½" 300.00
Vase, #1710, 1927, poppies on bl mat, 11x6" 425.00
Vase, #1710, 1928, poppies on brn mat, 11x6" 600.00
Vase, #1712, 1929, daffodils, yel mat, 9" 400.00
Vase, #1795, 1930, rook design, 5-sided, caramel mat, 5" 260.00
Vase, #1885, 1914, Arts & Crafts decor, brn on gr mat, 4" 250.00
Vase, #1894, 1920, lg dragonflies, rose mat, 6½" 400.00
Vase, #1906, 1915, fish/seaweed at base, gr to pk mat, 7½" 400.00
Vase, #1908, 1931, leaves at rim, olive on aqua mat, 5½" 200.00
Vase, #2090, 1929, Arts & Crafts decor, bl mat, 4½" 190.00
Vase, #2124, 1925, sea horse on bl & tan, 6" 375.00
Vase, #2135, 1924, geometric twisting panels, brn mat, 6" 260.00
Vase, #2141, 1928, floral in V panel, yel mat, 6½" 375.00
Vase, #2144, 1914, flowers & leaves, bl mat, 6½" 220.00
Vase, #2155, 1914, Arts & Crafts shoulder decor, 2½x4½" 140.00
Vase, #2216, 1930, stylized shoulder decor, bl mat, 5" 210.00
Vase, #2322, 1922, rooks in sqs, emb strapwork, 7½" 375.00
Vase, #2324, 1932, floral shoulder band, pk & gr mat, 8" 180.00
Vase, #2331, 1922, swirl-emb cylinder w/hdls, bl mat, 8" 300.00
Vase, #2354, 1929, rooks/leaves band, curdled pk mat, 7½" 350.00
Vase, #2380, 1932, floral w/5 butressed hdls, 6" 300.00
Vase, #2394, 1920, geometric panels in lower half, 9" 350.00
Vase, #2396, 1921, emb leaves, yel mat, 11" 280.00
Vase, #2401, 1927, eliptic medallions, med bl mat, 7" 280.00
Vase, #2410, 1917, buttresses at rim, gr over rose mat, 8" 300.00
Vase, #2422, 1920, point band under flared rim, bl mat, 11" 400.00
Vase, #2437, 1925, geometric shoulder band, med bl mat, 5½" ..190.00
Vase, #2586, 1922, blk hi-glaze, 8" 250.00
Vase, #2593, 1922, berries & leaves, yel mat, 7" 250.00
Vase, #2831, 1927, floral shoulder band, D Workum, 6" 800.00
Vase, #2855, 1927, stylized floral, aqua mat, 4½" 130.00

Vase, #2907, 1927, stylized swirl & panel, pk mat, 9" 250.00
Vase, #2949, 1926, wht mat, hdls, 9½x9" 270.00
Vase, #354, 1923, mustard yel mat, 3-hdld, 3½" 180.00
Vase, #5433, 1935, floral, wht mat, 3" 100.00
Vase, #6006, 1931, poppies/wheat on caramel tan, 12" 700.00
Vase, #607C, 1916, bl mat, integral hdls, 5" 275.00
Vase, #6215, 1931, fish & seaweed, mottled bl mat, 7" 325.00
Vase, #6342, 1942, flowers on stems, mint gr mat, 4" 160.00
Vase, #6431, 1943, floral w/lg leaves, molded/pnt, 3½" 300.00
Vase, #6433, 1934, emb floral w/leaves, bl mat, 2½" 100.00
Vase, #6893, 1946, lg floral, aqua hi-glaze, 9" 260.00
Vase, #7057, 1957, floral on wht, rectangular, 6" 125.00
Vase, #881F, 1913, cvd leaves, shaded tan mat, 3½" 160.00
Vase, #934, 1912, geometric-based panels, rose w/gr, 12½" 950.00
Vase, #942 F, 1907, incised/twisted geometrics, pk mat, 3½" 290.00
Vase, #969D, 1905, Greek Key band, pk/gr mat, gourd form, 5" 500.00
Wall pocket, #1036, 1938, lily form, gr on pk mat, 15½", NM ...260.00
Wall pocket, #2279, 1916, rook w/grapes, 3-color mat, 12" 550.00

Rorstrand

The Rorstrand Pottery was established in Sweden in 1726 and is today Sweden's oldest existing pottery. The earliest ware, now mostly displayed in Swedish museums, was much like old Delft. Later types were hard-paste porcelains that were enameled and decorated in a peasant style. Contemporary pieces, such as we've listed, are often described as Swedish Modern. Rorstrand is also famous for their Christmas plates.

Bowl, cvd decor, ochre to blk, 3-lobe rim, Nyland, 5" 210.00
Vase, beige mottle on gr mottle, teardrop form, 11x3⅞" 200.00
Vase, bl gloss, hourglass form, Stalhane, 9x2" 260.00
Vase, bl gloss crackle, CH Stalhane, teardrop form, 8" 230.00
Vase, bl/yel mottle, long neck, Stalhane, 11x3" 275.00

Rose Mandarin

Similar in design to Rose Medallion, this Chinese Export porcelain features the pattern of a robed mandarin, often separated by florals, ladies, genre scenes, or butterflies in polychrome enamels. It is sometimes trimmed in gold. Elaborate in decoration, this pattern was popular from the late 1700s until the early 1840s.

Brush box, 2840, 7¾" L, EX 875.00
Coffeepot, 1800s, 10¼" 1,500.00
Garden seat, keg design, mid-19th C, 19" 2,600.00
Plate, 9½" 135.00
Platter, oval, 1850s, 16½" 350.00
Platter, 1800s, 18" 600.00

Punch bowl, 19th century, 14½" dia, $1,850.00 at auction.

Shrimp dish, 1800s, 10⅝" dia 700.00
Temple jar, dome lid, foo dog finial, 1800s, 24" 3,850.00
Tray, pheasant/butterfly/fruit/florals, cut corners, 9¾x6¾" 220.00
Urn, gilt foo dog finial, 11½" 500.00
Vegetable dish, 1800s, w/lid, 9½" L 850.00
Wash basin, 16¼" 865.00
Wash basin, 1800s, 17", +water bottle, 16", both VG 1,200.00

Rose Medallion

Rose Medallion is one of the patterns of Chinese export porcelain produced from before 1850 until the second decade of the 20th century. It is decorated in rose colors with panels of florals, birds, and butterflies that form reserves containing Chinese figures. Pre-1850 ware is unmarked and is characterized by quality workmanship and gold trim. From about 1850 until circa 1860, the kilns in Canton did not operate, and no Rose Medallion was made. Post-1860 examples (still unmarked) can often be recognized by the poor quality of the gold trim or its absence. In the 1890s the ware was often marked 'China'; 'Made in China' was used from 1910 through the 1930s.

Bowl, chestnut; pierced basket & underplate, 11" 925.00
Bowl, court figures, roses, birds, insects, 5½x11½" 1,000.00
Bowl, figures in landscape panels, mid-1800s, 3¾x9", EX 600.00
Bowl, footed lozenge form w/scalloped edge, 19th C, 14" L 500.00
Bowl, marquise form, ftd, monogrammed, 19th C, 15¼", pr ..1,495.00
Bowl, sq, lobed, rstr, 9⅜" 520.00
Bowl, vegetable; firing blemishes, 9¼" 230.00
Brush pot, cylindrical, cvd lid, wood stand, 5¾" 525.00
Charger, birds/figures on terrace in 6 panels, 19th C, 18¼" 770.00
Garden seat, glaze wear, 19th C, 19" 1,265.00
Garden seat, rprs, 19th C, 18¾" 475.00
Garden seat, 19th C, 18¾", EX 2,500.00
Leaf dish, 7", pr 285.00
Pitcher, 19th C, 6½" 400.00
Pitcher, late, 6" 80.00
Platter, 19th C, 18¼" L 1,095.00
Punch bowl, 19th C, 13¾", EX 860.00
Punch bowl, 19th C, 14½" 1,380.00
Tureen, sauce; ftd, twist hdls, w/lid, late, 6" 495.00
Umbrella jar, 24", EX 920.00
Vase, baluster, appl dragons & foo dogs, scalloped, 18" 700.00
Vase, Ku form, 19th C, rstr rim, 13" 600.00
Vegetable stand, rectangular w/notched corners, w/lid, 9¼" 425.00

Roselane

Founded in California in 1938 by William and Georgia Fields, the Roselane company at first produced only figurines for the local florist. But by the '40s they offered candle holders, wall pockets, vases, and a line of modernistic animals mounted on wooden bases. In the '50s their 'Sparklers' — small stylized animal and bird figures with rhinestone eyes became popular. (Today these are worth from $10.00 to $25.00, depending on size.) The company closed in 1977. A variety of marks was used; all incorporate the Roselane name.

Ashtray, gray & rose 12.50
Bowl, fish design, turq & blk, w/stand, 13" dia 75.00
Bowl, pk & gray, A-11, 11" 24.00
Dealer sign, Roselane, deep aqua gloss, 3x12½" 275.00
Figurine, Balinese dancers, gray & mauve, 10x8", pr 130.00
Figurine, deer, brn & wht, Sparkler, 4x3½" 14.00

Pho'o courtesy Lee Garmon

Figurine, elephants with sparkler eyes and headpieces, 5½" to 6", $12.00 each.

Figurine, fawn, stylized, on ½-dome base, 5" 32.00
Figurine, giraffe, recumbent, looking bk, #264, 9" 40.00
Figurine, pheasant, brn on wht matt, tail up, 7¾" 22.50
Figurine, pug dog, Sparkler, 4" 18.00
Planter, Chinese Coolie atop rectangular form 22.50
Sculpture, elephant, stylized, brn lustre, wood base, 8" 150.00
Vase, Chinese Modern, emb decor base, ftd, 9¾" 40.00

Rosemeade

Rosemeade was the name chosen by Wahpeton Pottery Company of Wahpeton, North Dakota, to represent their product. The founders of the company were Laura A. Taylor and R.J. Hughes, who organized the firm in 1940. It is most noted for small bird and animal figurals, either in high gloss or a Van Briggle-like matt glaze. The ware was marked 'Rosemeade' with an ink stamp or carried a 'Prairie Rose' sticker. The pottery closed in 1961. Our advisor for this category is Bryce L. Farnsworth; he is listed in the Directory under North Dakota. For more information we recommend *Collector's Encyclopedia of the Dakota Potteries* by Darlene Hurst Dommel.

Animal dish, turkey, w/spoon notch 145.00
Ashtray, Blk Angus cow figurine 185.00
Ashtray, fox figurine 190.00
Ashtray, gopher figurine, Minnesota-Gopher State 125.00
Ashtray, horse figurine, gr 160.00
Ashtray, puma figurine 360.00
Ashtray, rooster figurine, strutting 120.00
Ashtray, turkey figurine 125.00
Bank, bear 375.00
Bank, hippo 650.00
Bell, tulip, pk 150.00
Cotton holder, rabbit, bl 220.00
Creamer & sugar bowl, corn, 2½" 45.00
Creamer & sugar bowl, tulip 50.00
Dealer sign 1,250.00
Figurine, duck, mini 100.00
Figurine, elephant, blk, sm 100.00
Figurine, frog, solid 260.00
Figurine, penguins, set of 3 ....200.00
Figurine, pheasant hen, 11½" 600.00
Figurine, pheasant rooster, 10¾" 450.00
Figurine, pheasant rooster, 12½" 250.00
Figurine, pheasant rooster, 14½" 450.00
Figurine, seals, set of 3 ....45.00
Planter, dove 210.00
Planter, elephant 90.00
Planter, lamb, standing 95.00
Planter, sleigh 90.00

Planter, squirrel on log 50.00
Plate, mouse in relief 95.00
Shakers, bears, pr 75.00
Shakers, buffalo, pr 120.00
Shakers, bull & cow, pr 250.00
Shakers, coyote pups, pr 275.00
Shakers, dog heads, Chihuahua, pr 425.00
Shakers, dog heads, English Setter, pr 45.00
Shakers, dog heads, Fox Terrier, pr 40.00
Shakers, dog heads, Pekinese, pr 55.00
Shakers, dog heads, Scottie, pr 50.00
Shakers, donkey heads, pr 75.00
Shakers, ducklings, pr 60.00
Shakers, elephants, pr 95.00
Shakers, flamingos, pr 195.00
Shakers, horse heads, pr 100.00
Shakers, kangaroos, papa & mama w/baby in pouch, pr 425.00
Shakers, pheasants, Golden, pr 140.00
Shakers, pheasants, tails down, pr 110.00
Shakers, pheasants, tails up, pr 35.00
Shakers, potatoes, pr 180.00
Shakers, Prairie Rose, pr 45.00
Shakers, roadrunners, pr 220.00
Shakers, turkeys, pr 75.00
Spoon rest, pheasant 80.00
Spoon rest, pheasant, Mann's-Devils Lake 220.00
Spoon rest, Prairie Rose 50.00
TV lamp, panther, bronze 450.00
TV lamp, pheasant 500.00
Wall plaque, mountain goat, dbl 525.00

Rosenthal

In 1879 Phillip Rosenthal established the Rosenthal Porcelain Factory in Selb, Bavaria. Its earliest products were figurines and fine tablewares. The company has continued to operate to the present decade, manufacturing limited edition plates.

Plate, multicolored flowers with gold on white, scalloped rim, 13" dia, $85.00.

Bowl, fruit; blkberries, sgn Butler, gold hdls, 6½x14" 575.00
Cup & saucer, coffee; wht porc w/Nouveau silver o/l, 6 for 750.00
Figurine, bird on branch, 4½" 50.00
Figurine, boy w/lamb 145.00
Figurine, dachshund, recumbent, 10x6" 425.00
Figurine, dachshund, sitting, 6x6" 250.00
Figurine, dachshund, sitting on bk legs, 9½x3½" 370.00
Figurine, dachshund, standing, 4¾" 150.00
Figurine, French poodle, wht, EX detail, 7x7" 350.00
Figurine, German shepherd, Fritz, 5¾x4¼" 325.00
Figurine, Harlequin Great Dane Fritz Diller, 8x9¼" 750.00
Figurine, nude boy holds dog by collar, 6¾" 395.00
Figurine, pointer, 5x10½" 550.00

Figurine, Russian wolfhound, wht, head up, 9¼x4½" 380.00
Plate, Delft bl windmill scene, hdls, 10½" 150.00

Roseville

The Roseville Pottery Company was established in 1892 by George F. Young in Roseville, Ohio. Finding their facilities inadequate, the company moved to Zanesville in 1898, erected a new building, and installed the most modern equipment available. By 1900 Young felt ready to enter into the stiffly competitive art pottery market. Roseville's first art line was called Rozane. Similar to Rookwood's Standard, Rozane featured dark blended backgrounds with slip-painted underglaze artwork of nature studies, portraits, birds, and animals. Azurean, developed in 1902, was a blue and white underglaze art line on a blue blended background. Egypto (1904) featured a matt glaze in a soft shade of old green and was modeled in low relief after examples of ancient Egyptian pottery. Mongol (1904) was a high-gloss oxblood red line after the fashion of the Chinese Sang de Boeuf. Mara (1904), an iridescent lustre line of magenta and rose with intricate patterns developed on the surface or in low relief, successfully duplicated Sicardo's work. These early lines were followed by many others of highest quality: Fudjiyama and Woodland (1905-06) reflected an Oriental theme; Crystalis (1906) was covered with beautiful frost-like crystals. Della Robbia, their most famous line (introduced in 1906), was decorated with designs ranging from florals, animals, and birds to scenes of Viking warriors and Roman gladiators. These designs were accomplished by sgraffito with slip-painted details. Very limited but of great importance to collectors today, Rozane Olympic (1905) was decorated with scenes of Greek mythology on a red ground. Pauleo (1914) was the last of the artware lines. It was varied — over two hundred glazes were recorded — and some pieces were decorated by hand, usually with florals.

During the second decade of the century until the plant closed forty years later, new lines were continually added. Some of the more popular of the middle-period lines were Donatello, 1915; Futura, 1928; Pine Cone, 1931; and Blackberry, 1933. The floral lines of the later years have become highly collectible. Pottery from every era of Roseville production — even its utility ware — attests to an unwavering dedication to quality and artistic merit.

Examples of the fine art pottery lines present the greatest challenge to evaluate. Scarcity is a prime consideration. The quality of artwork varied from one artist to another. Some pieces show fine detail and good color, and naturally this influences their values. Studies of animals and portraits bring higher prices than the floral designs. An artist's signature often increases the value of any item, especially if the artist is one who is well recognized. For further information consult *The Collector's Encyclopedia of Roseville Pottery, First and Second Series*, by Sharon and Bob Huxford (Collector Books).

Apple Blossom, ewer, #318, 15" 550.00
Apple Blossom, hanging basket 225.00
Apple Blossom, tea set, #371, 3-pc 425.00
Aztec, vase, cylindrical, 9½" 275.00
Baneda, bowl, console; 6-sided, red, 13" 425.00
Baneda, jardiniere, red, 9½" 750.00
Baneda, vase, tapered w/low hdls, red, 8" 475.00
Bittersweet, basket, #808, 6" 150.00
Bittersweet, ewer, #816, 8" 225.00
Bittersweet, planter, #868, 8" 125.00
Bittersweet, vase, dbl bud; #873, 6" 150.00
Blackberry, bowl, console; ovoid w/angled hdls, 13" 375.00
Blackberry, candle holders, 4½", pr 375.00
Blackberry, jardiniere, 6" 325.00
Blackberry, vase, bulbous w/angled hdls, 4" 275.00

Blackberry, wall pocket 775.00
Bleeding Heart, ewer, #972, 10" 300.00
Bleeding Heart, pitcher, #1323 ....275.00
Bleeding Heart, wall pocket, #1287, 8" ...300.00
Burmese, candle holders/bookends, #80-B, wht, pr ...250.00
Bushberry, basket, #369, 6½" 150.00
Bushberry, basket, #370, 8" 200.00
Bushberry, ewer, #2, 10" 225.00
Bushberry, vase, #29, 6" 125.00
Carnelian, bowl, console; 14" 125.00
Carnelian, loving cup, 5" 125.00
Carnelian, vase, fan; 8" 125.00
Carnelian II, vase, squatty rnd shape w/ear hdls, 6½" ...325.00
Ceramic Design, wall pocket, Persian type ...275.00
Cherry Blossom, candle holders, ring hdls, flared bases, 4", pr ...425.00
Cherry Blossom, jardiniere, 10" 750.00
Cherry Blossom, vase, cylindrical w/sm upper ring hdls, 7½" ...325.00
Cherry Blossom, vase, jug; 7" 375.00
Clemana, vase, flat-sided w/angled hdls, ftd, 7" ...225.00
Clematis, cookie jar, #3, 10" 375.00
Clematis, cornucopia, #140, 6" 90.00
Clematis, tea set, #5, 3-pc 300.00
Clematis, vase, bud; #187, 7" 85.00
Clematis, wall pocket, #1295, 8" 200.00
Columbine, basket, #365, 7" 200.00
Columbine, bowl, #655, 3" 100.00
Columbine, ewer, #18, 7" 175.00
Columbine, vase, #20, 8" 150.00
Corinthian, candle holder, 10" 95.00
Corinthian, compote, 5x10" 125.00
Cosmos, ewer, #951, 15" 550.00
Cosmos, vase, #954, 4" 100.00
Cosmos, vase, bowl; #376, 6" 200.00
Creamware, chocolate pot, cherry decal & gold line ...375.00
Cremona, vase, flat-sided, 7" 100.00
Cremona, vase, tapered w/flared rim, 10½" ...200.00
Dahlrose, bowl, oval, 10" 175.00
Dahlrose, vase, dbl bud 125.00
Dahlrose, vase, triple bud; 6" 150.00
Dawn, vase, #826, 6" 200.00

Della Robbia, vase, oak trees and oversized acorns, signed GB, 3-handled, 9¼x4", $10,000.00.

Decorated Utility Ware, pitcher, 7" 60.00
Dogwood I, wall pocket 250.00
Dogwood II, basket, 8" 150.00
Dogwood II, jardiniere, 8" 225.00
Donatello, flowerpot, w/saucer, 5" 150.00
Donatello, frog, rnd 15.00
Donatello, pitcher, 6½" 300.00
Dutch, pitcher, 9½" 175.00

Dutch, soap dish, 3" 225.00
Earlam, vase, bulbous w/ring hdls, 6" 175.00
Egypto, compote, emb floral design, w/seal, 9" ...500.00
Egypto, pitcher, bulbous, w/seal, 5" 375.00
Elsie the Cow, plate, #B2, 7½" 275.00
Falline, lamp, hdld & ftd rnd bowl shape w/2 lights ...750.00
Falline, vase, tapered w/sm ring hdls, 8" ...425.00
Ferella, bowl, ftd, 12" 450.00
Ferella, vase, above-shoulder hdls, 9" 425.00
Ferella, vase, tapered w/hdls, 6" 325.00
Florane, Late Line; bowl, #61, 9" 95.00
Florane, Late Line; vase, #80, 6" 60.00
Florane, vase, bowl; 3½" 85.00
Florane, vase, cylindrical w/sm angled hdls at rim, 6" ...85.00
Florentine, vase, dbl bud; 6" 100.00
Florentine, wall pocket, 9½" 200.00
Foxglove, basket, #373, 8" 225.00
Foxglove, cornucopia, #164, 8" 125.00
Foxglove, ewer, #6, 15" 375.00
Foxglove, vase, #42, 4" 95.00
Foxglove, vase, dbl bud; #160, 4½" 135.00
Freesia, bookends, #15 ....200.00
Freesia, candle holder, #1161, 4½" 95.00
Freesia, cookie jar, #4, 10" 425.00
Freesia, pitcher, #20, 10" 225.00
Fuchsia, pitcher, #1322, w/ice lip, 8" 400.00
Fuchsia, vase, #903, 12" 425.00
Fuchsia, vase, bowl; #645, 3" 125.00
Futura, planter, flat-sided, 7" 175.00
Futura, vase, cylindrical w/sq hdls, 6" 225.00
Futura, vase, fluted, pk & gray high gloss, 8" ...425.00
Gardenia, basket, #609, 10" 275.00
Gardenia, bowl, #600, 4" 95.00
Gardenia, cornucopia, #621, 6" 125.00
Gardenia, ewer, #616, 6" 150.00
Imperial I, basket, bowl shape, 6" 125.00
Imperial I, vase, triple bud; 8" 150.00
Imperial II, wall pocket, triple 250.00
Iris, basket, #354, 8" 250.00
Iris, jardiniere, #359, 5" 150.00
Iris, vase, bowl; #2117, 4" 100.00
Ivory II, candelabrum, #116, Velmoss II shape, 5½" ...175.00
Ixia, basket, #346, 10" 300.00
Ixia, bowl, #387, 6" 175.00
Jonquil, basket, shouldered bowl w/tall pointed hdl, 9" ...425.00
Jonquil, vase, bud; low hdls, 7" 150.00
Juvenile, mug, w/rabbit, 3" 100.00
Juvenile, pitcher w/saucer, w/chicks 175.00
Juvenile, plate, w/chicks, 7" 150.00
La Rose, bowl, 9" 100.00
La Rose, vase, dbl bud 125.00
Landscape, planter, 4½" 95.00
Laurel, bowl, plain rim, 7" 175.00
Laurel, vase, cylindrical w/closed hdls, 6" ...175.00
Lotus, candle holders, #L5, 2½", pr 125.00
Lotus, vase, #L3, 10" 225.00
Luffa, vase, cylindrical w/angled hdls, 6" ...250.00
Luffa, vase, tapers to flared base, angled hdls, 13" ...550.00
Lustre, vase, cylindrical, 10" 75.00
Magnolia, basket, #385, 10" 225.00
Magnolia, bowl, #665, 3" 75.00
Magnolia, mug, #3, 3" 150.00
Magnolia, pitcher, cider; #132, 7" 325.00
Magnolia, planter, #389, 8" 125.00

Mayfair, pitcher, #1105, 8" 125.00
Mayfair, tankard, #1107, 12" 175.00
Ming Tree, bowl, console; #528, 10" 150.00
Ming Tree, vase, #581, 6" 85.00
Mock Orange, basket, #909, 8" 200.00
Mock Orange, ewer, #916, 6" 125.00
Moderne, #794, 7" 125.00
Moderne, lamp, #799, 9" 425.00
Monticello, basket, bulbous vase w/arched hdl, 6½" 550.00
Monticello, vase, hdls above defined shoulder, 4" 175.00
Morning Glory, vase, ball shape w/angled hdls, 6" 425.00
Morning Glory, vase, concave w/angled hdls, 6" 350.00
Moss, bowl, candle holders, #1107, 4½", pr 200.00
Moss, vase, #774, 6" 175.00
Mostique, bowl, glossy beige exterior, 2½" H 75.00
Mostique, jardiniere, 10" 275.00

Mostique, jardiniere and pedestal, multicolor geometric floral decoration on neutral gray, 29", $700.00.

Orian, vase, bowl; 6" 225.00
Orian, vase, 12" 300.00
Panel, vase, dbl bud 150.00
Panel, vase, fan; w/nude, 6" 550.00
Panel, vase, pillow; 6" 125.00
Pasadena, bowl, #L24, 3" 65.00
Pasadena, flowerpot, #L36, 4" 60.00
Peony, bowl, #427, 4" 125.00
Peony, cornucopia, #172, dbl 150.00
Peony, ewer, #7, 6" 125.00
Peony, wall pocket, #1293, 8" 225.00
Persian, jardiniere 275.00
Pine Cone, basket, #339, 9x13" 850.00
Pine Cone, basket, #408, 6" 275.00
Pine Cone, candle holder, #1106, 5½" 275.00
Pine Cone, pitcher, ball shape w/ice lip, 8" 550.00
Pine Cone, vase, #109, 10" 500.00
Poppy, ewer, #876, 10" 225.00
Poppy, wall pocket/candle holder, #1281, 9" 475.00
Primrose, vase, #765, 8" 200.00
Primrose, vase, #767 ....250.00
Raymor, bean pot, #195 ....60.00
Raymor, hot plate, #159 ....40.00
Raymor, plate, dinner; #152 ....25.00
Rosecraft, candle holder, 8" 225.00
Rosecraft, frog 15.00
Rosecraft, jardiniere, 5" 150.00
Rosecraft, vase, cylindrical w/sm angled hdls, 8" 125.00
Rosecraft Black, vase, 10" 175.00
Rosecraft Hexagon, bowl, 4" 300.00
Rozane, bowl, #927, 2½" 125.00
Rozane, ewer, #828, 7" 325.00
Rozane, vase, #821, 9½" 325.00
Rozane, vase, pillow; #882, 9" 300.00

Rozane Royal, jug, cherries on deep brn, w/seal, J Imlay, 7" 250.00
Rozane Royal, mug, #886, 4½" 200.00
Rozane Royal, vase, #842, 8" 150.00
Rozane Royal, vase, floral on shaded cream & gray, J Imlay, 6" ..475.00
Rozane 1917, champagne bucket, mc floral & leaf design on ivory 325.00
Rozane 1917, compote, mc floral & leaf design on lt gr, 5" 125.00
Russco, vase, bud; 8" 150.00
Russco, vase, 14½" 250.00
Silhouette, basket, #708, 6" 175.00
Silhouette, cigarette box 150.00
Silhouette, planter, #731, 14" 150.00
Silhouette, vase, fan; #783, 7" 425.00
Snowberry, ashtray 85.00
Snowberry, bowl, #1RB, 5" 95.00
Snowberry, candle holders, #2CS-1, pr 85.00
Sunflower, jardiniere, 9" 650.00
Sunflower, vase, 6" 325.00
Teasel, basket, #349, 10" 275.00
Teasel, bowl, #342, 4" 150.00
Teasel, ewer, #890, 18" 475.00
Teasel, vase, #348, 6" 175.00
Thornapple, basket, #342, 10" 275.00
Thornapple, planter, #262, 5" 125.00
Topeo, bowl, plain rim, tapers to flat bottom, 2½" 150.00
Topeo, vase, shouldered, 6" 275.00
Tourmaline, planter, ovoid, ftd, 5x12½" 275.00
Tourmaline, vase, bowl; 5" 95.00
Tuscany, bowl, console, 11" 150.00
Tuscany, vase, flower arranger; 5" 100.00
Velmoss II, cornucopia, dbl, 8½" 225.00
Velmoss II, vase, dbl bud; 8" 175.00
Velmoss Scroll, bowl, rose & leaf design on wht, 2½x9" ..100.00
Velmoss Scroll, compote, rose & leaf design on wht, 4x9" 175.00
Water Lily, basket, #381, 10" 200.00
Water Lily, bowl, #663, 3" 85.00
Water Lily, cornucopia, #178, 8" 125.00
Water Lily, ewer, #12, 15" 550.00
White Rose, bowl, #387, 4" 125.00
White Rose, ewer, #990, 10" 300.00
White Rose, pitcher, #1324 ....250.00
White Rose, vase, #147, 8" 175.00
Wincraft, basket, #208, 8" 150.00
Wincraft, planter set, #1051/#1050, 6", 3-pc 150.00
Wincraft, vase, #285, 10" 175.00
Wincraft, vase, circle; #1053, 8" 150.00
Windsor, candlesticks, ftd cups w/dbl hdls, 4½", pr 275.00
Windsor, vase, bulbous w/hdls, ferns on bl, 9" 800.00
Wisteria, vase, bulbous w/ring hdls, 6" 375.00
Wisteria, vase, cylindrical w/angled hdls, 10" 650.00
Zephyr Lily, ashtray 60.00
Zephyr Lily, basket, #394, 8" 175.00
Zephyr Lily, console boat, #475, 10" 150.00
Zephyr Lily, ewer, #23, 10" 200.00
Zephyr Lily, tea set, #7, 3-pc 325.00

Rowland and Marsellus

Though the impressive back stamp seems to suggest otherwise, Rowland and Marsellus were not Staffordshire potters but American importers who commissioned various English companies to supply them with the transfer-printed historical ware that had been a popular import item since the early 1800s. Plates (both flat and with a rolled edge), cups and saucers, pitchers, and platters were sold as souvenirs from 1890 through the 1930s. Though other importers — Bawo & Dotter and A. C. Bosselman & Co., both of New York City — commissioned the manufacture of similar souvenir items, by far the largest volume carries the R. & M. mark, and Rowland and Marsellus has become a generic term that covers all 20th-century souvenir china of this type. Their mark may be in full or 'R. & M.' in a diamond. Though primarily made with blue transfers on white, other colors may occasionally be found as well. Our advisor for this category is David Ringering; he is listed in the Directory under Oregon.

Key:
r/e — rolled edge   v/o — view of
s/o — souvenir of

Cup & saucer, Chicago, s/o 95.00
Cup & saucer, farmer's 65.00
Cup & saucer, Lenox MA, s/o 85.00
Cup & saucer, Niagara Falls NY, w/o 75.00
Cup & saucer, Yale, s/o 95.00
Plate, Albany (NY), s/o, State Capital, r/e, 10" 70.00
Plate, Baltimore IN, Courthouse, s/o, r/e, 10" 65.00
Plate, Battle of Bunker Hill, fruit & flower border, 9¾" ...60.00
Plate, Battle of Lake Erie, fruit & flower border, 9¾" 60.00
Plate, Bethleham PA, Moravian College, v/o, 9" 35.00
Plate, Charles Dickens, r/e, 10½" 75.00
Plate, coupe; Am Poets, 7 portraits, v/o, 10" 60.00
Plate, coupe; Chicago, v/o, Marshall Field & Co, 6" 50.00
Plate, coupe; Jamestown Expo, Expo building, s/o, 1907, 6" 50.00
Plate, coupe; Miami, s/o, Chief Osceola, 10" 60.00
Plate, coupe; Salem, v/o, witch & 5 scenes, Daniel Low, 6" 60.00
Plate, coupe; San Francisco Harbor Scene, v/o, 10" 45.00
Plate, Denver Co, s/o, Capitol Building, r/e, 10" 70.00
Plate, Henry Addressing VA Assembly, fruit/flower border, 9¾" .60.00
Plate, Hermitage, fruit & flower border, 9¾" 50.00
Plate, Jackson MI, New Capitol Building, s/o, r/e, 10" ...75.00
Plate, Lookout Mountain, TN, s/o, r/e, 10" 70.00

Plate, Old Y Bridge, souvenir of Zanesville, 10⅛", $100.00.

Plate, Pilgrim Hall, fruit & flower border, 9¾" 55.00
Plate, Ride of Paul Revere, fruit & flower border, 9¾" ...55.00
Plate, Sacramento CA, w/o, 9" 40.00
Plate, Whirlpool Rapids, fruit & flower border, 9¾" 55.00
Tumbler, Ottawa Canada 85.00
Tumbler, Thousand Islands, v/o 85.00

Royal Bayreuth

Founded in 1794 in Tettau, Bavaria, the Royal Bayreuth firm originally manufactured fine dinnerware of superior quality. Their figural items, produced from before the turn of the century until the onset of WWI, are highly sought after by today's collectors. Perhaps the most abundantly produced and easily recognized of these are the tomato and lobster pieces. Fruits, flowers, people, animals, birds, and vegetables were also made. Aside from figural items, pitchers, toothpick holders, cups and saucers, humidors, and the like were decorated in florals and scenic motifs. Some, such as the very popular Rose Tapestry line, utilized a cloth-like tapestry background. Transfer prints were used as well. Two of the most popular are Sunbonnet Babies and Nursery Rhymes (in particular, those decorated with the complete verse).

Caution: Many pieces were not marked; some were marked 'Deponiert' or 'Registered' only. While marked pieces are the most valued, unmarked items are still very worthwhile. Our advisors for this category are Larry Brenner from New Hampshire and Dee Hooks from Illinois; they are listed in the Directory under their home states.

Figurals

Ashtray, clown, wht pearlized, bl mk 750.00
Ashtray, devil, red, bl mk, 2½x3¼" 275.00
Bowl, Art Nouveau lady, bl mk, 3½x6" 1,300.00
Bowl, berry; oak leaf, wht pearlized, bl mk, 6" 50.00
Bowl, lobster & leaf, ftd, bl mk, 6" 75.00
Bowl, oak leaf, wht pearlized, bl mk, 9" 300.00
Bowl, poppy, opal, bl mk, 6" 200.00
Bowl, poppy, red, bl mk, 6" 150.00
Bowl, poppy, red, bl mk, 8" 295.00
Bowl, salad; lobster, bl mk, lg 325.00
Bowl, shell, bl mk, 8½" 335.00
Candlestick, clown, red, sitting, bl mk 550.00
Candlestick, clown, red, standing, bl mk, tall 1,900.00
Candlestick, elk, low, bl mk 450.00
Candlestick, pansy, bl mk 395.00
Candlestick, poppy, red, bl mk, rare 675.00
Candy dish, clown, wht pearlized w/gold, bl mk 425.00
Candy dish, lobster, bl mk, 5½" 180.00
Celery dish/relish, elk, bl mk 225.00
Celery tray, tomato, bl mk 295.00
Cracker jar, tomato, bl mk 550.00

Cracker jar, grapes, green, blue mark, 7¾", $700.00.

Cup, demitasse; Devil & Cards, bl mk 95.00
Cup & saucer, pansy, pearlized w/gold, bl mk 350.00
Cup & saucer, shell, bl mk 200.00
Demitasse pot, poppy, red, bl mk 1,200.00
Hatpin holder, penguin, bl mk 850.00
Hatpin holder, poppy, red, bl mk 625.00
Humidor, clown (lady), red, bl mk, sm 950.00
Humidor, clown (male), red, bl mk, lg 1,100.00
Humidor, coachman, bl mk 1,350.00

Humidor, lobster, bl mk 650.00
Match holder, chimpanzee, bl mk, wall hanging 875.00
Match holder, Devil & Cards, bl mk, wall hanging 600.00
Match holder, eagle, red, wall hanging, bl mk, rare 600.00
Mayonnaise, poppy, red, w/underplate, bl mk 300.00
Mug, beer; Devil & Cards, commemorative, bl mk 200.00
Mug, beer; elk, bl mk, tall 495.00
Mug, shaving; elk, bl mk 600.00
Mustard jar, grapes, pearlized, bl mk 300.00
Mustard jar, lobster & leaf, bl mk 125.00
Mustard jar, murex shell, unmk 75.00
Mustard jar, poppy, red, bl mk 200.00
Mustard jar, shell, bl mk 135.00
Mustard jar, tomato, bl mk 80.00
Nappy, lettuce leaf, bl mk 48.00
Nappy, lobster & leaf, bl mk 55.00
Nappy, poppy, red, bl mk 150.00
Nappy, tomato & leaf, bl mk 45.00
Nut dish, poppy, red, bl mk, sm 50.00
Nut set, radish, unmk, 7-pc 750.00
Pitcher, apple, red, bl mk, cream sz 150.00
Pitcher, apple, red, bl mk, water sz 900.00
Pitcher, apple, yel, bl mk, cream sz 200.00
Pitcher, bull, blk, bl mk, cream sz 300.00
Pitcher, bull, gray, bl mk, cream sz 295.00
Pitcher, bull, orange, bl mk, cream sz, from $150 to 300.00
Pitcher, bull, rust-brn, bl mk, cream sz 300.00
Pitcher, butterfly, open wings, bl mk, cream sz 425.00
Pitcher, cat, blk w/yel eyes, bl mk, cream sz, 5" 250.00
Pitcher, cat, gray, bl mk, cream sz 275.00
Pitcher, cat hdl, orange/gray on bl mug, bl mk, cream sz 425.00
Pitcher, chick, bl mk, cream sz 350.00
Pitcher, chimpanzee, bl mk, cream sz 600.00
Pitcher, clown, gr, bl mk, cream sz 295.00
Pitcher, clown, orange, bl mk, cream sz, NM 350.00
Pitcher, clown, red, bl mk, cream sz 350.00
Pitcher, coachman, bl mk, cream sz 300.00
Pitcher, coachman, bl mk, water sz 1,200.00
Pitcher, coral & shell, bl mk, cream sz 110.00
Pitcher, corn, bl mk, cream sz 375.00
Pitcher, cow, red, bl mk, cream sz 315.00
Pitcher, crow, blk, bl mk, cream sz 200.00
Pitcher, dachshund, bl mk, cream sz 275.00
Pitcher, Devil & Cards, bl mk, cream sz 250.00
Pitcher, Devil & Cards, bl mk, water sz 600.00
Pitcher, duck, bl mk, cream sz 300.00
Pitcher, eagle, bl mk, water sz, rare 1,650.00
Pitcher, eagle, mouth open, bl mk, cream sz 285.00
Pitcher, elk, bl mk, water sz 600.00
Pitcher, fish, open mouth, bl mk, milk sz 300.00
Pitcher, grapes, lav satin, bl mk, water sz 495.00
Pitcher, grapes, pearlized, unmk, cream sz 80.00
Pitcher, grapes, pearlized, unmk, water sz 525.00
Pitcher, lemon, bl mk, cream sz 295.00
Pitcher, lobster, bl mk, cream sz 150.00
Pitcher, lobster, bl mk, milk sz 300.00
Pitcher, lobster, bl mk, water sz 500.00
Pitcher, mtn goat, bl mk, cream sz 335.00
Pitcher, oak leaf, bl mk, cream sz 300.00
Pitcher, oak leaf, pearlized, bl mk, cream sz 325.00
Pitcher, oak leaf, pearlized gr, bl mk, water sz 1,300.00
Pitcher, Old Man of the Mountain, bl mk, cream sz 125.00
Pitcher, Old Man of the Mountain, gr mk, cream sz 125.00
Pitcher, oyster & pearl, bl mk, cream sz 225.00

Pitcher, pansy, gr mk, cream sz 300.00
Pitcher, parakeet, bl mk, cream sz 295.00
Pitcher, pelican, bl mk, cream sz 350.00
Pitcher, pelican, bl mk, water sz 815.00
Pitcher, pig, gray, bl mk, cream sz 600.00
Pitcher, pig, red, bl mk, cream sz 750.00
Pitcher, poppy, red, bl mk, cream sz 200.00
Pitcher, poppy, red, bl mk, milk sz 325.00
Pitcher, robin, bl mk, cream sz 395.00
Pitcher, robin, bl mk, water sz 880.00
Pitcher, rooster, blk, bl mk, cream sz 325.00
Pitcher, rooster, mc, bl mk, cream sz 400.00
Pitcher, rose, pk, bl mk, cream sz 295.00
Pitcher, rose, pk & yel, bl mk, milk sz 550.00
Pitcher, seal, bl mk, cream sz 300.00
Pitcher, seal, bl mk, water sz 1,400.00
Pitcher, shell, bl mk, milk sz 195.00
Pitcher, shell, low, bl mk, cream sz 175.00
Pitcher, shell, tall, bl mk, cream sz 180.00
Pitcher, shell w/lobster hdl, bl mk, water sz 600.00
Pitcher, shell w/lobster hdl, unmk, cream sz 75.00
Pitcher, shell w/sea-horse hdl, unmk, cream sz 285.00
Pitcher, snake, bl mk, cream sz 900.00
Pitcher, spikey shell, bl mk, cream sz 200.00
Pitcher, St Bernard, bl mk, water sz 850.00
Pitcher, St Bernard, blk, bl mk, cream sz 400.00
Pitcher, strawberry, bl mk, cream sz 250.00
Pitcher, tomato, red, bl mk, cream sz 175.00
Pitcher, turtle, bl mk, cream sz 750.00
Pitcher, water buffalo, blk, bl mk, cream sz 200.00
Pitcher, water buffalo, gray, bl mk, water sz 295.00
Plate, lobster & leaf, bl mk, 4" 54.00
Plate, lobster & leaf, bl mk, 6" 65.00
Plate, poppy, red, bl mk, 7½" 125.00
Plate, shell, bl mk, 8" 150.00
Relish, poinsettia, bl mk 500.00
Relish, radish, bl mk 280.00
Relish, tomato, bl mk, leaf spoon 80.00
Shakers, elk, bl mk, pr 200.00
Shakers, grapes, pearlized, bl mk, pr 200.00
Shakers, grapes, purple, bl mk, pr 150.00
Shakers, lobster, bl mk, pr 220.00
Shakers, lobster, unmk, pr 80.00
Shakers, lobster & leaf, bl mk, pr 225.00
Shakers, shell, bl mk, pr 75.00
Shakers, strawberry, bl mk, pr 400.00
Shakers, tomatoes, bl mk, pr 110.00
Shoe, lady's boot, brn & tan, bl mk 195.00
Shoe, lady's high-top, bl mk 215.00
Shoe, man's, brn, bl mk 195.00
Shoe, man's, wht, bl mk 235.00
Sugar bowl, apple, bl mk 200.00
Sugar bowl, lobster, bl mk 175.00
Sugar bowl, orange, bl mk 375.00
Sugar bowl, shell, bl mk 100.00
Sugar bowl, tomato, bl mk 150.00
Tea strainer, pansy, mc, mk Deponiert 395.00
Teapot, orange, bl mk 375.00
Teapot, poppy, red, bl mk 425.00
Teapot, strawberry, bl mk 385.00
Teapot, tomato, bl mk 250.00
Teapot, tomato, bl mk, mini 200.00
Toothpick holder, bellringer, bl mk 400.00
Toothpick holder, elk, bl mk 225.00

Vase, Art Nouveau lady, bl mk, sm 800.00

Nursery Rhymes

Bowl, Jack & the Beanstalk, flat, bl mk, sm 285.00
Bowl, Jack & the Beanstalk, ftd, bl mk, sm 265.00
Cake plate, Ring Around the Rosie, bl mk 265.00
Candlestick, Jack & Jill, w/underplate, bl mk 300.00
Candlestick, Jack & the Beanstalk, bl mk 235.00
Candlestick, Little Boy Blue, bl mk 235.00
Coffeepot, Jack & Jill, bl mk 365.00
Creamer, Jack & Jill, bl mk 195.00
Cup & saucer, Jack & the Beanstalk, bl mk 215.00
Feeding dish, Jack & the Beanstalk, bl mk 250.00
Hair receiver, Ring Around Rosie, bl mk 365.00
Leaf dish, Little Jack Horner, bl mk 150.00
Pin dish, Jack in the Beanstalk, bl mk 115.00
Pin dish, Little Miss Muffett, bl mk 95.00
Pitcher, Jack & the Beanstalk, bl mk, milk sz 195.00
Pitcher, Little Jack Horner, bl mk, cream sz 135.00
Pitcher, Little Jack Horner, bl mk, milk sz 215.00
Pitcher, Little Miss Muffett, bl mk, milk sz 215.00
Pitcher, Little Miss Muffett, dbl hdld, bl mk, milk sz 250.00
Plate, Jack & Jill, bl mk, 7½" 175.00
Plate, Little Boy Blue, bl mk, 7⅝" 185.00
Plate, Little Jack Horner, bl mk, 7¾" 115.00
Plate, Ring Around Rosie, bl mk, 6" 115.00
Relish, Little Boy Blue, bl mk 250.00
Sugar bowl, Little Boy Blue, bl mk 215.00
Sugar bowl, Little Miss Muffett, bl mk 215.00
Toothpick holder, Little Boy blue, 3 gold hdls, bl mk 275.00

Scenics and Action Portraits

Bell, lady & chickens, wooden clapper, bl mk, 3" 265.00
Bowl, Snow Baby, ruffled rim, bl mk 195.00
Bowl, Snow Baby, sq, bl mk 195.00
Candlestick, Snow Baby, funnel shape, bl mk, rare 295.00
Cup & saucer, Beach Baby, bl mk 215.00
Hair receiver, Snow Baby, bl mk 375.00
Match holder, Snow Baby, wall hanging, bl mk 275.00
Pitcher, Babes in the Woods, flow bl, bl mk, cream sz 325.00
Pitcher, Beach Baby, bl mk, cream sz 175.00
Pitcher, girl w/dog, bl mk, cream sz 125.00
Pitcher, Snow Baby, bl mk, cream sz 235.00
Rose bowl, Snow Baby, hdls, bl mk 300.00
Sugar bowl, girl w/dog, bl mk, mini 175.00
Sugar bowl, Snow Baby, bl mk 225.00
Tea tile, Snow Babies, bl mk 145.00
Toothpick holder, cows in pasture, gold on hdl, bl mk 150.00
Vase, boy & donkeys, bl mk, 8¼" 165.00
Vase, cows, hdls, SP rim, bl mk, 3¼x2⅝" 60.00
Vase, hunt scene, 4-hdld, unmk, 3⅝x2" 45.00
Vase, musicians on gray, SP rim, bl mk, 3¼x2⅛" 60.00

Sunbonnet Babies

Bell, sewing, unmk 400.00
Cake plate, 2 hdls, bl mk 350.00
Candy dish, mending, 8-sided, loop hdl, bl mk 395.00
Cup & saucer, fishing, bl mk 350.00
Pitcher, sweeping, tankard shape, cream sz, 3½" 225.00
Pitcher, washing, jug form, bl mk, 4¼" 325.00
Plate, ironing, bl mk, 6" 175.00

Rose bowl, washing, bl mk 375.00
Sugar bowl, fishing, bulbous, bl mk, w/lid 250.00
Tumbler, cleaning, bl mk, 3½" 375.00
Vase, cleaning, bbl shape, bl mk, 5½" 325.00
Vase, fishing, bbl shape, bl mk, 5" 375.00

Tapestries

Basket, lady w/horse, bl mk, 5½" 595.00
Basket, Rose Tapestry, pk & yel on yel, bl mk, mini 285.00
Basket, Rose Tapestry, red to pk, bl mk 250.00
Basket, Rose Tapestry, sterling rose, bl mk, 2½x4¼" 950.00
Box, dresser; castle, bl mk 285.00
Cake plate, Rose Tapestry, 3-color, open hdls, bl mk, 10" 395.00
Chocolate set, Rose Tapestry, 3-color, pot +4 c/s 2,800.00
Cookie plate, Rose Tapestry, 3-color, bl mk, lg 450.00
Creamer, cows, pinch nose, bl mk 265.00
Creamer, Rose Tapestry, pk, bl mk, 4¼" 250.00
Creamer, Rose Tapestry, 3-color, 3½" 195.00
Creamer & sugar bowl, Prince & His Lady, bl mk 550.00
Creamer & sugar bowl, Rose Tapestry, pk to yel, bl mk 450.00
Cup & saucer, chocolate; Rose Tapestry, 3-color, bl mk 325.00
Dish, Rose Tapestry, bl mk, 1½x4½x2" 95.00
Hair receiver, Rose Tapestry, 3-color, bl mk, 3" 295.00
Hatpin holder, Rose Tapestry, gold at top, hexagonal, bl mk 300.00
Hatpin holder, Rose Tapestry, orange, unmk 595.00
Hatpin holder, Rose Tapestry, pk, bl mk 400.00
Hatpin holder, Rose Tapestry, 3-color, bl mk, 5" 450.00
Hatpin holder, violets, bl mk 500.00
Match holder, caveliers, hanging, bl mk 300.00
Nappy, Rose Tapestry, orange, clover leaf, bl mk 350.00
Nappy, sheep scenic, cloverleaf, hdld, bl mk 225.00
Nut set, Rose Tapestry, pk, 1 lg+6 sm bowls, bl mk, rare 1,400.00

Pitcher, Rose Tapestry, blue mark, cream size, 4½", $300.00.

Pitcher, Rose Tapestry, corset form, bl mk, milk sz 385.00
Powder jar, Rose Tapestry, yel, bl mk 325.00
Relish, Rose Tapestry, pk, open hdl, bl mk, 8" 250.00
Relish, Rose Tapestry, 3-color, open hdls, 8x4" 275.00
Ring tree, Rose Tapestry, 2-color, bl mk 375.00
Salt cellar, Rose Tapestry, 3-ftd, bl mk 245.00
Shaker, Rose Tapestry, 3-color, bl mk 135.00
Shoe, high-top; Rose Tapestry, gr leaves at top, bl mk, 3¼" 600.00
Shoe, Rose Tapestry, pk, orig lace, bl mk 400.00
Shoe, violets, low style, orig lace, gr mk 650.00
Sugar shaker, Rose Tapestry, orange w/gold 450.00
Teapot, Prince & His Lady, bl mk 400.00
Toothpick holder, goat scenic, scuttle form, unmk 300.00
Tray, Colonial Curtsy, bl mk, 11¾x8¼" 450.00
Tumbler, lake scene w/deer, bl mk 350.00
Vase, goats, bl mk, 6½" 495.00
Vase, Prince & His Lady, bl mk, 4" 180.00

Vase, Rose Tapestry, bl mk, 4½" 375.00
Vase, Rose Tapestry, bl mk, 5" 425.00
Vase, Rose Tapestry, 3-color, reverse cone shape, 4½" 195.00

Royal Bonn

Royal Bonn is a fine-paste porcelain, ornately decorated with scenes, portraits, or florals. The factory was established in the mid-1800s in Bonn, Germany; however, most pieces found today are from the latter part of the century.

Charger, floral decoration on earthenware, marked, 15½", VG, $150.00.

Ewer, floral tapestry w/brick fence, gold handle, 6½" 150.00
Umbrella stand, roses, yel on shaded gr, bulb bottom, 23", EX ...400.00
Vase, cavalier portrait, sgn M Wallraff, gold rococo, 12½" 525.00
Vase, Egyptian Revival, mc & gilt, hdls, mk/#d, 8¼x6" 200.00
Vase, lady's portrait, sgn Muller, 10½" 650.00
Vase, lady's portrait on dk bl, 8½" 625.00
Vase, Nouveau sailing scene w/flowers, mc, 13½" 325.00
Vase, parrot among branches, 2-hdld amphora form, 16", pr 550.00
Vase, peasant girl by wall, Muller, much gold, 14" 1,055.00
Vase, roses, deep pk on deep green, 20½x8½" 275.00
Vase, roses & river scene, bulbous, 10½x9½" 495.00

Royal Copenhagen

The Royal Copenhagen Manufactory was established in Denmark in about 1775 by Frantz Henrich Muller. When bankruptcy threatened in 1779, the Crown took charge. The fine dinnerware and objects of art produced after that time carry the familiar logo, the crown over three wavy lines. See also Limited Edition Plates.

Coffeepot, Quaking Grass, #884/9544 ....78.00
Compote, fruit; Floridian pattern, sgn Potentilla Nivea L 350.00
Figurine, baby bird, #1519 ....45.00
Figurine, boy w/broom 200.00
Figurine, Classical youth feeding eagle, parian, 8x10½" 880.00
Figurine, girl w/doll, #3539, 5½" 250.00
Figurine, girl w/goose, #528, 7½" 200.00
Figurine, Jason w/golden fleece, parian, 19th C, 13½" 770.00
Figurine, lovebirds, #402 ....75.00
Figurine, nude on rock, #4027 ....200.00
Figurine, otter, lt brn, #2936, 4½x7½" 270.00
Figurine, Pan on stump, #1738 ....110.00
Figurine, Pan sitting on post, looking down on rabbit, #456 ......255.00
Figurine, Pan w/parrot, #752, 7" 428.00
Figurine, rabbits w/long pk ears, #518, 3¼" L 120.00
Figurine, Sandman, #1145 ....165.00
Figurine, soldier & witch 450.00

Figurine, 2 ladies in Scandinavian costumes, 8¾" 525.00
Plate, Hans Christian Anderson Tales, set of 12 ....480.00
Vase, Apple Blossoms, #1752, 9", pr 190.00
Vase, hollyhocks, mc on bl w/faux crackle, 13½x7" 375.00

Royal Copley

Royal Copley is a decorative type of pottery made by the Spaulding China Company in Sebring, Ohio, from 1942 to 1957. They also produced two other major lines — Royal Windsor and Spaulding. Royal Copley was primarily marketed through five-and-ten cent stores; Royal Windsor and Spaulding were sold through department stores, gift shops, and jobbers. Items trimmed in gold are worth 25% to 50% more than the same item with no gold trim.

For more information we recommend *Royal Copley* and *More About Royal Copley* by Leslie and Marjorie Wolfe, edited by our advisor for this category, Joe Devine. (Both books are currently out of print; look for revised editions in 1998.) Mr. Devine is listed in the Directory under Iowa.

Photo courtesy Joe Devine

Figurines, Royal Windsor Green-Winged Teal Hen and Drake, from The Game Birds of North America series, designed by A.D. Priolo, 8½", 7½", $200.00 to $250.00 for the pair.

Ashtray, lily pad w/bird, gr stamp, 5" dia 12.00
Bank, pig, paper label or gr stamp, lg, 7½" 65.00
Bank, pig w/bow tie, paper label, 6¼" 35.00
Bank, teddy bear, blk & wht, paper label, 7½" 125.00
Bank, teddy bear, brn, paper label, 7½" 90.00
Figurine, cat, brn, paper label, 8" 75.00
Figurine, cockatoos, emb mk, 8¼" 35.00
Figurine, doe & fawn, emb mk, 8½" 30.00
Figurine, finches, paper label, 5" 30.00
Figurine, rooster, wht, paper label, 8" 75.00
Figurine, teddy bear w/bl sucker, paper label, 5½" 60.00
Figurine, thrush, paper label, 6½" 18.00
Figurine, titmouse, paper label, 8" 25.00
Lamp, figural; Oriental figure, w/shade 50.00
Lamp base, cocker spaniel, erect, 10" 85.00
Planter, big apple & finch, paper label, 6½" 20.00
Planter, birdhouse w/bird, paper label, 8" 75.00
Planter, coach shape, gr stamp, 3¼x6" 16.00
Planter, cocker spaniel head, emb mk, 5" 15.00
Planter, dog pulling wagon, paper label, 5¾" 35.00
Planter, dog w/string bass, paper label, 7" 90.00
Planter, Dutch boy or girl, w/bucket, paper label, 6", ea 15.00
Planter, girl w/wheelbarrow, paper label, 7" 28.00
Planter, Indian boy & drum, paper label, 6½" 18.00
Planter, ivy decor, paper label, 4" 10.00
Planter, kinglet, paper label, 5" 20.00
Planter, Peter Rabbit, paper label, 6½" 60.00
Planter, Plain Jane, emb mk, 3¼" 9.00

Planter, pony, raised letters, 5¼" 18.00
Planter, poodle prancing on gr, paper label, 6" 35.00
Planter, poodle resting, paper label, 6½x8½" 48.00
Planter, pup in basket, paper label, 7" 25.00
Planter, salmon jumping (3), paper label, 6½x11½" 55.00
Planter, salt box, raised letters, 5½" 30.00
Planter, Siamese cats (2), basketweave planter in bk, 9" 125.00
Planter, tanager, gr stamp or raised letters, 6¼" 15.00
Planter, teddy bear, open mouth, holds sucker, paper label, 8" 50.00
Planter, woodpecker, gr stamp or raised letters, 6¼" 15.00
Planter/vase, ram head, paper label, 6½" 20.00
Sugar bowl, leaf form, hdld, gr stamp 18.00
Vase, bud; warbler, gr stamp or raised letters, 5" 14.00
Vase, Carol's Corsage; floral decor, gr stamp, 7" 18.00
Vase, Dragon, Oriental style, paper label, 5½" 10.00
Vase, Floral Elegance, raised letters, 8" 18.00
Vase, floral hdl, gold stamp, 6¼" 18.00

Royal Crown Derby

The Royal Crown Derby company can trace its origin back to 1848. It first operated under the name of Locker & Co. but by 1859 had became Stevenson, Sharp & Co. Several changes in ownership occured until 1866 when it became known as the Sampson Hancock Co. The Derby Crown Porcelain Co. Ltd. was formed in 1876, and these companies soon merged. In 1890 they were appointed as a manufacturer for the Queen and began using the name Royal Crown Derby.

In the early years considerable 'Japan ware' decorated in Imari pattern using red, blue, and gold was popular. The company excelled in their ability to use gold in the decoration, and some of the best flower painters of all time were employed. Nice vases or plaques signed by any of these artists will bring thousands of dollars: Gregory, Mosley, Rouse, Gresley, and D'esir'e Leroy. If you find signed pieces and are not sure of your values, it would be best if possible to have it appraised by someone very knowledgeable regarding current market values.

As is usual among most other English factories, nearly all of the vases produced by Royal Crown Derby came with covers. If they are missing, deduct 40% to 45%. There are several well-illustrated books available from antique booksellers to help you learn to identify this ware. The back stamps used after 1891 will date every piece except dinnerware. The company is still in business, producing outstanding dinnerware and Imari-decorated figures and serving pieces. They also produce custom (one only) sets of table service for the wealthy of the world.

Plate, hawk with gold decoration, blue rim with gold, marked, 9½", $325.00.

Ewer, florals w/gold on pk, ca 1892, 8½", pr 525.00
Vase, bulbous, Tiffany & Co silver trim/hdls, 1885, 9½" 1,100.00
Vase, gold enamel on pk, 3-hdld, 8½" 350.00

Royal Doulton, Doulton

The range of wares produced by the Doulton Company since its inception in 1815 has been vast and varied. The earliest wares produced in the tiny pottery in Lambeth, England, were salt-glazed pitchers, plain and fancy figural bottles — all utility-type stoneware geared to the practical needs of everyday living. The original partners, John Doulton and John Watts, saw the potential for success in the manufacture of drain and sewage pipes and during the 1840s concentrated on these highly lucrative types of commercial wares. Watts retired from the company in 1854, and Doulton began experimenting with a more decorative product line. As time went by, many glazes and decorative effects were developed, among them Faience, Impasto, Silicon, Carrara, Marqueterie, Chine, and Rouge Flambe. Tiles and architectural terra cotta were an important part of their manufacture. Late in the 19th century at the original Lambeth location, fine artware was decorated by such notable artists as Hannah and Arthur Barlow, George Tinworth, and J.H. McLennan. Stoneware vases with incised animal drawings, gracefully shaped urns with painted scenes, and cleverly modeled figurines rivaled the best of any competitor.

In 1882 a second factory was built in Burslem which continues even yet to produce the famous figurines, character jugs, series ware, and table services so popular with collectors today. Their Kingsware line, made from 1899 to 1946, featured flasks and flagons with drinking scenes, usually on a brown-glazed ground. Some were limited editions, while others were commemorative and advertising items. The Gibson Girl series, twenty-four plates in all, was introduced in 1901. It was drawn by Charles Dana Gibson and is recognized by its blue and white borders and central illustrations, each scene depicting a humorous or poignant episode in the life of 'The Widow and Her Friends.' Dickensware, produced from 1911 through the early 1940s, featured illustrations by Charles Dickens, with many of his famous characters. The Robin Hood series was introduced in 1914; the Shakespeare series #1, portraying scenes from the Bard's plays, was made from 1914 until World War II. The Shakespeare series #2 ran from 1906 until 1974 and was decorated with featured characters. Nursery Rhymes was a series that was first produced in earthenware in 1930 and later in bone china. In 1933 a line of decorated children's ware, the Bunnykin series, was introduced; it continues to be made to the present day. About one hundred fifty 'bunny' scenes have been devised, the earliest and most desirable being those signed by the artist Barbara Vernon. Most pieces range in value from $60.00 to $120.00.

Factors contributing to the value of a figurine are age, color, and detail. Those with a limited production run and those signed by the artist or marked 'Potted' (indicating a pre-1939 origin) are also more valuable. After 1920 wares were marked with a lion — with or without a crown — over a circular 'Royal Doulton.' Our advisor for this category is Nicki Budin; she is listed in the Directory under Ohio.

Animals and Birds

Airedale, HN1023, Cotsford Topsail, med 235.00
Airedale, HN1028 ....155.00
Airedale, K-5 ....295.00
Alsatian, HN1115, Benign of Picardy, lg 700.00
Alsatian, HN1116 ....165.00
American Foxhound, HN2525, med 340.00
Antelope, HN1157, gr matt 565.00
Bluebird, K-30 ....495.00
Boxer, HN2643, Warlord of Mazelaine, tan, med 145.00
Buffalo, HN172 ....875.00
Bulldog, HN1074, wht, sm 235.00
Bulldog, K-1 ....125.00

Bulldog, Union Jack, HN6407, sm 265.00
Cairn, HN1035, Charming Eyes, sm 120.00
Calf, HN1146, gr matt 525.00
Cat, HN2581, recumbent 75.00
Cat, HN444, blk & wht 150.00
Cat on cushion, HN993 ....925.00
Chow, K-15 ....130.00
Cocker Spaniel, HN1002, liver & wht, lg 365.00
Cocker Spaniel, HN1020, blk, sm 150.00
Cocker Spaniel, HN1036, liver & wht, med 165.00
Cocker Spaniel, HN1037, liver & wht, sm 115.00
Cocker Spaniel, K-9A 100.00
Cocker w/Pheasant, HN1028 ....190.00
Dachshund, HN1128 ....150.00
Dalmatian, HN1113 ....215.00
Duckling, HN235 ....165.00
English Setter, HN1050, med 155.00
Fox Terrier, HN1014 ....115.00
Foxhound, K-17 ....90.00
Hare, K-39, ears up 160.00
Irish Setter, HN1055 ....160.00
Kingfisher, HN2573 ....160.00
Kitten, HN2584 ....65.00
Kittens, HN2583, licking pr 65.00
Lamb, HN2505, wht 220.00
Lion on rock, HN1119, earthenware 1,250.00
Monkey, HN118 ....350.00
Owl, HN155 ....265.00
Parrot, HN877 ....215.00
Pekinese, HN1012, Biddie of Ifield, sm 120.00
Puppies (3) in basket, HN2588 ....100.00
Robin, HN2617 ....165.00
Sealyham, K-4 ....295.00
Swiss goat, HN1178 ....565.00
Tiger, HN1084, stalking, sm 450.00
Welsh Corgi, HN1559, sm 80.00
Yel Bird, HN145 ....265.00

Bunnykins

Cup, saucer, and bowl,
$55.00 for the 3-piece set.

Bowl, cereal; Television Time 40.00
Bowl, oatmeal; Bathtime 40.00
Bowl, SF15, sgn 50.00
Collector's sign 50.00
Egg cup, ped ft, sgn 110.00
Family photograph, DB1 ....35.00
Figurine, Ace 175.00
Figurine, Clean Sweep 75.00
Figurine, Dollie 60.00
Figurine, Grandpa's Story 375.00
Figurine, Magician 115.00

Figurine, Milkman 295.00
Figurine, Rise & Shine 135.00
Figurine, Santa 35.00
Figurine, Schoolmaster 55.00
Figurine, Susan 55.00
Figurine, Touchdown 125.00
Mug, bunnies swing, bunny jumps rope, B Vernon, 3x3⅛" 45.00
Mug, Dancing Around the Barrel Organ 50.00
Plate, Christmas Tree, baby's, 7½" 85.00
Plate, Letter Box, 7½" 40.00
Plate, Watering the Flowers, 7½" 55.00
60th Anniversary bunny, DB137 ....50.00

Character Jugs

'Ard of 'Earing, D6588, lg 1,250.00
'Arriet, D6250, mini 75.00
Abraham Lincoln, ltd edition, 1992, 6¾" 190.00
Alfred Hitchcock, lg 150.00
Apothecary, D6574, sm 70.00
Auld Mac, D6527, tiny 145.00
Beefeater, D6251, GR, mini 60.00
Best Is Not Too Good, D6107 ....425.00
Bill Sykes, D6981, lg 175.00
Cap'n Cuttle, odd sz 165.00
Captain Ahab, D6500, lg 120.00
Captain Ahab, sm 45.00
Captain Hook, D6601, sm 360.00
Cardinal, D6258, tiny 225.00
Cavalier, sm 80.00
Chelsea Pensionier, lg 155.00

Clown, brown hair, gray
handle, 6¼", $2,500.00.

Dick Turpin, D2168, mini 60.00
Dick Turpin, D5495, mask up, gun hdl, lg 150.00
Falconer, D6540, sm 50.00
Falstaff, D6385, sm 50.00
Farmer John, D5788, lg 160.00
Fat Boy, D5840, sm 120.00
Fireman, lg 135.00
Gaoler, D6570, lg 150.00
Gardener, D6630, 1st version, lg 135.00
Genie, 7" 200.00
George Washington, ltd ed 200.00
Gone Away, D6545, mini 60.00
Guardsman, D6568, lg 125.00
Henry VIII, sm 75.00
Jimmy Durante, retired 150.00
John Barleycorn, hdl inside, sm 70.00
John Peel, D6130, mini 50.00
Jolly Toby, D6109 ....125.00
London Bobby, emb, lg 175.00

March Hare, lg 185.00
Mephistopheles (devil), D5758, sm 925.00
Mine Host, D6513, mini 55.00
Monty, D6202, lg 145.00
Monty, lg 150.00
Mr Pickwick, D6260, tiny 210.00
Night Watchman, D6583, mini 80.00
North American Indian, Canadian Centennial Series, 7½" 250.00
Old King Cole, D6036, lg 265.00
Paddy, D6145, tiny 95.00
Paddy, tiny 95.00
Parson, sm 80.00
Parson Brown, D5486, lg 150.00
Poacher, 6⅜" 150.00
Punch & Judy Man, D6593, sm 465.00
Reagan, lg 450.00
Red Queen, lg 150.00
Regency Beau, D6562, sm 635.00
Robin Hood, D6205, 1st version, lg 155.00
Robinson Crusoe, D6539, sm 60.00
Sairey Gamp, D6045, mini 55.00
Sam Weller, lg 150.00
Sancho Panza, D6518, mini 65.00
Sancho Panza, D6546, lg 125.00
Santa Claus, doll hdl, D6668, 1981 only, lg 175.00
Scaramouche, D6558, lg 775.00
Scaramouche, old, lg 650.00
Simon the Cellarer, D5504, lg 150.00
Sleuth, ltd ed, sm 125.00
Smuggler, D6616, 1st, lg 120.00
St George, D6618, retired 1975, lg 295.00
Toby Philpots, D5737, sm 75.00
Ugly Duchess, D6607, mini 255.00
Veteran Motorist, D6633, lg 135.00
Victoria, lg 150.00
Viking, D6496, lg 200.00
Walrus & Carpenter, D6600, lg 165.00
Winston Churchill, '92 Jug of Year, lg 225.00
Winston Churchill, sm 65.00
Yachtsman, D6622, lg 125.00

Figurines

A La Mode, HN2544 ....165.00
Adrienne, HN2304 ....175.00
Amy, HN2958 ....125.00
Anthea, HN1669 ....1,400.00
Auctioneer, HN2988 ....195.00
Baby Bunting, HN2108 ....350.00
Balloon Man, HN1954 ....230.00
Beachcomber, HN2487 ....185.00
Bell o' the Ball, HN1997, 1947-79 ....350.00
Bess, HN2002 ....300.00
Bluebeard, HN2105 ....450.00
Bonjour, HN1879 ....1,500.00
Boudoir, HN2542 ....450.00
Boy From Williamsburg, HN2183 ....165.00
Bride, HN2166 ....225.00
Bridesmaid, HN2196 ....130.00
Bridget, HN2070 ....325.00
Broken Lance, HN2041 ....495.00
Carpet Seller, HN1464 ....340.00
Cavalier, HN2716 ....175.00
Christine, HN1840 ....1,050.00

Clarissa, HN2345 ....180.00
Clown, HN2890 ....235.00
Coachman, HN2282 ....485.00
Debutante, HN2110 ....250.00
Do You Wonder?, HN1544 ....1,300.00
Dreamweaver, HN2283 ....200.00
Elyse, HN2429 ....280.00
Ermine Coat, HN1981 ....275.00
Fair Lady, HN2835 ....235.00
Falstaff, HN2054 ....120.00
Fiona, HN2694 ....185.00
Fleur, HN2368 ....290.00
Flora, HN2349 ....295.00
Forty Winks, HN1974 ....225.00
Geisha, HN1223 ....1,200.00
Golliwog, HN2040 ....195.00
Helen, HN1509 ....1,500.00
Hilary, HN2335 ....130.00
Ivy, HN1768 ....125.00
Jack, HN2060 ....165.00
Janine, HN2461 ....255.00
Jasmine, HN1863 ....1,400.00
Jean, HN2032 ....325.00
Jennifer, HN2392 ....225.00
Judge, HN2433 ....120.00
Karen, HN1994 ....485.00
Kathleen, HN1279 ....1,250.00
Lady Anne Nevill, HN2006 ....795.00
Last Waltz, HN2315 ....185.00
Laurianne, HN2719 ....150.00
Little Boy Blue, HN2062 ....150.00
Lorna, HN2311 ....175.00
Lunch Time, HN2485 ....185.00
Lynne, HN2329 ....230.00
Make Believe, HN2225 ....130.00
Margaret of Anjou, HN2012 ....795.00
Marion, HN1582 ....1,450.00
Mask Seller, HN2103 ....240.00
Masquerade, HN2259 ....270.00
Merry Christmas, HN3096 ....130.00
Miss Fortune, HN1897 ....495.00
Miss Muffett, HN1937 ....285.00
Modesty, HN2744 ....195.00
Monica, HN1458, old 100.00
News Vendor, HN2891 ....140.00
Nina, HN2347 ....185.00
Old Mother Hubbard, HN2314 ....325.00
Orange Lady, HN1953 ....265.00
Organ Grinder, HN2173 ....800.00
Owd Willum, HN2042 ....260.00
Pensive Moments, HN2704 ....200.00
Premiere, HN2343 ....165.00
Prince of Edinburgh, HN2386 ....425.00
Professor, HN2281 ....175.00
Punch & Judy Man, HN2765 ....285.00
Rendezvous, HN2212 ....350.00
Reverie, HN2306 ....285.00
Rocking Horse, HN2072 ....2,750.00
Rosabell, HN1620 ....1,275.00
Rosalind, HN2393 ....200.00
Rose, HN1368 ....70.00
Rosebud, HN1983 ....450.00
Royal Governor's Cook, HN2233 ....450.00
Sabbath Morn, HN1982 ....295.00

Sandra, HN2275, yel 130.00
Secret Thoughts, HN2382 ....275.00
Shore Leave, HN2254 ....225.00
Soiree, HN2312 ....130.00
Spanish Lady, HN1294 ....1,500.00
Spring Flowers, HN1807 ....400.00
St George, HN2051 ....500.00
Stitch in Time, HN2352 ....170.00
Stop Press, HN2683 ....165.00
Sunday Best, HN2206 ....185.00
Sunday Morning, HN2184 ....325.00
Sweeting, HN1935 ....135.00
Thank You, HN2732 ....165.00
Town Crier, HN2119 ....250.00
Uncle Ned, HN2094 ....450.00
Viking, HN2375 ....285.00
Wayfarer, HN2362 ....235.00

Winsome, HN2220, $245.00.

Wistful, HN2396 ....235.00
Yvonne, HN3038 ....130.00

Flambe

Bowl, free-form, wht/yel crackle runs over flambe, 1920s, 5" 575.00
Bowl, Veined Sung, 8" 785.00
Cup & saucer, demitasse 185.00
Figurine, alligator, rouge 1,550.00
Figurine, ballerina clown, 3½", on alabaster base 1,200.00
Figurine, bear, laughing, 5¼" 400.00
Figurine, cat, 4¾" 165.00
Figurine, Confucious, HN3314, 9" 95.00
Figurine, Dog of Fo, 5" 165.00
Figurine, dragon, HN3552, 5½" 145.00
Figurine, drake, rouge, 6" 125.00
Figurine, elephant, trunk up, 4x7½" 300.00
Figurine, elephant, tusks down, 9" 400.00
Figurine, fish, 6½" 500.00
Figurine, fox, #14, 4½" 100.00
Figurine, hippo, 6¾" 1,350.00
Figurine, monkeys, 2 embrace, 2¾" 350.00
Figurine, penguin, 6" 250.00
Figurine, quail, 5½" L 115.00
Figurine, rhino, Veined Sung, 12" 1,450.00
Figurine, tiger, 13½" L 750.00
Figurine, tortoise, 3" 575.00
Figurine, turtle, 4¼" L 300.00
Figurine, wizard, HN3121, 10" 195.00
Humidor, elephant, sgn Sung & SM 2,600.00
Inkwell, rectangular tray w/tapered well & lid, 1900s, 6" L 400.00

Memo holder, rabbit figural 235.00
Vase, coastal landscape w/cottage & horses, ca 1925, 11" 575.00
Vase, hunter transfer, woodcut, ca 1950s, 7¾" 230.00
Vase, landscape w/castle, early 1900s, 11" 260.00
Vase, red & gr mottle, Fred Moore monogram, ca 1930, 7¼" ...290.00
Vase, red & gr mottle, hdls, Fred Moore monogram, 6" 400.00
Vase, red & yel mottle, sgn H Nixon, ca 1930, 6¾" 315.00
Vase, Sung, bl mottle to red, Noke/Fred Moore, 1930s, 8½" 635.00
Vase, Veined, bl mottle & textured to red, 1950s, 11", pr 460.00
Vase, Veined Sung, bl mottle & textured to red, 1850s, 8½" 350.00
Vase, woodcut, boat scene, 7½" 285.00
Vase, yel & gr mottle to red, ca 1930, 6", EX 300.00

Series Ware

Punch bowl, Watchman, What of the Night, English night scene, $900.00.

Ashtray, Gnomes, bl underglaze 250.00
Biscuit jar, Royal Mail Coach, 8" 450.00
Bowl, Bobby Burns, 7½" 150.00
Bowl, Dickensware, Bill Sykes, Noke, rectangular, 1x9x7¾" 150.00
Candlesticks, Dutch People, D1881, pr 200.00
Coffeepot, Moorish Gate, merchants, 7x3¾" 150.00
Creamer & sugar bowl, Gnomes, w/lid 235.00
Cup & saucer, Under the Greenwood Tree, Robin Hood 75.00
Ewer, Babes in Woods, girl w/cape in woods, 9" 1,250.00
Flask, Kingsware, Scotsman 250.00
Jardiniere, Shakespeare, Ophelia & Hamlet, mk, 8¾x10" ...325.00
Match holder, Monks, profile on front, 2½" 75.00
Mug, Kingsware, Drink Wisely 200.00
Pitcher, Cavaliers, Better So Than Worse, 8" 95.00
Pitcher, Dickensware, Curiosity Shop, sq 195.00
Pitcher, Egyptian, geometric border, mk, 6⅜" 100.00
Pitcher, Polar Bear, D3128 ....100.00
Pitcher, Ye Canterbury Pilgrims 145.00
Plate, Coaching Days, William, Ye Driver, 10" 130.00
Plate, Deer, under tree, D5193, 10¼" 120.00
Plate, Dickensware, Artful Dodger, D5175, 10½" 125.00
Plate, Don Quixote, 10" 80.00
Plate, Gibson Girl, 1904, 10½" 130.00
Plate, Hunting Scenes, Fox Hunting, D5104, 1½x7x9¾" 135.00
Plate, King of Hearts, 10½" 150.00
Plate, Old English Proverbs, Fine Feather 75.00
Plate, Pan, flute player, D4794, 10¼" 125.00
Plate, Proverbs, vintage border, 10" 65.00
Sugar shaker, Jackdaw of Rheims, SP lid, mk, 6¾x2½" 175.00
Teapot, Reynard the Fox 250.00
Tray, sandwich; Cecil Alden's Dogs, mk, 11x5" 140.00
Tray, Shakespeare, Katharine, 15½" 165.00
Vase, Babes in Woods, lady picking berries, 5¼" 300.00

Vase, Babes in Woods, 2 girls/pixie, gold on hdls, 8x3½" 350.00
Vase, Dickensware, Fagin, Noke, 4½" 95.00
Vase, Shakespeare, Romeo & Juliet, mk, 11⅞x3⅛", pr 425.00
Vase, Welsh Ladies, 2 ladies by fence, mk, 3⅜" 120.00

Stoneware

Cup & saucer, mice frieze, H Barlow, Lambeth, 2⅛", 4½" 400.00
Figurine, Combat, frogs ride mice, Tinworth, Lambeth, rstr, 4" .260.00
Figurine, mouse on bun, Tinworth, Lambeth, 1884, 2¾", EX 115.00
Jardiniere, Florals & bl bands on gr, 1900s, w/ped, 42" 750.00
Jug, commemorative; coronation of Edward VII, SP trim, 7¼" ..350.00
Jug, dog in landscape, H Barlow, Lambeth, 7", EX 350.00
Jug, horses & farmer frieze, H Barlow, Lambeth, 7⅛" 575.00
Pitcher, donkeys frieze, H Barlow, Lambeth, 5¼" 550.00
Trump indicator, dk brn, Lambeth, ca 1910, 4" 260.00
Vase, bl & wht slip on salt glaze, E Simmance, Lambeth, 7¼" ...320.00
Vase, deer frieze, H Barlow/FC Roberts, Lambeth, 15⅞" 1,380.00
Vase, emb mottled foliage, early 1900s, 15" 230.00
Vase, horses frieze, H Barlow/FE Lee, Lambeth, 10½", EX 700.00
Vase, Nouveau mc florals & fruit on bl, early 1900s, 16", pr 775.00

Royal Dux

The Duxer Porzellan Manufactur was established by E. Eichler in 1860. Located in what is now Duchcov, Czechoslovakia, the area was known as Dux, Bohemia, until WWI. The war brought about changes in both the style of the ware as well as the mark. Prewar pieces were modeled in the Art Nouveau or Greek Classical manner and marked with 'Bohemia' and a pink triangle containing the letter 'E.' They were usually matt glazed in green, brown, and gold. Better pieces were made of porcelain, while the larger items were of pottery. After the war the ware was marked with the small pink triangle but without the Bohemia designation; 'Made in Czechoslovakia' was added. The style became Art Deco, with cobalt blue a dominant color.

Bowl, coupe; lady w/flowing hair, florals, hdls, 8½x12" 650.00
Figurine, camel w/rider & boy, pk/brn/gr, 17½x14" 700.00
Figurine, classic Roman couple w/gilt, #2140/#2141, 14¾", pr ...500.00
Figurine, cockatoo on perch, wht w/mc details, glossy, 15" 200.00
Figurine, German shepherd on base, pk triangle mk, 11½" L 225.00
Figurine, lady kneeling, man w/shovel, 4-color w/gold, 18x10" ..550.00
Figurine, owl, 1950s, 3¼" 65.00
Figurine, peasant boy on horsebk, #1693, 13x15" 600.00
Figurine, seated nude, flesh/maroon/brn w/gold, #1895/12, 18¾" ..635.00

Royal Flemish

Royal Flemish was introduced in the late 1880s and was patented in 1894 by the Mt. Washington Glass Company. Transparent glass was enameled with one or several colors and the surface divided by a network of raised lines suggesting leaded glasswork. Some pieces were further decorated with enameled florals, birds, or Roman coins. Our advisors for this category are Betty and Clarence Maier; they are listed in the Directory under Pennsylvania.

Biscuit jar, concentric circles/gold chrysanthemums, #4408, 8" ..2,200.00
Biscuit jar, Roman coins, ornate metal mts, 8¼x5½" 1,700.00
Bride's bowl, mc chrysanthemums w/gold, cherub std, 16½x11" ...3,000.00
Cracker barrel, Roman coins, blk/gr on Fall tones, 5¾" 1,200.00
Ewer, crowned lion & dbl-headed phoenix, EX detail, 12" 2,875.00
Jar, Roman coins w/gold scrolls on pk, dome lid, 7x5½" 3,000.00

Jar, temple; St George & Dragon w/gold, eagle band, w/lid, 16" ..8,500.00
Lamp, banquet; gulls/plants/creatures w/gold, #2657, 22½" 4,000.00

Parlor lamp, Garden of Allah, men at worship, camels included in scene, naturalistic colors, white metal mounts, 19", $16,250.00.

Pitcher, fish & aquatic plants, scrolled rim, rope hdl, 8x7" 3,500.00
Sugar bowl, apple blossoms w/gold, hdls, 2¾x4" 1,050.00
Vase, autumn leaves & berries, bulbous, 11½x6" 1,000.00
Vase, griffin/dragon/stars, mc w/gold, appl leaves, 10x6" 5,385.00
Vase, Guba duck, frost/lt yel w/gold stars, crown rim, 16" 5,000.00
Vase, mc pansies w/gold on clear/frost, #565, 12" 1,725.00
Vase, mythical winged head w/gold, bulbous, 4¼x4½" 1,750.00
Vase, pansies & vines, non-sectioned decor, bulbous, 6½x7" ..1,950.00
Vase, raised gold dragon, gold scrolls, 8x6" 3,000.00
Vase, Roman coins (3), gold on 'ldgl' ground, 3 ball ft, 6x6" ...1,500.00
Vase, Roman coins & figures w/gold sections, 7¾x8½" 4,250.00
Vase, Roman coins w/gold & jewels, stick neck, 14x7¼" 3,700.00
Vase, wild roses/mums w/gold, stick neck, 14x8" 2,750.00
Vase, 5 birds in flight, gold sections & stars, 6" 1,750.00

Royal Haeger, Haeger

In 1871 David Henry Haeger, a young son of German immigrants, purchased a brick factory at Dundee, Illinois, and began an association with the ceramic industry that his descendants have pursued to the present time. David's bricks had rebuilt Chicago after their great fire in 1871. By 1914 he had ventured into the field of commerical artware. Vases, figurines, lamp bases, and gift items in a pastel matt glaze carried the logo of the company name written over the bar of an 'H.' From 1929 to 1933, they produced a line of dinnerware which they marketed through Marshall Fields. Ware produced before the mid-'30s sometimes is found with a paper label; these are of special interest. 'Royal Haeger,' their premium line designed in 1938 by Royal Hickman, is highly desirable with collectors today. The mark 'Royal Haeger' (in raised lettering) was used during the '30s and '40s; later a paper label in the shape of a crown was used.

Fast becoming popular with today's collectors is the Earth Graphic Wraps line, first introduced in the mid-'70s. These one-of-a-kind pieces consist are decorated with raised formations on backgrounds of marigold, white, fern, and brown, in both matt and glossy finishes.

The Macomb plant, built in 1939, primarily made ware for the florist trade. A second plant, built there in 1969, produces lamp bases. For those interested in learning more about the subject, we recommend *Collecting Royal Haeger* by our advisors, Lee Garmon and Doris Frizzell (both are listed in the Directory under Illinois) and *Haeger Potteries Through the Years* by David Dilley (L-W Book Sales).

R-104, standing deer flower block, 11½" 35.00

R-107, dragon vase, oblong, 12" **20.00**
R-117, tropical fish planter, 9" **25.00**
R-127, bowl, floral cutouts, 13½" W **45.00**
R-158, Inebriated Duck, fallen, 10" **45.00**
R-159, Inebriated Duck, leaning, 10" L **45.00**
R-160, Inebriated Duck, upright, 10" L **45.00**
R-166, greyhound head, down, 9" **65.00**
R-167, greyhound head, up, 9" **65.00**
R-178, horse, head up, sm, 4" **20.00**
R-178-D, horse, head down, sm, 4" **20.00**
R-180, parrot (Macaw), 14" **150.00**
R-188, cookie jar, w/lid, 10" **75.00**
R-192, vase, bird perched on side, wings up, 11" **55.00**
R-196, vase, side design, 9" **35.00**
R-200, candy box, 2 birds on lid, 5" W **35.00**
R-218, giraffes, 15", pr **75.00**
R-227, lily bowl w/3 lilies, lg, 13" W **30.00**
R-237, 3 ducks/geese, wings down, beaks out, 11" **55.00**
R-270, tropical fish on waves (also in Boko finish), 15" **250.00**
R-309, Ruching bowl, 14½" **25.00**
R-313, tigress, 8" **150.00**
R-315, girl kneeling, 12" L **45.00**
R-329, conch shell bowl, 7" L **45.00**
R-334, fantail pigeon vase, 9" **65.00**
R-36, swan vase, neck down, bill on base, 16" **45.00**
R-370, Dutch cup bowl, 19" L **25.00**
R-373, console bowl, curved w/appl fruit **65.00**
R-375-D, polar bear, sitting, 7" L **125.00**
R-376-D, polar bear, standing, 5½" L **125.00**
R-377, Cabbage Rose (flowers appl), 16" **45.00**
R-379, bull on sq base, 7½" **275.00**
R-406, calla lily w/appl decor, 13" **30.00**
R-424, bucking horse & cowboy, 13" **150.00**
R-481, seashell on base, 11¼" **75.00**
R-65, window box, oblong, 24" **25.00**
R-740, giraffe & young (head & neck) **200.00**

Royal Rudolstadt

The hard-paste porcelain that has come to be known as Royal Rudolstadt was produced in Thuringia, Germany, in the early 18th century. Various names and marks have been associated with this pottery. One of the earliest was a hay-fork symbol associated with Johann Frederich von Schwarzburg-Rudolstadt, one of the first founders. Variations, some that included an 'R,' were also used. In 1854 Earnst Bohne produced wares that were marked with an anchor and the letters 'EB.' Examples commonly found today were made during the late 1800s and early 20th century. These are usually marked with an 'RW' within a shield under a crown and the words 'Crown Rudolstadt.' Items marked 'Germany' were made after 1890.

Bowl, mc florals, scalloped gold rim, sgn F Kahn, 9½" **75.00**
Chocolate set, Nouveau poppies w/gold, sgn F Kahn, pot+6 c/s .**500.00**
Ewer, floral w/gold on yel, gold hdl about neck, 10½" **135.00**
Ice cream set, bluebirds, 12½x7½" tray+6 5½" sq bowls **180.00**
Lamp, Delft, windmill pnt on globe, 23" **700.00**
Vase, mc morning glories w/gold, relief scrolls, 12½x5¾" **135.00**

Royal Vienna

In 1719 Claude Innocentius de Paquier established a hard-paste porcelain factory in Vienna where he made highly ornamental wares

similar to the type produced at Meissen. Early wares were usually unmarked; but after 1744, when the factory was purchased by the Empress, the Austrian shield (often called 'beehive') was stamped on under the glaze. In the following listings, values are for hand-painted items unless noted otherwise. Decal-decorated items would be considerably lower.

Note: An influx of Japanese reproductions on the market have influenced values to decline on genuine old Royal Vienna. Buyer beware! On new items the beehive mark is over the glaze, the weight of the porcelain is heavier, and the decoration is obviously decaled. Our advisor for this category is Madeleine France; she is listed in the Directory under Florida.

Portrait plates: Bonaparte lady, signed Wagner, cobalt and gold rim, NM, $450.00; Rembrandt, gold and floral rim, $450.00.

Candlesticks, scenes on maroon & gold, Kauffman, 5½", pr **495.00**
Cup & saucer, HP grapes w/gold sgn P Aauphin **75.00**
Dish, center portrait reserve: fairies/girls, hdls, 12" L **450.00**
Pitcher, rnd portrait reserve on cobalt, ornate shape/hdl, 12" **900.00**
Pitcher, rnd portrait reserve on cobalt, ornate shape/hdl, 6½" ...**400.00**
Plaque, Wasserrose, Grecian lady/columns, 6x8", +gilt fr **1,500.00**
Plate, Waldesflustern, lady sits, cherub on shoulder, Wagner, 9½" ..**450.00**
Urn, Jupiter & Calerti, sgn K Wek, hdls, beehive mk, 11" **1,100.00**
Vase, lady w/long hair reserve on maroon w/gold, Wagner, 12" ..**1,550.00**
Vase, maidens dancing w/sm cherub, urn form, beehive mk, 8" ..**350.00**

Roycroft

Near the turn of the century, Elbert Hubbard established the Roycroft Printing Shop in East Aurora, New York. Named in honor of two 17th-century printer-bookbinders, the print shop was just the beginning of a community called Roycroft, which came to be known worldwide. Hubbard became a popular personality of the early 1900s, known for his talents in a variety of areas from writing and lecturing to manufacturing. The Roycroft community became a meeting place for people of various capabilities and included shops for the production of furniture, copper, leather items, and a multitude of other wares which were marked with the Roycroft symbol, an 'R' within a circle below a stylized cross. Hubbard lost his life on the Lusitania in 1915; production in the community continued until the Depression.

Interest is strong in the field of Arts and Crafts in general and in Roycroft items in particular. Copper items are evaluated to a large extent by the condition of the original patina that remains. In the listings that follow, values reflect the worth of items retaining their original dark brown patina unless condition is otherwise described. Our advisor for this category is Bruce Austin; he is listed in the Directory under New York.

Key: h/cp — hammered copper

Andirons, #69, Secessionist-style spirals, 25½" **4,000.00**
Armchair, #28, incised Roycroft across front seat stretcher **2,000.00**
Armchair, 6-slat sides, magazine holder (rpl), rfn, 40x36" **1,100.00**
Bench, Ali Baba, split log, mk, minor wear, 44" L **5,000.00**
Bench, Ali Baba, split log top, inscr Pillars, 42", EX **7,500.00**
Blotter corners+desk pad, h/cp w/tooled floral, 14x20" **300.00**
Book, Dreams, O Schriner, 1901, half-levant binding, #d, EX ...**450.00**
Book, King Lear, Wm Shakespeare, 1904, tooled, #d, VG **425.00**
Book, Self Reliance, Emerson, 1905, tooled half-levant binding ...**375.00**
Book trough, semi-oval sides w/cutouts, keyed tenons, 25" **150.00**
Bookcase, like #085, 3 glazed doors, 53x68", VG **5,000.00**
Bookcase, 5-shelf, base drw w/copper pull & orb, rfn, 66x34" .**7,000.00**
Bookends, h/cp, arched strap on rectangle base, 3½x6" **180.00**
Bookends, h/cp, beehive shape w/curled top edge, design, 3" **50.00**
Bookends, h/cp, cross-like design, mk, 4¾", pr **55.00**
Bookends, h/cp, emb galleons, triangular w/brass wash, 5½" **125.00**
Bookends, h/cp, emb trefoils, mk, 5x3½" **300.00**
Bookends, h/cp, sq w/strap & ring hdls, 5" **300.00**
Bookends, h/cp, tall beehive form w/center design, 4" **80.00**
Bookends, h/cp fr w/flowers, lightened patina, 8½x5¾" **150.00**
Bookends, h/cp w/brass wash, lg tooled poppy, ½-rnd, 5½" **350.00**
Bookends, hammered brass w/rolled tip, ship in reserve, 5" **170.00**
Bookshelf, #087½, slatted sides/bk, orb mk, 39x32", EX **5,000.00**
Bowl, h/cp, flaring rim, str sides, 4x6" **425.00**
Bowl, h/cp, lobed incurvate rim, 2½x6½" **275.00**
Bowl, h/cp, tooled line at rim, 2½x6½" **325.00**
Bowl, h/cp, 2½x4½" **250.00**
Bud vase holder, h/cp, riveted base, early, rfn, 1½x2¾" **175.00**
Calendar, in h/cp fr w/oval top, 3¼", VG **70.00**
Candle holder, push-up, octagonal, no patina, early, 10", pr ...**2,700.00**
Candlesticks, h/cp, sq base w/2-strap std, mk, 8", VG, pr **500.00**
Candlesticks, h/cp, wide rippled ft, 2x3½", pr **200.00**
Chair, hall; #31, tall bk w/3 vertical slats, 47" **5,250.00**
Chair, side; #30, mahog, tall bk, Macmurdo ft, cvd orb, 44" ...**1,100.00**
Chamberstick, h/cp, cupped bobeche, flaring base, w/hdl, 3½" ..**170.00**
Chamberstick, h/cp, wide base, squat hdl, 1½x5½" **150.00**

Chandelier, hammered copper with 3 arms, each holding a torch-shaped light, originally kerosene, now electrified, EX original patina, unmarked, VG, 39x47", $4,750.00.

Crumber set, h/cp w/tooled floral, 8½x6", 2 pcs **150.00**
Desk set, h/cp w/floral, curled edges, bookends/tray+3 pcs, EX ...**500.00**
Frame, h/cp, dome shape w/sq window, 3½" **130.00**
Frame, h/NP/cp, scalloped, mk, 11x9", VG **175.00**
Frame, wood, orb mk, 17½x13½" **275.00**
Humidor, h/cp w/emb band on lid, 9½" L **400.00**
Inkwell, h/cp, flared base, linear tooling, no mk/insert, 2x4" **175.00**
Inkwell, h/cp, floriform top, no insert, 2¾x3" **100.00**
Inkwell, h/cp, riveted, flared sides, appl knob, 2½x3½" **150.00**
Jug/bean pot, ceramic, brn **50.00**
Lamp, h/cp, helmet shade, 13½x6", M **2,200.00**
Letter holder, h/cp, 2 compartments, shaped tops, 4" **175.00**
Letter opener, h/cp, stylized hdl, linear tooling, 9½" **100.00**

Letter rack+blotter, h/cp, ½-sand-$ design, 3½x5", 2 pcs **160.00**
Plates, gr/brn border & Roycroft monogram, 8", 8 for **1,000.00**
Sconce, h/cp w/open basket, curl ea side strap support, 10½" **425.00**
Stand, Little Journeys, 2-shelf, keyed-through tenons, +14 books ..**475.00**
Tabouret, #50½, 12" sq top w/flaring legs, rfn, 19" **1,400.00**
Tray, h/cp, octagonal, hdls, orb mk, 10" dia, VG **150.00**
Tray, h/cp, octagonal w/emb rim design, hdls, 17", VG **325.00**
Tray, pen; h/cp, emb trefoil on gr matt, 2¼x7¼" **100.00**
Tray, SP, riveted hdls, minor wear, 15" **250.00**
Vase, Am Beauty, tube neck, squat/shouldered base, 6½x3" **900.00**
Vase, Am Beauty, wide angle body, cylinder neck, rfn, 19x7½" ..**1,800.00**
Vase, h/cp, cylinder w/flared & riveted base, no patina, 11" **1,000.00**
Vase, h/cp, ovoid w/flaring rim, 5x4¼" **425.00**
Vase, h/cp, scalloped edge, ovoid, 8½x3½" **700.00**
Vase, h/cp, squat w/flared neck, wear, 4½x6" **400.00**
Vase, h/cp, stylized floral at top, str sides, 5" **450.00**
Vase, h/cp, tapered, 4½x3" **250.00**
Vase, h/cp w/appl silver bands etc, cylinder, 6" **1,100.00**
Vase, h/cp w/tooled floral & trailing stems, 10x3", M **2,100.00**

Rubena

Rubena glass was made by several firms in the late 1800s. It is a blown art glass that shades from clear to red. See also Art Glass Baskets; Cruets; Sugar Shakers; Salts; specific manufacturers.

Finger bowl, swirled zippers, gold florals/scrolls, +plate **150.00**
Pitcher, Invt T'print, clear hdl, Hobbs & Brockunier, 4" **150.00**
Tumbler, mc mixed flowers, 3¾x2¾" **55.00**

Rubena Verde

Rubena Verde glass was introduced in the late 1800s by Hobbs, Brockunier, and Company of Wheeling, West Virginia. Its transparent colors shade from red to green. Our advisor for this category is Mike Roscoe; he is listed in the Directory under Michigan. See also Art Glass Baskets; Cruets; Sugar Shakers; Salts.

Butter dish, vaseline knob hdl, 5¾x7" **650.00**
Celery vase, Invt T'print **165.00**

Pitcher, Diamond Quilted with hand-painted decor, 7¼", $500.00.

Decanter, wht floral, gr hdl/swirl stopper, ribbed/ftd, 15" **300.00**
Pitcher, ribbed/netted, bulbous, sq rim, yel hdl, 7¾" **175.00**
Vase, mc florals w/gold, flared/crimped top, 12" **500.00**

Ruby Glass

Produced for over one hundred years by every glasshouse of note in this country, ruby glass has been used to create decorative items such as one might find in gift shops, utilitarian bottles and kitchenware, figurines, and dinnerware lines such as were popular in the Depression era. For further information and study, we recommend *Ruby Glass of the 20th Century* by our advisor, Naomi Over; she is listed in the Directory under Colorado.

Basket, Blenko, yel hdl on 4½" H body	65.00
Bowl, cereal; Old Cafe, Anchor Hocking, 1940s, 5½"	12.00
Bowl, Oyster & Pearl, Anchor Hocking, 1938-40, 6½"	20.00
Candlestick, Viking, swan neck, 6¼"	27.50
Candy dish, Sweetheart, LG Wright, 3¾"	20.00
Comport bonbon, Dmn Optic, #1502, 7½"	38.00

Photo courtesy Naomi Over

Cornucopia, unknown maker, 5¾x5", $85.00.

Cup, measuring; unknown maker, 16-oz	27.50
Cup, Sweetheart, Macbeth-Evans, 1930-36, rare	100.00
Doorstop, Alley Cat, 11¾"	40.00
Figurine, bird, Swedish Glass, 4"	17.50
Figurine, seal, Mirror Images, Viking Glass, 4¼"	45.00
Figurine, swan, Summit Art Glass (Cambridge mold), 1986, 13"	80.00
Lamp, fairy; Sweetheart, LG Wright, 1974-81, 4½"	30.00
Lamp, oil; Rose Wreath, Pittsburgh, 8¼"	750.00
Nappy, Royal Ruby, Anchor Hocking, 6½"	10.00
Paperweight, apple, Viking, 3¾"	20.00
Pickle dish, Royal Ruby, Anchor Hocking, 7"	15.00
Pitcher, Blenko, #3750, 16-oz	22.00
Pitcher, Blenko, #93P, ca 1952, 14"	60.00
Plate, Oyster & Pearl, Anchor Hocking, 13½"	42.50
Saucer, American, Macbeth-Evans, 1930-36, scarce	25.00
Sherbat, plain stem, Anchor Hocking, ca 1942	6.00
Tray, Anchor Hocking, 14"	25.00
Tumbler, Hobnail, Anchor Hocking, 1930s, 4½"	6.50
Tumbler, iced tea; Provincial, Anchor Hocking, 1963, 16-oz	15.00
Vase, Blenko, #404M, 11x8¼"	57.50
Vase, Elite, Westmoreland, 1981, 8½"	28.00
Vase, Knotted Beads, slim form, 11"	65.00
Vase, Rachel, Anchor Hocking, 1940s, 10"	45.00
Vase, swan hdls, Venetian, 12"	130.00

Ruby-Stained Glass

Ruby-flashed or ruby-stained glass was made through the application of a thin layer of color over clear. It was used in the manufacture of some early pressed tableware and from the Victorian era well into the 20th century. These items were often engraved on the spot with the date, location, and buyer's name. Our advisors for this category are Bill and Marilyn Moore; they are listed in the Directory under Washington.

Cake stand, Millard	200.00
Creamer, Heart Band, Compliments of...	35.00

Goblet, Dakota, Midwinter Fair, 1894	50.00
Mug, Heart Band	25.00
Pitcher, Carnation, +6 tumblers	675.00
Sugar bowl, Heart Band	28.00
Toothpick holder, Gaelic	18.50
Toothpick holder, Ruby Thumbprint	45.00
Tumbler, Dakota, World's Fair, 1893	50.00
Wine, Button Arches	26.00
Wine, Dakota, Masonic Temple, 1893	50.00
Wine set, Loop & Block, 7-pc	350.00

Rugs

Hooked rugs are treasured today for their folk-art appeal. It was a craft that was introduced to this country in about 1830 and flourished its best in the New England states. The prime consideration is not age but artistic appeal. Scenes with animals, buildings, and people; patriotic designs; or whimsical themes are preferred. Those with finely conceived designs, great imagination, interesting color use, etc., demand higher prices. Condition is, of course, also a factor. Marked examples bearing the stamps of 'Frost and Co.,' 'Abenakee,' 'C.R.,' and 'Ouia' are highly prized. Note: the rugs listed here are rag unless noted otherwise. See also Orientalia, Rugs.

Angel slaying devil, w/cross/eye/shield/etc, mc, 40x29"	415.00
Cabin in snow, 6-color, rebound, 24½x33½"	300.00
Cats, pigs & dogs among flowers, mc on gray, 1924, 21x35"	450.00
Cobbler/lady spinning, cat/fireplace/etc, mc on yel, 19x69"	580.00
Cornucopias on brn w/gr borders, Am, 19th C, 68x36½"	1,725.00
Cottage in hollyhocks, mc, lt wear, rebacked, 24x33"	50.00
Cow, brn tones on bl & gr w/mc leafy border, 23x37"	385.00
Cows & sheep in landscape w/barn/etc, 7-color, 20x36"	415.00
Dog, gray on red w/purple borders, ca 1900, 33x44"	350.00
Dog amid scrolled foliage, 6-color, 40x24"	140.00
Dog w/floral border, 6-color, some wear, 19x40"	65.00
Geometric in style of Caucasian prayer rug, 1900s, 77x47½"	980.00
Grenfell, dog sled in Arctic landscape, 12x25½"	260.00
Grenfell, flying geese & pines, mc w/blk border, 27x39"	685.00
Grenfell, puffin on rocks, demilune shape, 39x26"	2,070.00
Horse & cart w/boy driver, 7-color on gray, 17x34"	415.00
Horse running w/in vine border, 4-color, 26x41"	550.00
Horse-drawn sleigh in winter scene, mc, 27x40", EX	275.00
Lions among palm trees, mc, 36x65", EX	425.00
Peacock w/tail spread wide, 6-color, 35" sq in 40" sq fr	770.00
Roosters crowing, mc on brn, segmented border, 19x34"	495.00
Stag, does & fawn w/mc stripes, button eyes, 28x40"	350.00
Stag & doe in restful scene, 6-color, 36x66", EX	245.00
Stylized flowers, red/bl/brn/wht on brn, 72x25", EX	250.00
Stylized flowers (detailed), 7-color, rprs/rebacked, 33x37"	160.00
Stylized leaves, 7-color, bright, some wear, 22x68"	140.00
Stylized tulips & 1919 on mc stripes, rebound, 25x58"	475.00
Waldoboro type, 3-D mc sculpted floral & birds, 1910, 37x21"	1,430.00
16-pointed star, 4-color on lt bl w/mc striped border, 45x27"	200.00
2 blk dogs by wht picket fence & flowers, 26x48", EX	330.00
3 kittens w/red ball of yarn, mc striped ground, 23x32"	770.00
3-masted ship w/Am flag, mc w/ornate star border, 40x59"	1,150.00

RumRill

George Rumrill designed and marketed his pottery designs from 1933 until his death in 1942. During this period of time, four different companies produced his works. Today the most popular designs are those made by the Red Wing Stoneware Company from 1933 until 1936 and Red Wing Potteries from 1936 until early 1938. Some of these lines include Trumpet Flower, Classic, Manhattan, and Athena, the Nudes.

For a period of months in 1938, Shawnee took over the production of RumRill pottery. This relationship ended abruptly and the Florence Pottery took over and produced his wares until the plant burned down. The final producer was Gonder. Pieces from each individual pottery are easily recognized by their designs, glazes, and/or signatures. It is interesting to note that the same designs were produced by all three companies. They may be marked RumRill or with the name of the specific company that made them. Our advisors for this category are Wendy and Leo Frese; they are listed in the Directory under Texas.

Bookends, #333, bl-blk, orig shape/color sticker, pr, minimum ...**300.00**
Bowl, console; #338, Pompeian, Continental Group, hdls, 13" **65.00**
Bowl, console; #377, Seashell, Fern Group, 12" **65.00**
Bowl, console; #614, Pompeian, Vintage Group, 12" **60.00**
Bowl, console; #618, Pompeian, Vintage Group, 12" **55.00**
Candle holder, #564, Athena Group, rare, minimum value **700.00**
Canoe, #317, ivory w/pk lining **60.00**
Ewer, #184, Goldenrod, wide base, narrow cylinder body **50.00**
Ewer, #184, Scarlet & Bay, Indian Group **40.00**
Ewer, #295, Marigold (yel), angle hdl, unmk **35.00**
Grape cluster, #627, lt gr, Vintage Group, pre-1938, 7½" **40.00**
Ivy ball, #601, Dutch Bl, 3 openings, 8", rare sz **190.00**
Ivy ball, #601, Eggshell, 6" **35.00**
Pitcher, #207, Scarlet & Bay (orange w/brn o/l), bulbous **50.00**
Planter, #315, Dutch Bl, 4½" **40.00**
Planter, #354, Dutch Bl **40.00**
Planter, #584, turq, modernistic style, 7" **25.00**
Shakers, P-15/P-16, gr w/P hdl & rose w/S hdl, stickers, pr **30.00**
Vase, $630, antique bl, 7" **80.00**
Vase, #C-5, blended yel, orange & brn, 4" **20.00**
Vase, #J-27, cornucopia, bl **35.00**
Vase, #J-27, cornucopia, lt gr **50.00**
Vase, #258, Jade, Fluted Group, 3-ftd, 1930s, 8½" **60.00**
Vase, #290, Apple Blossom (2 tone: gr over rose), hdls, 9" **50.00**
Vase, #310, Dutch Bl, Mandarin Group, 7" **40.00**
Vase, #311, Dutch Bl, 5" **35.00**
Vase, #349, Apple Blossom (2-tone: gr over rose) **45.00**
Vase, #368, Ripe Wheat, Grecian Group, (2-tone: beige over brn), 7" ..**40.00**
Vase, #387, Goldenrod, Fluted Group, gr over brn, 7½" **40.00**
Vase, #502, Scarlet & Bay, 7½" **30.00**
Vase, #505, Ripe Wheat, mk, 1930s **25.00**
Vase, #514, lg leaves, Ripe Wheat, Sylvan Group **35.00**
Vase, #525, ivory, 8" **60.00**
Vase, #528, Dutch Bl, Renaissance Group **50.00**
Vase, #570, Eggshell, Athena, 3 nude supports, 10" w/bowl **950.00**
Vase, #587, lt gr, hdls **40.00**
Vase, #631, Riviera (wht w/bl int), 7½" **30.00**
Vase, #631, 7½" **30.00**
Vase, #711, gray-gr, ftd **55.00**

Ruskin

This English pottery operated near Birmingham from 1989 until 1935. Its founder was W. Howson Taylor, and it was named in honor of the reknown author and critic, John Ruskin. The earliest marks were 'Taylor' in block letters and the initials 'WHT,' the smaller W and H superimposed over the larger T. Later marks included the Ruskin name.

Candlesticks, mottled lemon, caramel & wht lustre, 6½", pr **150.00**
Vase, bl crystalline drip on gray, salmon & tan, thrown, 9½" **230.00**

Vase, blue Oriental style, with lid, 1906, 8½", NM, $175.00.

Vase, bl crystalline on ivory to gr to bl, bulbous, 9x6" dia **300.00**
Vase, royal-bl drip matt on orange gloss, 5½x6" **130.00**
Vase, turq lustre/mustard flambe, 6x3¼" **250.00**
Vase, yel & orange lustre drip on wht gloss, thrown, 10" **30.00**

Russel Wright Dinnerware

Russel Wright, one of America's foremost industrial designers, also designed several lines of ceramic dinnerware, glassware, and aluminum ware that are now highly sought-after collectibles. His most popular dinnerware then and with today's collectors, American Modern, was manufactured by the Steubenville Pottery Company from 1939 until 1959. It was produced in a variety of solid colors in assortments chosen to stay attune with the times. Casual (his first line sturdy enough to be guaranteed against breakage for ten years from date of purchase) is relatively easy to find today — simply because it has held up so well. During the years of its production, the Casual line was constantly being restyled, some items as many as five times. Early examples were heavily mottled, while later pieces were smoothly glazed and sometimes patterned. The ware was marked with Wright's signature and 'China by Iroquois.' It was marketed in fine department stores throughout the country. After 1950 the line was marked 'Iroquois China by Russel Wright.' For those wanting to learn more about the subject, we recommend The *Collector's Encyclopedia of Russel Wright Designs* by our advisor, Ann Kerr. She is listed in the Directory under Ohio.

American Modern

To calculate values for items in American Modern, add 100% for Cedar, Black Chutney, and Seaform. Add 200% for White, Bean Brown, Cantelope, and Glacier Blue.

Ashtray, coaster **15.00**
Bowl, child's **75.00**
Bowl, salad **80.00**
Butter dish **200.00**
Casserole, w/lid, 12" **50.00**
Coffeepot, AD **75.00**
Creamer **12.00**
Icebox jar **165.00**
Mug (tumbler) **75.00**
Plate, chop **30.00**
Plate, chop **30.00**
Plate, salad; 8" **10.00**
Platter, 13¼" **25.00**
Salad fork & spoon **90.00**
Shakers, pr **16.00**
Stack server **260.00**
Sugar bowl, w/lid **15.00**

Casual

In Casual, Brick Red and Aqua items go for around 200% more than any other color (or 2x our suggested values), while those in Avocado Yellow are priced lower.

Asbestos pad	25.00
Bowl, cereal; 5"	10.00
Bowl, open vegetable; 10"	40.00
Bowl, soup; 11½-oz	20.00
Butter dish, regular colors, restyled, ¼-lb	200.00

Butter dish, Aqua, restyled, $225.00.

Casserole, deep, 4-qt, 8"	150.00
Casserole, open, 10"	40.00
Coffeepot, AD; 4½"	75.00
Cookware, 6-qt	200.00
Creamer, lg family sz	40.00
Creamer, restyled	15.00
Cup & saucer, restyled	18.00
Dutch oven	225.00
Lid for open divided vegetable bowl	25.00
Mug, 13-oz	75.00
Plate, chop; 13⅞"	30.00
Plate, dinner; 10"	10.00
Plate, party w/cup	75.00
Platter, oval, 10¼"	50.00
Shakers, stacking, pr	20.00
Sugar bowl, restyled	25.00
Sugar bowl, stacking, 4"	15.00

Glassware

Unless otherwise described, values are given for glassware in Coral and Seafoam; other colors are 10% to 15% less.

American Modern, chilling bowl, 12-oz, 3x5½"	100.00
American Modern, cocktail, 3-oz, 2½"	25.00
American Modern, cordial, 2"	38.00
American Modern, dbl old-fashioned, rare	40.00
American Modern, dessert dish, 2"	40.00
American Modern, goblet, 4"	40.00
American Modern, pilsner, rare, 7"	125.00
American Modern, sherbet, 2½"	25.00
American Modern, tumbler, iced tea; 13-oz	30.00
American Modern, tumbler, juice; 4"	30.00
American Modern, tumbler, water; 4½"	25.00
American Modern, wine, 3"	25.00
Eclipse, old-fashioned	15.00
Eclipse, shot glass	20.00
Flair, tumbler, iced tea; 14-oz	65.00
Flair, tumbler, juice; 6-oz	50.00
Flair, tumbler, water; 11-oz	50.00
Pinch, tumbler, iced tea; 14-oz	35.00
Pinch, tumbler, juice; 6-oz	35.00
Pinch, tumbler, red, any sz	125.00
Pinch, tumbler, water; 11-oz	35.00
Snow Glass, bowl, salad/vegetable; rnd	175.00
Snow Glass, plate, salad	100.00
Snow Glass, sugar bowl, w/lid	100.00
Snow Glass, tumbler, iced tea; 14-oz	150.00
Snow Glass, tumbler, juice; 5-oz	150.00

Highlight

Bowl, oval vegetable; Citron or Nutmeg	75.00
Creamer, White, Pepper or Blueberry	40.00
Plate, bread & butter; Citron or Nutmeg	10.00
Shakers, Citron or Nutmeg, lg or sm, pr	65.00
Sugar bowl, high gloss	50.00

Spun Aluminum

Russel Wright's aluminum ware may not have been especially well accepted in its day — it tended to damage easily and seems to have had only limited market appeal — but today's collectors feel quite differently about it, as is apparent in the suggested values noted in the following listings.

Bowl	75.00
Flower ring	125.00
Gravy boat	150.00
Muffin warmer, wire insert, w/lid	75.00
Relish rosette, lg	200.00
Smoking stand	450.00
Tray, tidbit	85.00
Vase, 12"	150.00
Wastebasket	125.00

Sterling

AD cup and saucer, $50.00.

Bowl, bouillon; 7-oz	15.00
Bowl, onion soup; 10-oz	20.00
Bowl, soup; 6½"	15.00
Coffee bottle	110.00
Creamer, ind, 3-oz	12.00
Cup & saucer, demitasse; 3½-oz	65.00
Pitcher, water; 2-qt	65.00
Plate, bread & butter; 6¼"	5.00
Plate, dinner; 10¼"	12.00
Platter, oval, 10½"	17.00
Teapot, 10-oz	100.00

Miscellaneous

Bauer, ash dish, #10A, 5½" sq	300.00
Bauer, ashtray, Pinch, 6½"	350.00
Bauer, bowl, mantlepiece; #9A, 24" L	825.00
Bauer, vase, oval, #18A, 12"	850.00
Book, Guide to Easy Living, R Wight, 1st edition, w/jacket, EX	150.00
Flair, plate, salad	8.00

Flair, tumbler **15.00**
Frosted Oak, bowl, serving **300.00**
Harker White Clover, bowl, vegetable; 7½" **20.00**
Harker White Clover, plate, jumbo; clover decor, 10" **16.00**
Home Decorator, tumbler **15.00**
Ideal Adult Kitchen Ware, butter dish **50.00**
Ideal Children's Toy Dishes, serving items, ea **20.00**
Knowles, plate, dinner; 10¾" **15.00**
Knowles, platter, oval, 13" **35.00**
Knowles, teapot **175.00**
Mary Wright, cup & saucer **100.00**
Mary Wright, wooden cheese board **150.00**
Meladur, bowl, fruit; 6-oz **8.00**
Meladur, cup & saucer **15.00**
Meladur, plate, compartmented, 9½" **15.00**
Oceana, relish rosette **800.00**
Price list of American Modern **35.00**
Residential, bowl, fruit **13.00**
Residential, plate, dinner **8.00**
Swan, nut cup **150.00**
Theme Formal, cup & saucer **100.00**
Torcheres, spun aluminum trumpet shade, chrome bases, 65", pr ...**1,000.00**
Wave, bowl, salad **700.00**

Russian Art

Before the Revolution in 1917, many jewelers and craftsmen created exquisite marvels of their arts, distinctive in the extravagant detail of their enamel work, jeweled inlays, and use of precious metals. These treasures aptly symbolized the glitter and the romance of the glorious days under the reign of the Tsars of Imperial Russia. The most famous of these master jewelers was Carl Faberge (1852-1920), goldsmith to the Romanovs. Following the tradition of his father, he took over the Faberge workshop in 1870. Eventually Faberge employed more than five hundred assistants and set up workshops in Moscow, Kiev, and London as well as in St. Petersburg. His specialties were enamel work, clockwork automated figures, carved animal and human figures of precious or semiprecious stones, cigarette cases, small boxes, scent flasks, and his best-known creations, the Imperial Easter Eggs — each of an entirely different design. By the turn of the century, his influence had spread to other countries, and his work was revered by royalty and the very wealthy. The onset of the war marked the end of the era. Very little of his work remains on the market, and items that are available are very expensive. But several of his contemporaries were goldsmiths whose work can be equally enchanting. Among them are Klingert, Ovchinnikov, Smirnov, Ruckert, Loriye, Cheryatov, Kuzmichev, Nevalainen, Adler, Sbitnev, Third Artel, Wakewa, Holmstrom, Britzin, Wigstrom, Orlov, Nichols, and Plincke. Most of them produced excellent pieces similar to those made by Faberge between 1880 and 1910.

Perhaps the most important bronze Russian artist was Eugenie Alexandrovich Lanceray (1847-87). From 1875 until 1887, he modeled many equestrian groups of falconers and soldiers ranging in height from about 20" to 30". Some of them bear the Chopin foundry mark; they are presently worth from $4,000.00 up. Other excellent artists were Schmidt Felling (19th century), who specialized in mounted figures of cossacks wearing military uniforms, and Nicholas Leiberich (late 19th century), who also specialized in equestrian groups. Most of the pieces made by the above artists were signed and had the foundry mark (Chopin, Woerfell, etc.).

Russian porcelain is another field where Imperial connections have undoubtedly added to the interest of collectors and museums worldwide. The most important factories were: Imperial Russian Porcelain, St. Petersburg (or Petrograd or Leningrad, 1744-1917); Gardner,

Moscow (1765-1872); Kuznetsoff, St. Petersburg and Moscow (1800-1900); Korniloff, St. Petersburg (1800-1900); and Babunin, St. Petersburg (1800-1900).

Beaker, silver gilt and enamel, lady beside broken jar in oval niello vignette, I.P. Khlebnikov, Assaymaster in Cyrillic 'IK,' Moscow, 1887, 4¼", 6.9-oz, $1,200.00.

Bowl, champleve, Khlebnikov, 1883, sm **300.00**
Box, gilt silver & enamel, pre-revolution, Cyrillic mk **1,100.00**
Box, silver vermeil w/pearls & semiprecious stone, hallmk, 4½" ...**700.00**
Candlesticks, ruby glass, brass stick/prisms, 1800s, 21", pr **400.00**
Cigarette case, silver, Ivanov, 1873 ....**300.00**
Cup, christening; glass, etched Peter the Great/1905, 5½" **400.00**
Cup, Kiddish; silver niello, mk Ak/AC, 1874/84, 1¾" **200.00**
Figurine, man in wht tunic leaning on stump, 1700s, 9½" **800.00**
Icon, Assumption of Virgin Mary/angels/etc, wooden, 1850s, 5x7" ..**200.00**
Icon, Mary & Jesus w/2 saints/2 angels/2 cherubs, 19th C, 10" ...**200.00**
Icon, Presentation of Christ in Temple, wood, 1850s, 10½x9" ...**200.00**
Icon, St Mark, wooden, late 1800s, 10½x12¼" **200.00**
Icon, St Panteleimon, wooden, late 1800s, 9½x11¾" **200.00**
Icon, Virgin of Joy & Saints, wooden, 1850s, 7x8¾" **200.00**
Icon, Virgin of 3 Hands, wooden, 4x5¼" **100.00**
Lampada, brass w/3 hdls, votive candle, 1890s, suspended **100.00**
Salt cellar, enamel on silver, #84, AA 1895 EK, 1¼x2½" **500.00**
Salt cellar, enameled, Ovchinikov, 1895 ....**300.00**
Spoon, enameled, JV Aarne, assayer Lebedkin, 1896-03, 3¾" ...**200.00**
Spoon, enameled, mk MC, Semenova, assayer Lebedkin, 1896, 4½" .**200.00**
Spoon, salt; enameled, mk Moscow #84, ca 1880, 3" **200.00**
Sweetmeat basket, silver, Odessa hallmks, 19th C, 5x6x5" **400.00**
Tea set, enameled & gilded silver, hallmk, 4½" pot+cr/sug **1,000.00**
Triptych, bronze central panel, bl/wht enamel, folds, 7" **100.00**
Urn, ormolu-mtd/patinated bronze, plinth base, 1820s, 14", pr ..**2,200.00**
Wine cup, silver w/foliate eng, mk AP, ca 1876, 2¼" **100.00**

Sabino

Sabino art glass was produced by Marius-Ernest Sabino in France during the 1920s and '30s. It was made in opalescent, frosted, and colored glass and was designed to reflect the Art Deco style of that era. In 1960 using molds he modeled by hand, Sabino once again began to produce art glass using a special formula he himself developed that was characterized by a golden opalescence. Although the family continued to produce glassware for export after his death in 1971, they were never able to duplicate Sabino's formula.

Box, powder; Petalia, med sz **125.00**
Charger, 3 swimming nudes, spirals, 11¾" **560.00**
Figurine, Chabot, fish **100.00**
Figurine, Gazelle, 4x6" **65.00**
Figurine, L'i Lole, nude seated in lotus position, 8½" **2,200.00**
Figurine, La Carpe **2,800.00**

Figurine, lady & doves **400.00**
Figurine, nude w/flowing hair, 7" **400.00**
Figurine, nude w/graceful cloak, 9½" **425.00**
Figurine, nude w/long flowing hair, opal, 7" **500.00**
Figurine, rooster, lg **385.00**
Figurine, squirrel on log, 2⅜x3⅜" **48.00**
Figurine, woodpecker **60.00**
Flacon, perfume; 5 draped nudes on oval opal form, mk, 6" **250.00**
Lamp base, Les Oiseaux, birds on branches, gilt mts, #449, 32" ..**3,850.00**
Plate, Birth of Star, 3 nude maids drift around rim, 12" **650.00**
Vase, Algues Marines **400.00**
Vase, Art Decoratifs, dancing nude on ea of 4 sides, 10" **2,750.00**
Vase, Enlacements, blown, 5" **350.00**
Vase, La Danse **1,500.00**
Vase, sparrow band, stylized feathers on body, opal, 8" **1,200.00**
Vase, Vallon, 10¾" **1,100.00**
Vase, 6 lg concave dahlias, turq, ca 1930, 7½x7½" **1,650.00**

Salesman's Samples and Patent Models

Salesman's samples and patent models are often mistaken for toys or homemade folk art pieces. They are instead actual working models made by very skilled craftsmen who worked as model-makers. Patent models were made until the early 1900s. After that, the patent office no longer required a model to grant a patent. The name of the inventor or the model-maker and the date it was built is sometimes noted on the patent model. Salesman's samples were occasionally made by model-makers, but often they were assembled by an employee of the company. These usually carried advertising messages to boost the sale of the product. Though they are still in use today, the most desirable examples date from the 1800s to about 1945.

Many small stoves are incorrectly termed a 'salesman's sample'; remember that no matter how detailed one may be, it must be considered a toy unless accompanied by a carrying case, the indisputable mark of a salesman's sample.

Wooden platform wagon with green and yellow paint, brass, metal and wooden undercarriage, patent dated 1874, 8½x26", $2,000.00.

Bed, brass, w/bedding & antique doll quilt **375.00**
Calendar, Marilyn Monroe, 1959, 8¼x11", EX **135.00**
Canoe, Old Town Canoe Co, gr w/red lettering, 50", EX+ **8,500.00**
Case, Heinz Pickles, 6 pnt zinc pickles in leather case, EX **1,840.00**
Fire extinguisher, Minimax Ltd, 1919, w/canvas case, 6", EX **220.00**
Gate, wood, orig pnt, Farmers Handy... Pat...1876, 17x29" **330.00**
Hat & hat box, Knox New York, trade-in for full-sz, NM **45.00**
Hoosier cabinet, Eureka, pnt & stained wood, 16", VG **1,540.00**
Ice box, Klean Kold, wood w/metal hardware, 12", VG **1,265.00**
Lawn-mowing machine, working & articulated, orig pnt, 1900 ..**595.00**
Mowing machine prototype, mahog/brass, 19th C, w/5x12x8½" box ..**750.00**

Saleman's Sample Book, Kaeser & Blair Inc, 1946-47, 26-pg, EX ..**105.00**
Water well pump, brass, orig red pnt, 1880s, 16¼", NM **750.00**

Salt Glaze

As early as the 1600s, potters used common salt to glaze their stoneware. This was accomplished by heating the salt and introducing it into the kiln at maximum temperature. The resulting gray-white glaze was a thin, pitted surface that resembles the peel of an orange.

Vegetable bowl, with lid and related tray, 14" long, VG, $1,500.00.

Bottle, England, ca 1750s, stain, 9" **525.00**
Dish, emb dots/diapers/stars/basketweave in panels, 1750s, 10" ..**435.00**
Plate, detailed molded surface w/rtcl panels, English, 12" **440.00**
Plate, press-molded seed-pattern border, ca 1760, 5¼" **230.00**
Teapot, appl vines/berries, crabstock hdl/spout, 1750s, 3½", EX ...**350.00**
Teapot, bulbous, lion finial, appl ft, rprs, 1750s, 5" **575.00**
Teapot, emb vintage, heart shape, serpent spout, 1750s, 3¾" .**2,550.00**
Teapot, incised band/appl vintage, foo lion finial, 4¾", EX **975.00**
Teapot, mc bird on branch & house, 1760s, rstr, 4½" **1,035.00**
Teapot, mc floral, crabstock hdl/spout, 1750s, 3½", VG **635.00**
Teapot, mc floral, crabstock hdl/spout, 1760s, 4¼", EX+ **1,265.00**
Teapot, mc floral, crabstock hdl/spout, 1760s, 5¼", EX **975.00**
Teapot, mc floral & fence, crabstock hdl, 1750s, 3¼", EX **550.00**

Salt Shakers

The screw-top salt shaker was invented by John Mason in 1858. In 1871 when salt became more refined, some ceramic shakers were molded with pierced tops. 'Christmas' shakers, so called because of their December 25, 1877, patent date, were fitted with a rotary agitator designed to break up any lumps in the salt. There are four types: Christmas Barrel (rare in cranberry and amethyst); Christmas Panel (rare in colors); Christmas Pearl (opaque, pearly white with painted decor); and Octagon Waffle (clear, thick glass made in three sizes with a rotary agitator, sometimes having undated tops). The dated tops and patented agitators were produced by Dana K. Alden of Boston, who contracted with various glasshouses to make the glass bodies. The Christmas Barrel and Christmas Panel patterns were produced by Boston and Sandwich (though the Christmas Barrel was made elsewhere as well). Alden contracted with Mt. Washington to make the Christmas Pearl pattern, and Waffle Octagon was made by several glass factories, McKee and Federal among them. Both of the latter patterns were made as late as 1900. Identical shakers which have no agitator or dated top are the companion peppers; these fetch about 30% less than the salts on today's markets.

Today's Victorian salt shaker collectors' interest primarily encompasses art glass, decorated cranberry and ruby, and custard and colored opalescent examples. (See also specified categories.) If you would like to learn more abut Victorian glass salt shakers, we recommend *The World of Salt Shakers, Second Edition,* by Mildred and Ralph Lechner; their address may be found in the Directory under Virginia. Be sure to watch for their upcoming third edition. (Mildred and Ralph deal only in Victorian shakers; please do not contact them with questions pertaining to novelty types.) In the following listings, prices are for single shakers unless noted 'pair.' Values are for old, original shakers. Some of these may have been reproduced, and this will be noted in the description.

Alaska (Foggy Bottom), bl to wht opal, blown, ca 1897, 2⅜" 75.00
Aster (tall), bl opaque, blown, 1902-05, 3½" 42.00
Aster & Leaf, bl, rare 95.00
Barrel Tapered, wht opalware, HP mc floral, 1897-1905, 3" 35.00
Beaded Twist, wht opalware, blown, ca 1890, 3¾" 30.00
Block (Duncan), ruby stained, pressed, ca 1887, 2⅜" 50.00
Block & Star, bl opaque, pressed, 1955-56, 2¾" 28.00
Bow & Tassel, wht opalware, blown, 1899-1901, 3⅛" 18.00
Brownie, lt gr opaque, blown, 1894-1900, 2" 225.00
Bubble Lattice, cranberry opal, blown, 1885-87, 2⅞" 125.00
Bulbous Base, cranberry, blown, 1889-91, 3" 50.00
Bulging Leaf, bl opaque, blown, 1894-96, 2" 45.00
Cane Woven, opaque custard, blown, 1901-04, 2½" 50.00
Centennial Boot 80.00
Chrysanthemum Sprig, custard, w/gold & decor, pr 300.00
Circle (dbl), (Jefferson #231), gr, blown, ca 1920, 3⅛" 60.00
Circled Scroll, gr, blown, 1902-05, 2⅞" 75.00
Colorado, gr w/gold, pr 395.00
Cone, bl opaque, blown, 1894-1904, 2⅞" 70.00
Creased Waist, yel opaque, blown, 1902-07, 3⅜" 45.00
Cube (tall), wht opal, floral decor, 1903-07, 2¾" 75.00
Daisy & Fern, cranberry, blown, 1894-1905, 2¾" 110.00
Dewey, gr, blown/pressed, 1900-01, 2⅞" 100.00
Diamond w/Peg, custard, souvenir, pr 175.00
Doodad, gr opaque, blown, 1896-1902, 3⅝" 40.00
Ear, gr opaque, blown, 1894-1900, 3" 40.00
Epaulette, wht opalware w/gold decor, blown, 1900-05, 2⅜" 13.00
Fish, pk cased, blown, 1894-1900, 3⅛" 50.00
Fish Pond, bl, HP fish decor, blown, 1900-10, 3¾" 180.00
Flora, emerald gr, gold decor, blown/pressed, 1895, 3½" 90.00
Floral Spray, wht opaque, HP floral, 1885-90, 2⅜" 78.00
Flower Band, pigeon blood, blown, 1901-02, 2⅝" 80.00
Flower Bouquet, bl opaque, blown, 1891, 3" 45.00
Forget-me-not (Eagle's), wht opalware, blown, ca 1901, 2⅜" 27.00
Gargoyle, wht opalware, blown, 1905, 2¼" 60.00
Globule, ruby, blown, ca 1901, 3⅛" 70.00
Grape, Imperial's, red, 1965-70, 3⅜" 23.00
Half Ribbed, wht opaque, blown, 1897-1903, 2⅜" 42.00
Hexagon Block, ruby stain, pr 125.00
Hobnail in Square, crystal & wht opal, ca 1887, 2⅞" 60.00
Holly Clear, crystal, blown/pressed, 1902-03, 3" 200.00
Jewel & Flower, bl, opal base, blown/pressed, 1904-06, 2⅞" 80.00

Leaf and Rib, clear blue, ca 1885-1891, 2⅝", $80.00.

Photo courtesy Mildred and Ralph Lechner

Leaf (3-Ftd), wht opalware, blown/pressed, 1900-07, 3⅛" 9.00
Liberty Bell, crystal, blown/pressed, 1875-77, rare, 2⅛" 100.00
Little Shrimp, custard, blown, 1895-1901, 1½" 65.00
Lobe, Four; opalware, HP floral, 1891-94, 2⅝" 50.00
Loop & Daisy, HP daisies on salmon opaque, 1887-94, 2⅝" 85.00
Many Petals, pk opaque, blown, 1902-06, 2½", pr 110.00
Opal Ribbon (short), cranberry opal, blown, 1887-1990, 2¼" 90.00
Ovals, Interlocking; bl, blown/pressed, 1891-97, 1⅞" 25.00
Pillar, Optic; bl, wht HP decor, blown, 1885-90, 3½" 155.00
Pineapple, variegated pk & wht opaque, blown, 1984-98, 3" 48.00
Poppy, Imperial's, pk irid carnival, 1975-82, 3" 15.00
Radiance, ruby, blown, 1936-39, 2½", pr 80.00
Rainbow satin, bulbous, 3¾", pr 5,000.00
Reverse Swirl, cranberry opal, blown, 1901-02, 3¼" 110.00
Rib, Scroll; bl opaque, blown, 1891-99, 2½" 40.00
Rib & Swirl, wht opaque opal, blown, 1878-87, 4" 50.00
Robin Hood, crystal, blown/pressed, ca 1898, 3⅛" 23.00
Scroll (4-ftd), wht opalware, blown/pressed, 1899-1902, 3⅛" 9.00
Scroll & Net, pk cased, blown, 1897-1903, 3" 50.00
Shuttle, crystal, blown/pressed, 1896, 2⅝" 49.00
Sphinx, crystal, blown/pressed, 1910-20, 2¾" 120.00
Spider Web, pk opaque cased, blown, 1894-1897, 2⅜" 40.00
Square S, bl opaque, blown, 1890, 3¼" 40.00
Swag w/Brackets, amethyst w/gold decor, ca 1904, 3" 70.00
Tangerine, Orange Side, clear to orange-red, pressed, 1930s, 2" .175.00
Tomato, pk flowers on bl, Mt WA, 1½", pr 175.00
Versailles, wht opalware, blown, ca 1900, 2¾" 28.00
Vine w/Flower, pk opaque cased, blown, 1902-08, 3" 55.00

Novelty

Those interested in novelty shakers will enjoy *Salt and Pepper Shakers, Volumes I, II, III*, and *IV*, by Helene Guarnaccia, and *The Collector's Encyclopedia of Salt and Pepper Shakers, Figural and Novelty, Volumes I* and *II*, by Melva Davern. Both are available at your local library or from Collector Books. Note: 'Mini' shakers are no taller than 2". Instead of having a cork, the user was directed to 'use tape to cover hole.' Our advisor for novelty salt shakers is Judy Posner; she is listed in the Directory under Pennsylvania. See also Regal; Rosemeade; Occupied Japan; Shawnee; other specific manufacturers.

Advertising, Budweiser, Bud Man, bl shoes, pr, from $200 to 250.00
Advertising, Budweiser, Bud Man, red shoes, pr 55.00
Advertising, Coca-Cola, bottle form, pr 12.00
Advertising, Harvestore Silos, pr 35.00
Advertising, Lone Star Beer, pr 25.00
Advertising, Mitchell's Dairy, milk bottles, pr 65.00
Advertising, Old Milwaukee, can form, pr 10.00
Advertising, Tipo Sherry, pr 18.00
Advertising, TWA, pr 18.00
Advertising, Virginia Dare Beverages, pr 18.00
Advertising, Wade's Dairy, milk bottles, pr 65.00
Animal, bear holding 2 fish, set 15.00
Animal, birds w/long beaks, stylized, mc, pr 24.00
Animal, creel of fish, set 15.00
Animal, dapper foxes w/top hat & canes, pr 24.00
Animal, donkey w/jugs on cart, set 10.00
Animal, elephant w/circus tent, pr 18.00
Animal, English bulldogs, pr 30.00
Animal, gray mouse w/cheese wedge, pr 8.00
Animal, hippo, mouth open, pr 12.00
Animal, lions, male & female, bone china, mk HP Relco, pr 28.00
Animal, mice, dressed, pr 30.00
Animal, monkey in car, set 45.00

Animal, owls on tray, mc, set 12.00
Animal, oxen pulling hay wagon, set 15.00
Animal, rabbit w/carrot, pr 12.00
Animal, rainbow trout, pr 10.00
Animal, Scotties, heavy metal, pr 70.00
Animal, seal, bone china, pr 15.00
Animal, Siamese cat, bsk, pr 15.00
Animal, starfish, maroon, bl & yel, pr 10.00
Animal, swan, lg, 5½x4½", pr 12.00
Animal, zebra, stylized, pr 10.00
Character, cow & moon, pr 35.00
Character, Garfield & Odie, pr 95.00
Character, Humpty Dumpty, plastic, pr 25.00
Character, Popeye & Olive Oyl, 1930s, pr, from $250 to 300.00
Character, Popeye & Olive Oyl, 1980s, pr 95.00
Character, Puss in Boots 25.00
Character, Rockabye Baby, pr 55.00
Character, Woody & Winnie Woodpecker, 1980s, pr 50.00

Corn people, painted ceramic,
$15.00 for the pair.

Food, cupcakes, pr 16.00
Food, squash people, pr 28.00
Travel, airplanes, on stands, metal, pr 55.00
Travel, Idaho, Mr & Mrs Spud, pr 75.00
Travel, Minnesota, state form, pr 25.00
Travel, Missouri, state form, w/mule, pr 35.00
Travel, Ozarks, jugs, pr 8.00
Travel, Reno, slot machines, pr 22.00
Travel, suitcases, NY City, pr 12.00
Travel, USS Alabama, pr 25.00

Salts, Open

Before salt became refined, processed, and free-flowing as we know it today, it was necessary to serve it in a salt cellar. An innovation of the early 1800s, the master salt was placed by the host and passed from person to person. Smaller individual salts were a part of each place setting. A small silver spoon was used to sprinkle it onto the food.

If you would like to learn more about the subject of salts, we recommend *5,000 Open Salts*, written by William Heacock and Patricia Johnson, with many full-color illustrations and current values. Our advisor for this category is Chris Christensen; he is listed in the Directory under California. In the listings below, the numbers refer to *Open Salts* by Johnson and Heacock and *Pressed Glass Salt Dishes* by L.W. and D.B. Neal. Lines with 'repro' within the description reflect values for reproduced salts.

Key:
EPNS — electroplated nickel silver   HM — hallmarked

Animals, Figurals, and Novelties

Rooster, clear glass with gold paint, double, NM, $50.00.

Bird and Berry, unmk Degenhart, HJ-933, colors, minimum 25.00
Duck, pressed, heavy, HJ-4677 ....45.00
Sleigh, Fostoria, HJ-3735, ca 1940 ....45.00
Swan, str neck, Crown Tuscan, Cambridge, HJ-935 ....100.00
Swan pulling cart, bl carnival, HJ-941, 1970s repro 25.00

Art Glass

Daum Nancy, flowers, mk, HJ-11 ....1,500.00
English Victorian, cranberry ruffled, clear rigaree, HJ-1312 ....115.00
Monot Stumpf, HJ-19 to HJ-22, ea 110.00
Steuben, bl, mk Aurene, HJ-14, 2" dia 400.00
Tiffany, ruffled, sgn LCT Favrille, HJ-32 ....200.00

Cameo, Art Glass, and Miscellaneous

Daum Nancy, winter scene 950.00
Intaglio, animals or butterfly HP, sgn, HJ-159 ....45.00
Lutz, red/wht/gold striping, blown, ftd master, 1½x⅞" 60.00
Moorcroft, sterling HM rim, London, HJ-1762, ca 1920 ....65.00
Opal w/vaseline ruffles, HJ-72 ....110.00
Royal Doulton, sterling HM rim, HJ-1870, ca 1873 ....115.00
Sowerby, cream opaque, HJ-385 ....75.00
Steuben, Calcite, ped ft, HJ-34 ....225.00
Webb, Burmese, HJ-75, ca 1890, 1¾" dia 650.00
Wedgwood, sterling rim, sgn, HJ-1850, ca 1897 ....160.00

China and Porcelain

Austrian or French, HP, HJ pg 78, ind, ea 12.00
Belleek, HP, ruffled top, mk, HJ-1310, rnd, ind 35.00
Dresden, attached flowers, HJ-1689, ind 45.00
Elfinware, basket, German, HJ-1253 ....15.00
Elfinware, wheelbarrow, sgn German, HJ-1244, ind 65.00
Haviland, factory decor, HJ-1397 to HJ-1400, ea 30.00
HP, artist sgn, scalloped ft, HJ-1390, ind 20.00
KPM, dbl, w/cherub, mk, HJ-1107 ....295.00
Meissen, HJ-1595, sq, ind 60.00
Nippon, HP, JJ-1365, ind 10.00
Nippon, HP floral tub, HJ-1454, ind 20.00
Pickard, sq, HJ-1569 ....55.00
Royal Bayreuth, figural claw, HJ-1667, ind 75.00
Royal Worcester, HJ-1861, ca 1870 ....150.00

Cut Glass

Amber, ped ft, English, ca 1880, master, pr 250.00
Bl cut to clear, ped ft, HJ-67 ....110.00
Clear, ped ft, mk Libbey 65.00
Clear, rnd, nappy style, HJ-3170 ....55.00
Cranberry, ped ft, etched, HJ-123, ca 1890 ....110.00

English Strawberry & Dmn Cut, oval tub, HJ-2857 ....35.00
Fan & Dmn, HJ-3416 or HJ-3417, ea 15.00
Heart, spade, dmn, club, HJ-3034 to HJ-3035, 4 for 160.00
J Hoare, sgn, HJ-3166 ....45.00
Waterford type, ped ft, HJ-3699, ca 1860 ....75.00

Lacy Sandwich Glass

Barlow/Kaiser #1462, aqua, beaded scroll & leaves, 1¾" 240.00
Barlow/Kaiser #1462, cobalt, beaded scroll & leaves, 1¾" 400.00
Barlow/Kaiser #1471, red-amber, sunburst base, sm chip, 1⅝" 375.00
Barlow/Kaiser #3276, milk glass, sawtooth, w/lid, 5¼" 110.00
Barlow/Kaiser #1459, yel w/amber-tone stag's horn, 1¾", EX 140.00
Neal BF-1, basket of flowers, #3462, VG 75.00
Neal BF-1d, basket of flowers, wht opaque, EX 250.00
Neal BS-3, beaded scroll, dk opaque violet 750.00
Neal BT-8, Lafayette Boat, med bl, NM 500.00
Neal CD-3, w/lid, NM 700.00
Neal CN-1, Crown, clear, rare 150.00
Neal CN-1a, opaque opal, NM 275.00
Neal CN-1b, Crown, fiery opal, NM 300.00
Neal DI-18, divided, French, NM 175.00
Neal EE-3b, eagles on 4 corners, VG 175.00
Neal NE-4, clear, NE Glass 85.00
Neal NE-5, lt gr, NE Glass, NM 300.00
Neal OL-24, oval, att Pittsburgh, NM 275.00
Neal PP-2c, Peacock Eye, clear, ped ft, flake 100.00
Neal SD-2, Strawberry Dmn, clear w/pale bl tint 100.00
Neal SD-2a, Strawberry Dmn, paw ft, NM 50.00
Neal SD-5a, Strawberry Dmn, dk brn-amber, rare 750.00
Neal SD-7, Strawberry Dmn, pk (amethystine), att Sandwich ...900.00
Neal SD-9, Strawberry Dmn, violet-bl, att Sandwich, chip 350.00
Neal SL-18, shell ped, rare 2,000.00
Neal SN-1, bl, staghorn, att Sandwich, EX 275.00
Neal WN-1, wagon, EX 450.00

Pottery, Porcelain, Semiporcelain

Niloak, rnd, HJ-1735, 1½" 45.00
Quimper, dbl, w/dog, HJ-1134 ....105.00
Royal Doulton, pyramid shape, HJ-1870, ca 1873 ....140.00
Wedgwood, HM, HJ-1871, ca 1900 ....145.00

Pressed Glass, Clear

Applied Bands, HJ-2934 ....25.00
Beaded Acorn Medallion, HJ-3533 ....45.00
Bearded Head, HJ-3636, master 40.00
Bow Tie, HJ-2548, ind 25.00
Candlewick, HJ-2642 ....10.00
Chicken, covered, sgn Vallerysthal, HJ-958 to HJ-960, ind 55.00
English Hobnail, HJ-2680, ind 8.00
Fancy Arch, HJ-3058 ....30.00
Hawaiian Lei, HJ-2577, ind 12.00
Heisey, Fancy Loop, HJ-2674, ind 25.00
Heisey, tub, sgn, HJ-2850 ....25.00
Liberty Bell 1776-1876, HJ-2689, ind 55.00
Loop & Dart, ped ft, HJ-2955 ....45.00
Panelled Grape Band, HJ-3516, master 35.00
Pillows, HJ-2697 ....35.00
Sawtooth Circle, HJ-3540, master 25.00
Turtle, HJ-3758, ind 35.00
Urn, Heisey, master 65.00
3-Face, HJ-4430 to HJ-4431, repro, ea 10.00

Pressed Glass, Colored

Bagware, HJ-449 ....15.00
Beatty Rib, wht opal, HJ-196 ....25.00
Bird & Berry, McKee, vaseline, amber or bl, HJ-997, ind, ea 55.00
Chippendale, amber, ped ft, HJ-596 ....35.00
Jersey Swirl, bl, HJ-426, ind 25.00
Lords & Ladies, bl, English, HJ-137 ....75.00
Tree Stump, Xd logs, milk glass, HJ-4473 ....55.00
Two-Panel, bl, gr or amber, HJ-429, ind, ea 20.00
Two-Panel, bl, gr or vaseline, HJ-564, master, ea 25.00

Silverplate

American, boat shape on ped ft, cobalt liner, HJ-661, VG 45.00
American, ruby liner, mk Derby, HJ-319 ....75.00
American, tulip on leaf, HJ-4155, VG 30.00
American, Victorian, crackle glass liner, Meriden, HJ-4215 ....85.00
English, oval, 4-ftd, clear liner, HJ-3945, VG 40.00
English, ruby liner, paw ft, ca 1900 ....75.00
English, vaseline ruffled Webb insert, HJ-95, ca 1880 ....225.00
Meriden, wolf-like dogs w/bowl on bk, HJ-4322, VG 125.00
Pairpoint, dolphin holds shell, HJ-4382, master, VG 110.00
Whiting, rams' heads, rnd, HJ-4252, VG 55.00

Sterling, Continental Silver, and Enamel

Albert Cole, Medallion, HJ-4208, ca 1836-76, 2¼", $450.00 for the pair.

Austria-Hungary, wht opal cut-bk bowl, sterling ped, HJ-138 ....150.00
Dutch, cobalt liner, HM, HJ-713, ca 1880, 4-pc set 300.00
English, boxed set of 2, apostle spoon, HJ-4794 ....200.00
French, liner & spoon, HJ-3937, ind 135.00
German, oval, ftd, cobalt liner, HJ-724 ....55.00
Gorham, medallion, ped ft, HJ-3976, ca 1860 ....175.00
Kerr, Art Nouveau, ped ft, cobalt liner, HJ-702, 1880 ....95.00
Russian, HP over sterling, 3 ball ft, HJ-2004 ....450.00
Swan, cut glass w/835 sterling wings, old, HJ-4287 ....55.00
Viking 900, Norway boat, enameled, HJ-2002 ....125.00

Samplers

American samplers were made as early as the colonial days; even earlier examples from 17th-century England still exist today. Changes in style and decorative motif are evident down through the years. Verses were not added until the late 17th century. By the 18th century, samplers were used not only for sewing experience but also as an educational tool. Young ladies, who often signed and dated their work, embroidered numbers and letters of the alphabet and practiced fancy stitches as well. Fruits and flowers were added for borders; birds, animals, and Adam and Eve were popular subjects. Later houses and other buildings were included. By the 19th century, the American Eagle and the little red schoolhouse had made their appearances.

Many factors bear on value: design and workmanship, strength of color, the presence of a signature and/or a date (both being preferred over only one or the other, and earlier is better), and, of course, condition.

ABC/s/verse/flowers, homespun, 5-color, sgn, 18x19", NM **600.00**
ABCs/birds/flowers, homespun, sgn/1841, fr, 17x11" **415.00**
ABCs/florals, homespun, worn, fr, 15x19" **100.00**
ABCs/florals, sgn/1807, 11x17", w/provenance, EX **800.00**
ABCs/flowers/birds/etc, needlepoint canvas, 1880, 16x22" **440.00**
ABCs/flowers/buildings/etc, wool on canvas, 48x18" **490.00**
ABCs/flowers/fruit basket, homespun, sgn/1820, 16x17", VG **800.00**
ABCs/flowers/house/dog, homespun, sgn, 9½x11½", EX **225.00**
ABCs/house/flowers/trees, homespun, sgn, bright colors, 17x17" ...**3,100.00**
ABCs/verse/birds/tree, homespun, sgn/1784, 14x11", EX **2,185.00**
ABCs/verse/crowns/birds/flowers, homespun, sgn/1856, 21x12" .**360.00**
ABCs/verse/flowers/animals, homespun, sgn/1825, 17x18" **1,955.00**
ABCs/verse/names of authors/flowers, sgn/1833, 17x13" **525.00**
ABCs/verse/strawberries, homespun, sgn/1852, walnut fr, 22x21" ...**1,375.00**
ABCs/vining florals/verse, homespun, Boston/1816, 18x19" ...**4,600.00**
ABCs/10 Commandments in verse/house/etc, sgn/1799, 19x23" ...**825.00**
Birds/flowers/etc, beads/sequins, LH/1842, 21¼x20¾" **1,725.00**
Flowers/building/birds/deer, homespun, sgn/1822, 20x19" **600.00**
Landscape/verse/vines, homespun, sgn/1805, damage, fr, 17x14" ..**330.00**
Landscape/verse/vines, homespun, sgn/1841, stain, fr, 17x11" **415.00**
Strawberries/flowers/house/verse, homespun, 18x17" **825.00**

Sandwich Glass

The Boston and Sandwich Glass Company was founded in 1820 by Deming Jarves in Sandwich, Massachusetts. Their first products were simple cruets, salts, half-pint jugs, and lamps. They were attributed as being one of the first to perfect a method for pressing glass, a step toward the manufacture of the 'lacy' glass which they made until about 1840. Many other types of glass were made there — cut, colored, snakeskin, hobnail, and opalescent among them. After the Civil War, profits began to dwindle due to the keen competition of the Western factories which were situated in areas rich in natural gas and easily accessible sand and coal deposits. The end came with an unreconcilable wage dispute between the workers and the company, and the factory closed in 1888. See also Cup Plates; Lacy Glass; Salts, Open; other specific types of glass.

Bottle, scent; amethyst, 12-panel tapered form, 6½" **155.00**
Bottle, scent; Baby T'print, vaseline, orig stopper **395.00**
Bottle, scent; dk amethyst, waisted form, pewter cap, 2½" **45.00**
Bottle, scent; emb fans & dmns, faceted stopper, 7½" **30.00**
Bottle, scent; gr-canary, oval, paneled, lily top, 6⅝" **550.00**
Bottle, scent; Loop, bl, att, 1850s, 8¼" **1,265.00**
Bottle, scent; monument form, peacock, smooth base, 1850s ..**1,250.00**
Bottle, scent; ruby, 8 cut panels w/gold trim, 5¾" **525.00**
Bottle, scent; Star & Punty, canary, matching cut stopper, 7" **525.00**
Bottle, scent; violet, waisted, 8-sided, pewter cap, 2½" **60.00**
Bottle, scent; 8 cut panels, ruby w/gold, cut/decor stopper, 6" **525.00**
Bottle, toilet water; GI-7, cobalt, pontiled **175.00**
Bowl, Short Loop, canary, scalloped, 2⅛x8¾", NM **750.00**
Candlestick, bl opaque w/wht opaque looped base, 7", EX **650.00**
Candlestick, clambroth & bl dolphin form, 9¾", pr, EX **1,500.00**
Candlestick, clambroth/alabaster, columnar base, 9⅛", EX **130.00**
Candlestick, clambroth/alabaster, petal socket/loop base, 7" **185.00**
Candlestick, cobalt, hexagonal socket & base, 7⅞", EX **475.00**
Candlestick, fiery wht opal dolphins w/bl candle font, 10", pr ...**1,150.00**

Candlestick, lacy crossbar base, multiple wafers, 7", pr **200.00**
Compote, Elongated Loop, wht opaque, 8⅞x9⅝", NM **325.00**
Compote, Loop, moonstone/clambroth, flared bowl, 7x9⅝" ...**1,300.00**
Creamer, GI-29, sapphire bl, appl base & hdl, 4⅜" **1,800.00**
Decanter, bk bar; canary yel, pontiled, 10" **725.00**
Decanter, bk bar; emerald gr, 8-panel, pontiled, 11", NM **3,600.00**
Lamp shade, cranberry threaded on opal, 4x5¼x4¼" **195.00**
Salt cellar, yel canary, Tulip pattern, 6-sided base, 1¾" **275.00**
Spooner, amber, att, 1850s, 4¾" **860.00**
Sugar bowl, GI-29, sapphire bl, rolled lip, 1820s, 2½x5" **3,250.00**
Syrup, Chrysanthemum Leaf, heavy hdl, orig dtd lid **75.00**

Vase, purplish blue, tulip form with octagonal foot, ca 1850-1870, 10¼", $1,550.00.

Vase, amethyst, tulip form, 8-sided base, 1850s, 9½" **800.00**
Vase, emerald gr, trumpet form, knopped stem/rnd base, 13⅜" ..**2,250.00**
Vase, emerald gr, tulip form, wafered base, 10" **1,150.00**
Vase, fiery opal w/bl & gilt enamel, Greek revival style, 4¼" **180.00**
Vase, gr, flared rim, wafer connector, pontiled, 4½" **85.00**
Vase, Loop, canary, gauffered rim, rnd base, 10¼", pr **545.00**
Vase, Loop, canary, scalloped rim, 6⅜", NM **375.00**
Vase, trumpet form, baluster stem, att, 16x5⅛" **400.00**
Vase, tulip form, scalloped, 8-sided base, 1850s, 9⅞", pr **4,500.00**
Wine, dk teal gr w/fluted panels, stemmed, 5" **300.00**

Sarreguemines

Sarreguemines, France, is the location of Utzschneider and Company, founded in 1770, producers of majolica, transfer-printed dinnerware, figurines, and novelties which are usually marked 'Sarreguemines.'

Bank, tuba player, early mk, 5½" **200.00**
Basket, lt gr crystalline on textured surface, 9" **150.00**
Candlesticks, silver lustre on classic form, 7", NM, pr, ...**175.00**
Ewer, gray & tan crystalline on rose & mauve, ormolu mts, 11½" ...**250.00**
Jardiniere, oak leaves, branch hdls, majolica, 17x17½" **1,600.00**
Pitcher, Etna, mauve w/gr & gold crystalline, 5½x7½" **225.00**
Pitcher, man's face w/sideburns, 7½" **275.00**
Pitcher, pig figural, chip on ear, 9¼" **325.00**
Plate, country woman, pierced for hanging **100.00**
Plate, Fr country scenic transfer, floral rim, 6" **60.00**
Vase, gr crystalline, flared/folded tricorner rim, 5½x6½" **150.00**
Vase garniture, pk lustre w/blk bands, 3-pc, 1820s, 10", EX **700.00**

Satin Glass

Satin glass is simply glassware with a velvety matt finish achieved through the application of an acid bath. This procedure has been used by many companies since the 20th century, both here and abroad, on many types of colored and art glass. See also Mother-of-Pearl; Webb.

Ewer, blue with white interior, gold florals, clear twist handle, ruffled rim, 10", $110.00.

Ewer, tan w/bl matsu-no-ke, camphor trim, mc/gold leaves, 6" ...**375.00**
Ewer, wht w/gold floral limbs, ruffled rim/camphor hdl, 11¼" **120.00**
Pitcher, bl, camphor reed hdl, Mt WA, 3½" **90.00**
Rose bowl, bl, HP florals, 8-crimp, 3¾x4⅜" **135.00**
Rose bowl, yel seashell shape w/orange HP florets **85.00**
Vase, apricot, hummingbird/branch, egg form, camphor ft, 6½" ...**140.00**
Vase, yel, wht int, stick form, 7½x3½" **145.00**

Satsuma

Satsuma is a type of fine cream crackle-glaze pottery or earthenware made in Japan as early as the 17th century. The earliest wares, made at the original kiln in the Satsuma province, were enameled with only simple florals. By the late 18th century, a floral brocade (or nishikide design) was favored, and similar wares were being made at other kilns under the direction of the Lord of Satsuma. In the early part of the 19th century, a diaper pattern was added to the florals. Gold and silver enamels were used for accents by the latter years of the century. During the 1850s, as the quality of goods made for export to the western world increased and the style of decoration began to evolve toward becoming more appealing to the Westerners, human forms such as Arhats, Kannon, geisha girls, and samurai warriors were added. Today the most valuable pieces are those marked 'Kinkozan,' 'Shuzan,' 'Ryuzan,' and 'Kozan.' The genuine Satsuma 'mon' or mark is a cross within a circle — usually in gold on the body or lid, or in red on the base of the ware. Character marks may be included.

Caution: Much of what is termed 'Satsuma' comes from the Showa Period (1926 to the present); it is not true Satsuma but a simulated type, a cheaper pottery with heavy enamel. Collectors need to be aware that much of the of the 'Satsuma' today is really Satsuma style and should not carry the values of true Satsuma. Our advisor for this category is Norma Angelo; she is listed in the Directory under New York.

Koro, gr foo dog hdls to lid & sides, florals on bl, 17½" **425.00**
Plate, mtn landscape w/Mt Fuji, earthenware, 19th C, 9½" **130.00**
Vase, emb & pnt figures on blk field, earthenware, 8½" **350.00**
Vase, immortal figure w/decor, Japan, 15" **250.00**
Vase, Samurai scene, paneled baluster, Kyoto, 12" **400.00**
Vase (now lamp), court ladies/mtn scenes, 28" w/socket, pr **425.00**

Scales

In today's world of pre-measured and pre-packaged goods, it is difficult to imagine the days when such products as sugar, flour, soap, and candy first had to be weighed by the grocer. The variety of scales used at the turn of the century was highly diverse; at the Philadelphia Exposition in 1876, one company alone displayed over three hundred different weighing devices. Among those found today, brass, cast-iron, and plastic models are the most common. Fancy postal scales in decorative wood, silver, marble, bronze, and mosaic are also to be found.

A word of caution on the values listed: these values range from a low for those items in fair to good condition to the upper values for items in excellent condition. Naturally, items in mint condition could command even higher prices, and they often do. Also, these are **retail** prices that suggest what a collector will pay for the object. When you sell to a dealer, expect to get much less. These estimated values have been prepared by a committee of the International Society of Antique Scale Collectors under the direction of Robert Stein and George Mallis. The values noted are averages taken from various auction and other catalogs in the possession of the Society members. Among these, but not limited to, are the following: Joel L. Malter & Co., Inc., Encino, CA; *Collectors Journal of Ancient Art,* Joel L. Malter & Co., Inc.; Nobody's Bizness But Our Own, Storrs, CT; Craig A. Whitford Numismatic Auctions; *Auktion Alt Technic,* Auction Team, Koln, Germany; *Waaqgen Auktion Essen,* Auktion Karla W. Schenk-Behrens, Essen, Germany.

Those seeking additional information concerning antique scales are encouraged to contact the International Society of Antique Scale Collectors, whose address can be found in the Directory under Clubs, Newsletters, and Catalogs.

Key:
ap — arrow pointer	hcp — hanging counterpoise
bal — balance	hh — hand held
bm — base metal	l+ — label with foreign coin values
br — brass	lb w/i — labeled box with
Brit — British s	instruction
Can — Canadian	lph — letter plate or holder
Col — Colonial	pend — pendulum
h — hanging	PP — Patent Pending
CW — Civil War	st — sterling
cwt — counterweight	tt — torsion type
Engl — English	ua — unequal arm
eq — equal arm	wt — weight
Euro — European	
FIS — Fairbanks Infallible	
Scale Co.	

Dayton platform scale, 'Moneyweight' marque, very rare, 32", EX restored, $800.00.

Analytical (Scientific)

Am, eq, mahog w/br & ivory, late 1800s, 14x16x8", $200 to **400.00**

Assay

Am, eq, mahog box w/br & ivory, plaque/drw, 1890s, $250 to ...**350.00**

Coin: Equal Arm Balance, American

Blk japanned metal, eagle on lid, late 19th C, $125 to **225.00**
Col, oak 6-part box, Col moneys, Boston, 1720-75, $600 to ...**1,200.00**
Post Col to CW, oak 6-part box, 1+, 1843, $400 to **1,000.00**

Coin: Equal Arm Balance, English

Charles I, wooden box w/11 Brit wts, 1640s, $900 to **1,500.00**
1-pc wood box, rnd wts, label, Freeman, 1760s, $250 to **450.00**
6-pc oak box, coin wts label, Thos Harrison, 1750s, $200 to **450.00**

Coin: Equal Arm Balance, French

Solid wood box, 12 sq wts, J Reyne, Bourdeau, 1694, $400 to .**1,000.00**
Solid wood box w/recesses, 5 sq wts, A Gardes, 1800s, $250 to ..**800.00**
1-pc oval box, nested/fractional wts, label, 18th C, $250 to **400.00**
1-pc oval box, no wts, label of Fr/Euro coins, 18th C, $150 to **250.00**
1-pc walnut box, nested wts, Charpentier label, 1810, $275 to ..**675.00**

Coin: Equal Arm Balance, Miscellaneous

Amsterdam, 1-pc box, 32 sq wts, label, late 1600s, $850 to **2,500.00**
Cologne, full set of wts & full label, late 1600s, $1,200 to **2,800.00**

Counterfeit Coin Detectors, American

Allender Pat, lb w/i, cwt, Nov 22, 1855, 8½", $350 to **650.00**
Allender PP, rocker, labeled box, cwt, 1850s, 8½", $450 to **750.00**
Allender PP, rocker, no box or cwt, 1850s, 8½", $250 to **375.00**
Allender PP, space for $3 gold pc, lb w/i, cwt, 1855, $350 to **750.00**
Allender PP, space for $3 gold pc, no box or cwt, 1855, $275 to ...**375.00**
Allender Warranted, rocker, no box or cwt, 1850s, 8½", $350 to .**475.00**
McNally-Harrison Pat 1882, rocker, cwt, JT McNally, $275 to ..**500.00**
McNally-Harrison Pat 1882, rocker, cwt & box, FIS, $400 to **750.00**
McNally-Harrison...1882, rocker, CI base, no cwt/box, $250 to .**400.00**
Thompson, Z-formed rocker, Berrian Mfg, 1877 Pat, $175 to **350.00**

Counterfeit Coin Detectors, English

Folding, Guinea, self-rising, labeled box, 1850s, $175 to **225.00**
Folding, Guinea, self-rising, wood box/label, ca 1890s, $125 to ..**175.00**
Folding, Guinea, self-rising, wooden box, pre-1800, $175 to **275.00**
Rocker, simple, no maker's name or cb, end-cap box, $85 to **125.00**
Rocker, w/maker's name & cb, end-cap box, $120 to **150.00**

Postal

In the listings below an asterisk (*) was used to indicate that any one of several manufacturers' or brand names might be found on that particular set of scales. Some of the American-made pieces could be marked Pelouze, Lorraine, Hanson, Kingsbury, Fairbanks, Troemner, IDL, Newman, Accurate, Ideal, B-T, Marvel, Reliance, Victor, Liberty, Gem, Superior, Landers-Frary-Clark, Chatillon, Triner, American Bank Service, or Weiss. European/U.S.-made scales marked with an asterisk (*) could be marked Salter, Peerless, Pelouze, Sturgis, L.F.&C., Alderman, G. Little, or S&D. English-made scales with the asterisk (*) could be marked Josh. & Edmd. Ratcliff, R.W. Winfield, S. Mordan, STS (Samuel Turner, Sr.), W.&T. Avery, Parnall & Sons, S&P, or H.B. Wright. There may be other manufacturers as well.

Brit/Can Bal, eq, br or CI on base, *, 4"-15", $100 to **750.00**
Engl Bal, eq/Roberval, gilt or st, on stand, *, 3"-8", $500 to **2,500.00**
Engl Bal, eq/Roberval, plain to ornate, *, 3"-8", $100 to **2,500.00**

Engl Spring, candlestick, br or st, *, 3½"-15", $100 to **500.00**
Engl Spring, CI, br or NP fr, Salter, ozs/lbs, 7"-10", $25 to **200.00**
Engl Steelyard, ua, 1- or 2-beam, h lph, *, 4"-15", $100 to **1,500.00**
Euro pend, gravity, br, CI or NP fr on base, oz/grams, $75 to **350.00**
Euro pend, gravity, 2-arm, bm, br or NP, *, 6"-9", $50 to **300.00**
Euro/US Spring, br or NP, pence/etc, h or hh, *, 4"-17", $10 to ..**100.00**
US Pend, gravity, metal, pnt face, ap, hcp, sm, $20 to **100.00**
US Spring, pnt bm, *, mtd on inkstand, 2½"-8", $75 to **250.00**
US Spring, pnt bm, rnd glass-covered face, *, 8"-10", $25 to **100.00**
US Spring, SP, oblong base, *, 2½"-8", $100 to **200.00**
US Spring, st, oblong base, *, 2½"-8", $200 to **500.00**
US Steelyard, ua, CI, *, 5"-13" beam, 4½"-12" base, $25 to **100.00**

Schafer and Vater

Established in 1890 by Gustav Schafer and Gunther Vater in the Thuringia region of southwest Germany, by 1913 this firm employed over two hundred workers. The original factory burned in 1918 but was restarted and production continued until WWII. In 1972 the East German government took possession of the building and destroyed all of the molds and the records that were left.

You will find pieces with the impressed mark of a nine-point star with a script 'R' inside the star. On rare occasions you will find this mark in blue ink under glaze. The items are sometimes marked with a four-digit design number and a two-digit artist mark. In addition or instead, pieces may have 'Made in Germany' or in the case of the Kewpies, 'Rose O'Neil copyright.' The company also manufactured items for sale under store names and those would not have the impressed mark.

Schafer and Vater used various types of clays. Items made of hard-paste porcelain, soft-paste porcelain, jasper, bisque, and majolica can be found. The glazed bisque pieces may be multicolored or have a colored slip wash applied that highlights the intricate details of the modeling. Gold accents were used as well as spots of high-gloss color called jewels. Metallic glazes are coveted. You can find the jasper in green, blue, pink, lavender, and white. New collectors gravitate toward the pink and lavender shades.

Since Schafer and Vater made such a multitude of items, collectors have to compete with many cross-over collections. This includes collections of shaving mugs, hatpin holders, match holders, figurals, figural pitchers, Kewpies, tea sets, bottles, naughties, etc.

Reproduction alert: In addition to the crudely made Japanese copies, some English firms are beginning to make figural reproductions. These seem to be well marked and easy to spot.

Ashtray, Waiting for the Smacks, Dutch boy & girl, 3¾x3" **150.00**
Candy container, pig playing flute, from Pig & Whistle, 5" **395.00**
Figurine, googly-eyed boy & girl w/doves & rabbits, 4x3⅜" **135.00**
Figurine, Scotsman drinking mug of ale, 4¼x2⅛" **145.00**

Photo courtesy Dawn Ricker

Hatpin holder, Egyptian head, brown jasper with pink cameo and flowers, jeweled, $450.00.

Hatpin holder, comical seated Chinaman 200.00
Hatpin holder, Nouveau bust of lady on ped base 250.00
Pitcher, Dutch girl, sm 75.00
Pitcher, smiling pear, sm 100.00
Pitcher, wht roses on gray to gr, 4¾" 45.00
Pitcher, William Taft, 5" 115.00
Stickpin holder, bell shape 150.00
Teapot, smiling apple, child sz 175.00
Toothpick holder, well-dressed gentleman 125.00
Vase, jasper, bl w/wht Classical lady, 7½" 45.00
Vase, jasper, gr w/wht lady playing harp, 9" 45.00
Vase, pk to bronze w/pnt jewels, 5" 85.00

Scheier

The Scheiers began their ceramics careers in the late 1930s and soon thereafter began to teach their craft at the University of New Hampshire. After WWII they cooperated with the Puerto Rican government in establishing a native ceramic industry, an involvement which would continue to influence their designs. In the '50s they retired and moved to Mexico; they currently reside in Arizona.

Bowl, lt/dk gr w/brn flambe, brn speckled/swirled center, 12" 175.00
Bowl, mocha w/brn specks, ribbed ext, brn central swirl, 12" 100.00
Cup, brn & teal w/brn int swirl, mfg flaw, +teal saucer 50.00
Vase, abstract, mc flowing lustre, ribbed, bottle neck, 6" 225.00
Vase, faces, brn gloss w/olive & bl, wide ftd U-form, 9½" 950.00
Vase, fish drawn on brn-specked ivory/tan matt, ribbed, 5½" 400.00
Vase, stylized figures/lg fish cvd in bl on bl/aqua, 8x4" 475.00
Vase, tan/gray/mustard/brn w/blk highlights, 6½x5" 250.00

Schlegelmilch Porcelain

Authority Mary Frank Gaston, who is our advisor, has completed four volumes of *The Collector's Encyclopedia of R.S. Prussia* with full-color illustrations and current values. Mold numbers appearing in some of the listings refer to these books. You will find Mrs. Gaston's address in the Directory under Texas.

Key:
BM — blue mark   SM — steeple mark
GM — green mark   RM — red mark

E.S. Germany

Fine chinaware marked 'E.S. Germany' or 'E.S. Prov. Saxe' was produced by the E.S. Schlegelmilch factory in Suhl in the Thuringia region of Prussia from sometime after 1861 until about 1925.

Bowl, masted schooner & lighthouse, scalloped rim, mk 85.00
Bowl, 3 maidens & cherub, Kauffmann, mk, 9" 75.00
Box, 3 maidens & man playing harp, Kauffmann, brass closure, sm ..80.00
Chocolate set, roses, hexagonal pot+4 c/s 150.00
Nappy, hunt scene, mk 85.00
Plate, luncheon; Madame DuBoise, 4-leaf clovers w/gold 75.00
Platter, maidens, Kauffmann, teal border w/gold, hdls, 14½" 210.00
Teapot, Victorian ladies cameos & flowers on leaf mold 175.00
Vase, lady w/swallows on wht w/turq & gold, 9½" 475.00

R.S. Germany

In 1869 Reinhold Schlegelmilch began to manufacture porcelain in Suhl in the German province of Thuringia. In 1894 he established another factory in Tillowitz in upper Silesia. Both areas were rich in resources necessary for the production of hard-paste porcelain. Wares marked with the name 'Tillowitz' and the accompanying 'R.S. Germany' phrase are attributed to Reinhold. The most common mark is a wreath and star in a solid color under the glaze. Items marked 'R.S. Germany' are usually more simply decorated than R.S. Prussia. Some reflect the Art Deco trend of the 1920s. Certain hand-painted floral decorations and themes such as 'Sheepherder,' 'Man With Horses,' and 'Cottage' are especially valued by collectors — those with a high-gloss finish or on Art Deco shapes in particular. Not all hand-painted items were painted at the factory. Those with an artist's signature but no 'Hand Painted' mark indicate that the blank was decorated outside the factory.

Basket, orchids & daisies w/gold, low, twisted hdl, 4¼x8" 55.00
Basket, pheasants, brn tones, mk, 6¼" 200.00
Bowl, florals on lettuce mold w/lustre, mk, 10" 325.00
Bowl, Madame LeBrun as paintress, hdls, mk 900.00
Bowl, wild roses & berries, irregular shape, mk, 10" 125.00
Candlestick, lt bl flowers, mk, 6" 90.00
Cup & saucer, demitasse; floral, ftd 30.00
Plate, molded Indian chief hdl, 6½" 95.00
Toothpick holder, flowers, 3-hdld, mk 110.00
Toothpick holder, lilies on gr, 3-hdld, mk 45.00
Tray, wht & gr poppies, ornate hdls, mk, 15¼" 250.00
Vase, cottage scene, salesman's sample 100.00
Vase, sleeping maiden w/cherub, gold hdls, mk, 10" 350.00

R.S. Poland

'R.S. Poland' is a mark attributed to Reinhold Schlegelmilch's factory in Tillowitz, Silesia. It was in use for a few years after 1945.

R.S. Poland vase, single blossom, gold trim, 3¼", $100.00.

Bowl, berry; pheasants, unmk, 2¼x9⅜" 145.00
Bowl, Rembrandt's Nightwatch on gray-gr, mk, 1½x5⅜" 145.00
Cake plate, floral, floral border, hdls, 10" 135.00
Planter, floral medallions, mk, 5½x7½" 235.00
Server, lav & pk roses w/gold, center hdl, RM, 11" dia 515.00
Tray, bird on branch, floral/geometric border, mk, 14" 115.00
Vase, crowned cranes, salesman's sample, 3½x1½" 815.00
Vase, lady, sheep & cottage scene, ornate gold hdls, mk, 10" 635.00

R.S. Prussia

Art porcelain bearing the mark 'R.S. Prussia' was manufactured by Reinhold Schlegelmilch from the late 1870s to the early 1900s in a Germanic area known until the end of WWI as Prussia. The vast array of mold shapes in combination with a wide variety of decorations is the basis for R.S. Prussia's appeal. Themes can be categorized as figural (usually based on a famous artist's work), birds, florals, portraits, scenics, and animals.

Biscuit jar, pk roses, emb florals, SP rim/lid/hdl, unmk, 7" 225.00

Biscuit jar, scattered flowers on satin, iris mold, RM 650.00
Bowl, berry; mixed florals, 5-lobed, mk, lg+4 sm 356.00
Bowl, berry; red roses, iris mold, 9", +6 5½" bowls 495.00
Bowl, Dice Throwers, mk, 10¼" 895.00
Bowl, Easter lily, rare plume mold, mk, 3x10" 225.00
Bowl, Flora portrait, Tiffany border & gold, shallow, 10" 950.00
Bowl, floral, carnation mold, ftd, 3x6" 175.00
Bowl, floral, emb Nouveau scrolls, 4-lobed, unmk, 10½" 200.00
Bowl, floral, sunflower mold, 3x11" 450.00
Bowl, forget-me-nots & roses on satin, mk, 10½" 315.00
Bowl, fruit decor, circle mk, 10½" 175.00
Bowl, fruit; pk roses, RM, 9" 180.00
Bowl, jonquils on cobalt, 10" 595.00
Bowl, lady w/dog, cobalt border, SM 1,600.00
Bowl, lilies on orange/purple lustre, fishscale mold, 3x11" 325.00
Bowl, pale gr flowers & rosettes, iris mold, unmk, 9¾" 255.00
Bowl, pk roses on pearlized, fancy border w/gold, RM, 10" 425.00
Bowl, yel flowers & gold on maroon Tiffany finish, unmk 350.00

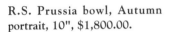

R.S. Prussia bowl, Autumn portrait, 10", $1,800.00.

Cake plate, floral on satin, fleur-de-lis mold, mk, 11" 190.00
Cake plate, floral w/4 Cupid medallions, Tiffany finish, 10½" ...890.00
Cake plate, hanging baskets, RM, 10" 345.00
Cake plate, mc roses, carnation mold, RM 295.00
Cake plate, poppies on satin, iris mold 525.00
Cake plate, snapdragons on pastel, mk, 11½" 345.00
Cake plate, Spring Season, fleur-de-lis mold, RM, 9¾" 1,550.00
Cake plate, swan scene, open hdls, scalloped, mk, 10" 495.00
Cake plate, water lilies reflecting, medallion mold, mk, 10½" 165.00
Cake plate, wild roses on satin, mk, 11" 325.00
Celery dish, pk & yel roses, carnation mold, RM 350.00
Celery dish, roses & snowballs, cobalt rim, mk 295.00
Celery tray, dogwood on pearlized lustre, mk, 12¼" L 200.00
Celery tray, gold & yel roses, lily mold, unmk, 13½x8½", NM ..175.00
Celery tray, pk & wht floral w/gold, open hdls, RM, 12½" L 225.00
Celery tray, pk & wht roses, gold leaves, Tiffany border, RM 270.00
Chocolate pot, florals, flower finial, steeple mold, RM 150.00
Chocolate pot, Madame Recamier, 10½", +6 c/s 7,500.00
Chocolate pot, mc roses w/gold, RM 395.00
Chocolate pot, turkeys & swallows, mk 1,195.00
Coffeepot, Dice Throwers, cobalt & gold, RM, 11" 750.00
Cracker jar, Deco swan on satin w/gold, RM 600.00
Cracker jar, 7 Scattered Flowers w/gold & red, RM 450.00
Creamer, Madame Lebrun, wht hat, gr base, mk 235.00
Creamer & sugar bowl, pk roses & pale bl band w/gold, RM 215.00
Cup & saucer, chocolate; pk & wht poppies, ftd egg shape 110.00
Cup & saucer, demi; pk roses, scalloped, mk, 1¾", 4½" 120.00
Ferner, floral on pastel, ribbed/scalloped, mk, 8x4" 250.00
Mug, scuttle; dogwood on pearlized w/gold, swirled, unmk 150.00
Mug, scuttle; wildflowers w/gold, 6-sided, unmk 175.00
Mustard pot, wht flowers on shiny gr, RM 150.00
Plate, Dice Throwers, flower border, gold rim, 2 mks, 9⅛" 450.00
Plate, pk poppies, gr border, RM, 8½" 175.00

Plate, pk roses on pk, carnation mold, unmk, 7½" 165.00
Plate, poppies, iris mold, open hdls, mk, 11" 175.00
Plate, poppies, reflecting, medallion mold, RM, 7½" 85.00
Plate, Spring, fleur-de-lis mold, RM, 9¾" 1,500.00
Plate, yel roses on pk, RM, 8½" 180.00
Relish, forget-me-nots/carnations/jewels, unmk 125.00
Shaving mug, stippled floral, mirror front, yel roses 400.00
Slipper, turq w/gold trim, roses & lily of the valley, mk, 8" 245.00
Syrup, Dogwood & Pine, RM 175.00
Syrup, swan on satin, RM, 4" 325.00
Tankard, bronze & orange mums, unmk, 14" 325.00
Tankard, hanging basket of roses on satin, mk, 10" 725.00
Tankard, roses, stipple mold, mk, 13¼" 625.00
Teapot, orange & wht poppies on gr, mk, +cr/sug 525.00
Teapot, roses, +4 c/s, child sz 625.00
Toothpick holder, floral, star mk 135.00
Toothpick holder, wht to pk, flower-form rim, no hdls, unmk 135.00
Tray, red & pk roses, pierced hdl, mk, 11x8" 250.00
Vase, lady w/dog, unmk, 4" 325.00
Vase, lilies on gr, gold hdls, mk, salesman's sample, 4" 145.00
Vase, mill scene, RM, 7" 325.00
Vase, pheasant scene, unmk, 6¾x2¾" 125.00
Vase, Summer Season portrait, gold hdls & beads, RM, 10½" ..1,100.00
Vase, village scene, salesman's sample, RM 325.00

R.S. Suhl, Suhl

Porcelains marked with this designation are attributed to Reinhold Schlegelmilch's Suhl factory.

Box, floral, w/beveled mirror, mk 200.00
Coffee set, Angelica Kauffmann scene, 9" pot+cr/sug+6 c/s 1,675.00
Cup & saucer, Nightwatch, brn tones 55.00
Vase, Melon Boys, flared sides, mk, 9½" 1,150.00
Vase, sunflowers on brn, hdls, mk, 6¾" 110.00
Wall plaque, daisies, 10½" 125.00

R.S. Tillowitz

R.S. Tillowitz-marked porcelains are attributed to Reinhold Schlegelmilch's factory in Tillowitz, Silesia.

Berry set, Acorn & Oak Leaf w/gold, mk, 7-pc 250.00
Bowl, pheasants, scalloped, oval, open hdls, mk, 10" L 265.00
Cake set, fuchsia on gr w/tan shadows, open hdls, 7-pc 350.00
Chocolate pot, Deco decor w/gold on yel, mk 150.00
Gravy boat, wht flowers on shaded cream, mk 70.00
Plate, poinsettias, pk on ivory to gr, hdls, 9¾" 60.00
Plate, stylized butterfly border w/gold, gold hdls, mk, 7" 35.00

Schneider

The Schneider Glass Company was founded in 1914 at Epinay-sur-seine, France. They made many types of art glass, some of which sandwiched designs between layers. Other decorative devices were applique and carved work. These were marked 'Charder' or 'Schneider.' During the '20s commercial artware was produced with Deco motifs cut by acid through two or three layers and signed 'LeVerre Francais' in script or with a section of inlaid filigrane. Our advisor for this category is Don Williams; he is listed in the Directory under Missouri. See also Le Verre Francais.

Bowl, mottled red-orange/cobalt on amethyst ft, 6¼x8" 550.00
Compote, canary opal tray w/tri-pulled edge, orange base, 2½" ..350.00

Compote, mottled magenta to opal, amethyst base, 4¾x13½" ...**600.00**
Finger bowl, tangerine mottle w/scattered wine & yel, +plate **250.00**

Vases, tomato red mottled with burgundy, blown into a wrought-iron footed armature, 8¼", NM, $1,600.00 for the pair.

Vase, Majorelle, mottled orange/cobalt, vertical bars, 9¾" **2,000.00**
Vase, maroon spots on orange to lt peach, ovoid, 14" **635.00**
Vase, rose/wht mottle w/yel splashes, 3 yel nodules, 20" **1,375.00**

Schoolhouse Collectibles

Schoolhouse collectibles bring to mind memories of a bygone era when the teacher rang her bell to call the youngsters to class in a one-room schoolhouse where often both the 'hickory stick' and an apple occupied a prominent position on her desk. Our advisor for this category is Kenn Norris; he is listed in the Directory under Texas.

Book, Along the Way, Winston Co, EX **20.00**
Book, Arithmetic for You, Lyons, 1945, VG **10.00**
Book, Children's Own Reader, 1936, EX **20.00**
Book, Dick & Jane, Before We Read, soft cover, VG **175.00**
Book, Dick & Jane, Fun w/Our Friends, 1962, VG **25.00**
Book, Dick & Jane, Good Times w/Our Friends, 1941, VG **45.00**
Book, Dick & Jane, Look/See, soft cover, M **150.00**
Book, Dick & Jane, More Friends & Neighbors, 1946, EX **25.00**
Book, Dick & Jane, Our New Friends, hard cover, 1942, VG **45.00**
Book, Dick & Jane, pre-primer, soft cover, 1936, G **65.00**
Book, Dick & Jane, The New Our New Friends, hardcover, 1956, EX ..**50.00**
Book, Dick & Jane, We Work & Play, yel soft cover, EX **30.00**
Book, Friends & Neighbors, Scott Foresman, 1946, VG **25.00**
Book, Pete's Family, 1942, EX **25.00**
Book, We Are Neighbors, Ginn, 2nd edition, 1948, EX **15.00**
Book, We Are Neighbors, Ginn Co, 1949, VG **10.00**
Book, World of Science, Scribner, 1940, VG **10.00**
Desk, child's, cherry, lift top, low gallery, rprs, 26x27" **165.00**
Desk, child's, hardwood w/dk varnish, 34x19x14" **60.00**
Desk, master's, ash/cherry Co Hplwht, lift lid, 34x30x25" **275.00**
Desk, master's, cherry Co Sheraton, 3 dvtl drws, 33x33x21" **770.00**
Desk, master's, rfn walnut, dvtl drw & gallery, 42x32" **715.00**
Desk, schoolmaster's, cherry, slant top, trn legs, 33x28x22" **650.00**
Globe, Joslin's Six Inch Terrestrial, Boston 1854, CI base **1,300.00**
Globe, Wilson's Terrestrial, SR Gray...NY, 1859, 18" H **3,000.00**
Ink jar, ceramic, wire lock, Sanford's Ink, 9" **125.00**
Lunch box, pail type, metal, bail hdl, 4x4½" **15.00**
Pencil sharpener, automobile form, sheet metal, Japan, 1¾" **30.00**
Pencil sharpener, pistol form, CI, Germany **20.00**
Slate, peg-constructed fr, 9x13" **50.00**
Spelling board, heavy red cb, letters & #s, 1916, 14" dia **125.00**

Pencil Boxes

Among the most common of school-related collectibles are the many classes of pencil boxes. Generally from the period of the 1870s to the 1940s, these boxes were made in many hundred different styles.

Materials included tin, wood (thin frame and solid hardwood), and leather; later fabric and plastics were used. Most pencil boxes were in a basic, rectangular configuration, though rare examples were made to resemble other objects. These included rolling pins, ball bats, and nightsticks. Pencil boxes are still to be found at reasonable prices, though collectors have lately noticed this field. All boxes listed below are in very-good to near-mint condition. Our advisors for pencil boxes are Sue and Lar Hothem, authors of *School Collectibles of the Past*; they are listed in the Directory under Ohio.

Cardboard, snap lid, 1 lg compartment, 7¼x1x2½" **15.00**
Frame box, ABC on lid paper, orig key, 8⅜" L **22.50**
Wood, Bronsdon hardware, sliding top, 9" L **45.00**
Wood, combination lock, twin knobs at end, 8⅝x1½x2½" **30.00**
Wood, ruler on side, sliding top, 1-compartment, extra long **55.00**
Wood, Schumacher's Cash Store, sliding top, 9" L **50.00**
Wood, sliding top, pull-out ruler, 2-compartment, 9⅜" L **65.00**

Schoop, Hedi

Swiss-born Hedi Schoop started her ceramics business in North Hollywood in 1940. With a talented crew of about twenty decorators, she produced figurines, figure-vases, console sets, TV lamps, and other decorative housewares — much of which was accented with gold or platinum trim. Schoop's pottery closed after a fire destroyed the building in 1958. Marks are impressed or printed. For further information we recommend *The Collector's Encyclopedia of California Pottery* by our advisor, Jack Chipman; he is listed in the Directory under California.

Photo courtesy Pat and Kris Secor

Tray, lady figural, flowing skirt forms tray, 10x13", from $175.00 to 225.00.

Ashtray, ballerina on triangular form, 10" W **175.00**
Box, faux marble, pnt details, w/lid **75.00**
Cookie jar, Darner Doll **350.00**
Cookie jar, King **600.00**
Darner Doll, pk & gr stripes **250.00**
Figurine, Asian musician (& dancer), pr **200.00**
Figurine, ballerina, HP, no gold, 11½" **260.00**
Figurine, clown, ft wide apart, holds barbell aloft, 13" **185.00**
Figurine, Conchita, 13" **145.00**
Figurine, Debutante, flower holder, HP, 12½" **150.00**
Figurine, Dutch man & woman, pk/cream/bl gloss, 11", 9½", pr ..**125.00**
Figurine, girl w/ponytail in pk & wht, flower basket holder **85.00**
Figurine, Josephine, HP, no gold, 13" **225.00**
Figurine, lady w/flowers, cream/brn/yel/peach, 13" **120.00**
Figurine, Oriental girl, #215, 11½" **100.00**
Figurine, Oriental girl w/basket on hip, 12½" **125.00**
Figurine, Oriental girl w/bowl, #216 ....**100.00**
Figurine, Oriental girl w/umbrella, gr, #220, 12" **110.00**
Figurine, Repose, heavy gold, 13" **125.00**

Figurine, rooster, 13" **165.00**
Lamp, peasant lady figural **225.00**
Planter, pinched irregular rim, 12" L **75.00**
Vase, butterflies, bulbous, pk int, 9½" **85.00**
Vase, duck form **75.00**

Scouting Collectibles

Scouting was founded in England in 1907 by a retired Major General, Lord Robert Baden-Powell. Its purpose is the same today as it was then — to help develop physically strong, mentally alert boys and to teach them basic fundamentals of survival and leadership. The movement soon spread to the United States, and in 1910 a Chicago publisher, William Boyce, set out to establish Scouting in America. The first World Scout Jamboree was held in 1911 in England. Baden-Powell was honored as the Chief Scout of the World. In 1926 he was awarded the Silver Buffalo Award in the United States. He was knighted in 1929 for distinguished military service and for his Scouting efforts. Baden-Powell died in 1941. For more information you may contact our advisor, R.J. Sayers, author of *Guide to Scouting Collectibles*, whose address (and ordering information regarding his book) may be found in the Directory under North Carolina.

Boy Scouts

Medal, Eagle Scout, Be Prepared, eagle, and BSA, with red, white, and blue ribbon, Stange #3, 1974-78, $35.00.

Axe, BSA, #1002, w/sheath #1003, Collins **50.00**
Badge, tenderfoot; TH Foley Mfg, long knot, lg, 1912-17 ....**50.00**
Belt buckle, Nat'l Jamboree, Max Silber, brass, 1960 ....**35.00**
Boatswain's pipe, Sea Scout, #1086 ....**10.00**
Bookends, BSA, brass, #1726, 1933-37 ....**20.00**
Breeches, Official Scout; #598, lace-up leg **30.00**
Buckle, BSA leader, sterling w/leather belt, #514, 1923-32 ....**30.00**
Bugle, BSA, Conn, brass, #1277, 1925-32 ....**22.00**
Calendar, BSA, #3018, 1912-17 ....**25.00**
Camera, BSA, Brownie, #1395, 1933-37 ....**15.00**
Canteen, BSA, Wearever, cork plug/screw top, 1924-29 ....**12.00**
Card, membership; Lone Scout, 1918, 3x5" **10.00**
Cards, motto; BSA, #3024, 1933-37 ....**30.00**
Coin, Nat'l Jamboree, brass, 1957 ....**5.00**
Compass, BSA, flip-top, #1076, 1925-32 ....**12.00**
Compass, BSA, Magnapole, #1204, wht enamel dial, 1918-24 .....**20.00**
Cook kit, BSA, Wearever Aluminum, #1200, 6-pc, 1924-29 ....**20.00**
Creamer & sugar bowl, Nat'l Jamboree, 1964 ....**7.00**
Cuff links, Nat'l Jamboree, souvenir, enamel logo, 1964 ....**10.00**
Cup, BSA, adjustable, full logo, brass/NP, 1912-17 ....**20.00**
Desk flag set, Nat'l Jamboree, wood base, 1957 ....**6.00**
Drum, street; BSA, logo, lg, #1154, 1933-37 ....**25.00**

Eating kit, BSA, Shrade, leather pouch, 1925-32, 3-pc **17.50**
Field glass, BSA, #1077, 1912-17 ....**50.00**
Fire-making equipment, BSA, 1930s, EX in graphic box **60.00**
Fire-making kit, BSA, bow & leather thong, #1532, 1925-32 ....**15.00**
First Aid Kit, Hospital Corps, #1101, 1912-17 ....**40.00**
Flag, troop; Nat'l Jamboree, w/logo, 3x5', 1957 ....**50.00**
Flashlight, BSA, 90-degree type, gr-over-brass, #1278, 1925-32 ...**10.00**
Flint & steel kit, BSA, #1505, 1925-32 ....**7.50**
Guide rope, BSA, #1276 ....**5.00**
Handbook, Lone Scout, 1918 ....**20.00**
Harmonica, BSA Marine Band, #1256 ....**25.00**
Knickerbockers, BSA, #513, scarce, 1918-24 ....**65.00**
Knife, BSA, #1005, ebony hdl, brass lining, w/shackle **90.00**
Lantern, camp; BSA, Baldwin, 1912-17 ....**22.00**
Lantern, folding; BSA, #1258, 1925-32 ....**10.00**
Lighter, Nat'l Jamboree Appreciation, Zippo, 1969 ....**7.00**
Mess kit, BSA, Urton, #1535, 1925-32, lg, 7-pc **22.00**
Microscope, BSA, brass, #1085, 1912-17 ....**100.00**
Mug, Nat'l Jamboree, 1960 ....**2.00**
Neckerchief, Leaders; Nat'l Jamboree, stenciled logo, 1935 ....**85.00**
Neckerchief, Nat'l Jamboree, bl, full sq, w/logo, 1935 ....**45.00**
Pants, BSA, gr cotton, 1933-37 ....**5.00**
Paperweight, Nat'l Jamboree, Lucite, Ladies Appreciation, '64 ....**7.00**
Patch, Committee; Nat'l Jamboree, bl felt, wide dmn, 1935 ....**135.00**
Patch, scribe; Second Class, gold emblem, on tan sq, 1918-24 ...**100.00**
Patch, shirt; BSA, 2-line **100.00**
Patch, Special Ushers; Nat'l Jamboree, felt, 1935 ....**145.00**
Patch, tenderfoot; BSA, #47, on tan sq **20.00**
Pedometer, 100-mile; BSA, #1192, 1925-32 ....**10.00**
Pin, Assistant Scoutmaster; First Class, red enamel, 1½" **120.00**
Pin, First Class, miniature, #36 ....**15.00**
Pin, monogram; Lone Scout, 1915-24 ....**50.00**
Pin, Press Club; BSA, #347, 1933-37 ....**10.00**
Pin, Quill Award; Lone Scout, highest award pin, 1915-24 ....**400.00**
Pin, scarf; Deputy Commissioner, #63, bl enamel, 1918-24 ....**100.00**
Pocketwatch, BSA, Triumph, #1268, silver case, 1918-24 ....**50.00**
Ring, Nat'l Jamboree, sterling silver, 1950 ....**15.00**
Scarf, ladies; Nat'l Jamboree, silk, 1953 ....**11.00**
Sewing kit, BSA, #1061, 1912-17 ....**22.00**
Souvenir book, Nat'l Jamboree, 1953 ....**10.00**
T-shirt, Nat'l Jamboree, 1950 ....**7.00**
Tie rack, BSA, compo wood, #1742, 1933-37 ....**10.00**
Wall plaque, BSA, compo wood, #5096 ....**3.00**
Watch, stop; BSA, Excelsior, #1289 ....**25.00**
Watch, Sun; BSA, #1488, 1933-37 ....**15.00**
Watch fob, BSA, #305, leather strap, 1925-32 ....**50.00**
Watch fob, Tenderfoot patrol leader, 1912-17 ....**75.00**
Whistle, BSA, police type, chrome-over-brass, #1006, 1925-32 .....**4.00**
Wristwatch, BSA, 6-jewel, leather strap, #1547, 1925-32 ....**25.00**

Girl Scouts

Collecting Girl Scout memorabilia is a hobby that is growing nationwide. When Sir Baden-Powell founded the Boy Scout Movement in England, it proved to be too attractive and too well adaped to youth to limit its great opportunities to boys alone. The sister organization, known in England as the Girl Guides, quickly followed and was equally successful. Mrs. Juliette Low, an American visitor to England and a personal friend of the father of Scouting, realized the tremendous future of the movement for her own country, and with the active and friendly cooperation of the Baden-Powells, she founded the Girl Guides in America, enrolling the first patrols in Savannah, Georgia, in March 1912. In 1915 National Headquarters were established in Washington, D.C., and the name was changed to Girl Scouts. The first National

Convention was held in 1914, and each succeeding year has shown growth and increased enthusiasm in this steadily growing army of girls and young women who are learning in the happiest ways to combine patriotism, outdoor activities of every kind, skill in every branch of domestic science, and high standards of community service. Today there are over 400,000 girl Scouts and more than 22,000 leaders. Mr. Sayers is also our Girl Scout advisor.

Armband, GSA, embr GSM on khaki, pre-uniform 100.00
Belt buckle, GSA, 1936 ....10.00
Book, Nature; GSA, for leaders 5.00
Camera, GSA, Brownie, box type, 1957 ....15.00
Camera, GSA, Univex, bellows type, 1938 ....50.00
Cap, Den Mother's, Garrison type, bl, w/pin, 1960s 5.00
Compact, unofficial, bronze, w/mirror, 1½" sq 20.00
Cup, collapsible; GSA, aluminum, 1950 ....5.00
Diary, GSA, 1929 ....15.00
Doll, GSA, Sylvia, 1940 era 50.00
Doll, uniform; GSA, Terri Lee, hard plastic, 1949-53, 16" 20.00
Emblem, GSA, Hospital Aide 20.00
Flag, GSA, Brownie, sm, 1930s 25.00
Flag, troop; GSA, wool, 1930s 30.00
Locket, unofficial, brass, opens to hold picture, sm 20.00
Medal, GSA, Honorable Mention, 1920s 100.00
Medal, Silver; Life Saving, Maltese cross, gr ribbon, 1916 ....300.00
Patch, GSA, Treasurer's, gr twill, 1937 ....10.00
Plantation cookie jar, GSA, litho 40.00
Postcard, GSA, outdoors type, 1928, set of 6 ....25.00
Poster, GSA, Cookie Drive, color litho, 1923 ....100.00
Poster, GSA, 25th Anniversary, 1937 ....40.00
Scarf, Nat'l Jamboree, silk, w/logo, 1960 ....7.00
Uniform, GSA Brownie, middy & bloomers, 1918 ....200.00
Whistle, cylinder, GSA, 1920s 20.00

Scrimshaw

The most desirable examples of the art of scrimshaw can be traced back to the first half of the 19th century to the heyday of the whaling industry. Some voyages lasted for several years, and conditions on board were often dismal. Sailors filled the long hours by using the tools of their trade to engrave whale teeth and make boxes, pie crimpers (jagging wheels), etc., from the bone and teeth of captured whales. Eskimos also made scrimshaw, sometimes borrowing designs from the sailors who traded with them.

Beware of fradulent pieces; fakery is prevalent in this field. Many carved teeth are of recent synthetic manufacture (examples engraved with information such as ship's or captain's names, dates, places, etc., should be treated with extreme caution) and have no antique or collectible value. A listing of most of these plastic items has been published by the Kendall Whaling Museum in Sharon, Massachusetts. If you're in doubt or a novice collector, it's best to deal with reputable people who **guarantee** the items they sell. Our advisor for this category is John Rinaldi; he is listed in the Directory under Maine. See also Powder Horns.

Busk, whalebone w/eng hearts/flowers/etc, 12" 660.00
Fid, cvd whalebone, faced bipyramidal, mushroom hdl, 1800s 275.00
Mallet, whalebone, incised decor, 19th C, 4½" head, 12½" hdl .590.00
Panbone, folky whaling scene w/longboats, 1840s, 16x2½" 2,395.00
Panbone, frigate starboard view, 1830s, EX color, 6¾x11", VG ...990.00
Pie crimper, whale ivory, 2-pc hdl, 1840s, 1¾" wheel, 7" 1,100.00
Seam rubber, cvd whalebone, 1800s, 5" 275.00
Swift, trn/incised/stained whale ivory, 1850s, opens to 20" 2,650.00

Tooth, Am ship w/flags/portrait/etc, mc stain, 1840-50, 6¾" ..4,750.00
Tooth, lady's portrait, deep patina, 1840s, 5¾x2¾" 975.00
Tooth, military camp/Zachary Taylor in uniform, ca 1845, 6½" ...1,875.00
Tooth, Neptune King of the Sea/Am frigate, 1840s, 5x2¾" 2,950.00
Tooth, Scottish highlander man & woman, mc, 1830s, 7¼", pr ..1,785.00
Tooth, ship/whaling scene/lighthouse, mc stain, 1860s, 5¼" ..2,350.00
Tooth, ship w/Am eagle/banner/lady's portrait/Turk, 1850s, 6¾" .1,290.00
Tooth, The Day Is Ours, sailor, border, red stain, 1860s, 6" 2,490.00
Tooth, warship, Victory From Traffalgar Ad Nelson, 8½x3" ..2,875.00
Walking stick, rope-cvd whalebone shaft, horn hdl, 1850s, 35" 985.00

Sebastians

Sebastian miniatures were first produced in 1938 by Prescott W. Baston in Marblehead, Massachusetts. Since then more than six hundred have been modeled. These figurines have been sold through gift shops all over the country, primarily in the New England states. In 1976 Baston withdrew his Sebastians from production. Under an agreement with the Lance Corporation of Hudson, Massachusetts, one hundred designs were selected to be produced by that company under Baston's supervision. Those remaining were discontinued. In the time since then, the older figurines have become very collectible. Price is determined by three factors: 1) in production/out of production; 2) labels — color of oval label, i.e. red, blue, green, etc.; Marblehead label, a green and silver palette-shaped label used until 1977; or no label; 3) condition. If there is no label and the varnish coat is quite yellowed, then it is considered to be of the Marblehead era. Dates are merely copyright dates and have no particular significance in regard to value. (Signed) 'P.W. Baston' should only have impact on price when the signature is an actual autograph. Most pieces are manufactured with an imprinted 'P.W. Baston' on the base. Baston died in 1984; the miniatures are now being done by P.W. Baston, Jr.

John and Priscilla Alden, 2⅞", $35.00.

Basketball Hall of Fame 35.00
Budding Philatelist, pnt 40.00
Chiquita Banana 300.00
Christmas Morning 30.00
Diedrich Knickerbocker, Marblehead era 50.00
Elizabeth Monroe 115.00
First at Bat 35.00
George & the Hatchet 400.00
House of 7 Gables, Marblehead era 60.00
Ice Sleigh, St Paul Carnival 5.00
James Madison, pewter 65.00
John Monroe 115.00
Mark Antony, Marblehead era 65.00
Mrs Obocell 400.00
Paul Revere, Masons 225.00
Penny Shop, Marblehead label 50.00

Romeo, Marblehead era **70.00**
Sampling the Stew, Marblehead era **55.00**
Scrooge **25.00**
Sir Frances Drake **250.00**
Stagecoach, Marblehead era **65.00**
Swanboat, Masons **300.00**
Uncle Sam, Marblehead era **50.00**
Wickford Weavers **300.00**

Sevres

Fine-quality porcelains have been made in Sevres, France, since the early 1700s. Rich ground colors were often hand painted with portraits, scenics, and florals. Some pieces were decorated with transfer prints and decalcomania; many were embellished with heavy gold. These wares are the most respected of all French porcelains. Their style and designs have been widely copied, and some of the items listed below are Sevres-type wares.

Vase, florals on white with gilt-traced olive rim and foot, gilt handles, plinth base, dated 1809, 13", $2,000.00.

Box, jewel; bouquet among gold scrolls, hinged lid, 3¾x8" **350.00**
Box, trinket; cobalt w/gold, musical, hinged lid, 4¼x3¾" **550.00**
Centerpc, 4 mc vignettes on yel, ornate hdls/gold, 5x13x8" **1,500.00**
Jar, courtiers & floral panels on yel, w/lid, 21" **990.00**
Lamp, lady's portrait on bl, goat's-head hdls, 20" **200.00**
Plate, Cupid & maiden allegorical, much gold, 9½", pr **330.00**
Plate, Marechal Duroc (Mm Foix), sgn Rochelle, 9⅜", pr **660.00**
Plate, Queen Louise portrait, gold trim, 10" **125.00**
Urn, lovers & landscape reserves, amphora form, w/lid, 26", pr ..**1,650.00**
Urn, romantic couples in oval reserve, mtd as lamp, 24", pr **375.00**
Vase, earthenware, Beaux Arts-style decor, silver mts, 7", pr **495.00**

Sewer Tile

Whimsies, advertising novelties, and other ornamental items were sometimes made in potteries where the primary product was simply tile.

Figure, cat, seated, EX detail & some hand tooling, 5¾" **770.00**
Figure, cat sleeping, hand molded, 7" L **360.00**
Figure, dog on rectangular base, firing crack, 7¼" **150.00**
Figure, dog seated, gr-brn mottle, dtd 1939, 10¼" **385.00**
Figure, frog on rnd base, 5¾" **127.50**
Figure, lion battling serpent, old chips, 8x11" **220.00**
Figure, lion on rectangular base, 9" **140.00**
Figure, owl, gray mottle w/blk pnt details, 6¾" **245.00**
Figure, owl w/wht clay eyes, sgn/dtd 1935, 8¾" **355.00**
Figure, rooster, appl stone eyes, sgn/dtd 1979, 18", EX **220.00**
Lady's shoes, old dk bl ribbon laces, 5", pr **140.00**
Plaque, dog's head on dmn bk w/initials, 8¼" L **200.00**

Sewing Items

Sewing collectibles continue to intrigue collectors, and fine 19th-century and earlier pieces are commanding higher prices due to increased demand and scarcity. Complete needlework boxes and chatelaines in original condition are rare. But even though they may be incomplete, as long as boxes contain fittings of the period and the chains of the chatelaine are intact and contemporary with the style and the individual holders original and matching the brooch, they should be considered prime additions to any collection. As 19th-century items become harder to find, new trends in collecting develop. Among them are needlebooks, many of which were decorated with horses, children, beautiful ladies, etc. Some were giveaways printed with advertisements of products and businesses. Even early pins are collectible; the earliest were made in two parts with the round head attached separately. Pin disks, pin cubes, and other pin holders make interesting additions to a sewing collection as well.

Tape measures are now popular. Victorian figurals command premium prices. Early wooden examples of transferware and Tunbridge ware have gained in popularity as have figurals of vegetable ivory, celluloid, and other early plastics. From the 20th century, tatting shuttles made of plastics as well as bone, brass, sterling, and wood decorated with Art Nouveau, Deco, and more modern designs are in demand; so are darning eggs, stillettos, and thimbles. Because of the decline in the popularity of needlework after the 1920s (due to increased production of machine-made items), novelty-type items were made in an attempt to regain consumer interest, and many collectors today find them appealing.

Watch for reproductions. Sterling thimbles are being made in Holland and in the U.S. and are available in many designs from the Victorian era. But the originals are usually plainly marked, either in the inside apex or outside on the band. Avoid testing gold and silver thimbles for content; this often destroys the inside marks. Instead, research the manufacturer's mark; this will often denote the material as well. Even though the reproductions are well finished, they do not have the manufacturers' marks. Many thimbles are being made specifically for the collectible market; reproductions of porcelain thimbles are also found. Prices should reflect the age and availability of these thimbles. Our advisor for this category is Marjorie Geddes; she is listed in the Directory under Oregon. See also Mauchline Ware.

Lady's chatelaine, multipurpose type, silverplated brass set with green brilliants, seven matching tools on chains, unmarked, $950.00.

Bodkin, whale ivory, trn/scribed head, puzzle rings, 5¼" **250.00**
Box, bird's-eye maple vnr, appl cvgs/moldings, 1843, 12" L **990.00**
Box, wood w/flags/geometrics/medallion inlays, 10½" L **395.00**
Buttonhole cutter, steel **45.00**
Chatelaine, Nouveau style w/5 tools, sterling silver, EX **1,100.00**
Clamp, hemming; iron w/ribbed design, 4¼" **95.00**

Crochet hook, flat ivory (not bone), graduated set of 3 ....90.00
Darner, clear glass w/mc spatter, 6¼" 160.00
Darner, milk glass w/pk & bl splotches cased in clear, 6⅜" 150.00
Darner, milk glass w/red star cased in clear, 4⅞" 350.00
Darning tool, ivory & lignum vitae, English, 19th C, 8" 175.00
Dressmaker's form, thin cardboard w/tabs & metal brads, M 85.00
Fabric weight, brn marble, eng sissors 1 side, eng initials 40.00
Gauge, knitting needle; bell shape 48.00

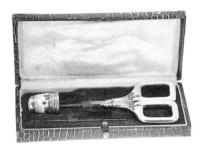

Kit, Delft-design enamel on sterling scissors and thimble, with needle in original velvet-lined box (probably German made), $195.00.

Kit, celluloid & NP brass, Olds Hotel, ¾x2¼" 35.00
Knitting sheath, cvd wood 145.00
Measure, brass, German inn 350.00
Measure, celluloid, bowl of flowers 120.00
Measure, celluloid, FAB advertising 22.00
Measure, celluloid, General Electric refrigerator, 1930s, EX 40.00
Measure, celluloid, Indian boy, broken tape 95.00
Measure, celluloid, kangaroo 120.00
Measure, celluloid, lady in cabana 295.00
Measure, celluloid, Little Red Riding Hood 195.00
Measure, celluloid, pig w/hat 35.00
Measure, celluloid, sunflower 125.00
Measure, celluloid, trout 85.00
Measure, plastic, dressmaker's dummy 45.00
Measure, vegetable ivory, bbl, M 125.00
Measure, vegetable ivory, w/up bbl, some wear 50.00
Measure/pincushion, celluloid, dress form, pk 45.00
Needle & thread holder, sterling w/inset, plain, 2½" 140.00
Needle case, ivory/blk Bakelite parasol shape 150.00
Needle case, vegetable ivory, 4" 85.00
Needle holder, rosewood, 6 compartments, brass-plated lid 135.00
Needle holder, vegetable ivory, EX cvg, 2½", EX 95.00
Needle sharpener, Dold Animal Foods, oval emery, 1¾x2¾" 65.00
Netting shuttle, brass, W Lord, 5½" 165.00
Pincushion, brn vegetable ivory ped base 85.00
Pincushion, elephant, metal w/cushion in bk, Germany 125.00
Pincushion, Mammy figural, w/spool holder 65.00
Quilt pattern, openwork leather star, 7½" 30.00
Sewing bird, brass, w/pincushion, EX 250.00
Tatting shuttle, bone, 3" 45.00
Tatting shuttle, celluloid, 4" 25.00
Thimble, aluminum, John Hancock Ins advertising 12.50
Thimble, brass, Scotch Gold, advertising 12.50
Thimble, sterling, Simons, mk Priscilla 40.00
Thimble, sterling, Simons, 10 panels at base 40.00
Thimble, 10k gold, floral band, Simons 145.00
Thimble, 800 silver w/5 bl stones, unmk 125.00
Thimble holder, vegetable ivory, acorn form 80.00
Thread winder, cvd MOP, rare 135.00

Sewing Machines

The fact that Thomas Saint, an English cabinetmaker, invented

the first sewing machine in 1790 was unknown until 1874 when Newton Wilson, an English sewing machine manufacturer and patentee, chanced on the drawings included in a patent specification describing methods of making boots and shoes. By the middle of the 19th century, several patents were granted to American inventors, among them Isaac M. Singer, whose machine used a treadle. These machines were ruggedly built, usually of cast iron. By the 1860s and '70s, the sewing machine had become a popular commodity, and the ironwork became more detailed and ornate.

Though rare machines are costly, many of the old oak treadle machines (especially these brands: Davis, Home, Household, National, New Home, Singer, Weed, Wheeler & Wilson, and Willcox & Gibbs) have only nominal value. Machines manufactured after 1875 are generally very common as most were mass produced. Values for these later sewing machines range from $50.00 to $100.00. Many children's machines have been marketed; refer to *Toy and Miniature Sewing Machines* by Glenda Thomas for more information. Our advisor for this category is Peter Frei; he is listed in the Directory under Massachusetts. In the listings that follow, unless noted otherwise, values are suggested for machines in excellent working order.

Child's, Betsy Ross, electric, ca 1949, 6¼x7¾x4½" 95.00
Child's, Casige, bl-gr metal, MIG, British Zone 125.00
Child's, Casige, eagle on gr metal, Germany, British Zone 100.00
Child's, FW Muller #12, cast metal, 8⅜x11⅜x6¾" 225.00
Child's, Gateway, red-pnt ltweight steel 50.00

Photo courtesy Peter Frei

Child's, Ideal, M, $1,700.00.

Child's, Jaymar, battery, 5½x7x4" 50.00
Child's, KAYanEE Sewmaster, pk sheet metal, 6x7⅛x4⅜" 75.00
Child's, KAYanEE Sewmaster, red & wht, 6¾x7¾x4⅜" 50.00
Child's, Little Mary Mix Up (unmk), gr metal, '30s, 7x7¾x4" 75.00
Child's, Little Modiste, red metal, batteries, Japan 75.00
Child's, Necchi, red plastic, 1950s, 5½x7¼x2½" 35.00
Child's, Olympia, manual or battery, Japan, 5½x7x4" 35.00
Child's, Princess, belt drive, Made in Japan, 5¾x8¾x3⅝" 175.00
Child's, Singer Model 20, gold decor on blk, 1910, 6¼x7x3" 225.00
General Electric Featherweight, gr, 1949, EX 400.00
Goodrich, treadle, quarter-sawn oak cabinet, EX 195.00
Peerless Automatic 495.00
Singer #3, portable, hand crank, dome case, 1898, NM 250.00
Singer Feather Weight, NM 325.00

Shaker Items

The Shaker community was founded in America in 1776 at

Niskeyuna, New York, by a small group of English 'Shaking Quakers.' The name referred to a group dance which was part of their religious rites. Their leader was Mother Ann Lee. By 1815 their membership had grown to more than one thousand in eighteen communities as far west as Indiana and Kentucky. But in less than a decade, their numbers began to decline until today only a handful remain. Their furniture is prized for its originality, simplicity, workmanship, and practicality. Few pieces were signed. Some were carefully finished to enhance the natural wood; a few were painted.

Although other methods were used earlier, most Shaker boxes were of oval construction with overlapping 'fingers' at the seams to prevent buckling as the wood aged. Boxes with original paint fetch triple the price of an unpainted box; number of fingers and size should also be considered.

Although the Shakers were responsible for weaving a great number of baskets, their methods are not easily distinguished from those of their outside neighbors, and it is nearly impossible without first-hand knowledge to positively attribute a specific example to their manufacture. They were involved in various commercial efforts other than woodworking — among them sheep and dairy farming, sawmilling, and pipe and brick making. They were the first to raise crops specifically for seed and to market their product commercially. They perfected a method to recycle paper and were able to produce wrinkle-free fabrics. Our advisor for this category is Nancy Winston; she is listed in the Directory under New Hampshire. Standard two-letter state abbreviations have been used throughout the following listings.

Key:
bj — bootjack
CB — Canterbury
EF — Enfield
NL — New Lebanon
PH — Pleasant Hill
ML — Mt. Lebanon
SDL — Sabbathday Lake
WV — Watervliet

Apple corer & slicer, wood, 4-blade, riveted, CB, 5x4⅝" dia 350.00
Armchair, maple w/stain, 3-slat bk/splint seat, ML/1950, 41" 700.00
Barrel, wooden staves, all wood, 16¼x17¼" 360.00
Basket, ash, ear hdls, dbl bottom, str sides, 8½x12½" 400.00
Basket, bl-gr stencil, sq bottom, 7½x10½" dia 175.00
Basket, blk ash, ear hdls, wrapped rim, CB, 5½x14x12½" 175.00
Basket, field; ash, rectangular, shaped hdl, CB, 10x23x17" 750.00
Basket, splint, bentwood rim hdls, sm break, 5x9" 300.00
Basket, splint, 4-hdl, 19th C, 14¾x19¼" dia, EX 500.00
Basket, utility; blk ash, wrapped rim, CB, 8½x12"+hdl 300.00
Basket, woven splint, bentwood hdl, oblong, 3½x6½x5¼" 165.00
Basket, woven splint, bl woven bands, oblong, 4¼x13¼x10½" ...95.00
Bed, trundle; oak, gr pnt, wooden wheels, ML, 68x31" 400.00
Bonnet, striped irid silk, EF, 19th C, 7¼", EX 430.00
Box, chip; dvtl pine, ash hdl, red stain, 9¼x15x9⅜" 1,840.00
Box, handkerchief; poplarware, kidskin & ribbon trim, 1950s 300.00
Box, pine, brn pnt, nailed, sm rpr, 15x26x16" 600.00
Box, pine/ash, bl-gr pnt, str seam, iron tacks, 4x8½" 230.00
Box, pine/birch, yel stain, satin lined, ML, 2x4½x2¾" 400.00
Box, wood; pine, old rpt, iron hinges, nailed, CB, 31x24x16" ..3,200.00
Box, 2 abbreviated fingers, maple/pine, bl pnt, 2¼x4⅜" 315.00
Box, 2-finger, pine/maple, orange stain, CB, 2⅛x5⅛x3¼" 1,500.00
Box, 2-finger, pine/maple, orig gr pnt, copper tacks, 6" L 800.00
Box, 2-finger, pine/maple, yel pnt/copper tacks, 1¼x3¼x2" ...5,175.00
Box, 3-finger, pine/maple, old red pnt, 2⅞x11x7¾" 350.00
Box, 3-finger, pine/maple, red rpt, copper tacks, 10¼" dia 520.00
Box, 3-finger, 19th C, 4¼x11½" 260.00
Box, 4-finger, bentwood, worn gr pnt, steel tacks, 10½" 1,045.00
Brush, wood & horsehair, red pnt, CB, 14¼" 150.00
Carrier, tin, rectangular, mid-point hdl, CB, 3x11¼x8" 345.00
Carrier, 3-finger, pine/birch, stained, swing hdl, 6⅜" L 495.00
Carrier, 3-finger, yel pnt, CB, 19th C, 6½x11" 500.00

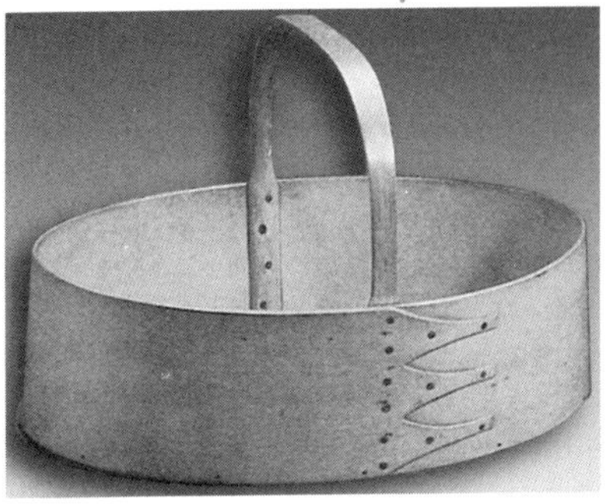

Carrier, 3-finger, yellow paint, fixed handle, Mt. Lebanon, New York, 19th century, 7¼x11¼", NM, $8,625.00.

Carrier, 3-finger, yel pnt, fixed hdl, ML, 19th C, 7¼x11" 1,200.00
Carrier, 4-finger, pine/ash w/stain, copper tacks, CB, 13" L 395.00
Chair, side; maple, salmon pnt, 3-slat, tape seat, CB, 41" 975.00
Chair, side; maple, slat bk, cane seat, CB, 1840s, 41", pr 675.00
Chair, side; maple, 3-slat bk, mc tape seat, CB, 40½" 750.00
Chair, side; maple, 3-slat bk, rush seat, ML, 38½" 800.00
Chair, side; maple, 3-slat bk, rush seat, ML, 41¼" 1,035.00
Chair, side; maple, 3-slat bk, splint seat, ML, 37" 115.00
Chair, work; maple/pine, old yel rpt, leather seat, 40¾" 1,800.00
Cup, wood, domed lid w/trn knob pnt blk, CB, 2⅞x4¼" 260.00
Cupboard, hanging; pine, red pnt, panel door, 1850s, 34x19" .1,000.00
Cupboard, hanging; pine, red stain, panel door, rprs, 31x20" 750.00
Cupboard, pine, old bl pnt, 1 door, SDL, 1790s, 37x36x17" .17,250.00
Cupboard, pine, yel stain, 2-shelf top, CB, 1870s, 28x25x17" .1,955.00
Cupboard, tool; pine, walnut drw fronts, gray pnt, MA, 45x39" .1,955.00
Dbl cupboard over case of drawers, pine, NY, 1840s, 37x37x17" .27,600.00
Desk, school; pine, orange grpt, slant top, MA, 32x66x31" 1,150.00
Dipper, heavy gauge tin, long hdl w/D-shaped ring, CB, 13" 345.00
Dust pan, commercially produced w/stencil decor, CB, 9" L 175.00
Engraving, Shakers...New York, unsgn, ca 1830, 8¾x12¾" 1,955.00
Firkin, pine staves, orig bl pnt, iron hoops, CB, 11x13" 1,600.00
Footstool, pine, brn stain, nailed, 5-board, 9½x15x8" 750.00
Lap desk, dvtl butternut/cherry/poplar, w/till, 3½x21x18" 3,735.00
Letter, death of loved one, CB, 1798, 12x7", EX 150.00
Lithograph, Shakers Near Lebanon, Pendleton, ca 1830, 9x13" ..1,035.00
Measure, grain; oak/pine, ME stencil, 1880-96, 4x7½" 60.00
Pail, pine staves, ochre-orange pnt, CB or EF, 7¼x10" 1,380.00
Pail, pine staves, orig yel pnt, iron hoops, 7x5⅜" 1,035.00
Pail, tongue-&-groove wood staves, bail hdl, lid, 9¾" dia 230.00
Pitcher, cream; heavy tin, soldered hdl, CB, 3¼x2⅞" 175.00
Rocker, #3, armless, old finish w/decal, NY, ca 1900, 33" 230.00
Rocker, #4, maple, ebony stain, 3-slat, tape seat, ML, 34¾" 400.00
Rocker, #6, maple, blk pnt, rpl seat, ML, 41¾" 1,380.00
Rocker, #7, armless, orig varnish, ML, 42" 500.00
Rocker, bentwood, orig finish, rpl tape seat, 37" 445.00
Rocker, maple, 3-slat bk, mc tape seat, CB, 39½" 600.00
Sack, grain; woven w/stencil, EF, 37½x18½", EX 115.00
Seed sower, pine/poplar w/galvanized metal, red pnt, EF, 10" 220.00
Sieve, stained wood, 19th C, 3⅝x6⅞" 115.00
Stove, CI, canted sides, hinged door, rnd hearth, 16x39x12" 460.00
Stove, CI, canted sides, 3-leg w/penny ft, 17x33x13" 500.00
Swift, maple, yel wash, trn cup, collapsible, MA, 24½" 420.00
Table, curly birch/pine, red wash, 1-drw, EF, 1840, 27x36x23" ...8,050.00
Table, drop leaf; pine/ash/birch, red traces, CB, 72" L 2,000.00
Table, pine, red pnt, 2-board top, 1-drw, NH/1850s, 61" L 2,300.00

Shaving Mugs

Between 1865 and 1920, owning a personalized shaving mug was the order of the day, with the occupationals enjoying their greatest popularity. Most men having occupational mugs would frequent the barber shop several times a week where their mugs were clearly visible for all to see in the barber's rack. As a matter of fact, this display was in many ways the index of the individual town or neighborhood.

During the first twenty years, blank mugs were almost entirely imported from France, Germany, and Austria and were hand painted in this country. Later on, some china was produced by local companies. It is noteworthy that American vitreous china is inferior to the imported Limoges and is subject to extreme crazing.

Artists employed by the American barber supply companies were for the most part extremely talented and capable of executing any design the owner required, depicting his occupation, fraternal affiliation, or preferred sport. When the mug was completed, the name and the gold trim were always added in varying degrees, depending on the price paid by the customer. This price was determined by the barber who added his markup to that of the barber-supply company. As mentioned above, the popularity of the occupational shaving mug diminished with the advent of World War I and the introduction by Gillette of the safety razor. Later followed the blue laws forcing barber shops to close on Sundays, thereby eliminating the political and social discussions for which they were so well noted.

Occupational shaving mugs are the most sought after of the group which would include those with sport affiliations. Fraternal mugs, although desirable, do not command the same price as the occupationals. Occasionally, you will find the owner's occupation together with his fraternal affiliation. This combination could add anywhere between 25% to 50% to the price, which is dependent on the execution of the painting, rarity of the subject, and detail. Some subjects can be done very simply; others can be done in extreme detail, commanding substantially higher prices. It is fair to say, however, that the rarity of the occupation will dictate the price. Mugs which have lost the gold through wear lose between 20% and 30% of their value immediately. This would not apply to the gold trim around the rim, but to the loss of the name itself. Our advisor for this category is Burton Handelsman; he is listed in the Directory under New York.

Bl opaline, Fr, NM 125.00
Decorative, florals HP on wht w/gold, VG 25.00
Decorative, sailboat on ocean, rocky shore & gulls, name in gold ..135.00
Decorative, seaport town transfer print, EX 45.00
Decorative, tree branch & birds in flight, EX 35.00
Fraternal, Civil War Sons Association, commemorative metal, VG ...120.00

Occupational, Brew Master, very fine design, gold trim, $1,750.00.

Occupational, bookkeeper, man at desk, MIG, EX 600.00
Occupational, butcher, steer head & tools, gold name, Germany ..90.00
Occupational, lathe operator, man at work, worn gilt, VG 400.00
Occupational, lawyer, justice holding scales, rising sun 175.00
Occupational, milk man, man & 2-horse wagon, TV Limoges, rpr ...450.00
Occupational, minister, open Bible, gold name, CA Smith, EX 1,600.00
Occupational, pharmacist, mortar & pestle w/gold, Austria, EX ..150.00
Occupational, piano salesman, upright piano w/gold, Austria 700.00

Occupational, tailor, man at table, gold lettering, VG 220.00
Occupational, tinsmith, smelter, worn gilt, Germany, VG 210.00
Occupational, trainman standing along side engine 1,400.00
Occupational, trollyman, trolly & operator, Limoges, EX 375.00
Patriotic, eagle w/shield & flags, EX gold, ca 1927, Germany 210.00

Shawnee

The Shawnee Pottery Company operated in Zanesville, Ohio, from 1937 to 1961. They produced inexpensive novelty ware (vases, flowerpots, and figurines) as well as a very successful line of figural cookie jars, creamers, and salt and pepper shakers.

They also produced three dinnerware lines, the first of which, Valencia, was designed by Louise Bauer in 1937 for Sears & Roebuck. A starter set was given away with the purchase of one of their refrigerators. Second and most popular was the King Corn line. It was produced from 1946 to 1954, when the colors were changed to a lighter yellow for the kernels and darker green for the shucks. This variation was called Queen Corn. (Our values are for yellow corn prices unless white is noted in the description.) Their third dinnerware line, produced after 1954, was called Lobsterware. It was made in either black, brown, or gray; lobsters were usually applied to serving pieces and accessory items.

For further study we recommend these books: *The Collector's Guide to Shawnee Pottery* by our advisors, Janice and Duane Vanderbilt, who are listed in the Directory under Indiana; and *Shawnee Pottery, An Identification and Value Guide,* by Jim and Bev Mangus, who are listed in Ohio.

Cookie Jars

Basketweave, hexagonal, gold trim, mk USA, minimum value ..100.00
Cottage, mk USA 6, minimum value 650.00
Drum Major, airbrushed colors, mk USA, minimum value 200.00
Dutch Boy, decals/stripes/gold trim, mk USA, minimum value ..250.00
Dutch Boy, Happy, decals/gold trim, mk USA, minimum value .225.00
Dutch Boy, wht w/bl pants & trim, mk USA, minimum value 80.00
Dutch Girl, blk hair, bl skirt & trim, mk USA, minimum value ...75.00
Dutch Girl, gold decals, mk USA, minimum value 250.00
Dutch Girl, gr, mk Great Northern 1026, minimum value 250.00
Dutch Girl, plain wht head & bodice, mk USA, minimum value ..50.00
Elephant, sitting, plain wht, mk USA, minimum value 75.00
Fernware, octagonal, mk USA, minimum value 75.00
Fruit Basket, mk USA, minimum value 125.00
Jug, Pennsylvania Dutch design, mk USA, minimum value 150.00
Jug, plain colors, mk USA, minimum value 75.00
Little Chef, wht w/bl, mk USA, minimum value 75.00
Little Chef, wht w/gold trim, mk USA, minimum value 175.00
Muggsy, decals/gold trim, mk Pat Muggsy USA, minimum value ..550.00
Muggsy, plain, mk USA, minimum value 325.00

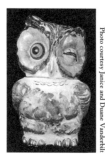

Owl, gold trim, marked USA, $225.00 minimum value.

Owl, wht w/mc trim, mk USA, minimum value 125.00
Puss 'N Boots, cold-pnt trim, minimum value 150.00
Puss 'N Boots, tail over ft, decals/gold trim, minimum value 375.00
Sailor Boy, decals/gold trim, mk USA, minimum value 550.00
Sailor Boy, plain wht, mk USA, minimum value 100.00
Smiley the Pig, bl bib, mk USA, minimum value 150.00
Smiley the Pig, clover buds, mk Pat Smiley USA, minimum value ...225.00
Smiley the Pig, mums, gold trim, mk USA, minimum value 325.00
Smiley the Pig, tulips, mk USA, minimum value 200.00
Snowflake, bean pot, yel, mk USA, minimum value 50.00
Winnie the Pig, clover bud, mk Pat Winnie USA, mimimum value ..300.00
Winnie the Pig, peach collar, minimum value 225.00
Winnie the Pig, red collar/gold trim, mk USA, minimum value ...350.00

Corn Line

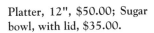
Platter, 12", $50.00; Sugar bowl, with lid, $35.00.

Bowl, cereal; mk #94 ....45.00
Bowl, fruit; mk #92 ....40.00
Bowl, mixing; mk #5, 5" 25.00
Bowl, mixing; mk #6, 6" 30.00
Bowl, vegetable; mk #95 ....35.00
Butter dish, #72 ....50.00
Casserole, mk #73, w/lid, sm, from $60 to 75.00
Casserole, mk #74, w/lid, lg 60.00
Cookie jar, mk #66 ....200.00
Corn holder, #79 ....32.00
Creamer, gold trim, mk USA 65.00
Creamer, mk #70 ....25.00
Cup, mk #90 ....30.00
Mug, mk #69 ....45.00
Pitcher, mk #71, lg 65.00
Plate, mk #68, 10" 35.00
Plate, mk #93, 8" 15.00
Platter, mk #96, 12" 50.00
Relish dish, mk #79 ....17.00
Saucer, mk #93 ....12.00
Shakers, Indian corn, pr 65.00
Shakers, lg, pr 30.00
Shakers, sm, pr 20.00
Shakers, wht corn, lg, pr 30.00
Shakers, wht corn, sm, pr 25.00
Sugar bowl, mk #78 ....35.00
Sugar bowl, wht corn, gold trim, mk USA 60.00
Sugar shaker, wht corn 60.00
Teapot, mk #65, 10-oz 175.00
Teapot, mk #75, gold trim, 30-oz 150.00
Teapot, mk #75, 30-oz 70.00

Kitchenware

Bowl, mixing; 5" 12.00

Bowl, mixing; 6" 15.00
Bowl, mixing; 7" 17.00
Coffeepot, Sunflower, mk USA 150.00
Creamer, elephant, decals/gold trim, mk Pat USA 175.00
Creamer, Flower & Fern, mk USA 17.00
Creamer, Pennsylvania Dutch, tilt jug, mk USA 10 ....80.00
Creamer, Puss 'N Boots, gold trim, mk Shawnee 85 ....250.00
Creamer, Sunflower, ball jug, mk USA 45.00
Creamer, Tulip, ball jug, mk USA 75.00
Lobster, plate, compartment 27.00
Lobster, range set, 4-pc 70.00
Lobster, relish pot, from $45 to 75.00
Lobster, salad set, 9-pc 275.00
Pie bird, wht w/mc trim 30.00
Pitcher, Bo Peep, airbrushing/gold trim, mk Shawnee 47 ....175.00
Pitcher, Bo Peep, bl bonnet, mk Pat Bo Peep 90.00
Pitcher, Charlie Chicken, pnt/decals/gold, mk Chanticleer 250.00
Pitcher, Fruit, ball jug, gold trim, mk Shawmee 80 ....125.00
Pitcher, Pennsylvania Dutch, ball jug, mk USA 64 ....95.00
Pitcher, Snowflake, ball jug, mk USA 50.00
Shakers, Bo Peep & Sailor Boy, sm, pr 20.00
Shakers, Charlie Chicken, gold trim, lg, pr 80.00
Shakers, Dutch Boy & Girl, decals/gold trim, lg, pr 110.00
Shakers, Farmer Pig, gold trim, sm, pr 47.00
Shakers, Flower & Fern, 4-sided, lg, pr 25.00
Shakers, flowerpots, gold trim, sm, pr 30.00
Shakers, fruit, mk USA, lg pr 30.00
Shakers, fruit, sm, pr 15.00
Shakers, jugs, bl, lg, pr 30.00
Shakers, jugs, Pennsylvania Dutch, lg, pr 55.00
Shakers, milk cans, sm, pr 15.00
Shakers, Muggsy, gold trim, sm, pr 100.00
Shakers, Muggsy, wht/bl trim, lg, pr 85.00
Shakers, Puss 'N Boots, gold trim, sm, pr 100.00
Shakers, Smiley, bl bib, lg 90.00
Shakers, Smiley, peach bib/decals/gold trim, lg, pr 150.00
Shakers, Smiley, peach bib/gold trim, sm, pr 85.00
Shakers, Winnie & Smiley, hearts, lg, pr 100.00
Shakers, Winnie & Smiley, hearts, sm, pr 60.00
Sugar bowl, bucket, mk Northern USA 1042 ....55.00
Sugar bowl, Flower & Fern, mk USA 20.00
Sugar bowl, Snowflake, mk USA 15.00
Teapot, elephant, gold trim, mk USA 175.00
Teapot, elephant, mc trim on wht, mk USA 130.00
Teapot, emb rose, pk w/gr leaves, mk USA 60.00
Teapot, emb rose, solid gold, mk USA 200.00
Teapot, Granny Ann, decals/gold trim, mk USA 225.00
Teapot, Granny Ann, purple/gr wash, mk Pat Granny Ann 90.00
Teapot, Pennsylvania Dutch, mk USA, 10-oz 70.00
Teapot, Snowflake, mk USA 25.00
Teapot, Tom Tom, airbrushed, mk Tom the Piper's Son Pat USA 100.00
Utility jar, Basketweave, wht/gold trim, mk USA 80.00
Valencia, bowl, onion soup; w/lid 22.00
Valencia, chocolate mug, 7-oz 17.00
Valencia, coaster 15.00
Valencia, egg cup 15.00
Valencia, jug, 2-pt 30.00
Valencia, tea saucer 10.00
Valencia, teacup 17.00

Miscellaneous

Ashtray, leaf form, mk USA 350 ....8.00
Ashtray, triangular w/3 flying geese, mk USA 403 ....18.00

Bank, Smiley the Pig, dk brn/gr bib, minimum value 300.00
Bank, Winnie the Pig, dk brn/gr trim, minimum value 300.00
Cigarette box, mk USA 225.00
Clock, pk sq w/textured gold X design at corners, rnd dial 110.00
Figurine, donkey, tan w/brn spots, 6½" 12.00
Figurine, gazelle, gold trim, mk USA 614, 5" 85.00
Figurine, lamb, wht w/floral lei & bow on tail, 6½" 25.00
Figurine, Muggsy, gold trim, mk USA, 5½" 85.00
Lamp, clown, cold pnt on wht 55.00
Lamp, Spanish dancers 40.00
Lamp, Victorian couple 100.00
Miniature, cornucopia, bl w/molded floral base, mk USA 12.00
Miniature, donkey w/cart, mk USA 15.00
Miniature, hand vase, mk USA 18.00
Miniature, pitcher, mk USA 10.00
Miniature, tumbling bear, gold trim 95.00
Miniature, tumbling bear, plain 50.00
Planter, Chinese man & basket, gold trim, mk USA 617 ....16.00
Planter, Colonial lady, mk USA 616 ....35.00
Planter, elephant, gold trim, mk USA 759 ....25.00
Planter, piano, mk USA 528 ....30.00
Planter, Polynesian girl's head, mk Shawnee 896 ....30.00
Planter, poodle on tricycle, mk USA 712 ....32.00
Planter/Vase, fish, gold trim, mk USA 717 ....55.00
Vase, leaf form, gold trim, mk Shawnee 823, 9" 45.00
Vase, Moor's head, gold trim, 8" 55.00
Vase, swan, gold trim, mk USA 806, 6" 26.00

Shearwater

Since 1928 generations of the Peter, Walter, and James McConnell Anderson families have been producing figurines and art-wares in their studio at Ocean Springs, Mississippi. Their work is difficult to date. Figures from the '20s and '30s won critical acclaim and have continued to be made to the present time. Early marks include a die-stamped 'Shearwater' in a dime-sized circle, a similar ink stamp, and a half-circle mark. Any older item may still be ordered in the same glazes as it was originally produced, so many pieces on the market today may be relatively new. However, the older marks are not currently in use. Currently produced Black and pirate figurines are marked with a hand-incised 'Shearwater' and/or a cypher formed with an 'S' whose bottom curve doubles as the top loop of a 'P' formed by the addition of an upright placed below and to the left of the S. Many are dated, '93, for example. These figures are generally valued at $35.00 to $50.00 and are available at the pottery or by mail order. New decorated and carved pieces are very expensive, starting at $400.00 to $500.00 for a 6" pot.

Vase, black with blue mottling, melon-ribbed sides, incised mark, 6", $85.00.

Bowl, yel/cream/bl gloss, 7" 80.00
Figurine, gull, stylized, tan matt, 11" W 70.00
Figurine, man on horse, blk matt, ink mk, 6½" 70.00

Figurine, pirate w/sword, yel, blk & gr gloss, 8" 40.00
Pitcher, aqua & gunmetal gloss, stylized hdl, 7" 20.00
Vase, emb men & dogs, gr & brn matt, 10½" 75.00
Vase, lt gr matt, mk, 5½" 95.00
Vase, stylized birds, 4¾" 300.00
Vase, turq over cream, imp mk, 6x8" 285.00

Sheet Music

Sheet music is often collected more for its colorful lithographed covers, rather than for the music itself. Transportation songs (which have pictures or illustrations of trains, ships, and planes), Ragtime and Blues, Comic characters (especially Disney), Sports, Political, and Expositions are eagerly sought after. Much of the sheet music on the market today is valued at under $5.00; some of the better examples are listed here. Values are given for examples in excellent to near-mint condition unless otherwise noted. Our advisor for this category is Jeannie Peters; she is listed in the Directory under Ohio.

Al-La-Carte, Abe Holzman, 1915 ....10.00
Always, Movie: Christmas Holiday, Irving Berlin photo, 1925 .....10.00
America First, Howard Kocian, 1916 ....15.00
And That Ain't All, sgn Sophie Tucker photo, 1919 ....50.00
Anniversary Song, Movie: Jolson Story, 1936 ....5.00
Back to Dixieland, Jack Yellen, 1914 ....10.00
Barney Google, Barney & Spark Plug photo, 1923 ....40.00
Big Red Shawl, Bob Cole & Billy Johnson, 1908 ....10.00
Blue Moon, Movie: Words & Music, cast photo, 1934 ....10.00
Can't You Be Good?, Geo W Meyer, 1909 ....10.00
Charge of the Light Brigade, ET Paull, 1898 ....35.00
Cheer Up Little Darling, Little Mildred photo, 1917 ....10.00
Custer's Last Charge, John Philip Sousa, 1922 ....45.00
Daddy Long Legs, Mary Pickford photo, 1919 ....15.00
Darling What More Can I Do, Gene Autry photo, 1945 ....5.00
Day After Forever, Movie: Going My Way, Bing Crosby photo 5.00
Deep in the Arms of Love, Lou Davis & Roy Ingraham, 1929 ......15.00
Dime a Dozen, Sammy Kaye photo, 1949 ....3.00
Drifting On, H Johnson & J Santly, Deco cover, 1919 ....10.00
Elite Syncopations, Scott Joplin, 1902 ....50.00
Evelina, Harold Arlen & EY Harburg, 1944 ....5.00
Fine Romance, Movie: Swing Time, Astaire/Rogers cover, 1936 .10.00
For the Good Times, Kris Kristofferson, 1968 ....4.00
Gather the Rose, Musical: White Eagle, 1931 ....10.00
Girl Upstairs, Movie: Seven Year Itch, M Monroe photo, 1955 ...20.00
Golden Girl of My Dreams, Geo Spink, 1927 ....10.00
Has Anybody Here Kissed Toodles, DJ Sullivan, 1915 ....10.00
Helen, Jacob Henry Ellis & Al Wilson, 1908 ....15.00
I Could Write a Book, Musical: Pal Joey, 1940 ....5.00
I'll Give the World for You, K Bainbridge & JS Zamecnik, 1925 .15.00
I Love You More Each Day, Fink, 1914 ....10.00
Jeanie w/the Light Brown Hair, Dale Evans photo, 1939 ....10.00
Keep the Home Fires Burning, Lena G Ford & Ivor Novello, 1915 ...10.00
Kinky Kids Parade, Gus Kahn & Walter Donaldson, 1925 ....25.00
Lady Bird, Cha Cha Cha, Rockwell cover, 1968 ....25.00
Let's Go Into a Picture Show, McRee & Von Tilzer, 1908 ....10.00
Magna Carta, John Philip Sousa, 1927 ....20.00
Mandy, Movie: White Christmas, cast photo, 1942 ....10.00
May I Never Love Again, Sano Marco & Jack Erickson, 1940 ....5.00
Mr Yankee Doodle, Clarke, Leslie & Schwartz, 1912 ....10.00
My Love Song to You, sgn Jackie Gleason photo, 1954 ....15.00
New Moon Is Over My Shoulder, Movie: Student Tour, 1934 ....5.00
Oceana Roll, Roger Lewis & Lucien Denni, 1911 ....10.00
Old Apple Tree, Movie: Swing Your Lady, cast photo, 1938 ....10.00

Paradise Street, C Fox Smith & Alec Rowley, 1933 ....**5.00**
Please Mr Sun, Sid Frank & Ray Geton, Johnnie Ray photo, 1951 .**5.00**
Princess Pocahontas March, full-figure photo cover, 1903 ....**40.00**
Queen of Hearts, JW Bratton, 1898 ....**15.00**
Ragtime Soldier Man, Irving Berlin, 1912 ....**15.00**
Red Roses for a Blue Lady, Perry Como photo, 1948 ....**5.00**
Roses & Thorns, HH Schultz & J Edwin Allemong, 1916 ....**10.00**
Scorcher, George Rosey, 1897 ....**25.00**
Seal It w/a Kiss, Movie: That Girl From Paris, Pons photo **5.00**
Short'nin Bread, sgn Eddy Nelson photo, 1928 ....**100.00**
Someone, Movie: Girl From Woolworths, 1929 ....**10.00**
Sugar Cane Rag, Scott Joplin, 1908 ....**50.00**
Thrill Is Gone, Musical: George White's Scandals, 1931 ....**10.00**
True Love Never Runs Smooth, Oscar Loraine, 1918 ....**15.00**
Under the Banana Tree, Lamb & O'Connor, 1905 ....**5.00**
Up in a Balloon, HB Farnie, 1869 ....**25.00**
Virginia From Virginia, David S Jacobs & Chas Roy Cox, 1917 ..**10.00**
Was It Rain, Movie: Hit Parade, F Langford/P Regan photo **5.00**
When You Wake Up Dancing, Musical: Toot Toot, 1918 ....**10.00**
You're Driving Me Crazy, Walter Donaldson, 1930 ....**5.00**

Shelley

In 1872 Joseph Shelley became partners with James Wileman, owner of Foley China Works, thus creating Wileman & Co. in Stoke-on-Trent. Twelve years later James Wileman withdrew from the company, though the firm continued to use his name until 1925 when it became known as Shelley Potteries, Ltd. Like many successful 19th-century English potteries, this firm continued to produce useful household wares as well as dinnerware of considerable note. In 1896 the beautiful Dainty White shape was introduced, and it is regarded by many as synonymous with the name Shelley. In addition to the original Dainty 6-Flute design, other lovely shapes were produced: 12-Flute, 14-Flute, Oleander, Queen Anne, and the more modern shapes of Vogue, Regent, and Eve.

Though often overlooked, striking earthenware was produced under the direction of Frederick Rhead and later Walter Slater and his son Eric. Many notable artists contributed their talents in designing unusual, attractive wares: Rowland Morris, Mabel Lucie Attwell, and Hilda Cowham, to name but a few.

In 1966 Allied English Potteries acquired control of the Shelley Company, and by 1967 the last of the exquisite Shelley China had been produced to honor remaining overseas orders. In 1971 Allied English Potteries merged with the Doulton group. Reports of Shelley China currently being produced have not been verified. Some Shelley patterns (Dainty Blue and Bridal Rose) have been seen on wares bearing the names Royal Albert and Queensware. Our advisors for this category are Lila and Fred Shrader; they are listed in the Directory under California.

Key:
MLA — Mabel Lucie Attwell   W — Wileman, pre-1910
QA — Queen Anne

Ashtray, Dog series (head & shoulders): Springer **75.00**
Ashtray, Harlequin Cigarettes (advertising), W, 5¾" sq **78.00**
Ashtray, Windflower, 6-flute, 3½" **35.00**
Biscuit jar, Intarsio, colorful stylized flowers on dk purple **635.00**
Bowl, cereal; Begonia, 6-flute, 6½" **35.00**
Bowl, cereal; Dainty Blue, 6-flute, 6½" **49.00**
Bowl, cream soup; Bridal Rose, Oleander shape, w/underplate **72.00**
Bowl, flat soup; Dainty White w/yel polka dots, 7½" **75.00**
Bowl, fruit; Cape Gooseberry, Regent shape, 5½" **22.00**
Bowl, fruit; Dainty Blue, 9" sq **255.00**

Bowl, fruit; Lily of the Valley, 5½" **35.00**
Bowl, fruit; Rose & Red Daisy, 6-flute, 5½" **45.00**
Bowl, rimmed soup; sm enameled roses on ¾" gold band **95.00**
Bowl, vegetable; Cottage pattern, QA, w/lid & hdls, 9½" **190.00**
Bowl, vegetable; Harebell, Oleander shape, hdls/domed lid, 9½" **365.00**
Bowl, vegetable; Shamrocks, 6-flute, 9" **255.00**
Box, Heavenly Blue, Dainty shape, w/lid, 5x4" **225.00**
Box, Keepe Sake..., w/lid, W, 3" dia **35.00**
Butter dish, Bridal Rose, 6-flute, w/lid, 7½" dia **175.00**
Butter dish, Harebell, Oleander shape, 8½" dia **175.00**

Butter dish, Dainty Blue, 6-flute, 7½x6", $225.00.

Butter pat, Celandine, 6-flute **45.00**
Butter pat, Heavenly Blue, 6-flute **75.00**
Butter pat, Pansy (single, lg), 6-flute **75.00**
Butter pat, Rose & Red Daisy **42.00**
Butter pat, Summer Glory (Chintz) **65.00**
Butter tub, Harmony Ware, w/lid & underplate **110.00**
Cake plate, Archway of Roses, QA, 9" sq **95.00**
Cake plate, Cornflower, Alexandra shape, tab hdls, W, 8½" sq .**125.00**
Cake plate, Old Sevres, ped ft, w/gold, 8" **158.00**
Cake plate, Rosebud, 6-flute, 3" ped ft, 8" **210.00**
Candlestick, flower & butterfly decor pnt on blk matt, 10" **72.00**
Candlesticks, Cloisello, 3½", pr **155.00**
Candy dish, Dainty Mauve, 6-flute, 5" **75.00**
Candy dish, Dainty Yellow, 6-flute, 4½" **65.00**
Candy dish, Regency, 5½" sq **42.00**
Chamberstick, daisies on wht, w/finger ring, W **75.00**
Cheese dish, Dainty Pink, oblong, w/domed lid, 7¼" L **465.00**
Children's ware, bowl, cereal; MLA, Boo-Boos & airplane, 6½" **135.00**
Children's ware, egg cup, Teddy bear **65.00**
Children's ware, mug, MLA, Donkey in cart w/Boo-Boos, 3½" ..**110.00**
Children's ware, mug, steam engine & train, 3½" **65.00**
Children's ware, pitcher, MLA, rabbit w/coat & scarf, 5½" **715.00**
Cigarette holder, Windflower, 6-flute, 2" **45.00**
Coffeepot, Iris (lg), Regent shape, lg **195.00**
Coffeepot, Lily of the Valley, Dainty shape, ind **175.00**
Coffeepot, Violets, Dainty shape, 8-cup **265.00**
Commemorative mug, Queen Victoria's Dmn Jubilee, W **110.00**
Commemorative plate, Elizabeth II Coronation, Dainty shape, 8" ..**75.00**
Creamer, Scenes of Auld Wynebrooke, squat, 1-pt **45.00**
Creamer & sugar bowl, Blue Rock, 6-flute, med **75.00**
Creamer & sugar bowl, Bridal Rose, 6-flute, w/tray, ind **135.00**
Creamer & sugar bowl, Harmony, w/tray, med **95.00**
Creamer & sugar bowl, Primrose Chintz, w/tray, med **165.00**
Creamer & sugar bowl, Rosebud, ind **75.00**
Cup & saucer, Begonia Spray inside cup, Oleander shape **65.00**
Cup & saucer, Blue Rock, 14-flute **55.00**
Cup & saucer, Chester Pastels **50.00**
Cup & saucer, Daffodil Time **52.00**
Cup & saucer, Dainty White, 6-flute **48.00**
Cup & saucer, demitasse; Begonia, 6-flute **55.00**

Cup & saucer, demitasse; flowers & rich gold on blk matt **58.00**
Cup & saucer, demitasse; Sheraton, Mocha shape **55.00**
Cup & saucer, Heather, Henley shape **49.00**
Cup & saucer, Honeysuckle, 6-flute **59.00**
Cup & saucer, ivy decor, Empire shape, W **62.00**
Cup & saucer, Maytime (Chintz), Henley shape **65.00**
Cup & saucer, Melody (Chintz) inside cup, Oleander shape **75.00**
Cup & saucer, Morning Glory, 6-flute **75.00**
Cup & saucer, Pole Star, QA shape **58.00**
Cup & saucer, Stocks, Gainsborough shape w/pk ft **58.00**
Cup & saucer, Summer Glory (Chintz), Ripon shape w/gold ped .**75.00**
Egg cup, Bridal Rose, 6-flute, lg **75.00**
Egg cup, Dainty White, lg **28.00**
Egg cup, Harebell, Oleander shape, lg **75.00**
Egg cup, Harmony Drip Ware, sm **35.00**
Egg cup, Wildflowers, 6-flute, sm **65.00**
Gravy boat, Phlox, Regent shape **55.00**
Hatpin holder, Cloisonne, 5½" **165.00**
Heraldic ware, ashtray, crested shield shape, W, 2½x3" **20.00**
Heraldic ware, box, crested, 2¼" dia **65.00**
Honey pot, Countryside (Chintz), w/lid **142.00**
Jam container, Harmony, w/lid, in metal stand **110.00**
Menu plaque, Menu in blk script w/gold decor, 5x7" **105.00**
Mould, food; Armadillo shape, 2-pt **125.00**
Mould, food; Star shape, 1½-pt **55.00**
Muffin dish, Lilac Time, 6-flute, w/lid, 9" **186.00**
Mustard, white dogwood & turq roses, 6-flute, w/lid **65.00**
Napkin ring, Dainty Blue, unmk (could be Royal Albert), ea **65.00**
Plate, American Brookline, 6-flute, 8" **57.00**
Plate, Archway of Roses, QA, 7" **55.00**
Plate, Begonia, 6-flute, 10½" **110.00**
Plate, Blue Poppy, 6-flute, 8" **54.00**
Plate, Chester Pastels, 8" **40.00**
Plate, Dainty Blue, 6-flute, 10½" **120.00**
Plate, Honeysuckle, 6-flute, 6" **34.00**
Plate, Maytime (Chintz), 8" **57.00**
Plate, Rose & Red Daisy, 14-flute, 8" **45.00**
Plate, Serenity, 9" **35.00**
Plate, Stocks, 6-flute, 9" **75.00**
Plate, Summer Glory (Chintz), 8" **65.00**
Platter, Drifting Leaves, 12x9" **90.00**
Platter, Glorious Devon, 6-flute, 16x13½" **295.00**
Platter, Violets, 6-flute, 12x10" **148.00**
Powder jar, Melody (Chintz), w/lid **195.00**
Relish dish, Forget-Me-Not, 6-flute, 3½x6" **95.00**
Shakers, Bridal Rose, cylindrical, 6-flute, 3½", pr **148.00**
Snack set, Regency, cup+indented 8" sq plate **75.00**
Tea & toast set, Hibiscus, 6-flute, cup+6x9" plate **88.00**
Tea & toast set, Wild Anenome, 6-flute, cup+5x8" plate **75.00**
Teapot, Daffodil Time, pear shape, 6-cup **155.00**
Teapot, Harebell, Oleander shape **235.00**
Teapot, Japan pattern, Empire shape, W, 6-cup **250.00**
Teapot, Lilac Time, Dainty shape, 8-cup **325.00**
Teapot, Old Sevres, 6-cup **185.00**
Toast rack, Bridal Rose, Dainty shape, 3-bar **175.00**
Toast rack, Primrose (Chintz), 3-bar **185.00**
Tray, sandwich; Begonia, 6-flute, tab hdls, 11½x4½" **195.00**
Tray, sandwich; Wild Anenome, 6-flute, tab hdls, 7½x4½" **145.00**
Tray, triple; Regency, 6-flute, gold hdl, 12½" **295.00**
Vase, Cloisello, cylindrical, 7½" **167.00**
Vase, Intarsio, daffodils/leaves on vertical ground, W, 10½" **675.00**
Vase, Japanese Fruit, rose bowl shape, 6½" **235.00**
Vase, Moonlight, jug style w/hdl, W, 6½" **55.00**
Vase, violets pnt on blk matt, 16" **300.00**

Wall pocket, Melody (Chintz), 7x6" **345.00**

Silhouettes

Silhouette portraits were made by positioning the subject between a bright light and a sheet of white drawing paper. The resulting shadow was then traced and cut out, the paper mounted over a contrasting color and framed. The hollow-cut process was simplified by an invention called the Physiognotrace, a device that allowed tracing and cutting to be done in one operation. Experienced silhouette artists could do full-length figures, scenics, ships, or trains freehand. Some of the most famous of these artists were Charles Peale Polk, Charles Wilson Peale, William Bache, Doyle, Edouart, Chamberlain, Brown, and William King. Though not often seen, some silhouettes were completely painted or executed in wax. Examples listed here are hollow-cut unless another type is described and assumed to be in excellent condition unless noted otherwise.

Key:
bk — backing
c/p — cut and pasted
fl — full length
p — profile
wc — watercolor

Man in a library, cut full-length profile in watercolor and ink background, unsigned, restored, framed, 1800s, 9¾x7½", $300.00.

Lady, fl, gold brushed details, identified, ca 1850s, 14x10" **360.00**
Lady, p, eglomise decor glass w/blk cloth bk, gilt fr, 6x5" **115.00**
Lady, p, gilt details, cut...by Mr W Seville on label, 6x5" **245.00**
Lady, p, identified, PA, molded fr, 5¾x4⅞" **355.00**
Lady, p, ink details, emb brass fr, New England, 5¼x4⅜" **385.00**
Lady, p, ink details, oval, emb brass-on-wood fr, 5x4" **300.00**
Lady dancing, fl, Edouart, 1830, 12x10", EX **385.00**
Lady in bonnet in chair, ink, reeded fr, 7x6½" **110.00**
Lady w/fancy collar & bodice, p, stains, fr, 5⅛x4" **350.00**
Man, p, blk ink details, late, brass fr, 4x3" **50.00**
Man, p, gilt details, artist's label, blk lacquer fr, 6x5" **275.00**
Man, p, gilt highlights, in gilt-brass fr, 5x4" **100.00**
Man, p, litho torso, blk cloth bk, fr, 8x7" **275.00**
Man, p, wht & gold details, leather-trimmed fr, 4x4" **95.00**
Man & lady, fl, identified, Edouart, 1841, fr, 17x13" **2,800.00**
Man & lady, fl, identified, Edouart, 1844, 15x12" **2,000.00**
Man w/paper & scissors, fl, ink wash bkground, fr, 14x13" **550.00**
Man w/walking stick & top hat, fl, gilt details, fr, 12x9" **385.00**
Old lady, p, blk cloth bk, emb brass on wood fr, 7x6" **115.00**

Silver

Coin Silver

During colonial times in America, the average household could not afford items made of silver, but those fortunate enough to have accumulations of silver coins (900 parts silver/100 parts alloy) took them to the local silversmith who melted them down and made the desired household article requested. These pieces bore the owner's monogram and often the maker's mark, but the words 'Coin Silver' did not come into use until 1830. By 1860 the standard was raised to 925 parts silver/75 parts alloy and the word 'Sterling' was added. Our advisor for Coin Silver is Betty Bird; she is listed in the Directory under California.

Key:
gw — gold washed   t-oz — troy ounce

Gorham for E.A. Tyler of New Orleans, ewer, tapered baluster with foliate decoration, framed repousse reserve, ca 1860-70, 18 troy ounces, 22", $770.00.

Am, goblet, paneled bowl, eng name, wide ft, 6½", 6-t-oz 225.00
Am, pitcher, pear form w/scroll hdl, wide base, 18th C, 4-t-oz ...175.00
Am, porringer, eng initials, keyhole hdl, 1790s, 9-t-oz 750.00
Anthony Rasch & Co, tablespoon, grape & palmette, 3-t-oz 125.00
Bigelow Bros & Kennard, pitcher, eng scenes, 8-sided, 11" 900.00
C Dahl, spoon, may be a salesman's sample, 16" 400.00
Continental, serving spoon, early, 11½" 70.00
Daniel Henchman, Boston; spoon, 8" 250.00
E Benjamin & Co, spoons, shell bks, ca 1835, 9", 4 for 175.00
E Stebbins, NY; cream jug, urn form w/S-scroll hdl, 1825, 7¾" ..275.00
G Eoff, NY City; creamer, 2-t-oz 220.00
Garner & Winchester, Lex, KY; julep cup, eng AD, 3.6-t-oz 495.00
Gorham, cup, appl insects, child sz 800.00
Gorham, ladle, Fiddle Thread, mid-19th C, 11", 4-t-oz 275.00
Gorham, salt cellar, Medallion, boat shape, pr 395.00
Gorham, salver, Greek Key border 250.00
H Haddock, Boston; pitcher, chased florals, 1850s, 21-t-oz 750.00
J Crawford, NY/Phila; creamer/sugar bowl, 8", 8¾", 20-t-oz 495.00
James Mix, NY; soup ladle, fiddle hdl (eng), ca 1850, 13½" 330.00
JB Jones, Boston; sugar bowl, acanthus bands/bud finial, 25-t-oz ...230.00
JB Jones Jr, Boston; coffeepot, chased decor, 47-t-oz 690.00
JD, creamer, eng monogram, beaded trim, 5.4-t-oz 220.00
Jones-Ball, Boston, dinner fork, Fiddle Thread, 1850, 6 for 180.00
Leonard & Wilson, Phila; presentation mug, chased/repousse, 4" ..300.00
Lincoln & Reed, teapot, hammered, ca 1835, 7¼x10½" 500.00
Obadiah Rich, Boston; presentation ewer, 1848, 13", 16-t-oz .1,265.00
PLK Standard, mug, repousse lilies/cattails, ear hdl, 65-t-oz 195.00
Polhemus for Tiffany, dinner forks, Fiddle Thread, 6 for 175.00
R Swan, creamer, resoldered hdl, 5.6-t-oz 220.00
R&W Wilson, Phila; dinner forks, Fiddle Thread, 1830s, 6 for ..175.00
W Jenkins, Phila or NY; tea set, gadrooning, 3-pc, 66-t-oz 2,000.00
Wm Adams, NY; hot water kettle w/stand, 1831-43, 16", 79-t-oz ...1,400.00

Flatware

Silver flatware is being collected today either to replace missing pieces of heirloom sets or in lieu of buying new patterns, by those who admire and appreciate the style and quality of the older ware. Prices vary

from dealer to dealer; some pieces are harder to find and are therefore more expensive. Items such as olive spoons, cream ladles, lemon forks, etc., once thought a necessary part of a silver service, may today be slow to sell; as a result, dealers may price them low and make up the difference on items that sell more readily. Many factors enter into evaluation. Popular patterns may be high due to demand though easily found, while scarce patterns may be passed over by collectors who find them difficult to reassemble. If pieces are monogrammed, deduct 30% (rare, ornate patterns) to 40% (common, plain pieces). Place settings generally come in three sizes: dinner, place, and luncheon, with the dinner size generally more expensive. Our advisor for this category is Rick Spencer; he is listed in the Directory under Utah. (See also Tiffany, Silver.)

Key:
fh — flat handle   hh — hollow handle

Acorn, cream soup spoon, George Jensen 75.00
Acorn, demitasse spoon, George Jensen 45.00
Acorn, dinner fork, George Jensen 105.00
Acorn, sauce ladle, George Jensen 95.00
American Victorian, cold meat fork, Lunt 55.00
American Victorian, gumbo soup, Lunt 28.00
American Victorian, 4-pc set, Lunt, place sz 79.00
Baltimore Rose, lemon fork, Schofield 40.00
Baltimore Rose, tablespoon, pierced, Schofield 75.00
Baltimore Rose, teaspoon, Schofield 22.00
Ben Franklin, berry spoon, Towle 120.00
Ben Franklin, dinner knife, Towle 32.00
Ben Franklin, iced tea spoon, Towle 30.00
Bridal Bouquet, ind butter spreader, fh, Alvin 20.00
Bridal Bouquet, poultry shears, Alvin 80.00
Bridal Bouquet, sugar tongs, Alvin 32.00
Bridal Bouquet, 4-pc set, Alvin, luncheon sz 76.00
Buttercup, cocktail fork, Gorham 25.00
Buttercup, coffee spoon, Gorham 15.00
Buttercup, jelly server, Gorham 38.00
Buttercup, 4-pc set, Gorham, dinner sz 115.00
Candlelight, bouillon spoon, Towle 30.00
Candlelight, tomato server, Towle 75.00
Candlelight, 4-pc set, Towle, place sz 85.00
Chantilly, bonbon server, Gorham 42.00
Chantilly, fruit spoon, Gorham 24.00
Chantilly, ice cream fork, Gorham 25.00
Chantilly, oval soup spoon, Gorham 40.00
Chantilly, sugar spoon, Gorham 30.00
Chateau Rose, place fork, Alvin 26.00
Chateau Rose, place knife, Alvin 22.00
Chateau Rose, serving spoon, Alvin 55.00
Chippendale, butter spreader, hh, Towle 20.00
Chippendale, cream soup, Towle 30.00
Chippendale, salad fork, Towle 32.00
Chippendale, strawberry fork, Towle 22.00
Corsage, pickle fork, Stieff 30.00
Corsage, sugar spoon, Stieff 25.00
Corsage, 4-pc set, Steiff, luncheon sz 78.00
Damask Rose, baby spoon, Oneida 24.00
Damask Rose, gravy ladle, Oneida 55.00
Damask Rose, teaspoon, Oneida 20.00
Dawn Star, oval soup spoon, Wallace 28.00
Dawn Star, place fork, Wallace 28.00
English Shell, demitasse spoon, Lunt 15.00
English Shell, iced tea spoon, Lunt 25.00
Etruscan, fruit spoon, Gorham 20.00
Etruscan, sardine fork, Gorham 150.00

Etruscan, 4-pc set, Gorham, luncheon sz 85.00
Fairfax, breakfast knife, Durgin 38.00
Fairfax, lettuce fork, Durgin 120.00
Fairfax, mustard ladle, Durgin 40.00
Fairfax, 4-pc set, Durgin, dinner sz 118.00
Federal Cotillion, roast carving set, F Smith, 3-pc 265.00
Federal Cotillion, strawberry fork, F Smith 24.00
Federal Cotillion, 4-pc set, F Smith, luncheon sz 109.00
Francis I, asparagus server, Reed & Barton 325.00
Francis I, ice tongs, Reed & Barton 195.00
Francis I, soup ladle, Reed & Barton 245.00
Francis I, tablespoon, Reed & Barton 68.00
Francis I, 4-pc set, Feed & Barton, place set 120.00
French Provincial, butter knife, hh, Towle 25.00
French Provincial, dinner knife, Towle 32.00
French Provincial, teaspoon, Towle 16.00
Frontenac, chocolate spoon, International 40.00
Frontenac, dessert fork, 3-tine, International 42.00
Frontenac, master salt spoon, International 35.00
Frontenac, 4-pc set, International, dinner sz 152.00
George & Martha, cocktail fork 18.00
George & Martha, 4-pc set, Westmoreland, luncheon sz 80.00
Grand Baroque, olive fork, Wallace 28.00
Grand Baroque, pea spoon, Wallace 195.00
Grand Baroque, 4-pc set, Wallace, dinner sz 138.00
Joan of Arc, gravy ladle, International 65.00
Joan of Arc, place knife, International 25.00
King Richard, ice cream fork, Towle 26.00
King Richard, soup ladle, hh, Towle 185.00
King Richard, youth set, Towle 82.00
King Richard, 4-pc set, Towle, luncheon sz 109.00
Lancaster Rose, bouillon spoon, Gorham 30.00
Lancaster Rose, tablespoon, pierced, Gorham 62.00
Lily, cream soup, Whiting 34.00
Lily, 4-pc set, Whiting, luncheon sz 125.00
Louis XIV, sauce ladle, Towle 30.00
Louis XIV, 4-pc set, Towle, dinner sz 120.00

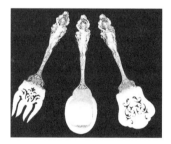

Love Disarmed, 3-piece serving set, Reed and Barton, 21 troy ounces, $1,500.00.

Lucerne, cream soup spoon, Wallace 35.00
Lucerne, dinner fork, Wallace 36.00
Lucerne, dinner knife, Wallace 28.00
Lucerne, fish server, Wallace 275.00
Marlborough, bouillon spoon, Reed & Barton 34.00
Marlborough, salad serving set, Reed & Barton 225.00
Marlborough, 4-pc set, Reed & Barton, luncheon sz 95.00
Meadow Rose, 4-pc set, Watson, dinner sz 98.00
Milburn Rose, 4-pc set, Westmoreland, place sz 75.00
Modern Victorian, jelly server, Lunt 25.00
Modern Victorian, strawberry fork, Lunt 28.00
Modern Victorian, 4-pc set, Lunt, dinner sz 105.00
Old Master, cream soup spoon, Towle 34.00
Old Master, salt spoon, Towle 14.00
Old Master, soup ladle, hh, Towle 195.00

Old Master, 4-pc set, Towle, place sz 100.00
Old Orange Blossom, ice cream spoon, Alvin 62.00
Old Orange Blossom, 4-pc set, Alvin, dinner sz 225.00
Plymouth, butter spreader, fh 22.00
Plymouth, cheese scoop, Gorham 105.00
Plymouth, salad fork, Gorham 32.00
Prelude, fish fork, International 42.00
Prelude, fish knife, International 42.00
Prelude, pie server, International 45.00
Prelude, 4-pc set, International, luncheon sz 75.00
Primrose, gravy ladle, Kirk 78.00
Primrose, place fork, Kirk 34.00
Primrose, teaspoon, Kirk 25.00
Rambler Rose, cream soup spoon, Towle 26.00
Rambler Rose, serving spoon, Towle 48.00
Rambler Rose, teaspoon, Towle, sm 15.00
Rambler Rose, 4-pc set, Towle, place sz 78.00
Repousse, berry spoon, Kirk 135.00
Repousse, cucumber server, Kirk 125.00
Repousse, iced tea spoon 30.00
Repousse, tablespoon, Kirk 55.00
Repousse, 4-pc set, Kirk, dinner sz 125.00
Richelieu, berry spoon, International 125.00
Richelieu, 4-pc set, International, dinner sz 139.00
Romance of the Sea, cocktail fork, Wallace 28.00
Romance of the Sea, demitasse spoon, Wallace 20.00
Romance of the Sea, steak knife, Wallace 42.00
Rose, olive spoon, pierced, Stieff 40.00
Rose, 4-pc set, Stieff, luncheon sz 98.00
Royal Danish, baby-food pusher, International 35.00
Royal Danish, ice cream fork, International 27.00
Sir Christopher, pie server, Wallace 55.00
Sir Christopher, tomato server, Wallace 70.00
Sir Christopher, 4-pc set, Wallace, place sz 105.00
Stately, lobster fork, State House 32.00
Stately, viande fork, State House 24.00
Stately, 4-pc set, State House, luncheon sz 72.00
Tara, salad fork, Reed & Barton 32.00
Tara, sugar spoon, Reed & Barton 26.00
Versailles, berry spoon, Gorham 150.00
Versailles, ice cream spoon, Gorham 56.00
Versailles, stuffing spoon, Gorham 475.00
Versailles, 4-pc set, Gorham, dinner sz 200.00
Violet, asparagus fork, Wallace 425.00
Violet, cold meat fork, Wallace 65.00
Violet, teaspoon, Wallace 20.00
Wedgewood, demitasse spoon, International 18.00
Wedgewood, 4-pc set, International, luncheon sz 87.00
William & Mary, gumbo soup spoon, Lunt 36.00
William & Mary, nut spoon, Lunt 34.00
William & Mary, 4-pc set, Lunt, place sz 80.00
1810, teaspoon, International 18.00
1810, 4-pc set, International, dinner sz 110.00

Hollow Ware

Until the middle of the 19th century, the silverware produced in America was custom made on order of the buyer directly from the silversmith. With the rise of industrialization, factories sprung up that manufactured silverware for retailers who often added their trademark to the ware. Silver ore was mined in abundance, and demand spurred production. Changes in style occurred at the whim of fashion. Repousse decoration (relief work) became popular about 1885, reflecting the ostentatious preference of the Victorian era. Later in the century,

Greek, Etruscan, and several classic styles found favor. Today the Art Deco styles of this century are very popular with collectors.

In the listings that follow, manufacturer's name or trademark is noted first; in lieu of that information, listings are by country. Weight is given in troy ounces. See also Tiffany, Silver.

Key:

t-oz — troy ounce	gw — gold washed

B Laver, London, serving dish, greyhound/dragon eng, 22-t-oz ..**715.00**
Bailey & Co, mustard scoop, gw, Victorian lady hdl **90.00**
BR Hampel, cake server, Deco birds/scrolls/etc, 11" **90.00**
Charles Wright, tankard, George III, 1777, 8½" **2,000.00**
Dodge, mug, hand-hammered, mk #925/1000, #313, 3", EX **60.00**
Dominick & Haff, coffee service, 9¾" pot+cr/sug, 52-t-oz **300.00**
English, basket, swing hdl, pierced/fluted ped ft, 18th C, 3" **85.00**
English, tea/coffee set, eng/chased cartouches, 4-pc, 79-t-oz ...**1,760.00**
Frank Smith, coffeepot, Fiddle Thread **650.00**
Frank Smith, teapot, Fiddle Thread **650.00**
Geo Jensen, bowl, pod & floral support, domed base, 6x10½" ...**2,165.00**
Geo Jensen, compote, appl vintage/twist stem, 7⅜x7¼", pr **4,000.00**
Geo Jensen, creamer, #71B, w/ladle, 1933, 6-t-oz **1,100.00**
Geo Jensen, pitcher, vasiform, hdl w/wooden grip, 8¾" **1,952.00**
Geo Jensen, salad fork & spoon, ca 1914, 8-t-oz, 9¾" **750.00**
George III, creamer, repousse florals, lyre hdl on pear form **230.00**
German, candlesticks, vintage bands, sq base, 1815-25, 11", pr ...**2,000.00**
Gorham, bowl, vegetable; Plymouth, w/lid **395.00**
Gorham, candelabra, Chantilly, 3-light, pr **575.00**
Gorham, candlesticks, Strasbourg, 10", pr **420.00**
Gorham, fruit stand, floral & openwork repousse sides, 22-t-oz ..**625.00**
Gorham, pitcher, urn shape w/flower border, C hdl, 20-t-oz **475.00**
Gorham, tea set, Chantilly, 5-pc **3,200.00**
Gorham, tea set, Fairfax, 3-pc **1,200.00**
Gorham, vase, amphora form, scroll hdls, 16¾", 50-t-oz **1,800.00**
HC (Henry Cowper), George III, sugar basket, bright-cut, 6" **650.00**
Hillard & Thomas, Birmingham 1878, snuff box, eng leaves **240.00**
International, bowl, fruit; Royal Danish, rnd, #2102 ....**325.00**
International, bread tray, Prelude **160.00**
International, creamer & sugar bowl, Prelude **300.00**
International, tea & coffee set, Royal Danish, 5-pc **1,500.00**
International, tray, oval vegetable; Royal Danish, 12x7" **375.00**
J King, London; marrow scoop, Geo II, 1744, 9½", 2-t-oz **220.00**
J McKay, cake basket, Scottish Regency, 9x12", 30-t-oz **1,150.00**
J&N Richardson, Phila; can, pear shape w/lyre hdl, 12½-t-oz ..**2,200.00**
James Watts, Phila, porringer, Gothic pierced hdl, ca 1835 ....**500.00**
Jeffery Lang, Salem MA; can, pear shape, lyre hdl, 12-t-oz **1,500.00**
John Payne, tankard, George III, baluster, domed lid, 1760, 8" ..**2,300.00**
Kalo, bowl, 5-lobed, inscription, 1924, 8" **325.00**
Kalo, plate, hammered, 5-lobed, #320F, 9½" dia, VG **260.00**
Kalo, tray, hand-wrought, 8-lobed, initialed, 7x14" **475.00**
Kirk, chamberstick, sm **150.00**
Kirk, compote, repousse, #436F **220.00**
Kirk, creamer & sugar bowl, w/tray, repousse **250.00**
Kirk, mirror, bush & comb, repousse, 3-pc **525.00**
Kirk, salver, repousse, claw ftd, 12" **1,200.00**
Lebolt, salt & peppers shakers, hand-wrought, ped ft, 5", pr **200.00**
London, 1802, wine funnel, Geo III, 5⅝", 3-t-oz **440.00**
London hallmk for 1762, sauce boat, Geo III, 3¾x6" **500.00**
London hallmk for 1814, entree dish, Geo III, 32-t-oz **400.00**
London hallmk for 1837, castor, eng foliage/scrolls, 3½" **250.00**
Mexican, goblet, baluster support, dome base, 7", 6 for **265.00**
Mexican, tray, 4 scrolling ft, 14" dia, 50-t-oz **300.00**
Mulholland, porringer, hand-wrought, 5" **170.00**
Nathanial Mills, Birmingham 1850; vinaigrette on neck chain ..**220.00**

Reed & Barton, coffeepot, Georgian Rose **390.00**
Reed & Barton, creamer & sugar bowl, Hampton Court **400.00**
Reed & Barton, demitasse set, Hampton Court, 3-pc **675.00**
Reed & Barton, tea set, Hampton Court, 4-pc **1,700.00**
Richard Bayley, tankard, George II, 1730, 7¼" **1,840.00**
Shiebler, pitcher, appl florals, water sz **2,000.00**
Sterling, repousse vintage on urn w/branch hdl, 34-t-oz **1,550.00**
Stieff, compote, Rose, 5-oz **125.00**
Thomas Pitts, epergne, George III, 4-arm, 13x20" **13,800.00**
Thomkins & Black, pitcher, decor urn w/lyre hdl, 27-t-oz **1,600.00**
Towle, bowl, Silver Flutes, 9" **150.00**
Towle, candlesticks, Old Master, pr **175.00**
Towle, cookie tray, Silver Flutes, 10" **150.00**
Towle, cookie tray, Silver Flutes, 13" **300.00**
Towle, waste bowl, Old Master **375.00**
TW, tray, George III, Fide et Virtute eng, 26¼", 97-t-oz **3,165.00**
Wallace, tray, emb florals, ca 1925, 13⅝" **150.00**
Whiting, cup, Heraldic, child sz **525.00**
Wm Gale & Sons, centerpc, wirework bowl on std, 7¾x9½" .**2,000.00**
Wm Pitts, tea urn, Regency, paw ft, 1814, 18", 161-t-oz **4,600.00**
Wm Spratling, cordials, mk Sterling, 2", 8 for **550.00**

Silver Lustre Ware

Much of the ware known as silver lustre was produced in the 1800s in Staffordshire, England. This type of earthenware was entirely covered with the metallic silver glaze. It was most popular prior to 1840 when the technique of electroplating was developed and silverplated wares came into vogue. Later in the century, artisans used silver lustre to develop designs on vases and other decorative ware.

The process for decorating pottery with the silver-resist method involved first coating the design or that portion of the pattern that was to be left unsilvered with a water-soluble solution. The lustre was applied to the entire surface of the vessel and allowed to dry. Before the final firing, the surface was washed, removing only the silver from the coated areas. This type of ware was produced early in the 1800s by many English potteries, Wedgwood included.

Bust, Madonna on flared rnd base, 1820s, 13½" **1,150.00**
Jardiniere, dice banded borders reveal bl agate to wht, 7½" **300.00**
Jug, bird & stag among foliage, early 1800s, 5½" **180.00**
Jug, birds, blk transfer w/bl enamel, ca 1815, 6½", EX **635.00**
Jug, birds & florals, blk w/mc, ca 1815, 5½", EX **400.00**
Jug, bl vintage band over stiff leaf body, 1815, rpr, 6" **460.00**
Jug, florals & foliage w/banded border, ca 1815, 10", EX **635.00**
Jug, harvest scene bl transfer, ca 1815, 5½", NM **350.00**
Jug, HP birds on branches on panels, leafy lustre, 5¼" **400.00**
Jug, hunt scene in blk & brn, rim & lustre wear, 1810s, 5½" **400.00**
Jug, hunter w/dogs, bl w/mc, ca 1815, 5¼", EX **460.00**
Jug, huntsman, sepia transfer, ca 1815, rim line, 5¼" **230.00**
Jug, Mary Lloyd, man & horse/stag, bl w/mc, 1815, rstr, 7¼" **700.00**
Jug, sporting figures in wht relief, 1810s, 5½", EX **230.00**
Jug, Wellington battle scene, commemorative, 1812, 5", EX **800.00**
Model of a lion, ca 1820, sm rpr/chips, 10½" L **500.00**
Pitcher, overall decor, wht int, 7", NM **50.00**
Pitcher, overall lustre w/slight wear, 1850s, 6¾" **35.00**
Teapot, rooster form, att Geo Jones, ca 1875, rpr, 11" **700.00**

Silver Overlay

The silver overlay glass made since the 1880s was decorated with a cut-out pattern of sterling silver applied to the surface of the ware.

Decanter, Alpine dancers and floral devices on clear, 8½", $430.00; Perfume, scroll cut decor on red, Patented 999, 3½", $460.00; Decanter, vinyard scene with cherubs on blue, 12", $300.00.

Bottle, scent; red w/scroll o/l, mk Pat 999 Fine, 3½" 450.00
Decanter, emerald gr w/scroll o/l, squatty, 7¾" **775.00**
Pitcher, cranberry, floral o/l, invt bull's eye shoulder, 10" **625.00**
Vase, amber w/gold irid, floral o/l, 3⅞" **800.00**
Vase, amber w/gold irid, scrolling floral o/l, 2½" **745.00**
Vase, amethyst, repeated vine o/l, 4" **300.00**
Vase, blk amethyst, leafy o/l w/parrot medallions, trumpet, 9" **525.00**
Vase, gold irid w/lily o/l, A (Austrian) hallmks, 4¼" **460.00**
Vase, gr w/air-trapped dmn quilt, floral o/l, 6½" **1,265.00**
Vase, red irid, floral o/l mk Sterling, 2¾" **865.00**

Silverplate

Silverplated flatware is fast becoming the focus of attention for many of today's collectors. Pricing is based on pieces in excellent or restored/resilvered condition. Serving pieces are priced to reflect the values of examples in complete original condition, with knives retaining their original blades. If pieces are monogrammed, deduct 25% (for rare, ornate patterns) to 30% (for common, plain pieces). Our advisor for this category is Rick Spencer; he is listed in the Directory under Utah. See also Railroadiana, Silverplate.

Key:
hh — hollow handle   lh — long handle

Flatware

Adam, 1917, Community, cream ladle 15.00
Adam, 1917, Community, cream soup spoon 6.00
Adam, 1917, Community, dinner fork 6.00
Adam, 1917, Community, iced tea spoon 7.00
Adam, 1917, Community, salad fork 6.00
Adam, 1917, Community, sugar tong 16.00
Adoration, 1939, Community, berry spoon 20.00
Adoration, 1939, Community, ice cream fork 12.00
Adoration, 1939, Community, luncheon knife 6.00
Adoration, 1939, Community, roast carving set, 2-pc 50.00
Adoration, 1939, Community, sugar spoon 3.00
Adoration, 1939, Community, teaspoon 3.00
Ambassador, 1919, 1847 Rogers, berry spoon 24.00
Ambassador, 1919, 1847 Rogers, cold meat fork 12.00
Ambassador, 1919, 1847 Rogers, cream ladle 16.00
Ambassador, 1919, 1847 Rogers, dinner knife, hh 8.00
Ambassador, 1919, 1847 Rogers, ind butter spreader 6.00
Ambassador, 1919, 1847 Rogers, luncheon fork 6.00
Ambassador, 1919, 1847 Rogers, master butter spreader 4.00
Ambassador, 1919, 1847 Rogers, rnd soup spoon 7.00
Ambassador, 1919, 1847 Rogers, serving spoon 7.00
Arcadian, 1884, 1847 Rogers, berry spoon 40.00
Arcadian, 1884, 1847 Rogers, claret ladle 90.00
Arcadian, 1884, 1847 Rogers, demitasse spoon 7.00

Arcadian, 1884, 1847 Rogers, pastry fork, 3-tine 22.00
Arcadian, 1884, 1847 Rogers, pie server 40.00
Arcadian, 1884, 1847 Rogers, sugar tongs 25.00
Bride, 1909, Holmes & Edwards, dinner fork 8.00
Bride, 1909, Holmes & Edwards, rnd soup spoon 10.00
Bride, 1909, Holmes & Edwards, salad fork 12.00
Bride, 1909, Holmes & Edwards, soup ladle 110.00
Bride, 1909, Holmes & Edwards, teaspoon 6.00
Burgundy, 1934, Wm Rogers, baby spoon, curved hdl 12.00
Burgundy, 1934, Wm Rogers, cream soup spoon 5.00
Burgundy, 1934, Wm Rogers, dinner knife, hh 6.00
Burgundy, 1934, Wm Rogers, infant fork 7.00
Caprice, 1937, Nobility, cocktail fork 6.00
Caprice, 1937, Nobility, cold meat fork 10.00
Caprice, 1937, Nobility, dessert server, pierced 16.00
Caprice, 1937, Nobility, iced tea spoon 6.00
Caprice, 1937, Nobility, tomato server 14.00
Caprice, 1937, Nobility, viande fork 5.00
Caprice, 1937, Nobility, viande knife 5.00
Century, 1923, Holmes & Edwards, bouillon spoon 7.00
Century, 1923, Holmes & Edwards, cake serving fork 22.00
Century, 1923, Holmes & Edwards, cream ladle 12.00
Century, 1923, Holmes & Edwards, fruit knife, hh 10.00
Century, 1923, Holmes & Edwards, ice cream fork 15.00
Century, 1923, Holmes & Edwards, jelly server 10.00
Century, 1923, Holmes & Edwards, salad fork 6.00
Century, 1923, Holmes & Edwards, sugar tongs 15.00
Coronation, 1936, Community, bonbon server 8.00
Coronation, 1936, Community, cocktail fork 5.00
Coronation, 1936, Community, dinner fork 7.00
Coronation, 1936, Community, iced tea spoon 7.00
Coronation, 1936, Community, rnd soup spoon 5.00
Coronation, 1936, Community, sugar spoon 3.00
Coronation, 1936, Community, viande knife, hh 5.00
Daffodil, 1950, 1847 Rogers, berry spoon 18.00
Daffodil, 1950, 1847 Rogers, luncheon fork 7.00
Daffodil, 1950, 1847 Rogers, oval soup spoon 6.00
Daffodil, 1950, 1847 Rogers, relish spoon, pierced 9.00
Daffodil, 1950, 1847 Rogers, salad fork 6.00
Daffodil, 1950, 1847 Rogers, sugar spoon 4.00
Daffodil, 1950, 1847 Rogers, tomato server 20.00
Danish Princess, 1938, Holmes & Edwards, cold meat fork 10.00
Danish Princess, 1938, Holmes & Edwards, dinner knife, hh 8.00
Danish Princess, 1938, Holmes & Edwards, jelly knife 4.00
Danish Princess, 1938, Holmes & Edwards, salad set, olive wood ..70.00
Danish Princess, 1938, Holmes & Edwards, teaspoon 3.00
Danish Princess, 1938, Holmes & Edwards, 5 o'clock spoon 6.00
Dolly Madison, 1911, Holmes & Edwards, berry spoon 24.00
Dolly Madison, 1911, Holmes & Edwards, cake serving fork 23.00
Dolly Madison, 1911, Holmes & Edwards, iced tea spoon 10.00
Dolly Madison, 1911, Holmes & Edwards, pickle fork, lh 13.00
Dolly Madison, 1911, Holmes & Edwards, sugar spoon 5.00
Dolly Madison, 1911, Holmes & Edwards, teaspoon 5.00
First Love, 1937, 1847 Rogers, baby spoon/fork 20.00
First Love, 1937, 1847 Rogers, cocktail fork 8.00
First Love, 1937, 1847 Rogers, dessert fork 8.00
First Love, 1937, 1847 Rogers, dinner knife, hh 8.00
First Love, 1937, 1847 Rogers, gravy ladle 25.00
First Love, 1937, 1847 Rogers, iced tea spoon 9.00
First Love, 1937, 1847 Rogers, rnd soup spoon 7.00
First Love, 1937, 1847 Rogers, teaspoon 3.00
Georgian, Community, cake server, hh 20.00
Georgian, Community, cold meat fork 8.00
Georgian, Community, demitasse spoon 7.00

Georgian, Community, dinner fork 4.00
Georgian, Community, sauce ladle 8.00
Georgian, Community, soup ladle 65.00
Georgian, Community, tablespoon 7.00
Heraldic, 1916, 1847 Rogers, cheese knife, hh 24.00
Heraldic, 1916, 1847 Rogers, dinner fork 6.00
Heraldic, 1916, 1847 Rogers, oval soup spoon 6.00
Heraldic, 1916, 1847 Rogers, sugar spoon 4.00
Heraldic, 1916, 1847 Rogers, teaspoon 3.00
Heritage, 1953, 1847 Rogers, berry spoon 25.00
Heritage, 1953, 1847 Rogers, cocktail fork 7.00
Heritage, 1953, 1847 Rogers, dinner knife, hh 7.00
Heritage, 1953, 1847 Rogers, gravy ladle 18.00
Heritage, 1953, 1847 Rogers, nut scoop, pierced 6.00
Heritage, 1953, 1847 Rogers, pie server, pierced 18.00
Heritage, 1953, 1847 Rogers, punch ladle, hh 125.00
Heritage, 1953, 1847 Rogers, salad fork 7.00
Heritage, 1953, 1847 Rogers, serving spoon, pierced 12.00
Joan, 1896, Wallace, cake serving fork 30.00
Joan, 1896, Wallace, fish serving set 80.00
Joan, 1896, Wallace, fruit knife, hh 15.00
Joan, 1896, Wallace, ice cream fork 18.00
Joan, 1896, Wallace, ind butter spreader 7.00
Joan, 1896, Wallace, luncheon fork 6.00
Joan, 1896, Wallace, soup ladle 60.00
Lady Hamilton, 1932, Community, baby fork 6.00
Lady Hamilton, 1932, Community, jelly knife 6.00
Lady Hamilton, 1932, Community, luncheon knife 6.00
Lady Hamilton, 1932, Community, rnd soup spoon 6.00
Lady Hamilton, 1932, Community, sugar spoon 3.00
Lady Hamilton, 1932, Community, teaspoon 3.00
Lady Hamilton, 1932, Community, viande fork 5.00
Lovely Lady, 1937, Holmes & Edwards, berry spoon 18.00
Lovely Lady, 1937, Holmes & Edwards, cold meat fork 12.00
Lovely Lady, 1937, Holmes & Edwards, dinner fork 7.00
Lovely Lady, 1937, Holmes & Edwards, serving spoon 8.00
Lovely Lady, 1937, Holmes & Edwards, teaspoon 3.00
Milady, 1940, Community, bonbon server 6.00
Milady, 1940, Community, gumbo soup spoon 5.00
Milady, 1940, Community, jelly server 4.00
Milady, 1940, Community, master butter spreader 3.00
Milady, 1940, Community, oval soup spoon 4.00
Milady, 1940, Community, sauce ladle 12.00
Milady, 1940, Community, teaspoon 3.00
Noblesse, 1930, Community, demitasse spoon 5.00
Noblesse, 1930, Community, dinner knife, hh 6.00
Noblesse, 1930, Community, luncheon fork 4.00
Noblesse, 1930, Community, salad fork 5.00
Noblesse, 1930, Community, tablespoon, pierced 13.00
Old Colony, 1911, 1847 Rogers, bouillon spoon 8.00
Old Colony, 1911, 1847 Rogers, cocktail fork 8.00
Old Colony, 1911, 1847 Rogers, demitasse spoon 6.00
Old Colony, 1911, 1847 Rogers, fruit spoon 8.00
Old Colony, 1911, 1847 Rogers, ice cream spoon 30.00
Old Colony, 1911, 1847 Rogers, olive spoon 32.00
Old Colony, 1911, 1847 Rogers, punch ladle 150.00
Old Colony, 1911, 1847 Rogers, sugar tongs 20.00
Patrician, Oneida, dinner fork 4.00
Patrician, Oneida, fruit spoon 6.00
Patrician, Oneida, luncheon knife, hh 5.00
Patrician, Oneida, teaspoon 3.00
Patrician, Oneida, tomato server 16.00
Patrician, Oneida, 5 o'clock spoon 5.00
Paul Revere, 1927, Community, bouillon spoon 5.00

Paul Revere, 1927, Community, dinner fork 5.00
Paul Revere, 1927, Community, fruit spoon 7.00
Paul Revere, 1927, Community, master butter spreader 3.00
Paul Revere, 1927, Community, oval soup spoon 4.00
Paul Revere, 1927, Community, seafood fork 6.00
Paul Revere, 1927, Community, soup ladle 50.00
Queen Bess II, 1946, Tudor, berry spoon 10.00
Queen Bess II, 1946, Tudor, dinner fork 3.00
Queen Bess II, 1946, Tudor, dinner knife, hh 5.00
Queen Bess II, 1946, Tudor, gravy ladle 10.00
Queen Bess II, 1946, Tudor, tablespoon 3.00
Queen Bess II, 1946, Tudor, teaspoon 2.00
Queen Bess II, 1946, Tudor, youth fork 7.00
Remembrance, 1948, 1847 Rogers, ind butter spreader 7.00
Remembrance, 1948, 1847 Rogers, jelly server 7.00
Remembrance, 1948, 1847 Rogers, relish, pierced 10.00
Remembrance, 1948, 1847 Rogers, salad fork 7.00
Remembrance, 1948, 1847 Rogers, teaspoon 3.00
Remembrance, 1948, 1847 Rogers, tomato server 24.00
Remembrance, 1948, 1848 Rogers, steak knife 20.00
Sheraton, 1910, Community, berry spoon 22.00
Sheraton, 1910, Community, cheese server, hh 18.00
Sheraton, 1910, Community, cream soup 6.00
Sheraton, 1910, Community, pie fork, 3-tine 8.00
Sheraton, 1910, Community, salad fork 5.00
Sheraton, 1910, Community, soup ladle 45.00
Sheraton, 1910, Community, sugar tongs 20.00
Sheraton, 1910, Community, teaspoon 3.00

Tea set, chased and repousse floral motifs, Simpson, Hall and Miller, 6-piece set includes 14" coffeepot, teapot, creamer, sugar bowl with lid, waste bowl, and kettle on stand, $1,100.00.

Vanity Fair, 1924, Gorham, carving set, 2-pc 38.00
Vanity Fair, 1924, Gorham, dinner knife, hh 7.00
Vanity Fair, 1924, Gorham, gravy ladle 18.00
Vanity Fair, 1924, Gorham, ind butter spreader 5.00
Vanity Fair, 1924, Gorham, oval soup spoon 7.00
Vanity Fair, 1924, Gorham, pie server 16.00
White Orchid, 1953, Community, berry spoon 24.00
White Orchid, 1953, Community, cocktail fork 8.00
White Orchid, 1953, Community, dinner knife, hh 7.00
White Orchid, 1953, Community, feeding spoon 12.00
White Orchid, 1953, Community, oval soup spoon 7.00
White Orchid, 1953, Community, teaspoon 3.00
White Orchid, 1953, Community, viande knife 7.00
Youth, 1940, Holmes & Edwards, cold meat fork 10.00
Youth, 1940, Holmes & Edwards, oval soup spoon 4.00
Youth, 1940, Holmes & Edwards, rnd soup spoon 5.00
Youth, 1940, Holmes & Edwards, salad fork 6.00
Youth, 1940, Holmes & Edwards, sugar spoon 3.00
Youth, 1940, Holmes & Edwards, tablespoon 7.00
Youth, 1940, Holmes & Edwards, viande fork 4.00

Hollow Ware

Bowl, vegetable; Coronation, w/lid, Community, 1936 ....120.00

Bowl, vegetable; Daffodil, w/lid, 1847 Rogers, 1950 ....**75.00**
Bread tray, Bird of Paradise, 1926, Community, 14x7" **45.00**
Bread tray, Flair, 1847 Rogers, 1956 ....**40.00**
Cake basket, rtcl border/emb florals/loop hdl, 1890s, 10x12½" ..**140.00**
Cake dish, Remembrance, 1847 Rogers, 1948, 14" dia **60.00**
Cake tray, Eternally Yours, ftd, 1847 Rogers, 1941, 13x15" **70.00**
Candelabra, Heritage, 3-light, 1847 Rogers, 1953, 18" **165.00**
Candle holder, Queen Bess, dbl-arm, Tudor, 1946 ....**75.00**
Candlestick, Heritage, 1847 Rogers, 1953, 12" **40.00**
Coffee/tea set, English, Georgian style, wood hdls, 5-pc **440.00**
Coffeepot, Eternally Yours, 1847 Rogers, 1941, +cr/sug **275.00**
Coffeepot, Remembrance, 1847 Rogers, 1948, +cr/sug+lid **225.00**
Gravy boat, Adoration, w/underplate **75.00**
Lamp, Georgian-style urn form w/loop hdls, 28", pr **1,750.00**
Pitcher, water; Bird of Paradise, Community, 1926, 7½" **70.00**
Plateau mirror, Rococo-style florals/etc, 15½" dia+2 sticks **110.00**
Platter, well & tree; Remembrance, 1847 Rogers, 1948 ....**100.00**
Tea urn, unmk, English Regency, gadrooned, mask hdls, 17x11" ...**600.00**
Tray, eng shield under crown w/greyhounds/etc, 30x18" **770.00**
Tray, serving; ftd, C scrolls/florets, Towle, 25" L **220.00**
Tray, serving; Tupperware Rose, 14" dia **45.00**
Tureen & underplate, Edwardian, eng zigzags, 12x17" **990.00**

Sheffield

Candelabra, Queen Anne form, sq stepped bases, 20", pr **335.00**
Candlesticks, Geo III, urn form nozzle, 1790, 12", pr **400.00**
Candlesticks, telescopic, circular base, 7" closed, pr **700.00**
Hot water urn, George III, fluted lid, stepped base, 1890s **660.00**
Hot water urn, vine hdls, urn-shaped finial, vine hdls, 21" **500.00**
Inkstand, eng base, crystal wells, appl lappets, 1850s, 10" **300.00**
Lamp, spherical reservoir w/flame finial, early 1800s, 15¼" **715.00**
Tea service, Geo IV, repousse decor, ebony finial, 3-pc **550.00**
Tray, coat-of-arms/scrolls/etc eng, ftd, 19th C, 30x21" **715.00**
Tray, serpentine w/pierced gallery, cut-out hdls, 24½" **400.00**
Wine cooler, gadroon border, bracket hdls, w/liner/collar, 10" ...**1,150.00**

Sinclaire

In 1904 H.P. Sinclaire and Company was founded in Corning, New York. For the first sixteen years of production, Sinclaire used blanks from other glassworks for his cut and engraved designs. In 1920 he established his own glass-blowing factory in Bath, New York. His most popular designs utilize fruits, flowers, and other forms from nature. Most of Sinclaire's glass is unmarked; items that are carry his logo: an 'S' within a wreath with two shields.

Basket, cut, cornflowers, 6" dia **160.00**
Bowl, canoe form w/eng flowers, 11x7½" **175.00**
Bowl, dk amethyst, wide flat rim, #11703, 8" **45.00**
Candlesticks, amber, tulip cups, 10-prism bobeche, 9", pr **295.00**
Compote, amber & gr, rolled rim, #11915, 6½" **85.00**
Plate, luncheon; Colonial bl, sgn, 4 for **60.00**
Teapot, cut, florals & thistles, appl hdl & spout **400.00**
Vase, cut, geometrics & hobstars, rayed base, wide rim, 10" **195.00**
Vase, ribbed cutting, rose etching at top, 12½" **200.00**

Slag Glass

Slag glass is a marbleized opaque glassware made by several companies from about 1870 until the turn of the century. It is usually found in purple or caramel (see Chocolate Glass), though other colors were also

made. Pink is rare and very expensive. It was revived in recent years by several American glassmakers, L.E. Smith, Westmoreland, and Imperial among them. Our advisor for this category is Sharon Thoerner; she is listed in the Directory under California.

Blue, basket, cherries/leaves in relief, crimped/ruffled, 9" **75.00**
Blue, humidor, drum shape, cap-shaped finial, 6½x5¼" **250.00**
Pink, Invt Fan & Feather, bowl, master berry **800.00**
Pink, Invt Fan & Feather, butter dish, 7x7⅝" **1,300.00**
Pink, Invt Fan & Feather, creamer **425.00**
Pink, Invt Fan & Feather, cruet **1,400.00**
Pink, Invt Fan & Feather, jelly compote, scalloped, 4½x5" **550.00**
Pink, Invt Fan & Feather, pitcher, 7½" **1,200.00**
Pink, Invt Fan & Feather, punch cup **265.00**
Pink, Invt Fan & Feather, sauce dish, ball ft, 2½x4½" **265.00**
Pink, Invt Fan & Feather, sauce dish, shell ft, 2⅜x4" **600.00**
Pink, Invt Fan & Feather, shakers, rare, pr **1,200.00**
Pink, Invt Fan & Feather, spooner, 4¼" **425.00**
Pink, Invt Fan & Feather, sugar bowl, w/lid, 7¼" **900.00**
Pink, Invt Fan & Feather, toothpick holder **650.00**
Pink, Invt Fan & Feather, tumbler, average color, 4" **250.00**
Pink, Invt Fan & Feather, tumbler, EX color, 4" **435.00**
Purple, Beads & Bark, vase, novelty **50.00**
Purple, candy dish, Indiana Glass, ftd **55.00**
Purple, Flute, celery vase **85.00**
Purple, Jenny Lind, compote, 7¾x8½" **165.00**
Purple, oil lamp, emb spears, clear font, 13" **200.00**
Purple, Oval Medallion, spooner **85.00**
Purple, Panel & Waffle mold, compote, w/lid, 8x8" **125.00**
Purple, Panel & Waffle mold, vase, ftd, scalloped, 8" **90.00**
Purple, plate, lattice edge, 13" **125.00**
Purple, Scroll w/Acanthus, creamer & sugar bowl **100.00**
Purple, Scroll w/Acanthus, spooner **75.00**
Purple, vase, paneled sides, 8" **150.00**
Red, vase, mc/gold decor at top, 7" **60.00**

Smith Bros.

Alfred and Harry Smith founded their glassmaking firm in New Bedford, Massachusetts. They had been formerly associated with the Mt. Washington Glass Works, working there from 1871 to 1875 to aid in establishing a decorating department. Smith glass is valued for its excellent enameled decoration on satin or opalescent glass. Pieces were often marked with a lion in a red shield. Our advisors for this category are Betty and Clarence Maier; they are listed in the Directory under Pennsylvania.

Biscuit jar, gold floral vine decor on pale beige, #4402 on lid, 7x6", $500.00.

Biscuit jar, pk roses & gold leaves, melon ribs, 7" **800.00**
Biscuit jar, Roman coins/mc florals, melon ribs, SP trim, 6" **900.00**
Biscuit jar, wheat on melon ribs, metal fittings, 8½" **675.00**
Bowl, pansy bouquets, melon ribbed, 2½x5" **225.00**
Clock, floral/bird on pnt burmese, 6" dia, on 12" chain **275.00**

Mustard, bouquets, red on opal, ribbed, 2¼" 170.00
Sweetmeat, floral on pk, melon ribbed, SP mts, 3x4" 180.00
Toothpick holder, floral on wht opaque bbl form, 2¼" 265.00
Toothpick holder, Little Lobe, roses on bl opaque, 2½" 245.00
Vase, carnations, pk/lav w/gold, gold rim, global, 4" 150.00
Vase, daisies on leafy stems, gilt/enamel rim, pinched, 4½" 200.00
Vase, florals, emb rope around rim, rampant lion mk, 6" 295.00
Vase, wisteria on chalk wht w/gold, short neck, mk, 8¾" 750.00

Snow Babies

During the last quarter of the 19th century, snow babies — little figurals in white snowsuits — originated in Germany. They were made of sugar candy and were often used as decorations for Christmas cakes. Later on they were made of marzipan, a confection of crushed almonds, sugar, and egg whites. Eventually porcelain manufacturers began making them in bisque. They were popular until WWII. These tiny bisque figures range in size from 1" up to 7" tall. Quality German pieces bring very respectable prices on the market today. Beware of reproductions. Our advisor for this category is Linda Vines; she is listed in the Directory under New Jersey.

Photo courtesy Linda Vines

Baby feeding seal with a baby bottle, Germany, 2", $175.00.

Babies, 1 pulling another on sled, Germany, 2" 135.00
Babies, 2 holding Santa's hands, Germany, 2" 150.00
Babies, 3 on sled, Germany, 2" 175.00
Baby, jtd shoulders & hips, Germany, 3½" 200.00
Baby in sled pulled by huskies, Germany, 2" 165.00
Baby lying on side, blk face, brn eyes, Germany, 2" 250.00
Baby playing musical instrument, Germany, 2" 110.00
Baby sitting, snow ft, pointed hood, EX detail, Germany, 2" 150.00
Baby standing, yel fluorescent pnt, B Shackman, 1940s, 2½" 75.00
Baby standing on lg snowball, Japan, 2½" 30.00
Baby standing or sitting, Germany, 1" 40.00
Carollers, 3 w/snow hats & lantern on snow base, Germany, 2" .125.00
Child, girl or boy skater, snow hat & sweater, Germany, 2" 90.00
Child, no snow boy or girl pushing lg snowball, Germany, 2" 125.00
Children (2) sliding down brick wall, Germany, 2½" 100.00
Santa at ft of sleeping child's bed, Germany, 2" 125.00
Santa atop gray elephant, Germany, 2½" 175.00
Santa in red train w/golliwog & dolls, Germany, 2" 175.00
Santa in yel sailboat, Germany, 2" 125.00
Santa nodder, Germany, 3" 90.00
Santa place card holder, googly eyes, twig tree, Germany, 2" 75.00
Santa riding in yel car, Germany, 2" 150.00
Santa sitting on wht swing, Germany, 3" 135.00
Snow angel sits w/arms out, pk wings, loop in bk, Germany, 1½" 200.00

Snow bear sitting or walking, Germany, 2½" 75.00
Snow dog, rabbit or cat, Germany, 1", ea 50.00
Snow man sitting, blk top hat, Germany, 2" 110.00
Snow mother pushing twins in red carriage-sled, Germany, 2½" 175.00

Snuff Boxes

As early as the 17th century, the Chinese began using snuff. By the early 19th century, the practice had spread to Europe and America. It was used by both the gentlemen and the ladies alike, and expensive snuff boxes and bottles were the earmark of the genteel. Some were of silver or gold set with precious stones or pearls, while others contained music boxes. In the following listings, the dimension noted is length. See also Orientalia, Snuff Bottles.

Bird's eye maple, oblong w/hinged lid, 2x1¼x⅜" 100.00
Cvd hand form, EX detail, 19th C, 4" 275.00
Horn w/eng Am flag & British Jack, A Pinch For..., 3¾" L 875.00
Papier-mache, brn w/emb dmn design, ca 1860 ....75.00
Silver, eng eagle, Never To Be Forgotten..., mk DG, 1840s, 2½" 300.00
Silver, eng swags/urns/coat-of arms, English, 1793, 3⅜" 475.00
Silver, repousse hunt scene, rectangular, Continental 160.00
Tortoise shell & engr MOP, wht metal mts, 2⅝" L 220.00

Soap Hollow Furniture

In the Mennonite community of Soap Hollow, Pennsylvania, the women made and sold soap, the men made handcrafted furniture. Rare today, these pieces were stenciled, grain painted, and beautifully decorated with inlaid escutcheons. These pieces are becoming very sought after. When well kept, they are very distinctive and beautiful. The items described in these listings were sold through Merle S. Mishlers Auctions, RD 2, Hollsopple, Pennsylvania. All are in excellent condition unless otherwise noted. Our advisor for this category is Anita Levi; she is listed in the Directory under Pennsylvania.

Chest, blanket; feathers on mustard & brn, MB/1897, EX 1,100.00
Chest, blanket; grpt w/blk lid, fruit/florals w/gold, 1882 ....2,900.00
Chest, blanket; maroon w/gold stencil, rnd escutcheon, 1856 .2,000.00
Chest, blanket; poplar, orig red pnt w/blk/gold, att, 22x42" 3,850.00
Chest, blanket; rose decals, blk & brn graining, LK/1890, EX ..5,000.00
Chest, 4 lg/2 sm drws w/decor, enamel pulls, sgn, 1851, EX+ ..4,600.00
Chest, 4 lg/3 sm drws, stencil, enamel pulls, sgn, 1883, EX+ ...5,400.00
Chest of drws, bk brd, hidden lock, stencil, HS/1879, EX 5,500.00
Chest of drws, brn grpt w/stencil, pnt pulls, 1883, EX+ 5,400.00
Chest of drws, floral decals/fruit/gilt stencil/grpt, MH/1879, EX ..2,750.00
Chest of drws, redwood, 1841, EX 750.00
Chest of drws, stenciling w/decals, dk brn, fancy bk brd, EX ...7,200.00
Cradle, gilt stencils, mustard trim, maroon grpt, EX 1,100.00
Cupboard, corner; maroon w/blk, stencil, 1856, EX 11,500.00
Cupboard, Dutch; 4 doors/2 drws, stencil/old rpt, 1875, 84x65" ...6,000.00
Dresser, Empire style, columns on 3 drws, HF/1874, EX 2,200.00
Frame, gilt eagles, stenciled, blk, EX 1,050.00
Rope bed, cherry, red & brn finish, rare, EX 2,300.00
Stand, bedside; rpt mustard brn, EX 400.00

Soapstone

Soapstone is a soft talc in rock form with a smooth, greasy feel from whence comes its name. (It is also called Soo Chow Jade.) It is composed basically of talc, chlorite, and magnetite. In colonial times it was extracted from out-croppings in large sections with hand saws, carted by oxen to mills, and fashioned into useful domestic articles such as footwarmers, cooking utensils, inkwells, etc. During the early 1800s, it was used to make heating stoves and kitchen sinks. Most familiar today are the carved vases, bookends, and boxes made in China during the Victorian era.

Censer, dragon-mask/ring hdls, dragon finial, 3-leg, 8" **165.00**
Figurine, Lohan w/dbl-gourd bottle, 1800s, 2" **80.00**
Figurine, seated diety, 9" **85.00**
Figurine, Shoulao w/dragon-headed staff & peach, China, 16½" ..**225.00**
Foot warmer, oblong, heavy wire bail, EX **50.00**
Toothpick holder, tan/wht, cylindrical, 2" **28.00**
Vase, floral w/vintage rim, blk soapstone base, 11" **85.00**
Wax seal, cvd animals in landscape, late 19th C, 5" **200.00**
Wax seal, oxen, head bent down, brn, rstr, 2½" **165.00**

Soda Fountain Collectibles

The first soda water sales in the United States occurred in the very late 1790s in New York and New Haven, Connecticut. By the 1830s soda water was being sold in drug stores as a medicinal item, especially the effervescent mineral waters from various springs around the country. By this time the first flavored soda water appeared at an apothecary shop in Philadelphia.

The 1830s also saw the first manufacturer (John Matthews) of devices to make soda water. The first marble soda fountain made its appearance in 1857 as a combination ice shaver and flavor-dispensing apparatus. By the 1870s the soda fountain was an established feature of the neighborhood drug store.

The fountains of this period were large, elaborate marble devices with druggists competing with each other for business by having fountains decorated with choice marbles, statues, mirrors, water fountains, and gas lamps.

In 1903 the fountain completed its last major evolution with the introduction of the 'front' counter service we know today. (The soda clerk faced the customer when drawing soda.)

By this time ice cream was a standard feature being served as sundaes, ice cream sodas, and milk shakes. Syrup dispensers were just being introduced as 'point-of-sale' devices to sell various flavorings from many different companies. Straws were commonplace, especially those made from paper. Fancy and unusual ice cream dippers were in daily use, and they continued to evolve reaching their pinnacle with the introduction of the heart-shaped dipper in 1927.

This American business has provided collectors today with an almost endless supply of interesting and different articles of commerce. One can collect dippers, syrup dispensers, glassware, straw dispensers, milk shakers, advertising, and trade catalogs.

Collectors need to be made aware of decorating pieces that are fantasy items: copper ice cream cones, a large copper ice cream dipper, and a copper ice cream soda glass. These items have no resale value. Our advisors for this category are Joyce and Harold Screen; they are listed in the Directory under Maryland. See also Advertising; Coca-Cola.

Bottle holder, for rnd bottle, unusual sq base **75.00**
Bowl, crushed fruit; ftd, Heisey **300.00**
Carton, ice cream; Hendler's, w/holiday wrap, 1920s, 1-pt **75.00**
Catalog, Ice Cream Molds, color photos, orig **450.00**
Cone holder, clear glass, metal lid, NP base, 13½", EX **425.00**
Counter, oak w/marble top & front base, 36x72x24", EX **500.00**
Cup, Burham's Clam Bouillon, china **40.00**
Dipper, banana split; United **695.00**
Dipper, Benedict, 1¾", EXIB **40.00**
Dipper, Bohlig **1,600.00**

Dipper, conical bowl, squeeze hdl, rare **375.00**
Dipper, Dover Slicer, single trigger **350.00**
Dipper, Indestructo #4 ....**25.00**
Dipper, Pi-Alamoder **700.00**
Dipper, Polar Pak **695.00**
Dispenser, Armour's Vigoral, urn w/floral motif, w/base, EX ...**1,000.00**
Dispenser, Birchola, ceramic, ball shape, rpl pump, 14x9" dia .**1,500.00**
Dispenser, Buckeye, urn, dancing satyrs, scarce, 16", EX **2,000.00**
Dispenser, Buckeye, urn, mug & nut-bud decor, 16", EX **1,500.00**
Dispenser, Cherry Smash, potbelly, cherry branch, 14", VG+ .**1,400.00**
Dispenser, Cherry Smash 5¢, ftd ball, orig pump, 16x9" dia, EX ..**1,900.00**
Dispenser, Dr Swett's Root Beer, tree trunk, EX **4,180.00**
Dispenser, Fowler's Root Beer, potbelly, brn on wht, NM **1,075.00**
Dispenser, Grape-Julep, potbelly, orig pump, VG **900.00**
Dispenser, Hires Little Boy, brn trim, Mettlach **36,000.00**
Dispenser, Howel's Grape-Julep, potbelly, EX **900.00**
Dispenser, Howel's Orange-Julep, orange belly, w/pump, EX **900.00**
Dispenser, Miners Beef Malt, bull's head, EX **450.00**
Dispenser, Mission Orange, Deco style, tin, 16x9" dia, EX **600.00**
Dispenser, Murry's Root Beer, barrel atop tree stump, NM **400.00**
Dispenser, Rochester Root Beer, barrel on tree stump, NM+ **400.00**
Dispenser, Viccola, urn, gold trim, orig pump, EX **1,760.00**
Fountain glass, Cherry Smash, w/syrup line **250.00**
Fountain glass, Drink Birchola, flared, w/syrup line **125.00**
Fountain glass, flat banana split, Tea Room pattern, pk **200.00**
Fountain glass, Howel's Orange-Julep, milk glass, NM **250.00**
Fountain glass, Mah-Tay, syrup line **25.00**
Fountain glass, Zipps Grape-O, thin blown, acid etched **125.00**
Malted milk container, Thompson's, enamel **350.00**
Mixer, Hamilton Beach, single head, 2-speed **125.00**
Mug, Buckeye, V-shaped hdl, blk logo, 6", NM **75.00**
Mug, Dove Brand ginger ale, china **95.00**
Mug, Dr Swett's, emb image, cream, brn & bl, 6", EX **300.00**
Mug, Hires root beer, bl salt glaze **400.00**
Mug, Howell's Root Beer, glass, emb script lettering, NM **35.00**
Mug, Richardson's Liberty root beer, sm **295.00**
Paper napkin holder, Purity Ice Cream, ad ea side, oval **100.00**
Postcard, interior view of fountain, blk/wht, pre-1920 ....**12.50**
Pump only, for syrup dispenser, rnd ball type, orig **750.00**

Seltzer bottle, Parfay Sparkling Water, red and blue lettering on clear, 12", $45.00.

Sign, Cherry Chick, cb diecut w/hatchet & birds, 16x20", EX ...**850.00**
Sign, Hendler's Ice Cream flavors, rvpt glass, EX **300.00**
Straw holder, clear glass, 'cut' Illinois pattern, no lid **100.00**
Straw holder, clear glass, NP base & lid, 11", VG **140.00**
Straw holder, gr glass, 'cut' Illinois pattern, glass lid **400.00**
Straw holder, horizontal, Heisey **600.00**
Syrup bottle, Ginger Ale label, glass, orig cap, 11" **75.00**
Syrup bottle, Grape Smash, label under glass **575.00**
Syrup bottle, Orange-Julep, glass/alumimun cap, 12", EX **250.00**

Tray, C&M College Ices, tin, oval, EX 400.00

South Jersey Glass

As early as 1739, Caspar Wistar established a factory in Salem County, taking advantage of the large beds of sand suitable for glass blowing and the abundant forests available for fueling his furnaces. Scores of glassworks followed, many of which were short-lived. It is generally conceded that aside from the early works of Wistar and the Harmony Glass Works, which emerged from the Glassboro factory originally founded by the Strangers, the finest quality glassware was blown after 1800. In the 1850s coal was substituted for the wood as fuel. Though a more efficient source of heat, the added cost of transporting the coal inland proved to be the downfall of many of the smaller factories, and soon many had failed.

Glassware can be attributed to this area through the study of colors, shapes, and decorative devices that were favored there; but because techniques were passed down through generations of South Jersey blowers, without documentation it is usually impossible to identify the specific factory that produced it.

Our advisor for this category is Mark Vuono; he is listed in the Directory under Connecticut.

Carafe, appl pouring ring, eng presentation pc, 10⅝" 350.00
Creamer, dk amber, appl ft & hdl, 5⅜" 265.00
Creamer, lt bl w/bl-wht loopings, crimped ft, 3⅞" 575.00
Goblet, aqua, blown, hollow stem w/funnel-shaped base, 6⅛" ...400.00
Pitcher, aqua, blown, flared mouth, tooled rim, pontil, 5½" 350.00
Pitcher, aquamarine, 6 vertical pulls, threaded neck, 7⅜" 3,600.00
Pitcher, aquamarine/wht loopings, cylindrical, 9½" 1,700.00
Pitcher, olive-amber, urn-like form w/appl rings, 8½" 850.00
Pitcher, sapphire bl, free-blown, tooled rim, pontil, 6" 1,300.00
Vase, cobalt, flared rim, solid base, pontil, 11¼x4½" 180.00
Vase, cornflower bl, bulbous, hdls, 10¼" 280.00

Spangle Glass

Spangle glass, also known as Vasa Murrhina, is cased art glass characterized by the metallic flakes embedded in its top layer. It was made both abroad and in the United States during the latter years of the 19th century, and it was reproduced in the 1960s by the Fenton Art Glass Company.

Vasa Murrhina was a New England distributor who sold glassware of this type manufactured by a Dr. Flower of Sandwich, Massachusetts. Flower had purchased the defunct Cape Cod Glassworks in 1885 and used the facilities to operate his own company. Since none of the ware was marked, it is very difficult to attribute specific examples to his manufacture. See also Art Glass Baskets; Fenton.

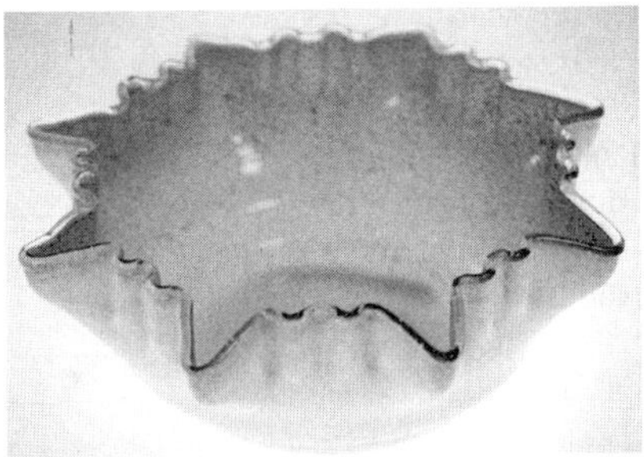

Bowl, blue cased with mica, clear crimped and folded rim, 9½" diameter, $145.00.

Pitcher, clear & rose w/silver mica, HP floral w/gold, 8" 500.00
Pitcher, mc spatter w/gold mica, ribbed hdl, sq mouth, 7½" 165.00
Rose bowl, end-of-day, 3½" 75.00
Rose bowl, pk w/silver mica, 8-crimp, 6¾x3⅞" 175.00
Rose bowl, rose w/silver mica, 8-crimp, 3¾x3½" 110.00
Tumbler, Invt T'print, orange & wht spatter w/mica, 3¾" 40.00
Vase, bl w/mica, ewer form, thorny hdl, 7⅜x3⅜" 115.00

Spatter Glass

Spatter glass, characterized by its multicolor 'spatters,' has been made from the late 19th century to the present by American glasshouses as well as those abroad. Although it was once thought to have been made entirely by workers at the 'end of the day' from bits and pieces of leftover scrap, it is now known that it was a standard line of production. See also Art Glass Baskets.

Bowl, bl/wht/clear, 8 deep crimps, 3⅛x9" 85.00
Creamer & sugar bowl, 4-color, wht cased, crimped ft, 4¼" 120.00
Sweetmeat, cased rainbow w/floral; metal rim/bail/lid, 3" 175.00
Vase, gr & wht, crimped rim, 3 horizontal ribs, 8½x4" 35.00
Vase, sapphire bl & wht opaque, clear ft, HP florals, 7x4" 225.00

Spatterware

Spatterware is a general term referring to a type of decoration used by English potters beginning in the late 1700s. Using a brush or a stick, brightly colored paint was dabbed onto the soft-paste earthenware items, achieving a spattered effect which was often used as a border. Because much of this type of ware was made for export to the United States, some of the subjects in the central design — the schoolhouse and the eagle patterns, for instance — reflect American tastes. Yellow, green, and black spatterware is scarce and highly valued by collectors.

In the descriptions that follow, the color listed after the item indicates the color of the spatter. The central design is identified next, and the color description that follows that refers to the design. Our advisor is Diane Patalano; she is listed in the Directory under New Jersey.

Bowl, bl, pineapple, 3-color, 3½x6½", EX 1,400.00
Bowl, sauce; bl, peafowl, 3-color, 12-sided, 5⅜", NM 350.00
Creamer, bl, fort, yel/red/brn/gr, lt wear, 5¾" 400.00
Creamer, bl, fort, 4-color, rare, mini, NM 625.00
Creamer, red, holly, red & gr, 3¾" 120.00
Creamer, yel/purple, rainbow, 4", EX 350.00
Cup & saucer, bl, holly berry, 3-color, NM 375.00
Cup & saucer, bl, rooster, 3-color, rare 1,100.00
Cup & saucer, bl & purple variegated, 2⅜", 5¾" 85.00
Cup & saucer, brn, peafowl, 3-color, prof rprs 625.00
Cup & saucer, gr, peafowl, mismatched colors 220.00
Cup & saucer, gr, peafowl, 5-color 335.00
Cup & saucer, gr stick stylized leaves, unmk, mini 50.00
Cup & saucer, red, open tulip, 3-color, NM 450.00
Cup & saucer, red, peafowl, 4-color 490.00
Cup & saucer, red & gr, star, 3-color, NM 550.00
Cup & saucer, yel, flying eagle brn transfer, NM 925.00
Cup plate, bl, boy w/hat blk transfer, rprs, 3¾" 85.00
Cup plate, bl, children w/kite transfer, 3¾" 220.00
Pitcher, bl, peafowl, 3-color, 6-sided, rprs, 6½" 425.00
Pitcher, purple, holly berry, 3-color, rprs, 11", VG 275.00
Pitcher, red, holly, red & gr, 6⅛" 400.00
Plate, bl, center star, 3-color, 9½", EX 55.00
Plate, bl, fort, 3-color, rprs, 9⅛" 160.00
Plate, bl, pomegranate, 4-color, 7¾" 700.00
Plate, bl & gr rainbow in alternating bands w/bl center, 8½" 325.00
Plate, purple, daisy, gr, 8½" 150.00

Plate, red, acorn, 4-color, rpr, 8½" 275.00
Plate, red, peafowl, 3-color, rpr, 9¼" 180.00
Plate, red, peafowl, 3-color, rprs, 8¼" 175.00
Plate, red, peafowl, 3-color, 9⅝", NM 825.00
Plate, red, thistle, red & gr, 8¼" 330.00
Plate, red & gr, rainbow, 9½", EX 250.00
Platter, red & gr, rainbow, bull's-eye center, 15¾" 2,255.00
Sugar bowl, bl, peafowl, 4-color, 7", EX 300.00
Sugar bowl, bl, pineapple, 4-color, w/rpl lid 1,600.00
Sugar bowl, bl, pomegranate, 4-color, w/lid, rpr 525.00
Sugar bowl, bl, sm chip to finial, 4¼" 200.00
Sugar bowl, bl, vining band, 3-color, 7⅝", EX 195.00
Sugar bowl, purple, beehive, 2-color, 3¾", NM 1,000.00
Sugar bowl, red, rooster, 3-color, 3¼x4½", NM 400.00
Tea set, gr, peafowl, 4-color, 4" pot+cr/sug+3 cups 350.00
Tea set, red, bl & gr, rainbow, 11-pc, child sz, EX 1,500.00
Toddy, red, tulip, 4-color, 5¾" 175.00
Wash bowl, bl, defiant eagle on shield, brn, rstr, 13¾" 350.00
Wash bowl, rainbow, 4-color, old rpr, 12¼" 1,045.00
Wash bowl, red & gr, peafowl, 3-color, scalloped, 13¼", EX 600.00
Wash bowl & pitcher, blk & purple, rainbow, 8-sided, NM 2,250.00

Cut-Sponge

Bowl, vegetable; red & gr, floral bands, Ironstone, 2x9x7" 90.00
Creamer, bl w/Gem pattern transfer, Hammersly, 4⅝" 275.00
Cup & saucer, Bull's Eye variant w/red & gr floral border 50.00
Cup & saucer, red, swags & tassels, England, NM 65.00
Cup & saucer, red & bl, flowers w/blk stems, 2", 4½" 95.00
Plate, bl, florets, HP mc decor, Auld Heather Ware, 9⅛" 85.00
Plate, bl, florets in clusters, 9⅛" 55.00
Plate, blk, leaf band, mc stripes, 8⅝" 30.00
Plate, blk, red & mc florals, 9" 190.00
Plate, Camellia, red & gr flower border, 8¾" 150.00
Plate, purple w/Gem pattern transfer, Hammersley, 7¾" 130.00
Plate, red, Dmn, blk striping, 9⅜", NM, pr 55.00
Plate, red & gr, leaves, bl & yel stripes, 9⅝" 55.00
Plate, red & gr, leaves & florettes w/gr stripe, 8¾" 55.00
Plate, red & gr, 8-pointed stars, Powell & Bishop, 9" 35.00
Plate, red/gr/bl, floral center w/gr leaves, 8½", NM 150.00

Spode-Copeland

The Spode Works was established in 1770 in England by Josiah Spode I and continued to operate under that title until 1843. Their earliest products were typical underglaze blue-printed patterns. After 1790 a translucent porcelain body was the basis for a line of fine enamel-decorated dinnerware. Stone China was introduced in 1805, often in patterns reflecting an Oriental influence. In 1833 William Taylor Copeland purchased the company, having been Spode's business partner. Copeland continued the business in much the same tradition as the Spode-Copeland partnership. Spode was the Royal Potter for years, providing many exquisite items for the Royal Families. They employed paintresses to decorate the merchandise by hand. Most of the Spode-Copeland wares were marked with one of several variations that incorporate the firm's name, making identification possible. The Spode Company merged with Worcester Royal Porcelain Company in 1976 and became Royal Worcester Spode Limited. This company was then purchased by Derby International in 1988. The two firms separated in 1989. The holding company is the Porcelain and Fine China Companies Limited, a division of Derby International. Spode china is still being manufactured today at exactly the same location where Josiah Spode I began in 1770. Robert Copeland, a descendent of William Taylor Copeland, resides in England. He writes books and gives lectures on Spode. Our advisor for this category is Don Haase; he is listed in the Directory under Washington.

Bathroom sink, Blue Tower 795.00
Bread & butter, Aster, 6¼" 25.00
Bread & butter, Billingsley Rose, 5½" 23.00
Butter dish, Buttercup, sq, w/lid 110.00
Butter dish, Mayflower, rectangular, w/lid 145.00
Butter pat, Buttercup 25.00
Butter pat, Mayflower 28.00
Cereal, Chelsea Garden, bone 49.00
Cereal, Christmas Tree, gr trim 28.00
Cereal, Christmas Tree, magenta trim 32.00
Cereal, Wildflower 32.00
Chop plate, Blue Tower, 15" dia 265.00
Chop plate, Florence, 13" dia 165.00
Chop plate, Pink Tower, 13" dia 195.00
Coffeepot, Billingsley Rose, 6-cup 185.00
Coffeepot, Forget-Me-Not, bone, 8-cup 315.00
Coffeepot, Irene, bone, 8-cup 295.00
Cream soup & saucer, Blue Italian 65.00
Cream soup & saucer, Blue Tower 75.00
Cream soup & saucer, Dresden Rose Savoy, bone 135.00
Creamer & covered sugar, Gainsborough, 3", 3½" 95.00
Creamer & covered sugar, Grey Fleur-de-Lis, bone, 3", 3½" 165.00
Creamer & covered sugar, Pink Tower, 4", 4½" 145.00
Demitasse cup & saucer, Roberta, bone 65.00
Demitasse cup & saucer, Rosalie 39.00
Demitasse cup & saucer, Valencia 39.00
Dessert plate, Buttercup, 8" 32.00
Dessert plate, Dresden Rose Savoy, bone, 8" 62.00
Dinner, Buttercup 39.00
Dinner, Castle (1815) 195.00
Dinner, Mayflower 45.00
Dinner, Ruins (1880) 75.00
Dish warmer, Filigree (1810-33) 345.00
Footed salad, Billingsley Rose 425.00
Footed salad, Ruins 495.00
Fruit, Byron 25.00
Fruit, Chadsworth 25.00
Fruit, Fairy Dell 25.00
Joke cup, Blue Fleur-de-Lis 145.00
Joke cup, Blue Tower 165.00
Jubilee dish, India Tree 165.00
Luncheon plate, Blue Tower, 8½" sq 45.00
Luncheon plate, Bridal Rose, 7½" sq 65.00
Luncheon plate, Fairy Dell, 8½" sq 42.00
Platter, Florence, 13" 115.00
Platter, Herring's Hunt, gr, 15" 185.00
Platter, Mayflower, 24" 595.00
Platter, Pink Tower, 17" 235.00
Platter, Tower, bl, 11" 170.00
Punch bowl, Wildflower, 15" 525.00
Rim soup, Castle (1815), 9" 225.00
Rim soup, Romney, 6½" 32.00
Rim soup, Ruins (1880), 9" 75.00
Salad plate, Indian Tree 28.00
Salad plate, Primrose, bone 59.00
Salt & pepper, Rosebud Chintz 95.00
Salt & pepper, Wickerdale 85.00
Soup tureen w/underplate & ladle, Billingsley Rose 1,120.00
Soup tureen w/underplate & ladle, Blue Tower, lg 1,295.00
Syrup, Wicker Lane, 6" 75.00

Teacup & saucer, Blue Ermine, tall 39.00
Teacup & saucer, Bridal Rose, bone, short 69.00
Teacup & saucer, Chelsea Wicker, tall 35.00
Teacup & saucer, Cowslip, tall 39.00
Teacup & saucer, Mayflower, short 45.00
Vegetable, Blue Trophies, covered/ftd, 11" 265.00
Vegetable, Hazel Dell, oval, 9½" 110.00
Vegetable, Lady Ann, oval, 8½" 85.00
Vegetable, Wickerdale, 10" sq 125.00
Vegetable, Wildflower, 10" 165.00

Spongeware

Spongeware is a type of factory-made earthenware that was popular during the last quarter of the 19th century. It was decorated by dabbing color onto the drying ware with a sponge, leaving a splotched design at random or in simple patterns. Sometimes a solid band of color was added. The vessel was then covered with a clear glaze and fired at a high temperature. Blue on white is the most preferred combination, but green on ivory, orange on white, or those colors in combination may also occasionally be found. For further informaton we recommend *Collector's Encyclopedia of Salt Glaze Stoneware* by Terry Taylor and Terry and Kay Lowrance, available from Collector Books.

Pitchers: Flared cylinder, 9", EX, $275.00; Barrel shaped, 8⅜", $220.00; Water size, hairline/stains, 9¾", $135.00; Bulbous with cylindrical neck, 8⅞", EX, $220.00.

Bowl, bl/wht w/wht band & bl stripes, 5½x10¾", EX 75.00
Bowl, mixing; bl & brn on cream, 5½x12½" 100.00
Cooler, bl/wht, #8, NP spigot, 18", EX 350.00
Cooler, bl/wht w/#2 & Ice Water, no spigot, w/lid, 9½" 110.00
Creamer, bl/wht, molded swirled ribs, 5½" 275.00
Crock, bl/wht, brn Albany slip int, 7¼x7¾", EX 125.00
Cuspidor, bl/wht, bl stripes, 3¼" 275.00
Jardiniere, bl/wht, spiral ribs, worn gold, 6¾" 55.00
Jug, bl/wht, emb leaf detail, wire bail, 5½", NM 550.00
Jug, bl/wht, Grandmother's Maple Syrup of 50 Yrs Ago, 6½", EX ..470.00
Pitcher, bl/brn w/brn stripes on cream, 7½", EX 85.00
Pitcher, bl/wht, bl flower, 9", EX 335.00
Pitcher, bl/wht, bulbous, 8¾" 470.00
Pitcher, bl/wht, emb florals, 7½", NM 300.00
Pitcher, bl/wht, molded shoulder & neck decor, rpr, 6¼" 110.00
Pitcher, bl/wht, stripes, bbl shape, hairlines, 8⅝" 300.00
Pitcher, bl/wht w/Albany slip int, 7" 350.00
Pitcher, milk; dk gray-bl/wht, swirled ribs, bulbous, 5⅝" 415.00
Plate, bl/wht, molded rim, 9¼" 110.00
Platter, bl/wht, 15" 300.00
Sugar bowl, bl/wht, att Buford Bros, rpr to lid, 7½" 165.00
Teapot, bl/wht, prof rpr, 7" 825.00
Tray, dk bl/wht, oblong leaf shape, 9½" 85.00
Vase, bl/wht, cylindrical, 5" 330.00
Vase, bl/wht, emb swirled ribs, 5½", EX 165.00

Spoons

Souvenir spoons have been popular remembrances since the 1890s. The early hand-wrought examples of the silversmith's art are especially sought and appreciated for their fine craftsmanship. Commemorative, personality-related, advertising, and those with Indian busts or floral designs are only a few of the many types of collectible spoons. In the following listings, spoons are entered by city, character, or occasion. Our advisor for this category is Margaret Alves; she is listed in the Directory under Connecticut.

Key:
B — bowl   ff — full figure
BR — bowl reverse   GW — gold wash
emb — embossed   H — handle
eng — engraved   HR — handle reverse

Albany NY State Capitol in B; scenes on H; scrolled HR; 5" 27.50
Am Bankers' Assoc 1904 w/scrolls on H; emb scene in GW B; 4¼" ..25.00
Am flag pnt on H; Library of Congress in GW B; Sterling, demi ..65.00
Atlantic City Casino, Boardwalk B; golfer ff H 85.00
Boston on H; The Hub in B; decor on HR; Shiebler, 4⅛" 18.00
Boston Public Library in B; bean-pot finial H; demi 20.00
Capitol Washington DC in B; 1901 on H; w/eagle finial; 5¾" 28.00
Capitol Washington DC on H; eng scene in B; scenes on HR 28.00
Centenary Collegiate Institute...NJ on H; building in B; 4⅛" 27.50
Christopher Columbus ff H; Santa Maria in B; Sterling, demi 28.00
Dayton OH eng in GW B; Colonial pattern H; Towle, 3⅞" 17.50
De Soto Hotel Savannah GA & scene in B; GA on H; 5⅜" 25.00
Duluth MN on H; Aerial bridge in B; seal on HR; 5½" 28.00
Eureka CA on H; courthouse eng in B; Watson-Newell, 5½" 30.00
Findlay OH in GW B; scrolled hdl w/1901; eng monogram on HR ..22.50
Frederick Douglass emb in B; emb links/dates on H; Sterling 325.00
I'm From MO-Show Me on H; farm scene in B; Watson-Newell .32.00
Kennebunkport ME & sailing scene in B; fish on oar-shaped H ...17.50
KY in banner & D Boone on H; eng scene in B; Watson 40.00
Los Angeles CA emb in B; Capitol on H; Carmel Mission on HR ...20.00
Mt Vernon scene entrance in B; Washington & scene on H; 5½" ..37.50
Niagara Falls on H; waterfall in B; Canada/etc on HR 25.00
NJ & coat of arms on H; plain B; Wendell, 5½" 24.00
NJ on H w/emb florals; Lakewood eng in B; Gorham, 4" 25.00
NY & waterfall on H: building & bridge on HR; plain GW B 18.00
Omaha brite-cut in B; rose finial on leafy H; demi 18.00
Pikes Peak & Cog Road on H: Manito Co on HR; eng scene in B 32.50
Pisces & carnations on H; eng name in B; 1909 on HR; Wallace 32.00
Pittsburgh courthouse in B; crest/eagle/PA on H; scrolled HR 22.50
Plymouth emb in B; Speak For... on H; M Standish on HR 18.00
Potter Hotel Santa Barbara CA on H; scene in GW B 16.50
Prosperity/Protection in B; man bust finial; eagle/etc on HR 18.00
Salem witch, cat & moon, Sterling, demitasse 65.00
Salem Witch H; plain citrus-shaped B; Durgin, 5¾" 48.00
Salt Lake City/eagle on H; tabernacle/etc on HR; Temple in B ...37.50
San Francisco H w/warrior/mtn finial; New Cliff House in B 27.50
San Gabriel Mission Los Angeles in B; Eureka/etc on H; 5½" 32.00
Sarasota emb in B; scrolled H; plain HR; Alvin, 3½" 12.50
Soldiers & Sailors monument eng in GW B; angel finial H 17.50
Statue of Liberty & flowers in B; flowers & beads on H; 4" 20.00
Topeka KS on H; Capitol building in B; scrolled HR; 5¼" 22.50
University of IA, Sterling 185.00
VA on H w/eagle finial; scrolled HR; plain B 22.50
Waco TX in lg cut-out letters on H; GW B; Sterling, demi 35.00
Washington's Headquarters...NY on H; NY/etc on HR; scene in B ..25.00
West VA/June 20 1863 on H; Capitol bldg in B; 5½" 28.00

Yellowstone Park, Old Faithful on H; plain B & HR 20.00

Sporting Goods

When sports cards became so widely collectible several years ago, other types of related memorabilia started to interest sports fans. Now they search for baseball uniforms, autographed baseballs, game-used bats and gloves, and all sorts of ephemera. Although baseball is America's all-time favorite, other sports have their own groups of interested collectors. Our advice for this category comes from Paul Longo Americana. Mr. Longo is listed in the Directory under Massachusetts. See also Target Balls.

Baseball, sgn by Gaylord Perry, M 25.00
Baseball, sgn by Hank Aaron, M 40.00
Baseball, sgn by Joe DiMaggio, M 200.00
Baseball, sgn by Rick Ferrell, M 35.00
Baseball, signed by 1986 World Champion Mets team 175.00
Book, Jack Nicklaus Instruction Book (golf), 1970s, EX 20.00
Book, Jackie Robinson, My Own Story, soft cover, EX 40.00
Book, Vest-Pocket Encyclopedia of Baseball, 1956, EX 20.00
Booklet, How To Pitch, Spalding, 1932 ....35.00
Button, pin-bk; Nat'l League Champions, Cinci Reds, 1939 ....35.00
Calendar/poster, Lou Gehrig, Hall of Fame, 1951, 22x24", EX ...125.00
Discus, wood/iron/brass, Drake University, 1930, 3¾" 60.00
Dumbbells, wood w/red-brn stain, mk Spalding, 10½", pr 45.00
Flag, Olympic, 1932, 48x96" 1,000.00
Helmet, football, leather, adjustable forehead, 1920s, EX 200.00
Lapel pin, Nascar International, ⅜x1" 5.00
Medal, Nat'l Bowling Association Tournament, 1911, w/ribbon ..75.00
Paperback, Story of Brooklyn Dodgers, Bantam, 1949, EX 35.00

Pennants, Boston Red Sox and N.Y. Giants, from game 2 of 1912 World Series, along with full ticket stub from game, $1,300.00 at auction.

Poster, World's Champions...of the...Ring, 1947, 23x28", EX 60.00
Program, baseball; 1951 World Series, EX 100.00
Program, basketball; Harlem Globetrotters, 1953 ....35.00
Program, boxing; Joe Lewis vs Jersey Joe Wolcot, 1948, EX 200.00
Program, racing; Danbury Auto Races, 1930 ....40.00
Program, tennis; Wembley, Riggs, 1949 ....45.00
Program, tennis; Wimbledon, Ashe cover, 1969 ....55.00
Ray-o-View card, Lou Gehrig, 1930 ....165.00
Score card, boxing; Sugar Costner title fighter, NJ, 6x9¼" 10.00
Scorer, baseball; Doelger Beer, celluloid 50.00
Shoes, baseball, metal cleats, ca 1920, EX, pr 50.00
Stein, University of KY Wildcats, 1952 ....100.00
Ticket, Am League baseball, Griffith Stadium, 1933 ....30.00
Token, tennis; 1984 Olympics in Los Angeles 4.00

Wastebasket, Joe Namath & Jet football team, 1960, M 50.00

St. Clair

The St. Clair Glass Company began as a small family-oriented operation in Elwood, Indiana, in 1941. Most famous for their lamps, the family made numerous small items of carnival, pink and caramel slag, and custard glass as well. Later, paperweights became popular production pieces; many command considerably high prices on today's market. Weights are stamped and usually dated, while small production pieces are often unmarked. For further information we recommend *St. Clair Glass Collector's Book* by Bonnie Pruitt, available from our advisor, Ted Pruitt, who is listed in the Directory under Indiana.

Animal dish, dolphin, bl, Joe St Clair 175.00
Animal dish, horse, bl, Joe St Clair 145.00
Bell, ACGA 10th Annual Convention, bl carnival 75.00
Bell, ACGA 10th Annual Convention, cobalt 75.00
Bell, Holly Carillion, cobalt carnival, sgn 35.00
Cordial, vaseline carnival 45.00
Creamer, Holly Band, aqua opal 85.00
Creamer & sugar bowl, Grape, red carnival, rare 200.00
Doorstop, mallard 375.00
Fez hat, Joe St Clair 200.00
Goblet, Hobstar, ice bl 25.00
Goblet, Rose in the Snow, amethyst carnival, 1969 ....40.00
Goblet, Roses in the Snow, cobalt 30.00
Goblet, Wild Flower, cobalt 25.00
Goblet, Wildflower, amethyst carnival 45.00
Lamp, 2-balled, sgn Joe & Bob St Clair 1,250.00
Lamp, 3-balled, sgn Joe & Bob St Clair 1,500.00
Paperweight, owl sulfide, Joe St Clair 120.00
Paperweight, rose, any color, Joe St Clair 1,000.00
Paperweight, rose, etched/windowed, Joe St Clair, $1,200 to ..1,500.00
Paperweight, 5-lily, controlled bubbles 95.00
Plate, Reagan/Bush '80 GOP, marigold carnival 20.00
Ring holder, clear w/yel flower 50.00
Statue, Scottie, any color other than dk amethyst, Bob St Clair ...175.00
Statue, Scottie, dk amethyst (blk), Bob St Clair 300.00
Toothpick holder, Bicentennial, bl or gr carnival, ea 30.00
Toothpick holder, cactus form, wht carnival 35.00
Toothpick holder, Holly, carnival glass, sgn Joe St Clair 45.00
Toothpick holder, Holly Band, red carnival 20.00
Toothpick holder, Indian, caramel lustre, sgn Joe St Clair 45.00
Toothpick holder, Indian figural, bl carnival 20.00
Toothpick holder, Indian figural, cobalt 25.00
Toothpick holder, Indian figural, yel carnival 25.00
Toothpick holder, kingfisher, amberina, 1970 ....35.00
Toothpick holder, kingfisher, cobalt carnival 18.00
Toothpick holder, Nixon, cobalt carnival 50.00
Toothpick holder, paneled, red carnival 25.00
Toothpick holder, S Repeat, purple, 1970s 35.00
Toothpick holder, Santa Claus, Joe St Clair 150.00
Toothpick holder, sheaf of wheat, red carnival 35.00
Toothpick holder, wheelbarrow form, caramel slag, Joe St Clair ..40.00
Tumbler, Cactus, cobalt carnival 28.00
Tumbler, Grape & Cable, red 30.00
Tumbler, Invt Fan & Feather, cobalt 25.00

Staffordshire

Scores of potteries sprang up in England's Staffordshire district in the early 18th century; several remain to the present time. (See also specific companies.) Figurines and groups were made in great numbers; dogs were favorite subjects. Often they were made in pairs, each a mirror image of the other. They varied in heights from 3" or 4" to the largest, measuring 16" to 18". From 1840 until about 1900, portrait figures were produced to represent specific characters, both real and fictional. As a rule these were never marked.

The Historical Ware listed here was made throughout the district; some collectors refer to it as Staffordshire Blue Ware. It was produced as early as 1820, and because much was exported to America, it was very often decorated with transfers depicting scenic views of well-known American landmarks. Early examples were printed in a deep cobalt. By 1830 a softer blue was favored, and within the next decade black, pink, red, and green prints were used. Although sometimes careless about adding their trademark, many companies used their own border designs that were as individual as their names.

This ware should not be confused with the vast amounts of modern china (mostly plates) made from early in the century to the present. These souvenir or commemorative items are usually marketed through gift stores and the like. (See Rowland and Marsellus.) See also specific manufacturers.

Key:
blk — black
gr — green
d/b — dark blue

l/b — light blue
m/b — medium blue
m-d/b — medium dark blue

Figures and Groups

Classical draped figures of man and woman, ca 1800, 25⅝", EX, $1,400.00.

Admiral Dundas beside cannon, cobalt coat, 19th C, 12"	385.00
Benjamin Franklin, bl coat w/gold buttons, rstr, 14¼"	1,100.00
Birds in branches, nest w/3 eggs, Wood, ca 1760, 7¾", NM	3,000.00
Calf nursing cow, spill vase, mc, minor rstr, 11½"	275.00
Cherub holding fruit basket, mc on gr mottle base, 9¼"	275.00
Christ's Agony, kneeling figure, mc, pearlware, rstr, 10½"	1,600.00
Commander Napier, standing in full uniform, 11¾"	440.00
Couple at well, he w/nest & she w/bird, mc, 10¼"	275.00
Couple in boat, he w/Fr flag/stands by anchor, 19th C, 7½"	275.00
Couple stand w/basket of fish, 19th C, 7¾"	550.00
Courting couple, mc w/gold, firing flaw, 8½"	235.00
Dog, reclining, brn splotches on creamware, 1790-1820, 3x4"	135.00
Dog holding a bird, blk/red/gold/cobalt, 6"	175.00
Donkey w/basket of flowers, mc w/gold, 7½"	250.00
Esmeralda & Gringoire, mc details, 10", EX	160.00
George Washington (civilian), mc w/gold, rare, 14½"	3,500.00
Husband/seated wife w/child under floral trellis, 19th C, 9"	415.00
King William III on horse, gold trim, 11"	170.00
Lady reading to child, mc w/EX detail, rstr, 8¼"	175.00
Lady w/watering can & flowers, mc, 8", EX	160.00
Lion on base, paw on ball, mc, pearlware, rstr, 5¾x5¾"	900.00
Lion Slayer, mc details & gold, 15½"	145.00

Little Red Riding Hood, bright colors, 6½"	175.00
Little Red Riding Hood, vase, mc, 10½"	325.00
Lord Dundonald seated on his horse, rare, 14¾"	1,500.00
Man beside tree (vase), lady w/lg fish & basket, 19th C, 8¼"	385.00
Man holding parrot, mc details, 12¼", NM	95.00
Man w/flower basket, mc w/gold, 7¾"	160.00
Naval officer (Farragut?), mc w/gold, sm hairline, 9½"	1,200.00
Nobleman & peasant girl, spill vase, mc w/gold, 8"	85.00
Peter Restoring the Lame Man, mc w/pk lustre, 1810s, 6¾"	400.00
Rabbit, long ears, wht w/mc details, ca 1850-70, 2¼x3¼"	225.00
Robin Hood & Little John, spill vase, mc w/EX detail, 15", NM	300.00
Sailor, bearded, bl jacket, by cannon, 19th C, 7½"	440.00
Sailor in bl jacket stands by capstan, 19th C, 7⅞"	415.00
Sailor in cobalt jacket, bright vest & hat, 19th C, 9"	330.00
Sailor w/blk hair & beard in wht pants, 19th C, 10"	880.00
Sailor w/bottle & cup stands near bbl, 19th C, 10"	440.00
Sampson & the Lion, well colored, coleslaw, 11⅜", NM	425.00
Spaniel, pnt details, gold traces, 13½", EX	225.00
Spaniels, blk & wht w/gilt collars, seated, 12", pr	1,400.00
Spaniels, inkwells: male & female w/pup on base, 19th C, 5"	1,100.00
Squirrel perched on branch, vase, mc details, 1850-70, 6"	425.00
Squirrel w/nut, dk maroon-brn on gr base, Wood, 7½"	2,750.00
Tom King on horse, mc details, blk lettering, 8", NM	300.00
Twin brothers flanked by waterfall, 19th C, 10¾"	250.00
Uncle Tom & Eva, she putting rose wreath around his neck, 8"	400.00
Victoria in robes of State, blk & gold trim, 10¾", EX	550.00
Wellington seated, much cobalt & gold, rare, 12"	1,500.00
Wounded Soldier, 2 sailors w/hats, capes/walking stick, 12¾"	440.00
Zebra, blk & gr, 6½"	275.00

Historical

Basket, Dorney Court Buckinghamshire, openwork, d/b, Wood	850.00
Bowl, Chinese Family, d/b, unmk, 1⅛x8"	70.00
Bowl, Lafayette at Franklins' Tomb, d/b, 3¼x6½", NM	375.00
Bowl, vegetable; Boston State house, d/b, Rogers, w/lid, 9" sq	1,400.00
Bowl, vegetable; Liberty Cap & Am Flag, m-d/b w/red/ochre, 10"	165.00
Bowl, vegetable; Oriental, red, Ridgway, 10¼" L	35.00
Bowl, vegetable; Ship of Line in Downs, d/b, 9⅝", EX	900.00
Bowl, vegetable; Upper Ferry Bridge..., brn, Jackson, 9⅛"	575.00
Coffeepot, Lafayette at Tomb..., d/b, Phillips, 10½", EX	500.00
Coffeepot, Lafayette at Tomb..., d/b, Phillips, 11¾"	1,500.00
Coffeepot, Sailboat w/Abbey Ruins, d/b, domed top, rstr, 9¾"	325.00
Coffeepot, Virginia Church, d/b, high dome, rstr, 11"	600.00
Compote, Rode Hall Cheshire, d/b, ftd, Hall, 3½x12"	350.00
Cup & saucer, Columbian Star...1840, d/b, Ridgway, mini	250.00
Cup & saucer, Wadsworth Tower, d/b, irregular shell border	650.00
Cup plate, Arms of South Carolina, d/b, unmk Mayer, 4"	700.00
Cup plate, Broadlands Hampshire, d/b, Halls Scenery, 4"	185.00
Cup plate, Chinoiserie-Pagoda, d/b, flake, 3¾"	50.00
Cup plate, French View...Stone Bridge, m/b, Wood, 2¾", EX	40.00
Cup plate, Fruit & Birds, d/b, Stubbs, 4¼"	90.00
Cup plate, Shield of US, brn w/l/b spatter border, 3⅞"	190.00
Cup plate, Ship Under Half Sail, d/b, irregular shell border	257.00
Cup plate, Thatched Huts, d/b, Adams, 4"	70.00
Cup plate, Unidentified English Manor, d/b, Riley, 3½"	60.00
Garden seat, Olympian/Bizantium, m-d/b, Ridgway, 21x15⅜"	3,500.00
Gravy boat, Elk, d/b, Wood Zoological series, 4½"	350.00
Gravy undertray, Cathedral at York, d/b, Wood, 7⅛"	190.00
Gravy undertray, Upper Ferry Bridge..., d/b, Stubbs, 9" W	225.00
Pitcher, Coronation, Clews Warranted Ironstone, 6½"	325.00
Pitcher, Lady of Lake, m/b, Careys, rstr, 6⅝"	145.00
Pitcher, Lafayette at Tomb of Franklin, d/b, Phillips, 6¼"	750.00
Pitcher, Mt Vernon Washington's Seat, d/b, 6¾"	1,800.00

Pitcher, Newburgh Hudson River, red, Clews, 9½" 300.00
Pitcher, States Mansion w/Winding Driveway, d/b, Clews, 6⅛" 600.00
Pitcher & bowl, Norwich Castle/Rivax Abbey, d/b, Clews, NM .1,600.00
Plate, Am & Independence, d/b, Clews, 10⅝", EX 300.00
Plate, Am & Independence, d/b, Clews, 8" 200.00
Plate, Am Marine, brn, Ashworth, 7½" 20.00
Plate, At Richmond VA, blk, Jackson, 7" 20.00
Plate, Batalha Portugal, d/b, 8¼" 65.00
Plate, British Views, d/b, fruit/flower border, 8¼", NM 85.00
Plate, Caldwell Lake George, l/b, Mellor Venerables, 10" 65.00
Plate, Capitol Washington, d/b, wht rim, RSW, 10" 350.00
Plate, Chinoiserie, d/b, att Stubbs, 7⅝" 50.00
Plate, Church at Point Levi, l/b, Morely, 8⅛" 50.00
Plate, City Hall NY, m/b, 9¾" 150.00
Plate, Clyde Scenery, blk w/red border, Jackson, 10½" 110.00
Plate, Columbian Star..., brn, Ridgway, 7½" 100.00
Plate, Commodore MacDonnough's Victory, d/b, Wood, 10¼" .385.00
Plate, Courthouse Baltimore, d/b, Henshall, spider, 8½" 300.00
Plate, Edinburgh, d/bl, floral/scroll border, 8¼" 150.00
Plate, Esholt House Yorkshire, d/b, grape border, 10¼" 170.00
Plate, Fairmount Ardens, d/b, Ridgway, 9" 90.00
Plate, Fairmount Near Phila, d/b, eagle border, Stubbs, 10", EX .100.00
Plate, Fairmount Water Works on Schuylkill, d/b, Wood, 9" 100.00
Plate, Faulkbourne Hall, d/b, Stevenson wild rose border, 8⅝" ..110.00
Plate, Faulkbourne Hall, d/b, wild rose border, 10¼" 170.00
Plate, Friburg, l/b, Davenport, 9¼" 35.00
Plate, Hanover Lodge Regent's Park, d/b, Wood, 9⅜" 145.00
Plate, Haxham Abbey, m-d/b, 10" 70.00
Plate, Kent East Indiaman, d/b, irregular shell border, 9¼" 400.00
Plate, La Grange Residence...Lafayette, d/b, 10¼", EX 300.00
Plate, Landing of Lafayette, d/b, Clews, flake, 9" 200.00
Plate, Liberty Cap & Am Flag, mulberry w/mc, 10¾" 185.00
Plate, lion, d/b, Hall Quadrupeds series, 10" 275.00
Plate, Mosaic Tracery, d/b, Clews, 7¼" 65.00
Plate, Moulin Sur La Marine A Charenton, d/b, Wood, 9⅛" 115.00
Plate, Orwell Park Suffolk, d/b, 7¾" 130.00
Plate, Pains Hill Surrey, d/b, Hall Select Views, 10" 140.00
Plate, Park Theatre NY, d/b, 10" 225.00
Plate, Pittsfield Elm, d/b, Clews, rstr, 10⅝" 125.00
Plate, Pittsfield Elm, m/b, Clews, 6¾" 225.00
Plate, Quebec, d/b, Davenport Cities series, 9" 225.00
Plate, Race Bridge Phila, red, Jackson, flake, 9" 120.00
Plate, Residence of Late Richard Jordan, blk, 10½" 195.00
Plate, Residence of Late Richard Jordan, purple, 7⅝" 150.00
Plate, Residence of Late Richard Jordan, red, 10⅜" 250.00
Plate, Schuylkill Water Works, d/b, Goodwin, 9¼" 160.00
Plate, Shells, d/b, Stubbs, sm rpr, 10¼" 170.00
Plate, Sheltered Peasants, d/b, Hall, 10", NM 160.00
Plate, Tomb of Washington..., l/b, Mellor Venerables, 7⅜" 30.00
Plate, Transylvania University Lexington, d/b, Wood, 9½" 360.00
Plate, unidentified cathedral, d/b, Clews scroll border, 7¾" 85.00
Plate, Upper Ferry Bridge..., d/b, eagle border, Stubbs, 8¾" 160.00
Plate, View Near Conway NH, red, Adams, 9" 35.00
Plate, View of Liverpool, d/b, irregular shell border, rpr, 10" 250.00
Plate, View of Trenton Falls, d/b, regular shell border, 7¾" 275.00
Plate, Villa in Regent's Park...Waverly, d/b, Wood, 8⅞" 145.00
Plate, Village of Little Falls, red, Meigh, 8⅛" 130.00
Plate, Wm Penn's Treaty, brn, T Green, 7¼" 60.00
Platter, Am & Independence, d/b, Clews, 12⅞", EX 770.00
Platter, Am Villa, d/b, rstr, 16½" 300.00
Platter, Beehive & Vases, d/b, Stevens & Wms, 14⅞" 475.00
Platter, Boston State House, d/b, Rogers, 14⅝" 550.00
Platter, Boston State House, d/b, Rogers, 18¾" 800.00
Platter, British Views, d/b, 19¼" 650.00

Platter, Celtic China...Grecian Scenery, d/b, Wood, 18½" 375.00
Platter, Chief Brigan's Death, l/b, crack, 21¾" 100.00
Platter, Columbus...Landing Scene, red, Adams, 15¼", NM 200.00
Platter, Commerce...Free Trade, blk, Phillips, 19" 325.00
Platter, Eastern Port Scene, m-d/b, Ridgway, 21", EX 450.00
Platter, Fairmount Near Phila, d/b, eagle border, 20½" 1,750.00
Platter, Florals & Geometrics, d/b, 20¾" 350.00
Platter, Hare Hall Yorkshire, d/b, passion flower border, 15" 450.00
Platter, Hermitage en Dauphine, d/b, Wood, rstr, 15" 500.00
Platter, Mendenhall Ferry, d/b, eagle border, Stubbs, 16½" 1,100.00
Platter, NY From Heights Near Brooklyn, d/b, Stevenson, 16¼" .1,200.00
Platter, PA Hospital Phila, d/b, Ridgway, 8-sided, 18½" 1,400.00
Platter, Peace & Plenty, d/b, Clews, prof rstr, 17¼" 550.00
Platter, University, gray-blk, Ridgway, 19½" 100.00
Platter, Upper Ferry Bridge..., d/b, eagle border, 18½" 1,350.00
Platter, well & tree; Coronation, m-d/bl, Clews, 20¾" 1,000.00
Platter, Wild Rose, brn, unmk, 14¼" 75.00
Platter, York, l/b, wht emb rim, Wood, 16¾" 300.00
Shakers, Am Eagle on an Urn, d/b, urn shape, Clews, 4½" 500.00
Soup, Arms of NY, d/bk, Mayer, 10" 635.00
Soup, Bridge at Lucano, d/b, att Spode, 9¾" 110.00
Soup, Chaudiere Bridge, l/b, Morely, 10¼" 50.00
Soup, Landing of Gen Lafayette, d/b, Clews, 9⅞", EX 275.00
Soup, Octagon Church Boston, d/b, Ridgway, chip, 9¾" 260.00
Soup, Pastoral, m/b, emb wht border, Stevenson, chip, 10½" 50.00
Soup, Pine Orchard House, Catskill Mtns, d/b, Wood, 9⅜" 525.00
Soup, St Peters Rome, d/b, Wood, 10¼" 200.00
Soup, US Hotel Phila, d/b, James, 10¼" 625.00
Soup, View Near Phila, d/b, Wood, 9¾" 310.00
Soup ladle, Lady of the Lake, m/b, Carey, rstr, 11" 140.00
Soup tureen, Lakes of Kilarney, m-d/b, scroll finial, 8x14" 750.00
Sugar bowl, Boston State House, d/b, Rogers, w/lid, rstr, 5½" 450.00
Sugar bowl, Eagle on Rock, red, Wood, w/lid, rstr 600.00
Sugar bowl, Lafayette at Tomb of Franklin, d/b, w/lid 275.00
Sugar bowl, Mt Vernon...Gen'l Washington, d/b, rstr, 5½" 300.00
Sugar bowl, Phila Water Works, l/b, 8-sided, flower finial 425.00
Tea bowl & saucer, Residence of Late Richard Jordan, blk 275.00
Teapot, Basket of Flowers, d/b, C hdl, rstr, 6½" 650.00
Teapot, Basket of Fruit & Flowers, d/b, Clews, 7x11¾", EX 350.00
Teapot, Boston Harber, d/b, unmk Rogers, rstr, 7" 800.00
Teapot, Coronation, ca 1819-35 ....350.00
Teapot, Man in Boat w/English Town..., d/b, rstr, 7½x12" 400.00
Tray, Girl Musician, d/b, Riley, scalloped oval, 10" 300.00
Tureen, Passaic Falls/Hudson River View, d/b, w/lid, 6⅜x8" 950.00
Tureen, sauce; Balloch Castle..., d/b, Riley, w/lid, EX 325.00
Tureen, sauce; Upper Ferry Bridge, Stubbs, w/underplate 220.00
Tureen, Trinity Hall..., d/b, w/lid, Ridgway, 6¼x8¼" 325.00
Undertray, Pass in Catskills, d/b, Wood, 8" 850.00
Wash bowl, Lafayette at Tomb of Franklin, d/b, Wood, 12" 1,250.00
Waste bowl, Lafayette at Tomb of..., d/b, Phillips, 6¼" 290.00

Stained Glass

There are many factors to consider in evaluating a window or panel of stained glass art. Besides the obvious factor of condition, intricacy, jeweling, beveling, and the amount of selenium (red, orange, and yellow) present should all be taken into account. Remember, repair work is itself an art and can be very expensive. Our advisor for this category is Carl Heck; he is listed in the Directory under Colorado.

Lamps

Ceiling, red grapes among amber & gr, bent crown above, 20" dia ...375.00

Chicago Mosaic, 24" water-lily shade; 3-socket std, 26½" **4,000.00**
Duffner-Kimberly, 18½" scrolled shade; 4-socket std, 23½" **8,000.00**
Duffner-Kimberly, 19" shell shade; 3-socket foliate std, 23" ..**11,500.00**
Duffner-Kimberly, 22" floral shade w/apron; 3-face std, 29" ..**13,800.00**
Duffner-Kimberly, 22" spider-web shade; 3-socket std, 24" **5,000.00**
Duffner-Kimberly, 24" peony shade w/apron; bronze std, 29" .**14,950.00**
Duffner-Kimberly, 31" vintage umbrella shade; bronze std, 70" .**17,250.00**
Jefferson, 18" pond lilies/pads, mc/bl shade; mk std, 21½" **3,738.00**
Seuss, 20" dogwood umbrella shade; 3-socket bronze std, 21" ..**3,500.00**
Seuss, 22" peony irregular-rim shade; bronze std, 30" **5,175.00**

Wilkinson, 22" floral shade; 3-socket gilt metal standard base, 29", $4,000.00.

Wilkinson, 22" floral/scroll dome shade; 4-socket std, 60" **8,165.00**

Windows

Foliate design surrounds central anchor, jewels, 112x39" **3,000.00**
Symmetrical Gothic-style design w/red/bl/amber panels, 33x28" ..**440.00**
Tree of Life scene ornate design, several layers, 56x37" **3,250.00**
Wisteria on trellis, encased in safety glass, 40x20" **2,250.00**

Stanford

The Stanford Pottery Co. was founded in 1945 in Sebring, Ohio. One of the founders was George Stanford, a former manager at Spaulding China (Royal Copley). They continued in operations until the factory was destroyed by a fire about 1961. They produced a Corn Line, similar to that of the Shawnee Company, that is today becoming very collectible. Most examples are marked (either Stanford Sebring Ohio or with a paper label), so there should be no difficulty in distinguishing one from the other.

In addition to their Corn line, they produced planters and figurines, many of which were black trimmed with gold, made to be sold as pairs or sets. Wall pockets and vases were made as well. In 1949 they introduced a line called Tomato Ware, consisting of a cookie jar, grease jar, salt and pepper shakers, creamer and sugar bowl, mustard jar, marmalade jar, etc. These were shaped as bright red tomatoes with green leaves and stems (often used as lid finials), and were marketed under the name 'The Pantry Parade.' Our advisor for this category is Joe Devine; he is listed in the Directory under Iowa.

Ashtray, free-form, orange w/wht 'stucco,' #270-D, mk, 10x7" **12.00**
Corn Line, butter dish **45.00**
Corn Line, casserole, 8" L **35.00**
Corn Line, creamer & sugar bowl **45.00**
Corn Line, pitcher, 7½" **55.00**
Corn Line, plate, 9" L **30.00**
Corn Line, relish tray **35.00**
Corn Line, shakers, sm, pr **25.00**
Corn Line, shakers, 4", pr **25.00**

Corn Line, spoon rest **25.00**
Corn Line, teapot **60.00**
Planter, drum major or majorette, ea **15.00**
Planter, Dutch boy or girl by tulip, blk w/gold trim, ea **15.00**
Planter, teddy bear, wht w/pk & bl trim, paper label, 7" **28.00**
Tomato Ware, casserole, w/lid, 6x9" **55.00**
Tomato Ware, cookie jar, 8" **60.00**
Tomato Ware, creamer **25.00**
Tomato Ware, grease jar, w/lid **30.00**
Tomato Ware, marmalade jar **25.00**
Tomato Ware, mustard jar **25.00**
Tomato Ware, pitcher, 6½" **50.00**
Tomato Ware, sugar bowl **25.00**
Wall pocket, bird, bl & cobalt w/gold trim **28.00**
Wall pocket, cherry branch, red pie-crust edge, #299, mk, 6¼" **20.00**

Stangl

Stangl Pottery was one of the longest-existing potteries in the United States, having its beginning in 1814 the Sam Hill Pottery, becoming the Fulper Pottery which gained eminence in the field of art pottery (ca. 1860), and then coming under the aegis of Johann Martin Stangl. The German-born Stangl joined Fulper in 1910 as chemical engineer, left for a brief stint at Haeger in Dundee, Illinois, and rejoined Fulper as general manager in 1920. He became president of the firm in 1928. Although Stangl's name was on much of the ware from the late '20s onward, the company's name was not changed officially until 1955. J.M. Stangl died in 1972; the pottery continued under the ownership of Wheaton Industries until 1978, then closed. Stangl is best known for its extensive Birds of America line, styled after Audubon; its brightly colored, hand-carved, hand-painted dinnerware; and its great variety of giftware, including the dry-brushed gold lines. For more information we recommend *Stangl Pottery* by Harvey Duke; for ordering information refer to the listing for Nancy and Robert Perzel, Popkorn Antiques (our advisors for this category), in our Directory under New Jersey.

Birds

#3250E, Drinking Duck **100.00**
#3274, Penguin **500.00**
#3275, Turkey, 3½" **500.00**
#3276D, Bluebirds, 8" **180.00**
#3285, Rooster, wht & blk w/red & yel, early version, 4½" **100.00**
#3286, Hen, late version **50.00**
#3400, Lovebird, revised version **60.00**
#3401, Wren, brn, revised version **60.00**
#3401, Wren, tan, old version **250.00**
#3401D, Wrens, early version, 6½" **250.00**
#3402D, Orioles, early version, 6½" **225.00**
#3402D, Orioles, revised **125.00**
#3404, Lovebirds Kissing **350.00**
#3405, Cockatoo **50.00**
#3405D, Cockatoos, old, 10" **190.00**
#3405D, Cockatoos, revised version, 9½" **150.00**
#3406D, Kingfishers, 5" **135.00**
#3408, Bird of Paradise, 8" **125.00**
#3444, Cardinal, dk red matt, 7" **135.00**
#3444, Cardinal, pk, 7" **100.00**
#3445, Rooster, lt yel **175.00**
#3446, Hen, gray **200.00**
#3447, Prothonatary Warbler, yel & gr, 5" **85.00**
#3448, Blue-Headed Vireo, 4" **85.00**
#3449, Parrot, dk gr w/mc, 5½" **150.00**

#3450, Passenger Pigeon 1,200.00
#3454, Key West Quail Dove, both wings up 1,000.00
#3454, Key West Quail Dove, single wing up, 10" 300.00
#3455, Shoveler Duck, rare, 12½x14" 1,200.00
#3458, Quail, old mk, 7½" 1,000.00
#3490D, Redstarts, 9½" 225.00
#3518D, White-Crowned Pigeons 750.00
#3581, Chickadees (group), blk & wht 275.00
#3581, Chickadees, 5½x8½" 225.00
#3582D, Parakeets, bl 125.00
#3583, Parula Warbler, 4" 55.00
#3585, Rufous Hummingbird, 3½" 65.00
#3591, Brewer's Blackbird, 4" 130.00
#3592, Titmouse, 3" 60.00
#3593, Nuthatch, 3" 60.00
#3596, Cardinal, gray, 5" 90.00
#3598, Kentucky Warbler, 3½" 60.00
#3599D, Hummingbirds 300.00
#3627, Rivoli Hummingbird, w/pk flower 150.00
#3628, Reiffers Hummingbird, 4½x6½" 125.00
#3629, Broadbill Hummingbird 125.00
#3635, Gold Finches, group of 4 ....185.00
#3715, Blue Jay, w/peanut, 10" 675.00
#3750, Western Tanager, 8½", $220 to 235.00
#3752D, Red-Headed Woodpeckers, pk glossy, 8½" 275.00
#3752D, Red-Headed Woodpeckers, red matt 300.00
#3754, White-Wing Crossbill 2,250.00
#3757, Scissor-Tailed Flycatcher, 11" 600.00
#3810, Blackpoll Warbler 155.00
#3811, Chestnut-Backed Chickadee, 5" 125.00
#3813, Evening Grosbeak, artist sgn, 5" 125.00
#3814, Black-Throated Green Warbler, 3" 135.00
#3848, Golden-Crowned Kinglet, 4½" 110.00
#3853, Gold-Crowned Kinglets, group: mother/2 babies, 5½x5" ..550.00
#3922, European Finch 1,000.00
#3924, Yellow-Throated Warbler, 6" 425.00

Miscellaneous

Dogwood, plate, 10", $11.00.

Apple Delight, mug 20.00
Apple Delight, plate, luncheon 10.00
Apple Delight, server, 2-tier 20.00
Ashtray, mallard duck, sq, #3915 ....50.00
Ashtray, pheasant, oval, #3926 ....25.00
Bachelor's Button, plate, 12" 30.00
Blueberry, bowl, fruit 15.00
Blueberry, bowl, vegetable; 10" 50.00
Blueberry, butter dish 40.00
Blueberry, cup & saucer 15.00
Blueberry, gravy boat 25.00
Blueberry, gravy liner 15.00

Blueberry, lug soup 15.00
Blueberry, plate, 10" 22.00
Blueberry, plate, 12" 40.00
Blueberry, plate, 6" 8.00
Blueberry, plate, 8" 16.00
Blueberry, sandwich tray, center hdl, 10" 8.00
Blueberry, shakers, pr 20.00
Carnival, bread tray, #420 ....25.00
Carnival, condiment tray, #415 ....15.00
Carnival, plate, 8" 7.50
Carnival, shakers, pr 8.00
Country Garden, bowl, lug soup 12.00
Country Garden, bowl, 12" 75.00
Country Garden, bowl, 8" 30.00
Country Garden, butter dish, ¼-lb 40.00
Country Garden, cup & saucer 16.00
Country Garden, plate, 10" 20.00
Country Garden, plate, 8" 14.00
Country Garden, sugar bowl, w/lid 12.50
Country Garden, teapot 65.00
Country Life, bowl, fruit; w/pony 75.00
Country Life, cup & saucer 65.00
Country Life, soup, mallard, 8" 150.00
Festival, bowl, cereal 12.00
Festival, bowl, divided vegetable 35.00
Festival, bowl, fruit 10.00
Festival, casserole, w/serving lid 50.00
Festival, cup & saucer, Terra Rose 15.00
Festival, plate, Terra Rose, 10" 15.00
Festival, plate, 6" 6.00
Fruit, bowl, cereal 18.00
Fruit, bowl, fruit 16.00
Fruit, bowl, oval vegetable; 2-part 40.00
Fruit, bowl, soup; 7½" 20.00
Fruit, casual plate 55.00
Fruit, chop plate, 12" 45.00
Fruit, chop plate, 14" 55.00
Fruit, creamer & sugar bowl 27.50
Fruit, cruet, w/stopper 35.00
Fruit, cup & saucer 17.00
Fruit, egg cup 15.00
Fruit, gravy boat 25.00
Fruit, pitcher, ½-pt 15.00
Fruit, plate, dinner 22.00
Fruit, plate, 6" 8.00
Fruit, plate, 8" 20.00
Fruit, relish tray 40.00
Fruit, shakers, pr 18.00
Golden Blossom, cup & saucer 11.00
Golden Blossom, egg cup 12.00
Golden Blossom, platter, 12" dia 27.50
Golden Harvest, bowl, salad; 10" 30.00
Golden Harvest, chop plate, 12" 20.00
Golden Harvest, creamer & sugar bowl, w/lid 15.00
Golden Harvest, cup & saucer 12.00
Golden Harvest, pitcher, 2-qt 35.00
Golden Harvest, shakers, pr 15.00
Kiddieware, ABC dish 115.00
Kiddieware, bowl, Little Bo Peep 100.00
Kiddieware, cup, Indian Campfire 100.00
Kiddieware, dish, Kitten Capers, 3-part 100.00
Kiddieware, plate, Gingerbread Boy 300.00
Kiddieware, plate, Little Boy Blue 100.00
Magnolia, bowl, centerpc; 12" 60.00

Magnolia, bowl, 5½" 8.00
Magnolia, creamer & sugar bowl, w/lid 22.00
Magnolia, plate, dinner; 10" 15.00
Magnolia, shakers, pr 20.00
Mediterranean, platter, Casual 45.00
Plate, factory outlet, Flemington, silk screened, 10" 125.00
Provincial, bowl, fruit; 5½" 9.00
Provincial, bowl, lug soup 12.00
Sculptured Fruit, bowl, 8" 30.00
Sculptured Fruit, cup & saucer 15.00
Sculptured Fruit, plate, 10" 14.00
Sportsmen, plate, Canvas Back, 11" 58.00
Terra Rose, fish vase, gr, #3569 ....200.00
Terra Rose, horse-head vase, gr, #3611 ....400.00
Terra Rose, mtn goat vase, gr & mauve, #3708 ....450.00
Terra Rose, wall planter, cosmos, gr, #2091 ....45.00
Thistle, bowl, casserole, knob lid, ind 15.00
Thistle, bowl, cereal 16.00
Thistle, bowl, fruit 12.00
Thistle, bowl, lug soup 15.00
Thistle, bowl, salad; 10" 40.00
Thistle, bowl, salad; 12" 65.00
Thistle, bowl, 5½" 10.00
Thistle, coaster 16.00
Thistle, condiment tray 28.00
Thistle, creamer & sugar bowl, w/lid 22.00
Thistle, cup & saucer 12.50
Thistle, gravy w/stand 38.00
Thistle, plate, 10" 15.00
Thistle, plate, 6" 6.00
Thistle, plate, 9" 14.00
Thistle, relish 25.00
Thistle, teapot 60.00
Town & Country, cheese & crackers, bl dustpan shape 100.00
Town & Country, plate, bl, 10" 45.00
Town & Country, spoon rest 30.00
Town & Country, teapot, bl 125.00
Wig stand, blond, wood base 450.00
Wig stand, brunette, ceramic base 350.00

Stanley Tools

The Stanley company was founded in Connecticut in 1854, and over the years has absorbed more than a score of tool companies already in existence. By the second decade of the 20th century, having long since solidified their position as *the* source for tools of the highest grade, the company enjoyed worldwide prestige. Through both World Wars, they were recognized as one of the nation's premier producers of wartime goods. Industrial arts classes introduced baby boomers to Stanley tools and provided yet another impetus to expansion and recognition. Overall, the company's growth and development has kept an easy pace along with the economy of the nation, and it continues today as a leader in the field of tool production.

Two factors to consider when evaluating a tool are age and condition. One of their earliest trademarks (1854-1857) is 'A. Stanley,' found only on rulers. In the early '20s, their now-familiar 'sweetheart' trademark, the letters SW and a heart shape within the confines of a modified rectangle, was adopted. They continued to use this trademark until it was discontinued in 1933. Many other variations were used as well, some of which contain a patent date. A study of these marks will help you determine the vintage of your tools. Condition is extremely important, and though a light cleaning is acceptable, you should never attempt to 'restore' a tool by sanding, repainting, or replacing parts that may be

damaged or missing. Tools listed below are for those in average 'as found' condition, ranging from very good to excellent.

For more information, we recommend *Antique and Collectible Stanley Tools,* written by our advisor, John Walter, who is listed in the Directory under Ohio.

Angle divider, #30, MIB 140.00
Beader, #66 ....285.00
Bevel, #25 ....150.00
Bit brace, #813G, heavy-duty chuck, 12" sweep 60.00
Bit brace, corner; #984 ....150.00
Butt gauge & mortiser, MIB 50.00
Carpenter's plumb & level, #98, rosewood, brass-bound, 12" 475.00
Clamp, cable splicing 50.00
Cutter & chisel grinder, #200 ....200.00
Hand drill, #624, NMIB 325.00
Hollow & Round set, #6 ....95.00
Level, machinist's; #34V, 4" L, M 75.00
Level sights, #2, MIB 95.00
Marking gauge, #65 ....60.00
Mortise gauge, #91 ....65.00

Plane/cutter, type 7, $185.00.

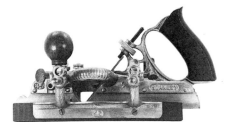

Plane, #3, rosewood hdld, MIB 250.00
Plane, block; #65 ....165.00
Plane, dovetail; #444 ....850.00
Plane, improved dado; #239, MIB 550.00
Plane, jack; #5 ....85.00
Plane, jointer; #7, NM 325.00
Plane, side rabbet; #79, NMIB 145.00
Plane, smooth; #2 ....495.00
Pliers, lead pipe expanding; #19 ....200.00
Plumb bob, #1 ....245.00
Rule, caliper; ivory, #38, 2-fold, 6" 325.00
Rule, carpenter's sliding; 2-ft, 2-fold, #15 ....295.00
Screwdriver, ratchet; #215 ....90.00
Spoke shave, chamfer; #65 ....160.00
Square, combination; #21, 12" 60.00
Square, improved mitre; #16 ....125.00
Square, try; gold lettering rosewood hdl, 10" bl blade, MIB 250.00
Trammel points, #2 ....150.00
Vantage rod, #44, 16½" long, hand stamped 150.00

Statue of Liberty

Long before she began greeting immigrants in 1886, the Statue of Liberty was being honored by craftsmen both here and abroad. Her likeness was etched on blades of the finest straight razors from England, captured in finely detailed busts sold as souvenirs to Paris fairgoers in 1878, and presented on colorfully lithographed trade cards, usually satirical, to American shoppers. Perhaps no other object has been represented in more forms or with such frequency as the universal symbol of America. Liberty's keepsakes are also universally accessible. Delightful souvenir models created in 1885 to raise funds for Liberty's pedestal are frequently found at flea markets, while earlier French bronze and terra cotta Liberties have been auctioned for over $100,000.00. Some collectors hunt for the countless forms of 19th-century Liberty memorabilia, while many collections were begun in anticipation of the 1986 Centennial with concentration on modern depictions. Our advisor for this category is Mike Brooks; he is listed in the Directory under California.

Booklet, Rays From Liberty's Torch, 1890 ....30.00
Bookmark, fabric, Bartholdi Souvenir, 1886 ....25.00
Bottle, milk glass, pewter lid, 10" 235.00
Bottle, seltzer; etched Liberty, A Doeink, Liberty NY 35.00
Box, Liberty Hair Clipper, 1930s 25.00
Candy container, glass miniature w/metal statue top, 1920s 130.00
Card, admission to inauguration, 1886 ....70.00
Card, eng, Visit to Gauthier et Cie, Paris Foundry, 1883, VG 75.00
Charm bracelet, NY World's Fair 40.00
Cigar box label, Victory Day, WWI 6.00
Clock, figural, United, animated, very rare 350.00
Cup, pewter, Germany, ca 1904 ....60.00
Cup, sterling, Windsor Club, 1907, 2" 22.00
Envelope, NY World newspaper, postmk 1885, Liberty logo 55.00
First Day Internat'l covers, Internat'l album of 50, 1986 ....75.00
Hanukkah menorah, Liberty-featured candle holders, M Anson 1,800.00
Harper's Weekly, various litho prints, 1880s, ea, from $10 to 25.00
Invitation to inauguration, by President Cleveland 150.00
Letter, teen to military father re: parade on Broadway, 1886 ....95.00
Magic lantern slide, harbor scene 30.00
Medal, Democratic National Convention, NY, 1924 ....30.00
Medal, Tasset, Paris, 1876 (earliest known) 100.00
Napkin holder, sterling 15.00
Paperweight, rnd, ca 1880s 100.00
Photo, Liberty sketch, Centennial Photographic Co, 1876, VG 40.00
Photo album, celluloid image on front, velvet bk, 10x8" 275.00
Photograph, Liberty nearing completion, 1886 ....85.00
Pin, enamel, 77th Div, WWI 12.00
Pipe, glazed clay, 1880s 90.00
Plate, Austrian, various NY scenes, ca 1900 ....45.00
Plate, glass, eng statue, heart shape 22.00
Plates, various makers, 1980s, ea, from $10 to 20.00
Playing cards, Allied Nations, WWI, complete deck 20.00
Radio speaker stand, wht metal casting, Palcone, 17" 175.00
Statue, cast metal on marble base, June 13, 1885 ....1,000.00
Stereo card, head of Liberty, Paris, 1878 ....80.00
Straight razor, Liberty-etched blade, Sheffield, ca 1880 ....75.00
Trade card, satirical, A&C Hams 70.00
Trade card, satirical, Moline Plow 30.00
Vase, frosted Liberty hand, Gillinder, 1876 Centennial 70.00
Watercolor, View of Liberty, JW Goppard, 21x15" 220.00

Steamship Collectibles

For centuries, ocean-going vessels with their venturesome officers and crews were the catalyst that changed the unknown aspects of our world to the known. Changing economic conditions, unfortunately, have now placed the North American shipping industry in the same jeopardy as the American passenger train. They are becoming a memory. The surge of interest in railroad collectibles and the railroad-related steamship lines has lead collectors to examine the whole spectrum of steamship collectibles. Our advisors for this category are Lila and Fred Shrader; they are listed in the Directory under California.

Key:
BS — back stamped   TL — top logo
NBS — no back stamp   TM — top mark
SL — side logo

Dinnerware

Bowl, Pacific Mail SS Co, wht w/SL in red & blk, 6" 125.00
Butter pat, Mobil 75.00
Butter pat, North Pacific SS Co, TM w/house flag 110.00
Butter pat, United Fruit, Antigua, house flag/name, 2¾" sq 172.00
Creamer, Zim Lines, house flag w/7 stars, 3¾" 22.00
Cup, bouillon; Am Export Lines, wht w/yel & bl stripes, +liner 39.00
Cup, demitasse; Livanos Shipping Co 20.00
Cup & saucer, demitasse; Am Mail Line, TM & SL 65.00
Cup & saucer, Ford, wht w/dk gr Ford logo 45.00
Cup & saucer, Pacific Far East..., cobalt house flag/yel bear 55.00
Egg cup, Cunard, wht w/gold & floral border 35.00
Egg cup, Texaco, house flag on side, lg 125.00
Plate, Merchants & Miners, swallowtail flag, M&MMT Co, 10" 75.00
Plate, Monticello SS Co, Vallejo, logo on wht, 6½" 88.00
Plate, Pacific Far East..., cobalt house flag/yel bear, 6" 32.00
Platter, Great Northern Pacific SS, flag w/Xd bars & star, 6x8" 125.00
Relish, Dollar Line, pinstripes & house flag on wht, 4½x7½" 65.00
Teapot, Hellenic Lines, Hellenic, bl & wht flag, NBS, ind 65.00
Toothpick holder, CP BC SS, verde gr, gold stamped logo, 2" 49.00

Glassware

Cocktail, Matson, w/logo 15.00
Cordial, Matson, w/logo 22.00
Cordial, White Star, swallowtail house flag logo cut in side 110.00
Tumbler, French Line silkscreened in brn, 5½" 9.00
Tumbler, United States Line, eng eagle in rope fr, 5" 59.00
Wine, Hellenic Lines, eng house flag, 5" 43.00

Silver

Ashtray w/matchbox holder, Union Castle Line, 5½" 78.00
Creamer, MM (Moore-McCormick), Int Silver Co, 2½" 60.00
Fork, serving; White Star, TM w/house flag, EX 128.00
Iced tea spoon, Alaska SS, TM logo 32.00
Spoon, serving; Dollar Line, TM logo 65.00
Sugar shell, Union Estates SS Co 28.00
Sugar tongs, White Star, w/talon-like tongs, TM, 5" 88.00
Teaspoon, Alaska SS, TM logo 24.00
Thermos bottle, Am Pres Lines, Reed & Barton, w/stopper, 8½" 150.00

Miscellaneous

Ashtray, Cunard, Queen Mary, brn Bakelite RMS Queen Mary, 3x4" 55.00
Ashtray/matchbox holder, CN SS, brass w/maple leaf logo, 5¼" dia 64.00
Baggage sticker, Union Castle Line, Art Deco, 3x4½" 9.00
Blanket, CN SS, bl leaf pattern, cotton, center logo, 48x80" 175.00
Bottle opener, Queen Mary, ship floats in hdl 32.00
Brochure, Dollar Line Rnd World Via Orient & Europe, 1926 ....22.00
Button, uniform; Dollar Line, ⅞" 8.00
Button, uniform; Royal Mail Steam Packet Co, ¾" 15.00
Desk set, Anchor line, fr, paper/pen holder, metal & Bakelite 135.00
Lap robe, No German Line, Kronprinzessin, woven, leather bound 225.00
Matchbook, Cunard, 1960s, unused 6.00
Menu, Cunard, Queen Mary, luncheon, 1937 ....11.00
Menu, Farrell Lines, SS Red Jacket, 1-sheet, 1981, 5½x9" 3.50
Mirror, frosted Drottningholm on bl w/bevel, 26" dia 385.00
Postcard, Cunard's RMS Carmania at sea, M 12.00
Postcard, Pacific Coast SS Spokane at Taku glacier, AK, 1913 ....15.00

Stationery, pre-1917 sheets & envelopes, unused, ea, from $10 to ..**25.00**
Stationery, 1918-40, sheets & envelopes, unused, ea, from $5 to .**20.00**
Towel, bath; Hamburg-Am Line, Deutschland in bl **57.00**

Steins

Steins have been made from pottery, pewter, glass, stoneware, and porcelain, from very small up to the four-liter size. They are decorated by etching, in-mold relief, decals, and occasionally they may be hand painted. Some porcelain steins have lithophane bases. Collectors often specialize in a particular type — faience, regimental, or figural — while others limit themselves to the products of only one manufacturer. Our advisor for this category is Ron Fox; he is listed in the Directory under New York. See also Mettlach.

Key:
L — liter   tl — thumb lift
lith — lithophane

Anheuser Busch by Ceramarte, bald eagle, w/lid, .5L **400.00**
Anheuser Busch by Ceramarte, Bud Girl, .5L, NM **325.00**
Anheuser Busch by Ceramarte, Clydesdales, .5L **235.00**
Anheuser Busch by Ceramarte, Orig Bud Man, lt bl, .5L, EX **300.00**
Anheuser Busch by Gerz, Adolphus Busch, A & eagle lid, .5L ...**145.00**
Bl salt glaze, etched decor, pewter lid, ca 1850, sm chop, 1.5L ...**220.00**
Bl salt glaze, relief: Minerva/Acamemnon/Achilles, 3L, EX **235.00**
Character, barmaid, porc, porc lid, Shierholz, rpr, .5L **1,485.00**
Character, cat w/fish & bottle, pottery, music box, .5L **500.00**
Character, Dutch boy, porc, porc lid, .5L **180.00**
Character, half-moon face, porc, rpl pewter lid, .25L **225.00**
Character, knight, majolica, pewter helmet lid, .5L, NM **330.00**
Character, Munich child, porc, inlaid lid, .5L **300.00**
Character, Munich child, porc, monument lith, .5L **695.00**
Character, Munich child, pottery, inlaid lid, Reinemann, 1L **385.00**
Character, owl, stoneware, inlaid lid, #922, .5L **400.00**
Character, pig, inlaid lid, R Merkelbach #1116, .5L, NM **210.00**
Character, roly-poly barmaid, pottery, inlaid lid, .5L, NM **535.00**

Character stein, Sailor, pottery, marked 1821, .5-L, $1,100.00.

Character, stepmother w/money bag, pottery, inlaid lid, .5L, EX ..**440.00**
Character, woman, pottery, inlaid, rprs, Diesinger #702, .5L **455.00**
Convention, pewter, Minneapolis 1979, 313, 1L **130.00**
Glass, blown, amber, HP floral traces, pewter lid, 1.5L **95.00**
Glass, blown, amber, pewter floral o/l, hdl & lid, .5L **145.00**
Glass, blown, amber w/bl hdl, HP hops/wheat, prism lid, 1.5L ...**525.00**
Glass, blown, cranberry, ribbed, pewter o/l base, .3L **275.00**
Glass, blown, cut circles, inlaid lid, dwarf tl, .3L **185.00**
Glass, blown, cut circles & stars, pewter base & lid, .5L **155.00**
Glass, blown, eng vintage, faceted, dwarf tl, 1870s, .5L **300.00**

Glass, blown, faceted at base, Munich child on porc lid, .5L **95.00**
Glass, blown, faceted/HP: 4-leaf clover/card suits, .5L **165.00**
Glass, blown, HP floral/gold verse, pewter lid, 1840s, 1L **600.00**
Glass, blown, HP house scene, faceted, pewter lid, .3L **125.00**
Glass, blown, HP leaping deer, pewter lid, flaw, .5L **145.00**
Glass, pressed, transfer: hunter coming home, pewter lid, .5L **80.00**
Military, porc, Conzer Medical Division 1963-66, w/lid, .5L **165.00**
Military, porc, transfer: Wallace Barracks 1958, w/lid, .5L **180.00**
Occupational, architect, stoneware, combed bbl shape, .5L **115.00**
Occupational, carpenter relief, pottery, tans, pewter lid, .5L **300.00**
Occupational, farmer, bl salt glaze, pewter lid, #3006, .5L **150.00**
Pewter, relief: farming scenes, dents, .5L **130.00**
Pewter, relief: lovers & cherubs, woman finial, .5L, NM **300.00**
Pewter, repousse: castle scene, lead cherub ft, 1870s, 1.5L **375.00**
Porc, transfer/HP: floral, pewter lid, man lith, .5L **140.00**
Porc, transfer/HP: Goldnes Eachel-Innsburck, lith, .3L, NM **140.00**
Porc, transfer/HP: hunter, inlaid lid, lady lith, .5L **110.00**
Porc, transfer/HP: Munich child, family lith, .5L **125.00**
Porc, transfer/HP: musician, inlaid lid, lith, 1896, .5L, EX **250.00**
Porc, transfer/HP: stag, tree trunk body, lith, .5L, NM **140.00**
Pottery, etched/HP: knight/innkeeper, Germscheid, rpl lid, 1L **90.00**
Pottery, etched/HP: Tasthaus scene, pewter lid, .5L **90.00**
Pottery, etched: Art Nouveau/verse, bl, Marzi & Remy, .5L **260.00**
Pottery, etched: musicians, Marzi & Remy, #1636, .5L **290.00**
Pottery, etched: people in boat, Hauber/Reuther #446, .5L **165.00**
Pottery, HP: Charles Wirth Restaurant/verse, pewter lid, .5L **95.00**
Pottery, relief: battle scenes, tans, Dumler/Breiden, 4L, EX **185.00**
Pottery, relief: book binding, owl inlaid lid, #1714, .5L **400.00**
Pottery, relief: cavaliers, tans, pewter lid, .5L **70.00**
Pottery, relief: family outing, tans, figural lid, rpr, .5L **130.00**
Pottery, relief: horseman & lady, tans, pewter lid, 1L **80.00**
Pottery, relief: HP blacksmith shop, Hauber/Reuther #461, .5L .**180.00**
Pottery, relief: HP couple, pewter lid, GK, #119/17, 2L **165.00**
Pottery, relief: HP hunter & puppies, pewter lid, #249, .5L **80.00**
Pottery, relief: HP tower form, pottery lid, .5L **250.00**
Pottery, relief: lovers, tans, pewter lid, #1158D, .5L **55.00**
Pottery, relief: men drink, tans, pewter lid, #1015, .5L **85.00**
Pottery, relief: men's portraits, tan, Diesinger, .5L, EX **155.00**
Pottery, relief: Munich child, pewter lid (rpr), #204, 1L **55.00**
Pottery, relief: Nouveau lady/etc, tans, music box, .5L **150.00**
Pottery, relief: Wilhelm Tell, tans, pewter lid, .5L **100.00**
Pottery, relief: 2 ladies, tan, Diesinger #192, 1L **140.00**
Pottery, transfer: HP shooting festival, pewter lid, .5L **200.00**
Pottery, transfer: HP stag leaps/hunters, metal lid, .5L **140.00**
Regimental, porc, 1 Artillery...1892-95, pewter lid, .5L, EX **250.00**
Regimental, porc, 2 Ulan...1903-06, lion tl, rpr, .5L **335.00**
Regimental, porc, 24 Dragoon...1892-95, lion finial, .5L **435.00**
Regimental, porc, 3 Train...1905-07, 4 scenes, lion tl, .5L **1,000.00**
Regimental, pottery, 8 Infantry...1906-08, lith, rprs, .5L **150.00**
Regimental, stoneware, 6 Infantry...1901-03, lion tl, .5L **750.00**
SP copper: florals & horned animals, coins in panels, 1L **800.00**
Stoneware, HP: floral, pewter lid, .5L **150.00**
Stoneware, octagon, gray/brn, pewter lid, #6117, .5L **120.00**
Stoneware, relief: lady w/cat, pewter lid, .5L **150.00**
Stoneware, relief: men in cellar, bl, Whites, #39, 1L, NM **350.00**
Stoneware, sculpted Nouveau decor, brn speckled, #2221, 1L, NM ..**100.00**
Stoneware, threading/bl salt glaze, frog inside, #877, .5L, NM ...**100.00**
Stoneware, transfer/HP: Munchener Burgerbrau, pewter lid, 1L ..**800.00**
Stoneware, transfer/HP: Wizen Bierbrauerei, pewter lid, 1L **940.00**
Terra cotta, relief/cold pnt: cavaliers, no lid, #101, 3L **115.00**
Wood, burned design: monk, wooden lid, finial gone, 1L **50.00**
Wood, Norwegian, cvd florals/circles, cvd lid, 1750s, 1.5L **4,900.00**
Wood w/repeating SP o/l design, St Louis Silver Co, .5L, EX **150.00**
Wood w/SP florals, SP lid, St Louis Silver Co, 1L, NM **235.00**

Steuben

Carder Steuben glass was made by the Steuben Glass Works in Corning, New York, while under the direction of Frederick Carder from 1903 to 1932. Perhaps the most popular types of Carder Steuben glass are Gold Aurene which was introduced in 1904 and Blue Aurene, introduced in 1905. Gold and Blue Aurene objects shimmer with the lustrous beauty of their metallic iridescence. Carder also produced other types of 'Aurenes' including Red, Green, Yellow, Brown, and Decorated, all of which are very rare. Aurene also was cased upon Calcite glass. Some pieces had paper labels.

Other types of Carder Steuben include Cluthra, Cintra, Florentia, Rosaline, Ivory, Ivorene, Jades, Verre de Soie; there are many more.

Frederick Carder's leadership of Steuben ended in 1932, and the production of colored glassware soon ceased. Since 1932 the tradition of fine Steuben art glass has been continued in crystal.

Our advisor for this category is Thomas P. Dimitroff; he is in the Directory under New York. In the following listings, examples are signed unless noted otherwise.

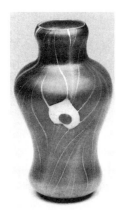

Vase, Green Aurene cased to white opalescent with iridescent Gold Aurene peacock eyes and swirling threads, #508, 7¾", $3,700.00.

Atomizer, Blue Aurene, cut floral/net on ft/acorn finial, 10" 850.00
Atomizer, Blue Aurene, gilt top w/scrolls, #6136, 7" 600.00
Basket, Blue Aurene, folded rim, berry prunts on hdl, #1468, 11" ..1,850.00
Bonbon, Gold Aurene, triangular, #531, 5" 250.00
Bottle, scent; Blue Aurene, #1404, pointed stopper, 6" 1,300.00
Bottle, scent; Blue Aurene, #1414, conical stopper, 4⅞" 865.00
Bottle, scent; Blue Aurene, #1455, teardrop stopper, 4½" 925.00
Bottle, scent; Blue Aurene, #2834, sgn Carder, 4¼" 1,495.00
Bottle, scent; Blue Aurene, #2885, button stopper, 3" 750.00
Bottle, scent; Blue Aurene, #3174, conical stopper, 7½" 1,265.00
Bottle, scent; Blue Aurene, #6237, conical stopper, 9¾" 1,375.00
Bottle, scent; clear opal w/pk-purple Cintra hdls, #3048, 5½" ...1,600.00
Bottle, scent; Gold Aurene, #3049, mk Haviland, 6½" 1,495.00
Bottle, scent; Gold Aurene, #6136, gold/blk onyx dauber, 7" 550.00
Bottle, scent; Verre-de-Soie, #1988, bl teardrop stopper, 7½" 325.00
Bowl, Amethyst, ribbed/ftd, 4¼x14" 250.00
Bowl, Blue Aurene, floral-etched rim, 3-ftd, #2586 ....1,150.00
Bowl, Blue Aurene, on std, #2799, 4x5" dia 850.00
Bowl, Bristol Yellow w/random bubbles, #6118, 5¼x10" 175.00
Bowl, Celeste Blue, scalloped trumpet form, 7⅜x11¾" 490.00
Bowl, centerpc, clear bubbly w/gr threads, 12", +gr frog 375.00
Bowl, centerpc; Gold Aurene on Calcite, 10¼" 575.00
Bowl, centerpc; Green Florentia, floral int, #3782, 4¼x12" 1,850.00
Bowl, centerpc; Grotesque, Ivorene, #7563, 6½x13¾x10½" 430.00
Bowl, flower; Blue Aurene w/silver irid, #2687, 3x5¾" 525.00

Bowl, Gold Aurene on Calcite, incurvate, like #3198, 2x12" 250.00
Bowl, Gold Aurene w/Calcite exterior, 10" 500.00
Bowl, Grotesque, Flemish Blue & clear, #7091, 6⅝x11½" 300.00
Bowl, pk & wht Cluthra center, #6887, 3¾x12" 865.00
Bowl, Verre-de-Soie, gr threading at top, flared, 8½" 225.00
Box, Grapevine, #800 ....2,500.00
Box, puff; Verre-De-Soie, bulbous w/SP chased floral lid, 4¼" ...230.00
Cake plate, Gold Aurene on Calcite, rope twist hdl, 11½" 700.00
Candlestick, Mat-Su-Noke, clear w/Celeste Blue rim, 10" 375.00
Candlestick, teardrop-vase shaft on bell-form base, 14" 275.00
Candlesticks, Alabaster & Jade Green, #5175, 11¾", pr 925.00
Candlesticks, bl rim wraps & flower prunts, 12", pr+lg bowl ...1,800.00
Candlesticks, Topaz & Pomona Green, #6154, 12", pr 700.00
Candlesticks, Verre-De-Soie w/gr threads on floral, 7", pr 520.00
Champagne, opal w/Cintra half-twist stem, #7160, 5½" 525.00
Champagne, Spinach Green crystal, thorny/leafy stem, #8316, 6" ..225.00
Compote, Blue Aurene on Calcite, incurvate, #5066, 6¼x6" ...525.00
Compote, Gold Aurene on Calcite, rolled rim, #5090, 3¼x7½" ...475.00
Compote, Gold Aurene w/bl irid, ruffled, ½-twist stem, #637, 6" ...500.00
Compote, Green Jade/Alabaster, ring hdl, ped ft, 8½x10¼" 700.00
Compote, Orange Cintra, cupped ft, clear wafer, 7x7" 1,100.00
Cordial, Blue Aurene, #2025, 3½" 500.00
Cordial, Gold Aurene, #2361 ....175.00
Creamer & sugar bowl, Celeste Blue, appl amethyst hdls 395.00
Dish, Gold Aurene, wide flat rim, 1x6½" 190.00
Finger bowl, Gold Aurene on Calcite, #2361, 2¼" H, +plate 300.00
Finger bowl, Pink Cluthra, hexagonal, +6" ruffled plate 850.00
Finger bowl, Verre-de-Soie, 2½" H, +plate, Carder, #2361 ....300.00
Goblet, Gold Aurene, domed ft, short stem, sgn/#d, 4½" 235.00
Goblet, Oriental Poppy, pk stripes to opal, gr stem/ft, 8" 1,095.00
Goblet, Oriental Poppy, Pomona Green ball stem, #6522, 8" 850.00
Goblet, Thistle, gr cut to clear, clear base, 6¼x4" 260.00
Lamp, Gold Aurene, gilt mts/pull switch, #915, 13½" 3,000.00
Lamp shade, Red & Blue Aurene on Calcite, hearts/vines, 6x14" 2,500.00
Plate, Audubon Barred Owl eng, wings spread, #2028, 10" 700.00
Plate, blk w/appl gr rim, 8½", 6 for 500.00
Plate, Camellias eng on crystal, #8194, 8¼" 460.00
Rose bowl, Blue Aurene, #2651, 2⅞x10" 450.00
Salt cellar, Blue Aurene, waisted rim, mk Haviland, 1x1¾" 400.00
Salt cellar, Celeste Blue, ribbed/ftd, #2653, 1½x2½" 250.00
Salt cellar, Gold Aurene w/red highlights, #2660, 1x2" 200.00
Sherbet, Celeste Blue 180.00
Tray, Topaz Dmn Quilt, appl blk reeded border, 14" dia 150.00
Vase, Alabaster, shiny bulbed trumpet form, ped ft, 9½", NM ...260.00
Vase, amber, 3-branch tree trunk, #2743, 6" 295.00
Vase, Aurene, hearts/vines, gold on ivory, +gr leaves, 7" 4,500.00
Vase, Blue Aurene, appl ft, #6034, 12" 1,955.00
Vase, Blue Aurene, ornate urn form w/cupped ft, #6047, 10" ..1,100.00
Vase, Blue Aurene, silver to peacock irid, #3283, 7¾" 635.00
Vase, Blue Aurene on Calcite, trumpet form, #1399, 13" 1,495.00
Vase, Blue Aurene w/gr striped base, 10-ribbed, 5⅜" 635.00
Vase, Blue Aurene w/silver irid, oval w/flared rim, 12" 925.00
Vase, Blue Jade (acid etched) on Alabaster, #6078, Sherwood ...950.00
Vase, bud; Green Jade w/Alabaster disk ft, #2556, 12½" 300.00
Vase, Calcite, trumpet form w/ruffled edge, 5" 175.00
Vase, cornucopia; Ivorene, #7579, 6" 425.00
Vase, French Blue crystal, vertical ribs, #236, 8" 250.00
Vase, Gold Aurene, #2556, 8¼" 400.00
Vase, Gold Aurene, bowl form w/3 hdls, #2706, 4⅛x10" 1,150.00
Vase, Gold Aurene, flared/scalloped trumpet form, #346, 6½" ...650.00
Vase, Gold Aurene, gr feathers/platinum irid, #690, 4" 1,265.00
Vase, Gold Aurene, stretched/scalloped, int ribs, #743, 10" 750.00
Vase, Gold Aurene, 4 pinched sides, cylindrical neck, 4⅛" 475.00
Vase, Gold Aurene w/violet shading, tapered ovoid, 4½" 430.00

Vase, Green Jade, diagonal optic ribs, 11½" 350.00
Vase, Green Jade, rectangular, 9" 400.00
Vase, Green Jade, 3-prong stump, 5" 700.00
Vase, Green Jade & Alabaster, bonsai cameo, #6078, 7x8" 980.00
Vase, Green Jade & Alabaster, etched exotic birds, #938, 9" 980.00
Vase, Green Jade & Alabaster, M hdls, #6795, 10", NM 800.00
Vase, Grotesque, amethyst, ruffled, floriform, #7090, 11½" 400.00
Vase, Grotesque, gold ruby to clear, #7276, 4½x8x7¾" 400.00
Vase, Grotesque, Ivorene, 4-pillar, #7171, 6½x12¼" 345.00
Vase, Ivorene, cut leaping deer/swirls, 10x9" 2,300.00
Vase, Ivorene, dbl-bulbed, ball stem, disk ft, #7320, 9¾" 800.00
Vase, Ivorene, 3-lily form on disk ft, #7595, 12½", pr 2,100.00
Vase, jack-in-the-pulpit; Gold Aurene, 6" 1,200.00
Vase, Lt Blue Jade on Alabaster, jardiniere form, 7¼x10" 1,725.00
Vase, Matzu, Jade Green, cut, global form, #6078, 7" 1,250.00
Vase, Mirror Black, #6989, foil label, 12" 575.00
Vase, Mirror Black, oval vasiform, #6989, 12" 1,095.00
Vase, Oriental Poppy, pk opal w/satin irid, #6030, 7" 1,840.00
Vase, Pink Cluthra, flared oval, #2683, 10x10⅜" 1,380.00
Vase, Pomona Green, floral, ftd, #938, 7" 230.00
Vase, Rosalene to Alabaster, dragon/Greek key, #6148, 7½" ..1,800.00
Vase, Spanish Green, 6-prong, disk base, 14½" 1,380.00
Vase, Topaz w/Pomona Green knobbed stem, ribbed fan form, 8" ..300.00
Vase, Verre-de-Soie aqua urn form, pear finial, #2968, 13½" 975.00
Vase, White Cluthra, classic oval, #2683, 6¼", NM 500.00
Vase, White Cluthra, wht internal bubbles, #7409, 11x9" 1,150.00
Whimsey card holder, Jade Green, 2½x3¼" 90.00
Whimsey darner, Blue Aurene, 9" 400.00

Stevengraphs

A Stevengraph is a small picture made of woven silk resembling an elaborate ribbon, created by Thomas Stevens in England in the latter half of the 1800s. They were matted and framed by Stevens, usually with his name appearing on the mat or, more commonly, the trade announcement on the back of the mat. He also produced silk postcards and bookmarks, all of which have 'Stevens' woven in silk on one of the mitered corners. Anyone wishing to learn more about Stevengraphs is encouraged to contact the Stevengraph Collectors' Association, whose address can be found in the Directory under Clubs, Newsletters, and Catalogs.

The Start, original mat and frame, NM, $250.00.

Are You Ready?, EX 300.00
Called to Rescue, Heroism at Sea, EX 250.00
Columbus Leaving Spain, matted & fr, G 200.00
Death of Nelson, G 195.00
Declaration of Independence, woven at Columbian Exhibition .225.00
Finish, orig cb mat, 6⅛x8¾" in fr, G 200.00
First Innings, G 325.00
God Speed the Plough, G 220.00
Good Old Days, orig mat, 6⅛x8¾" in fr, EX 220.00
Landing of Columbus, NM 250.00

Meet, orig mat, old fr, NM 250.00
Park in Coventry 75.00
Present Time (60 Miles an Hour), EX 175.00
Water Jump, fr, EX 225.00
Wellington & Blugher, EX 300.00

Miscellaneous

Bookmark, Behold the Man, blk fr, G 50.00
Bookmark, Friend's Blessings 45.00
Bookmark, Love's Remembrance 75.00
Bookmark, Lt Gen US Grant, Richmond, 1865 ....75.00
Bookmark, Prayer to a Bible Couple 100.00
Postcard, Ann Hathaway's Cottage 40.00

Stevens and Williams

Stevens and Williams glass was produced at the Brierly Hill Glassworks in Stourbridge, England, for nearly a century, beginning in the 1830s. They were credited with being among the first to develop a method of manufacturing a more affordable type of cameo glass. Other lines were also made — silver deposit, alexandrite, and engraved rock crystal, to name but a few. Our advisor for this category is Don Williams; he is listed in the Directory under Missouri.

Basket, pk o/l, amber hdl/ruffle, cranberry leaf, 7½x6" 265.00
Bowl, amethyst, optic ribs, vertical ridges, att, 3¼x12¾" 145.00
Bowl, bl opal, appl amber peach on leafy branch, 7¼x6½" 550.00
Finger bowl, bl, ribbed w/zipper motif, sqd/ruffled, +plate 150.00
Finger bowl, pk opal stripes, crimped, +6" plate 200.00
Rose bowl, brn shaded satin egg w/gold prunus, pleated, 5x3½" ..425.00
Rose bowl, gr w/opaque feathers/gold flecks, att, 3x3¼" 300.00
Rose bowl, Matsu-No-Ke floral vine, pk, w/base, #15353, 3x3½" .585.00
Vase, bl, wht & clear stripes, 3-sided w/dimples, 7½" 345.00
Vase, bl cased w/clear rim, HP florals w/gold, 7x6" 335.00
Vase, bl o/l w/amber cherry branch, red/gr leaves, sqd rim, 7" 525.00
Vase, butterscotch MOP swirl, bell form w/stick neck, 7" 450.00
Vase, moss agate craquelle, global w/appl ring, 4½" 900.00
Vase, Pompeian Swirl, verre-de-soie, bl/pk on wht opal, 13" 975.00
Vase, Silveria, twisted fan shape, 6x7¾" 3,950.00
Vase, swirled amber w/pk int, machine threads/gold floral, 9¼" ..900.00
Vase, teal bl w/gold MOP spirals, bottle form, 10" 800.00

Stickley

Among the leading proponents of the Arts and Crafts Movement, the Stickley brothers — Gustav, Leopold, Charles, Albert, and John George — were at various times and locations separately involved in designing and producing furniture as well as decorative items for the home. (See Arts and Crafts for further information.) The oldest of the five Stickley brothers was Gustav; his work is the most highly regarded of all. He developed the style of furniture referred to as Mission. It was strongly influenced by the type of furnishings found in the Spanish missions of California — utilitarian, squarely built, and simple. It was made most often of oak, and decoration was very limited or non-existent. The work of his brothers display adaptations of many of Gustav's ideas and designs. His factory, the Craftsman Workshop, operated in Eastwood, New York, from the late 1890s until 1915, when he was forced out of business by larger companies who copied his work and sold it at much lower prices. Among his shopmarks are the early red decal containing a joiner's compass and the words 'Als Ik Kan,' the branded mark with very similar components, and paper labels.

The firm known as Stickley Brothers was located first in Binghamton, New York, and then Grand Rapids, Michigan. Albert and John George made the move to Michigan, leaving Charles in Binghamton (where he and an uncle continued the operation under a different name). After several years John George left the company to rejoin Leopold in New York. (These two later formed their own firm called L. & J.G. Stickley.) The Stickley Brothers Company's early work produced furniture featuring fine inlay work, decorative cutouts, and leaned strongly toward a style of Arts and Crafts with an English influence. It was tagged with a paper label 'Made by Stickley Brothers, Grand Rapids,' or with a brass plate or decal with the words 'Quaint Furniture,' an English term chosen to refer to their product. In addition to his furniture, he made metal accessories as well.

The workshops of the L. & J.G. Stickley Company first operated under the name 'Onondaga Shops.' Located in Fayetteville, New York, their designs were often all but copies of Gustav's work. Their products were well made and marketed, and their business was very successful. Their decal labels contained all or a combination of the words 'Handcraft' or 'Onondaga Shops,' along with the brothers' initials and last name. The firm continues in business today. Our advisor for this category is Bruce Austin; he is listed in the Directory under New York. Note: When only one dimension is given for tables, it is length. Cleaning diminishes values; ours are for furniture and metals with excellent original finishes unless noted otherwise.

Key: h/cp — hammered copper

Side chair, #384, unmarked, EX original finish, 46", $2,000.00.

Gustav Stickley

Armchair, #310½, 3-slat bk, tacked seat, decal, cleaned 400.00
Armchair, #318, 5 vertical bk slats, corbels, decal, 38" 1,600.00
Armchair, #320, open arms, 4-slat bk, decal, rpl ropes/pads 1,200.00
Bed, #923, 3 wide vertical ft/head brd slats, decal, VG 800.00
Bookcase, 2 12-pane doors w/V pulls, decal, 56x60", VG 5,000.00
Bowl, nut; h/cp, 3 ft, no mk, 3½x7" 350.00
Box, shirtwaist; #95, 11-spindle ends, no mk, 16x16x30", VG ...3,750.00
Burner, chafing dish; copper, long wood hdl, 1¾x11½" 125.00
Cabinet, smoker; #89, drw/door, decal, strap hardware, 29x20" ..29,000.00
Chair, host; #1304 A, 2 horizontal bk slats, tacked seat 1,000.00
Chair, Morris; #346, mahog, angled open arms, corbels, decal ...1,300.00
Chair, Morris; #367, 16 spindles w/thru tenons, decal, VG 4,000.00
Chair, side; #1304, 2-slat bk, tacked seat, NM, 8 for 5,500.00
Chair, side; #304, 4-slat bk, rpl seat, cleaned, pr 800.00
Chair, side; #306½, 3-slat bk, cleaned, 36", VG 325.00
Chair, side; #349½, horizontal 3-slat bk, decal, rfn, pr 1,100.00
Chair set, #353, 3-slat bk, arched rail, 3 sides+1 bk, mk 3,500.00
Chest, #909, 2 sm drw over 3 w/wood knobs, mk, 42x36", VG ..2,400.00
China cabinet, #803, arched glazed door/apron, label, 60x36" ..6,000.00

China cabinet, #820, 1 12-pane door, overhanging top, 63x36" ..4,500.00
China cabinet, 2 8-pane doors, copper V pulls, 63x42" 5,000.00
Desk/table, overhang rfn top, 1-drw, no shelf, decal, 48", VG ..2,400.00
Dish/ashtray, h/cp, emb spades, mk, 5½" dia 350.00
Dresser, #902, 2 short drw over 4, decal, 54x42" 6,000.00
Dresser, child's; #921, swivel mirror w/3 short slats ea side 3,000.00
Footstool, fr shaped as X w/curled terminals, uphl, rpr, G 1,200.00
Lamp, table; wicker 18" shade; 4-corbel sq-base std, mk, 22" ..2,500.00
Letter rack, rotating, cut-out hdl, 4-compartment, dvtl, 11x13" ..1,000.00
Magazine stand, cvd Tree of Life on side, leather faced, 43" 800.00
Mirror, cheval; #918, splay legs, 2 stretchers, 70x30", VG 6,500.00
Mirror, swivels in fr mtd on platform, decal, cleaned, 20x26" .1,500.00
Rocker, #2603, open-arm, U-shape crestrail, 4-slat bk, 36" 1,000.00
Safe, 2 cabinet doors, strap hinges, decal, 30x36" 3,500.00
Sconce, h/cp strap w/rolled ends holds arm w/candle cup, 13" 800.00
Server, #802, splashbrd, overhang top, 2-drw, shelf, branded ..2,700.00
Settle, #222, even-arm, 22-slat bk/8 ea side, decal, 80" 15,000.00
Settle, child's; #215, maple, 2 horizontal bk slats, 42" 2,000.00
Sideboard, #800, center drw w/2 sm drw ea side over drw, mk ...6,000.00
Sideboard, #814, plate rail, cabinet door ea side 3 drw, decal ..2,000.00
Stand, #642, 2 drw over 1 w/wood knobs, decal, rfn top 2,300.00
Table, #446, stacked trumpet X-stretchers, 48" dia, G 1,800.00
Table, #601, arched X-stretchers, worn 14" dia top, mk 650.00
Table, #611, cut-corner 25" sq top, 2-tier, mks, VG 1,800.00
Table, #632, dining, 5-leg, 6 leaves in case, decal, 48" dia 5,000.00
Table, #636, X-stretchers, decal, 48" dia 6,500.00
Table, #647, upright stretcher w/tenon & keys, mk, 40x30" top ..2,600.00
Table, drop-leaf side w/gate legs, decal, cleaned, 25x26x22" ...1,400.00
Table, lamp; X stretchers w/keyed-through tenons, no mk, 24" 1,400.00
Table, library; #619, 3-drw, no mk, varnished, 66" 6,000.00
Table, library; #659, 3-drw, 13-spindle sides, decal, VG 6,000.00
Table, library; blind drw over stretcher, decal, 30x20x30", VG ..1,100.00
Table, tea; #605, arched X-stretchers, decal, 26" dia 1,900.00
Tray, h/cp, appl hdls, rolled edges, mk, 12x24" 700.00
Tray, h/cp, riveted hdls, 17" 1,200.00
Umbrella stand, triple; #55, tall posts/no pan, decal, varnish 475.00
Wood basket, like #236, slats in iron strap fr, no mk, 31" L 2,000.00

L. & J.G. Stickley

Armchair, #448, fixed bk, slats/corbels under arms, rfn, 42" 1,100.00
Armchair, 5 slats under arms/5 in bk, rfn/new leather, no mk .2,100.00
Bed, #92, 4 tall tapered posts, 7-slat head/ft brds, mk 8,000.00
Bookcase, #654, 2 12-pane doors, keyed, no mk, 55x54" 4,500.00
Bookcase, #728, 2 6-pane doors, decal, 54x48" 4,000.00
Chair, #446, open-arm, 4-slat bk, long corbels, mk, rpl uphl ...1,700.00
Chair, #808, 5-slat bk, curved crest rail, decal, rpl seat 450.00
Chair, Morris; #410, bent arms, 7-slat sides, new pads, decal ..8,000.00
Chair, Morris; #830, open arms, 5-slat bk, label, 40", VG 1,200.00
Chair, side; #800, 3 bk slats, no mk, cleaned, 4 for 1,600.00
Chair set, #1340, 3-slat bks, decal, rfn, 5 side+1 host 1,200.00
China cabinet, #727, 9-pane door, arched apron, mk, rfn, 55x34" ..3,750.00
Clock, mantel; wide beveled ft & overhang top, Hansen, 22x16" ..8,500.00
Daybed, #292, 4 vertical slats ea end, orig pad, 29x80x30" 3,000.00
Desk, #394, drop front, ash, no mk, rfn, 48x36" 650.00
Desk, #604, gallery top, 3-drw, arched apron, no mk, rfn, 40" 600.00
Desk, chalet; #370, chestnut, drop-front, no mk, rfn, 49x36" 750.00
Liquor cabinet, pull-out copper-lined shelf, drw, decal, 40" 1,200.00
Magazine stand, #45, 4-shelf, arched rails, no mk, rfn, 45x19" ...900.00
Magazine stand, #46, 3-slat sides, no mk, 42x21" 1,500.00
Magazine stand, #46, 4-shelf, curved toe-brd/rails, rfn, 42x21" ..1,000.00
Plant stand, #325, sq top, stretchers, decal, rfn, 22x13" sq 475.00
Rocker, #403, open arms, 5-slat bk, decal, new leather 1,900.00
Rocker, #817, open arms, 6-slat bk, orig cushion, mk, 36" 1,400.00

Rocker, armless; 3-slat bk, from Stickley estate, cleaned, 32" **300.00**
Rocker, Morris; #831, open arms w/corbels, decal, wear, 38" ...**1,800.00**
Rocker, open-arm, 4-slat bk, drop-in seat, new leather, no mk ...**650.00**
Settle, #225, open-arm, 13-slat bk, arch rail, no mk, VG, 53" .**1,200.00**
Settle, #232, even-arm, 1-slat sides/5 in bk, brand, 72" **4,250.00**
Settle, #263, slatted drop arms w/corbels, 7-slat bk, mk, 77" ...**2,500.00**
Settle, like #206, 13-slat bk, wood seat, brand, rfn, 68" **1,200.00**
Stand, drink; #22, flaring legs, X-stretcher, rfn, 28" dia **2,700.00**
Table, #554, open legs, brand, 18x15" sq **750.00**
Table, #562, clip-corner top, wide slat ea side, rfn, 20" sq **1,200.00**
Table, #577, rnd shelf on X-stretchers, rfn, 30" dia **950.00**
Table, #604, X-stretchers mortised through legs, rfn, 26" dia ..**1,400.00**
Table, dining; #713, ped w/4 flaring ft, no mk, 54" dia **2,800.00**
Table, library; #377, 1-drw w/wood pulls, keyed tenon, rfn **1,200.00**

Stickley Bros.

Book through, mahog, 2-shelf, through-tenons & keys, label, M **325.00**
Bookcase, #4776, 3 8-pane doors, rpl hdw, no mk, 47x62", VG ..**3,500.00**
Candlestick, #14, invt trumpet top on 3-prong support, 18" ...**2,000.00**
Chair, Morris; #631½, 3 slats under ea arm, label, rpl seat **2,000.00**
Chair, Morris; hip rail under open arm, no mk, 43", VG **700.00**
Chair, side; cut-out bk over 5 vertical slats, VG **400.00**
Chest of drw, 2 sm over 4 wide drw, wood knobs, brand, 53" **800.00**
Clock, tall case; brass face, pendulum, rpl top/rfn, 80" **3,100.00**
Footstool, #5674, through-tenons, drop-in seat, 9x12x19", EX ..**750.00**
Jardiniere, #302, copper w/Arts & Crafts design, 9x14" **1,500.00**
Jardiniere, att, copper, ring hdls, 3 brass knob ft, 9x13" **425.00**
Lamp, table; #506, oak/copper trestle base, no mk, 17" L **6,250.00**
Mirror, #7577, through-tenons, hooks, 32x43" **1,700.00**
Mirror, sq swivel fr mtd on stretcher platform, 20x19" **550.00**
Plant stand, #131, wide arched apron, X stretcher base, VG ...**1,300.00**
Plant stand, #73S, arched stretchers, blk finish, 24x16" sq **400.00**
Rocker, 5-slat sides under shaped arms, corbels, no mk, 35" **900.00**
Settle, #88889, 13-slat bk, 3 under arm, no mk, rfn, 72" **1,600.00**
Table, #2864, X-stretcher, no mk, 26x25" dia, EX **1,300.00**
Table, dining; #716, 5 legs over Xd base, mk, 42" dia **4,750.00**
Table, hall; #2720, 3-slat sides, dbl stretcher, rfn, 36" **1,000.00**
Table, library; #2896, 1 drw, through-tenons/corbels, tag, 40" **500.00**
Table, side; 3-slat sides, no mk, cleaned, 30" **1,500.00**
Table, 1-drw, 3-slat sides, lower shelf, no mk, 24x22" top **1,500.00**
Umbrella stand, rnd w/3 vertical pcs fastened to slats, no mk **175.00**

Stiegel

Baron Henry Stiegel produced glassware in Pennsylvania as early as 1760, very similar to glass being made concurrently in Germany and England. Without substantiating evidence, it is impossible to positively attribute a specific article to his manufacture. Although he made other types of glass, today the term Stiegel generally refers to any very early ware made in shapes and colors similar to those he is known to have produced — especially that with etched or enameled decoration. It is generally conceded, however, that most glass of this type is of European origin. Our advisor for this category is Mark Vuono; he is listed in the Directory under Connecticut.

Bottle, dk amethyst, expanded dmns, pontiled, 3½", NM **280.00**
Bottle, HP flowers, ½-post neck, no cap, att, 6" **385.00**
Bottle, HP flowers/lady/inscription, ½-post neck, att, 5⅝" **330.00**
Bowl, baptismal; bl, dmn mold, 4¼" **925.00**
Bowl, cobalt, 15-dmn, appl ft, pontil scar, 2½x3½" **3,500.00**
Bucket bowl, eng tulips, invt baluster stem, thick base, 6½" **225.00**
Creamer, bl, emb dmns, ftd, 3⅝" **450.00**

Creamer, deep cobalt, folded rim & spout, appl hdl/ft, 3⅞" **250.00**
Creamer, emerald gr, flint, ogival dmns, 3½" **425.00**
Cup, invt pear shape w/dmn mold on rnd base, 3" **350.00**
Flip, eng tulip & vines, pontil, wooden muller, 7x5¾" **200.00**
Flip, 12-panel, eng geometrics, pontil, 5⅝x4¼" **135.00**
Jigger, HP hands/heart/lovebirds, inscription/1720, att, 2½" **330.00**
Mug, HP floral band, appl hdl, att, 4¼" **550.00**
Mug, HP flowers & rooster, appl hdl, att, 5" **635.00**
Perfume flask, amethyst, chestnut w/12 ogival dmns, 5½" **3,250.00**
Perfume flask, med amethyst, Dmn Quilt, pontiled, 6" **1,600.00**
Pitcher, cobalt, tooled rim & spout, appl hdl/ft, 5⅝" **300.00**
Pocket flask, dk purple amethyst, 12-dmn, pontil scar, 5½" **2,400.00**
Sugar bowl, bl, emb dmns, 18th C, 4½" dia **625.00**
Sugar bowl, bl, rimmed base, 3¼" dia **500.00**
Tumbler, eng flowers, 8" **110.00**
Tumbler, HP flower & bird, flake, 4" **330.00**
Tumbler, HP flowers & man on horsebk, att, 3⅝" **635.00**
Tumbler, HP flowers w/bird on heart, att, 4¾" **525.00**
Tumbler, HP lady w/heart in hand w/flowers, att, 4¼" **470.00**

Stocks and Bonds

Scripophily (scrip-awfully), the collecting of 'worthless' old stocks and bonds, gained recognition as an area of serious interest around the mid-1970s. Today there are an estimated 5,000 collectors in the United States and 15,000 worldwide. Collectors who come from numerous business fields mainly enjoy its hobby aspect, though there are those who consider scripophily an investment. Some collectors like the historical significance that certain certificates have. Others prefer the beauty of older stocks and bonds that were printed in various colors with fancy artwork and ornate engravings. Even autograph collectors are found in this field, on the lookout for signed certificates.

Many factors help determine the collector value: autograph value, age of the certificate, the industry represented, whether it is issued or not, its attractiveness, condition, and collector demand. Certificates from the mining, energy, and railroad industries are the most popular with collectors. Other industries or special collecting fields include banking, automobiles, aircraft, and territorials. Serious collectors usually prefer only issued certificates that date from before 1910. Unissued certificates are usually worth one-fourth to one-tenth the value of one that has been issued. Inexpensive issued common stocks and bonds dated between the 1930s and 1980s usually retail between $1.00 to $10.00. Those dating between 1890 and 1930 usually sell for $10.00 to $50.00. Those over one hundred years old retail between $25.00 and $100.00 or more, depending on the quantity found and the industry represented. Some stocks are one of a kind while others are found by the hundreds or even thousands, especially railroad certificates. Autographed stocks normally sell anywhere from $100.00 to $1,000.00. A formal collecting organization for scripophilists known as The Bond and Share Society has an American chapter located in New York City.

Our advisor for this category is Warren Anderson; he is listed in the Directory under Utah. In many of the following listings, two-letter state abbreviations immediately follow company name. All are in fine condition unless noted otherwise.

Key:
I/C — issued/cancelled   U — unissued
I/U — issued/uncancelled   vgn — vignette

Annie C Gold Mining, NB/1896, mining vgn, blk on bl-gr, I/U ..**60.00**
Atlantic Nat'l Bank, MA/1932, boats/ships eng, I/U **30.00**
AZ Belmont Mining, AZ/1914, desert vgn/2 miner vgns, I/U **25.00**

Black Hills Copper, AZ Territory/1905, miners vgn, I/U 35.00
Boston-Cobalt Mining, MA/1906, miners vgn, gold seal, I/C 15.00
Bowie Leasing Corp, AZ/1926, train vgn, blk on orange, I/U 15.00
Buckeye Mining & Tunneling, CO/1880, 100 shares, miners vgn, I/C ..95.00
Buffalo, Niagara & Eastern Power, NY/1925, dynamo vgn, I/U ...15.00
Carmer Mining, CO/1890s, 3 miners & mtns in vgn, brn border, U ..10.00
Chicago, St Louis & Pittsburgh RR, IN/IL/1887, train vgn, I/C ...25.00
Chicago & Northwestern Rwy, 1937, train/state arms vgn, I/U ...15.00
Chicago Goldfields Mining, AZ Territory/1907, miner vgn, I/U ..30.00

Colonial Beach Improvement, Virginia, 1884, Washington's bust engraving, Columbia, eagle, sailor, anchor, and sails, ten shares, $100.00 minimum value.

Columbus & IN Central RR, OH/IN/1868, train vgn on bl, I/U ..22.00
Decatur Oil & Gas, NV/1931, eagle vgn, gray borders, I/U 12.50
Ely Consolidated Copper, UT/1917, 3 vgns, I/C 17.50
GA & FL RR, GA/SC/1925, $1,000, speeding train vgn, I/C 60.00
GMB Oil, KS/1929, oil depot & gusher vgns on gr, I/U 20.00
Green Mount Water Supply, PA/1905, allegorical vgn, I/C 10.00
Harvard Gold Mining, CO/1896, eagle vgn, ornate banner, I/U ..45.00
Housatonic RR, CT/1880, 2 train vgns/1 flag vgn, ABNCo, U 20.00
Ivanhoe Mining, CO/1882, miner vgn, I/U 65.00
Jupiter Oil Co, WY/1918, horse & wagon vgn, gold seal, I/U 15.00
La Zacupala-Hidalgo Rubber, NV/1916, eagle vgn, I/U 15.00
Leon Gold Mining, CO/1895, flowers/winged serpent vgn, I/U 45.00
Lone Pine Mining, WV/1902, miners vgn, brn, I/U 35.00
Lone Star Canal, TX/1905, gold seal, I/U 35.00
New London Ship & Engine, CT/1912, engine vgn, I/C 45.00
North Butte Extension Development, ME/1908, miner vgn, I/U .25.00
NV Copper Belt RR, ME/1909, $500 bond, gr/brn, I/U 30.00
NY Central & Hudson River RR, NY/1898, train vgn, I/C 30.00
NY Realty Owners, NY/1906, income bond, eagle on shield vgn, I/C ...35.00
Oil Lease Development, DE/1923, eagle vgn, ornate banner, I/U .10.00
PA Salt Mfg, PA/1888, eagle on shield vgn, I/U 45.00
Peerless Truck & Motor, VA/1923-25, women vgn, ABNCo, I/C .35.00
Pioneer Consolidated Mines, WY/1909, desert/mtn vgn, I/U 25.00
Pittsburgh Tin Plate & Steel, DE/1920, eagle vgn, IC 15.00
Progressive Placer, AZ/1913, Liberty vgn, fancy banner, I/U 20.00
Provo Mining, UT/1909, mining vgn, gold seal, I/U 25.00
Pure Gold Mines, AZ Territory/1904, 3 vgns, gold stripe, I/U 30.00
Santa Fe Dredging, NM/1914, bull elk & mtns vgn, I/C 20.00
Specialty Supply, SD/1904, eagle vgn, bold title, I/U 15.00
Swanton Coal & Iron, MD/1856, $500 bond, train vgn, I/C 70.00
Tonopah Belmont Development, NJ/1928, mining vgn, I/U 15.00
Traders Gold Mining, CO/1896, Liberty vgn, gold seal, I/U 45.00
Trinity Goldbar Mining, NV/1933, mining vgn, gold seal, I/U 15.00
Uintah Oil, UT/1901, horse & wagon+4 vgns, gold seal, I/U 25.00
Union Nat'l Bank, PA/1870s, eagle/Columbia/ship vgns, I/C 55.00
UT Bingham Mining, ME/1906, mining vgn, bold title, I/U 25.00
Village Bell Gold Mining, CO/1900, lady vgn, gold seal, I/C 30.00
West Chester & Philadelphia RR, PA/1858, blk on bl, I/U 15.00
Westinghouse Electric, PA/ca 1930, 3 women w/torch vgn, I/C ...35.00

Stoneware

There are three broad periods of time that collectors of American

pottery can look to in evaluating and dating the stoneware and earthenware in their collections. Among the first permanent settlers in America were English and German potters who found a great demand for their individually turned wares. The early pottery was produced from red and yellow clays scraped from the ground at surface levels. The earthenware made in these potteries was fragile and coated with lead glazes that periodically created health problems for the people who ate or drank from it. There was little stoneware available for sale until the early 1800s, because the clays used in its production were not readily available in many areas and transportation was prohibitively expensive. The opening of the Erie Canal and improved roads brought about a dramatic increase in the accessibility of stoneware clay, and many new potteries began to open in New York and New England.

Collectors have difficulty today locating earthenware and stoneware jugs produced prior to 1840, because few have survived intact. These ovoid or pear-shaped jugs were designed to be used on a daily basis. When cracked or severely chipped, they were quickly discarded. The value of handcrafted pottery is often determined by the cobalt decoration it carries. Pieces with elaborate scenes (a chicken pecking corn, a bluebird on a branch, a stag standing near a pine tree, a sailing ship, or people) may easily bring $1,000.00 to $12,000.00 at auction.

After the Civil War there was a need and a national demand for stoneware jugs, crocks, canning jars, churns, spittoons, and a wide variety of other pottery items. The competition among the many potteries reached the point where only the largest could survive. To cut costs, most potteries did away with all but the simplest kinds of decoration on their wares. Time-consuming brush-painted birds or flowers quickly gave way to more simply executed swirls or numbers and stenciled designs. The coming of home refrigeration and Prohibition in 1919 effectively destroyed the American stoneware industry. See also Bennington, Stoneware.

Batter pail, bird, c/s, att Whites Utica, 1870s, 10½", VG 150.00
Bottle, Albany glaze, W Richard Warren & Co, 1870s, 11" 100.00
Bowl, #1½/squiggles, c/s, att N Clark Lyons, 5½x11½" 440.00
Cake crock, #2/dbl flower, WA MacQuoid...NY, 6", EX 385.00
Cake crock, floral (brushed), c/s, J Swank...PA, 1½-gal, 7" 300.00
Churn, #2/bird on plume, c/s, unsgn, w/dasher & guide, 13" 770.00
Churn, #3/bird on plowed field, c/s, WH Farrar, rstr, 15" 2,200.00
Churn, #4/paddletail bird/floral, c/s, NA White..., rstr, 17" 900.00
Churn, #5/dbl flower (detailed), c/s, T...Lyons, rstr, 19" 2,650.00
Churn, #5/partridge, c/s, John Burger, rstr, 19" 5,050.00
Churn, #6/hen pecks corn, c/s, unsgn, crack, 18½" 850.00
Churn, #6/trumpet flower, c/s, Burger Bros, rstr, 20" 360.00
Churn, #6/8-point star w/face, c/s, T Harrington Lyons, 20" ...3,850.00
Cream pot, bird on floral, c/s, att Whites Utica, 8-qt, 9" 360.00
Crock, #1/bird (detailed), c/s, W Roberts Binghamton NY, rpr, 7" ..465.00
Crock, #1/flowers, c/s, Cowden & Wilcox...PA, lines, 6½" 230.00
Crock, #1/leaf (brushed), c/s, Taft & Co Keene NH, chips, 7½" ...135.00
Crock, #2/bird, c/s, Ottman Bros...Ft Edward NY, crack, 9" 415.00
Crock, #2/bird on floral branch, c/s, Edmands & Co, 9½", EX ...770.00
Crock, #2/bird on leaf, c/s, Whites Utica, 1870s, 9½", EX 450.00
Crock, #2/bird on twig, c/s, West Troy..., spots, 9" 465.00
Crock, #2/bird running, c/s, S Hart Fulton, crack, 9" 285.00
Crock, #2/flower (dbl), c/s, N Clark Jr, stains/chips, 9½" 100.00
Crock, #2/leaves, Seymour Bosworth, stain, 1880s, 9" 135.00
Crock, #2/tornado, c/s, Geddes, 1880s, 9", EX 110.00
Crock, #2/wreath, c/s, John Burger Rochester, chip, 11½" 385.00
Crock, #3/bird & plume, c/s, Haxstun...Ft Edward NY, chip, 11" ...465.00
Crock, #3/dbl hops (brushed), c/s, T Harrington Lyons, 12" 600.00
Crock, #3/hops (brushed), c/s, J Fisher...Lyons NY, 10", EX 250.00
Crock, #3/plume flower, c/s, Edmands & Co, stain, 10¼" 110.00
Crock, #4/bird on plume, c/s, Ft Edward NY, 1870s, 11½" 855.00
Crock, #4/bird on stump w/arrow, c/s, Whites Utica, rstr, 11" ..1,155.00

Crock, #4/flowers (brushed), c/s, C Hart Sherburne, 11½", EX ..135.00
Crock, #4/paddletail bird, c/s, NA White...Utica NY, 11", EX ..550.00
Crock, #5/banner (detailed), c/s, NY Stoneware..., 12½", EX 800.00
Crock, #5/dbl bird, c/s, Ottman Bros...NY, 12", NM 1,700.00
Crock, #6/bird, c/s, W Roberts Binghamton NY, 13½", EX 495.00
Crock, #6/trumpet flower/daisy, c/s, John Burger, rstr, 14" 415.00
Crock, #6/wreath, c/s, Burger & Co, line, 13½" 300.00
Jar, #1/running birds, c/s, att Whites Utica, chip, 1870s, 9" 450.00
Jar, #1/triple flower, c/s, Cortland, chip, 1870s, 8½" 190.00
Jar, #4/swags, cobalt on cinnamon clay, C Crolius...NY, 17" 600.00
Jar, Malted Beef/wheat shaft, Bristol, Whites Utica, 6" 330.00
Jar, preserve; #1/flower (slip), c/s, Olean NY, 9½", EX 175.00
Jar, preserve; #1/flower/dbl 1s, c/s, Lyons, 9", EX 360.00
Jar, preserve; #2/bird on branch, c/s, Whites Utica, rstr, 11" 225.00
Jar, preserve; #2/plume, c/s, Rullard & Scott, chip, 11½" 165.00
Jar, preserve; #2/triple fern, c/s, Harrington-Burger..., 12" 715.00
Jar, preserve; #3/dbl flower, c/s, F Stetzenmeyer..., rstr, 14" 1,425.00
Jar, preserve; #3/dbl flower, c/s, John Burger..., 13" 770.00
Jar, preserve; #5/bird on stump, c/s, unsgn, line, 15½" 770.00
Jar, preserve; cherries (stenciled), c/s, flakes, 6½" 2,145.00
Jar, preserve; flower, c/s, 8½" 275.00
Jar, preserve; foliage & wavy lines, c/s, 8" 715.00
Jug, #1/bird, c/s, Haxstun Ottman...Ft Edward NY, 11½", EX 350.00
Jug, #1/bird on twig, c/s, FT Wright & Son...Mass, line, 11½" ...255.00
Jug, #1/bird running, c/s, Whites Utica, rstr, 10½" 285.00
Jug, #1/dbl flower, c/s, Campbell Penn Yan, 10½", EX 440.00
Jug, #1/flamingo on stump, c/s, Whites Utica, rstr, 11" 360.00
Jug, #1/flower (stylized), c/s, NY Stoneware..., 11½" 200.00
Jug, #1/long-tail bird, c/s, Whites Utica, 1870s, 11", EX 525.00
Jug, #1/orchid, c/s, Whites Utica, 1870s, 11" 320.00
Jug, #1/poppies, c/s, Whites Binghamton, 1860s, 10½", VG 165.00

Jug, #2/Hamilton & Jones, Greensboro, PA, some free-hand decoration, cobalt on gray salt glaze, ca 1860-80, 14", EX, $500.00.

Jug, #2/bird (dotted) on branch, c/s, Whites Binghamton, 13" ...700.00
Jug, #2/bird on branch, c/s, T Harringon Lyons, rstr, 13½" 825.00
Jug, #2/bird on plume, c/s, Haxstun...Ft Edward NY, 14", EX 525.00
Jug, #2/bird on plume, c/s, JS Taft...Keene NH, line, 14" 850.00
Jug, #2/dbl flower, c/o, Edmands & Co, chips, 1870s, 13" 165.00
Jug, #2/dbl flower, c/s, Riedinger...NY, stains, 13½" 110.00
Jug, #2/dbl flower (brushed), c/s, Lyons, 1860s, 14", EX 220.00
Jug, #2/dotted leaf, c/s, NY Stoneware...Ft Edward NY, 14", EX .100.00
Jug, #2/flower (brushed), c/s, NA Seymour Rome, rstr, 13½" 265.00
Jug, #2/flower (ribbed), c/s, F Stetzenmeyer...NY, 14½" 1,550.00
Jug, #2/flower (simple), c/s, GF Brayton...NY, 10½", EX 265.00
Jug, #2/flower (triple), c/s, WH Farrar...Geddes NY, 14", EX 385.00
Jug, #2/flowers (brushed/dotted), c/s, Cortland, 14", EX 745.00
Jug, #2/triple fern, c/s, John Burger..., 1860s, 15" 600.00
Jug, #3/daisy, c/s, John Burger, stains, 16" 350.00
Jug, #3/flower (dbl), c/s, Harrington & Burger Rochester, 16" 635.00
Jug, #3/flower (slip), c/s, WA Lewis...NY, rstr, 15½" 330.00
Jug, #4/bird on berry branch, c/s, att Fulper Bros, 18" 580.00
Jug, #4/flowers/leaves (lg), c/s, Jordan in script, 18" 990.00

Jug, foliage scroll, c/s, Lyons, 12¼", NM 235.00
Match safe, Am Brew Co Rochester NY, c/s, 3" 190.00
Match safe, Westcott & Parcer Coal..., c/s, 3" 200.00
Mug, Am Patriot & bust, Bristol glaze, crazing, 3" 145.00
Mug, Iroquois Brewing...NY, c/s, stain/line, 5" 145.00
Pail, #2/flower (dotted), c/s, J Burger Jr...NY, line, 10" 450.00
Pitcher, #1/poppy, c/s, Whites Binghamton, squat, 9½" 1,375.00
Pitcher, bird singing, c/s, unsgn, 1880s, 1½-gal, 11" 800.00
Pitcher, brushed c/s, unsgn PA, nearly ½-gal, 8½", EX 470.00
Pitcher, deer hunt scene, Bristol glaze, Whites Utica, 7½" 200.00
Pitcher, Root Beer, Bristol glaze, Whites Utica, 11", EX 415.00
Pitcher, star & swags, c/s, tooled pewter lid, 12½" 300.00
Stein, lady tuba player, 2-color, salt glaze, Whites Utica, 12" 415.00
Stein, man & lady in relief, Bristol glaze, 1890s, 13" 385.00
Stein, nude scene, c/s, Whites Utica, rstr, 14½" 600.00
Stein, tavern scene, serpent hdl, Bristol, Whites Utica, 7½" 110.00
Syrup jug, #2/bird, c/s, Haxstun Ottman..., 1870s, 11½", EX 745.00
Syrup jug, #2/bird on plume, c/s, NY...Ft Edward NY, 15", EX ...550.00
Syrup jug, #2/grapes, c/s, AK Ballard...VT, chips, 12½" 660.00
Vase, butterflies/ferns, c/s, Whites Utica, line, 8" 120.00

Store

Perhaps more than any other yesteryear establishment, the country store evokes the most nostalgic feelings for folks old enough to remember its charms — barrels for coffee, crackers, and big green pickles; candy in a jar for the grocer to weigh on shiny brass scales; beheaded chickens in the meat case outwardly devoid of nothing but feathers. Today mementos from this segment of Americana are being collected by those who 'lived it' as well as those less fortunate! Our advisor for this category is Charles Reynolds; he is listed in the Directory under Virginia. See also Advertising; Scales.

Bag, homespun, stenciled S Kruger in blk, 58x21", EX 55.00
Bag holder, heavy wire, folds up 140.00
Bag rack, poplar w/red traces, wire nails, 14" 300.00
Bill clip, CIU duck head w/glass eyes, 1890s, 1x1x5" 120.00
Bill holder, National Cash Register 15.00
Box, biscuit; wood, hinged lid, Currier & Ives scene, 22" L 175.00
Butcher block, 16x19x33" 395.00
Cabinet, cheese display; glass & oak, 22x20x22", VG 350.00
Case, counter display; slanted glass top, oak fr, 34x21x10", EX ..210.00
Case, glass w/oak fr, Sun Mfg on brass plaque, 42x49x27", EX ...750.00
Cigar mold, wooden, 13" L 90.00
Cigar mold clamp, WD Zell, CI 125.00
Coffee bin, pine w/orig stencil, 33" H 550.00
Credit coin, Finder Please Return to...PA emb on German silver ...10.00
Dispenser, ribbon; oak, 21 metal spools, Lokner, 39x24" dia 525.00
Dispenser, tape; porc, butcher's type w/orig tape, lg 28.00
Dispenser, wrapping paper; CI/wood, counter-top type, 9x12x6" ...300.00
Fly paper holder, counter model, CI/steel 265.00
Fly swatter display, Acme, wooden, 5 swatters 165.00
Hog oiler, CI, single wheel 110.00
Ice-cream freezer, Hoxies, wooden 425.00
Jar, glass, paneled sides, w/lid, 12¼x5¾" dia 40.00
Lamp, hanging, kerosene burner, brass font, tin shade 345.00
Lantern, brass font, wire fr, tin shade, complete, 36" 275.00
Mannequin, cvd/pnt wood, bust length, Am, 19th C, 26", EX ...865.00
Mannequin, Wolfform Garment Co, NY, 44x10", VG 75.00
Peanut warmer, aluminum, peanut finial, 1930s, EX 160.00
Pigeon holes, ash & poplar, 20 holes, dk finish, 24x18x7" 140.00
Post office, wooden, 12x14x42" 320.00
Rack, broom display; CI, on casters, Pat 1885, 28x12", EX 245.00

Scoop, brass w/wood hdl, 8" 30.00
Tobacco plug cutter, Buzzsaw, CI 225.00

Stoves

Antique stoves' desirability is based on two criteria: their utility and their decorative value. It's the latter that adds an 'antique' premium to the basic functional value that could be served just as well by a modern stove. Sheer age is usually irrelevant. Decorative features that enhance desirability include fancy, embossed ornamentation, nickel-plated trim, mica windows, ceramic tiles, and (in cooking stoves) water reservoirs and high warming closets rather than mere high shelves. The less sheet metal and the more cast iron, the better. Look for crisp, sharp designs in preference to those made from worn or damaged and repaired foundry patterns. Stoves with a pastel porcelain finish can be very attractive; blue is a favorite, white is least desirable. Chrome trim dates a stove to circa 1933 or later and is a good indicator of a post-antique stove. Though purists prefer the earlier models trimmed in nickel rather than chrome, there is now considerable public interest in these post-antique stoves as well, and some people are willing to pay a good price for these appliance-era 'classics.'

Among stove types, base burners (with self-feeding coal magazines) are the most desirable. Then come the upright, cylindrical 'oak' stoves, kitchen ranges, and wood parlors. Cannon stoves approach the margin of undesirability; laundries and gasoline stoves plunge through it.

There's a thin but continuing stream of desirable antique stoves going to the high-priced Pacific Coast market. Interest in antique stoves is least in the Deep South. Demand for wood/coal stoves is strongest in areas where firewood is affordable and storage of it is practical. Demand for antique gas ranges has become strong, especially in metropolitan markets, and interest in antique electric ranges is starting to surface. The market for antique stoves is so limited and the variety so bewildering that a consensus on a going price can hardly emerge. They are only worth something to the right individual, and prices realized depend very greatly on who happens to be in the auction crowd. Even an expert's appraisal will usually miss the realized price by a substantial percent.

In judging condition look out for deep rust pits, warped or burnt-out parts, unsound firebricks, poorly fitting parts, poor repairs, and empty mounting holes indicating missing trim. Search meticulously for cracks in the cast iron. Our listings reflect auction prices of completely restored, safe, and functional stoves, unless indicated otherwise.

Base Burners

Burdette-Smith #44, swivel top, tiles, 38" 1,200.00
Favorite #30, Piqua OH, fancy CI, mica windows, 52"+14" urn ...2,000.00
Michigan Stove, Art Garland #400, gargoyles/NP/mica, 1889, rstr ..9,800.00
Thos Caffney Waverly #12, Boston MA, 40x20x22" 18,750.00

Box Stoves

A Belanger Barge #34, scrollwork, CI, 1905, sm 200.00
Bussey & McLeod Ajax 18, ornate CI, 1897, 53-lb, very sm 250.00
Unknown, parlor type, reeded-column sides, 1830s, 25x37x17" ..500.00
Walker & Pratt Laconia, ornate CI, NP foot rail, 1860s, 35" 125.00

Franklin Stoves

H Ransom Ben Franklin Air Tight, CI fireplace, Pat 1850 ....250.00
Iron Foundry...NH, ornate CI, grate missing, 1820s, 37x26x32" ...200.00
Magee Ideal #3, CI fireplace, 2 side trivets, 1892, 32x28" 250.00
Noyes & Nutter Kineo #16, fireplace, 1870s, 32x23x20" 185.00

Walker & Pratt Good Cheer #22, fireplace, 1850s, 32x27x31" ..300.00
Wyer & Noble, CI/brass-trim fireplace, very old, rstr/EX 2,000.00

Parlor

The term 'parlor stove' as we use it here is very general and encompasses at least eight distinct types recognized by the stove industry: cottage parlor, double-cased airtight, circulator, cylinder, oak, base burner, Franklin, and the fireplace heater.

1913 Round Oak 18 S-B (18" firepot diameter, square base), complete except with incorrect replaced urn, silver paint over the originally nickeled trim, footed iron base, 78x30", EX, $700.00.

Albany NY, ornate CI, 4-column, paw ft, 1820s, 42"+15" urn ...1,600.00
Fuller-Warren-Morrison Floral 32, CI, 1853, 45x22x17" 1,250.00
HJ Shear #2, Albany NY, 2-column, CI, 56" 850.00
Ilion #5, ornate CI, ca 1853, 33"+13" 2-pc urn 500.00
JS&M Peckham Rosedale #23, 1870s, 33"+10" swivel top dome ..250.00
Low/Hicks Gothic #4, 4 slide front doors, 1840s, 36"+6" urn 425.00
Morison & Manning (att), column type, 1830s, 42x21x32" 2,300.00
Rathbone Sard & Co Floral Acorn #38, ca 1894, 37"+9" urn 725.00
SH Ransom Parlor #3 Gem, ornate CI, Pat 1855, 32"+6" urn 625.00
Unknown, ornate CI, 2-column, missing urn, ca 1830s, 40" 725.00
Weir Modern Glenwood Oak #116, mica windows, 1908, 68x25x25" ..375.00
Wood/Bishop Ideal 23 Clarion, flat top, 1880s, 26x27x25" 900.00

Ranges (Gas)

Cribben-Sexton Universal, 4-burner, gr/cream, high oven, '27, VG ...375.00
Magic Chef, 6-burner/2-oven, warming closet, 1932, EX 2,500.00
Magic Chef, 6-burner/2-oven, warming closet, 1937, rstr 6,000.00
Weir Insulated Glenwood, 6-burner/2-oven, wht, 1932, rstr ...4,125.00

Ranges (Gas, Wood, and Coal Combination)

Magee New Republic, 1929, M, rstr 5,000.00

Ranges (Wood and Coal)

Cribben-Sexton Universal, bl porc, high closet/no reservoir ...2,750.00
Kalamazoo, tan enamel, 1937, EX 315.00
Portland Atlantic Grand, ornate bk shelf, 12x20x18", EX 2,125.00
Quick Meal, bl porc, EX 3,125.00
Taunton Quaker Standard 8-20, NP trim, trivets, shelf, 1890s ...850.00
Weir Glenwood C #280, 2-shelf bk, no trivets, 1900s 1,000.00
Wood/Bishop Home Clarion, CI, 1907, oven: 12x19x19" 750.00
Wood/Bishop New Clarion #8, low closet, 1882, 32x28x46" ..1,875.00
Wood/Bishop Popular Clarion, scrolling, trivets, 1890s 1,050.00

Stove Manufacturers' Toy Stoves

Buck's Jr Range, St Louis MO, new body/pnt/recast parts, 26" ...850.00
Charter Oak #503, GF Filley, St Louis MO, 14x12x25", EX ...2,050.00
Dainty, Reading Stove Works, PA, 7x13x8", VG 150.00
Karr, Qualified, bl porc w/NP, Belleville IL, 1925, EX 2,500.00
Karr Range, Belleville IL, bl porc, old model, 21½x13x9" 3,100.00
Little Eva T Southard, NYC, 8½x14x11", G 350.00
Little Fanny, CI, minor rust, EX 300.00
Little Willie, CI, EX 75.00
Royal American, Bridgeford, Louisville KY, 14x12x10", G 950.00

Toy Manufacturers' Toy Stoves

Arcade Hotpoint range, pnt CI, tan & gr, VG 150.00
Arcade Roper range, pnt CI, gas type, door opens, 4½", EX 70.00
Bing, cook stove, bl steel, brass trim, 16½", VG 600.00
Crescent, cook stove, bl steel, brass trim, 16½", VG 600.00
Eagle, Hubley, Lancaster PA, NP, recast parts 450.00
Eclipse, CI, EX 175.00
Kenton Royal, CI & steel, 4-burner, ornate, 10", VG 100.00
Little Giant, unmk/unidentified, 7½x8½x11", EX orig 675.00
Novelty, Kenton Hdwe, bl pnt/NP trim, rfn, 13x6½x8½" 600.00
Pet, The; Young Bros, Albany NY, 10½x6x8½" 165.00
Rival, J&E Stevens, Cromwell CT, 14x9x16", M, +2 kettles ..1,350.00
Royal, plated CI, stovepipe, shield shape, 16", G 85.00
Triumph, Kenton Hdwe, OH, 14x8½x19", G 195.00

Strawberry Soft Paste and Lustre Ware

Strawberry lustre is a general term for pearlware and semiporcelain decorated with hand-painted strawberries, veins, tendrils, and pink lustre trim. Strawberry soft paste is decorated creamware without the pink lustre trim. Both types were made by many manufacturers in England in the 19th century, most of whom never marked their ware.

Coffeepot, dome lid, soft paste, 12", NM 1,800.00
Cup & saucer, flared sides, 2⅜x3¾", 5⅞", EX+ 250.00
Cup & saucer, handleless; patterned in & out 195.00
Cup & saucer, prof rpr, 2⅜x3¾", 5⅞" 200.00
Plate, pearlware, wide pk/red rim bands, #8, 8" 425.00
Plate, soft paste, Davenport, ca 1810, 6½" 185.00
Sauce boat, lustre, 6" 175.00
Sugar bowl, ftd, scroll hdls, scalloped rim, w/lid, rprs, 6" 160.00
Teapot, baluster form, 11¼" 850.00
Teapot, ftd, scrolled hdl, scalloped rim, rpr, 11" 275.00
Teapot, squat, 1820s, 6", VG 525.00
Teapot, vine border, ftd, 11", EX 600.00

Stretch Glass

Stretch glass, produced from 1916 until after 1930, was made in an effort to emulate the fine art glass of Tiffany and Carder. The glassware was sprayed with a metallic salts mix while hot, then reshaped, causing a stretch effect in the iridescent finish. Pieces which were not reshaped had the iridized finish without the stretch, as seen on Fenton's #222 lemonade set and #401 guest set. Northwood, Imperial, Fenton, Diamond, Lancaster, and the United States Glass Company were the largest manufacturers of this type of glass. See also specific companies.

Basket, rose, Imperial #300, 10¼" 65.00
Bowl, amber irid, collar bottom, 3x10" 40.00

Bowl, amber irid, Imperial, 3½x12" 45.00
Bowl, aquamarine, Fenton #1609 ....275.00
Bowl, bl, ruffled rim, 3½x12" 50.00
Bowl, ivory, NW #617, 3¾x8" 85.00
Bowl, olive gr, flared, collar bottom, 3½x9½" 50.00
Bowl, vaseline, Fenton, 3¾x10" 85.00
Candlestick, pk, Fenton #316, 2¾x4½" 35.00
Candlestick, russet, NW #658 ....48.00
Candlestick, topaz, NW #649, 9¾" 100.00

Candy jar, blue, Fenton, #1532, 8", $80.00.

Cheese/cracker set, smoke, cut decor, Imperial #641 ....75.00
Compote, wht, HP florals, Lancaster, 4¼x6¾" 45.00
Flower bowl, bl, w/candle holders attached, dmn shape 85.00
Plate, amberina, Imperial #6724, 6" 45.00
Plate, bl, 8¾" 18.00
Plate, Colonial Panel, Iris Ice, 8" 14.00
Plate, purple, Imperial, 8" 18.00
Plate, vaseline, Fenton, 8" 18.00
Sherbet, purple, Imperial #6001 ....28.00
Vase, tangerine, Fenton #1531, 14" 150.00

String Holders

Today, if you want to wrap and secure a package, you have a variety of products to choose from: cellophane tape, staples, etc. But in the 1800s, string was about the only available binder; thus the string holder, either the hanging or counter type, was a common and practical item found in most homes and businesses. Chalkware and ceramic figurals from the 1930s and 1940s contrast with the cast and wrought iron examples from the 1800s to make for an interesting collection. Our advisor for this category is Charles Reynolds; he is listed in the Directory under Virginia. See also Advertising.

Apple w/berries, ceramic, 8" 40.00
Birds on branch, scissors in head, ceramic 85.00
Blk child w/pk bandana, ceramic 195.00
Bonnet girl, eyes to side, ceramic, EX 60.00
Boy w/pipe, chalkware 60.00
Bull, brn & wht, ceramic 225.00
Cat atop ball of red string, chalkware, 7" 45.00
Chef, pnt CI 65.00
Child sits on globe on beast-head base, brass, 1870s, 14" 325.00
Colonial lady in rocking chair, PY/Japan 100.00
Deco girl w/hands in front, flowers, ceramic 95.00
Deco woman's head, ceramic 165.00
Dog, Schnauzer, ceramic 110.00
Heinz Pickle, metal ceiling type for cone string 2,500.00
Mammy, blk face, red/wht polka-dot scarf, clay 450.00
Mammy, chalk face, wht bandana, red dots 250.00
Man between 2 Southern belles, ceramic 50.00
Pig face, pottery 125.00

Porter, ceramic **95.00**
Southern belle, ceramic, Japan, 6" **45.00**
Table top, aluminum **45.00**

Sugar Shakers

Sugar shakers (or muffineers, as they were also called) were used during the Victorian era to sprinkle sugar and spice onto breakfast muffins, toast, etc. They were made of art glass, in pressed patterns, and in china. See also specific types and manufacturers. Our advisors for this category are Jeff Bradfield and Dale MacAllister; they are listed in the Directory under Virginia.

Acorn, bl opaque **210.00**
Acorn, shaded pk w/enamel & gold **240.00**
Alba, bl opaque **180.00**
Argus Swirl, clear satin **130.00**

Chrysanthemum Swirl, cranberry satin opalescent, 4½", $400.00.

Coin Dot, bl opal, 9-panel **185.00**
Coin Spot, cranberry opal, wide waist **250.00**
Coin Spot, rubena opal **250.00**
Cone, bl **125.00**
Creased Teardrop, translucent bl slag **125.00**
Crown Milano, fall leaves/bl berries on bsk, floral-emb lid **325.00**
Daisy & Fern Northwood Swirl, cranberry opal **325.00**
Forget-me-not, pk **140.00**
Hobbs Optic, rubena **165.00**
Hobnail, amber **95.00**
Leaning Pillar, bl opaque **110.00**
Optic Panels (8), cranberry, bulbous, metal collar **175.00**
Parian Swirl, gr opaque **175.00**
Quilted Phlox, gr transparent **175.00**
Quilted Phlox, pk cased **250.00**
Ribbed Lattice, bl opal **195.00**
Ribbed Lattice, cranberry opal **275.00**
Ribbed Pillar, cranberry spatter **185.00**
Ring Neck Optic, cranberry **235.00**
Royal Ivy, rubena **275.00**
Spanish Lace, bl opal, wide waist **215.00**
Spanish Lace, vaseline opal, wide waist **215.00**
West Virginia, optic ribbed milk glass w/HP florals **95.00**

Sunderland Lustre

Sunderland lustre was made by various potters in the Sunderland district of England during the 18th and 19th centuries. It is often characterized by a splashed-on application of the pink lustre, which results in an effect sometimes referred to as the 'cloud' pattern. Some pieces are transfer printed with scenes, ships, florals, or portraits.

Bowl, God Speed the Plow, blk w/mc, lustre band, 10⅛" **635.00**

Cup, mask ea side, splash lustre ground, 1820s, 5" **700.00**
Egg cup stand, mottled splashes, 8¼", +6 1¾" egg cups **700.00**
Jug, Guernsey 1856 memorial & Masonic decor, LePage mk **350.00**
Jug, puzzle; house & landscape, 1820s, 6½", EX **750.00**
Jug, sailor's farewell & girl milking, old rpr/chips, 8" **500.00**
Loving cup, sailor's farewell & clipper, frog at bottom **395.00**
Mug, seagoing scene & verse, 19th C, 5" **110.00**
Pitcher, Ann Amelia Hamon Born..., blk transfer, rstr, 7¼" **315.00**
Pitcher, Capt Jones & Capt Hull, blk transfers w/lustre, 7" **5,000.00**
Pitcher, Hunting, blk transfer, gr leaf border, 4" **150.00**
Pitcher, Masonic Devices..., blk transfer, splash lustre, 7½" **325.00**
Pitcher, sailing ship & verses, blk transfer w/mc, 1820s, 9¼" **975.00**
Pitcher, 4 blk transfers, overall lustre, 9½x9", NM **550.00**
Plaque, Behold God Will Not... (Job 8:20), 8½" dia **500.00**
Plaque, May They Ever Be United, blk transfer w/mc **200.00**
Plaque, mottled fr around 2-masted ship, blk transfer, 7x8" **150.00**
Plaque, Thou God Seeth Me, ca 1830, 7½x8½" **245.00**
Vase, quintal; splash decor, wear to rim, 1820s, 7½", pr **900.00**

Surveying Instruments

The practice of surveying offers a wide variety of precision instruments primarily for field use, most of which are associated with the recording of distance and angular measurements. These instruments were primarily made from brass; the larger examples were fitted with tripods and protective cases. These cases also held accessories for the instruments, and these can sometimes play a key part in their evaluation. Instruments in complete condition and showing little use will have much greater values than those that appear to have had moderate or heavy use. Instruments were never polished during use, and those that have been polished as decorator pieces are of little interest to most avid collectors. Our advisor for this category is Dale Beeks; he is listed in the Directory under Iowa.

Abney level, K&E, ca 1910, w/case **65.00**
Alidade, folding sight vanes, leather case **50.00**
Alidade, telescopic, exploration type, 10" **425.00**
Alidade, telescopic, w/post, ca 1910 ....**350.00**
Barometer, pocket-watch type, 1½" dia, w/case **100.00**
Chain, Chesterman Sheffield, 100-ft, EX **175.00**
Chain, 4-pole, Gurley NY, dirty, rust **120.00**
Compass, B Pike & Sons NY, early 1800s, w/mahog case **550.00**
Compass, FW&R King Balto, 1860s, 5" needle, 6" L **700.00**
Compass, geologist's, w/inclinometer needle, 4" sq **150.00**
Compass, HM Poole, ca 1850 ....**850.00**
Compass, plain, B Pike & Son **750.00**
Compass, pocket type, wooden housing, 3" **110.00**
Compass, staff, folding sight vanes **110.00**
Compass, telescopic vernier, Randolf **650.00**
Compass, vernier, W&LE Gurley, ca 1880, 15" **750.00**
Compass, wooden, ca 1810, 12" **750.00**
Compass, 5" brass housing, mk France **85.00**
Jacob's staff, oak w/steel tip, octagonal **120.00**
Level, Bostrom, w/case & tripod, unused **120.00**
Level, dumpy, Brunson, blk pnt **200.00**
Level, dumpy, engineer's, CL Berger & Sons, 1931, 17" scope **25.00**
Level, engineer's, J Roach, ca 1875, 16½" scope **325.00**
Level, gravett; Troughton & Simms, ca 1875, 15", +compass **500.00**
Level, wye, architect's, ca 1915, 11½" scope, 5" vial **200.00**
Level, wye, architect's, Keuffer & Esser, ca 1885, 11" **400.00**
Level, wye, builder's, 12" telescope **210.00**
Level, wye, engineer's, E Brown & Sons NY, 1850s, 17" scope ...**400.00**
Level, wye, engineer's, Fennel Kassel, ca 1940, 18" scope **125.00**

Level, wye, Gurley, ca 1880, 18" 350.00
Level, wye, Young & Sons Phila, 1887, 18" scope, 7¼" vial 250.00
Level/transit, Henry Ware, Cincinnati OH, brass, 66"+stand 900.00
Plumb-bob, mining type w/wick & gimbals, in box 450.00
Plumb-bob, w/internal reel 200.00
Pocket transit, Brunton, Wm Ainsworth, 1893 ....150.00
Solar attachment, Saegmuller; Bubb & Buff, 1940s, 6" scope 600.00
Theodolite, triangulation; DF Sohne Cassel, 1906, 14" scope 900.00
Tranist, blk pnt, ca 1930 ....225.00
Transit, #7, Young & Sons, ca 1895, 11" scope, 6½", EX 750.00
Transit, CL Berger & Sons, 1945, 11" scope, 6¼" 450.00
Transit, exploration type, ca 1890, 8" 450.00
Transit, FE Brandis NY, 1895, 10" scope, 6", rfn 400.00
Transit, lt mtn, ca 1900 ....550.00
Transit, Mahn & Co MO, 1900, 11" scope, 4¼" compass, 6¼" ..225.00
Transit, preliminary survey; Keuffel & Esser, 1906, 5½" 450.00
Transit, R Seelig Chicago, 1900s, 11¼" scope, 6¼" vial 500.00
Transit, W&LE Gurley NY, 1890s, 11½" scope, 6¾" 450.00
Transit, W&LE Gurley Troy NY, #1235 ....450.00
Transit, Young & Sons #9405 ....550.00
Tripod, transit type, telescopic legs 45.00

Swarovski Crystal

The Swarovski family has been perfecting the glassmaker's art in Wattens, Austria, since 1895. Collectible figurines and desk items were introduced in 1977, and the Swarovski Collectors Society (SCS) was created in 1987. Featuring lead content of 30%+, these 'Silver Crystal' limited edition decorative accessories have attracted a following of over 200,000 dedicated collectors worldwide. Some designs were distributed regionally, making pursuit of retired items an interesting challenge that spans the globe. Most items have an etched mark on the underside. The first mark was a block-style SC. In 1989 the mark was changed to a Swan. Marks on larger items also include the name Swarovski. SCS figurines are further identified with the year and designer's initials. The periodical *Swan Seekers News*, published by Maret Webb, our advisor for this category, is available if you want more information about retired Swarovski items. Her address is listed in the Directory under Arizona. Prices listed below reflect the presence of complete original packing and enclosures, without which prices are compromised 10% to 35%.

do1x881, woodpeckers, from $1,300 to 1,450.00
do1x901, dolphins, from $1,000 to 1,200.00
do1x951, lion, from $450 to 540.00
003-8901707, dolphin pin, club item, from $155 to 170.00
7432nr57002, geometric paperweight, from $170 to 210.00
7454nr60, atomic paperweight, clear 1,980.00
7466nr063100, treasure box, butterfly, oval 275.00
7474nr000027, town hall, from $220 to 235.00
7475nr000007, shepherd, from $120 to 135.00
7504nr030R, apple photo stand, rhodium, sm, from $240 to 270.00
7507nr105002, pineapple, rhodium, lg, from $420 to 480.00
7522nr60, rhino, sm, from $110 to 130.00
7550nr30015, grapes, lg, from $1,650 to 1,680.00
7553nr200, bee, rhodium 2,280.00
7600nr106, candle holder, from $300 to 335.00
7600nr133, global candle holders, med, pr, from $140 to 155.00
7616nr000003, beaver baby, recumbent, from $90 to 95.00
7620nr100000, walrus, from $170 to 200.00
7621nr000001, kingfisher, from $130 to 145.00
7626nr65, hippopotamus, from $120 to 155.00
7630nr30, hedgehog, silver whiskers, sm, from $400 to 480.00
7631nr30, mouse, sm, from $105 to 120.00

7631nr52, cat, med, from $450 to 540.00
7632nr75, turtle, king sz, from $280 to 390.00
7635nr70, Pluto, standing, from $110 to 145.00
7642nr48, frog, blk eyes, from $130 to 145.00
7653nr75, duck, lg 360.00
7672nr42, dachshund, mini, from $130 to 170.00

Swastika Keramos

Swastika Keramos was a line of artware made by the Owens China Co., of Minerva, Ohio, around 1902-04. It is characterized either by a coralene type of decoration (similar to the Opalesce line made by the J.B. Owens Pottery Company of Zanesville) or by the application of metallic lustres, usually in simple designs. Shapes are often plain and handles squarish and rather thick, suggestive of the Arts and Crafts style.

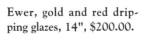

Ewer, gold and red dripping glazes, 14", $200.00.

Ewer, comet & tree landscape, mc sky bkground, 10½" 850.00
Pitcher, broad leaves, gr on gold gloss, #704-L, 10", NM 180.00
Vase, irises, gold w/blk on red & gold, #705A, 11", NM 130.00
Vase, purple lustre on red matt, wafer mk, #513, 8½" 110.00
Vase, textured gr decor on wht over gold gloss, #7066, 7½" 160.00

Syracuse

Syracuse was a line of fine dinnerware and casual ware which was made for nearly a century by the Onondaga Pottery Company of Syracuse, New York. Early patterns were marked O.P. Company. Collectors of American dinnerware are focusing their attention on reassembling some of their many lovely patterns. In 1966 the firm became officially known as the Syracuse China Company in order to better identify with the name of their popular chinaware. Many of the patterns were marked with the shape and color names (Old Ivory, Federal, etc.), not the pattern names. By 1971 dinnerware geared for use in the home was discontinued, and the company turned to the manufacture of hotel, restaurant, and other types of commercial tableware.

Arcadia, cup & saucer 28.00
Arcadia, gravy boat 65.00
Arcadia, plate, dessert; 7⅛" 18.00
Arcadia, platter, 14" 58.00
Bombay, bowl, vegetable; gold trim, w/lid 98.00
Bombay, coffeepot, ivory w/gold trim 95.00
Bombay, platter, gold trim, 16" 65.00
Bracelet, plate, dinner; 9¾" 40.00
Bracelet, platter, 12" 55.00
Briarcliff, bowl, cereal 32.00

Briarcliff, bowl, vegetable; w/lid 130.00
Briarcliff, plate, dessert; 7⅛" 17.50
Briarcliff, platter, 12" 57.50
Briarcliff, sugar bowl 37.50
Circus, bowl, cereal; dog & ball, Union Pacific RR, 6" 70.00
Circus, mug, horse & elephant, Union Pacific RR, 3½" 125.00
Circus, plate, clown face, Union Pacific RR, 1951, 8½" 70.00
Clover, plate, salad; 8" 16.00
Coralbel, soup 25.00
Gardenia, bowl, cereal 27.50
Jefferson, bowl, vegetable; w/lid 98.00
Jefferson, gravy boat 67.50
Jefferson, plate, dinner; 10¼" 30.00
Jefferson, teapot 98.00
Lady Mary, plate, dinner; 9¾" 22.00
Lady Mary, platter, 12" 57.50
Lady Mary, sugar bowl 36.00
Meadow Breeze, bowl, vegetable; rnd 88.00
Meadow Breeze, plate, bread & butter 20.00
Meadow Breeze, plate, salad 26.00
Minuet, cup & saucer 32.50
Minuet, plate, dinner 36.00
Orleans, cup, bouillon 12.00
Royal Court, plate, 10¼" 50.00
Sharon, bowl, vegetable; oval, 10" 47.50
Sharon, plate, salad 17.50
Sherwood, gravy boat 68.00
Sherwood, plate, salad 17.50
Sherwood, platter, 14" 65.00
Singing Cowboys, chop plate 38.00
Singing Cowboys, plate, 7½" 18.00
Stansbury, bowl, vegetable; oval, 9¼" 48.00
Stansbury, bowl, vegetable; w/lid 125.00
Stansbury, plate, dinner 25.00
Stansbury, plate, salad; 8" 16.00
Suzanne, bowl, vegetable; oval 68.00
Suzanne, gravy boat 75.00
Suzanne, rim soup 32.00
Sweetheart, creamer 37.50
Sweetheart, cup & saucer 26.00
Sweetheart, plate, dinner; 10¼" 24.00
Sweetheart, plate, salad; 8" 14.00
Sweetheart, sugar bowl 45.00
Victoria, platter, 12x9" 70.00
Virginia, bouillon, w/underplate 12.00
Whitby, cake plate, 1 hdl 65.00
Whitby, cup & saucer 30.00

Syrups

Values are for old, original syrups. Beware of reproductions! See also various manufacturers and specific types of glass. Our advisors are Jeff Bradfield and Dale MacAllister; they are listed in the Directory under Virginia.

Atlanta, frosted 225.00
Blocked T'print Band, ruby stain 225.00
Button Arches, ruby stain 275.00
Chrysanthemum Swirl, wht satin 250.00
Coin Spot & Swirl, bl opal 200.00
Coin Spot & Swirl, wht opal 150.00
Daisy & Fern, W VA Optic mold, bl opal 250.00
Diamond Spearhead, vaseline opal 425.00

Florette, pk satin 275.00
Forget-Me-Not, bl 190.00
Frosted Lion, 5¼" 350.00
Hercules Pillar, amber 150.00
Hexagon Block, amber flashed 250.00
Hexagon Block, ruby flashed 225.00
Inside Ribbed, bl 175.00
Invt T'print, bl, tapered 150.00
Late Block, ruby stain 250.00
Nail, ruby stain 325.00
O'Hara Dmn, ruby stain 325.00
Open Heart Arches, cobalt 395.00
Polka Dot, cranberry opal, clear hdl, orig top 600.00
Ring Band, custard, souvenir decor 275.00
Ring Neck Coin Spot, bl opal 200.00
Sunk Honeycomb, ruby stain 220.00
Swirled Windows, cranberry opal, orig lid 650.00
Thousand Eye, lt gr 175.00
Torpedo, ruby stain 250.00
Truncated Cube, ruby stain 225.00
Valencia Waffle, amber 135.00
Yoked Loop, ruby stain 245.00
Zipper Border, ruby stain, etched 250.00

Tamac Pottery

At the close of World War II, finding jobs almost nonexistent for home-coming military men, Leonard Tate and Allen Macauley decided to take advantage of an offer made by the state of Oklahoma which was trying to encourage industry by offering free factory sites for new businesses. Their wives had both worked as designers for the same company, so the foursome decided to combine efforts and past experiences and thus formed 'Tamac' pottery, a conglomeration of the two last names.

The company was organized in September 1946 in Henry and Zoma Tate's garage (they were Leonard Tate's parents) in Perry, Oklahoma; production was very limited. They expanded in 1948 and were able to produce over three hundred pieces of earthenware daily.

The Tates and Macauleys were directly responsible for all phases of Tamac production: designing and making the molds, mixing the Oklahoma and Kansas clays, final processing and shipping. They had customers in every state as well as foreign countries, and they operated an outlet store as well.

About seventy various pieces of Tamac pottery were produced, mainly buffet/dinnerware. Other 'specialty' pieces included candle holders, ashtrays, vases, and table centerpieces. One of their most popular sellers was the barbeque line, designed for casual entertaining and backyard dining. It consisted of tray-like plates with unique coffee mugs having nontraditional handles.

Six colors were produced, each with a 'frosted' rim of a different color. The six colors were Frosty Pine, Avocado, Frosty Fudge, Honey, Raspberry, and Butterscotch. The Frosty Pine and Avocado (both with dark green bases) are the most readily available. Few items, mainly 'specialty' pieces, were manufactured in Raspberry.

In 1950 the Macauleys sold their shares to the Tates. The business expanded and by 1952 required bank financing which proved impossible to obtain. As a result, the plant was sold in September of that year to Earl, Raymond, and Bettye Bechtold. (Earl was a brother to Zoma Tate.) With only eight employees, the pottery produced about 250,000 pieces a year, shipping their product to ten states and four foreign countries, those being Canada, Australia, Germany, and Belgium. Most of their sales, however, were made at the plant itself. The motto of the pottery was 'See it Made.'

Raymond Bechtold was the active manager of the business and added more than thirty-five pieces to the line, among them the juice pitcher and juice glasses, breakfast plate and mug, covered casserole, decanter and goblet set, teapot, demitasse line, chocolate pitcher, and bud vase. These items are now among the most sought after. Bechtold also experimented with new colors in the accessory and floral lines such as Raspberry, Sky Blue, and Bronze. Only Raspberry was popular, and the others were quickly phased out.

Raymond Bechtold assumed full control of the pottery in 1960 and operated it until February 1965, when he sold it to Mrs. Lenita Moore. Mrs. Moore's mother had been a long-time employee of the plant and was the active manager. The pottery operated until 1970 when it closed and the final auction was held. The building still stands and is used for storage.

Tamac pottery can easily be identified by its unique design and the stamp on the bottom of each piece: 'TAMAC Perry, Okla USA.' Some earlier pieces carry the etched 'TAMAC' mark.

Our advisors for this category are Bob and Dondee Klein. They are listed in the Directory under Oklahoma.

Ashtray, bridge	8.00
Ashtray, Oklahoma	15.00
Ashtray, rnd	15.00
Ashtray, 3-corner	8.00
Bird, 3-dimensional, any color, ea	30.00
Bowl, centerpc; dish garden	20.00
Bowl, centerpc; S-shape	17.50
Bowl, serving; 2-qt	18.00
Bowl, serving; 4-qt	30.00
Butter dish, no lid	9.00
Candle holder, dbl	25.00
Casserole, w/lid, 2-qt	30.00
Chocolate pot, tall & thin	55.00
Coffee cup, hdls	5.00
Coffee mug, w/finger insert	9.00
Creamer, demitasse	10.00
Creamer, 8-oz	8.00
Cup, demitasse	12.00
Decanter, wine; w/stopper	60.00
Goblet, wine; 6-oz	13.00
Pitcher, juice; 24-oz	15.00
Pitcher, 2-qt	25.00
Pitcher, 4-qt	35.00
Planter vase, no tray, 5x6" dia	20.00
Planter vase, w/tray & drain hole	15.00
Plate, barbecue; 15"	12.00
Plate, dinner; 10"	8.00
Platter, turkey; 18"	35.00
Saucer	3.00
Saucer, demitasse	7.00
Sugar bowl, w/lid	10.00
Teapot, short & squat	50.00
Toothpick holder	7.00
Tumbler, juice; 4-oz	10.00
Tumbler, 16-oz	8.00
Vase, free-form, 5½"	25.00
Violet planter, w/tray & drain hole	17.00
Wall vase/pocket, 5"	12.50

Target Balls

Prior to 1880 when the clay pigeon was invented, blown glass target balls were used extensively for shotgun competitions. Approximately 2¾" in diameter, these balls were hand blown into a three-piece mold. All have a ragged hole where the blowpipe was twisted free. Target balls date from approximately 1840 (English) to World War I, although they were most widely used in the 1870-1880 period. Common examples are unmarked except for the blower's code — dots, crude numerals, etc. Some balls are embossed in a dot or diamond pattern so they were more likely to shatter when struck by shot, and some have names and/or patent dates. When evaluating condition, bubbles and other minor manufacturing imperfections are acceptable; cracks are not. The prices below are for mint condition examples.

Amber w/emb ribs, horizontal or vertical	150.00
Bogardus' Glass Ball Pat'd April 10 1877, amber, Am	350.00
Bogardus' Glass Ball Pat'd April 10 1877, other than amber, Am	800.00
CTB Co, blk pitch, Pat dates on bottom, Am	250.00
Dmn Quilt w/plain center band, ground top, Am	150.00
Dmn Quilt w/shooter emb in 2 panels, clear, English	300.00
Dmn Quilt w/shooter emb in 2 panels, gr or purple, English	300.00
EE Eaton Guns & C 53 State St Chicago, golden yel-amber, 2⅝"	1,000.00
Flesschenfabriek Boers & CP Delft, emb dmns, lt olive, 2⅝"	300.00
For Hockey's Pat Trap, gr, English	500.00
Glasshuttenewotte un Charlottenburg, med yel-olive, 2⅝"	1,000.00
Great Western Gun Works, Pittsburgh, amber, Am	900.00
Gurd & Son, London, Ontario, amber, Canadian	500.00
Ilmenau (Thur) Sophiehutte, amber, Dmn Quilt, Germany	425.00
Ira Paine's Filled Ball Pat Oct 23 1877, amber, Am	250.00
Ira Paine's Filled Ball Pat Oct 23 1877, other than amber, Am	800.00
Man shooting, clear, 2⅝"	150.00
NB Glass Works Perth, other than pale gr, English	200.00
NB Glass Works Perth, pale gr, English	100.00
Plain, amber w/mold mks	65.00
Plain, clear w/mold mks	1,000.00
Plain, cobalt w/mold mks	150.00
T Jones, Gunmaker, Blackburn, pale bl, English	150.00
Van Cutsem, A St Quentin, cobalt, 2¾" dia	150.00
WW Greener, St Mary's Works, various colors, English, ea	250.00

Related Memorabilia

Ball thrower, dbl; old red pnt, ME Card, Pat...78, 79, VG	900.00
Clay birds, Winchester, Pat May 29 1917, 1 flight in box	100.00
Pitch bird, blk DUVROCK	1.00
Shell, dummy, w/single window, any brand	35.00
Shell, dummy shotgun, Winchester, window w/powder, 6"	125.00
Shell set, dummy, Gamble Stores, 2 window shells, 3 cut out	125.00
Shell set, dummy, Winchester, 5 window shells	175.00
Shell set, dummy shotgun, Peters, 6 window shells+full box	175.00
Shotshell loader, rosewood/brass, Parker Bros, Pat 1884	50.00
Target, Am sheet metal, rod ends mk Pat Feb 8 '21, set	25.00
Target, blk japanned sheet metal, Bussey Patentee, London	50.00
Target, BUST-O, blk or wht breakable wafer	20.00
Trap, DUVROCK, w/blk pitch birds	250.00
Trap, MO-SKEET-O, w/birds	150.00

Tartan Glass

Tartan glass is accredited to Henry G. Richardson at Wordsley Flint Glass Works near Stourbridge, England. Glass threads were arranged to form a plaid similar to Scotch Tartan. Tartan glass was registered February 24, 1886.

Bowl, triangular, mk, #46498, 3¾x8"	1,250.00
Gaslight shade, mk, #46498, 1½" dia end/base, 6" H	285.00

Tea Caddies

Because tea was once regarded as a precious commodity, special boxes called caddies were used to store the tea leaves. They were made from various materials: porcelain, carved and inlaid woods, and metals ranging from painted tin or tole to engraved silver. Our advisor for this category is Tina Carter; she is listed in the Directory under California.

Blk lacquered wood w/gold chinoiserie, 6⅝" 55.00
Burl inlay, 2-comparment, Sheraton, England, ca 1790 ....500.00
Burl veneer w/gilt brass strapping, dome top, 9", EX 275.00
Creamware, figures w/mc, w/lid, 1780s, 6¼" 1,000.00

Engraved ivory, views of Indian tea plantation and flowers, India (for English market), ca 1800, 7¼x10¼x6¼", EX, $2,750.00.

Mahog Chippendale w/inlay, 3-section interior, 1780s, 10" L 300.00
Mahog George III, oak-lined int, 1800s, 6⅛x11x6" 330.00
Mahog w/lt wood inlay, brass ft, lt wear, 8" 65.00
Old Sheffield, desert scene, oval, lion finial, ftd, 6x3" 250.00
Pearlware, bl chinoiserie, emb fluting on shoulder, 4¼" 190.00
Peking enamel on copper, mc flowers/Chinese characters, 5" 105.00
Rosewood Regency sarcophagus, MOP escutcheon, 1820s, 12" L ..300.00
Tole, orig gold crystallized pnt w/wht & gold edge, 5" 50.00
Wood, lacquer w/MOP inlay, Fr shape, VG 125.00
Wood veneer, chest, unmk, ca 1890, VG 225.00
Wood veneer w/MOP inlay, hinged lid, brass mts, 9x15x9", EX ...475.00

Tea Leaf Ironstone

Tea Leaf Ironstone became popular in the 1880s when middle-class American housewives became bored with the plain white stone china that English potters had been exporting to this country for nearly a century. The original design has been credited to Anthony Shaw of Longport, who decorated the plain ironstone with a hand-painted copper lustre design of bands and leaves. Originally known as Lustre Band and Sprig, the pattern has since come to be known as Tea Leaf Lustre. It was produced with minor variations by many different firms both in England and the United States. By the early 1900s, it had become so commonplace that it had lost much of its appeal.

Items marked Red Cliff are reproductions made from 1950 until 1980 for this distributing and decorating company of Chicago, Illinois. Hall China provided many of the blanks.

Our advice for this category comes from Home Place Antiques, whose address is listed in the Directory under Illinois.

Bone dish, scalloped edge, Wilkinson 75.00
Bowl, crimped edge, Wilkinson, 3⅜x9½" sq 75.00
Bowl, vegetable; Fish Hook, w/lid, Meakin, 10½x6½" 150.00
Bowl, vegetable; medallion finial & hdl, Mellor-Taylor 165.00
Bowl, vegetable; Pagoda, ribbed, hdls, w/lid, Wedgwood, 11x7" .225.00
Butter dish, Fish Hook, w/lid & drain, Meakin, EX 165.00

Butter dish, simple, w/lid & drain, Wedgwood, 5½" sq 165.00
Butter pat, sq, Meakin, 2¾" 14.00
Cake plate, 8-sided, Adams Microtex, 11⅛x8¾" 60.00
Coffeepot, Bamboo, Meakin, 9", EX 185.00
Coffeepot, Chinese shape, Shaw, 10" 275.00
Creamer, Adams Microtex, 11⅛x8¾" 60.00
Creamer, Morning Glory, Elsmore & Forster 285.00
Creamer, Wedgwood, 5¼" 95.00
Cup & saucer, Chelsea type, Johnson Bros, 3½x2⅝", EX 85.00
Cup & saucer, handleless; Meakin 95.00
Cup & saucer, Lily of the Valley, Shaw 140.00
Cup & saucer, ribbed below waist & around saucer, Wedgwood ..75.00
Cup & saucer, str sides, Meakin, 2¾", EX 75.00
Cup plate, unmk, 3½" 60.00
Gravy boat, Fish Hook, Meakin, 2¾x8" 70.00
Gravy boat, sq, unmk 55.00
Plate, Chinese Pattern, Shaw, 7⅞" 17.50
Plate, Chinese Pattern, Shaw, 9½" 35.00
Plate, Meakin, 7¾" 15.00
Plate, Meakin, 9¾" 30.00
Plate, Wedgwood, 9" 30.00
Plate, Wilkinson, 8" 16.00
Platter, Meakin, 12¾x9⅛" 45.00
Platter, oval, Shaw, 15x10½" 45.00
Relish, oval, Shaw 45.00
Sauce dish, rnd, Meakin, 4¾" 18.00
Shaving mug, Shaw, 3½x3⅜" 185.00
Sugar bowl, Bamboo, w/lid, Grindley 95.00
Sugar bowl, Fish Hook, w/lid, Meakin, 7" 85.00
Sugar bowl, Lily of the Valley, Shaw, 5½x6½" 150.00
Teapot, Fish Hook, Meakin, 8½" 185.00
Toothbrush holder, Mellor-Taylor 145.00

Teapots

Teapots have become popular collectibles in recent years with a surge in tea shops featuring tea, teapots, and afternoon tea. Collectors should be aware of modern teapots which imitate older similar versions. Study the types of pottery, porcelain, and china, as well as the marks. Multicolored, detailed marks over the glaze represent modern pieces. Teapots made in the last thirty years are quite collectible but generally don't demand the same prices as their antique counterparts.

A wide range of teapots can be found by the avid collector. Those from before 1880 are more apt to be found in museums or sold at quality auction houses. Almost every pottery and porcelain manufacturer in Asia, Europe, and America have produced teapots. Some are purely decorative and whimsical, while others are perfect for brewing a pot of tea. Tea drinkers should beware of odd-shaped spouts which sputter and drip. Reproductions to be aware of: majolica styles with modern marks, Blue Willow which has been made continuously for almost two centuries, and those marked Made in China (older teapots have 'chop marks' in Chinese).

Refer to various manufacturers' names for further listings. Our advisor for this category is Tina M. Carter, listed in the Directory under California. Her book, *Teapots*, is available at bookstores or direct from the author.

ALB, dripless, mottled, England, ca 1920 ....52.00
Anniversary, 50th; floral, Price Kensington 48.00
Automobile, silver lustre, Carlton Ware, England 495.00
Ballerina, music box & movement, Japan, ca 1960 ....30.00
Barge, brn, emb mk, Derbyshire, England, lg 75.00
Barge, emb floral decor, A Present..., ca 1800s 1,000.00

Basket, picnic teapot & 2 cups, hinged lid, padded, China 100.00
Belleek, American, ornate detail, palette mk, ca 1900 ....850.00
Beswick Ware, Dickens' characters, England, ca 1930 ....75.00
Boston Tea Party, commemorative, Davison Newman, +cr/sug 45.00

Bristol, floral sprays on barrel shape, leaf-molded handle, branch spout, ca 1772, 5¼", $300.00.

Cast metal, scenes, octagonal, China, ca 1920 ....65.00
Charles & Diana, brn pottery, Wales CM, 2½" 78.00
Cloisonne, animal or designs, China, mini 35.00
Copper, Art Deco style, enamel decor, ball ft, China 38.00
Crinoline Lady, Made in Czechoslovakia 75.00
Crinoline Lady (Cinderella), Sadler, England, ca 1930 ....65.00
Cube, fleur-de-lis, Royal Crownford, England 25.00
Cube, HP, Made in Japan, ca 1940 ....20.00
Cube, Los Angeles Steamship Co, Clews, England 38.00
Duck, Peking; HP, wicker hdl, no mk, China, ca 1920 ....75.00
Edward VII commemorative, pk lustre, England, 2-cup 250.00
Granny, mc, Lingard or HJ Wood, England, 1930 ....55.00
Granny, Queensware, modern 35.00
Granny Ann, mk USA, Shawnee 80.00
Iced tea dispenser, USA, 2-pc, lg 175.00
Jim Beam, characters, ltd ed, Wade 48.00
Lefton, cozy set, violets, ca 1950 ....32.00
Lipton's, oval, ribbed, Fraunfelter, ca 1930 ....35.00
Lipton's, rnd, various colors, Hall China Co 30.00
Meakin, Alfred; blk trim, china relief, England 38.00
Monterrey, Calif, Art Deco, pottery 42.00
Pewter, New Amsterdam Silver Co, USA 35.00
Pottery, pk, mk Ford, USA, 1-cup 25.00
Rough glaze, buff sharkskin, tan, slip decor, Japan, 1920s 28.00
RS Prussia, scalloped hdl/edge, HP decor, unmk 75.00
Sadler, folklore, Robin Hood/King Arthur/etc, ca 1990 ....35.00
Salada Tea, promotional item, USA, 1-cup 25.00
Silverplate, Rococo style, Community 70.00
Snow White w/Dwarfs, musical, Walt Disney Prod 75.00
Spode's Tower, bl/wht transfer, London shape, England, VG 58.00
Tiffin, tea liqueur, depot decanter, Germany, 1960 ....95.00
Weller, majolica, wooded scene, mk USA, ca 1930, VG 60.00
WWII, Esc to US by Royal Navy or Allied Fleets, brn, England ..45.00
Yxing, padded box, chop mk, China repro 45.00

Teco

Teco artware was made by the American Terra Cotta and Ceramic Company, located near Chicago, Illinois. The firm was established in 1886 and until 1901 produced only brick, sewer tile, and other redware. Their early glaze was inspired by the matt green made popular by Grueby. 'Teco Green' was made for nearly ten years. It was similar to Grueby's yet with a subtle silver-gray cast. The company was one of the first in the United States to perfect a true crystalline glaze. The only decoration used was through the modeling and glazing techniques; no hand painting was attempted. Favored motifs were naturalistic leaves and flowers. The company broadened their lines to include garden pottery and faience tiles and panels. New matt glazes (browns, yellows, blue, and rose) were added to the green in 1910. By 1922 the artware lines were discontinued; the company was sold in 1930.

Values are dictated by size and shape, with architectural and organic forms being more desirable. Teco is usually marked with a vertical impressed device comprised of a large 'T' to the left of the remaining three letters.

Bowl, emb floral on gr matt, 2½x9" 750.00
Bowl, gr, emb shoulder, incurvate, Albert design, 2x9" 325.00
Candlestick, pk, invt trumpet form w/sq hdl, 2½x5" 325.00
Garden urn, gr w/blk crazing, ovoid, sm nicks, 31x18" 2,100.00
Oil jar, oatmeal gloss, ovoid w/closed hdls, rpr lip, 30" 300.00
Paperweight, pelican, tan, rpr, 6½" 150.00
Pitcher, crystalline, #56, 4" 550.00
Pitcher, gr w/heavy charcoal, split whiplash hdl, 8½" 475.00
Pitcher, mint gr w/med charcoaling, integral hdl, Gates, 4" 350.00
Tile, sailing ship, deep cvg on oatmeal mottle, rpr, 26x17" 325.00
Vase, aventurine, yel/caramel/rose/violet/blk, 5½" 400.00
Vase, aventurine caramel/gold/blk, 4" 350.00
Vase, bl, cylinder w/4 emb ½-buttresses, #404, rpr lip, 7" 475.00
Vase, brn, pinched sides, 4" 425.00
Vase, brn, 4 bullet-nose columns atop cone body, 9" 750.00
Vase, brn, 4 sq buttresses cage bottle form, #488, 7x4" 1,000.00
Vase, caramel, incurvate, 2" 210.00
Vase, gold/orange/brn crystalline, teardrop form, 4", NM 210.00
Vase, gr, #202, 5x4¼" 550.00
Vase, gr, broad shoulder, #164, 10" 800.00
Vase, gr, broad shoulder, 5" 400.00
Vase, gr, broad-based cylindrical form, 4½" 450.00
Vase, gr, classic form w/2 thick buttress hdls, Gates, 7" 900.00
Vase, gr, gourd form w/flared neck, #164, 10x8" 800.00
Vase, gr, ovoid w/flared neck & closed sqd-off hdls, 7x5" 900.00
Vase, gr, shouldered ovoid w/flaring rim, Gates, 8" 425.00
Vase, gr, slim form w/sm closed shoulder hdls, 6" 700.00
Vase, gr, wide teardrop w/sm neck, 4x2¾" 375.00
Vase, gr, 2 open bar hdls, WD Gates, 8" 1,300.00
Vase, gr, 3 tapering sides, sqd shoulder, 7¾x4" 900.00
Vase, gr, 4 buttresses terminate 2" under rim, 10½x5" 1,300.00
Vase, gr, 4 lg Vs cradle shouldered body w/incurvate rim, 9x4" ..850.00
Vase, gr, 4 str vertical buttresses, WD Gates design, 6" 1,300.00
Vase, gr, 4 teardrop lobes over invt cone, scalloped base, 9" 850.00
Vase, gr, 6 swirled leaves disattached about neck, rstr, 14" 11,000.00
Vase, gr w/charcoal, long pointed pierced hdls, 11" 1,000.00
Vase, gr w/lt charcoal, dbl gourd w/4 curved buttresses, 8" 3,750.00
Vase, gr w/med charcoaling, long 4-lobe neck/wide base, 16" .2,100.00
Vase, mint gr, rnd w/pinched sides & rim, 4½" 300.00
Vase, mint gr w/charcoal, dbl gourd w/4 shaped buttresses, 6½" ..2,100.00
Vase, mustard, #392, 7" 500.00
Vase, purple, linear rim band & uprights, ovoid, 12x6" 1,400.00
Vase, red/orange metallic gloss, wide gourd form, 11x9" 3,500.00
Vase, tan gloss, closed hdls align w/rim & body, 9", EX 425.00
Vase, yel, spherical w/sm neck, 5" 350.00
Vase, yel, 4-lobed ovoid w/'windows' over rtcl ea side, 7" 1,300.00
Vase, yel/gr, tulip form w/in 4 buttresses, Moreau, 12" 1,600.00

Teddy Bear Collectibles

The story of Teddy Roosevelt's encounter with the bear cub has been oft recounted with varying degrees of accuracy, so it will suffice to say that it was as a result of this incident in 1902 that the teddy bear got his name. These appealing little creatures are enjoying renewed popularity with collectors today. To one who has not yet succumbed to their obvious charms, one bear seems to look very much like another. How to tell the older ones? Look for long snouts, jointed limbs, large feet and felt paws, long curving arms, and glass or shoe-button eyes. Most old bears have a humped back and are made of mohair stuffed with straw or excelsior. Cute expressions, original clothes, a nice personality, and, of course, good condition add to their value. Early Steiff bears in mint condition may go for a minimum of $100.00 per inch (for a small bear) up to $200.00 per inch (for one 20" high or larger). These are easily recognized by the trademark button within the ear. For further information we recommend *Teddy Bears, Annalees & Steiff Animals*, by Margaret Fox Mandel, available from Collector Books. See also Toys, Steiff.

Key: jtd — jointed

Bears

Am, gold mohair, jtd, bullet-shaped body, 1930s, 23", VG 175.00
Clemens, tan mohair, hump, glass eyes, felt pads, 9", M 95.00
Clemens, tan mohair, jtd, glass eyes, felt pads, 17", M 255.00
Clemens, Zotty type, squeaker, tan mohair, glass eyes, 11", EX 55.00

German, gold mohair, red muzzle, mechanical windup, 5½", EX, $500.00.

Germany, yel mohair, jtd, glass eyes, embr face, 1920s, 17", VG ...550.00
Hermann, gold mohair, jtd, plastic eyes, recent, 9", M 50.00
Hermann, growler, tan mohair, hump, no eyes, long nose, 11", VG ..200.00
Hermann, tan mohair, hump, jtd, glass eyes, sm rprs, 17", VG ...275.00
Hermann, Zotty type, brn mohair, hump, jtd, glass eyes, 12" 145.00
Ideal, gold mohair plush, button eyes, jtd, 1910s, 24", VG 320.00
Japan, mechanical, walking, molded fur, hump & tail, 1950s, 6" .50.00
Schuco, gold mohair, jtd, glass eyes, old, worn, 14" 350.00
Schuco, musical, yes/no, gold mohair, 16", M 2,000.00
Schuco, tan mohair, jtd metal-core body, bead eyes, 3½", EX 125.00
Schuco, yes/no, tan mohair, jtd, glass eyes, felt pads, 22" 1,000.00
Schuco, yes/no, tan mohair, jtd, glass eyes, 5", EX 465.00
Schuco, yes/no, wht mohair, jtd/swivel head, straw, 19", EX 750.00
Schuco, 2-faced golliwog/bear, tan mohair, jtd, 3¾", M 650.00
Steiff, blond mohair, jtd, button eyes, embr face, 1905, 13", EX ...1,100.00
Steiff, gold mohair, hump, jtd, plastic eyes, button, 8" 215.00
Steiff, gold mohair, jtd, claws, glass eyes, button, '40s, 14" 465.00
Steiff, mohair, jtd, sheared snout, glass eyes, button, '60s, 9" 130.00
Steiff, tan mohair, jtd, plastic eyes, button, 1940s, 11" 245.00
Steiff, yel mohair, jtd, glass eyes, '20s, button, 24", minimum .1,150.00
Steiff, 1983 Anniversary, growler, silver mohair, jtd, 12", MIB ..325.00
Unknown, bl fuzzy plush, jtd, glass eyes, ribbon, 8", M 45.00
Unknown, brn mohair, jtd, glass eyes, embr face, 1920s, 30", EX ...260.00
Unknown, brn mohair, jtd, glass eyes, long snout, 11", EX 135.00
Unknown, gold mohair, jtd, glass eyes/embr features, rprs, 25" ...275.00
Unknown, laughing type, tan mohair, glass eyes, 18", NM 150.00
Unknown, shaggy mohair, jtd, brn glass eyes, 16", NM 400.00
Unknown, wht baby type, growler, jtd, glass eyes, 16", NM 195.00
Unknown, wht fleecy, jtd, plastic eyes, 7", VG 200.00

Telephones

Since Alexander Graham Bell's first successful telephone communication, the phone itself has undergone a complete evolution in style as well as efficiency. Early models, especially those wall types with ornately carved oak boxes, are of special interest to collectors. Also of value are the candlestick phones from the early part of the century and any related memorabilia.

American Electric, oak, wall type, swivel mouthpc, EX 575.00
American Telecom, 1972, EX 40.00
American Telephone & Telegraph, candlestick, 1915, EX 130.00
Automatic Electric, dial, 1950s 25.00
Bell System, candlestick, operator's issue 90.00
Danish French, Bakelite, 1913, EX 75.00
Kellogg, metal, dial wall type, EX 95.00
National Cash Register, EX 145.00
Stromberg-Carlson, Bakelite, cradle style, 1920s 40.00
Stromberg-Carlson, candlestick type 110.00
Western Electric, oak, candlestick w/dial 275.00
Western Electric, oak, wall type, complete, EX 300.00
Western Electric, oval base, nondial cradle style 50.00
Western Electric, school wall intercom, brass/Bakelite, pr 100.00

Novelty Telephones

Beetle Bailey, 1983, MIB 95.00
Cabbage Patch Girl, 1980s, EX+ 85.00
Crest Sparkle, MIB 55.00
Garfield, Tyco 30.00
Joe Cook, Seika, 1992, M 60.00
Keeble Elf, NM 100.00
Mickey Mouse, pnt plastic, Am Telecomm Corp, 1975, 10", EX+ ..100.00
Raid Bug, EX+ 125.00
Snoopy & Woodstock, pnt plastic, Am Telecomm Corp, 1976, NM ..95.00
Snoopy as Joe Cool, 1980s, MIB 55.00
Winnie the Pooh, sq base, M, from $225 to 250.00
Ziggy, 1989, MIB 75.00

Related Memorabilia

Booklet, How To Build Rural Telephone Lines, ca 1900 ....15.00
Booth, Western Electric, wooden 600.00
Sign, Bell System, porc, flanged, roped bell, 16" sq, VG 200.00
Sign, New England Telephone...Bell System, bl/wht, 21x22" 145.00
Sign, Public Telephone, early bell, rnd, EX 190.00
Test box, portable, oak, w/carrying strap, all orig, EX 45.00

Blue Bell Paperweights

First issued in the early 1900s, bell-shaped glass paperweights were used as 'give-aways' and/or presented to telephone company executives as tokens of appreciation. The paperweights were used to prevent stacks of papers from blowing off the desks in the days of overhead fans. Over the years they have all but vanished — some taken by retiring employees, others accidently broken. The weights came to be widely used for advertising by individual telephone companies; and as the smaller companies merged to form larger companies, more and more new paperweights were created. They were widely distributed with the opening of the first transcontinental telephone line in 1915. The bell-shaped paperweight embossed 'Opening of Trans-Pacific Service, Dec. 23, 1931,' in peacock blue glass is very rare, and the price is negotiable. In 1972 the first Pioneer bell paperweights were made to sell to raise funds for the charities the Pioneers support. This has continued to the present day. These bell paperweights have also become 'collectibles.' For further study we recommend *Blue Bell Paperweights, 1992 Revised Edition,* and its accompanying *1995 Addendum* by Jacqueline C. Linscott; she is listed in the Directory under Florida.

Bell System, Peacock 225.00
Bell System C&P Telephone...Associated Companies, ice bl 225.00
Bell System The Central...Telegraph Company, Peacock 400.00
Local Long Distance (front & bk), Peacock 450.00
Nebraska Telephone Company, Peacock 375.00
Nevada Bell, blk glass w/silver etch 75.00
No embossing, cobalt 65.00
No embossing, ice bl 50.00
No embossing, Peacock 50.00
Opening of Trans-Pacific...Dec 23, 1931, Peacock...........................open
Southwestern Bell Telephone Company, ice bl 150.00
Telephone Pioneers of America-1988, Neodymium 45.00
Western Electric Company (inkwell), cobalt 200.00

Telescopes

Antique telescopes were sold in large quantities to sailors, astronomers, voyeurs, and the military but survive in relatively few numbers because their glass lenses and brass tubes were easily damaged. Even scarcer are antique reflecting telescopes, which use a polished metal mirror to magnify the world. Telescopes used for astronomy give an inverted image, but most old telescopes were used for marine purposes and have more complicated optics that show the world right-side up. Spyglasses are smaller, hand-held telescopes that collapse into their tube and focus by drawing out the tube to the correct length. A more compact instrument, with three or four sections, is also more delicate, and sailors usually preferred a single-draw spyglass. They are almost always of brass, occasionally of nickel siver or silver plate; and usually covered with leather, or sometimes a beautiful rosewood veneer. Solid wood barrel spyglasses (with a brass draw tube) tend to be early and rare. Before the middle of the 1800s, makers put their names in elaborate script on the smallest draw tube, but as 1900 approached, most switched to plain block printing. British instruments from WWI are commonly found, by a variety of makers but sharing a format of a 2" objective, 30" long with three draws extended, tapered main tube, and sometimes with low- and high-power oculars and a beautiful leather case. U.S. Navy WWII spyglasses are quite common but have outstanding optics and focus by twisting the eyepiece, which makes them weather-proof. The Quartermaster (Q.M.) 16x spyglass is 31" long, with a tapered barrel and a 2½" objective. The Officer of the Deck (O.D.D.) is a 23" cylinder with a 1½" objective. Very massive, short, brass telescopes are usually gunsights or ship equipment and have little interest to most collectors. World War II marked the first widespread use of coated optics, which can be recognized by a colored film on the objective lens. Collectible post-WWII telescopes include early refractors by Unitron or Fecker and reflectors by Cave or Questar. Modern spotting scopes often use a prism to erect the image and are of great interest if made by the best makers, including Nikon and Zeiss. Several modern makers still use lacquered brass, and many replica instruments have been reproduced.

A telescope with no maker's name is much less interesting than a signed instrument, and 'Made in France' is the most common mark on old spyglasses. Dollond of London made instruments for two hundred years and is probably the most common name on antiques, but because of their important technical innovations and very high quality, Dollond telescopes are always valuable. Bardou, Paris, telescopes are also very high quality. Bardou is another relatively common name, since they were a prolific maker for many years and their spyglasses were sold by

Sears. Alvin Clark and Sons were the most prolific early American makers, in operation from the 1850s to the 1920s, and their astronomical telescopes are of great historical import.

Spyglasses are delicate instruments that were subject to severe use under all weather conditions. Cracked or deeply scratched optics are impossible to repair and lower the value considerably. Most lenses are doublets, two lenses glued together, and deteriorated cement is common. This looks like crazed glaze and is fairly difficult to repair. Dents in the tube and damaged or missing leather covering can usually be fixed. The best test of a telescope is to use it, and the image should be sharp and clear. Any accessories, eyepieces, erecting prisms, or quality cases can add significantly to value. The following prices assume that the telescope is in very good to fine condition and give the objective lens (obj.) diameter, which is the most important measurement of a telescope.

Our advisor for this category is Peter Abrahams, who studies and collects telescopes and other optics. Please contact him, especially to exchange reference material. Mr. Abrahams is listed in the Directory under Oregon.

Key:
obj — objective lens   ODD — Officer of the Deck

Adams, George; brass, reflecting, 2" dia, cabriole tripod **2,300.00**
Bardou & Son, Paris, leather, 4-draw, 50mm obj, 35" **220.00**
Bausch & Lomb, wrinkle pnt, 1-draw, 45mm obj, 17" **90.00**
Brashear, brass, 3½" obj, tripod, w/eyepcs **4,000.00**
Brass, no name, spyglass, 2" obj, leather cover, $150 to **300.00**
Brass, no name, 2" obj, stand w/cabriole legs **1,200.00**
Brass, very heavy US military, complex housing, $100 to **300.00**
Cary, London (script), 2" obj, tripod, w/3 eyepcs **2,200.00**
Clark, Alvan; 4" obj, 48", iron mt on wood legs **4,500.00**
Dallmeyer, London (script), SP, 5-draw, 2½" obj, 49" **450.00**
Dolland, London (script), 2-draw, 2" obj, leather cover **200.00**
Dollond, London (block), 2-draw, 2" obj, leather cover **270.00**
Dollond, London (script), brass, 3" obj, 40", on tripod **2,500.00**
Dollond, London (script), 2-draw, 2" obj, leather cover **340.00**
France or Made in France, 3-draw, 30 mm obj, lens cap **80.00**
McAlister (script), brass, 3½" obj, 45", tripod **3,000.00**
Mogey, brass, 3" obj, 40", on tripod, w/4 eyepcs **2,400.00**
Queen & Co (script), wood vnr, 6-draw, 70mm obj, 50" **650.00**
Questar, reflecting, 1950s, 3½" dia, on astro mt **1,900.00**
Short, James; reflecting, 3" dia, brass cabriole tripod **2,500.00**

Student's, #52, converts from alt-azimuth into an equatorial, two eyepieces magnifying 36 and 72 diameters, on combination stand, with case, $400.00.

Tel Sct Regt Mk 2 S, many makers' names, UK, WWI **120.00**
Unitron, wht, 4" obj, 60", on tripod, w/many accessories **1,800.00**
US Navy, Bu Ships, Mk II, 10-Power, 1943 (ODD) **100.00**
US Navy, QM Spyglass, 16X, Mk II, in box **220.00**
Vion, Paris, leather, 40 Power, 3-draw, 40mm obj, 21" **110.00**
Wollensak Mirroscope, 1950s, 2" dia, 12" L, leather case **150.00**
Wood bbl, rnd taper, sgn, 1800s, 1½" obj **300.00**
Wood bbl, 8-sided, 1½" obj, 1700s, 30" **1,500.00**

Zeiss, brass w/eps & porro prism, 60mm obj, tripod **1,400.00**
Zeiss Asiola, 60mm obj prism spotting scope, pre-WWII **450.00**

Televisions

Many early TVs have escalated in value in the last few years. Pre-1943 sets (usually with only one to five channels) are often worth $500.00 to $5,000.00. Unusually styled small-screen wooden 1940s TVs are 'hot'; but most metal, Bakelite, and large-screen sets are still shunned by collectors. 1950s color TVs with 16" or smaller tubes are valuable; larger color sets are not. One of our advisors for this category is Harry Poster, author of *Poster's Radio & Television Price Guide 1920-1990, 2nd Edition*; he is listed in the Directory under New Jersey.

Key: t/t — table-top

Admiral, #17T12, mahog Bakelite, 1948, 7" **150.00**
Admiral, #19A11, Bakelite t/t, scarce Chinese grille, 1948, 7" ...**200.00**
Admiral, #24A12, Bakelite console, 1948, 12", minimum value ...**100.00**
Arvin, #4080T, metal w/mahog fr, 1950, 8" **350.00**
CBS-Columbus, #RX89, color (prototype), 1953, 15" **1,500.00**
Coronado, #FA 43-8965, t/t, 1949, 7" **200.00**
Crosley, #307TA, RCA 630 Chassis, 1947, 10" **200.00**
Crosley, #9-425, portable, 1949, 7" **175.00**
Delco, #TV-71A, wood t/t, 1948, 7" **125.00**
Fada, #799, t/t, 1948, 10" **125.00**
Garod, #930TV, w/AM/FM, 1948, 10" **175.00**
General Electric, #800, Bakelite portable, 1948, 10" **200.00**
Hallicrafters, #T-54, metal cabinet, 1948, 7" **200.00**
Hallicrafters, #T514, portable w/push-button selector, 1948, 7" ..**200.00**
HMV, #904, English, w/radio, 1938, 5", minimum value **3,000.00**
Hospix, t/t, 1950, 8" **225.00**
Meck, #XA-701, mahog, 1949, 7" **200.00**
Motorola, #V773, portable, leatherette, 1949, 7" **150.00**
Motorola, #17T32BZ, metal portable, 1958, 17" **75.00**
Motorola, VT71, t/t, 1947, 7" **175.00**
National, #TV-7W, mahog, 1949, 7" **200.00**
Philco, #H-2010, Safari, 1st transistor, 1960, 2" **150.00**
Philco, #10L60, Predicta Series, 1960, 21" **150.00**
Philco, #48-2500, projection, 1948 ....**150.00**
Philco, #49-1040, consolette, 1949, 10" **75.00**
Philco, #50-702, blk Bakelite, 1050, 7" **225.00**
Pilot, #TV-37, w/magnifier attachment, 1949, 3" **250.00**
Raytheon/Belmont, #22A21, 1947, 7" **400.00**
RCA, #TRK-120, w/radio, 1940, 12", minimum value **2,500.00**
RCA, #6TS30, 1st post-war mass-produced set, 1946, 10" **250.00**
RCA, #621 TS, walnut cabinet, 1946, 7" **400.00**
Scott, #6T11, projection, 1949 ....**300.00**
Sentinel, #400TV, portable, leatherette, 1948, 7" **200.00**
Silvertone, #9116, upright portable w/leatherette case, 7" **150.00**
Sony, #8-301W, 1st Japanese transistor TV, 1961, 8" **125.00**
Sparton, wooden t/t, 12" **75.00**
Sparton, 4900TVpt, mirror in lid, 1949 ....**225.00**
Stewart Warner, #AVC-1, mirror in lid, 1949 ....**250.00**
Stromberg Carlson, #TC-10H, Manhattan Porthole, 1958, 10" .**125.00**
Telephone, #TV-208, porthole, 1949, 7" **175.00**

Philco Predictas

Made in the years between 1958 and 1960, Philco Predictas have become one of the most sought-after lines of televisions from the post-war era. These TVs feature swivel or separate picture tubes and radical cabinet designs. Values given here are for average, clean, complete, and unrestored sets. Predictas that are missing parts or have damaged viewing screens will have a lower value. Above-average or restored Predictas will naturally be much higher. Our advisor for Predictas is David Weddington; he is listed in the Directory under Tennessee.

H4730 Danish Modern, mahogany-finished console, four fin-shaped legs, 21", $600.00.

Photo courtesy David Weddington

G4242 Holiday, wood t/t cabinet w/blond finish, 21" **325.00**
G4242 Holiday, wood t/t cabinet w/mahog finish, 21" **275.00**
G4654 Barber-Pole, blond console w/boomerang front leg, 21"...**500.00**
G4654 Barber-Pole, mahog console w/boomerang front leg, 21".**450.00**
G4710 Tandem, mahog finish, 21" separate screen w/25' cable...**475.00**
G4720 Stereo Tandem, mahog, 4 brass legs, 21" separate screen.**550.00**
G4720 Stereo Tandem, mahog w/matching #1606S phono & amp .**900.00**
H3406 Motel, metal t/t cabinet, cloth grill, no antenna, 17" **250.00**
H3408 Debutante, charcoal t/t w/cloth grill & antenna, 17" **250.00**
H3410 Princess, t/t w/metal grill, plastic tuner window, 17" **275.00**
H3410 Princess, t/t w/red finish, metal stand, 17" **350.00**
H3412 Siesta, gold-finish t/t, timer above tuner, w/clock, 17" **325.00**
H4730 Danish Modern, mahog-finish console, fin-shape legs, 21" ...**600.00**
H4744 Townhouse, room divider, brass w/walnut shelves, 21" **800.00**

Teplitz

Teplitz, in Bohemia, was an active art pottery center at the turn of the century. The Amphora Pottery Works was only one of the firms that operated there. (See Amphora.) Art Nouveau and Art Deco styles were favored, and much of the ware was hand decorated with the primary emphasis on vases and figurines. Items listed here are marked 'Teplitz' or 'Turn,' a nearby city. Our advisor for this category is Jack Gunsaulus; he is listed in the Directory under Michigan.

Bust, lady w/hair up, lacy gown, sgn/mk, 14" **1,800.00**
Vase, bl & gold irises, openwork hdls, RS&K, 9¼x5½" **575.00**
Vase, gold dragon, florals/beads, pierced top, rpr, 16x8" **785.00**
Vase, stylized leaves, bl w/gr-bl shadows, Stellmacher, 9⅜" **575.00**
Vase, stylized trees/pine needles, #2035, 15¾x8¼" **1,380.00**

Terra Cotta

Terra cotta is a type of earthenware or clay used for statuary, architectural facings, or domestic articles. It is unglazed, baked to durable hardness, and characterized by the color of the body which may range from brick red to buff.

Bust, Mary holding Christ, 30x26" 450.00
Bust, St Francis w/Animals, 30x26" 450.00
Jar, storage; w/lid, 39" 990.00
Plaque, B Franklin/American/1777, sm chip, 4½"+fr 425.00
Plaque, Nouveau lady in relief, Austrian, 1900s, 11" dia, pr 100.00
Urn, campana form, Bacchic masks, made in 6 parts, 90", pr ..3,300.00

Thermometers

Few objects man has invented have been so eloquently expressed both functionally and artistically as the ubiquitous thermometer. Developed initially by Galileo as a scientific device, thermometers slowly evolved into decorative objet d'art, functional household utensils, and eye-catching advertising specialties. Most American thermometers manufactured early in the 20th century were produced by Taylor (Tycos), and today their thermometers remain the most plentiful on the market. Decorative thermometers manufactured before 1800 are now ensconced in the permanent collections of approximately a dozen European museums. Because of their fragility, few devices of this era have survived in private collections. Nowadays most antique thermometers find their way to market through estate sales.

Insofar as sheer beauty, uniqueness, and scientific accuracy, decorative thermometers are far superior to the ordinary and inexpensive versions which carry advertising. Decorative thermometers run the gamut from plain tin household varieties to the highly ornate creations of Tiffany and Bradley and Hubbard. They have been manufactured from nearly every conceivable material — oak, sterling, brass, and glass being the favorites — and have tested the artistry and technical skills of some of America's finest craftsmen. Ornamental models can be found in free-hanging, wall-mounted, or desk/mantel versions. The largest collection of decorative thermometers — over 2,000 specimens — is housed in the National Thermometer Museum in Onset, Massachusetts.

Thermometer prices are based on age, ornateness, and whether mercury or alcohol is used as the filler in the tube. A broken or missing tube will cut at least 40% off the value. (Only three companies in the world makes replacement tubes.) Virtually all American-made thermometers available today as collectors' items were made between 1875 and 1940. The Golden Age of decoratives ended in the early 1940s as modern manufacturing processes and materials robbed them of their natural distinctiveness.

Key:
br — brass
F&C — Fahrenheit & Celsius
F&R — Fahrenheit & Reamer
hyg — hygrometer
mrc — mercury

pmc — permacolor
R&C — Reamer & Celsius
sc — scales
stl — stainless

Photo courtesy Joan Berman

Wise's Tunbridge thermometer,
stickware columns, $825.00.

Alexandre, desk, scimitar figural, br sc/mrc, 9" 430.00
Anonymous, Fr, desk, alabaster fr/sterling R sc/mrc, 1885, 6x3" ..920.00
Blk/Starr/Frost, desk, barometer, stl, F&C, mrc, 1910, 11" 2,100.00
Bradley & Hubbard, desk, br/ornate lion, br/sc/mrc, 9", VG 300.00
Brn & Bigelow, novelty desk, pot-metal fr/F sc/spirit, 1906, 6x1" ..375.00
Cheshire Silversmiths, desk, br candelabrum, mrc, 1875, 10" ..4,500.00
CW Wilder, desk, br figural fr, sterling R sc, mrc, 1870, 6x3" 950.00
CW Wilder...NH, bear & billboard br figural, mrc, 6½" 300.00
Dollard London, desk, sterling, br sc, mrc, 1908, 6" 850.00
Dring & Fage, desk, marble, ivory sc, mrc, 1880, 6" 1,600.00
G Staight, London, desk, tower br fr/ivory R&F/mrc/1890, 6x2" 850.00
M Comyns, Chelsea, desk, wood/ivory, R&F sc, mrc, 1880, 7x3" ..890.00
Negretti & Zambra, England, desk, wood w/ivory F sc, 1900, 7x2" ..650.00
Nova, desk, br/glass hex fr/br F sc/dial, 1925, rare 450.00
Pairpoint, desk, sterling picture fr, mrc, 1907, 5" 500.00
Reau, desk, ornate blk bronze, wood F&C sc, mrc 275.00
Seavers, English, desk, ivory fr, compass/R&F sc/mrc, 1890, 6x2" ...1,750.00
T Barton, desk, Tunbridge, wood fr, ivory F sc, mrc, 1875, 5x2" ..1,350.00
Thermindex Switzerland, desk, Bakelite stand, F sc, 5" 550.00
Tiffany, desk, horoscope, bronze, mrc, 1907, 4x7" 250.00
Tycos, desk/3-sided, sterling fr/br F sc/spirit, 1900, 7x2" 1,050.00
W Dixey, London, desk, br figural fr, F sc, mrc, 1865, 8x3" 930.00
Wise, desk, Tunbridge, twin columns, mrc, 1870, 5" 2,750.00

1000 Faces China

So named because of its many hand-painted faces, much of this chinaware was made during the '30s through the '50s (some even earlier). Though many pieces are unmarked, others are marked 'Made in Japan.' There are two primary patterns, 'Black Face' and the 'Gold' pattern, and variations exist. Both designs employ many colors. Dinner plates usually are decorated with an outer-most 'ring of color' (two or three hues) containing a simple design which is often flowers. The inner ring is usually comprised of many colors radiating from the center circle which may be done in a primary color (red, for instance) with a design such as a dragon or clouds painted in gold. 'Black Face' is distinguishable by its range of colors — primarily red, white, and yellow with some green and blue — and the black hand-painted faces. The 'Gold' pattern is also multicolored but is dominated by the gold throughout the design, and the faces themselves are gold as well. Other variations include '1000 Men in Robes' and '1000 Faces' with black or blue rims on the saucers and cups. These pieces seem to be very scarce. In the listings that follow, all items are marked 'Made in Japan' (MIJ) unless noted otherwise. Our advisor for this category is Suzi Hibbard; she is listed in the Directory under California.

Cup & saucer, bl faces, from $40 to 60.00
Cup & saucer, demitasse; gold 25.00
Cup & saucer, gold faces, bl rim 35.00
Cup & saucer, gold faces, from $30 to 50.00
Cup & saucer, men in robes 45.00
Egg cup, bl faces 15.00
Ginger jar, gold, from $75 to 100.00
Plate, bl faces, 6", from $8 to 10.00
Plate, gold, 10½", from $15 to 25.00
Salt cellar, bl faces, from $5 to 10.00
Shakers, bl faces, pr 20.00
Snack set, gold, kidney shaped 45.00
Soup set, gold, 3-pc 50.00
Sweetmeat set w/lacquer box, 12", 9-pc 125.00
Sweetmeat set w/lacquer box, 6", 6-pc 75.00
Tea set, demitasse; bl faces, 15-pc 125.00
Tea set, gold, 15-pc 150.00

Teapot, gold, dragon spout, 7" 50.00
Vase, gold, 8", from $75 to 100.00

Tiffany

Louis Comfort Tiffany was born in 1848 to Charles Lewis and Harriet Young Tiffany of New York. By the time he was eighteen, his father's small dry goods and stationery store had grown and developed into the world-renowned Tiffany and Company. Preferring the study of art to joining his father in the family business, Louis spent the next six years under the tutelage of noted artists. He returned to America in 1870 and until 1875 painted canvases that focused on European and North African scenes. Deciding the more lucrative approach was in the application of industrial arts and crafts, he opened a decorating studio called Louis C. Tiffany and Co., Associated Artists. He began seriously experimenting with glass, and eschewing traditionally painted-on details, he instead learned to produce glass with qualities that could suggest natural textures and effects. His experiments broadened, and he soon concentrated his efforts on vases, bowls, etc., that came to be considered the highest achievements of the art. Peacock feathers, leaves and vines, flowers, and abstracts were developed within the plane of the glass as it was blown. Opalescent and metallic lustres were combined with transparent color to produce stunning effects. Tiffany called his glass Favrile, meaning handmade.

In 1900 he established Tiffany Studios and turned his attention full time to producing art glass, leaded-glass lamp shades and windows, and household wares with metal components. He also designed a complete line of jewelry which was sold through his father's store. He became proficiently accomplished in silverwork and produced such articles as hand mirrors embellished with peacock feather designs set with gems and candlesticks with Favrile glass inserts.

Tiffany's work exemplified the Art Nouveau style of design and decoration, and through his own flamboyant personality and business acumen he perpetrated his tastes onto the American market to the extent that his name became a household word. Tiffany Studios continued to prosper until the second decade of this century when due to changing tastes his influence began to diminish. By the early 1930s the company had closed.

Serial numbers were assigned to much of Tiffany's work, and letter prefixes indicated the year of manufacture: A-N for 1896-1900, P-Z for 1901-1905. After that, the letter followed the numbers with A-N in use from 1906-1912; P-Z from 1913-1920. O-marked pieces were made especially for friends and relatives; X indicated pieces not made for sale.

Our listings are primarily from the auction houses in the East where Tiffany sells at a premium. All pieces are signed unless noted otherwise.

Glass

Vase, Tel el Amarna, turquoise cased to opal white, black foot and collar, white and gold iridescent medial zigzag motif, LC Tiffany Favrile 1820 E, 4¾", $4,025.00.

Bowl, amber w/violet irid, scalloped rim, 6⅜" 700.00
Bowl, feathers, wht on clear w/silver irid to gr, 3⅝" 900.00
Bowl, gold w/pk irid, ribbed, scalloped, #1284, 8¼" 460.00

Bowl, gold w/strong irid, ribbed w/wide flat rim, 4½x12" 700.00
Bowl, lt yel shaded w/gr stretch irid at rim, wht int, 8½" 700.00
Bowl, pulled lines, lt bl/gr in clear, flared rim, 9½" 300.00
Bowl, vines eng on gold stretch w/violet & bl irid, 11½" 1,265.00
Bowl, yel w/wht opal pulls to center, irid rim, 2½x8½" 635.00
Box, pk & clear opal, bronze mts w/openwork vintage, 6⅝" 415.00
Candlestick, Gr Pastel, flanged rim, opal stem/base, 3¾x4" 400.00
Candlesticks, Raspberry Pastel, wide wafer on stem, 4", pr 700.00
Champagne, gold irid, thin stem, 5½" 285.00
Champagne, Wisteria Pastel, ribbed morning-glory bowl, 7" 600.00
Compote, amber w/violet irid, scalloped, ftd, 4½x8⅛" 635.00
Compote, Bl Pastel, leaf-pattern floral-etched bowl, 4½x5" 650.00
Compote, Dmn Quilt, gold w/bl & violet, #N9329, 2¼x8" 440.00
Compote, gold irid, flared rim, 2⅛x7⅝" 350.00
Compote, gold w/mc irid, fluted/shallow, 3½x6" 450.00
Compote, gold w/mc irid, shallow, 4x8" 425.00
Compote, pulled decor on gold, cut stem, beveled ft, 6x8" 600.00
Cordial, gold w/bl irid, threaded band/appl pods, 3" 400.00
Cordial, pulled decor on gold, cut stem, beveled ft, 8 for 1,300.00
Cup & saucer, gold irid, cup w/7 appl lily pads & stems 425.00
Dish, bl w/purple & gr irid, scalloped, 1x4" 220.00
Dish, gold w/pk & bl irid, 8-rib, scalloped, 4" dia 200.00
Finger bowl, Bl Pastel ribbed, stretched border, +plate 700.00
Finger bowl, gold w/red irid, stretched/ruffled, +7"plate 450.00
Goblet, amber w/violet irid, invt bell form, 12 for 2,165.00
Goblet, Pk Pastel, yel opal melon ball on ribbed stem, 8¾" 750.00
Paperweight, gr irid damascene insert, bronze fr, #21566 ....2,070.00
Plate, Gr Pastel, ribbed rim w/scalloped edge, 10¾" 600.00
Plate, Wisteria Pastel, 8½" 650.00
Screen, dogwood, bl/wht/violet on amber, 3-fold, 11x19¼" 3,450.00
Sherbet, bl irid, tooled knobs on bowl, 3½" 425.00
Sherbet, gold w/vivid irid, 3½" 210.00
Shot glass, rose gold irid, dimpled, 1¾" 135.00
Tile, favrile tesserae in alabaster surround, #21458, 6" 1,400.00
Toothpick holder, gold, ftd urn form w/pulled hdls, 2¼" 400.00
Vase, bl irid, pinwheel hdls on angle shoulder, ftd, 4½x8" 1,200.00
Vase, bl irid, rolled rim, 6x4¼" 550.00
Vase, bl irid, trumpet form w/knob stem, 8" 950.00
Vase, bl w/EX irid, sm prunts on lt ribs, 3½" 500.00
Vase, bl w/violet & gr irid, 2 sm closed waist hdls, 3" 600.00
Vase, feathers, gold & olive w/violet-bl, LCT K13, 8¼" 1,200.00
Vase, feathers, gold/gr, trumpet form, in bronze ft, 12" 1,500.00
Vase, feathers, gr/gold on opal irid, dbl gourd, 6" 1,600.00
Vase, feathers, lt bl/cream on amber, long swollen neck, 10½" ..1,300.00
Vase, feathers, pk/red on platinum irid, tube neck, 3x3" 750.00
Vase, feathers, purple/dk pk irid, dbl-shouldered ovoid, 4½" ...1,000.00
Vase, floriform; feathers, elongated top, dome ft, 15½" 2,000.00
Vase, floriform; feathers, gr on wht, bowl-on-cone top, 12" 2,600.00
Vase, floriform; feathers, gr/wht on orange/wht, #3933A, 9½" ..1,600.00
Vase, floriform; feathers on gold/ivory irid, str rim, 11" 2,400.00
Vase, floriform; gold, lobed, in bronze holder mk #1048, 16" 900.00
Vase, floriform; gold w/mc irid, long ribbed bowl, 15" 1,100.00
Vase, floriform; gold w/mc irid, petal rim, long bowl, 11" 850.00
Vase, floriform; leaves, gr on gold irid, shallow bowl, 9" 2,000.00
Vase, gold w/mc irid, raised/pulled swirls, 1x1½" 200.00
Vase, gold w/mc irid, slim/flared, in short brass mt, 13" 900.00
Vase, gold w/pk & aqua irid, pinched sides, 5" 650.00
Vase, gold w/pk irid, dimpled ovoid, 4⅞" 800.00
Vase, Gr Pastel, clear ball-&-ft base, trumpet form, 6" 375.00
Vase, hooks/pulls, red/purple irid on gold to amber, 4x4" 850.00
Vase, hooks/swirls at low shoulder, turq/gr/gold/ivory, 5½" 2,100.00
Vase, intaglio gr ivy on amber, #6542, 9¼" 2,000.00
Vase, leaves/vines, chartreuse on gold, stick neck, 6" 800.00
Vase, paperweight jonqils, 3-color in clear, compote form, 5" .4,750.00

Vase, paperweight leaves/vines, yel/gr on amber, 6x5" **3,750.00**
Vase, pulls/hooks, gr/purple/bl on cypriote gr, 7½" **2,200.00**
Vase, red to amber, classic shouldered shape, 6" **2,000.00**
Vase, red to orange-red to gold irid at lip, #867A, 6½" **2,875.00**
Vase, Tel el Amarna, red cased w/zigzags, #6089E, 8½" **11,000.00**
Vase, Tel el Amarna, turq w/gold irid leaves, #1266E, 6¾" **4,600.00**
Vase, wavy shoulder band, gold on amber irid, #F2220, 7⅝" ...**2,070.00**
Vase, Yel Pastel, ribbed trumpet form, 9" **750.00**

Lamps

Lamp prices seem to be getting stronger, especially for leaded lamps with lighter colors (red, blue, purples). Bases that are unusual or rare have brought good prices and added to the value of the more common shades that sold on them. Bases with enamel or glass inserts are very much in demand. Our advisor for Tiffany lamps is Carl Heck; he is listed in the Directory under Colorado.

Key: c-b — counter-balance

Table lamp, 16 bright peacock-eye medallions among dark and emerald green, amber, and brown striated glass forming 16" dome shade; three-arm base with ribbed shaft and five ball feet, marked and numbered D795, 22", $26,000.00.

Candle, gold, baluster w/spreading ft, sgn/1927, 3¾" **200.00**
Candle, gold, ribbed shade on slim shaft w/dbl-ped base, 16" ..**1,000.00**
Candle, gold 7" ruffled shade/twist std, +gold candle, 12" **1,000.00**
Desk, amber 4-panel shade; pine needle #552 std, 8½" **2,000.00**
Desk, bell shade w/pulled waves (EX); harp std, 15" **1,800.00**
Desk, damascene 7" shade; c-b bronzed metal #416 std **5,000.00**
Desk, damascene 8" shade; gold dore #639 std w/swing arm **3,500.00**
Desk, Zodiac, geometric band on metal shade; harp #661 std ..**1,300.00**
Desk, 3 gold lily lights on bronze std, 16" **2,000.00**
Floor, bronze shade w/silver patina in harp #687 std, 56", M ..**1,100.00**
Floor, ldgl 10" Assoc Am shade; 5-leg dore #468 std, 51½" **3,450.00**
Floor, ldgl 12" acorn-band shade; harp #423 std w/arched ft ...**7,000.00**
Floor, ldgl 25" curtain-border shade; bronze #376 std, 78" **43,700.00**
Floor, pleated-panel shade; domical #577 std, 64" **2,400.00**
Floor, pulled waves 4-color 10" shade in harp #423H std, VG ...**4,250.00**
Lily, 10-light, amber irid shades; lily-pad #381 std, 21" **16,000.00**
Lily, 12-light, gold shades sgn LCT/#382; lily-pad std, 20¾" ...**23,000.00**
Lily, 3-light (sgn); height adjusts, #306 std, 22", VG **2,000.00**
Table, ldgl 14" acorn-band shade; #333 std, EX **5,500.00**
Table, ldgl 15" turtle-bk shade; verdigris urn-form std, 23" **6,000.00**
Table, ldgl 16" acorn shade; artichoke #21218 std, 18½" **11,000.00**
Table, ldgl 16" acorn-band shade; #6840 ftd/emb std **6,500.00**
Table, ldgl 16" apple blossom shade; 4-legged mk std, 20" **13,800.00**
Table, ldgl 16" feather shade; #444 std, 25" **5,175.00**
Table, ldgl 16" floral/medallion shade; gilt 3-arm #444 std ...**10,500.00**
Table, ldgl 16" Greek Key shade; ball-ftd bronze std, 21" **9,500.00**

Table, ldgl 16" peacock feather shade; 3-arm fluid std, 19½" ...**27,500.00**
Table, ldgl 16" swirling leaf/brickwork shade; 4-column std **5,000.00**
Table, ldgl 18" dogwood shade; scroll-ftd bronze std, 24" **22,000.00**
Table, ldgl 18" floral-band/brickwork shade; #522 bronze std ..**4,000.00**
Table, ldgl 18½" peony shade; cast base w/petal ft, 26" **52,900.00**
Table, ldgl 20" acorn border #1498 shade; bronze std, 29" **13,800.00**
Table, ldgl 20" dragonfly shade; gilt-bronze #1495 std, 27" **27,600.00**
Table, ldgl 20" shaded gr conical shade; hex #533 std, 24" **6,300.00**
Table, linenfold 17" 8-sided gold-amber shade; #629 std, 22" .**6,200.00**
Table, nautilus shell shade; HP dragonflies on mk base, 15" ...**5,500.00**
Table, 10½" gr/gold pulled-feather shade; mk oil std, 23" **10,925.00**

Metal Work

Items are bronze unless noted otherwise.

Ashtray, emb sailing ships, w/match holder, gilded, 5x6½" **625.00**
Blotter ends, Indian, #1181, 19½x2½", pr **160.00**
Bookends, animal relief, gilt w/gr beads, mk, 6" **515.00**
Bookrack, desk; rtcl vintage, gr/wht panels, adjusts, 6x14" **800.00**
Box, cigar; gilt/Azuriet mc enamel, #134, 3½x7x3¾" **1,265.00**
Box, cigarette; leaf in gr on gold dore, #314, 1½x2x4" **400.00**
Box, Grapevine, 2 velvet trays w/in, #830, 3x9x6" **1,200.00**
Box, Grapevine, 2x7" L **650.00**
Box, Pine Needle, 1½x4½" **250.00**
Candlestick, blown-in liner, flat rim, fluted base, 15" **1,600.00**
Candlestick, leaf base w/curving stem & tendril, #1203, 7½" **850.00**
Candlestick, leaves/stems support cup, pencil std, #1210, 10" **500.00**
Candlestick, organic 2-prong vine std, leaf base, 8", VG **650.00**
Candlesticks, bronze dore, LCT Favrile 43, 8¼", pr **300.00**
Clock, desk; Chinese, Gothic arch, acid etched, #1850, 5½" **750.00**
Clock, stylized swirl design, sqd/flaring sides, #1121, 6" **1,200.00**
Clock, Zodiac, gold dore, steeple shape, w/key, 5½" **925.00**
Compote, twisted wire/mc enamel on wide flat rim, #519, 3x8" .**550.00**
Desk set, Chinese, blotter & ends, pin & ashtrays, VG **750.00**
Desk set, Venetian, gold dore/mc enamel, 7 pcs **1,600.00**
Desk set, Zodiac, inkwell on tray/stamp box/calender+4 pcs **950.00**
Desk set, Zodiac, tray/bookends/box/knife+6 pcs, repatinated .**1,800.00**
Frame, Abalone, gold dore, #1179, 7½x9½" **1,600.00**
Frame, Grapevine, 11½x9½", EX **1,500.00**
Frame, Grapevine, 8½x7", EX **1,700.00**
Frame, Pine Needle, #947, 9½x8" **1,000.00**
Frame, Pine Needle, oval window, #949, 7x6" **1,200.00**
Frame, Zodiac, easel bk, 7½x7" **1,300.00**
Inkstand, repeating stylized trees, 3¾x3¾" **515.00**
Inkstand, Zodiac, dbl-disk style, hinged lid, #1073, 10x11" **750.00**
Inkwell, Chinese, cut corners, flaring sides, #1753, 4x6½" **500.00**
Inkwell, Grapevine, glass cracked, 4x4" sq **550.00**
Inkwell, Zodiac, gold dore, #842, 2x4" dia **200.00**
Letter holder, Am Indian, 2-tier, #1186, 11¼" **375.00**
Letter holder, Chinese, 3-compartment, #1765, 12" W **650.00**
Letter rack, Chinese, acid etched, #1755, 8x12x3" **750.00**
Mirror, vine-twisted oval fr w/lily-pad base, 19¾" **13,000.00**
Paperweight, puma, recumbent, gold patina, #932, 1¾x5" **435.00**
Paperweight, Shando dog, setter bust, solid, #889, 3½" **800.00**
Pen tray, pine-cone design w/caramel glass insert, 9½" **200.00**
Scale, desk; abalone inserts/mc enamel, #1170, 3½" **500.00**
Sconces, amorphic devices, 2-arm, unmk, 11", pr **2,500.00**
Tray, emb ray design, 2x8" dia **100.00**
Tray, sea shell form w/draped lady among waves, #2059, 6" L **550.00**

Pottery

Bowl, pumpkin form w/fruit branches, ivory w/gr int, LCT, 8" ..**3,750.00**

Vase, bronze w/silver wash, emb hollyhocks, 16½" 3,750.00
Vase, bronze w/silver wash, emb poinsettias, 12¾x4" 1,900.00
Vase, gr Old Ivory w/emb leaves, bottle shape, 8x4½" 1,900.00
Vase, olive/mint gr mottled matt, prof rpr, 14½x9" 1,300.00

Silver

Bowl, Am Trapshooting Assoc trophy, 7¾x12⅜", 22-t-oz 110.00
Bowl, fruit; emb rim & base, low, 15 troy ozs, 9" 350.00
Bowl, plain ftd form, #23648, stamped mk, 2x12" 330.00
Candlebra, repousse, 3-tier, 1897, pr 3,500.00
Candlesticks, Georgian style, urn-form nozzle, mks, 10", pr 2,300.00
Ladle, fiddle-shaped flat hdl, 13", 7 troy ozs 660.00
Ladle, King pattern, shell bowl 525.00
Salver, circular w/shell lozenge & leaf border, sm 280.00
Tea set, floral chased, monogrammed, 3-pc 3,900.00

Tiffin Glass

The Tiffin Glass Company was founded in 1887 in Tiffin, Ohio, one of the many factories composing the U.S. Glass Company. Its early wares consisted of tablewares and decorative items such as lamps and globes. Among the most popular of all Tiffin products was the black satin glass produced there during the 1920s. In 1959 U.S. Glass was sold, and in 1962 the factories closed. The plant was re-opened in 1963 as the Tiffin Art Glass Company. Products from this period were tableware, hand-blown stemware, and other decorative items.

Those interested in learning more about Tiffin glass are encouraged to contact the Tiffin Glass Collectors' Club, whose address can be found in the Directory under Clubs, Newsletters, and Catalogs. See also Black Glass; Glass Animals.

Vase, Mystic variant, 3" stem, 9½" overall, $225.00.

Bottle, seltzer; La Fleure, crystal, ftd 18.50
Bowl, finger; La Fleure, yel, ftd, #185 ....37.50
Bowl, salad; Cerise, 5x10" 48.00
Bowl, salad; June Night, #5209, 10" 150.00
Bowl, wishbone; Twilight, ftd, 6½" 135.00
Candy dish, Lois, gr, conical, w/lid, #345 ....95.00
Champagne, Byzantine, #15037 ....36.00
Champagne, Cherokee Rose, #17399 ....22.50
Champagne, Cherokee Rose, reeded stem 18.50
Champagne, Classic, crystal, tall 22.00
Champagne, Desert Rose/Wisteria 42.00
Champagne, Flanders, #15024 ....20.00
Champagne, Flanders, #15047 ....20.00
Champagne, Fuchsia, #15083 ....22.00
Champagne, June Night, #17358, 5½-oz 22.50
Champagne, June Night, #17392 ....19.00
Champagne, Persian Pheasant, 5½-oz 30.00
Claret, Fuchsia, 6-oz 20.00

Cocktail, Arcadian, pk/crystal, #024, 3-oz 35.00
Cocktail, Cherokee Rose, reeded stem 15.00
Cocktail, Cordelia 13.00
Cocktail, Desert Rose/Wisteria 42.00
Cocktail, Fuchsia, #15083 ....27.00
Cocktail, June Night, #17358 ....20.00
Cocktail, Persian Pheasant, 5¼" 27.50
Cocktail, Spiral Optic, crystal w/gr stem, 6" 22.50
Cordial, Cherokee Rose, #17399 ....50.00
Cordial, Flanders, pk 75.00
Cordial, June Beau 18.00
Cordial, June Night, #17358 ....45.00
Cordial, Persian Pheasant 55.00
Creamer, Fuchsia, #5902 ....28.00
Creamer & sugar bowl, La Fleure, Mandarin yel, ftd 75.00
Cup & saucer, Cadena, yel 59.00
Cup & saucer, Fontaine, Twilight, blown 125.00
Finger bowl, Palais Versailles 65.00
Flower arranger, Twilight, 13⅝" 125.00
Goblet, iced tea; June Night 27.50
Goblet, water; Byzantine, #15037 ....32.00
Goblet, water; Classic, crystal 27.00
Goblet, water; Desert Rose/Wisteria 45.00
Goblet, water; Flanders, #15047 ....22.00
Goblet, water; Fuchsia, #15083 ....34.00
Goblet, water; June Beau 15.00
Goblet, water; June Night 34.00
Goblet, water; Juno, gr 30.00
Goblet, water; Mandarin yel 30.00
Goblet, water; Palais Versailles 75.00
Goblet, water; Persian Pheasant 25.00
Goblet, water; Rosalind 23.00
Plate, Byzantine, #15037, 8" 18.00
Plate, Cadena, yel, 6" 10.00
Plate, Cadena, yel, 7¾" 14.00
Plate, Cadena, yel, 9¼" 40.00
Plate, Cerise, 14" 38.00
Plate, Cerise, 8" 10.00
Plate, Cherokee Rose, 8" 18.50
Plate, Classic, 8" 12.00
Plate, Desert Rose/Wisteria, 8" 28.00
Plate, Flanders, yel, 9½" 60.00
Plate, Fuchsia, 8" 22.50
Plate, Julia, amber, 10" 25.00
Plate, La Fleure, Mandarin yel, 6" 8.50
Plate, La Fleure, Mandarin yel, 7¼" 15.00
Plate, Palaise Versailles, 7½" 25.00
Plate, salad; Palais Versailles, half-moon 75.00
Relish, Cerise, oval, 10" 24.00
Relish, Fuchsia, 3-part, 12½" 60.00
Relish, Rambler Rose, etched crystal, 3-part, 11" 45.00
Server, Juno, pk, center hdl 75.00
Sherbet, Byzantine 20.00
Sherbet, Classic, crystal, low 17.00
Sherbet, Cordelia 6.00
Sherbet, June Beau 10.00
Sherry, June Night, #17403, 2-oz 45.00
Sugar bowl, Fuchsia, #5831 ....40.00
Sugar bowl, Juno, yel 37.50
Tumbler, bar; Classic, crystal, ftd 28.00
Tumbler, juice; Arcadian, pk/crystal, #185, 5-oz 45.00
Tumbler, juice; Cherokee Rose, reeded stem, 5" 18.50
Tumbler, juice; Desert Rose/Wisteria 48.00
Tumbler, juice; June Night, #17399 ....22.00

Tumbler, juice; June Night, ftd, #17403 ....25.00
Tumbler, water; Classic, crystal, ftd 20.00
Vase, bud; Cherokee Rose, 10½" 45.00
Vase, bud; June Night, #15082, 11" 45.00
Vase, Diana, etched, 10" 35.00
Vase, Oneida, 10¼" 150.00
Wine, Byzantine 35.00
Wine, Classic, crystal 30.00
Wine, June Beau 15.00
Wine, Palais Versailles 75.00
Wine, Rosalind, crystal 25.00
Wine, Rosalind, Mandarin yel 35.00

Tiles

The history of tile making dates back to ancient Egypt and Assyria. For centuries tiles have played an important role as a decorative art form, as well as having a utilitarian function. Places such as palace walls, Islamic mosques, Roman floors, and medieval English churches were all adorned with tiles or glazed ceramic surfaces. Remnants of these tile installations can still be seen throughout the world.

The heyday of tile making in England and the United States dates back to circa 1860 through 1930, and envelops the Victorian, Art Nouveau, and Arts & Crafts Movements in both countries. These tiles comprise most of those seen on today's market.

Tiles are being collected today as individual art objects and are increasingly used as decorative accessories. They are also sought in order to restore homes, buildings, and furniture to original period condition. Many people are now incorporating antique and collectible tiles into their home-rebuilding projects for gardens, kitchens, bathrooms, fireplaces, stair risers, and floors.

Tiles must be judged on an individual basis. The condition of the tile face; the quality of the design; the rarity of the artist, company, or series; and the size of the tile or tile panel are just some of the factors to consider when assessing value. People, animals, and scenes are generally more desirable than florals and geometrics. Some glaze colors, such as true pale pink or bright red majolica, add value to Victorian tiles. See also Batchhelder, Moravian, Grueby, and other specific manufacturers. Our advisor for this category is Karen Guido; she is listed in the Directory under New Jersey.

Key:
bkg — background
geo — geometric
maj — majolica glaze
plych — polychrome

prmld — press molded
srs — series
tbld — tube lined
tr-transfer printed

American

AETCO, Alhambra, mosaic, wht & gray, 6" 60.00
AETCO, thistle plants, mauve maj, prmld, 6" 40.00
Alhambra Kilns, floral, molded unglazed red clay, 4" 60.00
Claycraft, geo, mc high glaze, 6" 75.00
Enfield, Don Quixote, unglazed buff clay, molded, 4" 70.00
Franklin, faience, lion in shield, mc semimatt, prmld, 6" 145.00
Franklin, faience, sample bl, 4" 20.00
Franklin, female silhouette, pk & blk, 4" 45.00
Harris Strong, bay w/sailboats, maj HP panel, 6-tile, fr 457.00
Harris Strong, cave animal, gr linen & wood fr, 6" 95.00
Harris Strong, set of 4 owls on wood, tbld, 6x3" 325.00
Harris Strong, stylized jester, 2-tile, tbld, 48x12" 975.00
Kensington, floral, gold maj, prmld, 6" 50.00
Low, Ave Maria, sgn Osborne, plastic sketch, gr orig fr 1,475.00
Low, geo, bl high glaze, 4" 30.00
Low, woman's profile, lt gr maj, 6" dia 185.00

Malibu, flowers & leaves border, pastel mc, 4" 65.00
Malibu, Saracen line, leaves, mc, 2x4" 35.00
Mosaic, cottage, red clay, bl & wht tr, 4" 55.00
Mosaic, flying goose, mc, prmld, 6" 110.00
Mosaic, Lincoln bust, bl & wht, octagonal, 4" 45.00
Mueller, mosaic, geo bl matt recesses, sand bkg, unmk, 4" 55.00
Rookwood, phoenix trivet, pastels, dtd 1930, 6" 325.00
Solon & Schemmel, floral & geo, floor tile, mc, 6" 325.00
Solon & Schemmel, gravevine, unglazed buff clay, 3" 30.00
Taylor, geo, mc semimatt, 6" 55.00
Taylor, table, San Jose Mission, mc, 6 tiles 1,500.00
Trent, acorns in relief, brn maj, 4" 35.00
Trent, man/woman in Elizabethan costumes, gr maj, 6", fr pr 460.00
Tudor, house & mtn, bl matt w/brn & gr, 7½x3½" 250.00
US Encaustic, woman carying sticks in relief, gold maj, 6" 185.00

English

Copeland, floral center, geo bkg, brn maj, prmld, 6" 40.00
Maw, floral, cream/brn tr, 6" 25.00
Maw, Roman male head profile, low relief, gr maj, prmld, 6" 160.00
Minton Hollins, Seasons srs, Summer, brn & beige tr, 6" 85.00
Minton Hollins, sunflowers, terra cotta & blk tr, 6" 30.00

Mintons China Works, Astrology series, Gemini, Henry Stacey marks, hand painted over glaze, ca 1880, 6", $175.00.

Mintons China Works, fleur-de-lis, maroon & buff tr, 6" 40.00
Mintons China Works, highland cattle, brn & buff tr, 6" 135.00
Mintons China Works, Shakespeare srs, Othello, brn & buff tr, 6" 85.00
Mintons China Works, Waverley srs, Rob Roy, plych tr, 8" 245.00
Pilkingtons, Art Nouveau vines, mc high glaze, 6" 95.00
Sherwin & Cotton, Gladstone photo, sepia tones, orig fr, 9x6" 400.00
Wedgwood, floral, gold/wht tr, twisted wire trivet, 6" 35.00
Wedgwood, Months srs, October, brn & wht tr, 6" 145.00
Wm DeMorgan, BBB sunflower, HP/mc, 6" 295.00

Other Types

Cantagalli, geometric gold lustre, 6" 65.00
Mexican, geometric, mc, ca 1900, 4", set of 7 ....85.00
Royal Delft, flowers & windmill, mc, prmld, 4" 75.00
Tunisian, 8-pointed star, Cuenca bl & wht, 6" 50.00
Villeroy & Boch, (4) encaustic floor mosaic, mc, 6" 275.00

Tinware

In the American household of the 17th and 18th centuries, tinware items could be found in abundance, from food containers to foot warmers and mirror frames. Although the first settlers brought much of their tinware with them from Europe, by 1798 sheets of tin plate were being imported from England for use by the growing number of American tinsmiths. Tinwares were often decorated either by piercing or painted designs which were both freehand and stenciled. (See Tole-ware.) By the early 1900s, many homes had replaced their old tinware with the more attractive aluminum and graniteware.

In the 19th century, tenth wedding anniversaries were traditionally celebrated by gifts of tin. Couples gave big parties, dressed in their wedding clothes, and reaffirmed their vows before their friends and family who arrived bearing (and often wearing) tin gifts, most of which were quite humorous. Anniversary tin items may include hats, cradles, slippers and shoes, rolling pins, etc. See also Primitives and Kitchen Collectibles.

Anniversary, hat, admiral's type w/'ostrich' plume, 6½x16" 215.00
Anniversary, loving cup, 2 funnels soldered, ca 1900, 7⅜" 45.00

Baby rattle with whistle in the handle, ca 1850, 5½", EX, $85.00.

Cabinet, spice; 8-drw, orig blk pnt & stencils, hanging 280.00
Candle box, 2 tab hangers, 14x4½", EX 325.00
Candle lantern, pierced, Paul Revere type 190.00
Coffeepot, angular, C-hdl, curved spout, pewter finial, 10" 175.00
Coffeepot, tin w/copper bottom, lg 70.00
Colander, pierced, 2 open curved hdls, 3-ftd, mk, 2x11" 135.00
Downspout ornament, circle w/emb pineapple & cutouts, 27" ...250.00
Egg coddler, dk gray, ornate base, burner 200.00
Egg poacher, oval shape on 4 ft, wire stem w/loop hdl, 7" 22.00
Flour sifter, handmade, scoop shape, crank hdl 95.00
Pastry sheet, w/shelf, w/dk tin rolling pin 650.00
Sconces, oval crimped-edge reflector, 14", pr 725.00
Sconces, 13 tube receivers for flags, ca 1876, 16½", pr, G 750.00
Sieve, cottage cheese; heart form, ring ft & hdls, 4½" 250.00
Teakettle, slant spout, movable bail, ring finial, ca 1840 ....80.00
Toddy warmer, funnel shape, pouring lip, side hdl 100.00

Tobacciana

Tobacciana is the generally accepted term used to cover a field of collecting that includes smoking pipes, cigar molds, cigarette lighters, humidors — in short, any article having to do with the practice of using tobacco in any form. Perhaps the most valuable variety of pipes is the meerschaum, hand carved from hydrous magnesium, an opaque white-gray or cream-colored mineral of the soapstone family. (Much of this is today mined in Turkey which has the largest meerschaum deposit in the world, though there are other deposits of lesser significance around the globe.) These figural bowls often portray an elaborately carved mythological character, an animal, or a historical scene. Amber is sometimes used for the stem. Other collectible pipes are corn cob (Missouri Meerschaum) and Indian peace pipes of clay or catlinite. (See American Indian Art.)

Chosen because it was the Indians who first introduced the white man to smoking, the cigar store Indian was a symbol used to identify tobacco stores in the 19th century. The majority of them were hand carved between 1830 and 1900 and are today recognized as some of the finest examples of early wood sculptures. When found they command very high prices.

For further information on lighters, refer to *Collector's Guide to Cigarette Lighters* by James Flanagan. Our advisor for this category is Chuck Thompson; he is listed in the Directory under Texas. Chris Rossiter assisted with pipe listings; you will find him listed in the Directory under Wisconsin. See also Advertising; Snuff Boxes.

Ashtray, Camel Biker, pewter 10.00
Ashtray, Marlboro Unlimited, pewter 10.00
Cigar cutter, CI General Arthur figural, 7", NM 925.00
Cigar Cutter, Empire Tobacco Co, CI, gold trim, 17½", VG 50.00
Cigar cutter, horn, bottle shaped 110.00
Cigar cutter, pearl hdl 95.00
Cigar cutter, school boy figural, 7x4x3", VG 600.00
Cigar cutter, 3 holes, angle hdl, lg 175.00
Cigar cutter/watch fob, gold-filled blimp shape 110.00
Cigar cutter/watch fob, MOP 135.00
Cigarette box, German silver, classical figures, 5¼" 200.00
Cigarette card, Duke's, Honest Library, 1896, VG 60.00
Cigarette card, Duke's, NY From Brooklyn Bridge, 1885, EX 12.00
Cigarette card, Kalamazoo Bats, actress Annie Leslie, EX 20.00
Cigarette card, Kickapoo Plug, Red Cloud, EX 75.00
Cigarette carton, Lucky Strike, flat, man reading & pack, EX 55.00
Cigarette holder, Bakelite, gr or red 30.00
Cigarette holder, blk jet w/gold, horn shape 70.00
Cigarette holder, blk plastic w/rhinestones 35.00
Cigarette holder, Mathiss Parisenne, MOP, 1890s, 4", +case 95.00
Cigarette pack, Camel Menthol Slide-o-matic 5.00
Cigarette pack, Camel 75th Birthday 12.00
Cigarette pack, Eisenhower/Stevenson, pr 75.00
Cigarette pack, Fatima Turkish Blend, unopened, M 20.00
Cigarette papers, Duke's Mixture, #8, wht, NM 20.00
Cigarette papers, Golden Grain Smoking Tobacco, gummed, NM .5.00
Cigarette papers, Golden Grain Smoking Tobacco, plain, NM 6.00
Cigarette papers, Half & Half/A Cargo, NM 4.00
Cigarette papers, Half & Half/Lucky Strike, NM 10.00
Cigarette papers, Hi-Plane Smooth Cut Tobacco..., NM 20.00
Cigarette papers, Honest Long Cut, NM 30.00
Cigarette papers, Just Suits Cut Plug, NM 20.00
Cigarette papers, Pride of Reidsville, gr, NM 60.00
Cigarette roller, Bugler, w/Zig-Zag papers 8.00
Clock, Camel Joe pool player 50.00
Figure, Indian brave, cvd wood (rough hewn), rpt, 70" 2,800.00
Figure, Indian brave, wood & plaster, 72", EX 350.00
Figure, Indian lady, cvd wood, old rpt, late 1800s, 43", EX ...14,950.00
Figure, Indian princess, plaster, mc pnt, rprs, 62", VG 800.00
Figure, Indian scout, cvd wood, old rpt, 1880s, 74" 19,550.00
Humidor, emb dog's face, Staffordshire, pre-WWII, 5½" 425.00
Humidor, HP florals, pipe finial, ceramic, mk AK France 150.00
Humidor, La Palina Senators, brass 48.00
Humidor, monk figural, brns & tans, pottery, 9" 195.00
Humidor, monk's head form, brn & flesh tones, porc, 6" 65.00
Humidor, pewter, claw & ball ft, EX detail, 7½" 75.00
Humidor, Turkish man ¾-figure, tans & grs, Artware Ardall 95.00
Humidor, walnut burl veneer, brass mts, 2 doors/2 drws, 9" 875.00
Lighter, ATC cigarette case & lighter combo 20.00
Lighter, Camel, advertising, chrome & brass 12.50
Lighter, chromium, early 1940s, w/wick & instructions, 2¼", MIB ..90.00
Lighter, chromium rose form, table type, 1960s, 2½x1⅝" 35.00
Lighter, Dunhill, brass dueling pistol, 1930s, 4x6¼" 225.00
Lighter, Evans, blk w/HP florals, table model, EX 50.00
Lighter, figural Cupid stem, brass/dk copper, 8½" 95.00
Lighter, horse-head striker, USA 65.00
Lighter, Mastercase by Ronson, chromium/blk enamel, 1933, 4¾" ..40.00
Lighter, Ronson Spartan, Deco-style table model 15.00

Lighter, Shriner's hat, Boise ID, 1956 ....21.00
Lighter, telephone/clock, chrome, Alba Art 200.00
Lighter, Zippo style, Alcoa 16.00
Pipe, bone, man-in-moon cvg, EX details 150.00
Pipe, bone/wood, hag in bonnet cvg 150.00
Pipe, Charatan, Distinction, Duplain, extra long 155.00
Pipe, clay, nude figural stem, 1880s, 4" 75.00
Pipe, folk-art cvd calabash, animal head/hand, 18", VG 220.00
Pipe, meerschaum, animals fighting, amber stem, rpr, 20" 1,100.00
Pipe, meerschaum, lady's hand at bowl, silver ferrule, 5¾" 110.00
Pipe, meerschaum, lion, 4¾", NM, +case 175.00
Pipe, meerschaum, longhorn mtn goat, full figure, 6", EX 135.00
Pipe, meerschaum, nude around bowl, amber stem, 6½" 125.00
Pipe, meerschaum, rosettes/swirls, amber stem, 4½", +case 135.00
Pipe, meerschaum, turk's head, long stem, 16" 150.00
Plug cutter, Brighton #3, elf figural, 13" L, VG 275.00
Plug cutter, Evans Terry, CI, counter-top, 1914, NM 175.00
Plug cutter, Prize Cutter by S Lee, w/cork former 75.00
Plug cutter, Star, Pat 1885 ....75.00
Scissors, German silver, El Roi-Tan Perfect Cigars 75.00
Smoke stand/floor lamp/lighter, swing arm, base light, 1930s 195.00
Tobacco pouch, Duke's Mixture, cloth/paper label, ⅝-oz, NM 10.00
Tobacco pouch, George Washington Cut Plug, cloth, NM 28.00
Tobacco pouch, Golden Grain Smoking Tobacco, cloth, ⅞-oz, NM ..15.00
Tobacco pouch, Hambone Smoking Tobacco, cloth, 1-oz, VG ..105.00
Tobacco pouch, Horse Shoe Plug, leather, EX 15.00
Tobacco pouch, Old North State Tobacco, cloth, 1½-oz, NM 25.00
Tobacco pouch, Prince Albert, cloth, 1909, unopened, NM 115.00
Tobacco pouch, Ram's Horn Tobacco, EX 12.00
Tobacco pouch, Seal of North Carolina, cloth, EX 15.00
Tobacco pouch, Thumper Sun Cured Tobacco, cloth, NM 5.00
Tobacco pouch, U-Ta-Ka, cloth, EX 10.00
Tobacco tag, Lucky Strike, rnd, EX 8.00
Tobacco tag, Old Honesty, pictures dog, rnd, EX 18.00
Tobacco tag, Peerless, diecut P, EX 6.00
Tobacco tag, Pen-Point, diecut, gold, EX 6.00
Tobacco tag, Red Lion, oval, lg, EX 10.00
Tobacco tag, Sailor's Hope, EX 6.00
Tobacco tag, Sentinel, octagonal, EX 5.00
Tobacco tag, Toledo, frog, oval, EX 10.00
Tobacco tag, Tomahawk, diecut, P Lorillard Co, EX 6.00
Tobacco tag, Tuckahoe Plug, EX 4.00
Tobacco tag, Upper Ten, EX 3.00
Token, Ace Cigar Store, brass 3.00
Tool, cigar/pipe; stag hdl, cutter/knife blade/pick/etc 175.00

Toby Jugs

The delightful jug known as the Toby dates back to the 18th century, when factories in England produced them for export to the American colonies. Named for the character Toby Philpots in the song *The Little Brown Jug*, the Toby was fashioned in the form of a jolly fellow, usually holding a jug of beer and a glass. The earlier examples were made with strict attention to details such as fingernails and teeth. Originally representing only a non-entity, a trend developed to portray well-known individuals such as George II, Napoleon, and Ben Franklin. Among the most-valued Tobies are those produced by Ralph Wood I in the late 1700s. By the mid-1830s Tobies were being made in America. See also Doulton, Lenox, and Occupied Japan.

Admiral Beatty, Dread Naught, Wilkinson, ca 1915, 10¼" 500.00
Lady standing, yel apron & hat, brn coat, unmk, 1820s, 9½" 425.00
Lloyd George, titled Shellout, Wilkinson, ca 1915, 9¾" 700.00

Lord French, French Pour Les Francais, Wilkinson, 1915, 9½" ..700.00
Lord Kitchener, Bitter for the Kaiser, Wilkinson, 1915, 9¾" .1,035.00
Marshall Foch, Av Diable Le Kaiser, Wilkinson, 1915, 11¾" 700.00
Martha Gunn, translucent colors, England, 1800s, rpr, 9⅜" ...1,725.00
President Wilson, Welcome Uncle Sam, Wilkinson, 1915, 10¼" ...1,150.00

Seated men in typical colors: Sponged overcoat, tankard on knee, pipe at side, Pratt, ca 1800, restored, 9⅛", $1,300.00; Pitcher on knee, Walton, ca 1820, repairs, 10", $1,045.00.

Seated, blk hat, bl coat, yel pants, unmk, 1820s, 8½" 225.00
Seated, jug raised to lips, mc/lustre, Allertons, 9" 175.00
Seated w/jug, mc overglaze decor, 19th C, rprs, 9½" 345.00
Seated w/pitcher/mug, mc w/gold, Allertons Est 1831, 5¼" 60.00
Stands on gr base, EX detail, scene on jug, pearlware, 10", VG ..400.00

Toleware

The term 'toleware' originally came from a French term meaning 'sheet iron.' Today it is used to refer to paint-decorated tin items, most popular from 1800 to 1850s. The craft flourished in Pennsylvania, Connecticut, Maine, and New York state. Early toleware has a very distinctive look. The surface is dull and unvarnished; background colors range from black to cream. Geometrics are quite common, but florals and fruits were also favored. Items made after 1850 were often stenciled, and gold trim was sometimes added.

American toleware is usually found in practical, everyday forms — trays, boxes, and coffeepots are most common — while French examples might include candlesticks, wine coolers, jardinieres, etc. Be sure to note color and design when determining date and value, but condition of the paint is the most important worth-assessing factor. In the listings that follow, the dimension given for boxes and trays indicates length. Unless noted otherwise, values are for examples with average wear.

Box, deed; mc floral on dk japanning, dome top, 13", VG 165.00
Box, deed; orig tan w/grpt, brass lock/hdl, 10½" 165.00
Box, deed; red flowers w/gr leaves, wht swags on blk, 9" 260.00
Box, deed; strawberries on dk brn japanning, 8" 330.00
Box, floral on red-brn japanning, domed top, oval, 7½" 165.00
Box, gold floral on blk, drum shape, 5⅛" 55.00
Box, mc floral & pinwheels on dk brn japanning, 10", VG 185.00
Box, mc floral on dk brn japanning, dome top, 7" 125.00
Cheese rack, florals w/gold on boat form, early 19th C, 13" 220.00
Coffee urn, mc floral & city scene on blk w/gold stripes, 20" 360.00
Coffeepot, mc floral on blk, side spout, 11¾", VG 225.00
Coffeepot, mc floral on dk brn japanning, touch-ups, 10¾" 715.00
Jar, potpourri; gold florals/birds on blk, brass finial, 4½" 55.00
Mug, worn orig pnt w/stencil, child sz, 2¾", pr 110.00
Sugar bowl, mc florals on dk brn japanning, 3¾" 275.00
Tea caddy, mc floral on blk, bronze bail, 19th C, NM 425.00
Tea caddy, mc floral on blk, 5¼x3½x2⅝", EX 110.00
Teapot, mc floral on dk gr, rpr hdl, 8¼" 330.00

Tray, bread; mc floral on red, rtcl sides, open hdls, 13" 1,200.00
Tray, gilt chinoiserie on blk, rtcl gallery, oval, 24½" 250.00
Tray, gilt chinoiserie on Chinese red, 2⅜x27" 770.00
Tray, landscape w/peacocks, gold on blk, 19th C, 18x24" 360.00
Tray, mc floral on dk brn japanning w/gold striping, 14", VG 125.00

Tools

Before the Civil War, tools for the most part were handmade. Some were primitive to the point of crudeness, while others reflected the skill of those who took pride in their trade. Increasing demand for quality tools and the dawning of the age of industrialization resulted in tools that were mass produced. Factors important in evaluating antique tools are scarcity, usefulness, and portability. Those with a manufacturer's mark are worth more than unmarked items. When no condition is indicated, the items listed here are assumed to be in excellent condition. Our advisor for this category is Jim Calison; he is listed in the Directory under New York. See also Keen Kutter; Stanley; Winchester.

Auger, burn; point fired hot to penetrate wood, then twist for sz ..28.00
Auger, spiral; for bigger holes 45.00
Awl, cobbler's; thumb screws allow varied-sz points 18.00
Axe, grubbing; 2-headed, hand-forged, 1850s 38.00
Axe, Kent type, w/Fawnfoot hdl 95.00
Axe, Yankee; dbl-headed, 1850s 75.00
Baseball stitching vise 75.00
Broadaxe, Buzzard's wing 95.00
Caliper, logging; iron, long flattened hdl, some rust, 36" 25.00
Calipers, bronze, sgn TJ Smith, 1800s, 12¾" 110.00
Calipers, dbl; use on a lathe w/stock in motion 95.00
Calk remover, for horseshoes, factory stamped, eye to hang 20.00
Chalk-line reel, mortised, balanced hickory, freely spins, 1800s .110.00
Chisel, debarking; for cleaning logs, 1850s 95.00
Coach jack, hickory, iron joiners 110.00
Cooper's long jointer, bbl maker, 6" 175.00
Cooper's pull scraper, maple hdls, brass ferrule 45.00
Divider, carriage making; pearwood w/brass mts & wingtips, lg 45.00
Glut, oak w/iron band, very lg 16.00
Hacksaw, iron; brass color, wood hdl, cuts iron & wood 68.00
Hammer, bricklayer's 18.00
Knife, hoof; natural, bone hdl, 1890-99 ....28.00
Level, Davis, #9, 24" 85.00
Log roller 18.00
Log tongs, 4-man, all iron 45.00
Mallet, wheelwright's 19.00
Maul, 1-pc hickory 15.00
Measure, Lufkin #066D 7.50
Mortising gauge, cherry w/brass 65.00
Pick, cultivating; dbl-headed 19.00
Pick, prospector's 19.00
Plane, coach maker's, 7" 75.00
Rabbet, cherry, notched to fit wood 65.00
Saw, dvtl brass bk, trn wood hdl, 10½" 50.00
Saw, rip, #5, sm 20.00
Saw, trenching; maple, 1840s 85.00
Sawtooth bending tool, determines width of cut 22.00
Square, rosewood & brass 15.00
Tap & die auger, to cut wood threads 145.00
Trammel, wood & brass, 1890 ....98.00
Traveler, measured tires & wheels to match sz, 1800s 125.00
Wagon jack, wood & iron, sliding grip, New England origin 125.00
Wrench, steamboat engineer's, factory made 55.00

Toothbrush Holders

Most of the collectible toothbrush holders were made in prewar Japan and were modeled after popular comic strip and Disney characters. Since many were made of bisque and decorated with unfired paint, it's not uncommon to find them in less-than-perfect paint, a factor you must consider when attempting to assess their values. Our advisor for this category is Marilyn Cooper, author of *Pictorial Guide to Toothbrush Holders*; she is listed in the Directory under Texas.

Annie Oakley, Japan, 5¾" 125.00
Aviator, celluloid, 6⅛" 135.00
Baby Bunting, baby in bunny suit, Germany, 6¾" 395.00
Bonzo, lustreware, Japan, 5¾" 95.00
Children in auto, Japan, 5" 90.00
Clown w/mandolin, Japan, 6" 110.00
Dalmatian, Germany, 4" 175.00
Dog w/basket, Japan, 5¾" 90.00
Dwarfs in front of fence, Sleepy & Dopey, Japan, 3½" 1,275.00
Genie, Blk boy, Japan, 5¾" 125.00
Girl powdering nose, Japan, 6¼" 100.00
Girl w/umbrella, Japan, 4½" 75.00
Girl washing boy's face, Great Britain, 5" 90.00
Henry & Henrietta, Japan, 4½" 575.00
Indian Chief, bust in full headdress, Japan, 4½" 250.00
Kayo w/hands in pockets, Japan, 5" 125.00

Little Orphan Annie and Sandy on couch, bisque, back of couch holds two toothbrushes, FAS/Japan, 3¾", $125.00.

Little Red Riding Hood w/name on apron, Japan, 5¼" 110.00
Little Red Riding Hood w/Wolf, Germany, 6¼" 375.00
Mickey Mouse, Addis (English), w/orig toothbrush, MIB 145.00
Pluto, Japan, 4⅝" 325.00
Sailors on anchor, Japan, 5½" 70.00
Toonerville Trolley, Japan, 5½" 550.00

Toothpick Holders

Once common on every table, the toothpick holder was relegated to the china cabinet near the turn of the century. Fortunately, this contributed to their survival. As a result, many are available to collectors today. Because they are small and easily displayed, they are very popular collectibles. They come in a wide range of prices to fit every budget. Many have been reproduced and, unfortunately, are being offered for sale right along with the originals. These 'repros' should be priced in the $10.00 to $30.00 range. Unless you're sure of what you're buying, choose a reputable dealer. In addition to pattern glass, you'll find examples in china, bisque, art glass, and various metals. Toothpick holders in the listings that follow are glass unless noted otherwise. Values here are for originals. Our advisor for this category is Judy A. Knauer; she is listed in the Directory under Pennsylvania.

Alligator, amber	65.00
Atlas, ruby stain	65.00
Baby Chick, gr stippled, Vallerysthal	40.00
Baby's Bootie, amber	48.00
Basketweave, amber, mug form	45.00
Beaded Swag, ruby stain (+)	75.00
Beaded Swag w/Roses, wht opal (+)	65.00
Beaded Swirl & Disc	55.00
Beatty Ribbed, bl opal	30.00
Beatty Waffle, bl opal	45.00
Button Arches, clambroth, Mother (+)	25.00
Button Arches, ruby stain (+)	35.00
Button Panel, gold top	55.00
Carmen	55.00
Cherubs holding bbl, glass (+)	25.00
Chrysanthemum Sprig, custard	250.00
Coal Hod, amber	40.00
Colorado, gr, souvenir	45.00
Columbian Coin, ruby stain	450.00

Chick and basket, amber, 2½", $65.00. (Reproduced in a variety of colors with the original showing complete claw foot while repros do not.)

Croesus, purple (+)	110.00
Croesus, purple w/gold (+)	120.00
Daisy & Button, gr, coal scuttle shape	30.00
Daisy & Button w/advertising, pressed hat form w/gold (+)	45.00
Delaware, clear w/rose & gold	95.00
Delaware, rose stain w/gold	115.00
Diamond Quilt, amberina, sq rim, 2½"	175.00
Diamond Spearhead, cobalt opal	150.00
Diamond Spearhead, gr opal	70.00
Diamond Spearhead, vaseline opal	65.00
Esther, gr w/gold	180.00
Feather	75.00
Fine Cut Star & Fan	50.00
Footed Square, milk glass	20.00
Galloway	25.00
Gathered Knot, amethyst	85.00
Heart Band, ruby stain	38.00
Invt T'print, cranberry, bulging base	85.00
Invt T'print, sapphire bl, wht florals w/gold, bulbous	120.00
Iris w/Meander, bl opal	135.00
Iris w/Meander, gr opal	65.00
Kewpie (+)	60.00
King's Crown, ruby stain	30.00
Kitten on pillow, amber (+)	75.00
Ladder w/Dmn, EX gold	50.00
Madame Bovary, bl w/amber rim & ft	95.00
Michigan, bl stain w/yel enamel dots (+)	75.00
Mikado, bl	75.00
Minnesota	30.00
Monkey on tree stump (+)	25.00
New Hampshire, advertising	45.00

Oval Star	25.00
Paneled Sprig, wht opal	85.00
Pillar, pk & wht spatter	65.00
Pleating, ruby stain	50.00
Priscilla	65.00
Ribbed Swirl, wht opal	85.00
Riverside's Brilliant, yel flashed	160.00
Scalloped Swirl, ruby stain	60.00
Scroll w/Cane Band, ruby stain	110.00
Shamrock, ruby stain & gold	38.00
Shoshone, clear w/EX gold	30.00
Simplicity Scroll, souvenir, EX gold	30.00
Squirrel & Stump, bl (+)	60.00
Sunbeam, gr w/gold	80.00
Sunrise, ruby stain	45.00
Swag w/Brackets, purple w/gold	70.00
Swirl, frosted w/amber stain & HP decor, blown	75.00
Tacoma	25.00
Tarentum T'print, clear w/HP flowers, souvenir	40.00
Tarentum T'print, custard, souvenir	55.00
Texas	35.00
Vermont, gr w/gold (+)	70.00
Windsor Anvil, bl	35.00
Wreath & Shell, vaseline opal	225.00
York Herringbone, ruby stain	55.00
Zipper Slash, clear frosted w/decor	45.00

Torquay Pottery

Torquay is a unique type of pottery made in the South Devon area of England as early as 1867. At the height of productivity, at least a dozen companies flourished there, producing simple folk pottery from the area's natural red clay. The ware was both wheel turned and molded and decorated under the glaze with heavy slip resulting in low-relief nature subjects or simple scrollwork. Three of the best-known of these potteries were Watcombe (1867-1962); Aller Vale (in operation from the mid-1800s, producing domestic ware and architectural products); and Longpark (1890 until 1957). Watcombe and Aller Vale merged in 1901 and operated until 1962 under the name of Royal Aller Vale and Watcombe Art Pottery.

A decline in the popularity of the early classical terra-cotta styles (urns, busts, figures, etc.) lead to the introduction of painted and glazed terra-cotta wares. During the late 1880s white clay wares, both turned and molded, were decorated with colored glazes (Stapleton ware, grotesque molded figures, ornamental vases, large jardiniers, etc.). By the turn of the century, the market for art pottery was diminishing, so the potteries turned to wares decorated in colored slips (Barbotine, Persian, Scrolls, etc.).

Motto wares were introduced in the late 19th century by Aller Vale and taken up in the present century by the other Torquay potteries. This eventually became the 'bread and butter' product of the local industry. This was perhaps the most famous type of ware potted in this area because of the verses, proverbs, and quotations that decorated it. This was achieved by the sgraffito technique — scratching the letters through the slip to expose the red clay underneath. The most popular patterns were Cottage, Black Cockerel, Multi-Cockerel, and a scrollwork design called Scandy. Other popular decorations were Kerswell Daisy, ships, kingfishers, applied bird decorations, Art Deco styles, Egyptian ware, and many others. Aller Vale ware may sometimes be found marked 'H.H. and Company,' a firm who assumed ownership from 1897 to 1901. 'Watcombe Torquay' was an impressed mark used from 1884 to 1927.

Our advisors for this category are Jerry and Gerry Kline; they are listed in the Directory under Ohio. If you're interested in joining a Torquay club, the address of The North American Torquay Society is given under Clubs, Newsletters, and Catalogs.

Art Pottery

Bottle, scent; Devon Violets, unmk, 2½" 50.00
Bowl, Devon Tors, Cottage, 1½x10½" 250.00
Bowl, Fish & Seaweed, Dartmouth, no motto, 2½" 60.00
Candlestick, Scroll, Aller Vale, 4¼" 125.00
Candlesticks, Scroll, Longpark Tormohun, bl, 5½", pr 250.00
Creamer, Polka Dot, Babbacombe, 2¼" 25.00
Figure, cat, Aller Vale, Imp, 5¾" 650.00
Figure, cat, gr, Watcombe, 8½" 1,000.00
Hatpin holder, faience, unmk, 4½" 150.00
Jar, powder; Peacock, faience, dome lid, Lemon & Crute, 4½" dia ..135.00
Jardiniere, iris on gr, Longpark, 6½x8¾" dia 600.00
Pitcher, Scrolls on gr, Longpark, Imp, 8" 275.00
Pitcher, Sea Gull, Babbacombe, 3½" 30.00
Teapot, Scrolls on gr, 'Filling the Teapot...,' 4⅞" 175.00
Teapot stand, Kingfisher, motto, 5¾" dia 65.00
Tile, faience, cottage, Watcombe, 6" dia 95.00
Toby, unmk Devonmoor, mini, 1¾" 30.00
Vase, Cabbage Rose, ear hdls, faience, Lemon & Crute, 4" 145.00
Vase, floral on gr, Aller Vale, 4½" 135.00
Vase, Tintern Abbey, bottle form, Longpark, 7" 160.00
Vase, wht flowers on bl, unmk, mini, 2" 32.00
Wall pocket, floral, unmk, 6" L 240.00

Devon Motto Ware

Ashtray, Cottage, Watcombe, 'I'll Take Care...,' 4½" 60.00
Ashtray, Windmill & Cottage, Watcombe, 'Who Burnt...,' 4⅞" ..65.00
Bowl, Cottage, unmk Watcombe, scalloped, w/motto, 6½", EX .110.00
Bowl, junket; Scandy, Aller Vale, 'Take a Little...,' 7" 125.00
Bowl, Watcombe, ped ft, 'Actions Speak Louder...,' 3¼" H 65.00
Butter tub, Shamrock, Longpark, 'From Killarney...,' 4½" 75.00
Candlestick, Cottage, Longpark, 'Towyn Hear All...,' 110.00
Candlestick, Cottage, Torquay, no motto, 6½" 85.00
Candlestick, Scandy, Aller Vale, 'Many Are Called...,' 4¼" 95.00
Candlestick, Scandy, Longpark, 'Many Are Called...,' 3½" 85.00
Candlestick, Scandy, Tormohun Ware, 'Last in Bed...,' 6" 125.00
Candlestick, Scandy, unmk Watcombe, 'Daunt Lite Yer...,' 7¼" ..145.00
Candlestick, Shamrock, Longpark, 'Killarney...,' 4" 105.00
Candlestick, Shamrock, Longpark, 'None of Your Blarney,' 3" 85.00
Candlestick, Ship, unmk Barton, porc, 'Don't Burn the...,' 5" 110.00
Coffeepot, Cockerel, Longpark, 'Wishes Never Filled...,' 4¼" 135.00
Coffeepot, Cottage, Watcombe, 'Contrivance...,' 5¼" 135.00
Coffeepot, Cottage, Watcombe, 'If Your Lips...,' 7½" 210.00
Coffeepot, Cottage, Watcombe, 'Say Not Always...,' 6½" 170.00
Coffeepot, Cottage, Watcombe, 'Stitch in Time...,' 6" 155.00
Coffeepot, Cottage, Watcombe, w/motto, prof rstr, 7" 100.00
Coffeepot, Dbl Cottage, Watcombe, w/motto, 8½", EX 225.00
Coffeepot, Scandy, unmk, 'Du'ee Have a Cup...,' 6½" 185.00
Creamer, Dbl Cottage, Watcombe, 'Make Thisen...,' 2¼" 42.00
Cup & saucer, demi; Windmill, Watcombe, 'Have Another...' 60.00
Egg cup, Cottage, Babbacombe, 'Fresh Today,' 1960s 30.00
Gypsy pot, Scandy, Longpark, 'If You Can't Be Aisy...,' 3" 75.00
Hatpin holder, ship scene, 'I'll Take Care...,' 4½" 175.00
Humidor, Scandy, Aller Vale, 'As Pan Brot Music...,' 5" 185.00
Inkwell, Scandy, Tormorhun Ware, 'Us Be Always...,' 2⅜" dia 95.00
Inkwell & tray, Scandy, Longpark, motto 395.00
Jam jar, Cottage, 'Take a Little Marmalade,' 3¾x3" 55.00
Jardiniere, Scandy, unmk, 'Vessels Lg May Venture...,' 4½" 110.00

Jug, Cottage, Watcombe, 'Help Yourself...,' 4" 75.00
Jug, Cottage, Watcombe, 'Will'ee 'Elp Yerzel...,' 5¼" 150.00
Jug, Cottage, Watcombe, bbl form, 'I Cum From...,' 5" 150.00
Jug, puzzle; Black Cockerel, unmk, 'Within This Jug...,' 3⅝" 200.00
Jug, Shamrock, Longpark, bbl form, 'From Cushendall...,' 3½" 65.00
Match striker, Cottage, Watcombe, 'A Match for...,' 6½" L 165.00
Mug, Cottage, Royal Watcombe, wide mouth, w/motto, 4½" 85.00
Mug, Shamrock, Royal Watcombe, w/motto, child sz, 2½" 65.00
Mug, shaving; Multi Cockerel, Longpark, motto, 4" 300.00
Mustard pot, Scandy on gr, Aller Vale, 'Be Canny...,' wht clay 65.00
Pitcher, Cottage, Watcombe, ped ft, 'Give & Spend...,' 4" 110.00
Pitcher, Scandy, Aller Vale, side spout, 'Every Blade...,' 3" 60.00
Pitcher, Scandy, HM Exeter, 'Put a Stout Heart...,' 2½" 45.00
Pitcher & bowl, Fish & Seaweed, Dartmouth, no motto 260.00
Plate, Black Hen, 'Hear All, See All, Say Nothing,' 4⅝" 75.00
Plate, Cottage, Watcombe, 'Better Wait on...,' 8¼" 110.00
Plate, Cottage, Watcombe, 'Masters Two Will Never Do,' 5" 50.00
Shaker, Cottage, unmk, 'There's No Fun Like Work' 28.00
Sugar bowl, Scandy on gr, Aller Vale, wht clay, 4¼" 60.00

Teapot, Cottage, Watcombe, 'Take a Cup of Kindness for Auld Lang Syne,' 6", $195.00.

Teapot, Cottage, 'We'll Take a Cup...,' 3¾x3⅞" 120.00
Teapot, Cottage, Watcombe, 'Du'ee Zit Down...,' 5" 175.00
Teapot, Shamrock, Longpark, 'From Courtown Arrah...,' 3¾" ...130.00
Tile, Shamrock, Aller Vale, 'Chosen Leaf...,' 4¼" 85.00
Toast rack, Cottage, unmk Longpark, 'Crisp & Brown,' 1920s ...175.00
Vase, Scandy, Aller Vale, hdls, 'A Fellow Feeling...,' 5½" 115.00
Vase, Scandy, Longpark, 'When Down in the Mouth...,' 7" 175.00
Vase, Shamrock, hdl, 'If You Can't Be Aisy...,' 5½" 105.00

Tortoise Shell Glass

By combining several shades of glass — brown, clear, and yellow — glass manufacturers of the 19th and 20th centuries were able to produce an art glass that closely resembled the shell of the tortoise. Some of this type of glassware was manufactured in Germany, Italy, and Czechoslovakia. In America it was made by several firms, the most prominent of which was the Boston and Sandwich Glass Works.

Bottle, scent; silver collar, dk amber faceted stopper, 6" 125.00
Bowl, centerpiece; att Sandwich, 9½" 300.00
Cruet, melon ribbed, clear hdl, cut faceted stopper, 7" 95.00
Finger bowl, ruffled, +6" undertray, Sandwich 300.00
Pitcher, hand blown, pinched w/polished pontil, 10" 135.00
Vase, amber w/brn spots, appl amber serpentine, 12¼" 260.00
Vase, crimped & ruffled rim, 9" 70.00
Wig stand, 9½" 225.00

Toys

Toys can be classified into at least two categories: early collectible toys with an established history, and the newer toys. The antique toys are easier to evaluate. A great deal of research has been done on them, and much data is available. The newer toys are just beginning to be studied; relative information is only now being published, and the lack of production records makes it difficult to know how many may be available. Often warehouse finds of these newer toys can change the market. This has happened with battery-operated toys and to some extent with robots. Review past issues of this guide. You will see the changing trends for the newer toys. All toys become more important as collectibles when a fixed period of manufacture is known. When we know the numbers produced and documentation of the makers is established, the prices become more predictable.

The best way to learn about toys is to attend toy shows and auctions. This will give you the opportunity to compare prices and condition. The more collectors and dealers you meet, the more you will learn. There is no substitute for holding a toy in your hand and seeing for yourself what they are. If you are going to be a serious collector, buy all the books you can find. Read every article you see. Knowledge is vital to building a good collection. Study all books that are available. These are some of the most helpful: *Collecting Toys, Collecting Toy Soldiers*, and *Collecting Toy Trains, An Identification & Value Guide #3*, by Richard O'Brien; *Evolution of the Pedal Car and Other Riding Toys, 1844-1970s*, by Neil Wood; and *Toys of the Sixties, A Pictorial Guide*, by Bill Bruegman. Other informative books (published by Collector Books) are *Schroeder's Collectible Toys, Antique to Modern*, by Sharon and Bob Huxford; *Collector's Guide to Tinker Toys* by Craig Strange; *Classic Plastic Model Kits* by Rick Polizzi; *The Golden Age of Automotive Toys, 1925-1941*, by Ken Hutchinson and Greg Johnson; *Motorcycle Toys, Antique & Contemporary*, by Sally Gibson-Downs and Christine Gentry; *Mego Toys* by Wallace M. Chrouch; *Collector's Encyclopedia of Disneyana* by David Longest and Michael Stern; *Stern's Guide to Disney Collectibles* by Michael Stern; *Modern Toys, American Toys, 1830-1980*, by Linda Baker; *Character Toys and Collectibles, Antique and Collectible Toys, 1970-1950*, and *Toys, Antique & Collectible*, both by David Longest; *Collector's Guide to Tootsietoys* by David Richter; *Collectible Male Action Figures* by Paris and Susan Manos; *Matchbox Toys, 1948-1993, Matchbox Toys, 1974-1996, Second Edition* and *Diecast Toys and Scale Models*, all three by Dana Johnson. *The Dictionary of Toys Sold in America, Vol. I & II*, by Earnest and Ida Long are good for identification and dating.

Our advisor for all toys except Farm Toys, Guns, Steiff, Toy Soldiers, and Trains is Jon Thurmond; he is listed in the Directory under Missouri. In the listings that follow, toys are listed by manufacturer's name if possible, otherwise by type. Condition is given when known. Measurements are given when appropriate and available; if only one dimension is noted, it is the greater one — height if the toy is vertical, length if it is horizontal. See also Children's Things; Personalities. For toy stoves, see Stoves.

Key:
b/o — battery operated   NP — nickel plated
cl — celluloid   w/up — wind-up
jtd — jointed

Company or Country of Manufacturer

AC Williams, Coupe, CI, metal wheels, 5⅛", G	165.00
AC Williams, Fire Pumper, CI, w/driver, 6¼", G	140.00
AC Williams, Ford Model T Express Truck, CI, 7", VG	275.00
AC Williams, Lincoln Sedan, CI, metal spoke wheels, 9", G	255.00
AC Williams, Stake Truck, CI, NP spoke wheels, 5", G	90.00
Alps, Charlie the Drumming Clown, b/o, 9½", MIB	300.00
Alps, Circus Jet, b/o, circles & fires gun, MIB	150.00
Alps, Clown Magician, b/o, 12", EXIB	175.00
Alps, Coney Island Rocket Ride, b/o, rare, 14", MIB	1,000.00
Alps, Daisy the Drumming Duck, b/o, 9", MIB	375.00
Alps, Firebird III, b/o, red/wht, 11½", NMIB	200.00

Alps, Flutterbirds, b/o, litho tin/plush, 27", MIB	550.00
Alps, Mumbo Jumbo the Hawaiian Drummer, b/o, 10", MIB	375.00
Alps, Rodeo Cowboy, w/up, celluloid/tin, 9", NMIB	185.00
Alps, Santa in His Rocking Chair, b/o, rare, 21", EX	750.00
Alps, Smiling Sam the Carnival Man, w/up, 9", EXIB	200.00
Alps, Whirly Twirly Rocket Ride, b/o, 13", NM	325.00
Arcade, Andy Gump Car, CI, mk 348 on grille, 7", G	1,760.00
Arcade, Baby Dump Truck, CI, w/driver, metal wheels, rstr	175.00
Arcade, Camouflage Tank, CI, 8", M	875.00
Arcade, Chevrolet Roadster, CI, rstr, 6½"	420.00
Arcade, Fire Pumper, CI, 6 firemen, NP hose reel, 13", VG	935.00
Arcade, Greyhound Bus, mk Century of Progress 1933, CI, 8", EX	175.00
Arcade, Hathaway's Bakery Truck, CI, 9½", G	1,600.00
Arcade, Horse-Drawn Fire Pumper, CI, 4", EX	85.00
Arcade, Mack Gasoline Truck, CI, 1929, 13", EX	1,155.00
Arcade, Mack Ladder Truck, CI, rpl wheels, 20", G	255.00
Arcade, Mack T-Bar Dump Truck, CI, NP wheels, 1928, 12", VG	250.00
Arcade, White Ice Truck, CI, NP grille, 1941, VG	375.00
Arcade, Yellow Cab, CI, 1941, 8¼", G	200.00
Bandai, Buick Convertible, friction, wht, 6", MIB	200.00
Bandai, Cadillac Sedan, friction, lt brn, 1962, 8¼", MIB	55.00
Bandai, Ford T-Bird Convertible, b/o, red/blk, 11", MIB	200.00
Bandai, Rambler Station Wagon, friction, 11", NMIB	270.00
Bing, Ocean Liner Leviathan, pnt tin, 3 levels, 36", EX	3,750.00
Bing, Old Lady, w/up, HP tin, 7", G	200.00
Bing, Pigmyphone, w/up, gr litho tin, 3x6x6", EX	400.00
Bing, Steam Launch, w/up, pnt tin, brass boiler, 23", VG	600.00
Bing, Yellow Cab, w/up, 8½", EX	1,000.00
Bliss, Battleship, litho paper on wood, 16 guns, 36", EX	4,000.00
Bliss, block set, animal scenes w/alphabet, set of 12, EX	285.00
Bliss, block set, Read & Learn, set of 8, G in box	2,200.00
Bliss, Gunboat, paper litho on wood, 25½", G+	1,500.00
Bliss, Side-Wheeler Union, paper litho on wood, 23", EX	1,155.00
Borgfeldt, Mickey & Minnie Acrobats, w/up, 11½", EX	725.00
Buddy L, Aerial Ladder Truck, red w/NP ladders, 39", VG	955.00
Buddy L, Allied Van Lines Moving Van, orange/blk, 29", EX	715.00
Buddy L, Bus, gr w/gold stripe, 28", G	2,050.00
Buddy L, Caboose, red w/blk trucks, 10¼", G	550.00
Buddy L, Cement Mixer, gr w/blk crank & wheels, 11", EX	275.00
Buddy L, Dump Truck #10, blk/red, 1935, 25", G	545.00

Buddy L, Flivver Pickup Truck, pressed steel, black with decal, 1920s, 12", EX, $950.00.

Buddy L, Greyhound Bus, #955, NMIB	475.00
Buddy L, Ice Truck #207, blk/yel, 1926, rpt, 26", EX	1,650.00
Buddy L, Shell Gas Truck, orange/red, open cab, G	300.00
Buddy L, Steam Shovel, blk w/red roof & base, 13", G	245.00
Buddy L, Tugboat, type II, mk ...Navigation Co, 28", rstr	2,415.00
Buddy L, US Mail Truck, Buy Defense Bonds decal, 21", M	825.00
Carette, Battle Cruiser, w/up, pnt tin, 1908, 27", rstr	2,300.00
Carette, Limousine, w/driver, w/up, 1910, 13", VG	2,200.00
Carette, Phaeton, w/figures, w/up, ca 1905, 9", VG	2,300.00

Carette, Racing Boat, figure at helm, w/up, pnt tin, 8", G 625.00
Carette, Touring Car, w/up, wht, 13", EXIB 15,400.00
Chein, Barnacle Bill, w/up, 1930s, 6", VG 250.00
Chein, Ferris Wheel #172, w/up, 1930s, 17", NMIB 650.00
Chein, Happy Hooligan, w/up, 1932, 6", EXIB 1,550.00
Chein, Playland Merry-Go-Round, w/up, 11" dia, NMIB 800.00
Chein, Racer #5, w/up, 1930, scarce, 9½", EX 400.00
CIJ, Alpha Romeo Racer #2, w/up, bl/red, 21", EX 2,400.00
CIJ, Swimming Fish, w/up, tin, wood base, 17", EXIB 1,400.00
Cragstan, Crapshooting Monkey, b/o, NMIB 100.00
Cragstan, Lady Pup Tending Her Garden, b/o, 9", MIB 475.00
Cragstan, Mammal of the Sea, friction, 6", NMIB 225.00
Cragstan, Rock 'N Roll Monkey, w/up, NM 225.00
Cragstan, Sailboat, b/o, 12", NMIB 225.00
Cragstan, Shuttling Train Set, b/o, 38", MIB 215.00
Cragstan, Teddy the Champ Boxer, b/o, 9", NMIB 355.00
Cragstan, Trumpet Playing Monkey, b/o, tin/plush, MIB 275.00
Cragstan, Two-Gun Sheriff, b/o, 1950s, EXIB 200.00
Daiya, General Patton Tank M-107, b/o, 7", MIB 275.00
Daiya, Motorcycle Cop, b/o, litho tin, NMIB 375.00

Dayton, Roadster, painted tin, ca 1910-20, 14", M, $1,500.00.

Photo courtesy Dunbar Gallery

Dent, Horse-Drawn Sleigh, CI, w/rider, rpt, 15½" 910.00
Dent, Phaeton, CI, 2 figures, rpt, 8½" 195.00
Dent, Taxi, CI, w/driver, 7½", EX 1,265.00
Distler, Monkey Drummer, w/up, gr platform, 8", EX 650.00
Fallows, Elephant in Hoop, tin, rstr, 11½" dia 440.00
Fischer, Limousine, w/driver, w/up, 1910, 13", VG 3,400.00
Fischer, Touring Car, w/driver & passengers, w/up, 9", EX 900.00
Fisher-Price, Bunny Push Cart, #303, 1957, EX 75.00
Fisher-Price, Chatter Monk, #798, 1957, EX 100.00
Fisher-Price, Circus Wagon, #156, 1942, EX 400.00
Fisher-Price, Dr Doodle, #100, 1931, EX 700.00
Fisher-Price, Gabby Duck, #190, 1939, EX 350.00
Fisher-Price, Huckleberry Hound, #711, Sears only, 1961, EX ...300.00
Fisher-Price, Kriss Krickey, #678, 1955, EX 100.00
Fisher-Price, Looky Chug Chug, #161, 1949, EX 250.00
Fisher-Price, Mini Snowmobile, #705, 1971-73, EX 50.00
Fisher-Price, Musical Sweeper, #100, 1950, EX 250.00
Fisher-Price, Play Family Camper, #994, 1973-76, EX 75.00
Fisher-Price, Poodle Zilo, #739, 1962, EX 75.00
Fisher-Price, Puppy Back-Up, #365, w/up, 1932, EX 800.00
Fisher-Price, Strutter Donald Duck, #510, 1941, EX 300.00
Fisher-Price, Tuggy Turtle, #139, 1959, EX 100.00
Fisher-Price, Uncle Timmy Turtle, #125, red shell, 1956, EX ...100.00
Fisher-Price, Winky Blinky Fire Truck, #200, 1954, EX 100.00
Gilbert, Erector Set #4, 2 instruction book, metal box, G 50.00
Gunthermann, Bagpipe Player, w/up, HP tin, 10½", EX 465.00
Gunthermann, Clown Musicians, w/up, 1890s, EX 1,380.00
Gunthermann, Gordon Bennet Car, flywheel, 6", VG 2,300.00

Gunthermann, Organ Grinder & Monkey, w/up, 1900, 9", VG ...3,500.00
Gunthermann, Rabbit w/Cymbals, w/up, 9½", EX 375.00
Hartland, Brave Eagle, NM 200.00
Hartland, Bret Maverick w/gray horse, rare, NM 700.00
Hartland, Chief Thunderbird, rare shield, NM 150.00
Hartland, Dale Evans, rare bl version, NM 400.00
Hartland, Gil Favor, prancing, NM 800.00
Hartland, Lone Ranger, miniature series, NM 75.00
Hartland, Paladin, NMIB 350.00
Hartland, Tom Jeffords, NM 175.00
Hartland, Wyatt Earp, NM 200.00
Hubley, Bell Telephone Truck, CI, 12", EX 990.00
Hubley, Dump Truck, CI, NP dump, 7½", EX 455.00
Hubley, Harley-Davidson Motorcycle, CI, w/driver, 7", VG 600.00
Hubley, Horse-Drawn Sleigh, CI, w/rider, rpt, 13½" 660.00
Hubley, Mr Magoo Car, b/o, tin/cloth, 9", NMIB 425.00
Hubley, Penn-Yan Speedboat, CI, 1930, 14", VG 8,800.00
Hubley, Road Roller, CI, rpl figure, 7½", NM 525.00
Hubley, Royal Circus Band Wagon, CI, rpt, 29" 2,530.00
Hubley, Royal Circus Lion Cage, CI, w/driver, 15½", EX ...1,430.00
Hubley, Sedan, CI, NP grille, 4", EX+ 165.00
Hubley, Tri-Motor Airplane Am, CI, NP props, 17" wingspan, G ...4,100.00
Hubley, Wrecker, CI, 2 rpl tires, 4", G 100.00
Ives, Rowboat Mary, w/up, girl in boat, Pat 1869, 13", VG 4,300.00
Ives, Santa Walker, w/up, 1880, 9", EX 800.00
JEP, Bugatti Racer #2, w/driver, w/up, 9", EX 600.00
JEP, Street Bus, w/up, lists destinations, 10½", EX 800.00
Joustra, Circus Boy, w/up, litho tin, 6", EX 350.00
Kenner, Build-A-Home Set #16, NMIB 125.00
Kenner, Constructioneer Girder & Panel Set #08, VG 65.00
Kenner, Hydro-Dynamic Building Set #11, MIB, from $125 to ..200.00
Kenton, Contractor's Auto Coal Wagon, CI, w/driver, 8", VG ..525.00
Kenton, Horse-Drawn City Express Wagon, CI, Blk driver, 17", G ...525.00
Kenton, Horse-Drawn Farm Cart, CI, Blk driver, rpt, 13" 300.00
Kenton, Horse-Drawn Ice Wagon, CI, 1929, 16", VG 1,870.00
Kenton, Horse-Drawn Stake Wagon, CI, w/driver, 10½", G 195.00
Kenton, Overland Circus Bear Cage, CI, w/driver, 14", VG 245.00
Kenton, Police Patrol, CI, 4 figures, 1933, 9½", G 825.00
Kenton, Touring Car, CI, rpt, 6½" 165.00
Lehmann, Autobus, w/up, red w/yel stripes, 8", EX 1,475.00
Lehmann, Baldur Limousine, w/up, blk/yel, w/driver, 10", EX ...1,650.00
Lehmann, Crocodile, w/up, realistic color, 9½", NM 415.00
Lehmann, Dancing Sailor, w/up, cloth clothes, 7½", EXIB 900.00
Lehmann, Galop Racer #1, w/up, 5½", EX, minimum value 500.00
Lehmann, Lu Lu Delivery Van, w/up, 7", EX 3,600.00
Lehmann, Paddy the Pig, w/up, HP tin, cloth clothes, 5½", NM ...2,250.00
Lehmann, Rigi 900 Cable Car, w/up, w/passengers, 1950, EX ...300.00
Lehmann, Wild West Bucking Bronco, w/up, 6", NMIB 1,250.00
Lindstrom, Am Railway Express w/Trailer, w/up, 16", EX 675.00
Lindstrom, Dancing Dutch Boy, w/up, 1930s, 8", NMIB 300.00
Lindstrom, Johnny the Clown, w/up, 1930s, 8", EX 225.00
Linemar, Ball Playing Dog, b/o, tin/plush, 9", M 175.00
Linemar, Casper the Ghost Tank, w/up, 4", NMIB 725.00
Linemar, Concrete Mixer, b/o, 9", NMIB 240.00
Linemar, Donald Duck Dipsy Car, w/up, NMIB, minimum value ...825.00
Linemar, Huckleberry Aeroplane, friction, 1961, 10", NMIB 675.00
Linemar, Louie in His Dream Car, friction, 5", NMIB 575.00
Linemar, Popeye in Rowboat, remote control, 10", NMIB 9,000.00
Linemar, Sleeping Baby Bear, b/o, tin/plush, 9", NMIB 310.00
Linemar, Wild West Rodeo Bubbling Bull, b/o, 7", MIB 375.00
Marklin, Construction Set #1012, EXIB 135.00
Marklin, D-A LBA Transport Plane Kit #1151, EXIB 2,000.00
Marklin, Side-Wheeler Priscilla, pnt tin/canvas, 30", EX 17,600.00
Marklin, Submarine, w/up, pnt tin, gr/blk, 16", EX 1,100.00

Marx, Alley the Roaring Stalking Tiger, b/o, MIB **475.00**
Marx, Am-La France Fire Hose Truck, pressed steel, 21", EX **300.00**
Marx, Bedrock Express, w/up, litho tin, 1962, 12", EX **250.00**
Marx, BO Plenty, w/up, litho tin, tips hat, 8", MIB **350.00**
Marx, Brewster the Rooster, b/o, plush over tin, 10", MIB **225.00**
Marx, Dagwood the Driver, w/up, litho tin, 8", NMIB **1,400.00**
Marx, Dippy Dumper, w/up, erratic action, 1930s, 9", EXIB ...**1,800.00**
Marx, Disneyland Jeep, friction, litho tin, 9", EXIB **250.00**
Marx, Electric Robot & Son, b/o, plastic, 16", EXIB **450.00**
Marx, Flash Gordon Rocket Fighter, w/up, 1939, 12", G **300.00**
Marx, Futuristic Airport, remote control, EXIB **385.00**
Marx, Hootin' Hollerin' Haunted House, b/o, litho tin, NM ..**1,150.00**
Marx, Knockout Champs, w/up, tin/celluloid, 7x7" base, NMIB ...**350.00**
Marx, Little Orphan Annie Skipping Rope, w/up, 1930s, 6", EX ..**600.00**
Marx, Lizzie of the Valley Jalopy, w/up, litho tin, 7", VG **275.00**
Marx, Lumar Coal Truck, red/bl pressed steel, 11¼", G **40.00**
Marx, Magic Garage & Car, w/up, 10" garage, EXIB **300.00**
Marx, Marx-A-Haul Dump Truck, pressed steel, NMIB **125.00**
Marx, Masterbuilder Kit of the White House, MIB **185.00**
Marx, Mickey Mouse on Big-Wheel, b/o, NMIB **275.00**
Marx, Mighty Kong, remote control, plush/tin/vinyl, 11", NMIB ...**615.00**
Marx, Milton Berle Car, w/up, 1950, 5½", EXIB **450.00**
Marx, Moon Mullins & Kayo Handcar, w/up, 1930s, 6", VG **500.00**
Marx, Nutty Mad Car, b/o, litho tin/vinyl, 9", EX **285.00**
Marx, Public Utility Service Truck, pressed steel, 17", NMIB **425.00**
Marx, Red Cap Porter, Blk man, w/up, 1930, 8", VG **700.00**
Marx, Roadside Rest Service Station, litho tin, 14", VG **400.00**
Marx, Rollover Plane, w/up, litho tin, 6" wingspan, VG **175.00**
Marx, Super Sonic Jet, friction, 1960s, EX **50.00**
Marx, Tidy Tim, w/up, pushes bbl, 9", NM, minimum value **850.00**
Marx, Tom Corbett Space Cadet Rocket Ship, w/up, '30s, 12", EX .**600.00**

Photo courtesy Dunbar Gallery

Marx, Twin Engine Bomber, wind-up, 1930s, 18" wingspan, M in torn original box, $375.00.

Marx, US Army Command Car, friction, b/o siren, 19", EXIB ...**350.00**
Marx, Wacky Taxi, friction, litho tin, 7", VG **100.00**
Marx, Walking Pinocchio, w/up, 1939, 8½", EXIB **450.00**
Marx, Whistling Spooky Kooky Tree, b/o, tin/vinyl, 13", NMIB ..**2,000.00**
Marx, Whoopee Cowboy, w/up, litho tin, 1932, 8", NM **425.00**
Minic, Double-Decker Bus, w/up, ads on sides, 7½", NMIB **200.00**
Minic, Royal Mail Van, w/up, red w/decals, 3½", EX **110.00**
Modern Toys, College Bear, w/up, plush/tin, 6", EXIB **100.00**
Modern Toys, Expert Motorcyclist, b/o, EXIB **1,000.00**
Modern Toys, Grand-Pa Panda, b/o, 9", MIB **450.00**
Modern Toys, Police Sidecar Motorcycle, friction, 7", NMIB **325.00**
Modern Toys, Siren Patrol Motorcycle, b/o, 12", NMIB **330.00**
Modern Toys, Tom & Jerry Helicopter, b/o, EX **325.00**
Nifty, Barney Google & Spark Plug, w/up, 1920s, 7", VG **1,265.00**
Nifty, Katrinka Lifting Jimmie, w/up, 1923, 6½", EX **2,000.00**
Nifty, Maggie & Jiggs, w/up, 4-wheeled platform, 7", EX **1,550.00**
Nylint, Elgin Street Sweeper, w/up, 8½", EX **175.00**
Ohio Art, Automatic Airport, w/up, 9", NMIB **350.00**

Ohio Art, Giant Ride Ferris Wheel, w/up, 1950s, 17", NMIB **350.00**
Ohio Art, Mickey Mouse Washing Machine, w/up, 8", NMIB ..**1,100.00**
Reed, block set, cut-out ABCs, EXIB **3,000.00**
Reed, Clipper Ship Am, paper litho on wood, 1877, 42", EX ..**1,750.00**
Reed, Side-Wheeler Pilgrim, paper litho on wood, 1890s, 28", G ..**700.00**
Richter, Anchor Stone Fortress set #404, complete, VG **250.00**
Richter, Anchor Stone Fortress set #406A, complete, VG **400.00**
Richter, Anchor Stone set #05A, DS, complete, VG **150.00**
Richter, Anchor Stone set #07, KK-NF, complete, VG **100.00**
Richter, Anchor Stone set #09A, DS, complete, VG **250.00**
Richter, Anchor Stone set #10, GK-NF, complete, VG **300.00**
Richter, Anchor Stone set #102, Neue Reihe, complete, VG **75.00**
Richter, Anchor Stone set #108, Neue Reihe, complete, VG **250.00**
Richter, Anchor Stone set #11A, KK-NF, complete, VG **275.00**
Richter, Anchor Stone set #13A, DS, complete, VG **325.00**
Richter, Anchor Stone set #14A, GK-NF, complete, VG **200.00**
Richter, Anchor Stone set #22A, GK-NF, complete, VG **450.00**
Richter, Anchor Stone set #23A, DS, complete, VG **750.00**
Schuco, Angel, w/up, tin w/cloth robe, 5", VG **1,485.00**
Schuco, Charlie Chaplin, w/up, tin w/cloth outfit, 7", G **900.00**
Schuco, Mirako Peter Cycle, #1013, w/up, scarce, 5", EX **600.00**
Schuco, Mouse in Convertible, Sonny 2005, w/up, 6", G **220.00**
Schuco, Solisto Clown Drummer, w/up, 4½", NMIB **325.00**
Schuco, Tumbling Mouse, w/up, felt over tin, 4", EX **450.00**
Strauss, Chek-A-Cab #69, w/up, 8½", VG **650.00**
Strauss, Clock Blocks, paper litho on wood, 1904, EXIB **165.00**
Strauss, Jazzbo Jim, w/up, 1920s, 10", G, minimum value **350.00**
Strauss, Leaping Lena Car, w/up, 1930, 8", VG, minimum value **400.00**
Strauss, Wildfire Trotter, w/up, 8½", EX **250.00**
Structo, Cattle Truck #708, pressed steel, red/wht, MIB **225.00**
Structo, Motor Dispatch Tow Truck, pressed steel, bl, 24", VG .**525.00**
Structo, Steam Shovel, b/o, pressed steel, orange, EX **150.00**
Structo, Truck Fleet Set #725, pressed steel, NMIB **550.00**
TN, Dolly Dressmaker, b/o, 10 actions, 1950s, 7", NMIB **200.00**
TN, Grasshopper, w/up, litho tin/plastic, 6", MIB **125.00**
TN, Maxwell Coffee-Loving Bear, b/o, 10", NMIB **250.00**
TN, Pat O'Neill the Fun Lovin' Irishman, b/o, 11", NMIB **600.00**
TN, Shoe Shine Joe w/Lighted Pipe, b/o, 9", M **165.00**
TN, Topo Gigio Xylophone Player, b/o, 1960s, MIB **1,450.00**
Tootsietoy, Army Supply Truck #4634, 1939, M **75.00**
Tootsietoy, Buck Rogers Battle Cruiser #1031, 1937, 5", MIB ...**350.00**
Tootsietoy, Chevy El Camino Camper & Boat, 1962-64, NM ...**100.00**
Tootsietoy, Fire Watertower Truck #4653, 1927-33, NM **95.00**
Tootsietoy, Graham 6-Wheel Sedan #0613, M **150.00**
Tootsietoy, Jumbo Wrecker #1027, 1940s, 6", NM **55.00**
Tootsietoy, Mack Van Trailer #0803, gr/red, 1930s, NM **125.00**
Tootsietoy, Station Wagon #1046, 1940-41, M **75.00**
Tootsietoy, Tow Truck #2485, HO series, 1960s, M **45.00**
Tootsietoy, Wrigley's Box Van #1010, red w/decal, 1940-41, NM ...**100.00**
TPS, Animal's Playland, w/up, litho tin, NMIB **325.00**
TPS, Bear Golfer, w/up, 4½", NMIB, minimum value **225.00**
TPS, Dune Buggy, b/o, tin/plastic, 11", EX+ **100.00**
TPS, Fishing Monkey on Whale, w/up, litho tin, 9", NMIB **375.00**
TPS, Skating Chef, w/up, litho tin w/cloth pants, 7", MIB **350.00**
Unique Art, Capitol Hill Racer, w/up, 1930, 16", MIB **275.00**
Unique Art, GI Joe & His K-9 Pups, w/up, litho tin, 9", NMIB .**250.00**
Unique Art, Krazy Car, w/up, soapbox-type racer, orig box, G ...**700.00**
Wolverine, Drum Major, w/up, litho tin, 1930s, 14", EX **225.00**
Wolverine, Jet Roller Coaster, w/up, 12", NMIB **275.00**
Wolverine, Musical Merry-Go-Round, w/up, 1930s, 13", NM **450.00**
Wolverine, Sunny Andy Kiddie Kampers, w/up, rare, 14", EX ...**350.00**
Wyandotte, Humphrey Mobile, windup, 1950, 9", NM **650.00**
Wyandotte, Red Ranger Ride 'Em Cowboy, w/up, 7", EX **175.00**
Y, Acrobot, b/op, robot does acrobatics, plastic, MIB **525.00**

Y, Bubble Blowing Boy, b/o, litho tin, 7½", MIB 375.00
Y, Hungry Baby Bear, b/o, tin/plush, 10", MIB 275.00
Y, JTY Y53 Racer, w/driver, w/up, red/bl litho tin, 12", EX 600.00

Farm Toys

Farm set, Tootsietoy
#6800, 9-piece, NM
in torn box, $550.00.

Combine, Ertl, John Deere, #5601DA, Collector's Ed, MIB 45.00
Disk harrow, Ertl, 4½" 35.00
Disk harrow, red, Tru Scale, #D405, MIB 50.00
Dump rake, Arcade, McCormick-Deering, 5", G 75.00
Spreader, Arcade, McCormick-Deering, w/oxen, CI, 15", VG ...385.00
Thresher, Arcade, McCormick-Deering, CI w/NP wheels, 9", EX .465.00
Tractor, Advanced Prod, Co-op E3, orange, 7", EX 250.00
Tractor, Arcade, Allis Chalmers, w/hauler, CI, 1930, 8", MIB ...675.00
Tractor, Arcade, Farmall Model M, gr-pnt CI, 5½", VG 200.00
Tractor, Arcade, Fordson, w/hay rake, gr/red-pnt CI, 8½", EX ...475.00
Tractor, Arcade, Oliver 70, red, 7", VG 200.00
Tractor, Ertl, Case L, #252, 150 Year Collector's Ed, MIB 35.00
Tractor, Hubley, Allis Chalmers, w/driver, CI, 1939, 7", EX 320.00
Tractor, International Harvester, red, 5½" 50.00
Tractor, John Deere, gr, 8¼" 85.00
Wagon, Vindex, John Deere, CI, gr/red w/2 horses, rare, 7½" ...1,300.00

Guns: Cast-Iron Cap Guns (Caution: some reproductions exist.)

In years past, virtually every child played with toy guns, and the survival rate of these toys is minimal, at best. The interest in these charming toy guns has recently increased considerably, especially western-styled, as collectors discover their scarcity, quality, and value. Toy gun collectibles encompass the early and the very ornate figural toy guns and bombs though the more realistic ones with recognizable character names, gleaming finishes, faux jewels, dummy bullets, engraving, and colorful grips. This section will cover some of the most popular cast-iron and die-cast toy guns from the past one hundred years.

Our advisor is James Schleyer, internationally recognized collector and appraiser of toy guns. He has authored numerous books, articles, and newsletters on antique toy guns and holsters. He is the former editor for the Toy Gun Purveyors, an international newsletter that fostered the collecting of these valuable and rare toys. His current book Backyard Buckaroos — Collecting Western Toy Guns contains nearly 2,500 photographs. Mr Schleyer's address is listed in the Directory under Virginia. Please include a SASE when requesting information.

American, Kilgore, cylinder revolves, 1940, 8⅜", VG 375.00
Army 45 Auto, Hubley, 1945, 6½", M 145.00
Atta Boy, Hubley, single shot, 1935, 4", G- 50.00
Bango, Stevens, engr/jewels, 1940, 7½", VG 100.00
Big Bill, Kilgore, single shot, 1935, 4⅞", M 65.00
Big Horn, Kilgore, cylinder revolves, 1940, 8⅝", M 500.00
Big Scout, Stevens, single shot, 1930, 9⅜", VG 150.00

Billy the Kid, Stevens, single shot, 1940s, 6¾", G- 120.00
Border Patrol, Kilgore, automatic, 1935, 4½", VG 85.00
Buc-A-Roo, Kilgore, single shot, 1940, 7¾", M 125.00
Buffalo Bill, Kenton, single shot, 1930, 13½", rare, VG 550.00
Buffalo Bill, Stevens, single shot, 1890, 11¾", rare, G- 235.00
Bulldog, Hubley, single shot, 1935, 6", G 35.00
Bunker Hill, National, single shot, 1925, 5¼", M 95.00
Captain, Kilgore, automatic, 1940, 4¼", VG 85.00
Champ, Hubley, automatic, star medallion, 1940, 5", EX 100.00
Chief, Dent, single shot, 1935, 7½", VG 100.00
Colt, Stevens, single shot, 1900, 5½", EX 75.00
Cowboy, Hubley, 1940, 8", VG 120.00
Cowboy King, Stevens, 1940, 9", M 350.00
Dick, Hubley, automatic, 1930, 4⅛", VG 45.00
Doughboy, Kilgore, automatic, 1920, 4⅞", VG 100.00
Eagle, Hubley, single shot, 1935, 8½", VG 155.00
G-Man, Kilgore, automatic, 1935, 6", rare, M 185.00
Gene Autry, Kenton, Dummy, 1940, 8⅜", rare, M 350.00
Gene Autry, Kenton, eng, 1940, 6½", rare, VG 500.00
Gene Autry, Kenton, repeater, nickel, 1940, 8⅜", VG 250.00
Invincible, Kilgore, 1935, 5¼", G- 45.00
Lasso Em Bill, Kilgore, cylinder revolves, 1930, 9", EX 250.00
Lawmaker, Kenton, nickel, 1940, 8⅜", rare, M 300.00
Lone Eagle, Kilgore, cylinder revolves, 1930, 5¼", EX 150.00
Lone Ranger, Kilgore, nickel, 1940, 8¼", rare, M 345.00
Long Boy, Kilgore, single shot, 1920, 11⅛", VG 135.00
Long Tom, Kilgore, cylinder revolves, 1940, 10⅜", rare, M 600.00
Mohican, Dent, single shot, 1930, 6¼", EX 100.00
National Auto, National, 1915, 3¾", G- 25.00
Officers Pistol, Kilgore, automatic, 1940, 5", rare, M 375.00
Pawnee Bill, Stevens, 1940, 7⅝", VG 235.00
Peacemaker, Stevens, gold, 1940, 8½", M 175.00
Pirate, Hubley, dbl bbl, 1940, 8⅜", M 145.00
Presto, Kilgore, automatic, 1940, 5⅛", VG 65.00
Rodeo, Hubley, single shot, 1940, 7", EX 50.00
Roy Rogers, Kilgore, CI, 1940, 10¼", rare, EX 950.00
Scout, Stevens, single shot, 1890, 7", VG 75.00
Six Shooter, Kilgore, cylinder revolves, 1940, 6½", VG 85.00
Spitfire, Kilgore, automatic, 1940, 4⅝", EX 90.00
Texan, Hubley, cylinder revolves, NPCI, 9¼", M 175.00
Texan Jr, Hubley, CI, 1940, 8⅛", VG 85.00
Trooper Safety, Kilgore, repeater, 1925, 10¼", M 145.00
Two Time, Kenton, 1929, rubber band, 9¼", VG 155.00
Warrior, Kilgore, repeater, nickel, 1920s, EX 175.00
Wild West, Kenton, single shot, 1920s, 11½", rare, M 275.00
101 Ranch, Hubley, single shot, 1930, 11½", VG 245.00
2 in 1, Stevens, rubber band, 1930, 9¼", VG 150.00
49-er, Stevens, 1940, 9", M 350.00

Guns: Die-Cast and Miscellaneous Toy Guns

Alan Ladd, Geo Schmidt, 10¼", rare, EX 325.00
Army 45 Auto, Hubley, 6½", M 85.00
Atomic Disintegrator, Hubley, space gun, 8", VG 345.00
Bonanza, Leslie-Henry 44, revolving cylinder, 10½", M 175.00
Bronco, Kilgore, revolving cylinder, 9¼", VG 75.00
Buck'n Bronc, Geo Schmidt, 10½", EX 115.00
Buckle Gun, Mattel, derringer, 3", VG 95.00
Champion, Leslie-Henry, 9", VG 100.00
Colt .45, Hubley, revolving cylinder w/bullets, 14", VG 150.00
Cowboy, Hubley, revolving cylinder, gold, 12", rare, EX 250.00
Cowboy, Hubley, revolving cylinder, 12", M 175.00
Cowhand 250, Nichols, 8½", VG 70.00
Coyote, Hubley, 8¼", M 85.00

Dale Evans, Geo Schmidt, jewels, 10½", rare, VG 350.00
Davy Crockett, Hubley, flintlock buffalo rifle, 25", EX 175.00
Deputy-BB, Schmidt, copper grips, sm, 8½", EX 75.00
Dick Tracy Squad Shotgun, Mattel, cap & water, pump 125.00
Eagle, Kilgore, revolving cylinder, nickel, 8", M 125.00
Fanner Shootin' Shell, Mattel, bullets, 9", M 150.00
Fanner 45 Shootin' Shell, Mattel, 11¼", rare, EX 300.00
Fanner 50, Mattel, nickel, 10⅝", EX 125.00
Flip Rifleman Ring Rifle, Hubley, 32", VG 275.00
G-man, Marx, Sparkling Machine Gun, tin, 26", VG 175.00
Gene Autry, Leslie-Henry, nickel, 9", M 175.00
Gene Autry, Leslie-Henry 44, revolving cylinder/bullets, 11", EX ...165.00
Gray Ghost, Lone Star, nickel, silver grips, 9", rare, EX 300.00
Grizzly, Kilgore, revolving cylinder, gold, 10¼", M 250.00
Hawkeye, Kilgore, automatic, 4¼", M 45.00
Hopalong Cassidy, Geo Schmidt, cameo grips, 9", EX 325.00
Hopalong Cassidy, Wyandotte, gold, 9", M 450.00
Hopalong Cassidy, Wyandotte, nickel, 9", VG 325.00
Indian Scout Rifle, Mattel, bullets, 30", M 210.00
Lone Ranger, Actoy, antique bronze, 10", VG 175.00
Lone Ranger, Marx, tin clicker w/jewel, 8", M 95.00
Maires Leg, Marx, Winchester lever-pistol, 14", EX 135.00
Marshal, Halco, revolving cylinder, bullets, 10½", M 175.00

Maverick, Halco, revolving cylinder w/bullets, rare, $325.00.

Maverick, Leslie-Henry, 10½", VG 130.00
Model 61, Nichols, revolving cylinder, steel-bl finish, rare, M ...325.00
Mountie, Kilgore, automatic, 6", M 50.00
Mustang 500, Nichols, nickel, 12¼", EX 165.00
Paladin, Leslie-Henry, repeater, nickel, 9", rare, EX 235.00
Pioneer, Hubley, blk grips w/compass, 10¼", EX 130.00
Pioneer, Hubley, nickel, amber grips, 10¼", M 125.00
Pony Boy, Esquire-Actoy, nickel, 10", EX 85.00
Rebel Scattergun, Marx, dbl bbl, 21", rare, M 500.00
Red Ranger, Wyandotte, 7¾", VG 45.00
Remington 36, Hubley, revolving cylinder/bullets, 8¾", EX 75.00
Ric-O-Shay, Hubley, revolving cylinder/bullets, 12¼", M 150.00
Roy Rogers, G Schmidt, copper grips, 10¼", EX 225.00
Roy Rogers, Kilgore, die cast, nickel, 8", M 175.00
Roy Rogers, Kilgore, die cast, revolving cylinder, eng, 10", M 385.00
Roy Rogers, Leslie-Henry, gold, 9", EX 350.00
Stallion .32, Nichols, 8", VG 35.00
Stallion 38, Nichols, revolving cylinder/bullets, 9½", EX 115.00
Stallion 45 Mk II, Nichols, revolving cylinder/bullets, 12", M 325.00
Star, Hubley, single shot, nickel, 7", MIB 35.00
Sure Shot, Hubley, nickel, 8", EX 30.00
Texan, Hubley RC, die cast, gold, 9½", M 175.00
Texan, Jr, Hubley, die cast, side opener, 9½", M 70.00
Texan, Jr, Hubley, die cast, 9" VG 50.00
Thundergun, Marx, nickel, eng, 12½", M 225.00
US Marshal, Leslie-Henry RC, antique bronze, 11½", VG 130.00
Wagon Train, Leslie-Henry 44, antique bronze, 11¼", VG 135.00

Wells Fargo, Actoy, nickel, 11", M 155.00
Western, Hubley, nickel, 9", M 70.00
Wild Bill Hickok, Leslie-Henry, 9", VG 125.00
Wild Bill Hickok, Leslie-Henry 44, 11½", EX 165.00
Winchester Carbine, Mattel 26" Shootin' Shell, M 165.00
Winchester Saddle Gun, Mattel, 33", M 185.00
Wyatt Earp, Actoy, Buntline Special, 11", M 155.00
Wyatt Earp, Hubley, nickel, long bbl, 11", M 175.00
2-in-1, Hubley, 2 interchanging bbls, 6", EX 50.00
45 Colt, Hubley, revolving cylinder/ivory grips, nickel, 14", VG ..125.00

Guns: Early-Style Figural Guns and Bombs (Caution: reproductions exist.)

Admiral Dewey Bomb, CI, Grey Iron, 1900, 1¾", EX 300.00
Butting Match, CI, Ives, 1885, 5", EX 475.00
Cannon, Kenton, CI, 1900, 4⅞", VG 450.00
Chinese Must Go, CI, Ives, 1880, 4¾", G- 375.00
Clown on Powder Keg, CI, Ives, 1890s, 3¾", VG 400.00
Devil's Head Bomb, Ives, CI, 1880, 2⅛", EX 275.00
Dog's Head Bomb, Ives, CI, 1880, 2⅛", EX 250.00
Double Face Man, Ives, CI, 1890, 1⅝", VG 145.00
George Washington Bomb, CI, 1900, 1¼", EX 300.00
Hobo Bomb, Ideal, CI, 1890s, 2", G- 125.00
Liberty Bell Bomb, CI, 1876, 2⅜", EX 175.00
Lightening Express, CI, Kenton, 1800, 5", EX 650.00
Punch & Judy, CI, Ives, 1880s, 5¼", VG 750.00
Sea Serpent, CI, Stevens, 1890, 3½", EX 950.00
Yellow Kid Bomb, CI, Grey Iron, 1900, 1½", VG 175.00

Model Kits

Adams, Hawk Missile Batter #154, 1/40, 1958, MIB 75.00
Adams, Thor Rocket #162, 1/87, 1958, MIB 150.00
AMT, Flintstones' Sports Car, 1970s, MIB, sealed 90.00
AMT, Munsters' Coach, orig issue, 1964, NMIB 240.00
AMT, Star Trek Motion Picture Enterprise #970, 1/500, 1979, MIB ..60.00
AMT, 1949 Ford Sedan 2-Door #T149-149, 1/25, MIB 55.00
AMT, 1963 Buick Electra Convertible #06-513-149, 1/25, MIB ..150.00
Aurora, Alfred E Neuman, 1965, MIB, minimum value 300.00
Aurora, Am Astronaut #AMS409, 1/12, 1967, MIB, minimum value ..140.00
Aurora, Chitty-Chitty Bang-Bang, 1968, EXIB 55.00
Aurora, Customizing Monster Kit #1, 1963, MIB 140.00
Aurora, Dracula #424, Monsters of the Movies, 1962, MIB, sealed ...295.00
Aurora, Forgotten Prisoner, glow-in-the-dark, 1969, MIB 300.00
Aurora, Frankenstein, Monster Scenes, MIB, minimum value ...125.00
Aurora, Green Beret, 1966, MIB 85.00
Aurora, Hulk, Comic Scenes, MIB 75.00
Aurora, John F Kennedy #851, 1/8, 1965, EXIB 90.00
Aurora, Pendulum, Monster Scenes, MIB 125.00
Aurora, Rat Patrol, 1967, MIB 100.00
Aurora, Superboy, Comic Scenes, 1974, MIB 70.00
Aurora, Viking Ship #320, 1/80, 1962, MIB 60.00
Bachmann, Animals of the World, Lion #7101, 1/12, 1959, MIB 40.00
Bachmann, Dogs of the World, Wire-Haired Terrier, 1960s, MIB ...25.00
Bandai, Godzilla #0003526, 1/350, MIB 55.00
Bandai, Star-Blazers Space Cruiser #0031253, 1/500, MIB 75.00
Billiken, Creature From the Black Lagoon, MIB 120.00
Billiken, 7th Voyage of Sinbad, Cyclops, 1984, MIB 200.00
Fun Dimensions, Colossal Mantis, MIB 95.00
Fun Dimensions, Space: 1999, Alpha Moonbase, 1976, MIB 75.00
Hawk, Silly Surfers, Hodad Makin' the Scene, 1954, MIB, sealed ..125.00
Hawk, Vanguard Satellite #515, 1/5, 1958, MIB 75.00
Hawk, Weird-Ohs, Drag Hag #536, 1960s, MIB, sealed 150.00

Hawk, Weird-Ohs Customizing Set, 3 in 1, rare, MIB **795.00**
Horizon, Bride of Frankenstein #003, MIB **50.00**
Horizon, Terminator 2, T-800 Terminator #020, 1/5, MIB **55.00**
Lindberg, Satellite w/3-Stage Launching Rocket, 1950s, MIB **130.00**
Lindberg, 13th-Century Clock #339, 1969, MIB **30.00**
Monogram, Firecracker Fire Engine Show Rod, Tom Daniels, NMIB ..**80.00**
Monogram, Li'l Coffin, 1966, MIB **65.00**
Monogram, US Army Eager Beaver 2½-Ton Military Truck, MIB ..**80.00**
MPC, Beverly Hillbillies TV Truck, 1968, NMIB **100.00**
MPC, Hot Rodder Tall T, NMIB **180.00**
MPC, Mannix Roadster #609, 1968, MIB **170.00**
MPC, Welcome Back Kotter, Sweathog Car #641, 1/25, 1976, MIB ...**40.00**
MPC, Yellow Submarine, EXIB **200.00**
Palmer, Animals of the World, Atlantic Sailfish, 1950s, MIB **25.00**
Palmer, Spanish Conquistador #32, 1/5, 1950s, MIB **75.00**
Renwal, Human Skeleton #803, 1950s-60s, MIB **45.00**
Renwal, Visible Horse #807, 1/3, 1960s, MIB **145.00**
Revell, Dr Seuss' Horton the Elephant, 1960, NMIB **170.00**
Revell, Ed 'Big Daddy' Roth, Rat Fink, 1960s, MIB **150.00**
Revell, Gemini Astronaut, 1967, MIB, sealed **70.00**
Revell, Moon Ship #1825, 1/96, 1957, MIB **240.00**
Revell, Perri the Squirrel #1900, Disney, 1/1, 1956, MIB **100.00**
Revell, 1959 Ford Galaxie Skyliner #H-1227, 1/25, MIB **125.00**
Tsukuda, Alien #02, 1/5, 1984, MIB **215.00**
Tsukuda, Batman Returns, Penguin #07, 1/6, 1992, MIB **85.00**

Pedal Cars and Ride-On Toys

BMC Dump Truck, red w/silver-pnt grille & lights, 41", EX **600.00**
British Car, bl/wht, blk rubber tires, 42", G **600.00**
Eureka Racer, sleek bl body, disk wheels, 56", rstr **2,200.00**
Garton Station Wagon, maroon w/bl trim, 47", rstr **935.00**

Gendron 1938 Ford, 2-tone green, professionally restored, 45", $2,450.00.

Keystone Ride-'Em Shovel, VG+ **400.00**
Murray Atomic Missile, plane-type vehicle, 1950s, 44", M **2,500.00**
Murray Buick, bright bl w/chrome trim, 1949, 39", rstr **2,300.00**
Steelcraft Buick Roadster, tan/cream, chrome trim, 46", rstr ...**5,700.00**
Steelcraft Mack Dump Truck, red/blk, 62", rstr **3,300.00**
Toledo Roadster, orange/brn, gr stripes, 46", rstr **1,650.00**

Penny Toys

Airplanes on Rod, spring-activated, Germany, 7", EX **385.00**
Boy & Rabbit in Victorian Rocker, Meier, 3", EX **365.00**
Butting Goat, att George Fischer, 3", EX **525.00**
Carousel Whistle, children on horses, Kicko, 4", EX **300.00**
Charabanc, Henri Avoiron/France, 4", G **440.00**
Dancing Poodle Whistle, EC/France, 4", EX **275.00**
Dog Cart, Germany, 6", VG+ **440.00**

Duck on Wheels, Germany, 3", EX **230.00**
Gas Station & Car, Distler, 4", EX **600.00**
Horse-Drawn Military Cart, Meier, 4½", NM **220.00**
Limousine, KS/Japan, open driver's seat, 3", VG **360.00**
Puppy on 4-Wheeled Platform, Distler, 2½", G **300.00**
Sewing Machine, hand-crank needle, Fischer, 1920s, 3", G **55.00**
Steamship, 3 smokestacks & flag, Distler, 4¾", G **360.00**
Stutz Bearcat, figure in open car, Gesch, 4½", EX **330.00**

Pipsqueaks

Pipsqueak toys were popular among the Pennsylvania Germans. The earliest had bellows made from sheepskin. Later cloth replaced the sheepskin, and finally paper bellows were used.

Bird w/flapping wings, pnt compo/wood, 4", EX **1,200.00**
Chicken, papier-mache, wire legs, mk Germany, nonworking, 5" ...**120.00**
Circus wagon, 3 cages w/animal figures, Germany, silent, 9" **225.00**
Clown on donkey, papier-mache/wood/wire, oval base, 8½", VG ...**545.00**
Girl holding lamb, pnt papier-mache, nonworking, 4½", EX **745.00**
Horse, papier-mache, orig pnt, leather bellows, squeaks, 4¾" **220.00**
Horse in cage, dapple-gray flannel coat, glass eyes, 9", EX **475.00**
Parrot on stump, papier-mache, 4", EX **145.00**
Peacock, pnt papier-mache, nonworking, 5¾" **265.00**

Pull Toys

Clown on pig, bell toy, CI, Gong Bell, 1903, 6½", minumum **900.00**
Cow on platform, cowhide over papier-mache, moos, 11", EX ...**470.00**
Dog cart, HP CI, Wilkins, 6", VG **425.00**
Elephant on platform, bell toy, pnt tin, Fallows, 1880s, 7", EX ...**450.00**
Girl w/rod & paddle on platform, wood/wire figures, 12", EX **700.00**
Horse & rider on platform, pnt tin, Fallows, 1870, 6½", VG **525.00**
Horse-drawn dump cart, pnt tin, Merriam, 1870s, 16", EX **2,600.00**
Rooster & hen on platform, papier-mache, wood platform, 6", G ...**200.00**
St Nicholas in sleigh w/horses, CI w/mc pnt & gold, 16½" **200.00**
Steer on platform, rawhide cover, wood platform, 9", EX **415.00**

Schoenhut

Our advisor for Schoenhut Toys is Keith Kaonis, who has collected these toys for nearly twenty years. Because of his involvement with the publishing industry (currently the Inside Collector, Antique Doll World, and during the '80s, Collectors' Showcase), he has visited collections across the United States, produced several articles on Schoenhut toys, and served a term as president of the Schoenhut Collectors' Club. Keith is listed in the Directory under New York.

The listings below are for Humpty Dumpty Circus pieces. All rating conditions that follow are based on good to very good condition, i.e., very minor scratches and wear, good original finish, no splits, chips, no excessive paint wear or cracked eyes, and of course completeness.

Humpty Dumpty Circus Clowns and Other Personnel

Clowns with two-part heads (a cast face applied to a wooden head) were made from 1903-1915 and are most desirable — condition always is important. There have been nine distinct styles in fourteen different costumes recorded. Only eight costume styles apply to the two-part headed clowns. The later clowns had one-part heads whose features were pressed, and the later ones, ca. 1920, were no longer tied at the wrists and ankles.

Black Dude, reduced sz, from $300 to **600.00**
Black Dude, 1-part head, purple coat, from $250 to **800.00**

Black Dude, 2-part head, blk coat, from $500 to **800.00**
Chinese Acrobat, 1-part head, from $300 to **600.00**
Chinese Acrobat, 2-part head, rare, from $500 to **1,000.00**
Clown, early, G, from $150 to **500.00**
Clown, reduced sz, 1926-35, from $75 to **150.00**
Gent Acrobat, bsk head, rare, from $300 to **600.00**
Gent Acrobat, 2-part head, very rare, from $800 to **1,200.00**
Hobo, reduced sz, from $300 to **600.00**
Hobo, 1-part head, from $200 to **500.00**
Hobo, 2-part head, curved-up toes, from $700 to **1,200.00**
Hobo, 2-part head, facet toe ft, from $400 to **800.00**
Lady Acrobat, bsk head, from $300 to **500.00**
Lady Acrobat, 1-part head, from $200 to **400.00**
Lady Rider, bsk head, from $250 to **500.00**
Lady Rider, 1-part head, from $200 to **400.00**
Lady Rider, 2-part head, very rare, from $700 to **1,200.00**
Lion Trainer, bsk head, rare, from $350 to **600.00**
Lion Trainer, 1-part head, from $250 to **500.00**
Lion Trainer, 2-part head, early, very rare, from $600 to **1,200.00**
Ring Master, bsk, ca 1912-14, from $450 to **650.00**
Ring Master, 1-part head, from $200 to **450.00**
Ring Master, 2-part head, early, very rare, from $500 to **1,200.00**

Humpty Dumpty Circus Animals

Humpty Dumpty Circus animals with glass eyes, ca. 1903-1914, are more desirable and can demand much higher prices than the later painted-eye versions. A general rule is a glass-eye version is 30% to 40% more than a painted-eye version. (There are exceptions.) The following list suggests values for both GE (glass-eye) and PE (painted-eye) versions and reflects a low PE price to a high GE price.

There are other variations and nuances of certain figures: Bulldog — white with black spots or Brindle (brown), open- and closed-mouth zebras and giraffes; ball necks and hemispherical necks on some animals such as the pig, leopard, and tiger to name a few. These points can affect the price and should be judged individually.

Leopard, painted eyes, rope tail, 4¼x7½", VG-, $500.00; Camel, painted eyes, closed mouth, leather ears, cord tail, 6½", G+, $350.00.

Alligator, GE/PE, from $200 to **650.00**
Arabian Camel, 1 hump, GE/PE, from $250 to **750.00**
Bactrian Camel, 2 humps, GE/PE, from $200 to **1,500.00**
Brown Bear, GE/PE, from $200 to **900.00**
Buffalo, cloth mane, EG/PE, from $300 to **700.00**
Buffalo, cvd mane, GE/PE, from $200 to **1,200.00**
Bulldog, GE/PE, from $400 to **1,600.00**
Burro (made to go w/chariot & clown), GE/PE, from $200 to **700.00**
Cat, GE/PE, rare, from $600 to **3,000.00**
Cow, GE/PE, from $250 to **1,000.00**
Deer, GE/PE, from $300 to **1,000.00**
Donkey, GE/PE, from $75 to **200.00**
Donkey w/blanket, GE/PE, from $90 to **300.00**
Elephant, GE/PE, from $90 to **300.00**
Elephant w/blanket, GE/PE, from $200 to **500.00**

Gazelle, GE/PE, rare, from $700 to **3,000.00**
Giraffe, GE/PE, from $200 to **700.00**
Goat, GE/PE, from $150 to **400.00**
Goose, PE only, from $200 to **600.00**
Gorilla, PE only, from $1,200 to **2,500.00**
Hippo, GE/PE, from $300 to **1,000.00**
Horse, brn, saddle & stirrups, GE/PE, from $150 to **400.00**
Horse, wht, platform, GE/PE, from $125 to **400.00**
Hyena, GE/PE, very rare, from $1,000 to **3,700.00**
Kangaroo, GE/PE, from $400 to **1,400.00**
Lion, cloth mane, GE, from $500 to **1,200.00**
Lion, cvd mane, GE/PE, from $250 to **2,000.00**
Monkey, 1-part head, PE only, from $250 to **450.00**
Monkey, 2-part head, wht face, from $300 to **900.00**
Ostrich, GE/PE, from $200 to **850.00**
Pig, 5 versions, GE/PE, from $200 to **900.00**
Polar Bear, GE/PE, from $500 to **1,800.00**
Poodle, cloth mane, GE only, from $300 to **600.00**
Poodle, GE/PE, from $125 to **300.00**
Rabbit, GE/PE, very rare, from $1,000 to **4,000.00**
Rhino, GE/PE, from $250 to **1,200.00**
Sea Lion, GE/PE, from $400 to **1,000.00**
Sheep (lamb) w/bell, GE/PE, from $200 to **750.00**
Tiger, GE/PE, from $250 to **900.00**
Wolf, GE/PE, very rare, from $600 to **4,000.00**
Zebra, GE/PE, from $250 to **1,000.00**
Zebu, GE/PE, rare, from $1,000 to **3,000.00**

Humpty Dumpty Circus Accessories

There are many accessories: wagons, tents, ladders, chairs, pedestals, tight rope, weights, and more.

Menagerie tent, early, ca 1904, from $1,800 to **2,500.00**
Menagerie tent, later, ca 1914-20, from $1,200 to **2,000.00**
Oval lithograph tent, 1926, from $3,000 to **4,000.00**
Side show panels, 1926, pr, from $3,000 to **4,000.00**

Steiff

Margaret Steiff began making her stuffed felt toys in Germany in the late 1800s. The animals she made were tagged with an elephant in a circle. Her first teddy bear, made in 1903, became such a popular seller that she changed her tag to a bear. Felt stuffing was replaced with excelsior and wool; when it became available, foam was used. In addition to the tag, look for the 'Steiff' ribbon and the button inside the ear. For further information we recommend *Teddy Bears and Steiff Animals*, a full-color identification and value guide by Margaret Fox Mandel, available from Collector Books or your public library. See also Teddy Bears.

Boar, plastic tusks, no ID, 1950s, 8", VG **160.00**
Camel, mohair/felt, glass eyes, w/all ID, M **165.00**
Cat, brn/wht stripes, raised button, ribbon w/bell, 5", NM **100.00**
Cat, hand puppet, plush w/glass eyes, 1950s, 8½", EX **75.00**
Chow Dog, raised script button, rare, 4½", EX **375.00**
Cocker Spaniel, blk/wht, w/button & tags, 1950s, 4½", M **150.00**
Dinosaur Stegosauras, mohair/glass eyes, button/tag, 13", minimum ...**1,250.00**
Fawn, resting w/legs fully extended, ear tag, 16", EX **450.00**
German Shepherd, Arco, mohair, w/collar & tag, rare, 4", M **350.00**
Goat, Zicky, standing, w/button, 1950s, 12", EX **265.00**
Hedgehog, Joggi, w/chest tag, 5", M **100.00**
Horse on wheeled base, felt, ear button, 1930s, 15", EX **700.00**
Lady Bug on wheels, mohair, 1950s, no ID, 19", EX **500.00**
Lobster, felt, raised script button & stock tag, 1950s, 4", M **225.00**

Monkey, wht, fully jtd, w/all ID, 1950s, 4", NM, minimum value ...**145.00**
Mouse, Woolie, gray, inscr button & stock tag, 1½", M **45.00**
Orangutan, mk King Louie/Walt Disney, w/tag, 11", EX **375.00**
Pelican, Piccy, wht w/yel bill, chest tag, 6½", M **350.00**
Rabbit, Niki, raised script button & tags, 1950s, 7", M **500.00**
Rabbit, sitting, blond mohair, pk glass eyes, jtd, ca 1913, 12" **800.00**
Rooster, raised script button & chest tag, 6", NM **100.00**
Squirrel, Perri, w/all ID, 1950s, 5", M **100.00**
Squirrel, velvet & mohair, 4", NM **85.00**
Turtle, tan mohair, glass eyes, no ID, 5½", EX **65.00**
Zebra, mohair, incised button, 8", M **175.00**

Trains

Electric trains were produced as early as the late 19th century. Names to look for are Lionel, Ives, and American Flyer. The prices presented are the most common versions of each item. In many cases, there are several other variations often having a substantially higher value. Identification numbers given in the listings below actually appear on the item.

Key: Std Gauge — Standard Gauge

Am Flyer, #21130 Hudson engine w/tender, S gauge, 1959-60, EX ..**160.00**
Am Flyer, #24047 GN Plugdoor boxcar, S gauge, EX **85.00**
Am Flyer, #24191 Canadian Nat'l reefer car, S gauge, 1958, EX ...**230.00**
Am Flyer, #24812 T&P Baldwin locomotive, S gauge, EX **160.00**
Am Flyer, #326 Hudson set, S gauge, 1953-57, 4-pc, EX **360.00**
Am Flyer, #4006 hopper, Std gauge, red, EXIB **450.00**
Am Flyer, #752 Seaboard coal car, S gauge, 1946-50, EX+ **475.00**
Am Flyer, #795 station & terminal, S gauge, 1954, EX+ **400.00**
Am Flyer, #981 Central of Georgia boxcar, S gauge, 1956, EX ...**120.00**
Am Flyer, Century set w/#9915 locomotive, 4-pc, G **850.00**
Am Flyer, Minnie Ha-Ha set, 4-pc, EX **275.00**
Am Flyer, Nation Wide set w/#1093 locomotive, 3-pc, EX+ **575.00**
Am Flyer, Statesman set w/#4654 locomotive, Std gauge, 4-pc, VG ...**300.00**
Am Flyer, Warrior set #6512, Std gauge, 5-pc, EX+ **2,200.00**
Am Flyer, Washington set, S gauge, 5-pc, EX+ **600.00**
Ives, #10 steam engine w/tender, O gauge, 1930, G **75.00**
Ives, #1100 steam engine w/tender, O gauge, 1917-22, EX **175.00**
Ives, #3218 electric engine, O gauge, 1914-16, VG **275.00**
Ives, #3235 electric engine, Wide gauge, 1924-25, EX **200.00**
Ives, #3235 locomotive, Std gauge, 1924-25, G **100.00**
Ives, #64 Canadian Pacific boxcar, gray roof, EX **240.00**
Ives, US engine w/tender, blk/red, disk wheels, 13", EX **2,750.00**
Lionel, #155 freight station, 1930-42, VG+ **550.00**
Lionel, #165 magnetic crane w/controller, 1940-42, EX **525.00**
Lionel, #1800 Deluxe Gen, O27 gauge, 1959-62, complete, NMIB ...**1,200.00**
Lionel, #1912 locomotive, Std gauge, sq cab, 1910-12, EX **250.00**
Lionel, #2023 UP Alco AA engine, O gauge, 1950-51, EXIB **375.00**
Lionel, #214 boxcar, Std gauge, yel/orange, 1926-40, EX+ **350.00**
Lionel, #2322 Virginia FM engine, O gauge, 1965-66, NM **700.00**
Lionel, #2338 Milwaukee Road GP7 engine, O gauge, 1955-56, NM ...**375.00**
Lionel, #300 Hellsgate Bridge, 1928-42, EX+ **1,000.00**
Lionel, #3360 Burro crane car, O gauge, 1956-57, EXIB **325.00**
Lionel, #3494-150 MoPac boxcar, O gauge, 1956, EX **150.00**
Lionel, #3540 radar car, O gauge, 1959-60, NMIB **225.00**
Lionel, #421 WestPhal Pullman Blue Comet, Std gauge, 1936-38, VG ...**800.00**
Lionel, #442 Tempel Blue Comet car, Std gauge, 1930-40, EX ..**800.00**
Lionel, #445 oil derrick, O gauge, gr top, 1950-54, NMIB **250.00**
Lionel, #460 Piggyback Transport, O gauge, 1955-57, NMIB **230.00**
Lionel, #516 coal hopper, brass plates, 1928-40, EX **280.00**
Lionel, #611 Jersey Central NW2 switcher, O gauge, 1957-58, EX **250.00**
Lionel, #624 C&O NW2 switcher, O gauge, 1952-54, VG+ **350.00**

Lionel, #6557 caboose, O gauge, 1958-59, NMIB **240.00**
Lionel, #814 boxcar, O gauge, yel/brn, 1926-42, EX **400.00**
Lionel, Blue Streak set #265, O gauge, 1935-41, 4-pc, EX **725.00**
Lionel, Stephen Girard set, Std gauge, 1931-40, 5-pc, EX **4,000.00**
Marx, #M10000 set, 6-pc, VG **150.00**
Marx, Steam Line w/#M10005 engine, UP on cars, complete, EX **235.00**
Williams, Amtrak Amfleet passenger set, O gauge, 4-pc, MIB ...**210.00**
Williams, Lackawanna 3-Rail Camel-bk engine, O gauge, MIB .**400.00**
Williams, Pennsylvania Shark-nose Baldwin engine, O gauge, M ..**290.00**

Trade Signs

Trade signs were popular during the 1800s. They were usually made in an easily recognizable shape that one could mentally associate with the particular type of business it was to represent, especially appropriate in the days when many customers could not read!

Blacksmith at anvil, flat sheet iron, old black paint, early 1900s, 23x25½", some corrosion, $275.00.

Anchorage, federal shield w/anchor & chain, cvd/pnt, 23x23" ..**500.00**
Buckeye Pilsner Beer, pnt letters on wood, 57x24" **1,200.00**
Hen & eggs & Price of Eggs..., oak w/blk & red, 29x16" **1,650.00**
Indian, cvd/pnt wood, 19th C, 48" **3,100.00**
Indian warrior in canoe, cvd wood, Redmann Lodge, 1920s, 30" ..**2,000.00**
Insurance, Stock Insurance Mutual, pnt tin, 1890s, 13x61" **375.00**
Locksmith, blk letters on yel w/mc borders, 19th C, 84x25" **800.00**
Nightcrawlers, old wooden arrow shape w/red & silver pnt, 38" .**125.00**
Pocketwatch, cast metal, 28x30" dia **350.00**

Tramp Art

'Tramp' is considered a type of folk art. In America it was primarily made from the end of the Civil War through the 1930s though it employs carving and decorating methods which are much older, originating mostly in Germany and Scandinavia. 'Trampen' probably refers to the itinerant stages of Middle Ages craft apprenticeship. The carving techniques were also used for practice. Tramp art was spread by soldiers in the Civil War and primarily practiced where there was a plentiful and free supply of materials such as cigar boxes and fruit crates. The belief that this work was done by tramps and hobos as payment for room or meals is generally incorrect. The larger pieces especially would have required a lengthy stay in one place.

There is a great variety of tramp art, from boxes and frames which are most common to large pieces of furniture and intricate objects. The most common method of decoration is chip carving with several layers built one on top of another. There are several variations of that form as well as others such as 'Crown of Thorns,' an interlocking method, which are completely different. The most common finishes were lacquer or stain, although paints were also used. The value of tramp art varies according to size, detail, surface, and complexity. The new collector should be aware that tramp art is being made today. While some sell it as new, others are offering it as old. In addition, many people mistakenly use the term as a catchall phrase to refer to other forms of construction — expecially things they are uncertain about. Our advisor is Matt Lippa; he is listed in the Directory under Alabama.

Box, appl dbl horseshoes & birds, chip cvd, hinged, 7x10x6", EX ...**240.00**
Box, chip cvd (10-layer), ftd, dk lacquer, 1890s, 14x12x10", VG **475.00**
Box, chip cvd w/glass foil-lined panels w/scrap decor, 13x9x6" ..**225.00**
Box, sewing; chip cvd, dbl ped, 5-drw, 1900s, 18x11x7", EX **800.00**
Cabinet, children's prints in door panels, 12x21x6¾" **55.00**

Photo courtesy Matt Lippa

Combination piece: box with two drawers, two swivel frames and lamp, 1930s, 12x15x5½", $375.00.

Comb case, chip cvd (10 to 15 layers), brn pnt, 1900s, 36x18" ...**1,650.00**
Comb case, chip cvd (5-layer), mc pnt, 130s, 18x12½x5" **425.00**
Dresser, chip cvd (5 to 8 layers), porc pulls, 1900s, 28x12" **400.00**
Frame, simple chipping (8 layers), silver pnt, 1920, 12x13" **275.00**
Mirror, cvd hearts & vines, 1890s, 20¾x17" **750.00**
Mirror frame, simple notched bands, 12x13" **95.00**
Planter, 16-layer ped base, 8-sided (9-layer), 1900, 10x8" **350.00**

Traps

Though of interest to collectors for many years, trap collecting has gained in popularity over the past ten years in particular, causing prices to appreciate rapidly. Traps are usually marked on the pan as to manufacturer, and the condition of these trademarks is important when determining their value. Grading is as follows:

Good: one-half of pan legible.
Very Good: legible in entirety, but light.
Fine: legible in entirety, with strong lettering.
Mint: in like-new, shiny condition.

Our advisor for this category is Boyd Nedry; he is listed in the Directory under Michigan. Prices listed here are for traps in fine condition.

Acme, Shann Mfg Co, wood, mousetrap **20.00**
Alexander Clutch, trap sz B **450.00**
All-Steel #1, long spring **50.00**
Auto-Set, Victor, mousetrap **10.00**
Automatic World's Finest Mouse Trap, metal **20.00**
Beaten Path, metal rat trap **30.00**
Bigelow, Killer **12.00**
Blake-Lamb Co #2 dbl under spring **20.00**
Blake-Lamb Co #2 Milk Pattern 'Fox,' under spring **25.00**
Boyer, Winona, metal, snap mousetrap **10.00**
Cabela's Professional #2, coil spring **10.00**
Champion #1, single long spring **18.00**
Champion #1½ Cush-In-Grip, under spring **35.00**

Chasse, wood, 3-hole mousetrap **35.00**
Cinch mole trap **15.00**
Clincher #0, single long spring **85.00**
Cyclone, metal mousetrap **35.00**
Dauffer Killer **25.00**
Dearborne #3, dbl long spring **200.00**
Delusion Mouse Trap, self-setting **45.00**
Diamond #15, dbl under spring **65.00**
Diamond #51 Walloper, coil spring **45.00**
Dodd Safe-T-Set, wood, snap mousetrap **35.00**
Economy #1, single long spring **25.00**
Ejector, wood, mousetrap **15.00**
Eldgin, metal, mousetrap **20.00**
End-O-Mice, mousetrap **22.00**
Erie Rat Trap, wood **10.00**
Fairy Mouse Trap, w/exercise wheel **85.00**
Fatal Self Setting, tin & wood, mousetrap **125.00**
Gabriel, fish & game trap **90.00**
Gibbs, hawk trap **225.00**
Gibbs 'King Bee' #0 ....**65.00**
Gibbs Dope Trap #4 ....**450.00**
Halfmoon, metal, mousetrap **50.00**
Handforged #6, bear trap **550.00**
Herters #0, single long spring **70.00**
Herters #1 Stop Loss **75.00**
Hold Fast, wood, rat trap **6.00**
Hotchkiss #2, dbl long spring **80.00**
Ideal, claw type, gopher trap **85.00**
Ideal, scissors, mole trap **22.00**
Jackfrost Killer **25.00**
Ketchem Tile Trap #2 ....**35.00**
Kitty-Got-Cha, plastic, mousetrap **50.00**
Kleflock Killer **35.00**
Kompakt #0, under spring **35.00**
Kopper Kat, metal, mousetrap **22.00**
Lightning W-1290, wood, mousetrap **14.00**
Lines Trap Setter **30.00**
Little Champ, plastic, mousetrap **20.00**
Little Giant, fly trap **30.00**
Lohmar #3 ....**20.00**
McGill, metal, self-setter **8.00**
McGill Can't Miss, wood, mousetrap **6.00**
Montgomery #1½, coil spring **7.00**
Montgomery Digger, coil spring **125.00**
Newhouse #0, single long spring **65.00**
Newhouse #2½, single long spring **65.00**
Newhouse #50, bear trap **350.00**
Newhouse #81, single long spring **65.00**
NKAPS #1½, coil **10.00**
Northwoods, metal, mousetrap **3.00**
Northwoods #2, dbl coil spring **10.00**
Old Tom, fits on fruit jar, mousetrap **25.00**
Olmsteads, CI, mole trap **35.00**
Orvis, glass, minnow trap **90.00**
Perfection, metal, mousetrap **20.00**
Prott #1/4, single long spring **35.00**
PS Mfg Co #2, dbl long spring **50.00**
PS&W #1, single long spring **20.00**
PS&W Good Luck #1, single long spring **95.00**
PS&W Hector #2, dbl long spring **50.00**
Quigley Van Camp Hardware, wood, snap mousetrap **22.00**
Roy, gopher trap **18.00**
Sabo Den Trap **90.00**
Sargent #0, cast pan, single long spring **45.00**

Sargent #62, dbl under spring 150.00
Sav-A-Leg #210 ....60.00
Shene #2, coil spring 40.00
Star Mfg Co, Dina, Indiana, metal, snap mousetrap 20.00
Stopthief #1 Killer 30.00
Taylor Special #1½, single long spring 12.00
Tepee Runway, mousetrap 25.00
Trailzend #9, dbl long spring 700.00
Triumph #0, single long spring 20.00
Triumph #115X, single long spring 15.00
U-Neek, glass, mousetrap 85.00
Union Hardware #1, single long spring 45.00
Unique, plastic, coon trap 20.00
Verbail, chain trap 85.00
Victor #0, dogless, cast pan 80.00
Victor #33 Stop Loss, single long spring 20.00
Victor Easy Set, mousetrap 8.00
WA Reddick Mole Trap, Niles, Mich, Pat Aug 7, 1894 ......20.00
Webley #1½, single long spring 25.00
Winona, metal, mousetrap 10.00
Wire Cage, dome shape, rat trap 30.00
Woodward Death Clamp, 4" sz 40.00
X-Terminator, plastic, live mousetrap 6.00
ZIP, Sears RoeBuck Co, metal, snap mousetrap 15.00

Trenton

Trenton, New Jersey, was an area that supported several pottery companies from the mid-1800s until the late 1960s. A consolidation of several smaller companies that occured in the 1890s was called Trenton Potteries Company. Each company produced their own types of wares independent of the others.

Urn, wht, hdls, ped base, partial label, 8x7" 60.00
Vase, ivory, 2 long hdls, 7½x4½" 50.00
Vase, sea gr horn shape, 6x7½" 45.00
Vase, yel w/V-shaped top, flared/pointed sides, label, 6x6¼" 40.00

Trivets

Although strictly a decorative item today, the original purpose of the trivet was much more practical. They were used to protect table tops from hot serving dishes, and irons heated on the kitchen range were placed on trivets during use to protect work surfaces. The first patent date was 1869; many of the earliest trivets bore portraits of famous people or patriotic designs. Florals, birds, animals, and fruit were other favored motifs. Watch for remakes of early original designs. Some of these are marked Wilton, Emig, Wright, Iron Art, and V.M. for Virginia Metal-crafters. However, many of these reproductions are becoming collectible in the '90s. Expect to pay considerably less for these than for the originals, since they are abundant.

Brass

Cut-out heart designs, 3-ftd, 12" L 50.00
Flatiron shape, open center, 10x3¼" 110.00
Hearts & dmns cutouts, 9" 40.00
Horse in center, 3-leg fireplace type, 3½x6" dia 90.00
Horseshoe w/1888 in center, w/hdl 90.00
Repousse w/hand-stippled ground, Arts & Crafts era, 7" sq 80.00
Rtcl design, stamped flowers & 1849, blk wooden hdl, 11¼" 165.00
6-pointed star in hexagon, 3-ftd, 8½" 85.00

Cast Iron

Butterfly, 9½" 80.00
Cathedral pattern, 3¾x1⅝" 18.00
Floral scrolls, blk rpt, 10" 95.00

Good Luck to All Who Use This Stand, 8", $38.00; Sensible, 6", $35.00.

Lyre, 7¼" 40.00
Open star & fan, Cleveland Foundry, for flatiron 28.00
Star & braid, buffed, 8" 75.00
Star in circle w/in flatiron shape, 8¼" 40.00
Strauss Comfort Gas Iron, ornate w/legs, lg 30.00
Tulip, mk SB Miller, 8" 50.00
Uneedit, ornate, 7" 48.00

Wrought Iron

Circular w/twisted & tooled details, folding spit rest, 18" L 250.00
Dbl heart, shoe ft, blk pnt, 4½" 175.00
Foot shape, 4-ftd, 1700s, 3½x9x6" 85.00
Heart shape, long hdl, & penny ft, 10" L 350.00
Rope twist open quatrefoil, matching legs, shoe ft, 4½" 95.00
Round, 3 penny ft, 2¼x4½" dia 65.00
Simple spade shape w/curved hdl, general use, 1800s, 10" L 175.00
Triangular, high legs w/paw-like ft, 9" 50.00

Trolls

The first trolls to come to the United States were molded after a 1952 design by Marti and Helena Kuuskoski of Tampere, Finland. The first trolls to be mass produced in America were molded from wood carvings made by Thomas Dam of Denmark. As the demand for these trolls increased, several U.S. manufacturers were licensed to produce them. The most noteworthy of these were Uneeda Doll Company's Wishnik line and Inga Dykin's Scandia House True Trolls. Thomas Dam continued to import his Dam Things line. Today trolls are enjoying a renaissance as baby boomers try to recapture their childhood. As a result, values are rising.

The troll craze from the '60s spawned many items other than troll dolls such as wall plaques, salt and pepper shakers, pins, squirt guns, rings, clay trolls, lamps, Halloween costumes, animals, lawn ornaments, coat racks, notebooks, folders, and even a car.

In the '70s, '80s, and '90s new trolls were produced. While these trolls are collectible to some, the avid troll collector still prefers those produced in the '60s. Remember, trolls must be in mint condition to receive top dollar. For more information we recommend *Collector's Guide to Trolls, ID and Values*, by Pat Peterson. Our advisor for this category is Roger Inouye; he is listed in the Directory under California.

Ballerina, red mohair, gr eyes, orig outfit, MIP 55.00
Bank, mouse, Norfin, MIP 60.00
Batman, no hood, normal-sz eyes, Wishnik, 5", VG 15.00
Bijou Neanderthal, orig leopard clothes, 8" 28.00
Bride & Groom, dk bl mohair, Wishnik, 5", pr 35.00

Cheerleader, vinyl body, plastic eyes, Dam, 1964, 2½" **18.00**
Clown, pnt clothes, yel eyes/red nose, Dam, 1965, from $175 to ...**250.00**
Common, 10" **50.00**
Common, 12" **60.00**
Common, 15", minimum **80.00**
Common, 2½-3", minimum **15.00**
Common, 4", from $20 to **25.00**
Common, 7", from $30 to **40.00**
Cookie cutter, Mills, rare, 3½" **50.00**
Donkey, wht hair on mane/tail, amber eyes, Dam, 9" **50.00**
Elephant, hollow bl plastic, Japan, 1960s, 3" **25.00**
Elephant, wrinkled flesh-tone skin, orange hair, Dam, 1964, 6" .**175.00**
German character, nodder, gray body, inset eyes, paper sticker **60.00**
Giraffe, hollow body, posable head, Japan, 1960s **25.00**
Graduate, peach hair, orange spiral eyes, Wishnik, 5", NM **25.00**
Here Comes the Judge, wht hair, amber eyes, Wishnik, 5" **20.00**
Horse, solid body w/long mane & tail, felt saddle, Dam, 1964 .....**48.00**
Hula girl, flowers in hair, burgundy skirt, Wishnik, 5" **40.00**
Indian, orig headband, outfit & shoes, 1960s, 3½" **15.00**
Judge, gray hair, orange eyes, Uneeda Wishnik, 5½" **30.00**
Kool-Aid Troll, pk hair, 5" **15.00**
Lamp, Wishnik, rare, complete, 18" **250.00**
Leprechaun, w/jacket, 1969 ....**25.00**
Moonitik, mohair body, shake eyes, Uneeda Wishnik, rare, 18" ...**100.00**
Neanderthal Man, pnt eyes, Bijou Toy, 1963, 7½" **32.00**
Pencil topper, astronaut troll, Scandia House Ent, 1½", MIP **45.00**
Sailor, lt aqua hair, Wishnik, 3" **10.00**
Seal, brn body, wht chest, dk amber eyes, Norfin, 6½" **50.00**
She Nik, long wht mohair, yel eyes, S on dress, Wishnik, 5" **15.00**
Thumb sucker, long wht mohair, purple felt dress, Norfin, 18" **88.00**
Troll House, pnt wood, unmk, rare, 9x5½" **85.00**
Troll Village, Marx, MIB **300.00**
Turtle, Dam Things, 1964, 6" **250.00**
Viking, wht mohair, brn eyes, bl dress, Dam, from $150 to **200.00**
Voodoo doll, blk plastic, cloth outfit, wht hair/ruby eyes, '60s **15.00**
Werewolf Monster, 1960s, 3" **40.00**

Trunks

The first use of the term 'trunk' can be traced back to Egyptian times, when hollowed-out tree sections were used to transport goods of commerce. In the the days of steamboat voyages, stagecoach journeys, and railroad travel, trunks were used to transport clothing and personal belongings.

The most desirable trunks are flat-tops, 24" to 38" long, from the late 1800s, preferably in restored condition. Embossed dome-tops (rounded on top to better accommodate milady's finery) from the 1880s, 24" to 38" long, in complete original condition are very desirable as well. On the other hand, ca 1870s flush tin trunks, even in mint condition, inspire very little collector interest.

Unless the trunk is complete (retaining all original trays and compartments), its value is considerably lessened. If parts are absent or broken, the trunk is judged incomplete. All interiors differ; some had upper-lid compartments, others did not. Our advisor is Doris Harroff; she is listed in the Directory under Indiana.

Dome top, top and front painted with multicolor flowers on black, complete, mid-1800s, 12x27x14", $2,000.00.

Dome-top, emb decor, 1880s, 24" to 38", complete, from $75 to ..**175.00**
Flat-top, orig, 1880-1900, 24" to 38", complete, from $75 to **125.00**
Flat-top, orig, 1880-1900, 24" to 38", complete, rstr, $300 to **425.00**
Leather trim w/brass tacks on pine, 19x10x9" **110.00**
Stagecoach, flat or dome, pre-1860s, 24" to 38", rstr, up to **475.00**

Tuthill

The Tuthill Glass Company operated in Middletown, New York, from 1902 to 1923. Collectors look for signed pieces and those in an identifiable pattern. Condition is of utmost importance, and examples with brilliant cutting and intaglio (natural flowers and fruits) combined fetch the highest prices.

Bonbon, notching, eng flowers/leaves, star center, 8-sided **90.00**
Bowl, Primrose, cut, 4¼x9½" **950.00**
Bowl, vintage intaglio w/in hobnail gallery, oval, 9¾" **575.00**
Nappy, vintage cutting, blown blank, hdls, 5" **225.00**
Vase, bud; floral cuttings allover, flower cut into pontil, 8" **160.00**
Vase, intaglio, 3 fruits/geometrics, waisted, 3-ftd, 12½" **600.00**

Typewriters

The first commercially successful typewriter was the Sholes and Glidden, introduced in 1874. By 1882 other models appeared, and by the 1890s dozens were on the market. At the time of the First World War, the ranks of typewriter-makers thinned, and by the 1920s only a few survived.

Collectors informally divide typewriter history into the pioneering period, up to about 1890; the classic period, from 1890 to 1920; and the modern period, since 1920. There are two broad classifications of early typewriters: (1) Keyboard machines, in which depression of a key prints a character and via a shift key prints up to three different characters per key; (2) Index machines, in which a chart of all the characters appears on the typewriter; the character is selected by a pointer or dial and is printed by operation of a lever or other device. Even though index typewriters were simpler and more primitive than keyboard machines, they were none-the-less a later development, designed to provide a cheaper alternative to the standard keyboard models that were selling for upwards of $100.00. Eventually second-hand keyboard typewriters supplied the low-price customer, and index typewriters vanished except as toys. Both classes of typewriters appeared in a great many designs.

It is difficult, if not impossible, to assign standard market prices to early typewriters. Unlike postage stamps, carnival glass, etc., few people collect typewriters, so there is no active market place from which to draw stable prices. Also, condition is a very important factor, and typewriters can vary infinitely in condition. A third factor to consider is that an early typewriter achieves its value mainly through the skill, effort, and patience of the collector who restores it to its original condition, in which case its purchase price is insignificant. Some unusual-looking early typewriters are not at all rare or valuable, while some very ordinary-looking ones are scarce and could be quite valuable. No general rules apply. When no condition is indicated, the items listed below are assumed to be in excellent, unrestored condition. Our advisor for this category is Mike Brooks; he is listed in the Directory under California.

American, indicator type, M **85.00**
Automatic **1,000.00**
Bing #2, 1926, EX **135.00**
Blinkensderfer #5, EX **110.00**
Blinkensderfer Electric **7,000.00**
Boston, index **13,000.00**

Brooks	1,000.00
Caligraph	175.00
Coffman, index	175.00
Columbia, index	1,500.00
Crandall	1,000.00
Dollar, toy, index	1,200.00
Edison, index	1,000.00
Edland, index, pot metal	750.00
Fitch	1,000.00
Franklin	350.00
Geniatus Indicator	250.00
Hall, index	250.00
Hammond #12	75.00
Hammonia, German index	4,000.00
Jackson	2,500.00
Lasar	2,000.00
Manhattan	250.00
McCool	1,500.00
Molle	75.00
MW Indicator	125.00
National	1,200.00
Niagara, index	3,500.00
O'Dell #4, orig box	275.00
Oliver #5 Standard Visible Writer, old upright keys, M	85.00
Peoples, index	250.00
Practical #4, oak base	110.00
Rapid, minimum value	5,000.00
Remington-Rand #5, portable	35.00
Royal #10, 1922, EX	50.00
Salter #5	800.00
Sholes & Glidden, w/decor	2,500.00
Smith Corona, folding	45.00
Sun, index	600.00
Travis	1,200.00
Underwood Standard, gr, portable, in orig case, EX	45.00
Victor, index	700.00

Ungemach Pottery Company

Fred Ungemach began his career as a boy, jiggering for the Nelson McCoy Pottery of Roseville, Ohio. Later he worked for Thomas Watt in Hawthorne, Pennsylvania; then he returned to Roseville to work for the Ransbottom Pottery. In 1938 with the help of his daughter Mary who was an employee of the Brush Pottery, he opened his own company in Roseville. The business was first known as the South Fork Pottery, but after several years and a number of expansions, the name was changed to the Ungemach Pottery Company (UPCO).

In June 1950 a flood demolished the plant, but it reopened in three weeks and continued to expand. In April 1966 the plant was struck by lightning and destroyed again, but by September of the same year they were back in production. Then in 1984 the pottery was sold to Friendship Pottery of Roseville, Ohio.

Ungemach produced a full line of wares including kitchen items, planters, vases, and novelty pieces. During the 1940s and '50s they obtained an exclusive contract with Walt Disney Productions, Burbank, California, to produce Disney character planters. These pieces were marked with Disney copyrights only. Their other production pieces are marked in a variety of ways — 'Ungemach, UPCO, Roseville.' A few are not marked at all. Our advisors for this category are Brenda and Jerry Siegel; they are listed in the Directory under Missouri.

Bowl, fluted, rnd, brn, #762	7.00

Bowl, fruit; yel, #779, 7"	8.00
Bread server, brn, mk Roseville, #630, 10"	8.00
Bread server, rust & brn, oval, #797	9.00
Candy server, bl, 10"	11.00
Lamp, snowman's head, blk, red & gr pnt, no mk, 8½"	24.00

Planter, floral relief on sides, dark green glaze, pedestal base, marked Ungemach-USA-UPCO, 5¼", $12.00.

Planter, bonsai, wht, #289, 9x6x3½"	10.00
Planter, cactus, yel, 8"	8.00
Planter, chalice, brn, mk Flora Plant UPCO, rare, 8"	16.00
Planter, fluted star, tan, 5"	6.00
Planter, hand thrown, gr, #489, 8"	9.00
Planter, octagonal, tan, #755	6.00
Planter, rnd, tan, 6½"	4.00
Planter, rnd, wht, #610, 4½"	4.00
Strawberry pot, gr, 4"	6.00

Unger Brothers

Art Nouveau silver items of the highest quality were produced by Unger Brothers, who operated in Newark, New Jersey, from the early 1880s until 1909. In addition to tableware, they also made brushes, mirrors, powder boxes, and the like for milady's dressing table as well as jewelry and small personal accessories such as match safes and flasks. They often marked their products with a circle seal containing an intertwined 'UB' and '925 fine sterling.' In addition to sterling, a very limited amount of gold was also used. Note: This company made no pewter items; Unger designs may occasionally be found in pewter, but these are copies. Items dated in the mark or signed 'Birmingham' are English (not Unger).

Ashtray, man-in-moon, Nouveau lady formed by pipe smoke	525.00
Ashtray, smoking lady	395.00
Cuff links, lady figural, pr	195.00
Doll mirror, cherubs, mini	350.00
Flask, knight's head	795.00
Match safe, Nouveau-style decor	275.00
Pin, gargoyle, gold wash w/ruby eyes	365.00
Spoons, lady's head & children's heads, pr	150.00
Thimble case, walnut figural, chatelaine loop, unlined, 1"	265.00
Vanity set, He Loves Me, mirror+2 brushes+jar w/cut lid, 1904	1,300.00

Universal

Universal Potteries Incorporated operated in Cambridge, Ohio, from 1934 to 1956. Many lines of dinnerware and kitchen items were produced in both earthenware and semiporcelain. In 1956 the emphasis was shifted to the manufacture of floor and wall tiles, and the name was changed to the Oxford Tile Company, Division of Universal Potteries.

The plant closed in 1976. Our advisor for this category is Ted Haun; he is listed in the Directory under Indiana.

Ballerina, bowl, cereal	5.00
Ballerina, bowl, soup	6.00
Ballerina, chop plate	15.00
Ballerina, creamer & sguar bowl	20.00
Ballerina, cup & saucer, demitasse	20.00
Ballerina, egg cup	12.00
Ballerina, gravy boat	12.00
Ballerina, shakers, pr	12.00
Bittersweet, cup & saucer	14.00
Bittersweet, plate, salad; 7"	12.00
Bittersweet, platter, oval, 13½"	28.00
Calico Fruit, bowl, mixing; w/lid, 8¾"	47.00
Calico Fruit, bowl, utility; w/lid, 5"	35.00
Calico Fruit, creamer	11.00
Calico Fruit, cup	8.00
Calico Fruit, jug, w/lid	47.50
Calico Fruit, refrigerator jug, w/lid	35.00
Calico Fruit, shakers, pr	20.00
Calico Fruit, utility shaker	12.00
Cattail, bowl, berry; 5¼"	4.00
Cattail, bowl, mixing; 6"	15.00
Cattail, bowl, soup; 7¾"	7.00
Cattail, bowl, 6¼"	7.00
Cattail, cake lifter	12.00
Cattail, casserole, made for Sears, w/lid, 8½"	30.00
Cattail, cookie jar	75.00
Cattail, cup & saucer	10.00
Cattail, pie baker, 10"	25.00
Cattail, pie server	25.00
Cattail, scales, metal	37.00
Cattail, teapot	35.00
Woodvine, bowl, berry; 5¼"	8.00
Woodvine, bowl, mixing; 4"	19.00
Woodvine, bowl, mixing; 7½"	22.00
Woodvine, pitcher, milk; 6½"	35.00
Woodvine, sugar bowl, w/lid	18.00
Zinnias, casserole	13.00

Val St. Lambert

Since its inception in Belgium at the turn of the 19th century, the Val St. Lambert Cristalleries has been involved in the production of high-quality glass, producing some cameo. The factory is still in production. Our advisor for this category is Don Williams; he is listed in the Directory under Missouri.

Bowl, ruby cut to clear, repeated bull's eyes & bars, 5½x12"	300.00
Bowl, violets w/gold on textured green, ruffled rim, 5" H	225.00
Vase, clear w/int purple layer & agate trailings, 10½"	400.00
Vase, fishing scene, dk/lt bl on frost, sgn, 7¾"	1,200.00
Vase, flowering trees (3 repeats), ruby/clear, 7"	575.00

Valentines

Handmade valentines date back to the mid-1700s in the United States; as time went on, increased interest resulted in other types of valentine cards being made. Today valentine collectors are not the only ones who buy; valentines are often considered a desirable addition to other collections as well — Black memorabilia, advertising, trans- portation memorabilia, Walt Disney, cartoon and movie characters, etc. Besides examples representing these areas, three-dimensionals and mechanical valentines (1860s to the present) are becoming highly prized by many collectors. One category of valentines to collect are the Penny Dreadfuls. They can date from the 1800s. They reflected every facet of life, occupation, and often poked fun at someone's looks. These were usually done with a wood block and originally hand colored. As with all categories of valentines the Penny Dreadfuls can fit into anyone's collection. Please remember there are six qualifying specifications to consider when evaluating a valentine card: age, size, category, manufacturer, artist signature, and condition. Our advisor for this category is Katherine Kreider; she is listed in the Directory under California and Pennsylvania.

Key:
AS — artist signed   HCPP — honeycomb paper puff

Babe Ruth, caricature, 1940s, 4x3", VG	5.00
Bershire Stocking ad for Valentine's Day, AS, 8x10", NM	40.00
Big-eyed children, dimensional, w/rabbit pull toy, 6x8"	35.00
Big-eyed children in cart pulled by dogs, 10x6", VG	10.00
Big-eyed children talking on phone, HCPP, 10x6", EX	35.00
Black child, Dobbs, Kidd & Co, 1850s, 6x5", EX	175.00
Black messenger, Tuck, early 1900s, 9x5", EX	75.00
Boston Bull, flat, 9x5", NM	57.00
Civil War tent draped in Am flag, 1800s, 7x5", EX	350.00
Cobweb, all orig, 1840s, EX	250.00
Collie dog w/orig chain to doghouse, MIG, 6x5", EX	40.00
Comic, Flappers, 1920s, 5x6", EX, set of 24	50.00
Comic, Jimmy Durante, flat, 1930s, 8x10", EX	20.00
Commic, occupational, flat, USA, 1930s, 9x6", VG	15.00
Daguerreotype valentine, England, 1800s, 4x3", EX	50.00
Dimensional, airplane, crepe-paper wings, MIG, 14x6"	175.00
Dimensional, harp, easel bk, early 1900s, 7x5", EX	40.00
Dimensional, Pug, MIG, 5x3x3", EX	45.00
Dimensional, rowboat w/cherubs, MIG, 6x5x1", EX	50.00
Flat, child carrying box of hearts, easel bk, MIG	25.00
Flat, Golliwog, MIG, 1930s, 3x3", NM	20.00
Flat, Little Bo Peep, easel bk, 6x4", EX	10.00
Flat, Troll, USA, 1960s, 5x5", EX	15.00
Greeting card style, Victorian children, 1800s, EX	25.00
Hall Bros, dog w/felt ears, 1940s, 8x6", EX	15.00
Manuscript valentine, hand colored, 1840s, EX	75.00
Mechanical-flat, children at photo center, 1930s, 8x6", EX	30.00
Mechanical-flat, children skiing, MIG, 9x9", NM	35.00
Mechanical-flat, Humpty Dumpty, USA, 5x4", VG	5.00
Mechanical-flat, Jack Horner, Katz, 1929, 6x3", EX	10.00
Mechanical-flat, Jimmy Durante, 1930s, 8x4", NM	25.00
Mechanical-flat, Movie Director, 7x4", EX	10.00
Mechanical-flat, World, Tuck, early 1900s, 5x5", EX	10.00
Mechanical-flat novelty, scissors, 5x4", EX	15.00
Nister, hanging, nautical theme, AS, 9x10", EX	75.00
Novelty, dancing couple w/arm on spring, AS, 5x7", VG	10.00
Novelty, pig finger-puppet card, 6x3", NM	10.00
Paper doll, Cowboy, Ameri-card, 1950s, 5x5", NM	15.00
Penny Dreadful, Ugly, Fat & 40, 1900s, VG	15.00
Valentine sachet, England, late 1800s, 4x3", EX	50.00
Violin, celluloid, all orig, early 1900s, 6x4", VG	40.00
3-D grandfather clock, 1905, 5x6x3", EX	40.00

Van Briggle

The Van Briggle Pottery of Colorado Springs, Colorado, was

established in 1901 by Artus Van Briggle, whose early career had been shaped by such notables as Karl Langenbeck and Maria Nichols Storer. His quest for several years had been to perfect a completely flat matt glaze, and upon accomplishing his goal, he opened his pottery. His wife, Anne, worked with him, and they, along with George Young, were responsible for the modeling of the wares. Their work typified the flow and form of the Art Nouveau movement, and the shapes they designed played as important a part in their success as their glazes. Some of their most famous pieces were Despondency, Lorelei, and Toast Cup. Increasing demand for their work soon made it necessary to add to their quarters as well as their staff. Although much of the ware was eventually made from molds, each piece was carefully trimmed and refined before the glaze was sprayed on. Their most popular colors were Persian Rose, Ming Blue, and Mustard Yellow.

Van Briggle died in 1904, but the work was continued by his wife. New facilities were built; and by 1908, in addition to their art-ware, tiles, gardenware, and commercial lines were added. By the '20s the emphasis had shifted from art pottery to novelties and commercial wares. As late as 1970, reproductions of some of the early designs continued to be made. Until about 1920 most pieces were marked with the date and shape number; after that the AA mark was used.

Bookends, owl, bl on aqua matt, 5½", pr **180.00**
Bookends, pug dog, mulberry, pr **175.00**
Bowl, flowers cvd at shoulder, burgundy w/wht froth, 1907, 6" ..**400.00**
Bowl, Lady of Lake at side, bl on aqua, w/frog, 10½x16" **375.00**
Bowl, mermaid at side, bl & violet matt, w/frog, 9x13", NM **600.00**
Bowl, stylized leaves at shoulder, dk bl & violet matt, 5½" **210.00**
Bowl vase, dragonfly, 2-tone bl, 1920-30s, 3" **275.00**
Creamer, stylized geometrics, dk bl on burgundy matt, 4" **140.00**
Figurine, donkey, violet matt, 3½" **100.00**
Figurine, Hopi maiden grinds corn, bl on dk rose matt, 5½x7" ..**210.00**
Figurine, panther, seated, bl-gr matt, mk, 10½" **90.00**
Figurine, rabbit, dk gr on chocolate matt, 2½" **150.00**
Figurine, rabbit, dk red w/bl matt, 2½" **130.00**
Lamp, draped lady w/urn by tree, wht matt, pottery: 16½" **180.00**
Night light, owl figural, mulberry, all orig **400.00**
Pitcher, bell/Mission Inn emb, brn over mustard, 1941, 8½" **270.00**
Pitcher, thick pk matt, rnd form, #433, ca 1905, 4½" **180.00**
Shakers, penguins, bl on aqua matt, 4", pr **200.00**
Tile, clouds/trees on hillside, 5-color, 6", +oak fr **1,700.00**
Tile, landscape, 4-color, mk VBPC, #B115, 6x6" **865.00**
Vase, arrowhead leaves & stems, curdled gr, 1905, 9x4½" **1,900.00**
Vase, Arts & Crafts motif, gr, #915/187, 1915, 2" **130.00**
Vase, cranes, wht w/bl highlights, AA, #84, 16¾x8" **260.00**
Vase, daffodils/swirling stems, bl/maroon, 1940s, 9" **375.00**
Vase, daffodils/swirling stems, brn/gr, 1920, 9½" **650.00**
Vase, dandelion panels cvd in lower half, med gr, 1906, 9x7" .**1,200.00**
Vase, flamingos, bl & gr matt, paper label, 21½" **325.00**
Vase, floral, mottled gr matt, mk AA, #800, 9½x5½" **1,095.00**
Vase, floral, Persian rose w/dk bl, 1920, 17x8" **450.00**
Vase, floral (swirling), turq/med bl, ca 1930, 10" **375.00**
Vase, floral at swollen neck, long leaves, gr matt, 1930s, 6" **170.00**
Vase, floral emb at collar, charcoal gr, #696, 1907-12, 5" **425.00**
Vase, floral stems/draped rim, rose/bl, hdls/ftd, 1920s, 12" **375.00**
Vase, geometrics, deep wine w/dk bl highlights, 1920s, 4" **200.00**
Vase, Indian faces (3 in relief), dk rose/bl matt, 12" **415.00**
Vase, irises/leaves, bl-gray over rose, 1920, 14x8" **600.00**
Vase, Lady of Lily, bl on aqua matt, 14½x12" **500.00**
Vase, leaves at base, brn w/olive, cylinder neck, 1914, 11" **1,100.00**
Vase, lime/tan mottle, shouldered, #343, 1904-06, 4½" **240.00**
Vase, Lorelei, bl/maroon, 1930s, 10" **425.00**
Vase, Lorelei, mermaid wrapped around rim, rose & dk bl, 10" ..**550.00**

Vase, morning glories w/long stems, rose w/bl, 1919, 12" **1,500.00**
Vase, plain, lt bl matt, #306, 1905, 2⅞x4¾" **260.00**
Vase, poppies/whiplash stems, med bl/lt bl, post-1940, 9½" **180.00**
Vase, spade leaves & tall thin leaves, purple, #1903, 4½" **1,200.00**
Vase, stylized stems, powder wht matt w/exposed clay, 7x3¾" ...**700.00**
Vase, sunflowers at rim, leaves below, bl/aqua, 1920, 9x8" **1,000.00**
Vase, tulips on long stems, mint over aqua, 1907-12, 12" **1,100.00**
Vase, vertical design under pk to gr wax-matt, #687, 3x2¾" **175.00**
Vase, yucca leaves, vivid med bl matt, 1920s, 4½" **280.00**

Vance Avon

Although pottery had been made in Tiltonville, Ohio, since about 1880, the ware manufactured there was of little significance until after the turn of the century when the Vance Faience Company was organized for the purpose of producing quality artware. By 1902 the name had been changed to the Avon Faience Company, and late in the same year it and three other West Virginia potteries incorporated to form the Wheeling Potteries Company. The Avon branch operated in Tiltonville until 1905 when production was moved to Wheeling. Art pottery was discontinued.

From the beginning, only skilled craftsmen and trained engineers were hired. Wm. P. Jervis and Fredrick Hurten Rhead were among the notable artists reponsible for designing some of the early artware. Some of the ware was slip decorated under glaze, while other pieces were molded with high-relief designs. Examples with squeeze-bag decoration by Rhead are obviously forerunners of the Jap Birdimal line he later developed for Weller. Ware was marked 'Vance F. Co.'; Avon F. Co., Tiltonville'; or 'Avon W. Pts. Co.'

Jar, squeeze bag, roses, pk/gr on wht, mk Avon, 16", VG **1,300.00**
Vase, floral, squeeze-bag, WP&S Co, 5½x5½", NM **1,200.00**
Vase, shades of gr & brn, 11" **80.00**
Vase, stylized trees, squeeze-bag, bulbous w/can neck, 6" **550.00**

Vaseline

Vaseline, a greenish-yellow colored glass produced by adding uranium oxide to the batch, was produced during the Victorian era. It was made in smaller quantities than other colors and lost much of its popularity with the advent of the electric light. It was used for pressed tablewares, vases, whimseys, souvenir items, oil lamps, perfume bottles, drawer pulls, and doorknobs. Pieces have been reproduced, and some factories still make it today in small batches. Vaseline glass will flouresce under an ultraviolet light.

Compote, Daisy and Button, with lid, 13", NM, $195.00.

Bowl, Wildflower, 7½x7½" **30.00**
Butter dish, Oaken Bucket **275.00**
Candlestick, flint, Sandwich or NE Glass, 1890s, 10½x5" **140.00**
Candlestick, Swirl, short, 1938, pr **55.00**

Celery tray, Daisy & Button, Hobbs & Brockunier, 2x14" L 125.00
Creamer, Oaken Bucket 100.00
Knife rest, cut 6-panel Bar w/honeycomb-cut fct balls, 4⅜" 150.00
Match holder, Daisy & Button, umbrella w/wire hdl, Doyle & Co ..120.00
Pitcher, Daisy & Button w/Crossbars 120.00
Pitcher, milk; Zipper 55.00
Spooner, Log Cabin 225.00
Sugar bowl, Oaken Bucket 225.00
Sugar bowl, Starburst & Pinwheel, w/lid 45.00
Toothpick holder, Oaken Bucket, wire hdl, 2½" 30.00

Verlys

Verlys art glass, produced in France after 1931 by the Holophane Company of Verlys, was made in crystal with acid-finished relief work in the Art Deco style. Colored and opalescent glass was also used. In 1935 an American branch was opened in Newark, Ohio, where very similar wares were produced until the factory ceased production in 1951. French Verlys was signed with one of three mold-impressed script signatures, all containing the company name and country of origin. The American-made glassware was signed 'Verlys' only, either scratched with a diamond-tipped pen or impressed in the mold. There is very little if any difference in value between items produced in France and America. Though some seem to feel that the French should be higher priced (assuming it to be scarce), many prefer the American-made product.

In June of 1955, about sixteen Verlys molds were leased to the A.H. Heisey Company. Heisey's versions were not signed with the Verlys name, so if an item is unsigned it is almost certainly a Heisey piece. The molds were returned to Verlys of America in July 1957. Fenton now owns all Verlys molds, but all issues are marked Fenton. Our advisor for this category is Don Frost; he is listed in the Directory under Washington.

Bowl, Birds & Bees, clear frosted, 2½x11¾" 275.00
Bowl, Birds & Bees, frosted opal, 2x11¾" 325.00
Bowl, Cupid, clear frosted, 2x6" 145.00
Bowl, Orchid, frosted opal, 1½x14" 300.00
Bowl, Pine Cone, bl, 6" 185.00
Bowl, Pine Cone, opal 225.00
Bowl, Poppies, shallow, ftd, mk, 13¾" 325.00
Bowl, Thistle, topaz 250.00
Bowl, Water Lily, Dusty Rose (rare color) 500.00
Bowl, Wild Duck 175.00
Candle holders, Eagles, 3½", pr 500.00
Vase, Alpine Thistle, topaz, 9x9" 450.00
Vase, clear w/vertical amethyst ribbing, sgn, 9x8½" 350.00
Vase, crested bird pr/berries leaves, bl, cylinder, 7¾" 450.00
Vase, Eglantine, opal, base chips 250.00
Vase, floral, emb fiery opal, w/flower frog, mk, 6½" 345.00
Vase, Gems, amber, w/frog, 6½x6½" 350.00
Vase, Lovebirds, clear frosted, w/sticker, 4½x6½" 225.00
Vase, Mandarin, clear frosted, 9½" 500.00
Vase, Seasons, 8x5½" 800.00
Vase, Thistle, fiery opal, mk, 9¾", NM 450.00

Vernon Kilns

Vernon Potteries Ltd. was established by Faye G. Bennison in Vernon, California, in 1931. The name was later changed to Vernon Kilns; until it closed in 1958, dinnerware, specialty plates, and figurines were their primary products. Among its wares most sought after by collectors today are items designed by such famous artists as Rockwell Kent, Walt

Disney, Don Blanding, Jane Bennison, and May and Vieve Hamilton. Authority Maxine Nelson has compiled a lovely book, *Collectible Vernon Kilns*, with full-color photos, and current prices; you will find her listed in the Directory under Arizona.

Calico, chop plate, 14" 75.00
Calico, cup & saucer 20.00
Calico, pitcher, bulbous, 1-pt 35.00
Calico, plate, luncheon; 9½" 18.00
Chintz, bowl, fruit; 5½" 8.00
Chintz, creamer 20.00
Chintz, cup 8.00
Chintz, plate, dinner; 10" 13.00
Chintz, plate, luncheon; 9½" 10.00
Chintz, plate, salad; 7¼" 8.00
Chintz, saucer 4.00
Chintz, sugar bowl, w/lid 20.00
Coral Reef, cup & saucer 26.00
Decanter, penguin, 1930s 195.00
Desert Bloom, coffeepot 65.00
Early Days, soup tureen, w/15" underplate 250.00
Fantasia, bowl, goldfish, #121 ....375.00
Fantasia, bowl, mushroom, HP 375.00
Fantasia, bowl, Sprite, bl, #125 ....275.00
Fantasia, figurine, Satyr, 4½" 250.00
Fantasia, plate, salad; Nutcracker, 7½" 165.00
Fantasia, shakers, Hop Low, mushrooms, pr 150.00
Frontier Days, plate, chop; 14" 175.00
Gingham, butter pat 26.00
Gingham, casserole, ind; w/lid & stick hdl 35.00
Gingham, casserole, w/lid 45.00
Gingham, coaster 26.00
Gingham, flowerpot, w/saucer, 4" 40.00
Gingham, spoon rest 40.00
Gingham, teapot 50.00

Hawaiian Flowers, iced tea tumbler, $35.00; Lei Lani, chop plate, 14", $145.00.

Hawaiian Flowers, plate, chop; 12" 95.00
Hawaiian Flowers, plate, chop; 14" 125.00
Hawaiian Flowers, shakers, pr 35.00
Hawaiian Flowers, teapot 85.00
Homespun, creamer & sugar bowl, w/lid 25.00
Homespun, cup & saucer 12.00
Homespun, pitcher, 2-qt 47.50
Homespun, plate, chop; 12" 17.50
Homespun, plate, dinner; 10½" 12.00
Homespun, platter, 12½" 17.50
Homespun, shakers, pr 18.00
Lei Lani, cup & saucer, demi 35.00
Lei Lani, plate, chop; 14" 145.00
Lei Lani, plate, chop; 17" 215.00
Lei Lani, plate, dinner; 10" 45.00

Lei Lani, plate, salad; 7" 27.00
Mayflower, bowl, chowder; tab hdld, 6⅛" 12.00
Mayflower, bowl, salad; 12" 60.00
Mayflower, bowl, vegetable; oval 20.00
Mayflower, butter tray & lid 45.00
Mayflower, creamer & sugar bowl, w/lid 25.00
Mayflower, cup & saucer 15.00
Mayflower, plate, chop; 12" 25.00
Mayflower, plate, dinner; 10½" 12.50
Mayflower, plate, salad; 7½" 9.00
Mayflower, platter, 13½" 20.00
Mayflower, shakers, pr 15.00
Moby Dick, bowl, fruit; 5½" 50.00
Moby Dick, bowl, vegetable; 9" 165.00
Moby Dick, creamer & sugar bowl, ind 225.00
Moby Dick, cup & saucer, AD 50.00
Moby Dick, shakers, pr 145.00
Moby Dick, sugar bowl 75.00
Mojave, bowl, mixing; 5" 15.00
Mojave, butter tray & lid 35.00
Mojave, sugar bowl, w/lid 14.00
Orchard, bowl, 1-pt 40.00
Organdie, bowl, chowder; tab hdld, 6" 10.00
Organdie, casserole, w/lid, ind 25.00
Organdie, cup & saucer 7.00
Organdie, cup & saucer, demitasse 25.00
Organdie, egg cup 15.00
Organdie, plate, luncheon; 9½" 10.00
Organdie, teapot 45.00
Our America, bowl, chowder 100.00
Our America, cup & saucer 100.00
Our America, plate, dinner; 10½" 110.00
Our America, plate, 6" 50.00
Our America, plate, 7" 85.00
Plate, Alaska Scrimshaw, 10½" 45.00
Plate, Bits Mission, San Diego, 14" 95.00
Plate, Bits of the Old West, 8½" 25.00
Plate, Edvard Grieg, Composer, 8½" 40.00
Plate, Moor Man's, advertising, 10½" 45.00
Plate, Mt Rushmore, 10½" 15.00
Plate, St Louis 15.00
Plate, Texas, spindle top 45.00
Plate, Virginia 15.00
Salamina, bowl, fruit; 5½" 75.00
Salamina, cup & saucer 100.00
Salamina, plate, bread & butter; 6" 60.00
Salamina, plate, chop; 12" 285.00
Salamina, plate, chop; 14" 300.00
Salamina, plate, chop; 17" 800.00
Salamina, plate, dinner; 10" 175.00
Salamina, plate, luncheon; 9" 145.00
Salamina, plate, salad; 7½" 75.00
Santa Maria, bowl, serving; 9" 42.00
Shadow Leaf, pitcher, 1-qt 32.00
Shadow Leaf, syrup 65.00
Tam O' Shanter, bowl, mixing; 5" 20.00
Tam O' Shanter, bowl, vegetable; 8¾" 24.00
Tam O' Shanter, bowls, mixing; nesting set of 5 ...125.00
Tam O' Shanter, carafe, w/stopper 45.00
Tam O' Shanter, casserole, hdls, w/lid 50.00
Tam O' Shanter, pitcher, 2-qt 50.00
Tam O' Shanter, plate, bread & butter; 6¼" 6.00
Tam O' Shanter, plate, luncheon; 9¾" 11.00
Tam O' Shanter, plate, salad; 7½" 8.00

Tam O' Shanter, platter, oval, 12½" 22.00
Trade Winds, pitcher, 2-qt 40.00
Tweed, bowl, chowder 25.00
Tweed, plate, chop; 12" 55.00
Tweed, shakers, lg, pr 90.00
Tweed, sugar bowl, w/lid 40.00
Vernon's 1860, bowl, vegetable 25.00
Vernon's 1860, plate, chop; 14" 50.00
Winchester 73, bowl, divided, 10" 90.00
Winchester 73, cup & saucer 75.00
Winchester 73, mug 45.00
Winchester 73, plate, chop; 12" 100.00
Winchester 73, plate, dinner; 10" 75.00
Winchester 73, plate, 6" 32.00
Winchester 73, platter, oval, 12½" 130.00
Winchester 73, salt cellar & pepper mill, pr 125.00
Winchester 73, tumbler 45.00

Vistosa

Vistosa was produced from about 1938 through the early '40s. It was Taylor, Smith, and Taylor's answer to the very successful Fiesta line of their nearby competitor, Homer Laughlin. Vistosa was made in four solid colors: mango red, cobalt blue, light green, and deep yellow. 'Pie crust' edges and a dainty five-petal flower molded into handles and lid finials made for a very attractive yet nevertheless commercially unsuccessful product. For further information, we recommend *Collector's Guide to Lu-Ray Pastels* by Kathy and Bill Meehan (Collector Books). Our advisor for this category is Ted Haun; he is listed in the Directory under Indiana.

Bowl, coupe soup 25.00
Bowl, fruit; 5¾" 8.00
Bowl, lug soup 30.00
Bowl, nappy 50.00
Bowl, salad; pie-crust ft, rare 150.00
Chop plate, 12" 40.00
Chop plate, 14" 50.00
Creamer 20.00
Cup & saucer 15.00
Cup & saucer, demitasse 55.00

Photo courtesy Kathy and Bill Meehan

Egg cup, $35.00.

Pitcher, jug form 85.00
Plate, 6", from $10 to 15.00
Plate, 7", from $12 to 18.00
Plate, 9" 18.00
Sauce boat, rare 120.00
Shakers, pr 32.00
Sugar bowl, w/lid 25.00

Teapot 100.00

Volkmar

Charles Volkmar established a workshop in Tremont, New York, in 1882. He produced artware decorated under the glaze in the manner of the early barbotine work done at the Haviland factory in Limoges, France. He relocated in 1888 in Menlo Park, New Jersey, and together with J.T. Smith established the Menlo Park Ceramic Company for the production of art tile. The partnership was dissolved in 1893. From 1895 until 1902, Volkmar located in Corona, New York, first under the name Volkmar Ceramic Company, later as Volkmar and Cory, and for the final six years as Crown Point. During the latter period he made art tile, blue under-glaze Delft-type wares, colorful polychrome vases, etc. The Volkmar Kilns were established in 1903 in Metuchen, New Jersey, by Volkmar and his son. Wares were marked with various devices consisting of the Volkmar name, initials, or 'Crown Point Ware.'

Mug, gr matt, swollen form, ink mk, 4" 260.00
Plaque, cows by riverbank, sgn Chas, 9x7¾" 2,500.00
Vase, floral, mc Limoges glaze, Crown Point Ware, rstr, 7" 350.00
Vase, floral, mc Limoges glaze, flattened from, 10x7", EX 325.00
Vase, gr satin w/lg leaf panels, 10x9" 850.00
Vase, gr/brn mottled matt, 4 slightly flattened sides, 3x4" 200.00
Vase, gray lustre/pk irid over wht crackle, 1938/29D, 6½" 400.00

Volkstedt

There were several porcelain factories in and around Volkstedt, Province of Thuringia, the original and earliest one established in 1762 by George Heinrich Macheleid. Others soon followed, producing many fine porcelain figures and groups in the Scheib-Alsbach, Potschappel, and Sitzendorf style. The 'crossed hayforks' mark was used from 1787 to 1800 by Christian Nonne; it was later modified with the addition of a crown by R. Ekhart (1906-08). An 'M' crossed by a 'V' with a crown was used from 1907-47 by Muller, who used an oval-shaped diamond with an 'M,' 'V,' and a crown from 1910-1960. The Greiner Bros. mark was a double crossed 'G' and a crown, in use from 1850-1920.

Candlesticks, man & lady in period clothes, 1886 mk, 11", pr ...800.00
Figurine, man w/shovel, woman w/sprinkler, mc w/gold, 7½" 250.00
Figurine, 2 girls preceed bride/groom/page boy, 9x13" 1,300.00
Plaque, gr Jasper, dancing cherubs, floral fr, 11x9" 485.00

Wade

The Wade Group of Potteries originated in 1810 with a small, single-oven pottery near Chesterton, just west of Burslem, England. This pottery, first owned by a Henry Hallen, was eventually taken over by George Wade who had opened his own pottery in the latter part of the 19th century on Hall Street, Burslem. In the early 19th century, George Wade combined the two businesses into one pottery — the George Wade Pottery, located on High Street, Burslem. This pottery was named the Manchester Pottery; it still stands and is in business today.

Both the original Hallen Pottery and the newer George Wade Pottery specialized in pottery items for the textile industry, then booming in northern England. In 1906 Wade's son, George Albert Wade, joined the company, and in 1919 the pottery name was changed to George Wade and Son Ltd.

George Wade's brothers, Albert and William, had interests in two other potteries, Wade Heath & Co. Ltd., founded in 1867 as Wade, Colclough and Lingard (changed to Wade & Co. in 1887 and to Wade Heath & Co. Ltd. in 1927) and J.& W. Wade & Co., founded in the late 19th century with a name change also in 1927, to A.J. Wade & Co. Together the potteries manufactured decorative tiles, teapots, and other related dinnerware. In 1938 Wade Heath took over the Royal Victoria Pottery, also in Burslem, and began producing a wide range of figurines and other decorative items. The A.J. Wade & Co. pottery ceased production in 1970, but the main building was not sold and has reopened recently as The Pottery Store. The Royal Victoria Pottery is still in production but is now referred to as Hill Top.

In 1947 a new pottery was opened in Portadown, Northern Ireland, to produce both industrial ceramics and Irish porcelain giftware. In 1958 all the Wade potteries were amalgamated, becoming the Wade Group of Potteries. The most recent addition to the group is Wade (PDM) Limited, a marketing arm for the advertising ware made by Wade Heath at the Royal Victoria Pottery. Wade (PDM) Limited was incorporated in 1969. In 1989 the Wade Group of Potteries was bought out by Beauford Engineering. With this takeover, Wade Heath and George Wade & Son Ltd. were combined to form Wade Ceramics. Wade (Ireland) Ltd. and Wade (PDM) Ltd. became subsidiaries of Wade Ceramics. In 1990 Wade (Ireland) Ltd. changed its name to Seagoe Ceramics Limited. In April 1993, Seagoe Ceramics Limited ceased the production of table and gifware to concentrate on industrial ceramics. The pottery, although still owned by Beauford, is no longer part of the Wade Group.

For those interested in learning more about Wade pottery, we recommend *The World of Wade* and *The World of Wade Book 2* by Ian Warner and Mike Posgay; Mr. Warner is listed in the Directory under Canada.

Bell's Whiskey Decanter, Charles & Diana Wedding, 75cl, empty .120.00
Bell's Whiskey Decanter, Charles & Diana Wedding, 75cl, MIB .1,000.00
Birdbath Pitcher, 10¼" 80.00
Birdbath Pitcher, 6¼" 70.00
British Character, Fish Porter 220.00
British Character, Lawyer 230.00
British Character, Pearly King 175.00
British Character, Pearly Queen 170.00
Burslem the Factory Cat 75.00
Character Jug, Charrington's Beers 150.00
Character Jug, Highwayman 200.00
Character Jug, Pirate 200.00
Character Jug, Toby Jim Jug 120.00
Christmas Puppy, Wade Limited Edition 35.00
Grey Haired Rabbit, Wade Limited Edition 95.00
Minkins, various figures, ea 25.00
Novelty Animal Figure, Bernie & Poo 220.00
Novelty Animal Figure, Dustbin Cat 220.00
Novelty Animal Figure, Jonah & the Whale 1,050.00
Novelty Animal Figure, Jumbo Jim 220.00
Novelty Animal Figure, Kitten on the Keys 250.00
Red Rose Tea (US), Clown w/Drum 3.00
Red Rose Tea (US), Clown w/Pie 3.00
Red Rose Tea (US), Human Cannonball 3.00
Red Rose Tea (US), Ringmaster 3.00
Red Rose Tea (US), Strongman 3.00
Ringtons Ltd Mini Maling Jug w/lid 55.00
Ringtons Ltd Mini Maling Teapot 55.00
Ringtons Ltd Tea Caddy, 1991 ....70.00
Ringtons Ltd Tea Caddy, 1993 ....60.00
Romance Wall Plate, 10½" 75.00
Seattle Westie 30.00
Tea Tidy, Jim Beam/Wade 20.00
Van Money Box, bl, Jim Beam/Wade 95.00

Van Money Box, wht, Jim Beam/Wade 125.00
Wade (PDM) Ashtray, Beefeater Gin 10.00
Wade (PDM) Water Pitcher, Dewars Whiskey 30.00

Wallace China

Dinnerware with a Western theme was produced by the Wallace China Company, who operated in California from 1931 until 1964. Artist Till Goodan designed three lines, Rodeo, Pioneer Trails, and Boots and Saddle, which they marketed under the package name Westward Ho. When dinnerware with a western theme became so popular just a few years ago, Rodeo was reproduced, but the new trademark includes neither 'California' or 'Wallace China.'

Our advisor for this category is Marv Fogleman; he is listed in the Directory under California. If you'd like to learn more about this company, we recommend *The Collector's Encyclopedia of California Pottery* by Jack Chipman.

Boots & Saddles, bowl, oval, 12" 250.00
Chuck Wagon, creamer, 3" 45.00
Chuck Wagon, platter, 11½" 125.00
Chuck Wagon, shakers, 5", pr 95.00
El Rancho, coffee mug 20.00
El Rancho, plate, Hitching Post Cheyenne, 9½" 75.00
Rodeo, chop plate, 13" 295.00
Rodeo, cup & saucer, demi 50.00
Rodeo, plate, luncheon 125.00
Rodeo, plate, salad; 7¼" 60.00
Westward Ho, ashtray, Pioneer Trail 50.00
Westward Ho, plate, Little Buckaroo, boy on horse, 9" 180.00
Westward Ho Rodeo, bowl, salad; 5½x13" 400.00

Walrath

Frederick Walrath was a studio potter who worked from around the turn of the century until his death in 1920. He was located in Rochester, New York, until 1918 when he became associated with the Newcomb Pottery in New Orleans, Louisiana.

Bowl, floral on gray matt, shouldered, att, 2x8" 160.00
Bowl, gr matt, 3 frogs sit on leaves at rim, rprs, 3x8" 750.00
Bowl, leaves, olive on dk mustard, 1912, 1½x5" 190.00
Planter, stylized leaves, gr on olive, +insert, 3½x7½", NM 550.00
Vase, Arts & Crafts floral, lt gr/pk on med gr, 9x6" 4,750.00
Vase, cvd/rtcl tulips on gr matt w/ochre & rust, FW/1902, 8½" ...2,100.00
Vase, pendant berries/leaves, olive/pk on dk gr, 5½" 3,500.00
Vase, rnd leaves, impressionistic, yel/olive on gr, 7" 850.00

Walter, A.

Almaric Walter was employed from 1904 through 1914 at Verreries Artistiques des Freres Daum in Nancy, France. After 1919 he opened his own business where he continued to make the same type of quality objets d'art in pate-de-verre glass as he had earlier. His pieces are signed A. Walter, Nancy H. Berge Sc.

Bowl, lizard inside, gr on yel w/red, Berge, 3x7" 4,750.00
Covered dish, yel w/amber mouse on lid, 6¼" 2,875.00
Dish, bee at side, triangular, 1x4½" 2,650.00
Paperweight, brn 3" beetle amid oak leaves, 1½x4" 2,100.00
Paperweight, bumble bee moth on flowers, sgn Berge, 3¾" 2,100.00

Paperweight, crawfish on bl base, 1¾x3½" 3,000.00
Paperweight, fish/minnows, orange/teal, sgn Berge, 5" L 1,150.00
Paperweight, moth on flower cluster, 1¼x4" 1,700.00
Paperweight, royal beetle on yel base, 2x2¼" 2,250.00
Paperweight, sparrow, honey-amber on gr base, Berge mk, 4" .1,265.00
Tray, beetle at side, blk/brn on turq, 1½x3¾" 2,300.00
Tray, butterfly/pine cones, gr/tan, 7" dia 2,000.00
Tray, fish, emerald gr on sea gr oval, 7⅜" 4,025.00
Tray, fish in deep relief, gr w/emerald flecks, 6" 4,600.00
Tray, scarab, brn/blk on amber crescent form, 4" 3,100.00
Vase, bees among pine branches, sgn, 5¾" 4,485.00
Vase, berries/leaves on purple to peach, lug hdls, 5" 2,100.00
Vase, berry branches, gr/brn on cream opaque, hdls, 4½" 4,315.00

Wannopee

The Wannopee Pottery, established in 1892, developed from the reorganization of the financially insecure New Milford Pottery Company of New Milford, Connecticut. They produced a line of mottled-glazed pottery called 'Duchess' and a similar line in porcelain. Both were marked with the impressed sunburst 'W' with 'porcelain' added to indicate that particular body type.

In 1895 semiporcelain pitchers in three sizes were decorated with relief medallion cameos of Beethoven, Mozart, and Napoleon. Lettuce Leaf ware was first produced in 1901 and used actual leaves in the modeling. Scarabronze, made in 1895, was their finest artware. It featured simple Egyptian shapes with a coppery glaze. It was marked with a scarab, either impressed or applied. Production ceased in 1903.

Vase, Scarabronze, glossy caramel brown with nacreous metallic lustre overglaze, six buttressed handles, LO/1014H/21, 20¼x12", $2,100.00.

Bowl, Lettuce Leaf, #212, lg, nM 135.00
Ewer, brn, yel & gr gloss, mk, 9x7" 350.00
Vase, Scarabronze, appl scarab/emb Egyptian, rstr, 12x6" 200.00

Warwick

The Warwick China Company operated in Wheeling, West Virginia, from 1887 until 1951. They produced both hand-painted and decaled plates, vases, teapots, coffeepots, pitchers, bowls, and jardinieres featuring lovely florals or portraits of beautiful ladies done in luscious colors. Backgrounds were usually blendings of brown and beige, but ivory was also used as well as greens and pinks. Various marks were employed, all of which incorporate the Warwick name. For a more thorough study of the subject, we recommend *Warwick, A to W*, a supplement to *Why Not Warwick* by our advisor, Donald C. Hoffmann, Sr.; his address can be found in the Directory under Illinois. In an effort to inform the collector/dealer, Mr. Hoffmann now has a video available that identifies the company's decals and their variations by number.

Vase, A Beauty, gr, rose, F-2, 15" 325.00

Vase, A Beauty, wht, rose, D-2, 15" 330.00
Vase, Albany, brn, floral, A-27, 7" 215.00
Vase, Albany, matt tan, nuts, M-64, 7" 230.00
Vase, Alexandria, brn, floral, A-40, 12½" 320.00
Vase, Alexandria, red, poinsettia, E-2, 12½" 330.00
Vase, Bonnie, brn, floral, A-40, 10¼" 285.00
Vase, Bonnie, wht, roses, F-2, 10¼" 290.00
Vase, Bouquet #1, brn, portrait, A-17, 11½" 270.00
Vase, Bouquet #1, charcoal, floral, C-6, 11½" 280.00
Vase, Bouquet #1, matt tan, lady w/lg hat, M-1, 11½" ...290.00
Vase, Bouquet #1, red, orchid, E-2, 11½" 300.00
Vase, Bouquet #1, wht, birds, D-1, 11½" 295.00
Vase, Bouquet #2, Bonfits, hair up, A-17, 10½" 290.00
Vase, Bouquet #2, brn, Bonfits, rose in hair, A-17, 10½" ...280.00
Vase, Bouquet #2, brn, gypsy, A-17, 10½" 240.00
Vase, Bouquet #2, brn, lady w/orchid in hair, A-17, 10½" ...265.00
Vase, Bouquet #2, brn, lady w/sunflower in hair, A-17, 10½" 325.00
Vase, Bouquet #2, brn, lady w/violets, A-17, 10½" 280.00
Vase, Bouquet #2, brn, Madame Recamier, A-17, 10½" ...280.00
Vase, Bouquet #2, brn, older blond, A-17, 10½" 250.00
Vase, Bouquet #2, brn, redhead, A-17, 10½" 280.00
Vase, Bouquet #2, brn, redhead w/scarf, A-17, 10½" ...295.00
Vase, Bouquet #2, brn, sgn Carreno, A-33, 10½" 315.00
Vase, Bouquet #2, brn, sgn Carreno, younger, A-33, 10½" ...325.00
Vase, Bouquet #2, brn, sm roses, A-23, 10½" 250.00
Vase, Bouquet #2, brn, young blond, A-17, 10½" 240.00
Vase, Bouquet #2, charcoal, floral, C-6, 10½" 285.00
Vase, Bouquet #2, charcoal, sgn Carreno, A-33, 10½" ...300.00
Vase, Bouquet #2, gr, Madame Le Brun (child), F-3, 10½" ...290.00
Vase, Bouquet #2, gr, roses, B-30, 10½" 280.00
Vase, Bouquet #2, matt gr to tan, floral, M-15, 10½" ...280.00
Vase, Bouquet #2, matt tan to gr, portrait, M-1, 10½" ...275.00
Vase, Carnation, gr, roses, B-30, 9" 190.00
Vase, Carnation, matt tan, pine cones, M-2, 9" 170.00
Vase, Carnation, pk, lady w/boa, H-1, 9" 220.00
Vase, Carnation, pk, lady w/lg hat, H-1, 9" 235.00
Vase, Carnation, red, poinsettias, E-2, 9" 290.00
Vase, Carnation, yel/gr, floral, K-2, 9" 270.00
Vase, Carnation, yel/gr, portrait, K-1, 9" 280.00
Vase, Carol, brn, floral, A-40, 8" 250.00
Vase, Carol, pk, lady w/boa, H-1, 8" 300.00
Vase, Chicago, brn, floral, A-6, 8" 225.00
Vase, Chrys #1, brn, floral, A-40, 15" 185.00
Vase, Chrys #1, brn, floral, A-6, 15" 185.00
Vase, Chrys #2, charcoal, floral, C-6, 13" 190.00
Vase, Clematis, brn, floral, A-27 ....235.00
Vase, Clematis, wht, birds, D-1 ....290.00
Vase, Cloverleaf, matt, nuts, M-4 ....295.00
Vase, Cloverleaf, red, floral, poinsettias, E-2 ....285.00
Vase, Verbinia #1, brn, floral, A-6 ....195.00
Vase, Verbinia #2, charcoal, portrait, Carreno, C-1 ....230.00
Vase, Verbinia #2, wht, birds, D-1 ....225.00
Vase, Verona, brn, floral, A-16 ....175.00
Vase, Victoria, wht, birds, D-1 ....250.00
Vase, Violet, brn, floral, A-27 ....115.00
Vase, Violet, gr, floral, B-30 ....130.00
Vase, Virginia, matt, nuts, M-4 ....180.00
Vase, Virginia, pk, portrait, H-1 ....220.00
Vase, Warwick, brn, floral, A-40 ....290.00
Vase, Warwick, matt bl to pk, portrait, M-1 ....310.00
Vase, Warwick, pk, portrait, H-1 ....315.00
Vase, Windsor, brn, floral, mixed, A-25 ....295.00
Vase, Windsor, brn, nuts, A-64 ....285.00
Vase, Windsor, matt, pine cones, M-2 ....315.00

Vase, Windsor, pk, portrait, H-1 ....330.00

Wash Sets

Before the days of running water, bedrooms were standardly equipped with a wash bowl and pitcher as a matter of necessity. A 'toilet set' was comprised of the pitcher and bowl, toothbrush holder, covered commode, soap dish, shaving dish, and mug. Some sets were even more elaborate. Through everyday usage, the smaller items were often broken, and today it is unusual to find a complete set.

Porcelain sets decorated with florals, fruits, or scenics were produced abroad by Limoges in France; some were imported from Germany and England. During the last quarter of the 1800s and until after the turn of the century, American-made toilet sets were manufactured in abundance. Tin and graniteware sets were also made.

Alhambra, flow bl, Meakin, pitcher+bowl+soap dish+pot 1,100.00
English, bl-gr florals, pitcher+bowl+toothbrush holder+pot 350.00
Gertrud, semivitreous, Arts & Crafts floral, pitcher+bowl 600.00
Gr-striated opal glass, 19th C, pitcher+bowl+2 pcs 660.00
Ironstone, wht w/gold trim, pitcher+bowl 200.00
Minton, child's, gr ivy on cream, 7" pitcher, 9½" bowl 250.00
Myott, Bl Willow, 9½" pitcher+bowl+pot 600.00

P.H. Leonard, New York City Importer/Vienna, hand-painted forest scenes, 11" pitcher, 16¼" bowl, along with slop jar and lid, chamber pot and lid, shaving mug, toothbrush holder, small pitcher, and three-piece oval soap dish, $550.00.

Paris, porc, floral on blk w/gold, 8-sided, pitcher+bowl 825.00
Royal Doulton, Rosetti, pitcher+bowl 265.00
W Hall & Co, Oriental Gardens, brn transfer, pitcher+bowl 195.00

Watch Fobs

Watch fobs have been popular since the last quarter of the 19th century. They were often made by retail companies to feature their products. Souvenir, commemorative, and political fobs were also produced. Of special interest today are those with advertising, heavy equipment in particular. Some of the more pricey fobs are listed here, but most of those currently available were produced in such quantities that they are relatively common and should fall within a price range of $3.00 to $10.00. Our advisor for this category is Tony George; he is listed in the Directory under California.

Adamant Suit 55.00
Ahlberg Bearing Co, rnd, EX 210.00
Allis Chalmers, emb on textured ground, rectangular, EX 110.00
Alpha Portland Cement 30.00
Apex Ham, porc ham shape, EX 85.00
Armour & Co, steer's head 35.00

Atlas Explosives Safety Committee, porc/sterling, rnd, 1927, M ..25.00
Avery, tractor 75.00
Babe Ruth, celluloid (foxed) 75.00
Beck & Corbitt Iron Co, St Louis, anvil shape, VG 60.00
Boy's State Fair School Illinois, corn on oval, 1940, EX 105.00
Brobe Co Bread, rnd w/scalloped edge, EX 50.00
Bryan/Kern 1908, brass w/enameled flag in center, NM 55.00
Bucyrus Erie 55.00
Bulldog Cylinders 110.00
Burruss Engineering Co/Oil Mill Builders Atlanta, rnd, EX 100.00
Cadillac, 4-color cloisonne emblem on blk ribbon, EX+ 110.00
Case, eagle on globe 30.00
Chief Kokomo, Indian in headdress on arrowhead shape 65.00
Denver 1st Annual Fat Stock Show, 1903 ....225.00
Dominion Cartridge Co, porc on metal, EX 525.00
Elk's tooth, 10k mts 40.00
Engman-Matthews Range Co, celluloid, 2-sided, rnd, EX 22.00
Erie Foundry, foundry on shield, EX 35.00
Fish Bros Wagon Co 85.00
Floyd-Wells Co/Bengal Furnaces, tiger, rnd, VG 50.00
For President Al Smith, blk/wht celluloid, brass fr, NM 45.00
For President Herbert Clark, blk/wht celluloid, brass fr, NM 45.00
General Electric, stove, EX 40.00
Golden Shell Motor Oil, 1¼" dia, EX 65.00
Golden Shell Oil, rnd w/shell emblem, 1¼"dia, EX 195.00
Goodyear Tractor Tires, logo above tire shape, EX 20.00
Haynes Automobile, Kokomo Indiana 185.00
Heiden Tractor 120.00
Hoberg Tissue Paper, blk/flesh-tone porc, EX 130.00
Hudson Motor Car 70.00
International Harvester, emb IH/wheat border, rnd, EX 425.00
Iron Age Potato, potato shape 35.00
Jas E Pepper Whiskey/Joseph Spang Distributor, 17 & 80, EX 85.00
John Deere, bl porc oval w/emb deer, EX 160.00
John Deere, MOP, deer & plow 85.00
John Deere Centennial, cast bronze, 1937 ....95.00
Kentucky Whiskey 80.00
Michelin Earthmover Tires, tires & Mr Bib, rectangular, EX 25.00
National Cigar Stands 5¢ Cigars, w/cigar cutter 85.00
National Sportsman, elk & rifle 65.00
Old Ben Coal, w/cigar cutter 45.00
Opal Hair Tonic, Indianapolis 54.00
Panton Plows, rnd w/scalloped edge, NP, EX 125.00
Pathfinder Coffee, coffee can on celluloid center, EX 35.00
Richmond Rubber Co, bl on NP, rectangle w/arched top, EX 75.00
Robin Hood Flour, red/bl porc shield, EX 25.00
Rock Island Plow 95.00
Rock Island RR 70th Anniversary, 1922, w/strap 30.00
Roosevelt (Teddy) & Fairbanks to Washington, 1904, VG 40.00
Roosevelt (Teddy) & Johnson jugate, metal, 1912 ....180.00
Roosevelt 1904 Fairbanks, brass, sq, EX 30.00
Russell Grader Mfg, emb oval, EX 305.00
Russell Road Builders, emb eagle, rnd/scalloped edge, EX 305.00
Sears Roebuck & Co, David Bradley Plows, celluloid, mc, EX 95.00
Snowbird Flour, Galesburg Michigan 75.00
Taft/Sherman 1908, blk enamel on brass, VG 55.00
Theodore Hofeller, Oldest Dealer in Old Rubber..., rnd, EX 65.00
Turkey Coffee, emb turkey, rnd, M 85.00
TX Cattle Raisers Assoc, bronc rider & steer, 1903 ....325.00
Union Stock Yards & Transit Co, beehive, 1901, EX 120.00
US Secret Service 65.00
Velvet Tobacco, enamel, VG 45.00
White Rolls Cigarettes, porc pack, rnd w/scrolled edge, EX 100.00
Wichita Falls Brick & Tile Co Texas, suitcase, EX 125.00

Woodmen Accident Association, porc center, rnd, EX 75.00

Watch Stands

Watch stands were decorative articles designed with a hook from which to hang a watch. Some displayed the watch as the face of a grandfather clock or as part of an interior scene with figures in period costumes and contemporary furnishings. They were popular products of Staffordshire potters and silver companies as well.

Bust of lady, chalk, cloth & paper flowers in niche, 14", EX 900.00
Castle, turrets/stairs, Staffordshire, 12" 135.00
Moor figure, silver finish on bronze, Austrian, 6" 450.00
Mottled purple lustre, shelf over 2 columns, England, 1820s, 8" ...1,035.00
Oriental gong on hex base, wood, 1800s, 13" 325.00
Pearlware, Goddess of Truth on base, mc details, 9¼" 350.00
Pearlware, tall case clock form, mc, Fell, ca 1820, 8½" 300.00
Wax figure of mother & child behind glass, mc chalkware, 15" .285.00

Watches

First made in the 1500s in Germany, early watches were actually small clocks, suspended from the neck or belt. By 1700 they had become the approximate shape and size we know today. The first watches produced in America were made in 1810. The well-known Waltham Watch Company was established in 1850. Later, Waterbury produced inexpensive watches which they sold by the thousands.

Open-face and hunting-case watches of the 1890s were often solid gold or gold-filled and were often elaborately decorated in several colors of gold. Gold watches became a status symbol in this decade and were worn by both men and women on chains with fobs or jeweled slides. Ladies sometimes fastened them to their clothing with pins often set with jewels. The chatelaine watch was worn at the waist, only one of several items such as scissors, coin purses, or needle cases, each attached by small chains.

Most turn-of-the-century watch cases were gold-filled; these are plentiful today. Sterling cases, though interest in them is on the increase, are not in great demand. Please note: The price of gold has fallen since this time last year; consequently the values of solid gold pocket watches have gone down as well. Our advice for this category comes from Maundy International Watches, Antiquarian Horologists, price consultants, and researchers for many watch reference guides and books on Horology. Their firm is a leading purveyor of antique watches of all kinds. They are listed in the Directory under Kansas. For character-related watches, see Personalities.

Key:
adj — adjusted
brg — bridge plate design
d/s — double sunk dial
fbd — finger bridge design
g/f — gold-filled
g/j/s — gold jewel setting
h/c — hunter case
HCI#P — heat, cold,
   isochronism & position
   adjusted
j — jewel
k — karat

k/s — key set
k/w — key wind
l/s — lever set
mvt — movement
o/f — open face
p/s — pendant set
r/g/p — rolled gold plate
s — size
s/s — single sunk dial
s/w — stem wind
w/g/f — white gold-filled
y/g/f — yellow gold-filled

Am Watch Co, 0s, 7j, #1891, 14k, h/c, Am Watch Co 475.00
Am Watch Co, 12s, 17j, #1894, 14k, o/f, Royal 285.00

Am Watch Co, 12s, 21j, #1894, 14k, h/c 495.00
Am Watch Co, 16s, 11j, #1872, p/s, silver h/c, Park Road 425.00
Am Watch Co, 16s, 15j, #1899, y/g/f, h/c 190.00
Am Watch Co, 16s, 16j, #1884, 5-min, 14k, Repeater 5,000.00
Am Watch Co, 16s, 17j, #1888, Railroader 675.00
Am Watch Co, 16s, 19j, #1872, 14k, h/c, Am Watch Woerd's Pat ...3,250.00
Am Watch Co, 16s, 21j, #1888, o/f, 14k, Riverside Maximus .1,475.00
Am Watch Co, 16s, 21j, #1899, y/g/f, l/s, o/f, Crescent St 325.00
Am Watch Co, 16s, 21j, #1908, y/g/f, o/f, Grade #645 ....280.00
Am Watch Co, 16s, 23j, #1908, o/f, 18k, Premier Maximus, MIB ..10,000.00
Am Watch Co, 16s, 23j, #1908, y/g/f, o/f, adj, RR, Vanguard 325.00
Am Watch Co, 16s, 23j, #1908, y/g/f, o/f, Vanguard Up/Down ..825.00
Am Watch Co, 18s, #1857, silver h/c, Samuel Curtiss k/w 3,450.00
Am Watch Co, 18s, 11j, #1857, k/w, 1st run, PS Barlett 900.00
Am Watch Co, 18s, 11j, #1857, silver h/c, k/w, DH&D 1,425.00
Am Watch Co, 18s, 11j, #1857, silver h/c, k/w, s/s, Ellery, EX ...325.00
Am Watch Co, 18s, 15j, #1877, k/w, RE Robbins 295.00
Am Watch Co, 18s, 15j, #1883, y/g/f, 2-tone, Railroad King 675.00
Am Watch Co, 18s, 17j, #1883, y/g/f, o/f, Crescent Street 175.00
Am Watch Co, 18s, 17j, #1892, HC, Canadian Pacific Railway 950.00
Am Watch Co, 18s, 17j, #1892, y/g/f, o/f, Sidereal, rare 1,950.00
Am Watch Co, 18s, 17j, 25-yr, y/g/f, o/f, s/s, PS Bartlett 180.00
Am Watch Co, 18s, 21j, #1892, y/g/f, o/f, d/s, Crescent St 325.00
Am Watch Co, 18s, 21j, #1892, y/g/f, o/f, Grade #845 ....325.00
Am Watch Co, 18s, 21j, #1892, y/g/f, o/f, Pennsylvania Special 1,900.00
Am Watch Co, 18s, 7j, #1857, silver case, k/w, CT Parker 2,000.00
Am Watch Co, 6s, 7j, #1873, y/g/f, h/c, Am Watch Co 195.00
Auburndale Watch Co, 18s, 7j, k/w, l/s, Lincoln 1,000.00
Aurora Watch Co, 18s, 11j, k/w, silver h/c 495.00
Aurora Watch Co, 18s, 15 ruby j, y/g/f, s/w 750.00
Ball (Elgin), 18s, 17j, o/f, silver, Official RR Standard 550.00
Ball (Hamilton), 16s, 21j, #999, g/f, o/f, l/s 425.00
Ball (Hamilton), 16s, 23j, #998, y/g/f, o/f, Elinvar 1,000.00
Ball (Hamilton), 18s, 19j, #999, g/f, o/f, l/s 550.00
Ball (Hampden), 18s, 17j, o/f, adj, RR, Superior Grade 1,650.00
Ball (Illinois), 12s, 19j, w/g/f, o/f 250.00
Ball (Waltham), 16s, 17j, y/g/f, o/f, Commercial Std 225.00
Ball (Waltham), 16s, 21j, o/f, Offical Standard 440.00
Columbus, 18s, 11-15j, k/w, k/s 450.00
Columbus, 18s, 15j, o/f, l/s 225.00
Columbus, 18s, 15j, y/g/f, o/f, Jay Gould on dial 625.00
Columbus, 18s, 21j, y/g/f, h/c, train on dial, Railway King 675.00
Columbus, 18s, 23j, 14k h/c, Columbus King 1,900.00
Columbus, 6s, 11j, 14k h/c 495.00
Cornell, 18s, 15j, s/w, JC Adams 625.00
Cornell, 18s, 15j, silver h/c, k/w, John Evans 540.00
Dudley, 12s, #1, 14k, o/f, flip-bk case, Masonic 3,500.00
Elgin, 10s, 18k, h/c, k/w, k/s, s/s, Gail Borden 650.00
Elgin, 12s, 15j, 14k, h/c 450.00
Elgin, 12s, 17j, 14k, h/c, GM Wheeler 425.00
Elgin, 16s, 15j, doctor's, 4th model, 18k, 2nd sweep hand, h/c 1,400.00
Elgin, 16s, 15j, 14k, h/c 595.00
Elgin, 16s, 21j, g/f, 3 fbd, grade #91, scarce 2,250.00
Elgin, 16s, 21j, y/g/f, g/j/s, o/f, BW Raymond 325.00
Elgin, 16s, 21j, y/g/f, g/j/s, 3 fbd 395.00
Elgin, 16s, 21j, y/g/f, o/f, l/s, RR, Father Time 295.00
Elgin, 16s, 23j, up/down indicator, BW Raymond 975.00
Elgin, 17s, 7j, k/w, orig silver case, Leader 150.00
Elgin, 18s, 11j, silver, h/c, k/w, gilded, MG Odgen 225.00
Elgin, 18s, 15j, o/f, d/s, k/w, silveroid, RR, BW Raymond 1st run 950.00
Elgin, 18s, 15j, silver, k/w, k/s, h/c, HL Culver 275.00
Elgin, 18s, 15j, silver h/c, Penn RR dial, BW Raymond k/w mvt ..2,250.00
Elgin, 18s, 17j, silveroid, BW Raymond 150.00
Elgin, 18s, 21j, y/g/f, o/f, Father Time 325.00

Elgin, 18s, 23j, y/g/f, o/f, 5-position, RR, Veritas 485.00
Elgin, 6s, 11j, 14k, h/c 325.00
Elgin, 6s, 15j, 20-yr, y/g/f, h/c, s/s 110.00
Fredonia, 18s, 11j, y/g/f, h/c, k/w 425.00
Hamilton, #4992B, 16s, 22j, o/f, steel case 280.00
Hamilton, #910, 12s, 17j, 20-yr, y/g/f, o/f, s/s 110.00
Hamilton, #912, 12s, 17j, y/g/f, o/f, adj 110.00
Hamilton, #920, 12s, 23j, 14k, o/f 425.00
Hamilton, #922MP, 12s, 18k case, Masterpiece (sgn) 1,100.00
Hamilton, #925, 18s, 17j, y/g/f, h/c, s/s, l/s 220.00
Hamilton, #928, 18s, 15j, y/g/f, o/f, s/s 160.00
Hamilton, #933, 18s, 16j, h/c, nickel plate, low serial # 1,400.00
Hamilton, #938, 18s, 17j, 10k, y/g/f, adj 750.00
Hamilton, #940, 18s, 21j, nickel plate, coin silver, o/f 375.00
Hamilton, #946, 18s, 23j, y/g/f, o/f, g/j/s, EX 675.00
Hamilton, #947 (mk), 18s, 23j, 14k, h/c, orig/sgn, EX 7,450.00
Hamilton, #950, 16s, 23j, y/g/f, o/f, l/s, sgn d/s 675.00
Hamilton, #965, 16s, 17j, 14k, p/s, h/c, brg, scarce 1,200.00
Hamilton, #972, 16s, 17j, y/g/f, g/j/s, o/f, d/s, l/s, adj 200.00
Hamilton, #974, 16s, 17j, 20-yr, y/g/f, o/f, s/s 150.00
Hamilton, #992, 16s, 21j, y/g/f, o/f, adj, d/s, dbl roller 265.00
Hamilton, #992B, 16s, 21j, y/g/f, o/f, l/s, Bar/Crown 350.00
Hampden, 12s, 17j, w/g/f, o/f, thin model, Aviator 120.00
Hampden, 16s, 17j, o/f, adj 90.00
Hampden, 16s, 17j, y/g/f, h/c, s/w 185.00
Hampden, 16s, 21j, g/j/s, y/g/f, NP, h/c, Dueber, ¾-mvt 280.00
Hampden, 16s, 21j, o/f, adj, dbl roller, Special Railway 350.00
Hampden, 16s, 7j, gilded, nickel plate, ¾-mvt 85.00
Hampden, 18s, 15j, k/w, mk on mvt, Railway 800.00
Hampden, 18s, 15j, s/w, gilded, JC Perry 225.00
Hampden, 18s, 15j, silver, k/w, h/c, Hayward 240.00
Hampden, 18s, 15j, y/g/f, damascened, h/c, Dueber 165.00
Hampden, 18s, 21j, y/g/f, g/j/s, h/c, New Railway 280.00
Hampden, 18s, 21j, y/g/f, o/f, d/s, l/s, N Am Railway 325.00
Hampden, 18s, 23j, y/g/f, d/s, adj, New Railway 365.00
Hampden, 18s, 23j, 14k, h/c, Special Railway 950.00
Hampden, 18s, 7-11j, k/w, gilded, Springfield Mass 195.00
Howard, E; 16s, 15j, s/w, 14k h/c, Series V, L sz 1,350.00
Howard, E; 18s, 15j, h/c, silver case, k/w, Series I, N sz 2,400.00
Howard, E; 18s, 15j, 18k h/c, k/w, Series II, N sz 3,400.00
Howard, E; 18s, 17j, 25-yr, y/g/f, o/f, orig case 675.00
Howard, E; 6s, 15j, s/w, 18k h/c, Series VIII, G sz 1,200.00
Howard (Keystone), 12s, 23j, 14k, h/c, brg, Series 8 ....650.00
Howard (Keystone), 16s, 17j, y/g/f, o/f, Series 9 ....295.00
Howard (Keystone), 16s, 21j, y/g/f, o/f, RR Chronometer II 525.00
Howard (Keystone), 16s, 23j, y/g/f, o/f, Series 0, jeweled bbl 695.00
Illinois, 0s, 7j, 14k, l/s, h/c 325.00
Illinois, 12s, 17j, y/g/f, o/f, d/s dial 95.00
Illinois, 16s, 17j, y/g/f, o/f, d/s, Bunn, EX 225.00
Illinois, 16s, 19j, y/g/f, o/f, d/s, 60-hr, Sangamo Special 1,200.00
Illinois, 16s, 21j, g/j/s, h/c, Burlington 295.00
Illinois, 16s, 21j, o/f, d/s, Santa Fe Special 395.00
Illinois, 16s, 21j, y/g/f, o/f, s/s, Bunn Special 325.00
Illinois, 16s, 23j, y/g/f, stiff bow, o/f, Sangamo Special 795.00
Illinois, 18s, 11j, #1, silver, k/w, Alleghany 190.00
Illinois, 18s, 11j, #3, o/f, s/w, l/s, Comet 250.00
Illinois, 18s, 11j, Forest City 225.00
Illinois, 18s, 15j, #1, adj, y/g/f, k/w, h/c, gilt, Bunn 775.00
Illinois, 18s, 15j, #1, k/w, k/s, silver hunter, Stuart 675.00
Illinois, 18s, 15j, k/w, k/s, gilt, Railway Regulator 675.00
Illinois, 18s, 15j, s/w, silveroid 95.00
Illinois, 18s, 17j, g/j/s, adj, B&O RR Special (Hunter), h/c 1,375.00
Illinois, 18s, 17j, h/c, s/w, nickel plate, coin silver, Bunn 375.00
Illinois, 18s, 17j, o/f, d/s, adj, silveroid case, Lakeshore 175.00

Illinois, 18s, 17j, o/f, s/w, 5th pinion, Miller 225.00
Illinois, 18s, 21j, g/j/s, g/f, o/f, A Lincoln 340.00
Illinois, 18s, 21j, g/j/s, o/f, adj, B&O RR Special 1,625.00
Illinois, 18s, 21j, 14k, g/j/s, h/c, Bunn Special 900.00
Illinois, 18s, 23j, g/j/s, Bunn Special 625.00
Illinois, 18s, 24j, g/j/s, adj, o/f, Chesapeake & Ohio 2,400.00
Illinois, 18s, 24j, g/j/s, Bunn Special 825.00
Illinois, 18s, 26j, g/j/s, o/f, Ben Franklin USA 6,500.00
Illinois, 18s, 26j, 14k, Penn Special 6,000.00
Illinois, 18s, 7j, #3, Interior 150.00
Illinois, 18s, 7j, #3, silveroid, America 100.00
Illinois, 18s, 9-11j, o/f, k/w, s/s, silveroid case, Hoyt 150.00
Illinois, 8s, 13j, 3/4-mvt, Rose LeLand, scarce 275.00
Ingersoll, 16s, 7j, wht base metal, Reliance 45.00
Lancaster, 18s, 7j, o/f, k/w, k/s, eng silver case 150.00
Marion US, 18s, h/c, k/w, k/s, ¾-plate, Asa Fuller 350.00
Marion US, 18s, 15j, nickel plate, h/c, s/w, Henry Randel 400.00
Melrose Watch Co, 18s, 7j, k/w, k/s 375.00
New York Watch Co, 18s, 7j, silver, h/c, k/w, Geo Sam Rice 375.00
New York Watch Co, 19j, low sz #, wolf's teeth wind 1,495.00
Patek Philippe, 12s, 18j, 18k, o/f 1,650.00
Patek Philippe, 16s, 20j, 18k, h/c 2,650.00
Rockford, 16s, 17j, y/g/f, h/c, brg, dbl roller 190.00
Rockford, 16s, 21j, #515, y/g/f 275.00
Rockford, 16s, 21j, g/j/s, o/f, grade #537, rare 800.00
Rockford, 16s, 23j, 14k, o/f, mk Doll on dial/mvt 2,000.00
Rockford, 18s, 15j, o/f, k/w, silver case 250.00
Rockford, 18s, 17j, silveroid w/mc dial, fancy mvt/hands 375.00
Rockford, 18s, 17j, y/g/f, o/f, Winnebago 250.00
Rockford, 18s, 21j, o/f, King Edward 395.00
Seth Thomas, 18s, 17j, #2, g/j/s, adj, Henry Molineux 625.00
Seth Thomas, 18s, 17j, Edgemere 100.00
Seth Thomas, 18s, 25j, g/j/s, g/f, Maiden Lane 2,450.00
Seth Thomas, 18s, 7j, ¾-mvt, bk: eagle/Liberty model 150.00
South Bend, 12s, 21j, dbl roller, Grade #431 ....225.00
South Bend, 12s, 21j, orig o/f, d/s, Studebaker 250.00
South Bend, 18s, 21j, g/j/s, h/c, Studebaker 925.00
South Bend, 18s, 21j, 14k, h/c 800.00
Swiss, 18s, 18k, h/c, 1-min, Repeater, High Grade 3,650.00

Waterford

The Waterford Glass Company operated in Ireland from the late 1700s until 1851 when the factory closed. One hundred years later (in 1951) another Waterford glassworks was instituted that produced glass similar to the 18th-century wares — crystal glass, usually with cut decoration. Today Waterford is a generic term referring to the type of glass first produced there.

Bottle, scent; Lismore, w/4" dauber 98.00
Bowl, dessert; Colleen, stemmed, 4⅜x4½" 120.00
Bowl, dessert; Powercourt, stemmed 120.00
Champagne, Powercourt, 8-oz, 5½" 98.00
Cocktail, Colleen, 5½-oz 85.00
Compote, Colleen, ftd, lg 99.00
Compote/candy dish, Glandore, stemmed, 5½" 90.00
Cordial, Lismore 45.00
Dealer's sign, 8½" 67.50
Decanter, Baltray, star base, paneled neck, rnd stopper, 10½" 200.00
Decanter, invt arches w/t'print centers, honeycomb stopper 200.00
Decanter, Lismore, 13" 298.00
Flute champagne, Lismore 55.00
Goblet, Alana, 10-oz, 7" 59.00

Goblet, Powercourt, 10-oz 98.00
Jar, overall cuttings, cylinder w/galleried rim, inset lid 85.00
Jar, pineapple shape, cut, heavy, w/lid, 8½" 90.00
Old-fashioned, dbl; Lismore, 14½" 65.00
Pitcher, Lismore 115.00
Shakers, Lismore, ftd, pr 185.00
Tumbler, Boyne, 10-oz 80.00
Tumbler, highball; Colleen, 12-oz, 5½" 75.00
Tumbler, water; Colleen, 10-oz 60.00
Vase, cut/stylized flowers & geometrics, ftd, 10x6½" 165.00
Vase, ornate cutting, scalloped top, sgn, 9½" 225.00
Wine, Castletown, 7⅛" 185.00
Wine, Colleen, 4" 79.00
Wine, Powercourt, 6-oz, 7⅛" 98.00

Watt Pottery

The Watt Pottery Company was established in Crooksville, Ohio, on July 5, 1922. From approximately 1922 until 1935, they manufactured hand-turned stone containers — jars, jugs, milk pans, preserve jars, and various sizes of mixing bowls, usually marked with a cobalt blue acorn stamp. In 1936 production of these items was discontinued, and the company began to produce kitchen utilityware and ovenware such as mixing bowls, spaghetti bowls and plates, canister sets, covered casseroles, salt and pepper shakers, cookie jars, ice buckets, pitchers, bean pots, and salad and dinnerware sets. Most Watt ware is individually hand painted with bold brush strokes of red, green, or blue contrasting with the natural buff color of the glazed body. Several patterns were produced: Apple, Autumn Foliage, Cherry, Dutch Tulip, Morning Glory, Rio Rose, Rooster, Tear Drop, Starflower, and Tulip, to name a few. Much of the ware was made for advertising premiums and is often found stamped with the name of the retail company.

Tragedy struck the Watt Pottery Company on October 4, 1965, when fire completely destroyed the factory and warehouse. Production never resumed, but the ware they made has withstood many years of service in American kitchens and is today highly regarded and prized by collectors. The vivid colors and folk art-like execution of each cheerful pattern create a homespun ambiance that will make Watt pottery a treasure for years to come.

For further study we recommend *Watt Pottery, An Identification and Price Guide,* by our advisors for this category, Sue and Dave Morris; they are listed in the Directory under Oregon. For the address of the *Watt's News* newsletter, see the section on Clubs, Newsletters, and Catalogs.

Apple, bowl, cereal; #94 ....45.00
Apple, bowl, ribbed, #04 ....65.00
Apple, bowl, w/advertising, #7 ....45.00
Apple, casserole, Fr hdl, w/lid, #18, ind 225.00
Apple, casserole, ribbed, #601, w/lid 125.00
Apple, cookie jar, w/lid, #503 ....425.00
Apple, creamer, #62 ....90.00
Apple, ice bucket, w/lid 250.00
Apple, mug, #121 ....175.00
Apple, pie plate, w/advertising, #33 ....125.00
Apple, pitcher, #15 ....75.00
Apple, pitcher, w/ice lip, #17 ....225.00
Apple, shakers, hourglass form, pr 250.00
Apple, sugar bowl, w/lid, #98 ....400.00
Autumn Foliage, baker, w/lid, #96 ....90.00
Autumn Foliage, bowl, mixing; #6 ....35.00
Autumn Foliage, pie plate, w/advertising, #33 ....125.00
Autumn Foliage, pitcher, #15 ....65.00
Autumn Foliage, shakers, hourglass form, pr 175.00

Banded, casserole, bl & wht bands, w/lid, 8" dia 55.00
Basketweave, bowl, mixing; gr, #8 ....30.00
Brown glaze, dog dish, #7 ....145.00
Cherry, bowl, cereal; #52 ....55.00
Cherry, bowl, salad; #55 ....175.00
Cherry, bowl, spaghetti; #39 ....125.00
Cherry, cookie jar, w/lid, #21 ....250.00
Cherry, pitcher, w/advertising, #15 ....175.00
Cherry, shaker, bbl shape 90.00
Dutch Tulip, bowl, mixing; #6 ....100.00
Dutch Tulip, casserole, w/lid, #66 ....250.00
Dutch Tulip, cheese crock, w/lid, #80 ....475.00
Dutch Tulip, pitcher, #15 ....225.00
Dutch Tulip, refrigerator pitcher, sq, #69 ....600.00
Eagle, bowl, mixing; ribbed, #7 ....125.00
Esmond, Happy & Sad Face cookie jar, wooden lid 275.00
Goodies Jar, w/lid, #59 ....350.00
Kitch-N-Queen, bowl, mixing; #7 ....30.00
Kitch-N-Queen, pitcher, w/ice lip, #17 ....165.00
Morning Glory, bowl, mixing; #7 ....85.00
Morning Glory, pitcher, w/ice lip, #17 ....375.00
Rio Rose, bowl, berry; 4" 25.00
Rio Rose, bowl, spaghetti; #39, 13" 80.00
Rio Rose, casserole, stick hdl, w/lid, ind 100.00
Rio Rose, cut-leaf, casserole, w/lid, 8" 75.00
Rio Rose, cut-leaf, plate, dinner; 8½" 45.00

Rooster baking dish, rectangular, 2½x10x5¼", $1,000.00.

Rooster, bowl, mixing; #7 ....65.00
Rooster, creamer, w/advertising, #62 ....225.00
Rooster, ice bucket, w/lid 275.00
Rooster, pitcher, #16 ....160.00
Starflower, bowl, cereal; #74 ....25.00
Starflower, bowl, mixing; #8 ....35.00
Starflower, mug, bbl shape, #501 ....90.00
Starflower, pitcher, #15 ....65.00
Tear Drop, bean server, #75, ind 25.00
Tear Drop, bowl, ribbed, #07 ....40.00
Tear Drop, casserole, w/lid, #66 ....85.00
Tear Drop, pitcher, #15 ....65.00
Tulip, bowl, deep mixing; #63 ....75.00
Tulip, casserole, ribbed, w/lid, #601 ....265.00
Tulip, creamer, #62 ....225.00
Tulip, pitcher, w/ice lip, #17 ....300.00
White Daisy, casserole, w/lid, 8" 145.00

Wave Crest

Wave Crest is a line of decorated opal ware (milk glass)
patented in 1892 by the C.F. Monroe Co. of Meriden, Connecticut. They made a full line of items for every room of the house, but they are probably best known for their boxes and vases. Most items were hand painted in various levels of decoration, but more transfers were used in the later years prior to the company's demise in 1916. Floral themes are common; items with the scenics and portraits are rarer and more highly prized. Many pieces have ornately scrolled ormolu and brass handles, feet, and rims attached. Early pieces were often signed with a black mark; later a red banner mark was used, and occasionally a paper label may be found. However, the glass is quite distinctive and has not been reproduced, so even unmarked items are easy to recognize. Our advisors for this category are Dolli and Wilfred Cohen; they are listed in the Directory under California. Note: There is no premium for signatures on Wave Crest. Values are given for hand-decorated pieces (unless noted 'transfer') that are *not* worn.

Biscuit jar, daisies HP, emb leaves, 7½" dia 595.00
Biscuit jar, lilac transfer on pk, tapered, rtcl finial, 6" 175.00
Biscuit jar, pk roses transfer on tulip mold, metal trim, 8" 300.00
Biscuit jar, wild roses transfer, pk & bl on lt yel, 7x6" 175.00
Box, Egg Crate, mc floral/scrolls w/gold, metal mts, 5x3" 450.00
Box, lake-side cottage on lid, 2½x3½" dia 225.00
Box, orange/yel bouquets, dotted banner w/pk edge, 4x5½x3½" 650.00
Box, Puffy, bl forget-me-nots, lav scrolls, 3½x6½" 700.00
Box, Puffy, clover/daisies, red/wht on tan, ormolu ft, 6x5" 450.00
Box, Puffy, Collars & Cuffs, daisies & foliage, 7½x5" 1,250.00
Box, Swirl, bl floral bouquet w/mc details, 7" 595.00
Box, Swirl, forget-me-nots in bl/lav on lid, 4½" dia 225.00
Box, village/camel on lid, ivy on base, 2¼x4½" dia 300.00
Cigar holder/smoke set, hunting dog/cherub, 5x7" 600.00
Creamer & sugar bowl, bird on fence transfer, 3x4" 175.00
Match holder, floral, bl on wht, metal base, 3¾x3" 225.00
Photograph holder, Puffy, bl flowers, ornate rim, 4" 495.00
Photograph holder, Puffy, mc floral, brass rim, 4½x5½" 495.00
Shaker, Erie Twist, mc floral, 2½" 125.00
Spooner, floral transfer, rare 285.00
Sugar shaker, Swirl, colorful arrow leaves on bl 525.00
Vase, asters & emb scrolls on yel, gilt rim, 13¾" 975.00
Vase, floral, bl on gr w/wht beads, bulbous, ftd, 4¾x4½" 350.00
Vase, pastel florals cascade from gilt rim, cylindrical, 6¼" 300.00
Vase, pk flowers, ormolu hdls, 6½" 500.00
Vase, stylized floral on bl w/gold, scroll hdls, 12½x9½" 1,950.00

Weapons

Among the varied areas of specialization within the broad category of weapons, guns are by far the most popular. Muskets are among the earliest firearms; they were large-bore shoulder arms, usually firing black powder with separate loading of powder and shot. Some ignited the charge by flintlock or caplock, while later types used a firing pin with a metallic cartridge. Side arms, referred to as such because they were worn at the side, include pistols and revolvers. Pistols range from early single-shot and multiple barrels to modern types with cartridges held in the handle. Revolvers were supplied with a cylinder that turned to feed a fresh round in front of the barrel breech. Other firearms include shotguns, which fired round or conical bullets and had a smooth inner barrel surface, and rifles, so named because the interior of the barrel contained spiral grooves (rifling) which increased accuracy. For further study we recommend *Modern Guns, Eleventh Edition*, by Russell Quertermous and Steve Quertermous, available at your local bookstore. All weapons but swords are under the advisement of Steve Howard, see the Directory under California. See also Militaria.

Key:
bbl — barrel
cal — caliber
conv — conversion
cyl — cylinder
f/l — flintlock
f/s — full stock
ga — gauge
hdw — hardware
h/s — half stock

mag — magazine
mgn — magnum
mod — modified
oct — octagon
o/u — over/under
p/b — patch box
perc — percussion
/s — stock

Carbines

Burnside 4th Model Civil war, 54 cal perc, 1-shot, 21" bbl, G- ..**375.00**
Greene British, 54 cal, perc single shot, walnut/s, p/b, G **850.00**
IBM Line-Out M-1, 30 cal, flip sight, bbl dtd 43, NM **300.00**
Inland Line-Out Rock-Ola M-1, 30 cal, flip sight, flat bolt, EX .**400.00**
Inland M1, 30 cal, cannons on stock, bbl dtd 12-44, EX orig **500.00**
Irwin Pederson M-1, 30-cal, Rock-Ola bbl, flat bolt, EX **500.00**
Kentland & Co f/l, brass Brn Bess trigger, 1760-80, 25" bbl, VG **500.00**
Krag 1895, 30-40 cal, 22" bbl w/integral front sight, EX **850.00**
Nat'l Postal Meter M-1, 30 cal, IBM bbl, flip sight, EX **700.00**
Rock Island 1903 Bushmaster, 30-06 cal, 20" bbl, EX **450.00**
Saginaw M-1, 30 cal, steering gear, flat bolt & sight, NM **750.00**
Smith Civil War, 50 cal, perc breech loader, walnut/s, G **1,400.00**
Spencer Civil War Repeating, 52 cal rimfire, 22" rnd bbl, G ..**1,300.00**
Springfield US 1873 Trap Door, 45-70 cal, 22" rnd bbl, G- **350.00**
Springfield 1903 Experimental, 30-06 cal, ca 1921, 20" bbl, M **1,000.00**
Underwood M-1, 30 cal, dog-leg hammer/flat bolt/flip sight, EX **300.00**
Winchester M-1 Sniper, 30 cal, flat bolt, WRA proofed stock, NM .**550.00**
Winchester Model 94 Flat Band, 30 cal, str/s, NM **250.00**
Winchester M3, 30 cal, sniper scope, NM **850.00**
Winchester Post 64 Model 94, 30-30 cal, take down, 20" bbl, NM **300.00**

Muskets

AW Spies Warranted, 72 cal, smooth bore 40" bbl w/bayonet, VG ...**450.00**
Colt 1855 Martial, 56 cal, unique period fr, 31¼" bbl, VG **2,750.00**
Colt 1861 Special, Am Machine Wks, 50 cal perc, 1-shot, NM **4,000.00**
Dutch perc military, 69 cal, 40" rnd bbl w/bayonet, VG **600.00**
E India Brn Bess, f/l mk/dtd 1801, 37¼" rnd bbl, VG **450.00**
Russian f/l, Cyrillic mks, dtd 1834, iron ramrod, G **300.00**
Savage US 1861 Contract Rifle-Musket, 58 cal, 1863, 40" bbl, EX .**2,700.00**
Springfield 1863, 58 cal perc, std issue, tulip-head ramrod, G **450.00**
Tower British Indian Pattern Brn Bess, 70 cal, smooth bore, G ..**700.00**
Winchester 1885 Hi-Wall Winder, 22 cal, 28" rnd bbl, NM **600.00**

Pistols

Beretta 1934 Military, 32 ACP cal, rubber grips, eagle on fr, EX **300.00**
Colt Gold Cup Target, 45 cal, NP fr, checkered grips, NM **750.00**
Colt 1849 Pocket, 31 cal, 5-shot, 5" 8-sided bbl, VG **500.00**
High std S-101 Supermatic USMC, 22 cal, 6¾" bbl, EX **300.00**
Lugar 1916 DWM Artillery, 9mm cal, rebuilt/rstr, w/tool/holster **450.00**
Reising Semi-Auto Target, 22 cal, rubber grips, 6¾" bbl, EX **225.00**
Remington Vest Pocket, 22 cal rimfire, 1-shot, 3¼" bbl, VG **500.00**
Remington 1865 Navy, 50 cal rimfire, rolling block, VG **1,250.00**
Remington 51, 32 cal, rubber grips, EX **425.00**
Ruger Hawkeye Single Shot, 256 cal, 8½" bbl, w/scope, NM **750.00**
Savage 1905 Semi-Auto, 32 cal, metal grips, 3¾" bbl, EX **300.00**
Savage 1910 Pocket, 32 cal, rubber grips, 3½" bbl, VG **110.00**

Stevens 35 Offhand Target, 22 cal, 6" part rnd bbl, NP fr, G **110.00**

Revolvers

Smith & Wesson Model 29-2 double-action revolver, 44 Mag. caliber, blued 4" barrel, target trigger and hammer, magnum grips, M unfired, $500.00 to $600.00.

Colt Frontier Scout, 22 mgn cal, single action, 4¾" bbl, NM **350.00**
Colt New Frontier, 22/22 mgn cal, single action, EX **300.00**
Colt 1849 Pocket, 31 cal, 6-shot, 4" 8-sided bbl, G **450.00**
Merwin & Hulbert Army, 44-40 cal, 7" bbl, late production, EX **650.00**
Remington Smoot New Model #1, 30 cal rimfire short, 5-shot, EX ...**650.00**
Rogers & Spencer Army, 44 cal, 6-shot, 7½" 8-sided bbl, VG ...**700.00**
Smith & Wesson Model 10, 38 special cal, 4-screw, EX **170.00**
Smith & Wesson New Departure Safety Hammerless, 32 cal, NP, EX .**125.00**
Smith & Wesson 2nd Model Schofield Single Action, 45 cal, G **1,125.00**
Smith & Wesson 5-screw K22 Masterpiece, 22 cal, 6" bbl, EX ...**200.00**

Rifles

Browning Repro 1886, 45-70 cal, std grade, 26" 8-sided bbl, EX **650.00**
Enfield Pattern 14, 303 British cal, std issue, NM **350.00**
Krag 1896, 30-40 cal, 3-pc cleaning kit in butt trap, NM **450.00**
Krag 1896 Bolt Action, 30-40 cal, cleaning kit in butt trap, NM **500.00**
Remington 1903A3 Bolt Action, 30-06 cal, mk bbl, M **200.00**
Rock Island 1903 Bolt Action, 30-06 cal, mk bbl, EX **150.00**
Springfield M-1 Garand Semi-Auto, 308 cal, rstr, NM **450.00**
Springfield U S 1888 Trap Door, 45-70 cal, w/bayonet, VG **500.00**
Springfield 1903 Sniper, 30-06 cal, w/A-5 scope/silencer, NM **600.00**
Stevens Visible Loader Pump, 22 cal, ⅔-mag, 22" rnd bbl, EX ...**200.00**
Winchester Pre-64 100 Semi-Auto, 308 cal, walnut stock, NM .**250.00**
Winchester 1890 Pump, 22 cal, 24" 8-sided bbl, VG **500.00**
Winchester 92 Lever Action, 38 cal, 24" 8-sided bbl, EX **750.00**

Shotguns

Browning Sweet 16 A-5 Semi-Auto, 16 ga, 38" bbl, pistol grip, NM ...**375.00**
Dakin, 20 ga, 26" dbl bbls, eng receiver, VG **175.00**
LC Smith Featherweight Field Grade, 20 ga, 28" dbl bbls, NM **2,000.00**
LC Smith Grade 2, 12 ga, 28" dbl bbls, rstr **400.00**
Marlin LC Smith, 12 ga, 28" dbl bbls w/full/mod chokes, NM ...**750.00**
Marlin 90, 410 ga, 26" o/u dbl bbls, rpl stock/forearm, EX **325.00**
Parker, 12 ga, 30" dbl bbls, beavertail forearm, str/s, rstr **750.00**
Parker VHE, 12 ga, 30" dbl bbls w/chokes, splinter forearm, NM **800.00**
Smith & Wesson 916A Stainless Steel Pump, 12-ga, 20" bbl, NM ...**600.00**
Weatherby Orion II, 20 ga, 26 o/u bbls, screw chokes, NM **700.00**
Winchester Model 12 Pump, 20 ga, 28 full choke plain bbl, NM **700.00**
Winchester Model 42 Pump, 410 ga, 26" mod bbl, NM **750.00**

Swords

All swords listed below are priced 'with scabbard,' unless otherwise noted.

British Pattern 1853 Infantry officer, 32½" str blade, EX 125.00
Franco-Prussian War Era Cavalry, brass hilt, 1974 on 36" blade 300.00
French Artillery officer, brass hilt, much eng, 33" blade, EX ...1,600.00
French Dragoon Cavalry, brass 4-branch hilt, 36" str blade 300.00
US 1840 Cavalry, brass 3-branch basket hilt, leather grip, 36" ...375.00
US 1840 Cavalry officer, brass 3-branch hilt, curved blade, EX .600.00
US 1860 Light Cavalry, 3-branch guard, dtd 1862, 34" blade 375.00
US 1860 Staff/Field officer presentation, 1880s, EX+ 1,150.00
US 1861 Naval Cutlass repro, brass guard, 26" curved blade, EX 185.00
US 1872 Artillery officer, P-shaped guard, etched blade, EX 225.00

Weather Vanes

The earliest weather vanes were of handmade wrought iron and were generally simple angular silhouettes with a small hole suggesting an eye. Later copper, zinc, and polychromed wood with features in relief were fashioned into more realistic forms. Ships, horses, fish, Indians, roosters, and angels were popular motifs. In the 19th century, silhouettes were often made from sheet metal. Wooden figures became highly carved and were painted in vivid colors. E.G. Washburne and Company in New York was one of the most prominent manufacturers of weather vanes during the last half of the century. Two-dimensional sheet metal weathervanes are increasing in value due to the already heady prices of the full-bodied variety. Originality, strength of line, and patination help to determine value. When no condition is indicated, the items listed below are assumed to be in excellent condition.

Key:
fb — full-bodied   f/fb — flattened full-bodied

Arrow, copper, zinc & iron, w/directionals, 24½x35½" 3,200.00
Arrow, pine w/old yel pnt, old rprs, OH, 65" 1,700.00
Banner, copper, geometric cutouts, late 1800s, 28½" 460.00
Beaver, copper, primitive style, 20th C, 61" H on base 275.00
Bull, copper w/gilt & verdigris, f/fb, rpr, 19th C, 24" 2,100.00
Cow, copper, fb, rpr bullet holes, early 1900s, 28" 2,875.00
Cow, copper & CI, fb, early 1900s, 26" 2,185.00
Cow, copper w/cast-zinc head, fb, gilt traces, 18x26"+base 3,850.00
Eagle, copper & zinc w/verdigris, ca 1900, 10½" 1,150.00
Eagle, copper w/old gilt, early 1900s, Am, 12" 1,380.00
Eagle, gilt copper, ca 1890s, 18x24" 900.00
Eagle in flight, copper w/gold pnt, 7x14" 600.00
Horse, running, copper, att AL Jewell, MA, 26", EX 2,750.00
Horse, running, copper, ca 1900, 22x42" 1,955.00
Horse, running, copper, f/fb, rpr, late 1800s, 37" 1,725.00
Horse, running, copper, fb, EX detail, gilt traces, 28" 1,100.00
Horse, running, copper, gold/silver/blk rpt, CI arrow, 71" H 270.00
Horse, running, copper, rpt, detached tail, 1890s, 42" 1,600.00
Horse, running, copper & CI, gilt & verdigris, 1890s, 29" 2,750.00
Horse, running, copper w/cast-zinc head, rprs, 44" L 2,200.00
Horse, running, copper w/verdigris, late 1800s, 31¼", EX 1,380.00
Horse, running, hollow copper w/cast-zinc head, 27" L 825.00
Indian shooting arrow, copper, 20th C, soldered, 41" 165.00
Lyre-form banner, gilt copper, verdigris, 19th C, 65" 3,450.00
Merino ram, copper & zinc, fine verdigris, 19th C, rpr, 29" 6,900.00
Rooster, cvd wood w/gilt & mustard pnt traces, 18x26" 800.00
Rooster, gilt copper, 19th C, 19" 3,220.00
Rooster, gilt copper w/verdigris, red pnt traces, 22" 2,500.00
Rooster, gilt copper w/verdigris, 19th C, 21" 1,955.00
Rooster, sheet metal, low relief, rust, 20½" L 150.00
Rooster & arrow w/James in hollow shaft, CI/zinc, rprs, 25" L 870.00
Rooster on arrow, zinc, red rpt over silver, on base, 26" 95.00
Ship, copper & wood, 3-masted, old pnt, ca 1900, 40" 575.00

Stag, running, sheet iron, 40x49½" 1,600.00
Swordfish, copper w/verdigris, Am, 20th C, 43" 980.00

Weaving

Early Americans used a variety of tools and a great amount of time to produce the material from which their clothing was made. Soaked and dried flax was broken on a flax brake to remove waste material. It was then tapped and stroked with a scutching knife. Hackles further removed waste and separated the short fibers from the longer ones. Unspun fibers were placed on the distaff on the spinning wheel for processing into yarn. The yarn was then wound around a reel for measuring. Three tools used for this purpose were the niddy-noddy, the reel yarn winder, and the click reel. After it was washed and dyed, the yarn was transferred to a barrel-cage or squirrel-cage swift and fed onto a bobbin winder.

Today flax wheels are more plentiful than the large wool wheels since they were small and could be more easily stored and preserved. The distaff, an often-discarded or misplaced part of the wheel, is very scarce. French spinners from the Quebec area painted their wheels. Many have been stripped and refinished by those unaware of this fact. Wheels may be very simple or have a great amount of detail, depending upon the owner's ethnic background and the maker's skill. Our advisor for this category is Rosella Tinsley; she is listed in the Directory under Kansas.

Photo courtesy Aston Americana

Tape loom, walnut, cut-out decorative handle, 18th century, $380.00 to $450.00.

Flax wheel, oak, Am, early 19th C, EX 175.00
Loom, tape; wooden fish form, early 1800s, 19½x7¼", EX 300.00
Loom, wrought iron, T-shaped hanger, complete, 23" 715.00
Niddy noddy, wooden w/bent wood support ea end, trn shaft, 18" 65.00
Spinning wheel, hardwoods, dk patina, branded, AK, 33", EX ...165.00
Spinning wheel, maple/ash/pine, pegged, 12-spoke, 1820s, EX ...600.00
Spinning wheel, N Wolf T, old blk pnt, distaff missing, 21½" ...220.00
Spinning wheel, rfn hardwood, rpl parts, 39" 215.00
Swift, brass, marble base, acorn finial, 14¼" 250.00

Webb

Thomas Webb and Sons have been glassmakers in Stourbridge, England, since 1837. Besides their fine cameo glass, they have also made enameled ware and pieces heavily decorated with applied glass ornaments. The butterfly is a motif that has been so often featured that it tends to suggest Webb as the manufacturer. Our advisor for this category is Don Williams; he is listed in the Directory under Missouri. See also specific types of glass such as Alexandrite, Burmese, Mother of Pearl, and Peachblow.

Cameo

Bottle, lay-down, butterfly/palm fronds, wht on citron, 10" **1,800.00**
Bottle, lay-down; fuchsia/butterfly, wht on red, gilt cap, 3" **1,300.00**
Bottle, lay-down; leafy stalks, wht on bl, emb Starr lid, 7" **1,700.00**
Bottle, scent; wild roses, wht on bl, bulbous, 4" **2,200.00**
Bottle, scent; wild roses, wht on yel, bulbous, 4" **1,500.00**
Bowl, berry vines/insect, gold on pk fish scales, ribbed, 6" **550.00**
Bowl, foxglove floral branch/butterfly, wht on bl, 1⅛x6" **750.00**
Rose bowl, clematis on leafy vine/butterfly, wht on red, 4" **1,800.00**
Sweetmeat, morning glories, wht on citron, silver mts, 3x5" ...**1,500.00**
Tray, violets/grasses/etc, wht on raisin, ruffled, 6" dia **1,200.00**
Vase, apple branch on faux ivory, gourd form, 6" **1,000.00**
Vase, butterfly/fuchsia/vine, wht on red, cup rim, 6" **2,000.00**
Vase, cascading vines/clematis, wht on citron, 4" **950.00**
Vase, clematis/butterfly, wht on bl, neck ring, 7x7" **2,700.00**
Vase, floral, leaf band/bk: insects, wht/yel, stick neck, 17" **3,500.00**
Vase, floral/leaves, wht on citron, tapered, 3¼" **800.00**
Vase, floral, wht on amber, bulbous, att, 5", NM **800.00**
Vase, floral on honeycomb, purple on clear, ftd, 6¾x7" **700.00**
Vase, floral/3 geometric bands, wht on bl, 10½" **2,450.00**
Vase, floral/2 butterflies, 3-color att Woodall, 10x7" **4,750.00**
Vase, geraniums/butterfly, red/wht/yel frost, sgn, 9" **3,000.00**
Vase, gloxinia/dragonfly, wht on red, 5¾" **1,250.00**
Vase, mixed florals/geometrics, wht on sapphire bl, 4½" **700.00**
Vase, morning glories, wht on amber, shouldered, 5" **1,500.00**
Vase, morning glories/butterfly, wht on red, 8¼" **2,250.00**
Vase, roses, 3-color, bottle form, att Woodall, 13½ **6,000.00**
Vase, roses/butterfly, wht on bl, flattened oval, 7½" **1,265.00**
Vase, upright leaves form petal rim, faux ivory, 2½x2½" **950.00**

Miscellaneous

Bottle, lay-down; bl MOP Dmn Quilt, teardrop, 5½" **575.00**
Bowl, Rock Crystal, cut/eng lattice w/lanterns/vines, 7x9" **1,800.00**
Jardiniere, cranes/gilt/jeweled flowers on satin, 12x13" **650.00**
Pitcher, brn satin, bulbous, frosted hdl, 3¾x2½" **245.00**
Sweetmeat, heavy gold florals on aqua, SP lid/etc, 5x3⅜" **295.00**
Vase, floral, mc on shaded pk w/amber ruffle, 5¾x3⅛" **195.00**
Vase, gold lotus, floral branch on satin, 9½" **225.00**
Vase, gold seedlings/pk & wht flowers, stick neck, shiny, 8" **275.00**
Vase, heavy gold prunus on ivory opaque, stick form, 7½" **175.00**

Wedgwood

Josiah Wedgwood established his pottery in Burslem, England, in 1759. He produced only molded utilitarian earthenwares until 1770 when new facilities were opened at Etruria for the production of ornamental wares. It was there he introduced his famous Basalt and Jasper ware. Jasper ware, an unglazed fine stoneware decorated with classic figures in white relief, was usually produced in blues, but it was also made in ground colors of green, lilac, yellow, black, or white. Occasionally three or more colors were used in combination. It has been in continuous production to the present day and is the most easily recognized of all the Wedgwood lines. Jasper dip is a ware with a solid-color body or a white body that has been dipped in an overlay color. It was introduced in the late 1700s and is the type most often encountered on today's market. Though Wedgwood's Jasper ware was highly acclaimed, on a more practical basis his improved creamware was his greatest success. Due to the ease with which it could be potted and because its

lighter weight significantly reduced transportation expenses, Wedgwood was able to offer 'chinaware' at affordable prices. Queen Charlotte was so pleased with the ware that she allowed it to be called 'Queen's Ware.' Most creamware was marked simply 'Wedgwood.' ('Wedgwood & Co.' and 'Wedgewood' are marks of other potters.) From 1769 to 1780, Wedgwood was in partnership with Thomas Bentley; artwares of the highest quality may bear the 'Wedgwood & Bentley' mark indicating this partnership. Moonlight Lustre, an allover splashed-on effect of pink intermingling with gray, brown, or yellow, was made from 1805 to 1815. Porcelain was made, though not to any great extent, from 1812 to 1822. Bone china was produced before 1822 and after 1872. These types of wares were marked 'WEDGWOOD' (with a printed 'Portland Vase' mark after 1872). Stone china and Pearlware were made from about 1820 to 1875. Examples of either may be found with a printed or impressed mark to indicate their body type. During the late 1800s, Wedgwood produced some fine parian and majolica. Creamware, hand painted by Emile Lessore, was sold from about 1860 to 1875. From the 20th century, several lines of lustre wares — Butterfly, Dragon, and Fairyland (designed by Daisy Makeig-Jones) — have attracted the collector and, as their prices suggest, are highly sought after and admired.

Nearly all of Wedgwood's wares are clearly marked. 'WEDGWOOD' was used before 1891, after which time 'ENGLAND' was added. Most examples marked 'MADE IN ENGLAND' were made after 1905. A detailed study of all marks is recommended for accurate dating. See also Majolica.

Key:
WW — Wedgwood   WWMIE — Wedgwood Made in
WWE — Wedgwood England   England

Bust, black Basalt, Mercury, after John Flaxman, impressed late 19th century mark, 17⅝", $1,000.00.

Basket, Creamware, Twig, w/underplate, WW, 1830s, 11x9½" ..**850.00**
Biscuit barrel, Jasper, cobalt, baluster, WW, 5¼" **250.00**
Biscuit barrel, Jasper, gr, melon shape, WW, 6" **265.00**
Biscuit barrel, Jasper, lilac, SP lid/hdl, MIE **600.00**
Bowl, Bronze Lustre, fruit, MOP int, Z5458, ca 1928, 6½" **230.00**
Bowl, Creamware, Victoria Ware, SP rim, WW, 9½" **455.00**
Bowl, Dragon Lustre, WWE, 2½" **225.00**
Bowl, Fairyland Lustre, Elves, blk, WWE, 8⅞" **2,995.00**
Bowl, Fairyland Lustre, Elves, Empire shape, Z4968, WW, 4½" ..**2,250.00**
Bowl, Fairyland Lustre, Gargoyles, Z4968, WW, 7¾" **2,750.00**
Bowl, Fairyland Lustre, K'ang Hsi, sgn DMJ 3 times, WWE, 8" ..**4,500.00**
Bowl, Fairyland Lustre, Woodland Elves VI, WW, 8" **1,150.00**
Bowl, Fairyland Lustre, 8-sided, Z011, WW, 9½" **3,680.00**
Bowl, Hummingbird Lustre, Empire shape, WWE, 4½" **425.00**
Bowl, Hummingbird Lustre, orange, WWE, 8¼" **545.00**
Bowl, Jasper, lt gr, Dancing Hours, MIE, 10" **800.00**
Bowl, Lustre, Bl Fruit, 8-sided, Z5457 24, WW, 9½" **435.00**
Bowl, Lustre, Flame Daventry, Z5413, WW, 8¾" **1,265.00**
Bowl, Lustre, Lahore, Z5226 11, WW, 10" **2,760.00**
Bowl, punch; Fairyland Lustre, Sycamore Trees/etc, WWE, 11½" ..**5,500.00**

Bowl, punch; Fairyland Lustre, Woodland Elves V, WW, 11½" **4,375.00**
Bowl, salad; Jasper, gr, SP rim, WW, 8" dia **250.00**
Box, Basalt, Cupid sharpening arrow in gold, WWE, 2" oval **100.00**
Box, Basalt, Tutankhumun in gold, scalloped, WWE, 3½" dia ..**150.00**
Box, Creamware, bl printed, Ferrare, WW, 1880s, 3" dia **150.00**
Box, Creamware, lt bl, fish decor, WWE, 3½x5" **95.00**
Box, Jasper, bl, scalloped, WWE, 5" dia **95.00**
Box, Jasper, Portland Bl, Camilla, WWE, 2½" dia **95.00**
Box, pomade; Jasper, cobalt, WW, 1850s, 3½" dia **170.00**
Bust, Basalt, Dwight Eisenhower, #2271, WWE, 8½", MIB **175.00**
Bust, Basalt, Lord Nelson **1,100.00**
Bust, Basalt, Milton, WW, 13¾" **1,500.00**
Bust, Basalt, Wesley, WW, 8" **500.00**
Cake plate, Jasper, cobalt, MIE, 9" sq **125.00**
Calendar plate, Creamware, December, WW, 1895 ....**225.00**
Cameo, Jasper, blk, in 18k brooch **225.00**
Cameo, Jasper, lt bl, in gold-washed sterling w/sm dmn, WWE ..**125.00**
Cameo, Jasper, lt bl, WW, in sterling pendant **125.00**
Cameo, Jasper, lt bl, WW, in 9k gold bracelet **375.00**
Chamberstick, Jasper, cobalt, England, 6" dia **250.00**
Cheese keeper, Jasper, cobalt, England, 6½x8¼" **850.00**
Cigarette jar, Jasper, lt bl, WWE, w/lid **125.00**
Cigarette jar, Jasper, sage gr, w/lid, WWE **125.00**
Cigarette lighter, Bone China, Florentine, WWE **55.00**
Coffeepot, Basalt, widow finial, WW, 7" **650.00**
Coffeepot, Jasper, cobalt, Muses, England, 5½" **350.00**
Compact, Jasper, lt bl, Stratton, Aurora in Chariot, WWE **100.00**
Comport, Gr Glaze, Victorian yel-gr, WW, 4½" **230.00**
Comport, Jasper, terra cotta, WWE, 3¾x6" **245.00**
Comport, Moonlight Lustre, nautilus shell, WW, ca 1810, 8" **700.00**
Creamer, Creamware, Eastern Flowers, WW, ca 1860 ....**75.00**
Creamer, Drabware, molded thistle/rose/etc, WW, 2½x5" **175.00**
Creamer & sugar bowl, Jasper, cobalt, WWE, w/lid, sm **250.00**
Creamer & sugar bowl, Jasper, terra cotta, MIE **175.00**
Cup, custard; Creamware, Armorial decor, WW, ca 1800 ....**200.00**
Cup, melba; Fairyland Lustre, Elves on MOP, Z4968, WW, 3¼" .**1,000.00**
Cup & saucer, AD; Jasper, cobalt, Boston shape, WWE **100.00**
Cup & saucer, AD; Jasper, terra cotta, WWE **120.00**
Cup & saucer, Drabware, Bute shape, gold line, bl int, WW **95.00**
Cup & saucer, Jasper, cobalt, pear shape, WWE, ca 1937 ....**100.00**
Cup & saucer, Jasper, lt bl, pear shape, WWE, ca 1980 ....**60.00**
Cup & saucer, Pearlware, Strawberry Lustre, WWE, ca 1900 ....**75.00**
Custard cup, Jasper, lilac, teardrop shape, WW **750.00**
Ferner, Jasper, cobalt, 3 ball ft, WW, 7¾x8" **425.00**
Figure, Basalt, cat, gr eyes, WW, 4¾" **500.00**
Figure, Basalt, Hercules, WWE, ca 1978, 11½" **425.00**
Flowerpot, Jasper, cobalt, WW, 1870s, 2¾" **195.00**
Goblet, glass w/Martha Washington cameo, MIE, ca 1975 ....**175.00**
Incense burner, Moonlight Lustre, WW, ca 1810, 7½" **750.00**
Jam jar, Jasper, cobalt, WW **125.00**
Jar, Bone China, red printed decor, apple finial, WW, 18801 ....**225.00**
Jar, cigarette; Jasper, lt gr, WWE **125.00**
Jardiniere, Jasper, cobalt, England, 6⅛x7" **300.00**
Jardiniere, Jasper, crimson, England, 6½x7½" **1,250.00**
Jug, Majolica, Doric, gr/brn splashes, WW, 1870s, 8¼" **425.00**
Jug, Majolica, yel/brn/gr ivy band, WW, 8¼" **380.00**
Jug, Stoneware, salt glaze, Bacchanalian boys, WW, 9", EX **275.00**
Matchbox holder, Jasper, olive gr, England, 3½" **300.00**
Medallion, cobalt, Petrarch, unmk, 19th C, 5x3¼" **200.00**
Mold, Creamware, Corncob, WW **275.00**
Mold, Creamware, Ram & Crown, WW, 1880s, 6½x5½" **450.00**
Mug, Creamware, Royal Wedding, WWE **45.00**
Napkin ring, Bone China, Clementine, WWE, 4 for **75.00**
Pie holder, Jasper, cobalt, WW **345.00**

Pitcher, Jasper, cobalt, Cupid & Psyche, WW, 8" **350.00**
Pitcher, Jasper, dk bl, tankard, WWE, 4⅛x2¾" **88.00**
Plaque, Creamware, Hanging Basket of Yel Orchids, WW, 11½" ...**375.00**
Plaque, Jasper, lt gr, Muses, England, 11x4" **1,750.00**
Plate, Bone China, HP shells, WW, ca 1878 ....**95.00**
Plate, Creamware, Knave of Clubs, tan border, ca 1910 ....**125.00**
Plate, Creamware, Stratford Hall, MIE, 9½" **40.00**
Plate, Jasper, lt bl, Statue of Liberty, WWE, 6¾" **75.00**
Plate, Pearlware, Moonlight Lustre, shell shape, WW, 1810 ......**200.00**
Plate, tea; Jasper, cobalt, England, 6¼" **125.00**
Pot, Malfrey; Fairyland Lustre, Candlemas, WWE, w/lid, 8⅛" **2,300.00**
Shell dish, Majolica, mc splashes, WW, 12x6½" **195.00**
Shell dish, Moonlight Lustre, oval, WW, ca 1810, 11⅜", pr **635.00**
Spill vase, Jasper, blk, Muses, WW, 5¾" **235.00**
Spill vase, Jasper, gr, Bellflower, England, 7¾" **300.00**
Sugar bowl, Drabware, cobalt, WW, w/lid **350.00**
Sweetmeat jar, Jasper, dk bl, SP lid/trim, WWE, 4x3¼" **145.00**
Tankard, Basalt, Quebec Coat of Arms, England, 2¾" **75.00**
Tankard, Jasper, cobalt, England, ca 1900, 8¼" **300.00**
Tankard, Jasper, cobalt, WW, ca 1880, 4½" **100.00**
Tankard, Jasper, lt bl, WWE, 4" **125.00**
Tankard, Jasper, olive gr, WWE, 7¼" **250.00**
Tea bowl & saucer, Jasper, lt bl, Bacchanalian, WW **1,100.00**
Teakettle, Creamware, prunus & gold, W **450.00**
Teapot, Basalt, #146 shape, MIE, sz 30 ....**145.00**
Teapot, Basalt, Capri, WW, lg **650.00**
Teapot, Creamware, honey, printed/pnt florals, WWE **95.00**
Teapot, Jasper, cobalt, shape #146, WWE, sz 24 ....**125.00**
Teapot, Jasper, cobalt, St Louis Shape, England **250.00**
Teapot, Jasper, dk bl, classical ladies, WWE, 4½x4½" **195.00**
Teapot, Jasper, dk bl, WWE, +cr/sug **325.00**
Teapot, Jasper, lilac, Brewster, WW **445.00**
Teapot, Jasper, Royal Bl, Coronation, WWE, ca 1953 ....**375.00**
Teapot, Rockingham, widow finial, WW, 1840s, 4½" **265.00**
Teapot, stoneware, wht, WW, ca 1810 ....**250.00**
Tray, Fairyland Lustre, Z4968, WW, 12¾" **4,375.00**
Tray, Jasper, lt bl, Churchill, MIE, 4¼" **75.00**
Tray, Jasper, lt bl, Josia Wedgwood, WW Collector's Society **50.00**
Tray, Jasper, Royal Bl, Queen Elizabeth II, MIE, 4¼" **50.00**
Tray, Lustre, Nizami, 3 claw ft, WW, 6½" **4,025.00**
Vase, Basalt, Capri, 1-hdl, WW, 5½" **650.00**
Vase, bud; Jasper, cobalt, England, 5¼" **125.00**
Vase, bud; Jasper, lt bl, Arcadian, England, 5¼" **125.00**
Vase, bud; Jasper, lt gr, Arcadian, England, 5" **125.00**
Vase, Butterfly Lustre, WW, mini, 4¼" **350.00**
Vase, Caneware, gray Jasper, Bacchanalian Boys, WW, 5" **995.00**
Vase, Dragon Lustre, MOP ground, Z4829, WW, 16¾" **2,760.00**
Vase, Dragon Lustre on bl mottle, #2355, WWE, Z-4829, 8¾" ..**430.00**
Vase, Fairyland Lustre, baluster, Z5360, WW, 12½" **6,325.00**
Vase, Fairyland Lustre, blk, #2810, WWE, Z4968, 9¾" **3,000.00**
Vase, Fairyland Lustre, Castle on Road, #2442, WWE, Z-5125, 7¾" .**700.00**
Vase, Fairyland Lustre, Jewelled Tree, baluster, Z4968, WW, 11" ...**4,800.00**
Vase, Fairyland Lustre, MOP int, trumpet form, WW, rstr, 9½" **260.00**
Vase, Fairyland Lustre, trumpet form, WW, 9½" **3,675.00**
Vase, Jasper, cobalt, stick neck, WW, ca 1867, 7¼" **175.00**
Vase, Jasper, lt bl, Cupid finial, WW, 9½" **1,250.00**
Vase, Lustre, Daventry, baluster, Z5440, 8⅛" **2,185.00**

Weil Ware

Max Weil came to the United States in the 1940s, settling in California. There he began manufacturing dinnerware, figurines, cookie jars, and wall pockets. American clays were used, and the dinnerware was all hand decorated. Weil died in 1954; the company closed two years later. The last backstamp to be used was the outline of a burro with the words 'Weil Ware — Made in California.' Many unmarked pieces found today originally carried a silver foil label; but you'll often find a four-digit handwritten number series, especially on figurines. For further study we recommend *The Collector's Encyclopedia of California Pottery* by our advisor, Jack Chipman. He is listed in the Directory under California.

Planter, lady with fan (head and shoulders only), hand-painted flowers, $50.00.

Bowl, cream soup; Rose 10.00
Bowl, divided vegetable; Rose 15.00
Coffeepot, Bamboo, w/lid 75.00
Cup & saucer, Rose 10.00
Dealer's plaque 75.00
Dish, Dogwood, divided, sq, 10½" 15.00
Figurine, girl carries long tapered bucket ea side, 8" 35.00
Figurine, girl in bl gown w/pk shawl, 10½" 45.00
Figurine, sailor boy w/flower stands before vase, 11" 45.00
Vase, girl in loose dress, hands to hair, vase behind, 11" 42.00
Wall pocket, Oriental girl 40.00

Weller

The Weller Pottery Company was established in Zanesville, Ohio, in 1882, the outgrowth of a small one-kiln log cabin works Sam Weller had operated in Fultonham. Through an association with Wm. Long, he entered the art pottery field in 1895, producing the Lonhuda Ware Long had perfected in Steubenville six years earlier. His famous Louwelsa line was merely a continuation of Lonhuda and was made in at least five hundred different shapes until 1924. Many fine lines of artware followed under the direction of Charles Babcock Upjohn, art director from 1895 to 1904: Dickens Ware (1st Line), under-glaze slip decorations on dark backgrounds; Turada, featuring applied ivory bands of delicate openwork on solid dark brown backgrounds; and Aurelian, similar to Louwelsa, but with a brushed-on rather than blended ground. One of their most famous lines was 2nd Line Dickens, introduced in 1900. Backgrounds, characteristically caramel shading to turquoise matt, were decorated by sgraffito with animals, golfers, monks, Indians, and scenes from Dickens novels. The work is often artist signed. Sicardo, 1903, was a metallic lustre line in tones of rose, blue, green, or purple with flowing Art Nouveau patterns developed within the glaze.

Frederick Hurten Rhead, who worked for Weller from 1903 to 1904, created the prestigious Jap Birdimal line decorated with geisha girls, landscapes, storks, etc., accomplished through application of heavy slip forced through the tiny nozzle of a squeeze bag. Other lines to his credit are L'Art Nouveau, produced in both high-gloss brown and matt pastels, and 3rd Line Dickens, often decorated with Cruikshank's illustrations in relief. Other early artware lines were Eocean, Floretta, Hunter, Perfecto, Dresden, Etched Matt, and Etna.

In 1920 John Lessel was hired as art director, and under his supervision several new lines were created. LaSa, LaMar, Marengo, and Besline attest to his expertise with metallic lustres. The last of the art-

ware lines and one of the most sought after by collectors today is Hudson, first made during the early 1920s. Hudson, a semimatt glazed ware, was beautifully artist decorated on shaded backgrounds with florals, animals, birds, and scenics. Notable artists often signed their work, among them Hester Pillsbury, Dorothy England Laughead, Ruth Axline, Claude Leffler, Sarah Reid McLaughlin, E.L. Pickens, and Mae Timberlake.

During the '30s Weller produced a line of gardenware and naturalistic life-sized figures of dogs, cats, swans, geese, and playful gnomes. The Depression brought a slow, steady decline in sales, and by 1948 the pottery was closed. For a more thorough study we recommend *The Collector's Encyclopedia of Weller Pottery* by Sharon and Bob Huxford, available at your local library or from Collector Books.

Ardsley, console bowl w/fish frog, cattails, mk, 3½x12" 500.00
Ardsley, fan vase, cattails, mk, 8" 175.00
Athens, vase, swagged design w/cat's head on tan, unmk, 10" 900.00
Athens, vase, wht swagged design w/figures on bl, unmk, 10" 700.00
Aurelian, ewer, floral, sgn MP, 6" 200.00
Aurelian, pillow vase, dog w/game in mouth, mk, 7½" 1,500.00
Aurelian, vase, berries & leaves, sgn EA, 7" 275.00
Aurelian, vase, jonquils, sgn TJW, 16" 1,800.00
Auroro, vase, goldfish, artist Hattie Mitchell, 9" 1,300.00
Baldin, Blue; bowl, band of yel apples, unmk, 4" 225.00
Baldin, bowl, band of red apples, unmk, 4" 150.00
Barcelona, ewer, stylized flower, mk, 9½" 250.00
Bedford Matt, umbrella stand, flower heads at rim, 20x11", NM 475.00
Blue & Decorated, tropical birds & branches, 1920, 13¼x4½" 1,380.00
Blue Drapery, planter, unmk, 4" 75.00
Blue Ware, comport, swagged fruit, mk, 5½" 225.00
Blue Ware, jardiniere, 4 angels, mk, 9" 300.00
Blue Ware, vase, roses around 4 bl fancy oval panels, ftd, 10" 500.00
Bonito, bowl, stylized flowers on cream, sgn CF, 3½" 135.00
Bonito, vase, stylized flowers on cream, sgn NC, 10" 400.00
Brighton, bluebird on apple & branch pedestal, mk, 7½" 700.00
Brighton, canary, unmk, 2½" 200.00
Brighton, crow on pedestal, unmk, 6½" 900.00
Brighton, pheasant, 7x11½" 750.00
Burntwood, vase, birds & stylized flowers, unmk, 8½" 225.00
Burntwood, vase, stylized flowers, 7" 150.00
Cameo Jewel, mug, mk, 6½" 475.00
Chase, fan vase, wht fox hunt scene on bl, mk, 8½" 375.00
Chase, vase, wht fox hunt scene on tan, hand-mk, 10½" 425.00
Chengtu, covered jar, mk, 8" 200.00
Chengtu, vase, mk, 16" 300.00
Chengtu, vase, 6-sided incurvate form, mk, 9" 100.00
Claywood, mug, stylized flowers, cylindrical, unmk, 5" 100.00
Claywood, vase, butterflies, unmk, 3" 60.00
Claywood, vase, spider web, cylindrical, unmk, 5½" 85.00
Coppertone, ashtray, frog on rim, mk, 6½" 225.00
Coppertone, basket, flower & leaves w/twig hdl, 8½" 225.00
Coppertone, pillow vase, ftd, unmk, 7" 200.00
Coppertone, vase, spherical w/2 closed hdls, 7x9" 475.00
Coppertone, vase, swollen cylinder w/lg ear hdls, mk, 15½" 700.00
Coppertone, vessel w/lid, hdls, 11x9" 750.00
Copra, basket, floral design, mk, 11" 275.00
Copra, jardiniere, dbl tulips, mk, 8" 200.00
Corleone, vase, pods & leaves, sgn HP, 17" 1,350.00
Cretone, vase, brn stylized gazelle & flowers on cream, mk, 8" ...350.00
Cretone, vase, wht gazelle & flowers on blk, sgn HP, 7" 375.00
Dickens I, jardiniere, floral on dk brn, tan interior, mk, 8½" 400.00
Dickens I, jug, corn, mk, 6½" 350.00
Dickens I, mug, floral, sgn MM, 4½" 150.00
Dickens I, pillow vase, lady's portrait, ftd, mk, 7" 2,200.00
Dickens II, ewer, deer head, sgn MA, 11" 750.00

Dickens II, mug, Black Bird (Indian portrait), sgn UJ, 6" 900.00
Dickens II, pitcher, 2 gents playing game, sgn CW, 4" 500.00
Dickens II, tobacco jar, captain's head, 7" 1,700.00
Dickens II, vase, Bald Eagle, sgn Anna Dautherty, 9" 2,050.00
Dickens II, vase, cherubs, flat-sided, ftd, mk, 11½" 1,200.00
Dickens II, vase, Chief Hollow Horn Bear, sgn AD, 13" 2,500.00
Dickens II, vase, Don Quixote & Sancho, sgn EL Pickens, 16" 3,250.00
Dickens II, vase, hunter w/gun over shoulder, sgn Dunlavy, 16" 2,250.00
Dickens II, vase, hunting dog, sgn EL Pickens, 9" 1,700.00
Dickens III, creamer, cameo, #0034, 4" 200.00
Dickens III, ewer, Carker, Squeers, sgn LM, 12½" 750.00
Dickens III, inkwell, cameo lid, sgn R, #0038, 2½" 500.00
Dresden, mug, windmills, sgn LJB, 5½" 500.00
Dresden, vase, windmills, cylindrical, sgn LJB, 10½" 650.00
Eocean, basket, floral, short pedestal ft, unmk, 6½" 350.00
Eocean, candlestick, floral, sgn LJB, 9" 300.00
Eocean, vase, floral, sgn M Rauchfuss, 12½" 600.00
Eocean, vase, floral branch, sgn LJB, 13" 850.00
Eocean, vase, owl on tree branch, sgn EB, 10½" 1,500.00
Etna, bowl, w/mouse, mk, 2½" 400.00
Etna, pitcher, floral, mk, 6" 150.00
Etna, vase, frog & snake, mk, 6½" 600.00
Etna, vase, pansies, thick neck on squatty bulbous body, 6½" 150.00
Fairfield, vase, cherubs, unmk, 9½" 120.00
Flemish, comport, roses, w/lid, mk, 8½" 175.00
Flemish, jardiniere, floral design on panels, unmk, 7½" 150.00
Flemish, tub, roses, rnd bowl w/hdls, mk, 4½" 125.00
Fleron, bowl, ruffled rim, mk, 4" 110.00
Fleron, vase, plain flared rim, ear hdls, mk, 19½" 750.00
Florala, console bowl, flowers & ribs on wht, unmk, 11" 75.00
Florala, wall pocket, flowers & ribs on wht, mk, 10" 175.00
Floretta, ewer, floral, mk, 6" 90.00
Floretta, tankard, apples on a branch, matt, sgn CD, 13½" 550.00
Forest, basket, mk, 8½" 225.00
Forest, hanging basket, unmk, 8" 200.00
Forest, window box, mk, 5½x14½" 400.00
Geode, vase, comets & stars, wht on lt bl, HP, 5¾x6" 650.00
Glendale, plate w/flower frog, gulls around nest, mk, 15½" 500.00
Glendale, vase, lovebirds on a branch, unmk, 8½" 400.00
Greenbriar, ewer, marbleized, dbl-loop hdl, no mk, 11½" 225.00
Greenbriar, pitcher, marbleized effect, no mk, 10" 225.00
Hobart, candle holder, draped nude kneeling, unmk, 6" 300.00
Hudson, vase, blk-lined irises, sgn McLaughlin, 15" 1,600.00
Hudson, vase, branches on wht, 6-sided tapering form, mk, 11" .250.00
Hudson, vase, floral design, 2-hdld, sgn Timberlake, 6" 350.00
Hudson, vase, lg iris, cylindrical, sgn Axline, 8½" 550.00
Hudson, vase, orchids on bl to wht gloss, Timberlake, 27x11" ...21,850.00
Hudson, vase, owl/moon on bl, tapered cylinder, mk, 13½" 1,500.00
Hudson, vase, parrot on flowering branch, sgn Timberlake, 14" 2,500.00
Hudson, vase, roses, mc on gr to pk, E Hood, 1920, 8¾x4½" 400.00
Hudson, vase, scenic, cylindrical, sgn Pillsbury, 9" 2,000.00
Hudson, vase, scenic, sgn McLaughlin, cylindrical, mk, 9" 1,750.00
Hudson, vase, wht & bl lilacs on bl-gray, sgn McLaughlin, 12" 1,500.00
Hudson, vase, 2 birds on a branch on wht, mk, 15" 1,800.00
Hudson, vase, 2 swans under tree, sgn Pillsbury, 14½" 2,500.00
Hudson-Perfecto, vase, pine cones, sgn Leffler, 10" 450.00
Hunter, vase, deer head in profile, #343, 6½" 750.00
Hunter, vase, gulls soaring, sgn UJ, #413, 7½" 950.00
Ivoris, ginger jar, mk, 8½" 90.00
Ivory, pillow vase, swags & tassels w/ribbing, ftd, unmk, 5" 120.00
Jap Birdimal, mug, Oriental lady & wht cat on brn, mk, 5" 1,000.00
Jap Birdimal, vase, ducks on gray, twisted teardrop, unmk, 11" ..800.00
Jap Birdimal, vase, ducks soaring, 6 indented sides, mk, 4" 500.00
Kenova, vase, morning glories, mk, 6½" 300.00

Klyro, basket, flowers & berries, ftd, unmk, 7" 100.00
Klyro, wall pocket, flowers & berries, label, 7½" 125.00
Knifewood, covered jar, bluebird & branches, ovoid, mk, 8" 350.00
Knifewood, urn, daisies & butterflies, unmk, 8" 175.00
L'art Nouveau, bank, corn, unmk, 8" 550.00
L'art Nouveau, mug, floral, mk, 5" 250.00
L'art Nouveau, vase, grapes, mk, 16" 600.00
L'art Nouveau, vase, grapes, 4-sided, mk, 12" 650.00
Lamar, vase, palm trees, blk on dk berry red, unmk, 8½" 250.00
Lamar, vase, scenic, deep red, teardrop shape, mk, 14½" 550.00
LaSa, vase, landscape, shouldered ovoid, 6½" 500.00
LaSa, vase, landscape, 4-sided cone form, unmk, 6½" 200.00
LaSa, vase, pine trees/mtns/lake, ovoid, EX color, 7x3" 490.00
LaSa, vase, trees/lake/clouds, shouldered, 5¼" 400.00
LaSa, vase, trees/mtns/lake, gr/lav/brn on ivory & gr, mk, 12x6" 500.00
Lebonon, vase, camel rider, cone shape, unmk, 9" 450.00
Lonhuda, pillow vase, man & herd of cattle, #275, 11½" 4,400.00
Lonhuda, vase, floral, 2-hdld, sgn AH, 4½" 200.00
Lorbeek, bowl, futuristic form, mk, 5" 100.00
Lorbeek, wall pocket, futuristic form, mk, 8½" 135.00
Louella, basket, mk, 6½" 100.00
Louella, vase, flowers on drapery ground, mk, 8" 130.00
Louwelsa, bowl, floral, half-circle seal, 2" 100.00
Louwelsa, jardiniere, floral, ruffled rim, mk, 9½" 325.00
Louwelsa, mug, Blk man, artist Turner, 7" 1,600.00
Louwelsa, mug, smiling gent, #432, sgn Ferrell, 6½" 1,000.00
Louwelsa, pillow vase, floral, ftd, sgn M, 4" 150.00
Louwelsa, tobacco jar, blackberries, w/lid, sgn CA, 5½" 550.00
Louwelsa, vase, dog's head, sgn A Wilson, 10½" 1,700.00
Louwelsa, vase, floral on bl, cylindrical, mk, 10½" 1,100.00
Louwelsa, vase, grapevines, sgn Haubrich, 23½" 1,550.00
Louwelsa, vase, pansies w/silver o/l, mk, 6½" 3,000.00
Malverne, circle vase, leaves & pods, mk, 8" 95.00
Malverne, pillow vase, leaves & pods, unmk, 8½" 115.00
Marbleized, vase, trumpet shape, mk, 7½" 100.00
Marbleized, vase, 6-sided, mk, 10½" 165.00
Marengo, vase, no mk, 8" 300.00
Marengo, wall pocket, stylized tree & mtns, unmk, 8½" 225.00
Marvo, hanging basket, mk, 5" 150.00
Marvo, pitcher, allover flower/leaf design, mk, 8" 125.00
Matt Green, vase, cvd Arts & Crafts motif, 4 buttresses, 10" 600.00
Matt Green, vase, cvd cherries, lg rtcl hdls, 12x6½" 1,200.00
Matt Green, vase, emb stems, paneled w/angle shoulder, 7½" 375.00
Matt Green, vase, poppy band under rim, cylindrical, 10½" 1,100.00
Melrose, basket, grapes & roses, mk, 10" 200.00
Melrose, console bowl, roses on a branch, hdld, mk, 5x8½" 115.00
Minerva, vase, cranes, cylindrical, mk, 8½" 500.00
Minerva, vase, sm figure on galloping horse, mk, 8½" 550.00
Mirror Black, strawberry jar, no mk, 6½" 85.00
Mirror Black, vase, unmk, 12" 200.00
Muskota, boy in boat, mk, 3½x10½" 550.00
Muskota, gate w/pots & cats, mk, 7" 600.00
Noval, candlestick, applied apples, mk, 9½" 150.00
Noval, comport, applied apples, w/lid, unmk, 9½" 120.00
Patra, basket, mk, 5½" 125.00
Patra, vase, mk, 8" 150.00
Patricia, bowl, 8 duck heads around rim, mk, 13" dia 135.00
Patricia, planter, pelican form, mk, 5" 90.00
Pearl, basket, swagged pearls & roses on cream, unmk, 6½" 150.00
Pearl, vase, swagged pearls & roses on cream, unmk, 7" 110.00
Perfecto, ewer, corn, sgn A Haubrich, #580/4, 12" 750.00
Perfecto, pillow vase, horse head, sgn Hester Pillbury, 10½" ...3,750.00
Pumila, vase, lily pads form rim, mk, 12" 100.00
Pumila, wall pocket, lily pads form rim, unmk, 7" 135.00

Rhead Faience, cvd flowers on gr matt w/bl highlights, 5½" 450.00
Roba, ewer, flowering branch on wht & gr, mk, 11" 135.00
Roba, wall pocket, flowering branch on wht & bl, 10" 125.00
Roma, comport, flower/leaf swag, sq bowl on sq pedestal, 9½" ...175.00
Roma, console bowl, grapevines, w/liner, unmk, 6½x18" 200.00
Roma, tobacco jar, ftd, w/lid, no mk, 7½" 350.00
Roma, wall pocket, roses & grapes, no mk, 8" 250.00
Rosemont, jardiniere, bluebird on flowering branch on wht, 7" .325.00
Rosemont, jardiniere, bouquets of daisies on blk, rnd, mk, 7" 200.00
Sabrinian, basket, shells & sea horses, mk, 7" 300.00
Sabrinian, console bowl w/sea horse frog, mk, 3½x11½" 225.00
Sabrinian, window box, shell & sea horses, mk, 3½x9" 225.00
Sicardo, mug, allover design, cylindrical, unmk, 3½" 500.00
Sicardo, vase, bulbous, trumpet neck, 2-hdld shoulder, 12½" .2,500.00
Sicardo, vase, copper drips over wine/bl-gr, tiny neck, 4½" 475.00
Sicardo, vase, cylindrical w/rolled lip, flat bottom, 9" 950.00
Sicardo, vase, flat-sided, ftd, sgn Weller Sicardo, 2½" 300.00
Sicardo, vase, floral, dbl gourd, 6x4½" 450.00
Sicardo, vase, peacock feathers, X mk, 1905, 5⅝x4⅛" 635.00
Sicardo, vase, peacock feathers, 4¾x2¾" 500.00
Sicardo, vase, plume fans, teardrop form, unmk, 4½" 400.00
Silvertone, basket, grapevine, mk, 13" 350.00
Silvertone, vase, floral, ball/ruffled rim, hdld, mk, 8½" 350.00
Silvertone, vase, floral, 2 lg twisted hdls, 6½" 300.00
Sydonia, cornucopia, mottled gr, no mk, 8½" 70.00
Sydonia, dbl candle holder w/bud vase, bl, mk, 11½" 135.00
Tivoli, vase, floral decor around ftd base, unmk, 9½" 125.00
Turada, mug, emb design, mk 762/7, 6" 325.00
Turada, oil lamp base, ftd, emb design, mk, 8" 1,000.00
Turada, tobacco jar, brn w/wht emb design around neck, 5½" ...350.00
Turkis, vase, angled body & hdls, mk, 5½" 100.00
Turkis, vase, ruffled rim, mk, 8" 150.00
Velva, bowl, berries & leaves on tan, hdld, 3½x12½" 65.00
Velva, vase, berries & leaves on turq, hdld, mk, 9½" 65.00
Warwick, basket, tree trunk w/flowering branches, mk, 7" 150.00
Warwick, vase, tree trunk w/flowering branches, mk, 10" 225.00
Woodcraft, ashtray, oak leaves on tree trunk, unmk, 3" 90.00
Woodcraft, basket, acorn shape w/twig hdl, 9½" 250.00
Woodcraft, lamp, owls on tree-trunk pedestal, 12½" 300.00
Woodcraft, planter w/flower frog, 3 foxes in tree trunk, 6" 325.00
Woodcraft, wall pocket, owl, mk, 10" 350.00
Zona, comport, incised flowers on textured ground, mk, 5½" 70.00
Zona, pitcher, apples on a branch, unmk, 7" 150.00

Western Americana

The collecting of Western Americana encompasses a broad spectrum of memorabilia and collectibles. Examples of various areas within the main stream would include the following fields: weapons, bottles, photographs, mining/railroad artifacts, cowboy paraphernalia, farm and ranch implements, maps, barbed wire, tokens, Indian relics, saloon/gambling items, and branding irons. Some of these areas have their own separate listings in this book. Western Americana is not only a collecting field but is also a collecting *era* with specific boundries. Depending upon which field the collector decides to specialize in, prices can start at a few dollars and run into the thousands.

Our advisor for this category is Bill Mackin, author of *Cowboy and Gunfighter Collectibles* (order from the author); he is listed in the Directory under Colorado.

Book, History of Wild Wild West, WF Cody, 1888, EX 50.00
Branding iron, wrought iron, wood hdl attached w/nails, EX 40.00
Cartridge/money belt, pig skin, 40x3⅝", 2" NP buckle, EX 600.00
Chaps, batwing style, German silver conchos, 1920, 38x15" 175.00

Chaps, wooly, dk brn angora, shotgun style, Clark/Portland, G ..650.00
Cuffs, cvd & studded leather, 5⅝" L, EX, pr 135.00
Gauntlets, fringed deerskin w/beadwork, M, pr 450.00
Hat, cowboy; TX Centennial 550.00
Hitching post, CI, acorn finial w/ring, worn pnt, 45" 245.00
Lock, Wells Fargo & Co Express, brass & steel 475.00
Mail bag, haversack; Wells Fargo & Co Express 250.00
Saddle, handmade/tooled, silver conchos, padded seat, 1940, lg 300.00
Saddlebags, russet leather, 1-pc, 36x13½", VG 250.00
Sign, Wells Fargo...Express Office, hand pointing, porc, EX ...1,500.00
Spurs, Buermann, drop-shank silver stars, pr 475.00
Spurs, Buermann, str-shank Xs, pr 165.00
Spurs, Crockett, silver mtd 2" rowels, early, pr 365.00
Spurs, North & Judd, anchor, bronze, 1920, 7x4" 175.00
Spurs, Regulation US Army 1911 Model (cavalry) 55.00
Tether, horse; Wells Fargo & Co Express 300.00

Western Pottery Manufacturing Company

This pottery was originally founded as the Denver China and Pottery Company; William Long was the owner. The company's assets were sold to a group who in 1905 formed the Western Pottery Manufacturing Company, located at 16th Street and Alcott in Denver, Colorado. By 1926, one hundred eighty-six different items were being produced, including crocks, flowerpots, kitchen items, and other stoneware. The company dissolved in 1936.

Seven various marks were used during the years, and values may be higher for items that carry a rare mark. Numbers within the descriptions refer to specific marks, see the line drawings. Prices may vary depending on demand and locale. Our advisors for this category are Cathy Segelke and Pat James; they are listed in the Directory under Colorado.

Churn, #2, hdl, 4-gal, M 75.00
Churn, #2, hdl, 5-gal, M 65.00
Churn, #2, no lid, 5-gal, G 80.00
Crock, #4, bail lip, 4-gal, G 55.00
Crock, #4, hdl, no lid, 8-gal, M 90.00
Crock, #4, ice water; bl/wht sponge pnt, 3-gal, NM 30.00
Crock, #4, 2-gal, M 32.00
Crock, #4, 6-gal, EX 72.00
Crock, #4b, 20-gal, M 200.00
Crock, #4b, 22x17½", 15-gal, NM 150.00
Crock, #5, bail lip, 1½-gal, M 45.00
Crock, #5, no lid, 6-gal, M 70.00
Crock, #6, wire hdl, 10-gal, NM 100.00
Crock, #6, 3-gal, M 40.00

Crock, #6, 4-gal, M 50.00
Crock, #6, 5-gal, NM 60.00
Foot warmer, #6, M 50.00
Jug, #6, brn/wht, 1-gal, EX 25.00
Jug, #6, brn/wht, 5-gal, M 75.00
Rabbit feeder, #1, EX 25.00
Rabbit waterer, #1, M 25.00

Westmoreland

Originally titled the Specialty Glass Company, Westmoreland began operations in East Liverpool, Ohio, producing utility items as well as tableware in milk glass and crystal. When the company moved to Grapeville, Pennsylvania, in 1890, lamps, vases, covered animal dishes, and decorative plates were introduced. Prior to 1920 Westmoreland was a major manufacturer of carnival glass and soon thereafter added a line of lovely reproduction art glass items. High-quality milk glass became their speciality, accounting for about 90% of their production. Black glass was introduced in the 1940s, and later in the decade ruby-stained pieces and items decorated in the Mary Gregory style became fashionable. By the 1960s colored glassware was being produced, examples of which are very popular with collectors today. Early pieces were marked with a paper label; by the 1960s the ware was embossed with a superimposed 'WG.' The last mark was a circle containing 'Westmoreland' around the perimeter and a large 'W' in the center. The company closed in 1985, and on February 28, 1996, the factory burned to the ground. See also Animal Dishes with Covers; Carnival Glass. Note: Though you may find pieces very similar to Westmoreland's, their Della Robbia has no bananas among the fruits relief.

Candy dish, Sea Shells, shell finial, dolphin feet, green frost, ca 1960s-80s, 6½x6", $65.00.

Ashtray, Beaded Grape, milk glass, 4" **14.00**
Ashtray, Beaded Grape, milk glass, 5" **20.00**
Bottle, toilet; Panelled Grape, milk glass, 5-oz **55.00**
Bowl, Beaded Grape, milk glass, #1884, ftd, 9" **45.00**
Bowl, Beaded Grape, milk glass, flared, ftd, w/lid, 5" **25.00**
Bowl, belled; Panelled Grape, milk glass, 12½" **95.00**
Bowl, console; Dolphin, amber, #1820, 11" **95.00**
Bowl, English Hobnail, crystal, 4¾" **6.00**
Bowl, finger; English Hobnail, crystal, 4¾" **7.00**
Bowl, fruit; Old Quilt, milk glass, crimped, ftd, 9" **45.00**
Bowl, Old Quilt, milk glass, octagonal, ftd, 7½" **25.00**
Bowl, Thousand Eye, crystal w/stain, crimped, 12" L **48.00**
Bowl, Thousand Eye, milk glass, 11" **45.00**
Bowl, wedding; Roses & Bows, milk glass, 10" **95.00**
Box, Beaded Grape, milk glass, #1884, w/lid, 4" sq **35.00**
Box, cigarette; Beaded Grape, milk glass **40.00**
Cake salver, Doric, milk glass **22.00**
Candle holders, blk, 3-ball, #1067, pr **39.00**
Candlesticks, Beaded Grape, milk glass, #1884, pr **25.00**
Candlesticks, dbl; Thousand Eye, crystal w/stain, pr **75.00**
Candlesticks, Panelled Grape, milk glass, 4", pr **20.00**
Candlesticks, Thousand Eye, ruby stain, 3-ball, pr **40.00**

Candy dish, Bl opaque w/wht Beaded Bouquet lid, #1700 .....20.00
Candy dish, Panelled Grape, pk, 3-ftd 25.00
Candy dish, Roses & Bows, Della Robbia, ftd 50.00
Candy urn, Waterford, ruby stain, ftd, w/lid, 9" 50.00
Champagne, English Hobnail, crystal, rnd ft 7.00
Coaster, English Hobnail, crystal, 3⅛" 4.50
Cocktail, English Hobnail, crystal, sq base 9.00
Cocktail, Panelled Grape, crystal 15.00
Cocktail, Princess Feather, crystal 10.00
Cocktail, Thousand Eye, crystal w/stain 15.00
Compote, Dolphin, milk glass, 8x7" dia 48.00
Creamer, English Hobnail, amber, ftd 15.00
Creamer, Princess Feather, crystal 15.00
Creamer & sugar bowl, Old Quilt, milk glass, lg 30.00
Creamer & sugar bowl, Panelled Grape, milk glass, w/lid, sm 25.00
Cruet, Old Quilt, milk glass, w/stopper 35.00
Cruet, Princess Feather, crystal, w/stopper 24.00
Cup & saucer, Princess Feather, crystal 12.50
Egg cup, chick, milk glass, ftd, hdls 18.00
Egg cup, milk glass w/yel chick on side 25.00
Figurine, owl on books, lilac, glass eyes, #10 ....18.00
Goblet, water; Ashburton, gr 8.00
Goblet, water; Beaded Grape, milk glass, 8-oz 25.00
Goblet, water; Della Robbia, milk glass 16.00
Goblet, water; Old Quilt, milk glass 15.00
Goblet, water; Panelled Grape, amber 22.00
Goblet, water; Panelled Grape, bl opal 25.00
Goblet, water; Panelled Grape, crystal 15.00
Honey dish, Beaded Grape, gold fruit, w/lid 35.00
Honey dish, Beaded Grape, milk glass, #1884, w/lid, 5" 28.00
Lamp, English Hobnail, gr, 9¼" 125.00
Marmalade, English Hobnail, crystal, metal lid 20.00
Mayonnaise, Panelled Grape, milk glass, w/ladle, 3-pc 40.00
Parfait, Panelled Grape, crystal 25.00
Plate, blue jay decal on milk glass, beaded edge, 7" 18.00
Plate, Della Robbia, crystal, 6" 8.00
Plate, salad; Della Robia, crystal 15.00
Plate, torte; Thousand Eye, milk glass, 14" 60.00
Rose bowl, Doric, milk glass, flared rim 27.00
Shakers, Old Quilt, milk glass, flat, pr 25.00
Shakers, Panelled Grape, crystal/ruby stain, pr 55.00
Sherbet, Della Robbia, crystal 20.00
Sherbet, Thousand Eye, crystal (plain), 4¼" 12.00
Sherbet, Thousand Eye, crystal w/stain, 4¼" 15.00
Spoon holder, Old Quilt, milk glass 28.00
Spoon holder, Ring & Petal, milk glass 28.00
Sugar bowl, Thousand Eye, ruby stain, ftd 20.00
Tray, #1820, dk bl mist, heart shape 35.00
Tumbler, Thousand Eye, crystal w/stain, ftd, 6¾" 20.00
Tumbler/toothpick holder, Panelled Grape, crystal, 3¾" 18.50
Vase, bud; pk opal, #1921, 4½" 10.00
Vase, ivy ball; Panelled Grape, milk glass 45.00
Vase, milk glass, blown teardrop form, #231 ....69.00
Wine, Princess Feather, milk glass 12.50

Wheatley, T. J.

In 1880 after a brief association with the Coultry Works, Thomas J. Wheatley opened his own studio in Cincinnati, Ohio, claiming to have been the first to discover the secret of under-glaze slip decoration on an unbaked clay vessel. He applied for and was granted a patent for his process. Demand for his ware increased to the point that several artists were hired to decorate the ware. The company incorporated in

1880 as the Cincinnati Art Pottery, but until 1882 it continued to operate under Wheatley's name. Ware from this period is marked 'T.J. Wheatley' or 'T.J.W. and Co.,' and it may be dated.

Matt green pieces dominate today's market place and will bring much more than the decorated pieces. The matt green pieces are seldom, if ever, marked or dated.

Bowl, broad vertical leaves on gr matt, mks, 2½x9" 450.00
Lamp base, floral, wht on bl/wht striated ground, 7" dia 400.00
Tile, faux stone, gr/orange matt, 6", +fr 220.00
Vase, appl florals on Limoges-style ground, 8x6", EX 700.00
Vase, curdled gr w/silver o/l, waisted, 4-lobe top, 7½" 1,600.00
Vase, daisies, wht w/mc details on blk & wht, 1880, 7½" 475.00
Vase, daisies, wht/gr on bl mottle, pillow form, 13x11" 650.00
Vase, floral, brn shades w/gr on cream to brn, 1880, 8", EX 280.00
Vase, floral, mc on shaded gr, 1880, #73, rprs, 12½" 600.00
Vase, floral, pk/wht on cobalt, appl leaves, 1880, rprs, 13" 400.00
Vase, floral in Limoges style, #50, 1880, 12x7¾" 430.00
Vase, Greek Key band at shoulder, (feathered) gr matt, 10x7" 500.00
Vase, leaves, swastika-emb protruding sqs, gr matt, 14½" 3,250.00
Vase, leaves/buds emb on textured gr matt, squat bottom, 11x11" ..3,500.00
Vase, upright leaves, gr matt, 3 curved buttress ft, 12x10", NM 2,300.00

Whieldon

Thomas Whieldon was regarded as the finest of the Staffordshire potters of the mid-1700s. He produced marbled and black Egyptian wares as well as tortoise shell, a mottled brown-glazed earthenware accented with touches of blue and yellow. In 1754 he became a partner of Josiah Wedgwood. Other potters produced similar wares, and today the term Whieldon is used generically.

Plate, lattice rim, dot & basketweave border, 1770, 9¼", EX 400.00
Plate, tortoise shell, brn/gr/teal/yel, 18th C, 9¾", EX 270.00
Plate, tortoise shell, emb rope edge, 8-sided, 9", EX 115.00
Plate, tortoise shell, scalloped/emb rim, 1750s, 9", NM, pr 600.00
Platter, gr mottle, scalloped, ca 1750, chip, 11¾" 325.00
Tea canister, cauliflower form, cream & gr, 1780s, 4½", EX 400.00
Teapot, creamware, appl vines, gilt traces, 3½", G 230.00
Teapot, serpent spout, 1760s, 3¾", G 345.00

Wicker

Wicker is the basket-like material used in many types of furniture and accessories. It may be made from bamboo cane, rattan, reed, or artificial fibers. It is airy, lightweight, and very popular in hot regions. Imported from the Orient in the 18th century, it was first manufactured in the United States in about 1850. The elaborate, closely-woven Victorian designs belong to the mid- to late 1800s, and the simple styles with coarse reedings usually indicate a post-1900 production. Art Deco styles followed in the '20s and '30s. The most important consideration in buying wicker is condition — it can be restored, but only by a professional. Age is an important factor, but be aware that 'Victorian-style' furniture is being manufactured today.

Armchair, tight machine weave, simple style, uphl seat, pr 300.00
Armchair rocker, tight weave, Heywood Bros & Wakefield, 1900, 39" .255.00
Armchair rocker, w/balls & scrolls, late 1800s, child's, 35" 155.00
Baby stroller, tight weave, scrolling trim, wht pnt, EX 700.00
Bassinet, tight weave, ornate trim, Am, late 1800s 200.00
Bench, vanity, kidney shape, EX 25.00
Bench, window; tight weave, scrolled apron, wht pnt, EX 300.00
Book stand, tight weave, 4-shelf, 37½" 240.00
Chair, high spider-web bk, w/rabbit-ear finials, ornate 200.00

Chair, lounge; ornate scrolled bk & arm, padded seat, NM 800.00
Chair, photographer's corner; ornate scrolled bk & apron 300.00
Chair, side; rolled bk, stick & ball decor, EX 175.00
Chair, side; scalloped top, woven seat, trn legs, 20th C 300.00
Chair, tight weave fan-bk w/curliques, 1-arm style, 1890s, EX ...250.00
Chaise lounge, flat arms, Heywood-Wakefield 500.00
Couch & chair set, natural, uphl bk/seat, aprons 600.00
Cradle, open weave, wooden rockers, doll sz, 18x23½" 115.00
Desk, letter holder, glass top, 1 drw/4 side shelves, 37" L 400.00
Desk, letter holder, wooden top & legs, 1 drw, 30½" L 200.00
Desk, simple tight-weave design, kidney shape w/1 drw, 38" 300.00
Etagere, arched top, simple, 5 glass shelves, 82x28½", EX 165.00
Hamper, Haywood Bros & Wakefield, late 1800s, EX 50.00
Lamp, floor; sq std w/30" shade, Am, 20th C 285.00
Lamp, openwork 20" shade (no liner), woven std, 1890s, 30", VG 550.00
Ottoman, padded top, NM 150.00
Platform rocker, arm-to arm style w/openwork bk, 43" 400.00
Porch swing, X design on bk 850.00
Potty chair, orig finish, w/play tray 195.00
Rocker, child's, wicker seat & bk 85.00
Rocker, flat arms, apron, very simple 110.00
Rocker, flat arms w/openwork, scrolls/curlicues, cane seat, 40" ...450.00
Rocker, lady's, rolled edges, cane seat, EX 130.00
Rocker, platform; rabbit-ear finials, rolled arms, blk pnt 500.00
Rocker, rolled edges, dmn bk, flared sides, EX 200.00
Screen, dressing; oak stick-&-ball decor, Victorian 130.00
Settee, high bk, rolled arms & bk, EX 475.00
Settee, lift-top seat, skirted, EX 250.00
Settee, spindle bk w/curlique crest & apron, 31x35" 425.00
Settee, tight machine weave, no arms, uphl seat, 31x37" 265.00
Sofa, Lloyd loom tight weave, 3-cushion, 33x72", EX 325.00
Sofa, tight machine weave w/uphl seat/bk, metal springs, 84" 295.00
Suitcase, w/compartments, EX 25.00
Tea cart, glass tray top, late 1800s, EX 300.00
Vase, trumpet form w/hdls, floor sz 65.00

Will-George

In 1934, after years of working in the family garage (in Los Angeles, California), William and George Climes founded the Will-George Company. They manufactured high-quality artware of porcelain and earthenware. Both brothers, motivated by their love of art pottery, had completed extensive education and training in manufacturing and decoration. In 1940 actor Edgar Bergen, a collector of pottery, developed a relationship with the brothers and invested in their business. With this new influx of funds, the company relocated to Pasadena. There they produced an extensive line of art pottery, but it was the bird and animal figurines they created that made them so well known. In addition they molded a large line of human figurines similar to Royal Doulton. The brothers, now with a staff of decorators, precisely molded their pieces with great care. They placed added emphasis on originality and detail, and as a result the products they created were high quality works of art that were only carried by exclusive gift stores.

In the late 1940s, after a split with Bergen, the company moved to San Gabriel to a larger, more modern location and renamed themselves The Claysmiths. There they mass produced many items, but due to the cheap, postwar imports from Italy and Japan that were then flooding the market, they liquidated the business in 1956. Our advisor for this category is Marty Webster. He is listed in the Directory under Michigan.

Bird figurine, Baltimore oriole 135.00
Bird figurine, cardinal on a branch, 10" 65.00
Bird figurine, cardinal on a branch, 12½" 95.00
Bird figurine, eagle on rock, wht & brn, 10" 85.00

Bird figurine, flamingo, head to rear, 10" 75.00
Bird figurine, flamingo, head up to rear, 7½" 40.00
Bird figurine, mallard duck w/spread wings, 7x11" 65.00
Bird figurine, pheasant hen 110.00
Figurine, artist holding palette, mc, 8" 75.00
Figurine, boy holding frog on base, mc, 9" 95.00
Figurine, girl holding doll on base, mc, 9" 95.00
Figurine, hula dancer, wht skirt, 12" 125.00
Figurine, monk, brn bsk, 4½" 30.00
Figurine, monk, brn bsk, 5½" 55.00
Pitcher, chicken figural, mc, 7" 125.00
Tumbler, chicken figural, mc, 4½" 50.00
Wine glass, chicken figural, mc, 5" 55.00

Willets

The Willets Manufacturing Company of Trenton, New Jersey, produced a type of belleek porcelain during the late 1880s and 1890s. Examples were often marked with a coiled snake that formed a 'W' with 'Willets' below and 'Belleek' above. Not all Willet's is factory decorated. Items painted by amateurs outside the factory are worth considerably less. In the listings below, all items are belleek unless noted otherwise. Our advisor for this category is Mary Frank Gaston. You will find her address in the Directory under Texas.

Bowl, HP peaches & flowers w/gold, sgn EN Rewalt, ca 1885 ....225.00
Creamer & sugar bowl, floral on shell forms w/gold, w/lid 275.00
Mug, Indian chief portrait, hdl, mk, 5¾x4" 55.00
Mug, no decor, lizard hdl, mk, 5½" 115.00
Pitcher, cider; grapes & band, purple/gr on ivory, 6x6½" 150.00
Pitcher, cider; purple & gr leaves, red/gr/gold border, 6¼" 250.00
Stein, drunken men/castle/lake, gold & blk berry bands, 5½" 350.00
Tankard, monk drinking/resting on dk gr, 15" 195.00
Teapot, floral border on mauve 95.00
Vase, lady blowing bubbles, 15½" 1,450.00
Vase, mc orchids w/gr leaves on mc ground, mk, 30" 600.00
Vase, peacocks in landscape, snake mk, 10" 295.00

Willow Ware

Willow Ware, inspired no doubt by the numerous patterns of the blue and white Nanking imports, has been popular since the late 18th century and has been made in as many variations as there were manufacturers. English transfer wares by such notable firms as Allerton and Ridgway are the most sought after and the most expensive. Japanese potters have been producing Willow-patterned dinnerware since the late 1800s, and American manufacturers have followed suit. Although blue is the color most commonly used, mauve, black, and even multicolor Willow Ware may be found. Complementary glassware, tinware, and linens have also been made. For further study we recommend the book *Blue Willow*, with full-color photos and current prices, by Mary Frank Gaston. You will find her address in the Directory under Texas. In the following listings, if no manufacturer is noted, the ware is unmarked. See also Buffalo.

Bowl, child's, Japan, 3½" 10.00
Bowl, English, ped ft, 5x9¼" 150.00
Bowl, fruit; Royal, 5½" 3.00
Bowl, salad; 10" 35.00
Bowl, soup; Allerton, 6¾" 12.50
Bowl, soup; English, red 18.50
Bowl, soup; Japan, red, 8" 8.00
Bowl, soup; Japan, 6½" 4.00

Bowl, soup; Meakin 50.00
Bowl, soup; Ridgway, flat 22.00
Bowl, soup; Royal, 8½" 6.50
Bowl, unmk English, rtcl sides, hdls, 10" L 900.00
Bowl, vegetable; Allerton, red, scalloped, w/lid, 6x12" sq 250.00
Bowl, vegetable; Allerton, w/lid, 9¼" L 250.00
Bowl, vegetable; Booth's, oval 200.00
Bowl, vegetable; Booth's, w/lid, 9½" 200.00
Bowl, vegetable; Japan, red, oval, 11" 25.00
Bowl, vegetable; Japan, w/lid, child's, 3¼x4¼" 40.00
Bowl, vegetable; Meakin, rnd 35.00
Bowl, vegetable; Royal, 10" 18.00
Butter dish, English, 3x8" dia 145.00
Coffee set, child's, 3⅝" pot+ cr & sug 60.00
Coffeepot, Allerton, scalloped, 7½" 250.00
Coffeepot, Japan, cylindrical, 7" 115.00
Creamer, child's, Japan, 1¾" 10.00
Creamer, Staffordshire, cow form, Kent, M 1,250.00
Creamer & sugar bowl, unmk Japan, gold trim, w/lid, 3½" 55.00
Cruet set, 6 pcs in wooden holder 280.00
Cup, England 12.00
Cup, red, Japan 10.00
Cup & saucer, child's, unmk 12.00
Cup & saucer, design inside 6.00
Cup & saucer, Wilkinson, 1907 ....17.50
Egg cup, dbl; Booth's 40.00
Gravy boat, English, 7" 60.00
Lamp, flow bl, mini 60.00
Measuring cups, hanging, set of 4+ceramic holder 265.00
Mug, Japan 15.00
Mug, unmk, thick, design inside 15.00
Mush cup & saucer 65.00
Pitcher, Allerton, 8¼" 250.00
Plate, bread & butter; Maastricht, 6" 10.00
Plate, bread & butter; Staffordshire, 6½" 9.00
Plate, child's, Japan, 3½" 6.00
Plate, child's, Japan, 4¼" 8.00
Plate, dinner; Booth's, 10½" 35.00
Plate, dinner; Japan 12.00
Plate, dinner; Ridgway, 10½" 22.00
Plate, dinner; Staffordshire, 10" 12.00
Plate, dinner; unmk, rolled rim, 10" 3.00
Plate, grill; child's 48.00
Plate, grill; Moriyama 10.00
Plate, grill; Shenango 11.50
Plate, grill; Sterling, 9¼" 15.00
Plate, luncheon; Japan, red, 9¼" 7.00
Plate, luncheon; Japan, 9" 7.00
Plate, salad; Ridgway, 7" 13.00
Platter, Allerton, 11x9" 45.00
Platter, American Mfg, 11½" 20.00
Platter, English, pearlware, ca 1830, 24¾" 600.00
Platter, New Wharf mk, 11¾" 60.00

Platter, medium blue, English, ca 1820-40, 24¾", $600.00.

Platter, Ridgway, 11½x9"	45.00
Platter, unmk, 14x11½"	45.00
Platter, Wedgwood, 11x9"	45.00
Sugar bowl, Japan, child's, w/lid	20.00
Sugar bowl, unmk, w/lid	30.00
Teapot, child's, Japan, 3¾", +cr & sug w/lid	65.00
Teapot, child's, unmk, w/lid	35.00

Winchester

The Winchester Repeating Arms Company lost their important government contract after WWI and of necessity turned to the manufacture of sporting goods, hardware items, tools, etc., to augment their gun production. Between 1920 and 1931, over 7,500 different items, each marked 'Winchester Trademark U.S.A.,' were offered for sale by thousands of Winchester Hardware stores throughout the country. After 1931 the firm became Winchester-Western. Unless noted otherwise, values are for examples in EX condition. See also Knives. Our advisor for this category is James Anderson; he is listed in the Directory under Minnesota.

Ad, As Good As the Gun, 1920s, 17x22"+fr	95.00
Barrel stamp, from factory	100.00
Baseball, VG	275.00
Baseball cap, EX	550.00
Box, ammunition; wooden, dvtl, VG	60.00
Box, fishing tackle; EX mks	150.00
Box, lure; for 3 hooks, empty, EX	50.00
Boxing gloves, VG	450.00
Bullet mold, #44-WCF, G	70.00
Calendar, 1914, w/all pages, EX	950.00
Can, gun oil; red, blk & yel, 1940s	20.00
Can opener	100.00
Catalog, No 77, Oct 1911, 202-pg, EX	125.00
Clothes wringer, hand crank, clamps on, 1920s, rare	650.00
Cutlery set, 2-pc	110.00
Diecut, cb counter stand-up, shells, 1920s, NM	175.00
Envelope, from Winchester to customer, dtd 1908, w/letter	125.00
Fan, electric, 8"	250.00
Fish hooks, in cello pack, EX mks	60.00
Fishing line on orig spool	100.00
Fishing reel, #2242, EX	135.00
Flashlight, focusing	40.00
Flashlight, 1960s, MIB	90.00
Fly rod, dry fly action, 1 tip prof rpr, #6151, 5-oz, 8½"	275.00
Fly rod, 3-pc, 2 tips w/tip tube, 8½-ft, EX	425.00
Food chopper, #W32	75.00
Football, EX	325.00
Golf club, #7 iron, Mashie Niblick wood shaft	150.00
Golf club, putter, #6651	150.00
Hammer, ball pein; orig hdl, 16-oz	85.00
Hatchet, orig hdl, EX	110.00
Head lamp, twin service; MIB	185.00
Head lamp, w/tube-shaped battery pack, EX	115.00
Heater, #W600, ca 1920s, EX	210.00
Hockey puck, VG	150.00
Ice pick, VG	75.00
Ice skates, high tops, mk Arena, man's, pr, M	165.00
Ice skates, high tops, mk Lake Placid, lady's, pr, VG	90.00
Level, wood; #9821, 24"	150.00
Lure, Fluted Spinner #9642, feathered tail, VG	45.00
Lure, wooden, 5-hook, M	650.00
Pin, service; 5-yr, mk 10k gold on bk, 1920s	75.00

Plane, bottom; steel, #W-3, 9", VG	125.00
Plane, bottom; steel, #3006, 10", EX	135.00
Plane, bottom; steel, #3010, 14", EX	135.00
Plane, bottom; steel, #3025, corrugated bottom, 14", EX	180.00
Plane, bottom; wood, #3040	180.00
Pliers, slip-joint; NP, #2499, 10"	65.00
Poster, ad; Model 94 Carbine, full color, 34x13"	145.00
Poster, Bird Busters III, 17x28", EX	45.00
Poster, lithograph, Winchester Hounds, sgn HH Poore, 1907	1,750.00
Printer's block for Model 1895 rifle	85.00
Roller skates, VG	45.00
Ruler, wood, 4-fold, #W68	145.00
Salesman's dummy cartridge display, 1950s	185.00
Saw, hand; EX	145.00
Saw, keyhole; rare, VG	185.00
Scabbard, leather, full fringe, 1" letters, 43"	130.00
Scale, family; open face	185.00
Screwdriver, #7113, 4"	45.00
Shears, 6", EX	65.00
Shot glass, horse & rider	35.00
Shovel, G	145.00
Sign, tin, features bullet heads, 1970s, 17½x11½"	95.00
Sign, tin, 2-sided, Winchester factory scene, 1892, EX	1,100.00
Steel, knife-sharpening; all orig	85.00
Straight razor, #8531	110.00
Tennis racquet, NM	550.00
Token, brass, from factory tool room	35.00
Wagon, Coaster, steel w/rubber tires, EX	1,250.00

Windmill Weights

Windmill weights were used to protect the windmill's plunger rod from damage during high winds by adding weight that slowed down the speed of the blades.

Bull, Fairbury, cast iron, no remaining paint, 22½", $700.00.

Bull, Boss Bull, worn pnt, 32-lb	1,800.00
Bull, Fairbury, CI w/old rpt over silver, 18"+base	990.00
Crescent moon, Eclipse, Fairbanks, Morse & Co Chicago, 10½"	385.00
Horse, att Demster (no casting #s), CI, 16⅝x17¼"	150.00
Horse, Demster, CI, pnt traces, 18⅜"	495.00
Horse, long tail, Demster #58, old pnt	650.00
Rooster, rainbow tail, Elgin, EX pnt, 60-lb, 18x16x3"	1,150.00
Squirrel, flattened full body, Elgin, old pnt/rust, 17½"	2,100.00

Wire Ware

Very primitive wire was first made by cutting sheet metal into strips which were shaped with mallet and file. By the late 13th century, craftsmen in Europe had developed a method of pulling these strips through progressively smaller holes until the desired gauge was obtained. During the Industrial Revolution of the late 1800s, machinery was developed that could produce wire cheaply and easily; and it became a popular commercial commodity. It was used to produce large items such as garden benches and fencing as well as innumerable small pieces for use in the kitchen or on the farm. Beware of reproductions. Our advisor for this category is Rosella Tinsley; she is listed in the Directory under Kansas.

Bacon rack, 6-prong, heavy wire, hook at top **18.00**
Basket, gathering; stationary hdl, 8½"+hdls, 7" dia **55.00**
Basket, petal-shaped sides, scalloped bottom, folding, 4½x7" **55.00**
Basket, potato boiling; wrapped-wire bail, 1800s, 14x15" **195.00**
Biscuit pricker, heavy wire spikes, loop hdl, 2¼" dia **70.00**
Bottle carrier, holds 6, twisted hdl, 4x9x14" **75.00**
Comb holder, twisted, fancy top, wall mt **125.00**
Compote, twisted wire, ped base **150.00**
Egg tongs, heavy oval circular wire, squeeze hdl, 11" L **45.00**
Fork, meat; heavy wire, 3 sharp prongs, loop hdl, 1800s, 15" **20.00**
Glove, butcher's, woven wire mesh **24.00**
Hanger, twisted w/looped design in center, 15x18½" **20.00**
Pie rack, heavy wire, holds 6 pies **110.00**
Pie rack, 4-tier **75.00**
Planter, corner; 3-tiered, wht pnt, 19th C, 49x28x20" **495.00**
Postcard holder, twisted wire, 2 rows of circles **110.00**
Rolling pin holder, fine twisted wire, 4 hearts, old, EX **95.00**
Scrubber, wire ringlets, twisted wire hdl **45.00**
Soap dish, twisted, ornate, wall mt **75.00**
Soap saver, oblong screen-wire shape, wire & wood hdl **18.00**
Sponge holder, twisted wire w/loop for hanging, rnd bottom **135.00**
Tea ball, egg shape, ½" tin band ea side, 2¾" **28.00**
Toaster, Maltese cross design, wood hdl **45.00**
Trivet, fine wire in circles, ftd, 14" dia **85.00**
Trivet, for ironing, 3-ftd, 10¼" w/hdl **60.00**
Trivet, woven dmn center, 8" dia **20.00**
Whisk, tined loop w/twisted hdl, Germany, 8", EX **25.00**

Wisecarver, Rick

Rick Wisecarver is a contemporary ceramic artist from Ohio who is well known not only for his renderings of Indian portraits and brown-glaze ware reminiscent of similar lines made by earlier Ohio potteries but for his figural cookie jars as well, most of which have a Black theme.

Cookie jar, Beauty & the Beast **250.00**
Cookie jar, Indian Maid **180.00**
Cookie jar, Saturday Bath, from $175 to **235.00**
Jug, Native Am brave w/feathers in hair, mc on gr to yel, 8½" ...**110.00**
Vase, deer in snow, 18x10" **295.00**
Vase, gladiator w/helmet, mc w/gold on brn, 14" **100.00**
Vase, Native Am brave on horse, brn & yel shades, 17" **210.00**
Vase, Native Am brave w/headdress, brns/yels/blk/bl, 9½" **150.00**
Vase, Native Am Chief, full headdress, mc on brn, 17" **450.00**
Vase, old prospector, mc on yel to wht, 7½" **60.00**

Witch Balls

Witch balls were a Victorian fad touted to be meritorious toward ridding the house of evil spirits, thus warding off sickness and bad luck. Folklore would have it that by wiping the dust and soot from the ball, the spirits were exorcised. It is much more probable, however, considering the fact that such beautiful art glass was used in their making, that the ostensive Victorians perpetrated the myth rather tongue-in-cheek while enjoying them as lovely decorations for their homes.

Red, white, and blue loopings on clear, free-blown, pontiled, 5½", M, $525.00.

Amethyst, 6½", +matching trumpet vase, free-blown, 13" **1,600.00**
Blk amethyst, sm sheared opening on 1 end, 1870-90, 4¼" **85.00**
Clear w/wht opaque loopings, 7" **495.00**
Cobalt, open pontil 1 end, many bubbles, 1860-90, 8" **150.00**
Nailsea, clear w/cranberry, bl & wht loopings, 4¾" **450.00**
Ruby flashed in striated ruby-flashed bowl, clear ft, 4" dia **850.00**

Wood Carvings

Wood sculptures represent an important section of American folk art. Wood carvings were made not only by skilled woodworkers such as cabinetmakers, carpenters, etc., but by amateur 'whittlers' as well. They take the form of circus-wagon figures, carousel animals, decoys, busts, figurines, and cigar store Indians. Oriental artists show themselves to have been as proficient with the medium of wood as they were with ivory or hardstone. See also Carousel Animals; Decoys; Tobacciana.

Boxers (J Johnson/Jess Willard), walnut, early 1900s, 17" **350.00**
Fish decoy, 4 tin side fins & tin tail, glass eyes, 1930s, 7" **80.00**
Fleur-de-lis, weathered gray, 23" **475.00**
Greyhound w/rabbit, old mc rpt w/flakes, 11" **935.00**
Horse w/leather saddle/etc, on base, 1930s, 9½x8½x3" **125.00**
Kingfisher, pnt & laminated, 21" **900.00**
Lady w/long skirt, articulated arms, worn patina, 7¼" **325.00**
Man in top hat & goatee, mahog w/dk varnish, OH, 11½" **110.00**
Nude man on chamber pot in archway, ca 1900, 5¾x4¾" **85.00**
Rooster, pine w/mustard pnt, ca 1900, 16x26" **2,400.00**
Sheep, old blk & wht pnt, rpr, 6¾" **60.00**
Uncle Sam, EX detail & pnt, ca 1970, 76" **400.00**

Woodenware

Woodenware (or treenware, as it is sometimes called) generally refers to those wooden items such as spoons, bowls, food molds, etc., that were used in the preparation of food. Common during the 18th and 19th centuries, these wares were designed from a strictly functional viewpoint and were used on a day-to-day basis. With the advent of the Industrial Revolution which brought new materials and products, much of the old woodenware was simply discarded. Today original handcrafted American woodenwares are extremely difficult to find. See also Mauchline Ware.

Apple peeler, all wood, 1830s, mtd on 22x6" board **250.00**
Bin, sugar dispensing; chestnut, stenciling, 1880s, 8x16x7" **260.00**
Board, bread; maple, cvd wheat at edge, ¾x11½" dia **65.00**
Board, cutting; pine, apple shape, pnt edge, 8¼x5¾x¾" **25.00**
Board, cutting; 15x11½"+wood hdl attached w/pegs **55.00**
Board, springerle; 6 designs in sqs, 3⅞x6", EX **80.00**
Bowl, ash burl, EX figure, cvd rim hdls, 7x17" **770.00**
Bowl, ash burl, ftd, scrubbed, 2½x5" **525.00**
Bowl, ash burl, ftd, 19th C, 3x6¼" **700.00**
Bowl, ash burl, trn, 18th C, 2¼x7¾" **375.00**

Bowl, ash burl, trn ring at base, sm putty rpr, 3½x8" 300.00
Bowl, ash burl, wear/knife mks, 19th C, 12⅝" 980.00
Bowl, ash burl w/EX figure, dk patina, cut-out hdls, 7x20x14" 2,100.00
Bowl, ash burl w/EX figure, dk patina, rim damage, 3½x13½" ...715.00
Bowl, ash burl w/faint red traces, 2¾x3¼" 770.00
Bowl, chopping; old bl pnt, 6x19" 400.00
Bowl, elongated oblong, scrubbed, 13½x44" 300.00
Bowl, hand trn, irregular-shaped top, 3¾x9" 80.00
Bowl, poplar, old varnish over orig grpt, 8" 250.00
Bowl, poplar w/orig red grpt, 8½x13" 550.00
Bowl, poplar w/red traces, undulating rim, rectangular, 28" L 470.00
Butter paddle, ash burl, crook end, old varnish, 10" 220.00
Butter scraper, handcvd, thin rnded-end blade, hook at hdl 25.00
Canteen, staved, dk red pnt, cvd stopper, rope hdl, 8½" dia 295.00
Cheese ladder, mortised hickory, worn patina, 31x13½" 75.00
Cheese ladder, pegged rungs mortised to sides, 26x10" 110.00
Cookie board, chip-cvd letters, beach w/worm holes, 4⅝x21" ...200.00
Cookie board, couple & cat, chestnut, EX patina, 17x5" 220.00
Cookie board, horseman w/flag, chickens on bk, birch, 10x6" 470.00
Cookie board, 18 bearded men, beech w/EX patina, 26½x4" 165.00
Cookie roller, maple, ca 1860, 12" 35.00
Curd breaker, sq hopper on drum w/knives, crank hdl, 1850s 225.00
Dipper, delicate long hdl, 16⅜" 95.00
Dish, mc flowers, paper label dtd 1888, wear, 2⅝" 1,045.00
Doughnut cutter, mellow color, VG 98.00
Egg cup, Lehnware, mc tulips, yel int, lt wear, 3" 880.00
Jar, ash burl, w/lid, 19th C, 4½" 800.00
Jar, Lehn ware, mc strawberries & foliage, 4¾" 1,265.00
Jar, mc flowers, strawberries on lid, ftd, 4½", EX 770.00
Jar, Peaseware, bulbous, EX patina, crack, 5¼" 220.00
Jar, Peaseware, orig varnish, wire bail w/wood hdl, 3⅞" 470.00
Jar, Peaseware, wire bale w/wood hdl, rprs, 7½" 550.00
Jar, Peaseware, wire bale w/wood hdl, 8¼x8½" 800.00
Lemon reamer, mushroom knob hdl, 5¾" L 98.00
Lemon squeezer, maple, hinged, trn hdl, 1840s, 10½" 50.00
Mallet, burl head, chestnut hdl, 12" 55.00
Pickle dipper, hand-cvd, 1-pc, 4¾x2½" oval w/long hdl 75.00
Pie lifter, maple hdl w/wire V grippers, 1870s 38.00
Pitcher, maple, hand-cvd, 1-pt, 6" 185.00
Rolling pin, curly maple, 21" 150.00
Rolling pin, rock maple, hand-trn, heavy, early 1800s, 18x2" 35.00
Rolling pin, tiger maple, 2 hdls, 20" 120.00
Scoop, apple butter; D-shaped hdl, 15½" L 90.00
Scoop, ash burl, cvd, 6x4" dia 100.00
Scoop, hand-cvd maple, 1-pc, 4¼x3¼" w/3½" hdl 65.00
Spoon, hand-cvd, early, tablespoon sz 18.00

Woodworking Machinery

Vintage cast-iron woodworking machines are monuments to the highly skilled engineers, foundrymen, and machinists who devised them, thus making possible the mass production of items ranging from clothespins, boxes, and barrels to decorative moldings and furniture. Though attractive from a nostalgic viewpoint, many of these machines are bought by the hobbyist and professional alike, to be put into actual use — at far less cost than new equipment. Many worth-assessing factors must be considered; but as a general rule, a machine in good condition is worth about 65¢ a pound (excluding motors). A machine needing a lot of restoration is not worth more than 35¢ a pound, while one professionally rebuilt and with a warranty can be calculated at $1.10 a pound. Modern, new machinery averages over $3.00 a pound. Two of the best sources of information on purchasing or selling such machines are *Vintage Machines — Searching for the Cast Iron Classics* by Tom Howell, and *Used Machines and Abused Buyers* by Chuck

Seidel from *Fine Woodworking*, November/December 1984. Prices quoted are for machines in good condition, less motors and accessories. Our advisor for this category is Mr. Dana Martin Batory, author of *Vintage Woodworking Machinery, An Illustrated Guide to Four Manufacturers*. See his listing in the Directory under Ohio for further information. No phone calls, please.

Photo courtesy Dana Martin Batory

Parks 'Ideal' 12" jointer, ca 1925, $400.00.

American Saw Mill Machinery Company, 1931

Band saw, Monarch Line, #X25, 30" built-in ball-bearing motor 770.00
Jointer, Monarch Line, #XII, ball-bearing, 16" 1,200.00
Mortiser, Monarch Line, #XI, hollow chisel, motorized 345.00
Planer, Monarch Line, single surface, 30" 2,600.00
Sander, Monarch Line, #X8, ball-bearing drum & disk 560.00
Table saw, Monarch Line, #X24, tilting arbor, 16" 425.00

Blue Star Products, 1939

Band saw, #1200, 12" floor model 85.00
Lathe, #1001, 72" bed, 12" swing 60.00
Table saw, #800, 8" 95.00

Boice-Crane Power Tools, 1937

Band saw, #800, 14" 100.00
Drill press, #1600, 15" 75.00
Lathe, #1100, gap bed 50.00
Scroll saw, #900, 24" 75.00

Crescent Machine Company, 1921

Band saw, 36" 975.00
Mortiser, hollow chisel 525.00
Universal Wood-Worker, #59, 5 machines in 1 ....2,050.00

Defiance Machine Works, 1910

Band saw, 28" 520.00
Table saw, #2, hand feed, 20" 650.00
Table saw, #2, power feed, 20" 1,100.00

Gallmeyer & Livingston Company, 1927

Band saw, Union, 20" 390.00
Jointer, Union, motor on arbor, 8" 370.00
Table saw, Union #7, 7" 210.00

G.N. Goodspeed Company, 1876

Boring machine, upright 225.00

Planer, New & Improved, Pony, 24" 900.00
Table saw, 12" 200.00

Greenlee Bros. & Company, 1925

Tenoner, #530, sash, door & cabinet, ball-bearing 1,530.00

Hoyt & Brother Company, 1888

Band saw & resawing machine, #1194, 20" 1,700.00
Cutoff saw, overhung, traversing, 14" 650.00
Jointer, Perfection, 8" 450.00
Mortiser & borer, #2 ....780.00
Planer, matcher & surfacer, New Combined, #2, 24" 5,200.00
Planing & matching machine, #7, 13" 3,250.00
Sandpapering machine, The Boss, #5, 24" 1,600.00
Scroll saw, #1 ....300.00
Shingle machine, Grand Mogul, 2-block, automatic feed 2,210.00
Table saw, #2, 14" 800.00
Tenoning machine, #2 ....650.00
Wood shaper, dbl spindle 850.00

J.A. Fay & Egan Company, 1900

Jointer, New #2, 16" 1,550.00
Jointer, New #2, 20" 1,625.00
Jointer, New #2, 30" 1,820.00
Jointer, New #4, extra heavy, 16" 1,625.00
Jointer, New #4, extra heavy, 20" 1,690.00
Jointer, New #4, extra heavy, 24" 1,885.00
Jointer, New #4, extra heavy, 30" 2,275.00
Molder, #1½, 4-sided, 4" 1,050.00
Molder, #2½, 4-sided, 7" 2,100.00
Mortiser, #2, hollow chisel, automatic horizontal 1,500.00
Mortiser, #5, dbl hollow chisel, horizontal 1,100.00
Planer, #2½, dbl-belted surface, med sz, 26" 1,850.00
Saw, rip; #2, Improved Standard 1,175.00
Saw, rip; #2, self-feeding, lg 1,775.00
Saw, rip; #3, self-feeding, X-lg 2,400.00

J.D. Wallace Company, 1940s

Band saw, 16" 210.00
Grinder & sander, disk; Wonder, 16" 165.00
Jointer, 4" 15.00
Lathe, 6x24" 115.00
Saw, circular (table saw); Universal, 7" 75.00
Saw, circular; plain, 7" 65.00

L. Power & Co., 1888

Mortiser & borer, #2 ....780.00
Shaper, single spindle, reversible 585.00
Table saw, self feed, 14" 715.00

Ober Manufacturing Company, 1889

Rip saw, self feed, 14" 725.00
Saw, swing cut-off, 18" 275.00
Shaper, saw & jointer combination 400.00

Oliver Machinery Company, 1922

Band saw, #17, 30" 925.00

Shaper, #483, high speed, dbl spindle 1,300.00
Table saw, #32, Variety, 12" 500.00

Parks Ball Bearing Machine Company, 1925

Sanding machine, H-165, Economy, 24" 230.00
Saw, H-97, swing cut-off, Alert, 12" 225.00

P.B. Yates Machine Company, 1917

Planer, #160, dbl surface, 20" 1,235.00
Saw, #232, swing cut-off, 16" 260.00

Powermatic, Inc., 1965

Band saw, #141, 14" 145.00
Band saw, #81, 20" 500.00
Jointer, #50, 6" 110.00
Jointer, #60, 8" 170.00
Lathe, #45, 12" 230.00
Lathe, #90, 12" 360.00
Mortiser, #10, hollow chisel 375.00
Mortiser, #15, chain saw 390.00
Planer, #100, 12" 200.00
Planer, #160, 16" 650.00
Planer, #180, 18" 685.00
Planer, #221, 20" 725.00
Planer, #225, 24" 1,600.00
Sander, #300-01, 12" disk & 6" belt combination 95.00
Sander, #33, 6" belt 90.00
Sander, #35, 12" disk 55.00
Scroll saw, #95, 24" 100.00
Shaper, #26, single spindle 240.00
Table saw, #62, 10" 135.00
Table saw, #66, 10" 230.00
Table saw, #72, 12" 515.00
Tenoner, #2-A, single end 620.00

S.A. Woods Machine Company, 1876

Circular resawing machine, Joslin's Improved, 50" 2,275.00
Planer, panel; Improved, 20" 520.00
Planer, Pat Improved, shop surface, 30" 1,430.00

Sprunger Power Tools, 1950s

Band saw, 14" 60.00
Jigsaw, 20" 40.00
Lathe, gap bed, 10" 50.00
Table saw, tilt arbor, 10¼" 75.00

Worcester Porcelain Company

The Worcester Porcelain Company was deeded in 1751. During the first or Dr. Wall period (so called for one of its proprietors), porcelain with an Oriental influence was decorated in underglaze blue. Useful tablewares represented the largest portion of production, but figurines and decorative items were also made. Very little of the earliest wares were marked and can only be identified by a study of forms, glazes, and the porcelain body, which tends to transmit a greenish cast when held to light. Late in the '50s, a crescent mark was in general use, and rare examples bear a facsimile of the Meissen crossed swords. The first period ended in 1783, and the company went through several changes in ownership during the next eighty years. The years from 1783-1792 are referred to as the Flight period. Marks were a small crescent, a crown with 'Royal,' or an impressed 'Flight.' From 1792-1807 the company was known as Flight and Barr and used the trademark 'F&B' or 'B,' with or without a small cross. From 1807-1813 the company was under the Barr, Flight, and Barr management; this era is recognized as having produced porcelain with the highest quality of artistic decoration. Their mark was 'B.F.B.' From 1813-1840 many marks were used, but the most usual was 'F.B.B.' under a crown to indicate Flight, Barr, and Barr. In 1840 the firm merged with Chamberlain, and in 1852 they were succeeded by Kerr and Binns. The firm became known as Royal Worcester in 1862. The production was then marked with a circle with '51' within and a crown on top. The date of manufacture was incised into the bottom or stamped with a letter of the alphabet, just under the circle. In 1891 Royal Worcester England was added to the circle and crown. From that point on each piece is dated with a code of dots or other symbols. After 1891 most wares had a blush-color ground. Prior to that date it was ivory. Most shapes were marked with a unique number.

During the early years they produced considerable ornamental wares with a Persian influence. This gave way to a Japanesque influence. James Hadley is most responsible for the Victorian look. He is considered the 'best ever' designer and modeller. He was joined by the finest porcelain painters. Together they produced pieces with very fine detail and exquisite painting and decoration. Figures, vases, and tableware were produced in great volume and are highly collectible. During the 1890s they allowed the artists to sign some of their work. Pieces signed on the face by the Stintons, Baldwyn, Davis, Raby, Austin, Powell, Sedgley, and Rushton (not a complete list) are in great demand. The company is still in production. There is an outstanding museum on the company grounds in Worcester, England.

Note: most pieces had lids or tops (if there is a flat area on the top lip, chances are it had one), if missing deduct 30% to 40%.

Key: ug — underglaze

Biscuit jar, florals on lobed melon form w/gold, 1889, 6½" **200.00**
Bowl, florals on lobed body w/gold, ca 1890, 9" **300.00**
Bowl, leaf mold w/floral sprays & butterflies, 1884, 6¾" **230.00**
Cheese dish, bamboo leaves on bamboo, Stilton, 1879, 9¾" **635.00**
Coffeepot, floral sprays, gold bamboo hdl, maroon mk, 8" **225.00**
Epergne, 3 cornucopias w/3 gold lion heads, HP floral, 9" **1,150.00**
Ewer, butterflies among tall gilt grass, ca 1884, 9½" **395.00**
Ewer, floral & leaf band, bamboo hdl, RW, crown/dmn mk, 4" ..**175.00**
Fern pot, boy beside stump figural, rstr, 1887, 7" **350.00**
Figurine, Bather Surprised, crackle w/gold, 1900s, 25¼" **700.00**
Figurine, Elizabeth, enamel decor w/gold, ca 1807, 6¼" **450.00**
Figurine, Golden Crown Kinglets/Noble Pine, Doughty, 7¾", pr ...**1,650.00**
Figurine, lady w/tambourine (cymbals), 1890s, 10", 10¾", pr ..**1,250.00**
Figurine, Monday's Child, #3519, 7½" **125.00**
Figurine, Red-Eyed Vireos & Swamp Azaleas, Doughty, 7", pr **1,200.00**
Figurine, Yel-Headed Blkbirds/Spiderwort, Doughty, '52, 10¼", pr ..**1,750.00**
Figurine, Yel-Throats/Water Hyacinths, Doughty, '58, 12", pr **1,980.00**
Jardiniere, basketweave w/gold, scrolled hdls, 1897, 6¾" **350.00**
Jardiniere, floral sprays/foliate borders w/gold, 1891, 8¼" **525.00**
Pitcher, daisies/flowers, gold hdl, maroon mk, #1094, 6" **160.00**
Pitcher, mc floral, gold hdl, maroon mk, #1094, 5" **155.00**
Pitcher, mc floral, pinched spout, mk/#1094, 7¾" **170.00**
Pitcher, mc floral w/gold vine-wrapped hdl, maroon mk, 9" **250.00**
Pitcher, pk clematis w/gold, gold hdl, maroon mk, #1094, 8" **185.00**
Platter, mixed floral, J Green & Nephew, London, 18x13½" **150.00**
Potpourri, water lilies on basketweave, 1883, rstr, 14½" **450.00**
Teapot, garden landscape, red w/gold, mk, 1765, 5", EX **575.00**
Teapot, mc floral, gold bamboo hdl, maroon mk, 7" **200.00**
Teapot, mc floral, gold bamboo loop hdl, purple mk, 8½" **300.00**

Vase, butterflies/flowers, gold-leaf hdls, maroon mk, 5", pr **400.00**
Vase, elephant figural w/gold trim, late 1800s, 5⅝" **650.00**

Vase, figures and tropical birds in reserves on cobalt with gold, handles, ca 1770, 8¾", base restored, chip to 1 handle, $635.00.

Vase, floral relief w/gold, mk, ca 1887, 7¼" **500.00**
Vase, florals on yel w/gold, w/lid, 1893, 14¾" **700.00**
Vase, moon/gold branch & sky, hdls, stick neck, gr mk, 6½" **375.00**
Vase, roses w/gold, rtcl hdls, open neck, #942, 17½" **850.00**
Vase, Tommy, sgn FG Doughty, 4½" **225.00**

World's Fairs and Expos

Since 1851 and the Crystal Palace Exhibition in London, World's Fairs and Expositions have taken place at a steady pace. Many of them commemorate historical events. The 1904 Louisiana Purchase Exposition, commonly known as the St. Louis World's Fair, celebrated the 100th anniversary of the Louisiana Purchase agreement between Thomas Jefferson and Napoleon in 1803. The 1893 Columbian Exposition, known as The Chicago World's Fair, commemorated the 400th anniversary of the discovery of America by Columbus in 1492. (Both of these fairs were held one year later than originally scheduled.) The multitude of souvenirs from these and similar events have become a growing area of interest to collectors in recent years. Many items have a 'crossover' interest into other fields: i.e., collectors of postcards and souvenir spoons eagerly search for those from various fairs and expositions. For additional information collectors may contact World's Fairs Collectors Society (WFCS), whose address is in the Directory under Clubs, Newsletters, and Catalogs, or our advisor, D.D. Woollard, Jr. His address is listed in the Directory under Missouri.

Key:
T&P — Trylon & Perisphere WF — World's Fair

1876 Centennial, Philadelphia

Bandana, linen, printed brn bldgs, red border, 26x25", NM **150.00**
Book, History of Centennial..., McCabe, 300 illus, 6x9", EX **75.00**
Cake plate, glass, Declaration of Independence 1776-1876, 10" **50.00**
Cup, china, mc view of Centennial Memorial Bldg, 3½", EX **95.00**
Ribbon, silk, Father of Our Country..., 10", EX **50.00**
View book, Centennial Pocket Album, red/blk/gold cover, EX **25.00**

1893 Columbian, Chicago

Bell, brass w/wood hdl, Liberty Bell w/expo mks, 2½", EX **35.00**
Charm, gold-plated brass, bust of Cleveland & expo mks, rnd **35.00**
Cup, china, Government Bldg scene, gold trim, mk England, EX **60.00**
Handkerchief, mc scene embr on blk silk, 13x14", EX **35.00**
Paperweight, glass, mc, Woman's Bldg, 2½x4" **50.00**
Plate, china, To Castille & Leon...1492, mc, 9", EX **50.00**
Shaker, egg shape, frosted milk glass, Col 1893 Exhibition, EX ..**100.00**
Spoon, demi; sterling silver, heart-shaped bowl, 4", M **28.00**

Spoon, sterling, Children's Home emb in bowl, 4½" **45.00**
Tray, SP metal, Columbus & bldgs w/floral border, ftd, 7" dia, EX **75.00**

1901 Pan American

Ad card, Heide's Licorice Pastiles..., boy in fancy clothes **10.00**
Booklet, sketches of Niagara Falls/Buffalo/expo scenes, NM **20.00**
Coin, Electric Tower design, elongated, EX **15.00**
Doll, Kewpie type, celluloid, mk Pan-Am on ft, all orig, 3" **50.00**
Dresser jar, milk glass w/US Government Bldg decal, 3x3½", EX **60.00**
Letter opener, SP metal, mk Pam Am Souvenir on hdl, NM **16.00**
Napkin ring, aluminum, buffalo design, mk Pan-Am 1901, 1½" ..**20.00**
Pocket mirror, celluloid, Electric Tower, 2¼" **60.00**
Shot glass, When You Drink–Do of Me Think, 2½" **30.00**
Token, aluminum, World's Greatest Niagara Falls, EX **7.50**

1904 St. Louis

Cup, aluminum, Cascade Gardens, collapsible, 2½", EX **40.00**
Invitation, to dedication ceremonies, 8x10", NM **75.00**
Mirror, celluloid, mc, US Government Bldg, 2½", NM **100.00**
Mug, General Grant's log cabin transfer, NM **75.00**
Napkin ring, emb fair bldg on metal, EX **35.00**
Pin-bk, Kansas, w/Kansas Day ribbon, 9/30/04, VG **90.00**
Plate, china, mc scene of Palace Liberal Arts, 6¼", EX **40.00**
Pocketknife, emb views on aluminum hdl, 2¾" **75.00**
Skillet, Home Comfort Ranges, CI, 2½x3½", EX **40.00**
Stein, stoneware, Balance of Electricity, ½-liter, M **200.00**
Toothpick holder, ceramic, cream & orange, 2¼", EX **40.00**

Tray, Have Some Junket, girl heating product, 4½" dia, $250.00.

Tray, brass, floral border, emb mule, 3½", EX **35.00**
Tumbler, triple scene on china, 4", EX **45.00**

1905 Lewis and Clark

Pin-bk, celluloid, mc Lewis & Clark, 1½" **35.00**
Pin-bk, celluloid, 2 frogs, Mt Hood, 1¾" **40.00**
Poster stamps, various scenes, 4½x6½" sheet of 12 ....**20.00**

1909 Alaska Yukon Pacific

Bowl, ceramic, mc multi-scene, 5" **50.00**
Plate, china, mc scene, Rowland & Marsellus, 10" **100.00**

1915 Panama Pacific

Award ribbon, expo seal & lettering, gold/purple, 7x3½", EX **50.00**
Badge, celluloid, Admit One, Opening Day..., w/ribbon, EX **35.00**
Book, Architecture & Landscape Gardening of the Expo, 202 pgs, EX ..**40.00**
Book, What We Saw at Madame World's Fair, 86 pgs, EX **25.00**
Napkin ring, celluloid, cutout design around Tower of Jewels, EX **20.00**
Pan, metal, emb Tower of Jewels, 2¼", EX **15.00**
Table cover, bl felt, view of expo & poppies, 16x25", EX **35.00**

Tin, Ridgway's Tea, mc fair scene, 6x4x4", EX **50.00**
Trivet, brass, eng design of Tower of Jewels, 5½" sq, EX **25.00**

1926 Sesquicentennial

Certificate of Membership, w/seal, 11x8½", NM **40.00**
Medal, Washington, Liberty Bell, 1⅜", EX **10.00**
Paperweight, Liberty Bell shape, 1½x3x3", EX **25.00**
Pin-bk, celluloid, mc, Liberty Bell, 1776/1926, 1", NM **12.50**

1933 Chicago

Book, Color Beauties of a Century of Progress, 32 pgs, M **20.00**
Book, Official Book of Views, RH Donnelley Co, 64 pgs, EX **22.50**
Candle holders, metal, emb Hall of Science/Federal Bldg, 4", pr ..**45.00**
Catalog, Official Catalog of Exhibits...Hall of Science, VG **20.00**
Lamp, brass, mc design of fair bldgs on glass cylinder, 5", EX **125.00**
Paperweight, glass, mc scene, mk Night View of WF..., 4x3x1", NM ...**35.00**
Plate, china, Carillon Tower, blk on wht, 8¼", NM **40.00**
Program, Opening Day, illus, 24 pgs, VG **22.50**
Ring, comet design, silver on bl, adjustable **10.00**
Spoon, emb Chinese Temple/Carillon Tower on hdl, mk Sterling, 6" .**40.00**
Tapestry, aerial view of the fair, 25x41", M **75.00**
Tray, litho tin, Fort Dearborn, mc, 4" dia, EX **25.00**
Umbrella, bamboo spokes w/bl & red swirl on paper cover, VG ...**35.00**
Watch fob, brass, overview of fair, Leonard Refrigeration..., EX ...**25.00**

1935 California Pacific

Folder, Come to San Diego 1935, EX+ **7.50**
Matchbox holder, bl enamel expo scenes on brass, 1½x1½", EX **20.00**
Medal, brass, emb bldgs & state seal, mk State of CA Souvenir, VG ...**7.50**
Program, Official Guide, w/map, illus, 1936 issue, 56 pgs **20.00**
Tile, ceramic, raised image & lettering, mk Arts & Crafts..., NM **60.00**

1939 New York

Ashtray, clear glass w/Food Bldg design & lettering in red, NM ...**28.00**
Ashtray, emb T&P design & date, Syrocco wood base, 3" sq, EX **25.00**
Book, NY WF Views, T&P on cover, 48 pgs, NM **35.00**
Book, Official Souvenir Guide & Picture Book, EX **25.00**
Bookends, marble w/T&P design, 4½", NM, pr **200.00**
Box, brn felt cover w/US Steel Bridge design & date, 6x4x2", EX **20.00**
Camera, Kodak WF Bullet, blk/brass-colored, T&P logo, MIB ...**500.00**
Fan, paper w/wood hdl, mk Pavilion Japan NY WF, 18" sq, VG ...**65.00**
Hot pad, silver-colored metallic finish w/emb building, EX **20.00**
Lamp base, ceramic, T&P shape, mk Made in England **100.00**
Letter opener, metal w/image of Christian Science Bldg, 9", EX ..**20.00**
Scarf, cloth w/US flag, stars & NY WF 1939, red/wht/bl, 24x22", M ..**50.00**
Sheet music, Yours for a Song, T&P pictured, Robbins Music, NM **30.00**
Tray, metal w/T&P design, 18x11", EX **100.00**

1939 San Francisco

Bookmark, butterfly form, yel on acetate w/paper, MIP **25.00**
Compact, brushed brass, eng Golden Gate Internat'l Expo, MIB **30.00**
Folder, Kirkland Travel Service, folded: 4x9", EX **5.00**
Pillow sham, mc fair scenes, 17" sq, EX **25.00**
Plate, china, Bay Bridge & Tower design, mk Homer Laughlin, M .**100.00**
Ticket folder, WF Premiere, w/pin-on badge, M **35.00**

1964 New York

Booklet, Look's Guide to NY WF, w/color map, 34 pgs, EX **5.00**

Bumper sticker, I've Seen NY State at the Fair 1964-65, 4x8", NM **15.00**
Magazine, NY Vacation Lands 1965 WF Edition, 80 pgs, EX **10.00**
Puzzle, fr-tray; fair scene, Milton Bradley, NM **15.00**
Record, Triumph of Man, 45 rpm, shows Traveler's Ins Co exhibit, M ...**10.00**
Ring, flasher; plastic, shows Unisphere & NY WF 1964-65, M **10.00**
Spoon, demi; SP metal, Unisphere & 1964-65 NY WF on hdl, 4", NM ..**8.00**
Tray, metal, mc Unisphere scene, 12" dia, EX **12.50**

Wright, Frank Lloyd

Born in Richland Center, Wisconsin, in 1869, Wright became a pioneer in architectural expression, developing a style referred to as 'prairie.' From early in the century until he died in 1959, he designed houses with rooms that were open, rather than divided by walls in the traditional manner. They exhibited low, horizontal lines and strongly projecting eaves, and he filled them with furnishings whose radical aesthetics complemented the structures to perfection. Several of his homes have been preserved to the present day, and collectors who admire his ideas and the unique, striking look he achieved treasure the stained glass windows, furniture, chinaware, lamps, and other decorative accessories made by Wright.

Cabinet, Heritage Henredon, open bin above/below drw, 26x22" **800.00**
Cabinet, 2-doors w/recessed hdls, Taliesin edge, T base, 28" **275.00**
Cabinet, 3-drw, Taliesin edge, T base, 28x22" **550.00**
Card table, mahog, 2 wide slabs set at angle ea side, VG **2,100.00**
Chair, mahog angle fr, uphl sq bk/seat, 1955, rfn, VG **2,000.00**
Chair, side; hexagonal bk w/uphl chevron, 3-beam support **5,000.00**
Print, exterior drawing for office, emb FLW, 12½x21" **325.00**
Sculptures, Nakomis & Nakoma, blk gloss, 1929, 16", EX, pr .**7,000.00**
Sideboard, raised platform shelf, 11-drw, Taliesin edge, 62" **2,100.00**
Table, church; plywood triangle top/shelf, 3 slab legs, 25x46" **700.00**
Table, coffee; bench style w/drop sides, Taliesin edges, 60" W **2,400.00**
Table, mahog, 3 wide slabs form base, rpr, 28x36x24", VG **1,600.00**
Table, side; #452, sq top, cube base, Taliesin edge, 13x27" **1,400.00**
Table, side; divided open shelf over 2 drw, Taliesin edge **700.00**
Table, side; sq top on cube base, Taliesin edge, 13x27", VG **900.00**
Typewriter stand, Taliesin edge, 24x24x19", VG **600.00**

Wrought Iron

Until the middle of the 19th century, almost all the metal hand forged in America was made from a material called wrought iron. When wrought iron rusts it appears grainy, while the mild steel that was used later shows no grain but pits to an orange-peel surface. This is an important aid in determining the age of an ironwork piece.

Bench, strapwork w/scrolled crest & arms, 19th C, 33x48" **825.00**
Broiler, sq shape, rust, ca 1800, 25½" L **125.00**
Camp stove, hinged top grate, 8½x8½"+6" trn wood hdl **470.00**
Candlestand, tripod base, 1800s, 28½" **600.00**
Cookie peel, dbl rams' head curl, heart-shaped top, 28½" **260.00**
Dough scraper, peaned button top, 4" blade, 1870s, 5½" H **85.00**
Meat fork, cut-out dmn design, 18", EX **50.00**
Meat fork, wraparound loop hdl, 2-tine, 1860s, 21" **60.00**
Peel, sgn Preble, ca 1800, 36" **300.00**
Spatula, heart cutout, sgn H Hants on hdl, 18" **440.00**
Splint holder, twisted detail, trn wood base, 10⅜" **300.00**
Toaster, tooled initials & dtd 1778 on hdl, 15" **220.00**
Warming shelf, circular openwork, 8 hooks, 18th C, 21½" **500.00**

Yellow Ware

Ranging in color from buff to deep mustard, yellow ware which almost always has a clear glaze can be slip banded, plain, Rockingham decorated, flint enamel glazed, or mocha glazed. Mocha-decorated pieces, especially those which are red or black decorated, are usually the most expensive and desirable pieces to own. The majority of pieces are plain and do not bear a manufacturer's mark. Yellow ware which was primarily produced in the United States, England, and Canada was popular from the mid-19th century to the early 20th century. A utilitarian ware, it was first domestically produced in New York, Pennsylvania, and Vermont. With more than thirty active potteries, East Liverpool, Ohio, became the center for yellow ware production. Although other wares have become more popular, yellow ware is still being produced today in both England and the United States. Because of advanced collectors attempting to complete their collections, prices continue to rise. Note: Because this is a utilitarian ware, it is often found with damage and heavy wear; this would of course decrease the value of a piece. For further information we recommend *Collector's Guide to Yellow Ware* by Lisa S. McAllister and *Collecting Yellow Ware, An Identification and Value Guide,* written by our advisor, John Michel and Lisa S. McAllister. Mr. Michel's address is in the Directory under New York.

Baker, deep rim & strong color, 14" **275.00**
Bank, pig form w/bl & brn sponging, 5¾" L **150.00**
Beater jar, w/wht banding & advertising **135.00**
Bed warmer, Am, 19th C, 1¼x8x6" **250.00**
Colander, brn & wht bands, 13" **800.00**
Corn holder, plain, Am, ca 1910 ....**125.00**
Cradle, plain, 4" L, EX **500.00**
Creamer, cow figural, Rockingham decor, EX **450.00**
Egg cup, brn & wht bands, England, ca 1900 ....**475.00**
Jar, canning; octagonal, plain, 7¼" **185.00**
Mold, Centennial 1776-1876 (impressed), 5½" **650.00**
Mold, frog figural, plain, 5" **550.00**
Mold, turk's head, Rockingham decor exterior **165.00**
Mug, 2 wht slip bands, foliate hdl, 2" **190.00**

Mustard pot, blue seaweed, with lid, 2¼", EX, $500.00.

Pepper pot, bl & wht bands **675.00**
Pepper pot, bl seaweed mocha decor, bl bands **950.00**
Pepper pot, gr seaweed mocha decor, brn bands **750.00**
Pitcher, basketweave & morning glory emb, plain **250.00**
Pitcher, red & bl seaweed mocha, 10", EX **1,250.00**
Salt crock, Salt stamped in blk on wht slip, wall mt **295.00**
Sugar bowl, bl & wht slip bands, w/lid, 4½" **600.00**
Teapot, emb basketweave, Windsor Baking Powder giveaway, 5" **435.00**

Zanesville Glass

Glassware was produced in Zanesville, Ohio, from as early as 1815 until 1851. Two companies produced clear and colored hollow ware pieces in five characteristic patterns: 1) diamond faceted, 2) broken swirls, 3) vertical swirls, 4) perpendicular fluting, 5) plain, with scalloped or fluted rims and strap handles. The most readily identified product is perhaps the whiskey bottles made in the vertical swirl pattern, often called globular swirls because of their full, round bodies. Their necks vary in width; some have a ringed rim and some are collared. They were made in several colors; amber, light green, and light aquamarine are the most common. Our advisor for this category is Mark Vuono; he is listed in the Directory under Connecticut.

Bottle, amber, 24 swirled ribs, globular, 8⅞" 350.00
Bottle, amber, 24 swirled ribs, globular, 9⅝" 525.00
Bottle, amber, 24 swirled ribs, slightly clubbed shape, 8¼" 330.00
Bottle, aqua, 24 swirled ribs, globular, rolled lip, 9" 250.00
Bottle, deep amber, unpatterned, globular, 11½" 415.00
Bottle, golden amber, 24 swirled ribs, globular, 7½" 468.00
Bottle, golden amber, 24 swirled ribs, globular, 8½" 660.00
Bottle, golden amber, 24 swirled ribs, globular, 9½" 1,400.00
Bottle, med red-amber, 24 swirled ribs, globular, 8" 325.00
Bottle, olive-apricot, 24 swirled ribs, globular, 7½", EX 1,250.00
Chestnut flask, dk citron, 24 vertical ribs, teardrop, 5⅛" 375.00
Chestnut flask, dk red-amber, type 2, swirled ribs, 5½", NM 50.00
Chestnut flask, golden amber, 10-dmn, 5½" 935.00
Chestnut flask, golden amber, 24 vertical ribs, 4½" 275.00
Chestnut flask, golden amber, 24 vertical ribs, 5⅛" 300.00
Flip, clear w/bl tint, 10-dmn, pontil scar, 1820s, 6" 290.00
Inkwell, clear funnel type w/24 vertical ribs, 1⅜x1⅝" 250.00
Salt cellar, amethyst, 24 ribs, ogee shape, 2½" 1,350.00
Salt cellar, clear, 24 ribs, sheared mouth, ftd, 2⅞x3¼" 425.00

Zell

The Georg Schmider United Zell Ceramic Factories has a long and colorful history. Affectionately called 'Zell' by those who are attracted to this charming German-Dutch type tin-glazed earthenware, this type of ware came into production in the latter part of the last century.

While Zell has created some lovely majolica-like examples, it is the German-Dutch scenes that are collected with such enthusiasm. Typical scenes are set against a lush green background with windmills on the distant horizon. Into the scenes appear typically garbed girls (long dresses with long white aprons and lowland bonnet head-gear) being teased or admired by little boys attired in pantaloon-type trousers and short rust-colored jackets. There are variations on this theme, and occasionally a collector may find an animal theme or even a Kate Greenaway-like scene.

A similar ware in both theme, technique, and quality but bearing the mark Haag or Made in Austria is included in this listing.

While Zell produced a wide range of wares and even quite recently (1970s) introduced an entirely hand-painted hen/rooster line, it is this early charming German-Dutch theme pottery that is coveted and collected in increasing numbers by devoted collectors. Our advisors for this category are Fred and Lila Shrader; they are listed in the Directory under California.

Key: MIA — Made in Austria

Bowl, chickens, flat, Haag, 5½" 35.00
Bowl, porridge or sugar; boy & girl strolling, Zell, 3½" 22.00
Bowls, boy/girl scenes, Zell, nested set of 3: 7", 9½", 12" 275.00
Butter pat, girl on path, Zell 45.00
Creamer, 2 dolls gazing toward town, Haag, 4" 55.00
Cup & saucer, 2 sm girls, Zell, doll sz 55.00
Pitcher, barnyard scene w/roosters crowing, Haag, 8" 65.00
Plaque, boy & girl kissing, copper rtcl fr, 14" 295.00
Plate, cat in boots carries hare, Variety's the..., MIA, 10" 55.00

Tankard, girl standing, boy seated at harbor, Zell, 12½" 225.00
Teapot, boy extends hand to girl, Zell, 4-cup 175.00

Zsolnay

Only until the past decade has the production of the Zsolnay factory become more correctly understood. In the beginning they produced only cement; industrial and kitchen ware manufacture began in the 1850s, and in the early 1870s a line of decorative architectural and art pottery was initiated which has continued to the present time.

The city of Pecs (pronounced Paach) is the major provincial city of southwest Hungary close to the Yugoslav border. The old German name for the city was Funfkirchen, meaning 'Five Churches.' (The 'five-steeple' mark became the factory's logo in 1878.)

Although most Americans only think of Zsolnay in terms of the bizarre, reticulated examples of the 1880s and '90s and the small 'Eosine' green figures of animals and children that have been produced since the 1920s, the factory went through all the art trends of major international art potteries and produced various types of forms and decorations. The 'golden period,' circa 1895-1920, is when its Art Nouveau (Sezession in Austro-Hungarian terms) examples were unequaled. Vilmos Zsolnay was a Renaissance man devoted to innovation, and his children carried on the tradition after his death in 1900. Important sculptors and artists of the day were employed (usually anonymously) and married into the family, creating a dynasty.

Nearly all Zsolnay is marked, either impressed 'Zsolnay Pecs' or with the 'five steeple' stamp. Variations and form numbers can date a piece fairly accurately. For the most part, the earlier ethnic historical-revival pieces do not bring the prices that the later Sezession and second Sezession (Deco) examples do. Our advisor for this category is John Gacher; he is listed in the Directory under Rhode Island.

Bowl, mc floral, rtcl, 4-ftd, 5x7½" 260.00
Ewer, allover irid yel Persian motif on blk, bulbous, 5½" 450.00
Ewer, lg satyr hdl, gold w/scenic, #6102/36, EB/68751, 8½" 1,850.00
Ewer, rtcl Persian form, crescent finial, Pecs, 10", NM 190.00
Figurine, crying nude, classic bl/gr irid, gold stamp/mk, 10" 200.00
Inkwell, conch shell form, red/blk lustre, rpr hdl, #6576, 4½" 300.00
Pitcher, bird form, long crest as hdl, brn/gr w/gold, 9½" 1,700.00
Planter, lg cockatoo peers into bowl, jeweled/irid, 15" L 2,500.00
Salt cellar, seated toddler holds basket, gr irid, 2¾x4½" 200.00
Stein, repeating relief w/gold, mk/#2661/16, 1½-liter 200.00
Vase, allover floral, purple/bl/gold/red on blk, dome lid, 11" 800.00

Vase, maids in relief encircle recessed cylinder, the whole surrounded by hand-built and applied trees; opaque, metalescent, and colored eosin glazes, sculptured by Mihaly Kapas Nagy, ca 1900, 22x9", EX, $14,375.00.

Vase, appl dots & drips, gr/gold irid on mottled matt, 4x4½" 950.00
Vase, floral w/openwork, 4-color w/gold, stamped mk, 6x6½" 350.00
Vase, red w/mc irid floral, sphere w/horizontal ribs, 3" 200.00
Vase, repeating floral shoulder decor, gr/bl/red, 2⅝x3⅜" 85.00
Vase, scrolling flowers on elongated melon form, Pecs, 8" 100.00
Vase, 3-D nude hugs rim of acorn shape, red irid, 8" 1,850.00

Advisory Board

The editors and staff take this opportunity to express our sincere gratitude and appreciation to each person who has in any way contributed to the preparation of this guide. We believe the credibility of our book is greatly enhanced through their efforts. See each advisor's Directory listing for information concerning their specific areas of expertise.

You will notice that at the conclusion of some of the narratives the advisor's name is given. This is optional and up to the discretion of each individual. Simply because no name is mentioned does not indicate that we have no advisor for that subject. Our board grows with each issue and now numbers nearly 450; if you care to correspond with any of them or anyone listed in our Directory, you must send a SASE with your letter. If you are seeking an appraisal, first ask about their fee, since many of these people are professionals who must naturally charge for their services. Because of our huge circulation, every person who allows us to publish their name runs the risk of their privacy being invaded by too many phone calls and letters. We are indebted to every advisor and very much regret losing any one of them. By far, the majority of those we lose give that reason. Please help us retain them on our board by observing the simple rules of common courtesy. Take the differences in time zones into consideration; some of our advisors tell us they often get phone calls in the middle of the night. For suggestions that may help you evaluate your holdings, see the Introduction.

AAA Antique Shop
Nappanee, Indiana

Peter Abrahams
Lake Oswego, Oregon

Charles and Barbara Adams
Middleboro, Massachusetts

Geneva D. Addy
Winterset, Iowa

Charles Alexander
Indianapolis, Indiana

Margaret Alves
Shelton, Connecticut

James Anderson
New Brighton, Minnesota

Suzy McLennan Anderson
Holmdel, New Jersey

Tim Anderson
Provo, Utah

Warren R. Anderson
Cedar City, Utah

Dorothy Malone Anthony
Fort Scott, Kansas

John Apple
Racine, Wisconsin

Dick and Ellie Archer
Sarasota, Florida

Una Arnbal
Ames, Iowa

Bruce A. Austin
Pittsford, New York

Bobby Babcock
Austin, Texas

Rod Baer
Vienna, Virginia

Wayne and Gale Bailey
Dacula, Georgia

Roger Baker
Woodside, California

Robert Banks
Brookeville, Maryland

Jim Barker
Bethlehem, Pennsylvania

Kit Barry
Brattleboro, Vermont

Henry Bartsch
Rockaway, Oregon

Mark Bassett
Lakewood, Ohio

Daniel J. Batchelor
Oswego, New York

Dana Martin Batory
Crestline, Ohio

Joyce Bee
Sandy, Oregon

D.R. Beeks
Mt. Vernon, Iowa

Scott Benjamin
LaGrange, Ohio

Phyllis and Tom Bess
Tulsa, Oklahoma

Robert Bettinger
Mt. Dora, Florida

John E. Bilane
Union, New Jersey

Betty Bird
Mt. Shasta, Georgia

Brenda Blake
York Harbor, Maine

Clarence H. Bodine, Jr.
New Hope, Pennsylvania

Sandra V. Bondhus
Unionville, Connecticut

Clifford Boram
Monticello, Indiana

Jeff Bradfield
Dayton, Virginia

Larry Brenner
Manchester, New Hampshire

William J. Brinkley
McLeansboro, Illinois

Mike Brooks
Oakland, California

Jim Broom
Effingham, Illinois

David L. Brown
Victoria, British Columbia, Canada

Marcia Brown
White City, Oregon

Rick Brown
Newspaper Collector's Society of America
Lansing, Michigan

Nicki Budin
Worthington, Ohio

Richard M. (Dick) Bueschel
Mt. Prospect, Illinois

Robert C. Butz
Newbury Park, California

Jim Calison
Wallkill, New York

Carol and Jim Carlton
Englewood, Colorado

Fran Carter
Coos Bay, Oregon

Tina M. Carter
El Cajon, California

Cerebro
East Prospect, Pennsylvania

Mick and Lorna Chase
Cookeville, Tennessee

Pat and Chris Christensen
Costa Mesa, California

Jack Chipman
Venice, California

Joan Cimini
Belmont, Ohio

Debbie and Randy Coe
Lafayette, Oregon

Wilfred and Dolli Cohen
Santa Ana, California

Lillian M. Cole
Flemington, New Jersey

Marilyn Cooper
Houston, Texas

J.W. Courter
Kevil, Kentucky

Susan Cox
El Cajon, California

Rosalind Cranor
Blacksburg, Virginia

Ron Damaska
New Brighton, Pennsylvania

John Danis
Rockford, Illinois

Patricia M. Davis
Portland, Oregon

Gael deCourtivron
Sarasota, Florida

Richard K. Degenhardt
Hendersonville, North Carolina

Loretta DeLozier
Bedford, Iowa

Joe Devine
Council Bluffs, Iowa

Doug Dezso
Maywood, New Jersey

Thomas P. Dimitroff
Corning, New York

Ginny Distel
Tiffin, Ohio

Rod Dockery
Ft. Worth, Texas

L.R. 'Les' Docks
San Antonio, Texas

Rebecca Dodds
Ft. Lauderdale, Florida

Maryanne Dolan
Pleasant Hill, California

Pat Dole
Birmingham, Alabama

Ron Donnelly
Tuscaloosa, Alabama

Robert A. Doyle, CAI, ISA
Fishkill, New York

James Dryden
Hot Springs National Park, Arkansas

Louise Dumont
Coventry, Rhode Island

Ken and Jackie Durham
Washington, DC

William Durham
Belvidere, Illinois

Rita and John Ebner
Columbus, Ohio

Bill Edwards
Madison, Indiana

R.J. Sayers
Pisgah Forest, North Carolina

Elizabeth Schaaf
Mentone, Alabama

Nancy and Jim Schaut
Glendale, Arizona

Roselle Schleifman
Spring Valley, New York

Jim Schleyer
Burke, Virginia

Roger R. Scott
Tulsa, Oklahoma

Virgil Scowden
Williamsport, Indiana

Joyce and Harold Screen
Baltimore, Maryland

Cathy Segelke
Merino, Colorado

Lila and Fred Shrader
Crescent City, California

Brenda and Jerry Siegel
St. Louis, Missouri

Karen Silvermintz
Dallas, Texas

David Smies
Manhattan, Kansas

Allan Smith
Sherman, Texas

Pat Smith
Independence, Missouri

Carole and Richard Smyth
Huntington, New York

Charlie and Rose Snyder
Independence, Kansas

Dick Spencer
O'Fallon, Illinois

Rick Spencer
Salt Lake City, Utah

Greg Spiess
Joliet, Illinois

Bob Stein
International Society of Antique
Scale Collectors
Chicago, Illinois

Nancy Steinbock
Albany, New York

Stella's Collectibles
Torrance, California

Ron Stewart
Combs, Kentucky

Donna and Craig Stifter
Naperville, Illinois

Dick Strickfaden
Pekin, Illinois

Pamela and Joseph Tanner
Spokane, Washington

Jenny Tarrant
St. Peters, Missouri

Terry Taylor
East Bend, North Carolina

Bruce Thalberg
Weston, Connecticut

Sharon Thoerner
Bellflower, California

Chuck Thompson
Houston, Texas

Don Thornton
Sunnyvale, California

Phil and Nyla Thurston
Cortland, New York

Rosella Tinsley
Osawatomie, Kansas

Marlena Toohey
Longmont, Colorado

Veronica Trainer
Cleveland, Ohio

Leon Travis
Sterling, Virginia

Dan Tucker
Toledo, Ohio

Valerie and Richard Tucker
Argyle, Texas

Robert Tuggle
New York, New York

John Tutton
Front Royal, Virginia

Hobart D. Van Deusen
Watertown, Connecticut

Barry L. Van Hook
Chase Collectors Society
Mesa, Arizona

Jean and Dale Van Kuren
Clarence, New York

Joan F. Van Patten
Rexford, New York

Janice and Duane Vanderbilt
Indianapolis, Indiana

Norm Vigue
Stoughton, Massachusetts

Linda L. Vines
Upper Montclair, New Jersey

Stephen Visakay
West Caldwell, New Jersey

Mark Vuono
Stamford, Connecticut

John W. Waddell
Mineral Wells, Texas

Jim Waite
Farmer City, Illinois

John Walter
Marietta, Ohio

Judith and Robert Walthall
Huntsville, Alabama

Ian Warner
Brampton, Ontario, Canada

Cara Washburn
Willard, Wisconsin

Kitty Watson
Guthrie, Oklahoma

Maret Webb
Phoenix, Arizona

Marty Webster
Ann Arbor, Michigan

David Weddington
Murfreesboro, Tennessee

Pastor Frederick S. Weiser
New Oxford, Pennsylvania

BA Wellman
Westminster, Massachusetts

Rosalie Wells
Canton, Illinois

Kaye and Jim Whitaker
Lynnwood, Washington

John 'Grandpa' White
Denver, Colorado

Douglass White
Orlando, Florida

Margaret and Kenn Whitmyer
Gahanna, Ohio

Steven Whysel
Bella Vista, Arkansas

Doug Wiesehan
St. Charles, Missouri

James R. Wilkins
Duncanville, Texas

Don Williams
Kirksville, Missouri

Ron L. Willis
Moore, Oklahoma

Roy M. Willis
Lebanon Junction, Kentucky

Jack D. Wilson
Chicago, Illinois

Grant S. Windsor
Richmond, Virginia

Ralph Winslow
Overland Park, Kansas

Nancy Winston
Northwood, New Hampshire

Jo Ellen Winther
Arvada, Colorado

Raphael C. Wise
West Palm Beach, Florida

Wendy L. Woodworth
Ann Arbor, Michigan

D.D. Woollard, Jr.
Bridgeton, Missouri

Bill Wright
New Albany, Indiana

Libby Yalom
Adelphi, Maryland

Darlene Yohe
Stuttgart, Arkansas

Mary Young
Dayton, Ohio

Catherine Yronwode
Forestville, California

Charles S. Zayic
Ellsworth, Maine

Audrey Zeder
Long Beach, California

Auction Houses

We wish to thank the following auction houses whose catalogs have been used as sources for pricing information. Many have granted us permission to reproduce their photographs as well.

A-1 Auction Service
P.O. Box 540672, Orlando, FL 32804;
407-839-0004. Specializing in American antique sales

Absolute Auction & Realty,
Inc./Pleasant Valley Auction Hall
Robert Doyle
P.O. Box 658, 348 Main St., Beacon,
NY 12524. Antique and estate auctions the 4th Saturday of every month at their Beacon gallery, twice a month at Pleasant Valley Auction Hall; Free calendar of auctions

Alex G. Malloy, Inc.
P.O. Box 38, South Salem, NY 10590;
203-438-0396. Specializing in ancient and medieval coins, antiquities, numismatic literature; 4 mail bid auctions per year

America West Archives
Anderson, Warren
P.O. Box 100, Cedar City, UT 84721;
801-586-9497. Publishes 26-page illustrated catalog 6 times a year that includes auction section of scarce and historical early western documents, letters, autographs, stock certificates, and other important ephemera, Subscription: $15 per year

Andre Ammelounx
The Stein Company
P.O. Box 136, Palatine, IL 60078; 708-991-5927 or (Fax) 708-991-5947. Specializing in steins, catalogs available

Anthony J. Nard & Co.
US Rt. 220, Milan, PA 18831; 717-888-9404 or (Fax) 717-888-7723

Arman Absentee Auctions
16 Sixth St., Stamford, CT 06905;
203-928-5838. Specializing in American glass, Historical Staffordshire, English soft paste, paperweights

The Arts & Crafts Emporium
434 N. La Brea Ave.
Los Angeles, CA 90036; 213-935-3777

Aston Americana Auctions
2825 Country Club Rd., Endwell, NY 13760-3349; Phone or Fax 607-785-6598. Specializing in and appraisers of Americana, folk art, other primitives, furniture, fine glassware and china

Bill Bertoia Auctions
2413 Madison Ave., Vineland, NJ 08360; 609-692-4092 or Fax 609-692-8697. Specializing in toys, dolls, advertising, and related items

Bider's
241 S. Union St., Lawrence, MA 01843; 508-688-4347 or 508-683-3944. Antiques appraised, purchased, and sold on consignment

Brian Riba Auctions Inc.
P.O. Box 53, Main St., S. Glastonbury, CT 06073; 203-633-3076

Butterfield & Butterfield
220 San Bruno Ave., San Francisco, CA 91043; 415-861-7500 or (Fax) 415-861-8951.
Also located at: 7601 Sunset Blvd., Los Angeles, CA 90046; 213-850-7500 or (Fax) 213-850-5843. Fine Art Auctioneers and Appraisers since 1865

Cerebro
P.O. Box 327, E. Prospect, 17317-0327; 717-252-2400 or 800-69-LABEL. Specializing in antique advertising labels, especially cigar box labels, cigar bands, food labels, firecracker labels; Holds semiannual auction on tobacco ephemera; Consignments accepted

Charles E. Kirtley
P.O. Box 2273, Elizabeth City, NC 27096; 919-335-1262. Specializing in World's Fair, Civil War, political, advertising and other American collectibles

Cincinnati Art Gallery
635 Main St., Cincinnati, OH 45202; 513-381-2128. Specializing in American art pottery, American and European fine paintings, watercolors

Col. Doug Allard
P.O. Box 460, St. Ignatius, MT 59865-0460; 406-745-2951 or (Fax) 406-745-2961

Collector's Auction Services
326 Seneca St., Oil City, PA 16301; 814-677-6070. Specializing in advertising, oil and gas, toys, rare museum and investment-quality antiques

Collector's Sales & Service
P.O. Box 4037
Middletown, RI 02842; 401-849-5012 or (Fax) 401-846-6156

Country Girls Estate & Appraisal Service
Diane Patalano
P.O. Box 144,
Saddle River, NJ 07458

David Rago
Auction hall: 333 N. Main, Lambertville, NJ 08530; 609-397-7330
Gallery: 17 S. Main St., Lambertville, NJ 08530. Specializing in American art pottery and Arts & Crafts

Dunbar's Gallery
Leila and Howard Dunbar
76 Haven St., Milford, MA 01757;
508-634-8697 or (Fax) 508-634-8698

Dunning's
755 Church Road
Elgin, IL 60123; 708-741-3483 or 312-664-8400

Dynamite Auctions
Franklin Antique Mall & Auction Gallery
1280 Franklin Ave., Franklin, PA 16323; 814-432-8577 or 814-786-9211

Du Mouchelles
409 Jefferson Ave.,
Detroit, MI 48226

Early American Numismatics
Dana Linett, President
P.O. Box 2442, La Jolla, CA 92038.

Early Auction Co.
123 Main St., Milford, OH 45150

Freeman Fine Arts
1808 Chestnut St. Philadelphia, PA 19103; 215-563-9275 or (Fax) 215-563-8236

Garth's Auctions Inc.
2690 Stratford Rd., Box 369, Delaware, OH 43015; 614-362-4771

Glass-Works Auctions
James Hagenbuch
102 Jefferson, East Greenville, PA 18041; 215-679-5849. America's leading auction company in early American bottles and glass

Hake's Americana & Collectibles
Specializing in character and personality collectibles along with all artifacts of popular culture for over 20 years. To receive a catalog for their next 3,000-item mail/phone bid auction, send $5 to Hake's Americana, P.O. Box 1444M, York, PA 17405

Hanna-Whysel Auctioneers & Appraisers
Steven Whysel
3403 Bella Vista Way, Bella Vista, AR, 72714; 501-855-9600. Antiques and art auctions

Harmer Rooke Galleries
32 E. 57th St, 11th Floor New York, NY 10022; 212-751-1900 or (Fax) 212-758-1713

Henry/Pierce Auctioneers
1456 Carson Court, Homewood, IL 60430; 708-798-7508. Specializing in bank auctions

Horst Auctioneers
Horst Auction Center
50 Durlach Rd. (corner of Rt. 322 & Durlach Rd., West of Ephrata), Ephrata, Lancaster County, PA 17522; 717-859-1331 or 717-738-3080. Voices of Experience

Jack Sellner
Sellner Marketing of California
P.O. Box 308, Fremont, CA 94536;
415-745-9463

Jackson's, Auctioneers & Appraisers of Fine Art
2229 Lincoln St.
Cedar Falls, IA 50613; 319-277-2256 or (Fax) 319-277-1252. Specializing also in art pottery, jewelry, and decorative arts

James D. Julia
P.O. Box 210, Showhegan Rd., Fairfield, ME 04937

James R. Bakker Antiques, Inc.
James R. Bakker
370 Broadway, Cambridge, MA 02139; 617-864-7067. Specializing in American paintings, prints and decorative arts

John Toomey Gallery
818 North Blvd., Oak Park, IL 60301; 708-383-5234 or (Fax) 708-383-4828. Specializing in furniture and decorative arts of the Arts & Crafts, Art Deco and Modern Design movements; Modern Design Expert: Richard Wright

Joy Luke Fine Arts Brokers and Auctioneers
The Gallery
300 East Grove St., Bloomington, IL 61701; 309-828-5533

Ken Farmer Realty & Auction Company
1122 Norwood St., Radford, VA 24141; 703-639-0939 or (Fax) 703-639-1759

Kerry & Judy's Toys
7370 Eggleston Rd., Memphis, TN 38125-2112; 901-757-1722. Specializing in toys, 1900-1960s; Consignments always welcome

Kit Barry Ephemera Auctions
68 High St., Brattleboro, VT 05301;
802-254-3634. Tradecard and ephemera auctions, fully-illustrated catalogs with prices realized; Consignment inquiries welcome

Kurt R. Krueger
160 N. Washington St., P.O. Box 275, Iola, WI 54945-0275

L.R. 'Les' Docks
Box 691035, San Antonio, TX 78269-1035. Providing occasional mail-order record auctions, rarely consigned; The only consignments considered are exceptionally scarce and unusual records

Litchfield, Auction Gallery
425 Bantam Rd., P.O. Box 1337, Litchfield, CT 06759; 203-567-3126 or (Fax) 203-567-3266

Lloyd Ralston Toys
447 Stratford Rd., Fairfield, CT 06432

Manion's International Auction House, Inc.
P.O. Box 12214, Kansas City, KS 66112; 913-299-6692 or (Fax) 913-299-6792; E-mail: manions@qnicom URL: www.manions.com

Maritime Auctions
R.R. 2, Box 45A, York, ME 03909; 207-363-4247

Michael John Verlangieri
20th Century Arts & Design
P.O. Box 844
Cambria, CA 93428; 805-927-4428. Specializing in fine mid-century California pottery; holds cataloged auctions (video tapes available); E-mail: INTERNET:71332.3017@compuserve.com

McMasters Doll Auctions
P.O. Box 1755, 5855 Glenn Highway Rd., Cambridge, OH 43725; 614-432-4320 or (Fax) 614-432-3191

Mid-Hudson Auction Galleries
One Idlewild Ave., Cornwall-on-Hudson, NY 12520; 914-534-7828 or (Fax) 914-534-4802

Monsen & Baer, Annual Perfume Bottle Auction
Monsen, Randall; and Baer, Rod
Box 529, Vienna, VA 22183; 703-938-2129 or (Fax) 703-242-1357. Cataloged auctions of perfume bottles; Will purchase, sell, and accept consignments; Specializing in commercial, Czechoslovakian, Lalique, Baccarat, Victorian, crown top, factices, miniatures

Neal Auction Company
4038 Magazine St.; New Orleans, LA 70115; 504-899-5329 or 1-800-467-5329 or 504-897-3803

Noel Barrett Antiques & Auctions
P.O. Box 1001, Carversville, PA 18913; 215-297-5109 or (Fax) 215-297-0457

New England Absentee Auctions
16 6th St., Stamford, CT 06905; 203-975-9055. Specializing in Quimper pottery

Nostalgia Co.
21 S. Lake Dr., Hackensack, NJ 07601; 201-488-4536

Phillips
406 E. 79th St., New York, NY 10021

Postcards International
P.O. Box 2930, New Haven, CT 06515-0030; 203-865-0814 or (Fax) 203-495-8005

Rafael Osona, Auctioneer & Appraiser
P.O. Box 2607, Nantucket, MA 02584; 508-228-3942. Specializing in Americana, Fine Arts, Continental & Marine Antiques

Refinders
737 Barberry Rd., Highland Park, IL 60035; 708-831-1102 or 708-831-1160. Refinders will find your wants from 1860-1960

Rex Stark Auctions
49 Wethersfield Rd., Bellingham, MA 02019

Richard A. Bourne Co. Inc.
Estate Auctioneers & Appraisers
Box 141, Hyannis Port, MA 02647; 617-775-0797

Richard Opfer Auctioneering, Inc.
1919 Greenspring Dr., Timonium, MD 21093; 301-252-5035

Roan, Inc.
Box 118, R.D. 3, Cogan Station, PA 17728

Ron Fox Auctions
Ron Fox
P.O. Box 4025, Farmingdale, NY 11735; 516-420-9214 or (Fax) 516-243-0412. Specializing in steins; Auctions with illustrated catalogs and video tapes

Shot Glass Exchange
P.O. Box 219, Western Springs, IL, 60558; 706-246-1559. Publishes mail-auction catalog twice yearly

Skinner, Inc.
Auctioneers & Appraisers of Antiques and Fine Arts
The Heritage on the Garden, 63 Park Plaza, Boston, MA 02116; 617-350-5400 or (Fax) 617-350-5429. Second address: 357 Main Street, Boston, MA 01740; 508-779-6241 or (Fax) 508-779-5144

Smith & Jones, Inc.
12 Clark Lane; Sudbury, MA 01776; 508-443-5517 or (Fax) 508-443-8045. Specializing in Dedham dinnerware, Buffalo china and important American art pottery; Full-color catalogs available

Soldiers Trunk
60 Craigs Rd., Windsor, CT 06095; 203-688-0580. Specializing in American and foreign military items; 4 catalog issues for $20

Sotheby Parke Bernet, Inc.
980 Madison Ave., New York, NY 10021

Steffen Historical Militaria
Roger S. Steffen
14 Murnan Rd., Cold Springs, KY 41076; 606-431-4499. Specializing in quality militaria, military art, rare books, antique firearms

Three Rivers Collectibles
Wendy and Leo Frese
P.O. Box 551542, Dallas, TX 75355; 214-341-5165. Annual Red Wing and RumRill pottery and stoneware auctions

Tradewinds Auctions
Henry and Nancy Taron
24 Magnolia, Ave., Manchester-By-The-Sea, MA 01944

Treadway Gallery, Inc.
2029 Madison Rd., Cincinnati, OH 45208; 513-321-6742 or (Fax) 513-871-7722. Specializing in American Art Pottery; American and European art glass; European ceramics; Italian glass; fine American and European paintings and graphics; and furniture and decorative arts of the Arts & Crafts, Art Nouveau, Art Deco and Modern Design Movements. Modern Design expert: Thierry Lorthioir. Members: National Antique Dealers Association, American Art Pottery Association, International Society of Appraisers, American Ceramic Arts Society, Ohio Decorative Arts Society, Art Gallery Association of Cincinnati

Vicki and Buce Waasdorp
P.O. Box 434; 10931 Main St.; Clarence, NY 14031; 716-759-2361. Specializing in decorated stoneware

Weschler's
Adam A. Weschler & Son
905 E. St. N.W., Washington, DC 20004

Willis Henry Auctions
22 Main St., Marshfield, MA

Directory of Contributors

When contacting any of the buyers/sellers listed in this part of the Directory by mail, you must include a SASE (stamped, self-addressed envelope) if you expect a reply. As hectic as our lifestyles are, the time it saves them is probably worth more to them than the price of a stamp. Not only that, but trying to decipher someone's handwritten name and address can be very frustrating. Sometimes even zip codes are unreadable, and even more time is required to double check zip code numbers. And in the end, if 'Rosen' becomes 'River' and 'Ave. 5' becomes 'Ave. S,' even if the person you contacted was gracious enough to answer you, you probably won't ever know he did. Many of these people are professional appraisers and there will be a fee for their time and service. Find out up front. Include a clear photo if you want an item identified. Most items cannot be described clearly enough to make an identification without a photo.

If you call and get their answering machine, when you leave your number so that they can return your call, tell them to call back collect. And please take the differences in time zones into consideration. 7:00 a.m. in the Midwest is only 4:00 a.m. in California! And if you're in California, remember that even 7:00 p.m. is too late to call the East Coast. Most people work and are gone during the daytime. Even some of our antique dealers say they prefer after-work phone calls. Don't assume that a person who deals in a particular field will be able to help you with related items. They may seem related to you when they are not.

Please, we need your help. This book sells in such great numbers that allowing their names to be published can create a potential nightmare for each advisor and contributor. Please do your part to help us minimize this, so that we can retain them on our board and in turn pass their experience and knowledge on to you through our book. Their only obligation is to advise us, not to evaluate your holdings. Many of our people tell us that even with the occasional problem, they feel that the good outweighs the bad and makes all their hard work worthwhile.

Alabama

Dole, Pat
9825 Red Mill Rd.
Birmingham, 35215; 205-833-9853.
Specializing in Purinton pottery

Donnelly, Ron
Saturday Heroes
6302 Championship Dr., Tuscaloosa, 35405. Specializing in Big Little Books, movie posters, premiums, western heroes, Gone With the Wind, character collectibles, early Disney; Inquiries require SASE; No free appraisals

Lippa, Matt; and Schaaf, Elizabeth
Artisans
P.O. Box 256, Mentone, 35984; 205-634-4037. Specializing in folk art, quilts, painted and folky furniture, tramp art, whirligigs, windmill weights; Further contacts: artisans@vistech.net or http://www.vistech.net/users/artisans

Luckey, Carl
Carl F. Luckey Communications
R.R. 4, Box 301, Lingerlost Trail, Killen, 35645. Freelance writer specializing in art, antiques, and collectibles. No telephone calls will be accepted; SASE required for correspondence

Walthall, Judith and Robert
P.O. Box 4465, Huntsville, 35815; 205-881-9198. Judith founded Peanut Pals in 1978. Robert is serving second term as President of Peanut Pals. Specializing in Planters Peanuts memorabilia; also Old Crow collectibles

Arizona

Chase Collectors Society
Van Hook, Barry L.
2149 Jibsail Loop, Mesa, 85202-5524; 602-838-6971. Publishes (6 issues per year) newsletter, *Art Deco Reflections* (sample copy: $1); Membership: $5

Ellwood, J.M.
7077 E. Main #4, Scottsdale, 85251; 602-947-9679. Specializing in cast-iron banks, toys, irons, trivets, doorstops, and miscellaneous cast iron

Nelson, Maxine
7657 E. Hazelwood St., Scottsdale, 85251. Specializing in Vernon Kilns; Author of *Collectible Vernon Kilns*; Autographed copies available from the author for $24.95+$2.50 postage & handling (CA sale tax: $1.93); SASE appreciated for inquiries

Schaut, Jim and Nancy
Aquarius Antiques
P.O. Box 10781, Glendale, 85318; 602-878-4293. Specializing in Automobilia, racing memorabilia, auto toys; Authors of *American Automobilia*, 1994

Webb, Maret
Swan Seekers Network
4118 E. Vernon Ave., Phoenix, 85008-2333; 602-957-6294 or (Fax) 602-957-1631. Business hours: 9:00 a.m. - 5:00 p.m., M.S.T., Mon. — Fri.; Publishes *Swan Seekers News* and *Swan Seekers Marketplace* periodicals ($28 in US per year, $38 foreign); Specializing in Swarovski crystal

Arkansas

Dryden, James
Dryden Pottery
P.O. Box 603, Hot Springs National Park, 71902; 501-627-4201. Specializing in hand-thrown artware vases, mugs, ovenware, etc.

Gifford, David Edwin
P.O. Box 7617, Little Rock, 72217; 501-664-0902. Author of *Collector's Encyclopedia of Niloak Pottery* (out of print) and *The Collector's Encyclopedia of Camark Pottery, Volume 1* (early art pottery production); Autographed copies of Camark book available from author for $25 (includes shipping, handling, and tax)

Musgrave, Marge
Look Nook Antiques
10757 Hwy. 5-S, Salesville, 72653-9698; 501-499-5283. Specializing in colored Victorian glass

Whysel, Steven
Steven Whysel, L.L.C.
3403 Bella Vista Way, Bella Vista, 72714; 501-855-9600. Specializing in Art Nouveau, 19th- and 20th-century art, and Judaica

Yohe, Darlene
Timberview Antiques
P.O. Box 343, Stuttgart, 72160; 501-673-3437. Specializing in American pattern glass, historical glass, Victorian pattern glass, carnival glass, and custard glass

California

Aldrich, Jon Wm.
Jon Aldrich Antique Aero
P.O. Box 706, Groveland, 95321; 209-962-6121. Specializing in vintage aviation

Baker, Roger
Baker's Lady Luck Emporium
Box 620417, Woodside, 94062. Specializing in Saloon Americana — advertising, gambling, bar bottles, cigar lighters, match safes, bowie knives (1830-1900), dirks, daggers, cowboy hats, spurs, chaps, saddles, barber items: bottles, shaving mugs, razors

Berg, Paul
P.O. Box 8895, Newport Beach, 92620; Author of *Nineteenth Century Photographica Cases and Wall Frames*

Brooks, Mike
7335 Skyline, Oakland, 94611; 510-339-1751 (evenings). Specializing in typewriters, transistor radios, early televisions, Statue of Liberty

Bueschel, Richard M.
414 N. Prospect Manor Ave., Mt. Prospect, 60056-2046; 847-253-0791. Specializing in saloon, coin-operated machines, trade catalogs

Butz, Robert C.
Collector's Wedgwood
P.O. Box 462, Newbury Park, 91319. Specializing in Wedgwood; SASE required for reply

Carter, Tina M.
882 S. Mollison, El Cajon, 92020; 619-440-5043. Specializing in teapots, tea-related items, tea tins, children's and toy tea sets, plastic cookie cutters, etc.; Book on teapots available. Send $16 (includes postage) or $17 for CA residents, Canada: add $5, to above address

Chipman, Jack
California Spectrum
P.O. Box 1079, Venice, 90294-1079. Specializing in California ceramics; author of *Collector's Encyclopedia of California Pottery*, autographed copies available from author for $24.95+$3.50 postage and handling+(CA) tax of $2.35; Also look for *Collector's Guide to Bauer Pottery: Identification & Values* (due fall of 1997)

Christensen, Pat and Chris
1067 Salvador St., Costa Mesa, 92626. Specializing in open salts

Cohen, Wilfred and Dolli
Antiques & Art Glass
P.O. Box 27151, Santa Ana, 92799; 714-545-5673 (best to phone after 6:00 p.m. Pacific time). Specializing in Wave Crest (C.F. Monroe), Victorian Era art and pattern glass (salt shakers, toothpick holders, syrups, cruets, sugar shakers, tumblers, biscuit jars, table and pitcher sets), art and cameo glass open salts, ruby-stained, burmese, peachblow and amberina, pottery by Moorcroft (pre-1935 only), Buffalo (Deldare and Emerald ware), and Polia Pillin; Please include SASE for reply

Cox, Susan N.
237 E. Main St., El Cajon, 92020; 619-447-0800. Specializing in California pottery and Frankoma

Dolan, Maryanne
138 Belle Ave., Pleasant Hill, CA 94523. Specializing in and author of several informative books on vintage clothing; E-mail: 72144,1353@compuserve.com

Ehrhard, J. David
Psycho-Ceramic Restorations
7212 Valmont St., Tujunga, 91042. Specializing in restoration of ceramics, collects Susie Cooper and British pottery, Mabel Lucie Attwell, 'Old Bill' china by Grimades, etc., Artist: Bruce Bairsfather

Enge, Delleen
Franciscan Dinnerware Matching Service
323 E. Matilija, Ste. 112, Ojai 93023

Escoe, Adrienne S., Member
Glass Knife Collectors Club
4448 Ironwood Ave., Seal Beach, 90740-2926; 562-598-1585; Specializing in glass knives; E-mail: escoebliss@earthlink.net

Fogleman, Marv
Marv's Memories
1814 W. Carriage Dr., Santa Ana, 92704. Specializing in Western Dinnerware, Metlox, Mikasa, and Franciscan

George, Tony
22431-B160 Antonio Pkwy., #252, Rancho Santa Margarita, 92688; 714-589-6075. Specializing in watch fobs

Giacomini, Mary Jane
P.O. Box 404, Ferndale, CA 95536-0404; 707-786-9464. Author of *American Bisque, A Collector's Guide With Prices*; Specializing in American Bisque Pottery, cookie jars

Gibson, Pat
38280 Guava Dr., Newark, 94560; 510-792-0586. Specializing in R.A. Fox

Harrison, Gwynne
P.O. Box 1, Mira Loma, 91752-0001; 909-685-5434. Specializing in Autumn Leaf (Jewel Tea)

Hibbard, Suzi
WanderWares
2570 Walnut Blvd. #20, Walnut Creek, 94596. Specializing in Dragonware, 1000 Faces china, other Orientalia. Inquiries should be accompanied by SASE; E-mail: HMBK24A@Prodigy.com

Howard, Steve
101 1st St., Suite 404, Los Altos, 94022; 510-484-4488. Specializing in antique American firearms, bowie knives, Western Americana, old advertising, and vintage gambling items

Inouye, Roger
2622 Valewood Ave, Carlsbad, 92008-7925. Specializing in Trolls

Main Street Antique Mall
237 E Main Street
El Cajon, 92020; 619-447-0800

Maurer, Oveda L.
Oveda Maurer Antiques
34 Greenfield Ave., San Anselmo, 94960; 415-454-6439. Specializing in 18th-century and early 19th-century American furniture, lighting, pewter, hearthware, glass, folk art, and paintings

Pardini, Dick
3107 N. El Dorado St., Dept. SAPG, Stockton, 95204-3412; 209-466-5550 (recorder may answer). Specializing in California Perfume Company items dating from 1886 to 1928 and 'go-with' related companies: buyer and information center. Not interested in items that have Avon, Perfection, or Anniversary Keepsake markings. California Perfume Company offerings must be accompanied by a photo, Xerox copy, or sketching along with a condition report and, most important, price wanted. Inquiries require large SASE; not necessary if offering items for sale

Roller, Gayle
P.O. Box 222, San Marcos, 92079-0222. Specializing in Hagen-Renaker

Sanford, Steve and Martha
230 Harrison Ave., Campbell, 95008; 408-978-8408. Specializing in Brush McCoy

Shrader, Fred and Lila
Shrader Antiques
2025 Hwy. 199, Crescent City, 95531; 707-458-3525. Specializing in railroad, steamship and other transportation memorabilia; Shelley china (and its predecessor, Foley China); Buffalo china and Buffaly Pottery including Deldare; Niloak; and Zell (and Haag)

Stella's Collectibles
Pieces of the Past
19032 S. Vermont Ave., Torrance (Space 11), 90503; 310-316-7198; Julie's Antiques, Long Beach (Space 24); Santa Monica Antique Market (Space 113); Westchester Faire Mall (Space 320); Enchanted Treasures, Lake Elsinore (Space 25). Specializing in quality glass, china, and figurines

Thoerner, Sharon
15549 Ryon Ave., Bellflower, 90706; 562-866-1555. Specializing in covered animal dishes, powder jars with animal and human figures, slag glass

Thornton, Don
1345 Poplar Ave., Sunnyvale, 94087. Specializing in egg beaters; author of *Beat This: The Eggbeater Chronicles* ($28.95 including postage and handling)

Webb, Frances Finch
1589 Gretel Lane, Mountain View, 94040. Specializing in Kay Finch ceramics

Yronwode, Catherine
6632 Covey Rd., Forestville, 95436; 707-887-2424. Specializing in pre-1950 collectible plastic

Zeder, Audrey
6755 Coralite St. S., Long Beach, 90808 (appointment only). Specializing in British Royal Commemorative Souvenirs (mail-order catalog available); Author (Wallace-Homestead) of *British Royal Commemoratives*

Canada

Brown, David L.
Stevengraph Collectors Assn.
2103-2829 Arbutus Rd., Victoria, British Columbia, V8N 5X5; 250-477-9896. Specializing in Stevengraphs

Melis, Mirko
Marcelle Antiques
P.O. Box 53039, 5100 Erin Mills Pkwy., Mississauga, Ontario, L5M 4Z5; 905-689-1648. Specializing in American and European art glass, Russian works of art (enamels, porcelains, silver, etc.), English and Continental glass and china, member of Antique Appraisal Association of America, Inc., and AADA (Associated Antique Dealers of America, Inc.)

Warner, Ian
P.O. Box 93022, 499 Main St. S., Brampton, Ontario, L6Y 4V8; 905-453-9074 or (Fax) 905-453-2931. Specializing in Wade porcelain and Swankyswigs, author of *The World of Wade*, *The World of Wade Book 2*, *Wade Price Trends*, and *The World of Head Vase Planters*, Co-author: Mike Posgay

Colorado

Carlton, Carol and Jim
8115 S. Syracuse St., Englewood, 80112; 303-773-8616. Specializing in Broadmoor, Coors and other Colorado pottery

Heck, Carl
Carl Heck Decorative Arts
Box 8416, Aspen, 81612; Phone/Fax: 970-925-8011. Specializing in original Tiffany lamps, art glass, windows and chandeliers; Also reverse-painted and leaded-glass table lamps, stained and beveled glass windows, bronzes, paintings, etc.; Buy and sell; Fee for written appraisals. Please include SASE for reply

Mackin, Bill
Author of *Cowboy and Gunfighter Collectibles*; available from author: 1137 Washington St., Craig, 81625; 970-824-6717, Paperback: $25; Other titles available; Specializing in old and fine spurs, guns, gun leather, cowboy gear, Western Americana (Collection in the Museum of Northwest Colorado, Craig)

Over, Naomi L.
8909 Sharon Lane, Arvada, 80002; 303-424-5922. Specializing in ruby glassware, author of *Ruby Glass of the 20th Century*, available from author for $24.50 soft bound or $32.50 hard bound (includes shipping and handling); Naomi will attempt to make photo identifications for all who include a SASE with correspondence

Segelke, Cathy; and James, Pat
970-847-3759 (Pat). Specializing in crocks, Western Pottery Mfg. Co. (Denver, CO)

Toohey, Marlena
703 S. Pratt Pky., Longmont, 80501; 303-678-9726. Specializing in black glass; Book available from author for $20 (includes shipping and handling)

White, John 'Grandpa'
Grandpa's Depot
1616 17th St., Suite 267, Denver, 80202; 303-628-5590 or (Fax) 303-628-5547. Specializing in railroad-related items; Catalogs available

Winther, Jo Ellen
8449 W. 75th Way, Arvada, 80005; 800-872-2345 or 303-421-2371. Specializing in Coors

Connecticut

Alves, Margaret
84 Oak Ave., Shelton, 06484; 203-924-4768. Specializing in spoons: plated, sterling, silver, pre-1920s

Bondhus, Sandra V.
Box 100, Unionville, 06085; 860-678-1808. Author of *Quimper Pottery: A French Folk Art Faience*; Specializing in Quimper pottery

FDS Antiques, Inc.
62 Blue Ridge Dr., Stamford, 06903-4923. Publishes *The 'No Nonsense' Antique Mall Directory*, a directory of antique malls, centers, and multi-dealer co-ops; Over 4,700 listings listed according to state

Kilbride, Mrs. Richard J.
81 Willard Terrace, Stamford, 06903; 203-322-0568. Has available for sale: *Art Deco Chrome, The Chase Era*, and *Art Deco Chrome, Book 2, A Collector's Guide, Industrial Design in the Chase Era*

MacSorley, Earl
823 Indian Hill Rd., Orange, 06477; 203-387-1793 (after 7:00 p.m.). Specializing in nutcrackers, Bessie Pease Gutmann prints, figural lift-top spittoons

Postcards International
Shapiro, Marty
P.O. Box 2930, New Haven, 06515-0030; 203-865-0814 or (Fax) 203-495-8005. Specializing in vintage picture postcards

Roenigk, Martin
Mechantiques
26 Barton Hill, E. Hampton, 06424;
800-671-6333. Specializing in
mechanical musical instruments,
music boxes, band organs, musical
clocks and watches, coin pianos,
orchestrions, monkey organs, automata, mechanical birds and dolls, etc.

Thalberg, Bruce
Mountain View Dr., Weston, 06883;
203-227-8175. Specializing in canes
and walking sticks: novelty, carved,
and Black

Van Deusen, Hobart D.
28 The Green, Watertown, 06795;
203-945-3456. Specializing in Canton, SASE required when requesting information

Vuono, Mark
306 Mill Rd., Stamford, 06903; 203-357-0892 (10 a.m. to 5:30 p.m. E.S.T.).
Specializing in historical flasks, blown
3-mold glass, blown American glass

District of Columbia

Durham, Ken and Jackie (By appointment)
909 26 St. N.W., Suite 502, Washington, D.C. 20037. Specializing in
counter-top arcade machines, trade
stimulators, and vending machines;
16-page illustrated list: $2; Send
SASE for free list of books on coin-operated machines; E-mail:
http://www.GameRoomAntiques.com

Florida

Archer, Dick and Ellie
Artiques
5676 Pipers Waite, Sarasota, 34235-0923; 941-378-9116. Specializing in
Victorian silverplate: figurals, fancy
hollow ware, and collectibles

Bettinger, Robert
P.O. Box 333, Mt. Dora, 32757; 352-735-3575. Specializing in American
art pottery

Cohen, Joel
Cohen Books & Collectibles
P.O. Box 810310, Boca Raton, 33481;
407-487-7888. Specializing in Disneyana

deCourtivron, Gael
Cocaholics
4811 Remington Dr., Sarasota, 34234;
941-355-2652 or 813-359-2652. Specializing in Coca-Cola memorabilia

Dodds, Rebecca
Silver Flute
Box 39644, Ft. Lauderdale, 33339.
Specializing in jewelry

Elsner, Dr. Robert
29 Clubhouse Lane, Boynton Beach,
33436; 561-736-1362. Specializing in
antique barometers and nautical
instruments

France, Madeleine
P.O. Box 15555, Ft. Lauderdale,
33318; 305-584-0009. Specializing in
top-quality perfume bottles: Rene
Lalique, Steuben, Czechoslovakian,
DeVilbiss, Baccarat, Commercials;
French dore bronze and decorative arts

Hudson, Hardy
Our Antiques Market
5453 Lake Howell Rd., Winter Park,
32792; 407-657-2100 from 11:00 a.m.
to 6:00 p.m. Specializing in majolica,
American art pottery (buying one
piece or entire collections); Also buying Weller (garden ornaments, birds,
Mammy, Hudson, Sicard, Sabrinian,
or animal related), Roseville, Grueby,
Newcomb, Overbeck, Kay Finch,
Clewell, Tiffany, etc.

Kamm, Dorothy
P.O. Box 7460, Port St Lucie, 34985-4760. Author of American Painted
Porcelain: Identification and Value
Guide (Collector Books)

Lawrence, Judy and Cliff
1169 Overcash Dr., Dunedin, 34698.
Specializing in fountain pens and
mechanical pencils

Linscott, Jacqueline C.
3557 Nicklaus Dr., Titusville, 32780.
Specializing in Blue Bell paper-weights; Author of 1992 Revised Edition, Blue Bell Paperweights, and 1995
Addendum, complete with history,
illustrations, and price guide; Available from author for $17 (includes
postage and handling)

Linscott, Len
Line Jewels
3557 Nicklaus Dr., Titusville, 32780.
Specializing in glass insulators and
other telephone items. Distributor of
the only known set of books dealing
specifically with insulators, North
American Glass Insulators (2 volumes),
and accompanying Price Guide; long
SASE required for information

McNerny, Kathryn
118 Creek Hollow Lane, Middleburg,
32068. Author (Collector Books) on blue
and white stoneware, primitives, tools

New World Maps, Inc.
Charles R. Neuschafer
1123 S. Broadway, Lantana, 33462-4522; 407-586-8723. Buys and sells
antique and collectible maps, specializing in 20th-century road maps;
Columnist for Paper Collectors Marketplace and member of International
Map Dealers Association

Posner, Judy
November-April: 4195 S. Tamiami
Trail, #183SC, Venice 34293; 941-497-7149. May-October: R.D. 1, Box
273SC, Effort, PA 18330; 717-629-6583. Specializing in figural pottery,
salt and peppers, Black memorabilia,
Disneyana, character and advertising
collectibles, cookie jars; Buy, Sell,
Collect; Appraisals: $25

Roush, Peggy E.
Peggy's Matching Service
P.O. Box 476, Ocala, 34478; 352-629-3954. Specializing in discontinued
Noritake patterns

Supnick, Mark
2771 Oakbrook Manor, Ft. Lauderdale, 33332. Author of Collecting
Hull Pottery's Little Red Riding Hood
($12.95 postage paid). Specializing in
American pottery

White, Douglass
Classic Interiors & Antiques
2042 N. Rio Grande Ave., Suite E,
Orlando, 32804; 407-839-0004. Specializing in Fulper, Arts & Crafts furniture (photos helpful)

Wise, Raphael C.
The Collector's Stop
12018 Suellen Circle, West Palm
Beach, 33414; 407-793-0986. Specializing in Wedgwood Jasper Ware,
Rosenthal, Moorcroft, Buffalo Deldare
and Emerald Ware, Heisey, contemporary paperweights, English porcelains

Georgia

Bailey, Wayne and Gale
P.O. Box 173, Dacula, 30211; 770-963-5736. Specializing in Goebels
(Friar Tuck)

Bird, Betty
Memory Land & Antiques, Etc.
107 Ida St, Mt. Shasta, 96067; 916-926-4331. Specializing in coin silver
and open salts

Glenn, Walter
Geode Ltd.
3393 Peachtree Rd., Atlanta, 30326;
404-261-9346. Specializing in Frankart

Hartley, Glenn, Sr.
Fire Mark Circle of the Americas
2859 Marlin Dr., Chamblee, 30341-5119; 404-451-2651. Specializing in
fire marks, Methodist, Masonic, Foremost Dairies, Goodyear

Joiner, John R.
Aviation Collectors
173 Green Tree Dr., Newnan, 30265;
770-502-9565. Specializing in commercial aviation collectibles

Illinois

Ammelounx, Andre
The Stein Auction Company
P.O. Box 136, Palatine, 60078; 708-991-5927 or (Fax) 708-991-5947. Specializing in steins, catalogs available

The Barrel Antique Mall
5850 S St. Road, I-55 Exit 90, Springfield, 62707; 217-585-1438

Brinkley, Wm. J.
Brinkley Galleries
401 S. Washington Ave., McLeansboro, 62859. Specializing in Meissen,
Dresden, European porcelains, American porcelains (Cybis)

Broom, Jim
Box 65, Effingham, 62401. Specializing in opalescent pattern glassware

Bueschel, Richard M. (Dick)
414 N. Prospect Manor Ave., Mt.
Prospect, 60056-2046; 847-253-0791
or (Fax) 847-253-7919. Specializing
in coin machines, trade catalogs, pre-prohibition saloon, prohibition
speakeasy, screen doors, fretwork,
advertising folding chairs, food can
openers. Author of books relating to
coin-operated machines and saloon
collectibles (available from author)

Danis, John
11028 Raleigh Ct., Rockford, 61115;
815-877-6004 or (Fax) 815-877-6042.
Specializing in R. Lalique, Norse pottery; E-mail: danis6033@aol.com

Feldman, Arthur M.
Arthur M. Feldman Gallery
1815 St. Johns Ave., Highland Park,
60035; 847-432-8858 or (Fax) 847-266-1199. Specializing in Judaica, fine
art, and antiques

Frizzell, Doris
Doris' Dishes
5687 Oakdale Dr., Springfield, 62707;
217-529-3873. Specializing in Royal
Haeger, and Depression Glass; Co-author (Collector Books) of Royal
Haeger book

Garmon, Lee
1529 Whittier St., Springfield, 62704;
217-789-9574. Specializing in Royal
Haeger, Royal Hickman, glass animals; Co-author (Collector Books) of
Glass Animals and Figural Flower Frogs
of the Depression Era

Griffith, Woody
4132 N. Clarenden Ave., Chicago,
60613; 773-975-1957. Specializing in
DeVilbiss perfumes and perfume
lamps of the Deco period

Hall, Doris and Burdell
B&B Antiques
210 W. Sassafras Dr., Morton, 61550-
1245. Authors of *Morton's Potteries:
99 Years* (Vols. I and II); Specializing
in Morton pottery, American dinnerware, early American pattern glass,
historical items

Hastings, Mary Jane
310 West 1st South, Mt. Olive,
62069; Phone or Fax: 217-999-7519.
Specializing in Chintz dinnerware

Hilst, Randy
1221 Florence #4, Pekin, 61554; 309-
346-2710. Specializing in general line
including fishing and hunting collectibles

Hoffmann, Pat and Don, Sr.
1291 N. Elmwood Dr., Aurora,
60506; 630-859-3435. Authors of
Warwick, A to W, a supplement to
Why Not Warwick?; video regarding
Warwick decals currently available.
P.C.: http://www.skognet.com/nwar-
wick/ or E-mail: warwick@skognet.com

The Home Place Antiques
Durham, William; Galaway, William
615 S. State St., Belvidiere, 61008;
815-544-0577. Specializing in Tea
Leaf ironstone and white ironstone

Hooks, Dee
Dee's China Shop
P.O. Box 142, Lawrenceville, 62439-
0142; 618-943-2741. Specializing in
R.S. Prussia, Royal Bayreuth, Havi-
land, other fine china

Hopp, Dennis Carl
Midcentury
Chicago, 773-935-7872. Specializing
in 20th-century design, glass, pottery,
enamels, metal, art

Hurney, George and Mary
Glass Connection (Mail-order only)
312 Babcock Dr., Palatine, 50067;
847-359-3839. Specializing in Depression Glass and Paden City glass (not
advising on pottery)

The Illinois Antique Center
320 S.W. Commercial St.
Peoria, IL 61602

International Society of Antique
   Scale Collectors
Bob Stein, President
176 W. Adams, Suite 1706, Chicago,
60603; 312-263-7500. Publishes *Equilibrium* Magazine; President's newsletter; Annual membership directory;
Out-of-print catalogs; Annual convention

John Toomey Gallery
818 N. Blvd, Oak Park, 60301

Long, Dee
112 S. Center, Lacon, 61540. Specializing in reamers

Lubliner, Larry
Refinders mail/telephone auction
737 Barberry Rd., Highland Park, IL
60035; 708-831-1102 or 708-831-
1160. Refinders will find your wants
from 1860-1960

Martin, Jim
R.R. 1, 1091 215th Ave., Monmouth,
61462; 309-734-2703. Specializing in
Old Sleepy Eye, Monmouth pottery,
Western Stoneware

Meyer, Larry
4001 Elmwood, Stickney, 60402; 708-
749-1564. Specializing in fire
grenades and extinguishers

Miller, Larry; and Strickfaden, Dick
218 Devron Circle, E. Peoria, 61611-
1605. Specializing in German and
Czechoslovakian Erphila

Ochsner, Grace
Grace Ochsner Doll House
1636 E. County Rd. 2700, Niota,
62358; 217-755-4362. Specializing in
piano babies, bisque German dolls

Owen, Larry and Sally
Specializing in Morten Studio dogs, etc.

Pollack, Frank and Barbara (Appointment only)
1214 Green Bay Rd., Highland Park,
60035; 708-433-2213. Specializing in
American country antiques and art

Randy's Ol' Time Collectibles
Illinois Antique Center
308 S.W. Commercial, Peoria, 61602;
309-346-2710. Specializing in general
line, including hunting and fishing
collectibles

Rastello, Lisa
Milkweed Antiques
5N531 Ancient Oak Lane, St.
Charles, 60175; 708-377-4612. Specializing in Depression-Era collectibles

Rhoden, Joan and Charles
Memories/Rhoden's Antiques
605 N. Main, Georgetown, 61846;
217-662-8046. Specializing in
Heisey and other Elegant Glass-
ware, general line antiques. Co-
authors of *Those Wonderful
Yard-Long Prints and More*, and
*More Wonderful Yard-Long Prints,
Book II*, and *Yard-Long Prints, Book
III*, illustrated value guides

Rodrick, Tammy
1509 N. 300th St., Sumner, 62466.
Specializing in antiques and collectibles

Spencer, Dick
Glass and More (Shows only)
1203 N. Yale, O'Fallon, 62269; 618-
632-9067. Specializing in Cambridge,
Fenton, Fostoria, Heisey, etc.

Spiess, Greg
230 E. Washington, Joliet, 60433;
815-722-5639. Specializing in Odd
Fellows lodge items

Stifter, Donna and Craig
P.O. Box 6514, Naperville, 60540;
630-789-5780. Specializing in Coca-
Cola, Pepsi-Cola, Orange Crush, Dr.
Pepper, Hires, and other soda-pop
brand collectibles

Stretch Glass Society
Attention: Joanne Rodgers
P.O. Box 573, Hampshire, 60140.
Membership: $12 per year; quarterly
newsletter, annual convention

TV Guide Specialists
Box 20, Macomb 61455; 309-833-1809

Waite, Jim
112 N. Main St., Farmer City, 61842;
800-842-2593. Specializing in Sebastians

Wells, Rosalie J. 'Rosie'
22341 E. Wells Rd. S., Canton,
61520; 1-800-445-8745. Publishes *The
Ornament Collector,*™ *Precious Collectibles,*® and *Collectors' Bulletin*™.
Rosie also publishes the *Weekly Collectors' Gazette* and annual price
guides for Precious Moments® Collectibles, Hallmark Ornament Collectibles, Boyds Bears & Friends and
Cherished Teddies. Internet site:
http://www.RosieWells.com Rosie has
hosted eight International Conventions for Precious Moments Collectors
and hosts the semiannual Midwest
Collectibles Fest, held in Westmont,
IL, each March and October. For hot
tips and to record Voice Ads Rosie
offers a touch-tone 900 line (1-900-
740-7575) Call Rosie at 309-668-
2211 for information on limited
edition collectibles. E-mail:
Rosie@RosieWells.com

Wilson, Jack D.
P.O. Box 81974, Chicago, 60681-
0974; 773-282-9553. Specializing in
Phoenix and Consolidated glass; Buy-
ing Ruba Rombic; Author of *Phoenix
& Consolidated Art Glass: 1926-1980*;
Email: jdwilson@earthlink.net; Web
site: http://home.earthlink.net/~jdwilsonl/

Yester-Daze Glass
c/o Illinois Antique Center
320 S.W. Commercial St., Peoria,
61604; 309-347-1679. Specializing in
glass from the 1920s, '30s and '40s;
Fiesta; Hall; Pie Birds; Sprinkler Bottles; and Florence figurines

Indiana

AAA Antique Shop
US 6 West, Nappanee, 46550; 219-
773-4912. Specializing in trunks

Alexander, Charles
221 E. 34th St., Indianapolis, 46205;
317-924-9665. Specializing in American dinnerware.

Boram, Clifford
Antique Stove Information Clearing-
   house
Monticello; Free consultation by
phone only: 219-583-6465

Crossroads Antique Mall
311 Holiday Square, Seymour, 47274;
812-522-5675. Open 7 days a week

Edwards, Bill
620 W. 2nd, Madison, 47250. Author
(Collector Books) on Carnival Glass

Fred, James A.
Antique Radio Labs
5355 So. 275W, Cutler, 46920; 765-
268-2214. Specializing in radios made
from 1922 to 1950

Garrett, Jerry and Sandi
Jerry's Antiques (Shows only)
1807 W. Madison St., Kokomo,
46901; 765-457-5256. Specializing in
Greentown glass, old postcards

Gilley's Antique Mall and Collectibles
1209 W. Main (US 40), Plainfield,
46168; 317-839-8779. Open daily
from 10 a.m. to 5 p.m., features booths
with over 250 dealers; Outdoor summer weekend flea market

Haun, Ted
2426 N. 700 East, Kokomo, 46901;
317-628-3640. Specializing in American pottery and china, '50s items,
Russel Wright designs

Highfield, James
1601 Lincoln Way East, South Bend,
46613; 219-288-0300. Specializing in
Capo-di-Monte (Doccia, Ginori and
Royal Naples). Look for upcoming book

Heiss, Virginia
7777 N. Alton Ave., Indianapolis,
46268; 317-875-6797. Specializing in
Muncie, AMACO, Brandt Steele,
Marblehead, Kenton Hills

Howey Auction Center
Howey & Co. Auuctioneers
Kevin Howey
112 W. Washington St., Waynetown,
47990; 765-234-1020 or 1-800-495-7653

Keagy, William and June
P.O. Box 106, Bloomfield, 47424;
812-384-3471. Co-authors of *Those
Wonderful Yard-Long Prints and More*,
*More Wonderful Yard-Long Prints,
Book II*, and *Yard-Long Prints, Book
III*, illustrated value guides

Leslie, Beverly
Secretary/Treasurer of Uhl Collectors
   Society
801 Poplar St., Boonville, 47601; 812-
897-3681. Contact for newsletter and
membership information

McQuillen, Michael J. and Polly
McQuillen's Collectibles
P.O. Box 11141, Indianapolis, 46201;
317-322-8518. Writer of column,
Political Parade, which appears monthly in *AntiqueWeek* newspapers; Specializing in political campaign
memorabilia, Kentucky Derby items,
sports memorabilia; Buys and sells

Old Storefront Antiques
P.O. Box 357, Dublin, 47335; 317-
478-4809. Specializing in country
store items, tins, primitives, pharma-
ceuticals, advertising, etc.; Active in
mail order with catalogs available;
Information requires LSASE

Pruitt, Ted
3350 W. 700 N., Anderson, 46011. *St.
Clair Glass Collector's Book,* available
($15 ea) from Ted at above address

Scowden, Virgil
Williamsport, 47993; 317-762-3408
or 317-762-3178. Antiques museum,
general line, tours

Slater, Thomas D.
Slater's Americana
1325 W. 86th St., Indianapolis,
46260; 317-257-0863. Specializing in
political and sports memorabilia

Stofft, Jeanette
Marnette Antiques
Tell City, 47586; 812-547-5707. Specializing in Ohio art pottery, buy and
sell; no phone appraisals; SASE required

Swayzee Antique Mall
115 N. Washington St., Swayzee,
46986; 317-922-7903

Vanderbilt, Duane and Janice
4040 W. Over Dr., Indianapolis,
46268; 317-875-8932. Authors (Collector Books) of *Collector's Guide to
Shawnee Pottery*

Webb's Antique Mall
over 400 Quality Dealers
200 W. Union St., Centerville, 47330

Wright, Bill
325 Shady Dr., New Albany, 47150.
Specializing in knives: Bowie, hunting, military, and pocketknives

Iowa

Addy, Geneva D.
P.O. Box 124, Winterset, 50273;
515-462-3027

Arnbal, Una
Woodland Antiques
242 Trail Ridge Rd., Ames, 50014;
515-292-1005. Specializing in china,
glass, Lomonosov figurines, Danish
collector plates

Beeks, Dale
P.O. Box 117, Mt. Vernon, 52314;
319-895-0506. Specializing in instruments of science technology and
medicine, also surveying instruments
and microscopes

DeGood, Hal and Meredith
The Baggage Car
3100 Justin Dr., Suite B, Des Moines,
50322; 515-270-9080. Specializing in
Hallmark collectibles; publishers of
Hallmark newsletter

DeLozier, Loretta
1101 Polk St., Bedford, 50833;
Monday - Friday: 9:00 a.m. to 4:00
p.m., 712-523-2289 or Fax: 712-523-
2624. Author (Collector Books) of
*Collector's Encyclopedia of Lefton
China, Identification & Values,* Books
I and II; Specializing in Lefton
China; Buy, Sell & Consign; Fee for
written appraisals; Price list available for each pattern or series; E-
mail: Leftonlady@AOL.com

Devine, Dennis; Norman; and Joe
D & D Antique Mall
1411 3rd St., Council Bluffs, 51503;
712-323-5233 or 712-328-7305. Specializing in furniture, phonographs,
collectibles, general line. Joe Devine:
Royal Copley collector

Jaarsma, Ralph
De Pelikaan Antieks
812 Washington St., c/o Red Ribbon
Antique Mall, Pella, 50219. Specializing in Dutch antiques

Picek, Louis
Main Street Antiques
110 W. Main St., Box 340, West
Branch, 52358. Specializing in folk
art, country Americana, the unusual

Westmoreland Glass Society
Jim Fisher, President
513 5th Ave., Coralville, 52241; 319-
354-5011. Membership: $15 (single)
or $25 (household)

Kansas

Anthony, Dorothy Malone
World of Bells Publications
802 S. Eddy, Fort Scott, 66701; 316-
223-3404. Specializing in publishing
and selling books on all types of
small bells

Maundy International
P.O. Box 13028-GG, Shawnee Mission, 66282; 1-800-235-2866. Specializing in watches — antique pocket
and vintage wristwatches

McCormick, John and Marilyn
P.O. Box 3174, Shawnee, 66226; 913-
441-0793. Specializing in Gonder pottery

Rash, Jim
135 Alder Ave., Pleasantville, 08232;
609-646-4125. Specializing in advertising, cereal, and cartoon figures

Smies, David
Pops Collectibles
Box 522, 315 So. 4th, Manhattan, 66502;
913-776-1433. Specializing in coins,
stamps, cards, tokens, Masonic collectibles

Snyder, Charlie and Rose
Charlie's Collectables
R.R. 4, Box 79, Independence, 67301;
316-331-6259. Specializing in cookie
jars and accessories, salt and pepper
shakers, pottery

Street, Patti
Currier & Ives Newsletter
P.O. Box 504, Riverton, 66770; 316-
848-3529

Tinsley, Rosella
105 15th St., Osawatomie, 66064;
913-755-3237. Specializing in primitives, kitchen, farm, woodenware, and
miscellaneous (phone calls only, no
letters please)

Winslow, Ralph
4008 W. 100 Terrace, Overland Park,
66207. Specializing in Dryden Pottery

Kentucky

Courter, J.W.
3935 Kelly Rd., Kevil, 42053; 502-
488-2116. Specializing in Aladdin
lamps; Author of *Aladdin — The
Magic Name in Lamps, Revised Edition,*
hardbound, 304 pages; and *Aladdin
Electric Lamps,* softbound, 229 pages

Florence, Gene
Box 7186H, Lexington, 40522.
Author (Collector Books) on Depres-
sion Glass, Occupied Japan; Elegant
Glass, Kitchen Glassware

Hornback, Betty
Betty's Antiques
707 Sunrise Lane, Elizabethtown,
42701; 502-765-2441. Specializing in
Kentucky Derby glasses

Johnson, Wes, Sr.
RFD, Glenview, 40025. Specializing
in Cracker Jack: toys, point of sale,
packages, etc.; Checkers Confection,
Schoenhut toys, Victor Toy Oats,
Universal Theatre (Chicago), old
toys; Please include SASE

Ritchie, Roy B.
P.O. Box 384, Hindman, 41822; 606-
785-5796. Author of *Standard Knife
Collector's Guide* and *Standard Guide
to Razors;* Specializing in razors and
knives, all types of cutlery

Stewart, Ron
P.O. Box 151, Combs, 41729; 606-
436-5917. Author of *Standard Knife
Collector's Guide* and *Standard Guide
to Razors;* Specializing in razors and
knives, all types of cutlery

Willis, Roy M.
Heartland of Kentucky Decanters and
   Steins
P.O. Box 428, Lebanon Jct., 40150;
Huge selection of limited edition
decanters and beer steins — open
showroom. Include large self-
addressed envelope (two stamps) with
correspondence. Fee for appraisals.
Decanter price guide (listings only, no
pictures): $5.00 ppd.

Louisiana

Langford, Paris
Kollecting Kiddles
415 Dodge Ave., Jefferson, 70121;
504-733-0667. Specializing in all
small vinyl dolls of the '60s and '70s;
Author of *Liddle Kiddles Identification
and Value Guide* (Collector Books)

Maine

Blake, Brenda
Box 555, York Harbor, 03911; 207-363-
6566. Specializing in egg cups; E-mail:
Eggcentric@AOL.com

Hathaway, John
Hathaway's Antiques
3 Mills Rd., Bryant Pond, 04219; 207-
665-2124. Specializing in fruit jars;
Mail order a specialty

Rinaldi, John
Nautical Antiques and Related Items
Box 765, Dock Square, Kennebunkport, 04046; 207-967-3218. Specializing in nautical antiques,
scrimshaw, naval items, marine paintings, naval items, etc.; Fully-illustrated catalog: $5

Zayic, Charles S.
Americana Advertising Art
P.O. Box 57, Ellsworth, 04605; 207-
667-7342. Specializing in early magazines, early advertising art, illustrators

Maryland

Banks, Robert
18901 Gold Mine Court, Brookeville,
20833. Specializing in American flags
of historical significance and exceptional design

Ezell, Elaine; and Newhouse, George
Cruets Cruets Cruets
P.O. Box 1609, Pasadena, 21123-1609; 410-255-6777. Specializing in cruets, glass, porcelain and pottery

Humphrey, George C.
4932 Prince George Ave., Beltsville, 20705; 301-937-7899. Specializing in John Rogers groups

Meadows, John, Jean and Michael
Meadows House Antiques
919 Stiles St., Baltimore, 21202; 410-837-5427. Specializing in antique wicker, furniture (rustic, twig, and old hickory), quilts and tramp art

Michels, John
Jamm Enterprises
1658 Hardwick Rd., Baltimore, 21286; 410-825-3636. Specializing in watch stands, small clocks, dollar watches

Rudisill's Alt Print Haus
Rudisill, John and Barbara
P.O. Box 199, Worton, 21678; 410-778-9290. Specializing in Currier & Ives

Screen, Harold and Joyce
2804 Munster Rd., Baltimore, 21234; 410-661-6765. Specializing in soda fountain 'tools of the trade' and paper: catalogs, *Soda Fountain* Magazine, etc.

Welsh, Joan
7015 Partridge Pl., Hyattsville, 20782; 301-779-6181. Specializing in Chintz; Author of *Chintz Ceramics*

Yalom, Libby
The Shoe Lady
P.O. Box 7146, Adelphi, 20783; 301-422-2026. Specializing in glass and china shoes: Author of book

Massachusetts

Adams, Charles and Barbara
Middleboro, 02346; 508-947-7277. Specializing in Bennington (brown only)

Dunbar's Gallery
Leila and Howard Dunbar
76 Haven St., Milford, 01757; 508-634-8697 or (Fax) 508-634-8698. Specializing in advertising and toys

Frei, Peter
P.O. Box 500, Brimfield, 01010; 1-800-942-8968. Specializing in sewing machines (pre-1875, non-electric only), adding machines, typewriters, and hand-powered vacuum cleaners; SASE required with correspondence

Hess, John A.
Fine Photographic Americana
P.O. Box 3062, Andover, 01810. Specializing in 19th-century photography

Dedham/CKAW Antiques
Kaufman, James D.
248 Highland St., Dedham, 02026; 800-283-8070. Specializing in Dedham and Chelsea Art Works; Publishes *The Dedham Pottery Collectors Pottery Newsletter*, Subscription: $18 (published quarterly)

Longo, Paul J.
Paul Longo Americana
Box 5510, Magnolia, 01930; 508-525-2290. Specializing in political pins, ribbons, banners, autographs, old stocks and bonds, baseball and sports memorabilia of all types

MacLean, Dale
183 Robert Rd., Dedham, 02026; 617-326-3010 or 617-329-1303 (evenings). Specializing in Dedham and Dorchester potteries

Mallis, A. George
208 Reeds Landing, 807 Wilbraham Rd., Springfield, 01109-2055. Specializing in antique scales

Morin, Albert
668 Robbins Ave. #23, Dracut, 01826; 508-454-7907. Specializing in miscellaneous Akro Agate and Westite

Owings, K.C., Jr.
Antiques Americana
Box 19, N. Abington, 02351; 617-857-1655. Specializing in Civil War, Revolutionary War, autographs, documents, books, antiques

Vigue, Norm
62 Bailey St., Stoughton, 02072; 617-344-5441. Buying and selling TV, western, cartoon-show collectibles, animation art and 1-sheets, radio cereal premiums, and board games

Wellman, BA
P.O. Box 673, Westminster, 01473-1435. Specializing in all areas of American ceramics, dinnerware, figurines, and art pottery

Michigan

Brown, Rick
Newspaper Collector's Society of America
Box 19134-S, Lansing, 48901; 517-887-1255. Specializing in newspapers

Gunsaulus, Jack
Gray's Gallery/Jack's Corner Bookstore
583 W. Ann Arbor Trail, Plymouth, 48170. Specializing in porcelain, books, jewelry, glass

Haas, Norman
264 Clizbe Rd., Quincy 49802; 517-639-8537. Specializing in American art pottery

Hogan & Woodworth
Walter P. Hogan and Wendy L. Woodworth
520 N. State, Ann Arbor, MI, 48104; 313-930-1913. Specializing in Kellogg Studio

Iannotti, Dan
212 W. Hickory Grove Rd., Bloomfield Hills, 48302-1127S. Specializing in modern mechanical cast-iron banks; Member of The Mechanical Bank Collectors of America

Krupka, Rod
2615 Echo Lane, Ortonville, 48462; 810-627-6351. Specializing in lightning rod balls

Kurella, Elizabeth M.
The Lace Merchant
Box 222, Plainwell, 49080; 616-685-9792. Publisher of newsletter and books on lace and linens. Specializing in lace and linens

Marsh, Linda K.
1229 Gould Rd., Lansing, 48917. Specializing in Degenhart glass

Nedry, Boyd W.
728 Buth Dr., Comstock Park, 49321; 616-784-1513. Specializing in traps (including mice, rat, and fly traps) and trap-related items

Newbound, Betty
4567 Chadsworth, Commerce, 48382. Author (Collector Books) on Blue Ridge dinnerware, milk glass, wall pockets, and figural planters and vases; Specializing in collectible china and glass

Nickel, Mike
A Nickel's Worth
P.O. Box 456, Portland, 48875; 517-647-7646. Specializing in Roseville art pottery and juvenile pieces, Weller, Rookwood, Kay Finch, Ceramic Arts Studio, Josef, and Florence figurines

Oates, Joan
685 S. Washington, Constantine, 49042; 616-435-8353. Specializing in Phoenix Bird chinaware

Webster, Marty
6943 Suncrest Drive, Saline, 48176; 313-944-1188 or Fax: 313-944-2171. Specializing in California porcelain and pottery

Minnesota

Anderson, James
Box 120704, New Brighton, 55112; 612-484-3198. Specializing in old fishing lures and reels, also tackle catalogs, posters, calendars, Winchester items

Gallagher, Jerry
420 1st Ave. N.W., Plainview, 55964; 507-534-3511. Specializing in Morgantown research; matching service for Morgantown, Heisey, Fostoria, Cambridge, Duncan, and Tiffin. Publisher of *A Handbook of Old Morgantown Glass* and Price Guide ($35+$4 shipping & handling), Morgantown 1931 catalog reprint (sold out), *Morgantown Colors* placard ($4 post paid), and *The Morgantown Newscaster*, tri-annual research journal of the Morgantown Collectors of America, Inc. (subscription: $18 per year)

Harrigan, John
1900 Hennepin, Minneapolis, 55403; 612-872-0226 or (in winter) 407-732-0525. Specializing in Battersea (English enamel) boxes, Moorcroft, and Toby jugs. In winter call: 561-732-0525

Ketcham, Steve
Steve Ketcham Antiques
(Shows and mail order only)
Box 24114, Edina, 55424; 612-920-4205. Specializing in and buying early American bottles; Red Wing stoneware (no dinnerware); advertising signs, trays, trade cards, pocket mirrors, etched beer and shot glasses; Please include SASE for reply

Miller, Clark
4444 Garfield Ave., Minneapolis, 55409-1847; 612-827-6062. Specializing in Anton Lang pottery, American art pottery, Scandinavian glass and pottery

Nelson, C.L.
Box 222, Spring Park, 55384; 612-473-5625. Specializing in 18th-, 19th- and 20th-century English pottery and porcelain, among others: Gaudy Welsh, ABC plates, relief-molded jugs, Staffordshire transfer ware

Podpeskar, Doug
624 Jones St., Eveleth, 55734-1631; 218-744-4854. Specializing in Red Wing dinnerware. Prefers letters with clear photos of items to be identified along with SASE for return

Missouri

Heuring, Jerry
R.R. #1, Box 1110, Scott City, 63780; 573-264-3947. Specializing in Keen Kutter

International Rose O'Neill Club
Contact Karen Stewart
P.O. Box 668, Branson, 65616. Dues: $7 (single) or $10 (family) includes newsletter *Kewpiesta Kourier*, published quarterly

Old World Antiques
1715 Summit, Kansas City, 64108
Branch Location: 4436 State Line
Rd., Kansas City, 66103. Specializing
in 18th- and 19th-century furniture,
paintings, accessories, clocks, chandeliers, sconces, and much more

Roberts, Brenda
Country Side Antiques
R.R. 2, Marshall, 65340. Specializing in
Hull pottery and general line. Author
of *Collectors Encyclopedia of Hull Pottery*, *Roberts' Ultimate Encyclopedia of
Hull Pottery* and *The Companion Guide
to Robert's Ultimate Encyclopedia of Hull
Pottery*, all with accompanying price
guides; SASE required

Siegel, Brenda and Jerry
Tower Grove Antiques
3308 Meramec, St. Louis, 63118;
314-352-9020. Specializing in
Ungemach pottery

Scott, John and Peggy
Scotty's Antiques
4640 S. Leroy, Springfield, 65810;
417-887-2191. Specializing in Depression-era glassware and pottery

Smith, Pat
Independence
Author (Collector Books) of doll
book series

Tarrant, Jenny
Holly Daze Antiques
4 Gardenview, St. Peters, 63376. Specializing in early holiday items, Halloween, Christmas, Easter, etc.;
Always buying Halloween collectibles
(except masks and costumes) and
German rabbits and Santas

Wiesehan, Doug
D & R Farm Antiques
4535 Hwy. H, St. Charles, 63301.
Specializing in salesman's samples and
patent models, antique toys, farm toys,
metal farm signs

Williams, Don
P.O. Box 147, Kirksville 63501; 816-
627-8009 (between 8 a.m. and 6
p.m.). Specializing in art glass; SASE
required with all correspondence

Woollard, D.D., Jr.
11614 Old St. Charles Rd.,
Bridgeton, 63044; 314-739-4662.
Specializing in World's Fair & Exposition memorabilia

Nebraska

Larsen, Robert V.
3214 19th St., Columbus, 68601.
Specializing in old hatpins and hatpin holders

Neely, Nancee P.
16592 Hascall, Omaha, 68130; 402-
330-7033. Specializing in Fairing boxes

New Hampshire

Brenner, Larry
Brenner Antiques
1005 Chestnut St., Manchester,
03104; 603-625-8203. Specializing in
Royal Bayreuth

Holt, Jane
Jane's Collectibles
P.O. Box 115, Derry, 03038. Specializing in Annalee Motilitee Dolls;
Extensive list sometimes available

Winston, Nancy
Willow Hollow Antiques
648 1st N.H. Turnpike, Northwood,
03261; 603-942-5739. Specializing in
Shaker baskets, primitives, country
smalls, paper Americana, iron and copper

New Jersey

Anderson, Suzy McLennan
Heritage Antiques & Appraisal Services
65 E. Main St., Holmdel, 07733; 908-
946-8801 or (Fax) 908-946-1036.
Specializing in American furniture
and decorative accessories

Bilane, John E. (Mail order only)
2065 Morris Ave., Apt. 109, Union,
07083. Specializing in antique glass
cup plates

Cole, Lillian M., Editor of *Piebirds
Unlimited* Newsletter
14 Harmony School Rd., Flemington,
08822; 908-782-3198. Specializing in
pie birds, pie funnels, pie vents

Dezso, Doug
864 Paterson Ave., Maywood, 07607-
2119; 201-488-1311. Specializing in
nodders (German), glass candy containers, Tonka

Doorstop Collectors of America
Doorstopper newsletter
Jeanie Bertoia
2413 Madison Ave., Vineland, 08630;
609-692-4092. Membership: $20 per
year, includes 2 newsletters and convention. Send 2-stamp SASE for sample

George, Dr. Joan M.
ABC Collector's Circle
67 Stevens Ave., Old Bridge, 08857.
Specializing in educational china
(particularly ABC plates and mugs)

Guido, Karen
Karen Michelle
64 Kingwood Ave., Frenchtown,
08825. Specializing in tiles; Buy and
sell; Books on tiles available, many
out of print; Fee for written appraisal;
Please include SASE for inquiries

Litts, Elyce
P.O. Box 394, Morris Plains, 07950;
201-361-4087. Author (Collector
Books) of *Collector's Encyclopedia of
Geisha Girl Porcelain* (Out of print.
Ask your reference librarian or used
bookstore to secure you a copy)

Lockwood, Howard J.; Publisher
Vetri: Italian Glass News
Box 191, Fort Lee, 07024; 201-969-
0373. Specializing in Italian glass of
the 20th century ADVI

Meschi, Edward J.
129 Pinyard Rd., Monroeville, 08343;
Phone/Fax: 609-358-7293. Specializing in Durand art glass, Icart etching,
Maxfield Parrish prints, Rookwood
pottery, occupational shaving mugs,
oil paintings, and other fine arts

Patalano, Diane. I.S.A.
Appraisals, Liquidations and Auctions
P.O. Box 144, Saddle River 07458.
Specializing in banks, Black Americana, cookie jars, furniture, spatterware, various antiques and collectibles

Perzel, Robert and Nancy
Popkorn
4 Mine St. (near Main St.), P.O. Box
1057, Flemington, 08822; 908-782-
9631. Specializing in Stangl dinnerware,
birds, and artware; Depression Glass

Poster, Harry
Vintage TVs
Box 1883, S. Hackensack, 07606;
Days: 201-794-9606; 24-Hour Fax:
201-794-9553. Writes *Poster's Radio
and Television Price Guide*; Specializes
in vintage televisions, transistor
radios, 3-D stereo cameras

Rago, David
17 S. Main St., Lambertville, 08530;
609-397-9374. Specializing in Arts &
Crafts, art pottery

Rash, Jim
135 Alder Ave., Egg Harbor Township, 08234; 609-646-4125. Specializing in advertising dolls

Rosen, Barbara
6 Shoshone Trail, Wayne, 07470.
Specializing in figural bottle openers
and antique dollhouses

Vines, Linda L.
Yesterday Once More
P.O. Box 43721, Upper Montclair,
07043; 201-748-4990. Specializing in
Snow Babies, all holidays (Christmas,
Easter, Halloween), dolls, toys, and Steiff

Visakay, Stephen
Vintage Cocktail Shakers (By
appointment)
P.O. Box 1517, W. Caldwell, 07007-
1517. Specializing in vintage cocktail shakers

New Mexico

Hardisty, Don
Artistic Restorations
3020 E. Majestic Ridge, Las Cruces,
88011; 505-522-3721 or (Fax) 505-522-
7909. Specializing in Bossons, Hummels, postcards, rare coins, and Legend
Artware. Don's Collectibles carries a
full line of current issues and most discontinued Bossons and Hummel figurines of all marks. Postcard inventory
inclues over 500,000 with many original photo cards, and all current issues of
Legend. When mail ordering, you may
dial toll free 800-267-7667

Manns, William
P.O. Box 6459, Santa Fe, 87502; 505-
995-0102. Co-author of *Painted
Ponies*, hard-bound edition (226
pages), available from author for
$39.95+$5 shipping; Specializing in
carousel art and western antiques

Moyer, Patsy
Box 311, Denning, 88031; 505-546-4019
or 505-546-2525; Fax 505-546-2500.
Collector Books author on dolls; E-mail:
sctrading@zianet.com

New York

Austin, Bruce A.
1 Hardwood Hill Rd., Pittsford,
14534; 716-387-9820 (evenings);
716-475-2879 (week days). Specializing in clocks and Arts & Crafts furnishings and accessories including
medalware, pottery, and lighting; E-mail: baagll@rit.edu

Batchelor, Daniel J.
Batchelor's Auction Service
7307 Rt. 104 West, Oswego, 13126.
Specializing in Pairpoint, Handel,
Bradley and Hubbard lamps; Photo
and SASE required with all correspondence. No phone calls please

Calison, Jim
Tools of Distinction
Wallkill, 12589; 914-895-8035. Specializing in antique and collectible
tools, buying and selling

Dimitroff, Thomas P.
Dimitroff's Antiques (Appointment only)
140 E. First St., Corning, 14830; 607-
962-6745. Specializing in Steuben
and cut glass

Doyle, Robert A.
Absolute Auction & Realty,
Inc./Pleasant Valley Auction Hall
P.O. Box 658, 348 Main St., Beacon
12524. Antique and estate auctions
the 4th Saturday of every month at
their Beacon gallery, twice a month at
Pleasant Valley Auction Hall; Free
calendar of auctions available

Fer-Duc Inc.
Ferrara, Joseph
P.O. Box 1303, Newburgh, 12550; 212-627-5023. Specializing in American art pottery (Ohr and Rookwood), 19th- and 20th-century American paintings

Fox, Ron
Ron Fox Auctions
P.O. Box 4026, Farmingdale 11735; 516-420-9214 or (Fax) 516-243-0412.

Gerson, Roselyn
P.O. Box 40, Lynbrook, 11563; 516-593-8746. Author/collector specializing in unusual, gadgetry, figural compacts and vanity bags/purses

Greguire, Helen
Helen's Antiques
103 Trimmer Rd., Hilton, 14468; 716-392-2704. Specializing in graniteware (any color), Carnival Glass lamps and shades, Carnival Glass lighting of all kinds; Author (Collector Books) of *The Collector's Encyclopedia of Graniteware, Colors, Shapes & Values*, (updated values, $28.45 postage paid); Second book on graniteware now available with prices updated to 1997 (same price); Also available is *Carnival in Lights*, featuring Carnival Glass, lamps, shades, etc. ($13.45 postage paid, all available from author); Also interested in unusual and rare toasters; Author of new book on toasters and related items. Note: Anyone requesting information on any of the above subjects, please send a SASE

Handelsman, Burton
18 Hotel Dr., White Plains, 10605; 914-428-4480 (home) and 914-761-8880 (office). Specializing in occupational shaving mugs, accessories

Herley, Patrick J.
P.O. Box 606, E. Setauket, Long Island, 11733; 516-928-6052. Specializing in Goss china

Jordan, Ruth E.
Meridale, 13806; 607-746-2082. Specializing in cut glass, American Brilliant period

Kaonis, Keith, Publisher
Inside Collector and *Doll World*
60 Cherry Lane, Huntington, 11743; 516-351-0982. Specializing in Schoenhut toys

Laun, H. Thomas and Patricia
Little Century
215 Paul Ave., Syracuse, 13206; 315-437-4156. Summer residence: 35109 Country Rte. 7, Cape Vincent, 13618; 315-654-3244. Specializing in firefighting collectibles

Malitz, Lucille
Lucid Antiques
Box KH, Scarsdale, NY 10583; 914-636-7825. Specializing in lithophanes, kaleidoscopes, stereoscopes, medical and dental antiques

Malloy, Alex G.
Alex G. Malloy, Inc.
P.O. Box 38, South Salem, 10590; 203-438-0396. Specializing in ancient and medieval coins; antiquities, numismatic literature

Michel, John and Barbara
Americana Blue
200 E. 78th St., 18E, New York City, 10021; 212-861-6094. Specializing in yellow ware, cast iron, and tramp art

Owens, Lowell
Owens' Collectibles
12 Bonnie Ave., New Hartford, 13413. Specializing in beer advertising

Rifken, Blume J.
Author of *Silhouettes in America — 1790-1840 — A Collector's Guide*. Specializing in American antique silhouettes from 1790 to 1840

Safir, Charlotte F.
1349 Lexington Ave., 9-B, New York City, 10128; 212-534-7933. Specializing in cookbooks, children's books (out-of-print only)

Schleifman, Roselle
Ed's Collectibles/The Rage
16 Vincent Rd., Spring Valley, 10977; 914-356-2121. Specializing in Duncan & Miller, Elegant Glass

Smyth, Carole and Richard
Carole Smyth Antiques
P.O. Box 2068, Huntington, 11743; 516-673-8666. Authors of *The Burning Passion — Antique and Collectible Pyrography*, available from authors at above address for $19.95+$3 postage (New York State residents add 8.5% sales tax)

Steinbock, Nancy
Nancy Steinbock Posters
518-438-1577. Specializing in posters: travel, war, literary, advertising

Thurston, Phil and Nyla
82 Hamlin St., Cortland, 13045; 607-753-6770. Specializing in figural American pottery

Tuggle, Robert
105 W. St., New York City, 10023; 212-595-0514. Specializing in John Bennett, Anglo-Japanese china

Van Kuren, Jean and Dale
Ruth's Antiques, Inc.
9060 Main St., Clarence, 14031; 716-741-8001. Specializing in Buffalo pottery, chocolate molds, Noritake Azalea, general line

Van Patten, Joan F.
Box 102, Rexford, 12148. Author (Collector Books) of books on Nippon and Noritake

North Carolina

Degenhardt, Richard K.
Carriage Park
302 High Point Lane, Hendersonville, 28791; 704-696-9750. Author of *Belleek, The Complete Collectors' Guide and Illustrated Reference*, 1st and 2nd editions. Specializing in Belleek (The only Belleek is the Irish. Established by legal action in 1929)

Hughes, Kathy (Mrs. Paul)
Tudor House Galleries
1401 E. Blvd., Charlotte, 28203; 704-377-4748. Specializing in relief-molded jugs, 18th- and 19th-century English pottery and 19th-century oil paintings

Hussey, Billy Ray and Susan
1828 N. Howard Mill Road, Robbins, 27325. Specializing in Southern folk pottery contemporary face jugs.

Iannantuoni, Jean-Paul
P.O. Box 563072, Charlotte, 28256-3072; 704-547-9951 (Monday-Thursday from 7:00 p.m. to 10:00 p.m. EST, Saturday and Sunday from 1:00 p.m. to 8:00 p.m.). Specializing in Royal Doulton secondary market

Kirtley, Charles E.
P.O. Box 2273, Elizabeth City, 27096; 919-335-1262. Specializing in monthly auctions and bid sales dealing with World's Fair, Civil War, political, advertising, and other American collectibles

Sayers, R.J.
Southeastern Antiques & Appraisals
14 Longbranch Rd., Pisgah Forest, 28768. Specializing in Boy Scout collectibles, Pisgah Forest pottery, primitive American furniture; Author of *Guide to Scouting Collectibles, Revised 1996 Edition*, available from author for $26.95+$4 postage

Taylor, Terry
East Bend, 27018. Co-author of *Collector's Encyclopedia of Salt Glaze Stoneware* (Collector Books). Specializing in salt glaze stoneware

North Dakota

Farnsworth, Bryce
1334 14 1/2 St. South, Fargo, 58103; 701-237-3597. Specializing in Rosemeade pottery; If writing for information, please send a picture if possible, also phone number and best time to call

Ohio

Bassett, Mark
P.O. Box 771233, Lakewood, 44107. Author of *Cowan Pottery and the Cleveland School*, researcher with specialties in American art pottery, Cleveland artists, Art Deco and other 20th century design movements and designers.

Batory, Mr. Dana Martin
402 E. Bucyrus St., Crestline, 44827. Specializing in antique woodworking machinery, old and new woodworking machinery catalogs; Author of *Vintage Woodworking Machinery, an Illustrated Guide to Four Manufacturers*, currently available from Astragal Press, P.O. Box 239, Mendham, NJ 07945 for $21.95+$3.50 shipping. In order to prepare a definitive history on American manufacturers of woodworking machinery, Dana is interested in acquiring by loan, gift, or photocopy, any and all documents, catalogs, manuals, photos, personal reminiscences, etc., pertaining to woodworking machinery and/or their manufacturers. NO phone calls please

Benjamin, Scott
411 Forest St., LaGrange, 44050; 216-355-6608. Specializing in gas globes; Co-author of *Gas Pump Globes* and several other related books, listing nearly 4,000 gas globes with over 400 photos, prices, rarity guide, histories, and reproduction information (currently available from author); Also available: *Petroleum Collectibles Monthly* magazine, please inquire

Blair, Betty
Golden Apple Antiques
216 Bridge St., Jackson, 45640; 614-286-4817. Specializing in art pottery, Watt, cookie jars, chocolate molds, general line

Budin, Nicki
Curio Cabinet
679 High St., Worthington, 43085; 614-885-1986. Specializing in Royal Doulton

Business Recollections, Antiques and Collectibles
Nada Sue Knauss
1211 Potter Rd, Weston, 43569; 419-669-4735. Specializing in pottery, postcards

China Specialties, Inc.
19238 Dorchester Circle, Strongsville, 44136; 216-238-2528. Specializing in Autumn Leaf

Cimini, Joan
63680 Centerville-Warnock Rd., Belmont, 43718. Specializing in Imperial glass; Candlewick matching service

Cincinnati Auction Gallery
635 Main St., Cincinnati, 45202; 513-381-2128. Specializing in American art pottery (especially Rookwood), American and European fine paintings, watercolors

Collectors of Findlay Glass
P.O. Box 256, Findlay, 45840. An organization dedicated to the study and recognition of Findlay glass; *The Melting Pot* Newsletter published quarterly; Convention held annually; Membership: $10 per year

Distel, Ginny
Distel's Antiques
4041 S.C.R. 22, Tiffin, 44883; 419-447-5832. Specializing in Tiffin glass

Ebner, Rita and John
Cracker Barrel Antiques
4540 Helen Rd., Columbus, 43232. Specializing in door knockers, cast-iron bottle openers, Griswold

Ferguson, Maxine
1380 Bussemer, Zanesville, 43701

Forsythe, Ruth A.
Box 327, Galena, 43021. Author of *Made in Czechoslovakia*, books I and II; SASE required

Graff, Shirley
4515 Grafton Rd., Brunswick, 44212. Specializing in Pennsbury pottery

Guenin, Tom
Box 454, Chardon, 44024. Specializing in antique telephones and antique telephone restoration

Hamlin, Jack and Treva
R.R. 4, Box 150, Kaiser St., Proctorville, 45669; 614-886-7644. Specializing in Currier and Ives by Royal China Co.

Hothem, Lar
Hothem House
Box 458, Lancaster, 43130. Specializing in books about Indians and artifacts

Kao, Fern Larking
P.O. Box 312, Bowling Green, 43402; 419-352-5928. Specializing in jewelry, sewing implements, ladies' accessories

Kerr, Ann
P.O. 437, Sidney, 45365; 937-492-6369. Author (Collector Books) of *Collector's Encyclopedia of Russel Wright Designs*; Specializing in work of Wright; Interested in 20th-century decorative arts

Kier, Don and Anne
2022 Marengo St., Toledo, 43614; 419-385-8211. Specializing in general glass and china, 19th-century antiques, autographs, Brownies, Royal Bayreuth

Kitchen, Lorrie
Toledo, 419-478-3815. Specializing in Depression-era glass, Hall china, Fiesta, Blue Ridge, Shawnee

Klender, James and Grace
Town & Country Antiques & Collectibles
P.O. Box 447, Pioneer, 43554; 419-737-2880. Specializing in Depression Glass, and general line

Kline, Mr. and Mrs. Jerry and Gerry
Members of North American Torquay Society and Torquay Pottery Collectors' Society
604 Orchard View Dr., Maumee, 43537; 419-893-1226. Specializing in collecting Torquay pottery

Maggard, Deborah
P.O Box 211, Chagrin Falls, 44022; 216-247-5632. Specializing in elegant glassware, china, and Victorian art glass

Mathes, Richard
P.O. Box 1408, Springfield, 45501-1408; 513-324-6917. Specializing in buttonhooks

Moore, Carolyn
445 N. Prospect, Bowling Green, 43402. Specializing in primitives, yellow ware, graniteware, collecting stoneware

Murphy, James L.
1023 Neil Ave., Columbus, 43201; 614-297-0746. Specializing in Radford, Vance Avon

National Imperial Glass Collectors' Society, Inc.
P.O. Box 534, Bellaire 43906. Dues: $15 per year (plus $1 for each additional member in the same household); Quarterly newsletter; Convention every June

Nelson, Norman
2267 E. Erie, Lorain, 44052; 216-288-4977. Specializing in jukeboxes

Peters, Jeannie L.
Mt. Washington Antiques
3742 Kellogg, Cincinnati, 45226; 513-231-6584. Specializing in sheet music

Pierce, David
27544 Black Rd., P.O. Box 248, Danville, 43014; 614-599-6394. Specializing in Glidden pottery; Fee for appraisals

Rees, Debbie
Zanesville. Specializing in Watt, Roseville juvenile and other Roseville pottery, Zanesville area pottery, cookie jars, and Steiff

Riebel, James; Krause, Terry
Pottery Peregrinators
Zanesville, 614-452-7687. Specializing in American art pottery, Nicodemus, and Carnival Glass

Roscoe, Mike
3351 Lagrange, Toledo, 43608; 419-244-6935. Specializing in toys, advertising, coin-operated machines, furniture, and miscellaneous

Trainer, Veronica
Bayhouse
Box 40443, Cleveland, 44140; 216-871-8584. Specializing in beaded and enamelled mesh purses

Tucker, Dan
Toledo, 419-478-3815. Specializing in Depression-era glass, Hall china, Fiesta, Blue Ridge, Shawnee

Walker, Bunny
Box 502, Bucyrus, 44820; 419-562-8355. Specializing in Steiff teddy bears, penny toys, pottery

Walter, John
The Old Tool Shop
208 Front St., Marietta, 45750; 614-373-9973. Specializing in all types of antique tools

Whitmyer, Margaret and Kenn
Box 30806, Gahanna, 43230. Author (Collector Books) on children's dishes. Specializing in Depression-era collectibles

Wilkins, Juanita
The Bird of Paradise
Lima. Specializing in R.S. China, Old Ivory china, colored pattern glass, lamps, and jewelry

Young, Mary
Box 9244, Wright Brothers Branch, Dayton, 45409; 937-298-4838. Specializing in paper dolls; Author of several books

Oklahoma

Bess, Phyllis and Tom
14535 E. 13th St., Tulsa, 74108; 918-437-7776. Authors of *Frankoma Treasures*, and *Frankoma and Other Oklahoma Potteries*. Specializing in Frankoma and Oklahoma pottery

Klein, Bob and Dondee
1002 Walnut Court, Guthrie, 73044; 405-282-6545. Specializing in Tamac pottery

Moore, Art and Shirley
2145 S. Norfolk Ave., Tulsa, 74114; 918-747-4164. Specializing in Lu Ray Pastels, Depression Glass

Scott, Roger R.
4250 S. Oswego, Tulsa, 74135; 918-742-8710 or (Fax) 918-583-1226. Specializing in Victor and RCA Victor trademark items along with Nipper

Watson, Kitty
Kitty's Kewpie-Corner
201 Dena Dr., Guthrie, 73044; 405-282-2287. Specializing in Rose O'Neill items; Kewpies, Scootles and other related works.

Willis, Ron L.
2110 Fox Ave., Moore, 73160. Specializing in militaria

Oregon

Abrahams, Peter
1948 Mapleleaf Rd., Lake Oswego, 97034; 503-636-2988 (or e-mail: telscope@europa.com). Specializing in telescopes, binoculars, microscopes. Peter studies and collects optics: telescopes, binoculars, hand magnifiers, and microscopes and especially seeks reference material on these subjects, including books, catalogs, repair manuals, and histories

Bartsch, Henry
Antique Registers
2050 N. Hwy. 101, Rockaway Beach, 97136; 503-355-2932. Specializing in antique cash registers; Co-author of *Antique Cash Registers 1880-1920*. Written insurance appraisals are provided by Mr. Bartsch for a $25 fee; Please include register's model, serial number, condition and 3 keeper photographs

Brown, Marcia
Sparkles
P.O. Box 2314
White City; 541-826-3030 or Fax: 541-830-5385. Specializing in rhinestones

Carter, Fran (Appointment only)
Box 3220, Coos Bay, 97420; 503-888-5780. Specializing in estate sales

Coe, Debbie and Randy
Coe's Mercantile
Lafayette School House Mall #2, 748 3rd (Hwy. 99W), Lafayette, 97127. Specializing in elegant and Depression Glass, art pottery

Davis, Patricia M.
4326 NW Tam-O-Shanter Way, Portland, 97229-8738; 503-645-3084

Foland, Doug
1811 N.W. Couch #303, Portland, 97209. Author of *The Florence Collectibles, an Era of Elegance*, available at your local bookstore or from Schiffer publishers

Geddes, Marjorie
5955 W.W. 179th Ave., Beaverton 97007; 503-649-1041. Specializing in sewing items, open salts, Florence ceramics, California figurines, tea-related items, miscellaneous small and elegant collectibles; In space 21, Lafayette Schoolhouse Antique Mall, 503-864-2720

Hirshman, Susan and Larry
Everyday Antiques
2011 E. Main St., Medford, 97504;
541-608-9594. Specializing in china,
glassware, kitchenware

Main Antique Mall
30 N. Riverside, Medford, 97501.
Quality products and services for the
serious collector, dealer, or those just
browsing

Medford Antique Mall
Jim & Eileen Pearson, Owners
1 West 6th St., Medford 97501

Miller, Don and Robby
541-535-1231. Specializing in milk
bottles, TV Siamese cat lamps, seltzer
bottles, red cocktail shakers

Morris, Sue and Dave
3388 Merlin Rd., Suite 351, Grants
Pass, 97526. Specializing in Watt pot-
tery and Purinton pottery; Author of
*Watt Pottery — An Identification and
Value Guide*, and *Purinton Pottery —
An Identification and Value Guide*

Morris, Thomas G.
Prize Publishers
P.O. Box 8307, Medford, 97504.
Author of *The Carnival Chalk Prize*,
Books I and II, pictorial price guides
on carnival chalkware figures with
brief histories and values for each

Ringering, David
Belle Ringer Antiques
1480 Tumalo Dr. S.E., Salem, 97301;
503-585-8253. Specializing in Rowland & Marsellus and other sou-
venir/historical china with scenes of
buildings, parks, and other tourist
attractions of the 1890s-1930s. Feel
free to contact David if you have any
questions about Rowland & Marsellus
or other souvenir china. He will be
happy to answer questions about souvenir china

Roberts, Fred and Marilyn
Bah Humbug Collectibles
2663 Aldersgate Rd., Medford, 97504.
Specializing in Hummels; E-mail:
bahhumbug@juno

Pennsylvania

Barker, Jim
Toastermaster Antique Appliances
P.O. Box 41, Bethlehem, 18016; 610-
439-0751. Specializing in early electric toasters and fans, Porcelier and
Royal Rochester; Unusual electric
toasters always wanted

Barrett, Noel
Rosebud Antiques
P.O. Box 1001, Carversville, 18913;
215-297-5109. Specializing in toys

Bodine, Clarence H., Jr., Proprietor
East/West Gallery
41B Ferry St., New Hope, 18938. Specializing in antique Japanese wood-
block prints, netsuke, inro, porcelains

Cerebro
P.O. Box 327, East Prospect, 17317-
0327; 717-252-2400 or 800-69-
LABEL;   Fax: 717-252-3685.
Specializing in antique advertising
labels, especially cigar box labels, cigar
bands, food labels, firecracker labels

Damaska, Ron
738 9th Ave., New Brighton, 15066;
412-843-1393. Specializing in Fry
cut glass, match holders, oil lamps,
silver; SASE required when requesting information

Garvin, Joann
P.O. Box 182, Beaver Falls, 15010;
412-843-3999. Specializing in Fiesta

Gottuso, Bob
Bojo
P.O. Box 1403, Cranberry Township,
16066-0403; Phone/Fax: 412-776-
0621. Specializing in Beatles, Elvis,
KISS, Monkees, licensed Rock 'n Roll
memorabilia

Goyda, Cheryl
Box 192, E. Petersburg, 17520; 717-
569-7149. Specializing in SMF/Whee-
lock   Black   Forest   and
Czechoslovakian pottery

Hagenbuch, James
Glass-Works Auction
102 Jefferson, East Greenville, 18041;
215-679-5849. America's leading auction company in early American bottles and glass

Hain, Henry F., III
Antiques & Collectibles
2623 N. Second St., Harrisburg,
17110; 717-238-0534. Lists available
of items for sale

Hartz, Ray
120 Amberwood Ct., Bethel Park,
15102; 412-833-6777. Specializing
in old, unusual playing cards: U.S.
and Foreign, war, transformation,
advertising

Hinton, Michael C.
246 W. Ashland St., Doylestown,
18901; 215-345-0892. Owns/operates
Bucks County Art & Antiques Company and Chem-Clean Furniture
Restoration Company; Specializing
in quality restorations of a wide range
of art and antiques from colonial to
contemporary

Holland, William
William Holland Fine Arts
1708 E. Lancaster Ave., Paoli, 19301;
610-648-0369 or (Fax) 610-647-4448.
Specializing in Louis Icart etchings and
oils, Art Nouveau and Art Deco items;
Author of *Louis Icart: The Complete Etchings* and *The Collectible Maxfield Parrish*

Irons, Dave
Dave Irons Antiques
223 Covered Bridge Road, Northamp-
ton, 18067; 610-262-9335. Author of
Irons By Irons and *More Irons By Irons*
(both soft-cover); Available from
author (both containing pictures of
over 1,600 irons pictured, current
information and price ranges, collecting hints, news of trends, and information for proper care of irons);
Specializing in pressing irons, country
furniture, primitives, quilts, accessories

Ivankovich, Michael
P.O. Box 2458, Doylestown, 18901.
Specializing in Wallace Nutting,
author of *The Collector's Guide to Wal-
lace Nutting Pictures*, $17.95; *The Wal-
lace Nutting Expansible Catalog*, $14.95;
*The Alphabetical and Numerical Index to
Wallace Nutting Pictures*, $14.95; and
The Guide to Wallace Nutting Furniture,
$14.95. Also available: *Wallace Nutting
General Catalog, Supreme Edition*
(reprint), $13.95; *Wallace Nutting: A
Great American Idea* (reprint), $13.95;
and *Wallace Nutting's Windsor's: Correct Windsor Furniture* (reprint),
$13.95. Related books available are:
*The Guide to Wallace Nutting-Like Pho-
tographers of the Early 20th Century*,
$13.95; and *The History of Sawyer Pic-
tures* by Carol Begley Gray, $14.95. All
these books are currently available
from Diamond Press, P.O. box 2458,
Doylestown, PA, 18901, Shipping is
$3.75 for the first item ordered and
$1.50 for each additional item

Kamm, George
George Kamm Paperweights
106 River Bend Park, Lancaster,
17602; 717-295-7575 or (Fax) 717-
295-7576. Specializing in antique and
contemporary paperweights — color
brochure published bimonthly; $5
annual fee (refundable); Sample on
request (#10 SASE required)

Knauer, Judy A.
National Toothpick Holder Collectors Society
1224 Spring Valley Lane, West
Chester, 19380; 610-431-3477. Specializing in toothpick holders and
Victorian glass

The Krauses
Krause, Gail
97 W. Wheeling St., Washington,
15301; 412-228-5034. Author of book
on Duncan glass

Kreider, Katherine
Kingsbury Antiques
P.O. Box 7957, Lancaster, 17604-
7957; 717-892-3001. Author of
Valentines With Values, available
post-paid by sending $22.90
($24.09 Pennsylvania residents);
No free appraisals. Stop by Booth
#315 at Black Angus, in
Adamstown (new section) and talk
about valentines

Kurau, William
Box 457, Lampeter, 17537; 717-464-
0731. Specializing in historical
Staffordshire; SASE required when
requesting information

Levi, Anita
Allegheny Mountain Antique Gallery
5151 Clear Shade Dr., Windber,
15963; 814-467-8539. Specializing in
novelty clocks, advertising tins,
primitives, holiday decorations,
quilts, purses, Black memorabilia,
linens, stoneware, Roseville, kitchenware, Art Deco

Lindsay, Ralph
P.O. Box 21, New Holland, 17557.
Specializing in target balls. SASE
required with correspondence

Lowe, James Lewis
Kate Greenaway Society
P.O. Box 8, Norwood, 19074; E-mail:
JLewisLowe@juno.com. Specializing
in Kate Greenaway

Maier, Clarence and Betty
Mail order: The Burmese Cruet
Box 432, Montgomeryville, 18936;
215-855-5388. Specializing in Victorian art glass

Marks, Mariann Katz
1416 Main, Honesdale, 18431.
Author (Collector Books) of *Majolica Pottery, Second Series*; Specializing in collecting, buying, and selling
American and English majolica of
the Victorian period; LSASE
required for mail-order list; Enclose
photo and price wanted with offers
to sell

Merchants Square Mall
Jim & Annetta Vitez, Managers
1901 S. 12th St., Allentown, 18103;
610-797-7743

Oster, Frederick
Frederick W. Oster Fine Violins
1529 Pine St., Philadelphia, 19102;
215-545-1100 or (Fax) 215-735-
3634. Specializing in rare and
antique instruments of the violin
family, as well as antique stringed
and wind instruments

Posner, Judy
May-October: R.D. 1, Box 273SC, Effort, 18330; 717-629-6583 or November-April: 4195 S. Tamiami Trail, #183SC, Venice, FL 34293; 941-497-7149. Specializing in figural pottery, salt and peppers, Black memorabilia, Disneyana, character and advertising collectibles, cookie jars. E-mail: Judyandjef@aol.com. Buy, Sell & Collect; Appraisals: $25

Rosso, Philip J. and Philip Jr.
Wholesale Glass Dealers
1815 Trimble Ave., Port Vue, 15133; 412-678-7352. Specializing in Westmoreland glass

Weiser, Pastor Frederick S.
55 Kohler School Rd., New Oxford, 17350; 717-624-4106. Specializing in frakturs and other Pennsylvania German documents

Rhode Island

Dumont, Louise
579 Old Main St., Coventry, 02816; Alternative address: 319 Hawthorne Blvd, Leesburg, FL 34748. Specializing in cookie jars, Abingdon

Gacher, John
The Zsolnay Store
152 Spring St., Newport, 02840; 401-841-5060. Specializing in Zsolnay, Fischer, Amphora, and Austro-Hungarian art pottery; E-mail: http://www.drawrm.com

The Occupied Japan Club
c/o Florence Archambault
29 Freeborn St., Newport, 02840-1821. Publishes bimonthly newsletter, *The Upside Down World of an O.J. Collector;* SASE required when requesting information

South Carolina

Roerig, Fred and Joyce
R.R. 2, Box 504, Walterboro, 29488; 803-538-2487. Specializing in cookie jars; Authors of *Collector's Encyclopedia of Cookie Jars, an Illustrated Value Guide,* publishers of *Cookie Jarrin' with Joyce: The Cookie Jar Newsletter*

Tennessee

Chase, Mick and Lorna
Fiesta Plus
380 Hawkins Crawford Rd., Cookeville, 38501; 615-372-8333. Specializing in Fiesta, Harlequin, Riviera, Franciscan, Metlox, other American dinnerware

Grist, Everett
P.O. Box 91375, Chattanooga, 37412-3955; 423-510-8052. Specializing in covered animal dishes and marbles

Hudson, Murray
Murray Hudson Antiquarian Books & Maps
109 S. Church St., Box 163, Halls, 38040; 901-836-9057 or 800-748-9946; Fax: 901-836-9017. Specializing in antique maps, globes and books with maps, atlases, explorations, travel guides, geographies, surveys, etc.

Weddington, David
Predicta Sales
2702 Albany Ct.; Murfreesboro, TN 37129; 615-890-7498. Specializing in vintage Philco Predicta TVs

Texas

Babcock, Bobby
Jubilation Antiques
11109 Barrington Way, Austin, 78759; 512-258-2272. Specializing in Maxfield Parrish, Black memorabilia, and brown Roseville Pine Cone

Cooper, Marilyn
8408 Lofland Dr., Houston, 77055; 713-465-7773. Specializing in figural toothbrush holders, Pez, candy containers

Dockery, Rod
4600 Kemble St., Ft. Worth, 76103; 817-536-2168. Specializing in milk glass; SASE required with correspondence

Docks, L.R. 'Les'
Shellac Shack; Discollector
Box 691035, San Antonio, 78269-1035. Author of *American Premium Record Guide.* Specializing in vintage records

Frese, Leo and Wendy
Three Rivers Collectibles
Box 551542, Dallas, 75355; 214-341-5165. Specializing in RumRill, Red Wing pottery and stoneware

Gaston, Mary Frank
Box 342, Bryan, 77806. Author (Collector Books) on china and metals

Gibbs, Carl, Jr.
P.O. Box 131584, Houston, 77219-1584; 713-521-9661. Author of *Collector's Encyclopedia of Metlox Potteries,* autographed copies available from author for $24.95 plus $3 shipping and handling; Specializing in American ceramic dinnerware

Groves, Bonnie
402 North Ave. A, Elgin, 78621. Specializing in boudoir dolls

Horn, Glen
2016 Main, #2211, Houston, 77002. Specializing in Old Ivory dinnerware

Malowanczyk, Abby and Wlodek
Collage-20th Century Classics
3017-B Routh St., Dallas, 75201; 214-880-0020 or (Fax) 214-351-6208. Specializing in architect-designed furniture and decorative arts from the modern movement

Norris, Kenn
Schoolmaster Auctions
P.O. Box 4830, 513 N. 2nd St., Sanderson, 79848; 915-345-2640. Specializing in school-related items, barbed wire, related literature, and L'il Abner

Pringle, Joyce M.
Antiques and Moore
3708 W. Pioneer Pkwy., Arlington, 76013. Specializing in Boyd, Summit, and Mosser glass

Silvermintz, Karen
6164 Ravendale Lane, Dallas, 75214; 214-826-1107. Specializing in American dinnerware

Smith, Allan
1806 Shields Dr., Sherman, 75092; 903-893-3626. Specializing in children's lunch boxes, Coca-Cola, Dr. Pepper, Pepsi Cola, RC Cola, and western stars' items

Thompson, Chuck
Chuck Thompson & Associates
10802 Greencreek Dr., Suite 703, Houston, 77070. Send LSASE for free list of Chuck's tobacciana publications; Thompson specializes in smokers' ashtrays with and without advertising imprints. His research includes ashtrays designed for homes, automobiles, ocean liners, hotels, trains, and any place where 'ash receivers' were provided to accommodate smokers

Tucker, Richard and Valerie
Argyle Antiques
P.O. Box 262, Argyle, 76226; 817-464-3752. Specializing in windmill weights, shooting gallery targets, figural lawn sprinklers, cast-iron advertising paperweights, unusual figural cast iron. E-mail: millwt@pop.intex.net

Turner, Danny and Gretchen
Running Rabbit Video Auctions
P.O. Box 701, Waverly, 37185; 615-296-3600. Specializing in marbles

Waddell, John
2903 Stan Terrace, Mineral Wells, 76067. Specializing in buggy steps

Wilkins, James R.
Olden Year Musical Museum
Box 381951, Duncanville, 75138-1951; 972-298-5587. Specializing in music boxes, phonographs, grind organs, nickelodeons

Woodard, Dannie
The Aluminist
P.O. Box 1347, Weatherford, 76086; 817-594-4680. 6 issues per year; Back issues or sample copy: $2 each

Utah

Anderson, Tim
Box 461, Provo, 84603. Specializing in autographs; Buys single items or collections — historical, movie stars, US Presidents, sports figures, and pre-1860 correspondence. Autograph questions? Please include photocopies of your autographs if possible and enclose a SASE for guaranteed reply

Anderson, Warren R.
America West Archives
P.O. Box 100, Cedar City, 84721; 801-586-9497. Specializing in old stock certificates and bonds, western documents and books, financial ephemera, autographs, maps, photos; Author of *Owning Western History,* with 75+ photos of old documents and recommended reference guide (available for $18 soft cover or $28 hardback, postpaid, from author)

Spencer, Rick
Salt Lake City, 801-973-0805. Specializing in silverware, Old McDonald by Regal, Shawnee, Van Telligen, salt and pepper shakers. No free appraisals

Vermont

Barry, Kit
68 High St., Brattleboro, 05301; 802-254-3634. Author of *Reflections 1* and *Reflections 2.* Specializing in advertising trade cards and ephemera in general

Marie Miller's American Quilts
P.O. 968, Dorset, 05251; 802-867-5969

Virginia

Bradfield, Jeff
Jeff's Antiques
90 Main St., Dayton, 22821; 540-879-9961. Also located in Pat's Antique Mall (I-81), Exit 227, Verona, and Rolling Hills Antique Mall, I-81, Exit 247B, Harrisburg. Specializing in candy containers, toys, postcards, sugar shakers, lamps, furniture, pottery, and advertising items

Cranor, Rosalind
P.O. Box 859, Blacksburg, 24063. Specializing in Elvis collectibles; Author of *Elvis Collectibles* and *Best of Elvis Collectibles,* currently available from author for $19.95+$1.75 postage each

Flanigan, Vicki
Flanigan's Antiques
P.O. Box 1662, Winchester, 22604. Specializing in antique dolls and hand fans

Friend, Terry
839 Glendale Rd., Galax, 24333; 540-236-9027 after 9:30 p.m. E.S.T. Specializing in coffee mills; SASE required

Haigh, Richard
10607 Baypines Lane, Richmond, 23233; 804-741-5770. Specializing in Locke Art, Steuben

Lechner, Mildred and Ralph
Box 554, Mechanicsville, 23111; 804-737-3347. Author (Collector Books) on glass salt shakers; Specializing in art and pattern glass salt shakers circa 1870-1940; Directors of Antique and Art Glass Salt Shakers Collectors Society Club, 1991-92; **Please note:** Mildred and Ralph have absolutely **NO** involvement or dealings concerning novelty salt shakers or their values

MacAllister, Dale
P.O. Box 46, Singers Glen, 22850. Specializing in sugar shakers and syrups

Monsen, Randall; and Baer, Rod
Monsen & Baer
Box 529, Vienna, 22183; 703-242-1357. Specializing in perfume bottles, Roseville pottery, Art Deco

Reynolds, Charles
Reynolds Toys
2836 Monroe St., Falls Church, 22042; 703-533-1322. Specializing in limited-edition mechanical and still banks, figural bottle openers

Schleyer, Jim
Box 243-W, Burke, 22015. Former editor for Toy Gun Perveyors, an international newsletter that fostered the collecting of these valuable and rare toys; Author of *Backyard Buckaroos — Collecting Western Toy Guns*, which contains nearly 2,500 photographs. Toy gun inquires that include a SASE will be graciously answered

Travis, Leon
Goofus Glass Gazette
9 Lindenwood Ct., Sterling, 20165. Specializing in Goofus glass

Tutton, John
1967 Ridgway Rd., Front Royal, 22630; 540-635-7058. Specializing in milk bottles

Windsor, Grant S.
P.O. Box 3613, Richmond, 23235-7613; 804-320-0386. Specializing in Griswold cast-iron cookware

---

Washington

Frost, Donald M.
Country Estate Antiques (Appointment only)
14800 N.E. 8th St., Vancouver, 98684; 360-604-8434. Specializing in art glass and earlier 20th-century American glass

Haase, Don (Mr. Spode)
D&D Antiques
P.O. Box 818, Mukilteo, 98275; 425-348-7443. Specializing in Spode-Copeland China; E-mail: mrspode@aol.com or mrspode@msn.com

Jackson, Denis C., Editor
The Illustrator Collector's News
P.O. Box 1958, Sequim, 98382; 206-683-2559. Copy of recent sample: $3. Specializing in old magazines & illustrations such as: Rose O'Neill, Maxfield Parrish, pinups, Marilyn Monroe, Norman Rockwell, etc.

Moore, Bill and Marilyn
Mukilteo, 296-290-9055, Specializing in ruby-stained glass

Payne, Sharon A.
Antiquities & Art
9104 163rd Ave. NE, Granite Falls, 98252; 360-691-4847. Specializing in Cordey

Rothe, Linda
10020A, Main St. #422, Bellevue, 98004. Specializing in Black Americana

Weldin, Bob
Miner's Quest
W. 3015 Weile, Spokane, WA 99208; 509-327-2897. Specializing in mining antiques and collectibles (mail-order business)

Wheeler-Tanner Escapes
Tanner, Joseph and Pamela
3024 E. 35th Ave., Spokane, 99223; 509-448-8457. Specializing in handcuffs, leg shackles, balls and chains, restraints and padlocks of all kinds (including railroad) locking and non-locking devices; Also Houdini memorabilia: autographs, photos, posters, books, letters, etc.

Whitaker, Jim and Kaye
Eclectic Antiques
P.O. Box 475 Dept. S, Lynnwood, 98046. Specializing in Josef Originals and motion lamps; SASE required

---

West Virginia

Fostoria Glass Society of America, Inc.
Box 826, Moundsville, 26041. Specializing in Fostoria glass

Wisconsin

Apple, John
John Apple Antiques
1720 College Ave., Racine, 53403; 414-633-3086. Specializing in brass cash registers and parts

Helley, Phil
Old Kilbourne Antiques
629 Indiana Ave., Wisconsin Dells, 53965; 608-254-8770. Specializing in premiums, German and Japan tin toys, Cracker Jack, toothbrush holders, radio premiums, pencil sharpeners and comic strip toys

Knapper, Mary
Phoneco, Inc.
207 E. Mill Rd., P.O. Box 70, Galesville, 54630; 608-582-4124. Specializing in telephones, antique to modern

Matzke, Gene
Gene's Badges & Emblems
2345 S. 28th St., Milwaukee, 53215; 414-383-8995. Specializing in police badges, leg irons, old police photos, fire badges (old), patches, old handcuffs, and memorabilia

Rice, Ferill J.
302 Pheasant Run, Kaukauna, 54130. Specializing in Fenton art glass

Washburn, Cara
Washburn Antiques
N. 8527 Lakeside Rd., Willard, 54493; 715-267-7322 (M-F). Specializing in glass

Clubs, Newsletters, and Catalogs

Abingdon Pottery Collectors Club
Elaine Westover, Membership and
   Treasurer
210 Knox Hwy. 5, Abingdon, IL
61410; 309-462-3267. Specializing in
collecting and preservation of Abingdon pottery

ABC Collectors' Circle (Quarterly
   newsletter)
Dr. Joan M. George
67 Stevens Ave., Old Bridge, NJ
08857. Specializing in ABC plates
and mugs

Akro Agate Collectors Club and
   Clarksburg Crow Newsletter
Roger Hardy
10 Bailey St., Clarksburg, WV 26301-
2524; 304-624-4523 (evenings) or West
End Antiques, 97 Milford St., Clarksburg, WV 26301; 304-624-7600 (week
days). Annual membership fee: $20

The Akro Arsenal quarterly catalog
Larry D. Wells
6301 Walnut Valley Dr., Ft. Wayne,
IN 46818; 219-489-5842

The Aluminist
Dannie Woodard, Publisher
P.O. Box 1346, Weatherford, TX
76086. Subscription: $12 (for 6 issues)

America West Archives
Anderson, Warren
P.O. Box 100, Cedar City, UT 84721;
801-586-9497. 26-page illustrated catalogs issued 6 times a year; Has both
fixed-price and auction sections offering early western documents, letters,
stock certificates, autographs, and
other important ephemera; Subscription: $15 per year

American Antique Deck Collectors
52 Plus Joker Club
Clear the Decks, quarterly publication
Ray Hartz, Past President
P.O. Box 1002, Westerville, OH
43081; 614-891-6296.
Rhonda Hawes, Membership
204 Gorham Ave., Hamden, CT
06514 ($25 in U.S. and Canada, $35
foreign). Specializing in antique playing cards

American Bell Association, Int., Inc.
c/o The Bell Tower
P.O. Box 19443, Indianapolis, IN
46219. Dorothy Malone Anthony,
Past President

American Hatpin Society
Virginia Woodbury, President
20 Montecillo, Rolling Hills Estates,
CA 90274; 310-326-2196. Newsletter
published quarterly; Meetings also
quarterly

Antique and Art Glass Salt Shaker Collectors' Society (AAGSSCS)
7317 Hallbrook Rd., Knoxville, TN
37918-9448

Antique & Collectors Reproduction
   News
Antiques Coast to Coast
c/o Lorna Bambrook
Box 71174, Des Moines, IA 50325;
515-270-8994 or (subscriptions only)
800-227-5531. Monthly newsletter,
subscription: $32 per year in US; $41
in Canada.

Antique Advertising Association of
   America (AAAA)
P.O. Box 1121, Morton Grove, IL
60053; 708-466-0904. Publishes *Past
Times* Newsletter; Subscription: $35

Antique Bottle & Glass Collector Magazine
Jim Hagenbuch, Publisher
102 Jefferson St., P.O. Box 180, East
Greenville, PA 18041. Published
monthly for $3 per copy and $19
annual subscription ($22 in Canada)

Antique Bowie Knife Collectors Assn.
Roger Baker, Member
Box 620417, Woodside, CA 94062

Antique Comb Collectors Club International
Antique Comb Collector Newsletter
Belva Green, Editor
3748 Sunray Dr., Holiday, FL 34691-
3239; 813-942-7554

Antique Journal
Michael F. Shores, Publisher; Jeffrey
Hill, Editor/General Manager
1684 Decoto Road, Suite #166,
Union City, CA 50191-8592

Antique Purses Catalog: $4
Bayhouse
P.O. Box 40443, Cleveland, OH
44140; 216-871-8584. Includes colored photos of beaded and enameled
mesh purses.

Antique Souvenir Collectors' News
Gary Leveille, Editor
P.O. Box 562, Great Barrington, MA
01230

Antique Stove Association
Clifford Boram, Secretary
417 N. Main St., Monticello, IN 47960.
Inquiries should be accompanied by
SASE and marked 'Urgent' in red

Antique Telephone Collectors Association
Box 94, Abilene, KS 67410; 913-263-
1757. An international organization
associated with the Museum of Independent Telephony

Antique Trader Weekly
Julie Hoppensteadt, Editor
P.O. Box 1050, Dubuque, IA
52004-1050. Featuring news about
antiques and collectibles, auctions
and events; Listing over 165,000
buyers and sellers in every edition;
Subscription: $32 (52 issues) per
year; Toll free for subscriptions
only: 800-334-7165

Antique Wireless Association
Ormiston Rd., Breesport, NY 14816

Appraisers National Association
120 S. Bradford Ave., Placentia,
CA 92670; 714-579-1082. Founded
in 1982 by Dr. David Long, Ph.D.,
President of the College for
Appraisers, to provide for a stan-
dardization of educational require-
ments for certification of its
appraiser members and assure the
public that A.N.A. appraisers not
only have a broad range of knowledge in personal property valuation, but are held to the highest
ethical and professional standards
in the industry

Alex G. Malloy, Inc.
P.O. Box 38, South Salem, NY
10590; 203-438-0396. Specialized
catalogs on antiquities, and ancient
and medieval coins

Arkansas Pottery Collectors' Society
P.O. Box 7617, Little Rock, AR 72217

Arts & Crafts Quarterly/Style: 1900
17 S. Main St., Lambertville, NJ
08530; 609-397-9374

Ashtray Collectors Directory
Chuck Thompson
10802 Greencreek Dr., Suite 703,
Houston, TX 77070. Annual publication listing all known ashtray collectors with addresses and specialties,
$9.95 postage paid

Association of Coffee Mill Enthusiasts
c/o John E. White, Treasurer
5941 Wilkerson Road, Rex, GA
30273. Annual dues: $30, covers
cost of quarterly newsletter and
copy of membership roster

Autograph Times
2303 N. 44th St., #225, Phoenix AZ
85008; 602-947-3112 or (Fax) 602-
947-8363. Subscription: $15 (U.S.)
per year

Autographs of America
Tim Anderson
P.O. Box 461, Provo, UT 84603; 801-
226-1787 (please call in the afternoon). Free sample catalog of
hundreds of autographs for sale

Avon Times (National Newsletter Club)
c/o Dwight or Vera Young
P.O. Box 9868, Dept P., Kansas City,
MO 64134. Inquiries should be
accompanied by large SASE

Beatlefan
P.O. Box 33515, Decatur, GA 30033.
Subscription: $15 (U.S.) for 6 issues
or $18 (Canada and Mexico)

The Beer Stein Journal
Gary Kirsner, Publisher
P.O. Box 8807, Coral Springs, FL
33075; 305-344-9856 or (Fax) 305-
344-4421. Published quarterly; Subscriptions $20 per year in USA

Black Memorabilia Illustrated Sales
   List
Judy Posner
May-October: R.D. 1, Box 273 SC,
Effort, PA 18330; 717-629-6583 or
November-April: 4195 S. Tamiami Trail,
#183SC, Venice, FL 34293; 941-497-
7149; Send $2 and LSASE. Buy-Sell-
Collect; E-mail: Judyandjef@aol.com
URL: http://www.tias.com/stores/jpc

Bojo
P.O. Box 1403, Cranberry Township,
PA 16066. Send $3 for 28 pages of
Beatles, toys, dolls, jewelry, auto-
graphs, Yellow Submarine items, etc.

Boyd's Art Glass Collectors Guild
P.O. Box 52, Hatboro, PA 19040-0052

Boyd's Crystal Art Glass
*Jody & Darrell's Glass Collectibles
   Newsletter*
P.O. Box 180833, Arlington, TX
76096-0833. Publishes 6 times a year.
Subscription includes an exclusive
glass collectible produced by Boyd's
Crystal Art Glass. LSASE for current
subscription rates. Sample copy of
newsletter: $3

British Royal Commemorative Souvenirs Mail Order Catalog
Audrey Zeder
6755 Coralite St. S, Long Beach, CA
90808

Buckeye Marble Collectors Club
437 Meadowbrook Dr., Newark, OH
43055

The Buttonhook Society
Box 287, White Marsh, MD 21162.
Publishes bimonthly newsletter *The Boutonneur*, which promotes collecting of buttonhooks and shares research and information contributed by members

California Perfume Company
For information contact Dick Pardini
3107 North El Dorado St., Dept. SAPG, Stockton, CA 95204-3412. Information requires large SASE; not necessary when offering items for sale

Candy Container Collectors of America
P.O. Box 352, Chelmsord, MA 01824-0352
Or contact: Jeff Bradfield
90 Main St., Dayton, VA 22821

The Cane Collector's Chronicle
Linda Beeman
15 2nd St. N.E., Washington, D.C. 20002; $30 for 4 issues

The Carnival Pump
International Carnival Glass Assoc., Inc.
Lee Markley
Box 306, Mentone, IN 46539. Dues: $15 per family per year payable each July 1st

The Carousel News & Trader
87 Parke Ave. W., Suite 206, Mansfield, OH 44902. A monthly magazine for the carousel enthusiast. Subscription: $22 per year; Sample: $3

The Carousel Shopper Resource Catalog
Box 47, Dept PC, Millwood, NY 10546. Only $2 (+50¢ postage); A full-color catalog featuring dealers of antique carousel art offering single figures or complete carousels, museums, restoration services, organizations, full-size reproductions, books, cards, posters, auction services and other hard-to-find items for carousel enthusiasts

Central Florida Insulator Collectors
557 Nicklaus Dr., Titusville, FL 32780

Ceramic Arts Studio Collector's Association
P.O. Box 46, Madison, WI 53701; 608-241-9138. Publishes newsletter, *CAS Collector*, a 22-page bimonthly; Annual membership: $15; Sample copy: $3; Inventory record and price guide also available

Character and Advertising Collectibles Illustrated Sales List
Judy Posner
May-October: R.D. 1, Box 273SC, Effort, PA 18330; 717-629-6583, or November-April: 419 S. Tamiami Trail, #183SC, Venice, FL 34293; 941-497-7149; E-mail: Judyandjef@aol.com
Internet: http://www.tias.com/stores/jpc
Send $2 and LSASE. Buy-Sell-Collect

Chase Collectors Society
c/o Barry L. Van Hook
2149 W. Jibsail Loop, Mesa, AZ 85202-5524; 602-838-6971. Publishes newsletter *Art Deco Reflections*, Membership: $10, Sample copy of newsletter: $1

Chicagoland Antique Amusements Slot Machine & Jukebox Gazette
Ken Durham, Editor
909 26 St., N.W., Suite 502, Washington, DC 20037. 20-page newspaper published twice a year; Subscription: 4 issues for $10; Sample: $5; Send SASE for free list of books; http://www.GameRoomAntiques.com

Chintz Connection Newsletter
P.O. Box 222, Riverdale, MD 20738. Dedicated to helping collectors share information and find matchings; Subscription: 4 issues per year for $25

Coin-Op Newsletter
Ken Durham, Publisher
909 26th St. N.W., Suite 502, Washington, D.C. 20037. Subscription: $15 per year; Sample: $5; Send SASE for free list of books; E-mail: http://www.GameRoomAntiques.com

The Cola Clan
Alice Fisher, Treasurer
2084 Continental Drive N.E., Atlanta, GA 30345

Collectors of Findlay Glass
P.O. Box 256, Findlay, OH 45840. An organization dedicated to the study and recognition of Findlay glass; Newsletter *The Melting Pot*, published quarterly; Convention held annually; Membership: $10 per year

The Compact Collectors Chronicles
Roselyn Gerson
P.O. Box S, Lynbrook, NY 11563. Publishes *Powder Puff* Newsletter, which contains articles covering all aspects of compact collecting, restoration, vintage ads, patents, history, and articles by members and prominent guest writers; Seeker and sellers column offered free to members

Cookie Crumbs
Cookie Cutter Collectors Club
Ruth Capper, Secretary/Treasurer
1167 Teal Road S.W., Dellroy, OH 44620. Subscription $12 per year (4 issues); Payable to CCCC

Cookie Jars and Go Withs Illustrated Sales List
Judy Posner
May-October: R.D. 1, Box 273SC, Effort, PA 18330; 717-629-6583 or November-April: 4195 S. Tamiami Trail, #183SC, Venice, FL 34293; 941-497-7149. E-mail: Judyandjef@aol.com
Internet: http://www.tias.com/stores/jpc
$2 and LSASE; Buy-Sell-Collect

Cookie Jarrin' With Joyce: The Cookie Jar Newsletter
R.R. 2, Box 504, Walterboro, SC 29488

Cookies
Rosemary Henry
9610 Greenview Lane, Manassas, VA 20109-3320. Subscription: $12 per year (6 issues); Payable to Cookies

The Copley Courier
1639 N. Catalina St., Burbank, CA 91505

Cracker Jack® Collector's Assoc.
The Prize Insider Newsletter
Larry White
108 Central St., Rowley, MA 01969; 508-948-8187. Subscription: $18 per year or $24 per year for family membership

Creamers Newsletter
P.O. Box 11, Lake Villa, IL 60046-0011. Subscription: $5 per year (issued quarterly)

Currier & Ives Catalog
Rudisill's Alt Print Haus
P.O. Box 199, Worton, MD 21678. Please include LSASE

Currier & Ives China by Royal Newsletters
c/o Jack and Treva Hamlin
R.R. 4, Box 150, Kaiser St., Proctorville, OH 45669; 614-886-7644. 2 different newsletters and book soon to be available

Currier & Ives Quarterly Newsletter
c/o Patti Street
P.O. Box 504, Riverton, KS 66770; 316-848-3529. Subscription: $12 per year (includes 2 free ads)

Czechoslovakian Collectors Guild International
P.O. Box 901395, Kansas City, MO 64190

The Dedham Pottery Collectors Society Newsletter
Jim Kaufman, Publisher
248 Highland St., Dedham, MA 02026; 800-283-8070. Subscription $18 per year (issued quarterly)

Depression Glass Daze
Teri Steel, Editor/Publisher
Box 57, Otisville, MI 48463; 810-631-4593. The nation's market place for glass, china, and pottery

Disneyana Illustrated Sales List
Judy Posner
May-October: R.D. 1, Box 273SC, Effort, PA 18330; 717-629-6583, or November-April: 4195 S. Tamiami Trail, #183SC, Venice, FL 34293; 941-497-7149. E-mail: Judyandjef@aol.com
Internet: http://www.tias.com/stores/jpc
Send $2 and LSASE. Buy-Sell-Collect

Docks, L.R. 'Les'
Shellac Shack
Box 691035, San Antonio, TX 78269-1035. Send $2 for a 72-page catalog of 78s that Docks wants to buy, the prices he will pay, and shipping instructions

Doorstop Collectors of America
Doorstopper Newsletter
Jeanie Bertoia
2413 Madison Ave., Vineland, NJ 08630; 609-692-4092. Membership: $20 per year, includes 2 newsletters and convention; Send 2-stamp SASE for sample

Dragonware Club
c/o Suzi Hibbard
2570 Walnut Blvd. #20, Walnut Creek, CA 94596; HMBK24A@Prodigy.com. Inquiries should be accompanied by long SASE; All contributions welcome

Drawing Room of Newport
Gacher, John
152 Spring St., Newport, RI 02840; 401-841-5060. Book on Zsolnay available; On the Web: http://www.drawrm.com

Eggcup Collector's Corner
67 Stevens Ave., Old Bridge, NJ 08857. Issued quarterly; Subscriptions: $18 per year (checks made out to Joan George). Sample copies: $5

The Elegance of Old Ivory Newsletter
Box 1004, Wilsonville, OR 97070

Fenton Art Glass Collectors of America, Inc.
Williamstown, WV 26187

Fiesta Club of America
P.O. Box 15383, Loves Park, IL, 61132-5383; 815-282-2585

Fiesta Collector's Quarterly Newsletter
19238 Dorchester Circle, Strongsville, OH 44136. Subscription: $12 per year

Figural Bottle Opener Collectors
c/o Nancy Robb
3 Avenue A, Latrobe, PA 15650. Please include SASE

Fire Mark Circle of Americas
Glen Hartley, Sr.
2859 Marlin Dr., Chamblee, GA 30341-5119; 404-451-2651. Specializing in fire marks, Methodist, Masonic, Foremost Dairies, Goodyear

Florence Collector's Club Newsletter
Rita Bee, Editor; Beth Dunigan, Publisher; c/o Florence Collector's Club Membership Chairman
P.O. Box 122, Richland, WA 99353. 6 issues per year for $20.

Fostoria Glass Society of America, Inc.
P.O. Box 826, Moundsville, WV 26041

Frankoma Family Collectors Association
c/o Nancy Littrell
P.O. Box 32571, Oklahoma City, OK 73123-0771. Membership dues: $25; Includes quarterly newsletter, annual convention

Friar Tuck Collectors Club
Bob Furman
P.O. Box 262, Oswego, NY 13827. Quarterly newsletter, annual convention, write for membership application and information

Friends of Degenhart
c/o Degenhart Museum
P.O. Box 186, Cambridge, OH 43725; 614-432-2626. Membership: $5 ($10 for family) includes *Heartbeat* Newsletter (printed quarterly) and free admission to museum

H.C. Fry Society
P.O. Box 41, Beaver, PA 15009. Founded in 1983 for the sole purpose of learning about Fry glass; Publishes *Shards*, quarterly newsletter

George Kamm Paperweights
106 River Bend Park, Lancaster, PA 17602; 717-259-7575 or (Fax) 717-295-7576. Specializing in antique and contemporary paperweights; Color brochure published bimonthly, $5 annual fee (refundable); Sample on request (requires #10 SASE)

GAB! (Glass Animal Bulletin!)
P.O. Box 143
N Liberty, IA 52317. Subscription: $16 for 12 monthly issues, ads free to subscribers

The Glass Post newsletter
P.O. Box 205, Oakdale, IA 52319; phone or FAX 319-626-3216. Issued monthly, subscription $25 per year, ads free to subscribers

The Glass Menagerie, bimonthly newsletter
Susan Candelaria, Editor
5440 El Arbol, Carlsbad, CA 92008

Goofus Glass Gazette
c/o Leon Travis
9 Lindenwood Ct., Sterling, VA 20165-5646. Subscription: $20 per year; Sample: $5

Gonder Pottery Collectors' Newsletter
c/o John and Marilyn McCormick
P.O. Box 3174, Shawnee, KS 66226

Glass Knife Collectors' Club
Adrienne Escoe
4448 Ironwood Ave. Seal Beach, CA 90740; 562-430-6479. SASE for information

Grandpa's Depot
John 'Grandpa' White
1616 17th St., Suite 267, Denver, CO 80202; 303-628-5590 or (Fax) 303-628-5547. Publishes catalogs on railroad-related collectibles

Griswold & Cast Iron Cookware Association
Grand Windsor P.O. Box 3613, Richmond, VA 23235; 804-320-0386. Membership: $10 payable to club ($5 initiation fee/$5 dues — per person)

Haeger Pottery Collectors of America
Lanette Clarke
5021 Toyon Way, Antioch, CA 94509; 510-776-7784. Monthly newsletter available

The Hagen-Renaker Collector's Club Newsletter
c/o Jenny Palmer
13975 Litzen Rd., Copemish, MI 49625. Subscription: $20 per year; Sample copy: $4

Hake's Americana & Collectibles
Specializing in character and personality collectibles along with artifacts of popular culture for over 20 years. To receive a catalog for their next 3,000-item mail/phone bid auction, send $3 to: Hake's Americana; P.O. Box 1444M, York, PA 17405

Hall China Collector's Club Newsletter
P.O. Box 360488
Cleveland, OH 44136

Head Hunters Newsletter
c/o Maddy Gordon
P.O. Box 83HScarsdale, NY 10583. Subscription: $20 yearly for 4 quarterly issues

Homer Laughlin Eagle
c/o Richard Racheter
1270 63rd Terrace South, St. Petersburg, FL 33705

How To Open and Operate a Home-Based Antiques Business; How To Recognize and Refinish Antiques for Pleasure and Profit
Jacquelyn Peake, author
Globe Pequot Press
P.O. Box 833, Old Saybrook, CT 06475 or any book store

Ice Screamer
c/o Duvall Sollers
P.O. Box 132, Monkton, MD 21111. Published bimonthly; Dues: $15 per year; Annual convention held in late June

The Illustrator Collector's News
Denis C. Jackson, Editor
P.O. Box 1958, Sequim, WA 98382; Fax 206-683-2559. Subscription: $17 per year; $3 for sample copy of bimonthly publication; Publishes price and identification guides on various illustrators and magazines, write for further information

Indiana Historical Radio Society
245 N. Oakland Ave., Indianapolis, IN 46201

International Association of Calculator Collectors, *International Calculator Collector* Newsletter
Guy Ball, Co-editor
P.O. Box 345, Tustin, CA 92781-0345; E-mail: mrcalc@usa.net. Subscription: $16 per year ($20 foreign); sample copy available by sending $3

International Association of R.S. Prussia, Inc.
Frances Coy, Secretary
212 Wooded Falls Rd., Louisville, KY 40243. Membership: $20 per household; Yearly convention

International Nippon Collectors Club (INCC)
c/o Phil Fernkes
112 Oak Ave N., Owatonna, MN 55060. Publishes newsletter 6 times a year; Holds annual convention

International Perfume and Scent Bottle Collectors Association
Randall B. Monsen, President
P.O. Box 529, Vienna, VA 22183 or (Fax) 703-242-1357. Membership: $35 (USA) or $48 (Foreign); Newsletter published quarterly

International Rose O'Neill Club
Contact Karen Stewart
P.O. Box 668, Branson, MO 65616. Publishes quarterly newsletter *Kewpiesta Kourier*. Dues: (includes newsletter) $7 (single) or $10 (family)

International Society of Antique Scale Collectors
Bob Stein, President
176 West Adams, Suite 1706, Chicago, IL 60603; 312-263-7500. Publishes *Equilibrium* Magazine; Quarterly President's Newsletter; Annual membership directory and out-of-print scale catalogs; Holds annual convention

Iron Talk
Jimmy Walker, Editor
P.O. Box 68, Waelder, TX 78959. Journal of antique pressing irons; News of prices, patents, markets, collectibles, collectors, history, reference, advice and much more; One-year bimonthly subscription: $25 in U.S. (Texans add $1.94 tax); $30 foreign

Josef Originals Newsletter
Jim and Kaye Whitaker
P.O. Box 475, Dept. S, Lynnwood, WA 98046. Subscription (4 issues): $10 per year

Kay Finch Collectors Club and Newsletter
Mike Nickel and Cindy Horvath, Editors
Box 456, Portland, MI 48875. Dues $25 per year, includes 4 issues of full-color newsletter and free ads

Kitchen Antiques & Collectibles News Newsletter
Kollectors of Old Kitchen Stuff
Dana & Darlene DeMore, Editors
4645 Laurel Ridge Dr., Harrisburg, PA 17110; 717-545-7320. Subscription: $24 per year for 6 issues of *Kitchen Antiques & Collectibles News*

The Lace Merchant
Elizabeth M. Kurella, Publisher
Box 222, Plainwell, MI 49080; 616-685-9792

The Lady's Gallery Color-glossy magazine of fashion, decorative arts, and collectibles. Subscription: $15.95 (U.S., 4 issues) per year; Call 800-622-5676 or 216-871-4479 for further information

The Laughlin Eagle
Joan Jasper, Publisher
Richard Racheter, Editor
1270 63rd Terrace S., St. Petersburg, FL 33705. Subscription: $14 (4 issues) per year; Sample: $4

License Plate Collectors Hobby Magazine
Drew Steitz, Editor
P.O. Box 222, East Texas, PA 18046; Phone or Fax 610-791-7979. Bimonthly publication with many photographs, classifieds, etc.; $18 pr year (1st class, U.S.); Sample: $2

Line Jewels, NIA #255
3557 Nicklaus Dr., Titusville, FL 32780.

Mabel Lucie Attwell Catalogs
J. David Ehrhard
7212 Valmont St., Tujunga, CA 91042

Majolica International Society
Suite #103, 1275 First Ave., New York, NY 10021. Dues: $30 per year, entitles member to attend annual meeting and to receive the quarterly newsletter *Majolica Matters*

Majolica Mail Order Catalog
Items from the collection of Mariann Katz Marks
P.O. Box 750, Honesdale, PA 18431. Please send LSASE for majolica listing

Marble Collectors' Society of America
Claire Block, Secretary
P.O. Box 222, Trumbull, CT 06611. Publishes *Marble Mania*; Gathers and disseminates information to further the hobby of marbles and marble collecting; $12 adds your name to the contributor mailing list ($21 covers 2 years)

Marble Collectors Unlimited
P.O. Box 206, Northboro, MA 01532

Mason's Ironstone Collectors Club
c/o Susan Hirshman
2011 E. Main St., Medford OR 97504; 541-608-9594. Membership: $25 per year (includes 6 newsletters)

Mid-West Open Salt Society
Dave Dillingham
2620 Middlebelt Rd., W. Bloomfield,
MI 48324

Mike's General Store
52 St. Anne's Rd., Winnepeg, Manitoba, Canada R2M 2Y3; 204-255-3464. Catalog subscription: $6 per issue or next 4 issues for $20

Miniature Bottle Club of the Great
Lakes
39145 Marne, Sterling Heights, MI
48313; 810-566-0891. Dues $5 per
year; 4 meetings per year

Morgantown Collectors of America
Jerry Gallagher
420 1st Ave. N.W., Plainview, MN
55964; 507-534-3511. *The Morgantown Newscaster*, triannual journal for research of Morgantown Glass only; affiliated with no club; Subscription: $18 per year; *Morgantown Colors* placard: $4 postpaid; *A Handbook of Old Morgantown Glass, Volume I*, (A Guide to Identification and Shape): 256 pages, includes 8 color plates, 1,800+ illustrations, and price guide, $35+$4 insured shipping and handling; Order autographed copies from the author at above address; SASE required for answers to queries

Mt. Washington Art Glass Society
P.O. Box 24094, Fort Worth, TX
76124-1094. Publishes *MWAGS Review*, to educate, inform and provide helpful information to anyone interested in art glass; Holds annual convention; Subscription/membership: $20 per individual or $25 for 2 persons in 1 household

Murray Hudson Antiquarian Books
and Maps
109 S. Church St., Box 163, Halls, TN
38040; 800-748-9946 or 901-836-9057;
Fax: 901-836-9017. Buyer and seller of antiquarian maps (especially pocket, wall, U.S. Civil War, and railroad maps) and books with maps (atlases, travel guides, geographies, gazetteers, explorations, land surveys, etc.), especially of Southeastern and Southwestern U.S. prior to 1900; Also world globes, map jigsaw puzzles and gameboards prior to 1950; Contact for catalog

Mystic Lights of the Aladdin Knights
Newsletter
c/o J.W. Courter; 3935 Kelley Rd.,
Kevil, KY 40253; 502-488-2116. Information requires LSASE

National Association of Avon Collectors
c/o Connie Clark
6100 Walnut, Dept. P, Kansas City, MO
64113. Information requires large SASE

National Association Breweriana
Advertising
2343 Met-To-Wee Lane, Wauwatosa,
WI 53226; 414-257-0158. Membership: $20 (U.S.), $30 (Canada) or $40 (Overseas); Publishes *The Breweriana Collector* and Membership Directory; Holds annual convention

National Association of Watch &
Clock Collectors, Inc. (NAWCC)
514 Poplar St., Columbia, PA 17512-2130 (Headquarters, Museum, Library). Featured on national live FX Collector's program 1/24/96; Information/membership application available; Dues $40 per year, $50 outside U.S.; Benefits include subscriptions to 2 publications

National Association of Miniature
Enthusiasts (N.A.M.E.)
Box 2621, Anaheim, CA 92804-0621;
714-871-NAME

National Autumn Leaf Collectors' Club
c/o Gwynne Harrison
P.O. Box 1, Mira Loma, CA 91752-0001; 909-685-5434

National Blue Ridge Newsletter
Norma Lilly
144 Highland Dr., Blountville, TN 37617.
Subscription: $15 per year (6 issues)

National Cambridge Collectors, Inc.
P.O. Box 416, Cambridge, OH 43725

National Depression Glass Association
Anita Woods
P.O. Box 69843, Odessa, TX 79769;
915-337-1297. Publishes *News and Views*

National Graniteware Society
P.O. Box 10013, Cedar Rapids, IA 52410

National Greentown Glass Association
1807 W. Madison, Kokomo, IN 46901

National Imperial Glass Collectors'
Society, Inc.
P.O. Box 534, Bellaire, OH 43906.
Dues: $15 per year (+$1 for each additional member of household); Quarterly newsletter; Convention every June

National Insulator Association
1315 Old Mill Path, Broadview
Heights, OH 44147

National Milk Glass Collectors' Society
and *Opaque News*, quarterly newsletter
c/o Helen D. Storey
46 Almond Dr., Cocoa Townes, Hershey, PA 17033. Please include SASE

National Reamer Association
c/o Debbie Gillham
47 Midline Ct., Gaithersburg, MD 20878

National Shaving Mug Collectors
Association
Penelope G. Nader, Treasurer
320 S. Greenwood St, Allerton, PA
18104; 610-437-2534. To stimulate the study, collection and preservation of shaving mugs and all related barbering items; Provides quarterly newsletter, bibliography, and directory; Holds 2 meetings per year; Dues: $15 per year

National Society of Arkansas Pottery
Collectors
P.O. Box 7617, Little Rock, AR 72217.
Quarterly Newsletter dealing with Arkansas' three early pottery companies (Ouachita, Niloak, and Camark). Membership: $20 per year

National Society of Lefton Collectors
c/o Loretta DeLozier
1101 Polk St., Bedford, IA 50833;
712-523-2289 (Mon. - Fri. 9:00 a.m. - 4:00 p.m.). Quarterly newsletter, annual convention; Dues: $25 per year

National Toothpick Holder Collectors Society
Toby Shugart, Membership
P.O. Box 417, Safety Harbor, FL
34695-0417. Dues: $15 (single) or $20 (couple) per year (includes bimonthly *Toothpick Bulletin;*) Annual convention held in August; Exclusive toothpick holder annually

National Valentine Collectors Association
Evalene Pulati
P.O. Box 1404, Santa Ana, CA
92702; 714-547-1355. Specializing in Valentines and love tokens

The Nelson McCoy Express
Carol Seman
7670 Chippewa Rd., Ste. 406,
Brecksville, OH 44141-2320

New England Society of Open Salt
Collectors
Chuck Keys
21 Overbrook Lane, East Greenwich,
RI 02818. Dues: $7 per year

New York Decorative Ceramic Society
17 S. Main St., Lambertville, NJ
08530. Meetings held 4-6 times a year in New York and New Jersey, at museums, galleries, and collectors' homes

Newspaper Collector's Society of America
Rick Brown
Box 19134-S, Lansing, MI 48901;
517-887-1255 or (Fax) 517-887-2194

North American Torquay Society
Jerry and Gerry Kline, Archivists
604 Orchard View Dr., Maumee, OH
43537. Quarterly newsletter sent to members; Information and membership form requires #10 SASE

North American Trap Collectors'
Association
c/o Tom Parr
P.O. Box 94, Galloway, OH 43119-0094. Dues: $15 per year; Publishes bimonthly newsletter

Nutcracker Collectors' Club and
Newsletter
Susan Otto, Editor
12204 Fox Run Dr., Chesterland,
OH 44026. $10 for membership and quarterly newsletters, free classifieds for members

The Occupied Japan Club
c/o Florence Archambault
29 Freeborn St., Newport, RI 02840-1821. Publishes *The Upside Down World of an O.J. Collector,* a bimonthly newsletter. Information requires SASE

Old Sleepy Eye Collectors Club of
America, Inc.
P.O. Box 12, Monmouth, IL 61462.
Membership: $10 per year with additional $1 for spouse (if joining)

Old Stuff
Donna and Ron Miller, Publishers
336 N. Davis, P.O. Box 1084,
McMinnville, OR 97128. Published 6 times annually; Copies by mail: $3 each; Annual subscription: $12 ($20 in Canada)

On the LIGHTER Side Newsletter
(bimonthly publication)
International Lighter Collectors
Judith Sanders, Editor
136 Circle Dr., Quitman, TX 75783;
903-763-2795 or (Fax) 903-763-4953.
Annual convention held in different cities in the US; Subscription fees: Overseas rate, U.S. and Canada rate, and a Junior and Senior Citizen rate. Please include SASE when requesting information

Open Salt Collectors of the Atlantic
Regions (O.S.C.A.R.)
Lee Anne Gommer, Secretary
56 Northview Dr., Lancaster, PA,
17601. Dues: $10 per year

Open Salt Seekers of the West,
Northern California Chapter
Sara Conley
84 Margaret Dr., Walnut Creek, CA
94596. Dues: $7.50 per year

Open Salt Seekers of the West,
Southern California Chapter
Janet Hudson
2525 E. Vassar Court, Visalia, CA
93292. Dues: $5 per year

Pacific Northwest Fenton Assoc.
8225 Kilchis River Rd., Tillamook,
OR 97141; 503-842-4815. Newsletter subscription: $20 per year (published quarterly, includes annual piece of glass made only for subscribers)

Paper Collectors' Marketplace
P.O. Box 128, Scandinavia, WI 54977-0128; 715-467-2379 or (Fax) 715-467-2243 (8:00 a.m. to 5:00 p.m. Mon. - Fri.). Subscription: $19.95 per year in U.S. (12 issues)

Paper Pile Quarterly Magazine
Ada Fitzsimmons, Editor
P.O. Box 337, San Anselmo, CA 94979; 619-322-3525. Sales and features magazine serving paper collectors and dealers since 1980, quarterly cataloged sales, large advertising section. Subscription: $17 per year (shipped 1st class)

Paperweight Collectors' Association, Inc.
P.O. Box 1263, Beltsville, MD 20704; 410-828-5722. Membership: $15 per person or $25 per couple; Publishes 5 newsletters a year; Biannual conventions to promote and study paperweights; Annual bulletin not included with dues

Peanut Pals
Robert Walthall, President
P.O. Box 4465, Huntsville, AL 35815; 205-881-9198. Associated collectors of Planters Peanuts memorabilia, bimonthly newsletter *Peanut Papers*; Annual directory sent to members; Annual convention and regional conventions; Dues: $20 per year (+$3 for each additional household member); Membership information: P.O. Box 652, St. Clairsville, OH, 43950. Sample newsletter: $2

Pen Collectors of America
P.O. Box 821449, Houston, TX 77282-1449; Phone/Fax: 713-496-2290. Published quarterly newsletter, *Pennant*; Annual membership fee: $25 (Includes publication and access to extensive reference library)

Pen Fancier's Club
1169 Overcash Dr., Dunedin, FL 34698. Publishes bimonthly catalog of vintage pens and mechanical pencils, books, parts, and information; Subscription: $20 per year; Sample: $4

Pepsi-Cola Collectors Club Express
Bob Stoddard, Editor
P.O. Box 1275, Covina, CA 91723.

Petroleum Collectibles Monthly
Scott Benjamin and Wayne Henderson, Publishers
411 Forest St., LaGrange, OH 44050; 216-355-6608. Suscription: $29.95 per year (Samples $5). Scott advises on Gasoline Globes and is devoted to gas and oil collectibles.

Phoenix and Consolidated Glass Collectors' Club
Scott Montroy, Secretary
P.O. Box 182082, Arlington, TX 76096-2082. Membership: $25 (single) or $35 (couple) per year (check payable to the club); E-mail: connix@flash.net

Phoenix Bird Collectors of America (PBCA)
685 S. Washington, Constantine, MI 49042; 616-435-8353. Membership: (payable to Joan Oates) $10 per year, includes *Phoenix Bird Discoveries*, published 3 times a year, Also available: 1996 Updated Value Guide to be used in conjunction with Books 1-IV: $6 ppd

Pickard Collectors Club, Ltd.
Membership office: 300 E. Grove St., Bloomington, IL 61701; 309-828-5533 or (Fax) 309-829-2266. Membership: $20 a year (single) or $25 (family); Membership includes club newsletter

Pie Birds Unlimited Newsletter
Lillian M. Cole
14 Harmony School Rd., Flemington, NJ 08822; 908-782-3198. Specializing in pie birds, pie funnels, pie vents

The Prize Insider Newsletter for Cracker Jack Collectors
Larry White
108 Central St., Rowley, MA 01969
508-948-8187

Political Collectors of Indiana Club
Michael McQuillen
P.O. Box 11141, Indianapolis, IN 46201; 317-322-8518. Official APIC (American Political Items Collectors) Chapter comprised of over 100 collectors of presidential and local political items

The Political Gallery
Thomas D. Slater
1325 W. 86th St., Indianapolis, IN 46260; 317-257-0863. Specializing in political and sports memorabilia

Porcelain Collector's Companion c/o Dorthy Kamm
P.O. Box 7460, Port St. Lucie, FL 34985-4760; 561-464-4008 or Fax: 561-460-9050

Porcelier Collectors Club
21 Tamarac Swamp Rd., Wellingford, CT 06492. Publishes *Porcelier Paper* Newsletter, $2.50 for sample copy which contains much information and classified ads

Pottery Today
Bimonthly publication by Paradise Publications, P.O. Box 221, Mayview, MO 60471. Subscription: $15 (6 issues) per year

Powder Puff Compact Collectors' Chronicle
P.O. Box 40, Lynbrook, NY 11563; 516-593-8746

Purinton Pastimes
P.O. Box 9394, Arlington, VA 22219. Newsletter for Purinton pottery enthusiasts; Subscription: $10 per year

R. Lalique
John Danis
11028 Raleigh Ct., Rockford, IL 61115; 815-877-6004 or (Fax) 815-877-6042; E-mail: danis6033@aol.com

Red Wing Collectors Society
Doug Podpeskar, membership information
624 Jones St., Eveleth, MN 55734-1631; 218-744-4854. Please include SASE when requesting information

Ribbon Tin News Newsletter (quarterly publication)
Hobart D. Van Deusen, Editor
28 The Green, Watertown, CT 06795; 203-945-3456

Rosevilles of the Past Newsletter
Jack Bomm, Editor
P.O. Box 656, Clarcona, FL 32710-0656. $19.95 per year for 6 to 12 newsletters

Rosie Wells Enterprises, Inc.
22341 E. Wells Rd. S., Canton, IL 61520. Write for free literature; Publishes secondary market price guides for Precious Moments® collectibles, Hallmark ornaments, Boyds Bears & Friends, and Cherished Teddies. Check out rosies internet site! http://www/RosieWells.com Rosie has hosted International Conventions for Precious Moments Collectors and hosts the semiannual Midwest Collectibles Fest, both held in Westmont, IL. For Hot Tips and to record Voice Ads, Rosie offers a touch-tone 900 line (1-900-740-7575). Call 309-668-2211 for information on limited edition collectibles, Ask about the informational kit available to clubs for writing constitutions, planning meetings, etc. E-mail: Rosie@RosieWells.com

Salt & Pepper Illustrated Sales List
Judy Posner
May-October: R.D. 1, Box 273SC, Effort, PA 18330; 717-629-6583, or November-April: 4195 S. Tamiami Trail, #183SC, Venice, FL 34293; 941-497-7149; E-mail: Judyandjef@aol.com Internet: http://www.tias.com/stores/jpc Send $2 and LSASE. Buy-Sell-Collect

Salt & Pepper Novelty Shakers Club
Irene Thornburg
581 Joy Road, Battle Creek, MI 49017; 616-963-7953. Publishes quarterly newsletter; Holds annual convention; Dues: $20 per year in US, Canada and Mexico ($5 extra for couple)

Schoenhut Collectors Club
c/o Pat Girbach
1003 W. Huron St., Ann Arbor, MI 48103-4217 for membership information

Shawnee Pottery Collectors' Club
P.O. Box 713, New Smyrna Beach, FL 32170-0713. Monthly nation-wide newsletter. SASE (c/o Pamela Curran) required when requesting information. Optional: $3 for sample of current newsletter

Shelley National China Club
c/o LaDonna Douglass
P.O. Box 580, Chokoloskee, FL 34138. Membership: $25 per year; 4 quarterly newsletters, plus many other benefits; 7 years old, 400 members and growing, 1997 National convention in San Francisco; building large Shelley database and links to international Shelley clubs. E-mail: cleiser@compuserve.com

Society of Inkwell Collectors
5136 Thomas Ave. South, Minneapolis, MN 55410. Membership: $22.50 per year, includes subscription to *The Stained Finger*, a quarterly publication

Southern California Marble Club
18361-1 Strothern St., Reseda, CA 91335

Southern Folk Pottery Collectors Society Newsletter
c/o Billy Ray & Susan Hussey
1828 N. Howard Mill Rd., Robbins, NC 27325; 910-454-3961 or Fax 910-464-2530. Wednestay-Saturday 10:00 - 5:00 or by appointment. Dues are $25 per year. Membership includes biannual absentee auction catalogs, access to member pieces, opportunities to meet potters, participate in events, newsletter information and more

Southern Oregon Antiques & Collectibles Club
P.O. Box 508, Talent, OR 97540; 503-535-1231. Meets 1st Wednesday of the month; Promotes 2 shows a year in Medford, OR

Spoonville Scoop
Alves, Margaret
84 Oak Ave., Shelton, 06484; 203-924-4768. Specializing in spoons: plated, sterling, silver, pre-1920s; Subscription: $8 per year (published bimonthly); Sample: $2

Stangle/Fulper Collectors Club
P.O. Box 538, Flemington, NJ 08822; Yearly membership: $25 (includes quarterly newsletter)

Stanley Tool Collector News
c/o The Old Tool Shop
208 Front St., Marietta, OH 45750. Features articles of interest, auction results, price trends, classified ads, etc.; Subscription: $20 per year; Sample: $6.95

Stevengraph Collectors Assn.
David L. Brown
2103-2829 Arbutus Rd., Victoria, British Columbia, Canada, V8N 5X5; 250-477-9896

Still Bank Collectors Club of America
c/o Larry Egelhoff
4175 Millersville Rd., Indianapolis, IN 46205. Membership: $35 per year

Stretch Glass Society
P.O. Box 573, Hampshire, IL 60140. Membership: $12; Quarterly newsletter; Annual convention

Surveyors Historical Society Identification Committee
D.R. Beeks
P.O. Box 117, Mt. Vernon, IA 52314; 391-895-0506

Susie Cooper Catalogs
J. David Ehrhard
7212 Valmont St., Tujunga, CA 91042

Swan Seekers Network
Maret Webb
4118 E. Vernon Ave., Phoenix, AZ 85008-2333; 602-957-6294 or (Fax) 602-957-1631, 9:00 a.m. - 5:00 p.m. M.S.T., Mon. — Fri. Publishes *Swan Seekers News* and *Swan Seekers Marketplace* periodicals ($28 per year U.S., $38 foreign). Specializing in Swarovski crystal

Table Toppers
1340 West Irving Park Rd., P.O. Box 161, Chicago, IL 60613; 312-769-3184. Membership: $18 (single) per year, which includes *Table Topics*, a bimonthly newsletter for those interested in table-top collectibles

The Tanner Restraints Collection
3024 E. 35th, Spokane, WA 99223; 509-448-8457. 40-page catalog of magician/escape artist equipment from trick and regulation padlocks, handcuffs, leg shackles and straight jackets to picks and pick sets; Books on all of the above and much more; Catalog: $3

Tea Leaf Club International
222 Powderhorn Dr., Houghton Lake, MI 48629. Publishes *Tea Leaf Readings* Newsletter; Membership: $20 (single) or $25 (couple) per year

Tea Talk
Tina M. Carter, Teapot Columnist
Diana Rosen and Lucy Roman, Editors
P.O. Box 860, Sausalito, CA 94966; 415-331-1557

The TeaTime Gazette
Linda Ashley Leamer
P.O. Box 40276, St. Paul, MN 55104

Texas Gun Collectors Assn.
Roger Baker, Member
Box 620417, Woodside, CA 94062

Thermometer Collectors' Club of America
Richard Porter, Vice President
P.O. Box 944, Onset, MA 02558

Thimble Collectors International
6411 Montego Rd., Louisville, KY 40228

Three Rivers Depression Era Glass Society
Meetings held 1st Monday of each month at DeMartino's Restaurant, Carnegie, PA; For more information call: Edith A. Putanko at John's Antiques & Edie's Glassware Rte. 88 & Broughton Rd., Bethel Park, PA 15102; 412-831-2702

Tiffin Glass Collectors
P.O. Box 554, Tiffin, OH 44883. Meetings at Seneca Cty. Museum on 2nd Tuesday of each month

Tins 'n' Signs
Box 440101, Aurora, CO 80044. Subscription: $25 per year

Tobacco Antiques and Collectibles Market
Chuck Thompson, Publisher
P.O. Box 11652, Houston, TX 77293. Subscription: $9.95 (12 issues); $19.95 in Canada and Mexico; All other foreign countries: $30 for 6 issues

Tops & Bottoms Club (Rene Lalique perfumes only)
c/o Madeleine France
P.O. Box 15555, Ft. Lauderdale, FL 33318

Toy Gun Collectors of America Newsletter
Jim Buskirk, Editor & Publisher
175 Cornell St., Windsor, CA 95492; 707-837-9949. Published quarterly, covers both toy and BB guns; Dues: $15 per year

Toy Gun Purveyors
c/o Jim Schleyer
Box 243-S, Burke, VA 22015. An international club that fosters the collecting of valuable and rare toy guns; SASE required for information

Uhl Collectors' Society
Beverly Leslie, Secretary/Treasurer
801 Poplar St., Boonville, IN, 47601; 812-897-3681.
Dave Swick, Newsletter
Newton, IL

Vaseline Glass Newsletter
Jerry Chambers
2163 Pomona Place, Fairfield, CA 94533; 707-425-6166 after 4:30 p.m. P.S.T.

Vernon Views, newsletter for Vernon Kilns collectors
P.O. Box 945, Scottsdale, AZ 85252. Published quarterly beginning with the spring issue, $10 per year

Vetri: Italian Glass News
Howard Lockwood, Publisher
P.O. Box 191, Fort Lee, NJ 07024; 201-969-0373. Quarterly newsletter about 20th-century Italian glass

Vintage Fashion & Costume Jewelry Newsletter/Club
P.O. Box 265, Glen Oaks, NY 11004; 718-969-2320 or 718-939-3095. Year's subscription (4 issues): $15 in US; $20 in Canada; $25 International. Back issues available at $5 each

Visakay, Stephen
P.O. Box 1517, W. Caldwell, 07007. Writes monthly column for cyber-space magazine: *Shaken Not Stirred*, at: http://www.martinis.com/key/

The Wade Watch
Collector's Corner
8199 Pierson Ct.
Arvada, CO 80005; 303-421-9655 or 303-424-4401; Fax 303-421-0317. Year's subscription (4 issues): $8 in US; $10 International; Articles and photos welcome, but if to be returned, enclose SASE

Walking Stick Notes
Cecil Curtis, Editor
4051 E. Olive Rd., Pensacola, FL 32514. Quarterly publication with limited distribution

The Wallace Nutting Collector's Club
c/o Michael Ivankovich
P.O. Box 2458, Doylestown, PA 18901. Established in 1973, holds annual conventions, usually in the northeastern portion of the country; generally recognized national center of Wallace Nutting-like activity are Michael Ivankovich's *Wallace Nutting & Wallace Nutting-Like Specialty Auctions*; Held 3-4 times each year, these Auctions provide the opportunity for collectors and dealers to compete for the largest variety of Wallace Nutting and Wallace Nutting-Like pictures available anywhere. These Auctions also give sellers the opportunity to place their items in front of the country's leading enthusiasts; When writing for information please enclude a close-up photograph which includes the picture's frame, and a SASE

Watt's News Newsletter, for Watt pottery enthusiasts
c/o Watt Collectors Association
P.O. Box 184, Galesburg, IL 61402-0184. Subscription: $10 per year; quarterly newsletter, annual convention

The Wedgwood Society of New York
5 Dogwood Court, Glen Head, NY 11545. Membership: $27.50 (individual) or $32.50 (family). Publishes newsletter (6 times per year) and a scholarly magazine of original articles published by the Society; 6 meetings per year

Westmoreland Glass Collector's Newsletter
P.O. Box 143, North Liberty, IA 52317. Subscription: $16 per year. This publication is dedicated to the purpose of preserving Westmoreland Glass and its history

Westmoreland Glass Society
Jim Fisher, President
513 5th Ave., Coralville, IA 52241; 319-354-5011. Membership: $15 (single) or $25 (household)

The Whimsey Club
c/o Christopher Davis
522 Woodhill, Newark, NY 14513. *Whimsical Notions*, quarterly newsletter; Dues: $5 per year; Annual meeting in Rochester, NY, in April during Genessee Valley Bottle Collectors' Show

The White Ironstone China Association, Inc.
R.D. #1, Box 23, Howes Cave, NY 12092. Newsletter available for: $25 (single) or $30 (2 persons at same address)

The Willow Word
Mary Lina Berndt, Publisher
P.O. Box 13382, Arlington, TX 76094. Each bimonthly issue contains 20 pages of articles, photographs and full-color 'centerfold'; Subscription: $20 in U.S., $22 in Canada, $25 overseas (U.S. funds only)

World's Fair Collectors' Society, Inc.
Fair News Newsletter (monthly publication for members)
Michael R. Pender, Editor
P.O. Box 20806, Sarasota, FL 34276-3806; 941-923-2590. Dues: $17 per year in U.S., $18 in Canada, and $27 overseas

The Zsolnay Store
152 Spring St., Newport, RI 02840; 401-841-5060. Zsolnay book available; On the Web: http://www.drawrm.com

Invention Patents

Invention patents cover the unique mechanical workings of inventions which produce utilitarian results. An invention patent is in effect, with exclusive rights for the inventor, for 17 years from date of issuance.

A GUIDE FOR DATING INVENTION PATENT NUMBERS

Patent Numbers		Date	Patent Numbers		Date	Patent Numbers		Date
1 thru	109	1836	236,137	251,684	1881	1,568,040	1,612,789	1926
110	545	1837	251,685	269,819	1882	1,612,790	1,654,520	1927
546	1,060	1838	269,820	291,015	1883	1,654,521	1,696,896	1928
1,061	1,464	1839	291,016	310,162	1884	1,696,897	1,742,180	1929
1,465	1,922	1840	310,163	333,493	1885	1,742,181	1,787,423	1930
1,923	2,412	1841	333,494	355,290	1886	1,787,424	1,839,189	1931
2,413	2,900	1842	355,291	375,719	1887	1,839,190	1,892,662	1932
2,901	3,394	1843	375,720	395,304	1888	1,892,663	1,941,448	1933
3,395	3,872	1844	395,305	418,664	1889	1,941,449	1,985,877	1934
3,873	4,347	1845	418,665	443,986	1890	1,985,878	2,026,515	1935
4,348	4,913	1846	443,987	466,314	1891	2,026,516	2,066,308	1936
4,914	5,408	1847	466,315	488,975	1892	2,066,309	2,104,003	1937
5,409	5,992	1848	488,976	511,743	1893	2,104,004	2,142,079	1938
5,993	6,980	1849	511,744	531,618	1894	2,142,080	2,185,169	1939
6,981	7,864	1850	531,619	552,501	1895	2,185,170	2,227,417	1940
7,865	8,621	1851	552,502	574,368	1896	2,227,418	2,268,539	1941
8,622	9,511	1852	574,369	596,466	1897	2,268,540	2,307,006	1942
9,512	10,357	1853	596,467	616,870	1898	2,307,007	2,338,080	1943
10,358	12,116	1854	616,871	640,166	1899	2,338,081	2,366,153	1944
12,117	14,008	1855	640,167	664,826	1900	2,366,154	2,391,855	1945
14,009	16,323	1856	664,827	690,384	1901	2,391,856	2,413,674	1946
16,324	19,009	1857	690,385	717,520	1902	2,413,675	2,433,823	1947
19,010	22,476	1858	717,521	748,566	1903	2,433,824	2,457,796	1948
22,477	26,641	1859	748,567	778,833	1904	2,457,797	2,492,943	1949
26,642	31,004	1860	778,834	808,617	1905	2,492,944	2,536,015	1950
31,005	34,044	1861	808,618	839,798	1906	2,536,016	2,580,378	1951
34,045	37,265	1862	839,799	875,678	1907	2,580,379	2,624,045	1952
37,266	41,046	1863	875,679	908,435	1908	2,624,046	2,664,561	1953
41,047	45,684	1864	908,436	945,009	1909	2,664,562	2,698,433	1954
45,685	51,783	1865	945,010	980,177	1910	2,698,434	2,728,912	1955
51,784	60,657	1866	980,178	1,013,094	1911	2,728,913	2,775,761	1956
60,658	72,958	1867	1,013,095	1,049,325	1912	2,775,762	2,818,566	1957
72,959	85,502	1868	1,049,326	1,083,266	1913	2,818,567	2,866,972	1958
85,503	98,459	1869	1,083,267	1,123,211	1914	2,866,973	2,919,442	1959
98,460	110,616	1870	1,123,212	1,166,418	1915	2,919,443	2,966,680	1960
110,617	122,303	1871	1,166,419	1,210,388	1916	2,966,681	3,015,102	1961
122,304	134,503	1872	1,210,389	1,251,457	1917	3,015,103	3,070,800	1962
134,504	146,119	1873	1,251,458	1,290,026	1918	3,070,801	3,116,486	1963
146,120	158,349	1874	1,290,027	1,326,898	1919	3,116,487	3,163,864	1964
158,350	171,640	1875	1,326,899	1,364,062	1920	3,163,865	3,226,728	1965
171,641	185,812	1876	1,364,063	1,401,947	1921	3,216,729	3,295,142	1966
185,813	198,732	1877	1,401,948	1,440,361	1922	3,295,143	3,360,799	1967
198,733	211,077	1878	1,440,362	1,478,995	1923	3,360,800	3,419,096	1968
211,078	223,210	1879	1,478,996	1,521,589	1924	3,419,907	3,487,469	1969
223,211	236,136	1880	1,521,590	1,568,039	1925	3,487,470	3,551,908	1970

Design Patents

Design patents cover unique, ornamental exterior shapes or structures of an invention. A Design patent is in effect, with exclusive rights for the inventor, for 14 years from date of issuance.

A GUIDE FOR DATING DESIGN PATENT NUMBERS
Design patent numbers are preceded with the letters D or DES

Patent Numbers			Date	Patent Numbers		Date	Patent Numbers		Date
1	thru	14	1843	16,451	17,045	1886	77,347	80,253	1929
15		26	1844	17,046	17,994	1887	80,254	82,965	1930
27		43	1845	17,995	18,829	1888	82,966	85,902	1931
44		102	1846	18,830	19,552	1889	85,903	88,846	1932
103		162	1847	19,553	20,438	1890	88,847	91,257	1933
163		208	1848	20,439	21,274	1891	91,258	94,178	1934
209		257	1849	21,275	22,091	1892	94,179	98,044	1935
258		340	1850	22,092	22,993	1893	98,045	102,600	1936
341		430	1851	22,994	23,921	1894	102,601	107,737	1937
431		539	1852	23,922	25,036	1895	107,738	112,764	1938
540		625	1853	25,037	26,481	1896	112,765	118,357	1939
626		682	1854	26,482	28,112	1897	118,358	124,502	1940
683		752	1855	28,113	29,915	1898	124,503	130,988	1941
753		859	1856	29,916	32,054	1899	130,989	134,716	1942
860		972	1857	32,055	33,812	1900	134,717	136,945	1943
973		1,074	1858	33,813	35,546	1901	136,946	139,861	1944
1,075		1,182	1859	35,547	36,186	1902	139,862	143,385	1945
1,183		1,365	1860	36,187	36,722	1903	143,386	146,164	1946
1,366		1,507	1861	36,723	37,279	1904	146,165	148,266	1947
1,508		1,702	1862	37,280	37,765	1905	148,267	152,234	1948
1,703		1,878	1863	37,766	38,390	1906	152,235	156,685	1949
1,879		2,017	1864	38,391	38,979	1907	156,686	161,403	1950
2,018		2,238	1865	38,980	39,736	1908	161,404	165,567	1951
2,239		2,532	1866	39,737	40,423	1909	165,568	168,526	1952
2,533		2,857	1867	40,424	41,062	1910	168,527	171,240	1953
2,858		3,303	1868	41,063	42,072	1911	171,241	173,776	1954
3,304		3,809	1869	42,073	43,414	1912	173,777	176,489	1955
3,810		4,546	1870	43,415	45,097	1913	176,490	179,466	1956
4,547		5,451	1871	46,098	46,812	1914	179,467	181,828	1957
5,452		6,335	1872	46,813	48,357	1915	181,829	184,203	1958
6,336		7,082	1873	48,358	50,116	1916	184,204	186,972	1959
7,083		7,968	1874	50,117	51,628	1917	186,973	189,515	1960
7,969		8,883	1875	51,629	52,835	1918	189,516	192,003	1961
8,884		9,685	1876	52,836	54,358	1919	192,004	194,303	1962
9,686		10,384	1877	54,359	56,843	1920	194,304	197,268	1963
10,385		10,974	1878	56,844	60,120	1921	197,269	199,994	1964
10,975		11,566	1879	60,121	61,747	1922	199,995	203,378	1965
11,567		12,081	1880	61,748	63,674	1923	203,379	206,566	1966
12,082		12,646	1881	63,675	66,345	1924	206,567	209,731	1967
12,647		13,507	1882	66,346	69,169	1925	209,732	213,083	1968
13,508		14,527	1883	69,170	71,771	1926	213,084	216,418	1969
14,528		15,677	1884	71,772	74,158	1927	216,419	219,636	1970
15,678		16,450	1885	74,159	77,346	1928			

Index

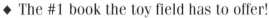
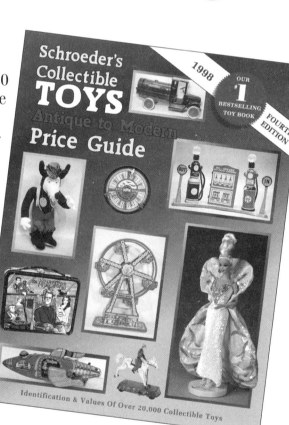